Merriam-Webster's
Crossword Puzzle
Dictionary

Merriam-Webster's Crossword Puzzle Dictionary

Third Edition

Merriam-Webster, Incorporated
Springfield, Massachusetts, U.S.A.

A GENUINE MERRIAM-WEBSTER

The name Webster alone is no guarantee of excellence. It is used by a number of publishers and may serve mainly to mislead an unwary buyer.

Merriam-Webster™ is the name you should look for when you consider the purchase of dictionaries or other fine reference books. It carries the reputation of a company that has been publishing since 1831 and is your assurance of quality and authority.

Preface to the Third Edition

This new edition of MERRIAM-WEBSTER'S CROSSWORD PUZZLE DICTIONARY represents a significant revision of those that have preceded it. Every entry has been reconsidered, the content has been thoroughly updated, and the page design has been enhanced for legibility.

In updating the work, we have added many terms that have recently entered the general English vocabulary: the names of computer languages (*Java, Perl*), new national currencies (*vatu, nakfa*), contemporary slang (*slacker, schlep, hoser, chill out, go-to guy, brewski, nebbish*), and much more. And numerous individuals and institutions that have emerged in recent years—soccer stars (*Hamm, Ronaldo*), auto companies (*Kia, Daewoo*), Nobel Prize winners (*Annan, Naipaul*), actors and actresses (*Depp, Swank*), and so on—have naturally also been added.

Drawing extensively on actual crossword puzzles, we have made a special effort to add examples of "crosswordese," words that show up unusually often in puzzle grids. Thus, you will find such distinctive words and names as those for Prince Valiant's wife (*Aleta*) and son (*Arn*), a former newspaper columnist (*Eda*), a sharp mountain ridge (*arête*), a hare's tail (*scut*), an eminent golfer (*Els*), Peer Gynt's mother (*Ase, Aase*), a puzzle-cube inventor (*Erno*), and a Scottish uncle (*eme*)—many of which might have been omitted if frequency of use in everyday English had been our only criterion.

While crossword clues have gotten cleverer in recent years, crossword answer words have gotten simpler, and archaic and obscure terms have gradually been disappearing from puzzle grids. For this new edition, it seemed unnecessary to retain words that were unlikely to show up in even the most challenging modern puzzles, and consequently a number of words that have fallen out of use have been deleted. Their absence has been more than made up for by additional entries and answer words, which now total substantially over 300,000.

We hope our revised edition, with its new orientation, will prove to be the most useful dictionary of its kind for a new century of puzzle solving.

The principal editors of this dictionary's first two editions were James G. Lowe and Michael G. Belanger. Editorial work on the new edition was carried out by Mark A. Stevens and C. Roger Davis with freelance help from Jocelyn White Franklin, Mike Nichols, Francesca M. Forrest, and Doris Maxfield. Eileen M. Haraty and Dr. Thomas W. Adams made valuable vocabulary contributions, and Robert D. Copeland and Ted Atanowski provided essential electronic assistance. The pages were typeset by Dianna Logan at Dedicated Business Services of Clarinda, Iowa.

Mark A. Stevens
Editor

Explanatory Notes

This dictionary is organized to make it easy to find answer words with a specific number of letters. Every answer word follows a numeral indicating the number of letters it contains. These words generally run from three to 13 letters. Two-letter words are omitted because such words almost never appear in crossword puzzles, and words longer than 13 letters are omitted because, when a puzzle calls for a longer answer, the answer is usually a phrase or part of a phrase rather than a single word or term. An exception to the 13-letter limit is made for multi-word titles of works, which occasionally run as long as 25 letters. The exception allows for those frequent crossword clues that omit one or two words from a title, perhaps enough for a five- or ten-letter answer.

As in any crossword dictionary, a single list of answer words will often include words representing various parts of speech. The entry for **quiet**, for example, includes synonyms for the noun *(silence),* the adjective *(placid),* and the verb *(soothe),* all in a continuous list. Since clues are often intentionally ambiguous as to what part of speech or meaning is intended, listing all the possible synonyms together is probably ideal for the puzzle solver.

Words that share a root with their entry word have usually been omitted from the answer lists, since puzzle creators rarely choose a clue that is related in this way to its answer. Therefore, *singular* does not appear at **single**, *basal* does not appear at **basic**, and *papa* does not appear at **pop**. On the other hand, since clues do occasionally share a standard prefix or suffix (such as *re-* or

-*ness*) with an answer word, we have retained many clue/answer-word pairs of this kind.

When one entry word simply adds a suffix to another entry word, as when **truthfulness** follows **truthful**, the answer list for the suffixed entry word will generally omit all the words that merely add the same suffix to a word in the stem word's list. For example, since **truthful** includes such answer words as *frank* and *candid,* the list at **truthfulness** omits *frankness* and *candidness.* When encountering a clue with a common suffix, therefore, the user will occasionally want to look at a neighboring entry to find all the possible synonyms.

When a personal name is entered as an answer-term, the first name generally appears in parentheses and is ignored in the letter count. In cases where the first name is the one normally encountered—e.g., for historical figures such as Michelangelo and Raphael or fictional characters such as Tess Durbeyfield and Angel Clare—the last name is generally parenthesized instead. When a title begins with an article *(A, An,* or *The),* the article is parenthesized and omitted from the letter count. In a list of geographic entities such as mountains (lakes, gulfs, etc.), the generic word *Mount (Lake, Gulf,* etc.*)* is similarly omitted from the letter count. If you find that none of the answers as listed fits the blanks for a given puzzle clue, you should naturally check to see if any of the parenthesized or omitted elements might help provide the desired answer.

Many entries are broken into subentries by means of subheadings. Subheadings often consist of a single word, which is usually to be read as either preceding or following the main entry word. Thus, in the entry for **hair**, the subheadings include **animal** (which should be read as "animal hair") and **ornament** (which should be read as "hair ornament"). The subentry **combining form** lists the kinds of word fragments, usually Greek or Latin in origin, that are commonly called *roots.*

The dictionary is best used somewhat imaginatively.

If you fail to find a word at its own entry, look up a synonym; only rarely will you fail to find one. If a clue takes a form such as **Australian tree**, **garden tool**, or **Southeast Asian lake** and the dictionary provides no such entry, check at the entry for the generic term—**tree**, **tool**, **lake**, etc.—for a list, perhaps broken down by subheadings.

A

A1
4 best, tops 5 prime 7 optimal, perfect 8 superior 9 excellent, first-rate, front-rank, matchless, top-drawer 10 blue-ribbon, first-class

Aaron
brother: 5 Moses
father: 5 Amram
sister: 6 Miriam

aback
7 unaware 8 suddenly, unawares 10 by surprise 12 unexpectedly

abaft
4 back 5 after 6 astern, behind 8 rearward 9 sternward

abalone
7 mollusc, mollusk 9 gastropod

abandon
4 cede, drop, dump, ease, jilt, junk, play, quit 5 cease, chuck, ditch, leave, let go, scrap, yield 6 desert, disown, give up, laxity, maroon, reject, resign, strand, vacate 7 back out, bail out, cast off, discard, drop out, forsake, freedom, liberty, license, pull out, retreat 8 abdicate, give over, hand over, renounce, wildness, withdraw 9 looseness, repudiate, surrender, throw over 10 enthusiasm, exuberance, relinquish, wantonness 11 discontinue, leave behind, naturalness, spontaneity, unrestraint 12 carelessness, heedlessness, intemperance, recklessness, unconstraint 13 impulsiveness

abandoned
4 free, lewd, lorn, wild 5 loose 6 gave up, jilted, vacant, wanton 7 cast off, corrupt, given up, outcast, uncouth 8 cast away, depraved, derelict, deserted, desolate, forsaken, stranded 9 cast aside, debauched, destitute, discarded, dissolute, lecherous, neglected, reprobate, shameless 10 degenerate, dissipated, eliminated, friendless, lascivious, left behind, licentious, profligate, unoccupied 11 uninhibited 12 incorrigible, relinquished, uncontrolled, unrestrained

abase
5 lower, shame 6 debase, defame, demean, demote, grovel, humble, lessen, reduce 7 cheapen, degrade, devalue, put down 8 belittle 9 denigrate, discredit, disparage, downgrade, humiliate 10 depreciate, undervalue

abash
4 faze 5 mix up, shame, upset 6 dismay, puzzle, rattle 7 confuse, mortify, mystify 8 confound 9 discomfit, embarrass 10 discompose, disconcert

abashment
6 unease 7 chagrin 8 disquiet 9 confusion 12 discomfiture, discomposure 13 embarrassment

abate
3 ebb, end 4 ease, fade, fall, omit, slow, void, wane 5 allay, annul, close, let up, quash, taper 6 deduct, lessen, negate, recede, reduce, relent, weaken 7 abolish, decline, deprive, die down, dwindle, ease off, nullify, slacken, subside 8 decrease,

abatement

diminish, mitigate, moderate **9** alleviate, eradicate **10** invalidate

abatement

6 ebbing, rebate, waning **8** decrease, discount **9** declining, deduction, dwindling, exemption, lessening, reduction, shrinkage **10** diminution, subsidence **11** subtraction

abattoir

8 shambles

abbey

6 friary **7** convent **8** cloister **9** monastery

abbot

female: 6 abbess

abbreviate

3 cut **4** clip, trim **5** prune **6** cut out, reduce **7** abridge, curtail, cut back, shorten **8** compress, condense, contract, cut short, truncate

abbreviation

5 brief **6** digest, précis, sketch **7** acronym, cutting, outline **8** abstract, clipping, synopsis, trimming **10** abridgment, shortening **11** curtailment **12** condensation

abdicate

4 cede, drop, quit **5** evade, forgo, leave, waive, yield **6** abjure, give up, reject, resign **7** abandon, cast off, discard **8** abnegate, disclaim, hand over, renounce, withdraw **9** repudiate, surrender **10** relinquish

abdomen

3 gut, pot **5** belly, tummy **6** middle, paunch **7** midriff, stomach **8** potbelly **9** bay window **10** midsection **11** breadbasket
depression: 5 navel

abduct

4 grab, take **5** seize **6** kidnap, remove, snatch **8** carry off, draw away, take away **9** carry away, steal away **10** spirit away **11** make off with

Abduction from the Seraglio composer

6 Mozart (Wolfgang Amadeus)

abecedarian

4 tyro **6** novice **7** amateur, dabbler, learner **8** beginner, initiate, neophyte **9** beginning, smatterer **10** apprentice, dilettante, elementary **11** rudimentary **12** alphabetical

Abel

brother: 4 Cain, Seth
father: 4 Adam
mother: 3 Eve
slayer: 4 Cain

Abelard

son: 9 Astrolabe
wife: 7 Heloise

abele

6 poplar

aberrant

3 odd **7** deviant, strange, unusual **8** abnormal, atypical, peculiar, straying **9** anomalous, deviating, different, eccentric, irregular, unnatural, untypical **11** exceptional, nonstandard

aberration

4 slip **5** quirk **6** change, oddity **7** anomaly, mistake **8** mutation, straying **9** curiosity, deviation, exception, wandering **10** deflection, difference, distortion, divergence **11** abnormality, peculiarity **12** eccentricity, irregularity

abet

3 aid, egg **4** ally, back, help, prod, spur, urge **5** boost, egg on **6** assist, exhort, foment, incite, second, stir up **7** condone, endorse, forward, promote, support **8** advocate **9** encourage, instigate **11** countenance

abettor

4 aide, ally **6** backup, cohort, helper **7** inciter, partner **8** fomenter **9** accessory, supporter **10** accomplice, instigator **11** confederate, conspirator **12** collaborator

abeyance

4 lull, rest **5** break, lapse, pause **6** recess **7** respite, time-out, waiting

8 breather, interval **10** inactivity, quiescence, suspension **12** intermission, interruption

abeyant
7 dormant **8** deferred, inactive, recessed **9** postponed, quiescent, suspended **11** interrupted

abhor
4 hate **5** scorn **6** detest, loathe, reject, revile, vilify **7** contemn, despise, disdain, dislike **8** execrate **9** abominate, excoriate, repudiate

abhorrence
4 evil, hate **6** hatred, horror **7** disgust **8** aversion, distaste, loathing **9** repulsion, revulsion **10** repugnance **11** abomination, detestation

abhorrent
4 base, foul, vile **5** awful **6** horrid, odious **7** beastly, hateful, heinous **8** damnable, horrible, horrific **9** atrocious, execrable, invidious, loathsome, monstrous, obnoxious, repellent, repugnant, repulsive, revolting **10** abominable, deplorable, despicable, detestable, disgusting **12** contemptible **13** reprehensible

abide
4 bear, last, live, stay, wait **5** await, brook, dwell, exist, stand, tarry **6** accede, accept, comply, endure, keep on, linger, remain, reside, stay on, suffer **7** consent, hang out, inhabit, persist, sojourn, stomach, subsist, swallow, wait for **8** continue, live with, stand for, tolerate **9** put up with, withstand

abiding
4 fast, firm, sure **6** steady **7** durable, eternal, lasting, staying **8** constant, enduring, timeless **9** complying, perpetual, steadfast **10** continuing, persistent, persisting, unchanging **11** everlasting, unfaltering

abigail
4 maid

Abigail
brother: **5** David

husband: **5** David, Nabal
mother: **5** Amasa
son: **7** Chileah

ability
4 bent, gift **5** craft, flair, knack, might, savvy, skill **6** talent **7** aptness, command, faculty, know-how, mastery, prowess **8** aptitude, capacity, facility **9** adeptness, dexterity, expertise, handiness, ingenuity, potential **10** adroitness, capability, cleverness, competence, efficiency **11** proficiency, skillfulness **13** qualification

abject
3 low **4** base, mean, poor, vile **5** lowly, sorry **6** dismal, humble, shabby, sordid **7** debased, fawning, forlorn, ignoble, pitiful, servile **8** cast down, degraded, dejected, downcast, hopeless, pathetic, pitiable, rejected, resigned, wretched **9** afflicted, destitute, groveling, miserable, worthless **10** deplorable, obsequious, spiritless, submissive **11** deferential, downtrodden, subservient **12** contemptible, dishonorable, ingratiating

abjure
4 cede, deny **5** avoid, spurn **6** desert, disown, recall, recant, reject, refuse, revoke **7** abandon, disavow, decline, forsake, retract **8** disclaim, forswear, renounce, take back, withdraw **9** repudiate, surrender **10** relinquish **11** abstain from

ablaze
5 afire, aglow, fiery **6** aflame, alight, on fire **7** blazing, burning, flaming, excited, flaring, ignited, radiant

able
3 apt, fit **4** keen **5** adept, alert, sharp, smart **6** adroit, clever, expert, facile, suited **7** capable, skilled **8** skillful, talented **9** competent, effective, effectual, efficient, qualified **10** proficient **11** intelligent, resourceful **12** accomplished, enterprising

able-bodied
3 fit **4** hale **5** hardy, lusty, sound, stout **6** brawny, hearty, robust,

strong, sturdy **7** capable **8** stalwart, vigorous **9** strapping

ablution
6 laving **7** bathing, washing **8** lavation **9** cleansing, immersion **12** purification

abnegate
4 cede, deny, drop **5** forgo, waive, yield **6** abjure, give up, recant, revoke, vacate **7** disavow, gainsay **8** disallow, disclaim, forswear, renounce, withdraw **9** repudiate, surrender **10** contradict, contravene, relinquish

abnegation
6 denial **9** surrender **10** abstinence, self-denial **12** renouncement, renunciation

Abner
cousin: 4 Saul
father: 3 Ner
slayer: 4 Joab

abnormal
3 odd **5** freak, undue, weird **6** offkey **7** bizarre, deviant, unusual **8** aberrant, atypical, freakish, peculiar **9** anomalous, divergent, eccentric, irregular, unnatural **11** heteroclite **13** heteromorphic, preternatural

abnormality
4 flaw **6** oddity **7** anomaly **8** deviance **9** deviation, exception **10** aberration, difference **12** irregularity

abode
4 home, nest **5** house **7** address, lodging, sojourn **8** domicile, dwelling **9** residence **10** habitation

abolish
3 end **4** undo, kill, void **5** abate, annul, erase, quash **6** cancel, negate, recall, repeal, revoke, vacate **7** destroy, nullify, rescind, retract, reverse, wipe out **8** abrogate, disallow, dissolve, overturn, prohibit **9** eliminate, eradicate, terminate **10** do away with, extinguish, invalidate

abolitionist
4 Mott (Lucretia), Weld (Theodore) **5** Brown (John), Child (Lydia), Lundy (Benjamin), Smith (Gerrit), Stowe (Harriet Beecher) **6** Birney (James), Lowell (James Russell), Parker (Theodore), Tappan (Arthur), Tubman (Harriet) **7** Lincoln (Abraham) **8** Douglass (Frederick), Garrison (William Lloyd), Phillips (Wendell), Whittier (John Greenleaf)

abominable
5 awful, nasty **6** cursed, horrid, odious **7** hateful **8** horrible, shocking, terrible, wretched **9** abhorrent, loathsome, offensive, repellent, repugnant, repulsive, revolting **10** deplorable, despicable, detestable, disgusting **12** contemptible

abominable snowman
4 yeti

abominate
4 damn, hate **5** abhor, curse, scorn **6** detest, loathe, revile **7** despise **8** execrate **9** repudiate

abomination
4 evil, hate **5** scorn **6** hatred, horror, plague **7** disdain, disgust, dislike **8** anathema, aversion, contempt, distaste, loathing **9** repulsion, revulsion **10** abhorrence, repugnance, repugnancy **11** detestation

aboriginal
5 first **6** native **7** ancient, endemic, primary **8** earliest, original, primeval **9** primitive **10** indigenous, primordial **13** autochthonous

aborigine
6 native **7** ancient **8** indigene **10** autochthon

abort
4 drop, halt, stop **5** check, expel, scrap, scrub **6** arrest, cancel **7** abandon, call off **8** cut short **9** interrupt, terminate

abortive
4 vain **5** empty **6** futile, unripe **7** failing, useless **8** immature, unformed **9** fruitless, worthless **10** unavailing, unfruitful

11 ineffective, ineffectual, unavailable, undeveloped **12** unproductive, unsuccessful

abound
4 flow, teem **5** burst, crawl, crowd, flood, swarm, swell **6** be full, throng **7** bristle, jam with **8** overflow, pack with **9** crawl with **11** be plentiful

abounding
4 full, rife **5** laden **6** filled, full of, jammed, packed **7** copious, profuse, replete, stuffed, teeming **8** abundant, swarming, thronged **9** alive with, bristling, plenteous, plentiful **11** overflowing

about
4 as to, back, in re, near, nigh, over **5** again, anent, circa, round **6** almost, around, moving, nearby, nearly **7** apropos, close to, roughly, through **8** backward **9** as regards, engaged in, haphazard, in general, in reverse, regarding **10** as concerns, concerning, encircling, in regard to, more or less, on all sides, oppositely, relating to, respecting **11** any which way, dealing with, on every side, practically, referring to, relative to, surrounding **12** here and there, with regard to **13** approximately, concerned with, in reference to, with respect to

about-face
4 turn **7** reverse **8** reversal **9** turnabout, volte-face

above
3 o'er **4** over, past **5** aloft, supra **6** beyond **8** overhead **9** exceeding **prefix: 4** over **5** hyper, super, supra

above all
7 chiefly **9** primarily **10** especially **11** principally **12** particularly

aboveboard
4 free, open **5** frank **6** candid, honest, openly **7** frankly, up front **8** candidly, honestly, straight **10** truthfully, forthright, scrupulous

abracadabra
5 charm, magic **6** babble, jargon **9** gibberish **10** double talk, mumbo jumbo **11** incantation **12** gobbledygook **13** mystification

abrade
3 bug, irk, rub **4** burn, fret, gall, rasp, wear **5** annoy, chafe, erode, grate, graze, upset, weary **6** bother, ruffle, scrape **7** corrode, eat away, perturb, provoke, roughen **8** irritate, wear away, wear down **9** aggravate, grind down

Abraham
brother: 5 Haran, Nahor
concubine: 5 Hagar
father: 5 Terah
grandfather: 5 Nahor
grandson: 5 Esau
nephew: 3 Lot
son: 5 Isaac, Medan, Shuah
6 Midian, Zimran **7** Ishmael
well: 9 Beer-Sheba
wife: 5 Sarah **7** Keturah

abrasion
5 chafe, scuff **6** scrape **7** chafing, erosion, grating, rubbing, scratch **8** friction, grinding, scraping, scuffing **10** irritation, scratching

abrasive
5 emery, rough, sharp **6** biting, pumice **7** wearing **8** annoying **9** smoothing, polishing **10** irritating, unpleasant

abreast
6 beside, next to, versed, with-it **7** versant **8** familiar, informed, up-to-date **9** au courant **10** acquainted, conversant **13** knowledgeable

abridge
3 cut **4** pare, trim **5** limit, prune **6** lessen, narrow, reduce **7** curtail, cut back, shorten **8** boil down, compress, condense, cut short, diminish, restrict, truncate **9** summarize **10** abbreviate

abridgment
5 brief **6** digest **7** capsule, cutting, summary **8** abstract, synopsis **9** reduction, short form **10** diminution,

abroad

lessening, shortening **11** compression, contraction, curtailment, restriction **12** abbreviation, condensation

abroad

4 afar, away **5** about **6** afield, astray, widely **7** touring **8** overseas **9** elsewhere, traveling

abrogate

3 end **4** undo, void **5** abate, annul, quash **6** cancel, negate, repeal, revoke, vacate **7** abolish, blot out, nullify, rescind, reverse **8** dissolve **9** discharge **10** extinguish, invalidate, obliterate

abrupt

4 curt **5** bluff, blunt, brief, brisk, crisp, gruff, hasty, sharp, sheer, short, steep **6** cut off, snippy, sudden **7** arduous, brusque, hurried, rushing **8** headlong **9** broken off, impetuous **10** unexpected **11** precipitant, precipitate, precipitous **13** unceremonious

abruptly

5 short **6** curtly **7** quickly, steeply **8** suddenly **12** unexpectedly **13** precipitately, precipitously

abruptness

8 curtness **9** steepness **10** brusquerie **12** precipitance

Absalom

commander: **5** Amasa
father: **5** David
mother: **7** Maachah
sister: **5** Tamar
slayer: **4** Joab

abscess

4 boil, sore **5** botch, ulcer **6** lesion, pimple, trauma **7** blister, pustule **8** furuncle **9** carbuncle

abscond

4 bolt, flee, quit **5** break, leave **6** decamp, escape, run off **7** run away, take off **8** slip away, sneak off **9** disappear, sneak away, steal away

absence

4 AWOL, lack, need, void, want **6** dearth, defect, vacuum **7** default,

drought, failure, vacancy **9** privation **10** deficiency, inadequacy **11** absenteeism, inattention **13** insufficiency

absent

4 away, AWOL, gone, lost **6** noshow **7** bemused, faraway, lacking, missing, omitted, wanting, without **8** distrait, heedless **9** elsewhere, forgetful, wandering **10** abstracted, distracted, not present **11** inattentive, preoccupied **12** not attentive

absentminded

4 lost **7** bemused, faraway **8** distrait, dreaming, heedless, unseeing **9** forgetful, oblivious, unheeding, unmindful **10** abstracted, distracted, unnoticing **11** inattentive, inconscient, preoccupied, unconscious, unobserving **12** unperceiving

absent without leave

4 AWOL

absolute

4 full, pure, real, true **5** ideal, sheer, total, utter **6** actual, entire, simple **7** eternal, genuine, perfect, supreme, unmixed **8** autarkic, complete, despotic, flawless, infinite, outright, positive, ultimate, simplest, thorough, unflawed **9** arbitrary, autarchic, boundless, downright, embodying, imperious, masterful, sovereign, unalloyed, unlimited **10** autocratic, autonomous, consummate, impeccable, monocratic, tyrannical **11** categorical, dictatorial, domineering, fundamental, independent, unequivocal, unmitigated, unqualified **12** indefectible, indisputable, totalitarian, unrestrained, unrestricted **13** authoritarian, incontestable, unconditional

absolutely

5 fully **6** wholly **7** utterly **8** entirely **9** doubtless, perfectly **10** completely, definitely, positively, thoroughly **11** doubtlessly **13** unequivocally

absolution

6 pardon **7** amnesty, freeing, release **9** releasing, remission **10** letting off

11 exculpation, exoneration, forgiveness 12 dispensation

absolutism
9 Caesarism, despotism
12 dictatorship

absolve
4 free 5 clear, let go, remit, spare 6 acquit, excuse, exempt, let off, pardon 7 forgive, release, relieve, set free 8 dispense 9 discharge, exculpate, exonerate, vindicate

absorb
4 bear, blot 5 imbue, learn, sop up, use up 6 assume, embody, endure, engage, imbibe, infuse, ingest, soak up, sponge, suck up, take in, take up 7 acquire, consume, drink in, engross, immerse, involve, receive, sustain 8 permeate 9 preoccupy, transform 10 assimilate
11 incorporate

absorbed
4 deep, into, lost, rapt 6 intent 7 engaged, wrapped 8 caught up, immersed, involved 9 engrossed, wrapped up 10 captivated, fascinated 11 preoccupied

absorbing
9 arresting, consuming 10 engrossing, intriguing 11 captivating, fascinating, interesting 12 monopolizing, preoccupying

abstain
4 curb, deny, diet, fast, keep, pass, stop 5 avoid, forgo, spurn 6 abjure, eschew, give up, pass up, refuse, reject 7 decline, forbear, refrain 8 abnegate, forswear, hold back, keep from, renounce, swear off, teetotal, withhold 9 constrain, do without 11 deny oneself

abstemious
5 sober 6 strict 7 ascetic, austere, chaste, sparing 9 abstinent, continent, temperate 10 restrained 11 self-denying

abstinence
6 denial 7 fasting 8 chastity, sobriety

9 soberness 10 continence, self-denial, temperance 12 renunciation 13 self-restraint

abstract
5 brief, ideal 6 detach, digest, précis 7 epitome, neutral, outline, shorten, summary, utopian 8 academic, breviary, condense, detached, notional, separate, synopsis 9 disengage, summarize 10 abridgment, conceptual, conspectus, disconnect, dissociate, impersonal 11 appropriate, impractical, speculative, theoretical 12 condensation, hypothetical, transcendent 13 disinterested

abstracted
4 lost, rapt 6 absent, intent 7 bemused, faraway 8 absorbed, distrait, heedless 9 engrossed, oblivious, unheeding, unmindful, unminding, withdrawn 11 inattentive, inconscient, preoccupied, unconscious 12 absentminded

abstruse
4 deep 5 heavy 6 knotty, occult 7 complex 8 esoteric, hermetic, involved, profound 9 difficult, intricate, recondite 11 complicated

absurd
5 balmy, comic, crazy, droll, funny, inane, loony, potty, silly, wacky 6 insane 7 asinine, fatuous, foolish, idiotic 8 farcical 9 illogical, laughable, ludicrous 10 irrational, ridiculous 11 harebrained 12 preposterous, unreasonable

absurdity
5 farce, folly 7 inanity 8 insanity, nonsense 9 craziness, dottiness, silliness 11 foolishness, incongruity, witlessness 12 irrationality, ludicrousness, senselessness

abundance
6 bounty, excess, plenty, riches, wealth 9 affluence, profusion 10 lavishness; prosperity 11 prodigality **Scottish:** 5 routh

abundant
4 full, lush, rich, rife 5 ample, thick

abuse

6 filled, lavish, plenty 7 copious, crammed, crowded, liberal, profuse, replete 8 adequate, fruitful, generous, prolific 9 abounding, bounteous, bountiful, extensive, luxuriant, plenteous, plentiful 10 sufficient

abuse

3 mar 4 harm, hurt, rail 5 anger, decry, shame, spoil, wrong 6 damage, debase, deride, impair, injure, misuse, revile, vilify 7 calumny, corrupt, cursing, exploit, obloquy, oppress, outrage, pervert, profane, pollute 8 belittle, berating, derision, derogate, discount, disgrace, ill-treat, maltreat, mistreat, reviling, swearing 9 blaspheme, contumely, desecrate, disparage, dispraise, harshness, invective, manhandle, mishandle, persecute, profanity, vehemence 10 defamation, depreciate, impose upon, malignment, revilement, scurrility 11 disapproval 12 billingsgate, condemnation, denunciation, vilification, vituperation

abusive

5 dirty, harsh 6 odious 7 corrupt 8 scurrile 9 injurious, insulting, invective, offending, offensive, truculent 10 calumnious, defamatory, scurrilous 11 blasphemous, castigating, opprobrious 12 calumniating, contumelious, sharp-tongued, vituperative, vituperatory

abut

4 join, link 5 flank, touch, verge 6 adjoin, border, butt on 8 border on, neighbor 9 lie beside 11 butt against, communicate

abutting

4 next 6 beside, joined, next to 7 joining, verging 8 adjacent, next door, touching 9 adjoining, bordering, impinging 10 connecting, contiguous, juxtaposed 11 bordering on, coextensive, coterminous, neighboring 12 conterminous

abysm

see **abyss**

abysmal

4 deep, vast 7 endless 8 infinite, profound, unending, wretched 9 boundless, cavernous, plumbless, soundless, unplumbed 10 bottomless, fathomless, unmeasured 11 illimitable, measureless 12 immeasurable, unfathomable

abyss

3 pit 4 gulf, hell, hole, void 5 abysm, chasm, depth, gorge, hades, Sheol 6 Tophet 7 fissure, Gehenna, inferno 8 crevasse, deepness 9 perdition 10 underworld

academia

10 university 12 professoriat

academic

3 don 5 pupil, tutor 6 closet, fellow, master 7 bookish, learned, scholar, student 8 abstract, gownsman, lecturer, pedantic 9 professor, scholarly 10 scholastic 11 book-learned, conjectural, impractical, speculative, theoretical 12 conventional, hypothetical

academic period

4 term 7 quarter 8 semester 9 trimester

academy

6 lyceum 7 college, society 9 institute 10 prep school 12 conservatory

Academy Award winner

picture:

1927–28: 5 Wings
1928–29: 14 Broadway Melody
1929–30: 25 All Quiet on the Western Front
1930–31: 8 Cimarron
1931–32: 10 Grand Hotel
1932–33: 9 Cavalcade
1934: 18 It Happened One Night
1935: 17 Mutiny on the Bounty
1936: 16 The Great Ziegfeld
1937: 15 Life of Emile Zola
1938: 20 You Can't Take It with You
1939: 15 Gone with the Wind
1940: 7 Rebecca
1941: 19 How Green Was My Valley
1942: 10 Mrs. Miniver

1943: 10 Casablanca
1944: 10 Going My Way
1945: 11 Lost Weekend (The)
1946: 19 Best Years of Our Lives (The)
1947: 19 Gentleman's Agreement
1948: 6 Hamlet
1949: 14 All the King's Men
1950: 11 All About Eve
1951: 15 American in Paris (An)
1952: 19 Greatest Show on Earth (The)
1953: 18 From Here to Eternity
1954: 15 On the Waterfront
1955: 5 Marty
1956: 26 Around the World in Eighty Days
1957: 20 Bridge on the River Kwai (The)
1958: 4 Gigi
1959: 6 Ben-Hur
1960: 9 Apartment (The)
1961: 13 West Side Story
1962: 16 Lawrence of Arabia
1963: 8 Tom Jones
1964: 10 My Fair Lady
1965: 12 Sound of Music (The)
1966: 16 Man for All Seasons (A)
1967: 19 In the Heat of the Night
1968: 6 Oliver
1969: 14 Midnight Cowboy
1970: 6 Patton
1971: 16 French Connection (The)
1972: 9 Godfather (The)
1973: 5 Sting (The)
1974: 9 Godfather (Part Two)(The)
1975: 25 One Flew over the Cuckoo's Nest
1976: 5 Rocky
1977: 9 Annie Hall
1978: 10 Deer Hunter (The)
1979: 14 Kramer vs. Kramer
1980: 14 Ordinary People
1981: 14 Chariots of Fire
1982: 6 Gandhi
1983: 17 Terms of Endearment
1984: 7 Amadeus
1985: 11 Out of Africa
1986: 7 Platoon
1987: 11 Last Emperor (The)
1988: 7 Rain Man
1989: 16 Driving Miss Daisy
1990: 16 Dances with Wolves
1991: 17 Silence of the Lambs (The)
1992: 10 Unforgiven
1993: 14 Schindler's List
1994: 11 Forrest Gump
1995: 10 Braveheart
1996: 14 English Patient (The)
1997: 7 Titanic
1998: 17 Shakespeare in Love
1999: 14 American Beauty
2000: 9 Gladiator
2001: 13 Beautiful Mind (A)
2002: 7 Chicago
2003: 14 Lord of the Rings

actor:

1927–28: 8 Jannings (Emil)
1928–29: 6 Baxter (Warner)
1929–30: 6 Arliss (George)
1930–31: 9 Barrymore (Lionel)
1931–32: 5 Beery (Wallace), March (Fredric)
1932–33: 8 Laughton (Charles)
1934: 5 Gable (Clark)
1935: 8 McLaglen (Victor)
1936: 4 Muni (Paul)
1937: 5 Tracy (Spencer)
1938: 5 Tracy (Spencer)
1939: 5 Donat (Robert)
1940: 7 Stewart (James)
1941: 6 Cooper (Gary)
1942: 6 Cagney (James)
1943: 5 Lukas (Paul)
1944: 6 Crosby (Bing)
1945: 7 Milland (Ray)
1946: 5 March (Fredric)
1947: 6 Colman (Ronald)
1948: 7 Olivier (Laurence)
1949: 8 Crawford (Broderick)
1950: 6 Ferrer (José)
1951: 6 Bogart (Humphrey)
1952: 6 Cooper (Gary)
1953: 6 Holden (William)
1954: 6 Brando (Marlon)
1955: 8 Borgnine (Ernest)
1956: 7 Brynner (Yul)
1957: 8 Guinness (Alec)
1958: 5 Niven (David)
1959: 6 Heston (Charlton)
1960: 9 Lancaster (Burt)
1961: 6 Schell (Maximilian)
1962: 4 Peck (Gregory)
1963: 7 Poitier (Sidney)

1964: 8 Harrison (Rex)
1965: 6 Marvin (Lee)
1966: 8 Scofield (Paul)
1967: 7 Steiger (Rod)
1968: 9 Robertson (Cliff)
1969: 5 Wayne (John)
1970: 5 Scott (George C.)
1971: 7 Hackman (Gene)
1972: 6 Brando (Marlon)
1973: 6 Lemmon (Jack)
1974: 6 Carney (Art)
1975: 9 Nicholson (Jack)
1976: 5 Finch (Peter)
1977: 8 Dreyfuss (Richard)
1978: 6 Voight (Jon)
1979: 7 Hoffman (Dustin)
1980: 6 De Niro (Robert)
1981: 5 Fonda (Henry)
1982: 8 Kingsley (Ben)
1983: 6 Duvall (Robert)
1984: 7 Abraham (F. Murray)
1985: 4 Hurt (William)
1986: 6 Newman (Paul)
1987: 7 Douglas (Michael)
1988: 7 Hoffman (Dustin)
1989: 8 Day-Lewis (Daniel)
1990: 5 Irons (Jeremy)
1991: 7 Hopkins (Anthony)
1992: 6 Pacino (Al)
1993: 5 Hanks (Tom)
1994: 5 Hanks (Tom)
1995: 4 Cage (Nicholas)
1996: 4 Rush (Geoffrey)
1997: 9 Nicholson (Jack)
1998: 7 Benigni (Roberto)
1999: 6 Spacey (Kevin)
2000: 5 Crowe (Russell)
2001: 10 Washington (Denzel)
2002: 5 Brody (Adrien)
2003: 4 Penn (Sean)
actress:
1927–28: 6 Gaynor (Janet)
1928–29: 8 Pickford (Mary)
1929–30: 7 Shearer (Norma)
1930–31: 8 Dressler (Marie)
1931–32: 5 Hayes (Helen)
1932–33: 7 Hepburn (Katharine)
1934: 7 Colbert (Claudette)
1935: 5 Davis (Bette)
1936: 6 Rainer (Luise)
1937: 6 Rainer (Luise)
1938: 5 Davis (Bette)

1939: 5 Leigh (Vivien)
1940: 6 Rogers (Ginger)
1941: 8 Fontaine (Joan)
1942: 6 Garson (Greer)
1943: 5 Jones (Jennifer)
1944: 7 Bergman (Ingrid)
1945: 8 Crawford (Joan)
1946: 11 de Havilland (Olivia)
1947: 5 Young (Loretta)
1948: 5 Wyman (Jane)
1949: 11 de Havilland (Olivia)
1950: 8 Holliday (Judy)
1951: 5 Leigh (Vivien)
1952: 5 Booth (Shirley)
1953: 7 Hepburn (Audrey)
1954: 5 Kelly (Grace)
1955: 7 Magnani (Anna)
1956: 5 Bergman (Ingrid)
1957: 8 Woodward (Joanne)
1958: 7 Hayward (Susan)
1959: 8 Signoret (Simone)
1960: 6 Taylor (Elizabeth)
1961: 5 Loren (Sophia)
1962: 8 Bancroft (Anne)
1963: 4 Neal (Patricia)
1964: 7 Andrews (Julie)
1965: 8 Christie (Julie)
1966: 6 Taylor (Elizabeth)
1967: 7 Hepburn (Katharine)
1968: 7 Hepburn (Katharine)
       9 Streisand (Barbra)
1969: 5 Smith (Maggie)
1970: 7 Jackson (Glenda)
1971: 5 Fonda (Jane)
1972: 8 Minnelli (Liza)
1973: 7 Jackson (Glenda)
1974: 7 Burstyn (Ellen)
1975: 8 Fletcher (Louise)
1976: 7 Dunaway (Faye)
1977: 6 Keaton (Diane)
1978: 5 Fonda (Jane)
1979: 5 Field (Sally)
1980: 7 Spacek (Sissy)
1981: 7 Hepburn (Katharine)
1982: 6 Streep (Meryl)
1983: 8 MacLaine (Shirley)
1984: 5 Field (Sally)
1985: 4 Page (Geraldine)
1986: 6 Matlin (Marlee)
1987: 4 Cher
1988: 6 Foster (Jodie)
1989: 5 Tandy (Jessica)

1990: 5 Bates (Kathy)
1991: 6 Foster (Jodie)
1992: 8 Thompson (Emma)
1993: 6 Hunter (Holly)
1994: 5 Lange (Jessica)
1995: 8 Sarandon (Susan)
1996: 9 McDormand (Frances)
1997: 4 Hunt (Helen)
1998: 7 Paltrow (Gwyneth)
1999: 5 Swank (Hilary)
2000: 7 Roberts (Julia)
2001: 5 Berry (Halle)
2002: 6 Kidman (Nicole)
2003: 6 Theron (Charlize)

accede

3 let 5 admit, agree, allow, grant, yield
6 accept, assent, comply, concur, give
in, permit 7 agree to, approve, concede, consent 9 acquiesce, cooperate, subscribe

accelerando

6 faster 7 speed up 10 speeding up

accelerate

3 gun, rev 4 grow, roll 5 hurry, impel, rev up, speed 6 hasten, open
up, step up 7 quicken, speed up
8 expedite, go faster, increase 9 fast
track, gain speed 10 move faster,
peel rubber

acceleration

7 speedup 8 hurrying, spurring
9 hastening, revving up 10 increasing, quickening, speeding up,
stepping up 12 moving faster

accent

4 beat, lilt, tone 5 acute, grave, meter, pulse, throb 6 rhythm, stress,
weight 7 cadence 8 emphasis
9 diacritic, pulsation 10 inflection,
intonation
Irish: 6 brogue
Scottish: 4 burr
Southern: 5 drawl

accept

3 bow, buy, see 4 bear, gain, okay,
take 5 admit, adopt, agree, catch,
favor, go for, grasp, yield 6 accede,
admire, affirm, assent, endure, follow,
take in, take on 7 agree to, approve,

believe, receive, respect, swallow,
welcome 8 assent to, bear with,
hold with, live with, stand for, tolerate, tough out 9 acquiesce, agree
with, undertake 10 capitulate, comprehend, concur with, understand
11 acknowledge, countenance, subscribe to

acceptable

4 good, okay 6 decent, worthy
7 average, welcome 8 adequate, all
right, bearable, ordinary, passable,
pleasing, standard, suitable 9 endurable, tolerable 10 sufficient 11 commonplace, respectable, supportable
12 satisfactory 13 unexceptional,
unimpeachable

acceptably

4 well 5 amply, right 7 capably
8 properly, suitably 9 fittingly, tolerably 10 adequately, becomingly, fairly
well 11 competently 12 sufficiently
13 appropriately

acceptant

4 open 8 amenable, friendly,
swayable 9 favorable, receptive, recipient, welcoming 10 open-minded,
responsive 11 persuadable, persuasible, susceptible 13 influenceable

acceptation

4 gist 5 point, sense 6 import
7 meaning, message, purport 9 intention 10 intendment 12 significance, significancy 13 signification,
understanding

accepted

5 usual 6 common, normal, proper
7 correct, regular, routine 8 approved, everyday, expected, habitual,
ordinary, orthodox, received 9 customary 10 accustomed, recognized,
sanctioned 11 established, traditional 12 conventional

access

3 fit, way 4 adit, door, gust, pang,
path, road, turn 5 burst, entry, get
at, onset, route, sally, spell, throe
6 attack, avenue, entrée 7 contact,
flare-up, ingress, passage, seizure

8 approach, entrance, eruption, increase, outburst **9** admission, explosion **10** admittance

accessible

4 near, open **5** handy **6** public, usable **8** possible **9** available, operative, reachable **10** attainable, employable, obtainable **11** practicable **12** approachable, unrestricted

accession

4 rise **5** raise **8** addition, approach, increase, outburst, taking on **9** accretion, adherence, increment, induction **10** admittance, assumption, attainment, succession **11** acquisition **12** augmentation, inauguration

accessory

3 aid **4** aide, trim **5** extra, frill **6** helper **7** abettor, adjunct, fitting, insider, partner **8** addition, adjuvant, appendix **9** accretion, adornment, ancillary, appendage, assistant, associate, auxiliary, increment, secondary, tributary **10** accomplice, coincident, collateral, concurrent, decoration, incidental, subsidiary **11** appurtenant, concomitant, confederate, conspirator, subordinate, subservient **12** appurtenance, contributory **13** accompaniment, coconspirator, supplementary

accident

3 hap, lot **4** fate, luck, odds **5** fluke **6** chance, gamble, hazard, kismet, mishap **7** bad luck, destiny, fortune, lottery **8** calamity, casualty, fortuity, incident **9** adventure, mischance **10** misfortune **12** misadventure

accidental

3 odd **5** fluky **6** casual, chance, random **7** unmeant **8** by chance, careless **9** chromatic, dependent, extempore, impromptu, unplanned, unwitting **10** coincident, contingent, fortuitous, incidental, undesigned, unexpected, unforeseen, unintended, unpurposed **11** conditional, inadvertent **12** coincidental, nonessential, uncalculated **13** unintentional

acclaim

4 hail, clap, laud **5** cheer, éclat, exalt, extol, glory, honor, kudos, roose **6** homage, praise, salute **7** applaud, approve, commend, glorify, magnify, ovation, root for **8** applause, plaudits **10** compliment

acclimate

5 adapt **6** adjust, change, harden, season **7** toughen **9** condition, habituate

accolade

4 bays, fame **5** award, badge, honor, kudos **6** praise **7** laurels, tribute **8** approval **10** decoration **11** distinction

accommodate

3 fit **4** hold, rent, suit **5** adapt, alter, board, defer, favor, house, humor, lodge, put up, yield **6** adjust, attune, bestow, billet, change, encase, harbor, modify, oblige, please, submit, tailor, take in **7** cater to, conform, contain, enclose, furnish, indulge, quarter, receive, shelter **8** accustom, allow for, domicile **9** entertain, harmonize, integrate, reconcile **11** domiciliate, make room for

accommodating

7 amiable, helpful, willing **8** gracious, obliging **9** adaptable **10** hospitable, solicitous, thoughtful **11** considerate, cooperative

accommodations

4 digs, keep, room **5** hotel, motel **7** housing, lodging, shelter **8** lodgment, quarters **9** residence **12** room and board

accompaniment

4 back, mate **6** fellow, backup **7** adjunct, comrade, consort, partner **8** addition **9** accessory, associate, attendant, colleague, companion, corollary **10** assistance, complement, enrichment, equivalent, supplement **11** concomitant, enhancement **12** augmentation

accompany
 4 join 5 bring, guide, pilot 6 attend, convoy, escort, go with 7 combine, conduct, consort 8 chaperon, come with 9 associate 10 appear with, go together 11 perform with

accompanying
 8 incident 9 accessory, ancillary, attendant, attending, secondary 10 associated, coincident, collateral 11 concomitant

accomplice
 4 aide, ally 5 aider 6 flunky, helper, stooge 7 abettor, partner 9 accessory, assistant, associate 11 confederate, conspirator, subordinate 13 coconspirator

accomplish
 3 win 4 gain 5 reach, score 6 attain, effect, fulfil, rack up 7 achieve, execute, fulfill, perfect, pull off, realize, succeed 8 bring off, carry out, complete 9 discharge 10 bring about

accomplished
 4 able 5 adept 6 expert 7 skilled 8 finished, masterly, skillful, talented 9 perfected, practiced 10 proficient 11 beyond doubt

accomplishment
 3 act, art 4 deed, feat 5 craft, doing, skill 6 action, effort, finish, talent 7 ability, exploit 9 adeptness, expertise 10 attainment, capability, completion, expertness 11 achievement, acquirement, acquisition, proficiency

accord
 4 deal, fuse, give, jibe, pact 5 agree, award, blend, chime, fit in, grant, match, merge, tally, union 6 affirm, assent, concur, confer, treaty 7 compact, concert, concord, conform, empathy, harmony, rapport 8 affinity, coalesce, coincide, dovetail, sympathy 9 agreement, harmonize, reconcile, vouchsafe 10 attraction, conformity, consonance, correspond, solidarity 11 concordance 13 understanding

accordant
 8 agreeing 9 congruous, consonant 10 conforming, harmonious 13 correspondent

accordingly
 4 duly, ergo, then, thus 5 hence 9 therefore, thereupon 12 consequently

accost
 3 dog 4 call, dare, face, hail 5 annoy, cross, front, hound, worry 6 bother, call to 7 affront, apply to, bespeak, outface, outrage 8 approach, confront 9 challenge 10 buttonhole 11 memorialize

accouchement
 7 lying-in 8 childbed, delivery 10 childbirth 11 confinement, giving birth, parturition

account
 3 tab, use 4 bill, deem, note, rate, view 5 avail, basis, favor, score, story, track, value, worth 6 assess, client, esteem, reason, reckon, record, regard, report, repute 7 analyze, explain, expound, history, invoice, justify, recital, respect, service, utility, version 8 appraise, consider, customer, estimate 9 advantage, chronicle, narrative, probe into, rationale, reckoning, relevance, statement, valuation 10 admiration, estimation, exposition, importance, reputation, usefulness 11 consequence, distinction, explain away, explanation, performance, rationalize 13 consideration, justification
 book: 6 ledger

accountable
 6 liable 8 amenable 10 answerable 11 explainable, responsible

accounting
 11 bookkeeping

accoutre
 3 arm, rig 4 deck, gear 5 adorn, dress, equip, fix up, ready 6 attire, fit out, outfit, supply 7 appoint, furnish, prepare, provide, turn out 9 provision

accoutrement

3 kit 4 gear 6 outfit, tackle 7 regalia
8 tackling 9 accessory, apparatus,
equipment, machinery, trappings
10 provisions 11 furnishings, habiliments 12 appointments 13 paraphernalia

accredit

3 lay 4 okay 5 refer 6 assign, attest,
charge, credit, enable 7 approve, ascribe, certify, commend, empower,
endorse, license, warrant 8 sanction,
validate, vouch for 9 attribute, authorize, recognize, recommend 10 commission, credential

accretion

4 rise 5 raise 6 growth 7 buildup
8 addition, increase 9 accession, appendage, increment 10 attachment
11 enlargement 12 accumulation,
augmentation

accrue

4 grow 5 amass 6 gather, pile
up 7 build up, collect, compile
8 increase 10 accumulate, amalgamate 11 agglomerate

accumulate

4 heap, grow, mass, pile 5 add to,
amass, hoard, lay by, lay in, lay up,
stock, store 6 accrue, garner, gather,
pile up, rack up, roll up 7 acquire,
backlog, collect, compile, lay down,
stack up, store up 8 assemble, increase 9 stockpile

accumulation

4 bank, heap, mass, pile 5 hoard,
stock, store, trove 6 growth 7 buildup, reserve 8 increase 9 accretion,
amassment 10 collection 11 aggregation, enlargement 13 agglomeration

accumulative

6 heaped 7 growing 8 additive, ad-
ditory 9 summative 10 collective, increasing 11 aggregative 12 aug-
mentative

accuracy

8 veracity 9 certainty, exactness,
precision 10 definition, exactitude
11 correctness, preciseness
12 definiteness

accurate

4 just, nice, true 5 exact, right
6 actual, proper 7 certain, correct,
factual, precise 8 definite, reliable,
rigorous 9 authentic, error-free, errorless 10 dependable

accursed

4 vile 6 odious 7 hateful
8 damnable 9 abhorrent, execrable,
loathsome, offensive, repugnant, revolting 10 abominable, despicable,
detestable

accusation

3 rap 6 charge 9 complaint
10 allegation, indictment
12 denunciation
false: 7 calumny

accuse

3 tax 5 blame, brand 6 allege,
charge, delate, finger, impute, indict
7 arraign, ascribe, censure, impeach
8 admonish, denounce, reproach
9 criminate, criticize, inculpate, reprobate 10 denunciate 11 incriminate

accustom

3 use 4 wont 5 adapt, inure 6 adjust, harden, season 7 conform
9 habituate 11 acclimatize, familiarize

accustomed

3 set 5 usual 6 normal 7 chronic,
regular, routine 8 accepted, everyday, familiar, habitual, ordinary, standard 9 customary 10 habituated
11 commonplace, established, traditional 12 conventional

ace

3 bit, jot, pip, top 4 atom, hair, iota,
mite, star 5 crumb, minim, point,
score, speck 6 defeat, master, winner 7 whisker 8 molecule, particle
9 first rate, hole in one 11 hairbreadth, tennis score

ace and face card

7 natural 9 blackjack

acedia
6 apathy 7 boredom

acerbate
3 vex 5 anger, annoy, peeve
6 madden 7 incense, inflame
8 embitter, irritate 9 aggravate
10 exasperate

acerbic
4 acid, sour, tart 5 acrid, harsh,
rough, sharp 7 caustic, cutting,
satiric 8 stinging 9 acidulous, corrosive, sarcastic 10 astringent

acerbity
7 acidity, sarcasm 8 acrimony, asperity, sourness, tartness 9 harshness, roughness, surliness 10 bitterness, causticity

Achates' companion
6 Aeneas

ache
3 yen 4 hurt, long, pain, pang, pine,
pity, sigh 5 crave, smart, throb, yearn
6 hanker, hunger, stitch, suffer, thirst,
twinge 8 yearning 11 commiserate
Scottish: 6 stound

Acheron
5 Hades, river

achieve
3 get, win 4 gain 5 reach, score
6 attain, effect, finish, obtain, rack up,
secure 7 acquire, execute, fulfill, get
done, perform, realize, succeed
8 carry out, complete, conclude
9 actualize 10 accomplish

achievement
4 deed, feat 6 finish 7 exploit, success 10 attainment, completion
11 acquisition, tour de force

Achilles
adviser: 6 Nestor
companion: 9 Patroclus
father: 6 Peleus
horse: 7 Xanthus
lover: 7 Briseis
mother: 6 Thetis
slayer: 5 Paris
victim: 6 Hector
vulnerable part: 4 heel

aching
4 hurt, sore 6 in pain 7 hurtful, hurting, painful 8 yearning 9 disturbed
10 afflictive, distressed 13 compassionate

acicular
5 acute, peaky, piked, sharp
6 peaked, pointy, spiked 7 pointed

acid
4 sour, tart 5 acerb 7 acerbic, acetose, caustic 8 stinging 9 corrosive,
sarcastic, vitriolic
bleaching: 6 oxalic
fatty: 6 capric 7 caproic, stearic
8 caprylic
found in apples: 5 malic
found in cranberries: 7 benzoic
found in grapes: 8 tartaric
found in lemons: 6 citric
found in rhubarb: 6 oxalic
found in sour milk: 6 lactic
indicator: 6 litmus
kind: 5 amino, boric, iodic, malic,
oleic 6 acetic, bromic, formic, nitric,
oxalic, tannic 7 nitrous, silicic
8 carbolic, carbonic, muriatic, sulfuric
9 aqua regia 12 hydrochloric
neutralizer: 4 base 6 alkali
tanning: 6 tannic 8 catechin
vinegar: 6 acetic

acidulous
3 dry 4 sour, tart 5 acerb, harsh,
sharp 6 biting 7 acerbic, acetose,
cutting, piquant, pungent 9 sarcastic

Acis
lover: 7 Galatea
slayer: 10 Polyphemus

acknowledge
3 own 4 avow, deem, tell, view
5 admit, agree, allow, grant, let
on, own up 6 accede, accept, fess
up, reveal 7 concede, confess, declare, divulge, profess 8 announce,
consider, disclose, proclaim
9 recognize

acknowledgment
6 assent, avowal, credit, notice
9 admission 10 confession 11 affirmation, declaration, recognition

acme

3 cap, top 4 apex, peak 6 apogee, climax, summit, tiptop, vertex, zenith 8 capstone, pinnacle, ultimate 9 high point 10 perfection 11 culmination

acorn sprouter

3 oak

acoustic

5 aural 6 audile 8 auditory 9 unplugged

acquaint

4 clue, tell, warn 6 advise, fill in, inform, notify, orient, reveal, wise up 7 apprise, divulge, present 8 accustom, disclose 9 enlighten, habituate, introduce 11 familiarize

acquaintance

4 mate 5 amigo, crony, grasp 6 friend 7 comrade, contact 9 associate, colleague, companion 10 cognizance, experience 11 familiarity

acquainted

6 versed 7 abreast, in touch 8 familiar, informed, up-to-date 9 au courant 10 conversant

acquiesce

3 bow, yes 5 agree, allow, bow to, yield 6 accede, accept, assent, comply, concur, give in, submit 7 consent, go along 9 reconcile, subscribe

acquiescence

6 assent 7 consent 8 giving in, yielding 9 deference 10 acceptance, compliance, conformity, submission 11 resignation

acquiescent

6 docile 7 passive 8 resigned, yielding 10 submissive 11 unresistant, unresisting 12 nonresistant, nonresisting

acquire

3 add, buy, get, win 4 earn, form, gain, land 5 amass, annex 6 garner, obtain, pick up, secure 7 bring in, collect, develop, procure 10 accumulate

acquirement

8 addition 9 accretion 11 acquisition

acquisition

4 gain 5 prize 7 winning 8 addition, learning, property, purchase 9 accretion

acquisitive

5 eager, itchy 6 grabby, greedy 8 covetous, desirous, grasping 10 avaricious

acquit

3 act 4 bear, free 5 carry, clear, let go 6 behave, deport, let off 7 absolve, comport, conduct, perform, release, set free 8 liberate 9 discharge, exculpate, exonerate, vindicate

acres

4 area, land 5 lands 6 estate 7 demesne, expanse, holding 8 property

acrid

4 acid, sour 5 harsh, nasty, sharp 6 biting, bitter 7 austere, burning, caustic, cutting, pungent 8 stinging 9 trenchant 10 astringent, irritating 11 acrimonious

acrimonious

3 mad 5 angry, cross, irate, sharp, testy 6 biting, bitter, cranky, ireful 7 acerbic, caustic, cutting 9 indignant, irascible, rancorous 11 belligerent, contentious, quarrelsome

acrimony

5 anger, spite 6 animus, malice, rancor 7 ill will 8 acerbity, asperity, mordancy 9 animosity, antipathy, harshness, virulence 10 bitterness 11 malevolence

Acrisius

daughter: 5 Danaë
slayer: 7 Perseus

acrobat

7 gymnast 9 aerialist, trapezist 11 funambulist

across

4 over 6 beyond 7 athwart
12 transversely
prefix: 5 trans

act

3 law, run 4 bear, bill, deed, fake, feat,
mime, play, pose, sham, work 5 bluff,
feign, front, put-on, serve, stunt 6 affect, appear, behave, shtick 7 exploit,
operate, perform, portray, pretend,
routine, statute 8 function, pretense,
simulate 9 officiate 10 masquerade
11 counterfeit, impersonate

acting

6 pro tem 7 interim, playing 9 ad interim, dramatics, imitating, portrayal,
temporary 10 pro tempore 12 entertaining

action

4 case, deed, move, step, stir, suit,
work 5 battle, bustle 6 battle, bustle,
combat 7 lawsuit, process, service
8 activity, behavior, conflict, fighting,
function 9 execution, operation, procedure 10 engagement, proceeding
11 performance

action painting

7 tachism

activate

4 stir, wake 5 rally, rouse, set up,
waken 6 arouse, awaken, call up,
turn on 8 energize, mobilize, motivate, vitalize 9 stimulate

active

4 busy, live, spry 5 agile, alert,
alive, brisk, going 6 at work, in play,
lively, moving 7 driving, dynamic,
flowing, running, working 8 animated, bustling, emitting, erupting,
spirited, vigorous 9 effective, energetic, operating, operative, sprightly
11 functioning, industrious 12 enterprising

activity

6 action, bustle, motion 7 process,
pursuit, venture 8 exercise, exertion
10 exercising, liveliness 11 undertaking

actor

4 mime, star 5 mimic 6 mummer,
player 7 trouper 8 thespian 9 performer 11 participant 12 impersonator

name: 3 Cox (Wally), Fox (James,
Michael J.), Lee (Bruce), Lom (Her-
bert), Mix (Tom), Ray (Aldo) 4 Alda
(Alan, Robert), Bean (Orson), Blue
(Ben), Bond (Ward), Caan (James),
Cage (Nicholas), Cobb (Lee J.),
Coco (James), Culp (Robert), Dean
(James), Depp (Johnny), Dern
(Bruce), Duff (Howard), Egan (Rich-
ard), Falk (Peter), Ford (Glenn, Harri-
son), Foxx (Redd), Geer (Will), Gere
(Richard), Grey (Joel), Hill (Arthur),
Hope (Bob), Hurt (John, William),
Ives (Burl), Kaye (Danny), Kean (Ed-
mund), Keel (Howard), Ladd (Alan),
Lahr (Bert), Lord (Jack), Lowe (Rob),
Lunt (Alfred), Marx (Chico, Groucho,
Harpo, Zeppo), Muni (Paul), Ngor
(Haing S.), Peck (Gregory), Penn
(Sean), Pitt (Brad), Raft (George),
Roth (Tim), Ryan (Robert), Shaw
(Robert), Tati (Jacques), Tone (Fran-
chot), Torn (Rip), Tune (Tommy),
Wahl (Ken), Webb (Clifton, Jack),
Wynn (Ed, Keenan), York (Michael)
5 Adler (Luther), Allen (Fred, Tim,
Woody), Arkin (Adam, Alan), Asner
(Ed), Autry (Gene), Ayres (Lew),
Bacon (Kevin), Barry (Gene), Bates
(Alan), Beery (Wallace), Benny
(Jack), Berle (Milton), Boone (Rich-
ard), Booth (Edwin), Boyer (Charles),
Brand (Neville), Burns (George),
Caine (Michael), Candy (John),
Chase (Chevy), Clift (Montgomery),
Cosby (Bill), Dafoe (Willem), Davis
(Clifton, Ossie, Sammy Jr.), Delon
(Alain), Donat (Robert), Evans (Mau-
rice), Ewell (Tom), Finch (Peter),
Firth (Colin, Peter), Flynn (Errol),
Fonda (Henry, Peter), Franz (Den-
nis), Gabin (Jean), Gable (Clark),
Gould (Elliot), Grant (Cary, Hugh),
Gwenn (Edmund), Hanks (Tom),
Hardy (Oliver), Hauer (Rutger),
Hawke (Ethan), Hayes (Gabby),

Irons (Jeremy), Jaffe (Sam), Jones (Dean, James Earl, Tommy Lee), Kazan (Elia), Keach (Stacy), Keith (Brian, David), Kelly (Gene), Kiley (Richard), Kline (Kevin), Kotto (Yaphet), Lamas (Fernando, Lorenzo), Lanza (Mario), Lewis (Jerry, Richard), Lloyd (Harold), Lorre (Peter), Lukas (Paul), Lynde (Paul), March (Fredric), Mason (James), McCoy (Tim), Mills (John), Mineo (Sal), Moore (Dudley, Roger, Victor), Neill (Sam), Nimoy (Leonard), Niven (David), Nolte (Nick), Olmos (Edward James), O'Neal (Patrick, Ryan), Payne (John), Perry (Luke, Matthew), Pesci (Joe), Power (Tyrone), Price (Vincent), Pryce (Jonathan), Quaid (Dennis, Randy), Quayle (Anthony), Quinn (Aidan, Anthony), Rains (Claude), Reeve (Christopher), Scott (Campbell, George C., Randolph), Segal (George), Sheen (Charlie, Martin), Smits (Jimmy), Stack (Robert), Stamp (Terence), Sydow (Max von), Tracy (Spencer), Wayne (John), Wilde (Cornel), Wills (Chill), Woods (James), Young (Gig, Robert) 6 Abbott (Bud), Albert (Eddie), Ameche (Don), Arness (James), Backus (Jim), Balsam (Martin), Barker (Lex), Baxter (Warner), Beatty (Ned, Warren), Begley (Ed), Blades (Ruben), Bogart (Humphrey), Bolger (Ray), Brando (Marlon), Brooks (Albert, Mel), Burton (Richard), Caesar (Sid), Cagney (James), Cantor (Eddie), Cariou (Len), Carney (Art), Carrey (Jim), Carvey (Dana), Chaney (Lon), Cleese (John), Coburn (Charles, James), Colman (Ronald), Conrad (Robert, William), Conway (Tim, Tom), Coogan (Jackie), Cooper (Gary), Cotten (Joseph), Coward (Noël), Crabbe (Buster), Crenna (Richard), Cronyn (Hume), Crosby (Bing), Cruise (Tom), Culkin (Macaulay), Curtis (Tony), Dailey (Dan), Dalton (Timothy), Danson (Ted), Danton (Ray), Darren (James), De Niro (Robert), de Sica (Vittorio), De Vito (Danny), Dillon (Matt), Downey (Robert), Dulea (Keir), Duryea (Dan), Duvall (Robert), Ferrer (José, Mel), Fields (W.C.), Finney (Albert), Garcia (Andy), Garner (James), Gibson (Hoot, Mel), Glover (Danny), Graves (Peter), Greene (Lorne), Grodin (Charles), Harris (Ed, Richard), Harvey (Laurence), Hayden (Sterling), Heflin (Van), Heston (Charlton), Hingle (Pat), Holden (Bill), Hopper (Dennis, William), Howard (Leslie, Ron, Trevor), Hudson (Rock), Hunter (Jeffrey, Tab), Huston (John, Walter), Hutton (Jim, Timothy), Irving (Henry), Jacobi (Derek, Lou), Jagger (Dean), Keaton (Buster, Michael), Keitel (Harvey), Kilmer (Val), Knotts (Don), Landau (Martin), Landon (Michael), Laurel (Stan), Lemmon (Jack), Liotta (Ray), Lugosi (Bela), MacRae (Gordon), Malden (Karl), Martin (Dean, Steve), Marvin (Lee), Massey (Raymond), Mature (Victor), McCrea (Joel), Meeker (Ralph), Menjou (Adolphe), Mifune (Toshiro), Modine (Matthew), Morley (Robert), Mostel (Zero), Murphy (Audie, Eddie), Murray (Bill, Don), Neeson (Liam), Nelson (Ozzie), Newley (Anthony), Newman (Paul), O'Brian (Hugh), O'Brien (Edmund, Pat), Oldman (Gary), O'Toole (Peter), Pacino (Al), Parker (Fess), Poston (Tom), Powell (Dick), Reeves (Keanu, Steve), Reiner (Carl, Rob), Reiser (Paul), Rennie (Michael), Ritter (John, Tex), Rogers (Roy, Wayne, Will), Romero (Cesar), Rooney (Mickey), Rourke (Mickey), Schell (Maximilian), Seagal (Steven), Sharif (Omar), Slezak (Walter), Snipes (Wesley), Spacey (Kevin), Spader (James), Swayze (Patrick), Taylor (Robert, Rod), Thomas (Danny, Richard), Turpin (Ben), Vallee (Rudy), Vaughn (Robert), Voight (Jon), Wagner (Robert), Walker (Robert), Warden (Jack), Wayans (Damon, Keenen Ivory), Weaver (Dennis, Fritz), Welles (Orson), Werner (Oskar), Wilder (Gene), Willis (Bruce) 7 Abraham (F. Murray),

Andrews (Dana), Astaire (Fred), Aykroyd (Dan), Baldwin (Alec, Daniel, Stephen, William), Bellamy (Ralph), Bogarde (Dirk), Branagh (Kenneth), Bridges (Beau, Jeff, Lloyd), Bronson (Charles), Brosnan (Pierce), Brynner (Yul), Burbage (Richard), Bushman (Francis X.), Buttons (Red), Calhern (Louis), Calhoun (Rory), Cameron (Rod), Carroll (Leo G.), Chaplin (Charlie), Clooney (George), Connery (Sean), Connors (Chuck), Conried (Hans), Costner (Kevin), Crystal (Billy), Daniels (Jeff), da Silva (Howard), DeLuise (Dom), Dennehy (Brian), Donahue (Troy), Donlevy (Brian), Douglas (Kirk, Melvyn, Michael, Paul), Dreyfuss (Richard), Durante (Jimmy), Edwards (Vince), Feldman (Marty), Fiennes (Ralph), Freeman (Morgan), Garrick (David), Gazzara (Ben), Gielgud (John), Gleason (Jackie), Goodman (John), Gossett (Lou), Grammer (Kelsey), Granger (Farley, Stewart), Guinness (Alec), Hackman (Gene), Henreid (Paul), Hoffman (Dustin), Homolka (Oscar), Hopkins (Anthony), Hoskins (Bob), Janssen (David), Johnson (Ben, Don, Van), Jourdan (Louis), Jurgens (Curt), Karloff (Boris), Kennedy (Arthur, George), Klugman (Jack), Lawford (Peter), Leonard (Robert Sean, Sheldon), Lithgow (John), MacLane (Barton), Maharis (George), Mathers (Jerry), Matthau (Walter), McCarey (Leo), McGavin (Darren), McQueen (Steve), Milland (Ray), Mitchum (Robert), Montand (Yves), Navarro (Ramon), Newhart (Bob), O'Connor (Carroll, Donald), Olivier (Laurence), Palance (Jack), Paulsen (Pat), Peppard (George), Perkins (Anthony), Pickens (Slim), Pidgeon (Walter), Poitier (Sidney), Preston (Robert), Randall (Tony), Redford (Robert), Rickman (Alan), Robards (Jason), Robbins (Tim), Robeson (Paul), Roberts (Pernell, Tony), Sanders (George), Savalas (Telly), Scourby (Alexander), Selleck (Tom), Sellers (Peter),

Shatner (William), Shepard (Sam), Silvers (Phil), Sinatra (Frank), Skelton (Red), Skinner (Otis), Steiger (Rod), Stewart (James, Patrick), Stooges (Three), Tamblyn (Russ), Ustinov (Peter), Van Dyke (Dick, Jerry), Wallach (Eli), Widmark (Richard), Wilding (Michael), Winters (Jonathan), Woolley (Monty) **8** Banderas (Antonio), Barrault (Jean-Louis), Basehart (Richard), Belmondo (Jean-Paul), Berenger (Tom), Blackmer (Sidney), Borgnine (Ernest), Buchanan (Edgar), Buchholz (Horst), Chandler (Jeff), Costello (Lou), Crawford (Broderick, Michael), Cummings (Robert), Day-Lewis (Daniel), DiCaprio (Leonardo), Eastwood (Clint), Forsythe (John), Garfield (John), Goldblum (Jeff), Griffith (Andy), Harrison (Noel, Rex), Hemmings (David), Holbrook (Hal), Holloway (Stanley), Houseman (John), Jannings (Emil), Kingsley (Ben), Langella (Frank), Laughton (Charles), Marshall (E.G., Herbert), McDowall (Roddy), McDowell (Malcolm), McLaglen (Victor), Meredith (Burgess), Rathbone (Basil), Redgrave (Michael), Reynolds (Burt), Ritchard (Cyril), Robinson (Edward G.), Sarrazin (Michael), Scofield (Paul), Seinfeld (Jerry), Stallone (Sylvester), Stroheim (Erich von), Sullivan (Barry), Travolta (John), Turturro (John), Van Damme (Jean-Claude), Von Sydow (Max), Whitmore (James), Williams (Robin) **9** Amsterdam (Morey), Barrymore (John, Lionel), Brandauer (Klaus Maria), Broderick (Matthew), Carnovsky (Morris), Carradine (David, John, Keith, Robert), Courtenay (Tom), Depardieu (Gérard), Fairbanks (Douglas), Fishburne (Larry), Franciosa (Anthony), Hardwicke (Cedric), Harrelson (Woody), Hyde-White (Wilfrid), Lancaster (Burt), MacMurray (Fred), Malkovich (John), Montalban (Ricardo), Nicholson (Jack), Pleasance (Donald), Robertson (Cliff, Dale), Strasberg (Lee),

Tarantino (Quentin), Valentino (Rudolph), Zimbalist (Efrem) **10** Fitzgerald (Barry), Hasselhoff (David), Montgomery (Robert), Richardson (Ralph), Sutherland (Donald, Kiefer), Washington (Denzel) **11** Chamberlain (Richard), Greenstreet (Sydney), Mastroianni (Marcello), Trintignant (Jean-Louis) **13** Kristofferson (Kris)

actor's
quest: 4 part, role
signal: 3 cue

actress
3 Bow (Clara), Cox (Courtney), Day (Doris), Dee (Ruby, Sandra), Dru (Joanne), Gam (Rita), Loy (Myrna), May (Elaine), Rae (Charlotte) **4** Ball (Lucille), Bara (Theda), Barr (Roseanne), Cass (Peggy), Cher, Coca (Imogene), Cruz (Penelope), Dahl (Arlene), Daly (Tyne), Dern (Laura), Diaz (Cameron), Dors (Diana), Down (Lesley-Ann), Duke (Patty), Duse (Eleonora), Eden (Barbara), Foch (Nina), Garr (Teri), Gish (Dorothy, Lillian), Grey (Jennifer), Gwyn (Nell), Hawn (Goldie), Holm (Celeste), Hunt (Helen, Linda, Marsha), Hurt (Mary Beth), Hyer (Martha), Ivey (Judith), Kahn (Madeline), Kerr (Deborah), Lake (Veronica), Lisi (Virna), Main (Marjorie), Mayo (Virginia), Neal (Patricia), Olin (Lena), Page (Geraldine), Raye (Martha), Rigg (Diana), Ross (Diana, Katharine), Rush (Barbara), Ryan (Meg, Peggy), Shue (Elisabeth), Weld (Tuesday), West (Mae), Wood (Natalie, Peggy), Wray (Fay), York (Susannah) **5** Adams (Maude), Aimee (Anouk), Allen (Joan, Gracie, Karen), Alley (Kirstie), Arden (Eve), Astor (Mary), Bates (Kathy), Berry (Halle), Black (Karen), Bloom (Claire), Blyth (Ann), Booth (Shirley), Brice (Fanny), Britt (May), Bruce (Virginia), Buzzi (Ruth), Caron (Leslie), Close (Glenn), Crain (Jeanne), Danes (Claire), Davis (Bette, Geena, Judy), Dench (Judi), Derek (Bo), Dunne (Irene), Eggar (Samantha),

Evans (Edith), Falco (Edie), Field (Sally), Fonda (Bridget, Jane), Gabor (Eva, Zsa Zsa), Garbo (Greta), Gless (Sharon), Grant (Lee), Greer (Jane), Grier (Pam), Hagen (Uta), Hasso (Signe), Hayek (Salma), Hayes (Helen), Heche (Anne), Henie (Sonja), Howes (Sally Ann), Jones (Cherry, Jennifer, Shirley), Kazan (Lainie), Kelly (Grace, Patsy), Kurtz (Swoosie), Lahti (Christine), Lange (Hope, Jessica), Leigh (Janet, Jennifer Jason, Vivien), Lenya (Lotte), Lewis (Juliette), Loren (Sophia), Mason (Marsha, Pamela), Meara (Anne), Miles (Sarah, Vera), Moore (Demi, Julianne, Mary Tyler, Terry), North (Sheree), Novak (Kim), O'Hara (Maureen), Olson (Nancy), O'Neal (Tatum), Perez (Rosie), Picon (Molly), Pitts (Zasu), Reese (Della), Ricci (Christina), Roman (Ruth), Ruehl (Mercedes), Ryder (Winona), Saint (Eva Marie), Scott (Lizbeth, Martha), Shire (Talia), Smith (Alexis, Maggie), Stone (Sharon), Storm (Gale), Swank (Hilary), Tandy (Jessica), Terry (Ellen), Tomei (Marisa), Tyler (Liv), Tyson (Cicely), Watts (Naomi), Welch (Raquel), Wiest (Dianne), Wyatt (Jane), Wyman (Jane), Young (Sean, Loretta) **6** Adjani (Isabelle), Angeli (Pier), Arthur (Beatrice, Jean), Ashley (Elizabeth), Bacall (Lauren), Bardot (Brigitte), Barkin (Ellen), Barrie (Wendy), Baxter (Anne), Bening (Annette), Bergen (Candice, Polly), Bisset (Jacqueline), Blaine (Vivian), Brooks (Louise), Bujold (Genevieve), Butler (Brett), Cannon (Dyan), Carter (Dixie, Lynda, Nell), Cooper (Gladys), Crouse (Lindsay), Curtin (Jane), Curtis (Jamie Lee), Danner (Blythe), Davies (Marion), Delaney (Dana), Del Rio (Dolores), Dennis (Sandy), Diller (Phyllis), Draper (Ruth), Dumont (Margaret), Duncan (Sandy), Durbin (Deanna), Duvall (Shelley), Ekberg (Anita), Ekland (Britt), Fabray (Nanette), Farmer (Frances), Farrow (Mia), Feldon (Barbara), Fisher (Carrie), Foster (Jodie),

Garner (Peggy Ann), Garson (Greer), Gaynor (Mitzi), Gordon (Ruth), Grable (Betty), Grimes (Tammy), Hannah (Daryl), Harlow (Jean), Harper (Jessica, Tess, Valerie), Harris (Barbara, Julie, Rosemary), Hedren (Tippi), Hiller (Wendy), Hunter (Holly, Kim), Hussey (Ruth), Huston (Anjelica), Hutton (Betty), Irving (Amy), Keaton (Diane), Keeler (Ruby), Kidman (Nicole), Kinski (Nastassja), Knight (Shirley), Lamarr (Hedy), Lamour (Dorothy), Lasser (Louise), Laurie (Piper), Lillie (Beatrice), Louise (Tina), Lupino (Ida), MacRae (Sheila), Malone (Dorothy), Martin (Mary), Matlin (Marlee), McGraw (Ali), Merkel (Una), Merman (Ethel), Midler (Bette), Miller (Ann), Mirren (Helen), Monroe (Marilyn), Moreau (Jeanne), Moreno (Rita), Oberon (Merle), O'Brien (Margaret), Oliver (Edna May), Palmer (Lili), Paquin (Anna), Parker (Eleanor, Mary-Louise, Sarah Jessica, Suzy), Peters (Bernadette), Powers (Stephanie), Prowse (Juliet), Rainer (Luise), Rashad (Phylicia), Remick (Lee), Ritter (Thelma), Rivera (Chita), Rogers (Ginger), Scales (Prunella), Seberg (Jean), Sidney (Sylvia), Somers (Suzanne), Sommer (Elke), Spacek (Sissy), Streep (Meryl), Taylor (Elizabeth), Temple (Shirley), Theron (Charlize), Thomas (Marlo), Tiffin (Pamela), Tomlin (Lily), Turner (Kathleen, Lana), Walker (Nancy), Warren (Lesley Ann), Watson (Emily), Weaver (Sigourney), Wilson (Marie), Winger (Debra), Wright (Teresa), Wynter (Dana) **7** Allyson (June), Andress (Ursula), Andrews (Julie), Aniston (Jennifer), Bassett (Angela), Bennett (Constance, Joan), Bergman (Ingrid), Binoche (Juliette), Blethyn (Brenda), Buckley (Betty), Bullock (Sandra), Burnett (Carol), Burstyn (Ellen), Campbell (Mrs. Patrick), Colbert (Claudette), Collins (Joan, Pauline), Cornell (Katherine), Cushman (Charlotte), Darnell (Linda), DeCarlo (Yvonne), Deneuve (Catherine), Dukakis (Olympia), Dunaway (Faye),

Dunnock (Mildred), Fawcett (Farrah), Fleming (Rhonda), Fricker (Brenda), Gardner (Ava), Garland (Judy), Gingold (Hermione), Goddard (Paulette), Grahame (Gloria), Grayson (Kathryn), Hayward (Susan), Heckart (Eileen), Hepburn (Audrey, Katharine), Hershey (Barbara), Jackson (Anne, Glenda, Kate), Langtry (Lillie), Learned (Michael), Lombard (Carole), MacGraw (Ali), Madonna, Magnani (Anna), Mangano (Silvana), McGuire (Dorothy), McKenna (Siobhan), McQueen (Butterfly), Meadows (Audrey, Jayne), Mimieux (Yvette), Miranda (Carmen), Mulgrew (Kate), Natwick (Mildred), Parsons (Estelle), Perlman (Rhea), Perrine (Valerie), Plummer (Amanda), Podesta (Rosanna), Portman (Natalie), Roberts (Julia), Russell (Jane, Rosalind, Theresa), Scacchi (Greta), Sevigny (Chloë), Shearer (Norma), Shields (Brooke), Siddons (Sarah), Simmons (Jean), Sorvino (Mira), Sothern (Ann), Stevens (Connie, Stella), Stritch (Elaine), Swanson (Gloria), Swinton (Tilda), Thaxter (Phyllis), Thurman (Uma), Tierney (Gene), Ullmann (Liv), Winfrey (Oprah), Winslet (Kate), Winters (Shelley), Withers (Jane), Woodard (Alfre) **8** Anderson (Judith, Loni, Melissa Sue), Arquette (Patricia, Rosanna), Ashcroft (Peggy), Bancroft (Anne), Bankhead (Tallulah), Basinger (Kim), Blondell (Joan), Byington (Spring), Caldwell (Zoe), Channing (Carol, Stockard), Charisse (Cyd), Christie (Julie), Crawford (Joan), DeMornay (Rebecca), Dewhurst (Colleen), Dietrich (Marlene), Dressler (Marie), Fletcher (Louise), Fontaine (Joan), Fontanne (Lynn), Goldberg (Whoopi), Griffith (Melanie), Hayworth (Rita), Holliday (Judy), Lansbury (Angela), Lawrence (Gertrude), Leachman (Cloris), Leighton (Margaret), Lindfors (Viveca), Lockhart (June), Lovelace (Linda), MacLaine (Shirley), McDaniel (Hattie),

Mercouri (Melina), Minnelli (Liza), Nelligan (Kate), Neuwirth (Bebe), O'Donnell (Rosie), Pfeiffer (Michelle), Pickford (Mary), Prentiss (Paula), Redgrave (Lynn, Vanessa), Reynolds (Debbie), Roseanne, Rowlands (Gena), Sarandon (Susan), Shepherd (Cybill), Signoret (Simone), Stanwyck (Barbara), Straight (Beatrice), Sullavan (Margaret), Talmadge (Norma), Thompson (Emma, Sada), Van Doren (Mamie), Williams (Esther), Woodward (Joanne) **9** Alexander (Jane), Barrymore (Drew, Ethel), Bernhardt (Sarah), Blanchett (Cate), Cardinale (Claudia), Christian (Linda), Clayburgh (Jill), Dandridge (Dorothy), DeGeneres (Ellen), Dickinson (Angie), Fairchild (Morgan), Henderson (Florence), Kellerman (Sally), Mansfield (Jayne), McDonnell (Mary), Moorehead (Agnes), O'Sullivan (Maureen), Pleshette (Suzanne), Plowright (Joan), Schneider (Romy), Singleton (Penny), Stapleton (Jean, Maureen), Strasberg (Susan), Streisand (Barbra), Struthers (Sally), Thorndike (Sybil), Vera-Ellen, Zellweger (Renée) **10** Ann-Margret, Lanchester (Elsa), Montgomery (Elizabeth), Richardson (Miranda, Natasha), Rossellini (Isabella), Rutherford (Margaret), Tushingham (Rita) **11** de Havilland (Olivia), McCambridge (Mercedes), Riefenstahl (Leni), Silverstone (Alicia), Steenburgen (Mary) **12** Bonham-Carter (Helena), Lollabrigida (Gina), Mastrantonio (Mary Elizabeth)

actual
4 hard, live, real, true **5** exact **6** extant, living **7** certain, current, factual, genuine **8** absolute, bona fide, concrete, definite, existent, existing, material, physical, positive, tangible **9** authentic, objective **10** legitimate, phenomenal, undeniable **12** indisputable

actuality
4 fact **5** being, truth **7** reality **9** existence, substance **10** embodiment **11** incarnation, materiality

actually
4 very **5** truly **6** indeed, in fact, really **7** de facto, no doubt **9** genuinely, in reality, veritably **10** absolutely

actuate
4 move, spur, stir **5** drive, impel, rouse **6** arouse, excite, propel, set off, turn on **7** provoke, trigger **8** activate, energize, mobilize, motivate, vitalize

act up
5 cut up **7** show off **9** misbehave **11** misfunction

acumen
3 wit **6** acuity, vision, wisdom **7** insight **8** keenness **9** acuteness, sharpness **10** astuteness, perception, shrewdness **11** discernment, penetration, percipience **12** perspicacity

acute
4 dire, keen **5** sharp **6** urgent **7** crucial, exigent, intense, pointed **8** critical, incisive, piercing, shooting, stabbing **9** knifelike, observant, trenchant **10** perceptive **11** penetrating, quick-witted, sharp-witted

ad ____
3 hoc, lib, rem **7** hominem, interim, nauseam **9** infinitum

adage
3 saw **4** rule **5** axiom, maxim, motto **6** byword, saying, truism **7** proverb **8** aphorism, apothegm

adagio
4 slow **5** tempo

Adah
husband: **4** Esau **6** Lamech
son: **5** Jabal, Jubal **7** Eliphaz

Adam
grandson: **4** Enos **5** Enoch
rib: **3** Eve
son: **4** Abel, Cain, Seth
wife: **3** Eve **6** Lilith

Adam ____
4 Bede **5** Smith

adamant
3 set **4** firm, hard **5** rigid, stiff, stone, tough **6** flinty **8** immobile, obdurate,

resolute **9** immovable, unbending, unswaying **10** determined, inflexible, unbendable, unyielding **11** unbreakable

adapt

3 fit **4** suit **5** alter, shape, yield **6** adjust, change, modify, revise, square, tailor **7** arrange, conform, remodel **9** acclimate, habituate, reconcile **11** acclimatize, accommodate

adaptable

6 mobile, pliant, supple **7** ductile, plastic, pliable **8** flexible, moldable **9** alterable, malleable, versatile **10** adjustable, modifiable **11** conformable

adaptation

6 change **8** revision **9** reworking **10** adjustment, alteration **12** modification

ad astra per _____

6 aspera

add

3 sum, tot **4** cast, foot, join, tote **5** affix, annex, count, tally, total, unite **6** append, attach, figure, reckon, tack on, take on **7** augment, compute, count up, enlarge, improve, include **8** compound, increase, totalize **9** build onto, calculate **10** supplement

added

3 new **4** else, more **5** extra, fresh, other **7** another, farther, further **8** appended **9** accessory, increased **10** additional **13** supplementary

addendum

5 extra, rider **8** addition **10** supplement

adder

5 snake, viper **10** calculator **12** hognose snake

addict

3 fan, nut **4** bias, buff **5** hound, lover **6** abuser, devote, junkie, zealot **7** booster, devotee, fanatic, groupie, habitué **9** habituate, surrender **10** aficionado, enthusiast

addition

4 plus, rise **5** annex, extra, raise, rider **7** accrual, adjunct **8** addendum, appendix, increase **9** accession, accessory, accretion, extension, increment **10** supplement **11** enlargement **12** appurtenance, augmentation

additional

see **added**

additionally

3 too **4** also, more, then **5** again **6** as well **7** addedly, besides, further **8** likewise, moreover **9** along with **11** furthermore

additive

5 extra **8** extender **9** summative, substance

addle

5 mix up, spoil **6** muddle, puzzle **7** confuse, fluster, nonplus, perplex **8** befuddle, bewilder, confound, distract, throw off **9** dumbfound

add-on

7 adjunct **9** accessory **11** enhancement

address

3 aim, air, set, URL **4** hail, send, tact, talk **5** apply, court, grace, greet, level, place, point, poise, remit, route, skill, speak, treat **6** call to, devote, direct, pursue, relate, salute, speech **7** bearing, consign, deliver, forward, know-how, lecture, speak to, write to **8** appeal to, approach, converse, deal with, deftness, delivery, demeanor, dispatch, identify, location, petition, position, presence, talk with, transmit **9** attention, dexterity, diplomacy, expertise **10** adroitness, competence, directions, efficiency **11** communicate, comportment, designation, proficiency, savoir faire, tactfulness

adduce

3 lay **4** cite **5** claim, offer **6** allege, submit, tender **7** advance, present, proffer, propose, refer to, suggest **8** document **9** exemplify **10** illustrate

add up
3 sum   5 count, tally, total   6 amount, reckon   7 compute   9 make sense

add up to
4 mean   5 spell   6 amount, denote, import, intend   7 compute, connote, express, signify

A Death in the Family author
4 Agee (James)

adept
3 pro   4 deft, whiz   5 crack, savvy   6 adroit, expert, master, wizard   7 skilled   8 masterly, skillful, virtuoso   9 dexterous, masterful   10 proficient   11 crackerjack   12 professional

adequacy
5 might   6 enough   7 ability   8 capacity   10 capability, competence, sufficient   11 sufficiency   13 qualification

adequate
6 common, decent, enough   8 all right, passable, pleasing, standard, suitable   9 competent, sufficing   10 acceptable, sufficient   11 comfortable   12 satisfactory   13 unexceptional, unimpeachable

adequately
4 well   5 amply, right   6 enough   8 all right, passably, properly, suitably   9 fittingly, tolerably   12 sufficiently   13 appropriately

adhere
4 glue   5 cling, paste, stick   6 attach, bind to, cement, cleave, cohere, fasten   7 stick to   8 hold fast

adherence
4 bond   5 cling   7 loyalty   8 adhesion, clinging, cohesion, fidelity, sticking   9 constancy   10 attachment   12 faithfulness

adherent
6 cohort, votary   7 devotee, sectary   8 disciple, follower, henchman, partisan, stalwart   9 satellite, supporter   10 aficionado

adhering
6 clingy, gluing, sticky   7 binding   8 clinging, sticking   9 attaching, cementing

adhesive
4 glue   5 gluey, gooey, gummy, stamp, tacky   6 cement, clingy, gummed, sticky   7 holding, stickum   8 adhering, fastener, mucilage, sticking   9 attaching

adieu
5 congé   6 bye-bye, so long   7 cheerio, good-bye, parting   8 farewell   11 leave-taking

ad interim
6 acting, pro tem   9 temporary   10 pro tempore   11 temporarily

adios
4 by-by, ciao, ta-ta   5 adieu, later   6 bye-bye, so long   7 cheerio, good-bye, toodles   8 farewell, toodle-oo   10 hasta luego

adipose
3 fat   4 oily   5 fatty   6 greasy   7 fatlike

adit
3 way   4 door   5 entry   6 access, entrée, tunnel   7 ingress, passage   8 entrance   9 mine entry   10 passageway   12 mine entrance

adjacent
4 near   5 close   6 beside, nearby, next to   8 abutting, next door, touching   9 adjoining, alongside, bordering   10 contiguous, juxtaposed, near-at-hand   11 close-at-hand, neighboring   12 conterminous

adjoin
3 add   4 abut, link, line, meet   5 annex, touch, verge   6 append, attach, border, butt on, couple   7 connect, impinge   8 neighbor   11 communicate

adjourn
4 move, rise, stay   5 defer, delay   6 hold up, put off, recess, shelve   7 hold off, suspend   8 dissolve, hold over, postpone, prorogue   9 prorogate

adjudge
4 deem, rule   5 award, grant   6 decide, settle, umpire   7 mediate, referee   9 arbitrate   10 adjudicate

adjunct

5 added, affix **6** joined **8** addendum, addition, appanage, appendix, attached **9** accessory, accretion, appendage, assistant, associate, auxiliary **10** attachment **12** appurtenance

adjure

3 beg, bid **4** urge **6** exhort **7** beseech, entreat, command, implore, require **9** importune **10** supplicate

adjust

3 fit, fix, rig **4** suit, tune **5** adapt, order, right **6** accord, attune, modify, orient, settle, square, tailor, tune up **7** arrange, conform, correct, rectify, resolve **8** modulate, regulate **9** habituate, harmonize, reconcile **11** accommodate

adjuvant

4 aide **6** aiding, helper **8** enhancer, modifier **9** accessory, ancillary, assisting, auxiliary **10** collateral, subsidiary **11** appurtenant **12** contributory

ad-lib

9 extempore, improvise, impromptu **10** improvised, off-the-cuff, unprepared **11** extemporize, spontaneous, unrehearsed

Admetus

father: **6** Pheres
wife: **8** Alcestis

administer

3 run **4** boss, deal, give, head **5** issue **6** direct, govern, head up, manage **7** conduct, control, deal out, deliver, dole out, execute, give out, mete out, oversee, perform, provide **8** carry out, dispense, share out **9** apportion, supervise **10** distribute, portion out

administration

6 regime **7** control **9** direction **10** governance, presidency
system of: **11** bureaucracy

administrator

4 boss, exec, head **5** chief **7** manager, officer **8** director, official, overseer **9** executive **10** supervisor

admirable

6 august, worthy **8** laudable **9** deserving, estimable, excellent, meritable **11** commendable, meritorious, outstanding **12** praiseworthy

admiral

American: **4** Byrd (Richard), Sims (William) **5** Dewey (George), Stark (Harold) **6** Halsey (Bull), Nimitz (Chester) **7** Zumwalt (Elmo) **8** Farragut (David), Rickover (Hyman), Spruance (Raymond)
Confederate: **6** Semmes (Raphael)
Dutch: **5** Tromp (Maarten)
English: **5** Drake (Francis) **6** Nelson (Horatio), Rodney (George), Vernon (Edward) **7** Hawkins (John) **8** Beaufort (Francis), Jellicoe (John), Villiers (George) **11** Mountbatten (Louis)
French: **10** Villeneuve (Pierre-Charles)
German: **4** Spee (Graf Maximilian von) **6** Dönitz (Karl), Raeder (Erich) **7** Doenitz (Karl), Tirpitz (Alfred von)
Japanese: **4** Togo (Hideki) **5** Yonai (Mitsumasa) **8** Yamamoto (Isoroku)
Spanish: **8** Menéndez (Pedro)

admiration

5 favor **6** esteem, praise, regard **7** account, delight, respect **8** applause, approval, pleasure **9** affection **10** estimation **11** approbation **12** appreciation

admire

5 adore, honor, prize, value **6** esteem, praise, regard, relish, revere **7** adulate, applaud, approve, cherish, commend, respect **8** consider, treasure **9** delight in **10** appreciate

admirer

3 fan **4** beau, buff **7** booster, devotee, fancier **8** believer, follower, partisan **9** supporter **10** enthusiast

admission

3 way **4** door **5** entry **6** access, assent, entrée **7** ingress **8** entrance **10** admittance, concession, confession **11** affirmation

admit

3 own **4** avow, take **5** agree, allow,

enter, grant, let in, let on, lodge,
own up **6** accept, fess up, harbor,
permit, suffer, take in **7** concede,
confess, receive, shelter, welcome
9 entertain, introduce, recognize
11 acknowledge

admix

5 blend, merge **6** mingle **7** combine
8 comingle, compound, immingle
9 commingle **11** intermingle

admixture

5 alloy, blend, combo **6** fusion
7 amalgam **8** compound **9** aggregate, composite **12** amalgamation

admonish

4 warn **5** alert, chide **6** lesson, monish, rebuke, talk to **7** caution, counsel,
reprove, speak to **8** call down, forewarn, reproach **9** criticize, reprimand

admonition

3 tip **6** caveat, rebuke **7** caution,
chiding, reproof, warning **8** reproach
9 criticism, reprimand **11** disapproval, forewarning

ado

4 fuss, stir **5** tizzy, whirl, worry
6 bother, bustle, flurry **7** concern,
problem, trouble, turmoil **9** confusion
10 difficulty

adolescence

5 youth **7** puberty **8** minority
9 greenness **10** juvenility, pubescence **12** youthfulness

adolescent

4 teen **5** minor **6** teener **7** teenage
8 immature, preadult, teenager,
youthful **9** pubescent

Adonai

3 God **4** YHWH **6** Elohim, Yahweh

Adonijah

brother: 5 Amnon **7** Absalom,
Chileab
father: 5 David
mother: 7 Haggith
slayer: 7 Benaiah

Adonis

lover: 5 Venus **9** Aphrodite

mother: 5 Myrrh **6** Myrrha
slayer: 4 boar

adopt

4 pick, take **5** raise **6** accept, affect,
assume, choose, select, take on,
take up **7** care for, embrace, endorse, espouse

adoption

6 choice **7** raising, support **8** espousal, taking in **9** embracing, selection **11** embracement

adorable

4 cute, dear **7** darling, lovable, winsome **8** charming, pleasing, precious **9** appealing **10** attractive, delightful

adoration

4 love **5** ardor, honor **6** esteem,
praise **7** passion, worship **8** devotion, idolatry **9** adulation, affection,
reverence **10** admiration **11** idolization

adore

4 love **5** honor, prize **6** admire, dote
on, esteem, revere **7** cherish, idolize, respect, worship **8** dote upon,
treasure, venerate **9** affection, delight in, reverence

adorn

4 deck, trim **5** fix up, grace
6 bedeck, enrich, pretty **7** dress up,
enhance, enliven, furbish, garnish,
smarten **8** beautify, decorate, ornament, prettif **9** embellish

adornment

5 decor, frill **6** finery **7** garnish
8 ornament, trimming **9** accessory,
caparison **10** decoration **13** embellishment

ad rem

3 apt **7** apropos, fitting, germane
8 apposite, material, relevant **9** pertinent **10** applicable, relevantly, to the
point **11** applicative, applicatory

adrift

4 asea, lost **5** at sea, loose **6** afloat
7 aimless, mixed up **8** confused,

floating, unmoored **10** anchorless, bewildered **11** disoriented, purposeless

adroit

3 apt **4** able, deft **5** adept, canny, handy, savvy, smart **6** astute, clever, expert, nimble, shrewd **7** cunning, skilled **8** skillful, talented **9** dexterous, ingenious **11** intelligent, quick-witted, resourceful **13** perspicacious

adroitness

3 art **4** gift **5** craft, flair, knack, savvy, skill **7** address, cunning, know-how, prowess **8** deftness **9** adeptness, dexterity, expertise, ingenuity, readiness **10** cleverness, expertness **12** intelligence

adulation

7 acclaim, baloney, blarney, fawning, tribute, worship **8** applause, flattery, soft soap **9** servility, sweet talk **10** overpraise **11** false praise **12** blandishment

adulatory

7 buttery, fawning **8** unctuous **9** kowtowing **10** flattering, obsequious, oleaginous **11** bootlicking, sycophantic

adult

4 aged, ripe **5** grown **6** mature **7** grown-up, matured, ripened **9** full-blown **10** fully grown **11** full-fledged

adulterate

3 cut **4** thin **5** alloy, dirty, taint, water **6** debase, defile, dilute, doctor, dope up, impair, weaken **7** cheapen, corrupt, defiled, degrade, devalue, diluted, falsify, pollute, tainted, thinned **8** degraded, denature, impurify, polluted, spurious **9** water down **10** tamper with **11** contaminate

adumbrate

3 dim, fog **4** bode, call, hint, mist, veil **5** augur, cloud **6** darken, shadow, sketch **7** becloud, bespeak, betoken, obscure, outline, portend, predict, presage, suggest **8** block out, disclose, forebode, forecast, foretell, indicate, intimate, prophesy **9** obfuscate, prefigure **10** foreshadow, overshadow **11** prefigurate **12** characterize

adumbration

4 hint, sign **5** shade, umbra **6** shadow **7** outline **8** penumbra **10** indication, intimation, suggestion

advance

3 aid **4** cite, help, lend, loan, move, rise **5** get on, march, money, raise, serve **6** assist, course, foster, mature, prefer, supply, uplift **7** deposit, develop, elevate, forward, furnish, further, headway, ongoing, present, proceed, promote, propose, upgrade **8** approach, get along, heighten, increase, progress **9** encourage, evolution, provision **10** accelerate, bring about **11** development, furtherance, improvement, progression **12** breakthrough

advanced

3 old **5** first **6** far out **7** forward, in front, leading, liberal, radical **8** far ahead, foremost **9** developed **10** precocious **11** broad-minded, progressive

advancement

4 gain, rise **5** boost **6** growth **7** headway **8** progress **9** elevation, promotion **10** betterment, preference **11** improvement, progression

advantage

4 boon, edge, gain, good, help, lead, odds **5** asset, avail, serve **6** better, profit **7** account, benefit, mastery **8** blessing, interest, leverage **9** allowance, head start, upper hand **10** ascendancy, domination, leadership, prosperity **11** superiority **12** running start

advantageous

4 good **6** timely, toward, useful **7** benefic, gainful, helpful **8** favoring, salutary **9** conducive, desirable, expedient, favorable, fortunate, promising **10** beneficial, profitable, propitious, worthwhile

advent
5 onset 6 coming 7 arrival 8 approach 9 beginning

adventitious
5 fluky 6 casual, chance 8 by chance 9 unplanned 10 accidental, contingent, fortuitous, incidental, unexpected

adventure
3 try 4 feat, risk, trip 5 quest, wager 6 chance, gamble, hazard 7 exploit 8 escapade 9 undertake 10 enterprise, experience

adventurous
4 bold, rash 5 brash, risky 6 daring 8 intrepid, reckless 9 audacious, dangerous, daredevil, foolhardy, hazardous, impetuous, imprudent 10 innovative 12 enterprising

adversary
3 con, foe 4 anti 5 enemy, rival 7 opposer 8 opponent, opposing 10 antagonist, competitor

adverse
3 bad 4 anti 7 counter, harmful, hostile, hurtful, opposed 8 contrary, damaging, negative, opposing, opposite 9 injurious 11 deleterious, detrimental, obstructive, unfavorable 12 antagonistic, antipathetic

adversity
4 dole 5 trial 6 misery, mishap 7 bad luck, bad news, trouble 8 bad break, distress, hard time, hardship 9 mischance, suffering 10 difficulty, ill fortune, misfortune

advert
4 cite, note 5 refer 6 allude, notice, remark 7 bring up, mention, observe 8 indicate, point out

advertent
5 aware 7 heedful, mindful 9 attentive, intentive, observant, regardful

advertise
4 drum, hype, plug, puff, push 5 boost, pitch 6 blazon, herald, inform, notify, report 7 advance, apprise, build up, declare, promote, publish, sponsor 8 announce, ballyhoo, proclaim 9 broadcast, publicize 10 annunciate, promulgate

advertisement
4 bill, plug, sign 5 blurb, flyer, promo 6 notice, poster, want ad 7 affiche 8 circular 9 billboard, broadcast, promotion, publicity 10 commercial 11 declaration, publication 12 announcement, proclamation

advice
3 aid, tip 4 help, news, view, word 5 input 6 notice 7 caution, counsel, opinion, tidings, warning 8 guidance, teaching 10 admonition, suggestion 11 information, instruction 12 intelligence

advisable
4 wise 5 sound 6 seemly 7 politic, prudent 8 sensible, suitable, tactical 9 desirable, expedient, practical 10 worthwhile 11 recommended 12 advantageous

advise
3 tip 4 tell, tout, urge, warn 5 guide 6 clue in, confer, enjoin, fill in, inform, notify, tip off, wise up 7 apprise, caution, consult, counsel, suggest 8 acquaint, forewarn, instruct, point out 9 encourage, prescribe, recommend

Advise and Consent author
5 Drury (Allen)

advised
7 studied, weighed 8 designed, intended 10 calculated, considered, deliberate, thought out 11 intentional 12 premeditated

adviser
5 coach, guide 6 mentor 7 counsel, tipster 9 counselor 10 consultant, instructor

advisory
7 guiding, helping 9 educative 10 counseling 12 consultative 13 informational

advocacy
3 aid 6 urging 7 backing, defense, support 9 promotion

advocate
4 back, push, tout, urge 5 favor 6 backer, defend, preach, uphold 7 promote, propose, support 8 argue for, backstop, champion, exponent, plump for, side with 9 encourage, expounder, proponent, recommend, spokesman, supporter 11 countenance

Aeacus
father: 4 Zeus
mother: 6 Aegina
son: 6 Peleus 7 Telamon

Aedon
brother: 7 Amphion
sister-in-law: 5 Niobe
son (victim): 6 Itylus

Aeëtes
daughter: 5 Medea
father: 6 Helios

aegis
4 care, ward 5 armor, guard 6 charge, shield 7 backing, control, defense, support 8 auspices, guidance, security 9 influence, patronage, safeguard 10 protection 11 sponsorship

Aegisthus
father: 8 Thyestes
lover: 12 Clytemnestra
mother: 7 Pelopia
slayer: 7 Orestes
victim: 6 Atreus 9 Agamemnon

Aeneas
companion: 7 Achates
father: 8 Anchises
mother: 5 Venus 9 Aphrodite
son: 5 Iulus 8 Ascanius
wife: 6 Creusa 7 Lavinia

Aeneid
author: 6 Vergil, Virgil
first words: 16 arma virumque cano
hero: 6 Aeneas

Aeolus
daughter: 7 Alcyone 8 Halcyone
father: 8 Poseidon

aeon
3 age 4 time 6 period 8 blue moon, duration

aerate
7 lighten, freshen, refresh 9 oxygenate, ventilate

aerial
4 high 5 lofty 6 flying, vapory 7 antenna, soaring 8 birdlike, elevated, ethereal, fanciful, towering, vaporous 9 pneumatic 10 impalpable 11 atmospheric, forward pass

aerie
4 nest 7 citadel, lookout 9 penthouse

aeronaut
4 Fogg (Phileas) 5 pilot 7 aviator 8 Zeppelin (Ferdinand, Graf von) 10 balloonist

Aerope
husband: 6 Atreus
lover: 8 Thyestes
son: 8 Menelaus 9 Agamemnon

aery
see **aerial**

Aesculapius
daughter: 6 Hygeia 7 Panacea
father: 6 Apollo
slayer: 4 Zeus 7 Jupiter
teacher: 6 Chiron
wife: 6 Epione

Aeson
brother: 6 Pelias
son: 5 Jason

aesthete
4 buff 6 expert 7 devotee 9 authority 10 dilettante 11 appreciator, cognoscente, connoisseur

aesthetic
6 artful 8 artistic, creative, pleasing 9 beautiful, sensitive 10 attractive, harmonious

afar
5 apart 6 remote 7 distant

affable

4 kind, open, warm 6 at ease, genial, gentle, kindly, polite 7 amiable, cordial 8 friendly, gracious, obliging, pleasant, sociable 9 congenial, courteous

affair

4 case, love 5 amour, worry 6 action, matter 7 concern, liaison, palaver, romance 8 business, function, interest, intrigue, occasion 9 happening, procedure 10 proceeding 12 relationship

affect

3 act 4 fake, move, sham, stir, sway 5 adopt, alter, bluff, fancy, feign, haunt, put on, touch 6 assume, change, strike 7 act upon, disturb, impress, inspire, pretend 8 frequent, simulate 9 cultivate, influence 11 counterfeit

affectation

3 air 4 airs, pose, sham, show 6 facade 8 pretense 9 mannerism 10 pretension 13 artificiality

affected

5 false, moved, put-on 6 phoney 7 altered, assumed, changed, feigned, stilted 8 disposed, inclined, involved, mannered, precious, spurious 9 concerned, conscious, contrived, insincere, pretended, unnatural 10 artificial 11 overrefined, pretentious 13 self-conscious

affecting

3 sad 6 lively, moving 7 pitiful 8 exciting, poignant, touching 9 thrilling 10 disturbing, impressive 11 distressing, influential

affection

4 bias, love 5 trait 6 doting, liking, malady, virtue, warmth 7 ailment, concern, disease, emotion, feature, feeling, illness, leaning, passion, quality 8 devotion, disorder, fondness, interest, penchant, property, sickness, sympathy 9 attention, attribute, character, complaint, condition, sentiment 10 attachment, propensity, tenderness 12 predilection

affectionate

4 dear, fond, warm 6 caring, doting, loving, tender 7 devoted 8 friendly 11 sympathetic

affective

6 moving 7 emotive 8 stirring, touching 9 emotional

affectivity

7 emotion, feeling, passion 9 sentiment

affianced

7 engaged, pledged 8 intended, plighted, promised 9 betrothed, committed 10 contracted

affiche

4 bill, list 6 notice, poster 7 placard 8 handbill

affidavit

4 oath 9 testimony 11 affirmation, declaration

affiliate

4 ally, join 5 annex, unite 6 branch 7 combine, connect, partner 9 associate

affiliated

4 akin 5 bound 6 allied, joined, linked 7 kindred, related 9 connected, dependent 10 associated

affiliation

4 club 5 tie-in, union 6 hookup, league 7 cahoots, company, joining 8 alliance 10 connection, fellowship 11 association, combination, conjunction, partnership

affinity

6 simile 7 analogy, kinship, rapport 8 likeness, relation, sympathy 9 alikeness 10 attraction, similarity, similitude 11 resemblance 13 compatibility

affirm

3 say, yes 4 aver, avow, okay 5 state, swear, vouch 6 assent, assert, attest, depose, ratify, uphold 7 certify, confirm, declare, profess,

protest, testify, witness **8** dedicate, validate **9** guarantee

affirmative
3 aye, yea, yes **4** yeah **6** assent **8** approval, positive **9** affirming, approving, asserting, assertion, endorsing, favorable, ratifying **10** confirming, supporting **11** affirmation

affix
3 add, tag **4** bind, glue, join, nail, tack **5** annex, paste, put on, rivet, stick, tag on **6** append, attach, fasten, tack on **7** impress, stick on, subjoin **8** addition **9** appendage **10** attachment

afflict
3 try, vex **4** pain, rack **5** annoy, beset, harry, press, smite, worry, wound, wring **6** bother, burden, harass, harrow, injure, martyr, pester, plague, strike, suffer **7** agonize, anguish, torment, torture, trouble **8** distress

afflicted
6 pained, rueful, woeful **7** doleful, injured, unhappy, worried **8** dolorous, stricken, troubled, wretched **9** disturbed, miserable, sorrowful, tormented **10** distressed

affliction
3 woe **4** care **5** cross, grief, trial **6** ordeal, plague, sorrow **7** anguish, illness, scourge, torment, trouble **8** distress, hardship, sickness **9** adversity, heartache, infirmity **10** misfortune **11** tribulation

afflictive
3 sad **4** dire, sore **6** aching, bitter, woeful **7** galling, hurtful, hurting, painful **8** grievous, mournful **9** sorrowful **10** calamitous, deplorable, lamentable **11** distasteful, distressing, regrettable, troublesome, unfortunate, unpalatable **13** heartbreaking

affluence
5 means, worth **6** bounty, influx, plenty, riches, wealth **8** opulence,

property, richness **9** abundance, plenitude, profusion, resources **10** prosperity

affluent
4 full, rich **5** flush **6** loaded **7** copious, flowing, moneyed, opulent, wealthy, well-off **8** abundant, well-to-do **9** bountiful, plentiful, tributary, well-fixed **10** prosperous

afford
4 able, bear, give **5** allow, grant, incur, offer, spare, stand **6** bestow, confer, donate, impart, manage, supply **7** furnish, present, support, sustain

affordable
5 cheap **6** modest **7** low-cost **8** bearable **10** manageable, reasonable **11** inexpensive

affray
3 row **5** clash, fight, melee, scrap **6** fracas, rumpus **7** dispute, quarrel, ruction, scuffle **8** disorder, skirmish

affront
3 vex **4** face, meet, slap, slur **5** abuse, anger, annoy, wrong **6** injury, insult, offend, slight **7** offense, outrage, put down **8** contempt, rudeness **9** aspersion, criticize, encounter, indignity

Afghanistan
capital: **5** Kabul
city: **5** Herat **8** Kandahar **12** Mazar-i-Sharif
ethnic group: **7** Pashtun
language: **4** Dari **6** Pashto
monetary unit: **7** Afghani
neighbor: **4** Iran **5** China **8** Pakistan **10** Tajikistan, Uzbekistan **12** Turkmenistan

aficionado
3 fan **4** buff **5** hound, lover **6** expert **7** admirer, devotee, habitué **10** enthusiast **11** appreciator

afield
4 afar, away, awry **5** amiss, badly, wrong **6** abroad, astray **8** straying **9** elsewhere, off course

afire

3 hot 5 aglow, fiery 6 ablaze,
aflame, alight, red-hot 7 blazing,
burning, excited, flaming, flaring, ignited 8 inflamed, in flames 9 energized, excitable 10 passionate
11 conflagrant

afloat

4 asea 5 at sea 6 adrift, buoyed
9 supported, sustained

afraid

4 wary 5 chary, jumpy, loath, scary,
sorry, timid 6 averse, scared, trepid
7 anxious, fearful, uneager, worried
8 cautious, hesitant, skittish, timorous 9 concerned, regretful, reluctant, unwilling 10 frightened 11 disinclined 12 apprehensive

afresh

3 new 4 anew, over 5 again, newly
6 de novo, encore 8 once more, repeated 9 once again

Africa

country: 4 Chad, Mali, Togo
5 Benin, Congo, Egypt, Gabon,
Ghana, Kenya, Libya, Niger, Sudan,
Zaire 6 Angola, Gambia, Guinea,
Malawi, Rwanda, Uganda, Zambia
7 Algeria, Burundi, Comoros, Eritrea,
Lesotho, Liberia, Morocco, Namibia,
Nigeria, Senegal, Somalia, Tunisia
8 Botswana, Cameroon, Djibouti,
Ethiopia, Tanzania, Zimbabwe
9 Cape Verde, Mauritius, Swaziland
10 Ivory Coast, Madagascar, Mauri-
tania, Mozambique, Seychelles
11 Burkina Faso, Côte d'Ivoire,
Sierra Leone, South Africa
12 Guinea-Bissau
ethnic group: 3 Ibo 4 Akan, Arab,
Boer, Copt, Fula, Issa, Moor, Zulu
5 Bantu, Fulah, Galla, Hausa, Kongo,
Mande, Pygmy, Swazi, Wolof 6 Berber, Fulani, Hamite, Herero, Kikuyu,
Nubian, Somali, Tuareg, Ubangi,
Yoruba 7 Ashanti, Bedouin, Bushman, Malinke, Swahili 8 Egyptian,
Mandingo 9 Hottentot
language: 3 Ibo 5 Bantu, Galla,
Hausa 6 Arabic, Berber, Somali,
Yoruba 7 Amharic, Bambara, Swahili
8 Malagasy 9 Afrikaans

aft

5 after 6 astern 8 rearmost, rearward 9 sternward

after

3 aft, for 4 back, hind, next, past,
rear 5 below, later, since 6 astern,
back of, behind, beyond, hinder 7 by
and by, ensuing 8 hindmost, in view
of 9 following, posterior, sternward
10 subsequent 12 subsequently

after all

3 yet 5 still 6 at last, though 7 finally, however 8 in the end 11 nonetheless 12 nevertheless

aftereffect

5 issue 6 result, upshot 7 fallout,
outcome 11 consequence, eventuality

afterlife

6 beyond 8 eternity 9 hereafter

aftermath

4 wake 6 effect, result, upshot
12 consequences, repercussion

afterward

4 next, soon, then 5 later 6 behind
7 by and by, thereon 8 latterly
9 hereafter 10 thereafter 12 subsequently

afterword

8 epilogue

Agag

kingdom: 6 Amalek
slayer: 6 Samuel

again

4 also, anew, back, over 6 afresh,
de novo, encore 8 once more

again and again

3 oft 4 much 5 often 8 ofttimes
10 frequently, oftentimes, repeatedly

against

6 contra, facing, versus 7 vis-à-vis
8 fronting, opposite, touching
prefix: 4 anti 6 contra 7 counter

Agamemnon
avenger: 7 Orestes
brother: 8 Menelaus
daughter: 7 Electra 9 Iphigenia
father: 6 Atreus
slayer: 9 Aegisthus
son: 7 Orestes
wife: 12 Clytemnestra

agape
4 love, open 6 amazed, gaping
7 yawning 8 wide open 9 astounded,
love feast 10 astonished, confounded 11 dumbfounded, overwhelmed 13 thunderstruck

agate
3 taw 4 type 6 marble, quartz
7 shooter 8 type size

Agave
father: 6 Cadmus
husband: 6 Echion
mother: 8 Harmonia
sister: 3 Ino 6 Semele 7 Autonoë
son: 8 Pentheus

age
3 eon, era 4 aeon, grow, span, time
5 epoch, ripen, stage 6 grow up,
mature, mellow, period 7 develop,
grow old 8 blue moon, division, interval, lifetime, long time, majority,
maturate 9 become old 10 generation

aged
3 old 4 ripe, worn 5 cured, hoary,
olden 6 mellow, senior 7 ancient,
antique, elderly, matured, ripened
8 grown old, timeworn 9 developed,
senescent, venerable 11 patriarchal
12 antediluvian

ageless
7 endless, eternal, lasting 8 date-
less, enduring, immortal, timeless
9 immutable 11 everlasting

agency
4 firm 5 cause, force, means, organ,
power 6 action, bureau, medium,
office 7 company, channel, vehicle
8 activity, auspices, business, division, function, ministry 9 mechanism, operation 10 department,
instrument 12 organization
13 establishment

agenda
6 docket, lineup 7 program 8 calendar, schedule 9 timetable
entry: 4 item

Agenor
brother: 5 Belus
daughter: 6 Europa
father: 7 Antenor, Neptune 8 Poseidon
mother: 5 Libya
son: 6 Cadmus

agent
3 fed, spy 4 tool 5 actor, means, organ, proxy, spook 6 deputy, factor,
medium 7 channel, proctor, steward,
vehicle 8 assignee, attorney, executor, minister, ministry 9 activator, go-
between, middleman, operative
10 instrument, procurator

age-old
5 olden 7 ancient, antique, elderly,
forever 8 timeworn 9 venerable
10 immemorial 11 time-honored, traditional

agglomerate
4 heap, mass, pile, rock 6 gather
7 cluster 9 aggregate 10 collection
11 aggregation

agglomeration
4 heap 5 hoard, trove 7 cluster
9 aggregate, amassment, gathering
10 collection, cumulation 11 aggregation

aggrandize
4 hype 5 boost 6 beef up, expand,
extend, praise 7 augment, build up,
enhance, enlarge, ennoble, glorify,
inflate, magnify 8 heighten, increase, multiply 11 distinguish

aggravate
3 vex 4 gall 5 anger, annoy, grate,
mount, peeve, pique, rouse, upset
6 burn up, deepen, nettle, worsen
7 bedevil, disturb, enhance, inflame,
magnify, perturb, provoke 8 heighten,
increase, irritate 9 intensify
10 exacerbate

aggravation
4 pain 5 worry 6 bother 8 increase
9 annoyance, worsening 10 irritation
11 provocation

aggregate
3 all, sum 4 body, bulk, floc 5 add up,
gross, total, whole 6 amount 8 entirety, quantity, totality 9 composite
10 cumulative 11 agglomerate
12 conglomerate 13 agglomeration

aggregation
4 body, mass 5 crowd, group, hoard,
total, trove 7 cluster, company 8 assembly 9 amassment, gathering
10 assemblage, collection, cumulation 11 agglomerate 12 accumulation

aggression
4 push, raid 5 fight, onset 6 attack
7 assault, offense 8 invasion 9 hostility, incursion, offensive, onslaught,
pugnacity 10 assailment 12 belligerence 13 combativeness

aggressive
5 pushy 6 fierce, severe 7 hostile,
scrappy, vicious, warlike 8 emphatic,
forceful, militant 9 assertive, attacking, combative, energetic, intrusive,
offensive 11 belligerent, contentious,
domineering, hard-hitting 12 enterprising

aggrieve
4 hurt, pain 5 annoy, harry, upset,
worry, wrong 6 harass, injure, plague
7 afflict, oppress, torment, trouble
8 distress 9 constrain, persecute

aghast
4 agog, awed 6 afraid, amazed,
scared 7 anxious, fearful, shocked,
stunned 8 appalled, dismayed,
startled 9 awestruck, horrified, terrified 10 astonished, confounded,
frightened 11 dumbfounded, overwhelmed 13 thunderstruck

agile
4 deft, spry 5 alert, brisk, catty, lithe,
quick, zippy 6 active, adroit, limber,
lively, nimble, supple 7 lissome
9 adaptable, dexterous, sprightly

agitate
4 move, rile, rock, stir, toss 5 argue,
churn, peeve, shake, upset 6 arouse,
bother, excite, flurry, joggle, ruffle, stir
up 7 discuss, dispute, disturb, fluster,
perturb, provoke, tempest, trouble,
unhinge 8 disquiet, irritate 9 thrash
out 10 discompose

agitation
4 flap, fuss, stir, to-do 5 clash
6 bustle, clamor, debate, flurry,
lather, tumult 7 dispute, tempest,
turmoil 9 commotion, confusion
10 turbulence 11 disturbance

agitator
5 rebel 6 shaker 7 inciter, stirrer
8 fomenter, inflamer 9 disrupter
10 instigator 11 provocateur

Aglaia
see **Graces**

Aglauros
father: 7 Cecrops
sister: 5 Herse 9 Pandrosos

aglow
4 warm 5 afire 6 bright, aflame,
alight 7 excited, radiant, shining
8 gleaming, luminous

agnate
4 akin, like 5 alike 6 allied, joined,
linked 7 cognate, connate, kindred,
kinsman, related, similar 8 relation,
relative 9 analogous 10 affiliated
11 consanguine 13 corresponding

agnostic
7 doubter, skeptic 8 doubting
10 questioner, undogmatic 11 uncommitted 12 noncommittal

Agnus _____
3 Dei

ago
4 back, gone, past, yore 5 since
6 before

agog
4 avid, keen 5 eager 6 roused
7 excited, fervent 8 desirous
9 expectant, impatient
12 enthusiastic

agon
5 clash 6 battle 7 contest 8 conflict, struggle

agonize
4 fret, gall, hurt, pain, rack 5 chafe 6 harrow, squirm, suffer, writhe 7 afflict, torment, torture, trouble 8 distress, stew over, struggle 10 excruciate

agonizing
6 fierce 7 extreme, intense, painful, racking, tearing 9 harrowing, suffering, torturing, torturous 10 tormenting 12 excruciating

agony
4 pain 5 dolor, pangs 6 misery 7 anguish, passion, torment, torture 8 distress, outburst, struggle 9 suffering 10 affliction

agora
11 marketplace 12 meeting place

agrarian
5 rural 6 rustic 8 pastoral 10 campestral 12 agricultural

agree
3 buy, set, yes 4 jibe, okay, suit 5 admit, check, equal, fit in, match, tally 6 accede, accept, accord, assent, concur, settle, square 7 buy into, comport, concede, concert, concord, conform, consent 8 check out, coincide, dovetail, side with 9 acquiesce, harmonize, recognize, subscribe 10 correspond 11 acknowledge

agreeable
4 nice, open 5 ready 7 affable, welcome, willing 8 amenable, in accord, pleasant, pleasing 9 approving, congenial, congruous, consonant, favorable, receptive 10 acceptable, compatible, concurring, consenting, consistent 11 pleasurable, sympathetic

agreed
3 aye, yea, yep, yes 4 okay 6 surely 8 all right, of course 9 certainly 10 definitely, positively

agreement
4 bond, deal, pact 6 accord, assent, treaty 7 bargain, compact, concord, consent, entente, harmony 8 contract, covenant 9 concordat 10 acceptance, consonance 11 arrangement, concordance, concurrence

agree with
3 fit 4 suit. 5 befit 6 assist, become 7 support 10 go together

agricultural
7 bucolic 8 agrarian, pastoral

agriculture
7 farming, tillage 8 agronomy, ranching 9 husbandry 11 cultivation, soil culture

Agrippina
brother: 8 Caligula
husband: 8 Claudius
son: 4 Nero

aground
5 stuck 6 ashore, on land 7 beached, on shore 8 disabled, stranded

ague
3 flu 5 fever 7 malaria, shivers 9 influenza, shivering 10 blackwater

Ahab
daughter: 8 Athaliah
father: 4 Omri
wife: 7 Jezebel

Ahasuerus
kingdom: 6 Persia
wife: 6 Esther, Vashti

Ahaz
kingdom: 5 Judah
son: 8 Hezekiah
wife: 3 Abi

Ahaziah
father: 4 Ahab 5 Joram 7 Jehoram
kingdom: 5 Judah 6 Israel
mother: 7 Jezebel 8 Athaliah
sister: 9 Jehosheba 11 Jehosobeath

ahead
4 ante, fore 6 before, onward 7 earlier, forward, in front, leading,

Ahinoam

onwards 8 foremost, forwards, previous 9 in advance 10 beforehand 11 precedently

Ahinoam
father: 7 Ahimaaz
husband: 4 Saul 5 David
son: 5 Amnon

aid
4 abet, care, hand, help, lift 6 assist, helper, relief, rescue, succor 7 backing, comfort, help out, support, sustain 9 assistant, attendant, subsidize 10 assistance, benefactor, mitigation 11 alleviation

Aida
composer: 5 Verdi (Giuseppe)
father: 8 Amonasro
lover: 7 Radames
rival: 7 Amneris

aide
6 deputy, helper, second 7 orderly 8 adjutant. 9 assistant, attendant, coadjutor 10 coadjutant, lieutenant

aikido
10 martial art

ail
4 hurt, pain 5 upset, worry 6 bother 7 afflict, disturb, trouble 8 distress

ailing
3 ill, low 4 down, sick, weak 6 in pain, poorly, sickly, unwell 8 below par, diseased 9 enfeebled 10 indisposed 11 debilitated

ailment
6 malady, unrest 7 disease, ferment, illness, turmoil 8 disorder, disquiet, sickness, syndrome 9 affection, complaint, condition, infirmity 10 inquietude, uneasiness 11 disquietude, restiveness 12 restlessness

aim
3 end, try 4 cast, goal, head, mark, mean, plan, want, wish 5 angle, essay, focus, level, point, slant, train 6 aspire, design, desire, direct, intend, object, strive, target, zero in 7 address, attempt, propose,

purpose 8 ambition, endeavor 9 objective 11 contemplate

aimless
6 random 7 wayward 8 goalless 9 desultory, haphazard, hit-or-miss, irregular, pointless, unplanned 10 designless 11 purposeless

air
3 sky 4 aura, mien, mood, song, tune, vent 5 style 6 manner, melody, reveal, strain 7 bearing, divulge, express, feeling, quality 8 demeanor 9 broadcast, character, ventilate 10 atmosphere, deportment

aircraft
5 blimp, drone, plane 6 glider 7 airship, balloon, chopper 8 aerodyne, aerostat, airplane, jetliner, zeppelin 9 dirigible 10 helicopter
carrier: 7 flattop
designer: 6 Fokker (Anthony), Martin (Glenn) 7 Junkers (Hugo), Tupolev (Andrei) 8 Northrop (Jack), Sikorsky (Igor), Yakovlev (Alexander) 13 Messerschmitt (Willy)

airless
5 close 6 stuffy, sultry 8 stagnant, stifling 11 suffocating

airline
3 JAL, KLM, LOT, TWA 4 BOAC, El Al 5 Delta, Pan Am, USAir, Varig 6 Iberia, Qantas, United, Virgin 7 Eastern, JetBlue, Olympic 8 Aeroflot, Alitalia, American, Swissair 9 Air France, Lufthansa, Northwest, Southwest, U.S. Airways 11 Continental, Pan American

airman
5 flier, flyer, pilot 6 flyboy 7 aviator 8 aeronaut

air movement
4 gust, wind 5 draft 6 breath, breeze 7 updraft 9 downdraft

air navigation system
5 loran, navar, radar

airplane
3 jet 5 avion 6 bomber 7 fighter 8 autogiro, autogyro 9 transport

A-bomb-dropper: 8 Enola Gay
battle: 8 dogfight
body: 8 fuselage
engine: 3 jet 6 fanjet 7 propjet
8 turbofan, turbojet 9 turboprop
engine casing: 7 nacelle
engineless: 6 glider
instrument: 5 radar, radio 7 compass 9 altimeter, gyroscope
10 tachometer 11 transponder
maneuver: 4 buzz, dive, loop, roll
8 nosedive 9 chandelle 10 barrel
roll
movement: 3 yaw 4 bank, spin
5 pitch 8 tailspin
part: 3 fin 4 flap, nose, prop, tail,
wing 5 cabin, wheel 6 engine, rudder 7 aileron 8 airscrew, elevator
9 empennage, propeller 10 stabilizer
pilotless: 5 drone
shelter: 6 hangar
target: 6 drogue
vapor: 8 contrail

air plant
6 orchid 8 epiphyte 9 bromeliad,
kalanchoe 11 Spanish moss
12 strangler fig

airport
5 field 7 helipad 8 heliport 9 aerodrome
building: 8 terminal
flag: 8 windsock
name:
　Atlanta: 10 Hartsfield
　Boston: 5 Logan
　Chicago: 5 O'Hare 6 Midway
　Dublin: 7 Shannon
　London: 7 Gatwick 8 Heathrow
　New York: 3 JFK 7 Kennedy 9 La
　Guardia
　Paris: 4 Orly 8 DeGaulle 9 Le
　Bourget
　Rome: 7 Da Vinci
　Washington: 6 Dulles, Reagan
　8 National
part: 5 apron, tower 6 runway
7 taxiway

airs
4 pose, show 5 front 6 vanity
7 hauteur 8 pretense 9 loftiness,
mannerism, vainglory 10 pretension
11 affectation, insincerity, ostentation
13 artificiality

airship
3 jet 5 blimp, plane 8 zeppelin 9 dirigible

airtight
4 shut 6 closed, sealed 7 certain
8 hermetic, ironclad 10 impervious
11 impermeable, irrefutable 12 indisputable, invulnerable 13 incontestable

airy
4 open, rare, thin 5 blowy, fresh,
gusty, light, lofty, proud, windy
6 aerial, bouncy, breezy, dainty, unreal 7 buoyant, gaseous, soaring,
tenuous 8 affected, animated, delicate, ethereal, graceful, illusory, rarefied, spirited, towering, vaporous,
volatile 9 expansive, frivolous, pneumatic, resilient, sprightly, vivacious
10 diaphanous, ventilated 11 atmospheric, skyscraping 12 effervescent, high-spirited

A Is for Alibi author
7 Grafton (Sue)

Ajax
4 hero 5 Greek 7 warrior
father: 6 Oileus 7 Telamon
opponent: 6 Hector
participant: 9 Trojan War

akin
4 like, same 5 alike 6 allied 7 kindred, related, similar, uniform 8 parallel 9 analogous, consonant 10 affiliated, comparable, compatible
11 consanguine 13 corresponding

Alabama
capital: 10 Montgomery
city: 5 Selma 6 Mobile
10 Birmingham, Huntsville, Tuscaloosa 12 Muscle Shoals
college, university: 6 Auburn
8 Tuskegee
mountain: 6 Cheaha
nickname: 6 Cotton (State)
12 Heart of Dixie

river: 6 Mobile 7 Alabama
9 Tombigbee
state bird: 12 yellowhammer
state flower: 8 camellia
state tree: 12 longleaf pine

alacrity
8 dispatch 9 briskness, eagerness,
quickness, readiness 10 enthusiasm, expedition, liveliness, promptness 11 promptitude, willingness
12 cheerfulness

alamo
6 poplar 10 cottonwood

a la mode
4 chic, tony 6 trendy 7 dashing,
stylish 8 up-to-date 9 exclusive
11 fashionable 12 with ice cream

alarm
3 SOS 4 bell, fear, horn 5 alert,
dread, panic, scare, siren, spook,
upset 6 dismay, excite, fright, signal,
terror, tocsin 7 anxiety, disturb, startle, terrify, unnerve, warning
8 distress, frighten 9 terrorize
11 forewarning, trepidation 12 apprehension 13 consternation

alas
3 heu, woe 4 darn, drat 5 alack,
oy vey 7 woe is me

Alaska
capital: 6 Juneau
city: 4 Nome 5 Sitka 6 Barrow
9 Anchorage, Fairbanks 10 Prudhoe
Bay
island group: 6 Kodiak 8 Aleutian,
Pribilof
mountain, range: 6 Brooks
8 McKinley, Wrangell
nickname: 12 Last Frontier
park: 6 Denali, Katmai
river: 5 Yukon
state bird: 9 ptarmigan
state flower: 11 forget-me-not
state tree: 11 sitka spruce

alb
4 gown 8 vestment

Albania
capital: 6 Tirana, Tiranë
city: 5 Korçë, Vlorë 6 Durrës
7 Shkodër
ethnic group: 4 Gheg, Tosk
monetary unit: 3 lek
neighbor: 6 Greece, Serbia 9 Macedonia
part of: 7 Balkans
peninsula: 6 Balkan
sea: 8 Adriatic

albatross
5 check, goony, worry 6 burden,
gooney 7 anxiety, seabird 9 hindrance, millstone, restraint 11 encumbrance

Albee play
7 Sandbox (The) 8 Seascape, Zoo
Story (The) 9 Tiny Alice 13 American Dream (The) 14 Three Tall
Women 16 A Delicate Balance
25 Who's Afraid of Virginia Woolf?

albeit
5 still, while 6 even if, much as,
though 7 despite, whereas 8 although 10 even though

Alberta
capital: 8 Edmonton
city: 5 Banff 7 Calgary
lake: 6 Claire, Louise 9 Athabasca
mountain, range: 7 Rockies 8 Columbia
provincial flower: 8 wild rose
river: 4 Milk 5 Peace 9 Athabasca

Albion
7 England

album
4 book 6 jacket, record 7 garland,
omnibus 8 notebook, pictures, register 9 anthology, portfolio, scrap-
book 10 collection, miscellany,
recordings

Alcestis
father: 6 Pelias
husband: 7 Admetus
rescuer: 8 Heracles, Hercules

alchemist
10 Paracelsus

alchemy
5 charm, magic 7 panacea, sorcery
8 wizardry 9 conjuring 10 necromancy

Alcina
sister: 7 Morgana 10 Logistilla
victim: 6 Rogero 8 Astolpho, Ruggiero

Alcinous
daughter: 8 Nausicaa
wife: 5 Arete

Alcmaeon
father: 10 Amphiaraus
mother: 8 Eriphyle
wife: 10 Callirrhoe

Alcmene
husband: 10 Amphitryon
son: 8 Heracles, Hercules

alcohol
4 grog 5 booze, hooch, juice, sauce
6 hootch, liquor, red-eye, rotgut, tipple 7 spirits 8 home brew 9 aqua
vitae, firewater, moonshine
name: 4 amyl 5 butyl, cetyl, ethyl
6 glycol, methyl, sterol 7 butanol,
ethanol, mannite, menthol 8 glyc-
erin, glycerol, inositol, mannitol,
methanol 9 isopropyl 11 cholesterol
used in perfumes: 5 nerol 7 bor-
neol 8 geraniol, linalool

alcoholic
4 hard 5 drunk 6 brewed 8 drunkard 9 distilled, fermented, inebriant,
inebriate, spiritous 10 spirituous
11 dipsomaniac, inebriating 12 in-
toxicating

alcoholic drink
see under **beverage**

alcove
4 nook 5 niche 6 gazebo, recess
9 belvedere 11 summerhouse
Japanese: 8 tokonoma

Alcyone
father: 5 Atlas 6 Aeolus

husband: 4 Ceyx
mother: 7 Pleione
sisters: 8 Pleiades

ale
3 nog 4 beer, nogg

aleatory
4 iffy 5 dicey, risky, shaky 6 chancy
9 hazardous, uncertain 10 contingent, precarious, vulnerable 11 problematic, speculative 13 unpredictable

alehouse
3 bar, pub 6 bistro, saloon, tavern
7 taproom 8 beer hall 10 beer garden 11 rathskeller

alembic
5 still 6 filter 9 distiller

alert
3 SOS 4 keen, warn 5 alarm, quick,
ready, sharp, smart 6 brainy, bright,
clever, lively, notify, tip off, tocsin
7 heedful, mindful, on guard, red flag,
wakeful 8 animated, forewarn, open-
eyed, vigilant, watchful 9 attentive,
mercurial, sprightly, wide-awake
10 perceptive 11 intelligent, quick-
witted
Scottish: 4 gleg 8 wakerife

Aleutian island
3 Fox 4 Adak, Atka, Attu, Near
5 Amlia, Kiska 6 Unimak
8 Unalaska 9 Andreanof
town: 11 Dutch Harbor

alewife
4 fish 7 herring 8 menhaden

Alexander
birthplace: 5 Pella
conquest: 4 Tyre 5 Egypt, Issus
6 Greece, Persia 7 Parthia
8 Granicus
father: 6 Philip
general: 9 Antipater
horse: 10 Bucephalus
kingdom: 9 Macedonia
mother: 8 Olympias
teacher: 9 Aristotle
wife: 6 Roxana

alfalfa
3 hay 5 plant 6 forage, legume
7 lucerne 9 perennial

alfresco
7 open-air, outdoor, outside 8 outdoors 9 out-of-door 10 out-of-doors

alga
6 desmid, diatom 7 seaweed
blue-green: 6 nostoc
brown: 4 kelp 5 fucus 8 rockweed
green: 9 chlorella
red: 4 nori

algebra term
4 root 6 factor 8 binomial, equation,
monomial, variable 9 quadratic
10 polynomial

Algeria
capital: 7 Algiers
city: 4 Bône, Oran 6 Annaba
11 Constantine
coast: 7 Barbary
desert: 6 Sahara
ethnic group: 4 Arab 6 Berber
language: 6 Arabic, Berber
monetary unit: 5 dinar
mountain range: 5 Atlas 12 Saharan Atlas
neighbor: 4 Mali 5 Libya, Niger
7 Morocco, Tunisia 10 Mauritania

Algren novel
17 Walk on the Wild Side (A)
19 Man with the Golden Arm (The)

Ali
son: 5 Hasan 6 Husayn
wife: 6 Fatima

alias
3 AKA 6 anonym, handle 7 moniker,
pen name 8 nickname 9 false name,
pseudonym, stage name 10 also
called, nom de plume 11 nom de
guerre

alibi
4 plea 5 clear, cover, proof 6 answer, excuse 7 account, cover up,
defense, pretext 9 assertion, exonerate 11 explanation

alien
6 exotic 7 foreign, opposed, strange
8 estrange, outsider, stranger, transfer 9 estranged, extrinsic, foreigner,
outlander 10 extraneous, outlandish
12 incompatible

alienate
4 part 5 repel 6 assign, convey, divide, offend, oppose 7 break up, turn
off 8 disunify, disunite, estrange,
separate, sign over, transfer 9 disaffect 10 drive apart, relinquish

alienation
5 break 6 breach 7 discord, divorce,
rupture 8 division 10 conveyance,
separation 11 breaking off 12 disaffection, estrangement

alight
4 land 5 fiery 6 arrive, bright, on
fire, settle 7 blazing, burning, deplane, descend, detrain, flaming,
flaring, get down, glowing, ignited,
shining 8 dismount 9 touch down
11 conflagrant

align
4 ally, join, line, true 5 agree, array,
order, range 6 adjust, follow, line
up 8 regulate 9 affiliate, associate
10 straighten

alike
4 akin, same 7 similar 8 parallel
9 analogous, consonant
10 comparable 13 corresponding

alikeness
6 simile 7 analogy 8 affinity, alliance, relation 9 closeness, semblance 10 comparison, connection,
similarity, similitude 11 resemblance

aliment
4 eats, fare, feed, food, grub 7 nourish, nurture, sustain 9 nutriment
10 sustenance 11 nourishment

alimentary
9 nutritive 10 nourishing, sustaining
11 nutritional

alimentary canal
7 enteron

alimony
4 keep 5 bread 6 living, upkeep

7 support 9 allowance, provision
10 livelihood, sustenance 11 maintenance, subsistence

alive

4 rife, spry 5 alert, awake, aware, brisk, fresh, quick, ready, vital 6 active, extant, living, moving, viable 7 animate, dynamic, knowing, replete, running, teeming, working, zestful 8 animated, existent, existing, sensible, sentient, swarming, thronged 9 abounding, breathing, cognizant, conscious, energetic, operative, sensitive, wide-awake 11 functioning, overflowing

alkali

4 base, salt 9 substance 11 soluble salt
metal: 6 cesium, sodium 7 lithium 8 francium, rubidium 9 potassium 10 monovalent
opposite: 4 acid

alkaline

5 acrid, basic, salty 6 bitter 7 antacid, caustic, soluble 8 chemical

alkaline substance

3 lye 4 lime, soda 5 borax 6 potash 7 ammonia, antacid 8 pearl ash, saltwort 11 caustic soda

alkaloid

4 base
medicinal: 5 ergot 7 codeine, emetine, eserine, quinine 8 atropine, caffeine, lobeline, morphine 9 ephedrine, quinidine, reserpine 11 scopolamine
narcotic: 6 heroin 7 cocaine, codeine 8 morphine
poisonous: 8 atropine, nicotine, solanine 11 scopolamine

all

3 sum 4 each 5 every, gross, total, whole 6 entire, in toto, purely, wholly 7 exactly, totally, utterly 8 complete, entirety, everyone, outright, totality 9 aggregate, everybody 10 altogether, everything

all-around

7 general, overall, skilled

8 complete, sweeping, synoptic 9 adaptable, competent, many-sided, panoramic, universal, versatile 10 consummate, proficient 11 wide-ranging 12 encompassing 13 comprehensive

allay

4 balm, calm, ease, lull 5 abate, quiet, still 6 lessen, reduce, settle, soothe, subdue 7 assuage, compose, lighten, mollify, quieten, relieve 8 decrease, diminish, mitigate, moderate 9 alleviate 11 tranquilize

all but

4 most, much, nigh 5 about 6 almost, nearly 8 as much as, in effect 9 just about, virtually 11 essentially, practically 13 approximately

All Creatures Great and Small author

7 Herriot (James)

allegation

5 claim 6 charge, report 9 assertion, statement 10 contention, profession 11 declaration

allege

3 say 4 avow, cite 5 claim, offer, state 6 adduce, assert, attest, charge, submit 7 advance, contend, declare, present, profess 8 maintain 10 put forward

alleged

6 stated 7 accused, dubious, reputed, suspect 8 asserted, declared, doubtful, so-called, supposed 9 described, pretended, professed, purported, soi-disant 10 ostensible, self-styled 12 questionable

allegiance

4 duty 5 ardor, piety 6 fealty, homage 7 loyalty 8 devotion, fidelity 9 adherence, constancy, obedience 10 dedication, obligation 11 devotedness 12 faithfulness

allegiant

4 firm, true 5 liege, loyal 6 ardent, steady 7 devoted, dutiful, staunch 8 constant, faithful, resolute 9 steadfast 10 dependable

allegorical

allegorical
5 moral **6** fabled **8** mythical, symbolic **9** legendary, spiritual **10** emblematic, exegetical, fictitious, figurative **12** iconographic, illustrative, metaphorical

allegory
4 myth, tale **5** fable, story **6** emblem, symbol **7** parable **8** apologue **9** symbolism **10** figuration **12** typification

allegro
5 brisk **6** bouncy, lively **8** animated, spirited **9** sprightly

allergy
5 dread **6** hatred **7** disgust, dislike **8** aversion, distaste **9** antipathy, disliking, rejection, repulsion

alleviate
4 cure, ease **5** allay **6** lessen, reduce, remedy **7** assuage, lighten, mollify, relieve **8** decrease, diminish, mitigate

alleviation
4 ease **6** relief **7** decline **8** decrease, easement **9** lessening, reduction **10** diminution, mitigation

alley
4 lane, walk **6** marble, street **7** passage **10** backstreet

all-fired
7 totally, utterly **9** extremely **10** absolutely, completely **11** excessively

alliance
3 tie **4** bond, pact **5** union **6** accord, league, treaty **7** compact, concord **8** affinity, relation **9** coalition **10** connection, federation **11** affiliation, association, combination, confederacy, conjunction, partnership, unification **12** relationship **13** confederation

allied
4 akin **5** bound **6** agnate, joined, linked, united **7** cognate, connate, kindred, related, unified **8** in league **9** connected **10** affiliated, associated, connatural **11** consanguine

alligator
11 crocodilian
relative: **4** croc **6** caiman, cayman **9** crocodile

alligator pear
7 avocado

all in
4 dead, used, worn **5** spent, tired **6** bushed, done in, used up **7** drained, far-gone, worn-out **8** depleted **9** dead tired, exhausted, washed-out

all in all
5 in all **6** mainly **7** en masse, largely **9** generally **10** altogether, by and large, on the whole

allocate
4 give **5** allot, slice **6** assign, divide **7** dish out, divvy up, dole out, earmark, mete out **8** set apart **9** admeasure, apportion, designate **10** distribute

allocution
4 talk **5** spiel **6** sermon, speech **7** address, lecture, oration, oratory, pep talk **11** exhortation

allot
4 give **5** grant, share **6** accord, assign **7** deal out, divvy up, dole out, mete out **8** allocate, dispense, set aside **9** admeasure, apportion **10** distribute

allotment
3 cut, lot **4** bite, part **5** chunk, piece, quota, share, slice **6** ration **7** measure, portion **9** allowance, provision **13** apportionment

all-out
4 full **5** total **6** entire, utmost **7** maximum **8** absolute, complete, thorough **9** full-blown, full-scale, unlimited **12** totalitarian **13** thoroughgoing

all over
8 wherever **9** all around **10** everyplace, everywhere, far and near, far and wide, high and low, thoroughly, throughout

allow
3 let, lot, own **4** avow, give **5** admit,

allot, brook, grant, leave, let on, stand 6 assign, endure, permit, suffer 7 concede, confess, consent, forbear, mete out 8 allocate, tolerate 9 apportion 11 acknowledge

allowance
3 aid, cut, lot, pay, sum 4 bite, edge, help, part 5 grant, leave, piece, quota, share, slice 6 amount, permit, ration 7 consent, measure, partage, portion, quantum, subsidy, vantage 8 handicap, pittance, quantity, sanction 9 advantage, allotment, head start, reduction 10 adjustment, allocation, assistance, concession, permission, sufferance, toleration 13 accommodation, apportionment, authorization

alloy
5 blend 6 fusion 7 amalgam, mixture 8 compound 9 admixture, composite 10 adulterant 11 interfusion 12 amalgamation, intermixture
brass-like: 6 latten
copper-sulfur: 6 niello
copper-tin: 6 bronze
copper-zinc: 5 brass 6 tombac
gold-like: 6 ormolu
gold-silver: 8 electrum
iron-carbon: 5 steel
iron-nickel: 5 invar
mercury: 7 amalgam
tin-lead: 5 terne 6 pewter, solder
used in jewelry: 6 tombac

all-powerful
6 mighty 7 supreme 8 absolute, almighty 10 invincible, omnipotent 11 controlling

all right
3 aye, yea, yep, yes 4 good, okay, safe, well 6 agreed, decent, proper, surely 7 average 8 adequate, of course, passable, passably, pleasing, standard, very well 9 agreeable, certainly, tolerable, tolerably 10 , acceptably, adequately, definitely, positively, sufficient, well enough 12 satisfactory

all round
see **all-around**

All the King's Men author
6 Warren (Robert Penn)

All the Way Home author
4 Agee (James)

allude
4 hint 5 imply, point, refer 7 bring up, suggest 8 indicate, intimate

allure
4 draw, pull 5 charm, tempt 6 appeal, entice, lead on, seduce 7 attract, beguile, enchant, glamour, win over 8 charisma, inveigle, persuade 9 captivate, fascinate, magnetism, magnetize 10 attraction 11 enchantment, fascination

alluring
6 lovely 7 winning, winsome 8 charming, inviting, pleasing 9 appealing, beguiling, glamorous, seductive 10 appetizing, attractive, bewitching, enchanting 11 captivating, fascinating

ally
4 join 5 unite 6 friend, helper 7 comrade, partner 8 federate 9 accessory, affiliate, associate, auxiliary, bedfellow, colleague, supporter 10 accomplice 11 confederate 12 collaborator

almighty
4 very 6 hugely, mighty 7 awfully, godlike, supreme 8 absolute 9 extremely 10 invincible, omnipotent 11 all-powerful, exceedingly

almost
4 nigh 5 about 6 all but, nearly 8 as good as, as much as, not quite, well-nigh 9 just about, virtually 11 essentially, practically 13 approximately
Scottish: 6 feckly

alms
4 gift 6 relief 7 present 8 donation, offering 10 assistance 11 benefaction, beneficence 12 contribution

aloe
9 emollient, succulent

Aloeus
father: 7 Neptune 8 Poseidon

mother: 6 Canace
son: 4 Otus 9 Ephialtes
wife: 9 Iphimedia

aloft
4 high, over 5 above 6 on high, upward 7 skyward 8 in flight, overhead

aloha
4 by-by, ciao, hail 5 hello, howdy 6 bye-bye, good-by, so long 7 goodbye, welcome 8 farewell, greeting 9 greetings
State: 6 Hawaii

alone
4 only, sole, solo, stag 5 apart 6 singly, solely, unique, wholly 7 isolate, removed 8 detached, entirely, isolated, peerless, singular, solitary 9 matchless, unequaled, unmatched, unrivaled 10 nothing but, unequalled, unexampled, unexcelled 11 exclusively, unsurpassed 12 incomparable, unparalleled, unrepeatable 13 unaccompanied

aloneness
8 solitude 9 isolation, seclusion 10 uniqueness

along
3 too, yet 4 also, near, with 5 forth, there 6 as well, at hand, on hand, onward 7 besides, forward 8 likewise, moreover 11 furthermore 12 accompanying, additionally

alongside
6 beside, next to 8 touching 9 adjoining, bordering

aloof
3 shy 4 cold, cool 5 apart, proud 6 casual, chilly, frigid, offish, remote 7 distant, haughty, removed, stuck up 8 arrogant, detached, reserved, reticent, solitary 9 incurious, unbending, uncurious, withdrawn 10 disdainful, restrained, unfriendly, unsociable 11 constrained, indifferent, standoffish, unconcerned 12 uninterested 13 disinterested

alopecia
8 baldness

alp
4 peak 5 mount 8 mountain

alpaca
4 wool 5 cloth 6 mammal
habitat: 4 Peru 5 Andes 7 Bolivia

alpha
4 dawn 5 first, start 6 outset 7 dawning, genesis, opening 9 beginning 12 commencement

alphabet
4 ABC's 7 letters
Arabic: 3 ayn, dad, dal, gaf, jim, kaf, kha, lam, mim, nun, qaf, sad, sin, tha, waw, zay 4 alif, dhal, shin 5 ghayn
Greek: 3 chi, eta, phi, psi, rho, tau 4 beta, iota, zeta 5 alpha, delta, gamma, kappa, omega, sigma, theta 6 lambda 7 epsilon, omicron, upsilon
Hebrew: 3 mem, nun, sin, taw, tet, vav, waw, yod 4 alef, ayin, beth, heth, kaph, koph, qoph, resh, shin, teth 5 aleph, gimel, lamed, sadhe, tsade, zayin 6 daleth, samekh
Old Irish: 4 ogam 5 ogham
runic: 7 futhark

Alpheus
beloved: 8 Arethusa
father: 7 Oceanus
form: 5 river
mother: 6 Tethys

Alpine
animal: 4 ibex 7 chamois
dress: 6 dirndl
house: 6 chalet
lake: 4 Como, Iseo 5 Garda 6 Geneva 7 Lucerne 8 Bodensee, Maggiore 7 Constance, Neuchâtel
pass: 3 col 5 Cenis 7 Brenner, Simplon 9 St. Bernard
peak: 5 Blanc, Eiger 7 Bernina 8 Jungfrau 10 Matterhorn
plant: 9 edelweiss
primrose: 8 auricula
resort: 5 Davos 7 Bolzano, Zermatt 8 Chamonix, Grenoble 9 Innsbruck 10 Interlaken 11 Saint Moritz
river: 5 Rhine, Rhône
snowfield: 4 firn, névé
staff: 10 alpenstock

state: 5 Tirol, Tyrol 7 Bavaria
tunnel: 5 Blanc, Cenis 7 Arlberg, Simplon 10 St. Gotthard
wind: 4 bora, föhn 5 foehn

already

4 even, once 5 by now, prior 6 before, by then 7 earlier, just now 8 formerly 9 before now 10 by this time, heretofore, previously

also

3 and, too 4 more, plus 5 again, along 6 as well 7 besides, further 8 likewise, moreover 9 along with, including, similarly 10 in addition 11 furthermore 12 additionally

also-ran

3 dud 5 loser 7 failure, washout 8 defeated

altar

6 shrine
boy: 6 server 7 acolyte
cloth: 4 pall 7 frontal
constellation: 3 Ara
hanging: 6 dorsal, dossal
platform: 8 predella
screen: 7 reredos
shelf: 7 retable
site: 4 apse, bema
vessel: 5 cruet, paten 7 chalice 8 ciborium 10 monstrance

alter

3 fix 4 geld, spay, turn, vary 5 adapt 6 adjust, change, doctor, modify, mutate, neuter, revamp 7 remodel 8 castrate, moderate, modulate 9 refashion

alteration

4 turn 5 shift 6 change 8 mutation, revision 9 variation 10 adaptation, adjustment, changeover, conversion, remodeling, transition 12 modification

altercate

4 spat, tiff 5 argue, scrap 6 bicker, hassle 7 dispute, quarrel, wrangle 8 squabble 9 caterwaul

altercation

3 row 4 beef, flap, spat, tiff 5 brawl 6 blowup, combat, fracas, hassle

7 contest, dispute, quarrel, rhubarb, wrangle 8 argument, squabble 9 bickering 10 falling-out 11 controversy, embroilment

alternate

3 sub 5 proxy 6 backup, by turn, change, fill-in, rotate, second 7 another, relieve, stand-in 8 periodic, rotating 9 change off, fluctuate, recurrent, recurring, replacing, surrogate 10 equivalent, every other, periodical, substitute 11 every second, pinch hitter, replacement 12 intermittent

alternately

6 in lieu, rather 7 instead 10 preferably

alternative

5 other, proxy 6 backup, choice, option, second 7 another 8 atypical, druthers, election 9 different, selection, surrogate 10 preference, substitute 11 contingency, nonstandard, possibility

Althaea

father: 8 Thestius
husband: 6 Oeneus
son (victim): 8 Meleager

although

4 when 5 still, while 6 albeit, even if, much as 7 despite, howbeit, whereas

altitude

6 height 8 eminence 9 elevation, high level

altitudinous

4 high, tall 7 eminent 8 elevated

altogether

4 nude, well 5 fully, in all, quite 6 in toto, wholly 7 all told, en masse, exactly, totally, utterly 8 all in all, entirely 9 generally, perfectly 10 absolutely, by and large, completely, on the whole, thoroughly

altruism

7 charity 8 sympathy 10 compassion, generosity 11 benevolence 12 philanthropy, selflessness 13 unselfishness

altruistic

3 big **6** humane **8** generous **9** unselfish **10** benevolent, bighearted, charitable, open-handed **11** considerate, magnanimous, noble-minded **12** humanitarian **13** philanthropic

alum

4 grad **6** emetic **7** styptic **8** graduate **10** astringent

always

4 ever **7** forever **8** evermore, for keeps **9** at any rate, endlessly, eternally **10** at all times, constantly, in any event, invariably **11** continually, forevermore, in perpetuum, perpetually, unceasingly **12** consistently, continuously

Amahl and the Night Visitors composer

7 Menotti (Gian Carlo)

amalgamate

3 mix **4** ally, fuse, meld, pool **5** admix, alloy, merge, unify, unite **6** mingle **7** combine **8** coalesce, compound, intermix **9** commingle, integrate **11** consolidate, intermingle

amalgamation

5 alloy, blend, union **6** fusion, merger **7** joining, melding, merging, mixture, uniting **8** alliance, compound **9** admixture, coalition, composite **10** commixture **12** intermixture **13** consolidation

Amalthea

form: **4** goat
horn: **10** cornucopia
nursling: **4** Zeus

amanita

8 death cap, mushroom **9** fly agaric

amanuensis

6 scribe **7** copyist **9** scrivener, secretary **11** transcriber **12** stenographer

amass

4 bulk, heap, make, pile **5** hoard, lay up, store, uplay **6** accrue, garner, gather, pile up, roll up **7** acquire, collect, compile, round up, store up **8** assemble, cumulate **9** aggregate, stockpile **10** accumulate **12** come together

amassment

4 pile **5** clump, group, hoard, stack, stock, store, trove **7** cluster **8** assembly, quantity **9** gathering, stockpile **10** assemblage, collection, cumulation **11** aggregation **12** accumulation **13** agglomeration

amateur

4 tyro **6** layman, novice, tinker, votary **7** admirer, dabbler, devotee, learner **8** aspirant, beginner, neophyte, putterer **9** greenhorn, smatterer **10** apprentice, dilettante, enthusiast, uninitiate **11** abecedarian

amateurish

3 raw **5** green **6** simple **7** artless **8** dabbling, inexpert **9** deficient, unskilled, untutored **10** dilettante, unfinished, unpolished, unskillful **12** dilettantist, unproficient **13** inexperienced

amative

see **amorous**

amatory

6 ardent, erotic, loving, tender **7** sensual **8** romantic **9** erogenous, seductive **10** passionate **11** aphrodisiac

amaze

4 daze **5** floor **6** wonder **7** astound, perplex, startle **8** astonish, bewilder, blow away, bowl over, confound, surprise **9** dumbfound **10** admiration **11** flabbergast

amazement

3 awe **6** marvel, wonder **8** surprise **9** marveling **10** admiration, perplexity, wonderment **12** astonishment, bewilderment, confoundment

amazing

7 awesome **8** striking, stunning, wondrous **9** marvelous, startling, wonderful **10** astounding, impressive, miraculous, stupendous, surprising **11** astonishing, bewildering, spectacular **12** breathtaking

Amazon
6 parrot **7** warrior **8** giantess **12** woman warrior

ambassador
5 agent, envoy **6** legate **8** diplomat, emissary **9** messenger
papal: 6 nuncio

amber
5 ocher, ochre, resin, rosin **6** orange, yellow **7** saffron

ambience
4 mood, tone **6** flavor, medium, milieu **7** climate **10** atmosphere **11** environment **12** surroundings

ambient
5 music **6** milieu **7** general, setting **8** everyday **9** prevalent **10** atmosphere, prevailing **11** atmospheric, environment, mise-en-scène **12** encompassing, surroundings **13** environmental

ambiguity
5 doubt **6** enigma, puzzle **7** evasion **9** equivoque, obscurity, vagueness **11** incertitude, uncertainty **12** doubtfulness, equivocality, equivocation **13** double meaning

ambiguous
5 vague **6** opaque, unsure **7** cryptic, dubious, inexact, obscure, unclear **8** doubtful, puzzling **9** enigmatic, equivocal, tenebrous, uncertain, unsettled **10** indefinite, inexplicit **11** problematic **12** inconclusive, questionable

ambit
4 area, room **5** field, limit, orbit, range, reach, scope, space, sweep **6** border, bounds, extent, limits, radius, sphere **7** breadth, circuit, compass, expanse, purview **8** boundary, confines **9** extension, perimeter, periphery **13** circumference

ambition
3 aim **4** goal, hope, itch, push, wish, zeal **5** ardor, dream, drive, vigor

6 desire, energy, hunger, spirit, target, thirst **7** avidity, craving, purpose **8** appetite, striving, yearning **9** eagerness, intention, objective **10** aspiration, enterprise, enthusiasm, get-up-and-go, initiative, pretension

ambitious
4 avid, bold, keen **5** eager, pushy **6** driven, hungry, intent **7** driving, zealous **8** aspiring, desirous, striving **9** energetic **10** aggressive **11** hardworking **12** enterprising, enthusiastic

ambivalent
5 mixed **6** unsure **7** warring **8** clashing, wavering **9** equivocal, uncertain, undecided **10** unresolved **11** fluctuating, vacillating **13** contradictory

amble
4 gait, walk **5** dally, drift, mosey **6** dawdle, linger, stroll, wander **7** meander, saunter

ambrosia
6 dainty, regale **7** dessert, perfume **8** delicacy, ointment

ambrosial
5 balmy, spicy, sweet **6** savory **7** scented **8** aromatic, fragrant, heavenly, luscious, perfumed, pleasing, redolent **9** delicious **10** delectable, delightful **11** scrumptious

ambulate
4 hoof, move, pace, step, walk **5** tread, troop **6** foot it, hoof it **7** traipse

ambulatory
6 moving, on foot, roving **7** nomadic, roaming, walking **8** vagabond **9** itinerant **11** peripatetic

ambush
4 jump, lurk, trap **5** snare **6** assail, attack, entrap, lay for, waylay **7** assault, ensnare **8** surprise **9** ambuscade **11** concealment

ameliorate
3 fix **4** help, lift, mend **5** amend, raise **6** better, perk up, remedy,

reform **7** elevate, enhance, improve, lighten, relieve, upgrade **8** mitigate **9** alleviate **10** convalesce, recuperate

amenable
4 open, tame **6** docile, liable, pliant, suited **7** plastic, pliable, subdued, subject, willing **8** biddable, in accord, obedient, yielding **9** adaptable, agreeable, complying, malleable, receptive, tractable **10** answerable, consenting, responsive, submissive **11** accountable, acquiescent, cooperative, responsible

amend
3 fix **4** help **5** alter, right **6** better, change, modify, reform, remedy, repair, revise, square **7** correct, improve, rectify **8** put right **9** meliorate **10** ameliorate

amendment
5 rider **6** change, remedy, reform **7** codicil, repair **8** addendum, revision **10** alteration, attachment, correction **11** enhancement, improvement, reformation **12** modification **13** rectification

amends
7 redress **8** reprisal **9** indemnity, quittance **10** recompense, reparation **11** restitution **12** compensation

amenities
5 mores **6** polish **7** decorum, manners **8** civility, courtesy **9** etiquette, propriety **12** social graces

amenity
5 charm, frill **6** luxury **7** comfort, quality **8** civility, courtesy, facility **9** advantage, etiquette, geniality, pleasance **10** affability, amiability, betterment, cordiality, enrichment, pleasantry, politeness **11** convenience, enhancement, improvement, sociability **12** agreeability, graciousness, pleasantness

ament
6 catkin

amerce
3 tax **4** dock, fine, levy **5** exact, mulct **6** punish **7** hit with, make pay **8** penalize

amercement
4 fine **5** mulct **7** damages, forfeit, penalty **10** assessment, punishment, reparation

American League
Baltimore: 7 Orioles
Boston: 6 Red Sox
Anaheim: 6 Angels
Chicago: 8 White Sox
Cleveland: 7 Indians
Detroit: 6 Tigers
Kansas City: 6 Royals
Milwaukee: 7 Brewers
Minnesota: 5 Twins
New York: 7 Yankees
Oakland: 9 Athletics
Seattle: 8 Mariners
Tampa Bay: 9 Devil Rays
Texas: 7 Rangers
Toronto: 8 Blue Jays

American Samoa
capital: 8 Pago Pago
island, island group: 4 Rose **5** Aunuu, Manua **6** Swains **7** Tutuila
language: 6 Samoan

America, the Beautiful
music: 4 Ward (Samuel Augustus)
words: 5 Bates (Katherine Lee)

Amfortas
father: 7 Titurel
opera: 8 Parsifal

amiability
7 amenity **9** geniality, pleasance **10** cordiality **11** sociability **12** complaisance, congeniality, friendliness, pleasantness, sociableness **13** agreeableness, enjoyableness

amiable
4 kind, warm **6** genial, gentle, kindly **7** affable, cordial, likable **8** cheerful, friendly, gracious, likeable, obliging, sociable **9** agreeable, congenial, courteous **10** responsive **11** com-

plaisant, good-humored, good-natured, warmhearted

amicable
7 cordial, pacific 8 empathic, friendly, peaceful, sociable 9 congenial, peaceable 10 harmonious, like-minded, neighborly 11 sympathetic 13 understanding

amid
4 over 5 among, midst 6 during 7 amongst, between 10 throughout

amigo
3 pal 4 chum, mate, pard 6 friend 7 comrade, partner 8 sidekick 9 companion, confidant 12 acquaintance

amino acid
4 dopa 6 leucin, lysine, serine, toluid, valine 7 cystein, cystine, glycine, leucine, proline, toluide 8 cysteine, dopamine, histidin, thyroxin, toluidin, tyrosine

Amis, Kingsley
novel: 8 Lucky Jim
son: 6 Martin

amiss
3 bad 4 awry, poor 5 badly, wrong 6 afield, astray, faulty, flawed 7 wrongly 8 erringly, faultily 9 defective, imperfect 10 improperly, mistakenly, out of place 11 erroneously, imperfectly, incorrectly, unfavorably 12 inaccurately 13 inappropriate

amity
5 union 6 accord, comity, unison 7 concert, concord, harmony 8 alliance, goodwill 9 agreement 10 cordiality, friendship, kindliness 11 concurrence 12 friendliness

Ammonite
6 Semite
god: 6 Molech, Moloch

ammunition
4 shot 5 bombs 6 rounds, shells 7 charges 8 armament, grenades, missiles, ordnance 10 cartridges 11 projectiles

Amneris's rival
4 Aïda

amnesty
6 pardon 7 freeing, release 8 immunity, reprieve 9 discharge 10 absolution 11 forgiveness 12 dispensation

Amnon
father: 5 David
half sister: 5 Tamar
mother: 7 Ahinoam

amoeba
4 blob 8 rhizopod 9 protozoan

Amon
father: 8 Manasseh
son: 6 Josiah

Amonasro's daughter
4 Aïda

among
3 mid 4 amid 5 midst 6 amidst, within 7 between
prefix: 5 inter

amorist
4 rake, wolf 5 lover, Romeo 7 Don Juan, gallant, playboy 8 Casanova, lothario, paramour 9 womanizer 12 heartbreaker

amorous
6 ardent, erotic, in love 7 amative, amatory, lustful 8 enamored, romantic 10 infatuated, passionate 11 aphrodisiac, impassioned

amorousness
4 love, lust 5 amour, ardor 6 desire 7 passion 9 eroticism

amorphous
7 unclear 8 formless, inchoate, nebulous, unformed, unshaped 9 shapeless, undefined 10 indistinct 11 nondescript 12 disorganized 13 characterless

amortize

5 repay 6 pay off, reduce 7 pay down 8 write off

amount

4 bulk, dose 5 add up, equal, price, total 6 dosage, matter, number, upshot 7 purport, quantum 8 quantity 9 aggregate, substance

owed: 4 debt

small: 3 bit, jot 4 atom, drop, iota, mite, whit 5 minim, spark, speck, trace 7 modicum, smidgen 8 molecule, particle 9 scintilla

amour

4 love 5 fling, lover 6 affair 7 liaison, passion, romance 8 intimacy, intrigue 9 dalliance 10 love affair 12 entanglement, relationship

amour propre

5 pride 6 egoism, vanity 7 conceit, egotism 8 self-love, vainness 9 vainglory 10 narcissism, self-esteem, self-regard 11 self-conceit, self-respect 12 pridefulness 13 conceitedness

amphetamines

5 speed 6 dexies, hearts, uppers 7 bennies, Dexoxyn 8 greenies, pep pills, Preludin 9 Dexedrine 10 Benzedrine, Methedrine

amphibian

burrowing: 9 caecilian

legless: 9 caecilian

tailed: 3 eft 4 newt 10 salamander

tailless: 4 frog, toad 8 bullfrog, tree toad 10 batrachian

wormlike: 9 caecilian

young: 7 tadpole 8 polliwog

Amphion

brother: 6 Zethus

conquest: 6 Thebes

father: 4 Zeus

mother: 7 Antiope

sister: 5 Aedon

wife: 5 Niobe

amphitheater

4 bowl 5 arena 7 stadium 8 coliseum 10 auditorium, hippodrome

Amphitrite

father: 6 Nereus

husband: 7 Neptune 8 Poseidon

mother: 5 Doris

son: 6 Triton

Amphitryon's wife

7 Alcmene

amphora

3 jar, jug, urn 4 ewer, vase 5 crock, flask 6 carafe, flagon, vessel

ample

4 wide 5 buxom, great, large, roomy 6 lavish, plenty, portly 7 copious, liberal, profuse 8 abundant, generous, handsome, spacious 9 bounteous, bountiful, capacious, expansive, extensive, plenteous, plentiful 10 commodious, sufficient 11 substantial

amplify

5 boost, raise, swell 6 dilate, expand, extend, jack up 7 augment, develop, distend, enhance, enlarge, inflate, magnify 8 increase 9 elaborate, intensify 10 supplement

amplitude

4 size 5 range, scale, scope, space 6 amount, extent, spread 7 bigness, breadth, expanse, stretch 8 distance, fullness, wideness 9 abundance, expansion, greatness, largeness, magnitude, roominess 12 spaciousness 13 capaciousness

amulet

4 juju, luck 5 charm 6 fetish, grigri, mascot 7 periapt 8 gris-gris, talisman 10 lucky piece, phylactery 11 rabbit's-foot

amuse

4 wile 5 charm, cheer 6 appeal, divert, engage, occupy, please, regale, tickle 7 animate, beguile, delight, enchant, enliven, gladden 8 distract, interest, recreate 9 entertain, fascinate

amusement

3 fun 4 play 7 delight, pastime 8 pleasure 9 diversion, enjoyment 10 recreation 11 distraction 13 entertainment

amusing
3 fun 5 droll, funny 7 comical, risible
8 engaging, humorous, pleasing
9 diverting, enjoyable 9 laughable
12 entertaining

Amycus
father: 7 Neptune 8 Poseidon
friend: 8 Heracles, Hercules
mother: 5 Melia

ana
5 varia 7 sayings 9 anecdotes
10 collection, miscellany 11 mem-
orabilia, miscellanea

anabasis
5 march 7 advance, headway, retreat 8 progress 11 advancement,
progression

anagogic
6 arcane, hidden, mystic, occult, secret 7 obscure 8 esoteric, mystical,
telestic 9 spiritual 10 symbolical
11 allegorical

analects
5 album 6 digest 7 garland, omnibus 8 treasury 9 anthology, selection 10 compendium, miscellany
11 compilation, florilegium

analgesic
6 opiate 7 anodyne 10 anesthetic,
painkiller

analogous
4 akin, like 5 alike 7 kindred, similar,
related, uniform 8 parallel 9 consonant 10 comparable, equivalent, resembling

analogue
5 match 7 cognate 8 parallel
9 correlate 10 similarity 11 correlation, counterpart, equivalence
13 correspondent

analogy
6 simile 8 affinity, likeness, metaphor,
parallel, relation 9 agreement, alikeness, semblance 10 comparison,
similarity, similitude 11 correlation,
equivalence, resemblance

analysis
5 assay, audit, proof, study 6 method,
review, report, survey 7 finding,
inquiry 8 division 9 breakdown,
partition, statement 10 dissection,
inspection, resolution, separation
11 examination 13 clarification

analytic
6 cogent, subtle 7 logical, testing
8 studious 9 organized 10 diagnostic, scientific, systematic 11 proposition, questioning 13 investiga-
tive, ratiocinative

analyze
4 part, test 5 assay, study 6 divide
7 dissect, examine, inspect, resolve
8 classify, consider, separate 9 anatomize, break down, decompose, interpret 10 decompound, scrutinize
11 deconstruct, distinguish, investigate

analyze grammatically
5 parse

Ananias
4 liar 9 falsifier 12 prevaricator
father: 9 Nedebaeus
wife (coconspirator): 8 Sapphira

anarchism
4 riot 6 theory 7 misrule 8 disorder
9 distemper, rebellion 11 lawlessness

anarchist
5 rebel 6 rioter 8 agitator, mutineer,
provoker, revolter 9 dissident, insurgent 10 malcontent 11 provocateur
13 revolutionary

anarchy
4 riot 5 chaos 7 misrule, mob rule,
turmoil 8 disarray, disorder 9 confusion, distemper, mobocracy, rebellion 10 ochlocracy, revolution
11 lawlessness 13 nongovernment

anathema
3 ban 4 bane 5 curse, enemy,
odium, taboo 6 pariah 7 bugbear,
censure, malison, outcast, reproof
8 loathing 9 damnation, bête noire
10 black beast, execration 11 abomination, commination, detestation, imprecation, malediction
12 condemnation, denunciation

anathematize

3 ban 4 damn, oust 5 curse, expel
6 banish 7 condemn 8 denounce,
execrate 9 objurgate, proscribe
13 excommunicate

anatomical depression

5 fossa, fovea

anatomical tube

3 vas 4 duct 5 canal

anatomist

5 Wolff (Kaspar) 6 Harvey (William)
8 Vesalius (Andreas)

anatomize

5 cut up 7 analyze, dissect 8 separate 9 break down, decompose

anatomy

5 frame, mummy 6 makeup 8 analysis, division, skeleton 9 framework,
histology, structure 10 dissection,
morphology, physiology 11 examination

Anaxo

brother: 10 Amphitryon
daughter: 7 Alcmene
father: 7 Alcaeus
husband: 9 Electryon

ancestor

8 forebear, foregoer 9 ascendant,
precursor, prototype 10 antecedent,
antecessor, forefather, forerunner,
progenitor 11 predecessor 12 primogenitor

ancestral

6 family, inborn, inbred, lineal
7 genetic 8 familial 9 inherited
10 bequeathed, hereditary 11 consanguine, patrimonial
sequence: 8 pedigree 9 bloodline,
genealogy

ancestry

4 line, race 5 blood, breed, stock
6 family, origin, source 7 descent,
history, kindred, lineage 8 heritage,
pedigree 9 parentage 10 derivation,
extraction

Anchises' son

6 Aeneas

anchor

4 moor 6 secure 7 grapnel, mooring
8 mainstay
part: 5 crown, fluke, shank

anchorage

4 port 5 haven, roads 6 harbor,
refuge, riding 7 mooring, shelter
9 harborage, roadstead

anchorite

5 loner 6 hermit 7 recluse 8 solitary

anchors ____

6 aweigh

ancient

3 old 4 aged 5 hoary, olden 6 age-
old, primal 7 antique, archaic,
elderly 8 Noachian, old-timer,
primeval, timeworn 9 venerable
10 primordial 12 antediluvian

ancient capital

4 Susa 5 Aksum, Balkh, Calah,
Isker, Kalhu, Ninus, Pella, Petra,
Sibir 6 Angkor, Bactra, Nimrud,
Sardis 7 Babylon, Knossos, Mem-
phis, Nineveh, Samaria, Shushan
10 Persepolis

ancient city

Asia Minor: 4 Nice, Teos 5 Tyana
6 Edessa, Nicaea 7 Antioch
13 Halicarnassus
Babylonia: 4 Sura 5 Agade, Akkad,
Eridu, Larsa 7 Ellasar
Bengal: 4 Gaur 9 Lakhnauti
Canaan: 5 Gezer
Cyprus: 7 Salamis
Egypt: 5 Tanis 6 Thebes
7 Memphis 10 Heliopolis
Etruria: 4 Veii
Euphrates River: 7 Babylon
Greece: 5 Crisa 6 Athens, Sparta
7 Calydon 10 Lacedaemon
Ionia: 4 Myus, Teos 5 Chios,
Samos 6 Priene 7 Ephesus, Lebe-
dos, Miletus, Phocaea 8 Colophon,
Erythrae 10 Clazomenae
Italy: 5 Locri 7 Pompeii 8 Siracusa,
Syracuse 11 Herculaneum
Latium: 5 Gabii 9 Alba Longa
Mayan: 4 Cobá 5 Tikal, Tulum,
Uxmal 8 Palenque 11 Chichén Itzá

Nile River: 5 Meroë
North Africa: 5 Utica 8 Carthage
Palestine: 4 Gaza 5 Ekron, Endor, Sodom 6 Beroea, Bethel, Gilead, Hebron 7 Jericho, Samaria 8 Ashkelon 9 Capernaum, Jerusalem
Peloponnesus: 5 Tegea 6 Sparta 7 Corinth
Sumeria: 4 Kish, Uruk 5 Erech, Larsa 6 Lagash
Turkey: 5 Assos, Assus 9 Byzantium

ancient country
Adriatic coast: 7 Illyria
Africa: 10 Mauretania
Arabian Peninsula: 5 Sheba
Asia: 4 Aram 5 Media, Minni, Syria 7 Armenia, Ash Sham, Bactria
Asia Minor: 5 Lydia, Mysia 6 Aeolis, Pontus 7 Cilicia, Phrygia 8 Bithynia
Balkan: 7 Macedon 9 Macedonia
Black Sea: 7 Colchis
Dead Sea: 4 Edom
Euphrates River: 9 Babylonia
Europe: 4 Gaul 5 Dacia 6 Gallia
gold-rich: 5 Ophir
Italy: 6 Latium 7 Etruria
Nile valley: 4 Cush
Peloponnesus: 4 Elis 7 Arcadia
Syria: 9 Phoenicia

ancient empire
6 Median 7 Hittite, Persian 8 Assyrian, Athenian, Chaldean, Seleucid 9 Ptolemaic 10 Babylonian

ancient kingdom
Anglo-Saxon: 6 Wessex
Asia: 4 Ghor, Ghur
Celtic: 7 Cumbria
China: 3 Shu
Euphrates valley: 4 Hira 7 Al-Hirah
Greece: 8 Pergamon, Pergamum
North Of Assyria: 3 Van 6 Ararat, Urartu
Palestine: 5 Judah 6 Israel
Persian Gulf: 4 Elam
Portugal: 7 Algarve
Spain: 4 Leon 6 Aragon 7 Castile, Galicia, Granada, Navarre

Syria: 4 Moab
Welsh: 5 Powys
West Sahara: 4 Gana 5 Ghana

ancient monument
6 sphinx 7 obelisk, pyramid

ancient royal forest
4 Dean 8 Sherwood

ancient town
Africa: 4 Zama
Armenia: 4 Dwin, Tvin
Asia Minor: 4 Soli 5 Derbe, Issus, Soloi
Attica: 6 Icaria
Black Sea: 5 Olbia 9 Apollonia
Greece: 4 Abae, Opus 8 Marathon
Italy: 4 Elea, Luna 5 Cumae, Velia
Latium: 5 Ardea, Cures
Macedonia: 5 Pydna, Stobi 9 Apollonia
Peloponnesus: 5 Asine
Persia: 6 Hormuz 8 Harmozia
Sicily: 5 Hybla
Spain: 5 Munda
Tatar: 5 Isker, Sibir
Wendish: 5 Julin

ancilla
3 aid 4 aide, ally, hand, help 6 helper 9 assistant, attendant, supporter

ancillary
5 extra 8 adjuvant, incident 9 accessory, attendant, attending, auxiliary, satellite, secondary 10 additional, coincident, collateral, subsidiary, supporting 11 appurtenant, concomitant, subordinate, subservient 12 accompanying, contributory 13 supplementary

andante
4 slow 5 tempo 7 relaxed, walking 8 moderate

Anderson, Maxwell
play: 7 High Tor 8 Key Largo 9 Winterset 11 Valley Forge 14 What Price Glory

Anderson, Sherwood
book: 9 Poor White 12 Dark Laughter 13 Winesburg Ohio

Andes native
4 Inca

andiron
7 firedog

Andorra
capital: 7 Andorra
language: 7 Catalan
liberator: 11 Charlemagne
monetary unit: 4 euro
mountain range: 8 Pyrenees
neighbor: 5 Spain 6 France
river: 6 Valira

Andrea _____
5 Doria 8 del Sarto

androgynous
7 epicene 8 bisexual 9 unisexual

android
5 robot 9 automaton

Andromache
husband: 6 Hector
son: 8 Astyanax, Molossus

Andromeda
father: 7 Cepheus
husband: 7 Perseus
mother: 7 Cassiopeia
rescuer: 7 Perseus

_____ and warp
4 weft, woof

anecdote
4 tale, yarn 5 story 7 account,
episode, recital 8 relation 9 narration, narrative 12 recollection,
reminiscence

anemic
3 wan 4 pale, thin, weak 5 pasty
6 feeble, pallid, sickly, watery 7 insipid 8 ischemic 9 bloodless, colorless 10 spiritless

anemone
9 buttercup 10 windflower

anent
4 as to, in re 5 about, as for 7 apropos 8 touching 9 as regards 10 concerning 13 with respect to

anesthetic
6 opiate 7 anodyne 9 analgesic
10 painkiller, palliative

medical: 5 ether 6 spinal 8 morphine, procaine 9 halothane, novo-
caine 10 benzocaine, chloroform,
tetracaine 11 scopolamine
suffix: 5 caine

anesthetize
4 numb, stun 6 benumb, deaden
8 etherize, knock out 9 narcotize
11 desensitize

anesthetized
4 dead, numb 5 inert 6 asleep,
torpid 10 insensible 11 insensitive,
unconscious

anew
4 over 5 again 6 afresh, de novo,
lately, of late 8 once more, recently

angel
6 backer, cherub, patron, seraph,
surety 7 sponsor 8 backer-up,
guardian 9 celestial, guarantor,
supporter 10 benefactor 11 underwriter
biblical: 5 Uriel 7 Gabriel, Michael,
Raphael
fallen: 7 Lucifer
hierarchy: 6 powers 7 thrones,
virtues 8 cherubim, seraphim
9 dominions
Mormon: 6 Moroni
of death: 6 Azrael

Angel Clare's bride
4 Tess

angelic
4 holy, pure 5 godly 6 divine
7 saintly 8 cherubic, ethereal,
heavenly 9 celestial 11 beneficient

Angelica
father: 9 Galaphron
husband: 6 Medoro
lover: 7 Orlando

Angelou work
13 Heart of a Woman (The) 25 I
Know Why the Caged Bird Sings

anger
3 ire, irk, vex 4 bile, boil, burn, fume,
fury, gall, huff, rage, rant, rave, rile
5 annoy, pique, storm, upset, wrath
6 blow up, choler, dander, enrage,
madden, nettle, offend, seethe, stir

up **7** affront, bristle, dudgeon, flare up, incense, outrage, provoke, steam up, umbrage **8** acrimony, boil over, irritate **9** aggravate, annoyance, animosity, displease, infuriate **10** antagonism, antagonize, exasperate **11** displeasure, indignation, infuriation **12** exasperation

angle
3 aim, bow **4** axil, bend, bias, fish, hand, skew, turn **5** facet, slant **6** aspect, corner, crotch, dogleg **7** flexure, outlook, turning **9** direction, viewpoint **10** standpoint

angler
6 fisher **8** monkfish **9** fisherman, goosefish

Anglo-Saxon
assembly: 4 moot **5** gemot **6** gemote
council: 9 heptarchy
county: 5 shire
court: 4 moot **5** gemot **6** gemote
crown tax: 4 geld
epic: 7 Beowulf
free servant: 5 thane, thegn
god: 3 Ing
goddess of fate: 4 Wyrd
historian: 4 Bede
king: 3 Ine, Ini **4** Edwy **5** Edgar, Edred **6** Alfred, Edmund, Edward, Egbert **8** Ethelred
kingdom: 4 Kent **5** Essex **6** Mercia, Sussex, Wessex **10** East Anglia **11** Northumbria
king's council: 5 witan
letter: 3 edh, eth, wen, wyn **4** wynn **5** thorn
nobleman: 4 earl
poet: 4 scop
prince: 8 atheling
sheriff: 5 reeve
slave: 4 esne
warrior: 5 thane, thegn

Angola
capital: 6 Luanda
city: 6 Huambo **7** Lubango **8** Benguela
exclave: 7 Cabinda
language: 10 Portuguese
monetary unit: 6 kwanza

neighbor: 5 Congo **6** Zambia **7** Namibia **11** South Africa
river: 5 Congo

angora
3 cat **4** goat, hair, wool, yarn **6** mohair, rabbit

angry
3 hot, mad **4** sore **5** irate, riled, riley, upset, vexed, wroth **6** fuming, heated, ireful, wrathy **7** enraged, furious, riled up **8** choleric, incensed, inflamed, maddened, wrathful **9** indignant, irritated **10** aggravated, infuriated **11** acrimonious, exasperated

angst
4 fear **5** worry **6** unease **7** anxiety, concern **8** distress **10** insecurity **11** disquietude, fretfulness **12** apprehension

Anguilla
island, island group: 3 Dog **4** Seal **5** Scrub **7** Leeward
language: 7 English
location: 10 West Indies
territory of: 7 Britain

anguish
3 rue, woe **4** ache, care, dole, hurt, pain, pang **5** agony, dread, grief, throe, worry **6** misery, regret, sorrow, throes **7** anxiety, torment, torture **8** distress, hardship **9** heartache, suffering **10** affliction, heartbreak **12** wretchedness

angular
4 bony, edgy, lank, lean, thin **5** gaunt, lanky, spare, stiff **6** forked, skinny, zigzag **7** pointed, scraggy, scrawny **8** cornered, rawboned, ungainly **9** roughhewn **10** unfinished, ungraceful, unpolished **13** sharp-cornered

ani
6 cuckoo

anima
4 soul **6** psyche, spirit **9** inner self

animadversion
4 slam, slur **7** censure, obloquy

9 aspersion, criticism **10** accusation, imputation, reflection **11** insinuation **12** reprehension

animadvert
6 notice **7** observe **9** criticize

animal
5 beast, brute, feral **6** brutal, carnal, ferine **7** beastly, bestial, brutish, critter, fleshly, sensual, swinish, wilding **8** creature, wildling
antlered: 3 elk **4** axis, deer **5** moose **7** caribou **8** reindeer
aquatic: 3 eel **4** fish, frog, seal **5** otter, whale **6** dugong, sea cow, walrus **7** dolphin, manatee, octopus **8** bryozoan, porpoise **9** alligator, crocodile
arboreal: 4 bird **5** chimp, coati, koala, lemur, sloth **6** gibbon, monkey **7** opossum, tarsier **8** kinkajou, marmoset, squirrel **9** orangutan
burrowing: 4 mole **5** brock, ratel **6** badger, gopher, marmot, rabbit **7** echidna **9** armadillo, groundhog, woodchuck
castrated: 5 capon, steer **6** barrow, wether **7** gelding
draft: 3 yak **4** mule, oxen (plural) **5** horse **6** donkey **8** elephant
exhibit: 3 zoo
extinct: 3 moa **4** dodo, urus **6** quagga **7** mammoth **8** dinosaur, eohippus, mastodon **9** trilobite
female: 3 cow, dam, doe, ewe, hen, pen, roe, sow **4** mare, puss **5** bitch, goose, jenny, nanny, vixen **6** jennet **7** lioness
four-footed: 9 quadruped
four-limbed: 8 tetrapod
free-swimming: 6 nekton
hibernating: 4 bear, frog, toad **5** skunk, snake **7** polecat **8** chipmunk **9** groundhog, woodchuck
horned: 3 ram, yak **4** bull, goat, ibex, kudu **5** addax, bison, eland, rhino **6** cattle, koodoo **7** buffalo, gazelle, giraffe, unicorn **8** antelope
humped: 3 elk, yak **4** zebu **5** bison, camel, moose
imaginary: 5 snark
insect-eating: 4 mole, newt

5 gecko, shrew **7** echidna **8** aardvark, anteater, hedgehog, pangolin, tamandua **10** salamander
male: 3 cob, ram, tom **4** boar, buck, bull, cock, stag, stud **5** billy, steer **6** gander **7** gobbler, rooster **8** bachelor, stallion
many-celled: 8 metazoan
many-footed: 9 centipede, millipede
marsupial: 5 koala **6** wombat **7** opossum, wallaby **8** kangaroo **9** bandicoot, phalanger
meat-eating: 9 carnivore
mythical: 5 Hydra **6** dragon, kraken, sphinx **7** centaur, griffin, mermaid, Pegasus, unicorn **8** basilisk, Cerberus, Minotaur
one-celled: 9 protozoan
Peruvian: 5 llama **6** alpaca, vicuña
plant-eating: 9 herbivore
skin disease: 5 mange
snouted: 5 coati, tapir **8** mongoose
(see also **animal insect-eating**)
spotted: 4 axis, paca **6** calico, jaguar, ocelot **7** cheetah, leopard, piebald **8** skewbald **9** dalmatian
striped: 4 kudo **5** tiger, zebra **6** koodoo, quagga
trail: 3 pug **4** foil, slot **5** spoor
tusked: 6 walrus **7** warthog **8** elephant
two-footed: 5 biped
web-footed: 4 duck, frog, toad **5** goose, otter **6** beaver **8** duckbill, platypus
young: 3 cub, kid, kit, pup **4** calf, colt, fawn, foal, joey, lamb **5** bunny, chick, kitty, poult, shoat, stirk, whelp **6** cygnet, farrow, heifer, kitten, piglet **7** bullock, gosling, lambkin **8** suckling, yeanling, yearling **9** fledgling

animal behavior
study of: 8 ethology

animal fat
4 suet **6** tallow

animalism
4 lust **7** abandon **8** vitality **9** carnality **10** sensualism, sensuality **11** lustfulness, physicality, unrestraint

animalize
4 warp 6 debase 7 corrupt, deprave, pervert, vitiate 9 brutalize 10 bestialize, demoralize

animal life
5 fauna

animal sound
3 arf, baa, bay, caw, coo, low, mew, moo 4 bark, bray, buzz, crow, hiss, hoot, howl, meow, purr, roar, yelp 5 bleat, chirp, croak, drone, growl, grunt, miaow, neigh, quack 6 bellow, gibber, gobble, warble 7 screech, twitter

animate
4 fire, live, move, spur, stir, urge 5 alert, alive, cheer, drive, exalt, impel, liven, nerve, spark, steel, vital 6 active, arouse, excite, inform, kindle, lively, living, viable, vivify 7 actuate, chirk up, dynamic, enliven, hearten, inspire, quicken, refresh 8 activate, embolden, energize, inspirit, motivate, spirited, vitalize 9 breathing, encourage, energized, enhearten, make alive, stimulate 10 invigorate

animated
3 gay 4 keen 5 alert, alive, peppy, quick, vivid, vital 6 lively, living 7 dynamic, excited, vibrant, zestful 8 spirited, vigorous 9 activated, energetic, energized, exuberant, sprightly, vitalized, vivacious 12 high-spirited

animation
3 pep, vim 4 brio, dash, élan, life, zing 5 oomph, verve 6 energy, esprit, gaiety, spirit 8 dynamism, vitality, vivacity 10 liveliness

animato
5 brisk, tempo 6 lively 8 spirited 9 energetic, sprightly

animosity
4 hate 5 venom 6 animus, enmity, hatred, rancor 7 dislike, ill will 8 acrimony 9 antipathy, hostility 10 antagonism, resentment

animus
4 plan, soul 6 design, enmity, intent, pneuma, psyche, rancor, spirit 7 dislike, ill will, meaning, purpose 9 antipathy, élan vital, hostility, intention 10 antagonism, intendment, opposition, vital force 11 disposition, malevolence

Anjou
4 pear
capital: 6 Angers
native: 7 Angevin

ankle
6 tarsus

annals
6 record 7 account, history 8 archives, register 9 chronicle

annelid
4 worm 5 leech 9 earthworm

annex
3 add, arm, cop, ell, win 4 gain, hook, join, land, take, wing 5 add on, affix, seize, tag on 6 adjoin, append, attach, fasten, obtain, pick up, secure, tack on, take on 7 acquire, connect, preempt, procure, subjoin 8 accroach, addition, appendix, arrogate, superadd, take over 9 extension 10 attachment, commandeer, subsidiary, supplement 11 appropriate, expropriate, incorporate

Annie Oakley
4 pass 10 free ticket, markswoman

annihilate
4 do in, kill, raze, rout, ruin, undo 5 abate, annul, crush, erase, quash, quell, wrack, wreck 6 murder, negate, quench, rub out, squash, uproot, vanish 7 abolish, blot out, destroy, expunge, nullify, put down, root out, vitiate, wipe out 8 abrogate, demolish, massacre, suppress, vanquish 9 eradicate, extirpate, liquidate, slaughter 10 extinguish, invalidate, obliterate 11 exterminate

annihilation
7 killing 8 massacre 9 abolition

anniversary

11 destruction, elimination, liquidation, termination 12 obliteration
13 extermination

anniversary

hundredth: 9 centenary 10 centennial
tenth: 9 decennial
thousandth: 10 millennial

annotate

5 gloss 6 remark 7 comment, explain 8 footnote 9 elucidate, interpret 10 commentate

announce

4 call, tell 5 augur, issue, sound, state 6 attest, blazon, herald, impart, report, reveal, signal 7 bespeak, declare, divulge, forerun, give out, portend, predict, presage, present, publish, release, signify, trumpet 8 disclose, forecast, foreshow, foretell, indicate, proclaim 9 advertise, broadcast, harbinger, make known, publicize 10 give notice, make public, promulgate 11 preindicate

announcement

4 news 6 notice, report 7 message, release 8 briefing, bulletin
9 broadcast, statement
10 communiqué, disclosure
11 declaration, publication
12 proclamation, promulgation
13 advertisement, communication

announcer

5 emcee 6 deejay, herald, veejay 9 anchorman, voice-over 10 disc jockey, disk jockey, newscaster 11 anchorwoman, broadcaster, commentator 12 anchorperson, sportscaster

annoy

3 bug, irk, vex 4 bait, fret, gall, miff 5 chafe, chivy, harry, peeve, tease, upset, worry 6 badger, bother, harass, heckle, hector, needle, nettle, pester, plague, ruffle 7 agitate, bedevil, disturb, hagride, perturb, provoke, tick off 8 distress, irritate 9 beleaguer
Scottish: 4 fash

annoyance

4 drag, to-do 5 trial, upset, worry 6 bother, nettle, plague, strain 7 problem, trouble 8 distress, headache, irritant, nuisance, vexation 10 affliction, harassment, irritation 11 aggravation, botheration, disturbance, indignation, provocation
12 exasperation

annoying

5 pesky 8 tiresome 9 troubling, vexatious 10 disturbing, irritating 11 aggravating, distressing, troublesome 12 exasperating

annual

5 plant 6 flower, yearly 7 almanac 8 each year, yearbook, yearlong
9 every year

annul

4 undo, void 5 abate, erase, quash 6 cancel, delete, efface, negate, revoke, vacate 7 abolish, blot out, expunge, nullify, redress, rescind, retract, reverse, vitiate, wipe out 8 abrogate, dissolve 9 cancel out, discharge, frustrate 10 annihilate, counteract, extinguish, invalidate, neutralize, obliterate
11 countermand

annunciate

see **announce**

anodyne

4 balm 5 bland 6 opiate, relief, remedy 7 soother 8 narcotic, nepenthe, painless, sedative 9 analgesic, calmative, innocuous, soporific 10 anesthetic, depressant, pain-killer, palliative 11 inoffensive, unoffending
12 tranquilizer

anoint

3 rub 4 daub, laud, name 5 anele, apply, bless, honor, smear 6 choose, hallow, ordain 7 confirm, massage 8 dedicate, sanctify, set apart, venerate 9 designate 10 consecrate

anomalous

3 odd 6 off-key 7 deviant, strange, unusual 8 aberrant, abnormal, atypical, peculiar 9 deviating, devia-

tory, divergent, irregular, unnatural, untypical **10** unexpected **11** heteroclite, incongruous, paradoxical **12** inconsistent **13** nonconforming, preternatural

anomaly
5 freak, quirk **6** oddity **9** departure, deviation, exception **10** aberration, divergence **11** abnormality, incongruity, peculiarity **12** idiosyncrasy, irregularity **13** inconsistency

anomie
4 flux **6** unrest **7** anxiety, inertia **10** alienation, insecurity **11** disquietude, instability, uncertainty **12** disaffection, estrangement, indifference, restlessness

anon
4 soon **5** later **7** by and by, shortly **8** directly **9** presently **10** before long **11** after a while

anonym
5 alias **6** handle **7** pen name **8** nickname **9** pseudonym **10** nom de plume **11** assumed name, nom de guerre

anonymous
7 unknown, unnamed **8** nameless, not named, unsigned **9** incognito **10** innominate **11** unspecified **12** undesignated, unidentified, unrecognized

anorak
5 parka

another
3 new **4** else, more **5** added, fresh **7** farther, further, one more **9** different **10** additional **11** alternative, someone else **13** something else

anschluss
5 union **6** league **8** alliance **9** coalition **10** federation **11** confederacy **13** confederation

answer
4 fill, meet, plea **5** atone, plead, rebut, reply, serve, solve **6** come in, refute, rejoin, result, retort, return **7** conform, defense, explain, fulfill, respond, satisfy **8** antiphon, rebuttal, response, solution **9** rejoinder **10** refutation **11** recriminate **13** countercharge

answerable
5 bound **6** liable **7** obliged, subject **8** amenable **9** compelled, duty-bound, obligated **11** accountable, constrained, responsible

ant
5 emmet **9** carpenter
relating to: 6 formic

Antaean
4 huge **5** giant **6** heroic **7** mammoth, titanic **8** colossal, enormous, gigantic **9** cyclopean, Herculean **10** gargantuan

Antaeus
father: 7 Neptune **8** Poseidon
mother: 4 Gaea
slayer: 8 Heracles, Hercules

antagonism
3 con **6** animus, enmity, hatred, rancor **7** discord **8** conflict, friction **9** animosity, antipathy, hostility **10** antithesis, contention, dissension, opposition, resistance **11** contrariety **12** disagreement

antagonist
3 con, foe **4** anti **5** enemy, match **6** muscle **7** opposer **8** chemical, opponent **9** adversary, contender

antagonistic
4 anti **6** averse **7** adverse, hostile, opposed **8** clashing, contrary, inimical, opposing **9** bellicose, combative, rancorous, truculent, vitriolic **10** discordant **11** belligerent, conflicting, contentious **12** antipathetic

Antarctica sea
4 Ross **7** Weddell **8** Amundsen

ante
3 bet, pay, pot **4** cost, risk **5** level, pay up, price, put up, stake, wager **6** stakes **7** produce

anteater
see **animal** *insect-eating*

antecede

7 forerun, precede, predate 8 fore-
date, go before

antecedence

8 priority 10 precedence, precession,
preference

antecedent

4 fore, line 5 cause, prior 6 former,
reason 7 earlier 8 ancestor, anterior, forebear, foregoer, occasion,
previous 9 condition, foregoing,
precedent, preceding, precursor,
prototype 10 forerunner, progenitor
11 determinant, predecessor

antedate

7 forerun, precede 11 anachronize
12 occur earlier

antediluvian

3 old 4 aged, fogy 5 hoary, passé
6 age-old, fogram, fossil, square
7 ancient, antique, archaic 8 mossback, Noachian, obsolete, outdated,
outmoded, primeval, timeworn 9 out-
of-date, primitive 10 antiquated,
fuddy-duddy 12 old-fashioned
13 stick-in-the-mud

antelope

3 gnu 4 kudu, oryx 5 addax, bongo,
eland, nyala, serow 6 dik-dik, duiker,
impala, koodoo, lechwe 7 blesbok,
chamois, gazelle, gemsbok, gerenuk,
sassaby 8 bushbuck, reedbuck,
steinbok 9 springbok, waterbuck
10 hartebeest
female: 3 doe
male: 4 buck
young: 3 kid
(see also **gazelle**)

antenna

4 wire 6 aerial, device, dipole,
sensor 8 monopole, receiver

antennae

4 ears 11 sensitivity
13 receptiveness

anterior

4 past 5 prior 6 former 8 previous
9 foregoing, precedent, preceding
10 antecedent

anteroom

5 entry, foyer, lobby 6 alcove 9 vestibule

Anteros

brother: 4 Eros
father: 4 Ares, Mars
mother: 5 Venus 9 Aphrodite
opposite: 4 Eros

anthem

4 hymn, song 5 chant, paean, psalm
8 canticle

anthology

3 ana 5 album 6 digest, reader
7 garland, omnibus 8 analects,
treasury 9 selection 10 assortment,
collection, compendium, miscellany
11 compilation, florilegium

anthropoid

3 ape 5 biped 6 monkey 7 bipedal,
gorilla, manlike, primate 8 hominoid,
humanoid 10 chimpanzee

anthropologist

4 Boas (Franz), Dart (Raymond),
Mead (Margaret) 5 Sapir (Edward),
Tylor (Edward Burnett) 6 Frazer
(James George), Geertz (Clifford),
Leakey (Louis), Morgan (Lewis
Henry) 7 Bateson (Gregory), Kroe-
ber (Alfred Louis) 8 Benedict (Ruth)
10 Malinowski (Bronisław) 11 Lévi-
Strauss (Claude)

anti

3 con 6 averse 7 adverse, against,
counter, opposed, opposer 8 contrary, opponent, opposing 9 adversary, opposed to 10 antagonist
12 antagonistic, antipathetic, in
opposition

antiaircraft fire

4 flak

antibiotic

7 colicin 8 neomycin, viomycin
9 polymyxin 10 bacitracin, novo-
biocin, penicillin 11 bacteriocin,
tyrothricin 12 streptomycin, tetracy-
cline

antic

3 gag 4 dido, joke, lark, romp

5 caper, comic, prank, trick 6 frisky, frolic, lively 7 comical, foolish, playful 8 escapade, farcical, prankish, spirited 9 high jinks, laughable, ludicrous, sprightly 10 frolicsome, rollicking, shenanigan, tomfoolery 11 mischievous, monkeyshine 12 monkeyshines 13 practical joke

anticipate
3 see 4 wait 5 await, check 6 divine, expect 7 counter, count on, foresee, prepare, presage, prevent, wait for 8 forecast, foreknow, foretell 9 apprehend, forestall, prevision, visualize 10 prepare for

anticipation
7 inkling, outlook, promise 8 awaiting, forecast, prospect 9 awareness, foresight, foretaste 10 expectancy 11 expectation, realization 12 apprehension 13 visualization

Anticlea
father: 9 Autolycus
husband: 7 Laertes
son: 7 Ulysses 8 Odysseus

antidote
4 cure, drug 6 remedy 7 negator 8 medicine 9 nullifier 10 corrective, counteract, preventive 11 counterstep, neutralizer 12 counteragent 13 counteractant, counteractive

Antigone
brother: 9 Polynices 10 Polyneices
father: 7 Oedipus
mother: 7 Jocasta
sister: 6 Ismene
uncle: 5 Creon

Antigua and Barbuda
capital: 7 St. Johns
island: 7 Antigua, Barbuda, Redonda
language: 7 English
monetary unit: 6 dollar

Antilochus
father: 6 Nestor
friend: 8 Achilles
slayer: 6 Memnon

Antiope
father: 6 Asopus

husband: 5 Lycus 7 Theseus
queen of: 7 Amazons
son: 6 Zethus 7 Amphion
10 Hippolytus

antipasto
9 appetizer 11 hors d'oeuvre 12 hors d'oeuvres

antipathetic
5 loath 6 averse, loathe 7 adverse, hostile, opposed 8 aversive, clashing, contrary, inimical, opposing, opposite 9 abhorrent, disliking, loathsome, repellent, repugnant, repulsive 10 discordant, unfriendly 11 conflicting, distasteful, ill-disposed, uncongenial 12 antagonistic 13 contradictory

antipathy
4 hate 6 animus, enmity, hatred, rancor 7 allergy, dislike, ill will 8 aversion, distaste, loathing 9 animosity, hostility 10 abhorrence, antagonism, opposition, repellency

antiphon
5 psalm, reply, verse 6 answer, anthem, return 7 respond 8 response

antipodal
5 polar 7 adverse, counter, opposed, reverse 8 contrary, converse, opposite 9 diametric 11 conflicting, contrasting, diametrical 12 antithetical 13 contradictory

antipode
6 contra 7 counter, reverse 8 contrary, converse, flip side, opposite 9 other side 10 antithesis 11 counterpole

antiquate
7 make old, outdate, outmode 8 obsolete 9 obsolesce 12 superannuate

antiquated
3 old 4 aged 5 dated, fusty, hoary, moldy, passé 6 old hat 7 ancient, antique, archaic 8 obsolete, old-timey, outmoded 9 out-of-date 10 old-fangled, out-of-style 11 discredited,

obsolescent **12** antediluvian, old-fashioned **13** inappropriate, superannuated

antique

3 old **4** aged **5** dated, hoary, olden, passé, relic **6** age-old, bygone, rarity **7** ancient, archaic, vintage **8** artifact, heirloom, old-timey, outdated, outmoded, timeworn **9** ancestral, objet d'art, out-of-date, venerable **10** antiquated, oldfangled **12** antediluvian, old-fashioned

antiseptic

6 iodine **7** alcohol, sterile **8** hygienic, peroxide, sanitary **9** boric acid, carvacrol, germicide, merbromin **10** gramicidin, sterilized **12** carbolic acid, disinfectant
pioneer: 6 Lister (Joseph)

antisocial

7 ascetic, austere, hostile **8** eremitic, solitary **9** alienated, reclusive, withdrawn **10** unfriendly **11** standoffish **12** antagonistic, misanthropic

antithesis

3 con **6** contra **7** counter, reverse **8** antipode, antipole, contrary, contrast, converse, opposite **10** antagonism, opposition **11** counterpole

antithetical

5 polar **7** counter, reverse **8** contrary, converse, opposite **9** antipodal, diametric **10** antipodean **11** diametrical **13** contradictory

antitoxin

4 sera (plural) **5** serum **11** neutralizer

antiwar

6 irenic **8** pacifist **10** nonviolent, pacifistic

Antony, Mark

defeat: 6 Actium
friend: 6 Caesar
lover: 9 Cleopatra
wife: 7 Octavia

anxiety

4 care, fear **5** doubt, dread, panic, worry **6** unease **7** concern **8** distress, mistrust, suspense **9** self-doubt, suffering **10** uneasiness **11** disquietude, uncertainty **12** apprehension

anxious

4 avid, keen **5** eager **6** afraid, ardent, scared, uneasy **7** alarmed, fearful, worried **8** agitated, desirous, troubled, worrying **9** impatient, perturbed, terrified **10** breathless, disquieted, frightened **12** apprehensive

any

3 all **4** a bit, some **5** at all, every **7** a little, several **8** whatever

anyhow

6 random **7** however **8** at random, randomly **9** hit-or-miss **10** carelessly, regardless **11** any which way, haphazardly **13** helter-skelter

anymore

3 now **5** today **8** nowadays **9** presently, these days

anyone

3 all **9** everybody

anything

5 at all

anytime

4 ever **5** at all **8** whenever

anyway

4 ever, once **5** at all **7** however **12** nevertheless

anywhere

5 at all **7** all over **10** at any point

anywise

5 at all

apace

4 fast **6** versed **7** abreast, flat-out, hastily, quickly, rapidly, swiftly **8** informed, up-to-date, speedily **9** posthaste **12** lickety-split **13** expeditiously

Apache

chief: 7 Cochise **8** Geronimo
subgroups: 7 Cibecue **9** Jicarilla, Mescalero **10** Chiricahua

apart

5 alone, aside **6** singly **7** asunder, removed **8** detached, isolated, one by one **9** severally **10** separately **12** individually **13** independently, unaccompanied
prefix: 3 dis

apart from

3 bar, but **4** save **6** except, saving **7** barring, besides **9** except for, excepting, excluding, other than, outside of **11** exclusive of

apartheid

8 division **9** partition **10** separation, separatism **11** segregation **12** separateness

apartment

4 flat, room **5** rooms, suite **6** rental **7** chamber, housing, lodging **8** building, dwelling **9** residence **13** accommodation

apathetic

4 dull, flat, limp **5** inert **6** stolid, torpid **7** languid, passive, unmoved **8** sluggish **9** impassive, untouched **10** anesthetic, insensible, phlegmatic, spiritless **11** emotionless, indifferent, insensitive **12** unresponsive **13** disinterested

apathy

6 torpor **8** coldness, dullness, lethargy, obduracy, stoicism **9** aloofness, disregard, inertness, lassitude, passivity, stolidity, torpidity, unconcern **10** detachment, dispassion **11** callousness, disinterest, impassivity **12** heedlessness, indifference, listlessness **13** insensibility, insensitivity

ape

4 copy, mime, mock **5** mimic **6** baboon, bonobo, gibbon, monkey, parody, pongid, simian **7** copycat, emulate, gorilla, imitate, siamang, take off **8** simulate, travesty **9** burlesque, orangutan **10** anthropoid, caricature, chimpanzee **11** impersonate

aperçu

5 brief **6** digest, précis, sketch, survey **7** insight, outline **8** syllabus **10** compendium, impression

aperitif

4 whet **5** drink **8** cocktail **9** appetizer

aperture

3 gap **4** hole, vent **6** outlet **7** opening, orifice, pinhole

apery

7 mimicry **9** imitation

apex

3 cap, tip, top **4** acme, cusp, peak, roof **5** crest, crown, limit, point **6** apogee, climax, summit, vertex, zenith **8** capstone, pinnacle, ultimate **9** crescendo, sublimity **11** culmination, ne plus ultra **12** quintessence

aphorism

3 saw **4** rule **5** adage, axiom, maxim, moral **6** dictum, saying, truism **7** precept, proverb **8** apothegm

aphrodisiac

6 erotic **7** amative, amatory, amorous, lustful **8** excitant **10** passionate

Aphrodite

Roman counterpart: 5 Venus
consort: 4 Ares **6** Vulcan **10** Hephaestus
father: 4 Zeus **7** Jupiter
goddess of: 4 love
mother: 5 Dione
son: 4 Eros **6** Aeneas **7** Priapus

apiarist

9 beekeeper

apical

3 top **7** highest, topmost **8** loftiest **9** uppermost

apiculture

10 beekeeping

apiece

3 per **4** a pop, each **6** singly, to each **7** for each **8** one by one **9** per capita, severally **10** separately **12** individually, respectively

apish
5 phony, silly 7 slavish 8 affected
9 emulative, imitative 10 artificial

aplenty
4 full 5 ample 6 galore, indeed
7 copious, greatly 8 abundant, very
much 9 extremely

aplomb
4 ease 5 poise 6 polish 8 coolness,
easiness 9 assurance, certainty,
certitude, composure 10 confidence,
equanimity 11 nonchalance, savoir
faire 12 self-reliance 13 self-
assurance

apocalypse
6 augury, oracle, vision 8 disaster,
prophecy 10 Armageddon, prediction, revelation

apocalyptic
4 dire 5 awful 7 baleful, baneful,
fateful, fearful, ominous 8 Delphian,
dreadful, oracular, terrible 9 appalling, climactic, grandiose, prophetic
10 foreboding, predicting 11 foretelling, prophetical, threatening
12 inauspicious
book: 10 Revelation 11 Revela-
tions

apocryphal
5 false, wrong 6 untrue 7 dubious
8 doubtful, spurious 9 incorrect,
ungenuine 10 ficticious, inaccurate,
unverified 11 unauthentic 12 questionable

apogee
4 acme, apex, peak 6 climax, summit, zenith 8 capstone, meridian,
pinnacle 9 high point 11 culmination

Apollo
6 Helios 7 Phoebus
beloved: 6 Cyrene, Daphne 8 Calliope
birthplace: 5 Delos
father: 4 Zeus 7 Jupiter
mother: 4 Leto 6 Latona
oracle: 6 Delphi
sister: 5 Diana 7 Artemis
son: 3 Ion 7 Orpheus
temple: 6 Delphi

apologetic
5 sorry 6 rueful 8 contrite, penitent
9 regretful, repentant 10 remorseful
11 penitential 12 compunctious

apologia
4 plea 6 excuse, reason 7 defense
8 argument 11 elucidation, explanation 13 clarification, justification

apologize
5 atone 6 lament, regret, repent
7 confess 9 beg pardon 10 make
amends

apologue
4 myth, tale 5 fable, story 7 parable
8 allegory

apology
4 plea 6 amends, excuse 7 redress,
regrets 8 mea culpa 9 admission,
makeshift 10 concession, confession

apostasy
7 perfidy 9 defection, desertion,
disavowal, falseness, rejection
11 abandonment, repudiation
12 disaffection, renunciation

apostate
7 heretic, traitor 8 defector, deserter,
recreant, renegade, turncoat 9 turnabout

apostatize
4 turn 6 defect, desert 7 abandon,
forsake, sell out 8 renounce 9 repudiate

a posteriori
9 inductive

apostle
4 John, Jude, Paul 5 James, Judas,
Peter, Silas, Simon 6 Andrew, Philip,
Thomas 7 Matthew 8 Barnabas,
disciple, follower, Matthias, preacher
9 missioner 10 colporteur, evangelist, missionary 11 Bartholomew
12 propagandist
of Germany: 8 Boniface
of Ireland: 7 Patrick
of the English: 9 Augustine
of the French: 5 Denis
of the Gauls: 8 Irenaeus

of the Gentiles: 4 Paul
of the Goths: 7 Ulfilas
to the Indians: 9 John Eliot

apothecary
7 chemist **8** druggist, pharmacy
9 drugstore **10** pharmacist

apothegm
see **aphorism**

apotheosis
6 height **7** epitome **8** exemplar, last word, ultimate **9** archetype, elevation **10** embodiment, exaltation **11** deification, ennoblement, idolization, lionization **12** enshrinement, quintessence **13** glorification

appall
3 awe **4** faze **5** alarm, shake, shock **6** dismay **7** horrify, outrage, overawe, perturb **8** confound, distress **10** disconcert **11** consternate

appalled
6 aghast **11** dumbfounded

appalling
5 awful **6** horrid **7** fearful **8** daunting, dreadful, horrible, horrific, shocking, terrible **9** atrocious, dismaying, frightful, loathsome **10** disgusting, formidable, horrifying

appanage
5 grant, right **7** adjunct **8** property **9** endowment, privilege **10** birthright, perquisite **11** prerogative

apparatus
4 gear, tool **5** gizmo **6** device, outfit, tackle **7** utensil **8** matériel, tackling **9** equipment, implement, machinery **10** instrument **11** contraption, habiliments **13** accouterments, accoutrements, paraphernalia

apparel
4 clad, duds, garb, gear, robe, suit, togs **5** adorn, array, dress, getup, habit **6** attire, clothe, outfit **7** clothes, costume, garment, raiment, threads **8** clothing, enclothe, glad rags, vestment **9** embellish **11** habiliments

apparent
5 clear, plain **6** patent **7** evident, obvious, seeming, visible **8** distinct, manifest, palpable **9** succedent **10** noticeable, observable **11** discernible, perceivable, unambiguous, unequivocal **12** successional

apparition
5 ghost, shade, umbra **6** shadow, spirit, vision, wraith **7** phantom, specter **8** illusion, phantasm **10** appearance, phenomenon **13** hallucination

appeal
3 ask, beg, bid **4** call, lure, plea, pray, pull, suit, urge **5** apply, brace, charm, crave, plead **6** accuse, allure, charge, excite, invoke, sue for **7** attract, beseech, entreat, glamour, implore, request **8** call upon, charisma, entreaty, interest, intrigue, petition **9** fascinate, importune, magnetism, seduction **10** allurement, attraction, supplicate **11** application, fascination, imploration **12** drawing power, solicitation, supplication

appealing
8 alluring, charming, pleading, pleasant, pleasing **9** agreeable, imploring **10** attracting, attractive, bewitching, enchanting, entreating **11** captivating, fascinating

appear
4 come, look, loom, rise, seem, show **5** arise, issue, occur, sound **6** arrive, emerge, show up **7** be clear, emanate **8** look like, resemble **9** be evident, come forth **10** be manifest **11** materialize

appearance
3 air **4** face, form, look, mien, pose, show **5** debut, dress, front, guise, image **6** advent, aspect, facade, manner **7** arrival, bearing, display, seeming **8** attitude, demeanor, illusion **9** semblance **10** impression, occurrence, simulacrum **11** countenance **13** manifestation

appease
4 calm, ease **5** allay, quiet **6** buy off, pacify, soothe **7** assuage, concede,

appellation

content, gratify, mollify, placate, relieve, satisfy, sweeten **10** conciliate, propitiate

appellation

4 name **5** brand, label, nomen, style, title **7** moniker **8** cognomen **10** identifier **11** designation **12** denomination

append

3 add **5** add on, affix, annex, tag on **6** adjoin, attach, tack on **7** subjoin **10** supplement

appendage

3 arm, fin, leg, tab, tag **4** barb, flap, horn, limb, seta, tail, wing **5** extra **6** cercus, member **7** adjunct, antenna, elytron, stipule **8** pedipalp, pendicle, tentacle **9** accessory, auxiliary, extremity **10** attachment, collateral, incidental, projection, supplement **12** appurtenance, nonessential, protuberance

appendix

5 notes, rider **7** adjunct, codicil **8** addendum, addition **9** accessory, appendage **10** attachment, supplement **12** appurtenance

apperception

5 grasp **9** awareness **10** cognizance **11** realization, recognition **12** apprehension, assimilation **13** comprehension, introspection, understanding

appertain

4 bear **5** apply, refer **6** bear on, belong, relate **8** bear upon **10** be relevant **11** be connected, be pertinent

appetence

3 yen **5** taste **6** desire, hunger, relish, thirst **7** craving, longing, stomach **8** fondness

appetent

4 agog, avid, keen **5** eager **6** ardent **7** anxious, craving, lusting, thirsty **8** desirous, yearning **9** impatient **10** breathless

appetite

3 yen **4** bent, itch, lust, urge **5** taste **6** desire, hunger, liking, relish **7** craving, leaning, longing, passion, stomach **8** cupidity, fondness, gluttony, penchant, soft spot, voracity, weakness, yearning **9** hankering **10** preference, proclivity, propensity **11** inclination

appetizer

4 whet **5** snack **6** canapé, savory, tidbit **8** aperitif, cocktail, stimulus **9** antipasto **11** hors d'oeuvre

appetizing

5 tasty **6** savory **8** saporous, tempting **9** agreeable, appealing, aperitive, flavorful, palatable, relishing, toothsome **10** delectable, flavorsome **11** tantalizing **13** mouthwatering

applaud

4 clap, hail, laud, root **5** bravo, cheer, extol **6** praise, rise to **7** acclaim, approve, commend **9** recommend **10** compliment

applause

4 hand **5** round **6** bravos, cheers, praise **7** acclaim, hurrahs, ovation, rooting **8** accolade, approval, cheering, clapping, plaudits **11** acclamation **12** commendation

apple

4 crab, Fuji, Gala, pome **6** Empire, pippin, russet **7** Baldwin, costard, Duchess, Winesap **8** Braeburn, Cortland, greening, Jonagold, Jonathan, McIntosh **9** Delicious **10** Rome Beauty **11** Granny Smith, Gravenstein, Northern Spy, Transparent
dessert: 5 crisp
juice: 5 cider

applejack

5 cider **6** brandy, liquor **8** calvados **9** hard cider

apple knocker

see **rustic**

apple-polish

4 fawn **5** toady **6** kowtow **7** cater to,

flatter, honey up, truckle **8** butter up
10 curry favor, ingratiate

apple-polisher
5 toady **6** yes-man **8** bootlick,
groveler, lickspit **9** flatterer, sycophant **11** lickspittle

applesauce
5 hooey **6** bunkum **7** baloney,
rubbish, twaddle **8** malarkey, nonsense **9** poppycock

appliance
6 device **7** utensil **9** implement
10 instrument **11** application
kitchen: 4 oven **5** mixer, range,
stove **6** fridge **7** blender, toaster
9 can opener, microwave **10** dishwasher **12** refrigerator

applicability
3 use **7** account, fitness, utility
9 advantage, relevance **10** usefulness

applicable
3 apt, fit **4** just, meet **5** ad rem
6 seemly, suited, useful **7** apropos,
fitting, germane **8** apposite, material,
relevant, suitable **9** befitting, pertinent **10** felicitous **11** appropriate

applicant
6 seeker **7** hopeful **8** aspirant,
inquirer **9** candidate, job-hunter,
job-seeker

application
3 use **4** form, heed, plea, suit
5 study **6** appeal, debate, effort,
letter **7** request **8** entreaty, exercise, exertion, industry, petition
9 assiduity, attention, diligence, operation, treatment **10** dedication, employment **11** requisition, utilization
12 solicitation **13** concentration, consideration

appliqué
5 decal

apply
3 dab, use **4** bend, give, turn, urge
5 press, refer **6** accost, affect,
appeal, assign, bear on, bestow,
devote, direct, employ, engage,

handle, relate, resort, take on
7 address, beseech, concern,
entreat, execute, implore, involve,
pertain, utilize **8** approach, bear
upon, exercise, petition, set about
9 appertain, implement, importune,
undertake **10** administer, buckle
down

appoint
3 arm, fix, rig, set, tap **4** gear, name
5 equip **6** assign, decide, fit out,
outfit, supply **7** dress up, furbish,
furnish, provide, turn out **8** accouter,
accoutre, accredit, delegate, nominate **9** authorize, designate, determine, embellish, provision **10** commission

appointment
3 job **4** date, meet, post, spot
5 berth, place, tryst **6** billet, choice,
office **7** meeting **8** election, position
9 equipment, selection, situation
10 assignment, connection, engagement, rendezvous **11** arrangement,
assignation, designation

appointments
7 fitting **8** equipage **9** equipment,
trappings **12** furnishings **13** accouterments, accoutrements

apportion
3 cut, lot **4** give, mete, part **5** allot,
allow, cut up, divvy, quota, serve,
share, slice, split **6** assign, bestow,
divide, parcel, ration **7** deal out, dish
out, divvy up, dole out, measure,
mete out, prorate, split up **8** allocate,
dispense, separate, share out
9 admeasure, partition **10** administer, distribute

apportionment
3 cut, lot **4** part **5** piece, quota,
share, slice, split **6** ration **7** measure, quantum **9** allotment, allowance **10** allocation, assignment

apposite
3 apt **4** just **5** ad rem **6** proper,
suited, timely **7** apropos, fitting,
germane, right on **8** material, on target, relevant, suitable **9** pertinent
10 applicable **11** appropriate

appositeness

7 aptness, fitness **9** relevance
10 pertinence, timeliness **11** suitability

appraisal

5 stock **6** rating, survey **7** pricing
8 estimate, judgment **9** valuation
10 assessment, estimation, evaluation

appraise

3 eye, fix, set **4** rate, size **5** assay,
audit, gauge, judge, price, set at,
value **6** assess, figure, size up,
survey **7** adjudge, examine, inspect,
measure, valuate **8** estimate, evaluate, look over **9** calculate, figure out

appreciable

5 clear, plain **6** marked **7** evident,
obvious **8** apparent, clear-cut,
concrete, manifest, material, palpable, sensible, tangible **10** detectable,
measurable, noticeable, observable
11 discernible, perceptible, substantial **12** considerable

appreciate

4 gain, go up, grow, know, like, love,
rise **5** enjoy, grasp, judge, prize,
savor, value **6** admire, esteem,
fathom, regard, relish **7** apprize,
cherish, cognize, enhance, improve,
inflate, realize, respect **8** evaluate,
increase, treasure **9** apprehend,
delight in, recognize **10** comprehend, understand

appreciation

4 gain, rise **6** growth, regard, thanks
7 tribute **8** increase, judgment
9 awareness, gratitude, inflation
10 evaluation, perception **11** recognition, sensitivity, testimonial **12** gratefulness

apprehend

3 dig, get, nab, see **4** bust, fear,
grab, know, nail, read, take, twig
5 catch, grasp, pinch, run in, seize,
sense **6** absorb, accept, arrest,
collar, detain, digest, divine, fathom,
pick up, take in, wise up **7** capture,
catch on, cognize, compass, foresee,

make out, preknow, previse, realize
8 conceive **9** penetrate, recognize,
visualize **10** anticipate, appreciate,
understand

apprehensible

5 clear, lucid, plain **7** evident, obvious **8** distinct, explicit, knowable,
luminous **9** graspable **10** fathomable

apprehension

3 ken **4** care, fear, idea **5** alarm,
angst, dread, grasp, pinch, worry
6 arrest, notion, pickup, unease
7 anxiety, capture, concern, seizure,
thought **8** disquiet, judgment **9** agitation, awareness, detention, knowledge, misgiving, suspicion **10** conception, foreboding, perception,
solicitude, uneasiness **11** disquietude, premonition **13** comprehension, understanding

apprehensive

5 alive, awake, aware, sharp **6** afraid,
astute, scared, uneasy **7** anxious,
fearful, knowing, worried **8** sensible,
sentient, troubled **9** cognizant,
conscious, observant, sensitive
10 discerning, disquieted, insightful,
perceptive

apprentice

4 bind, tyro **5** pupil, serve **6** novice,
rookie **7** learner, starter, student,
trainee, work for **8** beginner, freshman, neophyte, newcomer **9** novitiate **10** tenderfoot

apprenticed

5 bound **7** obliged, pledged **8** articled **9** obligated **10** indentured

apprise

4 clue, post, tell, warn **6** advise, clue
in, fill in, impart, inform, notify, reveal,
wise up **7** let know **8** acquaint, announce, describe, disclose **9** make
known **11** communicate

apprize

5 value **6** admire, esteem, regard,
relish **7** cherish **8** hold dear, treasure **10** appreciate, rate highly

approach
4 near, nigh **5** reach, rival, touch, verge **6** access, advise, amount, avenue, border, gain on **7** address, advance, apply to, attempt, consult, descent, request **8** come up to, draw near, endeavor, overture **9** come close **11** approximate

approachable
7 affable **8** friendly, sociable **9** agreeable, congenial, reachable, receptive **10** accessible, attainable

approaching
6 coming **7** nearing **8** expected, imminent, oncoming, upcoming **11** forthcoming

approbate
4 back, like **5** favor **6** accept, assent, praise **7** applaud, approve, commend, consent, endorse, support **8** sanction **9** recommend **11** countenance

approbation
3 nod **4** okay **5** favor **6** esteem, praise **7** acclaim, consent, support **8** applause, approval, sanction **10** admiration, permission **11** endorsement, recognition **12** commendation

appropriate
3 apt, cop, due, fit **4** grab, just, lift, meet, take, true **5** allot, annex, claim, exact, filch, grasp, pinch, right, seize, steal, swipe, usurp **6** assign, assume, budget, devote, pilfer, proper, snatch, snitch, timely, useful, worthy **7** apropos, desired, earmark, fitting, germane, merited, preempt, purloin **8** accroach, apposite, arrogate, deserved, eligible, entitled, relevant, rightful, set apart, set aside, suitable **9** befitting, opportune, pertinent, requisite **10** acceptable, admissible, applicable, commandeer, compatible, confiscate, convenient, felicitous, seasonable

appropriately
4 well **5** amply, aptly, right **8** properly, suitably **9** fittingly
10 acceptably, adequately, becomingly

appropriateness
3 use **5** order **7** account, aptness, fitness, service, utility **8** meetness **9** advantage, propriety, relevance, rightness **10** expediency, usefulness **13** applicability

appropriation
5 grant **7** funding, stipend, subsidy **9** allotment, allowance **10** allocation, assignment, earmarking, subvention

approval
4 okay **5** favor, leave **6** assent **7** consent, go-ahead, license, support **8** applause, blessing, sanction, suffrage **10** acceptance, compliment, green light, permission **11** approbation, benediction, concurrence, endorsement **12** commendation, ratification **13** authorization, confirmation

approve
4 okay **5** clear, favor, go for **6** accept, back up, praise, ratify, uphold **7** applaud, certify, commend, condone, confirm, endorse, initial, mandate, stand by, support, sustain **8** accredit, hold with, sanction **9** approbate, authorize, encourage **10** compliment **11** countenance

approximate
4 near **5** close, rough, touch **6** almost **7** similar, verge on **8** approach, come near **10** resembling **11** comparative

approximately
4 most, nigh **5** about, circa **6** all but, almost, nearly **7** close to **8** well-nigh **9** just about, very close **11** practically

approximation
8 likeness, nearness **9** closeness **10** similarity **11** resemblance

appurtenance
7 adjunct **8** addition, appendix, ornament **9** accessory, apparatus, appendage **10** attachment **11** furnishings **13** accompaniment

appurtenant

5 extra 8 adjuvant 9 accessory,
ancillary, auxiliary 10 additional,
collateral, subsidiary 11 subordinate,
subservient 12 accompanying,
contributory

a priori

8 provable, reasoned 9 deducible,
deductive, derivable, inferable
11 inferential, presumptive

apron

5 stage 6 shield 7 garment 8 pinafore 9 extension

apropos

3 apt 4 as to, in re, meet 5 about,
ad rem, anent, aptly, as for 6 proper,
timely 7 fitting, germane, related
8 apposite, material, pointful, relevant, suitable, suitably, touching
9 as regards, opportune, pertinent,
regarding 10 applicable, as respects, concerning, relevantly, respecting, seasonably 11 applicative,
applicatory, bearing upon, in respect
to, opportunely, pertinently 13 with
respect to

apt

3 fit 4 just 5 alert, given, prone,
quick, ready, savvy, smart 6 bright,
clever, liable, likely, prompt, proper
7 apropos, fitting, germane, tending
8 apposite, disposed, inclined,
relevant, suitable 9 befitting, pertinent, qualified 10 felicitous, responsive 11 appropriate, intelligent

aptitude

4 bent, gift 5 flair, knack, savvy
6 genius, liking, talent 7 ability,
faculty, fitness 8 capacity, tendency
10 capability, cleverness, proclivity,
propensity 11 disposition, inclination, suitability 12 predilection

aptness

4 bent, gift 5 flair, knack, skill 6 genius, talent 7 ability, faculty, fitness
8 tendency 9 propriety, readiness
10 capability, cleverness, expediency, likelihood 11 inclination,
suitability 12 intelligence

aquanaut

5 diver 10 scuba diver

aqua vitae

4 grog 5 booze, drink, hooch 6 liquor, tipple 7 alcohol, spirits

aqueduct

5 canal 6 course 7 channel, conduit, passage 8 waterway 11 watercourse

aqueous

5 fluid 6 liquid, watery 9 liquefied

Aquila

13 constellation
representation: 5 eagle
star: 6 Altair

Aquitaine

7 Guienne
queen: 7 Eleanor

aquiver

5 shaky 7 quaking, shaking, trembly
9 shivering, trembling, tremulant,
tremulous

Arab

chief: 4 emir 5 sheik 6 sheikh,
sultan
country: 4 Iraq, Oman 5 Egypt,
Libya, Qatar, Sudan, Syria, Yemen
6 Jordan, Kuwait 7 Algeria, Bahrain,
Lebanon, Morocco, Tunisia 11 Saudi
Arabia

arable

7 fertile 8 fruitful, tillable 10 cultivable, productive

Arachne

father: 5 Idmon
form: 6 spider
mother: 6 Cyrene
rival: 6 Athena 7 Minerva

arachnid

4 mite, tick 6 acarus, spider 8 scorpion 9 arthropod, phalangid, taran-
tula 10 harvestman 13 daddy longlegs

arbiter

5 judge 6 expert, umpire 7 referee
8 mediator 9 authority, moderator
11 adjudicator

arbitrary
4 rash 6 chance, random 7 erratic, offhand, wayward, willful 8 fanciful, heedless 9 frivolous, impetuous, whimsical 10 capricious, subjective 10 irrational 12 unreasonable 13 discretionary

arbitrate
5 judge 6 settle, umpire 7 adjudge, mediate, referee 9 intervene 10 adjudicate 12 intermediate

arbitrator
5 judge 6 umpire 7 referee, settler 8 mediator 9 moderator 11 adjudicator

arbor
4 axle, beam 5 bower, frame, shaft 7 pergola, shelter, spindle

arc
3 bow, lob 4 arch, bend, path 5 curve, round 7 rainbow 9 curvation, curvature 11 measurement, progression

arcade
6 arches 7 gallery 10 passageway

arcadia
4 Eden, Zion 6 heaven, utopia 7 Elysium, nirvana 8 paradise 9 fairyland, Shangri-la 10 wonderland 12 promised land

arcane
6 hidden, mystic, occult, opaque, secret 7 obscure, unknown 8 esoteric 9 recondite 10 cabalistic, mysterious, unknowable 11 inscrutable 12 impenetrable 13 unaccountable

Arcas
father: 4 Zeus 7 Jupiter
mother: 8 Callisto

arch
3 bow, coy, sly 4 bend, hump, pert 5 curve, fresh, saucy, vault 6 camber, cheeky, impish 7 playful, roguish, waggish 8 flippant, malapert 9 curvature 10 coquettish 11 mischievous
inner curve: 8 intrados
kind: 4 ogee 5 ogive, round, Tudor 6 lancet 7 rampart, trefoil

9 horseshoe, primitive, segmental 10 shouldered 11 equilateral
outer curve: 8 extrados
part: 6 impost 8 keystone, springer, voussoir

archaeological site
Africa: 8 Zimbabwe 13 Great Zimbabwe
Britain: 7 Avebury 9 Skara Brae, Sutton Hoo 10 Stonehenge
Cambodia: 6 Angkor 9 Angkor Wat
Crete: 7 Knossos
Egypt: 4 Giza 5 Luxor 6 Abydos, Karnak, Naqada, Thebes 7 Memphis 9 El-Bahnasa 11 Oxyrhynchus
Greece: 6 Delphi 7 Mycenae, Olympia
Guatemala: 5 Tikal
Honduras: 5 Copán
Indonesia: 9 Borobudur
Iran: 10 Persepolis
Iraq: 4 Isin, Nuzi 6 Nimrud 7 Babylon, Nineveh, Samarra
Israel: 7 Jericho
Italy: 7 Pompeii 11 Herculaneum
Lebanon: 6 Byblos 7 Baalbek
Mexico: 5 Mitla, Tulum, Uxmal 8 Palenque 10 Monte Albán 11 Chichén Itzá
Peru: 11 Machu Picchu
Syria: 7 Palmyra
Tunisia: 8 Carthage, Kairouan
Turkey: 4 Troy 6 Knidos 8 Hisarlik, Pergamon 9 Hissarlik
Uzbekistan: 9 Samarkand

archaeologist
4 Dart (Raymond) 5 Evans (Arthur) 6 Carter (Howard), Childe (V. Gordon), Kidder (Alfred), Petrie (Flinders) 7 Thomsen (Christian), Woolley (Leonard), Worsaae (Jens) 8 Breasted (James Henry), Goodyear (William) 10 Schliemann (Heinrich) 11 Champollion (Jean-François), Winckelmann (Johann)

archaic
3 old 5 dated, olden, passé 6 bygone 7 ancient, antique 8 obsolete, outdated 9 out-of-date, primitive, unevolved 10 antiquated 11 undeveloped 12 old-fashioned

archangel
5 Uriel 7 Gabriel, Michael, Raphael

arched
4 bent 5 bowed, round 6 curved
7 curving, rounded

archer
4 Tell (William) 5 Cupid 6 bowman
9 Robin Hood 11 Sagittarius

archery
9 toxophily

archetypal
5 ideal, model 7 classic, perfect,
typical 9 classical, exemplary
10 consummate 12 paradigmatic,
prototypical

archetype
4 idea 5 ideal, model 6 mirror
7 epitome, essence, example,
pattern 8 exemplar, original, paradigm, standard 9 beau ideal, prototype 10 apotheosis, embodiment,
protoplast 12 quintessence

archfiend
5 demon, devil, Satan 6 diablo
7 Lucifer

Archimedes
5 Greek 8 inventor
cry: 6 eureka
discovery: 5 screw 8 buoyancy
9 principle 11 water raiser

archipelago
Asian: 5 Malay
Canada: 6 Arctic
Japan: 4 Goto 9 Gotoretto
Norway: 11 Spitsbergen
Papua New Guinea: 8 Bismarck
9 Louisiade
Philippines: 4 Sulu
off Scotland: 7 Orcades, Orkneys
United States: 9 Alexander

architect
5 maker 7 creator 8 designer,
inventor 9 generator 10 origi-
nator
American: 3 Pei (I. M.) 4 Hood
(Raymond), Kahn (Louis) 5 Gehry
(Frank), McKim (Charles),
Meier (Richard), Roche (Kevin),
Stone (Edward Durell), Weese
(Harry), White (Stanford) 6 Breuer
(Marcel), Fuller (Buckminster),
Graves (Michael), Morgan (Julia),
Neutra (Richard), Rogers (Isaiah),
Soleri (Paolo), Upjohn (Richard),
Walter (Thomas), Warren (William),
Wright (Frank Lloyd) 7 Burnham
(Daniel), Gilbert (Cass), Johnson
(Philip), Latrobe (Benjamin), Olmsted
(Frederick Law), Renwick (James),
Sturgis (John Hubbard), Venturi
(Robert) 8 Bulfinch (Charles), Saari-
nen (Eero, Eliel), Sullivan (Louis),
Thornton (William), Yamasaki (Mi-
noru) 10 Richardson (Henry Hobson)
Austrian: 4 Loos (Adolf) 6 Wagner
(Otto)
Brazilian: 8 Niemeyer (Oscar)
Canadian: 6 Safdie (Moshe)
Dutch: 8 Rietveld (Gerrit)
English: 4 Nash (John), Shaw
(Richard), Wood (John), Wren
(Christopher) 5 Jones (Inigo), Scott
(George Gilbert), Wyatt (James)
6 Foster (Norman), Rogers (Richard),
Street (George Edmund), Voysey
(Charles) 7 Lutyens (Edwin)
8 Vanbrugh (John)
Finnish: 5 Aalto (Alvar) 8 Saarinen
(Eero, Eliel)
French: 6 Perret (Auguste)
7 Garnier (Tony), L'Enfant (Pierre-
Charles) 11 Le Corbusier 12 Viollet-
le-Duc (Eugène)
German: 8 Schinkel (Karl) 10 Men-
delsohn (Erich)
German-American: 7 Gropius (Wal-
ter)
Israeli: 6 Safdie (Moshe)
Italian: 5 Nervi (Pier Luigi) 6 Ro-
mano (Giulio), Soleri (Paolo) 7 Al-
berti (Leon Battista), Bernini (Gian
Lorenzo), da Vinci (Leonardo),
Orcagna, Peruzzi (Baldassare),
Raphael, Vignola (Giacomo da)
8 Bramante (Donato), Leonardo (da
Vinci), Palladio (Andrea), Sangallo
(Giuliano da), Terragni (Giuseppe)
9 Borromini (Francesco), Sansovino
(Jacopo) 12 Michelangelo

Japanese: 5 Tange (Kenzo)
Roman: 9 Vitruvius
Scottish: 10 Mackintosh (Charles Rennie)
Spanish: 5 Gaudí (Antonio)
Swedish: 7 Asplund (Erik Gunnar)

architecture
6 design, makeup 9 formation
11 composition 12 constitution, construction
ornament: 4 boss, fret 5 gutta
6 finial, volute 7 cabling, console, crocket, diglyph 8 triglyph, vignette
9 arabesque, modillion
style: 5 Doric, Ionic, Tudor
6 Gothic, Norman, Rococo 7 Baroque 8 Colonial, Georgian 9 Byzantine, Victorian 10 Corinthian, Romanesque

archive
4 file 6 record 7 collect, history, library, records 8 document, register
9 chronicle 10 collection, repository

archon
10 magistrate

arctic
3 icy 4 cold 5 chill, gelid 6 chilly, frigid, frosty, wintry 7 glacial, numbing 8 freezing, hibernal 11 hyperborean
animal: 3 auk, fox 4 bear, hare, seal, vole 5 sable, whale 6 ermine, marten 7 caribou, lemming 8 reindeer 9 polar bear, ptarmigan
base: 4 Etah 5 Thule 6 Barrow
11 Point Barrow
bird: 3 auk
cetacean: 7 narwhal
current: 8 Labrador
dog: 5 husky 7 Samoyed
8 malamute
explorer: 4 Byrd (Richard), Cook (Frederick) 5 Bylot (Robert), Davis (John), Peary (Robert) 6 Baffin (William), Bering (Vitus), Henson (Matthew), Hudson (Henry), Nansen (Fridtjof), Nobile (Umberto) 7 Barents (Willem), Bennett (Floyd), Wilkins (George), Wrangel (Ferdinand)
8 Amundsen (Roald) 9 Ellsworth

(Lincoln), Mackenzie (Alexander), MacMillan (Donald) 10 Stefansson (Vilhjalmus)
forest: 5 taiga
jacket: 5 parka 6 anorak
people: 4 Lapp 5 Aleut, Inuit, Yakut
6 Eskimo, Tungus 7 Chukchi, Samoyed
sea: 4 Kara 6 Laptev 7 Barents, Chukchi 8 Beaufort
transport: 7 dogsled
treeless plains: 6 tundra

ardent
3 hot 4 agog, avid, keen, true
5 eager, fiery, loyal 6 fervid, fierce, heated, intent, red-hot, strong, torrid
7 blazing, burning, devoted, earnest, fervent, flaming, glowing, intense, shining, staunch, zealous 8 constant, desirous, faithful, powerful, resolute, sizzling, vehement, white-hot 9 allegiant, impatient, impetuous, impulsive, perfervid, scorching, steadfast 10 breathless, hot-blooded, passionate 11 impassioned
12 enthusiastic

ardor
4 fire, heat, zeal, zest, zing 5 gusto, verve, vigor 6 energy, fealty, fervor, spirit, warmth 7 avidity, loyalty, passion 8 devotion, fidelity 9 eagerness, intensity, vehemence 10 allegiance, enthusiasm, excitement
12 faithfulness

arduous
4 hard 5 harsh, rough, sheer, steep, tight, tough 6 severe, taxing, tiring, trying, uphill 7 labored 8 grueling, rigorous, toilsome 9 difficult, effortful, gruelling, laborious, punishing, strenuous 10 formidable 11 precipitate, precipitous

area
4 belt, turf, zone 5 field, place, range, realm, scene, space, tract
6 domain, locale, region, sector, sphere 7 expanse, stretch 8 district, locality, province, vicinity 9 bailiwick, territory 12 neighborhood
unit: 4 acre 7 hectare

arena

5 field, scene, stage 6 sphere
7 stadium, theater 8 activity, building, coliseum, province 10 hippodrome 12 amphitheater

Ares

Roman counterpart: 4 Mars
consort: 9 Aphrodite
father: 4 Zeus
mother: 4 Enyo, Hera
sister: 4 Eris
son: 5 Remus 7 Romulus

arête

5 crest, ridge

Arethusa

5 nymph 6 spring 9 wood nymph
pursuer: 7 Alpheus

argent

6 silver 7 silvern, silvery
9 whiteness

Argentina

capital: 11 Buenos Aires
city: 6 Paraná 7 Córdoba, La Plata, Rosario, Santa Fe 11 Mar del Plata
desert: 9 Patagonia
language: 7 Spanish
leader: 5 Perón (Juan)
monetary unit: 4 peso
mountain, range: 5 Andes
9 Aconcagua
neighbor: 5 Chile 6 Brazil
7 Bolivia, Uruguay 8 Paraguay
plain: 6 Pampas
river: 5 Plata (Río de la) 6 Paraná
8 Colorado 12 Río de la Plata
volcano: 5 Maipo 9 Tupungato

Arges

7 Cyclops
brother: 7 Brontes 8 Steropes
father: 6 Uranus
mother: 4 Gaea

Argonaut

4 hero 10 adventurer 13 paper nautilus
leader: 5 Jason

argosy

4 ship 5 fleet 6 armada, supply
8 flotilla

argot

4 cant 5 idiom, lingo, slang 6 jargon, patois, patter 7 dialect 10 vernacular

arguable

4 moot 7 dubious 8 doubtful 9 debatable, in dispute, uncertain 10 disputable 11 contestable, problematic
12 questionable

argue

5 claim, clash, prove 6 assert, attest, bicker, debate, differ, induce, object, reason 7 agitate, canvass, contend, discuss, dispute, dissent, justify, protest, quarrel, quibble, stickle, testify, witness, wrangle 8 announce, conflict, consider, disagree, indicate, maintain, persuade, polemize, squabble 9 thrash out 10 polemicize 11 expostulate, remonstrate

argument

3 row 4 case, feud, flap, fuss
5 claim, proof, set-to, theme, topic
6 debate, dustup, hassle, motive, reason, rumpus, thesis 7 defense, dispute, polemic, sorites, subject, summary, wrangle 8 abstract, evidence, rebuttal 9 amplitude, assertion, discourse 10 contention, discussion, dissension, squabbling
11 controversy, disputation, embroilment 12 disagreement

argumentation

6 debate 7 dispute, oratory 8 forensic, rhetoric 9 dialectic, reasoning
10 discussion 11 controversy, disputation

argumentative

4 moot 9 in dispute, litigious, polemical 11 contentious, quarrelsome
12 disputatious, questionable
13 controversial

Argus

father: 4 Zeus
mother: 5 Niobe
slayer: 6 Hermes

Argus-eyed
5 alert 9 all-seeing

argyle
4 sock 6 design 7 diamond, pattern
8 Campbell

aria
3 air, lay 4 hymn, lied, solo, song,
tune 5 ditty 6 melody 7 descant

Ariadne
father: 5 Minos
husband: 7 Theseus
island home: 5 Naxos
mother: 8 Pasiphaë

arid
3 dry 4 drab, dull, sere 5 dusty, vapid 6 barren, boring, desert, dreary,
jejune 7 bone-dry, insipid, parched,
sterile, tedious, thirsty 8 droughty,
lifeless, weariful 9 dryasdust, infertile, unwatered, waterless, wearisome 10 lackluster, spiritless,
unfruitful 12 moistureless
13 uninteresting

Ariel
6 spirit
master: 8 Prospero

Aries
3 ram 13 constellation

aright
4 well 5 fitly 6 justly, nicely
8 decently, properly 9 correctly,
fittingly, precisely 10 accurately,
decorously

Arioso epic
14 Orlando Furioso

arise
4 go up, lift, soar, wake 5 awake, begin, get up, issue, mount, occur, start
6 appear, ascend, aspire, come up,
crop up, emerge, spring, uprear,
wake up 7 emanate, proceed
8 commence 9 originate

Aristaeus
father: 6 Apollo
mother: 6 Cyrene
son: 7 Actaeon
wife: 7 Autonoe

aristocracy
5 elite, state 6 gentry, jet set 7 who's
who 8 nobility, noblesse 9 beau
monde, blue blood, gentility, haut
monde 10 government, patricians,
patriciate, upper class, upper crust

aristocrat
9 blue blood, gentleman, patrician
ancient Greek: 8 eupatrid
Russian: 5 boyar 6 boyard

aristocratic
5 aloof, elite, noble 6 lordly 7 courtly,
elegant, genteel, haughty, refined,
stately 8 highborn, well-born, well-
bred 9 dignified, exclusive, patrician
10 privileged, upper-class, upper-
crust 11 blue-blooded

Aristophanes play
5 Birds (The), Frogs (The), Wasps
(The) 6 Clouds (The), Plutus

arithmetic
4 math 8 addition, counting, figuring
9 ciphering, reckoning 10 estimation
11 calculation, computation, mathematics

Arizona
capital: 7 Phoenix
city: 4 Mesa, Yuma 5 Tempe
6 Bisbee, Sedona, Tucson
8 Glendale, Prescott 9 Flagstaff
10 Scottsdale
mountain: 9 Humphreys (Peak)
nickname: 11 Grand Canyon (State)
park: 15 Petrified Forest
river: 4 Gila, Salt 8 Colorado
state bird: 10 cactus wren
state flower: 7 saguaro (cactus)
state tree: 9 palo verde

ark
3 den 4 ship 5 chest, haven 6 adytum, asylum, refuge 7 convent,
retreat, shelter 8 hideaway 9 safe
house, sanctuary 10 repository,
Torah chest
landfall: 6 Ararat
wood: 6 gopher 7 cypress

Arkansas
capital: 10 Little Rock
city: 4 Hope 9 Fort Smith, Pine Bluff

arm

10 Hot Springs **11** Bentonville
12 Fayetteville
mountain, range: 5 Ozark
8 Magazine
nickname: 17 Land of Opportunity
river: 3 Red **8** Arkansas
state bird: 11 mockingbird
state flower: 12 apple blossom
state tree: 12 loblolly pine

arm

3 bay, ell, gun, rig **4** cove, gear,
gulf, wing **5** annex, bayou, equip,
firth, force, inlet, power **6** fit out,
harbor, muscle, outfit, slough, weapon **7** appoint, furnish, turn out
8 accouter, strength **9** extension
bone: 4 ulna **6** radius **7** humerus
combining form: 6 brachi **7** brachio
muscle: 6 biceps **7** triceps

armada

4 navy **5** boats, fleet, force, group,
ships **7** vessels **8** flotilla, warships

armadillo

relative: 5 sloth **8** anteater

armament

4 arms **5** armor **6** weapon **7** defense **8** ordnance, security, weaponry **9** munitions, safeguard **10** ammunition, protection

armamentarium

4 fund **5** stock, store **6** supply
9 inventory

armchair

6 remote **8** fauteuil **9** vicarious
11 theoretical

armed forces

4 army, navy **6** troops **8** air force,
military **10** servicemen

Armenia

capital: 7 Yerevan
city: 6 Gyumri **8** Vanadzor
lake: 5 Sevan
monetary unit: 4 dram
mountain, range: 7 Aragats
8 Caucasus
neighbor: 4 Iran **6** Turkey
7 Georgia **10** Azerbaijan
river: 5 Araks

armistice

5 truce **9** agreement, cease-fire
10 suspension

armor

4 mail **5** aegis, cover, guard **6** shield
7 buckler **8** security **9** safeguard
10 protection
arm: 8 brassard
body: 7 cuirass
armpit: 8 pallette
buttocks: 5 culet
coat: 7 hauberk **10** brigandine
face: 5 visor **6** beaver
flexible: 4 mail
foot: 8 solleret
hand: 7 gantlet **8** gauntlet
head: 6 helmet
horse: 4 bard **5** barde **8** chamfron
leg: 6 greave **7** jambeau
mail: 4 coif **7** hauberk
suit: 7 panoply
thigh: 5 tasse **6** tuille
throat: 6 gorget

armory

4 dump **5** depot, plant, range,
store **7** arsenal, factory **8** magazine **10** collection, storehouse

armpit

6 axilla **8** underarm
Scottish: 5 oxter

arms

7 ensigns, warfare **8** weaponry

army

4 host **5** flock, horde **6** legion
7 militia **9** multitude
combat arm: 5 armor **8** infantry
9 artillery
commission: 6 brevet **7** reserve
Fort: 3 Dix, Lee, Ord **4** Drum,
Hood, Knox, Myer, Polk, Sill **5** Bliss,
Bragg, Irwin, Lewis, McCoy, Meade,
Riley, Story **6** Carson, Eustis,
Gillem, Gordon, Greely, McNair,
Monroe, Rucker **7** Belvoir, Benning,
Detrick, Jackson, Ritchie, Shafter,
Stewart **8** Buchanan, Campbell,
Hamilton, Holabird, Huachuca,
Monmouth **9** McClellan, McPherson
10 Richardson, Sam Houston,
Wainwright **11** Leavenworth

mascot: 4 mule
meal: 4 chow, mess
mine layer: 6 sapper
NCO: 8 corporal, sergeant
officer: 5 major 7 captain, colonel,
general, warrant 10 lieutenant
post: 4 base, camp, fort
postal abbreviation: 3 APO
relating to: 7 martial 8 military
school: 3 OCS, OTS 7 academy
9 West Point
store: 10 commissary 12 post
exchange
unit: 5 corps, squad, troop 7 brigade, cavalry, company, platoon
8 division, regiment 9 battalion
vehicle: 4 jeep, tank 6 Abrams,
Humvee 7 Bradley 9 half-track

aroma
4 balm, odor 5 scent, smell, spice
6 flavor 7 bouquet, incense, perfume
9 fragrance, redolence

aromatic
5 balmy, spicy, sweet 6 savory
7 odorous, perfumy, pungent, scented
8 fragrant, perfumed, redolent
9 ambrosial

around
4 near, nigh 5 about, circa 6 nearby
7 through
prefix: 4 ambi, peri 5 amphi
6 circum

around-the-clock
8 constant, unending 9 ceaseless,
continual, incessant, perpetual,
unceasing 10 continuous 11 unremitting 13 uninterrupted

arouse
4 fire, stir, wake, whet 5 alert, awake,
pique, rally, waken 6 awaken, bestir,
excite, fire up, foment, incite, kindle,
work up 7 agitate, inflame 9 challenge, stimulate

arraign
3 tax, try 5 blame 6 accuse, charge,
indict, summon 9 criminate, inculpate 11 incriminate

arrange
4 plan, sort 5 adapt, array, chart,

order, score, unify 6 assort, codify,
design, devise, lay out, line up, map
out, scheme, set out, settle 7 dispose, marshal, prepare, work out
8 organize, sequence 9 blueprint,
harmonize, integrate, methodize
10 bring about, categorize, instrument, symphonize, synthesize
11 choreograph, orchestrate, systematize

arrangement
5 array, order, setup 6 format,
layout, lineup, series 8 grouping,
ordering, sequence 9 structure
10 adaptation 11 disposition 12 distribution
floral: 4 posy 7 bouquet, garland

arrant
4 rank 5 gross, total, utter 6 brassy,
brazen 7 blatant, extreme, flat-out
8 absolute, complete, impudent,
infernal, overbold 9 barefaced,
downright, egregious, out-and-out,
shameless, unabashed 10 immoderate, unblushing

arras
6 screen 7 drapery 8 curtains,
tapestry

array
3 lot 4 clad, garb, pomp, show
5 adorn, batch, bunch, clump, dress,
group, order 6 attire, bundle, clothe,
draw up, finery, lineup, parade
7 apparel, arrange, cluster, display,
dispose, garment, marshal, militia,
panoply, raiment, variety 8 clothing,
decorate, enclothe, organize, spectrum 9 formation 10 assortment
11 systematize

arrears
3 due 4 debt 5 claim, debit 7 deficit
9 liability 10 balance due, obligation
12 indebtedness

arrest
3 nab, tab, tag 4 bust, grab, halt,
hold, jail, slow, snag, stay, stem, stop
5 block, catch, check, pinch, run in,
seize, stall 6 collar, detain, haul in,
lock up, pick up, pull in, retard, take in

arresting

7 capture, contain, seizure **8** imprison, obstruct, restrain **9** apprehend, detention, interrupt **11** incarcerate **12** apprehension

arresting

6 marked, signal **7** salient **8** striking **9** affective, appealing, prominent **10** attractive, compelling, enchanting, impressive, noticeable, remarkable **11** conspicuous, eye-catching, outstanding

arrival

6 advent, coming **7** landing, success **8** entrance, incoming **9** emergence **10** appearance

arrive

4 come, land, show **5** get in, get to, reach **6** appear, show up, thrive, turn up **7** prosper, succeed **8** flourish

arriviste

7 parvenu, upstart **8** roturier **12** nouveau riche

arrogance

3 ego **4** airs, gall **5** brass, cheek, pride **6** hubris **7** conceit, disdain, hauteur **8** self-love **9** loftiness **11** haughtiness

arrogant

5 cocky, proud **6** lordly, snooty **7** haughty, pompous **8** cavalier, fastuous, insolent, superior **9** egotistic **10** disdainful, high-handed, peremptory **11** domineering, magisterial, overbearing **12** supercilious **13** high-and-mighty, self-important

arrogate

4 grab, take **5** annex, claim, seize, usurp **6** assume, demand **7** ascribe, preempt **8** accroach, take over **9** sequester **10** commandeer, confiscate **11** appropriate, expropriate

arrow

4 dart **5** shaft
poison: 4 inée, upas **6** curare

arrowroot

5 plant, tuber **6** starch **7** coontie

Arrowsmith's wife

5 Leora

arroyo

3 gap **4** draw **5** brook, chasm, cleft, clove, creek, gorge, gulch, gully **6** coulee, ravine **7** channel **11** watercourse

arsenal

4 dump **5** depot, stock, store **6** armory, supply **7** factory, weapons **8** magazine, ordnance **9** stockpile **10** depository, repertoire, repository, storehouse

arson

6 firing **8** torching **9** pyromania **12** incendiarism

arsonist

5 firer, torch **7** firebug **10** incendiary

art

5 craft, skill **6** métier **7** finesse, know-how **8** artifice, painting, vocation **9** dexterity, expertise, sculpture **10** handicraft
faddish: 6 kitsch
style: 3 pop **4** dada **6** cubist, rococo **7** fauvist, realist, surreal **8** abstract, futurist **9** classical **10** naturalist, surrealist **12** naturalistic, surrealistic **13** expressionist, impressionist

art deco

5 style **6** design
designer: 4 Erté

Artemis

Roman counterpart: 5 Diana
birthplace: 5 Delos
brother: 6 Apollo
father: 4 Zeus
mother: 4 Leto
priestess: 9 Iphigenia

artery

3 way **4** duct, line, path, road, tube **5** aorta, track **6** avenue, course, street, vessel **7** carotid, channel, conduit, highway, passage, pathway **8** coronary **9** boulevard **12** thoroughfare

artful

3 sly **4** foxy, wily **5** adept, sharp, slick, smart, suave **6** adroit, astute, clever, crafty, shrewd, smooth, tricky

7 cunning **8** guileful, skillful **9** dexterous, ingenious **10** artificial, diplomatic

arthropod

3 bee, fly **4** crab, mite, moth, tick
6 beetle, insect, shrimp, spider
7 lobster **8** arachnid, barnacle, diplopod, myriapod, scorpion
9 butterfly, centipede, cockroach, millipede, trilobite **10** crustacean
body segment: 6 somite, telson
8 metamere

Arthur

see **King Arthur**

article

3 the **4** bind, item, part **5** essay, paper, piece, point, theme, thing
6 matter, object **7** element, feature, passage, section **10** particular
11 composition, stipulation

articled

5 bound **10** indentured

articulate

3 say **4** join, link, oral, talk **5** clear, hinge, joint, lucid, shape, speak, state, utter, vocal, voice **6** couple, fluent, prolix, relate, spoken, voiced **7** connect, express, jointed **8** coherent, definite, distinct, eloquent, vocalize **9** effective, enunciate, harmonize, integrate, pronounce, verbalize **10** coordinate, expressive
11 concatenate **12** intelligible, smooth-spoken

artifact

5 curio, relic **6** legacy, rarity, trophy
7 remnant, spin-off, vestige **8** creation, heirloom **9** by-product, handcraft, handiwork **10** handicraft
11 contrivance, fabrication

artifice

4 play, ploy, ruse, wile **5** craft, feint, guile, skill, trick **6** deceit, device, gambit **7** cunning, slyness
8 facility, foxiness, trickery, wiliness
9 adeptness, canniness, chicanery, duplicity, ingenuity, stratagem
10 adroitness, artfulness, cleverness, craftiness

artificial

4 fake, faux, mock, sham **5** bogus, dummy, faked, false, phony, put-on
6 ersatz, forced, hollow, unreal
7 assumed, feigned, in vitro, labored, man-made, plastic, pretend **8** affected, mannered, spurious **9** contrived, imitation, insincere, simulated, synthetic, unnatural **10** fabricated, factitious, fictitious, substitute

artillery

4 arms **5** canon, force **6** rocket
7 battery, bazooka, gunnery, weapons **8** cannonry, howitzer, ordnance, weaponry **9** munitions

artisan

6 worker **7** builder, workman **8** producer **9** carpenter, craftsman
12 craftsperson

artist

7 painter **8** sculptor, virtuoso
garb: 5 smock
knife: 7 spatula
medium: 3 oil **5** paint **6** pastel
7 tempera **9** charcoal **10** watercolor
pigment board: 7 palette
stand: 5 easel
workshop: 6 studio **7** atelier
(see also **painter**)

artless

4 free, open, pure, true **5** crude, naive, plain **6** direct, honest, simple **7** genuine, natural, sincere, unaware
8 trusting **9** childlike, guileless, ingenuous, unstudied **10** aboveboard, forthright, unaffected, uncultured, unschooled **12** unartificial, unsuspicious

arty

5 showy **6** pseudo **8** affected, imposing **9** overblown **11** pretentious **12** high-sounding

Aruba

capital: 10 Oranjestad
language: 5 Dutch **10** Papiamento
monetary unit: 6 florin
part of: 11 Netherlands

as

3 for, who **4** coin, like, that, when

5 being, since, which, while
6 though **7** because **11** considering,
for instance

_____ as a pin
4 neat

as a rule
6 mainly, mostly **7** usually **8** commonly **9** generally **10** frequently,
ordinarily

Ascanius
5 Iulus
father: 6 Aeneas

ascend
4 go up, lift, rise, soar **5** arise, climb,
crest, mount, scale **6** aspire, move
up, occupy **7** lift off, take off **8** escalade, escalate, surmount

ascendancy
4 rule **5** power, reign **7** command,
control, mastery **8** dominion **9** authority, dominance, influence, supremacy **10** domination, prepotency
11 preeminence, sovereignty **13** preponderance

ascendant
6 master, rising **7** regnant **8** ancestor, dominant, forebear, relative,
superior **9** paramount, precursor,
prevalent, sovereign **10** commanding, forefather, forerunner, prevailing, progenitor **11** controlling, overbearing, predecessor, predominant,
predominate **12** preponderant,
primogenitor

ascension
4 rise **6** rising **7** going up, scaling
8 climbing, mounting

ascent
4 ramp, rise **5** climb, grade, slope
6 rising **7** advance, incline
8 gradient, progress **9** acclivity,
elevation, uplifting

ascertain
5 learn **7** catch on, find out, unearth
8 discover, make sure **9** determine,
establish, figure out

ascetic
5 stoic **6** hermit, severe **7** austere,
eremite, recluse **9** abstinent,

anchoress, anchorite, mortified
10 abstemious, astringent, forbearing, restrained **11** disciplined, self-
denying
ancient Hebrew: 6 Essene
Buddhist: 5 bonze
early Christian: 7 stylite
Hindu: 4 yogi **5** fakir, Yogin

Asclepius
see **Aesculapius**

ascribe
3 lay **4** cite **5** infer, refer **6** assign,
charge, credit, impute **8** accredit
9 attribute, reference **10** conjecture

Asenath
husband: 6 Joseph
son: 7 Ephraim **8** Manasseh

aseptic
4 cool, flat **5** clean **7** sterile **8** germ-
free, hygienic, sanitary **9** unfeeling
10 restrained, sterilized **11** emotionless, unemotional

asexual
6 agamic

as for
4 in re **5** about, anent **7** apropos
9 regarding **10** concerning, respecting **12** with regard to

as good as
4 nigh **6** all but, almost, nearly
8 in effect, well-nigh **9** basically,
in essence, just about, virtually
11 essentially, practically

ash
4 soot, tree, wood **7** cinders, residue
8 clinkers

ashamed
6 abased, abject, guilty **7** abashed,
humbled **8** contrite, penitent **9** chagrined, mortified, repentant **10** humiliated **11** discomfited, embarrassed

ashen
3 wan **4** gray, pale **5** faded, pasty,
waxen **6** doughy, pallid, sallow,
sickly **7** ghostly **8** blanched,
bleached **9** bloodless, colorless
10 corpselike

Asher
daughter: **5** Serah
father: **5** Jacob
mother: **6** Zilpah
son: **4** Isui **6** Beriah, Ishuah, Jimnah

ashes
5 ruins **6** pallor **7** remains

ashy
3 wan **4** drab, pale **5** livid, waxen
6 doughy, leaden, pallid **7** ghastly,
greyish **8** blanched **9** bloodless,
colorless, washed-out **10** cadaverous

Asia
country: **4** Laos **5** Burma, China,
India, Japan, Korea, Nepal **6** Bhutan,
Russia, Taiwan **7** Armenia, Georgia,
Myanmar, Vietnam **8** Cambodia,
Malaysia, Mongolia, Pakistan, Sri
Lanka, Thailand **9** Indonesia, Kam-
puchea, Kazakstan, Singapore
10 Azerbaijan, Bangladesh, Kazakh-
stan, Kyrgyzstan, North Korea,
South Korea, Tajikistan, Uzbekistan
11 Afghanistan, Philippines
12 Turkmenistan
ethnic group: **3** Han, Lao, Tai
4 Arab, Kurd, Moor, Shan **5** Karen,
Khmer, Malay, Tajik, Tamil, Uzbek
6 Burman, Lepcha, Manchu, Mongol,
Sindhi **7** Baluchi, Bengali, Persian,
Punjabi, Tibetan **8** Armenian, Assyrian, Javanese **9** Dravidian, Indo-
Aryan, Sinhalese **10** Circassian,
Montagnard, Singhalese
language: **3** Lao **4** Urdu **5** Hindi,
Malay, Tamil, Uzbek **6** Arabic,
Bahasa, Korean, Nepali **7** Bengali,
Burmese, Khalkha, Kurdish, Persian,
Tibetan, Turkish **8** Armenian, Japan-
ese, Javanese, Mandarin **9** Cambo-
dian **10** Vietnamese

Asia Minor
8 Anatolia
country: **6** Turkey

Asian inland sea
4 Aral

aside
4 away **5** apart **7** tangent **8** away
from **9** in reserve, privately **10** digression, discursion **11** parenthesis

aside from
3 bar, but **4** save **6** bating, except
7 barring, besides **9** excepting,
excluding, other than, outside of
11 exclusive of

Asimov, Isaac
forte: **5** sci-fi
work: **6** I Robot **9** Nightfall **10** Foundation (Trilogy) **14** Gods Themselves
(The)

asinine
5 crazy, daffy, silly **6** absurd, simple
7 fatuous, foolish, idiotic, puerile, witless **8** mindless **9** brainless **10** irrational, ridiculous **11** nonsensical

ask
3 beg, bid **4** pray, quiz, seek **5** crave,
exact, grill, plead, query **6** appeal,
demand, desire, invite **7** beseech,
call for, canvass, consult, enquire,
entreat, examine, implore, inquire,
request, require, solicit **8** petition,
question **9** catechize, importune
10 supplicate **11** interrogate
Scottish: **5** speer, speir

askance
8 sidelong, sideways **9** cynically,
obliquely **10** critically, doubtfully,
doubtingly, scornfully **11** skeptically
12 suspiciously **13** distrustfully,
mistrustfully

asker
6 beggar, prayer, suitor **7** speaker
9 suppliant **10** petitioner, questioner,
supplicant **11** supplicator

askew
4 awry **6** turned **8** cockeyed
9 crookedly

aslant
4 awry **5** askew **7** crooked **8** cockeyed, sideways, sidewise **9** obliquely

asleep
4 dead, idle, numb **5** inert **6** dozing,
numbed **7** defunct, dormant, nap-
ping **8** benumbed, deadened, inactive, in repose, not alert, sluggish
9 senseless, unfeeling **10** insensible,
slumbering, unanimated **11** indifferent, unconscious **12** anesthetized

as long as
3 for **5** since **6** seeing **7** because, whereas **10** inasmuch as **11** considering **12** provided that

as much as
6 all but, almost **8** well-nigh **11** essentially, practically

aspect
3 air **4** look, mien, side **5** angle, facet, phase, scene, slant **6** regard, status **7** bearing, seeming **8** exposure, position **9** direction **10** appearance **11** perspective

aspen
4 tree **6** poplar

asperity
5 rigor **8** acerbity, acrimony, grimness, hardness, hardship, mordancy, severity, tartness **9** harshness, roughness, sharpness **10** bitterness, difficulty, unevenness **12** irregularity, irritability

asperse
4 slur **5** libel, smear, sully **6** attack, defame, insult, malign, vilify **7** baptize, slander, tarnish, traduce **8** bad mouth, dishonor, sprinkle **9** denigrate, insinuate **10** calumniate

aspersion
4 muck, slam, slur **5** abuse **7** calumny, obloquy, slander **9** invective, stricture **10** defamation, detraction **11** denigration **12** vilification, vituperation **13** animadversion

asphalt
4 pave **7** bitumen, surface **8** blacktop, pavement

asphyxiate
4 kill **5** choke, drown **6** stifle **7** smother **8** strangle, throttle **9** suffocate

aspirant
6 seeker **7** hopeful, seeking **9** applicant, candidate, contender

aspiration
3 aim **4** goal, urge, wish **5** dream **6** desire, intent, object **7** craving, longing, passion, pursuit **8** ambition, striving, yearning **9** breathing, objective **10** pretension **13** ambitiousness

aspire
3 aim, try **4** long, pant, rise, seek, soar, want, wish **5** arise, mount, yearn **6** ascend, desire, hunger, strive, thirst

aspiring
7 longing, seeking, wanting, wishful **8** striving, vaulting, yearning **9** ambitious

as regards
4 in re **7** apropos **8** touching **10** concerning, respecting

ass
4 dolt, fool, jerk, moke, mule **5** burro, dunce, idiot **6** donkey, nitwit **8** bonehead, imbecile **10** nincompoop
female: 5 jenny
male: 4 jack
wild Asian: 5 kiang **6** onager

assai
4 very

assail
4 bash, beat **5** abuse, beset, blast, pound, storm **6** attack, berate, buffet, charge, fall on, malign, oppugn, pummel, revile, strike, vilify **7** assault, bombard **8** fall upon, lambaste **9** break down

assassin
3 gun **5** bravo **6** gunman, hit man, killer **7** torpedo **8** murderer **9** cutthroat **10** hatchet man, triggerman
of Caesar: 6 Brutus **7** Cassius
of Garfield: 7 Guiteau (Charles Julius)
of J. F. Kennedy: 6 Oswald (Lee Harvey)
of M. L. King: 3 Ray (James Earl)
of Lincoln: 5 Booth (John Wilkes)
of Marat: 6 Corday (Charlotte)
of McKinley: 8 Czolgosz (Leon)
of R. F. Kennedy: 6 Sirhan (Sirhan)

assassinate
4 do in, kill, slay **6** finish, murder, rub out **7** bump off, execute, gun down,

put away, take out **8** dispatch, knock off **9** eliminate, liquidate

assault

3 mug, war **4** raid **5** beset, fight, onset, set-to, storm **6** assail, attack, charge, fall on, strike, threat **7** aggress, besiege, mugging, offense **8** fall upon, invasion, storming **9** incursion, offensive, onslaught, violation **10** aggression

assay

3 try **4** rate, seek, test **5** judge, offer, prove, trial, value, weigh **6** assess, result, rating, strive, survey **7** analyze, attempt, examine, inspect, measure, valuate, venture **8** analysis, appraise, endeavor, estimate, evaluate, struggle **9** appraisal, undertake, valuation **10** assessment, evaluation, inspection, measurement **11** examination

assemblage

5 crowd, group **6** muster **7** company, turnout **8** audience **9** gathering **10** collection **11** aggregation, composition, convergence **12** congregation

assemble

4 call, form, make, mass, meet, mold **5** amass, build, clump, group, shape, unite **6** gather, muster, summon **7** cluster, collect, convene, convoke, fashion, marshal, produce, round up **8** congress, contrive **9** aggregate, forgather **10** accumulate, congregate **11** fit together, manufacture, put together **12** call together, come together **13** bring together

assembly

4 bevy **5** bunch, covey, crowd, flock, group, party, rally, set-up **6** muster, troupe **7** cluster, meeting **8** conclave **9** congeries, gathering **10** collection **11** association, fabrication, get-together, manufacture **12** congregation, construction
American Indian: 6 powwow
ancient Greek: 8 ecclesia
ancient Roman: 7 comitia
Anglo-Saxon: 4 moot **5** gemot **6** gemote **8** folkmoot, folkmote

ecclesiastical: 5 synod **10** consistory
legislative: 4 diet **6** senate **8** congress **10** parliament
place: 4 hall, room **5** agora **10** auditorium
Russian: 4 duma
witches': 6 sabbat **7** sabbath

assent

3 nod, yes **4** okay **5** agree **6** accede, accord, concur, say yes **7** approve, consent, embrace **8** approval, sanction, thumbs-up **9** accession, acquiesce, admission, agreement, subscribe **10** acceptance, permission **11** affirmation, concurrence **12** acquiescence

assert

3 say **4** aver, avow **5** argue, claim, posit, state, utter, voice **6** adduce, affirm, allege, attest, avouch, defend, depose, insist, submit **7** advance, contend, declare, express, justify, profess, protest, publish, warrant **8** announce, maintain, proclaim **9** broadcast, postulate, predicate **10** promulgate

assertion

6 avowal **8** averment **9** affidavit, statement **10** allegation, avouchment, contention, deposition, disclosure, insistence, profession **11** affirmation, attestation, declaration **12** asseveration **13** pronouncement

assertive

4 firm, sure **5** pushy **6** strong **7** assured, certain, decided, pushing **8** cocksure, emphatic, forceful, positive **9** confident, energetic, insistent **10** aggressive, resounding **11** affirmative, distinctive, self-assured **13** self-confident

assess

3 fix, tax **4** deem, levy, rate **5** assay, exact, judge, put on, set at, value, weigh **6** charge, figure, impose, reckon, survey **7** account, compute, subject, valuate **8** appraise, consider, estimate, evaluate **9** determine

assessment

3 fee, tax 4 duty, levy, toll 6 charge,
impost, rating, tariff 8 estimate,
judgment 9 appraisal, valuation
10 estimation, evaluation 12 ap-
praisement

asset

4 boon, good 5 merit 6 credit
7 benefit 8 blessing, resource
9 advantage 11 distinction
opposite: 9 liability

assets

5 items, means, money 6 wealth
7 capital 8 bankroll, property
9 resources, valuables 11 possessions

asseverate

4 aver, avow 5 state 6 affirm,
assert, attest, avouch, depose, insist
7 certify, contend, declare, profess
8 maintain, proclaim 9 pronounce

assiduous

4 busy 5 eager 6 active 7 moiling,
zealous 8 diligent, sedulous, tireless
9 attentive, laborious 10 persistent,
unflagging 11 hard-working, industrious 13 indefatigable

assiduously

4 hard 6 busily 9 earnestly, intensely 10 diligently, thoroughly
11 intensively 12 exhaustively,
meticulously, persistently 13 painstakingly, unremittingly

assign

3 fix, lay, set 4 cede, deed, give,
name 5 allot, allow, refer 6 charge,
convey, credit, define, impute, remise,
settle 7 appoint, ascribe, earmark, lay
down, mete out, specify, station
8 accredit, allocate, delegate, make
over, relegate, sign over, transfer
9 admeasure, apportion, attribute,
designate, establish, prescribe
10 pigeonhole

assignation

4 date 5 tryst 7 meeting 9 allotment 10 engagement, rendezvous
11 appointment, get-together

assignee

5 agent, proxy 6 deputy, factor
7 officer 8 attorney, delegate

assignment

3 job 4 beat, duty, post, task, work
5 chore, stint 6 office 8 homework,
position, transfer 9 allotment 10 allocation, delegation, obligation 11 designation

assimilate

5 adapt, adopt, grasp, learn, liken,
match 6 absorb, adjust, digest,
equate, imbibe, soak up, take in,
take up 7 blend in, compare, conform 8 parallel 10 comprehend,
understand 11 incorporate

assimilation

8 taking in 9 awareness 10 absorption, conversion 11 mindfulness,
recognition 12 apperception 13 consciousness, incorporation

assist

3 aid 4 abet, back, help, lift 5 boost,
do for, serve, stead 6 relief, succor
7 backing, benefit, comfort, help out,
secours, service, support, work for
8 benefact, work with 9 cooperate,
open doors

assistance

3 aid 4 hand, help, lift 5 boost
6 relief, succor 7 backing, benefit,
comfort, secours, service, subsidy,
support 8 abetment 9 upholding
10 subvention, supporting 11 cooperation

assistant

3 aid 4 aide, ally, help 5 aider
6 backer, backup, deputy, flunky,
helper, second 7 acolyte, ancilla,
orderly 8 adjutant, henchman
9 attendant, auxiliary, coadjutor
10 accomplice, aide-de-camp,
coadjutant, lieutenant 12 right-hand
man

assistive

6 aiding, useful 7 helpful 10 beneficial 11 serviceable

assize

3 law 4 rule, writ 5 canon, edict

6 decree 7 finding, inquest, precept, statute, verdict 8 standard 9 ordinance, prescript 10 regulation

associate

3 pal 4 ally, chum, join, link, mate, pair, yoke 5 blend, buddy, crony, group, match, merge, unite 6 cohort, comate, couple, fellow, friend, hobnob, relate, worker 7 bracket, combine, compeer, comrade, conjoin, connect, consort, partner 8 confrere, coworker, employee, familiar, federate, identify, intimate 9 affiliate, bedfellow, colleague, companion, copartner, secondary 10 accomplice, amalgamate, compatriot, complement 11 concomitant, confederate, correlative, counterpart, running mate, subordinate 12 acquaintance 13 accompaniment

association

3 tie 4 band, bloc, bond, clan, club, crew, hint 5 group, guild, order, tie-up, union 6 hookup, league 7 circuit, concert, linkage, linking, society 8 alliance, congress, overtone, relation, sodality, teamwork 9 coalition, undertone 10 conference, connection, federation, fellowship, fraternity, mental link, suggestion 11 affiliation, brotherhood, combination, conjunction, connotation, cooperation, implication, partnership 12 conjointment, organization, relationship, togetherness 13 collaboration

assort

5 class, group, order 6 codify, divide 7 arrange 8 classify, stratify 9 associate, designate, harmonize, methodize 10 categorize, distribute, pigeonhole 11 systematize

assorted

4 like 5 mixed 6 fitted, motley, suited, sundry, varied 7 adapted, diverse, matched, similar, various 9 different 11 diversified, conformable 12 conglomerate, multifarious 13 heterogeneous, miscellaneous

assortment

4 olio 5 array, group 6 choice,

jumble, medley 7 mélange, mixture, variety 8 mishmash, mixed bag, pastiche 9 diversity, potpourri, selection 10 collection, hodgepodge, miscellany 11 gallimaufry

assuage

4 calm, cool, ease 5 allay, quiet 6 lessen, pacify, quench, reduce, soften, soothe, temper 7 appease, lighten, mollify, placate, relieve, sweeten 8 decrease, mitigate, moderate 9 alleviate 10 conciliate, propitiate

as such

5 per se 8 by itself 9 in essence, virtually 11 essentially 12 by definition 13 fundamentally, intrinsically

assumably

6 likely, surely 7 no doubt 8 probably 9 doubtless 10 most likely, presumably

assume

3 act, don 4 fake, sham, take 5 adopt, bluff, feign, put on, seize, usurp 6 affect, draw on, expect, reckon, slip on, take in, take on, take up 7 believe, imagine, preempt, premise, presume, pretend, receive, suppose, suspect 8 accroach, arrogate, shoulder, simulate, take over 9 undertake 10 commandeer, presuppose, understand 11 appropriate, counterfeit

assumed

4 fake, sham 5 bogus, false, put on, tacit 6 made-up, phoney 7 feigned 8 affected, delusory, putative, spurious, supposed 9 deceptive, pretended, simulated 10 artificial, fictitious

assumption

5 posit 6 belief, thesis 7 conceit, premise, seizure, surmise 8 takeover 9 arrogance, postulate 10 acceptance, arrogation, conjecture, pretension, usurpation 11 expectation, supposition, undertaking 13 appropriation

assurance

4 oath, word **5** nerve, troth **6** aplomb, parole, pledge, safety, surety **7** promise, support, warrant **8** audacity, boldness, safeness, security, sureness, temerity, warranty **9** assertion, brashness, certainty, certitude, cockiness, composure, guarantee, hardiness, self-trust **10** brazenness, confidence, conviction, equanimity, profession **11** affirmation, presumption

assure

4 aver **5** bet on, cinch, swear **6** affirm, attest, ensure, insure, pledge, secure, soothe **7** certify, comfort, confirm, promise, satisfy **8** convince, persuade **9** guarantee **11** make certain

assured

3 set **4** cool **5** fixed **6** secure **7** certain, decided, settled **8** clear-cut, composed, definite, positive, sanguine **9** assertive, collected, confident, undoubted, unruffled **10** guaranteed, pronounced **11** beyond doubt, made certain, unflappable **13** imperturbable, self-confident, self-satisfied

assuredly

9 certainly, doubtless **10** positively **11** confidently, undoubtedly, without fail

assuredness

6 surety **9** certainty, certitude **10** confidence, conviction

Assyria

capital: 5 Calah **7** Nineveh
city: 5 Ashur, Assur
god: 3 Sin **4** Nabu **5** Ashur, Nusku **6** Tammuz **7** Ninurta
goddess: 6 Ishtar
king: 3 Pul **6** Sargon **11** Sennacherib, Shalmaneser **12** Ashurbanipal
language: 7 Aramaic
queen: 9 Semiramis
river: 6 Tigris
writing: 9 cuneiform

asterisk

4 star **6** symbol **9** character

astern

3 aft **4** rear, tail **5** abaft **6** back of, behind **8** backward, rearmost, rearward

asteroid

5 Ceres

Asterope

father: 5 Atlas
mother: 7 Pleione
sisters: 8 Pleiades

asthma

7 allergy **8** disorder

as to

4 in re **5** about, anent **7** apropos **9** regarding **10** concerning, respecting **11** according to

astonish

4 daze, stun **5** amaze, floor, shock **7** astound, stagger, startle, stupefy **8** blow away, bowl over, confound, dumfound, surprise **9** dumbfound, take aback **11** flabbergast

astonishing

7 amazing **8** stunning, wondrous **9** marvelous, startling, wonderful **10** astounding, miraculous, prodigious, staggering, stupendous, surprising **11** spectacular **12** breathtaking

astonishment

3 awe **5** shock **6** wonder **8** surprise **9** amazement, confusion **10** perplexity, wonderment **12** bewilderment, stupefaction **13** consternation

astound

4 daze, stun **5** amaze, shock **7** confuse **8** astonish, bewilder, confound, dumfound, surprise **9** dumbfound, overwhelm, take aback **11** flabbergast

Astraea

father: 4 Zeus **7** Jupiter
mother: 6 Themis

astral

6 dreamy, starry **7** exalted, highest,

stellar **8** elevated, sidereal **9** celestial, top-drawer, unworldly, visionary **10** top-ranking **11** high-ranking **12** otherworldly

astray
4 awry **5** amiss, badly, wrong **6** adrift, afield **7** in error **9** off course

astride
8 bridging, spanning **10** on each side, straddling

astringent
4 acid, keen **5** acerb, acrid, harsh, sharp, stern **6** biting, bitter, severe, strict **7** acerbic, ascetic, austere, caustic, cutting, puckery, pungent, styptic **8** incisive, stinging **10** irritating **11** contracting **12** constrictive

astrolabe successor
7 sextant

astrologer
5 Dixon (Jeane), Faust **9** stargazer, Zoroaster **11** horoscopist, Nostradamus

astrological aspect
5 trine **7** sextile **8** quartile **10** opposition **11** conjunction

astronaut
4 Ride (Sally) **5** Glenn (John), White (Edward), Young (John) **6** Aldrin (Edwin), Cooper (Gordon), Lovell (James), Worden (Alfred) **7** Bluford (Guion), Collins (Michael), Gagarin (Yuri), Grissom (Gus), Jemison (Mae), Schirra (Walter), Shepard (Alan), Yegorov (Boris) **8** Stafford (Thomas), Armstrong (Neil), Carpenter (Scott), McAuliffe (Christa) **10** Tereshkova (Valentina)

astronomer
American: 3 See (Thomas Jefferson) **5** Sagan (Carl) **6** Hubble (Edwin), Lowell (Percival) **7** Langley (Samuel), Newcomb (Simon), Shapley (Harlow) **8** Bowditch (Nathaniel), Mitchell (Maria), Tombaugh (Clyde) **9** Pickering (Edward) **11** Schlesinger (Frank)

Austrian: 13 Schwarzschild (Karl)
Danish: 5 Brahe (Tycho)
Dutch: 4 Oort (Jan Hendrik) **6** Sitter (Willem de) **7** Huygens (Christiaan)
English: 4 Ryle (Martin), Wren (Christopher) **6** Halley (Edmond), Lovell (Bernard) **7** Lockyer (Joseph), Parsons (William) **8** Herschel (Caroline, John, William)
French: 6 Picard (Jean) **7** Laplace (Pierre-Simon de), Messier (Charles)
German: 4 Wolf (Maximilian) **5** Vogel (Hermann) **6** Kepler (Johannes), Müller (Johann), Struve (Otto)
Greek: 12 Eratosthenes
Italian: 7 Galileo (Galilei) **12** Schiaparelli (Giovanni)
Persian: 11 Omar Khayyám
Polish: 10 Copernicus (Nicolaus)
Swedish: 7 Celsius (Anders)
Swiss: 6 Zwicky (Fritz)

astute
3 sly **4** deep, foxy, keen, wily **5** cagey, canny, heady, quick, savvy, sharp **6** artful, clever, crafty, shrewd, tricky **7** cunning, knowing **8** guileful **9** insidious, sagacious **11** calculating **13** perspicacious

astuteness
3 wit **6** acumen **8** keenness, wiliness **9** canniness **10** craftiness, shrewdness **11** discernment, percipience **12** perspicacity

Astyanax
father: 6 Hector
mother: 10 Andromache

asunder
4 torn **5** apart, split **7** divided **9** into parts, separated

as usual
8 normally, wontedly **9** routinely **10** habitually, ordinarily **11** customarily **12** consistently

as well
3 and, too, yet **4** also, even, just, more, plus **7** besides, further **8** likewise, moreover **9** along with, including, similarly **10** in addition **11** furthermore **12** additionally

as well as
3 and **4** plus **7** besides **9** along with **11** not counting **12** in addition to, together with

as yet
5 so far, to now **7** earlier, thus far **8** hitherto, until now **10** to this time **12** to the present

asylum
4 home, port **5** cover, haven **6** covert, harbor, refuge **7** retreat, shelter **8** hospital, security **9** harborage, safe house, sanctuary **10** protection, sanatorium **11** institution

asymmetric
6 uneven **7** not even, unequal **8** lopsided **9** irregular **10** unbalanced **12** overbalanced

Atalanta
husband: 8 Melanion
suitor: 10 Hippomenes

at all
4 ever, once **6** anyway **7** anytime

atavism
9 reversion, throwback **10** recurrence

ataxia
5 chaos, snarl **6** huddle, muddle **7** clutter **8** disarray, disorder **9** confusion

atelier
6 studio **8** workroom, workshop

Athamas
daughter: 5 Helle
father: 6 Aeolus
son: 7 Phrixos, Phrixus **8** Learchus
wife: 3 Ino **7** Nephele

Athena
Roman counterpart: 7 Minerva
attribute: 3 owl **5** Aegis **7** serpent
city: 6 Athens
father: 4 Zeus
names: 4 Nike **6** Pallas **9** Parthenos
shield: 5 Aegis
statue: 9 Palladium
temple: 9 Parthenon

athenaeum
6 museum **7** library **8** archives **10** repository

Athens
citadel: 9 Acropolis
founder: 7 Cecrops
last king: 6 Codrus
marketplace: 5 agora
rival: 6 Sparta
senate: 5 boule
temple: 9 Parthenon

athirst
4 avid, keen **5** eager **6** ardent **7** anxious **8** desiring, desirous, yearning **9** impatient

athlete
4 jock **5** sport **6** player **7** acrobat, gymnast, tumbler **8** sportsman **10** competitor **11** sportswoman

athlete's foot
8 ringworm **10** tinea pedis

athletic
6 brawny, robust, sinewy **8** sporting, vigorous **9** strapping, strenuous
contest: 5 agon, game **5** match
field: 4 oval, ring, rink **5** arena, court **7** diamond, stadium **8** gridiron
prize: 3 cup **5** medal **6** trophy, wreath

athletics
5 games, races **6** events, sports **7** contest **8** exercise **9** exercises **10** gymnastics, recreation **12** calisthenics

athwart
4 over **5** cross **6** across, beyond **9** crossways, crosswise, opposed to **12** transversely

Atlanta's civic center
4 Omni

Atlas
brother: 10 Prometheus
daughter: 5 Hyads **6** Hyades **8** Pleiades **10** Atlantides
father: 7 Iapetus
mother: 7 Clymene
race: 5 Titan
wife: 7 Pleione

at last
7 finally

Atli
wife (slayer): 6 Gudrun

atmosphere
3 air 4 aura, mood, tone 6 medium,
milieu 7 ambient, climate, feeling,
quality 8 ambiance, ambience
11 environment, mise-en-scène
12 surroundings
stratum: 9 exosphere
10 ionosphere, mesosphere
11 chemosphere, ozonosphere,
troposphere 12 stratosphere,
thermosphere
sun's: 12 chromosphere

atmospheric
4 airy 6 aerial 8 ethereal

atoll
6 island
equatorial area: 5 Baker
Indian Ocean: 4 Male
Kiribati: 4 Beru
Marshall Islands: 6 Bikini
8 Eniwetok
Tuamotu: 4 Anaa 5 Chain
Tuvalu: 8 Funafuti

atom
3 bit, jot 4 iota, mite, whit 5 minim,
speck, touch, trace 6 tittle 7 modicum, smidgen 8 particle 9 scintilla
charged: 3 ion 5 anion
group: 7 radical

atomic particle
3 ion 4 beta, muon, pion 5 alpha,
boson, meson 6 baryon, hadron,
lepton, proton 7 fermion, hyperon,
neutron, nucleon 8 electron, mesotron, neutrino, positron, thermion
hypothetical: 5 quark 6 parton

atomize
4 nuke, ruin 5 smash, wreck 6 divide,
rub out 7 break up, destroy, shatter
8 demolish, destruct, disperse,
dynamite, fragment, nebulize
9 break down, devastate, pulverize
10 disconnect

at once
3 now 4 away, both 6 pronto

8 directly, first off, right now, together 9 forthwith, instantly, right
away 11 immediately, straightway
12 concurrently, straightaway, without delay

atone
3 pay 6 redeem, repair, repent
7 correct, expiate, rectify, redress,
satisfy 10 compensate, make
amends, recompense

atoner
8 penitent

atop
4 upon

Atossa
father: 5 Cyrus
husband: 6 Darius 7 Smerdes
8 Cambyses
son: 6 Xerxes

at random
5 about 6 anyhow 7 anywise 8 by
chance 9 aimlessly, haphazard
10 carelessly 11 any which way,
haphazardly 12 accidentally
13 helter-skelter

at rest
4 dead 5 still 8 inactive, lifeless,
reposing, sleeping, tranquil, unmoving 9 quiescent 10 motionless,
stationary, untroubled 11 trouble-
free

Atreus
brother: 8 Thyestes
father: 6 Pelops
mother: 10 Hippodamia
slayer: 9 Aegisthus
son: 8 Menelaus 9 Agamemnon
11 Pleisthenes
victim: 11 Pleisthenes
wife: 6 Aerope

atrocious
4 foul, vile 5 awful, cruel 6 brutal, horrid, odious, savage, wicked 7 heinous, noisome, obscene 8 barbaric,
horrible, shocking, terrible 9 appalling, desperate, execrable, loathsome,
monstrous, offensive, repulsive,
revolting, sickening 10 abominable,

despicable, detestable, disgusting, horrifying, outrageous, scandalous **12** contemptible

atrocity

4 evil **5** crime **6** horror, infamy **7** cruelty, outrage **8** enormity, savagery **9** barbarity, brutality **11** abomination, heinousness **13** monstrousness

atrophy

7 decline, wasting **9** decadence, waste away **10** devolution **11** declination **12** degeneration **13** deterioration

attach

3 add, fix, tie **4** bind, hook, link, take **5** affix, annex, latch, rivet, stick, unite **6** adhere, append, assign, fasten, secure **7** ascribe, connect **8** make fast **9** associate, attribute

attached

5 fixed **7** sessile

attachment

3 tie **4** bond, link, love **6** fealty **7** loyalty, seizure **8** addition, adhesion, devotion, fastener, fidelity, fondness **9** accessory, adherence, affection, connector, constancy **10** allegiance, connection **12** faithfulness

attack

4 bout, jump, raid, rush **5** beset, blitz, drive, fight, foray, onset, sally, siege, spasm, spell, storm, throe **6** access, ambush, assail, banzai, battle, charge, fall on, harass, have at, invade, irrupt, onrush, sortie, strike, tackle **7** aggress, assault, barrage, besiege, bombard, offense, seizure **8** fall upon, invasion, outbreak, paroxysm **9** beleaguer, incursion, offensive, onslaught, pugnacity **10** aggression, blitzkrieg

attain

3 get, win **4** gain **5** reach, score **6** arrive, come to, effect, make it, obtain, rack up **7** achieve, fulfill, pull off, realize, succeed **8** bring off, complete **10** accomplish

attainment

4 feat **6** finish **7** arrival **10** completion **11** achievement, acquirement, acquisition, fulfillment, realization

attempt

3 bid, try **4** seek, shot, stab **5** assay, crack, essay, offer, trial **6** attack, effort, strive, tackle **7** assault, venture **8** endeavor, striving, struggle **9** undertake **11** undertaking **12** make an effort

attend

3 aid, see **4** be at, go to, hear, heed, help, mark, mind, note **5** apply, catch, nurse, see to, serve, visit, watch **6** assist, convoy, doctor, drop in, escort, go with, listen, notice, show up, turn up, wait on **7** be there, care for, conduct, hearken, oversee, pay heed, work for **8** chaperon, stay with, wait upon **9** accompany, chaperone, companion, look after, supervise **11** concentrate

attendant

4 aide **5** valet **6** escort, helper, lackey **7** orderly, servant **9** ancillary, assistant **10** bridesmaid, coincident **11** chamberlain, concomitant **12** accompanying
ancient Roman: 6 lictor
in court: 7 bailiff **8** tipstaff

attendants

5 suite, train **7** cortege, retinue **9** entourage

attendee

4 goer

attention

4 care, heed, mark, note **5** study **6** notice, regard, remark **7** amenity, command, concern, respect, service, thought **8** civility, courtesy, industry, scrutiny **9** assiduity, awareness, deference, diligence, gallantry, spotlight, treatment **10** absorption, cognizance, observance, politeness **11** application, mindfulness, observation, sensibility **12** deliberation **13** concentration, consciousness, consideration

attention getter
4 ahem 5 gavel

attentive
4 kind 5 alert, awake, aware, civil
6 intent, polite 7 devoted, gallant,
heedful, mindful 8 gracious, obliging,
open-eyed 9 advertent, courteous,
observant, regardful 10 interested,
respectful, solicitous, thoughtful
11 considerate 13 concentrating

attenuate
3 sap 4 rare, slim, thin 5 abate,
blunt, reedy 6 lessen, rarefy, shrink,
slight, stalky, subtle, twiggy, weaken
7 cripple, deflate, disable, reduced,
slender, squinny, subtile, tenuous,
unbrace 8 contract, enfeeble, mitigate, rarefied, tapering, wiredraw
9 constrict, dissipate, undermine
10 become thin, become fine, become less, debilitate

attest
4 aver, show 5 argue, prove, swear,
vouch 6 adjure, affirm, assert, verify
7 certify, confirm, declare, display,
exhibit, point to, support, sustain,
swear to, testify, warrant, witness
8 announce, indicate, manifest
9 establish 10 asseverate 11 bear
witness, demonstrate 12 authenticate

attestation
5 proof 7 witness 8 evidence 9 testament, testimony 10 validation 11 declaration, testimonial 12 confirmation

attic
4 loft, room 6 garret 7 storage
8 cockloft

Attica
6 Greece
division: 4 deme

at times
9 sometimes 10 now and then,
on occasion 11 now and again
12 here and there, occasionally

attire
4 clad, duds, garb, gear, togs, wear
5 array, drape, dress, getup, habit,

tog up 6 clothe, fit out, outfit 7 apparel, clothes, costume, garment,
raiment, threads 8 clothing, garments, glad rags 11 habiliments

attitude
4 pose, view 5 angle, stand 6 manner, stance 7 bearing, mind-set, outlook, posture 8 carriage, demeanor,
position, pretense 10 standpoint
11 inclination, perspective, point of
view

attitudinize
4 mask, pose, sham 6 affect 7 pass
for, pass off, posture, pretend, show
off 10 masquerade

attorney
5 agent, proxy 6 deputy, factor,
lawyer 7 counsel 8 advocate,
assignee 9 barrister, counselor,
solicitor 10 counsellor, legal eagle,
mouthpiece

attract
4 draw, lure, wile 5 charm, court,
tempt 6 allure, appeal, beckon, draw
in, entice, invite, seduce 8 beguile,
bewitch, enchant, solicit 8 appeal to,
interest, intrigue, inveigle 9 captivate, fascinate, influence, magnetize

attraction
4 bait, call, draw, lure, pull 5 charm
6 allure, appeal, liking 8 affinity,
cynosure, sympathy 9 affection,
chemistry, magnetism, seduction
10 allurement 12 drawing power

attractive
4 cute, fair, sexy 5 bonny, dishy
6 comely, lovely, luring, pretty
7 Circean, likable, winsome 8 alluring, charming, engaging, enticing,
fetching, handsome, inviting, magnetic, mesmeric, tempting 9 appealing, beauteous, beautiful, beckoning,
glamorous, seductive 10 bewitching,
enchanting 11 captivating, fascinating, good-looking, tantalizing
13 prepossessing

attractiveness
5 charm 6 appeal, beauty, glamor
7 glamour

attribute

3 lay **4** mark, sign **5** apply, facet, pin on, point, refer, trait **6** aspect, assign, charge, credit, emblem, impute, symbol, virtue **7** ascribe, connect, earmark, explain, feature, quality **8** accredit, classify, property **9** adjective, character, designate

attrition

3 rue **4** ruth, wear **6** sorrow **7** erosion, penance, remorse, rubbing, wearing **8** abrasion, friction, grinding **9** penitence, penitency, reduction, weakening **10** repentance **12** contriteness

attritional

5 sorry **6** rueful **8** contrite, penitent **9** regretful, repentant **10** apologetic, remorseful **11** penitential

attune

6 accord, adjust **7** balance, conform **9** harmonize, integrate, reconcile **10** coordinate, proportion **11** accommodate

atypical

3 odd **5** queer **7** deviant, strange, unusual **8** aberrant, abnormal, peculiar **9** anomalous, deviative, different, divergent, irregular, unnatural **11** exceptional, heteroclite, nonstandard **13** preternatural

auberge

3 inn **5** hotel, lodge **6** hostel, tavern **7** hospice **8** hostelry **9** roadhouse **11** caravansary, public house

Auber opera

10 Fra Diavolo

auburn

4 rust **5** henna **6** russet **8** chestnut **11** burnt sienna **12** reddish-brown

au courant

3 mod **4** up on **5** awake, aware, hep to, hip to, savvy **6** modern, modish, versed **7** abreast, current, in touch, knowing, stylish, versant, witting **8** familiar, informed, sentient, up-to-date **9** cognizant, conscious, plugged in **10** acquainted, conversant

11 fashionable **12** contemporary **13** up-to-the-minute

auction

4 sale, sell

audacious

4 bold, rash **5** brash, brave, cocky, risky, saucy **6** brazen, cheeky, daring **7** valiant **8** arrogant, fearless, impudent, insolent, intrepid, reckless, unafraid, uncurbed **9** daredevil, dauntless, foolhardy, shameless, undaunted, venturous **10** courageous, ungoverned, unhampered **11** adventurous, impertinent, temerarious, uninhibited, untrammeled, venturesome **12** unrestrained **13** adventuresome

audacity

4 gall **5** brass, cheek, moxie, nerve, spunk **6** mettle, spirit **7** courage **8** boldness, chutzpah, rashness, temerity **9** assurance, arrogance, brashness, cockiness, disregard, hardihood, hardiness, impudence, insolence **10** brazenness, effrontery **12** recklessness

audible

5 aural, clear, heard **8** distinct **9** auricular

audibly

5 aloud **7** aurally, clearly, out loud

audience

5 crowd, group, house **6** public **7** hearing, gallery, hearers, meeting **8** admirers, assembly, audition, devotees **9** clientele, following, gathering, interview, listeners **10** assemblage, spectators

audile

see **auditory**

audio

5 sound

audit

4 scan **5** check, probe **6** go over, report, review, survey, verify **7** analyze, balance, checkup, examine, inspect **8** analysis, scrutiny

10 inspection, scrutinize **11** examination **13** investigation

audition
4 test **5** trial **6** tryout **7** hearing, reading

auditor
8 examiner, listener **9** inspector **10** accountant, controller **11** comptroller

auditory
5 aural **8** acoustic

au fait
4 able **5** right **6** decent, proper, versed **7** abreast, capable, correct, versant **8** becoming, decorous, familiar, informed, relevant **9** befitting, competent, qualified **10** acquainted, conforming, conversant, to the point

au fond
8 at bottom **9** basically, in essence **11** essentially **13** fundamentally

Augean
9 difficult **10** formidable **11** distasteful
stable: 3 sty **4** sink **5** filth, Sodom **7** cesspit **8** cesspool

auger
3 bit **5** borer, drill, screw **6** gimlet, trepan, wimble **9** corkscrew

Auge's son
8 Telephus

aught
3 all, nil, nix, zip **4** nada, zero **5** zilch **6** cipher **7** nothing **8** anything, goose egg **10** everything

augment
3 wax **4** grow, hike, rise **5** add to, boost, build, exalt, mount, raise **6** beef up, expand, extend **7** build up, develop, enhance, enlarge, magnify **9** intensify, reinforce **8** compound, heighten, increase, multiply **10** aggrandize, supplement **11** make greater

augmentation
4 rise **5** annex, extra, raise **7** adjunct, buildup **8** addition, increase **9** accession, accretion, increment **10** complement, enrichment **11** enhancement, enlargement

augur
4 bode, seer **6** herald, oracle **7** betoken, diviner, portend, predict, presage, promise, prophet, suggest **8** forebode, forecast, foreshow, foretell, indicate, prophesy, soothsay **9** adumbrate, foretoken, harbinger, predictor, prefigure **10** forecaster, foreshadow, foreteller, prophesier, soothsayer, vaticinate **11** Nostradamus **13** prognosticate

augury
4 omen, sign **5** token **6** herald **7** auspice, portent, presage, warning **8** bodement, forecast, prophecy **9** foretoken, harbinger **10** divination, forerunner, prediction, prognostic **11** forewarning

august
5 grand, noble, regal **6** lordly **7** eminent, stately **8** baronial, imposing, majestic, princely, splendid **9** dignified, grandiose **11** magnificent

auk
5 alcid **7** seabird
genus: 4 Alca

_____ **au lait**
4 café

au naturel
3 raw **4** nude **5** naked, plain **6** unclad **8** stripped **9** unclothed, undressed **10** stark naked

aura
3 air **4** feel, glow, halo, mood, tone, vibe **5** aroma, vibes **6** nimbus **7** aureole, feeling, quality **8** ambience, mystique, radiance, stimulus **9** emanation, semblance, sensation **10** atmosphere

aural
6 audile **7** audible **8** acoustic, auditory **9** auricular

aureate
6 florid, golden **7** flowery, orotund

aureole
8 sonorous 9 bombastic, grandiose, overblown 10 euphuistic, rhetorical 11 declamatory 13 grandiloquent

aureole
4 aura, halo, ring 5 crown, light 6 circle, corona, nimbus 8 radiance

au revoir
4 by-by, ciao, ta-ta 5 adieu, adios 6 bye-bye, so long 7 good-bye 8 farewell 11 arrivederci

auricular
see **aural**

Auriga star
7 Capella

aurora
4 dawn, morn 7 dawning, morning, sunrise 8 cockcrow, daybreak

Aurora
Roman counterpart: 3 Eos
goddess of: 4 dawn
husband: 8 Tithonus
son: 6 Memnon

auslander
5 alien 7 inconnu 8 outsider, stranger 9 foreigner

auspice
4 omen, sign 10 divination

auspices
5 aegis 6 charge 7 backing, support 8 guidance 9 influence, patronage 11 sponsorship, supervision

auspicious
5 lucky 6 bright, timely 7 hopeful 9 favorable, fortunate, opportune, promising, well-timed 10 prosperous 11 encouraging, propitious

Austen, Jane
novel: 4 Emma 10 Persuasion 13 Mansfield Park 15 Northanger Abbey 17 Pride and Prejudice 19 Sense and Sensibility

Auster
see **Notus**

austere
4 bare, cold, dour, firm, grim, hard 5 acrid, bleak, grave, harsh, plain, rigid, sharp, spare, stern 6 bitter, severe, simple, somber, strict 7 ascetic, serious, spartan 8 exacting 9 stringent, unadorned, unfeeling 10 astringent, restrained 11 self-denying

austerity
5 rigor 6 thrift 7 economy 8 acerbity, asperity, coldness, grimness, hardness, rigidity, severity 9 harshness, parsimony, privation, solemnity, spareness, sternness, stiffness 10 self-denial, simplicity, strictness, stringency 11 unadornment 13 self-restraint

Australia
capital: 8 Canberra
city: 5 Perth 6 Darwin, Sydney 8 Adelaide, Brisbane 9 Melbourne, Newcastle
desert: 10 Great Sandy 13 Great Victoria
ethnic group: 9 Aborigine
island: 6 Fraser 8 Kangaroo, Melville, Tasmania
lake: 4 Eyre
monetary unit: 6 dollar
mountain, range: 9 Ayers Rock 9 Kosciusko 13 Great Dividing
reef: 12 Great Barrier
river: 4 Swan 6 Murray 7 Darling 8 Flinders 11 Cooper Creek 12 Coopers Creek
strait: 4 Bass 6 Torres

Austria
capital: 6 Vienna
city: 4 Graz, Linz 8 Salzburg 9 Innsbruck 10 Klagenfurt
lake: 10 Neusiedler
monetary unit: 4 euro
mountain: 13 Grossglockner
mountain range: 4 Alps
neighbor: 5 Italy 7 Croatia, Germany, Hungary 8 Slovakia, Slovenia 11 Switzerland 13 Czech Republic, Liechtenstein
river: 3 Ems 6 Danube

autarchy
see **autocracy**

autarkic

4 free　8 separate　9 sovereign
10 autonomous, self-ruling　11 independent, self-reliant　13 self-governing

autarky

7 freedom　8 autonomy
12 independence, self-reliance

authentic

4 real, true　5 legit, pukka, right, solid, sound, valid　6 actual, trusty
7 certain, factual, for real, genuine
8 accurate, bona fide, credible, faithful, reliable　9 undoubted, veritable
10 convincing, dependable, legitimate, sure-enough　11 indubitable, trustworthy　12 questionless

authenticate

5 prove, vouch　6 adduce, attest, verify　7 bear out, certify, confirm, justify, voucher, warrant　8 accredit, validate　11 corroborate　12 substantiate

author

5 maker　6 penman, scribe, writer
7 creator　8 inventor, novelist, prosaist　9 generator　10 originator
American: 3 Bly (Robert), Fox (Paula), Nin (Anaïs), Poe (Edgar Allan), Tan (Amy)　**4** Agee (James), Baum (L. Frank), Buck (Pearl S.), Cook (Robin), Dana (Richard Henry), Fast (Howard), Ford (Richard), Grey (Zane), Jong (Erica), Mann (Thomas), Puzo (Mario), Rand (Ayn), Rice (Anne), Roth (Philip), Shaw (Irwin), Uris (Leon), West (Nathanael), Wouk (Herman)　**5** Aiken (Conrad), Alger (Horatio), Banks (Russell), Barth (John), Benét (Stephen Vincent), Blume (Judy), Boyle (T. Coraghessan), Brown (Rita Mae), Clark (Mary Higgins), Crane (Hart, Stephen), Dunne (Dominick, John Gregory), Elkin (Stanley), Ellis (Bret Easton), Foote (Horton), Harte (Bret), Henry (O.), Jakes (John), James (Henry), Levin (Ira), Lewis (Sinclair), Lurie (Alison), Mason (Bobbie Ann),
Oates (Joyce Carol), O'Hara (John), Ozick (Cynthia), Paine (Thomas), Paley (Grace), Potok (Chaim), Price (Reynolds, Richard), Steel (Danielle), Stein (Gertrude), Stone (Irving), Stout (Rex), Stowe (Harriet Beecher), Turow (Scott), Twain (Mark), Tyler (Anne), Vidal (Gore), Welty (Eudora), White (Edmund, E. B., T. H.), Wolfe (Thomas, Tom), Wylie (Elinor)　**6** Alcott (Louisa May), Asimov (Isaac), Auster (Paul), Bellow (Saul), Berger (Thomas), Bierce (Ambrose), Bowles (Paul), Cabell (James Branch), Capote (Truman), Cather (Willa), Chopin (Kate), Clancy (Tom), Conroy (Pat), Cooper (James Fenimore), Dickey (James), Didion (Joan), Ellroy (James), Ferber (Edna), French (Marilyn), Gaddis (William), Gaines (Ernest J.), Gilroy (Frank), Godwin (Gail), Hailey (Arthur), Harris (Frank, Joel Chandler), Hawkes (John), Heller (Joseph), Hersey (John), Hinton (S. E.), Holmes (Oliver Wendell), Hughes (Langston), Irving (John, Washington), Jewett (Sarah Orne), Kidder (Tracy), Koontz (Dean), Krantz (Judith), L'Amour (Louis), L'Engle (Madeleine), Le Guin (Ursula K.), London (Jack), Mailer (Norman), McBain (Ed), Miller (Arthur, Henry, Joaquin, May), Morley (Christopher), Morris (Wright), Mosley (Walter), Norrie (Frank), Parker (Dorothy), Piercy (Marge), Porter (Katherine Anne, William Sydney), Proulx (E. Annie), Runyon (Damon), Sarton (May), Singer (Isaac Bashevis), Smiley (Jane), Styron (William), Taylor (Peter), Updike (John), Walker (Alice), Waller (Robert James), Warren (Robert Penn), Wilder (Laura Ingalls, Thornton), Wilson (August, Edmund, Harriet, Lanford), Wister (Owen), Wright (James, Richard)　**7** Baldwin (Faith, James), Beattie (Ann), Cheever (John), Clemens (Samuel Langhorne), Collins (Jackie), Connell (Evan), Cozzens (James Gould), DeLillo (Don),

Dreiser (Theodore), Ellison (Ralph), Erdrich (Louise), Farrell (James T.), Francis (Dick), Franzen (Jonathan), Gardner (Erle Stanley), Garland (Hamlin), Glasgow (Ellen), Goldman (William), Grafton (Sue), Grisham (John), Hammett (Dashiell), Heyward (DuBose), Howells (William Dean), Hurston (Zora Neale), Jackson (Shirley), Jarrell (Randall), Johnson (Diane, James), Keillor (Garrison), Kennedy (William), Kerouac (Jack), Kincaid (Jamaica), Lardner (Ring), Leonard (Elmore), Malamud (Bernard), Marquis (Don), Masters (Edgar Lee), McCourt (Frank), Mumford (Lewis), Nabokov (Vladimir), O'Connor (Flannery), Pynchon (Thomas), Rexroth (Kenneth), Richter (Conrad), Roberts (Elizabeth Madox, Kenneth, Nora), Saroyan (William), Sheehan (Neil), Sheldon (Sidney), Theroux (Paul), Thoreau (Henry David), Thurber (James), Wallace (Lew), Wharton (Edith) **8** Anderson (Maxwell, Poul, Regina, Sherwood), Benchley (Peter), Bradbury (Ray), Bradford (Barbara Taylor), Caldwell (Erskine), Chandler (Raymond), Cornwell (Patricia), Crichton (Michael), Doctorow (E. L.), Faulkner (William), Kingston (Maxine Hong), Marquand (John P.), McCarthy (Cormac, Mary), McMillan (Terry), McMurtry (Larry), Melville (Herman), Michener (James), Mitchell (Donald Grant, Margaret, S. Weir), Morrison (Toni), Remarque (Erich Maria), Rinehart (Mary Roberts), Salinger (J. D.), Sandburg (Carl), Sinclair (Upton), Spillane (Mickey), Stockton (Frank R.), Vonnegut (Kurt), Wambaugh (Joseph) **9** Burroughs (Edgar Rice, John, William S.), Dos Passos (John), Hawthorne (Nathaniel), Hemingway (Ernest), Hillerman (Tony), Isherwood (Christopher), McCullers (Carson), Steinbeck (John), Wodehouse (P. G.), Woollcott (Alexander) **10** Cunningham (Michael), Fitzgerald (F. Scott), Kingsolver (Barbara), Tarkington (Booth) **11** Auchincloss (Louis), Matthiessen (Peter)

Argentinian: 6 Borges (Jorge Luis)

Australian: 4 West (Morris L.) **5** Stead (Christina), White (Patrick) **6** Davies (Robertson) **7** Clavell (James) **8** Keneally (Thomas) **10** McCullough (Colleen), Richardson (Henry Handel)

Austrian: 5 Kafka (Franz) **7** Jelinek (Elfriede), Suttner (Bertha) **8** Bernhard (Thomas) **10** Schnitzler (Arthur)

Canadian: 3 Roy (Camille, Gabrielle) **5** Kirby (William), Moore (Brian), Munro (Alice) **6** Atwood (Margaret), Davies (Robertson) **7** Leacock (Stephen), Raddall (Thomas), Richler (Mordecai), Service (Robert), Shields (Carol) **8** Woodcock (George) **9** de la Roche (Mazo), MacLennan (Hugh)

Chilean: 6 Donoso (José) **7** Allende (Isabel)

Chinese: 5 Han Yu

Colombian: 7 Márquez (Gabriel García)

Czech: 5 Capek (Karel), Hasek (Jaroslav) **7** Kundera (Milan)

Danish: 4 Rode (Helge), Wied (Gustav) **6** Jensen (Johannes Vilhelm) **7** Dinesen (Isak), Holberg (Ludwig)

Dutch: 6 Vondel (Joost van den)

Egyptian: 7 Mahfouz (Naguib)

English: 4 Amis (Kingsley, Martin), Dahl (Roald), Ford (Ford Madox, John), Lyly (John), Saki, Snow (C. P.), Ward (Mrs. Humphry), West (Rebecca) **5** Byatt (A. S.), Defoe (Daniel), Doyle (Authur Conan), Eliot (George, Thomas Stearns), Evans (Mary Ann), Frayn (Michael), Hardy (Thomas), James (Henry, P. D.), Lewis (C. S., Monk, Wyndham), Lowry (Malcolm), Milne (A. A.), Munro (H. H.), Powys (John Cowper, Llewelyn, Theodore Francis), Reade (Charles), Spark (Muriel), Waugh (Alec, Evelyn), Wells (Charles Jeremiah, H. G.), White (T. H.), Wilde (Oscar), Woolf (Leonard, Virginia),

Young (Arthur, Edward, Francis Brett) **6** Ambler (Eric), Archer (Jeffrey), Austen (Jane), Belloc (Hilaire), Brontë (Anne, Charlotte, Emily), Bunyan (John), Butler (Samuel), Clarke (Arthur C.), Conrad (Joseph), Fowles (John), Graves (Robert), Greene (Graham, Robert), Hilton (James), Hudson (W. H.), Huxley (Aldous), Malory (Thomas), McEwan (Ian), O'Brian (Patrick), Orwell (George), Potter (Beatrix), Powell (Anthony), Sayers (Dorothy L.), Sterne (Laurence), Stoker (Bram), Storey (David), Walton (Izaak) **7** Ballard (J. G.), Burgess (Anthony), Burnett (Frances Hodgson), Carroll (Lewis), Collins (Wilkie), Dickens (Charles), Dodgson (Charles), Durrell (Lawrence), Fleming (Ian), Follett (Ken), Forster (E. M.), Forsyth (Frederick), Golding (Louis, William), Kipling (Rudyard), Le Carré (John), Lessing (Doris), Lofting (Hugh), Maugham (Robin, W. Somerset), Murdoch (Iris), Naipaul (V. S.), Rendell (Ruth), Rowling (J. K.), Sassoon (Siegfried), Shelley (Mary Wollstonecraft, Percy Bysshe), Sitwell (Edith, Osbert, Sacheverell), Southey (Robert), Stewart (Mary), Surtees (Robert Smith), Tolkien (J. R. R.), Walpole (Horace, Hugh), Wyndham (John) **8** Christie (Agatha), Fielding (Henry), Forester (C. S.), Koestler (Arthur), Lawrence (D. H., T. E.), Macaulay (Rose, Thomas Babington), Meredith (George), Sillitoe (Alan), Smollett (Tobias), Strachey (Lytton), Trollope (Anthony), Zangwill (Israel) **9** De Quincey (Thomas), Du Maurier (Daphne, George), Goldsmith (Oliver), Isherwood (Christopher), Mansfield (Katherine), Masefield (John), Priestley (J. B.), Radcliffe (Ann), Stevenson (Robert Louis), Thackeray (William Makepeace), Wodehouse (P. D.) **10** Chesterton (Gilbert Keith), Galsworthy (John), Richardson (Dorothy, Samuel) **12** Quiller-Couch (Arthur Thomas)

Finnish: 7 Waltari (Mika) **9** Sillanpää (Frans Eemil)
French: 4 Gide (André), Hugo (Victor), Kock (Charles-Paul de), Sade (Marquis de), Sand (George), Zola (Emile) **5** Beyle (Marie Henri), Camus (Albert), Dumas (Alexandre), Genet (Jean), Sagan (Françoise), Staël (Germaine de), Verne (Jules), Vigny (Alfred-Victor) **6** Balzac (Honoré de), Daudet (Alphonse), France (Anatole), Proust (Marcel), Sartre (Jean-Paul) **7** Cocteau (Jean), Colette, Gautier (Léon, Théophile), Malraux (André), Mauriac (Claude, François), Maurois (André), Merimée (Prosper), Rolland (Romain), Romains (Jules), Simenon (Georges) **8** Beauvoir (Simone de), Flaubert (Gustave), Marivaux (Pierre), Rabelais (François), Stendhal, Voltaire **9** Giraudoux (Jean) **10** Maupassant (Guy de), Saint-Simon (Duke de) **12** Robbe-Grillet (Alain), Saint-Exupéry (Antoine de)
German: 4 Böll (Heinrich), Mann (Thomas) **5** Grass (Gunter), Hesse (Hermann), Kafka (Franz), Storm (Theodor), Tieck (Ludwig), Zweig (Stefan) **6** Goethe (Johann Wolfgang von), Toller (Ernst) **7** Fontane (Theodor), Richter (Jean Paul), Wieland (Christoph Martin) **8** Hoffmann (E. T. A., Heinrich), Remarque (Erich Maria), Schlegel (August Wilhelm von, Friedrich von, Johann Elias) **9** Hauptmann (Gerhart), Sudermann (Hermann) **10** Wassermann (Jakob)
Greek: 6 Lucian **11** Kazantzakis (Nikos)
Hungarian: 5 Jókai (Mór)
Icelandic: 7 Laxness (Halldór)
Indian: 7 Rushdie (Salman)
Irish: 5 Behan (Brendan), Doyle (Roddy), Joyce (James), Moore (Brian), Wilde (Oscar) **6** O'Brien (Edna), Stoker (Bram) **7** Beckett (Samuel), O'Connor (Frank), Russell (George William) **8** O'Faolain (Julia, Sean), Stephens (James) **9** O'Flaherty (Liam)

Italian: 3 Eco (Umberto) 5 Verga (Giovanni) 6 Silone (Ignazio) 7 Calvino (Italo), Manzoni (Alessandro), Moravia (Alberto) 9 Boccaccio (Giovanni), Vittorini (Elio) 10 Pirandello (Luigi), Straparola (Gianfrancesco)

Japanese: 7 Mishima (Yukio) 8 Kawabata (Yasunari), Murakami (Haruki), Murasaki (Shikibu) 9 Yokomitsu (Riichi), Yoshikawa (Eiji)

Lebanese: 6 Gibran (Khalil) 7 Fuentes (Carlos)

Nigerian: 6 Achebe (Chinua) 7 Soyinka (Wole), Tutuola (Amos)

Norwegian: 3 Lie (Jonas) 6 Hamsun (Knut), Undset (Sigrid) 7 Rolvaag (Ole) 8 Bjornson (Bjornstjerne), Kielland (Alexander)

Peruvian: 11 Vargas Llosa (Mario)

Polish: 7 Reymont (Wladyslaw) 8 Zeromski (Stefan) 11 Sienkiewicz (Henryk)

Portuguese: 6 Pessoa (Fernando) 8 Saramago (José)

Roman: 5 Pliny, Varro (Marcus Terentius)

Russian: 5 Gogol (Nikolai), Gorki (Maxim), Gorky (Maxim) 7 Chekhov (Anton), Pushkin (Alexander), Tolstoy (Leo) 8 Andreyev (Leonid), Turgenev (Ivan), Zamyatin (Yevgeny) 9 Ehrenburg (Ilya), Lermontov (Mikhail), Pasternak (Boris), Sholokhov (Mikhail) 10 Dostoevsky (Fyodor) 11 Dostoyevsky (Fyodor), Yevtushenko (Yevgeny) 12 Solzhenitsyn (Alexander)

Scottish: 4 Lang (Andrew) 5 Scott (Alexander, Walter) 6 Barrie (James M.), Buchan (John) 8 Urquhart (Thomas) 9 Stevenson (Robert Louis)

South African: 6 Fugard (Athol) 8 Gordimer (Nadine)

Spanish: 6 Baroja (Pio) 7 Alarcón (Pedro Antonio de) 9 Cervantes (Miguel de)

Swedish: 7 Johnson (Eyvind), Rydberg (Viktor) 8 Lagerlöf (Selma) 10 Lagerkvist (Pär), Strindberg (August)

Swiss: 4 Wyss (Johann Rudolf) 5 Spyri (Johanna) 6 Frisch (Max) 9 Spitteler (Carl)

Trinidadian: 7 Naipaul (V. S.)

Welsh: 4 Owen (Alun, Daniel, Goronwy, John) 5 Evans (David, Evan), Wynne (Ellis)

Yiddish: 4 Asch (Sholem) 6 Singer (Isaac Bashevis) 8 Aleichem (Sholem)

authoritarian

5 harsh, rigid 6 despot, severe, strict, tyrant 8 absolute, autocrat, despotic, dictator, dogmatic 9 imperious, stringent 10 absolutist, autocratic, oppressive, totalistic, tyrannical 11 dictatorial, doctrinaire, domineering, magisterial 12 totalitarian

authoritative

4 sure, true 5 legal, legit, sound 6 lawful, proven 7 factual 8 accepted, accurate, approved, attested, dogmatic, official, orthodox, reliable, verified 9 canonical, cathedral, confirmed, imperious, trustable, validated 10 autocratic, commanding, definitive, dependable, documented, dominating, ex cathedra, legitimate, sanctioned 11 dictatorial, doctrinaire, domineering, irrefutable, magisterial, overbearing, trustworthy 12 indisputable

authority

4 rule, sway 5 clout, force, power, right, say-so 6 agency, charge, credit, expert, master, weight 7 command, control, grounds, license, mastery, warrant 8 citation, decision, dominion, prestige 9 influence, testimony 10 domination, governance, government, management 12 jurisdiction

authorization

4 okay, word 5 leave 6 permit 7 consent, go-ahead, mandate 8 approval, sanction 9 agreement, allowance, clearance 10 green light, permission, sufferance 11 approbation

authorize

3 let **4** okay, vest **5** allow **6** affirm, enable, invest, permit **7** approve, confirm, empower, endorse, entitle, license, qualify, warrant **8** accredit, sanction, vouch for **9** give leave, recognize **10** commission **11** countenance

auto

see **automobile**

autobahn

7 highway **8** turnpike **10** expressway **12** superhighway

autobiography

4 life, vita **5** diary **6** memoir **7** account, journal **9** life story **11** confessions **13** reminiscences

autochthonous

6 native **7** endemic **8** original **10** aboriginal, indigenous

autocracy

7 czarism, tyranny **8** monarchy **9** despotism, monocracy **12** absolute rule, dictatorship

autocrat

4 czar, duce, emir, lord, raja, shah, tsar, tzar **5** mogul, rajah, ruler **6** caliph, despot, sultan, tyrant **7** magnate, monarch **8** dictator, oligarch, overlord **9** potentate, sovereign **10** absolutist

autocratic

7 haughty **8** absolute, arrogant, despotic **9** arbitrary, imperious, tyrannous **10** monocratic, tyrannical **11** dictatorial, domineering, overbearing

autodidactic

10 self-taught **12** self-educated

autograph

3 ink, pen **4** sign **5** write **7** endorse **8** original **9** signature, subscribe **11** endorsement, John Hancock

Autolycus

daughter: **8** Anticlea
father: **6** Hermes **7** Mercury

automated

7 robotic **9** by machine, motorized **10** electrical, electronic, mechanical, mechanized, programmed **12** computerized

automatic

6 reflex **8** habitual **9** impulsive, reflexive **10** mechanical, self-acting, unprompted **11** instinctive, involuntary, perfunctory, spontaneous, unmeditated
prefix: **4** self

automaton

5 droid, golem, robot **7** android, machine **9** mechanism

automobile

3 bus, car **5** buggy, coupe, racer, sedan **6** jalopy, tourer, wheels **7** flivver, hardtop, machine **8** dragster, motorcar, roadster, runabout **9** hatchback, limousine **11** convertible
American: **3** Reo **4** Cord, Ford, Jeep, Nash **5** Buick, Dodge, Eagle, Essex, Lexus **6** DeSoto, Hudson, Model A, Model T, Saturn, Willys **7** LaSalle, LeBarón, Lincoln, Maxwell, Mercury, Mustang, Packard, Pontiac, Rambler, Seville **8** Cadillac, Chrysler, Corvette, Eldorado, Franklin, Plymouth **9** Chevrolet, Hupmobile **10** Duesenberg, Oldsmobile, Studebaker **11** Continental, Pierce-Arrow, Thunderbird **12** Kaiser-Frazer
British: **4** Mini **6** Anglia, Austin, Cooper, DeSoto, Jaguar, Morris **7** Bentley, Daimler, Hillman, Sunbeam, Triumph **8** Vauxhall **10** Range Rover, Rolls-Royce **11** Aston Martin, Land Rover **12** Austin-Healey
French: **5** Simca **7** Citroën, Peugeot, Renault
German: **3** BMW **4** Audi, Benz, Opel **7** Daimler, Porsche **8** Mercedes **10** Volkswagen **12** Mercedes-Benz
Italian: **4** Fiat **6** Lancia **7** Bugatti, Ferrari **8** Maserati **9** Alfa-Romeo **11** Lamborghini

Japanese: 5 Honda, Isuzu, Mazda
6 Datsun, Nissan, Subaru, Toyota
10 Mitsubishi
Korean: 3 Kia 6 Daewoo 7 Hyundai
Swedish: 4 Saab 5 Volvo

automotive pioneer
4 Benz (Carl Friedrich), Ford (Henry),
Olds (Ransom), Otto (Nikolaus),
Pope (Albert) 5 Evans (Oliver),
Rolls (Charles), Roper (Sylvester)
6 Cugnot (Nicholas Joseph), Duryea
(Charles E., J. Frank), Lenoir (Eti-
enne), Winton (Alexander) 7 Bugatti
(Ettore), Citroën (André-Gustave),
Daimler (Gottlieb), Peugeot (Ar-
mand), Stanley (Francis, Freelan)
8 Morrison (William) 10 Lanchester
(Frederick William)

Autonoë
father: 6 Cadmus
husband: 9 Aristaeus
mother: 8 Harmonia
sister: 5 Agave
son: 7 Actaeon

autonomous
4 free 8 autarkic, separate 9 sovereign 10 self-ruling 11 independent,
self-reliant 12 self-governed, uncontrolled 13 self-contained, self-
governing

autonomy
7 autarky, freedom 8 home rule,
self-rule 11 sovereignty 12 independence

autopsy
6 assess 7 examine 8 evaluate,
necropsy 10 assessment, dissection, evaluation, postmortem
11 examination

auto racer
4 Foyt (A. J.), Hill (Graham) 5 Clark
(Jim), Mears (Rick), Petty (Richard),
Unser (Al, Bobby) 6 Carter (Pancho), Fangio (Juan), Vogler (Rich)
7 Brabham (Jack), Stewart (Jackie)
8 Andretti (Mario, Michael), Johncock
(Gordon) 9 Earnhardt (Dale)
10 Rutherford (Johnny)

autumn
4 fall 6 season 8 maturity

auxiliary
4 aide 5 spare 6 backup, helper
7 reserve 8 adjutant, adjuvant
9 accessory, ancillary, assistant,
coadjutor, secondary 10 accomplice,
additional, collateral, subsidiary
11 appurtenant, subservient 12 contributory 13 complementary, supplementary
verb: 3 are, can, did, had, has, may,
was 4 been, does, have, must,
were, will 5 could, might, ought,
shall, would 6 should

avail
3 aid, use 4 gain, good, help
5 asset, serve 6 profit 7 account,
benefit, fitness, satisfy, service
9 advantage, relevance
10 usefulness 13 applicability

available
5 handy, on tap, ready, valid 6 at
hand, on hand, usable 7 present, willing 8 prepared 9 qualified 10 accessible, attainable, convenient, obtainable, procurable 11 purchasable

avalanche
4 mass, rush 5 drown, flood, slide
6 deluge 7 overrun, smother 8 inundate, mudslide, overflow, rockfall
9 landslide, overwhelm, rockslide,
snowslide 10 inundation 12 accumulation

Avalon
8 paradise

avant-garde
7 radical 8 advanced, contempo
10 innovative, pioneering 11 cutting-
edge, leading-edge, progressive
12 experimental 13 up-to-the-minute

avarice
5 greed 7 avidity 8 cupidity, rapacity, voracity 10 greediness 12 covetousness

avaricious
6 grabby, greedy, stingy 7 miserly
8 covetous, esurient, grasping, ravenous 9 mercenary, rapacious
11 acquisitive

avatar
4 type 5 image 7 epitome 8 exem-

plar **9** archetype **10** apotheosis, embodiment, expression **11** incarnation, reification **13** manifestation

avaunt

4 away **5** hence, leave, scram **6** beat it, depart, get out

ave

4 hail **8** farewell, greeting

avenge

5 repay, right **6** punish **7** get even, pay back, redress, requite **9** fight back, retaliate, vindicate

avenue

3 way **4** path, road **5** drive, means, route, track **6** access, artery, course, street **7** channel, parkway, pathway **8** approach **9** boulevard **10** passageway **12** thoroughfare

aver

4 avow **5** prove, state, swear **6** affirm, allege, assert, attest, avouch, depose, insist, verify **7** declare, profess, protest, testify, warrant **8** maintain **9** guarantee, predicate

average

3 par **4** fair, mean, norm **5** usual **6** common, divide, equate, figure, median, medium, middle, normal **7** balance, even out, typical **8** everyday, midpoint, moderate, ordinary **12** intermediate

averagely

4 so-so **6** enough, fairly, rather **8** passably **9** tolerably **10** moderately

averse

5 balky, loath **6** afraid **7** hostile, opposed, uneager **8** allergic, hesitant **9** reluctant, resistant, unwilling **10** indisposed **11** disinclined **12** antipathetic

aversion

4 fear, hate **5** dread **6** hatred, horror **7** allergy, disgust, dislike **8** disfavor, distaste, loathing **9** antipathy, disliking, repulsion, revulsion **10** abhorrence, antagonism, repugnance **11** abomination, detestation, displeasure **13** indisposition

aversive

8 ungenial **9** repellent, repugnant **11** uncongenial **12** antipathetic **13** unsympathetic

avert

4 foil, halt, turn, veer, ward **5** avoid, check, deter **6** thwart **7** deflect, fend off, forfend, obviate, prevent, rule out, ward off **8** go around, stave off, turn away **9** forestall, turn aside

avian

6 flying, winged **8** birdlike, ornithic

aviary

4 cage **8** birdcage, dovecote **9** birdhouse, enclosure

aviator

3 ace **4** Post (Wiley) **5** flier, pilot **6** airman, flyboy, Wright (Orville, Wilbur), Yeager (Chuck) **7** birdman, Earhart (Amelia) **8** aeronaut **9** bush pilot, Lindbergh (Charles) **10** Richthofen (Manfred von) **12** Rickenbacker (Eddie)

avid

4 agog, keen **5** eager **6** ardent, greedy, hungry **7** anxious, athirst, craving, fervent, thirsty, zealous **8** appetent, covetous, desirous, grasping **9** impatient **10** breathless, insatiable **12** enthusiastic

avidity

4 zeal **5** greed **6** fervor, thirst **7** avarice, craving **8** cupidity, keenness, rapacity **9** eagerness **10** greediness

Avis

competitor: 5 Hertz

_____ avis

4 rara

avocation

5 hobby **7** pastime, pursuit **8** sideline **9** amusement, diversion **10** recreation

avoid

4 bilk, duck, miss, shun, snub **5** annul, avert, dodge, elude, evade, shirk, skirt **6** bypass, divert, escape, eschew, pass up **7** abstain, prevent, refrain **8** preclude, sidestep, stay away, withdraw **9** keep clear **11** refrain from **12** keep away from

avoidance

5 dodge **6** escape **7** dodging, elusion, evasion **8** escaping, escapism, eschewal, shirking, shunning **9** runaround **10** abstinence

avouch

3 own **4** aver, avow **5** admit, claim, state, swear **6** affirm, assert, depose, insist **7** certify, confess, confirm, declare, profess, testify **9** predicate, pronounce **11** acknowledge, corroborate

avow

3 own **4** aver **5** admit, allow, grant, let on, own up, state, swear **6** affirm, assert, avouch, depose **7** concede, confess, declare, profess, protest **8** disclose, maintain, proclaim **9** predicate **11** acknowledge

avowal

6 assent **9** admission, assertion, statement **10** profession **11** affirmation, attestation, declaration

avowedly

6 openly **7** frankly **8** candidly **9** allegedly **10** apparently, ostensibly, supposedly

await

4 bide, hope, stay **5** abide **6** expect **7** count on, look for **8** watch for **10** anticipate, hang around

awake

4 stir **5** alert, alive, aware, rouse **6** active, arouse, bestir, excite, revive, roused, stir up **7** animate, aroused, excited, on guard **8** activate, sensible, sentient, vigilant, watchful **9** attentive, cognizant, conscious, observant, stimulate, stirred up

award

4 gift, give, kudo **5** allot, badge, endow, grant, honor, kudos, medal, prize **6** accord, bestow, confer, donate, trophy **7** concede, laurels; tribute **8** accolade, citation, donation **9** vouchsafe **10** blue ribbon, decoration, distribute **11** distinction
motion picture: **5** Oscar **7** Academy **11** Golden Globe
mystery novel: **5** Edgar
record: **6** Grammy
science-fiction: **4** Hugo
television: **4** Emmy
theater: **4** Tony

aware

4 onto **5** alert, alive, awake **7** heedful, knowing, mindful, tuned in, witting **8** informed, sensible, sentient, vigilant **9** attentive, au courant, cognizant, conscious, observant **10** conversant, perceptive **12** apprehensive **13** knowledgeable

awash

4 full **6** afloat, filled, jammed, loaded, packed **7** brimful, covered, crammed, crowded, flooded, run-over, stuffed **8** brimming, chockful **9** chock-full **11** overflowing

away

3 far, fro, now, off, out **4** afar, gone **5** along, apart, aside, forth, hence **6** abroad, absent, afield, far off **7** distant, lacking, missing, not here **9** elsewhere **11** incessantly **12** continuously

away from

6 beyond

awe

5 alarm, amaze, scare **6** wonder **7** inspire, startle **8** astonish **9** amazement, reverence **10** veneration, wonderment **11** flabbergast **12** astonishment

aweless

4 bold **5** brave **7** valiant **8** fearless, intrepid, unafraid **9** dauntless, undaunted **10** courageous

awesome

6 august **7** amazing, sublime **8** imposing, terrific, wondrous **10** formidable, impressive **11** astonishing **12** breathtaking **13** extraordinary

awful
3 bad 4 very 5 nasty 6 odious
7 hateful 8 dreadful, horrible, horrific, shocking, terrible, terrific 9 appalling, atrocious, extremely, frightful,
loathsome, offensive 10 deplorable,
disgusting, formidable

awfully
4 much, very 6 hugely, vastly
7 greatly 8 terribly, whopping 9 extremely, immensely 10 dreadfully,
enormously 11 exceedingly

awhile
7 briefly 8 for a time 11 temporarily

awkward
5 gawky, inept, messy, nerdy, splay
6 clumsy, gauche, klutzy, wooden
7 artless, gawkish, halting, lumpish,
unhandy, unhappy 8 bumbling,
bungling, tactless, ungainly 9 graceless, ham-handed, ill-chosen, inelegant, lumbering, maladroit 10 blundering, ungraceful, unskillful 11 heavy-
handed, unfortunate 12 embarrass-
ing, incommodious, inconvenient,
infelicitous

awl
4 tool 7 piercer

awning
6 canopy 7 marquee 8 sunshade
ancient Roman: 8 velarium

awry
5 amiss, askew, wrong 6 astray
7 askance, crooked 8 cockeyed
9 cock-a-hoop, crookedly
Scottish: 5 agley

ax, axe
3 can, hew 4 adze, boot, chop, fire,
sack 6 bounce 7 boot out, chopper,
cleaver, dismiss, hatchet, kick out
8 tomahawk 9 discharge, terminate
blade: 3 bit
handle: 5 helve

axiom
3 law 4 rule 5 adage, maxim, moral,
truth 6 dictum, truism 7 precept,
theorem 8 aphorism, apothegm

9 postulate, principle 10 principium
11 fundamental

axiomatic
5 given 7 assumed, certain, obvious
8 accepted, absolute, manifest,
provable 10 aphoristic, understood
11 fundamental, indubitable, self-
evident 12 unquestioned

axis
4 line, pole, stem 5 point, pivot
8 alliance 9 continuum, plant stem
11 partnership 12 straight line,
turning point

axle
3 bar, pin, rod 4 beam 5 bogie,
shaft 7 spindle, support

aye
3 yea, yep, yes 4 amen, okay,
ever, vote 6 agreed, always 8 all
right 11 affirmative, continually

Azerbaijan
capital: 4 Baku
city: 5 Gäncä 8 Sumqayit
exclave: 8 Naxçivan
11 Nakhichevan
monetary unit: 5 manat
neighbor: 4 Iran 6 Russia
7 Armenia, Georgia
river: 4 Kura 5 Araks
sea: 7 Caspian

Azores
capital: 12 Ponta Delgada
city: 5 Horta
island: 4 Pico 5 Corvo, Faial, Lajes
6 Flores 8 São Jorge, Terceura
9 São Miguel 10 Santa Maria
part of: 8 Portugal

Aztec
capital: 12 Tenochtitlán
conqueror: 6 Cortés, Cortéz
emperor: 9 Moctezuma, Montezuma
god: 4 Xipe 5 Tlaloc 9 Xipetotec
12 Quetzalcoatl
hero: 4 Nata
language: 7 Nahuatl
temple: 8 teocalli

azure
3 sky 4 blue 5 color 7 sky blue

B

baa
5 bleat

Babbitt
10 conformist, middlebrow, philistine
author: 5 Lewis (Sinclair)

babble
3 gab, jaw, yak, yap 4 blab, chat, go
on, gush, rant, rave 5 clack, prate,
run on 6 burble, drivel, gibber,
gossip, jabber, murmur, patter, piffle,
rattle, yammer 7 blabber, blather,
chatter, maunder, palaver, prattle,
twaddle 8 nonsense, idle talk 9 gibberish 11 jabberwocky

babe
3 cub, tot 4 doll, girl 5 bairn, child,
chick, cutie, woman 6 infant, hottie
7 bambino, papoose, neonate, newborn 8 bantling, nursling

babel
3 ado, din, row 4 to-do 5 hoo-ha
6 bedlam, clamor, hubbub, jangle,
outcry, racket, ruckus, tumult, uproar
7 clangor, discord, ferment, turmoil
8 brouhaha, clangour, foofaraw
9 cacophony, commotion, confusion
10 dissonance, hullabaloo, hurly-
burly, turbulence 11 pandemonium
12 vociferation

baboon
3 oaf 4 clod, dolt, goon, lout
6 chacma, galoot, simian 7 palooka
8 lunkhead, mandrill, meathead
9 hamadryas

babushka
6 granny 7 bandana 8 bandanna,
kerchief

baby
3 pet, tot 4 tiny 5 bairn, sissy, spoil
6 cocker, coddle, cosset, dote on,
infant, pamper 7 bambino, cater to,
indulge, neonate, newborn, papoose,
toddler 8 bantling, dote upon,
nursling, suckling, weanling
11 mollycoddle
ailment: 5 colic, croup
bed: 4 crib 6 cradle 8 bassinet
bedroom: 7 nursery
breechcloth: 6 diaper
cap: 6 biggin, bonnet
carriage: 4 pram 5 buggy 8 stroller
12 perambulator
doctor: 12 pediatrician
food: 3 pap 4 milk 6 pablum
7 pabulum
garment: 7 rompers
Italian: 7 bambino
napkin: 3 bib
outfit: 7 layette
powder: 4 talc
shoe: 6 bootee
Spanish: 4 bebé, nene

baby grand
5 piano

babyhood
7 infancy 10 diaper days, immaturity

babyish
5 petty 7 foolish, puerile, spoiled
8 childish, immature, juvenile 9 infantile, infantine

Babylonian
6 lavish 9 luxurious
abode of the dead: 5 Aralu
capital: 7 Babylon
chaos: 4 Apsu

city: 5 Akkad **6** Cunaxa
crown prince: 10 Belshazzar
division: 5 Akkad, Sumer
earth mother: 6 Ishtar
first ruler: 6 Nimrod
god: 3 Bel **6** Marduk, Tammuz
goddess: 5 Belit **6** Ishtar
hero: 9 Gilgamesh
king: 6 Sargon **9** Hammurabi
12 Ashurbanipal
river: 6 Tigris **9** Euphrates
sun god: 3 Bel **7** Shamash
tower: 5 Babel **8** ziggurat
waters: 4 Apsu **6** Tiamat
winged dragon: 6 Tiamat

baccalaureate
6 degree **9** bachelor's **10** graduation

bacchanal
6 maenad
see also **bacchanalia**

bacchanalia
4 bash, orgy **5** binge, revel, spree
6 bender, excess **7** blowout, carouse,
debauch, revelry, wassail **8** carnival,
festival, wingding **11** celebration,
dissipation, merrymaking

bacchanalian
4 wild **7** drunken, riotous **8** frenzied
9 debauched, orgiastic **12** intoxi-
cating
cry 4 evoe **5** evohe

Bacchus
8 Dionysus
attendant: 6 maenad **9** bacchante
father: 4 Zeus **7** Jupiter
lover: 5 Venus **9** Aphrodite
mother: 6 Semele
son: 7 Priapus
staff: 7 thyrsus

Bach, Johann Sebastian
birthplace: 8 Eisenach
genre: 5 fugue, motet, suite **6** sonata **7** cantata, chorale, partita,
prelude, toccata **8** concerto, fantasia, oratorio, sinfonia
home: 7 Leipzig
instrument: 5 organ **11** harpsichord
musical style: 7 baroque
religion: 8 Lutheran

back
3 aft, aid **4** abet, fund, help, hind, rear
5 abaft, about, dorsa (plural), spine,
stake **6** assist, astern, dorsum,
hinder, recede, uphold **7** endorse,
finance, promote, retract, retreat,
reverse, sponsor, support **8** advocate, bankroll, champion, rearward,
side with **9** in reverse, posterior,
retrocede, subsidize **10** retrograde
ailment: 7 lumbago **10** rheumatism
of an arthropod: 6 tergum
of an insect: 5 notum
of the neck: 4 nape **6** scruff
prefix: 4 post **5** retro
relating to: 6 dorsal

back answer
3 lip **6** retort **7** riposte **8** comeback,
repartee **9** rejoinder, wisecrack
10 return shot **11** parting shot

backbite
4 slam, slur **5** abuse, decry, knock,
libel, smear, sully, taint **6** defame,
defile, malign, vilify **7** asperse, put
down, run down, slander, traduce
8 bad-mouth, belittle, besmirch,
derogate, diminish **9** denigrate, discredit

backbiter
6 gossip **7** defamer, traitor
9 detractor, slanderer **10** talebearer

backbiting
5 abuse, smear, spite **6** gossip
7 abusing, calumny, obloquy, scandal, slander **8** libelous, smearing
9 aspersion, cattiness, gossiping,
invective, maligning, traducing,
vilifying **10** calumnious, defamation,
defamatory, scandalous, slandering,
slanderous **11** denigration **12** belittlement, depreciation, spitefulness,
vituperation **13** disparagement

backbone
4 base, grit, guts, will **5** basis,
moxie, nerve, spine, spunk **6** mettle,
pillar, rachis **7** resolve, support
8 mainstay, tenacity **9** character,
fortitude, framework, toughness,
vertebrae **10** foundation, moral fiber,

resolution **12** spinal column
13 determination, steadfastness

backbreaking
6 taxing, tiring **7** arduous, onerous
8 grueling, toilsome **9** fatiguing,
gruelling, laborious, punishing,
strenuous, torturous, wearisome
10 burdensome, exhausting

backchat
6 banter, gossip **10** persiflage

backcomb
5 tease

backcountry
4 bush **6** sticks **7** boonies, outback
8 frontier, interior **9** boondocks
10 hinterland

backcourtman
5 guard

back down
4 balk **5** admit, demur, welsh, yield
6 beg off, bow out, cry off, give in,
give up, recall, recant, renege **7** concede, disavow, retract, retreat **8** take
back, withdraw **9** surrender, weasel
out **10** chicken out

backdrop
6 milieu **7** climate, context, scenery,
setting **8** stage set **10** atmosphere,
background **11** environment, mise-
en-scène **12** surroundings

backer
4 ally **5** angel **6** patron, surety
7 sponsor **8** advocate, defender,
exponent, follower, investor, promoter **9** auxiliary, guarantor, proponent, supporter **10** bankroller, benefactor, meal ticket

backfire
4 fail **5** blast **6** fizzle, go awry **7** go
amiss, go wrong **8** miscarry, ricochet
9 boomerang, discharge, explosion
10 disappoint, spring back **11** fall
through **13** counteraction

backgammon
board section: 5 table
piece: 5 stone
wedge: 5 point

background
4 base, tone **6** milieu **7** history,
scenery, setting **8** heritage, training
9 education **10** experience, supporting **13** circumstances, qualification

backhanded
7 devious, oblique **8** indirect, derisive, sneering **9** insulting, sarcastic
10 roundabout **12** disingenuous
13 condescending
compliment: 6 insult, slight **7** put-
down **9** aspersion

backing
3 aid **4** help **5** aegis, funds **7** harmony, support **8** auspices **9** patronage, promotion **10** assistance
11 endorsement, sponsorship **13** accompaniment, encouragement

backland
see **backcountry**

backlash
5 slack **6** recoil **8** kickback, reaction,
response, ricochet **11** retaliation
12 repercussion

backlog
4 pile **5** hoard, stock, store **6** pile
up, supply **7** nest egg, reserve
9 inventory, reservoir, stockpile
12 accumulation

back of
5 abaft **6** behind **9** following

back off
see **back down**

back out
4 quit **5** leave, welsh, yield **6** beg
off, desert, give up, renege **7** forsake
8 withdraw **9** surrender

backpack
4 gear, hike **5** tramp **6** duffel,
ramble **8** knapsack, rucksack
9 haversack

backpedal
see **back down**

backset
see **setback**

backside
3 bum 4 butt, rear, rump, seat, tail,
tush 5 fanny, hiney, stern 6 behind,
bottom, breech, far end, heinie
8 buttocks, derriere, haunches
9 fundament, posterior 12 hindquarters

backslide
4 fall, sink, slip 5 lapse 6 return,
revert 7 go wrong, regress, relapse
9 retrovert 10 degenerate, go downhill, recidivate 11 deteriorate

backstabbing
4 slur 5 smear 6 malice 7 calumny, scandal, slander 8 betrayal
9 treachery 10 defamation, detraction, traitorous 11 treacherous
12 belittlement, depreciation, vilification 13 disparagement

backstairs
6 covert, secret, sneaky, sordid
7 furtive 8 hush-hush 9 secretive
10 scandalous 11 clandestine,
underhanded 13 surreptitious

backstop
5 fence 6 screen, uphold 7 bolster,
support 8 advocate, champion, side
with

back talk
3 lip 4 guff, sass 5 cheek, mouth,
sauce 9 freshness, impudence,
insolence 12 impertinence

backtrack
7 regress, retrace, retreat, reverse
8 turn tail

backward
4 dull, slow, rear 5 abaft, dense
6 averse, astern, behind, stupid
7 awkward, delayed, moronic
8 ignorant, inverted, rearward, retarded, reversed, stagnant 9 benighted, dim-witted, in reverse
10 half-witted, retrograde, slow-
witted, uncultured 11 thickheaded,
turned around, undeveloped
12 feebleminded, simpleminded,
uncultivated 13 unprogressive

backwoods
see **backcountry**

backwoodsman
4 hick, rube 5 swain, yokel 6 rustic
7 bumpkin, hayseed 9 hillbilly
10 clodhopper, country boy, provincial 11 mountaineer

bacon
side: 6 flitch, gammon
slice: 6 rasher

Bacon, Francis
work: 12 Novum Organum

bacteria
5 cocci 7 bacilli, vibrios 8 spirilla
culture medium: 4 agar
destroyer: 10 antibiotic

bacterial disease
6 plague, typhus 7 anthrax, leprosy,
tetanus, typhoid 8 botulism, syphilis
9 gonorrhea, infection, pneumonia
10 diphtheria, meningitis 11 shigel-
losis

bacteriologist
American: 6 Enders (John
Franklin) 7 Noguchi (Hideyo),
Theiler (Max)
British: 7 Fleming (Alexander)
French: 5 Widal (Fernand)
7 Nicolle (Charles-Jean-Henri),
Pasteur (Louis)
German: 4 Cohn (Ferdinand
Julius), Koch (Robert) 5 Klebs (Ed-
win) 7 Behring (Emil von), Löffler
(Friedrich) 10 Wassermann (August
von)
Japanese: 8 Kitasato (Shibasaburo)
Russian: 11 Metchnikoff (Elie)
Swiss: 6 Yersin (Alexandre-Emile-
John)

bad
3 ill, low 4 evil, foul, sour 5 amiss,
awful, lousy, wrong 6 crummy,
putrid, rancid, rotten, sinful, wicked
7 harmful, hateful, hurtful, immoral,
naughty, noisome, noxious, spoiled,
tainted, vicious 8 damaging, dreadful, inferior, perverse, terrible,
wretched 9 abhorrent, defective,
execrable, injurious, loathsome,
obnoxious, offensive, putrefied,
reprobate, repulsive, sickening

10 disgusting, iniquitous 11 deleterious, detrimental, distasteful, intolerable 12 unacceptable 13 objectionable
comparative: 5 worse
prefix: 3 dys, mis
superlative: 5 worst

Badebec
husband: 9 Gargantua
son: 10 Pantagruel

Baden
3 spa 6 resort 9 hot spring

badge
3 pin 4 arms, logo, mark, seal, sign 5 award, honor, kudos, medal, token 6 button, emblem, ensign 7 laurels 8 accolade, hallmark, insignia 10 coat of arms, decoration 11 distinction, purple heart

badger
3 bug, nag 4 bait, goad, ride 5 annoy, brock, chivy, harry, hound 6 chivvy, harass, hassle, heckle, hector, needle, pester, plague 7 torment 8 bullyrag 9 importune

Badger State
9 Wisconsin

badinage
4 play 6 banter, joking 7 jesting, joshing, kidding, ribbing, teasing 8 backchat, chitchat, repartee 9 cross talk 10 persiflage

badland
4 wild 5 waste, wilds 6 barren, desert 7 outback 8 wildness 10 wilderness 11 hill country

bad mark
3 gig 7 demerit 9 poor grade

bad-tempered
4 dour, sour 5 cross, sulky, surly, testy 6 crabby, cranky, crusty, grumpy, ornery, sullen, touchy 7 grouchy, peevish 8 choleric, petulant 9 crotchety, dyspeptic, irascible, irritable, splenetic 10 ill-humored, ill-natured, unpleasant 11 quarrelsome 12 cantankerous, curmudgeonly, disagreeable, misanthropic

Baedeker
5 guide 6 manual 8 handbook 9 guidebook, vade mecum 10 compendium 11 enchiridion, travel guide

baffle
4 balk, foil 5 addle, block, floor, mix up, stump 6 bemuse, hinder, impede, muddle, puzzle, thwart 7 barrier, confuse, flummox, mystify, nonplus, perplex 8 befuddle, bewilder, confound 9 deflector, dumbfound, frustrate 10 circumvent, disappoint, disconcert

bafflement
9 confusion 10 bemusement, perplexity 12 bewilderment

bag
3 cop, nab, kit, net, sag, win 4 flop, grip, hook, kill, land, nail, poke, sack, tote, trap 5 biddy, bulge, catch, crone, forgo, pouch, purse, seize, shoot, snare, steal, udder 6 beldam, collar, duffel, duffle, give up, secure, valise 7 abandon, acquire, capture, satchel 8 backpack, knapsack, reticule, suitcase 9 apprehend, haversack 12 protuberance

bagatelle
6 trifle, whimsy 9 plaything

baggage
4 gear 5 hussy, stuff, tramp, trull, wench 6 burden, things, wanton 7 carry-on, effects, jezebel, luggage, parcels, trollop 8 obstacle, matériel, slattern, strumpet 9 equipment, hindrance 10 impediment, prostitute 11 impedimenta 13 paraphernalia

baggy
5 loose

Baghdad
founder: 6 Mansur
river: 6 Tigris

bagnio
4 crib, stew 7 brothel, lupanar 8 bordello, cathouse 10 bawdy house, whorehouse

bagpipe
part: 5 drone 7 bourdon, chanter
sound: 5 skirl

Bahamas
capital: 6 Nassau
island: 3 Cat 5 Abaco 6 Andros, Inagua 7 Watling 9 Eleuthera, Mayaguana 11 Grand Bahama, San Salvador 13 New Providence
language: 7 English
monetary unit: 6 dollar
neighbor: 4 Cuba

Bahrain
capital: 6 Manama
island: 6 Sitrah 7 Bahrain 10 Al Muharraq
language: 6 Arabic
monetary unit: 5 dinar

bail
3 bar, dip 4 bond, flee, lade 5 ladle, scoop 6 handle, pledge, surety 7 release 8 guaranty, security, warranty 9 guarantee 10 collateral 12 recognizance

bailiwick
4 area, turf, zone 5 field, realm 6 domain, sphere 7 demesne, purview, terrain 8 district, dominion, province 9 champaign, specialty, territory 10 discipline 12 jurisdiction

bailout
3 aid 6 relief, rescue 7 subsidy 11 benefaction, deliverance

bairn
3 kid, tot 4 babe, baby, tyke 5 child 6 infant

bait
3 nag, try, vex 4 lure, ride, trap 5 abuse, chase, chivy, decoy, harry, hound, leger, snare, taunt, tease, tempt, worry 6 allure, badger, come-on, entice, entrap, harass, heckle, hector, lead on, molest, pester, seduce 7 beguile, torment, torture 8 bullyrag, inveigle, ridicule 9 persecute, seduction, sweetener 10 attraction, allurement, enticement, temptation
and switch: 4 lure 5 trick 8 inveigle 10 substitute

bake
4 burn, char, cook, fire, kiln 5 broil,

roast, toast 6 scorch 7 scallop, scollop, swelter

baked clay
7 ceramic

baker's dozen
8 thirteen

bakers' yeast
6 leaven 9 leavening

baking
3 hot 5 fiery 6 red-hot, torrid 7 burning 8 broiling, scalding, sizzling, white-hot 9 scorching
chamber: 4 kiln, oven

baksheesh
3 tip 4 alms 5 bribe, favor 6 grease, reward 7 payment 8 gratuity 9 emolument 12 compensation

Balaam
beast: 3 ass 6 donkey
father: 4 Beor

balance
4 rest 5 level, scale, weigh 6 adjust, excess, make up, offset, set off, square, stasis 7 harmony, remains, remnant, residue 8 atone for, equalize, outweigh, residual, residuum, symmetry 9 composure, congruity, equipoise, harmonize, remainder, stability 10 compensate, counteract, difference, equanimity, neutralize, proportion, steadiness 11 consistency, countervail, equilibrium, self-control 12 counterpoise

balanced
4 fair 5 equal 6 offset, stable, steady 7 equable, weighed 9 equitable, impartial 10 evenhanded, harmonized, stabilized

balcony
6 piazza 7 catwalk, gallery 8 platform 9 mezzanine
section: 4 loge

bald
4 bare, nude 5 blunt, naked, plain, stark 6 barren, severe, shaven, smooth 8 glabrous, hairless, palpable, treeless 9 depilated, unadorned,

uncovered **10** deforested, forthright **11** undisguised, unvarnished

baldachin
4 silk **6** canopy, fabric

Balder, Baldur
father: 4 Odin
mother: 5 Frigg **6** Frigga
slayer: 3 Höd **4** Hoth, Loke, Loki **5** Hoder, Hothr
wife: 5 Nanna

balderdash
3 rot **4** bosh, bull, bunk **5** bilge, crock, hooey **6** blague, bunkum, drivel **7** baloney, eyewash, garbage, hogwash, palaver, rubbish, twaddle **8** buncombe, claptrap, malarkey, nonsense, tommyrot **9** poppycock **10** tomfoolery **11** foolishness **13** horsefeathers

bald-faced
4 bold **6** arrant, brazen **7** blatant, defiant **8** impudent, insolent **9** audacious, shameless, unabashed **11** impertinent

baldness
8 alopecia **12** hairlessness

baldpate
7 widgeon **8** skinhead

Baldwin, James
essay: 17 Nobody Knows My Name, Notes of a Native Son
novel: 12 Fire Next Time (The) **13** Giovanni's Room **14** Another Country **21** Go Tell It on the Mountain
play: 21 Blues for Mister Charlie

balefire
6 beacon **9** watchfire

baleful
4 dire, evil **6** deadly, malign **7** direful, fateful, harmful, hostile, malefic, ominous **8** menacing, sinister **9** ill-boding, ill-omened, malignant **10** maleficent, malevolent, pernicious **11** apocalyptic, threatening **12** unpropitious

balk
3 bar, gag, jib, shy **4** beam, dash,

foil, ruin **5** block, check, demur, plank, stall **6** baffle, boggle, desist, flinch, hinder, rafter, refuse, thwart **7** prevent, scruple, stumble **8** hang back, hesitate, obstruct **9** frustrate, hindrance **10** circumvent, disappoint

balky
5 loath **6** averse, ornery, mulish, unruly **7** froward, restive, wayward, willful **8** contrary, hesitant, perverse, stubborn **9** immovable, obstinate, reluctant **10** unreliable **11** intractable, wrongheaded **12** cross-grained, recalcitrant **13** uncooperative, unpredictable

ball
3 orb, wad **4** prom **5** dance, globe, round **6** sphere **8** spheroid
batted high: 3 fly
batted straight: 5 liner
of thread or yarn: 4 clew
ornamental: 6 pom-pom, pompon
tiny: 7 globule

ballad
3 lay **4** poem, song
singer: 8 minstrel **10** troubadour

ballast
4 load **5** poise **6** steady **7** balance, freight **8** balancer **9** stabilize, weigh down **10** dead weight, stabilizer **12** counterpoise **13** counterweight

ballerina
6 dancer **8** coryphée, danseuse **9** toe dancer **11** dancing girl
see **dancer**

ballet
4 Agon **6** Apollo, Jewels, Sylvia **7** Giselle, Orpheus **8** Bayadère (La), Coppélia, Firebird (The), Raimonda, Raymonda, Swan Lake, Sylphide (La) **9** Fancy Free, Petrushka, Sylphides (Les) **10** Don Quixote, Nutcracker (The), Petrouchka **12** Rite of Spring (The)
costume: 4 tutu **6** tights **7** leotard
dancer: 7 danseur **8** coryphée, danseuse **9** ballerina
for two: 9 pas de deux

handrail: **5** barre
jump: **4** jeté **9** entrechat
knee bend: **4** plié
position: **6** pointe **8** attitude
9 arabesque
step: **3** pas **8** glissade
turn: **6** chaîné **9** pirouette

ball game
see at **game**

Ballo in Maschera composer
5 Verdi (Giuseppe)

balloon sail
9 spinnaker

ball-shaped
7 globoid, globose **8** globular,
spheroid **9** globulous, spherical

ball up
4 clew, daze **5** addle **6** fuddle,
jumble, muddle, puzzle, tangle
7 confuse, fluster **8** befuddle,
bewilder, bollix up, confound, distract, throw off **9** disorient

ballyhoo
4 hype, tout **6** blazon, herald,
hoopla, hubbub, tumult **7** promote,
trumpet **8** brouhaha **9** commotion,
publicity **12** extravaganza

balm
4 lull **5** aroma, cream, quiet, salve,
scent, spice **6** chrism, relief, remedy,
solace **7** anodyne, bouquet, comfort,
incense, perfume, soother, unction,
unguent **8** easement, ointment
9 emollient, fragrance, redolence
10 palliative **11** consolation, restorative

balmacaan
8 overcoat

balm of Gilead
6 poplar **7** soother **8** restorer **9** balsam fir **11** restorative **12** balsam
poplar

balmy
4 calm, daft, mild, nuts, soft **5** crazy,
loony, nutty, potty, silly, sweet, wacky
6 gentle, insane, smooth **7** cracked,
foolish, lenient, summery

8 aromatic, deranged, fragrant,
perfumed, peaceful, pleasant,
pleasing, redolent, soothing, tropical
9 agreeable, ambrosial, temperate

baloney
3 rot **4** bosh, bull, bunk **5** bilge,
hokum, hooey **6** bunkum, humbug
7 hogwash, rubbish **8** buncombe,
claptrap, nonsense **9** poppycock
10 balderdash **11** foolishness

balsam poplar
9 tacamahac **12** balm of Gilead

Balthazar's gift
5 myrrh

Baltic
native: **4** Lett **7** Latvian **8** Estonian
10 Lithuanian
state: **6** Latvia **7** Estonia
9 Lithuania

Baltic native
4 Lett, Sorb, Wend **7** Latvian
8 Estonian, Prussian **10** Lithuanian

balustrade
4 rail **5** fence **7** railing **8** banister,
handrail

Balzac character
4 Pons (Cousin) **5** Bette (Cousin)
6 Goriot (Père), Vidocq **7** Chabert
(Colonel), Eugénie (Grandet),
Grandet, Vautrin **8** Rubempré
(Lucien de) **9** Birotteau, Rastignac
(Eugène de) **13** Henri de Marsay

Bambi author
6 Salten (Felix)

bambino
3 kid, tot **4** babe, baby, tyke **5** bairn,
child **6** cherub, Christ, infant, moppet, nipper **7** toddler

bamboozle
3 con **4** bilk, dupe, fool, gull, hoax,
scam **5** stump, trick **6** baffle, befool,
diddle, puzzle **7** chicane, confuse,
deceive, defraud, mislead, perplex,
swindle **8** befuddle, confound, flimflam, hoodwink, throw off **9** frustrate
11 hornswoggle

ban

3 bar 5 curse, taboo 6 enjoin, forbid, outlaw 7 censure, exclude 8 anathema, prohibit, suppress 9 damnation, interdict, proscribe 10 injunction 11 forbiddance, malediction, prohibition, suppression 12 denunciation, interdiction, proscription

Ban

ally: 6 Arthur
son: 8 Lancelot

banal

4 blah, dull, flat 5 bland, corny, ho-hum, tired, trite, usual, vapid 6 common, jejune, stupid 7 clichéd, humdrum, insipid, prosaic, sapless, trivial 8 ordinary 9 hackneyed, quotidian, wearisome 10 namby-pamby, pedestrian, uninspired, wishy-washy 11 commonplace

banality

5 ennui 6 cliché, old saw, truism 7 bromide, inanity, old song 8 chestnut, monotony, prosaism 9 platitude 10 dreariness, shibboleth, triviality 11 commonplace, old chestnut, tediousness

banausic

4 blah, drab, dull, poky 6 dreary, earthy, stodgy 7 humdrum, mundane, routine, secular, sensual, tedious, worldly 8 everyday, material, plodding, temporal, workaday 9 practical, pragmatic 10 monotonous, pedestrian 11 acquisitive, utilitarian 13 materialistic, uninteresting

band

4 belt, bevy, club, crew, gang, gird, sash, tape 5 bunch, corps, covey, group, horde, party, strap, strip, troop, unite 6 concur, fillet, girdle, league, outfit, ribbon, team up, troupe 7 cluster, combine, company, coterie 8 cincture, engirdle, ensemble, symphony 9 cooperate, orchestra 10 federation
Mexican: 8 mariachi
neck: 6 torque
small: 5 combo

bandage

4 bind 5 cover, dress, gauze, truss 6 swathe 7 plaster, swaddle 8 compress, dressing

bandanna

8 babushka, kerchief 9 headscarf 11 neckerchief

bandeau

3 bra 5 strip 6 fillet, ribbon, stripe 7 tube top 8 swimwear 9 brassiere

banderilla

4 dart

banderole

4 flag, jack 6 banner, burgee, colors, ensign, pennon, scroll 7 pennant 8 bannerol, standard, streamer

bandicoot

3 rat

bandit

6 outlaw, raider, robber, sacker 7 brigand, cateran, forager, ravager 8 marauder, pillager 9 cutthroat, desperado, holdup man, plunderer 10 freebooter, highwayman 11 bushwhacker

bandleader

7 maestro 9 conductor

bandolier

4 belt, sash

bandwagon

3 fad 4 chic, mode, rage 5 craze, style, trend, vogue 7 fashion

bandy

3 bat 4 flip, swap, toss 5 argue, bowed 6 banter 7 discuss, shuffle 8 exchange 9 bowlegged, pass about 11 interchange

bane

3 woe 4 pest, ruin 5 curse, death, venom, virus 6 blight, burden, plague, poison 7 bugaboo, bugbear, scourge, torment, undoing 8 anathema, calamity, downfall, nuisance 9 bête noire, contagion, destroyer, ruination 10 affliction, pestilence 11 destruction

baneful
4 dire, evil 5 fatal 6 deadly 7 fateful, harmful, hurtful, malefic, noxious, ominous 9 ill-boding, ill-omened, injurious, malignant, pestilent, unhealthy 10 disastrous, pernicious 11 apocalyptic, deleterious, pestiferous, threatening 12 pestilential, unpropitious

bang
3 bat, box, hit, pop, rap 4 bash, beat, belt, blow, boom, bump, clap, peal, push, rape, shot, slam, sock, wham, whop 5 blast, burst, crack, crash, noise, pound, punch, smack, smash, sound, vigor, whack 6 fringe, report, strike, thrill, wallop 7 collide, exactly, resound 8 smack-dab, squarely 9 explosion 10 detonation

banger
7 athlete, sausage

Bangkok native
4 Thai

Bangladesh
capital: 5 Dacca, Dhaka
city: 6 Khulna 10 Chittagong
former name: 6 Bengal
language: 7 Bengali
monetary unit: 4 taka
neighbor: 5 Burma, India
7 Myanmar
river: 5 Padma 6 Ganges, Jamuna
11 Brahmaputra

bangle
4 disk 5 charm 6 anklet, bauble 7 pendant, trinket 8 bracelet, wristlet

bang-up
3 ace 4 fine 5 dandy, primo, super 6 far-out, superb 7 capital 8 champion, fabulous, five-star, splendid, top-notch 9 excellent, first-rate 10 first-class 11 spectacular

banish
3 ban 4 oust 5 debar, eject, evict, exile, expel 6 deport, dispel, put out, run out 7 cast out, dismiss, exclude, shut out, turn out 8 drive out, relegate, send away 9 discharge, ostracize, rusticate, transport 10 expatriate 13 excommunicate

banishment
5 exile 7 banning 8 eviction 9 discharge, expulsion, ostracism 10 dispelling, relegation 11 deportation, dissolution 12 displacement

banister
3 bar 4 rail 7 railing 10 balustrade

bank
3 row 4 edge, heap, hill, mass, pile, rank, save, tier, tilt 5 amass, array, beach, coast, group, hoard, levee, mound, pitch, shore, slope, stack, stash 6 coffer, dealer, invest, margin, rivage, strand 7 deposit, incline, lay away, pyramid 8 lakeside, lay aside, salt away, seafront, set aside, sock away, squirrel, treasury 9 riverside 10 repository, storehouse 11 credit union 12 squirrel away

bank on
5 trust 7 believe

bankroll
4 back, fund 5 endow, funds, stake 6 pay for 7 capital, finance, sponsor, support 9 grubstake, subsidize 10 capitalize, underwrite

bankrupt
4 bare, bust, do in, ruin 5 break, drain, empty, strip, spent, use up, wreck 6 broken, divest, failed, fold up 7 deplete, deprive, exhaust, lacking, sterile 8 depleted, indebted 9 destitute, exhausted, pauperize, penniless 10 impoverish 12 impoverished

bankruptcy
4 lack, ruin 6 penury 7 failure 9 depletion, ruination, sterility, total loss 10 barrenness, exhaustion, insolvency 11 destitution, liquidation

banned
5 taboo 6 barred 7 illegal, illicit, tabooed 8 enjoined, verboten 9 forbidden 10 contraband, disallowed, prohibited, proscribed 11 interdicted

banner

4 flag, jack **6** burgee, ensign, pennon **7** pendant, pennant **8** banderol, gonfalon, standard, streamer **9** banderole
Roman: 7 labarum **8** vexillum

bannerol

see **banderole**

banquet

4 feed **5** feast **6** dinner, regale, repast, spread

banquette

4 seat, sofa **5** bench, shelf **8** platform, sidewalk

Banquo

5 ghost
murderer: 7 Macbeth

banshee

6 keener, wailer

bantam

3 wee **4** arch, fowl, mini, pert, runt, tiny **5** dwarf, saucy, small **6** cheeky, little, petite **8** insolent, malapert **9** combative, undersize **10** diminutive, undersized

banter

3 fun, kid, rag, rib, wit **4** fool, jest, jive, joke, josh, razz **5** chaff, dally, jolly, tease **7** jesting, joshing, kidding, mockery, ragging, razzing, ribbing, teasing **8** backchat, back talk, badinage, chitchat, drollery, exchange, repartee **9** challenge, small talk **10** persiflage, pleasantry **11** give-and-take

bantling

4 babe, baby **5** bairn **6** infant **7** bambino, newborn, papoose

baptize

3 dip, dub **4** call, name, soak **5** douse, title **6** anoint, drench, purify **7** asperse, cleanse, entitle, immerse **8** christen, dedicate, initiate, sprinkle **9** designate **10** consecrate, denominate, regenerate

bar

3 ban, dam, pub, rod, tap **4** curb,

dive, halt, save, stop **5** block, court, estop, ingot, limit, stick, strip **6** bistro, except, impede, lounge, saloon, tavern **7** barrier, cantina, delimit, exclude, gin mill, rule out, taproom **8** alehouse, blockade, count out, obstacle, obstruct, restrict, tribunal **9** barricade, eliminate, honky-tonk, nightclub, roadhouse **11** obstruction, rathskeller **12** circumscribe, watering hole
type: 3 raw **4** cash, fern, open, roll, tiki **6** sports

barb

3 dig **4** dart, hook **5** quill, shaft, thorn

Barbados

capital: 10 Bridgetown
language: 7 English
location: 10 West Indies
monetary unit: 6 dollar

barbarian

3 Hun **4** Goth, lout, rude, wild **5** beast, crude, brute **6** savage, Vandal **7** lowbrow, uncouth **8** Visigoth **9** foreigner, Ostrogoth, primitive **10** uncultured **11** uncivilized **12** uncultivated

barbaric

4 wild **5** crude, rough **6** brutal, coarse, savage **7** beastly, boorish, brutish, loutish, uncouth **8** churlish **9** atrocious, monstrous, primitive, unrefined **11** uncivilized

barbarism

8 malaprop, rudeness, solecism **9** vulgarism, vulgarity **10** coarseness, corruption **11** impropriety, malapropism **12** backwardness, unseemliness

barbarity

7 cruelty **8** atrocity, savagery **9** brutality, depravity **10** inhumanity, savageness **11** viciousness **12** ruthlessness **13** monstrousness

barbarous

4 base, fell, grim, rude, vile, wild **5** cruel, harsh **6** brutal, fierce,

Gothic, savage, unholy, vulgar,
wicked **7** brutish, Hunnish, inhuman,
lowbrow, uncivil, ungodly, vicious,
wolfish **8** backward, fiendish, inhumane, ruthless, sadistic **9** benighted,
ferocious, graceless, heartless,
merciless, monstrous, primitive,
tasteless, truculent **10** abominable,
outlandish, outrageous, philistine,
unmerciful **11** unchristian, uncivilized **12** uncultivated

Barbary state
  5 Tunis **7** Algiers, Morocco, Tripoli

barbecue
  5 grill, roast **7** cookout, roaster

barber
  3 bob, cut **4** clip, crop, trim **5** shave,
  shear **6** shaver **7** clipper, cropper
  8 coiffeur **9** coiffeuse **10** beautician,
  haircutter **11** hairdresser, hair stylist

Barber of Seville
  author: **12** Beaumarchais (Pierre-Augustin)
  character: **6** Figaro, Rosina, Rosine
  7 Bartolo, Basilio **8** Almaviva,
  Bartholo
  composer: **7** Rossini (Gioacchino)
  9 Paisiello (Giovanni)

bard
  4 muse, poet, scop **5** skald **8** jongleur, minstrel **9** balladist **10** Parnassian, troubadour

Bard of Avon
  11 Shakespeare (William)

bare
  4 bald, mere, nude, void **5** empty,
  naked, shorn, stark, strip **6** barren,
  denude, devoid, expose, peeled,
  reveal, unclad, unveil, vacant **7** denuded, disrobe, emptied, exposed,
  uncover **8** bankrupt, disclose,
  stripped **9** unclothed, uncovered,
  undressed

barefaced
  4 bald, bold, open **5** blunt, naked
  6 arrant, brassy, brazen **7** blatant,
  glaring, obvious **8** flagrant, impudent, overbold **9** audacious, beardless, shameless, unabashed
10 unblushing **11** temerarious,
unconcealed

barefoot
  6 unshod **8** shoeless **9** discalced

bareheaded
  7 hatless

barely
  4 just **6** hardly, scarce **7** faintly
  8 meagerly, scarcely

bargain
  3 buy **4** bond, deal, pact, swap
  5 agree, steal, trade, truck, value
  6 barter, confer, dicker, haggle,
  higgle, palter, pledge **7** chaffer,
  compact, savings, traffic **8** closeout,
  contract, covenant, exchange,
  giveaway, good deal, huckster,
  markdown, transact **9** agreement,
  good value, negotiate, reduction
  10 compromise, convention, loss
  leader, pennyworth **11** arrangement,
  transaction **13** understanding

barge
  4 scow **5** clump, stump **6** lumber
  7 galumph, stumble

baritone
  4 Prey (Hermann) **5** Gobbi (Tito)
  6 Bailey (Norman), London (George),
  Milnes (Sherrill), Terfel (Bryn),
  Warren (Leonard) **7** Hampson
  (Thomas), MacNeil (Cornell), Merrill
  (Robert), Tibbett (Lawrence)
  8 Raimondi (Ruggero), Warfield
  (William)

bark
  3 arf, bay, yap, yip **4** snap, woof,
  yelp **5** snarl **6** bellow

barkeeper
  see **bartender**

barker
  6 hawker **8** pitchman

Barlow epic
  9 Columbiad

barman
  see **bartender**

Barmecidal
5 empty, false 6 unreal 7 fictive
8 apparent, illusive, illusory 9 imaginary 10 chimerical, ostensible
13 insubstantial

barn
6 stable
area of: 4 loft 7 hayloft

barnacle
5 leech 7 sponger 8 hanger-on,
nuisance, parasite 9 dependent, free
rider 10 crustacean, freeloader

barnstorm
8 campaign

Barnum
elephant: 5 Jumbo
midget: 8 Tom Thumb
partner: 6 Bailey

barnyard
4 foul, rude 5 crass, crude, dirty,
nasty 6 coarse, earthy, filthy, ribald,
smutty, vulgar 7 obscene, raunchy,
uncouth 8 indecent 9 tasteless
10 indelicate 12 scatological

baron
4 lord, peer 5 mogul, noble 6 tycoon
7 kingpin, magnate 8 overlord
13 industrialist

baronial
5 ample, grand, noble 6 august,
lordly 7 stately 8 imposing, majestic, princely 9 grandiose 10 commanding, impressive 11 magnificent,
resplendent

baroque
6 florid, ornate, rococo 7 complex
8 dramatic 9 excessive, grotesque,
irregular 10 flamboyant, ornamented
11 embellished, extravagant 12 ostentatious 13 overdecorated

Baroque
architect: 4 Wren (Christopher)
7 Bernini (Gian Lorenzo), Guarini
(Guarino), Maderno (Carlo)
9 Borromini (Francesco)
composer: 4 Bach (Johann Sebastian) 5 Lully (Jean-Baptiste)

6 Handel (George Frideric), Rameau
(Jean-Philippe), Schütz (Heinrich)
7 Corelli (Arcangelo), Purcell
(Henry), Vivaldi (Antonio) 8 Albinoni
(Tommaso), Couperin (François),
Telemann (Georg Philipp) 9 Pachelbel (Johann), Scarlatti (Alessandro,
Domenico) 10 Monteverdi
(Claudio)
painter: 4 Hals (Frans) 5 Steen
(Jan) 6 Claude (Lorrain), Rubens
(Peter Paul) 7 El Greco, Holbein
(Hans), Poussin (Nicolas), Van Dyck
(Anthony), Vermeer (Jan) 8 Carracci
(Agostino, Annibale, Lodovico),
Ter Borch (Gerard) 9 Rembrandt
(van Rijn), Velázquez (Diego)
10 Caravaggio
sculptor: 5 Puget (Pierre) 7 Bernini
(Gian Lorenzo), Coustou (Guillaume,
Nicholas), Pigalle (Jean-Baptiste)
8 Coysevox (Antoine), Girardon
(François)

barrack
4 jeer, root 5 cheer, scoff, taunt
6 billet, casern, deride, hector 7 caserne 8 quarters

barrage
3 dam 4 fire, hail, mass 5 blitz,
burst, salvo, storm, surge 6 deluge,
shower, stream, volley 7 gunfire,
torrent 8 drumfire, shelling 9 broadside, cannonade, crossfire, fusillade,
onslaught 11 bombardment

barranca
4 bank 5 bluff, gully 6 arroyo

barrel
3 keg, tun, vat 4 butt, cask, drum,
peck, race, rush, tear 5 hurry
6 firkin, hasten 8 hogshead
maker: 6 cooper
part: 4 hoop 5 stave
stopper: 4 bung
support: 6 gantry

barrelhouse
4 dive 5 hurry, joint 7 hangout
9 honky-tonk

barren
3 dry 4 arid, bare, poor 5 bleak,

empty, stark, stony, waste **6** desert, devoid, effete, futile, fallow **7** badland, lacking, parched, sterile, wanting **8** desolate, heirless, impotent **9** childless, fruitless, infertile, unbearing, unfertile, wasteland **10** unfruitful, untillable **11** unrewarding **12** hardscrabble, unproductive, unprofitable

barricade
5 block, fence **7** barrier **8** blockade **9** roadblock
of trees: 6 abatis

Barrie character
4 John, Nana **5** Peter, Tommy, Wendy **7** Michael **8** Crichton **9** Tiger Lily **10** Tinker Bell **11** Captain Hook

barrier
see **barricade**

barring
3 but **4** save **6** bating, except, saving **7** besides, without **9** aside from, excluding, excepting, outside of **11** exclusive of

barrio
4 slum, turf, ward **6** ghetto **7** quarter, section **8** district, precinct **12** neighborhood

barrister
6 lawyer **7** counsel **8** advocate, attorney **9** counselor

barroom
3 pub **6** lounge, saloon, tavern **7** gin mill, rum room, taproom **8** alehouse, beer hall, dramshop, drinkery, groggery, grogshop **9** beer joint, roadhouse **12** watering hole

bartender
7 tapster **8** boniface **10** mixologist **12** saloonkeeper

barter
4 swap **5** trade, truck **7** bargain, traffic **8** exchange

Bartered Bride composer
7 Smetana (Bedrich)

Barth novel
7 Chimera **12** Giles Goat-Boy **13** Sot-Weed Factor (The)

Baruch
father: 6 Neriah, Zabbai
occupation: 6 scribe

basal
5 basic, vital **6** bottom, lowest **7** minimal, primary, radical **8** simplest **9** beginning, essential, undermost **10** bottommost, elementary, primordial, underlying **11** fundamental, preliminary, rudimentary **12** foundational

base
3 bad, bed, fix, key, low **4** camp, evil, foot, foul, home, mean, poor, post, prop, rest, root, seat, site, ugly, vile **5** build, cheap, dirty, found, hinge, lousy, lowly, nadir, plant, set up, sorry, stand **6** bottom, coarse, common, depend, derive, filthy, ground, humble, menial, origin, paltry, scurvy, shoddy, sleazy, sordid, source, trashy, wicked **7** bedrock, caitiff, essence, footing, ignoble, lowborn, low-down, pitiful, servile, squalid, support **8** beggarly, buttress, cowardly, garrison, inferior, pedestal, plebeian, recreant, unwashed, unworthy, wretched **9** construct, dastardly, degrading, establish, framework, loathsome, low-minded, predicate, principle **10** abominable, despicable, foundation, groundwork, substratum, unennobled **11** disgraceful, humiliating, ignominious **12** contemptible, meanspirited, substructure, underpinning

baseball
abbreviation: 3 ERA, LOB, MVP, RBI
reputed founder: 9 Doubleday (Abner)
glove: 4 mitt
official: 3 ump **6** umpire
pitch: 4 drop, heat **5** curve, smoke **6** change, heater, sinker, slider, slurve **7** spitter **8** change-up, fadeaway, fastball, fork ball, knuckler, palm ball, spitball **9** brushback, screwball **11** knuckleball **12** change of pace, knuckle curve
player: 6 batter **7** baseman, catcher, fielder, pitcher **9** infielder,

shortstop **10** outfielder **11** left fielder **12** right fielder **13** center fielder **term: 3** bag, bat, box, fan, fly, out, run, tag, tap, tip **4** balk, ball, base, bean, bunt, cage, deck, foul, hook, line, mitt, pill, pole, save, walk **5** alley, apple, bench, bloop, clout, count, drive, error, flare, fungo, glove, homer, liner, mound, pop-up, slide, swing **6** assist, clutch, double, dugout, groove, ground, inning, inside, pop fly, pop-out, powder, putout, rubber, runner, single, strike, triple, windup **7** battery, blooper, bullpen, cleanup, diamond, floater, fly ball, home run, infield, manager, outside, pickoff, rhubarb, sidearm, squeeze, stretch **8** baseline, beanball, delivery, foul ball, grounder, keystone, outfield, pinch-hit, rosin bag, southpaw **9** full count, home plate, hot corner, line drive, sacrifice, strikeout, two-bagger **10** double play, frozen rope, ground ball, scratch hit, strike zone **11** knuckleball, pinch hitter, squeeze play, three-bagger

baseballer
3 Ott (Mel) **4** Bell (George), Cobb (Ty), Cone (David), Dean (Dizzy), Fisk (Carlton), Ford (Whitey), Foxx (Jimmy), Kaat (Jim), Mays (Willie), Rice (Jim), Rose (Pete), Ruth (Babe), Ryan (Nolan), Sosa (Sammy) **5** Aaron (Henry), Anson (Cap), Banks (Ernie), Belle (Albert), Bench (Johnny), Berra (Yogi), Boggs (Wade), Bonds (Barry), Brett (George), Brock (Lou), Brown (Kevin), Carew (Rod), Clark (Will), Damon (Johnny), Davis (Mark), Green (Shawn), Grove (Lefty), Gwynn (Tony), Henke (Tom), Jeter (Derek), Kiner (Ralph), Maris (Roger), Mauer (Joe), Paige (Satchel), Perez (Tony), Perry (Gaylord), Smith (Lee), Spahn (Warren), Staub (Rusty), Tiant (Luis), Viola (Frank), Weeks (Rickie), Young (Cy), Yount (Robin) **6** Dawson (Andre), Feller (Bob), Foster (George), Franco (John), Garvey (Steve), Gehrig (Lou), Gibson (Bob,

Josh, Kirk), Gooden (Dwight), Herzog (Whitey), Hunter (Catfish), Koufax (Sandy), Lajoie (Nap), Maddux (Greg), Mantle (Mickey), Morgan (Joe), Murphy (Dale), Murray (Eddie), Musial (Stan), Palmer (Jim), Piazza (Mike), Raines (Tim), Ripken (Cal), Seaver (Tom), Sisler (George), Sutter (Bruce), Sutton (Don), Thomas (Frank), Vaughn (Mo), Wagner (Honus), Walker (Larry) **7** Bagwell (Jeff), Canseco (José), Carlton (Steve), Clemens (Roger), Coleman (Vince), Collins (Eddie), Delgado (Carlos), Fingers (Rollie), Griffey (Ken), Hornsby (Roger), Hubbell (Carl), Jackson (Joe, Reggie), Johnson (Randy, Walter), Justice (David), Leonard (Buck), McGwire (Mark), Mondesi (Raul), Puckett (Kirby), Reardon (Jeff), Schmidt (Mike), Simmons (Al), Speaker (Tris) **8** Anderson (Sparky), Blyleven (Bert), Clemente (Roberto), DiMaggio (Joe), Guerrero (Vladimir), Martinez (Pedro), Mitchell (Kevin), Righetti (Dave), Robinson (Brooks, Frank, Jackie), Williams (Bernie, Ted), Winfield (Dave) **9** Alexander (Grover), Eckersley (Dennis), Gehringer (Charlie), Greenberg (Hank), Henderson (Rickey), Hernandez (Willie), Hershiser (Orel), Killebrew (Harmon), Mathewson (Christy), Mattingly (Don), Rodriguez (Alex), Sheffield (Gary) **10** Campanella (Roy), Conigliaro (Tony), Strawberry (Darryl), Valenzuela (Fernando) **11** Garciaparra (Nomar), Yastrzemski (Carl)

baseball team
see **American League; National League**

baseboard
7 molding **8** skirting

baseless
4 idle, thin, vain **5** empty, false, wrong **6** feeble, flimsy **9** frivolous, pointless, senseless, unfounded, untenable **10** fallacious, gratuitous, groundless, inadequate, incredible,

ungrounded **11** uncalled-for, uncon-
firmed, unnecessary, unsupported,
unsustained, unwarranted **12** indefensible, contemptible, unpersuasive
13 unjustifiable

basement
6 bottom, cellar, ground **7** bedrock
10 foundation, groundwork, substratum **12** substructure

base on balls
4 walk

bash
3 bat, hit **4** belt, blow, fete, gala,
slam, whop **5** blast, crack, crash,
party, pound, smack, smash, thump,
whack **6** attack, pummel, soiree,
strike, wallop **7** blowout, shindig
8 wingding

Bashemath
father: **7** Ishmael
husband: **4** Esau
sister: **8** Nebaioth

bashful
3 coy, shy **5** chary, mousy, timid
6 demure, modest **7** abashed,
nervous **8** blushing, reserved,
retiring, timorous **9** diffident, reluctant, shrinking, unassured **11** unassertive

basic
3 key **4** main **5** chief **6** bottom
7 capital, central, element, minimum,
primary, radical **8** cardinal, inherent,
rudiment **9** beginning, elemental,
essential, intrinsic, primitive, principal, unadorned **10** elementary,
underlying **11** fundamental **12** foundational

basically
6 au fond, mainly, mostly **7** at heart,
chiefly, firstly, overall **8** in effect
9 generally, in essence, primarily

basic point
4 crux, gist, pith **5** heart **6** kernel
7 essence

basilica
6 church **7** minster **9** cathedral

basin
3 dip, pan, sag **4** bowl, sink **6** cirque,
hollow **7** sinkage **8** sinkhole, wash-
bowl **9** concavity **10** depression
liturgical: **5** stoup **7** piscina

basis
3 bed **4** crux, root, seat, seed
5 heart, nexus **6** bottom, ground,
reason **7** bedrock, essence, footing,
grounds, nucleus, premise, support,
warrant **9** authority, postulate,
principle **10** assumption, foundation,
groundwork, substratum **11** fundamental, presumption **12** substructure, underpinning **13** justification

bask
3 sun **4** loll **5** glory, revel, relax
6 lounge, wallow, welter **7** indulge
8 sunbathe **9** luxuriate

basket
6 bushel, gabion **7** pannier
angler's: **5** creel

basketball
inventor: **8** Naismith (James)
official: **6** umpire **7** referee
player: **5** cager, guard **6** center
7 forward **8** hoopster, swingman
10 point guard
team: **4** five **7** quintet
term: **3** gun, jam, key **4** cage, dunk,
pass **5** board, lay-up, press, shoot,
tip-in **6** freeze, tap-off, tip-off, travel
7 dribble, keyhole, rebound, throw-in,
time-out **8** alley-oop, jump ball, slam
dunk **9** backboard, backcourt, field
goal, free throw **11** ball control

basketballer
3 Bol (Manute) **4** Bird (Larry), Ming
(Yao), Nash (Steve), Redd (Michael),
Reed (Willis), West (Jerry, Mark)
5 Allen (Ray), Barry (Rick), Brand
(Elton), Cousy (Bob), Davis (Baron),
Ewing (Patrick), Mikan (George),
O'Neal (Shaquille), Price (Mark)
6 Baylor (Elgin), Blount (Mark),
Boozer (Carlos), Bryant (Kobe),
Carter (Vince), Cowens (Dave),
Duncan (Tim), Erving (Julius),
Gervin (George), Jordan (Michael),

Malone (Jeff, Karl, Moses), McAdoo (Bob), McHale (Kevin), Miller (Brad, Reggie), Parish (Robert), Pierce (Paul, Ricky), Pippin (Scottie), Rodman (Dennis), Skiles (Scott), Thomas (Kenny), Thorpe (Otis), Walton (Bill), Worthy (James) **7** Barkley (Charles), Billups (Chauncey), Dampier (Erick), Dawkins (Darryl), Edwards (James), Frazier (Walt), Garnett (Kevin), Hilario (Nene), Houston (Allan), Iverson (Allen), Jackson (Lauren), Jamison (Antawn), Johnson (Magic), McGrady (Tracy), Russell (Bill), Rollins (Tree), Taurasi (Diana), Wallace (Ben), Wilkins (Dominique) **8** Auerbach (Red), Cardinal (Brian), Havlicek (John), Olajuwon (Akeem), Magloire (Jamaal), Nowitzki (Dirk), Randolph (Zach), Robinson (David), Stockton (John), Thompson (Tina), Williams (Buck) **9** Donaldson (James), Ferdinand (Marie), Holdsclaw (Chamique), Robertson (Oscar) **10** Stojakovic (Predrag), Williamson (Corliss) **11** Abdul-Jabbar (Kareem), Chamberlain (Wilt)

Basmath's father
7 Solomon

Basque
6 bodice
cap: **5** beret
game: **6** pelota **7** jai alai
mountains: **8** Pyrenees
province: **5** Alava **7** Vizcaya
9 Guipúzcoa

bass
3 low **4** deep **6** singer **8** cabrilla
famous: **5** Hines (Jerome), Pinza (Ezio), Ramey (Samuel), Siepi (Cesare), Tozzi (Giorgio) **6** Hotter (Hans), London (George), Morris (James) **7** Plishka (Paul), Robeson (Paul), Talvela (Martti) **8** Flagello (Ezio), Ghiaurov (Nicolai), Raimondi (Ruggero) **9** Chaliapin (Fyodor), Christoff (Boris)

Bassanio's beloved
6 Portia

bassinet
6 cradle, basket

bastard
5 cross **6** by-blow, hybrid **7** mongrel
9 love child **12** natural child
combining form: **4** noth **5** notho

bastardize
4 warp **5** taint **6** debase, defile
7 corrupt, debauch, degrade, deprave, pervert, pollute, vitiate **9** brutalize **10** adulterate, bestialize, demoralize, depreciate **11** contaminate

baste
3 sew **4** beat, drub, lash, mill, pelt, rail, tack, whip **5** paste, scold **6** batter, berate, larrup, pummel, revile, stitch, thrash, wallop **7** bawl out, belabor, chew out, clobber, moisten, tell off, trounce, upbraid **8** bless out, chastise **9** dress down **10** tonguelash

bastille
4 jail **6** prison **9** bridewell

bastinado
3 bat, rod **4** bash, beat, blow, cane, club **5** birch, crack, pound, smack, smash, stick, whack **6** cudgel, paddle, strike, switch, thwack, wallop **8** bludgeon **9** truncheon

bastion
5 tower **7** bulwark, citadel, parapet, rampart, redoubt **8** fastness, fortress **10** breastwork, stronghold **13** fortification

bat
3 bag, bop, hag **4** belt, biff, blow, bust, club, slam, sock, swat, whop, wink **5** biddy, blink, crone, smack **6** cudgel, thwack **7** meander **8** bludgeon **9** flying fox, truncheon **10** knobkerrie, shillelagh **11** pipistrelle

batch
3 lot, set **5** array, bunch, clump, crowd, group **6** bundle, clutch, parcel **7** cluster **8** quantity, shipment **10** assemblage, assortment, collection **11** aggregation **12** accumulation

bate
3 bar 4 omit 5 check 6 deduct, except, reduce 7 cut back, exclude, suspend 8 diminish, moderate, restrain, subtract

bateau
4 boat, dory 5 craft, skiff 6 dinghy, launch 7 shallop

bath
3 spa, tub 4 soak, wash 5 hydro, wells 6 shower 7 springs 8 ablution 13 watering place

bathe
3 dip, lap, lip, sop, tub, wet 4 bask, lave, soak, soap, swim, wash 5 clean, douse, flood, rinse, flush, souse, steep 6 shower 7 cleanse, immerse, pervade, suffuse 8 irrigate

bathetic
5 mushy, soppy, stale, tired, trite 6 drippy 7 clichéd, cloying, gushing, maudlin, mawkish 9 emotional, hackneyed, schmaltzy 10 lachrymose 11 commonplace, sentimental, stereotyped, tear-jerking 13 anticlimactic, overemotional, stereotypical

bathhouse
5 sauna 6 cabana

bathing suit
6 bikini, trunks 7 bandeau, maillot

bathos
7 letdown 8 banality, comedown 9 triteness 10 anticlimax

bathroom
3 loo 4 john 5 privy 6 toilet 8 lavatory, outhouse

Bathsheba
father: 5 Eliam
husband: 5 David, Uriah
son: 7 Solomon

bathtub gin
5 hooch 6 rotgut 7 bootleg 8 homebrew 9 moonshine 11 mountain dew

Batman creator
4 Kane (Bob)

baton
3 rod 4 club, mace, wand 5 billy, staff, stick 6 cudgel 7 war club 8 bludgeon 9 billy club, truncheon 10 nightstick

_____ Bator
4 Ulan

batrachian
4 frog, toad 9 amphibian

battalion
4 army, host, unit 5 force, horde 6 legion, throng, troops 8 squadron 10 contingent, detachment

batter
4 bash, beat, drub, hurt, maul, mush 5 baste, break, dough, paste, pound, wreck 6 bruise, buffet, bung up, hitter, mangle, pommel, pummel, thrash, wallop 7 assault, belabor, bombard, clobber, coating, contuse, cripple, lambast 8 demolish, lambaste

battery
3 lot, set 4 body, guns 5 abuse, array, batch, bunch, clump, group, suite 6 bundle, cannon, series 7 assault, beating, cluster 8 thumping 9 artillery, onslaught 10 energy cell 11 gunnery unit

battery terminal
5 anode 7 cathode

battle
4 fray 5 brush, clash, fight 6 action, assail, attack, combat, sortie 7 assault, contend, contest 8 conflict, skirmish, struggle 9 encounter, onslaught, scrimmage 10 engagement 11 hostilities

battle-ax
5 harpy, scold, shrew 6 virago 8 harridan 9 termagant, Xanthippe

Battle Born State
6 Nevada

battle cry
6 banzai

battlement
4 wall 7 barrier, bastion, bulwark, parapet, rampart 10 protection

batty

3 mad 4 daft, nuts, zany 5 barmy,
crazy, kooky, loony, nutty, potty,
wacky 6 crazed, cuckoo, insane,
maniac, screwy, whacko 7 bananas,
bonkers, cracked, idiotic, lunatic
8 deranged 9 bedlamite

bauble

3 toy 5 curio 6 gewgaw, trifle
7 bibelot, novelty, trinket, whatnot
8 gimcrack, ornament 9 objet d'art,
plaything 10 knickknack

Baucis's husband

8 Philemon

Bavaria

6 Bayern
capital: 6 Munich
city: 8 Augsburg, Bayreuth, Würzburg 9 Nuremberg
king: 6 Ludwig
patron saint: 6 Rupert

bawd

4 drab, moll, tart 5 madam, tramp,
whore 6 floozy, harlot, hooker
7 trollop 8 strumpet 10 prostitute
11 nightwalker 12 streetwalker

bawdy

4 blue, lewd 5 crude, dirty 6 coarse,
erotic, ribald, risqué, smutty, vulgar
7 obscene 8 indecent, prurient
9 lecherous, offensive, salacious
10 lascivious, libidinous, licentious,
suggestive

bawdy house

4 crib, stew 6 bagnio 7 brothel,
lupanar 8 bordello

bawl

3 cry, sob 4 howl, roar, rout, wail,
weep, yell, yowl 5 shout 6 bellow,
berate, boohoo, clamor, holler, outcry, scream, shriek, squall 7 blubber,
bluster

bawl out

3 wig 4 lash 5 baste, scold 6 berate, rebuke 7 censure, chew out,
condemn, tell off, upbraid 8 bless
out, denounce, tear into 9 castigate,
dress down, reprimand 10 tongue-
lash

bay

3 arm 4 cove, gulf, howl, nook, wail
5 award, bight, crown, firth, honor,
inlet, niche 6 harbor, laurel, recess
7 garland, laurels 8 accolade
10 decoration
Aegean Sea: 5 Anzac
Africa: 6 Walvis
Alaska: 7 Glacier
Antarctica: 3 Ice 8 Amundsen
Argentina: 6 Blanca
Australia: 5 Anson, Shark
6 Botany, Sharks 9 Discovery
Baltic: 4 Hano, Kiel 6 Danzig,
Kieler 9 Pomerania 10 Pomeranian,
Pommersche
Beaufort Sea: 7 Prudhoe
9 Mackenzie
Brazil: 9 Guanabara
Bristol Channel: 10 Carmarthen
California: 5 Morro 8 Monterey,
San Diego
Canada: 5 Fundy
Capetown: 5 Table
Caribbean Sea: 5 Limon
8 Chetumal
Central America: 7 Fonseca
Cuba: 10 Guantánamo
East River: 8 Flushing
Egypt: 6 Abu Qir
Eire: 4 Clew 7 Brandon
English Channel: 3 Tor 4 Lyme
Europe: 6 Biscay
Florida: 8 Biscayne
Greenland: 6 Baffin 8 Melville
Gulf of Alaska: 12 Resurrection
Gulf of California: 5 Adair
Gulf of Guinea: 5 Benin 6 Biafra
Gulf of Mexico: 5 Tampa 6 Mobile
7 Aransas 8 Campeche, Sarasota
9 Matagorda, Pensacola 10 San An-
tonio, Terrebonne 11 Atchafalaya,
Ponce de Leon 12 Apalachicola
13 Corpus Christi
Gulf of St. Lawrence: 5 Bonne,
Gaspé
Hawaii: 5 Koloa, Lawai
Hong Kong: 4 Deep
Honshu: 3 Ise 5 Mutsu, Osaka,
Owari, Tokyo 6 Atsuta, Sagami
Indian Ocean: 6 Bengal
Indonesia: 8 Humboldt
Irish Sea: 4 Luce 7 Dundalk

Jamaica: 4 Long
Japan: 4 Tosa
Java Sea: 7 Batavia 8 Djakarta
Lake Erie: 8 Sandusky
Lake Huron: 7 Saginaw, Thunder
Lake Michigan: 5 Green 13 Grand Traverse
Lake Ontario: 11 Irondequoit
Lake Superior: 5 Huron
8 Keweenaw 9 Whitefish
Long Island Sound: 6 Oyster
Maine: 5 Casco 7 Machias
9 Penobscot
Maryland-Virginia: 10 Chesapeake
12 Chincoteague
Massachusetts: 6 Boston 7 Cape
Cod 8 Buzzards, Plymouth
New Brunswick:
13 Passamaquoddy
Newfoundland: 4 Hare 5 White
7 Fortune
New Jersey: 5 Great 6 Newark
7 Raritan 8 Barnegat
New York: 7 Jamaica
North Carolina: 6 Onslow
Northwest Territories: 5 Wager
7 Repulse 8 Franklin 9 Frobisher
Oregon: 4 Coos
Puerto Rico: 5 Sucia
Quebec: 6 Ungava
Rhode Island: 12 Narragansett
Sea of Japan: 13 Peter the Great
South Carolina: 4 Bull, Long
South China Sea: 5 Subic
7 Camranh
Spain: 5 Cadiz
Strait of Gibraltar: 7 Tangier
Sydney: 6 Botany
Tasmania: 5 Storm
Texas: 7 Trinity
Tyrrhenian Sea: 6 Naples
7 Paestum
Wales: 10 Caernarfon, Caernarvon
Washington: 5 Dabob 6 Skagit
West Indies: 5 Coral

bayou
5 creek, marsh 6 slough
9 everglade, tributary
Louisiana: 5 Macon 9 Barataria,
Lafourche 10 Terrebonne
Mississippi: 9 Chickasaw

Bay State
13 Massachusetts

bay window
3 gut, pot 5 oriel, tummy 6 paunch
8 potbelly 9 beer belly, spare tire
11 corporation, breadbasket

bazaar
4 fair, mall, mart, souk 6 market
7 benefit 8 emporium, exchange
11 marketplace

bazooka's target
4 tank

be
4 live 5 exist

beach
4 bank 5 Cocoa, coast, shore
6 Malibu, Pebble, strand, Venice
7 seaside, shingle, Waikiki 8 cast
away, lakeside, littoral, seashore
9 lakeshore 10 Clearwater, Copaca-
bana, oceanfront, run aground

_____ Beach
3 Amy 4 Long, Palm, Vero 5 Dover,
Miami, Omaha 6 Delray, Myrtle,
Ormond 7 Daytona, Riviera, Waikiki
8 Imperial, Virginia

beached
6 ashore 7 aground 8 grounded,
marooned, stranded 9 abandoned

beachhead
8 foothold

beachwear
see **bathing suit**

beacon
4 buoy, sign 5 flare, guide 6 pharos,
signal 7 bonfire, lantern 8 balefire
9 watchfire 10 lighthouse, signal fire
11 inspiration, transmitter 12 guiding
light

bead
3 dab, dot, pea 4 blob, drop 6 bubble
7 driblet, globule 8 spherule

beak
3 neb, nib 4 bill, nose 5 snoot,
snout, spout 6 pecker, schnoz
7 schnozz 8 mandible 9 proboscis,
schnozzle

beaker

3 cup 6 carafe, goblet, vessel
8 decanter

beaklike part

7 rostrum

be-all and end-all

3 sum 4 pith, root, soul 5 total, whole
6 bottom 7 essence 8 entirety, sum
total, totality 9 aggregate, substance
10 prime cause 12 quintessence

beam

3 bar, ray 4 balk, boom, burn, glow,
grin, spar 5 flare, flash, gleam, joist,
plank, shaft, shine, shoot, smile, strut
6 girder, lintel, rafter, signal, streak,
stream, timber 7 radiate 8 transmit
9 broadcast

beaming

6 bright, joyful, lucent 7 fulgent, lambent, radiant 8 animated, cheerful,
luminous 9 brilliant, effulgent, refulgent 12 incandescent

bean

3 soy, wax 4 bush, conk, dome,
head, lima, mung, navy, pate, pole,
poll, snap, soya 5 baked, brain,
broad, horse, jelly, pinto 6 belfry,
coffee, frijol, kidney, legume, noddle,
noggin, noodle, string 7 jumping
9 headpiece 10 stringless
of India: 3 urd

beanery

4 café 5 diner, grill 9 hash house
10 coffee shop, restaurant 11 greasy
spoon 12 luncheonette

beano

5 bingo

Bean Town

6 Boston

bear

3 lug 4 tote 5 abide, allow, beget,
bring, brook, bruin, carry, stand,
touch 6 accept, behave, convey,
deport, endure, permit, suffer 7 comport, condone, conduct, deliver,
stomach, support, sustain, swallow,
undergo 8 engender, generate,

shoulder, tolerate 9 procreate,
propagate, reproduce, transport
10 bring forth 11 countenance
Alaskan: 5 polar 6 Kodiak
Australian: 5 koala
genus: 5 Ursus
kind: 3 sun 5 black, brown, honey,
koala, polar, sloth 6 Kodiak 7 grizzly
10 spectacled
relating to: 6 ursine
young: 3 cub

bearable

7 livable, tenable 8 adequate,
passable 9 allowable, endurable,
tolerable 10 acceptable, admissible,
good enough, manageable, sufferable 11 supportable, sustainable

bearcat

5 panda

beard

4 dare, defy, face, fuzz 5 brave, front
6 goatee 7 outface, stubble, Vandyke 8 confront, imperial, whiskers
9 challenge
on grain: 3 awn

bearded

5 bushy, fuzzy, hairy 6 shaggy,
tufted 7 bristly, goateed, hirsute,
stubbly 8 unshaven 9 whiskered
11 bewhiskered

bear down

4 rout 5 crush, quell 6 burden, defeat, reduce, subdue 7 conquer,
overrun, trample 8 overcome, vanquish 9 emphasize, overpower,
overwhelm, subjugate

bearer

4 mule 5 envoy 6 coolie, porter,
runner 7 carrier, courier 8 conveyor,
emissary 9 go-between, messenger
11 internuncio

bear hug

6 clinch

bearing

3 air, set 4 look, mien, pose 5 poise
6 aspect, manner, stance 7 address,
conduct, display, posture 8 attitude, behavior, carriage, delivery,

demeanor, presence, relation **9** demeanour, direction **10** connection, deportment **11** comportment

bearish
4 curt **5** gruff, rough, terse, surly **6** cranky, ornery **7** anxious, dubious, prickly, uncouth **8** cautious, vinegary **9** crotchety, irascible **10** ill-humored **11** pessimistic **12** cantankerous

bearlike
6 ursine

bear out
4 show **5** prove **6** attest, uphold, verify **7** certify, confirm, justify **8** validate, vouch for **9** vindicate **11** corroborate, demonstrate **12** authenticate, substantiate

bear up
4 cope, fare, prop **5** brace, get by **6** endure, uphold **7** bolster, support, sustain **8** buttress, get along, maintain, underpin

beast
5 brute **6** animal **7** critter, monster, varmint **8** behemoth, creature

beastly
4 foul, mean, vile **5** awful, brute, feral, nasty **6** animal, brutal, odious **7** bestial, brutish, inhuman, ogreish, swinish **8** horrible, terrible **9** barbarous, revolting **10** abominable, detestable

beat
3 box, get, gyp, hit, lam, rap, tan, top **4** balk, belt, best, cane, dash, drub, drum, dump, flap, flog, foil, lash, lick, maul, pelt, rout, ruin, stir, tick, trim, whip, whop **5** baste, cheat, cozen, excel, forge, lay on, meter, outdo, paste, pound, pulse, punch, rhyme, route, scoop, scour, smear, stick, stump, swing, throb, tread, tromp, whack, whisk **6** baffle, batter, better, buffet, cudgel, defeat, diddle, exceed, forage, hammer, larrup, muss up, patrol, pummel, rhythm, rounds, strike, thrash, thresh, thwart, wallop **7** belabor, clobber, circuit, conquer, exhaust, fashion, fatigue, lambast,

lay down, prevail, pulsate, ransack, rough up, shellac, surpass, swindle, triumph, trounce **8** bewilder, bludgeon, Bohemian, lambaste, outshine, outsmart, outstrip, overcome, precinct **9** exhausted, frustrate, palpitate, pulsation, transcend, vibration **10** circumvent, pistol-whip **11** oscillation

beating
4 rout **5** lumps **6** defeat, hiding, mayhem **7** assault, setback **9** hammering, pulsation, throbbing **11** palpitation, shellacking

beatitude
3 joy **5** bliss **7** delight, ecstasy, rapture **8** euphoria, gladness, rhapsody **9** happiness, transport **10** exaltation, joyfulness **11** blessedness **12** blissfulness

Beatles
4 John (Lennon), Paul (McCartney) **5** Ringo (Starr) **6** George (Harrison)

beatnik
5 rebel **6** hippie **7** radical **8** Bohemian **9** dissident **11** flower child **13** nonconformist

beat-up
6 shabby **7** rickety, worn-out **8** decrepit, tattered **9** crumbling **10** broken-down, ramshackle, tumbledown **11** dilapidated

beau
5 dandy, flame, lover, swain, wooer **6** steady, suitor **7** admirer, beloved **8** paramour, truelove, young man **9** boyfriend **10** sweetheart

Beau Brummell
3 fop **5** dandy, swell **7** coxcomb, gallant **8** macaroni **11** petit-maître **12** lounge lizard

beau ideal
5 guide, model **6** mirror **7** epitome, example, paragon, pattern **8** exemplar, paradigm, standard **9** archetype **12** quintessence

Beaumarchais hero
6 Figaro

beau monde

5 elite 6 gentry, jet set 7 society
8 smart set 10 glitterati, upper crust

beauteous

see **beautiful**

beautiful

4 fair 5 bonny 6 comely, lovely,
pretty 7 radiant 8 glorious, gorgeous, handsome, splendid, stunning
9 exquisite 10 attractive 11 good-
looking, resplendent, well-favored

beautiful people

6 jet set 8 smart set 9 haut monde
10 glitterati 11 high society

beautify

4 deck, gild, trim 5 adorn, array, fix
up, grace, prank, primp 6 bedeck,
doll up 7 dress up, festoon, garland,
garnish, gussy up, enhance, improve
8 decorate, ornament, prettify, spruce
up 9 embellish, glamorize

beauty

5 asset, belle, dream, merit, peach
6 appeal, eyeful, looker, lovely
7 charmer, dazzler, stunner 8 knockout 9 eye-opener, good looks
10 good-looker, loveliness

beaver

6 rodent
project: 3 dam
home: 5 lodge
young: 3 kit, pup

Beaver State

6 Oregon

becalm

4 hush, lull, stop 5 allay, quiet, stall,
still 6 arrest, pacify, sedate, settle,
soothe, steady, subdue 7 assuage,
compose, quieten 11 tranquilize

because

3 for, now 4 that 5 since 7 being
as, whereas 8 being how, as long
as, seeing as 10 inasmuch as

because of

4 over 5 due to 7 owing to, through
8 thanks to 10 by reason of 11 on
account of

Beckett work

4 Not I, Play, Watt 6 Molloy, Murphy
7 Endgame 9 Happy Days, Un-
namable (The) 10 Eleutheria, Malone Dies 14 Krapp's Last Tape
15 Waiting for Godot

beckon

3 bid, nod 4 lure, wave 6 allure,
entice, invite, motion, signal, summon 7 attract

becloud

3 dim, fog 4 blur, hide, veil 5 addle,
bedim, befog, cloak, muddy 6 impair,
darken, muddle, puzzle, shroud
7 confuse, eclipse, obscure, perplex
8 befuddle 9 obfuscate 10 overshadow

become

3 fit, get, wax 4 grow, suit 5 befit
6 go with 7 enhance, flatter 8 turn
into

becoming

3 apt 5 right 6 decent, proper,
seemly 7 correct, fitting 8 decorous, suitable, tasteful 9 befitting
10 attractive, flattering, well-chosen
11 appropriate, comme il faut

bed

3 cot 4 base, bunk, crib, sack,
twin 5 basis, berth, layer 6 bottom,
cradle, double, ground, Murphy,
pallet 7 bedrock, stratum, trundle
8 rollaway 10 foundation, substratum
of India: 7 charpoy

bedaub

4 coat 5 cover, smear 6 smudge
7 overlay, plaster

bedazzle

4 daze 5 blind

bedcover

5 duvet, quilt 6 afghan, spread
7 blanket 8 coverlet 9 comforter
11 counterpane

bedeck

4 trim 5 adorn, array, prank 6 attire,
bedaub, jazz up 7 appoint, bedizen,
dress up, festoon, furbish, garland,

garnish, gussy up **8** accouter, accoutre, beautify, decorate, ornament, prettify **9** embellish

bedevil
  5 annoy, harry, spoil, tease, worry **6** harass, needle, nettle, pester, plague **7** hagride, provoke, torment, trouble **8** bewilder **10** exasperate

bedevilment
  6 bother **7** torment, trouble **8** disorder, vexation **9** annoyance, confusion **10** irritation **11** aggravation **12** bewilderment

bedfellow
  4 ally **5** crony **7** comrade **9** associate, colleague **10** compatriot **11** confederate **12** collaborator

bedim
  3 fog **4** blur, mask, veil **5** befog, blear, cloud, gloom, shade **6** darken, muddle, shadow, shroud **7** becloud, confuse, eclipse, obscure **9** obfuscate

bedizen
  4 deck, garb, gild **5** adorn, array, endue **6** doll up, dude up, invest, outfit, rig out **7** costume, dandify, dress up, garnish, gussy up, turn out **8** beautify, ornament **9** caparison, embellish

bedlam
  3 ado **5** chaos, furor **6** asylum, clamor, furore, hubbub, tumult, uproar, welter **7** turmoil **8** foofaraw, madhouse, upheaval **9** commotion, maelstrom **10** hurly-burly **11** pandemonium

bedlamite
  3 mad, nut **4** loon, nuts **5** batty, crazy, loony **6** insane, madman, maniac **7** cracked, lunatic **8** demented, deranged

bedouin
  4 Arab **5** nomad

bedraggled
  5 faded, seedy **6** shabby, ragtag, untidy **7** muddied, rundown, unkempt **8** decrepit, dripping, slovenly, tattered

10 disheveled, disarrayed, disordered, down-at-heel, ramshackle, threadbare **11** dilapidated

bedridden
  6 laid up, shut-in **8** confined **12** hospitalized

bedrock
  4 base, core, foot, root **5** axiom, basic, basis, floor, nadir **6** bottom, depths, ground **7** footing, support **10** foundation, groundwork, substratum **11** fundamental **12** substructure, underpinning

bedroom
  7 boudoir, chamber

bedspread
  8 coverlet **11** counterpane

bed-wetting
  8 enuresis

bee
  food: **6** nectar
  glue: **8** propolis
  group: **5** swarm **6** colony
  house: **4** hive **6** apiary
  kind: **5** drone, mason, queen **6** mining, sewing, worker **8** quilting, spelling **9** carpenter
  nest: **4** hive, skep
  product: **3** wax **5** honey
  relating to: **8** apiarian
  wax cells: **9** honeycomb

beechnuts
  4 mast

beef
  4 crab, fuss, meat **5** bitch, brawn, gripe **6** grouse, muscle **7** grumble **9** bellyache, complaint, grievance
  cut: **3** rib **4** loin, rump, side **5** chuck, flank, plate, round, shank **7** brisket, sirloin **10** tenderloin **11** porterhouse
  grade: **5** prime **6** choice **7** utility **8** standard **10** commercial
  order: **4** rare **6** medium **8** well-done

beefeater
  5 guard **6** sentry, warder, yeoman

beefy

5 bulky, burly, hefty, husky, meaty
6 brawny, fleshy, robust, stocky, sturdy **7** massive **8** muscular, thickset **9** strapping **11** substantial

Beehive State

4 Utah

beekeeper

8 apiarist **12** apiculturist

beekeeping

10 apiculture

beeline

3 fly, nip, zip **4** race, whiz **5** hurry, speed **6** bullet, hasten, hustle, rocket **7** hotfoot **8** expedite, highball **10** make tracks **12** shortest path

Beelzebub

5 devil, fiend, Satan **6** diablo **7** Evil One, Lucifer, Old Nick, serpent **8** Apollyon **9** adversary, archfiend

beer

3 ale **4** bock, brew, suds **5** draft, lager, stout, weiss **6** porter **7** brewski, cerveza, pilsner **8** pilsener
vessel: **3** mug **4** toby **5** stein **6** flagon, seidel **7** tankard **8** schooner **9** blackjack
drinking place: **3** bar, inn, pub **6** saloon, tavern
ingredient: **4** hops, malt **5** yeast **6** barley
maker: **6** brewer
mythical inventor: **9** Gambrinus
plant: **7** brewery
Russian: **5** kvass
Scottish: **10** barley-bree

beer hall

3 pub **6** saloon, tavern **7** taproom **8** alehouse **11** public house, rathskeller

Beeri

daughter: **6** Judith
son: **5** Hosea

beet

5 chard **6** mangel, wurzel **10** Swiss chard
family: **9** goosefoot

Beethoven, Ludwig van

birthplace: **4** Bonn
opera: **7** Fidelio
overture: **6** Egmont **7** Leonore **10** Coriolanus, Prometheus
sonata: **7** Tempest **8** Kreutzer **9** Moonlight, Waldstein **10** Pathétique **12** Appassionata
symphony: **6** Choral, Eroica **8** Pastoral

beetle

3 bug, jut **5** bulge **6** insect, scarab, scurry **7** project **8** overhang, protrude, stand out, stick out
click: **6** elater **7** firefly
dung: **6** scarab **9** tumblebug
front wing: **6** elytra (plural) **7** elytron
fruit-eating: **8** curculio
insect-eating: **7** ladybug **8** ladybird
kind: **4** bean, dung, fire, June, stag **5** click, flour, grain, tiger, water **6** carpet, chafer, ground, May bug, museum **7** blister, cadelle, carabid, firefly, goldbug, goliath, June bug, vedalia **8** ambrosia, Japanese **9** longicorn, potato bug **10** cockchafer, rhinoceros
order: **10** Coleoptera
snouted: **6** weevil **7** billbug **8** curculio **9** wood borer
young: **4** grub **5** larva **6** larvae (plural) **8** wireworm

beet soup

6 borsch **7** borscht

befall

3 hap **5** ensue, occur **6** betide, chance, follow, happen **7** come off, develop, fall out **8** happen to **9** come about, eventuate, transpire

befit

4 meet, suit **6** become, go with **9** agree with, chime with **10** accord with, be right for **11** be proper for

befitting

3 apt **4** just, meet **5** happy, right **6** decent, proper, seemly **7** correct **8** becoming, decorous, suitable **10** conforming, felicitous **11** appropriate, comme il faut

befog
3 dim 4 blur, hide, veil 5 bedim, blear, cloak, cloud, muddy 6 darken, puzzle 7 becloud, confuse, eclipse, envelop, obscure, perplex 8 bewilder, confound 9 obfuscate, overcloud 10 overshadow

befool
4 dupe, gull, hoax, play 5 cozen, trick 6 delude, chicane, deceive, mislead 8 hoodwink 9 bamboozle, victimize 11 hornswoggle

before
3 ere 4 ante, once, till, up to 5 ahead, until 6 facing, sooner, up till 7 ahead of, already, earlier, prior to 8 formerly 9 in advance, in front of, preceding 10 previously 11 in advance of
prefix: 3 pre, pro 4 ante, fore

befoul
3 mar, tar 4 slur, soil 5 dirty, smear, spoil, sully, taint 6 defame, defile, malign, smudge 7 blacken, pollute, profane, spatter, tarnish, traduce 8 besmirch 9 bespatter, denigrate 10 adulterate 11 contaminate

befuddle
4 daze 5 addle, mix up 6 ball up, baffle, bemuse, muddle 7 confuse, fluster, perplex, stupefy 8 bewilder, confound, distract, throw off 9 disorient

befuddlement
3 fog 4 daze, haze, maze 5 mix-up 6 muddle, stupor 9 confusion 10 perplexity, puzzlement 11 distraction

beg
3 ask, bum, dun, nag, sue 4 pray, urge 5 apply, brace, cadge, crave, evade, hit on, mooch, plead, press, worry 6 adjure, appeal, call on, demand, invoke, pester 7 beseech, besiege, conjure, entreat, implore, request, solicit 8 petition, sidestep 9 importune, panhandle 10 supplicate

beget
4 bear, sire 5 breed, bring, cause, forge, hatch, spawn, yield 6 create, effect, father 7 produce 8 engender, generate, multiply, result in 9 procreate, propagate, reproduce 10 bring about

beggar
4 hobo, defy, ruin 5 tramp 6 bummer, cadger, fellow, pauper, prayer, sponge, suitor 7 moocher, sponger 8 bankrupt, deadbeat, vagabond 9 overwhelm, pauperize, schnorrer, suppliant 10 down-and-out, freeloader, impoverish, panhandler, petitioner, supplicant 11 bindle stiff, supplicator 12 street person

beggared
4 flat, poor 5 broke, needy 6 ruined 7 drained 8 bankrupt, dirt poor, indigent, strapped, wiped out 9 destitute, insolvent, penniless, penurious, tapped out 10 pauperized 11 impecunious, overwhelmed 12 dispossessed, impoverished

beggarly
3 low 4 base, mean, poor 5 cheap, lowly, nasty, petty, sorry 6 cheesy, meager, measly, paltry, scanty, scurvy, shabby, shoddy, trashy 7 ignoble, miserly, pitiful, squalid 8 pitiable, inferior, wretched 9 miserable, niggardly 10 despicable, despisable 11 ignominious 12 contemptible, parsimonious

Beggar's Opera
music: 7 Pepusch (John)
painting: 7 Hogarth (William)
text: 3 Gay (John)

beggarweed
6 dodder 9 knotgrass 11 tick trefoil

beggary
4 need, want 6 penury 7 bumming, cadging, poverty 8 mooching, pleading 9 indigence, neediness, pauperism, privation 10 meagerness, mendicancy 11 destitution, panhandling

begin

4 dawn, open, rise **5** arise, cause, dig in, enter, found, mount, set to, start **6** appear, attack, be born, broach, create, effect, emerge, get off, induce, invent, launch, spring, sprout, tackle, take up, tee off **7** break in, emanate, jump off, kick off, lead off, prepare, usher in **8** activate, commence, embark on, engender, initiate **9** establish, instigate, institute, introduce, originate **10** embark upon, inaugurate, issue forth **11** break ground

beginner

4 colt, tiro, tyro **6** newbie, new kid, novice, rookie **7** recruit, starter, student, trainee **8** freshman, neophyte, newcomer **9** fledgling, greenhorn, novitiate **10** apprentice, catechumen, tenderfoot **11** abecedarian

beginning

4 dawn, font, rise, root **5** alpha, basal, birth, fount, onset, start **6** day one, origin, outset, primal, source, spring **7** dawning, genesis, infancy, initial, kickoff, nascent, opening **8** creation, exordium, outstart, prologue, rudiment, simplest **9** elemental, emergence, inception, incipient **10** appearance, elementary, incipiency, initiative, initiatory, opening gun, rudimental **11** origination, rudimentary **12** commencement, inauguration, introductory

begird

3 hem **4** belt, bind, ring **5** beset, fence, hem in, round **6** circle, corral, girdle, immure **7** confine, enclose, wreathe **8** encircle, engirdle, surround **9** encompass **12** circumscribe

beg off

5 demur, welsh **6** bow out, cop out, opt out, pass up, refuse, renege **7** back out, bail out, decline, drop out, pull out **8** back down, withdraw

begone

5 leave, scram, split **6** beat it, decamp, depart, get out **7** buzz off, get lost, skiddoo, take off, vamoose **8** clear out, hightail, shove off **9** skedaddle **10** make tracks

begrime

3 tar **4** foul, soil, spot **5** dirty, muddy, smear, spoil, sully, taint **6** defile, mess up, muck up, smirch, smooch, smudge, smutch **7** blacken, corrupt, pollute, tarnish **8** besmirch **11** contaminate

begrudge

4 envy **6** resent

beguile

3 con **4** draw, dupe, fool, hoax, lure, play, snow, wile **5** bluff, charm, fleet, trick **6** beckon, betray, delude, divert, entice, humbug, seduce, take in **7** attract, bewitch, deceive, enchant, engross, exploit, finesse, mislead **8** distract, hoodwink, intrigue, maneuver **9** captivate, fascinate, while away **10** manipulate **11** doublecross

beguiling

4 wily **5** false **6** artful, subtle **8** alluring, deluding, delusive, delusory **9** deceitful, deceiving, deceptive, insidious, seductive **10** bewitching, chimerical, enchanting, fallacious, misleading **11** enthralling

Behan's autobiography

10 Borstal Boy

behave

3 act, run **5** carry, react **6** acquit, be good, deport, direct, manage **7** comport, conduct, disport, perform **8** function

behavior

3 act, air, way **4** mien, tone, ways **6** action, aspect, custom, habits, manner **7** bearing, conduct **8** demeanor, presence, response **10** deportment **11** comportment

behead

4 head, kill **7** execute **9** decollate **10** decapitate, guillotine

beheaded noblewoman

8 Jane Grey (Lady) **9** Catherine (Howard) **10** Anne Boleyn

behemoth
5 giant, jumbo, whale 7 goliath, mammoth, monster 8 colossus 9 leviathan 11 monstrosity

behemothic
4 huge 5 jumbo 7 mammoth, massive, titanic 8 colossal, gigantic, towering 9 Herculean, monstrous 10 gargantuan 11 elephantine

behest
3 say 4 will, wish, word, writ 5 edict, order 6 charge, demand, urging 7 bidding, command, dictate, mandate, precept, request 9 direction, enjoinder, ordinance, prescript, prompting 10 injunction 11 commandment, exhortation, instruction 12 solicitation

behind
3 can 4 late, next, rump 5 after, fanny 6 back of, bottom, heinie 7 backing 8 backside, buttocks, derriere, trailing 9 following, posterior 10 supporting 12 subsequent to
prefix: 4 post 5 retro

behindhand
3 lax 4 late, slow 5 slack, tardy 6 in debt, lesser, remiss 7 belated, delayed, laggard, overdue 8 backward, careless, derelict, sluggish 9 in arrears, negligent, unmindful 10 delinquent, neglectful, regardless, unpunctual 11 subordinate, undeveloped 13 unprogressive

behold
3 see 4 espy, note, view 6 descry, notice 7 discern, observe, witness
French: 5 voilà
Latin: 4 ecce

beholden
5 bound 7 obliged 8 grateful, indebted 9 duty-bound, obligated

beholder
4 seer 6 gawker, viewer 7 watcher, witness 8 observer, onlooker, passerby 9 bystander, spectator 10 eyewitness 12 rubbernecker

beige
3 tan 4 buff, ecru 7 vanilla

being
3 man 4 body, life, self, soul 5 human, stuff, thing 6 entity, matter, mortal, nature, object, person, spirit 7 essence 8 creature, existent, material 9 actuality, character, existence, personage, something, substance 10 individual 11 personality 12 essentiality 13 individuality

bejeweled
7 studded 8 sequined, spangled 9 encrusted 10 bespangled, gem-studded, ornamented

Bel
Sumerian counterpart: 5 Enlil
wife: 5 Belit 6 Beltis

Bel _____
3 Air 5 Paese

bel _____
5 canto 6 esprit

Bela
father: 4 Beor 8 Benjamin
son: 3 Ard

belabor
4 beat, drub, flog 5 baste, pound, scold 6 batter, berate, buffet, pummel, thrash, wallop 7 lambast, scourge, tell off, upbraid 8 chastise, lambaste, tear into 9 criticize, fulminate, overstate 10 flagellate 11 overexplain

Belarus
capital: 5 Minsk
city: 6 Homyel 7 Vitebsk 8 Mahilyow 9 Vitsyebsk
language: 7 Russian 10 Belarusian 11 Belarussian
monetary unit: 5 rubel, ruble
neighbor: 6 Latvia, Poland, Russia 7 Ukraine 9 Lithuania
river: 3 Bug 5 Neman 7 Dnieper, Pripyat

belated
4 late, slow 5 tardy 6 remiss 7 delayed, laggard, overdue 10 behindhand, behind time, unpunctual

Belau
see **Palau**

belch

4 burp, emit, gush, spew, vent, void
5 eject, eruct, erupt, expel, issue,
spout, spurt, vomit 6 hiccup, irrupt
7 explode, extrude 8 disgorge
10 eructation 11 expectorate

beldam

3 hag 5 crone 8 old woman

beleaguer

3 bug, dog, hem, nag, vex 4 gnaw
5 annoy, beset, harry, hound, siege,
storm, tease, worry 6 assail, attack,
badger, bother, fall on, harass,
invest, pester, plague 7 bedevil,
besiege, hagride, put upon, set upon,
trouble 8 blockade, fall upon

belfry

7 steeple 8 carillon 9 bell tower,
campanile
dweller: 3 bat

Belgium

capital: 8 Brussels
city: 4 Gent 5 Ghent, Liège 7 Antwerp 9 Charleroi
ethnic group: 7 Fleming, Flemish,
Walloon
language: 5 Dutch 7 Flemish
monetary unit: 4 euro
neighbor: 6 France 7 Germany
10 Luxembourg 11 Netherlands
plain: 8 Flanders
port: 7 Antwerp 8 Oostende
river: 4 Yser 5 Meuse 7 Schlede
sea: 5 North

belie

4 deny, hide, warp 5 color, twist
6 expose, doctor, garble 7 conceal,
confute, distort, falsify, gainsay,
pervert, trump up 8 confront, denounce, disagree, disguise, disprove,
miscolor, misstate, negative 9 disaffirm, gloss over, repudiate 10 contradict, contravene, controvert
11 dissimulate 12 misrepresent

belief

3 ism 4 idea, mind, view 5 axiom,
credo, creed, dogma, faith, hunch,
tenet, trust 6 assent, avowal, credit,
surety, theory, thesis 7 concept,

feeling, opinion, precept, surmise,
theorem 8 credence, doctrine,
firmness, religion, sureness 9 assurance, certainty, certitude, intuition,
postulate, principle, sentiment
10 acceptance, assumption, confidence, contention, conviction,
hypothesis, impression, persuasion
11 supposition

believable

5 solid, sound, valid 6 cogent, likely,
smooth, steady, trusty 7 logical,
swaying, tenable, up front 8 credible, possible, probable, rational,
reliable 9 authentic, colorable,
plausible 10 convincing, creditable,
impressive, meaningful, persuasive,
presumable, reasonable, satisfying,
supposable 11 conceivable, substantial, trustworthy 12 satisfactory

believe

3 buy 4 deem, hold, know 5 lap up,
think, trust 6 accept, affirm, assume,
credit, expect, reckon 7 fall for,
imagine, profess, suppose, suspect,
swallow 8 conceive, consider
10 conjecture, presuppose, understand

belittle

3 cut, pan 5 abuse, decry, knock,
scorn 6 deride, insult, jeer at, revile
7 cut down, put down, run down,
sneer at 8 bad-mouth, derogate,
diminish, discount, minimize, write off
9 criticize, discredit, disparage,
dispraise, downgrade, underrate
10 depreciate, undervalue 13 underestimate

belittlement

5 abuse, scorn 7 calumny, jeering,
scandal, slander 8 derision, ridicule
9 aspersion 10 backbiting, defamation, detraction 11 denigration
12 backstabbing, depreciation
13 disparagement

Belize

capital: 8 Belmopan
city: 10 Belize City
ethnic group: 4 Maya 5 Mayan

language: 7 English, Spanish
monetary unit: 6 dollar
mountain: 8 Victoria
neighbor: 6 Mexico 9 Guatemala
river: 5 Hondo
sea: 9 Caribbean

bell
4 peal 5 chime, knell 6 tocsin

belle
5 siren 6 beauty, eyeful 7 charmer
8 knockout, ornament 11 enchantress, femme fatale

Bellerophon
father: 7 Glaucus 8 Poseidon
grandfather: 8 Sisyphus
horse: 7 Pegasus
victim: 7 Chimera

belles lettres
10 literature

belletrist
8 novelist 4 poet 6 author, writer
9 dramatist 10 playwright

bellflower
9 campanula

_____ belli
5 casus

bellicose
6 ornery 7 hawkish, hostile, martial,
scrappy, warlike 8 factious, fighting,
militant 9 assertive, combative,
truculent 10 aggressive, pugnacious, rebellious 11 belligerent,
contentious, hot-tempered, quarrelsome 12 disputatious, gladiatorial

belligerence
5 fight 6 attack, enmity, rancor,
spleen 7 ill will 9 hostility, militancy,
petulance, pugnacity 10 aggression,
antagonism, truculence 11 bellicosity 12 churlishness 13 combativeness

belligerent
6 ardent, fierce 7 fighter, hostile,
scrappy, soldier, warlike, warring,
warrior 8 battling, churlish, fighting,
invading, militant, opponent, petulant

9 aggressor, attacking, bellicose,
combatant, combative, disputant,
splenetic, truculent 10 aggressive,
antagonist, pugnacious 11 contentious, hot-tempered, quarrelsome
12 antagonistic, disputatious

Bellini
opera: 5 Norma 6 Pirata (Il)
8 Puritani (I) 10 Sonnambula (La)
sleepwalker: 5 Amina

bell metal
6 bronze

bellow
3 bay, cry, moo 4 bark, bawl, bray,
howl, roar, rout, yowl 5 shout
6 clamor, holler 7 bluster

Bellow character
4 Rose (Billy) 5 Chick 6 Herzog
(Moses E.) 7 Citrine (Charlie),
Sammler (Arthur) 8 Humboldt,
Fonstein (Harry) 9 Henderson
10 Ravelstein (Abe), Augie March

bell ringer
6 toller 9 Quasimodo
12 carillonneur 13 campanologist

bell ringing
11 campanology

bell-shaped
11 campanulate

bell sound
4 bong, boom, ding, dong, peal,
ring, ting, toll 5 chime, clang, knell
6 tinkle

bell tower
6 belfry 7 clocher 8 carillon
9 campanile

_____ bellum
4 ante, post

bellwether
4 dean, lead 5 doyen, guide, pilot
6 leader 7 pioneer 8 lodestar
9 harbinger 10 forerunner 11 trend
setter

belly
3 gut, pot 5 tummy 6 paunch, venter 7 abdomen, midriff, stomach

bellyache

9 bay window 10 front porch, midsection 11 breadbasket
Scottish: 4 wame

bellyache

4 beef, carp, crab, fret, fuss, moan, yawp 5 bitch, bleat, colic, gripe, whine 6 grouse, snivel, squawk, yammer 7 grumble 8 complain 11 let off steam 12 collywobbles

bellyacher

4 crab 5 crank 6 griper, grouch, whiner 7 grouser 8 grumbler, sourpuss 10 complainer, crosspatch, malcontent 11 faultfinder

belly button

5 navel

belong

3 fit, set 4 suit, vest 5 agree, apply, befit, chime, fit in, match, tally 6 accord, attach, become, reside 7 pertain 9 correlate, harmonize 10 correspond

belongings

3 kit 4 gear 5 goods, stuff 6 assets, estate, legacy, things 7 baggage, effects 8 chattels, movables, property 9 patrimony 11 attachments, impedimenta, inheritance, possessions 13 appurtenances

beloved

3 pet 4 baby, beau, dear, idol, love 5 flame, honey, lover, swain, sweet 6 adored, steady 7 darling, dearest, dear one, doted on, sweetie 8 favorite, idolized, ladylove, old flame, precious, truelove 9 boyfriend, cherished, inamorata, treasured 10 girlfriend, heartthrob, sweetheart, sweetie pie

below

5 infra, under 7 beneath 10 underneath
prefix: 3 sub 5 infra

belt

3 bat, bop 4 area, band, bash, biff, blow, gird, loop, ring, sash, slam, slug, sock, whap, whop, zone 5 smack, smash, strap, strip 6 begird, cestus, circle, engird, girdle, region, wallop 7 baldric, clobber, stretch 8 begirdle, ceinture, cincture, encircle, engirdle 9 bandoleer, bandolier, territory, waistband 10 cummerbund
celestial: 6 zodiac

beltway

8 ring road

Belus

brother: 6 Agenor
daughter: 4 Dido
father: 7 Neptune 8 Poseidon
mother: 5 Libya
son: 6 Danaus 7 Cepheus, Phineus 8 Aegyptus

belvedere

6 alcove, cupola, gazebo, pagoda 7 balcony, terrace 10 widow's walk 11 garden house, summerhouse, observatory

bemedaled

9 decorated 10 beribboned

bemired

4 miry, oozy 5 boggy, dirty, grimy, gummy, gunky, muddy, stuck 6 filthy, soiled, swampy 7 swamped

bemoan

3 rue 4 wail, weep 6 bewail, grieve, lament, oppose, regret 7 deplore 8 complain, object to 10 sorrow over 12 disapprove of

bemuse

4 daze 5 addle 6 absorb, muddle, puzzle 7 confuse, mystify, nonplus, perplex 8 bewilder, distract 10 disconcert

bemused

3 wry 4 lost 6 absent, remote 7 faraway 8 distrait 9 distraite 10 abstracted, distracted 11 preoccupied 12 absentminded 13 lost in thought

bench

5 court 6 settee, settle, thwart 7 counter 8 platform 9 worktable
church: 3 pew
outdoor: 6 exedra
upholstered: 9 banquette

benchmark
4 norm 5 basis, gauge, guide, model, scale 7 measure 8 exemplar, paradigm, standard 9 criterion, guideline, milestone, yardstick 10 touchstone

bend
3 arc, bow, sag 4 arch, bank, cave, curl, flex, hang, hook, lean, mold, sway, tend, tilt, turn, veer, warp 5 angle, crook, curve, round, shape, shift, stoop, twist, yield 6 compel, corner, buckle, direct, double, fasten, kowtow, subdue, submit, zigzag 7 deflect, dispose, distort, flexure, turning 8 lean over 9 curvature, deviation, genuflect 10 compromise, predispose

bendable
5 lithe 6 limber, pliant, supple 7 elastic, plastic, pliable 8 flexible, moldable 9 malleable, tractable 11 manipulable

bender
see **binge**

_____ **bene**
4 nota

beneath
5 below, under
prefix: 3 hyp, sub 4 hypo 5 infra

_____ **Benedict**
4 eggs

benediction
4 boon, okay 5 favor, grace 6 orison, thanks 7 benefit, benison, godsend 8 approval, blessing 9 advantage 11 approbation 12 consecration, thanksgiving

benefaction
4 alms, care, fund, gift, help 5 favor, grant 6 relief 7 charity, comfort, handout, largess, service, subsidy 8 donation, largesse, oblation, offering, windfall 9 endowment, patronage 10 assistance 12 contribution, ministration

benefactor
5 angel, donor 6 backer, patron

7 grantor, sponsor 9 supporter, sustainer 11 contributor, underwriter

beneficence
see **benefaction**

beneficent
4 kind 6 benign, caring, giving 8 generous 10 altruistic, bighearted, charitable, ungrudging 11 kindhearted, magnanimous 13 compassionate, philanthropic

beneficial
4 good 5 brave, tonic 6 benign, toward, useful 7 helpful 8 favoring, salutary, valuable 9 favorable, healthful, nurturing, wholesome 10 profitable, propitious, salubrious 12 advantageous, constructive

beneficiary
4 heir 5 donee, payee 7 grantee, heiress, legatee 8 assignee 9 inheritor, recipient

beneficiate
5 treat 6 reduce 7 prepare, process

benefit
3 aid 4 boon, gain, good, help, perk, sake 5 avail, extra, favor, serve 6 assist, behalf, better, profit, relief, succor 7 account, advance, charity, further, godsend, improve, promote, relieve, welfare 8 blessing, interest 9 advantage, well-being 10 ameliorate, fund-raiser, prosperity 11 good fortune 12 contribute to

benevolence
4 boon, gift, help 5 amity, favor, grant 6 comity, relief 7 caritas, charity 8 altruism, clemency, goodness, goodwill, humanity, kindness 10 compassion, compliment, kindliness 11 magnanimity

benevolent
4 good, kind, warm 6 caring, dogood, humane, kindly 7 helpful, liberal 8 generous, tolerant 10 altruistic, beneficent, bighearted, charitable, openhanded 11 considerate, magnanimous, warmhearted

12 eleemosynary, humanitarian
13 compassionate, philanthropic,
tenderhearted

Ben Hur author
7 Wallace (Lew)

benighted
6 obtuse, unread 8 backward,
ignorant, untaught 9 untutored,
unwitting 10 illiterate, uneducated,
uninformed, unlettered, unschooled
11 know-nothing 12 uncultivated
13 unenlightened, unprogressive

benign
4 kind, mild 6 genial, gentle, humane,
kindly, mellow 7 amiable, clement
8 gracious, harmless, merciful, pleasant 9 favorable, fortunate, healthful,
temperate, wholesome 10 auspicious, benevolent, charitable, forbearing, propitious, remediable
11 good-hearted 12 noncancerous

Benin
capital: 9 Porto-Novo
city: 7 Cotonou
coast: 5 Slave
ethnic group: 3 Fon 6 Fulani,
Yoruba
former name: 7 Dahomey
language: 3 Fon 6 French
monetary unit: 5 franc
neighbor: 4 Togo 5 Niger 7 Nigeria
11 Burkina Faso
river: 5 Ouémé

benison
5 grace 8 blessing 11 benediction
12 consecration

Benjamin
brother: 6 Joseph
father: 5 Jacob
mother: 6 Rachel

bent
3 set 4 bias, gift 5 arced, bowed,
flair, knack 6 arched, curved, intent,
talent 7 decided, faculty, leaning
8 aptitude, capacity, penchant, resolute, resolved, tendency 10 determined, proclivity, propensity 11 disposition, inclination 12 predilection

benumb
4 daze, dull, stun 5 blunt, chill
6 deaden, freeze 7 petrify, stupefy
8 etherize, paralyze 10 immobilize
11 desensitize

benumbed
4 cold 6 frozen 9 unfeeling 10 insensible 11 insensitive 12 anesthetized

Beowulf
drink: 4 mead
monster: 7 Grendel

bequeath
4 gift, will 5 endow, grant, leave
6 bestow, commit, confer, devise,
hand on, impart, legate, pass on
7 furnish, present 8 hand down,
make over, transmit

bequest
3 lot 4 gift 5 share, trust 6 devise,
estate, legacy 7 portion 8 heritage
10 settlement 11 inheritance

berate
3 jaw 4 rail, rate 5 chide, scold
6 rebuke, revile 7 bawl out, chew
out, condemn, reprove, tell off, upbraid 8 admonish, chastise, reproach 9 castigate, criticize, reprimand 10 tongue-lash, vituperate

berceuse
7 lullaby 10 cradlesong

bereave
3 rob 4 lose 5 seize, strip 6 divest,
remove 7 deprive 8 take away
10 confiscate, disinherit, dispossess
11 appropriate, requisition

bereaved
8 mourning 9 sorrowful, sorrowing
10 distressed 11 heartbroken
13 grief-stricken

bereavement
3 rue, woe 4 loss 5 dolor, grief
6 misery, pining, regret, sorrow
7 anguish, despair, remorse, sadness 8 grieving, mourning 9 dejection, heartache 10 affliction, depression, desolation 11 deprivation,
despondency, lamentation, tribulation

bereft
5 shorn 6 devoid, robbed 7 fleeced, forlorn, wanting 8 beggared, deprived, desolate, divested, stripped 9 destitute 10 despondent 12 disconsolate, dispossessed, impoverished

Bergen's dummy
7 Charlie (McCarthy) 8 Mortimer (Snerd)

Berger novel
12 Little Big Man

Bergman role
4 Ilsa

berm
4 path 5 ledge, mound, shelf 8 shoulder

Bermuda
capital: 8 Hamilton
territory of: 7 Britain

Bernice
brother: 7 Agrippa
father: 5 Herod
husband: 6 Polemo
lover: 5 Titus 9 Vespasian

berry
5 cubeb, fruit, grape 7 currant, madrona, madrone 8 allspice 9 saskatoon

berserk
3 ape 4 amok 5 amuck, crazy 6 crazed, insane 7 bonkers, lunatic 8 demented, deranged, frenzied

berth
3 bed, cot 4 dock, moor, pier, port, post, quay, slip, spot 5 cabin, jetty, levee, place, wharf 6 billet, office 8 position 9 anchorage, situation 10 connection 11 appointment, compartment 13 accommodation

beseech
see **beg**

beset
3 dog, hem, try, vex 4 gird, ring 5 harry, hem in, storm, worry 6 assail, attack, badger, circle, fall on, harass, infest, pester, plague, strike 7 assault, besiege, overrun, trouble, torture 8 blockade, encircle, fall upon, surround 9 beleaguer, encompass, overswarm

besetment
3 nag 4 bane, pain, pest 5 curse, trial 6 blight, bother, gadfly, pester, plague 7 torment 8 irritant, nuisance, vexation 9 annoyance 10 affliction, botherment, holy terror 11 aggravation, botheration

besetting
6 urgent 7 driving 8 dominant 9 obsessive 10 compelling, persistent 11 omnipresent 12 overwhelming

beside
4 near, nigh 6 next to

besides
3 too 4 also, else, plus, save 5 added, extra 6 and all, as well, beyond, except, to boot 7 barring, farther, further, without 8 as well as, likewise, moreover, more than 9 aside from, along with, exceeding, excluding, other than, otherwise, outside of 10 in addition 11 exclusive of, furthermore, not counting 12 additionally, together with

besiege
3 nag 4 ring, trap 5 beset, hem in, hound 6 assail, attack, circle, girdle, harass, pester, plague 7 assault, confine, environ, trouble 8 blockade, encircle, surround 9 beleaguer, encompass

besmear
see **smear**

besmirch
4 blot, foul, slur, soil 5 dirty, libel, stain, sully, taint 6 defile, damage, impugn, malign 7 asperse, slander, tarnish 8 disgrace, dishonor

besom material
5 twigs

besotted
5 dotty, drunk 7 charmed, muddled,

smitten **8** enamored **9** enchanted
10 captivated, fascinated, infatuated,
spellbound **11** intoxicated

bespatter
see **spatter**

bespeak
3 ask **4** book, hire, show **5** imply
6 accost, attest, desire, evince,
reveal **7** address, apply to, betoken,
connote, lecture, portend, request,
reserve, signify, solicit, suggest,
testify, witness **8** announce, approach, foretell, indicate, intimate,
petition **9** preengage **10** prearrange

bespoke
8 tailored **10** custom-made

best
3 gem, top **4** beat, pick, tops **5** cream,
elite, excel, model, outdo, pride,
prime, prize **6** choice, defeat, exceed,
finest **7** conquer, leading, optimal,
optimum, paragon, premium, supreme, surpass **8** exemplar, foremost, greatest, nonesuch, outshine,
outstrip, overcome **9** matchless,
nonpareil, number-one, paramount,
transcend, unequaled **11** outstanding
12 incomparable
combining form: 6 aristo

bestial
4 vile, wild **5** brute, cruel, feral
6 animal, brutal, carnal, fierce,
malign, savage **7** beastly, brutish,
inhuman, swinish, vicious **8** depraved, inhumane **9** ferocious
10 degenerate

bestialize
4 ruin, warp **5** abase **6** debase,
defile **7** corrupt, debauch, degrade,
deprave, pervert, pollute, subvert,
vitiate, violate **9** brutalize **10** bastardize, demoralize

bestir
3 fly, rip **4** dash, flit, goad, race,
rush, spur, stir, tear, urge, wake,
whet **5** rally, rouse, scoot, waken,
whirl **6** arouse, awaken, hasten,
hustle, kindle **8** get going, scramble
9 challenge

bestow
4 give **5** apply, award, grant
6 confer, devote, donate, lavish
7 hand out, present **8** bequeath,
give away
Scottish: 7 propine

bestower
5 donor, giver **6** patron **7** donator
8 altruist **9** conferrer, patroness,
presenter **10** benefactor **12** bene-
factress **13** good Samaritan

bestrew
3 dot, sow **6** pepper, shower **7** diffuse, disject, scatter, speckle, stipple
8 disperse, sprinkle **9** broadcast,
interlard **10** distribute **11** disseminate

bestride
5 mount, tower **8** dominate, loom
over, straddle **9** stand over

bet
3 pot **4** ante, game, play, risk, shot
5 put on, stake, wager **6** gamble,
hazard, parlay, pledge **7** lay odds,
venture
racing: 6 exacta **8** perfecta,
quinella, quiniela
taker: 6 bookie

Betelgeuse
4 star
constellation: 5 Orion

betel palm
5 areca

bête noire
4 hate, ruin **5** trial **6** animus, horror
7 bugbear, scourge, torment, undoing **8** anathema, aversion, downfall
9 ruination **10** black beast

bethink
4 cite, mind **6** call up, recall, remind,
retain, review, revive **7** flash on
8 hark back, look back, remember,
summon up **9** conjure up, recollect,
reminisce **10** call to mind, retrospect

Bethuel
daughter: 7 Rebekah
father: 5 Nahor

mother: 6 Milcah
son: 5 Laban
uncle: 7 Abraham

betide
4 fall 5 break, ensue, occur 6 befall, chance, happen 7 come off, develop, fall out 8 commence 9 come about, transpire

betimes
4 anon, soon 5 early 6 pronto, seldom, timely 7 too soon 8 directly, far ahead, fitfully, promptly 9 presently 10 before long, now and then, on occasion, seasonably 11 prematurely 12 occasionally, sporadically

betoken
4 bode, omen, show, warn 5 argue, augur 6 attest, denote, hint at 7 bespeak, point to, portend, presage, promise, signify, suggest, testify, witness 8 announce, forebode, evidence, foreshow, foretell, indicate, intimate, prophesy 9 prefigure 10 foreshadow 13 prognosticate

betray
4 dupe, jilt, name, sell, show, tell, trap 5 bluff, cheat, knife, rat on, snare, spill, split 6 delude, desert, entrap, evince, finger, inform, reveal, seduce, take in, tattle, tell on, turn in, unmask, unveil 7 abandon, beguile, betoken, deceive, divulge, ensnare, forsake, let down, let slip, mislead, sell out, traduce, uncover 8 blurt out, denounce, disclose, discover, evidence, give away, indicate, manifest 9 deliver up 10 apostatize, break faith, lead astray 11 demonstrate, double-cross 13 inform against

betrayal
4 leak 7 perfidy, treason 8 exposure 9 duplicity, falseness, Judas kiss, treachery 10 disclosure, infidelity, revelation 13 faithlessness

betrayer
3 rat 4 fink, nark 5 Judas 6 snitch 7 stoolie, tattler, traitor 8 apostate, defector, informer, quisling, renegade, squealer, turncoat
10 talebearer, tattletale 11 backstabber, stool pigeon

betroth
3 wed 5 marry 6 pledge 7 espouse 8 affiance

betrothal
6 pledge 8 espousal 10 engagement

betrothed
6 fiancé 7 engaged, fiancée, pledged 8 intended, plighted, promised, wife-to-be 9 affianced, bride-to-be, spoken for 10 contracted 11 husband-to-be

better
3 fix, top, win 4 beat, help, mend, more, well 5 amend, cured, elder, excel, finer, outdo 6 exceed, fitter, repair 7 advance, correct, enhance, further, greater, improve, largest, mending, rectify, success, surpass, triumph, victory 8 greatest, improved, outshine, outstrip, stronger, superior, whip hand, worthier 9 advantage, desirable, excellent, healthier, improving, meliorate, preferred, transcend, upper hand 10 ameliorate, preferable, preferably, recovering, surpassing

bettor
7 gambler, wagerer

between
4 amid 5 among, twixt 6 within 7 betwixt
prefix: 5 inter, intra

betweentimes
11 at intervals

bevel
4 bias, cant 5 angle, grade, slant, slope 7 chamfer, incline, oblique 8 diagonal

beverage
3 ade, nog, pop, tea 4 cola, maté, milk, soda 5 cider, cocoa, drink, juice, mocha, shake 6 coffee, eggnog, frappe, malted, nectar 7 potable, soda pop 8 lemonade, libation, potation 9 drinkable, milk shake

alcoholic: 3 ale, gin, rum 4 beer, grog, mead, wine 5 cider, julep, negus, punch, stout, toddy, vodka 6 bishop, brandy, caudle, cooler, liquor, rickey, shandy, sherry, whisky 7 liqueur, martini, sangria, tequila, whiskey 8 cocktail, highball, sillabub, syllabub, vermouth
Arab: 4 arak 6 arrack
Australasian: 4 kava
Balkan: 9 slivovitz
British: 5 perry, stout
carbonated: 4 cola, soda 6 rickey 7 soda pop 8 root beer 9 ginger ale
central Asian: 6 kumiss 7 koumiss
Dutch: 7 schnaps 8 schnapps
from milk: 5 kefir 6 kumiss 7 koumiss
Greek: 4 ouzo 7 retsina
Irish: 6 poteen 10 usquebaugh
medicinal: 6 elixir
Mexican: 6 pulque 7 tequila
of the gods: 6 nectar
Oriental: 4 arak, sake, saki 6 arrack
Russian: 5 kefir, kvass, vodka
Scottish: 6 scotch
South American: 4 maté 5 yerba 9 yerba maté
Swedish: 5 glogg
Turkish: 4 raki
West Indies: 3 rum

bevy
3 mob 4 band, club, crew, gang, herd, knot, pack 5 bunch, covey, crowd, drove, flock, group, horde, party, swarm 6 clutch, gaggle, troupe 7 cluster, company, coterie 8 assembly 9 menagerie, multitude 10 assemblage, collection

bewail
3 rue 4 keen, moan, weep 5 mourn 6 bemoan, grieve, lament, regret 7 deplore

beware
4 heed, mark, mind, note, shun 5 avoid, watch 6 attend, notice 7 look out 8 take heed, watch out

bewhiskered
5 bushy 7 bearded, goateed, hirsute, stubbly 8 unshaven

bewilder
3 fog 4 daze, stun 5 addle, amaze, befog, mix up, stump 6 baffle, ball up, bemuse, fuddle, muddle, puzzle, rattle 7 confuse, fluster, mystify, nonplus, perplex, stumble 8 befuddle, confound, distract 9 disorient, dumbfound 10 disconcert

bewilderment
3 awe 4 daze 6 wonder 8 surprise 9 amazement, confusion 10 perplexity, puzzlement 11 distraction 12 astonishment, discomfiture, stupefaction 13 consternation

bewitch
3 hex 4 draw, pull, snow, take, wile 5 charm, spell, trick 6 allure, dazzle, seduce, voodoo 7 attract, bedevil, beguile, control, delight, enchant, possess 8 demonize, ensorcel, enthrall, entrance, intrigue, overlook 9 captivate, enrapture, ensorcell, fascinate, hypnotize, magnetize, mesmerize, spellbind

bewitching
4 foxy 5 siren 8 alluring, charming, engaging, enticing, magnetic, mesmeric 9 seductive 10 attractive 12 irresistible

bewitchment
3 hex 4 jinx 5 charm, magic, spell 6 trance 7 evil eye, sorcery 8 black art, wizardry 9 conjuring 10 necromancy 11 conjuration, enchantment, incantation, thaumaturgy

beyond
4 over, past 5 above, after 6 across, beside, yonder 7 besides, further, outside 8 as well as 9 afterlife, hereafter, otherwise 10 afterworld 12 over and above
prefix: 4 meta, over, para 5 extra, hyper, super, trans, ultra 6 preter

Bhutan
capital: 7 Thimphu
ethnic group: 6 Bhutia 8 Assamese, Nepalese 9 Mongolian, Sharcrops
language: 8 Dzongkha

monetary unit: 8 ngultrum
mountain range: 8 Himalaya
13 Great Himalaya
neighbor: 5 China, India, Tibet
plain: 5 Duars

bias

4 bend, bent, skew, sway, tilt, turn
5 angle, bevel, slant 7 beveled, bigotry, dispose, distort, incline, leaning,
oblique, slanted 8 diagonal, penchant, slanting, tendency 9 crosswise, inclining, influence, prejudice,
proneness, viewpoint 10 diagonally,
favoritism, partiality, propensity,
predispose, prepossess, proclivity,
standpoint, transverse 11 disposition,
inclination 12 one-sidedness, predilection 13 preconception

biased

6 racist, swayed, unfair, warped
7 bigoted, colored, partial, slanted
8 disposed, inclined, one-sided,
partisan, slanting 9 jaundiced, sectarian, unneutral 10 influenced,
interested, prejudiced 11 opinionated, predisposed, tendentious

bibelot

5 curio 6 bauble, gewgaw, trifle
7 memento, novelty, trinket, whatnot
8 gimcrack, ornament 9 objet d'art
10 knickknack

Bible -

abbreviation: 3 Col, Cor, Dan,
Eph, Gal, Gen, Hab, Heb, Hos, Jas,
Jer, Jon, Lam, Lev, Mal, Mic, Neh,
Num, Pet, Rev, Rom, Sam, Tim, Tit
4 Deut, Ezek, Josh, Judg, Obad,
Phil, Prov, Zech, Zeph 5 Chron,
Thess 6 Eccles, Philem
Apocrypha book: 5 Tobit
6 Baruch, Esdras, Esther, Judith
7 Susanna 8 Manasseh, Manasses
9 Maccabees
New Testament book: 4 Acts, John,
Jude, Luke, Mark 5 James, Peter,
Titus 6 Romans 7 Hebrews, Matt-
hew, Timothy 8 Philemon 9 Ephe-
sians, Galatians 10 Colossians,
Revelation 11 Corinthians, Philippi-
ans 13 Thessalonians

Old Testament book: 3 Job
4 Amos, Ezra, Joel, Ruth 5 Hosea,
Jonah, Kings, Micah, Nahum
6 Daniel, Esther, Exodus, Haggai,
Isaiah, Joshua, Judges, Psalms,
Samuel 7 Ezekiel, Genesis, Malachi,
Numbers, Obadiah 8 Habakkuk,
Jeremiah, Nehemiah, Proverbs
9 Leviticus, Zechariah, Zephaniah
10 Chronicles 11 Deuteronomy
12 Ecclesiastes, Lamentations
13 Song of Solomon
part: 4 book 5 verse 7 chapter
9 testament
translator: 4 Knox (Ronald Arbuth-
nott) 5 Eliot (John) 6 Jerome, Luther
(Martin) 7 Erasmus (Desiderius),
Tyndale (William), Zwingli (Huldrych)
8 Andrewes (Lancelot), Wycliffe
(John) 9 Coverdale (Miles)
version: 5 Douay 6 Coptic, Gothic,
Syriac 7 Vulgate 9 Jerusalem, King
James, Masoretic 10 New English,
Septuagint

Biblical

animal: 8 behemoth
ascetic order: 6 Essene
battle: 7 Jericho
battle site: 10 Armageddon
charioteer: 4 Jehu
city, town: 4 Cana, Gaza, Tyre, Zoar
5 Endor, Golan, Haifa, Joppa, Sidon,
Sodom 6 Asshur, Bethel, Emmaus,
Gilgal, Hebron, Mizpah, Shiloh,
Smyrna, Tarsus 7 Antioch, Baalbec,
Bethany, Corinth, Ephesus, Ephraim,
Jericho, Magdala, Nineveh, Samaria
8 Caesarea, Damascus, Gomorrah,
Nazareth, Philippi, Tiberias 9 Beer-
sheba, Bethlehem, Capernaum,
Jerusalem
coin:
(see at **Hebrew**)
desert: 5 Sinai
garden: 4 Eden 8 Paradise
giant: 7 Goliath
giant slayer: 5 David
hill: 4 Zion 7 Calvary
hunter: 6 Nimrod
judge: 3 Eli 4 Ehud 6 Gideon,
Samson, Samuel 7 Deborah, Jephtha 8 Jephthah

king: 3 Asa 4 Ahab, Amon, Elah, Jehu, Saul 5 David, Herod, Hiram 6 Josiah 7 Azariah, Menahem, Solomon 8 Hezekiah, Jeroboam, Manasseh, Rehoboam, Zedekiah 9 Zechariah 11 Jehoshaphat

land: 3 Nod 4 Aram, Elam, Moab, Seba 5 Judah, Judea 6 Canaan, Goshen, Israel 7 Chaldea, Galilee, Samaria 9 Palestine

land of plenty: 6 Goshen

measure:
(see at **Hebrew**)

mountain: 5 Horeb, Sinai 6 Ararat, Carmel, Gilboa, Gilead, Hermon, Moriah, Olivet, Pisgah 7 Lebanon

name: 3 Asa, Bel, Dan, Eli, Eve, Gad, Ham, Ira, Job, Lot, Uri 4 Abel, Adam, Ahab, Amon, Boaz, Cain, Elam, Enos, Esau, Jael, Jehu, Joel, John, Lael, Leah, Levi, Mark, Mary, Mica, Moab, Noah, Omar, Onan, Paul, Reba, Ruth, Sara, Saul, Seth, Shem 5 Aaron, Abner, Amram, Asher, Caleb, David, Dinah, Elias, Enoch, Ethan, Hagar, Heman, Herod, Hosea, Isaac, Jacob, James, Jared, Jesse, Jonah, Jubal, Judah, Judas, Laban, Micah, Moses, Naomi, Peter, Rufus, Sarah, Sheba, Simon, Tamar, Tubal, Uriah, Uriel, Zadok 6 Ashhur, Balaam, Baruch, Canaan, Daniel, Elijah, Elisha, Esther, Gideon, Gilead, Hannah, Hebron, Isaiah, Israel, Jeshua, Jethro, Joanna, Joseph, Joshua, Josiah, Judith, Martha, Miriam, Nathan, Nimrod, Pasach, Philip, Pilate, Rachel, Reuben, Salome, Samson, Samuel, Simeon, Thomas, Tobias

patriarch:
(see at **Hebrew**)

people: 6 Kenite, Levite 7 Amorite, Edomite, Elamite, Moabite 9 Israelite

plains: 6 Sharon 7 Jericho

plotter: 5 Haman

poem: 5 psalm

pool: 8 Bethesda

priest: 3 Eli 4 Levi 5 Aaron, Annas 8 Caiaphas

Promised Land: 6 Canaan

pronoun: 3 thy 4 thee, thou 5 thine

prophet:
(see **prophet**)

Psalmist: 5 David

punishment: 7 stoning

queen: 5 Sheba 6 Esther 7 Jezebel

river: 4 Nile 6 Jordan

sacred object: 4 urim 7 thummin

scribe: 6 Baruch

sea: 3 Red 4 Dead 7 Galilee

sea monster: 9 Leviathan

spice: 5 aloes, myrrh 6 cassia 7 calamus 8 cinnamon 12 frankincense

spy: 5 Caleb

temptress: 3 Eve 7 Delilah

thief: 8 Barabbas

tree: 5 cedar

valley: 4 Baca, Elah 6 Hinnon, Kidron, Shaveh, Siddim

witch's home: 5 Endor

bibliography

4 list 7 catalog, history 8 book list 13 reference list

bibliopole

7 bookman 10 book dealer, bookseller

bibulous

6 spongy 7 thirsty 8 drinking 9 absorbent 10 absorptive

bicker

3 row 4 spar, spat, tiff 5 argue, clack, fight, scrap 6 gurgle, hassle 7 brabble, clatter, contend, dispute, fall out, flicker, quarrel, quibble, wrangle 8 squabble

bickering

3 row 4 spat 5 brawl, run-in 6 blowup, fracas, hassle, ruckus, rumpus, strife 7 discord, dispute, quarrel, rhubarb, wrangle 8 squabble 11 altercation, embroilment

bicycle

4 bike

brake: 7 caliper, coaster

for two: 6 tandem

gear shift: 10 derailleur

rider: 6 cycler 7 cyclist

bid
3 ask, say, try 4 call, tell, warn, wish
5 essay, greet, offer, order 6 amount,
charge, direct, effort, enjoin, invite,
render, summon, tender 7 attempt,
command, proffer, request, require,
venture 8 endeavor, instruct, proposal 10 invitation, submission
11 proposition

biddable
4 mild 6 docile, pliant 7 amiable,
pliable, willing 8 amenable, obedient, obliging 9 tractable 10 gov-
ernable, manageable 11 acquiescent, cooperative, good-natured
13 accommodating

bidding
4 call, word 5 offer, order 6 behest,
charge, demand, notice, tender
7 auction, command, dictate, mandate, request, summons 9 ordinance, summoning 10 injunction,
invitation 11 commandment, instruction 12 proclamation

biddy
3 bag, bat, hag, hen 4 drab, trot
5 crone, witch 6 beldam 7 chicken

bide
4 live, stay, wait 5 await, dwell, tarry
6 hang in, linger, remain, reside
7 hang out, sojourn 8 continue,
sit tight, tolerate 10 hang around
11 stick around

bier
10 catafalque

biff
3 bop, box, hit, jab, zap 4 bash, belt,
blow, clip, ding, nail, slam, slug, sock,
swat, whop 5 blast, catch, clout,
pound, slosh, smack, thump, whack
6 strike, thwack, wallop

bifurcate
3 cut 4 fork 5 halve, split 6 bisect,
branch, cleave, divide 8 separate
9 branch out 11 dichotomize, dichot-
omous

bifurcation
4 fork 6 branch 8 division

9 dichotomy, partition, radiation
10 separation

big
3 fat 4 full, hard, huge, main, tall,
vast 5 adult, ample, chief, great,
grown, heavy, hefty, husky, large,
lofty, major, proud, roomy 6 bumper,
hugely 7 capital, copious, crammed,
crowded, eminent, grown-up, hulking, leading, liberal, mammoth,
massive, monster, notable, popular,
replete, sizable, stuffed, swollen,
weighty 8 colossal, enormous,
generous, gracious, imposing,
inflated, material, oversize, princely,
spacious, swelling 9 capacious,
chock-full, distended, extensive,
heavy duty, humongous, important,
momentous, overblown, paramount,
ponderous, principal, prominent, unselfish 10 commodious, large-scale,
preeminent, prodigious, voluminous
11 heavyweight, magnanimous,
major-league, overflowing, significant, substantial 12 considerable
13 comprehensive, consequential

big bang theorist
5 Gamow (George)

Big Bertha's birthplace
5 Essen

Big ____, Cal.
3 Sur

Big Dipper
constellation: 9 Ursa Major
star: 5 Alcor, Dubhe, Merak, Mizar

bigfoot
9 Sasquatch

biggety
4 bold, vain, wise 5 fresh, nervy,
sassy 6 cheeky, snippy, snooty,
uppity 7 forward, stuck-up 8 impudent, insolent, puffed up, snobbish
9 conceited 11 smart-alecky 13 self-
important

bighearted
6 giving 7 liberal 8 generous
9 forgiving 10 altruistic, benevolent,
charitable, munificent, openhanded
11 magnanimous 13 compassionate

big house
3 can, jug, pen 4 coop, jail 5 clink, joint 6 cooler, lockup, prison 7 slammer 8 bastille, hoosegow, stockade 9 bridewell 11 reformatory 12 penitentiary

bight
3 arm, bay 4 cove, gulf 6 harbor

bigmouthed
4 loud, rude 8 boastful 10 boisterous

bigness
4 size 5 scale, scope 6 extent, volume 9 amplitude, immensity, magnitude 10 dimensions, importance

bigot
6 racist 8 jingoist 9 extremist, racialist 10 chauvinist 11 supremacist

bigoted
6 biased, narrow, unfair 9 hidebound, illiberal, sectarian 10 brassbound, intolerant, prejudiced 11 smallminded 12 narrow-minded

bigotry
4 bias 6 racism 9 apartheid, prejudice 10 xenophobia 11 intolerance

big shot
3 VIP 4 czar 5 celeb, mogul, nabob 6 bigwig, fat cat, tycoon 7 kingpin, notable, pooh-bah 8 higher-up, luminary, top brass 9 celebrity, dignitary, personage 13 high-muck-a-muck

big-time
5 major 7 eminent, greatly, leading 8 renowned 9 high-level, important, paramount, prominent 10 largescale 11 influential, major-league

big top
4 tent 6 circus

bigwig
3 VIP 5 heavy, mogul, nabob 6 honcho, kahuna 7 kingpin, magnate, notable 8 luminary, somebody 9 dignitary, personage 11 heavy hitter, muckety-muck 13 high-muck-a-muck

bijou
3 gem 5 jewel 8 gemstone

bijouterie
6 jewels 7 jewelry 8 trinkets 10 decoration

bike
5 cycle 7 scooter 10 motorcycle 12 motorscooter

bilge
3 rot 4 bull, bunk, guff 5 hooey, trash 6 bunkum 7 baloney, garbage, hogwash, malarky, rubbish, twaddle 8 claptrap, nonsense 9 poppycock, silliness 10 balderdash 11 foolishness

bilk
3 con, gyp 4 balk, beat, dash, duck, dupe, foil, fool, hoax, hose, kite, milk, ruin, scam, take 5 avoid, cheat, cozen, dodge, elude, evade, shake, shaft, skirt, stiff, trick 6 baffle, chisel, chouse, diddle, double, escape, eschew, fleece, rip off, sucker, thwart 7 deceive, defraud, prevent, swindle 8 flimflam, hoodwink, sidestep, stave off 9 frustrate 10 circumvent

bill
3 dun, fin, neb, nib, tab 4 beak, bone, buck, chit, list, note, skin 5 check, score, visor 6 charge, damage, dollar, notice, poster, roster 7 account, charges, invoice, placard, program, sawbuck, smacker 8 mandible 9 greenback, reckoning, smackeroo, statement

billet
3 bar, bed, gig, hut, job, rod 4 post, slab, spar, spot 5 berth, board, house, ingot, lodge, place, put up, stick, strip 6 bestow, canton, harbor, office 7 quarter 8 domicile, position, quarters, vocation 9 entertain, situation 10 assignment, connection, employment, encampment, livelihood, profession, occupation 11 appointment

billet-doux
8 mash note 10 love letter

billfold
6 wallet

billiards term
3 cue 4 foot, head, jaws, kiss, long, peas, pool, race, rack, spot 5 break, carom, chalk, count, masse 6 bridge, cannon, corner, crotch, inning, miscue, nurses, pocket, stance, string 7 bricole, cue ball, ferrule, kitchen, pyramid, scratch, shooter, snooker 8 apex ball, balkline, bank shot, cue stick, dead ball, jump shot, rotation, triangle 9 clean bank, eight ball 10 chuck nurse, head string, object ball 12 balance point

billingsgate
5 abuse 6 tirade 7 obloquy 9 contumely, invective 10 revilement, scurrility 12 vilification, vituperation

billion
British: 8 milliard
combining form: 4 giga

billionth
combining form: 4 nano

bill of fare
4 menu 7 program 11 carte du jour

billow
4 mass, wave 5 bulge, cloud, surge, swell 6 puff up, roller 7 balloon, upsurge

Billy Budd's captain
4 Vere

billy club
4 cane 5 baton 6 cudgel, paddle 8 bludgeon 9 bastinado, truncheon 10 knobkerrie, nightstick

bin
4 crib 5 frame, stall 6 bunker, hamper, trough 9 container 10 receptacle

binary
4 twin, dual 5 duple 6 double, duplex, paired 7 coupled, matched, twofold 9 dualistic

bind
3 tie 4 frap, gird, tape, wrap 5 chain, cinch, strap, tie up, truss 6 cement, commit, fasten, fetter, ligate, pinion 7 bandage, confine, enchain, shackle, trammel 8 enfetter, restrain 9 constrain, constrict, indenture

binder
4 file 5 cover 6 folder, jacket 7 wrapper

binding
8 required 9 mandatory, requisite 10 obligatory

bindlestiff
4 hobo

binge
3 jag 4 orgy, riot, soak, tear, time, toot 5 blast, booze, fling, party, revel, souse, spree, stint 6 bender 7 blowoff, blowout, carouse, debauch, rampage, revelry, shindig, splurge, surfeit, wassail 8 carousal, gluttony 9 bacchanal, brannigan 10 debauchery, indulgence 11 bacchanalia, celebration 12 intemperance

bingo
3 yes 5 beano 7 correct

biographer
American: 5 Weems (Parson) 6 Parton (James) 7 Freeman (Douglas) 8 Bradford (Gamaliel), Sandburg (Carl) 10 McCullough (David)
English: 6 Aubrey (John), Morley (John), Walton (Izaak) 8 Strachey (Lytton)
French: 7 Maurois (André)
German: 6 Ludwig (Emil)
Greek: 8 Plutarch
Italian: 6 Vasari (Giorgio)
Roman: 9 Suetonius
Scottish: 7 Boswell (James)

biography
3 bio 4 life, obit, vita 5 diary, story 6 memoir 7 history, profile 8 obituary 11 confessions

biological category
5 class, genus, order 6 family, phylum 7 kingdom, species, variety 10 subspecies

bionomics
7 ecology

Bip's creator
7 Marceau (Marcel)

bird
African: 6 barbet, bulbul, jabiru, turaco 7 courser, marabou, ostrich, touraco 8 hornbill, oxpecker, parakeet 9 broadbill, francolin
Antarctic: 4 skua 7 penguin 10 sheathbill
aquatic: 3 auk, mew 4 coot, duck, erne, gull, loon, skua, swan, teal, tern 5 booby, cahow, goose, grebe, murre 6 fulmar, gannet, petrel, puffin, scoter, wigeon 7 anhinga, dovekie, mallard, moorhen, pelican, penguin, skimmer, widgeon 8 baldpate, dabchick, murrelet 9 albatross, cormorant, gallinule, guillemot, kittiwake 10 shearwater, sheathbill
arctic: 3 auk 4 knot, skua 5 murre 6 fulmar, jaeger 7 dovekie 9 guillemot, gyrfalcon
Asian: 4 myna, ruff, smew 5 mynah, pewit 6 chukar, drongo, dunlin, hoopoe, peewit 7 courser, lapwing, peacock 8 dotterel, hornbill, parakeet, tragopan, wheatear 9 francolin
Australian: 3 emu 4 lory 5 galah 6 drongo 7 bustard 8 bellbird, cockatoo, lorikeet, lyrebird, parakeet 9 cassowary
blackbird: 3 ani, daw 4 crow, rook 5 merle, ousel, ouzel, raven 6 chough, magpie, thrush 7 grackle, jackdaw, redwing
carrion-eating: 6 condor 7 buzzard, vulture
Central American: 4 guan, ibis 5 booby, macaw 6 barbet, jabiru, toucan 7 bittern, jacamar, quetzal, tinamou 8 curassow, troupial
chimney-nesting: 5 swift
class: 4 Aves
colony: 5 roost 7 rookery
combining form: 5 ornis 6 ornith 7 ornitho 8 ornithes (plural)
crow family: 3 daw, jay 4 rook 5 raven 6 chough, corbie, magpie 7 jackdaw
diving: 3 auk 4 smew 5 grebe, murre 6 petrel 8 murrelet 9 guillemot, merganser

European: 3 mew 4 rook, smew, wren 5 crake, egret, finch, merle, ousel, ouzel, pewit, pipit 6 cuckoo, hoopoe, linnet, martin, merlin, redleg, thrush 7 bustard, jackdaw, kestrel, lapwing, martlet, ortolan, redwing, sparrow, wagtail 8 blackcap, dabchick, nightjar, nuthatch, redstart, starling, throstle, whimbrel, woodcock 9 chaffinch, crossbill, stonechat 10 chiffchaff, goatsucker, kingfisher 11 lammergeier
extinct: 3 moa 4 dodo 9 aepyornis, solitaire
fabulous: 3 roc 7 phoenix
fish-eating: 4 erne 6 osprey
flightless: 3 emu, moa 4 dodo, kiwi, rhea 6 kakapo, ratite, takahe 7 apteryx, ostrich, penguin 9 cassowary
game: 4 duck, rail, teal 5 brant, goose, quail, snipe 6 chukar, grouse, turkey 7 bustard, mallard, pintail, widgeon 8 baldpate, bobwhite, moorfowl, pheasant, shoveler, tragopan, wildfowl, woodcock 9 merganser, partridge, ptarmigan
ground-dwelling: 5 quail 6 grouse, peahen, turkey 7 chicken, peacock, peafowl 8 bobwhite, moorfowl, pheasant 9 partridge, ptarmigan
Indian: 6 bulbul 7 peacock 8 adjutant, tragopan
Jamaican: 7 vervain
large: 3 emu, moa 5 eagle 6 curlew 7 bustard, ostrich, pelican 8 curassow, shoebill
largest: 7 ostrich
Madagascar: 6 drongo 7 anhinga
marsh: 4 coot, rail 5 crane, snipe, stilt 9 gallinule
Mexican: 6 jacana
mythical: 3 roc 7 phoenix
New Zealand: 3 kea 4 kiwi 6 kakapo 7 apteryx
nocturnal: 3 owl 5 owlet 7 oilbird 8 guacharo, nightjar 9 nighthawk 10 goatsucker
North American: 3 ani, tit 4 coot, wren 5 booby, crane, egret, junco, murre, robin, swift, veery, vireo 6 dunlin, fulmar, grouse, phoebe,

towhee, turkey, verdin, willet **7** anhinga, blue jay, catbird, flicker, grackle, tanager **8** bobolink, bobwhite, cardinal, killdeer, nuthatch, thrasher, titmouse **9** chickadee, crossbill, nighthawk, partridge, snakebird **10** bufflehead **12** whippoorwill

of Arabian Nights: 3 roc

of brilliant plumage: 4 lory **5** macaw **6** oriole, parrot, toucan, trogon **7** jacamar **8** lorikeet, parakeet, pheasant, tragopan

of peace: 4 dove

of prey: 3 owl **4** hawk, kite **5** buteo, eagle, harpy **6** condor, falcon, osprey, raptor **7** buzzard, goshawk, harrier, kestrel, vulture **8** caracara **9** accipiter **11** lammergeier

passerine:
(see **songbird** below)

razorbilled: 3 auk

relating to: 5 avian **8** ornithic

shore: 3 auk **4** gull, tern **5** snipe, stilt **6** avocet, curlew, dunlin, plover, puffin, willet **7** lapwing, skimmer **8** killdeer, whimbrel, woodcock **9** phalarope, sandpiper, turnstone

small: 3 tit **4** wren **5** finch, pewee, pipit, vireo **6** canary, tomtit, verdin **7** sparrow **8** titmouse **9** chickadee

songbird: 3 jay, tit **4** chat, crow, lark, wren **5** finch, pipit, robin, veery, vireo **6** bulbul, canary, linnet, oriole, shrike, thrush **7** catbird, creeper, kinglet, redwing, skylark, sparrow, swallow, tanager, titlark, wagtail, warbler, waxwing **8** bobolink, brantail, cardinal, nuthatch, Philomel, redstart, starling, thrasher, woodlark **9** chickadee, stonechat **10** chiffchaff, flycatcher **11** nightingale

South American: 4 guan, loro, rhea **5** egret, macaw **6** jabiru, toucan **7** jacamar, limpkin, oilbird **8** caracara, curassow, guacharo, screamer, troupial **9** trumpeter

talking: 4 myna **5** mynah **6** parrot

tropical: 3 ani **6** barbet, drongo, toucan, trogon **7** jacamar, quetzal, sawbill, waxbill **8** troupial

turkey-like: 8 curassow

unfledged: 4 eyas **5** chick **8** nestling

wading: 4 ibis, rail **5** crane, egret, heron, stork **6** godwit, jabiru, jacana **7** bittern, limpkin, tattler **8** flamingo, shoebill **9** spoonbill

web-footed: 3 auk **4** duck, loon, swan **5** goose, murre **6** avocet, fulmar, gannet, petrel, puffin **7** anhinga, pelican, penguin **8** shoveler **9** albatross, cormorant, guillemot, merganser, razorbill, snakebird **10** shearwater

West Indian: 3 ani

birdbrain
4 dodo, goof **5** dummy, dunce, idiot, moron, ninny **6** nitwit **7** airhead, dullard, halfwit **8** dumbbell, imbecile, meathead, numskull **9** dumb bunny, ignoramus, numbskull, simpleton **10** nincompoop **11** featherhead

birdcage
6 aviary

birdlife
8 avifauna

bird pepper
9 chiltepin

birds' eggs
study of: 6 oology

birth
4 dawn, stem **5** arise, issue, onset, start **6** create, outset, spring **7** emanate, genesis, lineage, opening **8** delivery, generate, geniture, nascence, nascency, nativity, pedigree **9** beginning, originate **10** extraction **11** parturition **12** commencement

birth-control leader
6 Sanger (Margaret)

birth flower
April: 5 daisy
August: 9 gladiolus
December: 10 poinsettia
February: 8 primrose
January: 9 carnation
July: 8 sweet pea

birthmark

June: **4** rose
March: **6** violet
May: **15** lily of the valley
November: **13** chrysanthemum
October: **6** dahlia
September: **5** aster

birthmark
4 mole **5** nevus, point, trait **7** feature
13 discoloration

Birth of a Nation director
8 Griffith (D. W.)

birthright
3 due, lot **6** legacy **7** bequest,
portion **8** appanage, heirloom,
heritage **9** patrimony **11** entitlement,
inheritance

birthroot
8 trillium

birthstone
April: **7** diamond **8** sapphire
August: **7** peridot **8** sardonyx
December: **6** zircon **9** turquoise
February: **8** amethyst
January: **6** garnet
July: **4** ruby
June: **5** agate, pearl **11** alexandrite
March: **6** jasper **10** aquamarine,
bloodstone
May: **7** emerald
November: **5** topaz
October: **4** opal **10** tourmaline
September: **8** sapphire **10** chrysolite

biscuit
4 rusk, snap **6** cookie **7** cracker
8 cracknel, hardtack

bishop
district: **7** diocese
headdress: **5** miter, mitre
seat of office: **3** see
skullcap: **9** zucchetto
staff: **7** crosier, crozier
throne: **8** cathedra

bishopric
3 see **7** diocese

bison
European: **6** wisent **7** aurochs
family: **7** Bovidae
North American: **7** buffalo

bistered
4 dark **5** brown, dusky, swart, tawny
6 brunet, tanned **7** swarthy **8** brunette **11** dark-skinned

bistro
3 bar, pub **4** café **5** joint **6** nitery,
tavern **7** barroom, cabaret, hot
spot, niterie, taproom **8** snack bar
9 coffee bar, nightclub, night spot
10 coffee shop **11** rathskeller
13 watering place

bit
3 dab, dot, end, jot, tad **4** atom,
dash, drop, iota, lump, mite, part,
rein, tick, time, whet **5** borer, flake,
grain, minim, pinch, scrap, shard,
shred, slice, space, speck, spell,
trace, while **6** minute, moment,
morsel, rather, second **7** portion,
segment, smidgen, stretch, trickle
8 fraction, fragment, molecule,
mouthful, particle, somewhat

bit by bit
6 evenly **9** by degrees, gradually,
piecemeal **12** continuously **13** slow
and steady

bitch goddess
7 success

bite
3 cut, eat, lot, nip **4** chaw, chew,
edge, etch, food, gnaw, kick, meal,
pain, part, rust, snap, tapa, zest
5 champ, chomp, erode, munch,
piece, quota, share, slice, snack,
stink, taste, tooth **6** crunch, morsel,
nibble **7** corrode, portion, eat away, eat into,
engrave, portion **8** dissolve, mouthful, piquancy **9** allotment, allowance,
masticate, occlusion **10** laceration
11 refreshment

biting
3 raw **4** cold **5** bleak, crisp, harsh,
nippy, sharp **6** bitter, severe **7** acerbic, caustic, cutting, mordant, satiric
8 freezing, incisive, piercing, scathing **9** sarcastic, trenchant **11** penetrating

bitter
4 acid, tart **5** acerb, acrid, harsh,

sharp **6** severe **7** acerbic, caustic, galling, hostile, painful **8** grievous, ruthless, virulent **9** rancorous, vexatious, vitriolic **11** acrimonious, unpalatable **12** antagonistic

bitterness
4 gall **6** rancor **7** ill will **8** acridity, acrimony, asperity, coldness **9** animosity, antipathy **10** resentment

bittersweet
4 vine **8** poignant **10** nightshade

bitumen
3 tar **5** pitch **7** asphalt **8** blacktop

bivalve
4 clam, spat **6** cockle, mussel, oyster **7** geoduck, mollusk, piddock, scallop **9** lampshell **10** brachiopod

bivouac
4 camp, tent **6** billet, encamp, laager, maroon **7** shelter, sojourn **10** encampment

bizarre
3 odd **5** antic, queer, weird **7** curious, oddball, strange, uncanny, unusual **8** abnormal, atypical, freakish, peculiar, quixotic, singular **9** anomalous, eccentric, fantastic, grotesque, unearthly, unnatural **10** outlandish, outrageous **11** extravagant

bizarrerie
5 freak **6** oddity **7** anomaly, caprice, oddness **9** curiosity, weirdness **10** aberration

Bizet opera
6 Carmen

blab
3 gab, gas, jaw, yak **4** chat, leak, talk, tell **5** run on, spill **6** babble, betray, burble, gabble, gossip, inform, jabber, reveal, snitch, squeal, tattle, tell on, yammer **7** blather, chatter, divulge, let slip, palaver, prattle **8** blurt out, disclose, give away, go public

blabber
3 gab, rat **4** chat, fink **5** clack, drool,

prate **6** babble, canary, drivel, gabber, gabble, gossip, jabber, magpie, prater, ramble **7** blather, chatter, palaver, prattle, twaddle **8** idle talk, jabberer, prattler **9** chatterer **10** chatterbox, tattletale

blabbermouth
3 rat **4** fink **6** canary, gabber, gossip, magpie, prater, snitch **7** windbag **8** busybody, jabberer, prattler **10** chatterbox, talebearer, tattletale **11** stool pigeon

black
3 jet **4** ebon, inky, noir, onyx **5** ebony, raven, sable **6** pitchy **8** charcoal, funereal **9** pitch-dark **combining form: 3** mel **4** atro, mela, melo **5** melam, melan **6** melano

blackball
3 bar **4** veto, shun, snub **5** block, spurn **6** ice out, refuse, reject, strike **7** boycott, exclude, keep out, rule out **9** interdict, ostracize **11** vote against

black bass
7 sunfish

black beast
see **bête noire**

Black Beauty author
6 Sewell (Anna)

blackbird
see **bird**

black cohosh
7 bugbane

black crappie
7 sunfish **10** calico bass

black death
6 plague **13** bubonic plague

black diamond
4 coal **8** hematite **9** carbonado

blacken
3 dim, fog, ink **4** blot, burn, char, sear, slur, soil, soot **5** cloud, libel, shade, singe, smear, sully, taint **6** bruise, darken, defame, defile, malign, scorch, vilify **7** asperse,

black eye
cloud up, eclipse, slander, traduce
8 besmirch, dishonor 10 calumniate

black eye
4 blot, onus, slur 5 stain 6 bruise,
defeat, shiner, stigma 7 setback

blackfish
5 whale 6 tautog 10 pilot whale

Black Forest
11 Schwarzwald
city: 10 Baden-Baden
peak: 8 Feldberg
river: 5 Rhein, Rhine 6 Danube,
Neckar

black gold
3 oil 9 petroleum

blackguard
4 heel, punk 5 abuse, cheat, knave,
rogue 6 rascal 7 hoodlum, lowlife,
ruffian, villain 8 hooligan, scalawag
9 charlatan, miscreant, reprobate,
scoundrel 10 delinquent, mountebank 11 rapscallion

blackhead
3 zit 4 spot 5 sebum 6 pimple
10 larval clam

blackjack
3 oak, sap 4 bash, club, cosh
6 coerce 7 pontoon, tankard
8 bludgeon 9 twenty-one, vingt-et-un
10 sphalerite

black lead
8 graphite

black letter
6 Gothic 10 Old English

blacklist
3 bar 4 oust 5 expel, purge, smear
6 banish, impugn 7 boycott, condemn, exclude, shut out 8 denounce
9 ostracize, proscribe 10 stigmatize

blackmail
5 bleed 6 extort, payoff 7 milking,
squeeze 8 chantage, coercion
9 extortion, hush money, shake down

black out
4 edit, wipe 5 annul, erase, faint,
swoon 6 cancel, censor, cut off,

darken, delete, efface, excise 7 conceal, eclipse, expunge 8 collapse,
make dark, sanitize, suppress
9 eradicate, expurgate 10 blue-
pencil, obliterate

blackpoll
7 warbler

Black Prince
6 Edward

Black Sea
city: 5 Yalta 6 Odessa 9 Constanta
peninsula: 6 Crimea 7 Crimean

Blackshirt
7 fascist

blacksmith
6 forger 7 farrier, striker
10 horseshoer

blacktail
8 mule deer

blackthorn
4 plum, sloe

black widow
6 spider

bladder
3 sac 4 cyst 5 pouch 7 blister,
vacuole 7 vesicle

blade
4 beau, buck, dude, edge, leaf
5 knife, sword 6 runner 9 swordsman

blah
4 bosh, dull, flat, tame 5 ho-hum,
hooey, tired, vapid 6 boring,
bunkum, dreary, humbug, stodgy
7 humdrum 8 banausic, lifeless,
mediocre, nonsense, plodding
10 balderdash, lackluster, monotonous, pedestrian 11 indifferent,
uninspiring 13 uninteresting

blamable
see **blameworthy**

blame
3 rap 4 onus 5 fault, guilt, knock
6 accuse, charge, finger, indict
7 censure, condemn 8 denounce,

reproach **9** criticize, liability, reprehend, reprobate **10** accusation, imputation **11** culpability **12** condemnation, denunciation, reprehension

Scottish: **4** wite, wyte **6** dirdum

blameless

4 good, pure **5** clean, moral **7** perfect, upright **8** innocent, unguilty, virtuous **9** crimeless, exemplary, faultless, guiltless, honorable, lily-white, righteous, unsullied **10** immaculate, impeccable, inculpable **13** unimpeachable

blameworthy

3 lax **5** amiss **6** guilty, liable, sinful **7** at fault **8** criminal, culpable, derelict **9** negligent **10** answerable, censurable, delinquent, indictable, punishable **11** disgraceful, inexcusable, responsible **12** dishonorable **13** reprehensible, objectionable

blanch

4 fade, pale **5** quail, scald, start **6** bleach, shrink, whiten **7** decolor, lighten, parboil **8** etiolate

blanched

3 wan **4** ashy, pale **5** ashen, faded, livid, peaky, waxen, white **6** anemic, doughy, pallid, peaked **7** ghostly **9** bloodless, colorless, washed out **10** cadaverous

Blancheflor's beloved

6 Flores, Floris

bland

4 dull, flat, blah, mild, soft **5** balmy, banal, vapid **6** boring, gentle, pablum **7** insipid, restful, sapless **8** soothing **9** calmative **10** complacent, flavorless, monotonous, namby-pamby, wishy-washy **12** ingratiating **13** nonirritating

blandish

3 con, woo **4** coax, fawn, urge **5** cozen **6** cajole, stroke **7** blarney, flatter, wheedle **8** butter up, inveigle, soft-soap **9** importune, sweet-talk **10** curry favor

blandishment

3 oil **5** honey **7** blarney, eyewash, incense, promise **8** flattery, soft soap **9** adulation, seduction, sweet talk **10** allurement, compliment, inducement, sycophancy, temptation

blank

3 gap **4** bare, dull, seal, skip, void **5** chasm, dazed, empty, space **6** stupid, vacant, virgin **7** deadpan, obscure, unfilled, vacuous **8** complete, omission, outright, spotless **9** impassive **10** empty space, interstice, obliterate **11** featureless **12** inexpressive, unexpressive

blanket

4 bury, hide **5** cover, quilt, throw **6** afghan, stroud **7** overlay **8** coverlet, mackinaw, sweeping **10** overspread

blankness

6 vacuum **7** nullity, vacancy, vacuity **9** emptiness **10** desolation

blare

4 roar **5** blast, shout **6** clamor, jangle **7** trumpet

blaring

4 loud **5** sharp **6** brassy, shrill **7** clarion, jarring, roaring **8** blinding, piercing, strident **9** deafening, dissonant **10** stentorian **11** ear-piercing, penetrating, stentorious **12** earsplitting

blarney

3 con, oil **4** coax, bunk **5** charm, honey, hooey **6** bunkum, cajole, humbug **7** baloney, incense, wheedle **8** blandish, buncombe, cajolery, flattery, inveigle, nonsense, soft soap **9** adulation, sweet-talk **11** compliments **12** blandishment, inveiglement

blasé

4 cool **5** bored, jaded, sated **6** breezy **7** knowing, offhand, unmoved, worldly **9** apathetic, incurious, surfeited, unexcited **10** worldweary **11** indifferent, unconcerned,

blaspheme

worldly-wise **12** disenchanted, uninterested **13** disillusioned, sophisticated

blaspheme

4 cuss **5** abuse, curse, swear **6** revile **7** pollute, profane **8** denounce, execrate **9** castigate, excoriate

blasphemous

6 coarse, sinful **7** godless, impious, obscene, profane, ungodly **10** irreverent **12** sacrilegious **13** disrespectful

blasphemy

3 sin **5** abuse, error **6** heresy **7** cursing, cussing, impiety, mockery **8** swearing **9** profanity, sacrilege, violation **10** execration, heterodoxy, iconoclasm **11** desecration, imprecation, irreverence, malediction, profanation

blast

3 din **4** bang, beat, blow, boom, clap, dash, gale, gust, kill, peal, ruin, slam, toot **5** blare, burst, crack, crash, salvo, shoot, smash, wreck **6** attack, blight, blow up, damage, squall, wallop **7** destroy, lambast, shatter, shrivel, trumpet **8** dynamite, lambaste, outburst **9** explosion, castigate, discharge, overwhelm, shock wave **10** annihilate, detonation

blat

4 bray **5** blurt **6** cry out **7** exclaim **8** blurt out

blatant

4 bald, loud **5** clear, gaudy, naked, noisy, overt, saucy **6** arrant, brassy, brazen, crying, flashy, garish, patent, tawdry, vulgar **7** glaring, jarring, obvious **8** flagrant, immodest, impudent, insolent, manifest, overbold, strident **9** barefaced, clamorous, obtrusive, shameless, unabashed **10** boisterous, outrageous, scurrilous, unblushing, vociferous **11** conspicuous, loudmouthed, transparent **12** ear-splitting, obstreperous

blather

3 gab, gas, jaw, rot, yak **4** bosh, gush, rave, stir **5** bleat, drool, hokum, prate **6** babble, bunkum, drivel, effuse, gabble, jabber, natter, yammer **7** blabber, chatter, enthuse, palaver, prattle, rubbish, twaddle **8** chitchat, claptrap, idle talk, nonsense **9** commotion **10** balderdash, double-talk, flapdoodle **12** gobbledygook

blaze

4 burn, fire **5** burst, flame, flare, glare, shine **7** flare up **8** eruption, outburst **10** incandesce **13** conflagration

Scottish: 3 low **4** lowe

blazer

6 marker, reefer **9** sport coat **10** sports coat **12** sports jacket

blazes

4 hell **5** abyss, Hades, Sheol **6** Tophet **7** Gehenna, inferno **9** perdition **11** netherworld

blazing

4 keen **5** afire, fiery **6** aflame, alight, ardent, fervid, on fire, red-hot **7** burning, fervent, flaming, flaring, furious, glowing, ignited, intense, lighted **8** dazzling, feverish, powerful, speeding, white-hot **9** brilliant, perfervid **11** conflagrant, impassioned **12** incandescent **13** scintillating

blazon

4 deck **5** adorn, sound **7** declare, display, publish, trumpet **8** announce, proclaim **9** advertise, broadcast **10** coat of arms, promulgate **11** ostentation

bleach

3 dim **4** fade, pale **5** white **6** blanch, blench, purify, whiten **7** decolor, launder, wash out **8** etiolate, peroxide, sanitize **9** whitewash

bleak

3 raw, sad **4** bare, cold, dour, drab, grim, wild **5** chill, drear, empty, harsh, stark **6** barren, chilly, dismal, dreary, gloomy, lonely, severe, somber, wintry **7** austere, exposed, joyless **8** blighted, desolate, funereal, hopeless **9** cheerless, windswept, woebegone **10** depressing, despondent, oppressive, melancholy

blear

3 dim, fog **4** blur, dull, mist, murk, veil **5** bedim, faint, vague **6** hidden, shroud **7** becloud, obscure, shadowy, unclear **10** indistinct

bleary

3 dim **5** all in, faint, filmy, fuzzy, milky, spent, tired, vague **6** pooped, sapped, used-up, wasted **7** blurred, drained, obscure, shadowy, unclear, worn-out **8** depleted **9** enervated, exhausted, washed-out **10** indistinct

bleat

3 baa **4** blat, carp, crab, fuss, yawp **5** gripe, whine **6** bellow, grouse, squawk, yammer **7** blather, grumble, whimper **8** complain **9** bellyache

bleed

3 sap, run **4** milk, ooze, pity, seep **5** drain, exude, leech, mulct **6** extort, fleece **7** diffuse, extract **9** blackmail **10** hemorrhage

blemish

3 mar **4** blot, flaw, harm, mark, maim, mole, scar, spot, vice, wart **5** fault, nevus, spoil, stain **6** blotch, damage, deface, defect, impair, injure, pimple, stigma **7** blacken, distort, freckle, pervert, tarnish, vitiate **8** impurity, mutilate, pockmark **9** birthmark **12** imperfection **13** disfigurement

blench

3 shy **4** balk, duck, fade **5** blink, cower, quail, quake, start, wince **6** flinch, purify, recoil, shrink, whiten **7** launder, shy away, squinch, tremble **8** draw back, etiolate **9** whitewash

blend

3 fit, mix **4** brew, fuse, meld, weld **5** admix, alloy, merge, unify, union, unite **6** commix, fusion, go with, hy-
brid, mingle **7** amalgam, combine, mélange, mixture **8** beverage, coalesce, compound, conflate, immingle, infusion, intermix, mishmash **9** admixture, commingle, composite, harmonize, integrate **10** amalgamate, commixture, concoction, synthesize **12** adulteration, amalgamation, intermixture

blender setting

3 mix **4** whip **5** puree **7** liquefy

blesbok

8 antelope

bless

4 laud **5** exalt, extol, endow, favor, grace **6** anoint, bestow, hallow, praise, uphold **7** approve, beatify, glorify, magnify, make holy, sanctify **10** consecrate

blessed

4 holy **5** happy, lucky **6** joyous, sacred **7** saintly **8** beatific, hallowed **9** beatified, fortunate, venerated **10** inviolable, sacrosanct, sanctified **11** consecrated

blessedness

5 bliss **8** felicity, sanctity **9** beatitude, godliness, happiness **12** blissfulness

blessing

4 boon, good, okay **5** asset, favor, grace **6** assent, bounty, thanks **7** benefit, benison, consent, fortune, godsend, support **8** approval, good luck, windfall **9** advantage **10** invocation, permission **11** approbation, benediction, endorsement, good fortune, valediction **12** commendation, consecration, thanksgiving **13** encouragement

"_____ bleu!"

5 Sacré

blight

3 mar, nip **4** dash, ruin **5** blast, decay, spoil, wreck **6** canker, wither **7** disease, scourge, shrivel **9** withering **10** pestilence **13** deterioration

blimp
7 airship 8 zeppelin 9 dirigible

blind
4 daze, dull 5 decoy, front, shade, shill 6 dazzle 7 eyeless, muddled, shutter 8 bedazzle, unseeing 9 sightless 10 visionless

blind alley
6 pocket 7 dead end, impasse 8 cul-de-sac, deadlock 9 stone wall 10 standstill 11 obstruction

blind god
4 Eros, Hodr, Hoth 5 Cupid, Hoder, Hodur, Hothr

blindworm
8 slowworm

blink
3 bat 4 wink 5 flash, yield 6 give in, squint 7 flicker, flutter, nictate, twinkle 9 nictitate 11 scintillate

blink at
4 omit 5 clear, let go 6 bypass, excuse, forget, ignore, slight 7 condone, connive, let pass, neglect 8 discount, overlook, pass over 9 disregard, exonerate, whitewash

blip
6 censor, screen 9 deviation, expurgate, radar spot 10 bowdlerize

bliss
3 joy 4 Zion 6 Canaan, heaven 7 ecstasy, elysium, nirvana, rapture 8 empyrean, euphoria, paradise 9 beatitude, happiness 10 exaltation 11 blessedness

blissful
5 happy 6 divine, elated, joyful, joyous 8 beatific, ecstatic, euphoric 9 ambrosial, delighted, entranced, rapturous 10 delightful, entrancing

blissfulness
3 joy 7 ecstasy 8 euphoria 9 beatitude, happiness 10 exaltation 11 contentment

blister
4 bleb, flay, lash 5 blain, bulla, slash 6 assail, canker, scathe, scorch

7 lambast, scarify, scourge, vesicle 8 lambaste 9 castigate, excoriate

blithe
3 gay 4 boon 5 happy, jolly, merry, sunny 6 bouncy, casual, cheery, chirpy, jaunty, jocund, jovial 7 gleeful 8 carefree, careless, cheerful, chirrupy, gladsome, heedless, mirthful 9 lightsome, sprightly, unworried, vivacious 10 untroubled 11 thoughtless 12 lighthearted

blithesome
see blithe

blitz
4 raid, rush 7 air raid, bombard, bombing 8 shelling 9 onslaught 10 mass attack 11 bombardment

blitzkrieg
6 attack 7 assault, bombing 9 offensive, onslaught 11 bombardment

blizzard
4 gale 5 squall 8 whiteout 9 snowstorm

bloat
5 bulge, swell 6 billow, expand, fatten, puff up 7 balloon, distend, enlarge, inflate 10 distension

bloated
5 puffy 6 puffed 7 pompous, swollen 8 arrogant, enlarged, inflated 9 distended, overblown, overlarge 11 pretentious 13 self-important

bloc
4 band, ring 5 cabal, party, union 6 clique, league 7 combine, faction 8 alliance 9 coalition 10 consortium, contingent, federation 11 association, combination 13 confederation

block
3 bar 4 clog, fill, hunk, plug, slab, stop, wall, wing 5 brick, choke, chunk, close, ingot 6 cut off, hinder, impede 7 barrier, congest, occlude, stopper 8 obstacle, obstruct 9 barricade, hindrance, intercept

blockade
3 bar 4 stop, wall 5 beset, hem in,

siege **6** shut in **7** barrier, besiege **8** close off, encircle, obstruct, stoppage **9** barricade, beleaguer, blank wall, hindrance, roadblock **10** impediment **11** obstruction

blockage
3 bar **4** clog, halt **7** barrier **8** obstacle, stoppage **10** impediment **11** obstruction

blockbuster
4 bomb **11** spectacular

blockhead
3 oaf **4** clod, dolt, dope, fool **5** dummy, dunce, idiot, moron, ninny **6** nitwit **7** halfwit, imbecile **8** clodpole, clodpoll, dumbbell, numskull **9** ignoramus, lamebrain, numbskull, simpleton **10** nincompoop **12** featherbrain

blockheaded
4 dull, dumb **5** dense, thick **6** obtuse, stupid **7** doltish **9** brainless, dim-witted **10** slow-witted

block out
4 mark **5** chart, close, draft, frame **6** hinder, screen, sketch **7** obscure, outline, prepare, repress, shut off **8** indicate, obstruct **9** adumbrate, formulate

block up
3 dam **4** clog, fill, plug, stop **5** choke **7** congest

bloke
3 guy, man **4** chap, gent **6** fellow **9** gentleman

blond
4 fair, gold, pale **5** light, sandy, straw, tawny **6** flaxen, golden **7** towhead **8** platinum **9** champagne, towheaded **10** fair-haired **11** sandy-haired **12** honey-colored

blood
4 gore **7** descent, kindred, kinship, lineage **8** ancestry **10** extraction
cancer of: 8 leukemia
cell: 3 red **5** white **8** hemocyte, monocyte, platelet **9** corpuscle, leukocyte **10** lymphocyte **11** erythrocyte, granulocyte

clot: 8 thrombus
coloring matter: 10 hemoglobin
disease: 6 anemia **8** leukemia **10** hemophilia
fluid part: 5 serum **6** plasma
of the gods: 5 ichor
particle in: 7 embolus
poisoning: 6 pyemia **7** toxemia **10** septicemia
pressure: 8 systolic **9** diastolic
relating to: 5 hemic
serum: 6 plasma
study of: 10 hematology
sugar: 7 glucose

bloodbath
7 carnage, slaying **8** butchery, massacre **9** slaughter **10** decimation **12** annihilation **13** extermination

bloodless
3 wan **4** ashy, dull, pale, weak **5** ashen, waxen **6** anemic, feeble, pallid, sallow, torpid **8** listless **9** insensate, unfeeling **10** insensible, nonviolent **11** coldhearted, passionless, unemotional

bloodletting
4 gore **7** carnage, killing **8** butchery, shambles, violence **9** slaughter **10** phlebotomy **11** venesection

bloodline
6 family, strain **7** descent, lineage **8** ancestry, pedigree **10** family tree

bloodroot
7 puccoon

bloodshed
4 gore **7** carnage **9** slaughter

bloodstained
4 gory **6** grisly **7** imbrued, wounded **8** sanguine **10** sanguinary **11** ensanguined, sanguineous

bloodstone
10 chalcedony

bloodsucker
4 tick **5** lamia, leech **6** lizard, sponge **7** sponger, vampire **8** hanger-on, parasite **10** freeloader **12** lounge lizard

bloodthirsty

5 rabid **8** ravening, sanguine
9 cutthroat, homicidal, murdering,
murderous, predatory, voracious
10 sanguinary **11** sanguineous

blood vessel

4 vein **5** aorta **6** artery **7** jugular
9 capillary
combining form: 3 vas **4** angi,
vasi, vaso **5** angio

bloody

4 gory, grim, very **5** cruel **6** damage,
damned, deadly, grisly **7** blasted,
hateful, imbrued, wounded **8** accursed, infernal, sanguine **9** cutthroat, homicidal, murdering, murderous **10** detestable, sanguinary
11 ensanguined, sanguineous
12 death-dealing, slaughtering

bloom

4 blow, glow, open, posy **5** blush
6 floret, flower, thrive, unfold **7** blossom, burgeon, coating, develop,
dusting, prosper **8** flourish, rosiness
10 cloudiness, effloresce **13** discoloration

blooper

4 goof, slip, trip **5** boner, break,
error, fluff, lapse **6** boo-boo,
bungle, howler, slipup **7** blunder,
faux pas, fly ball, misstep, mistake,
offense **8** solecism **9** indecorum,
false step **11** impropriety **12** indiscretion

blossom

3 bud, wax **4** blow, glow, grow,
open, posy **5** bloom, blush, flush
6 expand, flower, mature, thrive,
unfold **7** burgeon, develop, prosper **8** flourish, floweret, progress
10 effloresce, peak period **13** efflo-
rescence

blot

4 blur, mark, onus, slur, smut, soil,
spot **5** brand, odium, smear, speck,
stain, sully **6** absorb, smudge,
stigma **7** bestain, blemish, spatter,
tarnish **8** black eye, discolor, disgrace **9** bespatter, moral flaw

blotch

4 mark, spot **5** stain **6** macula,
macule, mottle, smudge **7** blemish,
splotch **12** imperfection

blot out

4 raze, void **5** annul, crush, erase,
quash, quell, scrub **6** cancel, delete,
efface, squash **7** abolish, destroy,
expunge **9** eliminate, eradicate,
extirpate **10** annihilate, extinguish,
obliterate **11** exterminate

blotto

see **drunk**

blouse

5 middy, shell, shirt, smock, tunic
6 guimpe

bloviate

4 rail, rant, rave **5** mouth, orate,
spout **7** bluster, carry on, declaim,
inveigh, soapbox, talk big **8** harangue, perorate, sound off, splutter
9 hold forth **10** vociferate

blow

3 bop, fan, hit, jar **4** bang, bash, belt,
biff, bump, cuff, damn, fail, gasp,
gust, huff, pipe, puff, slam, slug,
swat, toot, whop, wind **5** boast,
botch, crack, drive, erupt, leave,
pound, punch, shock, slosh, smack,
smash, sound, spend, waste, whack
6 buffet, depart, impact, mishap,
thwack, wallop **7** assault, breathe,
chagrin, consume, debacle, explode,
flutter, fritter, trumpet **8** calamity, disaster, flounder, knockout, squander
9 bombshell, collision, dissipate,
throw away **10** concussion, misfortune, trifle away **11** catastrophe

blow-by-blow

4 full **5** fussy **6** minute **7** careful,
precise **8** detailed, itemized, thorough **10** exhaustive, meticulous,
scrupulous **13** thoroughgoing

blowhard

see **boaster**

blow in

4 land **5** pop by **6** appear, arrive,
drop by, show up, turn up **7** hit town
11 materialize

blowout
 4 bash, fete, gala, riot, tear **5** binge, blast, break, party, split, spree **6** frolic, shindy **7** shindig, victory **8** carousal, flat tire **9** festivity

blowsy
 5 dingy, ruddy **6** florid, frowsy, sloppy, untidy **7** flushed, healthy, unkempt **8** blooming, blushing **10** bedraggled

blow up
 4 bomb, burn, fume, rage **5** bloat, burst, erupt, flare, go off, storm, swell **6** expand, seethe **7** bristle, distend, enlarge, explode, inflate, magnify, rupture, shatter **8** boil over, demolish, detonate, dynamite, heighten, mushroom **9** discredit, fulminate, overstate **10** aggrandize

blowy
 4 airy, wild **5** fresh, gusty, windy **6** breezy, stormy **7** squally **8** blustery **9** windswept **11** tempestuous

blubber
 3 cry, fat, sob **4** bawl, flab, keen, lard, pipe, wail, weep **5** flesh **6** snivel **7** carry on **8** whale fat

bludgeon
 3 bat **4** club **5** baton, billy, bully **6** attack, cudgel, hector **7** bluster, war club **8** browbeat, bulldoze, bullyrag **9** bastinado, billy club, blackjack, strong-arm, truncheon **10** intimidate, nightstick
 British: 4 cosh

blue
 3 low, sad, sea **4** down, glum, lewd, navy, racy **5** bawdy, ocean, royal, salty, spicy **6** cobalt, gloomy, risqué **7** naughty, profane, unhappy **8** dejected, downcast, indecent, off-color **9** depressed, woebegone **10** despondent, dispirited, melancholy, suggestive **11** downhearted
 combining form: 4 cyan **5** cyano
 dark: 5 perse **6** indigo
 grayish: 5 merle, slate
 greenish: 4 aqua, cyan, teal **5** beryl **6** cobalt **7** azurite **9** turquoise
 reddish: 5 smalt **6** marine, purple, violet **7** cyanine, gentian, lobelia
 sky: 5 azure **8** cerulean

_____ Blue
 3 Ben **9** Little Boy

blue blood
 4 lady, lord, peer **5** elite, noble **6** aristo **7** royalty **8** nobleman **9** gentility, gentleman, patrician **10** aristocrat, noblewoman **11** gentle birth, gentlewoman

bluebonnet
 4 Scot **11** Texas lupine

Blue Boy painter
 12 Gainsborough (Thomas)

bluecoat
 3 cop, law **4** fuzz **5** bobby **6** copper **9** constable, patrolman, policeman

Bluegrass State
 8 Kentucky

Blue Grotto site
 5 Capri

bluejacket
 4 mate, salt, swab **5** limey **6** sailor, seaman **7** swabbie **9** sailorman

blue jeans
 5 Levis **6** denims

blue moon
 3 age, eon, era **4** aeon **5** epoch **7** dog's age **8** eternity, lifetime **10** generation

bluenose
 4 prig **5** prude **7** puritan **9** Mrs. Grundy, nice Nelly **10** goody-goody

bluenosed
 4 prim **5** rigid **6** prissy, proper, square, stuffy **7** prudish **8** overnice, priggish **9** Victorian **10** scrupulous, tight-laced **11** puritanical, straitlaced

blue-pencil
 3 cut **4** edit, trim **5** emend **6** cut out, delete, excise, remove, revise **7** clean up **8** boil down, cross out **9** strike out, tighten up

bluepoint
 6 oyster

blueprint

3 map **4** cast, plan, plot **5** chart, draft, frame, model, trace **6** design, devise, rubric, scheme, set out, sketch **7** arrange, diagram, outline, picture, project **8** game plan, strategy **9** delineate **10** conception, rough draft **11** description

blue-ribbon

3 top **5** prime **6** Grade A, tip-top **7** capital, premier **8** five-star, top-notch, superior **9** excellent, first-rate, top-drawer **10** first-class, top-quality, world-class **11** outstanding **12** prize-winning

blues

4 funk **5** dumps, gloom, grief **6** lament **7** sadness, trouble **8** doldrums, glumness **9** dejection, pessimism **10** depression, desolation, low spirits, melancholy, woefulness **11** despondency, melancholia, unhappiness **12** hopelessness, mournfulness

bluff

3 act, con **4** curt, fake, fool, jive, ruse, sham, show **5** blunt, cliff, feign, frank, gruff, rough, trick **6** abrupt, betray, candid, crusty, delude, direct, hearty, humbug **7** beguile, brusque, deceive, fake out, mislead, playact, pretend **8** headland, pretense **9** deception, outspoken, precipice, steep bank **10** escarpment, forthright, no-nonsense, promontory, subterfuge **11** counterfeit, double-cross, plainspoken, short-spoken **13** unceremonious

blunder

4 bull, gaff, goof, mess, muff, slip, trip **5** boner, botch, error, fluff, gaffe, gum up, lapse, lurch **6** bobble, bollix, bumble, bungle, foul up, fumble, goof up, howler, mess up, wander **7** blooper, failure, faux pas, louse up, misstep, mistake, screw up, stumble **8** disaster, flounder **12** indiscretion, misadventure

blunderbuss

3 gun **4** dolt **5** klutz **6** galoot,

lummox **7** bungler, firearm **8** bonehead, numskull **9** blockhead, numbskull **10** stumblebum **13** butterfingers

blunt

4 bald, calm, curt **5** allay, bluff, brief, frank, gruff, plain, rough, terse **6** abrupt, benumb, candid, crusty, deaden, direct, lessen, obtuse **7** brusque, rounded, uncivil **8** enfeeble, not sharp, snippety **10** forthright **11** desensitize, insensitive, plainspoken, unvarnished **12** discourteous **13** unceremonious

blur

3 dim, fog **4** blot, dull, mist **5** befog, blear, cloud, muddy, smear, stain, taint **6** smudge, stigma **7** becloud, besmear, confuse, tarnish **8** besmirch, discolor
in printing: 6 mackle

blurb

4 hype, plug, puff **5** press **6** notice **7** write-up **8** good word **9** promotion **12** commendation

blurry

4 hazy **5** vague **6** cloudy **7** clouded, unclear **9** undefined, unfocused **10** indistinct

blurt

4 blab, blat, bolt **5** spill **6** cry out, let out **7** divulge, exclaim, let slip, spit out **8** disclose, give away **9** ejaculate

blush

4 burn, glow, rose, view **5** bloom, color, flame, flush, rouge **6** mantle, pinken, redden **7** blossom, crimson, redness, turn red **8** mantling, rosiness

bluster

4 bawl, crow, gust, huff, rage, roar, rout **5** blast, bully, prate, storm, strut, vaunt **6** bellow, clamor, hector, lean on **7** bombast, bravado, dragoon, roister, swagger, talk big **8** boasting, browbeat, bulldoze, bullyrag, domineer **9** gasconade **10** grandstand, intimidate **11** braggadocio

blustery
4 wild 5 blowy, gusty, rough
6 drafty, raging, raving, stormy
7 furious, squally, violent 9 truculent,
tumultuous, turbulent 10 boisterous
11 tempestuous

boa
5 scarf, snake

boar
3 pig 4 male 5 swine

board
4 fare, feed, food, lath, slab, slat
5 catch, get on, hop on, house,
lodge, meals, panel, plank, put up,
table 6 billet, embark 7 emplane,
entrain, quarter 9 directors 11 direc-
torate
artist's: 7 palette

boarder
5 guest 6 lodger, renter, roomer,
tenant

board game
see at **game**

boarding house
6 hostel 7 hospice, lodging, pension
8 pensione

boardwalk
7 gangway 9 esplanade, promenade

boast
3 own 4 blow, brag, crow, have,
puff 5 exalt, exult, glory, mouth,
prate, preen, strut, vaunt 6 parade 7 bluster, bombast, bravado,
contain, enlarge, exhibit, inflate,
possess, show off, swagger, talk big
9 gasconade 10 exaggerate, grandstand 11 rodomontade 12 exaggeration

boaster
6 gascon 7 egotist, peacock,
show-off 8 big mouth, blowhard,
braggart 11 braggadocio, rodomontade

boastful
4 vain 5 cocky 6 braggy 8 arrogant,
braggart, puffed-up, vaunting
9 bigheaded, conceited, egotistic

11 egotistical, pretentious, swell-
headed 12 vainglorious 13 swelled-
headed
Scottish: 6 vaunty

boat
3 ark, hoy, tug 4 dhow, dory, junk,
pram, prau, proa, punt, scow, ship,
yawl 5 barge, canoe, coble, ferry,
kayak, ketch, scull, shell, skiff, sloop,
smack, umiak, yacht 6 bateau,
bugeye, caïque, cutter, dinghy,
hooker, lateen, lugger, packet,
sampan, vessel, wherry 7 caravel,
coracle, currach, curragh, gondola,
lighter, pinnace, pirogue, pontoon,
shallop, steamer, trawler, vedette,
vidette 8 schooner, trimaran 9 catamaran, hydrofoil
bottom projection: 4 keel
captain: 5 pilot 6 master 7 skipper
dock, basin: 6 marina
front end of: 3 bow 4 fore, prow
motor: 7 cruiser, inboard 8 outboard, runabout
on a ship: 3 gig 6 launch 7 pinnace
race: 7 regatta
rear end of: 3 aft 5 stern
song: 6 chanty, shanty 7 chantey
9 barcarole 10 barcarolle

boatman
4 mate 5 limey 6 Charon, sailor
7 mariner, oarsman, paddler 8 deckhand, water dog 9 gondolier, navi-
gator

boat-shaped
8 scaphoid 9 navicular

Boaz's wife
4 Ruth

bob
3 jig, nod, rap, tap 4 buff, clip, crop,
dock, trim 5 bunch, float 6 bounce,
curtsy, jiggle, jounce, polish, trifle,
wobble 7 cluster, curtsey, nosegay
8 shilling 9 genuflect

bobbery
3 ado, din, row 4 fray, riot 5 babel,
noise 6 bedlam, hubbub, racket,
ruckus, rumpus 7 ferment, ruction

bobbin

9 commotion, confusion 10 hulla-baloo, hurly-burly 11 disturbance, pandemonium

bobbin

4 pirn 5 quill, spool, wheel 7 spindle 8 cylinder

bobble

3 bob, dud 4 flub, goof, mess, muff 5 botch, error, fluff, gum up 6 ball up, bollix, bumble, bungle, flub up, fumble, goof up, muff up 7 blooper, failure, louse up, mistake

bobby

3 law 6 copper, peeler 7 officer 9 constable, patrolman, policeman

bobwhite

5 quail 9 partridge

Boccaccio

beloved: 9 Fiammetta
tales: 9 Decameron

bode

4 hint 5 augur 6 signal, warn of 7 betoken, portend, presage, promise, signify, suggest 8 foreshow, indicate 9 foretoken, prefigure 10 foreshadow

bodega

3 bar, pub 6 saloon 7 barroom, grocery 8 wineshop 12 general store

bodement

4 omen, sign 5 hunch 6 augury 7 portent, presage 8 prophecy 9 foretoken, harbinger 10 foreboding, intimation, prediction, prognostic 11 premonition 12 presentiment

bodiless

7 ghostly 8 ethereal, spectral 9 unfleshly 10 discarnate, immaterial, unphysical 11 disembodied, incorporeal, nonmaterial 12 apparitional 13 insubstantial

bodily

6 carnal 7 en masse, earthly, fleshly, sensual, somatic, totally 8 corporal, entirely, physical, visceral 9 corporeal 10 altogether, completely 11 unspiritual

bodkin

4 shiv 5 blade, knife, shank 6 dagger, lancet, needle 7 poniard 8 stiletto

_____ bodkins

4 odds

body

4 bulk, core, form, hull, mass, soma 5 frame, stiff, stock, torso 6 corpse, corpus 7 anatomy, cadaver, carcass, chassis, corpora (plural), remains 8 physique 9 aggregate, substance
combining form: 4 dema, soma, some, somi (plural) 5 somat, somia, somus 6 somata (plural), somato

body cavity

5 cecum, sinus 6 coelom 7 abdomen 8 hemocoel

body check

5 block

bodyguard

7 retinue 9 attendant, protector

body of water

3 bay, sea 4 cove, gulf, lake, pond, pool 5 bight, brook, creek, fiord, firth, fjord, inlet, ocean, river 6 harbor, lagoon, puddle, stream 7 channel, estuary 9 reservoir

body passage

4 duct, vein 5 canal 6 artery, meatus, ureter, vagina, venule, vessel 7 trachea, urethra 8 bronchus 9 arteriole, capillary, esophagus, intestine 10 bronchiole 13 bronchial tube, fallopian tube

body politic

5 state 6 nation 11 nation-state

boffo

3 gag, gas, hit 4 wild 5 laugh 6 scream 7 sold-out 8 smash-hit, smashing 10 successful 11 sensational

bog

3 fen 4 mire, quag 5 delay, marsh, swamp 6 impede, morass, muskeg, slough, slow up 8 quagmire 9 swampland

Bogart, Humphrey

film: 6 Sahara 7 Dead End, Sabrina 8 Big Sleep (The), Key Largo 10 Casablanca, High Sierra 11 Caine Mutiny (The) 12 African Queen (The) 13 Maltese Falcon (The) 15 Petrified Forest (The) 16 To Have and Have Not 24 Treasure of the Sierra Madre (The)

wife: 6 Bacall (Lauren)

bog down

4 flag, mire 5 choke, delay, stall 6 detain, falter, hang up, hinder, impede, retard, slow up 7 embroil, set back, slacken 8 encumber, keep back, obstruct, slow down 9 lose steam 10 decelerate

bogey

5 ghost, haunt, shade, spook 6 scarer, shadow, spirit, wraith 7 phantom, specter 8 phantasm, revenant 10 apparition

bogeyman

5 spook 7 bugbear, chimera, monster, phantom, specter, spectre 10 apparition

boggle

4 balk, mess, muff, stun 5 amaze, botch, fudge, gum up, shock, wreck 6 bollix, bungle, cobble, goof up, mess up, strain 7 astound, louse up, nonplus, stagger, stumble, stupefy 8 astonish, bewilder, bowl over, confound 9 dumbfound, mishandle, mismanage, overwhelm, take aback 11 flabbergast

bogus

4 fake, mock, sham 5 false, phony, snide 6 ersatz, forged, pseudo 7 fictive, pretend 8 invented, specious, spurious 9 brummagem, concocted, imitation, pinchbeck, simulated, trumped up 10 artificial, fabricated, fraudulent, mendacious 11 counterfeit

Bohème, La

character: 4 Mimi 7 Rodolfo
composer: 7 Puccini (Giacomo)
setting: 5 Paris

bohemian

5 artsy, gypsy, hippy 6 hippie 7 beatnik, dropout, oddball, offbeat 8 maverick, vagabond, wanderer 9 eccentric 10 avant-garde, iconoclast, unorthodox 13 nonconformist

boil

3 jet 4 bolt, brew, burn, cook, dash, foam, fume, gush, moil, race, rage, rush, spew, spot, stew, vent 5 anger, churn, erupt, fling, froth, poach, shoot, storm, swirl 6 blow up, bubble, charge, canker, coddle, pimple, seethe, simmer 7 abscess, agitate, bristle, ferment, flare up, pustule, smolder 8 furuncle 9 carbuncle, discharge 10 effervesce 11 excrescence

boil down

4 pare, trim 6 amount, reduce 7 distill 8 compress, condense, simplify, truncate 9 summarize, synopsize 10 streamline 11 concentrate, encapsulate

boiler suit

8 coverall

boiling

3 hot 5 fiery 6 baking, red-hot, sultry, torrid 7 burning, febrile 8 agitated, roasting, scalding, sizzling, tropical 9 scorching 10 blistering

boil over

4 burn, fume, rage 5 erupt 6 blow up, bridle, see red, seethe 7 bristle, flare up

boisterous

4 loud, wild 5 noisy, rowdy 6 lively, stormy, unruly 7 blatant, raucous, riotous 8 strident 9 clamorous, convivial, turbulent 10 disorderly, disruptive, rollicking, tumultuous, uproarious, vociferous 11 loudmouthed, tempestuous 12 high-spirited, obstreperous, rambunctious, ungovernable, unrestrained

Boito opera

11 Mefistofele

bold

4 free, pert, rude 5 bluff, brave, fresh, gutsy, nervy, sassy, saucy, sheer, showy, steep 6 arrant, bright, brazen, cheeky, daring, heroic 7 doughty, forward, glaring, obvious, valiant 8 cocksure, fearless, impudent, insolent, intrepid, resolute, unafraid, valorous 9 audacious, dauntless, intrusive, prominent, shameless, undaunted 10 courageous, pronounced 11 adventurous, impertinent, smart-alecky, venturesome 12 enterprising, presumptuous

boldness

4 gall, grit 5 drive, nerve, valor 6 aplomb, mettle, spirit 8 audacity, backbone, chutzpah, temerity 9 arrogance, challenge, hardihood, impudence, insolence 10 brazenness, disrespect, effrontery 11 discourtesy 12 impertinence

Bolero composer

5 Ravel (Maurice)

Bolivia

ancient culture: 4 Inca 10 Tiahuanaco
capital: 5 La Paz, Sucre
city: 6 El Alto 9 Santa Cruz 10 Cochabamba
conqueror: 7 Pizarro (Hernando)
Indian people: 6 Aymara 7 Quechua
lake: 5 Poopó 8 Titicaca
language: 6 Aymara 7 Quechua, Spanish
monetary unit: 9 boliviano
mountain, range: 5 Andes 6 Sajama
neighbor: 4 Peru 5 Chile 6 Brazil 8 Paraguay 9 Argentina
river: 4 Beni 5 Abuna 6 Mamoré 7 Guaporé 9 Pilcomayo

bollix

4 flub, mess, muff, ruin 5 botch, gum up, spoil, upset 6 bobble, bumble, bungle, foul up, fumble, goof up, jumble, mess up, muck up, muddle, muff up 7 confuse, louse up, screw up 8 dishevel, disorder, scramble, unsettle 9 mishandle, mismanage

bolo

5 knife 7 machete

Bolshevik

3 Red 6 commie 7 comrade 8 Leninist, tovarich, tovarish 9 communist

bolshevism

7 Marxism 8 Leninism 9 communism

bolster

3 aid 4 buoy, gird, help, prop 5 boost, brace, carry, cheer 6 assist, bear up, buoy up, pillow, upbear, uphold 7 bulwark, cushion, fortify, hearten, shore up, support, sustain 8 backstop, buttress, maintain 9 encourage, reinforce 10 strengthen 12 underpinning 13 reinforcement

bolt

3 bar, fly, rod, run 4 cram, dash, dart, flee, gulp, jump, lock, race, rush, tear, wolf 5 arrow, blurt, bound, chase, dowel, flush, rivet, scarf, scoot, shoot, skirr, slosh, start 6 charge, decamp, devour, gobble, guzzle, secure, spring 7 abscond, exclaim, hotfoot, make off, missile, rigidly, scamper, startle, take off 8 blurt out, hightail 9 skedaddle 10 make tracks, take flight 11 ingurgitate 13 thunderstroke

bomb

3 dud, hit 4 bust, dull, fail, flop, sink, zero 5 blast, blitz, lemon, loser, pound, shell 6 blow up 7 debacle, destroy, failure, home run, success, washout, wipe out 8 detonate, disaster, fall flat, long pass, long shot, spray can

bombard

4 pelt 5 blast, blitz, shell, storm 6 attack, assail, cannon, hammer, pepper, shower, strafe, strike 7 assault, barrage 8 catapult 9 cannonade

bombardment

4 hail 5 burst, salvo 6 attack, shower, volley 7 barrage, battery 8 drumfire 9 broadside, cannonade, fusillade, onslaught

bombardon
4 bass 8 bass tuba

bombast
4 rant 6 hot air 7 bluster, fustian,
oration 8 rhapsody, tumidity 9 fancy
talk, pomposity, turgidity 10 pretension 11 rodomontade

bombastic
5 wordy 6 prolix 7 aureate, flowery,
orotund, pompous, swollen 8 inflated,
puffed-up 9 overblown 10 euphuistic, rhetorical 11 declamatory, overwrought 12 magniloquent 13 grandiloquent

bombed
4 high 5 drunk, fried, stiff, tight
6 blotto, stoned, wasted 8 comatose,
tanked up 9 plastered 10 inebriated
11 intoxicated

bombinate
3 hum 4 buzz, purr, whir 5 drone,
strum, thrum 6 bumble, rumble
7 grumble

bombshell
4 blow, jolt 5 shock 6 marvel
8 surprise 9 curveball, sensation
10 revelation 11 thunderbolt

bona fide
4 real, sure, true 5 valid 6 actual
7 earnest, genuine, sincere 8 sterling 9 authentic, undoubted, veritable 10 legitimate, sure-enough
11 indubitable, in good faith 13 au-
thenticated

bona fides
6 candor 7 probity 8 goodwill
9 good faith, sincerity 10 reputation
11 reliability, sincereness

bonanza
4 mine 5 catch, hoard 7 pay dirt
8 Golconda, gold mine, treasure,
treasury, windfall 12 extravaganza
13 treasure trove

bonbon
5 candy, sweet 7 fondant 9 sweetmeat, sugarplum 10 confection

bond
3 tie 4 bail, fuse, knot, link, pact,
yoke 5 nexus 6 cement, fetter,
pledge, surety 7 bargain, compact,
linkage, promise, shackle, warrant
8 adhesive, affinity, cohesion, contract, covenant, guaranty, ligament,
ligature, security, vinculum, warranty
9 adherence, agreement, coherence,
guarantee 10 attachment, connection, connective, obligation

bondage
4 yoke 6 chains, thrall 7 durance,
fetters, helotry, peonage, serfage,
serfdom, slavery 9 captivity, detention, servitude, thralldom, vassalage,
villenage 10 subjection 11 enslavement, subjugation 12 imprisonment

bondsman
4 peon, serf 5 helot, slave 6 surety
7 chattel

bone
ankle: 5 talus 6 tarsus
arm: 4 ulna 6 radius 7 humerus
back: 5 spine 8 vertebra 9 vertebrae (plural)
breast: 7 sternum
calf: 6 fibula
cavity: 5 fossa
change into: 6 ossify
cheek: 5 malar 6 zygoma
chest: 3 rib
collar: 8 clavicle
face: 5 malar, nasal 7 frontal
finger: 7 phalanx 8 phalange
foot: 6 tarsus 9 calcaneum, calcaneus 10 astragalus, metatarsus
hand: 10 metacarpus
head: 5 skull, vomer 7 cranium
8 parietal, sphenoid 9 occipital
heel: 9 calcaneum, calcaneus
hip: 5 ilium, pubis 6 pelvis
7 ischium
jaw: 7 maxilla 8 mandible
kneecap: 7 patella
leg: 5 femur, tibia 6 fibula 7 patella
lower back: 6 coccyx, sacrum
middle ear: 5 anvil, incus 6 hammer, stapes 7 malleus, stirrup
pelvis: 5 ilium
relating to: 6 osteal
shin: 5 tibia
shoulder blade: 7 scapula

small: 7 ossicle
substance: 6 ossein
thigh: 5 femur
toe: 7 phalanx 8 phalange
U-shaped: 5 hyoid
wrist: 6 carpus

bonehead
4 clod 5 dunce, moron 6 cretin,
dimwit, nitwit 7 halfwit 8 clodpole,
clodpoll, lunkhead, numskull 9 ignoramus, lamebrain, numbskull
12 featherbrain

bonelike
7 osseous, osteoid

boner
see **blooper**

bone up
4 cram 5 study 6 review, revise
8 pore over

bong
4 bell, dong, peal, ring, toll 5 chime,
knell, sound 6 hookah, strike 7 resound 9 water pipe 11 reverberate

boniface
7 barkeep 8 publican, taverner
9 barkeeper, innkeeper
12 saloonkeeper

bonkers
3 ape, mad 4 daft, loco, nuts, wild
5 batty, crazy, giddy, loony, potty
6 cuckoo, insane 7 bananas, haywire 8 demented, deranged, unhinged

bon mot
4 jest, quip 5 crack, sally 7 epigram,
riposte 8 one-liner, repartee 9 witticism

bonny
4 fair, fine 6 comely, lovely, pretty
7 winsome 8 pleasing 9 beauteous,
beautiful, excellent 10 attractive,
delightful 11 good-looking

bon ton
4 élan 5 flair, style 6 gentry, jet set
7 fashion, society 8 elegance, smart
set 9 haut monde, propriety 11 high
society

bonus
4 gift, plus 6 reward 7 benefit,
payment, premium 8 dividend
12 compensation 13 fringe benefit

bon vivant
7 epicure, flaneur, gourmet, trifler
8 aesthete, gourmand 10 aficionado,
dilettante, gastronome 11 cognoscente, connoisseur 12 boulevardier, gastronomist, man-about-town

bony
4 lank, lean, thin 5 gaunt, lanky,
spare 6 barren, skinny, twiggy
7 angular, osseous, scraggy, scrawny,
starved 8 rawboned, skeletal, underfed 9 emaciated 10 cadaverous

boo
4 hiss, hoot, jeer, razz 6 bellow,
deride, heckle, revile 7 catcall
9 raspberry, shout down

boob
3 oaf 4 dolt, dope, goof, goon, boor
5 chump, dunce, goose, ninny
6 breast, dumb ox 7 blunder,
fathead, mistake, tomfool 8 lunkhead 9 simpleton 10 dunderhead,
philistine

boo-boo
see **blooper**

booby hatch
6 asylum, bedlam 8 bughouse,
loony bin, madhouse, nuthouse
9 funny farm 11 institution

booby trap
4 mine 5 snare 6 hazard 7 pitfall,
springe 8 deadfall, land mine

boodle
3 wad 4 bilk, haul, heap, loot, mint,
perk, take 5 booty, prize, spoil
6 bundle, packet, payola, spoils
7 fortune, plunder, present 8 kickback 9 incentive 10 bribe money,
inducement

book
4 list, text, tome 5 album, bible,
codex, enter, folio, novel, tract
6 charge, engage, enroll, folder, line
up, manual, octavo, quarto, record,

script, volume **7** catalog, edition, reserve **8** hardback, inscribe, register, schedule, softback, treatise **9** hardcover, monograph, paperback, preengage **10** compendium **11** publication
combining form: 6 biblio
of hours: 5 Horae
of psalms: 7 psalter

bookie
see **bookmaker**

bookish
5 nerdy **6** formal **7** erudite, learned **8** academic, cerebral, literary, pedantic, studious, well-read **9** scholarly **10** longhaired **12** intellectual, professorial

bookkeeping term
4 loss **5** asset, audit, check, debit, entry, yield **6** budget, credit, equity, income, ledger, margin, profit, return **7** account, accrual, balance, expense, invoice, revenue, voucher **8** discount, dividend, interest, write off **9** inventory, liability **10** appreciate, depreciate, fiscal year **11** double entry **12** amortization, appreciation, balance sheet, depreciation, variable cost

booklet
8 brochure, opuscule, pamphlet

bookmaker
6 binder, bookie, editor **7** printer **9** bet holder, oddsmaker, publisher

book of account
6 ledger, record **7** journal **8** register

bookplate
5 label **8** ex libris

bookstall
5 kiosk **9** newsstand

boom
3 wax **4** bang, clap, grow, rise, slam, spar, wham **5** blast, boost, burst, crack, crash, sound, smash, swell **6** do well, expand, growth, rumble, thrive **7** explode, prosper, resound, thunder **8** flourish, kick hard, long

beam **9** expansion **10** bull market, detonation, prosperity **11** reverberate

boomerang
6 recoil **7** rebound **8** backfire, backlash, come back, kick back, ricochet **10** bounce back

booming
4 bass, deep **6** robust **7** roaring **8** affluent, resonant, sonorous, thriving **9** deafening **10** prospering, prosperous, successful **11** flourishing

boon
3 aid, gay **4** gift, good, help **5** asset, grant, favor, jolly, merry, token **6** blithe, bounty, jocund, jovial **7** benefit, festive, gleeful, godsend, largess, present **8** blessing, largesse, mirthful, windfall **9** advantage, convivial, privilege **10** indulgence **11** benediction, benefaction

boondocks
5 wilds **6** sticks **7** outback **8** backland, frontier **9** backwater, backwoods, provinces, rural area **10** hinterland **11** backcountry, countryside **12** back of beyond

boondoggle
4 cord, hoax, scam **5** fraud, hokum **6** hustle **7** fast one, hatband, lanyard, swindle **8** flimflam **10** fool around, mess around **11** horse around

boor
3 cad, oaf **4** lout, hick, rube **5** brute, chuff, churl, clown, yahoo, yokel **6** lummox, rustic **7** buffoon, bumpkin, hayseed, peasant **9** ignoramus, vulgarian **10** clodhopper, philistine, provincial

boorish
4 rude **5** crass, crude, rough **6** coarse, common, rugged, vulgar **7** ill-bred, loutish, lowbred, lumpish, uncivil, uncouth **8** churlish, cloddish, clownish, impolite, insolent, lubberly, swainish **9** graceless, offensive, tasteless, unrefined **10** philistine,

provincial, robustious, uncultured, ungracious, unmannerly, unpolished, unsociable **11** bad-mannered, clodhopping, ill-mannered, uncivilized **12** discourteous, uncultivated **13** disrespectful

boost

3 aid **4** hike, lift, jump, plug, push, rise **5** raise, steal **6** assist, beef up, expand, extend, foster, jack up **7** advance, amplify, augment, elevate, magnify, promote, support **8** heighten, increase, shoplift **9** advertise, encourage, expansion, promotion **10** assistance **11** helping hand **13** encouragement

booster

3 fan **4** hypo, shot **6** backer, patron, rocket, rooter **7** vaccine **8** champion, defender, promoter, upholder **9** amplifier, expositor, injection, proponent, supporter **10** shoplifter **11** inoculation

boot

3 can **4** bang, fire, kick, sack **5** chuck, eject, evict, expel, start **6** bounce, thrill **7** dismiss, kick out, start up **8** throw out **9** discharge, dismissal, terminate
kind: 5 wader **6** arctic, chukka, gaiter, galosh, mukluk **7** jodhpur, shoepac **8** balmoral, cothurni (plural), overshoe, shoepack **9** cothurnus **10** Wellington

Boötes star

8 Arcturus

booth

4 nook **5** berth, bower, kiosk, stall, stand **6** carrel **9** enclosure **11** compartment

bootleg

3 hot, run **5** hooch **6** pirate **7** illicit, smuggle **9** irregular, moonshine **10** bathtub gin, contraband **11** black market, mountain dew **12** unauthorized

bootless

4 vain **5** empty **6** futile, hollow **7** useless **8** abortive, impotent,

nugatory **9** fruitless, valueless, worthless **10** profitless, unavailing **11** ineffective, ineffectual **12** unproductive, unprofitable, unsuccessful

bootlick

4 fawn **5** cower, crawl, creep, toady **6** cringe, grovel, kowtow, stroke **7** cater to, flatter, truckle **8** blandish **9** brownnose, importune, seek favor **10** curry favor **11** apple-polish **12** bow and scrape

bootlicker

4 toad **5** toady **6** lackey, lapdog, minion, yes-man **7** doormat, spaniel **8** hanger-on **9** sycophant **11** lickspittle

booty

4 haul, lift, loot, pelf, swag, take **5** prize, spoil, yield **6** spoils **7** pillage, plunder, rear end, seizure, takings **8** buttocks

booze

4 brew, grog, swig **5** binge, drink, hooch, juice, quaff, sauce, souse, swill **6** guzzle, imbibe, liquor, rotgut, tank up, tipple **7** alcohol, carouse, put away, spirits, swizzle **8** cocktail, liquor up **9** aqua vitae, firewater, knock back, moonshine

boozehound

3 sot **4** lush, wino **5** drunk, hoser, souse **7** guzzler **8** drunkard **9** alcoholic, inebriate **11** dipsomaniac

boozer

see **boozehound**

bop

3 bat, box, hit, jab, pop, rap **4** bash, bean, belt, biff, boff, blow, clip, cuff, jive, slug, sock, swat, whop **5** clock, pound, smack, thump, whack **8** plant one

borax

4 junk

Bordeaux wine

district: 5 Médoc **6** Graves
grape: 6 Malbec, Merlot **8** Cabernet
name: 5 Arsac, Ludon, Macau

6 Moulis **7** Labarde, Margaux, Pomerol **8** Cantenac, St. Julien, Pauillac **9** St. Emilion, St. Estèphe, St. Laurent
red: 6 claret

bordello
see **brothel**

border
3 hem, lip, rim **4** abut, brim, edge, join, line, pale, trim **5** bound, brink, flank, frame, limit, march, skirt, touch, verge **6** adjoin, bounds, butt on, define, fringe, limbus, margin, trench **7** contour, outline, selvage **8** approach, boundary, frontier, neighbor, sideline, surround **9** marchland, perimeter, periphery **11** butt against, communicate
inlaid: 8 purfling
raised: 7 coaming

bordereau
4 note **6** record **7** account **10** memorandum

bordering
4 nigh **5** close **6** almost, next to **7** meeting, verging **8** abutting, adjacent, touching **9** adjoining, alongside, close upon, impinging **10** approximal, contiguous, juxtaposed **11** coterminous, neighboring, practically

borderland
5 march **6** fringe, margin **8** frontier **9** marchland

borderline
4 pale **6** almost, nearly **7** dubious, unclear **8** boundary, doubtful, marginal, unstable **9** ambiguous, debatable, dubitable, equivocal, perimeter, uncertain, undecided, unsettled **11** demarcation, problematic **12** intermediate **13** indeterminate

border state
8 Delaware, Kentucky, Maryland, Missouri, Virginia

bore
3 irk **4** drag, drip, mine, peer, pill, ream, sink, tire, yawn **5** auger, drill, drone, gouge, prick, punch **6** burrow,

pierce, tunnel **7** bromide, caliber, fatigue **8** diameter, puncture **9** penetrate, perforate, soporific **10** dullsville

boreal
3 icy **4** cold, cool **5** chill, gelid, polar **6** arctic, bitter, chilly, frosty, frigid, tundra **7** glacial, wintery **8** freezing, northern **9** northerly

Boreas
beloved: 8 Orithyia
brother: 5 Notus **8** Hesperus, Zephyrus
father: 8 Astraeus
mother: 3 Eos
son: 5 Zetes **6** Calais

boredom
5 blahs, ennui **6** apathy, stupor, tedium, torpor **7** fatigue **8** doldrums, dullness, flatness, monotony **9** lassitude, weariness **11** incuriosity, tediousness **12** indifference

Borgia
4 Juan **6** Alonso, Cesare **7** Alfonso, Rodrigo **8** Lucrezia

boring
3 dry **4** arid, drab, dull, flat, zero **5** ho-hum, vapid **6** dreary, stodgy, tiring **7** humdrum, tedious **8** bromidic, drudging, lifeless, tiresome **9** wearisome **10** lackluster, monotonous, pedestrian, unexciting **13** uninteresting

boring tool
5 drill, auger **6** trepan

Boris Godunov composer
10 Mussorgsky (Modest)
11 Moussorgsky (Modest)

born
3 née **6** innate, native **8** destined, inherent **9** intrinsic **10** congenital, deep-seated
combining form: 3 gen **4** gene **6** genous **7** genetic

borne by the wind
6 aeolic, eolian **7** aeolian

Borneo
ethnic group: 4 Dyak **5** Dayak

mountain: 8 Kinabalu
nation: 6 Brunei
river: 6 Rabang

Borodin opera
10 Prince Igor

borough
4 town 5 burgh 7 village 8 township

bosh
see **bunkum**

Bosnia-Herzegovina
capital: 8 Sarajevo
language: 7 Serbian 8 Croatian
13 Serbo-Croatian
monetary unit: 4 mark 5 dinar
neighbor: 6 Serbia 7 Croatia
part of: 7 Balkans
sea: 8 Adriatic

bosom
4 bust, core, soul, teat 5 chest,
close, heart 6 breast 7 embrace
8 feelings, intimate 10 affections,
conscience

bosomy
5 built, busty, buxom, curvy 6 chesty
7 shapely, stacked 9 Junoesque
11 full-figured

boss
4 head, stud 5 chief 6 direct, honcho, leader, manage, master, survey
7 command, foreman, headman,
oversee 8 director, employer, overlook, overseer, superior 9 chieftain,
supervise 10 supervisor, taskmaster
11 superintend
African: 5 bwana

bossy
3 cow 4 calf 7 studded 8 despotic,
imperial 9 arbitrary, assertive, imperious, masterful 10 autocratic, high-
handed, imperative, oppressive,
peremptory, tyrannical 11 controlling, dictatorial, domineering,
magisterial, overbearing

botanist
American: 4 Gray (Asa) 5 Sears
(Paul B.) 6 Bailey (Liberty), Bessey
(Charles), Carver (George Washing-
ton) 7 Bartram (John, William), Bur-
bank (Luther) 9 Fairchild (David)
Austrian: 6 Mendel (Gregor)
British: 6 Sloane (Sir Hans)
Danish: 7 Warming (Johannes)
Dutch: 7 De Vries (Hugo)
French: 7 Lamarck (Chevalier de)
German: 4 Cohn (Ferdinand), Mohl
(Hugo von) 5 Sachs (Julius von)
Irish: 6 Harvey (William)
Scottish: 5 Brown (Robert)
Swedish: 8 Linnaeus (Carolus)
Swiss: 6 Nägeli (Karl) 8 Candolle
(Augustin)

botany branch
7 ecology 8 algology, bryology, my-
cology 9 phycology 10 morphology,
palynology, physiology 11 hydro-
ponics, paleobotany, pteridology,
systematics 12 bacteriology

botch
4 blow, flop, flub, foul, goof, mess,
muck, muff, ruin 5 fluff, gum up,
mix-up, snarl, spoil 6 bobble, boggle, bollix, bumble, bungle, fiasco,
fumble, goof up, mess up, muddle
7 blunder, confuse, louse up, washout 8 bugger up, disaster, disorder,
dishevel, shambles 9 mishandle,
mismanage, patchwork 10 discompose, hodgepodge, misconduct,
mishmash

botchy
5 messy 6 blowzy, frowsy, frowzy,
sloppy, untidy 7 chaotic 8 careless,
confused, slapdash, slipshod,
slovenly

both
combining form: 3 bis
prefix: 4 ambi, amph 5 amphi

bother
3 ado, bug, irk, nag, vex 4 drag, fret,
fuss, gall, pest, pain 5 annoy, eat at,
harry, trial, upset 6 badger, flurry,
harass, needle, pester, plague, ruffle
7 afflict, agitate, anxiety, bedevil,
concern, disturb, fluster, perturb,
provoke, torment, trouble 8 disquiet,
headache, irritant, nuisance, vexation
9 aggravate, annoyance 10 discompose, exasperate, irritation 11 aggravation, intrude upon 12 exasperation 13 inconvenience

botheration

4 damn, pain, pest 5 trial 6 plague
7 torment 8 headache, irritant,
nuisance, vexation 9 annoyance
10 difficulty, irritation 11 aggravation,
provocation 12 exasperation
13 inconvenience

Botswana

capital: 8 Gaborone
city: 11 Francistown
desert: 8 Kalahari
former name: 12 Bechuanaland
language: 6 Tswana 7 English
monetary unit: 4 pula
neighbor: 7 Namibia 8 Zimbabwe
11 South Africa
river: 5 Chobe 6 Molopo 7 Limpopo 8 Okavango

bottle

4 vial 5 cruet, cruse, flask, phial
6 ampule, carafe, fiasco, flacon,
magnum, vessel 7 ampoule 8 decanter, jeroboam 9 container

bottle gourd

8 calabash

bottleneck

5 choke 6 hinder, impede, narrow
7 impasse 8 obstacle, obstruct,
paralyze, slowdown, throttle 9 hindrance 10 choke point, congestion,
traffic jam 11 obstruction

bottom

3 bum 4 base, boat, core, foot, root,
pith, rump, seat, ship, sole, soul, tail,
tush 5 basal, basic, basis, fanny,
found, nadir 6 behind, breech,
heinie, lowest, source 7 bedrock,
essence, footing, primary, rear end
8 backside, buttocks, derriere,
pedestal, pediment 9 establish,
fundament, lowermost, posterior,
predicate, principle, underbody, undermost, underside 10 foundation,
nethermost, underbelly, underlying,
underneath 11 fundamental, lowest
point 12 undersurface

bottomless

4 deep, vast 7 abysmal, endless
8 baseless, enduring, profound,
unending 9 boundless, unlimited

10 gratuitous, groundless, unfillable,
ungrounded 11 everlasting, inestimable, never-ending 12 immeasurable, incalculable, unfathomable
13 inexhaustible

bottommost

4 last 5 least 6 lowest 7 deepest

bough

3 arm 4 limb 5 shoot 6 branch
8 offshoot

boulevard

4 road 6 artery, avenue, street
7 terrace 8 main drag 9 esplanade, promenade 10 high street
12 thoroughfare

boulevardier

7 flaneur, trifler 9 bon vivant 10 aficionado, dilettante 11 cognoscente,
connoisseur 12 man-about-town

bounce

3 can, hop, pep, vim, zip 4 fire,
jump, leap, oust, sack, zest 5 expel,
vault, verve, vigor 6 energy, hurdle,
spirit, spring 7 bluster, boot out,
dismiss, kick out, rebound, saltate,
sparkle 8 buoyancy, ricochet, vitality
9 animation, discharge, eliminate,
terminate 10 ebullience, elasticity,
liveliness

bounce back

5 rally 6 perk up, pick up, recoil,
return, revive 7 cheer up, improve,
rebound, recover 8 backfire 9 boomerang 10 recuperate, turn around

bounce off

5 carom 7 rebound 8 ricochet

bouncer

4 goon 5 guard 8 houseman,
sentinel, watchman 9 muscleman

bouncy

3 gay 4 airy 5 peppy, perky
6 blithe, cheery, jaunty, jocund, lively
7 buoyant, elastic 8 animated,
volatile 9 ebullient, energetic, expansive, exuberant, resilient, sprightly
10 unsinkable 12 effervescent, high-
spirited 13 irrepressible

bound

3 end, hem, hop, rim **4** bolt, edge, jump, leap, term, skip **5** caper, frisk, hem in, limit, skirt, vault, verge **6** border, bounce, define, demark, driven, finite, fringe, gambol, hurdle, margin, spring, sprint **7** confine, delimit, enclose, hotfoot, limited, mark out, obliged, pledged, rebound, saltate **8** articled, beholden, confined, confines, enslaved, resolved, restrain, surround **9** compelled, demarcate, obligated **10** determined, indentured, limitation **11** apprenticed, responsible **12** circumscribe

boundary

3 hem **4** mete, pale **5** ambit, limit **6** limits, margin **7** compass, outline **8** confines, environs, purlieus **9** perimeter, precincts **10** borderline **13** circumference

bounder

3 cad, cur, dog **4** boor, worm **5** knave, louse, rogue **6** rascal, rotter

boundless

4 vast **5** great **7** endless **8** infinite **9** excessive, limitless, unbounded, unlimited **10** indefinite, unconfined, unmeasured **11** illimitable, measureless **12** immeasurable, unrestricted **13** inexhaustible, unsurpassable

bounteous

5 ample **6** benign, lavish **7** copious, liberal, profuse **8** abundant, generous, handsome, prodigal **9** bountiful, capacious, expansive, extensive, plenteous, plentiful, unsparing **10** beneficent, big-hearted, free-handed, munificent, openhanded, voluminous **11** magnanimous, overflowing

bountiful

see **bounteous**

bounty

5 grant, prize, yield **6** deluge, plenty, reward, wealth **7** payment, premium **8** richness **9** abundance, affluence, plenitude, profusion **10** cornucopia, generosity, induce-

ment, liberality, luxuriance, prosperity **11** benevolence, copiousness **12** compensation

Bounty captain

5 Bligh (William)

bouquet

4 balm, kudo, odor, posy **5** aroma, kudos, scent, spice, spray **6** eulogy, medley **7** acclaim, corsage, essence, garland, incense, nosegay, perfume **8** accolade, encomium **9** fragrance, redolence **10** compliment **11** arrangement, boutonniere **12** commendation

bourgeois

7 burgher **8** ordinary **10** conformist, philistine **11** middle-class **12** conventional

bourgeoisie

11 middle class, third estate

Bourne Identity author

6 Ludlum (Robert)

bout

3 jag, run **4** game, meet, term, tour, turn **5** match, round, shift, siege, spell, spasm, spree, stint, throe, trick **6** attack **7** contest, session **8** outbreak **10** engagement

boutique

4 shop **8** emporium

bovine

3 cow, yak **4** anoa, bull, calf, gaur, neat, zebu **5** bison, steer, stirk **6** heifer, placid, torpid, wisent **7** aurochs, banteng, buffalo, bullock, cowlike **8** longhorn
genus: 3 Bos
sound: 3 low, moo

bow

3 arc, bob, dip, nod **4** arch, bend, knot, lout, prow, turn **5** angle, crook, curve, debut, defer, hunch, round, stoop, yield **6** archer, congee, curtsy, give in, kowtow, relent, salaam, salute, submit **7** concede, curtsey, flexure, incline, rainbow, succumb, turning **9** curvation, curvature,

genuflect, obeisance, surrender
10 capitulate **11** buckle under
12 knuckle under

Bow, Clara
6 It girl

bowdlerize
4 blip, edit **6** censor, excise, purify,
screen **7** abridge, cleanse, distort,
launder **8** sanitize **9** expurgate
10 adulterate, blue-pencil

bowed
4 bent **5** arced, bandy **6** arched,
curved **11** bandy-legged, curvilinear

bowel
3 gut **6** paunch **9** intestine

bower
5 arbor **6** anchor **7** enclose, pergola,
retreat **9** apartment

bowery
7 skid row

bowfin
4 amia **7** mudfish

bowl
5 arena, basin, jorum, mazer, stade,
tazza **6** tureen, vessel **7** stadium
8 coliseum **12** amphitheater

bowlegged
5 bandy

bowler
3 hat **5** derby **6** kegler

Bowl game
5 Super
Abilene: **5** Pecan
Anaheim: **7** Freedom
Atlanta: **5** Peach
Dallas: **6** Cotton
El Paso: **3** Sun
Fresno: **7** California
Honolulu: **5** Aloha
Houston: **10** Bluebonnet
Jacksonville: **5** Gator
Memphis: **7** Liberty
Miami: **6** Orange **8** Carquest
Mobile: **6** Senior
New Orleans: **5** Sugar
Orlando: **13** Florida Citrus
Pasadena: **4** Rose

San Diego: **7** Holiday
Shreveport: **12** Independence
Tampa: **10** Hall of Fame
Tempe: **6** Fiesta
Tucson: **6** Copper

bowling
7 kegling
British: **8** skittles
Italian: **5** bocce, bocci **6** boccie
term: **3** pin **4** hook, lane, spot
5 curve, frame, spare, split **6** gutter,
strike, string, turkey **7** duckpin
9 candlepin

bowl over
3 awe, wow **4** daze, fell, stun
5 floor, shock, throw **6** boggle,
dismay **7** astound, flatten, impress,
stupefy **8** blow away, surprise
9 bring down, dumbfound, knock
down, overwhelm **10** disconcert

bow out
4 exit, fold, quit **5** leave, welsh
6 beg off, give up, retire **8** withdraw
9 surrender

box
3 bin **4** case, cell, chop, cuff, duke,
loge, slap, sock, spar **5** booth, chest,
clout, crate, fight, punch, smack,
stall, trunk **6** buffet, carton, casket,
coffer, coffin, encase, hopper, packet
7 confine, enclose, package **9** container, enclosure, rectangle **10** pigeonhole, receptacle **11** compartment

boxer
7 fighter, palooka **8** pugilist **9** fly-
weight **11** heavyweight, light-
weight **12** bantamweight, mid-
dleweight, welterweight **13** feather-
weight
champ: **3** Ali (Muhammad) **4** Bowe
(Riddick) **5** Bruno (Frank), Jones
(Roy), Lewis (Lennox), Louis (Joe),
Moore (Archie), Tyson (Mike)
6 Hagler (Marvin), Hearns
(Thomas), Holmes (Larry), McCall
(Oliver), Moorer (Michael), Seldon
(Bruce), Spinks (Leon, Michael),
Tunney (Gene), Walker (Mickey)
7 Charles (Ezzard), Corbett (James),
Dempsey (Jack), Douglas (Buster),

Foreman (George), Frazier (Joe), Johnson (Jack), LaMotta (Jake), Leonard (Sugar Ray), Sharkey (Jack), Walcott (Joe) **8** Marciano (Rocky), Robinson (Sugar Ray), Sullivan (John L.) **9** Armstrong (Henry), Holyfield (Evander), Patterson (Floyd), Schmeling (Max)

boxing

8 pugilism **10** fisticuffs **13** prizefighting
term: 3 jab, TKO **4** blow, bout, duck, foul, hook, ring, rope, spar **5** break, count, feint, glove, match, parry, punch, round, swing **6** bucket, canvas, corner **7** low blow, referee **8** heavy bag, knockout, uppercut **9** knockdown **11** punching bag

boy

3 lad, son, tad **5** gamin, puppy, sonny **6** laddie, nipper, shaver **9** shaveling, stripling, youngster
combining form: 3 ped **4** paed, paid, pedo **5** paedo, paido
errand: 5 gofer **8** lobbygow
French: 6 garçon
Latin: 4 puer
mischievous: 6 urchin
Spanish: 4 niño

boyfriend

4 beau **5** swain **6** fiancé, old man, suitor **7** main man **9** inamorato

Boy Scout

founder: 11 Baden-Powell (Robert)
gathering: 8 jamboree
motto: 10 be prepared
rank: 4 Life (Scout), Star (Scout) **5** Eagle (Scout) **10** Tenderfoot
unit: 5 troop **6** patrol

Boys Town

founder: 8 Flanagan (Edward)
state: 8 Nebraska

bozo

3 oaf **4** boob, clod, dodo, dolt, dope, fool, goof, jerk, mutt, simp, yo-yo **5** chump, dummy, dunce, idiot, moron, ninny, noddy, stupe **6** dimwit, donkey, dum-dum, nitwit, noodle **7** airhead, dullard, pinhead **8** bonehead, clodpoll, dumbbell, dumbhead, imbecile, lunkhead, meathead, numskull **9** birdbrain, blockhead, ignoramus, lamebrain, numbskull, simpleton, thickhead **10** dunderhead, hammerhead, nincompoop **11** chowderhead, chucklehead, knucklehead

B.P.O.E. member

3 Elk

Brabantio's daughter

9 Desdemona

brabble

3 row **4** beef, feud, flap, riot, spat, tiff **5** argue, scrap, set to **6** bicker, blowup, fracas, grouse **7** dispute, fall out, palaver, quarrel, rhubarb, scuffle, wrangle **8** argument, squabble **9** altercate, bickering, brannigan, caterwaul, wrangling **10** falling-out **11** altercation, disputation, embroilment

brace

3 arm, bar, duo, tie **4** dyad, gird, pair, prop, stay **5** clamp, ready, shore, steel, strut, truss **6** accost, bear up, column, couple, demand, splint, steady, uphold **7** bolster, bracket, enliven, fortify, freshen, prepare, refresh, shore up, support, sustain, tighten, twosome **8** buttress **9** reinforce **10** cantilever, exhilarate, invigorate, strengthen **12** underpinning **13** underpropping

bracelet

6 bangle **7** manacle **8** wristlet

bracing

4 keen **5** brisk, crisp, fresh, nippy, sharp, tonic **6** biting, chilly **7** rousing **8** stirring **9** animating **10** energizing, quickening **11** restorative, stimulating, stimulative **12** exhilarating, invigorating

bracken

4 fern **5** brake, brush, scrub **11** undergrowth

bracket

3 arm **4** join, link, omit **5** brace

6 couple, relate, remove 7 combine, compare, conjoin, connect, embrace, enclose, include, support 8 buttress, encircle, leave out, put aside, set aside 9 associate, encompass 11 parenthesis 12 strengthener

brackish
4 sour 5 acrid, briny, salty 6 saline, salted 9 repulsive, sickening 10 nauseating

bract
4 leaf 5 glume 6 paleat, spathe 8 phyllary

brad
4 nail

Bradamant
brother: 7 Rinaldo
husband: 6 Rogero 8 Ruggiero

Bradbury's forte
5 sci-fi 7 fantasy

brae
4 bank, hill 5 slope 8 hillside

brag
3 gas 4 blow, crow, puff 5 boast, mouth, prate, vaunt 7 show off, swagger, talk big 9 cockiness, gasconade 10 grandstand 11 rodomontade

braggadocio
6 hot air 7 boaster, bombast, bravado, conceit, puffery, swagger, windbag 8 blowhard, boasting, braggart, bragging 9 arrogance, cockiness, pomposity 10 cockalorum, pretension, swaggering 11 fanfaronade

braggart
6 blower 7 boaster, egotist, vaunter, windbag 8 big mouth, blowhard 9 big talker, know-it-all, swaggerer, vulgarian 11 braggadocio

Brahmin
8 highbrow 9 blueblood, patrician 10 aristocrat

braid
4 plat 5 plait, queue 7 galloon, pigtail 8 soutache 9 interlace 10 intertwine, interweave

brain
3 wit 4 bean, conk, mind 7 concuss 9 intellect 10 gray matter 12 intelligence
bone: 5 skull 7 cranium
clot: 10 thrombosis
gland: 6 pineal 9 pituitary
layer: 6 cortex
lobe: 6 limbic, vermis 7 frontal 8 parietal, temporal 9 occipital
membrane: 3 pia 4 dura 6 meninx 8 pia mater 9 arachnoid, dura mater
part: 4 lobe 7 medulla 8 cerebrum, thalamus 9 sensorium, ventricle 10 cerebellum, hemisphere 12 diencephalon
relating to: 8 cerebral 10 encephalic
ridge: 4 gyri (plural) 5 gyrus
vertebrate: 10 encephalon
wave record: 3 EEG

brainchild
4 idea, opus, work 6 animus, scheme, theory 7 coinage 9 handiwork, invention 10 hypothesis, innovation 11 achievement, chef-d'oeuvre, contrivance

brainiac
4 whiz 6 genius 7 prodigy

brainless
3 dim 5 dense, silly, thick 6 simple, stupid 7 asinine, foolish, idiotic, moronic, vacuous, witless 9 dimwitted, nitwitted 10 acephalous 12 feebleminded

brainpower
3 wit 5 sense 6 smarts 8 aptitude, capacity, sagacity 9 intellect, mentality, mother wit 10 perception 11 discernment, penetration 12 intelligence 13 comprehension

brainsick
3 mad 4 daft 5 batty, crazy, manic, potty 6 crazed, insane, mental 7 cracked, haywire, lunatic 8 aberrant, demented, deranged, maniacal, unhinged 9 bedlamite, delirious, disturbed 10 disordered, incoherent, irrational, unbalanced

brainstorm
3 rap, jaw 4 idea 6 confer, huddle

7 dream up, think up 8 cogitate,
discuss, mull over 9 mental fit
10 groupthink, kick around, toss
around 11 inspiration, put together

brainteaser
5 poser, rebus 6 puzzle, riddle
7 stumper 9 conundrum 10 cryptogram

brainwashing
10 propaganda 11 mind control,
reeducation

brainy
4 keen 5 quick, savvy, sharp, smart
6 adroit, astute, bright, clever 9 egg-
headed, brilliant, sagacious 10 discerning, precocious 11 intelligent,
quick-witted, ready-witted 13 knowledgeable, perspicacious

brake
4 curb, slow, stop 5 block 6 damper,
hinder, impede, retard, slough 7 barrier, bracken, slacken 8 blockade,
obstacle, obstruct, slow down 9 deterrent, hindrance 10 constraint,
decelerate 11 bracken fern

bramble
4 burr 5 brier, furze, gorse, hedge,
shrub, thorn 6 nettle 7 thistle

branch
3 arm 4 fork, limb, rami (plural), wing
5 bough, ramus 6 ramify 7 diverge,
outpost 9 division 9 tributary
10 subsidiary

branched
6 ramate, ramose

brand
4 blot, blur, logo, make, mark, onus,
sear, slur, sort, spot, type 5 badge,
class, odium, stain, stamp, sword,
taint, torch 6 accuse, charge,
impute, stigma, stripe 7 species,
variety 8 black eye, disgrace,
insignia, logotype 9 trademark
10 stigmatize

brandish
4 wave 5 flash, shake, sport, swing,
wield 6 flaunt, parade 7 display,
exhibit, show off 8 flourish

brand-new
4 mint 5 fresh 6 latest, unused,
virgin 8 up-to-date 9 untouched
11 cutting-edge 13 inexperienced

brandy
4 marc, ouzo, raki 5 Pisco 6 cognac,
grappa, kirsch, Metaxa 7 liqueur
8 Armagnac, calvados, digestif, eau-
de-vie 9 applejack, framboise,
slivovitz

brannigan
3 row 4 bust, flap, spat, tiff 5 binge,
fight, set-to, spree 6 bender, blowup
hassle, ruckus 7 brabble, discord,
dispute, quarrel, wassail, wrangle
8 squabble 10 falling-out 11 altercation

brash
4 bold, flip, pert 5 cocky, gutsy, hasty,
nervy, saucy 6 brassy, brazen,
cheeky, madcap, uppish, uppity
7 brittle, forward 8 arrogant, cocksure, flippant, impudent, insolent,
reckless, tactless 9 audacious,
bumptious, ebullient, energetic,
exuberant, hot-headed, impetuous,
impolitic, maladroit, unabashed,
untactful 10 ill-advised, incautious
11 overweening, thoughtless
12 high-spirited, presumptuous,
undiplomatic, unrestrained
13 disrespectful, inconsiderate, irrepressible, self-assertive

brashness
4 gall, grit, guts 5 brass, cheek,
crust, nerve, pluck 6 aplomb, daring,
mettle, spirit 8 audacity, chutzpah,
temerity 9 assurance 10 confidence.
effrontery 11 presumption

brass
4 gall 5 cheek, nerve 8 audacity,
chutzpah 9 brashness, impudence,
insolence 10 confidence, effrontery
11 presumption 12 impertinence

brassbound
3 set 5 brash, rigid 6 brazen, narrow 7 adamant, bigoted, forward
8 obdurate 9 illiberal, presuming,
obstinate, unbending 10 implacable,

inflexible, intolerant, relentless, unswayable, unyielding **11** opinionated, small-minded, unrelenting **12** narrow-minded, presumptuous, single-minded **13** dyed-in-the-wool, self-asserting, self-assertive

brasserie
10 restaurant

brass hat
3 VIP **4** boss **5** elder **6** better, senior **7** big shot **8** big whell, higher-up, superior

brassica
4 kale, rape **5** colza **6** turnip **7** cabbage, mustard **8** broccoli, collards, kohlrabi, rutabaga **11** cauliflower

brass tacks
5 facts **7** details **11** nitty-gritty, particulars

brass worker
7 brazier

brassy
see **brazen**

brat
3 imp **4** punk **6** urchin **10** holy terror

bravado
5 bluff **6** hot air **7** bluster, bombast **8** audacity, boasting, boldness, bragging, defiance, vaunting **9** gasconade **10** blustering, pretension, swaggering **11** braggadocio, grandiosity **12** boastfulness

brave
4 bold, dare, defy, face, game, meet, risk **5** beard, gutsy, hardy, manly, nervy, noble, stout **6** daring, heroic, manful, plucky, spunky, take on **7** defiant, doughty, gallant, valiant, venture **8** confront, face down, fearless, intrepid, reckless, resolute, spirited, splendid, stalwart, unafraid, valorous **9** audacious, challenge, dauntless, excellent, steadfast, undaunted, withstand **10** courageous **11** boldhearted, indomitable, lionhearted, undauntable, unflinching, venturesome **12** stouthearted **13** adventuresome

Brave New World author
6 Huxley (Aldous)

bravery
4 grit, guts **5** nerve, pluck, valor **6** daring, mettle, spirit **7** courage, heroism **8** audacity, boldness, temerity **9** derring-do, fortitude, gallantry **11** intrepidity **12** fearlessness, intrepidness
false: 7 bravado

bravo
3 olé **4** rave **5** cheer **6** gunman, hit man, killer **7** ovation, plaudit, villain **8** applause, assassin **9** desperado

bravura
4 bold **5** showy **6** daring, florid, ornate **8** dazzling, skillful, virtuoso **9** brilliant

brawl
3 row **4** feud, flap, fray, fuss, maul, riot, spar, spat, tiff **5** clash, broil, fight, melee, scrap, set-to **6** affray, battle, bicker, dustup, fracas, rumble, tussle **7** bobbery, brabble, contend, quarrel, rhubarb, ruction, scuffle, wrangle **8** dogfight, eruption, skirmish, slugfest, squabble, upheaval **9** fistfight, imbroglio, scrimmage **10** donnybrook, fisticuffs, free-for-all **11** altercation, disturbance **13** confrontation

brawn
4 beef, meat, thew **5** clout, flesh, might, power, sinew **6** muscle **8** strength **9** puissance **10** headcheese

brawny
5 beefy, burly, husky, lusty, tough **6** robust, sinewy, stocky, strong, sturdy **8** athletic, muscular, powerful, thickset, vigorous **9** strapping, well-built **10** able-bodied

bray
4 mill **5** crush, grind, pound **6** bellow, pestle, powder **7** atomize, trumpet **9** pulverize

brazen
4 bold, loud **5** brash, gaudy, noisy,

showy **6** arrant, brassy, cheeky
7 blatant, defiant, forward, glaring,
jarring **8** flagrant, impudent, insolent
9 audacious, barefaced, obtrusive,
shameless, unabashed **10** outrageous, procacious, unblushing **11** conspicuous, impertinent **12** contumelious, presumptuous **13** disrespectful

Brazil

capital: 8 Brasília
city: 5 Belém **6** Recife **8** Salvador,
São Paulo **12** Rio de Janeiro
13 Belo Horizonte
discoverer: 6 Cabral (Pedro)
island: 6 Marajó **7** Caviana
language: 10 Portuguese
monetary unit: 4 real
neighbor: 4 Peru **6** Guyana
7 Bolivia, Uruguay **8** Colombia,
Paraguay, Suriname **9** Argentina,
Venezuela **12** French Guiana
river: 6 Amazon **8** Parnaíba
10 Alto Paraná **12** São Francisco

breach

3 gap **4** gash, hole, open, rent, rift,
slit **5** break, chasm, cleft, crack, split
6 hiatus, lacuna, schism **7** break in,
discord, disrupt, fissure, infract,
interim, opening, rupture, violate
8 aperture, disunity, division, fracture, infringe, interval, trespass
9 disregard, severance, violation
10 alienation, contravene, infraction,
separation, transgress **11** delinquency, dereliction **12** disaffection,
disobedience, estrangement, infringement, interruption **13** contravention, discontinuity, noncompliance, nonobservance, transgression

bread

3 bun **4** food, pita, rusk **5** bagel,
money, toast **6** living, muffin, sippet
7 biscuit, crouton, edibles, stollen
8 victuals, zwieback **9** provender
10 livelihood, provisions, sustenance
11 comestibles, maintenance,
subsistence
communion: 4 host **5** wafer
9 Eucharist
from heaven: 5 manna

ingredient: 4 meal **5** flour, yeast
6 leaven
Jewish: 5 matzo **6** hallah, matzoh
7 challah
maker: 5 baker
Scottish: 7 bannock
spread: 3 jam **4** oleo **5** jelly
6 butter **9** margarine
unleavened: 5 matzo **6** matzoh

bread and butter

4 keep, work **6** basics, living **7** support **8** mainstay, victuals **10** employment, livelihood, occupation, sustenance **9** nutriment **11** maintenance, necessities, subsistence
12 alimentation

breadbasket

3 gut **5** belly, tummy **6** paunch
7 abdomen, stomach **8** potbelly
9 bay window, beer belly

breadth

4 area, size, span **5** range, reach,
scope, space, sweep, width **6** extent, spread **7** compass, expanse,
stretch **8** distance, fullness, latitude,
vastness, wideness **9** amplitude,
expansion, magnitude **10** liberality

break

3 gap **4** bust, dash, halt, leak, luck,
rest, rift, ruin, tame **5** burst, clear,
crack, inure, sever, solve, spell
6 breach, chance, decode, divide,
escape, exceed, hiatus, impair,
lacuna, refute, relief, reveal
7 destroy, divulge, fall out, interim,
lighten, opening, respite, rupture,
shatter, surpass, suspend, time-out,
violate **8** accustom, bankrupt,
breather, decipher, disclose, division,
downtime, fracture, good luck, interval, moderate **9** interlude, interrupt
10 annihilate, controvert, impoverish
11 discontinue, disjunction, dislocation, opportunity, suspensions
12 intermission, interruption **13** discontinuity

breakable

4 weak **5** frail **6** flimsy **7** brittle,
fragile, friable **8** delicate **9** frangible

breakaway
4 prop 7 escapee 8 offshoot, renegade, seceding

break down
4 fail, fold, sort, wilt 5 class, decay, index 6 cave in, digest, give in 7 analyze, clarify, crumble, crumple, elucidate, give out, give way, go crazy, succumb 8 classify, collapse, dissolve 9 anatomize, decompose, fall apart 12 disintegrate·

breakdown
5 crash, decay, smash, study, wreck 6 mishap 7 crack-up, debacle, failure, smashup 8 analysis, collapse, taxonomy 9 cataclysm, partition 10 disruption, dissection, resolution 11 dysfunction, examination, prostration

breaker
4 wave 6 billow, comber, roller

Breakfast at Tiffany's author
6 Capote (Truman)

breakfront
7 cabinet 8 bookcase

break in
4 tame 5 train 6 breach, burgle, gentle, invade 7 intrude 8 initiate 9 condition, habituate, interfere, interpose, interrupt

breakneck
4 fast 5 fleet, hasty, quick, rapid, swift 6 racing, speedy, unsafe 8 meteoric 10 harefooted 11 precipitous

break off
3 end 4 drop, halt, kill, stop 5 abort, cease, scrub, sever 6 cancel, detach 7 curtail, scratch, suspend 8 cut short 9 terminate 11 discontinue

break out
4 bolt, flee 5 arise, erupt, flare 6 emerge, escape 7 explode 8 mushroom, separate

break through
5 burst 6 breach, emerge, pierce 7 rupture, surface 8 overcome 9 penetrate

breakthrough
4 find, gain, hike, leap, rise 5 boost 7 advance, radical, upgrade 8 advanced, increase, landmark 9 invention, milestone 10 avant-garde, innovation 11 cutting-edge, development, exceptional, progressive, quantum leap

break up
3 end 4 halt, part 6 divide, sunder 7 destroy, disband, disjoin, disrupt, rupture, scatter, shatter 8 disperse, dissever, dissolve, disunite, separate 9 decompose, dismantle, pulverize, terminate 12 disintegrate

breakup
4 rift 5 split 7 divorce, parting 8 analysis 9 dispersal 10 dissection, separation 11 dissolution

breakwater
5 jetty

breast
5 bosom, chest, heart
animal: 7 brisket
combining form: 3 maz 4 mast, mazo 5 masto, stern, steth 6 mastia (plural), sterno, stetho

breastbone
7 sternum

breast-feed
5 nurse 6 suckle 7 nourish

breastwork
7 barrier, bastion, bulwark, defense, parapet, rampart 9 barricade, earthwork 10 embankment 13 fortification, reinforcement

breath
4 gasp, gust, hint, puff 5 let-up, pause, trace, whiff 6 breeze 7 respite 10 exhalation, inhalation, suggestion

breathe
4 emit, sigh 5 exude, utter, voice 6 endure, exhale, expire, inhale, murmur 7 confide, express, give off, inspire, persist, radiate, respire, subsist, survive, whisper

breather
    4 lull, rest, stay, vent 5 break,
    let-up, pause, spell 6 hiatus, recess
    7 caesura, respite 8 downtime
    9 remission 12 interruption

breathing
    labored: 7 dyspnea
    normal: 6 eupnea
    rapid: 8 polypnea

breathing apparatus
    10 respirator
    underwater: 5 scuba

breathing orifice
    4 nose 5 mouth 8 blowhole, spiracle

breathless
    4 agog, avid, keen 5 eager 6 ardent
    7 anxious, gasping, intense 8 grip-
    ping 9 expectant, impatient 11 short-
    winded 13 on tenterhooks

breathtaking
    6 moving 7 awesome 8 dramatic,
    exciting, imposing, stunning, won-
    drous 9 panoramic, thrilling 10 im-
    pressive, staggering 11 astonishing,
    magnificent, spectacular 12 awe-
    inspiring, overwhelming 13 heart-
    stirring

Brecht play
    4 Baal 13 Life of Galileo (The),
    Mother Courage 15 Seven Deadly
    Sins (The), Threepenny Opera (The)
    20 Caucasian Chalk Circle (The)

breech
    3 bum 4 duff, rear, rump, seat, tail
    5 fanny 6 behind, bottom, heinie
    7 keester, keister, rear end 8 back-
    side, buttocks, derriere, haunches
    9 fundament, posterior 12 hind-
    quarters

breechclout
    9 loincloth

breed
    3 ilk 4 bear, grow, kind, make, mate,
    race, rear, sire, sort, type 5 beget,
    brand, cause, class, cross, genus,
    hatch, likes, raise, stock, yield
    6 couple, create, father, induce,
    nature, strain, stripe 7 bring up,
    develop, educate, lineage, nurture,

produce, species, variety 8 copulate,
engender, generate, mate with,
multiply 9 cultivate, procreate,
propagate, reproduce 10 discipline,
extraction, give rise to, impregnate,
inseminate

breeding
    4 line 5 grace, taste 6 polish
    7 culture, decorum, lineage, manners
    8 ancestry, civility, courtesy, pedigree
    9 genealogy, gentility, propriety
    10 refinement, upbringing 11 cultiva-
    tion

breeding ground
    6 hotbed, origin 8 hothouse 10 forc-
    ing bed, mating spot 12 forcing
    house

breeze
    3 zip 4 flit, sail, snap, waft 5 cinch,
    draft, waltz 6 zephyr 8 duck soup,
    kid stuff 10 child's play

breezy
    4 airy, cool 5 fresh, gusty, windy
    6 blithe, casual, drafty 7 offhand,
    relaxed 8 carefree, careless,
    detached, informal 9 easygoing
    10 insouciant, nonchalant 11 uncon-
    cerned 12 devil-may-care, light-
    hearted

Breton
    4 Celt

_____ breve
    4 alla.

breviary
    5 brief 6 digest, précis 7 epitome,
    essence, outline, rundown, summary
    8 abstract, boildown, synopsis
    9 reduction 10 abridgment, conspec-
    tus, prayer book 11 abridgement
    12 condensation, divine office

brevity
    7 economy 8 laconism 9 briefness,
    concision, crispness, pithiness,
    shortness, terseness 10 transience

brew
    3 ale, tea 4 beer, loom, mull, plan,
    plot 5 drink 6 cook up, foment,
    gather, impend, infuse, scheme, stir
    up 7 concoct, ferment 8 contrive

briar
4 burr, pipe 5 furze, gorse, shrub, thorn 6 nettle 7 bramble, thistle

Briareus
7 Aegaeon
father: 6 Uranus
mother: 4 Gaea

bribe
3 buy, fix, sop 6 buy off, payoff, payola, square, suborn 7 corrupt 9 incentive 10 enticement, inducement, tamper with

bric-a-brac
6 curios 8 trinkets 9 ornaments 10 objets d'art 11 gingerbread, knickknacks 13 embellishment

brick
5 block
layer: 5 mason
laying: 7 masonry
material: 4 clay, marl
oven: 4 kiln
row: 6 course
sun-dried: 5 adobe
trough for carrying: 3 hod

bridal
7 nuptial, spousal 8 conjugal 9 connubial 11 matrimonial

bridal wreath
6 spirea

bridewell
3 can, jug, pen 4 coop, jail 5 clink, joint 6 lockup, prison 7 slammer 8 bastille 12 penitentiary

bridge
4 join, link, span 5 unite 7 connect 8 overpass, traverse
great: 8 Brooklyn 10 Golden Gate
kind: 4 arch, draw, rope 5 swing, truss 7 bascule, covered, natural, pontoon, trestle, viaduct 10 cantilever, suspension
term: 3 bid 4 book, east, pass, ruff, slam, suit, void, west 5 bonus, dummy, north, raise, south, trick, trump 6 double, renege, rubber 7 auction, finesse, no-trump, overbid 8 contract, jump call, redouble 9 grand slam, overtrick, singleton 10 little slam, undertrick, vulnerable

bridgelike game
5 whist 6 hearts

bridle
3 bit 4 curb, fume, rein, rule 5 check, flare, quell 6 govern, halter, hold in, manage, master, rein in, ruffle, seethe, subdue 7 bristle, control, flare up, inhibit, repress 8 hold back, moderate, restrain, suppress, withhold 9 constrain, deterrent, hackamore, restraint

brief
4 curt 5 pithy, short, terse 6 abrupt, digest, inform 7 brusque, concise, epitome, laconic, outline, passing, summary 8 abstract, breviary, fleeting, succinct, synopsis 9 momentary, transient 10 abridgment, conspectus 11 abridgement, compendious 12 condensation 13 short and sweet

brig
3 can, jug, pen 4 coop, jail 5 clink 6 cooler, lockup, prison 7 slammer 8 stockade 9 guardroom 10 guardhouse

brigade
4 army, unit 5 force, group 6 troops 10 contingent, detachment

brigand
6 bandit, bummer, looter, pirate, raider 7 cateran, corsair, forager, rustler 8 marauder, pillager 9 buccaneer, plunderer 10 freebooter, highwayman

brigandage
7 pillage, sacking 10 despoiling, ransacking 11 depredation

bright
4 fair, keen 5 aglow, alert, clear, light, lucid, quick, shiny, smart, sunny, vivid 6 brainy, cheery, clever, lively, lucent 7 beaming, blazing, flaming, fulgent, glowing, lambent, lighted, radiant 8 cheerful, dazzling, gleaming, luminous, lustrous, sunshiny 9 brilliant, effulgent, favorable, refulgent, sparkling 10 auspicious, glittering, precocious, propitious,

brighten

shimmering **11** illuminated, intelligent, quick-witted **12** incandescent **13** scintillating

brighten

4 buoy **5** cheer, clear, shine **6** look up, perk up, polish, revive, solace **7** burnish, cheer up, clear up, enhance, enliven, furbish, gladden, hearten, improve **8** illumine **10** illuminate

brightness

5 éclat, shine **6** luster, lustre **8** radiance, splendor **10** brilliance, effulgence, luminosity
measure of: 3 lux **5** lumen **6** candle **7** candela **10** foot-candle

brilliance

see **brightness**

brilliant

6 ablaze, brainy, genius, lucent, superb **7** beaming, fulgent, lambent, radiant, shining, stellar **8** dazzling, luminous, masterly, striking **9** effulgent, ingenious, refulgent, sparkling **10** glittering **11** exceptional **12** incandescent

brilliantine

6 pomade **9** hair cream

brim

3 hem, lip, rim **4** edge, fill, well **5** brink, skirt, verge, visor **6** border, fill up, fringe, margin **7** run over **8** overflow, well over **9** perimeter, periphery **13** circumference

brimful

see **brimming**

brimming

4 full **5** awash, flush **6** filled, jammed, loaded, packed **7** crammed, crowded, replete, stuffed, teeming, welling **8** bursting, overfull, suffused, swarming, swelling **9** chock-full, jam-packed **11** chockablock, running over

brimstone

6 sulfur

brine

3 sea **4** deep, main **5** ocean **8** seawater **9** salt water

bring

3 lug **4** lead, pack, tote **5** carry, fetch, gross, yield **6** convey **7** attract, produce **9** transport

bring about

3 win **5** beget, cause **6** create, draw on, effect, secure **7** procure, produce, trigger **8** engender, generate, result in **10** accomplish, effectuate, give rise to

bring around

4 hook, sway, turn **7** convert, win over **8** convince, persuade, talk into **9** argue into, prevail on, sweet-talk **11** prevail upon

bring back

5 renew **6** recall, recoup, return, revive **7** recover, reprise, restore, salvage **8** retrieve, revivify **9** reinstate **10** repatriate **11** reestablish

bring down

3 bag, hew **4** drop, fell, raze **5** floor, level, shoot **6** defeat, depose, ground, humble, lay low, reduce **7** depress, flatten **8** demolish, overturn **9** humiliate, overthrow, prostrate, undermine

bring forth

4 bear **5** beget, yield **6** create, elicit, invent **7** deliver, produce **8** generate **9** propagate, reproduce **10** give rise to

bring forward

6 adduce, submit, tender, unveil **7** advance, present, produce, proffer **9** introduce

bring in

3 pay, net, win **4** draw, earn, gain, sell **5** fetch, gross, yield **6** garner, return, secure **7** acquire, be worth, realize **9** introduce

bring off

6 effect, finish, rescue **7** achieve, execute, realize, succeed **8** carry out **9** discharge, implement **10** accomplish, consummate, effectuate **12** carry through

bring out
4 cull 5 educe, utter, voice 6 elicit,
reveal 7 declare, enhance, explain,
extract 8 disclose, showcase
9 elucidate, highlight, introduce

bring together
3 mix, wed 4 herd, join, link, yoke
5 amass, batch, blend, group, marry,
merge, rally, unify, unite 6 corral,
muster 7 collect, compact, compile,
convene, round up 8 assemble
9 aggregate, integrate, reconcile,
stockpile 10 synthesize 11 consolidate

bring up
4 moot, rear 5 breed, raise, refer,
teach, train, vomit 6 advert, allude,
broach, foster, school 7 advance,
educate, mention, nurture, propose,
suggest, touch on 8 point out,
instruct 9 cultivate, introduce 10 put
forward 11 regurgitate

brink
3 hem 4 bank, brim, edge 5 point,
skirt, verge 6 border, fringe, margin
9 extremity, perimeter, periphery,
threshold

briny
5 salty 6 saline

brio
3 pep, vim, zip 4 dash, élan, fire, life,
zest, zing 5 ardor, flair, gusto,
oomph, style, verve, vigor 6 bounce,
esprit, fervor, spirit 7 panache,
passion, sparkle 8 dynamism,
vivacity 9 animation

brioche
4 roll

Briseis' lover
8 Achilles

brisk
4 busy, fast, keen, spry, yare 5 agile,
fresh, nippy, quick, sharp, zippy
6 lively, nimble, snappy, speedy
7 bracing 8 animated, bustling,
vigorous 9 energetic, sprightly
10 refreshing 11 stimulating 12 invigorating

bristle
4 boil, burn, fume, seta 5 anger,
quill, setae (plural), spine 6 arista,
chaeta, seethe 7 chaetae (plural)
Scottish: 5 birse

British
air force: 3 RAF
cathedral city: 3 Ely 4 York
5 Ripon, Truro, Wells 6 Durham,
Exeter 7 Chester, Lincoln 8 Coventry, Hereford, St. David's 9 Lichfield,
Salisbury, Wakefield, Worcester
10 Canterbury, Gloucester
Channel Island: 4 Sark 6 Jersey
8 Alderney, Guernsey
coin, current: 5 pence (plural),
penny, pound
coin, old: 3 bob 5 crown, groat,
noble 6 bawbee, florin, George,
guinea, tanner, teston 8 farthing,
shilling 9 halfcrown, halfpenny,
sovereign 10 threepence
colony, former: 4 Aden, Cape
5 Adana, Kenya, Malta, Natal
6 Ceylon, Cyprus, Gambia 7 Jamaica, Sarawak 9 Gold Coast,
Singapore, Transvaal
10 Basutoland, New Zealand
11 Orange River, Sierra Leone
12 Bechuanaland
county: 4 Avon, Kent, York
5 Derby, Devon, Essex, Gwent
6 Dorset, Durham, Oxford, Surrey,
Sussex 7 Bedford, Cumbria, Norfolk, Rutland, Suffolk, Warwick
8 Cheshire, Cornwall, Hereford, Hertford, Somerset, Stafford 9 Berkshire,
Cleveland, Hampshire, Lancaster,
Leicester, Wiltshire, Worcester
10 Cumberland, Gloucester, Hum-
berside, Lancashire, Merseyside,
Shropshire 11 Westmorland
12 Lincolnshire
court, local: 8 hustings
court, medieval: 4 eyre
forest: 5 Arden, weald 8 Sherwood
king, legendary: 3 Lud 4 Beli, Bran
6 Arthur 7 Artegal, Belinus, Elidure
8 Brannius
language, ancient: 6 Celtic, Cymric
9 Brythonic

legislature: 10 Parliament
news agency: 7 Reuters
nobleman: 4 duke, earl, peer
5 baron 6 prince 8 marquess,
viscount
order: 6 Garter
people, early: 5 Celts, Iceni, Jutes,
Picts 6 Angles, Saxons
political party: 4 Tory, Whig
6 Labour 12 Conservative
pope: 8 Adrian IV
prince: 5 Harry 6 Andrew, Edward
7 Charles, William
princess: 4 Anne 5 Diana
8 Margaret
prison: 5 Tower (of London)
7 Newgate 8 Dartmoor
queen, ancient: 8 Boadicea,
Boudicca
resort: 4 Bath 7 Margate 8 Brighton
9 Blackpool
royal house: 4 York 5 Tudor
6 Stuart 7 Hanover, Windsor
9 Lancaster 11 Plantagenet
royal residence: 7 Windsor
8 Balmoral 10 Buckingham
school: 4 Eton 5 Rugby 6 Harrow
10 Winchester
school, military: 9 Sandhurst
spa: 4 Bath 5 Epsom 6 Buxton
7 Malvern, Matlock 8 Brighton
9 Harrogate 10 Cheltenham

British Columbia

capital: 8 Victoria
city: 6 Surrey 7 Burnaby 8 Richmond 9 Vancouver
mountain: 11 Fairweather
provincial flower: 7 dogwood
(Pacific)

British Honduras

6 Belize

brittle

4 curt 5 crisp, frail, stiff 6 infirm
7 crumbly, fragile, friable 9 breakable,
frangible, inelastic, irritable, sensitive
10 perishable, transitory

broach

3 tap 4 moot 6 open up 7 bring up,
mention, propose, suggest 8 initiate
9 introduce 10 put forward

broad

4 wide 7 general, liberal 8 extended,
generous, spacious, sweeping,
tolerant 9 expansive, extensive
combining form: 4 eury, lati, plat
5 platy

broadcast

3 air, sow 4 beam, show 5 radio,
strew 6 blazon, report, spread
7 bestrew, declare, publish, scatter
8 announce, proclaim, televise,
transmit 9 advertise, publicize
10 bruit about, promulgate 11 communicate, declaration, disseminate,
publication 12 announcement,
proclamation, promulgation, transmission

broaden

4 open 5 swell, widen 6 dilate,
expand, extend, fatten, spread
7 amplify, augment, distend, enlarge,
thicken 8 increase 10 supplement

broadloom

6 carpet

broad-minded

4 open 7 liberal 8 catholic, eclectic,
flexible, tolerant, unbiased 9 accepting, indulgent, unbigoted 10 forbearing, undogmatic 11 progressive
12 unjudgmental, unprejudiced

broadsheet

7 tabloid 9 newspaper

broadside

4 hail 5 burst, salvo, sheet, storm
6 shower, volley 7 barrage, torrent
8 at random 9 cannonade, fusillade, laterally, obliquely 11 bombardment

broadtail

4 hawk 5 sheep 7 karakul 8 lambskin

Brobdingnagian

4 huge 5 giant, jumbo 7 hulking, immense, mammoth, massive, titanic
8 colossal, gigantic, towering 9 cyclopean, humongous, monstrous
10 gargantuan, prodigious 11 elephantine

brochette
4 spit 6 skewer

brochure
5 flier, flyer 7 booklet 8 pamphlet

brogue
4 lilt, shoe 6 accent, oxford 7 dialect

broil
3 row 4 bake, burn, char, cook, fray, riot, sear 5 brawl, clash, fight, grill, melee, roast, run-in, toast 6 affray, fracas, scorch, tumult 7 bobbery, rhubarb, ruction, swelter, wrangle 8 disorder, squabble 10 donnybrook, free-for-all 11 disturbance

broiling
3 hot 5 fiery 6 baking, red-hot, torrid 7 blazing, burning 8 ovenlike, scalding, sizzling, white-hot 9 scorching 10 blistering, oppressive, sweltering

broke
4 poor 5 needy, spent 6 busted, ruined 7 drained 8 bankrupt, beggared, dirt poor, indigent, strapped, wiped out 9 destitute, insolvent, out of cash, penniless, penurious, played out 10 cleaned out 11 impecunious

broke-in
4 tame 5 tamed 6 docile

broken
4 shot 5 tamed 6 beaten, busted, cut off, faulty 7 crushed, haywire, humbled, subdued 8 bankrupt, defeated, violated, weakened 9 depressed, disrupted, fractured, heartsick, shattered, sorrowful 11 discouraged, demoralized, interrupted 12 disconnected, disheartened 13 discontinuous

broken-down
7 rickety 8 battered, decaying, decrepit 9 crumbling, neglected 10 threadbare, ramshackle 11 debilitated, dilapidated 12 deteriorated

brokenhearted
7 crushed, unhappy 8 dejected, dolorous, hopeless, wretched

9 depressed, heartsick, sorrowful 10 despairing, despondent 12 inconsolable 13 grief-stricken

broker
5 agent 6 factor 8 diplomat, mediator 9 financier, go-between, middleman 10 interagent, interceder, matchmaker, negotiator 11 intercessor 12 intermediary 13 intermediator

brolly
8 umbrella

bromide
4 bore, drip, lump, pill, yawn 5 drone, grind 6 cliché, old saw, truism 7 proverb 8 banality, chestnut, prosaism, sedative 9 platitude, soporific 10 shibboleth, triviality 11 commonplace, rubber stamp

bromidic
3 dry 4 arid, dull 5 banal, bland, dusty, stale, trite 6 boring 7 humdrum, insipid, tedious 8 shopworn, tiresome 9 dryasdust, moth-eaten, wearisome 10 monotonous, pedestrian, unoriginal 11 commonplace 13 unimaginative, uninteresting

bronco
5 horse 6 cayuse 7 mustang
Australian: 6 brumby

Brontë
character: 9 Catherine, Rochester 10 Heathcliff
novel: 7 Shirley 8 Jane Eyre, Villette 16 Wuthering Heights
sisters: 4 Anne 5 Emily 9 Charlotte

Bronx cheer
3 boo 4 hoot, jeer, razz 5 taunt 7 catcall 9 raspberry

brooch
3 pin 4 clip 5 clasp 8 fastener

brood
3 set, sit 4 fret, mope, muse, stew, sulk 5 cover, flock, gloom, hatch, worry 6 litter, ponder, repine 7 despond, progeny 8 children, meditate, ruminate 9 offspring

brook
4 bear, burn, gill, race, rill 5 abide, creek, stand 6 arroyo, endure, rillet, runnel, stream, suffer 7 rivulet, stomach, swallow 8 stand for, tolerate
Scottish: 6 burnie

Brookner novel
10 Hotel du Lac

broom
5 besom, brush, shrub, sweep, whisk 7 heather

broth
5 stock 8 bouillon, consommé

brothel
4 crib, stew 6 bagnio 7 lupanar 8 bordello, cathouse 9 call house 10 bawdy house, whorehouse

brother
3 kin 4 monk 5 friar 7 comrade, sibling
French: 5 frère
Italian: 3 fra 5 frate 8 fratello
Latin: 6 frater
relating to: 9 fraternal
Spanish: 7 hermano

brotherhood
4 club, gang 5 amity, guild, order, union 6 league 7 kinship, society 8 alliance, sodality 10 fellowship, fraternity, friendship 11 association, camaraderie, comradeship, confederacy 12 togetherness 13 consanguinity, secret society

brotherly
9 fraternal

Brothers Karamazov
4 Ivan 5 Mitya 6 Alexei, Alexey, Dmitri, Dmitry 7 Alyosha 10 Smerdyakov

brouhaha
3 din 4 coil, flap, fuss, riot, to-do 5 babel, broil, hoo-ha, whirl 6 bedlam, clamor, fracas, furore, hubbub, hurrah, jangle, pother, racket, ruckus, rumpus, shindy, tumult, uproar 7 ferment 8 foofaraw 9 agitation, commotion 10 excitement, hullabaloo, hurly-burly 11 pandemonium

brow
3 top 4 mien 5 front, crest, crown 8 forehead 9 gangplank 10 expression 11 countenance

browbeat
3 cow 5 beset, bully, harry, press 6 badger, carp at, coerce, harass, hector, lean on 7 bluster, dragoon 8 bludgeon, bulldoze, bullyrag, domineer, overbear, pressure 9 tyrannize 10 intimidate

brown
4 sear 5 dusky, toast 6 scorch, tanned 7 swarthy
dark: 5 sepia, umber 9 chocolate
grayish: 3 dun 6 bister, bistre
light: 3 tan 4 ecru, fawn 5 beige, hazel, khaki, tawny
moderate: 4 teak 6 sienna
reddish: 3 bay 4 roan 5 henna 6 auburn, russet, sorrel, titian 8 chestnut
yellowish: 6 bronze 12 butterscotch

Brown Bomber
5 Louis (Joe)

brown coal
7 lignite

brownie
3 elf, fay 5 fairy, pixie 6 sprite

Browning poem
8 Prospice, Sordello 11 Aurora Leigh, Pippa Passes 12 Rabbi Ben Ezra 13 Fra Lippo Lippi, My Last Duchess 14 How Do I Love Thee?

brown recluse
6 spider

brownshirt
4 Nazi 12 storm trooper

browse
4 crop, feed, scan, shop, skim 5 graze, munch 6 forage, nibble, peruse 7 dip into, pasture 8 glance at, look over 10 glance over 11 flip through, leaf through, look through, skim through 12 thumb through

bruin
4 bear

bruise
 5 pound, wound 6 batter, damage, injure, injury 7 contuse 8 abrasion, discolor 9 contusion 13 discoloration

bruit about
 6 blazon, gossip, report, spread 7 declare, publish 8 announce, proclaim 9 advertise, broadcast, circulate 10 annunciate, pass around, promulgate 11 blaze abroad

brume
 3 fog 4 film, haze, mist, murk 5 vapor 6 miasma 8 haziness 11 obscuration

brummagem
 4 fake, sham 5 bogus, false, gaudy, phony, showy 6 ersatz, pseudo, tinsel, tawdry 7 chintzy 8 spurious 9 imitation, pinchbeck, tasteless 10 fabricated, fictitious 11 counterfeit, make-believe

Brunei
 capital: 17 Bandar Seri Begawan
 island: 6 Borneo
 language: 5 Malay
 monetary unit: 6 dollar
 neighbor: 8 Malaysia
 sea: 10 South China

brunet
 3 jet 4 dark, onyx 5 dusky, ebony, raven, sable, sooty, swart 6 swarth 7 swarthy 8 bistered, obsidian 10 dark-haired 11 brown-haired

Brunhild
 5 queen 7 heroine 8 Valkyrie
 husband: 6 Gunnar 7 Gunther
 lover: 9 Siegfried

brunt
 4 jolt 5 shock 6 burden, impact

brush
 4 clip, kiss, skim 5 broom, clash, graze, run-in, scrap, scrub, shave, sweep, whisk 6 glance, scrape, tussle 7 contact, thicket 8 skirmish 9 encounter, shrubbery, sideswipe 11 undergrowth

brusque
 4 curt, tart 5 bluff, blunt, brief, gruff,
rough, short, surly, terse 6 abrupt, crusty, snippy 7 uncivil 8 impolite, snippety, succinct 10 peremptory, ungracious 11 ill-mannered 12 discourteous

brutal
 4 hard 5 cruel, feral, harsh 6 rugged, savage, severe 7 beastly, bestial, callous, inhuman, swinish, vicious 8 barbaric, pitiless, ruthless, sadistic 9 barbarous, ferocious, merciless 10 relentless 11 cold-blooded, remorseless 12 bloodthirsty

brutalize
 5 abuse 6 debase, harden 7 corrupt, debauch, deprave, pervert, roughen, subvert, vitiate 8 maltreat, mistreat 9 manhandle 10 bestialize

brute
 4 ogre 5 beast, cruel, feral 6 animal, savage 7 beastly, bestial, inhuman, piggish, swinish, varmint 8 creature 10 troglodyte 11 instinctive

brutish
 3 low 4 base, vile 5 crude, feral, gross, rough, stony 6 animal, carnal, coarse, scurvy, strong 7 beastly, bestial, boorish, inhuman, obscene, piggish, swinish, uncivil, uncouth 8 barbaric, degraded, depraved, inhumane, physical, sadistic 9 primitive, truculent, unrefined 11 animalistic, uncivilized

bryophyte
 4 moss 8 hornwort 9 liverwort

Brythonic
 see **Cymric**

bubble
 3 sac 4 blob, boil, dome, fizz, foam, moil 5 churn, froth, slosh, spume, swash 6 burble, gurgle, seethe, simmer 7 ferment, globule, vesicle 10 effervesce

bubbly
 5 alive, fizzy, foamy, jolly, perky 6 cheery, frothy, lively 7 buoyant, excited 8 animated, effusive 9 champagne, ebullient, exuberant, sparkling 10 carbonated

buccaneer

5 rover 6 cowboy, pirate, sea dog
7 corsair, sea wolf 8 picaroon, sea
rover 9 sea robber 10 freebooter

buck

3 fop, guy, lad, lug 4 balk, bear, bill,
chap, dude, jerk, load, move, note,
oner, pack, stag, tote, trip 5 cadet,
carry, dandy, ferry, fight, money,
pitch, repel, stark, throw 6 combat,
dollar, fellow, oppose, resist, unseat
7 coxcomb, trestle 8 antelope, bank
note, sawhorse, traverse 9 greenback, withstand, workhorse 10 completely 11 Beau Brummel

bucket

3 fly, run 4 pail, rush, whiz 5 hurry,
speed 6 barrel, basket, hasten,
hustle, vessel 9 clamshell 10 receptacle

Buckeye State

4 Ohio

buckle

4 bend, clip, fold, hasp, kink, warp
5 catch, clamp, clasp, heave, yield
6 cave in, fasten 7 contort, crumple,
harness 8 collapse 9 fastening
10 coffee cake

buckle under

3 bow 4 cave, fold, give 5 defer,
yield 6 cave in, submit 7 concede,
succumb 8 collapse 9 surrender
10 capitulate 11 admit defeat

Buck novel

9 Good Earth (The)

buckram

4 taut 5 stiff 6 wooden 8 starched
9 cardboard, unbending 10 inflexible
11 interlining

bucks

4 kale 5 bread, dough, money,
moola 6 dinero, do-re-mi, moolah
7 lettuce 10 greenbacks

buck up

4 buoy, lift 5 cheer, rally 6 solace
7 comfort, console, gladden, improve, refresh, smarten 8 brighten
9 encourage 10 strengthen

_____ buco

4 osso

bucolic

5 rural 6 rustic 7 georgic, halcyon,
idyllic 8 agrarian, arcadian, pastoral
10 campestral, provincial 11 countrified, picturesque

bud

4 germ, seed 5 gemma, spark
6 sprout 7 burgeon 9 pullulate
10 primordium
combining form: 5 blast 6 blasto

Buddha

7 Gautama 10 Siddhartha
dialogues: 5 sutra
disciple: 6 Ananda
enemy: 4 Mara
Japanese: 5 Amida, Amita
mother: 4 Maya
son: 6 Rahula
teachings: 6 dharma
wife: 9 Yasodhara

Buddhism

3 Son, Zen 4 Chan 5 Kegon
6 Huayan, Tendai 7 Tiantai
8 Hinayana, Mahayana, Nichiren,
Pure Land 9 Theravada, Vajrayana

Buddhist

chant: 6 mantra
dialogues: 5 sutra
enlightenment: 6 satori
evil spirit: 4 Mara
fate: 5 karma
language: 4 Pali
monk: 4 lama 5 arhat, bonze
sacred city: 5 Lhasa
saint: 5 arhat
scripture: 5 sutra 6 sutras 9 Pali
canon
sect: 3 Zen
shrine: 4 tope 5 stupa 7 chorten
spell: 6 mantra
spiritual leader: 4 guru 9 Dalai
Lama
state of happiness: 7 nirvana
temple: 6 pagoda
title: 7 mahatma
tree of enlightenment: 5 bodhi,
pipal

buddy
3 mac, pal 4 chum, mate 5 crony
6 comate, fellow, friend 7 compeer,
comrade, partner 8 coworker, playmate, sidekick 9 associate, companion 10 accomplice 11 confederate

buddy-buddy
5 close, pally, thick, tight 6 chummy
8 intimate 10 palsy-walsy 11 insep-
arable

budge
4 move 5 shift, yield 7 give way

budgerigar
6 parrot 8 parakeet

budget
5 funds, means 6 amount, ration,
supply 8 allocate, estimate 9 allowance, apportion, resources

Buenos ____
5 Aires

buff
3 fan, nut, rub, tan 4 fawn, sand,
wipe 5 beige, brush, fiend, freak,
glaze, gloss, lover, shine 6 addict,
expert, polish, votary 7 admirer,
burnish, devotee, fanatic, fancier,
furbish, groupie, habitué 8 follower
9 yellowish 10 aficionado, altogether, enthusiast 11 connoisseur,
yellow-brown

buffalo
4 bilk, faze 5 bison, bovid, stump
6 baffle, muddle, rattle 7 carabao,
confuse, defraud, flummox, fluster,
nonplus, perplex, swindle 8 befuddle,
bewilder, confound, hoodwink
9 bamboozle, dumbfound

buffalo grass
5 grama

buffer
6 screen, shield 7 buckler, bulwark,
cushion 8 absorber, mediator,
polisher 9 safeguard 10 protection
12 intermediary

buffet
3 box, hit, rap 4 beat, blip, blow,
bump, chop, cuff, drub, jolt, move,

poke, slap, sock 5 clout, drive, force,
pound, punch, smack, spank 6 batter, hammer, pummel, thrash, wallop
7 belabor, clobber, counter, lambast
8 lambaste, salad bar 9 sideboard

buffoon
3 wag 4 dolt, fool, goof, lout, zany
5 antic, clown, comic, droll, dunce,
joker, yokel 6 jester 7 bumpkin,
dullard 8 bonehead 9 blockhead,
harlequin 10 clodhopper 11 merry-
andrew

bug
3 fad, fan, irk, nag, nut, spy, tap, vex
4 buff, flaw, fret, gall, germ, rage
5 annoy, bulge, craze, fiend, freak,
mania, peeve 6 badger, bother, defect, insect, malady, needle, nettle,
pester, plague, zealot 7 disease,
fanatic, microbe, provoke, wiretap
8 irritate, listen in, protrude, sickness
9 eavesdrop, infection, obsession
10 enthusiast 12 imperfection
13 microorganism

bugaboo
see **bugbear**

bugbear
4 bane, bogy, fear, ogre 5 bogey,
bogie, poser 6 goblin, teaser 7 bugaboo, problem, specter, spectre
8 anathema, bogeyman, phantasm
9 bête noire, boogerman, boogeyman, hobgoblin 10 black beast
11 abomination

buggy
4 cart, tram 6 go-cart, jalopy 8 carriage

bugle
call: 4 mess, taps 5 drill 6 sennet,
tattoo 7 fanfare, retreat, tantara
8 assembly, reveille
relative: 6 cornet 7 trumpet
10 flugelhorn

build
3 wax 4 body, form, make, mode,
mold, rise 5 boost, erect, forge,
frame, habit, mount, put up, raise,
set up, shape, swell 6 expand, figure
7 amplify, augment, compose,

enlarge, fashion, magnify, produce, upsurge **8** assemble, compound, engineer, escalate, heighten, increase, multiply, physique **9** construct, establish, fabricate, institute, intensify, originate **10** accelerate, inaugurate, strengthen **11** fit together, manufacture **12** conformation, constitution

builder
5 mason **9** carpenter **10** bricklayer, contractor

builder's knot
10 clove hitch

building
3 hut **5** house **7** edifice **8** dwelling **9** structure
addition: 3 ell **4** wing **5** annex
compartment: 3 bay **4** room **6** office
connector: 9 breezeway
farm: 4 barn, crib, shed, silo
for apartments: 8 tenement
for arms: 7 arsenal
for gambling: 6 casino
for grain: 4 silo **7** granary **8** elevator
for horses: 6 stable
for manufacture: 4 shop **5** plant **7** factory
for music: 10 auditorium
for sports: 3 gym **4** bowl **5** arena **7** stadium **8** coliseum **9** gymnasium **10** hippodrome
material: 4 iron, wood **5** adobe, brick, glass, steel, stone **6** cement **8** concrete
projection: 3 bay, ell **4** wing **5** annex **6** dormer **7** cornice
round: 7 rotunda

building kit
5 Legos **10** Erector set **11** Lincoln Logs

build up
4 hype, plug, puff **5** boost, brace, erect **6** accrue, expand, extend, praise **7** collect, develop, enhance, fortify, improve, promote **8** buttress, heighten, increase **9** advertise, construct, establish, intensify, publicize

10 accumulate, aggrandize, strengthen

buildup
4 hype, puff, to-do **6** growth, hoopla **8** increase, ballyhoo **9** accretion, expansion, promotion, publicity **10** escalation **11** development, enhancement, enlargement **12** accumulation, augmentation **13** strengthening

built-in
6 inborn, inbred, innate **8** included, inherent **9** essential, ingrained, intrinsic **10** congenital, deep-seated, indwelling **11** established, fundamental **12** constitutive, incorporated

bulb
4 leek, lily, sego **5** onion, tulip **6** allium, garlic, squill **8** daffodil, hyacinth **9** amaryllis, narcissus
segment: 5 clove

bulb-like bud
4 corm **5** tuber **7** rhizome

Bulgaria
capital: 5 Sofia
city: 4 Ruse **5** Stara, Varna **6** Burgas, Pleven, Zagora **7** Plovdiv
monetary unit: 3 lev
mountain, range: 6 Balkan, Musala **7** Rhodope
neighbor: 6 Greece, Serbia, Turkey **7** Romania **9** Macedonia
part of: 7 Balkans
river: 6 Danube **7** Maritsa
sea: 5 Black

bulge
3 bag, jut, sac, sag **4** blob, bump, edge, lump, poke **5** bloat, pouch, swell **6** beetle, billow, bubble, bug out, dilate, excess, expand **7** balloon, distend, inflate, project, puff out **8** overhang, protrude, stand out, stick out, swelling **9** allowance, head start **10** distension, projection, promontory, protrusion **11** excrescence, protuberate **12** protuberance

bulk
4 body, core, loom, mass **5** fiber, swell, total **6** amount, corpus,

expand, volume **7** bigness, quantum **8** majority, quantity, stand out **9** aggregate, magnitude, substance

bulky

3 fat **5** beefy, hefty, husky, large, obese, stout **7** massive **8** cumbrous, unwieldy **9** corpulent, ponderous **10** cumbersome, overweight **11** substantial

bull

4 bunk, male, slip, toro, trip **5** boner, edict, error, fluff, force, hooey, lapse **6** bovine, bungle, decree **7** baloney, blooper, blunder, hogwash, mistake **8** nonsense **9** detective
combining form: 4 taur **5** tauri, tauro

bulldoze

3 cow **4** move, push, raze **5** abash, bully, clear, cream, elbow, force, level, press, scare, shove **6** coerce, hector, hustle, jostle, lean on, menace, propel, thrust **7** bluster, clobber, dragoon, flatten, oppress, trounce **8** bludgeon, browbeat, bullyrag, demolish, domineer, restrain, shoulder **9** terrorize, tyrannize **10** intimidate, obliterate

bullet

6 dumdum, tracer **9** cartridge **10** projectile
size: 7 caliber, calibre

bulletin

4 news **5** flash, scoop **6** notice, report **7** account, catalog, gazette, message, missive, release **8** briefing, calendar, dispatch, magazine, register **9** catalogue, statement **10** communiqué, periodical **12** announcement

bull fiddle

10 contrabass, double bass

bullfighter

6 torero **7** matador, picador **8** toreador **11** cuadrillero **12** banderillero
famous: 6 Arruza **7** Ordóñez **8** Belmonte, Joselito, Manolete **9** Dominguin **10** El Cordobés

bullfighting

arena: 5 plaza
cheer: 3 olé
hero: 6 torero **7** matador **8** toreador
lancer: 7 picador
red cloth: 6 muleta
Spanish: 7 corrida
team: 9 cuadrilla

bullheaded

6 mulish **7** adamant, willful **8** contrary, obdurate, perverse, stubborn **9** insistent, obstinate, pigheaded **10** headstrong, refractory, self-willed, unyielding **11** intractable, stiff-necked **12** intransigent, pertinacious, strong-willed

bullish

4 rosy **6** brawny, rising, upbeat **7** booming **9** advancing, expanding, favorable **10** optimistic

bully

3 cow **4** goon, pimp, punk, thug **5** abuse, heavy, meany, tease, tough **6** harass, hector, meanie, menace, pander, pick on, rascal **7** bluster, buffalo, dragoon, harrier, oppress, ruffian, torment, torture **8** bludgeon, browbeat, bulldoze, bullyrag, harasser, threaten **9** bulldozer, persecute, victimize, tormenter, tyrannize **10** browbeater, corned beef, intimidate, persecutor **11** intimidator

bullyrag

see **bulldoze**

bulrush

4 reed **5** sedge **7** cattail, papyrus

bulwark

4 wall **6** screen, shield **7** barrier, bastion, parapet, rampart, seawall **8** buttress, fortress, palisade **9** earthwork, safeguard **10** breakwater, breastwork, embankment, stronghold **13** fortification

bum

3 beg, vag **4** bust, hobo, idle, laze, lazy, loaf, loll, slug **5** binge, cadge, drunk, hit up, mooch, tramp **6** bottom, dawdle, loafer, loiter, lounge, slouch, unfair **7** depress,

bumbershoot

drifter, feel low, goof off, rear end, vagrant, wheedle **8** buttocks, derelict, fainéant, slugabed, sluggard, vagabond **9** do-nothing, goldbrick, importune, lazybones, panhandle, transient

bumbershoot
8 umbrella

bumble
3 mar **4** blow, flub, muff **5** botch, fluff, gum up, lurch **6** bobble, bollix, bungle, falter, fumble, mess up, muck up, rumble, slip up, teeter, totter **7** blunder, screw up, stagger, stumble **8** flounder

bumbling
5 inept, gawky **6** clumsy, gauche, klutzy **7** awkward, halting, unhandy **8** ungainly **9** all thumbs, graceless, ham-handed, maladroit, unskilled **11** heavy-handed, incapable, incompetent **13** butterfingers, uncoordinated

bummer
3 dud **4** drag, flop, hobo **5** tramp **6** beggar, cadger, downer, sponge, too bad **7** failure, forager, moocher, sponger **8** deadbeat, vagabond **9** tough luck **10** freebooter, panhandler, rotten luck, wet blanket

bump
3 bop, hit, jar, ram, rap, wen **4** bang, bash, bust, jolt, knot, lump, oust, slam **5** break, carom, clash, crack, crash, gnarl, knock, prang, shift, shock, shove, wound **6** demote, growth, impact, injury, jostle, jounce, nodule, remove, strike, wallop **7** collide, degrade, demerit, pothole, run into **8** demotion, dislodge, displace, swelling **9** carbuncle, collision, contusion, convexity **10** concussion, projection, protrusion **12** protuberance

bumpkin
3 oaf **4** boor, hick, lout, rube **5** clown, swain, yokel **6** rustic **7** hayseed, peasant **9** chawbacon, hillbilly, simpleton **10** clodhopper, country boy, countryman, provincial

bump off
3 ice **4** do in, kill, slay **5** erase, snuff **6** murder, rub out **7** butcher, execute, take out **8** knock off **9** eliminate, liquidate **11** assassinate

Bumppo, Natty
alias: 7 Hawkeye **10** Deerslayer, Pathfinder
creator: 6 Cooper (James Fenimore)

bumptious
5 cocky, pushy **8** arrogant, impudent **9** audacious, obnoxious, obtrusive, officious **13** self-assertive

bumpy
5 jerky, nubby, ridgy, rough **6** bouncy, jouncy, knobby, knotty, patchy, pimply, uneven **7** jolting, nodular **9** difficult, irregular

bun
4 load, roll **6** pastry

bunch
3 lot, set, wen **4** band, bevy, bump, clot, crew, knot, lump, mass, push **5** batch, clump, covey, crowd, flock, group, party, spray, stack, swell **6** bundle, circle, clutch, gather, huddle, parcel, throng **7** bouquet, collect, cluster **8** assembly, protrude, swelling **9** gathering **10** assemblage, assortment, collection, congregate **11** aggregation **12** accumulation

bunco steerer
3 gyp **6** con man **7** cheater, diddler, grifter, sharper **8** swindler **9** defrauder, trickster **12** double-dealer **13** confidence man

bundle
3 lot, pot, set, wad **4** bale, body, heap, mint, pack, pile, wrap **5** array, batch, bunch, clump, group, sheaf, truss **6** fardel, packet, parcel **7** cluster, fortune **10** assortment

bungalow
5 cabin, lodge **6** chalet **7** cottage

bungle
4 flub, goof, mess, muff, slip, trip **5** boner, botch, error, fluff, gum up,

lapse, mix up, spoil **6** bollix, bumble, fiasco, foozle, foul up, fumble, goof up, mess up, muck up, muddle **7** blooper, blunder, failure, louse up, misstep, mistake, stumble **9** mishandle, mismanage

bungler
3 oaf **4** clod, dolt, goof **5** klutz **7** screw-up, tomfool **8** bonehead, goofball, shlemiel **9** blunderer, schlemiel **10** stumblebum **11** blunderbuss, incompetent **13** butterfingers

bunglesome
6 clumsy, klutzy **7** awkward **8** bumbling **9** all thumbs **13** uncoordinated

bung up
4 beat, hurt **5** abuse, pound **6** batter, bruise, injure **7** contuse, disable **9** disfigure, manhandle

bunion
4 lump **8** swelling **10** protrusion, turnescence **11** enlargement

bunk
3 bed, cot, kip, rot **4** bosh, bull, guff, jazz **5** bilge, board, crash, hokum, hooey, house, lodge, put up **6** humbug, pallet, piffle **7** eyewash, baloney, hogwash, rubbish, twaddle **8** claptrap, domicile, flimflam, malarkey, nonsense, tommyrot **9** poppycock **10** balderdash

bunker
3 bin **6** dugout **7** bastion, chamber **10** embankment, stronghold **11** compartment

bunkum
3 rot **4** bosh, bull, guff, jazz **5** bilge, hokum, hooey **6** humbug, piffle **7** baloney, hogwash, rubbish, twaddle **8** claptrap, flimflam, malarkey, nonsense, tommyrot **9** poppycock **10** balderdash

bunting
5 flags **9** streamers

Bunyanesque
4 huge **5** giant, jumbo **7** mammoth, massive, titanic **8** behemoth,

colossal, gigantic, towering **9** Herculean **10** gargantuan, prodigious

Bunyan's ox
4 Babe

buoy
4 lift, prop **5** boost, cheer, float, raise **6** assist, beacon, bear up, buck up, signal, solace, uphold, uplift **7** bolster, comfort, gladden, hearten, support, sustain **9** encourage

buoyancy
6 bounce, levity **7** jollity **8** airiness **10** ebullience, exuberance, exuberancy, liveliness, resilience **12** floatability **13** effervescence

buoyant
3 gay **4** airy **5** sunny **6** afloat, bouncy **7** elastic **8** cheerful, floating, volatile **9** expansive, floatable, resilient **10** unsinkable, weightless **12** effervescent, lighthearted

burble
3 gas, yak **4** blab, chat, gush, talk, wash **5** clack, plash, run on, slosh, swash **6** babble, bubble, gabble, gurgle, murmur, rattle, splash, yammer **7** chatter, prattle, sparkle

burden
3 tax, try **4** care, clog, core, duty, gist, haul, lade, load, onus, pile, pith, task, text **5** brunt, cargo, press, theme, weigh **6** amount, charge, chorus, cumber, hamper, lading, lumber, saddle, strain, stress, thrust, upshot, weight **7** afflict, anxiety, freight, oppress, payload, refrain, purport **8** encumber, handicap, obligate, overload **9** millstone, substance, weigh down **10** deadweight **11** encumbrance

burdensome
5 tough **6** taxing, trying **7** arduous, exigent, irksome, onerous, weighty **8** crushing, exacting, grievous **9** demanding, difficult, fatiguing, ponderous **10** exhausting, oppressive **11** troublesome **12** backbreaking, unmanageable

bureau
4 unit 5 chest 6 agency 7 dresser, section 8 ministry 10 department, chiffonier 11 writing desk

bureaucrat
8 mandarin, minister, official 11 functionary 12 civil servant, officeholder

burg
4 city, town 7 borough 8 fortress 10 metropolis, walled town 12 municipality

burgee
4 flag 6 banner, ensign, pennon 7 pendant, pennant 8 standard, streamer

burgeon
4 blow, boom, open 5 bloom, build, mount, run up 6 emerge, expand, flower, sprout, thrive, unfold 7 augment, blossom, develop, enlarge, fill out, prosper, run riot 8 flourish, heighten, increase, multiply, mushroom, snowball 9 germinate 10 burst forth, effloresce

burghal
5 civic, urban 8 citified 9 municipal 12 metropolitan

burgher
7 citizen, denizen 8 townsman

burglar
4 yegg 5 thief
loot: 4 swag

burglarize
see burgle

burglary
5 heist, theft 7 larceny

burgle
3 rob 4 lift, loot 5 heist, steal, strip 6 rip off, thieve 7 despoil, plunder, ransack 9 break into, knock over 10 housebreak

burgomaster
5 mayor 10 magistrate

Burgundy wine
grape: 5 Gamay 9 Pinot Noir 10 Chardonnay

red: 8 Mercurey 10 Beaujolais
white: 5 Rully 6 Chagny 7 Chablis 10 Montrachet 13 Pouilly-Fuissé

burial
4 tomb 5 grave 7 funeral 9 interment, obsequies, sepulcher, sepulchre, sepulture 10 entombment, inhumation
box: 6 casket, coffin
ceremony: 7 funeral, obsequy 9 obsequies
mound: 6 barrow 7 tumulus
tomb: 9 mausoleum, sepulcher, sepulchre

burial ground
8 boot hill, cemetery 8 boneyard, God's acre 9 graveyard 10 churchyard, necropolis 12 memorial park, potter's field
early Christian: 8 catacomb

Burkina Faso
capital: 11 Ouagadougou
ethnic group: 3 Gur 5 Mossi 7 Voltaic
former name: 10 Upper Volta
language: 4 Moré 5 Dyula 6 French
monetary unit: 5 franc
neighbor: 4 Mali, Togo 5 Benin, Ghana, Niger 10 Ivory Coast
river: 5 Volta (Black, Red) 6 Nazion 7 Mouhoun, Nakanbe 8 Red Volta 10 Black Volta

burlap
5 gunny 6 fabric 7 bagging, sacking
fiber: 4 hemp, jute

burlesque
3 ape 4 mock, sham 5 farce, spoof 6 parody, satire, send-up 7 lampoon, mockery, mocking, takeoff 8 pastiche, skin show, travesty 10 caricature, distortion, girlie show, lampoonery

burly
4 hale 5 beefy, hefty, husky, tough 6 brawny, robust, strong, stocky 8 athletic, heavyset, muscular, powerful, stalwart, thickset, vigorous 9 strapping

Burma
see **Myanmar**

burn
4 bake, char, cook, fire, fume, rage, sear 5 anger, blaze, broil, creek, flame, flare, gleam, roast, scald, singe, smart, smoke, sting, toast 6 ignite, kindle, scorch, seethe 7 bristle, combust, consume, cremate, flare up, inflame, radiate, smolder, swelter 8 smoulder 9 carbonize, cauterize 10 incinerate

burnable
8 volatile 9 flammable, ignitable 10 incendiary 11 combustible, inflammable

burned-out
4 beat, shot 5 spent, weary 6 sapped 7 drained, worn-out 8 consumed, fatigued 9 destroyed, exhausted, played-out 10 broken-down 11 debilitated 12 extinguished

burner
3 hob

burning
3 hot 5 afire, aglow, fiery 6 ablaze, aflame, alight, ardent, fervid, heated, hectic, red-hot, torrid, urgent 7 blazing, fervent, fevered, glowing, ignited, kindled, searing 8 broiling, feverish, pressing, sizzling, white-hot 9 scorching 10 imperative, passionate 11 conflagrant, impassioned 12 incandescent
combining form: 4 igni
malicious: 5 arson

burnish
3 rub, wax 4 buff 5 glaze, gloss, scour, sheen, shine 6 luster, patina, polish, smooth 7 furbish, varnish 8 brighten

burnished
5 shiny 6 glossy, satiny, sheeny 7 lambent, radiant, shining 8 gleaming, lustrous, polished 9 brilliant 10 glistening 11 resplendent

burnsides
8 whiskers 9 sideburns 10 side-boards 11 dundrearies, mutton-chops 12 side-whiskers

burp
5 belch, eruct, expel

burro
3 ass 6 donkey 7 jackass

Burroughs hero
6 Tarzan

burrow
3 den, dig 4 hole, lair, mine, nook, snug 5 delve, gouge, lodge 6 cavity, cuddle, nestle, nuzzle, tunnel 7 snuggle 10 excavation

burst
3 pop, run 4 bang, boom, clap, gush, gust, rive, rush, slam, wham 5 blast, crack, crash, erupt, flare, go off, lunge, sally, salvo, smash, spasm, split, storm, surge 6 access, blow up, emerge, launch, plunge, shiver, spring, shower, volley 7 assault, barrage, explode, flare-up, fly open, rupture, shatter, torrent 8 detonate, drumfire, eruption, fragment, outbreak, splinter, splitter 9 broadside, cannonade, explosion, fusillade, onslaught 11 bombardment

Burundi
capital: 9 Bujumbura
ethnic group: 4 Hutu 5 Tutsi
former name: 6 Urundi
lake: 10 Tanganyika
language: 5 Rundi 6 French 7 Kirundi
monetary unit: 5 franc
neighbor: 5 Congo 6 Rwanda 8 Tanzania

bury
4 hide, sink, stow 5 cache, cover, embed, inter, plant, stash 6 absorb, entomb, inhume, mantle, shroud 7 blanket, conceal, cover up, implant, lay away, overlay, put away, secrete 8 ensconce, submerge

bus
5 clear 7 missile, trolley, vehicle 9 hand truck 10 spacecraft

bush

4 rose **5** lilac, shrub, wahoo **6** azalea, cassis, privet **7** currant, thicket, weigela **8** backland, barberry, hazelnut **9** backwater, backwoods, forsythia, manzanita **10** gooseberry, hinterland, wilderness **11** pussy willow **12** rhododendron

bushel

3 ton **4** heap, load, pile **6** basket, hamper **7** pannier

bush-league

5 minor **6** junior, two-bit **8** inferior, mediocre, small-fry **9** small-time **10** inadequate, second-rate **11** lightweight **13** insignificant

bushranger

6 outlaw **8** woodsman **12** frontiersman

bushwhack

4 trap **6** ambush, assail, attack, entrap, waylay **7** assault **8** surprise **9** blindside

bushwhacker

6 bandit, outlaw, raider, sniper **8** guerilla, woodsman **9** guerrilla **10** highwayman

bushy

5 bosky, fuzzy, hairy, leafy **6** fluffy, woolly **7** hirsute, unkempt **9** bristling, luxuriant, overgrown **10** disordered **11** flourishing

business

3 job **4** firm, line, work **5** trade **6** affair, custom, matter, métier, office, outfit, racket **7** calling, company, concern, pursuit, traffic **8** commerce, function, industry **9** patronage **10** employment, enterprise, livelihood, occupation **11** corporation **13** establishment
expense: 8 overhead
syndicate: 6 cartel

businesslike

6 formal **7** orderly, serious **8** diligent, thorough **9** competent, efficient, practical, pragmatic **10** impersonal, methodical, no-nonsense, purposeful, systematic **11** disciplined, hardworking **12** professional

businessman

6 broker, dealer, trader, tycoon **7** magnate **8** investor, merchant **9** bourgeois, financier, tradesman, executive **10** capitalist, trafficker **12** entrepreneur, merchandiser **13** industrialist

busker

8 minstrel, musician **11** entertainer

buss

4 kiss, peck **5** smack **6** smooch **8** osculate

bust

3 bag, cop, dud, hit, jag, nab, net **4** bomb, bump, fail, flop, fold, raid, ruin, slug, sock, tear, tour **5** binge, bosom, break, broke, burst, catch, chest, crash, lemon, loser, punch, smash, spell, spree, stint, torso, trash **6** arrest, bender, breast, collar, demote, pick up **7** break up, carouse, degrade, demerit, destroy, exhaust, failure, rupture, wear out **8** bankrupt, demolish, fracture **9** apprehend, break down, destitute, downgrade, penniless **10** impoverish, police raid

bustle

3 ado, fly, run **4** flit, fuss, rush, stir, tear, teem, to-do **5** hurry, whirl, whisk **6** action, be busy, bestir, clamor, flurry, furore, hassle, hasten, hubbub, hustle, motion, pother, scurry, tumult, uproar **7** ferment, turmoil **8** activity, to-and-fro **9** commotion, whirlpool, whirlwind **10** hurly-burly, excitement, liveliness

bustling

4 busy, rife **5** brisk, fussy, peppy **6** active, hectic, lively **7** dynamic, festive, hopping, humming, jumping **8** animated, swarming, vigorous **9** energetic **10** tumultuous **11** hardworking, industrious

busty

5 ample, buxom, curvy **6** bosomy,

chesty, zaftig **7** shapely, stacked
10 curvaceous, voluptuous **11** full-
bosomed, well-rounded

busy
5 brisk, fussy **6** active, at work,
lively, on duty, tied up **7** crowded,
engaged, hopping, humming,
swamped, teeming, working
8 bustling, diligent, employed, hustling, meddling, occupied, overdone,
sedulous **9** assiduous, congested,
elaborate, energetic, intrusive,
obtrusive, officious **10** meddlesome,
overworked **11** impertinent, industrious, interfering, unavailable

busybody
5 prier, pryer, snoop, yenta **6** butt-in,
gossip, old hen **7** meddler **8** informer,
kibitzer, quidnunc **9** pragmatic
10 chatterbox, newsmonger, pragma-
tist, talebearer, tattletale **11** nosey
parker, rumormonger **12** gossipmonger, rubbernecker, troublemaker

but
3 bar, yet **4** just, only, save **5** alone
6 except, merely, saving, unless
7 barring, besides, however **8** entirely **9** aside from, excepting,
excluding, outside of **13** on the
contrary

butcher
4 ruin, slay **5** botch, carve, clean,
spoil, wreck **6** bollix, killer, mess up,
slayer **7** cut meat, destroy, meat man
8 mutilate **9** slaughter **11** slaughterer

butcher-bird
6 shrike

butcherly
5 cruel **6** bloody, clumsy, savage
7 awkward **8** sadistic **9** ferocious,
merciless **10** unskillful

butchery
7 carnage **8** abattoir, genocide,
massacre **9** bloodbath, bloodshed,
holocaust, slaughter **10** mass murder **12** annihilation **13** extermination

buteo
4 hawk **7** buzzard

butler
5 valet **7** steward **10** manservant

Butler, Samuel
novel: 7 Erewhon **13** Way of All
Flesh (The)
poem: 8 Hudibras

butt
3 end, keg, tip, ram, tun, vat **4** base,
cask, drum, dupe, join, push, rump,
stub, tail **5** chump, fanny, patsy,
stump, touch, verge **6** adjoin, barrel,
border, bottom, firkin, pigeon, sucker,
target, thrust, victim **7** collide, fall
guy, rear end, run itno **8** derriere,
hogshead, neighbor **9** cigarette,
fundament, lie beside, pilgarlic,
posterior, remainder **11** communicate, sitting duck **12** hindquarters
13 laughingstock

butter
artificial: 4 oleo **9** margarine
13 oleomargarine
Indian: 4 ghee
piece: 3 pat
semifluid: 4 ghee
tree: 4 shea

butterball
5 blimp, whale **8** dumpling, elephant
10 bufflehead

butterfish
6 gunnel

butterfly
4 blue **5** diana, satyr, zebra **6** copper, morpho **7** admiral, buckeye,
monarch, satyrid, skipper, sulphur,
vanessa, viceroy **8** crescent,
grayling, milkweed, victoria **9** aphrodite, metalmark, nymphalid, wood
nymph **10** fritillary, hairstreak
11 swallowtail
bush: 8 buddleia
fish: 6 blenny, chiton **7** gurnard
larva: 11 caterpillar
lily: 8 mariposa
order: 11 Lepidoptera
plant: 8 oncidium
pupa: 9 chrysalis
scientist: 13 lepidopterist

butter up
4 coax 5 charm 6 cajole, kowtow, praise, stroke 7 adulate, beguile, blarney, flatter, massage, wheedle 8 blandish, bootlick, soft-soap 9 brownnose, sweet-talk 10 over-praise

butt in
6 kibitz, meddle 7 intrude, obtrude 8 busybody, overstep 9 interfere, interlope, interpose, interrupt

buttinsky
7 meddler 8 busybody, kibitzer, quidnunc 9 loudmouth 10 trespasser 12 troublemaker

buttocks
4 rear, rump, seat, tail 5 fanny, nates 6 behind, bottom, breech, heinie 7 hind end, hunkers, keister, rear end, tail end 8 backside, derriere, haunches 9 fundament, posterior

buttonball
8 sycamore 9 plane tree

button-down
6 square, stuffy 8 decorous, orthodox, straight 10 restrained 11 straitlaced, traditional 12 conservative, conventional

buttonwood
8 sycamore 9 plane tree

buttress
4 pier, prop, stay 5 brace, carry, shore, strut, truss 6 back up, bear up, hold up, column, uphold 7 bolster, bulwark, fortify, shore up, support, sustain 9 reinforce, stanchion 10 strengthen 12 underpinning 13 fortification, reinforcement

buxom
5 ample, busty, curvy 6 bosomy, chesty, zaftig 7 shapely, stacked 10 curvaceous, voluptuous 11 full-bosomed, full-figured, well-rounded

buy
5 bribe 6 obtain, ransom, redeem 7 acquire, bargain, believe 8 purchase

buy back
6 ransom, recoup, redeem, regain 8 retrieve 10 repurchase

buyer
6 client, patron, vendee 7 shopper 8 consumer, customer 9 purchaser

buy off
3 fix, sop 5 bribe 6 settle 7 corrupt, silence 9 influence 10 manipulate, tamper with

buzz
3 fad, hum 4 call, fizz, high, hiss, news, purr, ring, talk, whir, whiz 5 craze, drone, hurry, rumor, strum, thrum, whirr, whish 6 bumble, fizzle, gossip, murmur, natter, report, rumble, sizzle, summon, wheeze, whoosh 7 chatter, scandal, whisper 8 sibilate 9 bombinate 11 reverberate, scuttlebutt

buzzard
5 buteo 7 vulture 13 turkey vulture

by
3 per, via 4 away, near, nigh, past 5 along, aside 6 at hand, beside, next to 7 through 9 alongside 10 incidental 11 according to 12 not later than

by and by
4 anon, soon 5 after, later 7 shortly 8 directly, latterly 9 afterward, presently 10 before long 12 subsequently

by and large
7 all told, broadly, en masse, overall, usually 8 all in all, normally 9 generally, typically 10 altogether, on the whole, ordinarily 11 principally

by dint of
see **by means of**

bye-bye
4 ciao, ta-ta 5 adieu, adios 6 so long 7 cheerio 8 au revoir, farewell, sayonara, toodle-oo

bygone
3 old 4 dead, late, lost, once, past 5 dated, of old, olden 6 former, fossil, of yore, remote, whilom

7 antique, archaic, belated, defunct, extinct, old-time, onetime, quondam, vintage **8** departed, sometime, obsolete, outdated, outmoded, vanished **9** erstwhile, out-of-date **10** antiquated, oldfangled **12** antediluvian, old-fashioned

by means of
3 per, via **4** with **5** using **7** through **9** employing, utilizing

byname
6 handle **7** epithet, moniker **8** cognomen **9** sobriquet **10** diminutive, hypocorism **11** appellation

bypass
4 omit **5** avoid, burke, shunt, skirt **6** detour, ignore **7** highway **8** outflank, ring road, sidestep **10** circumvent, pass around **11** deviate from

by-product
5 yield **6** effect, result **7** outcome, residue, spin-off **8** offshoot **9** outgrowth **10** derivative, descendant **11** aftereffect, consequence **12** repercussion

Byron work
4 Cain, Lara **5** Beppo **6** Giaour (The), Werner **7** Corsair (The), Don Juan, Manfred **12** Childe Harold

bystander
6 gawker, viewer **7** watcher, witness

8 beholder, observer, onlooker, passerby **9** spectator **10** eyewitness **12** rubbernecker

by stealth
5 slyly **7** sub rosa **8** covertly, in secret, secretly **9** furtively, privately **10** under cover **11** insidiously **13** clandestinely

by virtue of
see **by means of**

by way of
see **by means of**

byword
3 saw **5** adage, axiom, maxim, motto, nomen **6** dictum, phrase, saying, slogan, truism **7** epigram, epithet, precept, proverb, refrain **8** aphorism, cognomen, nickname **9** platitude, prescript, sobriquet **10** hypocorism, shibboleth **11** catchphrase, commonplace, rallying cry

Byzantine
6 daedal, knotty **7** complex, devious **8** involved **9** elaborate, intricate **10** convoluted **11** complicated **12** labyrinthine **13** sophisticated, surreptitious
emperor: **3** Leo **4** Zeno **5** Basil **6** Bardas, Justin, Phocas **7** Michael, Romanus **9** Heraclius, Justinian **10** Nicephorus, Theodosius
empress: **3** Zoe **5** Irene **8** Theodora

C

cab
4 hack, taxi 6 jitney 7 hackney
8 carriage

cabal
3 mob 4 clan, club, plot, ring 5 coven,
group, junta, mafia 6 cartel, circle,
clique 7 coterie, faction, in-group
8 intrigue 9 camarilla 10 conspiracy
11 machination

cabaletta
4 aria, song

cabalistic
6 arcane, mystic, occult 8 esoteric
9 recondite 10 mysterious 11 inscrutable 12 impenetrable

caballero
6 knight 7 paladin 8 cavalier,
horseman 9 chevalier

cabana
3 hut 5 shack 7 shelter

cabaret
4 café 6 bistro, nitery 7 hot spot
9 nightclub, nightspot 10 supper
club 12 watering hole

cabbage
3 nab, nip 4 cash, hook, lift, palm
5 bread, dough, filch, kraut, money,
moola, pinch, steal, swipe 6 dinero,
do-re-mi, moolah, pilfer 7 purloin,
scratch 10 greenbacks, sauerkraut
disease of: 6 mildew, mosaic 7 root
rot, yellows 8 blackleg, club root
family: 4 cole, kale, rape 5 colza,
savoy 6 turnip 7 collard, mustard
8 broccoli, colewort, kohlrabi,
rutabaga 11 cauliflower

cabbagehead
see **dunce**

cabdriver
4 hack 5 cabby 6 cabbie

cabin
3 hut 4 camp, shed 5 berth, hovel,
lodge, shack 6 cabana, chalet,
lean-to, shanty 7 bivouac, cottage
9 stateroom

cabin cruiser
5 yacht 9 motorboat, powerboat

cabinet
4 case 6 bureau 7 armoire, chamber, commode, console, council,
dresser 8 advisers, advisors,
cupboard, ministry 9 presidium
10 chiffonier, collection, counselors

cabinetmaker
American: 5 Eames (Charles),
Phyfe (Duncan) 6 Belter (John
Henry) 7 Goddard (John, Stephen,
Thomas) 8 McIntire (Samuel),
Townsend (Christopher, Edmund,
James, Job, John)
English: 4 Adam (James, Robert),
Hope (Thomas), Kent (William)
8 Sheraton (Thomas)
11 Chippendale (Thomas), Hepple-
white (George)
French: 6 Boulle (André-Charles)
8 Caffieri (Jacques, Jean-Jacques,
Philippe), Cressent (Charles)
German: 10 Weisweiler (Adam)

cable
4 rope, wire 5 braid, chain 6 stitch
8 transmit 9 telegraph

cabriolet
 5 coupe 8 carriage

cache
 4 bury, hide 5 cover, plant, stash, store 6 memory, wealth 7 conceal, lay away, nest egg, put away, reserve, secrete 8 ensconce, treasure 9 stockpile 10 accumulate 11 hiding place

cachet
 4 rank, seal 5 motto, state 6 slogan, status 7 dignity, stature 8 approval, position, prestige, standing 11 consequence

cachinnate
 4 crow, howl, roar 5 laugh, whoop 6 guffaw, shriek

cackle
 3 gab, jaw 4 blab, chat, crow 5 clack, cluck 6 babble, burble, gabble, gaggle, gobble 7 blabber, blatter, chatter, prattle

cacoëthes
 4 zeal 5 mania 6 desire 9 obsession

cacomistle
 5 civet 7 raccoon 8 civet cat, ringtail

cacophonic
 5 harsh 8 tuneless 9 dissonant, unmusical 10 discordant 11 unmelodious 12 unharmonious

cacophony
 9 harshness 10 dissonance

cactus
 5 nopal 6 cereus, cholla, mescal, peyote 7 opuntia, saguaro 11 prickly pear

cad
 3 cur, dog 4 boor, heel, lout, rake 5 creep, knave, louse, rogue 6 rascal, rotter 7 bounder 9 conductor, scoundrel

cadaver
 4 body, mort 5 stiff 6 corpse 7 carcass, remains 8 deceased

cadaverous
 5 ashen, gaunt, livid 6 pallid, wasted 7 deathly, ghastly, ghostly, shadowy 8 skeletal, spectral 9 deathlike, emaciated, ghostlike 10 corpselike

caddy
 3 bin, box 4 aide 5 toter 6 casket 8 canister, tea chest

cadence
 4 beat, flow, lilt 5 meter, pulse 6 rhythm 9 pulsation 10 conclusion, inflection, intonation

cadet
 4 pimp 5 plebe 7 student, trainee

cadge
 3 beg, bum 5 mooch 6 hustle, sponge 8 freeload, scrounge 9 panhandle

Cadmus
 daughter: 3 Ino 5 Agave 6 Semele 7 Autonoë
 father: 6 Agenor
 sister: 6 Europa
 victim: 6 dragon
 wife: 8 Harmonia

cadre
 4 cell, core 5 frame, staff 6 cohort 7 in-group 9 framework

caducity
 3 age 6 dotage, old age 8 senility 10 senescence 11 senectitude

Caesar
 assassin: 6 Brutus (Marcus Junius) 7 Cassius (Gaius)
 battle: 4 Zela 9 Pharsalus
 conquest: 4 Gaul 7 Britain
 eulogist: 6 Antony (Marc) 7 Anthony (Mark) 8 Antonius (Marcus)
 message: 12 Veni vidi vici
 river: 7 Rubicon
 utterance: 9 Et tu Brute
 wife: 7 Pompeia 8 Cornelia 9 Calpurnia

Caesarism
 7 tyranny 9 authority, autocracy, despotism 10 absolutism 12 dictatorship

caesura
 5 break, pause 12 interruption

café
5 diner 6 bistro, nitery 7 barroom, beanery, cabaret, hot spot 8 cookshop 9 lunchroom, nightclub, nightspot 10 coffee shop, restaurant, supper club 12 luncheonette, watering hole 13 watering place

café _____
4 noir 6 au lait, filtre 7 society

caftan
4 gown, robe 6 muumuu 12 dressing gown

cage
3 hem, pen 4 cell, coop, jail 5 score 6 corral, immure, lock up, shut in 7 close in, enclose, impound 8 imprison 9 enclosure 11 incarcerate

cagey
3 sly 4 foxy, wary, wily 5 canny, sharp 6 astute, clever, crafty, shrewd

cahier
6 record, report, review

cahoots
6 hookup, league 8 alliance 9 collusion 10 complicity 11 partnership

caiman
9 crocodile 11 crocodilian

Cain
brother: 4 Abel, Seth
father: 4 Adam
land: 3 Nod
mother: 3 Eve
nephew: 4 Enos
son: 5 Enoch
victim: 4 Abel

Caine Mutiny author
4 Wouk (Herman)

Cain novel
8 Serenade 13 Mildred Pierce 23 Postman Always Rings Twice (The)

cajole
3 con 4 coax, dupe 6 entice, seduce 7 beguile, blarney, deceive, wheedle 8 blandish, inveigle, maneuver, persuade, soft-soap 9 sweet-talk

cake
3 dry, set 4 coat, loaf, rime 5 cover, crust 6 harden, pastry 7 congeal, encrust, incrust 8 solidify
almond: 8 macaroon
flat: 5 cooky 6 cookie
oatmeal: 4 farl 5 scone 7 bannock
ring-shaped: 5 donut 6 jumble 8 doughnut
rum-soaked: 4 baba
Scottish: 4 farl 5 scone
shell-shaped: 9 madeleine
topping: 5 icing 8 frosting, streusel
without flour: 5 torte
without shortening: 6 sponge

Cakes and Ale author
7 Maugham (W. Somerset)

cakewalk
4 romp, rout, snap 5 cinch, dance, strut 6 breeze, prance 8 pushover, walkover

calaboose
3 can 4 brig, coop, jail, tank 5 clink, pokey 6 cooler, lockup, prison 7 slammer 8 hoosegow 9 jailhouse

calamitous
4 dire 5 fatal 6 woeful 7 ruinous 8 grievous 10 disastrous, lamentable 11 cataclysmic, devastating, unfortunate 12 catastrophic 13 heartbreaking

calamity
4 ruin 5 wreck 7 tragedy 8 disaster, downfall 9 cataclysm 11 catastrophe, tribulation

Calamity _____
4 Jane

calculate
4 rely 5 assay, count, gauge, judge, solve, tally, tot up, value 6 assess, cipher, figure, intend, reckon 7 compute, measure, work out 8 appraise, estimate, evaluate, forecast 9 ascertain, determine, figure out

calculated
6 likely 7 planned 8 intended 9 worked out 10 deliberate 12 aforethought, premeditated

calculating

3 sly 4 wary, wily 5 canny, chary, sharp 6 artful, crafty, shrewd 7 careful, cunning, devious, politic 8 cautious, discreet, guileful, scheming 9 designing 11 circumspect

calculating device

6 abacus
Peruvian: 5 quipu

calculation

8 analysis, counting, estimate, figuring, prudence 9 ciphering, reckoning 10 arithmetic, estimation, prediction 11 computation

Caledonia

8 Scotland

calendar

3 log 4 card, sked 6 agenda, docket 7 almanac, program 8 schedule 9 timetable
abbreviation: 3 Apr, Aug, Dec, Feb, Fri, Jan, Mar, Mon, Nov, Oct, Sat, Sep, Sun, Tue, Wed 4 Sept 5 Thurs
ecclesiastical: 4 ordo

calenture

4 fire, zeal 5 ardor, fever 6 fervor 7 passion 10 enthusiasm

calf

hide: 3 kip
leather: 3 elk
meat: 4 veal
stray: 5 dogie
unbranded: 8 maverick

Caliban

5 slave
master: 8 Prospero
witch-mother: 7 Sycorax

caliber

4 bore 5 class, gauge, grade, merit, value, worth 6 virtue 7 ability, quality, stature 8 diameter

calibrate

3 set 6 adjust, polish 7 measure 8 fine-tune, regulate 9 ascertain 11 standardize

California

capital: 10 Sacramento
city: 4 Napa 6 Fresno, Sonoma 7 Anaheim, Oakland, San Jose 8 San Diego, Santa Ana 9 Long Beach, Santa Cruz 10 Los Angeles 12 San Francisco
college, university: 3 USC 4 UCLA 5 Mills 6 Pomona 8 Berkeley, Stanford, Whittier 9 Loma Linda 10 Golden Gate, Occidental, Pepperdine, Santa Clara
desert: 6 Mohave
fault zone: 10 San Andreas
lake: 5 Owens, Tahoe 9 Salton Sea
lowest spot: 11 Death Valley
motto: 6 Eureka
mountain, range: 5 Coast 6 Lassen (Peak), Shasta 7 Whitney 12 Sierra Nevada
nickname: 6 Golden (State)
park: 7 Sequoia 8 Yosemite 11 Kings Canyon 14 Channel Islands
river: 10 Sacramento, San Joaquin
state bird: 5 quail
state flower: 11 golden poppy
state tree: 7 redwood, sequoia
wine region: 4 Napa 6 Sonoma

caliginous

3 dim 4 dark, dusk 5 dusky, foggy, misty, murky 6 gloomy 7 obscure, sunless 8 nebulous 9 lightless, tenebrous

Caligula's mother

9 Agrippina

caliph's name

3 Ali 7 Abu Bakr

Calista's seducer

8 Lothario

calisthenics

7 workout 9 exercises

call

3 bid, cry 4 buzz, hail, lure, name, page, ring, yell 5 phone, pop in, shout, visit 6 bellow, come by, drop by, drop in, holler, salute, stop by, stop in, summon 7 convene, convoke, summons 8 estimate 9 designate, telephone

calla

4 lily

call down
5 chide, scold 6 rebuke 7 censure, reprove 8 admonish, reproach 9 reprimand

called
5 named 6 chosen, picked, yclept 7 ycleped 8 selected

caller
5 guest 6 suitor 7 visitor

call for
3 ask, beg 4 seek 5 crave, plead 6 demand, entail, pick up 7 beseech, entreat, implore, involve, require 11 necessitate

call forth
5 awake, educe, evoke, rouse 6 arouse, elicit 7 conjure, provoke 9 conjure up

calligrapher
6 penman, scribe 7 copyist 9 engrosser, scrivener

calligraphy
4 hand 6 script 7 writing 8 longhand 10 penmanship 11 handwriting

call in
5 phone 6 summon 7 convene, reclaim 8 retrieve, withdraw 9 repossess, telephone

calling
3 job 4 duty, work 5 craft, trade 6 career, métier 7 mission, pursuit, yelling 8 business, lifework, shouting, vocation 10 employment, obligation, occupation, profession

call in sick
7 book off

Calliope
4 Muse
father: 4 Zeus 7 Jupiter
mother: 9 Mnemosyne
son: 7 Orpheus

Callisto
lover: 4 Zeus 7 Jupiter
son: 5 Arcas

Call It Sleep author
4 Roth (Henry)

call off
4 halt 5 abort, scrub 6 cancel, divert 8 distract

Call of the Wild
author: 6 London (Jack)
dog: 4 Buck

call on
5 visit 6 oblige 7 require

callosity
8 hardness 9 thickness

callous
5 stony 8 hardened, obdurate, uncaring 9 heartless, indurated, unfeeling 10 hard-bitten, hard-boiled 11 coldhearted, hardhearted, insensitive, unemotional 12 casehardened, stonyhearted 13 unsympathetic

callow
3 raw 5 fresh, green, naive, young 7 puerile 8 immature, juvenile, youthful 9 unfledged 10 unseasoned 13 inexperienced, unexperienced

call's partner
4 beck

call up
5 draft, evoke 6 summon 8 mobilize, retrieve 9 conscript

calm
4 cool, ease, hush, lull 5 allay, peace, quiet, relax, salve, still 6 hushed, pacify, placid, poised, repose, sedate, serene, settle, smooth, soothe, stable, steady, stilly 7 appease, assuage, compose, halcyon, mollify, pacific, placate, restful, resting 8 composed, inactive, peaceful, reposing, serenity, tranquil 9 collected, composure, easygoing, impassive, possessed, quiescent, unruffled 10 phlegmatic, untroubled 11 tranquility, tranquilize, unflappable 12 even-tempered, self-composed, tranquillity 13 imperturbable, selfpossessed

calmative
8 quietive, relaxing, sedative 9 soporific 12 tranquilizer

calmness
4 lull 5 quiet 6 phlegm 8 coolness, serenity 9 composure, placidity, sangfroid 10 equanimity 11 tranquility 12 tranquillity

calumet
4 pipe 9 peace pipe

calumniate
5 libel, smear 6 defame, malign, vilify 7 asperse, slander, tarnish, traduce 8 besmirch 9 denigrate 10 scandalize

calumnious
8 libelous 9 maligning, traducing, vilifying 10 backbiting, defamatory, detracting, scandalous, slanderous

calumny
7 scandal, slander 9 aspersion 10 backbiting, defamation, detraction 11 denigration 12 backstabbing, belittlement, depreciation 13 disparagement

calvados
6 brandy 9 applejack

calvary
5 agony, cross, trial 6 misery, ordeal 7 anguish 8 distress 9 suffering 10 affliction, visitation 11 tribulation

Calypso
beloved: 7 Ulysses 8 Odysseus
island: 6 Ogygia

calyx part
3 cup 5 sepal

camaraderie
5 cheer 7 jollity 10 affability, fellowship 12 conviviality

camarilla
3 mob 4 camp, clan, ring 5 cabal, mafia 6 circle, clique 7 coterie, ingroup

Cambodia
9 Kampuchea
capital: 9 Phnom Penh
city: 10 Battambang 11 Kompong Cham
ethnic group: 8 Mon-Khmer
lake: 8 Tonle Sap

language: 5 Khmer
leader: 6 Pol Pot
monetary unit: 4 riel
neighbor: 4 Laos 7 Vietnam 8 Thailand
river: 6 Mekong
ruin: 9 Angkor Wat

camel
one-humped: 9 dromedary
two-humped: 8 Bactrian

camel-hair fabric
3 aba

camelopard
7 giraffe

Camelot
6 palace
lord: 6 Arthur

Camembert
6 cheese

cameo
6 brooch, relief, walk-on 8 portrait

cameraman
6 photog 7 lensman 12 photographer

Cameroon
capital: 7 Yaoundé
ethnic group: 4 Fang 5 Duala, Pygmy 6 Fulani 8 Bamileke
largest city: 6 Douala
monetary unit: 5 franc
neighbor: 4 Chad 5 Congo, Gabon 7 Nigeria
river: 5 Nyong 6 Sanaga

Camille's creator
5 Dumas (Alexandre)

Camino ____
4 Real

camouflage
4 mask 5 cloak 7 conceal, deceive 8 disguise 9 dissemble 11 dissimulate

camp
3 hut 4 bloc, shed 5 cabin, lodge, shack 6 clique, shanty 7 bivouac, coterie, cottage, faction 10 settlement

campaign
4 push 5 blitz, drive, fight, lobby,

stump **6** attack **7** agitate, canvass, crusade **8** movement, politick **9** barnstorm, offensive **10** engagement, expedition **11** electioneer, whistle-stop

campaigner
   8 activist **9** candidate

campanile
   6 belfry **8** carillon **9** bell tower

campesino
   6 farmer **7** peasant

campestral
   5 rural **6** rustic, sylvan **7** bucolic, country, idyllic **8** agrarian, pastoral **10** provincial **11** countrified

campus
   see **college**

Camus work
   4 Fall (The) **5** Rebel (The) **6** Plague (The) **8** Caligula, Stranger (The)

can
   3 may, tin **4** boot, fire, sack **5** let go, put up **7** dismiss **9** container, discharge **10** receptacle

Canaan
   4 Zion **12** Promised Land
   father: 3 Ham
   grandfather: 4 Noah

Canaanite god
   3 Mot **4** Baal **6** Molech, Moloch

Canada
   bay: 5 Fundy, James **6** Baffin, Hudson, Ungava **8** Georgian **9** Frobisher
   capital: 6 Ottawa
   city: 6 London, Oshawa, Quebec, Regina, Surrey **7** Burnaby, Calgary, Halifax, Moncton, Toronto, Windsor **8** Edmonton, Hamilton, Montreal, Moose Jaw, Victoria, Winnipeg **9** Longueuil, North York, Saskatoon, Vancouver **10** Lethbridge, Thunder Bay **11** Fredericton, Scarborough **13** Charlottetown, Mississisauga
   district: 6 riding
   explorer: 6 Hudson (Henry) **7** Cartier (Jacques) **9** Champlain (Samuel de)
   Indian people: 4 Cree, Inuk

5 Blood, Haida, Huron, Inuit, Métis, Niska, Slave **6** Abnaki, Beaver, Eskimo, Micmac, Mohawk, Nootka, Ojibwa, Ojibwe, Ottawa, Piegan, Seneca, Stoney **7** Kutenai, Naskapi, Ojibway, Siksika, Wyandot **8** Algonkin, Chippewa, Iroquois, Kootenai, Kootenay, Kwakiutl, Salishan, Tsattine **9** Algonkian, Algonquin, Blackfeet, Blackfoot, Chipewyan, Tsimshian **10** Algonquian, Athapascan, Gros Ventre, Montagnais **11** Assiniboine
   island, island group: 5 Banks, Devon **6** Baffin **7** Belcher **8** Melville, Victoria **9** Anticosti, Ellesmere, Vancouver **10** Cape Breton **11** Southampton **12** Newfoundland, Prince Edward
   lake: 6 Louise **7** Nipigon **8** Reindeer, Winnipeg **9** Athabasca, Champlain, Great Bear **10** Great Slave
   language: 6 French **7** English
   monetary unit: 6 dollar
   mountain, range: 5 Coast, Logan, Rocky **10** Laurentian
   national park: 5 Banff, Fundy **6** Jasper **7** Glacier, Nahanni **8** Kootenay **9** Gros Morne **10** Grasslands, Point Pelee **11** Georgian Bay, Wood Buffalo
   peninsula: 5 Bruce, Gaspé **6** Ungava **8** Labrador
   prime minister: 4 King (W. L. Mackenzie) **5** Clark (Joe) **6** Abbott (John), Borden (Robert Laird), Bowell (Mackenzie), Martin (Paul), Tupper (Charles), Turner (John) **7** Bennett (Richard Bedford), Laurier (Wilfrid), Meighen (Arthur), Pearson (Lester), Trudeau (Pierre Elliott) **8** Campbell (Kim), Chrétien (Jean), Mulroney (Brian), Thompson (John) **9** MacDonald (John), Mackenzie (Alexander), St. Laurent (Louis) **11** Diefenbaker (John)
   province: 6 Quebec **7** Alberta, Nunavut, Ontario **8** Manitoba **10** Nova Scotia **12** New Brunswick, Newfoundland (and Labrador), Saskatchewan **15** British Columbia **18** Prince Edward Island

provincial park: 3 Gas 7 Rondeau
9 Garibaldi
river: 3 Red 5 Liard, Slave, Yukon
6 Albany, Fraser, Nelson, Ottawa,
Severn 8 Columbia, Saguenay
9 Athabasca, Churchill, Mackenzie
10 St. Lawrence
sea: 8 Beaufort, Labrador
symbol: 9 maple leaf
territory: 5 Yukon 9 Northwest

Canadian insurgent
4 Riel (Louis)

canaille
3 mob 6 masses, rabble 8 riffraff,
unwashed 9 hoi polloi 11 proletarian,
proletariat

canal
4 duct 6 course 7 channel, conduit
8 aqueduct 11 watercourse
Africa: 4 Suez 8 Ismailia
Belgium: 6 Albert
Canada: 7 Welland
Central America: 6 Panama
China: 7 Da Yunhe
Florida: 10 Saint Lucie
Germany: 4 Kiel
Greece: 7 Corinth
Michigan: 3 Soo
New York: 4 Erie 6 Oswego
9 Champlain
Ontario: 6 Rideau
Venice: 5 Grand

canapé
6 morsel 9 appetizer 11 hors
d'oeuvre
spread: 4 paté

canard
3 fib, lie 4 tale, yarn 5 fraud, rumor,
spoof 6 deceit 7 falsity, untruth
8 chestnut 9 falsehood

canary
3 rat 4 fink, wine 5 finch 6 snitch
7 rat fink, stoolie 8 informer, squealer
11 stool pigeon

Canary Islands
5 Ferro, Lobos, Palma 6 Gomera,
Hierro 7 Inferno 8 Graciosa, Tenerife 9 Alegranza, Lanzarote

cancel
3 end 4 drop, undo, x out 5 abort,

annul, erase, scrub 6 delete, efface,
negate, offset, repeal, revoke 7 blot
out, call off, destroy, expunge, nullify,
rescind, wipe out 8 black out,
deletion 9 terminate 10 invalidate,
neutralize, obliterate

cancer
5 tumor 9 carcinoma 10 malignancy
treatment: 5 chemo, X rays 9 radiation 12 chemotherapy

cancer-causing
12 carcinogenic
substance: 10 carcinogen

candescent
7 glowing 8 dazzling 9 refulgent

Candia
5 Crete

candid
4 fair, just, open 5 blunt, frank, plain
6 honest 7 sincere 8 unbiased
9 equitable, guileless, impartial,
objective 10 aboveboard, forthright,
scrupulous, unreserved 11 openhearted, unconcealed, undisguised
12 unprejudiced 13 dispassionate

candidate
6 seeker 7 hopeful, nominee,
stumper 8 aspirant 9 applicant,
contender 10 campaigner, contestant

Candide
author: 8 Voltaire
lover: 9 Cunegonde
tutor: 8 Pangloss
valet: 7 Cacambo

candle
5 taper 6 bougie
holder: 6 sconce 7 menorah,
pricket 9 girandole 10 candelabra
11 candelabrum
material: 3 wax 4 wick 6 tallow
7 beeswax, stearin 8 paraffin
religious: 6 votive 7 paschal

candlefish
8 eulachon
relative: 5 smelt

candlelit service
5 vigil

candlepins
7 bowling

candor
7 honesty 8 fairness, openness
9 frankness, sincerity, whiteness
11 artlessness 13 guilelessness

candy
7 sweeten 9 sugarcoat 10 confection
kind: 4 rock 5 fudge, lolly, sweet,
taffy 6 bonbon, comfit, dragée,
jujube, nougat, toffee 7 brittle,
caramel, fondant, gumdrop, penuche,
praline 8 licorice, lollipop, lollypop,
marzipan, sourball 9 chocolate, jelly
bean, nonpareil, sweetmeat
10 confection 12 butterscotch
medicated: 7 lozenge 9 cough drop

cane
3 rod 4 beat, drub, flog, lash, reed,
stem, swat 5 flail, grass, spank,
staff, stave, stick, weave, whale
6 batter, buffet, cudgel, larrup, paddle,
rattan, thrash, wallop 7 lambast,
sorghum 8 lambaste 12 walking
stick

Canea's land
5 Crete

canine
3 dog 4 tyke 5 hound, pooch

caning material
5 istle

Canis Major star
6 Sirius

Canis Minor star
7 Procyon

canker
4 rust, sore 5 stain 6 debase, infect
7 corrupt, debauch, deprave, pervert,
vitiate 8 necrosis 10 demoralize

cankered
8 infested, infected

canker sore
5 ulcer 6 lesion 10 ulceration

cannabis
3 pot 4 hemp 5 bhang, ganja, grass
7 hashish 9 marijuana

canned
5 drunk, fired 6 potted 11 prere-
corded

Cannery Row author
9 Steinbeck (John)

canniness
7 caution, cunning, slyness 8 prudence, wiliness 9 cageyness,
foresight 10 artfulness, cleverness,
craftiness, discretion, precaution,
providence, shrewdness 11 forethought

cannon
6 pom-pom 8 howitzer, ordnance
9 artillery
part: 5 chase 6 breech 8 cascabel,
trunnion

cannonade
4 bomb 5 blitz, burst, salvo, shell
6 shower, volley 7 barrage, bombard
8 drumfire, shelling 9 broadside,
fusillade 11 bombardment

cannonball
4 dive 5 speed 7 missile

cannoneer
6 gunner

cannon fodder
6 troops 8 infantry, soldiers

canny
3 sly 4 wary, wise 5 acute, cagey,
chary, quick, sharp, smart 6 adroit,
clever, frugal, saving, shrewd 7 cunning, knowing, prudent, thrifty 9 ingenious, provident 10 economical 11 quick-witted, sharp-witted
12 nimble-witted

canoe
6 dugout 7 pirogue
ancient: 7 coracle
Eskimo: 5 kayak, umiak

canon
3 law 4 list, rule 5 dogma, edict,
round, tenet 6 decree 7 precept,
statute 8 doctrine, standard
9 clergyman, criterion, ordinance
10 regulation

canonical
 5 sound 6 lawful 7 classic 8 accepted, approved, official, orthodox, received 10 authorized, recognized, sanctioned 13 authoritative

canonical hour
 4 none, sext 5 lauds, prime, terce 6 matins, tierce 7 vespers 8 compline

canonicals
 9 vestments

canoodle
 3 hug, pet 5 spoon 6 caress, cuddle, fondle

can opener
 9 church key

canopy
 5 cover, shade 6 awning 7 marquee, shelter 8 covering, sunshade 9 baldachin 10 baldachino
 canvas: 4 tilt

cant
 3 tip 4 heel, lean, list, tilt 5 angle, argot, bevel, idiom, lingo, piety, slang, slant, slope 6 humbug, jargon, patois, patter, speech 7 dialect, diction, incline, lexicon, palaver, recline 8 language, singsong 9 hypocrisy 10 dictionary, pharisaism, sanctimony, vernacular 11 inclination, insincerity 12 pecksniffery

cantaloupe
 5 melon 9 muskmelon

cantankerous
 4 dour, sour 5 cross, huffy, testy, waspy 6 crabby, cranky, crusty, grumpy, morose, ornery 7 bearish, crabbed, grouchy, peevish, prickly, waspish 8 cankered, liverish, petulant, snappish, stubborn, vinegary 9 crotchety, difficult, dyspeptic, irascible, irritable, obstinate 10 ill-natured, irritating, vinegarish 12 cross-grained

canter
 3 bum 4 gait, hobo, lope 5 tramp 6 beggar 7 drifter, vagrant 8 derelict, vagabond 11 bindle stiff

Canterbury
 Archbishop: 3 Oda 6 Anselm, Becket (Thomas á), Parker (Matthew) 7 Cranmer (Thomas), Dunstan 9 Augustine

Canterbury Tales
 author: 7 Chaucer (Geoffrey)
 character: 8 Griselda, pardoner, summoner 10 wife of Bath
 inn: 6 Tabard

canticle
 3 ode 4 hymn, song 6 Te Deum 10 Benedicite, Benedictus, Magnificat 12 Nunc Dimittis

canticles
 11 Song of Songs 13 Song of Solomon

cantilever
 4 beam 6 bridge 7 bracket, support

cantillate
 4 sing 5 chant 6 intone, recite

cantina
 3 bar, pub 6 saloon, tavern 7 barroom

canton
 5 state 6 billet 7 quarter, section 8 district, division

cantor
 5 hazan 6 singer 9 precentor

canvas
 4 duck, sail, tarp, tent 7 tenting 8 painting 9 sailcloth, tarpaulin

canvasback
 4 duck

canvass
 3 con, vet 5 argue, study 6 debate, survey 7 discuss, dispute, examine, inspect, solicit 8 campaign 9 check over 10 scrutinize 11 electioneer 12 authenticate

canyon
 4 Glen, Zion 5 Bryce, chasm, gorge, Grand, gulch, Hells 6 Copper, coulee, ravine, valley

cap
 3 tam, top 4 best 5 beret, cover,

crest, crown, limit, trump **6** beanie, exceed, top off **7** calotte **9** culminate
clergyman's: 7 biretta **9** zucchetto
hoodlike: 4 coif
hunter's: 7 montero
jester's: 7 coxcomb **9** cockscomb
Jewish: 8 yarmulke
knitted: 5 toque, tuque **9** balaclava
military: 4 kepi
mushroom: 6 pileus
part: 4 bill, brim, flap, peak **5** visor **7** earflap
Roman: 6 pileus
Scottish: 3 tam **8** balmoral **9** glengarry **11** tam-o'-shanter
Turkish: 6 calpac **7** calpack

capability
5 craft, means, skill **7** ability, potency **8** adequacy, aptitude, capacity, efficacy, facility **9** potential **10** competence, efficiency **12** potentiality **13** effectiveness, qualification

capable
3 apt **4** able **5** adept **6** adroit, au fait **9** competent, efficient, qualified **10** proficient **11** susceptible

capacious
4 wide **5** ample, roomy **7** sizable **8** abundant, spacious **9** extensive **10** commodious **11** substantial

capacitance
unit of: 5 farad

capacity
4 bent, gift, rank, role, room **5** knack, range, reach, scope, skill, space **6** output, status, talent **7** ability, caliber, faculty **8** adequacy, aptitude, facility, position, standing **10** capability, competence **11** proficiency **13** qualification
unit of: 4 gill, peck, pint **5** liter, litre, minim, quart **6** bushel, gallon **10** fluid ounce, milliliter

Capaneus
slayer: 4 Zeus
wife: 6 Evadne

caparison
5 adorn **6** finery **7** apparel, panoply, raiment **9** adornment, trappings

cape
4 cope, ness **5** cloak, point **6** capote, mantle, tabard, tippet **7** manteau, pelisse **8** foreland, headland, mantelet, mantilla, pelerine **9** peninsula **10** promontory
clergyman's: 8 mozzetta

Cape
Africa: 4 Juby, Yubi **5** Blanc **6** Blanco **7** Agulhas
Alaska: 3 Icy **4** Nome **11** Krusenstern
Algeria: 3 Fer
Antarctica: 3 Ann **4** Dart **5** Adare
Arctic: 8 Nordkaap
Asia: 5 Aniva
Australia: 5 Byron, Otway, Sandy, Smoky **6** Arnhem **9** Van Diemen
Baffin Island: 4 Dyer
Black Sea: 5 Yasun
Borneo: 4 Datu **6** Datoek
Brazil: 4 Frio, Raso
California: 9 Mendocino
Colombia: 5 Aguja
Costa Rica: 5 Velas
Crete: 5 Plaka
Croatia: 5 Ploca **6** Planka
Cuba: 4 Cruz **5** Maisi
Desolación Island: 5 Pilar **6** Pillar
Djibouti: 3 Bir
Egypt: 5 Banas
England: 8 Bolerium, Lands End
Florida: 5 Sable **7** Kennedy **9** Canaveral
Greece: 4 Busa **5** Gallo, Malea, Papas, Vouxa **6** Araxos, Maleas **7** Akritas
Guinea: 5 Verga
Gulf of California: 5 Lobos
Gulf of Guinea: 5 Lopez
Gulf of Mexico: 4 Rojo
Hawaii: 5 Ka Lae **10** South Point **11** Diamond Head
Hispaniola: 5 Beata
Honshu: 3 Iro, Oma **5** Inubo, Kyoga, Nyudo
Indonesia: 4 Vals **5** False
Japan: 4 Esan, Nomo, Sata, Soya **5** Erimo, Kamui

Libya: 3 Tin 4 Milh
Long Island Sound: 10 Throgs Neck
Malay Peninsula: 5 Bulat
Malaysia: 4 Piai 5 Sirik
Massachusetts: 3 Ann, Cod
Mediterranean: 5 Ajdir
Mexico: 4 Buey
Morocco: 3 Sim 4 Guir, Rhir
Namibia: 4 Fria
Newfoundland: 5 Bauld
New Jersey: 3 May
New Zealand: 3 Brett
North Carolina: 4 Fear 7 Lookout
8 Hatteras
Northwest Territories: 8 Bathurst
Nova Scotia: 5 Canso 6 Breton
Oman: 3 Nus 4 Hadd
Ontario: 4 Hurd, Rich
Pakistan: 5 Monze, Muari
Portugal: 4 Roca
Puerto Rico: 4 Rojo
Quebec: 5 Gaspé
Red Sea: 5 Kasar
Sicily: 4 Boeo, Faro 7 Lilibeo,
Passero, Pelorus
Solomon Islands: 5 Zelee
Somalia: 4 Asir 5 Assir, Hafun
South Africa: 8 Good Hope
South America: 4 Horn
Spain: 3 Nao 4 Gata 5 Creus,
Penas
Syria: 5 Basit
Taiwan: 5 O-luan 7 Garam Bi
Tierra del Fuego: 5 Penas
Tunisia: 5 Blanc
Turkey: 3 Boz 4 Baba, Ince, Kara,
Krio 6 Lectum 8 Bozburun
9 Inceburun, Karaburun
Vancouver Island: 5 Scott
Virginia: 5 Henry
Washington: 5 Alava

Căpek, Karel

coinage: 5 robot
play: 3 R.U.R.

caper

4 dido, lark, leap, romp 5 antic,
frisk, prank, revel, shine, theft, trick
6 cavort, frolic, gambol, prance
7 roguery, rollick 8 escapade,
mischief 10 shenanigan, tomfoolery
11 monkeyshine

Cape Town's famous son

5 Smuts (Jan)

Cape Verde

capital: 5 Praia
city: 7 Mindelo
island: 3 Sal 4 Fogo, Maio 5 Brava
8 Boa Vista, São Tiago 10 São
Vicente, São Nicolau, Santa Luzia,
Santo Antão
language: 7 Crioulo 10 Portuguese
monetary unit: 6 escudo

capillary

4 tube 6 tubule 8 hairlike 11 blood
vessel

capital

4 main 5 basic, chief, funds, major,
prime 6 assets, lethal, wealth
8 cardinal 9 essential, excellent,
financing, first-rate, principal, re-
sources 10 first-class, investment,
preeminent, underlying 11 funda-
mental, outstanding, predominant,
wherewithal
Afghanistan: 5 Kabul
Albania: 6 Tirana, Tiranë
Alberta: 8 Edmonton
Algeria: 7 Algiers
Angola: 6 Luanda
Antigua and Barbuda: 7 St. John's
10 Saint John's
Argentina: 11 Buenos Aires
Armenia: 7 Yerevan
Assam: 6 Dispur
Australia: 8 Canberra
Austria: 4 Wien 6 Vienna
Azerbaijan: 4 Baku
Bahamas: 6 Nassau
Bahrain: 6 Manama
Bangladesh: 5 Dhaka
Barbados: 10 Bridgetown
Belarus: 5 Minsk
Belgium: 8 Brussels
Belize: 8 Belmopan
Benin: 9 Porto-Novo
Bhutan: 7 Thimphu
Bolivia: 5 La Paz
Bosnia and Herzegovina:
8 Sarajevo
Botswana: 8 Gaborone
Brazil: 8 Brasília

Bulgaria: 5 Sofia
Burkina Faso: 11 Ouagadougou
Burma: 6 Yangon **7** Rangoon
Burundi: 9 Bujumbura
Cambodia: 9 Phnom Penh
Cameroon: 7 Yaoundé
Canada: 6 Ottawa
Cape Verde: 5 Praia
Central African Republic: 6 Bangui
Chad: 8 N'Djamena
Chile: 8 Santiago
China: 6 Peking **7** Beijing
Colombia: 6 Bogotá
Comoros: 6 Moroni
Congo (Zaire): 8 Kinshasa
Costa Rica: 7 San José
Côte d'Ivoire: 7 Abidjan **12** Yamoussoukro
Croatia: 6 Zagreb
Cuba: 6 Havana
Cyprus: 7 Nicosia
Czech Republic: 6 Prague
Denmark: 10 Copenhagen
Dominica: 6 Roseau
Dominican Republic: 12 Santo Domingo
East Timor: 4 Dili
Ecuador: 5 Quito
Egypt: 5 Cairo
El Salvador: 11 San Salvador
Equatorial Guinea: 6 Malabo
Eritrea: 6 Asmara
Estonia: 7 Tallinn
Ethiopia: 10 Addis Ababa
Faeroe Islands: 8 Tórshavn
Falkland Islands: 7 Stanley
Fiji: 4 Suva
Finland: 8 Helsinki
France: 5 Paris
French Guiana: 7 Cayenne
Gabon: 10 Libreville
Galápagos Islands: 12 San Cristóbal
Gambia: 6 Banjul
Georgia, Republic of: 6 Tiflis **7** Tbilisi
Germany: 6 Berlin
Ghana: 5 Accra
Greece: 6 Athens
Greenland: 8 Godthaab
Grenada: 9 St. George's **12** Saint George's

Guam: 5 Agana
Guinea: 7 Conakry
Guyana: 10 Georgetown
Haiti: 12 Port-au-Prince
Honduras: 11 Tegucigalpa
Hungary: 8 Budapest
Iceland: 9 Reykjavík
India: 8 New Delhi
Indonesia: 7 Jakarta **8** Djakarta
Iran: 6 Tehran **7** Teheran
Iraq: 7 Baghdad
Ireland: 6 Dublin
Israel: 7 Tel-Aviv **9** Jerusalem
Italy: 4 Rome
Jamaica: 8 Kingston
Japan: 5 Tokyo
Jordan: 5 Amman
Kazakhstan: 6 Astana **7** Alma-Ata
Kenya: 7 Nairobi
Kiribati: 6 Tarawa **11** South Tarawa
Korea, North: 9 Pyongyang
Korea, South: 5 Seoul
Kuwait: 10 Kuwait City
Kyrgyzstan: 7 Bishkek
Laos: 9 Vientiane
Latvia: 4 Riga
Lebanon: 6 Beirut
Lesotho: 6 Maseru
Libya: 7 Tripoli
Liechtenstein: 5 Vaduz
Lithuania: 7 Vilnius
Macedonia: 6 Skopje
Madagascar: 12 Antananarivo
Malawi: 8 Lilongwe
Malaysia: 11 Kuala Lumpur
Maldives: 4 Male
Mali: 6 Bamako
Malta: 8 Valletta
Manitoba: 8 Winnipeg
Marshall Islands: 6 Majuro
Mauritania: 10 Nouakchott
Mauritius: 9 Port Louis
Micronesia: 7 Palikir
Moldova: 8 Chişinău, Kishinev
Mongolia: 9 Ulan Bator
Montserrat: 8 Plymouth
Morocco: 5 Rabat
Mozambique: 6 Maputo
Myanmar: 6 Yangon **7** Rangoon
Namibia: 8 Windhoek
Nauru: 5 Yaren
Nepal: 8 Katmandu **9** Kathmandu

Netherlands: 9 Amsterdam
Newfoundland: 10 Saint Johns
New Zealand: 10 Wellington
Nicaragua: 7 Managua
Niger: 6 Niamey
Nigeria: 5 Abuja
Northern Ireland: 7 Belfast
Northern Territory: 6 Darwin
**North-West Frontier Province:
8** Peshawar
Northwest Territories: 11 Yellow-
knife
Norway: 4 Oslo
Nova Scotia: 7 Halifax
Oman: 6 Muscat
Pakistan: 9 Islamabad
Palau: 5 Koror **10** Babelthuap
Papua New Guinea: 11 Port
Moresby
Paraguay: 8 Asunción
Peru: 4 Lima
Philippines: 6 Manila
Poland: 6 Warsaw
Portugal: 6 Lisbon
Prince Edward Island: 13 Char-
lottetown
Puerto Rico: 7 San Juan
Qatar: 4 Doha
Queensland: 8 Brisbane
Réunion: 7 St. Denis **10** Saint Denis
Romania: 9 Bucharest
Russia: 6 Moscow
Rwanda: 6 Kigali
Saint Helena: 9 Jamestown
Saint Kitts and Nevis: 10 Basse-
terre
Saint Lucia: 8 Castries
Samoa: 4 Apia
Saskatchewan: 6 Regina
Saudi Arabia: 6 Riyadh
Scotland: 9 Edinburgh
Senegal: 5 Dakar
Serbia and Montenegro: 8 Belgrade
Seychelles: 8 Victoria
Shetland: 7 Lerwick
Sicily: 7 Palermo
Sierra Leone: 8 Freetown
Sikkim: 7 Gangtok
Sind: 7 Karachi
Slovakia: 10 Bratislava
Slovenia: 9 Ljubljana
Solomon Islands: 7 Honiara

Somalia: 9 Mogadishu
South Africa: 8 Cape Town, Preto-
ria **12** Bloemfontein
South Australia: 8 Adelaide
South-West Africa: 8 Windhoek
Spain: 6 Madrid
Sri Lanka: 7 Colombo
Sudan: 8 Khartoum
Suriname: 10 Paramaribo
Swaziland: 7 Mbabane
Sweden: 9 Stockholm
Switzerland: 4 Bern **5** Berne
Syria: 8 Damascus
Tahiti: 7 Papeete
Taiwan: 6 Taipei
Tajikistan: 8 Dushanbe
Tanzania: 6 Dodoma **11** Dar es
Salaam
Tasmania: 6 Hobart
Thailand: 7 Bangkok
Tibet: 5 Lhasa
Tirol: 9 Innsbruck
Togo: 4 Lomé
Tonga: 9 Nuku'alofa
Trinidad and Tobago: 11 Port-of-
Spain
Tunisia: 5 Tunis
Turkey: 6 Ankara
Turkmenistan: 8 Ashgabat
9 Ashkhabad
Tuvalu: 8 Funafuti
Uganda: 7 Kampala
Ukraine: 4 Kiev
United Arab Emirates: 8 Abu Dhabi
United Kingdom: 6 London
Uruguay: 10 Montevideo
Uttar Pradesh: 7 Lucknow
Uzbekistan: 8 Tashkent
Vanuatu: 4 Vila
Venezuela: 7 Caracas
Victoria: 9 Melbourne
Vietnam: 5 Hanoi
Wales: 7 Cardiff
Western Australia: 5 Perth
Yemen: 4 Sana **5** Sanaa
Yugoslavia: 8 Belgrade
Yukon: 10 Whitehorse
Zambia: 6 Lusaka
Zimbabwe: 6 Harare

capitalist
6 backer, tycoon **7** magnate

capitalistic
8 investor 9 bourgeois, financier, plutocrat 12 entrepreneur

capitalistic
9 bourgeois

capitalize
4 back, fund 5 stake 6 profit 7 convert, finance, promote, sponsor, support 8 bankroll 9 grubstake, subsidize

capital sin
see **deadly sin**

capitation
3 tax 7 payment, poll tax

Capitol Hill sound
3 aye, nay

capitulate
3 bow 4 cave 5 defer, yield 6 cave in, give in, give up, relent, submit 7 concede, succumb 9 acquiesce, surrender 12 knuckle under

capitulation
9 surrender 10 submission

capo
3 bar 4 boss, head 5 chief 9 godfather

capote
4 cope 5 cloak 6 mantle, tabard 7 manteau, pelisse 8 overcoat

capper
4 lure 5 blind, decoy, shill 6 climax, finale 8 clincher

capriccio
4 whim 5 caper, fancy, prank 6 notion, vagary, whimsy 7 impulse

caprice
3 bee 4 mood, vein, whim 5 fancy, freak, humor 6 foible, maggot, megrim, notion, vagary, whimsy 7 conceit 8 crotchet

capricious
4 iffy 5 flaky, moody 6 chancy, fickle 7 erratic, flighty, wayward 8 fanciful, unstable, variable, volatile 9 arbitrary, impulsive, mercurial, uncertain, whimsical 10 changeable, inconstant 12 effervescent, incalculable 13 temperamental, unpredictable

caprid
4 goat

capriole
4 leap 5 caper

capsize
4 keel, roll, sink 5 upset 7 founder, tip over 8 collapse, overturn, turn over

capstone
4 acme, apex, peak 6 apogee, climax, coping, summit, zenith 8 pinnacle 9 high point 11 culmination

capsule
6 canned, pocket, potted 7 compact, outline 9 condensed

capsulize
6 reduce 7 enclose 8 compress, condense 9 summarize, synopsize

captain
6 master 7 skipper
fictional: 4 Ahab, Nemo 5 Queeg
historical: 5 Bligh (William)
pirate: 4 Kidd (William)

Captains Courageous author
7 Kipling (Rudyard)

caption
5 title 6 legend, rubric 7 cutline, heading 8 subtitle 9 underline

captious
5 testy 7 carping, peevish 8 caviling, contrary, critical, exacting, petulant, snappish 9 demanding, irritable 10 censorious, nit-picking 12 faultfinding, overcritical 13 hypercritical

captivate
4 draw, grip, hold, take 5 charm 6 allure, dazzle, please, ravish, seduce 7 attract, beguile, bewitch, delight, enchant, gratify 8 enthrall 9 enrapture, fascinate, hypnotize, infatuate, magnetize, mesmerize, spellbind

captivating
8 charming, enticing, fetching, magnetic, riveting 9 appealing, glamorous, seductive 10 bewitching,

engrossing, intriguing **11** enthralling, fascinating

captive
5 bound, caged, taken **6** jailed **7** hostage **8** confined, detainee, internee, prisoner **10** enthralled, hypnotized, imprisoned

captivity
7 bondage, custody, slavery **9** detention **10** internment **11** confinement **12** imprisonment

capture
3 bag, get, nab, net, win **4** nail, take, trap **5** catch, lasso, prize, seize, snare **6** arrest, collar, entrap, occupy, secure **7** conquer, ensnare **8** preserve

Capuan
4 lush **5** plush **6** deluxe **7** opulent **8** luscious, palatial **9** luxuriant, luxurious, sumptuous **11** upholstered

car
4 auto, heap **5** buggy, coach, crate, sedan, wreck **6** jalopy, junker, wheels **7** clunker, flivver **8** roadster **10** automobile
(see also **automobile**)

carafe
4 ewer **5** cruet **6** bottle, flacon, flagon **8** decanter

caravan
6 convoy, safari

caravansary
3 inn **4** khan **5** hotel, lodge, serai **6** hostel, tavern **10** campground

carbohydrate
5 sugar **6** starch **7** amylose, glucose, lactose, maltose, sucrose **8** fructose, glycogen **9** cellulose, galactose

carbolic acid
6 phenol

carbon
4 coal, coke, soot **8** charcoal, graphite, plumbago **9** lampblack

carbonate
6 aerate

carbon copy
4 dupe, twin **5** clone, ditto, mimeo, repro, Xerox **7** replica **8** knockoff **9** duplicate, facsimile **10** dead ringer **11** replication **12** reproduction

carbonize
4 burn, char, sear **5** singe, toast **6** scorch

carbuncle
4 boil, sore **5** ulcer **6** garnet, pimple **7** abscess, pustule **8** cabochon

carcass
4 body, hulk, mort **5** frame, shell, stiff **6** corpse **7** cadaver, remains **8** skeleton

carcinoid
5 tumor **8** neoplasm

carcinoma
5 tumor **6** cancer **8** neoplasm

card
3 wag, wit **4** menu, sked **5** joker **6** agenda, docket **7** program **8** calendar, comedian, humorist, schedule **9** timetable
fortune-telling: 5 tarot
performer's: 3 cue
spot: 3 pip

cardboard
5 stiff **6** unreal, wooden **7** bristol, buckram, stilted **8** lifeless **10** unlifelike **11** stereotyped, unrealistic

card-carrying
4 true **7** genuine **8** bona fide **9** authentic, certified **11** full-fledged

card game
see at **game**

cardiac stimulant
7 ouabain **9** digitalis

cardinal
3 key **4** main **5** basic, chief, prime, vital **6** ruling **7** central, leading, pivotal, primary **9** essential, important, principal **10** overriding, overruling **11** fundamental **12** constitutive
point: 4 east, west **5** north, south
suffix: 4 teen

care

virtue: **7** justice **8** prudence
9 fortitude **10** temperance

care

3 rue, woe **4** fear, heed, mind, tend,
ward **5** alarm, grief, nurse, pains,
serve, trust, watch, worry **6** attend,
charge, dismay, effort, mother,
regard, regret, sorrow, strain, stress,
unease, wait on **7** anguish, anxiety,
concern, conduct, custody, keeping,
trouble **8** disquiet, exertion, handling, interest, suspense **9** attention,
curiosity, misgiving, oversight,
vigilance **10** affliction, foreboding,
management, solicitude, uneasiness
11 disquietude, heedfulness, maintenance, safekeeping, supervision
12 apprehension, guardianship,
watchfulness **13** consciousness,
consideration, consternation

careen

4 race, sway, tilt **5** lurch, pitch,
speed, swing, weave **6** repair,
wobble **7** stagger

career

3 job **4** race, rush, tear, work
5 chase, speed **6** charge, course
7 calling, passage **8** lifework, vocation **9** encounter **10** livelihood,
profession

care for

4 like, love, mind, tend **5** nurse, treat
6 attend, foster **7** cherish, nurture
8 preserve **9** cultivate, look after

carefree

4 wild **6** blithe, breezy, jaunty
8 reckless **10** insouciant, untroubled
12 happy-go-lucky, lighthearted
13 irresponsible

careful

4 safe, wary **5** chary, exact, fussy
7 dutiful, guarded, precise, prudent,
studied **8** accurate, cautious, critical,
discreet, gingerly, thorough **9** attentive, provident **10** deliberate,
meticulous, particular, scrupulous
11 calculating, circumspect, considerate, foresighted, painstaking,
punctilious **13** conscientious

carefully

6 warily **8** gingerly **10** cautiously,
discreetly **12** meticulously, scrupulously **13** painstakingly, punctiliously

careless

3 lax **5** hasty, messy, slack **6** casual,
remiss, sloppy, untidy **7** cursory,
offhand, unkempt **8** feckless, heedless, reckless, slapdash, slipshod,
slovenly **9** forgetful, negligent,
oblivious, unheeding, unmindful,
unstudied **10** disheveled, inaccurate,
incautious, neglectful, unthinking,
untroubled **11** inadvertent, inattentive, indifferent, perfunctory, spontaneous, thoughtless, unconcerned
12 uninterested, unreflective **13** irresponsible

caress

3 pat, pet, toy **4** kiss, love **5** dally,
touch **6** coddle, cosset, cuddle,
dandle, fondle, nuzzle, pamper,
stroke **7** cherish, indulge **8** canoodle **10** endearment

caressive

7 calming **8** soothing

caretaker

6 warden **7** curator, janitor **9** custodian

careworn

3 wan **5** drawn, faded, jaded **7** haggard, pinched, wearied **8** fatigued,
troubled **9** exhausted **10** distressed

cargo

4 haul, load **6** burden, lading
7 freight, payload **8** shipload,
shipment **11** consignment

caribe

7 piranha

caribou

4 deer **8** reindeer

caricature

4 mock, sham **5** farce, phony
6 parody **7** cartoon, lampoon,
mockery, takeoff **8** travesty

9 burlesque 10 distortion, pasquinade 12 exaggeration

Carlsbad feature
4 cave 6 cavern

Carmen
author: 7 Mérimée (Prosper)
composer: 5 Bizet (Georges)
lover: 7 Don José 9 Escamillo

carnage
4 gore 8 butchery, hecatomb, massacre 9 bloodbath, bloodshed, slaughter

carnal
4 lewd 6 animal, bodily, coarse, earthy, sexual, vulgar, wanton 7 earthly, fleshly, lustful, mundane, obscene, sensual, worldly 8 corporal, material, physical, sensuous, temporal 9 corporeal 10 lascivious

carnation
4 pink 5 color 6 flower

carnival
4 fair, fete 6 fiesta
attraction: 4 ride 6 midway 8 sideshow 10 concession
character: 5 shill 6 barker, hawker 7 grifter, spieler
New Orleans: 9 Mardi Gras
performer: 4 geek

carnivore
9 meat-eater 10 flesh-eater

carol
4 song 6 ballad
Christmas: 4 noel

carom
6 bounce, glance 7 rebound 8 ricochet

Caron role
4 Gigi, Lili 5 Fanny

carotid's relative
5 aorta

carousal
3 bat, jag 4 bash, tear 5 binge, booze, drunk, fling, revel, spree

6 bender, frolic 7 blowout, debauch, shindig 8 wingding 9 brannigan
Scottish: 6 splore

carouse
5 revel 6 cavort, frolic 7 roister
Scottish: 4 birl

carp
3 nag 4 fuss 5 bream, cavil, scold 6 peck at, pester 7 henpeck 8 complain, cyprinid, sea bream 9 complaint, criticize, find fault

carpe ___
4 diem

carpenter
3 ant, bee 6 joiner, wright 7 builder, workman 10 woodworker

carpentry
7 joinery 10 timberwork

carper
6 critic, nagger 7 caviler, knocker 9 nitpicker 10 complainer, criticizer 11 faultfinder

carpet
3 mat, rug 4 Agra 5 Herat, Heriz, Koula, Ladik, Sarok, tapis 6 Herati, Kerman, Keshan, Kirman, Sarouk, Tabriz, Wilton 8 moquette 9 Axminster, broadloom

carpet beetle
10 buffalo bug

carping
7 blaming, fussing, nagging, railing 8 captious, caviling, critical, scolding 9 pestering 10 censorious, upbraiding 11 criticizing, reproachful 12 faultfinding, overcritical

carrageen
7 seaweed 9 Irish moss

carrefour
5 plaza 6 square 10 crossroads

carriage
3 rig 4 pose 5 coach 6 stance 7 posture, transit 8 attitude 9 transport 10 conveyance, deportment

American: 5 buggy 8 rockaway 9 buckboard
attendant: 6 flunky 7 footman
baby: 4 pram 5 buggy 8 stroller 12 perambulator
driver: 4 hack 5 cabby 8 coachman
folding top: 6 calash
four-wheeled: 4 trap 5 buggy, coupe 6 calash, fiacre, landau, surrey 7 hackney, phaeton 8 barouche, brougham, carryall, rockaway, stanhope, victoria 9 buckboard
Indian: 6 gharry
man-drawn: 8 rickshaw 10 jinricksha, jinrikisha
Russian: 6 troika 7 droshky
stately: 7 caroche
three-horse: 6 troika
two-wheeled: 3 gig 4 shay, trap 5 buggy, sulky 6 chaise, hansom 7 calèche, dogcart, tilbury 9 cabriolet
with attendants: 8 equipage

carriage trade
5 elite 6 gentry 7 quality 9 blue blood, gentility 10 upper class, upper crust 11 aristocracy

carrick bend
4 knot

carrier
4 mule 5 envoy 6 bearer, porter, runner, vector 7 airline, courier, shipper, vehicle 8 conveyor, emissary 9 go-between, messenger 11 internuncio, transporter

Carroll character
5 Alice, Bruno, snark 6 boojum, Sylvie 8 Dormouse, Red Queen 9 Mad Hatter, March Hare 10 Mock Turtle 11 White Rabbit 12 Humpty Dumpty

carrot
5 prize 6 reward 9 incentive 10 inducement

carry
3 get, lug 4 bear, haul, have, hump, keep, move, pack, send, take, tote, wear 5 bring, ferry, fetch, range, stock 6 affect, bear up, convey, uphold 7 comport, conduct, portage, possess, support, sustain 8 buttress, transfer, transmit 9 influence, transport

carrying case
7 holdall, satchel 8 carryall

carry off
4 kill 6 abduct, kidnap, remove 7 achieve, destroy, execute, perform, realize 8 complete, conclude, dispatch, shanghai 10 accomplish, spirit away

carry on
3 run 4 go on, keep, rant, rave, wage 6 direct, endure, manage, ordain 7 conduct, operate, persist, prattle, proceed 8 continue, sound off 9 persevere

carry out
6 effect, govern, render 7 achieve, execute, fulfill, oversee, perform, realize 8 bring off, complete, finalize, transact 9 discharge, prosecute 10 accomplish, administer, effectuate 12 administrate

carry over
6 deduct 7 persist 8 postpone, transfer

carry through
4 last 5 abide 6 effect, endure 7 execute, perdure, perform, persist, survive 8 bring off, complete, continue 10 accomplish, effectuate

Carson work
11 Sea Around Us (The) 12 Silent Spring

cart
3 gig 4 dray, haul 5 buggy, carry 6 barrow, convey, schlep 7 schlepp, trundle, tumbrel, tumbril 8 carriage 9 transport 11 wheelbarrow
Indian: 5 tonga
racing: 5 sulky

_____ carte
3 à la

_____ Carte
5 D'Oyly

carte blanche
3 say **5** power, right, say-so **7** freedom, license **8** free hand, free rein **9** authority **10** blank check **11** prerogative

carte du jour
4 menu

cartel
4 bloc, pool **5** trust **7** combine **9** syndicate **10** consortium **12** conglomerate

Carthaginian
goddess of the moon: 5 Tanit **6** Tanith
queen: 4 Dido **6** Elissa

cartilage
7 gristle

cartographer
English: 5 Smith (William)
Flemish: 6 Kremer (Gerhard) **8** Mercator (Gerardus), Ortelius
German: 13 Waldseemüller (Martin)
Greek: 7 Ptolemy

cartography
9 mapmaking

carton
3 box **4** pack

cartoonist
3 Lee (Stan) **4** Capp (Al), Kane (Bob), Nast (Thomas), Szep (Paul) **5** Adams (Scott), Booth (George), Chast (Roz), Crumb (R.), Davis (Jim), Gould (Chester), Hanna (Bill), Jones (Chuck), Kelly (Walt), Steig (William), Young (Chic) **6** Addams (Charles), Caniff (Milton), Disney (Walt), Larson (Gary), Martin (Don), Schulz (Charles), Walker (Mort) **7** Barbera (Joe), Feiffer (Jules), Ketcham (Hank), Mauldin (Bill), Thurber (James), Trudeau (Garry) **8** Goldberg (Rube), Groening (Matt), Herblock, Hokinson (Helen), MacNelly (Jeff), Oliphant (Pat) **9** Fleischer (Max) **10** Hirschfeld (Al)

cartouche
5 frame **6** shield **9** cartridge

cartridge
4 case, tube **5** shell **8** cassette, cylinder **9** cartouche, container

cartwheel
4 coin **6** dollar, tumble **10** handspring

carve
3 cut, hew **4** chip, etch, form, hack **5** shape, slice **6** chisel, cleave, incise, sculpt **7** dissect, engrave, whittle **9** sculpture

Casablanca
actor: 5 Lorre (Peter), Rains (Claude) **6** Bogart (Humphrey) **7** Bergman (Ingrid) **11** Greenstreet (Sydney)
character: 4 Ilsa (Lund), Rick (Blaine) **6** Laszlo (Victor)
director: 6 Curtiz (Michael)

Casanova
4 rake, roué, wolf **5** Romeo **6** lecher, masher, tomcat **7** amorist, Don Juan, gallant, playboy, seducer **8** lothario, paramour **9** adulterer, ladies' man, libertine, womanizer **10** lady-killer, voluptuary **11** philanderer

cascade
4 fall, gush, lace, pour, spew **5** chute, falls, flood, spill **6** deluge, plunge, rapids, shower, tumble **7** Niagara, torrent **8** cataract **9** avalanche, waterfall **10** outpouring

Cascade Mountains peak
6 Lassen, Shasta **7** Rainier

case
3 box, con, vet **4** etui, hull, husk, skin, suit **5** cause, event, shell **6** action, sample, sheath **7** episode, examine, example, inspect, lawsuit **8** argument, covering, incident, instance, sampling, specimen **9** check over, condition, situation **10** occurrence, proceeding, scrutinize **11** eventuality **12** circumstance
grammatical: 6 dative **8** ablative, genitive, vocative **9** objective **10** accusative, nominative, possessive

casebearer
5 larva 11 caterpillar

case-hardened
5 tough 7 callous 8 obdurate
9 indurated, insensate, toughened,
unfeeling 11 insensitive 12 thick-skinned

casement
4 sash 6 window

Casey at the Bat poet
6 Thayer (Ernest Lawrence)

cash
4 coin, jack 5 bread, dough, money,
scrip 6 dinero, redeem, wampum
7 cabbage, lettuce, scratch 8 currency 10 greenbacks, ready money
11 legal tender

cashier
3 can 4 boot, fire, oust, sack 5 clerk,
eject, expel, scrap 6 banker, bounce,
bursar, reject, teller 7 boot out,
discard, dismiss, kick out 8 jettison,
throw out 9 discharge, eliminate,
terminate, throw away 10 bookkeeper 11 bean counter, comptroller

cash in
3 die 4 conk, drop 5 croak 6 expire,
pop off, redeem, retire 7 kick off,
succumb 8 check out, drop dead,
pass away, settle up 9 liquidate

casing
4 hull, husk, pipe, rind, skin, tire
5 frame, shell, space 7 wrapper
8 membrane

casino
attendant: 6 dealer 8 croupier
game: 4 faro 5 craps, monte,
poker 6 tierce 8 baccarat, roulette
9 blackjack

cask
3 keg, tun 4 butt, drum, pipe 6 barrel,
firkin 8 hogshead

casket
3 box 5 chest 6 coffer, coffin 8 jewel
box

Caspian Sea
city: 4 Baku
feeder: 4 Ural

Cassandra
4 seer 7 prophet, seeress 8 doomster 9 doomsayer, pessimist,
worrywart 10 prophetess
brother: 7 Helenus
father: 5 Priam
lover: 9 Agamemnon
mother: 6 Hecuba
slayer: 12 Clytemnestra

casserole
4 dish 5 crock 6 tureen

Cassiopeia
13 constellation
daughter: 9 Andromeda
husband: 7 Cepheus

Cassio's mistress
6 Bianca

cassock
4 robe 7 soutane 8 vestment

cast
3 add, hue, sum, tot 4 drop, face,
fire, form, hurl, kind, look, mold,
shed, sort, tint, tone, toss, turn, type
5 color, fling, heave, leave, pitch,
range, shade, shape, strew, throw,
tinge, total, touch 6 actors, design,
devise, direct, figure, nature, reject,
slough, troupe, visage 7 arrange,
company, quality, replica, scatter
8 abdicate, disperse, jettison, sprinkle 9 character, prognosis, throw
away 10 appearance, conjecture,
distribute, expression, prediction,
strabismus, suggestion 11 countenance
a spell on: 3 hex 5 charm
7 beguile, bewitch 8 enthrall
9 captivate, enrapture, fascinate,
hypnotize, infatuate, mesmerize,
spellbind
overboard: 7 deep-six 8 jettison

cast about
4 hunt, seek 5 grope 6 search
7 seek out 8 contrive 9 search for,
search out

castaway
5 leper, tramp 6 beggar, maroon,
pariah 7 Ishmael, outcast, vagrant
8 deadbeat, derelict 10 Ishmaelite

cast down
see **downcast**

caste
5 class 6 degree, estate, status
7 station 8 division, prestige

cast head
4 bust

castigate
4 beat, flay, rail, whip 5 baste,
chide, scold, slash 6 berate,
pummel, punish, rebuke, scorch,
thrash 7 belabor, blister, chasten,
chew out, lambast, reprove, scarify,
scourge, upbraid 8 chastise, lambaste, penalize 9 criticize, dress
down, excoriate, reprimand 10 discipline, tongue-lash

castigation
3 rod 6 rebuke 7 reproof 8 punition,
scolding 10 correction, discipline,
punishment 12 chastisement

castle
5 manor, villa 7 alcazar, château,
citadel, mansion 8 fortress
10 stronghold
adjunct: 4 moat
gate: 10 portcullis
ledge: 7 rampart
structure: 6 turret
tower: 4 keep 6 donjon
wall: 6 bailey 10 battlement

cast off
5 fling, flung, let go, loose, untie
6 jilted, untied 7 unhitch 8 cut loose,
forsaken, rejected, unfasten, unmoored 9 discarded, unhitched
10 left behind, unfastened

Castor
brother: 6 Pollux 10 Polydeuces
constellation: 6 Gemini
father: 4 Zeus 9 Tyndareus
mother: 4 Leda
sister: 5 Helen
slayer: 4 Idas

castor oil
8 laxative 9 cathartic, lubricant,
purgative

cast out
4 oust 5 eject, evict, exile, expel
6 banish, deport 7 discard 9 eliminate, ostracize

castrate
3 fix 4 geld, spay 5 alter, unman,
unsex 6 neuter 7 unnerve 8 enervate, mutilate 9 sterilize 10 emasculate 11 desexualize

castrato singer
9 Farinelli

casual
5 light, minor 6 breezy, chance,
random, remote 7 natural, offhand,
relaxed, trivial, unfussy 8 detached,
informal, laid-back 9 easygoing,
impromptu, irregular, uncurious,
unplanned, unserious 10 accidental,
contingent, fortuitous, improvised,
incidental, insouciant, nonchalant,
occasional 11 indifferent, low-
pressure, spontaneous, unconcerned, unimportant 12 uninterested
13 disinterested, insignificant

casualty
4 prey 5 death 6 mishap, victim
8 accident, calamity, disaster, fatality
9 mischance 10 misfortune 11 catastrophe 12 misadventure

casuistry
7 sophism 9 deception, sophistry
12 equivocation, speciousness
13 deceptiveness

casus ____
5 belli

cat
4 lion, lynx, puma, puss 5 felid,
kitty, liger, ounce, pussy, tiger, tigon
6 cougar, feline, jaguar, mouser,
ocelot 7 caracal, cheetah, leopard,
panther 12 mountain lion
Alice's: 5 Dinah
catlike animal: 5 civet, genet
7 linsang
combining form: 5 ailur 6 ailuro
disease: 9 distemper
domestic: 3 Mau, Rex 4 Manx
5 tabby 6 Angora, Birman, calico,

exotic, Ocicat, Somali **7** bobtail,
Burmese, Persian, Ragdoll, Siamese
8 longhair, Wirehair **9** Himalayan,
Maine coon, shorthair, Tonkinese
10 Abyssinian
extinct: 10 saber-tooth
fastest: 7 cheetah
female: 5 queen **7** lioness, tigress
9 grimalkin
genus: 5 Felis
grinning: 8 Cheshire
male: 3 gib, tom
relating to: 6 feline
ring-tailed: 6 serval
sound: 3 mew **4** hiss, meow, purr,
roar **9** caterwaul
spotted: 4 pard **6** jaguar, margay,
ocelot, serval **7** cheetah, leopard,
panther
striped: 5 tiger
tailless: 4 Manx
young: 6 kitten

cataclysm
5 flood **6** deluge **7** Niagara, torrent,
tragedy **8** calamity, cataract, disaster, flooding **10** inundation **11** catastrophe, devastation

cataclysmic
5 fatal **7** ruinous **10** calamitous,
disastrous **11** devastating **12** catastrophic

catacomb
5 crypt, vault **8** cemetery **10** necropolis, undercroft

catafalque
4 bier

catalog
4 list, roll **5** enter, index, tally **6** enroll, roster **7** itemize, program
8 classify, inscribe, register, roll call,
schedule, syllabus **9** enumerate,
inventory **10** prospectus
of books: 11 bibliotheca
of saints: 9 hagiology

catalyst
4 goad, spur **7** impetus, impulse
8 stimulus **9** incentive, stimulant
10 incitation, incitement, motivation

catamaran
4 boat, raft

catamount
4 lynx, puma **6** bobcat, cougar
7 panther, wildcat

cataract
5 falls, flood, rapid **6** deluge, rapids
7 cascade, Niagara, torrent **8** downpour **9** waterfall **10** inundation

catastrophe
3 woe **6** deluge, fiasco **7** debacle,
tragedy **8** calamity, disaster, melt-
down **9** cataclysm, emergency
11 devastation

catastrophic
5 fatal **6** deadly, tragic **7** ruinous
10 calamitous, disastrous **11** cataclysmic

Catawba
4 wine **5** river **6** Indian

catcall
4 hiss, hoot, jeer, razz **9** criticism,
raspberry **10** Bronx cheer

catch
3 bag, get, nab, net, see, wed
4 dupe, find, fool, grab, grip, gull,
haul, hoax, hook, nail, snag, sock,
spot, take, trap **5** block, clasp, clout,
grasp, hit on, marry, reach, round,
seize, smite, snare, stick, stump,
trick, watch, whack **6** accept,
anchor, arrest, clutch, collar, cut off,
descry, detect, engage, entrap,
fasten, flurry, follow, put out, rattle,
secure, snatch, strike, take in, tangle
turn up **7** capture, confuse, deceive,
disturb, ensnare, grapple, hit upon,
perplex, receive **8** confound, contract, entangle, flimflam, fragment,
hoodwink, kick over, meet with,
overhaul, overtake **9** apprehend,
bamboozle, embarrass, encounter,
intercept **10** comprehend, understand **12** come down with

Catch-22 author
6 Heller (Joseph)

catchall term
3 etc.

Catcher in the Rye
author: 8 Salinger (J. D.)
character: 9 Caulfield (Holden)

catcher's glove
4 mitt

catching
6 taking 10 contagious, infectious
12 communicable

catch on
3 see 4 hear 5 learn 7 find out
8 discover 9 ascertain, determine,
figure out

catchphrase
see **catchword**

catch up
4 hold 6 gain on 7 close in, ensnare
8 entangle, enthrall 9 fascinate,
mesmerize, spellbind

catchword
5 maxim, motto 6 slogan 10 shibboleth

catchy
6 fitful, spotty, tricky 7 erratic
8 sporadic 9 appealing, desultory,
irregular, memorable, spasmodic

catechist
7 teacher

catechize
3 ask 4 quiz 5 grill, query, train
7 examine, inquire 8 instruct, question 9 inculcate 11 interrogate

catechumen
6 novice 7 convert, student, trainee
8 initiate, neophyte

categorical
7 certain, decided, express 8 absolute, clear-cut, definite, emphatic,
explicit, positive 9 downright
10 definitive, forthright 11 unambiguous, unequivocal, unqualified

categorize
3 peg 4 sort 5 class, group 7 put

down 8 classify, identify 10 pigeonhole

category
4 rank, tier 5 class, genre, grade,
group 6 league 7 section 8 division,
grouping 10 pigeonhole

catenation
4 link 5 chain 6 series, string
7 linkage 10 connection, succession

catercorner
9 obliquely, slantways, slantwise
10 cornerwise, diagonally

caterpillar
5 larva 7 cutworm, webworm
8 armyworm, silkworm 10 casebearer

cater to
5 humor 6 pamper, supply 7 furnish,
gratify, indulge

caterwaul
4 howl, meow, yowl 5 miaow 6 squall

catfish
see **fish**

catharsis
5 purge, tonic 7 purging 8 curative
9 cleansing, purgation, purgative
10 lustration 11 expurgation, restorative 12 purification

cathartic
5 purge, tonic 8 curative 9 castor
oil, purgative 11 restorative, therapeutic

Cathay
5 China

cathedral
5 duomo 6 church 8 basilica
feature: 4 apse, nave 5 altar
6 chapel 7 chancel 10 clerestory
8 buttress, transept

Cather novel
8 Lost Lady (A) 9 My Antonia, One
of Ours, O Pioneers 13 Song of the
Lark 15 Professor's House (The)
16 Shadows on the Rock 23 Youth
and the Bright Medusa

catholic

5 broad 6 global 7 general, liberal
8 eclectic, tolerant 9 expansive,
inclusive, undivided, universal,
worldwide 10 ecumenical 12 cosmopolitan 13 comprehensive

catholicity

7 breadth 9 tolerance 10 liberality
11 magnanimity 12 universality

catholicon

6 elixir 7 cure-all, nostrum, panacea

catkin

5 ament

catlike

6 feline 7 furtive 8 stealthy

catnap

3 nap 4 doze 6 siesta, snooze
10 forty winks

Cato

title: 6 aedile, censor, consul
7 praetor, tribune 8 quaestor

Cat on a _____ Tin Roof

3 Hot

cat's-paw

4 dupe, knot, pawn, tool 5 patsy
6 puppet, stooge

cattail

4 reed, rush

cattle

4 cows, kine, neat, oxen 7 bovines
9 livestock
breed: 5 Angus, Devon, Kerry
6 Durham, Jersey, Sussex 7 Brahman, Hariana, Red Poll 8 Ayrshire,
Galloway, Guernsey, Hereford, Highland, Holstein, Limousin, Longhorn
9 Charolais, Red Polled, Shorthorn,
Simmental 10 Brown Swiss
11 Dutch Belted
catching rope: 5 lasso 6 lariat
cry: 3 low, moo
dehorn: 4 poll
disease: 4 loco 5 bloat 6 nagana
7 anthrax, locoism, measles, murrain
8 blackleg, lumpy jaw, mastitis,
staggers 10 rinderpest, Texas fever
11 brucellosis

extinct breed: 9 Teeswater
family: 7 Bovidae
feed: 6 fodder
genus: 3 Bos
goddess: 6 Bubona
grazing land: 5 range 7 pasture
group: 4 herd 5 drove
herdsman: 6 cowboy, drover,
gaucho 7 vaquero 8 wrangler
10 cowpuncher
identification: 5 brand
pen: 6 corral
round up: 7 wrangle
stable: 4 barn, byre
steal: 6 rustle
wild flight: 8 stampede

catty

4 mean 5 nasty 6 barbed, bitchy,
feline 7 furtive, vicious 8 spiteful,
stealthy 9 malicious 10 backbiting,
malevolent

Caucasian

capital: 4 Baku 6 Tiflis 7 Tbilisi,
Yerevan
republic: 7 Armenia, Georgia
10 Azerbaijan

Caucasus

peak: 6 Elbrus
people: 5 Osset

caucus

4 bloc, sect 5 cabal, lobby 6 parley,
powwow 7 faction

caudal appendage

4 tail

caudillo

6 despot, tyrant 8 dictator
9 strongman

cauldron

3 pot 6 boiler, kettle 8 crucible

cause

4 case, make, root 5 evoke, hatch
6 compel, effect, elicit, induce, motive, origin, reason, source, spring
7 produce, provoke 8 engender,
generate, movement 9 necessity,
principle 10 antecedent, bring about,
inducement, originator 11 determinant, precipitate 13 consideration

cause _____
7 célèbre

causerie
4 chat 5 essay 6 column 7 article, feature 8 colloquy, dialogue 12 conversation

caustic
4 acid, keen, tart 5 acerb, acrid, sharp 6 biting, bitter, ironic 7 acerbic, cutting, mordant, pungent 8 scathing, stinging 9 corrosive, sarcastic, trenchant 10 astringent
solution: 3 lye

cauterize
4 burn, numb, sear 6 deaden 11 anesthetize

caution
4 warn 6 caveat 7 warning 8 forewarn, monition, prudence 9 canniness, chariness, foresight, vigilance 10 admonition, discretion, providence 11 carefulness, forethought, forewarning 12 admonishment, discreetness

cautionary
7 warning 8 monitory 10 admonitory

cautious
4 wary 5 alert, cagey, canny, chary, leery 6 shrewd 7 careful, guarded, politic, prudent 8 discreet, gingerly, vigilant, watchful 9 judicious, provident 11 circumspect, considerate, foresighted

cavalcade
6 parade, series 7 cortege 8 sequence 10 procession, succession

cavalier
5 lofty, proud 6 casual, knight, lordly 7 gallant, haughty, offhand 8 arrogant, debonair, horseman, scornful, superior 9 caballero, gentleman 10 disdainful, dismissive, insouciant, nonchalant 12 aristocratic, supercilious

cavalryman
6 lancer 7 dragoon, trooper
Algerian: 5 spahi
horse: 5 waler

Prussian: 5 uhlan
Russian: 7 cossack
Turkish: 5 spahi
weapon: 5 lance, saber 7 carbine

cave
3 bow, den 4 bend, drop, give, grot, lair 5 antre, break, defer, yield 6 fold up, grotto, hollow, submit 7 crumple, knuckle, succumb 8 collapse 9 break down 10 capitulate, subterrane 11 buckle under 12 knuckle under, subterranean
dweller: 3 bat 4 bear, lion 6 hermit 9 Cro-Magnon 10 troglodite 11 Neanderthal
explorer: 9 spelunker
formation: 10 stalactite, stalagmite
France: 7 Lascaux 10 Rouffignac
Iceland: 7 Singing
Indiana: 9 Wyandotte
Iraq: 8 Shanidar
Kentucky: 7 Mammoth
New Zealand: 7 Waitomo
rock: 8 dolomite 9 limestone
Scotland: 7 Fingal's
South Africa: 5 Cango
Spain: 8 Altamira
study of: 10 speleology

caveat
6 notice 7 caution, warning 8 monition 10 admonition 11 explanation, forewarning

caveat _____
6 emptor

caveman
5 brute 6 savage 9 barbarian, Cro-Magnon 10 troglodyte

cavern
6 grotto 12 subterranean
Capri: 10 Blue Grotto
Montana: 13 Lewis and Clark
New Mexico: 8 Carlsbad
Tennessee: 10 Cumberland
Virginia: 7 Luray

cavernous
4 vast 6 gaping, hollow 7 yawning

caviar
3 roe 4 eggs 6 relish
source: 6 beluga 8 sturgeon

cavil
4 carp 7 nitpick, quibble 9 criticize, find fault

caviler
6 carper, critic 7 knocker 8 quibbler 10 criticizer 11 faultfinder

caviling
5 fussy 7 carping, finicky, nagging 8 captious, contrary, critical, exacting, niggling 10 censorious, nitpicking 12 faultfinding 13 hairsplitting

cavity
3 pit 4 bore, hole, void 5 decay 6 caries, hollow 7 vacuity 10 interstice
body: 5 antra (plural), sinus 6 antrum 8 follicle, hemocoel

cavort
4 leap, romp 5 caper, cut up, frisk, sport 6 frolic, gambol, prance 7 carry on, rollick 10 roughhouse 11 horse around

cavy
4 paca 6 rodent 9 guinea pig

caw
4 crow, yawp 6 squall, squawk

cay
3 key 4 isle, reef 5 islet 6 island

cayenne
6 pepper
genus: 8 Capsicum

cayman
see **caiman**

Cayman Islands
capital: 10 George Town
discoverer: 8 Columbus (Christopher)
territory of: 7 Britain

Cayuga chief
5 Logan (James)

cease
3 die, end 4 halt, quit, stop 5 close 6 desist, ending, finish 8 conclude, give over, knock off, leave off 9 terminate 10 conclusion 11 discontinue, termination

cease-fire
5 truce 9 armistice 10 suspension

ceaseless
7 endless, eternal, nonstop 8 constant, immortal, unending 9 continual, incessant, perennial, perpetual, sustained, unabating 10 continuing, continuous 11 everlasting, neverending, unremitting 12 interminable 13 uninterrupted

Cecrops' daughter
5 Herse 8 Aglauros, Aglaurus 9 Pandrosos, Pandrosus

cede
4 deed 5 grant, leave, yield 6 assign, convey, give up 7 abandon, concede 8 alienate, hand over, make over, part with, renounce, sign over, transfer 9 surrender, vouchsafe 10 relinquish

ceinture
4 belt, sash 6 girdle 9 waistband

Celaeno
father: 5 Atlas
mother: 7 Pleione
sisters: 8 Pleiades

celebrate
4 fete, hold, hymn, keep, laud 5 bless, cry up, exalt, extol, honor, party, revel 6 praise 7 carouse, glorify, maffick, observe, perform, rejoice 8 eulogize 9 solemnize 11 commemorate

celebrated
5 famed, great, noted 6 famous 7 eminent, notable, partied 8 caroused, rejoiced, renowned 9 prominent, well-known 11 illustrious 13 distinguished

celebration
4 bash, fete, gala 5 party 6 fiesta 7 blowout, jubilee, revelry 8 ceremony, festival, jamboree, wingding 10 observance

_____ célèbre
5 cause

celebrity
3 VIP 4 fame, hero, lion, name, star

5 éclat, glory 6 renown, repute
7 notable 8 eminence, luminary,
prestige, somebody 9 notoriety,
personage, superstar 10 notability,
prominence, reputation

celerity
4 pace 5 speed 8 alacrity, dispatch,
rapidity, velocity 9 briskness,
fleetness, quickness, swiftness
10 speediness

celestial
6 divine 7 blessed, elysian, sublime
8 beatific, empyreal, empyrean,
ethereal, heavenly, Olympian,
supernal 9 unearthly 12 otherworldly

celestial body
3 sun 4 moon, star 5 comet
6 meteor, nebula, planet 8 asteroid
9 satellite

Celestial Empire
5 China

celibate
5 unwed 6 chaste, single, virgin
8 virginal, virtuous 9 abstinent,
continent

cell
4 room 5 cubby, zooid 6 alcove
7 chamber, cubicle 9 corpuscle,
cubbyhole 11 compartment
blood: 8 hemocyte
disease: 6 cancer
division: 7 meiosis, mitosis
fertilized egg: 6 zygote
material: 3 DNA, RNA 7 protein
9 chromatin, cytoplasm 10 proto-
plasm
nerve: 6 neuron
part: 4 gene 7 nucleus, vacuole
8 ribosome 9 centriole 10 chromosome
reproductive: 3 egg 4 germ,
ovum 5 sperm 6 gamete 8 gonidium

cellar
5 store 7 shelter 8 basement

cellist
American: 4 Rose (Leonard)
6 Lesser (Laurence), Parnas (Leslie)
7 Nelsova (Zara), Parisot (Aldo),
Starker (Janos) 8 Fournier (Pierre),
Schuster (Joseph) 10 Greenhouse
(Bernard)
English: 5 du Pré (Jacqueline)
Russian: 11 Piatigorsky (Gregor)
12 Rostropovich (Mstislav)
Spanish: 6 Casals (Pablo)

cellophane
4 wrap 7 wrapper 8 wrapping
9 packaging

celluloid
4 film 7 plastic

Celt
4 Gael, Scot 6 Breton 8 Irishman,
Welshman 10 Cornishman, High-
lander

Celtic
deity: 4 Bran 5 Epona, Lugus,
Macha 6 Brigit 8 Rhiannon
9 Cernunnos
festival: 7 Beltane, Samhain

cement
4 bind, glue, join 5 grout, unify, unite
6 mortar 8 concrete
ingredient: 4 lime 6 silica
7 alumina 8 magnesia, pozzolan
9 iron oxide, pozzolana

cemetery
8 boneyard, boot hill 8 God's acre
9 graveyard 10 churchyard, necropolis 12 burial ground, memorial park,
potter's field
underground: 8 catacomb

cenotaph
4 tomb 6 marker 8 memorial,
monument

censer
8 thurible
carrier: 8 thurifer

censor
3 ban, cut 4 blip, edit 5 bleep,
purge 6 cut out, delete, excise, purify, screen 7 clean up 8 black out,
restrict, suppress, withhold 9 expurgate, red-pencil 10 blue-pencil,
bowdlerize

censorious
6 severe 7 carping 8 captious,

critical **10** accusatory, condemning
11 reproachful **12** condemnatory,
denunciatory, disapproving, faultfinding, overcritical, reprehending
13 hypercritical

censurable
5 wrong **6** guilty, sinful **7** heinous
8 blamable, blameful, culpable,
improper, wrongful **9** incorrect
10 deplorable, despicable, detestable **11** blameworthy, disgraceful,
impeachable **12** unacceptable
13 discreditable, objectionable,
reprehensible

censure
5 blame, scold **6** rebuke, strafe
7 condemn, reprove, upbraid
8 chastise, denounce, disallow,
reproach **9** castigate, criticize,
reprehend, reprimand, reprobate
10 disapprove

centaur
6 Chiron, Nessus

Centaurus star
4 Beta **5** Alpha

Centennial State
8 Colorado

center
3 hub, mid **4** axis, core, crux, mean,
pith, root, seat **5** focus, heart, midst,
pivot **6** inside, medial, median,
middle, source **7** central, essence
8 interior, midpoint, omphalos
10 focal point **11** equidistant
12 intermediary, intermediate

centerboard
4 keel

centerfold
7 foldout **8** gatefold

central
3 hub, key, mid **4** main, mean
5 basic, chief, focal **6** medial,
median, middle **7** leading, pivotal,
primary, salient **8** cardinal, dominant,
exchange, foremost, moderate
9 essential, paramount, principal
10 overriding **11** fundamental,
outstanding, predominant **12** intermediate

Central African Republic
capital: 6 Bangui
former name: 11 Ubangi-Shari
language: 5 Sango, Zande
6 French
monetary unit: 5 franc
neighbor: 4 Chad **5** Congo, Sudan
8 Cameroon

Central America
country: 6 Panama **8** Honduras
9 Costa Rica, Guatemala, Nicaragua
10 El Salvador
language: 7 Nahuatl, Spanish

centralize
5 focus, unify **11** concentrate, consolidate

centripetal
8 afferent, focusing, unifying
10 converging **11** integrative
12 centralizing **13** concentrating,
consolidating

centurion
7 officer **9** commander

century plant
5 agave

cephalopod
5 squid **7** mollusc, mollusk, octopus
10 cuttlefish

Cepheus
daughter: 9 Andromeda
kingdom: 8 Ethiopia
wife: 10 Cassiopeia

cerate
4 balm **5** cream, salve **6** chrism
7 unction, unguent **8** dressing, liniment, ointment **9** demulcent, emollient

Cerberus
5 guard **8** guardian, sentinel, watchdog
father: 6 Typhon
form: 3 dog
mother: 7 Echidna

cereal
4 meal, mush, samp **5** gruel **6** farina
7 oatmeal **8** cornmeal, porridge
grass: 3 rye **4** corn, oats, ragi, rice
5 emmer, maize, spelt, wheat

6 barley, millet 7 sorghum 9 buck-
wheat
North African: 8 couscous
Russian: 5 kasha

cerebral
6 mental 7 bookish 8 highbrow
9 scholarly 10 highbrowed 12 intellectual

cerebrate
5 think 6 reason 7 reflect .8 cogitate
9 speculate 10 deliberate

cerebration
7 thought 9 brainwork 10 cogitation,
reflection 11 speculation 12 deliberation

ceremonial
6 august, formal, ritual, solemn
7 courtly, stately, studied 8 mannered, stylized 10 liturgical 11 ritual-
istic 12 conventional

ceremonious
6 formal, proper, seemly, solemn
7 courtly, stately 8 decorous, imposing, majestic 9 dignified, grandiose 10 impressive 11 punctilious
12 conventional

ceremony
4 form, pomp, rite 6 ritual 7 decorum, liturgy, service 8 protocol
9 formality 10 observance
Jewish: 8 habdalah, havdalah
10 bar mitzvah, bat mitzvah
university: 8 encaenia

Ceres
Greek counterpart: 7 Demeter
daughter: 10 Persephone, Proserpina, Proserpine
father: 6 Cronus, Saturn
mother: 3 Ops 4 Rhea

certain
3 set 4 firm, some, sure, true
5 fated, fixed 6 divers, stated,
sundry 7 assured, settled, several,
various 8 cocksure, credible, definite, destined, positive, provable,
reliable, sanguine, specific, surefire,
unerring 9 authentic, certified,
confident, convinced, necessary,
plausible, warranted 10 conclusive,

dependable, guaranteed, inarguable,
inevitable, infallible, stipulated, undeniable, verifiable 11 confirmable,
indubitable, ineluctable, inescapable,
trustworthy, unavoidable 12 demonstrable, indisputable, well-grounded
13 incontestable, predetermined,
uncontestable

certainty
5 faith 6 surety 8 firmness, sureness 9 assurance, certitude, sure
thing 10 confidence, conviction
11 assuredness, staunchness
12 absoluteness, definiteness, posi-
tiveness

certificate
7 diploma, license, voucher 8 contract, document 9 affidavit 10 credential

certifier
6 notary 7 auditor 9 registrar

certify
4 aver, avow, okay 5 state, swear,
vouch 6 assert, assure, attest, verify
7 approve, confirm, endorse, license,
testify, warrant, witness 8 accredit,
guaranty, notarize 9 authorize, guarantee, recognize 10 commission
12 authenticate

Cervantes' hero
10 Don Quixote

cessation
3 end 4 halt, rest, stop 5 break,
cease, close, letup, pause 6 ending,
finish, freeze, hiatus, period, recess
7 respite 10 conclusion, suspension
11 termination 12 interruption

cesspool
3 den, pit, sty 4 sink 5 sewer,
Sodom 6 cloaca, gutter, pigsty
8 Gomorrah 12 Augean stable

cetacean
5 whale 7 dolphin 8 porpoise

Cetus star
4 Mira

Ceylon
8 Sri Lanka

cgs unit

3 erg 4 dyne, gram, phot 5 gauss, poise, stilb 6 second, stokes 7 lambert, maxwell, oersted 10 centimeter

Chablis

4 wine 8 Burgundy 9 white wine

Chad

capital: 8 N'Djamena
city: 4 Sarh 6 Abéché 7 Moundou
lake: 4 Chad
language: 6 Arabic, French
monetary unit: 5 franc
neighbor: 5 Libya, Niger, Sudan 7 Nigeria 8 Cameroon
river: 5 Chari 6 Logone

chafe

3 irk, rub, vex 4 fret, gall, peel, rage, skin, wear 5 annoy, erode 6 abrade, bother, scrape 7 provoke 8 irritate, vexation

chaff

3 kid, rag, rib 4 jest, joke, josh, razz 5 dregs, husks, tease 6 banter, debris, refuse 7 remains 8 detritus 9 sweepings

chaffer

6 barter, dicker, haggle, higgle, palter 7 bargain, chatter 8 exchange, huckster

chagrin

3 ire, irk, vex 5 abash, annoy, peeve, pique, upset 6 dismay 7 perturb 8 disquiet, distress, unsettle, vexation 9 annoyance, discomfit, displease, embarrass, humiliate, petulance 10 disappoint, discompose, disconcert, irritation 11 frustration, humiliation 12 discomfiture

chagrined

4 hurt 5 upset, vexed 6 shamed 7 ashamed 8 dismayed 9 disturbed, mortified, perturbed, unsettled 10 distressed, humiliated 11 discomposed, embarrassed 12 disappointed, disconcerted

chain

3 row 4 bind, bond, gyve 5 group, train, trust 6 cartel, catena, fetter, hobble, series, string, tether 7 combine, manacle, shackle 8 handcuff, sequence 9 syndicate 10 succession 11 concatenate, progression 12 conglomerate 13 concatenation
adjunct: 8 sprocket
collar: 6 torque
gang: 6 coffle
ornamental: 10 chatelaine
sound: 5 clank

chain ___

3 saw 4 gang, mail 5 store 6 letter 8 reaction

Chained Lady

9 Andromeda

chair

4 seat 5 stool 6 rocker, settee, settle 7 preside
back: 5 splat
bishop's: 8 cathedra
designer: 5 Eames
portable: 5 sedan
reclining: 12 chaise longue, chaise lounge
royal: 6 throne
type: 4 club, easy 6 morris 7 rocking 8 captain's, electric 9 director's, reclining 10 Adirondack, ladder-back

chaise

4 sofa 5 chair, coach, divan 8 carriage

chalcedony

4 onyx, sard 5 agate, chert 6 jasper, quartz 9 carnelian, cornelian 10 bloodstone 11 chrysoprase

chalet

3 hut 4 camp 5 lodge 7 cottage

chalice

3 cup 5 grail 6 goblet

chalk out

5 draft 6 sketch 7 outline 8 block out, rough out 11 skeletonize 12 characterize

chalk up

3 get, win 4 gain 6 attain, credit, impute, obtain, secure 7 achieve, acquire, ascribe, procure, realize 9 attribute

challenge
3 try 4 dare, defy, face, stir, wake
5 brave, claim, demur, doubt, exact,
rouse, waken 6 arouse, awaken,
demand, impugn, invite, kindle
7 calling, dispute, protest, require,
solicit, venture 8 confront, defiance,
demurral, demurrer, question,
struggle 9 objection, postulate,
stimulate 10 difficulty, insistence
12 remonstrance

challenger
5 rival 8 aspirant, opponent 9 adversary, contender 10 antagonist,
competitor, contestant

chamber
4 cell, hall, room 5 haven, house
7 cubicle 9 apartment, enclosure
11 compartment
underground: 8 hypogeum

chambered seashell
8 nautilus

chamberlain
6 priest 7 officer, servant 9 attendant, treasurer

chameleon
6 lizard

chameleonic
6 fickle 7 protean 9 mercurial
10 changeable, inconstant

chamfer
5 bevel 6 groove

chamois
6 shammy 7 leather 8 antelope,
ruminant
habitat: 4 Alps
Old Testament: 6 aoudad

chamois-like animal
4 goat, ibex

champ
3 gum 4 bite, chew, mash 5 gnash,
munch 7 trample 8 macerate,
ruminate 9 masticate

champagne
4 wine 6 bubbly
center: 5 Reims 6 Rheims

Champagne
capital: 6 Troyes

champaign
5 field, plain 7 expanse, terrain
11 battlefield

champignon
6 fungus 8 mushroom

champion
4 back, hero 5 first, prime 6 uphold,
victor, winner 7 capital, contend,
leading, paladin, premier, support,
titlist 8 advocate, defender, exponent, fight for, foremost, medalist,
unbeaten 9 excellent, nonpareil,
number one, principal, proponent,
protector, supporter 11 illustrious,
outstanding, titleholder, white knight

championship
5 crown, title 6 laurel, trophy 7 contest, defense, laurels, pennant 8 advocacy 10 blue ribbon

chance
3 hap, hit, lot, odd 4 fate, luck, meet,
odds, risk, shot 5 break, fluke, light,
wager 6 befall, casual, gamble,
happen, hazard 7 fortune, offhand,
stumble, venture 8 accident, fortuity,
occasion, prospect 9 advantage,
transpire 10 accidental, fortuitous,
incidental, likelihood 11 contingency,
opportunity, possibility, probability
even: 6 toss-up

chancellor
5 judge 8 minister 9 secretary
German: 4 Kohl (Helmut) 6 Brandt
(Willy), Erhard (Ludwig), Hitler (Adolf)
7 Schmidt (Helmut) 8 Adenauer
(Konrad), Bismarck (Otto von)
9 Schroeder (Gerhard)

chancy
4 iffy 5 dicey, fluky, hairy, risky
6 touchy, tricky 8 perilous, ticklish
9 dangerous, haphazard, hazardous,
uncertain 10 capricious, precarious
11 speculative, treacherous 12 incalculable 13 unpredictable

Chandler, Raymond
character: 7 Marlowe (Philip)
novel: 8 Big Sleep (The) 11 Long
Good-Bye (The) 13 Murder My
Sweet 16 Farewell My Lovely

screenplay: 10 Blue Dahlia (The)
15 Double Indemnity

change

3 fix 4 swap, turn, vary 5 alter, coins,
money, morph, shift, trade 6 adjust,
evolve, modify, mutate, reform,
remake, revamp, revert, revise,
switch 7 commute, convert, novelty,
replace, reverse 8 exchange, mutation, revision, transfer 9 alternate,
deviation, diversify, fluctuate, refashion, transform, transmute, transpose,
variation 10 alteration, conversion,
divergence, innovation, substitute
11 interchange, permutation, transfigure, vicissitude 12 metamorphose,
modification, transmogrify 13 metamorphosis, transmutation
sudden: 8 peripety 10 peripeteia

changeable

5 fluid 6 fickle, labile, pliant, shifty
7 flighty, mutable, plastic, protean,
unfixed, varying 8 restless, shifting,
slippery, ticklish, unstable, unsteady,
variable, volatile 9 adaptable, alterable, impulsive, mercurial, uncertain,
unsettled, whimsical 10 capricious,
inconstant 11 chameleonic, fluctuating, vacillating 13 kaleidoscopic,
temperamental, unpredictable

change decor

4 redo 10 redecorate

changeless

5 fixed 6 steady 7 abiding, regular,
uniform 8 constant, enduring, resolute 9 immutable, perpetual, steadfast, unvarying 10 invariable

change off

6 rotate 9 alternate

change of heart

8 reversal

change of life

9 menopause 11 climacteric

change of pace

5 pitch, shift 9 slow pitch

changeover

5 shift 10 alteration, conversion,
transition

channel

3 way 4 band, duct, pass, path, pipe
5 agent, canal, carry 6 agency,
convey, course, funnel, groove,
gutter, medium, siphon, strait, trough,
tunnel 7 conduct, conduit, passage,
vehicle 8 aqueduct, pipeline, trans-
mit 10 instrument 11 watercourse
Africa-Madagascar:
10 Mozambique
Atlantic-Nantucket Sound: 8 Mus-
keget
Atlantic-North Sea: 7 English
Ellesmere-Greenland: 7 Robeson
Ganges: 5 Hugli 7 Hooghly
Hawaii: 5 Kaiwi, Kauai
Japan: 5 Bungo
Northwest Territories: 9 M'Clintock
Pakistan: 4 Nara
Scotland: 5 Minch
Tierra del Fuego: 6 Beagle
Tigris-Euphrates: 11 Shatt al Arab
Virginia: 12 Hampton Roads
West Indies: 9 Old Bahama

channel bass

4 drum 7 red drum, redfish

Channel Islands

capital: 8 St. Helier 11 St. Peter
Port
dependency of: 7 Britain
island: 4 Sark 6 Jersey 8 Alderney,
Guernsey

chanson

4 song

"Chanson ____"

6 Triste

chanson de ____

5 geste

chant

4 sing, tune 5 drone 6 intone
8 vocalize 10 cantillate
Gregorian: 9 plainsong 12 cantus
firmus
Jewish: 6 Hallel

chanteuse

6 singer 7 artiste 10 cantatrice

chanticleer

4 cock 7 rooster

chaos
6 bedlam, muddle **7** anarchy, clutter, entropy, turmoil **8** disarray, disorder **9** confusion **11** lawlessness

Chaos
daughter: 3 Nox, Nyx **4** Gaea
son: 6 Erebus

chaotic
7 jumbled, lawless **8** anarchic, confused, formless **9** amorphous, haphazard, scrambled **10** disordered, disorderly, topsy-turvy, tumultuous **11** harum-scarum, unorganized **12** disorganized **13** helter-skelter, unpredictable

chap
3 guy **4** gent **5** bloke **6** fellow

chaparral
5 scrub **7** thicket

chaparral cock
10 roadrunner

chapeau
3 hat **6** topper

chapel
6 bethel, church, shrine **7** chantry **9** sanctuary

chaperone
5 guide **6** attend, duenna, escort, matron **7** oversee **9** accompany, companion, supervise **11** superintend

chapfallen
see **crestfallen**

chaplain
5 padre **6** pastor **8** minister, sky pilot

chaplet
5 crown **6** anadem, laurel, rosary, wreath **7** coronal, coronet, garland

chapter
4 unit **5** phase, stage **6** branch, period **7** episode, section **8** division **9** affiliate

char
4 burn **9** carbonize

character
3 ilk **4** bent, case, cast, kind, mark, mind, name, rank, role, sign, sort, type **5** state, trait **6** cipher, device, letter, makeup, nature, oddity, repute, spirit, status, stripe, symbol, temper, virtue **7** feature, oddball, persona, quality, station, variety **8** capacity, eminence, identity, position, standing **9** attribute, eccentric, rectitude, situation **10** reputation, uniqueness **11** description, disposition, personality, temperament **13** individuality
chief: 4 hero **11** protagonist
defect: 8 hamartia

character assassination
5 libel **7** calumny, scandal, slander **10** backbiting, defamation **12** backstabbing

characteristic
4 mark, sign **5** badge, point, token, trait **6** aspect, innate, normal, proper **7** feature, natural, quality, special, typical **8** especial, peculiar, property, specific, tendency **9** attribute, birthmark, component, mannerism, trademark **10** diagnostic, emblematic, individual, particular **11** distinction, distinctive, peculiarity, singularity **12** idiosyncrasy **13** idiosyncratic

characterize
4 mark **5** draft **6** define, sketch, typify **7** outline, portray **8** describe, identify **10** constitute, pigeonhole **11** distinguish, individuate, personalize **12** discriminate **13** differentiate, individualize

characterless
4 flat **5** mousy **7** humdrum, insipid, vacuous **8** mediocre **9** colorless **10** namby-pamby, wishy-washy **11** nondescript

charade
4 sham **5** farce, put-on **6** parody **8** disguise, pretense, travesty **9** deception **11** make-believe

chare
see **chore**

charge
3 ask, bid, fee, lay, tab, tax **4** bill,

care, cost, duty, fill, heap, kick, load, onus, race, rate, rush, task, tell, toll, warn **5** choke, debit, order, place, price, refer, trust **6** accuse, assign, attack, burden, credit, direct, enjoin, exhort, impugn, impute, indict, saddle, thrill **7** arraign, ascribe, bidding, command, conduct, entrust, expense, impeach, mandate, request, solicit **8** accredit, handling, instruct, price tag, reproach, stampede **9** attribute, committal, electrify, inculpate **10** accusation, allegation, commitment, injunction, management, obligation **11** incriminate, instruction, requirement, supervision

chargeable
6 liable **7** subject **11** accountable, responsible

chargeless
4 free **6** gratis **8** costless **10** gratuitous **13** complimentary

charger
5 horse, mount, steed **6** salver **7** courser, platter **8** trencher, warhorse

chariness
7 caution **8** prudence **9** integrity **10** discretion

chariot
8 carriage
four-horse: 8 quadriga

charioteer
6 Auriga, driver

charisma
5 charm **6** allure, appeal, duende **7** glamour **9** magnetism **10** attraction **11** fascination

charitable
6 benign, giving, humane, kindly **7** clement, lenient, liberal **8** generous, merciful, obliging, tolerant **9** forgiving, indulgent **10** altruistic, beneficent, benevolent, forbearing, thoughtful **11** considerate, kindhearted, sympathetic **12** eleemosynary, humanitarian **13** philanthropic

charity
4 alms, love **5** grace, mercy **6** lenity, relief **7** caritas **8** altruism, clemency, donation, goodwill, leniency, offering **10** generosity, humaneness, kindliness **11** benefaction, beneficence, benevolence **12** contribution

charivari
5 babel, melee **6** jangle, jumble, medley, racket, ruckus, uproar **7** farrago **8** serenade, shivaree **9** cacophony, confusion **10** hodgepodge **11** celebration

charlatan
4 sham **5** bluff, faker, fraud, quack **6** con man **8** imposter, impostor, swindler **10** mountebank **11** quacksalver **13** confidence man

Charlemagne
brother: 8 Carloman
father: 5 Pepin
knight: 6 Oliver, Roland **7** Olivier, paladin **8** douzeper
nephew: 6 Roland **7** Orlando
sword: 8 Joyeuse
traitor: 4 Gano **7** Ganelon

Charles's Wain
9 Big Dipper, Ursa Major

charleston
5 dance

Charley's Aunt author
6 Thomas (Brandon)

Charlie and the Chocolate Factory author
4 Dahl (Roald)

Charlie Brown creator
6 Schulz (Charles)

Charlie McCarthy
5 dummy **6** stooge
friend: 5 Snerd (Mortimer)
voice: 6 Bergen (Edgar)

charm
3 hex **4** juju, lure, mojo, rune, take, wile **5** grace, quark, spell **6** allure, amulet, appeal, enamor, fetish, mascot, seduce, voodoo **7** attract, beguile, bewitch, enchant, glamour

8 enthrall, entrance, talisman, witchery 9 captivate, enrapture, ensorcell, fascinate, hypnotize, magnetism, mesmerize 10 allurement, attraction, phylactery, witchcraft 11 fascination, incantation 13 agreeableness

charmed

5 lucky 7 blessed 8 enamored 9 bewitched, enchanted, entranced, fortunate 10 captivated, fascinated, infatuated

charmer

4 roué 5 magus 6 wizard 7 seducer, warlock 8 conjurer, lothario, magician, sorcerer 9 enchanter 11 spellbinder

charming

7 winsome 8 adorable, alluring, inviting, magnetic 9 appealing, glamorous, seductive 10 attractive, delightful, enchanting, entrancing 11 captivating

Charon

7 boatman 8 ferryman
father: 6 Erebus
mother: 3 Nox
river: 4 Styx

Charpentier opera

6 Louise

charpoy

3 bed, cot

chart

3 map 4 plan, plat, plot 5 graph, table 6 design, lay out, map out, sketch 7 arrange, diagram, outline, project 9 blueprint 10 tabulation

charter

3 let 4 deed, hire, rent 5 grant, lease 10 conveyance 12 constitution

Chartreuse

7 liqueur

chary

4 wary 5 cagey, canny 6 frugal, stingy 7 careful, guarded, miserly, prudent, sparing, thrifty 8 cautious, discreet, gingerly, hesitant 9 provident, reluctant 10 economical,

restrained, suspicious, unwasteful 11 calculating, circumspect, constrained, disinclined

Charybdis

9 whirlpool
rock associated with: 6 Scylla

chase

3 run 4 bolt, dash, game, hunt, prey, race, rush, tear 5 chivy, drive, eject, evict, hound, shoot, speed, trail 6 career, charge, course, follow, hasten, pursue, quarry 7 boot out, hunting, kick out, pursuit 8 run after, throw out

chase away

4 rout, shoo

chaser

4 wolf 6 masher 7 Don Juan 8 Casanova 9 ladies' man, womanizer 10 lady-killer 11 philanderer

chasm

3 gap 4 gulf, rift 5 abyss, cleft, clove, flume, gorge, gulch, split 6 ravine 8 crevasse

chasmal

6 gaping 7 echoing, yawning 9 cavernous

chassepot

5 rifle

chaste

4 pure 5 clean, moral 6 decent, modest, proper, seemly, vestal, virgin 7 austere, prudish 8 celibate, decorous, innocent, maidenly, platonic, spotless, virginal, virtuous 9 abstinent, continent, stainless, undefiled, unsullied 10 immaculate 11 unblemished

chasten

5 abase, scold 6 humble, punish, rebuke, refine, subdue 7 correct, upbraid 8 chastise 9 castigate, humiliate, reprimand 10 discipline

chastise

4 beat, flog, whip 5 scold 6 punish, rebuke, thrash 7 belabor, censure, chasten, correct, reprove, scourge, upbraid 9 castigate 10 discipline

chastisement
3 rod 7 reproof 8 punition 10 correction, discipline, punishment
11 castigation

chastity
6 purity, virtue 7 modesty 8 celibacy
9 innocence, integrity, virginity
10 abstention, continence, maidenhood

chasuble
8 vestment

chat
3 gab, jaw, rap, yak, yap 4 blab,
gush, talk 5 prate, visit 6 babble,
confab, gossip, jabber, natter, parley,
patter, yak-yak 7 chatter, palaver,
prattle, twaddle 8 causerie, colloquy,
converse, dialogue, schmooze
9 tête-à-tête, yakety-yak 11 confabulate 12 conversation, tittle-tattle
13 confabulation

château
5 manor, villa 6 castle, estate
7 mansion 8 fortress 12 country
house

chateaubriand
5 steak 10 tenderloin

Chateaubriand novel
4 René 5 Atala

chatelain
6 warden 8 governor 9 castellan

chatelaine
4 hook, wife 5 clasp 8 mistress

chattel
4 serf 5 slave 7 bondman 8 bondsman, property

chatter
3 gab, jaw, yak 4 blab, bull 5 prate
6 babble, gabble, gibber, gossip,
jabber, natter, patter, yak-yak, yammer 7 blabber, blather, palaver,
prattle, vibrate 9 small talk, yaketyyak 12 tittle-tattle

chatterbox
6 gabber, gossip, magpie, prater
7 blabber 8 jabberer, prattler
12 blabbermouth

chatty
5 gabby 7 voluble 9 garrulous,
talkative 10 loquacious

Chaucer pilgrim
4 Cook, Monk 5 Clerk, Friar, Reeve
6 Miller, Parson, Squire 8 Franklin,
Manciple, Merchant, Summoner
10 Nun's Priest, Wife of Bath

chauffeur
5 drive 6 driver 9 transport

chauvinism
6 sexism 8 jingoism 10 partiality,
patriotism 11 nationalism

cheap
4 mean, poor 5 junky, tight 6 cheesy,
common, cruddy, flashy, measly, paltry, shabby, shoddy, sleazy, stingy,
tawdry, trashy 7 chintzy, cut-rate,
low-cost, reduced, thrifty 8 inferior,
trifling, uncostly 9 brummagem, lowpriced 10 economical 11 inexpensive 12 contemptible, meretricious

cheapen
5 decry, lower 6 debase, reduce
7 devalue 8 mark down 9 devaluate, downgrade 10 depreciate,
undervalue

cheapjack
5 junky 6 hawker, cheesy, cruddy,
shoddy, sleazy, tawdry, trashy
7 haggler, higgler, packman, peddler 8 huckster, inferior, rubbishy
9 worthless 13 opportunistic

cheapskate
5 miser 7 niggard, scrooge 8 tightwad 9 skinflint 11 cheeseparer

cheat
3 con, gyp 4 bilk, burn, dupe, fool,
gull, hoax, milk, ream, scam 5 bunco,
cozen, crook, fraud, fudge, gouge,
hocus, put-on, screw, shaft, short,
slick 6 chisel, chouse, con man,
deceit, delude, diddle, extort, fleece,
humbug, rip-off, sucker, take in
7 beguile, chicane, deceive, defraud,
diddler, mislead, sharper, shyster,
swindle, two-time 8 flimflam, hoodwink, swindler, trickery 9 bamboozle,

chicanery, deception, defrauder, imposture, overreach, trickster **11** double-cross **12** double-dealer **13** confidence man
on a check: 4 kite

check

3 tab, try **4** bill, curb, halt, jibe, stay, stop, test, tick **5** block, brake, draft, prove, score, stall **6** accord, arrest, baffle, bridle, damage, desist, hold in, square, thwart, verify **7** compare, conform, control, examine, inhibit, repress, setback **8** dovetail, hold back, hold down, preclude, restrain, reversal, suppress **9** constrain, criterion, interrupt, restraint **10** correspond, inspection **11** examination **13** investigation

checkered

5 plaid **6** motley **7** mutable, spotted **9** patchwork, patterned **10** variegated **11** diversified

checklist

7 catalog **9** catalogue, inventory **11** enumeration

checkmate

4 beat **6** corner, defeat **7** outplay **8** vanquish **9** finish off

check out

3 die, eye **5** leave **6** assess **7** examine, inspect **8** appraise, evaluate, look over

check over

3 con, vet **4** scan **5** audit, study **6** review, survey **7** analyze, canvass, examine, inspect **10** scrutinize

checkup

4 exam **8** physical **10** inspection **11** examination

cheek

4 gall **5** brass, nerve **8** audacity, chutzpah, temerity **9** brashness, impudence, insolence **10** confidence, effrontery **11** presumption **12** impertinence

cheekbone

5 malar

cheeky

4 bold, flip, pert, wise **5** brash, cocky, fresh, nervy, sassy, saucy, smart **6** brazen **7** forward **8** flippant, impudent, insolent **11** impertinent, smart-alecky **12** presumptuous

cheep

4 peep **5** chirp, tweet **7** chirrup, chitter, twitter

cheer

3 rah **4** buoy, hail, root **5** bravo, huzza, nerve **6** buck up, gaiety, hoorah, hooray, hurrah, hurray, huzzah, solace, spirit **7** animate, applaud, comfort, console, enliven, gladden, hearten **8** embolden, inspirit **9** animation, encourage **10** strengthen
corrida: 3 olé

cheerful

3 gay **4** glad, rosy **5** jolly, merry, perky, sunny **6** blithe, bouncy, bright, chirpy, hearty, jaunty, jocund, lively **7** beamish, buoyant, radiant **8** animated, carefree, chirrupy **9** vivacious **12** lighthearted

cheerio

3 bye **4** ta-ta **5** adieu **6** bye-bye, good-by, so long **7** good-bye, toodles **8** farewell, toodle-oo

cheerless

4 dour, drab, grim **5** bleak **6** dismal, dreary, gloomy, somber, sombre **7** forlorn, joyless **8** desolate, dolorous, funereal, mournful **9** dejecting **10** depressing, melancholy, oppressive, tenebrific **11** dispiriting

cheers

5 salud, skoal **6** cincin, l'chaim, prosit **7** l'chayim, sláinte **8** applause, approval, chinchin **9** bottoms up **10** jubilation **11** acclamation, approbation

cheery

5 happy, jolly, merry, sunny **6** blithe, bouncy, chirpy, lively, upbeat **7** buoyant, chipper, festive, gleeful **8** animated, carefree, gladsome **9** convivial, sparkling **12** lighthearted

cheese

3 pot 4 blue, jack 5 brick, cream
6 farmer 7 cottage, process, ricotta
9 smearcase
American: 8 Longhorn
11 Liederkranz 12 Monterey Jack
Belgian: 9 Limburger
curdling agent: 6 rennet, rennin
Danish: 7 Havarti
dish: 6 fondue 7 rarebit, soufflé
Dutch: 4 Edam 5 Gouda 6 Leyden
English: 7 cheddar, Stilton 8 Cheshire 10 Lancashire
French: 4 Brie 7 fromage, Livarot
9 Camembert, Reblochon, Roquefort
10 Neufchâtel 11 Pont l'Évêque,
Port du Salut
German: 6 Tilsit 7 Munster 8 Muenster, Tilsiter
Greek: 4 feta
green: 7 sapsago
Italian: 6 Asiago, Romano 7 fontina, ricotta 8 Bel Paese, Parmesan, pecorino 9 provolone
10 Gorgonzola, mozzarella
lover: 9 turophile
main ingredient: 6 casein
Norwegian: 9 Jarlsberg
protein: 6 casein
Scottish: 6 Dunlop, Orkney 7 kebbock, kebbuck
Swiss: 6 Saanen 7 Gruyère,
sapsago 8 Vacherin 10 Emmentaler
11 Emmenthaler
uncured: 7 cottage
Welsh: 10 Caerphilly

cheesecloth

5 gauze

cheeselike

6 caseic 7 caseous

cheeseparer

5 miser 7 niggard, scrooge 8 tightwad 9 skinflint 10 cheapskate,
pinchpenny

cheeseparing

4 mean 5 chary, cheap, mingy, tight
6 frugal, shabby, stingy 7 chintzy,
miserly, thrifty 8 grudging, skimping
9 niggardly, penurious 11 closefisted, tightfisted 12 parsimonious
13 penny-pinching

cheesy

4 poor 5 cheap 6 common, shabby,
shoddy, sleazy, tawdry, trashy
7 caseous 8 rubbishy

Cheever, John

novel: 8 Falconer 14 Wapshot
Scandal (The) 16 Wapshot Chronicle
(The)
story: 7 Swimmer (The)

chef

4 cook

chef d'oeuvre

7 classic 9 showpiece 10 magnum
opus, masterwork 11 masterpiece,
tour de force

Chekhov, Anton

play: 6 Ivanov 7 Seagull (The)
10 Uncle Vanya 12 Three Sisters
13 Cherry Orchard (The)
story: 9 Black Monk (The)

chelonian

6 turtle 8 tortoise

chemical

agent: 8 catalyst
combining power: 7 valence
compound: 4 acid, base, diol, enol,
imid, oxim, salt, tepa, urea 5 amide,
amine, diene, ester, imide, imine,
indol, orcin, oxime, purin, pyran,
salol, tolan, triol 6 alkali, benzin,
benzol, diamin, emodin, guanin,
halide, hydrid, indole, inulin, ionone,
isatin, isolog, isomer, ketone, lactam,
maltol, metepa, natron, nitril, pterin,
purine, pyrone, pyrrol, quinol, retene,
silane, skatol, tannin, tetryl, thiram,
thymol, tolane, triene, trimer, uracil,
ureide, yttria, zeatin 7 barilla, benzene, benzole, cumarin, diamide,
diamine, diazine, diazole, diester,
flavone, guanine, heptose, hydride,
indamin, indican, indoxyl, isatine,
levulin, metamer, monomer, naphtol,
nitrile, orcinol, oxazine, phytane,
picolin, polyene, polymer, pyrrole,
quinoid, quinone, salicin, skatole,
steroid, taurine, terpene, thiazin,
thiazol, thymine, tolidin, triazin,
urethan, uridine, vitamer, xylidin

8 cephalin, cyanamid, disulfid, elaterin, fluorene, furfural, guaiacol, hematein, hexamine, indamine, isologue, kephalin, lichenin, limonene, melamine, naloxone, naphthol, palmitin, phenazin, phosphid, phthalin, picoline, piperine, pristane, quinolin, resorcin, salicine, santonin, siloxane, sodamide, sorbitol, spermine, squalene, stilbene, strontia, tautomer, thiazine, thiazole, thiophen, thiotepa, thiourea, tolidine, triazine, triazole, triptane, tyramine, urethane, vanillin, warfarin, xanthene, xanthine, xanthone, xylidine, ytterbia, zaratite, zirconia
(see at **element**)
quantity: 4 mole
radical: 4 acyl, amyl, cyan **5** allyl, butyl, ethyl, tolyl **6** acetyl, formyl, methyl, oxalic, phenyl, propyl, toluyl **7** benzoyl
reaction: 5 redox
salt: 5 niter, nitre, urate, ziram **6** haloid, humate, malate, oleate, phytin **7** ferrate, formate, gallate, maleate, pectate, persalt, picrate, tannate, toluate, zincate **8** fumarate, pyruvate, racemate, selenate, silicate, stearate, tartrate, thionate, titanate, valerate, vanadate, xanthate
suffix: 3 ane, ase, ate, ein, ene, ide, ile, ine, ite, ium, oic, oin, one, ose, ous, yne **4** eine, idin, itol, oate, olic, onic **5** idine, onium, oside, ylene
warfare agent: 7 tear gas **8** vesicant **10** mustard gas

chemin de fer
5 train **7** railway **8** railroad

chemise
4 slip

chemist
7 analyst **8** druggist **10** apothecary, pharmacist
American: 4 Urey (Harold)
6 Remsen (Ira), Sumner (James)
7 Onsager (Lars), Pauling (Linus), Seaborg (Glenn) **8** Hoffmann (Roald), Langmuir (Irving), Mulliken (Robert), Richards (Theodore), Woodward (Robert)

Austrian: 4 Kuhn (Richard) **5** Pregl (Fritz)
British: 4 Abel (Frederick), Davy (Humphry), Todd (Alexander)
5 Boyle (Robert), Soddy (Frederick)
6 Dalton (John), Ramsay (William)
7 Faraday (Michael) **8** Smithson (James) **9** Priestley (Joseph), Wollaston (William) **10** Williamson (Alexander)
Dutch: 8 van't Hoff (Jacobus)
French: 5 Curie (Irene, Marie, Pierre) **7** Moissan (Henri), Pasteur (Louis) **8** Sabatier (Paul) **9** Gay-Lussac (Joseph), Lavoisier (Antoine), Berthelot (Marcellin)
German: 5 Haber (Fritz) **6** Bunsen (Robert), Liebig (Justus von), Nernst (Walther), Wittig (Georg), Wohler (Friedrich) **7** Fischer (Emil, Ernst, Hans), Hofmann (August), Ostwald (Friedrich), Wallach (Otto), Wieland (Heinrich), Windaus (Adolf), Ziegler (Karl) **9** Zsigmondy (Richard) **10** Erlenmeyer (Richard), Staudinger (Hermann) **11** Willstatter (Richard)
Italian: 5 Natta (Giulio) **8** Avogadro (Amedeo)
Russian: 8 Semyonov (Nikolay), Zelinsky (Nikolay) **10** Mendeleyev (Dmitry)
Swedish: 8 Svedberg (The, Theodor) **9** Berzelius (J. J.)
Swiss: 6 Karrer (Paul), Werner (Alfred)
(see also under **Nobel Prize winner**)

chemist's vessel
4 vial **5** flask, phial **6** ampule, beaker, mortar, retort **7** ampoule **8** crucible, test tube

chemoreceptor
8 taste bud

cheongsam
5 dress

Cheops
5 Khufu

cherish
4 keep, save **5** adore, guard, honor, nurse, prize, value **6** admire, cosset, defend, dote on, esteem, foster,

harbor, relish, revere, shield **7** apprize, care for, nourish, nurture, shelter, worship **8** conserve, hold dear, preserve, treasure, venerate **9** cultivate, delight in, entertain, reverence, safeguard **10** appreciate

Cherokee
chief: 4 Ross (John)
historian: 7 Sequoia, Sequoya **8** Sequoyah

cherry
dark: 4 bing
family: 4 rose **8** Rosaceae
genus: 6 Prunus
hybrid: 4 Duke
sour: 7 morello
sweet: 4 bing **7** mazzard, oxheart
wild: 7 mazzard **10** maraschino

cherry bomb
11 firecracker

Cherry Orchard author
7 Chekhov (Anton)

cherrystone
4 clam **6** quahog

Chersonese
9 peninsula

cherub
4 babe, baby **5** angel, child, cupid, putto **6** infant **7** bambino **8** amoretto, innocent

cherubic
4 cute, rosy **6** chubby **7** angelic **8** adorable, innocent

chess
champion: 3 Tal (Mikhail) **4** Euwe (Max) **6** Karpov (Anatoly), Lasker (Emanuel) **7** Fischer (Bobby), Kramnik (Vladimir), Smyslov (Vassily), Spassky (Boris) **8** Alekhine (Alexander), Kasparov (Garry), Steinitz (Wilhelm) **9** Botvinnik (Mikhail), Petrosian (Tigran) **10** Capablanca (José)
draw game: 9 stalemate
goal: 4 mate **9** checkmate
move: 6 castle, gambit
opening: 6 gambit

piece: 4 king, pawn, rook **5** queen **6** bishop, knight
risk: 6 gambit
term: 5 check **7** capture, endgame

chest
3 box **4** kist **5** bosom, torso, trunk **6** breast, bureau, coffer, thorax **7** cabinet **8** cupboard, treasury **9** exchequer

chesterfield
4 sofa **5** divan **8** overcoat **9** davenport

chestnut
4 tree **5** color, horse **6** cliché, marron **10** chinquapin
extract: 6 tannin
water: 4 ling

cheval glass
6 mirror

chevalier
5 noble **6** knight **8** horseman **9** caballero, gentleman

chevet
4 apse

chevron
6 stripe

chew
3 eat, gum **4** bite, gnaw **5** champ, chomp, munch **6** crunch, devour, nibble **7** consume **8** ruminate **9** masticate

chewing gum
6 chicle

chew out
3 jaw **5** scold **6** rebuke, revile **7** bawl out, reprove, tell off, upbraid **8** lambaste, reproach **9** castigate, criticize, reprimand **10** tongue-lash, vituperate

Chiang _____
7 Kai-shek

chic
4 mode, rage, tony **5** smart, style, swank, swish, vogue **6** modish, trendy, with-it **7** dashing, elegant, fashion, stylish **10** dernier cri **11** fashionable

chicane
  4 dupe, fool, gull, hoax, ploy, ruse, wile **5** cavil, cheat, feint, fraud, trick **6** gambit **8** artifice, flimflam, hoodwink, trickery **9** bamboozle, deception, duplicity, stratagem, victimize **10** dishonesty, hanky-panky **13** double-dealing

chicanery
  4 plot, ruse **5** fraud, trick **6** gambit **8** intrigue, trickery **9** deception, duplicity **10** subterfuge **11** machination, skulduggery

chichi
  4 arty **5** gaudy, showy, swank **6** dressy, frilly, la-di-da **7** splashy **8** affected, précieux, precious **10** flamboyant, preciosity **11** affectation, fashionable, overrefined, pretentious **12** ostentatious **13** ornamentation

chick
  3 kid, tot **4** girl **5** child **6** moppet, nipper, pullet **7** toddler **8** juvenile, young one **9** youngster

chickadee
  8 titmouse
  family: 7 Paridae

chicken
  4 fowl, funk **5** sissy, timid **6** coward, craven **7** dastard, gutless **8** cowardly, poltroon **11** lily-livered, yellowbelly **13** pusillanimous
  breed: 4 Java **6** Cochin **7** Cornish, Leghorn **9** Dominique, Orpington, Wyandotte **11** Jersey Giant, Rock Cornish
  castrated: 5 capon
  cooking: 5 fryer **7** broiler, roaster
  disease: 8 pullorum **11** coccidiosis
  female: 3 hen **6** pullet
  genus: 6 Gallus
  male: 4 cock **7** rooster **8** cockerel
  pen: 4 coop
  small: 6 bantam
  sound: 6 cackle

chicken feed
  7 peanuts **8** pittance **11** chump change

chicken pox
  9 varicella

chickpea
  4 gram **8** garbanzo

chickweed
  4 pink **7** potherb

chicle
  3 gum **10** chewing gum

chicory
  6 endive **7** witloof **9** radicchio

chide
  3 kid **5** scold **6** berate, rebuke **7** chew out, lecture, reprove, upbraid **8** admonish, call down, reproach **9** castigate, reprimand

chiding
  6 rebuke **7** reproof **8** reproach **9** reprimand **10** admonition **12** admonishment

chief
  3 key **4** arch, boss, duce, head, lion, main, star **5** first, major, prime **6** führer, honcho, leader, master, primal, ruling, sachem **7** fuehrer, headman, highest, leading, premier, primary **8** cardinal, champion, dictator, dominant, eminence, foremost **9** number-one, principal, prominent **10** preeminent **11** outstanding, predominant
  commander: 4 CINC
  prefix: 4 arch
  Spanish: 4 jefe

Chief Justice
  3 Jay (John) **4** Taft (William Howard) **5** Chase (Salmon), Stone (Harlan Fiske), Taney (Roger), Waite (Morrison), White (Edward) **6** Burger (Warren), Fuller (Melville), Hughes (Charles Evans), Vinson (Fred), Warren (Earl) **8** Marshall (John), Rutledge (John) **9** Ellsworth (Oliver), Rehnquist (William)

chiefly
  6 mainly, mostly **7** largely, notably, overall **9** generally, primarily **10** especially **11** principally **12** preeminently **13** predominantly

chiffchaff
4 bird 7 warbler

chiffonier
5 chest 6 bureau 7 armoire, dresser

chigger
4 mite 6 chigoe, red bug

chignon
3 bun 4 knot

chilblain
4 sore 8 swelling 12 inflammation

child
3 kid 4 brat 5 minor, youth 6 cherub, infant, moppet, nipper, shaver, urchin 7 bambino, toddler 8 juvenile, small fry 9 youngling, youngster
combining form: 3 ped 4 paed, pedo 5 paedo
gifted: 7 prodigy
homeless: 4 waif
parentless: 6 orphan
Scottish: 5 bairn
spoiled: 4 brat
young: 3 tot 4 baby, tike, tyke 6 infant, kiddie 8 bantling, weanling

childish
5 naive 7 puerile 8 arrested, immature 9 infantile

childless
6 barren 7 sterile

childlike
5 naive 6 docile, filial 7 natural, puerile 8 innocent, trustful, trusting 9 ingenuous

children
4 kids, seed 5 brood, heirs, issue 6 scions 7 progeny 9 offspring, posterity 11 descendants

child's play
4 snap 5 cinch, setup 6 breeze, picnic 8 cakewalk, duck soup, kid stuff, pushover 11 piece of cake

Chile
capital: 8 Santiago
city: 6 Temuco 10 Concepción, Talcahuano, Valparaíso, Viña del Mar 11 Antofagasta
conqueror: 7 Almagro (Diego de) 8 Valdivia (Pedro de)
desert: 7 Atacama
island: 6 Easter 13 Juan Fernández
lake: 10 Llanquihue
language: 7 Spanish
leader: 7 Allende (Salvador) 8 Pinochet (Augusto)
monetary unit: 4 peso
mountain range: 5 Andes
neighbor: 4 Peru 7 Bolivia 9 Argentina
passage: 5 Drake
river: 6 Bío-Bío
strait: 8 Magellan

Chileab
father: 5 David
mother: 7 Abigail

chili con ____
5 carne

Chilion
father: 9 Elimelech
mother: 5 Naomi

chill
3 icy, raw 4 ague, cold, cool, hang 5 gelid, nippy 6 arctic, formal, freeze, frigid, frosty, wintry 7 distant, glacial, hostile 8 dispirit, freezing 10 demoralize, discourage, dishearten 11 emotionless, refrigerate

chiller
7 shocker 8 thriller

chilly
3 raw 4 cold 5 algid, brisk, crisp, nippy 6 frigid 7 bracing, coldish, hostile 10 unfriendly

chilopod
9 centipede

chime
3 din 4 bell, bong, dong, peal, ring, toll, tune 5 agree, clang, knell, sound 6 accord, strike 7 concord, harmony 8 carillon 9 agreement, harmonize 10 consonance, correspond

chime in
3 say 4 tell 5 state, utter 6 inject 7 break in, declare 9 interrupt

chimera

5 dream, fancy 7 fantasy, figment, monster, specter, spectre 8 illusion, phantasy 9 nightmare, pipe dream

Chimera

father: 6 Typhon
mother: 7 Echidna
slayer: 11 Bellerophon

chimerical

6 absurd, unreal 7 fictive, utopian 8 delusive, delusory, fabulous, fanciful, illusory, mythical, spurious 9 ambitious, beguiling, deceptive, fantastic, fictional, imaginary, visionary 10 far-fetched, fictitious, improbable, outlandish 11 extravagant, unrealistic 12 preposterous, supposititious

chiming

8 harmonic 9 consonant 10 harmonious

chimney

3 lum 4 flue, tube, vent 5 stack 10 smokestack
corner: 8 fireside 9 inglenook
output: 4 soot 5 fumes, smoke

chimpanzee

3 ape 7 primate 10 anthropoid
kin: 6 bonobo, gibbon 7 gorilla 9 orangutan

chin

3 gab, jaw, rap, yak 4 blab, chat, talk 8 converse

china

6 dishes 7 ceramic 8 crockery 9 porcelain, tableware 11 earthenware
maker: 3 Bow 5 Hizen, Imari, Spode 6 Doccia, Sèvres 7 Bristol, Chelsea, Dresden, Limoges, Meissen 8 Caughley, Haviland, Wedgwood

China

bay: 8 Hangzhou
capital: 7 Beijing
city: 4 Sian, Xi'an 5 Wuhan 6 Canton, Harbin, Mukden 7 Nanjing, Nanking, Tianjin 8 Shanghai, Shenyang, Tientsin 9 Chongqing, Guangzhou
desert: 4 Gobi 10 Taklimakan
dynasty: 3 Han, Sui 4 Ch'in, Chou, Ming, Sung, Tang, Yüan 5 Ch'ing, Shang 6 Manchu
ethnic group: 3 Han
gulf: 5 Bo Hai
heritage site: 9 Great Wall
island: 6 Hainan 8 Hong Kong
lake: 5 Tai Hu 8 Hongze Hu, Poyang Hu 10 Dongting Hu
language: 8 Han 8 Mandarin
leader: 9 Mao Zedong, Sun Yat-sen 10 Kublai Khan, Mao Tse-tung 12 Deng Xiaoping 13 Chiang Kai-shek, Teng Hsiao-p'ing
monetary unit: 4 yuan
monetary unit, former: 4 tael
mountain, range: 6 Kunlun 8 Himalaya 9 Altai Shan, Altay Shan, Himalayan 10 Gongga Shan
old name: 6 Cathay
peninsula: 7 Leizhou 8 Liaodong, Shandong
province: 5 Anhui, Gansu, Hevei, Henan, Hubei, Hunan, Jilin 6 Fujian, Shanxi, Yunnan 7 Guizhou, Jiangsu, Jiangxi, Qinghai, Shaanxi, Sichuan 8 Liaoning, Shandong, Szechuan, Szechwan, Zhejiang 9 Guangdong 12 Heilongjiang
region: 5 Tibet 6 Xizang 10 Nei Monggol 12 Ningxia Huizu 13 Inner Mongolia, Xinjiang Uygur
river: 4 Amur 5 Chang, Huang, Tarim 6 Mekong, Yellow, Zangbo 7 Salween, Yangtze

china clay

6 kaolin

chinchilla

3 fur 6 rodent

chine

5 crest, ridge, spine 7 hogback 8 backbone

Chinese

aromatic root: 7 ginseng
bamboo: 7 whangee
boat: 4 junk 6 sampan
bow: 6 kowtow
cabbage: 7 bok choy, pak choi
card game: 6 fan-tan

cauterizing agent: 4 moxa
prefix: 4 Sino
conveyance: 7 pedicab **8** rickshaw
10 jinricksha, jinrikisha
date: 6 jujube
dialect: 4 Amoy **8** Mandarin
9 Cantonese, Pekingese
dictator: 9 Mao Zedong **10** Mao
Tse-tung **12** Deng Xiaoping **13** Teng
Hsiao-p'ing
dog: 4 chow, Peke **8** chow chow
9 Pekingese
dynasty: 3 Ch'i, Han, Qin, Sui,
Wei, Yin **4** Ch'en, Ch'in, Chou,
Hsia, Ming, Qing, Song, Sung, T'ang,
Tsin, Yuan **5** Ch'ing, Liang, Shang
6 Manchu, Mongol, Shu Han
fabric: 6 pongee, tussah **8** shantung
feminine principle: 3 yin
feudal state: 3 Wei
food: 6 dim sum, lo mein, mantou,
subgum, wonton **8** chop suey, chow
mein **9** fried rice **10** egg foo yong,
egg foo yung, Peking duck **11** egg
foo young
fruit: 6 lichee, litchi, lychee, loquat
7 kumquat **9** mandarin
gambling game: 6 fan-tan
gong: 6 tam-tam
gruel: 6 congee
herb: 7 ramie **7** ginseng
idol: 4 joss
laborer: 6 coolie
legendary emperor: 7 Huangdi,
Huang-ti
mandarin's residence: 5 yamen
masculine principle: 4 yang
money, silver: 5 sycee
musical instrument: 4 pipa
nurse: 4 amah
official: 8 mandarin
official seal: 4 chop
oil: 4 tung
ox: 4 zebu
porcelain: 4 Ming **7** celadon, Nankeen **8** mandarin
pottery: 4 Kuan, Ming **5** Chien
puzzle: 7 tangram
race: 9 Mongoloid
religion: 6 Taoism **8** Buddhism
12 Confucianism

sauce: 3 soy
secret society: 4 tong
sheep: 5 urial
silkworm: 6 tussah
tea: 5 bohea, hyson **6** congou,
oolong **8** souchong
temple: 6 pagoda
tree: 4 tung **6** ginkgo, loquat
7 kumquat
vine: 5 kudzu

chink
4 rift, slit **5** caulk, cleft, crack, split
6 cranny **7** crevice, fissure, opening
8 aperture

chinquapin
3 nut **8** chestnut

chintzy
4 loud **5** cheap, gaudy, showy, tacky
6 flashy, garish, stingy, tawdry, vulgar
9 tasteless **12** meretricious

chip
4 flaw, nick **5** flake, notch, shard,
slice, split, wafer, wedge **6** chisel,
defect, paring, sliver **7** counter

chip in
6 ante up, kick in **7** pitch in **10** contribute **11** come through

chipper
4 spry **5** alert, brisk, perky, zesty
6 bright, lively, nimble **8** animated,
spirited **9** sprightly, vivacious

chirk
4 buoy **5** cheer **7** animate, enliven,
hearten **8** energize, inspirit **9** encourage **10** strengthen

chirography
6 script **8** longhand **10** penmanship
11 calligraphy, handwriting

chiromancy
9 palmistry

Chiron
7 centaur
father: 6 Cronus
mother: 7 Philyra
pupil: 5 Jason **8** Achilles, Heracles,
Hercules **9** Asclepius **11** Aesculapius

chiropody
8 podiatry

chiropractic founder
6 Palmer (Daniel)

chirp
4 chip, peep, sing 5 cheep, trill, tweet 6 warble 7 chirrup, twitter

chirpy
3 gay 5 sunny 6 blithe, cheery, sparky 7 buoyant, sparkly 8 cheerful, sunbeamy 9 lightsome

chirrup
4 chip, peep, sing 5 cheep, tweet 6 warble 7 chipper, twitter

chisel
3 gyp, hew 4 beat, bilk, scam 5 carve, cheat, cozen, cut in, gouge, trick 6 butt in, diddle, fleece, horn in, sculpt 7 defraud, engrave, intrude, swindle

chit
3 IOU, kid 4 memo, note, slip 5 child 6 moppet 7 invoice, voucher 8 notation 9 youngster 10 memorandum

chitchat
3 gab 5 chaff 6 babble, banter, gossip 7 chatter, palaver, prattle 8 badinage 9 small talk 12 tittle-tattle

chitter
4 chip, peep, sing 5 cheep, chirp, tweet 6 warble 7 chatter, chirrup, twitter

chivalric
see **chivalrous**

chivalrous
5 lofty, manly, noble 7 courtly, gallant, valiant 8 generous, gracious, knightly 9 honorable 10 benevolent, courageous 11 considerate, gentlemanly, magnanimous

chivy, chivvy
4 bait, ride 5 annoy, tease 6 badger, heckle, hector 7 torment 8 bullyrag

Chloe
11 shepherdess
beloved: 7 Daphnis

chlordane
11 insecticide

Chloris
father: 7 Amphion
husband: 6 Neleus 8 Zephyrus
mother: 5 Niobe
son: 6 Nestor

chloroform
7 anodyne, solvent 10 anesthetic 11 anaesthetic

chockablock
4 full 6 jammed, loaded, packed 7 brimful, crammed, crowded, stuffed 9 jam-packed

chocolate
5 brown, cacao, cocoa

Chocolate Soldier composer
6 Straus (Oscar)

chocolate tree
5 cacao

choice
3 top 4 best, pick, rare, vote 5 cream, elite, prime, prize 6 chosen, dainty, option, rating, select 7 elegant, verdict 8 decision, delicate, druthers, election, judgment, selected, superior, volition 9 exquisite, selection 9 selection 10 preference 11 alternative 13 determination
even: 6 toss-up

choir
6 chorus 7 chorale
area: 4 loft 7 chancel, gallery
leader: 6 cantor 8 choragus 9 precentor
member: 9 chorister
section: 4 alto, bass 5 tenor 7 soprano
vestment: 4 gown, robe 5 cotta 8 surplice

choke
3 gag 4 clog, plug, stop 5 block, close 6 stifle 7 congest, occlude, silence, smother 8 obstruct, strangle, throttle 9 constrict, suffocate 10 asphyxiate

choking
8 quashing, stifling 10 repression,

smothering, squelching, strangling
11 suppression

choleric
5 angry, fiery, irate 6 fierce, heated
7 enraged 8 incensed, wrathful
9 irascible, splenetic 10 infuriated
11 hot-tempered 13 quick-tempered

cholla
6 cactus 7 opuntia

Chomolungma
7 Everest (Mt.)

chomp
4 bite, chew 5 munch 6 crunch
9 masticate

choose
3 opt 4 cull, mark, pick, take, want
5 adopt, elect, favor 6 decide, desire,
opt for, prefer, select 7 embrace,
pick out 8 decide on, handpick
9 single out

choosy
5 fussy, picky 7 finical, finicky
9 finicking, selective 10 fastidious,
particular, pernickety 11 persnickety

chop
3 cut, hew 4 dice, fell, hack, hash,
seal, veer 5 cut up, grade, mince
7 quality

chop-chop
4 fast 5 quick 6 presto, pronto
7 quickly, rapidly 8 promptly, speedily 9 posthaste 12 lickety-split

chophouse
10 restaurant

Chopin, Frédéric
birthplace: 6 Poland
instrument: 5 piano
lover: 4 Sand (George)
work: 7 mazurka 8 nocturne
9 polonaise

choppy
4 wavy 5 jerky, rough 6 ripply,
stormy, uneven 7 erratic 8 variable
9 turbulent, unsettled

choral section
5 altos 6 basses, tenors 8 sopranos

chord
5 triad 6 tetrad 7 harmony
sequence: 7 cadence 11 progression

chore
3 job 4 duty, task 5 stint, trial
6 devoir, effort 7 routine 10 assignment, obligation 11 tribulation

choreograph
6 devise, direct, map out 7 arrange,
compose 11 orchestrate

choreographer
American: 4 Feld (Elliot), Holm
(Hanya), Lang (Pearl) 5 Ailey
(Alvin), Fosse (Bob), Limón (José),
Shawn (Ted), Tharp (Twyla)
6 Duncan (Isadora), Dunham
(Katherine), Fokine (Michel), Graham
(Martha), Morris (Mark), Taylor
(Paul), Tetley (Glen) 7 de Mille
(Agnes), Jamison (Judith), Joffrey
(Robert), Martins (Peter), Massine
(Leonide), Robbins (Jerome),
St. Denis (Ruth), Tamiris (Helen),
Weidman (Charles) 8 Champion
(Gower, Marge), Humphrey (Doris),
Nikolais (Alwin), Villella (Edward)
10 Balanchine (George), Cunning-
ham (Merce)
Australian: 8 Helpmann (Robert)
Cuban: 6 Alonso (Alicia)
Danish: 5 Bruhn (Erik) 7 Martins
(Peter) 12 Bournonville (August)
English: 5 Dolin (Anton), Tudor
(Antony) 6 Ashton (Frederick),
Weaver (John) 7 Markova (Alicia),
Rambert (Marie) 8 de Valois
(Ninette), Helpmann (Robert)
9 MacMillan (Kenneth)
French: 5 Lifar (Serge) 6 Béjart
(Maurice), Perrot (Jules), Petipa
(Marius) 7 Camargo (Marie), Mas-
sine (Léonide), Noverre (Jean-
Georges)
German: 5 Jooss (Kurt)
Hungarian: 5 Laban (Rudolf)
Mexican: 5 Limón (José)
Russian: 5 Lifar (Serge) 6 Fokine
(Michel), Petipa (Marius) 8 Nijinska
(Bronislava), Nijinsky (Vaslav)

chorography
3 map 7 mapping 8 features
9 mapmaking

chortle
5 laugh 6 giggle, guffaw, hee-haw,
titter 7 chuckle, snicker

chorus
5 choir 7 refrain

chorus girl
7 chorine

chosen
4 pick 5 elect, elite, named 6 called,
marked, pegged, picked, select
7 blessed 8 selected 9 appointed,
delegated, exclusive

Chou ____
5 En-lai

chouse
3 gyp 4 bilk, clip, dupe, herd 5 cheat,
cozen, drive, trick 6 diddle, fleece
7 defraud, swindle 8 flimflam

chow
4 eats, feed, food, grub, meal

chowchow
6 medley, relish 7 mélange

chowderhead
4 boob, clod, dodo, dolt, dope,
fool 5 chump, dunce, idiot, noddy
6 dimwit, nitwit, noodle 7 halfwit,
schnook 8 dumbbell, numskull
9 lamebrain, numbskull

chowhound
7 glutton 8 gourmand

chrism
3 oil 4 balm 5 cream, salve 6 cerate 7 unction, unguent 8 ointment

christen
3 dub 4 call, name, term 5 title
7 asperse, baptize, immerse 8 dedicate, sprinkle 9 designate

christening
7 baptism

Christian
denomination: 6 Mormon, Quaker
7 Baptist, Friends 8 Anglican,
Catholic, Lutheran, Moravian,
Nazarene, Reformed 9 Calvinist,
Episcopal, Mennonite, Methodist,
Unitarian 10 Anabaptist 11 Pentecostal 12 Episcopalian, Presbyterian, Universalist
Eastern rite: 5 Uniat 6 Uniate
Egyptian: 4 Copt
love feast: 5 agape
martyr, first: 7 Stephen
symbol: 3 IHS 4 fish, rood 5 cross
6 Chi-Rhos 7 ichthus

Christiania
4 Oslo

Christian Science founder
4 Eddy (Mary Baker)

Christie, Agatha
character: 6 Marple (Jane), Poirot
(Hercule)
novel: 14 Death on the Nile
24 Murder on the Orient Express
play: 9 Mousetrap (The) 24 Witness for the Prosecution

Christina's World painter
5 Wyeth (Andrew)

Christmas
4 Noel, yule 8 Nativity, yuletide
symbol: 7 Yule log

Christmas Carol, A
author: 7 Dickens (Charles)
character: 7 Scrooge (Ebenezer),
Tiny Tim 8 Cratchit (Bob)

Christogram
6 Chi-Rho

Christopher Robin creator
5 Milne (A. A.)

chromatic
8 colorful 10 accidental

chromatin thread
7 spireme

chromosome component
3 DNA 4 gene 8 telomere 10 cen-
tromere, chromomere

chronic
5 usual 6 wonted 7 routine

chronicle

8 constant, enduring, habitual
9 ceaseless, confirmed, continual, customary, incessant, perennial, perpetual, recurrent, recurring
10 accustomed, continuing, habituated, inveterate, persisting
11 unrelenting

chronicle

4 list 6 annals, record, relate, report
7 account, history, narrate, recital, recount 8 describe 9 narration, narrative

chronicler

8 narrator, recorder, reporter 9 historian

chronograph

5 clock, watch 9 timepiece

chronology

5 annal 6 annals, record 7 history
8 calendar, register, schedule 9 timetable

chronometer

5 clock, watch 9 timepiece

chrysalis

4 pupa 8 covering

Chryseis

captor: 9 Agamemnon
father: 7 Chryses

Chrysippus

father: 6 Pelops
slayer: 6 Atreus 8 Thyestes

chthonic

6 Hadean, nether 7 hellish, satanic
8 accursed, infernal, plutonic 9 plutonian, Tartarean 10 sulphurous

chubby

5 hefty, husky, plump, podgy, pudgy, round, tubby 6 chunky, fleshy, portly, rotund, stocky, zaftig 8 plumpish, roly-poly

chuck

3 pat, tap 4 beef, cast, hurl, junk, oust, shed, toss 5 ditch, fling, heave, nudge, pitch, scrap, throw 6 give up, reject 7 abandon, boot out, discard, dismiss, kick out 8 jettison, throw out
9 throw away

chucker

7 bouncer

chuckle

5 laugh 6 giggle, guffaw, hee-haw, titter 7 chortle, snicker

chucklehead

see **chowderhead**

chuff

3 oaf 4 boor, lout, rube 5 churl, clown, yahoo, yokel 7 bumpkin, hayseed 10 clodhopper

chum

3 pal 4 mate 5 buddy, crony 6 friend, salmon 7 comrade 8 sidekick
9 companion

chummy

4 cozy 5 close, pally, palsy, thick
8 familiar, intimate 10 buddy-buddy, palsy-walsy

chump

3 oaf, sap 4 boob, dolt, dope, dupe, fool, goof, goon, gull, mark 5 booby, dummy, dunce, patsy 6 pigeon, sucker, turkey 7 fall guy, fathead
8 dolthead, lunkhead

chunk

3 sum, wad 4 clod, hunk, lump, slab
5 clump 6 nugget

chunky

5 beefy, dumpy, hefty, husky, plump, pudgy, squat, stout 6 chubby, fleshy, portly, rotund, stocky, stubby, stumpy
8 heavyset, thickset

church

4 cult, fane, kirk, sect 5 creed, faith
6 temple 7 minster 8 basilica, religion 9 cathedral, communion
10 tabernacle 12 denomination
adjunct: 6 belfry 7 steeple 9 bell tower
basin: 4 font 5 stoup
bench: 3 pew
bishop's: 9 cathedral
calendar: 4 ordo
caretaker: 6 sexton
chapel: 7 oratory
council: 5 synod

court: 4 rota 10 consistory
creed: 6 Nicene 8 Apostles'
district: 6 parish 7 diocese
father: 5 Basil 6 Jerome, Justin, Origen 7 Ambrose, Clement 8 Ignatius 9 Augustine 10 Chrysostom, Tertullian, theologian
fund-raiser: 6 bazaar
governing body: 5 curia 7 classis 10 consistory, presbytery
head: 4 pope 7 pontiff
law: 5 canon
member: 11 communicant
of a monastery: 7 minster
officer: 5 elder, vicar 6 beadle, deacon, sexton, verger, warden 9 presbyter, sacristan
part: 4 apse, bema, loft, nave 5 aisle, altar, choir 6 vestry 7 chancel, gallery, narthex, steeple 8 sacristy, transept 9 baptistry, sanctuary 10 baptistery, clerestory
porch: 6 parvis 7 galilee
reader: 6 lector
recess: 4 apse
revenue: 5 tithe
room: 6 vestry 8 sacristy
Scottish: 4 kirk
seats for clergy: 7 sedilia
service: 4 mass 6 matins 7 vespers 8 evensong 9 communion
small: 6 chapel
tribunal: 4 rota
vault: 5 crypt

Churchill, Winston
daughter: 4 Mary 5 Diana, Sarah
father: 8 Randolph
mother: 6 Jennie
Order: 6 Garter
phrase: 11 Iron Curtain
son: 8 Randolph
trademark: 5 cigar
wife: 10 Clementine

church key
9 can opener

churchman
6 bishop, cleric, divine, parson, pastor, priest 8 minister, preacher, reverend 9 clergyman 12 ecclesiastic

churl
3 oaf 4 boor, clod, lout, rube 5 chuff, clown, yahoo, yokel 6 mucker 7 bumpkin, hayseed 10 clodhopper

churlish
4 base, curt, dour, rude 5 blunt, crude, gruff, surly 6 coarse, crusty, oafish, vulgar 7 boorish, brusque, loutish, lowbred, uncivil 8 cloddish, clownish 10 unmannerly 11 clodhopping, uncivilized 12 discourteous

churn
4 boil, foam, roil, stir 5 froth, swirl 6 bubble, seethe, simmer, stir up 7 agitate, ferment, smolder

chute
4 fall, ramp 5 falls, rapid, slide, spout 6 rapids 7 cascade, channel, descent 8 cataract 9 spinnaker, waterfall

chutzpah
4 gall 5 brass, cheek, moxie, nerve, spunk 8 audacity, temerity 10 effrontery

CIA
predecessor: 3 OSS

ciao
4 by-by, ta-ta 5 adieu, adios, aloha, hello, howdy 6 bye-bye, good-by, so long 7 good-bye, welcome 8 farewell 9 greetings

cicatrix
4 scar 13 scarification

Cicero
forte: 7 oratory
target: 8 Catiline 10 Mark Antony

cicerone
4 guru 5 coach, guide, tutor 6 docent, escort, mentor 7 adviser 9 counselor, tour guide

Cid, El (Le)
4 epic, hero, play, poem 5 opera
composer: 8 Massenet (Jules)
meaning: 4 lord
name: 4 Díaz (Rodrigo, Ruy) 5 Bivar
playwright: 9 Corneille (Pierre)
sword: 6 Colada, Tizona
wife: 6 Jimena, Ximena

cigar
5 stogy 6 corona, Havana, stogie
7 cheroot 8 panatela, perfecto
case: 7 humidor
color: 5 claro 6 maduro 8 colorado

cigarette
3 fag 4 butt 5 smoke 6 gasper
10 coffin nail

cilium
4 hair, lash 7 eyelash

Cimmerian
4 dark 5 dusky, murky 6 gloomy
7 hellish, shadowy, stygian 8 infernal, plutonic 9 plutonian

cinch
4 snap 5 girth, setup 6 assure,
breeze, ensure, fasten, insure,
picnic, secure, shoo-in 8 duck soup,
kid stuff, pushover 9 certainty
10 child's play

cinchona bark extract
7 quinine

cincture
4 band, belt, sash 6 girdle 9 waistband

cinders
3 ash 4 coal, lava, slag 5 ashes,
dross 6 embers 8 clinkers

cinema
4 film, show 5 flick, movie 6 movies
7 picture, theater, theatre 12 silver
screen 13 motion picture

cinereous
4 ashy, gray, grey 5 ashen 7 ashlike

cinnabar
3 ore 7 mineral, pigment 9 vermilion
color: 3 red

cinnamon bark
6 cassia

cinnamon stone
6 garnet 8 essonite

cipher
4 code, zero 5 aught, count, digit
6 figure, naught, nobody, number,
reckon, symbol 7 compute, integer,
numeral 8 estimate, monogram
9 calculate, nonentity 11 whole
number

ciphering
8 figuring 9 computing, reckoning
10 arithmetic 11 calculation, computation

circa
4 near, nigh 5 about 6 around
7 roughly 13 approximately

circadian
5 daily 6 cyclic 7 diurnal, regular
9 quotidian

Circe
5 siren 9 sorceress
brother: 6 Aeëtes
father: 3 Sol 6 Helios
home: 5 Aeaea
lover: 7 Ulysses 8 Odysseus
niece: 5 Medea
son: 5 Comus 9 Telegonus

Circean
6 luring 8 alluring, enticing, fetching,
tempting 10 bewitching

circinate
6 coiled 7 rounded

circle
4 belt, gyre, hoop, loop, ring
5 crowd, cycle, group, orbit, wheel,
whorl 6 clique, corona, girdle,
gyrate, rotary, rotate 7 compass,
coterie, cronies, friends, revolve,
rondure 8 surround 9 encompass
10 associates, companions, revolution
bisector: 8 diameter
colored: 6 areola
combining form: 3 gyr 4 cycl, gyro
5 cyclo
graph: 8 pie chart
luminous: 4 aura, halo 6 corona,
nimbus 7 aureole
part: 3 arc 6 sector 8 quadrant
small: 4 disk 7 annulet

circlet
4 band, ring 6 bangle, diadem
8 bracelet, headband
for head or helmet: 7 coronal

circuit
3 lap, way 4 loop, tour, trip, turn
5 ambit, cycle, orbit, round, route,
track 6 course, hookup, league
7 compass, journey, pathway, travels
8 district, rotation 9 perimeter,
periphery, round trip 10 revolution,
roundabout 11 association, circulation 13 circumference

circuitous
7 devious, oblique, winding 8 circular, indirect, tortuous 10 collateral,
convoluted, meandering, roundabout

circuit rider
5 judge 8 minister, preacher 9 clergyman

circular
4 bill 5 flier, flyer, round 7 annular,
cycloid, discoid, handout, leaflet
8 handbill 9 throwaway
file: 11 wastebasket
motion: 4 eddy, gyre, spin 5 whirl
8 gyration, rotation 10 revolution
plate: 4 disc, dish, disk

circularize
4 poll 6 survey 7 canvass 9 advertise, publicize

circulate
4 flow 6 rotate, spread 7 diffuse,
radiate, revolve 8 disperse 9 propagate 10 distribute 11 disseminate

circulation
4 flow 6 spread 8 currency 9 diffusion 11 propagation 12 transmission 13 dissemination

circumciser
5 mohel

circumcision, Jewish
4 bris 9 Brit Milah

circumference
3 rim 5 ambit 6 border, bounds,
limits, margin 7 circuit, compass
8 boundary, confines 9 perimeter,
periphery

circumflex
9 diacritic

circumjacent
11 surrounding

circumlocution
8 pleonasm, verbiage 9 euphemism,
loquacity, prolixity, verbosity, wordiness 10 redundancy 11 periphrasis,
verboseness

circumnavigate
5 skirt 6 bypass, detour 8 sidestep

circumnavigator
4 Cook (James) 5 Drake (Francis)
8 Magellan (Ferdinand), van Noort
(Olivier) 9 Cavendish (Thomas)

circumscribe
5 cramp, limit 6 fetter, hamper
7 confine, delimit, enclose, mark off,
outline, trammel 8 restrict, surround
9 constrict

circumscribed
5 bound, fixed 6 finite, narrow,
strait 7 bounded, cramped, limited,
precise 8 confined, definite, ham-
pered 10 restrained, restricted
11 determinate

circumscription
5 cramp, limit, stint 6 border, margin
8 boundary 9 perimeter, restraint,
stricture 10 constraint, definition,
limitation 11 confinement, restriction
12 ball and chain, delimitation
13 constrainment

circumspect
4 safe, wary 5 chary 7 careful,
guarded, prudent 8 cautious, discreet, gingerly 11 calculating

circumstance
4 fact, item 5 event, thing 6 detail,
factor 7 adjunct, element, episode,
feature 8 accident, incident, occasion 9 component, condition,
happening 10 occurrence, particular 11 concomitant, constituent,
eventuality

circumstantial
4 full 5 close, exact 6 strict 7 precise, replete 8 accurate, complete,
detailed, thorough 9 elaborate,
pertinent 10 blow-by-blow, ceremonial, exhaustive, incidental, particular

circumvent

5 avoid, elude, evade, hem in, skirt
6 bypass, detour 8 outflank, sidestep

circumvolution

4 gyre, turn 5 wheel, whirl 8 gyration,
rotation 10 revolution

circus

4 ring 5 arena 6 big top 9 spectacle
12 amphitheater
animal: 4 bear, flea, lion, seal
5 horse, tiger 8 elephant
attraction: 5 freak 8 sideshow
owner: 6 Bailey (James), Barnum
(P. T.) 8 Ringling (Bros.)
performer: 5 clown, tamer 7 acrobat, athlete, juggler, tumbler 9 aerialist, fire eater
worker: 10 roustabout

citadel

4 fort 7 redoubt 8 fastness, fortress
10 stronghold
of Carthage: 5 Bursa, Byrsa
Russian: 7 kremlin

citation

5 quote 6 eulogy 7 excerpt, mention, summons, tribute 8 accolade,
encomium 9 panegyric, quotation,
reference 12 commendation

cite

4 name, tell 5 offer, quote 6 adduce,
recall, summon 7 arraign, mention,
present, refer to, specify 8 point out,
remember 9 recollect

citizen

7 burgess, burgher, subject 8 civilian, national, resident, townsman
10 inhabitant

Citizen Kane director

6 Welles (Orson)

citron

4 tree 5 melon

citrus

family: 3 rue 8 Rutaceae
fruit: 4 lime, ugli 5 lemon 6 citron,
orange, pomelo 7 kumquat, tangelo
8 bergamot, mandarin, shaddock
9 tangerine 10 grapefruit

city

4 burg 5 urban 7 burghal 9 municipal 10 metropolis
combining form: 5 polis
Eternal: 4 Rome
French: 5 ville
heavenly: 4 Sion, Zion
Latin: 4 urbs
Motor: 7 Detroit
of Bells: 10 Strasbourg
of Bridges: 6 Bruges
of Brotherly Love: 12 Philadelphia
of David: 9 Jerusalem
official: 5 mayor 7 manager
8 alderman 10 councilman
of God: 6 heaven 8 paradise
of Gold: 8 Eldorado
of Kings: 4 Lima
of Lights: 5 Paris
of Lilies: 8 Florence
of Masts: 6 London
of Rams: 6 Canton
of Refuge: 6 Medina
of Saints: 8 Montreal
of Seven Hills: 4 Rome
of the dead: 10 necropolis
of Victory: 5 Cairo
planner: 8 urbanist
section: 4 slum, ward 5 block,
plaza 6 barrio, ghetto, square,
uptown 8 business, downtown,
red-light 11 residential
slicker: 4 dude
windy: 7 Chicago

city-state, Greek

5 Argos, polis 6 Athens, Delphi,
poleis (plural), Sparta, Thebes
7 Corinth

city, town, village

(see also **capital**)
Afghanistan: 5 Balkh, Farah, Herat,
Kushk 6 Konduz 8 Kandahar, Qan-
dahar 9 Jalalabad
Alabama: 3 Opp 4 Arab, Boaz,
Elba 5 Selma 6 Athens, Dothan,
Mobile 7 Decatur, Florala 8 Prichard
10 Birmingham, Huntsville, Scotts-
boro, Tuscaloosa 12 Muscle Shoals
Alaska: 4 Nome 5 Kenai, Sitka
6 Barrow, Bethel, Kodiak, Valdez
9 Anchorage, Fairbanks, Ketchikan
11 Point Barrow

Albania: 4 Fier 5 Berat, Korçë, Kukës, Vlorë

Alberta: 4 Olds 5 Hanna, Leduc, Taber 7 Calgary 8 Edmonton 10 Lethbridge 11 Medicine Hat

Algeria: 4 Bône, Oran 5 Batna, Blida, Médéa, Saïda, Sétif 6 Annaba, Bechar 11 Constantine

Angola: 6 Huambo 7 Lubango 8 Benguela

Argentina: 4 Azul, Goya 5 Junin, Lanus, Lujan, Merlo, Salta, Tigre 6 Parana 7 Córdoba, La Plata, La Rioja, Mendoza, Rosario, San Juan, Santa Fe 9 Catamarca 11 Bahía Blanca, Mar del Plata

Arizona: 3 Ajo 4 Eloy, Mesa, Yuma 5 Globe, Tempe 6 Tucson 7 Sun City, Winslow 8 Glendale, Prescott 9 Flagstaff, Tombstone 10 Casa Grande, Scottsdale

Arkansas: 4 Mena 5 Beebe, Cabot, Earle, Ozark, Wynne 9 Fort Smith, Pine Bluff, Texarkana 10 Hot Springs

Armenia: 6 Gyumri 8 Vanadzor

Australia: 3 Ayr 5 Dalby, Dubbo, Perth, Unley 6 Darwin, Sydney 8 Adelaide, Brisbane, Randwick 9 Bankstown, Blacktown, Gold Coast, Melbourne, Newcastle 10 Kalgoorlie, Parramatta, Sutherland, Wollongong 12 Alice Springs

Austria: 4 Enns, Graz, Linz, Wels 5 Steyr, Traun 8 Salzburg 9 Innsbruck 10 Klagenfurt

Azerbaijan: 5 Gänca 8 Sumqayit 9 Kirovabad

Bahamas: 8 Freeport

Bangladesh: 5 Bogra, Pabna 6 Khulna, Sylhet 7 Barisal, Comilla, Jessore, Rangpur, Saidpur 10 Chittagong

Belarus: 5 Brest, Gomel, Mozyr, Pinsk 6 Grodno, Homyel', Hrodna 7 Mogilev, Vitebsk 8 Babruysk, Mahilyow 9 Vitsyebsk

Belgium: 3 Ath, Hal, Huy, Mol 4 Amay, Dour, Geel, Genk, Gent, Hoei, Luik, Mons, Vise 5 Aalst, Arlon, Diest, Evere, Ghent, Halle, Ieper, Jumet, Leuze, Liège, Namur, Ronse, Theux, Wavre, Ypres

6 Bruges, Brugge 7 Antwerp, Hasselt, Louvain 8 Oostende 9 Charleroi

Benin: 5 Kandi 6 Abomey 7 Parakou

Bolivia: 5 Oruro, Uyuni 6 Potosí 9 Santa Cruz 10 Cochabamba

Bosnia and Herzegovina: 5 Bihac, Brcko, Jajce, Tuzla 6 Mostar, Zenica 9 Banja Luka

Botswana: 4 Maun 5 Kanye 11 Francistown

Brazil: 4 Codo, Pará 5 Bahia, Bauru, Belém, Ceara, Natal 6 Campos, Canoas, Caxias, Ilheus, Maceio, Manaus, Olinda, Recife, Santos 7 Aracaju, Caruaru, Goiania, Jundiai, Marilia, Niteroi, Pelotas, São Luis, Uberaba, Vitória 8 Campinas, Colatina, Curitiba, Londrina, Salvador, Santarém, São Paulo, Sorocaba, Teresina 9 Caratinga, Fortaleza, Guarulhos, Rio Grande 10 Guarapuava, Joao Pessoa, Juiz de Fora, Nova Iguaçu, Pernambuco, Petropolis, Piracicaba, Pôrto Velho, Santa Maria, Santo André, São Gonçalo, Uberlândia 11 Campo Grande, Caxias do Sul, Ponta Grossa, Pôrto Alegre 12 Montes Claros, Rio de Janeiro, Teófilo Otoni, Volta Redonda 13 Belo Horizonte, Campina Grande, Duque de Caxias, Florianopolis, Mogi das Cruzes, Riberião Prêto

British Columbia: 5 Comox 6 Surrey 7 Burnaby 8 Richmond 9 Vancouver

Bulgaria: 3 Lom 4 Ruse 5 Varna, Vidin 6 Burgas 7 Plovdiv 11 Stara Zagora

California: 4 Brea, Galt, Lodi, Ojai 5 Arvin, Azusa, Ceres, Chico, Chino, Dixon, Hemet, Indio, Norco, Ripon, Ukiah, Wasco, Yreka 6 Downey, Encino, Fresno, Oxnard, Pomona, Sonoma 7 Anaheim, Burbank, Compton, Fremont, Hayward, Modesto, Oakland, San Jose, Seaside, Soledad, Van Nuys 8 Berkeley, Glendale, Palo Alto, Pasadena, San Diego, Santa Ana, Stockton, Torrance, Yuba City 9 El Segundo, Hollywood, Long Beach, Menlo Park,

Riverside, Sausalito **10** Chula Vista, Culver City, Los Angeles, San Leandro, Santa Clara **11** Bakersfield, Laguna Beach, Pebble Beach, Redwood City, San Clemente, Santa Monica **12** Beverly Hills, Mission Viejo, Redondo Beach, San Francisco, Santa Barbara **13** San Bernardino, San Luis Obispo
Cambodia: 8 Siem Reap **10** Battambang **11** Kompong Cham
Cameroon: 4 Buea, Edea **5** Kribi, Lomie **6** Douala **7** Bamenda, Foumban **9** Bafoussam
Canada: 4 York **5** Banff **6** London, Oshawa, Ottawa, Regina, St. John **7** Brandon, Burnaby, Calgary, Halifax, Iqaluit, Red Deer, St. John's, Sudbury, Toronto, Windsor **8** Hamilton, Montreal, Moose Jaw, North Bay, Victoria, Winnipeg **9** Dartmouth, Kitchener, Longueuil, North York, Saint John, Saskatoon, Vancouver **10** Lethbridge, Saint John's, Sherbrooke, Thunder Bay, Whitehorse **11** Fredericton, Medicine Hat, Mississauga, Scarborough, Yellowknife **12** Peterborough, Prince Albert, Prince George **13** Charlottetown, Trois-Rivières
Central African Republic: 5 Bouar **7** Bambari
Chad: 4 Sarh **6** Abéché
Chile: 4 Lebu, Lota, Tomé **5** Ancud, Angol, Arica, Maipu, Penco, Rengo, Talca **6** Temuco **7** Copiapó, Iquique **8** Rancagua **10** Concepción, Talcahuano, Valparaíso **11** Antofagasta
China: 4 Amoy, Jian, Luan, Xi'an, Yaan **5** Hefei, Jilin, Jinan, Lhasa, Qinan, Ssuan, Wuhan, Yibin, Yumen **6** Andong, Anqing, Anshan, Anshun, Anyang, Beihai, Canton, Dalian, Datong, Foshan, Fushun, Fuzhou, Guilin, Haikou, Handan, Harbin, Hohhot, Hoihao, Jilong, Luzhou, Mukden, Ningbo, Pengbu, Suzhou, Ürümqi, Xiamen, Xining, Xuzhou, Yanggu, Yichun, Yining, Zhangi, Zhaoan **7** Baoding, Changan, Chengdu, Dandong, Guiyang, Huainan, Jiamusi, Jiaxing, Kaifeng,

Kunming, Lanzhou, Luoshan, Luoyang, Nanking, Nanjing, Nanning, Shantou, Tianjin, Taiyuan, Wanxian, Weifang, Yizhang, Zhuzhou **8** Changchi, Changsha, Dangshan, Hangzhou, Hanzhong, Hengyang, Huangshi, Jiangmen, Jiujiang, Kueiyang, Liaoyang, Nanchang, Shanghai, Shangrao, Shaoyang, Shenyang, Tianshui, Yinchuan, Zhenjing **9** Changchun, Chenjiang, Chongqing, Chungking, Guangzhou, Huangshih, Zhengzhou, Zhenjiang **10** Jingdezhen, Laojunmiao **11** Qinhuangdao, Zhangjiakou
Colombia: 4 Buga, Cali **5** Bello, Mocoa, Neiva, Ocaña, Pasto, Tuluá, Tunja **6** Cúcuta, Ibagué **7** Ciénaga, Palmira, Pereira, Popayán **8** Medellín, Montería **9** Cartagena, Manizales **10** Santa Marta **11** Bucaramanga **12** Barranquilla
Colorado: 6 Arvada, Aurora, Golden, Salida **7** Alamosa, Boulder, Durango, Greeley, La Junta **8** Brighton, Gunnison, Lakewood, Longmont, Loveland, Montrose, Thornton **9** Englewood, Estes Park, Leadville, Littleton, Rocky Ford, Telluride **10** Broomfield, Castle Rock, Fort Lupton, Fort Morgan, Monte Vista, Northglenn, Wheat Ridge **11** Fort Collins **13** Grand Junction
Congo (Zaire): 4 Boma **6** Bukavu **7** Kolwezi **8** Bandundu **9** Kisangani **10** Lubumbashi **12** Stanleyville
Congo-Brazzaville: 11 Pointe-Noire
Connecticut: 5 Byram **6** Darien, Easton, Granby, Groton, Haddam **7** Ansonia, Bethany, Danbury, Enfield, Meriden, Milford, Newtown, Niantic, Norwalk, Norwich, Old Lyme, Pomfret, Windham **8** Branford, Cromwell, East Lyme, Guilford, New Haven, Simsbury, Stamford, Suffield, Westport **9** Greenwich, New Canaan, Newington, New London, Rocky Hill, Southbury, Waterbury, Waterford **10** Bridgeport, Brookfield, East Haddam, Farmington, Kensington, Litchfield, New Britain, New

Milford, North Haven, Plainville, Ridgefield, Stonington, Torrington 11 Beacon Falls, Glastonbury, Middlefield, Old Saybrook, Southington, Wallingford, Willimantic 12 Wethersfield

Costa Rica: 8 Alajuela 10 Puntarenas 11 Puerto Limón

Croatia: 4 Pula 5 Sisak, Split, Zadar 6 Osijek, Rijeka, Zagreb 9 Dubrovnik

Cuba: 5 Banes, Bauta 6 Bayamo 7 Holguín 8 Camagüey, Marianao, Matanzas, Santiago 10 Cienfuegos, Guantánamo 11 Pinar del Río

Cyprus: 7 Kyrenia, Larnaca, Nicosia 8 Limassol 9 Famagusta

Czech Republic: 4 Brno, Zlín 5 Plzen 7 Liberec, Olomouc, Ostrava 10 Bratislava

Delaware: 5 Lewes 7 Seaford 10 Harrington, Wilmington, Winterthur

Denmark: 5 Arhus, Skive, Vejle 6 Alborg, Odense, Viborg 13 Frederiksberg

Dominican Republic: 4 Azua, Bani, Moca 5 Bonao, Nagua 8 Barahona, Santiago

Ecuador: 4 Loja 5 Canar, Daule, Manta, Pinas 7 Machala 8 Riobamba 9 Guayaquil

Egypt: 4 Giza, Idfu, Isna, Qena 5 Aswan, Asyut, Benha, Disuq, Girga, Luxor, Minuf, Tahta, Tanta 6 Helwan 7 El Arish, Zagazig 8 Damanhur, Damietta, El Faiyum, Ismailia, Port Said 10 Alexandria

Eire: 4 Athy, Birr, Cobh, Cork, Naas, Tuam 5 Ennis, Sligo 6 Carlow, Galway, Tralee 7 Dundalk, Kildare, Wexford, Wicklow 8 Drogheda, Kilkenny, Limerick, Monaghan 9 Castlebar, Killarney, Tipperary, Waterford 10 Balbriggan

El Salvador: 7 La Unión 8 Santa Ana 9 Sonsonate

England: 4 Bath, Eton, Hove, Ryde, York 5 Brent, Brigg, Colne, Corby, Cowes, Derby, Dover, Egham, Eling, Esher, Eston, Goole, Leeds, Leigh, Lewes, Luton, Poole, Ryton, Wigan

6 Bexley, Bolton, Dudley, Durham, Exeter, Merton, Oldham, Oxford, Torbay, Warley, Welwyn 7 Bristol, Bromley, Croydon, Hackney, Ipswich, Malvern, Norwich, Salford, Seaford, Walsall 8 Abingdon, Basildon, Bradford, Brighton, Coventry, Hastings, Hatfield, Havering, Hertford, Kingston, Lewisham, Plymouth, Wallsend 9 Aylesbury, Blackpool, Cambridge, Islington, Leicester, Liverpool, Newcastle, Sheffield, Stratford 10 Birkenhead, Birmingham, Canterbury, Colchester, Manchester, Nottingham, Portsmouth, Sunderland 11 Bournemouth, Northampton, Southampton 12 Peterborough, Stoke-on-Trent, West Bromwich 13 Southend-on-Sea, Wolverhampton

Estonia: 5 Narva, Pärnu, Tartu

Ethiopia: 5 Aksum, Harer 6 Nazret 8 Dire Dawa

Finland: 4 Kemi, Oulu, Pori 5 Espoo, Hango, Kotka, Lahti, Rauma, Turku, Vaasa 6 Vantaa 7 Tampere

Florida: 5 Largo, Miami, Ocala, Ocoee, Oneco, Tampa 6 DeLand, Naples 7 Hialeah, Key West, Orlando, Sebring 8 Gulfport, Key Largo, Lakeland, Opa-Locka, Sarasota 9 Boca Raton, Bradenton, Fort Myers, Hollywood, Kissimmee, Palm Beach, Pensacola, Vero Beach 10 Clearwater, Cocoa Beach, Fort Pierce, Miami Beach, Punta Gorda, Titusville 11 Coral Gables, Gainesville, Key Biscayne, St. Augustine, Winter Haven 12 Apalachicola, Daytona Beach, Ft. Lauderdale, Jacksonville, Pompano Beach, St. Petersburg 13 Chattahoochee

France: 3 Dax, Pau 4 Agde, Agen, Albi, Ales, Auch, Caen, Gien, Laon, Lyon, Metz, Nice, Orly, Rezé, Sens, Sète, Vire 5 Arles, Arras, Auray, Auton, Avion, Berck, Blois, Bondy, Brest, Creil, Digne, Dijon, Douai, Dreux, Flers, Gagny, Laval, Le Puy, Lille, Lunel, Lyons, Mâcon, Meaux, Melun, Muret, Nîmes, Niort, Noyon, Reims, Revin, Rodez, Rouen,

Royan, Tours, Tulle, Vichy, Vitre
6 Amiens, Angers, Calais, Cannes,
Dieppe, Evreux, Le Mans, Nantes,
Nevers, Rennes, Rheims, Thiers,
Toulon, Troyes **7** Ajaccio, Antibes,
Avignon, Béthune, Bourges, Le
Havre, Limoges, Lorient, Lourdes,
Orléans, Roubaix **8** Beauvais, Be-
sançon, Biarritz, Bordeaux, Chartres,
Gentilly, Grenoble, Nanterre, Poitiers,
Toulouse **9** Cherbourg, Dunkerque,
Le Creusot, Marseille, Montreuil,
Perpignan **10** Draguignan, Mar-
seilles, Strasbourg, Versailles
11 Carcassonne, Montpellier
12 Saint-Etienne **13** Aix-en-Provence
Gabon: 4 Oyem **5** Bitam **10** Port-
Gentil **11** Franceville
Gambia: 9 Serekunda
Georgia: 4 Adel, Alma, Arco
5 Jesup, Macon, McRae **6** Albany,
Athens **7** Augusta, Calhoun **8** Amer-
icus, Columbus, Marietta, Savannah,
Valdosta **9** Brunswick
Georgia, Republic of: 6 Batumi
7 Kutaisi, Rustavi, Sukhumi
Germany: 3 Aue, Hof, Ulm **4** Bonn,
Gera, Goch, Hamm, Jena, Kehl, Kiel,
Köln, Mari, Suhl **5** Aalen, Ahlen,
Borna, Bruhl, Calbe, Celle, Düren,
Emden, Essen, Forst, Fulda, Furth,
Gotha, Greiz, Hagen, Halle, Hanau,
Herne, Hurth, Kleve, Lemgo, Lobau,
Mainz, Neuss, Peine, Pirna, Riesa,
Stade, Thale, Trier, Wesel, Zeitz
6 Aachen, Bremen, Coburg, Dachau,
Dessau, Erfurt, Kassel, Lübeck,
Munich, Rheydt **7** Cologne, Cottbus,
Dresden, Hamburg, Hanover,
Koblenz, Krefeld, Leipzig, München,
Munster, Potsdam, Rostock, Zwickau
8 Augsburg, Bayreuth, Chemnitz,
Cuxhaven, Dortmund, Duisburg,
Freiburg, Hannover, Mannheim,
Nürnberg, Würzburg **9** Bielefeld,
Brunswick, Darmstadt, Frankfurt,
Göttingen, Karlsruhe, Magdeburg,
Nuremberg, Offenbach, Oldenburg,
Osnabrück, Remscheid, Stuttgart,
Wiesbaden, Wuppertal **10** Baden-
Baden, Düsseldorf, Heidelberg,
Oberhausen, Regensburg, Salzgitter

11 Brandenburg, Bremerhaven,
Saarbrücken **12** Braunschweig
13 Gelsenkirchen
Ghana: 4 Axim, Keta, Tema
5 Lawra, Yendi **6** Kumasi
Greece: 3 Kos **4** Arta **5** Argos,
Lamia, Nemea, Volos **6** Sparta,
Thebes **7** Corinth, Khalkis, La-
rissa, Piraeus, Tríkala **8** Salonika
12 Thessaloniki
Guatemala: 5 Cobán **13** Quezal-
tenango
Guinea: 4 Labé **6** Kankan, Kindia
Haiti: 8 Gonaïves **10** Cap Haitien
Hawaii: 4 Aiea, Hilo, Laie **5** Kapaa,
Lihue, Maili **6** Kailua **7** Kaneohe,
Waikiki, Wailuku
Honduras: 5 Danlí **7** La Ceiba
12 San Pedro Sula
Hong Kong: 7 Kowloon
Hungary: 3 Ozd **4** Eger, Györ, Pécs
5 Abony, Bekes **6** Szeged **7** Miskolc
8 Debrecen
Idaho: 4 Buhl **5** Nampa **6** Dubois,
Moscow **7** Gooding, Payette,
Rexburg **8** Caldwell **9** Blackfoot,
Pocatello, Sandpoint, Sun Valley,
Twin Falls **11** Coeur d' Alene,
Grangeville **12** Mountain Home,
Saint Anthony
Illinois: 6 DeKalb, Galena, Hardin,
Joliet, Macomb, Moline, Paxton,
Peoria, Skokie, Urbana **7** Chicago,
Decatur, Glencoe, Oak Lawn, Oak
Park, Tuscola, Watseka, Wheaton
8 Carthage, Evanston, Kankakee,
La Grange, Monmouth, Rockford,
Vandalia, Waukegan **9** Belvidere,
Effingham, Galesburg, Park Ridge,
Yorkville **10** Belleville, Carbondale,
Carrollton, Des Plaines, Metropolis,
Northbrook, Rock Island **11** Carlin-
ville, Jerseyville, Lindenhurst, Mur-
physboro, Taylorville **12** Highland
Park, Mount Carroll
India: 3 Mau **4** Agra, Ahwa, Bhuj,
Durg, Gaya, Kota, Mhow, Pune, Puri,
Rewa, Tonk, Ziro **5** Adoni, Aimer,
Akola, Alwar, Arcot, Arrah, Banda,
Barsi, Bidar, Bihar, Churu, Damoh,
Delhi, Dewas, Eluru, Gonda, Jalna,
Jammu, Karur, Miraj, Morvi, Nasik,

Patan, Patna, Poona, Sagar, Satna, Sikar, Simla, Surat, Thana 6 Baroda, Bhopal, Bombay, Cochin, Guntur, Howrah, Indore, Jaipur, Jhansi, Kanpur, Madras, Meerut, Mysore, Nagpur, Raipur, Rajkot, Ranchi, Ujjain 7 Aligarh, Asansol, Belgaum, Bikaner, Burdwan, Cuttack, Gauhati, Gwalior, Jodhpur, Kurnool, Lucknow, Madurai, Mathura, Nellore, Patiala, Vellore 8 Amritsar, Bhatpara, Cal-. cutta, Dehra Dun, Kolhapur, Ludhiana, Sholapur, Srinagar, Varanasi 9 Ahmadabad, Allahabad, Bangalore, Hyderabad 10 Ahmadnagar, Chandigarh, Trivandrum 11 Pondicherry
Indiana: 4 Gary 5 Berne, Paoli, Vevay 6 Delphi, Kokomo, Marion, Muncie, Tipton 7 Bedford, Corydon, Elkhart, La Porte, Winamac 8 Bluffton, Kentland 9 Boonville, Fort Wayne, New Albany, Rushville, South Bend, Vincennes 10 Crown Point, Evansville, Logansport, Scottsburg, Terre Haute, Valparaiso 11 Bloomington, Greencastle, Noblesville, Shelbyville 12 Connersville, Lawrenceburg, Martinsville
Indonesia: 4 Pati 5 Ambon, Bogor, Garut, Kudus, Medan, Tegal, Turen 6 Batang, Kediri, Madiun, Malang, Manado, Padang 7 Bandung, Kendari 8 Semarang, Surabaja, Surabaya, Tjirebon 9 Palembang, Pontianak, Surakarta 10 Pekalongan 11 Tasikmalaja 12 Bandjarmasin
Iowa: 5 Onawa, Pella 6 Eldora, Harlan, Keokuk, Le Mars, Red Oak 7 Allison, Anamosa, Carroll, Clinton, Corydon, Denison, Dubuque, Marengo, Osceola, Waverly 8 Clarinda, Ida Grove, Waterloo 9 Davenport, Fort Dodge, Indianola, Mason City, Muscatine, Oskaloosa, Sioux City, Storm Lake, West Union, Winterset 10 Emmetsburg, Rock Rapids, Spirit Lake 11 Cedar Rapids, Fort Madison 13 Council Bluffs
Iran: 3 Qom, Qum 4 Amul, Arak, Khoi, Sari, Yazd, Yezd 5 Ahvaz,

Ahwaz, Babol, Rasht 6 Abadan, Meshed, Shiraz, Tabriz 7 Esfahan, Hamadan, Isfahan, Mashhad 9 Bakhtaran
Iraq: 3 Ana, Kut 4 Kufa 5 Al Kut, Amara, Basra, Erbil, Hilla, Mosul, Najaf, Rutba 6 Amarah, Hillah, Kirkuk, Ramadi, Rutbah 7 Falluja, Samarra 8 Fallujah, Nasiriya 9 Nasiriyah
Ireland: (see *Eire*, above)
Israel: 5 Afula, Haifa, Holon, Jaffa 7 Rehovot 8 Ashqelon, Nazareth, Ramat Gan 9 Beersheba
Italy: 4 Acri, Alba, Asti, Bari, Enna, Este, Fano, Gela, Iesi, Lodi, Lugo, Pisa 5 Adria, Agira, Anzio, Aosta, Arola, Cantù, Capua, Carpi, Crema, Cuneo, Eboli, Fermo, Fondi, Forli, Gaeta, Genoa, Imola, Ivrea, Lecce, Lecco, Lucca, Massa, Melfi, Menfi, Milan, Monza, Padua, Parma, Prato, Siena, Turin 6 Ancona, Assisi, Foggia, Mantua, Milano, Modena, Naples, Napoli, Rimini, Torino, Venice, Verona 7 Bergamo, Bologna, Bolzano, Brescia, Catania, Firenze, Leghorn, Messina, Palermo, Perugia, Pescara, Potenza, Ravenna, Salerno, San Remo, Taranto, Trieste, Venezia 8 Brindisi, Cagliari, Florence, La Spezia, Piacenza, Siracusa, Syracuse
Ivory Coast: 6 Bouaké
Jamaica: 6 May Pen 10 Montego Bay
Japan: 3 Ina, Ise, Ito, Ota, Tsu, Ube, Uji, Yao 4 Ageo, Anan, Gifu, Hagi, Himi, Hofu, Iida, Joyo, Kaga, Kobe, Kofu, Kure, Miki, Mito, Naha, Nara, Noda, Oita, Otsu, Saga, Saku, Soka, Tosu, Ueda, Yono 5 Akita, Atami, Beppu, Chiba, Imari, Itami, Iwaki, Iwata, Izumi, Izumo, Kiryu, Kochi, Kyoto, Minoo, Odate, Ogaki, Okawa, Okaya, Omiya, Omuta, Osaka, Otaru, Oyama, Sabae, Saiki, Sakai, Sanjo, Suita, Tenri, Urawa 6 Akashi, Aomori, Himeji, Kadoma, Kurume, Matsue, Mitaka, Nagano, Nagoya, Numazu, Sasebo, Sendai, Suzuka, Toyama, Yonago 7 Fukuoka, Hitachi,

Ibaraki, Imabari, Muroran, Niigata, Niihama, Nobeoka, Obihiro, Odawara, Okayama, Okazaki, Sapporo **8** Ashikaga, Fujisawa, Fukuyama, Hirakata, Hirosaki, Ichihara, Ichikawa, Kakogawa, Kamakura, Kanazawa, Kawasaki, Miyazaki, Nagasaki, Onomichi, Shizuoka, Takasaki, Toyonaka, Wakayama, Yamagata, Yokohama, Yokosuka **9** Fukushima, Funabashi, Hiroshima, Kawaguchi, Yamaguchi, Yokkaichi

Jordan: 5 Aqaba, Irbid

Kansas: 4 Gove, Iola **5** Colby, Hoxie, Lakin, Leoti, Paola, Pratt **6** Atwood, Beloit, Girard, Holton, Salina **7** Abilene, Emporia, Garnett, Kinsley, Wichita **8** Cimarron, Goodland, La Crosse, Sublette **9** Coldwater, Fort Scott, Great Bend, Oskaloosa **10** Hutchinson **11** Leavenworth **12** Council Grove, Overland Park **13** Medicine Lodge

Kazakhstan: 5 Semey **6** Almaty, Aqtöbe, Guryev, Uralsk **7** Alma-Ata, Zhambyl **8** Balkhash, Chimkent, Dzhambul, Kyzl Orda, Pavlodar, Shymkent **9** Karaganda **10** Aktyubinsk

Kentucky: 4 Inez **5** Cadiz, Hyden, McKee **6** Elkton, Harlan **7** Ashland, Campton, Greenup, Hindman, Paducah, Stanton **8** Fort Knox, Mayfield **9** Bardstown, Covington, Cynthiana, Lexington, Maysville, Owensboro, Pikeville, Pineville, Southgate, Vanceburg **10** Booneville, Hawesville, Louisville, Whitesburg **11** Hardinsburg, Harrodsburg, Hodgenville, Leitchfield, Morganfield **12** Bowling Green

Kenya: 4 Embu **5** Nyeri **6** Kisumu, Nakuru **7** Mombasa

Kyrgyzstan: 3 Osh **5** Naryn

Laos: 5 Pakse **11** Savannakhet

Latvia: 7 Jelgava, Liepaja **9** Ventspils **10** Daugavpils

Lebanon: 4 Tyre **5** Sidon, Zahlé **7** Juniyah, Tripoli

Libya: 4 Homs **5** Derna, Zawia **7** Tobruk **8** Benghazi, Misratah

Lithuania: 6 Kaunas **8** Klaipeda

Louisiana: 4 Jena **5** Amite, Arabi, Houma, Mamou, Norco, Rayne **6** Colfax, Edgard, Gretna, Minden, Ruston **7** Arcadia, Bastrop, Marrero, Oberlin **8** Bogalusa, De Ridder, Metairie, New Roads, Oak Grove, Westwego **9** Abbeville, Chalmette, Hahnville, Leesville, New Iberia, Opelousas, Port Allen, Thibodaux, Winnfield, Winnsboro **10** New Orleans, Plaquemine, Shreveport **11** Lake Charles **12** Natchitoches

Macedonia: 6 Bitola, Prilep, Tetovo

Maine: 4 Saco **5** Orono **6** Auburn, Bangor, Gorham **7** Berwick, Kittery, Machias, Rumford **8** Lewiston, Portland, Rockland **9** Bar Harbor, Biddeford, Brunswick, Ellsworth, Kennebunk, Skowhegan, Wiscasset **11** Millinocket, Presque Isle **13** Kennebunkport

Malawi: 5 Mzuzu, Zomba **8** Blantyre

Malaysia: 4 Ipoh **5** Gemas, Klang **6** Kelang, Penang, Pinang **11** Johore Bahru

Mali: 5 Kayes, Mopti, Ségou **7** Sikasso

Malta: 10 Birkirkara

Maryland: 5 Bowie **6** Denton, Elkton, Towson **8** Bethesda, Landover, Snow Hill **9** Baltimore, Rockville **10** Beltsville, Hagerstown **11** Chestertown, College Park, Leonardtown **12** Havre de Grace, Silver Spring

Massachusetts: 4 Ayer **5** Acton, Lenox, Salem **6** Agawam, Boston, Dedham, Lowell, Malden, Monson, Natick, Saugus, Woburn **7** Amherst, Danvers, Duxbury, Holyoke, Hyannis, Medford, Methuen, Needham, Swansea, Taunton, Walpole, Waltham, Wareham **8** Brockton, Chicopee, Falmouth, Plymouth, Rockport, Scituate, Yarmouth **9** Attleboro, Braintree, Brookline, Cambridge, Edgartown, Fall River, Fitchburg, Haverhill, Lexington, Nantucket, Southwick, Wilbraham, Worcester **10** Barnstable, Framingham, Gloucester, Greenfield, Leominster,

New Bedford, North Adams, Pitts-
field, Somerville, Swampscott
11 Northampton, Springfield
12 Mattapoisett, Provincetown,
Williamstown
Mauritania: 4 Atar **5** Kaedi **6** Dakhla
Mexico: 4 León **5** Ameca, Choix,
Tepic **6** Cancún, Celaya, Colima,
Jalapa, Juárez, Mérida, Oaxaca,
Puebla, Toluca, Tuxtla **7** Durango,
Guasave, Morelia, Obregón, Rey-
nosa, Tampico, Tijuana, Tlalpán,
Torreón, Uruapan, Zapopan
8 Chetumal, Coyoacán, Culiacán,
Ensenada, Mazatlan, Mexicali,
Saltillo, Tuxtepec **9** Chihuahua,
Fresnillo, Ixtacalco, Monterrey,
Querétaro, Salamanca, Tapachula,
Zacatecas **10** Cuernavaca, Her-
mosillo, Ixtapalapa, Xochimilco
11 Guadalajara, Nuevo Laredo
13 San Luis Potosí
Michigan: 4 Alma, Holt **5** Flint,
Ionia, L'Anse, Niles **6** Otsego, Paw
Paw, Warren **7** Allegan, Corunna,
Detroit, Gladwin, Livonia, Midland,
Saginaw **8** Ann Arbor, Bessemer,
Dearborn, Escanaba, Grayling,
Hastings, Houghton, Muskegon,
Newberry, Petoskey, Sandusky
9 Cheboygan, Coldwater, Hillsdale,
Kalamazoo, Menominee, Port Huron,
Roscommon, Ypsilanti **10** Charlevoix,
Grand Haven, West Branch, White
Cloud **11** Battle Creek, Grand
Rapids, Harrisville, Saint Ignace
12 Highland Park, Iron Mountain
Minnesota: 3 Ely **4** Mora **5** Anoka,
Edina, Osseo **6** Aitkin, Benson,
Duluth, Waseca, Windom, Winona
7 Glencoe, Hibbing, Mankato,
Red Wing, St. Louis, Wabasha
8 Brainerd, Elk River, Moorhead,
Shakopee **9** Caledonia, Crookston,
Faribault, Pipestone, Rochester,
Saint Paul, Silver Bay **10** Park
Rapids, Saint Cloud, Saint James,
Saint Peter, Stillwater, Two Harbors
11 Bloomington, Fergus Falls, Long
Prairie, Minneapolis, Worthington
12 Breckenridge, Granite Falls,
Redwood Falls

Mississippi: 4 Iuka **5** Amory
6 Biloxi, Leland, McComb, Purvis,
Sardis, Sumner, Tupelo, Winona
7 Belzoni, Brandon, Okolona, Quit-
man, Wiggins **8** Gulfport, Hernando,
Meridian, Paulding, Rosedale,
Walthall **9** Greenwood, Indianola,
New Albany, Pittsboro, Vicksburg
10 Batesville, Booneville, Brook-
haven, Clarksdale, Ellisville, Green-
ville, Hazlehurst, Pascagoula, Port
Gibson, Starkville, Waynesboro
11 Coffeeville, Hattiesburg, Poplar-
ville **12** Holly Springs
Missouri: 3 Ava **4** Linn **5** Eldon,
Hayti, Ladue, Rolla **6** Galena,
Neosho, Potosi **7** Hermann, Ironton,
Kennett, Linneus, Osceola, Palmyra,
Sedalia, St. Louis **8** Gallatin,
Hannibal **9** Boonville, Hartville,
Hillsboro, Maryville, Pineville, Tus-
cumbia, Warrenton **10** Kansas City,
Kirksville, Marble Hill, Marshfield,
Perryville, Saint Louis, Springfield,
Steelville, Unionville, West Plains
11 Poplar Bluff, Saint Joseph,
Warrensburg **12** Independence,
Saint Charles
Moldova: 5 Balti **7** Tighina
8 Tiraspol
Mongolia: 5 Kobdo **6** Darhan
10 Choybalsan
Montana: 5 Butte, Havre, Libby
6 Hardin, Polson **7** Bozeman
8 Billings, Missoula, Red Lodge
10 Great Falls
Montenegro: 8 Titograd
9 Podgorica
Morocco: 3 Fès **4** Safi, Salé, Taza
5 Nador, Oujda **6** Agadir, Meknès
7 Kenitra, Tangier **9** Marrakech,
Marrakesh **10** Casablanca
Mozambique: 5 Beira **7** Chimoio,
Nampula **9** Quelimane, Quilimane
Myanmar: 3 Pyu **4** Paan **5** Akyab,
Bhamo, Chauk, Katha, Magwe,
Minbu, Mogok, Tavoy **7** Bassein
8 Mandalay, Moulmein
Namibia: 5 Outjo **6** Tsumeb
8 Oshakati **12** Keetmanshoop
Nebraska: 3 Ord **5** Cozad, Omaha,
Ponca, Tryon, Wahoo **6** Elwood,

Gering, McCook, Minden, Wilber
7 Burwell, Fremont, Kearney, Kimball, Osceola, Tekamah **8** Beatrice, Fairbury, Hastings, Ogallala, Red Cloud, Schuyler, Tecumseh, Thedford **9** Fullerton, Papillion **10** Springview, Stockville **11** Grand Island, Hayes Center, North Platte, Plattsmouth
Netherlands: 3 Ede, Epe, Oss **4** Echt, Tiel, Uden **5** Aalst, Assen, Breda, Delft, Emmen, Hague, Soest, Vaals, Venlo, Vught, Weert, Weesp, Zeist **6** Arnhem **7** Haarlem, Tilburg, Utrecht **8** Enschede, Nijmegen, The Hague **9** Apeldoorn, Eindhoven, Groningen, Rotterdam, Zandvoort **10** Maastricht
Nevada: 3 Ely **4** Elko, Reno **6** Fallon, Minden, Pioche **7** Tonopah **8** Las Vegas, Lovelock **9** Goldfield, Yerington **10** Winnemucca
New Brunswick: 5 Minto **6** St. John **7** Moncton **9** Dalhousie, Saint John **10** Edmundston, Richibucto **12** Hopewell Cape, Perth Andover, Saint Andrews
Newfoundland: 5 Burin **6** Wabana **10** Mount Pearl **11** Corner Brook
New Hampshire: 5 Derry, Dover, Keene **6** Berlin, Exeter, Gorham, Nashua **7** Hanover, Laconia, Lebanon, Ossipee **8** Hinsdale, Seabrook **9** Littleton, Merrimack **10** Manchester, Portsmouth, Woodsville
New Jersey: 4 Atco, Lodi **6** Camden, Newark, Nutley, Rahway, Rumson **7** Bayonne, Cape May, Clifton, Hoboken, Paramus, Passaic, Raritan, Teaneck **8** Freehold, Metuchen, Paterson, Vauxhall, Woodbury **9** Belvidere, Bridgeton, Elizabeth, Glassboro, Lakehurst, Maplewood, Menlo Park, Montclair, Princeton, Riverside, Toms River **10** Asbury Park, Bloomfield, Cherry Hill, East Orange, Flemington, Hackensack, Jersey City, Morristown, Mount Holly, Perth Amboy, Piscataway, Plainfield, Somerville, West Orange **11** Mays Landing, South Orange **12** Atlantic City, New Brunswick **13** Palisades Park

New Mexico: 4 Taos **5** Belen, Hobbs, Raton **6** Clovis, Deming, Grants **7** Roswell, Socorro **8** Estancia, Los Lunas, Portales **9** Carrizozo, Las Cruces, Los Alamos, Lovington, Tucumcari **10** Alamogordo, Bernalillo, Fort Sumner **11** Albuquerque
New York: 4 Elma, Ovid, Troy **5** Depew, Ilion, Islip, Le Roy, Nyack, Olean, Owego, Utica **6** Attica, Cohoes, Delmar, Elmira, Hudson, Ithaca, Oneida **7** Batavia, Buffalo, Corning, Geneseo, Katonah, Mineola, Penn Yan, Suffern, Yonkers **8** Bay Shore, Cortland, Herkimer, Hyde Park, Kingston, Lockport, Mayville, Ossining, Syracuse, Valhalla **9** Greenport, Hempstead, Patchogue, Riverhead, Rochester, Scarsdale, Schoharie **10** Binghamton, Glens Falls, Haverstraw, Huntington, Lackawanna, Lake George, Lake Placid, Mamaroneck, Massapequa, Mount Kisco, Plattsburg, Rensselaer, Watervliet **11** Canajoharie, Canandaigua, Cooperstown, Farmingdale, Hudson Falls, Plattsburgh, Port Chester, Saint George, Schenectady, Southampton, Watkins Glen, White Plains **12** Lake Pleasant, Poughkeepsie **13** Mechanicville, Port Jefferson
New Zealand: 4 Hutt, Tawa **5** Levin, Taupo, Waihi **7** Dunedin, Manukau **8** Auckland **12** Christchurch
Nicaragua: 4 León **5** Boaco, Rivas **6** Masaya **7** Granada
Nigeria: 3 Aba, Ado, Ede, Ife, Ila, Iwo, Jos, Owo, Oyo **4** Kano, Ondo **5** Akure, Enugu, Gusau, Lagos, Okene, Zaria **6** Ibadan, Ilesha, Ilorin, Kaduna, Mushin, Sokoto **7** Onitsha, Oshogbo **8** Abeokuta **9** Maiduguri, Ogbomosho **12** Port Harcourt
North Carolina: 4 Dunn **5** Ayden, Elkin, Erwin, Oteen, Sylva **6** Dobson, Durham, Lenoir, Manteo, Marlon, Shelby, Winton **7** Bayboro, Brevard, Edenton, Kinston, New Bern, Newland, Roxboro, Sanford, Tarboro **8** Asheboro, Beaufort,

Gastonia, Hatteras, Snow Hill
9 Albemarle, Asheville, Charlotte, Currituck, High Point, Kitty Hawk, Louisburg, Lumberton, Morganton 10 Chapel Hill, Greensboro, Mocksville, Smithfield, Wilkesboro 11 Statesville, Yanceyville 12 Murfreesboro, Winston-Salem
North Dakota: 4 Mott 5 Cando, Fargo, Minot, Rolla 6 Amidon, Ashley, Bowman, Formon, Lakota, Linton, Medora, Mohall 8 Wahpeton, Washburn 9 Dickinson, Williston 10 Devils Lake, Grand Forks
Northern Ireland: 5 Derry, Larne, Newry, Omagh 6 Antrim, Armagh 9 Bally-mena, Coleraine, Craigavon, Dungannon 10 Ballymoney 11 Ballycastle, Downpatrick, Enniskillen, Londonderry 13 Carrickfergus
North Korea: 5 Haeju, Nampo 6 Wonsan 7 Hamhung, Kaesong, Sinuiju 8 Ch'ongjin, Kimchaek 9 P'yongyang
Northwest Territories: 6 Dawson 10 Whitehorse 11 Yellowknife
Norway: 4 Bodo 5 Hamar, Skien, Vardo 6 Bergen, Tromso 8 Kirkenes 9 Stavanger, Trondheim 10 Hammerfest 12 Kristiansand
Nova Scotia: 5 Digby 6 Pictou 7 Arichat, Baddeck 8 Port Hood 9 Dartmouth, Kentville, Lunenburg, Shelburne, Westville 10 Antigonish 11 Guysborough
Ohio: 4 Kent 5 Akron, Berea, Bryan, Carey, Eaton, Heath, Logan, Niles, Parma, Piqua, Solon, Xenia 6 Canton, Celina, Dayton, Elyria, Euclid, Kenton, Lorain, Marion, Medina, Sidney, Tiffin, Toledo 7 Ashland, Batavia, Bucyrus, Chardon, Findlay, Ironton, Oakwood, Pomeroy, Ravenna, Wauseon, Wooster 8 Conneaut, Marietta, Sandusky 9 Ashtabula, Cleveland, Coshocton, Mansfield 10 Cincinnati, Gallipolis, Wapakoneta, Zanesville 11 Chillicothe, Circleville, Millersburg, Mount Gilead, Painesville, Port Clinton 12 Steubenville 13 Bellefontaine, Cuyahoga Falls

Oklahoma: 3 Ada 4 Alva, Enid 5 Altus, Atoka, Sayre, Tulsa 6 Durant, El Reno, Guymon, Idabel, Lawton, Okemah, Poteau, Wewoka 7 Antlers, Ardmore, Cordell, Eufaula, Newkirk, Purcell, Sapulpa, Watonga 8 Anadarko, Okmulgee, Pawhuska, Sallisaw, Stilwell 9 Chickasha, Claremore, Frederick, McAlester, Wilburton 10 Stillwater, Tishomingo 11 Pauls Valley 12 Bartlesville
Oman: 3 Sur 6 Matrah 7 Salalah
Ontario: 4 Ajax, Wawa, York 6 Barrie, Guelph, Kenora, London, Oshawa, Sarnia, Simcoe 7 Cobourg, Markham, Napanee, Sudbury, Windsor 8 Brampton, Cochrane, Goderich, Hamilton, North Bay, Pembroke, Prescott 9 Brantford, Etobicoke, Kitchener, L'Original, Newmarket, North York, Owen Sound, Walkerton 10 Belleville, Brockville, Burlington, Haileybury, Parry Sound, Thunder Bay 11 Bracebridge, Fort Frances, Mississauga, Scarborough 12 Peterborough, St. Catharines
Oregon: 5 Canby, Nyssa 6 Eugene 8 Coquille, La Grande, Portland, Roseburg 9 Clackamas, Corvallis, Gold Beach, Pendleton, The Dalles, Tillamook 10 Grants Pass 12 Klamath Falls
Pakistan: 5 Bannu, Bhera, Kasur, Kohat 6 Gujrat, Lahore, Mardan, Multan, Quetta, Sukkur 7 Karachi, Sialkot 8 Lyallpur, Peshawar, Sargodha 9 Hyderabad 10 Bahawalpur, Faisalabad, Gujranwala, Rawalpindi
Paraguay: 3 Itá 4 Yuty 5 Luque, Pilar 7 Caacupé, Caazapa 9 Paraguarí 10 San Lorenzo
Papua New Guinea: 3 Lae 10 Mount Hagen, Popondetta
Pennsylvania: 4 Erie, York 5 Avoca, Darby, Muncy, Paoli 6 Easton 7 Altoona, Bedford, Clarion, Hanover, Hershey, Latrobe, Reading, Ridgway, Sunbury 8 Carlisle, Edinboro, Hazleton, Montrose, Scranton, Somerset 9 Allentown, Ebensburg, Honesdale, Jim Thorpe, Lancaster,

Lewisburg, Lock Haven, Meadville, New Castle, Wellsboro **10** Bloomsburg, Brookville, Carbondale, Clearfield, Gettysburg, Greensburg, Huntingdon, Kittanning, McKeesport, Middleburg, Pittsburgh, Pottsville, Waynesburg **11** Stroudsburg, Valley Forge, West Chester, Wilkes-Barre **12** Philadelphia, State College, Williamsport

Peru: 3 Ica, Ilo **5** Ancon, Cuzco, Jauja, Junin, Lamas, Pisco, Piura, Tacna **6** Callao **8** Arequipa, Chiclayo, Chimbote, Trujillo

Philippines: 3 Iba **4** Bago, Bais, Boac, Bogo, Cebu, Daet, Jolo, Lipa, Mati **5** Basco, Bulan, Cadiz, Danao, Davao, Digos, Gapan, Gubat, Iriga, Laoag, Ormoc, Pasay, Silay, Tagum, Vigan **6** Butuan, Iloilo, Quezon **7** Angeles, Bacolod, Basilan **8** Batangas, Calbayog, Caloocan **9** Zamboanga **10** Quezon City

Poland: 4 Lodz, Nysa, Pila, Zary **5** Bytom, Bytow, Chelm, Kutno, Lomza, Luban, Lubin, Plock, Radom, Torun, Tychy **6** Elblag, Gdansk, Gdynia, Kalisz, Kielce, Krakow, Lublin, Poznan, Rybnik, Zabrze **7** Chorzow, Dabrowa, Gliwice, Rzeszow, Wroclaw **8** Gornicza, Katowice, Szczecin **9** Bialystok, Bydgoszcz, Sosnowiec, Walbrzych **11** Czestochowa

Portugal: 4 Faro **5** Braga, Evora, Porto **6** Almada, Oporto, Queluz **7** Amadora **8** Barreiro, Santarém

Prince Edward Island: 10 Summerside

Puerto Rico: 5 Ponce **6** Caguas **7** Arecibo, Bayamón **8** Carolina, Guaynabo, Mayagüez

Quebec: 4 Alma **5** Amqui, Anjou, Gaspé, Laval, Lévis, Magog, Percé, Rouyn **6** Granby, Ham Sud, Matane, Ste.-Foy, Val d'Or **7** Bedford, Lachute **8** Beauport, Cap Santé, Joliette, Lac Brome, Maniwaki, Montreal, Rimouski, Roberval, Sept-Iles, Waterloo **9** Bécancour, Cookshire, Iberville, Inverness, La Malbaie, La Prairie, Longueuil, Montmagny, Sainte-Foy,

Saint Jean, Tadoussac, Vaudreuil **10** Baie-Comeau, Chicoutimi **11** Beauharnois, Louiseville, Mont-Laurier **12** Charlesbourg **13** Trois-Rivières

Rhode Island: 7 Newport, Rumford, Warwick **8** Apponaug, Coventry, Cranston, Tiverton, Westerly **9** Hopkinton, Pawtucket **10** Woonsocket **12** Narragansett, West Kingston

Romania: 3 Dej **4** Aiud, Arad, Cluj, Deva, Husi, Iasi **5** Anina, Bacau, Buzau, Carei, Lugoj, Sibiu, Turda **6** Braila, Brasov, Galati, Oradea **7** Craiova **8** Ploiesti **9** Constanta, Timisoara **10** Cluj-Napoca

Russia: 3 Kem, Ufa **4** Inta, Luga, Okha, Omsk, Orel, Orsk, Perm, Tula, Tura, Zima **5** Aldan, Artem, Chita, Ishim, Kansk, Kazan, Lysva, Onega, Penza, Pskov, Rzhev, Salsk, Serov, Sochi, Sokol, Tomsk, Tulun, Volsk, Yurga **6** Bratsk, Grozny, Kaluga, Kovrov, Kurgan, Rostov, Ryazan, Samara, Syzran, Tambov, Tyumen, Vyborg, Yelets **7** Irkutsk, Ivanovo, Izhevsk, Kalinin, Kolomna, Lipetsk, Magadan, Norilsk, Rybinsk, Saransk, Saratov, Shakhty, Vologda, Yakutsk, Zhdanov **8** Belgorod, Kemerovo, Kostroma, Murmansk, Nakhodka, Novgorod, Orenburg, Smolensk, Taganrog, Vladimir, Volzhski, Voronezh **9** Archangel, Astrakhan, Berezniki, Krasnodar, Serpukhov, Stavropol, Ulyanovsk, Volgograd, Yaroslavl **10** Cheboksary, Dzerzhinsk **11** Arkhangel'sk, Chelyabinsk, Cheremkhovo, Cherepovets, Kaliningrad, Krasnoyarsk, Novosibirsk, St. Petersburg, Vladivostok **13** Yekaterinburg

Saskatchewan: 8 Moose Jaw **9** Saskatoon **10** Assiniboia **12** Prince Albert

Saudi Arabia: 4 Jauf, Taif **5** Jedda, Jidda, Mecca, Tabuk **6** Jeddah, Jiddah, Medina **8** Buraydah

Scotland: 3 Ayr **4** Alva, Caol, Dyce, Oban **5** Alloa, Annan, Beith, Cowie, Cupar, Dalry, Ellon, Kelso, Kelty, Largs, Leven, Nairn, Patna, Troon

6 Dundee 7 Glasgow, Paisley
8 Aberdeen, Greenock, Hamilton
9 Inverness, Lockerbie 10 Kilmar-
nock 11 Dunfermline, John o'Groats
Senegal: 5 Thiès 6 Kaolak
7 Kaolack 10 Saint-Louis
Serbia: 3 Bor, Nis, Pec 4 Ruma
5 Becej, Cacak, Pirot, Sabac, Senta,
Vrbas, Vrsac 7 Novi Sad 8 Subotica
10 Kragujevac
Slovakia: 5 Nitra 6 Kosice, Presov,
Zilina
Slovenia: 4 Bled 5 Celje, Koper,
Kranj 7 Maribor
Somalia: 3 Eil 5 Afgoi, Alula, Brava,
Burao, Marka, Obbia 7 Berbera,
Kismayu 8 Hargeysa, Kismaayo
South Africa: 5 Brits, Ceres, De
Aar, Nigel, Paarl 6 Benoni, Durban,
Soweto 7 Springs 8 Boksburg,
Mafeking 9 Germiston, Kimberley,
Ladysmith, Uitenhage 10 East Lon-
don 11 Krugersdorp, Vereeniging
12 Johannesburg 13 Port Elizabeth
South Carolina: 5 Aiken, Cayce,
Saxon 6 Sumter 7 Gaffney, Lau-
rens, Manning, Pickens 8 Beaufort,
Newberry, Rock Hill, Walhalla
9 Abbeville, Allendale, Greenwood,
Kingstree, McCormick, Winnsboro
10 Charleston, Darlington, Green-
ville, Hilton Head, Orangeburg, Wal-
terboro 11 Bishopville, Myrtle
Beach, Spartanburg 12 Moncks
Corner
South Dakota: 7 Sturgis, Yankton
8 Deadwood, Elk Point 9 Brookings,
Rapid City 10 Sioux Falls
South Korea: 3 Iri 4 Yosu 5 Cheju,
Masan, Mokpo, Pusan, Suwon,
Taegu, Ulson, Wonju 6 Chinju,
Chonju, Inchon, Kunsan, Taejon
7 Kwangju
Spain: 4 Adra, Baza, Elda, Jaca,
Jaén, León, Loja, Lugo, Olot, Reus,
Vich, Vigo 5 Albox, Alcoy, Alora,
Baena, Cádiz, Ceuta, Cieza, Ecija,
Eibar, Elche, Gijón, Ibiza, Jodar,
Lorca, Mahon, Oliva, Osuna, Palma,
Ronda, Soria, Ubeda 6 Bilbao,
Burgos, Cuenca, Huelva, Lérida,
Málaga, Mérida, Murcia, Oviedo,

Toledo 7 Almadén, Almería, Cáceres,
Córdoba, Durango, Granada, Sego-
via, Sevilla, Seville, Tarrasa, Vitoria
8 Albacete, Alicante, La Coruña,
Pamplona, Sabadell, Valencia,
Zaragoza 9 Algeciras, Barcelona,
Salamanca, Santander, Saragossa,
Tarragona 10 Hospitalet, Valladolid
12 San Sebastián
Sri Lanka: 5 Galle, Kandy 6 Jaffna
8 Dehiwala, Moratuwa 10 Batticaloa
Sudan: 4 Juba 5 Kodok, Kosti 7 El
Obeid, Kassala 8 Omdurman
Sweden: 4 Lund, Täby, Umea
5 Falun, Gävle, Lulea, Malmö, Växjö,
Visby 6 Orebro 7 Uppsala 8 Göte-
borg, Halmstad 9 Jönköping,
Linköping 12 Kristianstad
Switzerland: 3 Zug 4 Biel, Chur,
Sion, Thun 5 Aarau, Arbon, Baden,
Basel, Koniz 6 Geneva, Lugano,
St. Gall, Zürich 7 Lucerne, Zermatt
8 Lausanne, Montreux, St. Moritz
9 Neuchâtel, Saint Gall 11 Saint
Moritz
Syria: 4 Hama, Homs 5 Idlib
6 Aleppo, Tartus 7 Latakia
Taiwan: 5 Chia-i 6 T'ai-nan 7 Chi-
lung, Hsin-chu 8 Feng-shan, Pan-
ch'iao, San-ch'ung, T'ai-chung
9 Kao-hsiung
Tanzania: 5 Lindi, Mbeya, Tanga
6 Arusha, Dodoma, Kigoma, Mwanza
8 Morogoro, Zanzibar 11 Dar es
Salaam
Tennessee: 5 Alcoa, Erwin, Rives
6 Loudon, Ripley, Selmer 7 Memphis,
Waverly 8 Gallatin, Oak Ridge,
Rutledge, Tazewell, Wartburg
9 Dandridge, Dyersburg, Jacksboro,
Jonesboro, Knoxville, Lewisburg,
Maryville 10 Cookeville, Crossville,
Somerville, Waynesboro 11 Blount-
ville, Chattanooga, Clarksville,
Greeneville, McMinnville, Rogers-
ville, Sevierville, Shelbyville 12 Eli-
zabethton, Lawrenceburg, Madison-
ville, Murfreesboro
Texas: 4 Azle, Waco 5 Alvin,
Anson, Baird, Bowie, Bryan, Clute,
Cuero, Emory, Ennis, Freer, Hondo,
Marfa, Mexia, Olney, Pampa, Pecos,

Pharr, Plano, Sealy, Vidor, Wylie
6 Belton, Boerne, Bonham, Burnet,
Conroe, Dallas, Del Rio, Denton,
El Paso, Gilmer, Goliad, Jayton,
Lamesa, Laredo, Linden, Lufkin,
Odessa, Seguin, Sinton, Uvalde
7 Abilene, Anahuac, Bandera,
Bastrop, Brenham, Denison, Dimmitt,
Houston, Kaufman, Kountze, Lub-
bock, Midland, Wharton **8** Amarillo,
Angleton, Beaumont, Beeville,
Cleburne, Eastland, Giddings,
Gonzales, Granbury, Groveton,
Hemphill, La Grange, Lampasas,
Longview, McKinney, Monahans,
Montague, Pearsall, Rockwall,
Stinnett **9** Arlington, Ballinger,
Bellville, Big Spring, Brownwood,
Corsicana, Crosbyton, Eagle Pass,
Fort Worth, Galveston, Groesbeck,
Henrietta, Hillsboro, Kerrville, Level-
land, Palo Pinto, Plainview, San
Angelo, San Marcos, Woodville
10 Brownfield, Coldspring, Gates-
ville, Jourdanton, Kingsville, Port
Arthur, Port Lavaca, San Antonio,
Sweetwater, Waxahachie **11** Browns-
ville, Floresville, Littlefield, Nacog-
doches, Weatherford **12** Brecken-
ridge, Daingerfield, Fort Stockton,
New Braunfels, Raymondville,
Stephenville, Wichita Falls **13** Corpus
Christi, Hallettsville
Thailand: 3 Nan, Tak **5** Phrae, Roi
Et, Surin **8** Songkhla **9** Chiang Mai
10 Nonthaburi
Tunisia: 4 Béja, Sfax **5** Gabès,
Gafsa, Susah **6** Ariana **7** Bizerte,
Safaqis
Turkey: 5 Adana, Bursa, Izmir,
Konya, Sivas **6** Edirne, Erzurm,
Samsun **7** Antakya, Antalya, Anti-
och, Kayseri, Malatya **8** Istanbul
9 Eskisehir, Gallipoli, Gaziantep
10 Diyarbakir
Turkmenistan: 8 Nebit Dag
9 Chardzhou, Dashhowuz
Uganda: 5 Jinja, Mbale **7** Entebbe
Ukraine: 4 Lviv, Lvov, Sumy
5 Lutsk, Rovno, Yalta **6** Odessa
7 Donetsk, Kharkiv, Kharkov, Kher-
son, Luhansk, Poltava **8** Mariupol,

Vinnitsa, Zhitomir **9** Chernigov,
Chernobyl, Krivoy Rog, Krivyy Rih,
Nikolayev **10** Kirovograd, Sebasto-
pol, Sevastopol, Simferopol, Zaporo-
zhye
United Arab Emirates: 5 Ajman,
Dubai **6** Dubayy **8** Fujairah,
Fujayrah
Uruguay: 4 Melo **5** Minas, Pando,
Rocha, Salto **6** Rivera **8** Paysandú
10 Las Piedras
Utah: 3 Loa **4** Lehi, Orem **5** Manti,
Ogden, Provo, Sandy **6** Dugway,
Tooele **7** Parowan **8** Duchesne
9 Coalville **11** Saint George
Uzbekistan: 5 Nukus **6** Kokand
7 Bukhara, Fergana **8** Andizhan,
Chirchik, Namangan **9** Samarkand,
Samarqand
Venezuela: 4 Coro **5** Anaco, Cagua
6 Cumaná, Mérida, Petare **7** Cabi-
mas, Guayana, Maracay **8** Valencia
9 Maracaibo **12** Barquisimeto, San
Cristóbal
Vermont: 5 Barre **7** Rutland **8** St.
Albans **10** Bennington, Burlington,
Middlebury **11** Brattleboro, Saint
Albans, St. Johnsbury
Vietnam: 3 Hue **4** Vinh **5** Da Lat,
Hoi An, My Tho **6** Can Tho, Da
Nang, Saigon **7** Bien Hoa, Narr
Dinh, Qui Nhon **8** Haiphong, Nha
Trang, Thanh Hoa **9** Long Xuyᥫ n
Virginia: 4 Tabb **5** Luray **6** Grundy
7 Accomac, Boydton, Fairfax, Hamp-
ton, New Kent, Norfolk **8** Abingdon,
Culpeper, Leesburg, Manassas,
Montross, No⸀oway, Poquoson,
Powhatan, Rustburg, Tazewell
9 Arlington, Clintwood, Courtland,
Dinwiddie, Eastville, Farmville,
Fincastle, Goochland, Lunenburg,
Lynchburg **10** Alexandria, Appomat-
tox, Berryville, Front Royal, Hillsville,
Jonesville, King George, Lovingston,
Pearisburg, Portsmouth, Rocky
Mount, Wytheville **11** Heaths-
ville, King William, Newport News
12 Chesterfield, Prince George,
Spotsylvania, Williamsburg
Wales: 4 Rhyl **5** Neath, Risca,
Tenby, Tywyn **7** Cardiff, Cwmbran,

Denbigh, Harlech, Newport, Swansea **8** Aberdare, Bridgend **10** Caernarfon, Caernarvon, Llangollen **11** Aberystwyth
Washington: **4** Omak **5** Brier, Camas, Kelso, Lacey, Pasco, Selah **6** Asotin, Colfax, Tacoma, Yakima **7** Ephrata, Everett, Prosser, Redmond, Seattle, Spokane **8** Bellevue, Chehalis, Colville, Okanogan **9** Montesano, Ritzville, Snohomish, Wenatchee **10** Bellingham, Coupeville, Ellensburg, Goldendale, Walla Walla, Waterville **11** Port Angeles, Port Orchard **12** Friday Harbor, Port Townsend
West Virginia: **5** Nitro, Welch **6** Elkins, Hamlin, Hinton, Keyser, Ripley **7** Beckley, Weirton **8** Kingwood, Philippi, Wheeling **9** Pineville, Wellsburg **10** Buckhannon, Clarksburg, Huntington, Moorefield, Morgantown, Petersburg, Williamson **11** Harrisville, Martinsburg, Moundsville, Parkersburg **12** Harpers Ferry, Summersville **13** New Cumberland, Point Pleasant
Wisconsin: **4** Kiel **5** Ripon, Tomah **6** Antigo, Barron, Oconto, Racine, Wausau **7** Baraboo, Chilton, Elkhorn, Hayward, Kenosha, Mauston, Merrill, Oshkosh, Shawano, Viraqua, Waupaca, Wautoma **8** Appleton, Green Bay, Kewaunee, La Crosse, Montello, Phillips, Washburn, Waukesha, West Bend **9** Eau Claire, Ellsworth, Fond du Lac, Green Lake, Ladysmith, Manitowoc, Marinette, Menomonie, Milwaukee, Sheboygan, Shell Lake, Wauwatosa, West Allis, Whitehall **10** Balsam Lake, Darlington, Dodgeville, Eagle River, Grantsburg, Janesville **11** Neillsville, Sturgeon Bay **12** Stevens Point, Whitefish Bay
Wyoming: **6** Casper, Lander **7** Laramie, Rawlins **8** Gillette, Kemmerer, Sheridan **10** Green River **11** Rock Springs
Yemen: **4** Aden **5** Taizz **7** Hodeida, Mukalla **8** Hudaydah
Zambia: **5** Kabwe, Kitwe, Mansa,

Mbala, Mongu, Ndola **6** Kasama **7** Chipata
Zimbabwe: **5** Gweru **6** Hwange, Kadoma, Kwekwe, Mutare, Umtali **7** Mashava **8** Bulawayo, Masvingo

civet
3 cat
Madagascar: **5** fossa
relative: **5** genet

civic
5 urban **6** public, social **8** communal, national, societal **9** municipal

civil
6 polite, public, seemly, urbane **7** affable, cordial, courtly, genteel, refined **8** decorous, gracious, mannerly, national, obliging, wellbred **9** courteous, political **10** diplomatic **12** well-mannered **13** accommodating

civility
6 comity **7** amenity, decency, decorum, manners **8** courtesy **9** etiquette, gentility, propriety **10** politeness **11** correctness

civilization
7 culture

civilized
6 decent, proper, urbane **7** genteel, refined **8** decorous, mannerly, tasteful **9** courteous **10** cultivated **13** sophisticated

civil rights
leader: **4** King (Martin Luther)
organization: **4** ACLU, CORE **5** NAACP

Civil War
admiral: **8** Buchanan (Franklin), Farragut (David)
battle: **6** Shiloh **7** Bull Run **8** Antietam, Manassas **9** Mobile Bay, Nashville, Vicksburg **10** Cold Harbor, Gettysburg **11** Chattanooga, Chickamauga
general: **3** Lee (Robert E.) **4** Hood (John Bell), Pope (John) **5** Bragg (Braxton), Buell (Don Carlos),

Ewell (Richard Stoddart), Grant (Ulysses S.), Meade (George), Sykes (George) **6** Hooker (Joseph) **7** Forrest (Nathan Bedford), Jackson (Thomas "Stonewall"), Sherman (Thomas West, William Tecumseh) **8** Burnside (Ambrose), Johnston (Albert Sidney, Joseph Eggleston), Sheridan (Philip) **9** McClellan (George Brinton), Rosecrans (William), Schofield (John) **10** Beauregard (Pierre)

ship: 7 Monitor **9** Merrimack

civil wrong

4 tort

clabber

5 curds

clack

3 gab, jaw, yak **4** blab, chat **5** prate **6** babble, cackle, gabble, gossip, jabber, rattle **7** blabber, chatter, clatter, palaver, prattle **9** yakety-yak

clad

4 face, side, skin **5** dress, faced **6** clothe, decked, garbed, outfit **7** attired, clothed, covered, dressed, overlay, sheathe **8** costumed, overlaid, sheathed **9** outfitted

claim

4 call, dibs, hold, plea, take **5** argue, exact, right, share, stake, title **6** adduce, allege, assert, defend, demand, insist **7** advance, call for, contend, declare, justify, profess, purport, require, solicit, warrant **8** interest, maintain **9** assertion, challenge, postulate, privilege **10** allegation, birthright **11** affirmation, declaration, prerogative, requisition **12** protestation

clairvoyance

3 ESP **7** insight **9** intuition, telepathy **10** sixth sense **11** penetration, second sight **12** precognition

clairvoyant

4 seer **5** sibyl **7** diviner **8** telepath **10** soothsayer

clam

4 buck **5** razor **6** dollar, quahog **7** bivalve, coquina, geoduck, mollusc, mollusk, smacker, steamer **11** cherrystone

genus: 3 Mya

clamant

4 dire **6** crying, urgent **7** blatant, burning, exigent **8** pressing **9** insistent **10** compelling, imperative

clamber

5 climb, crawl, scale, swarm **8** scrabble, scramble, struggle

clammy

4 cool, dank, damp **5** close, moist, slimy **6** sticky

clamor

3 cry, din **4** bawl, roar, to-do **5** babel, hoo-ha, noise **6** bellow, demand, hubbub, jangle, outcry, racket, ruckus, tumult, uproar **7** agitate, dispute, ferment, protest, turmoil **8** brouhaha, shouting **9** agitation, commotion **10** hullabaloo, hurlyburly **11** pandemonium

clamorous

5 noisy, vocal **6** crying, shrill, urgent **7** blatant, exigent, raucous, voluble **8** strident, vehement **9** insistent **10** boisterous, imperative, tumultuous, vociferous **11** importunate **12** obstreperous

clamp

4 grip, hold, vise **5** clasp, grasp **6** clench, clinch, clutch, fasten, secure **7** grapple

clamshell

6 bucket **7** grapple

clan

3 mob **4** camp, folk, ring, sept **5** cabal, house, stock, tribe **6** circle, clique, family **7** coterie, kindred, lineage **9** camarilla

emblem: 5 totem

Clancy novel

12 Patriot Games **13** Sum of All Fears (The) **17** Hunt for Red October (The) **21** Clear and Present Danger

clandestine
6 covert, secret, sneaky 7 furtive,
illicit 8 hush-hush, stealthy 10 undercover, under wraps 11 underhanded
12 hugger-mugger, illegitimate
13 surreptitious, under-the-table

clang
3 cry, din 4 ding, peal, slam 6 jangle
8 ding-dong

clangor
3 din 5 noise 6 clamor, jangle,
racket, rattle, tumult, uproar 7 clatter, ringing 9 stridency 13 reverberation

clangorous
5 noisy 7 booming, rackety, ringing
8 clattery, sonorous 9 deafening
12 earsplitting

clap
3 pat 4 bang, blow, boom, slam, slap
5 blast, burst, crack, crash, whack
6 strike 7 applaud 8 applause

claptrap
4 bull, bunk 5 cheap, hokum, showy,
trash 6 bunkum, drivel, humbug,
vulgar 7 baloney, eyewash, hogwash, twaddle 8 malarkey, nonsense 9 poppycock 10 balderdash,
flapdoodle

Clara Bow
6 It girl

Clare Boothe _____
4 Luce

claret
3 red 4 wine 8 Bordeaux

clarify
5 clean, clear 6 define, filter, purify
7 analyze, cleanse, clear up, explain,
resolve 8 simplify 9 elucidate
10 illuminate 13 straighten out

clarion
5 clear 7 ringing, rousing, trumpet
8 gleaming, stirring 9 brilliant

clarity
6 purity 8 accuracy, lucidity 9 clearness, limpidity, precision 10 exactitude, simplicity 12 transparency

Clarke novel
10 Earthlight 19 Fountains of Paradise (The)

clash
4 bump, jolt 5 brawl, crash, melee,
set-to, smash 6 battle, fracas,
impact, jangle 7 collide 8 conflict,
mismatch, skirmish 9 collision,
encounter 10 engagement 11 embroilment

clasp
3 hug, pin 4 clip, grip, hold 5 clamp,
grasp, press 6 brooch, buckle,
clench, clinch, clutch, enfold 7 embrace, grapple, squeeze 10 chatelaine

class
3 ilk 4 hold, kind, mark, part, rank,
rate, sort, tier, type 5 allot, brand,
caste, gauge, genre, genus, grade,
grain, group, judge, order, score,
stamp, style 6 assess, assign, assort, branch, course, league, nature,
reckon, regard, stripe 7 bracket,
caliber, quality, section, species,
variety 8 appraise, category, consider, division, evaluate, grouping,
separate 10 categorize, pigeonhole
11 description 12 denomination
middle: 11 bourgeoisie
school: 6 junior, senior 8 freshman
9 sophomore
working: 11 proletariat

classic
5 ideal, model, prime 7 capital,
typical, vintage 8 champion, enduring, standard, superior, top-notch
9 authentic, canonical, classical,
excellent, exemplary, memorable,
tradition 10 magnum opus, masterwork 11 chef d'oeuvre, masterpiece,
tour de force, traditional 12 paradigmatic, prototypical 13 authoritative

classical
4 pure 5 Attic, Greek, ideal, Latin,
Roman 7 ancient, fitting, Grecian,
perfect, typical, vintage 8 Hellenic,
standard, sterling 9 canonical,

exemplary **10** consummate **11** traditional **13** authoritative

classical musician

4 Böhm (Karl), Hess (Myra), Lind (Jenny), Muti (Riccardo), Pons (Lily), Shaw (Robert) **5** Arrau (Claudio), Biggs (E. Power), Borge (Victor), Boult (Adrian), Davis (Colin), du Pré (Jacqueline), Gould (Glenn), Masur (Kurt), Mehta (Zubin), Melba (Nellie), Ozawa (Seiji), Patti (Adelina), Pinza (Ezio), Price (Leontyne), Ramey (Samuel), Sills (Beverly), Stern (Isaac), Szell (George) **6** Abbado (Claudio), Battle (Kathleen), Boulez (Pierre), Callas (Maria), Caruso (Enrico), Casals (Pablo), Galway (James), Levine (James), Maazel (Lorin), Midori, Norman (Jessye), Peters (Roberta), Previn (André), Rampal (Jean-Pierre), Rattle (Simon), Reiner (Fritz), Serkin (Peter, Rudolf), Terfel (Bryn), Tucker (Richard), Upshaw (Dawn), Walter (Bruno) **7** Bartoli (Cecilia), Beecham (Thomas), Bocelli (Andrea), Brendel (Alfred), Cliburn (Van), Corelli (Franco), Domingo (Plácido), Farrell (Eileen), Fiedler (Arthur), Fleming (Renée), Glennie (Evelyn), Haitink (Bernard), Heifetz (Jascha), Karajan (Herbert von), Menuhin (Yehudi), Nilsson (Birgit), Ormandy (Eugene), Perlman (Itzhak), Pollini (Maurizio), Sargent (Malcolm), Segovia (Andrés), Tebaldi (Renata) **8** Anderson (Marian), Argerich (Martha), Bergonzi (Carlo), Carreras (José), Flagstad (Kirsten), Horowitz (Vladimir), Kreisler (Fritz), Marriner (Neville), Oistrakh (David), Schnabel (Artur), Te Kanawa (Kiri), Zukerman (Pinchas) **9** Barenboim (Daniel), Bernstein (Leonard), Chaliapin (Feodor), Klemperer (Otto), Landowska (Wanda), Pavarotti (Luciano), Stokowski (Leopold), Toscanini (Arturo) **10** Rubinstein (Arthur), Sutherland (Joan), Tetrazzini (Luisa) **11** Furtwängler (Wilhelm), Kostelanetz (André), Schwarzkopf (Elisabeth) **12** Rostropovich (Mstislav)

classification

4 sort, type **5** genre, genus, grade, order **6** family, phylum, rating **7** sorting, species **8** category, division, grouping, ordering, taxonomy, typology **11** arrangement, cataloguing

classified

6 secret, sorted **7** divided, ordered **9** top secret **11** categorized **12** confidential

classify

4 rank, rate, sort **5** grade, group **6** assort **7** arrange **9** break down **10** categorize, pigeonhole

classy

4 chic, tony **5** swank **6** modish **7** dashing, elegant, refined, stylish **8** gracious, tasteful, well-bred **9** courteous **11** fashionable

clatter

4 to-do **6** clamor, hubbub, pother, rattle, tumult, uproar **7** turmoil **9** commotion **10** hurly-burly **Scottish: 7** brattle

clattery

5 noisy **7** rackety **10** clangorous

Claudia's husband

6 Pilate

Claudio's beloved

4 Hero

Claudius

nephew: 6 Hamlet
predecessor: 8 Caligula
slayer: 6 Hamlet **9** Agrippina
successor: 4 Nero
wife: 8 Gertrude **9** Agrippina

Clavell novel

6 Gai-Jin, Shogun, Tai-Pan **7** King Rat

claw

3 dig **4** nail, rake, tear **5** chela, talon, uncus **6** scrape **7** scratch

clay

3 cob **4** loam, lute, marl **5** argil, brick, earth, gault, loess, ocher, ochre **6** kaolin **10** terra-cotta
baked: 4 tile **5** adobe, brick

box: 6 saggar, sagger
building: 5 adobe
ceramic: 10 terra-cotta
constituent: 6 silica 8 feldspar,
silicate 9 kaolinite
in glass: 4 tear
made of: 7 fictile
porcelain: 6 kaolin
red: 8 laterite
rock: 5 shale
tobacco pipe: 6 dudeen
watery mixture: 4 slip
white: 6 kaolin

clay pigeon
6 target

clean
4 dust, fair, pure, swab, tidy, wash,
wipe 5 bathe, fresh, groom, purge,
scour, scrub, sweep 6 bright, chaste,
decent, neaten, purify, spruce,
vacuum, washed 7 clarify, launder,
sinless 8 hygienic, innocent, sanitary, sanitize, spotless, unsoiled
9 blameless, faultless, sparkling,
stainless, undefiled, unsullied,
untainted, wholesome 10 antiseptic, immaculate 11 unblemished
12 spick-and-span

clean-cut
4 trim 7 defined, precise 8 definite,
explicit, specific 9 wholesome
10 definitive 11 categorical, unambiguous, well-groomed

cleaner
see **cleanser**

cleanhanded
8 innocent 9 blameless

clean-limbed
4 trim 7 shapely 8 handsome
10 statuesque

cleanse
4 wash 5 purge, rinse 6 purify,
refine 7 clarify, launder 8 lustrate,
sanitize 9 disinfect, expurgate,
sterilize

cleanser
3 lye 4 soap 9 detergent 10 antiseptic 12 disinfectant

cleansing
7 purging 8 ablution 9 catharsis,
purgation 10 lustration 11 expurgation 12 purification

clear
3 get, net, pay, rid, win 4 earn, fade,
fair, fine, free, gain, leap, lose, make,
pure, well 5 close, empty, exact,
fully, glean, lucid, overt, pay up,
plain, quite, repay, solve, stark,
sunny 6 acquit, gather, hurdle,
limpid, obtain, pay off, pick up,
secure, settle, simple, square,
vacant, vacate, vanish 7 absolve,
acquire, approve, audible, clarify,
clarion, cleanse, clean up, defined,
evident, explain, improve, legible,
obvious, precise, rule out, satisfy,
utterly 8 apparent, definite, distinct,
entirely, explicit, knowable, luminous,
manifest, palpable, pleasant, scot-
free, shake off, surmount 9 authorize, cloudless, discharge, eliminate,
elucidate, evaporate, exculpate,
exonerate, extricate, liquidate,
meliorate, negotiate, perfectly,
unblurred, unclouded, vindicate
10 ameliorate, completely, illuminate,
illustrate, openhanded, see-through
11 conspicuous, disentangle, open-
and-shut, perceptible, translucent,
transparent, unambiguous, unequivocal 12 recognizable, unmistakable
13 uncomplicated

clearance
3 gap 4 sale 7 go-ahead, removal
8 approval 10 green light, permission 13 authorization

clear away
6 remove 7 take out

clear-cut
5 crisp, exact, plain 7 decided,
precise 8 definite, distinct, explicit,
manifest 10 definitive, pronounced,
undisputed 11 categorical, indubitable, unambiguous, unequivocal
12 unquestioned

clear-eyed
6 astute 9 judicious, observant
10 discerning, perceptive

clearheaded
4 calm, cool 10 perceptive

clearing
3 gap 5 field, glade 7 opening
10 settlement

clear out
5 scoot, scram, split 6 beat it, begone, bug off, decamp, depart 7 buzz
off, skiddoo, take off, vamoose
8 shove off 9 drive away, skedaddle
10 hightail it

clear-sightedness
6 acuity, acumen 8 keenness, sagacity 10 astuteness, shrewdness
11 discernment, penetration, percipience 12 perspicacity

clear up
5 solve 6 cipher, unfold 7 clarify,
dope out, explain, resolve, unravel
8 decipher 9 elucidate, figure out
10 illuminate

clearwing
4 moth

cleat
4 bitt 5 chock 6 batten 7 bollard,
dolphin

cleavage
4 rift 5 chasm, cleft, split 6 schism
7 fissure 8 crevasse 9 splitting

cleave
3 cut, hew 4 chop, join, link, rend,
rive 5 carve, cling, sever, slice, split,
stick, unite 6 adhere, divide, sunder
7 combine 8 dissever, separate

cleft
3 gap 4 rift 5 chasm, chink, clove,
crack, gorge, gulch, split 6 clough,
ravine, schism 7 crevice, fissure
8 cleavage

clemency
5 grace, mercy 6 lenity 7 caritas,
charity 8 kindness, lenience,
leniency, mildness 9 tolerance
10 compassion, gentleness, indulgence, sufferance, toleration 11 forbearance

clement
4 fair, kind, mild 5 balmy 6 benign,
humane, kindly 7 lenient 8 merciful,
tolerant 9 indulgent 10 benevolent,
charitable, forbearing 13 compassionate

clench
4 grip, grit, hold 5 clamp, clasp,
grasp 6 clutch 7 grapple

Cleopatra
attendant: 4 Iras 8 Charmian
brother: 7 Ptolemy
husband: 7 Ptolemy
killer: 3 asp
lover: 6 Antony (Marc), Caesar
(Julius) 7 Anthony (Mark)
river: 4 Nile

Cleopatra's Needle
7 obelisk

clepsydra
9 timepiece 10 water clock

clerestory
7 gallery

clergy
7 canonry 8 ministry 9 churchmen,
diaconate, pastorate, rabbinate
10 priesthood 11 cardinalate 13 ec-
clesiastics

clergyman
5 clerk, padre, vicar 6 bishop,
cleric, curate, divine, father, parson,
pastor, priest, rector 7 dominie,
prelate 8 chaplain, clerical, minister,
preacher, reverend, shepherd,
sky pilot 9 churchman, pulpiteer
10 evangelist, missionary, sermonizer 12 ecclesiastic
American: 4 Hale (Edward Everett),
King (Martin Luther, Thomas Starr)
5 Eliot (John), Moody (Dwight),
Stone (Barton Warren), Weems
(Parson) 6 Dwight (Timothy), Finney
(Charles), Graham (Billy), Holmes
(John Haynes), Hooker (Thomas),
Mather (Cotton, Increase, Richard),
Merton (Thomas), Parker (Samuel,
Theodore), Sunday (Billy), Taylor
(Edward, Graham, Nathaniel William)
7 Beecher (Henry Ward, Lyman),

Edwards (Jonathan), Harvard (John), Russell (Charles Taze) **10** Muhlenberg (Frederick Augustus, Henry Melchior, John Peter Gabriel)
English: 4 Ward (Nathaniel, Seth, William George) **5** Donne (John), Paley (William), Smith (Henry "Silver-Tongued," John "The Sebaptist," Sidney) **6** Cotton (John), Fuller (Andrew, Thomas), Taylor (Jeremy, Rowland), Wesley (Charles, John) **7** Cranmer (Thomas), Parsons (Robert) **8** Kingsley (Charles) **10** Whitefield (George)
home: 5 manse **6** priory **7** rectory **8** vicarage **9** monastery, parsonage
traveling: 12 circuit rider

cleric
see **clergyman**

clerisy
8 literati **10** illuminati **13** intellectuals

clerk
7 cashier **8** salesman **9** secretary **10** accountant, bookkeeper **11** salesperson **12** stenographer

clever
3 apt, sly **4** able, deft, good, keen **5** adept, alert, canny, funny, handy, quick, savvy, sharp, smart, witty **6** adroit, astute, brainy, bright, crafty, expert, shrewd, tricky **7** amusing, capable, cunning, knowing, skilled **8** fanciful, humorous, pleasing, skillful, talented **9** competent, dexterous, ingenious **10** proficient **11** intelligent, quick-witted, resourceful **12** entertaining

cliché
3 saw **6** truism **7** bromide **8** banality, buzzword, chestnut **9** platitude **10** shibboleth, stereotype **11** commonplace

clichéd
5 banal, bland, musty, stale, tired, trite, vapid **6** old-hat **7** humdrum, insipid, worn-out **8** bromidic, shopworn, timeworn **9** hackneyed **10** pedestrian, unoriginal **11** stereotyped **13** platitudinous, unimaginative

click
3 fit **4** snap, tick, work **5** agree, match **6** go over, pan out **7** come off, succeed

client
6 patron **7** patient, protégé **8** customer **9** dependent

clientele
4 fans **5** trade, train **6** custom, market, public **7** patrons, traffic **8** audience, patients, regulars, shoppers **9** customers **10** purchasers, supporters **12** constituency

cliff
4 crag **5** bluff, scarp **8** headland, palisade **9** precipice **10** escarpment

climacteric
4 apex, crux, cusp **5** acute **6** crisis **7** crucial **8** critical **9** menopause **11** culmination **12** change of life, turning point

climactic
4 peak **7** crucial, pivotal **8** critical, decisive, dramatic **9** momentous **10** definitive **11** culminating, determining

climate
6 medium, milieu **7** ambient **8** ambience **10** atmosphere **11** environment **12** surroundings

climax
3 cap **4** acme, apex, peak **5** crown **6** apogee, summit, top off **8** capstone, meridian, pinnacle **9** culminate **11** culmination

climb
4 go up, rise, soar **5** mount, scale, slope **6** ascend **7** clamber **8** escalate, increase

climbing
8 scandent

climbing iron
7 crampon

clinch
3 hug **4** grip, hold, seal **5** clamp, clasp, grasp, sew up **6** clutch, decide, ensure, lock up **7** confirm, embrace, grapple, squeeze **8** nail down

clincher

4 tire **5** proof **6** kicker **7** quietus **9** deathblow **10** smoking gun **11** affirmation, attestation, coup de grâce **12** confirmation **13** corroboration

cling

4 bond **5** stick **6** adhere, cleave, clutch, hold on, linger **8** adhesion **9** adherence

clingstone

5 peach

clink

3 can, jug, pen **4** brig, cell, coop, jail, stir **5** pokey, pound **6** cooler, jingle, lockup, prison, tingle, tinkle **7** slammer **8** hoosegow **9** calaboose

clinker

3 dud **4** bomb, bust, flop, goof, slag **5** botch, brick, error, lemon, loser **6** bummer, bungle, fiasco, howler, turkey **7** bloomer, blunder, failure, faux pas, mistake

clinkers

3 ash **4** slag **5** ashes **7** cinders

clinquant

5 gaudy **6** flashy, garish, tawdry, tinsel **8** specious **10** glittering **11** superficial

Clio

see **Muse**

clip

3 bob, cut, mow, pin **4** crop, hasp, pare, snip, sock, trim **5** block, clasp, prune, punch, shave, shear, slash **6** broach, brooch, fleece, reduce **7** curtail, cut back, cut down, shorten **8** magazine, truncate **10** abbreviate, overcharge

clique

3 set **4** camp, clan, club, gang, ring **5** cabal, crowd, mafia **6** circle **7** coterie, faction, in-group **9** camarilla

cloak

4 cape, mask, robe, veil, wrap **5** cover, guise **6** facade, joseph, mantle, screen, shroud, veneer **7** blanket, conceal, curtain, dress up, manteau, obscure **8** disguise **9** dissemble, semblance **10** camouflage **11** dissimulate
ancient Greek: 7 chlamys
ancient Roman: 7 pallium
Arab: 3 aba
fur: 7 pelisse
hooded: 6 capote **7** burnous **8** burnoose
liturgical: 4 cope
Moroccan: 8 djellaba
over armor: 6 tabard **7** surcoat
Spanish: 5 manta

clobber

4 belt, drub, flay, lick, slam, slug, whip, whup **5** blast, brain, clout, pound, smash **6** hammer, thrash, wallop **7** shellac, trounce **8** demolish, lambaste

clochard

3 bum, vag **4** hobo **5** tramp **6** beggar, canter **7** drifter, floater, moocher, vagrant **8** deadbeat, derelict, vagabond **9** transient **10** freeloader, panhandler **11** bindle stiff

cloche

3 hat **5** cover, toque, tuque

clock

4 time **9** timepiece **11** chronometer
water: 9 clepsydra

clocklike

5 exact **6** minute, prompt, strict, timely **7** precise, regular **8** accurate, punctual, reliable, thorough **9** assiduous **10** dependable, meticulous, scrupulous **11** painstaking **13** conscientious

clockmaker

10 horologist

clockwise

6 deasil **7** dextral **11** right-handed

Clockwork Orange author

7 Burgess (Anthony)

clod

3 gob, wad **4** boob, dolt, dope, hunk, lump, soil **5** chump, chunk, clump, dummy, dunce, earth **6** dimwit **8** dumbbell **9** blockhead, lamebrain

cloddish

7 boorish, ill-bred, loutish, uncouth
8 churlish, clownish 9 unrefined
10 uncultured, unpolished 11 uncivilized

clodhopper

4 boor, boot, hick, lout 5 chuff, churl,
clown, yokel 6 rustic 7 bumpkin,
hayseed, redneck 9 chawbacon

clog

3 gum, jam, tax 4 fill, glut, load, plug,
stop 5 block, choke, close, stuff
6 hamper, hinder 7 congest 8 encumber, obstruct, overload 10 impediment 11 encumbrance

cloister

5 abbey, court 6 arcade, garden
7 convent, retreat, seclude, shelter
9 courtyard, monastery, sequester

Cloister and the Hearth author

5 Reade (Charles)

cloistered

7 recluse 8 confined, hermetic,
secluded 9 seclusive, withdrawn
11 sequestered

cloistered one

3 nun 4 monk

clone

4 copy 5 ditto 6 double, carbon
7 replica 9 duplicate, facsimile,
replicate, reproduce 10 carbon copy,
simulacrum 12 reproduction

Clorinda

beloved: 7 Tancred
father: 6 Senapo
guardian: 6 Arsete
slayer: 7 Tancred

close

3 end 4 near, nigh, shut, slam
5 block, cease, choke, humid, muggy,
tight 6 ending, finale, finish, narrow,
nearby, sticky, stuffy, sultry, windup,
wrap up 7 airless, compact, crowded,
stopper 8 abutting, adjacent, complete, conclude, finalize, intimate,
obstruct, stifling 9 adjoining, cessation, condensed, terminate 10 con-

clusion, consummate, convenient,
near-at-hand 11 constricted, neighboring, termination 12 confidential

closed-minded

4 deaf 6 narrow 8 obdurate 9 hidebound, obstinate, pigheaded, unbending 10 bullheaded, hardheaded
11 intractable

closefisted

5 cheap, mingy 6 frugal, stingy
7 miserly, thrifty 9 niggardly, penurious 13 penny-pinching

close in

3 hem 4 cage 5 fence, hedge
6 corral, immure 7 advance, confine, enclose, envelop, impound
8 approach, converge, encircle,
enshroud, imprison, surround

close-knit

8 intimate

closely

4 hard 7 sharply 8 intently, minutely
9 carefully 11 searchingly 12 meticulously, scrupulously, thoughtfully
13 punctiliously

close match

6 toss-up

closemouthed

3 mum 4 mute 6 silent 7 laconic
8 reserved, reticent, taciturn
12 tight-mouthed

closeness

8 intimacy

close off

4 clog, plug 5 block 6 stop up
7 isolate, occlude 8 insulate 9 segregate, sequester

closet

6 covert, inside, office 7 cabinet,
chamber, furtive, private 8 wardrobe
11 speculative, theoretical

closing

3 end 4 last, stop 5 final 6 ending,
finish, latest, period, windup, wrap-
up 7 curtain 8 eventual, terminal,
ultimate 9 cessation 10 concluding
11 termination

closure

3 cap, end, lid **6** ending, finish
8 fastener **9** cessation

clot

3 gel, set **4** curd, glob, jell, lump
5 clump **6** curdle, gelate **7** congeal
8 coagulum, thrombus **9** coagulate
10 gelatinize
combining form: 6 thromb
7 thrombo

cloth

see **fabric**

clothe

3 tog **4** deck, do up, garb, robe
5 array, cloak, couch, drape, dress,
endow, equip **6** attire, bedeck, outfit,
swathe **7** apparel, costume, dress
up **8** accouter

clothes

3 rig **4** duds, garb, rags, togs **5** array,
dress, getup, habit **6** attire, outfit,
things **7** apparel, costume, raiment,
rigging, threads, toggery, vesture
8 garments, glad rags **9** vestments
11 habiliments
basket: 6 hamper
civilian: 5 mufti

clothes-moth genus

5 Tinea

clothespress

7 armoire **8** wardrobe

cloud

3 dim, fog, tar **4** blur, haze, mist,
murk **5** addle, befog, brume, gloom,
muddy, plume, smear, sully, taint
6 muddle, nebula, puzzle, shadow,
smudge **7** besmear, confuse, obscure, perplex, tarnish **8** befuddle,
besmirch, discolor, distract, overcast
9 obfuscate
type: 6 cirrus, nimbus **7** cumulus,
stratus **11** altocumulus, altostratus
12 cirrocumulus, cirrostratus, cumu-
lonimbus, nimbostratus **13** stratocu-
mulus

cloudburst

6 deluge, shower **7** monsoon, torrent **8** downpour, drencher, rainfall
10 outpouring

clouded

5 dusky, murky, shady **6** dreary,
gloomy, somber, sombre **7** dubious,
ominous, sunless, unclear **8** doubtful, overcast **9** ambiguous, equivocal, uncertain, unsettled **11** problematic

cloudless

4 fair, fine **5** clear, sunny **7** clarion
8 pleasant, rainless, sunshiny

cloud-like mass

6 nebula

cloudy

4 dull, hazy **5** dusky, foggy, heavy,
misty, murky, vague **6** gloomy,
opaque, somber, sombre **7** louring,
obscure, tainted, unclear **8** confused,
darkened, lowering, nebulous,
overcast, vaporous **10** indistinct

clout

3 box, hit, rag **4** blow, cuff, poke,
pull, slam, slap, slug, sock, swat,
sway **5** paste, power, punch, smack,
smite, whack **6** strike **9** influence

clove

4 bulb **5** spice **7** chopped, severed

clove hitch

4 knot

clover

5 lotus **6** alsike, ladino, lucern
7 alfalfa, berseem, lucerne, melilot,
trefoil **8** four-leaf, shamrock **9** lespedeza
family: 3 pea
genus: 9 Trifolium

clown

3 wag **4** mime, zany **5** cutup, joker,
Punch **6** jester, mummer **7** buffoon
8 comedian, jokester **9** harlequin,
prankster **11** merry-andrew
French: 7 Pierrot
operatic: 5 buffo
Spanish: 8 gracioso

clownish

4 rude **6** clumsy, gauche, oafish
7 awkward, boorish, ill-bred, loutish,
lumpish, uncouth **8** churlish, cloddish **9** unrefined

cloy
4 fill, glut, jade, pall, sate   **5** gorge
6 sicken   **7** satiate, surfeit   **8** overfill

cloying
4 icky   **5** gushy, mushy, sappy, soppy
6 sticky, sugary   **7** fulsome, gushing,
maudlin, mawkish   **9** excessive,
schmaltzy, sickening   **10** disgusting,
lovey-dovey, nauseating, saccharine
11 distasteful, sentimental

club
3 bat, sap   **4** beat, cosh, iron, mace
5 baton, billy, guild, lodge, order,
union   **6** cudgel, league   **7** society
8 bludgeon, sodality, sorority   **9** blackjack, truncheon   **10** fellowship, fraternity, knobkerrie, nightstick   **11** association, brotherhood
Australian: **5** waddy
Irish: **10** shillelagh

clubfoot
7 talipes

cluck
4 dodo, dolt, dope, fool   **5** dunce
6 dimwit, nitwit   **7** pinhead

clue
3 cue   **4** hint, idea, lead, sign, tell,
warn   **6** advise, inform, notify, notion,
tip-off   **7** inkling   **8** evidence, telltale
10 indication, intimation, suggestion

clump
3 gob, wad   **4** clod, hunk, lump,
mass, mess, plod   **5** batch, bunch,
chunk, group, stomp, tramp   **6** bumble, bundle, lumber, parcel   **7** cluster,
galumph, stumble

clump of grass
4 tuft   **6** tuffet   **7** tussock

clumsy
5 bulky, gawky, inept, splay   **6** clunky,
gauche, klutzy, wooden   **7** awkward,
hulking, lumpish, uncouth, unhandy
8 bumbling, bungling, tactless,
ungainly, unsubtle, unwieldy   **9** all
thumbs, graceless, ham-handed,
inelegant, lumbering, maladroit
11 heavy-handed, inefficient

clumsy one
3 oaf   **4** clod, goon, lout, slob   **5** klutz

6 baboon, galoot, lummox   **7** bumpkin, bungler, palooka   **13** butterfingers

clunk
4 thud   **5** clout, thump, whack
6 thwack, wallop

clunker
4 bomb, heap   **5** crate, wreck   **6** jalopy,
junker   **7** stinker   **10** rattletrap

cluster
3 lot, set   **4** band, bevy, crew, knot,
pack   **5** array, batch, bunch, clump,
covey, group   **6** bundle, clutch,
gather   **7** collect, package   **8** assemble, assembly   **9** aggregate, associate, gathering   **10** accumulate

cluster bean
4 guar

clutch
4 grab, grip, hold, keep   **5** catch,
clamp, clasp, grasp, pinch, seize
6 bundle, clench, clinch, snatch
7 cluster, grapple

clutter
4 hash, mash, mess, muss, ruck
5 chaos, snarl, strew   **6** jumble,
litter, muddle   **7** mélange, rummage
8 disarray, disorder, mishmash,
shambles   **9** confusion   **10** hodgepodge

Clydesdale
5 horse   **10** draft horse

Clymene
father: **7** Oceanus
husband: **7** Iapetus
mother: **6** Tethys
son: **5** Atlas   **10** Epimetheus,
Prometheus

Clytemnestra
brother: **6** Castor, Pollux   **10** Polydeuces
daughter: **7** Electra   **9** Iphigenia
father: **9** Tyndareus
husband: **9** Agamemnon
lover: **9** Aegisthus
mother: **4** Leda
slayer: **7** Orestes
son: **7** Orestes
victim: **9** Agamemnon, Cassandra

Clytie
beloved: **6** Apollo
form: **9** sunflower **10** heliotrope

coach
3 bus, car **5** drill, stage, train, tutor
6 chaise, mentor **7** prepare, trainer
8 carriage, instruct **10** instructor

coadjutor
3 aid **4** aide **6** bishop, deputy **9** assistant **10** aide-de-camp, lieutenant

coagulate
3 gel, set **4** clot, jell **6** curdle **7** congeal, jellify, thicken **8** coalesce,
condense, solidify **10** gelatinize,
inspissate **11** concentrate, consolidate

coal
distillate: **3** tar
dust: **4** smut, soot **5** slack
element: **6** carbon
fused leavings: **4** slag **7** clinker
glowing: **5** ember, gleed
hard: **10** anthracite
lump: **3** cob
miner: **7** collier
region: **4** Saar
residue: **4** coke
soft: **6** cannel **10** bituminous

coalesce
3 mix **4** fuse, join, link **5** blend,
merge, unite **6** mingle **7** combine,
conjoin **10** amalgamate

coalition
4 bloc, ring **5** party, union **6** fusion,
league, merger **7** combine, melding,
merging **8** alliance **9** anschluss
10 federation **11** affiliation, association, combination, confederacy, integration, unification **13** confederation,
consolidation

coarse
3 raw **4** rude **5** bawdy, crass, crude,
dirty, gross, rough, tacky **6** common,
filthy, grainy, ribald, smutty, vulgar
7 boorish, obscene, raffish, raunchy,
uncouth **8** granular, indecent **9** inelegant, roughneck, unrefined
10 uncultured **11** particulate **12** uncultivated

coast
4 bank **5** beach, drift, shore, slide
6 strand **7** seaside **8** littoral, seashore
of Antarctica: **4** Knox

coastal
7 seaside **8** littoral, riverine

coaster
4 sled, tray **6** trader

coat
5 crust, glaze, gloss, layer, parka,
plate, tunic **6** blazer, duster, finish,
jacket, patina, raglan, reefer, ulster,
veneer **7** cutaway **8** covering,
mackinaw, tegument **9** newmarket,
redingote **10** integument, mackintosh **11** windbreaker
animal: **3** fur **4** hide, pelt, wool
6 pelage
fur-lined: **7** pelisse
kind: **3** pea, top **5** frock **6** trench
Levantine: **6** caftan
of arms: **5** crest **6** blazon, emblem,
shield, tabard **8** blazonry **10** escutcheon
of egg white: **5** glair **6** glaire
of mail: **7** hauberk
soldier's: **5** frock, tunic **6** capote
waterproof: **7** slicker **10** mackintosh

coating
4 film, leaf, scum, skin **5** glaze,
gloss, layer **6** finish, patina, veneer
7 dusting, lacquer, overlay, surface,
varnish **8** covering

coax
4 lure, urge **5** cable, press, tempt
6 cajole, entice, induce **7** blarney,
wheedle **8** blandish, butter up,
inveigle, persuade, soft-soap
9 importune, sweet-talk

cob
3 ear **4** swan **5** adobe, horse

cobble
4 make, mend **5** patch, stone
6 repair **11** paving stone

cobbler
3 pie **5** drink **8** cocktail **9** shoemaker

cobbler's form
4 last

cobelligerent
4 ally

cobweb
3 net 4 mesh, trap 8 gossamer
9 confusion, spiderweb 12 entanglement

coccyx
8 tailbone

cochineal
3 dye 6 insect

cock
3 tap 4 boss, head, heap, hill, lord,
mass, pile, rick, tilt 5 chief, mound,
stack, strut, valve 6 faucet, honcho,
leader, master, spigot 7 headman,
hydrant, rooster, swagger 11 chanticleer

cock-a-hoop
4 awry 5 askew 7 askance, crooked
8 boastful, exultant, exulting, jubilant
9 triumphal 10 triumphant

Cockaigne
6 utopia 7 arcadia 9 Shangri-la
10 wonderland

cockalorum
7 bluster, bombast, bravado 8 blowhard, boasting, braggart, leapfrog
11 braggadocio

cockamamy
5 batty, crazy, daffy, flaky, kooky,
loony, nutty, wacky 6 absurd 9 ludicrous 10 incredible, ridiculous
11 harebrained

cock-and-bull story
5 crock 6 canard 7 whopper 9 fairy
tale

cockcrow
4 dawn, morn 5 sunup 7 morning,
sunrise 8 daybreak, daylight

cocker
4 baby 5 humor, spoil 6 coddle,
cosset, pamper 7 indulge, spaniel
11 mollycoddle

cockeyed
4 awry 5 askew 8 lopsided 11 harebrained

cockle
5 shell 6 dimple, furrow, groove,
pucker, ripple 7 bivalve, mollusc,
mollusk, wrinkle

cockleshell
4 boat

cockscomb
see **coxcomb**

cocksure
5 brash 6 cheeky 9 bumptious
13 overconfident

cocktail
5 Bronx, drink 6 gibson, gimlet,
mai tai, mimosa, mojito, Rob Roy,
zombie 7 gin fizz, martini, sidecar,
stinger 8 aperitif, daiquiri, pink lady,
salty dog, sombrero 9 Cuba libre,
manhattan, margarita, mint julep,
rusty nail 10 Bloody Mary, Tom
Collins, wallbanger 11 grasshopper,
screwdriver, whiskey sour 12 black
russian, cosmopolitan, old-fashioned
fruit: 9 macedoine
gasoline: 7 Molotov

Cocktail Party author
5 Eliot (T. S.)

cocky
4 bold, sure 5 brash, pushy, sassy,
saucy 6 brassy, cheeky, jaunty
8 arrogant, impudent, insolent 9 conceited 10 swaggering 11 self-
assured 12 enterprising 13 over-
confident, self-confident

coconspirator
7 abettor 9 accessory 10 accomplice 11 confederate

coconut
husk fiber: 4 coir
meat: 5 copra

coda
5 envoi, envoy 6 ending, finale
7 summary 8 epilogue, follow-up
9 afterword 10 conclusion

coddle
4 baby 5 humor, spoil 6 cosset, pamper 7 cater to, indulge

code
6 cipher, symbol 7 encrypt 8 encipher
kind: 3 zip 4 area 5 Morse, legal, penal
message in: 10 cryptogram 11 cryptograph

code word
see **communications code word**

codger
6 duffer, fellow

codicil
5 rider 8 addendum, addition, appendix 10 postscript, supplement

codswallop
see **nonsense**

coefficient
6 factor 7 measure 8 constant

coelenterate
5 coral 7 anemone, hydroid 9 cnidarian, jellyfish 10 sea anemone

coerce
3 cow 5 bully, force, impel, press 6 compel, menace, oblige 8 browbeat, bulldoze, dominate, threaten 9 blackjack, constrain, strong-arm, terrorize 10 intimidate

coercion
5 force 6 duress, menace, threat 8 pressure 10 compulsion, constraint

Coeur d'____
5 Alene

coeval
see **contemporary**

coexistent
see **contemporary**

coffee
alkaloid: 8 caffeine
bean: 3 nib
cake: 6 kuchen
cup: 9 demitasse
French: 4 café
grinder: 4 mill
kind: 4 drip, java 5 decaf, latte, mocha 7 arabica, instant 8 espresso 9 Americano, macchiato 10 café au lait, cappuccino
maker: 10 percolator
pot: 3 urn

coffee shop
4 café 5 diner 8 snack bar 9 cafeteria, hash house, lunchroom 11 greasy spoon 12 luncheonette

coffer
5 chest 6 casket 8 treasury 9 exchequer, strongbox

coffin
3 box 4 kist 6 casket
carrier: 6 hearse 10 pallbearer
nail: 9 cigarette
stand: 4 bier 10 catafalque

cogency
5 force, point, power, punch 7 potency 8 strength, validity 9 relevance 10 conviction, pertinence 13 effectiveness

cogent
5 solid, sound, valid 6 potent 7 telling, weighty 8 forceful, powerful, relevant 9 pertinent 10 compelling, convincing, meaningful, persuasive 11 influential, well-founded 12 well-grounded 13 consequential

cogitate
4 muse 5 think 6 ponder, reason 7 reflect 8 conceive, consider, meditate, mull over, ruminate 9 cerebrate, speculate 10 deliberate

cogitation
7 thought 10 meditation, reflection, rumination 11 cerebration, speculation 12 deliberation 13 consideration

cogitative
7 pensive 10 meditative, reflective, ruminative, thoughtful 11 speculative 13 contemplative

Cogito ____ sum
4 ergo

cognac
6 brandy

cognate
4 akin, like 5 alike 6 allied, common
7 kindred, related, similar 8 parallel
10 affiliated, associated

cognition
9 awareness, knowledge, sentience
10 perception

cognizance
4 heed, note 6 notice 9 attention,
awareness, knowledge 12 jurisdiction

cognizant
5 aware 7 knowing, mindful 8 informed, sensible 9 conscious
13 knowledgeable

cognize
4 know 5 grasp 6 fathom 7 realize
8 perceive 9 apprehend 10 appreciate, comprehend, understand

cognomen
4 name 5 alias, title 7 epithet,
moniker, surname 8 nickname
11 appellation, appellative, designation 12 denomination

cognoscente
5 judge 6 critic, expert 7 epicure
8 aesthete 9 authority 10 specialist
11 connoisseur

cognoscible
8 knowable 10 fathomable 13 apprehensible

cohere
4 fuse, join 5 agree, blend, cling,
merge, stick, unite 6 accord 7 combine, comport, conform, connect
8 coalesce, dovetail 10 correspond
11 consolidate

coherence
4 bond 5 union, unity 8 adhesion,
cohesion 9 agreement, congruity,
integrity 10 conformity, connection,
consonance, solidarity 11 consistency, integration

coherent
5 sound 7 logical, ordered, unified
8 rational 10 consistent, integrated,
meaningful 11 coordinated

cohesion
see **coherence**

coho
6 salmon 12 silver salmon

cohort
3 pal 4 ally, band, chum, crew, mate
5 buddy, crony, group 6 fellow, friend
7 comrade, partner 8 adherent,
confrere, disciple, follower, henchman, sidekick 9 assistant, associate,
colleague, companion, supporter
10 accomplice 11 demographic
12 collaborator

coif
3 cap, cut 4 hood, perm 6 hairdo
7 haircut 8 skullcap

coiffeur
6 barber 10 haircutter 11 hairdresser, hairstylist

coiffure
6 hairdo
aid: 3 net, rat 5 snood

coil
4 curl, loop, ring, turn, wind 5 helix,
twine, twist 6 rotate, spiral 7 entwine, revolve, wreathe 8 curlicue
9 corkscrew

coiled
6 spiral, volute 7 helical, voluted,
whorled 9 circinate

coin
4 mint 6 invent, make up, strike
Afghanistan: 3 pul 7 afghani
Albania: 3 lek 9 quindarka
Algeria: 5 dinar 7 centime
ancient Greek: 4 obol
ancient Muslim: 5 dinar
ancient Roman: 8 denarius
Argentina: 4 peso 7 centavo
Austria: 4 euro 8 groschen 9 schilling
Bahrain: 4 fils 5 dinar
Belgium: 4 euro 5 franc 7 centime
Benin: 5 franc 7 centime
Bhutan: 7 chetrum 8 ngultrum
Bolivia: 7 centavo 9 boliviano
Botswana: 4 pula 5 thebe
Brazil: 4 real 7 centavo 8 cruzeiro

Bulgaria: 3 lev 8 stotinka
Burundi: 5 franc 7 centime
Cameroon: 5 franc 7 centime
Canada: 6 loonie, toonie, twonie
Cape Verde Islands: 6 escudo 7 centavo
Chile: 4 peso 7 centavo
China: 3 fen 4 jiao, yuan
Columbia: 4 peso 7 centavo
Costa Rica: 5 colón 7 centimo
Cuba: 4 peso 7 centavo
Czech Republic: 5 haler 6 koruna
defective: 4 fido
Denmark: 3 ore 5 krone
Dominican Republic: 4 peso 7 centavo
Ecuador: 5 sucre 7 centavo
edge: 7 milling
Egypt: 7 piastre
European gold: 5 ducat
Finland: 4 euro 5 penni 6 markka
former: 3 ecu, mil, pie, sol, sou 4 anna, besa, doit, duit, kran, para, pice, reis (plural) 5 fanam, litas, mohur, paisa, rupia, shahi, soldo, toman 6 centas, denier, heller, macuta, pagoda, tangka 7 santims, sapeque 8 maravedi, skilling 9 rigsdaler 10 Indian head, reichsmark 13 reichspfennig
France: 4 euro 5 franc 7 centime
Gambia: 5 butut 6 dalasi
Germany: 4 euro, mark 7 pfennig
Ghana: 4 cedi 6 pesewa
Great Britain: 3 bob 5 crown, penny 6 guinea 7 ha'penny 8 farthing, shilling, sixpence 9 halfpenny, sovereign 10 threepence
Greece: 4 euro 5 lepton 7 drachma
Guatemala: 7 centavo, quetzal
Guinea-Bissau: 4 peso
Haiti: 6 gourde 7 centime
Honduras: 7 centavo, lempira
Hungary: 5 pengo 6 filler, forint
Iceland: 5 aurar (plural), eyrir, krona
India: 5 paisa, rupee
Indonesia: 3 sen 6 rupiah
Iran: 4 rial 5 dinar
Iraq: 4 fils 5 dinar
Ireland: 4 euro 5 penny 8 farthing
Israel: 4 agora 6 shekel
Italy: 4 euro, lira 5 scudo

Japan: 3 rin, sen, yen
Jordan: 4 fils 5 dinar
Kenya: 8 shilling
Korea, North and South: 3 won 4 chon
Kuwait: 4 fils 5 dinar
large: 9 cartwheel
Lebanon: 5 livre 7 piastre
Lesotho: 4 loti 7 licente, lisente
Libya: 5 dinar 6 dirham
Luxembourg: 4 euro 5 franc
Madagascar: 5 franc
Malawi: 6 kwacha 7 tambala
Mauritania: 5 khoum 7 ouguiya
Mauritius: 5 rupee
Mexico: 4 peso 7 centavo
Monaco: 4 euro 5 franc
Morocco: 6 dirham
Mozambique: 7 metical
Nepal: 5 paisa, rupee
Netherlands: 4 euro 6 florin, gulden 7 guilder
Nicaragua: 7 centavo, córdoba
Nigeria: 4 kobo 5 naira
Norway: 3 ore 5 krone
Oman: 4 rial 5 baiza
Pakistan: 5 paisa, rupee
Panama: 6 balboa 9 centesimo
Papua New Guinea: 4 kina, toea
Paraguay: 7 centimo, guarani
Peru: 3 sol 7 centimo
Philippines: 4 piso 7 sentimo
Poland: 5 grosz, zloty
Portugal: 4 euro 6 escudo 7 centavo
Qatar: 5 riyal 6 dirham
Roman: 6 aureus, bezant 7 solidus
Romania: 3 ban, leu
Russia: 5 kopek, ruble 6 kopeck
San Marino: 4 lira
Saudi Arabia: 4 rial 6 halala
Seychelles: 5 rupee
side of a: 7 obverse
Slovakia: 5 haler 6 koruna
South Africa: 4 rand 10 Krugerrand
Spain: 4 euro 6 peseta 7 centimo
Sri Lanka: 5 rupee
stamping metal: 8 planchet
Suriname: 6 florin, gulden 7 guilder
Swaziland: 9 lilangeni
Sweden: 3 ore 5 krona 8 skilling

Switzerland: 5 franc **6** rappen
Syria: 7 piastre
Tanzania: 8 shilling
Thailand: 4 baht **5** tical **6** satang
Tonga: 6 pa'anga, seniti
Tunisia: 5 dinar
Turkey: 4 lira **5** kurus
Uganda: 8 shilling
United Arab Emirates: 6 dirham
United States: 4 dime **5** penny
6 dollar, nickel **7** quarter **10** half-dollar
Uruguay: 4 peso **9** centesimo
Vatican City: 4 lira
Venezuela: 7 bolivar
Samoa: 4 sene, tala
Zambia: 5 ngwee **6** kwacha

coinage
7 new word **8** creation, currency
9 invention, neologism **10** brainchild
11 contrivance

coincide
4 jibe **5** agree, equal, match, tally
6 accord, concur, square **7** comport,
conform **8** dovetail **9** harmonize
10 correspond

coincident
7 similar **9** consonant **10** concurrent
11 concomitant, synchronous **12** accompanying, contemporary, simultaneous

coincidentally
8 by chance, together **12** accidentally, concurrently, fortuitously

coin-shaped
8 nummular

col
4 pass **5** ridge **6** saddle

_____ colada
4 piña

colander's cousin
5 sieve **6** sifter **8** strainer

cold _____
3 war **4** call, cash, cuts, feet, fish,
sore, wave **5** cream, frame, front,
patch, steel, sweat, water **6** turkey
7 comfort, storage **8** shoulder

cold
3 icy, raw **4** cool, dead, iced **5** aloof,
chill, crisp, frore, gelid, nippy, polar
6 arctic, biting, chilly, frigid, frosty,
frozen, wintry **7** bracing, glacial,
shivery **8** chilling, comatose, freezing, lifeless **11** emotionless, passionless, unconscious, unemotional
12 unresponsive
combining form: 4 cryo, kryo
common: 6 coryza
symptom: 5 cough, fever **6** sneeze
7 catarrh

cold-blooded
5 cruel **6** brutal **7** callous **8** hardened, obdurate, pitiless, ruthless
9 heartless, impassive, unfeeling
10 hard-boiled, impersonal **11** emotionless, hard-hearted **12** matter-of-fact, stonyhearted **13** dispassionate,
unimpassioned

cold feet
4 fear **5** alarm, doubt, dread, panic,
worry **6** dismay, fright, terror **7** anxiety, jitters **8** timidity **9** cowardice
11 trepidation **12** apprehension

coldhearted
see **cold-blooded**

cold-shoulder
3 cut **4** snub **6** ignore, slight **9** ostracize

cold storage
8 abeyance, dormancy **10** quiescence, suspension **12** intermission,
interruption

cole
4 kale, rape **7** cabbage **8** brassica,
broccoli, kohlrabi **11** cauliflower

Coleridge poem
9 Dejection, Kubla Khan **10** Christabel

Colette character
4 Gigi **5** Cheri **8** Claudine

colewort
4 kale **7** cabbage

colic
5 gripe **9** bellyache **11** stomachache **12** collywobbles

coliseum

4 bowl 5 arena, stade 6 circus
7 stadium

collaborate

6 team up 7 collude 8 conspire
9 cooperate

collaborator

4 ally 6 helper 7 abettor, partner,
traitor 8 coworker, henchman,
quisling 9 accessory, assistant,
associate, auxiliary, colleague
10 accomplice 11 confederate,
conspirator

collapse

4 cave, drop, fail, ruin 5 break, crash,
smash, wreck 6 buckle, cave in, fold
up 7 breakup, crack-up, crumple,
debacle, deflate, downfall, failure,
founder, give out, give way, pass
out, shatter, smashup, succumb
8 condense 9 breakdown, cataclysm, fall apart, ruination 10 disruption 11 catastrophe, destruction,
prostration 12 disintegrate

collar

3 bag, nab 4 grab, hook, nail, take
5 catch, seize 6 arrest, secure
7 capture 9 apprehend
armor: 6 gorget
boy's: 4 Eton
chain: 4 torc 6 torque
jeweled: 8 carcanet
lace-edged: 6 rebato
metal: 4 torc 6 torque
pleated: 4 ruff

collarbone

8 clavicle

collate

5 group, order 7 arrange, collect,
compare, compile 8 assemble,
contrast, organize 9 integrate

collateral

4 bond 6 allied, lineal, pledge, surety
7 cognate, kindred, oblique, related,
subject 8 indirect, parallel, security
9 accessory, ancillary, attendant,
auxiliary, dependent, secondary,
tributary 10 coincident, coordinate,
reciprocal, subsidiary 11 concomitant, subordinate, subservient
12 accompanying, confirmatory,
contributory 13 complementary,
corresponding, corroborative

colleague

4 aide 6 cohort, fellow, helper
7 partner 8 confrere, coworker,
teammate 9 assistant, associate,
companion 10 compatriot 11 confederate 12 collaborator

collect

4 draw 5 group, infer, raise 6 deduce, derive, gather, muster, prayer
7 build up, compile, compose,
convene, dispose, marshal, round up
8 assemble, conclude, converge
10 accumulate, congregate, rendezvous

collected

4 calm, cool 5 quiet, still 6 poised,
serene 7 assured 8 complete,
composed, sanguine, tranquil 9 as-
sembled, confident, unruffled 11 unflappable 13 imperturbable, self-
possessed

collection

3 ana, kit, lot 4 band, bevy, crew,
olio, ruck 5 bunch, crowd, hoard,
trove 6 medley, muster 7 cluster,
variety 8 assembly, caboodle
9 aggregate, anthology, congeries,
gathering, stockpile 10 assemblage,
assortment, cumulation, miscellany
11 aggregation 12 accumulation,
congregation 13 agglomeration
miscellaneous: 4 hash, olio 6 jumble, medley 7 mélange, mixture
8 mishmash, pastiche 9 potpourri
10 hodgepodge, salmagundi 11 olla
podrida
of anecdotes: 3 ana
of animals: 3 zoo 9 menagerie
of artistic works: 6 museum
7 gallery
of clothes: 8 wardrobe
of dried plants: 9 herbarium
of literary pieces: 8 analects
9 anthology
of reports: 4 file 7 dossier
of trinkets: 10 bijouterie

collective
5 joint 7 commune, kibbutz, kolkhoz
11 cooperative

collector
of bird's eggs: 8 oologist
of books: 11 bibliophile
of coins: 11 numismatist
of fares: 9 conductor
of phonograph records: 10 discophile
of stamps: 11 philatelist

colleen
4 girl, lass 6 maiden
country: 4 Eire, Erin 7 Ireland

college
building: 3 gym, lab 4 dorm, hall
campus area: 4 quad 10 quadrangle
class meeting: 3 lab 7 lecture,
seminar 8 tutorial, workshop
degree: 3 BLS, DST, LLB, LLD,
MBA, MEd, MFA, MLS, PhD 5 LittD
graduate: 6 alumna, alumni (plural)
7 alumnae (plural), alumnus
official: 4 dean 5 prexy 6 bursar,
regent 7 proctor, provost 9 registrar
oldest in U.S.: 7 Harvard
oldest women's in U.S.: 12 Mount
Holyoke
relating to: 8 academic 10 collegiate
social group: 4 frat 8 sorority
10 fraternity
song: 9 alma mater
student class: 4 soph 5 frosh
6 junior, senior 8 freshman 9 sophomore
teacher: 3 don 4 prof 8 academic
9 professor
term: 7 quarter, session 8 semester
9 trimester
VIP: 4 BMOC
woman: 4 coed

college team
Air Force: 7 Falcons
Alabama: 11 Crimson Tide
Arizona: 8 Wildcats
Arizona State: 9 Sun Devils
Arkansas: 10 Razorbacks
Arkansas State: 7 Indians

Army: 6 Cadets
Auburn: 6 Tigers
Baylor: 5 Bears
Boston College: 6 Eagles
Boston University: 8 Terriers
Brigham Young: 7 Cougars
Brown: 5 Bears
California: 11 Golden Bears
Central Michigan: 9 Chippewas
Cincinnati: 8 Bearcats
Citadel: 8 Bulldogs
Clemson: 6 Tigers
Colgate: 10 Red Raiders
Colorado: 9 Buffaloes
Colorado State: 4 Rams
Columbia: 5 Lions
Connecticut: 7 Huskies
Cornell: 6 Big Red
Dartmouth: 8 Big Green
Davidson: 8 Wildcats
Delaware State: 7 Hornets
Drake: 8 Bulldogs
Duke: 10 Blue Devils
Eastern Kentucky: 8 Colonels
Eastern Michigan: 6 Eagles
Florida: 6 Gators
Florida State: 9 Seminoles
Fresno State: 8 Bulldogs
Furman: 8 Palidans
Georgia: 8 Bulldogs
Georgia Tech: 13 Yellow Jackets
Harvard: 7 Crimson
Hawaii: 15 Rainbow Warriors
Holy Cross: 9 Crusaders
Houston: 7 Cougars
Howard: 6 Bisons
Idaho: 7 Vandals
Idaho State: 7 Bengals
Illinois: 14 Fighting Illini
Illinois State: 8 Redbirds
Indiana: 8 Hoosiers
Indiana State: 9 Sycamores
Iowa: 8 Hawkeyes
Iowa State: 8 Cyclones
Kansas: 8 Jayhawks
Kansas State: 8 Wildcats
Kent State: 13 Golden Flashes
Kentucky: 8 Wildcats
Lehigh: 9 Engineers
Louisiana State: 6 Tigers
Louisiana Tech: 8 Bulldogs
Maine: 10 Black Bears

Maryland: 5 Terps 9 Terrapins
Massachusetts: 9 Minutemen
Miami (Florida): 10 Hurricanes
Miami (Ohio): 8 Redskins
Michigan: 10 Wolverines
Michigan State: 8 Spartans
Minnesota: 7 Gophers
Mississippi: 6 Rebels
Mississippi State: 8 Bulldogs
Missouri: 6 Tigers
Montana: 9 Grizzlies
Montana State: 7 Bobcats
Navy: 10 Midshipmen
Nebraska: 11 Cornhuskers
Nevada: 6 Rebels 8 Wolfpack
New Hampshire: 8 Wildcats
New Mexico: 5 Lobos
New Mexico State: 6 Aggies
North Carolina: 8 Tar Heels
North Carolina State: 8 Wolfpack
Northeastern: 7 Huskies
Northwestern: 8 Wildcats
Notre Dame: 13 Fighting Irish
Ohio State: 8 Buckeyes
Ohio University: 7 Bobcats
Oklahoma: 7 Sooners
Oklahoma State: 7 Cowboys
Oregon: 5 Ducks
Oregon State: 7 Beavers
Pennsylvania: 7 Quakers
Pennsylvania State: 12 Nittany
Lions
Pittsburgh: 8 Panthers
Princeton: 6 Tigers
Purdue: 12 Boilermakers
Rhode Island: 4 Rams
Rice: 4 Owls
Rutgers: 14 Scarlet Knights
San Diego State: 6 Aztecs
San Jose State: 8 Spartans
South Carolina: 9 Gamecocks
South Carolina State: 8 Bulldogs
Southern California: 7 Trojans
Southern Illinois: 7 Salukis
Southern Methodist: 8 Mustangs
Stanford: 9 Cardinals
Syracuse: 9 Orangemen
Temple: 4 Owls
Tennessee: 10 Volunteers
Tennessee State: 6 Tigers
Tennessee Tech: 12 Golden Eagles
Texas: 9 Longhorns

Texas A&M: 6 Aggies
Texas Christian: 11 Horned Frogs
Texas Southern: 6 Tigers
Texas Tech: 10 Red Raiders
Toledo: 7 Rockets
Tulane: 9 Green Wave
UCLA: 6 Bruins
UNLV: 12 Runnin' Rebels
Utah: 4 Utes
Utah State: 6 Aggies
Vanderbilt: 10 Commodores
Villanova: 8 Wildcats
Virginia: 9 Cavaliers
VMI: 7 Keydets
VPI: 8 Gobblers
Wake Forest: 12 Demon Deacons
Washington: 7 Huskies
Washington State: 7 Cougars
West Virginia: 12 Mountaineers
William & Mary: 5 Tribe
Wisconsin: 7 Badgers
Wyoming: 7 Cowboys
Yale: 4 Elis 8 Bulldogs

collide
3 hit, ram 4 bump 5 clash, crash,
smash 6 impact, strike 7 impinge
8 conflict

collision
4 bump, jolt 5 clash, crash, shock,
smash, wreck 6 impact 7 crack-up,
smashup 10 concussion

collocate
7 arrange 8 position 9 juxtapose

collogue
6 confer, huddle, parley, powwow
7 consult

colloid
3 gel, sol 4 agar 7 mixture 8 hydro-
gel, hydrosol

colloquial
6 casual, vulgar 7 demotic 8 familiar,
informal 9 idiomatic 10 vernacular

colloquium
5 forum 7 palaver, seminar 9 symposium 10 conference, roundtable

colloquy
4 chat, talk 5 forum 6 debate, parley
7 palaver, seminar 8 dialogue

9 symposium **10** conference, discussion, roundtable **12** conversation **13** confabulation

collude
4 plot **6** devise, scheme **7** connive **8** conspire, contrive, intrigue **9** machinate

collusion
4 plot **8** intrigue, skin game **10** conspiracy

collywobbles
5 colic, gripe **9** bellyache **11** stomachache

Colombia
capital: 6 Bogotá
city: 4 Cali **6** Ibagué **8** Medellín **9** Cartagena **12** Barranquilla
language: 7 Spanish
liberator: 7 Bolivar (Simón)
monetary unit: 4 peso
mountain, range: 5 Andes, Chita **6** Puracé, Tolima **9** Cristóbal
neighbor: 4 Peru **6** Brazil, Panama **7** Ecuador **9** Venezuela
river: 6 Chauca **7** Orinoco **9** Magdalena
sea: 9 Caribbean

Colonel Blimp
4 fogy, Tory **6** fossil **7** old fogy **8** mossback **10** fuddy-duddy **11** reactionary

colonnade
4 stoa **9** peristyle

colony
7 outpost **9** satellite **10** settlement

color
3 dun, dye, hue, red, tan **4** aqua, blue, cast, glow, gold, gray, grey, jade, lime, navy, pink, puce, rose, teal, tint, tone **5** amber, azure, beige, belie, black, blush, brown, coral, ebony, flush, green, hazel, henna, ivory, khaki, lilac, mauve, ocher, ochre, olive, paint, peach, rouge, shade, stain, taupe, tinge, umber **6** auburn, bronze, canary, copper, indigo, maroon, orange, purple, redden, salmon, sienna, silver, violet, yellow **7** crimson, emerald, magenta, pigment, saffron, scarlet **8** chestnut, dyestuff, lavender, tincture **9** embellish, embroider, turquoise, vermilion **10** aquamarine, exaggerate **12** pigmentation
band: 5 facia, vitta **6** fascia
combining form: 5 chrom **6** chromo **7** chromat **8** chromato
primary: 3 red **4** blue **6** yellow
relating to: 9 chromatic
secondary: 5 green **6** orange, purple
soft: 6 pastel

Colorado
capital: 6 Denver
city: 4 Vail **5** Aspen **6** Aurora, Pueblo **7** Boulder **8** Lakewood **11** Fort Collins
college, university: 5 Regis **9** Fort Lewis
mountain, range: 5 Longs (Peak), Pikes (Peak), Rocky **6** Elbert **7** Rockies
nickname: 10 Centennial (State)
park: 9 Mesa Verde
river: 8 Arkansas, Colorado **9** Rio Grande
state bird: 11 lark bunting
state flower: 9 columbine
state tree: 10 blue spruce

colorant
3 dye **5** stain **7** pigment **8** dyestuff, tincture

colored
6 biased, warped **8** one-sided, partisan **9** jaundiced **10** prejudiced **11** tendentious

colorful
3 gay **5** gaudy, showy, vivid **6** bright, flashy, florid, garish, motley **7** splashy

coloring
4 cast, tint **5** front, tinge **6** facade, nuance **7** pigment **8** overtone **10** camouflage, complexion **12** embroidering **13** embellishment

colorless
3 wan **4** ashy, drab, dull, flat, pale **5** ashen, pasty, prosy, waxen, white

Color Purple author
6 albino, doughy, pallid 7 insipid,
neutral, prosaic 8 abstract,
blanched, bleached 10 achromatic,
lackluster

Color Purple author
6 Walker (Alice)

colossal
4 huge, vast 7 immense, mammoth,
massive, titanic 8 enormous, gigantic 9 cyclopean, monstrous 10 gargantuan, stupendous 11 astonishing, elephantine

colossus
5 giant, titan 6 statue 7 goliath,
mammoth, monster 8 behemoth
9 leviathan

Colossus of ___
6 Rhodes

colporteur
10 evangelist, missionary 12 propagandist

colt
4 foal, tyro 6 novice, rookie 8 beginner, freshman, neophyte, newcomer
9 fledgling 10 tenderfoot

coltish
6 frisky, impish 7 playful 10 frolicsome

Columbine
beloved: 9 Harlequin
father: 9 Pantaloon

Columbus, Christopher
birthplace: 5 Genoa
patron: 8 Isabella 9 Ferdinand
ship: 4 Niña 5 Pinta 10 Santa
Maria
son: 5 Diego
starting point: 5 Palos

column
3 row 4 pier 5 shaft, stela 6 pillar
7 obelisk 8 pilaster
angle: 5 arris
base: 4 ordo 5 socle 6 plinth
9 stylobate
bulge: 7 entasis
female figure: 8 caryatid
male figure: 5 atlas 7 telamon
8 atlantes (plural)
style: 5 Doric, Ionic 10 Corinthian
top: 7 capital 8 chapiter

coma
6 stupor, torpor 8 blackout, hebetude, lethargy 9 lassitude

comate
3 pal 4 chum 5 buddy, crony
7 comrade, partner 9 associate,
colleague, companion

comatose
5 dopey 6 stupid, torpid 7 out cold
8 sluggish 9 lethargic 10 insensible
11 unconscious

comb
4 rake, sift, sort 5 crest, curry, probe,
scour, sweep, tease 6 search,
winnow 7 ransack 8 untangle
10 straighten 11 investigate

combat
3 war 4 buck, duel, fray 5 fight,
repel 6 action, battle, oppose, resist,
strife 7 contend, contest, dispute
8 skirmish, struggle 9 withstand
11 controversy

combatant
7 battler, fighter, soldier, warrior
8 militant, opponent 9 adversary,
aggressor, assailant, contender,
disputant, mercenary 10 antagonist,
challenger, competitor, contestant
11 belligerent

combative
6 feisty 7 scrappy, warlike 8 militant
9 agonistic, bellicose, truculent
10 aggressive, pugnacious 11 belligerent, contentious, quarrelsome
12 disputatious, militaristic

combativeness
9 pugnacity 10 aggression, truculence 11 bellicosity 12 belligerence

combe
4 dale, dell, glen, vale 6 dingle,
valley

combination
3 mix 4 bloc, pool, ring 5 blend,
union 6 fusion, hookup, merger
7 melding, merging 8 alliance

9 aggregate, coalition, composite, synthesis 10 connection 11 affiliation, association, conjunction, partnership, unification 13 consolidation

combine

3 add, mix, wed 4 band, bloc, fuse, join, link, pool, ring 5 blend, chain, group, marry, merge, trust, unify, union, unite 6 cartel, league, mingle 7 bracket, conjoin, connect, faction 8 coadjute, coalesce 9 associate, coalition, commingle, cooperate, integrate, syndicate 10 amalgamate 11 consolidate, incorporate 12 conglomerate
Japanese: 8 keiretsu, zaibatsu
Korean: 7 chaebol, jaebeol

combined action

7 synergy 9 synergism

combo

4 band, trio 5 group 6 septet, sextet 7 quartet, quintet 8 ensemble

combust

4 burn 6 ignite, kindle 10 incinerate

combustible

4 edgy, fuel 8 burnable, volatile 9 excitable, flammable, ignitable 11 inflammable
material: 3 gas, oil 4 coal, peat, wood 6 tinder

combustion

4 riot 7 burning 8 eruption, ignition, kindling 9 explosion, oxidation 13 thermogenesis

come

4 flow, hail, stem 5 arise, issue, occur 6 arrive, derive, show up, spring, turn up 7 advance, emanate, proceed 8 approach 9 originate
a cropper: 4 fail, fall
across: 4 find, meet 8 discover 9 encounter
apart: 12 disintegrate
at: 6 attack
away: 5 leave 6 depart
before: 7 precede
clean: 7 confess
forth: 5 issue 6 appear, emerge

forward: 7 advance 9 volunteer
into: 5 enter 7 acquire
near: 5 verge 8 approach
round: 5 rally 7 get well, recover
to pass: 5 occur 6 happen
up: 5 arise
upon: 4 find, meet 8 discover 9 encounter

comeback

5 rally 6 answer, retort, return 7 rebound, revival, riposte 8 rebuttal, recovery, repartee, response 11 improvement 12 counterclaim, recuperation

come by

4 call 5 pop in, visit 6 drop in, look in 7 acquire, collect, inherit

comedian

3 wag, wit 4 card 5 clown, comic, droll, joker 6 jester 7 farceur 8 funnyman, humorist, jokester, quipster 11 entertainer

comedo

9 blackhead

comedown

4 dive, fall, ruin 5 crash 7 decline, descent, failure, setback 8 collapse 9 ruination

come down with

3 get 5 catch 7 develop 8 contract

comedy

5 farce, humor 6 levity 8 drollery, hilarity 9 drollness, wittiness

come in

5 enter, reply 6 answer 7 respond

comely

4 fair 5 bonny, sonsy 6 lovely, pretty, proper, sonsie 7 winsome 8 becoming, decorous, handsome, pleasing 9 beauteous, beautiful, befitting 10 attractive 11 good-looking

come off

4 fare, seem 5 click, occur 6 appear, go over, happen, pan out 7 develop, succeed 8 prove out 9 transpire

come-on
4 bait, lure, trap 5 decoy, snare
9 seduction 10 allurement, enticement, inducement, invitation, temptation 12 blandishment, inveiglement, solicitation

come out
4 leak 5 break, debut, end up
6 emerge 9 transpire

come out with
3 say 4 tell 5 state, utter 6 report
7 declare, deliver, publish, release
8 announce, proclaim

comestible
6 edible 7 eatable 8 esculent

comestibles
4 feed, food 6 viands 7 edibles
8 victuals 9 provender 10 provisions

come through
6 chip in, endure 7 pitch in, prevail,
survive 8 transmit 10 contribute

come together
4 mass, meet 5 merge, swarm
6 gather, huddle 7 cluster, collect,
combine, convene 8 assemble,
converge 10 congregate

come upon
4 find 7 run into, uncover, unearth
8 bump into, discover, trip over
9 encounter, run across

comeuppance
3 due 5 lumps 7 deserts

comfort
3 aid 4 help 5 cheer 6 assist, buck
up, luxury, relief, solace, soothe,
succor 7 amenity, cheer up, console,
relieve, support 8 reassure, sympathy 10 assistance, sympathize
11 commiserate, consolation, contentment

comfortable
4 cozy, easy, homy, snug, soft
5 ample, cushy, homey, roomy
7 content, easeful, restful, well-off
8 adequate, homelike, pleasant,
pleasing, spacious, well-to-do
9 agreeable, satisfied, well-fixed
10 commodious, prosperous, sufficient, well-heeled 11 substantial
12 satisfactory

comforter
4 down, pouf, puff 5 duvet, quilt
9 eiderdown

comfy
4 cozy, homy 5 cushy, homey

comic
3 wag, wit 5 antic, droll, funny, joker
6 jester 7 risible 8 comedian,
farcical, funnyman, humorist, jokester, quipster 9 laughable, ludicrous
10 ridiculous

comical
4 zany 5 droll, funny, goofy, silly
6 absurd 7 amusing, foolish, risible,
waggish 8 farcical 9 laughable,
ludicrous 10 ridiculous

comic strip
4 Pogo, Shoe 5 Hazel, Henry, Nancy
6 Archie, Popeye 7 Blondie, Dilbert,
Far Side (The), Peanuts 8 Alley
Oop, Andy Capp, Garfield, Krazy Kat,
Li'l Abner, Superman 9 Betty Boop,
Dick Tracy, Marmaduke, Mary Worth,
Spider-Man, Yellow Kid (The)
10 Doonesbury, Joe Palooka, Little
Nemo 11 Bloom County, Brenda
Starr, Flash Gordon, Mutt and Jeff,
Rex Morgan M.D., Steve Canyon
12 Beetle Bailey 13 Captain Marvel,
Gasoline Alley, Prince Valiant

coming
3 due 4 next 5 fated, onset 6 advent, future 7 arrival, ensuing,
nearing 8 approach, expected,
foreseen, imminent 9 following,
impending 11 approaching
forth: 7 issuant

comity
5 amity 7 concord, harmony 8 goodwill 10 friendship 11 benevolence,
camaraderie 12 friendliness

comma
4 lull 5 pause 8 interval

command
3 bid 4 rule, sway 5 order 6 adjure,
behest, charge, compel, direct,
enjoin 7 bidding, conduct, control,

dictate, mandate, mastery, precept **9** authority, direction, directive, expertise, ordinance **10** domination, injunction **11** instruction **12** jurisdiction

to go: 4 mush **6** avaunt, begone **7** giddyap, giddyup

to stop: 4 whoa **5** avast

commandeer
4 take **5** annex, seize, usurp **6** assume, hijack **7** preempt **8** accroach, arrogate **9** conscript, sequester **10** confiscate **11** appropriate, expropriate, requisition

commander
4 boss, head **6** honcho, leader, master **7** captain, general, headman, officer

commandment
3 law **4** fiat, rule **5** edict, order **6** decree **7** mitzvah, precept, statute

commedia dell' ____
4 arte

comme il faut
6 decent, polite, proper, seemly **7** correct **8** becoming, decorous, suitable

commemorate
4 keep **7** observe **8** eulogize, monument **9** celebrate, solemnize **11** memorialize **13** monumentalize

commemorative
8 memorial **10** dedicatory **11** celebratory

commence
5 begin, start **6** launch, set out **7** kick off **8** embark on, initiate **10** embark upon, inaugurate

commencement
4 dawn **5** birth, onset, start **6** outset **7** dawning, genesis, opening **9** beginning, inception **10** graduation **12** inauguration

commend
4 hail, laud **5** extol **6** commit, kudize, praise, salute, tender **7** acclaim, applaud, approve, consign, entrust **8** hand over, relegate, turn over **10** compliment

commendable
6 worthy **8** laudable **9** admirable, deserving, estimable, meritable, venerable **10** creditable **11** meritorious **12** praiseworthy

commensurable
see **commensurate**

commensurate
4 even **5** equal **10** comparable **11** coextensive **12** proportional **13** corresponding, proportionate

comment
4 note **5** opine **6** remark **7** mention, observe **8** critique, point out **9** criticism, interject **10** animadvert **11** observation **12** obiter dictum

commentary
5 gloss **6** review **8** analysis, critique, exegesis **9** editorial, narration, voice-over **10** annotation, exposition **11** explanation, observation **12** appreciation, obiter dictum

commerce
5 trade **7** contact, traffic **8** business, congress, dealings, exchange, industry **9** communion **11** interchange **13** communication

commercial
6 advert **8** economic **10** mercantile **13** advertisement

commie
3 Red **5** pinko **6** bolshy **7** bolshie **9** Bolshevik

commination
5 curse **8** anathema **10** accusation, execration **11** imprecation, malediction **12** denunciation

commingle
3 mix **4** meld **5** blend, merge, unify **8** compound, intermix **9** integrate **10** amalgamate

comminute
4 bray **5** crush, grind **9** granulate, pulverize

commiserate
4 pity **7** condole, feel for **9** empathize **10** sympathize **13** compassionate

commiseration

4 pity, ruth **7** empathy **8** sympathy **10** compassion, condolence

commission

3 bid, fee **4** name **5** board, order **6** agency, assign, charge, enable, engage, enjoin, enlist **7** appoint, command, council, empower, license, warrant **8** accredit, delegate, deputize **9** authorize, designate **10** delegation, deputation, percentage **11** certificate

commit

4 bind **5** allot, grant, refer **6** assign, convey, invest, ordain, pledge, record, reveal **7** achieve, consign, deposit, entrust, execute, perform, promise, pull off, trustee **8** allocate, carry out, hand over, obligate, relegate, turn over **10** accomplish, perpetrate

commitment

3 vow **4** bond, deal, duty **6** charge, devoir, pledge **7** promise **8** contract **9** agreement, assurance, guarantee **10** obligation **11** undertaking

committal

see **commitment**

commixture

5 blend **6** fusion **7** amalgam, melange **8** compound, mingling **9** composite

commodious

4 wide **5** ample, roomy **8** spacious **9** capacious, expansive, luxurious **11** comfortable

commodities

5 goods, items, wares **8** articles, products **9** vendibles **11** merchandise

common

4 park **5** banal, daily, joint, plaza, trite, usual **6** mutual, normal, shared **7** general, generic, prosaic, regular, routine, typical **8** adequate, communal, conjoint, conjunct, déclassé, everyday, familiar, frequent, habitual, ordinary, standard, workaday **9** customary, prevalent, tolerable, universal **10** collective, pedestrian, prevailing, unexciting, widespread **12** conventional, run-of-the-mill, satisfactory **13** unexceptional, uninteresting

commonalty

3 mob **5** plebs **6** masses, people, plebes, public, rabble **7** commune **8** populace **9** hoi polloi, multitude, plebeians **11** proletariat, rank and file, third estate

commoners

see **commonalty**

commonplace

5 stale, tired, trite, usual **6** cliché, normal, truism **7** bromide, clichéd, humdrum, mundane, obvious, prosaic, regular, routine, typical **8** banality, bromidic, chestnut, everyday, habitual, mediocre, ordinary, well-worn, workaday **9** hackneyed, platitude, prevalent **10** pedestrian, shibboleth, stereotype, uneventful **11** stereotyped **12** conventional, run-of-the-mill, unremarkable **13** stereotypical, unexceptional, uninteresting

common sense

6 wisdom **8** judgment, prudence **10** shrewdness

Common Sense author

5 Paine (Thomas)

commotion

3 ado, din, row **4** flap, fuss, moil, riot, stew, stir, to-do **5** storm, whirl **6** bustle, clamor, dither, flurry, fracas, furore, hoopla, hubbub, hurrah, lather, outcry, pother, racket, ruckus, rumpus, shindy, tumult, uproar, upturn **7** ferment, tempest, turmoil **8** brouhaha, foofaraw **9** agitation, confusion **10** convulsion, hullabaloo, hurly-burly, turbulence **11** pandemonium

commove

5 rouse **6** excite **7** agitate, inspire, provoke **9** electrify, galvanize, stimulate

communal
5 civil, joint 6 common, mutual, public, shared 10 collective 11 socialistic

commune
10 collective
Israeli: 7 kibbutz
Russian: 3 mir 7 kolkhoz

communicable
8 catching 10 contagious, infectious 13 transmissible, transmittable

communicate
4 tell 6 convey, impart, inform, pass on, relate, reveal, signal 7 connect, contact, divulge 8 disclose, transmit 9 make known

communication
4 talk 7 contact, message, missive, talking 8 converse, exchange 9 directive 10 discussing, discussion 11 interchange, intercourse 12 conversation
means: 3 Web 4 drum, mail, note 5 e-mail, media, phone, radio 6 letter, medium, pigeon, speech 8 Internet 9 telegraph, telephone 10 television
system: 8 language

communications code word
4 Alfa, Echo, Golf, Kilo, Lima, Mike, Papa, Xray, Zulu 5 Alpha, Bravo, Delta, Hotel, India, Oscar, Romeo, Tango 6 Quebec, Sierra, Victor, Yankee 7 Charlie, Foxtrot, Juliett, Uniform, Whiskey 8 November

communicative
5 vocal 6 fluent, prolix 7 verbose, voluble 8 eloquent 9 expansive, garrulous, talkative 10 articulate, expressive, loquacious

communion
7 rapport, sharing 9 Eucharist, sacrament 10 connection, fellowship
cloth: 8 corporal
cup: 7 chalice
plate: 5 paten

communism
7 Marxism 8 Leninism 10 bolshevism 12 collectivism

Communist
3 red 5 lefty, pinko 6 bolshy, Maoist 7 bolshie, comrade, Marxist 8 Leninist 9 Bolshevik, Stalinist 10 Bolshevist, Trotskyist

Communist leader
Chinese: 3 Mao 4 Deng 5 Jiang 8 Hu Jintao 9 Mao Zedong 10 Jiang Zemin, Mao Tse-tung 12 Deng Xiaoping 13 Teng Hsiao-p'ing
Russian: 5 Lenin (Vladimir Ilyich) 6 Stalin (Joseph) 7 Kosygin (Aleksey), Trotsky (Leon) 8 Andropov (Yuri), Brezhnev (Leonid) 9 Chernenko (Konstantin), Gorbachev (Mikhail) 10 Khrushchev (Nikita)

community
4 town 7 enclave, society 12 neighborhood
ecological: 10 biocenosis 11 biocoenosis

commute
5 alter 6 change, make up, modify, soften, travel 7 convert, curtail, shorten, shuttle 8 decrease, exchange, mitigate, transfer 9 transform, translate, transmute, transpose 10 compensate, substitute 11 interchange

Como está _____?
5 usted

Comoros
capital: 6 Moroni
island: 6 Mohéli 7 Anjouan 12 Grande Comore
language: 6 Arabic, French 8 Comorian
monetary unit: 5 franc
volcano: 8 Karthala

compact
4 bond 5 close, dense, unify 7 bargain, bunched, crowded, pressed 8 compress, condense, contract, covenant 9 agreement, concordat 10 convention 11 concentrate, consolidate, transaction

compadre
3 pal 4 chum, mate 5 amigo, buddy,

companion

crony 6 friend 7 comrade, partner
8 confrere, sidekick, intimate 9 associate, colleague, companion

companion

3 pal 4 chum, mate 5 buddy, crony
6 cohort, escort 7 comrade, consort,
partner 8 sidekick 9 associate,
attendant, colleague

companionable

6 genial, social 7 affable, amiable
8 outgoing, sociable 9 agreeable,
congenial, convivial 10 gregarious
11 good-natured

companionship

7 company, society 8 intimacy
10 fellowship 11 camaraderie

company

4 band, club, crew, firm, gang, team
5 corps, group, party, troop 6 circle,
clique, guests, outfit, troupe 7 concern, coterie, retinue, society, visitor
8 assembly, business, ensemble,
visitors 9 gathering 10 assemblage,
enterprise, fellowship 11 association,
camaraderie, corporation 12 congregation 13 companionship, establishment

comparable

4 akin, like 5 alike 6 agnate 7 similar,
uniform 8 parallel 9 analogous
10 equivalent, homologous 12 commensurate 13 corresponding

comparative

4 near 8 relative 11 approximate

compare

5 liken, match 6 equate, relate
7 collate 8 contrast, parallel 9 correlate 10 assimilate

comparison

6 simile 7 analogy 8 affinity, contrast, likeness 9 collation, semblance 10 similarity, similitude
11 correlation, resemblance

compartment

3 bay 4 cell, nook, part, slot 5 berth,
booth, niche, stall 6 alcove, carrel,
locker 7 chamber, cubicle, section
8 division 9 cubbyhole 10 pigeonhole 11 subdivision

compass

3 hem 4 ring 5 ambit, field, grasp,
orbit, range, reach, scope, sweep
6 bounds, circle, domain, extent,
girdle, limits, radius, sphere 7 circuit,
environ, purview 8 boundary, confines, environs 9 enclosure, extension, perimeter, periphery 13 circumference
kind: 4 gyro 5 solar 8 magnetic
stand: 8 binnacle

compassion

4 pity, ruth 5 mercy 7 charity, empathy 8 clemency, humanity, kindness,
sympathy 10 condolence, humaneness 11 benevolence 13 commiseration, fellow feeling

compassionate

4 pity, warm 6 humane, tender
7 clement 8 merciful 10 benevolent,
charitable, solicitous 11 commiserate, kindhearted, softhearted, sympathetic, warmhearted

compassionless

5 stony 7 callous 8 obdurate
9 heartless, unfeeling 11 cold-
blooded, hard-hearted, ironhearted
12 stonyhearted

compass point

3 ENE, ESE, NNE, NNW, SSE,
SSW, WNW, WSW 4 east, west
5 north, rhumb, south 7 bearing
Scottish: 4 airt

compatible

6 proper 8 suitable 9 agreeable,
congenial, congruous, consonant
10 consistent, harmonious, like-
minded 11 appropriate, sympathetic

compatriot

8 confrere 9 associate, colleague,
companion

compeer

see **companion**

compel

4 hale, urge 5 drive, force 6 coerce,
impose, oblige 7 enforce 9 constrain

compelling

4 dire 5 acute 6 cogent, crying,
urgent 7 clamant, exigent, telling,

weighty **8** forceful, pressing **10** convincing, persuasive **11** importunate, significant **12** well-grounded **13** authoritative

compendious
5 brief, pithy, short **7** compact, concise, summary **8** succinct **9** condensed **11** abbreviated

compendium
4 list **5** brief, guide **6** aperçu, digest, manual, précis, sketch, survey **7** epitome, summary **8** abstract, Baedeker, handbook, overview, syllabus, synopsis **9** anthology, guidebook, vade mecum **10** abridgment, collection, conspectus **11** abridgement, compilation, enchiridion

compensate
3 pay **5** atone, repay **6** make up, offset, pay off, redeem, set off **7** balance, guerdon, requite, satisfy **8** outweigh **9** indemnify, reimburse **10** counteract, neutralize, recompense, remunerate **11** countervail

compensation
6 amends, reward, salary **7** damages, payment, redress **8** earnings, reprisal, requital, solatium **9** atonement, indemnity, quittance, repayment **10** recompense, reparation **11** restitution **12** remuneration

compete
3 vie **4** spar **5** fight **6** battle, strive **7** contend, contest **8** struggle

competence
5 skill **7** ability, know-how **8** adequacy, aptitude, capacity, facility **9** expertise **10** capability **11** proficiency, sufficiency **13** qualification

competent
3 fit **4** able **5** adept **6** au fait, decent, proper **7** capable, skilled **8** adequate **9** efficient, qualified **10** proficient, sufficient **12** satisfactory

competition
4 bout, game, meet, race **5** clash, fight, match, rival **6** strife **7** contest,

matchup, rivalry **8** concours, conflict, striving, struggle, tug-of-war **10** antagonism, contention, tournament

competitor
5 enemy, rival **8** opponent **9** adversary **10** antagonist, contestant, opposition

compile
4 edit **5** amass **6** gather, select **7** build up, collate, collect **8** assemble **9** construct **10** accumulate **11** anthologize

complacency
5 pride **7** conceit **8** smugness **10** narcissism

complacent
4 smug **6** serene **7** assured **9** conceited, confident **11** self-assured, unconcerned **13** self-confident, self-contented, self-possessed, self-satisfied

complain
3 nag **4** beef, crab, fret, fuss, wail **5** gripe, grump, whine **6** grouch, grouse, lament, yammer **7** grizzle, grumble, protest **9** bellyache

complainer
4 crab **5** crank **6** griper, grouch **7** grouser **8** grumbler, sourpuss **10** malcontent **11** faultfinder

complaint
5 gripe **6** grouse, lament, malady **7** ailment, disease, protest **8** disorder, sickness, syndrome **9** condition, criticism, grievance, infirmity, objection **10** affliction, allegation **12** protestation

complaisant
4 easy, mild **7** amiable, lenient **8** generous, obliging **9** agreeable, compliant, easygoing, indulgent **11** deferential, good-humored, good-natured **12** good-tempered **13** accommodating

complement
4 crew, rest **9** correlate, remainder **10** supplement **11** counterpart

complete
3 end **4** done, full, halt **5** close,

ended, total, utter, whole **6** entire, finish, intact, wind up, wrap up **7** achieve, fulfill, perfect, perform, plenary **8** absolute, conclude, finalize, finished, integral, round out, thorough **9** concluded, out-and-out, terminate **10** accomplish, consummate, exhaustive, unabridged **11** categorical, unmitigated **13** thoroughgoing

completed

4 done, over **5** ended **7** through **8** done with, executed, finished **9** concluded, fulfilled **10** terminated **11** consummated **12** accomplished

completion

3 end **6** finish, windup, wrap-up **8** fruition **10** conclusion

complex

6 daedal, knotty, system, varied **7** chelate, gordian, network **8** abstruse, compound, involved, syndrome, tortuous **9** aggregate, Byzantine, composite, elaborate, intricate **10** convoluted **11** complicated **12** conglomerate, labyrinthine **13** heterogeneous, sophisticated

complexion

3 hue **4** cast, tint, tone **5** color, humor, tinge **6** aspect, makeup, nature, temper **8** tincture **9** character **10** appearance, coloration **11** disposition, temperament **12** pigmentation **13** individuality

compliance

7 consent **8** docility **9** agreement, deference, obedience **10** acceptance, conformity, submission **11** amenability, flexibility, resignation **12** acquiescence, tractability

complicate

5 mix up, ravel, snarl **6** jumble, muddle, tangle **7** confuse, involve **8** confound, disorder, entangle **9** aggravate, convolute **10** disarrange, exacerbate

complicated

6 daedal, knotty **7** complex, gordian, tangled **8** abstruse, involved, tortu-

ous **9** Byzantine, elaborate, intricate, recondite **10** convoluted **12** labyrinthine **13** heterogeneous, sophisticated

complicity

8 abetment **9** collusion **10** connivance **11** involvement

compliment

4 hail, kudo, laud **5** extol, honor, kudos **6** praise, salute **7** acclaim, applaud, bouquet, commend, regards, tribute **8** accolade, encomium **9** laudation, recommend **11** recognition **12** appreciation, commendation, congratulate

complimentary

4 free **6** gratis **8** costless **9** favorable, laudatory **10** chargeless, gratuitous **12** appreciative

comply

4 obey **5** yield **6** accede, submit **7** conform **9** acquiesce

component

4 part **5** piece **6** factor **7** element, segment **10** ingredient **11** constituent

comport

4 bear, jibe **5** agree, carry, fit in, match, tally **6** accord, acquit, behave, demean, square **7** conduct **8** coincide, dovetail **9** harmonize **10** correspond

comportment

3 air **4** mien **7** address, bearing, conduct **8** attitude, behavior, carriage, demeanor, presence

compose

4 calm, cool, form, lull, make **5** forge, quiet, relax, still, write **6** becalm, create, devise, draw up, indite, invent, make up, settle, solace, soothe **7** collect, console, contain, control **8** comprise **9** construct, fabricate, formulate, originate **10** constitute
type: **3** set

composed

4 calm, cool **5** staid **6** poised,

sedate, serene **9** collected, unruffled
11 unflappable **13** imperturbable,
self-possessed

composer

6 scorer **8** melodist **9** balladist,
songsmith, tunesmith **10** songwriter
American: 3 Kay (Hershy, Ulysses)
4 Bock (Jerry), Cage (John), Hill
(Edward Burlingame), Ives (Charles),
Kern (Jerome), King (Carole), Lane
(Burton), Monk (Thelonious), Work
(Henry Clay) **5** Adams (John),
Arlen (Harold), Beach (Amy), Blake
(Eubie), Bland (James A.), Bloch
(Ernest), Cohan (George M.), Friml
(Rudolf), Glass (Philip), Gould
(Morton), Grofé (Ferde), Handy
(W. C.), Loewe (Frederick), Mason
(Daniel Gregory, Lowell), Moore
(Douglas), Reich (Steve), Sousa
(John Philip), Still (William Grant),
Styne (Jule), Zappa (Frank) **6** Barber
(Samuel), Berlin (Irving), Carter
(Elliott), Cowell (Henry), Emmett
(Daniel), Foster (Stephen), Hanson
(Howard), Harris (Roy), Herman
(Jerry), Joplin (Scott), Kander (John),
McHugh (Jimmy), McKuen (Rod),
Menken (Alan), Morton ("Jelly Roll"),
Oliver ("King"), Parker (Charlie "Bird,"
Horatio), Piston (Walter), Porter
(Cole), Previn (André), Seeger
(Pete), Taylor (Deems), Varèse
(Edgard), Warren (Harry) **7** Babbitt
(Milton), Brubeck (Dave), Copland
(Aaron), Gilbert (Henry F.), Gilmore
(Patrick), Goldman (Edwin Franko),
Herbert (Victor), Loesser (Frank),
Mancini (Henry), Menotti (Gian
Carlo), Rodgers (Richard), Romberg
(Sigmund), Schuman (William),
Thomson (Virgil), Tiomkin (Dimitri),
Willson (Meredith), Youmans (Vin-
cent) **8** Anderson (Leroy), Billings
(William), Burleigh (Henry Thacker),
Damrosch (Leopold, Walter), Gersh-
win (George), Hamlisch (Marvin),
Herrmann (Bernard), Korngold (Erich
Wolfgang), Kreisler (Fritz), Marsalis
(Wynton), Schuller (Gunther), Ses-
sions (Roger), Sondheim (Stephen),

Williams (John) **9** Bacharach (Burt),
Bernstein (Elmer, Leonard), Donald-
son (Walter), Ellington (Duke), Hov-
haness (Alan), MacDowell (Edward)
10 Blitzstein (Marc), Carmichael
(Hoagy), Gottschalk (Louis Moreau)
Argentinian: 9 Ginastera (Alberto)
Australian: 8 Grainger (Percy)
Austrian: 4 Berg (Alban), Wolf
(Hugo) **5** Haydn (Franz Joseph)
6 Czerny (Karl), Mahler (Gustav),
Mozart (Leopold, Wolfgang Ama-
deus), Straus (Oscar), Webern
(Anton) **7** Strauss (Eduard, Johann,
Josef) **8** Bruckner (Anton), Schubert
(Franz) **10** Schoenberg (Arnold)
Belgian: 5 Ysaÿe (Eugène)
6 Franck (César)
Brazilian: 5 Jobim (Antonio Carlos)
10 Villa-Lobos (Heitor)
Czech: 3 Suk (Josef) **6** Dvořák
(Antonín) **7** Janáček (Leoš), Martinu
(Bohuslav), Smetana (Bedřich)
Danish: 7 Nielsen (Carl)
Dutch: 9 Sweelinck (Jan Pieter-
szoon)
English: 4 Arne (Thomas Augus-
tine), Byrd (William) **5** Elgar (Ed-
ward), Holst (Gustav) **6** Delius
(Frederick), Morley (Thomas), Tallis
(Thomas), Walton (William), Wesley
(Charles, Samuel) **7** Britten (Ben-
jamin), Dowland (John), Gibbons
(Orlando), Purcell (Henry), Weelkes
(Thomas) **8** Sullivan (Arthur) **9** Dun-
stable (John) **11** Lloyd Webber
(Andrew)
Finnish: 8 Palmgren (Selim),
Sibelius (Jean)
Flemish: 5 Dufay (Guillaume),
Lasso (Orlando di) **6** Lassus (Or-
lande de) **8** Willaert (Adriaan)
French: 4 Indy (Vincent d'), Lalo
(Edouard) **5** Auber (Esprit), Bizet
(Georges), Dukas (Paul), Fauré
(Gabriel), Ibert (Jacques), Jarre
(Maurice), Lully (Jean-Baptiste),
Ravel (Maurice), Satie (Erik), Widor
(Charles-Marie) **6** Boulez (Pierre),
Campra (André), Franck (César),
Gounod (Charles), Rameau (Jean-
Philippe), Thomas (Ambroise)

7 Berlioz (Hector), Debussy (Claude), Delibes (Léo), Machaut (Guillaume de), Milhaud (Darius), Poulenc (Francis) **8** Chabrier (Emmanuel), Couperin (François, Louis), Honegger (Arthur), Massenet (Jules), Messiaen (Olivier) **9** Meyerbeer (Giacomo), Offenbach (Jacques) **10** Saint-Saëns (Camille)

German: 4 Bach (C. P. E., Johann Christian, Johann Sebastian, Wilhelm Friedemann), Orff (Carl) **5** Bruch (Max), Gluck (Christoph Willibald von), Reger (Max), Spohr (Louis, Ludwig), Weber (Carl Maria von), Weill (Kurt) **6** Brahms (Johannes), Handel (George Frideric), Schütz (Heinrich), Vogler (Abt), Wagner (Richard) **7** Hassler (Hans Leo), Strauss (Richard) **8** Korngold (Erich Wolfgang), Schumann (Robert), Telemann (Georg Philipp) **9** Beethoven (Ludwig van), Buxtehude (Dietrich), Hindemith (Paul), Meyerbeer (Giacomo), Pachelbel (Johann) **10** Praetorius (Michael) **11** Humperdinck (Engelbert), Mendelssohn (Felix), Stockhausen (Karlheinz)

Hungarian: 5 Léhar (Franz), Liszt (Franz) **6** Bartók (Béla), Kodály (Zoltán), Ligeti (György) **8** Dohnányi (Erno)

Italian: 4 Peri (Jacopo), Rota (Nino) **5** Berio (Luciano), Boito (Arrigo), Verdi (Giuseppe) **6** Busoni (Ferruccio) **7** Bellini (Vincenzo), Caccini (Giulio), Corelli (Arcangelo), Martini (Padre), Puccini (Giacomo), Rossini (Gioacchino), Salieri (Antonio), Tartini (Giuseppe), Vivaldi (Antonio) **8** Albinoni (Tomaso), Clementi (Muzio), Gabrieli (Andrea, Giovanni), Mascagni (Pietro), Paganini (Niccolò), Respighi (Ottorino) **9** Cherubini (Luigi), Donizetti (Gaetano), Pergolesi (Giovanni Battista), Scarlatti (Alessandro, Domenico), Tommasini (Vincenzo) **10** Boccherini (Luigi), Monteverdi (Claudio), Palestrina (G. P. da), Ponchielli (Amilcare), Zingarelli (Niccolò) **11** Frescobaldi (Girolamo), Leoncavallo (Ruggero) **12** Dallapiccola (Luigi)

Mexican: 6 Chávez (Carlos)
Norwegian: 5 Grieg (Edvard)
Polish: 6 Chopin (Frédéric) **7** Gorecki (Henryk) **10** Paderewski (Ignacy Jan), Penderecki (Krzysztof), Wieniawski (Henryk) **11** Lutoslawski (Witold), Szymanowski (Karol)
Romanian: 7 Xenakis (Iannis)
Russian: 6 Glinka (Mikhail) **7** Borodin (Aleksandr) **8** Glazunov (Aleksandr), Scriabin (Aleksandr) **9** Balakirev (Mily), Prokofiev (Sergey), Schnittke (Alfred) **10** Kabalevsky (Dmitri), Mussorgsky (Modest), Rubinstein (Anton), Stravinsky (Igor), Tcherepnin (Nikolay) **11** Tchaikovsky (Pyotr Ilich) **12** Khachaturian (Aram), Rachmaninoff (Sergey), Shostakovich (Dmitry)
Spanish: 5 Falla (Manuel de) **7** Albéniz (Isaac), Rodrigo (Joaquin) **8** Granados (Enrique), Victoria (Tomas Luis de)

composite
3 mix **5** blend **6** fusion, hybrid **7** amalgam, complex, mixture **8** compound **11** combination **12** amalgamation

composition
4 opus **5** essay, paper, theme **6** design, layout, makeup **7** article **9** formation **11** arrangement **12** architecture, constitution, construction
choral: 4 mass **5** motet **8** oratorio
for eight: 5 octet
for five: 7 quintet
for four: 7 quartet
for nine: 5 nonet
for one: 4 aria, solo
for seven: 6 septet
for six: 6 sextet
for three: 4 trio
for two: 4 duet
instrumental: 3 jig **4** reel **5** étude, fugue, gigue, march, rondo, suite **6** sonata **7** caprice, partita, prelude, scherzo **8** concerto, fantasia, overture, rhapsody, saraband, sinfonia, symphony, tone poem **9** allemande, capriccio, sarabande **10** intermezzo
vocal: 4 aria, lied, mass, song **5** carol, chant, motet, opera, round

6 arioso, ballad, chanty 7 cantata, chanson, chantey, chorale, lullaby, requiem 8 berceuse, madrigal, oratorio 9 plainsong, spiritual

compos mentis
4 sane 5 lucid, sound 6 normal

composure
4 calm 5 poise 7 balance, dignity 8 calmness, coolness, evenness, serenity, sobriety 9 sangfroid 10 equanimity 11 equilibrium

compound
3 mix 4 join, link 5 admix, alloy, blend, union, unite 6 expand, extend, fusion, make up, mingle 7 amalgam, augment, complex, compost, enlarge, magnify, mixture 8 coalesce, comingle, heighten, increase, intermix, multiply 9 admixture, aggravate, associate, commingle, composite, intensify, synthesis 10 commixture, exacerbate 11 intermingle 12 amalgamation
chemical:
(see at **chemical**)
medicinal: 8 magnesia
protein: 7 peptone
sulfur: 5 thiol 7 sulfide, sulfone 8 sulfonyl, sulfuryl, sulphide

comprehend
4 know 5 catch, grasp 6 absorb, accept, embody, fathom, take in 7 cognize, compass, contain, discern, embrace, include, involve, subsume 8 comprise, perceive 9 encompass 10 appreciate, understand

comprehensible
8 knowable 9 graspable 10 fathomable 12 intelligible

comprehension
3 ken 5 grasp 9 awareness, knowledge 10 cognizance, conception, perception 11 discernment 12 apperception 13 understanding

comprehensive
4 full, wide 5 broad 6 global 7 general, overall 8 catholic, complete, sweeping 9 all-around, extensive, inclusive, universal 10 exhaustive 12 all-inclusive, encyclopedic

comprehensiveness
5 range, reach, scope 7 breadth 8 fullness 9 amplitude

compress
3 jam 4 cram, push 5 crush, press 6 reduce, shrink, squash, squish, shrink 7 bandage, compact, squeeze 8 condense, contract 11 concentrate

comprise
4 form 6 make up 7 compose, contain, embrace, include, subsume 10 comprehend, constitute

compromise
4 mean, pact, risk 6 settle 7 bargain, compact 8 contract, endanger, trade off 9 agreement, middle way 10 concession, golden mean, jeopardize, settlement 12 middle ground

compulsion
4 itch, need, urge 5 drive, force 8 coercion 9 necessity 10 constraint

compulsive
7 driving 9 besetting, obsessive 12 irresistible, overwhelming

compulsory
7 binding 8 coercive, enforced, required 9 mandatory, requisite 10 imperative, obligatory

compunction
4 pang 5 demur, qualm 6 regret, unease 7 remorse, scruple 8 distress 9 hesitancy, misgiving 10 conscience, hesitation

compunctious
5 sorry 8 contrite, penitent 9 regretful, repentant 10 apologetic, remorseful 11 penitential

computation
8 figuring 9 ciphering, reckoning 10 arithmetic, estimation 11 calculation

compute
5 tally, total 6 cipher, figure, reckon 8 estimate 9 calculate, determine

computer
6 abacus, laptop 7 desktop 9 mainframe 10 calculator

component: 3 CPU 4 chip
5 mouse, tower 7 monitor 8 keyboard 9 hard drive
information: 4 data
instruction: 5 macro
inventor: 7 Babbage (Charles)
language: 3 Ada, APL 4 Java, Lisp, Perl 5 ALGOL, BASIC, COBOL
6 Pascal 7 FORTRAN
type: 6 analog 7 digital

comrade
3 pal 4 ally, chum, mate 5 buddy, crony 6 cohort, comate, fellow
7 consort 8 sidekick, tovarich, tovarish 9 associate, colleague, companion

con
3 gyp, vet 4 anti, bilk, coax, dupe, fool, hoax, rook, scam 5 cheat, fraud, learn, study, trick 6 cajole, fleece, gammon, inmate, survey
7 against, blarney, canvass, chicane, convict, deceive, defraud, examine, inspect, swindle, wheedle 8 blandish, flimflam, hoodwink, inveigle, jailbird, memorize, negative, opponent, persuade, prisoner, soft-soap
9 bamboozle, check over, sweet-talk
10 antithesis, manipulate, scrutinize
11 hornswoggle 12 tuberculosis

concatenate
4 join, link 5 unite 7 connect

concavity
3 dip, sag 4 bowl, dent, sink 5 basin
6 crater, hollow, trough 7 sinkage
8 sinkhole 10 depression

conceal
4 bury, hide, mask, veil 5 cache, cloak, cover, stash 6 screen 7 obscure, secrete 8 ensconce, enshroud, palliate 10 camouflage

concealed
5 privy 6 buried, covert, hidden, secret 7 obscured, shrouded, ulterior 11 clandestine

concede
3 own 4 avow, fold 5 admit, allow, award, grant, yield 6 accept, accord

7 confess 9 surrender, vouchsafe
10 capitulate, relinquish 11 acknowledge

conceit
4 idea, whim 5 fancy, pride 6 egoism, megrim, notion, vagary, vanity 7 caprice, egotism, thought 8 crotchet, metaphor, self-love, smugness, snobbery 9 self-pride, vainglory
10 narcissism, self-esteem 11 complacence, complacency, self-opinion, swelled head

conceited
4 vain 6 snobby, snooty 7 pompous, stuck-up 8 immodest, puffed up, snobbish 12 narcissistic, vainglorious

conceitedness
6 vanity 8 self-love 9 vainglory
10 narcissism

conceivable
8 possible 9 plausible, thinkable
10 imaginable, supposable

conceive
4 form 5 beget, fancy, grasp, think
6 accept, assume, devise, expect, follow, gather, ideate, ponder 7 believe, dream up, feature, imagine, realize, suppose, suspect, think up
8 cogitate, envisage, envision, meditate, ruminate 9 apprehend, formulate, originate, speculate, visualize
10 comprehend, excogitate, understand

concentrate
4 mass 5 focus 6 gather, shrink
7 collect, compact 8 assemble, compress, condense, contract, converge 10 accumulate 11 consolidate

concentrated
5 thick 6 intent, strong 7 focused, intense 8 vehement 9 intensive, undiluted, undivided 12 undistracted

concentration
5 field, major, study 9 attention
10 absorption 11 application

concept
4 idea 5 image 6 notion, theory
7 conceit, thought 10 impression,
perception

conception
4 idea 5 birth, image, start 6 notion,
origin, outset, theory 7 conceit,
genesis, thought 9 beginning 10 impression, perception

conceptual
5 ideal 8 abstract, notional 9 imaginary, visionary 10 ideational 11 theoretical 12 hypothetical, intellectual

concern
4 care, firm, heed 5 doubt, worry
6 affair, bear on, bother, engage,
gadget, matter, occupy, outfit, regard,
unease 7 anxiety, company, disturb,
involve, perturb, trouble 8 business,
deal with, disquiet, interest, mistrust
9 attention, curiosity, misgiving,
suspicion 10 enterprise, skepticism,
solicitude, uneasiness 11 carefulness, contrivance, uncertainty
12 apprehension 13 consciousness,
consideration, establishment

concerned
7 anxious, worried 8 affected,
involved 10 implicated, interested

concerning
4 as to, in re 5 about, anent, as for
7 apropos 9 as regards, regarding
10 relating to, relative to, respecting

concert
5 agree, union 6 accord, concur,
settle, soiree 7 arrange, concord,
harmony, recital 8 coincide, musi-
cale 9 agreement, cooperate,
harmonize, negotiate 11 performance

concerted
5 joint 6 mutual, united 7 unified
8 combined 11 coordinated 13 collaborative

concert hall
5 arena, odeum 7 theater, theatre
10 auditorium

concession
5 favor, grant 8 giveback 9 admission, allowance, privilege 10 compromise 12 acquiescence

conch
5 shell 7 mollusc, mollusk

concierge
6 porter, warden 7 doorman, janitor
9 custodian 10 doorkeeper

conciliate
4 calm, ease 6 disarm, pacify, soothe
7 appease, assuage, mollify, placate,
sweeten, win over 9 reconcile
10 propitiate

concise
5 brief, pithy, short, terse 7 compact,
laconic, summary 8 abridged, succinct 9 condensed 10 compressed,
contracted 11 compendious 13 short
and sweet

conclave
5 synod 6 caucus, powwow 7 meeting, session 8 assembly 9 gathering
10 conference, consistory, convention 11 convocation

conclude
3 end 4 halt, stop 5 close, infer,
judge 6 decide, deduce, derive,
effect, figure, finish, gather, reason,
settle, wind up, wrap up 7 collect,
resolve 8 complete 9 determine,
terminate

concluding
4 last 5 final 6 latest, latter 7 closing
8 eventual, terminal, ultimate

conclusion
3 end 4 stop 5 cease, close 6 ending, epilog, finale, finish, period,
result, windup 7 closing, closure,
outcome, verdict 8 decision, epilogue, judgment, sequitur 9 cessation, deduction, inference, summation 10 completion, denouement,
resolution, settlement 11 culmination, termination 13 determination

conclusive
4 last 5 final 6 cogent 8 deciding, decisive, ultimate 9 clinching

10 compelling, convincing, definitive, undeniable **11** determinant, determinate, irrefutable **12** irrefragable, unanswerable **13** determinative

concoct

3 mix **4** brew, cook **5** frame, hatch **6** cook up, create, devise, invent **7** dream up **8** conceive, contrive **9** fabricate, formulate, originate

concoction

4 brew, plan **5** blend **7** mixture, project **8** compound, creation **9** invention **11** combination, contrivance, fabrication, preparation

concomitant

7 adjunct **8** adjuvant **9** accessory, ancillary, associate, attendant, attending, companion, satellite **10** coincident, collateral **12** accompanying **13** accompaniment, supplementary

concord

4 pact **5** amity, peace, unity **6** accord, comity, treaty **7** concert, entente, harmony, rapport **8** goodwill **9** agreement **10** consonance

concordant

8 agreeing **9** congruous, consonant **10** compatible, consistent, harmonious **11** appropriate

concourse

5 foyer **6** throng **7** joining, meeting **8** junction **9** gathering **10** confluence, crossroads

concrete

5 solid **6** actual **8** specific, tangible **10** particular **11** substantial **component: 4** sand **5** water **6** gravel

concubine

7 hetaera, hetaira **8** mistress **9** courtesan, odalisque

concupiscence

4 lust **5** ardor **6** desire **7** lechery, passion **9** prurience, pruriency **11** lustfulness **13** lickerishness

concupiscent

3 hot **7** aroused, goatish, lustful

8 prurient **9** lecherous, lickerish, salacious **10** lascivious, libidinous, lubricious, passionate

concur

4 jibe **5** agree, unite **6** accord, assent **7** approve, combine, concord, consent, go along **8** coincide **9** cooperate, harmonize

concurrent

6 coeval **8** parallel **10** coexistent, coexisting, convergent, synchronic **11** synchronous **12** contemporary, simultaneous

concurrently

6 at once **8** together **12** coincidently

concuss

3 jar **4** rock, stun **5** shake, shock **7** agitate

concussion

3 jar **4** bump, jolt **5** clout, crash, shock **6** impact **7** jarring, jolting, shaking **8** pounding **9** agitation, collision

condemn

3 rap **4** damn, doom **5** blame, decry, knock, seize **7** censure, convict, deplore **8** denounce, sentence **9** criticize, deprecate, proscribe, reprehend, reprobate **10** denunciate

condensation

3 dew **5** brief **6** digest, précis **7** epitome, outline, summary **8** abstract, synopsis **9** reduction **10** abridgment, conspectus **11** abridgement

condense

5 sum up **6** digest, reduce, shrink **7** abridge, compact, shorten **8** boil down, compress, contract **9** constrict, epitomize, summarize, synopsize **10** abbreviate **11** concentrate, consolidate, precipitate

condensed

7 concise, summary **10** boiled down **11** compendious

condescend

5 deign, stoop **6** unbend

condescending

5 lofty **6** lordly, snobby, snooty, uppish, uppity **7** haughty, pompous **8** affected, arrogant, cavalier, snobbish, superior **10** disdainful **11** patronizing, pretentious **12** supercilious

condign

3 apt, due, fit **4** fair, just **5** right **6** proper **7** fitting, merited **8** deserved, rightful, suitable **9** equitable, justified **11** appropriate

condiment

5 curry, sauce, spice **6** catsup, relish, tamari **7** chutney, ketchup, mustard **8** dressing, soy sauce **9** seasoning **10** mayonnaise

____ con Dios!

4 Vaya

condition

5 shape, state, terms **6** fettle, malady, status **7** ailment, disease, fitness, proviso **8** syndrome **9** complaint, essential, exception, necessity, provision, requisite, situation **10** limitation, sine qua non **11** requirement, reservation, stipulation **12** prerequisite **13** qualification

conditional

7 reliant **8** relative **9** dependent, provisory, qualified, tentative, uncertain **10** contingent, restricted **11** provisional

condolence

3 rue **4** pity, ruth **6** solace **7** comfort **8** sympathy **10** compassion **13** commiseration

condonable

7 tenable **9** excusable, tolerable **10** acceptable, defensible, pardonable **11** justifiable

condone

5 remit **6** excuse, pardon **7** forgive **8** overlook

conduce

4 lead, tend **7** redound **10** contribute

conducive

7 helpful, leading, tending **9** favorable **10** beneficial, salubrious **11** efficacious, serviceable, stimulating **12** advantageous, contributory, instrumental **13** accommodating

conduct

3 act, run **4** bear, head, lead, show **5** guide, pilot, steer, usher **6** attend, behave, charge, convey, demean, deport, direct, escort, handle, manage **7** arrange, bearing, comport, control, manners, operate, oversee **8** behavior, demeanor, handling, shepherd, transmit **9** accompany, oversight, supervise **10** administer, deportment, management **11** comportment, supervision

conductor

5 guide **6** escort, leader **7** maestro **8** motorman **10** bandleader
American: **4** Shaw (Robert) **5** Stock (Frederick), Szell (George) **6** Levine (James), Maazel (Lorin), Previn (André), Reiner (Fritz), Thomas (Theodore, Michael Tilson), Walter (Bruno) **7** Fennell (Frederick), Fiedler (Arthur), Monteux (Pierre), Ormandy (Eugene), Schwarz (Gerard), Slatkin (Leonard) **8** Damrosch (Leopold, Walter), Williams (John) **9** Bernstein (Leonard), Leinsdorf (Erich), Rodzinski (Artur), Steinberg (William), Stokowski (Leopold) **11** Kostelanetz (André), Mitropoulos (Dimitri)
Argentinian: **7** Kleiber (Carlos) **9** Barenboim (Daniel)
Australian: **7** Bonynge (Richard)
Austrian: **4** Böhm (Karl) **6** Mahler (Gustav) **7** Karajan (Herbert von) **11** Weingartner (Felix)
Belgian: **5** Ysaÿe (Eugene)
British: **5** Solti (Georg)
Canadian: **6** Dutoit (Charles) **9** MacMillan (Ernest)
Czech: **7** Kubelik (Jan, Rafael)
Dutch: **7** Haitink (Bernard) **10** Mengelberg (Willem)
English: **4** Wood (Henry) **5** Boult (Adrian), Davis (Colin) **6** Rattle (Simon) **7** Beecham (Thomas), Leppard (Raymond), Malcolm (George),

Pinnock (Trevor), Sargent (Malcolm)
8 Goossens (Eugene), Marriner
(Neville) 9 Mackerras (Charles)
10 Barbirolli (John)
Finnish: 7 Salonen (Esa-Pekka)
French: 5 Munch (Charles) 6 Boulez
(Pierre), Prêtre (Georges) 7 Monteux
(Pierre)
German: 4 Muck (Carl, Karl)
5 Masur (Kurt) 6 Jochum (Eugen)
7 Kleiber (Erich) 9 Klemperer (Otto),
Scherchen (Hermann) 10 Sawallisch
(Wolfgang) 11 Furtwängler (Wil-
helm), Mendelssohn (Felix)
Greek: 11 Mitropoulos (Dimitri)
Hungarian: 5 Seidl (Anton) 6 Doráti
(Antal), Reiner (Fritz) 7 Nikisch
(Arthur), Ormandy (Eugene), Richter
(Hans)
Indian: 5 Mehta (Zubin)
Italian: 4 Muti (Riccardo) 6 Abbado
(Claudio) 7 Chailly (Riccardo),
Giulini (Carlo Maria) 8 Cantelli
(Guido), Sinopoli (Giuseppe) 9 Tos-
canini (Arturo)
Japanese: 6 Ozawa (Seiji)
Polish: 9 Rodzinski (Artur)
Russian: 7 Gergiev (Valery) 10 Te-
mirkanov (Yuri) 12 Koussevitzky
(Serge)
Spanish: 6 Iturbi (José)
Swiss: 8 Ansermet (Ernest)
stick: 5 baton

conduit

4 duct, main, pipe 5 canal 6 course
7 channel 8 aqueduct, penstock,
pipeline 11 watercourse

coney

4 pika 5 hyrax, lapin 6 rabbit 10 butterfish

confab

4 chat, talk 6 confer, huddle, parley,
powwow 7 consult 8 collogue,
colloquy, dialogue 10 conference,
discussion 12 conversation, deliberation

confabulate

see **confab**

confabulation

see **confab**

confection

see **candy**

confederacy

5 cabal, union 6 league 7 compact
8 alliance 9 coalition, syndicate
10 conspiracy, federation

confederate

3 reb 4 ally 5 rebel, unite 6 fellow
7 abettor, partner 9 accessory,
associate, colleague, Johnny Reb
10 accomplice 11 conspirator
12 collaborator 13 coconspirator
admiral: 6 Semmes
capital: 8 Richmond
color: 4 gray
general: 3 Lee (Robert E.) 4 Hill
(Ambrose), Hood (John Bell) 5 Bragg
(Braxton), Ewell (Richard Stoddart),
Price (Sterling), Smith (Edmund
Kirby) 6 Morgan (John Hunt), Stuart
(J. E. B.) 7 Forrest (Nathan Bedford), Hampton (Wade), Jackson
(Thomas Jonathan "Stonewall"),
Pickett (George) 8 Johnston (Albert
Sidney, Joseph Eggleston) 9 Pemberton (John Clifford) 10 Beauregard
(Pierre G. T.), Longstreet (James)
president: 5 Davis (Jefferson)
soldier: 9 butternut
spy: 4 Boyd (Belle)
vice-president: 8 Stephens (Alex-
ander)

confederation

see **confederacy**

confer

4 give, meet, talk 5 allot, award,
grant, speak 6 accord, advise,
bestow, confab, donate, huddle,
parley, powwow 7 consult, discuss,
present 8 collogue, converse
10 deliberate 11 confabulate

conference

4 talk 5 forum, synod 6 caucus,
league, parley, powwow 7 meeting,
palaver, seminar 8 assembly, colloquy, congress 9 symposium 10 colloquium, discussion, round-robin,
roundtable 11 association, convocation 12 consultation, deliberation
13 confabulation

confess

3 own 4 avow, sing 5 admit, allow, grant, let on, own up 6 reveal 7 concede, divulge, profess 8 disclose 9 come clean 11 acknowledge

confession

5 creed 6 avowal 7 peccavi 9 admission, statement 10 disclosure

confidant

8 familiar, intimate

confide

4 tell 5 trust 6 bestow, commit, reveal 7 commend, consign, entrust, whisper 8 hand over, relegate, turn over

confidence

5 faith, poise, stock, trust 6 aplomb, surety 8 credence, reliance, sureness 9 assurance, certainty, certitude 10 conviction, equanimity
game: 4 scam 5 bunco, bunko, grift, sting 7 swindle 8 flimflam

confidence man

3 gyp 5 shark 7 diddler, grifter, scammer, sharper, sharpie 8 swindler 9 charlatan, defrauder, trickster 11 bunco artist

confident

4 bold, sure 5 brash, brave, cocky 6 secure 7 assured, certain 8 cocksure, fearless, intrepid, positive, sanguine, unafraid 9 dauntless, undaunted 10 courageous, undoubtful 11 self-assured, self-reliant 13 self-assertive, self-possessed

confidential

5 close, privy 6 hushed, inside, secret 7 private 8 familiar, hush-hush, intimate 9 auricular 10 classified

configuration

4 cast, form 5 shape 6 figure, layout, makeup 7 contour, gestalt, outline, pattern 9 structure 12 conformation

confine

3 box, mew, pen 4 cage, coop, crib, jail, term 5 bound, cramp, hem in, limit 6 immure, intern, lock up, shut in, shut up 7 delimit, enclose, impound, put away 8 encircle, imprison, localize, restrict 9 constrain 11 incarcerate 12 circumscribe

confinement

7 custody, lying-in 8 childbed 9 captivity, detention, restraint 10 constraint 12 accouchement, imprisonment 13 incarceration

confines

6 bounds, limits 7 borders, compass 8 boundary, environs, purlieus 9 precincts 10 boundaries

confirm

3 fix, set 5 check, prove, vouch 6 attest, ratify, uphold, verify 7 approve, bear out, certify, concede, endorse, justify, support 8 buttress, check out, validate 9 ascertain, reinforce 10 strengthen 11 corroborate 12 authenticate, substantiate

confirmation

5 proof 7 support, witness 8 approval, evidence 9 testimony 10 validation 11 attestation, endorsement, testimonial 12 ratification, verification 13 certification, corroboration

confirmed

3 set 5 fixed, sworn 6 proven 7 chronic, settled 8 deep-dyed, definite, habitual, hardened, ratified 10 accustomed, deep-rooted, deep-seated, entrenched, habituated, inveterate, persistent 13 bred-in-the-bone, dyed-in-the-wool

confiscate

4 grab, take 5 annex, seize, usurp 7 escheat, impound, preempt 8 arrogate 9 sequester 10 commandeer 11 appropriate, expropriate

confiture

3 jam 8 conserve, preserve 9 marmalade, preserves

conflagrant

5 afire, fiery 6 ablaze, aflame, alight 7 blazing, burning, flaming

conflagration
3 war 4 fire 5 blaze 7 inferno
8 conflict 9 holocaust

conflate
3 mix 4 fuse, join, meld, weld
5 blend, merge, mix up 6 mingle,
muddle 7 combine, confuse, mistake
8 coalesce, confound 9 commingle

conflict
3 row, war 4 bout, duel, rift, vary
5 brawl, clash, fight, set-to 6 battle,
combat, differ, fracas, strife 7 contend, contest, discord, dispute,
rivalry, warfare 8 argument, disagree, mismatch, struggle, tug-of-
war, variance 9 encounter, rencontre
10 contention, engagement 11 competition

conflicting
6 at odds 7 opposed, warring
8 clashing, contrary, opposing 9 dissonant 10 contending, discordant,
discrepant 11 incongruent, incongruous, inconsonant 12 antagonistic,
antipathetic, incompatible, inconsistent, inharmonious 13 contradictory

confluence
6 merger 7 joining, meeting, merging 8 junction 9 concourse, gathering 11 convergence

conform
3 fit 4 jibe, obey, suit 5 adapt,
agree, fit in, match, yield 6 accord,
adjust, attune, comply, follow, square,
submit, tailor 8 dovetail 9 acquiesce, harmonize, reconcile 10 coordinate, correspond, proportion
11 accommodate

conformable
6 fitted, suited 7 adapted, matched
8 amenable, obedient, suitable
9 agreeable, compliant, congenial,
consonant 10 submissive

conformation
4 cast, form 5 shape 6 figure
7 anatomy 9 structure 10 adaptation 11 arrangement 13 configuration

conforming
3 apt 6 decent, proper, seemly
7 correct, uniform 8 becoming,
decorous, suitable 9 befitting,
civilized 10 compatible, consistent
11 comme il faut

conformity
6 accord 7 decorum, harmony
9 agreement, coherence, congruity,
obedience, orthodoxy 10 accordance, allegiance, compliance,
consonance, observance, submission 11 consistency 12 acquiescence

confound
4 damn, faze 5 befog, mix up, stump
6 baffle, puzzle, rattle, refute 7 confuse, mistake, mystify, nonplus,
perplex, stupefy 8 befuddle, bewilder, disprove 9 discomfit, dumbfound, embarrass, frustrate 10 controvert, disconcert 11 misidentify

confounded
5 utter 6 blamed, cursed, cussed,
damned 7 blasted, blessed, doggone, shocked 8 absolute, accursed, dismayed, infernal, outright 9 consarned, dad-blamed,
execrable, out-and-out 11 dumbfounded, overwhelmed, unmitigated
13 thunderstruck

confrere
see **colleague**

confront
4 defy, face, meet 5 beard, brave,
cross 6 accost, breast, oppose, take
on 9 challenge, encounter

Confucian way of life
3 tao

confuse
3 fog 4 blur, daze, faze 5 abash,
addle, befog, cloud, dizzy, mix up,
muddy, stump, upset 6 baffle, ball
up, bemuse, flurry, foul up, fuddle,
garble, jumble, mess up, muddle,
puzzle, rattle 7 agitate, becloud,
derange, disrupt, distort, flummox,
fluster, mislead, mistake, mystify,

nonplus, perplex, perturb, snarl up
8 bedazzle, befuddle, bewilder,
confound, disorder, disquiet, distract,
throw off, unsettle **9** discomfit,
disorient, embarrass **10** complicate,
disarrange, discompose, disconcert
11 disorganize, misidentify **12** misrepresent

confused
4 lost **5** dazed, messy, muddy,
muzzy, vague **6** addled **7** at a loss,
chaotic, mixed up, muddled, puzzled
9 flustered, perplexed, unsettled
10 bewildered, nonplussed, topsy-
turvy **11** disoriented **12** disconcerted

confusion
3 ado, din **4** flap, mess, stew **5** babel,
chaos, havoc, mix-up, snafu, snarl
6 bedlam, dither, foul-up, hubbub,
huddle, jumble, lather, muddle,
tumult, unease **7** anarchy, clutter,
turmoil **8** disarray, disorder, shambles **9** abashment, agitation, commotion, imbroglio **10** hullabaloo,
perplexity, puzzlement, turbulence,
uneasiness **11** derangement, disturbance, pandemonium **12** bewilderment **13** embarrassment

confute
4 deny **5** evert, rebut **6** defeat,
negate **8** confound, disprove, puncture **10** controvert, disconfirm

congé
3 bow **5** adieu **6** good-by **7** goodbye, molding, parting, sendoff **8** farewell **9** dismissal **11** leave-taking

congeal
3 dry, gel, set **4** clot, jell **5** jelly
6 curdle, harden **7** stiffen, thicken
8 solidify **9** coagulate **10** gelatinize

congener
6 agnate **7** cognate, sibling **8** relation, relative

congenial
4 nice **6** social **7** affable, amiable,
cordial, kindred, welcome **8** amicable, friendly, gracious, pleasant,

pleasing, sociable, suitable **9** agreeable, congruous, consonant, favorable **10** compatible, consistent,
gratifying, harmonious **11** cooperative, pleasurable, sympathetic
13 companionable

congenital
6 inborn, inbred, innate, native
7 natural **8** inherent **9** essential,
ingrained, intrinsic **10** deep-seated,
indigenous, indwelling

conger
3 eel

congeries
5 group **7** company **8** assembly
9 gathering **10** assemblage, collection **11** aggregation **12** congregation

congest
3 jam **4** clog, fill, plug, stop **5** block,
choke, close, crowd **6** plug up
7 occlude **8** obstruct

conglobate
4 ball **6** sphere **8** ensphere
9 spherical

conglomerate
4 mass, pool **5** chain, group, mixed,
trust **6** cartel, motley **7** chaebol,
combine **8** keiretsu, zaibatsu
9 aggregate, syndicate **11** aggregation **12** multifarious **13** heterogeneous

conglomeration
5 hoard, trove **8** mishmash **9** aggregate **10** collection, cumulation,
hodgepodge, miscellany **11** agglomerate, aggregation **12** accumulation

Congo, Democratic Republic of the
capital: **8** Kinshasa
city: **7** Kolwezi **9** Mbuji-Mayi
10 Lubumbashi
explorer: **7** Stanley (Henry Morton)
former name: **5** Zaire **12** Belgian
Congo
lake: **4** Kivu **5** Mweru **6** Albert,
Edward **10** Tanganyika

Congo, Republic of
language: 6 French 7 English
monetary unit: 5 franc
neighbor: 5 Congo, Sudan 6 Angola, Rwanda, Uganda, Zambia
7 Burundi 8 Tanzania
river: 5 Congo

Congo, Republic of
capital: 11 Brazzaville
city: 11 Pointe-Noire
former name: 11 Middle Congo
language: 6 French
monetary unit: 5 franc
neighbor: 5 Congo, Gabon 6 Angola 7 Cabinda 8 Cameroon
river: 5 Congo

congratulate
4 laud 6 salute 10 compliment, felicitate

congregate
4 meet 5 swarm 6 gather, muster
7 collect, convene 8 assemble, converge 9 forgather, foregather, rendezvous

congregation
4 mass 5 crowd, flock, group
7 meeting 8 assembly, audience
9 gathering 10 assemblage, collection 11 churchgoers 12 parishioners

congress
4 diet 5 synod 6 league 7 meeting, society 8 assembly, conclave
10 convention, parliament 11 association, Capitol Hill, legislature

congressman
5 solon 7 senator 8 delegate, lawmaker 10 legislator 14 representative

congruity
9 agreement, coherence 10 conformity 11 consistency

congruous
3 apt, fit 7 fitting 9 agreeable, befitting, congenial, consonant 10 compatible, concordant, consistent, harmonious 11 appropriate, sympathetic

conifer
3 fir, yew 4 pine 5 cedar, larch
6 spruce 7 cypress, hemlock, juniper
8 softwood 9 evergreen 10 arborvitae

conjectural
7 reputed 8 putative, supposed
11 speculative, theoretical 12 hypothetical, suppositious 13 suppositional

conjecture
5 guess, infer 6 assume, theory
7 presume, suppose, surmise, suspect 8 theorize 9 inference, speculate 11 hypothesize, proposition, speculation, supposition

conjoin
3 wed 4 band, link, yoke 5 unite
6 couple 7 combine, connect
8 federate 9 affiliate, associate, cooperate 11 consolidate

conjoint
6 common, mutual, public, shared, united 7 unified 8 combined, communal 9 concerted 10 collective
11 coefficient, cooperative, intermutual

conjointly
8 mutually, together

conjugal
6 wedded 7 marital, married, nuptial, spousal 8 hymeneal 9 connubial
11 matrimonial

conjugality
7 wedlock 8 marriage 9 matrimony

conjugate
4 fuse, join, link, pair, yoke 5 yoked
6 couple, joined, linked 7 bracket, combine, conjoin, connect, coupled
9 associate, connected

conjunct
5 joint 6 common, joined, mutual, shared, united

conjunction
3 and, but, for, nor, yet 4 lest, once, than, then, when 5 after, since, union, until, where, which, while 6 before, either, though, unless 7 because, however, neither,

whereas, whether 8 alliance, although, moreover, whenever 9 therefore 10 connection 11 affiliation, association, combination, concurrence

conjuration

4 oath 5 charm, spell, trick 7 sorcery 10 adjuration, hocus-pocus, invocation 11 abracadabra, incantation

conjure

3 beg 4 urge 6 appeal, invoke, summon 7 beseech, entreat, imagine, implore 8 contrive 9 importune 10 supplicate

conjurer

4 mage, seer 5 magus 6 Magian, wizard 7 warlock 8 magician, sorcerer 9 enchanter, trickster 11 illusionist, necromancer

conjuring

5 magic 7 sorcery 8 wizardry 10 hocus-pocus, necromancy 11 abracadabra, legerdemain, thaumaturgy

conk

3 die, hit, rap 4 belt, swat 5 croak, faint, knock, thump, whack 8 knock out

con man

see **confidence man**

connate

4 akin 6 allied, inborn, native 7 kindred, related 8 inherent 9 congenial, elemental, essential, ingrained, inherited, intrinsic 10 affiliated, congenital, indigenous, indwelling 11 consanguine

connect

3 tie, wed 4 ally, bind, join, link, yoke 5 marry, unite 6 attach, bridge, couple, fasten, relate 7 combine, conjoin 8 transfer 9 affiliate, associate, interlock

Connecticut

capital: 8 Hartford
city: 4 Avon 6 Darien 8 New Haven, Stamford 9 Greenwich, New London, Waterbury 10 Bridgeport
college, university: 4 Yale 7 Trinity 8 Wesleyan 9 Fairfield 10 Quinnipiac
nickname: 6 Nutmeg (State) 12 Constitution (State)
river: 6 Thames 10 Housatonic 11 Connecticut
state bird: 5 robin (American)
state flower: 14 mountain laurel
state tree: 8 white oak

connection

3 tie 4 bond, link 5 joint, nexus, tie-in, union 6 hookup 7 joining, kinship, network 8 affinity, alliance, coupling, junction, juncture 9 coherence, communion, fastening 10 attachment, catenation, continuity 11 affiliation, association, combination, conjunction, partnership 12 relationship

connective

3 and, nor, not 4 then 6 either 7 neither 8 syndetic 11 conjunction, conjunctive

conniption

3 fit 4 bout 5 furor, spasm, spate, spell, throe 6 attack, frenzy 7 seizure, tantrum 6 outburst, paroxysm 10 convulsion

connivance

8 intrigue 9 collusion 10 complicity, conspiracy

connive

4 plot, wink 5 blink 6 devise, scheme, wink at 7 blink at, collude 8 conspire, contrive, intrigue 9 machinate

connoisseur

4 buff 6 expert 7 epicure, gourmet 8 aesthete, gourmand, highbrow 9 authority, bon vivant 10 dilettante, gastronome 11 cognoscente

connotation

4 hint 7 meaning 8 overtone 9 undertone 10 intimation, suggestion 11 association, implication 13 signification

connote

4 hint, mean 5 imply, spell 6 hint at,

intend **7** betoken, express, signify, suggest **8** indicate, intimate **9** insinuate

connubial
6 wedded **7** marital, married, nuptial, spousal **8** conjugal, hymeneal **11** matrimonial

connubiality
7 wedlock **8** marriage **9** matrimony **11** conjugality

conquer
4 beat, best, lick, tame, whip **5** crush **6** defeat, master, subdue **8** overcome, surmount, vanquish **9** checkmate, overpower, overthrow, overwhelm, subjugate

conquest
3 win **4** rout **7** triumph, victory **9** overthrow, seduction **11** subjugation

Conrad, Joseph
character: **3** Jim **4** Axel, Lena **5** Flora, Kurtz **6** Marlow, Verloc **7** Almayer **8** MacWhirr, Nostromo work: **5** Youth **6** Chance **7** Lord Jim, Typhoon, Victory **8** Nostromo **11** Secret Agent (The) **13** Almayer's Folly **15** Heart of Darkness

Conroy novel
10 Beach Music **11** Water Is Wide (The) **12** Great Santini (The) **13** Prince of Tides (The) **17** Lords of Discipline (The)

consanguineous
4 akin **6** agnate **7** cognate, connate, kindred, related

conscience
5 demur, honor, qualm **6** ethics, virtue **7** decency, remorse, scruple **8** morality, scruples **9** integrity **10** contrition **11** compunction

conscienceless
6 amoral **7** immoral **9** unethical **12** unprincipled, unscrupulous

conscientious
4 fair, just, true **5** exact **6** honest **7** careful, dutiful, upright **8** diligent, reliable, studious **9** honorable **10** high-minded, meticulous, principled, scrupulous **11** hard-working, painstaking, punctilious

conscious
5 alive, awake, aware **7** knowing, mindful, witting **8** sensible, sentient **9** attentive, cognizant **10** deliberate, perceptive

consciousness
4 heed, mind **6** regard **7** concern **9** alertness, awareness, knowledge **10** cognizance, perception **11** realization, recognition

conscribe
5 draft, limit **6** call up, enlist, enroll, muster **7** recruit

conscript
5 draft, elect **6** called, choose, chosen, enlist, enroll, induct, select **7** drafted, dragoon, impress, recruit, soldier **8** selected

consecrate
5 bless **6** anoint, devote, hallow, ordain, pledge **8** dedicate, sanctify

consecrated
4 holy **6** sacred **7** blessed **8** hallowed **10** sanctified
oil: **6** chrism

consecution
see **sequence**

consecutive
4 next **5** later **6** serial **7** ensuing, ordered, sequent **9** following, succedent **10** sequential, subsequent, succeeding, successive **11** progressive **12** successional

consent
3 yes **4** okay **5** agree, allow, leave, yield **6** accede, accord, assent, comply, concur, permit **7** approve, go-ahead **8** approval, sanction **9** acquiesce, agreement, allowance, subscribe **10** compliance, permission **12** acquiescence **13** authorization, understanding

consequence
4 fame, note, rank **5** issue, state

6 cachet, effect, import, moment, renown, repute, result, sequel, status, upshot, weight 7 account, conceit, dignity, fallout, outcome, stature 8 eminence, interest, position, prestige, reaction, standing 9 aftermath, inference, magnitude 10 importance, reputation 11 after-effect, weightiness 12 repercussion, significance 13 momentousness

consequent
5 later, sound 7 ensuing, logical 8 rational 9 deduction, following, resulting

consequential
3 big 5 major 7 serious, weighty 8 egoistic, indirect, material 9 conceited, egotistic, important, momentous 10 collateral, incidental, meaningful, subsidiary 11 significant, substantial 12 considerable 13 self-important

consequently
4 ergo, thus 5 hence 9 as a result, therefore, thereupon 10 inevitably 11 accordingly

conservation
4 care 7 control 9 attention, husbandry 10 management, protection 11 safekeeping 12 guardianship, preservation

conservative
4 tory 6 proper 7 diehard, old-line 8 cautious, discreet, old-guard, orthodox, rightist, standpat 9 right-wing, temperate 10 restrained 11 circumspect, reactionary, right-winger, standpatter, traditional

conservatory
6 school 7 academy, nursery 8 hothouse 10 greenhouse 11 music school

conserve
3 can, jam 4 keep, save 5 hoard, lay up, put up, skimp, store 6 keep up 7 husband, protect, support, sustain 8 maintain, set aside, withhold 9 confiture, economize, safeguard, sweetmeat

consider
3 see 4 deem, feel, mind, muse, note, rate, view 5 fancy, judge, sense, study, think, weigh 6 credit, look at, notice, ponder, reason, reckon, regard 7 account, believe, examine, imagine, inspect, reflect, respect, suppose 8 appraise, cogitate, conceive, conclude, envisage, meditate, mull over, ruminate 9 speculate, think over 10 deliberate, excogitate, scrutinize, think about 11 contemplate

considerable
3 big 5 ample, hefty, large, major 7 notable, sizable, weighty 8 material, sensible, sizeable 9 extensive, important, momentous, plentiful 10 large-scale, meaningful 11 respectable, significant, substantial 13 consequential

considerably
3 far 4 well 5 quite 6 rather 7 notably 8 somewhat 10 noticeably 11 appreciably 13 significantly, substantially

considerate
4 kind 6 kindly, polite, tender 7 amiable, careful, patient, tactful 8 discreet, generous, obliging 9 attentive 10 chivalrous, forbearing, solicitous, thoughtful 11 circumspect, complaisant, sympathetic, warmhearted 13 compassionate

consideration
3 fee 4 heed, tact 5 cause, favor, issue, study 6 esteem, factor, motive, reason, regard 7 account, concern, payment, respect, thought 8 kindness 9 attention, awareness 10 admiration, cogitation, discussion, estimation, inducement, recompense, reflection, solicitude 11 application, forbearance, mindfulness 12 deliberation 13 attentiveness, concentration

considered
7 advised, studied, weighed 8 studious 10 deliberate, thought-out

11 intentional 12 aforethought, premeditated

consign

4 give, send, ship 5 agree, allot, award, remit, yield 6 commit, convey, devote, submit 7 address, commend, confide, deliver, entrust, forward 8 dispatch, hand over, relegate, transmit, turn over 9 surrender

consist

3 lie 4 rest 5 abide, agree, dwell, exist, fit in 6 accord, inhere, reside 7 comport, conform, consort, subsist 8 dovetail 10 correspond

consistency

7 aptness, concord, density, fitness, harmony, texture 8 evenness, firmness, likeness 9 agreement, coherence, congruity, thickness, viscosity 10 conformity, consonance, similarity 11 suitability

consistent

4 even, true 6 steady 7 regular, uniform 8 constant 9 accordant, agreeable, congenial, congruous, consonant, unfailing, unvarying 10 compatible, conforming, dependable, invariable, unchanging 11 homogeneous, sympathetic, undeviating

consistently

8 wontedly 9 regularly, routinely 10 habitually, invariably 11 customarily

console

4 calm, case 5 cheer 6 buck up, solace 7 cabinet, comfort, hearten

consolidate

3 mix, set 4 fuse, join, meld, pool 5 blend, merge, unify, unite 6 firm up, secure 7 compact, fortify 8 compress, condense, federate, solidify 9 integrate 10 amalgamate, strengthen 11 concentrate

consolidation

5 union 6 merger 7 melding, merging 8 coalition 11 combination, integration, unification 12 amalgamation

consonance

6 accord 7 concord, harmony 9 agreement, congruity, resonance 10 congruence

consonant

4 akin, like 6 agnate 7 musical, similar 8 blending, harmonic, resonant 9 congruous 10 compatible, harmonious 11 conformable 13 corresponding

kind: 4 stop, surd 5 nasal, velar 6 atonic, voiced 7 lateral, palatal, spirant 8 alveolar, bilabial, unvoiced 9 fricative, voiceless

consort

3 set 4 mate, wife 5 agree, group, tally, unite 6 accord, attend, fellow, spouse, square, troupe 7 company, comport, conform, husband, partner 8 assembly, chaperon, dovetail 9 accompany, associate, companion, harmonize 10 correspond

consortium

4 bloc, club, ring 5 guild, trust, union 6 cartel, league 7 combine, society 8 alliance, congress 9 coalition, syndicate 10 federation 11 association 12 conglomerate

conspectus

5 brief 6 digest, précis, sketch, survey 7 epitome, outline, summary 8 abstract, overview, synopsis 9 reduction 10 abridgment 11 abridgement 12 condensation

conspicuous

5 clear, overt, showy 6 marked, patent, signal 7 blatant, evident, glaring, notable, obvious, pointed, salient 8 apparent, distinct, flagrant, manifest, striking 9 arresting, egregious, notorious, obtrusive, prominent 10 celebrated, noticeable, pronounced, remarkable 11 eye-catching, illustrious, outstanding 12 ostentatious

conspiracy

4 plan, plot 5 cabal 6 scheme 8 intrigue 11 machination

conspirator

7 abettor, plotter, schemer 9 accessory, intriguer 10 accomplice 11 confederate

conspire

4 plot 5 cabal 6 scheme 7 collude, connive 8 intrigue 9 machinate

constable

6 deputy, lawman, warden 7 marshal, sheriff

constancy

5 faith 6 fealty 7 loyalty, resolve 8 adhesion, devotion, fidelity, firmness 9 adherence, diligence, endurance, fortitude 10 allegiance, attachment, dedication, resolution, steadiness 11 staunchness 12 faithfulness, perseverance 13 dependability, steadfastness

constant

4 even, fast, firm, true 5 fixed, loyal 6 dogged, stable, steady, trusty 7 abiding, chronic, endless, equable, lasting, nonstop, staunch, uniform 8 enduring, faithful, habitual, resolute, unending 9 ceaseless, confirmed, continual, immovable, immutable, incessant, obstinate, perpetual, steadfast, sustained, unceasing, unfailing, unmovable, unvarying 10 changeless, consistent, continuous, dependable, inflexible, invariable, inveterate, persistent, persisting, unchanging, unwavering 11 everlasting, inalterable, unalterable, unrelenting, unremitting 12 interminable, unchangeable

Constantine

birthplace: 4 Nish
mother: 6 Helena
son: 7 Crispus
victim: 6 Fausta 7 Crispus
wife: 6 Fausta

constantly

4 ever 5 often 6 always 7 forever 9 eternally 10 frequently, invariably, repeatedly 11 incessantly, perpetually 12 continuously

constellation

5 group 7 pattern 10 assemblage, collection 11 arrangement
Altar: 3 Ara
Archer: 11 Sagittarius
Arrow: 7 Sagitta
Balance: 5 Libra 9 Ursa Major
Bear, Little: 9 Ursa Minor
Big Dipper: 9 Ursa Major
Bird of Paradise: 4 Apus
Bull: 6 Taurus
Centaur: 9 Centaurus
Chained Lady: 9 Andromeda
Chameleon: 10 Chamaeleon
Champion: 7 Perseus
Charioteer: 6 Auriga
Clock: 10 Horologium
Colt: 8 Equuleus
Crab: 6 Cancer
Crane: 4 Grus
Cross: 4 Crux
Crow: 6 Corvus
Crown: 6 Corona
Cup: 6 Crater
Dolphin: 9 Delphinus
Dove: 7 Columba
Dragon: 5 Draco
Eagle: 6 Aquila
Fishes: 6 Pisces
Fly: 5 Musca
Flying Fish: 6 Volans
Furnace: 6 Fornax
Graving Tool: 6 Caelum
Great Bear: 9 Ursa Major
Greater Dog: 10 Canis Major
Hare: 5 Lepus
Herdsman: 6 Boötes
Horned Goat: 11 Capricornus
Hunter: 5 Orion
Indian: 5 Indus
Keel: 6 Carina
Lady in the Chair: 10 Cassiopeia
Larger Bear: 9 Ursa Major
Larger Dog: 10 Canis Major
Lesser Dog: 10 Canis Minor
Lion: 3 Leo
Little Bear: 9 Ursa Minor
Little Dipper: 9 Ursa Minor
Little Fox: 9 Vulpecula
Lizard: 7 Lacerta
Lyre: 4 Lyra
Mariner's Compass: 5 Pyxis

Monarch: 7 Cepheus
Net: 9 Reticulum
Painter's Easel: 6 Pictor
Pair of Compasses: 8 Circinus
Peacock: 4 Pavo
Pump: 6 Antlia
Ram: 5 Aries
Rescuer: 7 Perseus
River Po: 8 Eridanus
Sails: 4 Vela
Scorpion: 8 Scorpius
Serpent: 7 Serpens
Serpent Holder: 9 Ophiuchus
Sextant: 7 Sextans
Shield: 6 Scutum
Smaller Bear: 9 Ursa Minor
Square: 5 Norma
Stern: 6 Puppis
Swan: 6 Cygnus
Table: 5 Mensa
Toucan: 6 Tucana
Triangle: 10 Triangulum
Twins: 6 Gemini
Unicorn: 9 Monoceros
Virgin: 5 Virgo
Water Carrier: 8 Aquarius
Water Monster: 5 Hydra
Water Snake: 6 Hydrus
Whale: 5 Cetus
Winged Horse: 7 Pegasus
Wolf: 5 Lupus

consternate
5 alarm, daunt, shake, shock
6 appall, dismay 7 horrify, unnerve
8 distress

consternation
4 fear 5 alarm, dread, panic, shock
6 dismay, fright, horror, terror 11 trepidation 12 bewilderment

constituent
4 part 5 piece, voter 6 factor, member 7 element, portion 8 division,
fraction 9 component, elemental,
principal 10 ingredient

constitute
4 form, make 5 enact, found, set up,
start 6 create, embody, make up
7 appoint, compose 8 complete,
comprise, organize 9 establish,
institute, represent

constitution
3 law 4 code 5 build, canon 6 design, makeup, nature 7 charter
8 physique 9 formation, structure
11 composition 12 architecture,
construction

constitutional
4 walk 6 inborn, inbred, innate,
lawful 7 built-in, organic 8 inherent
9 essential, ingrained, intrinsic
10 congenital, deep-seated

Constitution State
11 Connecticut

Constitution, U.S.S.
12 Old Ironsides

constitutive
5 vital 8 cardinal 9 essential 11 fundamental 12 constructive

constrain
3 bar 4 curb, deny, jail 5 chain,
check, crush, force, impel, limit,
press 6 bridle, coerce, compel,
enjoin, oblige, secure, squash,
squish 7 confine, deprive, inhibit,
refrain, squeeze 8 compress, hold
back, hold down, imprison, restrain,
restrict 11 incarcerate

constraint
4 bond 5 check, force 6 duress
8 coercion, pressure 9 captivity,
detention, restraint 10 compulsion,
diffidence, inhibition, limitation,
repression 11 confinement, restriction, suppression 13 embarrassment

constrict
4 curb 5 cramp, limit, pinch, strap
6 hamper, narrow, shrink 7 confine,
inhibit, squeeze, tighten 8 compress,
condense, contract, restrain, strangle, stultify 9 constrain 12 circumscribe

constrictor
3 boa 5 snake 6 muscle 8 anaconda 9 sphincter, strangler

construct
4 form, make 5 build, erect, forge,
frame, put up, raise, set up, shape
6 create, devise 7 build up, compile,

fashion, produce **8** assemble,
engineer **9** establish, fabricate
11 manufacture, put together

construction
6 design, makeup **7** edifice, shaping
8 assembly, building **9** formation
10 fashioning **11** arrangement,
engineering, fabrication, manufacture
12 architecture, constitution

constructive
6 useful **7** helpful, implied, virtual
8 implicit, positive, valuable **9** practical **10** beneficial

construe
5 educe, gloss, parse **6** induct **7** analyze, explain, expound **9** explicate,
interpret **10** paraphrase, understand

consuetude
5 habit, usage **6** custom, manner
8 practice **10** convention

consult
3 ask **6** advise, confer, huddle,
parley **7** examine, refer to **8** collogue, consider **11** confabulate

consume
3 eat, use **4** down, gulp, ruin **5** drain,
drink, eat up, gorge, spend, use up,
waste **6** absorb, devour, expend,
finish, ingest, obsess, take up **7** deplete, destroy, engross, exhaust, put
away, put down, swallow **8** squander
9 dissipate, finish off, polish off
10 annihilate, extinguish, monopolize, run through

consumer
4 user **5** buyer **6** client **7** shopper,
end user **8** customer **9** purchaser

consumer advocate
5 Nader (Ralph)

consuming
6 ardent **7** fervent, intense **8** gripping, riveting **9** absorbing **10** engrossing **11** enthralling **12** monopolizing

consummate
3 end **4** ripe **5** close, crown, ideal,
utter **6** finish, superb, wind up, wrap

up **7** achieve, perfect, supreme
8 absolute, complete, conclude,
finished, flawless, peerless, ultimate
9 faultless, matchless, perfected,
virtuosic **10** accomplish, impeccable,
inimitable **11** superlative **12** accomplished **13** thoroughgoing

consumption
3 use **5** decay, waste **6** intake
7 wasting **8** phthisis **9** depletion,
ingestion **10** absorption ·**11** dissipation **12** tuberculosis

contact
4 meet **5** reach, touch **8** tangency,
touching **9** closeness, communion,
proximity **10** connection, contiguity
11 association, contingence **13** communication

contagion
3 pox **4** bane, meme **5** taint, venom,
virus **6** miasma, plague, poison
7 disease, scourge **8** epidemic
9 infection, pollution **10** corruption,
pestilence **13** contamination

contagious
6 catchy **8** catching, epidemic
9 spreading **10** infectious **12** communicable, pestilential **13** transmissible, transmittable

contain
4 hold, keep **5** check, house **6** embody, take in **7** collect, control,
embrace, enclose, include, receive,
repress, subsume **8** comprise,
restrain **9** encompass **10** comprehend **11** accommodate

container
3 bag, bin, box, can, cup, jar, keg,
mug, pod, pot, tin, tub, urn, vat
4 cage, case, cask, drum, etui, ewer,
pail, sack, silo, tank, vase, vial, well
5 chest, crate, cruet, flask, glass,
gourd, phial, pouch **6** basket, bottle,
carafe, carton, casket, coffin, cooler,
goblet, hamper, hatbox, holder,
inkpot, shaker **7** bandbox, capsule,
chalice, inkwell, package, pitcher,
thermos **8** canister, catchall, decanter, envelope, hogshead, jerrican,
puncheon **10** receptacle

contaminate

liturgical: 3 pyx **7** chalice **8** ciborium

contaminate

4 foul, soil **5** dirty, spoil, stain, sully, taint **6** befoul, debase, defile, infect, injure, poison **7** corrupt, deprave, pervert, pollute, profane, tarnish, vitiate **9** desecrate **10** adulterate

conte

4 tale **5** story **9** narrative

contemn

4 snub **5** abhor, scorn, spurn **6** deride **7** deplore, despise, disdain **8** ridicule **10** look down on

contemplate

4 mull, muse, view **5** study, think, weigh **6** behold, debate, gaze at, intend, look at, ponder, regard **7** examine, inspect, propose, reflect **8** consider, gaze upon, look upon, meditate, mull over, ruminate, think out **9** think over **10** deliberate, excogitate, scrutinize

contemplation

5 study **6** musing **7** thought **8** thinking **9** intention, pondering **10** cogitation, meditation, reflection, rumination **11** cerebration, expectation, speculation **12** deliberation **13** consideration

contemplative

6 musing **7** pensive **10** cogitative, meditative, reflecting, reflective, ruminative, thoughtful **11** speculative **13** introspective

contemporary

3 new **6** coeval, extant, modern, recent **7** current, present, topical **8** existent, existing, up-to-date **9** au courant **10** coexistent, coexisting, coincident, concurrent, present-day, synchronic **11** synchronous **12** simultaneous

contempt

5 scorn, shame **7** despite, disdain, mockery **8** aversion, defiance, disfavor, disgrace, dishonor, distaste, ignominy **9** antipathy, discredit, disesteem, disrepute **10** disrespect, opprobrium, repugnance **12** disobedience, stubbornness

contemptible

3 low **4** base, mean, poor, vile **5** cheap, sorry **6** abject, odious, paltry, scummy, scurvy, shabby, sordid **7** hateful, ignoble, pitiful, squalid **8** inferior, pitiable, shameful, unworthy, wretched **9** abhorrent, loathsome **10** despicable, detestable, disgusting **11** ignominious **12** dishonorable

contemptuous

7 haughty **8** arrogant, derisive, scornful **10** disdainful **12** supercilious **13** condescending, disrespectful

contend

3 vie, war **4** aver, avow, cope, face, urge **5** argue, brawl, claim, fight **6** affirm, allege, assert, battle, charge, combat, debate, defend, insist, oppose, report, strive **7** compete, contest **8** confront, maintain, struggle **9** encounter, withstand

contender

5 match, rival **6** player **8** opponent **9** adversary, candidate, combatant **10** antagonist, challenger, competitor, contestant

—— contendere

4 nolo

content

4 cozy, gist **5** happy **6** at ease, serene **7** appease, gratify, meaning, placate, satisfy **9** gratified, satisfied, substance **11** comfortable **12** significance

contention

3 war **4** beef, feud **6** combat, rumpus, strife, thesis **7** discord, dispute, dissent, quarrel, rivalry, wrangle **8** argument, conflict, disunity, squabble **10** difference, dissension, dissidence **11** altercation, competition, controversy
Scottish: 5 sturt

contentious

5 fiery **7** carping, froward, peppery, scrappy, warlike **8** captious, caviling, contrary, militant, perverse **9** bellicose, combative, hotheaded, litigious, polemical, truculent **10** pugnacious **11** belligerent, quarrelsome **12** disputatious, faultfinding **13** argumentative, controversial

conterminous

10 coincident **11** coextensive

contest

3 vie **4** bout, duel, feud, fray, game, meet, race, tilt **5** clash, fight, match, repel, rival, trial **6** battle, combat, debate, oppose, resist, strife, strive **7** compete, dispute, rivalry, warfare **8** argument, conflict, endeavor, skirmish, struggle, tug-of-war **9** challenge, encounter, rencontre **10** engagement, tournament **11** competition

contiguity

9 adjacency, immediacy, proximity **11** propinquity

contiguous

4 next **8** abutting, adjacent, touching **9** adjoining, bordering **10** juxtaposed

continence

6 purity, virtue **8** chastity, sobriety **9** austerity **10** abnegation, abstinence, asceticism, chasteness, moderation, temperance **11** forbearance **12** renunciation **13** self-restraint

continent

4 Asia, mass **5** sober **6** Africa, chaste, Europe **8** celibate, mainland **9** abstinent, Australia, temperate **10** abstemious, Antarctica, restrained **11** abstentious **12** North America, South America
lost: 8 Atlantis

contingence

5 touch **7** contact **8** tangency, touching

contingency

4 pass **5** event **6** chance, crisis **8** exigency, juncture, occasion

9 emergency **10** likelihood **11** opportunity, possibility, probability, uncertainty

contingent

3 odd **4** band **5** group, party, troop **6** casual, chance, likely **7** reliant **8** possible, probable, relative **9** dependent, empirical, entourage, uncertain **10** accidental, delegation, deputation, detachment, fortuitous, incidental, unforeseen **11** conditional **13** unanticipated, unforeseeable, unpredictable

continual

6 steady **7** abiding, endless, nonstop, regular, running **8** constant, enduring, timeless, unbroken, unending **9** ceaseless, incessant, perpetual, perennial, recurrent, recurring, unceasing, unfailing, unvarying **10** persistent, persisting, relentless, unchanging, unflagging **11** everlasting, unremitting **12** interminable **13** uninterrupted

continually

4 ever **6** always **7** forever **8** steadily, together **9** endlessly **10** constantly **11** incessantly, night and day **12** interminably, persistently, relentlessly, successively **13** consecutively

continuance

3 run **4** stay **5** delay **6** sequel **8** duration, survival **9** longevity **10** permanence **11** adjournment, persistence **12** postponement, prolongation

continuation

3 run **4** coda **6** sequel **8** appendix, duration, epilogue **9** endurance, extension **10** resumption **11** persistence, protraction **12** prolongation

continue

4 go on, last, stay **5** abide, renew, run on **6** endure, hang in, keep at, keep on, keep up, pick up, push on, remain, reopen, resume, retain, take up **7** carry on, persist, press on, proceed, prolong, restart, survive **8** maintain, postpone **9** carry over, persevere **10** recommence

continuing

5 fixed **6** steady **7** abiding, chronic, durable, eternal, lasting, ongoing **8** constant, enduring, lifelong, stubborn **9** long-lived, obstinate, perennial, prolonged, steadfast, tenacious, unabating **10** inveterate, persistent, persisting **11** long-lasting

continuity

4 flow **6** script **8** duration, scenario, sequence **9** endurance **11** persistence, progression

continuous

see **continual**

continuously

see **continually**

contort

4 knot, warp **5** twist, wring **6** deform, wrench, writhe **7** distort, grimace, torture **9** convolute, corkscrew, disfigure

contortionist

7 acrobat

contour

4 form, line **5** curve, lines, shape **6** figure **7** outline, pattern, profile **9** lineament, lineation **10** silhouette **11** delineation

contra

6 facing, toward **7** against, counter, reverse, vis-à-vis **8** converse, fronting, opposite **10** conversely

contraband

3 hot **5** taboo **6** banned **7** bootleg, illegal, illicit, smuggle **8** unlawful **9** forbidden **10** prohibited, proscribed **11** black market, bootlegging, trafficking

contract

4 bond, hire, pact, sink **5** catch, incur, lease **6** engage, induce, lessen, reduce, shrink, treaty, weaken **7** abridge, acquire, afflict, bargain, decline, dwindle, shorten, shrivel **8** compress, condense, covenant, decrease, diminish **9** agreement, constrict, succumb to **11** concentrate, transaction **12** come down with **part: 6** clause **7** article, proviso

contraction

3 he'd, he's, I'll, it's, I've, tic **4** ain't, can't, don't, flex, he'll, isn't, let's, she'd, she's, won't, you'd **5** aren't, cramp, didn't, hadn't, hasn't, she'll, spasm, they'd, wasn't, you'll, you're, you've **6** haven't, mustn't, needn't, they'll, they've, weren't **7** couldn't, elision, mightn't, wouldn't **8** shouldn't **9** reduction, shrinkage **10** abridgment **12** abbreviation
heart's: 7 systole
poetic: 3 e'en, e'er, o'er, 'tis **4** ne'er, 'twas **5** 'twere, 'twill

contradict

4 deny **5** belie, cross, rebut **6** impugn, negate, refute, take on **7** confute, dispute, gainsay **8** negative, traverse **9** challenge, disaffirm

contradiction

6 denial **7** paradox **8** antinomy, negation, rebuttal, variance **9** disparity **10** gainsaying, opposition, refutation **11** discrepancy, incongruity **12** disagreement, protestation **13** inconsistency

contradictory

7 counter, reverse **8** contrary, converse, negating, opposite **9** antipodal **10** antipodean, antithesis, nullifying **12** antithetical

contraption

3 rig **5** gizmo **6** device, doodad, gadget **7** machine **9** apparatus, doohickey **11** contrivance

contrariety

10 antagonism, antithesis, opposition, perversity, unlikeness

contrariwise

9 vice versa **10** conversely, oppositely

contrary

5 balky **6** averse, ornery, unruly **7** adverse, counter, froward, reverse, wayward **8** converse, opposite, perverse, stubborn **9** antipodal, diametric, dissident, obstinate, vice versa **10** conversely, discordant, headstrong, oppositely, rebellious,

refractory 11 conflicting, intractable, wrongheaded **12** antagonistic, antipathetic, antithetical, contumacious, cross-grained, recalcitrant
prefix: 7 counter

contrast
6 differ **7** collate, compare, diverge **8** conflict, disagree **9** disparity, diversity **10** comparison, difference, divergence **11** distinction, distinguish **13** dissimilarity

contravene
4 defy, deny **5** break, cross, fight **6** abjure, breach, disown, impugn, negate, offend, oppose, reject **7** disobey, gainsay, violate **8** disclaim, infringe, renege on **9** disaffirm, go against, repudiate **10** contradict, transgress

contravention
6 breach **7** offense **8** trespass **9** violation **10** infraction **12** infringement **13** nonobservance, transgression

contretemps
3 row **4** slip, tiff **5** clash, run-in **6** dustup, mishap, slip-up **7** dispute, quarrel **8** argument **9** mischance **10** falling-out, misfortune

contribute
3 add **4** give, help, tend **5** grant **6** chip in, donate, kick in, submit, supply **7** conduce, pitch in, redound **9** subscribe **11** come through

contribution
4 alms, gift **5** input, share **7** charity, payment, present **8** donation, offering **11** benefaction, beneficence

contributory
8 adjuvant **9** accessory, ancillary, auxiliary **10** collateral, subsidiary, supporting **11** appurtenant, subservient

contrite
5 sorry **8** penitent **9** regretful, repentant **10** apologetic, remorseful **11** penitential

contriteness
see contrition

contrition
3 rue **4** ruth **6** regret **7** penance, remorse **9** penitence **10** repentance **11** compunction **12** self-reproach

contrivance
4 ruse **6** device, gadget **7** gimmick **8** artifice **9** apparatus, expedient, invention, stratagem **10** brainchild **11** contraption

contrive
3 rig **4** fake, make, move, plan, plot **5** frame, hatch **6** cook up, devise, invent, make up, manage, scheme, vamp up, wangle **7** arrange, concoct, connive, develop, dream up, fashion, project, work out **8** cogitate, conspire, engineer, intrigue **9** construct, elaborate, fabricate, formulate, machinate

contrived
5 hokey **6** forced **7** labored **8** strained **9** concocted, insincere **10** artificial, fabricated, factitious

control
3 run **4** curb, rein, rule, sway **5** guide, power, steer **6** bridle, direct, govern, handle, manage, master, rein in, subdue **7** command, conduct, mastery, oversee, repress, reserve **8** dominate, dominion, regulate, restrain **9** authority, direction, restraint, supervise, supremacy **10** discipline, domination, management **11** supervision **12** jurisdiction

controlled
8 discreet, reserved **9** temperate **10** restrained

controversial
5 risky **6** touchy **7** awkward, charged, eristic **8** delicate, disputed, ticklish **9** explosive, litigious, polemical **11** contentious, problematic **12** disputatious **13** argumentative

controversy
3 row **5** clash **6** debate, rumpus, strife **7** dispute, quarrel, wrangle **8** argument, squabble **10** contention, falling-out **11** altercation, disputation, embroilment

controvert

4 deny 5 rebut 6 debate, oppose, oppugn, refute 7 confute, counter, dispute, gainsay 8 disprove, question 9 challenge, repudiate

contumacious

7 froward 8 contrary, insolent, mutinous, obdurate, perverse 9 obstinate 10 rebellious, refractory 11 disobedient, intractable 12 recalcitrant 13 insubordinate

contumacy

8 contempt, defiance 9 insolence 10 perversity 12 stubbornness 13 recalcitrance

contumelious

7 abusive 8 derisive, insolent, scornful 9 insulting, truculent 10 disdainful, scurrilous 11 opprobrious 12 vituperative

contumely

5 abuse 6 insult 7 affront, mockery, obloquy 8 contempt, ridicule, sneering 9 aspersion, invective 10 scurrility 12 vituperation

contuse

6 batter, bruise, injure 7 blacken

conundrum

5 poser 6 enigma, puzzle, riddle 7 baffler, mystery, problem, puzzler, stumper 10 puzzlement 13 Chinese puzzle

convalesce

4 heal, mend 7 improve, recover 10 recuperate

convene

4 call, meet 6 call in, gather, muster, summon 7 convoke, summons 8 assemble 9 forgather 10 congregate 12 come together

convenience

4 ease 7 amenity, benefit, comfort, leisure 8 facility 9 handiness 10 assistance 13 accessibility

convenient

3 fit 4 near 5 close, handy, ready 6 at hand, nearby, proper, useful 7 close by, helpful 8 suitable 9 available, immediate, opportune 10 accessible 11 appropriate, comfortable 12 advantageous

convent

5 abbey 6 priory 7 nunnery 8 cloister 9 monastery, sanctuary

convention

3 law 4 bond, code, pact, rule 5 canon, usage 6 accord, custom, treaty 7 compact, meeting, precept 8 assembly, congress, contract, covenant, practice, protocol 9 agreement, concordat, formality, gathering, propriety, tradition 11 convocation 13 understanding

conventional

5 trite, usual 6 formal, normal, proper, seemly, solemn, square 7 correct, regular, routine, typical 8 everyday, habitual, moderate, ordinary, orthodox, standard, straight 9 bourgeois, customary 10 button-down, conforming, prevailing, restrained, unoriginal 11 commonplace, traditional 12 conservative

conventionalize

5 adapt 7 conform, stylize

converge

4 join, meet 5 focus, merge, unite 11 concentrate 12 come together

conversant

8 familiar 9 au courant 10 acquainted 11 experienced

conversation

4 chat, talk 6 confab, debate, parley 7 palaver, talking 8 causerie, colloquy, dialogue, duologue, exchange, repartee 9 discourse, tête-à-tête 10 discussion 13 confabulation

conversation piece

5 curio 6 oddity 9 curiosity

converse

3 gab 4 chat, chin, talk 5 speak, visit 6 confer, contra, parley 7 chatter, counter, reverse 8 antipode, contrary, opposite 9 antipodal, diametric 10 antithesis 12 antithetical 13 contradictory

conversely
9 vice versa 10 oppositely 12 contrariwise

conversion
5 shift 6 change, switch 7 novelty, rebirth, turning 8 mutation, reversal 9 about-face 10 alteration, changeover 11 permutation 12 modification, regeneration 13 metamorphosis, transmutation

convert
4 sway 5 alter 6 change, modify, redeem, reform, switch 7 commute, remodel 8 persuade, renovate 9 proselyte, transform, translate, transmute, transpose 11 transfigure 12 metamorphose, transmogrify
Christian: 10 catechumen

convex
5 bowed, toric 6 arched, curved 7 bulging, curving, gibbous, rounded

convey
3 lug 4 bear, cart, cede, deed, pack, send, tell, tote 5 bring, carry, ferry 6 assign, impart, pass on 7 channel, conduct, consign, deliver, express, project 8 make over, sign over, transfer, transmit 9 transport 11 communicate

conveyance
3 car 4 auto, cart, deed, sled 5 coach, sedan, stage, title, wagon 7 charter, trailer, transit, vehicle 8 carriage, carrying 9 transport 10 automobile 12 transporting
public: 3 bus, cab 4 taxi, tram 5 plane, train 6 subway 7 trolley 8 airplane, monorail, railroad, rickshaw 9 streetcar 10 jinricksha, jinrikisha

convict
5 felon, lifer 6 inmate, send up 7 condemn, put away 8 criminal, jailbird, prisoner, sentence, yardbird 10 find guilty

conviction
4 view 5 creed, faith 6 belief, surety 7 opinion 8 doctrine, sentence, sureness 9 assurance, certainty, certitude, sentiment 10 confidence, persuasion 12 condemnation

convince
6 assure, induce, prompt 7 satisfy, win over 8 persuade, talk into 9 influence, prevail on 11 bring around, prevail upon

convincing
5 solid, sound, valid 6 cogent 8 credible, faithful 9 plausible 10 believable, conclusive, persuasive, satisfying 11 trustworthy

convivial
3 gay 5 jolly, merry 6 hearty, jocund, jovial, lively, social 7 festive 8 mirthful, sociable 9 fun-loving, vivacious 10 gregarious 13 companionable

convocation
5 synod 7 council, meeting 8 assembly, conclave 9 gathering 10 assemblage 12 congregation

convoke
4 call 6 gather, invite, muster, summon 7 collect, convene 8 assemble 12 call together

convoluted
6 coiled 7 complex, tangled, winding 8 involved, tortuous 9 intricate 10 circuitous 11 anfractuous, complicated 12 labyrinthine

convoy
6 attend, escort 7 conduct 9 accompany

convulse
4 rock 5 shake 7 agitate, concuss 8 tetanize

convulsion
3 fit 5 spasm 6 attack, tumult, uproar 7 quaking, rocking, seizure, shaking 8 disaster, paroxysm, upheaval 9 commotion, trembling

cook
3 fix, fry 4 bake, boil, chef, heat, melt, stew 5 broil, grill, poach, roast, sauté, steam 6 braise, doctor, simmer 7 falsify, parboil, prepare, swelter

cooked
4 done, sham 5 bogus, faked, phony

cookery

6 made-up 7 altered 8 doctored, spurious 10 fictitious

cookery

7 cuisine

expert: 3 Yan (Martin) 4 Chen (Joyce), Kerr (Graham), Puck (Wolfgang), Root (Waverley) 5 Beard (James), Child (Julia), David (Elizabeth), Hines (Duncan), Smith (Jeff) 6 Bocuse (Paul), Carême (Marie-Antoine), Farmer (Fannie), Fisher (M. F. K.), Franey (Pierre), Waters (Alice) 7 Crocker (Betty), Stewart (Martha) 8 Bourdain (Anthony), Rombauer (Irma) 9 Claiborne (Craig), Escoffier (Auguste), Prudhomme (Paul)

cookie

4 snap 7 biscuit, brownie 10 gingersnap

cooking

appliance: 4 oven 5 mixer, range, stove 7 blender, toaster 9 microwave 10 rotisserie
implement: 3 cup, pan, pot, wok 4 olla 5 ladle, sieve, spoon, whisk 6 grater, masher, sifter, tureen 7 griddle, skillet, spatula, steamer 8 colander, teaspoon 9 eggbeater, frying pan 10 rolling pin, tablespoon 12 measuring cup
room: 6 galley 7 kitchen

Cook Islands

capital: 6 Avarua
dependency of: 10 New Zealand
island: 9 Rarotonga

cool

3 hep, hip, icy 4 calm, cold 5 abate, aloof, chill, gelid, nippy 6 arctic, chilly, frigid, frosty 7 assured, compose, control, decline, distant, dwindle, repress, subside 8 composed, decrease, detached, diminish, reserved, suppress 9 collected, confident, impassive, unruffled 10 nonchalant, phlegmatic, unsociable 11 indifferent, standoffish, unflappable 13 imperturbable, self-possessed

cooler

3 fan, jug, pen 4 brig, coop, jail 5 clink, pokey 6 fridge, icebox, lockup, prison 7 freezer, slammer 9 calaboose 11 refrigerant 12 refrigerator

cooling device

3 fan 6 fridge, icebox 7 freezer 12 refrigerator

coolness

5 chill, poise 6 aplomb, phlegm 7 reserve 9 composure, frigidity, sangfroid 10 dispassion, equanimity 11 nonchalance, self-control

coop

3 hem, jug, mew, pen 4 brig, cage, jail 5 cramp, fence, pokey 6 cooler, corral, lockup, prison, shut in 7 close in, confine, enclose, slammer 9 calaboose, enclosure

cooperate

5 agree, unite 6 concur, league 7 combine, conjoin, pitch in 8 coincide, conspire 11 collaborate, participate 12 work together

cooperation

8 alliance, teamwork 13 confederation

cooperative

5 joint 6 common, mutual, shared 8 coactive, conjoint, obliging 9 collegial, concerted 10 collective, synergetic 11 coordinated 13 accommodating, collaborative, uncompetitive

Cooper hero

7 Hawkeye 10 Deerslayer, Pathfinder 11 Natty Bumppo

coordinate

4 mate, mesh 5 align, equal, match, order 6 adjust, relate 7 coequal, conform 8 organize, parallel 9 companion, correlate, harmonize, integrate, reconcile 10 proportion, reciprocal 11 accommodate, correlative, counterpart

coot

4 bird, fogy 6 dotard, duffer, fellow, oddity, scoter, weirdo 7 oddball 9 character, eccentric

cootie

5 louse 9 body louse

cop
3 nab **4** lift, take **5** adopt, catch, filch, pinch, steal, swipe **6** pilfer **7** capture, officer **8** bluecoat **9** patrolman, policeman

copacetic
3 A-OK **4** fine, jake, okay **5** dandy, great, nifty **8** all right **9** excellent **12** satisfactory

cope
4 cape, hack **5** cloak, cover, get by, match, vault **6** canopy, endure, make do, manage, mantle **7** carry on, survive **8** vestment

copestone
5 crown

copious
4 lush, rich **5** ample **6** lavish, plenty **7** liberal, profuse, replete **8** abundant, generous **9** abounding, bounteous, bountiful, exuberant, luxuriant, plenteous, plentiful

Copland work
5 Rodeo **11** Billy the Kid **17** Appalachian Spring

cop-out
5 dodge **6** excuse **7** evasion, pretext, retreat

copper
4 cent, coin **5** metal, penny, token **9** butterfly, policeman
item: 4 cent **5** penny **6** kettle
sulfate: 7 vitriol **9** bluestone **11** blue vitriol

copperhead
5 snake, viper **8** pit viper

coppice
4 bosk, wood **5** copse, grove, woods **6** bosque, forest, growth **7** thicket **9** brushwood, underwood

copse
see **coppice**

Copt
8 Egyptian

copula
4 bond, link **5** joint, union **7** coupler

copy
3 ape **4** echo, fake, mock, sham **5** clone, ditto, forge, mimic, model **6** carbon, parrot, repeat **7** emulate, forgery, imitate, replica, takeoff **8** knockoff, likeness, simulate **9** duplicate, facsimile, imitation, replicate, reproduce **10** impression, simulacrum, simulation, transcribe, transcript **11** counterfeit, counterpart, reduplicate, replication **12** reproduction

copyist
5 clerk **6** scribe **8** imitator **9** engrosser **10** plagiarist **11** transcriber

copyread
4 edit

coquet
3 toy **4** fool, vamp **5** dally, flirt, tease **6** trifle

coquette
4 vamp **5** flirt, tease

coquettish
3 coy **6** fickle **9** frivolous, kittenish **11** flirtatious

coral
3 red **4** pink, rosy **5** polyp **9** limestone

coral reef
3 cay, key **5** atoll
off Australia: 5 Wreck
world's largest: 12 Great Barrier

cord
3 tie **4** band, lace, pile, rope, whip, yarn **5** cable, nerve, stack **6** strand, string, tendon
twisted: 7 torsade

cordage
4 rope **5** ropes **7** rigging
fiber: 4 bast, hemp, jute, pita **5** sisal

Corday's victim
5 Marat (Jean-Paul)

Cordelia
father: 4 Lear
sister: 5 Regan **7** Goneril

cordial

4 warm 6 genial, hearty, jovial, tender 7 affable, liqueur, sincere 8 cheerful, friendly, gracious, sociable 9 congenial, convivial, heartfelt 10 hospitable 11 sympathetic, warmhearted 12 wholehearted

cordiality

6 warmth 7 amenity 9 geniality 10 amiability 12 agreeability, friendliness

cordon

4 lace, line, ring 5 braid 6 circle, ribbon 7 barrier 8 espalier
bleu: 4 chef, cook 6 ribbon 10 blue ribbon, decoration, master chef

core

3 hub, nub 4 base, crux, gist, meat, pith, root 5 basis, focus, heart, midst 6 center, depths, kernel, middle, upshot 7 essence, nucleus 8 interior, midpoint 9 substance 10 foundation

corium

5 cutis 6 dermis

cork

4 bark, plug, seal, stop 5 float 6 bobber 7 stopper, stopple

corker

4 lulu 5 beaut, dandy, dilly, doozy 6 doozie, killer 8 jim-dandy, knockout 9 humdinger 11 crackerjack 12 lollapalooza

corkscrew

4 coil, wind 5 helix, twist 6 spiral

cormorant

4 bird, shag 7 glutton

corn

5 grain, maize 6 hominy 9 granulate
bread: 4 pone 7 bannock
Indian: 5 maize 6 mealie
kind: 3 pop 5 flint, flour, sweet 6 Indian
pest: 5 borer
piece: 3 cob, ear 5 spike 6 kernel, nubbin

Corncracker State

8 Kentucky

corner

3 box, fix, jam, nab 4 hole, nook, trap, tree 5 angle, catch, coign, niche, seize 6 collar, cranny, dogleg, pickle, plight, recess, scrape 7 capture, dilemma, impasse, trouble 8 bottle up, monopoly 10 bring to bay 11 predicament 12 intersection
of eye: 7 canthus

cornerstone

4 base 5 basis 7 support 8 rudiment 10 foundation, groundwork

cornet

4 cone, horn 7 officer, trumpet 10 instrument

Cornhusker State

8 Nebraska

cornice

3 cap 4 band, eave 5 crown 7 molding

cornmeal

4 masa, samp 5 grits 6 hominy 7 hoecake
mush: 7 polenta

cornucopia

4 cone, horn 6 bounty, plenty, wealth 9 abundance, profusion 12 horn of plenty

Cornwallis, Charles

adversary: 6 Greene (Nathanael)
surrender site: 8 Yorktown

corny

5 banal, sappy, stale, trite 6 old hat 7 clichéd, mawkish 8 shopworn 9 hackneyed, schmaltzy 11 sentimental, stereotyped

corollary

6 effect, result, sequel, upshot 8 parallel, sequence 9 resulting 10 associated, end product, equivalent 11 aftereffect, consequence

corona

4 aura, glow, halo 5 cigar, crown, glory 6 circle, nimbus 7 aureola, aureole

coroner

8 examiner

coronet
5 crown, tiara 6 anadem, circle, diadem, wreath 7 chaplet, circlet, garland 8 headband

Coronis
form: 4 crow
son: 9 Asclepius 11 Aesculapius

corporal
3 NCO 6 bodily, carnal 7 fleshly, somatic 8 physical

corporate
7 unified 8 combined 9 aggregate

corporeal
6 bodily, carnal, mortal 7 fleshly, somatic 8 material, physical, tangible 9 objective 10 phenomenal 11 substantial

corps
4 band, body 5 group, party, troop 6 outfit, troupe 7 company

corpse
4 body 5 bones, stiff 7 cadaver, carcass, carrion, remains
combining form: 4 necr 5 necro

corpselike
4 dead 5 gaunt 7 deathly, ghastly, macabre 8 lifeless, skeletal 10 cadaverous

corpulence
7 fatness, obesity 9 adiposity, rotundity 10 fleshiness

corpulent
3 fat 5 bulky, gross, heavy, obese, plump, stout 6 fleshy, portly, rotund 7 porcine, weighty 9 overblown 10 overweight

corpus
4 body, bulk, core, mass 6 oeuvre 9 principal, substance 10 collection 11 compilation

corpuscle
4 cell 8 hemocyte, monocyte 9 blood cell, leukocyte 10 lymphocyte 11 erythrocyte, granulocyte

corral
3 mew, pen 5 fence 6 gather, shut in 7 close in, collect, confine, enclose, round up 8 surround 9 enclosure

correct
3 fit, fix 4 edit, just, mend, true 5 amend, emend, exact, right 6 adjust, decent, proper, punish, reform, remedy, repair, revise, seemly 7 chasten, fitting, improve, perfect, precise, rectify, redress 8 accurate, becoming, chastise, decorous, flawless, set right 9 castigate, faultless 10 conforming, discipline, impeccable, legitimate, meticulous, scrupulous 11 appropriate, comme il faut, punctilious 12 conventional
combining form: 4 orth 5 ortho

correction
3 rod 6 rebuke 7 reproof 8 revision 9 amendment 10 adjustment, discipline, emendation, punishment 11 castigation

corrective
4 cure 6 remedy 8 antidote, punitive, remedial 10 beneficial 11 counterstep, restorative 12 counteragent 13 counteractive

correctness
7 decorum 8 accuracy, fidelity 9 precision, propriety 10 exactitude

correlate
5 match 6 analog 7 pendant 8 analogue, coincide, dovetail, parallel 9 harmonize 10 complement, correspond 11 counterpart

correlative
3 and, nor 4 both, then 6 either 7 neither, related 10 complement, reciprocal 11 counterpart 13 complementary, corresponding

correspond
4 jibe 5 agree, equal, match, write 6 accord, concur 7 comport, conform 8 dovetail 9 harmonize 11 communicate

correspondence
4 mail 7 analogy, letters 8 symmetry

correspondent

9 agreement, congruity 10 conformity, similarity 11 consistency, correlation
mathematical: 7 mapping 8 function

correspondent

5 match 6 analog, pen pal, writer 7 fitting 8 analogue, parallel, reporter, suitable 9 correlate 10 conforming, journalist 11 commentator, contributor, counterpart

corresponding

4 akin, like 5 alike 6 agnate 7 related, similar 8 matching, parallel 9 analogous, consonant 10 comparable 11 correlative

correspondingly

4 also 7 equally 8 likewise 9 similarly 11 analogously

corrida

9 bullfight
shout: 3 olé

corridor

4 hall, lane, path 5 aisle, route, strip 6 artery, avenue 7 hallway, passage 10 passageway

corroborate

5 prove 6 uphold, verify 7 approve, bear out, certify, confirm, endorse, justify, support 8 document, validate 9 vindicate 12 authenticate, substantiate

corroborative

9 ancillary, auxiliary 10 collateral, supporting, supportive 12 confirmatory

corrode

4 rust 7 eat away, eat into, oxidize 8 wear away 9 undermine

corrosive

5 acerb 6 biting 7 acerbic, caustic, cutting 9 sarcastic

corrosiveness

7 sarcasm 8 acerbity

corrugation

4 fold, ruck 5 plica, ridge 6 crease, furrow, groove 7 crinkle, wrinkle

corrupt

3 rot 5 bribe, decay, spoil, stain, taint, venal 6 befoul, debase, defile, molder, rotten, smirch 7 crooked, debauch, degrade, deprave, pervert, putrefy, tarnish, vitiate 8 bribable, degraded, depraved, infected, perverse 9 decompose, dishonest, miscreant, reprobate, unethical 10 bastardize, degenerate 12 unprincipled, unscrupulous 13 untrustworthy

corruptible

5 venal 7 buyable 8 bribable

corruption

4 vice 5 decay, fraud, graft 7 bribery, jobbery 9 barbarism, depravity, turpitude 10 immorality, wickedness 11 impropriety

corsair

5 rover 6 pirate 8 picaroon, sea rover 9 buccaneer, pickaroon, privateer 10 freebooter

corset

5 stays 6 bodice, girdle 7 support

cortege

5 train 6 parade 7 retinue 9 entourage 10 attendants, procession

cortex

4 bark, husk, peel, rind 6 casing 8 peridium

Cortland

5 apple

corundum

4 ruby 5 emery, topaz 7 emerald 8 abrasive, amethyst, sapphire

coruscate

5 flash, gleam, glint, shine 7 glisten, glitter, sparkle, twinkle 11 scintillate

corvid

3 jay 4 crow 5 raven 6 magpie 9 passerine

Corvino's wife

5 Celia

corybantic

3 mad 4 wild 5 rabid 6 crazed

7 frantic, furious **8** ecstatic, frenetic, frenzied **9** delirious

coryphée
6 dancer **8** danseuse **9** ballerina

Cosí Fan Tutte composer
6 Mozart (Wolfgang Amadeus)

cosmetic
4 kohl **5** blush, rouge **6** ceruse, makeup, powder **7** blusher, bronzer, mascara **8** lip gloss, lipstick **9** eye shadow **10** decorative, nail polish, ornamental **11** beautifying, superficial

cosmetologist
10 beautician

cosmic
4 huge, vast **7** immense **8** infinite **9** planetary, spiritual, unbounded, universal **12** astronomical, metaphysical

cosmopolitan
6 global, urbane **7** worldly **8** catholic, cultured, polished **9** civilized, universal, worldwide **10** cultivated, ecumenical **11** worldly-wise **13** sophisticated

cosmos
6 flower **8** creation, universe

Cossack
army: 3 Don **4** Ural **5** Kuban
land: 7 Ukraine
leader: 5 Razin (Stenka) **6** ataman, hetman, Mazepa (Ivan) **7** Bulavin (Kondraty) **8** Pugachov (Yemelyan)
novel: 10 Taras Bulba

cosset
3 pet **4** baby, lamb, love **5** humor, spoil **6** caress, cocker, coddle, cuddle, dandle, dote on, fondle, pamper **7** cater to, indulge **11** mollycoddle

cost
3 tab **4** rate, toll **5** price **6** charge, damage, outlay, tariff **7** expense, payment **8** price tag **9** sacrifice **11** expenditure **12** disbursement
business: 8 overhead

Costa Rica
bay: 8 Coronado
capital: 7 San José
city: 8 Alajuela **10** Puntarenas **11** Puerto Limón
discoverer: 8 Columbus (Christopher)
language: 7 Spanish
leader: 5 Arias (Oscar)
monetary unit: 5 colón
neighbor: 6 Panama **9** Nicaragua
peninsula: 3 Osa **6** Nicoya
river: 7 San Juan
volcano: 5 Barba, Irazú **9** Turrialba

costermonger
6 hawker **7** peddler **9** barrow boy

costive
4 mean, slow **5** bound, close, tight **6** frugal, stingy **7** miserly **9** penurious **10** hardfisted, pinchpenny **11** closefisted **12** cheeseparing, parsimonious

costless
4 free **6** gratis **10** gratuitous **13** complimentary

costly
4 dear, rich **5** fancy **6** lavish, pricey **7** opulent, premium **8** precious, splendid, valuable **9** expensive, luxurious, priceless **10** exorbitant, high-priced, invaluable **11** extravagant

costume
3 rig **4** duds, garb, mode **5** dress, getup, guise, habit, style **6** attire, outfit **7** apparel, clothes, fashion, threads, turnout, uniform **8** disguise, ensemble, garments **9** trappings

cot
3 bed, hut **4** camp **5** cabin, lodge, shack **6** shanty
wheeled: 6 gurney

coterie
4 band, camp, clan, club, ring **5** cabal **6** circle, clique **7** in-group **9** camarilla

cotillion
4 ball, prom **5** dance

cottage
3 hut 4 camp 5 cabin, lodge, shack
6 shanty 8 bungalow
Russian: 5 dacha
Swiss: 6 chalet

cotton
cleaner: 3 gin 6 linter
cloth: 4 duck, jean, mull 5 baize,
chino, denim, drill, khaki, scrim, terry,
wigan 6 calico, canvas, chintz,
dimity, muslin, oxford, sateen, velour
7 batiste, etamine, fustian, gingham,
jaconet, nankeen, organdy, percale
8 corduroy, dungaree, moleskin,
nainsook, tarlatan 9 grenadine,
percaline, stockinet, swansdown
10 balbriggan 11 stockinette
cloth, Indian: 5 surah 6 madras
7 dhurrie, khaddar
comb: 4 card
fuzz remover: 6 linter
measure: 4 hank, pick, yard 5 count,
skein
pad: 7 pledget
pod: 4 boll
refuse: 5 flock
seed separator: 3 gin
sheet: 4 batt
thread: 5 lisle

Cotton State
7 Alabama

cottonwood
5 alamo 6 poplar

cottony
4 soft 6 fluffy

_____ Coty
4 René

couch
3 den, put 4 lair, sofa, word 5 divan,
lodge 6 burrow, chaise, daybed,
lounge, phrase 7 express, lie down,
recline 9 davenport, formulate
12 chesterfield

couch potato
7 slacker

cougar
3 cat 4 puma 7 panther
9 catamount 12 mountain lion

cough
4 hack, hawk

cough drop
6 troche 7 lozenge

cough up
3 pay 5 spend 6 lay out, pay out
7 deliver, dole out, fork out 8 fork
over, hand over, shell out

couloir
5 chasm, gorge, gulch, gully 6 ravine

council
4 diet 5 board, junta 6 powwow,
senate 7 cabinet, meeting 8 assembly, conclave, congress, ministry
10 conference, federation 12 consultation
ancient Greek: 5 boule
church: 5 synod 10 consistory
medieval English: 4 moot 5 gemot
6 gemote 8 hustings
Muslim: 5 divan
Russian: 4 duma 6 soviet
secret: 5 cabal, junto 9 camarilla
Spanish: 7 cabildo

counsel
4 urge, warn 6 advice, advise,
charge, direct, enjoin, lawyer 7 consult, suggest 8 advocate, attorney
9 prescribe, recommend 10 advise-
ment 12 deliberation
British: 9 barrister, solicitor

count
3 add, sum, tot 4 bank, earl, mean,
rely, tote 5 issue, score, tally, total,
tot up, weigh 6 census, charge,
depend, expect, figure, matter,
number, reckon, result, tote up
7 compute, signify 8 estimate,
militate, numerate, quantify 9 calculate, enumerate 10 allegation

countenance
3 mug 4 back, cast, face, look, mien,
phiz 5 favor, go for 6 accept, visage
7 approve, commend, condone,
endorse, support 8 advocate,
features, hold with, sanction, tolerate
9 approbate, composure, encourage
10 expression 11 physiognomy

counter
3 pit, vie 4 anti 5 asset, check, match, polar, shelf 6 offset, oppose 7 adverse, against, hostile, obverse, opposed, reverse 8 antipode, contrary, converse, opposing, opposite 9 antipodal, diametric 10 antipodean, antithesis, contravene 12 antagonistic, antipathetic, antithetical 13 contradictory

counteract
3 fix 4 foil 5 annul 6 cancel, negate, oppose, resist, thwart 7 balance, correct, nullify, prevent, rectify, redress 8 negative 9 cancel out, frustrate 10 balance out, neutralize

counteragent
4 cure 6 remedy 8 antidote 9 antitoxin, antivenin 10 corrective

counterbalance
6 cancel, make up, offset, redeem, set off 7 ballast, correct, even out, rectify, redress 8 equalize, outweigh 10 compensate

counterblow
7 revenge 8 reprisal, requital, revanche 9 vengeance 11 retaliation, retribution

counterclockwise
4 levo 12 levorotatory

counterfeit
4 copy, fake, hoax, sham 5 bluff, bogus, dummy, false, feign, forge, fraud, mimic, phony 6 affect, assume, deceit, ersatz, forged, pseudo 7 feigned, imitate, pretend 8 delusive, delusory, knock off, simulate, spurious 9 brummagem, deception, deceptive, fabricate, imitation, imposture, insincere, pinchbeck, pretended, simulated 10 fraudulent, misleading, simulacrum
prefix: 5 pseud 6 pseudo

counterpane
4 pouf, puff 5 duvet 6 spread 8 bedcover, coverlet 9 bedspread, comforter, eiderdown

counterpart
4 like, twin 5 equal, match 6 analog,

double 7 vis-à-vis 8 analogue, parallel 9 correlate, duplicate 10 complement, coordinate, equivalent 11 correlative 13 correspondent

counterpoise
6 make up, offset, redeem, set off 7 balance, ballast 8 outweigh 9 stabilize 10 compensate

countersign
8 password 9 watchword

countervail
4 foil 6 cancel, offset, oppose, redeem, set off, thwart 7 balance, correct, nullify, rectify 8 outweigh 9 frustrate 10 compensate, neutraliz

countless
6 legion, myriad, untold 7 umpteen 11 innumerable

Count of Monte Cristo
6 Dantès (Edmond)
author: 5 Dumas (Alexandre)

count out
5 expel 6 except 7 exclude 9 disregard, eliminate

countrified
5 rural 6 rustic 7 bucolic 8 homespun, pastoral 10 campestral

country
4 home, land, soil 5 rural 6 nation, region, rustic, sticks 7 boonies, bucolic, outland 8 homeland, pastoral 9 backwoods, boondocks 10 campestral, fatherland, motherland, provincial
dance: 3 jig 4 reel 10 strathspey
home: 5 manor, ranch, villa 8 hacienda
music: 9 bluegrass
road: 4 lane, path 5 byway

coup
4 blow, feat 5 upset 6 putsch, stroke 8 takeover

couple
3 duo 4 bond, dyad, fuse, join, link, mate, pair, span, team, yoke 5 brace, hitch, marry, merge, unite 6 hook up, link up 7 bracket, combine, conjoin, connect, doublet, harness, twosome

coupler

4 link, ring **5** hitch, joint **6** hookup
7 shackle **8** ligature
railroad: 7 drawbar

couplet

3 duo **4** dyad, pair **5** twins **7** distich,
doublet, twosome

coupling

4 link, seam **5** joint, union **7** joining,
pairing **8** junction, juncture **9** connector **10** connection

courage

4 dash, grit, guts **5** heart, moxie,
nerve, pluck, spunk, valor **6** daring,
mettle, spirit **7** bravery, heroism
8 audacity, backbone, boldness,
firmness, temerity, tenacity, valiance,
valiancy **9** assurance, fortitude,
gallantry **10** resolution **11** doughti-
ness, intrepidity **12** fearlessness
13 dauntlessness

courageous

4 bold **5** brave, gutsy, nervy, stout
6 daring, heroic, manful, plucky,
spunky, strong **7** doughty, gallant,
valiant **8** fearless, intrepid, resolute,
stalwart, unafraid, valorous **9** audacious, dauntless, tenacious, undaunted **11** venturesome **12** stouthearted

courier

5 envoy **6** legate, runner **8** emissary
9 go-between, messenger **11** internuncio

course

3 row, run, way **4** dart, dash, duct,
flow, line, path, plan, race, road,
rush, tack, tear **5** canal, chain,
chase, class, hurry, orbit, order,
range, route, scoot, scope, speed,
surge, track, trend **6** career, design,
hasten, hustle, manner, policy, polity,
scheme, sequel, series, string,
system **7** advance, channel, circuit,
conduit, passage, pattern, program,
regimen, routine, seminar **8** aqueduct, duration, progress, sequence,
syllabus **9** procedure, racetrack
10 curriculum, succession **11** progression

dinner: 4 soup **5** salad **6** entrée
7 dessert **9** appetizer, blue plate

courser

4 bird **5** horse **7** charger **8** huntsman, warhorse

court

3 bar, woo **4** date, quad, yard
5 charm, motel, spark, suite, tempt
6 allure, homage, invite, palace,
pursue **7** address, flatter, justice,
retinue, romance, solicit **8** assembly,
cloister, tribunal **9** captivate, curtilage, enclosure, entourage **10** magistrate, parliament, quadrangle
11 legislature
action: 4 suit **5** trial **6** appeal,
assize **7** hearing, inquest, lawsuit
10 proceeding
calendar: 6 docket
call to: 7 summons **8** subpoena
11 arraignment
circuit: 4 eyre
crier's call: 4 oyez
decision: 6 assize **7** finding, verdict
8 judgment
ecclesiastical: 4 rota **5** Curia
10 consistory
Indian: 6 durbar
kind: 4 moot **5** civil **6** county, family
7 circuit, customs, federal, supreme
8 chancery, criminal, district, juvenile,
kangaroo, superior **9** appellate, municipal **11** territorial
medieval English: 4 eyre, moot
5 gemot **6** gemote **8** hustings
of equity: 8 chancery
officer: 5 clerk, crier, judge **7** bailiff,
justice, marshal, sheriff **10** prosecutor
order: 4 writ **5** edict **6** decree
7 summons **8** mandamus, subpoena
panel: 4 jury
relating to: 8 judicial **9** juridical
session: 6 assize **7** sitting **8** sederunt

courteous

5 civil **6** polite **7** courtly, gallant,
genteel **8** mannerly, well-bred
9 attentive **10** chivalrous, thoughtful
11 considerate **12** well-mannered

courtesy
  7 amenity, decorum, manners, service **8** chivalry, civility **9** attention, etiquette, gallantry **10** cordiality, indulgence **11** courtliness **12** graciousness **13** attentiveness, consideration

court game
  see under **game**

courtly
  5 noble **6** august, formal, urbane **7** elegant, gallant, refined, stately **8** gracious **9** dignified **10** chivalrous, flattering **11** ceremonious

courtship
  4 suit **6** dating, wooing **7** romance **10** flirtation
  former custom of: 8 bundling

courtyard
  4 quad **5** garth, patio **9** curtilage **10** quadrangle

cousin
  3 kin **7** kinsman **8** relative

Cousteau, Jacques
  ship: 7 Calypso
  vehicle: 11 bathysphere

couturier
  8 clothier, costumer, designer **10** dressmaker

cove
  3 arm, bay **4** nook **5** bight, firth, inlet, niche **6** harbor, recess **9** concavity

covenant
  3 vow **4** bond, pact **5** agree, swear **6** pledge, treaty **7** compact, promise **8** contract **9** agreement **10** convention

Covent Garden offering
  5 opera

cover
  3 cap, lid **4** bury, hide, hood, mask, wrap **5** alibi, cloak, front, guise, stash, track **6** enfold, enwrap, facade, hiding, insure, refuge, screen, secure,

shield, shroud, travel **7** blanket, conceal, embrace, enclose, envelop, obscure, overlay, protect, secrete, shelter, write up **8** disguise, ensconce, enshroud, traverse **9** encompass, safeguard, sanctuary, superpose **10** overspread **11** concealment, superimpose
  rooflike: 6 awning, canopy
  the eyes: 9 blindfold
  the face: 4 mask, veil
  the mouth: 6 muzzle
  with asphalt: 4 pave
  with cloth: 5 drape
  with dirt: 7 begrime, blacken **8** besmirch
  with straw: 6 thatch

coverall
  8 jumpsuit **10** boilersuit

covered wagon
  9 Conestoga

covering
  anatomical: 5 theca, velum **6** tegmen **7** velamen **8** tegument **10** integument
  close-fitting: 6 sheath **9** sheathing
  cloth: 5 sheet
  flap: 9 operculum
  for a book: 4 case **6** jacket
  for a cigar: 7 wrapper
  for a coffin: 4 pall
  for a corpse: 6 shroud **8** cerement
  for a package: 7 wrapper
  for concealment: 10 camouflage
  for food: 4 cosy, cozy
  for soil: 5 mulch
  metal: 4 mail **5** armor
  of a diatom: 7 lorica
  of a plant ovary: 8 pericarp
  of a seed: 4 aril, case **5** testa
  of fruits: 4 peel, rind
  of gloom: 4 pall
  of grain: 4 hull, husk **5** chaff
  shell-like: 8 carapace
  thin: 4 film **6** patina, veneer
  waterproof: 4 tarp **9** tarpaulin

coverlet
  4 pouf, puff **5** duvet **6** spread **8** bedcover **9** bedspread, comforter **11** counterpane

covert

4 lair **5** haven, privy **6** hidden, masked, refuge, secret, veiled **7** feather, furtive, retreat, shelter, sub-rosa, thicket **8** hush-hush, shrouded, stealthy **9** concealed, disguised, sanctuary, sheltered **10** undercover **11** camouflaged, clandestine, hiding place, underhanded **12** hugger-mugger **13** surreptitious, under-the-table

covertly

7 sub-rosa **9** by stealth **12** hugger-mugger

covet

4 want **5** crave **6** desire

covetous

4 avid, keen **5** itchy **6** grabby, greedy **7** envious **8** desirous, esurient, grasping, ravenous **9** rapacious, voracious **10** avaricious, gluttonous **11** acquisitive

covey

4 band, bevy, crew, nest **5** brood, bunch, flock, group, party, troop **6** gaggle, troupe **7** cluster, company

cow

(see also **cattle**)
4 faze, kine (plural), neat **5** abash, bossy, bully, daunt **6** appall, bovine, dismay, hector, rattle **7** bluster, dragoon **8** bludgeon, browbeat, bulldoze, bullyrag **9** discomfit, embarrass, strong-arm **10** disconcert, intimidate
cud: 5 rumen
French: 5 vache
hornless: 5 muley **7** pollard
mammary gland: 5 udder
pen: 6 corral
shed: 4 barn, byre
Spanish: 4 vaca
young: 4 calf **5** stirk **6** heifer

coward

6 craven **7** caitiff, chicken, dastard, milksop, nebbish **8** poltroon, recreant **9** jellyfish **10** scaredy-cat **11** yellowbelly

_____ Coward

4 Noël

cowardly

5 timid, wimpy **6** afraid, craven, yellow **7** caitiff, chicken, fearful, gutless **8** poltroon, recreant, timorous **9** dastardly **11** lily-livered, milk-livered, poltroonish **12** apprehensive, fainthearted, poor-spirited, white-livered **13** pusillanimous

cowboy

5 rogue, waddy **6** drover, herder, waddie **7** puncher, rancher **8** buckaroo, herdsman, maverick, wrangler **9** cattleman, ranch hand **10** cowpuncher **12** broncobuster
contest: 5 rodeo
gear: 5 cuffs, quirt, spurs **6** duster **7** bedroll, slicker, Stetson
legendary: 9 Pecos Bill
leggings: 5 chaps
movie: 3 Mix (Tom) **4** Hart (William S.) **5** Autry (Gene), Wayne (John) **6** Gibson (Hoot), McCrea (Joel), Murphy (Audie), Ritter (Tex), Rogers (Roy, Will) **8** Cisco Kid, Eastwood (Clint)
rope: 5 lasso, reata, riata **6** lariat
Spanish-American: 6 charro, gaucho **7** vaquero

cower

5 quail, wince **6** blench, cringe, flinch, recoil, shrink

cowfish

6 dugong, sea cow **7** grampus, manatee **8** sirenian

cowl

4 cape, hood **5** cloak **6** mantle **7** capuche

cowpox

8 vaccinia

cowpuncher

see **cowboy**

coxcomb

3 fop **4** beau, buck, dude, fool **5** blood, dandy, swell **7** peacock **8** macaroni **9** exquisite **11** Beau Brummel **12** clotheshorse, fashion plate, lounge lizard

coy
3 shy 4 arch, cute, pert 5 saucy,
timid 6 demure, modest 7 bashful,
evasive, playful 8 blushing, decorous, skittish 9 diffident, kittenish
10 capricious, coquettish 11 flirtatious, mischievous 12 noncommittal

Coyote State
11 South Dakota

coypu
6 rodent
fur: 6 nutria

cozen
3 gyp 4 bilk, scam 5 cheat, trick
6 diddle, fleece, take in 7 beguile,
deceive, defraud, swindle, wheedle
8 flimflam 9 bamboozle 11 double-
cross

cozy
4 safe, snug, soft 5 comfy, cushy,
pally, tight 6 chummy, secure
8 familiar, intimate 11 comfortable

crab
3 nag 4 beef, fuss, yawp 5 gripe,
sidle 6 grinch, griper, grouch,
kvetch, squawk, yammer 7 decapod,
grouser, growler 8 arthropod, complain, grumbler, sourpuss 9 bellyache, shellfish 10 bellyacher, complainer, crosspatch, crustacean,
curmudgeon 11 faultfinder
claw: 5 chela 6 nipper
constellation: 6 Cancer
genus: 3 Uca 6 Birgus 7 Limulus,
Pagurus
kind: 3 pea 4 blue, king, pine, rock
5 ghost, purse 6 hermit, spider
7 fiddler 9 Dungeness, horseshoe
king, horseshoe: 7 limulus

crabbed
4 dour, glum, grim, sour 5 gruff, surly
6 crusty, gloomy, morose, sullen
9 illegible, irascible, saturnine,
splenetic

crablike
8 cancroid

crabwise
8 sidelong, sideward, sideways
9 laterally

crack
3 gag, gap, rap, try 4 bang, bash,
belt, blow, boom, clap, flaw, jest,
joke, open, peal, quip, rift, roll, shot,
slam, slap, snap, stab, wham, whop
5 adept, break, burst, chink, cleft,
crash, craze, knock, smack, smash,
solve, split, whack, whirl, wreck
6 breach, cranny, decode, expert,
master, moment, thwack 7 break up,
crevice, decrypt, destroy, fissure,
instant, shatter, skilled 8 crevasse,
decipher, disorder, interval, masterly,
skillful, superior 9 break into, excellent, interrupt, masterful, witticism
10 percussion, proficient

crackbrain
3 nut 4 kook 5 crank, wacko 6 cuckoo 7 dingbat, lunatic 9 ding-a-ling,
fruitcake, screwball

crackdown
5 purge 8 quashing 10 repression
11 suppression

cracked
3 mad 4 daft, nuts 5 balmy, batty,
crazy, daffy, loony, nutty 6 broken,
crazed, cuckoo, insane, screwy
7 bonkers, lunatic, smashed 8 demented, deranged

cracker
5 wafer 6 hacker, rustic 7 biscuit, saltine, snapper 8 Georgian
9 Floridian

crackerjack
3 ace 4 lulu 5 dandy, nifty, sharp
6 corker, killer 8 jim-dandy, knockout
9 humdinger 12 lollapalooza

crackle
4 snap 7 glitter, sparkle, twinkle
9 crepitate 10 effervesce 13 effervescence

crackpot
3 nut 4 case, kook, loon 5 crank,
loony, wacko 6 cuckoo, madman
7 dingbat, lunatic, oddball 9 ding-a-
ling, eccentric, fruitcake, harebrain,
screwball

crack-up, crack up
5 crash, smash, wreck 6 fiasco

7 debacle **8** accident, collapse, disaster **9** breakdown **11** catastrophe

cradlesong

7 lullaby **8** berceuse

craft

3 art, job **5** guile, knack, skill, trade, wiles **6** career, deceit, métier **7** ability, calling, cunning, know-how, slyness **8** artifice, caginess, foxiness, vocation, wiliness **9** adeptness, canniness, dexterity, duplicity, expertise, ingenuity, technique **10** adroitness, artfulness, competence, occupation, profession, shrewdness **11** proficiency

craftiness

5 guile **7** cunning **8** artifice, subtlety

craftsman

5 smith **6** carter, carver, potter, weaver, wright **7** artisan, builder, cobbler, jeweler **9** carpenter **10** blacksmith

crafty

3 sly **4** foxy, keen, wily **5** acute, cagey, canny, sharp, slick **6** adroit, artful, astute, clever, shrewd, tricky **7** cunning, devious, fawning, vulpine **8** guileful, scheming, skillful, slippery **9** deceitful, designing, ingenious, insidious **11** calculating, duplicitous **Scottish: 7** sleekit

crag

3 tor **4** hill **5** cliff

craggy

5 harsh, rocky, rough **6** jagged, rugged, uneven

cram

3 jam, ram **4** bolt, fill, gulp, heap, load, pack, wolf **5** crowd, crush, drive, force, press, shove, study, stuff, wedge **6** gobble, review, squash, thrust **7** jam-pack, overeat, squeeze

crammed

4 full **5** awash, flush **7** brimful **8** brimming **9** chock-full

cramp

4 kink, pain, pang **5** crick, limit, spasm **6** hamper, stitch **7** confine, inhibit, shackle **8** confined, restrain, restrict **9** restraint, stricture **10** constraint, limitation **11** confinement, restriction

cramped

5 close, tight **6** narrow **9** confining, two-by-four

crane

4 bird, boom, rail **5** heron **7** derrick, stretch
arm: 3 jib
genus: 4 Grus
ship's: 5 davit

Crane hero

12 Henry Fleming

cranium

5 skull **9** braincase

crank

3 nut **4** crab, kook **5** fancy **6** griper, grouch, notion, rotate, turn up, vagary **7** caprice, conceit, fanatic, grouser, oddball **8** crackpot, crotchet, grumbler, sourpuss **9** eccentric, screwball **10** bellyacher, crosspatch

cranky

5 cross, testy **6** crabby, crusty, cussed, grumpy, ornery, tetchy, touchy **7** bearish, crabbed, peevish, prickly **8** contrary, petulant, tortuous, vinegary **9** crotchety, irascible, irritable, obstinate **10** bad-humored, ill-humored **12** cantankerous, disagreeable **13** unpredictable

cranny

3 gap **4** nook, slit **5** chink, crack, niche **6** corner **7** crevice

crash

3 din, jar, ram **4** bang, boom, bump, bust, clap, fail, fold, jolt, peal, slam, wham **5** blast, break, burst, crack, shock, smash, wreck **6** impact, pileup **7** collide, crack-up, debacle, decline, failure, smashup **8** accident, collapse **9** breakdown, collision **10** concussion

crass

4 rude 5 crude, gross 6 coarse, vulgar 7 boorish, loutish, uncouth 8 churlish 9 unrefined 13 materialistic

crate

3 box 4 heap 5 wreck 6 jalopy, junker 7 clunker

crater

3 pit 4 dent, hole, pock 5 crash 6 cavity, dimple, hollow, trough 7 caldera 8 collapse 10 depression
Hawaiian: 7 Kilauea

cravat

3 tie 4 band 5 ascot, scarf 7 necktie

crave

3 ask, beg 4 need, want, wish 5 covet 6 demand, desire 7 call for, entreat, implore, long for, require 8 yearn for

craven

4 funk 6 abject, coward 7 caitiff, chicken, dastard, fearful, gutless, ignoble 8 cowardly, cringing, poltroon, recreant 9 dastardly 11 lily-livered, poltroonish, yellowbelly 13 pusillanimous, yellowbellied

craving

4 itch, lust, urge 6 desire, hunger, thirst 7 longing, passion 8 appetite, yearning 9 hankering

crawl

4 flow, inch, teem 5 creep, swarm 6 abound, grovel 7 slither, wriggle 9 pullulate

crawling

6 repent

craze

3 fad 4 chic, rage 5 crack, fever, furor, mania, trend, vogue 6 dement, enrage, frenzy, furore, madden 7 derange, fashion, unhinge 9 unbalance 10 dernier cri, enthusiasm

craziness

5 folly, mania 6 lunacy 8 hysteria, insanity 9 absurdity

crazy

3 fey, mad 4 daft, gaga, loco, nuts, wild 5 balmy, barmy, batty, daffy, dotty, goofy, kooky, loony, loopy, nutty, rabid, silly, wacko, wacky 6 absurd, cuckoo, fruity, insane, mental, psycho, screwy, teched, whacky 7 berserk, bonkers, cracked, foolish, frantic, lunatic, smitten, tetched, touched, unsound 8 cockeyed, crackpot, demented, deranged, frenetic, frenzied, maniacal, unhinged 9 bedlamite, delirious, eccentric, fanatical, foolhardy, ludicrous, possessed, screwball, senseless 10 crackbrain, moonstruck, ridiculous, unbalanced 11 harebrained, nonsensical 12 preposterous
British: 5 potty 6 scatty
Scottish: 3 wud

creak

4 rasp 5 grate, grind 6 scrape, squeak, squeal 7 grating, screech 9 squeaking

creaky

4 aged 5 rusty 7 rickety, run-down, squeaky, unsound, worn-out 8 decrepit 9 tottering 10 broken-down, ramshackle

cream

3 top 4 balm, beat, best, drub, pick, whip, whup 5 blast, elite, prime, salve 6 cerate, choice, defeat, finest, thrash 7 clobber, destroy, trounce, unguent 8 lambaste, liniment, ointment

crease

4 fold, ruck 5 graze, plica, ridge 6 furrow, groove, rumple 7 crinkle, wrinkle

create

3 dub 4 form, make, sire 5 beget, build, cause, forge, found, hatch, set up, spawn, start 6 author, design, devise, father, invent 7 compose, concoct, develop, fashion, produce 8 conceive, engender, generate, occasion 9 construct, establish, fabricate, formulate, institute, originate 10 constitute

creation

5 birth, world **6** cosmos, nature **7** genesis **8** universe **9** inception, macrocosm **10** conception **11** macrocosmos

creative

7 fertile **8** artistic, inspired, original **9** deceptive, demiurgic, ingenious, inventive **10** innovative, innovatory **11** imaginative **12** innovational

creator

3 god **6** author **8** inventor **9** architect, generator, patriarch **10** originator, progenitor

creature

3 man **5** beast, being, brute, human **6** animal, mortal, person **7** critter, varmint
fabled: 3 elf, imp, orc, roc **4** ogre, puck, yeti **5** dwarf, fairy, ghost, giant, gnome, harpy, nymph, pixie, troll **6** dragon, goblin, gorgon, kraken, merman, sphinx, sprite **7** bigfoot, brownie, bugbear, centaur, chimera, gremlin, griffin, mermaid, monster, unicorn, vampire, wendigo **8** minotaur, werewolf **9** hobgoblin, manticore, sasquatch **10** cockatrice, hippogriff, leprechaun
(see also **monster**)

credence

5 faith, trust **6** belief, credit **8** reliance **9** sideboard **10** acceptance, confidence

credentials

6 papers **9** documents **10** references **12** certificates, testimonials **13** documentation

credenza

6 buffet **8** bookcase **9** sideboard

credible

5 solid, sound, valid **6** trusty **8** reliable **9** authentic, colorable, plausible **10** believable, convincing, persuasive, reasonable **11** trustworthy **12** satisfactory

credit

4 deem, feel **5** asset, faith, honor, refer, sense, think, trust **6** accept, assign, belief, charge, impute, notice, weight **7** ascribe, believe **8** consider, credence, prestige, reliance **9** attribute, authority, influence **10** confidence, reputation **11** recognition

creditable

6 worthy **8** laudable, reliable **9** colorable, deserving, estimable, plausible, reputable **10** believable **11** commendable, meritorious, respectable **12** praiseworthy

credo

5 canon, creed, dogma, tenet **6** belief, tenets **7** beliefs, precept **8** doctrine, ideology **9** catechism, principle

credulous

5 naive **6** unwary **8** gullible, trustful, trusting **9** believing **12** unsuspecting, unsuspicious **13** unquestioning

creed

4 sect **5** canon, dogma, faith, tenet **6** belief, church, tenets **7** beliefs, precept **8** doctrine, ideology, religion **9** catechism, communion, principle **12** denomination

creek

4 burn, rill **5** brook **6** arroyo, rillet, runlet, runnel, stream **7** freshet, rivulet **8** brooklet **9** streamlet

creep

4 drag, edge, inch, lurk, slip **5** crawl, glide, shirk, skulk, slide, slink, snake, sneak, steal **6** spread, tiptoe **7** gumshoe, slither, wriggle **9** pussyfoot

creeping

6 repent **7** gradual **9** prostrate

creepy

5 eerie, weird **6** spooky **7** anxious, macabre, ominous, strange, uncanny **8** ghoulish, menacing, sinister **9** unnerving **10** disturbing, unpleasant, unsettling **11** hair-raising

crème de la crème

4 best **5** elect, elite **6** finest **8** very best

Cremona family
5 Amati 8 Guarneri

Creon
daughter: 6 Creusa, Glauce, Glauke
sister: 7 Jocasta
son: 6 Haemon
victim: 8 Antigone

crescendo
4 acme, apex, peak, rise 5 crest,
surge, swell 6 apogee, climax,
growth, height, zenith 8 increase,
pinnacle 9 high point 11 culmination

crescent-shaped
5 bowed 6 lunate, sickle 7 falcate
body or surface: 8 meniscus

crest
3 cap, top 4 acme, apex, comb,
noon, peak, roof, tuft 5 arête, chine,
crown, plume, ridge 6 apogee,
climax, summit, vertex 7 hogback
8 pinnacle, surmount 9 high point
10 coat of arms, prominence 11 culmination
of a wave: 8 whitecap

crestfallen
3 low 4 blue, down 6 droopy 8 dejected, downcast, drooping 9 depressed 10 dispirited 11 discouraged, downhearted 12 disappointed,
disconsolate, disheartened

Crete
ancient city: 7 Cnossus, Knossos
8 Phaistos
ancient name: 6 Candia
capital: 5 Canea
goddess: 8 Dictynna 11 Britomartis
guard: 5 Talos
king: 5 Minos 9 Idomeneus
maze: 9 labyrinth
monster: 8 Minotaur
mountain: 3 Ida
princess: 7 Ariadne

cretin
3 oaf 4 boob, clod, dolt, dope, fool,
lout 5 dumbo, dummy, dunce, idiot,
moron 6 dimwit, nitwit 7 half-wit
8 imbecile, lunkhead, numskull
9 lamebrain, numbskull, simpleton

Creusa
father: 5 Priam
husband: 6 Aeneas
mother: 6 Hecuba
son: 3 Ion 8 Ascanius

crevice
3 gap 4 seam, slit 5 chink, cleft,
crack 6 cranny 7 fissure 8 cleavage
10 interstice

crew
4 band, bevy, gang, team 5 bunch,
covey, group, party 6 rowers, rowing
7 company, sailors

crib
3 bed, bin, box, hut, key 4 pony, trot
5 cheat, crate, hovel, shack, stall,
steal, theft 6 cradle, crèche, manger,
pilfer 7 barrier, brothel 8 bassinet,
bedstead, bordello 9 enclosure
10 plagiarism, plagiarize

Crichton novel
11 Terminal Man (The) 12 Jurassic
Park 15 Andromeda Strain (The)

cricket
period of play: 7 innings
team: 6 eleven
term: 3 leg, off, rot 4 bowl 5 pitch
6 bowler, wicket, yorker 7 batsman,
striker 9 fieldsman
turn at bat: 4 over

crime
3 sin 4 evil, tort, vice 5 caper
6 breach, delict, felony 7 misdeed,
offense 8 atrocity, iniquity 9 diablerie,
violation 10 corruption, illegality,
infraction, wrongdoing 11 misdemeanor 13 transgression
instructor: 5 Fagin

Crimea
city: 5 Kerch, Yalta 10 Sebastopol,
Sevastopol, Simferopol
river: 4 Alma
sea: 4 Azov
strait: 5 Kerch

criminal
4 hood, thug 5 crook, felon, shady
6 outlaw 7 convict, corrupt, crooked,
hoodlum, illegal, illicit, lawless,

criminate

mobster **8** culpable, fugitive, gangster, jailbird, offender, scofflaw, unlawful, wrongful **9** desperado, felonious, miscreant, nefarious, racketeer, wrongdoer **10** delinquent, lawbreaker, malefactor, trespasser **12** illegitimate, transgressor
habitual: 8 repeater **10** recidivist

criminate

see **incriminate**

crimp

4 bend, curb, wave **5** frizz **6** crease, hamper, hold in **7** crinkle, inhibit, wrinkle **8** hold back, obstacle, restrain **9** constrain, restraint **10** impediment **11** obstruction

crimson

3 red **4** rose **5** blush, color, flush **6** redden

cringe

4 duck **5** cower, hunch, quail, wince **6** blench, flinch, recoil, shrink

crinkle

4 ruck **5** crimp, plica, ridge **6** crease, furrow, pucker, ruck up, rumple, rustle **7** crackle, crumple, scrunch, wrinkle **11** corrugation

crinkly

5 crepy **6** crepey, frizzy **7** frizzed **8** wrinkled

cripple

4 lame, maim **6** mangle **7** disable **8** mutilate, paralyze **9** hamstring, undermine **10** debilitate **12** incapacitate

crippled

4 halt, lame **6** maimed **7** gnarled, mangled **8** battered, deformed, disabled, weakened **9** enfeebled, misshapen, mutilated, paralyzed **11** debilitated, handicapped

crisis

4 crux, pass **5** pinch **6** climax, crunch, height, strait **7** impasse, straits **8** disaster, exigency, juncture, zero hour **9** emergency, extremity **10** crossroads **11** catastrophe, contingency **12** turning point

crisp

4 cold, cool, curl, deft, keen, neat, wavy **5** brisk, clean, crimp, curly, fresh, nippy, pithy, sharp, short **6** biting, chilly, lively, ripple, spruce **7** bracing, brittle, crunchy, cutting, wrinkle **8** clean-cut, clear-cut, incisive **9** trenchant **11** stimulating **12** invigorating

crisscross

3 net **4** grid, mesh **5** weave **7** network, overlap **8** reticule **9** confusion, decussate, intersect, reticular **10** reticulate

criterion

4 norm **5** canon, gauge, ideal, model, tenet **7** measure, precept **8** exemplar, paradigm, standard **9** benchmark, yardstick **10** touchstone

critic

5 judge **6** carper, pundit **7** arbiter, caviler **8** caviller, censurer, quibbler, reviewer **9** belittler, nitpicker **10** disparager, mudslinger **11** commentator, connoisseur, faultfinder

critical

4 dire **5** acute, fussy **7** carping, crucial, finicky, pivotal, weighty **8** captious, caviling, decisive **9** desperate, important, momentous **10** belittling, censorious, conclusive, precarious **11** disparaging, significant **12** faultfinding **13** consequential, determinative, hairsplitting
study: 6 examen **8** exegesis

criticism

4 flak, slap **5** blame, cavil, swipe **6** rebuke, review **7** censure, comment, opinion, reproof **8** analysis, judgment, reproach **9** appraisal, objection **10** assessment, commentary, evaluation, nitpicking **11** examination, observation **12** faultfinding

criticize

3 pan, rap **4** bash, carp **5** blame, blast, cavil, chide, fault, judge, knock, roast, scold **6** assess, rebuke, review, scathe **7** censure, condemn, nitpick, reprove **8** appraise, bad-mouth, chastise, denounce, evaluate, lambaste **9** castigate, disparage, dress down, excoriate, find fault, reprehend, reprimand, reprobate

critique
see **criticism**

critter
5 beast **6** animal **7** varmint

Crius
father: **6** Uranus
mother: **4** Gaea
son: **8** Astraeus

croak
3 die **6** cackle, expire, squawk
7 grumble

croaky
5 gruff, husky, raspy **6** hoarse
8 gravelly

Croatia
capital: **6** Zagreb
city: **5** Split **6** Osijek, Rijeka **9** Dubrovnik
monetary unit: **4** kuna
neighbor: **7** Hungary **8** Slovenia
part of: **7** Balkans
region: **8** Dalmatia, Slavonia

crock
3 jar, lie, pot **4** tale **6** tureen **7** cripple, disable, fiction **9** break down
11 fabrication

crocked
3 lit **4** high **5** drunk, lit up, oiled,
tipsy **6** bashed, blotto, bombed,
juiced, potted, soaked, soused,
stewed, stoned, tanked, wasted,
zonked **7** drunken, pickled, pie-
eyed, sloshed, smashed **9** plastered
10 inebriated, liquored up **11** intoxicated

crocodile
7 reptile
bird: **6** plover
Indian: **6** gavial **7** gharial
relative: **9** alligator
South American: **6** caiman, cayman
Southeast Asian: **6** mugger

Croesus' kingdom
5 Lydia

croft
4 farm **5** field

crofter
4 hind **6** farmer

Cromwell, Oliver
13 lord protector
battle: **6** Naseby **11** Marston Moor
regiment: **9** Ironsides
son: **7** Richard

crone
3 hag **4** trot **5** biddy, witch **6** beldam
7 beldame

Cronus
5 Titan **6** Saturn
daughter: **4** Hera **6** Hestia
7 Demeter
father: **6** Uranus
mother: **4** Gaea
sister: **4** Rhea **6** Cybele, Tethys
son: **4** Zeus **5** Hades **7** Jupiter,
Neptune **8** Poseidon
wife: **4** Rhea **6** Cybele

crony
3 pal **4** chum **5** buddy **6** cohort
7 comrade **8** sidekick **9** associate,
companion **10** accomplice **11** confederate

crook
3 bow **4** bend, flex, hook, wind
5 angle, curve, staff, thief **6** bandit,
robber **7** burglar, crosier, hoodlum,
pothook **8** criminal

crooked
4 awry **5** askew, lying, shady, venal
6 curved, errant, jagged, shifty,
skewed, zigzag **7** bending, corrupt,
devious, illegal, illicit, slanted **8** cockeyed, criminal, ruthless, tortuous,
twisting **9** deceitful, dishonest,
nefarious, underhand, unethical
10 fraudulent, mendacious, untruthful
11 duplicitous, underhanded **12** unscrupulous **13** double-dealing

croon
4 sing **6** murmur, warble

crooner
4 Cole (Nat "King"), Como (Perry)
5 Laine (Frankie), Tormé (Mel)
6 Crosby (Bing), Martin (Dean),
singer, Vallee (Rudy) 7 Astaire
(Fred), Bennett (Tony), Sinatra
(Frank) 8 Eckstine (Billy), vocalist,
Williams (Andy)

crop
3 bob, cut, hew, lop, mow 4 chop,
clip, pare, snip, trim 5 prune, shave,
shear, stock, yield 6 gullet, handle,
output 7 harvest, produce 8 fruit-
age, truncate 10 collection

croquet
5 roque

crosier
5 crook, staff

cross
3 mad 4 mule, rood, span 5 angry,
surly, testy, trial 6 betray, bridge,
crabby, cranky, grumpy, hybrid,
negate, oppose, ordeal, tetchy, touchy
7 athwart, calvary, carping, gainsay,
grouchy, mongrel, peevish 8 captious, choleric, confront, traverse
9 decussate, half blood, half-breed,
hybridize, intersect, irascible, irritable, querulous, splenetic 10 affliction,
contradict, contravene, interbreed,
transverse 11 tribulation 12 cantankerous 13 quick-tempered
a river: 4 ford
bearer: 8 crucifer
decoration: 4 iron 8 Victoria
Egyptian: 4 ankh
kind: 3 tau 5 Greek, Latin, papal
6 Celtic, fleury, formée, moline,
pommée, potent 7 avellan, botonée,
Calvary, Maltese 8 crucifix, fourchée,
Lorraine, quadrate 11 patriarchal
12 Saint Andrew's 13 Saint Anthony's
section: 5 slice
stroke of a letter: 5 serif

crossbow
8 arbalest, arbalist

crossbreed
4 mule 6 hybrid 7 bastard, mongrel
9 half blood, half-breed, hybridize
10 interbreed

cross-eye
6 squint 10 strabismus

crossing
8 junction, overpass, traverse 9 traversal, underpass 10 transverse
11 decussation, interchange, trans-
versal 12 intersection

cross out
5 erase 6 cancel, delete, efface,
excise 7 expunge

crosspatch
4 crab 5 crank, grump 6 griper,
grouch 7 grouser 8 grumbler,
sorehead, sourpuss 10 complainer,
curmudgeon

crossroads
4 crux, pass 5 pinch 6 crisis, strait
8 exigency, juncture, zero hour
9 carrefour, emergency 11 contingency 12 intersection, turning
point
goddess: 6 Hecate, Hekate, Trivia

cross-shaped
8 cruciate 9 cruciform

crossways
6 aslant 7 athwart, oblique 8 diagonal
9 obliquely 10 diagonally, transverse
11 kitty-corner 12 transversely

crotchet
3 bee 4 whim 5 fancy, freak, quirk,
trick 6 foible, megrim, notion, vagary
7 caprice, conceit 11 quarter note
12 eccentricity

crotchety
5 testy 6 crabby, cranky, crusty,
ornery, tetchy, touchy 7 bearish,
peevish, prickly 8 contrary, snappish, vinegary 9 difficult, eccentric,
irascible 10 vinegarish 11 ill-
tempered 12 cantankerous, cross-
grained

crouch
4 bend, duck 5 cower, hunch, squat,
stoop 6 cringe, huddle, shrink
10 hunker down

croup
3 bum 4 butt, hack, rear, rump, seat,
tail 5 cough, edema, whoop 6 be-

hind **7** keister, rear end, tail end
8 backside, buttocks, derriere,
haunches **9** posterior

crow
4 blow, brag, puff **5** boast, exult, gloat,
prate, vaunt **6** cackle **7** bluster
9 gasconade, humble pie
colony: **7** rookery
cry: **3** caw
family: **6** corvid **8** Corvidae
genus: **6** Corvus
relating to: **7** corvine
relative: **3** daw, jay **4** rook **5** raven
6 chough, magpie **7** jackdaw

crowbar
3 pry **5** jimmy, lever

crowd
3 jam, mob **4** army, bear, cram, fill,
herd, host, mass, pack, pile, push,
rout, ruck **5** bunch, crush, drove,
flock, flood, group, horde, hurry,
press, serry, shove, surge, swarm,
troop **6** circle, clique, gaggle, huddle, jostle, legion, rabble, squash,
squish, stream, throng **7** cluster,
collect, company, coterie, squeeze
8 assembly **9** gathering, multitude
10 assemblage, collection **11** aggregation **12** congregation

crowded
4 full **5** awash, close, dense, thick,
tight **6** loaded **7** brimful, compact,
teeming **8** brimming, populous,
swarming **9** chock-full, congested,
jam-packed

crow-like
7 corvoid

crown
3 cap, top **4** acme, apex, peak, roof
5 cover, crest, tiara **6** climax, diadem, laurel, summit, top off, vertex,
wreath, zenith **7** chaplet, coronal,
coronet, garland, overlay, perfect
8 pinnacle, round off, surmount
9 culminate, finish off **10** consummate **11** culmination

crucial
4 dire **5** acute, vital **6** urgent **7** central, pivotal **8** critical, deciding,
decisive **9** desperate, essential,

important, momentous, necessary
10 imperative **11** climacteric, significant

crucible
4 test **5** trial **6** ordeal **8** acid test
10 melting pot

crucifix
4 rood **5** cross

crucifixion site
7 Calvary **8** Golgotha

crucify
4 rack **6** impale, martyr **7** mortify,
pillory, torment, torture **10** excruciate

crud
3 goo **4** glop, gook, gunk, junk, muck
5 dreck, filth, slime, trash **6** debris,
sludge **7** deposit, garbage, rubbish
12 incrustation

crude
3 raw **4** poor **5** crass, dirty, gross,
rough **6** coarse, earthy, gauche,
impure, ribald, risqué, vulgar **7** boorish, ill-bred, loutish, lowbred, obscene, obvious, raunchy, uncivil,
uncouth **8** backward, cloddish,
homespun, ignorant, indecent,
inferior **9** elemental, graceless,
inelegant, makeshift, primitive, roughhewn, unrefined **10** amateurish,
unfinished, unpolished

cruel
4 fell, grim, mean **5** harsh **6** brutal,
fierce, savage **7** bestial, brutish,
callous, heinous, vicious **8** inhumane, ruthless, sadistic **9** atrocious,
barbarous, ferocious, heartless,
merciless, monstrous, truculent
12 bloodthirsty

cruise
4 roam, rove, sail, surf, tour **5** drift,
jaunt **6** junket, voyage **9** excursion

cruiser
4 boat **5** yacht **7** warship **8** squad
car **9** patrol car, powerboat

crumb
3 bit **4** iota **5** ounce, scrap, shred
6 morsel, sliver **7** smidgen **8** fragment, particle

crumble

5 decay 8 collapse 9 break down, decompose 11 deteriorate 12 disintegrate

crumbly

7 friable

crummy

4 poor 5 dingy, lousy, seedy, tacky 6 cruddy, flimsy, shoddy, sleazy 8 inferior

crumple

3 wad 4 cave 5 crimp 6 buckle, cave in, ruck up 7 crinkle, scrunch, wrinkle 8 collapse

crunch

4 chew 5 champ, chomp, grind, munch, sit-up 6 crisis 7 compute, process, squeeze 8 shortage, showdown

crusade

5 cause, drive 6 appeal 7 holy war 8 campaign, movement 9 offensive 10 expedition 11 undertaking

Crusader

English: 7 Richard (Lionheart)
French: 5 Louis (IX) 6 Philip, Robert 7 Baldwin, Charles, Godfrey, Raymond, Raymund 8 Boniface, Montfort, Philippe, Theobald
German: 6 Conrad 9 Frederick, Friedrich 10 Barbarossa
Norman: 7 Tancred 8 Bohemund
Preacher: 5 Peter (the Hermit), Urban (II) 7 Adhémar, Bernard 8 Innocent (III), Pelagius

crusading

11 evangelical 12 evangelistic

crush

3 jam, mob 4 cram, mash, pulp, push, ruin 5 crowd, drove, grind, horde, pound, press, quash, quell, smash, wreck 6 bruise, burden, defeat, reduce, squash, squish, subdue, throng 7 conquer, destroy, mortify, oppress, passion, put down, repress, scrunch, squeeze, squelch, trample 8 bear down, beat down, demolish, overcome, suppress,

vanquish 9 humiliate, multitude, overpower, overwhelm, pulverize, puppy love, subjugate 10 annihilate, extinguish, obliterate 11 infatuation

crust

4 cake, coat, rime, scab 7 coating, deposit 8 covering

crustacean

4 crab, flea 5 louse, prawn 6 isopod, shrimp, slater, sow bug 7 copepod, daphnia, decapod, lobster, pill bug 8 amphipod, barnacle, crawfish, crayfish, ostracod, sand flea 9 arthropod, beach flea, shellfish, water flea, wood louse 10 stomatopod, whale louse 11 branchiopod
aggregate of: 5 krill
appendage: 7 pleopod
body segment: 6 somite, telson 8 metamere
claw: 5 chela 6 pincer
covering substance: 6 chitin
larva: 8 nauplius

crusty

4 curt 5 bluff, blunt, gross, gruff, short, surly 6 cranky 7 brusque, crabbed, prickly 8 choleric 9 irascible, irritable, saturnine, splenetic

crux

3 nub 4 core, gist, meat, pith 5 focus, heart 6 kernel, thrust 7 essence, purport 9 substance

cry

(see also **exclamation**)
3 sob 4 bawl, blub, call, howl, keen, mewl, moan, pule, wail, weep, yawp, yell, yowl 5 bleat, motto, mourn, shout, whine, whoop 6 boohoo, furore, holler, lament, scream, snivel, squall, squawk, squeak, squeal 7 blubber, screech, ululate, whimper 10 vociferate
bacchanals': 4 evoe
calf: 5 bleat
cat: 3 mew 4 meow 5 miaow
cattle: 3 low, moo
chick: 4 peep 5 cheep
court: 4 oyez
crane: 5 clang

crow: 3 caw
dog: 3 arf 4 bark, woof
donkey: 4 bray 6 hee-haw
duck: 5 quack
frog: 5 croak
goat: 5 bleat
goose: 4 honk 5 clang
hen: 6 cackle
horse: 5 neigh 6 nicker, whinny
7 whicker
lion: 4 roar
owl: 4 hoot
pig: 4 oink 5 grunt
raven: 5 croak
sheep: 5 bleat
songbird: 5 chirp, tweet
turkey: 6 gobble

cry down
5 decry 6 defame, deride, malign,
revile, vilify 7 condemn 8 belittle,
denounce, derogate, diminish
9 denigrate, deprecate, discredit,
disparage 10 calumniate, depreciate
11 detract from, opprobriate

crying
4 dire 5 acute, vital 6 urgent 7 blatant, burning, clamant, exigent,
heinous 8 flagrant, pressing, shocking 9 atrocious, clamorous, desperate, monstrous, notorious 10 compelling, imperative, outrageous,
scandalous 11 importunate

crypt
5 vault 7 chamber 8 catacomb
9 mausoleum 10 undercroft

cryptic
5 vague 6 arcane, occult, opaque,
secret 7 Delphic, obscure, unclear
8 abstruse, Delphian, esoteric,
puzzling 9 ambiguous, enigmatic,
recondite, tenebrous 10 mysterious,
mystifying 12 unfathomable

crystal
4 lens 5 clear, lucid 6 limpid, lucent,
quartz 8 clear-cut, luminous, pellucid
9 glassware, unblurred 11 translucent, transparent 12 transpicuous
gazer: 4 seer 7 psychic 11 clairvoyant

Cry, the Beloved Country author
5 Paton (Alan)

cry up
4 laud, puff 5 boost, extol 6 praise
7 acclaim

cub
3 pup 4 baby, tyro 6 novice, rookie
8 neophyte 9 offspring, youngster
10 apprentice

Cuba
capital: 6 Havana
city: 7 Holguín 8 Camagüey,
Santiago 10 Guantánamo, Santa
Clara
discoverer: 8 Columbus (Christopher)
language: 7 Spanish
leader: 6 Castro (Fidel) 7 Batista
(Fulgencio)
monetary unit: 4 peso 6 dollar
sea: 9 Caribbean

cubbyhole
5 niche 6 alcove, recess 7 cubicle

cube
4 dice 5 mince

Cub Scout
rank: 4 Bear, Lion, Wolf 6 Bobcat
7 Webelos
unit: 3 den 4 pack

Cuchulain
father: 3 Lug 4 Lugh 5 Lugus
foe: 4 Medb 5 Maeve
kingdom: 6 Ulster
lord: 9 Conchobar
mother: 8 Dechtire
son: 8 Conlaoch
victim: 8 Conlaoch
wife: 4 Emer

cuckoo
3 mad, nut 4 daft, kook, nuts 5 batty,
crank, crazy, daffy, loony, loopy, nutty,
potty, silly, wacko, wacky 6 crazed,
fruity, insane, screwy, whacky
7 bonkers, cracked, idiotic, lunatic,
nutcase 8 crackpot, demented
9 ding-a-ling, harebrain, screwball
12 crackbrained
bird: 3 ani

cucumber
4 pepo 7 gherkin

cuddle
3 hug, pet 4 neck, snug 5 spoon
6 burrow, caress, clinch, cosset,
dandle, fondle, nestle, nuzzle 7 embrace, snuggle, squeeze 8 canoodle

cuddlesome
7 lovable, snuggly 8 huggable
11 embraceable

cudgel
3 bat, sap 4 club, cosh, mace
5 baton, billy 7 war club 8 bludgeon
9 bastinado, billy club, blackjack,
truncheon 10 knobkerrie, nightstick,
shillelagh

cue
3 key, nod, rod, tip 4 clue, hint, lead,
prod, sign 6 insert, notion, prompt,
signal, tip-off 7 inkling, warning
8 high sign, reminder, telltale 10 indication, intimation, suggestion

cuff
3 box, hit 4 belt, blip, clip, poke,
slap, sock 5 clout, fight, punch,
smack, whack 6 bangle, buffet,
wallop 7 clobber, scuffle 8 bracelet,
wristlet

cul-de-sac
5 pouch 6 pocket 7 dead end, impasse 10 blind alley 12 diverticulum

cull
4 pick, sift, thin 5 elect, glean
6 choose, garner, gather, select,
winnow 7 extract, thin out

culminate
4 peak 5 crest 6 climax

culmination
3 top 4 acme, apex, peak 6 apogee,
capper, climax, height, payoff, summit, zenith 8 capstone, pinnacle
11 ne plus ultra 12 consummation

culpability
4 onus 5 blame, fault, guilt

culpable
6 guilty, liable, sinful 7 at fault
8 blamable, blameful 10 censurable,

delinquent 11 blameworthy, impeachable, responsible 13 reprehensible

cult
3 fad 4 sect 5 creed, faith 6 church
8 religion 10 persuasion 12 denomination

cultivable
6 arable 8 tillable

cultivate
4 farm, grow, tend, till 5 breed,
nurse, raise 6 enrich, foster, refine
7 cherish, develop, further, improve,
nourish, nurture, produce, promote
9 encourage, propagate

cultivated
6 urbane 7 genteel, refined 8 cultured, polished, well-bred

cultivation
6 polish 7 culture 8 breeding
10 refinement 11 development

culture
4 grow 5 taste 6 foster 7 nurture
9 cultivate, erudition, gentility 10 refinement 11 cultivation 12 civilization
13 enlightenment

cultured
6 urbane 7 erudite, genteel, learned,
refined 8 educated, highbrow,
literate, polished, well-bred 9 civilized
10 cultivated 11 enlightened

culture medium
4 agar

cum ____ salis
5 grano

cumber
4 clog, lade, load 6 burden, hinder,
hobble, impede, saddle 7 clutter
8 handicap 9 hindrance

cumbersome
5 bulky, heavy, hefty 6 clumsy
7 awkward 8 unwieldy 9 lumbering,
ponderous 10 slow-moving

cumbrous
see **cumbersome**

cumshaw
3 fee, tip 5 bribe 6 payoff 7 present
8 gratuity, largesse 9 lagniappe,
pourboire 10 perquisite

cumulate
4 heap 5 amass, hoard, lay up, store
6 garner, gather, pile up 7 collect,
combine, store up 9 stockpile

cumulation
4 heap, mass, pile 5 cache, hoard,
trove 9 stockpile 10 collection
11 aggregation 13 agglomeration

cumulative
8 additive, compound 9 summative
10 compounded, increasing

cunning
3 sly 4 cute, foxy, keen, wary, wily
5 acute, cagey, canny, craft, guile,
savvy, sharp, skill, slick, smart
6 adroit, artful, astute, clever, crafty,
deceit, shifty, tricky 7 finesse, know-
how, slyness 8 artifice, deftness,
facility, foxiness, guileful, slippery,
subtlety, wiliness 9 adeptness,
cageyness, canniness, dexterity,
dexterous, duplicity, ingenious, ingenuity, insidious, sharpness, slickness
10 adroitness, artfulness, cleverness,
craftiness, shiftiness, shrewdness,
trickiness

cup
3 mug 4 toby 5 grail, jorum, stein
6 beaker, goblet, seidel 7 chalice,
tankard 8 schooner
handle: 3 ear, lug
liturgical: 5 calix 7 chalice
small: 6 noggin 8 cannikin, pan-
nikin 9 demitasse
sports: 5 Davis, Ryder, World
6 Curtis, Nextel 7 Stanley 8 America's, Wightman

cupbearer of the gods
4 Hebe 8 Ganymede

cupboard
5 ambry, cuddy 6 buffet, closet,
larder, pantry 7 armoire, cabinet
8 credence, credenza 9 sideboard

Cupid
4 Amor, Eros 5 putto 6 cherub
8 amoretto

beloved: 6 Psyche
brother: 7 Anteros
father: 6 Hermes 7 Mercury
mother: 5 Venus 9 Aphrodite
title: 3 Dan

cupidity
4 lust 5 greed 6 desire 7 avarice,
avidity, craving, lechery, passion
8 rapacity, voracity 9 eagerness,
esurience 10 greediness 11 infatuation 12 covetousness 13 rapacious-
ness

cupola
4 dome 5 vault 6 turret 7 furnace,
lookout

cur
3 dog 4 mutt 7 mongrel

curate
6 cleric, priest 9 churchman, clergyman

curative
4 pill 5 tonic 6 elixir, relief, remedy
7 healing, nostrum, panacea, therapy
8 antidote, remedial, salutary, sanative, solution 9 healthful, medicinal,
remedying, treatment, wholesome
10 beneficial, corrective 11 restorative, therapeutic 12 health-
giving

curator
6 keeper, warden 9 caretaker,
custodian 11 conservator

curb
3 bit 4 deny 5 check, frame, leash,
tie up 6 border, bridle, edging, fetter,
hamper, hobble, hold in, subdue
7 abstain, contain, control, inhibit,
refrain, repress 8 hold back, hold
down, restrain, suppress, withhold
9 constrain, entrammel, restraint
British: 4 kerb

curdle
4 clot, sour, turn 5 spoil 7 clabber,
congeal, thicken 9 coagulate

cure
3 age, spa 4 heal, mend 5 treat
6 elixir, kipper, physic, pickle, relief,
remedy 7 rectify, relieve, restore,

therapy **8** antidote, medicant, medicine, preserve, recovery, solution **10** ameliorate, corrective **12** counteragent **13** counteractive

cure-all

6 elixir **7** nostrum, panacea **10** catholicon

curio

6 oddity, whimsy **7** novelty

curiosity

5 freak **6** marvel, oddity, rarity, whimsy, wonder **7** anomaly, concern, novelty **8** interest, nonesuch

curious

3 odd **4** nosy **5** nosey, novel, queer, weird **6** exotic, prying, quaint, snoopy **7** bizarre, oddball, strange, unusual **8** meddling, peculiar, puzzling, singular **9** inquiring, intrusive **11** inquisitive, questioning

curl

4 coil, kink, wind **5** frizz, twine, twist **6** spiral **7** contort, crinkle, entwine, frizzle, ringlet, wreathe **9** corkscrew

curling

match: 8 bonspiel
period of play: 3 end
team: 4 four
term: 3 tee **4** hack, rink **5** house, stone

curly

4 wavy **5** kinky **6** frizzy

currency

4 cash, coin **5** dough, lucre, money, scrip **7** coinage **8** banknote **10** acceptance, prevalence **11** legal tender
unit:
(see **individual country**)

current

4 eddy, flow, flux, rush, tide **5** drift, flood, spate, tenor, trend **6** extant, modern, strain, stream **7** instant, ongoing, popular, present, regnant, topical **8** accepted, existent, existing, tendency, up-to-date **9** prevalent **10** present-day, prevailing, widespread **11** fashionable **12** contemporary

air: 4 gale, gust, wind **5** blast, draft **6** breeze, squall, zephyr **7** cyclone, indraft, updraft **9** downdraft **10** slipstream
ocean: 7 riptide **8** undertow **9** maelstrom, whirlpool
unit: 3 amp **6** ampere

Currier's partner

4 Ives (James)

curry

4 beat, comb, seek, whip **5** groom **6** thrash

curse

4 bane, cuss, damn, evil, jinx, oath **5** swear **6** blight, plague, whammy **7** afflict, damning, malison, scourge, torment **8** anathema, cussword, execrate **9** bête noire, blaspheme, blasphemy, expletive, imprecate, profanity, swearword **10** affliction, execration, misfortune, pestilence **11** commination, imprecation, malediction, profanation **12** anathematize, denunciation

cursed

6 damned **7** blasted, dratted **8** damnable, infernal **9** execrable **10** confounded **13** blankety-blank

cursive

6 fluent, smooth **7** flowing, running

cursory

5 hasty, quick, rapid **6** casual **7** hurried, shallow, sketchy **8** careless **10** uncritical **11** perfunctory, superficial

curt

4 rude **5** bluff, blunt, brief, gruff, short, terse **6** abrupt, crusty **7** brusque, concise **8** succinct **10** peremptory

curtail

3 cut **4** clip, dock, trim **5** prune, slash **6** lessen, reduce **7** abridge, cut back, shorten **8** diminish, pare down, retrench, truncate **10** abbreviate

curtain

4 drop, veil **5** drape **6** screen **7** barrier
doorway: 8 portiere

holder: 3 rod
Indian: 6 purdah
rod concealer: 7 valance
sash: 7 tieback
stage: 4 drop 5 scrim 8 backdrop

curtains
  3 end 4 ruin 5 death 6 demise,
finish 7 decease 8 disaster

curtilage
  4 quad, yard 5 court 8 cloister
9 courtyard, enclosure 10 quadrangle

curvaceous
  5 buxom 7 rounded, shapely 9 Junoesque 10 statuesque, voluptuous
13 well-developed

curvature
of the spine: 8 kyphosis, lordosis
9 scoliosis

curve
  3 arc, bow 4 arch, bend, turn, veer,
wind 5 crook, round, twist 6 convex,
spiral, swerve 7 concave, flexure,
rondure
of an arch: 8 extrados, intrados
pitcher's: 4 hook
plane: 7 cycloid, limaçon
8 parabola, sinusoid, trochoid 9 hyperbola
S-shaped: 3 ess 4 ogee 7 sigmoid

curved
  4 bent 5 arced, bowed, round
6 arched 7 arcuate, bending, embowed, falcate, rounded, sigmoid,
sinuous, twisted
implement: 6 sickle
molding: 4 ogee
sword: 5 kukri, saber, sabre 7 cutlass 8 scimitar

curvilinear
  see **curved**

curvy
  see **curvaceous; curved**

Cush
father: 3 Ham
son: 6 Nimrod

cushion
  3 mat, pad 5 squab 6 absorb,

buffer, pillow, soften 7 bolster,
hassock, pillion 8 palliate, woolsack

cushy
  4 cozy, easy, soft 11 comfortable,
undemanding

cusp
  3 tip 4 apex, edge, peak 5 point,
verge 12 turning point

cuspid
  6 canine 8 eyetooth

cuspidate
  5 sharp 6 peaked, pointy 7 pointed

cuss
  3 guy, man 4 chap, damn, dude,
oath 5 curse, swear 6 fellow
9 expletive

cussed
  4 dour 5 crude, gruff 6 crusty,
cursed, grumpy, ornery 7 boorish,
brusque, grouchy 8 churlish 9 obstinate 10 unyielding 11 contentious
12 antagonistic, cantankerous

cussword
  4 oath 5 curse 9 expletive, swearword

custard
  4 flan 7 pudding

custodian
  5 super 6 keeper, porter, warden
7 curator, steward 8 guardian,
overseer, watchdog, watchman
9 caretaker, concierge, protector
10 supervisor 11 conservator

custody
  4 care, ward 5 guard, trust 6 charge
7 keeping 9 captivity, detention
10 caretaking, management, protection 11 confinement, safekeeping,
supervision 12 guardianship

custom
  3 use 4 norm 5 habit, mores
(plural), trade, usage 6 groove,
manner, praxis, ritual 7 folkway,
precept, routine, traffic 8 business,
habitude, practice 9 patronage
10 consuetude, convention

customary

5 usual 6 common, normal, wonted
7 general, regular, routine 8 accepted, everyday, familiar, frequent, habitual, ordinary, orthodox, standard
10 accustomed 11 established, traditional 12 conventional

custom-built

7 bespoke 10 tailor-made 11 made-to-order

customer

5 buyer 6 client, patron 7 shopper
8 consumer 9 purchaser
frequent: 7 habitué

customized

see **custom-built**

custom-made

see **custom-built**

cut

3 bob, hew, lop, mow, saw 4 bite, chop, clip, crop, dice, dock, fell, gash, hack, nick, pare, reap, sawn, slit, snip, snub, trim 5 carve, filet, lathe, lower, mince, notch, piece, prune, quota, sawed, sever, share, shave, shear, slash, slice, split, wound 6 cleave, delete, dilute, divide, excise, fillet, incise, reduce, scythe, sickle, sunder 7 abridge, curtail, dissect, operate, portion, scissor, section, segment, shorten
8 amputate, decrease, dissever, division, mark down, separate, truncate 9 allotment, allowance, reduction 10 abbreviate 12 cold-shoulder
of beef: 3 rib 4 loin, rump 5 chine, chuck, flank, roast, shank, steak, T-bone 6 saddle 7 brisket, sirloin
9 aitchbone 11 porterhouse

cut across

6 bisect 8 transect 9 transcend

cut-and-dried

5 stock 7 routine 9 formulaic
10 unoriginal 11 predictable 13 unimaginative

cutaneous

6 dermal

cutaway

4 coat, dive 5 tails

cut back

3 zag 4 clip, curb, dock, pare, trim 5 lower, prune, shave, slash
6 lessen, reduce 7 abridge, curtail, shorten 8 decrease, retrench, truncate 10 abbreviate

cut down

3 axe 4 chop, clip, fell, pare 5 lower, shave, slash 6 digest, reduce
7 abridge, shorten 10 abbreviate

cute

6 dainty, pretty 7 cunning 8 affected
10 attractive 11 impertinent, smart-alecky

cut in

7 include, intrude, obtrude 9 introduce

cutlass

5 saber, sabre, sword 7 machete
8 scimitar

cut off

3 axe, bar, end, lop 4 halt, kill, stop
5 abort, block, sever 6 disown
7 curtail, destroy, isolate, suspend
8 amputate, obstruct, renounce, separate, truncate 9 intercept, interrupt, terminate 10 disinherit
11 discontinue

cut out

3 end 4 halt 5 leave, scram, usurp
6 beat it, delete, depart, escape, excise, remove, resect 7 defraud, deprive, take off 8 displace, supplant
9 eliminate, extirpate 10 disconnect

cutpurse

5 thief 10 pickpocket

cut short

3 bob 4 clip, crop, dock, halt, poll 5 abort, check, scrub, shear
7 abridge, curtail 8 break off 9 interrupt, terminate 10 abbreviate

cuttable

7 sectile 8 scissile

cutthroat

5 bravo 6 gunman, hit man, killer

7 torpedo 8 assassin, murderer
10 hatchet man, triggerman

cutting
8 incisive, piercing 9 sarcastic,
trenchant 11 penetrating
edge: **5** blade
remark: **3** dig **4** barb **5** taunt
tool: **3** axe, hob, saw **4** adze
5 knife, lathe, mower, plane, razor
6 reaper, scythe, shears, sickle
7 hatchet 8 scissors, tomahawk

cuttlefish
7 mollusc, mollusk 10 cephalopod
ink: **5** sepia
relative: **5** squid **7** octopus

cut up
4 dice, hash, romp 5 caper, clown,
mince, slash 6 cavort 7 carry on,
show off 9 misbehave 10 roughhouse

cutup
3 wag 4 zany 5 clown, joker 6 madcap 7 buffoon, farceur 8 jokester

cyan
4 blue

Cybele
4 Rhea
beloved: **5** Attis
brother: **6** Cronus
father: **6** Uranus
husband: **6** Cronus
mother: **4** Gaea
son: **4** Zeus **7** Jupiter, Neptune
8 Poseidon

cyber
5 wired 10 electronic

cybernetics founder
6 Wiener (Norbert)

cycle
3 age, lap, set 4 bike, loop, ring
5 chain, orbit, recur, round, wheel
6 circle, course, period, series 7 circuit 8 rotation, sequence 9 vibration
10 revolution, succession, two-
wheeler, velocipede 11 oscillation

cyclic
7 regular 8 periodic, repeated, rhyth-

mic 9 iterative, recurring, repeating
10 isochronal 12 intermittent

cyclone
7 tornado, twister

cyclopean
4 huge 7 immense, mammoth,
massive, titanic 8 colossal, enormous, gigantic 9 monstrous 10 gargantuan, tremendous 11 elephantine

Cyclops
5 Arges 7 Brontes 8 Steropes
10 Polyphemus

Cycnus
father: **4** Ares, Mars
slayer: **8** Heracles, Hercules

cygnet
4 swan
dam (mother): **3** pen
sire (father): **3** cob

Cygnus
form: **4** swan
friend: **7** Phaeton
star: **5** Deneb

cylinder
4 drum, pipe, tube 5 spool 6 barrel,
bobbin, platen, roller

cylindrical
6 terete 7 tubular 8 tubelike

Cymbeline
daughter: **6** Imogen
son: **9** Arviragus, Guiderius
son-in-law: **9** Posthumus

Cymric
5 Welsh 6 Celtic 9 Brythonic
bard: **8** Taliesin
Elysium: **6** Annwfn
god: **5** Lludd
  of Elysium: **5** Arawn
  of the dead: **5** Pwyll
  of the seas: **3** Ler **4** Llyr **5** Dylan
  of the sky: **7** Gwydion
  of the sun: **4** Lleu, Llew
  of the underworld: **4** Gwyn
goddess: **3** Don **9** Arianrhod
magician: **6** Merlin

Cymru
5 Wales

cynical
8 derisive, sardonic, scornful 12 misanthropic

Cynthia
4 Luna, moon 5 Diana 7 Artemis

cyprian
4 bawd, jade, slut, tart 5 hussy, tramp 6 floozy, harlot, hooker, wanton 7 jezebel, trollop 8 slattern, strumpet 10 prostitute

Cyprus
capital: 7 Nicosia 8 Lefkosia
city: 7 Larnaca 8 Limassol
language: 5 Greek 7 Turkish
monetary unit: 4 lira 5 pound
mountain: 7 Olympus
port: 9 Famagusta
sea: 13 Mediterranean

Cyrano de Bergerac
4 poet 7 duelist 8 duellist
author: 7 Rostand (Edmond)
beloved: 6 Roxane
feature: 4 nose
rival: 9 Christian

Cyrus
conquest: 5 Lydia, Media 7 Babylon
daughter: 6 Atossa
empire: 7 Persian
father: 8 Cambyses
son: 8 Cambyses

cyst
3 sac, wen 4 sore 5 pouch, spore 6 growth 7 abscess, blister, capsule, vesicle 8 swelling

Cytherea
4 isle 5 Venus 6 island 9 Aphrodite

czar
5 chief, mogul 6 despot, honcho, tycoon, tyrant 7 emperor, kingpin, magnate 8 autocrat
Russian: 4 Ivan 5 Basil, Boris, Peter 6 Alexis, Dmitry, Feodor, Fyodor, Vasily 7 Dimitri, Michael, Romanov 8 Nicholas, Romanoff, Theodore 9 Alexander 12 Boris Godunov

czar's wife
7 czarina

Czech Republic
capital: 6 Prague
city: 4 Brno 7 Ostrava
monetary unit: 6 koruna
neighbor: 6 Poland 7 Austria, Germany 8 Slovakia
region: 7 Bohemia, Moravia
river: 4 Labe, Oder 5 March 6 Morava

D

dab
3 bit, pat 4 blob, blow, daub, peck, poke, spot 5 smear, touch 6 bedaub 7 besmear, plaster, splotch 8 flatfish

dabble
3 dip, dot, toy 4 fool, stud 5 fleck 6 dampen, fiddle, monkey, pepper, putter, splash, tinker 7 freckle, spatter, stipple 8 sprinkle 9 bespeckle, muck about 10 muck around

dabbler
4 duck, tyro 7 amateur 8 putterer, tinkerer 9 smatterer 10 dilettante

dabchick
5 grebe

dacha
5 villa 7 cottage 12 country house

dad
3 pop 4 papa 5 padre, pater 6 father, old man, parent

Dadaist
3 Arp (Jean), Ray (Man) 4 Ball (Hugo) 5 Ernst (Max), Grosz (George), Tzara (Tristan) 7 Duchamp (Marcel), Picabia (Francis) 10 Schwitters (Kurt)

daedal
6 knotty 7 complex 8 artistic, involved, skillful 9 elaborate, intricate 11 complicated 12 labyrinthine 13 sophisticated

Daedalus
7 builder 9 architect, artificer
construction: 9 Labyrinth
father: 6 Metion
son: 6 Icarus
victim: 5 Talos 6 Perdix

daffy
see **daft**

daft
3 mad 4 loco, nuts 5 balmy, crazy, dopey, flaky, loony, nutty, potty, silly, wacko, wacky 6 absurd, crazed, cuckoo, insane, screwy 7 cracked, foolish, idiotic, lunatic, witless 8 demented 10 unbalanced 11 harebrained

Dag
father: 7 Delling
horse: 9 Skinfaksi
mother: 4 Nott

Dagda
chief god of the: 5 Gaels, Irish
daughter: 6 Brigit
instrument: 4 harp
son: 6 Aengus
wife: 5 Boann

dagger
4 dirk 5 skean, skene 6 bodkin, stylet 7 dudgeon, poniard 8 stiletto
handle: 4 hilt
Malay: 4 kris

_____ Dahl
5 Roald 6 Arlene

daikon
6 radish

daily
7 diurnal 8 everyday 9 circadian, quotidian

dainty
5 goody, tasty, treat 6 choice, morsel, select, tidbit 7 elegant, fragile 8 delicacy, delicate, ethereal, graceful, kickshaw 9 exquisite, recherché 10 delightful

dairy
8 creamery

dais
5 stage 6 podium 7 rostrum 8 platform

daisy
5 oxeye 6 Shasta
British: 10 moonflower
Scottish: 5 gowan

Daisy Miller author
5 James (Henry)

Dakota dialect
5 Teton

Daksha's father
6 Brahma

dale
4 dell, glen, vale 6 dingle, valley

dally
3 lag, pet, toy 4 drag, idle, play
5 delay, flirt, tarry 6 coquet, dawdle, diddle, linger, loiter, trifle 8 lollygag
9 hang about, waste time 10 fool around

dam
4 weir 5 block, check 7 barrier
8 hold back, restrain
major: 4 Oahe 6 Hoover 7 San Luis 8 Fort Peck, Garrison, Oroville 10 Bonneville, Glen Canyon
11 Grand Coulee

damage
3 mar 4 blot, harm, hurt, loss, maim, ruin 5 abuse, burst, cloud, spoil, stain, wound 6 blight, deface, impair, injure, injury, mangle, ravage, scathe 7 blemish, destroy, marring, tarnish, vitiate 8 maltreat, mischief, mistreat, mutilate, sabotage 9 devastate, vandalism 10 impairment 11 devastation

damaged
4 hurt, rent 6 broken, busted, dinged, flawed, marred 7 injured, spoiled, totaled 8 battered, impaired, ruptured 9 blemished, fractured, imperfect, shattered 10 fragmented

damaging
6 nocent 7 harmful, hurtful, nocuous 9 injurious 11 deleterious, detrimental, prejudicial

dame
4 lady 5 woman 6 gammer, matron 7 dowager 9 matriarch

Damien's island
7 Molokai

Damkina's son
6 Marduk

damn
4 cuss, darn, doom, drat 5 curse, swear 7 condemn, doggone 8 execrate, sentence 9 imprecate 10 vituperate 12 anathematize

damnable
6 blamed, cursed, cussed 7 blasted, dratted 8 accursed, infernal 9 abhorrent, execrable 10 abominable, detestable

damned
5 utter 6 blamed, cursed, cussed, darned, dashed, doomed 7 awfully, blasted, doggone, dratted, goldarn 8 accursed, infernal 9 condemned 10 confounded 13 anathematized

Damocles' _____
5 sword

Damon's friend
7 Pythias

damp
3 wet 4 dank, dewy 5 check, choke, humid, moist, musty 6 clammy 7 bedewed 8 humidify, humidity

dampen
4 cool, curb 5 chill 6 deaden 7 depress, moisten 8 diminish

damsel
3 gal 4 girl, lass, maid, miss 5 filly, wench 6 lassie, maiden

Dan
father: 5 Jacob
mother: 6 Bilhah
son: 6 Hushim

Danaë
  father: 8 Acrisius
  lover: 4 Zeus
  son: 7 Perseus

Danaus
  brother: 8 Aegyptus
  daughters: 7 Danaïds 8 Danaïdes
  father: 5 Belus
  founder of: 5 Argos
  grandfather: 7 Neptune 8 Poseidon

dance
  3 hop, jig, tap 4 ball, flit, foot, heel,
  hoof, juba, leap, lope, reel, step, trip
  5 bamba, brawl, galop, gigue, hover,
  lindy, mambo, mixer, polka, rumba,
  stomp, swing, tread 6 ballet, bolero,
  boogie, Boston, cancan, chassé, foot
  it, formal, frolic, German, hoof it,
  rhumba, shimmy 7 beguine, coranto,
  courant, flicker, flitter, flutter, hoedown, one-step, shuffle 8 cakewalk,
  flamenco, galliard, glissade, rigadoon, rigaudon 9 allemande, cotillion, jitterbug, pas de deux
  art of: 12 choreography
  Austrian: 7 ländler
  ballroom: 5 rumba, tango 6 cha-
  cha, rhumba 7 fox-trot, mazurka,
  two-step 8 merengue 9 cotillion
  10 Charleston
  Bohemian: 5 polka
  Brazilian: 5 samba 6 maxixe
  7 lambada 8 capoeira 9 bossa nova
  combining form: 5 chore 6 choreo,
  chorio
  country: 4 reel 8 hornpipe
  couple: 5 polka 9 cotillion, malaguena 11 square dance
  court: 6 canary, pavane 8 saraband 9 allemande, sarabande
  Cuban: 5 conga, mambo, rumba
  6 rhumba 8 habanera
  designer: 13 choreographer
  English: 6 morris
  formal: 4 ball, prom 9 cotillion
  French: 6 cancan 7 bourrée,
  gavotte 9 allemande 10 carmagnole
  garment: 4 tutu 7 leotard
  Haitian: 4 juba 8 merengue
  Hungarian: 7 czardas

  Indian: 6 nautch 7 bhangra
  instrument: 8 castanet
  Israeli: 4 hora
  Italian: 10 saltarello, tarantella,
  villanella 11 passacaglia
  lively: 3 jig 4 reel, trot 5 galop,
  gigue, polka, rumba 6 rhumba
  7 bourrée 8 fandango, hornpipe,
  rigadoon, rigaudon 9 farandole,
  shakedown 10 Charleston, saltarello, tarantella
  movement: 4 plié, step 8 capriole,
  glissade 9 pirouette
  Muse of: 11 Terpsichore
  1920's: 10 Charleston
  Polish: 5 polka 7 mazurka 9 polonaise
  Polynesian: 4 hula
  Scottish: 3 bob 4 reel 5 fling
  10 strathspey 11 schottische
  13 Highland fling
  shoes: 5 pumps 8 slippers
  slipper: 7 toeshoe
  slow: 6 adagio, minuet, pavane
  8 habanera
  South American: 7 carioca
  Spanish: 4 jota 6 bolero 7 zapateo
  8 cachucha, chaconne, fandango,
  flamenco, saraband 9 malaguena,
  sarabande 10 seguidilla
  springy: 3 jig
  square: 7 hoedown, lancers 9 cotillion, quadrille
  stately: 5 pavan 6 pavane 8 saraband 9 polonaise, sarabande
  step: 3 pas
  woman's: 6 cancan

dancer
  6 hoofer 7 chorine, clogger, danseur,
  stepper 8 coryphée, danseuse
  9 ballerina, chorus boy 10 cake-
  walker, chorus girl
  American: 4 Feld (Elliot), Holm
  (Hanya), Lang (Pearl), Tune (Tommy)
  5 Ailey (Alvin), Fosse (Bob), Kelly
  (Gene), Shawn (Ted), Tharp (Twyla)
  6 Castle (Irene, Vernon), Duncan
  (Isadora), Dunham (Katherine),
  Graham (Martha), Morris (Mark),
  Taylor (Paul), Verdon (Gwen)
  7 Astaire (Fred), Bujones (Fernando),

de Mille (Agnes), Farrell (Suzanne), Gregory (Cynthia), Jamison (Judith), Joffrey (Robert), Martins (Peter), Massine (Leonide), McBride (Patricia), Robbins (Jerome), St. Denis (Ruth), Tamiris (Helen) **8** Champion (Gower, Marge), d'Amboise (Jacques), Humphrey (Doris), Kirkland (Gelsey), Mitchell (Arthur), Nikolais (Alwin), Villella (Edward) **9** Tallchief (Maria) **10** Cunningham (Merce)
Cuban: 6 Alonso (Alicia)
Danish: 5 Bruhn (Erik) **7** Martins (Peter) **8** Tomasson (Helgi)
English: 5 Dolin (Anton), Somes (Michael), Tudor (Antony) **7** Fonteyn (Margot), Markova (Alicia), Rambert (Marie) **8** de Valois (Ninette), Helpmann (Robert)
French: 5 Lifar (Serge) **6** Béjart (Maurice), Perrot (Jules), Petipa (Marius) **7** Camargo (Marie), Massine (Leonide)
German: 5 Jooss (Kurt)
Italian: 5 Grisi (Carlotta)
Mexican: 5 Limón (José)
Russian: 5 Lifar (Serge) **6** Fokine (Michel), Petipa (Marius) **7** Massine (Leonide), Nureyev (Rudolf), Pavlova (Anna), Ulanova (Galina) **8** Danilova (Aleksandra), Makarova (Natalia), Nijinska (Bronislava), Nijinsky (Vaslav), Vaganova (Agrippina) **9** Karsavina (Tamara), Semyonova (Marina) **11** Baryshnikov (Mikhail), Plisetskaya (Maya)
Scottish: 7 Shearer (Moira)

dancing
  6 ballet **12** choreography
  mania: 9 tarantism

dandle
  3 pet **4** play **6** caress, cosset, cradle, cuddle, pamper

dandruff
  5 scall, scurf

dandy
  3 fop **4** beau, buck, dude, fine, toff **5** nifty, swell **6** peachy **7** coxcomb, foppish **8** terrific **9** excellent, firstrate, hunky-dory **11** Beau Brummel, crackerjack **12** lounge lizard

dang
  4 damn, darn **6** cursed, cussed, damned, darned **7** blasted, dratted, goldarn **8** infernal **10** confounded

danger
  4 risk **5** peril **6** crisis, hazard, menace, plight, threat **7** pitfall, trouble **8** distress, jeopardy **9** emergency
  signal: 4 bell **5** alarm, siren **6** tocsin

dangerous
  5 risky **6** unsafe **7** parlous **8** insecure, menacing, perilous, unstable **9** hazardous **10** precarious **11** threatening

dangle
  4 hang **5** droop, swing **6** depend **7** suspend

Daniel _____
  pioneer: 5 Boone
  statesman: 7 Webster

Danish
  hero: 5 Ogier
  king: 9 Christian, Frederick
  queen: 9 Margrethe

dank
  3 wet **4** damp **5** humid, moist **6** clammy **8** dripping

Dante
  beloved: 8 Beatrice
  birthplace: 8 Florence
  daughter: 7 Antonia
  deathplace: 7 Ravenna
  party: 6 Guelph **7** Bianchi
  patron: 5 Scala
  teacher: 6 Latini
  wife: 5 Gemma
  work: 7 Inferno **8** Commedia, Paradiso **9** Vita Nuova **10** Purgatorio **12** Divine Comedy (The)

Dantean division
  5 canto

Danton's colleague
  5 Marat (Jean-Paul) **11** Robespierre (Maximilien)

Danzig
  6 Gdańsk

Daphne
  father: 5 Ladon **6** Peneus

form: 6 laurel 10 laurel tree
pursuer: 6 Apollo 9 Leucippus

Daphnis' lover
5 Chloe

dapper
4 neat, trim 5 doggy, natty, sassy, smart, swank 6 classy, jaunty, rakish, snazzy, spiffy, spruce, sprucy 7 bandbox, dashing, doggish, foppish, stylish 11 well-groomed

dapple
4 spot 5 fleck, patch 6 mottle 7 speckle, stipple

dappled
4 pied 6 motley 7 flecked, mottled, patched, piebald, spotted 8 brindled 10 variegated 11 varicolored

Dardanelles
10 Hellespont

Dardanus
descendants: 7 Trojans
father: 4 Zeus 7 Jupiter
mother: 7 Electra

dare
3 try 4 defy, risk 5 beard, brave 6 hazard 7 attempt, venture 8 confront, defiance 9 challenge

daredevil
see **daring**

darer
4 hero 6 risker

daring
4 bold, guts, rash 5 brash, brave, gutsy, moxie, nerve, nervy, pluck, valor 6 heroic, plucky 7 bravery, courage, heroism 8 audacity, boldness, fearless, reckless 9 audacious, derring-do, fortitude, venturous 10 courageous 11 adventurous, venturesome 13 adventuresome

Darius
battle: 8 Marathon
father: 9 Hystaspes
country: 6 Persia 7 Parthia
son: 6 Xerxes
wife: 6 Atossa

Darjeeling
3 tea

dark
3 dim 4 dusk, inky, murk 5 black, blind, cloud, dingy, dusky, ebony, murky, night, sable, shady, sooty, swart, umber, unlit, vague 6 brunet, cloudy, dismal, gloomy, opaque, somber, sombre, wicked 7 obscure, ominous, rayless, satanic, shadowy, stygian, subfusc, sunless, swarthy, unclear 8 bistered, brunette, infernal, sinister 9 enigmatic, lightless, secretive, tenebrous, unlighted 10 caliginous, indistinct, mysterious, mystifying, pitch-black 11 crepuscular 13 unilluminated
poetic: 4 ebon

darken
3 dim 5 bedim, cloud, gloom, lower, shade, sully, umber 6 shadow 7 becloud, blacken, eclipse, obscure, tarnish 8 melanize, overcast 9 obfuscate, overcloud 10 overshadow
Scottish: 5 gloam

dark-haired
female: 8 brunette
male: 6 brunet

darkness
4 dusk, evil, murk 5 black, gloom, night, shade 6 shadow 8 blackout 9 nightfall, obscurity

darling
3 hon, pet 4 dear, duck, love 5 angel, deary, ducky, flame, honey, loved, sugar, sweet 7 beloved, dearest, sweetie 8 adorable, charming, favorite, precious 10 sweetheart, sweetie pie

darn
4 knit, mend 5 patch 6 blamed, cursed, cussed, damned, shucks 7 blasted, doggone, dratted 8 infernal 9 embroider 10 confound

darn it
French: 3 zut

Darrow client
4 Debs (Eugene), Loeb (Richard) 6 Scopes (John) 7 Haywood (William), Leopold (Nathan)

dart
3 fly, run, zip 4 barb, bolt, buzz, dash, flit, leap, rush, sail, scud, skim, tear 5 arrow, bound, hurry, lance, pitch, scamp, scoot, shaft, shoot, skirr, spear, speed, spurt 6 glance, hasten, scurry, spring, sprint 7 javelin, missile, scamper **barbed:** 10 banderilla

D'Artagnan's friends
5 Athos 6 Aramis 7 Porthos 10 musketeers

Dartmouth location
5 Devon 7 Hanover 12 New Hampshire

darts term
3 leg 4 bust 5 split 6 double, flight, hockey, treble 8 bull's-eye

Darwin, Charles
colleague: 7 Wallace (Alfred Russel)
ship: 6 Beagle
theory: 9 evolution, selection

dash
3 fly, nip, run 4 bolt, brio, cast, damn, dart, élan, foil, hurl, race, ruin, rush, slam, tear, zing 5 break, chase, flair, fling, pinch, smash, style, trace 6 esprit, hyphen, pizazz, scurry, splash, sprint, thrust, thwart 7 bravura, depress, destroy, pizzazz, shatter, smidgen, spatter 8 confound 9 animation, frustrate

dashboard reading
4 fuel 5 speed 7 mileage 8 pressure 11 temperature

dashing
4 bold 5 smart 6 dapper, jaunty, lively, modish 7 gallant, stylish 8 animated, spirited 11 adventurous, fashionable

Das Kapital author
4 Marx (Karl)

dassie
4 pika 5 coney, hyrax

dastard
6 coward, craven 7 chicken, quitter 8 poltroon, recreant 9 scoundrel

dastardly
3 low 4 base, mean 6 craven, yellow 8 cowardly, shameful, skulking 11 treacherous, underhanded 13 pusillanimous

data
4 info 5 facts, input 7 figures 9 documents 11 information

date
3 age, era, woo 5 court, epoch, tryst 6 cutoff, escort 7 take out 8 deadline 9 accompany 10 engagement, rendezvous 11 anniversary, appointment, assignation

dated
3 old 5 passé 6 démodé, old hat 7 archaic, outworn 8 obsolete, outmoded 10 antiquated 12 old-fashioned 13 unfashionable

datum
4 fact

daub
4 blob, blot, spot 5 fleck, paint, smear 6 dapple, smudge, splash 7 besmear, dribble, plaster, speckle, splotch

daughter
Blythe Danner's: 7 Paltrow (Gwyneth)
Bruce Dern's: 5 Laura
Bush's: 5 Jenna 7 Barbara
Carter's: 3 Amy
Cash's: 7 Rosanne
Cher's: 8 Chastity
Clinton's: 7 Chelsea
Cole's: 7 Natalie
Coppola's: 5 Sofia
Danny Thomas's: 5 Marlo
Debbie Reynolds's: 6 Carrie (Fisher)
Eddie Fisher's: 6 Carrie
Elizabeth II's: 4 Anne
Elvis's: 9 Lisa Marie
Fonda's: 4 Jane
Ford's (Gerald): 5 Susan
Freud's: 4 Anna
Garland's: 12 Liza Minnelli
Goldie Hawn's: 10 Kate Hudson

Ingrid Bergman's: 8 Isabella
(Rossellini)
Janet Leigh's: 8 Jamie Lee (Curtis)
Joel Grey's: 8 Jennifer
Johnson's (Lyndon): 4 Lucy
5 Linda
Jon Voight's: 8 Angelina (Jolie)
Kennedy's (John F.): 8 Caroline
Klaus Kinski's: 9 Nastassja
Maureen O'Sullivan's: 3 Mia
(Farrow)
Naomi Judd's: 7 Wynonna
Nat King Cole's: 7 Natalie
Nixon's: 5 Julie **6** Tricia
Pat Boone's: 5 Debby
Ravi Shankar's: 10 Norah Jones
Reagan's: 5 Patti **7** Maureen
Richard Burton's: 4 Kate
Ryan O'Neal's: 5 Tatum
Sinatra's: 5 Nancy
Tony Curtis's: 8 Jamie Lee (Curtis)

Daughter of the Moon
7 Nokomis

daunt
3 cow **5** alarm, deter **6** dismay,
subdue **7** terrify **8** frighten **10** disconcert, discourage, dishearten,
intimidate

daunting
7 awesome **8** imposing **9** dismaying, unnerving **10** forbidding, formidable **11** dispiriting **12** discouraging,
intimidating, overwhelming

dauntless
4 bold, game **5** brave **6** daring
7 gallant, valiant **8** fearless, unafraid
9 unfearful, unfearing **10** courageous **11** lionhearted **12** stouthearted

dauntlessness
4 guts **5** heart, nerve, pluck, spunk,
valor **6** daring, mettle, spirit **7** bravery, cojones, courage **8** boldness
10 resolution **12** fearlessness

davenport
4 desk, sofa **5** couch, divan **6** daybed
12 chesterfield

David
commander: 4 Joab **5** Amasa
companion: 8 Jonathan

daughter: 5 Tamar
father: 5 Jesse
rebuker: 6 Nathan
son: 5 Amnon **7** Absalom, Solomon
8 Adonijah
wife: 6 Michal **7** Abigail, Ahinoam
9 Bathsheba

_____ David
4 Camp **5** Magen, Mogen **6** Star of

David Copperfield
author: 7 Dickens (Charles)
character: 4 Dora, Heep **5** Uriah
6 Barkis **8** Micawber, Peggotty
9 Murdstone **10** Steerforth

Da Vinci Code author
5 Brown (Dan)

davit
5 crane

dawdle
3 lag **4** idle, laze, loaf, loll **5** dally,
delay, tarry **6** diddle, linger, loiter,
lounge **8** lollygag **10** dillydally

dawn
4 morn **5** sunup **6** aurora **7** morning,
sunrise **8** cockcrow, daybreak, daylight **9** beginning **10** first light
goddess: 3 Eos **6** Aurora

day
abbreviation: 3 Fri, Mon, Sat,
Sun, Thu, Tue, Wed **4** Thur, Tues
5 Thurs
before: 3 eve
church calendar: 5 feria
French: 4 jour
German: 3 Tag
holy: 5 feast
hour: 4 noon
Latin: 4 dies
Spanish: 3 día

daybreak
4 dawn, morn **5** sunup **6** aurora
7 dawning, morning, sunrise **8** cockcrow, daylight

daydream
4 muse **5** fancy **6** vision **7** fantasy,
reverie **8** phantasy **9** fantasize
10 woolgather **13** woolgathering

daystar
3 Sol, sun 5 Venus 7 phoebus

daze
3 fog 4 haze, stun 5 amaze, blind
6 dazzle, stupor, trance 7 astound,
confuse, stupefy 8 astonish, bedazzle, befuddle, confound 9 dumbfound

dazed
5 woozy 6 groggy, punchy 7 dazzled,
stunned 8 confused 9 stupefied
10 punch-drunk

_____ **d'Azur**
4 Côte

dazzle
5 amaze, blind, éclat, glitz, shine
7 impress 8 astonish, bewilder,
confound, outshine 9 overpower

dazzling
6 flashy, garish 7 radiant 8 splendid,
stunning 9 brilliant 11 confounding,
resplendent 12 overpowering

deacon
6 clergy, cleric, layman 8 reverend
9 churchman

dead
4 cold, gone, late 5 passé, slain, stiff
6 buried, fallen 7 defunct, done
for, expired, extinct 8 deceased,
departed, lifeless 9 senseless
10 corpselike 11 unconscious
12 extinguished

deadbeat
3 bum 5 idler 6 debtor, loafer,
slouch 7 lounger, shirker, slacker
10 delinquent, malingerer

dead duck
5 goner 8 casualty, fatality

deaden
4 dull, kill, mute, numb, stun 5 blunt,
quiet 6 benumb, dampen, lessen,
muffle, obtund, reduce, stifle
7 smother, stupefy 8 suppress
11 anesthetize, desensitize

dead end
4 halt, stop 6 pocket, unruly

7 impasse 8 cul-de-sac, standoff
9 stalemate, terminate 10 blind alley,
bottleneck, standstill

deadened
4 numb 6 asleep, dulled, killed,
numbed 7 blunted 8 benumbed,
impaired 12 anesthetized

deadeye
5 block 8 marksman 12 sharpshooter

deadfall
4 trap 7 springe 9 booby trap,
mousetrap

deadliness
8 fatality 9 lethality, mortality

deadlock
3 tie 4 draw 7 impasse 8 standoff,
stoppage 9 checkmate, stalemate
10 standstill

deadly
5 fatal, toxic 6 lethal, mortal 7 capital,
killing 8 lethally, unerring 10 implacable 11 destructive 12 pestilential

deadpan
5 blank, empty 6 vacant 9 impassive
10 poker-faced 11 inscrutable
12 inexpressive, unexpressive

Dead Souls author
5 Gogol (Nikolay)

dead to rights
9 red-handed

deadweight
4 load 6 weight

deal
4 dole, sale, sell 5 allot, serve,
shake, share, trade, treat 6 barter,
dicker, parcel 7 bargain, deliver,
dish out, dole out, mete out, package, portion, traffic, wrestle 8 contract,
disburse, dispense, share out
9 agreement, apportion, negotiate
10 administer, compromise, distribute, measure out 11 arrangement,
transaction 13 understanding
great: 4 gobs, heap, lots, tons
5 heaps, horde, loads, scads
6 oodles, plenty, stacks

out: 8 disburse, dispense 9 apportion 10 administer, distribute
with: 5 serve, treat 6 handle, regard 7 concern, involve

dealer
5 agent 6 broker, seller, trader, vendor 8 chandler, merchant, operator 9 tradesman 10 negotiator, trafficker 11 businessman, distributer, distributor 12 merchandiser
British: 5 coper 6 draper, jobber, mercer 7 chapman

dealings
5 trade, truck 7 affairs, matters, traffic 8 business, commerce, concerns 11 intercourse 12 interactions, transactions, undertakings

dean
4 head 5 chief, doyen, elder 6 leader

dear
3 pet 4 fond, lamb, love 5 honey, loved, sweet 6 costly, doting, loving, prized, scarce 7 beloved, darling, devoted, lovable, machree, querida, tootsie 8 favorite, precious, valuable 9 cherished, expensive, heartfelt, treasured 10 fair-haired, honeybunch, sweetheart 12 affectionate
French: 4 cher 5 chère 6 cherie

dearth
4 lack, want 6 famine 7 absence, default, paucity 8 scarcity, shortage, sparsity 9 privation, scantness 10 deficiency, meagerness, scantiness

death
3 end 4 exit 6 demise, ending, expiry 7 decease, passing, quietus 8 casualty, curtains, fatality, necrosis, thanatos 9 bloodshed, departure 10 expiration, extinction, grim reaper 11 dissolution, termination 12 annihilation
after: 10 posthumous
combining form: 6 thanat 7 thanato
music: 5 dirge, elegy 8 threnody
notice: 4 obit 8 obituary 9 necrology
of tissue: 8 gangrene
personification: 10 grim reaper

put to: 3 gas, hit, ice, zap 4 do in, hang, kill, slay 5 drown, lynch, snuff, waste 6 murder, poison, rub out 7 bump off, butcher, execute, smother, wipe out 8 blow away, dispatch, immolate, knock off, strangle, throttle 9 slaughter, suffocate 10 asphyxiate 11 assassinate, electrocute
rate: 9 mortality
rites: 7 funeral 8 exequies 9 interment, obsequies

deathless
7 abiding, eternal, lasting, undying 8 enduring, immortal 11 everlasting 12 imperishable

deathlike
see **deathly**

deathly
5 fatal 6 lethal, mortal 7 macabre, stygian 12 pestilential

debacle
4 rout 6 defeat, fiasco 7 breakup, failure 8 collapse, disaster 9 breakdown, cataclysm 10 disruption

debar
3 ban 4 stop 6 forbid, outlaw 7 exclude, prevent, rule out 8 preclude, prohibit 9 interdict

debark
4 land 6 alight, get off 11 decorticate

debase
3 mar 4 harm 5 lower, stain 6 damage, defile, demean, dilute, impair, reduce, weaken 7 cheapen, corrupt, degrade, devalue, pervert, pollute, vitiate 8 dishonor 9 undermine 10 adulterate, depreciate 11 contaminate

debatable
4 iffy, moot 7 dubious 8 arguable, doubtful 9 contested, uncertain, undecided 10 disputable, unresolved 11 problematic 12 questionable

debate
4 moot 5 argue, bandy, plead 7 contend, contest, discuss, dispute, quarrel, wrangle 8 argument, consider,

forensic, question **9** dialectic, thrash out **10** controvert, toss around **11** application, controversy, disputation **12** deliberation **13** argumentation
art of: 9 forensics
expert: 7 eristic
place for: 5 forum

debauch
4 orgy, warp **6** seduce **7** corrupt, deprave, pervert, vitiate **9** bacchanal, brutalize **10** lead astray, saturnalia **11** bacchanalia

debauched
6 wanton **8** degraded, depraved, vitiated **9** corrupted, dissolute, libertine, perverted **10** degenerate, licentious

debilitate
3 sap **6** impair, weaken **7** cripple, disable **8** enfeeble **9** attenuate, undermine **10** devitalize

debilitated
4 weak **6** feeble, infirm, sapped **7** run-down, worn-out **8** weakened **9** enfeebled

debility
7 disease, malaise **8** weakness **9** infirmity **10** feebleness, infirmness, sickliness **11** decrepitude

Debir
kingdom: 5 Eglon
slayer: 6 Joshua

debit
4 bill, levy **6** charge **7** deficit **8** drawback **9** liability **11** encumbrance, shortcoming

debonair
5 suave **6** smooth, urbane **7** dashing, elegant **10** nonchalant **12** lighthearted

Deborah's husband
9 Lappidoth

debris
4 junk, slag **5** trash, waste **6** litter, refuse, rubble, spilth **7** garbage, rubbish **8** detritus, riffraff, wreckage
rock: 5 scree, talus **8** colluvia **9** colluvium

debt
3 due, sin **6** arrear, red ink **7** arrears, default, deficit **8** mortgage, trespass **9** arrearage, liability **10** obligation **11** delinquency
acknowledgment: 3 IOU **4** bill **5** check

debtless
7 solvent

debunk
6 expose, reveal, show up, unmask **7** lay bare, lay open, uncloak, uncover, undress **8** unshroud **9** demystify, discredit

Debussy's La _____
3 Mer

debut
3 bow **5** entry **6** entree **7** come out, opening, present **8** entrance, premiere **9** beginning, coming out, introduce **12** introduction, presentation

decadence
5 decay **7** decline **10** degeneracy, regression **11** degradation **12** degeneration **13** deterioration

decadent
6 effete **7** debased **8** decaying, degraded, depraved **9** debauched, declining, dissolute **10** degenerate **13** self-indulgent

Decalogue verb
5 shalt

Decameron, The
author: 9 Boccaccio (Giovanni)
heroine: 8 Griselda

decamp
4 blow, bolt, exit, flee **5** leave, scram, split **6** beat it, begone, cut out, escape, get out, retire **7** abscond, make off, pull out, run away, skiddoo, take off, vamoose **8** clear out, withdraw **9** skedaddle

decant
4 pour **7** draw off, pour out **8** transfer

decanter
5 cruet, flask **6** bottle, carafe, flagon, vessel

decapitate
4 head 6 behead 9 decollate 10 guillotine

decapod
7 mollusc, mollusk 10 crustacean

decathlon champ
6 Jenner (Bruce), Morris (Glenn), O'Brien (Dan), Schenk (Christian), Sebrle (Roman), Toomey (Bill), Zmelik (Robert) 7 Doherty (Ken), Johnson (Rafer), Mathias (Bob) 8 Campbell (Milton), Thompson (Daley)

decay
3 rot 4 ruin, wane 5 spoil, waste 6 molder, wither 7 atrophy, crumble, decline, putrefy, rotting 8 putresce, spoilage 9 decompose 11 deteriorate 12 dilapidation, putrefaction 13 deterioration

decayed
6 putrid, rotted, rotten, ruined 7 carious, spoiled 8 decadent, moldered, overripe 9 putrefied 10 decomposed, degenerate

decease
3 die, end 4 fail, pass 5 death, dying, sleep 6 demise, depart, expire, finish, pass on, perish 7 passing, quietus, release, succumb 8 pass away 9 departure 10 expiration

deceased
4 body, dead, late 6 corpse 7 cadaver, carcass, expired, remains 8 departed, lifeless 9 inanimate

deceit
3 gyp 4 hoax, ruse, sham 5 fraud, guile, trick 6 humbug 7 swindle 8 artifice, flimflam, trickery 9 chicanery, deception, duplicity, imposture 10 dishonesty 13 double-dealing

deceitful
3 sly 4 wily 5 false, lying 6 crafty, sneaky, tricky 7 cunning, knavish, roguish 8 guileful, two-faced 9 deceptive, dishonest, underhand 10 mendacious 11 underhanded 13 double-dealing

deceive
3 con 4 bilk, dupe, fool, gull, hoax 5 bluff, cozen, lie to, trick 6 delude, humbug, palter, take in 7 beguile, mislead, sandbag, two-time 8 flimflam, hoodwink 9 bamboozle, four-flush 11 double-cross

deceiving
5 false 6 tricky 8 deluding, delusive, delusory, guileful, two-faced 9 beguiling, deceptive 10 fallacious, misleading 11 duplicitous, underhanded

decelerate
4 slow 5 delay 6 retard, slow up 7 slacken 8 slow down

decency
7 decorum, dignity, fitness, modesty 8 civility 9 etiquette, propriety 10 conformity, seemliness

decennium
6 decade

decent
4 fair, good 5 right 6 honest, modest, proper, seemly 7 correct, fitting, upright 8 adequate, all right 9 competent, honorable, tolerable 10 acceptable, conforming, sufficient 11 comme il faut, presentable, respectable 12 satisfactory

deception
3 gyp 4 gaff, hoax, hype, ruse, sham, wile 5 cheat, fraud, guile, put-on, trick 6 deceit, dupery, humbug, mirage 7 chicane, cunning, fallacy, fantasm, knavery, sophism 8 flimflam, illusion, intrigue, phantasm, trickery, trumpery, wiliness 9 casuistry, chicanery, duplicity, imposture, sophistry, treachery 10 artfulness, dishonesty, hanky-panky, subterfuge 11 indirection 12 speciousness, spuriousness 13 double-dealing

deceptive
5 false, phony 6 tricky 8 deluding, delusory, illusory, specious 9 beguiling, deceitful, deceiving 10 fallacious, misleading

decide
3 opt 4 rule, will 5 judge 6 settle 7 adjudge, resolve 8 conclude 9 determine 10 adjudicate

decided

3 set 4 firm 5 fixed 6 intent 7 assured, certain, obvious, settled 8 definite, resolute, resolved 10 determined, pronounced 11 established, unequivocal

decimate

4 raze, ruin 5 wreck 7 abolish, destroy, wipe out 8 demolish, massacre 9 slaughter 10 annihilate, obliterate 11 exterminate

decipher

4 read 5 break, crack, solve 6 decode, reveal 7 decrypt, resolve, unravel 8 unriddle 9 figure out, interpret, puzzle out, translate 12 cryptanalyze

decision

4 fiat 6 choice, ruling 7 finding, resolve, verdict 8 firmness, judgment, sentence 9 selection 10 conclusion, resolution, settlement 13 determination
rabbinical: 9 responsum

decisive

3 set 7 crucial, settled 8 critical, resolute 10 conclusive, convincing, determined, imperative, peremptory 11 determining 12 unmistakable

deck

4 trim 5 adorn, array, dress, equip, floor, level, porch, prank 6 attire, blazon, clothe 7 apparel, appoint, furnish, garland, garnish, terrace 8 accouter, accoutre, beautify, decorate, emblazon, ornament, platform 9 embellish
chief: 4 bos'n 9 boatswain
high: 4 poop
lowest: 5 orlop
out: 5 array, fix up, slick, spiff, tog up 6 clothe, doll up 7 dress up, gussy up 8 spruce up
part: 7 scupper

deckhand

3 gob 4 jack, swab 6 sailor, seaman 7 jack-tar, rouster, swabbie 10 bluejacket

declaim

4 rant 5 mouth, orate, speak 6 recite 7 deliver, lecture 8 bloviate, harangue, perorate 9 hold forth

declamatory

5 tumid, windy, wordy 6 florid, turgid 7 aureate, flowery, fustian, orotund, pompous, ranting, verbose 8 sonorous 9 bombastic, high-flown, overblown 10 euphuistic, oratorical, rhetorical 12 magniloquent 13 grandiloquent

declaration

5 edict 6 avowal, notice, report 7 promise 8 document, pleading 9 affidavit, manifesto, statement, testimony 10 confession, deposition, disclosure, expression, profession 11 affirmation, attestation 12 announcement, notification, proclamation 13 advertisement, pronouncement

declare

3 say, vow 4 aver, avow, tell, vent 5 claim, sound, state, swear, utter, voice 6 affirm, allege, assert, avouch, blazon, depone, depose, herald, insist, ordain, report, reveal 7 certify, confirm, deliver, divulge, express, profess, signify, testify 8 announce, disclose, indicate, maintain, manifest, proclaim, propound 9 advertise, broadcast, enunciate, predicate, pronounce 10 annunciate, asseverate, promulgate 11 come out with, disseminate
a saint: 8 canonize
in cards: 3 bid 4 meld
invalid: 5 annul

declass

4 bump, bust 5 abase, lower 6 demote, reduce 7 degrade, set back 9 downgrade

déclassé

4 mean, poor 6 common, vulgar 7 ignoble, lowered 8 inferior, lowgrade, mediocre, middling 10 second-rate 11 second-class

declension

5 class, slope 7 decline, descent

8 downfall 9 downgrade 10 inflection 12 dégringolade 13 deterioration

declination
3 ebb 5 slant, slide 6 ebbing 7 refusal, incline 8 downturn 9 downgrade 10 deflection 12 dégringolade, turning aside 13 deterioration

decline
3 dip, ebb, jib, rot, sag, set 4 balk, dive, drop, fade, fail, fall, flag, loss, sink, slip, wane 5 abate, avoid, demur, droop, lapse, lower, say no, slide, slope, slump, spurn 6 ebbing, go down, recede, refuse, reject, renege, waning, weaken, worsen 7 abstain, atrophy, descend, descent, devolve, dismiss, drop-off, dwindle, failure, falloff, forbear, refrain, relapse, sell-off, sinkage, subside 8 comedown, decrease, downfall, downturn, languish, lowering, turn down 9 backslide, decadence, downgrade, downslide, downswing, downtrend, reprobate, repudiate, weakening 10 degeneracy, degenerate, depression, devolution, disapprove, falling off 11 backsliding, deteriorate 12 degeneration, dégringolade 13 deterioration

declivitous
5 steep 6 sloped 7 pitched, sloping 8 inclined 9 inclining 10 descending

declivity
3 dip 4 drop, fall 5 slope 7 decline, descent 8 downturn, gradient 9 downgrade 11 inclination

decode
see decipher

decollate
4 head, kill 6 behead 10 decapitate, guillotine

decolor
6 blanch, bleach, blench, whiten 7 wash out 11 achromatize

decompose
3 rot 5 decay, spoil, taint 6 fester, molder 7 analyze, break up, crumble, putrefy, resolve 8 dissolve, separate 9 anatomize, break down 12 disintegrate

decor
7 setting 8 backdrop, stage set 11 furnishings 13 ornamentation

decorate
4 do up, pink, trim 5 adorn, dress, frill 6 bedeck 7 bedizen, dress up, enhance, festoon, furnish, garnish 8 appliqué, beautify, emblazon, ornament 9 embellish
a border: 6 purfle

decorated
6 ornate 7 adorned, honored, wrought 9 bemedaled, decked out, garnished 10 beribboned, ornamented 11 embellished

decoration
4 bays 5 award, badge, honor, kudos, medal 6 doodad, plaque 7 garnish, laurels 8 accolade, filigree, fretting, fretwork, frippery, furbelow, ornament, trimming, vignette 11 distinction
cutout: 8 appliqué
furniture: 4 buhl 6 boulle

decorous
3 fit 4 meet, prim 5 right 6 au fait, comely, decent, proper, seemly 7 correct, elegant, fitting 8 becoming, mannerly, suitable, tasteful 9 befitting, civilized, de rigueur, dignified 10 conforming 11 appropriate, respectable, well-behaved

decorously
5 fitly 7 rightly 8 decently, properly, suitably 9 correctly, fittingly 11 befittingly, respectably

decorousness
7 decency 8 civility 9 propriety, rightness 10 seemliness 11 correctness, orderliness 12 correctitude

decorticate
4 bare, bark, flay, hull, husk, pare, peel, skin 5 scale, scalp, shell, shuck, strip 6 denude 9 lay bare, pull off

decorum

5 order **7** decency, dignity, fitness, modesty **8** protocol **9** etiquette, propriety **10** properness, seemliness **11** correctness, orderliness **12** correctitude

decoy

4 bait, fake, lure **5** plant, shill, tempt **6** allure, capper, delude, entice, lead on, pigeon, seduce **7** deceive, mislead **8** inveigle **10** red herring

decrease

3 cut, ebb **4** bate, drop, ease, fall, loss, wane **5** allay, lower **6** lessen, reduce, shrink **7** abridge, curtail, cut back, cutback, cut down, decline, die down, drop off, dwindle, fall off, lighten, shorten, slacken, subside **8** diminish, downturn, moderate, rollback, taper off **9** abatement, alleviate, reduction **10** abbreviate, depreciate, diminution, falling off

decree

4 fiat, rule **5** canon, edict, enact, judge, order, ukase **6** behest, charge, dictum, impose, ordain, ruling **7** adjudge, appoint, bidding, command, declare, dictate, lay down, mandate, precept, statute **8** judgment, proclaim, sentence **9** directive, judgement, ordinance, prescribe, prescript, pronounce **10** adjudicate, injunction, regulation **11** declaration **12** adjudication, announcement, proclamation, promulgation **13** pronouncement **Muslim: 5** fatwa

decrepit

4 aged, weak, worn **5** frail, seedy, tacky **6** creaky, feeble, infirm, senile, shabby, wasted, weakly **7** fragile, run-down, worn-out **8** battered, impaired, weakened **10** bedraggled, broken-down, down-at-heel, ramshackle **11** dilapidated

decrepitude

4 ruin **5** decay **7** frailty, wasting **8** collapse, debility, weakness **9** disrepair, infirmity **10** exhaustion, feebleness, infirmness **12** dilapidation, enfeeblement **13** deterioration

decretal

4 fiat, writ **5** edict, order, ukase **6** assize, dictum, letter, ruling **7** dictate **8** decision, judgment **11** declaration **13** pronouncement

decry

3 boo **4** bash, slam, slur **5** abuse **6** berate, malign, vilify **7** asperse, censure, condemn, degrade, devalue, put down **8** bad-mouth, belittle, denounce, derogate, reproach **9** criticize, deprecate, discredit, disparage, dispraise, reprehend, reprobate **10** depreciate, disapprove **11** rail against

decrypt

see **decipher**

decumbent

4 flat **5** prone **6** supine **9** lying down, prostrate, reclining **10** horizontal

decussate

5 cross **8** crosscut **9** intersect **10** crisscross, intercross

dedicate

3 vow **5** bless **6** commit, devote, hallow, pledge **7** address **8** inscribe, restrict, set apart **10** consecrate

deduce

5 infer, judge, trace **6** derive, evolve, gather, reason, reckon **7** discern, make out, surmise **8** conclude **9** figure out

deduct

4 bate **5** abate, infer, judge **6** gather, remove **7** make out, take off, take out **8** conclude, knock off, perceive, subtract, take away

deduction

3 cut **8** discount, illation, judgment, sequitur, write-off **9** abatement, inference, reasoning **10** conclusion **11** subtraction

deductive

7 a priori **8** dogmatic, illative, provable, reasoned **9** derivable, inferable **10** consequent **11** inferential **13** ratiocinative

deed
3 act 4 cede, fact, feat, pact 5 doing, title 6 action, assign, convey, escrow, remise 7 charter, exploit 8 alienate, contract, covenant, make over, sign over, transfer 9 adventure 10 conveyance, enterprise 11 achievement, performance, tour de force
brutal: 8 atrocity
evil: 3 sin 11 malefaction
good: 7 mitzvah

deem
4 feel, hold 5 judge, think 7 account, adjudge, believe 8 consider

de-emphasize
8 downplay, minimize, play down 9 gloss over, soft-pedal, underplay 13 underestimate

deep
3 low 4 bass, rapt, sunk 5 abyss, grave, ocean 6 occult, orphic, secret 7 abyssal, obscure 8 abstruse, esoteric, hermetic, profound 9 engrossed, recondite 10 bottomless, fathomless, mysterious
combining form: 5 bathy

deepen
6 darken, worsen 7 enhance, enlarge, magnify, thicken 8 heighten 9 aggravate, intensify 10 strengthen

deepness
5 abyss 9 intensity 10 profundity

deep-seated
6 inborn, inbred, innate 7 settled 8 inherent, lifelong, profound, stubborn 9 confirmed, ingrained, intrinsic 10 congenital, entrenched, indwelling, inveterate 11 established 12 longstanding 13 bred-in-the-bone, dyed-in-the-wool, thoroughgoing

deep-six
4 dump, toss 5 chuck, scrap 6 unload 7 discard 8 jettison 9 eliminate

deep water
7 trouble 8 distress 10 difficulty

deer
3 elk, roe 4 buck, musk, stag 5 moose 6 wapiti 7 caribou, venison

Asian: 4 axis 6 sambar 7 muntjac
British: 4 hart
female: 3 doe 4 hind
Japanese: 4 sika
male: 4 buck, hart, stag 7 roebuck
meat: 5 jerky 7 venison
path: 3 run 5 trail
red: 7 brocket
relating to: 7 cervine
track: 4 slot 5 spoor
young: 3 kid 4 fawn

Deerslayer (The)
author: 6 Cooper (James Fenimore)
character: 5 Harry (Hurry) 6 Hutter (Thomas), Judith (Hutter) 11 Natty Bumppo 12 Chingachgook

deface
3 mar 4 harm, ruin 6 damage, deform, impair, injure 9 disfigure, vandalize

de facto
6 actual, really 8 actually, existing

defalcation
7 default, failing, failure 10 embezzling, inadequacy, negligence 12 embezzlement

defamation
5 libel, smear 7 calumny, obloquy, slander 10 backbiting 11 traducement 12 backstabbing 13 disparagement

defamatory
8 libelous 9 maligning, traducing, vilifying 10 backbiting, calumnious, slanderous 11 denigrating

defame
5 abase, libel, smear 6 malign, vilify 7 asperse, blacken, blemish, slander, traduce 8 dishonor 9 denigrate, discredit 10 calumniate

default
4 fail 5 welsh 7 absence, exclude, failure, forfeit, neglect 9 selection

defeasance
4 deed 6 defeat 9 overthrow 11 termination

defeat
3 tan 4 beat, best, down, drub,

edge, foil, lick, loss, rout, sink, undo, whip, whup **5** crush, outdo, skunk, swamp, upset, waste, whomp **6** outgun, reduce, subdue, wallop **7** beating, conquer, destroy, failure, licking, mow down, nose out, nullify, outplay, overrun, setback, shellac, trounce, wipe out **8** knock out, outfight, outflank, overcome, vanquish, waterloo **9** frustrate, overpower, overthrow, overtrump, subjugate, thrashing, trouncing **10** obliterate **11** shellacking

defeatist

8 doomster **9** doomsayer, Gloomy Gus, pessimist, worrywart

defect

3 bug **4** flaw, lack, vice, want **5** botch, error, fault **6** damage, dearth, desert, foible, injury **7** blemish, default, failing **8** drawback, weakness **9** birthmark, deformity **10** apostatize, deficiency **11** shortcoming **12** imperfection, tergiversate
timber: 4 knot
visual: 6 myopia, squint **9** amblyopia, hyperopia **10** presbyopia, strabismus

defection

8 apostasy **9** desertion, forsaking, recreancy **10** disloyalty **11** abandonment

defective

5 amiss **6** broken, faulty, flawed **7** damaged, lacking, unsound, wanting **8** impaired **9** corrupted, deficient, imperfect **10** inaccurate, inadequate, incomplete **12** insufficient

defector

5 Judas **7** traitor **8** apostate, quisling, recreant, renegade, turncoat **9** turnabout **13** double-crosser

defend

4 back, hold, save **5** argue, cover, guard **6** screen, secure, shield, uphold **7** contend, justify, protect, support **8** advocate, champion, maintain, plead for, preserve **9** safeguard

defendable

see **defensible**

defendant

7 accused, libelee **8** libellee

defender

7 paladin, tribune **8** advocate, champion, guardian **9** protector **11** white knight

defense

4 fort, ward **5** aegis, alibi, armor, guard **6** excuse, sconce, shield **7** bulwark, rampart, shelter **8** apologia, armament, fastness, fortress, muniment, security **9** safeguard **10** protection, stronghold **11** exculpation, explanation **13** justification
organization: 4 NATO **5** NORAD, SEATO **10** Warsaw Pact

defenseless

4 open **7** exposed, unarmed **8** helpless, wide open **9** unguarded **10** vulnerable **11** unprotected

defensible

5 valid **7** tenable **8** passable **9** excusable, plausible **10** condonable, reasonable **11** justifiable

defer

3 bow **4** stay, wait **5** delay, remit, stall, table, yield **6** accede, hold up, put off, shelve, submit **7** hold off, lay over, put over, suspend **8** hold over, postpone, prorogue **9** acquiesce **13** procrastinate

deference

5 honor **6** esteem, homage, regard **7** respect **8** courtesy **9** obeisance **11** recognition

deferential

8 obliging **9** disarming, regardful **10** respectful **11** complaisant

defiance

4 dare **5** moxie **7** bravado **8** audacity, contempt **9** challenge, contumacy, impudence, insolence **10** brazenness, effrontery **12** contrariness, stubbornness

defiant

4 bold **5** brash, gutsy, sassy, saucy **6** brazen, cheeky, daring **8** arrogant, impudent, insolent 9 audacious, obstinate, resistant 10 refractory 12 recalcitrant

deficiency
4 flaw, lack, want 5 fault, minus 6 dearth 7 absence, blemish, demerit, failing, failure, paucity 8 scarcity, shortage, weakness 9 privation 10 inadequacy, scantiness 11 defalcation, shortcoming 12 imperfection
mental: 6 idiocy 7 amentia

deficient
3 shy 5 minus, scant, short 6 faulty, flawed, meager, meagre, measly, scanty, scarce 7 failing, lacking, unsound, wanting 8 exiguous, impaired 9 defective, imperfect 10 inadequate, incomplete

deficit
4 lack, loss 6 red ink 8 shortage 10 impairment, inadequacy 12 disadvantage 13 insufficiency

defile
3 tar 4 foul, pass, rape, soil 5 dirty, gorge, march, shame, smear, spoil, stain, sully, taint 6 befoul, debase, ravish 7 besmear, corrupt, pollute, profane, tarnish, violate 8 deflower, dishonor 9 desecrate 11 contaminate

defiled
5 raped 6 impure 7 stained, unclean 8 profaned, polluted, ravished, violated 9 corrupted 10 deflowered, desecrated 12 contaminated

define
3 fix, hem, rim, set 4 edge 5 limit 6 assign, border, detail 7 clarify, delimit, lay down, mark off, mark out, outline, specify 9 delineate, demarcate, determine, establish 11 distinguish 12 characterize

definite
3 set 4 sure 5 clear, final, fixed, sharp, solid 7 certain, decided, express, precise, settled 8 clear-cut, distinct, explicit, specific 10 conclusive, pronounced 11 unambiguous, unequivocal 12 unmistakable

definiteness
8 accuracy, sureness 9 certainty, certitude, exactness, precision 10 exactitude

definitive
5 final 7 express 8 clear-cut, complete, explicit, settling, specific, ultimate 10 concluding, conclusive, exhaustive 11 categorical, determining, unambiguous 13 authoritative

deflate
4 dash 6 humble, reduce, shrink 7 devalue, put down 8 contract, ridicule 9 humiliate, shoot down

deflect
5 avert, parry 6 divert 7 deviate, diverge, hold off 9 turn aside

deflection
3 yaw 4 bend, tack, turn, veer 5 carom, curve, shift 6 double, swerve 7 bending, rebound, turning, veering 8 swerving 9 departure, deviation, diversion 10 divergence

deflower
4 rape 5 spoil 6 defile, ravish 7 despoil, violate 9 desecrate

Defoe, Daniel
character: 6 Crusoe (Robinson), Friday, Roxana 12 Moll Flanders

deform
4 warp 5 spoil 6 deface 7 contort, distort 8 misshape 9 disfigure

deformed
4 awry, bent 5 askew, bowed 6 warped 7 buckled, crooked 8 crippled 9 contorted, misshapen, unshapely

deformity
4 flaw 6 defect 7 blemish 11 abnormality 12 imperfection, irregularity, malformation 13 disfigurement

_____ de France
3 Île

defraud
3 con, gyp 4 bilk, dupe, rook, scam 5 cheat, cozen, mulct, trick 6 fleece, rip off 7 swindle 8 flimflam 9 bamboozle

deft

3 apt **4** able **5** adept, agile, handy
6 adroit, clever **7** skilled **8** dextrous,
skillful **9** dexterous

deftness

5 knack, skill **7** address, prowess
8 facility **9** adeptness, dexterity
10 capability

defunct

4 cold, dead, late **5** kaput **7** extinct
8 deceased, departed, lifeless,
vanished

defy

4 dare, face, gibe, jeer, mock **5** beard,
brave, flout, stump **6** resist **7** affront,
outdare, outface **8** confront **9** challenge, disregard, withstand

dégagé

6 breezy, casual **7** relaxed, unfussy
8 informal **9** easygoing **10** nonchalant, unreserved **13** unconstrained

degeneracy

see **degeneration**

degenerate

4 sink **6** rotten, sunken, worsen
7 corrupt, debased, decayed, decline, descend, immoral, pervert,
vicious, vitiate **8** decadent, degraded, depraved **9** backslide,
dissolute **11** deteriorate

degeneration

7 atrophy, decline **8** downfall, lowering **9** decadence, depravity, downgrade **10** debasement, perversion,
regression **11** degradation **12** dégringolade **13** deterioration

degradation

4 fall **7** decline, descent **8** demotion
9 abasement, decadence, depravity,
downgrade, reduction **10** corruption,
debasement, degeneracy, perversion
11 downgrading **12** degeneration

degrade

4 bump, bust **5** abase, break, decry,
lower **6** debase, demean, demote,
impair, lessen, reduce **7** corrupt,
declass, pervert, put down **8** belittle,
cast down, derogate, diminish **9** decompose, discredit, disparage, downgrade, humiliate

degree

3 peg **4** heat, rank, rate, rung, step,
term, tier **5** grade, honor, notch,
order, pitch, point, ratio, scale, shade,
stage, stair **6** amount, extent, status
7 measure, station **8** standing
9 dimension, intensity, magnitude
10 proportion
academic: 3 BFA, BSc, DDS, LLB,
LLD, LLM, MBA, MFA, MSc, PhD
5 MPhil **7** master's **9** bachelor's,
doctorate
highest: 8 cum laude **13** magna
cum laude, summa cum laude
of combining power: 7 valence
of height: 5 grade
of importance: 7 caliber, calibre
of outward slope: 5 splay
seeker: 9 candidate
slight: 4 hair
utmost: 4 acme

dégringolade

see **degeneration**

_____ de guerre

3 nom

dehydrate

3 dry **4** sear **5** parch **9** desiccate,
exsiccate

Deianira

brother: 8 Meleager
father: 6 Oeneus
husband: 8 Heracles, Hercules
mother: 7 Althaea
victim: 8 Heracles, Hercules

deific

5 godly **6** divine **7** godlike

deification

8 idolatry **10** apotheosis, glorifying
13 glorification

deify

5 exalt **7** glorify, idolize, worship
8 sanctify, venerate **11** apotheosize

deign

5 stoop **7** descend **9** vouchsafe
10 condescend

Deiphobus
brother: **5** Paris **6** Hector
father: **5** Priam
mother: **6** Hecuba
wife: **5** Helen

Deirdre
beloved: **5** Noisi
father: **5** Felim

deity
3 god **4** Lord **7** goddess, godhead,
godhood **8** Almighty, divinity **12** supreme being
(see also at **Greek; Hindu; Norse;
Roman**)

deject
5 chill, cloud, daunt **6** dampen,
dismay **7** depress **8** dispirit **9** disparage **10** demoralize, discourage,
dishearten

dejected
3 low, sad **4** blue, down, glum, sunk
6 gloomy, morose, somber, sombre **7** doleful, hangdog, humbled,
unhappy **8** downcast, wretched
9 cheerless, depressed, woebegone
10 despondent, spiritless **11** crestfallen, downhearted **12** disconsolate,
disheartened

dejection
5 dumps, gloom **7** despair, sadness
10 melancholy **11** despondency,
unhappiness **12** mournfulness

Delaware
capital: **5** Dover
city: **10** Wilmington
nickname: **5** First (State) **7** Diamond
(State)
state bird: **14** blue hen chicken
state flower: **12** peach blossom
state tree: **13** American holly

delay
3 lag **4** drag, hold, slow, stay, wait
5 dally, defer, stall, tarry, trail **6** dawdle, detain, hang up, hinder, holdup,
impede, linger, loiter, put off, retard,
slow up **7** bog down, hold off, respite, set back, slacken, suspend
8 hesitate, hold over, postpone,

prorogue, reprieve, slow down
10 dillydally, moratorium, suspension
13 procrastinate

delaying
8 dawdling, dilatory **10** postponing,
putting off

delectable
5 tasty, yummy **6** choice, savory
8 charming, heavenly, luscious,
pleasing **9** ambrosial, delicious,
enjoyable, exquisite, toothsome
10 delightful, enchanting **11** scrumptious **13** mouthwatering

delectation
3 fun, joy **4** zest **5** gusto **6** relish
7 delight **8** gladness, pleasure
9 enjoyment

delegate
4 name, send **5** agent, envoy,
proxy **6** assign, depute, deputy,
legate **7** appoint, consign, entrust
8 deputize, emissary, transfer **9** authorize, catchpole, designate,
spokesman **10** commission, mouthpiece, procurator

delete
4 drop, omit, x out **5** erase, purge
6 cancel, censor, cut out, efface,
excise, remove **7** blot out, destroy,
expunge, take out, wipe out **8** black
out, cross out **9** eliminate, eradicate,
strike out **10** blue-pencil, obliterate

deleterious
3 bad **6** nocent **7** baneful, harmful,
hurtful, noxious, noxious, ruinous
8 damaging **9** injurious **10** pernicious **11** destructive, detrimental,
mischievous, prejudicial

deletion
7 erasure, voiding **9** canceling
10 deficiency **11** elimination **12** can-
cellation

deliberate
4 chaw, cool, muse, pore, slow
5 chary, meant, study, think, weigh
6 chew on, ponder, reason **7** careful,
heedful, planned, reflect, studied,
willful, willing, witting **8** cautious,

deliberately

cogitate, consider, intended, measured, meditate, mull over, ruminate, talk over 9 cerebrate, conscious, unhurried 10 calculated, considered, purposeful, thought-out 11 circumspect, intentional 12 premeditated

deliberately

9 knowingly, on purpose, purposely, willfully, wittingly 11 consciously 12 purposefully 13 intentionally

deliberation

5 study 6 debate 7 thought 10 conference, discussion, reflection 13 consideration

Delibes, Léo

ballet: 6 Sylvia 8 Coppélia, La Source
opera: 5 Lakmé

delicacy

5 goody, treat 6 dainty, luxury, morsel, nicety, tidbit 7 frailty 8 kickshaw, fineness 9 fragility, precision 10 daintiness, difficulty, indulgence, stickiness 11 awkwardness 12 ticklishness

delicate

4 fine, lacy, weak 5 frail 6 choice, dainty, flimsy, petite, queasy, sickly, slight, subtle, tender, touchy, tricky 7 elegant, fragile, refined, tactful, tenuous 8 ethereal, feathery, finespun, gossamer, graceful, pleasing, ticklish 9 exquisite, sensitive, squeamish 10 precarious

delicatessen

11 charcuterie

delicious

5 tasty, yummy 6 choice, divine, savory 8 heavenly, luscious 9 ambrosial, exquisite, toothsome 10 delectable, delightful 11 scrumptious 13 mouthwatering

delight

3 joy 4 glee 5 amuse, bliss, charm, enjoy, exult, glory, mirth, revel 6 divert, please, regale, relish 7 ecstasy, enchant, gladden, gratify, jollity, rapture, rejoice 8 enravish, en-

trance, fruition, hilarity, pleasure 9 delectate, enjoyment, enrapture, entertain 11 delectation
in: 4 love 5 adore, enjoy, savor 6 admire, relish 7 cherish 10 appreciate

delighted

4 glad 5 happy 6 joyful 8 ecstatic, euphoric

delightful

5 yummy 6 dreamy, lovely 8 charming, heavenly, luscious, pleasant, pleasing 9 congenial, enjoyable 10 delectable, enchanting, satisfying 11 captivating, fascinating, pleasurable, scrumptious 12 entertaining

Delilah's victim

6 Samson

DeLillo novel

5 Libra, Mao II 10 Underworld, White Noise

delimit

3 bar 5 bound, hem in 6 demark, define 7 confine, enclose 8 restrict 9 demarcate, determine 12 circumscribe

delineate

3 map 4 etch, limn 5 chart, image, trace 6 define, depict, detail, render 7 outline, picture, portray 8 describe, spell out 9 elucidate, interpret, represent 10 illustrate

delineation

5 draft, story 6 report 7 account, contour, drawing, outline, picture, profile 9 depiction, rendering 11 presentment

delinquency

4 debt 5 crime, fault, lapse 7 default, failure, misdeed, neglect, offense 8 omission 9 oversight 10 misconduct, nonpayment, wrongdoing 11 dereliction, misbehavior

delinquent

3 lax 5 slack 6 debtor 7 overdue 8 careless, offender 9 defaulter, in arrears, negligent 10 behindhand, neglectful

deliquesce
3 rot, run 4 flux, fuse, melt, thaw
5 decay 6 render, soften 7 liquefy,
putrefy 8 dissolve, fluidize 9 decompose, disappear, waste away 12 disintegrate

delirious
3 mad 4 wild 5 crazy 6 crazed,
insane, raving 7 frantic, lunatic
8 confused, demented, deranged,
ecstatic, frenetic, frenzied, rambling
9 rapturous 10 bewildered, corybantic, distracted, irrational 11 lightheaded, overexcited, overwrought

delirium
5 furor, mania 6 fervor, frenzy
7 ecstasy, jimjams, rapture, seizure
8 dementia, hysteria 13 hallucination

delirium ____
7 tremens

deliver
4 bear, deal, feed, find, give, hand,
save, send, ship, sing, take 5 bring,
serve, speak, state, throw, utter
6 convey, redeem, rescue, strike,
supply 7 consign, present, produce,
provide, set free, release 8 hand
over, liberate, turn over 9 pronounce,
surrender 10 bring forth, emancipate
11 come out with, come through

deliverance
6 rescue 7 freeing, opinion, release,
verdict 8 decision 9 acquittal,
discharge, salvation 10 absolution,
liberation

Deliverance author
6 Dickey (James)

delivery
4 drop 5 birth, labor 6 rescue 7 address, bearing 8 birthing, shipment
9 elocution, rendition, salvation
10 childbirth, conveyance, liberation
11 consignment, parturition, transferral 12 childbearing, transmission

dell
4 dale, glen, vale 6 dingle, hollow,
valley

Delphic
4 dark 5 vatic 6 arcane, hidden,
mantic, mystic, occult, veiled 7 cryptic, obscure 8 auguring, divining,
esoteric, mystical, oracular 9 ambiguous, enigmatic, equivocal, prophetic, recondite, sibylline, vaticinal
10 mystifying, portentous 11 prophesying, prophetical

delta
5 plain 6 letter, symbol 7 deposit
8 triangle 9 increment

delude
3 con 4 dupe, fool, gull, hoax 5 bluff,
cozen, trick 6 betray, humbug,
juggle, take in 7 beguile, deceive,
mislead 8 flimflam, hoodwink
11 double-cross

deluge
5 drown, flood, swamp 6 drench,
engulf 7 Niagara, torrent 8 cataract,
downpour, drencher, flooding, inundate, overflow 9 cataclysm, overwhelm 10 cloudburst, outpouring,
inundation

delusion
4 hoax, sham 5 dream, fancy,
snare 6 mirage 7 chimera, fallacy,
fantasy, figment, phantom, specter
8 daydream, phantasm 9 deception
10 apparition 11 ignis fatuus 13 hallucination

delusive
5 false 8 fanciful, illusory, specious
9 beguiling, deceiving, deceptive,
imaginary 10 chimerical, fallacious,
misleading

delusory
see **delusive**

deluxe
4 lush, posh 5 grand, plush, ritzy,
swank 6 choice, costly, swanky
7 elegant, opulent 8 luscious, splendid 9 expensive, exquisite, luxuriant,
luxurious, sumptuous 10 first class

delve
3 dig, dip 4 mine 5 probe 6 dredge,
fathom, hollow, quarry, search,
shovel 7 inquire 8 excavate

delving

into: 4 sift 5 probe 7 explore
8 prospect 11 investigate

delving
6 asking 7 inquest, inquiry, probing
8 research 9 inquiring, searching

demagnetize
7 degauss

demagogue
6 leader 7 inciter 8 agitator, fomenter 9 firebrand 10 instigator
11 provocateur 12 rabble-rouser

demand
3 ask, use 4 call, need, urge, want
5 claim, crave, exact, force, order
6 compel, direct, expect, insist 7 call
for, request, require 11 requirement,
requisition

demanding
4 hard 5 pushy, tough 6 taxing,
trying 7 exigent, onerous, weighty
8 exacting, forceful, rigorous 9 assertive, difficult, insistent, strenuous,
stringent 10 aggressive, burdensome, oppressive 11 challenging

demarcate
5 bound, limit 6 define, set off 7 delimit, mark off, outline 8 separate,
set apart 9 delineate, determine
11 distinguish 12 circumscribe
13 differentiate

demarcation
9 outlining 10 border line, separation
11 distinction 12 delimitation

démarche
4 plan, ploy, ruse 5 feint 6 action,
device, gambit, scheme, tactic
7 protest 8 artifice, maneuver,
petition 9 stratagem 10 initiative
11 contrivance, machination

demean
4 bear 5 abase, carry, decry, lower
6 acquit, behave, debase, deport,
humble 7 comport, conduct, degrade, detract 8 bad-mouth, belittle
9 disparage, humiliate

demeanor
3 air 4 look, mien 6 aspect, manner
7 address, bearing, conduct 8 behavior, carriage, presence 10 deportment 11 comportment

demented
3 mad 5 crazy, loony, nutty, wacko
6 crazed, insane, psycho 7 lunatic,
unsound 8 deranged, frenzied,
maniacal 9 delirious 10 hysterical,
unbalanced 12 psychopathic

_____ de mer
3 mal

demerit
4 mark 5 fault, stain 6 defect
7 blemish, penalty 9 downgrade
10 deficiency, punishment 11 shortcoming 12 imperfection

demesne
5 field, realm 6 domain, estate,
region, sphere 7 terrain 8 dominion,
province 9 bailiwick, champaign,
territory
house: 5 manor

Demeter
see **Ceres**

demigod
4 diva, idol 8 superman 9 superstar

demise
3 die, end 4 drop, pass 5 death,
dying, sleep 6 cash in, depart,
ending, expire 7 decease, passing,
quietus, release, silence, succumb
8 pass away 9 cessation, departure
10 expiration, extinction

demit
4 quit 6 bow out, give up, resign
8 abdicate, renounce, step down,
withdraw

demiurgic
8 creative, original 9 formative,
ingenious, inventive 10 innovative
11 originative 12 innovational

demobilize
7 break up, disband, dismiss, scatter
8 disperse, separate 9 discharge,
disengage, muster out

democratic
7 popular 8 populist 10 self-ruling
11 egalitarian 13 self-governing

Democrats' symbol
6 donkey

démodé
5 dated, passé 7 antique, archaic
8 old-timey, outdated 9 out-of-date
12 old-fashioned

demoiselle
6 damsel, lassie, maiden 10 damsel-
fish

demolish
4 raze, ruin 5 crush, level, smash,
total, wrack, wreck 7 destroy, flatten,
wipe out 8 decimate, tear down
9 finish off 10 annihilate, obliterate

demolition
6 razing 8 leveling, wrecking 10 bull-
dozing 11 destruction 12 annihilation

demolition bomb
11 blockbuster

demon
3 imp 5 devil, fiend, genie, ghoul,
jinni, Satan 7 hellion, incubus 9 archfiend
Arabic: 5 afrit 6 afreet
female: 5 lamia 7 succuba, succubi
(plural) 8 succubae (plural), succubus

demonic
6 wicked 7 satanic 8 devilish,
diabolic, fiendish, infernal 9 possessed 10 diabolical

demonize
6 malign, revile, vilify 7 bedevil,
censure, slander 8 denounce 9 dia-
bolize

demonstrate
3 try 4 mark, show, test 5 prove,
rally 7 confirm, display, exhibit,
explain, make out, protest 8 evidence, manifest, proclaim, validate
9 determine, establish 10 illustrate
12 authenticate

demonstration
4 expo, show, test 5 march, proof,
rally, trial 6 picket 7 display, protest
9 spectacle 10 exhibition, exposition, validation 12 presentation
13 corroboration, manifestation

demonstrative
4 open 8 effusive, outgoing, specific
9 emotional, expansive, exuberant,
outspoken 10 outpouring, unreserved, validating 12 affectionate,
unrestrained 13 unconstrained

demoralize
5 chill, daunt, shake, unman, upset
6 dampen, debase, deject, rattle,
weaken 7 corrupt, debauch, deprave, unnerve, vitiate 8 dispirit,
psych out 9 undermine 10 discourage, dishearten

Demosthenes
6 orator
oration: 9 Philippic

demote
4 bump, bust 5 lower 6 reduce
7 declass, degrade 9 downgrade

demulcent
4 balm 5 jelly, salve 7 unguent
8 liniment, ointment, soothing 9 softening

demur
5 qualm 6 object, oppose, resist
7 dispute, protest 8 question 9 challenge, hesitancy, objection 10 hesitation, indecision, reluctance 11 compunction, remonstrate

demure
3 coy, shy 5 timid 6 modest 7 bashful 8 reserved, reticent, retiring
9 diffident 11 unassertive 12 self-
effacing

demurral
7 protest 9 challenge, objection
12 remonstrance 13 remonstration

demurrer
see **demurral**

den
4 base, cave, home, lair, nest, room
5 study 6 burrow, cavern, hollow
7 dayroom, hideout, sanctum 8 hideaway, playroom
rabbit: 6 warren

denial
3 nay 6 heresy 7 refusal 8 disproof,
negation, rebuttal 9 disavowal,

denigrate

rejection **10** abnegation, gainsaying, refutation **11** repudiation **12** renunciation

denigrate

5 decry, libel, smear, stain, sully **6** darken, defame, defile, impugn, malign, vilify **7** asperse, devalue, put down, slander, tarnish, traduce **8** belittle, dishonor, tear down **9** discredit, disparage **10** calumniate, scandalize

denims

5 jeans **8** overalls **9** blue jeans, dungarees

denizen

5 liver **6** native **7** dweller, habitué, haunter, resider **8** habitant, occupant, resident **9** indweller, inhabiter **10** frequenter, inhabitant

Denmark

capital: 10 Copenhagen
city: 5 Århus **6** Ålborg, Odense **11** Helsingborg **13** Frederiksberg
island: 3 Fyn **7** Falster, Zealand **8** Bornholm **9** Sjaelland
monetary unit: 5 krone
neighbor: 6 Sweden **7** Germany
part of: 11 Scandinavia
peninsula: 7 Jutland
possession: 9 Greenland **12** Faroe Islands **13** Faeroe Islands
sea: 5 North **6** Baltic
strait: 5 Lille, Store **9** Langeland

denominate

3 dub **4** call, name, term **5** label, style, title **7** baptize, entitle **8** christen **9** designate

denomination

4 cult, name, sect **5** creed, faith, style, title **6** church **8** category, cognomen, religion **9** communion **10** persuasion
religious: 5 Amish **6** Mormon **7** Baptist **8** Lutheran, Moravian, Reformed **9** Adventist, Episcopal, Mennonite, Methodist, Unitarian **11** Pentecostal **12** Presbyterian, Universalist **13** Roman Catholic

denotation

4 name, sign **5** sense **6** import **7** meaning **10** indication, signifying **11** designation **13** signification, specification

denote

4 mark, mean, name, show **5** spell **6** import **7** add up to, betoken, express **8** announce, indicate **9** designate, represent

denouement

6 effect, result, upshot **7** outcome **10** conclusion **11** consequence, culmination

denounce

3 rap **4** skin **5** blame, blast, decry, knock **6** rebuke, scathe **7** censure, condemn, upbraid **8** derogate, reproach **9** castigate, criticize, dress down, excoriate, reprehend, reprobate **10** denunciate, vituperate **11** incriminate **12** anathematize

de novo

4 anew, over **5** again, newly **6** afresh **8** once more **9** over again **11** from scratch

dense

4 dull, dumb **5** close, heavy, solid, thick, tight **6** obtuse, opaque, stupid **7** compact, crammed, crowded, doltish, serried **9** fatheaded, jam-packed **10** numskulled **11** block-headed, numbskulled, thickheaded **12** impenetrable

dent

4 bash, ding, flaw, nick **5** tooth **6** dimple, hollow **10** depression, impression

denticulate

6 ridged **7** dentate, notched, serrate, serried, toothed **8** saw-edged, saw-tooth, serrated **10** saw-toothed

dentin

6 enamel

denude

4 bare **5** strip **6** divest **7** disrobe, uncover, undress **8** unclothe

denunciate
see **denounce**

deny
5 cross, rebut 6 disown, forbid, negate, refuse, refute, reject, renege 7 disavow, gainsay 8 abnegate, disallow, disclaim, forswear, renounce, traverse, withhold 9 disaffirm 10 contradict, contravene

depart
3 die 4 exit, flee, pass, quit 5 leave, scram, split 6 begone, decamp, demise, desert, escape, expire, go away, move on, pass on, perish, skidoo 7 decease, deviate, go forth, move out, pull out, skiddoo, take off, vamoose 8 pass away, shove off, slip away, withdraw 9 skedaddle, take leave

departing
6 egress, exodus 7 good-bye 8 farewell 9 desertion 11 leave-taking, valedictory

department
5 arena 6 branch, domain, sphere 7 section 8 category, division, province 9 bailiwick, territory 11 subdivision

departure
4 exit 5 adieu, break, congé, going 6 egress, exodus, flight 7 leaving 8 farewell 9 deviation, diversion 10 aberration, decampment, deflection, divergence, embarkment, setting-out, withdrawal 11 embarkation, leave-taking
of a ship: 6 sortie
point: 7 outport

dependable
4 sure, true 5 loyal, solid, tried 6 secure, steady, trusty 7 certain, staunch 8 accurate, constant, faithful, reliable, surefire 9 authentic, steadfast, unfailing 11 responsible, trustworthy 12 tried and true 13 authoritative
Scottish: 6 sicker

dependence
4 need 5 faith, habit, stock, trust 8 reliance 9 addiction 11 contingency, habituation

dependent
5 child 6 minion, vassal 7 reliant, relying 9 secondary 10 contingent, equivalent 11 conditional, subordinate

depend on
5 bet on, trust 6 bank on, hang on, look to, rely on, turn on 7 build on, count on, hinge on, stand on, swear by

depict
4 draw, limn, show 5 image, paint 6 relate, render, sketch 7 express, picture, portray 8 describe 9 delineate, represent 10 illustrate

depiction
5 image 6 sketch 7 drawing, picture 9 portrayal, rendering 11 delineation, portraiture, presentment 12 illustration, presentation

deplete
3 sap 4 milk 5 bleed, drain, eat up, empty, leech, use up 6 expend, lessen, reduce 7 consume, draw off, exhaust 8 decrease, diminish, draw down 9 undermine 10 run through

depleted
6 sapped, used up 7 drained, reduced 8 consumed, expended 9 exhausted, washed-out

deplorable
5 awful 6 rotten, woeful 8 dreadful, god-awful, grievous, terrible, wretched 9 execrable, miserable, sickening 10 calamitous, disastrous, lamentable 11 distressing, intolerable 12 contemptible, disreputable, heartrending 13 heartbreaking, reprehensible

deplore
3 rue 5 abhor, mourn 6 bemoan, bewail, grieve, lament, regret 7 condemn 8 denounce, object to 9 deprecate 10 disapprove

deploy

3 use 5 array 6 muster, unfold
7 arrange, display, dispose, marshal,
utilize 8 position

_____ de plume

3 nom

depone

5 state, swear 6 affirm, assert,
attest 7 certify, confirm, declare,
testify, warrant 11 corroborate
12 authenticate

deport

3 act 4 bear 5 carry, exile, expel
6 acquit, banish, behave, demean
7 conduct, displace, relegate
10 expatriate

deportee

5 exile 8 expellee

deportment

3 air, set 4 mien, port 6 aspect,
manner 7 address, bearing, conduct, manners 8 behavior, carriage,
demeanor, presence

depose

4 aver, avow, oust 5 state, swear
6 affirm, assert, avouch, remove,
topple, unmake 7 declare, profess,
testify, uncrown 8 dethrone, displace, throw out, unthrone 9 overthrow

deposit

3 lay 4 bank, drop, dump, fund,
lees, pawn, save, stow 5 cache,
chest, dregs, place, put by, stash,
store 6 settle 7 consign, grounds,
lay away 8 put aside, security,
sediment, sock away 9 settlings
11 precipitate 13 precipitation
alluvial: 5 delta
black: 4 soot
calcium carbonate: 10 stalactite,
stalagmite
containing gold: 6 placer
eggs: 5 spawn
geologic: 7 horizon
glacial: 4 till 5 drift, esker 7 moraine

loam: 5 loess
mineral: 4 lode 10 concretion
muddy: 6 sludge
sand: 4 bank 5 beach
sedimentary: 4 silt
skeletal: 5 coral
stolen goods: 5 fence
stream: 8 alluvium, sediment
tooth: 6 tartar

deposition

6 avowal 7 ousting, placing 9 affidavit, dismissal, testimony 10 testifying
11 attestation, declaration

depository

4 bank, dump, safe 5 attic, cache,
depot, store, vault 7 archive, arsenal
8 magazine 9 warehouse 10 storehouse
for bones: 7 ossuary

depot

4 dump 5 cache, store 6 armory,
garage 7 arsenal, station 8 magazine, terminal, terminus 9 warehouse 10 depository, repository,
storehouse 12 station house

deprave

4 warp 6 debase 7 corrupt, debauch, pervert, vitiate 9 brutalize
10 bastardize, bestialize, demoralize

depraved

3 bad, low 4 base, evil, ugly, vile
6 putrid, rotten, wanton, warped,
wicked 7 bestial, corrupt, debased,
immoral, twisted, vicious 8 degraded, perverse, vitiated 9 corrupted, debauched, miscreant,
nefarious, perverted, reprobate
10 degenerate

depravity

4 vice 8 baseness 9 abasement,
decadence 10 corruption, debasement, debauchery, degeneracy,
immorality, perversion 12 degeneration

deprecate

7 frown on, put down 8 belittle,
derogate, disfavor, object to, play

down, pooh-pooh **9** disparage
10 disapprove **12** disapprove of

depreciate
4 drop, fall. **5** abate, decry, erode,
lower **6** lessen, reduce, slight
7 cheapen, devalue, put down
8 belittle, decrease, derogate, diminish, discount, mark down, write off
9 devaluate, disparage, downgrade,
underrate **10** devalorize, undervalue
11 detract from

depreciation
8 discount **11** denigration **12** belittlement **13** disparagement

depreciative
9 slighting **10** derogatory, detracting,
pejorative **11** disparaging, underrating **12** undervaluing

depredate
4 sack **5** waste **6** ravage **7** despoil,
pillage, plunder **8** desolate, lay
waste, prey upon, spoliate **9** desecrate, devastate, vandalize

depredation
4 sack **5** havoc **7** pillage, plunder,
sacking **8** ravaging **9** marauding,
ruination **10** spoliation **11** desecration, destruction, devastation **12** despoliation

depredator
6 looter, raider, vandal **7** forager,
spoiler **8** marauder **9** plunderer
10 freebooter

depress
4 damp, dash, dent **5** chill, daunt,
lower **6** dampen, deject, dismay,
sadden **7** afflict, trouble **8** dispirit,
enfeeble **9** disparage, weigh down
10 discourage, dishearten

depressed
3 low, sad **4** blue, down, glum, sunk
6 broody, gloomy, glumpy, lonely,
somber **8** cast down, dejected,
downcast **9** bummed out, flattened,
woebegone **10** dispirited, lugubrious, melancholy, spiritless **11** crestfallen, downhearted, melancholic
12 disconsolate **13** disadvantaged

depressing
3 sad **5** bleak **6** dismal, dreary,
gloomy, somber, sombre **7** joyless
8 funereal, mournful **9** saddening
10 melancholy, oppressive **11** melancholic **13** disheartening

depression
3 dip, low, pit, sag **4** bust, drop, funk,
hole, sink, vale **5** basin, blues, dolor,
dumps, ennui, gloom, scoop, slump
6 cavity, crater, hollow, pocket, valley
7 cyclone, decline, sadness, sinkage
8 downturn, sinkhole **9** concavity,
dejection **10** desolation, melancholy
11 melancholia, unhappiness
anatomical: 5 fossa, fovea **6** foveae
(plural)
geographic: 7 Qattara
in ridge: 3 col
in snow: 8 sitzmark
small: 4 dent **6** dimple

depressive
4 blue, dour, glum **6** woeful **7** doleful
8 downbeat, downcast, mournful
9 miserable, woebegone **11** despondent, melancholy **11** low-spirited

deprivation
4 lack, loss **6** denial **7** forfeit, removal
10 forfeiture **11** bereavement,
divestiture **13** dispossession

deprive
3 rob **5** strip **6** divest **8** disseise,
disseize **10** disinherit, dispossess
of brilliancy: 4 dull **6** deaden
of courage: 7 unnerve
of sensation: 6 benumb

depth
4 base, drop, gulf **5** abyss, chasm,
gorge **7** lowness **10** profundity
measure: 6 fathom
of water: 5 draft **7** draught

depthless
7 cursory, shallow, sketchy **10** uncritical **11** superficial

Dept. of ___
5 Labor, State **6** Energy **7** Defense,
Justice **8** Commerce, Interior,
Treasury **9** Education **11** Agriculture

deputize

4 name 6 assign 7 appoint, empower, warrant 8 delegate 9 authorize, designate 10 commission

deputy

4 aide 5 agent, proxy 6 backup,
factor 8 delegate 9 assistant, catchpole, surrogate

derange

4 muss 5 craze, upset 6 madden,
mess up 7 confuse, perturb, unhinge
8 confound, disarray, disorder, distract, unsettle 9 interrupt, unbalance
10 discompose 11 disorganize

deranged

3 mad 4 loco 5 crazy, wacko
6 crazed, insane, maniac 7 berserk,
cracked, haywire, lunatic, unsound
8 demented, maniacal 9 disturbed
10 disordered, flipped out, unbalanced

derangement

4 mess 5 chaos, mania 6 lunacy,
muddle 7 madness 8 dementia,
disorder, insanity 9 confusion,
unbalance 10 hodgepodge 11 distraction, disturbance, psychopathy

derby

3 hat 4 race 7 contest 9 horse race

derelict

3 bum 4 hobo, lorn 5 tramp 6 remiss,
shabby 7 drifter, outcast, run-down,
uncouth, vagrant 8 careless, deserted, vagabond 9 abandoned,
negligent 10 neglectful 11 dilapidated 12 disregardful, undependable 13 irresponsible

dereliction

5 fault 7 default, failure, neglect
9 deviation, disregard, oversight
11 abandonment, delinquency,
shortcoming

deride

3 rag, rap 4 gibe, jeer, jibe, lout,
mock, quiz, razz, twit 5 fleer, rally,
scoff, scout, sneer, taunt 6 dump
on, insult 7 catcall 8 ridicule

de rigueur

5 right 6 au fait, decent, proper
7 correct 8 becoming, decorous,
required 9 essential, mandatory,
requisite 10 compulsory, obligatory,
prescribed 11 comme il faut

derision

5 abuse, scorn 7 disdain, mockery,
ribbing 8 contempt, raillery, ridicule,
scoffing 9 contumely, invective

derisive

7 abusive, jeering, mocking 8 sardonic, scoffing, scornful, taunting
9 insulting, sarcastic 10 disdainful
12 contemptuous

derivable

7 a priori 9 deducible, deductive,
traceable 10 obtainable 11 extract-
able 12 attributable, determinable

derivation

4 root 6 origin, source 7 descent
9 etymology 10 provenance, wellspring 11 origination, provenience

derivative

5 banal 7 spin-off 8 acquired,
offshoot 9 by-product, imitative,
outgrowth, secondary 10 descendant, unoriginal

derive

3 get 4 draw, flow, rise, stem, take
5 adapt, arise, educe, infer, issue,
trace 6 deduce, deduct, evolve,
gather, obtain 7 descend, emanate,
extract, proceed, work out 8 arrive
at, conclude 9 formulate, originate

dernier cri

3 fad 4 chic, rage 5 craze, vogue
8 last word

derogate

5 decry 6 berate, dump on, insult
7 put down 8 bad-mouth, belittle,
diminish, minimize, write off 9 disparage, dispraise 10 depreciate
11 detract from

derogatory

5 snide 8 decrying, scornful, spiteful
9 degrading, demeaning, maligning,

slighting **10** belittling, detracting, disdainful, pejorative **11** disparaging **12** contumelious, depreciative

derrick
5 hoist

derriere
3 bum **4** beam, butt, rear, rump, seat, tail **5** fanny **6** behind, bottom **7** rear end **8** backside, buttocks **9** posterior

derring-do
4 guts **5** nerve, pluck, spunk, valor **6** daring, mettle **7** bravado, bravery, bravura, courage **8** boldness **9** gallantry **12** fearlessness **13** dauntlessness

dervish
4 monk, Sufi **9** mendicant
in Arabian Nights: 4 Agib
practice: 7 dancing **8** whirling
wandering: 5 fakir **8** calender

descant
4 sing **6** melody, remark, treble **7** comment, discuss, melisma, melodia, oration, soprano **9** discourse, expatiate **12** counterpoint

Descartes's axiom
13 cogito ergo sum

descend
4 dive, drop, fall, pass, sink **5** slide, stoop, swoop **6** alight, derive, go down, plunge, worsen **7** decline **8** come down, dismount **9** originate **10** degenerate, retrograde
by rope: 6 rappel

descendant
4 heir **5** scion **7** progeny, spin-off **8** offshoot, relative **9** by-product, offspring, outgrowth **10** derivative

descendants
4 seed **5** brood, heirs, issue, spawn **6** litter **7** progeny **8** children **9** offspring, posterity **11** progeniture

descent
3 dip **4** drop, fall **5** birth, blood, slide, slope **6** origin, plunge, tumble **7** decline, drop-off, incline, lineage, sinkage **8** ancestry, comedown,

gradient, pedigree **9** declivity, downgrade **10** derivation, devolution, extraction
airplane: 8 approach
parachute: 4 jump **7** bailout

describe
4 limn **6** denote, depict, recite, relate, render, report **7** explain, express, mark out, narrate, outline, picture, portray, recount **9** delineate, represent **10** illustrate **12** characterize

description
3 ilk **4** kind, sort, type **6** nature, report **7** account, picture, species **9** character, depiction, narrative, portrayal **10** recounting

descry
3 see **4** espy, spot **6** behold, detect, spy out, turn up **7** discern, find out, hit upon **8** discover, meet with, perceive **9** encounter, recognize

Desdemona
father: 9 Brabantio
husband: 7 Othello
slanderer: 4 Iago
slayer: 7 Othello

desecrate
4 sack **5** stain, sully, waste **6** befoul, debase, defile, ravage **7** corrupt, degrade, despoil, pillage, pollute, profane, violate **8** spoliate **9** depredate, devastate

desecration
5 abuse **7** impiety **9** blasphemy, sacrilege **10** debasement, defilement, spoliation **11** profanation **12** despoliation

desensitize
4 dull, numb **5** blunt **6** benumb, dampen, deaden, freeze, sedate **11** anesthetize

desert
4 flee, quit **5** leave, waste **6** barren, betray, decamp, defect, escape, maroon, strand **7** abandon, abscond, badland, forsake **8** renounce **9** repudiate, wasteland **10** apostatize, wilderness **12** tergiversate

African: 5 Namib 6 Libyan, Sahara
7 Arabian 8 Kalahari
Arizona: 7 Painted
Asian: 4 Gobi, Thar 6 Syrian
7 Kara-Kum 8 Kyzyl Kum, Qizilkum
10 Great Sandy
basin bottom: 5 playa
beast: 5 camel 9 dromedary
California: 6 Mohave, Mojave
Chilean: 7 Atacama
clay: 5 adobe
dweller: 4 Arab 5 nomad 6 Berber,
Libyan, Malian, Nubian 7 bedouin
8 Algerian, Egyptian, Maghrebi,
Maghribi, Sudanese 11 Mauritanian
Egyptian: 7 Arabian
fertile area: 5 oases (plural), oasis
garb: 3 aba
hallucination: 6 mirage
Israeli: 5 Negev
region: 3 erg
Saudi Arabia: 7 Al-Nafud, An
Nafud
Sudan: 6 Nubian
travel group: 7 caravan
wind: 7 sirocco

deserted
4 bare, lorn 6 barren, vacant 8 derelict, desolate, forsaken, solitary
9 abandoned, neglected 11 uninhabited

deserter
3 rat 4 AWOL 6 bolter 7 runaway
8 apostate, defector, fugitive, renegade, runagate, turncoat

desertion
7 perfidy 8 apostasy 9 defection,
forsaking 11 abandonment, dereic-
tion

deserts
3 due 6 reward 8 requital 9 reckoning 10 recompense 11 comeuppance

deserve
3 win 4 earn, gain, rate 5 merit
6 demand 7 justify, warrant

deserved
3 apt, due 4 just 5 right 7 fitting,
merited 8 rightful, suitable 9 befitting
11 appropriate 13 rhadamanthine

deserving
3 due 6 worthy 8 laudable 9 admirable, estimable 10 creditable
11 commendable, meritorious, thankworthy 12 praiseworthy

desiccate
3 dry 5 dry up, parch, wizen 6 wither
7 shrivel 9 dehydrate 10 devitalize

desiderate
4 want, wish 5 covet, crave 6 desire
7 long for, wish for 8 yearn for

design
3 aim 4 cast, draw, form, mean,
mind, plan, plot, will 5 chart, draft,
frame, model, motif 6 create, device,
devise, figure, intend, intent, invent,
lay out, makeup, map out, motive,
scheme, set out, sketch, tailor
7 arrange, diagram, drawing, execute, fashion, meaning, outline,
pattern, prepare, project, propose,
tracing 8 contrive, creation, game
plan, intrigue, strategy, thinking
9 blueprint, construct, delineate,
direction, formation, intention,
invention 10 decoration, figuration
11 arrangement, composition 12 architecture, construction
book: 8 vignette
carpet: 3 gul 9 medallion
incised: 8 intaglio
Indonesian: 5 batik
inlaid: 6 mosaic
intricate: 9 arabesque
of squares: 5 check
openwork: 8 filigree
perforated: 7 stencil
raised: 8 repoussé
skin: 6 tattoo
textile: 8 polka dot
velvety: 8 flocking

designate
3 dub, tap 4 call, name, pick, term
5 allot, elect, label, style, title 6 assign, choose, denote, depute, select
7 appoint, declare, earmark, reserve,
signify, specify 8 allocate, christen,
delegate, identify, set aside, stand
for 9 apportion, stipulate 10 decide
upon 11 appropriate 12 characterize

designation
4 name, sign 5 class, nomen, style, title 6 naming 8 cognomen, monicker 11 appellation

designed
7 devised, planned 8 intended, resolved 9 contrived, patterned 10 considered, deliberate, determined, thought-out 12 premeditated

designedly
9 expressly, knowingly, on purpose, purposely, willfully, wittingly 11 consciously, purposively 12 deliberately 13 intentionally

desirable
8 enviable, fetching 9 advisable, agreeable, preferred 10 attractive, beneficial 12 advantageous

desire
3 aim, yen 4 envy, eros, itch, lust, want, wish 5 covet, crave, fancy, go for, greed 6 pining, thirst 7 avarice, craving, long for, longing, passion 8 appetite, cupidity, petition, yearn for, yearning 9 eroticism, hankering, prurience, pruriency 10 aphrodisia, attraction, preference 11 inclination, lustfulness 13 concupiscence, lickerishness

desired
6 wanted 8 hoped-for 9 preferred, requested

desirous
6 greedy 7 athirst, craving, envious, longing, wishful, wishing 8 covetous, grasping 10 solicitous

desist
4 halt, quit, stop 5 cease, yield 7 forbear, hold off, refrain 8 knock off, leave off, surcease 11 discontinue

desistance
3 end 4 halt, stop 5 cease, close 6 ending, finish, period 8 stoppage, stopping 9 cessation 10 conclusion 11 termination

desk
5 booth, stand, table 7 counter, lectern, rolltop 8 lapboard 9 secretary 10 escritoire

adjunct: 8 inkstand, standish
item: 3 pad 7 blotter, inkwell
library: 6 carrel

desolate
4 bare, lorn, sack 5 alone, bleak, drear, stark, waste 6 barren, devoid, dismal, dreary, gloomy, ravage 7 despoil, forlorn, joyless, pillage, plunder 8 dejected, derelict, deserted, desolate, downcast, forsaken, lay waste, lifeless, lonesome, solitary, spoliate 9 abandoned, cheerless, depredate, desecrate, destitute, devastate, sorrowful 10 despondent 11 dilapidated 12 inconsolable 13 disheartening

desolation
3 woe 4 ruin 5 gloom, grief, waste 6 misery, sorrow 7 anguish, despair, sadness 8 bareness 9 bleakness, dejection, wasteland 10 loneliness 11 abandonment, devastation 12 wretchedness

despair
6 give up 8 lose hope

despairing
7 anxious, doleful, forlorn 8 dejected, desolate, hopeless, wretched 9 depressed 10 despondent 11 downhearted 12 disconsolate 13 brokenhearted

desperado
6 bandit, gunman, outlaw 7 bandito, brigand, convict, ruffian 8 criminal 9 cutthroat 10 gunslinger, highwayman, lawbreaker

desperate
4 bold, dire, rash 5 acute, risky 6 daring, futile 7 crucial, forlorn, frantic, useless, violent 8 critical, headlong, hopeless, reckless, shocking 9 foolhardy, impetuous 10 despondent, frustrated, outrageous, scandalous 11 climacteric, precipitate 12 overpowering 13 irretrievable

desperation
5 agony 7 anguish, despair 8 distress 11 distraction 12 hopelessness, wretchedness

despicable
3 low 4 base, foul, grim, mean, ugly, vile 5 awful, cheap, gross, sorry 6 abject, scurvy, shabby, sordid 7 beastly, hateful, ignoble, pitiful 8 pitiable, shameful, wretched 9 degrading, loathsome 10 deplorable, detestable 11 disgraceful, ignominious 12 contemptible, disreputable 13 reprehensible

despise
4 hate, shun, snub 5 abhor, avoid, scorn, spurn 6 detest, loathe, reject 7 contemn 8 execrate 9 abominate

despised one
6 pariah 7 outcast

despisement
4 hate 5 scorn 6 hatred, malice 7 disdain, ill will 8 aversion, contempt, loathing 9 antipathy, contumely 10 abhorrence 11 detestation

despite
8 although 11 in the face of 12 regardless of

despiteful
4 evil, mean 5 catty 6 bitchy, horrid, malign, odious, wicked 7 baleful, baneful, hostile, vicious 8 vengeful 9 malicious, rancorous, repellent 10 despicable, malevolent

despoil
4 sack 5 blast, strip, waste, wreck 6 denude, devour, maraud, ravage 7 pillage, plunder 8 desolate, spoliate 9 depredate, desecrate, devastate, strip away, vandalize 10 wreak havoc

despoiler
6 looter, sacker, vandal 7 ravager, wrecker 8 marauder, pillager 9 plunderer, spoliator 10 depredator, freebooter

despond
4 fret, mope, wilt 5 brood, droop, worry 6 give up, sorrow 8 languish 9 dejection 12 hopelessness

despondency
5 blues, dumps, gloom 6 misery, sorrow 7 anguish, despair, sadness 8 glumness 9 dejection 10 depression, melancholy 11 desperation, unhappiness 12 hopelessness

despondent
3 low, sad 4 blue, down, glum 7 doleful, forlorn 8 cast down, dejected, downcast, grieving, hopeless, mourning 9 depressed, desperate, heartsick, heartsore, sorrowful, woebegone 10 dispairing, dispirited, melancholy 11 discouraged, downhearted 12 disconsolate, disheartened

despot
4 czar, duce, tsar, tzar 5 ruler 6 tyrant 7 autarch, emperor 8 autocrat, dictator 9 oppressor, strong man

despotic
8 absolute 9 arbitrary, autarchic, imperious, tyrannous 10 autocratic, monocratic, tyrannical 11 dictatorial 12 totalitarian

despotism
7 czarism, tsarism, tyranny, tzarism 8 autarchy 9 autocracy 10 absolutism, domination 12 dictatorship

desquamate
4 pare, peel 5 scale 7 peel off 8 flake off, scale off 9 exfoliate

dessert
3 ice, pie 4 cake, flan, fool, tart 5 Betty, bombe, crepe, crisp, fruit, grunt, halva, Jell-O, melba, s'more, sweet, torte 6 afters, blintz, Danish, éclair, fondue, frappe, gâteau, halvah, hermit, junket, kuchen, mousse, pastry, sorbet, sundae, trifle 7 brownie, cobbler, compote, custard, gelatin, parfait, pudding, sabayon, sherbet, soufflé, spumoni, strudel 8 ambrosia, Bismarck, crostata, flummery, ice cream, macaroon, meringue, napoleon, pandowdy, streusel, tiramisu, turnover 9 charlotte, cream puff, fruitcake, petit four, shortcake 10 blancmange, brown Betty, cheesecake, frangipane, icebox cake, zabaglione

11 baked Alaska, banana split, crème brûlée, gingerbread 12 hasty pudding, zuppa inglese
French: 5 bombe 6 éclair, frappe, gâteau, mousse 7 parfait, sabayon 9 petit four 10 blancmange, frangipane
frozen: 5 bombe 7 parfait, sherbet
German: 6 kuchen 7 strudel
Italian: 7 cannoli, spumoni 8 tiramisu 10 zabaglione 12 zuppa inglese
Turkish: 5 halva 6 halvah

destination
3 aim, end, use 6 object, target 7 purpose 8 terminus 9 objective 10 appointing

destine
4 fate 6 assign, direct, intend 8 dedicate, set aside 9 designate, determine, preordain 10 foreordain 12 predetermine

destiny
3 lot 4 doom, fate 5 karma 6 design, future, kismet, Moirai 7 fortune, portion 8 prospect 9 hereafter 12 circumstance

destitute
4 bare, poor, void 5 broke, empty, needy 6 bereft, devoid, ruined 7 drained, lacking 8 bankrupt, depleted, dirt poor, divested, indigent, strapped, stripped 9 deficient, exhausted, penurious 10 bankrupted, stone-broke 11 impecunious 12 impoverished

destitution
6 penury 7 poverty 9 indigence, privation

destroy
3 axe, zap 4 doom, down, kill, nuke, raze, ruin, sack, slay, undo 5 crush, erase, quash, quell, smash, total, trash, waste, wrack, wreck 6 finish, lay low, mangle, ravage, rubble, rub out 7 abolish, atomize, despoil, expunge, nullify, pillage, shatter, wipe out 8 decimate, demolish, dispatch, dynamite, lay waste, pull down, snuff out, stamp out, tear down 9 devastate, dismantle, eradicate, extirpate, liquidate, pulverize 10 annihilate, extinguish 11 exterminate

destroyer
4 bane, ruin 6 tin can, vandal 7 undoing, warship 8 downfall

destruction
4 loss, ruin 5 havoc 7 killing, sacking, undoing 8 downfall 9 ruination 10 extinction 11 devastation, liquidation 12 annihilation

destructive
7 baneful, harmful, ruinous 8 damaging 9 corrosive, injurious 10 shattering 11 deleterious, detrimental

desuetude
6 disuse 7 closure, neglect 9 cessation 11 abandonment

desultory
6 casual, chance, fitful, random, spotty 7 aimless, erratic, offhand, vagrant 8 shifting, slipshod, sporadic, wavering 9 haphazard, hit-or-miss, unplanned 10 capricious, digressive, disjointed 11 purposeless 12 unmethodical, unsystematic

detach
4 free, part, undo, wean 5 sever 6 cut off, remove, sunder 7 disjoin, divorce, release 8 separate, uncouple, withdraw 9 disengage 10 disconnect 12 disaffiliate

detached
5 alone, aloof, apart 6 remote 7 distant, neutral, removed, severed 8 abstract, isolated, separate, unbiased 9 incurious, withdrawn 10 impersonal 11 indifferent, unconcerned, unconnected 12 uninterested 13 disinterested, dispassionate, unaccompanied

detachment
5 squad 7 divorce, rupture 8 disunion, division 9 partition 10 neutrality, separation 11 dissolution

detail

4 item, list, part 5 point 6 assign,
nicety, relate, report 7 appoint,
article, element, itemize, listing,
minutia, specify 8 allocate, spell out
9 enumerate, stipulate 10 assignment, particular 12 circumstance
13 particularize

detailed

4 full 6 minute 8 itemized, complete, thorough 10 blow-by-blow,
exhaustive, meticulous, particular
13 thoroughgoing

detain

3 nab 4 bust, curb, hold, keep, mire,
snag 5 check, delay, run in 6 arrest,
collar, hang up, hinder, hold up,
impede, pick up, retard, slow up
7 bog down, reserve, set back 8 hold
back, keep back, restrain, slow down,
withhold 9 apprehend 10 buttonhole
in conversation: 10 buttonhole

detect

4 espy, find, spot 5 catch, dig up, hit
on, scent 6 descry, notice, turn up
7 discern, hit upon, uncover, unearth
8 discover, meet with 9 ascertain,
encounter, ferret out, track down

detectable

6 patent 7 evident, visible 8 sensible,
tangible 10 noticeable, observable
11 discernible, perceptible

detection

9 discovery 10 unearthing
system: 5 radar, sofar

detective

4 dick, G-man 6 shamus, sleuth
7 gumshoe 8 hawkshaw, informer,
sherlock 9 inspector 10 private eye
12 investigator
fictional: 4 Chan (Charlie), Gray
(Cordelia), Moto (Mr.) 5 Banks (Alan),
Bosch (Harry), Brown (Father), Dupin
(Auguste), Lecoq, Lupin (Arsène),
McGee (Travis), Morse (Inspector),
Queen (Ellery), Rebus (John), Saint,
Spade (Sam), Trent (Philip), Vance
(Philo), Wolfe (Nero) 6 Alleyn (Rod-
erick), Archer (Lew), Carter (Nick),
Hammer (Mike), Holmes (Sher-
lock), Marple (Miss Jane), McCone
(Sharon), Poirot (Hercule), Wimsey
(Peter) 7 Campion (Albert), Charles
(Nick, Nora), Maigret (Jules), Mar-
lowe (Philip) 8 Drummond (Bulldog),
Millhone (Kinsey) 9 Dalgleish
(Adam) 10 Robicheaux (Dave),
Warshawski (V. I.) 11 Father Brown

detective-story writer

3 Poe (Edgar Allan), Tey (Josephine)
4 Carr (John Dickson), Knox (Ronald)
5 Blake (Nicholas), Block (Law-
rence), Cross (Amanda), Doyle
(Arthur Conan), Green (Anna Kath-
erine), Innes (Michael), James
(P. D.), Marsh (Ngaio), Queen
(Ellery), Stout (Rex) 6 Bramah
(Ernest), Buchan (John), Hansen
(Joseph), McBain (Ed), Mosley
(Walter), Parker (Robert), Peters
(Ellis), Sayers (Dorothy L.) 7 Bentley
(E. C.), Biggers (Earl Derr), Collins
(Wilkie), Francis (Dick), Freeman
(Austin), Gardner (Erle Stanley),
Grafton (Sue), Hammett (Dashiell),
Hornung (E. W.), Rendell (Ruth),
Simenon (Georges), Van Dine (S. S.),
Wallace (Edgar) 8 Chandler (Ray-
mond), Christie (Agatha), Gaboriau
(Emile), Marquand (John), Paretsky
(Sara), Rinehart (Mary Roberts),
Spillane (Mickey) 9 Allingham
(Margery), Hillerman (Tony), Lock-
ridge (Frances, Richard), Macdonald
(Ross) 10 Chesterton (Gilbert Keith)

detention

6 arrest 7 holding 10 internment
11 confinement 12 imprisonment

deter

5 avert, block 6 divert, hinder,
impede, thwart 7 forfend, inhibit,
obviate, prevent, rule out, shut out,
ward off 8 dissuade, preclude,
restrain, stave off 9 forestall, turn
aside 10 discourage

deterge

4 wash 7 cleanse, wash off

detergent

4 soap 8 cleanser

deteriorate

3 rot **4** fade, fail, flag, sink, wear **5** decay, lapse, slide, spoil **6** weaken, worsen **7** decline, regress **8** languish **9** decompose, fall apart **10** debilitate, degenerate, depreciate, go downhill, retrograde, retrogress **12** disintegrate

deterioration

4 ruin **5** decay **6** ebbing, waning **7** atrophy, decline, erosion, failing, rotting **8** decaying, spoiling **9** crumbling, decadence, downgrade **10** debasement, degeneracy **12** degeneration, dégringolade

determinant

4 gene **5** agent, basis, cause, trait **6** factor, ground, reason **7** epitope, radical **9** attribute, influence

determinate

5 fixed **6** cymose **7** limited, precise, settled **8** constant, definite **10** definitive, restricted **11** established **13** circumscribed

determination

5 drive, spunk **6** fixing, mettle **7** finding, opinion, purpose, resolve, verdict **8** decision, firmness, judgment, tenacity **9** assurance, hardihood, impulsion, intention, resolving, willpower **10** conclusion, dedication, definition, doggedness, resolution, settlement **11** decidedness, intrepidity **12** perseverance, resoluteness, stubbornness **13** purposiveness

determine

3 fix, set **4** rule **5** bound, limit, prove **6** decide, figure, ordain, settle **7** control, delimit, find out, mark out, measure, preform, unearth **8** conclude, discover, regulate **9** ascertain, demarcate, establish, preordain, resolve on **10** delimitate, foreordain, predestine, predispose

determined

3 set **4** bent **5** fixed **6** driven, intent **7** decided, earnest, serious, settled **8** decisive, hellbent, resolute, resolved, stubborn **9** tenacious **10** persistent, purposeful, unwavering **11** established, persevering, unfaltering **12** foreordained, unhesitating

detest

4 hate **5** abhor, spurn **6** loathe **7** despise, dislike **8** execrate **9** abominate, repudiate

detestable

4 foul, vile **6** damned, horrid, odious **7** hateful, heinous **9** abhorrent, execrable, loathsome **10** abominable, despicable **12** contemptible

detestation

4 hate **6** hatred **8** anathema, aversion, loathing **9** repulsion, revulsion **10** abhorrence, execration, repugnance

dethrone

4 oust **6** depose **7** uncrown **8** displace

detonate

5 blast, burst, go off, spark **6** blow up, set off **7** explode **8** touch off

detonator

3 cap **4** fuse **9** explosive **11** blasting cap

detour

5 avoid, skirt **6** bypass **9** diversion

detract

6 divert, lessen, reduce **8** decrease, diminish, minimize **10** depreciate

detraction

9 aspersion, maligning, traducing **10** backbiting, belittling, derogation, slandering **11** denigration, deprecation, traducement **12** backstabbing, belittlement **13** disparagement

detractive

9 maligning, slighting, traducing, vilifying **10** defamatory, derogatory, pejorative **11** denigrating, disparaging **12** depreciative, depreciatory

detriment

4 harm, loss **6** damage, injury **7** marring **8** drawback **10** impairment **12** disadvantage

detrimental

3 bad, ill **7** adverse, harmful, hurtful, nocuous **8** damaging, negative **9** injurious **11** deleterious, unfavorable

detritus

4 tufa, tuff **5** scree, talus **6** debris, rubble **7** remains **11** odds and ends

Detroit

county: **5** Wayne
founder: **8** Cadillac (Sieur de)
lake: **4** Erie **10** Saint Clair
sobriquet: **6** Motown **9** Motor City

de trop

5 extra, spare **7** too much, surplus **9** excessive, redundant **10** gratuitous **11** superfluous **13** supernumerary

Deucalion

father: **10** Prometheus
kingdom: **6** Phthia
mother: **7** Clymene
son: **6** Hellen
wife: **6** Pyrrha

Deutschland über _____

5 alles

Devaki's son

7 Krishna

_____ De Valera

5 Eamon

devaluate

5 abase, decry, lower **6** reduce, weaken **7** cheapen, degrade **8** mark down, write off **9** undermine, underrate, write down **10** depreciate

devaluation

7 decline **10** debasement, declension **11** declination

devalue

see **depreciate**

devastate

4 raze, ruin, sack **5** waste **6** ravage **7** despoil, pillage, plunder **8** demolish, desolate, lay waste, overcome, spoliate **9** depredate, desecrate, overpower, overwhelm

devastation

4 loss, ruin **5** chaos, havoc, waste **6** ravage **7** pillage, plunder **8** disorder **9** confusion, ruination **10** demolition, desolation, spoliation **11** depredation

develop

3 age **4** form, grow **5** occur, reach, ripen **6** attain, dilate, evolve, expand, grow up, happen, mature, mellow, open up, thrive, unfold, unfurl **7** achieve, acquire, advance, burgeon, enlarge, expound, promote **8** flourish **9** actualize, elaborate, establish, transpire **11** come to light, materialize

development

5 phase **6** growth, result, spread **7** advance, buildup, outcome **8** ontogeny, progress, ripening **9** evolution, expansion, flowering, phylogeny, unfolding **10** maturation **11** elaboration, progression
of life: **10** biogenesis

Devi

7 goddess
consort: **5** Shiva
father: **7** Himavat
name: **3** Uma **4** Kali **5** Durga, Gauri, Chandi **7** Parvati

deviant

4 bent **5** kinky, queer **6** off-key **7** twisted, wayward **8** aberrant, abnormal, atypical, perverse **9** anomalous, different, divergent, irregular, unnatural **11** heteroclite

deviate

3 err, yaw **4** turn, vary, veer **5** sheer, stray **6** depart, swerve, wander **7** digress, diverge **8** aberrant **9** eccentric, turn aside

deviation

3 yaw **4** bend, tack, turn **5** error, shift **6** change **7** anomaly, turning, veering **8** variance **9** departure, diversion **10** aberration, alteration, deflection, divergence

device

4 ploy, tool **5** feint, gizmo, means, motif, motto, shift, thing, trick **6** dingus, doodad, emblem, figure,

gadget, gambit, hickey, jigger, medium, motive, symbol, widget **7** gimmick, machine, utensil, whatnot, whatsit **8** artifice, creation, insignia **9** apparatus, appliance, doohickey, expedient, implement, invention, makeshift, mechanism, thingummy **10** instrument **11** contraption, contrivance, inclination, thingamabob, thingamajig, thingumajig
automatic: 5 servo
binding: 5 clamp
fastening: 6 zipper
grasping: 4 tong
heating: 8 radiator
hoisting: 5 crane, lewis **8** windlass
holding: 4 vise **5** clamp

devil

5 beast, cloot, demon, fiend, rogue, Satan, scamp **6** Belial, diablo, dybbuk, rascal, spirit **7** Clootie, dickens, Lucifer, Old Nick, serpent, tempter, villain **8** Apollyon, Mephisto, scalawag, succubus **9** archfiend, Beelzebub, cacodemon, scoundrel, skeezicks **10** blackguard, Old Scratch **11** rapscallion

devilfish

3 ray **5** manta **7** octopus **8** manta ray **10** cephalopod

devilish

3 bad **4** evil **6** cursed, wicked **7** demonic, hellish, roguish, satanic **8** accursed, damnable, diabolic, fiendish, infernal, sinister **9** nefarious **10** diabolical, iniquitous, villainous **11** mischievous

devil-may-care

3 gay **4** rash, wild **6** rakish, sporty **7** raffish **8** carefree, rakehell, reckless **9** easygoing

devilry

7 knavery, roguery, sorcery, waggery **8** mischief **9** diablerie **10** wickedness, witchcraft **11** roguishness, waggishness **12** sportiveness

devious

3 sly **4** foxy, wily **6** artful, crafty, errant, erring, roving, shifty, sneaky, tricky **7** bending, crooked, cunning, curving, erratic, winding **8** aberrant, guileful, indirect, scheming, sneaking, twisting **9** deceptive, underhand, wandering **10** roundabout **11** out-of-the-way, underhanded

devise

4 form, plan, plot, will **5** chart, forge, frame, shape **6** cook up, create, design, invent, legacy, legate, scheme **7** arrange, bequest, concoct, connive, dope out, dream up, hatch up, project **8** bequeath, property **9** determine, formulate **11** inheritance

devitalize

3 sap **5** drain **6** deaden, weaken **7** exhaust **8** enfeeble **9** desiccate **10** eviscerate

devoid of

7 lacking, wanting **8** free from

devoir

3 job **4** duty, task, work **5** chore, stint **6** charge **9** committal **10** assignment, commitment, obligation

devolution

5 decay **7** decline, passing **8** receding, transfer **9** conferral, decadence, recession, surrender **10** conveyance, declension, degeneracy, regression, relegation, transferal **11** degradation **12** degeneration, dégringolade, retrograding, transference **13** retrogression

devolve

4 give, pass **6** pass on **8** hand down, hand over, relegate, transfer **10** degenerate

devote

5 apply **6** commit, direct, donate, hallow **7** reserve **8** dedicate, give over, sanctify **9** confirm in, habituate **10** consecrate

devoted

4 dear, fond, true **5** loyal **6** ardent, caring, doting, fervid, loving **7** dutiful, fervent, zealous **8** constant, faithful

devotee

9 dedicated 10 thoughtful 12 affectionate
religiously: 6 oblate

devotee

3 fan, nut 4 buff 5 hound, lover
6 addict, votary, zealot 7 admirer,
amateur, fanatic, fancier, habitué
8 follower 9 supporter 10 aficionado,
enthusiast

devotion

4 love, zeal 5 ardor, piety 6 fealty,
fervor, prayer 7 loyalty, passion
8 fidelity, fondness 9 adherence,
adoration, reverence 10 allegiance,
attachment, dedication, enthusiasm
12 faithfulness

devour

3 eat 4 eat up, enjoy 6 absorb,
feed on 7 consume, destroy, feast
on, pillage 8 prey upon, wolf down
9 delight in, feast upon, polish off,
swallow up 10 annihilate

devouring

4 avid 6 greedy 8 esurient, ravenous 9 voracious 10 gluttonous

devout

4 holy 5 godly, loyal, pious 6 ardent
7 earnest, fervent, serious, sincere,
zealous 8 faithful, reverent 9 pietistic, prayerful, religious

devoutness

4 zeal 5 ardor, piety 9 reverence
10 commitment

dew

5 sweat, tears 8 moisture 11 precipitate 12 perspiration 13 precipitation

dewy

3 wet 4 damp, pure 5 fresh, moist,
naive 7 artless, natural 8 innocent,
wide-eyed 9 credulous, guileless,
ingenuous, unworldly

dexter

5 right

dexterity

4 ease 5 craft, grace, skill 7 ability,
aptness, know-how, prowess, sleight
8 deftness, facility 9 adeptness,

expertise, readiness 10 adroitness,
nimbleness, smoothness 12 skillfulness

dexterous

3 apt 4 able, deft 5 adept, agile,
handy 6 adroit, artful, facile, nimble,
smooth 7 skilled 8 masterly, skillful
10 proficient

_____ Dhabi

3 Abu

diablerie

7 devilry, roguery, sorcery, waggery
8 deviltry, iniquity, mischief, satanism
9 devilment 10 black magic, wickedness, witchcraft, wrongdoing 11 roguishness, waggishness 12 sportiveness

diabolical

4 evil 5 awful 6 impish, wicked
7 beastly, demonic, heinous, hellish,
puckish, roguish, satanic 8 demoniac,
devilish, dreadful, fiendish, godawful, hellborn, infernal, rascally,
sinister 9 execrable, malicious,
monstrous, nefarious 10 degenerate, demoniacal, horrendous, iniquitous, scandalous, villainous 11 mischievous

diabolism

see **diablerie**

diacritic

5 acute, breve, grave, haček, tilde
6 macron, umlaut 7 cedilla 8 dieresis 9 diaeresis 10 circumflex
Arabic: 5 hamza 6 hamzah

diadem

5 crown 6 wreath 7 chaplet, coronal, coronet 8 headband

diagnose

4 spot 5 place 8 identify, pinpoint
9 determine, interpret, recognize
11 distinguish

diagnostic

8 analytic 10 analytical, expository,
indicating, indicative 11 explanatory,
exploratory 12 interpretive

diagonal

4 bias 5 bevel 6 biased 7 beveled,

oblique, slanted **8** inclined, slanting **9** inclining, slantways, slantwise

diagonally
9 slantways, slantwise **10** cornerwise **11** catercorner, kitty-corner

diagram
3 map **5** chart, graph **6** design, layout, sketch **7** drawing, isotype **9** represent

dial
4 call, face, knob, tune, turn **5** phone **6** rotate **7** control **10** manipulate

dialect
4 cant, jive **5** argot, idiom, koine, lingo, slang **6** creole, jargon, patois, patter, pidgin, speech, tongue **8** language, localism **10** vernacular **11** regionalism, terminology **13** provincialism
Georgia: 6 Gullah
London: 7 cockney

dialectic
5 logic **6** debate **8** dialogue, forensic **9** reasoning **10** discussion **11** disputation **13** argumentation, investigation

dialogue
4 chat, talk **6** confer, parley, script **8** colloquy, converse **12** conversation **13** confabulation

diameter
4 bore **5** chord, width **7** breadth, caliber **8** bisector, wideness **9** broadness

diametric
7 counter, opposed **8** contrary, converse, opposite **12** antithetical **13** contradictory

diamond
3 gem **5** field, stone
element: 6 carbon
famous: 4 Hope, Pitt **5** Sancy **6** Orloff, Regent **8** Braganza, Cullinan, Kohinoor **9** Excelsior **10** Great Mogul
inferior: 4 bort
oval: 9 briolette

pattern: 6 argyle
playing card: 7 lozenge
state: 8 Delaware
surface: 5 facet

Diana
see **Artemis**

diapason
4 peal, stop **5** range, scale, scope **7** compass, measure **8** spectrum **10** tuning fork

diaper
5 nappy **7** pattern **8** ornament

diaphanous
5 filmy, gauzy, sheer, vague **6** flimsy **8** ethereal, gossamer **11** transparent **13** insubstantial

diaphragm
4 stop **6** septum **8** membrane **9** partition

diarist
4 Gide (André) **5** Frank (Anne), Pepys (Samuel), Scott (Walter), Swift (Jonathan), Woolf (Virginia) **6** Burney (Fanny), Evelyn (John) **7** Boswell (James) **8** Robinson (Henry Crabb) **10** chronicler, journalist

diary
3 log **6** record **7** daybook, diurnal, journal, logbook **8** notebook, register **9** chronicle

diastase
6 enzyme **8** catalyst, reactant

diatribe
6 tirade **7** polemic **8** harangue, jeremiad **9** criticism, philippic **11** castigation **12** denunciation

dibs
4 gelt **5** claim, dough, money, title **6** rights **11** reservation

dice
4 cast, cube **5** bones, cubes, ivory, mince **11** devil's-bones
game: 5 craps
losing throw: 7 missout
singular: 3 die
throw: 7 boxcars **9** snake eyes

dicer
5 loser 6 risker 7 gambler

dicey
4 iffy 5 risky 6 chancy, tricky 8 ticklish 9 uncertain, whimsical 10 precarious, speculative 11 problematic 13 unpredictable

dichotomize
5 halve 7 dissect 8 hemisect 9 bifurcate

dichotomous
5 split 6 forked 7 pronged 9 bifurcate 10 bifurcated

dichotomy
7 forking 8 division 9 bisection, branching, splitting 11 bifurcation 13 contradiction

Dickens, Charles
birthplace: 10 Portsmouth
captain: 6 Cuttle
character: 3 Ada (Clare), Pip, Tim 4 Dick (Mr.), Dora, Gamp (Sairey), Heep (Uriah), Nell 5 Drood (Edwin), Emily, Fagin, Lucie (Manette), Sikes (Bill) 6 Barkis, Bumble (Mr.), Carton (Sydney), Cuttle (Capt.), Darnay (Charles), Dombey (Fanny, Florence, Paul), Dorrit (Amy), Oliver (Twist) 7 Barnaby (Rudge), Dedlock (Lady), Defarge, Gargery (Joe), Manette (Dr.), Scrooge (Ebenezer), Tiny Tim 8 Cratchit (Bob), Havisham (Miss), Jarndyce (John), Magwitch (Abel), Micawber (Mr.), Nickleby (Nicholas), Peggotty (Clara, Daniel, Ham), Pickwick (Mr.) 9 Bill Sikes, Gradgrind (Mr.), Murdstone (Mr.), Pecksniff (Mr.), Uriah Heep 10 Chuzzlewit (Anthony, Jonas, Martin), Steerforth 11 Copperfield (David)
hero: 6 Carton (Sydney)
nationality: 7 English
pen name: 3 Boz
villain: 5 Fagin
work: 9 Hard Times 10 Bleak House 11 Oliver Twist 12 Barnaby Rudge, Dombey and Son, Little Dorrit 14 Christmas Carol (A), Pickwick Papers (The) 15 Our Mutual Friend, Tale of Two Cities (A) 16 David Copperfield, Martin Chuzzlewit, Nicholas Nickleby 17 Great Expectations

dicker
4 deal, swap 5 argue, trade 6 barter, haggle, higgle, palter 7 bargain, chaffer 8 contract, huckster 9 negotiate

dickey
10 shirtfront

Dickey novel
11 Deliverance

dictate
3 set 4 lead, rule, word 5 edict, order, tenet 6 behest, decree, direct, enjoin, govern, impose, ordain, recite 7 bidding, command, control, lay down, mandate, read off, summons 9 determine, direction, directive, prescribe, principle, pronounce, verbalize 10 injunction 12 prescription

dictative
5 bossy 8 despotic, dogmatic 9 imperious 10 peremptory 11 doctrinaire, magisterial 13 authoritarian

dictator
4 czar, duce 6 caesar, despot, tyrant 8 autocrat, martinet 9 oppressor, strongman
German: 6 Hitler (Adolf)
Italian: 9 Mussolini (Benito)
military: 8 caudillo
Spanish: 8 Franco (Francisco)

dictatorial
5 bossy 8 despotic, dogmatic 9 arbitrary, imperious, masterful 10 autocratic, iron-handed, peremptory, tyrannical 11 doctrinaire, domineering, overbearing 12 totalitarian 13 authoritarian

dictatorship
7 tyranny 9 autocracy, Caesarism, despotism, supremacy 10 absolutism

diction
6 phrase, speech 7 wordage,

wording **8** delivery, language, parlance, phrasing, rhetoric, verbiage **9** elocution, verbalism **11** enunciation, phraseology

dictionary

7 lexicon **8** glossary, wordbook **10** repository **13** reference book
compiler: 7 Johnson (Samuel), Webster (Noah) **13** lexicographer
geographical: 9 gazetteer
of synonyms: 8 thesauri (plural) **9** thesaurus

dictum

4 fiat **5** adage, axiom, edict, maxim, moral **6** ruling **7** mandate, opinion, precept, proverb **11** declaration **13** pronouncement

didactic

5 moral **6** teachy **7** donnish, preachy **8** advisory, edifying, pedantic, sermonic, teaching **9** hortative, pedagogic, teacherly **10** moralizing **11** informative, instructive

diddle

3 con, gyp, toy **4** beat, bilk, dupe, hoax, fool, idle, laze, loaf, loll, rook, scam **5** cheat, cozen, delay, drone, trick **6** chisel, chouse, dabble, dawdle, delude, fiddle, fleece, loiter, lounge, rope in, take in **7** deceive, defraud, goof off, mislead, swindle **8** flimflam, fool with, hoodwink, lollygag **9** bamboozle, overreach, victimize, waste time **10** dilly-dally, fool around, hang around

diddler

3 gyp **4** sham **5** cheat, faker, fraud, rogue **6** con man **7** grifter, shammer, sharper **8** swindler **9** con artist, defrauder, trickster **11** flimflammer **12** double-dealer **13** confidence man

dido

4 jest, lark **5** antic, caper, curio, frill, prank **6** bauble, frolic, gewgaw, trifle, whimsy **7** bibelot, novelty, trinket **8** furbelow, gimcrack, kickshaw, mischief **9** bagatelle, plaything **10** knickknack, tomfoolery

Dido

6 Elissa
brother: 9 Pygmalion
city founded by: 8 Carthage
father: 5 Belus **6** Mutton
husband: 7 Acerbas **8** Sichaeus
lover: 6 Aeneas

Dido and Aeneas composer

7 Purcell (Henry)

die

4 drop, fall, mold, pass, stop, wane **5** cease, croak **6** cash in, demise, expire, go west, matrix, pass on, peg out, perish, pop off **7** decease, go south, kick off, snuff it, succumb **8** cash it in, check out, drop dead, pass away **9** disappear **10** buy the farm **12** join the choir **13** kick the bucket
from hunger: 6 starve
loaded: 6 fulham

____ die

4 sine

diehard

7 devoted, fanatic **8** true-blue **9** dogmatist **10** determined **11** bitterender, doctrinaire, reactionary, standpatter **12** conservative, intransigent **13** stick-in-the-mud

____ diem

3 per **5** carpe

Dies ____

4 Irae

diet

4 eats, fare, fast, feed, menu **6** ration, reduce, regime **7** regimen **8** assembly, victuals **10** parliament **11** legislature, nourishment

Diet of ____

5 Worms **6** Speyer, Spires **8** Augsburg

Dieu ____ (British motto)

10 et mon droit

____-dieu

4 prie

differ

4 vary **5** demur **7** deviate **8** disagree

difference

7 discord, dispute, dissent **8** conflict, contrast, variance **9** departure, deviation, disparity, otherness, variation **10** dissension, divergence, unlikeness **11** controversy, discrepancy, distinction **12** disagreement **13** dissimilarity

different

5 other **6** divers, single, sundry, unlike **7** another, deviant, distant, diverse, several, special, unalike, unequal, unusual, various **8** discrete, distinct, peculiar, separate **9** disparate, divergent **10** dissimilar, individual, particular **11** contrasting, distinctive

differentiate

4 vary **5** adapt **6** change, modify **8** contrast, separate **9** diversify, transform **11** distinguish, individuate **12** characterize, discriminate

difficult

4 hard **5** tough **6** thorny, uphill **7** arduous, awkward, labored, obscure, operose **8** exacting, perverse, puzzling, stubborn **9** demanding, effortful, herculean, laborious, strenuous **10** refractory **11** problematic

difficulty

3 ado, fix, jam **4** beef **4** pass, snag **5** hitch, nodus, pinch, rigor, worry **6** bother, hang-up, hassle, pickle, plight, scrape, strait **7** dilemma, pitfall, problem, trouble **8** distress, hardness, hardship, hot water, obstacle, quandary, quagmire, question, squabble **9** adversity, bickering, challenge, deep water, objection **10** falling-out, impediment **11** aggravation, altercation, arduousness, controversy, obstruction, predicament, vicissitude **12** complication, disagreement **13** embarrassment, inconvenience

diffidence

7 modesty, reserve, shyness **8** distrust, meekness, timidity **9** quietness, restraint, timidness **10** hesitation **11** bashfulness

diffident

3 shy **4** meek **5** timid **7** bashful **8** hesitant, reserved, retiring, timorous **9** reluctant, unassured **11** unassertive **12** self-effacing

diffuse

5 strew, wordy **6** prolix, spread **7** scatter, verbose **8** disperse, rambling **9** broadcast, dispersed, propagate, scattered, spreading, spread out **10** distribute, longwinded, widespread **11** disseminate, distributed

diffusion

6 spread **7** osmosis **9** broadcast, dispersal, prolixity, spreading **10** dispersion, scattering **11** circulation, propagation **12** broadcasting, promulgation

dig

3 jab **4** barb, grub, hole, like, mine, poke, prod, root, site, stab **5** delve, ditch, enjoy, gouge, nudge, probe, scoop, spade, taunt **6** burrow, plunge, quarry, relish, rootle, shovel, thrust, trench, tunnel **7** explore, root out, unearth **8** excavate, prospect **10** excavation **11** investigate
up: 6 exhume **7** unearth

digest

5 sum up **6** absorb, codify, précis **7** consume, stomach, summate, swallow **8** abstract, boil down, classify, compress, condense, syllabus, synopsis **9** summarize, summation, synopsize **10** abridgment **12** condensation

digger

4 plow **5** miner **6** shovel **7** soldier

digit

3 toe **5** thumb **6** cipher, figure, finger, number, pinkie **7** integer, numeral **9** character **11** whole number

dignified

4 prim **6** august, formal, proper, seemly **7** courtly, elegant, stately **8** cultured, decorous, ennobled, polished **9** distingué, patrician

dignify

5 adorn, exalt, grace, honor 7 ennoble, elevate, glorify, sublime
11 distinguish

dignitary

3 VIP 4 lion 5 chief, nabob 6 leader,
worthy 7 notable 8 eminence,
luminary 9 personage 10 notability
11 muckety-muck 13 high-muck-a-muck

dignity

4 rank 5 honor, merit, poise, pride,
worth 6 cachet, status, virtue 7 address, decorum, gravity, hauteur,
majesty, stature 8 grandeur, nobility, position, prestige, standing
9 propriety 10 augustness, seemliness 11 consequence, self-respect

digress

5 stray 6 depart, ramble, swerve,
wander 7 deviate, diverge 8 divagate

digression

5 aside 7 episode, tangent 8 drifting,
excursus, rambling, straying 9 deviation, wandering 10 deflection, divagation, divergence 11 parenthesis

dig up

4 find 6 expose, reveal 7 nose out,
root out, uncover, unearth 8 discover
9 ferret out, run across, search out,
track down

dik-dik

8 antelope

dike

3 dam 4 bank 5 ditch, drain, levee
7 barrier 8 causeway 10 embankment 11 watercourse

dilapidate

4 ruin 5 decay, wreck 7 break up,
crumble, decline, neglect 9 break
down, decompose, disregard 10 deliquesce 12 disintegrate

dilapidated

5 dingy, seedy 6 beat-up, ragtag,
ruined, shabby 7 decayed, run-down
8 battered, crumbled, decrepit
9 crumbling 10 broken-down, down-at-heel, ramshackle 12 deteriorated

dilapidation

4 ruin 5 decay 7 atrophy 8 collapse,
decaying 9 crumbling, decadence,
disrepair 11 decrepitude 13 decomposition, deterioration

dilate

5 swell, widen 6 expand, extend
7 distend, enlarge, expound 9 discourse, expatiate

dilatory

4 idle, slow 5 slack, tardy 7 laggard
8 dallying, delaying, sluggish 9 leisurely, lingering, unhurried 11 time-wasting

dilemma

3 box, fix, jam 4 bind, hole, spot
6 choice, corner, pickle, plight,
scrape 7 catch-22, problem 8 argument, quandary 10 difficulty 11 predicament

dilettante

4 tyro 7 amateur, dabbler 8 aesthete,
putterer 9 smatterer

dilettantish

see **amateurish**

diligence

4 zeal 8 industry 9 assiduity 10 commitment 11 application, persistence
12 perseverance, sedulousness
13 assiduousness

diligent

8 sedulous 9 assiduous 10 persistent, persisting, unflagging 11 hard-working, industrious, painstaking,
persevering

dilly

4 lulu 5 dandy, doozy, peach
6 corker, doozie, pippin, ripper, rouser
8 jim-dandy, knockout 9 humdinger
10 ripsnorter 11 crackerjack

dillydally

see **delay**

dilute

3 cut 4 thin, weak 5 water 6 watery,
weaken 8 diminish, weakened
9 attenuate, water down 11 watered-down

dim

4 dull, dumb, hazy, pale, slow
5 befog, blear, blind, cloud, dense,
dusky, faint, muddy, murky, muted,
thick, vague 6 bleary, gloomy, stupid
7 becloud, low beam, obscure, shadowy, subdued, unclear 9 tenebrous
10 ill-defined, indistinct, lackluster,
lusterless 11 unpromising

dime novel

4 pulp 7 chiller, shocker 8 dreadful,
thriller 12 bloodcurdler 13 penny
dreadful

dimension

4 size 5 reach, scale, scope, width
6 aspect, extent, spread 7 compass,
expanse, measure, quality 9 amplitude, magnitude

diminish

3 ebb 4 bate, wane 5 abate, peter,
quell, taper 6 lessen, reduce, subdue,
temper, weaken 7 curtail, dwindle,
subside 8 belittle, decrease, minimize, moderate, restrain, taper off
9 attenuate, disparage, dispraise
10 depreciate 11 detract from

diminishing

6 waning 8 receding 9 declining,
dwindling, lessening, subsiding,
weakening 10 curtailing, decreasing
11 attenuating 12 depreciating

diminutive

3 wee 4 tiny 5 bitsy, dwarf, pygmy,
small, teeny, weeny 6 bantam, little,
midget, minute, peewee, petite,
teensy 9 miniature, pint-sized,
undersize 10 teeny-weeny 11 lilliputian 12 teensy-weensy

_____ dimittis

4 Nunc

dimple

3 pit 4 dent, dint, fret, nick 5 notch
6 ripple 8 pockmark 10 depression
11 indentation

dimwit

3 oaf 4 clod, dodo, dolt, dope, fool,
simp, yo-yo 5 booby, chump, cluck,
dummy, dunce, idiot, moron, stupe
6 dum-dum 7 airhead, dullard,
fathead, pinhead 8 bonehead,
dumbbell, imbecile, lunkhead, meathead, numskull 9 birdbrain, blockhead, dumb bunny, dumb cluck,
ignoramus, lamebrain, numbskull,
simpleton 10 dunderhead, nincompoop 11 featherhead, knucklehead
12 featherbrain

dim-witted

4 dull, dumb, slow 6 stupid 7 doltish, foolish, idiotic, moronic 8 backward, imbecile, retarded 9 brainless,
half-baked, imbecilic 11 birdbrained,
lamebrained 12 feebleminded,
simpleminded

din

3 row 4 roar 5 babel, clash, noise
6 bedlam, clamor, deafen, hubbub,
racket, rattle, tumult, uproar 7 clangor, clatter, resound 8 brouhaha
9 commotion, stridency 10 hullabaloo, hurly-burly 11 pandemonium
13 clamorousness

Dinah

brother: 4 Levi 6 Simeon
father: 5 Jacob
mother: 4 Leah

dine

3 eat, sup 4 feed 5 feast 6 eat out
7 banquet, nourish

diner

4 café 5 eater 6 eatery 7 canteen
8 snack bar 9 hash house 10 coffee
shop, restaurant 11 greasy spoon
12 lunch counter, luncheonette,
sandwich shop

ding

3 mar 4 dent, nick 5 clang 7 blemish

ding-a-ling

3 nut 4 kook, yo-yo 5 flake, loony,
wacko 6 cuckoo, nitwit, weirdo
7 lunatic 8 crackpot 9 fruitcake,
harebrain, lamebrain, screwball
10 crackbrain 12 scatterbrain

dinghy

5 skiff 7 rowboat, shallop 8 lifeboat,
life raft, sailboat

dingle
4 dale, dell, glen, vale 6 ravine, valley

dingus
5 gizmo 6 doodad, gadget, jigger, widget 7 whatsit 9 doohickey, thingummy 11 thingamabob, thinga-majig, thingumajig

dingy
4 foul, mean 5 dirty, seedy, tacky 6 filthy, grubby, grungy, scuzzy, shabby, soiled, sordid 7 run-down, squalid, sullied, unclean 8 begrimed

dinky
3 toy 4 tiny 5 small, teeny 9 under-size 10 locomotive

"Dinner ____"
7 at Eight

dinner
4 meal 5 feast 6 regale, repast, spread, supper 7 banquet 8 lunch-eon 9 collation 10 table d'hôte
course: 4 meat, soup 5 salad 6 entrée 7 dessert 9 appetizer
jacket: 3 tux 6 tuxedo

dinosaur
6 fossil 7 has-been 8 theropod 11 anachronism

dinosauric
4 huge 5 passé 6 bygone 7 extinct, mammoth 8 colossal, enormous, obsolete, outmoded 9 cyclopean, leviathan, out-of-date 10 antiquated, behemothic, fossilized, gargantuan, mastodonic, oldfangled 11 elephan-tine 12 antediluvian, old-fashioned, out-of-fashion 13 anachronistic

dint
4 nick 5 force, might, power 6 dimple, virtue 7 drive in, impress 10 impres-sion 11 indentation

diocese
3 see 9 bishopric
Eastern Orthodox: 7 eparchy
subdivision: 6 parish

diode
9 rectifier 10 vacuum tube 12 elec-tron tube

component: 5 anode 7 cathode 9 electrode

Diomedes
city founded by: 4 Arpi
father: 4 Ares, Mars 6 Tydeus
foe: 6 Aeneas, Hector
slayer: 8 Hercules
victim: 6 Rhesus

Dione
5 Titan
cult partner: 4 Zeus
daughter: 5 Venus 9 Aphrodite
father: 7 Oceanus
lover: 4 Zeus
mother: 6 Tethys

Dionysus
see Bacchus

Dionyza's husband
5 Cleon

Dioscuri
5 twins 6 Castor, Gemini, Pollux
father: 4 Zeus 9 Tyndareus
mother: 4 Leda
sister: 5 Helen

dip
3 sag 4 bail, draw, drop, duck, dunk, fall, lade, sink, skid, slip, slue, swim 5 basin, ladle, lower, pitch, sauce, scoop, slope, slump, spoon, stoop 6 go down, hollow, plunge 7 decline, descend, descent, falloff, immerse, sinkage 8 decrease, downturn, sinkhole, submerge, submerse 9 concavity, declivity, downswing, downtrend, immersion 10 depression

diphthong
7 digraph 8 ligature

diploma
6 degree 7 charter 8 document 9 sheepskin 10 credential

diplomacy
4 tact 7 address, finesse 8 delicacy 10 artfulness, discretion, statecraft 11 negotiation, savoir faire, tactful-ness

diplomatic
4 deft 5 bland, suave 6 artful,

diplomat's office

astute, polite, smooth, urbane
7 courtly, politic, tactful 8 delicate,
discreet 9 courteous 12 conciliating,
conciliatory, paleographic 13 accommodating

diplomat's office

7 embassy, mission

diplopod

9 millipede

dipper

3 cup 4 bird 5 ladle, ouzel, scoop,
stars 6 bucket 10 pickpocket, water
ouzel

dippy

4 daft, zany 5 crazy, daffy, flaky,
goofy, kooky, loony, nutty, silly, wacky
6 stupid 7 doltish, foolish, witless
9 half-baked 11 harebrained 12 preposterous

dipsomania

10 alcoholism

dire

4 grim 5 acute, awful 6 dismal,
horrid, tragic, urgent, woeful 7 baleful, baneful, crucial, extreme, fateful,
ominous, ruinous 8 alarming, critical,
dreadful, grievous, horrible, horrific,
menacing, shocking, sinister, terrible
9 appalling, desperate, frightful, illboding 10 calamitous, deplorable,
depressing, foreboding, malevolent,
oppressing, oppressive, pernicious
11 apocalyptic, distressing, threatening

direct

4 head, lead, show 5 apply, frank,
guide, label, level, order, pilot, plain,
point, route, steer, train 6 assign,
charge, define, devote, divert, enjoin,
escort, extend, govern, lineal, linear,
manage, ordain, settle 7 address,
carry on, command, conduct, control,
genuine, nonstop, operate, oversee,
preside, project, request 8 dispatch,
instruct, regulate, shepherd, straight,
unbroken, verbatim 9 determine,
firsthand, immediate, prescribe
10 administer, contiguous, continu-

ous, inevitable 11 categorical, undeviating, unequivocal, word for word
a helmsman: 4 conn
proceedings: 7 preside

direction

3 way 4 east, line, path, side, west
5 angle, north, point, south, trend
6 course, design 7 bearing, channel,
command, purpose 8 guidance,
tendency 9 clockwise, oversight,
viewpoint 10 management, standpoint, trajectory 11 instruction,
supervision
blowing: 7 leeward 8 windward
horizontal: 7 azimuth
main line of: 4 axis
(see also **compass point**)

directive

4 fiat, memo, word, writ 5 edict,
order, ukase 6 charge, decree,
dictum, notice, ruling 7 bidding,
command, dictate, mandate 8 deciding, managing 9 presiding 10 assignment, injunction, memorandum
11 instruction, supervising, supervisory 12 policy-making 13 communication, pronouncement

directly

3 due 4 anon, soon 5 right, spang
6 at once, pronto 7 bluntly, by and
by, shortly 8 first off, in person,
promptly, squarely, straight, verbatim 9 forthwith, instanter, instantly,
presently, right away 10 face-to-face
11 immediately, straight off, straightway, word for word 12 contiguously,
straightaway

director

4 boss, head 5 chief 6 leader,
top dog 7 manager 8 overseer
9 conductor, organizer 10 head
honcho, supervisor

directory

4 list 5 guide, index 6 folder 7 catalog 8 register 9 catalogue 11 compilation

dirge

6 lament 7 requiem 8 threnody
11 lamentation
Gaelic: 8 coronach

dirigible
5 blimp 7 airship 8 zeppelin 9 steerable

dirk
4 stab 5 sword 6 dagger 7 poniard

dirt
3 mud 4 clay, dust, land, loam, mire, muck, porn, smut, soil, spot 5 earth, filth, fraud, grime, stain 6 gossip, ground 7 chicane, squalor 9 chicanery, excrement, indecency 10 corruption, hanky-panky 11 pornography

dirt-poor
4 bust 5 broke 8 beggared, indigent 9 destitute, flat broke, penniless, penurious 10 stone-broke 12 impoverished

dirty
3 low, tar 4 base, foul, lewd, smut, soil 5 bawdy, foggy, grimy, messy, mucky, muddy, murky, nasty, smear, sooty, stain, sully, taint 6 basely, befoul, coarse, debase, defile, filthy, grubby, impure, smudge, smutty, soiled, sordid, sully, vulgar 7 corrupt, defiled, hateful, immoral, obscene, raunchy, smutchy, spotted, squalid, squally, sullied, tainted, tarnish, unclean, unkempt 8 begrimed, besmirch, blustery, indecent, off-color, polluted, unchaste, unwashed 9 ill-gotten, uncleanly 10 abominable, blustering, scandalous, scurrilous 11 disgraceful, distasteful, distressing, tempestuous, unlaundered 12 contaminated, contemptible, disagreeable, dishonorable, scatological

Dis
see Pluto

disability
7 ailment 8 drawback, handicap 9 detriment, hindrance, infirmity, unfitness 10 affliction, impairment, impediment, incapacity 11 restriction, shortcoming 12 disadvantage

disable
3 sap 4 maim 5 spoil 6 hobble, weaken 7 cripple 8 enfeeble, handicap, paralyze, sabotage 9 hamstring, undermine 10 debilitate, immobilize 12 incapacitate
a racehorse: 6 nobble

disabled
7 hobbled 8 crippled 9 arthritic, paralyzed, rheumatic 11 handicapped 13 incapacitated

disabuse
4 free 5 emend, purge 7 correct, deliver, rectify, redress, release, relieve 8 liberate, unburden 9 enlighten, undeceive 10 illuminate 11 disencumber, disillusion

disaccharide
7 lactose, maltose, sucrose

disaccord
3 jar, war 4 vary 5 brawl, clash 6 combat, debate, differ 7 contest, contend, dispute, dissent, quarrel 8 conflict, disagree 12 disharmonize

disadvantage
3 bar 4 harm, loss 6 burden, damage, hamper 7 barrier, setback 8 drawback, handicap, obstacle 9 detriment, hindrance, liability, prejudice 10 impairment, impediment, imposition, limitation 11 deprivation, obstruction

disadvantaged
7 lacking 8 deprived 11 handicapped

disaffect
4 wean 5 alien, repel 8 alienate, disquiet, disunite, estrange 10 antagonize

disaffirm
4 deny 5 annul, belie, cross 6 abjure, impugn, negate, refute, reject 7 confute, explode, gainsay, reverse 8 disclaim, disprove, negative, traverse 9 repudiate 10 contradict, contravene

disagree
4 vary 5 argue, clash 6 bicker, differ, divide, haggle 7 contend, contest, dispute, dissent 8 conflict

disagreeable

4 ugly 7 peevish 8 annoying, petulant 9 offensive 10 unpleasant
11 disobliging, distressing, ill-tempered

disagreement

5 clash 6 debate 7 discord, dispute, quarrel, wrangle 8 argument, conflict, squabble, variance 9 disparity 10 contention, difference, dissension, divergence, unlikeness 11 altercation, controversy, discrepancy, incongruity

disallow

4 deny, veto 5 debar 6 enjoin, forbid, refuse, reject 7 disavow, dismiss, exclude, rule out, shut out 8 disclaim, prohibit 9 interdict, proscribe, repudiate

disallowance

4 veto 5 taboo 6 denial 7 refusal 9 disavowal, dismissal, exclusion, rejection 11 prohibition, repudiation 12 interdiction, proscription

_____-disant

3 soi

disappear

3 die 5 clear, leave 6 depart, die out, vanish 8 evanesce, fade away, melt away, pass away, slip away 9 evaporate, sneak away, steal away 13 dematerialize

disappoint

4 dash, foil, ruin 6 baffle, defeat, thwart 7 let down 9 frustrate 10 discourage, dishearten

disappointment

4 blow 6 bummer, defeat, downer 7 failure, letdown 8 comedown 9 bringdown 11 frustration

disapproval

4 veto 6 rebuke 7 censure, dislike, obloquy, reproof 8 reproach 9 criticism, objection, rejection
expression of: 3 boo 4 hiss, hoot, jeer 7 catcall 9 raspberry 10 Bronx cheer

disapprove

4 veto 6 oppose, reject 7 decline, dislike, dismiss, frown on 8 disfavor, turn down 9 dispraise

disarm

5 charm 6 allure 7 win over 8 sideline 9 captivate 10 neutralize

disarming

5 silky 6 silken 7 amiable, likable, winning, winsome 8 likeable, pleasing 9 endearing 10 convincing, persuasive, saccharine 11 deferential, insinuating 12 ingratiating

disarrange

4 mess 5 mix up, upset 6 jumble, mess up, mislay, muddle, muss up 7 confuse, disturb 8 disorder, displace, misplace, unsettle 10 discompose 11 disorganize

disarray

5 chaos 6 bedlam, jumble, mess up, muddle 7 clutter, undress 8 disorder, shambles, unsettle 9 confusion 10 discompose, dishabille

disassemble

6 detach 7 scatter 8 dismount, disperse, separate, take down, tear down 9 break down, come apart, dismantle, dismember, take apart

disassociate

5 sever, unfix 6 detach, sunder 7 back off 8 abstract, alienate, back down, disunite, liberate, separate, uncouple, withdraw 9 disengage 10 disconnect

disaster

3 woe 6 fiasco 7 debacle, failure, tragedy 8 calamity 9 cataclysm, ruination 11 catastrophe, devastation

disastrous

4 dire 5 fatal 6 tragic 7 fateful, ruinous 8 terrible 10 calamitous, horrendous 11 cataclysmic, destructive, devastating 12 catastrophic

disavow

4 deny 6 abjure, disown, impugn,

negate, recant, reject **7** forsake, gainsay, retract **8** abnegate, disclaim, forswear, negative, renounce **9** repudiate

disband

3 end **4** part **5** sever **6** divide, sunder **7** break up, dissect, divorce, scatter **8** disperse, dissolve, separate

disbelieve

5 doubt, scorn, scout **6** eschew, reject **7** scoff at, suspect **8** discount, distrust, mistrust, question **9** discredit, repudiate

disbeliever

5 cynic **7** doubter, sceptic, scoffer, skeptic **9** dissenter **10** questioner **11** freethinker

disbelieving

4 wary **5** leery **6** show-me **7** cynical, dubious **8** doubting **9** quizzical, skeptical **11** incredulous, mistrustful, questioning, unconvinced

disburden

4 shed **6** unlade, unload, unship, unstow **7** off-load, relieve **8** disgorge **9** discharge

disburse

3 pay **5** allot, issue **6** lay out, pay out, supply **7** deliver, dole out, furnish, provide **8** dispense, disperse **9** apportion, partition **10** distribute, measure out

disbursement

4 cost **5** funds **6** outlay **7** expense, payment **9** allotment **11** expenditure **12** distribution

discard

4 cast, drop, dump, junk, shed, toss, waif **5** chuck, ditch, eject, let go, scrap **6** reject **7** cast off, castoff, deep-six, jettison, shuck off, throw out **9** throw away, toss aside

discarnate

8 bodiless, ethereal, spectral **9** asomatous, unfleshly **10** immaterial,

unembodied, unphysical, wraithlike **11** disembodied, incorporeal, nonphysical **12** otherworldly **13** insubstantial

discern

3 see **4** know, note **5** grasp, sense **6** behold, detect, divine, notice **7** observe **8** identify, perceive **9** apprehend, ascertain, recognize **10** comprehend, understand **11** distinguish **12** discriminate **13** differentiate

discernible

7 visible **8** apparent, palpable **10** detectable, noticeable, observable **11** appreciable, perceivable **12** recognizable

discerning

4 keen **5** acute, aware **6** astute **7** knowing **9** clear-eyed, insighted, observant, sagacious **10** insightful, perceptive **12** clear-sighted **13** knowledgeable, perspicacious

discernment

6 acumen **7** insight **8** keenness, sagacity **9** intuition **10** astuteness, perception, shrewdness **11** penetration, percipience, recognition **12** perspicacity **13** comprehension, sagaciousness

discharge

3 can, pay **4** drop, emit, fire, free, gush, oust, quit, sack, spew, vent, void **5** annul, clear, demob, eject, empty, expel, exude, let go, loose, pay up, quash, salvo, shoot, utter **6** bounce, excuse, exempt, let fly, let off, loosen, outlet, remove, settle, unbind, unload, vacate **7** absolve, boot out, barrage, cashier, deliver, dismiss, exclude, excrete, execute, fulfill, give off, kick out, manumit, off-load, release, relieve, removal, satisfy, unchain **8** abrogate, aquittal, dispense, displace, dissolve, ejection, emission, get rid of, liberate, separate, throw off **9** acquittal, dismissal, eliminate, explosion, expulsion, muster out, pour forth,

send forth, terminate, unshackle
10 deactivate, demobilize, emancipate, inactivate, liberation, separation
11 exoneration, fulfillment
electrical: 5 spark **6** leader
8 streamer **9** lightning

disciple

3 fan **6** minion **7** apostle, devotee, learner **8** adherent, follower, henchman, partisan, retainer **9** supporter
10 enthusiast

disciplinarian

8 enforcer, martinet **10** taskmaster
11 slave driver

disciplinary

8 punitive **9** punishing **10** corrective

discipline

4 curb, rule, will **5** check, drill, field, guide, order, teach, train **6** bridle, direct, method, punish, school, subdue **7** chasten, conduct, control, correct, educate **8** approach, chastise, instruct, penalize, restrain, training **9** castigate, obedience, subjugate, will-power **10** correction, punishment **11** castigation, self-control, self-mastery **12** chastisement **13** self-restraint

disclaim

4 deny **6** abjure, reject **7** disavow, gainsay, retract **8** disallow, forswear, renounce, traverse **9** repudiate
10 contradict

disclose

3 own **4** avow, tell **5** spill **6** expose, impart, relate, report, reveal, unmask, unveil **7** display, divulge, uncover **8** discover, give away, unclothe **9** make known

disclosure

6 exposé **8** exposure **10** revelation
11 declaration

discolor

3 tar **4** blot, dull, fade, smut, soil
5 smear, stain, sully, taint, tinge
6 defile, smudge **7** besmear, bestain, tarnish **8** besmirch

discoloration

4 spot **5** stain, taint **6** blotch, bruise, smudge **7** blemish **9** birthmark

discomfit

3 irk, vex **4** faze **5** abash, annoy, upset **6** baffle, bother, defeat, rattle, thwart **7** fluster, nonplus, perturb, unnerve **8** confound **9** embarrass
10 discompose, disconcert

discomfiture

5 upset **6** unease **8** disquiet
9 abashment, agitation, confusion **10** uneasiness **11** frustration
12 discomposure, perturbation
13 embarrassment, inconvenience

discomfort

3 irk, vex **4** ache, pain **5** annoy
6 bother, unease **7** malaise **8** vexation **9** annoyance **10** uneasiness
13 embarrassment

discomforting

see **uncomfortable**

discommend

5 decry **7** censure, frown on, put down **8** admonish, disfavor, object to **9** criticize, deprecate, disesteem, disparage, reprehend **10** disapprove

discommode

3 irk, vex **5** annoy, upset **6** bother, burden, flurry, put out **7** disturb, fluster, perturb, trouble **8** encumber
9 aggravate, disoblige **13** inconvenience

discompose

3 irk, vex **5** annoy, harry, upset, worry **6** bother, dismay, flurry, harass, pester, plague, ruffle, untune
7 agitate, disturb, fluster, perturb, unhinge **8** disarray, disorder, unsettle **9** embarrass **10** disarrange
11 disorganize

discomposure

5 upset, worry **6** bother, unease
8 vexation **9** abashment, agitation, annoyance, confusion **10** discomfort, irritation, perplexity, uneasiness
11 disquietude **12** discomfiture, perturbation **13** consternation, embarrassment

disconcert

4 faze 5 abash, upset, worry 6 bemuse, bother, puzzle, rattle, ruffle 7 confuse, disturb, nonplus, perplex, perturb, trouble 8 bewilder, confound, disquiet 9 discomfit, embarrass, frustrate

disconfirm

4 deny 5 rebut 6 refute, negate 7 gainsay 8 abnegate, confound, disclaim, disprove 10 contradict, controvert

disconnect

3 cut, gap 5 break, sever, unfix 6 cut off, detach 7 disjoin 8 separate, uncouple 9 disengage 10 dissociate

disconnected

7 muddled 8 detached, separate 10 disjointed, incoherent, unattached 11 fragmentary, unorganized 13 discontinuous

disconsolate

3 low, sad 4 blue, down 5 bleak, drear 6 abject, dreary, gloomy, woeful 7 doleful, forlorn, joyless, unhappy 8 dejected, downcast, wretched 9 cheerless, depressed, miserable, sorrowful, woebegone 10 dispirited, melancholy 11 comfortless, crestfallen, downhearted

discontent

4 envy 9 dysphoria 10 depression, inquietude, uneasiness 11 displeasure 12 disaffection, restlessness

discontented

5 upset 6 uneasy 7 annoyed, fretful, unhappy 8 restless 9 disturbed, irritated, perturbed 10 displeased 11 complaining, disgruntled, ungratified, unsatisfied 12 dissatisfied

discontinuation

3 end 4 stop 5 cease, close, pause 6 ending, finish 7 closing 8 abeyance 9 cessation 10 conclusion, desistance, moratorium, suspension 12 postponement

discontinue

3 end 4 halt, quit, stay, stop 5 cease, close, sever 6 desist, give up, wind up, wrap up 8 break off, close out, conclude, knock off, leave off, shut down, surcease 9 terminate

discontinuity

3 gap 4 hole, rent, rift 5 break, cleft, crack, split 6 breach, lacuna 7 fissure, opening, rupture

discontinuous

6 fitful 7 muddled 8 discrete, separate 9 spasmodic 10 incoherent, incohesive 11 unconnected 12 disconnected, intermittent 13 nonsequential

discord

5 clash 6 enmity, rancor, strife 7 rupture 8 conflict, contrast, disunity, division, friction, mismatch, variance 9 animosity, antipathy, hostility 10 antagonism, contention, difference, dissension, dissidence, dissonance, opposition 12 inconsonance, polarization 13 inconsistency
goddess: 3 Ate 4 Eris

discordant

5 harsh 6 at odds 7 jarring 8 clashing, contrary, jangling, strident 9 dissonant 10 cacophonic, unpleasant 11 cacophonous, conflicting, disagreeing, inconsonant, quarrelsome, unmelodious 12 unharmonious

discotheque

6 bistro, nitery 7 hot spot 9 dance club, nightclub, night spot

discount

5 doubt, lower 6 deduct, ignore, reduce, slight 7 neglect, take off 8 belittle, derogate, decrease, diminish, knock off, mark down, markdown, minimize, overlook, roll back, rollback, subtract, take away 9 abatement, deduction, disregard, reduction, substract, underrate 13 underestimate

discountenance

4 faze 5 abash 6 rattle 7 frown on 8 confound, disfavor 9 deprecate,

discourage

discourage

398

discomfit, embarrass **10** disapprove, disconcert, discourage

discourage
4 damp **5** daunt, check, chill, deter **6** dampen, deject, divert, hinder, impede **7** depress, inhibit, trouble **8** disfavor, dissuade, suppress **10** demoralize, dishearten

discouraging
5 bleak **7** unhappy **8** daunting **9** deterring, troubling **10** depressing **11** unfavorable, unpromising **12** unpropitious **13** disappointing, disheartening

discourse
4 talk **5** argue, essay, orate, speak, spiel, voice **6** sermon, speech, thesis **7** amplify, descant, enlarge, explain, expound, lecture **8** converse, harangue, perorate, rhetoric, speaking, treatise **9** expatiate, hold forth, monograph, sermonize, utterance **10** expression **11** interchange **12** conversation **13** verbalization
art of: **8** rhetoric
religious: **6** homily, sermon

discourteous
4 rude **6** unkind **7** boorish, brusque, ill-bred, uncivil, uncouth **8** impolite **10** ungracious, unmannerly **11** ill-mannered, impertinent **13** disrespectful

discover
4 espy, find, spot **5** learn **6** betray, detect, expose, reveal, unmask **7** divulge, find out, observe, unearth **8** come upon, perceive, proclaim, unshroud **9** ascertain, determine, encounter, make known **10** come across

discovery
4 find **5** trove **6** espial, strike **7** finding **8** locating, sighting **9** detection **10** revelation, unearthing

discredit
4 slur, ruin **5** doubt, shame **6** defame, malign, show up **7** asperse, degrade, put down, run down, slander, traduce **8** disgrace, ignominy **9** dis-

parage, disrepute **10** disbelieve, opprobrium

discreditable
5 shady **6** shabby, shoddy **8** shameful, unworthy **9** degrading **10** inglorious **11** blameworthy, disgraceful, ignominious **12** contemptible, dishonorable, disreputable

discreet
4 wary **5** chary, muted, plain **6** modest, simple **7** careful, guarded, prudent, tactful **8** cautious, moderate **9** unadorned **10** controlled, reasonable, restrained **11** circumspect, considerate, unelaborate, unobtrusive **12** unnoticeable **13** unpretentious

discrepancy
3 gap **8** alterity, conflict, variance **9** disparity, otherness, variation **10** difference, divergence, divergency, unlikeness **12** disagreement **13** inconsistency

discrepant
6 unlike **7** diverse, varying **8** contrary **9** different, differing, disparate, divergent **11** conflicting, disagreeing **12** incompatible, inconsistent **13** contradictory

discrete
8 detached, distinct, separate **9** countable, different **12** disconnected **13** discontinuous, noncontinuous

discretion
4 care, tact **7** caution, reserve **8** delicacy, judgment, prudence, wariness **9** canniness, chariness, restraint **10** judiciousness

discriminate
5 judge **6** assess **7** compare, discern, make out **8** contrast, disfavor, evaluate, perceive, separate **9** segregate, tell apart **11** distinguish **13** differentiate

discriminating
6 choosy, select **7** finical, finicky **8** eclectic **9** judicious, selective **10** discerning **11** prejudicial

discrimination

5 taste 6 acumen 7 bigotry, insight 8 inequity, judgment 9 prejudice 10 astuteness, favoritism, partiality, perception 11 discernment, intolerance, penetration

discriminatory

6 biased 7 partial, unequal 8 partisan 9 jaundiced 10 prejudiced 11 inequitable, predisposed

discursive

5 windy, wordy 6 chatty, prolix 7 diffuse, logical, verbose 8 rambling, tortuous 9 desultory 10 analytical, circuitous, digressive, longwinded, meandering 11 wide-ranging

discuss

4 moot 5 argue, weigh 6 debate, parley 7 canvass, expound 8 consider, converse, hash over, talk over 9 elucidate, expatiate, interpret, talk about, thrash out, ventilate 10 deliberate, toss around
business: 8 talk shop
lightly: 5 bandy
thoroughly: 7 exhaust

discussion

3 rap 4 chat, talk 6 confab, debate, parley, powwow 7 canvass, palaver 8 argument, colloquy 10 conference, rap session 11 bull session, ventilation 12 conversation, deliberation 13 confabulation

discus thrower

6 Alekna (Virgilijus), Marten (Maritza), Oerter (Al) 10 discobolus 11 Rashchupkin (Viktor)

disdain

5 abhor, scorn, scout, spurn 6 deride, refuse, reject, slight 7 contemn, despise, despite, hauteur, put down 8 aversion, belittle, contempt, disprize, misprize 9 antipathy 10 repugnance, undervalue

disdainful

5 aloof, proud 6 averse, lordly, snooty, uppity 7 haughty 8 arrogant, cavalier, derisive, insolent, scorning, spurning, superior, toplofty 11 overbearing 12 antipathetic, contemptuous, supercilious 13 high and mighty

disease

3 bug, ill 5 upset, virus 6 blight, malady 7 ailment, anthrax, illness, malaise, mycosis, purpura 8 debility, disorder, epidemic, myxedema, pandemic, sickness, syndrome, zoonoses (plural), zoonosis 9 affection, black lung, complaint, condition, contagion, ill health, infection, infirmity, sclerosis 10 affliction, alteration, blackwater, bronchitis, feebleness, impairment, infirmness, sickliness 11 decrepitude, derangement 13 unhealthiness
animal: 5 mange, surra 6 rabies 7 bighead 8 enzootic, zoonosis 9 distemper, tularemia 10 rinderpest
blood: 8 leukemia, leukoses (plural), leukosis
cabbage: 8 clubroot
cattle: 6 cowpox 7 foot rot, locoism, murrain 8 blackleg, vaccinia 9 vibriosis 10 rinderpest 11 brucellosis
cereal grass: 4 bunt, smut 5 ergot
children's: 5 mumps 7 measles, rubella 10 chicken pox 13 whooping cough
citrus tree: 8 tristeza
classification: 8 nosology
combining form: 4 path 5 patho
communicable: 4 mono 5 mumps, polio 6 dengue, herpes, plague, rabies 7 cholera, leprosy, malaria, measles, rubella, tetanus, typhoid 8 impetigo 9 hepatitis, influenza 10 giardiasis 12 tuberculosis
deficiency: 6 scurvy 7 rickets 8 beriberi, pellagra
disseminator: 6 vector 7 carrier
eye: 8 glaucoma, trachoma 9 retinitis
hair follicle: 7 sycoses (plural), sycosis
heart: 11 cardiopathy
horse: 6 nagana, spavin 7 locosim, sarcoid 8 glanders 9 strangles
identification of: 9 diagnosis

industrial: 10 byssinosis
infectious: 4 mono, yaws **6** dengue, typhus **7** leprosy, malaria, tetanus, typhoid **9** tularemia, vibriosis **10** rinderpest **13** whooping cough
liver: 9 cirrhosis, hepatitis
livestock: 7 locoism **9** vibriosis **10** rinderpest
lung: 8 phthisic, phthisis **9** pneumonia **10** byssinosis **12** tuberculosis
lymph glands: 8 scrofula
metabolic: 4 gout
nervous system: 4 kuru **6** rabies **10** diphtheria
of beets: 8 heartrot
of mammals: 6 rabies **7** malaria **9** distemper **10** babesiosis, rinderpest
parasitic: 3 rot **4** smut **5** mange **7** malaria **8** hookworm, kala-azar **9** heartworm
plant: 4 rust, scab, smut, wilt **5** blast, edema, scald, scurf, stunt **6** blight, blotch, canker, mosaic, streak **7** blister, crinkle, foot rot, frogeye, red leaf, root rot **8** clubroot, curly top, fusarium, gummosis, leaf curl, leaf roll, leaf rust, leaf spot, ring spot, root knot, stem rust **9** chlorosis, crown gall, white rust **10** blackheart, leaf scorch
poultry: 8 leukosis
respiratory: 6 asthma, coryza **10** byssinosis
sheep: 3 gid **7** scrapie **9** vibriosis **10** bluetongue
skin: 4 acne, yaws **5** favus, hives, lupus, mange, pinta, tinea **6** eczema, tetter **7** leprosy, prurigo, sarcoid, scabies **8** impetigo, miliaria, pyoderma, ringworm, vitiligo **9** pemphigus, psoriasis **10** erysipelas **11** scleroderma
syphilitic: 5 tabes
throat: 5 croup
thyroid: 8 struma
tropical: 4 yaws **5** pinta, sprue, surra **6** dengue **8** kala-azar
venereal: 8 syphilis **9** chancroid, gonorrhea
viral: 3 flu **4** AIDS, noma **5** Ebola, mumps, polio **6** dengue, grippe, herpes, rabies, zoster **7** measles, rubella, rubeola, variola **8** morbilli, shingles, smallpox **9** hepatitis, influenza, varicella **13** poliomyelitis

diseased
3 ill **6** ailing, infirm, sickly, unwell **7** fevered, unsound **8** feverish, infected

disembark
4 land **6** alight **7** deplane, detrain **8** go ashore

disembarrass
3 rid **4** free **7** release, relieve **8** liberate, unburden, untangle **9** extricate **11** disencumber, disentangle

disembodied
7 ghostly **8** ethereal, spectral **9** asomatous, unfleshly **10** immaterial, unphysical, wraithlike **11** incorporeal, nonmaterial, nonphysical **13** insubstantial

disembogue
4 flow, gush, pour, spew **5** empty **7** pour out **9** discharge

disembowel
3 gut **10** eviscerate, exenterate

disenchanted
5 blasé, jaded **6** soured **7** cynical **9** jaundiced **10** undeceived **11** worldly-wise **12** disappointed, dissatisfied **13** disenthralled, disillusioned

disencumber
4 free **7** lighten, release, relieve, sort out **8** free from, liberate, unburden **9** alleviate, disburden, extricate

disengage
4 free, part **5** loose, unfix **6** detach, opt out, unbind **7** back up, drop out, release, unloose **8** cut loose, liberate, separate, uncouple, unfasten, unloosen, withdraw **10** disconnect

disentangle
5 untie **6** detach **7** resolve, sort out, unravel, unsnarl, untwine **8** separate **9** extricate **10** unscramble **11** disencumber **13** straighten out

disenthrall
4 free 7 manumit, release 8 liberate 10 emancipate

disfavor
7 dislike 8 aversion, distrust, mistrust 9 deprecate, disesteem, disregard, disrepute 10 disrespect 11 disapproval 12 disadvantage, unpopularity

disfigure
3 mar 4 maim, scar 6 deface, defile, deform, impair, injure, mangle 7 blemish, distort 8 mutilate

disfranchise
3 bar 7 exclude 8 take away 9 deprive of 10 disentitle

disgorge
4 barf, spew 5 belch, eject, eruct, erupt, expel, vomit 6 give up, irrupt, spit up 7 release, throw up, upchuck 9 discharge

disgrace
5 odium, shame 6 stigma 7 attaint, mortify, obloquy 8 black eye, contempt, dishonor, ignominy, reproach 9 discredit, disrepute, humiliate 10 opprobrium, stigmatize 11 degradation, humiliation

disgraceful
7 ignoble 8 shameful 9 degrading 10 deplorable, inglorious, unbecoming 11 humiliating, ignominious, reproachful 12 dishonorable, disreputable

disgruntled
5 vexed 6 cranky, put out 7 annoyed, beefing, griping 8 grousing 9 irritated 10 discontent, displeased, illhumored, malcontent 11 ungratified 12 discontented, malcontented

disguise
4 hide, mask, sham, veil 5 belie, cloak, feign, put on 6 facade 7 conceal, falsify, obscure 8 artifice, pretense 9 deception 10 camouflage, false front, pretension 12 misrepresent

disguised
6 masked, veiled 7 cloaked, feigned 9 incognito 10 undercover 11 camouflaged

disguisement
4 mask, veil 5 cloak, front 6 facade 8 pretense 9 deception 10 false front, pretention

disgust
6 nausea, offend, revolt, sicken 8 aversion, gross out, loathing, nauseate 9 antipathy, repulsion, revulsion 10 abhorrence, repugnance 13 squeamishness

disgusted
5 fed up 8 offended, repelled, repulsed, revolted, sickened 9 nauseated, squeamish 10 grossed out

disgusting
4 foul, icky, vile 5 gross, nasty, yucky 7 noisome 9 loathsome, offensive, repellent, repugnant, repulsive, revolting, sickening 10 nauseating

dish
4 bowl, buzz, food, talk, tray 5 plate 6 course, gossip, tureen 7 chatter, hearsay, platter, scandal, slander 9 casserole, container 11 scuttlebutt
baked: 7 soufflé
baking: 7 cocotte, scallop 9 casserole 12 scallop shell
cheese: 6 fondue 7 ramekin, rarebit 8 raclette, ramequin
Chinese: 6 dim sum, lo mein, subgum, wonton 8 chop suey, chow mein 10 egg foo yong, egg foo yung 11 egg foo young
deep: 9 casserole
Hungarian: 7 goulash
Italian: 5 penne, pesto, pizza 6 scampi 7 cannoli, lasagna, polenta, ravioli 8 calamari, linguine, linguini, osso buco, rigatoni 9 foccaccia, manicotti 10 cannelloni, scaloppine, tortellini 11 saltimbocca
Japanese: 7 sashimi, tempura 8 sukiyaki
Mexican: 4 taco 5 chili 6 fajita, flauta, nachos, tamale 7 burrito, chalupa 8 frijoles 9 enchilada, guacamole 10 carne asada 11 chimichanga 12 refried beans 13 chili con carne

Middle Eastern: 5 halva, kebab, kibbe, kibbi **6** halvah, hummus, kibbeh **7** baklava, falafel **8** couscous, moussaka **10** shish kebab **11** baba ghanouj **12** baba ghanoush
principal: 6 entrée
rice: 7 risotto
rice and meat: 5 pilaf
Scottish: 5 brose **6** haggis
shallow: 6 saucer
Thai: 7 pad thai

disharmonize
3 jar, war **5** clash **6** jangle **7** discord **8** conflict, mismatch **9** disaccord

disharmony
6 strife **7** discord **8** conflict, disunion, disunity, friction, variance **9** cacophony **10** contention, difference, dissension, dissonance

dishearten
3 cow **5** chill, crush, daunt, shake **6** dampen, deject, dismay, sadden **7** depress, unnerve **8** dispirit, distress **10** demoralize, discourage, intimidate

disheartening
8 daunting **9** dismaying, saddening **10** depressing **11** dispiriting **12** demoralizing, discouraging, intimidating

dishes
4 ware
clay: 7 pottery
porcelain: 5 china

dishevel
5 touse **6** muss up, rumple, tousle **8** disarray, disorder **10** disarrange, discompose

disheveled
5 messy **7** ruffled, rumpled, tousled, unkempt **8** ill-kempt, mussed up, uncombed **10** disarrayed, disordered **11** discomposed

dishonest
5 false, lying, rogue, snide **6** tricky, unfair **7** corrupt, crooked, knavish **8** cheating, cozening, two-faced **9** deceitful, deceiving, deceptive, swindling **10** defrauding, fraudulent,

mendacious, untruthful **13** double-dealing, untrustworthy

dishonesty
5 fraud, guile **6** deceit **7** falsity, knavery, roguery **8** flimflam, pretense, trickery **9** chicanery, deception, duplicity, falsehood, hypocrisy **10** corruption **11** crookedness **13** double-dealing

dishonor
see **disgrace**

dishonorable
see **disgraceful**

dish out
5 ladle, serve **6** pile on, supply **7** deliver, present, serve up **8** allocate, disburse, dispense **10** distribute

disillusioned
see **disenchanted**

disinclination
7 dislike **8** aversion, distaste **9** antipathy, objection **10** reluctance **13** indisposition, unwillingness

disinclined
5 loath **6** averse **7** balking, opposed **8** boggling, hesitant **9** reluctant, resistant, unwilling **10** hesitating, indisposed **12** antipathetic **13** unsympathetic

disinfect
6 purify **8** sanitize **9** autoclave, sterilize **13** decontaminate

disingenuous
3 sly **4** foxy, wily **5** false **6** artful, crafty, tricky **7** cunning, devious, feigned **8** delusive, guileful, indirect, specious **9** deceitful, deceiving, deceptive, dishonest, insidious, insincere, sophistic **10** misleading **11** calculating, casuistical, sophistical

disinherit
6 cut off **7** bereave, exclude **9** deprive of, repudiate **10** dispossess

disintegrate
3 rot **4** turn **5** break, burst, decay, spoil, taint **6** molder **7** crumble, scatter, shatter **8** splinter **9** break

down, decompose, fall apart **10** deliquesce

disinter
5 dig up **6** exhume, unbury **7** unearth **8** exhumate **9** resurrect

disinterest
6 apathy **7** neglect **8** coolness, lethargy **9** aloofness, disregard, unconcern **10** detachment, dispassion, neutrality **11** impassivity, inattention, insouciance, nonchalance, objectivity **12** indifference

disinterested
4 fair, just **5** aloof **6** candid **7** neutral **8** detached, unbiased **9** impartial, impassive, incurious, objective **10** even-handed, impersonal, neglectful, nonchalant **11** inattentive, indifferent, unconcerned

disjoin
4 part **5** sever, unfix **6** detach, divide, sunder, unlink **7** break up, divorce **8** disunite, separate, uncouple, unfasten **9** disengage, take apart **10** dissociate **12** disaffiliate, disassociate

disjointed
7 jumbled, muddled **8** confused, inchoate, rambling **9** displaced **10** disordered, incoherent, incohesive **11** unconnected, unorganized **13** discontinuous

disk
4 puck **5** wafer **6** record
metal: 4 slug
ornamental: 6 bangle, sequin

dislike
4 hate, shun **5** abhor, scorn, spurn **6** animus, detest, loathe, oppose, reject, resent **7** deplore, despise, frown on **8** aversion, disfavor, distaste, execrate **9** animosity, antipathy **10** alienation, disapprove, repugnance **11** detestation, disapproval **13** indisposition

dislimn
3 dim **5** bedim **6** darken **7** becloud, obscure **9** obfuscate

dislocate
5 break **7** disrupt, unhinge **9** disengage **10** disconnect **13** disarticulate

dislodge
4 oust **5** eject, evict, expel **6** remove, uproot **8** displace, drive out, force out

disloyal
5 false **6** untrue **8** apostate, recreant **9** alienated, faithless **10** perfidious, traitorous, unfaithful **11** disaffected, treacherous

disloyalty
7 falsity, perfidy, treason **8** apostasy **9** falseness, recreancy, treachery **10** alienation, infidelity **12** disaffection **13** faithlessness

dismal
5 bleak **6** dreary, gloomy, horrid, somber, sombre **7** joyless **8** desolate, dreadful, funereal, lowering **9** atrocious, cheerless, depressed, tenebrous **10** depressing, depressive **11** dispiriting **12** discouraging **13** disheartening

dismantle
4 raze, undo **5** strip, unrig, wreck **6** denude, divest **7** break up, destroy **8** demolish, pull down, take down **9** break down, knock down, take apart **11** disassemble

dismay
4 faze, fear **5** abash, alarm, daunt, dread, panic, scare, shake, upset **6** appall, fright, horror, rattle **7** agitate, fluster, horrify, perturb, unnerve **8** affright, bewilder, confound, dispirit, distress, frighten **9** discomfit, dumbfound, embarrass **10** discompose, disconcert, discourage, dishearten **11** trepidation **12** perturbation **13** consternation

dismayed
5 upset **6** afraid, aghast, scared, shaken **7** fearful, shocked **9** disturbed

dismember
4 maim **7** disjoin **8** mutilate **9** dismantle, take apart

dismiss

3 axe, can **4** drop, fire, oust, sack, shed **5** chuck, eject, evict, let go, scorn, spurn **6** bounce, depose, deride, lay off, reject, remove, retire, shelve, unseat **7** boot out, cashier, contemn, decline, disband, kick out, kiss off, turn off **8** displace, furlough, pooh-pooh, ridicule, throw out, turn away, turn down **9** discharge, repudiate, terminate **11** send packing

dismissal

5 congé **6** firing, layoff, ouster **7** removal **8** brush-off, bum's rush **9** discharge, expulsion **10** cashiering

dismount

6 alight, debark, get off **7** deplane, detrain **9** disembark **10** alight from **11** descend from

Disney, Walt

10 cartoonist
character: **4** Gyro, Huey, Lady **5** Ariel, Bambi, Daisy, Dewey, Dumbo, Goofy, Louie, Mulan, Pluto, Simba, Tramp **6** Beauty, Donald, Mickey, Minnie, Mowgli **7** Aladdin, Scrooge **9** Gladstone, Pinocchio **10** Beagle Boys, Clarabelle, Pocahontas
classic: **5** Bambi, Dumbo **8** Fantasia **9** Pinocchio **10** Jungle Book (The) **15** Lady and the Tramp

disobedient

6 unruly **7** naughty, wayward, willful **8** contrary **10** headstrong, ill-behaved, rebellious, refractory, uncompliant **11** misbehaving **12** contumacious, noncompliant, obstreperous, recalcitrant **13** insubordinate

disoblige

5 annoy **6** bother, offend, put out **7** affront, disturb, trouble **9** displease, incommode **10** discommode **13** inconvenience

disorder

3 ill **4** mess, riot **5** chaos, mix up, snarl, upset **6** ataxia, hubbub, jumble, malady, mess up, muddle, muss up, ruckus, rumple, tumble, tumult, unrest, uproar **7** ailment, anarchy, clutter, confuse, disease, embroil, illness, misdeed, shuffle, turmoil **8** disarray, sickness, syndrome, unsettle, upheaval **9** affection, agitation, commotion, complaint, confusion, infirmity **10** affliction, turbulence, untidiness
mental: **5** mania **8** delirium, insanity, neurosis, paranoia **9** psychosis **11** psychopathy **13** schizophrenia

disordered

6 roiled **7** jumbled, muddled **8** confused, inchoate, shuffled **9** displaced **10** disjointed, dislocated, incoherent, incohesive **11** disarranged, unconnected, unorganized **13** discontinuous

disorderly

5 rowdy **6** unruly, untidy **7** jumbled, raucous, unkempt **8** confused **9** cluttered, offensive, turbulent **10** boisterous, topsy-turvy, tumultuous **12** disorganized, rambunctious, unsystematic

disorganize

5 upset **6** jumble, mess up **7** break up, confuse, derange, disband, disrupt **8** disorder, disperse, unsettle **10** disarrange

disoriented

4 lost **7** mixed up **8** confused **9** displaced, perplexed, unsettled **10** bewildered

disown

4 deny, dump **6** desert, reject **7** cast off, disavow **8** disclaim, renounce **9** repudiate

disparage

5 decry **6** defame, slight **7** condemn, degrade, devalue, dismiss, put down, run down **8** bad-mouth, belittle, derogate, discount, downplay, minimize, pooh-pooh **9** denigrate, deprecate, discredit, dispraise, downgrade, underrate **10** demoralize, depreciate, undervalue **11** detract from

disparagement

5 scorn **7** calumny, censure, despite,

scandal, slander **8** contempt, despisal, reproach **9** aspersion, discredit, stricture **10** backbiting, defamation, derogation, detraction, diminution **11** degradation **12** backstabbing, depreciation **13** animadversion

disparate
6 at odds, divers, unlike, varied **7** diverse, unalike, unequal, various, varying **8** discrete, distinct, separate **9** different, divergent, unsimilar **10** dissimilar **11** distinctive, incongruous, inconsonant **12** incompatible, inconsistent

disparity
3 gap **8** contrast **9** imbalance **10** difference, divergence, divergency, inequality **11** discrepancy **13** disproportion, dissimilarity

dispassionate
4 calm, fair, just **7** neutral **8** composed, detached, unbiased **9** equitable, impartial, objective, unruffled **10** impersonal **11** unemotional **12** unprejudiced **13** disinterested

dispatch
4 kill, send, ship, slay **5** haste, hurry, scrag, speed **6** defeat, murder **7** bump off, execute, forward, killing, message, put away **8** alacrity, get rid of, shipment, transmit **9** dispose of, eliminate, swiftness **10** expedition, put to death, speediness **11** assassinate, promptitude

dispel
6 banish **7** cast out, scatter **8** disperse **9** clear away, dissipate, drive away

dispensable
5 minor **7** trivial **8** needless, unneeded **10** disposable, expendable, unrequired **11** superfluous, unessential, unimportant, unnecessary **12** nonessential

dispensary
6 clinic

dispensation
4 plan **5** favor, share **7** license,

portion, service **8** bestowal, courtesy, kindness, ordering **9** allotment, exception, exemption, privilege, remission **10** indulgence, management **12** disbursement, distribution **13** apportionment, authorization

dispense
5 allot, apply, wield **6** assign, divide, excuse, exempt, ration, supply **7** absolve, deal out, deliver, dish out, dole out, furnish, give out, mete out, portion, provide, release **8** allocate, carry out, disburse, share out, transfer **9** apportion, discharge, partition **10** administer, distribute, measure out, portion out

disperse
3 sow **5** spray, strew **6** dispel, divide, spread, vanish **7** break up, diffuse, disband, radiate, scatter **9** broadcast, dissipate, partition, propagate **10** distribute

dispersion
6 spread **7** breakup, colloid **9** diffusion, spreading **10** scattering **11** dissipation **12** distribution **13** dissemination

dispirit
3 cow **5** chill, daunt **6** deject, dismay, sadden **7** depress, oppress **8** distress **10** demoralize, discourage, dishearten

dispirited
3 low, sad **4** blue, down, glum **5** cowed **6** morose **7** daunted **8** cast down, dejected, dismayed, downcast, saddened **9** bummed out, depressed, oppressed, woebegone **10** distressed, melancholy **11** crestfallen, demoralized, discouraged, downhearted **12** disconsolate, disheartened

dispiriting
4 blue **6** dismal, dreary, gloomy **8** daunting, dolorous, funereal **9** cheerless, dismaying, saddening **10** depressing, oppressive **12** demoralizing, disconsolate, discouraging **13** disheartening

displace

4 oust, sack 5 exile, expel, usurp
6 banish, deport, depose, remove
7 succeed 8 dethrone, supplant
9 supersede, transport 10 expatriate,
substitute

display

4 pomp, show 5 array, model
6 evince, expose, flaunt, lay out,
parade, reveal, spread, unfold,
unfurl, unveil 7 exhibit, panoply,
present, showing, show off, trot out,
uncover 8 brandish, evidence,
manifest, showcase 9 showiness,
spectacle 10 exhibiting, exhibition
11 demonstrate, ostentation 13 demonstration, manifestation

displeasing

6 vexing 7 irksome 8 annoying
10 bothersome, unpleasant 12 disagreeable 13 objectionable

displeasure

8 aversion, disfavor, vexation 9 annoyance 10 discomfort, discontent,
irritation, uneasiness 11 indignation,
unhappiness 13 indisposition

disport

4 show 5 amuse 6 acquit, behave,
divert, expose, flaunt, frolic, parade
7 conduct, display, exhibit, show off,
trot out 9 entertain

disposal

5 order 7 removal 8 bestowal,
chucking, jettison, ordering, transfer
9 clearance 10 allocation, assignment, demolition, discarding, regulation, relegation 11 arrangement,
consignment, destruction, disposition
12 distribution, transference

dispose

4 bend, bias, rank 5 array, order,
range 6 settle 7 arrange, incline,
marshal, prepare 8 organize, regulate 9 make ready 11 systematize
of: 4 dump, junk, sell 5 chuck,
scrap 6 finish, handle, unload
7 deep-six, destroy, discard 8 deal
with, throw out, transfer 9 eighty-six,
eliminate 10 distribute

disposed

3 apt 4 fain, game 5 prone, ready
6 biased, minded 7 partial, willing
8 arranged, inclined 9 persuaded

disposition

4 bent, cast, mood, tone, type, vein
5 being, order, stamp 6 makeup,
nature, temper 7 control, leaning,
mind-set 8 ordering, penchant,
riddance, sequence, tendency,
transfer 9 character, direction
10 management, proclivity, propensity, settlement 11 arrangement,
inclination, personality, temperament 12 constitution, predilection
13 individuality
favorable: 8 optimism
unfavorable: 9 pessimism

dispossess

3 rob 4 oust 5 eject, strip 6 divest
7 bereave, deprive

dispossession

4 loss 6 ouster 7 seizure 9 privation 10 divestment 11 deprivation,
divestiture 13 expropriation

dispraise

3 pan 5 decry 6 censor, deride,
dump on 7 put down, run down
8 bad-mouth, belittle, derogate
9 criticize, deprecate, discredit,
disparage 10 depreciate, disapprove
11 detract from 12 depreciation

disproportion

8 imparity, mismatch 9 disparity
10 inequality, unevenness 12 lopsidedness

disproportionate

6 uneven 7 unequal 8 lopsided
10 unbalanced

disprove

5 belie, rebut 6 refute, negate
7 confute, explode 8 confound,
overturn, puncture, traverse 9 discredit, overthrow 10 invalidate

disputable

4 iffy, moot 7 dubious 8 arguable,
doubtful 9 debatable, uncertain,
unsettled 10 unresolved 11 problematic 12 questionable 13 controversial

disputation
6 debate 8 argument, forensic, polemics 9 dialectic 11 controversy 13 argumentation

dispute
4 buck, duel, moot, tiff 5 argue, fight, rebut, repel 6 bicker, combat, debate, hassle, impugn, negate, oppose, refute, resist, rumpus, strife 7 confute, contend, contest, discuss, gainsay, quarrel, quibble, wrangle 8 argument, conflict, question, squabble 9 bickering, challenge, thrash out, withstand 10 contention, controvert, falling-out 11 altercation, controversy, embroilment

disputed
7 debated 8 arguable 9 contested, uncertain 12 questionable 13 controversial

disqualified
5 unfit 8 unfitted 10 ineligible, unequipped

disqualify
3 bar 5 debar 6 except 7 exclude, rule out, suspend 9 eliminate
as judge: 6 recuse

disquiet
5 alarm, angst, upset, worry 6 bother, flurry, unease, unrest 7 agitate, anxiety, concern, disturb, ferment, fluster, perturb, trouble, turmoil 10 discompose, uneasiness 11 disturbance, restiveness 12 restlessness 13 Sturm und Drang

disquietude
4 care 5 worry 6 unease, unrest 7 anxiety, concern, ferment, turmoil 9 agitation, misgiving 10 foreboding, uneasiness 11 nervousness, restiveness 12 apprehension, restlessness 13 Sturm und Drang

Disraeli, Benjamin
novel: 5 Sybil 7 Lothair, Tancred 8 Endymion 9 Coningsby
opponent: 4 Peel (Robert) 9 Gladstone (William)
queen: 8 Victoria

disregard
6 forget, ignore, slight 7 neglect, tune out 8 overlook 9 unconcern 12 heedlessness, indifference

disregardful
3 lax 5 slack 6 remiss 8 careless, derelict, heedless 9 forgetful, unheeding, negligent, unmindful 10 neglectful, regardless, unthinking 11 indifferent, unconcerned 12 absent-minded

disremember
6 forget

disreputable
4 base 5 dingy, seamy, seedy, shady 6 scurvy, shabby, shoddy, sordid 7 run-down 8 decrepit, infamous, shameful 10 inglorious 11 dilapidated, disgraceful, ignominious 12 contemptible, unprincipled 13 discreditable, unrespectable

disrepute
5 odium, shame 7 obloquy 8 disfavor, disgrace, dishonor, ignominy 9 disesteem 10 opprobrium

disrespect
6 insult 7 disdain 8 boldness, contempt, rudeness 9 disregard, flippancy, impudence, insolence 10 incivility 11 discourtesy, presumption 12 impertinence, impoliteness

disrespectful
4 flip, rude 5 sassy, saucy 7 ill-bred, uncivil 8 flippant, impolite, impudent, insolent 10 ungracious 11 ill-mannered, impertinent 12 contemptuous, discourteous

disrobe
4 bare, peel 5 strip 6 denude, divest 7 undress 8 unclothe

disrupt
5 upset 6 mess up 7 break up, rupture 8 disorder, unsettle

dissatisfaction
6 dismay 9 annoyance, complaint 10 discontent, irritation, uneasiness 11 displeasure, frustration

dissatisfied
5 irked, vexed **7** annoyed **8** bothered **10** begrudging, discontent, displeased, malcontent **11** complaining, disaffected, unfulfilled **12** disappointed, discontented, malcontented

dissect
5 probe, study **7** analyze, examine, inspect **9** anatomize, break down, take apart **10** scrutinize

dissection
7 autopsy **8** analysis, necropsy of animals: **7** zootomy

dissemble
4 hide, mask **5** cloak, feign **7** conceal, cover up, dress up, falsify **8** disguise, simulate **9** whitewash **10** camouflage **11** counterfeit

dissembler
4 fake **5** faker, fraud, phony **8** deceiver, imposter, impostor, pharisee **9** hypocrite, pretender

disseminate
3 sow **5** strew **6** blazon, spread **7** bestrew, diffuse, publish, scatter, send out **8** announce, disperse, proclaim **9** advertise, broadcast, circulate, propagate, publicize **10** promulgate

dissension
5 fight **6** strife **7** discord, dispute, faction, quarrel, wrangle **8** argument, clashing, conflict, disunity, friction, variance **9** bickering **10** contention, difference, quarreling **11** altercation, controversy **12** disagreement

dissent
5 demur **6** differ, heresy, object **8** conflict, variance **9** misbelief **10** contention, difference, heterodoxy, opposition, resistance **11** unorthodoxy **12** nonagreement **13** nonconformism, nonconformity

dissenter
7 heretic **8** apostate, defector, deserter, partisan, recreant **10** schismatic, separatist **11** misbeliever, schismatist **13** nonconformist

dissertation
6 thesis **8** tractate, treatise **9** discourse, monograph **10** commentary, exposition **11** disputation **12** disquisition **13** argumentation

disservice
4 harm **6** damage, injury, insult **8** disfavor, meanness, mischief **9** detriment **10** misfortune

dissever
3 cut, hew **4** hack, part **5** carve, slice, split **6** cleave, detach, divide, sunder **7** disjoin, divorce **8** disjoint, disunite, separate, uncouple **10** disconnect

dissidence
6 heresy, schism, strife **7** discord, dispute, dissent, faction **8** conflict, friction, variance **10** contention, disharmony, dissension, heterodoxy, opposition **11** discordance, unorthodoxy **12** disagreement **13** nonconformism, nonconformity

dissident
7 heretic **8** partisan, recusant **9** differing, dissenter, heretical, heterodox, protestor **10** schismatic, separatist, unorthodox **11** contentious, disagreeing, misbeliever, nonbeliever, quarrelsome, schismatist **12** disputatious, unharmonious **13** nonconformist

dissimilar
6 unlike **7** diverse, unalike, unequal, various **8** distinct **9** different, disparate, divergent **13** heterogeneous

dissimilarity
8 contrast, variance **9** disparity, diversity, variation **10** difference, divergence, divergency, unlikeness **11** incongruity **13** heterogeneity, inconsistency

dissimulate
see **dissemble**

dissimulation
5 fraud, guile, lying **6** deceit **7** cunning **8** artifice, flimflam, pretense **9** deception, duplicity, hypocrisy,

mendacity, sophistry 10 craftiness, pharisaism 11 beguilement, smoke screen

dissipate

4 blow 5 use up, waste 6 burn up, spread, vanish 7 break up, scatter 8 disperse, evanesce, melt away, misspend, squander 9 evaporate, throw away 11 fritter away

dissipated

6 rakish, wanton, wasted 8 depraved 9 debauched, reprobate 10 degenerate, licentious, profligate 11 intemperate

dissociate

4 part 5 unfix 6 cut off, detach 7 disband, disjoin 8 alienate, disunite, estrange, separate, uncouple 9 disengage 10 disconnect

dissolute

3 lax 4 fast, wild 5 loose, slack 6 rakish, wanton 7 raffish, wayward 8 decadent, depraved 9 abandoned, debauched, indulgent, reprobate 10 degenerate, dissipated, licentious, profligate 12 unprincipled, unrestrained

dissolution

5 death, decay, split 6 demise 7 breakup, divorce, rupture, split-up 8 division 9 dispersal, partition 10 detachment, disbanding, profligacy 11 evaporation 12 liquefaction

dissolvable

7 soluble 8 meltable

dissolve

3 end 4 flux, melt, thaw, undo, void 5 annul, quash, recess, vacate, vanish 7 adjourn, break up, destroy, diffuse, disband, liquefy, resolve, shatter, unravel 8 abrogate, demolish, disperse, evanesce, fade away, get rid of, melt away, prorogue, separate 9 decompose, dissipate, evaporate, prorogate, terminate, waste away 10 deliquesce, do away with 12 disintegrate

dissonance

6 strife 7 discord 8 clashing, conflict 9 cacophony, harshness 10 contention, difference, disharmony 11 incongruity 12 disagreement 13 inconsistency

dissonant

5 harsh 7 grating, jarring, raucous 8 strident 9 unmusical 10 cacophonic, discordant, inharmonic 11 cacophonous, conflicting, incongruous 12 incompatible, inharmonious

dissuade

5 deter 7 turn off 10 discourage, disincline

distaff

6 female 8 maternal

distance

4 area 5 ambit, lapse, orbit, range, reach, scope, space, sweep 6 course, degree, extent, length, radius, remove, spread 7 breadth, compass, expanse, horizon, mileage, reserve, spacing, stretch 8 coldness, interval 9 amplitude, disparity, expansion, extension 10 divergence, divergency, remoteness, separation 11 distinction, perspective 13 dissimilarity
angular: 8 latitude 9 longitude
between levels: 4 drop
between rails: 4 gage
between supports: 4 span
from bottom to top: 6 height
geometric: 8 altitude
greatest perpendicular: 6 camber
measuring instrument: 8 odometer 9 pedometer, telemeter 11 range finder
minute: 4 hair
perpendicular: 5 depth
shortest: 7 beeline 12 straight line
the wind blows: 5 fetch

distant

3 far, shy 4 afar, cold, cool 5 aloof, apart 6 absent, far-off, remote 7 faraway, haughty, obscure, removed, spacial, spatial 8 far-flung,

distaste

isolated, outlying, reserved, secluded, solitary **9** separated, unsimilar, withdrawn **10** unsociable **11** out-of-the-way, sequestered, standoffish
combining form: 3 tel **4** tele, telo

distaste

7 disgust, dislike **8** aversion, loathing **9** antipathy, hostility, revulsion **10** abhorrence, repugnance **13** indisposition

distasteful

8 unsavory **9** loathsome, obnoxious, offensive, repellent, repugnant, repulsive **10** abominable, unpleasant **11** displeasing, unpalatable **12** disagreeable, unappetizing **13** objectionable

distemper

6 malady **7** ailment, disease **8** disorder **9** contagion, strangles **10** affliction **11** derangement **13** panleucopenia

distend

5 bloat, bulge, swell, widen **6** dilate, expand, extend, puff up **7** amplify, augment, enlarge, inflate, stretch **8** increase, lengthen **10** stretch out

distill

6 refine **7** extract **8** boil down **11** concentrate, precipitate

distinct

4 sole **5** clear, lucid, plain **6** marked, patent, single, unique **7** audible, defined, diverse, evident, express, notable, obvious, special, unusual **8** apparent, clear-cut, definite, discrete, especial, explicit, manifest, palpable, peculiar, separate, specific **9** different, divergent **10** individual, noticeable, particular **11** categorical, unambiguous, unequivocal **12** unmistakable

distinction

4 bays, rank **5** award, badge, grade, honor, kudos **6** nicety, renown **7** laurels **8** accolade, eminence, prestige **10** difference, divergence, divergency, prominence, unlikeness

11 differentia, peculiarity, preeminence, recognition **12** significance **13** dissimilarity

distinctive

6 proper, single, unique **7** special **8** peculiar, separate, singular **10** individual **13** idiosyncratic

distingué

6 classy, urbane **7** courtly, elegant, eminent, genteel, refined **8** cultured, decorous, highbrow, mannerly, polished, well-bred **9** dignified, high-class **10** cultivated **13** sophisticated

distinguish

4 mark, note, spot, view **5** honor, place **6** descry, notice, set off **7** dignify, make out, mark off, observe, pick out **8** classify, identify, perceive, separate **9** recognize, single out **10** categorize **12** characterize, discriminate **13** differentiate, individualize

distinguished

5 famed, noted **6** famous **7** eminent, notable, stately **8** esteemed, imposing, renowned **9** dignified, prominent **10** celebrated **11** illustrious

distort

4 bend, warp, wind **5** alter, color, twist **6** deform, garble **7** contort, falsify, pervert, torture **8** misstate **11** misconstrue **12** misinterpret, misrepresent

distortion

8 twisting **9** deformity

distract

5 addle, mix up **6** ball up, bemuse, divert, puzzle **7** confuse, fluster, mislead, perplex **8** befuddle, bewilder, confound, throw off **9** sidetrack, unbalance

distracted

8 confused, deranged, maddened, troubled **9** oblivious **10** nonplussed **11** disoriented, inattentive, preoccupied **12** absent-minded

distraction

5 upset 9 agitation, amusement, confusion, diversion 10 perplexity 12 interruption 13 entertainment

distrait

5 upset 7 anxious, bemused, faraway, worried 8 confused, deranged, harassed, maddened, troubled 9 tormented, withdrawn 10 abstracted, distracted, distraught 11 inattentive, preoccupied 12 absentminded, apprehensive

distraught

5 upset 6 addled, crazed 7 anxious, frantic, muddled, rattled, shook up, unglued, worried 8 agitated, confused, demented, deranged, frenzied, harassed, troubled, worked up 9 flustered, perturbed, tormented, wigged-out 10 distressed, bewildered, freaked out, nonplussed 11 overwrought

distress

3 ail, irk, mar, try, vex, woe 4 ache, care, hurt, pain, pang, rack 5 agony, annoy, cross, dolor, grief, rigor, throe, trial, upset, worry 6 bother, grieve, harass, misery, pester, plague, sorrow, strain, strait, twinge 7 afflict, anguish, anxiety, exhaust, torment, torture, trouble 8 aggrieve, calamity, exigency, hardship 9 adversity, constrain, hard times, suffering 10 affliction, difficulty, heartbreak, misfortune, visitation 11 tribulation, vicissitude
call: 6 Mayday
signal: 3 SOS 5 alarm

distressing

4 dire 6 woeful 8 alarming, grievous, shocking 9 offensive 10 deplorable, lamentable 11 dispiriting, regrettable, unfortunate 13 heartbreaking

distribute

4 deal, mete 5 allot, place, strew 6 assign, assort, divide, donate, parcel, ration, spread 7 deal out, deliver, diffuse, dish out, divvy up, dole out, dribble, give out, hand out, mete out, prorate, radiate, scatter, slice up 8 allocate, classify, disburse, dispense, position, separate 9 apportion, circulate, partition, propagate, spread out 10 administer, measure out 11 disseminate
in a tournament: 4 seed

distribution

7 density 8 delivery, dividend, grouping, ordering, sequence 9 allotment, allotting, diffusion, dispersal, marketing, placement, spreading 10 dispersion, scattering 11 arrangement, probability, propagation 12 apportioning, dispensation 13 apportionment, dissemination

distributor

5 agent 6 broker, jobber 7 carrier 10 wholesaler 12 intermediate

district

4 area, ward 5 tract 6 barrio, locale, parcel, region, sector 7 borough, quarter, section 8 division, locality, precinct, vicinage, vicinity 11 subdivision 12 neighborhood
ecclesiastical: 5 synod 6 parish 7 diocese
Greek: 4 deme
Indian: 6 tahsil
judicial: 7 circuit
London: 4 Soho 7 Chelsea, Mayfair 9 Docklands, Greenwich, Southwark 10 Kensington, Piccadilly 11 Canary Wharf, Notting Hill 13 Knightsbridge
New York: 4 Soho 7 Chelsea, Tribeca
theater: 6 rialto

District of Columbia

college, university: 6 Howard 8 American, Catholic 9 Gallaudet 10 Georgetown
motto: 13 E Pluribus Unum
official bird: 10 wood thrush
official flower: 18 American Beauty rose

distrust

5 doubt 7 suspect 8 question, wariness 9 disbelief, discredit, misgiving, suspicion 10 disbelieve

distrustful
4 wary **5** chary, leery **7** cynical, dubious, jealous **8** doubtful, doubting **10** suspicious **12** questionable

distrusting
4 wary **5** chary, leery **7** cynical, dubious, jealous **8** doubtful, doubting **10** suspicious

disturb
4 faze **5** alarm, daunt, rouse, upset, worry **6** bother, harass, meddle, mess up, pester, stir up **7** agitate, break up, disrupt, fluster, perplex, trouble, unnerve **8** bewilder, distress, unsettle **9** incommode, interrupt **10** discompose, disconcert, tamper with **13** inconvenience, interfere with

disturbance
4 flap, fuss, stir, to-do **5** stink **6** clamor, hubbub, rumpus, tumult, unrest, uproar **7** bobbery, turmoil **8** disorder **9** agitation, commotion, confusion **10** alteration, disruption, turbulence **11** derangement, distraction **12** interruption
atmospheric: **5** storm **7** cyclone, tornado **9** hurricane
mental: **6** frenzy **8** delirium, neurosis **9** psychosis
oceanic: **7** tsunami

disturbed
5 upset **6** insane, shaken **7** anxious, puzzled, rattled, worried **8** bothered, demented, deranged, troubled **9** concerned, psychotic, unsettled **10** distracted, distressed **12** disconcerted

disunion
7 divorce, rupture, split-up **8** division, severing, variance **9** partition **10** detachment, difference, separation **13** disconnection

disunite
4 part **6** divide, sunder **7** break up, disjoin, divorce, split up **8** dissever, separate, uncouple **9** disengage, fall apart **10** disconnect **12** disaffiliate

disunity
6 strife, schism **7** discord **8** conflict, division, variance **10** alienation, contention, disharmony, dissension **12** disaffection, disagreement, estrangement

disused
5 passé **8** obsolete, outdated, outmoded **9** abandoned, discarded **10** antiquated, superseded

ditch
3 dig, pit **4** drop, dump, foss, junk, moat **5** chuck, fosse, leave, scrap, swale **6** reject, trench, trough **7** abandon, cashier, discard, dismiss, forsake, foxhole **8** jettison, throw out **9** crash-land, dispose of, throw away **10** excavation

dither
4 fuss, stew **5** quake, shake, tizzy, waver **6** falter, flurry, quaver, shiver **7** flutter, tremble, twitter, whiffle **8** hesitate **9** agitation, commotion, confusion, vacillate **10** excitement, turbulence **12** shilly-shally

dithyramb
4 hymn, poem **5** chant

dithyrambic
6 ardent, fervid **9** perfervid, rhapsodic **10** boisterous, passionate **11** impassioned

ditto
4 copy, same **5** clone, me too, Xerox **6** carbon, repeat **7** replica, reprint, similar **9** duplicate, facsimile, photocopy **10** carbon copy, mimeograph **11** replication **12** reproduction **13** reduplication

ditty
3 air, lay **4** song, tune **5** carol, chant **6** ballad

diurnal
5 daily **7** daytime **8** daylight **9** circadian, ephemeral, quotidian

diva
7 goddess **10** prima donna **11** leading lady

divagate
4 turn, veer **5** drift, stray **6** depart, ramble, wander **7** deviate, digress, diverge

divan

  4 sofa 5 couch 6 settee 7 chamber, council 9 davenport 12 chesterfield

dive

  3 bar, pub 4 dash, dump, hole, jump, leap 5 joint, lunge, pitch, sound, swoop 6 header, lounge, plunge, saloon, tavern 7 barroom, decline, descend, descent, hangout, plummet, taproom 8 submerge 9 honkytonk, roadhouse 10 cannonball
  type: 4 pike, swan, tuck 6 gainer
  7 cutaway 9 belly flop, jackknife

diver

  4 loon

diverge

  4 part, vary 5 stray 6 depart, differ, swerve 7 deflect, deviate, digress 8 disagree, separate 9 bifurcate, branch off, draw apart

divergence

  7 parting 9 departure, deviation, differing 10 aberration, deflection, difference, digression, separation 11 disagreeing, discrepancy, distinction 12 disagreement

divergent

  6 unlike 8 aberrant, abnormal, atypical 9 anomalous, different, differing, disparate, irregular 10 dissimilar

divers

  6 sundry 7 several, various 8 assorted 9 different, disparate 13 miscellaneous

diverse

  5 mixed 6 motley, sundry, unlike, varied 7 several, unalike, unequal, various, varying 8 assorted, discrete, distinct, manifold, separate 9 different, differing, disparate, multiform, multiplex, unsimilar 10 contrasted, dissimilar 11 contrasting, contrastive 12 multifarious 13 contradictory, miscellaneous
  meanings: 8 polysemy

diversion

  5 sport 7 pastime, turning 8 pleasure, sideshow 9 amusement, deviation, enjoyment 10 aberration, deflection, recreation, red herring 11 distraction 13 entertainment

diversity

  7 variety 10 assortment, difference, unlikeness 11 variegation 12 multiformity 13 dissimilarity, heterogeneity

divert

  4 turn, veer 5 amuse 6 regale, swerve 7 beguile, deflect, delight, deviate, digress 8 distract, redirect 9 entertain, turn aside

divest

  3 rid, rob 4 free 5 spoil, strip 6 denude 7 bereave, deprive, despoil, disrobe, undress 8 take away 9 dismantle 10 disinherit, dispossess

divide

  3 cut 4 fork, part 5 allot, cut up, sever, share 6 assign, cleave, parcel, ration, sunder 7 break up, dissect, divorce, dole out, isolate, prorate, quarter, share in, split up 8 allocate, classify, dispense, disunite, separate 9 apportion, branch out, partition, watershed 10 distribute, measure out 11 dichotomize, distinguish
  into four parts: 7 quarter
  into three parts: 7 trisect
  into two parts: 5 halve 6 bisect
  9 bifurcate

divided

  4 rent 5 riven, split 6 cloven 7 asunder, partite 8 ruptured

dividend

  5 bonus, share 6 return, reward 7 benefit, guerdon, portion, premium 9 allotment 12 dispensation

divider

  6 border, screen 9 partition

divination

  6 augury 7 insight 8 prophecy 11 foretelling, soothsaying
  by communication with the dead:
  10 necromancy

by figures: 8 geomancy
by lots: 9 sortilege
by numbers: 10 numerology
by rods: 7 dowsing 11 rhabdo-mancy
by stars: 9 astrology

divine

4 holy 5 clerk, godly, infer 6 cleric, deduce, deific, intuit, parson, priest, sacred, superb 7 foresee, godlike 8 clerical, foreknow, heavenly, luscious, minister, preacher, prophesy, reverend 9 apprehend, churchman, clergyman, marvelous, religious, visualize 10 anticipate, conjecture, sanctified, superhuman, theologian 11 scrumptious 12 ecclesiastic

diviner

4 seer 5 augur, sibyl 6 oracle 7 palmist, prophet 8 haruspex 10 forecaster, prophetess, soothsayer

divinity

3 god 5 deity, fudge 7 goddess, godhead, godhood 8 theology

division

3 cut 4 part, unit 5 class, piece, slice, split 6 branch, moiety, parcel, schism, sector 7 breakup, discord, dissent, divorce, parting, portion, rupture, section, segment, split-up 8 category, conflict, district, disunion, disunity, variance 9 partition 10 detachment, difference, disharmony, dissidence, separation 11 dissolution 12 disagreement 13 apportionment
Bible: 5 verse
book: 7 chapter
British territorial: 5 shire
building: 4 wing
cell: 7 meiosis, mitosis
city: 4 ward 7 borough 8 precinct
contest: 4 heat 6 inning, period
corolla: 5 petal
country: 5 state 6 canton 8 province 10 department, prefecture
family: 4 side 6 branch

geologic time: 3 eon, era 5 epoch 6 period
hospital: 4 ward, wing
into two: 9 bisection 11 bifurcation, bipartition
meal: 6 course
music: 3 bar 4 beat 7 measure 8 movement
opera, play: 3 act 5 scena, scene
poem: 5 canto, verse 6 stanza
population: 7 segment, stratum
race: 3 lap 4 heat
social: 5 caste, class, tribe
state: 6 county, parish
term: 8 quotient
time: 3 day, eon 4 week, year 5 month 6 decade, minute, moment, second 7 century, weekend 9 fortnight 10 millennium
tribal: 4 clan
word: 8 syllable
zodiac: 4 sign

divisive

8 factious 11 disunifying

divorce

4 part 5 sever, split 6 divide, sunder 7 break up, breakup, disjoin, rupture 8 disjoint, dissever, disunion, disunite, separate 9 partition, severance 10 detachment, separation 11 dissolution

divot

3 sod 4 turf 5 clump

divulge

4 blab, leak, tell 5 spill 6 betray, expose, gossip, reveal, tattle 7 let slip, uncover 8 disclose, give away

Dixie composer

6 Emmett (Daniel D.)

dizziness

7 vertigo 9 giddiness

dizzy

5 addle, dazed, giddy, mix up, silly, tipsy 6 addled 7 confuse, dazzled, flighty, foolish, fuddled, muddled, puzzled, reeling 8 confused, swimming, whirling 9 befuddled, confusing 10 bewildered, confounded,

distracted, exorbitant, immoderate, inordinate **11** extravagant, light-headed, vertiginous

Djibouti
  capital: **8** Djibouti
  language: **6** Arabic, French
  monetary unit: **5** franc
  neighbor: **7** Eritrea, Somalia
  8 Ethiopia
  sea: **3** Red

DNA
  component: **7** adenine, guanine, thymine **8** cytosine **10** nucleotide **11** deoxyribose
  segment: **7** cistron

doable
  8 feasible, possible, workable
  9 realistic **10** achievable, attainable
  11 performable

do away with
  3 end, nix, zap **4** kill, slay **5** annul, erase, whack **6** cancel, finish, murder, remove, repeal, revoke, rub out **7** abolish, bump off, deep-six, destroy, discard, expunge, rescind, squelch, wipe out **8** abrogate, blow away, demolish, dispatch, dissolve, massacre, stamp out **9** dispose of, eliminate, eradicate, extirpate, finish off, liquidate, slaughter **10** extinguish, obliterate **11** discontinue, exterminate

docent
  5 guide **6** leader **7** teacher **8** lecturer **10** instructor

docile
  4 tame **6** pliant **7** ductile, pliable **8** amenable, biddable, obedient, yielding **9** adaptable, compliant, teachable, tractable **10** submissive **11** acquiescent

dock
  3 bob, cut **4** crop, fine, pier, quay, rump, slip **5** berth, jetty, levee, tie up, wharf **6** anchor, hangar, lessen, marina, reduce **7** abridge, landing, shorten **8** cut short, platform, truncate
  worker: **6** lumper **9** stevedore **12** longshoreman

docket
  4 card **6** agenda, lineup, record **7** program **8** abstract, calendar, caseload, register, schedule **9** timetable

doctor
  3 fix, vet **4** mend **5** adapt, alter, medic, treat **6** medico, repair **7** croaker, dentist, falsify, scholar, surgeon **8** sawbones **9** clinician, internist, physician **10** adulterate, specialist **11** medicine man, recondition, reconstruct
  animal: **3** vet **12** veterinarian
  children's: **12** pediatrician
  famous: **4** Koop (C. Everett) **5** Galen, Spock (Benjamin) **6** Atkins (Robert), Chopra (Deepak), Ornish (Dean) **9** Kevorkian (Jack) **10** Schweitzer (Albert) **11** Hippocrates, Livingstone (David)
  foot: **10** podiatrist **11** chiropodist
  heart: **12** cardiologist
  teeth: **7** dentist
  women's: **12** gynecologist

Doctor of the Church
  5 Basil **6** Jerome **7** Ambrose, Gregory **9** Augustine **10** Athanasius

Doctorow novel
  7 Ragtime **9** City of God (The) **10** Waterworks, World's Fair **12** Book of Daniel (The) **13** Billy Bathgate **18** Welcome to Hard Times

doctrinaire
  5 rigid **8** dogmatic **9** obstinate **10** unyielding **11** domineering, magisterial **13** authoritarian

doctrine
  3 ism **5** axiom, basic, canon, credo, creed, dogma, faith, tenet **7** precept **8** teaching **9** principle **11** fundamental

document
  4 deed **5** paper **6** record **8** evidence, monument **9** testimony **10** instrument **11** certificate
  travel: **8** passport

dodder
4 limp 5 shake 6 falter, hobble, totter 7 shamble, shuffle, stagger, tremble 12 morning glory

doddering
5 shaky 6 doting, feeble, senile 7 fragile 8 unsteady, weakened 9 faltering

dodge
4 duck, jink, ruse, slip 5 avoid, elude, evade, fence, parry, shirk, skirt, slide, trick 6 escape, scheme, weasel 7 evasion 8 sidestep 9 avoidance, deception, expedient

Dodger
5 Davis (Tommy) 6 Garvey (Steve), Karros (Eric), Koufax (Sandy), Piazza (Michael), Snider (Duke), Sutton (Don) 8 Newcombe (Don), Robinson (Jackie) 9 Hershiser (Orel) 10 Campanella (Roy)
field: 7 Ebbetts
manager: 6 Alston (Walter) 7 Lasorda (Tommy)

dodger
6 outlaw, screen 7 escapee 8 circular, deceiver, deserter, fugitive, handbill, runagate 9 throwaway

dodgy
4 iffy 5 fishy, vague 6 tricky 7 cryptic, obscure 8 doubtful, unproven 9 ambiguous, enigmatic, uncertain 10 indefinite, suspicious, unreliable 11 problematic 12 questionable 13 controversial

dodo
3 oaf 4 bird, boob, clod, dolt, dope, goof, yo-yo 5 chump, dummy, dunce, idiot, moron, ninny, noddy, stupe 6 dimwit, dum-dum, nitwit 7 airhead, dullard, pinhead 8 bonehead, dumbbell, imbecile, lunkhead, meathead, numskull 9 birdbrain, blockhead, ignoramus, lamebrain, numbskull, simpleton 10 dunderhead, nincompoop 11 chowderhead, chucklehead

doe
4 deer 6 female, rabbit 8 kangaroo

doff
4 shed 6 remove 7 take off

dog
3 cur, pug, pup, tag 4 bird, chow, fice, mutt, peke, puli, tail, tyke 5 Akita, boxer, feist, frank, hound, husky, lemon, pooch, puppy, spitz, trail 6 Afghan, beagle, bowwow, briard, canine, collie, detent, poodle, pursue, rascal, saluki, setter, shadow, vizsla, wiener, wretch 7 andiron, Maltese, mastiff, mongrel, pointer, Samoyed, spaniel, terrier, whippet 8 Airedale, Brittany, inferior, keeshond, papillon, Pekinese, pinscher, spurious, wirehair 9 Chihuahua, dachshund, dalmation, Great Dane, greyhound, Pekingese, retriever, schnauzer 10 bloodhound, Pomeranian, rottweiler, Weimaraner 11 bullmastiff, frankfurter, wienerwurst 12 Newfoundland, Saint Bernard 13 cocker spaniel
Alaskan: 8 malamute, malemute
Australian: 5 dingo
barkless: 7 basenji
bird: 6 setter 7 pointer, spaniel 9 retriever
Bush's: 6 Millie
Buster Brown's: 4 Tige
Charlie Brown's: 6 Snoopy
command: 3 sit 4 heel, stay
Dorothy's: 4 Toto
Eskimo: 5 husky
family: 7 Canidae
FDR's: 4 Fala
fictional: 4 Buck 5 Astro, Pluto 6 Big Red 8 McBarker 9 Marmaduke, Old Yeller, Scooby-Doo, White Fang
"Garfield": 4 Odie
genus: 5 Canis
Hungarian: 6 vizsla
hunting: 5 hound 6 beagle, borzoi, saluki, setter, Talbot, vizsla 7 harrier, pointer, redbone 8 elkhound, foxhound 9 wolfhound 10 bloodhound 11 basset hound
Indian: 5 dhole
L.B.J.'s: 3 Her
long-bodied: 9 dachshund

movie: 4 Asta, Toto 5 Benji, Tramp 6 Lassie 9 Beethoven, Old Yeller, Rin Tin Tin

name: 4 Fido, Spot 5 Rover 6 Bowser

Nixon's: 8 Checkers

Odysseus's: 5 Argos

of Hades: 8 Cerberus

Orphan Annie's: 5 Sandy

powerful: 11 bullmastiff

Roy Rogers's: 6 Bullet

Russian: 6 borzoi 7 Samoyed

shaggy-coated: 4 komondor, sheepdog 9 deerhound

short-legged: 5 corgi

small: 3 pom, pug, pup 4 peke 8 Pekinese 9 Chihuahua, Pekingese 10 Pomeranian

space traveler: 5 Laika

Steinbeck's: 7 Charley

television: 4 King 5 Eddie, Tramp 6 Lassie, Murray 8 Wishbone 9 Rin Tin Tin

terrier: 7 Scottie

three-headed: 8 Cerberus

Tibetan: 9 Lhasa apso

tiny: 9 Chihuahua

tooth: 4 fang

tracking: 10 bloodhound

two-headed: 6 Orthos

Wallace's: 6 Gromit

Welsh: 5 corgi

Wendy's: 4 Nana

wild: 5 dingo

young: 3 pup 5 puppy, whelp

dog days
6 August 9 canicular

dogfight
3 row 4 fray 5 brawl, broil, melee, set-to 6 fracas, ruckus 7 ruction 10 donnybrook, free-for-all

dogfish
6 bowfin, burbot 8 mud puppy

dogged
7 adamant 8 obdurate, resolute, stubborn 9 insistent, steadfast, obstinate, tenacious, unbending 10 bullheaded, hardheaded, persistent, persisting, unshakable, unyielding 11 persevering, unremitting 12 pertinacious

doggone
4 damn, dang, darn, rank 5 utter 6 cursed, damned, darned 7 blasted, blessed, dratted 8 absolute, accursed, infernal, outright 9 out-and-out 10 confounded 11 unmitigated 13 blankety-blank

dogma
4 code, rule 5 canon, credo, creed, tenet 6 belief, gospel 7 precept 8 doctrine, ideology 9 orthodoxy, postulate, teachings 10 conviction, persuasion

dogmatic
8 oracular, orthodox 9 assertive, canonical, doctrinal 11 dictatorial, doctrinaire, magisterial 13 authoritarian, authoritative

Dog of Flanders author
5 Ouida

dog-paddle
4 swim

dog's age
3 eon 4 aeon 8 blue moon, eternity

Dog Star
6 Sirius

dogwood
6 cornel, Cornus 8 red osier

do in
4 kill, ruin, slay 5 cheat, wreck 6 defeat, finish, murder, rub out 7 blot out, bump off, destroy, execute, exhaust, frazzle, take out, wear out, wipe out 8 dispatch, knock off, knock out 9 eliminate, liquidate, prostrate, run ragged, shipwreck 11 assassinate

doing
3 act 6 action 8 activity
good: 10 beneficent
evil: 10 maleficent

doit
3 bit, jot 4 coin, damn, dram, drop, hoot, iota, mite, whit 6 trifle 8 particle

doldrums
5 blahs, blues, dumps, ennui, gloom,

slump **6** apathy, tedium, torpor
7 boredom **9** dejection **10** depression, inactivity, quiescence, stagnation **12** listlessness

doleful

3 sad **4** down **7** forlorn, ruthful
8 cast down, dejected, dolorous, downcast, grieving, mournful, mourning **9** afflicted, cheerless, depressed, miserable, plaintive, sorrowful, sorrowing, woebegone **10** dispirited, lamentable, lugubrious, melancholy **11** crestfallen, downhearted **12** disconsolate

dole out

4 deal **5** allot **6** divide, parcel, ration **7** divvy up **8** disburse, dispense, disperse **9** apportion, partition **10** administer, distribute

doll

3 Ken **6** Barbie, figure, Kewpie, puppet **10** Betsy Wetsy, Raggedy Ann **11** Raggedy Andy
grotesque: 8 golliwog

dollar

3 one **4** bill, buck, clam, oner, peso
5 taler **6** single **7** ringgit, smacker **8** simoleon **9** cartwheel, greenback

dollop

4 blob, glob, lump **7** portion

Doll's House, A

author: 5 Ibsen (Henrik)
heroine: 4 Nora

dolly

4 cart **7** stirrer **8** platform **10** locomotive

dolomite

6 marble **9** limestone

dolor

5 agony, grief **6** misery, sorrow
7 anguish, passion **8** distress **9** suffering **10** affliction

dolorous

6 rueful, woeful **7** ruthful **8** grievous, mournful, wretched **9** afflicted, anguished, miserable, plaintive, sorrowful **10** lamentable, lugubrious, melancholy **13** heartbreaking

dolphin

5 whale **7** bollard **8** porpoise

dolt

3 ass, oaf **4** boob, clod, dodo, dork, fool, goof, goon, lout, yo-yo **5** booby, chump, dunce, idiot **6** nitwit **7** dullard, fathead, halfwit, jughead, saphead, schnook **8** bonehead, dumbbell, dummkopf, imbecile, lunkhead, meathead, numskull **9** blockhead, lamebrain, numbskull, simpleton

doltish

4 dull, dumb **5** dense, thick **6** oafish, obtuse, stupid **7** idiotic, moronic **8** ignorant, mindless **9** dim-witted, fatheaded, imbecilic

domain

4 land, rule, turf **5** field, realm
6 estate, sphere **7** kingdom, terrain **8** dominion, province **9** bailiwick, territory

dome

4 head, hill, roof **5** mound **6** cupola **7** ceiling **8** mountain

domestic

4 help, home, tame **6** family, native **7** servant **8** houseboy, internal, national **9** charwoman, household **10** indigenous **11** chambermaid

domesticate

4 tame **5** adapt, adopt, train
10 housebreak

domicile

3 pad **4** home **5** abode, house, lodge, put up **6** bestow, billet, harbor **7** quarter **8** dwelling, quarters **9** residence, residency **10** habitation

domiciliate

4 bunk, tame **5** house, lodge, put up **6** billet, harbor, reside **7** quarter

dominance

4 rule, sway **5** power **7** command, control **7** mastery **9** supremacy
10 ascendancy, prepotency **11** preeminence, sovereignty

dominant

4 main **5** chief, first, major **6** ruling

7 leading, supreme **8** foremost, powerful, reigning **9** ascendant, governing, number-one, paramount, prevalent, principal **10** commanding, preeminent, prevailing, successful, surpassing **11** controlling, outweighing, overbearing **12** preponderant

dominate

4 rule **5** reign **6** direct, govern, obsess **7** control, prevail, repress **8** bestride, hold sway, look down, loom over, overlook **9** subjugate, tower over, tyrannize **10** tower above

domination

4 rule, sway **5** might, power **7** command, control, mastery **9** authority, supremacy **10** ascendancy, prepotency, suzerainty **11** preeminence, sovereignty **13** preponderancy

dominator

4 boss, head **5** chief, ruler **6** honcho, leader, master, top dog **7** headman **8** director, hierarch, kingfish **9** chieftain, commander

domineer

5 bully **6** hector **7** swagger **8** browbeat, bulldoze **9** tyrannize **10** intimidate

domineering

5 bossy **6** lordly **8** arrogant, despotic **9** imperious, masterful **10** autocratic, high-handed, oppressive, tyrannical **11** dictatorial, magisterial, overbearing

Dominica

capital: **6** Roseau
discoverer: **8** Columbus (Christopher)
language: **7** English
location: **10** West Indies
monetary unit: **6** dollar
sea: **9** Caribbean

Dominican Republic

capital: **12** Santo Domingo
island: **10** Hispaniola
language: **7** Spanish
location: **10** West Indies
monetary unit: **4** peso
mountain: **6** Duarte
neighbor: **5** Haiti
sea: **9** Caribbean

dominion

3 raj **4** rule, sway, turf **5** realm, power **6** domain, empery, empire, regnum, sphere **7** demesne, kingdom, terrain **8** province **9** ascendant, ownership, supremacy, territory **10** ascendancy, possession **11** preeminence, sovereignty

domino

4 mask **5** amice, cloak, visor **6** vizard **8** disguise
spot: **3** pip

don

3 sir **4** lord **5** get on, put on, tutor **6** assume, fellow, take on **9** professor, undertake

Donalbain

brother: **7** Malcolm
father: **6** Duncan

donate

4 give **5** grant **6** chip in, supply **7** dish out, hand out, present, provide **8** give away, shell out, transfer **10** contribute

donation

3 aid **4** alms, gift **5** grant **7** bequest, handout **8** offering **9** endowment **11** benefaction, beneficence **12** contribution, philanthropy

Don Carlos

author: **8** Schiller (Friedrich von)
composer: **5** Verdi (Giuseppe)
father: **6** Philip

done

4 over **5** all in, ended, ready, spent **6** bushed, decent, doomed, gone by, proper, used up **7** correct, drained, dressed, far-gone, settled, through, worn-out **8** becoming, complete, depleted, finished, washed-up **9** befitting, completed, concluded, exhausted **10** terminated **12** accomplished
poetic: **3** o'er

donee
7 grantee **8** receiver **9** recipient
11 beneficiary

done for
4 gone, sunk **5** kaput **6** beaten,
doomed, ruined **7** wrecked **8** finished, stricken

done in
5 spent **6** effete, used up **7** far gone,
worn out **8** depleted **9** exhausted,
washed out

Don Giovanni composer
6 Mozart (Wolfgang Amadeus)

Donizetti, Gaetano
hero: **7** Roberto (Devereux)
opera: **5** Lucia (di Lammermoor)
10 Anna Bolena, La Favorita **11** Don
Pasquale **12** Maria Stuarda

Don Juan
4 rake, roué, wolf **5** Romeo **6** chaser,
masher **7** amorist, gallant, playboy,
seducer **8** Casanova, lothario,
paramour **9** ladies' man, libertine,
womanizer **10** lady-killer, profligate
11 philanderer
drama: **10** Stone Guest (The)
home: **7** Seville
mother: **4** Inez
poet: **5** Byron (Lord) **7** Pushkin
(Alexander)

donkey
3 ass **4** mule **5** burro **7** jackass
female: **5** jenny

donkeywork
4 moil, toil **5** grind, labor **7** travail
8 drudgery

donnybrook
3 row **4** fray **5** brawl, broil, fight,
melee, set-to **6** fracas, ruckus,
rumpus, tumult, uproar **7** dispute,
quarrel, rhubarb, ruction **10** free-for-
all **11** altercation

donor
5 giver **6** patron **7** granter, grantor
8 bestower **9** conferrer, presenter
10 benefactor **11** contributor

do-nothing
3 bum **4** slug **5** idler **6** loafer,
slouch **7** goof-off, slacker **8** deadbeat, fainéant, layabout, slugabed,
sluggard **9** lazybones, vegetable
11 couch potato

Don Pasquale composer
9 Donizetti (Gaetano)

Don Quixote
author: **9** Cervantes (Miguel de)
beloved: **8** Dulcinea
companion (squire): **11** Sancho
Panza
giant: **8** windmill
home: **8** La Mancha
horse: **9** Rocinante, Rosinante,
Rozinante

doodad
5 gizmo, thing **6** bauble, dingus,
entity, gadget, gewgaw, jigger, widget
7 trinket, whatsit **8** gimcrack **9** doohickey, thingummy **10** attachment,
decoration, knickknack **11** thingamabob, thingamajig, thingumajig

doodle
6 dabble, dawdle, fiddle, potter,
putter, sketch, tinker, trifle **7** cartoon,
drawing **8** scribble **10** mess around

doodlebug
7 ant lion, missile **8** buzz bomb

doohickey
see **doodad**

doom
4 damn, fate, ruin **5** death **6** decree,
demise, kismet **7** condemn, destiny,
tragedy **8** calamity, disaster, judgment, sentence **11** catastrophe
12 annihilation, last judgment

doomful
4 dire **7** baleful, baneful, direful,
fateful, malefic, ominous, unlucky
8 dreadful, ill-fated, sinister **10** foreboding, portentous **11** apocalyptic

doomsayer
7 killjoy **9** Cassandra, defeatist,
Gloomy Gus, pessimist

_____ Doone
5 Lorna

door
3 way **4** adit, exit **5** entry **6** access,

egress, entrée, portal 7 gateway, ingress, opening 8 entrance, entryway 9 admission 10 admittance 11 entranceway
rear: 7 postern

doorkeeper
6 porter

doorway
5 entry 6 portal 8 entrance, entryway 11 entranceway

doozy
3 ace, pip 5 dandy 7 paragon 8 standout 10 phenomenon 11 crackerjack

dope
3 oaf 4 clod, dodo, dolt, drug, goof, news, yo-yo 5 chump, drugs, dummy, dunce, facts, idiot, moron, ninny, noddy, stupe 6 dimwit, dumdum, heroin, nitwit, opiate, sedate, skinny 7 airhead, cocaine, details, dullard, lowdown, pinhead 8 bonehead, dumbbell, imbecile, lunkhead, meathead, narcotic, numskull 9 birdbrain, blockhead, ignoramus, lamebrain, marijuana, narcotize, numbskull, simpleton 10 dunderhead, nincompoop 11 anesthetize, chowderhead, chucklehead, information, preparation

doped
4 high 5 dazed 6 stoned, zonked 7 drugged, tuned-in 8 hopped-up, tripping, turned on, wiped out 9 spaced-out, strung out, stupefied 10 narcotized

dopey
4 dumb 5 silly 6 dulled, stupid, torpid 7 fatuous, fuddled, muddled 8 comatose, sluggish 9 lethargic, senseless, stupefied

Doris
brother: 6 Nereus
daughters: 7 Nereids
father: 7 Oceanus
husband: 6 Nereus

dormancy
5 sleep 6 repose 7 latency, slumber 8 abeyance, diapause, doldrums, downtime 9 torpidity 10 inactivity, quiescence, suspension 11 cold storage 12 intermission, interruption

dormant
5 inert 6 asleep, drowsy, fallow, latent, torpid 7 abeyant 8 comatose, inactive, sluggish 9 lethargic, potential, quiescent, suspended 10 slow-moving, slumbering

dormer
3 bay 4 nook 5 niche 6 window

dorsal
6 aboral 7 abaxial

_____ d'Orsay
4 Quai

dorsum
4 back

Dorus
brother: 6 Aeolus
father: 6 Hellen

dory
4 bark, boat 5 craft, skiff 6 barque, bateau 7 shallop 8 lifeboat

dose
3 fix, hit 4 dram, shot, slug 7 measure, portion 8 medicate, quantity

Dos Passos trilogy
3 U.S.A.

dossier
4 file 6 folder 9 portfolio

dot
4 mark, mote, stud 5 dower, dowry, point, speck 6 bestud, pepper, period 7 freckle, speckle, stipple 8 flyspeck, sprinkle 9 bespeckle 12 decimal point

dotage
8 senility 11 decrepitude, senectitude

dote on
5 adore, enjoy, fancy, prize 7 cherish, idolize 8 treasure 9 delight in

doting
4 dear, fond 6 loving 7 adoring, devoted 12 affectionate

dotted
6 spotty 8 punctate, stippled

dotty
4 gaga 5 crazy, loony, wacky
6 absurd, insane 7 foolish, smitten
8 enamored 9 eccentric 10 captivated, enraptured, infatuated 12 preposterous

double
4 copy, dual, fold, mate, tack, twin
5 clone, duple, image, match, twice
6 bifold, binary, duplex, paired, ringer
7 dualize, enlarge, magnify, replica, twofold 8 alter ego, geminate,
increase 9 companion, dualistic,
duplicate, look-alike, replicate
10 dead ringer, reciprocal, simulacrum, understudy 13 spitting image

double-barreled
4 dual 5 duple 6 bifold, binary,
duplex, paired 7 twofold 9 dualistic

double bass
10 bull fiddle

double-cross
3 con 4 dupe 5 cheat, trick 6 betray,
delude, humbug, juggle, take in
7 beguile, deceive, sell out, two-time
8 flimflam, hoodwink 9 four-flush

double dagger
6 diesis

double-dealer
3 gyp 5 cheat, knave 6 con man
7 cozener, diddler, sharper 8 deceiver, swindler 9 defrauder 11 flimflammer 13 confidence man

double-dealing
5 fraud 6 deceit 7 chicane 8 flimflam, trickery 9 chicanery, deceitful,
deception, duplicity, two-timing
10 hanky-panky 11 duplicitous

double-dome
7 egghead 8 Einstein, highbrow
10 pointy-head 12 intellectual

double-faced
9 deceitful, deceptive, equivocal, insincere 10 reversible 12 hypocritical
13 untrustworthy

doublet
3 duo 4 dyad, pair, span 5 brace
6 couple, jacket 7 twosome

double-talk
4 bosh, bunk 5 hokum, hooey
6 babble, bunkum, drivel, jabber
7 blather, hogwash, twaddle 8 flimflam, nonsense 9 gibberish, poppycock 10 balderdash 12 gobbledygook

double vision
8 diplopia

doubt
5 qualm 7 concern, dispute, dubiety,
suspect 8 distrust, mistrust, question 9 challenge, disbelief, misgiving, suspicion 10 skepticism
11 dubiousness, incertitude, incredulity, uncertainty

doubtable
4 hazy, iffy, moot 7 dubious, suspect
8 arguable 9 ambiguous, debatable,
equivocal, uncertain, undecided
10 disputable, borderline, indefinite
11 problematic 12 questionable

doubter
5 cynic 6 Thomas 7 skeptic 8 agnostic 10 Pyrrhonist, questioner,
unbeliever 11 freethinker

doubtful
4 hazy, iffy, moot 5 fishy, shady,
shaky 6 chancy, unsure 7 clouded,
dubious, obscure, suspect, unclear
8 arguable, unlikely 9 ambiguous,
debatable, dubitable, equivocal,
uncertain, undecided, unsettled
10 borderline, disputable, improbable 11 problematic, speculative
12 questionable

doubtfulness
7 concern, dubiety 8 mistrust
9 ambiguity, misgiving, suspicion
10 indecision, skepticism, uneasiness 11 dubiousness, incertitude,
uncertainty 13 indeterminacy

doubting Thomas
see **doubter**

doubtless
6 likely, surely 7 certain, clearly
8 of course, probably 10 absolutely,
definitely, positively, presumably
11 indubitably 12 indisputably
13 presumptively, unequivocally

douceur
3 tip 4 gift 5 bribe 7 present
8 gratuity

dough
4 cash 5 bread, money 6 dinero,
moolah 7 cabbage, lettuce, scratch
8 currency 11 legal tender
inflator: 5 yeast

doughboy
7 dogface 11 infantryman

doughty
4 bold 5 brave, gutsy, manly, stout
6 daring, heroic, plucky, spunky,
strong 7 gallant, valiant 8 fearless,
intrepid, resolved, stalwart, unafraid,
valorous 9 dauntless, undaunted
10 courageous 12 stouthearted

doughy
3 wan 4 pale 5 pasty, waxen
6 pallid 8 blanched 9 colorless

do up
3 can, fix 4 mend, wash, wrap
5 clean, patch 6 clothe, doctor,
fasten, repair, revamp 7 exhaust,
festoon, launder, package, prepare,
rebuild, wear out 8 decorate, gift
wrap, ornament, overhaul 9 embellish 11 recondition, reconstruct

dour
4 glum, grim 5 bleak, harsh, rigid,
stern, surly 6 gloomy, morose,
severe, strict, sullen 7 austere,
crabbed, peevish 9 obstinate,
saturnine, stringent 10 forbidding,
unyielding

douse
3 sop 4 duck, dunk, soak 5 bathe,
drown, plash, slosh, souse 6 drench,
put out, quench, splash, strike
7 immerse, slacken 8 inundate,
saturate, snuff out, submerge,
submerse 10 extinguish

dove
6 culver, pigeon 8 pacifist
call: 3 coo
genus: 7 Columba

dovecote
6 aviary 9 birdhouse

dovetail
3 fit 4 jibe, mesh 5 agree, match,
tally 6 accord, splice, square 7 comport, conform 8 check out 9 harmonize, interlock, intermesh 10 correspond

dovish
4 mild 6 gentle 7 antiwar, pacific
8 pacifist 9 peaceable 10 nonviolent, pacifistic 11 peace-loving
12 conciliatory

dowager
4 dame 5 widow 6 matron 9 matriarch 10 grande dame 11 grandmother

dowdy
4 drab 5 dated, frump, passé,
seedy, tacky 6 blowsy, bygone,
démodé, frowsy, frowzy, frumpy, old
hat, shabby 7 rundown, unkempt
8 frumpish, outdated, outmoded,
slattern, slovenly 9 out-of-date,
unstylish 10 antiquated, bedraggled,
slatternly 11 draggle-tail 12 old-
fashioned 13 draggletailed

dowel
3 bar, peg, pin, rod 5 stick

dower
4 gift 5 endow, endue 6 legacy,
talent 8 bequeath

dowitcher
5 snipe 9 sandpiper

do without
5 forgo, waive 6 abjure, eschew,
give up, pass up 8 renounce

down
3 eat, fur, ill, low, off, sad 4 blue, fell,
fuzz, lint, pile, sick 5 below, ended,
floor, floss, fluff, level, lower, under
6 defeat, fallen, finish, lay low, nether
7 conquer, consume, destroy, flatten,

swallow, unhappy **8** bowl over, complete, defeated, dejected, dispatch, feathers, finished, inferior, overcome, sluggish, surmount **9** completed, concluded, depressed, earthward, miserable **10** dispirited, groundward

down-and-out
5 broke, needy **6** hard-up, ruined **8** beggared, derelict, homeless **9** destitute, penniless, penurious **12** impoverished

down-and-outer
3 bum **6** beggar, pauper, wretch **7** have-not **9** mendicant **10** supplicant

down-at-heels
4 mean **5** dingy, ratty, seedy, tacky **6** ragged, ragtag, shabby, shoddy **7** ignoble, run-down, worn-out **8** decrepit, tattered **10** bedraggled, threadbare **11** dilapidated **12** deteriorated, disreputable

downbeat
3 low, sad **4** blue, glum **6** droopy, gloomy, morose **7** decline, doleful **8** dejected **9** depressed **10** dispirited, melancholy **11** discouraged, pessimistic **12** disconsolate, disheartened, heavyhearted

downcast
3 low, sad **4** blue, glum, sunk **5** moody, mopey **6** droopy, gloomy, morose **7** doleful, forlorn, unhappy **8** dejected, dismayed, listless, soul-sick, troubled **9** depressed, heartsick, heartsore, miserable, oppressed, woebegone **10** chapfallen, despondent, dispirited, distressed, melancholy, spiritless **11** crestfallen, discouraged, low-spirited **12** disconsolate, disheartened

downfall
4 bane, ruin **6** demise **7** decline, undoing **8** collapse, Waterloo **9** ruination **10** devolution **11** declination, destruction **12** degeneration, dégringolade **13** deterioration

downgrade
4 bump, bust **5** abase, lower **6** demote **7** decline, demerit, descent, devalue **8** belittle, diminish, discount, minimize, relegate **9** denigrate, deprecate, devaluate, discredit, disparage, humiliate **10** depreciate, undervalue **12** degeneration, dégringolade **13** deterioration

downhearted
see **downcast**

down-in-the-mouth
see **downcast**

down payment
5 token **6** pledge **7** advance, deposit, earnest

downplay
8 belittle, discount, minimize, pooh-pooh **11** de-emphasize

downpour
6 deluge **7** monsoon **8** drencher **9** drenching, rainstorm **10** cloudburst, inundation **11** gully washer

downright
5 blunt, gross, total, truly, utter **7** blatant, flat-out **8** absolute, complete, explicit, positive, thorough **9** out-and-out **10** absolutely, sure-enough **11** indubitable, unequivocal, unmitigated, unqualified **13** thoroughgoing

downslide
3 dip, sag **4** drop, slip **5** slump **7** decline, drop-off, falloff **8** decrease **9** declivity, reduction

downstairs
6 cellar **8** basement

down-to-earth
8 rational **9** practical, pragmatic, realistic **10** hard-boiled, hardheaded, no-nonsense, reasonable **11** common-sense, plain-spoken **12** matter-of-fact **13** unpretentious, unsentimental

downtrend
see **downslide**

downtrodden
6 abject, abused 9 oppressed
10 maltreated, mistreated, perse-
cuted, tyrannized

downturn
see **downslide**

downward
8 dropping 9 declining 10 descending

downy
4 soft 5 fuzzy 6 fleecy, fluffy 7 velvety
8 feathery
filler: 5 eider

dowry
4 gift 6 talent
French: 3 dot

doxy
4 moll, tart 5 wench 6 floozy, harlot
7 trollop 8 mistress 10 prostitute

doyen
4 dean, head 5 chief, maven 6 expert, leader, master, wizard 7 maestro 8 virtuoso 9 authority, patriarch
10 past master

Doyle's detective
6 Holmes (Sherlock)

D'Oyly Carte offering
8 operetta

doze
3 nap 5 sleep 6 catnap, drowse,
nod off, snooze 7 drop off, slumber
8 drift off 10 forty winks

dozy
see **drowsy**

DP
5 exile 6 émigré 7 evacuee, outcast, refugee 8 deportee, emigrant,
fugitive 10 expatriate

drab
4 dull, flat 5 bleak, brown, dingy,
faded, mousy, muddy, olive, vapid
6 dismal, dreary, mousey 7 subfusc
8 lifeless 9 cheerless, colorless
10 lackluster 11 dispiriting

draconian
5 cruel, harsh, rigid 6 severe,
strict 7 callous 8 ironclad, rigorous,
ruthless 9 merciless, stringent
10 inflexible, ironfisted, ironhanded

Dracula author
6 Stoker (Bram)

draft
3 tap 4 dose, haul, plan, plot, pull,
pump, swig 5 check, claim, drink,
frame, press, swill 6 breeze, call up,
demand, design, devise, enlist,
enroll, induct, potion, scheme, select,
siphon, sketch 7 compose, concoct,
current, outline, portion, prepare,
project, recruit 8 block out, contrive, rough out, skeleton, traction
9 adumbrate, allowance, blueprint,
conscribe, conscript, fabricate,
formulate, muster out 11 delineation,
skeletonize
avoider: 6 dodger
of a law: 4 bill

drag
3 lug, tow, tug 4 bore, haul, puff,
pull, swig 5 dally, delay, draft, tarry,
trail 6 burden, dawdle, harrow, loiter,
schlep, search, sledge 7 schlepp
8 friction, straggle 9 lag behind
13 procrastinate

dragging
4 beat, long 5 all in, spent, weary
6 pooped 7 drained, lengthy, tedious 8 drawn-out, extended, fatigued, overlong, sluggish, wiped out
9 exhausted, lethargic, long-drawn,
pooped out, prolonged, washed-out,
wearisome 10 protracted, slow-
moving 12 interminable, long-
drawn-out

draggle
3 lag 4 rove 5 stray, trail 8 straggle,
trail off 10 fall behind

draggle-tail
4 bawd, drab, slut 5 wench, whore
6 harlot 8 slattern 10 prostitute
11 nightwalker 12 streetwalker

draggletailed

6 blowsy, frowsy, frowzy, sordid, un-tidy 8 slattern, sluttish 10 slatternly

dragnet

4 trap 5 snare, trawl 7 network

drag off

4 cart, haul

dragon

5 beast 8 basilisk 10 cockatrice
biblical: 5 Rahab
Canaanite: 3 Yam 4 Yamm 5 Lotan
Chinese: 4 lung
French: 8 Tarasque
genus: 5 Draco
Greek: 5 Ladon 9 Eurythion
slayer: 4 Baal, Enki, Zeus 5 Indra
6 Cadmus, George (St.), Marduk,
Sigurd 7 Beowulf, Jupiter, Michael
(St.), Ninurta, Perseus 8 Margaret
(St.)
Sumerian: 3 Kur
Wagnerian: 6 Fafnir

dragoon

3 cow 5 bully 6 badger, coerce,
harass, hector 8 bludgeon, brow-beat, bulldoze, bullyrag, threaten
9 persecute, strong-arm, terrorize
10 cavalryman, intimidate

drain

3 dry, tap 4 pump, sink, sump, swig,
tire, vent, wear 5 bleed, draft, drink,
empty, leech, sewer, swill, use up,
weary 6 burden, gutter, siphon,
trench 7 conduit, culvert, deplete,
dwindle, draw off, exhaust, fatigue,
outflow 8 bankrupt, draw down,
wear down 9 discharge 10 impoverish 11 watercourse

drain away

3 ebb 4 drop, sink, wane 5 abate
6 lessen, reduce, remove 7 draw
off, dwindle, retreat, subside 8 de-crease, diminish, draw back, taper
off, withdraw

drained

4 beat 5 all-in, spent, weary 6 bleary,
pooped, used up 7 far-gone, worn-out 8 depleted, dragging, weakened,

wiped out 9 exhausted, pooped out,
washed-out

drainpipe

4 duct 5 sewer, spout 7 conduit
9 downspout

dram

3 bit, dab, nip, tot 4 atom, dash,
drop, iota, jolt, mite, shot, slug, spot,
swig, whit 5 crumb, grain, ounce,
pinch, scrap, shred, snort, speck
6 morsel, sliver 7 modicum, smidgen,
snifter, snippet, soupçon 8 particle

drama

4 play 7 pageant, theater, theatre,
tragedy
award: 4 Tony
former English: 6 masque
Japanese: 3 Noh
main part: 8 epitasis
musical: 5 opera 8 operetta
suspenseful: 11 cliff-hanger

dramatic

5 vivid 8 striking, thespian 10 his-trionic, theatrical
conflict: 4 agon

dramatis personae

4 cast 5 parts, roles 6 actors, troupe
7 company 10 characters

dramatist

10 playwright
American: 4 Hart (Moss), Inge
(William), Rabe (David), Rice
(Elmer), Uhry (Alfred) 5 Albee (Ed-ward), Barry (Philip), Foote (Horton),
Guare (John), Hecht (Ben), Mamet
(David), Odets (Clifford), Parks
(Suzan-Lori), Payne (John Howard),
Simon (Neil) 6 Ferber (Edna), Gur-ney (A. R.), Henley (Beth), Miller
(Arthur), Norman (Marsha), O'Neill
(Eugene), Thomas (Augustus),
Wilder (Thornton), Wilson (August,
Lanford, Robert) 7 Hellman (Lillian),
Kaufman (George S.), Kushner
(Tony), Shanley (John Patrick), Shep-ard (Sam) 8 Anderson (Maxwell,
Robert), Caldwell (Erskine), Connolly
(Marc), Sherwood (Robert), Williams
(Tennessee) 9 Chayefsky (Paddy),

Fierstein (Harvey), Hansberry (Lorraine) **11** Hammerstein (Oscar), Wasserstein (Wendy)
Austrian: 10 Schnitzler (Arthur)
Belgian: 11 Maeterlinck (Maurice)
Czech: 5 Havel (Vaclav)
English: 3 Fry (Christopher), Gay (John) **4** Hare (David), Rowe (Nicholas), Tate (Nahum) **5** Frayn (Michael), Milne (A. A.), Orton (Joe), Peele (George), Wilde (Oscar) **6** Barrie (James), Coward (Nöel), Dryden (John), Jonson (Ben), Pinero (Arthur Wing), Pinter (Harold), Steele (Richard), Storey (David) **7** Delaney (Shelagh), Marlowe (Christopher), Marston (John), Osborne (John), Shaffer (Anthony, Peter), Webster (John) **8** Congreve (William), Rattigan (Terrence), Shadwell (Thomas), Stoppard (Tom), Tourneur (Cyril), Vanbrugh (John), Zangwill (Israel) **9** Ayckbourn (Alan), Churchill (Caryl), Goldsmith (Oliver), Middleton (Thomas), Wycherley (William) **11** Shakespeare (William)
French: 5 Camus (Albert), Genet (Jean) **6** Musset (Alfred de), Racine (Jean), Sardou (Victorien), Sartre (Jean-Paul), Scribe (Eugène) **7** Anouilh (Jean), Ionesco (Eugène), Labiche (Eugène), Molière, Rostand (Edmond) **8** Marivaux (Pierre) **9** Corneille (Pierre), Crébillon, Giraudoux (Jean) **12** Beaumarchais (P. A. Caron de)
German: 5 Weiss (Peter) **6** Brecht (Bertolt), Goethe (Johann Wolfgang von), Kleist (Heinrich von) **8** Schiller (Friedrich von) **9** Hauptmann (Gerhart), Zuckmayer (Carl)
Greek: 8 Menander **9** Aeschylus, Euripides, Sophocles **12** Aristophanes
Hindu: 8 Kalidasa
Irish: 4 Shaw (George Bernard) **5** Behan (Brendan), Friel (Brian), Synge (John Millington), Yeats (William Butler) **6** O'Casey (Sean) **7** Beckett (Samuel), Gregory (Lady Augusta) **8** Sheridan (Richard Brinsley)
Italian: 5 Gozzi (Carlo), Verga (Giovanni) **7** Alfieri (Vittorio), Ariosto (Ludovico), Giacosa (Giuseppe), Goldoni (Carlo) **8** Trissino (Gian Giorgio) **9** D'Annunzio (Gabriele) **10** Metastasio (Pietro), Pirandello (Luigi)
Japanese: 5 Zeami
Nigerian: 7 Soyinka (Wole)
Norwegian: 5 Ibsen (Henrik) **8** Bjornson (Bjornstjerne)
Roman: 6 Seneca **7** Plautus, Terence
Romanian: 7 Ionesco (Eugene)
Russian: 7 Chekhov (Anton) **8** Zamyatin (Yevgeny)
South African: 6 Fugard (Athol)
Spanish: 4 Vega (Lope de) **5** Lorca (Federico García) **7** Alberti (Rafael), Arrabal (Fernando) **8** Quintero (Serafín, Joaquín) **9** Benavente (Jacinto) **11** García Lorca (Federico), Valle-Inclán (R. M. del)
Swedish: 5 Sachs (Nelly) **10** Strindberg (August)
Swiss: 6 Frisch (Max)

drape

4 fold, hang, roll **5** adorn, array, cloak, cover **6** clothe, enfold, enwrap, swathe, wrap up **7** curtain, swaddle **8** enswathe, envelope, swathe in

drapery

7 curtain, hanging **8** curtains, hangings

drastic

4 dire **5** harsh **6** severe **7** extreme, radical **9** desperate **10** exorbitant

draw

3 gut, tie, tow, tug **4** etch, haul, limn, lure, puff, pull, pump **5** draft, drain, infer, judge, trace **6** allure, appeal, deduce, depict, derive, elicit, entice, extend, gather, indite, inhale, pencil, siphon, sketch **7** attract, deplete, exhaust, extract, outline, portray, prolong, spin out, win over **8** conclude, contract, convince, dead heat, deadlock, lengthen, protract, standoff **9** delineate, formulate, represent,

stalemate **10** allurement, attraction, disembowel, eviscerate, exenterate
forth: **5** educe **6** elicit **7** extract
from: **4** milk, pump **5** bleed
together: **3** tie **4** join, lace

draw back
4 duck **5** cower, quail, wince **6** blench, flinch, recoil, shrink **7** back off, retreat, take off **9** turn aside

drawback
4 flaw, snag **5** fault, hitch **6** defect, refund **7** failing, trouble **8** weakness **9** detriment, hindrance **10** deficiency, difficulty, impediment **11** shortcoming **12** disadvantage **13** inconvenience

draw down
4 milk **5** drain, spend, use up **6** expend, reduce **7** deplete, exhaust **8** decrease, diminish **9** reduction, siphon off

drawer
9 draftsman
for money: **4** till

drawers
5 pants **6** undies **8** trousers **10** underpants

draw in
6 enmesh, entice, induce, prompt **7** involve, retract, win over **8** convince, persuade, pull back **9** prevail on **11** bring around, prevail upon

drawing
6 doodle, sketch **7** cartoon, outline

drawing power
4 lure, pull **6** appeal **9** magnetism **10** attraction

drawn
4 taut, worn **6** peaked **7** fraught, haggard, pinched **8** careworn, fatigued, pictured, strained, stressed **9** attracted **10** delineated

drawn-out
4 long **7** lengthy, tedious **8** extended, overlong **9** prolonged **10** protracted

draw off
3 tap **4** pump **5** bleed, draft, drain **6** siphon

draw out
6 extend **7** prolong, stretch **8** elongate, lengthen, protract

draw up
4 balk, halt, lift, make, stop **5** array, draft, frame, order, raise, write **6** deploy, map out **7** compose, concoct, dispose, marshal, prepare, set down **8** organize, write out **9** formulate

dray
4 cart, drag **5** wagon **6** barrow, sledge **7** travois **9** stoneboat

dread
4 fear **5** alarm, panic **6** dismay, fright, horror, phobia, terror **7** anxiety **10** foreboding **11** trepidation **12** apprehension **13** consternation

dreadful
5 awful **6** tragic **7** awesome, extreme, fearful, ghastly, hideous, ominous **8** alarming, horrible, horrific, shocking, terrible **9** appalling, frightful, revolting **11** distressing, frightening

dreadfully
7 awfully **8** horribly **9** decidedly, extremely, fearfully, hideously, seriously **10** strikingly, tragically **11** appallingly, exceedingly, frightfully

dreadnought
10 battleship

dream
4 ache, long, wish **5** crave, fancy, ideal **6** bubble, desire, hanker, vision **7** chimera, fantasy, imagine, rainbow, reverie, specter, spectre **8** ambition, delusion, illusion, phantasm, phantasy **9** fantasize, nightmare **10** aspiration
divination by: **11** oneiromancy
god: **8** Morpheus

dreamer
  7 utopian 8 idealist 9 visionary
  10 Don Quixote, lotus-eater
  13 castle-builder

dreamlike
  5 ideal, vague 6 unreal 7 shadowy,
  surreal 8 fanciful, illusory, nebulous
  9 imaginary, visionary 12 otherworldly

Dream of Gerontius composer
  5 Elgar (Edward)

dream up
  5 frame, hatch 6 cook up, create,
  devise, invent 7 concoct, imagine
  8 conceive, contrive, envisage,
  envision 9 formulate, visualize

dreamy
  7 pensive 9 unworldly, visionary
  10 idealistic 11 impractical 12 otherworldly 13 introspective

dreary
  4 blah, drab, dull 5 bleak 6 boring,
  dismal, gloomy, somber, sombre
  7 forlorn, humdrum, joyless, tedious
  8 banausic, tiresome, wretched
  9 cheerless 10 depressing, depressive, monotonous, oppressive,
  pedestrian 11 dispiriting 12 discouraging

dreck
  3 mud 4 junk, muck, slop 5 offal,
  swill, trash, waste 6 litter, refuse,
  sewage 7 garbage, rubbish 9 sweepings

dredge
  3 dig 5 barge, scoop 6 deepen, dig
  out, gather 8 excavate, scoop out
  9 hollow out, scrape out

dregs
  4 lees, scum 5 trash 6 grouts
  7 deposit, grounds, remains, residue
  8 sediment 9 settlings 11 precipitate

drei
  5 three

dreidel
  3 top

Dreiser, Theodore
  character: 5 Clyde (Griffiths)
  6 Carrie (Meeber), Eugene (Witla),
  Sondra (Finchley) 7 Roberta (Alden)
  9 Hurstwood (George) 10 Cowper-
  wood (Frank)
  novel: 5 Stoic (The), Titan (The)
  6 Genius (The) 9 Financier (The)
  12 Sister Carrie 14 Jennie Gerhardt
  15 American Tragedy (An)

drench
  3 sop 4 dunk, soak 5 douse, souse,
  steep, swill 6 deluge, seethe 7 immerse 8 inundate, saturate, submerge, waterlog

dress
  3 gut 4 bind, clad, deck, doll, duds,
  garb, gown, sack, togs 5 adorn,
  align, array, frock, getup, guise,
  habit, smock, weeds 6 attire, bedeck, caftan, clothe, dirndl, enrobe,
  outfit, sacque 7 apparel, bandage,
  bedizen, chemise, clothes, costume,
  garment, garnish, raiment, threads,
  turnout, uniform 8 beautify, clothing,
  covering, decorate, ensemble,
  ornament, wardrobe 9 embellish,
  make ready 11 habiliments
  a wound: 7 bandage
  designer: 4 Dior (Christian), Erté,
  Head (Edith) 5 Blass (Bill), Bohan
  (Marc), Karan (Donna), Klein
  (Calvin), Pucci (Emilio), Quant
  (Mary), Worth (Charles Frederick)
  6 Armani (Giorgio), Cardin (Pierre),
  Jacobs (Marc), Lauren (Ralph),
  Miyake (Issey), Poiret (Paul)
  7 Balmain (Pierre), Cassini (Oleg),
  Halston, Lacroix (Christian), Mizrahi
  (Isaac), Versace (Gianni) 8 Galliano
  (John), Givenchy (Hubert) 9 Cour-
  règes (André), de la Renta (Oscar),
  Gernreich (Rudi), Lagerfeld (Karl),
  Valentino 10 Balenciaga (Cristóbal)
  12 Saint-Laurent (Yves), Schiaparelli
  (Elsa)
  finically: 5 primp
  hair: 4 coif 6 barber
  line: 3 hem

mode of: 5 habit
oriental: 9 cheongsam
part: 5 skirt 6 bodice
South Seas: 6 sarong
with the beak: 5 preen
with vulgarity: 7 bedizen

dress down
5 chide, scold 6 berate, rail at, rebuke, revile 7 bawl out, reprove, tell off, upbraid 8 admonish, chastise, reproach 9 castigate, reprimand 10 tongue-lash

dresser
5 chest 6 bureau 7 commode, highboy 10 chiffonier
gaudy: 9 butterfly

dressing
5 sauce 6 catsup 7 bandage, catchup, ketchup 8 stuffing
salad: 5 ranch 6 French 7 Italian, Russian 10 blue cheese 11 vinaigrette 12 green goddess

dressing room
6 vestry 8 vestiary

dressmaker
7 modiste 9 couturier 10 couturiere, seamstress

dress up
6 attire, clothe, rig out, tog out 7 apparel, deck out 8 beautify, disguise, prettify, trick out 9 embellish 10 camouflage

dressy
4 chic 5 showy, smart 6 classy, formal, frilly, ornate 7 duded up, elegant, stylish 9 rigged out

Dreyfus's defender
4 Zola (Emile)

dribble
4 drip, leak, weep 5 drool 6 bounce, drivel, slaver 7 distill, drizzle, slobber, trickle 8 salivate, sprinkle

driblet
4 drop 6 gobbet 7 globule, smidgen 8 particle, pittance

dried grape
6 raisin

dried meat
5 jerky

dried plum
5 prune

drift
3 bat, gad 4 flow, flux, gist, roam, sail, skim, tide, waft, wash 5 amble, coast, creep, float, mosey, range, slide, stray, trend 6 bummel, linger, ramble, stream, stroll, wander 7 current, maunder, meander, meaning, saunter 8 movement, penchant, sideslip, tendency 9 deviation 10 propensity 11 disposition, inclination, progression 12 predilection

drifter
3 bum, vag 4 hobo 5 gypsy, nomad, tramp 7 floater, migrant, vagrant 8 derelict, vagabond 9 transient 11 beachcomber 12 rolling stone

drill
3 bit, dig 4 bore 5 auger, borer, punch, train 6 pierce, trepan, wimble 7 routine, wildcat, workout 8 exercise, practice, practise, rehearse 9 penetrate, rehearsal 10 discipline
command: 6 at ease 8 left face 9 about face, attention, right face

drink
3 ade, lap, nip, sea, sip, tea 4 belt, brew, deep, down, grog, gulp, soak, swig, tope, toss 5 booze, draft, drain, ocean, quaff, slurp, swill, toast 6 absorb, brandy, cognac, guzzle, imbibe, jigger, liquid, liquor, pledge, potion, tank up, tipple 7 consume, potable, schnaps, spirits, swallow, swizzle, toss off 8 aperitif, beverage, libation, liquor up, schnapps 9 aqua vitae
after-dinner: 6 frappé 7 cordial, liqueur
drugged: 6 Mickey 10 Mickey Finn
honey: 4 mead
hot: 5 negus, toddy
liquor: 5 booze, hooch 6 red-eye 9 firewater, moonshine
mixed: 3 nog 5 julep 6 Gibson, gimlet, mai tai, mimosa, mojito,

rickey, Rob Roy, zombie **7** gin fizz, martini, sidecar, stinger **8** daiquiri, pink lady **9** alexander, Cuba libre, manhattan, margarita, mint julep, rusty nail **10** Bloody Mary, piña colada, Tom Collins **11** gin and tonic, grasshopper, screwdriver, whiskey sour **12** black Russian, old-fashioned
mixer: 7 swirler
noisily: 5 slurp
of liquor: 4 dram, shot, slug **5** snort **8** highball
of the gods: 6 nectar
soft: 3 pop **4** cola, soda **5** tonic **7** soda pop **8** root beer **9** ginger ale **12** sarsaparilla
stimulating: 6 bracer
(see also **beverage**)

drinkable
6 liquor **7** potable **8** beverage, libation, potation

drinking
8 potation
fountain: 7 bubbler
horn: 6 rhyton
spree: 3 jag **4** tear, toot **5** binge, spree **6** bender **7** carouse **8** carousal

drip
4 leak, plop, weep **7** dribble, droplet, trickle **8** sprinkle

dripping
3 wet **5** runny, soppy **6** soaked, soused **7** drizzly, soaking, sopping **8** drenched **9** saturated **11** wringing-wet

drippy
5 mushy, rainy, sappy, sobby, soppy, soupy, teary, weepy **6** slushy, syrupy **7** drizzly, maudlin, mawkish, soaking, sopping, tearful **9** schmaltzy **11** sentimental

drive
3 pep, ram **4** goad, herd, push, spur, taxi, trip, urge **5** chase, force, guide, impel, jaunt, lunge, motor, moxie, oomph, pilot, pound, spunk, steer, surge, vigor **6** compel, convey,

exhort, hammer, outing, plunge, propel, strike, thrust **7** actuate, impetus, operate, produce **8** ambition, mobilize, momentum, navigate, shepherd, vitality **9** chauffeur, excursion, urge along **10** enterprise, get-up-and-go, initiative, motivation
away: 4 shoo **5** exile **6** aroint
back: 5 repel **6** defend **7** repulse
off: 6 dispel
out: 8 exorcise

drivel
3 rot **4** bosh, bunk **5** drool, hokum, hooey, prate **6** babble, bunkum, gabble, jabber, slaver **7** baloney, blabber, blather, dribble, hogwash, prattle, rubbish, slobber, twaddle **8** claptrap, flimflam, nonsense, salivate **9** gibberish, poppycock **10** balderdash, double-talk, flapdoodle **12** blatherskite, gobbledygook

driver
4 jehu **5** cabby **6** cabbie, cabman, hackie, mallet **7** hackman **8** coachman, motorist, muleteer, operator **9** chauffeur, dowitcher **10** taskmaster **11** tamping iron
of an elephant: 6 mahout
Roman: 10 charioteer
truck: 8 teamster

driving
7 dynamic, powered **8** forceful, vigorous **9** energetic, inspiring **10** compelling

drizzle
4 mist, rain **7** dribble, spatter **8** droplets, sprinkle **10** sprinkling **13** precipitation

Dr. Jekyll and Mr. _____
4 Hyde

droll
3 odd **5** comic, funny, nutty, witty **7** comical, risible **8** farcical, humorous **9** eccentric, laughable, ludicrous, whimsical

drollery
5 humor **6** comedy, joking, whimsy **7** jesting

dromedary
5 camel

drone
3 bee, hum 4 buzz, idle, laze, loaf, loll 5 idler 6 drudge, loiter, lounge, murmur 7 bagpipe 8 aircraft, parasite 9 bombinate 10 pedal point

drool
4 gush, rave 5 froth 6 dote on, drivel, saliva, slaver 7 blather, dribble, enthuse, slobber 8 salivate 10 rhapsodize

droop
3 sag 4 fall, flag, hang, loll, sink, swag, wilt 5 slump 6 dangle, slouch, weaken 7 decline, let down, subside 8 languish

droopy
4 blue, down, weak 5 baggy 6 gloomy 7 doleful, languid, sagging, slouchy, wilting 8 cast down, dejected, downcast 9 depressed 10 dispirited 11 downhearted

drop
3 dip, nip, sag, tot 4 down, drib, dump, fall, fell, jolt, lose, slip, slug, tear 5 cease, depth, lapse, lower, pitch, plump, scrub, slide, snort, speck, spend 6 cancel, cave in, demise, depart, expire, fumble, give up, go down, ground, plunge, reduce, smitch, topple, unload, vanish 7 abandon, decease, decline, deposit, descend, descent, distill, dribble, driblet, fall off, forfeit, give out, globule, pendant, plummet, trickle 8 bowl over, break off, collapse, comedown, downturn, keel over, nose-dive 9 declivity, discharge, downslide, downswing, downtrend, prostrate, reduction, terminate 10 depository

drop by
4 call 5 pop in, visit 6 stop in 8 come over

droplet
4 drib, tear 7 globule

drop off
3 nap, sag 4 doze, fall, slip 5 slide,
slump 6 catnap, drowse, lessen, snooze 7 decline, deliver, deposit, slacken 8 diminish, fall away, hand over 10 fall asleep

dropsical
5 puffy, tumid 6 turgid 7 swollen 8 inflated 9 edematous, tumescent

dropsy
5 edema 8 anasarca

dross
4 junk, scum, slag 5 dregs, offal, waste 6 debris, scoria 7 remains, residue, schlock 8 detritus, impurity, leavings

drossy
4 base 6 impure, scummy 7 trivial 8 inferior, unworthy 9 worthless

drought
4 lack, need, want 6 dearth 7 aridity, dryness 8 scarcity, shortage 10 deficiency

droughty
3 dry 4 arid, sere 7 bone-dry, dried up, parched, thirsty 10 desiccated

drove
3 mob 4 army, herd, host, mass, pack 5 crowd, flock, horde, troop 6 myriad, pushed, school, throng 7 phalanx 9 multitude

drover
6 cowboy 8 shepherd

drown
4 sink, soak 5 douse, flood, souse, swamp 6 deluge, drench, engulf 7 immerse, repress, smother 8 inundate, submerge 9 overpower, overwhelm, suffocate 10 asphyxiate, extinguish

drowse
3 nod 4 doze 5 sleep 6 catnap, snooze 7 doze off, drop off, shuteye, slumber 10 forty winks

drowsy
4 dozy 5 dopey 6 droopy, sleepy, torpid 7 languid 8 indolent, sluggish 9 lethargic, somnolent, soporific 10 slumberous 13 lackadaisical

Dr. Seuss
6 Geisel (Theodor Seuss)
book: 11 Cat in the Hat (The)
15 Green Eggs and Ham, Yertle the
Turtle 19 Horton Hatches the Egg
26 How the Grinch Stole Christmas

drub
3 tan, wax, zap 4 bash, beat, club,
deck, drum, flay, flog, lash, lick,
mash, maul, pelt, trim, whip 5 baste,
cream, crush, paste, pound, score,
slash, smash, smear, spank, stamp,
thump, wreck 6 batter, berate,
bruise, buffet, hammer, master, pummel, punish, revile, scorch,
thrash, thresh, wallop 7 belabor,
blister, censure, clobber, cripple,
lambast, scourge, shatter, shellac,
trounce 8 bulldoze, lambaste, lash
into, outclass, outshine 9 castigate,
excoriate, overwhelm

drubbing
4 loss, rout 6 defeat 7 setback
10 defeasance 11 shellacking

drudge
4 grub, hack, moil, peon, plod, slog
5 grind, slave 6 menial, slavey
7 grubber, plodder 8 dogsbody

drudgery
4 moil, toil 5 chore, grind 7 travail 9 grunt work 10 donkeywork
11 backbreaker

drudging
6 boring, tiring 7 irksome, tedious
8 dragging, tiresome 9 fatiguing,
laborious, wearisome 10 monotonous

drug
4 dope, lull 5 sulfa 6 downer,
ipecac, opiate, physic, poison,
potion, remedy, statin 7 fen-phen,
generic, stupefy 8 biologic, medicine, narcotic, nepenthe, relaxant,
sedative 9 ibuprofen, medicinal,
methadone 10 antibiotic, medicament, medication 11 thalidomide
addict: 6 junkie
agent: 4 narc
calming: 8 sedative

experience: 4 trip
illicit: 3 ice, kif, LSD, pot 4 acid,
coke, dope, hash, meth, scag, snow,
weed 5 crack, grass, opium, smack,
speed 6 heroin, peyote 7 cocaine,
crystal, hashish 8 cannabis, goofball
9 mescaline 10 methadrine, psilocybin
seller: 10 pharmacist
sleep-inducing: 8 hypnotic 9 soporific 11 barbiturate

drugged
4 high 5 dazed, doped, dopey
6 flying, loaded, stoned, zonked
8 benumbed, hopped-up, turned
on 9 spaced-out, stupefied 10 narcotized

druggist
7 chemist 10 apothecary, pharmacist

drugstore
8 pharmacy 10 apothecary

druid
4 Celt 6 priest 7 prophet
sacred object: 3 oak 9 mistletoe

drum
3 keg, vat 4 beat, cask 5 conga,
tabor 6 barrel, tom-tom, tympan
7 tambour, timpani (plural), tympani
(plural) 8 cylinder
Indian: 5 tabla 8 mridanga
Irish: 7 bodhran
large: 4 bass 7 timbale
small: 5 bongo, tabor 7 timbrel
string: 5 snare

drumbeat
4 flam, roll, tuck 6 ruffle, tattoo
7 booming, pit-a-pat, rat-a-tat 8 rataplan

drumfire
5 salvo 6 volley 7 barrage, booming
9 broadside, cannonade, fusillade
11 bombardment

drumhead
4 skin 7 summary

drummer
4 Rich (Buddy) 5 Krupa (Gene),
Roach (Max), Starr (Ringo), Watts

drum up

(Charlie) 6 Blakey (Art), hawker, Puente (Tito), vendor 7 peddler 8 pitchman, salesman

drum up

6 invent 7 canvass, solicit 9 originate
interest: 8 ballyhoo

drunk

3 lit, sot 4 lush, soak, wino 5 lit up, souse, tight, tipsy 6 blotto, boozer, juiced, soused, stewed, stinko, tiddly, wasted, zonked 7 crocked, guzzler, pie-eyed, sloshed, squiffy, tippler 8 squiffed 9 inebriate, plastered 10 boozehound, inebriated 11 intoxicated

drunkard

3 sot 4 lush, soak, wino 5 rummy, souse, stiff, toper 6 bibber, boozer, soaker 7 guzzler, swiller, tippler, tosspot 8 alcoholic, inebriate, juicehead 10 boozehound 11 dipsomaniac

Drusilla

brother: 8 Caligula
father: 5 Herod 10 Germanicus
husband: 5 Felix
mother: 9 Agrippina
sister: 8 Berenice 9 Agrippina

dry

3 set 4 arid, brut, dull, sere, sour, tart 5 baked, dusty, parch, stale, wizen 6 barren, desert, harden, stolid, thirst, wither 7 congeal, deadpan, parched, shrivel, sterile, thirsty 8 rainless, solidify, tearless, teetotal, withered 9 anhydrous, dehydrate, desiccate, evaporate, unwatered 10 dehydrated, desiccated 11 unemotional 12 matter-of-fact 13 uninteresting
combining form: 3 xer 4 xero
goods: 6 linens, napery 8 clothing, textiles
out: 5 sober 8 soberize
period: 7 drought
wine: 3 sec 4 brut

dryasdust

4 arid, dull 5 banal, inane, vapid

6 boring, stodgy 7 insipid, prosaic, tedious 9 wearisome 10 uninspired 13 uninteresting

dry measure

4 peck, pint 5 quart 6 bushel

Dryope

form: 5 lotus
husband: 9 Andraemon
sister: 4 Iole

dry up

4 wilt 5 wizen 6 wither 7 deplete, exhaust, mummify, shrivel 9 desiccate, disappear, evaporate

dual

3 two 4 twin 5 duple 6 bifold, binary, double, duplex, paired 7 coupled, matched, twofold 8 matching 9 duplicate

dualistic

5 duple 6 bifold, binary, double, duplex, paired 7 twofold 9 Manichean 10 Manichaean

dualize

4 copy, dupe 5 clone 6 double 9 duplicate, replicate, reproduce

dub

4 call, name, term, trim 5 style, title 6 duffer 7 baptize, bungler, entitle, fumbler 8 christen, nickname, rerecord 9 blunderer, designate 10 denominate

dubiety

5 doubt 7 concern 8 mistrust 9 confusion, suspicion 10 skepticism 11 incertitude, incredulity, uncertainty 12 doubtfulness

dubious

4 iffy 5 fishy 6 unsure 7 suspect, unclear 8 doubtful, hesitant, unlikely 9 equivocal, skeptical, uncertain, undecided 10 improbable, unreliable 11 mistrustful, problematic, questioning, unconvinced, unpromising 12 questionable, undependable, undetermined

dubitable

5 fishy 7 suspect 8 doubtful, mar-

ginal **9** ambiguous, uncertain, unsettled **10** borderline **11** problematic **13** indeterminate

duce
5 ruler **6** despot, leader, tyrant **8** dictator **9** Mussolini (Benito), oppressor, strongman

duck
3 bob, bow, dip, shy **4** bend, dive, dunk, shun **5** avoid, dodge, douse, elude, evade, fence, parry, shirk, stoop **6** escape, plunge **7** back out, immerse **8** sidestep, submerge, submerse **10** canvasback
Asian: 5 Pekin **8** mandarin
dabbling: 7 gadwall, mallard
diving: 4 smew **7** pochard **9** merganser **10** bufflehead
Eurasian: 4 smew
European: 8 shelduck
genus: 4 Anas
group: 4 team **5** brace, flock, skein **6** flight
hunter's screen: 5 blind
male: 5 drake
red-wattled: 7 Muscovy
river: 4 teal **6** wigeon **7** pintail, widgeon
scaup: 8 bluebill
sea: 5 eider, scaup **6** scoter

duckbill
8 platypus **9** hadrosaur, monotreme

duck soup
4 easy, snap **5** cinch **6** breeze, picnic, simple **8** kid stuff, painless, pushover **10** child's play **11** piece of cake

ducky
4 cute **5** swell **6** lovely, peachy **7** darling **9** hunky-dory **10** peachy-keen

duct
4 pipe, tube **5** canal **6** course, runway **7** channel, conduit **11** watercourse
anatomical: 3 vas **4** vasa (plural)

ductile
6 pliant, supple **7** plastic, pliable **8** flexible, moldable **9** adaptable, compliant, malleable, tractable
metal: 4 wire

ductless gland
see **endocrine gland**

dud
3 dog **4** bomb, bust, flop **5** lemon, loser **6** bummer, misfit, turkey **7** debacle, failure, washout **8** abortion **9** valueless **11** ineffective

dude
3 fop, guy **4** beau, buck, rake **5** blood, dandy **6** fellow **7** coxcomb **8** macaroni **9** exquisite **12** Beau Brummell, lounge lizard

dudgeon
3 ire **4** fury, huff, miff, rage **5** anger, pique, wrath **7** chagrin, offense, outrage, umbrage **8** vexation **10** resentment **11** indignation **12** exasperation

duds
3 rig **4** garb, gear, rags, togs **5** dress, getup, weeds **6** attire, things **7** apparel, clothes, raiment, threads, toggery **8** clothing, garments **9** trappings, vestments **11** habiliments

due
4 debt, just, owed **5** lumps, owing, right **6** direct, earned, lawful, proper, unpaid **7** arrears, condign, deserts, exactly, merited, payable, payment, regular **8** adequate, deserved, directly, expected, rightful, suitable **9** deserving, equitable, liability, requisite, scheduled **10** ascribable, obligatory, receivable, satisfying, sufficient **11** appropriate, outstanding **12** compensation, satisfaction

duel
4 tilt **5** fight, joust **6** combat **7** contest, dispute **8** conflict

duenna
8 chaperon **9** chaperone, companion, governess

duet
dancer's: 9 pas de deux

due to

4 over 7 owing to, through 9 because of 11 considering

duff

3 can 4 buns, butt, rear, rump, tail, tush 5 fanny, slack 6 bottom 7 keister, pudding, rear end 8 backside, buttocks, coal dust, derriere, fine coal

duffer

4 boob, clod, dolt, dope, yo-yo 5 chump, dunce, klutz 6 dimwit, dum-dum, lubber, nitwit 7 dullard, fumbler, peddler, pinhead 8 bonehead, dumbbell, lunkhead, numskull 9 blockhead, ignoramus, numbskull, simpleton 10 nincompoop, stumblebum 11 incompetent

dugout

5 canoe 6 trench 7 piragua, pirogue, shelter

duiker

8 antelope

dukedom

5 duchy 6 domain

dulcet

5 sweet 7 melodic, tuneful 8 charming, cheerful, engaging, euphonic, pleasant, pleasing, soothing 9 agreeable, melodious 10 euphonious 11 mellifluous

dulcimer

6 zither 8 psaltery
Hungarian: 8 cimbalom
Persian: 6 santir 7 santour

dull

3 dim, dun, mat 4 arid, blah, blur, drab, flat, numb 5 blunt, dense, dusty, faded, ho-hum, inert, matte, muddy, muted 6 benumb, blurry, boring, deaden, dreary, gloomy, leaden, obtuse, stodgy, stupid 7 blunted, humdrum, insipid, muffled, prosaic, stupefy, subdued, tarnish, tedious 8 banausic, bromidic, deadened, discolor, lifeless, listless, monotone, plodding, sluggish 9 bloodless, colorless, dim-witted, dryasdust, insensate, ponderous, wearisome 10 dispirited, indistinct, insensible, lackluster, lusterless, monotonous, pedestrian 11 commonplace, desensitize, insensitive, thickheaded, thick-witted, unsharpened 12 simpleminded 13 uninteresting

dullard

3 oaf 4 bird, boob, clod, dolt, dope, yo-yo 5 chump, dummy, dunce, idiot, moron, ninny, noddy, stupe 6 dimwit, dum-dum, nitwit 7 airhead, pinhead 8 bonehead, dumbbell, imbecile, lunkhead, meathead, numskull 9 birdbrain, blockhead, ignoramus, lamebrain, numbskull, simpleton 10 dunderhead 11 chowderhead, chucklehead

dullness

5 ennui 6 apathy, stupor, tedium, torpor 7 boredom, languor 8 hebetude, lethargy, monotony 9 bluntness, denseness, lassitude, stupidity, torpidity 12 indifference, listlessness, sluggishness

duly

8 properly, suitably 9 correctly, regularly 12 sufficiently 13 appropriately

duma

7 council 8 assembly, congress 11 legislature

Dumas character

5 Athos 6 Aramis, Dantès (Edmond) 7 Camille, Porthos 9 D'Artagnan

dumb

3 mum 4 dull, mute 5 dense, quiet, thick 6 deaden, obtuse, silent, stupid 7 doltish, foolish, idiotic, moronic 8 duncical, ignorant, taciturn, wordless 9 dim-witted, fatheaded, voiceless 10 speechless, tongue-tied 11 blockheaded, thick-witted, tight-lipped 12 closemouthed, inarticulate, simple-minded, tight-mouthed, unresponsive

dumbbell

see **dullard**

dumbfound

5 amaze **6** boggle, puzzle **7** astound, nonplus, perplex, stagger **8** astonish, bewilder, bowl over, confound, distract, surprise **9** take aback **11** flabbergast

dumbfounded

5 agape **6** amazed **7** puzzled, shocked **8** startled **9** astounded, perplexed, staggered, surprised **10** astonished, bewildered, bowled over, confounded, distracted, nonplussed, taken aback **13** thunderstruck

dummkopf

3 oaf **4** boob, clod, dodo, dolt, dope, fool, goof, jerk, mutt, simp, yo-yo **5** chump, dummy, dunce, idiot, moron, ninny, noddy, stupe **6** dimwit, donkey, dum-dum, nitwit, noodle **7** airhead, dullard, pinhead, schnook **8** bonehead, clodpoll, dumbbell, dumbhead, imbecile, lunkhead, meathead, numskull **9** birdbrain, blockhead, ignoramus, lamebrain, numbskull, simpleton, thickhead **10** dunderhead, hammerhead, nincompoop **11** chowderhead, chucklehead, knucklehead

dummy

4 boob, clod, dodo, dolt, mock, sham, yo-yo **5** chump, dunce, false, idiot, model, moron, ninny, noddy, stupe **6** dimwit, dum-dum, effigy, ersatz, layout, mock-up, nitwit, puppet, stooge **7** airhead, dullard, manikin, pinhead, stand-in **8** bonehead, dumbbell, imbecile, lunkhead, mannekin, meathead, numskull **9** birdbrain, blockhead, ignoramus, imitation, lamebrain, numbskull, simpleton, simulated **10** artificial, dunderhead, fictitious, nincompoop, substitute **11** chowderhead, chucklehead

dump

4 drop, junk **5** chuck, depot, ditch, scrap **6** armory, pigpen, pigsty, plunge **7** abandon, arsenal, deep-six, discard **8** jettison, magazine, throw out **9** stockpile, throw away **10** depository

dumpling

5 dough **8** quenelle **10** butterball

dumps

4 funk **5** blues, dolor, gloom, mopes, slump **7** sadness **8** doldrums **9** dejection **10** depression, gloominess, melancholy **11** despondency, unhappiness **12** mournfulness

dumpy

5 dingy, seedy, squat, stout **6** chubby, chunky, shabby, slummy, stocky, stubby, stumpy **7** run-down **8** heavyset, thickset **9** shapeless **10** broken-down **11** dilapidated, thick-bodied

dun

3 dim, fly **4** dull, drab, gray **5** annoy, brown, dusky, horse, murky, press **6** demand, gloomy, mayfly, needle, pester, plague, somber, sombre **9** ephemerid, importune

Duncan's slayer

7 Macbeth

dunce

3 oaf **4** boob, clod, dodo, dolt, dope, goof, mutt, simp, yo-yo **5** booby, chump, dummy, idiot, moron, ninny, noddy, stupe **6** dimwit, donkey, duffer, dum-dum, nitwit, noodle, stupid **7** airhead, dullard, fathead, pinhead **8** bonehead, clodpoll, dumbbell, imbecile, lunkhead, meathead, numskull **9** birdbrain, blockhead, ignoramus, lamebrain, numbskull, simpleton **10** dunderhead, hammerhead, nincompoop **11** chowderhead, chucklehead, knucklehead

Dunciad author

4 Pope (Alexander)

dundrearies

9 burnsides, sideburns **11** muttonchops **12** side-whiskers

dune

8 sandbank
area: 3 erg

dung

4 muck 6 manure, ordure 9 excrement

beetle: 6 scarab 9 tumblebug

dungeon

4 jail 5 vault 6 prison 9 black hole, oubliette

dunghill

6 midden

dunk

3 dip, sop 4 soak 5 douse, drown, souse 6 drench 7 immerse 8 saturate, submerge, submerse

dunlin

9 sandpiper

duo

4 duet, dyad, pair 5 brace 6 couple 7 doublet, twosome

dupe

3 con, kid, sap 4 butt, fool, gull, hoax, mark 5 cheat, chump, cozen, patsy, spoof, trick 6 befool, delude, double, outwit, pigeon, sucker 7 chicane, deceive, defraud, mislead 8 flimflam, hoodwink 9 bamboozle, victimize 11 double-cross, hornswoggle

dupery

3 con 4 scam, sham 5 cheat, fraud 6 deceit, humbug, hustle 7 chicane 8 cheating, flimflam, trickery 9 chicanery, deception, duplicity, imposture, swindling 10 dishonesty, hanky-panky 11 hoodwinking 13 double-dealing, sharp practice

duple

4 dual, twin 6 bifold, binary, double, duplex, paired 7 coupled, doubled, twofold 9 dualistic

duplex

see **duple**

duplicate

4 copy, fake, mate, redo, same, twin 5 clone, ditto, equal, match, mimeo, repro 6 carbon, double 7 dualize, imitate, replica 8 knockoff 9 companion, facsimile, identical, imitation, look-alike, replicate, reproduce 10 carbon copy, dead ringer, equivalent, reciprocal 11 counterfeit, counterpart, replication 12 reproduction

duplicitous

5 phony 6 shifty, sneaky 7 devious 8 delusive, guileful, scheming, sneaking, two-faced 9 deceitful, deceiving, deceptive, dishonest, underhand 10 fraudulent 11 underhanded 12 disingenuous 13 double-dealing

duplicity

5 fraud, guile 6 deceit 7 cunning, perfidy 8 scheming, trickery 9 chicanery, deception, treachery 10 dishonesty, doubleness 11 skulduggery 12 dissemblance, skullduggery 13 dissimulation, double-dealing

durability

4 wear 8 firmness 9 endurance, longevity, stability 10 permanence

durable

5 stout 6 stable, strong, sturdy 7 lasting 8 enduring 9 permanent, tenacious 10 dependable 11 longlasting

durance

7 bondage 9 captivity, detention, restraint 11 confinement 12 enthrallment, imprisonment 13 incarceration

duration

3 run 4 term, time 6 extent, period 7 interim 8 interval 11 persistence

duress

5 force 6 menace, threat 8 bullying, coercion, menacing, pressure 9 restraint 10 compulsion, constraint 11 restriction 12 intimidation

during

4 amid 10 throughout

durra

7 sorghum 12 grain sorghum

durum

5 wheat

dusk
4 dark 7 evening 8 darkness, eventide, gloaming, twilight 9 nightfall
12 semidarkness

dusky
3 dim 4 dark 5 murky, swart 6 brunet, gloomy, opaque, twilit 7 obscure, shadowy, swarthy 8 funereal,
nubilous, overcast, twilight 9 tenebrous 10 caliginous 11 dark-skinned

dust
4 grit, sand, sift, soot 5 ashes, grime
6 powder 8 sprinkle 10 besprinkle,
sprinkling

dustbowl victim
4 Okie

dustup
3 row 4 spat 5 fight, melee, run-in,
set-to 6 battle, fracas, hassle, tussle
7 dispute, quarrel, rhubarb, scuffle
8 argument, skirmish 9 bickering,
brannigan 10 falling-out 11 altercation

dusty
3 dry 4 arid, dull 5 stale 7 parched,
powdery, tedious, unswept

Dutch
7 trouble 8 hot water
African: 9 Afrikaans
ceramics: 5 delft
cheese: 4 Edam 5 Gouda
dog breed: 7 griffon 8 keeshond
painter: 3 Dou (Gerrit, Gerard)
4 Cuyp (Aelbert Jacobsz), Gogh
(Vincent van), Hals (Frans) 5 Bosch
(Hieronymus), Hooch (Pieter de),
Steen (Jan) 7 de Hooch (Pieter),
Hobbema (Meindert), van Gogh (Vincent), Vermeer (Jan) 8 Mondrian
(Piet), Ruysdael (Jacob van, Salomon van), Terborch (Gerard) 9 de
Kooning (Willem), Honthorst (Gerrit
van), Rembrandt (van Rijn)
philosopher: 7 Spinoza (Benedict de)
scholar: 7 Erasmus (Desiderius)

Dutch South African
4 Boer

dutiful
7 devoted 8 faithful 9 compliant
10 respectful 13 conscientious

duty
3 job, tax, use 4 levy, onus, role,
task, work 5 chare, chore, stint
6 burden, charge, devoir, impost,
office, tariff 7 respect, service
8 function 10 allegiance, assessment, assignment, commitment,
dedication, obligation

dwarf
4 runt 5 gnome, pygmy, stunt, troll
6 midget, peewee 7 manikin 8 Tom
Thumb 9 miniature 10 diminutive,
homunculus 11 hop-o'-my-thumb,
lilliputian
in Snow White: 3 Doc 5 Dopey,
Happy 6 Grumpy, Sleepy, Sneezy
7 Bashful
Scottish: 7 blastie

dwarfish
5 pygmy, small 6 midget 7 minikin,
stunted 8 inferior, pint-size 9 miniature, pint-sized 10 diminutive, undersized 11 lilliputian

dweeb
4 dork, drip, geek, nerd, wimp, wuss
5 loser 7 nebbish

dwell
3 lie 4 bide, live, stay 5 abide,
exist 6 locate, remain, repose,
reside, settle 7 hang out

dweller
7 citizen, denizen, settler 8 habitant,
occupant, resident 10 inhabitant

dwelling
3 pad 4 casa, digs, home, nest
5 abode, haunt, house 7 address,
habitat, lodging 8 domicile, quarters
9 residence 10 brownstone, habitation
American Indian: 4 tipi 5 hogan,
tepee 6 pueblo, teepee, wigwam
clergyman's: 5 manse 7 rectory
8 vicarage 9 parsonage
crude: 3 hut 4 camp 5 cabin,
hovel, shack 6 cabana, shanty
7 barrack 8 barracks

Eskimo: 5 igloo
grand: 5 manor, manse, villa 6 palace 7 château, mansion
Hindu: 6 ashram
Navajo: 5 hogan
Russian: 5 dacha
small: 3 cot, hut 5 hovel 7 cottage 8 bungalow

dwindle

3 ebb 4 fade, fall, wane 5 abate, taper 6 lessen, recede, reduce, shrink, weaken, wither 7 decline, die away, die down, shrivel, slacken, subside 8 decrease, diminish, taper off 9 attenuate, drain away

dyad

3 duo, two 4 pair, yoke 5 brace, twins 6 couple 7 doublet, twosome

dye

4 tint 5 color, stain, tinge 7 pigment 8 colorant, pyronine, tincture
blue: 4 woad 6 indigo 7 cyanine
for hair: 5 henna
plant: 4 woad 5 sumac 6 madder
red: 5 eosin, henna 6 kermes, ruddle 7 cudbear, fuchsin, magenta 8 alizarin, fuchsine, amaranth, safranin 9 cochineal, rhodamine, safranine 10 erythrosin
violet: 6 archil
yellow: 7 flavine 8 orpiment
yellowish red: 7 annatto

dyed-in-the-wool

5 loyal, sworn 7 devoted, die-hard, old-line, settled, staunch 8 faithful, hard-core, orthodox, standpat, true-blue 9 confirmed, hard-shell, steadfast 10 deep-rooted, deep-seated, entrenched, inveterate, unwavering 11 established 13 bred-in-the-bone, thoroughgoing

dyewood

6 fustic 10 brazilwood

dying

6 demise 7 done for, quietus 8 moribund 9 departure 10 extinction, in extremis 12 annihilation

dynamic

7 driving, intense 8 forceful, forcible, powerful, vigorous 9 energetic, strenuous 10 compelling, energizing

dynamite

4 raze 5 blast 6 blow up 7 destroy, explode, shatter 8 demolish 9 explosive 10 annihilate
inventor: 5 Nobel (Alfred)

dynamo

8 go-getter, live wire 9 generator 10 ball of fire 11 self-starter

dysentery

4 flux 6 scours 8 diarrhea

dyslogistic

7 adverse 10 derogatory, pejorative 11 deleterious, disparaging, prejudicial, unfavorable

dyspepsia

5 gloom 6 dismay 7 chagrin, pyrosis 8 glumness 9 dejection, heartburn 10 gloominess 11 frustration, indigestion

dyspeptic

5 cross, surly 6 crabby, morose, ornery 9 irritable 10 ill-humored, ill-natured 11 disgruntled, ill-tempered

dysphoria

4 funk 5 blues, dumps, gloom, mopes 6 sorrow 7 sadness 9 dejection 10 depression, gloominess, melancholy 11 unhappiness 12 mournfulness, wretchedness 13 cheerlessness

E

each
3 all, per 4 a pop 5 every 6 apiece
8 everyone 9 per capita, everybody

eager
3 hot 4 agog, avid, keen, wild
5 antsy, hyper, itchy, pushy, ready,
vital 6 ardent, fervid, gung ho,
heated, hungry, intent, pining, raring
7 anxious, athirst, burning, craving,
earnest, fervent, longing, restive,
thirsty, wishful 8 appetent, aspiring,
covetous, desirous, restless, striving,
vehement, yearning 9 ambitious,
energetic, hankering, impatient,
voracious 10 breathless, solicitous
11 impassioned 12 enthusiastic

eagerness
4 push, urge, zeal, zest, zing 5 ardor, gusto 6 desire, fervor, hunger,
spirit, thirst 7 avidity, craving, itching,
longing, passion 8 alacrity, ambition,
appetite, fervency, vitality, yearning
9 intensity, quickness, vehemence
10 enthusiasm, impatience, resolution

eagle
4 hawk 9 accipiter
nest: 4 aery 5 aerie, eyrie
North American: 4 bald 6 golden
sea: 4 erne 6 osprey

eagle-eyed
8 vigilant, watchful 9 attentive,
observant 10 perceptive 12 sharp-
sighted

ear
6 notice 7 auricle 9 attention
bone: 5 anvil, incus 6 hammer,
stapes 7 malleus, stirrup

canal: 5 scala
combining form: 3 aur, oto 4 auri,
otic
doctor: 9 otologist
inner: 9 labyrinth
middle: 8 tympanum
outer: 5 pinna
part: 4 drum, lobe 5 canal 6 tragus
7 cochlea
relating to: 5 aural 9 auricular
science: 7 otology

eardrum
8 tympanum

_____ **Earhart**
6 Amelia

earl
4 lord, peer 5 count, noble 8 nobleman, seigneur 9 patrician 10 aristocrat

earlier
3 ere, yet 4 once 5 as yet, so
far 6 before, sooner 7 already, thus
far 8 formerly, hitherto, previous
9 erstwhile, preceding 10 beforehand, heretofore, previously

earlier than
3 pre 6 before

earliest
5 first, prime 6 maiden, primal
7 initial, pioneer, primary 8 original,
primeval, pristine 10 aboriginal,
primordial

earlike projection
3 lug

early
3 old 5 first, prior 6 primal, timely

7 ancient, betimes **8** original, previous, primeval, pristine, untimely **9** preceding, premature, primitive **10** antecedent, antiquated, precocious, primordial **11** prematurely
prefix: 5 paleo

earn

3 bag, get, net, win **4** gain, make, rate, reap **5** amass, clear, gross, merit, score **6** attain, come by, obtain, pick up, rack up, secure, wangle **7** acquire, bring in, collect, deserve, harvest, procure, produce, realize, receive **8** pull down **9** bring home, knock down

earnest

3 vow **4** bond, busy, firm, keen, pawn, true, warm **5** grave, sober, token **6** active, ardent, intent, pledge, solemn, somber, surety **7** deposit, genuine, intense, serious, sincere, up front, warrant, zealous **8** contract, covenant, diligent, interest, security, sedulous, studious **9** assiduous, heartfelt **10** determined, nononsense, passionate, sobersided, thoughtful, unaffected **11** industrious **12** enthusiastic, wholehearted

earnestly

5 madly **7** for real, like mad

earnestness

6 fervor **7** gravity, honesty, passion, resolve **8** sobriety **9** sincerity **10** absorption, doggedness **11** engrossment, persistence **12** perseverance **13** concentration, determination

earnings

3 net, pay **4** gain **5** lucre, wages **6** income, profit, return, salary **7** profits **8** proceeds, take-home **9** emolument **10** bottom line

ear shell

see **abalone**

earshot

5 range, sound **7** hearing

earsplitting

4 loud **6** shrill **7** blaring, grating, raucous, roaring **8** piercing, strident **9** deafening, dissonant **10** screeching, stentorian **11** fullmouthed

earth

3 orb, sod **4** dirt, land, soil, turf **5** globe, world **6** ground, planet, sphere **7** dry land, terrain **8** creation **10** terra firma
combining form: 3 geo **4** geog **6** tellur **7** telluro
core: 12 centrosphere
god: 3 Geb, Keb, Seb **5** Dagan
goddess: 4 Erda, Gaea **5** Ceres, Nintu **6** Kishar **7** Demeter, Nerthus
relating to: 8 telluric **11** terrestrial
satellite: 4 moon
science: 7 geology **9** geography

earthenware

4 clay **5** china, delft **7** biscuit, faience, pottery **8** clayware, crockery, majolica **9** porcelain, stoneware **10** terra-cotta

earthlike

11 terrestrial

earthly

6 likely, mortal **7** mundane, worldly **8** feasible, material, physical, possible, probable, temporal **9** corporeal, potential, practical **10** imaginable **11** conceivable, terrestrial, unspiritual

earthquake

5 shake, shock **6** tremor **7** temblor
measuring device: 11 seismograph, seismometer
relating to: 7 seismic
science: 10 seismology **11** seismometry

earthwork

4 bank, wall **7** bulwark, rampart **10** embankment **13** fortification

earthworm

7 annelid **12** night crawler

earthy

3 low **4** base, real **5** crude, dirty, dusty, gross, muddy, sandy **6** clayey, coarse, common, simple **7** mundane, worldly **8** temporal **9** corporeal, inelegant, practical, pragmatic, realistic, unrefined **10** hard-boiled, hardheaded, indelicate, uncultured, unpolished **11** down-to-earth, terrestrial **12** matter-of-fact **13** materialistic, unsentimental

earwax
7 cerumen

ease
3 aid **4** bate, calm, dull, free, help, rest **5** allay, loose, peace, poise, relax, slack **6** assist, deaden, loosen, relief, repose, soften **7** assuage, comfort, fluency, improve, leisure, lighten, mollify, relieve, slacken **8** calmness, deftness, diminish, dispatch, facility, idleness, mitigate, moderate, pleasure, security, serenity **9** abundance, affluence, alleviate, expertise, reduction, untighten, well-being **10** ameliorate, artfulness, efficiency, expertness, facilitate, inactivity, mitigation, moderation, prosperity, relaxation, smoothness **11** alleviation, contentment, nonchalance, spontaneity, tranquility **12** satisfaction, skillfulness, tranquillity
off: 3 ebb **4** bate, fade, fall, flag, wane **5** abate, let up, loose, relax, slack **6** lessen, loosen, relent, unbend, unwind **7** die away, die down, slacken, subside **8** diminish, loosen up, moderate **9** untighten

easel
4 desk **5** frame, stand **7** support **9** workbench, worktable

easement
6 relief **7** comfort **10** mitigation, palliative **11** alleviation, consolation, restorative **13** mollification

easily
6 simply **7** handily, lightly, readily **8** facilely, smoothly **11** dexterously, efficiently **12** effortlessly

East
4 Asia **6** Levant, Orient

Easter
5 Pasch
relating to: 7 paschal
symbol: 3 egg **4** lamb **5** bunny **6** rabbit

eastern
8 oriental **9** Levantine
countries: 6 Orient

East Indian country
8 Malaysia **9** Indonesia, Singapore

East Timor
capital: 4 Dili
monetary unit: 6 dollar
neighbor: 9 Indonesia

easy
3 lax **4** calm, cozy, glib, mild, soft, snug **5** basic, clear, comfy, cushy, light, loose, naive, plain, suave **6** breezy, facile, fluent, kindly, placid, poised, polite, secure, serene, simple, smooth, urbane **7** amiable, courtly, cursive, evident, flowing, lenient, obvious, patient, relaxed **8** apparent, composed, familiar, graceful, gullible, in clover, informal, manifest, merciful, obliging, peaceful, pleasant, sociable, tolerant, tranquil, trusting **9** collected, credulous, forgiving, indulgent, possessed **10** charitable, diplomatic, effortless, elementary, forbearing, gregarious, permissive **11** comfortable, complaisant, good-humored, goodnatured, susceptible, sympathetic, unconcerned **12** good-tempered **13** compassionate, mollycoddling, self-possessed, uncomplicated

easygoing
3 lax **4** calm, cool, lazy **5** quiet **6** breezy, casual, dégagé, folksy, placid, poised, sedate, serene **7** affable, offhand, patient, relaxed, unfussy **8** amenable, carefree, composed, down home, fainéant, flexible, indolent, informal, laid-back, slothful, together, tranquil **9** apathetic, indulgent, offhanded, unhurried **10** nonchalant, permissive, unaffected **11** comfortable, complaisant, indifferent, low-pressure, pococurante, unconcerned, unflappable, uninhibited **12** devil-may-care, even-tempered, happy-go-lucky, lighthearted
13 self-possessed, unconstrained

easy mark

3 sap 4 butt, dupe, fool, gull 5 chump, patsy, sport 6 pigeon, softie, sucker, turkey, victim 7 fall guy 8 pushover 9 soft touch 11 sitting duck

eat

3 sup, vex 4 bite, chow, dine, gnaw, meal, pick, take, wolf 5 annoy, erode, feast, gorge, graze, hound, lunch, mouth, munch, scarf, scoff, scour, snack, use up 6 bother, devour, feed on, gobble, harass, hassle, ingest, inhale, nibble, pester, pick at, pig out, plague, take in 7 banquet, consume, corrode, exhaust, gorge on, swallow, torment 8 chow down, dissolve, take food, wear away 9 breakfast, decompose, masticate, partake of, polish off 10 break bread, gormandize, nibble away

eatable

6 edible 8 esculent, harmless 9 palatable 10 comestible, digestible

eatery

4 café 5 diner, grill 10 coffee shop, restaurant 11 greasy spoon 12 luncheonette

eating place

3 pub 4 café, mess 5 diner, grill, joint 6 bistro, tavern 7 automat, beanery, canteen, dinette, tearoom 8 cookshop, messroom, pizzeria, snack bar 9 brasserie, cafeteria, chophouse, hash house, lunchroom, trattoria 10 coffee shop, restaurant, steak house 11 greasy spoon 12 luncheonette

eavesdrop

3 bug, tap 4 lurk 7 monitor 8 listen in, overhear

ebb

4 drop, fade, fall, flag, tide, wane 5 abate, droop, let up 6 lessen, recede, reduce, relent, shrink, wither 7 decline, descent, die away, die down, ease off, retreat, slacken, subside 8 decrease, diminish, languish, moderate, withdraw 10 retrograde

Eblis

5 Satan

son: 3 Tir 4 Awar 5 Dasim 8 Zalambur

ebon, ebony

3 jet 4 inky 5 black, jetty, raven, sable 6 brunet 8 brunette, jet-black 9 pitch-dark 10 pitch-black

ebullience

3 vim, zip 4 brio, élan, zing 5 gusto 6 gaiety 7 abandon, elation 8 buoyancy, vitality, vivacity 9 animation 10 enthusiasm, excitement, exuberance, liveliness 11 high spirits 12 exhilaration, spiritedness 13 effervescence

ebullient

3 mad 4 gaga 5 brash, zingy, zippy 6 bouncy, bubbly, elated, frothy, geeked, pumped, raring 7 boiling, chipper, excited, gleeful, gushing, vibrant 8 hopped-up 9 sprightly, vivacious 11 exhilarated 12 enthusiastic, high-spirited 13 irrepressible

eccentric

3 odd, nut 4 coot, kook 5 crank, crazy, droll, flaky, freak, funky, funny, goofy, kooky, nutty, queer, wacky, weird 6 far out, oddity, quaint, quirky, screwy, weirdo, whacko, whacky 7 bizarre, curious, deviant, erratic, heretic, oddball, offbeat, strange, unusual 8 aberrant, abnormal, bohemian, cockeyed, crackpot, goofball, maverick, original, peculiar, singular, uncommon 9 anomalous, character, deviating, fantastic, fruitcake, grotesque, irregular, off-center, screwball, unnatural, whimsical 10 elliptical, off-balance, unbalanced, uncentered 11 exceptional 13 idiosyncratic, nonconformist

eccentricity

4 kink 5 quirk, twist 8 crotchet, quiddity 9 deviation, weirdness 10 aberration 11 strangeness 12 idiosyncrasy

ecclesiastic

see **clergyman**

ecclesiastical
4 holy 5 papal 6 church, sacred
8 churchly, clerical, pastoral, priestly
9 apostolic, canonical, episcopal,
spiritual, synagogal 10 churchlike,
pontifical, rabbinical, sacerdotal
11 ministerial, patriarchal, theological
12 episcopalian, evangelistic, taber-
nacular

ecdysiast
see **stripteaser**

echelon
3 row 4 file, line, rank, tier 5 grade,
group, level, order, queue 6 string
7 chevron 9 formation

echidna
8 anteater 9 monotreme 13 spiny
anteater

Echidna
father: 7 Phorcys 8 Chrysaor
mother: 4 Ceto 10 Callirrhoë
offspring: 5 Hydra 6 dragon,
Orthus, Sphinx 7 Chimera 8 Cerberus, Chimaera

echinoderm
6 urchin 7 crinoid, sea star 8 starfish
9 coelomate, sea urchin 11 sea
cucumber

echo
3 ape 4 mime, ring 5 evoke, mimic,
trace 6 mirror, parrot, repeat, result,
reverb, second 7 imitate, iterate,
reflect, resound, revoice, vestige
8 resonate, response 9 duplicate,
imitation, reiterate 10 reflection,
repetition 11 reverberate 12 repercussion 13 reverberation

Echo
5 nymph, oread
beloved: 9 Narcissus

echoic
7 mimetic 9 imitative 10 derivative 12 onomatopoeic 13 onomatopoetic

éclat
4 bang, dash, fame, pomp 5 glory,
honor, kudos 6 luster, lustre, praise,
renown, repute 7 acclaim, display,
laurels, stardom, success 8 applause, eminence, prestige, standing 9 celebrity, notoriety, publicity
10 brilliance, brilliancy, exaltation,
prominence, reputation 11 distinction, ostentation

eclectic
5 broad, fussy, mixed, picky 6 choosy,
select, varied 7 diverse, finicky,
mingled 8 assorted, catholic, elective 9 inclusive, selective 10 discerning, fastidious, particular 11 diversified 12 dilettantish, multifarious
13 heterogeneous

eclipse
3 dim 5 bedim, cloud, cover, excel,
outdo, shade 6 darken, exceed,
shadow 7 becloud, decline, obscure, surpass 8 downfall, outshine
9 adumbrate, obfuscate, overcloud
10 extinguish, overshadow

eclogue
3 ode 4 idyl, poem 5 idyll, lyric
8 pastoral

ecological
5 green 8 bionomic
community: 5 biome

ecology
9 bionomics 11 environment

economic
6 fiscal 8 material, monetary 9 budgetary, financial, pecuniary 10 mercantile, profitable
doctrine: 12 laissez-faire
system: 9 communism, socialism
10 capitalism 11 syndicalism 12 mer-
cantilism

economical
4 mean 5 canny, close, spare
6 frugal, saving, stingy 7 careful,
miserly, prudent, sparing, thrifty
8 skimping 9 efficient, niggardly,
penny-wise, penurious, provident,
scrimping 10 unwasteful 12 cheeseparing, parsimonious 13 penny-
pinching

economist

American: 5 Arrow (Kenneth), Simon (Herbert, Julian), Solow (Robert), Tobin (James) 6 Becker (Gary), George (Henry), Thurow (Lester), Veblen (Thorstein), Walker (Amasa), Weaver (Robert) 7 Krugman (Paul), Kuznets (Simon), Stigler (George), Volcker (Paul) 8 Friedman (Milton), Stiglitz (Joseph) 9 Galbraith (John Kenneth), Greenspan (Alan), Samuelson (Paul) 10 Schumpeter (Joseph)

Austrian: 5 Hayek (Friedrich von), Mises (Ludwig von)

Canadian: 7 Leacock (Stephen)

Dutch: 9 Tinbergen (Jan)

English: 3 Sen (Amartya) 4 Mill (John Stuart) 5 Coase (Ronald), Hayek (Friedrich von), Pigou (Arthur) 6 Engels (Friedrich), Keynes (John Maynard) 7 Bagehot (Walter), Malthus (Thomas), Ricardo (David)

French: 3 Say (Jean-Baptiste) 6 Monnet (Jean), Turgot (Anne-Robert-Jacques), Walras (Léon) 7 Quesnay (François)

German: 4 Marx (Karl) 5 Weber (Max) 6 Engels (Friedrich) 7 Schacht (Hjalmar)

Indian: 3 Sen (Amartya)

Scottish: 4 Mill (James) 5 Smith (Adam)

Swedish: 6 Myrdal (Gunnar)

Swiss: 8 Sismondi (Simonde de)

economize

4 save 5 skimp, stint 6 manage, scrimp 7 husband 8 conserve 10 cut corners 12 pinch pennies

economy

6 saving, thrift 8 prudence, skimping 9 concision, frugality, husbandry, parsimony, restraint, scrimping 10 discretion, efficiency, providence, stinginess 11 carefulness, conciseness, miserliness, thriftiness 13 niggardliness

Eco novel

13 Name of the Rose (The)
17 Foucault's Pendulum

ecru

see **beige**

ecstasy

3 joy 5 bliss 6 frenzy, heaven, trance 7 delight, elation, madness, rapture 8 euphoria, paradise, rhapsody 9 beatitude, transport 10 exaltation, joyfulness 11 blessedness, derangement, enchantment, high spirits, inspiration 12 blissfulness, exhilaration, intoxication 13 seventh heaven

ecstatic

6 elated, joyful 7 gleeful 8 euphoric, exultant, jubilant, thrilled 9 delirious, delighted, entranced, overjoyed, rapturous 11 exhilarated, transported

Ecuador

capital: 5 Quito
city: 6 Ambato, Cuenca 7 Machala 9 Guayaquil
Indian people: 7 Quechua
island group: 9 Galápagos
language: 7 Spanish
monetary unit: 5 sucre 6 dollar
mountain range: 5 Andes
neighbor: 4 Peru 8 Colombia
volcano: 6 Sangay 7 Cayambe 8 Cotopaxi 10 Chimborazo

ecumenical

6 cosmic, global 7 general, generic 8 catholic 9 inclusive, planetary, universal, worldwide 12 all-inclusive, cosmopolitan 13 comprehensive

ecumenical council

4 Lyon 5 Basel, Lyons, Trent 6 Nicene 7 Ephesus, Ferrara, Lateran, Vatican 8 Florence 9 Chalcedon, Constance

eczema

6 tetter

edacious

see **voracious**

eddy

4 purl 5 swirl, twirl, whirl, whorl 6 vortex 8 backwash 9 backwater, maelstrom, whirlpool 11 counterflow

edema

5 croup, tumor 6 dropsy 8 anasarca, swelling

Eden

6 heaven, utopia 7 arcadia, elysium 8 paradise
river: 5 Gihon 6 Pishon 8 Hiddekel 9 Euphrates

edentate

5 sloth 8 aardvark, anteater, pangolin 9 armadillo, toothless

Edessa's king

5 Abgar

edge

3 cut, end, hem, lip, rim 4 bank, bite, brim, cusp, draw, ease, hone, inch, lead, limb, line, pink, side, whet, worm 5 arris, bound, brink, bulge, force, ledge, picot, point, ridge, sidle, skirt, sting, strop, verge 6 border, fringe, margin, nosing 7 acidity, contour, chamfer, outline, serrate, sharpen, vantage 8 acerbity, acridity, boundary, emborder, handicap, keenness, surround, thinness 9 acuteness, advantage, extremity, harshness, head start, perimeter, periphery, sharpness, threshold, upper hand 10 causticity, shrillness, stringency 11 astringency 12 incisiveness 13 effectiveness

edge city

5 exurb 6 suburb

edged

4 acid, tart 5 acute, sharp 6 strong 7 cutting 8 incisive, piercing

edge in

6 inject 9 interject, interpose, insinuate 10 infiltrate 11 interpolate

edging

3 hem 4 lace 5 braid, frill, limit 6 border, flounce, fringe, lacing, margin, piping 7 selvage 8 rickrack, selvedge, trimming

edgy

3 hip 5 funky, nervy, sharp, tense, testy 6 daring, touchy, uneasy 7 excited, keyed up, offbeat, restive,

uptight 8 Bohemian, out-there, renegade, restless, skittery, skittish, volatile 9 excitable, impatient, irascible, irritable 10 high-strung, outlandish 11 provocative

edible

8 esculent 9 palatable 10 comestible
root: 3 oca, yam 4 beet, taro, yuca 6 carrot, daikon, ginger, jicama, potato, radish, turnip, wasabi 7 burdock, cassava, ginseng, malanga, parsnip, salsify 8 celeriac, galangal, kohlrabi, rutabaga 11 horseradish, sweet potato
seed: 3 nut, pea 4 bean 6 peanut

edibles

4 chow, eats, feed, food, grub 6 viands 7 aliment, goodies, nurture 8 victuals 9 provender 10 provisions, sustenance 11 comestibles

edict

3 law 4 bull, fiat, rule 5 canon, order, ukase 6 decree, dictum, ruling 7 command, dictate, mandate, precept, statute 9 directive, manifesto, ordinance, prescript 10 injunction, regulation 12 proclamation 13 pronouncement
Islamic: 5 fatwa
papal: 4 bull 8 decretal

Edict of _____

5 Milan, Worms 6 Nantes

edifice

4 pile 8 building, erection 9 structure

edify

5 teach 6 better, fill in, illume, inform, update, uplift 7 educate, elevate, enhance, improve 8 illumine, instruct 9 elucidate, enlighten 10 illuminate

edit

3 cut 4 cull, omit 5 adapt, alter, amend, emend, fix up 6 delete, doctor, excise, polish, redact, refine, review, revise, reword, select 7 abridge, compile, correct, rewrite 8 annotate, assemble, condense, copyread, fine-tune 9 proofread, rearrange 10 blue-pencil, bowdlerize

edition

4 copy, form 5 issue, print 7 reissue, reprint, version 8 printing, variorum 10 impression, reprinting 12 reproduction

editor

8 redactor 9 scrivener, wordsmith 10 copyreader 11 proofreader

Edomite's ancestor

4 Esau

educate

4 rear 5 brief, coach, drill, edify, nurse, teach, train, tutor 6 inform, school 7 explain, nurture 8 instruct 9 brainwash, enlighten 10 discipline 12 indoctrinate

education

7 culture, tuition 8 breeding, coaching, guidance, learning, literacy, pedagogy, teaching, training, tutelage, tutorage, tutoring 9 erudition, knowledge, schooling, tutorship 11 instruction, learnedness, scholarship 13 enlightenment

educational

11 informative, instructive 13 informational, instructional
institution: 6 school 7 academy, college 10 university 12 conservatory

educator

5 tutor 7 teacher 9 professor 10 instructor
American: 4 Mann (Horace) 5 Dewey (John) 6 Butler (Nicholas Murray), Conant (James Bryant), Harris (William Torrey) 7 Barnard (Henry), Beecher (Catharine), Peabody (Elizabeth) 8 Hutchins (Robert Maynard), McGuffey (William) 10 Washington (Booker T.)
Czech: 8 Comenius (John Amos)
English: 6 Arnold (Thomas) 7 Spencer (Herbert)
German: 7 Froebel (Friedrich), Herbart (Johann)
Italian: 10 Montessori (Maria)
Swiss: 10 Pestalozzi (Johann Heinrich)

educe

4 drag, draw, milk, pull 5 evoke, wrest, wring 6 derive, elicit, evince, evolve, extort, obtain, secure 7 distill, draw out, extract, procure 8 bring out 10 excogitate

eel

5 moray, siren 6 conger 7 hagfish, lamprey, sniggle
young: 5 elver

eelpout

6 blenny, burbot 10 muttonfish

eely

5 slimy 6 slippy, wiggly 7 elusive, wriggly 8 slippery, slithery 9 wriggling

eerie

5 scary, weird 6 creepy, spooky 7 bizarre, strange, uncanny 8 chilling, spectral 9 fantastic, grotesque, unearthly 10 mysterious 11 frightening, hair-raising 12 otherworldly

efface

4 dele, x out 5 annul, erase 6 cancel, delete, rub out 7 blot out, destroy, expunge, scratch, wipe out 8 black out, wear away 9 eliminate, eradicate, extirpate 10 obliterate

effect

3 end 4 make 5 cause, enact, event, fruit 6 create, draw on, induce, intent, invoke, render, result, secure, sequel, upshot 7 achieve, bring on, enforce, execute, fulfill, outcome, perform, produce, purport, realize, turn out 8 bring off, carry out, complete, conceive, generate, sequence 9 actualize, aftermath, corollary, discharge, implement, influence, operation, outgrowth, pursuance 10 accomplish, appearance, bring about, conclusion, consummate, denouement, effectuate 11 consequence, development, eventuality, precipitate 12 carry through, ramification, repercussion

effective

4 able 5 sound, valid 6 causal, cogent, direct, potent, useful 7 cap-

able **8** adequate **9** competent, operative **10** compelling, convincing, productive

effectiveness
5 clout, force, point, power, vigor **6** weight **7** cogency, potency **8** strength, validity **10** capability

effects
4 gear **5** goods, stuff **6** things **8** chattels, movables, property **9** equipment, moveables, trappings **10** belongings **11** impedimenta, possessions **13** accoutrements

effectual
5 sound, valid **6** potent, strong, useful **7** capable **8** decisive, powerful, workable **10** conclusive, fulfilling, productive **11** influential, practicable **13** authoritative, determinative

effectuate
see **effect**

effeminate
5 sappy, sissy **6** chichi, prissy **7** epicene, foppish **8** delicate, overnice, precious **9** sissified **10** old-maidish **11** overrefined

effervescence
5 giddy **7** fizzing, foaming, sparkle **8** bubbling, buoyancy, vivacity **9** animation **10** ebullience, ebullition, exuberance, exuberancy, liveliness **12** exhilaration

effervescent
3 gay **4** airy **5** jolly **6** bouncy, bubbly, lively **7** boiling, buoyant, excited **8** animated, mirthful, volatile **9** sparkling, sprightly, vivacious **10** carbonated **12** high-spirited **13** irrepressible

effete
4 soft, weak **5** frail, spent **6** barren **6** sickly **7** decayed, drained, sterile, worn-out **8** decadent, decaying, delicate, depleted, fatigued, pampered **9** declining, dissolute, enfeebled, exhausted, infertile, washed-out **10** degenerate, unfruitful **11** debilitated

efficacious
6 active, potent, strong **8** forceful, powerful, puissant **9** operative **10** productive **11** influential

efficacy
see **effectiveness**

efficiency
see **effectiveness**

efficient
4 able **5** adept **6** expert **7** capable, skilled **8** economic, masterly, skillful **9** competent **10** economical, productive

effigy
3 guy **4** icon, idol **5** dummy, image **6** figure **7** waxwork **8** likeness

effloresce
4 blow **5** bloom, burst **6** flower, sprout **7** blossom, burgeon **9** bear fruit

effluvium
3 air **4** odor, reek **5** smell, vapor, waste **6** miasma **7** exhaust **8** effusion, emission **9** by-product, discharge, emanation **10** exhalation

efflux
see **effluvium**

effort
3 job, try **4** feat, push, task, toil, work **5** chore, essay, force, labor, might, nisus, pains, sweat, while **6** energy, strain **7** attempt, travail, trouble, venture **8** endeavor, exertion, industry, struggle **11** application, elbow grease

effortful
4 hard **6** tiring, uphill **7** arduous, labored, operose **8** exacting, toilsome **9** ambitious, difficult, laborious, strenuous **11** challenging

effortless
4 easy **5** adept, light, ready **6** expert, facile, fluent, simple, smooth **8** masterly, skillful **10** proficient **11** undemanding

effrontery
4 face, gall **5** brass, cheek, nerve

effulgence

8 audacity, boldness, chutzpah, temerity 9 arrogance, assurance, brashness, hardihood, impudence, insolence 10 brazenness 11 presumption 12 impertinence

effulgence

4 glow 5 blaze, glory 6 luster, lustre 8 radiance, splendor 9 splendour 10 brightness, brilliance, brilliancy, luminosity

effulgent

5 vivid 6 bright, lucent 7 beaming, glowing, lambent, radiant, shining 8 dazzling, glorious, luminous, lustrous, splendid 9 brilliant 11 resplendent 12 incandescent

effuse

4 flow, gush, pour, shed 5 exude, issue 6 stream 7 emanate, enthuse, flow out, radiate

effusive

5 gushy 6 lavish, sloppy, smarmy 7 cloying, fulsome, gushing, profuse, verbose 9 expansive, exuberant 10 loquacious, outpouring, unreserved 11 extravagant 12 enthusiastic, unrestrained 13 demonstrative, unconstrained

eft

4 newt 6 triton 10 salamander

e.g.

10 for example 13 exempli gratia

egad

6 zounds 7 criminy 8 gadzooks 11 odds bodkins

egg

3 ova (plural) 4 ovum, seed 5 ovule
case: 5 shell 7 ootheca
combining form: 3 ovi, ovo
dish: 6 omelet 8 omelette
fertilized: 6 zygote 7 oospore
fish: 3 roe 6 caviar
French: 4 oeuf
immature: 6 oocyte
part: 4 yolk 5 glair, shell, white
shaped: 5 ovate, ovoid
white: 5 glair 7 albumen

egghead

6 pundit 8 highbrow 10 double-dome 12 intellectual

egg on

4 goad, prod, spur, urge 5 prick, rally 6 arouse, exhort, excite, incite, prompt, stir up 7 agitate 9 instigate, stimulate

eggplant

6 purple 9 aubergine 10 nightshade

egg-shaped

4 oval 5 ovate, ovoid 7 oviform

Eglah

husband: 5 David
son: 7 Ithream

eglantine

7 dog rose 10 sweetbriar, sweetbrier

Eglantine

father: 5 Pepin
husband: 9 Valentine

Eglon

king: 5 Debir
slayer: 4 Ehud

ego

4 self 5 pride 6 vanity 7 conceit 10 self-esteem

egocentric

7 selfish 9 conceited 10 self-loving 11 self-seeking 12 narcissistic, self-absorbed, self-affected, self-centered, self-involved, vainglorious 13 individualist, self-conceited, self-concerned, self-indulgent

egoism

5 pride 6 vanity 7 conceit 8 self-love 9 self-glory, self-pride, vainglory 10 narcissism, self-regard 11 selfishness, self-opinion

egoistic

4 smug, vain 7 selfish 9 conceited 12 self-absorbed, self-centered 13 self-concerned, self-contented, self-satisfied

egomaniacal

12 self-exalting, vainglorious

egotism

5 pride **6** vanity **7** conceit **8** boasting, bragging, self-love, vainness, vaunting **9** arrogance, pomposity, self-glory, self-pride, vainglory **10** narcissism, self-esteem **11** megalomania, self-opinion **12** boastfulness **13** conceitedness

egotistic

4 vain **5** cocky, proud **7** selfish, stuck-up **8** arrogant, boastful, inflated, puffed-up **9** conceited **11** pretentious, self-serving **12** self-absorbed, self-centered, self-involved **13** self-concerned, self-satisfied

egregious

4 rank **5** gross, stark **6** arrant, brazen **7** blatant, glaring, heinous **8** flagrant, infamous, outright, shocking **9** atrocious, notorious, shameless **10** deplorable, outrageous **11** conspicuous

egress, egression

4 door, exit **5** issue, leave **6** depart, escape, exodus, outlet **7** doorway, exiting, opening, passage **9** departure, emergence

egret

5 heron, wader

Egypt

ancient city: 6 Thebes **7** Memphis
capital: 5 Cairo
city: 4 Giza **8** Port Said **10** Alexandria
dam: 5 Aswan
desert: 6 Libyan **7** Arabian, Western
gulf: 4 Suez **5** Aqaba
lake: 6 Nasser
language: 6 Arabic
leader: 5 Sadat (Anwar el-) **6** Nasser (Gamal Abdul) **7** Mubarak (Hosni)
monetary unit: 5 pound
neighbor: 5 Libya, Sudan **6** Israel
oasis: 4 Siwa **6** Dakhla, Kharga **7** Farafra
peninsula: 5 Sinai
river: 4 Nile
sea: 3 Red **13** Mediterranean

Egyptian

burial jar: 7 canopic
Christian: 4 Copt
cross: 4 ankh
dam: 5 Aswan
dynasty: 5 Saite, Xoite **6** Hyksos, Tanite, Theban **7** Persian, Thinite **8** Memphite **9** Bubastite, Ethiopian **10** Diospolite
god:
  chief: 6 Amen-Ra
  crocodile-headed: 5 Sebek
  falcon-headed: 4 Ment **5** Horus, Mentu **6** Sokari **7** Sokaris
  ibis-headed: 5 Thoth **6** Dhouti
  jackal-headed: 6 Anubis
  of creation: 4 Ptah **5** Phtha
  of day: 5 Horus
  of earth: 3 Geb, Keb, Seb
  of evil: 3 Set **4** Seth **5** Sebek
  of life: 4 Amen, Amon **5** Ammon
  of magic: 5 Thoth **6** Dhouti
  of Memphis: 4 Ptah **5** Phtha **6** Sokari **7** Sokaris
  of the heavens: 5 Horus
  of the morning sun: 5 Horus **7** Khepera
  of the sun: 6 Amen-Ra
  of Thebes: 4 Amen **6** Khensu, Khonsu
  of the underworld: 6 Osiris
  of war: 4 Ment **5** Mentu
  of wisdom: 5 Thoth **6** Dhouti
  ram-headed: 4 Amen, Amon **5** Ammon, Khnum **6** Khnemu
  snake: 4 Apep **5** Apepi
goddess:
  cat-headed: 4 Bast **5** Pakht
  cow-headed: 4 Athor **6** Hathor
  lioness-headed: 4 Bast **5** Pakht **6** Sekhet
  of fertility: 4 Isis
  of love and mirth: 5 Athor **6** Hathor
  of motherhood: 4 Apet, Isis
  of Thebes: 3 Mut
  of the heavens: 3 Nut
  queen of the gods: 4 Sati
  vulture-headed: 3 Mut **7** Nekhebt **8** Nekhebet
king:
(see **king** entry)

eider

language: 6 Arabic, Coptic
native: 4 Arab, Copt 5 Nilot
president: 5 Sadat 6 Nasser
7 Mubarak
queen: 9 Cleopatra, Nefertiti
sacred bird: 4 ibis
solar disk: 4 Aten
sultan: 7 Saladin
talisman: 6 scarab
underworld: 4 Aaru, Duat 6 Amenti
wind: 7 khamsin, sirocco

eider

4 down, duck 7 sea duck

eidetic

5 exact, vivid 7 perfect, precise
8 absolute, lifelike

eidolon

4 icon 5 ghost, ideal, image, model,
shade 6 mirage, vision, wraith 7 epitome, fantasm, figment, paragon,
phantom, specter, spectre 8 exemplar, illusion, paradigm, phantasm
9 archetype, prototype 10 apparition

eight

group of: 5 octet 6 octave

eight bells

4 noon

eighth note

6 quaver

eighty-six

4 boot, toss 5 chuck, eject, evict,
scrap 6 bounce 7 discard, kick out
8 get rid of, jettison, throw out

Einstein, Albert

birthplace: 3 Ulm
theory: 10 relativity

Eire

see **Ireland**

eject

4 boot, bump, dump, fire, oust, sack
5 chuck, evict, expel 6 banish,
bounce 7 boot out, cast out, dismiss,
kick out 8 disgorge, throw out
9 discharge

eke out

6 extend 7 augment, enhance, fill
out, squeeze, stretch 8 increase
10 supplement

elaborate

4 busy 5 fancy, showy 6 daedal,
dressy, evolve, expand, knotty,
minute, ornate, refine, unfold 7 amplify, build up, careful, clarify, comment, complex, develop, discuss,
elegant, enlarge, explain, expound,
profuse, work out 8 detailed, involved, overdone, thorough 9 Byzantine, decorated, embellish,
extensive, interpret, intricate
10 overworked 11 complicated,
embellished, extravagant, painstaking 12 labyrinthine

Elaine

father: 6 Pelles
lover: 8 Lancelot 9 Launcelot
son: 7 Galahad

Elam

capital: 4 Susa 7 Shushan
father: 4 Shem
king: 12 Chedorlaomer

élan

3 pep, vim, zip 4 brio, dash, fire, life,
zeal, zest, zing 5 ardor, flair, gusto,
oomph, verve, vigor 6 energy, esprit,
fervor, spirit 7 impetus 8 vivacity
9 animation, eagerness, intensity
10 enthusiasm

élan vital

4 soul 5 anima 6 animus, pneuma,
psyche, spirit

elapse

4 go by, pass 6 expire, run out, slip
by 8 pass away

elastic

6 bouncy, limber, pliant, rubber,
supple 7 ductile, pliable, rubbery,
springy 8 animated, flexible, moldable, stretchy, volatile 9 adaptable,
expansive, malleable, resilient
10 extendable, extensible, rubber
band, rubberlike 11 stretchable

elate

4 buoy 5 cheer, exalt, flush, set up
6 excite, perk up, uplift 7 cheer up,
delight, enliven, gladden, gratify,
hearten, inspire, overjoy 8 brighten,
embolden, inspirit, spirit up 9 encourage 10 exhilarate, invigorate

elated
4 glad, high 5 happy 7 exalted, excited 8 ecstatic, euphoric, exultant, gladsome, jubilant 9 overjoyed 10 enraptured 11 exhilarated, intoxicated 12 high-spirited

elation
3 joy 4 glee 7 delight, ecstasy, rapture 8 buoyancy, euphoria 9 happiness, transport 10 exaltation, excitement, jubilation 12 exhilaration, intoxication

Elbe tributary
4 Eger, Iser, Ohre 5 Saale 6 Moldau, Vltava

elbow
4 push 5 joint, nudge, shove 6 hustle, jostle

eld
4 yore 6 old age 8 old times

elder
6 senior 8 old-timer 9 patriarch, presbyter 10 golden-ager

elderliness
3 age 6 old age 8 caducity 10 senescence 11 senectitude

elderly
3 old 4 aged, gray 5 aging, hoary 7 ancient 9 declining, venerable

eldritch
5 eerie, weird 7 uncanny

Eleanor's husband
7 Henry II 8 Franklin

elect
3 opt, tap 4 name, pick 5 co-opt, saved 6 choice, choose, chosen, decide, opt for, ordain, picked, vote in 7 resolve, vote for 8 destined, nominate, ordained, redeemed 9 delivered, designate, determine, exclusive, single out 10 designated, singled out

election
6 ballot, choice, voting 7 primary 8 choosing, decision 9 balloting 10 preference, referendum 11 alternative

electioneer
5 stump 7 canvass 8 campaign, politick 9 barnstorm

elective
6 chosen 8 optional 9 voluntary 11 sympathetic 13 discretionary, noncompulsory, nonobligatory

Electra
brother: 7 Orestes
father: 9 Agamemnon
husband: 7 Pylades
mother: 12 Clytemnestra
sister: 9 Iphigenia
victim: 9 Aegisthus 12 Clytemnestra

electric
appliance: 3 fan 4 iron, oven 5 clock, drier, dryer, mixer, range, stove 6 stereo, washer 7 blender, freezer, toaster 10 dishwasher, television 12 refrigerator
coil: 5 tesla 8 solenoid
device: 4 coil, fuse, plug 6 dynamo, magnet, switch 7 battery 8 resistor, rheostat, varistor 9 amplifier, capacitor, condenser, generator 11 transformer
generator: 6 dynamo
particle: 3 ion
unit: 3 amp, ohm 4 volt, watt 5 farad, henry, joule 6 ampere 7 coulomb, faraday 8 kilowatt

electric current
kind: 6 direct 11 alternating
power: 7 wattage
strength: 8 amperage

electricity
5 juice, spark 7 current 9 galvanism, lightning
kind: 6 static 7 current

electrify
3 jar 4 jolt, stun 5 amaze, power, shock 6 charge, excite, thrill 7 astound, enthuse, inflame, provoke, stagger, startle 8 astonish, energize

electrode
6 dynode
negative: 7 cathode
positive: 5 anode

electron

3 ion **7** polaron
stream: 10 cathode ray
tube: 6 triode **7** tetrode **8** dynatron,
klystron

Electryon

brother: 6 Mestor
daughter: 7 Alcmene
father: 7 Perseus
mother: 9 Andromeda
wife: 5 Anaxo

eleemosynary

6 humane **8** generous **10** altruistic,
beneficent, benevolent, charitable,
munificent, openhanded **12** humanitarian **13** philanthropic

elegance

4 chic, pomp, tone **5** charm, grace,
style, taste **6** luxury, polish **7** culture,
dignity **8** chicness, poshness, richness, splendor, urbanity **9** gentility,
precision **10** ornateness, refinement
11 cultivation **12** magnificence,
tastefulness **13** sumptuousness

elegant

4 chic, fine, posh **5** fancy, grand,
noble, swank **6** choice, classy,
dainty, lovely, modish, ornate,
swanky, urbane **7** courtly, genteel,
opulent, refined, stately, stylish
8 cultured, polished, splendid,
tasteful **9** exquisite, luxurious,
recherché, sumptuous **10** cultivated
11 fashionable

elegiac

7 pensive **8** dactylic **9** lamenting,
sorrowful **10** melancholy

elegy

4 poem, song **5** dirge **6** lament,
monody **8** threnody

_____ eleison

5 Kyrie

Elektra composer

7 Strauss (Richard)

element

4 item, part **5** basic, facet, piece,
point **6** aspect, detail, factor, member, sector **7** article, feature, portion,
section **8** division, particle, rudiment
9 component, essential, principle
10 ingredient, particular **11** constituent, fundamental
chemical: 3 tin **4** gold, iron, lead,
neon, zinc **5** argon, boron, radon,
xenon **6** barium, carbon, cerium,
cesium, cobalt, copper, curium,
erbium, helium, indium, iodine,
nickel, osmium, oxygen, radium,
silver, sodium **7** arsenic, bismuth,
bohrium, bromine, cadmium, calcium, dubnium, fermium, gallium,
hafnium, hassium, holmium, iridium,
krypton, lithium, mercury, niobium,
rhenium, rhodium, silicon, sulphur,
terbium, thorium, thulium, uranium,
yttrium **8** actinium, aluminum, anti-
mony, astatine, chlorine, chromium, europium, fluorine, hydrogen,
illinium, lutecium, masurium, nitrogen, nobelium, platinum, polonium,
rubidium, samarium, scandium,
selenium, tantalum, thallium, titanium, tungsten, vanadium **9** ameri-
cium, berkelium, beryllium, colum-
bium, germanium, lanthanum,
magnesium, manganese, neo-
dymium, neptunium, palladium,
plutonium, potassium, ruthenium,
strontium, tellurium, virginium,
ytterbium, zirconium **10** dysprosium,
gadolinium, lawrencium, meitnerium,
molybdenum, seaborgium **11** cali-
fornium, einsteinium, mendelevium,
phosphorous **12** darmstadtium,
praseodymium **13** rutherfordium,
protoactinium

elemental

3 key **4** pure **5** basal, basic, crude,
prime **6** inborn, innate, primal,
simple **7** central, connate, primary,
radical **8** cardinal, inherent, integral,
intimate, simplest **9** beginning,
essential, ingrained, intrinsic, primitive **10** deep-seated, primordial,
underlying **11** fundamental **13** uncomplicated

elementary

4 easy **5** basal, basic **6** simple
7 initial **9** beginning, essential,

primitive **10** rudimental, underlying **11** fundamental, preliminary, rudimentary **12** introductory

elemi
5 resin **9** oleoresin

elephant
6 tusker **9** pachyderm
boy: 4 Sabu
driver: 6 mahout
enclosure: 5 kraal
extinct: 7 mammoth **8** mastodon
female: 3 cow
group: 4 herd
keeper: 6 mahout
male: 4 bull
maverick: 5 rogue
nose: 5 trunk **9** proboscis
seat: 6 howdah
sound: 6 bellow **7** trumpet
tooth: 4 tusk
tusk: 5 ivory
young: 4 calf

elephant-headed god
6 Ganesa **7** Ganesha

elephantine
4 huge **6** clumsy **7** awkward, hulking, mammoth, massive **8** colossal, enormous, gigantic **9** graceless, humongous, monstrous, ponderous **10** gargantuan, mastodonic, prodigious, ungraceful **11** heavy-footed

Elephant Man
7 Merrick (Joseph)

elevate
4 lift, rear, rise **5** boost, elate, erect, exalt, hoist, raise **6** buoy up, jack up, lift up, pick up, uplift **7** advance, dignify, ennoble, glorify, hearten, improve, inspire, promote, upgrade **8** heighten **10** exhilarate

elevated
4 high **5** grand, lofty, moral, noble **6** aerial, formal, superb **7** ethical, refined, soaring, stately, sublime **8** eloquent, majestic, virtuous **9** dignified, grandiose, high-flown, honorable, righteous **10** highminded, upstanding **13** grandiloquent

elevation
4 hill, rise **5** boost **6** ascent, height, uplift **7** advance, raising **8** altitude, mountain **9** acclivity, promotion, upgrading **10** apotheosis, preference, preferment **11** advancement, ennoblement
indication: 9 benchmark

elevator
4 cage, lift, silo **5** hoist
maker: 4 Otis

elf
3 fay, imp **4** peri, puck **5** fairy, gnome, pixie, troll **6** goblin, sprite **7** brownie, gremlin **10** leprechaun

elfin
5 antic **6** frisky, impish **7** implike, playful, puckish **8** pixieish **11** mischievous

Elgin _____
7 Marbles

Eli
4 Yale **5** Yalie

Eli _____
4 Yale **5** Lilly **7** Whitney

Elia
4 Lamb (Charles)

Eliab
brother: 5 David
daughter: 7 Abihail
father: 5 Helon, Pallu
son: 6 Abiram, Dathan

Eliada
father: 5 David
son: 5 Rezon

Eliam's daughter
9 Bathsheba

elicit
5 educe, evoke **6** derive, evince, extort **7** extract, provoke **8** bring out **9** call forth, draw forth

elide
4 fail, omit, skip **6** excise, forget, ignore, remove, slight **7** abridge, curtail, neglect **8** condense, cross out, discount, overlook, pass over, suppress **9** disregard

eligible

3 fit 6 fitted, likely, nubile, seemly, suited, worthy 7 capable 8 entitled, suitable 9 desirable, qualified 10 acceptable 11 appropriate 12 marriageable

Elihu ____

4 Root, Yale

Elijah

5 Elias 7 prophet 8 Tishbite
father: 5 Harim 7 Jeroham

Elimelech's wife

5 Naomi

eliminate

3 bar 4 bate, drop, oust, void 5 debar, eject, erase, evict, expel, purge 6 delete, except, remove 7 discard, dismiss, exclude, expunge, obviate, rule out, take out 8 count out 9 clear away, eradicate, liquidate 11 exterminate

Eliot, George

lover: 5 Lewes (George Henry)
novel: 6 Romola 8 Adam Bede 11 Middlemarch, Silas Marner 13 Daniel Deronda 14 Mill on the Floss (The)
pseudonym of: 5 Evans (Mary Ann)

Eliot, T.S.

play: 13 Cocktail Party (The)
poem: 9 Gerontion, Hollow Men (The), Waste Land (The) 12 Ash Wednesday, Four Quartets

Eliphaz

father: 4 Esau
mother: 4 Adah
son: 5 Teman

Elisabeth

husband: 9 Zacharias
son: 4 John (the Baptist)

Elisha

father: 7 Shaphat
servant: 6 Gehazi

Elisheba

brother: 7 Nahshon
father: 9 Amminadab
husband: 6 Aaron
son: 5 Abihu, Nadab 7 Eleazar, Ithamar

elite

3 top 4 best, pick 5 cream, elect, pride, prime, prize 6 choice, flower, gentry, select 7 quality, society 9 exclusive, gentility, patrician 10 upper class, upper crust 11 aristocracy 12 aristocratic

elixir

4 balm, cure 6 potion 7 arcanum, cure-all, nostrum, panacea, philter 10 catholicon

Elizabeth I, name for

6 Oriana 8 Gloriana

elk

4 deer 5 moose 6 sambar, wapiti 7 red deer

ell

3 arm 4 wing 5 annex, elbow, joint 8 addition 9 extension

ellipse

4 oval 5 curve, orbit

elliptical

5 brief, ovate, short 6 gnomic 7 concise, cryptic, laconic, obscure, summary 9 condensed, enigmatic 11 abbreviated

elm

5 wahoo

elocution

7 diction, oratory 8 delivery, rhetoric 11 declamation, speechcraft

elongate

4 draw 6 extend 7 draw out, lengthy, spin out, stretch 8 extended, lengthen 10 lengthened

elope

4 flee 6 escape, run off 7 abscond, run away 9 steal away

eloquence

5 force, power 6 fervor, spirit 7 fluency, oratory, passion 8 rhetoric 10 expression 12 expressivity, forcefulness

eloquent

5 lofty 6 ardent, fervid, fluent, moving 7 fervent, voluble 8 elevated, forceful, powerful, stirring 9 affecting

10 articulate, expressive, impressive, meaningful, passionate, persuasive, rhetorical **11** impassioned, sententious **12** smooth-spoken **13** silver-tongued

El Salvador
capital: 11 San Salvador
city: 8 Santa Ana **9** San Miguel
ethnic group: 5 Pipil
lake: 8 Ilopango
language: 7 Spanish
monetary unit: 5 colón **6** dollar
neighbor: 8 Honduras **9** Guatemala
river: 5 Lempa

else
5 if not **7** besides, further **9** otherwise **10** additional **11** differently **12** additionally

elucidate
7 clarify, clear up, explain, expound **8** annotate, spell out **9** exemplify, explicate, interpret **10** illuminate, illustrate

elude
4 defy, duck, flee, foil **5** avert, avoid, dodge, evade **6** baffle, escape, outwit, thwart **8** confound **9** frustrate **10** circumvent

elusive
6 subtle, tricky **7** evasive, phantom **8** baffling, fleeting, fugitive, slippery **10** evanescent, intangible, mysterious **13** insubstantial

elute
7 extract

elver
3 eel

elvish
see **elfin**

Elysium
5 bliss **6** heaven **7** nirvana **8** empyrean, paradise

elytron
4 wing

emaciated
4 bony, lean, thin **5** gaunt **6** skinny, wasted **7** scrawny, starved, wizened **8** skeletal, underfed **10** cadaverous

emaciation
5 tabes **7** atrophy **8** marasmus **10** starvation **11** attenuation

emanate
4 emit, flow, rise, stem **5** arise, exude, issue **6** derive, emerge, spring **7** come out, give off, give out, proceed, radiate **9** originate **10** derive from

emanation
4 aura, flow **6** efflux **8** effusion, emission **9** effluence

emancipate
4 free **5** let go, loose **6** loosen, redeem, unbind **7** manumit, release, set free, unchain **8** liberate, unfetter **9** discharge, unshackle **11** enfranchise

emancipation
7 release **10** liberation **11** deliverance

emancipator
5 Moses **7** Lincoln (Abraham) **9** deliverer, liberator

emasculate
3 fix **4** geld **5** alter, unman **6** neuter, soften, weaken **7** unnerve **8** castrate, enervate, unstring **10** debilitate, devitalize

embalm
7 mummify, perfume **8** preserve

embankment
4 berm, bund, dike, quay **5** levee, mound

embargo
3 ban, bar **5** edict, order **8** blockade, stoppage **10** impediment **11** prohibition

embark
5 board, enter, start **6** set out **7** set sail **8** commence

embarrass
4 faze **5** abash, upset **6** flurry, hamper, hinder, impede, rattle **7** confuse, flummox, fluster, mortify,

nonplus, perturb **8** confound, distress **9** discomfit, humiliate **10** complicate, discomfort, discompose, disconcert

embarrassment

5 shame, upset **7** chagrin **8** distress **9** confusion **10** discomfort **11** humiliation **12** discomfiture, perturbation **13** mortification

embassy

5 envoy **7** mission **8** legation **10** ambassador, delegation, deputation

embay

4 trap **5** catch, seize **7** capture **8** encircle, surround

embed

3 fix, set **4** bury, root **5** infix, inlay, lodge **7** implant, ingrain **8** entrench

embellish

3 pad **4** deck, gild, trim **5** adorn, color **6** bedeck, blazon, emboss, enrich **7** amplify, dress up, enhance, festoon, garnish **8** beautify, decorate, ornament **9** elaborate, embroider **10** exaggerate **11** romanticize

embellishment

7 garnish, gilding, melisma, mordent **8** coloring, ornament **9** fioritura, floridity, hyperbole **10** decoration **11** elaboration **12** embroidering, exaggeration **13** ornamentation

ember

3 ash **6** cinder

embezzle

4 loot **5** filch, steal **6** pilfer **7** purloin **8** peculate **9** defalcate

embitter

4 sour **6** poison **7** envenom **9** acidulate

emblazon

4 laud **5** extol **7** glorify **8** inscribe **9** celebrate

emblem

4 arms, flag, logo, mace, seal, sign **5** badge, brand, crest, image, token **6** banner, device, symbol **7** pennant

8 colophon, hallmark, insignia, monogram, standard **9** attribute, trademark **10** coat of arms

emblematic

8 symbolic **10** figurative, indicative **11** allegorical **12** illustrative, metaphorical

embodiment

6 avatar **7** epitome **8** exemplar **9** archetype **11** incarnation **13** manifestation

embody

5 reify **6** evince, mirror, typify **7** compose, contain, exhibit, realize, subsume **8** manifest **9** actualize, encompass, epitomize, exemplify, incarnate, integrate, objectify, personify, represent, symbolize **10** constitute, illustrate **11** emblematize, externalize, hypostatize, incorporate, materialize **12** substantiate

embolden

5 steel **7** fortify, hearten, inspire **8** inspirit **9** encourage **10** strengthen

embolus

4 clog, clot

embosom

3 hug **7** embrace, enclose, envelop, shelter

embouchure

10 mouthpiece

embowel

3 gut **4** draw **10** eviscerate, exenterate

embrace

3 hug **4** hold, lock, love, wrap **5** admit, adopt, clasp, cling, press **6** accept, cradle, cuddle, embody, enfold, fondle, nuzzle, take in, take on, take up **7** cherish, contain, embosom, enclose, entwine, envelop, espouse, include, receive, snuggle, squeeze, subsume, welcome **8** comprise, encircle **9** encompass **10** comprehend **11** accommodate, incorporate **12** encirclement

embrangle

see **embroil**

embrocation
5 salve 7 unguent 8 liniment

embroider
3 pad, sew, tat 4 gild 5 color 6 expand, overdo, play up, stitch 7 amplify, build up, enhance, garnish, magnify, stretch 8 decorate, ornament 9 dramatize, elaborate, embellish 10 exaggerate 11 hyperbolize, romanticize

embroidery
6 crewel 7 cutwork, orphrey 8 bargello, couching, smocking, tapestry 10 crewelwork, needlework 11 needlepoint

embroil
4 mire 6 tangle 7 confuse, ensnare, involve 8 disorder, entangle 9 implicate

embroilment
4 tiff 6 fracas 7 dispute, quarrel, wrangle 8 squabble 9 bickering 10 falling-out 11 altercation, controversy

embryo
3 bud 4 germ, seed 5 fetus, spark 7 nucleus 8 blastula, gastrula

emend
4 edit 5 alter, right 6 polish, revise 7 correct, improve, rectify, retouch

emerald
3 gem 5 beryl, green, stone 8 gemstone

Emerald Isle
4 Eire, Erin 7 Ireland

emerge
4 flow, loom, rise, stem 5 arise, issue 6 appear, derive, evolve, spring 7 come out, develop, emanate, proceed, surface 9 originate, transpire 11 come to light, materialize

emergency
3 fix 4 hole, pass 5 pinch 6 climax, clutch, crisis, crunch, strait 7 squeeze 8 accident, exigency

emeritus
7 retired

Emerson, Ralph Waldo
essay: 12 Self-Reliance
forte: 5 essay
home: 7 Concord
friend: 7 Thoreau (Henry David)

emery
6 powder 8 abrasive, corundum

emetic
8 vomitive 9 cathartic, purgative

émeute
4 riot 6 mutiny, revolt, tumult 8 outbreak, upheaval, uprising 9 rebellion 12 insurrection

emigrant
7 pioneer, settler 8 colonist 10 expatriate

émigré
5 alien, exile, expat 7 evacuee, migrant, refugee 8 colonist 10 expatriate

Emilia
husband: 4 Iago 7 Palamon
slayer: 4 Iago

eminence
3 VIP 4 fame, peak, rise 5 honor, power 6 bigwig, esteem, height, leader, renown, repute 7 dignity, notable 8 altitude, big-timer, luminary, prestige, standing 9 authority, dignitary, elevation, greatness, loftiness 10 importance, projection, prominence, promontory, reputation 11 distinction, superiority

eminent
4 high 5 famed, grand, great, large, lofty, noble, noted 6 august, famous 7 exalted, notable 8 esteemed, renowned, towering 9 important, well-known 10 celebrated, noteworthy, projecting 11 conspicuous, illustrious, outstanding, prestigious 13 distinguished

eminently
4 very 6 highly 7 notably 9 extremely 10 remarkably, strikingly 11 exceedingly 12 surpassingly 13 exceptionally

emir

5 chief, ruler, sheik, title **6** sheikh
9 chieftain, commander

emissary

see **envoy**

emission

4 flow **7** venting **9** discharge,
effluvium, emanation, radiation

emit

4 beam, glow, ooze, pour, shed,
spew, vent, void **5** eject, expel,
exude, issue, loose, utter **6** exhale,
let out **7** emanate, excrete, extrude,
give off, give out, radiate, release,
secrete, send out **8** evacuate, throw
off **9** circulate, discharge

emmer

5 grain, spelt, wheat

emmet

3 ant **7** pismire

emollient

4 balm **5** salve **7** lenient **8** lenitive,
liniment, sedative, soothing
9 analgesic, softening **10** mollifying

emolument

3 fee, pay **4** wage **5** wages **6** income, reward, salary **7** guerdon,
stipend **8** earnings **10** recompense
11 pay envelope **12** compensation

emotion

3 ire, joy **4** fear, glee, hate, love
5 agony, ardor, grief, shame **6** affect, hatred, relief, sorrow, warmth
7 ardency, despair, disgust, ecstasy,
feeling, passion, sadness **8** jealousy,
surprise **9** affection, agitation, happiness, sentiment **11** affectivity, sensibility, sensitivity **12** excitability

emotional

4 warm **6** ardent, fervid, heated,
moving **7** feeling, fervent, intense,
soulful, zealous **8** effusive, stirring,
touching, vehement **9** affecting,
affective, excitable, heartfelt, impetuous, rhapsodic, sensitive **10** hysterical, passionate **11** impassioned,
overwrought, rhapsodical, softhearted, susceptible, sympathetic

emotionless

3 icy **4** cold, cool **5** chill, staid, stoic,
stony **6** frigid, remote, torpid **7** callous, deadpan, distant, glacial
8 detached, reserved **9** apathetic,
immovable, impassive, unfeeling
10 impersonal **11** cold-blooded,
indifferent **12** matter-of-fact **13** dispassionate, unimpassioned

empathy

4 pity **6** lenity, warmth **7** rapport
8 affinity, sympathy **9** communion
10 compassion **12** congeniality
13 compatibility, comprehension,
fellow feeling, understanding

emperor

4 czar, shah, tsar, tzar **5** ruler
6 caesar, kaiser **7** monarch **8** auto-
crat, dictator **9** potentate, sovereign
French: 8 Napoleon (Bonaparte)
9 Bonaparte (Napoleon) **11** Charlemagne
Indian: 5 Babur
Japanese: 6 mikado **7** Akihito
8 Hirohito
Mexican: 8 Iturbide (Agustín de)
10 Maximilian
Roman: 4 Nero **5** Galba, Nerva,
Titus **6** Decius, Julian, Trajan **7** Gra-
tian, Hadrian, Severus **8** Augustus,
Aurelian, Caligula, Claudius, Commodus, Domitian, Honorius, Tiberius,
Valerian **9** Antoninus, Caracalla,
Justinian **10** Diocletian, Elagabalus
11 Constantine

emphasis

5 focus, force **6** accent, stress,
weight **9** attention, intensity **10** insistence, prominence **12** accentuation

emphasize

6 accent, play up, stress **7** feature
8 pinpoint **9** highlight, italicize,
spotlight, underline **10** accentuate,
underscore

emphatic

4 firm **6** marked **7** decided, earnest,
pointed **8** accented, decisive, forceful, positive, stressed, vigorous

9 assertive, energetic, insistent
10 resounding, underlined 11 accentuated

empire
5 realm 6 domain 7 demesne, kingdom 8 dominion
ancient:
(see **ancient empire**)

Empire State
7 New York

empirical
7 factual 9 fact-based, pragmatic 12 experiential, experimental 13 observational

emplacement
7 battery 8 position

employ
3 job, use 4 busy, hire, work 5 apply, avail 6 devote, engage, occupy, retain, secure, take on 7 exploit, utilize 8 exercise, practice 9 make use of 10 occupation

employee
4 hand, help 5 agent 6 worker 7 servant 8 factotum 9 underling
bank: 5 clerk, guard 6 teller
hotel: 7 bellboy, bellhop, doorman 9 concierge, desk clerk 11 chambermaid

employer
4 boss 6 master 10 supervisor

employment
3 job, use 4 line, post, task, toil, work 5 trade, usage 6 hiring, métier, office 7 calling, mission, purpose, pursuit 8 business, exercise, function, position, vocation 9 appliance, operation, situation 10 engagement, occupation 11 application, recruitment, utilization 12 exploitation

emporium
4 mall, mart, shop 5 store 6 bazaar, market 8 exchange 11 marketplace

empower
5 endow 6 charge, enable, invest 7 entitle, entrust, license 8 accredit, delegate, deputize, sanction 9 authorize, privilege 10 commission

empress
5 queen
Byzantine: 3 Zoe
French: 7 Eugénie 9 Josephine
Japanese: 5 Suiko
of India: 8 Victoria
Mexican: 7 Carlota
Roman: 6 Fausta
Russian: 4 Anna 7 czarina, tsarina, tzarina 9 Alexandra, Catherine, Elizabeth

empressement
6 fervor, warmth 10 cordiality

emprise
4 feat, gest 5 geste 7 exploit, venture 9 adventure 11 undertaking

emptiness
4 void 5 blank 6 hunger, vacuum 7 inanity, vacancy, vacuity

emptor
5 buyer 6 vendee 8 consumer, customer 9 purchaser

_____ emptor
6 caveat

empty
3 rid 4 bare, dump, pour, vain, void 5 blank, clear, drain 6 barren, devoid, hollow, unload, vacant, vacate 7 deplete, drained, exhaust, vacated, vacuous 8 depleted, deserted, evacuate, forsaken 9 abandoned, destitute 10 unoccupied, untenanted
Scottish: 4 toom

empty-headed
6 simple, vacant 7 vacuous, witless 8 ignorant, untaught 9 benighted, brainless, frivolous 10 illiterate, uneducated, unlettered, unschooled 11 know-nothing 12 uninstructed 13 rattlebrained

empyreal
4 airy, holy 6 aerial, divine 7 sublime 8 beatific, ethereal, heavenly 9 celestial, spiritual, unearthly 12 transcendent

empyrean
3 sky 4 Zion 5 bliss, ether 6 heaven,

emu

welkin **7** Elysium, heavens, nirvana **8** paradise **9** firmament

emu

4 bird, rhea **6** ratite **9** cassowary

emulate

3 ape **4** copy **5** equal, mimic, rival **6** follow, mirror **7** compete, imitate **9** challenge

emulation

7 rivalry **8** striving, tug-of-war **9** imitation **10** contention **11** competition

emulous

5 vying **8** aspiring, striving, vaulting **9** ambitious **11** competitive

emulsifier

4 soap **5** algin

enable

3 fit, let **5** allow, ready **6** permit **7** empower, entitle, license, prepare, qualify **8** accredit, sanction **9** authorize, condition **10** commission, facilitate **12** make possible

enact

4 pass, play **6** decree, depict, effect, ordain, ratify **7** execute, perform, portray **8** proclaim **9** authorize, discourse, establish, institute, legislate, represent **10** accomplish, bring about, constitute, effectuate **11** impersonate

enactment

3 law **6** action, decree **7** statute **9** depiction, ordinance, portrayal **11** legislation, performance **12** ratification

enamel

5 glaze, gloss, japan, paint **7** lacquer

enamored

4 fond **6** loving **7** devoted, smitten **8** besotted **9** bewitched, enchanted, entranced, infatuate **10** captivated, infatuated

encamp

4 tent **6** settle **7** bivouac

encampment

6 billet, laager **7** bivouac, hutment

encase

3 box **4** pack **7** confine, enclose, envelop, sheathe

enceinte

6 gravid **8** pregnant **9** expectant, expecting **10** parturient

enchain

4 bind **6** fetter **7** manacle, shackle

enchant

3 hex **4** lure, wile **5** charm, spell, witch **6** allure, enamor, seduce, thrill, voodoo **7** attract, beguile, bewitch, delight **8** ensorcel, enthrall **9** captivate, enrapture, ensorcell, fascinate, hypnotize, magnetize, mesmerize, spellbind

enchanter

4 mage **5** magus **6** wizard **7** charmer, warlock **8** conjurer, conjuror, magician, sorcerer **11** necromancer, spellbinder

enchanting

5 siren **9** glamorous, seductive **10** attractive, delectable, delightful, intriguing

enchantment

3 hex **5** charm, magic, spell **6** allure **7** glamour, sorcery **8** witchery, wizardry **9** conjuring, seduction **10** necromancy, witchcraft **11** incantation

enchantress

3 hex **5** bruja, Circe, lamia, Medea, siren, witch **9** sorceress

enchiridion

4 text **5** guide **6** manual **8** Baedeker, handbook **9** guidebook, vade mecum

encipher

4 code

encircle

3 hem **4** band, gird, halo, hoop, ring **5** girth **6** begird, engird, enlace, girdle **7** compass, embrace, enclose, environ, wreathe **8** surround **9** encompass **12** circumscribe

enclave
6 colony, ghetto, sector 7 quarter
8 district, homeland

enclose
3 box, hem, mew, pen, rim 4 cage,
coop, mure, wall, wrap 5 bound,
fence, hedge, limit 6 circle, closet,
corral, hold in, immure, shroud, shut
in, wall in 7 compass, confine,
contain, embosom, include 8 fence
off, imprison, surround 9 capsulize
12 circumscribe

enclosed
6 obtect

enclosure
3 box, mew, pen, sty 4 cage, camp,
cell, coop, cote, fold, jail, pale, quad,
tank, trap, wall, weir, yard 5 court,
fence, kraal, pound, stall 6 aviary,
corral, cowpen, kennel, paling, prison
7 chamber, paddock 8 cloister,
stockade 9 courtyard 10 quadrangle

encomiast
7 praiser 8 eulogist 10 panegyrist

encomiastic
9 adulatory, laudative, laudatory
10 eulogistic 11 panegyrical

encomium
4 laud 5 kudos, paean 6 eulogy,
homage, praise 7 acclaim, plaudit,
tribute 8 accolade, citation, plaudits
9 laudation, panegyric 10 compliment, salutation 11 acclamation
12 commendation

encompass
3 hem 4 belt, gird, ring 5 bound
6 begird, circle, girdle, take in 7 contain, embrace, enclose, include,
subsume 8 encircle, surround
10 accomplish, bring about, comprehend

encore
6 recall, repeat, return 10 repetition

encounter
4 face, find, fray, meet 5 brush,
clash, fight, run-in, scrap, set-to
6 battle, engage, take on 7 collide,
contest, meeting, quarrel, run into
8 argument, bump into, come upon,
conflict, confront, meet with, skirmish, struggle 10 contention,
experience

encourage
4 abet, back, buoy, push, spur, stir,
urge 5 boost, cheer, egg on, rally,
rouse, serve, steel 6 assist, assure,
buck up, excite, foster, incite, induce,
praise 7 advance, animate, approve,
bolster, cheer up, endorse, fortify,
further, hearten, improve, inspire,
promote, provoke, quicken, support,
sustain 8 advocate, embolden,
energize, inspirit, reassure, sanction
9 enhearten, galvanize, instigate,
patronize, reinforce, stimulate,
subsidize 10 invigorate, strengthen

encouragement
4 lift, push 5 boost 7 backing,
support 8 approval 11 inspiration

encouraging
4 rosy 6 bright, likely 7 hopeful
9 favorable, promising 10 auspicious, propitious

encroach
5 poach 6 invade, meddle, trench
7 impinge, intrude 8 entrench,
infringe, overstep, trespass

encrypt
4 code 6 cipher, encode 7 convert
8 disguise, encipher

encumber
4 lade, load 6 burden, charge, fetter,
hamper, hinder, impede, saddle,
weight 7 freight, oppress 8 handicap, obstruct, overload 9 weigh
down 10 overburden 13 inconvenience

encumbrance
4 lien, load, onus 5 claim 6 burden
7 baggage 8 handicap, mortgage
9 albatross, millstone 10 impediment

encyclical
6 letter 7 general 8 circular

encyclopedic
5 broad 7 general 8 complete,

thorough **9** extensive, inclusive, universal **11** compendious, wide-ranging **12** all-embracing, all-inclusive **13** comprehensive

encyclopedist

7 Diderot (Denis)

end

3 aim, tip **4** coda, doom, goal, halt, quit, stop, tail, term **5** cease, close, death, finis, limit **6** demise, expire, finale, finish, object, period, result, scotch, windup, wrap up **7** abolish, closing, closure, extreme, lineman, outcome, purpose **8** boundary, complete, conclude, confines, curtains, finality, surcease, terminal, terminus **9** cessation, extremity, objective, terminate **10** borderline, completion, conclusion, denouement, expiration, extinction, limitation **11** culmination, discontinue, termination **12** consummation

endanger

4 risk **5** peril **6** expose **7** imperil **8** threaten **10** compromise, jeopardize

endeavor

3 aim, try **4** push, seek, toil, work **5** assay, essay, labor, trial **6** effort, intend, strain, strive **7** attempt, purpose, travail, venture **8** exertion, striving, struggle **9** determine, undertake **10** enterprise **11** undertaking

ended

4 done, over, past **7** through **8** complete

endemic

5 local **6** innate, native **8** homebred, inherent, primeval **9** homegrown, prevalent **10** aboriginal, indigenous, native-born

ending

4 stop **5** close **6** finale, finish, period, windup **7** closing, closure **8** terminus **9** cessation **10** completion, conclusion, denouement **11** termination

endive

7 lettuce, witloof **8** escarole

endless

7 eternal, undying **8** constant, enduring, immortal, infinite, unending **9** ceaseless, continual, incessant, limitless, perpetual, unbounded, unceasing, unlimited **10** continuous, indefinite, unmeasured **11** everlasting, illimitable, measureless **12** immeasurable, interminable

endmost

4 last **5** final **8** farthest, furthest, ultimate **10** concluding

endocrine gland

5 gonad, ovary **6** pineal, testis, thymus **7** adrenal, thyroid **8** pancreas **9** pituitary **11** parathyroid **12** hypothalamus

endomorphic

5 beefy, heavy, husky, stout **6** portly, pyknic, rotund

endorse

4 back, okay, sign **5** bless, vouch **6** attest, ratify, second, uphold **7** approve, certify, command, confirm, stand by, support, witness **8** accredit, advocate, champion, inscribe, make over, notarize, sanction **9** autograph, recommend **10** underwrite **12** authenticate

endorsement

7 backing, support **8** approval, sanction **9** signature **12** confirmation, ratification **13** authorization

endow

4 back, fund **5** found **6** bestow, confer, enrich, supply **7** empower, enhance, finance, furnish, promote, provide, sponsor, support **8** bequeath **9** subsidize

endowment

4 fund, gift **5** award, dower, dowry, grant, power, skill **6** legacy, talent **7** ability, bequest **8** appanage, aptitude, bestowal, capacity, donation **11** benefaction

end product
5 fruit, issue 6 effect, payoff, result, upshot 7 outcome 11 consequence

endue
3 don 4 vest 5 dower, equip, imbue, put on 6 clothe, invest, outfit 7 furnish, provide 8 accouter 9 crown with, transfuse

endurance
4 grit, guts, wind 5 moxie, pluck 6 mettle 7 stamina 8 patience, strength, tenacity 9 fortitude 10 permanence, resolution 11 persistence 12 perseverance

endure
4 bear, bide, go on, last 5 abide, brook, stand 6 accept, hold on, linger, pocket, remain, suffer 7 carry on, persist, ride out, stomach, survive, sustain, swallow, undergo, weather 8 continue, submit to, tolerate, tough out 9 withstand

enduring
3 old 4 fast, firm, sure 6 steady 7 abiding, durable, eternal, lasting, staunch 8 constant, lifelong 9 long-lived, perennial, permanent, steadfast 10 continuing, inveterate, persistent 11 long-lasting, unfaltering 12 never-failing

Endymion
father: 8 Aethlius
lover: 5 Diana 6 Selene
author: 5 Keats (John)

enemy
3 foe 5 rival 8 attacker, opponent 9 adversary, assailant 10 antagonist, competitor

energetic
4 spry 5 brisk, fresh, hardy, lusty, peppy, zippy 6 active, lively 7 driving, dynamic, vibrant 8 spirited, tireless, vigorous 9 sprightly, strenuous, vivacious 13 indefatigable

energize
3 pep 4 fuel, stir 5 liven, pep up, rouse, spark 6 enable, excite, stir up, turn on 7 empower, enliven, fortify, inspire, juice up 8 activate, inspirit, vitalize 9 electrify, galvanize, stimulate 10 invigorate, strengthen

energy
3 pep, vim, zip 4 dash, life, tuck 5 drive, force, juice, moxie, pluck, power, sinew, steam, verve, vigor 6 effort, muscle, spirit 7 current, potency, stamina, voltage 8 activity, dynamism, efficacy, exertion, strength, vitality 9 animation, intensity, puissance 10 enterprise, get-up-and-go, initiative 11 application
unit: 3 erg 4 dyne, volt 5 joule 7 quantum 10 horsepower

enervate
3 sap 4 jade, tire 5 weary 6 soften, weaken 7 disable, exhaust, fatigue, unnerve 8 enfeeble, unstring 10 debilitate, devitalize

enfant terrible
3 imp 5 scamp 6 urchin 9 skeezicks

enfeeble
3 sap 6 soften, weaken 7 deplete, disable, exhaust, fatigue 8 enervate 9 attenuate, undermine 10 debilitate, devitalize

enfold
3 hug 4 wrap 5 clasp, cover, press 6 shroud, swathe 7 contain, embrace, squeeze 8 surround

enforce
5 exact, impel 6 compel, effect, impose, invoke, oblige 7 execute, fulfill 8 carry out 9 constrain, discharge, implement, prosecute 10 accomplish, administer, strengthen

enfranchise
4 free 6 rescue 7 deliver, manumit, release, set free 8 liberate 10 emancipate

engage
4 bind, grip, hire, mesh 5 fight, troth 6 absorb, arrest, attack, battle, commit, employ, enlist, occupy, pledge, take on 7 assault, betroth, engross, immerse, involve, promise

8 affiance, enthrall, interact 9 captivate, encounter, fascinate, interlace, interlock, intermesh, interplay, preoccupy, undertake

engaged

4 busy, rapt 6 intent 7 working 8 absorbed, employed, immersed, intended, occupied, plighted 9 affianced, betrothed, committed, engrossed, wrapped up 10 contracted 11 preoccupied
  person: 6 fiancé 7 fiancée

engage in

4 wage 5 enter 6 pursue, tackle, take up 7 conduct 8 embark on, practice 9 prosecute, undertake

engagement

3 gig 4 date, fray, word 5 fight, troth, tryst 6 action, battle, combat, hiring, pledge, plight 7 booking, meeting, promise 8 espousal, skirmish 9 betrothal, encounter 10 commitment, employment, rendezvous 11 appointment, assignation

engaging

7 likable, winning, winsome 8 charming, pleasant, pleasing 9 appealing 10 attractive 13 prepossessing

engender

4 sire, stir 5 beget, breed, cause, hatch, rouse, spawn 6 arouse, create, excite, father, induce, lead to, work up 7 develop, produce, provoke 8 generate 9 originate, procreate, stimulate

engine

5 motor, turbo 7 turbine 10 locomotive
  kind: 3 gas, jet 5 steam 6 diesel 7 turbine 8 gasoline 9 hydraulic
  jet: 8 turbofan, turbojet
  part: 3 cam, rod 4 gear, plug, pump 5 choke 6 filter, piston, tappet 8 cylinder, manifold, throttle 9 condenser, crankcase 10 carburetor 12 transmission
  siege: 3 ram 6 onager 8 ballista, catapult 9 trebuchet 12 battering ram
  sound: 4 chug, roar 6 rattle

engineer

4 plan, plot 5 set up, swing 6 devise, driver, manage, scheme, wangle 7 arrange, finagle 8 contrive, intrigue, maneuver, motorman 9 machinate, negotiate 10 manipulate, mastermind 11 orchestrate
  kind: 5 civil 6 mining 8 chemical, sanitary 10 electrical, mechanical 12 aeronautical
  military: 6 sapper

engineers' group

  abbreviation: 4 IEEE

England

6 Albion 7 Britain 9 Britannia 12 Great Britain
see also **United Kingdom**

English

7 British
  cathedral city: 3 Ely 4 York 5 Wells 6 Durham, Exeter 7 Lincoln, Norwich 8 Coventry, Hereford 9 Salisbury, Worcester 10 Canterbury, Winchester
  coin: 5 crown, groat, pence 6 florin, guinea 8 farthing, shilling, sixpence, twopence 9 fourpence, half crown, halfpenny, sovereign 10 threepence
  combining form: 5 Anglo
  farm: 5 croft
  forest: 5 Arden 8 Sherwood
  letter: 3 zed
  measure: 3 rod, tun 4 gill, hand, peck, span 5 chain 6 barrel, bushel, fathom, firkin 7 furlong 8 hogshead 10 barleycorn
  military college: 9 Sandhurst
  patron saint: 6 George
  person: 4 chap, mate 5 bloke 6 Briton
  pirate: 4 Kidd (Capt. William) 5 Avery (Henry), Teach (Edward) 6 Morgan (Henry) 7 Dampier (William) 10 Blackbeard
  prince: 5 Harry 6 Andrew, Edward, Philip 7 Charles, William
  princess: 4 Anne 5 Diana 8 Margaret
  professor: 3 don
  royal family: 5 Tudor 6 Stuart 7 Hanover, Windsor

saint: 7 Dunstan 8 Cuthbert
spa: 4 Bath
sport: 5 rugby 7 cricket
tavern: 3 pub
university: 5 Leeds 6 Oxford
9 Cambridge
weight: 5 stone 6 firkin 7 quintal
8 quartern

English Channel swimmer
6 Ederle (Gertrude)

engrave
3 cut, fix 4 etch 5 carve, chase
6 incise, scrive 7 instill 8 inscribe

engraver
6 chaser, etcher
German: 5 Dürer (Albrecht)
10 Schongauer (Martin)
Italian: 8 Raimondi (Marcantonio)

engraving
7 etching, linecut, woodcut 8 dry-
point, intaglio 9 xylograph

engross
4 bury, busy, copy, grip 5 apply, write
6 absorb, engage, indite, occupy,
scribe 7 consume, immerse, involve
8 enthrall, inscribe 9 captivate,
preoccupy 10 transcribe

engrosser
6 scribe 7 copyist 9 scrivener
12 calligrapher 13 calligraphist

engulf
4 bury 5 drown, flood, swamp,
whelm 6 deluge, devour 7 immerse,
overrun, swallow 8 flow over, inundate, overflow, submerge 9 overwhelm, swallow up

enhance
4 lift 5 add to, adorn, exalt, raise
6 deepen 7 amplify, augment, build
up, elevate, enlarge, flatter, improve,
magnify 8 beautify, heighten, increase 9 aggravate, embellish,
embroider, intensify, reinforce 10 exaggerate, strengthen

enigma
4 crux, knot 5 poser, rebus 6 puzzle,
riddle, sphinx, teaser 7 mystery,
problem, puzzler 9 conundrum

10 closed book, perplexity, puzzlement 12 question mark 13 Chinese
puzzle, mystification

enigmatic
6 mystic 7 cryptic, Delphic, obscure 8 Delphian, oracular, puzzling
9 ambiguous 10 mysterious, mystifying, perplexing 11 inscrutable

enisle
6 cut off 7 isolate 8 insulate, separate 9 segregate, sequester

enjoin
3 ban, bid 4 deny, rule, tell, urge,
warn 5 order, taboo 6 adjure,
charge, decree, direct, forbid, impose, outlaw 7 caution, command,
counsel, dictate, inhibit 8 admonish,
disallow, forewarn, instruct, prohibit
9 interdict, prescribe, proscribe

enjoy
4 like, love 5 eat up, fancy, savor
6 relish 9 delight in 10 appreciate

enjoyable
3 fun 8 pleasant, pleasing 9 agreeable 10 delightful, satisfying 11 pleasurable 12 entertaining

enjoyment
4 zest 5 gusto, savor 6 relish
7 benefit, delight 8 felicity, fruition,
pleasure 9 diversion 10 indulgence,
recreation, relaxation 11 delectation
12 satisfaction 13 gratification

Enki
consort: 5 Nintu
son: 6 Ninsar

enkindle
4 fire 5 flame, light 6 ignite 7 inflame
8 touch off 9 set fire to

enlarge
3 wax 4 grow, rise 5 add to, boost,
build, mount, widen 6 beef up,
dilate, expand, extend 7 amplify,
augment, broaden, develop, greaten,
inflate, magnify, stretch 8 heighten,
increase, multiply 9 elaborate,
embroider 10 exaggerate

enlargement

4 node **5** tumor **6** blowup, growth, nodule **7** buildup **8** addition, increase, swelling **9** accretion, expansion, extension **12** augmentation **13** amplification

enlighten

5 edify, guide, teach **6** advise, illume, inform, uplift **7** educate, improve **8** illumine, instruct **10** illuminate

enlist

4 join **5** draft, enter **6** employ, enroll, join up, muster, sign on, sign up **7** attract, recruit **8** register **9** volunteer **11** participate

enliven

3 pep **4** buoy, fire, warm **5** amuse, cheer, pep up, renew, rouse **6** excite, jazz up, perk up, vivify, wake up **7** animate, cheer up, inspire, quicken, refresh, restore, spice up **8** energize, recreate **9** entertain, galvanize, stimulate **10** exhilarate, invigorate, rejuvenate

en masse

5 as one **6** bodily **8** together **12** collectively

enmesh

4 hook, mire, trap **5** catch, snare **6** draw in, tangle **7** embroil, ensnarl, involve, trammel **8** drag into, entangle **9** embrangle, implicate

enmity

4 hate **6** animus, hatred, rancor, spleen **7** ill will **8** aversion, bad blood, loathing **9** animosity, antipathy, hostility **10** abhorrence, antagonism **11** detestation

ennoble

5 exalt, honor, raise **6** uplift, uprear **7** dignify, elevate, glorify, magnify, sublime **10** aggrandize **11** distinguish

ennui

6 apathy, tedium **7** boredom, fatigue, languor **8** doldrums, dullness, lethargy **9** jadedness, lassitude, tiredness, weariness **11** languidness **12** listlessness

Enoch

father: 4 Cain
son: 10 Methuselah

Enoch Arden author

8 Tennyson (Alfred)

enormity

6 infamy **7** outrage **8** atrocity, hugeness, rankness, savagery, vastness **9** barbarity, depravity, flagrancy, graveness, greatness, grossness, immensity, magnitude **11** abomination, heinousness, massiveness, monstrosity, seriousness, weightiness

enormous

4 huge, vast **5** great **7** immense, mammoth, massive, titanic **8** colossal, gigantic **9** humongous, monstrous **10** astronomic, gargantuan, prodigious, stupendous, tremendous **12** astronomical

Enos

father: 4 Seth
grandfather: 4 Adam
grandmother: 3 Eve
uncle: 4 Abel, Cain

enough

5 ample **6** fairly, plenty **8** adequate, decently, passably **9** competent, tolerably **10** acceptably, adequately, sufficient **11** comfortable, sufficiency **12** satisfactory, sufficiently
poetic: 4 enow

enounce

3 say **5** state, utter **6** intone **8** proclaim, set forth **10** articulate

enrage

3 ire **4** rile **5** anger **6** madden **7** incense, inflame, steam up **9** infuriate

enrapture

5 charm, elate **6** ravish, trance **7** delight, enchant, rejoice **8** enthrall, entrance **9** captivate, transport

enraptured

6 elated **7** charmed **8** ecstatic, thrilled **9** bewitched, delighted, enchanted, entranced **10** captivated,

enthralled, mesmerized, spellbound
11 transported

enrich
5 adorn, endow 6 fatten 7 enhance,
improve 8 beautify, ornament
9 embellish, fertilize 10 supplement

enroll
4 book, file, join, list 5 draft, enter
6 enlist, induct, join up, muster,
record, sign on, sign up, wrap up
7 catalog, engross, recruit 8 inscribe,
register 9 conscript, subscribe
10 transcribe 11 matriculate

ensconce
4 bury, hide 5 cache, cover, place,
plant, stash 6 hole up, locate, settle
7 conceal, install, secrete, shelter
9 establish

ensemble
3 duo 4 band, crew, suit, trio 5 choir,
combo, decor, group, suite, troop,
whole 6 chorus, outfit, septet, sextet,
troupe 7 chorale, company, costume, en masse, quartet, quintet
8 together 9 aggregate, orchestra

enshrine
6 hallow, revere 7 cherish 8 dedicate, preserve, sanctify, treasure
10 consecrate 11 memorialize

enshroud
4 hide, veil, wrap 5 cloak 6 clothe,
enfold, enwrap, invest 7 blanket,
conceal, envelop, obscure

ensign
4 flag, jack, sign 5 badge, crest
6 banner, colors, emblem, pennon
7 officer, pennant 8 gonfalon, insignia, standard, streamer 9 oriflamme

enslave
4 yoke 5 chain 6 fetter, thrall 7 enchain, oppress, shackle, subject
8 dominate, enthrall 9 indenture,
subjugate 12 disfranchise

enslavement
4 yoke 6 thrall 7 bondage, helotry, peonage, serfdom, slavery
9 servitude, thralldom

ensnare
3 bag, net 4 hook, lure, mesh,
snag, trap 5 benet, catch, decoy
6 enmesh, entrap, tangle 7 capture
8 entangle, inveigle

ensnarl
4 mire 6 enmesh, tangle 7 embroil,
perplex, trammel 8 entangle 9 embrangle

ensorcell
3 hex 5 charm, spell, witch 6 allure,
voodoo 7 beguile, bewitch, enchant
8 enthrall 9 captivate, enrapture,
hypnotize, magnetize, mesmerize,
spellbind

ensorcellment
5 magic 7 sorcery 8 witchery, wizardry 9 conjuring 10 necromancy,
witchcraft 11 bewitchment, enchantment

ensphere
4 ball 8 conglobe 10 conglobate

ensue
4 stem 5 issue 6 attend, derive,
follow, result 7 emanate, proceed,
succeed 9 supervene

ensuing
4 next 5 later 9 resultant 10 consequent, subsequent, succeeding

ensure
5 cinch 6 clinch, secure 7 certify,
confirm, warrant 9 establish, guarantee

enswathe
4 roll, wrap 5 cloak, drape 6 bundle,
enwrap, shroud, wrap up 7 envelop,
swaddle

entail
5 imply 6 assign, confer, demand,
impose, lead to 7 call for, involve,
require 8 occasion, restrict, result in,
transmit 11 necessitate

entangle
4 mesh, mire, trap 5 catch, ravel,
snare, snarl, tie up, twist 6 enmesh,
entrap 7 capture, catch up, embroil,
ensnare, ensnarl, involve, perplex,
trammel 10 complicate, intertwine,
interweave

entanglement

3 web 4 knot, mesh, mess, toil
5 skein, snare 6 affair, cobweb,
muddle 8 intrigue 9 confusion,
imbroglio 11 embroilment, involvement 12 complication

entente

4 pact 6 league, treaty 7 compact
8 alliance, covenant 9 agreement,
coalition, concordat 13 understanding

enter

4 go in, join, list, open 5 admit, begin,
start 6 come in, enlist, enroll, go into,
insert, join up, muster, record, sign
on, sign up 7 intrude 8 come into,
embark on, inscribe, register 9 introduce, penetrate 10 embark upon

enterprise

4 deed, feat, firm, push, task 5 cause,
drive, pluck, vigor 6 action, daring,
effort, energy, hustle, outfit, scheme
7 attempt, company, concern, courage, exploit, project, pursuit, venture
8 activity, ambition, audacity, boldness, business, campaign, endeavor,
gumption, industry 9 adventure,
eagerness 10 enthusiasm, get-up-
and-go, initiative 11 corporation,
undertaking 12 organization, self-
reliance 13 establishment

enterprising

4 bold 5 eager 6 daring, hungry
7 driving, go-ahead 8 aspiring,
hustling 9 ambitious, audacious,
energetic 10 aggressive 11 adventurous, hardworking, industrious,
up-and-coming, venturesome

entertain

4 host 5 amuse 6 divert, regale
7 delight, receive 8 consider

entertainer

4 mime 5 actor, clown, comic
6 busker, dancer, jester, singer
7 actress, artiste, diseuse, trouper
8 comedian, minstrel 10 comedienne

entertaining

6 lively 7 amusing 8 engaging
9 diverting, enjoyable

entertainment

4 fete, play, show, skit 5 revue,
sport 6 circus 7 banquet, concert, pastime, ridotto 8 pleasure
9 amusement, diversion, enjoyment
10 recreation 11 distraction, performance

enthrall

4 grip 5 charm 6 absorb, subdue
7 beguile, bewitch, enchant, engross,
enslave 9 fascinate, hypnotize,
mesmerize, spellbind, subjugate

enthralling

8 exciting, gripping, riveting 9 absorbing, arresting 10 enchanting,
engrossing, entrancing 11 captivating, charismatic, provocative
12 spellbinding

enthuse

4 gush, rave 6 excite, thrill 7 animate, delight, inspire 8 energize
10 rhapsodize

enthusiasm

4 élan, fire, zeal, zest 5 ardor, craze,
fever, mania, verve 6 fervor, spirit
7 ardency, passion, rapture 9 eagerness, intensity 10 ebullience, excitement, fanaticism

enthusiast

3 bug, fan, nut 4 buff 5 fiend,
freak, lover, maven 6 addict, junkie,
maniac, votary, zealot 7 booster,
devotee, fanatic, groupie, habitué
8 believer, partisan 9 extremist
10 aficionado

enthusiastic

4 avid, gaga, keen 5 eager, rabid
6 ardent, fervid, gung ho, hearty,
hipped, raring 7 devoted, excited,
fervent, intense, zealous 8 hopped-
up, obsessed, spirited, vascular
9 fanatical 10 passionate

entice

4 bait, coax, draw, lure, toll, wile
5 charm, decoy, tempt 6 allure,
cajole, entrap, invite, lead on, seduce
7 attract, wheedle 8 inveigle, persuade

enticement
4 bait, lure, trap **5** decoy, snare **6** come-on **9** seduction **10** allure-ment, attraction, seducement, temptation **12** blandishment, in-veiglement

enticer
4 bait, vamp **5** Circe, decoy, siren **7** Lorelei **9** attractor, temptress **10** attraction, seductress **11** enchantress, femme fatale

enticing
5 siren **8** fetching, witching **9** seductive **10** attractive, bewitching, intriguing **11** captivating, fascinating

entire
3 all **4** full **5** gross, total, whole **6** intact **7** perfect, plenary, unified **8** complete, integral, outright **10** integrated **12** consolidated

entirely
5 fully, quite **6** wholly **7** utterly **9** perfectly **10** altogether, completely, thoroughly **11** exclusively

entirety
3 sum **5** total, whole **8** sum total, totality **9** aggregate, wholeness **10** everything **12** completeness, universality

entitle
3 dub, let **4** call, name, term **5** allow **6** enable, permit **7** baptize, empower, license, qualify **8** christen **9** authorize, designate **10** denominate

entity
3 sum **4** body, item, unit **5** being, thing, whole **6** object **7** article, integer **8** quiddity, totality **9** existence, something, substance **10** individual

entomb
4 bury **5** inter **6** inhume, shrine **7** mummify **8** enshrine **9** sepulcher, sepulchre

entombment
6 burial **7** obsequy **9** obsequies, sepulture **10** inhumation

entourage
5 staff, suite, train **6** escort, milieu **7** cortege, coterie, retinue **8** henchmen **9** courtiers, followers, following, hangers-on, retainers **10** associates, attendants **12** surroundings

entr'acte
8 interval **9** interlude **12** intermission

entrails
4 guts **5** pluck, tripe **6** bowels, tripes, vitals **7** giblets, innards, insides, viscera **8** stuffing **10** intestines

entrance
4 adit, door, gate, port **5** charm, foyer, inlet, lobby, mouth **6** access, portal, ravish **7** arrival, attract, bewitch, delight, doorway, enchant, gateway, ingress, opening **8** aperture, enthrall, open door **9** admission, captivate, enrapture, fascinate, hypnotize, mesmerize, spellbind, threshold, transport, vestibule **10** admittance, ingression **11** penetration

entrant
7 starter **10** competitor, contestant **11** participant

entrap
3 bag, net **4** bait, lure, toll **5** catch, decoy, snare, tempt **6** allure, ambush, entice, entoil, lead on, seduce, tangle **7** beguile, catch up, ensnare **8** entangle, inveigle

entre _____
4 nous

entreat
3 ask, beg, bid **4** pray, urge **5** crave, plead, press **6** adjure, appeal **7** beseech, implore, wheedle **8** blandish **9** importune **10** supplicate

entreaty
4 plea, suit **6** appeal, orison, prayer **7** request **8** petition **11** application, importunity **12** supplication

entrechat
4 leap

entrée
6 access 7 ingress 8 main dish
9 admission 10 admittance, main
course

entrench
3 fix 4 root 5 embed, lodge 6 define, furrow, ground, hole up, invade, settle 7 confirm, impinge, implant, intrude 8 encroach, ensconce, infringe, trespass 9 establish 10 strengthen

entrenched
3 set 4 firm 5 rigid, sworn 8 accepted, deep-dyed 9 hard-shell
10 deep-rooted, deep-seated, inveterate 13 bred-in-the-bone, dyed-in-the-wool

entrepôt
3 hub 4 mart 5 depot 6 bazaar, market 8 emporium, exchange
9 concourse, warehouse 10 depository, storehouse 11 marketplace

entrepreneur
10 capitalist, contractor, impresario

entresol
9 mezzanine

entropy
5 chaos, decay 7 decline 8 disorder
10 randomness 11 degradation

entrust
4 give 5 allot, leave 6 assign, charge, commit, confer, impose
7 commend, confide, consign, deliver, deposit 8 allocate, delegate, hand over, relegate, turn over

entry
3 way 4 adit, door, gate, item, port
5 debit, foyer, inlet, lobby 6 access, credit, portal, record 7 doorway, ingress, opening 8 headword
9 admission, threshold, vestibule
10 admittance, enlistment, enrollment, ingression

entryway
4 door, gate 5 foyer, lobby 6 portal
7 ingress, narthex, portico 9 vestibule

entwine
4 coil, wind 5 braid, plait, twist
6 enmesh 7 wreathe 8 entangle
9 interlace 10 interweave

enumerate
3 sum, tot 4 cite, list, tell, tote 5 add up, count, tally, total, tot up 6 detail, number, recite, reckon, tote up
7 compute, itemize, recount, specify, tick off 8 identify 9 calculate, inventory 13 particularize

enunciate
3 say 5 speak, state, utter, voice
6 affirm, intone 7 declare, express, lay down 8 announce, proclaim, propound, vocalize 9 formulate, postulate, pronounce, verbalize
10 articulate

envelop
3 hem 4 hide, roll, veil, wrap 5 cloak, cover, drape 6 cocoon, enfold, engulf, enwrap, invest, sheath, shield, shroud, swathe, wrap up
7 blanket, embrace, enclose, swaddle 8 encircle, enshroud, enswathe, surround 10 circumfuse

envenom
6 poison 8 embitter 10 exacerbate

envious
7 jealous 8 coveting, covetous, grudging 9 green-eyed, invidious, resentful 10 begrudging

environment
6 medium, milieu 7 ambient, climate, context, habitat, setting, terrain
8 ambiance, ambience, backdrop
9 situation 10 atmosphere, background 11 mise-en-scène 12 surroundings
science: 7 ecology

environmentalist
4 Muir (John) 6 Brower (David), Carson (Rachel), Nelson (Gaylord), Wilson (Edward O.) 7 Ehrlich (Paul), Thoreau (Henry David) 8 Commoner (Barry), Cousteau (Jacques-Yves)
9 ecologist, Roosevelt (Theodore)

environs
6 bounds, limits 7 compass, fringes, suburbs 8 boundary, confines, locality, purlieus, vicinity 9 districts, outskirts, precincts 12 neighborhood, surroundings

envisage
4 view 5 dream, fancy, grasp, image, think 6 regard, vision 7 dream up, feature, foresee, imagine, picture, realize 8 conceive, look upon, summon up 9 conjure up, objectify, visualize

envoy
5 agent 6 bearer, consul, deputy, legate, nuncio 7 attaché, carrier, courier 8 diplomat, emissary, minister 9 messenger 10 ambassador 11 internuncio 12 intermediary

envy
5 covet 6 grudge 8 begrudge, grudging, jealousy 10 resentment 12 covetousness 13 invidiousness

enwrap
4 roll, veil 5 clasp, drape 6 enfold, invest, shroud, swathe 7 enclose, engross, envelop, sheathe, swaddle 8 enshroud, enswathe

enzyme
3 ase 5 ficin, lyase, renin, urase 6 kinase, ligase, lipase, mutase, papain, pepsin, rennin, urease, zymase 7 amidase, amylase, cyclase, enolase, guanase, hydrase, inulase, isozyme, lactase, maltase, oxidase, pectase, pepsine, plasmin, ptyalin, rennase, sucrase, trypsin, zymogen 8 aldolase, diastase, elastase, esterase, fumarase, lyzozyme, nuclease, protease, steapsin, thrombin, zymogene 9 cellulase, invertase

eon
see **aeon**

Eos
see **Aurora**

épée
5 sword

epergne
5 stand 11 centerpiece

ephemeral
5 brief, short 7 passing 8 episodic, fleeting, fugitive, volatile 9 fugacious, momentary, temporary, transient 10 evanescent, short-lived, transitory 11 impermanent

Ephialtes
5 giant
brother: 4 Otus
father: 6 Aloeus 8 Poseidon
mother: 9 Iphimedia
slayer: 6 Apollo

Ephraim
brother: 8 Manasseh
father: 6 Joseph
grandfather: 5 Jacob
mother: 7 Asenath

epic
4 poem, saga 5 grand, Iliad 6 Aeneid, heroic 7 Beowulf, Odyssey 8 imposing, sweeping 9 Gilgamesh, narrative 12 Heimskringla

epicene
10 effeminate 11 intersexual 13 hermaphrodite

epicure
7 gourmet 8 aesthete, hedonist, sybarite 9 bon vivant 10 gastronome 11 connoisseur 12 gastronomist

epicurean
7 gourmet, sensual 8 aesthete, hedonist, sensuous, sybarite 9 bon vivant, luxurious 10 gastronome, voluptuous 11 connoisseur 12 gastronomist, sensualistic

epidemic
3 flu 4 rash, wave 6 plague 7 rampant, scourge 8 catching, outbreak 9 contagion, prevalent 10 contagious, pestilence

epidermis
4 skin 7 cuticle 10 integument

epigram
3 saw 4 poem 5 adage, axiom,

epigrammatic
maxim **6** bon mot, dictum, saying, truism **7** proverb **8** aphorism, apothegm

epigrammatic
5 meaty, pithy, terse, witty **6** cogent **7** compact, concise, marrowy, piquant, pointed

epigraph
5 motto **9** quotation **11** inscription

epilogue
4 coda **5** close **6** ending, finale, windup **7** closing **8** postlude **9** afterword **10** conclusion, postscript

Epimetheus
brother: **10** Prometheus
father: **7** Iapetus
wife: **7** Pandora

epiphany
6 aperçu, vision **7** insight **9** discovery, intuition **10** appearance, disclosure, revelation **11** inspiration, realization **13** manifestation

episode
5 event, phase **7** passage **8** incident, occasion **9** happening, interlude **10** occurrence **12** circumstance

episodic
5 brief **7** passing **8** fleeting, sporadic **9** ephemeral, irregular, temporary, transient **10** evanescent, occasional, short-lived **12** intermittent

epistaxis
9 nosebleed

epistle
4 note **6** letter **7** lection, missive **13** communication

epitaph
3 R.I.P. **5** elegy **6** eulogy **8** hic jacet **11** inscription

epithet
4 name **5** label, title **7** agnomen, moniker **8** cognomen, nickname **9** sobriquet **11** appellation

epitome
3 sum **4** acme, type **5** brief, short **6** digest, précis, résumé **7** essence, example, outline, summary **8** abstract, breviary, exemplar, synopsis, ultimate **9** archetype, summation, summing-up **10** abridgment, apotheosis, conspectus, embodiment **11** abridgement **12** condensation, quintessence

epitomize
5 sum up **6** digest, embody, mirror, typify **7** abridge, outline, summate **8** abstract, boil down, condense, manifest, tabulate **9** capsulize, exemplify, incarnate, inventory, objectify, personify, represent, summarize, symbolize, synopsize **10** abbreviate, illustrate **11** concentrate, emblematize, incorporate, personalize

epoch
3 age, eon, era **4** aeon, term, time **6** period **8** interval, time span

equable
4 calm, even, just **6** serene, stable, steady **7** orderly, regular, stabile, uniform **8** composed, constant **9** immutable, temperate, unvarying **10** consistent, invariable, unchanging **12** unchangeable

equal
3 tie **4** even, fair, like, mate, peer, same, twin **5** agree, alike, match **7** uniform **8** alter ego, amount to, parallel **9** duplicate, identical, impartial, objective **10** fifty-fifty **11** counterpart, symmetrical **12** commensurate, correspond to, proportional **13** commensurable, proportionate **combining form:** **3** iso **4** equi, pari **French:** **4** égal

equality
3 par **6** equity, parity **7** balance, égalité **8** evenness, fairness, sameness **10** uniformity

Equality State
7 Wyoming

equalize
4 even **5** level **6** square **7** balance **9** harmonize

equalizer
3 gun 6 pistol 8 handicap 10 tying score

equally
10 fifty-fifty 11 impartially

equanimity
4 calm, cool 5 poise 6 aplomb, phlegm 7 balance 8 calmness, coolness, evenness, serenity 9 assurance, composure, equipoise, placidity, sangfroid 10 detachment, steadiness 11 tranquility 12 tranquillity

equate
4 even 5 liken, match, treat 6 adjust, regard, relate, square 7 compare 8 consider, equalize, parallel 10 assimilate

Equatorial Guinea
capital: 6 Malabo
island, island group: 5 Bioko 6 Elobey, Pagulu 7 Corisco
language: 5 Bantu 6 French 7 Spanish
mainland: 5 Mbini 7 Río Muni
monetary unit: 5 franc
neighbor: 5 Gabon 8 Cameroon

equestrian
5 rider 6 horsey 8 horseman, knightly 10 horsewoman

equidistant
3 mid 6 medial, median, middle, midway 7 central, halfway, midmost

equilibrium
5 poise 6 aplomb, stasis 7 balance 8 evenness, symmetry 9 composure, stability 10 steadiness 12 counterpoise 13 stabilization

equine
4 colt, mare 5 filly, horse, steed 6 horsey 8 stallion 9 horselike

equip
3 arm, fit, rig 5 array, dress, endow, rig up 6 attire, fit out, outfit, rig out, supply 7 appoint, furnish, prepare, provide 8 accouter, accoutre 9 provision

equipment
3 rig 4 gear 5 traps 6 attire, outfit, tackle, things 7 baggage, panoply 8 fittings, material, matériel, ordnance, supplies, tackling 9 apparatus, endowment, machinery, trappings 10 provisions 11 accessories, attachments, habiliments, impedimenta 12 accouterment, accoutrement, provisioning 13 accouterments, accoutrements, appurtenances, paraphernalia

equitable
4 even, fair, just 5 level 6 proper, square 7 condign 8 balanced, deserved, unbiased 9 identical, impartial, objective, uncolored 10 evenhanded, impersonal 12 unprejudiced 13 dispassionate

equity
3 law 7 justice 8 equality, interest, justness

equivalence
3 par 6 parity, simile 7 analogy 8 equality, identity, likeness, sameness 10 conformity 11 correlation

equivalent
4 akin, copy, like, peer, same, twin 5 alike, match 6 agnate 7 identic, similar 8 parallel 9 analogous, duplicate, identical 10 comparable, homologous, substitute, tantamount 11 convertible, correlative, counterpart 12 commensurate 13 corresponding, proportionate

equivocal
4 hazy 5 fishy, vague 6 unsure 7 clouded, dubious, obscure, suspect, unclear 8 doubtful 9 ambiguous, debatable, enigmatic, uncertain, undecided 10 ambivalent, indecisive, indistinct, irresolute, unresolved 11 problematic 12 disreputable, inconclusive, questionable 13 indeterminate

equivocate
3 fib, lie 5 cavil, dodge, evade, fudge, hedge 6 palter, waffle, weasel 7 shuffle 8 sidestep 9 pussyfoot 11 prevaricate 12 tergiversate

equivocation
3 fib 7 evasion, fibbing, hedging, sophism 8 waffling 9 ambiguity, casuistry, duplicity, sophistry 12 speciousness

equivoque
3 pun 8 wordplay

era
3 age, day 4 date, term, time 5 epoch, stage 6 period

eradicate
4 dele, raze 5 abate, erase, purge 6 delete, efface, remove, uproot 7 abolish, blot out, destroy, expunge, root out, weed out, wipe out 8 demolish, stamp out 9 eliminate, extirpate, liquidate 10 annihilate, do away with, extinguish, obliterate 11 exterminate

erase
4 dele, void, x out 6 cancel, delete, efface, excise, remove, rub out 7 abolish, blot out, expunge, nullify, scratch, take out, wipe out 8 black out, blank out, cross off, cross out 9 eliminate, extirpate, sponge out, strike out 10 obliterate

Erato
see **Muse**

Erbin
father: 9 Custennin
nephew: 6 Arthur
son: 7 Geraint

ere
6 before

Erebus
daughter: 3 Day 6 Hemera
father: 5 Chaos
home: 5 Hades
sister, wife: 3 Nox, Nyx
son: 6 Aether, Charon

Erec et _____
5 Enide

Erechteus
daughter: 8 Chthonia
father: 6 Vulcan 10 Hephaestus
mother: 4 Gaea
slayer: 4 Zeus 7 Jupiter

erect
4 form 5 build, put up, raise, set up 6 create, raised 7 build up, stand-up, upright 8 assemble, elevated, standing, straight, vertical 9 construct, establish 10 upstanding 13 perpendicular

eremite
6 hermit 7 ascetic, recluse, stylite 9 anchoress, anchorite

Erewhon
6 utopia 7 nowhere
author: 6 Butler (Samuel)

ergo
4 then, thus 5 hence 9 therefore 11 accordingly 12 consequently

Erichthonius
father: 8 Dardanus
son: 4 Tros

Eridanus star
8 Achernar

Erin
see **Eire**

Erinyes
6 Alecto, Furies 7 Megaera 9 Eumenides, Tisiphone

Eris
brother: 4 Ares, Mars
daughter: 3 Ate
fruit: 5 apple
goddess of: 6 strife 7 discord
mother: 3 Nox, Nyx

Eritrea
archipelago: 6 Dahlak
capital: 6 Asmara
island: 5 Zuqar
monetary unit: 5 nakfa
neighbor: 5 Sudan 8 Djibouti, Ethiopia
river: 6 Baraka
sea: 3 Red

ermine
3 fur 5 stoat 6 weasel

erode
3 eat, rub 4 wear 5 decay, scour 6 abrade, rub off 7 consume, çor-

rade, crumble, eat away, rub away
8 wear away **9** scrape off **10** scrape away **11** deteriorate **12** disintegrate

Eroica composer
9 Beethoven (Ludwig van)

Eros
see **Cupid**

erose
6 jagged, uneven **9** irregular

erotic
4 lewd, racy, sexy **5** bawdy, spicy **6** carnal, earthy, ribald, risqué **7** fleshly, obscene, profane, sensual **8** off-color, prurient, sensuous **9** salacious **10** voluptuous **11** aphrodisiac, titillating

err
3 sin **4** goof, slip, trip **5** lapse, stray **6** bungle, foul up, mess up, slip up **7** blunder, deviate, screw up, stumble **8** trespass **10** transgress

errand
3 job **4** task **5** chore **7** mission **10** assignment

errand boy
4 page **5** gofer **7** bellboy, bellhop, courier **9** go-between

errant
5 stray **6** fickle, roving **7** aimless, deviant, erratic, naughty, ranging, roaming, wayward, willful **8** drifting, fallible, rambling, shifting, straying **9** deviating, itinerant, traveling, wandering **10** meandering, unreliable **11** mischievous

erratic
5 flaky **6** fitful **7** wayward **8** freakish, shifting, unstable, variable, volatile **9** arbitrary, desultory, eccentric, fluctuant, irregular, mercurial, spasmodic, uncertain, wandering, whimsical **10** capricious, changeable, inconstant, meandering **12** inconsistent **13** idiosyncratic, unpredictable

erring
see **errant**

erroneous
3 off **4** awry **5** amiss, askew, false, wrong **6** untrue **7** unsound **8** mistaken, specious, spurious **9** defective, incorrect, misguided **10** fallacious, inaccurate, misleading

error
4 flub, goof, muff, slip, trip **5** boner, botch, fault, fluff, gaffe, lapse **6** booboo, bungle, fumble, howler, miscue, slipup **7** blooper, blunder, fallacy, falsity, faux pas, misstep, mistake, screwup, stumble, untruth **8** delusion, illusion, screamer **9** falsehood, indecorum, oversight **10** inaccuracy, misreading **11** impropriety, misjudgment
printing: 4 typo **6** errata (plural) **7** erratum

ersatz
4 copy, fake, sham **5** bogus, dummy, faked, false, phony **6** pseudo **8** spurious **9** imitation, simulated, synthetic **10** artificial, factitious, simulacrum, substitute **11** counterfeit

Erse
5 Irish **6** Celtic, Gaelic

erstwhile
3 old **4** late, once, past **5** prior **6** before, bygone, former, whilom **7** already, earlier, onetime, quondam **8** formerly, previous **10** heretofore, previously

eruct
4 burp, emit, gush, spew **5** belch, eject, expel **7** explode **8** detonate, disgorge

erudite
7 bookish, learned **8** lettered, literate, studious, well-read **9** scholarly **10** scholastic

erudition
7 culture **8** learning, literacy **9** knowledge **11** bookishness, cultivation, learnedness, scholarship **12** studiousness **13** scholarliness

erupt
3 jet **4** spew **5** belch, burst, eject,

expel, go off, spout, spurt **7** explode
8 break out, burst out, detonate
9 discharge **10** break forth, burst
forth

eruption
4 gust, rush **5** blast, burst, flare,
sally **6** access **7** flare-up **8** outbreak,
outburst **9** commotion, explosion
skin: 3 zit **4** rash **6** pimple

Esau
brother: 5 Jacob
country: 4 Edom
descendant: 7 Edomite
father: 5 Isaac
father-in-law: 4 Elon
grandson: 6 Amalek
mother: 7 Rebekah
new name: 4 Edom
son: 5 Korha, Reuel **7** Eliphaz
wife: 4 Adah **10** Aholibamah

escalade
5 climb, mount, scale **6** ascend
7 scaling

escalate
4 grow, rise, soar **5** boost, climb,
mount, widen **6** expand, extend,
spread, step up **7** amplify, augment,
broaden, enlarge, inflate **8** heighten,
increase, multiply **9** intensify **11** proliferate

escapade
4 lark, romp **5** antic, caper, fling,
folly, prank, spree, stunt **6** frolic,
vagary **7** roguery, rollick **8** mischief
9 adventure

escape
3 fly, lam **4** bolt, duck, flee, shun,
skip, slip **5** avoid, break, dodge,
elude, evade, shake **6** bypass,
depart, eschew, flight, hegira, outlet
7 abscond, duck out, evasion, get
away, make off, release, run away,
skip out **8** breakout **9** avoidance,
desertion, disappear, steal away
10 circumvent, liberation **11** deliverance, evasiveness
artist: 7 Houdini (Harry)
narrow: 9 close call **10** close shave

escargot
5 snail

escarole
6 endive

escarpment
5 bluff, cliff, slope

eschar
4 scab **5** crust **6** lesion

eschew
4 shun **5** avoid, elude, evade, forgo,
spurn **6** abjure, forego, pass up,
refuse, reject **7** decline **8** turn down

eschewal
7 elusion, evasion, refusal **8** shunning, spurning **9** avoidance, rejection

escort
4 beau, date, lead, show **5** guard,
guide, pilot, steer, usher **6** attend,
convoy, direct, gigolo, squire **7** company, conduct, consort, retinue
8 cavalier, chaperon, henchman,
shepherd **9** accompany, bodyguard,
chaperone, companion, entourage,
safeguard **13** accompaniment

escritoire
4 desk **9** secretary **11** writing desk

escrow
4 bond, deed, fund **7** deposit

esculent
6 edible **7** eatable **10** comestible,
digestible

escutcheon
6 flange, shield

Eshcol
ally: 7 Abraham
brother: 4 Aner **5** Mamre

esker
4 kame **5** mound, ridge

Eskimo
4 Inuk **5** Aleut, Inuit
boat: 5 kayak, umiak
boot: 6 mukluk
dog: 5 husky **8** malamute
dwelling: 5 igloo
outer garment: 5 parka **6** anorak
sledge: 7 komatik

esophagus
6 gullet

esoteric
5 inner 6 arcane, mystic, occult, orphic, secret 7 cryptic, private 8 abstruse, hermetic, profound 9 recondite 10 cabalistic, mysterious 12 confidential

ESP
9 telepathy 10 sixth sense 12 clairvoyance, precognition

espadrille
4 shoe 6 sandal

espalier
7 lattice, railing, trellis

esparto
5 grass

especial
4 main 5 close 7 express, notable, unusual 8 dominant, intimate, peculiar, singular, specific, uncommon 9 paramount 10 individual, particular 11 exceptional

especially
7 notably 8 markedly 9 expressly, primarily, unusually 10 peculiarly, remarkably, singularly 11 principally 12 particularly, specifically 13 distinctively, exceptionally

espial
6 notice 9 detection, discovery 11 observation

espionage
6 spying 9 sleuthing 12 surveillance

espousal
5 troth, union 6 mating 7 embrace, support, wedding 8 adoption, advocacy, approval, ceremony, marriage 9 betrothal, embracing, matrimony, promotion 10 acceptance

espouse
3 wed 4 back 5 adopt, marry 6 accept, take on, take up 7 approve, embrace, support 8 advocate

esprit
3 vim, wit 4 brio, dash, élan, zest, zing 5 oomph, verve, vigor 6 fervor, gaiety, mettle, morale, spirit 7 courage, loyalty, panache, passion, sparkle 8 devotion, vibrancy, vitality 9 animation 10 brightness, enthusiasm, fellowship 11 camaraderie

esprit de corps
see **morale**

espy
3 see 4 mark, spot 5 sight 6 descry, detect, notice 7 discern, make out 9 recognize

_____ es Salaam
3 Dar

essay
3 try 4 seek, test 5 labor, paper, piece, study, theme, tract, trial 6 effort, strive, thesis 7 article, attempt, venture 8 endeavor, treatise 9 undertake 10 discussion, exposition 11 composition, undertaking 12 dissertation

essayist
American: 4 Agee (James), Will (George) 5 Baker (Russell), Cooke (Alistair), Gould (Stephen Jay), White (E. B.) 6 Brooks (Cleanth), Fisher (M. F. K.), Holmes (Oliver Wendell), Lowell (James Russell), Sontag (Susan), Thomas (Lewis) 7 Buckley (William F.), Cousins (Norman), Emerson (Ralph Waldo), Mencken (Henry Louis), Thoreau (Henry David) 8 Benchley (Robert), Lippmann (Walter), Repplier (Agnes) 10 Crèvecoeur (Jean de)
English: 4 Elia, Lamb (Charles) 5 Bacon (Francis), Cecil (Lord David), Pater (Walter), Smith (Sydney) 6 Arnold (Matthew), Cowley (Abraham), Morris (Jan), Ruskin (John), Steele (Richard) 7 Addison (Joseph), Hazlitt (William) 8 Beerbohm (Max) 9 De Quincey (Thomas) 12 Chesterfield (Lord)
French: 9 Montaigne (Michel de)
Scottish: 7 Carlyle (Thomas)

essence
3 nub 4 base, core, crux, gist, odor, pith, root, soul 5 basis, being, fiber,

essential

fibre, point, stuff **6** center, entity, kernel, marrow, nature, spirit **7** extract, perfume, quality **9** substance **10** distillate **12** distillation, significance

essential

4 main, must **5** basal, basic, chief, prime, vital **6** inborn, inbred, innate, primal **7** connate, crucial, element, primary **8** cardinal, foremost, inherent, required, rudiment **9** condition, elemental, intrinsic, necessary, necessity, principal, requisite, substance **10** congenital, deep-seated, elementary, idiopathic, imperative, sine qua non, underlying **11** fundamental, requirement **12** precondition, prerequisite **13** indispensable, part and parcel

essentially

6 almost, au fond, really **7** largely **8** actually, as good as, as much as, well-nigh **9** basically, virtually **11** practically **13** fundamentally, substantially

essonite

6 garnet **13** cinnamon stone

establish

3 fix, lay, put, set **4** base, form, root, show **5** build, enact, endow, erect, found, place, prove, set up, start **6** attest, create, decree, effect, ground, impose, secure, settle, verify **7** build up, certify, clarify, confirm, find out, implant, install, instill, provide, set down **8** document, ensconce, organize **9** authorize, construct, determine, formulate, institute, legislate, originate, prescribe **10** bring about, constitute, inaugurate **11** corroborate, demonstrate **12** authenticate, substantiate

establishment

4 firm **6** outfit **7** company, concern **8** business, old guard **9** institute, workplace **10** enterprise, foundation **11** institution, ruling class

estate

4 farm, land **5** manor, ranch, villa **6** domain, legacy, quinta **7** demesne **8** dominion, hacienda, property **10** plantation
feudal: 4 fief **7** fiefdom
first: 6 clergy
fourth: 5 press
manager: 7 steward **8** executor, guardian
second: 6 nobles **8** nobility
third: 7 commons

esteem

4 deem **5** favor, honor, prize, think, value **6** admire, liking, regard, revere **7** account, believe, cherish, idolize, respect, worship **8** approval, consider, treasure, venerate **9** valuation **10** admiration, appreciate **12** appreciation **13** consideration

ester

6 oleate **7** acetate **8** compound **9** phosphate

Esther

cousin: 8 Mordecai
enemy: 5 Haman
father: 7 Abihail
festival: 5 Purim
Hebrew name: 8 Hadassah
husband: 6 Xerxes **9** Ahasuerus

estimable

5 noble **6** august, valued, worthy **7** admired **8** laudable, sterling **9** admirable, deserving, honorable, reputable, respected, venerable **10** creditable **11** commendable, meritorious, respectable **12** praiseworthy

estimate

3 put **4** call, rank, rate **5** assay, gauge, guess, infer, judge, price, set at, value **6** assess, deduce, figure, rating, reckon, survey **7** imagine, opinion, project, suppose, surmise **8** appraise, conclude, discover, evaluate, forecast, judgment, round off **9** appraisal, calculate, determine, reckoning, valuation **10** assessment, conjecture, evaluation, impression, projection **11** approximate, calculation, measurement

estimation

4 fame 5 favor, honor, stock 6 esteem, regard 7 account, opinion, respect 8 figuring, judgment 9 appraisal, reckoning, valuation 10 admiration, assessment, evaluation, impression 11 calculation 13 consideration

Estonia

capital: 7 Tallinn
city: 5 Tartu
gulf: 4 Riga 7 Finland
island: 4 Muhu 6 Vormsi 7 Hiiumaa 8 Saaremaa
lake: 5 Pskov 6 Peipus 9 Vorts-Jarv
monetary unit: 5 kroon
neighbor: 6 Latvia, Russia
river: 5 Narva, Pärnu 6 Kasari
sea: 6 Baltic

estop

3 bar 6 enjoin, forbid 7 prevent 8 disallow, preclude, prohibit, restrain

estrange

4 part 5 split 7 break up, divorce 8 alienate, disunite, separate 9 disaffect

estrangement

4 rift 5 split 6 breach, schism 7 breakup, cooling, divorce, rupture 8 disunity, division 10 alienation, falling-out, withdrawal 12 disaffection

estuary

5 firth, frith, mouth 10 tidal river

esurient

4 avid 6 greedy, hungry 8 covetous, grasping, ravening, ravenous 9 rapacious, voracious 10 avaricious, gluttonous 11 acquisitive

étagère

7 cabinet, whatnot

Etats-_____

4 Unis

etch

3 cut 5 carve, stamp 6 depict, incise 7 engrave, impress, imprint, portray 8 inscribe 9 delineate, represent

etcher

American: 7 Pennell (Joseph) 8 Whistler (James McNeil)
Dutch: 9 Rembrandt (van Rijn)
French: 5 Redon (Odilon) 6 Villon (Jacques)
Italian: 8 Piranesi (Giambattista)
Spanish: 6 Ribera (José)
Swiss: 4 Zorn (Anders)

Eteocles

brother: 9 Polynices
father: 7 Oedipus
mother: 7 Jocasta
slayer: 9 Polynices

eternal

7 abiding, ageless, endless, lasting, undying 8 constant, enduring, immortal, infinite, timeless, unending 9 ceaseless, continual, deathless, immutable, incessant, permanent, perpetual, unceasing 10 immemorial, unchanging 11 amaranthine, everlasting, illimitable, inalterable, never-ending, unalterable, unremitting 12 imperishable, interminable

Eternal City

4 Rome

eternally

3 e'er 4 ever 6 always 7 forever 8 evermore, for keeps 11 forevermore, in perpetuum 12 in perpetuity

eternity

3 age, eon 4 aeon 7 dog's age 8 blue moon, coon's age, infinity 9 afterlife 10 infinitude, perpetuity 11 endlessness, immortality 12 infiniteness, timelessness

Etesian

4 wind 6 annual

Ethan _____

5 Allen, Brand, Frome

Ethbaal's daughter

7 Jezebel

ether

3 air, gas, sky 6 heaven 7 heavens 8 airwaves, empyrean 10 anesthetic, atmosphere

ethereal

4 aery, airy 5 filmy, light 6 aerial
7 fragile 8 delicate, empyreal,
empyrean, gossamer, heavenly,
rarefied, vaporous 9 celestial,
spiritual, unearthly, unworldly 10 immaterial, intangible 13 unsubstantial

ethical

4 good 5 moral, noble 6 decent
7 upright, virtual 8 elevated, virtuous
9 righteous 10 principled, upstanding 11 right-minded 13 conscientious

ethics

5 mores 6 morals, values 8 morality
9 moral code, standards 10 principles

Ethiopia

battle site: 5 Adowa
biblical name: 4 Cush
capital: 10 Addis Ababa
city: 6 Gonder 8 Dire Dawa
desert: 4 Haud 7 Danakil
emperor: 7 Menelik, Menilek
8 Selassie 9 Ras Tafari 13 Haile
Selassie
former name: 9 Abyssinia
language: 5 Oromo 7 Amharic
monetary unit: 4 birr
mountain: 9 Ras Dashen
neighbor: 5 Kenya, Sudan
7 Eritrea, Somalia 8 Djibouti
region: 5 Tigre 6 Ogaden, Tigray
7 Danakil
river: 4 Abay 5 Awash 6 Tekeze
8 Blue Nile

ethnic

6 racial, tribal 8 minority

etiolate

4 fade, pale 6 bleach, weaken
7 lighten, wash out 8 enfeeble

etiquette

4 code, form 5 mores 7 conduct,
customs, decency, decorum, manners 8 behavior, protocol 9 amenities, propriety 10 civilities, convention, deportment, seemliness
11 conventions, formalities, proprieties

Etruscan

city, town: 4 Roma, Veii 5 Caere,
Vulci 6 Arezzo 7 Clusium, Felsina,
Perugia 8 Volsinii 9 Florentia,
Tarquinia, Vetulonia
deity: 3 Tin, Tiv, Uni 4 Turm, Usil
5 Tinia, Turan, Turms 6 Menfra,
Menrva, Nethun, Trithn 7 Velchan
8 Sethlans, Voltumna
king: 7 Porsena, Tarquin 10 Tarquinius 11 Lars Porsena
kingdom: 7 Etruria

étude

5 study 8 exercise 11 composition

etui

4 case

etymology

11 word history

etymon

4 root 5 radix 6 source 8 morpheme

eucalyptus eater

5 koala

Eucharist

container: 3 pyx
plate: 5 paten
service: 4 Mass 9 Communion
vessel: 8 ciborium
wafer: 4 host 8 viaticum

Euclid

subject: 8 geometry
work: 8 Elements

_____ Eulenspiegel

4 Till, Tyll

eulogistic

9 adulatory, laudative, laudatory
11 encomiastic, panegyrical 12 commendatory 13 complimentary

eulogize

4 hymn, laud 5 cry up, exalt, extol
6 praise 7 acclaim, applaud, commend, glorify, magnify 9 celebrate
10 panegyrize

eulogy

5 paean 6 praise 7 oration, tribute
8 accolade, citation, encomium
9 laudation, panegyric 10 salutation
12 commendation 13 glorification

Eumenides

see **Erinyes**

eunuch
7 gelding 8 castrate, castrato

euphony
7 harmony 8 lyricism 9 sweetness
10 consonance

euphoria
3 joy 4 glee 5 bliss 7 ecstasy,
elation, rapture 9 transport 10 exaltation, jubilation 11 high spirits
12 exhilaration, intoxication

Euphrosyne
see **Graces**

euphuistic
5 fancy, tumid 6 florid, ornate, prolix,
purple, turgid 7 elegant, flowery,
fustian, orotund, verbose 8 colorful,
elevated, inflated, sonorous 9 bombastic, elaborate, high-flown, overblown 10 figurative, flamboyant,
rhetorical 11 highfalutin, overwrought
12 magniloquent 13 grandiloquent

eureka
3 aha

Euridice's husband
7 Orpheus

Euripides play
3 Ion 5 Helen, Medea 6 Hecuba
7 Bacchae (The), Cyclops, Electra,
Orestes 8 Alcestis 10 Andromache,
Hippolytus, Suppliants (The) 11 Trojan Women (The)

Europa
brother: 6 Cadmus
father: 6 Agenor 7 Phoenix
husband: 8 Asterius
son: 5 Minos 8 Sarpedon

Europe
9 continent
country: 4 Eire 5 Italy, Malta, Spain
6 France, Greece, Latvia, Monaco,
Norway, Poland, Russia, Sweden,
Turkey 7 Albania, Andorra, Armenia,
Austria, Belarus, Belgium, Croatia,
Denmark, Estonia, Finland, Georgia,
Germany, Hungary, Iceland, Ireland,
Moldova, Romania, Rumania,
Ukraine 8 Bulgaria, Portugal, Slova-
kia, Slovenia 9 Lithuania, Macedo-

nia, San Marino 10 Azerbaijan,
Luxembourg, Yugoslavia 11 Nether-
lands, Switzerland, Vatican City
13 Czech Republic, Liechtenstein,
United Kingdom
ethnic group: 4 Celt, Finn, Lapp,
Lett, Pole, Serb, Sorb, Turk, Wend
5 Croat, Czech, Dutch, Greek,
Gypsy, Irish, Latin, Swede, Swiss,
Welsh 6 Basque, Celtic, French,
German, Magyar, Polish, Scotch,
Slovak 7 Bosnian, Catalan, English,
Finnish, Fleming, Italian, Lettish,
Maltese, Russian, Slovene, Spanish,
Swedish, Walloon 8 Albanian,
Andorran, Armenian, Croatian,
Romanian 9 Belarusan, Bulgarian,
Hungarian, Ukrainian 10 Belarusian,
Macedonian, Monegasque, Phoeni-
cian 11 Belarussian 12 Byelorus-
sian, Scandinavian
language: 4 Lapp 5 Czech, Dutch,
Greek, Irish, Latin, Welsh 6 Basque,
Breton, Danish, French, Gaelic,
German, Magyar, Polish, Slovak
7 Catalan, English, Finnish, Flemish,
Italian, Maltese, Romansh, Russian,
Serbian, Slovene, Spanish, Swedish,
Turkish, Wendish 8 Albanian, Croat-
ian, Lusatian, Romanian, Rumanian
9 Bulgarian, Hungarian, Icelandic,
Norwegian 10 Macedonian, Portuguese 13 Serbo-Croatian
mountain range: 4 Alps 8 Pyrenees
11 Carpathians

Euryale
see **Gorgon**

Eurytus
daughter: 4 Iole
slayer: 8 Hercules

Euterpe
see **Muse**

evacuate
4 exit, void 5 clear, empty, expel,
leave 6 decamp, depart, remove,
vacate 7 abandon, excrete, exhaust,
pull out, retreat 8 clear out, pull
back, withdraw 9 eliminate

evacuee
6 émigré 7 refugee 8 fugitive

evade

4 duck, flee, foil 5 avoid, dodge, elude, hedge, parry, shirk, skirt 6 baffle, bypass, escape, eschew, outwit, thwart, weasel 7 sidestep, shuffle 8 sidestep, slip away 9 pussyfoot, turn aside 10 circumvent, equivocate 11 prevaricate 12 tergiversate

evaluate

4 rank, rate 5 assay, class, gauge, grade, set at, weigh 6 assess, figure, reckon, size up, survey 7 eyeball 8 appraise, classify, estimate 9 calculate, criticize

evaluation

6 rating 7 judging, opinion 8 estimate, judgment 9 appraisal 10 assessment 12 appreciation

Evander

father: 6 Hermes 7 Mercury
mother: 8 Carmenta 9 Carmentis
son: 6 Pallas

evanesce

4 fade 5 clear 6 vanish 7 scatter 8 disperse, dissolve, melt away 9 disappear, dissipate, evaporate 13 dematerialize

evanescent

6 fading 7 elusive, melting, passing 8 fleeting, fugitive, volatile 9 ephemeral, fugacious, momentary, transient, vanishing 10 dissolving, short-lived, transitory 12 disappearing

evangelical

6 ardent, fervid 7 fanatic, fervent, zealous 8 militant 9 crusading 10 missionary 13 proselytizing

Evangeline

author: 10 Longfellow (Henry Wadsworth)
beloved: 7 Gabriel
home: 6 Acadia

evangelist

4 John, Luke, Mark 5 Moody (Dwight) 6 Bakker (Jim, Tammy Faye), Graham (Billy, Franklin), Sunday (Billy), Wesley (John) 7 apostle, Edwards (Jonathan), Falwell (Jerry), Matthew, Roberts (Oral) 8 Schuller (Robert), Swaggart (Jimmy) 9 McPherson (Aimee Semple), missioner, Robertson (Pat) 10 colporteur, missionary, revivalist, Whitefield (George)

evangelistic

9 crusading, reforming 10 missionary, revivalist 13 proselytizing

evangelize

6 preach 7 convert 9 sermonize

evaporate

4 fade, melt 5 clear 6 vanish 8 diminish, disperse, dissolve, evanesce, melt away, vaporize 9 disappear, dissipate

evasion

5 dodge, fudge 6 escape, excuse 7 dodging, elusion, fudging 8 escaping 9 avoidance 13 circumvention

evasive

3 sly 5 cagey, dodgy, vague 6 shifty 7 elusive 8 slippery 9 ambiguous, equivocal

Eve

home: 4 Eden
husband: 4 Adam
son: 4 Abel, Cain, Seth
temptation: 5 apple, fruit

even

3 tie 4 fair, flat, just, same, tied 5 align, equal, exact, flush, grade, level, plane, still, truly 6 as well, equate, smooth, square, stable, steady 7 balance, equable, flatten, uniform 8 balanced, constant, equalize, smoothen, straight 9 equitable, expressly, identical, precisely, unvarying 10 absolutely, comparable, consistent, continuous, fifty-fifty, unchanging 13 fair and square, proportionate

evening

4 dusk 6 soiree, sunset 7 sundown 8 gloaming, twilight 9 nightfall
French: 4 soir
Italian: 4 sera
service: 7 vespers
star: 5 Venus 6 Vesper 8 Hesperus

evenness
6 equity, parity 7 balance 8 equality
9 stability 10 equanimity, uniformity
11 consistency, equilibrium

event
3 act 4 case, deed, fact, feat, meet
5 issue, match 6 action, affair,
chance, effect, result, upshot 7 contest, episode, outcome, product
8 accident, function, incident, occasion 9 aftermath, happening 10 occurrence, phenomenon 11 achievement, competition, consequence,
eventuality 12 circumstance, happenstance

eventful
4 busy 6 lively 9 important, momentous

eventual
4 last 5 final 6 ending 7 closing,
endmost, ensuing 8 terminal, ultimate 9 resulting 10 concluding,
consequent, inevitable, succeeding

eventuality
4 case 6 effect, result 7 outcome
11 consequence, contingency, possibility

eventually
6 at last, one day 7 finally, someday
8 sometime 9 hereafter 10 ultimately
13 sooner or later

eventuate
5 ensue, occur 6 befall, follow, happen, result 9 come about, take place

ever
4 once 5 at all 6 always 7 forever
9 at any time, eternally, regularly
10 constantly, invariably 11 perpetually 12 consistently, continuously

evergreen
3 fir, ivy, yew 4 ilex, pine, tree
5 cedar, holly, savin 6 laurel, myrtle,
spruce 7 conifer, cypress, hemlock,
juniper, lasting, redwood, sequoia,
undying 8 magnolia, mangrove,
timeless, unfading 9 mistletoe,
perennial 10 arborvitae 12 rhododendron

Evergreen State
10 Washington

everlasting
7 abiding, endless, eternal, forever,
lasting, undying 8 constant, immortal,
infinite, termless, timeless, unending
9 boundless, ceaseless, continual,
deathless, limitless, permanent,
perpetual, unceasing 10 continuous,
perdurable 11 amaranthine, never-
ending, unremitting 12 imperishable

evermore
6 always 7 for good 8 for keeps
9 eternally 12 in perpetuity

every
3 all 4 each
prefix: 3 pan

everybody
3 all 4 each

everyday
5 banal, plain, usual 6 common,
normal 7 mundane, prosaic, routine
8 familiar, habitual, ordinary 9 customary, quotidian 11 commonplace
12 conventional, run-of-the-mill,
unremarkable

everything
3 all
French: 4 tout
German: 5 alles

everywhere
7 all over, overall 8 all round, wherever 9 all around 10 far and near,
far and wide, high and low, throughout

evict
3 out 4 oust 5 eject, expel 6 bounce,
put out 7 boot out, dismiss, extrude,
kick out 8 dislodge, force out, throw
out 10 dispossess

evidence
4 clue, mark, show, sign 5 goods,
proof, prove 6 attest, evince, expose, reveal 7 confirm, display,
exhibit, symptom, testify, witness
8 indicate 9 testament, testimony
10 indication, smoking gun 11 attestation, demonstrate, testimonial
12 confirmation 13 documentation

evident

5 clear, overt, plain 6 marked, patent
7 obvious, visible 8 apparent, distinct, manifest, palpable, tangible
9 prominent 10 noticeable, pronounced 11 conspicuous, perceptible, unambiguous

evidently

9 outwardly, seemingly 10 officially, ostensibly

evil

3 bad, sin 4 foul, vice, vile 5 black
6 infamy, malice, sinful, wicked
7 badness, baleful, baneful, devilry, hateful, heinous, malefic, satanic, vicious 8 damnable, iniquity, satanism, villainy 9 atrocious, diablerie, diabolism, execrable, loathsome, malicious, malignant, nefarious
10 flagitious, iniquitous, maleficent, malevolent, pernicious, sinfulness, wickedness 11 maleficence
combining form: 3 mal

evildoer

6 sinner 7 villain 8 criminal 9 miscreant 10 malefactor

evil spirit

3 imp 5 demon, devil, fiend, Satan
6 daemon

evince

4 mark, show 5 educe, evoke, prove
6 attest, betray, elicit, expose, reveal
7 bespeak, betoken, confirm, display, exhibit, signify 8 evidence, indicate, manifest, proclaim 10 illustrate
11 demonstrate

eviscerate

3 gut 4 draw 5 bowel 7 embowel
8 protrude 10 disembowel, exenterate

evocative

6 moving 8 redolent, stirring 9 affecting, emotional, nostalgic 10 expressive, meaningful, suggestive
11 stimulating

evoke

4 cite, stir 5 educe, raise, waken
6 arouse, awaken, call up, elicit,
evince, excite, induce, recall 7 conjure 8 recreate, summon up 9 call forth, conjure up, stimulate 11 summon forth

evolution

6 change, growth 8 progress, upgrowth 9 flowering, phylogeny, unfolding 10 biogenesis, maturation
11 development, progression

evolve

4 grow 5 educe, ripen 6 change, derive, emerge, mature, open up, unfold 7 advance, develop, work out
8 progress 9 elaborate

ewe

5 sheep

ewer

3 jug 4 vase 7 pitcher

ex

4 from, past 5 prior 6 former
7 earlier, without 9 erstwhile

exacerbate

6 worsen 7 envenom, inflame, provoke 8 embitter, heighten 9 aggravate, intensify

exact

4 levy, true 5 claim, force, gouge, pinch, screw, wrest, wring 6 coerce, compel, dead-on, demand, extort, spot-on, strict 7 correct, extract, literal, precise, require, solicit, squeeze 8 accurate, rigorous, selfsame 9 identical, postulate, shake down 10 meticulous, scrupulous 11 painstaking, punctilious, requisition

exacting

5 fussy, rigid, stern, tough 6 severe, strict, taxing, trying 7 exigent, finicky, onerous 8 critical, rigorous 9 demanding, stringent 10 fastidious, nitpicking, particular, scrupulous
11 persnickety 13 hypercritical

exactitude

5 rigor 8 accuracy 9 precision
10 definitude 11 correctness, preciseness 12 definiteness

exactly
4 bang, just 5 quite, right, sharp, spang 6 bang on, square, to a tee, wholly 7 totally, utterly 8 entirely, smack-dab, squarely 9 on the nose, precisely 10 absolutely, accurately, altogether, completely, positively 12 specifically

exaggerate
6 overdo 7 amplify, enlarge, inflate, magnify, overact, romance 8 overdraw, overrate 9 embellish, embroider, overstate 11 hyperbolize 13 overemphasize

exaggeration
8 travesty 9 hyperbole 10 caricature, stretching 11 enlargement, overdrawing 12 embroidering 13 embellishment, overstatement

exalt
4 fete, laud, lift 5 boost, elate, extol, honor, raise 6 praise, uplift 7 acclaim, adulate, build up, dignify, elevate, enhance, ennoble, glorify, inspire, magnify, promote 8 eulogize, heighten, inspirit 9 intensify 10 aggrandize 13 apotheosize

exaltation
3 joy 5 bliss, glory 6 homage, praise 7 delight, ecstasy, elation, rapture, tribute 8 euphoria, rhapsody 9 panegyric, transport, uplifting 10 apotheosis, jubilation 11 deification 12 exhilaration, intoxication 13 glorification

exalted
4 high 5 grand, lofty, noble 6 august 7 eminent, highest, sublime 9 venerable 11 high-ranking, illustrious, outstanding, prestigious

examination
4 quiz, scan, test 5 assay, probe, trial 6 review, survey 7 canvass, checkup, hearing, inquest, inquiry, perusal, sifting, testing 8 analysis, scrutiny 9 breakdown, check-over, diagnosis 10 dissection, inspection 11 inquisition 13 catechization, investigation, perlustration

kind: 4 oral 5 final 7 medical, midterm 8 physical
of accounts: 5 audit
of a corpse: 7 autopsy 10 postmortem

examine
3 con, vet 4 pump, quiz, scan, sift, test 5 audit, check, grill, probe, query, study 6 go over, look at, peruse, survey 7 canvass, check up, inquire, inspect, observe 8 check out, look into, look over, question 9 catechize, check over 10 scrutinize 11 interrogate, investigate

examiner
6 censor 7 auditor, coroner 9 inspector 10 inquisitor, prosecutor 12 investigator

example
4 case 5 ideal, model 7 paragon, pattern 8 instance, paradigm, specimen, standard 9 archetype, precedent, prototype 11 case history 12 illustration

exanimate
4 dead 5 inert 8 lifeless, listless, sluggish, stagnant 9 lethargic 10 spiritless

exasperate
3 irk, vex 4 gall, rile, roil 5 anger, annoy, peeve, pique, upset 6 enrage, madden, nettle, rankle 7 agitate, incense, inflame, provoke 8 irritate 9 aggravate, infuriate

exasperation
8 vexation 9 annoyance 10 irritation 11 aggravation

ex cathedra
8 official 9 ex officio 13 authoritative

excavate
3 dig 4 grub 5 scoop, spade 6 dig out, dredge, expose, hollow, quarry, shovel 7 unearth 8 gouge out, scoop out 9 hollow out, scrape out

excavation
3 dig, pit 4 hole, mine 5 ditch, stope 6 dugout, hollow, quarry, trench, trough

exceed

3 cap, top 4 beat, best, pass 5 break, excel, outdo 6 better, outrun, overdo 7 eclipse, outpace, overrun, surpass 8 go beyond, outreach, outshine, outstrip, outweigh, overstep, overtake 9 overreach, transcend

exceedingly

4 very 6 hugely, vastly 7 awfully, notably, vitally 9 extremely 10 remarkably, strikingly 12 surpassingly 13 exceptionally
prefix: 5 ultra

excel

3 cap, top 4 beat, best, pass 5 outdo, shine 6 better, exceed, outrun, overdo 7 eclipse, outpace, overrun, surpass 8 go beyond, outclass, outreach, outshine, outstrip, outweigh, overstep, overtake 9 overreach, transcend

excellence

5 class, merit, value, worth 6 virtue 7 quality 8 fineness 9 greatness 10 perfection 11 distinction, superiority

excellent

3 top 4 fine 5 bully, prime 6 bangup, banner, famous, Grade A, superb, tip-top 7 capital, premium, supreme 8 champion, five-star, splendid, stunning, superior, terrific, top-notch 9 classical, first-rate, high-class, high-grade, marvelous, number one, wonderful 10 blue-ribbon, first-class 11 exceptional, magnificent, meritorious, sensational, superlative, unsurpassed 12 incomparable

except

3 bar, but, yet 4 omit, only, save 6 beside, exempt, object, reject, unless 7 barring, besides, exclude, however, outside, rule out, suspend 8 pass over 9 apart from, aside from, eliminate, excluding, outside of 11 exclusive of

exception

5 demur 7 anomaly, dissent 8 question 9 allowance, deviation, exclusion, objection 10 aberration

exceptionable

8 unwanted 9 unwelcome 10 unsuitable 11 regrettable, undesirable 12 unacceptable 13 objectionable

exceptional

4 rare 6 scarce, unique 7 notable, special, unusual 8 abnormal, atypical, distinct, singular, superior, uncommon, unwonted 9 anomalous, excellent, marvelous, wonderful 10 infrequent, noteworthy, phenomenal, remarkable 11 outstanding, uncustomary 13 extraordinary

exceptionally

4 very 6 hugely 7 notably 9 extremely 10 especially, remarkably, strikingly 11 exceedingly 12 particularly, stupendously

excerpt

4 cite, cull, pick 5 glean, quote 6 choose, sample, select 7 extract, passage, pick out, portion, snippet 8 fragment 9 quotation

excess

3 fat 4 glut, rest 5 extra, flood, spare, waste 7 nimiety, overage, surfeit, surplus 8 leavings, leftover, overflow, overkill, overmuch 9 indulgent, overstock, redundant, remainder 10 oversupply, surplusage 11 dissipation, prodigality, superfluity, superfluous, unessential 12 extravagance, immoderation, intemperance 13 overabundance, supernumerary

excessive

4 over 5 dizzy, steep, super, undue 6 too-too 7 extreme, sky-high 8 overmuch, prodigal 10 exorbitant, immoderate, inordinate, profligate 11 extravagant, intemperate, overweening, superfluous 12 supernatural, unrestrained

excessively

3 too 6 overly, unduly 8 overmuch
prefix: 5 hyper

exchange

4 swap, swop 5 bandy, trade, truck 6 barter, market, switch 7 bargain,

commute, convert, pay back, re-
place, traffic **8** displace **9** transpose
10 conversion, substitute **11** reciprocate

exchequer
5 funds **8** treasury

excise
3 fee, tax **4** toll **5** elide, slash **6** cut
out, delete, remove, resect **9** expur-
gate, extirpate, strike out, surcharge

excision
3 cut **7** removal, surgery **8** deletion
9 resection **11** extirpation

excitable
4 rash **8** volatile **9** impetuous
10 high-strung

excite
4 fire, goad, move, spur, stir **5** elate,
evoke, key up, pique, prime, rouse,
waken **6** appeal, arouse, elicit, fire
up, induce, kindle, stir up, thrill, turn
on **7** agitate, animate, commove,
inflame, inspire, provoke, quicken
8 activate, charge up, energize,
motivate **9** galvanize, impassion,
innervate, stimulate **10** exhilarate

excited
3 hot **4** avid **5** eager **6** aflame
7 fevered **8** aflutter, worked up
10 passionate **12** enthusiastic

excitement
3 ado **4** buzz, stir, to-do **5** fever,
furor **6** flurry, frenzy, furore, hubbub,
thrill **7** turmoil **8** delirium, hysteria
9 agitation, commotion **10** enthusiasm, hullabaloo **11** disturbance,
pandemonium **12** exhilaration

exclaim
4 blat, bolt **5** blurt **6** cry out **8** blurt
out, burst out **9** ejaculate

exclamation
3 aah, aha, bah, boo, cry, eek, feh,
fie, gee, hah, hey, huh, oho, ooh,
pah, tsk, tut, ugh, wow **4** ahem, alas,
amen, damn, dang, darn, drat, egad,
gosh, heck, hell, oops, ouch, phew,
pish, posh, rats, whew, yell **5** alack,
bravo, faugh, golly, humph, pshaw,
shout **6** clamor, hurrah, indeed, out-

cry, phooey, shucks **7** doggone, gee
whiz, hosanna, jeepers, whoopee
9 expletive **10** hallelujah **12** interjection
of disappointment: 4 damn, darn,
rats
of disapproval: 3 tsk **6** tsk-tsk
of disgust: 3 bah, boo, feh, fie,
ugh **4** yech, yuck **5** faugh, yecch
6 phooey
of dismay: 4 oh no, uh-oh **5** yikes
of enthusiasm: 4 whee **5** wahoo
7 whoopie
of fear: 3 eek
of pain: 4 ouch
of relief: 4 phew
of sorrow: 3 woe **4** alas **5** alack
of surprise: 3 wow **4** gosh **5** golly
of triumph: 3 aha, hah **5** yahoo
6 eureka
(see also **interjection**)

exclude
3 ban, bar **4** oust **5** block, debar
6 banish, disbar, reject **7** keep out,
lock out, obviate, prevent, rule out,
shut out, suspend **8** count out,
preclude, prohibit **9** blackball,
blacklist, eliminate, ostracize

excluding
3 bar, but **4** less, save **6** except
7 barring, besides **9** apart from,
aside from, other than, outside of

exclusion
3 bar **6** ouster **7** barring, lockout,
removal **8** ejection, eviction, omission **9** blackball, expulsion, ostracism **10** banishment **12** black-
balling, nonadmission

exclusive
4 lone, only, sole **5** elect, elite,
prime, scoop, smart, swank, swish
6 choice, chosen, picked, select,
single **7** cliquey, high-hat, stylish
8 clannish, cliquish, selected, snobbish **9** preferred, undivided **10** privileged **11** fashionable, prohibitive,
restrictive **12** aristocratic, concentrated, preferential

exclusively
4 only **5** alone **6** wholly **8** entirely
10 completely **12** particularly

excogitate
6 derive, devise, invent 7 develop, think up 8 contrive, think out

excommunicate
7 cast out 8 unchurch

excoriate
4 flay, lash, skin 5 roast, slash 6 abrade, scathe, scorch 7 blister, censure, scarify, scourge 8 chastise, lambaste, lash into 9 castigate

excrement
6 ordure
of animals: 4 dung, muck 6 manure
of sea birds: 5 guano

excrescence
4 blot, lump, mole, wart 5 tumor 6 growth, nodule, pimple 7 blemish, process 9 by-product, outgrowth

excrete
4 emit, spew 5 eject, expel, exude 9 discharge

excruciate
4 rack 6 martyr 7 afflict, crucify, torment, torture 9 martyrize

excruciating
5 acute, sharp 6 severe 7 extreme, intense 8 piercing, shooting, stabbing 9 agonizing, harrowing, torturous 10 unbearable 11 unendurable

exculpate
4 free 5 clear, remit 6 acquit, excuse, let off, pardon 7 absolve, amnesty, condone, forgive, justify 9 exonerate, vindicate 11 rationalize

excursion
4 ride, tour, trek, trip, walk 5 aside, drive, jaunt, paseo, sally, tramp 6 cruise, junket, outing, ramble, safari 7 day trip, journey 9 round trip 10 digression, divagation, expedition 11 parenthesis 12 pleasure trip

excusable
6 venial

excuse
3 out 4 plea 5 alibi, clear, remit 6 acquit, cop-out, defend, exempt, let off, pardon, reason, wink at 7 absolve, apology, condone, defense, forgive, justify, pretext, regrets, relieve 8 mitigate, overlook, palliate, pass over, shrug off, tolerate 9 discharge, exculpate, exonerate, extenuate, gloss over, makeshift, vindicate, whitewash 10 substitute 11 explanation, rationalize 13 justification

execrable
4 base, foul, vile 7 heinous 8 accursed, damnable, horrific, infernal, wretched 9 abhorrent, atrocious, loathsome, monstrous, repulsive, revolting 10 abominable, deplorable, despicable, detestable, horrifying

execrate
4 damn, hate 5 abhor, curse 6 detest, loathe, revile, vilify 7 censure, condemn, despise 8 denounce 9 abominate, imprecate 12 anathematize

execute
3 act 4 do in, kill, play, slay 5 cause, lynch 6 effect, finish, murder, render 7 achieve, bump off, conduct, enforce, fulfill, perform, realize 8 carry out, complete, dispatch, knock off, transact 9 discharge, eliminate, implement, liquidate 10 accomplish, administer, bring about, put through, put to death 11 assassinate 12 administrate

execution
6 murder 7 killing 11 performance

executioner
7 hangman, headman 8 headsman

executive
4 dean, suit 6 leader 7 manager 8 director, governor 9 president 10 supervisor 13 administrator

exegesis
5 gloss 8 analysis 9 construal 10 commentary, exposition 11 elucidation, explanation, explication 12 construction

exemplar
4 copy **5** ideal, model **7** epitome, paragon, pattern **8** instance, paradigm, specimen, standard **9** archetype, criterion, prototype **12** illustration

exemplary
4 pure **5** ideal, model **7** classic, typical **8** laudable, monitory, virtuous **9** admirable, blameless, classical, estimable, faultless, honorable, righteous **10** impeccable, inculpable, prototypal **11** commendable, meritorious **12** illustrative, paradigmatic, praiseworthy, prototypical

exemplify
4 copy **6** embody, mirror, typify **7** clarify **9** enlighten, epitomize, personify, represent, symbolize **10** concretize, illuminate, illustrate

exempt
4 free **5** spare **6** except, excuse, let off, spared **7** absolve, excused, relieve **8** dispense **9** discharge

exemption
7 freedom, release **8** immunity, impunity **9** discharge, exception

exenterate
3 gut **4** draw **7** embowel **10** disembowel, eviscerate

exercise
3 use, vex **4** fret, gall, hone **5** alarm, annoy, apply, drill, étude, exert, sit-up, train, upset, wield **6** chin-up, crunch, employ, pull-up, push-up **7** agitate, develop, exploit, improve, prepare, problem, provoke, utilize, work out **8** activity, maneuver, practice, rehearse **9** athletics, condition, cultivate, discharge, operation **10** employment **11** application **12** calisthenics

exert
3 use **5** apply, wield **6** employ, expend, put out, strain **8** exercise, put forth

exertion
4 toil, work **5** labor, pains **6** effort, strain **7** trouble **8** activity, exercise, striving **11** application, elbow grease

exfoliate
4 peel, shed **5** scale **7** cast off, leaf out **8** flake off **10** desquamate

exhalation
6 breath **8** emission **9** breathing, effluvium, emanation

exhale
4 blow, emit **6** expire, let out **7** breathe, respire **10** breathe out

exhaust
3 fag, sap **4** do in, tire **5** drain, eat up, empty, spend, use up, waste, weary **6** expend, finish, tucker, wash up, weaken **7** burn out, consume, deplete, fatigue, frazzle, tire out, wear out **8** draw down, enervate, squander, wear down **9** discharge, dissipate, prostrate, tucker out **10** debilitate, overextend, run through

exhausted
4 beat, limp, weak **5** all in, spent, tired **6** bushed **7** run-down, worn out **8** dog-tired

exhaustion
7 burnout, fatigue **8** collapse **9** lassitude, tiredness, weariness **11** prostration

exhaustive
8 complete, sweeping, thorough **9** full-blown, full-scale, intensive **10** scrupulous **11** painstaking **13** comprehensive, thoroughgoing

exhibit
4 fair, show **6** evince, expose, flaunt, parade, reveal **7** display, feature, show off **8** evidence, manifest, proclaim, showcase **10** exposition **11** demonstrate

exhibition
4 fair, show **7** display, pageant, showing **12** presentation **13** demonstration, manifestation

exhibitionist
3 fop **4** toff **6** hot dog **7** peacock, show-off **8** showboat **12** grandstander

exhilarate

4 buoy, lift 5 boost, cheer, elate, exalt, pep up 6 buck up, excite, thrill, uplift 7 animate, cheer up, commove, delight, enliven, gladden, inspire, refresh 8 inspirit, vitalize 9 stimulate 10 invigorate

exhilaration

3 joy 4 glee 7 ecstasy, elation 8 euphoria, gladness 10 exaltation, excitement 11 inspiration 12 vitalization, vivification 13 galvanization

exhort

4 goad, prod, spur, urge, warn 5 egg on, plead, press, prick 6 adjure, call on, incite, prompt, propel 7 beseech, entreat 8 admonish, call upon 9 stimulate

exhortation

4 plea 6 advice, urging 7 caution, warning 8 entreaty, jeremiad 10 admonition, incitement, injunction 11 inspiration 13 encouragement

exhume

5 dig up 6 redeem 7 reclaim, recover, unearth 8 disinter 9 resurrect

exigency

3 fix, jam 4 need, pass 5 pinch, rigor 6 crisis, demand, pickle, plight, strait 7 urgency 8 juncture, pressure, zero hour 9 extremity, necessity 10 compulsion, constraint, crossroads, difficulty, insistence 11 predicament, requirement

exigent

5 acute, vital 6 crying, taxing 7 burning, clamant, instant, onerous 8 exacting, grievous, pressing 9 clamorous, demanding, insistent, necessary 10 burdensome, imperative 11 importunate

exiguous

4 poor, puny, thin, tiny 5 scant, spare, token 6 meager, meagre, measly, paltry, scanty, shabby, skimpy, slight, sparse 7 minimal, scrimpy 9 miserable 10 inadequate, straitened

exile

4 oust 5 eject, expel 6 banish, deport, emigré 7 cast out, outcast, refugee 8 diaspora, displace, drive out, evacuate, expellee 9 exclusion, expulsion, extradite, migration, ostracism, ostracize 10 banishment, dispossess, expatriate, scattering 11 deportation, extradition 12 displacement, expatriation
place of: 4 Elba 7 Siberia

exist .

3 are, lie 4 live 5 occur

existence

4 life 5 being 7 reality 8 duration 9 actuality

existent

4 live, real 5 being, thing 6 actual, entity, extant, living 7 current, instant, present 10 present-day 12 contemporary

existentialist writer

5 Buber (Martin), Camus (Albert) 6 Marcel (Gabriel), Sartre (Jean-Paul) 7 Jaspers (Karl) 8 Beauvoir (Simone de) 9 Heidegger (Martin), Nietzsche (Friedrich) 11 Kierkegaard (Søren)

existing

5 alive, being, ontic 6 extant, living
from birth: 6 innate 10 congenital
Latin: 6 in esse

exit

3 die 4 door, gate, quit 5 death, going, leave, scram, split 6 depart, egress, escape, outlet, portal, retire 7 doorway, get away, off-ramp 8 withdraw 9 departure, egression 10 withdrawal

_____ ex machina

4 deus

exodus

6 flight 9 migration 10 emigration

Exodus author

4 Uris (Leon)

exonerate

4 free 5 clear, remit 6 acquit,

excuse, exempt, let off, pardon
7 absolve **8** reprieve **9** exculpate,
vindicate

exorbitant
5 undue **7** extreme **9** excessive
10 immoderate, inordinate, outrageous **11** extravagant, unwarranted
12 preposterous

exordium
5 intro, proem **6** lead-in **7** opening,
preface, prelude **8** foreword, overture, preamble, prologue **12** introduction, prolegomenon

exotic
4 rare **5** alien **7** bizarre, foreign,
strange, unusual **8** alluring, enticing,
imported, romantic **9** different,
glamorous, nonnative **10** introduced,
mysterious **11** fascinating

expand
3 wax **4** grow, open, rise **5** boost,
mount, swell, widen **6** beef up, bulk
up, dilate, pad out, spread, unfold
7 amplify, augment, bolster, develop,
distend, enlarge, inflate, magnify,
prolong, stretch **8** escalate, increase, lengthen, multiply, mushroom, protract **9** discourse, elaborate, expatiate, spread out

expanse
4 area, room **5** field, ocean, range,
reach, scope, space, sweep, tract
6 domain, extent, sphere, spread
7 breadth, stretch **8** distance **9** territory

expansion
6 growth, spread **8** increase **9** unfolding **11** enlargement **12** augmentation

expansive
3 big **4** wide **5** ample, broad, large,
roomy **6** lavish **7** buoyant, elastic,
liberal, sizable **8** effusive, extended, generous, outgoing, spacious **9** capacious, garrulous, talkative **10** gregarious, openhanded,
unreserved **11** extroverted **13** demonstrative

expatiate
6 ramble, wander **7** dissert, enlarge
8 dilate on, perorate **9** discourse,
elaborate, sermonize **10** dilate upon,
dissertate

expatriate
5 exile, expel **6** banish, deport,
émigré **8** displace, expellee, relegate

expect
4 feel, hope, take **5** await, sense,
think, trust **6** assume, divine, gather,
look to **7** believe, count on, foresee,
imagine, look for, predict, presume,
suppose, surmise **8** forecast, foreknow **9** apprehend, count upon
10 anticipate, presuppose

expectant
5 alert **6** gravid **7** anxious, hopeful **8** enceinte, pregnant, vigilant,
watchful **10** breathless, parturient
12 anticipatory, apprehensive

expectation
4 hope **5** hunch **8** prospect **9** assurance, intuition **10** assumption,
likelihood **11** presumption, probability **12** anticipation, presentiment

expectorate
4 spit

expediency
5 means **6** resort, tactic **7** aptness,
fitness, measure, stopgap **8** meetness, recourse, resource, strategy
9 makeshift, propriety, rightness
11 opportunism, suitability **12** appositeness, practicality, suitableness

expedient
3 fit **5** ad hoc, means, shift **6** resort,
timely, useful **7** fitting, politic, prudent, stopgap **8** feasible, recourse,
resource, suitable, tactical **9** advisable, judicious, makeshift, opportune
practical, pragmatic, well-timed
10 convenient **11** appropriate,
practicable, utilitarian **12** advantageous

expedite
4 send **5** hurry, issue, speed **6** hasten

expedition

7 quicken, speed up 8 dispatch
10 accelerate, facilitate

expedition

4 trek, trip 5 hurry, speed 6 voyage
7 journey 8 campaign, dispatch
9 excursion, swiftness 10 efficiency,
speediness 11 punctuality

expeditious

4 fast 5 brisk, quick, rapid, swift
6 prompt, speedy 9 efficient 11 efficacious

expeditiousness

5 hurry, speed 6 hustle 8 dispatch

expel

4 boot, oust, spew 5 eject, evict,
exile 6 banish, bounce, deport,
disbar 7 cast out, dismiss, drum
out, kick out, turn out 8 disgorge,
displace, throw out 9 discharge,
eliminate 10 expatriate

expellee

5 exile 6 émigré 7 outcast 8 deportee, emigrant

expend

3 pay, sap 4 blow 5 drain, spend,
use up, waste 6 lay out, outlay, pay
out 7 consume, deplete, dig into,
dole out, exhaust, fork out, utilize
8 disburse, dispense, shell out,
squander 9 dissipate 10 run through

expendable

10 disposable 11 dispensable,
inessential, replaceable 12 nonessential

expenditure

4 cost 6 outlay, payoff, payout
12 disbursement

expense

4 cost, loss, toll 5 debit, price 6 burden, charge, outlay 7 forfeit, payment 8 overhead 9 decrement,
sacrifice 10 forfeiture 12 disbursement

expensive

4 dear, high, posh 5 fancy, ritzy,
steep, stiff 6 costly, deluxe, lavish,
pricey 7 upscale 8 precious, valuable, wasteful 9 big-ticket, luxurious
10 exorbitant, high-priced, overpriced
11 extravagant 12 uneconomical

experience

4 know, live 5 event, savor, skill,
trial 6 ordeal, suffer, wisdom 7 episode, know-how, sustain, undergo
8 incident, practice 9 encounter, go
through 10 background 11 familiarity, savoir faire
anew: 6 relive

experienced

4 wise 6 mature, versed 7 old-line,
veteran, worldly 8 broken in, seasoned 9 practiced, qualified 12 accomplished

experiential

see **empirical**

experiment

3 try 4 test 5 assay, probe, trial
6 try out 7 test out 8 research, trial
run 13 trial and error

experimental

9 empirical, tentative 10 innovative
11 exploratory, preliminary, preparatory, provisional 13 developmental,
trial-and-error

experimentation

4 test 5 trial 7 testing 8 research,
trial run 13 trial and error

expert

3 ace, pro, wiz 4 deft, whiz 5 adept,
crack, doyen, maven 6 adroit,
master, wizard 7 skilled 8 masterly, skillful, virtuoso 9 authority,
dexterous, masterful, virtuosic
10 past master, proficient, specialist
11 crackerjack 12 passed master,
professional

expertise

5 craft, skill 7 ability, command,
know-how, mastery 8 facility
10 adroitness, competence 11 proficiency 12 skillfulness

expertness

see **expertise**

expiate

6 offset, pay for, redeem 7 redress
8 atone for

expiation
9 atonement, indemnity 10 recompense, reparation 11 restitution 12 satisfaction

expiatory
7 atoning, lustral 9 purgative 11 penitential, purgatorial 12 propitiatory

expiration
3 end 5 death 10 exhalation 11 termination

expire
3 die, end 4 pass 5 lapse 6 elapse, exhale, pass on, perish, run out 7 decease 8 pass away 9 terminate 10 breathe out

explain
5 gloss, solve 7 analyze, clarify, clear up, condone, expound, justify, resolve, unravel 8 construe, decipher, spell out, unriddle, untangle 9 break down, elucidate, interpret 10 account for, illuminate, illustrate, unscramble 11 disentangle, rationalize

explain away
6 excuse 7 justify 8 minimize 9 extenuate 10 account for 11 rationalize

explanation
3 key 5 gloss 6 excuse, motive, reason 7 account, example, grounds, meaning 8 exegesis 9 construal, rationale 11 elucidation 12 significance 13 clarification

explanatory
10 discursive, exegetical 12 enlightening, illuminating, illustrative, interpretive

expletive
4 cuss, oath 5 curse, swear 8 cussword 9 swearword 12 interjection (see also **exclamation**)

explicate
7 amplify, develop, explain, expound 8 construe, spell out 9 elucidate, interpret

explication
5 gloss 8 exegesis 9 construal 10 commentary 11 development

explicative
10 discursive, exegetical, scholastic 12 interpretive 13 hermeneutical

explicit
4 open, sure 5 clear, exact, frank, lucid, overt, plain 7 certain, correct, express, obvious, precise 8 clearcut, definite, distinct, specific 10 definitive 11 categorical, perspicuous, unambiguous, unequivocal

explode
3 pop 4 fire 5 blast, burst, erupt, go off 6 blow up, debunk, negate, refute 7 burgeon, deflate, disprove, dynamite, mushroom, puncture 9 discharge, discredit 10 burst forth 11 proliferate

exploit
3 act, use 4 coup, deed, feat, gest, play 5 abuse, geste, stunt 6 bestow, effort, employ, parlay, play on 7 emprise, utilize, venture 8 escapade, exercise 9 adventure, cultivate 10 enterprise, manipulate 11 achievement, performance, tour de force

explore
5 probe, scout 6 burrow, go into, search 7 dig into, examine 8 look into, prospect, traverse 9 delve into 11 inquire into, investigate

explorer
African: 3 Cam, Cão (Diogo) 4 Park (Mungo) 5 Grant (James), Laird (Macgregor), Speke (John Hanning) 6 Akeley (Carl, Mary), Burton (Richard), Lander (John, Richard) 7 Covilhâ (Pero da), Stanley (Henry) 8 Covilhão (Pero da) 10 Clapperton (Hugh) 11 Livingstone (David)
American: 4 Byrd (Richard), Hall (Charles Francis), Kane (Elisha Kent), Pike (Zebulon) 5 Beebe (Charles William), Clark (William), Lewis (Meriwether), Peary (Robert)

6 Henson (Matthew), Powell (John Wesley), Wilkes (Charles) 7 Frémont (John Charles)
Antarctic: 4 Byrd (Richard), Cook (Frederick), Ross (James Clark) 5 Fuchs (Vivian), Ronne (Finn), Scott (Robert Falcon) 6 Palmer (Nathaniel), Rymill (John Riddoch), Wilkes (Charles) 7 Weddell (James), Wilkins (George) 8 Amundsen (Roald), d'Urville (Dumont) 9 Ellsworth (Lincoln) 10 Shackleton (Ernest)
Arctic: 3 Rae (John) 4 Byrd (Richard), Cook (Frederick) 5 Davis (John), Peary (Robert) 6 Baffin (William), Bering (Vitus), Henson (Matthew), Hudson (Henry), Nansen (Fridtjof), Nobile (Umberto) 7 Barents (Willem), Bennett (Floyd), Wilkins (George), Wrangel (Ferdinand von) 8 Amundsen (Roald) 9 Mackenzie (Alexander), MacMillan (Donald) 10 Stefansson (Vilhjalmur)
Australian: 7 Wilkins (George)
Austrian: 9 Weyprecht (Carl)
Canadian: 9 Mackenzie (Alexander) 10 Stefansson (Vilhjalmur)
Danish: 9 Rasmussen (Knud)
Dutch: 6 Tasman (Abel Janszoon)
English: 4 Cook (James) 5 Cabot (John, Sebastian), Drake (Francis), Scott (Robert Falcon), Smith (John) 6 Baffin (William), Burton (Richard), Hudson (Henry) 7 Raleigh (Walter), Stanley (Henry) 9 Vancouver (George) 10 Shackleton (Ernest) 12 Younghusband (Francis)
French: 7 Cartier (Jacques), La Salle (Sieur de), Nicolet (Jean) 8 Cousteau (Jacques-Yves) 9 Champlain (Samuel de), La Perouse (Comte de), Marquette (Jacques)
French Canadian: 6 Joliet (Louis) 7 Jolliet (Louis) 9 Iberville (Sieur d')
German: 6 Peters (Carl) 8 Humboldt (Alexander von)
Italian: 5 Cabot (John) 6 Nobile (Umberto) 8 Vespucci (Amerigo)
New Zealand: 7 Hillary (Edmund)
Norwegian: 6 Nansen (Fridtjof)

8 Amundsen (Roald), Sverdrup (Otto) 9 Heyerdahl (Thor)
Portuguese: 4 Gama (Vasco da) 5 Cunha (Tristão da) 6 Cabral (Pedro) 8 Cabrilho (João Rodrigues), Magellan (Ferdinand)
Scottish: 3 Rae (John) 4 Park (Mungo), Ross (James Clark) 7 Thomson (Joseph) 11 Livingstone (David)
Spanish: 6 Balboa (Vasco Núñez de), Cortés (Hernán, Hernando), de Soto (Hernando), Pinzón (Martín Alonso, Vicente Yáñez) 7 Mendoza (Pedro de), Pizarro (Francisco) 8 Bastidas (Rodrigo de), Coronado (Francisco de) 11 Ponce de León (Juan)

explosion

3 pop, pow 4 bang, boom, clap 5 blast, burst, crack, crash, sally, salvo, storm 6 report, volley 7 barrage, blowout, torrent 8 eruption, outburst, paroxysm 9 discharge 10 detonation

explosive

3 TNT 5 nitro, tense 6 charge, petard, powder 7 cordite, violent 8 dynamite 9 gunpowder 13 nitroglycerin
device: 3 cap 4 bomb, mine 5 shell 6 petard 7 grenade 8 firework
expert: 5 Maxim (Hudson), Nobel (Alfred)
sound: 3 pop, pow 4 bang, boom 5 crack

exponent

6 backer 7 booster 8 advocate, champion, defender, partisan, promoter, upholder 9 supporter 12 practitioner

expose

3 air 4 bare, open, show 5 dig up, flash 6 debunk, flaunt, parade, reveal, show up, unmask, unveil 7 abandon, display, exhibit, lay open, publish, show off, subject, uncover, undress 8 brandish, disclose, discover, endanger, unclothe

exposé
10 disclosure, revelation, uncovering

exposed
4 bare, open 5 naked 6 liable
7 evident, subject, visible 8 manifest,
stripped, unhidden 9 uncovered
11 susceptible, unconcealed, unprotected

exposition
4 fair, show 6 bazaar 7 display,
exhibit

expostulate
5 argue 6 debate, reason 7 discuss,
dispute

exposure
4 risk 5 peril 6 airing, baring, danger
8 betrayal, jeopardy, openness
9 liability, publicity 10 revelation
12 helplessness 13 vulnerability

expound
5 state 6 defend 7 clarify, comment,
explain, present 8 construe, set
forth, spell out 9 discourse, explicate, interpret

expounder
7 teacher 8 advocate, champion,
defender, promoter 9 proponent,
supporter

express
3 air, say 4 mean, tell, vent 5 couch,
crush, frame, state, utter 6 broach,
convey, denote, impart, intend,
voiced 7 connote, declare, signify,
special, uttered 8 announce, clear-
cut, definite, disclose, explicit,
intended, proclaim, specific 9 enunciate, formulate, high-speed, pronounce, symbolize, ventilate 10 definitive, particular 11 categorical,
communicate, intentional, unambiguous
gratitude: 5 thank
regret: 9 apologize

expression
4 cast, face, form, look, mien, sign,
vent, word 5 idiom, issue, motto,
token, voice 6 symbol, visage
7 diction, gesture 8 locution 9 eloquence, statement, utterance, verbalism, vividness 10 embodiment,
indication 11 countenance, enunciation, observation 13 demonstration,
manifestation
facial: 4 grin, phiz, pout 5 frown,
scowl, smile, smirk, sneer, wince
7 grimace
of assent: 3 aye, nod, yea, yes
4 okay
of sorrow: 4 alas, tear
trite: 6 cliché 7 bromide 8 banality
witty: 4 quip 5 sally 6 bon mot

expressionless
5 blank 6 stolid, vacant, wooden
7 deadpan 9 impassive 10 poker-
faced 11 inscrutable

expressive
5 vivid 7 graphic 8 eloquent 9 re-
vealing 10 meaningful, passionate

expressly
9 precisely, purposely 10 explicitly
12 particularly, specifically 13 intentionally

expressway
4 road 7 freeway, highway, parkway
8 turnpike 12 thoroughfare

expropriate
4 take 5 annex, seize 7 impound,
preempt 8 arrogate 9 sequester
10 commandeer, confiscate, dispossess

expulse
see **expel**

expulsion
5 exile, purge 6 ouster 7 ousting,
removal 8 ejection, eviction 9 ostracism 10 banishment, relegation
11 deportation 12 displacement

expunge
4 dele, x out 5 annul, erase 6 cancel, delete, efface 7 blot out, destroy, exclude, wipe out 8 black out
9 eliminate, eradicate, strike out
10 annihilate, obliterate

expurgate
4 blip 5 bleep, purge 6 censor,

expurgation

purify, screen **7** cleanse **8** sanitize **10** bowdlerize

expurgation

8 ablution **9** catharsis, cleansing **10** lustration **12** purification

exquisite

3 fop **4** fine, keen, rare **5** acute, dandy, choice, dainty, select, superb **7** coxcomb, elegant, extreme, intense, refined **8** delicate, finished, flawless, macaroni **9** recherché **10** fastidious, immaculate, impeccable

exsiccate

3 dry **4** sear **5** parch

extant

4 live **5** alive **6** actual, living **7** current, present **9** surviving **10** present-day **12** contemporary

extemporaneous

5 ad-lib **6** casual **7** offhand **8** ad-libbed, informal **9** impromptu, impulsive, makeshift, unplanned **10** improvised, unprepared, unscripted **11** spontaneous, unrehearsed **12** unthought-out

extempore

see **extemporaneous**

extemporize

5 ad-lib **7** dash off, toss off **8** knock off **9** improvise

extend

4 draw, span, vary **5** award, grant, offer, range, reach **6** accord, attain, bestow, spread, tender, unbend, unfold **7** advance, amplify, augment, broaden, drag out, draw out, enlarge, further, hold out, present, proceed, proffer, project, prolong, spin out, stretch **8** continue, elongate, increase, lengthen, multiply, protract **10** outstretch, stretch out

extension

3 arm, ell **4** wing **5** annex, delay, range, reach, scope, sweep **6** radius, spread **7** adjunct, compass, purview **8** addition, increase **9** appendage, magnitude **10** broadening, elongation **11** enlargement, lengthening, protraction **12** augmentation, continuation, postponement, prolongation

extensity

5 ambit, orbit, range, reach, scope, sweep **6** radius **7** compass, purview

extensive

3 big **4** long, vast, wide **5** broad, large, major **7** general, immense, lengthy, sizable **8** far-flung, sizeable, spacious, sweeping, thorough **9** wholesale **10** large-scale, widespread **11** far-reaching, wideranging **12** considerable

extent

4 size **5** ambit, limit, orbit, range, reach, scope, sweep, width **6** amount, degree, domain, radius **7** breadth, compass, measure, purview **8** vicinity **9** magnitude **10** dimensions, proportion

extenuate

6 dilute, excuse, lessen, soften, temper, weaken **7** explain, justify, qualify, varnish **8** diminish, enervate, mitigate, moderate, palliate **9** gloss over **11** rationalize

exterior

4 skin **5** outer, shell **6** facade **7** outmost, outside, outward, surface **8** apparent **9** outermost **11** superficial

exterminate

4 kill **6** rub out **7** destroy, wipe out **8** massacre **9** eliminate, eradicate, finish off, liquidate, slaughter **10** annihilate, extinguish, obliterate

external

3 out **4** over **5** outer **7** foreign, outside, outward, surface **9** outermost **10** peripheral **11** superficial

externalize

4 show **6** embody, evince, excuse, expose, reveal **7** exhibit, justify **8** manifest **9** extenuate, incarnate, objectify, personify **11** rationalize **12** substantiate

extinct

4 cold, dead, gone, late **5** passé
6 bygone **7** archaic, defunct **8** deceased, departed, obsolete, perished, vanished **10** superseded

extinction

3 end **4** doom **5** death **6** demise
11 destruction, eradication, liquidation **12** annihilation, obliteration
13 disappearance, extermination

extinguish

3 end **5** crush, douse, erase, quash, quell **6** put out, quench, squash, stifle **7** abolish, blot out, blow out, destroy, eclipse, expunge, nullify, put down, wipe out **8** snuff out, stamp out, suppress **9** eliminate, eradicate, extirpate **10** annihilate, obliterate

extirpate

5 erase **6** cut out, efface, excise, resect, uproot **7** abolish, blot out, destroy, expunge, kill off, root out, wipe out **8** demolish **9** eliminate, eradicate **10** annihilate, deracinate, extinguish

extol

4 hymn, laud **5** cry up, exalt **6** praise **7** acclaim, applaud, commend, glorify, magnify **8** eulogize **9** celebrate **10** panegyrize

extort

5 wrest, wring **7** extract

extortion

8 exaction **9** blackmail

extra

3 odd **4** more, over **5** added, spare **6** de trop, rarely **7** reserve, surplus **8** leftover **9** lagniappe, redundant, unusually **10** additional, especially **11** superfluous **12** particularly, supplemental **13** supernumerary, supplementary

extract

4 pull, yank **5** evoke, glean, quote, wring **6** derive, eke out, elicit, remove **7** abridge, distill, essence, excerpt, passage, pull out, squeeze, take out **8** citation, condense, infusion **9** quotation, selection **11** concentrate

extraction

5 birth, blood, stock **6** origin **7** descent, essence, lineage **8** ancestry, pedigree **9** parentage **10** derivation **12** distillation

extraneous

5 alien, outer **6** exotic **7** foreign, outside **8** external **9** unrelated **10** immaterial, inapposite, incidental, irrelevant, peripheral **11** impertinent, inessential, superfluous, unessential **12** adventitious, inapplicable, nonessential

extraordinary

3 odd **4** rare **6** unique **7** amazing, notable, special, unusual **8** abnormal, atypical, singular, terrific, uncommon, unwonted **9** wonderful **10** noteworthy, phenomenal, remarkable, stupendous, tremendous **11** exceptional, outstanding

extravagance

5 frill, waste **6** excess, luxury **9** hyperbole, profusion **10** indulgence, lavishness **11** ostentation, prodigality, superfluity **12** immoderation, wastefulness

extravagant

4 wild **5** outré, undue **6** lavish **7** bizarre, extreme, profuse **8** overdone, prodigal, reckless, wasteful **9** elaborate, excessive, fantastic, grandiose, overblown **10** exorbitant, hyperbolic, immoderate, inordinate, profligate **11** exaggerated, implausible, intemperate, nonsensical **12** ostentatious, preposterous, unrestrained

extreme

3 top **4** apex, dire, last, peak, wild **5** crown, final, limit, ultra, undue **6** climax, excess, height, summit, utmost, zenith **7** drastic, fanatic, intense, maximal, maximum, outmost, radical, violent **8** farthest, furthest, pinnacle, remotest, ultimate **9** desperate, excessive, outermost,

extremely

uttermost **10** immoderate, inordinate, outlandish, outrageous **11** culmination, furthermost, unwarranted **12** unmeasurable, unreasonable **13** revolutionary
degree: 3 nth

extremely

4 very **5** ultra **6** highly, hugely, mighty, overly, plenty **7** acutely, awfully, greatly, utterly **8** severely, terribly **9** immensely, seriously, unusually **10** remarkably, strikingly **11** exceedingly **12** terrifically

extremist

5 rabid, ultra **6** zealot **7** die-hard, fanatic, radical **8** militant, ultraist **9** fanatical **10** monomaniac, ultraistic **11** reactionary **13** revolutionary

extremity

3 arm, end, leg, tip **4** acme, apex, foot, hand, tail **5** limit, verge **6** apogee, vertex; zenith **8** terminal, terminus

extricate

4 free **5** loose **6** detach, redeem, rescue **7** bail out, deliver, resolve, set free, untwine **8** liberate, untangle **9** disengage **11** disencumber, disentangle, distinguish, individuate **12** discriminate, disembarrass **13** differentiate

extrinsic

5 alien, outer **6** exotic **7** foreign, outside, outward **8** exterior, external, imported **10** incidental, extraneous

extrude

4 spew **5** eject **7** push out **8** press out **10** squeeze out

exuberance

4 glee, life, zest **5** ardor **6** gaiety, spirit **7** abandon **8** buoyancy, hilarity, vivacity **9** profusion **10** ebullience, enthusiasm, friskiness, liveliness **11** flamboyance, high spirits, zestfulness **12** exhilaration **13** effervescence, sprightliness

exuberant

3 gay **4** lush, rank **5** happy **6** bouncy, elated, fecund, lavish, lively **7** buoyant, profuse, rampant, riotous, zestful **8** fruitful, prodigal, prolific, spirited **9** ebullient, luxuriant, sprightly, vivacious **10** flamboyant **11** exhilarated **12** effervescent, enthusiastic, high-spirited

exude

4 emit, leak, ooze, seep, shed **5** issue **7** diffuse, display, emanate, excrete, exhibit, give off, ooze out, radiate, secrete **9** discharge

exult

4 crow **5** cheer, gloat, glory, revel **7** delight, rejoice **8** jubilate **9** celebrate

exultant

6 elated, joyful, joyous **7** gleeful **8** ecstatic, euphoric, jubilant **9** cock-a-hoop, overjoyed, rejoicing, triumphal **10** triumphant

exultation

3 joy **4** glee **7** delight, ecstasy, elation, rapture, triumph **8** euphoria, gloating **9** jubilance, rejoicing **10** jubilation

eye

3 orb **4** lamp, ogle, scan, view **5** sight, watch **6** behold, goggle, look at, ocular, oculus, peeper, regard, size up, vision **7** inspect **8** check out, consider, gaze upon, scrutiny **9** headlight **10** scrutinize
defect: 6 myopia **9** hyperopia **10** emmetropia, presbyopia **11** astigmatism
disease: 8 cataract, glaucoma, trachoma
doctor: 7 oculist **11** optometrist
opening: 5 pupil
part: 4 iris, lens, uvea **5** pupil **6** cornea, retina, sclera
relating to: 5 optic **7** optical
socket: 5 orbit
Spanish: 3 ojo

eyeball

4 scan **5** check, study **6** go over, look at, peruse, survey **7** examine, inspect, observe **8** appraise, check out, evaluate, pore over **10** scrutinize

eye-catching
4 bold **5** gaudy, showy **6** flashy **7** salient **8** striking **9** arresting, prominent **10** noticeable, remarkable **11** conspicuous

eyeful
6 looker **7** stunner **8** knockout

eyeglass
7 monocle

eyeglasses
5 specs **6** lenses **7** lorgnon **8** bifocals, pince-nez **9** lorgnette **10** spectacles

eyelash
6 cilium **11** hairbreadth

eyelet
4 hole **7** grommet **8** loophole, peephole

eyepiece
4 lens **6** ocular

eye-popping
7 amazing **8** exciting, stirring **9** thrilling **10** astounding **11** astonishing, mind-blowing, spectacular **12** breathtaking

eyesore
4 blot, dump, mess **6** blight **7** blemish **8** atrocity **11** monstrosity

eyespot
6 blight, fungus **7** ocellus

eyetooth
6 canine

eyewash
3 rot **4** bunk **5** bilge, hooey, tripe **6** bunkum **7** baloney, garbage, hogwash, rubbish, twaddle **8** malarkey, nonsense **9** poppycock **10** balderdash **13** horsefeathers

eyewitness
8 observer, onlooker **9** bystander, spectator

eyrie
see **aerie**

F

Fabergé product
3 egg 9 Easter egg

Fabian
4 Shaw (George Bernard), Webb
(Beatrice, Sidney) 7 politic 8 cautious, dilatory 9 socialist 11 circumspect, calculating

fable
4 myth, tale, yarn 5 story 6 legend
7 fantasy, fiction, figment, parable
8 allegory
animal: 8 bestiary

fabled
5 famed 6 famous, unreal 7 storied
8 fanciful, mythical, renowned
9 fictional, imaginary, legendary,
pretended 10 fictitious 11 make-
believe 12 mythological

fabric
3 aba, rep, web 4 lamé, repp 5 cloth,
fiber, grain 7 texture 8 building,
material, shirting 9 structure
coarse: 5 crash, gunny 6 burlap,
linsey, ratiné 7 cheviot, hopsack
8 homespun
corded: 3 rep 4 repp 5 piqué
6 calico, moreen, poplin 7 pinwale
8 corduroy, paduasoy 9 bengaline
cotton: 4 jean, leno 5 baize, chino,
domet, drill, scrim, wigan 6 chintz,
dimity, faille, madras, muslin 7 etamine, gingham, nankeen, percale,
ticking 8 chambray, dungaree,
nainsook, tarlatan
cotton and linen: 4 huck 7 fustian
9 huckaback
crepe: 8 marocain
dealer: 6 draper, mercer

durable: 4 huck, jean 5 chino,
denim, drill 6 frieze, moreen 7 lasting, ticking 8 cretonne, dungaree
embroidered: 9 baldachin 10 baldachino
finishing process: 8 lustring
9 mercerize
flag material: 7 bunting
glazed: 6 chintz 7 cambric, holland
knitted: 6 tricot 10 balbriggan
linen: 7 cambric, lockram
looped: 6 bouclé
lustrous: 4 silk 5 moiré, satin,
surah 7 taffeta 12 brilliantine
metallic: 4 lamé
net: 5 tulle 8 bobbinet, illusion
openwork: 4 lace 8 filigree
ornamental: 4 lace 5 braid 6 ribbon
7 bunting
pebbly-surface: 8 barathea
pile-surface: 5 panne, plush, terry
6 velour, velvet 7 duvetyn, velours
8 chenille, moleskin 9 velveteen
plaid: 6 tartan
printed: 5 batik, toile 6 calico,
chintz, damask 7 allover, challis
8 cretonne, jacquard 11 toile de Jouy
puckered: 6 plissé
raised pattern: 4 lamé 7 brocade
10 brocatelle
satin weave: 5 panne
sheer: 4 lawn, mull 5 gauze, ninon,
voile 6 dimity 7 batiste, chiffon,
organdy, organza, tiffany 8 tarlatan
silk: 6 faille, pongee, samite 7 foulard, grogram 8 paduasoy, sarcenet,
sarsenet, shantung 9 bombazine
striped: 3 aba 7 ticking 8 bayadere
synthetic: 5 ninon, nylon, Orlon,
rayon 6 Dacron

twill: **4** jean **5** chino, drill, serge **7** foulard, nankeen, ticking **8** dungaree, shalloon **9** bombazine **10** broadcloth

unfinished: **6** greige

waterproof: **7** oilskin

wool: **5** baize, loden, tweed **6** alpaca, caddis, camlet, duffel, duffle, melton, merino, wadmal, wadmel, wadmol, woolen **7** woollen **8** mackinaw, prunella **9** cassimere

wool, poor quality: **5** mungo **6** shoddy

wool mixture: **6** saxony **7** drugget, ratteen **8** moquette, shalloon, zibeline **9** zibelline

woven: **4** weft **7** textile

fabricate

4 form, make **5** build, erect, frame, set up, shape **6** cook up, create, devise, invent, make up **7** concoct, dream up, fashion, produce, think up **8** assemble, contrive **9** construct, structure **11** manufacture, put together

fabrication

3 fib, lie **4** bull, jive **6** canard, deceit **7** fiction, figment, hogwash, product, untruth **8** assembly, building, creation **9** deception, fairy tale, falsehood, invention **10** concoction, production **11** manufacture **12** construction

fabulist

French: **10** La Fontaine (Jean de)
Greek: **5** Aesop
Roman: **8** Phaedrus
Russian: **6** Krylov (Ivan)

fabulous

5 super **7** amazing **8** mythical, terrific, wondrous **9** fantastic, legendary, marvelous, wonderful **10** astounding, fictitious, incredible, outrageous, phenomenal, prodigious, remarkable, stupendous **11** astonishing, extravagant, spectacular **12** mythological

animal: **6** dragon **7** centaur, unicorn
bird: **3** roc
serpent: **8** basilisk **10** cockatrice

facade

4 face, mask **5** color, front, guise, put-on **6** veneer **8** disguise, exterior, frontage, pretense **10** appearance, camouflage, false front

face

3 mug, pan **4** dare, defy, dial, meet, phiz, puss, show, side **5** abide, brave, front, guise, honor, image, nerve **6** endure, facade, kisser, makeup, mazard, oppose, resist, suffer, take on, visage **7** compete, contend, dignity, surface **8** confront, cope with, deal with, disguise, features, prestige, war paint **9** assurance, encounter, lineament, semblance, withstand **10** appearance, confidence, experience, expression, maquillage, reputation **11** countenance, self-respect

face-off

5 clash, set-to **13** confrontation

facet

4 edge, item, part, side **5** angle, bezel, front, phase, plane, point, trait **6** aspect, detail **7** element, feature, surface **9** attribute, component **10** appearance, particular

facetious

4 flip **5** comic, droll, smart, witty **6** blithe, joking **7** amusing, comical, jesting, jocular, joshing, kidding, risible, waggish **8** flippant, humorous **9** ludicrous, unserious, whimsical **10** irreverent, ridiculous **12** wisecracking **13** tongue-in-cheek

face-to-face

6 direct **7** contact, present, vis-à-vis **8** directly, in person, personal **10** personally

facile

4 deft, easy, glib, snap **5** light, quick, ready **6** adroit, expert, fluent, poised, simple, smooth **7** assured, cursory, offhand, shallow, voluble **8** skillful, untaxing **9** dexterous **10** effortless, simplistic **13** uncomplicated

facilitate

3 aid **4** abet, ease, help **6** assist,

facility

enable, smooth **7** advance, forward, further, promote **8** expedite, make easy, simplify

facility

3 aid, wit **4** bent, ease **5** knack, privy, skill **6** talent, toilet **7** ability, amenity, comfort, fluency, leaning **8** aptitude, bathroom, building, capacity, lavatory, washroom **9** advantage, dexterity **10** adroitness, competence, smoothness **11** convenience, institution, proficiency **12** installation **13** accommodation, establishment

facing

5 front, panel **6** contra, lining, toward, veneer **7** surface, vis-à-vis **8** covering, opposite, paneling **11** over against
down: 5 prone
up: 6 supine

facsimile

4 copy, dupe, fake, twin **5** clone, ditto, match, repro **6** carbon, double **7** replica **8** knockoff, likeness **9** duplicate, imitation, photocopy **10** carbon copy, dead ringer, similitude **11** counterpart, duplication, replication **12** reproduction

fact

4 dope **5** datum, event, truth **6** detail, gospel, truism, verity **7** episode, reality **8** evidence, incident **9** actuality **10** occurrence, particular, phenomenon **11** information **12** circumstance, intelligence

faction

4 band, bloc, camp, part, ring, sect, side, wing **5** cabal, group, party **6** caucus, circle, clique, sector, strife **7** combine, coterie, discord, machine, section **8** alliance, disunity, splinter **10** contingent, disharmony

factious

7 warring **8** contrary, divisive, partisan **9** dissident, insurgent, sectarian, seditious, turbulent **10** contending, malcontent **11** contentious, disaffected, dissentious, quarrelsome **12** disputatious **13** troublemaking

factitious

4 sham **5** bogus, false, phony **6** ersatz, forced, made-up, unreal **7** assumed, created, feigned, manmade, shammed **8** affected, invented, spurious **9** concocted, contrived, fashioned, pretended, simulated, synthetic, unnatural **10** artificial, fabricated **11** constructed, counterfeit **12** manufactured **13** counterfeited

_____ facto

4 ipso **6** ex post

factor

4 gene, item **5** agent, cause, proxy **6** broker, lender, number, symbol **7** divisor, element, exclude, include, resolve **8** attorney, emissary, quantity **9** component, majordomo, substance **10** antecedent, ingredient, multiplier **11** determinant **12** intermediary

factory

4 mill, shop **5** plant, works **8** workshop **9** sweatshop **11** machine shop

factotum

4 grub **5** gofer **6** drudge **7** servant **9** assistant, operative **11** functionary

factual

4 real, true **5** exact, valid **6** actual **7** certain, genuine, literal **8** absolute, positive **9** authentic, undoubted **10** undisputed **12** indisputable

faculty

4 bent, body, gift **5** flair, knack, power **6** talent **7** ability, college **8** aptitude, capacity, facility, function, instinct **9** educators, lecturers **10** department, professors **11** instructors

fad

4 chic, kick, mode, rage, whim **5** craze, furor, style, trend **6** furore, latest, whimsy **7** caprice, fashion **9** bandwagon **10** dernier cri

faddish

3 hot **4** chic **5** today **6** modish, red-hot, trendy, with-it **7** stylish, voguish **8** contempo **9** au courant **11** cutting-edge, fashionable

fade
3 die, dim, ebb 4 fail, pale, wane, wilt 6 lessen, vanish, weaken, wither 7 decline, lighten, wash out 8 decrease, discolor, diminish 9 disappear, evaporate

faded
3 dim, wan 4 drab, dull, pale 6 pallid 8 bleached, vanished, withered 9 etiolated, washed-out

Faerie Queene, The
author: 7 Spenser (Edmund)
character: 3 Ate, Una 4 Alma 5 Guyon, Talus 6 Abessa, Amavia, Amoret, Arthur, Cambel, Duessa, Palmer 7 Artegal, Corceca, Fidessa, Maleger, Sansloy 8 Calidore, Florimel, Fradubio, Gloriana, Lucifera, Orgoglio, Satyrane 9 Archimago, Britomart 11 Britomartis

Fafnir
6 dragon
brother: 5 Regin 6 Fasolt, Reginn
father: 8 Hreidmar
slayer: 6 Sigurd 9 Siegfried
victim: 6 Fasolt 8 Hreidmar

fag
4 do in, moil, tire, toil 5 serve, smoke, stick, weary 6 drudge, overdo, tucker 7 exhaust, fatigue, servant, wear out 8 drudgery, knock out 9 cigarette

fag end
4 butt, edge, fray 7 remnant

faience
11 earthenware

fail
3 die, end 4 bomb, fade, lack, lose, miss, sink, slip, stop, wane 5 break, flunk 6 fizzle, forget, ignore, lessen, weaken 7 decline, default, founder, give out, go under, neglect 8 fall flat, languish, miscarry 9 break down, fall short 10 disappoint, go bankrupt 11 deteriorate

failing
4 flaw, vice 5 fault 6 defect 8 weakness 9 weak point 10 deficiency 11 shortcoming 12 imperfection

failure
3 bum, dud 4 bomb, bust, flop, miss 5 decay, loser 6 fiasco, fizzle, no-good, outage 7 default, washout 8 collapse, fracture, omission 9 breakdown, cessation, oversight, unconcern 10 bankruptcy, deficiency, insolvency, negligence 11 defalcation, dysfunction, miscarriage 12 interruption 13 deterioration

fain
3 apt 5 eager, prone, ready 6 gladly, minded 7 willing 8 amenable, inclined 9 agreeable

fainéant
3 bum 4 idle, lazy 5 idler, sloth 6 loafer, torpid 7 goof-off, slacker 8 deadbeat, inactive, indolent, layabout, slothful, sluggard, sluggish 9 do-nothing, lazybones, shiftless 11 couch potato, ineffectual 13 lackadaisical

faint
3 dim, low, wan 4 hazy, pale, soft, weak, wilt 5 dizzy, light, swoon, vague, woozy 6 feeble 7 conk out, obscure, pass out, shadowy, syncope, unclear 8 black out, collapse, keel over 9 undefined 10 ill-defined, indistinct

fair
3 due 4 even, expo, fine, join, just, mild, okay, open, so-so 5 ample, blond, bonny, clear, equal, fresh, light, sunny 6 bazaar, blonde, comely, decent, honest, kermis, lovely, market, pretty, square 7 cricket 8 adequate, all right, balanced, carnival, festival, mediocre, middling, pleasant, pleasing, rainless, rational, sunshiny, unbiased 9 beautiful, cloudless, equitable, favorable, fortunate, impartial, objective, tolerable, unclouded 10 aboveboard, acceptable, attractive, evenhanded, exhibition, exposition, open-minded, reasonable 11 good-looking, indifferent, nonpartisan, respectable, sportsmanly 12 satisfactory, unprejudiced 13 disinterested, dispassionate, sportsmanlike

fair food
10 candy apple, candy floss, fried dough, funnel cake **11** cotton candy, elephant ear

fair-haired
3 pet **5** blond **6** blonde **7** beloved, darling, favored **8** favorite **9** fortunate

fairly
5 quite **6** nearly, rather **7** plainly **8** passably, properly, somewhat **9** tolerably **10** acceptably, deservedly, distinctly, moderately, reasonably **11** practically

fairness
6 candor **7** honesty **8** justness **9** good faith **12** impartiality

fairy
3 elf, imp, nix **4** puck **5** elfin, nixie, nymph, pixie, sylph **6** goblin, kobold, sprite **7** brownie, gremlin **10** leprechaun
king: **6** Oberon
queen: **3** Mab **7** Titania **8** Gloriana
shoemaker: **10** leprechaun

fairy tale
author: **4** Lang (Andrew) **5** Grimm (Jacob, Wilhelm), Wilde (Oscar) **7** Kipling (Rudyard) **8** Andersen (Hans Christian), Perrault (Charles)
character: **4** Jack, Puck **6** Gretel, Hansel **8** Rapunzel, Tom Thumb **9** Snow White **10** Cinderella, Goldilocks, Thumbelina

faith
4 cult, sect **5** credo, creed, stock, troth, trust **6** belief, church, credit **8** credence, reliance, religion **9** certainty, certitude, communion, credulity **10** confidence, persuasion **12** denomination
article of: **5** tenet

faithful
4 fast, just, true **5** liege, loyal, pious, tried **6** steady, trusty **7** devoted, dutiful, staunch **8** constant, follower, reliable, resolute, true-blue **9** religious, steadfast **10** dependable, scrupulous, unwavering **11** truehearted, trustworthy

faithfulness
5 piety, troth **6** fealty **7** loyalty **8** devotion, fidelity **9** adherence, constancy **10** allegiance, attachment

faithless
5 false, Punic **6** fickle, untrue **8** disloyal, recreant **10** perfidious, traitorous **11** treacherous **13** untrustworthy

faithlessness
7 perfidy, treason **8** betrayal **9** falseness, treachery **10** disloyalty, infidelity

fake
3 act, gyp **4** hoax, mock, sham **5** bluff, bogus, false, feign, fraud, phony, put on, spoof **6** affect, doctor, ersatz, forged, framed, humbug, pseudo **7** falsify, pretend **8** impostor, invented, simulate, spurious **9** brummagem, charlatan, concocted, fabricate, imitation, imposture, pinchbeck, pretended, simulated **10** artificial, fabricated, fictitious, fraudulent, simulation **11** counterfeit
combining form: **5** pseud **6** pseudo

faker
4 sham **5** fraud, phony, quack **6** con man, hoaxer **8** deceiver, impostor **9** charlatan, con artist, pretender **10** mountebank **11** four-flusher **12** double-dealer **13** confidence man

fakir
7 ascetic, dervish **9** mendicant

falcon
4 hawk **5** hobby, saker **6** lanner, merlin **7** kestrel **9** peregrine
eye cover: **4** seel
male: **4** jack **6** tercel **7** tiercel **8** lanneret
mature: **7** haggard
young: **4** eyas

falcon-headed god
see at **Egyptian**

falconry
7 hawking
equipment: **4** bell, hood, jess, lure
procedure: **3** imp **4** cope, seel

Falkland Islands
 capital: 7 Stanley
 colony of: 7 Britain

fall
 3 dip, ebb, sag **4** dive, drip, drop,
 dump, hang, plop, sink, slip, trip,
 wane **5** abate, crash, lapse, slide,
 slump, spill **6** autumn, drowse, give
 up, go down, header, plunge, sprawl,
 tumble **7** cascade, decline, descend,
 descent, devolve, go under, plummet, scatter, stumble, subside
 8 collapse, decrease, diminish,
 keel over, nose-dive **9** hairpiece
 10 depreciate **11** precipitate

fallacious
 6 untrue **7** invalid **8** delusive,
 delusory **9** deceitful, deceptive,
 erroneous, sophistic **10** fraudulent

fallacy
 5 error **6** canard **7** falsity, sophism,
 untruth **8** delusion **9** falsehood
 11 non sequitur **13** misconception

fall apart
 6 lose it **7** crumble **9** break down,
 decompose **10** go to pieces **11** come
 unglued, deteriorate **12** disintegrate

fall back
 6 recede, recoil, retire **7** retract,
 retreat **8** withdraw **9** disengage,
 retrocede **10** retrograde

fall behind
 3 lag **4** drag **5** delay, tarry, trail
 6 dawdle, linger, loiter

fall flat
 4 bomb, fail, flop, miss **6** fizzle

fall guy
 4 dupe, fool, goat, gull **5** chump,
 front, patsy **6** stooge, sucker **8** front
 man **9** scapegoat **11** whipping boy

fallible
 4 iffy, weak **5** dicey, frail, human
 6 errant, erring, faulty **9** imperfect
 10 unreliable

falling-out
 3 row **4** beef, feud, fuss, spat, tiff
 5 break, run-in, words **6** bicker,

fracas, hassle **7** dispute, quarrel,
 rhubarb, wrangle **8** argument,
 conflict, squabble **9** brannigan
 11 altercation, controversy **12** disagreement, estrangement

falloff
 3 sag **4** drop, slip **5** slump **7** decline
 8 downturn **9** downslide, down-
 swing, downtrend **13** deterioration

fall out
 5 argue, break, leave, occur **6** bicker
 7 brabble, quarrel, wrangle **8** disagree, squabble

fallow
 4 idle **5** inert **6** unsown **7** dormant,
 resting **8** inactive, unseeded, untilled
 9 neglected, quiescent, unplanted
 12 uncultivated

false
 4 fake, mock, sham **5** bogus, dummy,
 hokey, lying, phony, wrong **6** ersatz,
 forged, hollow, pseudo, untrue
 7 crooked, devious, feigned, seeming, unloyal **8** apostate, apparent,
 deluding, delusive, delusory, disloyal,
 recreant, specious, spurious **9** brummagem, deceitful, deceiving, deceptive, dishonest, distorted, erroneous,
 faithless, illogical, imitation, incorrect,
 pinchbeck, simulated **10** artificial,
 fictitious, fraudulent, inaccurate,
 misleading, perfidious, traitorous,
 unfaithful, untruthful **11** counterfeit,
 treacherous
 combining form: 5 pseud **6** pseudo

falsehood
 3 fib, lie **5** fable **6** canard **7** fallacy,
 untruth, whopper **8** roorback **9** mendacity **11** fabrication **12** misstatement **13** prevarication

falseness
 7 fallacy, perfidy **8** apostasy
 9 treachery **10** disloyalty, infidelity
 11 insincerity

false teeth
 8 dentures

falsify
 3 fib, lie **4** cook, deny **5** belie, fudge,

falsity
slant 6 doctor, refute 7 deceive, distort, mislead 8 disprove, misstate 10 contradict 11 prevaricate 12 misrepresent

falsity
3 fib, lie 4 tale, yarn 5 fable 6 canard 7 untruth, whopper 9 falsehood, mendacity 11 fabrication 13 prevarication

Falstaff
companion: 3 Nym 4 Peto 6 Pistol 8 Bardolph
composer: 5 Verdi (Giuseppe)
creator: 11 Shakespeare (William)
play: 7 Henry IV
prince: 3 Hal
tavern: 9 Boar's Head

Falstaffian
3 fat 6 jovial 7 roguish 8 boastful 9 convivial, dissolute

falter
4 halt, limp, reel, sway, trip 5 quail, waver 6 flinch, teeter, totter, wobble 7 give way, stagger, stammer, stumble 8 hesitate 9 vacillate 12 shilly-shally

fame
4 note 5 éclat, glory, honor, kudos 6 esteem, regard, renown, repute 7 acclaim, stardom 8 standing 9 celebrity, notoriety 10 popularity, prominence, reputation 11 acclamation, immortality, recognition

famed
5 noted 6 marked 7 eminent, notable 8 renowned 9 notorious, prominent, well-known 10 celebrated 11 illustrious 13 distinguished

familiar
4 cozy 6 common, folksy 8 domestic, everyday, frequent, informal, intimate, standard 10 accustomed 11 comfortable, commonplace 12 conventional, recognizable 13 garden-variety

familiarity
4 ease 8 intimacy 9 closeness, knowledge 11 informality 12 acquaintance

family
3 kin 4 clan, folk, home, line, race 5 brood, folks, house, issue, stirp, stock, tribe 6 ménage, strain 7 dynasty, kindred, lineage, progeny 8 pedigree 9 bloodline, household, offspring
branch: 5 stirp
lineage: 4 tree 6 stemma 8 pedigree 9 genealogy

famine
4 want 6 dearth, hunger 10 starvation

famished
6 hungry 7 starved 8 ravenous, starving

famous
5 famed, noble, noted 6 fabled 7 eminent, notable, popular 8 historic, renowned 9 legendary, notorious, prominent, well-known 10 celebrated 11 illustrious, prestigious, redoubtable

fan
3 bug, nut 4 blow, buff, open, wind 5 lover, rouse 6 addict, arouse, expand, extend, kindle, rooter, ruffle, spread, stir up, unfold, votary, whip up, winnow 7 admirer, devotee, habitué 8 adherent, enkindle, follower, railbird 9 stimulate 10 aficionado, enthusiast
horseracing: 7 turfman
India: 6 punkah
movie: 7 cineast 8 cineaste

fanatic
3 bug, nut 4 buff 5 fiend, freak, rabid 6 addict, maniac, votary, zealot 7 devotee, die-hard, habitué 10 aficionado, enthusiast

fanatical
5 fiery, rabid 6 ardent, fervid 7 extreme, fervent, zealous 8 frenetic, frenzied, maniacal, obsessed 9 perfervid 10 passionate 11 impassioned

fanaticism
4 zeal 5 mania 6 frenzy 8 zealotry 9 extremism, monomania

fancier

6 grower 7 amateur, admirer, breeder, devotee

fanciful

6 absurd, unreal 7 bizarre, fictive 8 fabulous, illusory, imagined, mythical, notional, romantic 9 fantastic, fictional, grotesque, imaginary 10 chimerical, fictitious 11 fantastical 12 preposterous

fancy

3 bee 4 posh, whim 5 dream, ritzy, shine, smart, taste 6 liking, megrim, notion, relish, snazzy, swanky, vision, whimsy 7 caprice, chimera, conceit, concept, dream up, elegant, fantasy, feature, imagine, picture 8 conceive, daydream, envision, fondness, judgment, velleity 9 capriccio, elaborate, intricate, inventive, visualize, whimsical 10 decorative, ornamental, partiality, propensity 11 extravagant, highfalutin, imagination, inclination

fandango

5 dance 9 malaguena

fanfare

4 pomp, show 5 array 7 display, panoply 8 flourish
trumpet: 6 tucket

fanlike

7 plicate

fanny

3 bum, can 4 buns, butt, duff, moon, rear, rump, seat, tail, tush 5 booty, nates 6 behind, bottom, breech, heinie 7 caboose, hind end, keister, rear end, tail end 8 backside, buttocks, derriere 9 fundament, posterior

fantasia

6 vision 8 daydream, illusion, rhapsody 9 fairyland 10 apparition

fantasize

4 moon 5 dream, fancy 7 imagine 8 daydream 10 woolgather

fantastic

3 odd 4 wild 6 absurd, unreal 7 bizarre, surreal 8 fanciful, singular 9 eccentric, grotesque, imaginary, marvelous, monstrous, unearthly, whimsical 10 chimerical, far-fetched, improbable, incredible, outlandish, outrageous, prodigious, stupendous, tremendous 11 implausible, nonsensical, sensational, superlative 12 preposterous, unbelievable

fantasy

4 moon, whim 5 dream, fancy, freak 6 vagary, vision, whimsy 7 caprice, chimera, fiction, reverie 8 daydream, delusion, phantasm 9 imagining, invention, pipe dream 10 bizarrerie 11 imagination 12 grotesquerie

far

4 long 6 remote 7 distant 8 outlying
combining form: 3 tel 4 tele, telo

far and wide

7 all over 10 everyplace, everywhere, throughout

faraway

4 lost 5 moony 6 absent, dreamy, remote 7 distant, removed 8 outlying 9 oblivious, unheeding 10 abstracted, distracted 11 preoccupied, inattentive 12 absentminded

farce

6 comedy, satire 7 mockery 8 travesty 9 burlesque, slapstick 10 caricature

farceur

5 clown, cutup, joker 7 buffoon

farcical

5 comic 6 absurd 7 comical, foolish, risible 9 laughable, ludicrous 10 ridiculous 12 preposterous

fare

4 diet, dine, food, pass, rate, toll 5 get on, price, track 6 manage, travel 7 come off, journey, make out, proceed, succeed 8 get along, progress, victuals 9 passenger, surcharge 10 provisions 11 comestibles

farewell

3 ave, bye 4 ta-ta 5 adieu, adios,

aloha, congé **6** bye-bye, pip-pip, shalom, so long **7** aloha oe, cheerio, good-bye **8** swan song **9** bon voyage, departure **11** arrivederci, leave-taking, valediction, valedictory

far-fetched
5 fishy **6** absurd **7** dubious **8** doubtful, strained, unlikely **10** improbable, incredible **11** implausible, unrealistic **12** preposterous, unbelievable

far-flung
6 remote **7** distant, removed **8** outlying **10** widespread

farinaceous
5 mealy **6** floury **7** starchy
food: 4 meal **5** flour, grits **6** cereal, hominy **7** polenta, pudding, tapioca

farm
4 till **5** croft, ranch **6** grange, rancho **7** hennery **8** estancia, hacienda, hatchery **9** cultivate, farmstead **10** plantation
building: 4 barn, shed, silo
Dutch: 6 bowery
Israeli collective: 7 kibbutz
Russian: 7 kolkhoz, sovkhoz

farmer
6 grower, tiller, yeoman **7** granger, planter, rancher **8** ranchero, ranchman **13** agriculturist
Russian: 5 kulak
South African: 4 Boer
tenant: 6 cottar, cotter **7** crofter **12** sharecropper

farming
7 tillage **8** agronomy **9** husbandry **11** agriculture, cultivation

faro
5 monte
bet: 7 sleeper
card: 4 case, hock, soda

far-off
6 remote **7** distant, removed **8** outlying

far-out
3 rad **4** cool **5** outré, weird **6** groovy **7** bizarre, offbeat, radical **9** eccentric

10 avant-garde, off-the-wall, outlandish

farrago
4 hash, mess, olio **5** gumbo **6** jumble, medley, muddle **7** goulash, mélange, mixture **8** mishmash, shambles **9** potpourri **10** hodgepodge, miscellany

far-reaching
5 broad **8** sweeping **9** extensive, momentous, pervasive **10** portentous, widespread **11** significant, wide-ranging **13** comprehensive, consequential

farrier
5 smith **10** blacksmith, horseshoer

farsighted
4 sage, wise **9** hyperopic, prescient, sagacious **10** discerning

farthest
6 utmost **7** apogean, extreme, outmost **8** remotest, ultimate **9** outermost, uttermost

Fasching
8 carnival

fascinate
4 draw, wile **5** charm **6** allure, enamor, entice, please **7** attract, beguile, bewitch, enchant **8** enthrall, intrigue, transfix **9** captivate, enrapture, magnetize, mesmerize, spellbind

fascination
5 charm **6** allure, appeal **7** glamour **8** charisma **9** magnetism **10** attraction, witchcraft **11** enchantment **12** enthrallment

Fascist
4 Nazi **6** despot, Hitler (Adolf), tyrant **8** autocrat **9** Falangist, Mussolini (Benito) **10** Blackshirt

fashion
3 fad, fit, ton, way **4** chic, form, mode, mold, suit, tone, vein, wear **5** craze, shape, style, trend, usage, vogue **6** create, custom, design, devise, manner, method, sculpt, tailor

7 compose, costume, pattern **8** contrive **9** bandwagon, construct, fabricate **10** dernier cri **12** haute couture

fashionable
3 hip **4** chic, cool, posh, tony **5** fresh, ritzy, sharp, smart, swank, swish **6** chichi, du jour, modish, trendy, with-it **7** à la mode, current, dashing, faddish, popular, stylish, voguish **8** up-to-date **9** au courant, exclusive, happening **12** silk-stocking

fashion designer
American: 4 Head (Edith) **5** Beene (Geoffrey), Blass (Bill), Dache (Lilly), Ellis (Perry), Karan (Donna), Klein (Anne, Calvin) **6** Jacobs (Marc), Lauren (Ralph), Mackie (Bob) **7** Galanos (James), Halston, Mizrahi (Isaac) **8** Galliano (John), Hilfiger (Tommy) **9** Claiborne (Liz), de la Renta (Oscar), Gernreich (Rudi)
Anglo-French: 5 Worth (Charles Frederick)
Dominican: 9 de la Renta (Oscar)
English: 5 Quant (Mary) **8** Westwood (Vivienne)
French: 4 Dior (Christian) **5** Bohan (Marc) **6** Cardin (Pierre), Chanel (Coco), Poiret (Paul) **6** Ungaro (Emanuel) **7** Balmain (Pierre), Lacroix (Christian), Montana (Claude) **8** Givenchy (Hubert de) **9** Courrèges (André), Lagerfeld (Karl) **12** Saint-Laurent (Yves), Schiaparelli (Elsa)
German: 9 Lagerfeld (Karl)
Israeli: 7 Mizrahi (Isaac)
Italian: 5 Pucci (Emilio), Ricci (Nina) **6** Armani (Giorgio) **7** Cassini (Oleg), Versace (Gianni) **12** Schiaparelli (Elsa)
Japanese: 6 Miyake (Issey)
Spanish: 10 Balenciaga (Cristóbal)

fast
3 set **4** diet, easy, firm, Lent, soon, sure, true, wild **5** fixed, fleet, hasty, hitch, loose, loyal, quick, rapid, swift **6** firmly, prompt, snappy, speedy, stable **7** abstain, hastily, hurried, lasting, quickly, rapidly, staunch, swiftly **8** chop-chop, constant,

faithful, full tilt, immobile, promptly, resolute, speedily **9** breakneck, dissolute, immovable, libertine **10** abstinence, profligate, recklessly, stationary **11** expeditious, promiscuous **12** lickety-split **13** expeditiously

fasten
3 fix, peg, pin, set, sew, tie, zip **4** bind, bolt, clip, hook, join, lace, lash, link, lock, moor, nail, seal, shut, weld **5** affix, cable, catch, chain, cinch, clamp, clasp, close, cramp, dowel, girth, hitch, latch, rivet, screw, stake, stick, strap, tie up, truss **6** anchor, attach, batten, buckle, button, couple, secure, skewer, solder, staple, tether **7** connect, mortise **8** buckle up

fastener
3 nut, peg, pin, tie **4** bolt, brad, clip, cord, frog, hasp, link, lock, nail, rope, snap, stud, tack, tape **5** catch, clamp, clasp, dowel, girth, hinge, hitch, latch, rivet, screw, spike, stake, strap **6** buckle, button, cotter, skewer, staple, tether, toggle, zipper **7** grommet, padlock, netsuke, shackle **8** coupling, cuff link, handcuff, seat belt, shoelace **9** connector, cotter pin, safety pin, thumbtack **10** clothespin

fastidious
5 fussy, picky **6** choosy, dainty, queasy **7** choosey, finical, finicky, refined **8** exacting **9** demanding, squeamish **10** meticulous, particular, pernickety **11** persnickety

fastness
4 fort, hold, keep **6** bunker, castle, refuge **7** alcazar, bastion, citadel, crannog, redoubt, sanctum **8** casemate, fortress, presidio **10** stronghold, tower house **11** strongpoint

fast-talking
4 glib **5** slick **6** facile **8** slippery **13** silver-tongued

fat
3 big, oil **4** flab, lard, suet, wide **5** beefy, broad, bulky, burly, cream,

fatal

dumpy, gross, heavy, husky, large, lipid, obese, plump, pudgy, round, stout, thick, tubby 6 chunky, excess, fleshy, grease, portly, rotund, stocky, stubby, tallow 7 adipose, blubber, paunchy, porcine, surfeit, surplus, weighty 8 heavyset, oversize, thickset 9 corpulent 10 full-bodied, overweight, potbellied 11 superfluity

fatal

6 deadly, lethal, mortal 7 deathly, ruinous 8 terminal 9 incurable, pestilent 10 pernicious 12 pestilential

fatality

4 doom 5 death 8 casualty 10 deadliness

fata morgana

6 mirage 8 illusion

fat cat

5 mogul, nabob 6 big gun, bigwig, tycoon 7 big shot, magnate, poohbah 8 big wheel 9 moneybags, plutocrat 11 muckety-muck 13 high-muck-a-muck

fate

3 end, lot 4 doom, luck, ruin 5 death, karma 6 chance, kismet, upshot 7 destiny, fortune, outcome, portion 13 inevitability

fateful

6 deadly 7 ominous, ruinous 8 decisive 9 momentous, prophetic 10 portentous

Fates

see at **Greek; Norse; Roman**

fathead

3 ass, oaf 4 boob, clod, dodo, dope, dolt, gawk, goof, goon, jerk, lump, mutt, yo-yo 5 cluck, clunk, dummy, dunce, idiot, moron, stock, stupe, yahoo 6 cretin, dimwit, donkey, doofus, dum-dum, nitwit, noodle, schlub, turkey 7 buffoon, dullard, jackass, schnook 8 dumbbell, imbecile, numskull 9 birdbrain, ignoramus, lamebrain, numbskull, simpleton

fatheaded

4 dull, dumb 5 dense, dopey, thick 6 obtuse, simple, stupid 7 doltish, idiotic 8 gormless 9 brainless, dim-witted, imbecilic 10 numskulled 11 numbskulled, thick-witted

father

3 dad, pop 4 dada, papa, père, sire 5 beget, breed, daddy, hatch, padre, pappy, pater, poppa, spawn 6 author, create, old man, parent, priest 7 builder, creator, founder, produce 8 ancestor, engender, generate, inventor, producer 9 architect, initiator, originate, patriarch, procreate 10 originator, prime mover **combining form:** 4 patr 5 patri, patro

Father Brown creator

10 Chesterton (Gilbert Keith)

fatherland

4 home, soil 7 country

Father Time's implement

6 scythe

fathom

4 know 5 probe, sound 7 discern, explore, measure 9 apprehend, figure out, penetrate 10 comprehend, understand 11 investigate

fathomless

7 abysmal, abyssal 8 profound 12 immeasurable

fatidic

5 vatic 6 mantic 7 Delphic, sibylic 8 Delphian, oracular, sibyllic 9 prophetic, prescient, sibylline, vaticinal 10 divinatory, predictive

fatigue

3 fag 4 poop, tire, wear 5 drain, weary 6 tucker 7 deplete, burn out, exhaust, frazzle, wear out 8 drudgery, wear down 9 tiredness, weariness 10 enervation, exhaustion **combat:** 7 frazzle 10 shell shock

Fatima

father: 8 Mohammed, Muhammad **husband:** 9 Bluebeard **son:** 5 Hasan 6 Husayn **stepbrother:** 3 Ali

fatness
7 obesity 9 adiposity 10 corpulence, overweight

fatty
4 oily, rich 6 greasy 7 adipose 8 unctuous 10 oleaginous
combining form: 4 lipo 5 adipo

fatuous
4 dumb, fond 5 inane, sappy, silly 6 jejune, simple 7 asinine, foolish, puerile, witless

faucet
3 tap 4 bung, cock, gate 5 valve 6 spigot 7 hydrant, petcock 8 stop-cock

Faulkner, William
character: 3 Ike (Snopes), Joe (Christmas) 4 Eula (Varner Snopes), Flem (Snopes), Mink (Snopes) 5 Benjy (Compson), Caddy (Compson), Gavin (Stevens), Henry (Sutpen), Jason (Compson), Lucas (Beauchamp) 6 Dilsey, Temple (Drake) 7 Candace (Compson), Quentin (Compson) 8 Benjamin (Compson)
county: 13 Yoknapatawpha
family: 6 Benbow, Snopes, Sutpen 7 Compson 8 McCaslin, Sartoris 9 Beauchamp
novel: 4 Town (The) 6 Hamlet (The) 7 Mansion (The), Reivers (The) 8 Sartoris 9 Sanctuary, Wild Palms (The) 11 As I Lay Dying 13 Light in August 14 Absalom, Absalom 15 Sound and the Fury (The) 17 Intruder in the Dust

fault
3 err, nag, sin 4 flaw, rift, slip, spot, vice, want 5 blame, break, knock, error, scold 6 accuse, defect, foible, miscue 7 censure, demerit, failing, fissure, frailty, mistake, upbraid 8 fracture, weakness 9 criticize, infirmity 10 San Andreas 11 culpability, dereliction, shortcoming 12 imperfection
line: 4 rift 5 split 6 breach 7 fissure 8 crevasse

faultfinder
4 crab 5 grump 6 critic, griper, grouch, nagger, whiner 7 grouser 8 grumbler 10 bellyacher, complainer, criticizer, crosspatch

faultfinding
7 carping 8 captious, critical, nitpicky 9 criticism 10 censorious, nit-picking, pernickety 11 persnickety 12 over-critical 13 hypercritical

faultless
4 pure 7 perfect 8 innocent, unerring 9 guiltless 10 immaculate, impeccable, inculpable

faulty
4 awry 5 amiss, wrong 6 flawed, marred 7 botched, damaged, defaced, inexact, unsound 8 fallible, specious 9 blemished, defective, deficient, erroneous, imperfect, incorrect 10 fallacious, inaccurate
prefix: 3 dys

faun
5 satyr

fauna
7 animals

Faunus
grandfather: 6 Saturn
son: 4 Acis 7 Latinus

Faust
author: 6 Goethe (Johann Wolfgang von)
beloved: 8 Gretchen
composer: 6 Gounod (Charles)

faux
4 fake, sham 5 bogus, false, phony 6 ersatz 9 imitation, pretended, simulated, synthetic 10 substitute

faux pas
4 flub, goof, slip 5 boner, error, gaffe 6 boo-boo, howler, miscue, slipup 7 blooper, blunder, misstep, mistake, stumble 8 pratfall, solecism 9 gaucherie 11 impropriety

favor
4 baby, back, bias, boon, gift, okay 5 bless, bribe, grace, mercy, token,

favorable

value 6 accept, behalf, choose, oblige, pamper, prefer, regard 7 indulge, present, support, sustain 8 courtesy, goodwill, interest, keepsake, kindness, resemble, sanction, sympathy 9 attention, patronage, privilege, take after 10 admiration, facilitate, indulgence, partiality 11 approbation, benevolence, countenance

favorable

4 fair 5 lucky 6 benign, biased, golden, timely, toward, useful 7 helpful, partial 8 pleasant, pleasing, positive 9 agreeable, benignant, fortunate, promising 10 auspicious, benevolent, propitious, prosperous 11 affirmative 12 advantageous 13 complimentary

favoring

4 rosy 6 timely, toward, useful 7 helpful 9 opportune 10 auspicious, beneficial, propitious 12 advantageous
prefix: 3 pro

favorite

3 pet 7 dearest, popular, special 8 precious 9 preferred, well-liked 10 fair-haired, preference 11 frontrunner, teacher's pet, white-haired

favoritism

4 bias 8 cronyism, nepotism 10 partiality 12 one-sidedness

fawn

3 kid 4 deer, ecru 5 beige, toady 6 bister, grovel, kowtow 7 flatter, truckle, wheedle 8 blandish, bootlick 9 sweet-talk 11 apple-polish

fawning

6 smarmy 8 unctuous 9 parasitic 10 obsequious 11 sycophantic

fay

3 elf 4 puck 5 elfin, fairy, pixie 6 elfish, goblin, sprite 7 brownie 10 leprechaun

faze

3 cow 5 abash, daunt, throw 6 dismay, rattle 7 confuse, disturb, non-plus, perturb 8 befuddle, bewilder, confound, unsettle 9 discomfit, dumbfound, embarrass 10 disconcert 11 flabbergast

FBI director

5 Freeh (Louis) 6 Hoover (J. Edgar) 7 Mueller (Robert)

fealty

5 faith, troth 7 loyalty 8 devotion, fidelity 9 adherence, constancy, vassalage 10 allegiance, attachment 11 devotedness 12 faithfulness

fear

3 awe 5 alarm, angst, dread, panic, qualm, scare, worry 6 dismay, fright, horror, phobia, terror 7 anxiety, jitters 8 cold feet, disquiet, timidity 9 agitation, cowardice, misgiving 10 foreboding 11 disquietude, trepidation 12 apprehension, cowardliness, perturbation, presentiment, timorousness
of animals: 9 zoophobia
of being buried alive: 11 taphephobia
of cats: 12 ailurophobia
of crowds: 11 ochlophobia
of darkness: 11 nyctophobia
of dirt: 10 mysophobia
of fire: 10 pyrophobia
of heights: 10 acrophobia
of men: 11 androphobia
of new things: 9 neophobia
of open areas: 11 agoraphobia
of pain: 10 algophobia
of strangers: 10 xenophobia
of thunder: 12 brontophobia
of water: 11 hydrophobia
of women: 10 gynophobia

fearful

5 timid 6 afraid, aghast, scared, trepid 7 alarmed, anxious, jittery, panicky 8 alarmist, paranoid, timorous 9 terrified, tremulous 12 apprehensive

fearless

4 bold 5 brave 6 daring 7 gallant, valiant 8 intrepid, unafraid 9 dauntless 10 courageous 11 lionhearted 12 greathearted, stouthearted

Fear of Flying author
  4 Jong (Erica)

fearsome
  3 shy 5 scary, timid 6 afraid 7 extreme, intense 8 daunting, timorous 9 frightful 10 terrifying 11 frightening 12 intimidating

feasible
  6 doable, likely, viable 8 possible, suitable, workable 10 reasonable 11 practicable 12 tried-and-true

feast
  3 eat 4 dine, meal 5 gorge 6 dinner, regale, repast, spread 7 banquet, indulge 8 potlatch
  Hawaiian: 4 luau
  Scottish: 3 foy

Feast of Lights
  8 Hanukkah

Feast of Lots
  5 Purim

Feast of Tabernacles
  6 Sukkot 7 Sukkoth

feat
  3 act 4 deed, gest 5 stunt, trick 6 action 7 exploit 11 achievement, performance, tour de force

feather
  3 ilk 4 down, kind, sort, type 5 breed, order, pinna, plume, quill 6 fledge, fletch, pinion 7 species, variety
  kind: 4 down 6 covert 7 contour, plumule, rectrix 8 scapular
  part: 3 web 4 barb, vane 5 shaft 7 barbule, calamus 8 barbicel

featherbrained
  5 dizzy, giddy, silly 7 flighty, foolish 8 heedless 9 frivolous 11 lightheaded, thoughtless

feathered
  7 plumose

feathers
  4 down 7 plumage

feature
  4 item, mark, part 5 add-on, trait 6 aspect, detail, factor 7 article, element, fixture, gimmick, quality 8 hallmark, property 9 attribute, component, lineament 10 attraction, ingredient 11 drawing card, peculiarity

febrile
  3 hot 5 fiery 7 fevered, pyretic 8 feverish

feckless
  4 weak 7 useless 8 carefree, impotent 11 incompetent, ineffective, ineffectual 12 undependable 13 irresponsible

fecund
  4 rich 7 fertile 8 fruitful, prolific 9 inventive 10 productive

fecundity
  9 abundance, fertility 11 prodigality 12 fruitfulness, productivity

Federalist writer
  3 Jay (John) 7 Madison (James) 8 Hamilton (Alexander)

federation
  5 union 6 league, nation 7 council 8 alliance 10 government 11 confederacy

fed up
  4 sick 9 disgusted 11 exasperated

fee
  3 cut, pay, tax 4 bill, cost, dues, hire, toll, wage 5 price 6 charge 7 expense, payment, rake-off, stipend, tuition 8 retainer 9 emolument 10 commission, recompense
  minting: 10 seignorage 11 seigniorage
  wharf: 7 quayage

feeble
  4 puny, weak 5 frail 6 infirm, sickly, weakly 7 doddery 8 decrepit 9 doddering, unhealthy 10 inadequate

feebleminded
  4 daft, dull, slow 5 dense, thick 6 stupid 7 doltish, foolish, idiotic, moronic, witless 8 imbecile, retarded 9 brainless, dim-witted, imbecilic 10 half-witted, slow-witted 11 harebrained, thickheaded

feebleness
7 frailty 8 debility 9 fragility, infirmity 10 enervation, inadequacy 11 decrepitude

feed
3 eat 4 grub, hand, meal 5 feast, gorge, graze, stuff 6 browse, devour, fatten, fodder, ingest, regale, repast, supply, viands 7 banquet, consume, deliver, dish out, edibles, furnish, nourish, nurture, provide, sustain 8 dispense, hand over, victuals 9 partake of, provender, provision, refection 10 provisions

feedback
8 critique, reaction, response 9 criticism 10 evaluation

feed the kitty
4 ante

feel
5 grope, sense, touch 6 caress, fondle, handle, stroke 7 palpate

feeler
4 palp 5 probe 6 palpus 7 antenna 8 proposal, tentacle 12 trial balloon

feeling
3 air 4 aura, mood 5 hunch, sense, touch 6 notion, temper 7 emotion, inkling, opinion, outlook, passion, sensate 8 attitude, instinct, sentient 9 affection, emotional, intuition, semblance, sensation, sentiment, suspicion 10 atmosphere, impression, persuasion 11 affectivity, palpability, sensibility, sensitivity, tangibility

feign
3 act 4 fake, play, sham 5 bluff, put on 6 affect, assume 7 pretend 8 simulate 9 dissemble 11 counterfeit, make believe

feigned
4 fake, sham 5 false, phony, put-on 7 assumed 8 imagined 9 imitation, insincere, pretended, simulated 10 fabricated, fictitious 11 counterfeit

feint
4 fake, hoax, play, ploy, ruse, sham, wile 5 trick 6 gambit 8 maneuver 9 stratagem
hockey: 4 deke

feisty
6 frisky, plucky, spunky, touchy 7 bristly, fidgety 8 petulant, snappish, spirited 9 fractious, irascible 10 aggressive 11 quarrelsome

feldspar
6 albite 8 andesine 9 anorthite, moonstone 10 microcline, orthoclase 11 plagioclase
clay: 6 kaolin

felicitate
6 salute 7 commend 10 compliment 12 congratulate

felicitous
3 apt, fit 4 meet 5 happy 6 proper, timely 7 apropos, fitting 8 apposite, pleasant, suitable 9 agreeable 10 delightful 11 appropriate

feline
3 cat, sly, tom 4 lion, lynx, pard, puma, puss 5 catty, felid, pussy, sleek, tiger 6 bobcat, cougar, jaguar, margay, ocelot, serval, slinky, sneaky, tomcat 7 caracal, catlike, cheetah, furtive, leonine, leopard, lioness, panther, tigress, wildcat 8 pussycat, stealthy
hybrid: 5 liger, tigon 6 tiglon

fell
3 cut, hew, mow 4 down, drop, kill, raze 5 floor 6 poleax 7 cut down, flatten 8 knock off 9 bring down, knock down

Fellini film
8 Amarcord, Casanova, La Strada 9 Satyricon 10 I Vitelloni 11 La Dolce Vita 15 Nights of Cabiria 18 Juliet of the Spirits

fellow
3 bub, guy, joe, lad, man 4 buck, chap, dude, gent, mate, peer, twin 5 bloke, match 6 codger, cohort, hombre, person 7 comrade, consort, partner 8 confrere 9 associate, companion, copartner, gentleman 10 coordinate, reciprocal

fellow feeling
5 agape 7 concern, empathy, rapport 8 affinity, kindness, sympathy 9 affection 10 compassion, kindliness 11 consolation 13 understanding

fellowship
4 club 5 guild 6 league 7 coterie, society, stipend 8 sodality 9 communion, community 10 fraternity 11 association, brotherhood

felon
3 con 7 convict, whitlow 8 criminal 10 malefactor

felt
6 groped, sensed

felt hat
3 fez 5 derby, terai 6 fedora, trilby 7 homburg, stetson 8 snap-brim 9 wideawake

female
4 girl 5 woman 7 girlish, womanly 8 feminine
suffix: 3 ess 4 ette, trix

Feminine Mystique author
7 Friedan (Betty)

feminist
10 suffragist

femme fatale
5 siren 7 Lorelei 8 Mata Hari 9 temptress 10 seductress 11 enchantress

femur
9 thighbone

fen
3 bog 4 mire, quag, wash 5 marsh, swamp 6 morass, muskeg, slough 9 marshland

fence
3 bar, pen 4 cage, rail, pale, weir 5 hedge, parry 6 corral, paling, picket 7 barrier, enclose, railing 8 backstop, boundary, hoarding, palisade, receiver, sidestep, stockade 9 barricade, stone wall

fencer
7 duelist, épéeist 8 foilsman 9 swordsman

fencing
9 swordplay
attack: 5 lunge 6 thrust 7 reprise, riposte
cry: 6 touché
defense: 5 parry
movement: 4 volt
term: 4 jury 5 forte, lunge 6 flèche, foible, touché
touch: 3 cut, hit
weapon: 4 épée, foil 5 blade, guard, saber, sabre 6 pommel

fender
4 skid 5 guard 6 buffer, bumper, shield 7 cushion, railing 8 mudguard

fennec
3 fox

Fenrir
chain: 8 Gleipnir
father: 4 Loki
form: 4 wolf
mother: 9 Angerboda 10 Angerbotha
slayer: 5 Vidar 6 Vithar
victim: 4 Odin

Fenway Park site
6 Boston

feral
4 wild 5 brute 6 brutal, savage 7 beastly, bestial, brutish, inhuman, untamed

Ferber novel
5 Giant, So Big 8 Cimarron, Show Boat 9 Ice Palace 13 Saratoga Trunk

Ferdinand
beloved: 7 Miranda
father: 6 Alonso

Ferdinand, King
conquest: 7 Granada
daughter: 6 Joanna
wife: 8 Germaine, Isabella

fermata
4 hold 5 pause

ferment
4 boil, brew, stir 5 rouse, sweat 6 clamor, enzyme, excite, incite,

leaven, seethe, simmer, unrest, work up **7** smolder, turmoil **9** agitation, commotion **12** restlessness

fermentation
7 zymosis **13** bioconversion

fern
4 tree **5** brake, holly, royal **6** Boston **7** bracken **8** polypody **10** maidenhair, spleenwort
leaf: 5 frond

ferocious
4 fell, grim, wild **5** brute, cruel **6** brutal, fierce, savage **7** bestial, extreme, inhuman, intense, vicious, violent **8** barbaric, inhumane, ruthless **9** barbarous, rapacious, truculent

ferret out
4 find **5** dig up, flush **6** elicit **7** unearth **8** discover **9** ascertain

ferrule
3 cap, tip **4** band, ring, virl **6** collet

ferry
5 carry **6** convey **7** shuttle **9** transport

ferryman
6 Charon **9** gondolier

fertile
4 lush, rich **6** fecund **8** abundant, creative, fruitful, pregnant, prolific **9** bountiful, ingenious, inventive, luxuriant, plenteous **10** productive **12** reproductive

fertilize
5 beget, breed **6** enrich **8** generate **9** fecundate, pollinate **10** impregnate, inseminate

fertilizer
4 dung **5** guano, mulch **6** manure **7** compost **9** plant food

ferule
3 rod **5** stick

fervent
3 hot **4** keen **5** eager, fiery **6** ardent, devout, gung-ho **7** blazing, burning, earnest, glowing, intense, zealous **8** vehement **9** heartfelt **10** hot-blooded, passionate **11** impassioned, warm-blooded **12** enthusiastic, wholehearted

fervor
4 fire, heat, zeal **5** ardor **6** warmth **7** passion **8** devotion, violence **9** vehemence **10** devoutness, enthusiasm

fescennine
7 obscene **10** scurrilous

fess up
3 own **5** admit **9** come clean

fester
3 rot **6** rankle **7** inflame, putrefy **8** ulcerate **9** suppurate

festina ____
5 lente

festival
4 fair, fete, gala **5** feast **6** fiesta **7** jubilee **8** carnival, jamboree **11** celebration, merrymaking

festive
3 gay **4** gala **5** jolly, merry **6** joyful, joyous **7** gleeful **8** mirthful **11** celebratory

festivity
4 bash, fair, fete, gala **5** feast, party, revel **6** affair, frolic, gaiety **7** blowout, revelry, whoopee **8** carnival, jamboree **9** rejoicing, merriment **11** celebration, merrymaking

festoon
4 deck, hang **5** adorn **6** bedeck **7** garland **8** decorate, ornament **9** embellish

fetch
3 get **4** draw, earn **5** bring, yield **6** take in **7** attract, bring in, realize **8** retrieve

fetching
4 fair **6** comely, lovely, pretty **7** winsome **8** alluring, charming, enticing, engaging, handsome, pleasing **9** appealing **10** attractive

fete
4 ball, bash, fair, gala **5** feast, honor,

party **6** affair, fiesta, soiree **7** banquet, jubilee, shindig **8** carnival, festival, jamboree, wingding **9** celebrate, entertain **11** celebration, commemorate **13** entertainment

fetid
4 foul, high, rank **5** funky **6** putrid, rancid, smelly, strong **8** mephitic, stinking **10** malodorous

fetish
4 idol, juju, luck **5** charm **6** amulet **7** periapt **8** fixation, gris-gris, talisman **10** phylactery

fetor
4 odor, reek **5** stink **6** stench

fetter
3 tie **4** bind, bond, gyve **5** chain, check, irons **6** hobble, hog-tie, impede **7** enchain, manacle, shackle, trammel **8** handcuff, restrain **9** restraint

fettle
5 shape **6** health **7** fitness **9** condition **12** constitution

feud
6 enmity, strife **7** dispute, quarrel **8** argument, vendetta **9** hostility **11** controversy

feudal
estate: 3 fee **4** feud, fief
jurisdiction: 4 soke
laborer: 4 serf
lord: 5 laird, liege, thane **8** suzerain
status: 9 vassalage
tax: 7 tallage
tenant: 6 vassal **7** homager, socager, vavasor **8** vavasour
tenure of land: 6 socage
tribute: 6 heriot

feuilleton
5 essay

fever
4 ague, fire, heat **5** flush, Lassa **6** dengue, frenzy **7** ferment, passion, pyrexia **8** delirium **9** calenture
recurrent: 7 malaria, quartan, tertian

fevered
6 crazed, heated **7** burning, febrile, flushed **8** agitated, frenetic, restless **9** delirious **10** distracted, overheated **11** overwrought

feverish
3 hot **5** fiery **6** hectic **7** burning, febrile, flushed, pyretic **8** frenetic, frenzied **10** passionate **11** overwrought

fever tree
6 acacia **7** blue gum

few
4 rare **5** scant **6** meager, meagre, scanty, scarce, sparse **7** handful, limited **8** sporadic **9** scattered **10** infrequent, occasional, scattering, smattering, spattering, sprinkling
combining form: 4 olig **5** oligo

fey
4 daft **5** campy, crazy, vatic **7** touched **8** oracular, precious **9** pixilated, prophetic, sibylline, visionary **11** clairvoyant **12** otherworldly

———-fi
3 sci

fiasco
3 dud **4** bomb, flop **5** farce, flask **6** bottle, defeat **7** blunder, debacle, failure, washout **8** abortion, disaster **11** miscarriage **13** embarrassment

fiat
5 edict, order **6** decree **7** command, dictate, mandate, warrant **8** sanction **11** endorsement **12** proclamation **13** authorization

fib
3 lie **4** tale **5** story **7** falsify, falsity, untruth **9** falsehood, mendacity **10** taradiddle **11** fabrication, prevaricate

fiber
3 web **4** noil, pita **5** grain, istle **6** fabric, strand, thread **7** texture
basketry: 5 istle
brain: 4 pons

coarse: 4 jute 8 piassava
coconut husk: 4 coir
rope: 4 bast, hemp 5 sisal 8 henequen
silky: 5 kapok
small: 6 fibril
substructure: 7 micelle, spongin
synthetic: 5 nylon, Orlon, rayon, saran, vinal 6 Dacron 7 spandex
woody: 4 bast
woollike: 7 lanital

fibrous
4 ropy, wiry 5 tough, woody 6 sinewy 7 stringy

fibula
4 bone 5 clasp

fichu
5 scarf

fickle
7 flighty 8 unstable, variable, volatile 9 mercurial 10 capricious, changeable, inconstant, unfaithful, unreliable 12 undependable 13 temperamental, unpredictable

fiction
4 tale, yarn 5 fable, story 7 fantasy, figment 8 pretense 9 fish story, invention, narrative 10 concoction 11 fabrication

fictional
6 made-up, unreal 8 notional 9 imaginary 11 make-believe 12 supposititious

fictitious
4 fake, mock, sham 5 bogus, faked, false, phony 6 ersatz, made-up, unreal, untrue 7 assumed, created 8 cooked-up, fanciful, illusory, imagined, invented, mythical, spurious 9 concocted, fantastic, imaginary, simulated, trumped-up 10 apocryphal, artificial, chimerical, fabricated 11 make-believe 12 supposititious

fiddle
3 toy 4 play, rack 5 alter, cheat 6 dawdle, diddle, doodle, finger, meddle, monkey, potter, putter, tamper, tinker, trifle, violin 7 swindle 9 interfere 10 fool around, manipulate, mess around

fiddle-faddle
3 rot 4 bosh, bull, bunk, nuts 5 fudge, drool, hokum, hooey 6 bunkum, drivel, hoodoo, humbug, piffle 7 baloney, blarney, hogwash, rubbish, twaddle 8 nonsense, pishposh, tommyrot 9 poppycock 10 applesauce, balderdash, flapdoodle

_____ Fideles
6 Adeste, Semper

Fidelio
composer: 9 Beethoven (Ludwig van)
hero: 9 Florestan
heroine: 7 Leonora

fidelity
5 ardor, piety, troth 6 fealty 7 loyalty 8 devotion 9 adherence, constancy 10 allegiance, attachment 11 staunchness 12 faithfulness 13 dependability, steadfastness

fidget
6 fantod, fiddle, jitter, squirm, twitch 7 wriggle

fidgety
5 antsy, jumpy 6 uneasy 7 jittery, nervous, restive, squirmy, twitchy 8 restless

field
3 lea 4 area, mead, turf 5 green, milpa, orbit, range 6 domain, meadow, métier, region, sphere 7 demesne, pasture, purview, terrain 8 dominion, gridiron, precinct, vocation 9 bailiwick, champaign, specialty, territory 10 department, discipline, occupation

field crop
3 hay 4 corn, oats 5 grain, wheat 6 cotton 7 alfalfa 8 soybeans

field deity
3 Pan 4 Faun 5 Fauna 6 Faunus

field glasses
10 binoculars

field hand
4 hoer 5 sower 6 picker 7 laborer, planter

Fielding novel
6 Amelia 8 Tom Jones 13 Joseph Andrews

field marshal
Austrian: 8 Radetzky (Joseph)
British: 6 Napier (Robert), Raglan (Baron), Wavell (Archibald), Wilson (Henry) 7 Roberts (Frederick) 8 Wolseley (Garnet) 9 Kitchener (Horatio) 10 Montgomery (Bernard)
French: 4 Foch (Ferdinand) 6 Joffre (Joseph-Jacques-Césaire), Pétain (Philippe)
German: 6 Keitel (Wilhelm), Paulus (Friedrich), Rommel (Erwin), Rupert (Prince) 9 Mackensen (August von), Rundstedt (Karl von), Waldersee (Alfred von) 10 Kesselring (Albert)
Japanese: 8 Sugiyama (Hajime)
Prussian: 6 Moltke (Helmuth von)
Russian: 7 Kutuzov (Mikhail), Suvorov (Aleksandr) 8 Potemkin (Grigory)

field mouse
4 vole

field officer
5 major 7 colonel

fiend
3 bug, imp, nut 5 demon, devil, freak, Satan 6 addict, Belial, diablo, maniac, zealot 7 devotee, fanatic, habitué, Lucifer, monster, Old Nick, serpent 8 Apollyon, succubus 9 Beelzebub 10 enthusiast, Old Scratch 13 Old Gooseberry

fiendish
3 bad 4 evil 5 cruel 6 malign, savage, wicked 7 baleful, demonic, hellish, inhuman, malefic, satanic, vicious 8 demoniac, devilish, diabolic, infernal, sinister 9 barbarous, difficult, ferocious, malicious, malignant 10 diabolical

fierce
4 fell, grim, wild 5 cruel 6 brutal, savage, wicked 7 brutish, hostile, inhuman, intense, vicious, violent, wolfish 8 inhumane, pitiless, ruthless, terrible, vehement 9 barbarous, bellicose, ferocious, merciless, truculent 10 aggressive, determined

fiery
3 hot, red 5 afire 6 ablaze, aflame, ardent, fervid, fierce, heated, red-hot, torrid 7 burning, febrile, fervent, flaming, flaring, igneous, intense, peppery 8 broiling, feverish, spirited, vehement, white-hot 9 flammable, hotheaded, irritable, perfervid 10 mettlesome, passionate 11 combustible, inflammable, impassioned

fiesta
4 fete 5 party 6 frolic 8 carnival, festival, jamboree 9 merriment

fife
4 pipe 5 flute

fifth
combining form: 5 quint

fig
genus: 5 Ficus
sacred: 5 pipal
variety: 5 elemi 6 Smyrna

fight
3 row, war 4 bout, buck, duel, feud, fray, spat, tiff 5 brawl, broil, clash, joust, match, melee, repel, scrap, set-to 6 affray, attack, battle, combat, fracas, oppose, oppugn, resist, rumble, tussle 7 contend, contest, dispute, quarrel, scuffle, wrangle, wrestle 8 conflict, skirmish, slugfest, squabble, struggle, traverse 10 aggression, donnybrook, free-for-all 11 altercation

fighter
3 pug 5 boxer 7 brawler, soldier, warrior 8 champion, pugilist, scrapper 9 combatant, gladiator, man-at-arms, mercenary 11 interceptor

fighter plane
3 MiG, Roc 4 Zero 5 Sabre 6 bomber, Fokker, Hawker, Mirage, Voodoo 7 Corsair, Harrier 8 Spitfire 11 interceptor

fighting fish
5 betta

figment
5 dream, fable, fancy 7 chimera, fiction 8 daydream, illusion, phantasm 9 invention, unreality 11 contrivance, fabrication

figure
3 add, sum, tot 4 cast, form, mold, rule, tote 5 count, digit, frame, image, model, motif, shape, total 6 cipher, decide, design, device, effigy, motive, number, reckon, settle, symbol 7 compute, integer, numeral, outline, pattern, resolve 8 conclude, estimate, physique 9 calculate, character, determine, enumerate
geometric: 4 cone, cube 5 rhomb 6 circle, isogon, square 7 decagon, ellipse, hexagon, nonagon, octagon, polygon, rhombus 8 pentacle, pentagon, rhomboid, tetragon, triangle 9 rectangle 10 hexahedron, octahedron 11 icosahedron 12 dodecahedron, rhombohedron
human: 4 nude 5 atlas 7 telamon 8 caryatid
ornamental: 6 statue 8 gargoyle

figurehead
4 pawn, tool 5 front 6 minion, puppet 7 cat's-paw 8 creature 10 instrument, mouthpiece

figure of speech
5 trope 6 aporia, simile 7 litotes 8 metaphor, metonymy 10 synecdoche

figure out
5 crack, learn, solve 6 decide, decode, fathom 7 resolve, unravel 8 decipher, discover, unriddle 9 ascertain, determine

figure skating
jump: 4 axel, loop, lutz 5 split 6 rocker 7 bracket, counter, salchow 11 spreadeagle
spin: 5 camel

figurine
9 statuette

Fiji
capital: 4 Suva
explorer: 4 Cook (Capt. James) 6 Tasman (Abel)
island: 3 Gau 4 Koro 6 Ovalau 8 Viti Levu 9 Vanua Levu
island group: 3 Lau 6 Yasawa
language: 6 Fijian 7 English
monetary unit: 6 dollar
neighbor: 5 Samoa 7 Vanuatu

filch
3 cop, nip 4 crib, lift, take 5 boost, pinch, steal, swipe 6 pilfer, snitch 7 purloin

file
3 row, rub 4 line, rank, rasp, tier 5 lodge, march, place, queue 6 smooth 7 archive, arrange, corrupt, dossier 10 emery board

filial
5 sonly 7 duteous, dutiful

filibuster
5 delay, stall 10 adventurer

filigree
4 lace 6 design 7 pattern 8 fretwork, openwork, ornament 10 decoration 13 embellishment, ornamentation

fill
3 jam 4 clog, cloy, cram, glut, heap, lade, load, pack, pile, plug, sate, stop 5 block, choke, close, gorge, stock, stuff 6 charge, stodge 7 congest, engorge, inflate, occlude, pervade, satiate, satisfy, stopper, surfeit 8 permeate
interstices: 4 calk 5 caulk, chink, putty

filled
5 awash, flush, sated 6 packed 7 replete 9 saturated

filler
5 squib 7 packing, padding, tobacco, wadding 8 stuffing

fillet
4 band 5 slice, snood, strip 6 ribbon, stripe 7 bandeau, banding 8 headband

anatomical: 9 lemniscus
architectural: 6 listel, reglet, taenia
meat: 10 tenderloin

fill in
3 sub 4 clew, clue, post 6 advise, detail, insert, notify 7 apprise 8 acquaint, complete 10 substitute

fill-in
3 sub 4 temp 6 backup 7 stopgap 9 alternate, expedient, makeshift, surrogate, temporary 10 substitute 11 locum tenens, pinch hitter, replacement, succedaneum

fillip
3 tap 4 goad, kick, spur 5 boost, tonic 6 buffet, strike 7 impetus, wrinkle 8 catalyst, stimulus 9 incentive, stimulant, stimulate 10 inducement, motivation 13 embellishment

film
4 coat, scum, show, skim, skin 5 flick, glaze, layer, movie, Mylar, shoot 6 cinema, lamina, patina 7 tarnish 8 membrane, pellicle 9 celluloid, photoplay 11 picture show 13 motion picture, moving picture

filmy
4 hazy 5 gauzy, misty, sheer, wispy 6 dainty 8 delicate, gossamer 10 diaphanous 11 transparent

fils
3 son

filter
4 sift 5 clean, leach, sieve 6 purify, refine, screen, strain 7 clarify, cleanse 9 percolate

filth
4 crud, dirt, dung, muck, slop, smut 5 dreck, grime, slime, trash 6 ordure, refuse, sludge 7 squalor 9 obscenity

filthy
4 base, foul, vile 5 black, dirty, grimy, gross, gunky, mucky, muddy, nasty 6 coarse, cruddy, grubby, ribald, scuzzy, skanky, smutty, sordid 7 obscene, raunchy, squalid, unclean 8 indecent 9 loathsome, offensive, repulsive, revolting 12 scatological

filthy lucre
4 cash, loot, pelf 5 bread, bucks, dough, money, moola 6 boodle, riches, moolah, wampum 7 cabbage, scratch 8 currency

fin
3 arm 4 bill 5 fiver, pinna 7 airfoil, flipper
type: 6 caudal, dorsal 7 ventral 8 pectoral

finagle
5 cheat, trick 6 wangle 7 snaffle, swindle, wheedle 8 fast-talk, maneuver, scrounge 9 bamboozle, machinate

final
3 end 4 last 6 ending, latest 7 closing 8 hindmost, terminal, ultimate 10 concluding, conclusive, definitive 11 examination

finale
3 end 4 coda 5 close, finis 6 capper, climax, ending, payoff, windup, wrap-up 7 closing 10 conclusion, denouement 11 culmination, termination

finalize
3 end 5 close, sew up, tie up 6 decide, finish, wind up, wrap up 7 approve 8 complete, conclude, solidify 9 terminate 10 consummate

finally
6 at last, lastly 7 someday 8 at length 9 belatedly 10 at long last, eventually, ultimately 12 subsequently

finance
4 back, bank, fund 5 endow, funds, money, stake 6 credit 7 banking, promote, revenue, sponsor, support 8 bankroll 9 grubstake, patronize, subsidize 10 capitalize, investment, underwrite

financial
6 fiscal, pocket 8 business, economic, monetary 9 pecuniary 10 commercial
plan: 6 budget
statement: 12 balance sheet

financier

American: 4 Hill (James Jerome), Ryan (Thomas Fortune), Sage (Russell) 5 Astor (John Jacob), Baker (George Fisher), Eaton (Cyrus), Field (Cyrus West), Gould (Jay), Grace (William Russell), Green (Hetty) 6 Biddle (Nicholas), Boesky (Ivan), Girard (Stephen), Mellon (Andrew), Morgan (John Pierpont, Junius Spencer), Morris (Robert), Rogers (Henry Huttleston), Yerkes (Charles Tyson) 7 Peabody (George) 10 Vanderbilt (Cornelius, William)
British: 6 Baring (Alexander), Rhodes (Cecil) 7 Gresham (Thomas)
French: 6 Necker (Jacques) 7 Colbert (Jean-Baptiste)
German: 7 Schacht (Hjalmar) 10 Rothschild (Amschel, Jakob, Karl, Mayer, Nathan, Salomon)

finch

4 pape 5 junco, serin, zebra 6 canary, linnet, siskin, towhee 7 bunting, chewink, redpoll, sparrow 8 cardinal, grosbeak, longspur 9 crossbill, seedeater

find

3 gem 4 gain, meet, spot 5 catch, dig up, hit on, reach, sight 6 attain, detect, locate, supply, turn up 7 discern, furnish, scare up, uncover, unearth 8 bump into, come upon, discover, meet with, perceive, treasure 9 determine, discovery, encounter 10 experience 13 treasure trove

find out

4 hear 5 catch, learn 6 detect 7 catch on 8 discover, perceive 9 ascertain, determine

fine

3 end, top 4 fair, keen, levy, pure, thin 5 bonny, close, clear, dandy, mulct, sheer 6 amerce, choice, minute, ornate, punish, purify, subtle 7 clarion, damages, elegant, forfeit, penalty 8 all right, delicate, penalize, pleasant, splendid, superior 9 beautiful, enjoyable, excellent, first-rate 10 punishment, reparation

finery

5 array 6 attire 7 apparel, regalia 8 clothing, frippery, glad rags, ornament 9 caparison, full dress, trappings, trimmings 10 decoration, Sunday best

finesse

5 dodge, evade, skill, skirt 6 jockey 7 beguile, cunning, exploit 8 maneuver, subtlety 9 dexterity 10 adroitness, artfulness, manipulate

Fingal's Cave island

6 Staffa

finger

5 blame, digit, index, pinky, strum, touch 6 accuse, pinkie 7 palpate 8 identify, pinpoint
bone: 7 phalanx
combining form: 6 dactyl

finicky

5 fussy, picky 6 choosy, dainty, prissy 7 choosey 8 exacting 9 squeamish 10 fastidious, meticulous, particular, pernickety 11 persnickety

finis

3 end 5 close 6 finale 10 completion, conclusion

finish

3 end 4 do in, kill, slay, stop 5 cease, close, glaze, use up 6 cut off, ending, finale, murder, patina, polish, windup, wrap up 7 closing, consume, destroy, execute, exhaust, surface 8 complete, conclude, dispatch, finalize, terminus 9 cessation, liquidate, terminate 10 completion, conclusion, denouement, run through 11 termination
dull: 3 mat 4 matt 5 matte
second: 5 place
third: 4 show

finished

4 done, over, ripe 5 ideal 7 done for, perfect, refined, through 8 achieved, complete, over with, polished, washed-up 9 perfected 10 consummate

finite
5 bound, fixed 7 bounded, limited, precise 9 definable 10 restricted 12 determinable

fink
3 rat 5 Judas 6 betray, snitch, squeal 7 traitor 8 betrayer, informer, quisling, snitcher 11 backstabber 13 strikebreaker

Finland
5 Suomi
Arctic region: 7 Lapland
capital: 8 Helsinki
city: 5 Espoo, Turku 6 Vantaa 7 Tampere
ethnic group: 4 Lapp, Sami
gulf: 7 Bothnia
invader: 9 Alexander
island: 5 Karlö 6 Kimito 9 Vallgrund
island group: 5 Åland
lake: 5 Inari 6 Saimaa 7 Keitele 8 Pielinen
language: 7 Finnish, Swedish
monetary unit: 4 euro
monetary unit, former: 6 markka
neighbor: 6 Norway, Russia, Sweden

Finlandia composer
8 Sibelius (Jean)

Finnigans Wake author
5 Joyce (James)

Finnish
bath: 5 sauna
epic: 8 Kalevala
god: 6 Jumala

fir
4 pine 6 balsam, Fraser 7 conifer, Douglas 9 evergreen
genus: 5 Abies

fire
3 can, pep, vim, zip 4 bake, brio, burn, cast, dash, hurl, sack, stir, toss, zeal, zest, zing 5 ardor, blaze, drive, flame, flare, fling, glare, ingle, light, pitch, rouse, salvo, shoot, spark, throw, torch, verve, vigor 6 arouse, energy, excite, fervor, flames, ignite, kindle, spirit 7 animate, boot out, dismiss, enthuse, inferno, inflame, inspire, kick out, passion, provoke 8 enkindle 9 calenture, discharge, holocaust, terminate 10 combustion, enthusiasm, liveliness 13 conflagration
combining form: 3 pyr 4 igni, pyro
god: 4 Agni, Loki 6 Vulcan 10 Hephaestus

firearm
see **gun**

firebrand
8 agitator 10 incendiary, instigator

firebug
5 torch 8 arsonist 10 incendiary, pyromaniac

firecracker
5 squib 6 banger 9 explosive 10 cherry bomb, noisemaker

firedog
7 andiron

firedrake
6 dragon

firefly
12 lightning bug

fire opal
7 girasol

fireplace
5 grate, ingle
equipment: 6 fender, screen 7 andiron
part: 3 hob 6 hearth, mantel

fireplug
7 hydrant

fire up
5 anger, annoy, rouse, spark 6 excite, ignite, incite, kindle 7 enliven, inflame, inspire, provoke 8 enkindle, irritate

firework
6 petard, rocket 8 pinwheel, sparkler 11 pyrotechnic, Roman candle
cluster: 9 girandole

firkin
3 keg, tun, vat 4 butt, cask, pipe 6 barrel, vessel 8 hogshead

firm

3 set **4** fast, hard, sure **5** fixed, rigid, solid, sound, stiff, tight, tough **6** harden, outfit, secure, settle, stable, steady, strong, sturdy **7** abiding, adamant, certain, company, concern, improve, settled, staunch, unmoved **8** business, constant, definite, enduring, faithful, resolute, specific, vigorous **9** steadfast, tenacious **10** determined, enterprise, inflexible, stipulated, strengthen, unwavering, unyielding **11** established, partnership, substantial, unfaltering, well-founded **13** establishment

firmament

3 sky **5** vault **6** sphere, welkin **7** expanse, heavens **8** empyrean

firmness

7 resolve **8** decision, security, solidity, strength, tenacity **9** constancy, stability **10** durability, resolution **13** determination

first

4 arch, head **5** alpha, chief, prime **6** maiden, primal **7** highest, initial, leading, lead-off, opening, pioneer, premier, primary, supreme **8** champion, dominant, earliest, foremost, headmost, original **9** inaugural, initially, paramount, principal, sovereign **10** aboriginal, preeminent, primordial
prefix: 4 prot **5** proto

firstborn

4 heir **6** eldest, oldest

first-class

3 top **4** A-one, best, fine **5** prime **6** tip-top **7** capital, supreme **8** five-star, superior, top-notch **9** excellent, top-drawer

firsthand

6 direct **7** primary **9** immediate

first man in space

7 Gagarin (Yury)

first showing

5 debut **7** opening **8** premiere

First State

8 Delaware

firth

3 arm, bay **4** cove, gulf **5** inlet **6** harbor, slough **7** estuary

fiscal

8 monetary **9** budgetary, financial

fish

3 bob, net **4** cast, gill, hint **5** angle, seine, trawl, troll **7** gillnet, sniggle
angler: 9 goosefish
aquarium: 4 barb **5** betta, danio, guppy, platy, tetra **7** cichlid, gourami, rasbora **8** goldfish **9** angelfish
basket: 5 creel
catfish: 8 bullhead, hornpout
cod: 4 cusk, hake, ling **6** burbot, tomcod **7** pollack, pollock
combining form: 6 ichthy
croaker: 4 drum **7** corbina **8** kingfish, sea trout, weakfish **10** squeteague
eellike: 5 moray **6** conger **7** hagfish, lamprey
eggs: 3 roe **5** spawn
electric: 7 torpedo **9** stargazer
flatfish: 3 dab **4** butt, dace, sole **5** bream, brill, fluke **6** plaice, turbot **7** halibut **8** flounder
food: 3 cod, eel **4** bass, carp, cero, hake, ling, scup, shad, sole, tuna **5** jurel, perch, scrod, skate, smelt, trout **6** bonito, caviar, kipper, mullet, plaice, pompon, salmon, tautog, wrasse **7** alewife, catfish, cavalla, escolar, grouper, haddock, halibut, herring, pollack, pollock, pompano, sardine, sea carp, snapper **8** brisling, crevalle, flounder, mackerel
game: 4 bass, pike, tuna **5** cobia, perch, trout **6** grilse, marlin, salmon, tarpon **8** pickerel **9** swordfish
grunt: 7 pigfish
herring: 4 shad, sild **5** sprat **7** alewife, sardine **8** brisling, pilchard
kind: 3 gar, ray **4** bass, cero, chub, dory, goby, jack, opah, pike, rudd, scup, tuna **5** bream, cisco, loach, perch, porgy, shark, skate, smelt, snook, tench, tunny, wahoo **6** blenny, bonito, dorado, marlin, minnow,

mullet, permit, puffer, remora, sauger, sucker, tarpon, tautog, warsaw, wrasse 7 anchovy, buffalo, capelin, cavalla, chimera, cowfish, crappie, dolphin, grunion, haddock, hogfish, jewfish, mudfish, oarfish, piranha, pupfish, sardine, sawfish, sculpin, snapper, sunfish, tilapia, whiting 8 albacore, blowfish, bluefish, bluegill, bonefish, chimaera, filefish, gambusia, grayling, halfbeak, ladyfish, lookdown, lumpfish, lungfish, mackerel, menhaden, moonfish, pickerel, pipefish, rockfish, sailfish, seahorse, skipjack, stingray, sturgeon, tilefish, warmouth, wolffish 9 amberjack, barracuda, greenling, jacksmelt, killifish, mummichog, pilotfish, spadefish, swordfish, topminnow, trunkfish, whitebait, whitefish 10 butterfish, flying fish, needlefish, parrotfish, silverside, tripletail, yellowtail 11 muskellunge, pumpkinseed, stickleback, triggerfish 12 schoolmaster
luminescent: 11 hatchetfish, lanternfish
minnow: 3 koi 4 carp, chub, dace 6 shiner
pan: 5 bream, perch, trout 7 crappie, sunfish 8 bluegill, rock bass 11 pumpkinseed
porgy: 4 scup 7 pinfish 10 sheepshead
relating to: 7 piscine
rockfish: 8 bocaccio, lionfish, rosefish
salmon: 3 dog 4 chum, coho 6 sebago 7 chinook, sockeye
spear: 3 gig 7 harpoon, trident
stew: 8 cioppino, matelote 13 bouillabaisse
trap: 4 weir
trout: 4 char 5 charr 7 rainbow 9 cutthroat 11 Dolly Varden
voracious: 6 caribe 7 piranha
young: 3 fry 4 parr 5 larva, smolt 6 alevin, grilse

fisherman
6 angler

fish hawk
6 osprey

fishhook
adjunct: 5 snell
part: 4 barb 5 shank

fishing line
4 trot 7 setline 8 longline, trotline
float: 3 bob 5 quill
leader: 5 snell

fishing lure
3 fly 4 bait 5 spoon 7 spinner

fishing net
5 seine, trawl

fishlike mammal
4 orca 5 whale 6 dugong, sea cow 7 dolphin, grampus, manatee, narwhal 8 cetacean, porpoise

fish story
3 fib, lie 4 bunk, yarn 11 fabrication 12 exaggeration 13 overstatement

fishwife
5 harpy, scold, shrew, vixen 6 virago 9 termagant, Xanthippe

fishy
7 dubious, suspect 8 doubtful, unlikely 9 ambiguous, dubitable, equivocal, uncertain 10 suspicious 11 problematic 12 questionable

fission element
7 uranium 9 plutonium

fissure
3 gap 4 gash, hole, part, rent, rift 5 break, chasm, chink, cleft, crack, split 6 breach, cleave, divide, schism 7 crevice, discord, opening, rupture 8 crevasse, fracture 10 disharmony, separation

fist
4 duke, grip, hand 5 clamp, grasp 6 clench, clinch, clutch

fit
3 apt, set 4 hale, jibe, just, sane, suit, turn 5 adapt, agree, frame, ready, sound, spasm, spell, tally, throe 6 access, accord, adjust, attack, become, belong, decent, go with, proper, seemly, square, tailor, useful 7 capable, conform, healthy, prepare, qualify, seizure, tantrum

8 assemble, decorous, dovetail, eligible, paroxysm, suitable **9** agree with, congruous, consonant, harmonize, reconcile **10** applicable, convenient, correspond, felicitous, go together **11** accommodate, appropriate

fitful
6 random, spotty **7** erratic **8** periodic, sporadic, variable **9** haphazard, hit-or-miss, irregular, spasmodic, uncertain **10** changeable, convulsive, herky-jerky, inconstant **12** intermittent

fitness
4 trim **5** order, shape **6** fettle, health, kilter, repair **7** account, decorum, service, utility **8** capacity **9** condition, propriety, relevance **11** eligibility, suitability **13** applicability

fit out
3 arm, rig **5** equip **6** outfit **7** appoint, furnish **8** accouter, accoutre

fitting
3 apt, due **4** able, just, meet, part, true **5** happy, right **6** proper, seemly **7** apropos, germane **8** apposite, relevant, suitable **9** accessory, befitting, pertinent, qualified **10** applicable, attachment, felicitous, harmonious **11** appropriate

fit together
4 hook, join, mesh **6** hook up **7** connect **8** dovetail **9** integrate

Fitzgerald novel
10 Last Tycoon (The) **11** Great Gatsby (The) **16** Tender Is the Night **17** Tales of the Jazz Age **18** This Side of Paradise **17** All the Sad Young Men **21** Beautiful and the Damned (The)

five
combining form: **4** pent **5** penta **6** quinqu **7** quinque
group of: **6** pentad **7** quintet

five-dollar bill
3 fin

fivefold
9 quintuple

Five Nations
8 Iroquois
member: **7** Cayugas, Mohawks, Oneidas, Senecas **9** Onondagas

five-sided figure
8 pentagon

five-star
6 deluxe, superb **8** superior, top-notch **9** excellent, first-rate **10** first-class **11** outstanding

five-year period
6 luster, lustre **7** lustrum

fix
3 jam, rig, set **4** cook, cure, geld, mend, mess, moor, root, spay, spot, work **5** affix, alter, catch, patch, ready, renew, rivet, solve, state, stick **6** adjust, anchor, assign, attach, change, decide, doctor, fasten, neuter, pickle, plight, repair, revamp, scrape, secure, settle, square, steady **7** appoint, arrange, correct, dilemma, resolve, restore, specify, work out **8** castrate, discover, overhaul, position, renovate, solution **9** condition, establish, stabilize, sterilize **11** predicament

fixation
5 craze, mania **6** fetish **9** obsession **11** fascination, infatuation

____ fixe
4 idée, prix

fixed
3 pat, set **4** fast, firm, sure **6** frozen, secure, stable, stated, steady **7** abiding, certain, limited, precise, settled **8** constant, definite, enduring, immobile, resolute **9** exclusive, immovable, immutable, permanent, steadfast, tenacious **10** inflexible, invariable, restricted, stationary, stipulated, unswerving, unwavering **11** determinate, unalterable **12** concentrated, unchangeable **13** circumscribed

fizz
4 buzz, foam, hiss 5 froth 6 bubble, spirit 7 bubbles, sparkle, sputter 10 effervesce, liveliness 13 effervescence

fizzle
4 bomb, fail, flop 6 fiasco 7 failure, misfire 8 miscarry, peter out 10 effervesce 11 fall through

fjord
Baffin Island: 9 Admiralty
Denmark: 3 Ise, Lim 5 Lamme
Iceland: 4 Axar, Eyja 5 Horna, Skaga, Vopna
Norway: 3 Tys 4 Bokn, Nord, Salt, Stor, Tana, Vest 5 Lakse, Ranen, Sogne 9 Stavanger, Trondheim
Spitsbergen: 3 Ice
Svalbard: 4 Stor

flab
3 fat 4 bulk, lard 5 flesh 7 blubber, fatness 9 cellulite 10 corpulence 11 love handles

flabbergast
3 awe 4 stun 5 amaze, shock, throw 7 astound, nonplus 8 astonish, bowl over, surprise 9 dumbfound, overwhelm

flabby
see **flaccid**

flaccid
4 limp, soft, weak 6 feeble, flabby, floppy 8 flexible

flag
3 ebb, lag, sag, tag 4 fade, fail, hail, iris, jack, sign, swag, tail, tire, waft, wane, wave, wilt 5 abate, color, droop, stone 6 banner, burgee, colors, ensign, pennon, signal, weaken 7 bunting, decline, pendant, pennant 8 bannerol, gonfalon, languish, Old Glory, penalize, registry, standard, streamer, tricolor 9 banderole, blue peter, oriflamme, Union Jack 10 Jolly Roger 11 deteriorate 12 Stars and Bars

flagellate
4 beat, flog, hide, lash, whip 5 whale

6 larrup, lather, stripe, switch, thrash 7 scourge 9 horsewhip

flagitious
4 evil 6 sinful, wicked 7 corrupt, vicious 8 criminal, depraved, infamous, perverse, shameful 9 miscreant, nefarious, perverted 10 degenerate, scandalous, villainous 11 disgraceful

flagon
3 jug 4 ewer 5 stoup 6 vessel 7 tankard

flagpole
4 mast 5 staff
rope: 7 halyard

flagrant
4 bold, rank 5 gross 6 wanton 7 blatant, glaring, heinous, obvious 8 striking 9 atrocious, egregious, monstrous 10 outrageous 11 conspicuous

flagstone
5 shale, slate

flag-waver
7 patriot 8 jingoist, loyalist 10 chauvinist 11 nationalist 12 superpatriot

flail
4 club, beat, flog, whip 6 strike, thrash, thresh 7 scourge 8 flounder, thresher

flair
4 bent, chic, élan, gift 5 knack, style 6 genius, talent 7 ability, aptness, faculty 8 aptitude, tendency 10 proclivity 11 inclination

flak
4 fire 5 abuse 6 shells 7 censure, vitriol 9 brickbats, criticism, hostility 10 opposition 11 disapproval 12 condemnation, fault-finding

flake
3 bit 4 chip, kook, peel 5 scale 6 lamina 7 oddball 8 crackpot, fragment 9 eccentric

flake off
4 chip, peel 5 scale 9 exfoliate 10 desquamate

flaky
3 odd 5 goofy, nutty, wacky, weird 6 fickle, screwy 7 bizarre, erratic, offbeat 9 eccentric

flambé
6 ablaze, aflame, alight 7 blazing, flaming

flamboyant
4 loud 5 gaudy, showy 6 flashy, florid, ornate, rococo 7 baroque, splashy 8 colorful, luscious 10 over-the-top 12 ostentatious

flame
4 beau, dear, fire, glow, love 5 ardor, blaze, flare, flash, honey, light, lover 7 beloved, darling, passion, sweetie 8 ladylove, truelove 9 boyfriend, inamorata, inamorato 10 brilliance, brightness, girlfriend, heartthrob, sweetheart

flamen
6 priest

flaming
5 afire, fiery 6 ablaze, alight, ardent, red-hot 7 blazing, burning, fervent, flaring, ignited, intense 10 hot-blooded, passionate 11 conflagrant, impassioned

flammable
8 burnable 9 ignitable 10 incendiary 11 combustible
liquid: 3 gas, oil 7 acetone, alcohol, ethanol 8 gasoline, kerosene 9 petroleum 10 turpentine

Flanders
capital: 5 Lille
language: 7 Flemish

flaneur
12 boulevardier, man-about-town

flank
4 abut, side 6 adjoin, border

flap
3 tab, tap 4 beat, flog, fold, slap, stew, wave, wing 5 fling, panel 6 crisis, dither, lather, pother, tumult, uproar 7 aileron, flutter, turmoil 9 agitation, commotion, confusion

flapdoodle
3 rot 4 bosh, bull, nuts 5 drool, fudge, hokum, hooey 6 bunkum, drivel 7 baloney, blarney, hogwash, rubbish 8 malarkey, nonsense, tommyrot 9 poppycock 10 applesauce, balderdash 12 blatherskite, fiddle-faddle, fiddlesticks

flapjack
7 hotcake, pancake 11 griddle cake

flare
4 burn 5 blaze, burst, flame, flash 6 signal 7 flicker 8 outburst

flare-up
5 blaze, burst, flame, flash, surge 8 eruption, outburst 9 explosion

flaring
5 afire, fiery 6 ablaze, aflame, alight 7 blazing, burning 11 conflagrant

flash
3 ray 4 beam, rush, snap, show 5 blaze, blink, crack, flame, flare, glare, gleam, glint, jiffy, shake, shine, showy, spark, speed 6 dazzle, expose, flaunt, glance, minute, moment, second 7 display, disport, exhibit, flicker, glamour, glimmer, glisten, glitter, instant, pizzazz, shimmer, show off, spangle, sparkle, twinkle 8 brandish 9 coruscate 11 coruscation, scintillate, split second 13 scintillation

flashy
4 loud 5 gaudy, jazzy, showy 6 brazen, florid, garish, glitzy, ornate, snazzy, sporty, tawdry, tinsel 7 blatant, chintzy, glaring, insipid 9 sparkling 10 flamboyant, glittering 12 meretricious, ostentatious

flask
6 bottle, fiasco, flacon 7 ampulla, canteen, costrel, thermos

flat
3 dim, mat 4 dead, drab, dull, even 5 banal, bland, exact, fixed, flush, level, muted, plane, prone, rooms, stale, vapid 7 insipid, prosaic 8 lodgings, tenement, unsavory

9 apartment, colorless, innocuous
10 flavorless, lackluster, monotonous

flatfish
see at **fish**

flatland
4 mesa 5 plain 6 steppe, tundra
7 plateau 9 tableland

flat-out
8 absolute 9 downright 10 absolutely

flatten
4 deck, down, dull, even, fell, raze
5 crush, floor, level 6 smooth,
squash 9 knock down, prostrate

flattened at the poles
6 oblate

flatter
4 coax, suit 5 toady 6 become,
cajole, praise, stroke 7 adulate,
blarney, gratify, wheedle 8 blandish, bootlick, butter up, soft-soap
9 sweet-talk

flattery
5 smarm 6 butter, praise 7 blarney
8 cajolery, soft soap, toadyism
9 adulation, sweet talk 10 sycophancy 11 compliments 12 blandishment, ingratiation, unctuousness

Flaubert, Gustave
birthplace: 5 Rouen
heroine: 4 Emma (Bovary)
novel: 8 Salammbô 12 Madame
Bovary

flaunt
4 show, wave 5 flash, flout, vaunt
6 expose, parade 7 display, disport,
exhibit, show off 8 brandish, flourish

flavor
4 race, tang, zest, zing 5 smack,
spice, taste, tinge 6 relish, season
7 variety, version

flavorless
4 flat 5 bland, stale 7 insipid 8 unsavory 11 unpalatable

flavorsome
5 sapid, tasty, yummy 6 savory
9 delicious, palatable 10 appetizing,
delectable 11 good-tasting

flaw
3 gap, rip, sin 4 blot, chip, tear, vice
5 crack, fault 6 defect 7 blemish
8 weakness 9 deformity 12 imperfection

flawed
5 amiss 6 faulty, marred 7 damaged,
spoiled 8 impaired 9 defective,
imperfect

flawless
4 pure 5 ideal, model 6 intact
7 perfect 8 seamless, unmarred
9 exquisite 10 immaculate, impeccable 11 unblemished

flax
5 linen
fiber: 3 tow
prepare: 3 ret 4 card 5 dress
6 hackle, scutch

flaxen
4 fair 5 blond, straw 6 blonde,
golden, yellow 7 towhead

flay
4 beat, lash, peel, skin 7 blister,
censure, lambast, upbraid 8 lambaste 9 castigate, criticize, excoriate

flea
6 chigoe, jigger 7 chigger
water: 7 daphnid

Fleance's father
6 Banquo

flèche
5 spire

fleck
3 dot 4 mark, mote, spot 5 flake,
speck 6 dapple, mottle, streak,
stripe 7 spatter, speckle, stipple
8 particle 9 bespeckle

Fledermaus, Die
3 bat
character: 5 Adele, Falke, Frank
6 Alfred 9 Rosalinde 10 Eisenstein
composer: 7 Strauss (Johann)

fledge
4 rear 7 feather

fledgling
4 colt, tyro **6** novice, rookie **8** beginner, freshman, neophyte, newcomer **10** apprentice

flee
3 fly, lam, run **4** bolt, scat, skip **5** elude, scoot, scram, skirr, steal **6** decamp, escape **7** abscond, make off, run away, scamper, vamoose **8** stampede, turn tail **9** skedaddle **10** make tracks

fleece
3 rob **4** bilk, clip, gaff, milk, rook, skin, soak, wool **5** bleed, cheat, cozen, mulct, shear, stick, sweat **6** extort, hustle, rip off **7** defraud, swindle **8** flimflam **10** overcharge

fleecy
5 downy **6** fluffy, pilose, woolly **7** hirsute **9** whiskered **10** flocculent

fleer
4 gibe, gird, jeer, jest, mock, quip **5** flout, laugh, scoff, scout, sneer, taunt

fleet
4 fast, navy, spry **5** agile, brisk, group, hasty, quick, rapid, swift **6** argosy, armada, nimble, speedy **8** flotilla **9** breakneck **10** harefooted

fleeting
5 brief **7** passing **8** fugitive, volatile **9** ephemeral, fugacious, momentary, temporary, transient **10** evanescent, short-lived, transitory

Fleming, Ian
hero: **9** James Bond
novel: **4** Dr. No **9** Moonraker **10** Goldfinger **11** Thunderball **12** Casino Royale **13** Live and Let Die **16** You Only Live Twice **18** From Russia with Love

flesh
4 beef, meat, skin **5** stock **7** kindred **9** offspring, relatives, substance

fleshly
5 obese **6** animal, bodily, carnal **7** lustful, profane, secular, sensual **8** corporal, physical, sensuous, temporal **9** corporeal, epicurean, luxurious, sybaritic **10** voluptuous

fleshy
3 fat **5** ample, beefy, burly, gross, heavy, hefty, husky, meaty, obese, plump, pudgy, stout, tubby **6** chubby, chunky, portly, rotund **7** porcine, weighty **9** corpulent **10** overweight, well-padded
fruit: **4** pome **5** berry, drupe

Fletcher's partner
8 Beaumont (Francis)

fleur-de-lis
4 iris

flex
4 bend **5** tense

flexible
5 lithe, loose **6** docile, floppy, limber, pliant, supple **7** elastic, pliable, springy, willowy **8** amenable, bendable, stretchy, yielding **9** adaptable, compliant, malleable, tractable

flexion
3 bow **4** bend, fold, turn **5** angle

flexuous
5 fluid, lithe, snaky **7** sinuous, winding **8** tortuous **10** circuitous, convoluted, meandering, serpentine **11** anfractuous

flick
4 film, show **5** movie **13** motion picture, moving picture

flicker
4 bird, film, flit, hint **5** flash, gleam, glint, movie, waver **6** quiver **7** twinkle **10** woodpecker **13** motion picture, moving picture

flickering
7 lambent **8** unsteady

flier
3 ace **5** pilot **6** airman **7** aviator, birdman, handout **8** aviatrix, brochure, circular **9** throwaway

flight
3 hop, lam **4** rout, soar, slip, wing **5** flock, floor, flush, flyby, story **6** escape, flying, series **7** getaway **8** breakout

flighty
  5 dizzy, giddy, silly, swift 7 foolish
  8 freakish, skittish, unstable, volatile
  9 frivolous, mercurial, transient
  10 capricious, changeable, inconstant 11 empty-headed, harebrained
  13 irresponsible

flimflam
  3 con, gyp 4 bilk, dupe, fake, fool,
  gull, hoax, jazz, sham 5 cheat,
  cozen, fraud, hokum, trick 6 chouse,
  deceit, diddle, humbug 7 chicane,
  deceive, defraud, swindle 8 hoodwink, trickery 9 bamboozle, deception, moonshine 10 balderdash,
  double-talk 11 hornswoggle

flimflammer
  3 gyp 5 cheat 6 con man 7 diddler,
  sharper 8 swindler 9 defrauder
  11 four-flusher 12 double-dealer

flimsy
  4 limp, weak 5 cheap, filmy, frail,
  gauzy, sheer 6 feeble, flabby, sleazy,
  slight, spindly 7 flaccid, fragile, rickety, tenuous, unsound 8 decrepit,
  delicate, gossamer 10 diaphanous,
  improbable 11 implausible, transparent 12 unconvincing 13 insubstantial

flinch
  5 quail, start, wince 6 blench, cringe,
  recoil, shrink

fling
  3 peg 4 cast, emit, fire, flap, hurl,
  plop, rush, shot, slap, stab, tear, toss
  5 binge, chuck, heave, pitch, shoot,
  spree, throw 6 affair, charge, hurtle,
  launch 7 splurge 8 catapult

flip
  4 glib, leaf, pert, riff, toss, wise
  6 breezy, riffle, ruffle 8 turn over
  10 somersault 11 impertinent,
  smart-alecky

flip-flop
  5 U-turn, waver 6 sandal, switch,
  waffle 7 reverse 8 reversal 9 about-
  face, turnabout, vacillate, volte-face
  10 turnaround 11 vacillation

flippancy
  5 cheek 6 levity 8 archness, pert-
  ness 9 cockiness, freshness, frivolity 10 cheekiness, impishness
  11 roguishness

flippant
  4 glib, pert 5 sassy, saucy 6 breezy,
  cheeky 11 impertinent, smart-alecky
  13 disrespectful

flirt
  3 toy 4 flit, fool, minx, ogle, vamp
  5 dally, tease 6 coquet, trifle, wanton
  8 coquette 10 experiment, mess
  around

flit
  3 fly, zip 4 dart, pass, rush, sail,
  scud, whiz, wing 5 flash, hurry,
  scoot, speed 7 flicker, flutter, twinkle

flitter
  4 dart, flap, wing 5 hover, waver
  6 quiver 7 skitter 9 fluctuate

flivver
  6 jalopy 9 tin lizzie

float
  3 bob, fly 4 buoy, cork, hang, raft,
  ride, sail, scud, swim, waft 5 drift,
  hover 6 wander 7 pontoon, propose
  8 levitate 9 negotiate

floater
  3 bum, vag 4 hobo, raft 5 tramp
  7 drifter, vagrant 8 derelict, vagabond 10 roustabout

floating
  5 fluid, loose 6 adrift 7 buoyant,
  movable 8 moveable, shifting,
  variable 10 adjustable 11 fluctuating

flocculent
  5 flaky 6 fleecy, fluffy, woolly

flock
  3 mob 4 army, bevy, herd, host,
  mass, pack, rout 5 brood, bunch,
  cloud, covey, crowd, drove, group
  6 flight, gaggle, gather, legion, scores,
  throng 8 assemble, assembly,
  converge 9 multitude 11 aggregation 12 congregation

floe
  3 ice 4 berg 7 glacier, iceberg 8 ice
  field

flog

3 tan 4 beat, cane, flap, hide, lash, slog, whip 5 birch, drive, flail, whale 6 larrup, lather, stripe, switch, thrash 7 cowhide, leather, scourge 10 flagellate

flood

4 fill, flow, flux, glut, pour, rush, tide 5 burst, drown, float, spate, swamp 6 deluge, engulf, stream 7 current, freshet, immerse, Niagara, torrent 8 alluvion, cataract, inundate, overflow, submerge 9 avalanche, cataclysm, overwhelm 10 inundation, outpouring

floor

4 base, down, drop, fell 5 amaze, level, shock, story 6 ground 7 astound, flatten 8 astonish, audience, bowl down, bowl over, surprise 9 dumbfound, knock down 11 flabbergast

flop

3 dud 4 bomb, bust, fail, fall 5 lemon, loser 6 bummer, fizzle, turkey 7 clinker, failure

floppy

4 limp 6 flimsy 7 flaccid 8 diskette, flexible

flora

6 plants 10 vegetation

flora and fauna

5 biota

Florence

bridge: 12 Ponte Vecchio
cathedral: 5 Duomo
family: 6 Medici
museum: 6 Uffizi 8 Bargello
palace: 5 Pitti
river: 4 Arno

florid

3 red 5 flush, gaudy, ruddy, showy 6 ornate, rococo 7 baroque, flowery, flushed, glowing 8 rubicund, sanguine, sonorous 9 bombastic, elaborate, overblown 10 euphuistic, flamboyant, rhetorical 11 declamatory 12 magniloquent 13 grandiloquent

Florida

capital: 11 Tallahassee
city: 5 Miami, Tampa 6 Naples, Venice 7 Hialeah, Key West, Orlando 8 Sarasota 9 Palm Beach 11 St. Augustine 12 Jacksonville, St. Petersburg
college, university: 7 Rollins, Stetson
key: 4 Long, Vaca, West 5 Largo 7 Big Pine 9 Matecumbe, Sugarloaf
lake: 9 Kissimmee 10 Okeechobee
nickname: 8 Sunshine (State)
park: 10 Everglades
river: 6 Indian 7 St. Johns 8 Suwannee 12 Apalachicola
state bird: 11 mockingbird
state flower: 13 orange blossom
state tree: 9 sabal palm

florilegium

5 album 6 reader 7 garland, omnibus 8 analects 9 anthology 10 collection, miscellany

Florimel's husband

7 Marinel

floss

4 down, fuzz, lint 5 fluff 6 thread

flotilla

5 fleet 6 argosy, armada

Flotow opera

5 Indra 6 L'Ombre, Martha

flotsam

6 debris, jetsam 7 remains 8 wreckage 9 driftwood

flounce

5 frill, mince, strut, waltz 6 bounce, prance, ruffle, sashay

flounder

3 dab 5 slosh 6 fumble, muddle, splash, thrash, wallow 7 blunder, flounce 8 flatfish, struggle

flour

4 meal 6 pinole, powder
beetle: 6 weevil

flourish

3 wax 4 grow, wave 5 adorn, bloom 6 flower, stroke, thrive 7 blossom,

burgeon, develop, fanfare, prosper, succeed **8** brandish, curlicue, ornament **13** embellishment, ornamentation

flout
4 defy, mock **5** scorn, spurn **6** deride, insult **7** scoff at

flow
4 emit, flux, gush, ooze, pour, rill, rise, rush, stem, tide, well **5** arise, drift, flood, issue, spate, spill, surge, swarm **6** course, deluge, onrush, sluice, spring, stream **7** cascade, current, emanate, give off, outflow, proceed **8** inundate, sequence **9** discharge, originate **10** continuity, inundation, succession **11** progression **12** continuation

flower
4 best, blow, pick, posy **5** bloom, cream, elite, pride, prime, prize **6** choice, thrive **7** blossom, burgeon, develop **10** effloresce **13** inflorescence
buttonhole: 11 boutonniere
cluster: 4 cyme **5** spike, umbel **6** corymb, floret, raceme, spadix **7** panicle **8** spikelet **9** capitulum, dichasium, glomerule **11** monochasium **13** inflorescence
cup: 5 calyx
garden: 4 iris, lily, pink, rose **5** aster, canna, daisy, pansy, peony, phlox, poppy, tulip **6** azalia, cosmos, crocus, dahlia, orchid, violet **7** jonquil, petunia **8** camellia, daffodil, gardenia, geranium, gloxinia, hyacinth, larkspur, marigold, primrose **9** carnation, gladiolus, narcissus **10** delphinium, heliotrope **13** chrysanthemum
opening: 8 anthesis
part: 5 bract, calyx, ovary, ovule, petal, sepal, style **6** anther, pistil, spathe, stamen, stigma **7** corolla, nectary, pedicel, petiole **8** calyptra, filament, peduncle, perianth
spike: 5 ament **6** catkin, spadix
stalk: 7 pedicel **8** peduncle
type: 3 ray **4** disk **6** annual, simple **9** composite, perennial

wild: 4 flag **5** bluet, daisy, vetch **6** lupine **7** anemone, arbutus, cowslip, gentian, vervain **8** bluebell, hepatica, trillium **9** buttercup, columbine, dandelion, saxifrage **10** cinquefoil **12** lady's slipper

flower arranging
7 ikebana

flowering
6 growth **8** progress **9** evolution **11** development, florescence, progression

flowerless plant
4 fern, moss **6** lichen **9** liverwort

flowery
5 wordy **6** florid, ornate, prolix **7** aureate, diffuse, verbose **8** sonorous **9** overblown **10** euphuistic, rhetorical **11** declamatory **12** magniloquent **13** grandiloquent

Flowery Kingdom
5 China

flowing
4 easy **5** fluid **6** fluent, liquid, smooth **7** cursive, running **10** effortless
back: 6 reflux **8** refluent
in: 6 influx **8** influent
together: 7 conflux **9** confluent

flow regulator
4 cock, gate **5** valve **8** throttle

flub
4 goof, mess, muff, slip **5** boner, botch, error, fluff, gaffe, lapse, snarl **6** bollix, bungle, foul up, goof up, mess up **7** blunder, faux pas, louse up

fluctuate
4 sway, yo-yo **5** swing, waver **6** seesaw **8** undulate **9** alternate, oscillate, vacillate

flue
4 pipe, vent **6** funnel, uptake **7** channel, chimney, outtake

fluent
4 easy, glib **5** fluid **6** facile, liquid, smooth, supple **7** cursive, flowing, voluble **8** eloquent, polished **10** articulate, effortless

fluff
4 down, flub, fuzz, goof, lint, mess, muff, slip, trip 5 boner, botch, error, floss, gaffe, lapse, whisk 6 bobble, bollix, bungle, goof up, mess up 7 blooper, blunder, faux pas, louse up, mistake

fluffy
5 downy 6 flossy 7 cursory, shallow 8 puffed up 10 flocculent 11 superficial 13 unsubstantial

fluid
4 free 5 lymph, water 6 liquid, mobile, molten, serous, watery 7 mutable, protean 8 flexible, shifting, unstable, unsteady, variable 9 adaptable, changeful, unsettled 10 changeable
excessive: 5 edema

fluke
3 hap 4 lobe, worm 5 quirk 6 chance 8 flatfish, fortuity 9 trematode

fluky
3 odd 6 casual, chance, chancy, random 9 arbitrary 10 accidental, fortuitous

flume
5 chute 6 sluice, stream 7 channel 8 aqueduct 11 watercourse

flummox
5 abash, addle 6 baffle, rattle, stymie 7 confuse, fluster, perplex 8 befuddle, bewilder, confound 9 discomfit, embarrass 10 disconcert

flunk
4 fail

flunky
4 peon 5 gofer, toady 6 drudge, lackey, stooge, yes-man 7 footman, servant, steward 8 factotum, follower

flurry
3 ado, fit 4 fuss, gust, spit, stir, to-do 5 haste, whirl 6 bother, bustle, furore, pother, tumult 7 barrage, flutter, turmoil 8 snowfall 9 agitation, commotion, confusion, whirlpool, whirlwind 10 excitement, turbulence

flush
4 even, flat, glow, pink, rich, rose, wash 5 bloom, color, level, plane, raise, rinse, rouge 6 florid, filled, mantle, redden, sluice 7 cleanse, crimson, glowing, inflame, opulent, suffuse, wealthy 8 abundant, abutting, irrigate, rubicund, sanguine, squarely 9 turn color

fluster
5 addle, dizzy, shake, upset 6 ball up, bother, fuddle, muddle, rattle, ruffle 7 agitate, confuse, disturb, nonplus, perturb, unhinge 8 befuddle, bewilder, confound, disquiet, distract 10 discompose

flustered
5 upset 7 abashed, anxious, rattled 8 agitated, confused, troubled 9 chagrined, disturbed, flummoxed, perplexed, perturbed 10 bewildered, disquieted, distracted, distraught, distressed, nonplussed 11 discomposed, embarrassed 12 disconcerted

flute
4 fife, roll 5 pleat 6 goffer, groove 7 chamfer, channel, piccolo 8 recorder 9 wineglass
Japanese: 10 shakuhachi
player: 5 piper 7 flutist 8 flautist

flutist
American: 5 Baker (Julius), Baron (Samuel) 7 Robison (Paula) 8 Zukerman (Eugenia)
British: 6 Galway (James)
French: 6 Rampal (Jean-Pierre)

flutter
4 beat, flap, flit 5 hover, quake, shake 6 flurry, quaver, quiver, wobble 7 flicker, flitter, pulsate, tremble, vibrate 9 agitation, commotion, confusion, palpitate, vibration 11 fluctuation

flu type
5 Asian, swine

flux
3 run 4 flow, fuse, melt, rush, thaw, tide 5 drift, flood, spate 6 change,

stream **7** current, flowing, outflow
8 dissolve

fly
3 zip **4** bolt, dart, dash, flee, flit, lure,
scud, skip, soar, whiz, wing **5** fleet,
float, glide, hover, hurry, pilot, scoot,
shoot, skirr, sweep, whish, whisk
6 aviate, escape, hasten, hustle
7 abscond, flutter
insect: 4 gnat **5** midge **6** botfly,
gadfly, mayfly, tsetse **7** deerfly,
sandfly **8** blackfly, dipteron, horsefly,
housefly, tachinid **10** bluebottle
larva: 6 maggot

fly-by-night
5 shady **7** passing **9** transient
10 transitory, unreliable **12** disreputable, undependable **13** untrustworthy

flycatcher
5 pewee **6** phoebe, tyrant **8** bellbird,
kingbird **9** passerine

flying
5 aloft **6** volant **8** airborne

Flying Dutchman, The
composer: 6 Wagner (Richard)
heroine: 5 Senta

flying fish
7 gurnard

flying fox
3 bat **8** fruit bat

flying horse
7 Pegasus **10** hippogriff

flying island
6 Laputa

flying lemur
6 colugo

flying mammal
3 bat

flying saucer
3 UFO

fly in the ointment
5 catch **8** drawback

foam
4 head, scud, scum, suds, surf

5 churn, froth, spume **6** bubble,
lather, seethe **7** bubbles **10** effervesce

fob
4 seal **5** chain **6** pocket, ribbon
8 ornament

fob off
5 foist **6** put off **7** palm off, pass off

focus
3 fix, hub **4** zoom **5** heart, rivet
6 adjust, center, fixate, home in
8 converge, emphasis, meditate,
polestar **9** concenter, epicenter
10 hypocenter **11** concentrate,
nerve center

fodder
4 feed, food **6** forage, silage **9** provender
crop: 3 hay, oat, rye **4** corn **5** maize,
vetch, wheat **6** barley, clover, millet
7 alfalfa, sorghum
storage structure: 4 silo
store: 6 ensile

foe
5 enemy, rival **8** opponent **9** adversary **10** antagonist

fog
4 blur, daze, foam, haze, mist,
murk, soup **5** brume, cloud, vapor
6 miasma, muddle **7** pea soup,
pogonip

foggy
4 hazy **5** dirty, grimy, misty, murky,
soupy, vague **7** brumous, muddled,
obscure, tenuous **8** confused, pea
soupy, vaporous

fogy
6 fossil, square **7** diehard **8** mossback **10** fuddy-duddy **12** antediluvian, conservative **11** standpatter
13 stick-in-the-mud

fogyish
7 old-line **8** outmoded, standpat
9 hidebound, out-of-date **10** antiquated, fuddy-duddy, mossbacked
11 reactionary **12** conservative,
old-fashioned

foible

4 vice **5** fault **6** defect **7** failing, frailty **8** weakness **11** shortcoming **12** imperfection

foil

4 balk, beat, curb, dash, faze **5** check, sword **6** baffle, defeat, rattle, thwart **7** buffalo **8** contrast, restrain **9** discomfit, embarrass, frustrate **10** circumvent, disappoint, disconcert **11** straight man

foist

6 fob off **7** palm off, pass off

fold

3 pen, ply **4** bend, fail, tuck **5** drape, flock, pleat, plica, ridge **6** crease, double, furrow, pucker **7** flexure, plicate **9** plication **11** corrugation **skin:** 4 ruga **5** plica, rugae (plural) **6** dewlap, plicae (plural)

folder

4 file **6** binder **9** portfolio

foliage

6 growth, leaves **7** verdure **8** greenery, lushness **10** vegetation

folk

4 race **6** people **9** community

folklore

4 myth, tale **5** fable **6** belief, custom, legend, mythos, wisdom **9** mythology, tradition **12** superstition

folks

6 family **7** parents **9** relatives

folksinger

4 Baez (Joan), Ives (Burl) **5** Dylan (Bob), Niles (John Jacob), White (Josh) **6** Odetta, Seeger (Pete) **7** Collins (Judy), Guthrie (Arlo, Woody), Robeson (Paul) **9** Belafonte (Harry), Ledbetter (Huddie)

folksy

5 homey **6** casual, earthy, mellow, rustic, simple **7** natural **8** downhome, familiar, informal, laid-back, sociable **9** easygoing, ingenuous **10** unaffected, unpolished **13** unpretentious

folktale

4 myth **5** fable **6** legend **7** märchen

follow

3 dog, spy, tag **4** hunt, keep, obey, seek, tail, walk **5** catch, chase, ensue, grasp, hound, trace, track, trail **6** accept, comply, convoy, pursue, search, shadow, travel **7** conform, imitate, proceed, replace, succeed **8** postdate, practice, supplant **9** accompany, supersede **10** comprehend, understand

follower

3 fan **5** toady **6** addict, cohort, minion, sequel, votary **7** apostle, devotee, groupie, habitué, sectary, trailer **8** adherent, advocate, disciple, faithful, hanger-on, henchman, myrmidon, parasite, partisan, tagalong **9** dependent, satellite, supporter, sycophant **10** aficionado

following

4 next **5** after, below, later, since **6** behind, public **7** ensuing, retinue **8** audience **9** adherents, afterward, believers, disciples, entourage, partisans **10** afterwards, sequential, supporters, subsequent, succeeding, successive **12** subsequently, subsequent to

follow-up

6 sequel

folly

4 whim **6** lunacy, vanity **7** fatuity, foolery, inanity, madness **8** insanity, nonsense **9** absurdity, craziness, dottiness, silliness, stupidity **10** indulgence **11** foolishness **12** extravagance

foment

3 sow **4** brew, goad, spur **5** rouse, set on **6** arouse, excite, foster, incite, stir up, whip up **7** agitate, nurture, provoke **9** cultivate, encourage, instigate

fond

4 dear, warm **5** silly **6** doting, loving, tender **7** devoted, fatuous, foolish,

partial **8** desirous, enamored, romantic **9** indulgent **10** infatuated **11** sentimental **12** affectionate

fondle
3 paw, pet **5** grope, touch **6** caress, cosset, dandle, stroke **7** embrace **8** canoodle

fondness
4 love **5** fancy, taste **6** liking, relish **8** appetite, devotion, penchant, soft spot, weakness **9** affection, tendresse **10** attachment, partiality, preference, propensity **11** inclination **12** predilection

font
4 root, type **6** origin, source **8** fountain **10** receptacle

food
3 pap **4** chow, diet, eats, fare, grub, meal, meat **5** bread, manna **6** fodder, viands **7** aliment, cuisine, edibles, nurture, pabulum, vittles **8** delicacy, victuals **9** nutriment, provender **10** provisions, sustenance **11** comestibles, nourishment
disorder: 7 bulimia **8** anorexia
divine: 8 ambrosia
element: 5 fiber, fibre, sugar **6** starch **7** mineral, protein, vitamin **12** carbohydrate
from heaven: 5 manna
lover: 7 epicure, gourmet **8** gourmand
provision: 4 mess **6** ration **7** serving
scarcity: 6 famine
waste: 7 garbage

foofaraw
3 ado **4** fuss, stir, to-do **5** stink **6** bother, finery, frills, furore, hurrah, pother, ruckus, rumpus **8** brouhaha **9** commotion **11** disturbance

fool
3 ass, kid, oaf, rag, rib, sap, toy **4** boob, butt, clod, dolt, dope, dupe, fish, gull, hoax, jerk, jest, joke, josh, zany **5** chump, clown, comic, dally, dummy, dunce, goose, idiot, loser, moron, ninny, patsy, schmo, trick **6** banter, cretin, dawdle, delude, diddle, dimwit, doodle, galoot, gammon, jester, lead on, meddle, monkey, motley, nitwit, pigeon, schmoe, stooge, sucker, tamper, trifle, victim **7** beguile, buffoon, chicane, deceive, fake out, fall guy, fritter, half-wit, jackass, mislead, pinhead, saphead, schmuck **8** bonehead, comedian, dumbbell, flimflam, hoodwink, imbecile, lunkhead, numskull, pushover **9** bamboozle, birdbrain, blockhead, interfere, simpleton **10** nincompoop **11** hornswoggle, merry-andrew, string along **13** laughingstock
around: 4 futz, idle, laze, loaf, loll **5** flirt **6** dawdle, diddle, lounge **8** lollygag, womanize **9** philander

foolhardy
4 bold, rash **6** daring, madcap **8** headlong, reckless **9** audacious, daredevil, impetuous **11** precipitate, temerarious

foolish
3 mad **4** daft, gaga, rash, zany **5** balmy, batty, crazy, dippy, dizzy, dorky, dotty, goofy, inane, inept, kooky, loony, loopy, nutty, sappy, silly, wacky **6** absurd, insane, simple, stupid, unwise **7** asinine, doltish, fatuous, idiotic, lunatic, meshuga, moronic, witless **8** clueless, reckless, trifling **9** half-baked, brainless, fantastic, frivolous, half-baked, imbecilic, insensate, laughable, ludicrous, senseless **10** cockamamie, halfcocked, half-witted, irrational, ridiculous **11** harebrained, nonsensical **12** feebleminded

foolishness
4 bull, bunk **5** folly, fudge **6** bêtise, bunkum, lunacy **7** fatuity, inanity, rubbish **8** claptrap, drollery, insanity, nonsense, tommyrot **9** absurdity, craziness, silliness, stupidity **10** imbecility, imprudence **12** fiddle-faddle **13** horsefeathers

fool's gold
6 pyrite

foot

foot
3 paw 4 hoof
ailment: 4 corn 6 bunion, callus
animal: 3 pad, paw 4 hoof
bones of: 5 talus, tarsi (plural)
6 cuboid, tarsal, tarsus 7 phalanx
9 calcaneus, cuneiform, navicular,
phalanges (plural) 10 metatarsal
combining form: 3 ped, pod 4 podo
doctor: 10 podiatrist 11 chiropodist
metric: 4 iamb 5 arsis 6 dactyl,
thesis 7 anapest, pyrrhic, spondee,
trochee
part: 3 toe 4 arch, ball, claw, nail
5 ankle, digit, talon 6 hallux, instep

football
5 rugby 6 rugger, soccer 7 pigskin
field: 8 gridiron
foul: 7 holding, offside 8 clipping
12 interference
official: 6 umpire 7 referee 8 linesman 9 back judge, line judge 10 field
judge
play: 4 dive, trap 5 sneak, sweep
6 option, screen 7 audible, counter,
handoff, rollout, runback 8 dropback
9 crossbuck, off-tackle 10 buttonhook
player position: 3 end 4 back
5 guard 6 center, safety, tackle
7 flanker, lineman, wideout 8 fullback, halfback, slotback, split end,
tailback, tight end, wingback 9 noseguard 10 cornerback, linebacker,
nose tackle 11 quarterback 12 defensive end, wide receiver
scoring: 6 safety 9 field goal,
touchdown 10 conversion
starting play: 7 kickoff
team: 6 eleven
term: 4 down, kick, pass, punt, rush,
snap 5 blitz, block, squad 6 fumble,
huddle, kicker, onside, option, safety,
spiral 7 end zone, handoff, kickoff,
offside, pigskin, quarter, spinner,
tweener, yardage 8 clipping, crossbar, goal line, goalpost, gridiron, half-
time 9 backfield, defensive, field
goal, intercept, offensive, placekick,
scrimmage, touchback, touchdown
11 broken field 12 interception

footballer
3 end 4 half, Kemp (Jack), Long
(Howie), Lott (Ronnie), Levy (Marv),
Monk (Art), Moon (Warren), Reed
(Andre), Rice (Jerry), wing 5 Allen
(Marcus), Baugh (Sammy), Berry
(Raymond), Brady (Tom), Brown
(Bob, Jim), Clark (Gary), Ditka
(Mike), Elway (John), Eller (Carl),
Favre (Brett), Gibbs (Joe), Groza
(Lou), guard, Jones (Bert, Deacon),
Kelly (Jim), Kosar (Bernie), Leahy
(Pat), Lomax (Neil), Muñoz (An-
thony), Shula (Don), Simms (Phil),
Smith (Emmitt), Starr (Bart), Stram
(Hank), Swann (Lynn), Young (Steve)
6 Aikman (Troy), Blanda (George),
Butkus (Dick), Carter (Chris, Ki-
Jana), center, Csonka (Larry),
Dawson (Len), Ellard (Henry),
Graham (Otto), Grange (Red),
Greene (Joe), Harris (Franco),
Jaeger (Jeff), Joiner (Charlie), kicker,
Lofton (James), Lowery (Nick),
Marino (Dan), Murray (Eddie),
Namath (Joe), Payton (Walter),
player, Rypien (Mark), safety, Sayers
(Gale), Slater (Jackie), tackle, Taylor
(Lawrence), Thorpe (Jim), Tittle
(Y. A.), Turner (Jim), Unitas (Johnny),
Walker (Herschel) 7 Bledsoe (Drew),
Dorsett (Tony), Esiason (Boomer),
flanker, Gifford (Frank), Hornung
(Paul), Johnson (Norm), Largent
(Steve), lineman, Luckman (Sid),
Manning (Peyton), Montana (Joe),
Newsome (Ozzie), Riggins (John),
Sanders (Barry, Deion), Simpson
(O. J.), Stabler (Ken), Thurman
(Thomas), tweener 8 Andersen
(Morten), Anderson (Gary, Ottis),
Bradshaw (Terry), defender, full-
back, halfback, linesman, Nagurski
(Bronko), Plunkett (Jim), receiver,
scatback, split end, Staubach
(Roger), tailback, tight end, wingback
9 Dickerson (Eric), Jurgensen
(Sonny), Hostetler (Jeff), noseguard,
Tarkenton (Fran) 10 cornerback,
linebacker, Stallworth (John), Single-
tary (Mike), Stephenson (Dwight),
Youngblood (Jack) 11 ballcarrier,
placekicker, quarterback, running
back, snapper-back 12 strong
safety, triple threat, wide receiver

Foote play
15 Trip to Bountiful (The) 19 Young Man from Atlanta (The)

footfall
4 step 5 tread

footing
4 base, rank, seat, term 5 basis, place, state 6 bottom, ground, status 7 bedrock, seating, station, warrant 8 basement, capacity, pedestal, position, standing 9 character, situation 10 foundation, groundwork, substratum 12 underpinning

footless
4 dull, dumb 5 crass, dense, inept, unfit 6 stupid 7 foolish

foot lever
5 pedal 7 treadle

footman
7 servant 10 pedestrian 11 infantryman

footpad
5 thief 6 mugger, robber 8 criminal 10 highwayman, pickpocket

footprint
3 pug 4 sign, step 5 spoor, trace, track, tract 7 pugmark, vestige

footslog
4 plod, slop, toil 5 tramp, tromp 6 trudge

footstone
6 ledger, marker 8 monument 11 grave marker

footstool
7 cricket, hassock, ottoman

fop
3 jay 4 beau 5 blade, blood, dandy, spark, swell 7 coxcomb, gallant 8 cavalier, macaroni, popinjay 9 exquisite, ladies' man, pretty boy 10 lady-killer 11 Beau Brummel, petit-maître 12 fashion plate, lounge lizard

foppish
6 chichi 8 dandyish, peacocky 10 peacockish

for
3 pro

forage
4 beat, comb, grub, prog, raid, rake, sack 5 scour 6 browse, fodder, ravage, rustle, search 7 plunder, ransack, rummage 8 finecomb, scrounge 9 pasturage
(see also **fodder**)

foray
4 raid 6 inroad, sortie 8 invasion 9 incursion, irruption

forbear
4 shun 5 avoid, forgo, spare 6 endure, eschew, resist, suffer 7 abstain, decline, refrain 8 hold back, restrain, tolerate

forbearance
5 grace, mercy 6 lenity 7 charity 8 clemency, lenience, leniency, mildness, patience 9 restraint, tolerance 10 abstinence, toleration 13 consideration

forbearing
4 easy, kind, mild 6 gentle 7 clement, lenient, patient 8 merciful, tolerant 9 indulgent 10 charitable, thoughtful 11 considerate, magnanimous

Forbes hero
8 Tremaine (Johnny)

forbid
3 ban, bar, nix 4 curb, deny, halt, stop, veto 5 block, check, debar 6 enjoin, hinder, impede, outlaw, refuse 7 inhibit, prevent, rule out, shut out 8 disallow, obstruct, preclude, prohibit, restrain 9 interdict, proscribe

forbidden
5 taboo 6 banned 7 illegal, illicit 8 verboten 10 prohibited

Forbidden City
5 Lhasa 6 Gu Gong 7 Beijing

forbidding
4 grim 5 drear, harsh 6 dreary, severe 8 daunting, menacing, sinister 9 repellent 10 formidable 11 threatening

force

3 jam 4 cram, push 5 drive, foist, impel, might, power, press, vigor, wreak, wreck, wrest 6 coerce, compel, demand, duress, effort, energy, extort, impose, legion, muscle, oblige 7 command, impetus, inflict, potency, require, sandbag 8 coercion, manpower, momentum, obligate, pressure, shoehorn, strength, violence 9 constrain, intensity, puissance, strong-arm 10 compulsion, constraint

apart: 5 wedge
unit: 4 dyne

forced

8 strained 9 contrived, unnatural 10 artificial, compulsory 11 involuntary

forceful

5 stiff, stout 6 mighty, potent, punchy, strong, virile 7 dynamic 8 emphatic, powerful, puissant, vigorous 9 assertive 10 compelling

forceless

4 lame, weak 5 wimpy 6 feeble 8 impotent, nugatory 9 powerless 10 inadequate 11 ineffective, ineffectual

force out

see **expel**

forcible

8 coercive 9 compelled 10 compulsory, obligatory, peremptory

ford

5 cross

Ford's folly

5 Edsel

for each

3 per 6 apiece

forearm bone

4 ulna 6 radius

forebear

8 ancestor 9 precursor 10 antecedent, progenitor 11 predecessor 12 primogenitor

forebode

5 augur 7 betoken, portend, predict, presage 8 foretell, prophesy, soothsay 13 prognosticate

foreboding

4 omen, sign 5 dread 6 augury 7 anxiety, portent, presage, warning 10 prediction, prognostic 11 premonition 12 apprehension, presentiment

forecast

5 augur 6 divine 7 foresee, portend, predict, presage 8 estimate, foretell, indicate, prophecy, prophesy 9 adumbrate, calculate, prevision, prognosis 10 prediction 13 prognosticate

forecaster

4 seer 5 augur 6 oracle 7 diviner, prophet 8 haruspex 9 predictor 10 prophesier, soothsayer, weatherman 11 Nostradamus 13 meteorologist, weatherperson

foreclose

3 bar 5 debar 6 cut off, hinder 7 prevent, shut out 8 preclude

forefather

see **forebear**

forefeel

6 divine 9 apprehend, prevision

forefinger

5 index

forefront

3 van 4 lead 8 vanguard 10 avantgarde, firing line 11 cutting edge

foregoer

6 herald 8 ancestor, forebear 9 harbinger, precursor, prototype 10 antecedent, antecessor, forerunner, progenitor 11 predecessor 12 primogenitor

foregoing

5 prior 6 former 7 earlier 8 anterior, previous 9 precedent, preceding 10 antecedent

forehanded

7 prudent, thrifty 8 well-to-do 9 provident 10 prosperous

forehead
4 brow 5 frons, front 8 sinciput
9 sincipita (plural)

foreign
5 alien 6 exotic 7 strange 8 external, offshore, overseas 9 extrinsic, nonnative 10 accidental, extraneous, immaterial, irrelevant 11 incongruous 12 adventitious, inapplicable, incompatible, inconsistent 13 inappropriate
prefix: 4 xeno

foreigner
5 alien 8 outsider, stranger 9 outlander 10 tramontane

foreknow
6 divine 9 apprehend, prevision
10 anticipate

foreland
4 beak, cape, head, ness 5 point
10 promontory

forelock
5 bangs, quiff

foreman
4 boss 5 chief 6 gaffer, ganger, honcho, leader 7 captain, manager, steward 8 overseer 10 supervisor

foremost
4 arch, head, high, main 5 chief, first, front, grand 7 leading, premier, supreme 9 number one, paramount, principal 10 preeminent 11 cutting-edge, outstanding

forenoon
4 morn 7 morning 12 ante meridiem

forensic
8 judicial 9 debatable 10 rhetorical
13 argumentative

foreordain
4 doom, fate 9 determine 10 predestine 12 predetermine

forerunner
4 omen, sign 5 envoy 6 augury, herald 7 pioneer, portent, presage, symptom, warning 8 ancestor, exemplar, outrider 9 announcer,
harbinger, initiator, messenger
10 antecedent, originator, prognostic
11 anticipator, predecessor

foresee
6 divine 7 predict, presage 8 perceive, prophesy 9 apprehend, prefigure, prevision 10 anticipate
13 prognosticate

foreseer
5 augur 6 auspex, oracle 7 diviner, prophet 8 haruspex 9 predictor
10 soothsayer 11 Nostradamus

foreshadow
4 bode, hint 5 augur 6 herald
7 betoken, portend, predict, presage, promise, suggest 8 forecast, intimate 9 adumbrate, prefigure
13 prognosticate

foresight
6 vision 7 caution 8 prudence, sagacity 10 discretion, perception, precaution, prescience, providence

forest
4 bosk, wood 5 copse, grove, weald, woods 6 bosque 7 coppice, thicket, woodlot 8 wildwood, woodland
10 timberland, wilderness
deity: 5 dryad, sylvan 8 Sylvanus
English: 5 Arden 8 Sherwood
opening: 5 glade
relating to: 6 sylvan
subarctic: 5 taiga
tropical: 5 selva 6 jungle

forestall
5 avert, block, deter 6 hinder 7 obviate, preempt, prevent, rule out, ward off 8 preclude, stave off 10 anticipate

Forester, C. S.
hero: 10 Hornblower (Horatio)
novel: 12 African Queen (The)

foretell
4 bode, warn 5 augur 6 divine
7 portend, predict, presage, promise
8 proclaim, prophesy, soothsay
9 adumbrate, apprehend, prefigure
10 anticipate, vaticinate 13 prognosticate

forethought
8 judgment, planning, prudence
10 discretion, precaution 12 deliberation 13 premeditation

foretoken
4 bode, hint, omen, sign, warn
5 augur 6 augury, herald 7 portend, portent, presage, promise, symptom, warning 8 forecast 9 harbinger, precursor 10 intimation

forever
3 aye 6 always 7 endless 8 eternity, evermore 9 endlessly, eternally
10 in aeternum 11 ad infinitum, ceaselessly, continually, everlasting, incessantly, permanently, perpetually, unceasingly 12 in perpetuity 13 everlastingly

forewarning
6 caveat, tip-off 7 caution 8 monition
11 premonition

foreword
5 intro, proem 7 preface, prelude
8 exordium, overture, preamble, prologue 12 introduction, prolegomenon

for example
6 such as

for fear that
4 lest

forfeit
4 fine, lose 5 mulct 6 give up 7 penalty 9 sacrifice 10 amercement

forfend
4 ward 5 avert, deter 6 secure
7 obviate, prevent, protect, rule out, ward off 8 preclude, preserve, stave off

forge
4 copy, fake, form, make 5 pound, shape 6 smithy 7 advance, fashion, imitate, produce, turn out 8 continue
9 construct, fabricate 11 counterfeit, manufacture

forget
4 fail, omit 6 ignore, slight 7 neglect
8 discount, overlook, pass over
9 disregard

forgetful
3 lax 5 slack 6 absent, remiss
7 amnesic 8 amnesiac, careless, heedless 9 negligent, oblivious, unwitting 10 abstracted, neglectful
11 inattentive, thoughtless 12 absentminded

forgetfulness
5 lethe 7 amnesia 8 oblivion 10 negligence 11 inattention

forgivable
6 venial 10 remissible

forgive
5 remit 6 excuse, pardon 7 absolve, condone 8 overlook

forgiveness
6 pardon 7 amnesty 9 remission
10 absolution

forgo
3 bag 5 leave, waive, yield 6 eschew, give up, resign 7 abandon
8 abnegate, jettison, renounce
9 sacrifice, surrender 10 relinquish

fork
6 bisect, branch, crotch 7 diverge, utensil 9 branch off
prong: 4 tine

fork out
3 pay 5 spend 10 contribute

forlorn
5 alone 6 bereft, futile, lonely 8 desolate, forsaken, hopeless, lonesome, solitary, wretched 9 abandoned, depressed, destitute, miserable
10 despairing, despondent 12 disconsolate

form
3 way 4 body, cast, make, mode, mold 5 build, forge, found, frame, image, model, shape, style 6 create, design, devise, figure, make up, manner 7 compose, contour, develop, fashion, outline, process, produce, profile 8 comprise, organize, practice 9 construct, establish, fabricate, framework, procedure, structure, take shape 10 constitute, convention, regulation 11 materialize
13 configuration
combining form: 5 morph

formal
3 set 4 prim 5 exact, legal, rigid, stiff 6 dressy, lawful, proper, seemly, solemn 7 distant, orderly, regular, stately, starchy, stilted 8 abstract, black-tie, decorous, elevated, official, reserved 10 ceremonial, methodical, systematic 11 ceremonious, syntactical 12 conventional

formality
4 form, rite 6 ritual 7 liturgy, service 8 ceremony, insignia 10 ceremonial, convention, observance

formalize
6 codify 9 establish, normalize 10 regularize 11 standardize

format
4 plan, size 5 shape, style 6 makeup, method 11 arrangement 12 organization

formation
4 rank 6 design, makeup 9 structure 11 arrangement, composition, development 12 architecture, construction

former
3 old 4 late, once, past 5 prior 6 bygone, whilom 7 earlier, onetime, quondam 8 anterior, previous, sometime 9 erstwhile, precedent, preceding 10 antecedent

formerly
4 erst, once 6 before, whilom 7 already, earlier 9 erstwhile 10 heretofore, previously

formidable
8 daunting 9 difficult 10 impressive 11 redoubtable

formless
5 vague 7 chaotic, obscure, unclear 8 inchoate, nebulous, unshaped 9 amorphous, undefined, unordered 10 immaterial, indefinite, indistinct 11 unorganized

Formosa
6 Taiwan
capital: 6 Taipei

formula
4 rite, rule 5 canon, maxim, tenet
6 method, recipe, ritual 7 precept, theorem 8 equation 9 algorithm, blueprint, principle, yardstick 10 touchstone 12 prescription

formulate
5 couch, draft, frame, hatch 6 codify, devise, invent, make up, phrase 7 concoct, dream up, express, prepare, work out 8 contrive

forsake
4 quit 5 avoid, leave, spurn 6 defect, depart, desert, give up, reject, resign 7 abandon 8 abdicate, renounce 9 throw over 10 relinquish

forsaken
4 lorn 6 bereft 7 forlorn 8 derelict, deserted, desolate, solitary 9 abandoned

Forseti
father: 6 Balder
palace: 7 Glitnir

forswear
4 deny 5 unsay 6 abjure, recall, recant, reject 7 perjure, retract 8 renounce, take back, withdraw

fort
6 castle 7 bastion, bulwark, citadel, redoubt 8 fastness, fortress, garrison, martello, stockade 10 stronghold
Baltimore: 7 McHenry
California: 3 Ord
New Jersey: 3 Dix
New York: 7 Niagara, Stanwix 8 Schuyler 11 Ticonderoga
Ontario: 9 Frontenac
San Antonio: 5 Alamo
South Carolina: 6 Sumter
Spanish: 7 alcazar 8 presidio

forte
3 bag 4 loud 5 thing 6 métier 8 long suit, strength 9 specialty 10 strong suit 11 strong point

forthcoming
7 pending 8 imminent 9 impending, proximate 10 responsive 11 approaching

for the most part
9 generally, typically 10 on the whole

for the time being
3 now 6 pro tem 9 at present, currently, presently 10 pro tempore

forthright
4 open 5 blunt, frank, plain 6 candid, direct 7 up-front 8 straight 10 aboveboard, foursquare 11 openhearted, straight-out, undisguised, unvarnished

forthwith
3 now 6 at once 8 directly 9 instantly, right away, thereupon 11 immediately, straightway 12 straightaway

fortification
4 moat, wall 6 abatis, buffer, glacis 7 barrier, bastion, bulwark, citadel, parapet, rampart, redoubt 8 barbican, enceinte, fastness, garrison, palisade, presidio, stockade 9 barricade, earthwork 10 breastwork, stronghold
part: 7 salient

fortify
3 arm 4 gird, stir 5 brace, rally, ready, renew, rouse, steel 6 enrich, secure 7 hearten, prepare, protect, refresh, restore 8 embolden, energize 9 encourage, reinforce 10 invigorate, strengthen

fortitude
4 grit, guts, pith 5 fiber, heart, nerve, pluck, spunk, valor 6 mettle, phlegm, spirit 7 bravery, courage, stamina 8 backbone, boldness, strength, tenacity 9 constancy, endurance, tolerance 10 resolution 11 intrepidity 12 fearlessness, perseverance, resoluteness, staying power 13 dauntlessness, determination

fortress
see **fort**

fortuitous
5 fluky, happy, lucky 6 casual, chance 10 accidental, auspicious 12 providential

fortuity
3 hap 4 luck 5 fluke 6 chance 8 accident 9 happening 10 occurrence

Fortuna
5 Tyche
symbol: 5 wheel 6 rudder

fortunate
5 happy, lucky 9 favorable 10 auspicious, propitious 12 providential

Fortunate Islands
8 Canaries

fortune
3 lot, pot, wad 4 doom, fate, luck, mint, pile, ship 5 worth 6 boodle, bundle, chance, happen, hazard, packet, riches, wealth 7 destiny, success, weather 8 property 9 resources

Fortune founder
4 Luce (Henry)

fortune-teller
4 seer 5 augur, sibyl 7 diviner, palmist 9 wisewoman 10 soothsayer
(see also **foreseer**)

fortune-telling
see **divination**

forty winks
3 nap 6 catnap, siesta, snooze 7 shut-eye

forum
5 court, panel 6 medium 8 congress, tribunal 9 symposium 10 colloquium, conference, roundtable 11 convocation, marketplace

forward
3 aid 4 abet, bold, send, ship 5 ahead, brash, eager, pushy, ready, relay, remit, sassy, saucy 6 cheeky, foster, onward, uphold 7 address, advance, consign, further, promote, support 8 advanced, champion, dispatch, impudent, transmit 9 encourage, in advance 11 smart-alecky 12 presumptuous 13 self-assertive
prefix: 4 ante

For Whom the Bell Tolls
author: 9 Hemingway (Ernest)
character: 5 Maria, Pablo, Pilar 6 Jordan

Forza del Destino composer
 5 Verdi (Giuseppe)

fossa
 3 pit 5 fovea 6 cavity, groove
 10 depression

fosse
 4 dike, moat 5 canal, ditch 6 trench
 7 acequia, channel

fossil
 4 fogy 5 amber, relic 7 antique
 8 calamite, conodont, mossback
 10 antiquated, fuddy-duddy 12 antediluvian 13 stick-in-the-mud
 fuel: 3 gas, oil 4 coal, peat 9 petroleum 10 natural gas

foster
 4 back, help, rear, tend 5 nurse
 6 assist, harbor, parent 7 advance,
bring up, nourish, nurture, promote,
support, sustain 8 champion 9 cultivate, encourage

fou
 5 crazy, drunk

foul
 4 base, rank, soil, vile 5 botch, dirty,
fetid, funky, muddy, nasty, yucky
 6 coarse, defile, filthy, grubby, horrid,
impure, odious, putrid, rotten, scuzzy,
smutty, stormy, turbid, vulgar, wicked
 7 abusive, noisome, obscene,
pollute, profane, raunchy, squalid,
tarnish, unclean 8 indecent, obstruct, polluted, stinking, wretched
 9 collision, loathsome, obnoxious,
offensive, repellent, repugnant,
repulsive, revolting 10 abominable,
detestable, disgusting, malodorous
 11 contaminate, treacherous 12 dishonorable, scatological

foul play
 3 hit 5 blood 6 murder 7 killing, outrage 8 homicide, violence 12 manslaughter

found
 4 base, cast, rear 5 begin, erect,
raise, set up, start 6 bottom, create,
invent 7 fashion, support 8 commence, initiate, organize 9 establish,
institute, originate, predicate

foundation
 3 bed 4 base, rock 5 basis 6 bottom,
corset, makeup 7 bedding, footing,
support 8 pedestal 9 endowment
 10 groundwork, substratum 11 institution 12 organization, substructure,
underpinning

foundational
 5 basic 6 bottom 7 primary 10 supportive, underlying 11 fundamental

founder
 4 fail, sink 5 wreck 6 author, father,
go down 7 creator 8 collapse,
inventor, submerge, submerse
 9 architect, generator, patriarch,
shipwreck 10 originator

fountain
 3 jet 4 head, root 5 spout 6 geyser,
origin, source, spring 7 bubbler
 8 wellhead 9 inception, reservoir
 10 wellspring
 nymph: 6 Egeria

four
 6 tetrad 7 quartet 10 quaternion
 bagger: 5 homer 7 home run
 combining form: 4 tetr 5 quadr,
tetra 6 quadri, quadru, quater, tessar
 7 tessara, tessera
 gills: 4 pint
 hundred: 5 elite 10 upper crust
 inches: 4 hand
 pecks: 6 bushel
 quarts: 6 gallon

four-flush
 4 dupe 5 bluff 6 betray, delude,
humbug, take in 7 beguile, deceive
 11 doublecross

four-footed animal
 8 tetrapod 9 quadruped

Four Horsemen
 3 War 5 Death 6 Famine
 8 Conquest 10 Pestilence

four-in-hand
 3 tie 5 coach 7 necktie

fourpence
 5 groat

four-poster
 3 bed

fourscore
6 eighty

four-sided figure
5 rhomb 6 square 7 rhombus
9 rectangle 13 quadrilateral, parallelogram

foursquare
8 straight 10 forthright 13 quadrilateral

fourteen pounds
5 stone

fourth
7 quarter 8 quadrant, quartern
combining form: 5 quadr, quart
6 quadri, quadru

fowl
3 hen 4 bird, cock, duck 5 chick,
goose, poult 6 bantam, pullet, turkey
7 chicken, rooster
(see also **chicken; poultry**)

Fowles novel
5 Magus (The) 9 Collector (The)
22 French Lieutenant's Woman (The)

fox
4 fool 5 trick 6 baffle, outwit
7 confuse, reynard 8 bewilder
African: 4 asse
female: 5 vixen
kind: 3 kit, red 5 swift 6 arctic,
fennec, silver 8 bat-eared
Scottish: 3 tod
young: 3 cub

foxglove
9 digitalis

fox grape
9 muscadine 11 scuppernong

foxiness
4 wile 5 craft, guile 7 cunning,
slyness 8 wiliness 10 artfulness,
craftiness, cleverness

foxlike
7 vulpine

foxy
3 sly 4 wily 5 canny, slick 6 artful,
astute, clever, crafty, shrewd, tricky
7 cunning, vulpine 8 guileful 9 insidious

foyer
5 lobby 8 anteroom, entrance
9 vestibule

fracas
3 row 4 feud, fray 5 brawl, broil,
fight, melee, run-in, set-to 6 affray,
hassle, shindy, uproar 7 dispute,
quarrel, ruction 8 squabble 9 bickering 10 donnybrook, free-for-all
11 altercation

fraction
3 bit, cut 4 part 5 piece, scrap
6 divide, little 7 portion, section
8 fragment

fractious
4 wild 6 unruly 7 peevish, pettish,
willful 8 contrary 9 bellicose, irritable 10 headstrong, pugnacious,
refractory 11 belligerent, contentious, intractable, quarrelsome
12 recalcitrant, ungovernable,
unmanageable

fracture
4 rent, rift, tear 5 break, cleft, crack,
split 6 breach, schism 7 rupture

Fra Diavolo composer
5 Auber (Esprit)

fragile
4 weak 5 frail 6 feeble, flimsy,
infirm 7 brittle, friable, tenuous,
unsound 8 decrepit, delicate
9 breakable, frangible

fragment
3 bit 4 chip, iota, part, rive 5 burst,
crumb, flake, grain, piece, scrap,
shard, shred, smash 6 morsel,
shiver, sliver 7 break up, flinder,
shatter 8 fraction, particle, splinter
9 fall apart 12 disintegrate

fragmentary
6 broken 7 partial 10 fractional,
incomplete, unfinished

fragrance
4 musk, nose, odor 5 aroma, attar,
scent, smell, spice 7 bouquet,
cologne, incense, perfume 9 redolence 11 eau de parfum, toilet water
13 eau de toilette

fragrant

7 odorous, scented 8 aromatic, perfumed, redolent 11 odoriferous

frail

4 puny, slim, thin, weak 5 petty, reedy, wispy 6 feeble, flimsy, infirm, sickly, slight 7 brittle, fragile, slender, spindly, tenuous, unsound 8 decrepit, delicate 9 breakable, frangible

frailty

4 vice 5 fault 6 foible 7 failing 8 delicacy, weakness 9 infirmity 10 feebleness 11 tenuousness 12 imperfection

frame

4 body, form, mold, plan, sash 5 build, draft, erect, forge, mount, shape, shell 6 border, casing, cook up, devise, draw up, figure, invent, make up, sketch, system 7 arrange, chassis, concoct, fashion, imagine, prepare 8 assemble, casement, conceive, contrive, regulate, skeleton 9 cartouche, construct, fabricate, formulate, structure

part: 4 sill, stud 5 joist, plate

framework

4 rack 5 shell, truss 7 trestle 8 cribbing, cribwork, scaffold, skeleton, studding, studwork, trussing 9 bare bones, structure

of crossed strips: 7 lattice, trellis

France

bay: 6 Biscay
capital: 5 Paris
channel: 6 Manche (La) 7 English
city: 4 Caen, Lyon, Metz, Nice 5 Brest, Lyons 6 Amiens, Calais, Nantes, Rennes 8 Bordeaux, Grenoble, Toulouse 9 Marseille 10 Marseilles, Strasbourg, Versailles 11 Montpellier
conqueror: 6 Caesar (Julius)
emperor: 5 Pepin (III, the Short) 8 Napoleon (Bonaparte) 11 Charlemagne
enclave: 6 Monaco
former name: 4 Gaul 6 Gallia

historic province: 4 Foix 5 Anjou, Aunis, Bearn, Berry, Maine 6 Alsace, Artois, Marche, Poitou, Vendée 7 Gascony, Guyenne, Picardy 8 Auvergne, Bretagne, Brittany, Burgundy, Dauphine, Flanders, Gascogne, Limousin, Lorraine, Lyonnais, Normandy, Picardie, Provence, Touraine 9 Angoumois, Bourgogne, Champagne, Languedoc, Nivernois, Orléanais, Saintonge, Venaissin 10 Roussillon 11 Bourbonnais, Île-de-France 12 Franche-Comté
island: 3 Yeu 6 Hyères, Oléron, Ushant 7 Corsica 8 Belle-Île 11 Noirmoutier
monarch: 5 Henri, Henry, Louis 6 Philip 7 Charles 8 Philippe
monetary unit: 4 euro
monetary unit, former: 3 sou 5 franc
mountain, range: 4 Alps, Jura 6 Vosges 7 Auvergne, Pyrenees 9 Mont Blanc
neighbor: 5 Italy, Spain 7 Andorra, Belgium, Germany 10 Luxembourg 11 Switzerland
president: 8 de Gaulle (Charles) 10 Mitterrand (François)
region: 5 Corse 6 Alsace, Centre 7 Corsica, Picardy 8 Auvergne, Bretagne, Brittany, Burgundy, Limousin, Normandy, Picardie 9 Aquitaine, Bourgogne, Champagne, Languedoc, Normandie 10 Rhône-Alpes 11 Île-de-France 12 Franche-Comté, Midi-Pyrénées
river: 4 Aire, Aude, Oise 5 Adour, Isère, Loire, Marne, Rhone, Saône, Seine, Somme, Yonne 7 Garonne
sea: 13 Mediterranean
strait: 5 Dover

Francesca's lover

5 Paolo

franchise

4 vote 6 ballot 7 freedom, license 8 suffrage 9 privilege

frangible

7 brittle, fragile, friable 8 delicate 9 breakable

frank

3 dog **4** fair, free, open **5** blunt, plain **6** candid, direct, honest, hot dog, weenie, wiener, wienie **7** upright **8** man-to-man, out-front, straight **9** barefaced, outspoken **10** forthright, scrupulous, unreserved **11** openhearted, plainspoken, transparent, unconcealed, undisguised, uninhibited, unvarnished, wienerwurst **12** heart-to-heart, unmistakable

Frankenstein author

7 Shelley (Mary)

frankfurter

3 dog **6** hot dog, weenie, wiener, wienie **11** wienerwurst

Frankie's lover

6 Johnny

Frankish hero

6 Roland

Franklin, Benjamin

birthplace: 6 Boston
invention: 5 stove **8** bifocals
pen name: 11 Poor Richard

frankness

6 candor **7** honesty

frantic

3 mad **4** wild **5** upset, wired **7** fraught, shook up, unglued **8** feverish, frenetic, frenzied, maniacal, worked up **10** distraught **11** overwrought

Franzen novel

11 Corrections (The)

frappe

7 chilled, liqueur **9** milk shake

fraternal

6 clubby **8** sociable **9** brotherly, comradely, dizygotic **10** like-minded

fraternal society

3 FOE **4** BPOE, Elks **5** Lions, Moose **6** Eagles, Masons **7** Woodmen **8** Shriners **10** Freemasons, Hibernians, Odd Fellows

fraternity

4 club **5** guild, order, union **6** league **7** company **8** sodality **10** fellowship **11** association, brotherhood **13** brotherliness

fraud

3 gyp **4** fake, gaff, hoax, sham **5** cheat, faker, phony, quack, trick **6** deceit, dupery, humbug, hustle **7** chicane, swindle **8** cozenage, flimflam, impostor, operator, trickery **9** charlatan, chicanery, deception, imposture, pretender, shell game, trickster **10** dishonesty, mountebank, subterfuge **11** counterfeit **12** double-dealer **13** double-dealing, sharp practice

fraudulence

6 deceit **8** quackery, trickery **9** chicanery, deception, phoniness **10** dishonesty

fraudulent

4 fake **5** false, phony **7** crooked **8** cheating, guileful **9** deceitful, deceptive, dishonest **10** fallacious **11** duplicitous

fraught

4 full **5** laden, tense **6** filled, uneasy **7** charged, replete, stuffed **8** pregnant **9** stressful

fräulein

4 maid, Miss **6** maiden **9** governess **12** mademoiselle

fray

3 row **4** fret **5** brawl, broil, brush, clash, fight, melee, ravel, shred **6** combat, fracas, strain, strife **7** dispute, frazzle, ruction, scuffle **8** irritate, skirmish, struggle **9** commotion, scrimmage **10** donnybrook **11** disturbance

frayed

4 worn **6** ragged, shabby **8** tattered **9** moth-eaten **10** threadbare

frazzle

4 do in, fray, poop, tire, wear **5** upset **6** tucker **7** exhaust, fatigue, wear out

frazzled
4 beat 5 upset 6 bushed, sapped
7 drained, rattled 8 agitated, confused, fatigued, tired out 9 exhausted, fagged out, unsettled
10 distressed 11 overwrought
12 disconcerted

freak
3 bug, nut 4 buff, geek, whim 5 go
ape, fancy, fiend, maven 6 addict,
hippie, maniac, megrim, oddity,
vagary, weirdo, whimsy, zealot
7 anomaly, caprice, chimera, conceit,
deviate, fanatic, monster 8 crotchet,
flimflam 9 androgyne, curiosity
10 aberration, enthusiast 11 abnormality, monstrosity 12 lusus naturae,
malformation

freakish
3 odd 5 kooky, outré, weird 6 far-
out, quirky 7 bizarre, erratic, oddball,
strange 8 aberrant, abnormal 9 arbitrary, eccentric, grotesque, whimsical 10 capricious, outlandish

freckle
3 dot 4 mole, spot 5 fleck 7 speckle,
stipple

free
3 rid 4 comp, open 5 frank, loose,
untie 6 acquit, exempt, gratis, loosen,
unbind, untied 7 absolve, at large,
liberal, manumit, movable, release,
unbound, unchain, unleash, unloose
8 detached, generous, liberate,
relieved, separate, unburden, unfasten, unloosen 9 at liberty, discharge,
exculpate, exonerate, extricate,
sovereign, unchained, unchecked,
unimpeded, unshackle, unsparing
10 autonomous, democratic, emancipate, gratuitous, unconfined, unfastened, unfettered, unhampered,
unshackled, voluntary 11 disentangle, emancipated, independent,
spontaneous, untrammeled 12 unrestrained, unrestricted 13 complimentary, self-directing, self-governing,
unconstrained

freebie
4 gift, pass 7 present 8 giveaway

freebooter
5 rover 6 bandit, pirate, raider
7 brigand, corsair 8 marauder,
picaroon, pillager, rapparee, sea
rover 9 buccaneer, pickaroon,
plunderer, ransacker

freedom
5 right 7 liberty, license, release
8 autonomy, immunity, latitude
9 exemption, franchise, privilege
11 prerogative 12 emancipation,
independence 13 outspokenness

free-for-all
4 fray 5 brawl, broil, melee 6 affray,
fracas, rumble 7 ruction 10 donnybrook

freehanded
7 liberal 8 generous 9 bounteous,
bountiful 10 munificent

freeloader
3 bum 5 leech 6 sponge 7 moocher
8 barnacle, hanger-on, parasite
11 bloodsucker

Free State
8 Maryland

free ticket
4 pass 11 Annie Oakley

freeze
4 halt, stop 5 chill, stall 6 benumb
7 congeal 8 glaciate, solidify, stoppage 10 immobilize

freezing
3 icy 4 cold 5 chill, gelid, nippy,
polar 6 arctic, bitter, chilly, frigid,
frosty, wintry 7 glacial, shivery
combining form: 4 cryo, kryo

freight
4 haul, lade, load 5 cargo 6 burden,
charge, lading 7 payload 9 transport

freighter
4 scow, ship 7 carrier, shipper

Freischütz composer
5 Weber (Carl Maria von)

French

article: 3 les, une
attendant: 9 concierge
back: 3 dos
bed: 3 lit 6 couche
boy: 6 garçon
brother: 5 frère
cap: 5 beret
cardinal: 7 Mazarin (Jules) 9 Richelieu (Duc de)
castle: 7 château
cathedral city: 4 Albi 5 Paris, Reims, Rouen 6 Amiens, Nantes, Rheims 8 Chartres
clergyman: 4 abbé, curé, père
coin: 3 ecu
combining form: 5 Gallo 6 Franco
conjunction: 4 mais
daughter: 5 fille
day: 5 jeudi, lundi, mardi 6 samedi 8 dimanche, mercredi, vendredi
dear: 4 cher
department head: 7 prefect
direction: 3 est, sud 4 nord 5 ouest
down with: 4 à bas
dream: 4 rêve
drink: 5 boire
dynasty: 5 Capet 6 Valois 7 Bourbon
egg: 4 oeuf
emblem: 10 fleur-de-lis
empress: 7 Eugénie 9 Joséphine
evening: 4 soir
exclamation: 3 zut 4 eheu, hein 9 sacrebleu
farewell: 5 adieu 8 au revoir
father: 4 père
forest: 7 Argonne, Belleau
friend: 3 ami 4 amie
game: 3 jeu 4 jeux (plural)
God: 4 dieu
good: 3 bon 5 bonne
hat: 7 chapeau
here: 3 ici
income: 5 rente
king: 3 roi
language: 9 Provençal
month: 3 mai 4 août, juin, mars, mois 5 avril 7 février, janvier, juillet
mother: 4 mère
national anthem: 12 Marseillaise (La)

opera: 5 Faust, Lakmé, Manon, Thaïs 6 Carmen, Mignon 7 Werther
pancake: 5 crêpe
pastry: 6 éclair 8 napoleon
policeman: 4 flic 8 gendarme
porcelain: 6 Sèvres 7 Limoges
preposition: 3 par, sur 4 avec, dans, pour, sans, sous
pretty: 4 joli 5 jolie
prison: 8 Bastille
pronoun: 3 eux, ils, mes, moi, toi, une 4 elle, nous, vous
Protestant: 6 Calvin (John) 8 Huguenot
pupil: 5 élève
queen: 5 reine
rabbit: 5 lapin
railroad station: 4 gare
resort: 3 Pau 4 Nice 5 Vichy 6 Cannes, Menton 7 Antibes 8 Biarritz
resort area: 7 Riviera
restaurant: 6 bistro
revolutionist: 5 Marat (Jean-Paul) 6 Danton (Georges) 11 Robespierre (Maximilien)
Revolution party: 7 Gironde, Jacobin 8 Mountain
Revolution song: 5 Ça Ira
saint: 4 Joan (of Arc) 5 Denis 6 Martin (of Tours) 7 Thérèse (of Lisieux)
school: 5 école, lycée
sea: 3 mer
season: 3 été 5 hiver 7 automne 9 printemps
servant: 5 valet
shop: 8 boutique
shrine: 7 Lourdes
singer: 4 Piaf (Edith) 8 chanteur 9 chanteuse
sister: 5 soeur
small: 5 petit 6 petite
soldier: 5 poilu 6 soldat, Zouave 8 chasseur
son: 4 fils
song: 7 chanson
soup: 6 potage
star: 6 étoile
state: 4 état
stock exchange: 6 bourse
street: 3 rue

subway: 5 metro
there!: 5 voilà
too much: 4 trop
very: 4 très
wartime capital: 5 Vichy
water: 3 eau
well: 4 bien
wineshop: 6 bistro
wood: 4 bois
yesterday: 4 hier

French Guiana
capital: 7 Cayenne
department of: 6 France
ethnic group: 6 Creole
island: 6 Devil's
mountain range: 10 Tumac-Humac
neighbor: 6 Brazil 8 Suriname
river: 4 Mana 6 Maroni 7 Oyapock

French Polynesia
archipelago 7 Tuamotu
capital: 7 Papeete
island, island group: 6 Tahiti
7 Austral, Gambier, Society 9 Marquesas
territory of: 6 France

frenetic
3 mad 4 loco, wild 5 crazy, wired
6 crazed, hectic 7 berserk, frantic
8 agitated, feverish, frenzied, maniacal 9 delirious, orgiastic 10 corybantic

frenzied
see **frenetic**

frenzy
4 amok, fury, rage 5 amuck, craze,
furor, mania 6 madden 7 derange,
madness, unhinge 8 delirium, distract, hysteria, insanity, paroxysm
9 unbalance 11 derangement

frequency unit
5 hertz 7 fresnel 9 gigahertz

frequent
5 haunt, often, usual, visit 6 common, hourly 7 regular 8 everyday, familiar, habitual 9 customary

frequenter
7 denizen, habitué, haunter

frequently
5 often 8 commonly 9 routinely
10 oftentimes, repeatedly 11 customarily, recurrently

fresh
3 new, raw 4 rude 5 green, naive,
novel, sassy, saucy, smart 6 callow,
cheeky, recent, unused, vernal, virgin
8 brand-new, impudent, insolent,
original 9 unspoiled 11 impertinent,
smart-alecky 12 invigorating 13 inexperienced

freshet
5 flood, spate 6 influx

freshman
4 tyro 5 frosh, plebe 6 novice,
rookie 8 beginner, neophyte, newcomer 10 apprentice, tenderfoot
13 underclassman

fret
4 fume, fuss, stew 5 brood, chafe,
worry 6 dither, pother

fretful
5 angry, cross 6 crabby, cranky
7 carping, chafing, peevish, pettish,
whining 8 captious, caviling, critical,
perverse, petulant, restless, snappish 9 fractious, impatient, irascible,
irritable, querulous

Frey
father: 5 Njörd 6 Njörth
god of: 3 sun 4 rain 5 peace
9 fertility
sister: 5 Freya
wife: 4 Gerd 5 Gerda, Gerth

Freya
brother: 4 Frey
domain: 9 Folkvangr
father: 5 Njörd 6 Njörth
husband: 4 Odin

friable
5 mealy 7 brittle, crumbly, fragile
9 frangible

friar
7 brother 8 cenobite 9 mendicant

fribble
3 toy 5 dally, flirt 6 coquet, trifle

friction

7 trifler 8 trifling 9 dalliance, frivolity
10 dillydally, fool around

friction

4 drag 7 discord, rubbing 8 abrasion
9 animosity, attrition 10 disharmony,
dissension, resistance 12 disagreement

friction match

5 vesta 7 lucifer 8 vesuvian

Friday's rescuer

6 Crusoe (Robinson)

friend

3 pal 4 ally, chum, mate 5 buddy,
crony, matey, serve 6 cohort 7 comrade, partner 8 alter ego, compadre,
confrere, familiar, intimate, playmate,
sidekick 9 associate, colleague,
companion, confidant 10 confidante
11 cater-cousin 12 acquaintance
French: 3 ami 4 amie
Spanish: 5 amiga, amigo

Friend

6 Quaker
founder: 3 Fox (George)

friendly

5 happy 6 amical, chummy, folksy,
genial 7 affable, amiable, cordial
8 amicable, cheerful, familiar, sociable 9 congenial, favorable
10 buddy-buddy, compatible, hospitable, neighborly 12 affectionate,
well-disposed 13 accommodating

Friendly Islands

5 Tonga

friends and neighbors

4 kith

friendship

5 amity 6 accord, comity 7 concord, empathy, harmony 8 affinity,
alliance, goodwill

frigate bird

3 ioa, iwa 8 alcatras 11 man-o'-war
bird
genus: 7 Fregata

Frigga, Frigg

husband: 4 Odin
son: 6 Balder

fright

4 fear 5 alarm, dread, panic, scare,
shock 6 dismay, horror, terror
11 trepidation

frighten

3 cow 5 alarm, bully, daunt, scare,
shock, spook 6 appall, dismay
7 horrify, perturb, scarify, startle, terrify, unnerve 9 terrorize 10 intimidate

frightful

4 ugly 5 awful, scary 6 horrid
7 fearful, ghastly, hideous 8 alarming,
dreadful, fearsome, horrible, horrific,
shocking, terrible, terrific 9 appalling,
startling 10 formidable, horrendous,
terrifying

frigid

3 icy 4 cold 5 chill 6 arctic, chilly,
frosty 7 glacial 8 freezing 11 emotionless, indifferent, passionless,
unemotional 12 unresponsive

frijoles

5 beans

frill

4 ruff 5 jabot, ruche 6 doodad,
luxury, ruffle 7 flounce, ruching
8 furbelow 11 affectation, superfluity
12 extravagance

fringe

3 hem, rim 4 brim, ruff 5 bound,
brink, skirt, thrum, verge 6 border,
edging, margin 7 fimbria 8 penumbra, trimming 9 perimeter, periphery
10 borderland

frippery

6 finery, frills, tawdry 7 regalia
8 foofaraw, trumpery 9 trappings
11 ostentation

frisée

6 endive 7 lettuce

frisk

4 leap, play, romp, skip 5 caper,
dance 6 cavort, frolic, gambol,
search 7 disport, pat down, rollick

frisky

3 gay 5 antic 6 feisty, lively 7 coltish,
playful 8 animated, gamesome,

sportive **9** sprightly, vivacious **10** frolicsome

fritter away
4 blow **5** spend, waste **7** consume **8** squander **9** dissipate

frivolity
3 fun **4** play **6** gaiety, levity, whimsy **8** nonsense **12** childishness

frivolous
3 gay **5** dizzy, giddy, light, silly **6** frothy, yeasty **7** flighty, playful, shallow, trivial **8** carefree, careless, heedless, trifling **11** light-headed, superficial

frizzy
5 kinky **6** coiled, curled **7** twisted

frock
4 gown **5** dress, habit **6** jersey, mantle

frog
4 toad **5** ranid **6** anuran **7** croaker **9** amphibian **10** batrachian
family: 7 Ranidae
genus: 4 Rana
kind: 4 hyla **6** peeper **7** leopard **8** bullfrog, tree toad
larva: 7 tadpole

frolic
3 fun **4** lark, play, romp **5** antic, caper, dance, frisk, party, prank, revel, sport, spree **6** cavort, didoes, gaiety, gambol, prance **7** disport, skylark **8** escapade, hilarity **9** festivity, merriment **10** shenanigan, tomfoolery

frolicsome
3 gay **5** antic **6** frisky, impish **7** coltish, jocular, playful, roguish **8** sportful, sportive **9** sprightly **10** rollicking **11** mischievous

from
German: 3 von
Scottish: 4 frae

From Here to Eternity author
5 Jones (James)

frondeur
5 rebel **8** mutineer, renegade

9 anarchist, dissident, insurgent **10** malcontent

front
3 bow, van **4** face, fore, lend, look, mask, prow **5** beard **6** facade, facing **7** forward **8** anterior, disguise **9** challenge, encounter **10** appearance, figurehead **11** countenance

frontier
5 bound, field, march **6** border **8** backland, backwash, boundary **9** up-country **10** borderland, hinterland **11** backcountry

frontiersman
5 Boone (Daniel), Clark (George Rogers, William) **6** Carson (Kit) **7** pioneer, settler **8** Crockett (Davy) **10** bushranger

fronton game
7 jai alai

frontward
8 anterior

frost
4 hoar, rime **6** freeze

frostfish
5 smelt **6** tomcod

frost heave
5 pingo

frosting
5 icing **7** topping **8** trimming

Frost poem
11 Mending Wall **12** Road Not Taken (The) **18** Death of the Hired Man (The) **30** Stopping By Woods on a Snowy Evening

frosty
3 icy **4** cold, rimy **5** chill, frore, hoary, nippy **6** chilly, frigid **7** glacial **8** freezing **10** unfriendly

froth
4 foam, head, suds **5** cream, spume, yeast **6** lather **8** airiness **9** frivolity, lightness

froufrou
6 frills **8** rustling

froward
5 balky 6 mulish, ornery 7 peevish, restive 8 contrary, perverse, petulant, stubborn 9 obstinate 10 headstrong, refractory 11 disobedient

frown
4 pout, sulk 5 glare, lower, scowl 6 glower

frowsy
5 dowdy, funky, fusty, messy, musty, stale 6 shabby, smelly, sordid, untidy 7 squalid, unkempt 8 slattern, slovenly 10 disheveled, disordered, slatternly 13 draggletailed

frozen
4 cold, hard 5 fixed, frore, rigid, stiff 6 frigid, numbed 7 chilled 8 benumbed, immobile 9 congealed, petrified

frugal
4 mean 5 canny, scant, spare 6 Scotch, stingy 7 careful, prudent, scrimpy, sparing, thrifty 8 discreet, stinting 9 niggardly, penurious, provident 10 economical, unwasteful 12 cheeseparing, parsimonious 13 penny-pinching

frugality
6 thrift 7 economy 8 prudence 9 husbandry 10 providence 11 thriftiness

fruit
5 issue, young 6 result 7 outcome, progeny 9 offspring
citrus: 4 lime 5 lemon 6 citron, orange, pomelo 7 kumquat, tangelo 8 bergamot, mandarin, shaddock 9 tangerine 10 calamondin, grapefruit
dried: 5 prune 6 raisin
drink: 3 ade 5 juice, punch
fleshy: 7 syconia (plural) 8 syconium
hard-shelled: 3 nut 4 seed 5 gourd 7 coconut
residue: 4 marc 6 pomace
seed: 3 pip
study of: 8 pomology 9 carpology
subtropical: 3 fig 4 date, lime 5 lemon, olive 6 citron, orange

7 avocado, kumquat 9 tangerine 10 grapefruit
sugar: 7 glucose 8 fructose, levulose
temperate-zone: 4 pear, plum, sloe 5 apple, grape, melon, papaw, peach, prune 6 casaba, cherry, loquat, pawpaw, quince 7 apricot, currant 8 dewberry 9 blueberry, cranberry, muskmelon, nectarine, raspberry 10 blackberry, gooseberry, loganberry, strawberry 11 boysenberry, huckleberry, pomegranate
tropical: 5 guava, mango 6 banana, papaya 7 acerola 8 rambutan, tamarind 9 cherimoya, persimmon, pineapple 10 calamondin, mangosteen
type: 3 nut 4 pepo, pome 5 berry, drupe 6 achene, legume, loment, samara 7 capsule, silique, utricle 11 hesperidium
undeveloped: 6 nubbin

fruitful
6 fecund 7 copious, fertile 8 abundant, prolific 9 bountiful, fructuous, plenteous, plentiful 10 productive 11 proliferant

fruition
7 delight 8 pleasure 9 enjoyment 10 attainment, conclusion 11 achievement, delectation, fulfillment, realization

fruitless
4 vain 6 barren, futile 7 sterile, useless 8 abortive 10 unavailing 11 ineffective, ineffectual 12 unproductive, unsuccessful

frumpy
4 drab, dull 5 dated, dowdy, tacky 6 stodgy 8 outmoded 9 out-of-date, unstylish 12 old-fashioned

frustrate
4 balk, bilk, dash, foil, halt 5 block, check, stump 6 arrest, baffle, defeat, hinder, impede, stymie, thwart 7 inhibit, prevent 8 confound, obstruct, preclude, prohibit 9 discomfit, forestall, interrupt 10 disappoint

frustration
   6 defeat, dismay 7 chagrin, letdown 8 vexation 9 annoyance,
   hindrance 10 impediment, irritation
   11 displeasure, obstruction

fry
   4 burn, sear 5 frizz, grill, sauté
   6 fishes, picnic 7 frizzle 11 electrocute

frying pan
   6 spider 7 griddle, skillet

fuddle
   5 befog, booze 6 ball up, jumble,
   tipple 7 confuse, fluster, stupefy
   8 bewilder 10 intoxicate

fuddy-duddy
   4 fogy 6 fossil, square, stodgy
   8 mossback, outdated, outmoded
   12 antediluvian, Colonel Blimp,
   old-fashioned, stuffed shirt 13 stick-
   in-the-mud

fudge
   3 pad 4 blur, bosh, fake 5 candy,
   cheat, color, dodge, hedge, hooey,
   welsh 6 bunkum 7 distort, falsify,
   hogwash, penuche 8 contrive,
   divinity, nonsense 9 embellish,
   embroider, overstate, poppycock
   10 equivocate, flapdoodle 11 foolishness

fuel
   3 gas, oil 4 coal, coke, fire, peat,
   wood 5 stoke 6 biogas, diesel,
   petrol 7 ethanol, gasohol, inflame,
   propane 8 charcoal, gasoline,
   kerosene 9 petroleum, stimulate
   10 natural gas 13 reinforcement

fugacious
   7 brittle, passing 8 fleeting, fugitive,
   volatile 9 ephemeral, momentary,
   transient 10 evanescent, short-lived,
   transitory

fugitive
   5 exile 6 outlaw 7 escapee, lamster,
   nomadic, passing, refugee, runaway
   8 deserter, fleeting, runagate, vagabond 9 ephemeral, fugacious,
   momentary, transient, wandering
   10 evanescent, short-lived, transitory

fugue master
   4 Bach (Johann Sebastian)

Führer, der
   6 Hitler (Adolf)

fulcrum
   3 hub 4 axis, prop 5 hinge, nexus,
   pivot 7 support

fulfill
   4 meet 5 honor 6 effect, finish,
   redeem 7 achieve, execute, perform,
   satisfy 8 complete 9 discharge,
   implement 10 accomplish

fulgent
   6 bright 7 beaming, glowing, radiant, shining 8 luminous, lustrous
   9 brilliant

fuliginous
   4 dark 5 dingy, dusky, grimy, murky,
   sooty 7 obscure

full
   5 sated, total, whole 6 entire, gorged,
   jammed, loaded, packed, utmost
   7 crammed, crowded, glutted, maximum, plenary, replete, stuffed
   8 brimming, complete, satiated
   9 jam-packed, plentiful, surfeited
   11 chockablock

full-blooded
   4 rich 5 flush, ruddy 6 ardent,
   florid 7 flushed, genuine, glowing
   8 forceful, purebred, rubicund,
   sanguine 9 pedigreed, pureblood
   10 compelling 12 thoroughbred

full-blown
   4 lush, ripe 5 adult, total 6 all-out,
   mature 7 grown-up

full-bodied
   4 rich 5 husky, lusty, stout 6 potent,
   robust, strong 9 corpulent 10 meaningful 11 significant, substantial

full dress
   6 finery 7 regalia 8 frippery, glad
   rags 10 Sunday best

full-figured
   5 ample, buxom, plump 6 zaftig
   10 curvaceous, Rubenesque, statuesque, voluptuous

full-fledged
4 ripe 5 adult, grown, total 6 mature
7 genuine, grown-up 8 complete
9 full-blown

full-grown
4 ripe 5 adult 6 mature

fullness
6 plenty 7 satiety 9 abundance,
amplitude, repletion 10 perfection
12 completeness

full-scale
5 total 6 all-out 8 complete, life-size
9 unlimited

full tilt
7 flat-out, rapidly, swiftly 8 pell-mell,
speedily 9 posthaste 12 lickety-split

fulminate
4 boil, burn, foam, fume, rage, rave
5 curse, flare 7 bluster, explode,
inveigh

fulsome
4 oily 5 plump, slick, soapy, suave
6 lavish, smarmy, smooth 7 buttery,
cloying, copious, profuse 8 abundant, effusive, generous, overdone,
unctuous 9 excessive 10 flattering,
oleaginous 11 extravagant, pharisaical 12 ingratiating, Pecksniffian

Fulton's steamboat
8 Clermont

fumarole
4 vent

fumble
3 bob, paw 4 feel, flub, mess, muff
5 botch, grope 6 bobble, bollix,
bungle, muddle 7 blunder, misplay
8 flounder

fume
3 gas 4 boil, burn, odor, rage, rant,
rave, reek, snit, stew 5 smoke,
vapor 6 seethe, swivet 7 sputter

fun
4 play 5 sport 6 frolic, gaiety 7 amusing, jollity, pastime, whoopee 8 hilarity, pleasant, ridicule 9 amusement,
diversion, diverting, enjoyment,
frivolity, horseplay, jocundity, joviality,
merriment 10 pleasantry 12 entertaining 13 entertainment

function
3 act, job, run, use 4 duty, goal,
mark, role, task, work 5 party, power,
react, serve 6 affair, behave, object,
office, target 7 concern, faculty,
operate, perform, purpose, service
8 activity, behavior, business, capacity, ceremony, occasion, province
9 objective, officiate, operation,
reception
trigonometric: 4 sine 6 cosine,
secant 7 tangent 8 cosecant
9 cotangent

functional
5 handy, utile 6 useful 7 working
9 practical 11 practicable, serviceable, utilitarian 12 occupational

functioning
6 active 7 dynamic 9 operative

fund
4 bank, pool 5 endow, stake, stock,
store 6 coffer, supply 7 capital,
finance, reserve 8 bankroll, treasury
9 inventory, subsidize 10 accumulate, capitalize

fundament
4 butt, rear, rump, seat 5 basis,
fanny 6 behind, bottom 8 backside,
buttocks, derriere 9 posterior, principle 10 foundation, groundwork

fundamental
3 key 5 axiom, basal, basic, prime,
vital 6 bottom, factor, primal, simple
7 bedrock, organic, primary, radical,
theorem 8 absolute, cardinal, dominant, ultimate 9 component, essential, important, necessary, paramount, primitive, principal, principle,
requisite 10 deep-rooted, elementary, grassroots, primordial, rock-
bottom, underlying 11 constituent,
irreducible, nitty-gritty 12 constitutive, foundational

fund-raiser
8 telethon

funeral
6 burial 7 obsequy 9 obsequies
car: 6 hearse
director: 9 mortician 10 undertaker
oration: 6 eulogy 8 encomium
9 panegyric
procession: 7 cortege
service: 7 requiem 9 obsequies
song: 5 dirge, elegy 8 threnody

funereal
3 sad 4 dark 5 black, bleak, grave
6 dismal, dreary, gloomy, solemn,
somber, sombre 7 elegiac 8 mournful 9 deathlike, sorrowful 10 depressing, depressive, lugubrious,
oppressive, sepulchral

fungus
4 conk, mold, rust, smut 5 ergot,
yeast 6 agaric, dry rot, mildew
7 candida, truffle 8 mushroom,
puffball 9 earthstar, stinkhorn,
toadstool
combining form: 4 myco 5 myces,
mycet 6 mycete, myceto
part: 3 cap 4 gill 5 ascus, hypha,
stipe, volva 7 annulus 8 basidium,
conidium, mycelium

fungus disease
3 rot 4 mold, rust, scab, smut
5 ergot, tinea 6 blight, mildew,
thrush 7 mycosis 8 lumpy jaw,
ringworm 12 athlete's foot

funk
4 odor, reek 5 blues, dolor, dumps,
ennui, gloom, smell, stink, slump
6 recoil, stench 7 sadness 9 dejection 10 depression, melancholy

funky
3 hip, odd 4 foul, rank 5 fetid, reeky
6 earthy, frowsy, grungy, quaint,
quirky, smelly, stinky 7 natural, noisome, oddball, offbeat 8 down-home
10 malodorous

funnel
4 flue, pipe 5 stack 6 hopper
7 channel, conduct, tundish 8 transmit 10 smokestack

funny
3 odd 4 joke, zany 5 antic, comic,
droll, fishy, queer 7 amusing,
bizarre, comical, jocular, risible,
strange 8 farcical, humorous, peculiar 9 facetious, fantastic, hilarious,
laughable, ludicrous 10 ridiculous

Funny Girl
5 Brice (Fanny)
composer: 5 Styne (Jule)

funnyman
3 wag, wit 5 clown, comic, cutup, droll, joker 6 gagman, jester
8 comedian, humorist, jokester,
quipster 10 comedienne

fur
4 down, hide, pelt, pile 5 floss, fluff,
stole 6 pelage, peltry
kind: 3 fox 4 mink, seal 5 fitch,
otter, sable 6 ermine, fisher, marten,
nutria, tanuki 7 raccoon 10 chinchilla
lamb: 7 caracul, karakul 9 broadtail
medieval: 4 vair 7 miniver

furbelow
5 frill 7 flounce

furbish
4 buff 5 fix up, renew, shine 6 polish,
revive 7 burnish, refresh, restore
8 renovate

Furies
6 Alecto 7 Erinyes, Megaera 9 Eumenides, Tisiphone

furious
3 mad 4 wild 5 angry, livid, irate,
rabid, upset 6 crazed, fierce, insane
raging, stormy 7 enraged, excited,
extreme, frantic, intense, violent
8 feverish, frenetic, frenzied, incensed, maddened, vehement,
wrathful 9 impetuous, turbulent
10 boisterous, corybantic

furl
4 curl, fold, roll, wrap 6 take in

furlough
4 pass 5 leave 6 lay off 7 liberty
10 shore leave 13 authorization

furnace
4 kiln, oven 5 forge, stove 6 heater
7 smelter 8 tryworks 11 incinerator

furnish

part: 4 port, vent 6 tuyere
tender: 6 stoker

furnish

3 arm, rig 4 give, hand, lend 5 endow, endue, equip 6 fit out, outfit, supply 7 apparel, appoint, deliver, provide, turn out 8 accouter, accoutre, dispense, hand over, transfer 9 provision 10 contribute

furnishings

4 gear 5 decor 9 equipment, trappings 10 housewares 11 appointment 13 accouterments, accoutrements, paraphernalia

furniture designer

American: 5 Eames (Charles, Ray), Phyfe (Duncan) 7 Goddard (John, Stephen, Thomas), Haldane (William) 8 Stickley (Gustav)
British: 6 Morris (William) 7 Gibbons (Grinling), Shearer (Thomas) 8 Sheraton (Thomas) 11 Chippendale (Thomas), Hepplewhite (George)
French: 5 Marot (Daniel) 6 Boulle (André-Charles)
German: 6 Breuer (Marcel)
Scottish: 4 Adam (James, Robert)

furniture style

4 Adam 6 Empire, Shaker 7 Bauhaus, Federal, Mission 8 Colonial, Georgian, Jacobean, Sheraton, Stickley 9 Queen Anne 11 chinoiserie, Chippendale, Duncan Phyfe, Hepplewhite 13 Arts and Crafts

furor

3 ado, cry, fad, wax 4 chic, mode, rage, stir, to-do 5 anger, craze, mania, style, vogue 6 flurry, frenzy, pother, ruckus, rumpus, uproar 7 fashion, madness 8 foofaraw 9 commotion 10 dernier cri, excitement 11 controversy

furrow

3 rut 4 ruck 5 plica, ridge, sulci (plural) 6 course, crease, groove, sulcus, trench 7 channel, crinkle, wrinkle 8 entrench 9 corrugate 11 corrugation

furrowed

5 lined 6 rugose 7 grooved, sulcate 8 wrinkled 10 corrugated

further

4 abet, also, help 5 again, fresh 6 beyond 7 advance, besides, forward, promote 8 engender, moreover 9 encourage, propagate 10 additional, in addition 12 additionally

furthermore

3 and, too 4 also 6 as well, withal 7 besides 8 likewise, moreover 9 what's more 12 additionally

furthermost

4 last 7 extreme 8 farthest, remotest, ultimate

furtive

3 sly 4 foxy, wary, wily 6 artful, covert, crafty, feline, masked, secret, shifty, sneaky, stolen, tricky 7 catlike, cunning, evasive, sub-rosa 8 guileful, hush-hush, scheming, stealthy 9 disguised, insidious 11 circumspect, clandestine 12 hugger-mugger 13 surreptitious, under-the-table

look: 4 peek, peep

fur trader

8 voyageur

furuncle

4 boil 7 abscess

fury

3 ire 4 burn, rage 5 anger, furor, wrath 6 frenzy 7 madness, passion 8 violence 9 vehemence 10 fierceness

furze

4 whin 5 gorse
genus: 4 Ulex 7 Genista

fuse

3 mix 4 flux, meld, melt, weld 5 blend, merge, smelt, unify, unite 6 anneal, solder 7 liquefy 8 coalesce, conflate, dissolve, intermix 9 commingle, integrate 10 amalgamate 11 consolidate, incorporate

fusillade
4 hail 5 burst, salvo 6 shower, volley 7 barrage 8 drumfire, outburst 9 broadside, cannonade 11 bombardment

fusion
5 alloy, blend, union 6 merger 7 amalgam, mixture 8 compound 9 coalition, immixture, synthesis

fuss
3 ado, nag, row 4 beef, crab, flap, fret, miff, stew, stir, to-do, wail 5 gripe, stink, upset, whine, worry 6 bother, bustle, hassle, hurrah, pother, ruckus, rumpus, squawk 7 protest, quarrel 8 complain, foofaraw, squabble 9 commotion, complaint, kerfuffle, objection 10 excitement 11 controversy 12 perturbation

fussbudget
3 hen 6 granny 8 stickler 10 fuddy-duddy 13 perfectionist

fusspot
8 stickler 9 nitpicker, worrywart

fussy
5 picky 6 cranky, dainty, ornate 7 careful, finicky, fretful 9 crotchety, irritable, querulous 10 fastidious, meticulous, particular, pernickety, scrupulous 11 painstaking, persnickety, punctilious 13 conscientious

fustian
4 rant 7 bombast, pompous 8 affected, inflated 9 high-flown 11 exaggerated, highfalutin, pretentious 13 grandiloquent

fusty
4 rank 5 close, dated, fetid, moldy, passé, stale 6 bygone, old-hat, smelly 7 archaic 8 outdated 10 antiquated, malodorous 11 reactionary 12 old-fashioned 13 superannuated

futile
4 idle, vain 5 empty 6 hollow, otiose 7 useless 8 abortive, bootless, hopeless, nugatory 9 fruitless, worthless 10 unavailing 11 ineffective, ineffectual 12 unproductive, unsuccessful

future
5 later 6 offing, to come 7 by-and-by 8 oncoming, tomorrow 9 hereafter

Futurism
founder: 9 Marinetti (Filippo Tommaso)
painter: 5 Balla (Giacomo), Carra (Carlo) 7 Russolo (Luigi) 8 Boccioni (Umberto), Severini (Gino)
sculptor: 8 Boccioni (Umberto)

fuzz
3 cop 4 down, lint 6 police

fuzzy
3 dim 5 faint, gauzy, linty, vague, woozy 6 bleary, blurry 7 blurred, muddled, obscure, shadowy, unclear 8 confused 9 distorted, undefined 10 ill-defined, incoherent, indefinite, indistinct

fylfot
8 swastika

G

gab
3 jaw, rap, yak **4** blab, chat, talk **5** clack, drool, prate, speak **6** babble, drivel, gibber, gossip, jabber, natter, yammer **7** blabber, blather, chatter, palaver, prattle, twaddle **8** chitchat, converse, idle talk **9** gibberish, small talk

gabber
6 gossip, magpie **7** blabber **9** chatterer **10** chatterbox **12** blabbermouth, gossipmonger

gabby
4 glib **5** talky, windy **6** chatty **7** voluble **8** effusive **9** garrulous, talkative **10** long-winded, loquacious **11** loose-lipped **12** loose-tongued

gaberdine
4 coat, suit **5** cloak, cloth **6** capote, fabric **7** garment, manteau **8** material

gable
4 wall **8** pediment
ornament: **6** finial

Gabon
capital: **10** Libreville
city: **10** Port-Gentil
ethnic group: **4** Fang **5** Bantu
language: **6** French
monetary unit: **5** franc
neighbor: **5** Congo **8** Cameroon
river: **6** Ogooué

gad
3 bat **4** flit, roam, rove **5** amble, drift, mooch, range, stray, tramp **6** chisel, ramble, wander **7** maunder, meander, traipse **9** gallivant

Gad
brother: **5** Asher
father: **5** Jacob
mother: **6** Zilpah
son: **3** Eri **5** Ezbon, Haggi

Gaddis novel
12 Recognitions (The) **14** Frolic of His Own (A) **16** Carpenter's Gothic

gadfly
3 nag **4** pest, pill **6** bother, critic, insect, nudnik **8** nuisance

gadget
4 tool **5** gizmo, thing **6** device, dingus, doodad, hickey, jigger, widget **7** concern, gimmick, utensil **9** apparatus, appliance, doohickey, implement, mechanism **10** instrument **11** contraption, thingamabob, thingamajig, thingumajig

gadwall
4 bird, duck, fowl **9** waterfowl

gadzooks
4 drat, egad **6** crikey, zounds

Gaea
husband: **6** Uranus
offspring: **6** Furies, Giants, Titans, Typhon, Uranus **7** Erinyes **8** Cyclopes **9** Eumenides
parent: **5** Chaos

Gaelic
4 Erse **5** Irish **6** Celtic **8** Scottish
god: **3** Ler **5** Dagda
hero: **5** Oisin **6** Ossian **11** Finn MacCool
king: **9** Conchobar, Conchobor
language: **4** Manx
poet: **4** bard **6** Ossian

queen: 4 Medb
soldier: 4 kern 6 Fenian
spirit: 7 banshee

gaff
3 fix, rig 4 hoax, hook, spar, spur
5 abuse, fraud, spear, trick 6 fleece,
ordeal 7 deceive, gimmick 8 raillery
12 climbing iron

gaffe
4 flub, goof, muff 5 boner, error,
fault, fluff, lapse 6 bollix, boo-boo,
bungle, foul-up, howler, slipup
7 blooper, blunder, clinker, faux
pas, misstep, mistake 8 solecism
9 gaucherie 11 impropriety, misjudgment 12 indiscretion

gag
4 balk, gasp, hoax, jape, jest, joke,
quip 5 choke, crack, heave, prank,
retch, trick 6 muffle, muzzle, shtick,
stifle, strain 7 repress, silence,
squelch 8 throttle 9 restraint, wisecrack, witticism

gaga
4 agog, wild 5 crazy, giddy, nutty,
wacky 6 doting, fervid, gung ho
7 foolish, gushing, excited, smitten 8 animated, enamored, obsessed, thrilled 9 ebullient, exuberant 10 captivated, infatuated
12 enthusiastic

gage
3 vow 4 bond 5 token 6 pledge,
surety 8 gauntlet, security
(see also **gauge**)

gaggle
4 crew, gang, pack 5 array, bunch,
flock, group 6 clutch, number
7 cluster 10 assemblage, collection
11 aggregation

Gaheris
brother: 6 Gareth, Gawain
father: 3 Lot
mother: 8 Margawse, Morgause
uncle: 6 Arthur
victim: 8 Margawse, Morgause

gaiety
3 fun, joy 4 glee 5 mirth, revel
6 finery, frolic, hoopla 7 elation,

jollity, revelry, whoopee 8 elegance,
hilarity, reveling, vivacity 9 animation, festivity, happiness, joviality,
merriment 10 ebullience, exuberance, hullabaloo, joyousness, jubilation, liveliness 11 high spirits, merrymaking 12 conviviality

gain
3 get, net, win 4 earn, land, make,
reap 5 clear, cover, lucre, reach,
score 6 attain, expand, obtain, pick
up, profit, rack up, return, secure
7 achieve, acquire, advance, attract,
augment, benefit, bring in, enlarge,
procure 8 draw down, earnings,
increase, overtake, persuade, proceeds, traverse, windfall 10 accomplish 11 move forward

gainful
6 paying 8 fruitful, generous 9 lucrative, rewarding 10 beneficial, productive, profitable, well-paying,
worthwhile 12 advantageous, remunerative

gainsay
4 buck, defy, deny 6 impugn, negate,
oppose, refute, resist 7 dispute
8 disclaim, disprove, negative,
traverse 9 disaffirm, repudiate,
withstand 10 contradict, contravene,
controvert

Gainsborough painting
7 Blue Boy

gait
3 air, run 4 clip, dash, lope, pace,
rate, step, trot, walk 5 amble, speed,
strut, train, tread 6 canter, gallop,
stride 7 bearing 8 demeanor

gaiter
4 boot, shoe, spat 7 legging 8 overshoe

gal
4 babe, doll 5 chick

gala
4 ball, bash, fete, prom 5 merry,
party 6 lively 7 festive, jubilee,
pageant, shindig 8 festival, jamboree, wingding 9 festivity, spectacle
11 celebration 13 entertainment

galago
5 lemur 8 bush baby

Galahad
father: 8 Lancelot 9 Launcelot
mother: 6 Elaine
quest: 5 Grail 9 Holy Grail

Galatea
father: 6 Nereus
husband: 9 Pygmalion
lover: 4 Acis
mother: 5 Doris

galaxy
6 nebula 8 Milky Way, universe

Galba
predecessor: 4 Nero
successor: 4 Otho

gale
4 blow, gust, wind 5 blast, storm
6 squall 7 cyclone, tempest, typhoon
8 outburst 9 hurricane

galena
3 ore

Galen's forte
7 healing 8 medicine

galilee
5 porch 6 chapel

Galilee town
4 Cana 7 Gergesa 8 Nazareth,
Tiberias 9 Bethsaida, Capernaum

Galileo's birthplace
4 Pisa 5 Italy 7 Tuscany

gall
3 irk, nag, rub, vex 4 bile, fray, fret,
rile, roil, sore, wear 5 annoy, brass,
chafe, cheek, erode, grate, graze,
nerve 6 abrade, bother, burn up,
harass, pester, plague, rancor, ruffle,
scrape 7 conceit, disturb, frazzle,
inflame, provoke, scratch, torment
8 audacity, boldness, chutzpah,
irritate, temerity 9 aggravate, arrogance, brashness, impudence,
insolence 10 bitterness, effrontery

gallant
3 fop 4 beau, bold, buck, dude, hero
5 blade, blood, brave, civil, dandy,
lover, manly, Romeo, showy, suave,
swain, wooer 6 daring, heroic, suitor,
urbane 7 courtly, coxcomb, dashing,
Don Juan, stately, valiant 8 Casanova, gracious, lothario, paramour,
spirited, valorous 9 attentive, courteous, dauntless, ladies' man 10 chivalrous, courageous

gallantry
5 honor, poise, valor 6 daring,
mettle, spirit 7 amenity, bravery,
courage, heroism, prowess, suavity
8 boldness, chivalry, courtesy, urbanity, valiance, valiancy 9 attention,
manliness 10 resolution 11 courtliness 12 fearlessness

galleon
7 warship 12 square-rigger

gallery
5 patio, porch, salon 6 arcade,
loggia, museum, piazza 7 balcony,
passage, portico, veranda 8 audience, corridor, showroom 9 colonnade, onlookers, promenade
ancient Greek: 4 stoa

galley
3 gig 4 boat, mess, ship, tray
5 cuddy, proof 6 bireme 7 canteen,
kitchen, trireme, warship 8 scullery
9 cookhouse

Gallic
6 French

gallimaufry
3 mix 4 hash, mess, olio, stew
5 chaos 6 jumble, medley 7 clutter,
goulash, mélange, mixture, variety
8 mishmash, pastiche 9 patchwork,
potpourri 10 assortment, hodgepodge, hotchpotch, miscellany,
salmagundi

gallinaceous bird
3 hen 5 quail 6 grouse, turkey
7 chicken, hoatzin, peacock 8 curassow, pheasant 9 partridge
10 guinea fowl

galling
6 bitter, vexing 8 rankling 9 upsetting,
vexatious 10 afflictive, irritating,

nettlesome **11** aggravating, distressing, troublesome **12** exasperating

gallivant

3 bat, bum, gad **4** flit, roam, rove **5** amble, drift, jaunt, mooch, range, stray **6** cruise, ramble, travel, wander **7** meander, traipse **8** vagabond **10** knock about

gallop

4 dash, race **6** sprint

gallows

6 gibbet
bird: 7 villain **8** criminal

galore

4 full, lush, rich **5** ample, great **6** lavish **7** aplenty, copious, endless, profuse **8** abundant, generous **9** bountiful, expansive, plentiful **11** overflowing

galosh

4 boot, shoe **6** rubber **8** overshoe

Galsworthy work

7 Justice **11** Forsyte Saga (The)

galumph

4 plod **5** barge, clomp, clump, stomp, stump, tramp **6** lumber, trudge

galvanize

3 jar, zap **4** coat, fire, jolt, stir, spur, stun **5** pep up, pique, prime, react, rouse, shock **6** arouse, excite, perk up, thrill **7** animate, enliven, immerse, inspire, provoke, quicken **8** activate, astonish, energize, motivate, vitalize **9** electrify, innervate, magnetize, stimulate **10** invigorate

gam

3 leg, pin, pod, rap **4** chat, flap, limb, talk **5** visit **6** confab **9** drumstick **12** conversation

Gambia

capital: 6 Banjul
city: 9 Serekunda
language: 7 English
monetary unit: 6 dalasi
neighbor: 7 Senegal

gambit

3 con, jig **4** move, play, ploy, ruse,

wile **5** dodge, topic, trick **6** design, device, remark, tactic **7** gimmick **8** artifice, maneuver, trickery **9** expedient, stratagem **10** subterfuge

gamble

3 bet, lay, set **4** dare, game, play, punt, risk **5** put on, stake, wager **6** chance, hazard, plunge, raffle **7** imperil, lottery, venture **8** cast lots, long shot **9** crapshoot, speculate **10** jeopardize

gambler

5 dicer, shark, sharp **7** sharper **9** cardsharp **10** cardplayer **11** cardsharper

gambling place

3 den **4** club, dive, Reno **5** joint, Vegas **6** casino **8** Las Vegas, pool hall **9** roadhouse **10** Monte Carlo **12** Atlantic City, betting house

gambol

3 hop **4** jump, lark, leap, romp, skip **5** bound, caper, frisk, revel, sport **6** cavort, frolic, prance, spring **7** carry on, roister, rollick

Gambrinus' invention

3 ale **4** beer **5** lager

game

3 bet, fun, lay **4** bold, jest, joke, lark, play, prey, romp **5** brave, chase, eager, hardy, sport, stake, trick, wager **6** gamble, quarry, spunky **7** contest, pastime, valiant, willing **8** fearless, intrepid, resolute, unafraid, valorous **9** amusement, dauntless, diversion, undaunted **10** courageous, recreation
ball: 4 golf, polo, pool **5** fives, rogue, rugby **6** hockey, pelota, soccer, squash, tennis **7** cricket, croquet, jai alai **8** baseball, football, handball, hardball, lacrosse, racquets, rounders, softball **9** billiards **10** basketball, volleyball **11** racquetball
Basque: 6 pelota **7** jai alai
bird: 4 duck **5** quail **6** chukar, turkey **7** bustard **8** bobwhite, pheasant **9** partridge

board: 5 chess 7 pachisi
8 checkers, Scrabble 9 crokinole,
Parcheesi 10 backgammon
card: 3 gin, loo, Uno, war 4 faro,
fish, skat, solo 5 monte, ombre,
pitch, poker, rummy, whist 6 Boston,
bridge, casino, écarté, euchre, fan-
tan, hearts, piquet 7 auction, bez-
ique, canasta, Concan, old maid,
primero 8 baccarat, Canfield, con-
quian, cribbage, gin rummy, pinochle
9 blackjack, solitaire, twenty-one,
vingt-et-un 11 chemin de fer
child's: 3 tag 5 jacks 7 marbles
8 leapfrog, peekaboo 9 hopscotch
confidence: 4 scam 5 bunco,
bunko, sting
court: 5 roque 6 pelota, squash,
tennis 7 jai alai 8 handball, racquets
9 badminton 10 basketball, volleyball 11 racquetball
electric: 7 pinball
English: 5 rugby 7 cricket
8 draughts
Irish: 7 hurling
of chance: 4 faro, keno 5 beano,
bingo, boule, craps, lotto, rondo
6 fan-tan, hazard, policy, raffle 7 lottery, rondeau 8 roulette
parlor: 8 charades
racket: 6 squash, tennis 8 lacrosse,
ping-pong, racquets 9 badminton
11 racquetball, table tennis
roulette-like: 5 boule
rule maker: 5 Hoyle (Edmond)
string: 10 cat's cradle
table: 4 pool 5 craps 7 mah-jong,
snooker 8 dominoes, mah-jongg,
ping-pong, roulette 9 bagatelle,
billiards 11 table tennis
word: 5 rebus 6 crambo 7 anagram,
hangman 8 acrostic, charades,
Scrabble 9 crossword, logogriph

game plan
6 scheme, tactic 8 scenario, strategy
9 blueprint 10 big picture

gamete
3 egg 4 ovum 5 sperm 8 germ cell

gamin
3 elf, imp, tad 4 brat, tyke, waif
5 scamp 6 monkey, rascal, urchin
11 guttersnipe 12 street urchin

gamine
3 elf, imp 4 brat, waif 5 scamp
6 hoyden, rascal, tomboy, urchin
11 guttersnipe 12 street urchin

gaming cubes
4 dice 5 bones

gammon
3 ham 4 dupe, fool, rook 5 bacon,
feign 6 delude, fleece, humbug
7 deceive, pretend, swindle 8 flimflam, hoodwink 9 bamboozle
11 hornswoggle

gamut
5 range, scale, scope, sweep 6 extent, series, spread 7 compass
8 diapason, spectrum

gamy
3 off 4 foul, racy, rank, vile 5 brave,
fetid, funky 6 plucky, putrid, rancid,
rotten, smelly, sordid, stinky, strong
7 corrupt, decayed, noisome, noxious, reeking 10 decomposed,
malodorous, scandalous 12 disagreeable, disreputable

gander
4 look, peek 5 goose 6 glance
7 glimpse 9 simpleton, waterfowl

—— **Gandhi**
5 Rajiv 6 Indira 7 Mahatma 8 Mohandas

gandy dancer
10 railroader, tracklayer

ganef
5 thief 6 rascal 9 scoundrel

Ganesa, Ganesh
father: 4 Siva 5 Shiva
head: 8 elephant
mother: 7 Parvati

gang
3 lot, mob, set 4 band, clan, club,
crew, pack, ring, team 5 bunch,
crowd, group, horde 6 circle, clique,
outfit 7 arrange, cluster, collect,
combine, company, coterie 8 assemble 10 accumulate, assemblage
11 combination

gangling
4 bony, lean, slim 5 gaunt, lanky,

rangy 6 meager, meagre, skinny
7 angular, scrawny, slender, spindly,
stringy 8 rawboned 9 spindling

ganglion
5 tumor 7 nucleus

gangrene
3 rot 5 decay 7 mortify, putrefy
8 necrosis 9 decompose

gangster
4 goon, hood, thug 5 rough, thief,
tough 6 bandit, gunman 7 hoodlum,
mafioso, mobster, ruffian 8 criminal
9 cutthroat, racketeer
girlfriend: 4 moll

gangway
4 hall, path 5 aisle 7 passage, walkway 8 corridor 10 passageway

ganja
3 kef, kif, pot, tea 4 hemp, herb,
weed 5 grass, smoke 7 hashish
8 cannabis, Mary Jane 9 marijuana

gannet
4 bird 5 booby 7 seabird

ganoid fish
3 gar 6 beluga, bowfin 7 dogfish,
garfish, teleost 8 billfish, sturgeon
10 paddlefish

Ganymede
abductor: 4 Zeus 7 Jupiter
brother: 4 Ilus
father: 4 Tros
function: 9 cupbearer

gaol
3 jug, pen 4 jail 5 clink, joint, pokey
6 cooler, lockup, prison 7 slammer
8 bastille 9 calaboose, jailhouse
12 penitentiary

gap
3 cut, pit 4 gash, gulf, hole, lull, pass,
rent, rift, skip, slit, slot, tear, vent,
void, yawn 5 abyss, blank, break,
chasm, chink, cleft, clove, crack,
gorge, gulch, gully, pause, space,
split 6 arroyo, breach, canyon,
cavity, cranny, divide, hiatus, hollow,
lacuna, ravine, recess, schism, vacuum 7 caesura, crevice, fissure,
interim, opening, orifice, rupture,
vacancy, vacuity 8 aperture, cleavage, division, fracture, interval 9 disparity, interlude 10 deficiency,
difference, interstice, separation
12 intermission, interruption 13 discontinuity

gape
3 eye, yaw 4 bore, gawk, gawp,
gaze, glom, leer, look, ogle, open,
part, peer, yawn 5 crack, glare,
gloat, space, split, stare 6 glance,
goggle 7 eyeball 10 rubberneck

gaping
4 huge, open, vast, wide 5 broad,
great 7 chasmal 9 cavernous

gar
4 fish, pike 8 billfish 10 needlefish

garage
4 shop 7 cabinet, car park, carport,
shelter

Garand
5 rifle

garb
4 clad, duds 5 array, cover, dress,
getup, style 6 attire, clothe, outfit
7 apparel, clothes, garment, raiment,
threads 9 trappings 10 appearance

garbage
4 junk, muck, slop 5 dreck, dregs,
filth, offal, trash, waste 6 debris,
litter, refuse, sewage 7 rubbish
8 detritus, riffraff
heap: 6 midden

garble
4 sift, warp 5 alter, belie, color, twist
6 jumble, mangle, muddle 7 becloud,
confuse, contort, distort, falsify, obscure, pervert 8 miscolor, misstate,
mutilate 9 obfuscate 10 impurities
12 misrepresent

garçon
3 boy 6 waiter 7 servant

garden
4 Eden, park 7 nursery
shelter: 5 arbor 6 arbour

gardener
6 grower 7 yardman 9 topiarist

garden house
6 alcove, gazebo 9 belvedere

Garden State
9 New Jersey

garden tool
3 hoe 4 claw, fork, rake 5 mower, spade 6 dibble, pruner, scythe, shears, shovel, sickle, trowel, weeder 8 clippers

Gardner character
10 Perry Mason

Gareth
brother: 6 Gawain 7 Gaheris
father: 3 Lot
mother: 8 Margawse, Morgause
slayer: 8 Lancelot 9 Launcelot
uncle: 6 Arthur
wife: 6 Liones

Gargamelle's son
9 Gargantua

Gargantua
abbey: 7 Thélème
author: 8 Rabelais (François)
father: 12 Grandgousier
first word: 5 drink
mother: 10 Gargamelle
son: 10 Pantagruel

gargantuan
see **gigantic**

Garibaldi follower
8 redshirt

garish
4 loud 5 gaudy, showy, vivid 6 brassy, brazen, flashy, tawdry, tinsel, vulgar 7 blatant, chintzy, glaring, raffish 12 meretricious

garland
3 ana, lei 5 album, crown 6 anadem, digest, laurel, wreath 7 chaplet, coronal, coronet, laurels, omnibus 8 analects 9 anthology, selection 10 collection, compendium, miscellany 11 florilegium

garlic
4 moly, ramp 5 clove 6 allium

garment
4 garb, gear 5 array, habit 6 attire 7 apparel, raiment 8 clothing, vestment 10 habiliment
African: 6 kaross 7 dashiki
Arab: 3 aba 4 haik
British: 10 mackintosh
clergy's: 3 alb 4 cope 7 cassock, soutane 8 vestment
close-fitting: 6 girdle, tights 7 leotard
for sleeping: 6 pajama 7 nightie 9 nightgown
Greek: 5 tunic 6 chiton, peplos 7 chlamys 8 himation
Hindu: 4 sari
hooded: 8 djellaba
Japanese: 6 kimono
lace: 10 chemisette
Malay: 6 sarong
men's: 3 tie 4 vest 5 pants, shirt, socks 6 jacket, slacks 7 drawers 8 trousers
outer: 4 cape, coat, robe, wrap 5 cloak, parka, shawl, smock, stole 6 capote, jacket, kimono, poncho, sarong, ulster, wammus 7 overall, pelisse, surtout, sweater, topcoat 8 overcoat, pinafore, pullover, scapular 9 coveralls, gaberdine, polonaise
Polynesian: 5 pareo, pareu
rain: 6 poncho 7 oilskin, slicker
Roman: 4 toga 5 tunic
Scottish: 4 jupe, kilt 7 sporran
sleeveless: 3 aba 4 cape 6 mantle, tabard
Turkish: 6 dolman
women's: 4 gown 5 dress, skirt 6 blouse, vestee 7 blouson, nightie, partlet 8 negligee, peignoir, pelerine

garner
4 cull, earn, hive, reap 5 amass, glean, hoard, lay up, store 6 gather, pick up, roll up 7 collect, extract, harvest, store up 8 cumulate, ingather 9 stockpile 10 accumulate

garnet
5 jewel, stone 6 pyrope 8 essonite 9 hessonite
black: 8 melanite
red: 9 almandine, almandite

garnish
4 deck, trim 5 adorn 6 bedeck

7 dress up, enhance 8 beautify, decorate, ornament 9 embellish

garret
4 loft, room 5 attic 8 cockloft

garrison
4 camp, fort, post 6 assign, billet, occupy, troops 7 station 8 fortress 10 stronghold

garrote
5 choke 8 strangle, throttle 11 strangulate

garrulous
see **gabby**

garter
4 band, belt 5 strap 7 support 9 supporter

garth
4 yard 5 close 9 enclosure

gas
4 fuel, fume 5 fumes, steam, vapor 6 petrol 8 gasoline 9 petroleum
atmospheric: 4 neon 5 argon, oxide, ozone, xenon 6 helium, oxygen 7 krypton, methane 8 hydrogen, nitrogen
flammable: 6 butane, ethane, ethyne 7 methane, propane, propene 8 ethylene
inert: 4 neon 5 argon, radon, xenon 6 helium 7 krypton
mine: 8 firedamp 9 black damp
oxygen: 5 ozone
toxic: 5 sarin, soman, tabun 6 arsine, ketene 7 mustard 8 phosgene 9 phosphine

gasconade
4 brag 7 bravado 8 boasting, bragging 11 braggadocio

gash
3 cut, rip 4 rend, slit, tear 5 carve, cleft, gouge, slash, slice, split 6 incise 8 lacerate 10 depression, laceration

gasket
4 ring, seal 5 O-ring 6 sealer

gasoline
4 fuel 6 petrol
rating: 6 octane

gasp
4 blow, huff, pant, puff 5 heave 6 wheeze 11 exclamation

Gaspar
companion: 8 Melchior 9 Balthazar
gift: 12 frankincense

gassy
5 windy 7 verbose 8 inflated, vaporous 9 flatulent

gastronome
7 epicure, gourmet 8 gourmand 9 bon vivant 11 connoisseur

gastropod
4 slug 5 conch, murex, snail, whelk 6 cowrie, limpet, volute 7 abalone, mollusc, mollusk, sea slug 8 pteropod, univalve 10 periwinkle

gat
3 gun 6 pistol, roscoe 7 channel, firearm, handgun, passage 8 revolver

gate
3 tap 4 cock, door, exit, port 5 entry, hatch, toril, valve 6 faucet, portal, spigot, switch, wicket 7 hydrant, opening, petcock 8 entrance, entryway, stopcock 9 turnstile 10 attendance

gâteau
4 cake

gatefold
6 insert 7 foldout

Gates of Hercules
9 Gibraltar 12 promontories

gateway
4 arch, door, exit 5 pylon, toril 6 portal 7 archway, doorway, opening 8 entrance

gather
4 brew, cull, gain, grow, heap, herd, loom, mass, meet, pick, pile, pool, reap 5 amass, bunch, flock, glean, group, horde, infer, judge, pluck, shirr, swarm 6 assume, deduce, derive, expect, garner muster, pick up, pucker, summon, take in 7 cluster, collect, convene, extract, harvest, marshal, round up, suppose,

surmise, suspect **8** assemble, conclude, converge, increase **9** aggregate, intensify **10** accumulate, congregate, understand **11** concentrate

gathering
4 bevy, crew, gang, herd, mass, ruck **5** bunch, crowd, crush, drove, flock, group, horde, party, press, rally, swarm **6** caucus, klatch, muster, throng **7** company, harvest, klatsch, meeting, reunion, turnout **8** assembly, congress, junction **9** concourse, congeries **10** assemblage, collection, conference, confluence **11** aggregation, get-together **12** congregation

Gath's giant
7 Goliath **10** Philistine

gauche
5 crude, gawky, inept **6** clumsy **7** awkward, halting, loutish, uncouth **8** bumbling, tactless **9** graceless, ham-handed, inelegant, maladroit **10** blundering

gaucho
6 cowboy **8** herdsman
weapon: 4 bola **5** bolas **7** machete

gaudeamus _____
6 igitur

gaudy
4 loud **5** showy **6** brassy, brazen, coarse, flashy, garish, tawdry, tinsel, vulgar **7** blatant, chintzy, glaring **9** brummagem, tasteless **10** outlandish **12** meretricious, ostentatious

Gaugamela
loser: 6 Darius, Persia
victor: 9 Alexander (the Great)

gauge
4 bore, rule, size **5** check, judge, meter, scale, weigh, width **6** assess, degree **7** compute, measure **8** diameter, estimate, evaluate, quantify, standard **9** benchmark, criterion, dimension, thickness, yardstick **10** instrument, touchstone **11** measurement

Gauguin's island
6 Tahiti

Gaul
4 Celt **6** France **9** Frenchman

Gaulish
6 French
god: 4 Esus **7** Taranis
goddess: 8 Belisama
priest: 5 druid

gaunt
4 bare, bony, grim, lank, lean, thin **5** harsh, lanky, spare **6** barren, gangly, skinny, wasted **7** angular, scraggy, scrawny **8** gangling, rawboned, skeletal **9** emaciated **10** cadaverous

gauntlet
4 dare, test **5** glove, trial **6** attack, ordeal **9** challenge, onslaught

Gautama
6 Buddha **10** Siddhartha
mother: 4 Maya **8** Mahamaya
son: 6 Rahula
wife: 9 Yasodhara

gauze
4 film, haze, leno, mesh, mist **5** cloth, crepe, tulle **6** fabric, tissue **7** bandage, chiffon, tiffany **8** compress, dressing **11** cheesecloth

gauzy
4 thin **5** filmy, fuzzy, sheer, vague **6** flimsy **8** delicate, pellucid **9** gossamery **10** diaphanous **11** transparent

gavel
6 hammer, mallet

gavial
7 gharial, reptile **9** crocodile

gavotte
4 tune **5** dance

Gawain
brother: 6 Gareth **7** Gaheris
father: 3 Lot
mother: 8 Margawse, Morgause
slayer: 8 Lancelot **9** Launcelot
uncle: 6 Arthur
victim: 6 Uwayne **7** Lamerok
9 Pellinore

gawk

3 oaf 4 bore, gape, gaze, hick, look, lout, lump, peer, rube 5 churl, glare, gloat, klutz, looby, stare, yokel 6 goggle, lubber

gawky

5 inept, splay 6 clumsy, coarse, gauche, oafish 7 awkward, loutish, lumpish, uncouth 8 bumbling, bungling, lubberly, ungainly 9 graceless, ham-handed, lumbering, maladroit

gay

4 glad, keen, wild 5 bonny, brash, happy, jolly, merry, queer, showy, sunny, vivid 6 blithe, bouncy, bright, cheery, festal, frisky, jocund, jovial, joyful, joyous, lively, rakish, sporty 7 animate, chipper, excited, festive, forward, gleeful, lesbian, playful, raffish 8 animated, cheerful, colorful, mirthful, rakehell, spirited, sportive 9 brilliant, exuberant, homophile, sparkling, sprightly, vivacious 10 blithesome, frolicsome, homoerotic, homosexual, insouciant, licentious, nonchalant 12 light-hearted

_____ Gay

4 John 5 Enola

Gaza victor

7 Allenby (Edmund)

gaze

3 eye 4 bore, gape, gawk, leer, look, ogle, peer, pore, scan, view 5 glare, gloat, stare, watch 6 goggle 7 eyeball, observe 8 consider 10 rubberneck 11 contemplate

gazebo

6 alcove 8 pavilion 9 belvedere 11 garden house, summerhouse

gazelle

4 kudu, oryx 5 eland, nyala 7 gembok 8 antelope

gazette

5 paper 6 record 7 journal, publish 8 newspaper 10 periodical 11 publication 12 announcement

gazetteer

5 atlas, guide, index

Ge

see **Gaea**

gear

3 cam, cog, rig 5 dress, goods, shift, stuff, wheel 6 adjust, tackle, things 7 apparel, harness, rigging 8 clothing, cogwheel, garments, materiel, property, sprocket, tackling, trapping 9 apparatus, equipment, machinery 10 belongings 11 accessories, habiliments, possessions 13 accouterments, accoutrements, paraphernalia

Geats

king: 7 Hygelac
prince: 7 Beowulf

Geb

daughter: 4 Isis 8 Nephthys
father: 3 Shu
mother: 6 Tefnut
sister: 3 Nut
son: 3 Set 6 Osiris
wife: 3 Nut

gecko

6 lizard 7 reptile

Gedaliah

father: 6 Ahikam 7 Pashhur 8 Jeduthun
slayer: 7 Ishmael

gee

3 wow 4 gosh, turn 5 golly, right 8 goodness, gracious 9 turn right

geek

4 buff, guru, nerd, whiz 5 carny, fiend, freak 6 carney, carnie, expert, pundit, weirdo 7 devotee, egghead, fanatic, oddball 9 authority, eccentric 10 enthusiast 12 intellectual

Gehenna

3 pit 4 hell 5 abyss, hades, Sheol 6 Tophet 7 inferno 8 Tartarus 9 perdition 10 underworld 11 netherworld

Geisel pseudonym

7 Dr. Seuss

geisha wear
3 obi 6 kimono

gel
3 dry, set 4 clot 6 harden, mousse
7 colloid, congeal, thicken 8 solidify
9 coagulate

gelatin
3 jam 4 agar 5 jelly 7 sericin

geld
3 cut, fix, tax 5 alter, desex, unsex 6 change, neuter 7 deprive
8 castrate, mutilate 9 sterilize
10 emasculate 11 desexualize

gelid
3 icy 4 cold 5 chill, nippy, polar
6 arctic, chilly, frigid, frosty, frozen,
steely 7 glacial 8 freezing

gelt
5 money

gem
3 jet 4 jade, onyx, opal, rock, ruby,
sard 5 agate, amber, beryl, bijou,
coral, jewel, pearl, stone, topaz
6 amulet, garnet, jasper, scarab,
sphene, spinel, zircon 7 bejewel,
cat's-eye, citrine, diamond, emerald,
enjewel, olivine, peridot 8 amethyst,
corundum, diopside, fluorite, intaglio,
lazurite, obsidian, sapphire, sardonyx,
sparkler, tigereye 9 carnelian,
moonstone, phenakite, scapolite,
spodumene, tiger's-eye, turquoise
10 aquamarine, cordierite, tourmaline
11 alexandrite, chrysoberyl, chrysoprase, lapis lazuli, masterpiece
blue: 6 zircon 8 sapphire 9 turquoise 10 aquamarine 11 lapis
lazuli
carved: 8 intaglio
changeable: 9 chatoyant
cut: 7 marquis 8 baguette, cabochon, marquise 9 brilliant
face: 5 facet
green: 4 jade 7 emerald, peridot,
smaragd 10 chrysolite 11 chrysoprase
red: 4 ruby, sard 6 garnet, pyrope,
spinel 9 carnelian

support: 7 setting
weight: 5 carat
yellow: 5 amber, topaz 6 sphene
7 citrine

Gemini star
6 Castor, Pollux

gemmule
3 bud

gemsbok
4 oryx 8 antelope

Gem State
5 Idaho

gemütlich
see genial

gendarme
3 cop 5 bobby 7 officer, soldier
8 flatfoot 9 constable, patrolman,
policeman

gender
3 sex 4 kind, male, sort, type 5 class
6 female, neuter 8 feminine 9 masculine

genealogy
5 roots, stirp, stock 6 origin, stemma
7 descent, history, lineage 8 ancestry, heredity, pedigree 9 bloodline
10 family tree

general
4 wide 5 broad, usual, vague 6 common, global, normal, public 7 blanket, generic, overall, regular, routine,
typical 8 catholic, everyday, sweeping 9 all-around, inclusive, prevalent,
universal 10 collective, prevailing,
unspecific, widespread 11 commonplace 13 comprehensive
American: 3 Lee (Robert E.)
4 Haig (Alexander), Pike (Zebulon),
Wood (Leonard) 5 Clark (Mark,
Wesley, William), Grant (Ulysses S.),
Meade (George), Scott (Charles,
Hugh, Winfield), Smith (Andrew
Jackson, Giles, Holland, Morgan,
Samuel, Walter, Bedell), Stark
(John), Worth (William) 6 Abrams
(Creighton), Custer (George Arm-
strong), Franks (Tommy), Hooker

(Joseph), Kearny (Philip, Stephen), Patton (George S.), Porter (Fitz-John), Powell (Colin), Slocum (Henry), Spaatz (Carl), Taylor (Maxwell, Richard, Zachary) **7** Bradley (Omar), Frémont (John Charles), Houston (Samuel), Jackson (Andrew, Thomas "Stonewall"), Lejeune (John), Ridgway (Matthew B.), Sherman (William Tecumseh), Twining (Nathaniel), Wallace (Lewis), Wheeler (Joseph) **8** Burnside (Ambrose), Goethals (George Washington), Marshall (George), Mitchell (Billy), Pershing (John J.), Sheridan (Philip), Stilwell (Joseph) **9** MacArthur (Arthur, Douglas), McClellan (George), Rosecrans (William), Schofield (John), Wilkinson (James) **10** Beauregard (P. G. T.), Eisenhower (Dwight D.), Vandegrift (Alexander), Wainwright (Jonathan) **11** Schwarzkopf (Norman) **12** Westmoreland (William)

American Revolutionary: 4 Knox (Henry), Ward (Artemas) **5** Gates (Horatio), Wayne ("Mad Anthony") **6** de Kalb (Baron), Greene (Nathanael), Morgan (Daniel), Putnam (Israel, Rufus) **8** Moultrie (William), Sullivan (John) **10** Washington (George)

Austrian: 11 Wallenstein (Albrecht von)

British: 4 Gage (Thomas), Howe (William) **5** Clive (Robert), Monck (George), Wolfe (James) **6** Rupert (Prince) **7** Amherst (Jeffery), Wingate (Orde Charles, Reginald) **8** Burgoyne (John), Cromwell (Oliver) **10** Abercromby (Ralph, Robert), Cornwallis (Charles), Wellington (Duke of)

Carthaginian: 8 Hamilcar, Hannibal **9** Hasdrubal

Chinese: 3 Yan (Xishan), Yen (Hsi-shan) **4** Feng (Guozhang, Kuochang, Yü-hsiang, Yuxiang) **5** Chang (Tso-lin), Zhang (Zuolin)

Confederate: 3 Lee (Robert E.) **4** Hill (Ambrose), Hood (John Bell)

5 Bragg (Braxton), Ewell (Richard Stoddart), Price (Sterling), Smith (Edmund Kirby) **6** Morgan (John Hunt), Stuart (Jeb) **7** Forrest (Nathan Bedford), Hampton (Wade), Jackson (Thomas "Stonewall"), Pickett (George) **8** Johnston (Albert Sidney, Joseph Eggleston) **9** Pemberton (John) **10** Beauregard (Pierre G. T.), Longstreet (James)

French: 3 Ney (Michel) **4** Foch (Ferdinand) **6** Moreau (Victor), Pétain (Philippe) **7** Weygand (Maxime) **8** de Gaulle (Charles), Lefebvre (Pierre), Montcalm (Marquis de), Saint-Cyr (Laurent de Gouvion-) **9** Frontenac (Comte de) **10** Rochambeau (Comte de)

German: 4 Jodi (Alfred) **6** Kleist (Paul Ludwig von), Rommel (Erwin) **9** Rundstedt (Gerd von) **10** Kesselring (Albert), Ludendorff (Erich)

Greek: 6 Nicias **9** Miltiades **10** Alcibiades **12** Themistocles

Japanese: 4 Tojo (Hideki) **5** Koiso (Kuniaki) **6** Yasuda (Yoshisada) **8** Yamagata (Aritomo) **9** Yamashita (Tomoyuki)

Mexican: 9 Santa Anna (Antonio López de)

Prussian: 11 Scharnhorst (Gerhard von)

Roman: 5 Sulla (Lucius Cornelius) **6** Caesar (Julius), Fabius (Quintus), Marius (Gaius), Pompey (the Great), Scipio (Gnaeus Cornelius, Publius Cornelius) **7** Regulus (Marcus Atilius), Ricimer (Flavius) **8** Agricola (Gnaeus Julius), Lucullus (Lucius Licinius), Stilicho (Flavius) **9** Marcellus (Marcus Claudius), Sertorius (Quintus) **10** Theodosius (the Great) **11** Cincinnatus (Lucius Quinctius)

Russian: 6 Zhukov (Georgy) **7** Kutuzov (Mikhail), Trotsky (Leon), Wrangel (Pyotr), Zhdanov (Andrey) **9** Yeremenko (Andrey)

Spanish: 4 Alba (Duke of), Alva (Duke of) **6** Franco (Francisco)

Swedish: 7 Wrangel (Karl Gustav)

general assembly
4 diet 6 plenum 8 congress 10 parliament 11 legislature

generalize
5 infer, widen 6 derive, extend, induce, spread 7 broaden 8 conclude 12 universalize

generally
6 mainly, mostly, widely 7 all told, as a rule, broadly, chiefly, en masse, largely, overall, usually 8 all in all, commonly, normally 9 on average, primarily, typically 10 altogether, by and large, frequently, on the whole, ordinarily 11 customarily, principally 12 almost always 13 predominantly

generate
4 bear, make, sire 5 beget, breed, cause, get up, hatch, spawn, yield 6 create, effect, father, induce, whip up, work up 7 achieve, develop, produce, provoke 8 engender, initiate, multiply, muster up 9 originate, procreate, propagate, reproduce 10 bring about, bring forth

generic
5 broad 6 common, global 7 blanket 9 inclusive, unbranded, universal 10 indistinct 12 nonexclusive

_____ generis
3 sui

generosity
7 charity 8 altruism, kindness, largesse 9 abundance 10 liberality 11 beneficence, benevolence, magnanimity, munificence 12 philanthropy 13 unselfishness

generous
4 free, kind 5 ample 6 lavish 7 copious, helpful, liberal, profuse, willing 8 abundant 9 bounteous, bountiful, plenteous, plentiful, unselfish, unsparing 10 altruistic, benevolent, bighearted, charitable, munificent, openhanded, ungrudging, unstinting 11 considerate, kindhearted, magnanimous, overflowing 12 greathearted

genesis
4 dawn, root 5 alpha, birth, start 6 origin, outset, source 7 dawning, opening 8 creation 9 beginning, formation, inception 10 provenance 12 commencement

genetic
10 congenital, hereditary
material: 3 DNA, RNA 7 cistron 9 chromatid 10 chromosome
term: 8 synapsis 9 backcross

genial
4 kind, warm 5 jolly, merry 6 benign, blithe, hearty, jocund, jovial, kindly, mellow, social 7 affable, amiable, cordial 8 amicable, friendly, gracious, pleasant, sociable 9 agreeable, congenial, convivial, easygoing 10 neighborly 11 good-humored, good-natured, warmhearted

genie
3 imp 4 jinn, puck 5 afrit 6 afreet, spirit, sprite 7 servant

geniture
4 dawn 5 birth, start 6 origin 8 nativity 9 beginning, inception

genius
4 bent, gift, head, turn 5 flair, jinni, knack 6 acumen, brains, master, spirit, talent, wizard 7 aptness, faculty, prodigy 8 aptitude, capacity, penchant 9 ingenuity, intellect 10 brilliance, creativity, mastermind, propensity 12 intelligence 13 inventiveness

Genoa's liberator
5 Doria (Andrea)

genre
3 ilk 4 kind, sort, type 5 class, style 6 family, stripe 7 species, variety 8 category, division

gens
3 kin 4 clan 5 group 6 family, people 7 kinfolk 9 relations, relatives

Genseric's subjects
7 Vandals

genteel
4 nice, prim 5 civil 6 formal,

la-di-da, polite, prissy, strict, stuffy, urbane 7 courtly, elegant, prudish, refined, stilted, stylish 8 affected, cultured, graceful, gracious, ladylike, mannerly, polished, precious, priggish, well-bred 9 courteous 10 artificial, cultivated 11 fashionable, gentlemanly, pretentious, straitlaced, well-behaved 12 aristocratic, well-mannered 13 distinguished

gentile

3 goy 5 pagan 7 heathen 9 Christian, non-Jewish

gentility

5 elite 6 gentry 7 decorum, manners, quality, society 8 breeding, courtesy, nobility 9 blue blood 10 aristocrat, refinement, upper class, upper crust 11 aristocracy

gentle

4 calm, easy, kind, meek, mild, soft, tame 5 balmy, bland, quiet, tamed 6 benign, docile, genial, kindly, mellow, placid, serene, smooth, tender 7 amiable, lenient 8 delicate, merciful, peaceful, pleasant, pleasing, soothing, tranquil 9 agreeable 11 softhearted, sympathetic, warmhearted 13 compassionate
creature: 4 lamb

gentleman

3 sir 6 aristo, fellow, mister 8 cavalier 9 blue blood, chevalier, patrician 10 aristocrat
English: 6 milord
French: 8 monsieur
Hindu: 4 babu
Spanish: 3 don 5 señor

gentleman friend

4 beau 5 lover, swain 6 fiancé, squire, suitor 7 gallant

gentlemanly

5 civil, noble, suave 6 polite, urbane 7 elegant, gallant, genteel, refined 8 mannerly, well-bred 9 courteous, honorable 10 chivalrous, cultivated 11 considerate

gentry

5 elite, folks 7 quality, society

8 nobility 9 gentility, patrician 10 gentlefolk, patriciate, upper class, upper crust 11 aristocracy, high society, ruling class

genuflect

3 bow 4 fawn 5 kneel 6 kowtow

genuine

4 pure, real, true 5 plain, pukka, valid 6 actual, dinkum, honest, tested 7 factual, natural, sincere 8 absolute, bona fide, positive, trueborn 9 authentic, certified, unalloyed, undoubted, unfeigned, veritable 10 sure-enough, unaffected

genus

3 ilk 4 kind, mode, sort, type 5 class, group, order 6 family 7 species, variety 8 category

geode

4 rock 5 stone 6 cavity, nodule

geoduck

4 clam

geographer

American: 10 Huntington (Ellsworth)
Flemish: 8 Mercator (Gerardus)
German: 6 Ratzel (Friedrich)
Greek: 6 Strabo 7 Ptolemy
Italian: 8 Vespucci (Amerigo)

geologic period

5 azoic 6 Eocene, Hadean 7 Archean, Miocene, Permian 8 Cambrian, Cenozoic, Devonian, Holocene, Jurassic, Mesozoic, Pliocene, Silurian, Triassic 9 Oligocene, Paleocene, Paleozoic 10 Cretaceous, Ordovician 11 Phanerozoic, Pleistocene, Precambrian, Proterozoic 13 Mississippian, Pennsylvanian

geometer

6 Euclid 13 mathematician

geometric

coordinate: 8 abscissa, ordinate
curve: 3 arc 6 spiral 7 ellipse, evolute 8 parabola
figure: 5 rhomb 6 circle, oblong, square 7 ellipse, hexagon, octagon, polygon, rhombus 8 heptagon, pentagon, rhomboid, triangle 9 rectangle

geometry letters

solid: 4 cone, cube 5 prism
6 sphere 7 pyramid 8 cylinder,
spheroid, spherule
surface: 5 nappe, torus 6 toroid

geometry letters
3 QED

geophagy
4 pica

Georgia
capital: 7 Atlanta
city: 5 Macon 6 Albany, Athens
7 Augusta 8 Columbus, Savannah
college, university: 5 Clark, Emory
6 Mercer 7 Spelman 8 Valdosta
9 Morehouse
founder: 10 Oglethorpe (James)
nickname: 5 Peach (State) 21 Empire State of the South
river: 8 Ocmulgee 13 Chattahoochee
state bird: 13 brown thrasher
state flower: 12 Cherokee rose
state tree: 7 live oak
swamp: 10 Okefenokee

Georgia, Republic of
ancient kingdom: 6 Iberia 7 Colchis
capital: 6 Tiflis 7 Tbilisi
city: 7 Kutaisi, Rustavi
includes: 6 Ajaria 8 Abkhazia,
Adzharia 12 South Ossetia
monarch: 6 Tamara (Queen)
monetary unit: 4 lari
mountain range: 8 Caucasus
neighbor: 6 Russia, Turkey 7 Armenia 10 Azerbaijan
river: 4 Kura 5 Rioni
sea: 5 Black

Georgics author
6 Virgil

Geraint's wife
4 Enid

Gerda's husband
4 Frey

geriatric
3 old 4 aged 5 aging 6 senior
7 elderly 8 outmoded 12 old-fashioned 13 superannuated

germ
3 bud, bug 4 seed 5 spark, spore,
virus 6 embryo, origin, source
7 microbe, nucleus 8 pathogen
9 bacterium
cell: 3 egg 4 ovum 5 sperm

German
3 Hun 4 Goth 6 Teuton
article: 3 das, der, des, die
bomber: 5 Gotha, Stuka
child: 4 Kind
coin: 4 Mark 5 Taler 6 Thaler
7 Pfennig
empire: 5 Reich
head: 4 Kopf
highway: 8 Autobahn
leader: 6 Führer, Kaiser
measles: 7 rubella
mister: 4 Herr
no: 4 nein
nobleman: 6 Junker
pronoun: 3 ich, sie, wir
rifle: 6 Mauser
weight: 3 Lot 5 Pfund, Stein
8 Vierling
woman: 4 Frau 8 Fräulein

germane
3 apt 5 ad rem 7 apropos, fitting,
related 8 material, relevant 9 pertinent 10 applicable 11 appropriate

Germany
11 Deutschland
capital: 6 Berlin
city: 3 Ulm 4 Bonn, Jena, Kiel
5 Essen, Mainz 6 Bremen, Erfurt,
Lübeck, Munich 7 Cologne, Dresden, Hamburg, Hanover, Leipzig,
München, Potsdam 8 Augsburg,
Dortmund, Duisburg, Freiburg,
Hannover, Schwerin 9 Frankfurt,
Nuremberg, Stuttgart, Wiesbaden
10 Baden Baden, Düsseldorf
leader: 4 Kohl (Helmut) 6 Brandt
(Willy), Hitler (Adolf) 7 Schmidt
(Helmut), Wilhelm (Kaiser) 8 Bismarck (Otto)
monetary unit: 4 euro
monetary unit, former: 4 mark
5 taler 6 thaler 12 deutsche mark
mountain, range: 4 Harz 7 Brocken

neighbor: 6 France, Poland 7 Austria, Belgium, Denmark 10 Luxembourg 11 Netherlands, Switzerland 13 Czech Republic
region: 4 Ruhr 6 Saxony 7 Bavaria 11 Black Forest
river: 4 Eder, Elbe, Isar, Main, Oder, Ruhr 5 Rhein, Rhine 6 Danube 7 Moselle
sea: 5 North 6 Baltic
state: 5 Hesse 6 Saxony 7 Bavaria 8 Saarland 9 Thuringia 11 Brandenburg

germinate
3 bud 6 evolve, spring, sprout 7 blossom, develop 9 originate, pullulate

Gerontion poet
5 Eliot (T. S.)

Gershom, Gershon
father: 4 Levi
son: 5 Libni 6 Shimei

Gershwin
3 Ira 6 George
opera: 12 Porgy and Bess
piece: 14 Rhapsody in Blue 15 American in Paris (An)
show: 5 Oh Kay 9 Funny Face, Girl Crazy 10 Lady Be Good 11 Of Thee I Sing 15 Strike Up the Band
song: 10 I Got Rhythm, Summertime

Gertrude
husband: 8 Claudius
son: 6 Hamlet

Gervaise's daughter
4 Nana

Geryon
dog: 6 Orthus
father: 8 Chrysaor
mother: 10 Callirrhoë
slayer: 8 Hercules

gestalt
4 form 5 shape 6 figure 7 pattern 9 structure 13 configuration

Gestapo chief
7 Himmler (Heinrich)

geste
4 deed, feat 7 emprise, exploit, romance, venture 9 adventure 10 enterprise 11 undertaking

gesticulate
3 nod 4 move, wave 6 beckon, motion, signal

gesticulation
4 wave 6 motion 7 gesture 8 high sign 9 pantomime 12 body language, sign language

gesture
3 nod 4 sign, wave 5 shrug, token 6 motion, salute, signal 8 reminder 9 signalize 10 expression, indication
graceful: 9 beau geste

get
3 bag 4 draw, earn, gain, land 5 catch, cause, seize 6 access, attain, become, elicit, extort, obtain, pick up, secure 7 achieve, acquire, bring in, capture, chalk up, deliver, extract, procure, receive 8 contract 10 understand 12 come down with

get around
4 roam, rove, tour, trek, walk 5 avoid, dodge, elude, evade, skirt 6 cruise, detour, escape, ramble, travel, wander 8 ambulate, outflank, sidestep 10 circumvent

get away
see **get out**

getaway
3 lam 4 exit, slip 6 escape, flight 7 retreat 8 breakout, vacation

get back
6 go home, recoup, regain, return, revert 7 recover, reclaim, revenge, revisit 8 retrieve 9 repossess, retaliate

get by
4 cope, fare 5 slide 6 eke out, endure, manage 7 carry on, survive 8 maintain

get off
4 walk 5 leave 6 alight, depart, go free, launch 7 pull out 8 dismount 9 disembark 10 beat the rap

get out
4 exit, kite, leak 5 break, issue, leave, scram, split 6 alight, beat it, begone, decamp, depart, egress, escape 7 buzz off, publish, skiddoo, take off, vamoose 8 dispatch, hightail 9 circulate, skedaddle 10 make tracks

Gettysburg general
3 Lee (Robert E.) 5 Meade (George)

get up
4 gain 5 arise, breed, cause, dress, hatch, mount, raise, stand 6 create, induce, summon 7 acquire, prepare, produce 8 engender, generate 12 rise and shine

getup
3 rig 4 duds, garb, togs 5 array, dress, guise 6 outfit 7 costume, threads

get-up-and-go
3 pep, vim, zip 4 bang, push, snap, zeal, zest 5 drive, moxie, oomph, punch, spunk, steam, verve, vigor 6 energy, spirit, starch 8 ambition 10 enterprise, initiative

gewgaw
3 toy 4 dido 5 bijou, curio 6 bangle, bauble, doodad, trifle 7 bibelot, novelty, trinket, whatnot 8 gimcrack, kickshaw 9 bagatelle, objet d'art 10 knickknack

geyser
3 jet 5 fount, spout, spurt 6 gusher, spring 8 fountain 10 wellspring 11 Old Faithful

Ghana
capital: 5 Accra
city: 4 Tema 6 Kumasi, Tamale
ethnic group: 4 Akan 5 Mossi
former name: 9 Gold Coast
gulf: 6 Guinea
lake: 5 Volta
language: 7 English
monetary unit: 4 cedi
neighbor: 4 Togo 10 Ivory Coast 11 Burkina Faso
river: 5 Volta

ghastly
4 grim, pale 5 awful, lurid 6 grisly, horrid, pallid 7 ghostly, hideous, macabre 8 dreadful, ghoulish, gruesome, horrible, shocking, spectral, terrible 9 appalling, deathlike, frightful, ghostlike, repulsive, sickening 10 cadaverous, corpselike, disgustful, disgusting, horrifying, nauseating, terrifying 11 frightening

ghee
3 fat 6 butter

gherkin
4 vine 6 pickle 8 cucumber

ghetto
4 slum

ghost
4 soul 5 demon, haunt, shade, spook, trace 6 kelpie, shadow, spirit, wraith, zombie 7 eidolon, phantom, specter 8 phantasm 10 apparition 11 poltergeist

ghostly
5 eerie, scary 6 spooky 7 shadowy 8 ethereal, spectral 9 deathlike, spiritual, unearthly, unworldly 10 cadaverous, corpselike, phantasmal 12 supernatural

Ghosts author
5 Ibsen (Henrik)

ghoul
4 ogre 5 fiend 7 monster 11 grave robber

GI
5 grunt 7 dogface, fighter, soldier, warrior 8 doughboy 9 man-at-arms 10 serviceman

Gianni Schicchi composer
7 Puccini (Giacomo)

giant
4 huge, hulk, ogre, Otus, vast 5 gross, Gyges, Hymir, jumbo, titan, whale 6 Cottus, Typhon 7 Aloadae (plural), Antaeus, Cyclops, Goliath, immense, mammoth, monster, titanic, whopper 8 behemoth, Briareus, colossal, colossus, enormous, gigantic,

Orgoglio **9** cyclopean, Enceladus, Ephialtes, Gargantua, Herculean, humongous, leviathan, monstrous **10** gargantuan, prodigious **11** elephantine
biblical: 4 Anak **7** Goliath
cactus: 7 saguaro
killer: 4 Jack **5** David
one-eyed: 5 Arges **7** Cyclops **10** Polyphemus
100-armed: 9 Enceladus
100-eyed: 5 Argus
rime-cold: 4 Ymer, Ymir
sea god: 5 Aegir

Giant author
6 Ferber (Edna)

giaour
7 infidel **10** unbeliever **11** non-believer

gib
6 tomcat

gibber
3 gab, yak **4** blab **5** prate **6** babble, drivel, gabble, jabber, yammer **7** blabber, blather, chatter, palaver, prattle, twaddle

gibberish
3 gab **5** Greek, hokum **6** babble, bunkum, burble, drivel, gabble, jabber, yammer **7** blabber, blather, chatter, palaver, prattle, twaddle **8** claptrap, flimflam, nonsense **10** balderdash, double-talk, hocus-pocus, mumbo jumbo **11** abracadabra, jabberwocky **12** gobbledygook

gibbet
4 hang **5** lynch, noose, scrag **7** execute, gallows **8** string up

gibbon
3 ape **7** primate, siamang **10** anthropoid

gibbous
6 arched, convex, humped **7** bulging, rounded, swollen **10** humpbacked **11** protuberant

gibe
4 gird, jeer, jest, mock, quip, rail

5 fleer, flout, scoff, scorn, scout, sneer, taunt, tease **6** deride, insult **8** ridicule

Gibraltar
colony of: 7 Britain, England
conqueror: 5 Tarik, Tariq
neighbor: 5 Spain
opposite: 5 Ceuta

giddy
4 gaga **5** dizzy, inane, light, silly, woozy **6** elated, yeasty **7** flighty, foolish, vacuous **8** euphoric **9** frivolous, slaphappy **10** hoity-toity **11** empty-headed, harebrained, light-headed, vertiginous **12** bubble-headed **13** rattlebrained

—— **Gide**
5 André

Gideon
father: 5 Joash
servant: 5 Purah
son: 9 Abimelech

gift
3 set, tip **4** alms, bent, boon, head, turn **5** award, bonus, endow, favor, flair, forte, grant, knack **6** genius, legacy, reward, talent **7** ability, aptness, cumshaw, faculty, freebie, handout, present, subsidy **8** aptitude, bestowal, capacity, donation, gratuity, largesse, oblation, offering **9** endowment, lagniappe **11** benefaction, benevolence **12** contribution, presentation

gifted
4 able **5** smart **6** expert **7** hotshot, skilled **8** masterly, skillful, talented **9** ingenious, masterful

gig
3 jab, job, top **4** boat, fool, goad, prod, spur **5** annoy, freak, rotor, spear **6** chaise, harass **7** demerit, provoke, rowboat **8** carriage **10** engagement

gigantic
4 huge, vast **5** giant, jumbo **7** hulking, immense, mammoth, massive, titanic **8** behemoth, colossal,

enormous, king-size, whopping
9 cyclopean, humongous, king-sized, monstrous, walloping 10 gargantuan, prodigious, stupendous 11 elephantine

giggle

5 laugh 6 guffaw, hee-haw, titter
7 chortle, chuckle, snicker, snigger, twitter

Gigi author

7 Colette

Gilbert and Sullivan opera

6 Mikado (The) 8 Iolanthe, Patience, Sorcerer (The) 9 Grand Duke (The), Ruddigore 10 Gondoliers (The)
11 H.M.S. Pinafore, Princess Ida, Trial by Jury

Gil Blas author

6 Lesage (Alain-René)

gild

4 coat, deck 5 adorn, cover, tinge
6 bedeck, tinsel 7 enhance, overlay
8 brighten, ornament 9 embellish, embroider

Gilda's father

9 Rigoletto

Gilead

father: 6 Machir
grandfather: 8 Manasseh
son: 7 Jephtha 8 Jephthah

Gilgamesh

4 epic
companion: 6 Eabani, Enkidu
home: 4 Uruk 5 Erech
mother: 6 Ninsun
victim: 6 Huwawa 7 Humbaba

gill

4 race 5 brook, creek 6 runnel, stream, wattle 7 rivulet
relating to: 9 branchial

gillyflower

4 pink 9 carnation, clove pink

Gilroy play

15 Subject Was Roses (The)

gilt

3 hog, pig, sow 4 bond, gold 5 swine
6 gilded, golden 10 brilliance

gimcrack

5 cheap 6 bauble, gewgaw, shoddy, trifle 7 bibelot, chintzy, trinket
8 kickshaw 10 knickknack

gimlet

4 tool 5 drill, drink 8 cocktail
ingredient: 3 gin 5 vodka 9 lime juice

gimmick

3 con 4 ploy, ruse, wile 5 angle, catch, dodge, feint, gizmo, trick
6 device, gadget, gambit, jigger, scheme, widget 8 artifice, maneuver
9 stratagem 10 subterfuge

gimp

3 vim 4 cord, halt 5 braid, hitch
6 dodder, falter, hobble, spirit 7 cripple 8 lameness

gimpy

4 game, halt, lame 7 hobbled, limping 8 crippled

gin

3 net 4 sloe, trap 5 catch, rummy, snare 6 device, liquor 7 springe
8 beverage, generate, separate

ginger

3 fig, pep, vim, zip 4 herb, stir, zing
5 liven, spice, verve, vigor 6 energy, mettle, revive, spirit 7 sparkle
cookie: 4 snap

gingerly

4 safe, wary 5 canny, chary 7 careful, guarded 8 cautious, delicate, discreet

gingery

4 tart 5 fiery, peppy, sharp, spicy, tangy, zesty 6 snappy, spunky
7 peppery, piquant, pungent 8 spirited 10 mettlesome 12 high-spirited

gingham

5 cloth 6 fabric 7 textile 8 material

gingiva

3 gum

gin mill

3 bar, pub 4 dive 5 joint 6 saloon, tavern 7 barroom, taproom 8 alehouse 9 roadhouse 11 public house
12 watering hole

Ginsberg poem
4 Howl 7 Kaddish

ginseng
4 herb, root

Gioconda, La
8 Mona Lisa
composer: 10 Ponchielli (Amilcare)
painter: 7 da Vinci (Leonardo)

giraffe
8 ruminant 9 quadruped 10 camelo-
pard

girandole
7 earring 10 candelabra 11 candelabrum, candlestick, composition

girasol
3 gem 4 opal 5 jewel, stone 7 mineral 8 fire opal 9 artichoke

gird
3 hem 4 band, belt, bind, ring, wrap
5 brace, equip, hem in, ready, round,
steel 6 circle 7 bolster, enclose,
fortify, prepare, provide, shore up,
wreathe 8 buttress, cincture, encircle, surround 9 encompass, reinforce 10 strengthen

girder
4 beam 5 brace 7 support 8 crossbar 9 crossbeam 10 crosspiece,
transverse

girdle
4 band, belt, ring, sash 6 cestus,
circle 8 ceinture, cincture, encircle,
surround 9 encompass, waistband
of Aphrodite: 6 cestus

girl
4 babe, bird, coed, doll, lass, maid,
miss 5 chick, filly, missy, wench
6 damsel, lassie, maiden 8 daughter
10 sweetheart

girth
4 band, belt, bind, size 5 brace,
cinch, strap 6 circle, fasten, girdle
7 measure 8 cincture, encircle,
surround 9 thickness 10 dimensions
13 circumference

Giselle composer
4 Adam (Adolphe)

gist
3 nub, sum 4 core, meat, pith
5 sense 6 burden, ground, kernel,
marrow, matter, thrust, upshot
7 essence 9 main point, substance

give
3 pay 4 deal, hand 5 allot, allow,
award, grant, issue, offer, remit
6 accord, afford, assign, bestow,
commit, confer, convey, devote,
direct, donate, extend, market, pony
up, render, supply, tender 7 deliver,
dish out, display, dole out, fall out,
fork out, furnish, hand out, mete out,
present, produce, proffer, provide
8 allocate, bequeath, disburse,
dispense, give away, hand over, shell
out, turn over 9 apportion, sacrifice
10 administer, contribute, distribute

give-and-take
6 banter 8 exchange, repartee,
trade-off 10 compromise 11 cooperation, reciprocity

give away
4 blab, leak 5 award, grant, spill
6 bestow, betray, confer, devote,
donate, expose, reveal, tattle 7 deliver, divulge, hand out, let slip,
present 8 bequeath, disclose

giveaway
4 deal, gift, leak 5 steal, value 6 tip-
off 7 bargain, freebee, freebie,
premium, present, sellout 8 betrayal,
exposure 10 disclosure, revelation

give back
6 refund, retire, return 7 replace,
restore, retreat 8 withdraw 9 reinstate

give in
4 fold, quit, stop 5 yield 6 assent,
comply, desist, relent, submit 7 concede, deliver, indulge, succumb
8 back down, cry uncle 9 surrender
10 relinquish

given
5 prone 6 donnée 7 assumed,
granted 8 inclined 9 presented,
specified 10 particular 11 considering, susceptible

give off

4 beam, emit, flow, vent 5 exude,
issue 6 effuse 7 emanate, radiate,
release 9 discharge

give out

4 deal, dole, emit, fail, mete, vent
5 issue 6 cave in 7 declare, release,
succumb 8 collapse, throw off
9 break down 10 distribute

giver

5 donor 7 donator, grantor

give up

4 cede, quit 5 allow, cease, forgo,
waive, yield 6 abjure, devote, resign,
vacate 7 abandon, despair 8 abdicate, hand over, renounce, withdraw
9 sacrifice, surrender 10 relinquish

give way

5 yield 6 buckle, cave in 7 retreat,
succumb 8 collapse 9 surrender

gizmo

see **gadget**

glabrous

4 bald, bare 6 shaven, smooth
8 hairless 9 beardless 10 bald-
headed 12 smooth-shaven

glacial

3 icy, raw 5 chill, gelid, nippy, polar
6 arctic, biting, chilly, frigid, frosty,
frozen, wintry 8 freezing

glacier

3 ice 6 ice cap 8 ice field, ice sheet
Alaska: 4 Muir, Taku 6 Bering
10 Mendenhall
Antarctica: 9 Beardmore
deposit: 4 kame 5 esker 6 placer
7 moraine
fissure: 8 crevasse
fragment: 4 berg 7 iceberg
Greenland: 8 Humboldt
hill: 7 drumlin
Karakoram: 5 Biafo 7 Baltoro
New Zealand: 6 Tasman
pinnacle: 5 serac

glacis

5 grade, slope 7 incline 10 buffer
zone 11 buffer state

glad

3 gay 4 fain 5 happy, jolly, merry
6 blithe, bright, cheery, genial,
jocund, jovial, joyful, joyous 7 beaming, gleeful, pleased, radiant, tickled,
willing 8 cheerful, mirthful, pleasant,
rejoiced 9 delighted, gratified, overjoyed 11 exhilarated 12 lighthearted

gladden

4 buoy 5 cheer, elate 6 buck up,
perk up, please, uplift 7 cheer up,
delight, gratify, hearten

glade

6 meadow 8 clearing 9 open space

gladiator

7 fighter 9 combatant, Spartacus

gladly

4 fain, lief 6 freely 7 happily, readily
8 heartily 9 willingly 10 cheerfully,
with relish 12 with pleasure

gladness

3 joy 4 glee 5 bliss, cheer, mirth
6 gaiety 7 delight, jollity 9 happiness, merriment

gladstone

3 bag 8 suitcase

glamorous

7 elegant 8 alluring, charming,
dazzling, enticing, magnetic 9 seductive 10 attractive, bewitching,
enchanting 11 captivating, fascinating 13 sophisticated

glamour

5 charm, magic, spell 6 allure,
appeal 7 romance 8 charisma,
witchery 9 magnetism, sex appeal
10 attraction, witchcraft 11 fascination 12 razzle-dazzle

glance

4 peek, peep, skim, skip 5 brush,
carom, flash, glaze, graze, shine
6 bounce, careen 7 glimpse 8 ricochet
lascivious: 4 leer

gland

5 gonad, liver, organ 6 pineal,
thymus 7 adrenal, mammary,

parotid, thyroid **8** exocrine, pancreas, prostate, salivary **9** endocrine, pituitary **11** parathyroid
secretion: **7** hormone
swelling: **4** bubo

glare
4 gaze, glow, peer **5** blaze, flame, flash, frown, gleam, light, lower, scowl, shine, stare **6** dazzle, glower **7** obtrude **8** stand out **10** garishness

glaring
4 loud, rank **5** gaudy, plain, vivid **6** brazen, flashy, garish, tawdry, tinsel **7** blatant, obvious **8** blinding, flagrant **9** audacious, egregious, obtrusive **10** noticeable **11** conspicuous, outstanding **12** ostentatious

Glasgow's patron saint
5 Mungo **9** Kentigern

glass
4 lens, pane **5** image, lense, prism **6** mirror **7** reflect **9** barometer, telescope
combining form: **5** vitro
container: **3** jar **6** beaker, bottle
decorative: **7** schmelz **8** schmelze
drinking: **4** pony **5** flute **6** goblet, jigger, rummer, seidel **7** snifter, tumbler **8** schooner
gem: **5** paste **6** strass
magnifying: **5** loupe
milky: **7** opaline
volcanic: **7** perlite **8** obsidian

glasses
5 specs **6** shades **7** goggles **8** bifocals, pince-nez, tumblers **9** lorgnette, trifocals **10** spectacles

glass-like
5 clear **6** glazed, limpid, smooth **8** pellucid, vitreous **9** vitrified **11** translucent, transparent

glassmaker
6 Blenko (William) **7** Lalique (René), Tiffany (Louis Comfort) **9** Waterford

glassmaking tool
5 punty **6** pontil **8** blowpipe

Glass Menagerie author
8 Williams (Tennessee)

glassy
5 blank, dazed, shiny **6** glazed, smooth, vacant **7** hyaloid **8** polished, vitreous **9** burnished

glaucous
4 waxy **7** frosted, powdery

Glaucus
beloved: **6** Scylla
father: **5** Minos **8** Sisyphus
mother: **6** Merope **8** Pasiphaë
son: **11** Bellerophon

glaze
3 rub **4** buff, coat, film **5** cover, glint, gloss, sheen, shine **6** enamel, finish, luster, patina, polish **7** burnish, coating, furbish, lacquer, overlay

glazed
5 blank **6** glassy

gleam
3 ray **4** beam, burn, glow **5** flare, flash, glint, sheen, shine **6** glance **7** glimmer, glisten, glitter, radiate, shimmer, sparkle, twinkle **8** radiance **11** coruscation, scintillate **13** scintillation

gleaming
5 aglow, shiny **6** glossy, sheeny **7** beaming, burning, glowing, lambent, radiant, shining **8** flashing, luminous, lustrous, polished **9** brilliant, burnished, refulgent, sparkling, twinkling **10** glimmering, glistening, glittering, shimmering **13** scintillating

glean
4 cull, reap, sift **5** amass, learn **6** garner, gather, pick up **7** extract, find out, harvest

glebe
4 land **5** field, tract **7** acreage **8** cropland, farmland

glee
3 joy **5** mirth **6** gaiety, levity **7** delight, elation, jollity **8** gladness, hilarity, part-song **9** enjoyment, festivity, good cheer, happiness, jocundity, joviality, merriment **10** exuberance, joyfulness, jubilation **12** exhilaration

gleeful
3 gay **5** jolly, merry **6** blithe, elated, jocund, jovial, joyous **8** cheerful, exultant, jubilant, mirthful **9** exuberant **12** lighthearted

glen
4 dale, vale **5** swale **6** dingle, valley
deep: 5 gorge **6** ravine

glengarry
3 cap **6** bonnet

glib
4 easy **5** slick **6** facile, fluent, smooth **7** offhand, shallow, voluble **8** eloquent, flippant **10** articulate, nonchalant **11** superficial

glide
3 fly **4** flow, sail, skim, slip, soar, waft **5** coast, creep, drift, float, skate, skirr, skulk, slide, slink, sneak, steal **7** descend, slither **8** glissade, volplane **10** portamento

glimmer
4 glow, hint **5** blink, flash, gleam, glint, shine, spark, trace **6** glance **7** flicker, glisten, glitter, inkling, shimmer, sparkle, twinkle **9** coruscate **10** suggestion **11** coruscation, scintillate **13** scintillation

glimpse
4 peek, peep **5** flash, glint, stime **6** glance

glint
3 ray **5** flash, glaze, gleam, sheen, shine, trace **6** glance, luster **7** glimmer, glisten, glitter, shimmer, sparkle, twinkle **9** coruscate **11** coruscation, scintillate **13** scintillation

glissade
4 skim, slip **5** glide, slide

glissando
3 run **5** slide **7** gliding, sliding

glisten
4 glow **5** flash, gleam, glint, shine **6** glance **7** flicker, glimmer, glitter, shimmer, spangle, sparkle, twinkle **9** coruscate **11** coruscation, scintillate **13** scintillation

glitch
3 bug **4** flaw, snag **5** fault **6** defect **7** failing, failure, gremlin, problem **8** obstacle **10** difficulty **11** malfunction

glitter
5 flash, gleam, glint, shine **7** glimmer, glisten, shimmer, spangle, sparkle, twinkle **9** coruscate **11** coruscation, scintillate **13** scintillation

glittering
5 gaudy, shiny, showy **6** flashy **7** fulgent **9** brilliant, clinquant, coruscant, effulgent **11** spectacular

gloaming
3 eve **4** dusk **5** gloom **7** evening **8** eventide, twilight **9** nightfall

gloat
4 crow **5** exult, revel, vaunt **6** relish **7** triumph **9** celebrate

glob
4 clot, lump **6** dollop

global
5 grand **6** cosmic **7** blanket, general, overall **8** all-round, catholic **9** inclusive, planetary, spherical, universal, worldwide **12** encyclopedic **13** comprehensive

globe
3 orb **4** ball **5** earth, round, world **6** planet, sphere **7** rondure
half: 10 hemisphere

globule
4 ball, bead, drip, drop **6** gobbet, pellet **7** driblet, droplet **8** spherule

gloom
3 dim **4** dusk, funk, loom, murk **5** bedim, blues, cloud, dumps, frown, lower, mopes, scowl **6** darken, glower, shadow **7** becloud, despair, dimness, obscure, sadness **8** darkness, overcast, twilight **9** adumbrate, bleakness, dejection **10** blue devils, depression, melancholy, overshadow **11** despondency, unhappiness **12** mournfulness

gloomy
3 dim, dun, sad **4** cold, dark, dour,

down, drab, dull, glum **5** black, bleak, drear, dusky, mopey, murky, muzzy, sulky, surly **6** dismal, dreary, morose, solemn, somber, sullen **7** forlorn, joyless, obscure, stygian, unhappy **8** dejected, desolate, downcast, funereal, mournful **9** cheerless, depressed, mirthless, oppressed, saturnine, tenebrous, woebegone **10** caliginous, chapfallen, depressing, depressive, dispirited, despondent, forbidding, lugubrious, melancholy, oppressive, tenebrific **11** dispiriting, pessimistic **12** disconsolate, discouraging

glorify
4 hymn, laud **5** bless, cry up, erect, exalt, extol, honor **6** admire, praise, revere **7** acclaim, dignify, elevate, ennoble, light up, lionize, magnify, sublime, worship **8** eulogize, venerate **9** celebrate **10** aggrandize

glorious
5 grand, great, noble, proud **6** august, divine, superb **7** eminent, exalted, radiant, sublime **8** esteemed, gorgeous, lustrous, majestic, renowned, splendid, stunning **9** beautiful, brilliant, effulgent, excellent, marvelous, ravishing, wonderful **11** illustrious, magnificent, resplendent, splendorous

glory
4 crow, fame, halo, pomp **5** exalt, exult, gloat, honor, revel **6** heaven, praise, relish, renown **7** acclaim, aureole, delight, majesty, rejoice, triumph **8** eminence, eternity, grandeur, jubilate, radiance, splendor **9** greatness, hereafter **10** effulgence, exaltation, exultation **11** distinction **12** magnificence, resplendence

gloss
4 buff **5** glaze, glint, sheen, shine **6** define, enamel, facade, finish, luster, patina, polish, veneer **7** burnish, comment, explain, furbish, varnish **8** annotate **9** interpret, sleekness, slickness, translate **10** annotation, appearance, brilliance, commentary,

definition **11** elucidation, explanation, translation

glossary
7 lexicon **8** wordbook **9** word-hoard **10** dictionary, vocabulary

gloss over
4 mask **5** slant **6** veneer **7** conceal, cover up, distort, falsify, varnish **8** disguise, palliate **9** dissemble, extenuate, sugarcoat, whitewash **10** camouflage

glossy
5 shiny, sleek, slick **7** shining **8** gleaming, lustrous, polished **9** burnished **10** glistening
fabric: 4 silk **5** satin
paint: 6 enamel

glove
4 gage, mitt **5** catch, cover **6** mitten, sheath **8** covering, gauntlet

glow
4 burn, pink, rose **5** bloom, blush, flush, gleam, rouge, shine **6** mantle, redden **7** blossom, crimson, fox fire, glisten, glitter, radiate **8** brighten, radiance **10** brilliance, luminosity **13** incandescence

glower
5 frown, scowl, stare **11** look daggers

glowing
3 hot, red **4** avid **5** flush, ruddy, shiny **6** ardent, fervid, florid, heated, red-hot **7** beaming, burning, fervent, flushed, lambent, radiant, vibrant **8** blushing, dazzling, gleaming, luminous, lustrous, rubicund, sanguine, suffused **9** brilliant **10** candescent, hot-blooded, passionate **11** impassioned **12** enthusiastic, incandescent

Gluck opera
5 Orfeo **6** Armide **7** Alceste

glucose
5 sugar, syrup

glue
3 fix, gum **4** bind, join **5** epoxy, paste, stick **6** adhere, attach,

gluey

cement, fasten **7** plaster, stickum
8 adhesive, mucilage

gluey

5 gummy, tacky **6** sticky, viscid
7 viscous **8** adhesive **12** mucilaginous

glum

3 sad **4** blue, dour, down **5** moody,
sulky, surly **6** dismal, dreary, gloomy,
morose, sullen, woeful **7** crabbed
8 brooding, dejected, downcast,
taciturn **9** depressed, oppressed,
saturnine, sorrowful, woebegone
10 despondent, dispirited, melancholy **11** downhearted, melancholic

glut

4 clog, cloy, cram, fill, pack, pall, sate
5 feast, flood, gorge, stuff **6** deluge,
excess, stodge **7** satiate, surfeit,
surplus, swallow **8** saturate **10** oversupply **13** overabundance

glutinous

4 ropy **5** gluey, gooey, gummy,
pasty, tacky, thick **6** sticky, viscid
7 viscous **10** gelatinous **12** mucilaginous

glutton

3 hog, pig **8** gourmand **9** chowhound, wolverine **11** gormandizer

gluttonous

7 hoggish, piggish **8** edacious,
ravening, ravenous **9** dissolute,
indulgent, rapacious, voracious
10 insatiable **11** intemperate
13 overindulgent

gluttony

6 excess **7** edacity **8** gulosity,
rapacity, voracity **11** piggishness

glyph

6 figure, groove, symbol **7** graphic
9 character

G-man

3 fed **4** narc, Ness (Eliot) **5** agent
6 Hoover (J. Edgar)

gnarl

4 bend, knot, warp **5** growl, snarl,
twist **6** deform **7** contort, distort

gnash

4 bite **5** grind

gnat

3 bug, fly **4** pest **5** midge **6** insect
7 no-see-um

gnaw

3 eat, nag, vex **4** bite, chaw, chew
5 annoy, chomp, erode, munch,
scour, tease, worry **6** bother, crunch,
nibble, pester, plague, rankle **7** bedevil, corrode, eat away **8** irritate,
wear away **9** masticate

gnome

3 elf, saw **4** rule **5** adage, axiom,
dwarf, maxim, moral, troll, truth
6 dictum, goblin, saying, truism
7 proverb **8** aphorism, apothegm
10 shibboleth

gnostic

6 occult, secret **8** abstruse **10** mysterious

gnu

10 wildebeest

go

against: 4 defy **5** fight **6** oppose,
resist **7** counter, protest **10** contradict
ahead: 4 lead **7** precede, proceed
8 continue, progress
along: 5 agree, yield **6** accede,
comply, concur **7** consent **9** acquiesce
around: 5 avoid, skirt **6** bypass,
detour **7** compass **8** outflank,
sidestep **10** circumvent
at: 6 assail, attack, tackle **7** assault
away: 3 git **4** exit, scat, shoo
5 leave, scram, split **6** beat it, begone, cut out, depart, move on, retire
7 buzz off, get lost, pull out, take off
8 clear out, run along, shove off,
withdraw **9** skedaddle
back: 6 recede, return, revert
7 regress, retreat
back on: 6 betray, renege **7** abandon **8** abrogate
back over: 6 rehash, review, rework
7 recheck, retrace
before: 4 lead **7** precede, predate
8 antedate

beyond: 4 pass 5 excel, outdo 6 exceed, outrun 7 eclipse, surpass 8 outshine, outstrip, overtake 9 transcend
forward: 6 move on, push on 7 advance, press on, proceed 8 continue, progress
in: 5 enter 9 penetrate
out: 4 exit 5 leave 6 expire
Scottish: 3 gae
through: 4 bear 5 audit, brave, check, spend 6 endure, suffer 7 consume, deplete, examine, exhaust, ride out, survive, sustain, undergo 8 squander 9 penetrate, withstand 10 experience
together: 3 fit 4 date, jibe, suit 5 agree, match, tally 6 accord, square 7 conform 8 dovetail 9 accompany, harmonize 10 correspond
with: 4 suit 5 befit, match 9 accompany

goad

3 egg, rod, sic 4 prod, push, spur, urge 5 drive, egg on, impel, prick, thorn 6 coerce, exhort, incite, motive, needle, prompt, propel 7 impetus, impulse 8 catalyst, motivate, stimulus 9 encourage, impulsion, incentive, stimulant, stimulate 10 inducement

go-ahead

4 okay 7 consent 8 spirited 9 ambitious, authority, clearance, energetic 10 green light, permission 11 progressive, up-and-coming 12 enterprising 13 authorization

goal

3 aim, end, use 4 duty, hope, mark 5 score 6 design, intent, object, target 7 mission, purpose 8 ambition, function 9 intention, objective

goat

3 kid, ram 4 lech 5 billy, letch, nanny 6 alpaca, angora, lecher, Saanen 8 cashmere 10 Toggenburg
female: 3 doe 5 nanny
genus: 5 Capra
Himalayan: 4 tahr
male: 4 buck 5 billy
neutered: 6 wether
relating to: 7 caprine
wild: 4 ibex
wool: 6 mohair 8 pashmina

goat antelope

5 serow 7 chamois

goatee

5 beard 7 Vandyke 8 imperial, whiskers

goatfish

6 mullet

goatish

3 hot 4 lewd 6 carnal 7 caprine, lustful, satyric 8 prurient 9 indulgent, lecherous, lickerish 10 lascivious, libidinous, passionate 12 concupiscent

goat-man deity

3 Pan

goat nut

6 jojoba, pignut

gob

3 wad 4 blob, clod, glob, hunk, lump, mass 5 chunk, mouth 6 nugget, sailor 7 extract

gobbet

4 drib, drip, drop, hunk, lump, mass 5 chunk, piece 7 driblet, droplet, globule, portion 8 fragment

gobble

3 eat 4 bolt, cram, grab, glut, gulp, slop, wolf 5 gorge 6 devour, guzzle 7 swallow 11 ingurgitate

gobbledygook

see **gibberish**

go-between

5 agent, envoy, proxy 6 broker, deputy, factor 7 liaison 8 emissary, mediator, procurer 9 middleman 10 arbitrator, interagent, interceder, matchmaker, negotiator, procurator 11 intercessor 12 intermediary, intermediate

goblet

3 cup 5 glass, grail 6 vessel 7 chalice

goblin
3 elf, fay, hob, imp 4 puck 5 bogey, bogle, fairy, ghost, gnome 6 sprite 7 brownie, bugbear 8 bogeyman

_____ go bragh
4 Erin

gobs
4 lots, tons, wads 5 heaps, loads, lumps, piles, rafts, reams, scads 6 oodles 8 slathers 10 quantities

god
4 idol 5 deity 7 creator 8 Almighty, divinity, immortal
combining form: 4 theo
false: 4 baal
French: 4 dieu
Hebrew: 6 Elohim, Yahweh
Latin: 4 deus
Spanish: 4 dios
(see specific entries (as **Greek; Roman**) for names of specific gods and goddesses)

god-awful
4 foul 6 horrid, rotten 7 beastly 8 dreadful, horrible, shameful, shocking, terrible, wretched 9 appalling, atrocious, miserable 10 abominable, deplorable, despicable, detestable, disgusting, outrageous

God Bless America composer
6 Berlin (Irving)

goddess
4 idol 5 deity 8 divinity, immortal
Latin: 3 dea
(see note at **god**)

godfather
3 don 4 boss, capo 6 leader 7 sponsor

Godfather, The
8 Corleone (Don)
actor: 6 Brando (Marlon), De Niro (Robert), Pacino (Al)
author: 4 Puzo (Mario)
director: 7 Coppola (Francis Ford)

God-fearing
5 pious 6 devout 8 faithful, reverent 9 pietistic, religious, righteous

godforsaken
4 bare 5 bleak 6 barren, dismal, gloomy, remote 7 pitiful 8 deserted, desolate, pitiable, wretched 9 miserable, neglected 11 unfortunate

Godiva's husband
7 Leofric

godless
5 pagan 6 unholy, wicked 7 heathen, impious, infidel, profane 8 agnostic 9 atheistic 11 irreligious, unreligious

godlike
4 holy 6 divine 7 blessed, supreme 8 almighty, immortal 10 omniscient 11 all-powerful

godliness
5 piety 6 purity 8 devotion, divinity, holiness, sanctity 9 beatitude, reverence 10 devoutness, sacredness 11 religiosity, saintliness 12 spirituality, virtuousness 13 righteousness

godly
4 holy 5 pious 6 devout, divine 7 angelic, blessed, saintly, supreme 8 almighty, hallowed, immortal, virtuous 9 pietistic, prayerful, religious 10 omniscient 11 all-powerful

go down
3 dip, set 4 drop, fall, fold, lose, sink 5 ensue, lower, occur, pitch, slide, slump 6 cave in, happen, plunge, settle, topple, tumble 7 crumple, decline, descend, founder, succumb 8 collapse, keel over, submerge, submerse 9 surrender, take place

God's acre
8 boneyard, catacomb, cemetery 9 graveyard 10 churchyard, necropolis 12 burial ground, memorial park, potter's field

godsend
4 boon, gift, good 5 manna 7 benefit 8 blessing, windfall 9 advantage 11 benevolence, serendipity

Goethe work
5 Faust 6 Egmont, Stella 7 Clavigo 10 Prometheus

gofer
4 aide, peon 5 toady 6 drudge,

flunky, helper, lackey, menial
7 courier, servant **8** factotum
9 assistant, attendant

goffer
5 crimp, flute, pinch, plait, pleat

go-getter
6 dynamo **7** hustler, rustler **8** live
wire **10** ball of fire, powerhouse
11 self-starter

goggle
3 eye **4** bore, gape, gawk, gaze,
look, ogle, peer **5** glare, gloat, stare
10 rubberneck

goggles
5 specs **7** glasses **10** eyeglasses,
spectacles

go-go
5 hyper **6** hectic **7** frantic **8** frenetic,
frenzied

Gogol novel
novel: 9 Dead Souls
story: 8 Overcoat (The) **10** Taras
Bulba **14** Diary of a Madman

goiter
6 struma **8** swelling

Golconda
see gold mine

gold
4 gilt **5** money **6** riches, wealth,
yellow **7** bullion **8** treasure
bar: 5 ingot
combining form: 4 auri, auro
5 chrys **6** chryso
fool's: 6 pyrite
imitation: 6 ormolu
measure: 5 carat, karat
Spanish: 3 oro

goldbrick
3 bum **4** idle, laze, lazy, loaf, loll
5 cheat, dally, idler, shirk, slack
6 dawdle, loafer, loiter, lounge
7 lounger, shirker, slacker, swindle
8 lollygag, malinger, sluggard **9** lazybones **10** dillydally, malingerer

Gold Bug author
3 Poe (Edgar Allan)

gold cloth
4 lamé

gold-covered
4 gilt **6** gilded

golden
4 gilt, rich **5** auric, blond, shiny,
straw **6** blonde, flaxen, gilded,
mellow, superb, yellow **7** aureate,
honeyed, shining **8** glorious, lustrous, resonant **9** favorable **10** auspicious, prosperous **11** flourishing

golden-ager
5 elder **6** senior **7** ancient, oldster,
retiree **8** old-timer **13** senior citizen

golden-apples guardian
5 Ithun **6** Ithunn

golden bough
9 mistletoe

Golden Bough author
6 Frazer (James George)

Golden Boy playwright
5 Odets (Clifford)

golden-crowned accentor
7 warbler **8** ovenbird

goldeneye
3 bug **4** duck, fowl **6** insect **8** lacewing

Golden Fleece seeker
5 Jason **8** Argonaut

Golden Hind captain
5 Drake (Francis)

Golden Horde
6 Tatars **7** Mongols
leader: 4 Batu

golden horse
7 Trigger **8** palomino

golden shiner
4 dace, fish

Golden State
10 California

goldfinch
4 bird **8** songbird **12** yellowhammer

gold mine
7 bonanza, pay dirt **8** El Dorado,
Golconda, treasure, treasury
13 treasure trove

golem

golem

3 oaf 4 clod, dolt, dope 5 dunce,
idiot, robot 6 nitwit 7 halfwit, machine 8 imbecile 9 automaton,
blockhead 10 nincompoop 11 blun-
derhead

golf

assistant: 5 caddy 6 caddie
club: 4 iron, wood 5 billy, spoon,
wedge 6 driver, mashie, putter
7 niblick, pitcher 9 metal wood, sand
wedge
club part: 3 toe 4 face, grip, head,
heel, neck, sole 5 hosel, shaft
course: 5 links
cup: 5 Ryder 6 Curtis, Walker
hazard: 4 trap 6 bunker 8 sand
trap
mound: 3 tee
score: 3 ace, par 5 bogey, eagle
6 birdie
stroke: 4 baff, chip, draw, fade,
hook, putt 5 drive, pitch, shank, slice
6 sclaff
target: 3 cup, par, pin 4 flag 5 green
7 fairway
term: 3 lie 4 club, fore, hole, loft
5 divot, rough, swing 6 hazard,
marker, stance, stroke 8 foursome,
handicap 9 backswing, downswing,
flagstick

golfer

8 linksman
man: 3 Els (Ernie) 4 Daly (John),
Ford (Doug), Kite (Tom), Lyle (Sandy),
Mize (Larry), Tway (Bob) 5 Boros
(Julius), Faldo (Nick), Floyd (Ray),
Grady (Wayne), Green (Hubert),
Hagen (Walter), Hogan (Ben), Jones
(Bobby), Irwin (Hale), North (Andy),
Pavin (Corey), Peete (Calvin), Price
(Nick), Shute (Denny), Singh (Vijay),
Snead (Sam), Woods (Tiger)
6 Casper (Billy), Graham (David),
Janzen (Lee), Langer (Bernhard),
Miller (Johnny), Nelson (Byron,
Larry), Norman (Greg), Ouimet
(Francis), Palmer (Arnold), Player
(Gary), Sluman (Jeff), Sutton (Hal),
Vardon (Harry), Watson (Tom)
7 Azinger (Paul), Couples (Fred),

Guldahl (Ralph), Mayfair (Billy),
Sarazen (Gene), Simpson (Scott),
Stewart (Payne), Strange (Curtis),
Trevino (Lee), Woosnam (Ian),
Zoeller (Fuzzy) 8 Crenshaw (Ben),
Nicklaus (Jack), Olazabal (José),
Weiskopf (Tom) 9 Rodriguez (Chi
Chi), Elkington (Steve) 10 Middlecoff
(Cary) 11 Ballesteros (Seve)
woman: 4 Berg (Patty), King (Betsy)
5 Baker (Kathy), Lopez (Nancy),
Rawls (Betsy), Stacy (Hollis), Suggs
(Louise) 6 Alcott (Amy), Carner
(Joanne), Daniel (Beth), Davies
(Laura), Geddes (Jane), Mallon
(Meg), Merten (Lauri), Wright (Mickey)
7 Bradley (Pat), Inkster (Juli),
Mochrie (Dottie), Sheehan (Patty)
8 Zaharias (Babe) 9 Didrikson
(Babe), Sorenstam (Annika), Whit-
worth (Kathy) 10 Stephenson (Jan)

Golgotha

7 Calvary

Goliath

5 giant 10 Philistine
deathplace: 4 Elah
home: 4 Gath
slayer: 5 David

Gollum creator

7 Tolkien (J. R. R.)

gonad

5 gland, ovary 6 testis 8 testicle

gondola

3 car 4 boat 7 ski lift 11 railroad car

gone

4 away, dead, left, lost, past 5 flown
6 absent 7 defunct, extinct, lacking,
missing 8 departed, vanished

gonef

see **ganef**

goner

8 dead duck 9 lost cause

Goneril

father: 4 Lear (King)
husband: 6 Albany
sister: 5 Regan 8 Cordelia
victim: 5 Regan

Gone with the Wind
author: 8 Mitchell (Margaret)
character: 5 Rhett (Butler) 6 Ashley (Wilkes) 7 Melanie (Wilkes) 8 Scarlett (O'Hara)
plantation: 4 Tara

gonfalon
4 flag, jack 6 banner, ensign 7 pendant, pennant 8 banderol, standard 9 banderole

gong
6 cymbal, tam-tam

gonzo
6 far-out 7 bizarre, offbeat 9 wigged-out 10 outrageous

goo
4 crud, glop, guck, gunk, muck 5 slime

goober
6 peanut

good
4 pure 5 right, sound, whole 6 decent, humane, kindly, toward, worthy 7 benefit, healthy, upright, welfare 8 innocent, virtuous 9 admirable, advantage, blameless, exemplary, favorable, healthful, honorable, righteous, well-being, wholesome 10 altruistic, beneficent, beneficial, benevolent, charitable, worthwhile 11 respectable, well-behaved 12 humanitarian · 13 philanthropic
French: 3 bon 5 bonne
German: 3 gut
Spanish: 5 bueno

good-bye
4 ciao, ta-ta 5 adieu, congé, later 6 so long 7 cheerio, parting, send-off, toodles 8 farewell, toodle-oo 9 departing, departure 11 leave-taking, valediction, valedictory
French: 5 adieu 8 au revoir 9 bon voyage
German: 8 lebe wohl
Italian: 11 arrivederci
Japanese: 8 sayonara
Spanish: 5 adios 12 hasta la vista

Good Earth author
4 Buck (Pearl S.)

good-for-nothing
3 bum 6 rascal, waster 7 inutile, rounder, useless, wastrel 8 feckless, rascally, unworthy 9 dissolute, scoundrel, valueless, worthless 10 ne'er-do-well, profligate, scapegrace 11 purposeless

good-looking
4 cute, fair, foxy 5 bonny, dishy, hunky 6 comely, lovely, pretty 8 alluring, drop-dead, fetching, handsome 9 beauteous, beautiful, bodacious, ravishing 10 attractive

goodly
4 fair, tidy 5 ample, hefty, large 7 sizable 8 generous 9 bountiful, plentiful 11 significant, substantial 12 considerable

good-natured
4 easy, kind, mild, warm 6 genial, jovial, mellow 7 affable, amiable, cordial, lenient 8 cheerful, friendly, laid-back, obliging, pleasant, pleasing, sanguine 9 agreeable, congenial, easygoing, gemütlich 10 altruistic, benevolent, charitable 11 complaisant

goodness
5 honor, merit, worth 6 purity, virtue 7 decency, honesty, probity, quality 8 morality 9 integrity, rectitude 11 benevolence

goods
4 gear 5 cargo, stock, stuff, wares 7 effects 8 chattels, movables, property 9 vendibles 10 belongings 11 commodities, merchandise, possessions 13 paraphernalia
smuggled: 10 contraband
stolen: 4 loot, swag 5 booty 6 boodle, spoils 7 plunder
thrown overboard: 5 lagan 6 jetsam

good-tasting
5 sapid, yummy 6 delish, savory, toothy 8 luscious 9 delicious, palatable, relishing, toothsome 10 appetizing, delectable, flavorsome 11 scrumptious 13 mouthwatering

goodwill

5 amity, favor 6 comity 7 charity, rapport 8 altruism, kindness, sympathy 9 tolerance 10 compassion, friendship, generosity, kindliness 11 benevolence, helpfulness 12 friendliness

goody

5 candy, treat 6 bonbon, dainty, morsel, tidbit 8 delicacy, kickshaw

goody-goody

4 prig 5 prude 6 Grundy 7 prudish, puritan, uptight 8 bluenose, Comstock, priggish 9 Mrs. Grundy, nice-nelly 11 puritanical

gooey

5 gluey, gummy, mushy, sappy, soupy 6 cloggy, drippy, slushy, sticky, viscid 7 maudlin, viscous 8 adhesive 9 glutinous 11 sentimental 12 mucilaginous

goof

3 err, kid 4 boob, dolt, flub, fool, mess, muff 5 boner, booby, botch, chump, dunce, error, fluff, gaffe, gum up, idiot, put on 6 bobble, boggle, bollix, bumble, bungle, fumble, mess up, slip-up 7 blooper, blunder, fathead, louse up, mistake 8 dolthead, lunkhead 9 blockhead

go off

4 blow 5 blast, burst, erupt, leave, sound 6 blow up, depart 7 explode 8 detonate

goofy

5 balmy, batty, crazy, daffy, dippy, loony, nutty, potty, silly 6 simple, stupid 7 foolish, idiotic 9 ludicrous 10 ridiculous 11 harebrained

gook

4 crud, glop, gunk, muck 5 gumbo, slime 6 debris, sludge

go on

4 last, stay 5 occur 6 endure, happen, keep up 7 persist, proceed 8 continue 9 persevere

goon

3 oaf, sap 4 boob, dodo, dolt, dope, fool, hood, thug 5 dummy, idiot 6 dimwit, hit man, nitwit 7 hoodlum 8 dumbbell, enforcer 10 triggerman

gooney

7 seabird 9 albatross

goop

4 crud, gunk, muck 5 gumbo, tripe

Goops author

7 Burgess (Gelett)

goose

4 poke, spur 9 stimulate
cry: 4 honk 5 clang
flock: 3 vee 5 skein 6 gaggle
genus: 5 Anser
Hawaiian: 4 nene
male: 6 gander
wild: 5 brant 7 greylag 8 barnacle
young: 7 gosling

gooseberry

7 currant

Goosebumps author

5 Stine (R. L.)

goose egg

3 nil, zip 4 nada, zero 5 aught, zilch 6 cipher, naught, nought 7 no score, nothing

gooseflesh

5 bumps 7 pimples

go over

4 scan, skim 5 study 6 peruse, review 7 examine, inspect

gopher

6 rodent 8 tortoise

Gopher State

9 Minnesota

Gordian knot cutter

9 Alexander

Gordius' son

5 Midas

gore

3 jab 4 stab 5 blood, slime, wound 6 gusset, pierce 7 carnage 12 gruesomeness

gorge

3 gap 4 cloy, fill, glut, jade, pall, sate 5 abyss, chasm, cleft, clove, flume, gulch, stuff 6 arroyo, canyon, clough,

defile, pig out, ravine **7** couloir, overeat, satiate, surfeit **11** overindulge
Arizona: **11** Grand Canyon
Colorado: **5** Royal

gorgeous

5 grand, plush **6** comely, lavish, lovely, pretty, superb **7** opulent, sublime **8** alluring, dazzling, glorious, splendid **9** beautiful, brilliant, exquisite, luxurious, sumptuous **10** attractive, glittering **11** magnificent, resplendent, splendorous

gorgon

3 hag **5** crone, harpy, witch **6** Medusa, ogress, virago **8** battle-ax, fishwife, harridan, slattern **9** battleaxe, termagant
father: **7** Phorcus, Phorcys
mother: **4** Ceto

gorilla

3 ape **4** goon, hood, thug **5** tough **6** simian **7** primate **8** gangster **10** anthropoid

Gorky drama

11 Lower Depths (The)

gormless

4 dumb, slow **6** stupid

gorse

4 whin **5** furze, shrub **6** legume

gory

5 lurid **6** bloody, grisly **8** gruesome, sanguine **10** sanguinary **11** ensanguined, sanguineous, sensational **12** bloodstained **13** bloodcurdling

gosh

3 gee, wow **4** dang, darn, drat, egad, geez, heck **5** golly **6** crikey, cripes, shucks **7** doggone **8** goodness, gracious

gospel

5 truth **6** truism **7** message **8** doctrine **9** scripture **11** evangelical

gossamer

4 airy, film, fine, webs **5** filmy, gauzy, sheer **6** flimsy **7** cobwebs, tenuous **8** delicate **10** diaphanous **11** transparent

gossip

4 blab, buzz, chat, dirt, talk **5** clack, prate, rumor **6** babble, rumble, tattle **7** babbler, chatter, hearsay, prattle, tattler **8** bigmouth, busybody, informer, prattler, quidnunc, telltale **10** talebearer **11** rumormonger, scandalizer, scuttlebutt **12** blatherskite

gossipy

5 gabby, talky **6** chatty **8** babbling, blabbing **9** garrulous, talkative

Gotham

7 New York (City)

Gothic

4 dark, wild **5** crude **6** brutal, coarse, savage **7** uncouth **8** barbaric, Germanic, medieval, Teutonic **9** barbarian, barbarous, sans serif **11** black letter, uncivilized

Götterdämmerung composer

6 Wagner (Richard)

Gouda

6 cheese

gouge

3 dig **4** milk, ream, tool **5** cheat, exact, pinch, screw, wrest, wring **6** chisel, coerce, extort, groove, wrench **7** squeeze **8** scoop out **9** blackmail, extortion, shake down **10** overcharge

goulash

4 stew **6** jumble, medley **7** mélange **8** mishmash **9** potpourri **10** bridge hand, hodgepodge, salmagundi **11** gallimaufry

go under

4 fall, flop, fold, lose, sink **5** drown **6** plunge, submit **7** founder, immerse, succumb **8** collapse, submerge, submerse **9** surrender **10** capitulate

Gounod work

5 Faust **8** Ave Maria

gourd

4 pepo **5** fruit, melon **6** bottle, squash, vessel **7** chayote, gherkin, pumpkin **8** calabash, cucumber, cucurbit
instrument: **6** maraca

gourmand

see **glutton**; **gourmet**

gourmet

7 epicure **9** bon vivant **10** gastronome **11** connoisseur **12** gastronomist

gout

4 blob, clot, gush **5** spurt **6** splash **7** disease, podagra **8** eruption, swelling

govern

4 head, lead, rule **5** guide, order, reign, steer **6** direct, manage, master **7** command, conduct, control, execute, oversee **8** dominate, hold sway, regulate **9** supervise **10** administer **11** superintend

governess

5 nanny, nurse **6** duenna **8** mistress **9** nursemaid **10** babysitter **11** Mary Poppins

government

4 rule **5** power **6** polity, regime **7** regency, regimen **8** monarchy, republic, Uncle Sam **9** authority, autocracy, democracy, hierarchy, oligarchy **10** Big Brother **11** aristocracy, sovereignty
autocratic: 7 czarism, fascism, tyranny **9** despotism **10** absolutism **12** dictatorship
by a few: 9 oligarchy
by one: 8 monarchy
by three: 8 triarchy **11** triumvirate
by women: 8 gynarchy
official: 10 bureaucrat **11** functionary
without: 7 anarchy

government agency

3 ATF, BIA, BLM, CDC, CIA, DEA, EPA, FAA, FBI, FCC, FDA, FEC, FHA, GAO, GPO, HUD, ICC, INS, IRS, NBS, NEA, NIH, NRC, TVA **4** FDIC, FEMA, FEPC, NASA, NOAA, NTSB, OSHA

governor

3 bey **4** head **5** chief, nabob, ruler **6** leader, regent **7** manager, viceroy **8** director **9** executive, regulator **10** commandant, magistrate
Chinese: 6 tuchun
of a fort: 7 alcaide, alcayde **9** castellan, chatelain
Persian: 6 satrap

gown

4 robe, toga **5** dress, frock, habit, tunic **6** camise, kimono, kirtle, mantua **7** cassock, chemise **8** peignoir
dressing: 8 bathrobe
hospital: 6 johnny

goy

6 non-Jew **7** gentile

grab

3 nab **4** glom, grip, snag, take **5** catch, clasp, grasp, pluck, seize **6** clutch, collar, snatch, tackle **7** capture, grapple, seizure

grabby

6 greedy **8** covetous, desirous, grasping **9** rapacious **10** avaricious, prehensile **11** acquisitive

grace

4 ease **5** adorn, charm, favor, mercy, poise **6** allure, lenity, pardon, polish, prayer, thanks, virtue **7** charity, dignify, dignity, enhance **8** approval, blessing, clemency, easiness, elegance, goodness, kindness, leniency, petition, reprieve **9** embellish, privilege **10** indulgence, invocation, refinement **11** benediction, forbearance **12** thanksgiving

graceful

4 airy, deft, easy **5** agile, lithe **6** nimble, poised, seemly, smooth, urbane **7** elegant, flowing, genteel, refined **8** debonair, elegance, pleasing, polished

graceless

4 rude **5** crude, gawky, inept **6** clumsy, coarse, gauche, klutzy, vulgar **7** awkward, boorish, uncouth **8** barbaric, ungainly **9** barbarian, barbarous **10** outlandish, unmannered **12** infelicitous

Graces
6 Charis **8** Charites (plural)
brilliance: 6 Aglaia
bloom: 6 Thalia
joy: 10 Euphrosyne
mother: 5 Aegle

gracious
4 kind **5** suave **6** benign, genial,
kindly, urbane **7** affable, amiable,
cordial, courtly, gallant, stately, tactful
8 charming, generous, mannered,
merciful, obliging, sociable **9** congenial, courteous **11** complaisant,
good-natured **13** compassionate

grackle
5 mynah **7** jackdaw **8** starling
9 blackbird

gradation
4 rank, step **5** order, range, scale,
shade, stage **6** ablaut, change,
degree, nuance, series **8** ordering,
position, spectrum **9** continuum,
variation **10** difference, succession

grade
3 peg **4** cant, form, kind, lean, mark,
rank, rate, rung, sort, step, tier, tilt
5 blend, class, group, level, notch,
order, pitch, place, slant, slope, stage
6 assess, assort, degree, league,
rating **7** arrange, caliber, echelon,
incline, leaning, quality **8** appraise,
category, classify, division, evaluate,
grouping, position, standard **10** categorize **11** inclination

Grade A
3 ace, top **4** best, boss, fine, tops
5 grand, great, prime, primo, super
6 choice, tip-top **7** capital, supreme
8 five-star, superior, top-notch **9** excellent, first-rate, nonpareil, number one, top-drawer **10** first-class
11 outstanding **13** par excellence

gradient
4 lean, ramp, rise, tilt **5** angle,
pitch, slant, slope **7** incline, leaning
9 acclivity, declivity **11** inclination

gradual
4 even, slow **6** Psalms, steady
7 ongoing **8** bit-by-bit, creeping

9 piecemeal, prolonged **10** continuous, developing, protracted,
step-by-step **11** progressive

gradually
6 slowly **7** by steps **8** bit by bit **9** by
degrees, piecemeal **10** step by step
12 deliberately **13** imperceptibly,
incrementally

graduate
4 alum
female: 6 alumna **7** alumnae
(plural)
male: 6 alumni (plural) **7** alumnus

Graeae, Graiae
4 Enyo **5** Deino **8** Pephredo
father: 7 Phorcus, Phorcys
mother: 4 Ceto
sisters: 7 Gorgons

graft
4 join, mend, scam, skim **5** affix,
crime, fraud, scion, unite **6** attach,
boodle, fasten, payola, splice **7** implant, swindle, topwork **8** kickback
10 corruption

Grafton, Sue
character: 8 Millhone (Kinsey)
novel: 11 A Is for Alibi

Grahame, Kenneth
character: 3 Rat **4** Toad, Mole
6 Badger
novel: 16 Wind in the Willows (The)

grail
3 cup, end **4** goal **6** goblet, object,
target **7** chalice **9** objective

grain
3 bit, jot, rye **4** corn, flax, iota, meal,
mite, oats, rice **5** crumb, fiber, kamut,
maize, speck, spelt, trace, wheat
6 barley, cereal, millet, quinoa, tittle
7 granule, smidgen, sorghum, texture **8** amaranth, molecule, particle
9 buckwheat, triticale
bundle: 4 bale **5** sheaf
chute: 6 hopper
ear: 5 spike
elevator: 4 silo
mixture: 6 fodder
row: 5 swath **7** windrow

grainy
5 rough 6 coarse 8 granular 10 unfinished, unpolished

grammarian
Roman: 7 Donatus (Aelius)

grammatical case
6 dative 7 oblique 8 ablative, genitive, locative, vocative 9 objective 10 accusative, nominative, possessive, subjective

grampus
5 whale 7 dolphin 8 cetacean, porpoise, scorpion 9 blackfish 12 whip scorpion

Granada
building: 8 Alhambra
citadel: 8 Alcazaba
last Moorish king: 7 Boabdil

granary
3 bin 4 silo 9 grain area 10 repository, storehouse

grand
3 fab 4 epic, fine, huge, vast 5 gaudy, lofty, noble, regal, royal, showy, super 6 august, flashy, garish, lavish, lordly, mighty, ornate, superb 7 exalted, opulent, pompous, stately, sublime 8 baronial, elevated, foremost, gorgeous, imposing, majestic, princely, splendid 9 first-rate, inclusive, luxurious, principal, sumptuous, wonderful 10 first-class, impressive, monumental, prodigious, stupendous, tremendous 11 magnificent 12 ostentatious 13 comprehensive

Grand Canyon
explorer: 6 Powell (John Wesley)
state: 7 Arizona

grande dame
5 queen 6 matron 7 dowager 9 matriarch

grandee
4 duke, earl, king, lord, peer 5 baron, noble, pasha 6 bashaw, prince 8 mandarin, marquess, nobleman, viscount 11 muckety-muck

grandeur
4 pomp 5 glory 7 dignity, majesty 8 nobility, opulence, splendor, vastness 9 greatness, immensity, largeness, loftiness, nobleness, sublimity 10 augustness 11 stateliness 12 magnificence

grandiloquent
5 lofty 7 aureate, bloated, fustian, pompous 8 inflated 9 bombastic, flatulent, high-flown, overblown 10 histrionic, portentous 11 declamatory, highfalutin, pretentious 12 magniloquent

grand inquisitor
Spanish: 10 Torquemada (Tomás de)

grandiose
4 epic, vast 5 lofty, noble, regal, royal, showy 6 august, cosmic, lavish, lordly 7 pompous, stately, sublime, utopian 8 affected, imposing, majestic, princely, splendid 9 ambitious, high-flown 11 extravagant, highfalutin, magnificent, pretentious 12 ostentatious

grand mal
7 seizure 8 epilepsy

grandmother
Russian: 8 babushka

grange
4 farm 9 farmhouse, farmstead

granite
3 ore 4 rock 5 stone 6 aplite 7 mineral 11 igneous rock

Granite State
12 New Hampshire

grant
3 aid 4 alms, avow, cede, dole, gift, give 5 admit, allow, award, endow, yield 6 accord, assert, assign, assume, bestow, confer, convey, donate, permit 7 charity, concede, consent, entitle, handout, present, property, subsidy, suppose 8 bequeath, donation, transfer 9 endowment, vouchsafe 10 assistance, concession, relinquish, subvention 11 acknowledge, benefaction 12 contribution 13 appropriation

granular
5 rough, sandy 6 coarse, grainy
7 powdery 8 powdered 10 unfinished, unpolished

granule
3 bit, jot 4 iota, pill, spot 5 grain
6 pellet 8 fragment, particle

grape
3 fox, uva 4 Bual 5 Gamay, Pinot, Syrah 6 Arinto, Burger, Gentil, merlot, muscat, Shiraz 7 Albillo, Aligote, Barbera, Catawba, Concord, Furmint, Niagara, sultana 8 Aleatico, Cabernet, Charbono, Delaware, Friularo, Grenache, Isabella, malvasia, muscadel, Muscadet, Nebbiolo, Riesling, Semillon, Sylvaner, Thompson, Traminer, vinifera, Viognier 9 Carmenère, Chasselas, Lambrusco, Malvoisie, muscadine, Pinot Gris, pinot noir, Sauvignon, Trebbiano, zinfandel 10 chardonnay, Grignolino, muscadelle, pinot blanc, Sangiovese, Verdicchio 11 Chenin Blanc, Petite Sirah, pinot grigio, scuppernong
disease: 4 esca
dried: 6 raisin
drink: 4 wine
pulp: 4 rape 6 pomace
residue: 4 marc

grapefruit
6 pomelo

Grapes of Wrath, The
author: 9 Steinbeck (John)
family: 4 Joad
people: 5 Okies

grapevine
4 buzz 5 rumor 6 gossip 7 hearsay
9 rumor mill 11 scuttlebutt

graph
3 map 4 plot 5 chart 6 sketch
7 diagram, outline 8 nomogram, pie chart

graphic
3 map 5 clear, lucid, photo, vivid
6 cogent, visual 7 picture, precise, telling, written 8 clear-cut, definite, detailed, explicit, incisive, striking
9 pictorial, realistic 10 compelling, photograph 11 descriptive, picturesque

graphite
4 lead 6 carbon 8 plumbago

grapnel
4 hook 6 anchor

grappa
6 brandy

grapple
3 nab 4 bind, cope, grab, grip, hold
5 catch, clamp, clasp, fight, grasp, seize 6 battle, bucket, clench, clinch, clutch, fasten, tackle, tussle
7 contest, scuffle, wrestle 8 struggle

grasp
3 dig, ken, see 4 glom, grip, hold, know, take 5 catch, clamp, clasp, seize 6 accept, clench, clinch, clutch, fathom, follow, handle, take in, tenure 7 cognize, compass, control, embrace, grapple, realize 8 envisage, perceive 9 apprehend, awareness 10 appreciate, comprehend, take hold of, understand 12 apprehension 13 comprehension, understanding

graspable
5 clear, lucid 6 lucent 8 coherent, knowable, palpable 10 fathomable 11 perspicuous 12 intelligible 13 apprehensible

grasping
4 avid 6 grabby, greedy 8 covetous, desirous 9 rapacious 10 avaricious, prehensile 11 acquisitive

grass
3 pot, sod, tea 4 lawn, reed, turf, weed 6 redtop 7 herbage, panicum, pasture 8 cannabis, Mary Jane 9 cocksfoot, marijuana
African: 6 imphee
annual: 6 darnel 8 teosinte
Asian: 7 vetiver, whangee
Australian: 8 spinifex
beach: 6 marram
cereal: 3 oat, rye 4 milo, teff 5 kafir, maize, proso, sorgo, wheat 6 millet 7 sorghum 8 triticum

clump: 4 tuft 7 tussock
dried: 3 hay 5 straw
European: 7 Bermuda, timothy
fiber: 4 flax
fragrant: 10 citronella
pasture: 5 Bahia, grama
perennial: 6 fescue, quitch, zoysia
7 esparto, galleta
prairie: 8 bluestem
second growth: 5 rowen
tropical: 5 cogon 6 bamboo

grasshopper
6 locust 7 katydid 8 cocktail

grassland
3 lea 5 field 6 meadow 7 pasture,
prairie
African: 4 veld 5 veldt
flat: 7 savanna 8 savannah
South American: 5 pampa 6 pampas

Grass novel
7 Tin Drum (The)

grate
3 irk, jar, rub, vex 4 file, fray, fret,
gall, rasp, rile 5 annoy, chafe, gnash,
grind, peeve, pique 6 abrade, grille,
nettle, rankle, scrape 7 provoke,
scratch 8 irritate 9 aggravate,
fireplace

grateful
7 obliged, pleased, restful, welcome
8 beholden, indebted, pleasant,
pleasing, thankful 9 agreeable,
congenial, favorable 10 refreshing
11 restorative 12 appreciative

Gratiano
brother: 9 Brabantio
friend: 7 Antonio 8 Bassanio
niece: 9 Desdemona
wife: 7 Nerissa

gratify
4 baby, sate 5 favor, humor, spoil
6 coddle, oblige, pamper, pander,
please 7 appease, cater to, content,
delight, gladden, indulge, satisfy

gratin
5 crust

grating
3 dry 4 grid, rasp 5 grill, harsh,
rough 6 grille, hoarse 7 irksome,
jarring, lattice, rasping, raucous
8 gridiron, strident 9 vexatious
10 stridulous

gratis
4 comp, free 6 comped 8 costless
10 chargeless 13 complimentary,
without charge

gratitude
6 thanks 12 appreciation, gratefulness, thankfulness

gratuitous
6 wanton 8 baseless 9 unfounded,
voluntary 10 groundless, reason-
less, ungrounded 11 uncalled-for,
unnecessary, unwarranted 12 indefensible

gratuity
3 tip 4 gift, perk 5 bonus 6 reward
7 cumshaw, douceur 8 donation,
largesse, offering 9 baksheesh,
lagniappe, pourboire 10 perquisite
11 benefaction 12 contribution

grave
3 pit, sad 4 dire, dour, fell, grim,
tomb 5 acute, awful, crypt, fatal,
heavy, major, sober, staid, vault
6 burial, deadly, gloomy, sedate,
severe, solemn, somber, sombre,
urgent 7 austere, ghastly, ominous,
ossuary, serious, subdued, weighty
8 catacomb, critical, dreadful, perilous, pressing, terrible 9 dangerous,
mausoleum, momentous, ponderous,
saturnine, sepulcher, sepulchre,
sepulture, unsmiling
marker: 5 stela, stele 8 memorial,
monument 9 footstone, headstone,
tombstone 11 sarcophagus
mound: 6 barrow 7 tumulus
robber: 5 ghoul

gravel
4 dirt, grit, sand
ridge: 5 esker

gravelly
5 raspy, rough 6 gritty, hoarse

7 rasping, grating 8 abrasive, granular, gutteral, scratchy

graven image
4 icon, idol

graver
4 tool 5 burin 8 sculptor

graveyard
8 boot hill, catacomb, cemetery, God's acre 10 necropolis 12 burial ground, memorial park, potter's field

gravid
5 heavy 8 enceinte, pregnant 9 expectant, expecting, with child 10 parturient 12 childbearing

gravity
5 force 6 weight 7 dignity, urgency 8 sobriety 9 heaviness, solemnity 10 importance, somberness 11 consequence, seriousness 12 significance

gravlax
3 lox 6 salmon

gravy
4 perk 5 bonus, bribe, graft, juice, sauce 6 payola 8 dressing, windfall
French: 3 jus

gray
3 ash, old 4 aged, ashy, blah, drab, dull 5 ashen, bleak, color, hoary, slate, slaty 6 dismal, gloomy, leaden 7 elderly, grizzly, neutral 8 grizzled, gunmetal, overcast 9 cinereous, colorless
brownish: 5 taupe 7 fuscous

gray duck
7 gadwall, pintail

grayfish
5 shark 7 dogfish

gray matter
3 wit 4 head, mind 5 brain 6 brains, noddle, noggin, noodle 8 cerebrum 9 intellect 10 encephalon 12 intelligence, neural tissue

graze
3 eat, rub 4 feed, gall, kiss, skim, skip, wear 5 brush, chafe, erode, shave, touch 6 abrade, browse, bruise, forage, glance, scrape 7 contuse, corrade, pasture 8 abrasion, ricochet

grazier
7 rancher

grease
3 fat, oil 4 lard 5 smear 6 smooth 7 lanolin 9 lubricant, lubricate
combining form: 4 sebi, sebo

greasy
4 oily 5 fatty, slick 8 slippery, unctuous 10 lubricious, oleaginous

greasy spoon
4 café 5 diner, grill 6 eatery 7 beanery, hashery 9 chophouse, hash house, lunchroom 10 coffee shop 12 luncheonette

great
3 big, fat 4 huge, vast 5 famed, grand, jumbo, large, noble 6 famous, heroic 7 eminent, exalted, extreme, immense, mammoth, notable, sublime, supreme, titanic 8 colossal, enormous, gigantic, glorious, oversize, renowned, terrific, towering 9 excellent, fantastic, humongous, paramount, prominent, wonderful 10 celebrated, impressive, noteworthy, prodigious, remarkable, stupendous, surpassing, tremendous, voluminous 11 illustrious, magnificent, outstanding, superlative 13 distinguished
combining form: 4 mega 6 megalo

Great Bear
9 Big Dipper, Ursa Major 13 constellation

Great Britain
see **England**

Great Commoner, the
4 Pitt (William) 5 Bryan (William Jennings) 7 Lincoln (Abraham)

Great Emancipator, the
7 Lincoln (Abraham)

greater
4 more 5 metro 6 better, bigger, higher, larger 8 superior 9 exceeding 10 surpassing 12 metropolitan

greatest
4 best, most 6 utmost 7 maximum, supreme 8 foremost

Great Expectations
author: 7 Dickens (Charles)
character: 3 Joe (Gargery), Pip 5 Biddy 7 Estella, Jaggers 8 Havisham (Miss), Magwitch (Abel)

greathearted
4 bold, kind 5 brave, lofty, noble 6 heroic 7 gallant 8 fearless, generous, princely 10 benevolent, chivalrous, courageous, high-minded 11 considerate, magnanimous

Great Lake
4 Erie 5 Huron 7 Ontario 8 Michigan, Superior
acronym: 5 HOMES

Great Lake State
8 Michigan

greave
7 legging

grebe
4 bird, fowl 8 dabchick 10 diving bird

Greece
ancient city-state: 5 Argos 6 Athens, Sparta, Thebes 7 Corinth
capital: 6 Athens
city: 6 Patras 7 Larissa, Piraeus 8 Salonika 12 Thessaloníki
conqueror: 6 Philip (of Macedonia) 9 Alexander (the Great)
island, island group: 5 Crete 6 Aegean, Euboea, Ionian 8 Cyclades, Sporades
monetary unit: 4 euro
mountain, range: 3 Ida 4 Ossa 6 Pindus 7 Olympus 9 Parnassus
neighbor: 6 Turkey 7 Albania 8 Bulgaria 9 Macedonia
part of: 7 Balkans
peninsula: 6 Balkan 10 Chalcidice 11 Peloponnese
region: 6 Epirus, Thrace 8 Thessaly
sea: 6 Aegean, Ionian 13 Mediterranean

greed
6 excess, hunger 7 avarice, avidity, craving 7 edacity, longing 8 cupidity, gluttony, rapacity, voracity 12 covetousness, ravenousness

greedy
4 avid 5 itchy 6 grabby 7 hoggish, miserly, selfish 8 covetous, desirous, edacious, esurient, grasping 10 avaricious, gluttonous 11 acquisitive

Greek
6 babble, drivel, jabber 7 Achaean 8 Hellenic, nonsense 9 gibberish
assembly: 5 agora, boule
coin: 4 obol 6 lepton, stater
column: 5 Doric, Ionic 10 Corinthian
contest: 4 agon
counselor: 6 Nestor
dictator: 7 Metaxas (Ioannis)
dragon: 9 Eurythion
drink: 4 ouzo
epic: 5 Iliad 7 Odyssey
Fates: 6 Clotho, Moirae 7 Atropos 8 Lachesis
god:
  chief: 4 Zeus
  messenger: 6 Hermes
  of agriculture: 6 Cronus
  of death: 8 Thanatos
  of dreams: 8 Morpheus
  of fire: 10 Hephaestus
  of healing: 9 Asclepius 11 Aesculapius
  of love: 4 Eros
  of marriage: 5 Hymen
  of the sun: 6 Apollo
  of physicians: 6 Hermes
  of the sea: 6 Nereus, Triton 7 Oceanus 8 Poseidon
  of the sun: 6 Helios
  of the underworld: 5 Pluto
  of the winds: 5 Eurus, Notus 6 Aeolus, Boreas 8 Zephyrus
  of war: 4 Ares
  of wine: 8 Dionysus
  of woods: 3 Pan
goddess:
  of agriculture: 7 Demeter
  of beauty: 9 Aphrodite
  of dawn: 3 Eos

of discord: 4 Eris
of fertility: 6 Cybele
of flowers: 7 Chloris
of harvests: 4 Rhea
of hunting: 7 Artemis
of justice: 7 Astraea
of love: 9 Aphrodite
of marriage: 4 Hera
of night: 3 Nyx
of peace: 5 Irene
of retribution: 7 Nemesis
of ruin: 3 Ate
of the earth: 4 Gaea, Gaia
of the hearth: 5 Hestia
of magic: 6 Hecate, Hekate
of the moon: 6 Hecate, Hekate,
  Selena, Selene 7 Artemis, Astarte
of the rainbow: 4 Iris
of the seasons: 5 Horae
of the underworld: 6 Hecate,
  Hekate 10 Persephone
of vengeance: 7 Nemesis
of victory: 4 Nike
of wisdom: 6 Athena
of witchcraft: 6 Hecate, Hekate
of womanhood: 4 Hera
of youth: 4 Hebe
hero: 4 Aias, Ajax 5 Jason 7 Theseus 8 Achilles, Argonaut, Heracles,
Hercules, Odysseus 9 Achilleus
historian: 8 Xenophon 9 Herodotus
10 Thucydides
lawgiver: 5 Draco, Solon
leader: 6 Agamemnon
letter: 3 chi, eta, phi, psi, rho, tau
4 beta, iota, zeta 5 alpha, delta,
gamma, kappa, omega, sigma, theta
6 lambda 7 epsilon, omicron, upsilon
magistrate: 6 archon
marketplace: 5 agora
porch: 4 stoa
sandwich: 4 gyro
soldier: 7 hoplite
theater: 5 odeon, odeum
underworld: 5 Hades
war cry: 5 alala
warrior: 4 Ajax 7 Ulysses 8 Achilles, Diomedes, Odysseus 9 Agamemnon, Palamedes
wine: 7 retsina

green

3 raw 4 jade, lime, moss 5 alive,
fresh, kelly, leafy, naive, virid, young
6 callow, forest, unripe 7 avocado,
celadon, emerald, untried, verdant
8 immature, juvenile, unversed,
youthful 9 unfledged 10 unseasoned
11 unpracticed 13 inexperienced
bluish: 8 glaucous
combining form: 4 verd 6 chloro
grayish: 5 olive
yellowish: 7 luteous 10 chartreuse

greenbacks

4 cash, jack, loot 5 bread, bucks,
dough, lucre, money, moola 6 moolah, wampum 7 dollars, scratch
8 currency, smackers 11 legal
tender

greenery

7 foliage, leafage 8 verdancy

green-eyed

7 envious, jealous 9 invidious
monster: 8 jealousy

greenfly

5 aphid

greengage

4 plum

greenhead

3 fly 8 horsefly

greenheart

6 laurel 9 evergreen

greenhorn

4 babe, hick, jake, naif, rube, tyro
5 clown 6 newbie, novice, rookie
7 bumpkin, ingenue 8 beginner,
newcomer 10 clodhopper, provincial

greenhouse

7 nursery 12 conservatory

Greenland

capital: 4 Nuuk 7 Godthåb
city: 5 Thule
ethnic group: 5 Inuit 6 Eskimo
explorer: 4 Eric (the Red), Erik (the
Red), Leif (Eriksson) 9 Rasmussen
(Knud)
language: 6 Danish
monetary unit: 5 krone
possession of: 7 Denmark

green light
3 nod **4** okay **5** leave **6** assent
7 consent, go-ahead, mandate
8 approval, blessing, sanction,
thumbs-up **9** authority, clearance
10 permission **11** endorsement
13 authorization

Green Mansions
author: 6 Hudson (W. H.)
character: 4 Rima

green monkey
6 guenon, simian, vervet

Green Mountain State
7 Vermont

greenness
5 youth **6** spring **7** puberty **8** verdancy, viridity **9** youthhood **10** immaturity, juvenility, pubescence,
springtide, springtime **11** adolescence **12** inexperience

green osier
6 willow **7** dogwood

green plover
7 lapwing **9** shorebird

greenroom
6 lounge

greenstone
4 jade **7** diabase **8** nephrite **9** trem-
olite **10** actinolite

greet
3 bow **4** hail, meet **6** accost, call to,
salaam, salute **7** address, react to,
receive, welcome

greeting
3 ave, bow, nod **4** ciao, hail **5** aloha,
hello, howdy **6** salaam, salute
7 address, welcome **9** handshake,
reception **10** salutation

gregarious
6 clubby, genial, social **7** affable
8 outgoing, sociable **9** clubbable,
congenial, convivial **11** extroverted
13 companionable

gremlin
3 bug, elf, imp **5** dwarf, gnome
6 defect, glitch **7** brownie

Grenada
capital: 9 St. George's
discoverer: 8 Columbus (Christopher)
former name: 10 Concepción
language: 7 English
location: 10 West Indies
nickname: 11 Isle of Spice

grenade
4 bomb **5** shell **7** missile **9** explosive, pineapple

grenadier
7 rattail, soldier

grenadine
4 pink, yarn **5** syrup **6** fabric **9** carnation

Grendel's slayer
7 Beowulf

Gretchen's lover
5 Faust

greylag
5 goose

Grey's forte
7 Western

grid
3 net **5** grate, grill **6** grille **7** grating,
lattice, network, trellis

griddle
3 pan **5** grill

griddle cake
7 hotcake, pancake **8** flapjack

gridiron
3 net **5** field, grate, grill **7** grating,
network

grief
3 rue, woe **4** care **5** agony, dolor,
gloom, tears **6** mishap, regret,
sorrow **7** anguish, chagrin, sadness,
trouble **8** disaster, distress, hardship
9 adversity, heartache, suffering
10 affliction, heartbreak, misfortune
11 despondency

Grieg work
8 Peer Gynt

grievance
4 beef **5** cross, gripe, trial, wrong
6 burden, grouse, injury, squawk

8 hardship, jeremiad **9** complaint,
injustice **10** affliction, allegation,
unfairness **11** tribulation

grieve
3 cry **4** ache, keen, moan, wail, weep
5 mourn **6** burden, lament, sadden,
sorrow, suffer **7** afflict, agonize
8 distress

grievous
3 sad **4** dire, fell, sore **5** cruel,
grave, great, major **6** bitter, severe,
taxing, tragic, woeful **7** galling,
heinous, onerous, painful, serious,
weighty **9** egregious **10** abominable, burdensome, calamitous,
deplorable, lamentable, oppressive
11 distressing, regrettable, troublesome, unfortunate **12** heartrending

grift
3 con, gyp **4** bilk, rook **7** defraud,
swindle **8** flimflam

grifter
3 gyp **5** cheat, crook, thief **6** con
man, gouger **7** cheater, scammer,
sharper, slicker **8** swindler **9** defrauder, trickster **13** confidence man

grill
3 fry, vex **4** cook, grid, pump, quiz
5 broil, grate, sauté, toast **6** eatery
7 afflict, debrief, grating, griddle,
torment **8** gridiron, question **10** restaurant **11** interrogate **12** cross-
examine

grilse
6 salmon

grim
3 set **4** cold, dour, fell, firm, hard
5 bleak, cruel, fixed, grave, harsh,
rigid, stern **6** dismal, dogged, dreary,
fierce, grisly, intent, savage, severe,
somber **7** adamant, austere, inhuman, ominous **8** gruesome, inhumane, obdurate, resolute, ruthless,
stubborn **9** merciless, offensive,
truculent **10** determined, forbidding,
implacable, inevitable, inexorable,
inflexible, melancholy, relentless,
unyielding, vindictive **11** unforgiving,
unrelenting

grimace
3 mow, mug **4** face, moue, pout
5 frown, lower, mouth, scowl, sneer

grimalkin
3 cat **5** tabby **6** feline **9** female cat

grime
4 crud, dirt, gunk, muck, smut, soot
5 filth

grim reaper
5 death

grimy
5 dingy, dirty **6** filthy, grubby,
grungy, soiled, scuzzy, smutty
10 besmirched

grin
4 beam **5** smile, smirk

grind
3 rut, vex **4** chew, grub, mill, moil,
pace, plod, plug, rote, slog, toil, whet
5 crank, crush, gnash, grate, labor,
slave, sweat **6** abrade, crunch,
drudge, groove, harass, kibble,
powder, rotate **7** oppress, routine,
travail **8** drudgery, monotony, wear
down **9** pulverize, treadmill **10** donkeywork

grinder
3 sub **4** gyro, hero **5** molar, tooth
6 hoagie **8** sandwich **9** submarine

grinding
5 harsh **6** severe **7** arduous, grating, wearing **9** fatiguing, strenuous
stone: **4** mano **6** mortar, muller,
pestle

griot
11 storyteller

grip
4 glom, hold, take **5** clamp, clasp,
grasp, seize **6** clench, clinch, clutch,
handle, tenure, valise **7** grapple
8 enthrall, suitcase **9** fascinate,
mesmerize, restraint, spellbind,
stagehand **10** constraint

gripe
3 bug, vex **4** beef, carp, crab, fuss,
yawp **5** annoy, bitch, bleat, cavil,
croak, groan, whine **6** bother,
grouch, grouse, kvetch, murmur,

griper

mutter, object, squawk, yammer
7 afflict, grumble **8** complain, distress, irritate **9** bellyache, complaint, grievance, objection

griper

see **grumbler**

grippe

3 flu **9** influenza

gripper

4 clip, hand, vise **5** clamp, clasp, tongs **6** pliers

gris-gris

5 charm, spell **6** amulet, fetish **8** talisman **11** incantation

Grisham novel

4 Firm (The) **6** Broker (The), Client (The) **7** Chamber (The), Partner (The) **8** Brethren (The) **12** Pelican Brief (The)

grisly

4 gory, grim **5** awful, lurid **6** horrid **7** ghastly, hideous, macabre **8** fearsome, god-awful, gruesome, horrible, terrible **9** frightful, repellent, repulsive, sickening **10** disgusting, horrifying, terrifying

grist

3 lot **5** grain, input, stint **6** amount, output **7** product **8** quantity

gristle

9 cartilage

grit

4 guts, sand **5** grate, grind, heart, moxie, nerve, pluck, spunk **6** gravel, mettle, powder, smooth, spirit **7** bravery, courage, granule **8** backbone, tenacity **9** fortitude **10** doggedness **13** determination

gritty

4 game **5** dirty, gutsy, rough, sandy **6** dogged, plucky, spunky **8** abrasive, gravelly, resolute, spirited **9** steadfast, tenacious **10** courageous, determined

groan

4 beef, carp, moan **5** cavil, creak, gripe **6** bemoan, grouse, lament,
object, repine **7** grumble **8** complain **9** bellyache

grocery

5 store **11** supermarket
Spanish: 6 bodega

grog

3 rum **5** booze, drink, hooch, juice, sauce **6** liquor, tipple **7** alcohol, spirits **9** firewater

groggy

4 dull, hazy, logy, weak **5** dazed, dopey, foggy, muzzy, tired, woozy **6** dulled, sleepy **7** muddled **8** befogged, confused, sluggish **9** befuddled, slaphappy, stupefied **10** punchdrunk

groin

4 fold **6** crotch

grok

6 intuit

grommet

6 eyelet **7** cringle

groom

4 comb, tend, tidy **5** brush, clean, curry, primp, ready, shave **6** neaten, ostler, polish **7** hostler, prepare, servant **8** benedict **9** attendant
Indian: 4 syce

groove

3 rut **4** pace, rote, slot **5** canal, flute, glyph, gouge, grind, niche, score, stria **6** furrow, gutter, hollow, rabbet, rhythm **7** chamfer, channel, routine, top form **8** monotony **10** depression

groovy

3 hip **4** cool, neat **5** ducky, great, nifty, sharp, slick, super, swell **6** choice, gnarly, peachy **7** right-on **8** smashing **9** copacetic, excellent, hunky-dory, marvelous, wonderful **10** delightful, marvellous, peachy keen

grope

4 feel, grub, poke, root **6** fondle, fumble, search **7** grabble **8** scrabble

grosbeak

5 finch **8** hawfinch, songbird

gross

3 fat, raw, sum 4 earn, foul, mass, rude 5 brute, bulky, crude, obese, rough, utter, whole 6 carnal, coarse, entire, vulgar 7 blatant, boorish, capital, extreme, glaring, hulking, obscene, overall, porcine, uncouth 8 absolute, complete, flagrant, ignorant, improper, indecent, outright, sum total, tangible, totality 9 aggregate, before tax, corporeal, corpulent, downright, egregious, excessive, loathsome, offensive, out-and-out, repulsive, revolting, unrefined 10 disgusting, exorbitant, immoderate 11 twelve dozen

grotesque

6 absurd, rococo, unreal 7 baroque, bizarre, extreme 8 aberrant, abnormal, deformed, fanciful, freakish 9 distorted, fantastic, ludicrous, misshapen, monstrous 11 incongruous

grotto

4 cave, hole 5 crypt, vault 6 cavern
Capri: 4 Blue

grouch

4 beef, carp, crab, kick, sulk, yawp 5 crank, croak, growl, grump, pique 6 carper, griper, grouse, grudge, kicker, kvetch, murmur, mutter, repine, squawk, whiner, yawper 7 crabber, grouser, growler, grumble 8 complain, grumbler, kvetcher, sorehead, sourpuss, squawker 9 bellyache, complaint 10 bellyacher, complainer, crosspatch, malcontent

ground

3 bed, sod 4 base, dirt, land, root, seat, soil, turf 5 basis, cause, earth, floor, proof 6 bottom, reason 7 bedrock, dry land, footing, support, sustain, terrain 8 argument, buttress, evidence 9 establish, testimony 10 foundation, terra firma

groundbreaking

10 innovative, innovatory, pioneering 11 cutting-edge, leading-edge

grounded

6 stable 7 beached 8 marooned, sensible, stranded 9 realistic 13 unpretentious

groundhog

6 marmot 9 woodchuck

grounding

8 practice, training, tutelage 11 instruction, preparation

groundless

4 idle 5 empty, false 6 hollow 8 baseless 9 causeless, unfounded 10 gratuitous 11 uncalled-for, unjustified, unwarranted

groundwork

3 bed 4 base, foot, root 5 basis 6 bottom 7 bedrock, footing, support 8 basement 10 foundation, substratum 11 cornerstone, preparation 12 substruction, substructure, underpinning

ground zero

5 focus, get-go 6 center, outset, target 8 bull's-eye 9 epicenter, square one

group

3 lot, set 4 band, bevy, body, club, crew, gang, pack, push, ruck, sect, team, tier 5 array, batch, bunch, class, clump, covey, crowd, grade, horde, squad, suite, troop 6 adjust, assort, bundle, cartel, circle, clique, clutch, gather, huddle, league, passel 7 battery, brigade, cluster, combine, company, coterie, council, dispose, echelon, platoon 8 assemble, assembly, category, classify, ensemble, organize 9 congeries, gathering, syndicate 10 assemblage, categorize, collection
of angels: 4 host
of ants: 6 colony
of bees: 4 hive 5 swarm
of birds: 6 flight
of cats: 7 clowder, clutter
of cattle: 5 drove
of chicks: 5 brood 6 clutch
of clams: 3 bed
of crows: 6 murder
of ducks: 5 brace

of eight: 5 octet
of elephants: 4 herd
of elks: 4 gang
of fish: 5 shoal 6 school
of five: 5 quint 6 pentad 7 quintet
of four: 6 tetrad 7 quartet
of foxes: 5 leash, skulk
of geese: 5 flock, skein 6 gaggle
of gnats: 5 cloud, horde
of goats: 5 tribe
of gorillas: 4 band
of greyhounds: 5 leash
of grouse: 5 covey
of hares: 4 down, husk
of hawks: 4 cast
of hounds: 3 cry 4 mute, pack
of kangaroos: 3 mob 5 troop
of kittens: 6 litter
of larks: 10 exaltation
of lions: 5 pride
of locusts: 6 plague
of monkeys: 5 troop
of mules: 4 span
of nine: 5 nonet
of oysters: 3 bed
of partridges: 5 covey
of peacocks: 6 muster
of pheasants: 4 nest
of plovers: 4 wing 12 congregation
of quail: 4 bevy 5 covey
of seals: 3 pod 5 patch
of seven: 6 pleiad, septet
of sheep: 5 drove, flock
of six: 6 sextet
of swans: 4 bevy
of teals: 6 spring
of three: 4 trio 5 triad 7 ternary, trinity, triplet
of vipers: 4 nest
of whales: 3 gam, pod
of wolves: 4 pack

grouper
8 rockfish

grouse
4 beef, carp 5 croak, gripe, quail, scold 6 mutter, yammer 7 grumble 8 complain, pheasant 9 bellyache, blackcock, ptarmigan 12 capercaillie
extinct: 8 heath hen
red: 8 moorfowl
strut: 3 lek

grout
4 lees, lute 5 dregs 6 cement, filler, mortar 7 grounds, plaster 8 concrete

grove
4 holt, wood 5 copse 7 boscage, coppice, orchard, thicket

grovel
4 fawn 5 abase, cower, crawl, creep, toady 6 cajole, cringe, kowtow, snivel, wallow 7 eat dirt, truckle 8 blandish, bootlick 9 brownnose 10 curry favor, ingratiate 11 apple-polish

grow
3 age, wax 4 flow, gain, rise, tend 5 amass, breed, nurse, raise, ripen, swell 6 abound, become, expand, foster, mature, sprout, thrive 7 burgeon, care for, develop, enlarge, gestate, nurture, produce 8 escalate, flourish, increase, multiply, mushroom, spring up 9 cultivate, propagate

growl
4 beef, carp, crab, fuss, roar 5 bitch, gripe, groan, snarl 6 grouse, kvetch, mutter, repine, rumble, yammer 7 grumble 8 complain 9 bellyache

growler
3 can 4 crab, floe 5 crank, grump 6 grouch, vessel 7 ice floe, iceberg, pitcher 8 sorehead, sourpuss 9 container 10 crosspatch, malcontent 11 faultfinder

grown-up
5 adult 6 mature 8 seasoned 9 developed 11 full-fledged

grow old
3 age 4 wane 5 ripen, wizen 6 mature, mellow

growth
4 gain, rise 5 surge, swell, tumor 7 buildup 8 increase, progress, swelling 9 accretion, evolution, expansion, flowering, unfolding 11 development, enlargement, progression

malignant: 6 cancer
skin: 3 tag, wen 4 corn, cyst, mole, wart 5 nevus 6 bunion, callus, keloid 7 verruca

grow up
3 age 5 ripen 6 evolve, mature, mellow 7 advance, develop 8 maturate 9 come of age

grub
3 dig 4 chow, comb, eats, feed, food, hack, moil, plod, poke, rake, root, slog, toil 5 grind, larva, scour, slave, spade, stump 6 burrow, drudge, forage, menial, shovel, slavey, uproot, viands 7 edibles, ransack, rummage, unearth, vittles 8 excavate, hireling, victuals 9 provender 11 comestibles

grubby
4 foul 5 dirty, grimy, messy, seedy 6 filthy, frowsy, frowzy, grungy, scuzzy, shabby, sloppy, soiled 7 scruffy, squalid, unclean, unkempt 8 slovenly, unwashed

grubstake
3 aid 4 back, fund, help, loan 5 funds 6 assist 7 backing, capital, finance, support 8 bankroll 9 financing 10 assistance, capitalize, underwrite

grudge
4 deny, envy 5 spite 6 refuse, spleen 7 ill will 9 grievance 10 resentment 12 hard feelings, spitefulness

gruel
4 mush 5 atole, kasha 6 burgoo, congee, sowens 8 flummery, loblolly, porridge 9 stirabout

gruesome
see **grisly**

gruff
4 curt, dour 5 bluff, blunt, cross, harsh, husky, stern, surly 6 abrupt, crabby, crusty, hoarse, morose, sullen 7 bearish, brusque, crabbed, grating, grouchy 8 churlish, croaking, snappish, snippety 9 saturnine 10 ill-natured 11 bad-tempered

grumble
4 beef, carp, crab, fuss, moan, yawp 5 bitch, croak, gripe, groan, growl, snarl, whine 6 bemoan, grouch, grouse, murmur, mutter, repine, squawk 8 complain 9 bellyache

grumbler
4 crab 5 crank, grump 6 grouch 8 sorehead 10 crosspatch, malcontent

grump
3 pet 4 beef, carp, crab, pout, sulk 5 crank, gripe, growl 6 griper, grouch 7 growler, grumble 8 complain, sorehead, sourpuss 9 bellyache 10 bellyacher, malcontent

grumpy
4 dour, sour 5 cross, moody, sulky, surly, testy 6 crabby, cranky, sullen 7 crabbed, peevish 8 petulant, vinegary 9 crotchety, irascible 11 bad-tempered, ill-tempered 12 cantankerous

grunion
10 silverside

grunt
5 groan, growl, snort 7 dogface, draftee, soldier

guacharo
7 oilbird

Guadeloupe
capital: 10 Basse-Terre
department of: 6 France
dependency: 8 Désirade, St. Martin 12 Marie-Galante, St. Barthélemy
discoverer: 8 Columbus (Christopher)
island: 10 Basse-Terre 11 Grande-Terre
location: 10 West Indies
volcano: 9 Soufrière

Guam
capital: 5 Agana
ethnic group: 8 Chamorro
island group: 7 Mariana

guanaco
5 llama 6 alpaca
kin: 5 camel

guano
6 manure 9 excrement

guarantee
3 vow 4 bail, bond, oath, seal, word
5 token, vouch 6 assert, assure,
ensure, insure, pledge, surety 7 certify, earnest, promise, warrant 8 security, warranty 9 agreement, assurance, insurance, undertake 11 stand
behind, undertaking

guarantor
5 angel 6 backer, patron, surety
7 ensurer, insurer, sponsor 8 bondsman 11 underwriter

guard
4 fend, mind, tend, ward 5 aegis,
alert, armor, cover, watch 6 convoy,
defend, escort, jailer, keeper, minder,
patrol, picket, police, screen, secure,
sentry, shield, warden, warder
7 bulwark, defense, lookout, oversee,
protect, turnkey 8 chaperon, overseer, preserve, security, sentinel,
shepherd, watchdog, watchman
9 chaperone, custodian, look after,
patrolman, protector, watch over
10 protection

guarded
4 safe, wary 5 cagey, chary, leery
7 careful, politic, prudent 8 cautious,
discreet, gingerly, reserved 11 circumspect, considerate

guardhouse
4 brig, jail, keep 5 clink 6 lockup,
prison 8 stockade

guardian
6 escort, keeper, patron, warden,
warder 7 curator, trustee 8 Cerberus, defender, overseer, watchdog
9 custodian, protector 11 conservator

guardianship
4 care, keep, ward 5 aegis, trust
6 charge 7 custody, keeping
8 auspices 10 protection
11 safekeeping

Guare play
17 House of Blue Leaves (The)
22 Six Degrees of Separation

Guatemala
capital: 9 Guatemala (City)
ethnic group: 4 Maya 5 Mayan
lake: 6 Izabal 7 Atitlán 9 Petén Itzá
language: 7 Spanish
monetary unit: 7 quetzal
mountain, range: 6 Tacaná 9 Tajumulco 10 Acatenango, Santa
María 11 Sierra Madre
neighbor: 6 Belize, Mexico 8 Honduras 10 El Salvador
peninsula: 7 Yucatán
river: 7 Motagua 8 Polochic,
Sarstoon 10 Usumacinta

guck
3 bog, goo, mud 4 clay, crud, dirt,
glop, goop, mire, ooze, smut 5 filth,
slime 7 stickum

gudgeon
3 pin 4 fish 5 pivot 6 socket 7 journal

Gudrun
brother: 6 Gunnar 7 Gunther
father: 5 Hetel
husband: 4 Atli 5 Etzel 6 Sigurd
9 Siegfried

guerrilla
8 partisan 9 irregular
Greek: 6 klepht

guess
4 call, shot, stab 5 fancy, hunch,
infer 7 believe, predict, presume,
suppose, surmise 8 estimate
9 speculate 10 conjecture, prediction 11 presumption, supposition,
speculation

guest
6 caller, lodger, roomer 7 boarder,
company, visitor 9 sojourner

guff
3 jaw, lip 4 bosh, sass 5 bilge,
cheek, hokum, hooey, mouth, sauce,
trash 6 bunkum, drivel, hot air,
humbug 7 baloney, hogwash,
palaver, twaddle 8 back talk, claptrap, malarkey, nonsense, tommyrot 9 poppycock 10 balderdash
13 horsefeathers

guffaw
6 cackle, hee-haw 7 chortle

guidance

6 advice 7 control, counsel 8 handling 9 direction, oversight 10 leadership, management 11 instruction, supervision

guide

4 dean, guru, help, lead, show 5 doyen, pilot, route, steer, usher 6 beacon, convoy, direct, docent, escort, handle, leader, manage, manual, mentor 7 adviser, conduct, control, marshal, oversee 8 Baedeker, chaperon, director, handbook, instruct, maneuver, navigate, shepherd, signpost 9 accompany, chaperone, conductor, vade mecum, Sacagawea 10 bellwether, compendium, instructor, pathfinder 11 enchiridion

guidebook

6 Fodor's, manual 8 Baedeker, Frommer's, handbook, Michelin 9 itinerary, vade mecum 10 compendium 11 enchiridion

guided missile

3 ABM 4 Hawk, ICBM, IRBM, Nike, Thor, Zuni 5 Atlas, drone, Snark, Titan 6 Bomarc, cruise, Exocet, Falcon, Navaho, rocket 7 Bullpup, Matador, Polaris, Regulus, Terrier 8 Redstone, Tomahawk 9 Minuteman 10 projectile, Sidewinder

Guiderius

brother: 9 Arviragus
father: 9 Cymbeline

guidon

4 flag 6 banner, burgee, ensign, pennon

guild

4 club 5 lodge, order, union 6 cartel, league 7 society 8 sodality 10 fellowship, fraternity 11 association, brotherhood
medieval: 5 Hansa, Hanse

guile

4 wile 5 craft, fraud 6 deceit 7 cunning 8 artifice, trickery, wiliness 9 deception, duplicity, stratagem 10 cleverness 13 dissimulation

guileful

3 sly 4 foxy, wily 5 cagey, canny, slick 6 artful, astute, crafty, shifty, shrewd, sneaky, tricky 7 cunning, devious 8 indirect, slippery, sneaking 9 designing, insidious, underhand 11 calculating, duplicitous, underhanded

guileless

4 open 5 frank, naive 6 candid, direct, honest 7 genuine, natural, sincere, up-front 8 innocent, truthful 9 ingenuous 10 aboveboard, forthright

guillemot

3 auk 5 murre 7 seabird

guillotine

6 behead 9 decollate 10 decapitate

guilt

4 onus 5 blame, fault, shame 6 regret, stigma 7 offense, remorse 10 contrition 11 culpability 12 self-reproach

guiltless

4 pure 5 clean 6 chaste 8 innocent, virtuous 9 blameless, exemplary, faultless, righteous, stainless 10 immaculate, inculpable

guilty

6 liable, rueful, sinful 7 ashamed, at fault 8 blamable, contrite, culpable, indicted, penitent 9 impeached, regretful 10 answerable, remorseful 11 accountable, blameworthy, responsible

guimpe

6 blouse

Guinea

capital: 7 Conakry
city: 4 Labé 6 Kankan, Kindia 5 Tombo
ethnic group: 6 Fulani 7 Malinke
island, island group: 3 Los 5 Tombo
language: 6 French
monetary unit: 5 franc
mountain: 5 Nimba
neighbor: 4 Mali 7 Liberia, Senegal

10 Ivory Coast 11 Sierra Leone
12 Guinea-Bissau
river: 5 Niger 6 Gambia 7 Senegal

Guinea-Bissau
archipelago: 7 Bijagós
capital: 6 Bissau
ethnic group: 6 Fulani 7 Malinke
8 Mandyako
language: 10 Portuguese
monetary unit: 5 franc
neighbor: 6 Guinea 7 Senegal
river: 4 Gêba

guinea fowl
genus: 6 Numida
young: 4 keet

guinea pig
4 cavy 6 rodent
genus: 5 Cavia

Guinevere
court: 7 Camelot
husband: 6 Arthur
lover: 8 Lancelot 9 Launcelot

guise
4 mask 5 cloak, cover, dress, getup
6 aspect, facade, outfit, veneer
7 costume, pretext 8 coloring,
pretense 9 posturing, semblance
10 appearance, false front

guitar
accessory: 4 capo
Mexican: 5 tiple 6 cuatro 8 cha-
rango
part: 3 nut, peg 4 fret, neck 5 brace
6 bridge, string 7 peghead
small: 3 uke 7 ukulele
tool: 4 pick 8 plectrum

guitarist
American: 4 Byrd (Charlie), King
(B. B., Freddie), Page (Jimmy), Pass
(Joe) 5 Ellis (Herb), Isbin (Sharon)
6 Kessel (Barney), Kottke (Leo),
Watson (Doc) 7 Burrell (Kenny),
Hendrix (Jimi), Metheny (Pat),
Vaughan (Stevie Ray) 9 Christian
(Charlie), Parkening (Christopher)
10 Montgomery (Wes), Pizzarelli
(Bucky, John)
Australian: 8 Williams (John)

British: 4 Beck (Jeff) 5 Bream
(Julian) 8 Richards (Keith)
French: 9 Reinhardt (Django)
Italian: 7 Ghiglia (Oscar)
Spanish: 5 Yepes (Narciso)
6 Romero (Celedonio) 7 Segovia
(Andrés)

guitarlike instrument
3 uke 4 lute, vina 5 banjo, sitar
7 bandore, pandora, samisen,
ukulele 8 mandolin, shamisen

gulch
3 gap 4 glen 5 gorge, gully 6 arroyo, canyon, coulee, hollow, ravine,
valley 7 couloir

gules
3 red

gulf
3 bay, pit 4 cove 5 abysm, abyss,
bayou, bight, chasm, firth, gorge,
gulch, inlet 6 cavity, harbor, hollow,
ravine, slough 8 crevasse
Adriatic Sea: 6 Venice
Aegean Sea: 7 Saronic 8 Salonika
Africa: 6 Guinea
Arabian Sea: 4 Oman 7 Persian
Australia: 9 Van Diemen 11 Car-
pentaria
Baltic Sea: 4 Riga 6 Danzig,
Gdansk 7 Bothnia, Finland
Bering Sea: 6 Anadyr
Canada: 13 Saint Lawrence
Central America: 7 Fonseca
Djibouti: 6 Tajura 8 Tadjoura
Europe: 7 Bothnia, Gascony
8 Gascogne
Greece: 7 Corinth, Lepanto
Indian Ocean: 4 Aden
Ionian Sea: 4 Arta 7 Taranto
Iran: 7 Arabian
Italy: 5 Genoa
Mediterranean Sea: 5 Sidra, Tunis
8 Valencia 10 Khalij Surt 11 Syrtis
Major
New Guinea: 5 Papua 7 McCluer
New Zealand: 7 Hauraki
North America: 6 Mexico
Northwest Territories: 7 Boothia
8 Amundsen 9 Queen Maud

Philippines: 4 Asid **5** Davao, Leyte, Panay, Ragay
Red Sea: 4 Suez **5** Aqaba **11** Aelaniticus
Russia: 8 Sakhalin
Solomon Sea: 4 Huon, Kula **5** Vella
South China Sea: 4 Siam **6** Tonkin **8** Lingayen
Tyrrhenian Sea: 7 Paestum
Yellow Sea: 6 Chihli

Gulf State
5 Texas **7** Alabama, Florida **9** Louisiana **11** Mississippi

gull
3 con, mew, sap **4** bird, dupe, fool, hoax, scam **5** chump, cozen **6** fleece, pigeon, stooge, sucker, take in **7** chicane, fall guy **8** flimflam, hoodwink **9** bamboozle **11** hornswoggle

gullet
3 maw **4** crop, tube **6** dewlap, throat **7** channel **9** esophagus

gullible
4 easy **5** green, naive **8** innocent, trusting **9** believing, credulous **11** susceptible **12** unsuspecting

Gulliver's Travels
author: 5 Swift (Jonathan)
horses: 10 Houyhnhnms
land: 6 Laputa **8** Lilliput **11** Brobdingnag
people: 6 Yahoos

gully
3 gap **4** glen **5** gorge, gulch **6** arroyo, coulee, hollow, ravine, valley **7** couloir

gulp
4 bolt, chug, cram, glut, slop, swig, wolf **5** gorge, quaff, scarf, scoff, stuff, swill **6** devour, gobble, guzzle **7** swallow **8** mouthful **11** ingurgitate

gum
4 chew **5** botch **6** bobble, bollix, bungle, chicle, gluten, goof up, tupelo **7** exudate, gingiva, louse up **8** adhesive, mucilage **9** sapodilla **10** eucalyptus

kind: 6 acacia, Arabic, balata, bubble **7** chewing, dextrin
resin: 5 myrrh **7** gamboge **8** ammoniac, galbanum, scammony **9** asafetida **10** asafoetida **12** frankincense

gumbo
3 mud **4** okra, soil, soup **6** creole **7** mélange, mixture

gummy
5 gooey, pasty **6** cloggy, sticky, viscid **7** viscous **8** adhesive **9** glutinous **10** gelatinous **12** mucilaginous

gumption
5 drive, nerve, savvy **6** energy **8** industry **10** enterprise, get-up-and-go, initiative

gumshoe
3 cop **4** bull, dick, fuzz, G-man, heat, narc **6** copper, peeler, shamus, sleuth **7** officer **8** flatfoot, hawkshaw, Sherlock **9** detective, policeman **10** bloodhound, private eye **12** investigator

gun
3 gat, rod **4** Colt **5** rev up, rifle **6** cannon, Garand, heater, mortar, musket, pistol, weapon **7** bazooka, carbine, firearm **8** Browning, howitzer, revolver **9** derringer, Remington **10** Winchester
antiaircraft: 6 ack-ack, Bofors
Austrian: 5 Glock
British: 4 Sten
French: 8 arquebus **9** harquebus
German: 5 Glock, Luger
Italian: 7 Beretta
mount: 6 turret
part: 3 pin **4** bolt, bore, butt, lock **5** sight, stock **6** barrel, breech, hammer, muzzle, safety **7** chamber, trigger **8** cylinder, magazine **9** buttstock

gunfire
4 shot **5** blast, salvo **6** volley **7** barrage **9** broadside, discharge, fusillade

gung ho
4 avid, keen **6** ardent, fervid, raring

7 fervent, zealous 9 exuberant
11 impassioned 12 enthusiastic

Guni's father
8 Naphtali

gunk
3 goo 4 crud, glop, gook, goop,
muck 5 slime

gunman
5 bravo 6 hit man, killer 7 shooter,
torpedo 8 assassin, enforcer

Gunnar
brother-in-law: 6 Sigurd
father: 5 Hetel
sister: 6 Gudrun
wife: 8 Brunhild, Brynhild

gunner
6 sniper 7 shooter 8 marksman,
rifleman 9 musketeer 11 infantryman 12 artilleryman

Gunther
sister: 7 Gutrune 9 Kriemhild
slayer: 5 Hagen
uncle: 5 Hagen
wife: 8 Brunhild 9 Brynhilde

gurgle
3 lap 4 flow, purl, wash 5 plash,
slosh, swash 6 babble, bubble,
burble, ripple

Gurkha knife
5 kukri

gurney
3 cot 9 stretcher

guru
4 sage 5 guide, swami, tutor 6 expert,
leader, master, mentor 7 teacher
9 maharishi

gush
3 jet 4 emit, flow, pour, rave, roll,
rush, spew, teem, well 5 burst, flood,
flush, issue, spout, spurt, surge
6 babble, effuse, sluice, spring,
stream 7 cascade, emanate 10 effervesce, outpouring

gushy
5 gooey, mushy, sappy, soppy
6 sloppy, slushy, sticky 7 cloying,
maudlin, mawkish, tearful 8 bathetic,
effusive 9 schmaltzy, sickening

10 nauseating, saccharine 11 sentimental

gusset
4 fold, gore, tuck 5 armor, plate,
pleat 6 insert 7 bracket

gussy up
5 adorn 6 bedeck 7 furbish 8 decorate, renovate

gust
3 fit 4 blow, gale, rush, wind 5 blast,
burst, draft, sally, surge, whiff
6 breeze, flurry, squall 7 bluster,
delight, flare-up 8 eruption, outburst,
paroxysm

gusto
3 vim 4 brio, élan, zeal, zest 5 ardor,
heart, oomph, taste, verve 6 fervor,
palate, relish, spirit 7 delight, passion 9 enjoyment 10 enthusiasm

gusty
5 blowy, windy 6 breezy 8 blustery

gut
4 draw, loot 5 belly, bowel, dress,
empty, tummy 6 bowels, paunch
7 abdomen, ransack, stomach
8 clean out, entrails, visceral 9 intestine 10 disembowel, eviscerate,
exenterate, intestines 11 instinctive

Gutenberg, Johannes
city: 5 Mainz
invention: 11 movable type
partner: 4 Fust (Johann)

gutless
5 sissy, wimpy, wussy 6 coward,
craven, yellow 7 chicken, unmanly
8 cowardly, timorous 9 spineless,
spunkless, weak-kneed 11 lily-
livered, poltroonish 12 fainthearted
13 pusillanimous

guts
4 grit, sand 5 bowel, heart, moxie,
nerve, pluck, spunk, tripe 6 bowels,
mettle, spirit 7 bravery, courage,
innards, insides, stamina, viscera
8 backbone, entrails, stuffing 9 fortitude, intestine 10 intestines, resolution

gutsy
4 bold 5 brave 6 plucky, spunky

7 valiant **8** intrepid, resolute **10** courageous, determined, mettlesome

gutter
  5 chase, ditch, flume, gully **6** furrow, groove, trench, trough **7** channel, conduit

guttersnipe
  3 bum **4** hobo, scum, waif **5** gamin **6** beggar, gamine, urchin **7** outcast, vagrant, wastrel **8** derelict, riffraff, vagabond **10** ragamuffin

guttural
  4 deep **5** gruff, harsh, husky, rough, velar **6** croaky, hoarse **7** grating, palatal, rasping, throaty **8** gravelly

guy
  3 cat, lad, man **4** buck, chap, dude, male, rope, stud, wire **5** bloke, brace, chain, guide **6** effigy, fellow, steady **7** support

Guyana
  capital: **10** Georgetown
  language: **7** English
  monetary unit: **6** dollar
  mountain range: **9** Pacaraima
  neighbor: **6** Brazil **8** Suriname **9** Venezuela
  river: **9** Essequibo

Guys and Dolls
  author: **6** Runyon (Damon)
  composer: **7** Loesser (Frank)

guzzle
  4 belt, gulp, slop, soak, swig, toss, tope **5** booze, drink, quaff, slosh, swill **6** imbibe, tank up, tipple **7** consume, swizzle

Gwendolen's husband
  7 Locrine

gymnast
  7 acrobat, athlete, tumbler
  American: **4** Hamm (Paul) **5** Rigby (Cathy) **6** Conner (Bart), Miller (Shannon), Retton (Mary Lou), Thomas (Kurt)
  Romanian: **8** Comaneci (Nadia)
  Russian: **3** Kim (Nelly) **6** Korbut (Olga)

gymnastics
  5 sport **8** exercise, tumbling **9** athletics **10** acrobatics **12** calisthenics
  apparatus: **3** bar **4** bars, beam, buck, ring, rope **5** horse **11** balance beam
  feat: **3** kip **4** flip **5** vault **6** tumble **9** handstand, headstand **10** handspring, headspring, somersault

gyp
  3 con **4** bilk, dupe, fake, hoax, rook, scam, sham **5** bunco, cheat, cozen, cross, fraud, spoof, trick **6** chisel, chouse, con man, diddle, fleece, humbug, rip-off, rip off **7** cheater, deceive, defraud, diddler, finagle, sharper, swindle **8** chiseler, hoodwink, swindler **9** bamboozle, defrauder, imposture, trickster **10** mountebank **11** double-cross, flimflammer **12** double-dealer

gypsum
  7 drywall, mineral **8** selenite **9** alabaster, wallboard

gypsy
  3 Rom **5** caird, nomad, rover **6** roamer, Romany, tinker **7** drifter, tzigane **8** Bohemian, vagabond, wanderer
  Spanish: **6** gitano

gyrate
  4 coil, purl, roll, spin, turn, wind **5** orbit, twirl, whirl **6** circle, rotate **7** revolve **9** oscillate, pirouette

gyration
  4 coil, turn **5** cycle, orbit, twirl, wheel, whirl **6** circle, circuit, turning **8** rotation **10** revolution

gyre
  4 coil, gird, ring, spin, wind **5** cycle, orbit, twirl, whirl **6** circle, girdle, rotate, spiral, vortex **7** circuit, revolve **8** rotation **10** revolution

gyro
  8 sandwich

gyve
  4 bond, iron **5** chain **6** fetter **7** shackle **8** restrain **9** restraint

H

Habakkuk
  7 prophet

habeas corpus
  4 writ **5** right **7** mandate

habiliments
  4 gear **5** dress **6** attire, outfit **7** apparel, clothes **8** clothing **9** apparatus, equipment, trappings

habilitate
  5 dress **6** clothe **7** qualify

habit
  3 rut **4** bent, form, garb, mode, rote, wont **5** dress, quirk, style, usage **6** attire, clothe, custom, groove, manner, outfit **7** costume, fashion, pattern, routine **8** behavior, clothing, practice, tendency **9** addiction, mannerism **10** consuetude, convention, proclivity **11** disposition, inclination
  riding: **8** jodhpurs
  wearer: **3** nun **5** rider

habitable
  7 livable

habitant
  5 liver **7** denizen, dweller, resider **8** occupant, resident

habitat
  4 home, site, turf **5** abode, haunt, range **6** locale, milieu **7** terrain **8** domicile **9** territory **11** environment **12** surroundings

habitation
  3 pad **4** digs, flat, home, nest, seat **5** abode, haunt, haven, house, place, roost **7** housing, lodging, tenancy **8** domicile, dwelling, lodgment, quarters **9** homestead, residence, residency **10** settlement

habitual
  3 set **5** fixed, usual **6** addict, inborn, native, normal, steady, wonted **7** chronic, regular, routine, settled **8** accepted, addicted, constant, familiar, frequent, inherent **9** automatic, confirmed, continual, customary, ingrained **10** accustomed, inveterate, persistent **11** established, instinctive, involuntary

habitually
  8 commonly, normally, wontedly **9** generally, regularly, routinely **10** ordinarily **11** customarily **12** consistently

habituate
  4 bear **5** inure, train **6** addict, adjust, endure, harden, school, season, take to **7** break in, prepare, support **8** accustom, tolerate **9** acclimate, condition **11** familiarize

habitué
  3 fan **4** buff, user **5** hound, lover **6** addict, patron **7** denizen, devotee, haunter **8** adherent, customer **10** enthusiast, frequenter

hacienda
  4 farm **5** manor, ranch, villa **6** estate, quinta **8** dwelling **9** residence **10** plantation

hack
  3 cab, cut, hew, try, vex **4** blow, chip, chop, dull, gash, grub, jade, loaf, mean, ride, taxi **5** annoy, cabby, cough, grind, horse, petty,

sever, slave, usual **6** cabbie, cliché, drudge, lackey, mangle, stroke, writer **7** clichéd, grating, machine, plodder, taxicab, trivial, vehicle **8** inferior, low grade, mediocre, tolerate **9** cabdriver, mercenary, potboiler **10** second-rate, uninspired **11** commonplace

hacker
4 geek, nerd **6** duffer

hackney
3 cab **4** taxi **5** horse **6** jitney **7** taxicab **8** carriage

hackneyed
3 old **4** dull, worn **5** banal, corny, stale, stock, tired, trite **6** cliché, common, old hat, old saw **7** archaic, clichéd, worn-out **8** everyday, obsolete, outdated, overused, outmoded, timeworn **9** out-of-date **10** antiquated, overworked, pedestrian **11** commonplace, meaningless

Hadad
father: **5** Bedad **7** Ishmael
victim: **6** Midian

Hades
4 Hell **5** Pluto, Sheol **6** blazes, Tophet **7** Gehenna, inferno **8** Tartarus **9** perdition **10** underworld **11** netherworld
Babylonian: **5** Aralu
god: **3** Dis **5** Orcus, Pluto
goddess: **10** Persephone
guard: **8** Cerberus
lake: **7** Avernus
river: **4** Styx **5** Lethe **7** Acheron, Cocytus **10** Phlegethon

haft
4 grip, hilt, knob **5** helve **6** handle

hag
3 hex **5** biddy, crone, harpy, shrew, vixen, witch **6** beldam, gorgon, virago **8** battle-ax, fishwife, harridan, slattern **9** hobgoblin

Hagar
9 concubine
lover: **7** Abraham

rival: **5** Sarah, Sarai
son: **7** Ishmael

Hagen
father: **8** Alberich
nephew: **7** Gunther
slayer: **9** Kriemhild
victim: **9** Siegfried

haggard
3 wan **4** hawk, lank, pale, thin, weak, wild, worn **5** ashen, drawn, faded, gaunt, tired **6** fagged, pallid, skinny, wasted **7** angular, pinched, scraggy, scrawny, starved, wearied **8** careworn, fatigued, shrunken, worn-down **9** emaciated, exhausted

Haggard, H. Rider
novel: **3** She **17** King Solomon's Mines

Haggith
husband: **5** David
son: **8** Adonijah

haggle
4 deal **5** argue, cavil, trade **6** barter, bicker, dicker **7** bargain, dispute, quibble, stickle, wrangle **8** squabble **10** horse-trade

hagiography subject
5 saint

hail
3 ave **4** ahoy, call **5** greet, salvo, shout, storm **6** accost, call to, holler, praise, salute, shower, volley **7** acclaim, address, applaud, barrage, call out, commend **8** greeting **9** broadside, cannonade, fusillade, originate, recommend **10** salutation **11** acclamation, bombardment

Haile Selassie
9 Ras Tafari
follower: **11** Rastafarian
nation: **8** Ethiopia

hair
3 bit, jot **4** hint, mite, wool **5** cilia (plural), pilus, trace **6** cilium, trifle **7** eyelash, whisker **8** fraction, particle
animal: **3** fur **4** mane, pelt, wool **8** vibrissa **9** vibrissae (plural)
braid: **5** queue **7** pigtail

haircutter

clip: 8 barrette
coarse: 7 bristle
covering of: 3 wig
cream: 6 pomade 7 pomatum
12 brilliantine
facial: 5 beard, patch 6 goatee
7 Vandyke 8 mustache, whiskers
9 burnsides, handlebar, moustache,
sideburns, soul patch 11 muttonchops
fine: 6 lanugo
fringe: 4 bang
head of: 9 chevelure
knot: 3 bun
lock of: 4 curl 5 tress 7 cowlick
loose roll: 4 pouf
matted: 6 dreads 10 dreadlocks
ornament: 7 topknot
preparation: 3 gel 6 mousse,
pomade 12 brilliantine
root: 6 fibril
set: 4 perm
stiff: 4 seta 5 setae (plural)
style: 4 flip, pomp, shag 5 butch,
taper, wedge 6 Caesar, mullet
7 bowl cut, buzz cut, crew cut,
flattop, pageboy 8 ducktail 9 pompadour
tangled: 7 elflock
tuft of: 7 fetlock
unruly: 3 mop
without: 4 bald

haircutter

6 barber 7 stylist 8 coiffeur 9 coiffeuse

hairdo

3 bob, bun 4 afro, flip, perm, trim
5 bangs, braid 6 Mohawk, mullet
7 beehive, bowl cut, buzz cut, chignon, crew cut, flattop, pageboy
8 brush cut, coiffure, cornrows, ducktail, pigtails, ponytail, razor cut
9 permanent, pompadour 10 dreadlocks

hairdresser
see **haircutter**

hair-raising

5 eerie, scary 6 spooky 7 amazing,
awesome 8 exciting 9 thrilling
10 terrifying 11 astonishing, fright
ening

hairsplitting

7 finicky 8 exacting 9 quibbling
10 nit-picking 12 overcritical 13 hypercritical

hairstyle
see **hairdo**

hairy

5 bushy, downy, furry, fuzzy, nappy,
risky, rough 6 chancy, fleecy, fluffy,
shaggy, tufted, woolly 7 bristly,
hirsute, scraggy, unshorn, villous
8 perilous, strigose 9 dangerous,
difficult, hazardous, tomentose,
whiskered 11 treacherous

Haiti

capital: 12 Port-au-Prince
island: 7 Tortuga 10 Hispaniola
language: 6 Creole, French
leader: 8 Aristide (Jean-Bertrand),
Duvalier (François, Jean-Claude)
location: 10 West Indies
monetary unit: 6 gourde
passage: 8 Windward
peninsula: 7 Tiburon
river: 10 Artibonite

hake

4 fish, ling 7 codling, whiting
relative: 3 cod

halcyon

4 calm 5 happy, lucky, quiet, still
6 golden, hushed, placid, serene
8 affluent, peaceful, tranquil 9 favorable 10 auspicious, felicitous, kingfisher, prosperous, untroubled

Halcyone

father: 6 Aeolus
husband: 4 Ceyx

hale

3 fit 4 sane, well 5 sound, stout
6 hearty, robust 7 healthy 8 vigorous 9 strapping, wholesome

Hale character
5 Nolan (Philip)

Haley epic
5 Roots

half
6 moiety
prefix: 4 demi, hemi, semi

half-baked
 8 slapdash, slipshod 9 imbecilic, senseless, underdone 11 hare-brained, impractical, nonsensical, unrealistic 12 ill-conceived, short-sighted 13 irresponsible

half-cocked
 4 rash 5 brash 8 reckless 9 foolhardy, imprudent, impulsive, misguided, premature 10 incautious, unprepared 11 precipitate

halfhearted
 4 weak 5 tepid 6 feeble 8 lukewarm 12 uninterested

half-moon
 4 arch 5 curve 6 lunule 8 crescent

halfway
 3 mid 6 center, medial, median, middle 7 midmost 10 centermost 11 equidistant 12 intermediate

half-wit
 4 dolt, dope, fool 5 dunce, idiot, moron 6 cretin 8 imbecile 9 blockhead, simpleton

half-witted
 4 dull, slow 7 moronic 8 backward, imbecile 9 imbecilic 12 feebleminded, simpleminded

hall
 4 dorm 5 foyer, lobby 6 lyceum 7 passage 8 corridor 9 dormitory 10 auditorium, passageway
 exhibition: 5 salon
 Salvation Army: 7 citadel

Halley's ____
 5 comet

hallmark
 4 logo, seal, sign 5 badge, stamp, trait 6 device, emblem, symbol, virtue 7 feature, imprint, quality 8 logotype, property 9 attribute 11 distinction 13 certification

hallow
 5 bless, honor 6 anoint, devote, revere 8 dedicate, make holy, sanctify, venerate 10 consecrate

hallowed
 4 holy 6 sacred

hallucination
 4 trip 5 ghost 6 mirage, vision, wraith 7 fantasy, phantom, specter 8 delusion, illusion, phantasm 10 apparition 11 fata morgana, ignis fatuus

hallucinogen
 3 LSD 9 mescaline 10 psilocybin 11 scopolamine

halo
 4 aura 5 nimbi (plural) 6 corona, nimbus 7 aureole

halogen
 6 iodine 7 bromine, element 8 astatine, chlorine, fluorine

halt
 3 bar, end 4 lame, limp, quit, stay, stop 5 cease, check, close, hitch, lapse, stall, waver 6 arrest, desist, dither, falter, finish, pull up 7 adjourn, bring up, stagger, suspend 8 conclude, cut short, hesitate, knock off, leave off 9 determine, interrupt, terminate, vacillate 10 standstill 11 discontinue

halter
 3 bit 4 hang, rope 5 noose 6 blouse, bridle, hamper 8 restrain, trammels 9 hackamore, headstall, restraint

ham
 4 hock 5 bacon, emote, thigh 7 buttock, overact 8 overplay, strutter 10 scene-eater 13 exhibitionist

Ham
 brother: 4 Shem 7 Japheth
 father: 4 Noah
 son: 4 Cush, Phut 6 Canaan 7 Mizraim

Haman's adversary
 6 Esther

ham-handed
 5 inept 6 clumsy, gauche 8 bumbling 9 all thumbs, graceless, inelegant, maladroit 10 blundering, unskillful

Hamilcar
 conquest: 5 Spain
 home: 8 Carthage

hamlet
son: 8 Hannibal
surname: 5 Barca

hamlet
7 village
Irish, Scottish: 7 clachan

Hamlet
author: 11 Shakespeare (William)
beloved: 7 Ophelia
castle: 8 Elsinore
country: 7 Denmark
friend: 7 Horatio
mother: 8 Gertrude
slayer: 7 Laertes
uncle: 8 Claudius
victim: 7 Laertes 8 Claudius, Polonius

Hamlet, The
author: 8 Faulkner (William)
family: 6 Snopes

hammer
4 drub, maul, peen 5 forge, gavel, pound 6 batter, mallet, pummel, sledge 7 malleus 8 lambaste
type: 3 air 4 claw, maul 6 sledge 8 ball-peen 9 pneumatic

hammerhead
4 dolt, dope, fool 5 dunce, idiot, shark 8 clodpoll, numskull 9 numb-skull 10 thickskull

hamper
3 bin, tie 4 balk, curb, snag 5 block, check, cramp, crimp, leash, limit 6 baffle, basket, fetter, hinder, hobble, hold up, impede, retard, stymie, thwart 7 inhibit, manacle, pannier, prevent, trammel 8 encumber, handicap, obstacle, obstruct, restrain, restrict, slow down 9 frustrate

hamstring
4 lame 6 muscle, tendon 7 cripple, disable 10 immobilize 12 incapacitate

Hamutal
father: 8 Jeremiah
husband: 6 Josiah
son: 8 Jehoahaz, Zedekiah

hand
3 aid, paw 4 fist, pass 5 manus

.6 script, worker 7 deliver, dish out, laborer, workman 8 employee, transfer 10 assistance, penmanship 11 calligraphy, chirography
clenched: 4 fist
combining form: 4 chir 5 chiro
counting zero: 8 baccarat
covering: 5 glove 6 mitten
down: 8 bequeath
gesture: 5 mudra
on hip: 6 akimbo
part: 4 palm 5 thumb 6 finger
poker: 5 flush 8 straight 9 full house
protector: 5 glove 7 gantlet 8 gauntlet

handbag
4 grip 5 purse 6 clutch 8 reticule, suitcase 10 pocketbook

handbill
5 flier, flyer 6 poster 7 affiche, leaflet, placard 8 circular

handbook
5 guide 6 manual 8 Baedeker 9 vade mecum 10 compendium 11 enchiridion
religious: 9 catechism

handcuff
6 fetter 7 manacle, shackle
British: 7 darbies (plural)

hand down
4 will 6 bestow, pass on 7 deliver 8 bequeath, transmit

Handel, George Frideric
aria: 5 Largo
birthplace: 5 Halle 7 Germany
opera: 4 Nero 5 Serse 6 Admeto, Alcina, Almira, Ottone, Xerxes 7 Arminio, Orlando, Rinaldo, Rodrigo 8 Berenice 9 Agrippina, Ariodante 12 Giulio Cesare, Julius Caesar
oratorio: 4 Saul 6 Esther, Joshua, Samson, Semele 7 Athalia, Deborah, Jephtha, Messiah, Solomon 8 Theodora

handicap
4 edge, load, odds 6 burden, hamper, hinder, impede 8 drawback,

encumber, restrict **9** advantage, allowance, detriment, head start, hindrance **10** disability, limitation **11** encumbrance **12** disadvantage

handicraft
5 skill **8** artefact, artifact

hand in
6 submit, tender **7** deliver, present

handkerchief
5 hanky **6** hankie **7** bandana **8** bandanna, mouchoir **9** accessory

handle
3 paw, use **4** feel, grip, haft, hilt, knob, name, test **5** crank, touch, trade, treat, wield **6** manage **7** control, moniker, operate **8** deal with, doorknob, exercise, maneuver, nickname **10** manipulate
scythe: 5 snath **6** snathe

handling
4 care **6** charge **9** packaging, treatment
partner: 8 shipping

hand out
4 give, mete **6** bestow, donate **7** deliver, present, provide **8** disburse, dispense, give away **10** administer, distribute

hand over
4 cede, feed, give **5** leave, yield **6** commit, donate, fork up, give up, supply **7** commend, confide, consign, deliver, entrust, present **8** dispense, give back, relegate, transfer **9** deliver up, surrender **10** relinquish

handrail
8 banister

handsome
4 buff, cute, fair **5** ample, hunky, noble **6** comely, lavish **7** dashing, liberal, sizable, stately, stylish **8** abundant, generous, gracious, majestic **9** beautiful, bounteous, bountiful **10** attractive, munificent **11** fashionable, good-looking **12** considerable

handspring
6 tumble
lateral: 9 cartwheel

handwriting
6 script **8** longhand **10** autography, manuscript, penmanship **11** calligraphy, chirography
bad: 10 cacography
study of: 10 graphology

handy
4 able, deft, near **5** adept, close, utile **6** adroit, clever, nearby, nimble, useful **7** close-by, skilled **8** adjacent, skillful **9** adaptable, available, dexterous **10** accessible, convenient, proficient **11** practicable, within reach

handyman
6 helper **7** go-to guy **8** factotum

hang
3 jut, sag **4** hook, idle, loll **5** cling, drape, droop, float, hoist, knack, lynch, sling, swing **6** dangle, depend **7** suspend
back: 3 lag **4** drag, poke **5** trail **6** dawdle, schlep **7** schlepp **8** straggle
loosely: 3 sag **6** dangle

hang around
4 stay, wait **5** abide, dally, tarry **6** dawdle, linger, loiter **7** goof off **8** frequent

hangdog
3 sad **4** blue, glum **5** cowed **6** guilty **7** ashamed, pitiful, unhappy **8** dejected, sheepish **9** chagrined, depressed **11** embarrassed

hanger-on
5 leech **6** sponge, sucker **7** sponger **8** barnacle, follower, parasite **9** sycophant **10** freeloader **11** bloodsucker

hanging
5 arras, slope **7** curtain, drapery, pendant, pendent **8** covering, tapestry **9** declivity, execution, pendulous, suspended

Hanging Gardens
7 Babylon

hang on

4 grip 5 grasp 6 clutch, endure, remain 7 persist, survive 8 continue, hold fast 9 persevere

hang out

4 idle, loaf 5 chill, dally, relax 6 loiter, lounge 7 goof off

hangout

5 haunt, joint 6 resort 7 purlieu, retreat 10 rendezvous 12 watering hole

hang up

4 mire, snag 5 delay 6 detain, impede, retard 7 bog down, set back, suspend 8 slow down

hang-up

5 block 7 dilemma, problem 9 obsession 10 difficulty, inhibition

hank

4 clip, coil, loop, ring 6 bundle

hanker

3 yen 4 ache, itch, long, lust, want, wish 5 covet, crave, yearn 6 desire, hunger, thirst

hankering

3 yen 4 ache, itch, lust, urge 5 ardor 6 desire, hunger, pining, thirst 7 craving, longing, passion 8 appetite, yearning

hanky-panky

5 fraud, trick 7 chicane 8 mischief, trickery 9 chicanery, dalliance, deception 13 double-dealing, sharp practice

Hannibal

defeat: 4 Zama
father: 8 Hamilcar
home: 8 Carthage
surname: 5 Barca
vanquisher: 6 Scipio
victory: 6 Cannae

Hansa

5 guild 6 league

Hans Brinker author

5 Dodge (Mary Mapes)

Hanseatic League city

6 Bremen, Lübeck, Wismar 7 Cologne, Hamburg, Rostock

Hänsel und Gretel composer

11 Humperdinck (Engelbert)

Hansen's disease

7 leprosy

hansom

5 coach 8 carriage

haole

5 white

haphazard

6 casual, chance, random 7 aimless 8 at random, careless, slipshod 9 desultory, hit-or-miss, irregular, unplanned 10 accidental, willy-nilly 11 unorganized 12 unsystematic 13 helter-skelter

hapless

4 poor 6 woeful 7 unhappy, unlucky 8 ill-fated, wretched 9 miserable 10 ill-starred 11 star-crossed, unfortunate

happen

4 pass 5 occur 6 befall, betide 7 develop, fall out, turn out 8 bechance 9 transpire
again: 5 recur
together: 6 concur 8 coincide

happening

3 new 5 event, scene, thing 7 episode 8 incident, occasion 9 adventure 10 experience, occurrence, phenomenon 11 fashionable 12 circumstance

happen on

4 find 8 bump into, discover

happenstance

5 event 6 chance 8 incident, occasion 9 condition, situation 11 coincidence

happiness

3 joy 4 glee 5 bliss, cheer, mirth 6 gaiety 7 aptness, content, delight, elation, jollity 8 felicity, gladness, pleasure 9 enjoyment, well-being 11 contentment 12 satisfaction

happy

4 glad 5 jolly, lucky, merry 6 joyful, joyous, upbeat 7 blessed, content,

pleased **8** friendly, jubilant **9** contented, favorable, satisfied **12** enthusiastic, lighthearted

happy-go-lucky
4 easy **6** blithe, breezy, casual **8** carefree, careless, cheerful, heedless, laid-back, reckless **9** easygoing, unworried **10** insouciant, nonchalant **11** unconcerned **12** devil-may-care, light-hearted

hara-kiri
7 seppuku, suicide **8** felo-de-se

Haran
brother: **7** Abraham
daughter: **5** Iscah **6** Milcah
father: **5** Terah **6** Shimei
son: **3** Lot

harangue
4 rant, rave **5** orate, spiel **6** exhort, hassle, tirade **7** declaim, lecture, oration **8** bloviate, diatribe, jeremiad **9** discourse, philippic **11** declamation, exhortation

harass
3 irk, vex **4** bait, raid, ride **5** annoy, beset, bully, chivy, harry, hound, tease, worry **6** badger, chivvy, hassle, heckle, hector, pester, plague, stress **7** bedevil, exhaust, fatigue, torment, trouble **8** bullyrag, distress **9** beleaguer, persecute

harbinger
4 omen, sign **5** augur **6** augury, herald **7** apostle, portent **9** messenger, precursor **10** forerunner, indication

harbor
3 bay **4** cove, port **5** haven, inlet, lodge, put up **6** billet, refuge, shield, take in **7** nurture, protect, seaport, shelter **9** anchorage, safeguard, sanctuary
Hawaii: **5** Pearl

hard
4 firm, iron **5** cruel, harsh, solid, tough **6** brutal, knotty, packed, rugged, tiring, trying **7** arduous, callous, onerous **8** absolute, concrete, exacting, granitic, grinding,

indurate, pitiless, rigorous **9** demanding, difficult, fatiguing, intensely, intensive, laborious, unfeeling **10** adamantine, exhausting, spiritous, thoroughly, vigorously **11** complicated, intensively, intractable, troublesome, unrelenting, unremitting **12** backbreaking
to please: **7** finicky

hard-boiled
4 grim **5** rough, stoic, tough **6** coarse **7** callous **8** seasoned **9** impassive, pragmatic, unfeeling **11** insensitive, unemotional **12** stonyhearted, thick-skinned **13** unsympathetic

harden
3 dry, set **5** inure, steel **6** anneal, freeze, ossify, season, temper **7** calcify, compact, congeal, densify, lithify, petrify, stiffen, toughen **8** solidify **9** acclimate, fossilize, habituate **10** strengthen

hardfisted
4 mean **5** close, tight **6** stingy, strict **13** penny-pinching

hardheaded
5 sober, tough **6** mulish, shrewd **7** willful **8** obdurate, perverse, stubborn **9** obstinate, practical, pragmatic, realistic **10** determined **11** down-to-earth, intractable

hardhearted
4 cold **8** pitiless, uncaring **9** merciless, unfeeling

hard-hitting
6 strong **8** emphatic, forceful, powerful **9** effective

hardihood
3 pep **4** gall, grit, guts **5** cheek, moxie, nerve, pluck, vigor **6** daring **7** courage **8** audacity, boldness, temerity **9** assurance, brashness, cockiness, fortitude, impudence, insolence **10** brazenness, robustness

hard-line
4 firm **5** fixed, rigid, tough **8** obdurate **9** obstinate, unbending **10** inflexible, unyielding **11** stiff-necked **12** intransigent

hardness

5 rigor 7 density 8 rigidity, severity
10 difficulty, resistance

hardscrabble

6 barren 8 marginal 9 infertile,
unbearing, unfertile 12 impoverished, unproductive

hardship

4 need, toil 5 rigor, trial 6 burden
7 travail 8 asperity, distress, drudgery 9 adversity, privation, suffering
10 affliction, difficulty, discomfort,
misfortune 11 tribulation

Hard Times author

7 Dickens (Charles)

hard up

4 poor 5 broke, needy 6 bad off
8 beggared, bankrupt, deprived,
indigent, strapped 9 desperate,
destitute, penniless 10 down-and-
out 11 necessitous 12 impoverished

hardy

4 bold, hale 5 brave, tough 6 daring,
robust, rugged, strong 7 healthy
8 intrepid, resolute 9 audacious

Hardy, Thomas

character: 3 Sue (Bridehead)
4 Alec (D'Urberville), Clym (Yeo-
bright), Jude (Fawley), Tess (Durbeyfield) 5 Angel (Clare) 7 Gabriel
(Oak) 8 Arabella (Donn), Eustacia
(Vye), Henchard (Michael) 9 Bathsheba (Everdene)
novel: 11 Woodlanders (The)
14 Jude the Obscure 17 Return
of the Native (The) 19 Mayor of
Casterbridge (The) 21 Tess of
the D'Urbervilles 22 Far from the
Madding Crowd
setting: 6 Wessex

hare

5 lapin 6 rabbit
female: 3 doe
genus: 5 Lepus
male: 4 buck
tail: 4 scut
young: 7 leveret

harebrained

5 crazy, loony, silly, wacky 6 absurd,
insane, stupid 7 asinine, foolish
9 frivolous 10 ridiculous 12 preposterous

harem

5 serai 6 zenana 8 seraglio
concubine: 9 odalisque

haricot

3 pod 4 bean 10 kidney bean

hark

4 hear, heed, mind, note 6 attend,
listen, notice

harlequin

5 clown, joker 6 jester, mottle
7 buffoon 9 prankster

Harlequin

beloved: 9 Columbine
rival: 7 Pierrot

harm

3 mar 4 hurt, maim, ruin 5 abuse,
spoil, wound, wrong 6 damage,
ill-use, impair, injure, injury, misuse,
molest 7 tarnish 8 ill-treat, maltreat,
mischief, mistreat 9 undermine
10 disservice, misfortune

harmful

3 bad 4 evil 5 risky, toxic 6 malign,
unsafe 7 noisome, noxious 8 damaging 9 dangerous, hazardous,
injurious, malignant, unhealthy
10 pernicious 11 deleterious,
detrimental, unhealthful

harmless

4 safe 6 benign 8 innocent, non-
toxic 9 innocuous 11 inoffensive

Harmonia

daughter: 3 Ino 5 Agave 6 Semele
7 Autonoë
father: 4 Ares, Mars
husband: 6 Cadmus
mother: 5 Venus 9 Aphrodite
son: 9 Polydorus

harmonious

5 sweet 7 chiming, chordal, musical,
pacific 8 blending, friendly, in accord, peaceful, pleasing 9 agreeable, congenial, congruous, conso-

nant, symphonic **10** compatible, concordant **11** cooperative, symmetrical, sympathetic

harmonize
3 fit **4** jibe, sing **5** agree, blend, match **6** accord, attune **7** arrange, concert, conform **8** coincide, dovetail **9** integrate **10** coordinate, correspond, synthesize **11** orchestrate

harmony
5 grace, peace, unity **6** accord **7** balance, concert, concord, oneness, rapport **8** affinity, sonority, symmetry **9** agreement, congruity, polyphony **10** accordance, concinnity, conformity, consonance, proportion **11** concordance, consistency, cooperation
lack of: 7 discord **10** dissonance
of movement: 8 eurythmy

harness
4 curb, gear, yoke **5** hitch, leash **6** bridle, tackle **7** utilize **11** domesticate
part: 3 bit **4** rein **5** girth, trace **6** collar **7** blinder, crupper **9** bellyband, breeching, checkrein **12** breast collar
ring: 6 terret

harp
4 lyre **9** harmonica
Greek: 7 cithara, kithara

harpsichord
7 cembalo **8** clavecin

harpsichordist
American: 6 Fuller (Albert, David), Kipnis (Igor), Newman (Anthony) **7** Marlowe (Sylvia), Pinkham (Daniel), Pinnock (Trevor), Valenti (Fernando) **11** Kirkpatrick (Ralph)
English: 7 Malcolm (George)
German: 7 Richter (Karl) **9** Leonhardt (Gustav)
Italian: 7 Sgrizzi (Luciano)
Polish: 9 Landowska (Wanda)

harpy
3 nag **5** leech, scold, shrew, vixen **6** virago **8** fishwife, harridan **9** termagant

Harpy
5 Aello **7** Celaeno, Ocypete
father: 7 Thaumas
mother: 7 Electra
sister: 4 Iris

harridan
3 hag **4** fury **5** biddy, harpy, shrew, vixen, witch **6** dragon, gorgon, ogress, virago **7** hellcat **8** battle-ax, fishwife **9** battle-axe, termagant

harrier
3 dog **4** hawk **6** hector, runner **10** persecutor

harrow
3 try, vex **4** bait, rack **5** devil, tease **6** badger, heckle, hector, needle, pester, suffer **7** afflict, bedevil, torment, torture, trouble **8** distress, irritate **9** cultivate **10** excruciate

harry
3 dog, irk, vex **4** gnaw, raid, sack **5** annoy, tease, upset, worry **6** attack, badger, harass, hassle, pester, plague, ravage **7** assault, bedevil, despoil, perturb, pillage, plunder, torment **8** desolate, maltreat **9** beleaguer, deprecate

harsh
5 cruel, gruff, rough, stern **6** biting, brutal, coarse, severe, uneven, unkind **7** austere, caustic, grating, jarring, painful, pungent, raucous, stubbly **8** exacting, grinding, jangling, scraping, scratchy, strident, unsmooth **9** dissonant, inclement **10** discordant, irritating, unpleasant

hart
4 deer, stag **7** red deer
mate: 4 hind

hartebeest
8 antelope
family: 7 Bovidae

Harte story
17 Luck of Roaring Camp (The) **19** Outcasts of Poker Flat (The)

Hartford
college: 7 Trinity
specialty: 9 insurance

Hart, Moss
 autobiography: 6 Act One
 collaborator: 7 Kaufman
  (George S.)
 musical: 13 Lady in the Dark
 play: 15 Once in a Lifetime 18 Man
  Who Came to Dinner (The) 20 You
  Can't Take It with You

haruspex
 5 augur 7 diviner, prophet 8 foreseer 9 predictor 10 forecaster,
 foreteller, soothsayer

harvest
 4 crop, pick, reap 5 amass, cache,
 glean, hoard, stash, yield 6 garner,
 gather 7 collect, reaping, store up,
 vintage 8 ingather, squirrel, stow
 away 9 garnering, gathering
 bug: 4 mite 7 chigger
 fly: 6 cicada
 festival: 6 Lammas 7 Cerelia
 10 Michaelmas 12 Thanksgiving
 god, goddess: 3 Ops 5 Ceres
 6 Consus 7 Demeter

harvester
 7 gleaner
 grain: 6 header
 of grapes: 8 vintager

Harvey
 5 pooka 6 rabbit
 author: 5 Chase (Mary)
 character: 6 Elwood (P. Dowd)

hash
 4 chop, mess, stew 5 botch, mince,
 mix-up 6 jumble, medley, muddle,
 review 7 clutter, confuse, mélange,
 mixture 8 consider, shambles
 9 patchwork 10 assortment, hodgepodge, miscellany

hash house
 4 café 5 diner 6 bistro, eatery 7 pit
 stop 10 coffee shop 12 luncheonette

hashish
 5 bhang, ganja 6 charas 8 cannabis, narcotic
 plant: 4 hemp

hash out
 6 review 7 discuss 8 talk over
 9 talk about

hasp
 5 catch 6 fasten 8 fastener 9 fastening

hassle
 3 row 4 beef, to-do 5 annoy, argue,
 brawl, fight, run-in 6 bicker, clamor,
 harass, hubbub, tumult, uproar
 7 dispute, problem, quarrel, rhubarb,
 turmoil, wrangle 8 argument, squabble, struggle 9 commotion 11 altercation, controversy

hassock
 4 pouf 7 cushion, kneeler, ottoman
 9 footstool

haste
 3 run 4 dash, rush 5 hurry, speed
 6 barrel, bustle, flurry, hustle 7 beeline, hotfoot 8 celerity, dispatch,
 rapidity, velocity 9 fleetness, quickness, swiftness 10 speediness
 11 hurriedness, impetuosity

hasten
 3 fly, hie, run 4 rush, urge 5 hurry,
 press, speed 6 barrel, hustle, step
 up, urge on 7 hurry up, quicken,
 speed up 8 expedite 10 accelerate

hasty
 4 fast, rash 5 brisk, eager, fleet,
 quick, rapid, swift 6 abrupt, rushed,
 speedy, sudden 7 cursory, hurried,
 rushing 8 careless, fleeting, headlong, heedless, reckless, slapdash
 9 hotheaded, impatient, impetuous,
 irritable, quickened 10 ill-advised,
 incautious 11 expeditious, perfunctory, precipitate, precipitous, superficial, thoughtless

hat
 5 derby, tuque 6 boater, cloche,
 fedora, panama, topper 7 bicorne,
 chapeau, homburg, porkpie, Stetson,
 tricorn 8 sombrero, tricorne 9 headpiece 11 deerstalker
 ancient Greek: 7 petasos, petasus
 brimless: 7 pillbox
 close-fitting: 4 kufi 5 toque, tuque
 6 cloche, turban
 felt: 5 busby, derby 6 bowler, trilby
 fur: 5 busby 6 castor

helmetlike: 4 topi 5 topee
maker: 7 modiste 8 milliner
Middle Eastern: 3 fez
military: 4 kepi 5 busby, shako
Muslim: 3 fez 6 turban 8 tarboosh
sheepskin: 6 calpac 7 calpack
soft: 5 toque
straw: 6 boater, panama, sailor
7 bangkok, leghorn, skimmer 8 sombrero
sun: 5 terai
tall: 9 stovepipe
waterproof: 9 sou'wester
woman's: 4 coif 5 toque 6 bonnet
7 pillbox

hatch
4 door, plan, plot 5 breed, brood,
cover, inlay, spawn 6 cook up,
create, design, devise, emerge,
invent, make up, work up 7 concoct,
dream up, opening, produce, think
up 8 contrive, engender, generate,
incubate, occasion 9 floodgate,
formulate, give birth, give forth,
originate, procreate 11 compartment

hatchet
3 axe 8 tomahawk

hatchet man
6 killer 7 torpedo 8 assassin,
enforcer, murderer 9 attack dog,
cutthroat 10 eliminator

hate
5 abhor, scorn, spite 6 animus,
detest, enmity, horror, loathe, malice,
rancor 7 despise, disgust 8 aversion, execrate, loathing 9 abominate, animosity, antipathy, deprecate,
repulsion, revulsion 10 abhorrence,
repugnance 11 abomination, detestation

hateful
4 evil, foul, mean, vile 5 nasty
6 horrid, malign, odious, scurvy
7 vicious 8 accursed, damnable,
infamous 9 abhorrent, execrable,
malicious, obnoxious, repellent,
repulsive 10 abominable, despicable, detestable, malevolent 11 blasphemous, opprobrious, unspeakable
13 reprehensible

Hatfields vs. _____
6 McCoys

hatred
5 odium, spite 6 animus, enmity,
rancor 7 dislike 8 aversion, loathing
9 animosity, antipathy, hostility,
repulsion, revulsion 10 abhorrence,
repugnance 11 abomination, detestation, malevolence
of change: 9 misoneism
of humankind: 11 misanthropy
of marriage: 8 misogamy
of men: 8 misandry
of women: 8 misogyny

hats
9 millinery

hauberk
5 armor 9 chain mail, habergeon

haughtiness
4 airs 5 pride, scorn 7 conceit,
disdain, hauteur 9 arrogance,
insolence, pomposity 12 snobbishness

haughty
5 aloof, proud 6 lordly, sniffy 7 distant 8 arrogant, cavalier, scornful, snobbish, superior 9 egotistic
10 disdainful 11 overbearing 12 contemptuous, supercilious

haul
3 lug, tow, tug 4 cart, drag, draw,
hump, lift, load, loot, pull, swag, take,
tote 5 boost, booty, cargo, hoist,
raise, truck 6 burden, lading, schlep,
spoils 7 freight, payload, schlepp
with a tackle: 5 bowse

haul up
5 hoise, hoist
with a rope: 5 trice

haunch
3 hip 11 hindquarter

haunches
4 rump 7 hind end, rear end 8 backside, buttocks 9 posterior 12 hindquarters

haunt
4 site 5 spook 6 obsess, prey on

haunter

7 habitat, hang out, inhabit, torment, trouble 8 frequent 9 preoccupy 10 hang around, rendezvous, stay around, visit often

haunter

5 ghost 7 denizen, habitué

hautbois

4 oboe

hauteur

see **haughtiness**

haut monde

5 elite 6 jet set 7 society, who's who 10 glitterati, upper crust 11 aristocracy, high society 13 carriage trade

have

3 own 4 hold 7 contain, include, possess

haven

4 port, roof 5 house 6 asylum, harbor, refuge 7 retreat, shelter 9 anchorage, sanctuary

haversack

3 bag 4 pack 8 backpack

havoc

4 loss, ruin, sack 5 chaos, waste 6 mayhem 8 calamity, disorder, ravaging 9 confusion, ruination 11 catastrophe, destruction, devastation, pandemonium

haw

4 left, tree 5 berry, fruit, shrub 8 turn left 10 equivocate

Hawaii

author: 8 Michener (James A.)
capital: 8 Honolulu
city: 4 Hilo
coast: 4 Kona
discoverer: 4 Cook (Capt. James)
island: 4 Maui, Oahu 5 Kauai, Lanai 6 Niihau 7 Molokai
mountain: 7 Kilauea 8 Mauna Kea, Mauna Loa
nickname: 5 Aloha (State)
park: 9 Haleakala
state bird: 4 nene
state flower: 8 hibiscus
state tree: 5 kukui 9 candlenut

Hawaiian

dance: 4 hula
feast: 4 luau
food: 3 poi
god: 4 Kane, Lono 5 Wakea 7 Kanaloa
goddess: 4 Pele
goose: 4 nene
instrument: 3 uke 7 ukulele
neckwear: 3 lei
nonnative: 5 haole 8 malihini
resident: 8 kamaaina
shaman: 6 kahuna
soup: 6 saimin
tree: 3 koa

hawk

4 kite, sell, vend 5 buteo 6 falcon, monger, osprey, peddle 7 Cooper's, goshawk, haggard, harrier 8 caracara, huckster, roughleg 9 accipiter, red-tailed, warmonger 10 militarist 11 ferruginous, rough-legged
male: 6 tercel 7 tiercel
young: 4 eyas

hawker

6 coster, monger, seller, vendor 7 packman, peddler 8 pitchman 12 costermonger

hawkeyed

11 keen-sighted 12 sharp-sighted

Hawkeye State

4 Iowa

hawkish

7 martial, warlike 9 combative 10 aggressive 11 belligerent 12 militaristic

_____ Hawley Tariff

5 Smoot

Hawthorne, Nathaniel

birthplace: 5 Salem
character: 6 Hester (Prynne) 8 Clifford (Pyncheon), Hepzibah (Pyncheon), Pyncheon (Judge) 10 Dimmesdale (Rev. Arthur) 13 Chillingworth (Roger)
novel: 10 Marble Faun (The) 13 Scarlet Letter (The) 21 House of the Seven Gables (The)

hay

3 bed 4 feed 5 grass 6 fodder, reward 7 herbage
crops: 6 clover 7 alfalfa, timothy

Haydn oratorio

7 Seasons (The) 8 Creation (The)

hay fever

7 allergy 10 pollenosis, pollinosis
cause: 6 pollen 7 ragweed

haying machine

5 baler

haymaker

3 box 4 blow, sock 5 clout, punch 6 wallop

hayseed

see **hick**

haywire

4 amok, awry 5 amuck, crazy, upset 6 faulty 8 confused 10 out of order 12 out of control

hazard

3 bet, try 4 dare, game, luck, risk 5 peril, shoal, wager 6 chance, danger, gamble, menace 7 fortune, imperil, venture 8 accident, endanger, jeopardy, obstacle

hazardous

5 hairy, risky 6 chancy, unsafe 7 unsound 8 perilous 9 dangerous, unhealthy 10 precarious

haze

3 fog 4 film, mist, murk, smog 5 brume, cloud, drive, smoke, vapor 6 harass 7 dimness, obscure 8 dullness, initiate, overcast 9 mistiness, murkiness, vagueness 10 cloudiness

hazel

4 wood 5 birch, shrub 7 filbert

hazy

3 dim 5 faint, filmy, foggy, fuzzy, misty, murky, smoky, vague 6 cloudy, unsure 7 blurred, clouded, obscure, unclear 8 nebulous, vaporous 9 uncertain 10 indefinite, indistinct

head

3 nut 4 boss, john, main, pate, poll 5 brain, caput, chief, first, prime, privy, scalp, skull 6 climax, honcho, leader, master, noggin, noodle, set out, talent, toilet 7 cranium, faculty, latrine, leading, premier, proceed, supreme 8 director, foremost, lavatory, light out 9 chieftain, principal, strike out 10 promontory
area: 5 crown 6 temple
back part: 7 occiput
bone: 5 skull 7 cranium 8 parietal
combining form: 6 cranio 7 cephalo
covering: 3 cap, hat 6 bonnet 8 kerchief
monastery: 4 dean 5 abbot 8 superior
nunnery: 6 abbess 8 superior
of hair: 4 mane 6 fleece 9 chevelure
relating to: 8 cephalic
shaving of: 7 tonsure
skin: 5 scalp
top: 4 pate 5 crown

headache

4 pain 5 worry 6 bother, megrim 7 problem 8 migraine, nuisance, vexation 9 annoyance 10 irritation

headband

7 bandeau, circlet, coronal
ancient Greek: 6 taenia 7 taeniae (plural)

headdress

7 topknot
American Indian: 9 warbonnet
Arab: 8 kaffiyeh
bishop's: 5 miter, mitre
medieval: 4 barb
Eastern: 6 turban
nobleman's: 7 coronet
royal: 5 crown, tiara 6 diadem
Spanish women's: 8 mantilla
women's: 6 bonnet
(see also **hat**)

headland

4 cape 5 point 10 promontory

headline

6 banner 7 feature, promote 8 screamer 9 emphasize, publicize, spotlight 10 noteworthy

headlong
4 rash 5 hasty 6 abrupt, daring,
rashly, sudden 7 hurried, rushing
8 heedless, reckless 9 foolhardy,
impetuous, impulsive 10 heedlessly,
recklessly 11 precipitate, precipitous

headmaster
6 leader 9 principal

head off
4 stop 5 avert, block 6 thwart
7 deflect, obviate, prevent, ward
off 8 stave off, turn back 9 forestall,
intercept

headquarters
3 hub 4 base, seat 6 center

head start
4 edge, jump, lead, odds 5 boost
7 advance, vantage 8 handicap
9 advantage, allowance

headstone
8 memorial, monument 11 grave
marker

headstrong
6 dogged, mulish, unruly 7 willful
8 contrary, perverse, stubborn
9 obstinate 10 bullheaded, refractory, self-willed 11 intractable,
stiff-necked

heads-up
5 alarm, alert 6 signal, tip-off 7 warning 8 high sign 11 resourceful

headway
4 gain 6 growth 7 advance · 8 anabasis, progress 11 advancement,
improvement

heady
4 rash, rich 5 giddy 6 elated, potent
7 willful 8 exciting 9 impetuous
11 exhilarated, intoxicated 12 intoxi-
cating

heal
3 fix 4 cure, mend 5 sew up, treat
6 cement, remedy, repair 7 patch up,
restore 8 make well

healer
6 doctor, shaman

healing
8 curative, remedial, salutary, sanative 9 vulnerary, wholesome 10 salubrious 11 restorative, therapeutic
12 convalescent
goddess of: 3 Eir

health
7 fitness, welfare 8 haleness, vitality,
wellness 9 soundness, well-being,
wholeness
club: 3 gym, spa

healthful
8 curative, hygienic, remedial, salutary 9 favorable, wholesome
10 beneficial, corrective, profitable,
salubrious 11 restorative

healthy
3 fit 4 hale, spry, well 5 sound, tonic
6 benign, robust, strong, sturdy
7 chipper 8 blooming, hygienic,
positive, salutary, thriving, vigorous
9 wholesome 10 able-bodied,
beneficial, prosperous, salubrious
11 flourishing

heap
3 lot 4 cock, fill, gobs, hill, load,
lump, mass, much, pack, pile, rick,
scad 5 amass, bunch, clump, crate,
loads, mound, shock, stack, wreck
6 barrel, charge, gather, jalopy,
junker, lumber, oodles 7 clunker,
collect, deposit, jillion 8 assemble,
mountain, slathers 9 abundance,
great deal, profusion, stockpile
10 quantities
combustible: 4 pyre

hear
4 heed 5 learn 8 listen to, perceive
9 apprehend

hearing
4 test 5 trial 6 tryout 7 earshot,
inquiry 8 audience, audition 9 interview 10 conference, discussion
distance: 7 earshot

hearken
4 heed, mind, note 6 attend, listen,
notice 7 observe

hearsay
4 buzz, news, talk 5 rumor 6 gossip, report 7 account, chatter 9 grapevine 11 scuttlebutt

heart
3 hub 4 core, crux, gist, guts, love, pith, root, seat, soul, zest 5 ardor, bosom, focus, gusto, moxie, pluck, spunk 6 breast, center, kernel, mettle, relish, spirit, ticker 7 courage, resolve 8 feelings, sympathy 9 character, fortitude 10 affections, compassion, conscience, enthusiasm
combining form: 6 cardio
contraction: 7 systole
dilation: 8 diastole
part: 5 valve 6 atrium, septum 9 ventricle

heartache
3 rue, woe 4 care, pain, pang 5 grief 6 regret, sorrow 7 anguish, sadness 8 distress 10 affliction

heartbeat
5 flash, jiffy, pulse, throb, trice 6 moment, second 9 pulsation
irregular: 10 arrhythmia

heartbreak
3 rue, woe 5 agony, grief 6 misery, regret, sorrow 7 anguish, despair, torment, torture 9 suffering 10 desolation 12 wretchedness

heartbreaking
6 bitter, tragic 8 grievous 9 agonizing 10 calamitous, deplorable, lamentable 11 devastating, distressing

heartbroken
7 crushed, grieved 8 mournful, overcome, wretched 9 sorrowful 10 despairing, despondent 12 disconsolate

heartburn
7 pyrosis

hearten
4 buoy, stir 5 cheer, rally, rouse 6 arouse, buck up, buoy up, perk up 7 animate, cheer up, enliven, inspire 8 embolden, energize, inspirit 9 encourage

heartfelt
4 deep, true 6 honest 7 earnest, fervent, genuine, sincere 8 profound 9 unfeigned

hearth
4 home 5 abode 8 domicile, dwelling, fireside 9 fireplace, residence

heartily
6 wholly 9 sincerely, with gusto, zestfully 10 completely, thoroughly

heartless
4 cold, hard 5 cruel 6 unkind 7 callous 8 uncaring 9 unfeeling 10 hard-boiled 11 insensitive, unemotional 13 unsympathetic

Heart of Dixie
7 Alabama

heartsease
5 pansy, viola 6 violet 11 peace of mind, tranquility 12 johnny-jump-up, tranquillity

heart-shaped
7 cordate

heartsick
4 blue, down 8 dejected, desolate, dismayed, downcast 9 depressed 10 despondent, dispirited 11 demoralized 12 disconsolate

heartthrob
4 idol, love 5 flame, honey, sweet 7 beloved, darling, passion 10 sweetheart

heart-to-heart
4 open, talk 5 frank 6 candid, honest 7 sincere 8 truthful 12 conversation

hearty
4 hale, warm 5 ample 6 jovial, robust, sailor, strong 7 cordial, healthy, profuse, sincere 8 abundant, vehement, vigorous 9 approving, energetic, exuberant, flavorful, unfeigned 12 enthusiastic, unrestrained

heat
4 cook, rage, warm, zeal 5 ardor,

fever **6** fervor, simmer, warmth
7 caloric, inflame, passion, swelter
8 pyrolyze
combining form: 4 pyro **6** calori,
thermo **7** thermia
measuring device: 11 calorimeter,
thermometer
quantity: 3 BTU

heated

3 hot, mad **5** angry, fiery, irate
6 ardent, fervid, fierce, ireful, raging,
steamy **7** boiling, burning, fevered,
furious **8** broiling, feverish, scalding,
sizzling, vehement, wrathful **9** indignant, scorching **10** passionate
11 acrimonious

heater

3 gun, rod **5** stove **6** boiler, pistol
7 furnace **8** fastball, radiator

heath

4 moor **5** shrub **9** wasteland

heathen

5 pagan **7** infidel **8** barbaric **11** irreligious, uncivilized

heat-producing

9 calorific

heave

3 lob **4** cast, draw, fire, gasp, haul,
heft, huff, hurl, lift, pant, puff, pull,
push, toss **5** fling, hoist, labor, pitch,
raise, retch, sling, surge, throw, vomit
6 launch

heave-ho

4 boot **6** ouster **8** bum's rush
9 dismissal

heaven

3 God **4** Zion **5** bliss, glory **6** utopia
7 arcadia, delight, ecstasy, ely-
sium, nirvana, rapture **8** empyrean,
eternity, paradise **9** firmament,
Shangri-la **10** wonderland **11** immortality, kingdom come **12** promised land

heavenly

4 lush **6** divine, sacred **7** blessed
8 beatific, empyreal, empyrean, ethereal **9** ambrosial, celestial, delicious
10 delectable, delightful, enchanting

heavy

3 big, fat **4** rich **5** beefy, bulky,
gross, hefty, obese, stout **6** bad
guy, chunky, drowsy, fleshy, gravid,
leaden, portly **7** arduous, intense,
labored, massive, porcine, villain,
weighty **8** burdened, cumbrous,
enceinte, pregnant, sluggish, unwieldy **9** corpulent, expectant,
expecting, laborious, lumbering,
ponderous, strenuous **10** burdensome, cumbersome, formidable,
oppressive, overweight

heavy-handed

5 crude, harsh, inept **6** clumsy,
gauche, klutzy **7** awkward **8** bumbling, despotic **9** maladroit **10** oppressive **11** domineering, overbearing

heavyhearted

3 sad **4** glum **5** sorry **7** unhappy
8 dejected, downcast, mournful,
saddened **9** depressed, miserable,
sorrowful **10** despondent, dispirited,
melancholy

heavyset

5 beefy, husky, stout, thick **6** chunky,
portly, stocky **11** thick-bodied

heavyweight

3 VIP **4** lion **5** boxer, chief **6** big
gun, bigwig, leader **7** big shot,
notable **8** big-timer

Hebe

father: 4 Zeus **7** Jupiter
husband: 8 Hercules
mother: 4 Hera, Juno
successor: 8 Ganymede

hebetude

6 stupor, torpor **7** languor **8** dullness, lethargy **9** lassitude, torpidity
10 drowsiness

hebetudinous

4 dull, logy **5** dopey **6** drowsy,
stupid, torpid **8** listless, sluggish
9 lethargic

Hebrew

3 Jew **6** Jewish
coin: 6 lepton, shekel
festival: 5 Purim **6** Pesach, Sukkot

7 Hanukah, Sukkoth 8 Chanukah, Lag b'Omer, Passover, Shabuoth 9 Tishah-b'Ab, Yom Kippur 12 Rosh Hashanah, Simchas Torah
God: 6 Adonai, Elohim, Yahweh 7 Jehovah
judge: 6 Gideon
lawgiver: 5 Moses
letter:
(see at **alphabet**)
measure: 5 cubit, ephah
month: 4 Adar, Elul, Iyar 5 Nisan, Sivan, Tebet 6 Kislev, Shebat, Tammuz, Tishri 6 Veadar (in leap year) 7 Heshvan
patriarch: 3 Dan, Gad 4 Cain, Levi, Seth 5 Asher, David, Isaac, Jacob, Judah 6 Joseph, Reuben, Simeon 7 Abraham, Zebulun 8 Benjamin, Issachar, Naphtali
sacred city: 5 Safad, Safed 6 Hebron 8 Tiberias 9 Jerusalem
(see also **Jewish**)

Hebrides island
4 Eigg, Rhum, Skye, Uist 5 Lewis 6 Harris

Hecate
father: 6 Perses
goddess of: 5 night 10 underworld, witchcraft
mother: 7 Asteria

hecatomb
7 killing, slaying 8 butchery 9 bloodbath, sacrifice, slaughter

heck
4 darn, drat, geez, gosh, hell, jeez 5 golly 6 shucks

heckle
3 nag 4 bait, faze, gibe, ride 5 annoy, chivy, hound, tease, worry 6 badger, bother, harass, hassle, hector, molest, needle, pester, plague, rattle 7 disrupt, disturb, torment 9 interrupt 10 disconcert

hectic
3 red 6 fervid 7 burning, excited, fevered, flushed 8 confused, exciting, feverish, frenetic, restless 9 turbulent 10 persistent

hector
3 cow, nag 4 bait, ride 5 bully, chivy, hound 6 badger, harass, lean on 7 bedevil, swagger 8 browbeat, bullyrag, domineer 10 intimidate

Hector
brother: 5 Paris 7 Helenus, Troilus 9 Deiphobus, Polydorus
father: 5 Priam
mother: 6 Hecuba
sister: 6 Creusa 8 Polyxena 9 Cassandra
slayer: 8 Achilles
victim: 9 Patroclus
wife: 10 Andromache

Hecuba
daughter: 6 Creusa 8 Polyxena 9 Cassandra
father: 5 Dymas
husband: 5 Priam
son: 5 Paris 6 Hector 7 Helenus, Troilus 9 Deiphobus, Polydorus
victim: 11 Polymnestor

hedge
4 trim 5 avoid, evade, fence, guard, hem in, limit 6 hinder 7 barrier, defense, enclose, evasion, protect 8 boundary, encircle, restrict 9 shrubbery 10 protection

hedgehog
9 porcupine 10 stronghold

hedonist
4 rake 7 epicure, gourmet 8 gourmand, sybarite 9 bon vivant, epicurean, libertine 10 sensualist, voluptuary

heebie-jeebies
5 jumps 6 creeps, nerves, shakes 7 jitters, shivers, willies 11 nervousness

heed
4 care, hark, mark, mind, note, obey 5 watch 6 attend, harken, listen, notice, regard, remark 7 be aware, concern, hearing, hearken, observe, respect 8 consider, interest 9 attention 10 observance

heedful
5 alert, aware 7 on guard 8 vigilant

heedless

9 attentive, observant, observing
10 interested, meticulous, scrupulous
13 conscientious

heedless

9 negligent, oblivious, unmindful
10 unthinking 11 inadvertent, inattentive, unobservant 12 unreflective
13 inconsiderate

heedlessness

7 neglect 9 disregard, unconcern
11 disinterest, inattention, insouciance 12 indifference

hee-haw

4 bray 5 laugh 6 guffaw 10 horse laugh

heel

3 bum, cad, tip 4 cant, hock, lean, list, tilt 5 creep, knave, louse, rogue, skunk, slope 6 rascal, rotter 7 incline, lowlife, villain 9 scoundrel
bone: 8 calcanea (plural), calcanei (plural) 9 calcaneum, calcaneus

heft

4 lift, load 5 hoist, raise, weigh
6 weight 7 heave up 9 heaviness, influence 10 importance

hefty

3 big 5 beefy, burly, bulky, heavy, husky, large, major 6 brawny, mighty, rugged, strong 7 massive, sizable 8 imposing, powerful 9 extensive, good-sized, plentiful, ponderous, strapping 11 substantial

hegira

6 escape, exodus, flight 7 journey
10 emigration, evacuation 11 deliverance

Heidi

author: 5 Spyri (Johanna)
goatherd: 5 Peter
setting: 4 Alps

heifer

4 calf

_____ Heifetz

6 Jascha

height

3 top 4 acme, apex, cusp, peak, rise
6 apogee, climax, heyday, summit, vertex, zenith 7 stature 8 altitude, pinnacle 9 elevation, loftiness
10 prominence
combining form: 4 acro

heighten

3 wax 5 boost, mount, raise 6 beef up, expand, extend 7 amplify, augment, build up, elevate, enhance, enlarge, improve, magnify 8 increase 9 highlight, intensify 10 aggrandize

heinie

3 bum 4 butt, rear, rump 5 fanny
6 bottom 7 rear end 8 backside

heinous

4 evil 6 odious 7 hateful 8 infamous, shocking 9 abhorrent, atrocious, execrable, monstrous
10 abominable, detestable, outrageous

heinousness

4 evil 6 horror, infamy 8 atrocity, enormity 13 monstrousness

heir

5 scion 7 grantee, heritor, legatee
9 inheritor, successor 11 beneficiary
joint: 8 parcener 10 coparcener

heist

3 cop, rob 4 lift, loot 5 boost, caper, filch, pinch, steal, swipe, theft
6 holdup, rip off 7 larceny, purloin, robbery 8 burglary 9 strong-arm

Helen of Troy

abductor: 5 Paris
husband: 8 Menelaus

Helenus

brother: 5 Paris 6 Hector 7 Troilus
9 Deiphobus, Polydorus
father: 5 Priam
mother: 6 Hecuba
sister: 6 Creusa 8 Polyxena 9 Cassandra
wife: 10 Andromache

Hel, Hela

father: 4 Loki
hall: 7 Niflhel 8 Niflheim
mother: 9 Angerboda

helical
6 spiral

helicopter
7 chopper 9 eggbeater 10 whirlybird
armed: 7 gunship
blade: 5 rotor

Helios
6 Apollo
daughter: 5 Circe 8 Pasiphaë
father: 8 Hyperion
mother: 5 Theia
sister: 3 Eos 6 Aurora, Selene
son: 8 Phaethon

heliotrope
4 herb 5 shrub 6 borage 10 bloodstone

hell
5 hades, Sheol 6 blazes, Tophet
7 Gehenna, inferno 9 perdition

hell-bent
6 driven, intent 8 obsessed, resolved 10 determined

Hellen
father: 9 Deucalion
mother: 6 Pyrrha
son: 5 Dorus 6 Aeolus, Xuthus

hellhole
3 pit 8 dystopia, snake pit 9 mare's nest

hellion
3 elf, imp 4 puck, punk 5 demon,
rogue, scamp 6 rascal 7 gremlin

hellish
6 horrid 7 ghastly, hideous, satanic,
stygian 8 damnable, diabolic, dreadful, gruesome, horrible, infernal,
terrible 9 appalling, frightful, monstrous, plutonian 10 diabolical

Hellman play
11 Little Foxes (The) 13 Children's
Hour (The) 15 Watch on the Rhine

hello
3 hey 4 ciao, hail 5 aloha, howdy
7 hi there, welcome 8 greeting
9 greetings

helm
5 wheel 7 cockpit 8 controls

helmet
6 casque, sallet, tin hat 7 morrion
8 burgonet, headgear
medieval: 6 sallet 7 basinet
part: 7 ventail 8 aventail
sun: 4 topi 5 topee

helmsman
5 pilot

Heloïse
husband: 7 Abelard (Peter)
son: 9 Astrolabe

helot
4 peon, serf 5 slave 6 vassal
7 laborer, peasant, servant

helotry
4 yoke 6 thrall 7 bondage, peonage,
serfdom, slavery 9 servitude, thralldom 11 enslavement

help
3 aid 4 abet, back, mend 5 avail,
boost, guide, serve 6 assist, relief,
remedy, succor 7 advance, benefit,
bolster, further, promote, relieve,
secours, service, support 8 mitigate, palliate 9 alleviate, meliorate
10 ameliorate, assistance, facilitate
11 cooperation
forward: 7 further
hired: 5 labor

helper
4 aide 6 deputy, server 7 ancilla,
servant 8 employee 9 assistant,
associate, attendant, auxiliary
10 apprentice 11 subordinate

helpful
5 of use 6 usable, useful 8 salutary,
valuable 9 effective, favorable,
practical 10 beneficial, profitable,
propitious 11 encouraging 12 advantageous, constructive

helping
4 dose 5 share 7 portion, serving
9 auxiliary

helpless
4 weak 6 feeble, futile, unable
7 forlorn 8 desolate 9 abandoned,
dependent 11 unprotected

helter-skelter
6 anyhow 7 anywise, flighty, hastily, turmoil 8 at random, disorder, pell-mell, randomly 9 confusion, haphazard, hit-or-miss 11 any which way, haphazardly, in confusion, precipitate

helve
4 haft 6 handle

Helvetian
5 Swiss

hem
3 pen, rim 4 brim, edge, gird, ring, seam, shut 5 bound, brink, fence, hedge, skirt, verge 6 border, circle, corral, edging, fringe, immure, margin, stitch 7 close in, enclose, selvage, shorten 8 encircle, surround 9 encompass, perimeter, periphery
turned-back: 4 cuff

Heman
father: 4 Joel
grandfather: 6 Samuel

hematite
3 ore 7 mineral 12 black diamond

Hemingway, Ernest
novel: 9 In Our Time 12 Sun Also Rises (The) 13 Moveable Feast (A) 14 Farewell to Arms (A) 15 Old Man and the Sea (The) 16 To Have and Have Not 18 Islands in the Stream, Snows of Kilimanjaro (The) 19 For Whom the Bell Tolls
sobriquet: 4 Papa

hemlock
4 drug, herb, tree, wood 6 poison

hemophiliac
7 bleeder

hemp
3 kef, kif 7 hashish 8 cannabis 9 marijuana
fiber: 5 oakum
kind: 4 aloe

hen
5 biddy
broody: 6 sitter
spayed: 8 poularde
young: 6 pullet

hence
4 away, ergo, thus 5 since 9 as a result, from now on, therefore, thereupon 11 accordingly 12 consequently

henceforth
9 from now on, hereafter

henchman
6 cohort, lackey, minion, stooge 7 abettor 8 adherent, disciple, follower, partisan, retainer 9 attendant, supporter 10 accomplice

Henley poem
8 Invictus

henpeck
3 nag 4 carp, fuss 5 annoy 6 badger, carp at, harass, hector 8 domineer 9 find fault

Henry II
adversary: 6 Becket (Thomas à)
son: 7 Richard (Lionheart)
surname: 5 Anjou 11 Plantagenet
wife: 7 Eleanor

Henry IV
surname: 9 Lancaster
victim: 10 Richard III

Henry VIII
archbishop: 7 Cranmer (Thomas) 10 Thomas More
daughter: 9 Elizabeth
son: 6 Edward
surname: 5 Tudor
victim: 4 Anne (Boleyn) 9 Catherine (Howard) 10 Thomas More
wife: 4 Anne (Boleyn, of Cleves), Jane (Seymour) 9 Catherine (Howard, of Aragon, Parr)

hepatic
9 liverwort

Hephaestus
6 Vulcan
father: 4 Zeus 7 Jupiter
mother: 4 Hera, Juno
wife: 5 Venus 6 Charis 9 Aphrodite

Hephzibah
husband: 8 Hezekiah
son: 8 Manasseh

hepped up
5 eager 7 excited, fervent 12 enthusiastic

Hera
4 Juno
father: 6 Cronus, Saturn
husband: 4 Zeus 7 Jupiter
messenger: 4 Iris
mother: 4 Rhea

Heracles
beloved: 4 Iole
brother: 8 Iphicles
charioteer: 6 Iolaus
father: 4 Zeus 7 Jupiter
mother: 7 Alcmene
son: 6 Hyllus
victim: 5 Hydra, Ladon 6 Geryon, Megara, Orthus 10 Nemean lion
wife: 4 Hebe 6 Megara 8 Deianira

herald
4 hail, tout 5 crier, greet 6 signal
7 courier, declare, portend, precede, presage, trumpet 8 announce, ballyhoo, exponent, outrider, proclaim 9 advertise, harbinger, messenger, precursor, publicize, spokesman 10 forerunner, foreshadow

heraldic
border: 7 bordure
cross: 6 fleury, formée, moline, pommée 8 fourchée
term: 4 bend, fess, orle, pale, seme, vert 5 crest, flank, gules 6 argent, blazon, canton, charge, device, dexter, emblem, impale, manche, sejant, voided, volant 7 chevron, nombril, passant, purpure, rampant, saltire, statant 8 guardant, sinister, tincture 9 regardant 10 escutcheon

heraldry
6 armory 9 pageantry

herb
3 oca 4 dill, flax, forb, hemp, leek, mint, nard, sage, wort 5 basil, chive, tansy, thyme 6 allium, arnica, borage, catnip, endive, eryngo, fennel, garlic, hyssop, lovage, orpine, squill, yarrow 7 boneset, caraway, catmint, chervil, chicory, comfrey, episcia, ginseng, milfoil, mullein, oregano, parsley, pinesap, pussley, salsify, sanicle 8 angelica, camomile, capsicum, cardamom, centaury, cilantro, costmary, feverfew, freewort, hepatica, lungwort, mandrake, marjoram, origanum, pokeweed, purslane, rapeseed, selfheal, tarragon, turmeric, euphrasy, valerian, woodruff, wormwood 9 birthwort, bush basil, chamomile, patchouli, spikenard 10 basil thyme 12 balm of Gilead
mythical: 4 moly
poisonous: 7 aconite, dogbane, hemlock, henbane 8 veratrum 9 hellebore

herbicide
6 dioxin, diquat, diuron 7 monuron 8 picloram, simazine 11 Agent Orange

Herculean
4 huge, vast 5 giant 7 arduous, immense, mammoth, titanic 8 colossal, enormous, gigantic, powerful 10 formidable, superhuman

Hercules
see **Heracles**

herd
3 mob 4 bevy, lead 5 covey, crowd, drive, drove, flock, swarm 6 gather, throng 9 associate, multitude

herdsman
6 Boötes, cowboy 7 breeder 8 shepherd

here and there
6 passim 7 at times 9 sometimes 11 irregularly

hereditary
6 inborn, inbred, innate, lineal 7 genetic 9 ancestral, inherited 10 congenital 11 traditional, transmitted

heredity
7 lineage 8 ancestry 9 tradition 11 inheritance
unit: 4 gene

heresy
6 schism 7 dissent, fallacy, impiety

heretic
9 defection, deviation, misbelief
10 dissidence, heterodoxy, infidelity,
radicalism 11 revisionism, unorthodoxy 13 nonconformism, nonconformity

heretic
7 infidel 8 apostate, defector, recusant, renegade 9 dissenter, dissident 10 iconoclast, schismatic,
separatist, unbeliever 11 misbeliever, nonbeliever, revisionist 13 nonconformist

heretical
7 infidel 8 apostate 9 dissident,
heterodox, miscreant, sectarian
10 dissenting, schismatic, unorthodox 11 revisionism 12 misbelieving
13 nonconformist

heritage
6 legacy 7 bequest 9 patrimony,
tradition 10 birthright

Hermes
7 Mercury
attribute: 7 petasos, petasus 8 caduceus
father: 4 Zeus 7 Jupiter
mother: 4 Maia

hermetic
6 closed, occult, secret 7 recluse
8 abstruse, airtight, profound, secluded, solitary 9 recondite 10 cloistered, impervious 11 sequestered

Hermia
beloved: 8 Lysander
father: 5 Egeus

Hermione
father: 8 Menelaus
husband: 7 Orestes, Pyrrhus
11 Neoptolemus
mother: 5 Helen

hermit
5 loner 6 cookie 7 eremite, recluse
8 solitary 9 anchorite

hermitage
7 retreat 8 cloister, hideaway 9 monastery

hernia
6 breach 7 rupture 10 protrusion

support: 5 truss
type: 6 cystic, hiatal 7 femoral
9 umbilical 10 incisional

hero
4 idol 6 knight 7 demigod, paladin
8 champion 11 protagonist
American: 6 Bunyan (Paul) 8 Su-
perman
Armenian: 10 Skanderbeg
Babylonian: 9 Gilgamesh
Celtic-French: 7 Tristan 8 Tristram
Crusades: 7 Tancred 8 Tancredi
English: 6 Arthur 7 Beowulf
9 Robin Hood
French: 6 Roland 11 Charlemagne
German: 5 Etzel 8 Arminius
9 Siegfried
Greek: 4 Ajax 5 Jason 7 Perseus,
Ulysses 8 Achilles, Heracles, Her-
cules, Leonidas, Odysseus 11 Bel-
lerophon
Hebrew: 5 David 6 Daniel, Samson
Hungarian: 5 Arpad 7 Hunyadi
(János)
Irish: 9 Cuchulain, Cuchulinn,
Cuchullin
Italian: 7 Orlando
Roman: 5 Romulus 8 Horatius
Scandinavian: 6 Sigurd 9 Siegfried
Scottish: 5 Bruce (Robert) 6 Rob
Roy
Spanish: 5 El Cid
Spartan: 8 Leonidas
Trojan: 6 Aeneas, Hector

Herod
daughter: 6 Salome
father: 7 Antipas 9 Antipater
kingdom: 5 Judea 6 Judaea
mother: 6 Cyprus
son: 5 Herod (Antipas) 6 Joseph
7 Pheroas 9 Phasaelus

Herodias
daughter: 6 Salome
father: 11 Aristobulus
husband: 5 Herod (Antipas)

heroic
4 bold, huge 5 brave, noble 6 daring, mighty 7 drastic, extreme, radical, valiant 8 colossal, enormous,

fearless, gigantic, intrepid, unafraid, valorous **9** dauntless, Herculean, undaunted **10** courageous

heroin
  4 gear, skag **5** horse, smack **8** narcotic **11** diamorphine

heroism
  5 valor **6** daring, spirit **7** bravery, courage, prowess **8** boldness, chivalry, nobility, valiance **9** gallantry **11** intrepidity

heron relative
  5 egret **7** bittern

Hero's lover
  7 Leander

herring
  7 sardine **8** brisling, pilchard
  smoked: 7 bloater

Herse
  father: 7 Cecrops
  sister: 8 Aglauros
  son: 8 Cephalus

Hersey
  novel: 4 Wall (The) **12** Bell for Adano (A)
  town: 5 Adano

Hesione
  brother: 5 Priam
  father: 8 Laomedon
  husband: 7 Telamon
  rescuer: 8 Heracles, Hercules
  son: 6 Teucer

hesitant
  4 slow **5** chary, loath, timid **6** afraid, averse, unsure **7** halting, uneager **9** faltering, reluctant, tentative, uncertain, unwilling **10** irresolute **11** disinclined, vacillating

hesitate
  4 balk **5** delay, demur, hedge, pause, stall, stick, waver **6** dawdle, dither, falter, waffle **7** stammer, stutter **8** hang back, hold back **9** temporize, vacillate **12** shilly-shally

Hesperides
  6 nymphs

Hesperus
  5 Venus **11** evening star
  father: 8 Astraeus
  mother: 3 Eos

Hesse novel
  6 Demian **10** Siddhartha **11** Steppenwolf **12** Magister Ludi

Hestia
  5 Vesta
  father: 6 Cronus, Saturn
  mother: 4 Rhea

heterodox
  9 dissident, heretical, sectarian **10** schismatic, unorthodox **13** nonconformist

heterodoxy
  6 heresy, schism **7** dissent **9** misbelief **10** dissidence **13** nonconformism, nonconformity

heterogeneous
  5 mixed **6** motley, sundry, varied **7** diverse, various **8** assorted **9** disparate **12** conglomerate

het up
  5 irate, upset **7** excited **8** agitated

hew
  3 axe, cut **4** chop, fell, form **5** shape, stick **6** adhere **7** conform, cut down

hex
  4 jinx **5** charm, curse, spell, witch **6** voodoo, whammy **7** bad luck, bewitch, enchant **9** sorceress **11** enchantment, enchantress

heyday
  4 acme, peak **5** prime **6** height, zenith **9** high point

Hezekiah
  father: 4 Ahaz **7** Neariah
  mother: 3 Abi
  son: 8 Manasseh
  wife: 9 Hephzibah

hiatus
  3 gap **5** break, space **6** breach, lacuna **7** interim **8** aperture, downtime, interval **10** suspension **12** interruption **13** discontinuity

Hiawatha
author: 10 Longfellow (Henry Wadsworth)
grandmother: 7 Nokomis
mother: 7 Wenonah
tribe: 6 Ojibwa, Ojibwe 7 Ojibway
wife: 9 Minnehaha

hibernal
6 wintry 8 winterly

Hibernia
4 Eire, Erin 7 Ireland

hick
4 rube 5 yokel 6 rustic 7 bumpkin, hayseed 8 cornball 10 clodhopper, provincial

hidden
5 privy 6 buried, covert, occult, secret, veiled 7 obscure 8 obscured, shrouded, ulterior 9 concealed 11 undisclosed
combining form: 6 crypto, krypto

hide
3 fur 4 bury, lurk, mask, pelt, skin, veil 5 cache, cloak, cover, inter, shade, stash 6 harbor, lie low, screen, shroud 7 conceal, cover up, leather, obscure, seclude, secrete, shelter 8 ensconce

hideaway
see **hideout**

hidebound
8 obdurate 9 parochial 10 inflexible, provincial 11 reactionary, straitlaced 12 conservative, narrow-minded 13 straightlaced

hideous
4 ugly 5 awful, gross, lurid, nasty 6 grisly, horrid 7 ghastly, hateful 8 gruesome, horrible, shocking, terrible 9 appalling, dismaying, frightful, loathsome, monstrous, offensive, repellent, repugnant, repulsive, revolting, sickening 10 disgusting, horrifying

hideout
3 den 4 lair 5 cache, haven 6 covert, refuge 7 retreat, shelter 9 hermitage, safe house, sanctuary

hie
3 run 4 dash, push, trot 5 hurry, scoot 6 hasten, hustle

hierarch
4 boss, head 5 chief 6 honcho, leader, master 7 headman 9 chieftain 10 high priest

hierarchy
5 group, order, ranks 6 ladder, system 7 pyramid 9 food chain, structure 11 bureaucracy 12 pecking order

hieratic
6 formal 8 priestly, stylized 10 priest-like, sacerdotal

high
4 tall 5 drunk, giddy, grand, lofty, noble, tipsy 6 elated, raised, stoned, treble, zonked 7 drugged, keyed up, soaring, supreme 8 abstruse, elevated, eloquent, euphoric, hopped-up, piercing, towering 9 climactic, delirious, prominent, spaced-out 11 extravagant, intoxicated
combining form: 4 alti

high _____
3 hat, tea 4 five, noon, road, sign, tech, tide, time 5 chair, heels, jinks 6 priest, roller, school

high-and-mighty
5 bossy, proud 6 lordly 7 haughty 8 arrogant, cavalier, insolent, superior 9 imperious 10 disdainful 11 domineering, overbearing 12 supercilious

highball
3 fly, run 4 dash, rush, whiz 5 hurry, speed 6 barrel, hustle, signal 7 hotfoot 8 cocktail

highboy
5 chest 6 bureau 7 dresser 9 furniture

highbrow
4 snob 7 egghead 8 cerebral, cultured, educated 9 intellect 12 intellectual

high-class
7 elegant 8 five-star, superior

9 exclusive, exquisite, first-rate, patrician 11 fashionable 12 aristocratic 13 sophisticated

highest

3 top 5 chief 6 apical, upmost 7 exalted, supreme, topmost 9 top-drawer, uppermost 10 top-ranking
point: 4 acme, apex 5 crest 6 summit, zenith 8 pinnacle

highfalutin

5 fancy, windy 6 florid 7 aureate, flowery, fustian, orotund, pompous 8 affected 9 bombastic, grandiose, overblown, rhapsodic 10 oratorical, rhetorical 11 declamatory, pretentious

high-flown

5 showy, tumid, windy 6 turgid 7 aureate, flowery, fustian, orotund, pompous, swollen 8 elevated, inflated, sonorous 9 bombastic, grandiose, overblown 10 flamboyant 11 declamatory, pretentious 12 magniloquent, ostentatious 13 grandiloquent

high-handed

5 bossy 8 dogmatic, imperial 9 arbitrary, imperious 10 autocratic, disdainful, imperative, peremptory 11 dictatorial, domineering, magisterial, overbearing

high-hat

4 snub 6 slight, snobby, snooty 7 disdain, haughty 8 arrogant, snobbish 9 conceited, disregard 11 pretentious 12 supercilious

high jinks

3 fun 6 antics 7 fooling, revelry 9 horseplay, rowdiness, whoop-de-do

Highlander

4 Gael, Scot

highlight

4 mark 5 focus 6 accent, stress 7 feature 8 point out 9 emphasize, underline 10 accentuate, focal point

high-minded

5 lofty, moral, noble 7 ethical, upright 8 elevated 10 principled

high-muck-a-muck

3 VIP 5 nabob 6 bigwig 7 big shot, notable

high-pitched

6 shrill 7 excited 8 agitated, feverish, frenetic, piercing

high point

3 top 4 acme, peak 6 apogee, summit, zenith 8 best part, pinnacle

high-powered

6 driven, strong 7 dynamic 8 animated, forceful, vigorous 9 energetic, strenuous 10 aggressive, compelling 12 enterprising

high-pressure

8 forceful 9 insistent, stressful 10 aggressive

high roller

7 gambler, spender, wastrel 8 prodigal 10 big spender, profligate, squanderer 11 spendthrift

high sign

3 nod, tip 4 wink 5 alarm 6 signal, tipoff 7 gesture, warning

Highsmith novel

11 Ripley's Game 16 Talented Mr. Ripley (The)

high-sounding

7 pompous 8 affected, imposing, inflated, puffed-up 9 grandiose, overblown 11 pretentious

high-spirited

4 bold 5 brash, fiery, jolly, merry 6 bubbly, daring, joyful, lively, plucky, spunky 7 excited, gleeful 9 ebullient, energetic, exuberant, vivacious 12 effervescent, lighthearted

high-strung

4 edgy, taut 5 hyper, jumpy, nervy, tense, tight, wired 6 touchy 7 fidgety, jittery, keyed up, nervous, uptight 8 restless 9 excitable, sensitive

hightail it

3 run 4 bolt, dash, flee 5 scoot, scram 6 get out, run off 7 take off 8 clear out 9 skedaddle

highway
4 pike, road 5 track 6 artery 8 corridor, turnpike 10 interstate 12 thoroughfare
German: 8 autobahn
Italian: 10 autostrada

highwayman
5 thief 6 bandit, robber 7 brigand

hijack
5 seize, steal 6 abduct, kidnap 8 take over 10 commandeer 11 appropriate

hike
4 jump, rove, snap, trek, walk 5 boost, raise, tramp, tromp 6 jack up, rise up, travel 7 journey, traipse, upgrade 8 backpack, increase

hilarious
5 funny, merry 7 comical 8 humorous, mirthful 9 laughable, priceless 10 rollicking

hilarity
4 glee 5 cheer, mirth 6 gaiety 7 delight 8 jocosity, laughter 9 merriment 12 cheerfulness

hill
4 bank, bump, cock, dune, heap, knob, pile, rick, rise 5 bluff, butte, knoll, mound, ridge, shock, slope, stack 6 cuesta, height 7 hummock, incline 8 mountain 9 elevation, monadnock
African veld: 5 kopje 6 koppie
Boston: 6 Bunker
craggy: 3 tor
Cuba: 7 San Juan
D.C.: 7 Capitol
elongate: 7 drumlin
level-topped: 4 mesa 5 butte
of stratified drift: 4 kame
rounded: 5 swell
sand: 4 dune
small: 5 knoll, kopje, mound 6 koppie
surrounded by ice: 7 nunatak

hillbilly
4 rube 5 yokel 6 rustic 7 bumpkin, hayseed 10 clodhopper 12 backwoodsman

hillock
4 rise 5 knoll, mound

hillside
5 slope
Scottish: 4 brae

hilt
4 grip, haft 6 handle 8 handgrip

Himalayan country
5 Nepal 6 Bhutan

hind
3 doe 4 back, deer, rear 5 after 7 grouper 9 posterior
mate: 4 hart

hinder
4 balk, curb, mire 5 block, check, delay, deter 6 baffle, burden, fetter, hamper, hold up, impede, retard, thwart 7 inhibit, prevent, shackle, trammel 8 handicap, hold back, obstruct, restrain 9 frustrate, hamstring, interfere, interrupt

hindmost
3 end 4 back, last, rear 5 after, final 6 latter 7 closing 8 farthest, terminal, ultimate 9 posterior 10 concluding

hindquarters
8 haunches

hindrance
3 bar 4 snag 8 obstacle 9 impedance 10 impediment 11 obstruction

Hindu
age: 4 yuga
ascetic: 4 yogi 5 fakir, swami
caste (varna): 5 Sudra 6 Vaisya 7 Brahman 9 Kshatriya
class: 5 caste, varna
community: 6 ashram
demon: 4 Rahu 6 Ravana
essence: 5 atman
force: 5 karma
garment: 4 sari
gentleman: 4 babu
god: 4 deva, Siva 5 Shiva 6 Brahma, Vishnu
goddess: 4 devi
goddess of beauty: 7 Lakshmi

goddess of destruction: 4 Kali
god of destruction: 4 Siva 5 Shiva
god of fire: 4 Agni
god of love: 4 Kama
god of the heavens: 7 Krishna
god of war: 6 Skanda 10 Karttikeya
god of wisdom: 6 Ganesa, Ganesh
hell: 6 Naraka
holy man: 5 sadhu
instrument: 5 sitar, tabla
leader: 6 Gandhi (Mahatma)
lowest caste: 5 Sudra
nobleman: 4 raja 5 rajah
philosophy: 7 Vedanta
precept: 5 sutra
prince: 4 raja 5 rajah 8 maharaja
9 maharajah
queen: 4 rani 5 ranee 8 maharani
9 maharanee
salvation: 7 nirvana
scripture: 4 Veda 6 Purana 12 Bhagavad Gita
social group: 5 caste, varna
teacher: 4 guru 5 swami 9 maharishi
term of respect: 5 sahib
title: 3 sri
treatise: 9 Upanishad
twice-born: 6 Vaisya 7 Brahman
9 Kshatriya

hinge
4 pawl 5 joint, mount 12 turning
point
kind: 4 butt 5 piano 10 hook-and-eye

hint
3 cue, tip 4 clue, dash, sign, wisp
5 imply, taste, tinge, touch, trace
6 allude, notion, shadow, tipoff
7 inkling, soupçon, suggest 8 allusion, indicate, innuendo, intimate
9 insinuate, scintilla, suspicion
10 indication, intimation, suggestion
11 implication, insinuation

hinterland
4 bush 6 sticks 8 frontier, interior
9 backwater, backwoods, boondocks,
up-country 10 wilderness 11 backcountry

hip
3 hot 4 chic, coxa 5 aware, savvy
6 haunch, trendy, with-it 7 tuned in
11 fashionable
bone: 5 ilium, pubis 6 pelvis
7 ischium
cattle: 5 thurl
disorder: 8 sciatica

hippie
8 bohemian, longhair 11 flower child
13 nonconformist

Hippocratic ____
4 oath

Hippodamia
father: 8 Oenomaus
husband: 6 Pelops 9 Pirithous
10 Peirithous
son: 6 Atreus 8 Thyestes

Hippolytus
father: 7 Theseus
mother: 7 Antiope 9 Hippolyte
stepmother: 7 Phaedra

hire
3 fee, pay 4 rent, wage 5 lease,
wages 6 employ, engage, retain,
sign on, take on 7 charter, payment,
recruit 8 contract 10 employment
11 contract for

hireling
4 hack 6 worker 7 servant 8 employee 9 mercenary

Hirschfeld's daughter
4 Nina

hirsute
5 hairy 6 shaggy, woolly 9 whiskered

Hispania
6 Iberia 9 peninsula
part: 5 Spain 8 Portugal

Hispaniola country
5 Haiti

hiss
3 boo 4 hoot, jeer 5 decry 6 deride,
revile, sizzle, wheeze 7 catcall,
whisper, whistle 8 sibilate

historian
8 annalist 10 chronicler

historical period

American: 4 Webb (Charles Richard) 5 Adams (Brooks, Charles Kendall, Hannah, Henry, Herbert Baxter), Beard (Charles, Mary), Foote (Shelby) 6 Brooks (Van Wyck), Catton (Bruce), DeVoto (Bernard), Durant (Ariel, Will), Malone (Dumas), Miller (Perry), Muzzey (David), Nevins (Allen), Sarton (George Alfred), Shirer (William), Sparks (Jared), Turner (Frederick Jackson) 7 Ambrose (Stephen), Morison (Samuel Eliot), Parkman (Francis), Ridpath (John Clark), Tuchman (Barbara), Woodson (Carter G.) 8 Bancroft (George), Boorstin (Daniel), Channing (Edward), Commager (Henry Steele), Prescott (William H.), Robinson (James Harvey), Woodward (C. Vann) 10 McCullough (David) 11 Schlesinger (Arthur)
Arab: 10 Ibn Khaldun
Danish: 4 Saxo (Grammaticus)
Dutch: 8 Huizinga (Johan)
English: 4 Bede (Venerable), Stow (John), Ward (Adolphus) 5 Acton (Lord), Grote (George), Wells (Herbert George) 6 Camden (William), Gibbon (Edward), Keegan (John), Namier (Lewis Bernstein), Stubbs (William), Taylor (A. J. P.) 7 Hakluyt (Richard), Raleigh (Walter), Toynbee (Arnold), Whewell (William) 8 Geoffrey (of Monmouth), Macaulay (Thomas Babington) 9 Holinshed (Raphael), Trevelyan (George)
French: 5 Bloch (Marc), Renan (Ernest), Taine (Hippolyte) 6 Guizot (François), Thiers (Louis-Adolphe), Volney (Comte de) 7 Braudel (Ferdinand) 8 Hanotaux (Gabriel), Michelet (Jules)
German: 5 Ranke (Leopold von) 7 Mommsen (Theodor), Niebuhr (Barthold Georg) 8 Spengler (Oswald)
Greek: 8 Plutarch, Polybius, Xenophon 9 Dionysius, Herodotus 10 Thucydides
Italian: 4 Vico (Giovanni) 5 Croce (Benedetto) 9 Salvemini (Gaetano)
Jewish: 8 Josephus (Flavius)

Roman: 4 Livy 7 Sallust, Tacitus (Cornelius) 9 Suetonius
Scottish: 7 Carlyle (Thomas) 9 Robertson (William)
Swiss: 6 Müller (Johannes von)
Welsh: 7 Nennius

historical period
3 age, era 5 epoch

history
4 past, saga 5 diary 6 annals, memoir, record 7 account, done for, journal 9 chronicle, narrative, treatment 10 chronology

histrionic
5 showy, stagy 6 staged 8 affected, dramatic 10 artificial, theatrical

hit
3 bop, jab, rap 4 bang, bash, bean, biff, blow, bump, bunt, butt, conk, cuff, ding, lick, slap, slug, sock, swat 5 clout, knock, paste, pound, punch, smack, smash, smite, swipe, whack 6 batter, buffet, chance, larrup, strike, stroke, thwack, wallop 7 clobber, sellout, success 8 bludgeon, lambaste 9 collision, sensation
baseball: 5 homer, liner 6 double, single, triple 7 home run 9 line drive
golf ball: 5 shank

hitch
4 jerk, join, halt, hook, knot, lift, limp, snag, yoke 5 delay, thumb, unite 6 attach, couple, fasten, hobble, tether 7 connect, harness 8 make fast, stoppage 10 connection, difficulty, impediment 11 obstruction 12 entanglement

Hitchcock, Alfred
film: 4 Rope 5 Birds (The), Topaz 6 Frenzy, Marnie, Psycho 7 Rebecca, Vertigo 8 Lifeboat, Sabotage 9 Notorious, Suspicion 10 Rear Window, Spellbound 12 Lady Vanishes (The) 13 To Catch a Thief 14 Shadow of a Doubt 16 North by Northwest
forte: 8 suspense

hitchhike
5 thumb

hither
  4 here **6** nearer **11** to this place

hitherto
  5 as yet, so far **7** earlier, thus far, till now **8** formerly, until now **10** previously

Hitler, Adolf
  follower: 4 Nazi
  title: 6 Führer **7** Fuehrer
  wife: 5 Braun (Eva)

hit man
  5 bravo **6** killer **7** torpedo **8** assassin, enforcer, murderer **9** cutthroat

hit-or-miss
  6 casual, chance, random **7** aimless, erratic **8** careless **9** desultory, haphazard, irregular, unplanned

hive
  6 apiary, colony **7** cluster **9** stockpile

HMS Pinafore
  composer: 8 Sullivan (Arthur)
  librettist: 7 Gilbert (W. S.)

hoagie
  3 sub **4** hero **5** po'boy **7** grinder, torpedo **8** sandwich **9** submarine

hoar
  4 rime **5** frost

hoard
  4 save **5** amass, cache, lay by, lay up, stash, stock, store, trove **6** supply **7** collect, lay away, nest egg, reserve **8** squirrel, treasure **9** stockpile **10** accumulate, collection, cumulation **11** aggregation **12** accumulation

hoarder
  5 miser **7** scrooge

hoarse
  5 gruff, husky, rough, thick **6** croaky **7** grating, rasping, raucous, throaty **8** croaking, gravelly, guttural

hoary
  3 old **4** aged **5** stale **6** age-old **7** ancient, antique **8** timeworn **9** venerable

hoax
  3 con **4** dupe, fake, fool, gull, sham **5** fraud, phony, trick **6** befool, delude, humbug, take in **7** deceive, mislead **8** flimflam, hoodwink, trickery **9** bamboozle, deception, imposture

Hobbit creator
  7 Tolkien (J. R. R.)

hobble
  4 lame, limp **6** fetter, hamper, hinder, hog-tie, impede **7** cripple, trammel **8** handicap

hobby
  6 falcon **7** pastime, pursuit **8** activity, sideline **9** avocation, diversion

hobgoblin
  5 bogey **7** bugaboo

hobnob
  3 mix **6** mingle **7** consort **9** associate, rub elbows, socialize **10** fraternize **11** get together

hobo
  3 bum **5** gypsy, tramp **7** drifter, floater, swagman, vagrant **8** derelict, vagabond

hock
  4 debt, pawn **5** ankle **6** prison

hockey
  6 shinny
  arena: 4 rink
  cup: 7 Stanley
  implement: 4 puck **5** stick
  official: 7 referee **8** linesman
  player: 3 Orr (Bobby), Roy (Patrick) **4** Bure (Pavel), Fuhr (Grant), Howe (Gordie), Hull (Bobby, Brett), Jagr (Jaromir), wing **5** Bossy (Mike), Bucyk (John), Hasek (Dominik), Kurri (Jari), Maruk (Dennis), Sakic (Joe), Shore (Eddie), Shutt (Steve) **6** center, Clarke (Bobby), Coffey (Paul), Dionne (Marcel), Dryden (Ken), goalie, Harvey (Doug), Juneau (Joe), Kariya (Paul), Leetch (Brian), Mikita (Stan), Morenz (Howie), Parent (Bernie), Potvin (Denis), Recchi (Mark), Savard (Denis), Sundin (Mats) **7** Belfour (Ed),

Bourque (Ray), Brodeur (Martin),
Chelios (Chris), Fedorov (Sergei),
forward, Francis (Ron), Gretzky
(Wayne), Lafleur (Guy), Lemieux
(Claude, Mario), Lindros (Eric),
Messier (Mark), Mogilny (Alexander),
Richard (Maurice), Richter (Mike),
Selanne (Teemu), Stastny (Peter),
Yzerman (Steve) **8** Beliveau (Jean),
Esposito (Phil, Tony), Forsberg (Pe-
ter), Nicholls (Bernie), pointman,
Shanahan (Brendan), Trottier
(Bryan), Ysebaert (Paul) **9** Hawer-
chuk (Dale) **10** Carbonneau (Guy),
defenseman, goalkeeper
team: 4 Jets **5** Blues, Kings, Stars
6 Bruins, Devils, Flames, Flyers,
Oilers, Sabres, Sharks **7** Canucks,
Rangers, Whalers **8** Capitals,
Panthers, Penguins, Red Wings,
Senators **9** Canadiens, Islanders,
Lightning, Nordiques **10** Black
Hawks, Maple Leafs, North Stars
11 Mighty Ducks
term: 3 box **4** cage, goal, puck, rink
5 bandy, bench, check, icing, stick
6 charge, crease, shinny **7** face-off,
offside **8** blue line **9** back-check,
body-check **10** center line, penalty
box
variation of: 9 broomball

hocus-pocus
4 sham **8** artifice, nonsense, trickery
9 conjuring, deception, imposture
10 mumbo jumbo **11** abracadabra,
incantation, legerdemain **13** sleight
of hand

hod
4 tray **6** trough **7** scuttle **11** coal
scuttle

Hoder, Hoth
brother: 6 Balder
slayer: 4 Vali
victim: 6 Balder

hodgepodge
4 hash **6** jumble, medley **7** mélange, mixture **8** mishmash, mixed
bag **9** patchwork, potpourri **10** assortment, miscellany **11** gallimaufry

hoe
4 till, weed **6** tiller, weeder **9** cultivate

hoedown
9 barn dance **11** contra dance,
square dance

hog
3 pig, sow **4** boar **5** swine
family: 6 Suidae
female: 3 sow **4** gilt
genus: 3 Sus
red: 5 duroc
young: 5 shoat

hogback
5 crest, ridge

hogshead
3 keg, tun **4** butt, cask **6** barrel
9 container

hog-tie
4 bind **6** fetter **7** shackle, trammel

hogwash
3 rot **4** bunk, slop **5** bilge, hokum,
hooey, swill **6** piffle **7** baloney,
garbage, rubbish **8** nonsense
9 moonshine, poppycock **10** applesauce, balderdash, flapdoodle,
taradiddle **12** gobbledygook

hog wild
5 crazy **6** crazed, madcap **7** berserk

ho-hum
4 dull **5** bored **6** boring **7** tedious
8 tiresome **10** unexciting **11** indifferent

hoi polloi
3 mob **5** horde **6** masses **8** populace **9** multitude **10** lower class
11 proletariat

hoist
4 lift **5** drink, raise, winch **6** lift up,
pick up, take up **7** derrick, elevate
8 windlass

hoity-toity
4 smug **5** dizzy, giddy, silly **7** flighty,
pompous **9** conceited, frivolous
11 highfalutin

hokey
4 fake, mock, sham **5** banal, bogus,

corny, hammy, phony, stale, stagy,
trite **6** ersatz, pseudo **7** clichéd
8 cornball, outdated **9** contrived,
hackneyed **12** melodramatic

hokum

4 bosh **5** hooey **7** baloney, hogwash
8 malarkey, nonsense **9** moonshine,
poppycock **10** applesauce, balderdash, flapdoodle, taradiddle **11** foolishness **12** gobbledygook

hold

3 own **4** bear, deem, grab, grip,
keep **5** carry, clamp, clasp, cling,
grasp, gripe, judge, sense, think,
value **6** arrest, clench, clinch,
clutch, detain, harbor, regard, retain
7 contain, convene, convoke, fermata, grapple, keep out, possess,
reserve, support, sustain **8** keep
back, maintain, preserve, restrict
close: 6 cuddle
dear: 7 cherish
in check: 7 repress
in common: 5 share
out: 4 last **6** endure
together: 4 bond **5** clamp **6** fasten
wrestling: 6 nelson **8** headlock,
scissors **10** full nelson, half nelson

hold back

4 curb, keep, stop **5** check, delay
6 bridle, detain, impede, retain
7 inhibit, keep out, prevent, refrain,
reserve **8** restrain, suppress, withhold **9** constrain

hold forth

4 rant **5** orate, speak, spout **7** declaim, expound, lecture **8** harangue,
proclaim **9** expatiate **10** dilate upon

hold off

4 stay, wait **5** defer, delay, pause,
repel **6** rebuff, resist **7** abstain,
adjourn, repulse, suspend **8** hesitate, postpone, prorogue **9** withstand
11 discontinue

hold up

3 rob **4** halt, lift, stay **5** check, defer,
delay, raise **6** hinder, impede, put
off, retard **7** support, suspend
8 postpone, prorogue, slow down

hole

3 den, gap, jam, pit **4** cave, flaw,
lair, rent, spot, void **5** fault, niche
6 breach, burrow, cavity, cranny,
defect, eyelet, lacuna, outlet **7** dilemma, opening, orifice **8** aperture,
weakness **9** perforate **10** excavation, interstice **11** perforation,
predicament

hole in one

3 ace

holiday

5 leave **6** May Day **7** Flag Day
8 Labor Day, New Year's, vacation
9 Christmas, Halloween **10** Father's
Day, Mother's Day **11** Memorial Day,
Veterans Day **12** All Saints' Day,
Groundhog Day, Thanksgiving
13 Presidents' Day, St. Patrick's Day,
Valentine's Day
British: 9 Boxing Day
Canadian: 11 Dominion Day,
Victoria Day
Jewish: 8 Passover

holiness

5 piety **6** purity **8** devotion, divinity,
sanctity **9** beatitude **11** religiosity
12 consecration, spirituality

Holland

see **Netherlands**

holler

3 cry **4** call, yell **5** shout **6** bellow,
clamor, cry out, outcry **7** call out
8 complain **9** complaint

hollow

3 dip, sag **4** void **5** basin, empty,
false **6** cavity, ravine, sunken, vacant
7 concave, echoing, sinkage **8** sinkhole, thorough **9** cavernous, concavity **10** depression, sepulchral
out: 3 dig, gut **4** mine **5** gouge
8 excavate

holly

4 tree **5** shrub
genus: 4 Ilex

holocaust

4 fire **7** inferno **8** genocide **9** sacrifice **10** mass murder **11** destruction
13 conflagration

Holofernes' slayer
6 Judith

holy
6 adored, divine, sacred 7 angelic, blessed, revered, sainted, saintly, sublime 8 hallowed 9 glorified, religious, spiritual, venerated, worshiped 10 reverenced, sacrosanct, sanctified 11 consecrated
combining form: 5 hagio, hiero
communion: 9 Eucharist
oil: 6 chrism
person: 5 saint 6 zaddik 7 tzaddik
Spirit: 9 Paraclete
vessel: 5 grail 7 chalice 8 ciborium

holy place
6 church, shrine, temple 7 sanctum 9 sanctuary

Holy Roman Emperor
4 Karl, Otto 5 Adolf, Franz, Henry, Louis 6 Albert, Arnulf, Conrad, Joseph, Lothar, Ludwig, Philip, Rudolf, Rupert, Wenzel 7 Charles, Francis, Leopold, Lothair 8 Heinrich 9 Ferdinand, Frederick, Friedrich, Sigismund 10 Maximilian 11 Charlemagne

Holy Thursday
6 Maundy (Thursday) 9 Ascension (Day)

holy writ
5 Bible 9 Scripture

homage
5 honor 6 praise 7 respect, tribute 9 deference, obeisance, reverence

hombre
3 cat, guy, lad, man 4 buck, chap, dude, gent, stud 6 fellow, honcho 7 comrade

home
4 digs, land, site 5 abode, haunt, house, range 6 family, hearth 7 country, habitat, housing 8 domicile, dwelling, locality 9 household, residence 10 fatherland, habitation, motherland 12 headquarters
country: 5 cabin 7 cottage 8 bungalow

homeless
5 stray 6 exiled 7 outcast, vagrant 8 derelict 9 abandoned, displaced, wandering 12 dispossessed

homely
4 cozy 5 plain 6 direct, modest, simple 7 natural 8 familiar, ordinary 11 comfortable, commonplace 12 unattractive 13 unpretentious

Homer epic
5 Iliad 7 Odyssey

homesickness
7 longing 9 nostalgia

homespun
5 plain 6 fabric, folksy, simple 8 ordinary 9 practical 13 unpretentious

Home, Sweet Home
music: 6 Bishop (Henry)
words: 5 Payne (John Howard)

homicidal
6 bloody 8 sanguine 9 murdering, murderous 10 sanguinary 11 sanguineous 12 bloodthirsty

homicide
5 blood 6 killer, murder, slayer 7 killing 8 foul play, murderer 9 manslayer 12 manslaughter

homily
6 sermon 7 lecture 9 discourse

homogeneous
7 uniform 10 consistent

Homo sapiens
3 man 7 mankind 8 humanity 9 humankind, human race

homunculus
5 dwarf, pygmy 6 midget, peewee 7 manikin 8 Tom Thumb

honcho
4 boss, head 5 chief 6 leader, master 7 big shot, foreman, headman 8 hierarch, overseer 9 chieftain

Honduras
capital: 11 Tegucigalpa
city: 7 La Ceiba 9 Choluteca 10 El Progreso 12 San Pedro Sula
coast: 8 Mosquito

discoverer: 8 Columbus (Christopher)
Indian people: 4 Maya 5 Mayan
language: 7 Spanish
monetary unit: 7 lempira
neighbor: 9 Guatemala, Nicaragua 10 El Salvador
river: 4 Coco, Ulúa 5 Aguán 6 Patuca
sea: 9 Caribbean

hone
4 edge, whet 6 finish, polish, refine, smooth 7 perfect, sharpen 9 whetstone

honest
4 fair, just, open, real, true 5 frank, plain 6 candid, simple 7 genuine, sincere, upright 8 innocent, reliable, truthful 9 objective, reputable, unfeigned, veracious 10 creditable, forthright, legitimate, scrupulous 11 respectable 12 praiseworthy 13 conscientious, dispassionate, unimpeachable

honesty
4 herb 5 honor 6 candor, virtue 7 probity 8 fairness, goodness, justness, veracity 9 integrity, rectitude, sincerity 11 uprightness 12 truthfulness

honey
combining form: 4 meli, mell 5 melli
drink: 4 mead

honeybee genus
4 Apis

honeycomb
3 pit 4 fill, fret 5 cells 6 impair, infest, riddle, weaken 7 subvert 9 perforate

honeydew
5 melon

honeyed
5 sweet 6 golden, liquid, mellow 9 sweetened 10 flattering 11 mellifluous

honeysuckle
6 azalea 9 columbine 13 pinxter flower

honk
4 blow, toot 5 blare, blast 7 trumpet

honky-tonk
4 dive 5 joint 7 hangout 9 juke joint, roadhouse 11 barrelhouse

honor
4 fete, laud 5 adorn, asset, award, badge, exalt, glory, kudos, medal 6 credit, esteem, homage, praise, purity, regard, trophy 7 commend, dignify, ennoble, fulfill, glorify, laurels, respect 8 accolade, approval, carry out, chastity, decorate, devotion, good name 9 adulation, deference, integrity, privilege, recognize, reverence 10 admiration, decoration, reputation, veneration 11 distinction, distinguish, recognition 12 commendation

honorable
4 just, true 5 moral, right 6 honest, worthy 7 ethical, upright 8 laudable 9 dignified 10 creditable, scrupulous 11 illustrious 13 conscientious

honorarium
7 payment 8 gratuity 10 recompense 12 compensation 13 consideration

hooch
6 liquor, rotgut 7 bootleg 8 dwelling, home brew 9 firewater, moonshine 10 bathtub gin

hood
4 cowl, thug 5 tough 6 bonnet, helmet 7 capuche 8 covering, gangster, hooligan 10 delinquent

hoodlum
4 punk, thug 5 bully 7 mobster, ruffian 8 criminal, gangster, hooligan 10 delinquent

hoodoo
3 hex 4 jinx, juju, rock 5 curse, haunt, hokum, magic, spell, spook 6 harass, voodoo, whammy 7 bewitch, evil eye, sorcery, terrify, torment 8 nonsense 9 conjuring 10 black magic, hocus-pocus, mumbo jumbo, witchcraft

hoodwink
3 con **4** dupe, fool, gull, hoax **5** trick
6 befool **7** deceive, mislead **8** flimflam **9** bamboozle

hooey
3 rot **4** bunk **5** bilge **6** bunkum
7 baloney, hogwash **8** claptrap,
malarkey, nonsense

hoof
4 foot, walk **5** troop **7** traipse **8** ambulate
cloven: 5 cloot

hoofer
6 dancer **7** danseur **8** coryphée,
danseuse **9** ballerina, tap dancer

hooflike
6 ungual

hook
3 nab, nip **4** gore, hasp **5** catch,
curve, hitch, pinch, steal **6** anchor,
fasten, pilfer **7** hamulus **8** crotchet
a fish: 4 gaff, snag
for keys: 10 chatelaine

hooklike
7 falcate **8** unciform, uncinate
part: 5 uncus **7** hamulus

hookup
7 circuit, linkage **8** alliance **10** assemblage, connection **11** affiliation,
association, combination, conjunction, partnership

hooky
6 truant **7** truancy **8** truantry

hooligan
see hoodlum

hoop
4 band, ring **6** circle **7** circlet

hoopla
4 bash, fuss, stir, to-do **6** bustle,
frolic **7** revelry, shindig, whoopee
8 ballyhoo, wingding **9** commotion,
festivity, merriment, promotion
13 entertainment

hoops
5 b-ball **10** basketball

hooray
3 rah, yay **5** cheer, huzza **6** huzzah,
yippee **7** acclaim **10** hallelujah

hoosegow
3 jug, pen **4** brig, cage, coop, jail,
keep, stir **5** clink, pokey **6** cooler,
lockup, prison **7** slammer **8** bastille,
big house **9** calaboose, jailhouse
12 penitentiary

Hoosier State
7 Indiana

hoot
3 bit, boo, jot **4** hiss, iota, jeer,
whit **5** laugh, scrap, shout, whoop
6 assail, deride, heckle **7** catcall,
modicum **8** particle

hooter
3 owl **5** owlet

Hoover Dam lake
4 Mead

hop
4 jump, leap, trip, vine **5** bound,
dance **6** bounce, spring, wait on
7 rebound **8** jump over

hope
4 goal, wish **5** await, dream, faith,
trust **6** aspire, desire, expect **7** count
on, longing, promise **8** ambition,
optimism, prospect **9** count upon
10 anticipate, aspiration, confidence
loss of: 7 despair

hopeful
4 rosy **5** eager, sunny **6** bright,
cheery, golden, seeker, upbeat
7 assured **8** aspirant, aspiring
9 candidate, confident, expectant,
promising **10** auspicious, contestant,
optimistic, propitious **11** encouraging
12 advantageous

hopeless
4 glum, lost, vain **6** futile, gloomy,
morose **7** forlorn **8** downcast
9 desperate, incurable, insoluble
10 despairing, despondent, impossible **11** ineffectual, irreparable,
pessimistic **12** incorrigible, irredeemable, irremediable

hoper
7 truster 8 optimist 9 expectant, Pollyanna

hopped-up
4 high 5 giddy 6 stoned, zonked 7 drugged, excited 9 delirious 12 enthusiastic

hopper
3 box, mix 4 frog, hare, tank, toad 5 bunny, chute 6 rabbit 7 cricket 10 freight car, receptacle

_____ Hopper
5 Grace (Murray), Hedda 6 Edward

hopping
4 busy 5 irate, livid 6 lively 7 furious 9 extremely, violently 10 infuriated

Horae
4 Dike 6 Eirene 7 Eunomia, seasons

Horam
kingdom: 5 Gezer
slayer: 6 Joshua

horde
3 mob 4 army 5 crowd, crush, drove, press, swarm 6 throng 9 multitude

horizon
4 goal 5 limit, range, reach, scope, vista 6 extent 7 purview, skyline 8 prospect 11 perspective

horizontal
4 flat 5 level 8 parallel

hormone
4 ACTH 5 kinin 6 estrin 7 estriol, estrone, gastrin, insulin, relaxin 8 autacoid, estrogen, glucagon, kallidin, secretin
female: 8 estrogen
insect: 8 ecdysone
pituitary: 8 oxytocin

horn
4 toot 5 cornu 6 antler, klaxon, shofar 7 trumpet 10 cornucopia, projection
ancient Greek: 5 rhyta (plural) 6 rhyton
animal: 6 antler

_____ Hornblower
7 Horatio

horn in
6 meddle 7 intrude, obtrude 9 insinuate, interfere, interlope, interrupt

hornlike
8 corneous 10 keratinous

hornswoggle
3 con 4 dupe, fool, gull, hoax 5 trick 7 deceive 8 flimflam, hoodwink 9 bamboozle

horrendous
5 awful 7 fearful, ghastly, heinous, hideous 8 alarming, dreadful, gruesome, horrible, horrific, shocking, terrible 9 abhorrent, appalling, execrable, frightful, repugnant, revolting 11 distressing, unspeakable

horrible
4 grim 5 awful, lurid 6 grisly 7 fearful, ghastly, hateful, hellish, hideous 8 dreadful, gruesome, shocking 9 abhorrent, appalling, frightful, loathsome, repellent, repugnant, repulsive, revolting 10 abominable, disgusting, terrifying

horrid
5 nasty 7 noisome 8 shocking 9 loathsome, offensive, repulsive, sickening 10 detestable, disgusting

horrific
5 awful 7 fearful 8 dreadful, shocking, terrible 9 appalling, dismaying, frightful, harrowing

horrify
5 daunt, shock 6 appall, dismay 7 disgust

horrifying
4 grim 5 awful, lurid 6 grisly 7 ghastly, hideous 8 gruesome, terrible 9 appalling, atrocious

horror
4 fear, hate, pain 5 alarm, dread, panic, shock 6 dismay, fright, hatred,

hors d'oeuvre

terror 7 disgust 8 aversion, loathing
9 repulsion, revulsion 10 abhorrence, repugnance 11 abomination,
detestation, trepidation

hors d'oeuvre

4 whet 6 canape 7 crudité 9 antipasto, appetizer

horse

4 buck, roan 5 bronc, pacer, steed
6 bronco, brumby, equine 7 cavalry,
palfrey, sawbuck, trestle, trotter
8 footrope, jackstay, palomino,
skewbald, stallion, traveler
Australian-bred: 5 waler
battle: 7 charger
breed: 5 pinto 6 Morgan 7 Arabian,
Belgian, Iceland 8 Palomino, Shetland 9 Appaloosa, Percheron
10 Lippizaner 12 standardbred,
Thoroughbred
champion: 7 Man o' War 8 Affirmed, Citation 10 Seabiscuit
11 Seattle Slew, Secretariat, Smarty
Jones
collar part: 4 hame
color: 3 bay 6 sorrel 8 chestnut
combining form: 4 hipp 5 hippo
covering: 8 trapping
draft: 10 Clydesdale
extinct: 8 eohippus
farm: 6 dobbin
female: 4 mare 5 filly
foot part: 7 pastern
gait: 4 trot 6 canter, gallop
gear: 3 bit 4 rein 6 saddle 7 harness 9 checkrein
leg joint: 7 fetlock
leg part: 6 gaskin 7 gambrel
male: 4 colt 8 stallion
mark: 5 blaze
of the movies: 4 Fury 6 Flicka,
Silver 7 Trigger 8 Champion
11 Black Beauty
race: 5 Ascot, derby 7 Belmont
9 Preakness
rump: 7 crupper
small: 4 pony 6 garron, jennet
spotted: 5 pinto 7 piebald
tan: 8 palomino
thoroughbred: 8 hotblood
war: 8 destrier
wild: 7 mustang

horsefeathers

3 rot 4 bull, bunk 5 bilge, hokum,
hooey, trash 6 bunkum, drivel, piffle
7 baloney, garbage, hogwash,
rubbish, twaddle 8 claptrap, flimflam,
nonsense, tommyrot 9 poppycock
10 applesauce, balderdash

horseman

5 rider 6 cowboy 7 vaquero 8 cavalier 9 caballero, chevalier 10 equestrian

horsemanship

6 manège 10 equitation

horse opera

5 oater 7 western

horseplay

7 fooling 8 clowning, rowdyism
9 high jinks, rowdiness 10 buffoon-
ery, roughhouse 11 shenanigans
12 roughhousing

horseshoer

6 smithy 10 blacksmith

hortative

8 advisory 9 exhorting, homiletic

horticulturist

7 Burbank (Luther)

Horus

brother: 6 Anubis
father: 6 Osiris
mother: 4 Isis
victim: 3 Set 4 Seth

hose

4 sock, tube, wash 5 cheat, spray,
trick, water 6 tights 8 stocking

hoser

6 barfly, boozer 7 redneck

hospice

see **hostel**

hospitable

4 kind, open 6 social 7 cordial
8 friendly, generous, gracious
9 convivial, receptive, welcoming
10 gregarious

hospital

6 clinic 7 lazaret 9 infirmary, lazaretto
attendant: 7 orderly
ship's: 7 sickbay

Hospitallers' island
5 Malta 6 Rhodes

host
4 army 5 array, cloud, crowd, emcee, flock, horde 6 angels, legion, myriad, scores, server 7 present, receive 8 assemble 9 innkeeper, introduce, moderator, multitude, presenter

hostage
4 pawn 5 token 6 pledge, surety 7 captive, earnest 8 guaranty, prisoner, security 9 guarantee

hostel
3 inn 4 stay 5 lodge 6 tavern, travel 7 auberge, lodging 11 caravansary, public house

hostile
4 anti, mean 5 enemy 6 bitter, fierce 7 adverse, opposed, warlike 8 contrary, inimical, opposite 9 bellicose, combative, resistant, resisting 10 malevolent, pugnacious, unfriendly 11 belligerent, contentious 12 antagonistic 13 argumentative

hostility
3 war 6 animus, enmity, hatred, rancor 7 ill will 8 conflict 9 antipathy 10 aggression, antagonism, opposition, resistance 12 belligerence

hot
3 new 4 fast, heat, sexy 5 angry, close, eager, fiery, lucky, spicy 6 ardent, baking, banned, heated, hectic, on fire, raging, stolen, sultry, torrid, urgent 7 boiling, burning, excited, fevered, illicit, lustful, peppery, popular, pungent, zealous 8 broiling, feverish, in demand, scalding, sizzling, tropical, vehement 9 energized, lecherous, scorching 10 blistering, contraband, passionate, sweltering 11 radioactive

hot air
4 bosh 6 bunkum 7 blather, prattle, twaddle 8 malarkey, nonsense 9 empty talk, poppycock 10 double-talk

hotbed
3 hub 4 core, seat 5 heart 6 center 7 nucleus 10 focal point 11 nerve center

hot-blooded
5 fiery 6 ardent 7 burning, fervent, flaming 9 excitable, impetuous, impulsive 10 passionate 11 impassioned 12 high-spirited

hotchpotch
see **hodgepodge**

hot dog
5 frank 6 weenie, wiener, wienie 7 sausage, show-off 11 frankfurter, wienerwurst

hotel
3 inn 5 lodge 6 tavern 7 auberge, hospice, pension 8 motor inn 11 public house 12 lodging house, rooming house 13 boardinghouse
chain: 5 Hyatt 6 Hilton, Ramada, Westin 7 Days Inn 8 Marriott, Radisson, Sheraton, Stouffer 10 Holiday Inn 11 Best Western, Four Seasons
inferior: 7 fleabag 9 flophouse

hothead
5 rebel 7 fanatic, inciter, radical 8 agitator 9 demagogue, firebrand 10 incendiary 12 rabble-rouser, troublemaker 13 revolutionary

hotheaded
4 rash 5 brash, fiery, hasty 6 madcap 8 reckless 9 excitable, impetuous, imprudent, impulsive, irritable

hotshot
3 ace 4 star, whiz 5 comer 6 expert, master, wizard 8 virtuoso 10 powerhouse 11 heavyweight

hot-tempered
see **quick-tempered**

hot water
3 box, fix, jam 4 bind, hole 6 corner, pickle 7 dilemma, problem, trouble 9 tight spot 10 difficulty 11 predicament

_____ Houdini
5 Harry

hound

3 dog, fan **4** bait, buff, ride **5** chivy **6** badger, basset, beagle, bowwow, canine, harass, hassle, heckle, hector, pester, pursue, Talbot **7** devotee **8** bullyrag **9** dachshund, persecute **10** aficionado
Russian: 6 borzoi

hourglass

5 timer

house

3 cot, hut, ken **4** home, shed **5** abode, board, cabin, dwell, hovel, lodge, put up, shack **6** billet, chalet, harbor, shanty **7** contain, cottage, enclose, mansion, quarter, saltbox, shelter, theater **8** audience, bungalow, domicile, dwelling, quarters **9** residence
clergyman's: 5 manse **7** rectory **9** parsonage
country: 5 manor **7** cottage **8** bungalow
dog: 6 kennel
earth: 5 adobe
Eskimo: 5 igloo
mean: 5 hovel, shack
of prostitution: 4 crib **6** bagnio **7** brothel **8** bordello
religious: 5 abbey **6** priory **7** convent, nunnery **9** monastery
rooming: 5 lodge
Russian: 5 dacha
small: 4 camp **5** cabin, shack **6** shanty **7** cottage **8** bungalow
Spanish: 4 casa

housebreaker

4 yegg **5** thief **7** burglar, prowler **8** picklock

household

4 home **5** folks **6** family, ménage **8** domestic, familiar
gods (Roman): 5 lares **7** penates

house of worship

6 bethel, chapel, church, mosque, pagoda, shrine, temple **7** chantry, minster, oratory **8** basilica **9** cathedral, sanctuary, synagogue **10** tabernacle **11** conventicle

housing

4 case, room **7** shelter **8** barracks, quarters **9** enclosure

hovel

3 hut, sty **4** dump, shed **5** hutch, shack **6** burrow, pigpen, pigsty, shanty **7** shelter

hover

4 flit, hang **5** dance, drift, float, poise, waver **7** flitter, flutter, suspend **9** fluctuate, hang about

howbeit

3 yet **4** when **5** still, while **6** even if, much as, though **7** whereas **8** after all, although **11** nonetheless **12** nevertheless

however

3 but, yet **4** only **5** still **6** except, though **8** after all **11** nonetheless

howl

3 bay, cry **4** bark, keen, wail, yell, yelp **6** cry out **9** caterwaul

howler

4 flub, gaff, goof **5** boner, fluff, gaffe **6** boo-boo **7** blooper, blunder

huarache

6 sandal

hub

4 axis, core **5** focus, heart, pivot **6** center **8** polestar **10** focal point **11** nerve center
opposite: 3 rim

hubbub

3 din **4** fuss, stir, to-do **5** babel, furor, hoo-ha, noise **6** clamor, furore, hassle, jangle, pother, racket, rumpus, tumult, uproar **7** turmoil **8** brouhaha, foofaraw **9** commotion, confusion **10** hullabaloo, hurly-burly **11** disturbance, pandemonium

hubris

3 ego **4** gall **5** brass, cheek, nerve, pride **7** conceit, hauteur, swagger **8** audacity, chutzpah **9** arrogance, cockiness, vainglory **11** braggadocio

hubristic

4 vain **5** cocky, proud **7** haughty

8 arrogant, insolent, superior **11** overbearing, overweening **13** overconfident

Huckleberry Finn
   author: **5** Twain (Mark) **7** Clemens (Samuel)
   character: **3** Jim, Tom (Sawyer)
   4 Duke, King
   river: **11** Mississippi

huckster
   4 hawk, plug, vend **5** pitch **6** dicker, haggle, hawker, peddle, vendor **7** bargain, chaffer, haggler, packman, peddler, promote **8** pitchman

huddle
   4 lump, mass **5** bunch, crowd, group, hunch **6** confab, confer, crouch, curl up, gather, parley, powwow **7** cluster, consult, meeting **8** assemble **10** conference, discussion

Hudson's ship
   8 Half Moon

hue
   4 cast, tint, tone **5** color, shade, shape, tinge, value **6** aspect, manner **8** coloring, tincture **10** coloration, complexion

huff
   3 pet **4** blow, gasp, pant, rile, roil, snap, snit, tiff **5** annoy, grate, heave, peeve, pique, storm **6** nettle, put out **7** bluster, inflate **8** irritate

huffy
   5 angry, proud, testy **6** piqued, touchy **7** annoyed, fretful, haughty, peevish, prickly, waspish **8** arrogant, petulant, snappish **9** irritable, irritated, querulous

hug
   4 hold **5** clasp, press, prize, value **6** clinch, clutch, cuddle, enfold **7** cherish, embrace, envelop, squeeze **8** hold fast, hold onto **12** congratulate

huge
   4 vast, wide **5** bulky, giant, grand, great, jumbo **6** heroic, mighty, untold **7** immense, mammoth, massive, titanic **8** colossal, enormous, gigantic, whopping **9** extensive, monstrous **10** monumental, prodigious, stupendous, tremendous **11** magnificent, mountainous

hugeness
   8 enormity **9** immensity, magnitude

hugger-mugger
   4 hash **6** jumble, muddle, secret, tangle **7** clutter, furtive, jumbled, secrecy **8** confused, covertly, disorder, secretly **9** by stealth, confusion, furtively **10** disordered, disorderly, stealthily, undercover **11** clandestine **13** clandestinely

Hugo, Victor
   character: **6** Javert (Inspector) **7** Cosette, Fantine, Valjean (Jean) **9** Esmeralda, Quasimodo
   novel: **13** Les Misérables **20** Hunchback of Notre Dame (The)

Huguenot
   10 Protestant
   leader: **5** Condé (Prince de), Rohan (Henri) **6** Mornay (Philippe) **7** Coligny (Gaspard II de)

Huguenots composer
   9 Meyerbeer (Giacomo)

hulk
   4 body, loom, ship **5** shell, wreck **8** skeleton **9** shipwreck

hulking
   4 huge **5** beefy, bulky, burly, husky **7** immense, mammoth, massive **8** colossal, enormous, gigantic, oversize **9** humongous, lumbering, monstrous, ponderous, strapping **11** heavyweight

hull
   3 pod **4** bark, body, case, husk, peel, rind, skin **5** chaff, frame, shell, shuck **6** casing **8** covering **11** decorticate

hullabaloo
   3 din **4** to-do **5** hoo-ha, noise **6** clamor, hubbub, jangle, pother, racket, tumult, uproar **8** ballyhoo, foofaraw **9** commotion, hue and cry **11** pandemonium

hum
4 buzz, purr, sing, zing 5 drone
6 murmur 7 vibrate

human
5 being, party 6 mortal, person
7 hominid 8 hominoid 10 individual
race: 7 mankind

Human Comedy author
6 Balzac (Honoré de) 7 Saroyan
(William)

humane
4 kind 6 gentle, kindly, tender
8 merciful 10 altruistic, benevolent,
charitable 11 considerate, kindhearted, soft-hearted, sympathetic,
warmhearted 13 compassionate,
philanthropic

humanitarian
5 giver 8 generous 10 altruistic,
benefactor, beneficent, benevolent,
charitable 13 compassionate,
philanthropic

humanity
6 people 7 mankind 8 kindness,
sympathy 10 compassion, generosity 11 benevolence, Homo sapiens

humble
3 low 4 meek 5 abash, crush, lowly,
quiet 6 demean, modest, simple
7 chagrin, deflate, degrade, subdued
8 cast down, disgrace, ordinary
9 compliant, diffident, discomfit,
embarrass, humiliate 10 submissive,
unassuming 11 acquiescent, deferential 13 insignificant, unpretentious

humbug
3 con, rot 4 fake, fool, hoax, sham
5 faker, fraud, hokum, phony, spoof,
trick 6 bunkum, delude, drivel, take
in 7 beguile, deceive, mislead
8 flimflam, impostor, malarkey,
nonsense, pretense, quackery
9 deception, hypocrite, imposture,
pretender, trickster 10 balderdash

humdinger
3 gem 5 beaut, dandy, dilly, doozy,
jewel, prize 6 doozie 8 jim-dandy
11 crackerjack

humdrum
4 blah, dull, flat 6 boring, dreary,
stodgy 7 prosaic, tedious 8 monotone, monotony, plodding, unvaried,
workaday 10 monotonous, uneventful 13 uninteresting

humid
3 wet 4 damp, dank 5 close, moist,
muggy, soggy 6 clammy, sodden,
steamy, sticky, stuffy 10 oppressive

humidify
6 dampen 7 moisten

humiliate
5 abase, crush, lower, shame 6 be-
mean, debase, demean, humble
7 chagrin, degrade, mortify 8 belittle,
cast down, disgrace 9 embarrass

humiliation
5 shame 7 chagrin, put-down
8 disgrace, ignominy, reproach
9 abasement, disrepute, indignity
11 degradation 13 embarrassment,
mortification

humility
7 modesty, shyness 8 meekness
9 abasement, lowliness 10 diffidence, submission 12 subservience
13 self-abasement

humming
4 busy 5 brisk 6 active, lively
8 bustling, hustling 9 energetic

hummock
4 hump 5 couch, knoll, mound 7 hillock

humongous
4 huge, vast 5 giant, jumbo 7 immense, mammoth, massive, titanic
8 colossal, enormous, gigantic
9 monstrous 10 gargantuan, prodigious, tremendous

humor
3 wit 4 baby, bent, mind, mood,
tone, vein, whim 5 fancy, fluid, spoil,
yield 6 banter, coddle, comedy,
cosset, esprit, joking, levity, nature,
pamper, temper 7 caprice, cater to,
conceit, gratify, indulge, jesting,
kidding 8 crotchet, drollery, jocosity,

repartee 9 character, drollness, flippancy, funniness, witticism, wittiness 10 complexion, jocularity, pleasantry 11 disposition, temperament

humorist
3 Ade (George), wag, wit 4 card, Nash (Ogden), Shaw (Henry Wheeler), Ward (Artemus, Edward) 5 Adams (Franklin Pierce), Allen (Fred), Barry (Dave), clown, comic, cutup, droll, Dunne (Finley Peter), joker, Twain (Mark), White (E. B.) 6 Blount (Roy), Browne (Charles Farrar), Diller (Phyllis), gagman, jester, kidder, Parker (Dorothy), Rogers (Will), Rourke (P. J.), Runyon (Damon), Thorpe (Thomas Bangs) 7 buffoon, Bombeck (Erma), Burgess (Gelett), Clemens (Samuel Langhorne), gagster, Hubbard (Kin), Keillor (Garrison), Marquis (Don), punster, Sedaris (David), Thurber (James), Trillin (Calvin) 8 Aleichem (Shalom), Benchley (Robert), comedian, funnyman, jokester, Perelman (S. J.), quipster 9 jokesmith, prankster, Wodehouse (P. G.)
Canadian: 7 Leacock (Stephen)

humorous
5 comic, droll, funny, jokey, merry, witty 6 jocose 7 amusing, comical, jocular, risible, waggish 8 mirthful 9 facetious, laughable, whimsical

hump
3 lug 4 bump, race, tote 5 bulge, carry, hunch, mound, range 6 hustle, schlep 7 hummock, schlepp 8 mountain, obstacle, swelling 9 transport 10 protrusion

humpback
5 whale 8 kyphosis 10 pink salmon

humpbacked
6 convex, curved 7 gibbous

Humperdinck opera
15 Hansel and Gretel

humus
3 mor 4 mull, soil 7 compost 8 material

hunch
4 arch, clod, idea, lump, hump, push 5 chunk, clump, crook, squat, stoop 6 crouch, curl up, huddle, jostle, notion, nugget 7 feeling, inkling 9 intuition

Hunchback of Notre Dame
author: 4 Hugo (Victor)
character: 9 Esmeralda, Quasimodo

hundred
combining form: 5 centi, hecto

Hungary
capital: 8 Budapest
city: 4 Pécs 6 Szeged 7 Miskolc 8 Debrecen
ethnic group: 6 Magyar
lake: 7 Balaton
monetary unit: 6 forint
mountain range: 10 Carpathian
national hero: 5 Árpád
neighbor: 6 Serbia 7 Austria, Croatia, Romania, Ukraine 8 Slovakia, Slovenia
plain: 11 Great Alföld
river: 5 Tisza 6 Danube

hunger
3 yen 4 ache, itch, long, lust, need, pine, want 5 crave, greed, yearn 6 desire, hanker, thirst 7 craving, longing

hungry
4 avid, keen, poor 5 eager 6 barren 7 craving, starved, thirsty 8 desirous, famished, ravenous, starving, underfed, yearning 9 hankering, motivated

hunk
3 gob, wad 4 clod, lump 5 chunk, clump, piece, wedge 6 nugget 7 portion

hunker down
5 dig in, squat 6 crouch 8 settle in

hunky
4 buff 5 burly 6 buffed 8 athletic, muscular 9 strapping, well-built

hunky-dory
4 fine, okay 5 dandy, ducky, nifty, swell 6 peachy 10 peachy keen 12 satisfactory

Hunnish
4 rude, wild 6 savage 7 fearful, uncivil 9 barbarian, barbarous, ferocious 11 uncivilized

hunt
3 dog, run 4 hawk, seek 5 chase, hound, prowl, quest, shoot, snare, stalk, track, trail 6 battue, course, dig out, prey on, pursue, safari, search 7 explore, pursuit, rummage 9 ferret out, search for, search out
birds: 4 fowl
illegally: 5 poach

hunter
6 jaeger, nimrod 8 predator
biblical: 6 Nimrod
cap: 7 montero
constellation: 5 Orion
mythological: 5 Orion 7 Actaeon

hunting
5 chase 6 venery 7 gunning, hawking 8 coursing, falconry 9 predatory 10 predacious
bird: 6 falcon
call: 7 recheat
cry: 6 yoicks 7 tallyho 10 view halloo
dog: 5 hound 6 basset, beagle, borzoi, saluki, setter, vizsla 7 harrier, pointer, spaniel 9 ridgeback, wolfhound 10 bloodhound
expedition: 6 safari
horn: 5 bugle

huntress
5 Diana 7 Artemis 8 Atalanta

hurdle
3 bar 4 leap, snag 5 bound, clear, vault 6 hamper, spring 7 barrier 8 leap over, obstacle, overcome, overleap, surmount, traverse 9 negotiate 10 difficulty, impediment 11 obstruction

hurl
4 cast, fire 5 chuck, fling, heave, pitch, sling, throw, vomit 6 launch, thrust 8 catapult

hurly-burly
3 din 4 riot, to-do 5 melee 6 clamor, furore, hassle, hubbub, racket, rumpus, tumult, uproar 7 turmoil 8 confused 9 commotion, confusion

hurrah
4 fuss, to-do, zeal 5 cheer 6 fervor, rumpus 7 fanfare, ovation 8 approval 9 commotion 10 enthusiasm 11 acclamation

hurricane
7 typhoon

hurried
4 fast, sped 5 hasty, quick, swift 6 abrupt, rushed, sudden 7 cursory, rushing 8 headlong 9 impetuous 11 precipitant, precipitate

hurry
3 fly, hie, jog, run, zip 4 post, prod, push, rush 5 fleet, haste, scoot, speed, whirl, whish, whisk 6 barrel, breeze, bullet, bustle, hasten, hustle, rocket, rustle, step up, tumult 7 beeline, hotfoot, quicken, shake up, skelter, speed up, swiften 8 celerity, dispatch, expedite, highball, make time 9 commotion, make haste, swiftness 10 accelerate, speediness

hurt
3 mar 4 ache, blow, harm, pain 5 wound, wrong 6 damage, grieve, hamper, harmed, impair, injure, injury, in pain, misuse, offend, pained, suffer 7 afflict, anguish, blemish, damaged, wounded 8 aggrieve, distress, mischief, mistreat 9 constrain, detriment, prejudice, resentful, suffering 10 resentment

hurtful
4 mean, sore 6 aching, unkind 7 harmful, painful 8 damaging, wounding 9 injurious 11 deleterious, destructive, detrimental, distressing, prejudicial

hurtle
3 fly 4 race, rush, tear 5 fling, shoot, speed, throw 6 charge, plunge, rocket

husband
3 man 4 mate, save 6 manage,

mister, spouse **7** consort, partner
8 conserve, helpmate, helpmeet
9 economize, other half **10** bridegroom

husbandry
  6 thrift **7** control, economy, farming
  8 prudence **9** frugality **10** management **11** agriculture, thriftiness
  12 conservation, preservation

hush
  4 calm **5** quell, quiet **6** shut up, stifle
  7 cover up, mollify, secrecy, silence
  8 choke off, suppress **9** cessation,
  quietness, stillness

hush-hush
  6 covert, secret **7** private, sub-rosa
  9 top secret **11** clandestine **12** confidential **13** surreptitious, under-the-table

husk
  3 pod **4** case, peel, rind, skin **5** shell,
  shuck, strip **6** casing

husky
  3 big, dog **5** beefy, burly, great,
  hefty, large, rough, stout **6** brawny,
  croaky, hoarse, mighty, robust, strong,
  sturdy **7** throaty **8** muscular, oversize, stalwart, thickset **9** strapping

hustings
  5 stump

hustle
  3 fly, rob, run **4** earn, move, push,
  rush, sell, urge, work **5** cheat,
  elbow, fraud, haste, hurry, press,
  shove, speed **6** hasten **7** hotfoot,
  promote, solicit, swindle **8** bulldoze,
  deception, dispatch **9** swiftness

hustler
  4 doer **6** dynamo, vendor **8** go-getter, live wire **10** powerhouse

hustling
  4 busy **5** eager **6** active, lively,
  speedy **7** hopping, humming **9** energetic **10** aggressive

hut
  3 cot **4** camp, crib, shed **5** cabin,
  dacha, hooch, hovel, hutch, jacal,

lodge, roost, shack **6** cabana,
chalet, lean-to, shanty **7** cottage
8 bungalow
  American Indian: 6 wigwam
  7 wickiup
  Scottish: 5 bothy, shiel **8** shieling

hutch
  3 bin, pen **4** cage, coop **5** chest,
  shack, locker, shanty **8** cupboard
  9 enclosure

Huxley novel
  8 Antic Hay **11** Crome Yellow
  13 Brave New World, Eyeless in
  Gaza

Hyacinthus
  father: 7 Amyclas
  slayer: 6 Apollo

hybrid
  5 blend, cross, mixed **7** amalgam,
  mixture **8** combined, compound
  9 composite, crossbred **10** crossbreed **11** combination

hybridize
  4 join **5** blend, cross **7** combine
  10 crossbreed, interbreed, intercross

Hydra
  5 polyp **6** plague **7** monster, serpent
  13 constellation
  father: 6 Typhon
  mother: 7 Echidna
  slayer: 8 Heracles, Hercules

hydrant
  3 tap **4** pipe **5** valve **6** faucet,
  spigot **7** petcock **8** fireplug

hydraulic device
  3 ram **4** jack, lift, pump **5** brake,
  press **8** elevator

hydrocarbon
  5 xylol **6** dioxin, ethane, xylene
  7 benzene, methane, styrene, toluene **8** biphenyl, butylene, ethylene
  liquid: 6 octane **7** retinol, styrene
  8 menthene

hydroid
  5 polyp **6** medusa, obelia **9** jellyfish

hydrometer scale
  4 Brix **5** Baumé

hydrophobia
5 lyssa 6 rabies

hyena
5 dingo 6 jackal 9 scavenger

Hygeia
5 Salus
father: 9 Asclepius 11 Aesculapius
goddess of: 6 health

hygiene
6 health 10 sanitation 11 cleanliness

hygienic
5 clean 7 aseptic, healthy, sterile
8 sanitary 9 healthful 10 antiseptic, unpolluted

Hyllus' father
8 Heracles, Hercules

hymeneal
6 bridal, wedded 7 marital, married, nuptial, spousal 8 conjugal 9 connubial 11 matrimonial

hymn
4 laud, song 5 bless, carol, chant, extol, paean, psalm 6 anthem, choral, praise 7 chorale, glorify 8 canticle, doxology, eulogize

hype
4 plug, tout 5 boost, thump 7 acclaim, enliven, glorify, promote, puffery, trumpet 8 ballyhoo, increase 9 advertise, excellent, publicity, publicize, stimulate 11 advertising

hyper
4 edgy 5 antsy, jumpy, wired 6 on edge 7 anxious, frantic 8 agitated, frenetic, hopped-up 9 excitable 10 high-strung, overactive 11 overwrought

hyperbole
6 excess 12 embroidering, exaggeration 13 embellishment, overstatement

hypercritical
6 severe 7 carping 8 captious, exacting 10 censorious, nit-picking 12 faultfinding

Hyperion
daughter: 3 Eos 6 Aurora, Selene
father: 6 Uranus
mother: 4 Gaea
son: 6 Helios
wife: 5 Theia

hypnotic
6 opiate, sleepy 8 mesmeric, narcotic, sedative 9 somnolent, soporific 11 mesmerizing, somniferous 12 somnifacient, spellbinding

hypnotize
4 drug 5 charm 6 dazzle, trance 8 enthrall, entrance, overcome 9 captivate, mesmerize, overpower, spellbind

hypocorism
7 pet name 8 nickname 9 sobriquet

hypocrisy
4 cant, sham 6 deceit, humbug 7 falsity, pietism 8 quackery 9 deception, duplicity, phoniness 10 sanctimony 11 insincerity, religiosity

hypocrite
4 fake, sham 5 actor, faker, fraud, phony, poser 6 humbug, poseur 7 bluffer, pietist 8 deceiver, impostor, pharisee 9 charlatan, pretender 10 dissembler 11 masquerader 12 dissimulator

hypocritical
5 false 7 canting 8 affected, specious, two-faced 9 deceitful, insincere, pietistic 10 Janus-faced 11 dissembling, double-faced, duplicitous 12 mealymouthed, pecksniffian 13 sanctimonious

hypothesis
6 belief, theory 7 premise 8 position, supposal 9 condition, inference 10 antecedent, assumption, conjecture 11 explanation, speculation, supposition

hypothetical
7 assumed 8 abstract, academic, supposed 10 assumptive 11 conditional, conjectural, suppositous, theoretical 12 suppositious 13 suppositional

hyrax

4 cony   5 coney   6 dassie, mammal
8 ungulate

hysteria

4 fear   5 craze, furor, mania, panic
6 excess, frenzy   7 madness   8 delirium

hysterical

5 rabid   6 crazed, madcap, raving
7 berserk, frantic   8 agitated, frenzied, neurotic   9 delirious, disturbed, hilarious, impetuous   10 convulsive, distraught, uproarious   11 impassioned, overexcited, overwrought
13 side-splitting

I

Iago
  general: 7 Othello
  victim: 6 Cassio, Emilia 7 Othello
  9 Desdemona
  wife: 6 Emilia

Iapetus
  father: 6 Uranus
  mother: 4 Gaea
  son: 5 Atlas 9 Menoetius 10 Epimetheus, Prometheus
  wife: 7 Clymene

Iasion
  brother: 8 Dardanus
  father: 4 Zeus 7 Jupiter
  lover: 5 Ceres 7 Demeter
  mother: 7 Electra
  son: 6 Plutus

ibex
  4 tahr 8 wild goat
  family: 7 Bovidae
  genus: 5 Capra

Ibhar's father
  5 David

ibis-headed god
  5 Thoth

ibis relative
  5 heron, stork

Ibsen, Henrik
  character: 3 Ase 4 Nora (Helmer)
  5 Brack (Judge), Brand, Hedda
  (Gabler), Helen (Alving), Werle
  (Gergers) 6 Ejlert (Lovberg), Hedvig
  (Ekdal), Jorgen (Tesman), Oswald
  (Alving) 7 Solness (Halvard),
  Solveig, Torvald (Helmer) 8 Peer
  Gynt 9 Stockmann (Thomas)

  country: 6 Norway
  play: 6 Ghosts 8 Peer Gynt, Wild
  Duck (The) 10 Doll's House (A)
  11 Hedda Gabler, Little Eyolf, Rosmersholm 13 Master Builder (The)
  16 Enemy of the People (An)

Icarus' father
  8 Daedalus

ice
  area: 4 rink
  dessert: 6 sorbet 7 sherbet
  floating: 4 berg, floe
  hanging: 6 icicle
  pinnacle: 5 serac

icebox
  6 cooler, fridge 12 refrigerator

ice cream
  7 spumoni, tortoni
  dish: 6 sundae 11 baked Alaska
  drink: 4 soda 6 frappe

iced
  5 glacé 6 glazed 7 chilled

ice field
  4 floe 7 glacier

ice game
  6 hockey 7 curling

ice house
  5 igloo

Iceland
  capital: 9 Reykjavik
  monetary unit: 5 krona
  sea: 9 Norwegian
  snowfield: 11 Vatnajökull
  strait: 7 Denmark
  volcano: 5 Hekla

Icelandic
  epic: **4** Edda, saga
  hero: **5** Njáll **6** Gunnar **7** Grettir

Ichabod Crane's beloved
  7 Katrina

icing
  7 topping **8** frosting

icky
  4 vile **5** awful, gross, nasty **9** loathsome, offensive, repellent, repulsive, revolting, sickening **10** disgusting **11** distasteful

icon
  4 idol, sign **5** image **6** emblem, symbol

iconoclastic
  9 dissident, heretical **10** rebellious, unorthodox **13** nonconformist

icy
  4 cold **5** gelid, polar **6** arctic, chilly, frigid, frosty, steely **7** glacial **8** freezing **11** emotionless, unemotional

Idaho
  capital: **5** Boise
  city: **6** Moscow **9** Pocatello, Twin Falls **10** Idaho Falls **11** Coeur d'Alene
  mountain: **5** Borah (Peak)
  nickname: **3** Gem (State)
  river: **5** Snake **6** Salmon
  state bird: **8** bluebird
  state flower: **7** syringa
  state tree: **9** white pine

Idas
  brother: **7** Lynceus
  father: **8** Aphareus
  slayer: **4** Zeus
  victim: **6** Castor
  wife: **8** Marpessa

idea
  4 whim **5** fancy, guess, motif **6** belief, notion, theory, thesis, vagary **7** caprice, conceit, concept, inkling, meaning, opinion, subject, surmise, thought **8** estimate **9** sentiment, suspicion **10** assumption, brainstorm, conception, conclusion, conjecture, conviction, estimation, hypothesis, impression, perception, reflection **11** abstraction, formulation, supposition

ideal
  4 best, goal **5** model **7** chimera, classic, epitome, paragon, perfect, utopian **8** absolute, ensample, exemplar, flawless, nonesuch, paradigm, standard, ultimate **9** archetype, classical, exemplary, nonpareil **10** archetypal, conceptual, consummate **11** theoretical

idealist
  7 dreamer, quixote, utopian **9** ideologue, visionary

idealistic
  6 dreamy **7** utopian **8** poetical, quixotic, romantic **9** visionary **10** starry-eyed **11** impractical, unrealistic

idealize
  5 deify, exalt, extol **7** elevate, ennoble, glorify, worship **8** venerate

ideate
  5 think **7** imagine **8** conceive, envisage, envision

idée fixe
  5 mania **6** fetish, phobia **7** complex **8** fixation **9** obsession **13** preoccupation

identical
  3 one **4** like, same, very **5** alike, equal, exact **8** selfsame **9** duplicate **10** equivalent, synonymous

identification mark
  4 logo **5** badge, brand, label **6** emblem

identify
  3 tag **4** mark, name, spot **5** brand, place **6** finger, select **7** make out, pick out **8** pinpoint **9** determine, recognize **11** distinguish

identity
  4 name, self **7** oneness **8** sameness, selfhood **9** character **10** congruence, uniformity, uniqueness **11** personality, singularity **13** individuality, particularity

ideological

8 notional 10 conceptual, ideational
11 speculative 13 philosophical

ideologue

8 believer, idealist, partisan, theorist

ideology

3 ism 5 credo, creed 7 beliefs
8 doctrine 10 philosophy, principles

idiocy

7 fatuity 9 cretinism, stupidity 10 imbecility 11 foolishness

idiomatic

7 demotic 8 peculiar 9 dialectal
10 colloquial, vernacular

idiosyncrasy

5 quirk 6 oddity 7 anomaly 11 peculiarity, singularity 12 eccentricity

idiosyncratic

3 odd 5 kooky, queer, weird 6 quirky
7 erratic, oddball, offbeat, unusual
8 peculiar, singular 9 eccentric
11 distinctive

idiot

3 ass 4 dolt, fool, jerk, simp 5 dummy,
dunce, moron, ninny 6 cretin, nitwit,
stupid 7 airhead, dullard, half-wit,
jackass, natural, tomfool 8 dumbbell,
imbecile, numskull 9 ignoramus,
numbskull, simpleton 10 nincompoop

idiotic

5 dopey 6 stupid 7 foolish, moronic
8 ignorant 9 brainless, imbecilic,
senseless

idle

3 bum 4 laze, lazy, loaf, loll, rest,
vain 5 dally, drone, empty, inert,
slack, tarry 6 asleep, dawdle, diddle,
fallow, futile, linger, loiter, lounge,
otiose, unused, vacant 7 aimless,
dormant, passive 8 inactive, indolent, slothful 9 shiftless 10 unoccupied

idleness

4 ease 5 sloth 6 vanity 7 leisure,
loafing 8 lethargy 9 indolence
10 inactivity

idler

3 bum 4 slug 5 drone 6 loafer,
slouch 7 dawdler 8 deadbeat,
fainéant, loiterer, slugabed, sluggard
9 do-nothing, lazybones 11 couch
potato

Idmon

daughter: 7 Arachne
father: 6 Apollo
mother: 6 Cyrene

idol

3 god 4 hero, icon, star 5 deity,
image, totem 6 fetish, minion,
symbol 8 likeness
Chinese: 4 joss

idolatry

7 worship 8 devotion 9 adoration
10 exaltation, veneration 11 deification 13 glorification

idolize

5 adore, deify, exalt 6 revere 7 glorify,
worship 8 venerate

Idomeneo composer

6 Mozart (Wolfgang Amadeus)

idyllic

5 ideal 6 rustic 7 bucolic, halcyon,
perfect, utopian 8 arcadian, heavenly, pastoral, peaceful, romantic
9 idealized, unspoiled 11 picturesque, sentimental

Idylls of the King

author: 8 Tennyson (Alfred)
character: 4 Enid 6 Arthur, Elaine,
Gareth, Merlin, Vivien 7 Geraint,
Lynette 8 Lancelot

iffy

5 dicey, risky 6 chancy, unsure
7 dubious, erratic 8 doubtful 9 uncertain 10 unreliable 12 inconsistent
13 unpredictable

igneous rock

4 lava 5 magma 6 basalt, gabbro
7 diabase, granite 8 porphyry

ignis fatuus

6 mirage 7 chimera 8 delusion,
illusion, phantasm 9 pipe dream
12 will-o'-the-wisp 13 hallucination

ignitable
8 burnable **9** excitable, flammable **10** incendiary **11** combustible, inflammable

ignite
4 fire **5** light, spark **6** excite, kindle **7** inflame **8** enkindle, touch off

ignited
3 lit **5** afire, fiery **6** ablaze, aflame, alight **7** blazing, burning, flaming, flaring **11** conflagrant

ignoble
3 low **4** base, mean, poor, vile **5** lowly **6** abject, coarse, common, scurvy, sordid, vulgar **7** lowborn, servile **8** baseborn, indecent, inferior, plebeian, shameful, unwashed, wretched **10** despicable, inglorious **11** disgraceful **12** contemptible, dishonorable

ignominious
6 odious **8** infamous, shameful **9** degrading **10** despicable, inglorious **11** disgraceful, humiliating, opprobrious **12** contemptible, dishonorable, disreputable **13** discreditable, unrespectable

ignominy
5 odium, shame **6** infamy **7** obloquy, scandal **8** disgrace, dishonor **9** discredit, disesteem, disrepute **10** opprobrium **11** humiliation **13** mortification

ignoramus
4 dolt **5** dummy, dunce, idiot, moron **6** dimwit, nitwit, stupid **7** airhead, dullard, half-wit **8** dumbbell, imbecile, numskull **9** numbskull, simpleton

ignorance
7 naiveté **9** innocence, nescience, stupidity **10** illiteracy, simpleness, simplicity **11** unawareness **12** incognizance

ignorant
5 naive **6** simple **7** unaware **8** nescient, untaught **9** benighted, ingenuous, oblivious, unknowing, unlearned, untutored, unwitting

10 illiterate, uncultured, uneducated, uninformed, unlettered, unschooled **11** incognizant, know-nothing **12** uninstructed **13** unenlightened

ignore
4 omit, snub **5** avoid **6** forget, reject, slight **7** neglect **8** overlook **9** disregard

Igraine
husband: **5** Uther **7** Gorlois
son: **6** Arthur

iguana
5 anole **6** lizard **8** basilisk **10** chuckwalla

ilex
4 maté **5** holly **6** yaupon **7** holm oak **8** inkberry

Iliad
4 epic
author: **5** Homer
character: **4** Ajax **5** Helen, Paris, Priam **6** Aeneas, Hector **8** Achilles, Diomedes, Odysseus **9** Agamemnon, Patroclus
city: **4** Troy

Ilium
4 Troy

ilk
4 kind, sort, type **5** breed, class, genre **6** family, kidney, nature, stripe **7** variety

ill
4 sick **6** ailing, infirm, laid up, malady, peaked, queasy, unwell **7** ailment, disease, trouble, unlucky **8** diseased, disorder, distress, feverish, nauseous, scarcely, sickness, syndrome **9** afflicted, infirmity, nauseated, unhealthy **10** misfortune

ill-adapted
8 unfitted, unsuited **10** unsuitable

ill-advised
4 rash **5** brash, hasty **6** madcap, unwise **7** foolish **8** careless, heedless, reckless **9** foolhardy, impolitic, imprudent **10** incautious, indiscreet, unthinking **11** inexpedient, injudicious, thoughtless

ill at ease

3 shy 4 edgy 6 on edge 7 anxious, awkward, fidgety, nervous 8 insecure, restless 9 unsettled 11 discomfited 12 apprehensive 13 self-conscious, uncomfortable

ill-boding

4 dire 7 baleful, doomful, fateful, ominous, unlucky 8 sinister 10 portentous 11 apocalyptic 12 inauspicious, unpropitious

ill-bred

4 rude 5 crude 7 boorish, loutish, uncivil, uncouth 8 impolite 9 unrefined 10 uncultured, ungracious, unmannered, unmannerly, unpolished 11 uncivilized 12 discourteous

ill-defined

5 faint, fuzzy, vague 7 shadowy 10 indistinct

illegal

3 hot 6 banned 7 bootleg, illicit, lawless 8 criminal, outlawed, unlawful, wrongful 9 felonious, forbidden 10 actionable, prohibited, proscribed, unlicensed 12 illegitimate
act: 5 crime 6 felony
scheme: 4 scam

illegible

8 scrawled 10 unreadable 11 inscrutable

illegitimacy

8 bastardy 11 bar sinister 12 unlawfulness

illegitimate

7 bastard, bootleg, erratic, invalid, lawless, natural 8 criminal, improper, spurious, unlawful 11 misbegotten 12 unauthorized

ill-fated

6 cursed, doomed 7 unhappy, unlucky 8 accursed, luckless, untoward 10 disastrous 11 star-crossed, unfortunate

ill-favored

4 ugly 5 plain 6 homely 12 unattractive

ill-humored

4 dour, sour 5 cross, surly, testy 6 crabby, cranky, crusty, grumpy, morose, ornery, sullen, tetchy, touchy 7 crabbed, grouchy, peevish, prickly 8 choleric, churlish, snappish 9 dyspeptic, irascible, irritable, saturnine, splenetic 12 cantankerous, disagreeable, misanthropic

illiberal

6 biased, narrow 7 bigoted, insular 9 hidebound, parochial, penurious 10 intolerant, prejudiced, provincial 11 reactionary, small-minded 12 conservative, narrow-minded, uncharitable

illicit

7 bootleg, crooked, lawless 8 criminal, unlawful 9 forbidden 10 contraband, prohibited 11 black-market, clandestine 12 unauthorized

illimitable

7 endless 8 infinite, unending 9 boundless 11 measureless

Illinois

capital: 11 Springfield
city: 6 Aurora, Cicero, Joliet, Peoria 7 Chicago 8 Rockford
college, university: 4 Knox 6 DePaul 7 Wheaton 12 Northwestern
nickname: 7 Prairie (State)
river: 6 Wabash
state bird: 8 cardinal
state flower: 6 violet
state tree: 8 white oak

illiterate

6 unread 8 untaught 9 untutored 10 uneducated, unlettered, unschooled

ill-mannered

4 rude 6 coarse 7 boorish, loutish, uncivil, uncouth 8 churlish, impolite 10 ungracious 12 discourteous

ill-natured

4 sour 5 cross, huffy, surly, testy 6 bitchy, crabby, grumpy, ornery, tetchy 7 grouchy, peevish, waspish 8 choleric, churlish, snappish, spiteful 9 dyspeptic, fractious, irascible,

irritable **10** malevolent **11** belligerent, contentious, quarrelsome **12** cantankerous, disagreeable

illness

6 malady **7** ailment, disease, malaise **8** cachexia, disorder, sickness **9** infirmity **10** affliction **13** indisposition

illogical

6 absurd **7** invalid, unsound **8** specious **9** plausible, senseless, sophistic **10** fallacious, irrational, unreasoned **11** nonrational **12** preposterous, unreasonable

ill-starred

6 cursed, doomed, malign **7** fateful, ominous, unhappy, unlucky **8** luckless, untoward **10** disastrous, foreboding, portentous **11** unfavorable, unfortunate, unpromising **12** inauspicious, unpropitious

ill-tempered

4 sour **5** cross, huffy, surly **6** crabby, bitchy, grumpy, ornery, snippy **7** grouchy, peevish, waspish **8** choleric, churlish, petulant, shrewish, snappish, spiteful **9** dyspeptic, fractious, irascible, irritable **11** belligerent, contentious, quarrelsome **12** cantankerous, disagreeable

ill-timed

11 inopportune **12** unseasonable

ill-treat

4 harm, hurt **5** abuse **6** injure, misuse, molest **7** torment **8** aggrieve **10** traumatize

illuminate

5 clear, edify, exalt, gloss, light **6** uplift **7** clarify, clear up, explain, lighten **8** brighten, decorate **9** elucidate, embellish, enlighten, highlight, irradiate, spotlight

illuminati

5 elite **7** clerisy, scholar **8** academic **11** academician **13** intellectuals

illumination

8 lighting
unit of: 3 lux **4** phot **5** lumen **6** candle **7** candela **10** footcandle

illusion

4 myth **5** dream, fancy, ghost **6** facade, mirage **7** chimera, fantasy **8** phantasm, phantasy **9** invention, pipe dream, semblance **11** ignis fatuus **12** will-o'-the-wisp **13** hallucination

illusionist

8 conjurer, magician **9** trickster

illusive

see **illusory**

illusory

4 sham **6** unreal **7** seeming **8** apparent, fanciful **9** deceptive, fictional, imaginary, visionary **10** chimerical, fallacious, fictitious, misleading, ostensible

illustrate

4 mark, show **6** depict, evince, expose, reveal **7** clarify, display, exhibit, explain, picture, portray **8** decorate, describe, evidence, instance, manifest **9** elucidate, epitomize, exemplify **11** demonstrate

illustration

4 case **6** sample **7** diagram, drawing, example, picture, problem **8** instance

illustrative

7 graphic **9** pictorial **10** clarifying **11** descriptive **12** iconographic

illustrator

American: 4 Kent (Rockwell), Pyle (Howard) **5** Abbey (Edwin Austin), Flagg (James Montgomery), Smith (Jessie Willcox), Wyeth (Newell Convers) **6** Gibson (Charles Dana) **7** Burgess (Gelett), Parrish (Maxwell) **8** Rockwell (Norman) **9** Remington (Frederic)
English: 5 Crane (Walter) **6** Morris (William), Potter (Beatrix) **7** Nielsen (Kay), Rackham (Arthur), Tenniel (John) **9** Beardsley (Aubrey), Caldecott (Randolph), du Maurier (George), Greenaway (Kate)
French: 4 Doré (Gustave) **5** Dulac (Edmund)
German: 5 Dürer (Albrecht)

illustrious

5 famed, great, lofty, noted 6 famous
7 eminent, exalted, notable, sublime
8 glorious, renowned, splendid
9 acclaimed, prominent 10 celebrated, preeminent 11 outstanding,
prestigious 13 distinguished

illustriousness

4 fame 5 glory 6 renown 8 eminence, prestige 9 celebrity 10 prominence 11 distinction, preeminence

ill will

5 spite, venom 6 animus, enmity,
malice, rancor, spleen 7 despite,
dislike 8 acrimony, aversion, bad
blood 9 animosity, antipathy, hostility, malignity 10 resentment 11 malevolence 12 spitefulness 13 maliciousness

Ilus

father: 4 Tros
grandson: 5 Priam
mother: 10 Callirrhoë
son: 8 Laomedon

image

4 copy, form, icon, idea, idol 5 equal,
match 6 double, effigy, figure, mirror,
notion, ringer, vision 7 concept,
fantasm, feature, picture 8 likeness,
phantasm, portrait 9 facsimile,
semblance 10 conception, equivalent, impression, reflection, simulacrum 12 illustration
Polynesian: 4 tiki
Semitic: 6 teraph 8 teraphim
(plural)

imaginary

5 ideal 6 made-up, unreal 7 fancied,
fictive 8 abstract, fabulous, fanciful,
illusive, illusory, notional, quixotic
9 dreamlike, fantastic, fictional,
legendary, visionary 10 apocryphal,
chimerical, fictitious, phantasmal
11 make-believe 12 hypothetical,
suppositious

imagination

5 fancy 7 fantasy 8 phantasy
9 invention 10 creativity 11 inspiration 13 inventiveness

imaginative

5 false 7 blue-sky, fictive 8 artistic,
creative, fanciful, original, poetical
9 ingenious, inventive, visionary,
whimsical 11 resourceful 12 enterprising

imagine

5 dream, fancy 6 assume, invent,
make up 7 dream up, feature,
picture, suspect 8 conceive, envisage, envision 9 fabricate, visualize
10 conjecture

imbecile

4 dodo, dolt, dull, fool, jerk 5 dunce,
idiot, moron, ninny 6 cretin, dimwit,
nitwit 7 half-wit, jackass, moronie,
pinhead, tomfool 8 numskull 9 birdbrain, blockhead, numbskull 10 dunderhead, nincompoop

imbibe

3 sip, sup 4 chug, soak, swig, toss
5 booze, drink, quaff, swill 6 absorb,
guzzle, tipple 7 consume, swallow,
swizzle 10 assimilate

imbricate

3 lap 7 overlap, shingle 11 over-
lapping

imbroglio

3 row 4 maze, mess, spat, to-do
5 brawl, mix-up 6 fracas, muddle,
tangle 7 dispute, quarrel, rhubarb,
scandal, wrangle 8 argument,
disorder, squabble 9 confusion,
intricacy 10 falling-out 11 altercation, predicament 12 complication,
entanglement

imbrue

4 soil 5 stain 8 discolor

imbue

3 dye 4 soak 5 bathe, endow,
steep, tinge 6 infuse, invest, leaven
7 ingrain, instill, pervade, suffuse
8 permeate, saturate 9 influence,
inoculate

imitate

3 ape 4 copy, echo, mime, mock
5 forge, mimic, spoof 6 parody
7 emulate, take off 8 resemble,

simulate, travesty **9** burlesque, duplicate, replicate, reproduce **11** counterfeit, impersonate

imitation
4 copy, fake, mock, sham **5** clone, ditto, dummy, false, match, phony **6** ersatz, parody, ringer **7** forgery, replica **8** likeness, parallel, spurious, travesty **9** duplicate, semblance, simulated **10** artificial, simulacrum, simulation, substitute **11** counterfeit, counterpart **12** reproduction, substitution

imitative
4 mock **5** apish **6** echoic **7** copycat, mimetic, parodic, slavish **11** counterfeit **12** onomatopoeic **13** onomatopoetic

immaculate
4 pure **5** clean **6** chaste, virgin **7** cleanly, perfect, sinless **8** flawless, spotless, unsoiled, virtuous **9** stainless, undefiled, unsullied **11** spic-and-span, unblemished **12** spick-and-span

immaterial
7 trivial **8** bodiless, ethereal **10** extraneous, inapposite, intangible, irrelevant **11** disembodied, incorporeal, nonphysical, unimportant **12** inapplicable **13** insignificant, insubstantial, unsubstantial

immature
3 raw **5** crude, green, young **6** callow, infant, unripe **7** puerile **8** childish, juvenile, youthful **9** infantile, primitive, unfledged **10** unfinished **11** undeveloped

immaturity
6 nonage **7** infancy **8** minority **9** childhood, salad days **11** adolescence **12** juvenescence

immeasurable
4 vast **6** untold **7** endless **8** infinite **9** boundless, extensive, limitless, unbounded, unlimited **11** illimitable, inestimable, uncountable **12** incalculable, unfathomable

immediate
4 next, nigh **5** close **6** at hand, direct, nearby, urgent **7** current, instant, ongoing, primary **9** first-hand, proximate **10** unmediated **12** straightaway **13** instantaneous

immediately
3 now, PDQ **4** anon, stat **6** at once, presto, pronto **8** directly, promptly **9** forthwith, instanter, instantly, right away **11** straightway **12** straightaway

immense
4 huge, vast **5** great, large **6** mighty **7** mammoth, massive, titanic **8** colossal, enormous, gigantic **9** humongous, monstrous **10** gargantuan, monumental, prodigious, tremendous **11** elephantine

immensely
4 a lot **8** terribly **9** extremely **11** exceedingly **12** inordinately

immensity
8 enormity, hugeness, vastness **9** greatness **12** enormousness

immerse
3 dip **4** duck, dunk, sink, soak **5** bathe, douse **6** drench, engage, plunge **7** baptize, engross, involve **8** saturate, submerge

immigrant
5 alien **7** settler **8** newcomer **10** transplant
Japanese: 5 issei

imminent
6 at hand **6** coming **7** brewing, nearing, ominous, pending **8** upcoming **9** gathering, proximate **11** approaching, overhanging

immobile
3 set **5** fixed, inert, still **6** frozen, stable, static **9** unmovable **10** motionless, stationary

immobilize
5 still **7** cripple, disable **8** paralyze **9** hamstring **12** incapacitate

immoderate
5 undue **7** extreme **9** excessive

immoderation

10 exorbitant, inordinate, untempered **11** extravagant, intemperate **12** unreasonable, unrestrained **13** extraordinary, overindulgent

immoderation

6 excess **11** exorbitance, prodigality **12** extravagance, intemperance

immodest

4 lewd, vain **7** stuck-up **8** arrogant, boastful, indecent, puffed-up, unchaste **9** conceited, egotistic **11** pretentious

immolate

4 burn, kill **7** destroy **9** sacrifice

immoral

4 evil, vile **5** dirty, wrong **6** sinful, wanton, wicked **7** corrupt, unclean, vicious **8** depraved, indecent, unchaste **9** dissolute, reprobate, uncleanly **10** degenerate, iniquitous, licentious

immorality

3 sin **4** vice **8** iniquity **9** depravity **10** corruption, unchastity, wickedness

immortal

7 endless, eternal, godlike, undying **8** timeless, unending **9** ceaseless, deathless, perpetual **11** amaranthine, everlasting, sempiternal

immotile

5 fixed, inert **6** rooted, static **9** paralyzed **10** stationary

immovable

3 pat, set **4** fast, firm **5** fixed, rigid **6** rooted, stable **7** adamant **8** constant, obdurate, stubborn **9** steadfast **10** inflexible, invariable, stationary, unyielding

immune

4 free, safe **6** exempt, secure **9** protected **10** impervious **12** invulnerable, unassailable

immunity

7 defense, freedom **9** exemption, privilege **10** protection

immure

3 pen **4** cage, coop, jail, wall **6** entomb, intern, shut in **7** confine, enclose **8** imprison **11** incarcerate

immutable

4 firm **5** fixed **8** constant **9** permanent, steadfast **10** changeless, inflexible, invariable, unchanging **11** inalterable, unalterable **12** unchangeable

Imogen

father: **9** Cymbeline
husband: **9** Posthumus

imp

3 elf **4** brat, puck **5** demon, devil, fiend, gamin, gnome, pixie, scamp **6** goblin, kobold, sprite, urchin **7** gremlin **9** hobgoblin

impact

3 hit, jar, rap **4** blow, bump, jolt, rock, slam, slap **5** brunt, embed, pound, punch, shock, smash, smite **6** affect, buffet, strike, wallop **9** collision, influence **10** concussion, percussion

impair

3 mar, sap **4** harm, hurt **5** spoil **6** damage, injure, lessen, weaken, worsen **7** cripple, tarnish, vitiate **8** enfeeble **9** prejudice, undermine **10** debilitate

impala

8 antelope

impale

4 gore, spit, stab **5** lance, prick, spear, spike, stick **6** pierce, skewer **8** puncture, transfix **11** transpierce

impalpable

4 fine **7** powdery **8** ethereal **10** intangible **11** disembodied, incorporeal **12** imponderable **13** imperceptible, indiscernible

impart

4 cede, give, lend, tell **5** grant, share, yield **6** afford, bestow, confer, convey, pass on, relate, render **8** disclose, transmit **11** communicate
knowledge: **5** teach **6** inform **7** educate **8** instruct

impartial
4 even, fair, just 5 equal 7 neutral
8 detached, unbiased 9 equitable,
objective, uncolored 10 evenhanded
12 unprejudiced 13 disinterested,
dispassionate

impassable
6 closed 7 blocked 10 obstructed
12 impenetrable

impasse
3 box, fix, jam 6 aporia, corner,
logjam, pickle, pocket 7 catch-22,
dead end, dilemma 8 cul-de-sac,
deadlock, standoff 9 stalemate
10 blind alley, bottleneck

impassioned
3 hot 5 fiery 6 ardent, fervid, fierce,
heated, red-hot, torrid 7 blazing,
burning, fervent, flaming, intense,
violent, zealous 8 feverish, romantic,
vehement, white-hot 9 emotional,
perfervid 10 hot-blooded, overheated 11 dithyrambic 12 melodramatic 13 overemotional

impassive
4 calm, cold, cool 5 stoic 6 stolid,
vacant 7 deadpan 8 composed,
hardened, reserved, reticent, taciturn
9 heartless 10 insensible, insentient,
phlegmatic, poker-faced 11 cold-
blooded, emotionless, insensitive,
passionless, unconcerned, unemotional, unexcitable, unflappable
12 inexpressive, unexpressive,
unresponsive 13 dispassionate,
self-possessed, unsusceptible

impassivity
6 apathy, phlegm 8 stoicism 9 stolidity 12 indifference 13 insensibility

impatient
4 edgy 5 antsy, eager, hasty 7 anxious, fretful, restive 8 restless
9 irascible, irritable 10 intolerant

impeach
5 blame, doubt 6 accuse, charge,
indict 7 censure 9 inculpate, reprehend 11 incriminate

impeccable
4 pure 5 exact 7 perfect, precise
8 absolute, accurate, flawless, unerring 9 blameless, errorless, faultless,
guiltless 10 infallible 11 unblemished

impecunious
4 poor 5 broke, needy 7 pinched
8 bankrupt, beggarly, indigent 9 destitute, insolvent, penniless, penurious
10 down-and-out 11 necessitous

impecuniousness
4 need, want 6 penury 7 poverty
9 indigence, neediness, pauperism,
privation 11 destitution

impedance
3 bar 4 clog 5 block 8 blockage,
obstacle 9 hindrance 10 opposition
11 obstruction

impede
3 bar, dam 4 clog, slow 5 block,
check, debar, delay, deter, stall
6 hinder, hang up, hold up, stymie,
thwart 7 bog down 8 encumber,
obstruct 9 embarrass, interfere,
stonewall

impediment
3 bar 4 clog, snag 5 block, hitch
6 hurdle 7 barrier 8 obstacle 9 barricade, hindrance, roadblock 10 difficulty 11 encumbrance, obstruction

impel
4 goad, prod, push, spur, urge
5 drive, force, rouse 6 excite, incite,
prompt 7 actuate, inspire 8 mobilize, motivate 9 instigate, stimulate

impend
4 loom, near 6 menace 8 approach,
overhang, threaten

impenetrable
5 dense 6 arcane 7 obscure 9 enigmatic, recondite 10 impervious,
invincible, mysterious, unknowable
11 impermeable, bulletproof, inscrutable, ungraspable 12 unfathomable

imperative
4 duty, need, rule, writ 5 acute, vital

6 crying, urgent 7 burning, clamant, command, crucial, exigent 8 critical, pressing, required 9 clamorous, essential, insistent, mandatory, necessary, necessity, requisite 10 compulsory, obligation, obligatory 11 fundamental, necessitous 12 prerequisite

imperceptible

3 dim 5 faint, vague 6 slight, subtle 7 gradual 9 invisible 10 impalpable, indistinct, insensible, intangible, unapparent 12 undetectable, unnoticeable, unobservable 13 inappreciable, inconspicuous, indiscernible

imperceptive

4 dull 7 shallow, unaware 11 inattentive, insensitive

imperfect

6 faulty, flawed 9 defective, deficient, irregular 10 defeasible, inadequate

imperfection

3 sin 4 flaw, wart 5 fault 6 defect, foible 7 blemish, demerit, failing, frailty 8 weakness 10 deficiency 11 shortcoming

imperial

5 regal, royal 6 kingly, lordly 7 haughty 8 absolute, majestic 9 masterful, sovereign 10 highhanded, peremptory 11 domineering, magisterial, monarchical

imperil

4 risk 6 hazard, menace 7 venture 8 endanger, threaten 10 jeopardize

imperious

5 bossy 6 urgent 7 haughty 8 absolute, arrogant, despotic, dominant 9 arbitrary, masterful 10 autocratic, commanding, high-handed, oppressive, peremptory, tyrannical 11 dictatorial, domineering, heavy-handed, magisterial, overbearing

impermanent

7 passing 8 fleeting, fugitive 9 ephemeral, fugacious, momentary, temporary, transient 10 evanescent, short-lived, transitory

impersonal

4 cold 5 aloof 8 abstract, detached 11 cold-blooded, emotionless 13 dispassionate, unimpassioned

impersonate

3 ape 4 play 5 mimic 6 act out 7 imitate, playact, portray 9 represent 11 counterfeit

impersonator

4 mime 5 actor, mimic 6 mummer, player, ringer 7 actress, copycat 8 thespian

impertinence

3 lip 4 gall, guff, sass 5 brass, cheek 8 audacity, boldness, chutzpah, rudeness, temerity 9 brashness, impudence, insolence 10 brazenness, effrontery, incivility 11 discourtesy, irrelevance

impertinent

4 bold, busy, rude 5 brash, fresh, sassy, saucy 6 brazen, cheeky 7 uncivil 8 insolent, meddling 9 audacious, intrusive, obtrusive, officious 10 inapposite, irrelative, irrelevant, meddlesome 11 ill-mannered 12 discourteous, inapplicable, presumptuous

imperturbability

5 poise 6 aplomb, phlegm 8 calmness, coolness, serenity, stoicism 9 composure, placidity, sangfroid 10 dispassion, equanimity 11 equilibrium, nonchalance, tranquility 12 tranquillity

imperturbable

4 calm, cool 5 stoic 6 placid, poised, serene, smooth, steady, stolid 7 unmoved 8 composed, tranquil 9 collected, unruffled 10 nonchalant, phlegmatic, unaffected 11 unflappable

impervious

4 safe 6 immune 8 hardened 10 inviolable 12 inaccessible, invulnerable

impetuous

3 hot 4 rash, wild 5 fiery, hasty

6 ardent, fervid, madcap, sudden
8 headlong, vehement, volatile
9 hotheaded, mercurial 10 irrational,
passionate 11 precipitant, precipitate, precipitous, spontaneous
13 temperamental

impetus
4 goad, push, spur 5 force 6 motive
8 catalyst, momentum, stimulus
9 incentive, stimulant 10 incitement,
motivation 13 encouragement

impinge
5 press 6 border 7 intrude, obtrude
8 encroach

impious
6 sinful, unholy, wicked 7 godless,
infidel, profane, secular, ungodly
8 agnostic, apostate 9 atheistic
10 irreverent, unfaithful, unhallowed
11 blasphemous, irreligious, unrighteous 12 iconoclastic, sacrilegious
13 unconsecrated

impish
4 arch 5 elfin 6 elvish 7 playful,
puckish, roguish, waggish 11 mischievous

impishness
7 devilry, roguery, waggery 8 deviltry, mischief 9 devilment 11 roguishness, waggishness

implacable
4 grim 8 ruthless 9 merciless
10 inexorable, unyielding 11 intractable 12 unappeasable

implant
3 fix 4 root 5 embed, graft, infix
6 enroot, infuse, insert 7 ingrain,
inspire, instill 9 establish, inculcate,
inoculate, introduce 10 inseminate
12 augmentation

implausible
5 fishy 6 flimsy 7 dubious, suspect
8 doubtful, fanciful, unlikely 10 far-
fetched, incredible 12 questionable,
unbelievable, unconvincing

implement
4 tool 6 device, effect, enable,

gadget 7 enforce, execute, fulfill,
perform, realize, utensil 8 carry out,
complete, make good 9 actualize,
apparatus, appliance 10 accomplish,
instrument, supplement 11 contraption, contrivance
carpentry: 3 die, saw 4 file 5 brace,
clamp, drill, punch, tongs 6 chisel,
hammer, pliers, reamer, sander,
wrench 7 hacksaw, scraper 9 blow-
torch 11 screwdriver
cleaning: 3 mop 5 broom, brush,
whisk 6 duster, vacuum 7 sweeper
10 whiskbroom
cutting: 5 knife, mower, razor
6 scythe, shears, sickle 8 scissors
digging: 5 spade 6 dibber, dibble,
shovel
drawing: 3 pen 6 eraser, pencil
7 compass 8 template
eating: 4 fork 5 knife, spoon
engraving: 5 burin 6 graver
farm: 4 plow 6 binder, harrow,
plough, scythe, seeder, sickle
8 gangplow, reaphook, spreader,
thresher 9 pitchfork 10 cultivator
fireplace: 5 poker, tongs 7 andiron
fishing: 3 rod 4 hook, lure, reel
6 sinker 7 harpoon, trident
garden: 3 hoe 4 rake 5 spade
6 dibber, dibble, digger, tiller, trowel
7 mattock 11 wheelbarrow
grooming: 4 comb, file 5 brush,
razor 7 clipper 8 clippers, nail file,
tweezers 10 toothbrush
kitchen: 3 pan, pot 4 mold 5 mixer,
whisk 6 grater, kettle, mortar, pestle
7 blender, skillet, spatula 8 colander,
saucepan, stockpot
logging: 5 peavy 6 peavey 8 cant
hook
measuring: 3 cup 4 gage, rule
5 gauge, ruler, scale 7 caliper,
divider, trammel, T-square
10 micrometer, protractor
stone: 5 burin 7 neolith 9 paleolith

implicate
4 link, mire 5 blame 6 tangle 7 concern, embroil, entwine, include,
involve 8 entangle, intimate 11 incriminate

implication
4 hint 8 allusion, overtone 9 inference, undertone 10 connection, intimation, suggestion 11 association, connotation 12 significance

implicit
5 tacit 6 unsaid 8 inherent, unspoken 9 doubtless, potential, unuttered 10 undeclared, understood 11 unexpressed 13 unquestioning

implied
5 tacit 6 unsaid 8 unspoken 9 suggested 10 undeclared, understood 11 unexpressed

implore
3 ask, beg 4 coax, pray 5 crave, plead 6 adjure, appeal 7 beseech, entreat, solicit 10 supplicate

imply
4 hint, mean 7 connote, include, involve, signify, suggest 8 indicate, intimate 9 insinuate

impolite
4 rude 5 crude 7 ill-bred, uncivil, uncouth 10 ungracious, unladylike, unmannered, unmannerly 11 ill-mannered 12 discourteous 13 ungentlemanly

impolitic
5 brash 6 unwise 8 tactless 9 imprudent, maladroit, untactful 10 ill-advised, indiscreet 11 inadvisable, inexpedient, injudicious 12 short-sighted, undiplomatic

import
4 bear, gist, mean, pith 5 sense, value, worth 6 convey, denote, intend, intent, matter, moment, stress, thrust, weight 7 concern, connote, express, meaning, message, purpose, signify 8 emphasis, indicate, transfer 9 magnitude, substance 10 intendment 11 acceptation, consequence 12 significance 13 signification

importance
4 mark, note, pith 5 value, worth 6 moment, weight 7 account, gravity 8 eminence, priority, salience, standing 9 greatness, magnitude, substance 10 prominence, worthiness 11 consequence, distinction, seriousness, weightiness 12 significance

important
3 big 5 chief, grave, great, heavy, major, noted, vital 6 famous, marked, potent, urgent, worthy 7 big-time, capital, crucial, eminent, fateful, notable, salient, serious, telling, weighty 8 critical, eventful, foremost, material, powerful, pressing, valuable 9 essential, estimable, imperious, memorable, momentous, prominent 10 meaningful, noteworthy, pre-eminent, worthwhile 11 outstanding, significant, substantial 12 considerable 13 consequential, distinguished, indispensable

importune
3 beg 4 pray, urge 5 annoy, plead, worry 6 appeal, invoke, plague 7 beseech, besiege, entreat, solicit, trouble 8 petition

impose
3 fob 4 lade, levy 5 abuse, enact, exact, foist, force, order, place, put on, visit, wreak 6 assess, burden, charge, compel, decree, demand, enjoin, fob off, ordain, saddle 7 command, dictate, exploit, inflict, intrude, lay down, obtrude, palm off, pass off, require 8 encroach, encumber, infringe, trespass 9 authorize, constrain, establish

imposing
4 huge 5 grand, noble, regal, royal 6 august 7 awesome, massive, pompous, stately 8 baronial, majestic, towering 9 dignified 10 commanding, monumental 11 magnificent, outstanding 12 high-sounding 13 distinguished

imposition
3 tax 4 duty, fine, levy 6 burden, demand 7 penalty 9 deception 13 inconvenience

impossible

6 absurd 8 hopeless 10 infeasible,
unfeasible, unworkable 11 unthinkable 12 preposterous, unacceptable,
unattainable, unbelievable, unimaginable, unrealizable, unreasonable
13 inconceivable

impost

3 fee, tax 4 duty, levy, toll 6 charge,
tariff 7 tribute 9 surcharge 10 assessment

impostor

4 fake, sham 5 actor, cheat, faker,
fraud, mimic, phony, poser, quack
6 humbug, poseur 8 deceiver 9 charlatan, con artist, hypocrite, pretender
10 dissembler, mountebank 11 masquerader 12 impersonator

imposture

4 fake, hoax, sell, sham, wile 5 cheat,
fraud 6 deceit, humbug 8 flimflam
9 deception, mare's nest, stratagem
11 counterfeit

impotence

8 weakness 9 sterility 10 inadequacy
12 helplessness 13 powerlessness

impotent

4 lame, weak 6 effete, feeble 7 sterile 8 helpless 9 forceless, incapable,
powerless 11 ineffective, ineffectual
12 invertebrate

impound

5 seize 6 immure, lock up 7 confine, enclose, put away 8 imprison
10 confiscate

impoverish

4 bust, ruin 5 break 6 beggar
8 bankrupt 9 pauperize

impoverished

4 poor 5 broke, needy 8 bankrupt,
indigent 9 destitute, penniless,
penurious

impoverishment

4 need, want 6 penury 9 indigence,
neediness, privation 11 destitution

impracticable

8 unusable 10 infeasible, unfeasible,
unworkable 11 insuperable, unrealistic 12 inaccessible, unattainable

impractical

7 utopian 8 quixotic, romantic,
unusable 9 visionary 10 idealistic,
infeasible, ivory-tower, starry-eyed,
unfeasible, unworkable 11 theoretical, unrealistic

imprecation

3 hex 4 cuss 5 curse 7 malison
8 anathema 11 malediction

imprecise

5 rough, vague 7 inexact 9 esti-
mated 10 indefinite 11 approximate,
unspecified

impregnable

4 safe 6 immune, secure 9 protected 10 invincible, inviolable,
unbeatable 11 indomitable, insuperable 12 unassailable 13 unconquerable

impregnate

3 sop 4 fill, soak 5 imbue, souse,
steep 6 drench, infuse 7 pervade
8 conceive, permeate, saturate
9 fecundate, fertilize, penetrate,
transfuse 10 inseminate

impresario

4 Bing (Rudolf) 5 Carte (Richard
D'Oyly), Hurok (Sol) 6 Pastor
(Tony) 7 manager 8 director,
Kirstein (Lincoln), producer, promoter
9 Diaghilev (Sergei) 10 D'Oyly Carte
(Richard)

impress

3 fix, set 4 dent, etch, mark, move,
seal, sway 5 brand, carry, drive,
exert, force, grave, infix, print, stamp,
touch 6 affect, effect, excite, strike
7 engrave, ingrain, inspire 8 inscribe,
transfer, transmit 9 establish, influence, stimulate

impressible

8 gullible, immature, moldable
9 malleable, receptive, sensitive
10 affectable, susceptive, vulnerable
11 persuadable, suggestible, susceptible

impression

4 dent, idea, mark, sign 5 image, print, stamp, trace, track 6 effect, hollow, notion 7 concept, edition, feeling, reissue, thought, vestige 8 printing, reaction 9 influence

impressionable

8 sensible, sentient 9 malleable, receptive, sensitive 10 responsive 11 suggestible, susceptible

impressionist

composer: 5 Ravel (Maurice) 7 Debussy (Claude)
mimic: 6 Carvey (Dana), Little (Rich)
painter: 5 Degas (Edgar), Manet (Edouard), Monet (Claude) 6 Renoir (Auguste), Sisley (Alfred) 7 Cassatt (Mary), Morisot (Berthe) 8 Pissarro (Camille)
(see also **postimpressionist**)

impressive

5 grand, noble 6 moving, superb 7 amazing, awesome, notable, stately, sublime 8 dazzling, dramatic, gorgeous, majestic, powerful, splendid, stirring, striking, touching 9 admirable, affecting, arresting, inspiring 11 magnificent

imprimatur

6 permit 7 license 8 approval, sanction 10 permission 13 authorization

imprint

3 fix 4 dent, etch, mark 5 grave, press, stamp 6 dimple, effect 7 engrave 8 inscribe 9 engraving, influence 10 depression 11 indentation, inscription

imprison

3 jug 4 cage, jail 6 coop up, detain, immure, intern, send up 7 confine, enclose 8 restrain, restrict, stockade 9 constrain 11 incarcerate

improbable

5 fishy 7 dubious 8 doubtful, fanciful, unlikely 10 far-fetched 11 implausible

impromptu

5 ad-lib 7 offhand 9 extempore, makeshift, unplanned, unstudied 10 off-the-cuff, unprepared, unscripted 11 extemporary, spontaneous, unrehearsed

improper

5 inapt, inept, outré, undue, wrong 6 gauche, risqué 7 illicit, naughty 8 ill-timed, indecent, tactless, unseemly, untimely, untoward 9 incorrect, unethical, unfitting 10 inaccurate, inapposite, indecorous, indelicate, malapropos, unbecoming, undecorous, unsuitable 11 impertinent, unbefitting 12 illegitimate, inadmissible, inapplicable, infelicitous, unseasonable 13 inappropriate

impropriety

5 gaffe 7 blooper, blunder, faux pas 8 solecism 9 barbarism, gaucherie, indecorum, vulgarism 12 unseemliness 13 incorrectness

improve

4 edit, help, mend 5 amend, boost, edify, emend, raise 6 better, enrich, look up, perk up, refine, reform, remedy, revise, revive, uplift 7 advance, amplify, augment, build up, correct, develop, enhance, enlarge, further, perfect, recover, rectify, upgrade 8 increase, progress 9 cultivate, intensify, meliorate 10 aggrandize, ameliorate, recuperate, strengthen

improvident

4 rash 6 lavish 8 careless, feckless, heedless, prodigal, reckless, wasteful 9 impetuous, negligent, unthrifty 10 profligate 11 extravagant, spendthrift 12 shortsighted, uneconomical

improvise

5 ad-lib 6 cook up, invent, make up 7 concoct 8 contrive 9 fabricate 11 extemporize

improvised

7 offhand 9 extempore, unstudied 10 off-the-cuff, unprepared, unscripted 11 extemporary, unrehearsed

imprudent

4 rash 6 unwise 7 foolish 8 reckless 9 foolhardy 10 ill-advised,

incautious, indiscreet **11** inadvisable, inexpedient, injudicious **12** short-sighted

impudence
4 gall **5** brass, cheek, nerve **8** audacity, boldness, chutzpah, temerity **9** brashness, cockiness, hardihood, insolence, nerviness **10** disrespect, effrontery **11** presumption

impudent
4 bold, flip, pert, wise **5** brash, cocky, fresh, nervy, sassy, saucy, smart **6** brassy, brazen, cheeky **7** blatant, forward **8** flippant, insolent, overbold **9** audacious, bare-faced, bold-faced **11** brazen-faced, smart-alecky **12** contumelious **13** disrespectful

impugn
5 cross **6** assail, attack, defame, malign, oppose, vilify **7** asperse, gainsay, impeach **8** chastise, reproach, traverse **9** castigate, denigrate, deprecate, disparage, reprehend **9** criticize, denigrate

impugnable
5 fishy, shady **6** guilty **7** suspect **8** doubtful **9** equivocal, uncertain **10** assailable, suspicious **11** problematic **12** disreputable

impulse
4 goad, push, spur, urge, whim **5** drive, force **6** motive, thrust, whimsy **7** caprice, passion **8** catalyst, excitant, stimulus **9** actuation, incentive, stimulant **10** incitation, incitement, motivation **11** inspiration, instigation

impulsive
4 rash **5** hasty **6** abrupt, fickle, sudden **7** erratic, flighty, offhand **8** headlong, volatile **9** automatic, extempore, mercurial, unplanned, whimsical **10** capricious **11** instinctive, involuntary, precipitate, spontaneous

impunity
7 freedom, liberty, license **8** immunity **9** exception, exemption, indemnity, privilege **10** absolution, protection **12** dispensation

impure
3 raw **5** mixed **6** soiled, sordid, unholy **7** alloyed, defiled, profane, sullied, unclean **8** indecent, polluted, unchaste **9** uncleanly, unrefined **10** desecrated, unhallowed **11** adulterated

impute
3 lay **4** cite **5** blame, refer **6** accuse, adduce, assign, charge, credit, indict **7** ascribe **8** accredit **9** attribute, implicate

inaccessible
5 aloof **6** arcane, closed, far-off, remote **7** cryptic, distant, faraway, obscure **8** abstruse, esoteric, hermetic **9** recondite **11** unavailable, unreachable **12** unattainable, unobtainable

inaccurate
5 false, wrong **6** all wet, faulty, untrue **7** unsound **8** specious **9** distorted, erroneous **10** fictitious

inaction
6 repose **7** latency **8** dormancy, idleness, lethargy **9** indolence, passivity, slackness, torpidity **10** quiescence **12** slothfulness

inactive
4 idle, lazy **5** inert, quiet, slack, still **6** asleep, latent, sleepy, static, torpid **7** abeyant, dormant, passive, resting **8** slothful, sluggish **9** do-nothing, lethargic, quiescent, sedentary

in addition
4 also **6** as well, to boot, withal **7** besides, further **8** moreover **11** furthermore

inadequacy
4 lack, want **6** dearth **7** deficit, failure, paucity **8** shortage, weakness **9** impotence **10** deficiency, scantiness **11** shortcoming

inadequate
3 shy **5** scant, short **6** meager, scanty, scarce, skimpy **7** lacking, scrimpy, wanting **8** impotent **9** defective, deficient **10** emasculate

inadmissible
5 unapt, unfit 8 unusable, unworthy
9 unwelcome 10 unsuitable 11 unqualified 12 unacceptable

inadvertent
8 careless, heedless 9 negligent,
unmindful, unplanned, unwitting
10 accidental, unintended, unthinking
13 unintentional

inadvisable
4 rash 6 unwise 7 foolish 8 careless, reckless 9 foolhardy, impolitic,
imprudent, pointless 10 ill-advised
11 harebrained

inalterable
5 fixed 6 stable 8 constant 9 immovable, immutable, steadfast,
unmovable, unvarying 12 unchangeable

inamorata, inamorato
4 beau, dear 5 flame, honey, lover
6 steady 7 beloved, darling, squeeze,
sweetie 8 ladylove, mistress, paramour, truelove 9 boyfriend 10 girlfriend, heartthrob, sweetheart

inane
4 flat, idle, vain 5 blank, dotty,
empty, silly, vapid 6 absurd, hollow,
jejune, vacant 7 asinine, fatuous,
foolish, idiotic, insipid, lunatic, trivial,
vacuous, witless 8 mindless 9 frivolous, pointless, senseless

inanimate
4 dead, dull 5 inert 5 still 6 asleep,
torpid 7 dormant 8 immotile, lifeless
9 quiescent 10 motionless 11 unconscious

inanity
5 folly 6 idiocy, lunacy 7 fatuity,
vacuity 8 vapidity 9 absurdity,
dottiness, emptiness, silliness
10 hollowness 11 foolishness,
vacuousness, witlessness 13 senselessness

inappreciable
6 meager, scanty, skimpy, slight
10 impalpable, unapparent 13 imperceptible

inappropriate
5 amiss, undue, unfit 6 unmeet
8 improper, unseemly, untimely,
untoward 9 ill-suited 10 malapropos, unsuitable 11 impertinent

inapt
5 unfit 6 clumsy, gauche, jejune,
unmeet 7 awkward, unhandy
8 improper, unfitted, unsuited,
untimely 9 maladroit, unfitting,
unskilled 10 amateurish, irrelevant,
malapropos, unskillful, unsuitable

inarticulate
4 dumb, mute 5 tacit 6 silent
7 halting, unvocal 8 mumbling,
unspoken, wordless 9 voiceless
10 maundering, speechless, tongue-
tied, undeclared 11 unexpressed

inasmuch as
5 since 7 because, whereas 11 considering

inattentive
6 absent, remiss 8 distrait, heedless
9 forgetful, negligent, unheeding,
unmindful 10 abstracted, distracted,
unthinking 12 absentminded

inaugural
5 first 6 maiden, speech 7 address,
initial, leading, opening, premier
8 foremost 9 beginning

inaugurate
5 begin, set up, start 6 launch
7 kick off 8 commence, dedicate,
initiate 9 establish, institute, originate 10 consecrate

inauspicious
4 dire 7 adverse, baleful, direful,
fateful, ominous, unlucky 8 sinister
9 ill-boding 11 threatening, unfavorable, unpromising 12 unpropitious

inborn
6 innate, native 7 connate, natural
8 inherent 9 intrinsic 10 congenital,
connatural, hereditary, unacquired

inbred
7 connate, genetic, natural 8 inherent 9 intrinsic 10 congenital, connatural, deep-seated, hereditary

Inca
capital: 5 Cuzco
conqueror: 7 Pizarro (Francisco)
god: 4 Inti **9** Viracocha **10** Pacha-
camac
language: 7 Quechua
record: 5 quipu
ruler: 9 Atahualpa, Pachacuti
10 Atahuallpa

incalculable
4 huge, iffy, vast **6** untold **8** enormous **9** boundless, countless,
limitless, uncertain **10** tremendous,
unnumbered **11** illimitable, measureless, uncountable **12** immeasurable,
unmeasurable **13** unpredictable

in camera
7 privily, sub rosa **8** covertly, secretly
9 furtively, privately **10** stealthily
13 clandestinely

incandescent
3 hot **5** lucid **6** ardent, bright, lucent
7 beaming, fulgent, glowing, intense,
lambent, radiant **8** dazzling, luminous **9** brilliant, effulgent, refulgent
11 resplendent

incantation
3 hex **4** rune **5** chant, charm, magic,
spell **10** hocus-pocus, mumbo-
jumbo, necromancy **11** abracadabra,
conjuration, enchantment
Buddhist, Hindu: 6 mantra

incapable
5 unfit **6** unable **8** impotent, un-
expert, unfitted **9** powerless, unskilled **10** unequipped, unskillful
11 unqualified **12** disqualified

incapacitate
6 disarm **7** cripple, disable **8** paralyze **10** debilitate, devitalize, disqualify, immobilize

incapacity
9 impotence, unfitness **10** impairment
11 disablement **12** fecklessness

incarcerate
3 jug **4** jail **6** coop up, immure,
intern, send up **7** confine, enclose,
impound **8** imprison

incarnadine
3 red **4** rosy **5** ruddy **6** redden
7 pinkish **8** bloodred

incarnate
5 human, reify **6** embody **7** realize
8 embodied, manifest **9** actualize,
corporeal, personify **11** materialize,
personalize **12** substantiate

incarnation
6 avatar **10** embodiment **11** reification
of Christ: 7 kenosis

incautious
4 rash **5** brash, hasty **6** daring,
madcap, unwary **8** careless, heedless, reckless **9** daredevil, foolhardy,
impetuous, imprudent, negligent,
unmindful **10** ill-advised, neglectful,
regardless **11** precipitate, thoughtless

incendiary
5 fiery, torch **7** firebug **8** agitator,
arsonist, arsonous **9** explosive,
firebrand, ignitable **10** pyromaniac
12 pyromaniacal

incense
3 ire, mad, oil **4** balm, burn, rile
5 anger, aroma, scent, spice
6 arouse, enrage, homage, incite,
madden **7** inflame, provoke **8** irritate
9 infuriate
vessel: 6 censer **8** thurible

incentive
4 goad, spur **5** spark **6** motive
7 impetus, impulse **8** catalyst,
stimulus **9** stimulant **10** inducement,
motivation **11** provocation **13** encouragement

inception
4 root **5** birth, start **6** origin, outset,
source **7** genesis, kickoff, opening
9 beginning **10** derivation, provenance **11** provenience **12** commencement

inceptive
7 initial, leadoff, nascent **9** beginning
10 initiatory

incertitude

5 doubt **7** dubiety **8** mistrust **9** suspicion **10** skepticism **11** dubiousness, uncertainty, vacillation **12** irresolution

incessant

6 steady **7** endless, eternal, nonstop **8** constant **9** ceaseless, continual, perpetual, unceasing **10** continuous **11** everlasting, unremitting **12** interminable **13** uninterrupted

inch

3 bit **5** crawl, creep **7** modicum

inchoate

8 formless, immature, unformed, unshaped **9** amorphous, embryonic, incipient, potential, shapeless **10** disjointed, incoherent **11** rudimentary, unorganized **12** disconnected

incident

5 event **6** moment **7** episode **8** occasion **9** ancillary, attendant, happening, satellite **10** affiliated, collateral, consequent, occurrence **11** concomitant, subordinate **12** circumstance

incidental

5 fluky, minor **6** casual, chance **9** accessory **10** contingent, fortuitous **11** subordinate **12** nonessential

incidentally

7 by the by **8** by the bye, by the way, casually **12** fortuitously

incinerate

4 burn **7** cremate

incipient

7 nascent **9** beginning, embryonic **10** commencing

incipit

5 start **7** opening **9** beginning

incise

3 cut **4** etch, gash, kerf, slit **5** carve, slash, slice **6** chisel, pierce **7** engrave

incision

3 cut **4** gash, slit **5** blaze, notch **10** laceration

incisive

4 keen **5** acute, crisp, sharp, terse **6** direct **7** cutting, mordant **8** clear-cut, piercing, slashing, succinct **9** trenchant **11** penetrating **13** perspicacious

incite

3 egg **4** abet, goad, prod, spur, urge **5** egg on, raise, rouse, set on **6** arouse, exhort, foment, kindle, set off, spur on, stir up, whip up **7** actuate, agitate, provoke, trigger **8** motivate **9** instigate, stimulate

incitement

see **incentive**

inclement

3 raw **5** harsh, rough **6** bitter, brutal, severe, stormy **8** rigorous

inclination

3 bow, nod **4** bent, bias, lean, tilt, will **5** fancy, grade, pitch, slant, slope, taste, trend **6** ascent, liking **7** descent, incline, leaning **8** affinity, appetite, fondness, gradient, penchant, soft spot, tendency, velleity, weakness **9** affection **10** attachment, partiality, proclivity, propensity **11** disposition **12** predilection

incline

3 tip **4** bend, bias, cant, cast, heel, lean, list, sway, tend, tilt, turn **5** grade, impel, slant, slide, slope **6** affect, induce **7** dispose, leaning **8** gradient, persuade **9** influence, prejudice

inclined

3 apt **5** given, prone, raked **6** liable, likely, minded **7** dipping, leaning, oblique, sloping, tilting, willing **8** diagonal, pitching **11** predisposed
way: 4 ramp

include

5 admit, bound, cover **6** enfold, number, take in **7** confine, contain, embrace, enclose, receive, subsume **8** comprise, encircle **9** encompass **10** comprehend **11** accommodate

inclusive

5 broad **6** global **7** general, overall

8 complete, sweeping **9** all-around, embrace **11** compendious **12** encompassing, encyclopedic **13** comprehensive

incognito
6 veiled **7** cloaked **9** anonymous, disguised **11** camouflaged

incognizant
7 unaware **8** ignorant **9** oblivious, unknowing, unmindful, unwitting **10** unfamiliar, uninformed **11** unconscious **12** unacquainted

incoherent
5 loose **6** broken, raving **7** muddled, unclear **8** confused **9** illogical **10** disjointed, disordered, irrational, maundering, tongue-tied **11** unconnected, unorganized **12** disconnected, disorganized **13** discontinuous

incombustible
9 fireproof **10** unburnable **12** nonflammable

income
4 gain, take **5** wages **6** profit **7** revenue **8** entrance, proceeds, receipts **9** emolument

incommode
3 irk, vex **5** annoy, upset **6** bother, burden, hinder, plague, put out **7** disturb, perturb, trouble **8** disquiet, distress, irritate **9** disoblige **10** disconcert

incommodious
7 awkward, cramped, crowded **8** confined **9** congested

incommunicable
8 reserved, taciturn **9** ineffable, withdrawn **11** unspeakable, unutterable **13** undescribable, unexpressible

incomparable
6 unique **7** supreme **8** peerless, singular, ultimate **9** matchless, nonpareil, paramount, unequaled, unmatched, unrivaled **10** preeminent, surpassing, unequalled, unrivalled **11** outstanding, superlative, unequalable, unmatchable **12** transcendent, unparalleled **13** unsurpassable

incompatible
7 adverse, counter **8** contrary, opposite **9** dissonant, unmixable **10** discordant, discrepant **11** conflicting, disagreeing, uncongenial, unfavorable **12** antagonistic, antithetical **13** contradictory, unsympathetic

incompetence
9 unfitness **10** disability, ineptitude **12** fecklessness

incompetent
5 inept, unfit **6** clumsy **8** helpless, inexpert, unfitted **9** incapable, maladroit, unskilled **10** unequipped **11** inefficient, unqualified

incomplete
4 part **5** short **6** broken, undone **7** partial, sketchy **8** abridged, immature **9** truncated **10** unfinished **11** fragmentary

incompliant
5 rigid, stiff **6** mulish **7** defiant **8** perverse, stubborn **9** obstinate, pigheaded, resistant, unbending **10** bullheaded, headstrong, inflexible, self-willed, unyielding **11** intractable **12** pertinacious, recalcitrant

incomprehensible
7 cryptic, obscure, unclear **8** abstruse, baffling, esoteric **9** fantastic **10** fathomless, mysterious, mystifying, unknowable **11** ungraspable **12** impenetrable, unfathomable, unimaginable

inconceivable
10 improbable, unknowable **11** implausible, unthinkable **12** unbelievable, unconvincing, unimaginable

in conclusion
6 lastly **7** finally

inconclusive
4 open **9** equivocal, uncertain, undecided, unsettled **10** unfinished

incongruous

5 alien 6 absurd 7 foreign, variant 9 anomalous, dissonant 10 discordant, discrepant, unsuitable 11 conflicting, disagreeing 12 disconsonant

inconsequential

5 petty, small 6 measly, paltry 7 trivial 8 picayune, trifling 9 illogical, small-time 10 immaterial, irrelevant, negligible 11 impertinent, superficial, unimportant

inconsiderable

4 puny 5 minor, petty 6 meager, meagre, paltry, scanty, skimpy, slight 7 scrimpy, trivial 8 picayune, trifling 9 frivolous, small-beer 10 negligible 11 unimportant

inconsiderate

4 rash 5 brash, hasty 6 unkind 8 careless, heedless, impolite, reckless 9 hotheaded, impulsive 10 illadvised, ungracious 11 precipitate, thoughtless 12 discourteous, uncharitable

inconsistent

6 fickle 8 contrary 9 dissonant, illogical, mercurial 10 capricious, changeable, discordant, discrepant 11 conflicting 13 contradictory

inconsolable

7 forlorn 8 desolate 9 heartsick 11 comfortless, heartbroken

inconspicuous

6 hidden, subtle 7 obscure 9 concealed 11 unobtrusive 12 unnoticeable

inconstant

6 fickle, untrue 7 erratic, mutable, protean, vagrant 8 unstable, unsteady, variable, volatile, wavering 9 changeful, faithless, fluctuant, irregular, mercurial, uncertain, unsettled 10 capricious, changeable, irresolute, perfidious, unfaithful 11 chameleonic, vacillating 13 temperamental

incontestable

4 sure 7 certain 8 absolute, clearcut, ironclad, positive 9 apodictic, undoubted 10 conclusive, inarguable, undeniable 11 irrefutable, unequivocal 12 unassailable, undisputable 13 unimpeachable

incontinent

5 loose 6 wanton 9 dissolute 10 licentious, profligate 12 unrestrained

incontrovertible

4 sure 7 certain 8 absolute, clearcut, definite, positive 10 conclusive, undeniable 11 irrefutable, unequivocal 12 undisputable

inconvenience

3 irk, vex 5 annoy 6 bother, meddle, put out 7 disrupt, disturb, trouble 8 handicap, vexation 9 aggravate, annoyance, disoblige 10 discomfort, discommode, disruption, exasperate 11 aggravation, awkwardness 12 disadvantage, discomfiture, exasperation 13 embarrassment

inconvenient

7 awkward, unhandy 8 annoying 10 bothersome, unsuitable 11 pestiferous, troublesome

incorporate

3 mix 4 form, fuse, join 5 blend, merge, unite 6 absorb, embody, imbibe, mingle 7 combine 8 organize 9 establish 10 amalgamate, assimilate

incorporeal

8 bodiless, formless 9 spiritual 10 discarnate, immaterial, unphysical 11 disembodied, nonmaterial, nonphysical 12 metaphysical 13 unsubstantial

incorrect

5 false, wrong 6 faulty, untrue 7 unsound 8 improper, specious 9 erroneous, imprecise 10 fallacious, inaccurate, unbecoming

incorrigible

6 unruly 8 depraved 9 incurable 10 delinquent, inveterate 11 unalterable 12 irredeemable

increase
3 add, eke, wax 4 gain, grow, hike, jump, plus, push, rise, teem 5 boost, build, mount, put up, raise, run up, surge, swarm, swell 6 accrue, amount, beef up, dilate, expand, extend, gather, growth, jack up, markup 7 accrual, advance, amplify, augment, burgeon, distend, enhance, enlarge, inflate, magnify, prolong, upsurge 8 addition, compound, escalate, flourish, heighten, lengthen, manifold, multiply, protract, snowball 9 accession, accretion, aggravate, expansion, extension, increment, inflation, intensify, pullulate, reinforce 10 accelerate, accumulate, aggrandize, appreciate, strengthen 11 enlargement 12 augmentation, breakthrough 13 amplification

incredible
7 amazing, awesome 8 unlikely 9 cockamamy, fantastic 10 astounding, cockamamie, far-fetched, impossible, improbable, outlandish, phenomenal, remarkable 11 astonishing, implausible 12 preposterous, unbelievable, unconvincing, unimaginable 13 extraordinary

incredulity
7 unfaith 8 distrust, mistrust, unbelief 9 disbelief, nonbelief, suspicion 10 skepticism

incredulous
6 show-me 7 dubious 8 doubting 9 quizzical, skeptical 10 suspicious 11 distrustful, mistrustful, questioning, unbelieving, unconvinced 12 disbelieving

increment
4 gain, hike, rise, step 5 raise 6 degree, growth 7 quantum 8 addition 9 accession, accretion 11 enlargement 12 augmentation

incriminate
6 accuse, charge 7 arraign, impeach 9 implicate

incrustation
4 film, rime, scab 5 scale 6 tartar 7 coating

incubus
5 demon, fiend 9 nightmare

inculcate
5 teach, train 6 impart 7 educate, implant, impress, instill

inculpable
4 pure 5 clean 8 innocent, spotless, virtuous 9 blameless, guiltless, righteous 10 impeccable

incumbent
7 leaning, resting 8 occupant, required 9 overlying 10 obligatory 12 officeholder

incur
7 acquire, bring on 8 contract

incurable
5 fatal 6 deadly, lethal 8 hopeless, terminal 9 immutable 11 immedicable, irreparable 12 irremediable, unchangeable 13 uncorrectable

incursion
4 raid 5 blitz, foray, sally 6 attack, sortie 7 assault 9 irruption

incus
4 bone 5 anvil

indebted
5 bound 7 obliged 8 beholden 9 obligated

indebtedness
3 due, IOU 7 arrears 9 arrearage, gratitude, liability 10 obligation 11 delinquency 12 thankfulness

indecent
4 blue, foul, lewd, racy 5 bawdy, dirty, gross, nasty 6 coarse, filthy, impure, risqué, smutty, vulgar 7 obscene, profane, raunchy 8 immodest, improper, off-color, unseemly, untoward 9 offensive 10 malodorous, scurrilous 12 scatological 13 objectionable

indecision
5 doubt 8 wavering 9 hesitancy 11 ambivalence, uncertainty, vacillation 12 equivocation, irresolution, shilly-shally

indecisive

5 vague 6 unsure 7 dubious,
unclear 8 wavering 9 equivocal,
tentative, uncertain, undecided,
unsettled 10 irresolute 11 problematic, vacillating

indecorous

4 rude 5 gross, rough 6 coarse,
vulgar 7 uncivil 8 impolite, improper,
unseemly, untoward 9 graceless,
irregular, offensive, tasteless, unrefined 10 unbecoming 11 ill-
mannered, undignified 12 discourteous

indecorum

5 gaffe 6 breach 7 blooper, blunder,
faux pas, offense 8 solecism 11 impropriety

indeed

4 amen 5 truly 6 really, surely, verily
8 forsooth, honestly 9 assuredly,
certainly 10 positively, undeniably
11 doubtlessly, undoubtedly 13 unequivocally

indefatigable

6 dogged 8 tireless, untiring, vigorous 9 energetic, tenacious 10 persistent, relentless, unflagging, unwearying 11 unrelenting

indefensible

9 unguarded, untenable 10 assailable, vulnerable 11 unprotected
12 unforgivable, unpardonable
13 unjustifiable

indefinable

5 vague 7 elusive 9 uncertain
11 unspeakable, unutterable 13 undescribable

indefinite

4 wide 5 broad, loose, vague 7 endless, general, inexact, obscure,
unclear, unfixed 8 infinite 9 ambiguous, boundless, imprecise, limitless,
unbounded, uncertain, undefined,
unlimited 10 indistinct, inexplicit,
unmeasured, unspecific 12 inconclusive 13 indeterminate
pronoun: 3 all, any, few 4 each,
many, most, none, some 6 anyone,
nobody 7 anybody, several, someone 8 everyone, somebody 9 everybody

indehiscent fruit

3 key, nut 4 pepo 5 berry, grain,
grape, melon 6 achene, loment,
samara, squash 7 pumpkin 8 cucumber 9 caryopsis 10 schizocarp

indelible

4 fast 5 fixed 7 lasting 8 enduring
9 memorable, permanent 13 unforgettable

indelicate

3 raw 4 lewd, rude 5 crude, gross,
rough 6 coarse, vulgar 7 uncouth
8 impolite, improper, tactless, unseemly, untoward 9 unrefined
10 unbecoming

indemnify

5 repay 6 secure 7 redress, requite
9 reimburse 10 compensate, recompense, remunerate

indemnity

6 amends 7 redress 8 requital,
security 9 exemption, quittance,
reprisals 10 protection, recompense,
reparation 11 restitution 12 compensation, remuneration 13 fee-for-
service

indentation

4 dent, nick 5 notch 6 dimple,
recess 10 depression

indenture

4 nick 5 notch 8 contract 9 agreement 11 certificate

indentured

5 bound 10 controlled 11 apprenticed

independent

4 free 8 absolute, autarkic, separate 9 autarchic, sovereign 10 autonomous 11 self-reliant 13 self-
contained

indescribable

11 unspeakable, unutterable 13 unexplainable

indestructible
7 lasting 8 enduring, immortal
9 permanent 12 imperishable,
irrefragable, unperishable

indeterminate
5 vague 9 imprecise, uncertain,
unlimited

index
4 list, mark, sign 5 ratio, table
7 catalog, symptom 8 classify,
evidence, regulate 9 catalogue
11 systematize

India
bay: 6 Bengal
capital: 8 New Delhi
city: 5 Delhi 6 Bombay, Kanpur,
Madras, Mumbai, Nagpur 7 Chennai, Kolkata, Lucknow 8 Calcutta
9 Ahmadabad, Bangalore, Hyderabad
coast: 7 Malabar 10 Coromandel
European discoverer: 4 Gama
(Vasco da)
language: 5 Hindi
leader: 5 Nehru (Jawaharlal)
6 Gandhi (Indira, Mohandas, Rajiv)
monetary unit: 5 rupee
mountain range: 7 Vindhya 9 Himalayas
neighbor: 5 Burma, China, Nepal
6 Bhutan 7 Myanmar 8 Pakistan
10 Bangladesh
pass: 5 Bolan, Gumal 6 Khyber
plateau: 6 Deccan
river: 5 Indus 6 Ganges, Yamuna
7 Krishna 11 Brahmaputra
sea: 7 Arabian

Indian
bread: 3 nan 4 naan 7 chapati
butter: 3 ghi 4 ghee
caste: 5 Sudra 6 Vaisya 7 Brahman 9 Kshatriya
female dancer: 8 bayadere
groom: 4 syce
harem: 6 zenana
instrument: 4 vina 5 sarod, sitar,
tabla 7 tambura
lady: 4 bibi 5 begum 8 memsahib
nurse: 4 amah, ayah
outcast: 6 pariah

prince: 4 raja, rana 5 rajah 8 maharaja 9 maharajah
princess: 4 rani 5 begum, ranee
scholar: 6 pandit, pundit
screen: 6 purdah
seal, stamp: 4 chop
soldier: 4 peon 5 sepoy
teacher: 4 guru
viceroy: 5 nabob, nawab
weight unit: 3 ser 4 cash, dhan,
pank, pice, powe, rati, tank, tola
5 adpao, fanam, hubba, masha,
maund, pally, pouah, ratti 6 dhurra,
pagoda, pollam 7 chinnam, chittak

Indiana
capital: 12 Indianapolis
city: 4 Gary 6 Muncie 9 Fort
Wayne, South Bend 10 Evansville,
Terre Haute 11 Bloomington
college, university: 6 DePauw,
Purdue 9 Ball State, Notre Dame
nickname: 7 Hoosier (State)
river: 5 White 6 Wabash
state bird: 8 cardinal
state flower: 5 peony
state tree: 5 tulip

Indian, American
baby: 7 papoose
ball game: 8 lacrosse
carrier: 7 travois
Central and South American:
3 Ona 4 Cuna, Inca, Maya 5 Arara,
Aztec, Carib, Huave, Olmec, Yagua
6 Arawak, Aymara, Jivaro, Omagua,
Toltec, Yahgan 7 Chibcha, Quechua,
Zapotec 8 Tarascan, Yanomamo
10 Araucanian 11 Tupi-Guaraní
food: 4 samp 5 maize 8 pemmican
home: 5 hogan, lodge, tepee
6 pueblo, teepee, wigwam 7 wickiup
leader: 4 Popé 6 Wovoka 7 Cochise, Osceola, Pontiac, Sequoia,
Sequoya 8 Geronimo, Hiawatha,
Powhatan, Sequoyah, Tecumseh
9 Black Hawk, Massasoit 10 Crazy
Horse 11 Cornplanter, Sitting Bull
money: 6 wampum
North American: 3 Fox, Oto, Sac,
Ute 4 Cree, Crow, Erie, Hopi, Hupa,
Iowa, Otoe, Pima, Pomo, Sauk,
Taos, Yuma, Zuni 5 Aleut, Caddo,

Creek, Haida, Huron, Kansa, Kiowa, Maidu, Miami, Modoc, Omaha, Osage, Sioux, Uinta **6** Apache, Cayuga, Dakota, Lenape, Mandan, Micmac, Mohawk, Munsee, Navaho, Navajo, Nootka, Oglala, Ojibwa, Oneida, Paiute, Pawnee, Pueblo, Quapaw, Salish, Santee, Seneca, Siwash **7** Anasazi, Arapaho, Arikara, Bannock, Chilkat, Chinook, Choctaw, Dakotah, Esselen, Klamath, Kutenai, Mohican, Naskapi, Natchez, Ojibway, Pontiac, Shawnee, Tlingit **8** Chero-kee, Cheyenne, Chippewa, Coman-che, Delaware, Illinois, Iroquois, Kickapoo, Kwakiutl, Nez Percé, Onondaga, Powhatan, Seminole, Shoshoni **9** Blackfoot, Chickasaw, Menominee, Tsimshian, Tuscarora, Wampanoag, Winnebago **10** Assin-iboin, Chiricahua, Gros Ventre, Potawatomi **11** Massachuset, Narraganset
pipe: 7 calumet
spirit: 5 totem **6** manitu **7** kachina, manitou

Indian paintbrush
8 hawkweed **10** painted cup

indicate
4 bode, hint, mark, mean, show **5** augur, imply, point, prove **6** attest, convey, denote, evince, import, reveal **7** bespeak, betoken, connote, display, exhibit, express, presage, signify, suggest **8** disclose, evi-dence, foretell, manifest, register **9** designate **10** foreshadow, illustrate **11** demonstrate

indication
3 cue **4** clue, hint, mark, sign **5** proof, token, trace **6** augury, signal **7** ges-ture, inkling, portent, symptom **8** evi-dence, reminder, telltale **9** testimony **10** expression, suggestion **13** fore-shadowing, manifestation

indicative
10 expressive, suggestive **11** evi-dentiary, symptomatic **12** illustrative **13** demonstrative

indicia
5 marks, signs **8** imprints, markings

indict
5 blame **6** accuse, charge **7** arraign, censure, impeach **9** criticize

indifference
6 apathy **9** aloofness, unconcern **10** detachment, dispassion **11** dis-interest **12** carelessness, impartiality

indifferent
4 cold, cool, numb, so-so **5** aloof, blasé, stoic **6** casual, remote **7** av-erage, neutral **8** careless, detached, mediocre, middling, moderate, ordinary, passable, unbiased, un-caring **9** apathetic, impartial, impas-sive, objective **10** nonchalant, unaffected **11** unconcerned, unemo-tional **12** uninterested, unprejudiced **13** disinterested, dispassionate

indigence
4 need, want **6** penury **7** poverty **9** neediness, pauperism, privation **11** deprivation, destitution

indigene
6 native **9** aborigine **10** aboriginal

indigenous
6 native **7** endemic, natural **10** ab-original, congenital, connatural, unacquired **13** autochthonous

indigent
4 poor **5** broke, needy **9** destitute, penniless **11** impecunious, necessi-tous **12** impoverished

indigestion
9 dyspepsia, heartburn

indignant
3 mad **5** irate, riled, upset, vexed **6** galled, heated **7** annoyed **8** of-fended, outraged, provoked **9** af-fronted, irritated, resentful

indignation
5 pique **7** dudgeon **10** irritation, resentment

indignity
3 cut **4** slap **6** injury, insult, slight **7** affront, outrage **9** contumely,

grievance **10** disrespect **11** humiliation **13** disparagement, embarrassment

indigo
4 blue **8** deep blue

indigo bird
5 finch **7** bunting

Indira's father
5 Nehru (Jawaharlal)

indirect
7 devious, oblique, vagrant, winding **8** circular, sidelong, tortuous **9** deceitful, underhand, wandering **10** backhanded, circuitous, collateral, meandering, roundabout **11** duplicitous, underhanded

indiscreet
5 gabby **6** unwise **7** foolish, gossipy **8** tactless **9** impolitic, imprudent, untactful **10** ill-advised **11** loose-lipped

indiscretion
4 slip **5** folly, gaffe, lapse **7** blunder, faux pas, mistake, misstep **8** solecism **10** imprudence **11** impropriety

indiscriminate
5 mixed **6** hybrid, motley, random, varied **7** aimless, jumbled, vagrant **8** assorted, careless **9** arbitrary, desultory, haphazard, hit-or-miss, unplanned, wholesale **10** uncritical **11** promiscuous **12** conglomerate, multifarious, unrestrained **13** heterogeneous, miscellaneous

indispensable
5 basic, vital **6** needed **7** crucial, needful, pivotal **8** cardinal, critical **9** essential, necessary, requisite **10** imperative, obligatory **11** fundamental

indisposed
3 ill **4** down, sick **5** loath **6** ailing, averse, poorly, sickly, unwell **7** uneager **8** hesitant **9** reluctant, resistant, unwilling **11** disinclined

indisposition
6 malady **7** ailment, dislike, illness, malaise **8** aversion, disfavor, distaste, sickness, unhealth **10** affliction, reluctance

indisputable
4 sure, true **7** certain, evident, obvious **8** absolute, ironclad, positive **9** apodictic **10** undeniable **11** irrefutable, unequivocal **12** irrefragable, unassailable

indistinct
3 dim **4** hazy **5** faint, foggy, misty, murky, vague **6** bleary, blurry, cloudy **7** blurred, obscure, shadowy, unclear **8** confused **9** uncertain, undefined **12** undetermined

indistinguishable
4 same **5** alike, equal, vague **7** unclear **9** duplicate, identical **10** equivalent

indite
3 pen **5** write **6** record, scribe **7** compose, engross **10** transcribe

individual
3 one **4** body, lone, self, sole, soul, unit **5** being, human, party, thing **6** entity, mortal, person, proper, single **7** special **8** creature, discrete, distinct, peculiar, personal, separate, singular, solitary, specific **10** particular, respective **11** distinctive **13** idiosyncratic
combining form: 4 idio

individualist
5 loner **6** hermit **8** lone wolf, maverick **13** nonconformist

individuality
4 self **7** essence, oneness **8** identity, selfhood **9** character **10** uniqueness **11** personality, singularity **12** idiosyncrasy, separateness

individualize
4 mark **7** specify **9** customize **10** specialize **11** distinguish, personalize, singularize **12** characterize **13** differentiate, particularize

Indochinese country
4 Laos **5** Burma **7** Myanmar, Vietnam **8** Cambodia, Thailand **9** Kampuchea

indoctrinate
5 teach, tutor **7** educate, program
8 convince, persuade **9** brainwash,
inculcate

indolence
4 laze **5** sloth **7** inertia, languor
8 idleness, laziness, lethargy **9** torpidity **12** slothfulness, sluggishness
13 shiftlessness

indolent
4 idle, lazy **6** torpid **8** fainéant,
slothful, sluggish **9** lethargic, shiftless

indomitable
7 staunch **9** steadfast **10** invincible,
unbeatable **11** impregnable **13** unconquerable

Indonesia
archipelago: 5 Malay
capital: 7 Jakarta **8** Djakarta
city: 5 Medan **7** Bandung, Cilacap
8 Semarang, Surabaja, Surabaya
9 Palembang
island group: 5 Sunda **8** Moluccas
language: 6 Bahasa
leader: 7 Suharto, Sukarno
monetary unit: 6 rupiah
regions: 4 Bali, Java **5** Ceram,
Timor **6** Bangka, Borneo, Flores,
Lombok, Madura **7** Celebes, Sumatra **8** Sulawesi **9** Irian Jaya
volcano: 8 Krakatau, Krakatoa

indubitable
4 sure **6** patent **7** certain, evident,
obvious **8** definite, ironclad, positive
9 apodictic, veritable **10** undeniable
11 irrefutable, self-evident, unequivocal **12** irrefragable

induce
5 cause **6** effect, elicit, prompt
7 actuate, procure **8** convince,
engender, generate, motivate,
occasion, persuade **9** encourage

inducement
4 bait, lure **6** come-on, motive
10 attraction, motivation **13** consideration

induct
4 lead **5** admit **6** enlist, enroll
7 appoint, install

inductance unit
5 henry

induction
8 entrance **9** accession, reasoning
10 enlistment **11** appointment
13 ratiocination

inductive
7 logical **9** prefatory, prelusive **11** a
posteriori

indulge
3 pet **4** baby, bask **5** allow, favor,
humor, spoil **6** cocker, coddle,
cosset, oblige, pamper, permit,
please, wallow **7** cater to, delight,
gratify, satisfy **9** luxuriate **11** mollycoddle

indulgence
5 favor, mercy, treat **6** luxury **7** charity **8** clemency, courtesy, kindness,
lenience, leniency **9** allowance,
remission, tolerance **10** compassion, kindliness, permission, toleration **11** forbearance, forgiveness
12 dispensation, mercifulness
13 gratification

indulgence seller
5 Tezel (Johann) **6** Tetzel (Johann)

indulgent
4 easy, kind **7** clement, lenient
8 generous, merciful, tolerant **9** forgiving **10** charitable, permissive

indurate
6 harden **7** callous, confirm, congeal **8** hardened, solidify, stubborn
9 unfeeling **11** hard-hearted

industrialist
6 tycoon **7** magnate **12** manufacturer

industrious
4 busy **8** diligent, sedulous **9** assiduous, laborious

industry
4 work **5** labor **8** business, commerce **9** assiduity, diligence **10** enterprise

inebriant
see **intoxicant**

inebriate
3 sot 4 lush, soak 5 drunk, souse, tight, tipsy, toper 6 bibber, boozer 7 stupefy, tippler, tosspot 8 drunkard 10 intoxicate

inebriated
3 lit 5 drunk, lit up, oiled, stiff, tight, tipsy 6 blotto, juiced, loaded, plowed, potted, soused, stewed, tanked, wasted 7 crocked, pickled, pie-eyed, sloshed, smashed 8 polluted 9 plastered

inedible
9 poisonous 12 unappetizing

ineffable
5 taboo 9 forbidden 11 unspeakable, unutterable 13 undescribable

ineffaceable
7 lasting 8 enduring 9 indelible, permanent

ineffective
4 vain, weak 6 futile 7 useless 8 abortive, bootless, feckless, impotent 9 fruitless, powerless 10 emasculate, unavailing 12 unproductive, unsuccessful

ineffectiveness
8 futility 9 impotence

ineffectual
see **ineffective**

inefficient
5 slack 6 clumsy 8 careless, slipshod, wasteful 9 negligent

inelastic
5 rigid, stiff 7 brittle 9 unbending 10 unyielding

inelegant
5 crass, crude, gross, rough 6 coarse, gauche, vulgar 7 awkward, uncouth 9 graceless, unrefined 10 uncultured, ungraceful 12 uncultivated

ineligible
5 unfit 8 unfitted, unworthy 10 unequipped, unsuitable 11 unqualified 12 disqualified

ineluctable
4 sure 5 bound, fated 6 doomed 7 certain 8 destined 9 necessary 10 inevitable, unevadable 11 unavoidable, unescapable 13 unpreventable

inept
5 unfit 6 clumsy, gauche, klutzy 7 artless, awkward, foolish, halting, unhandy 8 bumbling, bungling 9 all thumbs, ham-handed, maladroit, unskilled 10 malapropos, unskillful, unsuitable 11 heavy-handed, undexterous, unfortunate

inequality
8 imparity 9 disparity 10 unevenness 12 irregularity, variableness 13 disproportion, heterogeneity

inequitable
6 biased, unfair, unjust 7 partial 10 prejudiced 11 unjustified, unrighteous

inequity
4 bias 5 wrong 9 prejudice 10 unfairness, unjustness

ineradicable
6 innate 7 chronic 8 constant, inherent, stubborn 9 ingrained 10 deep-rooted, deep-seated, entrenched, inveterate 11 established, ever-present, never-ending

inert
4 calm, dead, idle 5 quiet, still 6 asleep, sleepy 7 dormant, passive 8 immobile, lifeless, sluggish 9 apathetic, lethargic 10 motionless

inert gas
4 neon 5 argon, radon, xenon 6 helium 7 krypton

inertia
5 sloth 6 apathy, stupor, torpor 7 languor 8 idleness, laziness, lethargy 9 indolence, inertness, lassitude, passivity, torpidity 10 immobility, inactivity 11 disinterest 12 listlessness, sluggishness

inescapable
see **inevitable**

inessential
see **unessential**

inestimable
9 priceless 11 measureless 12 immeasurable, unmeasurable, unfathomable

inevitable
4 sure 5 bound, fated 6 doomed 7 certain 8 destined 9 necessary 11 unavoidable, unescapable 12 foreordained 13 unpreventable

inevitably
8 perforce 10 willy-nilly 11 like it or not, unavoidably

inexcusable
6 guilty 8 blamable, culpable 9 untenable 10 censurable 11 blameworthy, condemnable 12 criticizable, unforgivable, unpardonable 13 reprehensible, unjustifiable

inexhaustible
8 tireless, untiring 9 unfailing, weariless 10 bottomless, unflagging 13 indefatigable

inexorable
5 rigid 6 strict 7 adamant 8 immobile, obdurate, stubborn 9 immovable, unbending 10 relentless, unyielding 11 unrelenting

inexpensive
3 low 5 cheap 7 cut-rate 8 moderate 10 reasonable

inexperience
7 naïveté, rawness 8 verdancy 9 freshness, greenness 10 callowness

inexperienced
3 raw 5 fresh, green, naive, young 6 callow 7 untried 8 unversed 9 unskilled, untrained, unworldly 10 amateurish, unseasoned

inexpert
9 maladroit, unskilled, untrained 10 amateurish

inexplicable
6 arcane, obtuse, opaque 7 cryptic 9 enigmatic 10 mysterious, mystifying, unsolvable 11 undefinable

12 impenetrable, unfathomable 13 unaccountable, unexplainable

inexpressible
8 nameless 11 unspeakable, unutterable 13 undescribable, unexplainable

inexpressive
5 blank, stoic 6 stolid, vacant, wooden 7 deadpan 9 impassive 10 poker-faced 13 straight-faced

inextricable
9 insoluble 10 unsolvable

infallible
4 sure 5 exact 6 trusty 7 certain, correct, perfect 8 absolute, accurate, flawless, surefire, unerring 9 errorless, unfailing 10 dependable, impeccable 11 trustworthy 12 tried-and-true 13 unimpeachable

infamous
4 evil, vile 6 odious 7 hateful, heinous 8 flagrant, shameful 9 abhorrent, miscreant, nefarious, notorious 10 abominable, despicable, detestable, flagitious, scandalous, villainous 11 disgraceful, ignominious, opprobrious 12 contemptible, disreputable

infamy
5 odium, shame 7 obloquy 8 disgrace, dishonor, ignominy 9 disrepute, notoriety 10 opprobrium

infancy
8 babyhood 9 childhood

infant
4 babe, baby 5 bairn, child, green 7 bambino, neonate, newborn, papoose, toddler 8 bantling, immature, nursling 9 unfledged
bed: 4 crib 6 cradle 8 bassinet
food: 3 pap 4 milk 7 pabulum
room: 7 nursery

infanta
8 princess

infantile
7 babyish, puerile 8 childish, immature

infantryman
7 dogface 8 doughboy 11 foot soldier
Algerian: 6 Zouave

infatuated
5 dotty, silly 7 foolish 8 besotted, enamored, obsessed 9 bewitched, rapturous 10 captivated, passionate

infatuation
4 rage 5 ardor, craze, crush, folly 7 passion, rapture 8 devotion 9 obsession, puppy love 11 fascination

infect
5 taint 6 defile, poison 7 corrupt, pollute 11 contaminate

infection
3 bug 6 sepses (plural), sepsis
fungous: 8 mycetoma

infectious
8 catching, epidemic, virulent 9 pestilent 10 contagious, corrupting 12 communicable 13 contaminating, transmittable

infelicitous
5 unapt, unfit 6 unmeet 7 awkward, unhappy 8 improper 9 imperfect 10 malapropos, unsuitable 11 regrettable, unfortunate

infer
5 judge 6 deduce, deduct, derive, gather, reason 7 collect, make out, suppose, surmise 8 conclude, construe 10 conjecture 11 hypothesize

inference
7 surmise 8 illation, sequitur 9 deduction 10 assumption, conclusion, conjecture, derivation 11 presumption, supposition

inferior
3 low 4 base, fair, hack, mean, poor, puny 5 cheap, lousy, lower, minor, petty, scrub, sorry, under, worse 6 common, deputy, feeble, impure, junior, lesser, nether, no-good, paltry, satrap, shoddy, sleazy, tawdry, tinpot, vassal 7 average, subject, un-equal 8 déclassé, low-grade, mediocre, middling, ordinary, unworthy, wretched 9 attendant, auxiliary, no-account, satellite, secondary, subaltern, subjacent, underling, worthless 10 inadequate, second-rate 11 substandard
prefix: 3 sub 4 demi 5 infra

infernal
6 Hadean 7 hellish, satanic 8 chthonic, damnable, demoniac, devilish, diabolic, plutonic 9 chthonian, plutonian, Tartarean 10 diabolical, sulphurous

inferno
3 pit 4 fire, hell 5 Hades, Sheol 6 blazes, Tophet 7 Gehenna 9 holocaust, perdition 10 underworld 11 netherworld 13 conflagration

Inferno
division: 5 canto
poet: 5 Dante (Alighieri)
verse form: 9 terza rima

infertile
6 barren, effete 7 sterile 8 impotent 10 unfruitful 12 hardscrabble, unproductive

infest
4 teem 5 beset, swarm 6 plague 7 overrun 10 parasitize

infidel
5 pagan 7 atheist, heathen, heretic, skeptic 8 agnostic 10 unbeliever

infidelity
7 perfidy, treason 8 adultery, betrayal, cheating 9 disbelief, treachery 10 disloyalty 13 faithlessness

infinite
4 vast 7 endless, eternal, immense 8 unending 9 boundless, countless, limitless, perpetual, unlimited 11 everlasting, illimitable, measureless, sempiternal 12 immeasurable

infinity
8 eternity 10 perpetuity 11 endlessness 12 sempiternity 13 boundlessness, limitlessness

infirm

4 lame, sick, weak 5 frail 6 ailing,
feeble, sickly 7 failing, fragile,
unsound 8 decrepit, unstable
9 doddering 11 debilitated

infirmity

3 ill 4 flaw 5 decay 6 malady
7 ailment, disease, frailty, illness,
malaise 8 debility, disorder, sickness, syndrome, weakness 9 complaint, condition 10 affliction, feebleness, sickliness 11 decrepitude
12 debilitation, enfeeblement

infix

4 root 5 embed, lodge 6 fasten,
pierce 7 engrave, implant, impress

inflame

4 fire, gall, goad, rile, roil 5 anger,
light, rouse 6 arouse, enrage, excite,
foment, ignite, kindle, madden,
redden, stir up 7 provoke 8 enkindle, irritate 9 aggravate 10 exacerbate, exasperate

inflammable

5 fiery 6 ardent 8 burnable, volatile 9 excitable, ignitable, irascible
11 combustible

inflammation

4 gout, sore 6 otitis, quinsy 7 catarrh, colitis 8 adenitis, bursitis,
cystitis, neuritis, pleurisy, rachitis,
swelling 9 arthritis, chilblain, gastri-
tis, nephritis, phlebitis 10 bronchitis,
cellulitis, combustion, dermatitis,
gingivitis, laryngitis, tendinitis 12 en-
cephalitis 13 poliomyelitis
eye: 6 iritis 7 pinkeye 9 keratitis
horse: 7 fistula, quittor
intestines: 7 ileitis 9 enteritis
suffix: 4 itis

inflammatory

8 exciting 9 explosive, seditious
11 provocative 13 rabble-rousing,
revolutionary

inflate

4 fill 5 bloat, elate, swell 6 expand
7 amplify, distend 10 aggrandize

inflated

5 tumid, windy 6 turgid 7 bloated,
swollen, verbose 9 bombastic,
distended, dropsical, flatulent, overblown 10 heightened 11 exaggerated, pretentious

inflection

4 bend, tone 5 curve, pitch 6 accent,
change, stress, timbre 8 emphasis,
tonality 9 accidence 10 modulation

inflexible

3 set 4 grim, hard, iron 5 fixed, rigid,
stiff 6 strict 7 adamant, die-hard
8 granitic, hard-line, immobile, ironclad, obdurate, stubborn 9 immovable, immutable, obstinate, steadfast,
unbending 10 adamantine, brassbound, implacable, rock-ribbed
unbendable, unyielding 11 unalterable, unrelenting 12 unchangeable
13 dyed-in-the-wool

inflict

5 visit, wreak 7 mete out, subject
8 dispense 10 administer

inflow

4 rush 7 arrival

influence

4 move, pull, sway 5 alter, bribe,
clout, force, impel, lobby, touch
6 affect, compel, impact, modify,
moment, strike, weight 7 command,
control, impress, mastery 8 dominate, militate, persuade, prestige
9 authority, dominance

influenceable

8 gullible 9 malleable, receptive,
tractable 11 persuadable, persuasible, suggestible

influential

6 potent 8 forceful, powerful 9 effective 10 persuasive 13 authoritative

influx

7 arrival 8 entrance, invasion 9 accession

inform

3 rat 4 blab, clue, leak, post, tell,
warn 5 brief, edify, endow, endue,

imbue, teach **6** advise, betray, fill
in, impart, leaven, notify, reveal,
snitch, squeal, tattle, turn in, update
7 animate, apprise, caution, educate **8** acquaint, disclose, forewarn
9 advertise, enlighten **10** illuminate
11 familiarize

informal
6 casual, dégagé, folksy **7** natural,
offhand, relaxed **8** down-home,
familiar, laid-back **9** easygoing
10 colloquial, unofficial **13** unceremonious

information
4 data, fact, lore, news, poop, word
5 scoop **6** advice, notice, skinny,
wisdom **7** lowdown, tidings **9** knowledge **12** intelligence
secondhand: 7 hearsay

information bureau
abbreviation: 4 USIA, USIS

informative
8 edifying, exegetic **10** exegetical
11 educational, elucidative, explanatory **12** enlightening, illuminating

informed
4 wise **5** aware **6** au fait, versed
7 abreast, knowing **8** apprised,
educated **9** au courant, cognizant
10 acquainted, conversant **11** enlightened **13** knowledgeable

informer
3 rat, spy **4** fink, mole **5** stool
6 canary, gossip, snitch **7** rat fink,
stoolie, tattler, tipster **8** squealer,
telltale **10** deep throat, talebearer,
tattletale **11** stool pigeon **13** whistle-
blower

infra
5 after, below, later, under **7** beneath

infract
3 sin **6** breach, offend **7** violate
8 trespass **10** contravene, transgress

infraction
3 sin **4** foul **5** crime, error **6** breach
7 faux pas, misdeed, offense **8** tres-

pass **9** violation **12** encroachment
13 contravention, transgression

infrastructure
4 base **5** basis **9** framework **10** foundation, groundwork, substratum
12 underpinning

infrequent
3 odd **4** rare **6** scarce, seldom
7 unusual **8** isolated, sporadic,
uncommon, unwonted **10** occasional
11 exceptional

infringe
6 breach, impose, meddle, offend
7 disturb, obtrude, violate **8** encroach,
entrench, trespass **10** transgress

infuriate
3 ire, mad **4** rile **5** anger, pique
6 enrage, madden, rankle **7** incense,
inflame, outrage, provoke, steam up

infuse
4 fill, soak **5** imbue, steep **6** leaven
7 animate, implant, pervade, suffuse
8 permeate, saturate **10** impregnate

ingenious
5 acute, canny, sharp, smart **6** adroit,
clever, crafty **7** cunning, fertile
8 creative, original **11** imaginative,
resourceful

ingenuity
5 knack, savvy, skill **6** acumen,
smarts, talent **7** know-how, mastery
8 deftness, keenness **9** adeptness,
handiness **10** adroitness, capability,
cleverness, perception, shrewdness
11 proficiency **12** intelligence,
skillfulness **13** inventiveness

ingenuous
4 open **5** naive **6** simple **7** artless,
natural **8** innocent **9** childlike, guileless, unstudied **10** unaffected

ingest
3 eat **4** feed **6** devour **7** consume,
partake, swallow

Inge work
6 Picnic **7** Bus Stop **18** Splendor in
the Grass **19** Come Back Little
Sheba

inglorious
8 shameful **11** disgraceful, ignominious, opprobrious **12** dishonorable, disreputable **13** discreditable, unrespectable

ingot
3 bar, rod **4** mold **6** billet

ingrained
6 innate **8** inherent **9** essential **10** congenital, deep-rooted, deep-seated

ingratiating
5 silky **6** silken, smarmy **7** fawning **8** pleasing, unctuous **9** adulatory **10** flattering **11** sycophantic

ingredient
4 part **5** piece **6** factor **7** element **9** component **11** constituent

ingress
4 door **5** entry **6** access, entrée, portal **7** doorway, passage **8** entrance, entryway **9** admission, vestibule **10** admittance **11** entranceway

ingurgitate
4 bolt, cram, gulp, slop, wolf **5** gorge, scarf, stuff, swill **6** devour, gobble, guzzle **7** swallow

inhabit
4 live **5** dwell, haunt **6** occupy, people, settle, tenant **8** populate

inhabitant
5 liver **6** inmate, native **7** citizen, denizen, dweller, resider **8** indigene, resident **9** aborigine **10** autochthon
foreign: 5 alien
indigenous: 6 native **9** aborigine

inhale
7 breathe, consume, respire, swallow

inharmonious
6 atonal **7** jarring **9** dissonant, unmusical **10** discordant **11** cacophonous, conflicting, conflictive, disagreeing, quarrelsome, uncongenial **12** antagonistic

inhere
3 lie **5** dwell **6** belong, reside

inherent
4 born **5** basic **6** native **7** built-in, connate, natural **8** immanent **9** elemental, essential **10** congenital, deep-seated **11** fundamental

inherit
7 acquire, receive, succeed

inheritance
3 DNA **4** gene, gift **6** devise, estate, legacy **7** bequest **8** heirloom, heritage **9** patrimony, tradition **10** birthright **13** primogeniture

inherited
6 native **7** connate, genetic, natural **10** bequeathed, congenital, connatural, handed-down, hand-me-down

inheritor
4 heir **7** heiress, legatee **11** beneficiary

inhibit
4 curb, slow **5** check **6** arrest, bridle, enjoin, fetter, hamper, hinder, hobble, impede **7** prevent, repress, trammel **8** hold back, obstruct, restrain, suppress, withhold **9** constrain **10** discourage

inhibition
4 curb **5** taboo **6** hang-up **7** barrier **9** hindrance, restraint, stricture **10** impediment, repression **11** suppression

inhuman
5 cruel, feral **6** brutal, savage **7** beastly, bestial, brutish **8** fiendish **9** barbarous, monstrous **10** diabolical

inhumane
4 fell, grim **5** cruel **6** brutal, fierce, malign, savage **8** ruthless, sadistic **9** barbarous, ferocious, heartless, merciless, truculent

inhumation
6 burial **9** interment, sepulture **10** entombment

inhume
4 bury **5** plant **6** entomb **7** put away **9** lay to rest

inimical
7 adverse, harmful, hostile 10 malevolent, unfriendly 11 belligerent, contentious 12 antagonistic, antipathetic

iniquitous
3 bad 4 base, evil, vile 5 wrong 6 sinful, unjust, wicked 7 immoral, vicious 9 nefarious

iniquity
3 sin 4 evil 5 crime, wrong 7 offense 9 turpitude 8 trespass 10 immorality, wickedness, wrongdoing 13 transgression

initial
5 first, prime 6 anlage, letter, maiden 7 approve, engrave, leading, opening, primary 8 earliest, foremost, monogram, original 9 beginning

initiate
4 open 5 begin, enter, set up, start 6 enroll, get off, induct, invest, launch, take up 7 install, kick off, usher in 8 commence 9 originate 10 inaugurate

initiation
5 debut 7 baptism 9 admission, beginning, induction 10 admittance 11 investiture, origination 12 commencement, introduction

initiative
4 push 5 drive, spunk 6 energy 8 ambition, aptitude, gumption 9 beginning 10 enterprise, get-up-and-go

inject
3 add 6 insert 7 implant, instill 9 inoculate, introduce, vaccinate

injection
3 fix 4 hypo, shot 5 serum 7 booster, vaccine 10 hypodermic 11 inoculation, vaccination

injudicious
4 rash 5 hasty 6 unwise 8 heedless, reckless 9 ill-judged, impolitic, imprudent 10 ill-advised, indiscreet 11 inexpedient 12 shortsighted

injunction
3 ban, bar 4 writ 5 order 6 behest, charge 7 bidding, command, dictate, mandate 9 direction 11 prohibition

injure
3 mar 4 foul, harm, hurt, maim, pain 5 spoil, wound, wrong 6 blight, bruise, damage, deface, deform, foul up, impair, mangle 7 afflict, contort, cripple, disable, torture 8 distress, maltreat, mutilate 9 disfigure 12 incapacitate

injurious
6 nocent 7 abusive, adverse, harmful, hurtful 8 damaging 9 offensive 10 defamatory 11 detrimental

injury
3 ill 4 harm, hurt 5 wound, wrong 6 bruise, damage, trauma 8 distress 9 detriment

injustice
4 tort 5 crime, wrong 6 breach, damage 7 outrage 8 inequity, trespass 9 grievance, violation 10 favoritism, wrongdoing

ink
3 dye, pen 4 sign 8 inscribe 9 autograph, signature, subscribe

inkling
3 cue, tip 4 clue, hint, idea, lead, wind 5 hunch 6 notion, tip-off 8 telltale 9 suspicion 10 indication, intimation, suggestion

inky
3 jet 4 ebon 5 black, ebony, jetty, raven, sable 9 Cimmerian, pitch-dark 10 pitch-black

inlaid
5 piqué 6 boolle 7 hatched 8 enchased, nielloed 9 damascene, incrusted

Inland Empire
8 Illinois

inlet
3 arm, bay 4 cove, gulf 5 bayou, bight, creek, fiord, firth, fjord, sound 6 harbor, slough, strait 7 estuary

Admiralties: 4 Kali
Adriatic Sea: 5 Vlorë
Aegean Sea: 7 Saronic
Africa: 6 Walvis
Alaska: 4 Cook 5 Cross, Taiya
7 Glacier 8 Chilkoot
Aleutians: 5 Holtz, Nazan
Angola: 5 Bengo, Tiger 6 Tigres
Antarctica: 3 Ice 7 McMurdo
8 Amundsen 10 Shackleton
Arabian Sea: 4 Qamr 5 Kamar
Australia: 4 King 6 Botany 9 Discovery 10 Broad Sound
Baffin Bay: 8 Melville
Baffin Island: 9 Admiralty
Baltic Sea: 4 Hano 6 Danzig,
Gdansk 9 Pomerania 10 Pomeranian
Barents Sea: 4 Kola 7 Pechora
Beaufort Sea: 7 Prudhoe 9 Mackenzie
Bismarck Sea: 5 Kimbe
Brazil: 9 Guanabara
Bristol Channal: 10 Carmarthen
California: 5 Morro 8 Monterey
Canada: 5 Fundy 8 Howe Sound
Cape Breton Island: 4 Mira
Caribbean Sea: 5 Limón
Central America: 7 Fonseca
Chile: 5 Otway
Crete: 4 Suda 5 Canea
Denmark: 3 Ise
Djibouti: 6 Tajura 8 Tadjoura
East River: 8 Flushing
Ecuador: 5 Manta
Eire: 4 Clew 7 Brandon
English Channel: 3 Tor
Florida: 5 Biscayne 10 Saint Lucie
Georgia: 8 Altamaha
Greenland: 6 Baffin
Gulf of Alaska: 3 Icy 5 Woman
12 Resurrection
Gulf of Mexico: 7 Aransas 8 Suwannee 9 Matagorda, Pensacola
10 Terrebonne 11 Atchafalaya
12 Apalachicola
Gulf of St. Lawrence: 5 Bonne
Hawaii: 11 Pearl Harbor
Honshu: 3 Ise 5 Owari 6 Atsuta
Hudson Bay: 7 Repulse
Iceland: 4 Axar, Eyja, Huna 5 Horna,
Skaga, Vopna 8 Hunafloi

Indonesia: 4 Bima 5 Saleh
Ionian Sea: 7 Taranto
Irish Sea: 4 Luce 7 Dundalk
Japan: 4 Tosa
Java: 4 Lada 5 Peper
Java Sea: 7 Batavia
Kara Sea: 6 Enisei 7 Yenisei
Labrador: 8 Hamilton
Lake Erie: 8 Put-in-Bay, Sandusky
Lake Huron: 7 Saginaw, Thunder
Lake Ontario: 11 Irondequoit
Lake Superior: 5 Huron 8 Keweenaw 9 Whitefish
Long Island: 8 Rockaway
Long Island Sound: 6 Oyster
Madagascar: 8 Antongil
Maine: 5 Casco 7 Machias
Maryland-Virginia: 10 Chesapeake
Massachusetts: 8 Buzzards,
Plymouth 9 Annisquam
Massachusetts Bay: 10 Lynn
Harbor
Mediterranean Sea: 8 Valencia
9 Famagusta 10 Khalij Surt 11 Syrtis
Major
Mozambique: 5 Memba, Pemba
Nantucket Sound: 5 Lewis
Newfoundland: 4 Hare 5 White
7 Fortune
New Guinea: 3 Oro 5 Berau, Hansa
11 McCluer Gulf
New Jersey: 7 Raritan 8 Barnegat
9 Little Egg
New Zealand: 5 Hawke 6 Tasman
North Carolina: 9 Albemarle
Northern Ireland: 12 Belfast Lough
North Sea: 4 Lyse 9 Hardanger
Northwest Territories: 5 Wager
8 Bathurst, Franklin 9 Frobisher
12 Prince Albert
Norway: 3 Tys 4 Bokn, Tana
5 Lakse, Sogne
Norwegian Sea: 4 Nord, Salt, Stor,
Vest 5 Ranen 8 Scoresby 9 Trondheim
Ontario: 4 Owen
Oregon: 4 Coos
Philippines: 5 Baler, Pilar, Sogod
6 Butuan 9 Davao Gulf, Leyte Gulf,
Panay Gulf
Puget Sound: 4 Carr, Case
Quebec: 6 Ungava

Red Sea: 4 Foul
Rhode Island: 12 Narragansett
Russia: 5 Chaun **8** Sakhalin
Santo Cruz Islands: 8 Basilisk
Solomon Islands: 4 Deep **8** Huon Gulf
South Africa: 5 Table
South Carolina: 4 Bull
South China Sea: 4 Bias, Datu, Siam, Taya **5** Dasol, Subic, Subig **6** Brunei, Paluan **7** Camranh **8** Lingayen
Spain: 5 Cádiz
Spitsbergen: 3 Ice **4** Bell **5** Kings
Sumatra: 5 Bajur **10** Koninginne
Tyrrhenian Sea: 6 Naples **7** Paestum
Wales: 5 Burry
Washington: 5 Dabob **6** Skagit **11** Grays Harbor

inmate
7 convict **8** occupant, prisoner, resident **10** inhabitant

inmost part
4 core, pith **5** heart **6** center, depths, kernel, marrow **7** nucleus

inn
5 hotel, lodge, motel, serai **6** hostel, tavern **7** auberge, hospice, pension **8** hostelry **9** roadhouse **11** caravansary, public house **12** caravansarai **13** boardinghouse
German: 7 Gasthof **8** Gasthaus
Spanish: 5 fonda **6** posada **7** parador
Turkish: 6 imaret

innards
4 guts **5** belly **6** bowels, tripes **7** viscera **8** entrails, stuffing **10** intestines

innate
see **inherent**

inner
3 gut **5** focal **6** hidden, middle, secret **7** central, nuclear, private **8** familiar, interior, internal, personal, visceral **9** concealed, essential

innervate
4 jolt, move **5** pique, rouse **6** excite

7 animate, provoke, quicken **8** motivate, vitalize **9** electrify, galvanize, stimulate

Innisfail
4 Eire, Erin **7** Ireland

innkeeper
4 host **8** boniface, hosteler, hotelier, landlord, publican

innocence
6 purity **7** naiveté **8** chastity **10** simplicity **11** artlessness, sinlessness

innocent
4 good, lamb, naïf, pure, void **5** clean, legal, licit, naive **6** chaste, devoid, lawful **7** artless, natural, unaware **8** harmless, ignorant, virtuous **9** blameless, childlike, exemplary, faultless, guileless, guiltless, ingenuous, innocuous, righteous, stainless, unstained, unsullied, untainted **10** inculpable, legitimate **12** unsuspecting

innocuous
5 banal, bland **6** pallid **7** insipid **8** harmless **11** inoffensive, unoffending **13** insignificant

innovation
6 change **7** novelty

innovative
3 new **5** novel **8** creative, original **9** inventive **10** newfangled **11** cutting-edge, leading-edge **12** trailblazing

innovator
9 architect, developer **10** originator **11** trailblazer **13** revolutionary

innuendo
4 clue, hint, slur **7** calumny **8** allusion **9** aspersion **10** backbiting, intimation **11** implication, insinuation

innumerable
4 many **6** legion, myriad, untold **7** umpteen **9** countless, uncounted **10** numberless **13** multitudinous

Ino
brother: 9 Polydorus
father: 6 Cadmus
grandfather: 6 Agenor

husband: 7 Athamas
mother: 8 Harmonia
sister: 5 Agave 6 Semele 7 Autonoë
son: 8 Learchus, Palaemon 10 Melicertes

inobtrusive
5 muted, quiet 6 modest 7 subdued
8 discreet, tasteful 10 restrained

inoculate
5 imbue, shoot, steep 6 infuse
7 implant, suffuse 9 vaccinate

inoffensive
5 bland 7 neutral 8 harmless
9 innocuous, peaceable

inopportune
8 ill-timed, mistimed, untimely 12 unseasonable

inordinate
5 undue 6 wanton 7 extreme
8 overmuch 9 excessive 10 exorbitant, gratuitous, immoderate, irrational 11 extravagant, intemperate, superfluous, uncalled-for
12 unreasonable 13 extraordinary

inorganic
7 mineral 10 artificial

in passing
5 aside 6 obiter 7 by the by 8 by the bye, by the way 12 incidentally

in perpetuum
4 ever 6 always 7 forever, for good
8 evermore, for keeps 9 eternally
10 enduringly 11 forevermore

input
4 data 6 advice, energy 7 comment, counsel, opinion 8 feedback, guidance, material, stimulus 11 information

inquest
5 probe 7 hearing, inquiry 11 examination 13 investigation

inquietude
5 angst 6 unease, unrest 7 anxiety, ferment, turmoil 8 distress 10 uneasiness 11 restiveness 12 restlessness 13 Sturm und Drang

inquire
3 ask, pry 4 seek 5 probe, query
7 examine 8 question 9 catechize
11 interrogate, investigate

inquiry
5 audit, probe, query 7 hearing
8 grilling, question, research, scrutiny
11 examination, questioning 13 investigation

inquisition
4 hunt 5 probe, quest, trial 6 search
7 inquiry 8 grilling, research 11 examination 13 interrogation, investigation

inquisitive
4 nosy 6 prying, snoopy 7 curious
8 meddling, snooping 9 intrusive
10 meddlesome 11 questioning

inquisitor
10 Torquemada (Tomás de)

in re
4 as to 5 about, as for 7 apropos
9 as regards, regarding 10 as respects, concerning, respecting
12 with regard to 13 with respect to

in respect to
see **in re**

inroad
4 raid 5 foray 7 advance 8 invasion
9 incursion 12 encroachment

ins and outs
5 ropes 6 quirks 7 details 8 minutiae, oddities 11 incidentals, particulars 12 lay of the land 13 peculiarities, ramifications

insane
3 mad, off 4 daft, nuts 5 batty, crazy, daffy, dotty, loony, manic, nutsy, nutty, rabid, silly, wacky
6 absurd, crazed, cuckoo, maniac, raving, schizo, screwy, teched
7 berserk, bonkers, cracked, haywire, lunatic, tetched, touched, unsound 8 demented, deranged, unhinged 9 eccentric, psychotic
10 disordered, irrational, moonstruck, unbalanced 11 harebrained
12 crackbrained, preposterous, unreasonable

insane asylum
6 bedlam 8 loony bin, madhouse, nuthouse, snake pit 10 sanatorium, sanitarium

insanity
5 folly, mania 6 frenzy, lunacy 7 madness 8 delirium, delusion, dementia, hysteria, illusion 9 craziness, dottiness, psychosis 11 derangement, psychopathy

insatiable
6 crying, greedy, urgent 7 exigent 8 pressing, ravenous 9 clamorous, demanding, voracious 10 quenchless 11 importunate 12 unappeasable, unquenchable

inscribe
4 etch, list 5 carve, enter, print, write 6 enroll, record 7 engrave, engross, impress, imprint 8 dedicate, enscroll, register

inscription
5 title 6 legend 7 epigram, epitaph, heading 8 epigraph 10 dedication

inscrutable
6 arcane 7 deadpan 10 mysterious, poker-faced, sphinxlike, unknowable, unreadable 12 impenetrable, unfathomable

insect
3 bee, bug, fly 6 beetle
adult: 5 imago
antenna: 4 palp 6 feeler, palpus
combining form: 5 entom 6 entomo
covering: 6 chitin
immature: 4 grub, pupa 5 larva, nymph 6 larvae (plural), maggot 8 wriggler 9 chrysalis 11 caterpillar
kind: 3 ant, bee 4 flea, moth, wasp 5 aphid, scale 6 bedbug, beefly, beetle, cicada, earwig, hornet, mantid, mantis, mayfly 7 ant lion, cricket, firefly, June bug, katydid, ladybug, termite 8 honeybee, horsefly, housefly, lacewing, mosquito, stinkbug 9 bumblebee, butterfly, damselfly, dragonfly 10 silverfish,

springtail 11 grasshopper 12 walkingstick
luminous: 7 firefly 8 glowworm
molt: 7 ecdysis
moth: 4 luna 5 gypsy 6 miller, sphinx 7 noctuid, pyralid, tortrix, tussock 8 cecropia, cinnabar, forester, sphingid 9 clearwing, geometrid, saturniid, tortricid 10 Polyphemus
multi-legged: 8 diplopod 9 centipede, millipede
part: 4 palp 5 cerci (plural) 6 cercus, labium, labrum, ocelli (plural), palpus, thorax 7 antenna, maxilla, ocellus 8 antennae (plural), mandible, maxillae (plural) 9 proboscis, spiracles 10 ovipositor 11 exoskeleton
pest: 4 flea, lice (plural), mite 5 louse, midge, scale 7 blowfly, termite 8 horsefly, housefly, mealybug 9 cockroach, gypsy moth 10 boll weevil, Hessian fly, silverfish
science: 10 entomology
winged: 5 alate
wingless: 4 flea, lice (plural) 5 louse 8 firebrat 10 silverfish, springtail 11 bristletail

insecticide
3 DDT 5 mirex, naled 6 aldrin, endrin 7 lindane, phorate 8 carbaryl, dieldrin, rotenone 9 chlordane, malathion, parathion 10 permethrin

insecure
5 shaky 6 unsafe, unsure, wobbly 7 anxious 8 unstable 9 uncertain 10 precarious 11 unconfident 12 apprehensive

inseminate
7 implant, instill 9 fertilize, pollinate 10 impregnate

insensate
4 dull, hard, numb 5 stony 6 brutal, numbed 7 callous 8 comatose 9 bloodless, heartless, impassive, unfeeling

insensibility
4 coma 6 apathy, torpor 8 lethargy, stoicism 12 indifference

insensible

4 cold, dead, dull, hard, numb, rapt **5** stoic **6** asleep, intent, numbed, obtuse, stolid **7** callous **8** absorbed, comatose, deadened, hardened, obdurate **9** apathetic, bloodless, engrossed, impassive, unfeeling **11** unconscious **12** anesthetized

insensitive

4 dull, hard, numb, rude **5** crass **6** numbed, obtuse, unkind **7** callous **8** benumbed, deadened, hardened, tactless, uncaring **9** bloodless, heartless, unfeeling **10** anesthetic, impossible **11** indifferent, unconcerned **12** anesthetized, unresponsive

insert

5 enter **7** implant, obtrude **9** interpose **10** interleave **11** intercalate, interpolate

insertion

8 addendum, addition **13** interpolation

in short

7 briefly, tersely **9** concisely **10** succinctly

inside

6 closet, secret, within **7** private **8** hush-hush, interior **12** confidential **combining form: 4** endo

insidious

3 sly **4** foxy, wily **6** artful, crafty, subtle, tricky **7** cunning, gradual **8** creeping, guileful **9** deceitful **13** surreptitious

insight

6 acumen, aperçu, wisdom **8** sagacity, sapience **9** intuition **11** discernment, penetration **13** understanding

insightful

4 keen, sage, wise **7** gnostic, knowing **9** intuitive, sagacious **10** discerning, perceptive **11** penetrating

insignia

4 mark, sign **5** badge **6** emblem **8** brassard **10** decoration

insignificant

4 puny **5** dinky, minor, petty, small **6** casual, little, minute, paltry **7** minimal, trivial **8** nugatory, trifling **9** secondary, small-time **10** negligible **11** minor-league, unimportant

insincere

5 false, lying, phony **6** double, forced, hollow, shifty, tricky **7** feigned **8** mala fide, slippery, spurious **9** deceitful, deceptive, dishonest, pretended, simulated **10** left-handed, mendacious, untruthful **11** dissembling, double-faced **12** hypocritical

insinuate

4 hint **5** imply **6** inject, insert, work in, worm in **7** implant, instill, suggest **9** introduce

insipid

3 dry **4** arid, dull, flat, mild, pale, thin, weak **5** banal, bland, vapid **6** jejune, watery **7** mundane, prosaic, subdued, tedious **8** bromidic, lifeless, ordinary **9** innocuous, tasteless **10** flavorless, monotonous, namby-pamby, wishy-washy **11** commonplace

insist

4 hold **5** argue, claim, swear **6** affirm, assert, demand, stress **7** certify, contend, declare, require, testify **8** maintain

insistent

6 crying, dogged, urgent **7** adamant, burning, clamant, exigent **8** emphatic, forceful, pressing, resolute **9** assertive, clamorous, obtrusive **10** determined, imperative, relentless **11** persevering

insolence

4 gall, guff, sass **5** brass, cheek, nerve **8** audacity, boldness, chutzpah, contempt, rudeness **9** arrogance, impudence **10** brazenness, disrespect, effrontery **11** haughtiness, presumption **12** impertinence

insolent

4 bold, flip, pert, rude **5** cocky, lofty,

sassy, saucy 6 brazen, cheeky
7 haughty, uncivil 8 arrogant, cavalier, flippant, impolite, impudent,
superior 9 audacious, barefaced,
bold-faced 10 disdainful, peremptory 11 impertinent, overbearing
12 contumelious, discourteous,
supercilious 13 high-and-mighty

insouciance
6 aplomb 9 disregard, unconcern
10 breeziness 11 disinterest, nonchalance 12 carelessness, heedlessness, indifference

insouciant
4 airy, flip 6 blithe, breezy, casual,
jaunty 8 carefree, flippant, heedless
9 easygoing 10 nonchalant, untroubled 11 indifferent, thoughtless,
unconcerned 12 devil-may-care,
happy-go-lucky, lighthearted

inspect
3 con, vet 4 scan, view 5 audit,
check, probe, study 6 review, size
up, survey 7 canvass, examine,
observe 8 appraise, check out,
look over, question 9 check over
10 scrutinize 11 investigate

inspiration
4 muse 6 animus, genius, vision
7 insight 8 afflatus 9 brainwave,
influence 10 brainchild, brainstorm,
creativity 13 enlightenment

inspire
4 fire, stir 5 elate, exalt, imbue,
rouse 6 arouse, excite, foment,
incite, prompt, strike 7 animate,
enliven, impress, instill, quicken
8 motivate 9 encourage, galvanize,
influence, stimulate 10 exhilarate

inspiring
6 moving 7 awesome, rousing
8 exalting, stirring 9 animating,
uplifting 10 vitalizing

inspirit
4 fire, lift, spur, stir 5 cheer, exalt,
liven, rally, rouse, spark, steel
6 arouse, excite, incite, kindle, revive, uplift, vivify 7 animate, comfort,

console, delight, enliven, gladden,
hearten, nourish, quicken, refresh,
restore 8 activate, embolden, energize, revivify, vitalize 9 encourage,
stimulate 10 invigorate, strengthen

instability
8 fluidity 9 shakiness 10 insecurity,
volatility 11 inconstancy 12 un-
steadiness

install
4 seat, vest 5 put in, set up 6 induct, invest 8 ensconce, enthrone,
entrench 9 establish

instance
4 case, cite, item 6 detail, ground,
reason, sample 7 example 8 specimen 10 particular 12 illustration

instant
3 sec 4 wink 5 flash, jiffy, point,
shake, trice 6 moment, second,
urgent 7 current, exigent, present
8 existent, occasion, pressing
9 heartbeat, immediate, insistent,
twinkling 10 imperative, present-day

instantaneous
4 fast 5 quick, rapid 9 immediate,
lightning, momentary 11 hair-trigger,
split-second

instanter
3 now 6 at once 8 directly 9 forthwith, right away 11 immediately

instantly
3 now 6 at once 8 directly 9 forthwith, right away 11 immediately

instead
4 else 6 in lieu, rather 11 alternately
13 alternatively

instigate
4 abet, fire, goad, plan, plot, prod,
spur, urge 5 egg on, impel, raise
6 excite, foment, incite, stir up, whip
up 7 provoke, suggest 8 motivate
9 stimulate 10 bring about

instill
5 imbue 6 impart, infuse, inject
7 implant, suffuse 8 engender
9 inculcate, introduce

instinct

4 nose 5 hunch, sense 7 feeling, impulse 8 aptitude, behavior 9 intuition 10 proclivity, sixth sense 11 gut reaction

instinctive

3 gut 6 inborn, innate, normal 7 natural 8 habitual, inherent, visceral 9 automatic, ingrained, intrinsic, intuitive, reflexive, unlearned 10 congenital, unprompted 11 involuntary, spontaneous, unmeditated

instinctual

6 reflex 7 natural, routine 8 habitual, knee-jerk, untaught 9 automatic, impulsive, intuitive, reflexive 10 mechanical, unthinking 11 involuntary, spontaneous, unconscious

institute

5 begin, found, set up, start 6 decree, launch, ordain 7 academy, pioneer, usher in 8 initiate, organize 9 establish, introduce, originate 10 inaugurate 12 organization

institution

4 firm, rite 5 habit 6 custom 9 enactment 10 foundation 13 establishment
kind: 6 asylum, school 7 academy, college 8 hospital 10 sanatorium, sanitarium, sanitorium, university

instruct

4 show 5 coach, drill, guide, order, steer, teach, train, tutor 6 direct, enjoin, inform, school 7 apprise, command, counsel, educate, lecture 9 enlighten, prescribe

instruction

5 drill 6 advice, lesson 7 precept 8 coaching, guidance, teaching, training, tutelage 9 catechism, education, schooling 10 directions
place of: 6 school 7 academe, academy, college 10 university

instructive

8 didactic, edifying, pedantic 9 pedagogic 11 educational, explanatory, explicative, informative 12 enlightening

instructor

3 don 4 guru 5 coach, guide, swami, tutor 6 mentor 7 teacher, trainer 8 educator, lecturer 9 pedagogue, preceptor

instrument

4 deed, gear, mean, tool 5 agent, means, organ 6 agency, device, gadget, medium 7 utensil, vehicle 9 apparatus, appliance, machinery, mechanism 11 contraption, contrivance 13 paraphernalia
aircraft: 5 radar, radio 7 compass 9 altimeter, gyroscope 10 altazimuth, tachometer 11 transponder
calculating: 6 abacus 8 computer 9 slide rule
graphic: 6 camera 8 otoscope 9 telescope 10 binoculars, microscope 11 fluoroscope, stethoscope, stroboscope 12 bronchoscope, oscilloscope, spectrograph, spectroscope
measuring: 4 gage 5 clock, gauge, radar, scale, sonar 7 alidade, ammeter, balance, caliper, sextant, transit 8 quadrant 9 altimeter, astrolabe, barometer, bolometer, manometer, pedometer, sonometer, voltmeter 10 anemometer, Fathometer, hydrometer, hygrometer, micrometer, radiometer, radiosonde, spirometer, tachometer, theodolite 11 chronometer, lie detector, range finder, seismograph, speedometer, thermometer 12 electroscope, galvanometer, oscillograph, oscilloscope 13 Geiger counter, potentiometer
medical: 6 lancet, trocar 7 curette, forceps, specula (plural) 8 tenacula (plural) 9 tenaculum
radiation-producing: 5 laser, maser
(see also **implement; musical instrument; tool**)

instrumental

5 vital 6 useful 7 crucial, helpful 9 conducive, essential, necessary, requisite 10 imperative 13 indispensable

instrumentality
5 agent, force, means, organ
6 agency, energy, medium 7 channel, vehicle 8 ministry 9 mechanism

insubordinate
6 unruly 8 factious, mutinous 9 fractious, seditious 10 headstrong, rebellious, refractory 11 disobedient, intractable, uncompliant 12 contumacious, recalcitrant, ungovernable

insubstantial
4 airy, weak 5 frail 6 feeble, flimsy 7 fragile, tenuous 8 bodiless, ethereal 9 imaginary, unfleshly 10 intangible 11 disembodied 12 apparitional

insufferable
10 unbearable 11 intolerable, unendurable 13 insupportable

insufficiency
4 lack 6 dearth 7 paucity, poverty 8 scarcity, shortage 10 deficiency, inadequacy, scantiness, scarceness 11 defalcation

insufficient
5 scant 6 scanty, scarce, skimpy 7 lacking, wanting 10 inadequate, incomplete

insular
5 local 6 narrow 7 bigoted, limited 8 confined, isolated, secluded 9 illiberal, parochial, sectarian, small-town 10 prejudiced, provincial, restricted

insulate
6 cut off, ensile 7 isolate 8 close off 9 segregate, sequester

insult
4 gibe, jeer, mock, slap, slur 5 abuse, fleer, scoff, scorn, shame, sneer, taunt 6 debase, deride, offend, revile 7 affront, disdain, obloquy, offense, outrage 8 derision, disgrace, ignominy, ridicule 9 contumely, humiliate 10 opprobrium 12 vituperation

insurance
8 guaranty, warranty 10 protection

agency: 7 actuary 8 adjuster 11 underwriter
term: 6 policy 7 annuity 8 coverage 9 bordereau 11 beneficiary

insure
5 cinch, guard 6 shield 7 confirm, protect 9 guarantee, safeguard 10 underwrite

insurgent
5 rebel 6 anarch 8 factious, frondeur, mutineer, mutinous, revolter 9 anarchist, seditious 10 incendiary, rebellious 12 contumacious 13 insubordinate, revolutionary

insurrection
4 coup 6 mutiny, putsch, revolt, rising 8 uprising 9 rebellion

insurrectionist
5 rebel 6 anarch 8 frondeur, mutineer, revolter 10 malcontent

insusceptible
6 exempt, immune 9 resistant 10 impervious 11 unreceptive

intact
5 sound, whole 6 entire, unhurt, virgin 7 perfect 8 complete, unbroken, unmarred, virginal 9 undamaged, uninjured, untouched 10 unimpaired

intangible
4 airy 5 vague 7 elusive, ghostly 8 ethereal 10 evanescent, immaterial, impalpable 11 incorporeal

integer
4 unit 5 digit 6 entity, figure, number 7 numeral 11 whole number

integral
4 full 5 whole 6 entire 7 perfect 8 complete, inherent 9 composite, elemental, essential, necessary, requisite 11 constituent 13 indispensable

integrate
3 mix 4 fuse, join, link 5 blend, merge, unify, unite 6 embody, mingle 7 combine, conjoin 8 coalesce 9 harmonize, reconcile 10 amalgamate, assimilate, coordinate, synthesize 11 consolidate, desegregate

integrity
5 honor **6** virtue **7** honesty, probity
8 cohesion **9** coherence, constancy,
rectitude, soundness, wholeness
12 completeness

integument
4 coat **5** testa **7** coating, cuticle
8 covering, envelope

intellect
3 wit **4** mind **5** brain **6** acumen,
brains, genius, reason, smarts
9 intuition, mentality **12** intelligence
13 comprehension, understanding

intellectual
5 brain **6** brainy, mental, pundit
7 bookish, egghead, erudite, psychic,
thinker **8** academic, cerebral, highbrow, longhair **9** scholarly

intelligence
3 wit **4** dope, info, mind, news,
word **5** brain, savvy, sense **6** acuity,
acumen, brains, notice, reason,
smarts, wisdom **7** hearsay, tidings
8 aptitude, judgment, learning,
sagacity **9** knowledge, mentality,
mother wit **10** brainpower, shrewdness

intelligent
4 keen, wise **5** acute, alert, aware,
quick, sharp, smart, sound **6** adroit,
astute, brainy, bright, clever, shrewd
7 cunning, knowing, logical **8** rational,
sensible **9** brilliant, ingenious,
sagacious **10** reasonable **11** quick-
witted, ready-witted **13** perspicacious

intelligentsia
7 clerisy **8** literati, vanguard
10 avant-garde, illuminati

intelligible
5 clear, lucid, plain

intemperance
6 excess **7** license **9** depravity
10 debauchery, profligacy **11** dissipation, drunkenness **12** immoderation, incontinence

intemperate
5 harsh **6** bitter, brutal, severe
7 drunken, extreme, violent **8** bibu-
lous **9** crapulous, dissolute, excessive **10** dissipated, exorbitant,
gluttonous, immoderate, inordinate,
profligate **12** unrestrained **13** overindulgent

intend
3 aim, try **4** mean, plan **5** essay,
spell **6** assign, denote, design,
scheme, strive **7** attempt, connote,
propose, purpose, signify **8** endeavor **9** designate

intended
6 fiancé **7** engaged, fiancée **8** destined, plighted, promised, proposed
9 affianced, betrothed **10** calculated,
deliberate

intense
4 keen **5** acute, vivid **6** ardent,
fervid, fierce, severe, strong **7** extreme, fervent, furious, violent,
zealous **8** powerful, vehement
9 assiduous, excessive, exquisite
10 heightened **12** concentrated

intensify
4 rise **5** mount, rouse **6** accent, heat
up, stress **7** enhance, sharpen
8 escalate, heighten, increase,
redouble **9** aggravate, emphasize
10 accentuate, aggrandize, exacerbate **11** concentrate

intensity
6 energy, fervor **7** passion **8** emphasis, ferocity, fervency, loudness
9 vehemence

intensive
6 all-out **7** zealous **8** sweeping,
thorough **10** exhaustive **12** concentrated
pronoun: 6 itself, myself **7** herself,
himself **8** yourself **9** ourselves
10 themselves, yourselves

intent
3 aim, set **4** goal, plan, rapt, will
5 eager, fixed **6** design, import,
object **7** decided, earnest, engaged,
meaning, purport, purpose, riveted,
wrapped **8** absorbed, conation,
decisive, diligent, immersed, resolute, resolved, sedulous, volition

9 engrossed, objective, wrapped up
10 determined

intention
3 aim, end **4** goal, hope, plan, wish
6 design, desire, object **7** meaning,
purpose **8** ambition **9** objective
10 aspiration

intentional
5 meant **7** advised, studied, willful,
willing, witting **8** designed, proposed
9 voluntary **10** considered, deliberate
12 premeditated

intentionally
9 on purpose, purposely

inter
4 bury **5** plant **6** entomb, inhume
9 lay to rest

interact
9 cooperate **11** collaborate

interbreed
5 cross **9** hybridize **10** mongrelize

intercede
6 step in **7** mediate **9** arbitrate

intercept
4 grab **5** catch, seize, steal **6** cut
off, hijack

intercessor
5 agent **6** broker **8** advocate, mediator **9** go-between, middleman

interconnect
4 join, link **5** unite **6** couple, hook
up, link up

intercourse
3 sex **5** trade, truck **7** contact, dealing, traffic **8** business, commerce,
dealings **9** communion **10** connection, networking **11** give-and-take
12 conversation **13** communication

intercross
9 hybridize **10** mongrelize

interdict
3 ban, bar **4** veto **5** block, taboo
6 cut off, enjoin, forbid, outlaw
7 censure, condemn, embargo
8 disallow, prohibit, sanction **9** proscribe **11** prohibition

interest
4 gain, grab, hook, lure, pull **5** pique,
stake, tempt **6** appeal, arouse,
behalf, engage, profit, regard **7** attract, concern, engross, involve,
welfare **8** appeal to, intrigue **9** attention, curiosity, fascinate, tantalize,
well-being **10** prosperity

interested
4 rapt **5** drawn **7** curious, partial
8 invested, partisan **9** attentive

interface
3 GUI **6** border **8** boundary **9** cooperate **11** communicate

interfere
6 butt in, horn in, meddle, step in
7 barge in, intrude

interim
3 gap **5** break, pause **6** acting,
breach, hiatus, lacuna, pro tem
7 stopgap, time-out **8** downtime,
meantime **9** makeshift, temporary
10 pro tempore **11** provisional

interior
3 gut **4** pith **5** belly, bosom, heart,
inner **6** center, inland, inside, inward,
marrow **8** visceral **9** heartland
10 hinterland

interject
3 add **6** fill in, insert **7** throw in

interjection
agreement: 4 amen **5** roger
6 righto **7** right on
attention-getter: 3 hey **4** ahem,
ahoy, psst **6** yoo-hoo
calling pigs: 5 sooey
cheer: 3 rah **5** wahoo **6** hooray,
hurrah, hurray
contempt: 4 pooh **5** pshaw
disappointment: 4 rats **5** shoot
6 shucks
disapproval: 3 boo, fie
disbelief: 3 huh
disgust: 3 bah, boo, pah, ugh
4 rats, yuck **5** faugh, yecch **6** phooey
dismay: 4 oh no, uh-oh
dismissal: 3 git **4** shoo
farewell: 3 bye **4** ciao **5** adios
6 bye-bye, so long **7** cheerio

greeting: 4 ciao 5 aloha, hello, howdy
in golf: 4 fore
in hunting: 6 yoicks
in marching: 3 hup, hut
joy: 4 whee 6 hooray, hurrah, hurray, yippee 7 hosanna, whoopee 8 alleluia 10 hallelujah
mild apology: 4 oops 6 whoops
mild oath: 3 gad 4 darn, drat, egad, geez, gosh, heck, jeez 5 egads, golly, zooks 6 jiminy, zounds 7 begorra, gee whiz, jeepers 8 gadzooks 13 gee whillikers
O.K.: 5 roger, wilco
pain: 4 ouch
peace: 6 shalom
regret: 3 woe 4 alas 5 alack 8 lackaday
relief: 4 phew
request: 7 prithee
silence: 3 shh
sneeze: 5 achoo 6 atchoo 7 kerchoo
sorrow: 4 alas 5 alack 8 lackaday
stop: 4 whoa
surprise: 3 aha, huh, oho, wow 4 gosh, oops 5 blimy, yikes, yipes, zowie 6 blimey
to a horse: 4 whoa 7 giddyap
toast: 5 salud, skoal 6 cheers, prosit 6 l'chaim 7 l'chayim
triumph: 3 aha, hah 6 eureka
(see also **exclamation**)

interlace
3 mix 5 braid, plait, twine, weave 7 entwine 9 alternate

interlard
3 mix 6 mingle

interlocuter
4 host 5 emcee

interlope
6 butt in, horn in, meddle 7 intrude 8 encroach, infringe 9 interfere

interlude
4 halt, lull, rest 5 break, idyll, letup, pause, spell 6 recess 7 episode, respite 8 breather, entr'acte, meantime, stoppage 9 meanwhile 10 suspension

intermediary
3 mid 4 mean 5 agent, envoy, organ 6 agency, broker, center, medium, middle, midway 7 central, channel, vehicle 8 delegate, emissary, mediator, ministry 9 go-between, middleman

intermediate
3 mid 4 fair, mean, so-so 6 broker, center, medium, middle, midway, step in 7 average, between, central 8 middling 9 arbitrate, go-between, middleman

intermediator
6 broker 7 liaison, referee 9 go-between, middleman

interment
6 burial 9 sepulture 10 inhumation

intermesh
4 lock 6 engage 8 dovetail

interminable
7 endless, eternal, lasting 8 constant, infinite, unending 9 boundless, ceaseless, continual, limitless, permanent, perpetual, unceasing 10 protracted 11 everlasting, never-ending

intermission
4 lull, rest, stop 5 break, pause, spell 6 recess 7 latency, respite, time-out 8 abeyance, dormancy, interval 10 quiescence, suspension 11 parenthesis

intermit
4 halt, stay 5 break, defer, delay 6 arrest, hold up, put off 7 suspend 8 postpone, prorogue 9 interrupt 11 discontinue

intermittent
6 broken, cyclic, fitful, serial 8 cyclical, metrical, periodic, seasonal, sporadic 9 irregular, recurrent, recurring, spasmodic, stop-and-go 10 occasional

intermix
4 meld 5 blend 6 mingle 8 comingle, compound 9 commingle,

integrate 10 amalgamate 11 intermingle

intermixture
4 brew 5 blend 7 amalgam 8 compound 9 composite, synthesis
12 amalgamation 13 miscege-
nation

intern
4 jail 6 immure 7 confine, impound,
put away, trainee 8 imprison 11 incarcerate

internal
6 native 7 private 8 visceral 10 subjective
prefix: 5 intra

internal organs
4 guts 6 bowels, vitals 7 innards,
viscera 8 entrails 10 intestines,
penetralia

international organization
3 FAO, IAM, ICJ, ILO, ITO, ITU,
OAS, WHO, WMO, WTO 4 IAAF,
IABA, IAEA, IARU, IATA, ICAO, IFIP,
IMCO, NATO 5 ICFTU, SEATO
6 UNESCO, UNICEF

internuncio
5 envoy 6 bearer, legate 7 carrier,
courier 8 delegate, emissary 9 go-
between, messenger, middleman

interpolate
3 add 5 admit, annex, enter 6 append, fill in, inject, insert 7 throw in
9 introduce

interpose
6 butt in, fill in, insert, meddle, step
in 7 intrude, mediate, obtrude, throw
in 8 moderate 9 arbitrate, insinuate,
introduce, negotiate 11 come between

interpret
5 gloss 6 decode 7 explain, expound 8 annotate, construe 9 elucidate, explicate 10 paraphrase

interpretation
5 gloss 7 meaning, reading, version
8 exegesis 9 construal, rendering
11 explanation, translation

interpretive
8 exegetic 10 diagnostic, exegetical,
expository 11 explanatory, explica-
tory

interregnum
5 break, lapse, pause 6 hiatus
7 time-out

interrogate
3 ask 4 pump, quiz 5 grill, query
7 examine 8 question 9 catechize
12 cross-examine

interrupt
4 halt, stay, stop 5 abort, break, cut
in 7 break in, chime in, suspend
8 cut short

interruption
3 gap 4 halt 5 break, pause, split
6 breach, cutoff, hiatus, lacuna,
recess 7 caesura 8 stoppage

intersect
4 meet 5 cross 9 decussate
10 crisscross

intersection
8 crossing, junction 10 crossroads

intersperse
7 diffuse, scatter 8 sprinkle

interstice
3 gap 4 slit, slot, vent 5 chink, cleft,
crack, space 6 breach, cavity,
cranny 7 crevice, fissure, opening,
orifice 8 aperture

intertwine
4 mesh 5 braid, plait, twist, weave
7 network 9 convolute 10 crisscross

interval
3 gap 4 lull, wait 5 break, comma,
delay, letup, pause, space 6 breach,
hiatus, lacuna, interim, respite, time-out 8 downtime
9 pausation 11 parenthesis
music: 4 rest

intervene
6 butt in, meddle, step in 7 intrude,
mediate, obtrude

interweave
3 mix 4 fuse, join, knit, link, mesh

intestinal fortitude

5 blend, plait, twine 6 enmesh
7 entwine, wreathe

intestinal fortitude

4 grit, guts 5 nerve, pluck, spunk
6 mettle, spirit 7 courage 8 backbone 10 resolution

intestine

3 gut 4 tube 5 bowel, canal 7 viscera (plural)
combining form: 4 coli, colo
6 entero
part: 5 cecum, colon, ileum 7 jejunum 8 duodenum

in the same place

6 ibidem

intimacy

9 closeness 11 familiarity 12 acquaintance

intimate

3 gut 4 cozy, dear, fond, hint 5 amigo, close, crony, imply, inner, privy
6 attest, friend, impart, loving, secret
7 comrade, connote, devoted, nearest, suggest 8 familiar, inherent
9 close-knit, companion, confidant, ingrained, insinuate, intrinsic 12 confidential

intimation

3 cue 4 clue, hint 5 shade, tinge, trace 6 breath 7 inkling 8 telltale
10 suggestion

intimidate

3 awe, cow 4 bait 5 bully, chivy, daunt, scare 6 badger, coerce, hector 7 buffalo, overawe 8 browbeat, bulldoze, bullyrag 9 strongarm, terrorize

intolerable

10 unbearable 11 unendurable
12 insufferable 13 insupportable

intolerant

6 narrow 7 bigoted 8 dogmatic
9 hidebound, illiberal 10 inflexible, prejudiced 11 small-minded
12 narrow-minded

intonation

5 chant, pitch 6 accent, timbre
7 cadence 8 chanting 10 inflection, modulation, recitation

intone

5 chant, croon, drone 10 cantillate

in toto

3 all 6 wholly 7 all told, en masse
10 altogether

intoxicant

5 booze, drink, hooch, sauce
6 hootch, liquor, rotgut 7 alcohol, spirits 9 aqua vitae, firewater, moonshine

intoxicated

3 lit, wet 4 high 5 blind, drunk, fried, giddy, lit up, oiled, stiff, tight, tipsy
6 blotto, bombed, canned, elated, juiced, loaded, looped, potted, sodden, soused, stewed, stoned, tanked, tiddly, zonked 7 blitzed, crocked, drunken, excited, maudlin, muddled, pickled, pie-eyed, sloshed, smashed, sozzled 8 cockeyed, polluted, squiffed 9 crapulous, plastered 11 exhilarated

intoxication

3 joy 5 bliss 6 frenzy 7 ecstasy, elation, rapture 8 delirium, euphoria
9 transport 10 exaltation 11 drunkenness, inebriation

intractable

4 wild 5 balky 6 mulish, ornery, unruly 7 froward, willful 8 mutinous, obdurate, perverse, stubborn
9 fractious, obstinate, pigheaded, unbending 10 bullheaded, headstrong, inflexible, rebellious, refractory, unyielding 12 pertinacious, recalcitrant, ungovernable 13 undisciplined

intransigent

5 rigid, tough 7 willful 8 obdurate, resolute, stubborn 9 obstinate, unbending, unpliable 10 refractory, self-willed, unyielding 12 contumacious, pertinacious

intrepid

4 bold, game 5 brave, gutsy, hardy
6 daring, heroic 7 doughty, gallant, valiant 8 fearless, resolute, stalwart, unafraid, valorous 9 audacious, dauntless, undaunted 10 courageous 11 adventurous, temerarious

intricate
4 mazy 6 daedal, knotty 7 complex, gordian, tangled 8 abstruse, involved, tortuous 9 Byzantine, elaborate 10 circuitous, convoluted 11 complicated 12 labyrinthine 13 sophisticated

intrigue
4 plot, wile 5 amour, cabal, cheat, pique, trick 6 affair, appeal, excite, scheme 7 attract, beguile, collude, connive, liaison, romance 8 cogitate, conspire, contrive, interest 9 machinate 10 conspiracy 11 machination

intriguing
8 enticing 9 absorbing, beguiling 10 engrossing, entrancing 11 captivating, fascinating, stimulating

intrinsic
see **inherent**

intrinsically
5 per se 6 as such 7 at heart 10 inherently

introduce
5 begin, enter, found, set up 6 broach, fill in, insert, launch, unveil, work in 7 bring up, implant, install, instill, pioneer, precede, preface, present, throw in, usher in 8 initiate, innovate, organize 9 establish, insinuate, institute, interject, interpose, originate

introduction
5 debut, proem 6 lead-in 7 introit, opening, preface, prelude 8 entrance, exordium, foreword, overture, preamble, prologue, protases (plural), protasis 12 prolegomenon

introductory
5 basic 7 initial, nascent, opening 8 proemial 9 beginning, prefatory 10 elementary 11 preliminary, preparatory

intrude
5 cut in 6 butt in, horn in, impose, invade, meddle 7 barge in, burst in, presume 8 encroach, infringe, trespass 9 interfere, interlope, interrupt

intrusive
4 busy, nosy 5 nosey 6 prying, snoopy 7 curious 8 meddling, snooping 9 officious 10 meddlesome 11 impertinent

in truth
6 indeed, really, verily 8 actually, candidly 9 veritably

intuit
5 infer, sense 6 deduce, divine 7 surmise

intuition
5 hunch 7 feeling, inkling, insight 8 instinct 10 sixth sense 11 second sight 12 presentiment

intuitive
6 innate 7 natural 8 unwilled, visceral 10 unthinking 11 instinctive, instinctual, involuntary, spontaneous, unconscious

Inuit
6 Eskimo

inundate
4 glut 5 drown, flood, swamp, whelm 6 deluge, engulf 7 overrun 8 overflow, submerge 9 overwhelm

inundation
5 flood, spate 6 deluge 7 Niagara, torrent 8 cataract, flooding, overflow 9 avalanche, cataclysm, landslide 10 cloudburst

inure
5 steel, train 6 harden, season 7 prepare, toughen 8 accustom 9 acclimate, habituate 10 discipline 11 familiarize

inutile
6 no-good 7 useless 8 unusable 9 valueless, worthless

invade
4 loot, raid 6 breach, occupy, ravage 7 overrun, pillage, plunder 8 encroach, infringe, trespass 9 penetrate

invader
8 intruder 10 encroacher, interloper, trespasser 11 infiltrator

invalid

3 bad **4** null, sick, void **5** false **6** ailing, infirm, shut-in, sickly **7** unsound **8** baseless, disabled **9** bedridden, illogical, sophistic **10** fallacious, irrational **11** null and void **12** convalescent

invalidate

4 undo, void **5** annul, quash **6** cancel, offset, vacate **7** abolish, nullify **9** discredit, repudiate **10** counteract, disqualify, neutralize

invaluable

7 crucial **8** precious **9** essential, priceless **11** beyond price, inestimable **13** irreplaceable

invariable

4 same **5** fixed **6** static, steady **7** uniform **8** constant **9** continual, immovable, immutable, unfailing, unvarying **10** changeless, consistent, unchanging **11** inalterable, unalterable **12** unchangeable

invariably

4 ever **6** always **7** forever

invasion

4 raid **5** foray **6** attack, inroad **7** assault, offense **8** trespass **9** incursion, intrusion, offensive, onslaught **12** encroachment

invective

5 abuse **6** tirade **7** abusive, obloquy **8** diatribe, jeremiad **9** contumely, philippic, truculent **10** opprobrium, scurrility, scurrilous **11** opprobrious **12** billingsgate, contumelious, vituperation, vituperative

inveigh

4 kick, rail, rant **6** object **7** protest **8** complain **9** fulminate **11** expostulate, remonstrate

inveigle

4 coax, lure **5** decoy, snare, tempt **6** allure, cajole, entice, entrap, lead on, rope in, seduce, wangle **7** blarney, win over **8** blandish, butter up, maneuver, persuade

invent

4 coin, mint **6** cook up, create, design, devise, make up, patent, vamp up **7** concoct, dream up, fashion, hatch up, pioneer, think up **8** conceive, contrive, discover, engineer, envision **9** fabricate, formulate, originate

invention

7 coinage, fiction **8** creation **10** brainchild, innovation **11** contrivance

inventive

7 fertile, teeming **8** creative, fruitful, original **9** demiurgic, ingenious **10** innovative, innovatory **11** imaginative

inventor

5 maker **6** author, father, mother **7** creator, founder **8** engineer **9** architect, generator, innovator **10** discoverer, introducer, originator
air brake: **12** Westinghouse (George)
air conditioning: **7** Carrier (Willis)
automobile: **7** Daimler (Gottlieb)
ballpoint pen: **4** Loud (John)
barbed wire: **7** Glidden (Joseph Farwell)
barometer: **10** Torricelli (Evangelista)
bifocal lens: **8** Franklin (Benjamin)
camera: **7** Eastman (George)
cash register: **5** Ritty (James)
cotton gin: **7** Whitney (Eli)
cylinder lock: **4** Yale (Linus)
dirigible: **8** Zeppelin (Ferdinand von)
dynamite: **5** Nobel (Alfred)
electric battery: **5** Volta (Alessandro)
electric fan: **7** Wheeler (George)
electric organ: **7** Hammond (Laurens)
electric razor: **6** Schick (Jacob)
electric stove: **7** Hadaway (W. S.)
elevator: **4** Otis (Elisha)
fountain pen: **8** Waterman (Lewis)
friction match: **6** Walker (John)
gyrocompass: **6** Sperry (Elmer)
helicopter: **8** Sikorsky (Igor)

investigate

hot-air balloon: 11 Montgolfier (Jacques, Joseph)
incandescent lamp: 6 Edison (Thomas Alva)
induction motor: 5 Tesla (Nikola)
lawn mower: 5 Hills (Amariah)
Linotype: 12 Mergenthaler (Ottmar)
logarithm: 6 Napier (John)
machine gun: 7 Gatling (Richard)
microphone: 8 Berliner (Emile)
microwave oven: 7 Spencer (Percy)
movable type: 9 Gutenberg (Johannes)
parachute: 9 Blanchard (Jean-Pierre)
pendulum clock: 7 Huygens (Christiaan)
phonograph: 6 Edison (Thomas Alva)
photography: 6 Niepce (Nicéphore), Talbot (W. H. Fox) 8 Daguerre (Louis)
piano: 10 Cristofori (Bartolomeo)
radio: 7 Marconi (Guglielmo)
reaper: 9 McCormick (Cyrus)
revolver: 4 Colt (Samuel)
rocket engine: 7 Goddard (Robert)
safety pin: 4 Hunt (Walter)
safety razor: 8 Gillette (King)
sewing machine: 4 Howe (Elias)
sleeping car: 7 Pullman (George)
spinning jenny: 10 Hargreaves (James)
steamboat: 5 Fitch (John) 6 Fulton (Robert), Miller (Patrick), Rumsey (James) 8 Jouffroy (Claude de)
steam engine: 4 Watt (James)
steam locomotive: 10 Stephenson (George)
stethoscope: 7 Laënnec (René)
submarine: 7 Holland (John Philip)
synthesizer: 4 Moog (Robert)
tank: 7 Swinton (Ernest)
telegraph: 5 Morse (Samuel F. B.)
telephone: 4 Bell (Alexander Graham)
telescope: 10 Lippershey (Hans)
television: 5 Baird (John) 6 Nipkow (Paul) 8 Zworykin (Vladimir) 10 Farnsworth (Philo)
thermometer: 7 Galileo (Galilei)
torpedo: 9 Whitehead (Robert)

tractor: 5 Deere (John)
transistor: 7 Bardeen (John) 8 Brattain (Walter), Shockley (William)
vulcanized rubber: 8 Goodyear (Charles)
writing for the blind: 7 Braille (Louis)
zipper: 6 Judson (Whitcomb)

inventory
3 sum 4 fund, list 5 hoard, stock, store, tally 6 assets, digest, record, supply, survey 7 account, backlog, catalog, itemize, reserve, specify, summary 8 register, tabulate 9 catalogue, checklist, enumerate, reservoir, stockpile, summarize, synopsize

inverse
8 contrary, opposite

inversion
7 reverse 8 flipping, reversal, upending 9 about-face, turnabout, volteface

invert
4 flip 5 upend 7 reverse 8 overturn, turn over 9 transpose

invertebrate
4 weak 5 timid 7 chicken, doormat, milksop 8 boneless, impotent, weakling 9 jellyfish, spineless 10 namby-pamby 11 ineffectual, milquetoast
kind: 4 worm 6 insect, sponge 7 mollusc, mollusk 8 arachnid 9 arthropod 12 coelenterate

invest
4 gird, veil, wrap 5 adorn, array, dress, endow, imbue 6 clothe, confer, enfold, induct, infuse, ordain 7 empower, enclose, envelop, ingrain, install, suffuse

investigate
3 pry 4 sift 5 audit, probe, study 6 go into, search 7 dig into, examine, explore, inquire, inspect 8 check out, look into, muckrake, prospect, research 9 delve into 10 scrutinize 11 inquire into

investigation
5 audit, probe 6 survey 7 inquest, inquiry 8 research, scrutiny 11 fact-finding, inquisition

investigator
3 spy 4 dick 5 hound 6 shamus, sleuth 7 gumshoe 8 hawkshaw, sherlock 9 detective

investiture
9 inaugural, induction 10 initiation, ordination 12 inauguration, installation, ratification

inveterate
3 old, set 5 fixed, sworn 6 rooted 7 abiding, chronic, settled 8 deep-dyed, enduring, habitual, hard-core, hardened, lifelong 9 confirmed, ingrained, perennial 10 continuing, deep-rooted, deep-seated, entrenched, habituated, persistent, persisting 11 established 12 incorrigible 13 dyed-in-the-wool

Invictus author
6 Henley (William Ernest)

invidious
7 envious, envying, jealous 9 green-eyed, obnoxious, resentful

invigorate
4 stir 5 brace, pep up, rally, renew, rouse 6 perk up, vivify 7 animate, brace up, enliven, fortify, juice up, refresh, restore 8 energize, vitalize 9 reinforce, stimulate 10 rejuvenate, revitalize, strengthen

invincible
10 inviolable, unbeatable 11 impregnable, indomitable, insuperable 12 invulnerable, unassailable, undefeatable 13 unconquerable

in vino ____
7 veritas

inviolable
4 safe 6 secure 10 impervious, sacrosanct 11 consecrated, impregnable 12 unassailable 13 incorruptible

invisible
6 hidden 9 concealed 10 intangible 12 unnoticeable 13 imperceptible

Invisible Man
author: 5 Wells (H. G.) 7 Ellison (Ralph)
character: 7 Griffin

Invisible Man, The
author: 5 Wells (Herbert George)
character: 7 Griffin (Herbert)

invitation
4 call, lure 6 come-on 7 bidding, proffer 8 entreaty, proposal 10 enticement 11 proposition 12 solicitation

invite
3 ask, bid 4 call, lure 5 tempt 6 allure, call in, entice, summon 7 propose, request, solicit

inviting
8 engaging, enticing, tempting 9 appealing, beguiling, seductive 10 attractive, intriguing

invocation
6 appeal, prayer 8 entreaty, petition 11 conjuration, incantation 12 supplication

invoice
3 tab 4 bill, list 5 score 7 account 8 manifest 9 reckoning, statement 11 consignment

invoke
3 beg 4 pray 5 crave, plead 6 appeal, call on, effect 7 beseech, conjure, enforce, entreat, implore, solicit 8 call upon, petition 9 call forth, conjure up, implement, importune 10 supplicate

involuntary
6 forced, reflex 8 knee-jerk 9 automatic, impulsive, reflexive, unwitting 10 compulsory, unintended, unprompted 11 instinctive, spontaneous, unconscious, unmeditated 13 unintentional

involve
4 mire 6 affect, embody, engage, entail, take in 7 call for, concern, contain, embrace, embroil, include,

require, subsume **8** comprise, entangle **9** encompass, implicate **10** complicate, comprehend **11** necessitate

involved
6 daedal, knotty **7** complex, gordian **8** confused **9** Byzantine, elaborate, intricate **10** convoluted **11** complicated **12** labyrinthine

invulnerable
6 immune, secure **10** impervious, invincible, unbeatable **11** impregnable, indomitable **12** unassailable

Io
father: 7 Inachus
guard: 5 Argus
son: 7 Epaphus

iodine source
4 kelp

Iolanthe
composer: 8 Sullivan (Arthur)
librettist: 7 Gilbert (W. S.)

Iolcus king
5 Aeson **6** Pelias

Iole
captor: 8 Heracles, Hercules
father: 7 Eurytus
husband: 6 Hyllus

ion
6 ligand
kind: 5 anion **6** cation **8** thermion

Ion
father: 6 Apollo
mother: 6 Creusa
stepfather: 6 Xuthus

Ionesco, Eugène
play: 6 Chairs (The), Lesson (The) **10** Rhinoceros **11** Bald Soprano (The)

iota
3 bit, jot, ray **4** atom, hint, mite, whit **5** crumb, grain, ounce, scrap, shred, speck, trace **6** tittle **7** smidgen **8** molecule, particle **9** scintilla

IOU
4 chit, debt
part: 3 owe, you

Iowa
capital: 9 Des Moines
city: 4 Ames **7** Dubuque **8** Waterloo **9** Davenport, Sioux City **11** Cedar Rapids **13** Council Bluffs
college, university: 5 Drake **8** Grinnell
nickname: 7 Hawkeye (State)
river: 9 Des Moines
state bird: 9 goldfinch
state flower: 15 wild prairie rose
state tree: 3 oak

Iphicles
brother: 8 Heracles, Hercules
mother: 7 Alcmene
son: 6 Iolaus

Iphigenia
avenger: 12 Clytemnestra
brother: 7 Orestes
father: 9 Agamemnon
mother: 12 Clytemnestra
sister: 7 Electra

Iran
ancient civilization: 4 Elam **5** Medes, Media **6** Persia
capital: 6 Tehran **7** Teheran
city: 3 Qom, Qum **6** Shiraz, Tabriz **7** Esfahan, Isfahan, Mashhad
conqueror: 9 Alexander (the Great)
gulf: 4 Oman **7** Persian
island: 5 Qeshm
language: 5 Farsi **7** Persian
leader: 7 Pahlavi (Mohammad Reza, Reza Shah) **8** Khomeini (Ayatollah Ruholla)
monetary unit: 4 rial
mountain, range: 6 Elburz, Zagros **8** Damavand **9** Hindu Kush
neighbor: 4 Iraq **6** Turkey **7** Armenia **8** Pakistan **10** Azerbaijan **11** Afghanistan **12** Turkmenistan
river: 5 Atrek, Karun, Safid **7** Karkheh
sea: 7 Caspian
strait: 6 Hormuz

Iranian
7 Persian
parliament: 6 Majlis
religious movement: 5 Baha'i
sect: 4 Shia
sect member: 6 Shiite

Iraq

Iraq

ancient civilization: 5 Akkad, Sumer 8 Akkadian, Sumerian 9 Babylonia 10 Babylonian
ancient name: 11 Mesopotamia
capital: 7 Baghdad
city: 5 Basra, Mosul, Najaf 6 Kirkuk 7 Falluja, Karbala 8 Fallujah
conqueror: 9 Alexander (the Great)
desert: 6 Syrian
gulf: 7 Persian
leader: 6 Faisal 7 Hussein (Saddam)
monetary unit: 5 dinar
neighbor: 4 Iran 5 Syria 6 Jordan, Kuwait, Turkey 11 Saudi Arabia
river: 6 Tigris 9 Euphrates

irascible

4 tart 5 huffy, surly, testy 6 crabby, cranky, feisty, tetchy, touchy 7 bristly, grouchy, peevish, peppery, prickly 8 choleric, petulant, snappish 9 crotchety, fractious, irritable, querulous, splenetic 11 hot-tempered 12 cantankerous 13 quick-tempered

irate

3 mad 5 angry, livid, riled, vexed, wroth 6 fuming 7 enraged, furious, steamed 8 choleric, incensed, provoked, wrathful 9 indignant 10 infuriated

ire

4 fury, rage, rile 5 anger, wrath 6 choler, enrage, madden, temper 7 incense, steam up, umbrage 9 infuriate 10 exasperate 11 indignation 12 exasperation

Ireland

4 Eire, Erin 8 Hibernia
capital: 6 Dublin
city: 4 Cork 5 Kerry, Louth, Meath, Sligo 6 Galway 7 Donegal, Kildare, Wexford, Wicklow 8 Kilkenny, Limerick 9 Waterford 12 Dun Laoghaire
county: 4 Mayo 5 Clare 6 Galway 8 Limerick
island group: 4 Aran 8 Hibernia
lake: 3 Ree (Lough) 4 Derg (Lough) 5 Neagh (Lough) 6 Corrib (Lough)
language: 5 Irish 6 Gaelic 7 English

monetary unit: 4 euro
monetary unit, former: 5 pound
nickname: 11 Emerald Isle
river: 6 Barrow, Liffey 7 Shannon

Irene

3 Pax
father: 4 Zeus 7 Jupiter
mother: 6 Themis

irenic

4 calm 7 pacific 8 pacifist 9 peaceable, placative, placatory 10 nonviolent 12 conciliatory, propitiatory

Iris

father: 7 Thaumas
mother: 7 Electra

Irish

4 Erse 6 Celtic, Gaelic
accent: 6 brogue
cattle: 5 Kerry
clan: 4 sept
combining form: 7 Hiberno
coronation stone: 7 Lia Fail
cudgel: 10 shillelagh
death spirit: 7 banshee
dog: 6 setter 7 terrier
elf: 10 leprechaun
flag color: 5 green, white 6 orange
flower: 8 shamrock
girl: 4 lass 6 lassie 7 colleen
god: 3 Ler 5 Dagda 6 Aengus
goddess: 4 Badb, Bodb 6 Brigit 8 Morrigan
hero: 9 Cuchulain 10 Cú Chulainn
heroine: 7 Deirdre
king: 9 Brian Boru
lake: 5 lough
language: 6 Gaelic
legislature: 4 Dail
militant force: 3 IRA
nationalist: 4 Tone (Wolfe) 6 Pearse (Padraig) 7 Collins (Michael), Parnell (Charles) 8 De Valera (Eamon), O'Connell (Daniel) 9 Sarsfield (Patrick)
nationalist society: 8 Sinn Fein
patron saint: 7 Patrick
theater: 5 Abbey
writing system: 4 ogam 5 ogham (see also **Gaelic; Celtic**)

Irish moss
7 seaweed 9 carrageen

irk
3 try, vex 4 fret, gall, pain, rile 5 annoy, peeve, pique, upset 6 abrade, bother, harass, nettle, ruffle, strain, stress 7 provoke, trouble 8 exercise, irritate 10 exasperate

irksome
6 vexing 7 tedious 8 annoying, rankling 9 provoking, upsetting, vexatious 10 bothersome, irritating, nettlesome, unpleasant 11 aggravating, troublesome, unpalatable

iron
4 firm, gyve, hard 5 press, rigid 6 fetter, strong 7 adamant, manacle, shackle 8 handcuff, obdurate 9 unbending 10 inexorable, inflexible
combining form: 5 ferro 6 sidero
German: 5 Eisen
relating to: 6 ferric 7 ferrous

ironbound
5 harsh, rocky, rough, stern 6 craggy, jagged, rugged, severe, strict, uneven 7 scraggy 8 asperous, exacting, rigorous, scabrous 9 stringent 10 inflexible

Iron City
10 Pittsburgh

ironclad
5 fixed 7 binding 8 constant 9 immovable, immutable 10 inflexible, invariable 11 inalterable, irrefutable, unalterable 12 indisputable, irrefragable, unchangeable 13 unimpeachable

ironfisted
4 grim, hard, mean 5 harsh 6 brutal, severe, stingy 7 callous, miserly 8 pitiless, ruthless 9 penurious 10 implacable, unmerciful 11 hardhearted, intractable, remorseless 12 unappeasable

ironhanded
5 harsh, rigid 6 severe, strict 8 despotic, rigorous 9 draconian, stringent 10 tyrannical 12 unpermissive

ironhearted
5 stony 7 callous 8 hardened, obdurate, ruthless 9 merciless, unfeeling 10 hard-boiled 11 coldblooded 13 unsympathetic

iron horse
10 locomotive

ironic
3 wry 6 biting 7 caustic, cutting, cynical, mordant, satiric 8 sardonic 9 sarcastic, trenchant

iron ore
8 goethite, hematite, limonite, siderite, taconite 9 magnetite

Iron Pants
6 Patton (George)

irons
5 bonds, gyves 6 chains 7 bilboes, darbies, fetters 8 manacles, shackles

Iroquois tribe
6 Cayuga, Mohawk, Oneida, Seneca 8 Onondaga 9 Tuscarora

irradiate
4 beam, glow 5 edify, light, shine 6 uplift 7 light up 8 illumine 9 enlighten 10 illuminate

irrational
3 mad 5 crazy 6 absurd, insane 7 invalid 8 demented 9 illogical, senseless, sophistic 10 cockamamie, fallacious, ridiculous 12 preposterous, unreasonable

irrefutable
4 sure 6 proven 7 certain 8 airtight, ironclad, positive 9 apodictic, veracious 10 conclusive, inarguable 11 indubitable 12 indisputable 13 incontestable

irregular
3 odd 5 queer 6 fitful, patchy, random, spotty, uneven 7 aimless, erratic, unequal 8 aberrant, abnormal, atypical, informal, lopsided, peculiar, singular, sporadic, unstable, unsteady, variable 9 anomalous, desultory, divergent, eccentric,

guerrilla, haphazard, hit-or-miss, spasmodic, unregular, unsettled **10** asymmetric, capricious, changeable, inconstant, off-balance, unbalanced, unofficial **11** exceptional, fluctuating **12** intermittent, unsystematic

irregularity
5 freak, quirk **6** oddity **7** anomaly **8** deviance **9** deviation, roughness **10** aberration, inequality, unevenness **11** abnormality

irrelevant
5 inapt **9** unrelated **10** extraneous, immaterial, inapposite, peripheral **11** inessential, unessential, unimportant **12** inapplicable **13** insignificant

irreligious
6 unholy **7** godless, impious, profane, ungodly **11** blasphemous

irreparable
8 cureless, hopeless **9** incurable **11** immedicable **12** irredeemable, irremediable **13** irretrievable, unrecoverable

irreproachable
4 pure **8** flawless, innocent, spotless, virtuous **9** blameless, errorless, exemplary, faultless, guiltless, righteous **10** immaculate, impeccable, inculpable, unblamable

irresolute
5 shaky **6** fickle, unsure, wobbly **7** halting **8** doubtful, hesitant, unstable, waffling, wavering **9** equivocal, faltering, tentative, uncertain, undecided **10** ambivalent, changeable, inconstant, wishy-washy **11** fluctuating, half-hearted, vacillating

irresponsible
4 rash, wild **8** carefree, careless, feckless, reckless **10** incautious, unreliable **12** undependable **13** unaccountable, untrustworthy

irreverent
4 flip **7** impious, profane, ungodly **8** flippant **9** satirical **11** blasphemous **12** sacrilegious

irrevocable
4 firm **5** final **9** immutable **11** unalterable **12** irreversible, unchangeable **13** nonreversible

irrigation ditch
5 flume **6** sluice **7** acequia

irritability
5 pique **6** choler **8** edginess **9** petulance **10** crabbiness, impatience **11** fretfulness, peevishness
abnormal: 8 erethism

irritable
4 edgy, sour **5** cross, huffy, testy, waspy, whiny **6** crabby, cranky, crusty, grumpy, ornery, snappy, tetchy, touchy **7** fretful, grouchy, peevish, pettish, prickly, waspish **8** captious, choleric, petulant, snappish **9** crotchety, fractious, impatient, irascible, querulous, splenetic **12** cantankerous, disagreeable

irritant
4 itch, pest **5** nudge **6** bother, gadfly, noodge, nudnik, pester, plague **8** headache, nuisance, vexation **9** annoyance **11** botheration

irritate
3 bug, irk, rub, vex **4** fret, gall, goad, rile, roil **5** anger, annoy, chafe, grate, peeve, pique, spite **6** abrade, badger, bother, burn up, harass, hector, madden, needle, nettle, offend, ruffle **7** inflame, provoke **9** aggravate, stimulate **10** exacerbate, exasperate

irritated
5 irate, testy **7** fretful, peevish **8** choleric **9** impatient, irascible

irritation
4 itch, pest, rash, sore **6** bother, plague **7** chagrin **8** nuisance, vexation **9** annoyance

irrupt
5 belch, eruct, surge **6** invade **7** intrude

irruption
4 raid **5** foray **6** inroad **7** upsurge **8** invasion **9** incursion, intrusion

I.R.S. employee
7 auditor 10 accountant

Irving novel
15 Cider House Rules (The) 17 Hotel New Hampshire (The) 20 World According to Garp (The)

Isaac
father: 7 Abraham
mother: 5 Sarah
son: 4 Esau 5 Jacob
wife: 7 Rebekah

Isabella I
country: 5 Spain
home: 7 Castile
husband: 9 Ferdinand

Isaiah
7 prophet
father: 4 Amoz

Iscah
brother: 3 Lot
father: 5 Haran
sister: 6 Milcah

Iseult, Isolde
beloved: 7 Tristan 8 Tristram
husband: 4 Mark

Ishbak
father: 7 Abraham
mother: 7 Keturah

Ishbosheth's father
4 Saul

Ishmael
6 pariah 7 outcast 8 castaway, outsider 11 untouchable
father: 7 Abraham
mother: 5 Hagar

Ishtar
brother: 7 Shamash
father: 3 Anu, Sin
lover: 6 Tammuz

Ishui's father
4 Saul 5 Asher

Isis
brother: 6 Osiris
father: 3 Geb
husband: 6 Osiris
mother: 3 Nut
son: 4 Sept 5 Horus

Islam
adherent: 6 Moslem, Muslim
founder: 8 Mohammed, Muhammad
god: 5 Allah
holy city: 5 Mecca
holy month: 7 Ramadan
law: 6 Sharia
place of worship: 6 mosque
priest: 4 imam
scriptures: 5 Koran, Quran
sect: 4 Shia, Sufi 5 Sunni 6 Shiite, Sufism 7 Ismaili, Wahhabi
(see also **Muslim**)

island
3 ait, cay, key 4 holm 5 atoll, oasis 6 skerry 7 crannog
Admiralty group: 5 Manus
Adriatic Sea: 3 Vis 4 Brac, Cres, Hvar 5 Brach, Ciovo, Mljet, Solta 6 Lesina, Pharus
Aegean Sea: 4 Scio 5 Chios, Khios, Samos, Thira 6 Ikaria, Lemnos, Lesbos, Limnos 7 Nikaria 8 Mitilini, Mytilene, Santorin 10 Sakis-Adasi, Susam-Adasi
Alaska: 4 Adak, Atka, Attu, Kuiu 8 Wrangell
Aleutian group: 3 Rat 4 Adak, Akun, Attu 5 Amlia, Kiska, Umnak 6 Kanaga, Tanaga, Unimak 8 Amchitka, Unalaska
American Samoa: 3 Ofu, Tau 4 Rose 6 Swains
Andaman Sea: 4 Mali 5 Tavoy
Antarctica: 5 Scott, Young
Apostle group: 3 Oak 4 Long, Sand 5 Outer 8 Madeline, Michigan, Stockton
Arafura Sea: 5 Dolak
Arctic Archipelago: 6 Baffin 8 Victoria
Arctic Ocean: 5 Senja
Australian: 5 Cocos 8 Tasmania
Azores: 4 Pico 5 Corvo, Faial
Bahamas: 3 Cat, Rum 4 Long 5 Abaco, Exuma 6 Andros, Inagua 7 Acklins, Crooked 8 Watlings 9 Eleuthera, Mayaguana 11 San Salvador
Bahrain: 5 Sitra 8 Muharraq
Balearic group: 5 Ibiza 7 Majorca, Menorca, Minorca 8 Mallorca

Baltic Sea: 4 Moon, Muhu 5 Faron, Mukhu, Rugen, Worms 6 Vormsi 7 Gotland 8 Bornholm, Gothland, Gottland

Barents Sea: 4 Bear

Bay of Naples: 5 Capri

Bay of Panama: 4 Naos

Bering Sea: 5 Medny 7 Nunivak 10 Big Diomede 13 Little Diomede

Bismarck Archipelago: 5 Lihir 10 New Britain

Bristol Channel: 5 Lundy

Buzzards Bay: 9 Cuttyhunk

Canadian: 5 Banks, Devon 6 Baffin 8 Bathurst, Melville, Somerset, Victoria 9 Anticosti, Ellesmere 10 Cape Breton 11 Axel Heiberg, Southampton 12 Newfoundland, Prince Edward

Canaries: 6 Gomera 7 La Palma 8 Tenerife 9 Lanzarote

Cape Verde: 4 Fogo, Maio, Mayo 5 Brava, Rombo

Caribbean Sea: 4 Cuba 5 Aruba, Utila, Vache 6 Tobago 7 Antigua, Curaçao, Jamaica 8 Barbados, Dominica, Trinidad 10 Guadeloupe, Martinique, Puerto Rico (see also **Virgin group**)

Carolines: 5 Soroi 6 Ponape 9 Ascension

Chagos Archipelago: 11 Diego Garcia

Channel group: 4 Herm, Sark 5 Lihou, Sercq 6 Jersey 8 Guernsey

Chesapeake Bay: 4 Deal, Kent 5 Smith, Watts

Chukchi Sea: 6 Herald

Comoro group: 7 Mayotte

Congo River: 4 Bamu

Cook group: 4 Atiu 5 Mauke

Croatia: 3 Krk, Pag, Rab 5 Susak, Unije

Cyclades: 3 Ios, Kea, Nio 4 Ceos, Keos, Milo 5 Delos, Melos, Milos, Naxos, Paros, Siros, Syros 6 Andros, Dhilos 7 Amorgos, Cythnos, Kithnos, Kythnos, Mykonos

Denmark: 3 Als, Fyn, Mon 4 Aero, Fano, Moen, Mors 5 Alsen, Funen, Moers, Samso 6 Bornholm 13 Fanum Fortunae

D'Entrecasteaux group: 8 Kaluwawa 9 Fergusson

Dodecanese group: 3 Coo, Cos, Kos 4 Caso, Lero, Simi, Syme 5 Kasos, Leros, Lipso, Lisso, Patmo, Telos 6 Calino, Lipsos, Nisiro, Patmos 7 Calimno, Nisiros, Nisyros 8 Kalymnos

East River: 5 Ward's 7 Welfare 9 Roosevelt

England's: 7 Britain 9 Britannia 12 Great Britain

English Channel: 5 Wight

Faeroes: 4 Vago 5 Bordo, Sando

Fiji: 4 Koro 5 Mango, Vatoa

Florida Keys: 4 Long, Vaca, West 5 Largo 7 Big Pine 9 Matecumbe, Sugarloaf

Fox group: 5 Umnak 6 Akutan, Unimak 8 Unalaska

French: 7 Corsica 12 New Caledonia

French Polynesia: 4 Rapa, Reao, Ua Pu 5 Ua Pau

Frisian group: 3 Rom 4 Föhr, Sylt 5 Amrum, Juist, Mando, Texel 6 Borkum 7 Ameland 8 Langeoog, Pellworm, Vlieland 9 Helgoland, Norderney

Futunas: 5 Alofi

Galápagos: 5 Pinta 7 Chatham, Isabela 8 Abingdon 10 Albermarle

Georgia: 5 Tybee

Germany: 4 Fohr 7 Fehmarn 9 Helgoland 10 Heligoland

Greater Antilles: 4 Cuba 7 Jamaica 10 Hispaniola, Puerto Rico

Greece: 4 Milo, Rodi 5 Creta, Crete, Hydra, Idhra, Kriti, Rodos, Tenos, Tinos 6 Euboea, Evvoia, Hydrea, Lesbos, Rhodes, Rhodus 9 Negropont 10 Negroponte

Grenadines: 5 Union

Gulf of Alaska: 6 Kodiak

Gulf of Bothnia: 5 Karlö

Gulf of Carpentaria: 5 Maria 6 Groote 7 Eylandt

Gulf of Guinea: 7 Sao Tomé 8 Príncipe, Sao Thomé 11 Saint Thomas

Gulf of Mexico: 3 Cat 5 Lobos

Gulf of Panama: 3 Rey

Gulf of St. Lawrence: 5 Brion
Gulf of Thailand: 3 Kut 5 Samui
Haiti: 6 Gonâve
Hawaii: 4 Maui, Oahu 5 Kauai,
Lanai 6 Niihau 7 Molokai
9 Kahoolawe
Hudson Bay: 5 Coats
Indian Ocean: 4 Mahé, Nias
5 Heard, Pemba 7 La Dique,
Praslin, Réunion 8 Sri Lanka, Zanz-
ibar 9 Mauritius 10 Madagascar
Indonesia: 4 Bali, Biak, Java, Maja,
Muna, Nias, Rhio, Riau, Roma, Roti,
Savu, Sawu 5 Batam, Boano, Buton,
Djawa, Japen, Lakor, Moena, Riouw,
Rotti, Rupat, Sawoe, Solor, Sumba,
Wetar, Wokam 6 Butung, Flores,
Jappen, Lombok, Madura, Pa-
dang, Roepat, Romang, Soemba
7 Celebes, Madoera, Sumatra,
Sumbawa 8 Boetoeng, Soembawa,
Sulawesi 10 Bandanaira, Banda
Neira, Sandalwood
Inner Hebrides: 4 Coll, Eigg, Iona,
Jura, Muck, Mull, Skye 5 Canna,
Gigha, Islay, Tiree, Tyree
Ionian group: 5 Corfu, Paxos,
Zante 6 Cerigo, Ithaca, Leukas,
Levkas 10 Santa Maura
Iran: 5 Shahi
Ireland: 4 Aran
Irish Sea: 3 Man
Italy: 4 Elba 6 Sicily 8 Sardinia
Japan: 3 Iki, Uku 4 Naru, Yezo
5 Awaji, Fukae, Fukue, Hondo,
Shodo 6 Honshu, Kyushu 7 Shi-
koku 8 Hokkaido 10 Shodoshima
Java Sea: 4 Laut
Kiribati: 6 Tarawa
Kuril group: 4 Urup 5 Ketoi, Matua
6 Iturup 7 Etorofu, Matsuwa 8 Ku-
nashir 9 Kunashiri
Lake Champlain: 5 Grand
Lake Erie: 9 North Bass, South
Bass 10 Middle Bass
Lake Huron: 8 Drummond 10 Man-
itoulin
Lake Michigan: 3 Hog 4 High
6 Beaver
Lake Ontario: 5 Wolfe
Lake Superior: 4 Sand 6 Royale
7 Manitou

Lake Winnipeg: 5 Hecla
largest: 9 Greenland
Leeward group: 5 Nevis 7 Antigua,
Barbuda, Redonda 8 Anguilla,
Sombrero 10 Montserrat, Saint Kitts
13 St. Christopher
legendary: 7 Cipango
Lesser Sundas: 4 Alor 5 Ombai
Leti group: 3 Moa 5 Lakor
Line group: 5 Flint 6 Malden,
Vostok 7 Fanning, Palmyra 8 Star-
buck 9 Christmas
Long Island Sound: 4 City, Hart
5 Goose, Harts
Loyalty group: 3 Uea 4 Lifu, Maré,
Uvea 5 Lifou
Malay Archipelago: 5 Kisar, Larat,
Timor 6 Borneo 9 New Guinea
Malaysia: 6 Penang, Pinang
13 Prince of Wales
Malta: 4 Gozo
Marianas: 4 Maug, Rota 5 Pagan
6 Saipan
Marquesas group: 4 Eiào, Ua Pu
6 Hatutu, Hiva Oa, Ua Huka 7 Ta-
huata 8 Fatu Hiva, Nuku Hiva
Marshall group: 5 Wotho, Wotje
8 Eniwetok 9 Kwajalein
Massachusetts: 9 Nantucket
Mediterranean Sea: 4 Elba 5 Corfu,
Crete, Malta 6 Cyprus, Euboea,
Rhodes, Sicily 7 Corsica 8 Sardinia
Midway group: 4 Sand 7 Eastern
Moluccas: 4 Buru 5 Ambon,
Ceram, Seram 6 Boeroe
Mozambique channel: 10 Juan de
Nova
Myanmar: 5 Daung, Kadan, Lanbi
Narragansett Bay: 5 Rhode 8 Pru-
dence 9 Aquidneck, Conanicut
Netherlands: 5 Texel 7 Ameland
8 Vlieland
Netherlands Antilles: 7 Curaçao
New York: 4 Fire, Long 9 Gardiners,
Roosevelt
New York Bay: 5 Ellis 6 Staten
7 Liberty 9 Governors, Manhattan
New Zealand: 5 South, White
7 Chatham, Stewart 8 D'Urville
Niagara River: 4 Goat
Nile River: 4 Argo, Roda, Ruda
5 Rhoda 6 Rawdah 11 Elephantine

North Channel: 3 Mew
Northern Cook group: 7 Penrhyn
8 Manihiki 9 Tongareva
North Pacific: 4 Wake
Northwest Territories: 5 Banks,
Bylot, Devon 8 Bathurst, Melville
9 Ellesmere 10 Cornwallis, Resolution 13 Prince of Wales
Norwegian: 8 Jan Mayen
Norwegian Sea: 5 Donna, Smola,
Vikna
Nova Scotia: 5 Sable 10 Cape
Breton
off Alaska: 4 Dall 5 Kayak
off Albania: 5 Sazan 6 Saseno
off Australia: 4 Dunk
off Belize: 9 Ambergris
off Brazil: 4 Apeu 5 Rocas
off British Columbia: 4 King, Pitt
9 Vancouver
off Cape Cod: 8 Muskeget 9 Nantucket
off Chile: 5 Guafo, Mocha
off China: 4 Amoy 5 Ma-tsu
6 Hainan, Quemoy, Taiwan
off Crete: 3 Dia
off Ecuador: 4 Puna
off England: 3 Man 5 Wight
6 Walney
off Florida: 3 Dog 4 Pine 6 Amelia
7 Pelican, Sanibel 9 Anastasia
off French Guiana: 6 Devil's
off Georgia: 10 Cumberland
11 Saint Simons
off Germany: 4 Sylt
off Greenland: 5 Disko
off Guinea: 5 Tombo
off Hispaniola: 5 Beata
off Honduras: 5 Tigre
off Iceland: 7 Surtsey
off India: 5 Sagar
off Ireland: 4 Tory 5 Clare, Clear
off Kenya: 4 Lamu
off Long Island: 7 Fishers
off Louisiana: 5 Marsh
off Maine: 4 Deer, Orrs 5 Swans
8 Monhegan 11 Mount Desert
off Malay Peninsula: 6 Phuket
9 Singapore
off Maryland: 10 Assateague
off Massachusetts: 4 Plum 7 Naushon

off Mexico: 7 Cozumel
off Mississippi: 4 Horn, Ship
off Mozambique: 3 Ibo
off New Brunswick: 10 Campobello
off Newfoundland: 4 Bell
off Nigeria: 5 Lagos
off North Carolina: 5 Bodie
off Norway: 5 Bomlo, Froya, Hitra,
Sotra, Stord, Vardo 8 Hitteren
off Panama: 5 Coiba 6 Parida
off Poland: 5 Wolin 6 Wollin
off Puerto Rico: 4 Crab 7 Culebra,
Vieques
off Rhode Island: 5 Block
off Scotland: 4 Bute 5 Arran
off South Carolina: 5 North 6 Parris 10 Hilton Head
off Sri Lanka: 5 Delft
off Staten Island: 7 Hoffman
off Sumatra: 3 Weh
off Sweden: 5 Graso, Oland, Vaddo
off Syria: 5 Arvad, Arwad, Rouad
6 Aradus
off Tanzania: 5 Mafia, Pemba
off Tasmania: 5 Bruni, Bruny
off Tunisia: 5 Jerba 6 Djerba,
Meninx
off Venezuela: 5 Aruba 7 Bonaire
8 Buen Aire
off Virginia: 5 Wreck
off Wales: 5 Caldy 6 Caldey
Okinawa group: 4 Kume
Orkneys: 3 Hoy
Outer Hebrides: 5 Barra, Scarp
Palmer Archipelago: 6 Anvers
7 Antwerp, Brabant
Pearl Harbor: 4 Ford
Persian Gulf: 4 Qeys 5 Kharg,
Khark
Philippines: 4 Buad, Cebu, Fuga,
Ilin, Poro, Sulu 5 Balut, Batan,
Bohol, Coron, Daram, Leyte, Luzon,
Panay, Samal, Samar, Sugbu, Talim,
Ticao, Verde 6 Negros 7 Masbate,
Mindoro, Palawan, Paragua 8 Limasawa, Mindanao 10 Corregidor
Phoenix group: 4 Hull, Mary
6 Birnie, Canton 9 Enderbury
Puerto Rico: 4 Mona
Quebec: 4 Alma
Queen Charlotte group: 7 Moresby
Red Sea: 5 Tiran, Zugur, Zuqar

Russia: 7 Wrangel
Ryukyu group: 7 Okinawa
St. Lawrence River: 4 Hare 5 Jesus
8 Montreal
San Francisco Bay: 5 Angel
Santa Cruz: 5 Anuda, Ndeni
6 Cherry
Sea of Japan: 4 Sado 5 Rebun
Sea of Marmara: 4 Avsa
second largest: 9 New Guinea
Senegal: 5 Gorée
Seychelles: 4 Mahé 7 La Digue,
Praslin
Shetland archipelago: 4 Unst, Yell
5 Foula
Shumagin group: 4 Unga
Sierra Leone: 5 Tasso
Society group: 5 Eimeo, Tahaa,
Tahao, Taiti 6 Moorea, Tahiti 8 Ota-
heite
Solomon group: 4 Buka, Gizo,
Savo 7 Malaita 11 Guadalcanal
12 Bougainville
South Atlantic: 5 Gough
6 Gough's 11 Saint Helena
South Korea: 5 Cheju
South of Tokyo: 3 Iwo 7 Iwo Jima,
Naka Iwo
South Orkneys: 10 Coronation
South Pacific: 3 Hiu 4 Niue
5 Raoul 6 Savage, Sunday 7 Nor-
folk 8 Pitcairn
Spitsbergen archipelago: 4 Edge
Strait of Hormuz: 5 Qeshm, Qishm
Sulu Archipelago: 4 Jolo 5 Lapac
Svalbard: 4 Hope
Sverdrup: 11 Axel Heiberg
12 Amund Ringnes
Swedish: 3 Ven 4 Hven 5 Hveen,
Orust
Tanzania: 8 Zanzibar
Texas: 5 Padre
Thames River: 7 Sheppey
third largest: 6 Borneo
Tierra del Fuego: 5 Hoste
Tonga: 3 Eua, Foa 4 Uiha 5 Haano
Treasury group: 4 Mono
Truk group: 3 Tol 4 Haru, Moen,
Udot, Uman 5 Fefan
Tuamotu Archipelago: 4 Anaa
5 Chain
Turkish: 5 Imroz 6 Imbros

Tuvalu: 7 Nanumea 9 Nukufetau
Tyrrhenian Sea: 6 Ischia 11 Mon-
tecristo
Vanuatu: 3 Api, Epi, Oba 4 Aoba,
Gaua, Tana, Vate 5 Efate, Maewo,
Tanna
Venezuelan: 5 Patos 9 La Tortuga
Virgin group, American: 9 Saint
John 10 Saint Croix 11 Saint
Thomas
Virgin group, British: 5 Peter
6 Norman 7 Anegada, Tortola
11 Jost Van Dyke
volcanic: 5 Tofua 7 Iwo Jima
Wales: 8 Anglesea, Anglesey,
Holyhead
Weddell Sea: 4 Ross 6 Hearst
Western Samoa: 5 Upolu 6 Savaii
West Indies: 4 Mona, Saba, Salt
5 Nevis, Peter, Saona 6 Tobago,
Tortue 7 Grenada, Tortuga 8 Trini-
dad 9 Santa Cruz 10 Concepción,
Hispaniola, Montserrat, Saint Croix
(see also **Bahamas; Greater An-
tilles; Leeward group; Virgin
group; Windward group**)
West of England: 7 Ireland
West Pacific: 5 Dyaul, Fauro,
Ocean 6 Banaba, Marcus 7 Iwo
Jima, Kita Iwo 9 Minami Iwo
Windward group: 10 Martinique
with former penitentiary: 8 Alcatraz

island group

Alaska: 3 Rat 8 Aleutian, Pribilof
9 Andreanof, Catherine
Aleutians: 4 Near
American Samoa: 5 Manua
Arabian Sea: 9 Laccadive
Arctic Archipelago: 8 Sverdrup
Arctic Ocean: 8 Svalbard 12 No-
vaya Zemlya
Bahamas: 5 Berry, Exuma 6 Bimini
Banda Sea: 5 Damar
Bangladesh: 5 Hatia, Hatya
Bay of Bengal: 7 Andaman, Nicobar
between England and France:
7 Channel
Bismarck Archipelago: 4 Feni
5 Tabar, Tanga
Bismarck Sea: 4 Vitu
British: 7 Bermuda

Caribbean Sea: 4 Swan 5 Pearl 6 Cayman, Perlas, Pigeon 8 Pichones 10 Grenadines, West Indies
Carolines: 3 Uap, Yap 4 Truk 5 Nomoi 7 Hogoleu
Central Pacific Ocean: 4 Line 5 Samoa, Union 6 Danger, Midway 7 Phoenix, Tokelau 8 Manihiki 9 Polynesia 12 Northern Cook
Coral Sea: 4 Huon
Cuba: 8 Camagüey
east of Philippines: 10 Micronesia
East Siberian Sea: 4 Bear 8 Medvezhi
Ecuador: 5 Colón 9 Galápagos
England: 5 Farne
Fiji: 3 Lau 7 Eastern
Formosa Strait: 4 Hoko 6 Peng hu 10 Pescadores
French: 5 Salut 6 Safety 9 Kerguelen
French Polynesia: 3 Low 6 Tubuai 7 Austral, Paumotu, Société, Society, Tuamotu 9 Marquesas, Touamotou
Germany: 8 Halligen
Greece: 6 Aegean, Ionian 8 Cyclades 10 Dodecanese 11 Dodecanesus
Hudson Bay: 7 Belcher
Indian Ocean: 7 Aldabra
Indonesia: 4 Asia, Batu, Pagi, Sula 5 Babar, Batoe, Pagai, Pageh, Penju, Spice, Wakde 6 Maluku
Ireland: 4 Aran
Japan: 4 Osumi
largest: 5 Malay 8 Malaysia
Lesser Antilles: 8 Windward
Malay Archipelago: 5 Sunda 6 Soenda
Mediterranean Sea: 8 Baleares, Balearic
Moluccas: 3 Kai, Kei, Obi 4 Leti 5 Banda, Letti 8 Tanimbar 9 Timorlaut
New Caledonia: 7 Loyalty 9 Loyalties
north of Australia: 9 Melanesia
north of British Isles: 5 Faroe 7 Faeroes
north off Fiji: 5 Hoorn 6 Futuna
north of Madagascar: 7 Aldabra 8 Farquhar

north of New Caledonia: 5 Belep
north of New Guinea: 8 Bismarck 9 Admiralty 11 Admiralties
Northwest Territories: 5 Parry
off Alaska: 3 Fox
off Alaska Peninsula: 8 Shumagin
off Cape Cod: 9 Elizabeth
off eastern Asia: 5 Kuril 6 Kurile
off England: 6 Scilly
off Florida: 11 Dry Tortugas
off Guinea: 3 Los 4 Loos
off Honduras: 5 Bahia
off Morocco: 7 Madeira
off New Guinea: 3 Aru 4 Aroe
off Nicaragua: 4 Corn
off northern Africa: 6 Canary 8 Canaries
off northern Australia: 6 Wessel 7 Dampier
off Sicily: 5 Egadi 8 Aegadian
Outer Hebrides: 4 Uist
Papua New Guinea: 5 Green
Persian Gulf: 4 Tunb
Philippines: 4 Cuyo 5 Tapul 6 Lubang 7 Basilan, Bisayas, Visayan
Portuguese: 6 Azores
Quebec: 8 Magdalen 9 Madeleine
Ryukyus: 5 Amami
St. Lawrence River: 8 Thousand
Sea of Japan: 3 Oki
Sea of Marmara: 5 Kizil 7 Princes 11 Kizil Adalar
South Atlantic Ocean: 8 Falkland, Malvinas
South China Sea: 6 Hirata 7 Paracel, Spratly
south of New Zealand: 8 Auckland
South Pacific: 11 Austronesia
Sulu Sea: 7 Cagayan 9 Cagayanes
Tonga: 5 Vavau
Tyrrhenian Sea: 5 Ponza
Venezuelan: 4 Aves, Bird 9 Los Roques
West Europe: 12 British Isles
West Indies: 6 Virgin 10 Guadeloupe
west of French Polynesia: 4 Cook
west of Scotland: 7 Western 8 Hebrides
west Pacific Ocean: 4 Duff 5 Bonin, Mapia, Palau, Pelew 7 Ladrone, Mariana, Solomon, Vanuatu 8 Mar-

shall, Treasury **9** Ogasawara
10 Saint David

island nation
Atlantic Ocean: 9 Cape Verde
Indian Ocean: 8 Malagasy, Malgache, Sri Lanka **9** Mauritius
10 Madagascar, Seychelles
Mediterranean Sea: 6 Cyprus
Mozambique Channel: 6 Comoro
7 Comores
off southern China: 6 Taiwan
south of Greenland: 7 Iceland
West Indies: 4 Cuba **7** Jamaica
8 Barbados **10** Saint Lucia
West Pacific Ocean: 5 Nauru
Windward group: 8 Dominica

island province
12 Prince Edward

island state
6 Hawaii

isle
see **island**

Ismene
brother: 9 Polynices
father: 7 Oedipus
mother: 7 Jocasta
sister: 8 Antigone
uncle: 5 Creon

isochronous
7 regular **8** cyclical, periodic, rhythmic **9** recurrent, recurring **10** periodical **12** intermittent

isolate
6 cut off, detach, enisle **7** seclude
8 close off, insulate, pinpoint, separate, set apart **9** segregate, sequester **10** quarantine

isolated
5 alone **6** random, remote, unique
7 unusual **8** solitary, sporadic
9 separated, withdrawn **11** exceptional, quarantined

Isolde
see **Iseult**

Israel
ancient name: 4 Zion **5** Judea
6 Canaan, Judaea **9** Palestine
capital: 9 Jerusalem
city: 4 Acre **5** Haifa, Jaffa **7** Tel Aviv **9** Beersheba
desert: 5 Negeb, Negev
gulf: 5 Aqaba
lake: 8 Tiberias **12** Sea of Galilee
language: 6 Arabic, Hebrew
monetary unit: 6 shekel
neighbor: 5 Egypt, Syria **6** Jordan
7 Lebanon
plain: 9 Esdraelon
river: 6 Jordan
sea: 4 Dead **13** Mediterranean

Israeli
5 Sabra

Israelite
see **Hebrew; Jewish**

Issachar
father: 5 Jacob
mother: 4 Leah

issue
4 emit, flow, gush, pour, rise, seed, stem, vent **5** arise, birth, brood, child, fruit, scion, topic **6** affair, appear, effect, emerge, get out, matter, put out, result, scions, sequel, source, spring, upshot **7** concern, descent, edition, emanate, give off, give out, outcome, problem, proceed, progeny, publish, release, subject **8** bulletin, children, question, throw off **9** come forth, offspring, originate, posterity **10** derive from, distribute, end product, promulgate **11** consequence, descendants, progeniture, publication

Istanbul
ancient name: 9 Byzantium
business section: 6 Galata
country: 6 Turkey
foreign quarter: 4 Pera **7** Beyoglu
park: 8 Seraglio
residential section: 7 Uskudar

isthmus
Africa-Asia: 4 Suez
America: 6 Panama
Greece: 7 Corinth
Malay Peninsula: 3 Kra

Italian

automobile: 4 Fiat 6 Lancia 7 Ferrari 8 Maserati 9 Alfa Romeo 11 Lamborghini

cathedral: 5 duomo

dialect: 6 Tuscan 8 Sicilian

dictator: 9 Mussolini (Benito)

family: 4 Este 5 Cenci, Savoy 6 Borgia, Medici, Orsini, Pepoli, Savoia, Sforza 7 Colonna, Gonzaga, Spinola 8 Visconti

fascist: 10 Blackshirt

game: 5 bocce, bocci 6 boccie

gentleman: 6 signor 7 signore

highway: 10 autostrada

lady: 5 donna 7 signora 9 signorina

magistrate: 7 podestà

meat: 6 salami 8 pancetta 9 pepperoni, salsiccia 10 mortadella, prosciutto

opera house: 7 La Scala

patriot: 6 Cavour (Conte di), Rienzo (Cola di) 7 Mazzini (Giuseppe) 9 Garibaldi (Giuseppe)

religious reformer: 10 Savonarola (Girolamo)

resort: 4 Lido 5 Abano, Capri 8 Sorrento, Taormina

road: 6 strada

soup: 10 minestrone

square: 6 piazza

street: 3 via 5 corso

weight: 5 libra, oncia

Italy

bay: 6 Naples

capital: 4 Rome

city: 4 Asti, Bari, Pisa 5 Aosta, Genoa, Milan, Padua, Parma, Siena, Turin 6 Genova, Mantua, Milano, Modena, Naples, Napoli, Padova, Torino, Venice, Verona 7 Bergamo, Bologna, Bolzano, Catania, Cremona, Firenze, Leghorn, Livorno, Mantova, Palermo, Perugia, Ravenna, Salerno, Taranto, Trieste, Venezia 8 Florence, Siracuse, Syracuse

enclave: 9 San Marino 11 Vatican City

gulf: 5 Gaeta 7 Salerno, Taranto 11 Sant' Eufemia

island, island group: 4 Elba 5 Caprì 6 Ischia, Lipari, Sicily 7 Aeolian, Capraia 8 Sardinia

lake: 4 Como 5 Garda 7 Bolsena 8 Maggiore 9 Bracciano

leader: 9 Mussolini (Benito)

monetary unit: 4 euro

monetary unit, former: 4 lira

mountain, range: 4 Alps, Etna 9 Apennines, Mont Blanc, Monte Rosa 10 Monte Corno

neighbor: 6 France 7 Austria 8 Slovenia 11 Switzerland

peninsula: 9 Salentina

river: 4 Arno, Liri 5 Adige, Piave, Tiber 6 Isonzo, Tevere 8 Volturno

sea: 6 Ionian 8 Adriatic, Ligurian 10 Tyrrhenian 13 Mediterranean

strait: 7 Messina, Otranto

volcano: 4 Etna 8 Vesuvius

wine region: 4 Asti

itch

3 yen 4 ache, long, lust, pine 5 crave, yearn 6 desire, hanker, hunger, thirst 7 craving, longing 8 appetite, pruritus, yearning 9 hankering

itchy

4 avid, edgy, keen 5 antsy, eager, jumpy 7 fidgety, restive 8 prurient, pruritic, restless 9 impatient

item

3 bit 5 entry, point, scrap, story, thing, topic 6 detail, matter 7 account, article, element, feature, product 8 clipping 9 commodity 10 particular

itemize

4 list 5 count, tally 6 number 7 catalog, run down, specify, tick off 8 document, spell out 9 catalogue, enumerate, inventory

iterate

5 drill, recap, renew 6 rehash, repeat, replay, retell 7 reprise, restate 12 recapitulate

Ithaca king

8 Odysseus

Ithamar's father

5 Aaron

itinerant

5 gypsy, nomad **6** roving **7** migrant, nomadic, roaming, vagrant **8** drifting, rambling, traveler, vagabond, wanderer **9** migratory, transient, unsettled, wandering, wayfaring **11** peripatetic

itty-bitty

3 wee **4** tiny **5** teeny, weeny **6** teensy **10** teeny-weeny **12** teensy-weensy

Ivanhoe

author: **5** Scott (Walter)
character: **5** Isaac **6** Cedric, Rowena, Ulrica **7** Rebecca, Wilfred **9** Robin Hood

Ivory Coast

11 Côte d'Ivoire
capital: **7** Abidjan **12** Yamoussoukro
city: **6** Bouaké
language: **6** French
monetary unit: **5** franc
mountain: **5** Nimba
neighbor: **4** Mali **5** Ghana **6** Guinea **7** Liberia **11** Burkina Faso
river: **7** Bandama **9** Sassandra

ivory-tower

8 academic **11** conjectural, impractical, theoretical, unrealistic

J

jab
3 hit 4 blow, poke, prod, sock, stab
5 nudge, prick, punch 6 pierce,
strike, thrust 8 puncture

jabber
3 gab, jaw, yak 6 babble, drivel,
gabble 7 blather, chatter, prattle
8 nonsense 9 gibberish

jabberer
6 gabber, magpie 7 babbler, blabber, gabbler 8 prattler 9 chatterer
10 chatterbox

Jabberwocky author
7 Carroll (Lewis)

jabot
4 fall 5 frill 6 ruffle

_____ jacet
3 hic

jack
3 tar 4 bird, card, fish, flag, hike, lift,
move, salt 5 boost, brace, bread,
dough, knave, knife, money, put up,
raise 6 brandy, cheese, device,
donkey, rabbit, sailor, seaman 7 laborer, mariner, servant 8 increase,
standard 9 criticize, mechanism
10 take to task

jackal
4 dupe, pawn 5 agent, canid, patsy
6 canine, flunky, lackey, minion,
stooge 7 cat's-paw 9 accessory,
auxiliary 10 accomplice 11 stool
pigeon
god: 4 Anpu 6 Anubis

jackanapes
3 ape 4 brat, fool 6 monkey

jackass
4 dolt, dope, fool, jerk 5 burro,
dunce, idiot, schmo 6 donkey, nitwit
7 nebbish 8 bonehead, imbecile,
numskull 9 blockhead, numbskull
10 nincompoop
deer: 3 kob 8 antelope

jackdaw
7 grackle 9 blackbird

jacket
4 Eton 5 parka, tunic 6 anorak,
blazer, bolero, jerkin, reefer, sacque,
tuxedo 7 doublet, Norfolk, peacoat,
spencer 8 camisole 10 roundabout
armored: 7 hauberk 9 habergeon
sleeveless: 4 vest 6 bolero, jerkin
9 waistcoat

jackhammer
5 drill 9 rock drill

jackknife
4 dive 6 barlow
game: 11 mumblety-peg

jackleg
6 make-do, novice 7 amateur,
shyster, stopgap 9 dishonest,
greenhorn, makeshift, temporary,
unskilled 10 substitute 11 pettifogger 12 unscrupulous

jack-of-all-trades
6 tinker 7 go-to guy 8 factotum,
handyman

jack-o'-lantern
6 fungus 7 pumpkin

jackpot
3 sum 4 pool 5 award, kitty, prize
6 reward, stakes 7 bonanza, success 8 windfall

jackrabbit
4 hare

jackstay
3 bar, rod 4 rope 7 rigging, support

Jacob
brother: 4 Esau
daughter: 5 Dinah
father: 5 Isaac
father-in-law: 5 Laban
mother: 7 Rebekah
new name: 6 Israel
son: 3 Dan, Gad 4 Levi 5 Asher,
Judah 6 Joseph, Reuben, Simeon
7 Zebulun 8 Benjamin, Issachar,
Naphtali
variant: 5 James
wife: 4 Leah 6 Rachel

Jacobin
7 radical 9 Dominican, extremist

Jacob's ladder
4 herb 5 phlox 9 perennial

jade
3 gem, nag 4 bore, cloy, dull, minx,
pall, tire, wear 5 color, drain, flirt,
green, hussy, jewel, stone, tramp,
weary, wench 6 wanton 7 fatigue,
jezebel, mineral, trollop, wear out
8 gemstone, nephrite, strumpet, wear
down

jaded
4 worn 5 blasé, bored, sated, tired,
weary 6 dulled 7 cynical, wearied,
worn-out 8 fatigued, satiated, worn
down 9 apathetic, exhausted,
surfeited 10 overworked

jaeger
4 skua 6 hunter 8 huntsman

Jael
husband: 5 Heber
victim: 6 Sisera

jag
3 cut 4 barb, jerk, load, pink, tear
5 binge, notch, prick, spell, spree
6 bender, indent, thrill, thrust 7 serrate

jagged
5 harsh, rough, sharp 6 broken,
craggy, rugged, spiked, uneven
7 scraggy 8 serrated, unsmooth
9 irregular

_____ Jagger
4 Mick

jai alai
6 pelota
basket: 5 cesta
court: 6 cancha 7 fronton

jail
3 can, jug, pen 4 coop, gaol, poky
5 clink, pokey 6 cooler, lockup,
prison 7 confine, freezer, slammer
8 hoosegow, imprison, stockade
9 constrain 11 confinement, incarcerate

jailbird
3 con 5 felon, loser 7 convict
8 criminal, prisoner, repeater 10 recidivist

jailer
5 guard, screw 6 keeper, warden
7 turnkey 8 overseer

jakes
5 privy 8 outhouse 9 backhouse

jalopy
3 car 4 auto, heap 5 crate, wreck
6 beater, junker 7 clunker, vehicle
10 automobile, rattletrap

jalousie
5 blind 6 window 7 shutter

jam
3 box, fix 4 bind, clog, cram, dunk,
pack, push 5 block, crowd, crush,
force, jelly, press, stuff, wedge
6 bruise, impede, plight, scrape,
squash, squish 7 dilemma, squeeze
8 compress, conserve, obstacle,
preserve 9 confiture, preserves
10 difficulty 11 predicament

Jamaica
capital: 8 Kingston
cay: 5 Pedro 6 Morant
city: 10 Montego Bay 11 Spanish
Town
discoverer: 8 Columbus (Christopher)

language: 7 English
location: 10 West Indies
mountain range: 4 Blue 10 Dry Harbour
sea: 9 Caribbean

Jamaican

export: 3 rum 5 sugar
hair style: 10 dreadlocks
music: 3 dub, ska 6 reggae
musician: 5 Cliff (Jimmy) 6 Marley (Bob, Ziggy) 7 Wailers
nationalist: 6 Garvey (Marcus)

jambalaya

4 olio 5 gumbo 7 mélange, mixture 8 mishmash

jamboree

4 gala 5 revel 6 fiesta, frolic 7 carouse, shindig 8 carnival, festival, wingding 9 merriment 11 celebration 13 entertainment

James

brother: 4 John 5 Jesus, Joses
cousin: 5 Jesus
father: 7 Zebedee 8 Alphaeus
mother: 4 Mary 6 Salome

James novel

8 American (The) 9 Europeans (The) 10 Bostonians (The), Confidence, Golden Bowl (The), Tragic Muse (The) 11 Ambassadors (The), Daisy Miller 14 Turn of the Screw (The), Wings of the Dove (The) 15 Portrait of a Lady (The) 16 Washington Square

Jammu and _____

7 Kashmir

Jane Eyre

author: 6 Brontë (Charlotte)
lover: 9 Rochester

jangle

3 jar 4 ring 5 babel, clash 6 clamor, excite, hubbub 7 discord, quarrel 8 conflict 11 discordance, discordancy 12 disharmonize

jangling

5 harsh, noisy, tense 7 grating 9 dissonant 10 discordant, quarreling

janitor

5 super 6 porter 7 cleaner 9 caretaker, concierge, custodian 10 doorkeeper

japan

4 coat 7 coating, varnish 11 lacquerware

Japan

5 Nihon 6 Nippon
capital: 3 Edo 5 Tokyo
city: 4 Kobe 5 Kyoto, Osaka, Otaru 6 Nagoya 7 Fukuoka, Okinawa, Sapporo 8 Kawasaki, Nagasaki, Yokohama 9 Hiroshima
island: 6 Honshu, Kyushu 7 Shikoku 8 Hokkaido
lake: 4 Biwa 8 Chuzenji
monetary unit: 3 yen
mountain: 4 Fuji 8 Fujiyama

Japanese

aborigine: 4 Ainu
art: 6 bonsai 6 ukiyo-e
baron: 6 daimyo
battle cry: 6 banzai
Buddha: 5 Amida, Amita
cartoons: 5 anime
comics: 5 manga
dancing girl: 6 geisha
dish: 4 miso, soba 5 gyoza, katsu, kombu, sushi 7 sashimi, tempura 8 sukiyaki, teriyaki
drama: 3 Noh 6 Bugaku, Kabuki 7 Bunraku
drink: 4 sake, saki
emperor: 6 Mikado 7 Akihito 8 Hirohito
fencing: 5 kendo
festival: 3 Bon
fish: 4 fugu
flower arrangement: 7 ikebana
garment: 6 kimono
gateway: 5 torii
god: 5 Ebisu, Hotei 7 Daikoku, Jurojin 8 Bishamon
goddess: 6 Benten 9 Amaterasu
governor: 6 shogun
grill: 7 hibachi
immigrant: 5 issei
instrument: 4 biwa, koto 7 samisen 8 shamisen 10 shakuhachi

martial art: 4 judo 5 kendo 6 aikido, karate 7 jujitsu
martial artist: 5 ninja
money: 3 sen, yen
plum: 6 loquat
poem: 5 haiku, tanka
porcelain: 5 imari
pottery: 4 raku 7 satsuma
radish: 6 daikon
religion: 6 Shinto 8 Buddhism 9 Shintoism
rice wine: 4 sake, saki
robe: 6 kimono
samurai clan: 5 Taira 8 Minamoto
sash: 3 obi
song: 3 uta
suicide: 7 seppuku 8 hara-kiri, kamikaze
theater: 3 Noh 6 Bugaku, Kabuki 7 Bunraku
tidal wave: 7 tsunami
vehicle: 8 rickshaw
warrior: 7 samurai
warrior code: 7 bushido
wrestling: 4 sumo
writing: 4 kana 8 hiragana, katakana
zither: 4 koto

Japanese-American
5 Issei, Nisei
second-generation: 6 Sansei

jape
3 gag, kid, rib 4 gibe, jest, jibe, joke, mock, quip 5 crack, laugh, prank, tease 7 waggery 8 drollery 9 wisecrack, witticism

Japheth
brother: 3 Ham 4 Shem
father: 4 Noah
son: 5 Gomer, Javan, Madai, Magog, Tiras, Tubal 7 Meshech

jar
4 bump, jolt, olla 5 cruse, quake, shake, shock, upset 6 jangle, jounce 7 tremble, vibrate 8 mismatch 9 container
ancient: 6 krater 7 amphora
Egyptian: 7 canopic

jardiniere
5 stand 6 holder 7 garnish

jargon
4 cant 5 argot, idiom, lingo, slang 6 patois, pidgin 7 dialect, lexicon, palaver 8 language 9 gibberish 10 mumbo-jumbo, vernacular, vocabulary 11 terminology
lawyer's: 8 legalese

jarl
4 earl 5 noble 8 nobleman 12 Scandinavian

jarring
5 harsh, rough 6 hoarse, jangly 7 grating, rasping, raucous 8 strident 9 dissonant 10 discordant, unsettling

jasmine
3 tea 4 vine 5 shrub 6 flower, yellow 7 perfume

Jason
father: 5 Aeson
helper: 5 Medea
lover: 6 Creusa, Glauce, Glauke
quest: 6 Fleece 12 Golden Fleece
ship: 4 Argo
shipmate: 8 Argonaut
teacher: 6 Chiron 7 Cheiron
uncle: 6 Pelias
wife: 5 Medea

jasper
6 morlop, quartz 9 stoneware 10 chalcedony

jaundice
4 bias 7 disease, icterus 9 prejudice

jaundiced
6 biased, warped, yellow 7 colored, cynical, envious, hostile, jealous 9 distorted 10 suspicious

jaunt
4 ride, trip 5 drive, sally 6 junket, outing, ramble 7 journey 9 excursion

jaunty
4 airy, pert 5 fresh, light, peppy, perky 6 breezy, lively 7 buoyant 8 debonair 9 sprightly 10 nonchalant

java
6 coffee

Java
almond: 7 talisay
cotton: 5 kapok
jute: 5 kenaf
plum: 5 jaman 6 jambul 7 jambool

Javanese
civet: 5 rasse
orchestra: 7 gamelan
tree: 4 upas

Javan squirrel
8 jelerang

javelin
5 lance, shaft, spear 6 weapon
7 assagai, assegai, harpoon

Javert's prey
7 Valjean (Jean)

jaw
3 gab, yak 4 chat, rail, talk 5 clack,
prate 6 babble, gabble 7 chatter,
prattle 9 yakety-yak

jawbone
7 maxilla 8 arm-twist, mandible,
persuade, talk into

jawbreaker
9 hard candy

jay
4 bird, blue, hick, rube 5 dandy
6 rustic 7 bumpkin, hayseed 9 chatterer, greenhorn

Jayhawker
9 guerrilla
State: 6 Kansas 8 Missouri

jazz
3 bop 4 guff, jive 5 bebop, stuff,
swing 6 boogie 7 ragtime 8 malarkey, nonsense
up: 5 rouse 6 vivify 7 animate,
enliven 9 stimulate

jazz musician
4 Cole (Nat "King"), Getz (Stan), Hirt
(Al), Monk (Thelonious), O'Day
(Anita), Rich (Buddy), Shaw (Artie)
5 Baker (Chet), Basie (Count), Brown
(Clifford), Corea (Chick), Davis
(Miles), Evans (Bill, Gil), Hines (Earl
"Fatha"), Jones (Hank), Krall (Diana),
Krupa (Gene), McRae (Carmen),
Roach (Max), Smith (Jimmy), Sun
Ra, Tatum (Art), Tormé (Mel), Young
(Lester) 6 Bechet (Sidney), Blakey
(Art), Burton (Gary), Carter (Benny),
Dorsey (Jimmy, Tommy), Farmer
(Art), Garner (Erroll), Gordon (Dex-
ter), Herman (Woody), Jordan
(Louis), Kenton (Stan), Mingus
(Charles), Morton (Jelly Roll), Oliver
(King), Parker (Charlie), Pepper (Art),
Powell (Bud), Puente (Tito), Silver
(Horace), Waller (Fats) 7 Brubeck
(Dave), Coleman (Ornette), Connick
(Harry), Goodman (Benny), Hampton
(Lionel), Hancock (Herbie), Hawkins
(Coleman), Holiday (Billie), Jarrett
(Keith), Metheny (Pat), Rollins
(Sonny), Rushing (Jimmy), Shorter
(Wayne), Vaughan (Sarah), Webster
(Ben) 8 Adderley (Cannonball),
Calloway (Cab), Coltrane (John),
Eldridge (Roy), Marsalis (Wynton),
Mulligan (Gerry), Peterson (Oscar),
Williams (Mary Lou) 9 Armstrong
(Louis), Ellington (Duke), Gillespie
(Dizzy), Reinhardt (Django) 10 Fitz-
gerald (Ella), Montgomery (Wes),
Washington (Dinah) 11 Beiderbecke
(Bix)

jazzy
5 gaudy 6 brassy, flashy, glitzy,
lively, rakish 7 raffish, splashy
8 animated, colorful, exciting, spirited
9 vivacious 10 flamboyant

jealous
5 green 7 envious, hostile 8 doubting, vigilant 9 demanding, green-
eyed, invidious, resentful 10 intolerant, possessive, suspicious
11 distrustful, mistrustful

jeer
4 gibe, jibe, mock 5 fleer, flout, scoff,
scorn, sneer, taunt 6 deride, heckle,
hector, insult 7 contemn, laugh at,
mockery 8 derision, ridicule

Jeeves
creator: 9 Wodehouse (P. G.)
employer: 7 Wooster (Bertie)
position: 5 valet 6 butler

jeez
4 gosh, heck 5 golly, shoot 6 shucks
7 jeepers

jefe
4 boss, head, lord 5 chief, ruler
6 honcho, leader 9 chieftain, commander

Jefferson, Thomas
home: 10 Monticello
lover: 5 Sally (Hemings)
state: 8 Virginia

Jehoram
brother: 7 Ahaziah
father: 4 Ahab 11 Jehoshaphat
kingdom: 5 Judah
slayer: 4 Jehu
wife: 8 Athaliah

Jehoshaphat
father: 3 Asa 6 Ahilud, Nimshi,
Paruah
father-in-law: 4 Ahab
son: 4 Jehu 7 Jehoram
wife: 8 Athaliah

Jehovah
3 God 6 Adonai, Elohim, Yahweh

Jehu
6 driver
father: 6 Hanani 11 Jehoshaphat
grandfather: 6 Nimshi
son: 8 Jehoahaz
victim: 5 Joram 7 Jehoram

jejune
4 dull, flat 5 banal, bland, empty,
inane, silly, trite, vapid 7 insipid,
puerile 8 childish, juvenile, lifeless
9 colorless, innocuous 10 spiritless
13 uninteresting

Jekyll's alter ego
4 Hyde (Mr.)

jell
3 set 4 form 6 cohere, gelate
7 congeal, thicken 8 coalesce
9 coagulate, take shape

jelly
3 set 4 mass 5 aspic 6 spread
7 congeal, thicken 9 coagulate

jellyfish
6 coward, medusa 7 doormat,
medusan 8 medusoid, pushover,
weakling 10 ctenophore 12 coelenterate, invertebrate, siphonophore

je ne _____ quoi
4 sais

jennet
3 ass 5 hinny, horse 6 donkey

jenny
4 bird 6 donkey, female 7 machine

jeopardize
4 risk 5 peril 6 chance, expose,
hazard 7 imperil 8 endanger

jeopardy
4 risk 5 peril 6 danger, hazard,
menace 8 exposure 9 liability
12 endangerment

jeremiad
6 lament, tirade 7 lecture 8 diatribe,
harangue 9 complaint, philippic
11 declamation, lamentation

Jeremiah
scribe: 6 Baruch

Jericho's conqueror
6 Joshua

jerk
3 ass, lug, tic, tug 4 dolt, dope, fool,
jolt, pull, push, snap, twit, yank
5 brute, idiot, lurch, ninny, spasm,
twist, wrest 6 bounce, nitwit, thrust,
twitch, wrench 7 jackass 8 preserve
10 nincompoop

jerkin
6 jacket

jerky
4 meat 5 inane 6 abrupt, stupid,
sudden 7 foolish, idiotic, jolting
8 saccadic 9 senseless

Jerome's Bible
7 Vulgate

jersey
3 cow 6 fabric 7 garment, sweater
8 pullover

Jerusalem
4 Sion, Zion **5** Salem **8** Holy City
hill: 4 Sion, Zion **6** Moriah
mosque: 4 Omar **6** Al-Aqsa
13 Dome of the Rock
pool: 6 Siloam **8** Bethesda

Jerusalem artichoke
5 tuber **8** girasole **9** sunflower

Jerusalem thorn
5 shrub **9** horsebean

jess
5 strap

Jesse
daughter: 7 Abigail, Zeruiah
father: 4 Obed
grandfather: 4 Boaz
son: 4 Ozem **5** David, Eliab, Elihu
6 Raddai **7** Shammah **8** Abinadab,
Nethanel
youngest son: 5 David

Jessica
father: 7 Shylock
husband: 7 Lorenzo

jest
3 fun, gag, kid, rag, rib **4** butt, game,
gibe, jape, jeer, joke, josh, mock,
quip, razz **5** crack, fleer, flout, humor,
prank, scoff, sneer, spoof, sport,
tease **6** banter, gaiety **7** mockery,
waggery **8** derision, drollery, ridicule
9 merriment, wisecrack, witticism

jester
3 wag, wit **4** fool **5** actor, clown,
comic, joker **7** buffoon **8** comedian,
funnyman, humorist, jokester, quipster **9** prankster **11** entertainer

Jesuit
founder: 6 Loyola (Ignatius)
leader: 6 Xavier (St. Francis)

jet
4 coal, ebon, emit, gush, inky, rush,
spew **5** black, ebony, plane, spout,
spurt **6** engine, nozzle, squirt,
stream, travel **7** current, jewelry
8 airplane **9** pitch-dark **10** pitch-
black

Jethro
daughter: 8 Zipporah
son-in-law: 5 Moses

jetsam
7 flotsam **8** wreckage **9** driftwood

jet set
5 A-list, elite **9** beau monde, haut
monde **10** glitterati

jettison
4 drop, dump, junk, omit **5** eject,
forgo, scrap **6** reject, remove **7** deep-
six, discard **8** disposal, get rid of,
throw out **9** sacrifice, throw away

jetty
4 dock, ebon, inky, pier, quay **5** black,
ebony, groin, wharf **7** project **9** pitch-
dark **10** pitch-black

Jew
6 Essene, Hebrew, Semite **7** Israeli,
Judaist **9** Israelite

jewel
3 gem **4** rock **5** adorn, bijou, ideal,
prize, stone **7** bearing **8** gemstone,
ornament, treasure **9** embellish

jeweler
8 lapidary
famous: 7 Tiffany (Charles Lewis)

jewelry
10 bijouterie
artificial: 5 glass, paste **6** strass
7 costume
piece: 3 pin **4** ring **6** brooch **7** earring **8** bracelet, cufflink, necklace,
tieclasp **9** lavaliere
set: 6 parure

Jewish
bread: 5 matzo **6** matzoh
ceremony: 4 bris **8** havdalah
10 bar mitzvah, bas mitzvah
combining form: 5 Judeo **6** Judaeo
credo: 5 shema
doctrine: 6 Mishna **7** Mishnah
New Year: 12 Rosh Hashanah
organization: 8 Hadassah **9** B'nai
B'rith
prayer: 7 kaddish, kiddush
prayer book: 6 siddur
sabbath: 8 Saturday
scripture: 5 Torah **6** Talmud
synagogue: 4 shul
teacher: 5 rabbi, rebbe **6** Hillel
village: 6 shtetl
(see also **Hebrew**)

Jezebel
4 slut **5** hussy, tramp, trull, wench
6 wanton **7** trollop **8** slattern, strumpet
father: 7 Ethbaal
home: 5 Sidon
husband: 4 Ahab
slayer: 4 Jehu
victim: 6 Naboth

jib
3 arm, shy **4** balk, boom, sail, stop
5 demur **6** refuse **9** stop short

jibe
5 agree, fit in, match, shift, tally
6 accord, concur, square **7** conform
8 dovetail **9** harmonize **10** correspond, go together **12** change
course

jiffy
3 sec **4** tick, wink **5** flash, hurry,
shake, trice **6** minute, moment,
second **7** instant **11** split second

jig
4 fish, game, hoax, hook, jerk, play,
ploy, ruse, sham, wile **5** catch,
dance, feint, trick **6** device, gambit
7 gimmick **9** deception

jigger
4 jerk, mold, sail **5** alter, gizmo
6 device, dingus, doodad, gadget,
widget **7** gimmick, machine, measure **9** doohickey, rearrange, shot
glass, thingummy **10** manipulate

jiggle
4 jerk **5** shake **7** agitate **9** oscillate

jigsaw
3 cut **4** tool **6** puzzle **7** arrange,
machine

jihad
3 war **6** strife **7** crusade, holy war
8 campaign, struggle

jilt
4 drop **5** ditch, leave **6** desert, reject
7 abandon, cast off, discard

jim-dandy
5 great, ideal, nifty, super **7** perfect
8 knockout **9** excellent, first-rate,
humdinger **11** outstanding

jimmy
3 bar, pry **4** open **5** crack, force,
lever **7** crowbar **9** break open, force
open

jimsonweed
6 datura **10** thorn apple

jingle
4 call, ring, song **5** clink, rhyme,
sound, verse **6** tinkle

jingoistic
7 hawkish **11** belligerent **12** chauvinistic, militaristic **13** nationalistic

jinn
5 afrit, genie **6** afreet, spirit

jinx
3 hex **5** charm, curse, spell **6** plague,
whammy **7** bad luck, evil eye
8 foredoom **10** affliction, misfortune

jitters
5 jumps, panic **6** nerves, shakes
7 anxiety, shivers, willies **9** whimwhams **11** nervousness, stage fright
13 heebie-jeebies

jittery
5 jumpy, nervy **6** goosey, spooky
7 anxious, fearful, fidgety, nervous,
panicky **10** high-strung

jive
3 kid **4** fool, jazz, talk **5** dance,
music, swing, tease **6** cajole, hot air,
jargon

Joab
brother: 6 Asahel **7** Abishai
father: 7 Seraiah, Zeruiah
slayer: 7 Benaiah
uncle: 5 David
victim: 5 Abner, Amasa

Joan of Arc
birthplace: 7 Domremy
epithet: 7 Pucelle (La) **13** Maid of
Orléans
king: 10 Charles VII
victory: 7 Orléans

Joan's husband
5 Darby

Joash
father: 4 Ahab **7** Ahaziah **8** Jehoahaz

job

son: 6 Gideon 7 Amaziah 8 Jeroboam
victim: 9 Zechariah

job

4 duty, hire, item, post, role, spot, task, work 5 chore, stint, trade 6 effort, office 7 calling, deprive, posting, pursuit, robbery 8 business, function, penalize, position, vocation 9 situation, speculate, victimize 10 assignment, difficulty, employment, engagement, livelihood, occupation, profession 11 undertaking

Job

daughter: 6 Keziah 7 Jemimah
father: 8 Issachar
friend: 6 Bildad, Zophar 7 Eliphaz

jobber

6 broker, dealer, seller, trader 8 merchant 10 contractor, wholesaler

job-safety agency

4 OSHA

job-training program

4 JTPA

Jocasta

daughter: 6 Ismene 8 Antigone
husband: 5 Laius 7 Oedipus
son: 7 Oedipus 8 Eteocles 9 Polynices

jock

5 pilot 7 athlete

jockey

4 play 5 rider, trick 7 beguile, exploit, finesse 8 maneuver 10 manipulate
famous: 5 Baeza (Braulio) 6 Arcaro (Eddie), Bailey (Jerry), Murphy (Isaac), Pincay (Laffit) 7 Cauthen (Steve), Cordero (Angel), Hartack (Bill), Longden (Johnny), Stevens (Gary) 8 McCarron (Chris), McHargue (Darrel), Turcotte (Ron) 9 Shoemaker (Willie)

jocular

5 comic, funny, jolly, merry, witty 6 jocose, jocund, jovial, lively 7 amusing, comical, jesting, playful 8 cheerful, humorous 9 facetious

jocularity

3 fun, wit 4 glee 5 humor, mirth 6 gaiety 7 jollity 8 hilarity 9 jocundity, joviality, merriment 11 high spirits, playfulness

jocund

3 gay 5 happy, jolly, merry 6 elated, jovial, lively 7 festive, gleeful, playful 8 mirthful 12 lighthearted

joe

3 guy 4 java 6 coffee, fellow

jog

3 dig, jab, run 4 lope, move, pace, poke, prod, push, ride, stir, trot 5 nudge, punch, rouse, shake 6 bounce, change, jounce, prompt, remind

joggle

4 join, trot 5 dowel, joint, notch, shake, tooth 6 jostle

john

4 head 5 privy 6 toilet 7 latrine 8 bathroom, lavatory 11 water closet

John Hancock

9 autograph, signature

Johnson, Samuel

biographer: 7 Boswell (James)
work: 8 Rasselas 10 dictionary

John the Baptist

father: 9 Zacharias
mother: 9 Elisabeth

John the Evangelist

brother: 5 James
father: 7 Zebedee
mother: 6 Salome

join

3 tie, wed 4 abut, ally, bind, bond, fuse, line, link, mate, yoke 5 affix, align, blend, marry, merge, piece, touch, unify, union, unite 6 attach, border, couple, engage, enlist, enroll, sign on, sign up, splice 7 combine, connect 8 compound, side with 9 affiliate, associate, integrate 12 come together

joint

3 bar, ell, hip, tie 4 butt, crux, dive,

knee, link, node, seam **5** ankle, elbow, hinge, nexus, union, wrist **6** common, mutual, public, shared, suture, united **7** hangout, knuckle, shiplap **8** abutment, combined, communal, conjunct, coupling, junction, juncture, shoulder **9** concerted, honky-tonk **10** collective, connection **11** cooperative **12** articulation

combining form: 5 arthr **6** arthro, condyl **7** condylo

disease: 9 arthritis **10** rheumatism

joist
  4 beam **6** rafter, timber **7** support

joke
  3 gag, kid, pun, rag, rib, yak **4** fool, jape, jest, josh, quip, razz **5** crack, humor, prank, sally **6** banter, corker, parody **7** mockery, sarcasm, waggery **8** drollery, one-liner **9** burlesque, wisecrack, witticism **11** monkeyshine

  stale: 8 chestnut

joker
  3 guy, wag, wit **4** card, fool **5** catch, clown, comic, cutup **6** fellow, jester, kicker **7** proviso **8** comedian, humorist **9** condition **10** limitation **11** stipulation

jollity
  3 fun, joy **4** glee **5** cheer, mirth **6** gaiety, revels **7** revelry, whoopee **8** hilarity **9** festivity, jocundity, joviality, merriment **10** ebullience, jocularity, liveliness **11** high spirits, merrymaking **12** cheerfulness, conviviality

jolly
  3 fun, gay, kid **4** glad, jest, josh, very **5** humor, merry **6** banter, blithe, jocund, jovial, joyful, joyous **7** festive, gleeful, jocular, playful, roguish, waggish **8** cheerful, mirthful, splendid **9** convivial **10** frolicsome **12** lighthearted

Jolly Roger
  4 flag **6** ensign

  user: 6 pirate

jolt
  3 hit, jar **4** blow, bump, jerk, shot, slug, stun **5** check, clash, crash, knock, lurch, shake, shock, snort, upset **6** impact, jounce, rattle **7** disturb, reverse, shake up, startle **8** astonish, surprise **9** collision

Jonah
  7 prophet

  swallower: 4 fish **5** whale

Jonathan
  brother: 7 Johanan

  father: 4 Saul

  friend: 5 David

Jones, John Paul
  ship: 15 Bonhomme Richard

  victim: 7 Serapis

Jones novel
  11 Thin Red Line (The) **15** Some Came Running **18** From Here to Eternity

jongleur
  4 bard **6** singer **7** juggler **8** minstrel **10** troubadour **11** entertainer

jonquil
  8 daffodil **9** narcissus, perennial

Jonson play
  7 Volpone **9** Alchemist (The) **15** Bartholomew Fair

Joplin creation
  3 rag **7** ragtime

Joram
  brother: 7 Ahaziah

  father: 3 Toi **4** Ahab **11** Jehoshaphat

  slayer: 4 Jehu

  son: 7 Ahaziah

Jordan
  capital: 5 Amman

  city: 5 Irbid, Zarqa

  gulf: 5 Aqaba

  language: 6 Arabic

  monarch: 7 Hussein

  monetary unit: 5 dinar

  mountain: 4 Ramm

  neighbor: 4 Iraq **5** Syria **6** Israel **11** Saudi Arabia

  river: 6 Jordan

  sea: 4 Dead

jorum
   3 cup, jug 6 vessel

Joseph
   brother:
   (see **Jacob** son)
   buyer: 8 Potiphar
   father: 5 Asaph, Jacob 9 Zacharias
   10 Mattathias
   mother: 6 Rachel
   son: 5 Jesus 7 Ephraim 8 Manasseh
   wife: 4 Mary 7 Asenath

josh
   3 kid, rag, rib 4 jest, joke, razz
   5 chaff, jolly, tease 6 banter

Joshua's victory
   7 Jericho

Joshua tree
   5 yucca

joss
   4 idol 5 image

Jo's sister
   3 Amy, Meg 4 Beth

jostle
   3 jar, jog 4 bump, push 5 crowd,
   elbow, nudge, press, shove 7 agitate, collide, compete, contend, vie
   with 8 shoulder

jot
   3 bit 4 atom, iota, note, whit 5 grain,
   minim, speck, write 6 tittle 7 smidgen 8 particle

joule component
   3 erg

jounce
   3 bob, jar, jog 4 bump, jolt 5 shake,
   shock, thump 6 impact

journal
   3 log 5 diary, organ, paper 6 ledger, record, review 7 account,
   gazette, minutes 8 magazine,
   register 9 chronicle, newspaper
   10 periodical

journalist
   3 Bly (Nellie) 4 Dowd (Maureen),
   Drew (Elizabeth), King (Larry),
   Pyle (Ernie), Reed (John), Rose
   (Charlie), Will (George F.), Zahn
   (Paula) 5 Baker (Russell), Brown
   (George), Cooke (Alistair), Dunne
   (Finley Peter), Evans (Rowland),
   Hersh (Seymour), Novak (Robert),
   Rowan (Carl), Royko (Mike), Safer
   (Morley), Smith (Hedrick), Stahl
   (Lesley), Stone (I. F.), Szulc (Tad),
   White (William Allen), Wolfe (Tom)
   6 Arnett (Peter), Bierce (Ambrose),
   Broder (David), Brokaw (Tom),
   Ephron (Nora), Koppel (Ted), Kuralt
   (Charles), Lehrer (Jim), Moyers
   (Bill), Murrow (Edward R.), Osgood
   (Charles), Rather (Dan), Reston
   (James), Reuter (Paul Julius),
   Rivera (Geraldo), Runyon (Damon),
   Safire (William), Shirer (William L.),
   Thomas (Helen, Lowell), Zenger
   (John Peter) 7 Blitzer (Wolf), Bradlee (Benjamin), Breslin (Jimmy),
   Cousins (Norman), Greeley (Horace),
   Gunther (John), Huntley (Chet),
   Kempton (Murray), McGrory (Mary),
   Mencken (H. L.), Pearson (Drew),
   Royster (Vermont), Russert (Tim),
   Tarbell (Ida), Trillin (Calvin), Wallace
   (Chris, Mike), Walters (Barbara)
   8 Amanpour (Christiane), Anderson
   (Jack, Terry), Atkinson (Brooks),
   Brinkley (David), Cronkite (Walter),
   Garrison (William Lloyd), Jennings
   (Peter), Lippmann (Walter), Pulitzer
   (Joseph), Salinger (Pierre), Sevareid
   (Eric), Steffens (Lincoln), Thompson
   (Dorothy, Hunter), Winchell (Walter),
   Woodward (Bob) 9 Bernstein (Carl),
   Donaldson (Sam), Frederick (Pauline), Salisbury (Harrison), Schieffer
   (Bob)

journey
   3 hie 4 hike, roam, tour, trek, trip
   5 jaunt, quest 6 cruise, junket, push
   on, safari, travel, voyage 7 caravan,
   odyssey, proceed, travels 8 progress
   9 excursion 10 expedition, pilgrimage
   route: 9 itinerary
   stage: 3 leg

joust
   4 duel, feud, spar, tilt 5 clash, fight

6 combat **7** contest **8** conflict
10 tournament
arena: 5 lists **8** tiltyard

Jove
see **Jupiter**

jovial
5 happy, jolly, merry **6** cheery
7 amiable **8** cheerful **9** convivial
11 good-humored, good-natured

jowl
3 jaw **5** cheek **6** dewlap, wattle
8 mandible

joy
4 glee **5** bliss, mirth **6** gaiety **7** delight, elation **8** felicity, fruition, gladness, pleasure **9** enjoyment, happiness, merriment **11** delectation

Joyce, James
birthplace: 6 Dublin
character: 5 Bloom (Leopold),
Bloom (Molly) **7** Dedalus (Stephen)
work: 6 Exiles **7** Ulysses **9** Dubliners **13** Finnegans Wake

joyful
3 gay **4** glad **5** happy, jolly, merry
6 elated, jocund **7** buoyant, festive,
gleeful, pleased **8** ecstatic, jubilant,
mirthful **9** delighted, rapturous
12 lighthearted

jubilant
5 happy **6** elated, joyful, joyous
8 euphoric, exultant, exulting **9** cock-a-hoop, delighted, overjoyed, triumphal **10** triumphant

jubilate
5 exult, glory **7** delight, rejoice
9 celebrate

jubilation
3 joy **4** glee **7** ecstasy, rapture
8 euphoria, rhapsody **9** rejoicing,
transport **10** exaltation, exultation,
joyfulness, joyousness **11** celebration **12** exhilaration

jubilee
6 flambé **8** festival **9** festivity **10** indulgence **11** anniversary, celebration
13 commemoration

Judah
brother:
(see **Jacob** son)
father: 5 Jacob
king: 3 Asa **4** Ahaz, Amon **5** Joash
6 Abijam, Josiah, Jotham, Uzziah
7 Ahaziah, Amaziah, Jehoram **8** Hezekiah, Jehoahaz, Manasseh, Rehoboam, Zedekiah **9** Jehoiakim
10 Jehoiachin **11** Jehoshaphat
mother: 4 Leah
son: 4 Onan **6** Shelah

Judas
7 traitor **8** informer, turncoat
father: 5 Simon **7** Chalphi **10** Mattathias
replacement: 8 Matthias
suicide place: 8 Aceldama, Akeldama

judge
3 ref, try, ump **4** call, deem, rule,
test **5** infer **6** critic, decide, deduce,
jurist, reckon, settle, umpire **7** arbiter,
justice, mediate, referee **8** assessor,
critique, estimate, mediator **9** arbitrate, criticize, determine, moderator
10 adjudicate, arbitrator, chancellor,
magistrate, negotiator **11** conciliator
12 intermediary
bench: 4 banc
chamber: 6 camera
in Hades: 5 Minos **6** Aeacus
12 Rhadamanthus
mallet: 5 gavel
Muslim: 5 mufti

judgment
5 award, sense **6** acumen, decree,
ruling, result, wisdom **7** finding,
insight, opinion, verdict **8** decision,
sagacity, sentence **9** appraisal,
deduction, good sense, inference
10 assessment, conclusion, discretion, estimation, evaluation, horse
sense, punishment **11** common
sense, discernment **13** determination

judgmental
7 carping **8** captious, critical **10** belittling, censorious, derogatory
11 disparaging, reproachful **12** disapproving, faultfinding **13** hypercritical

Judgment Day
8 doomsday

_____ **judicata**
3 res

judicial
assembly: 5 court
document: 4 writ

judicious
3 apt 4 fair, just, sage, sane, wise
5 right, sound 6 astute 7 careful,
prudent, sapient 8 accurate, discreet, rational, sensible 9 equitable,
objective, sagacious 10 discerning,
reasonable

Judith
father: 5 Beeri
home: 8 Bethulia
husband: 4 Esau
victim: 10 Holofernes

judo
10 martial art
teacher: 6 sensei

Judy's husband
5 Punch

jug
3 jar, pen 4 coop, ewer, gaol, jail,
stew, stir, toby 5 pokey 6 cooler,
flagon, immure, intern, lockup,
prison, vessel 7 confine, pitcher,
slammer 8 demijohn, imprison
9 constrain, container 11 incarcerate

jug-band instrument
5 kazoo 6 bottle 7 washtub 9 stovepipe, washboard

juggernaut
11 steamroller

juggle
3 fix 4 fool, toss 5 bluff, trick
6 change, delude, doctor, handle,
humbug, take in 7 balance, beguile,
deceive, mislead, shuffle 9 rearrange
10 manipulate

juice
3 sap 4 fuel, must 5 fluid 7 current,
essence 8 vitality 10 succulence
11 electricity
fermented: 4 wine 5 cider, perry

juicy
3 fat 4 racy, rich 5 lusty, vital 7 piquant 8 colorful, dripping, exciting
9 delicious, rewarding, succulent
10 profitable 11 fascinating, sensational

juju
4 luck 5 charm, magic 6 amulet,
fetish, mascot 8 talisman 10 lucky
charm

jujube
4 tree 5 fruit 7 gumdrop, lozenge

julep
5 drink

Juliet
betrothed: 5 Paris
father: 7 Capulet
lover: 5 Romeo

July 14
11 Bastille Day

jumble
3 mix 4 cake, hash, mess, olio
5 chaos, mix up, shake 6 cookie,
medley, mess up, muddle, muss up
7 clutter, confuse, disturb, mélange,
rummage, shuffle 8 disarray, disorder, mishmash, pastiche, scramble
9 confusion, patchwork, potpourri
10 assortment, hodgepodge, hotchpotch, miscellany

jumbo
4 huge, vast 5 giant 6 mighty
7 immense, mammoth, massive
8 colossal, enormous, gigantic,
oversize 9 oversized 10 prodigious
11 elephantine

jump
3 hop 4 bolt, hike, leap, move, trip
5 avoid, begin, boost, bound, clear,
flush, hurry, leave, put up, raise,
shift, start, vault 6 attack, bounce,
bustle, change, hurdle, hustle, jack
up, pounce, spring 7 bail out, elevate, startle 8 increase, leap over
9 advantage

jumper
4 sled 5 dress, horse, smock
6 blouse, jacket

jumping-frog county
9 Calaveras

jumpy
6 on edge 7 anxious, jittery, nervous
9 excitable 10 high-strung

junction
4 seam 5 joint, union 7 joining,
meeting 8 coupling 9 interface
10 confluence, connection, crossroads 12 intersection

juncture
4 seam 5 joint, point, union 6 crisis,
moment 7 instant, joining 8 coupling
10 connection, crossroads 11 concurrence, convergence 12 turning
point

jungle
3 web, zoo 4 hash, mash, maze
5 snarl 6 jumble, morass, muddle,
tangle 7 clutter, thicket 8 mishmash
9 labyrinth

Jungle Books, The
author: 7 Kipling (Rudyard)
bear: 5 Baloo
boy: 6 Mowgli
panther: 8 Bagheera
python: 3 Kaa
tiger: 9 Shere Khan
wolf: 5 Akela

Jungle, The
author: 8 Sinclair (Upton)
locale: 7 Chicago 10 stockyards

junior
3 son 5 lower, minor, sonny, youth
6 lesser 7 student, younger 8 inferior, young man, youthful 9 secondary, youngster 11 subordinate

juniper
4 cone 5 cedar, fruit, savin, shrub
7 conifer 9 evergreen

junk
4 boat, dope, drug, ship 5 scrap,
trash, waste 6 debris, heroin, litter,
refuse, reject 7 cashier, clutter,
discard, rubbish, rummage 8 get rid
of, jettison, throw out 9 narcotics,
throw away

junker
4 heap 5 crate, wreck 6 jalopy

junket
4 trip 5 feast, jaunt, spree 6 outing,
picnic 7 banquet, dessert, journey
9 excursion

junk mail
4 spam

Juno
bird: 7 peacock
epithet: 6 Moneta
Greek equivalent: 4 Hera
husband: 7 Jupiter
(see also **Hera**)

Junoesque
7 stately 10 curvaceous, statuesque

junta
5 cabal, group 7 council, faction
9 committee

Jupiter
4 Jove, Zeus
angel: 7 Zadkiel
cupbearer: 8 Ganymede
daughter: 5 Venus 7 Minerva
epithet: 6 Fidius, Fulgur, Stator,
Tonans 7 Pluvius
father: 6 Saturn
lover: 6 Europa 8 Callisto
mother: 3 Ops
satellite: 6 Europa 8 Callisto,
Ganymede
son: 5 Arcas 6 Castor, Pollux
temple: 7 Capitol
wife: 4 Juno

Jurgen
author: 6 Cabell (James Branch)
trade: 10 pawnbroker

juridical
5 legal 6 lawful 8 juristic 10 legal-
istic

jurisdiction
3 law, see 4 sway, zone 5 might,
orbit, power, range, reach, scope,
venue 6 county, domain, parish,
sphere 7 circuit, command, compass, control, diocese, mastery,

purview **8** dominion, hegemony, province **9** authority, bailiwick, territory **10** domination **11** supervision

jurisprudence
3 law

jurist
5 judge

jury
5 panel
decision: 7 verdict

jury-rigged
6 make-do **7** stopgap **9** makeshift, temporary **10** improvised

just
3 apt, due, fit **4** even, fair, good, meet, only, true, very **5** equal, legal, quite, right **6** barely, hardly, honest, lawful, nearly, proper, simply, square **7** correct, ethical, exactly, fitting, merited, perhaps, precise, totally, upright **8** accurate, deserved, directly, possibly, recently, rightful, scarcely, squarely, suitable, unbiased **9** equitable, expressly, honorable, impartial, justified, objective, precisely, requisite, righteous **10** accurately, completely, legitimate, reasonable, scrupulous **11** appropriate, immediately, well-founded **12** unprejudiced **13** conscientious

justice
3 law **5** court, judge, right **6** equity **7** honesty **8** evenness, fairness, fair play **10** lawfulness, magistrate **11** correctness **12** impartiality

justification
6 excuse, reason **7** account, apology, defense, grounds **8** apologia

9 rationale **10** validation **11** explanation, vindication

justify
5 argue, claim, prove **6** assert, defend, uphold, verify **7** account, bear out, confirm, contend, explain, support, warrant **8** maintain, make even, validate **9** vindicate **10** legitimate, legitimize **11** corroborate, rationalize **12** authenticate, legitimatize, substantiate

jut
4 hang, poke **5** bulge, pouch **6** beetle, thrust **7** project **8** extend up, overhang, protrude, stand out, stick out **9** extend out, extension **10** projection, protrusion **12** protuberance

jute
5 gunny **6** burlap **7** sacking

Juvenal
4 poet **5** Roman
forte: 6 satire

juvenile
3 kid **5** actor, child, green, young, youth **6** callow, jejune, junior, moppet **7** preteen, puerile **8** childish, immature, youthful **9** childlike, fledgling, youngling, youngster **11** undeveloped

juvenility
5 youth **9** childhood, greenness **10** immaturity, springtide, springtime **12** youthfulness

juxtaposed
4 next **8** abutting, adjacent, neighbor, proximal, touching **9** adjoining, bordering **10** appositive, contiguous, side-by-side **11** coterminous, neighboring **12** conterminous

K

kabob
see kebab

kachina
4 doll 6 spirit 12 impersonator

kaddish
6 prayer

Kafka, Franz
character: 4 Olga 6 Gregor (Samsa), Joseph (K.)
novel: 5 Trial (The) 6 Castle (The) 7 Amerika
story: 8 Judgment (The) 12 Hunger Artist (A) 13 Metamorphosis (The)

kaiser
5 ruler 7 emperor, monarch 8 autocrat 9 sovereign

kaka
6 parrot

kale
4 cash, cole 5 bucks, money, moola 6 moolah 7 cabbage 8 colewort

kaleidoscopic
8 changing, colorful 10 variegated

Kali
aspect: 5 Durga 7 Parvati
husband: 4 Siva 5 Shiva

Kama
god of: 4 love
mount: 6 parrot 7 sparrow
wife: 4 Rati

kamikaze
7 suicide 8 suicidal

kampong
6 hamlet 7 village

Kampuchea
see Cambodia

kangaroo
6 leaper 7 wallaby 8 wallaroo 9 marsupial
herd: 3 mob
young: 4 joey

Kansas
capital: 6 Topeka
city: 6 Olathe, Salina, Topeka 7 Abilene, Emporia, Shawnee, Wichita 8 Lawrence
nickname: 9 Jayhawker (State), Sunflower (State)
prison: 11 Leavenworth
river: 8 Arkansas
state bird: 10 meadowlark
state flower: 9 sunflower
state tree: 10 cottonwood

kaolin
4 clay

kaput
5 spent 6 ruined 7 done for, useless 8 defeated, finished, outmoded 9 destroyed

karakul
5 sheep 9 broadtail

karma
4 fate 9 emanation

kaross
3 rug 7 garment

kasha
5 grain 8 porridge 9 buckwheat

Katharina
father: 8 Baptista
suitor: 9 Petruchio

Katrina's suitor
9 Brom Bones 12 Ichabod Crane

katydid
3 bug 6 insect 11 grasshopper

katzenjammer
3 din 5 noise 6 clamor, hubbub, racket 8 distress, hangover, headache 9 commotion

kava
5 shrub 6 pepper 8 beverage

kayo
6 defeat, finish 8 knockout 9 finish off 11 coup de grace

Kazakhstan
capital: 6 Akmola, Astana
city: 5 Semey 8 Pavlodar, Shymkent
lake: 6 Tengiz 8 Balkhash
language: 6 Kazakh 7 Russian
monetary unit: 5 tenge
mountain: 10 Khan-Tengri
neighbor: 5 China 6 Russia 10 Kyrgyzstan, Uzbekistan 12 Turkmenistan
river: 4 Ural 6 Irtysh 8 Syr Dar'ya
sea: 4 Aral 7 Caspian

Kazantzakis hero
5 Zorba (Alexis)

kea
6 parrot

Keats poem
5 Lamia 8 Endymion, Hyperion, Isabella, To Autumn 11 Ode to Psyche 12 Eve of St. Agnes (The) 16 Ode on a Grecian Urn 17 Ode to a Nightingale

kebab
8 shashlik

kedge
6 anchor

keel
4 boat, lean, ship 5 barge, pitch, ridge, slump 6 carina 7 capsize 8 overturn 11 centerboard

keen
4 avid, fine, wail, yowl 5 acute, alert, eager, honed, mourn, sharp, smart 6 ardent, astute, bewail, bright, clever, gung ho, intent, lament, shrewd 7 anxious, fervent, intense, whetted, zealous 8 animated, spirited 9 fine-edged, impatient, sensitive, wonderful 10 perceptive, razor-sharp 11 lamentation, penetrating, quick-witted, sharp-witted 12 enthusiastic, sharp-sighted

keenness
3 wit 4 edge, zeal 6 acuity, acumen 10 enthusiasm 11 discernment, penetration 12 incisiveness, perspicacity

keep
3 own 4 hold, jail, mind, obey, save, stay, tend 5 lodge, stock 6 castle, comply, detain, living, lockup, manage, prison, retain 7 abstain, conduct, confine, forbear, fulfill, possess, refrain, reserve 8 conserve, fortress, maintain, preserve, withhold 9 constrain 10 livelihood, sustenance 11 maintenance, subsistence

keep back
3 bar, dam 4 curb, hold, save, stay 6 detain, retain, retard, stifle 7 contain, inhibit, repress, reserve 8 restrain, restrict, suppress, withhold

keeper
5 guard 6 warden 7 big fish, curator 8 Cerberus, guardian, watchdog 9 custodian, protector

keeping
4 care, ward 5 aegis, trust 6 charge 7 custody, support 8 wardship 9 provision 10 caretaking, conformity, observance 11 maintenance 12 conservation, guardianship

keep on
4 last 5 abide 6 endure 7 persist 8 continue 9 hang tough, persevere

keep out
3 ban, bar 4 hold, stop 5 block, check, debar 6 forbid 7 embargo, exclude 8 prohibit, turn back 9 blackball

keepsake
5 token 6 trophy 7 memento 8 memorial, reminder, souvenir 11 remembrance

keep up
7 persist, prolong, sustain 8 continue, maintain, preserve 9 persevere

kef
4 hash, hemp 7 hashish 10 dreaminess 12 tranquillity

keg
3 tun 4 butt, cask, pipe 6 barrel, firkin, vessel 8 hogshead 9 container

kegler
6 bowler

keister
3 bum, end 4 buns, duff, rear, rump, seat, tail, tush 5 fanny 6 behind, bottom 8 backside, buttocks, derriere 9 posterior

keloid
4 scar

kelp
4 alga 7 seaweed

kelpie
3 dog 5 naiad, nixie 6 sprite

ken
4 view 5 grasp, range, reach, scope, sight 7 horizon, purview 9 knowledge 10 perception 13 comprehension, understanding

kenaf
5 fiber, plant 8 hibiscus

Kenilworth author
5 Scott (Walter)

Kennedy novel
8 Ironweed

kennel
4 pack 5 board 6 gutter 7 shelter 9 enclosure

keno
4 game
similar to: 5 beano, bingo, lotto

Kentucky
capital: 9 Frankfort
city: 9 Lexington 10 Louisville 12 Bowling Green
nickname: 9 Bluegrass (State)
park: 11 Mammoth Cave
racecourse: 14 Churchill Downs
river: 4 Ohio
state bird: 8 cardinal
state flower: 9 goldenrod
state tree: 11 tulip poplar

Kentucky bluegrass
3 Poa

Kenya
capital: 7 Nairobi
city: 6 Kisumu, Nakuru 7 Mombasa
lake: 7 Turkana 8 Victoria
language: 7 English, Swahili
monetary unit: 8 shilling
mountain: 5 Elgon, Kenya
neighbor: 5 Sudan 6 Uganda 7 Somalia 8 Ethiopia, Tanzania
river: 4 Tana

kepi
3 cap

kerchief
6 hankie 7 bandana 8 babushka, bandanna, kaffiyeh
Scottish: 5 curch

kerf
3 cut 4 nick, slit 5 cleft, notch 6 groove

kerfuffle
3 ado, row 4 flap, fuss, stir, to-do 5 hoo-ha 6 dust-up, ruckus, rumpus 7 turmoil 8 foofaraw 11 disturbance

kermis
4 fair 8 carnival, festival

kernel
3 nub, nut 4 core, crux, gist, meat, pith, seed 5 grain 6 nubbin, upshot 7 essence, nucleus 9 substance

Kerouac novel
6 Big Sur 9 On the Road 10 Dharma Bums (The) 13 Subterraneans (The)

Kesey novel
21 Sometimes a Great Notion
25 One Flew over the Cuckoo's Nest

kestrel
4 bird, hawk 6 falcon 9 windhover

ketch
4 boat 6 vessel 8 sailboat 10 watercraft

ketone
7 acetone, camphor

kettle
3 pot 6 hollow, vessel 7 caldron, marmite, pothole 8 cauldron

kettledrum
5 naker 7 timpani (plural), timpano

key
4 clue, isle, reef 5 basic, islet, vital 6 cotter, island, legend, master, opener, samara, spline, ticket, tip-off 7 central, crucial, digital, pivotal 8 critical, passport, password, skeleton, solution, tonality 9 essential, important 10 open sesame 11 fundamental
combining form: 5 clavi, clavo
notch: 4 ward

keyboard
6 manual 7 clavier

key fruit
6 samara

key man
5 chief 7 kingpin 9 locksmith

keynote
4 core, crux, gist, pith, tone 5 theme, tonic

keynoter
6 orator 7 speaker

Keystone State
12 Pennsylvania

khaki
3 tan 5 brown, cloth, color 7 garment, uniform

khamsin
4 wind

khan
5 chief, ruler 9 chieftain, sovereign 11 caravansary

khedive
5 ruler 7 viceroy

Khomeini
4 imam 9 ayatollah

Ki
mother: 5 Nammu
son: 5 Enlil

kiang
3 ass

kibble
4 meal 5 grain, grind 9 pulverize

kibbutz
4 co-op, farm 7 commune 10 collective, settlement 11 cooperative

kibe
4 heel, sore 8 swelling 9 chilblain

kibitz
4 chat 6 banter, butt in, meddle 7 comment, intrude, obtrude 9 interfere

kibitzer
7 meddler 8 busybody, observer 9 buttinsky, spectator 10 rubberneck

kibosh
3 hex 4 jinx, stop 5 check, curse

kick
4 bang, boot, carp, fuss, punt, wail 5 gripe, rebel, whine 6 object, recoil, repine, resist, thrill, wallop 7 grumble, protest 8 complain

kicker
5 catch 6 clause, punter 9 condition, fine print

kick in
3 die, pay 4 give 5 begin, put up, start 6 donate, pony up 7 cough up, fork out 8 fork over, hand over 10 contribute

kick off
3 die 4 open 5 begin, croak, start 6 launch 8 commence, drop dead, embark on, initiate 10 inaugurate

kick out
3 axe, can 4 fire, oust, sack 5 eject, evict 6 bounce 7 boot out, cashier, dismiss 8 throw out 9 discharge

kickshaw
5 goody, treat 6 bauble, dainty, gewgaw, morsel, tidbit, trifle 7 bibelot, trinket 8 delicacy 9 bagatelle

kid
3 guy, rag, rib 4 dupe, fool, gull, hoax, jest, joke, josh, razz 5 child,

jolly, trick, youth 6 banter, befool, moppet, nipper 7 deceive, younger 8 flimflam, hoodwink, juvenile 9 bamboozle, youngling, youngster

kidnap
6 abduct, snatch 8 shanghai

kidney
5 gland, organ
combining form: 4 reni, reno 5 nephr 6 nephro

kidney-shaped
8 reniform

kielbasa
7 sausage

kilderkin
3 keg 4 cask 6 barrel 9 container

kilim
3 mat, rug 6 carpet

kill
3 end, off, zap 4 do in, prey, slay, stop, veto 5 creek, croak, scrag, snuff, waste 6 defeat, delete, finish, murder, quarry, stifle 7 bump off, butcher, channel, destroy, execute 8 blow away, carry off, dispatch, knock off, massacre 9 sacrifice, slaughter 10 annihilate 11 assassinate, exterminate

killer
6 gunman, hit man 7 butcher, torpedo 8 assassin, homicide
combining form: 4 cide

Killer Angels author
6 Shaara (Michael)

killer whale
4 orca 8 cetacean

killing
5 blood, fatal 6 deadly, lethal, mortal, murder 7 carnage 8 butchery, foul play, homicide 9 bloodbath, bloodshed, slaughter 12 manslaughter
of a race: 8 genocide
of bacteria: 11 bactericide
of a brother: 10 fratricide
of a father: 9 patricide
of a king: 8 regicide
of a mother: 9 matricide

of a relative: 9 parricide
of a sister: 10 sororicide
of oneself: 7 suicide
of plants: 9 herbicide

killjoy
6 downer, grinch, grouch 7 spoiler 8 doomster, sourpuss 9 Cassandra, defeatist, doomsayer, gloomy Gus, pessimist, worrywart 10 spoilsport, wet blanket

Kilmer poem
5 Trees

kiln
4 oast, oven 7 furnace

kilt
5 skirt
accessory: 7 sporran
fabric: 5 plaid 6 tartan

kilter
4 trim 5 order, shape 6 fettle, repair 7 fitness 9 condition

kimono
4 gown, robe
sash: 3 obi

kin
3 sib 4 clan, folk, sept 5 blood, flesh, house, stock, tribe 6 family 7 lineage, related 8 relation, relative

kind
3 ilk 4 good, like, sort, type, warm 5 breed, class, genre 6 benign, genial, gentle, humane, loving, nature, stripe, tender 7 affable, amiable, clement, essence, feather, helpful, lenient, quality, species, variety 8 category, merciful, tolerant 9 character 10 altruistic, benevolent, charitable, forbearing, responsive 11 considerate, description, good-hearted, good-humored, good-natured, openhearted, softhearted, sympathetic, warmhearted 12 affectionate, good-tempered, humanitarian 13 compassionate, philanthropic

kindle
4 bear, fire, stir, wake, whet 5 light, rally, rouse, spark, start, waken

kindliness

6 arouse, awaken, bestir, excite, foment, ignite, incite **7** inflame, provoke **8** activate **9** instigate, stimulate **10** illuminate

kindliness

8 goodwill, sympathy **9** affection **10** solicitude **11** benevolence

kindly

6 benign, gentle **7** benefic **8** friendly, generous, gracious, pleasant **9** agreeable, attentive, benignant **10** beneficent, beneficial, neighborly **11** considerate, good-hearted, sympathetic

kindness

5 favor, mercy **7** service **8** clemency, courtesy, goodwill, sympathy **10** compassion, generosity, indulgence **11** benevolence **13** consideration

kind of

5 quite **6** fairly, pretty, rather **8** passably, somewhat **9** tolerably **10** more or less, reasonably, relatively

kindred

3 sib **4** clan, folk, like, sept **5** alike, blood, flesh, house, stock, tribe **6** agnate, allied, family **7** cognate, connate, lineage, related, similar **9** relatives **10** affiliated, connatural **11** consanguine

king

3 rex **4** czar, tsar **5** mogul, ruler **6** tycoon **7** magnate, monarch **9** sovereign
Albanian: 3 Zog **7** William
Assyrian: 6 Sargon **11** Sennacherib, Shalmaneser
Babylonian: 6 Sargon **9** Hammurabi **10** Belshazzar
Belgian: 6 Albert **7** Leopold **8** Baudouin
Bohemian: 9 Wenceslas **10** Wenceslaus
Bulgarian: 5 Boris **6** Simeon
Damascus: 8 Benhadad
Danish: 4 Abel, Eric, Gorm, Hans, John, Olaf **5** Sweyn **6** Canute, Harold, Magnus **8** Nicholas, Walde-

mar **9** Christian, Frederick **11** Christopher
Dutch: 7 William
Egyptian: 3 Tut **4** Pepi, Seti **5** Khufu, Menes, Necho **6** Cheops, Ramses **7** Harmhab, Osorkon, Psamtik, Ptolemy **8** Ikhnaton, Thothmes, Thutmose **9** Amenhotep, Sesostris **11** Tutankhamen
English: 4 John **5** Henry, James **6** Alfred, Canute, Edmund, Edward, Egbert, George, Harold **7** Charles, Richard, Stephen, William **8** Ethelred **9** Athelstan, Ethelbald, Ethelbert
French: 3 Odo, roi **4** Jean, John **5** Henri, Henry, Louis, Pepin, Raoul **6** Philip, Robert, Rudolf **7** Charles, Francis, Lothair **8** François **9** Hugh Capet **11** Charlemagne
German: 4 Carl, Karl **5** König, Louis **6** Lothar, Ludwig **7** Charles, Lothair
Greek (modern): 4 Paul **6** George **9** Alexander **11** Constantine
Hawaiian: 10 Kamehameha
Hungarian: 6 Attila
Indian: 4 raja **5** rajah
Irish: 9 Brian Boru
Italian: 7 Humbert, Umberto
Jordanian: 5 Talal **7** Hussein **8** Abdullah
Judah:
(see at **Judah**)
Judean: 5 Herod
Lydian: 5 Gyges **7** Croesus **8** Alyattes
Norwegian: 4 Eric, Erik, Inge, Olaf **5** Sweyn **6** Haakon, Harald, Harold, Magnus, Sigurd, Sverre
Ostrogothic: 9 Theodoric
Persian: 5 Cyrus **6** Darius, Xerxes
Portuguese: 4 John **5** Henry, Louis, Peter **6** Carlos, Edward, Manuel, Sancho **7** Alfonso **9** Ferdinand, Sebastian
Prussian: 7 Wilhelm, William **9** Frederick, Friedrich
relating to: 5 regal, royal
Saudi Arabian: 4 Saud **6** Faisal **9** Abdul-Aziz
Scottish: 4 John **5** David, Edgar, James **6** Duncan **7** Macbeth, Mal

colm, William 9 Alexander, Donalbane 10 David Bruce 11 Robert Bruce
Spanish: 3 rey 5 Louis 6 Philip 7 Alfonso, Amadeus, Charles 9 Ferdinand 10 Juan Carlos
Spartan: 8 Leonidas
Swedish: 4 Eric, John 5 Oscar 6 Birger, Gustav, Haakon, Magnus 7 Charles 8 Gustavus, Waldemar 9 Frederick, Sigismund, Sten Sture
Visigothic: 6 Alaric

King Arthur
birthplace: 8 Tintagel
chronicler: 8 Geoffrey (of Monmouth)
court site: 7 Camelot 8 Caerleon
deathplace: 6 Camlan
father: 5 Uther
father-in-law: 9 Laodogant, Leodegran 11 Leodegrance
foster father: 5 Ector
jester: 7 Dagonet
knight: 3 Kay 4 Bors 5 Balan, Balin 6 Gareth, Gawain, Modred 7 Galahad, Geraint, Lamerok, Mordred, Tristan 8 Bedivere, Lancelot, Parsifal, Percival, Tristram 9 Launcelot
lance: 3 Ron
last abode: 6 Avalon
last name: 9 Pendragon
magician: 6 Merlin
mother: 6 Ygerne 7 Igraine
nephew: 6 Gareth, Modred 7 Mordred
queen: 9 Guinevere
shield: 7 Pridwin
sister: 7 Morgain 11 Morgan le Fay
slayer: 6 Modred 7 Mordred
son: 6 Modred 7 Mordred
steward: 3 Kay
sword: 9 Excalibur
victim: 6 Modred 7 Mordred
wife: 9 Guinevere

king crab
7 limulus

kingdom
5 realm 6 domain, empire 7 demesne 8 monarchy

kingdom come
4 Zion 6 heaven 8 paradise 9 hereafter 10 afterworld

kingfish
4 boss 6 bigwig, honcho, master 7 big shot, croaker 8 mackerel

kingfisher
7 halcyon 10 kookaburra

kingly
5 regal, royal 6 august, lordly, regnal 7 exalted 8 imperial, majestic 9 imperious, masterful, monarchal, sovereign 10 monarchial 11 monarchical

King novel
6 Carrie 7 Shining (The) 8 Dead Zone (The) 9 Dark Tower (The), Green Mile (The), Salem's Lot 11 Firestarter, Pet Sematary

King Philip
9 Metacomet

kingpin
4 boss, guru, head 5 chief, mogul 6 bigwig, top dog 7 magnate 9 top banana 10 mastermind

Kings Peak range
5 Uinta

Kingu
consort: 6 Tiamat
slayer: 6 Marduk

kink
4 bend, curl, knot, whim 5 cramp, crick, quirk, snarl, spasm, twist 6 tangle 11 peculiarity 12 eccentricity, imperfection

kinky
3 odd 4 bent 5 curly, outré, ultra, weird 6 curled, far-out, frizzy, quirky 7 bizarre, deviant, knotted, strange, twisted 9 eccentric 10 outlandish

kiosk
5 booth 8 pavilion 9 newsstand 11 summerhouse

kip
3 bed, nap 4 hide, pelt, skin 5 sleep

Kipling, Rudyard

work: 3 Kim 6 L'Envoi 8 Gunga Din, Mandalay 10 Fuzzy Wuzzy 11 Jungle Books (The), Recessional 13 Just So Stories, Soldiers Three 15 Light That Failed (The), Puck of Pook's Hill 18 Captains Courageous

Kiribati

capital: 6 Tarawa
island, island group: 4 Line 6 Banaba 7 Gilbert, Phoenix
language: 7 English
location: 7 Oceania
monetary unit: 6 dollar

kirk

6 church

kirsch

6 brandy, liquor

kirtle

4 coat, gown 5 dress, tunic 7 garment

Kish

father: 3 Ner 4 Abdi 5 Abiel, Jeiel 6 Jehiel
son: 4 Saul

kismet

3 lot 4 doom, fate, luck 5 weird 6 Moirai 7 destiny, fortune

kiss

4 buss, neck, peck 5 graze, smack 6 cookie, glance, smooch 7 lip-lock 8 osculate, pucker up 10 osculation

kisser

3 mug 4 face, lips 5 mouth

Kiss sculptor

5 Rodin (Auguste)

kit

3 set 4 gear, pelt 5 group 6 outfit, tackle, violin 7 package 8 caboodle 9 container 10 collection

kitchen

4 mess 6 galley 7 cuisine 8 scullery
appliance:
(see at **appliance**)
boss: 4 chef
(see also **cooking**)

kite

4 hawk, sail, soar 5 check, glede, hurry, mosey 7 saunter, take off 8 clear out, hightail, predator 9 spinnaker

kith

3 kin, sib 4 clan, folk 6 family 7 friends, kindred, kinfolk 9 neighbors, relatives

kitsch

4 camp, junk 9 vulgarity

kittenish

3 coy 6 elvish, frisky, impish 7 coltish, playful 10 frolicsome 11 mischievous

kitty

3 cat, pot 4 fund, pool, puss 5 pussy 6 feline, stakes 7 jackpot

kiwi

4 bird 5 fruit 7 Apteryx 12 New Zealander

klatch

5 bunch, group 7 meeting 9 gathering 11 get-together

kleptomaniac

5 thief 7 booster 10 shoplifter

klutz

3 oaf 4 boob, clod, gawk, lout, lump 5 looby 6 lubber, lummox 7 bungler, palooka 8 shlemiel 9 schlemiel 10 stumblebum

klutzy

5 inept 6 clumsy 7 awkward 9 all thumbs, maladroit 10 blundering

knack

4 bent, gift, head 5 flair, forte, skill, trick 6 genius, talent 7 ability, aptness, command, faculty, know-how, mastery 8 aptitude, capacity, facility 9 dexterity, expertise, stratagem 10 expertness

knapsack

4 pack 8 backpack

knave

4 heel, jack 5 fraud, rogue, scamp 6 rascal, varlet 7 lowlife, villain

8 scalawag, swindler 9 scoundrel
10 blackguard 11 rapscallion

knavery
5 fraud 6 deceit 8 mischief, trickery,
villainy 9 chicanery, deception,
rascality 10 dishonesty

knavish
5 lying 6 shifty, tricky 7 devious,
roguish 8 rascally 9 deceitful,
deceptive, dishonest 10 mendacious
12 unscrupulous

knead
4 form, mold, work 5 press, shape
7 massage 10 manipulate

knee
5 joint
bend: 9 genuflect 12 genuflection
bone: 7 patella

kneeler
5 stool 7 cushion 8 prie-dieu 9 foot-stool

knell
4 bong, peal, ring, toll 5 chime
6 summon 7 warning 8 announce,
proclaim

knickknack
3 toy 4 dido 5 curio 6 bauble,
gadget, gewgaw, trifle 7 bibelot,
novelty, trinket, whatnot, whatsit
8 gimcrack, ornament, souvenir
9 bagatelle, bric-a-brac, objet d'art

knife
4 bolo, shiv, snee 5 blade, bowie,
panga, shank, sword 6 barong,
cutter, dagger, parang, sickle
7 cleaver, machete, scalpel 8 stiletto, yataghan 11 switchblade
case: 6 sheath
handle: 4 haft, hilt
maker: 6 cutler 7 grinder

knifelike
4 keen 5 acute, sharp 7 cutting
8 piercing, stabbing 11 penetrating

knight
3 dub, sir 5 eques 8 cavalier, chess-
man, horseman 9 caballero, chevalier

code: 8 chivalry
competition: 7 listing, tilting 8 joust-
ing 10 tournament
German: 6 Ritter
servant: 4 page 5 valet 6 squire
title: 3 sir
wife: 4 lady

knighthood
8 chivalry

knightly
4 bold 5 brave, noble 6 heroic
7 gallant, valiant 10 chivalrous

Knight of the Round Table
see **King Arthur**

Knight of the Rueful Countenance
10 Don Quixote

knit
4 bind, heal, join, link, mend, purl
5 plait, unite, weave 6 fabric, stitch
7 conjoin, crochet 8 contract 9 interlace 10 intertwine

knitting
material: 4 yarn
stitch: 3 rib 4 purl 6 garter
tool: 6 needle

knob
3 bun, bur, nub 4 bump, burl, burr,
dial, hill, hump, lump, node, umbo
5 bulge, gnarl, knoll, mound 6 button, finial, handle, nubble, pommel
7 hillock 12 protuberance

knobkerrie
3 bat 4 club, mace 5 billy 6 cudgel,
weapon 7 war club 8 bludgeon
9 billy club, truncheon

knock
3 bob, hit, rap, tap 4 bash, blow,
bump, cuff, lick, swat 5 blame, clout,
fault, pound, swipe, thump 6 strike
7 censure, condemn, setback 8 denounce, reversal 9 criticize 10 denunciate

knock down
4 drop, earn, fell, gain, raze 5 floor,
level, lower 6 lay low, reduce 7 acquire, bring in, flatten 9 dismantle
11 disassemble

knocker
6 carper, critic 7 caviler 8 quibbler 10 complainer, criticizer 11 fault-finder

knock off
3 rob 4 copy, do in, halt, kill, quit, slay, stop 5 cease 6 deduct, defeat, desist, finish, murder 7 execute, imitate, take out 8 discount, overcome, subtract 9 liquidate 11 assassinate, call it quits, counterfeit

knockout
4 kayo 5 dandy, final 6 beauty, eyeful, looker, lovely 7 stunner 8 decisive, jim-dandy, striking, stunning 9 deathblow, finishing, humdinger 10 attractive 11 coup de grace, crackerjack

knock over
3 rob 4 down, drop, fell 5 amaze, floor, steal, upset 6 boggle, hijack, hold up, lay low, topple 7 flatten, stick up 9 bring down, eliminate, overpower, overthrow, overwhelm, prostrate

knoll
4 hill, knob 5 mound 7 hillock

knot
3 bow, tie 4 bond, burr, link, loop, lump, node 5 bunch, gnarl, hitch, nexus 6 jungle, tangle 8 ligament, ligature, vinculum
in fiber: 3 nep
kind: 4 bend, loop, slip 5 hitch 6 granny, splice, square 7 bowline 9 sheet bend 10 clove hitch, sheepshank

knotty
4 hard 6 sticky 7 complex, gnarled, Gordian 8 involved 9 byzantine, difficult, elaborate, intricate 10 formidable 11 complicated, problematic

knout
4 flog, lash, whip 7 scourge

know
3 wot 5 grasp 6 fathom, intuit 7 discern, realize 9 apprehend, recognize 10 appreciate, comprehend, experience, understand
Scottish: 3 ken

knowable
9 graspable 10 cognizable, fathomable 12 intelligible 13 apprehensible

know-how
5 craft, knack, skill 6 talent 7 ability, cunning, faculty, mastery 8 aptitude 9 dexterity, expertise 10 adroitness, expertness 11 proficiency

knowing
3 hep, hip 4 sage, wise 5 aware, blasé, canny, smart 6 bright, clever 7 witting, worldly 8 sentient 9 cognizant, conscious, sagacious 10 conversant, discerning, insightful, perceptive 11 worldly-wise 13 sophisticated

know-it-all
6 smarty 7 wise guy 8 wiseacre 10 smart aleck 11 smarty-pants, wisenheimer

knowledge
3 ken 4 lore, news 5 facts 6 wisdom 7 science 8 learning 9 cognition, education, erudition 10 cognizance 11 information, scholarship 12 intelligence 13 enlightenment
lack of: 9 ignorance
mystical: 6 gnosis

knowledgeable
5 savvy 8 educated, informed

know-nothing
4 dolt, dope, fool 5 dummy, dunce, idiot, yahoo 6 dimwit 7 pinhead 8 agnostic, ignorant, numskull 9 benighted, blockhead, brainless, ignoramus, lamebrain, numbskull 10 illiterate, uneducated 11 empty-headed

knuckle
5 joint
combining form: 6 condyl 7 condylo

knucklehead
4 dolt, dope, fool 5 dummy, dunce, idiot, yahoo 6 dimwit 8 clodpole, numskull 9 ignoramus, lamebrain, numbskull

knuckle under
3 bow 4 cave 5 yield 6 cave in, give in, submit 7 succumb 8 say uncle 9 surrender 10 capitulate

knurl
3 nub 4 bead, knob 5 ridge 12 protuberance

KO
4 kayo 8 knockout

koan
7 paradox

kobold
5 dwarf, gnome 6 goblin, spirit, sprite

Kohinoor
3 gem 7 diamond

kohlrabi
7 cabbage

kola
3 nut 4 tree

komatik
4 sled 6 sledge

kook
3 nut 5 crank, loony, wacko 6 cuckoo, weirdo 7 dingbat, lunatic, oddball 8 crackpot 9 ding-a-ling, fruitcake, screwball 10 crackbrain

kooky
4 daft, nuts 5 batty, crazy, daffy, dotty, flaky, loony, nutty, silly, wacky, weird 6 freaky, fruity, insane, screwy 7 bizarre, idiotic, lunatic, offbeat, touched 8 demented 9 eccentric, fantastic 10 flipped out, freaked-out, off-the-wall, outlandish

kopeck
4 coin
one hundred: 5 ruble

Koran
chapter: 4 sura
revealer of: 7 Gabriel
scholar: 5 ulama, ulema

Korea
see **Korea, North; Korea, South**

Korean
dynasty: 5 Silla 7 Koguryo
national dish: 6 kimchi

Korea, North
capital: 9 P'yongyang
city: 7 Hamhung 8 Ch'ongjin
leader: 9 Kim Il-sung, Kim Jong Il 10 Kim Chong-Il
monetary unit: 3 won
mountain: 6 Paektu
neighbor: 5 China 6 Russia 10 South Korea
sea: 6 Yellow

Korea, South
captial: 5 Seoul
city: 5 Pusan, Taegu 6 Inch'on, Taejon 7 Kwangju
island: 5 Cheju
monetary unit: 3 won
neighbor: 10 North Korea
river: 3 Han 7 Naktong
sea: 5 Japan 6 Yellow

kosher
3 fit 4 pure 5 clean 6 proper 10 acceptable, legitimate, sanctioned 12 satisfactory

Kosinski novel
5 Steps 10 Being There 11 Painted Bird (The)

Koussevitzky
5 Serge 6 Sergei 9 conductor

kowtow
3 bow 4 fawn 5 cower, defer, kneel, toady 6 cringe, grovel 7 honey up, truckle 8 bootlick 11 apple-polish

kraal
3 pen 6 corral 7 village 9 enclosure

kraken
5 squid 9 leviathan 10 giant squid, sea monster

krater
3 jar 4 vase 6 vessel

Kriemhild
brother: 7 Gunther
husband: 5 Etzel 6 Attila 9 Siegfried
slayer: 10 Hildebrand
victim: 5 Hagen

kris
6 dagger

Krishna

avatar of: 6 Vishnu
brother: 8 Balarama
father: 8 Vasudeva
mother: 6 Devaki
uncle: 5 Kansa
victim: 5 Kansa

Krupp works site

5 Essen

kudos

4 bays, fame 5 award, glory, honor
6 honors, praise, renown 7 acclaim,
bouquet, laurels 8 accolade, bou-
quets 10 compliment 11 distinction,
recognition

kudu

8 antelope

kukri

5 sword

kumquat

5 fruit
kin: 6 orange

Kushner play

15 Angels in America

Kuwait

capital: 6 Kuwait
gulf: 7 Persian
island: 7 Bubiyan 8 Faylakah
language: 6 Arabic 7 Persian
monetary unit: 5 dinar
neighbor: 4 Iraq 11 Saudi Arabia
oasis: 8 Al-Jahrah

kvass

4 beer

kvetch

4 beef, crab, fret, fuss 5 gripe,
whine 6 grouch, grouse 7 grumble
8 complain 9 bellyache

_____ kwon do

3 tae

kyphosis

8 humpback 9 curvature, hunchback

Kyrgyzstan

capital: 7 Bishkek
city: 3 Osh
conqueror: 9 Jöchi Khan
lake: 8 Issyk-Kul
language: 6 Kyrgyz 7 Russian
monetary unit: 3 som
mountain, range: 4 Alai 6 Pobedy
7 Victory 8 Tian Shan 10 Khan-Tengri 11 Kok Shaal-Tau
neighbor: 5 China 10 Kazakhstan,
Tajikistan, Uzbekistan
river: 5 Naryn

L

Laadah
  father: 6 Shelah
  grandfather: 5 Judah

laager
  4 camp 6 encamp 7 bivouac

lab
  13 proving ground

Laban
  daughter: 4 Leah 6 Rachel
  father: 7 Bethuel
  grandfather: 5 Nahor
  sister: 7 Rebekah

label
  3 tag 4 band, mark 6 marker, ticket
  7 epithet, sticker 8 classify, hallmark,
  identify, insignia

labium
  3 lip

labor
  4 moil, task, toil, work 5 chore,
  grind, sweat 6 drudge, effort, strain,
  strive 7 slavery, travail 8 drudgery, endeavor, exertion, struggle
  10 birth pangs, childbirth, donkeywork 12 childbearing
  group: 3 AFL, CIO 5 ILGWU, union
  6 AFL-CIO
  leader: 5 Hoffa (James, Jimmy),
  Lewis (John L.), Meany (George)
  6 Chavez (Cesar) 7 Gompers (Samuel), Reuther (Walter), Sweeney
  (John J.) 8 Kirkland (Lane), Randolph (A. Philip)

laboratory
  device: 5 flask 6 beaker, mortar,
  pestle, retort 7 burette, pipette
  8 crucible, test tube 12 Bunsen
  burner

labored
  4 hard 6 forced, taxing, tiring 7 arduous 8 strained 9 difficult, effortful,
  fatiguing, strenuous

laborer
  4 hack, hand, peon 5 grind, navvy
  6 coolie, menial 7 workman 10 roustabout, workingman
  Mexican: 7 bracero

laborious
  4 hard 6 tiring, uphill 7 arduous,
  onerous, operose 8 diligent, grueling, sedulous, toilsome 9 assiduous,
  difficult, effortful, strenuous 10 burdensome, unflagging 11 hard-
  working, industrious, persevering
  12 backbreaking

La Brea
  4 pits 7 tar pits
  fossil: 7 mammoth 8 mastodon
  10 saber-tooth

labyrinth
  3 web 4 coil, knot, maze, mesh
  5 skein, snarl 6 jungle, morass,
  tangle
  builder: 8 Daedalus
  hero: 7 Theseus
  monster: 8 Minotaur

labyrinthine
  4 mazy 6 daedal, knotty 7 complex,
  gordian 8 involved, mazelike, tortuous 9 Byzantine, elaborate, intricate 10 convoluted, perplexing
  11 bewildering, complicated

lace
  3 net, tat, tie 4 cord, trim 5 adorn,
  braid, frill, plait, twine 6 fasten, string
  7 entwine, netting, tatting 8 filigree,

Lacedaemon

openwork **9** embroider **10** embroidery, intertwine **11** needlepoint
edge: 5 picot
ground: 6 reseau
into: 5 abuse **6** attack **7** condemn
kind: 6 bobbin **7** Alençon, guipure, macramé, Maltese, Mechlin, torchon **8** Brussels, Venetian **9** Chantilly **11** needlepoint **12** Valenciennes
make: 3 tat
pattern: 5 toilé

Lacedaemon
6 Sparta

lacerate
3 cut, rip **4** gash, rend, tear **5** slash, wound **6** mangle, pierce **7** afflict, mangled, torment **8** distress

lachrymose
3 sad **5** teary, weepy **7** doleful, tearful, weeping **8** dolorous, mournful **11** tear-jerking

lack
4 need, want **6** dearth, defect **7** absence, default, deficit, failure, paucity, poverty, require **8** scarcity, shortage **9** privation **10** deficiency, inadequacy, scantiness **13** insufficiency

lackadaisical
4 idle, lazy, limp, slow **5** moony **6** dreamy **7** languid, passive **8** fainéant, indolent, listless, slothful **9** apathetic, enervated **10** languorous, spiritless **11** daydreaming, halfhearted, languishing

lackey
5 toady **6** fawner, flunky, minion, vassal **7** footman, servant **8** truckler **9** attendant, sycophant

lacking
3 shy **4** sans **5** minus, short **6** absent, flawed, needed **7** missing, needing, omitted, wanting, without **8** devoid of, impaired **9** defective, deficient **10** deprived of, inadequate, incomplete **11** halfhearted **12** insufficient

lackluster
3 dim **4** arid, blah, drab, dull, flat **5** blind, ho-hum, matte, muted, prosy, rusty, vapid **6** boring, leaden **7** prosaic **8** lifeless, mediocre **9** colorless, tarnished, wearisome **10** uninspired **13** unimaginative

Laconian
7 Spartan
king: 5 Lelex, Myles **8** Menelaus

laconic
4 curt **5** bluff, blunt, brief, pithy, short, terse **7** brusque, concise **8** succinct

lacquer
5 glaze, gloss **6** enamel, finish **7** shellac, varnish

lacrosse
related game: 7 jai alai
term: 5 clamp **6** crease, crosse, pocket **7** face-off
team: 3 ten

lactate
4 salt **5** ester, nurse **6** suckle **7** secrete **8** wet-nurse **10** breastfeed

lacteal
5 milky **6** cloudy, pearly

lacuna
3 gap, pit **4** void **5** blank, break, space **6** breach, cavity, hiatus **7** caesura **10** deficiency **12** interruption **13** discontinuity

lacy
5 meshy **6** dainty **7** netlike **8** delicate, gossamer **9** filigreed

lad
3 boy, son, tad **5** youth **6** shaver **9** shaveling, stripling
Irish: 4 boyo **5** bucko
Scottish: 5 chiel **7** callant

ladder
3 run **5** ranks, scale **6** series **7** ranking **9** hierarchy
adjunct: 4 rung **6** rundle

ladderlike
6 scalar, scaled **7** stepped **11** scalariform

lade
3 dip, tax 4 bail, load, pack, ship, stow 5 ladle, scoop 6 burden, saddle, weight 8 encumber

la-di-dah
6 too-too 7 elegant, genteel, stuck-up 8 affected, snobbish 9 conceited, grandiose, high-flown 10 hoity-toity 11 pretentious

lading
4 haul, load 5 cargo, goods 6 burden 7 bailing, dipping, freight, loading, payload 8 shipment 11 consignment

ladle
3 dip 4 bail 5 scoop, spoon 6 dipper

Ladon
6 dragon
father: 7 Phorcus, Phorcys
mother: 4 Ceto
slayer: 8 Heracles, Hercules

lady
4 dame 5 madam, woman 6 female, matron
French: 4 dame
German: 4 Frau
Italian: 5 donna 7 signora
Muslim: 5 begum
Spanish: 4 doña 6 señora

lady ____
4 luck 5 apple 6 beetle, chapel

ladybug
6 beetle
Australian: 7 vedalia

Lady Chatterley's Lover
author: 8 Lawrence (David Herbert)
character: 6 Connie 7 Mellors (Oliver) 9 Constance

lady-killer
4 dude, hunk, roué, stud 7 playboy, seducer 8 Casanova, lothario 12 heartbreaker

Lady of the Lake, The
5 Ellen (Douglas), Nimue 6 Vivien
author: 5 Scott (Walter)

Lady Windermere's Fan
author: 5 Wilde (Oscar)

Laertes
father: 8 Acrisius, Polonius
sister: 7 Ophelia
son: 7 Ulysses 8 Odysseus
victim: 6 Hamlet
wife: 8 Anticlea

La Fontaine's forte
5 fable

lag
4 drag, flag, last, poke, slow, tire 5 dally, delay, tarry, trail 6 dawdle, linger, loiter 7 slacken 8 hang back, hindmost, interval 10 dillydally 13 procrastinate

lager
4 beer, brew, malt, suds 7 brewski

laggard
3 lax 4 slow 5 tardy 6 loafer 7 dawdler 8 dallying, dawdling, delaying, dilatory, flagging, lingerer, loiterer, slowpoke, sluggish, tarrying 9 apathetic, lazybones, lethargic, loitering, straggler 10 behindhand

La Gioconda
8 Mona Lisa
composer: 10 Ponchielli (Amilcare)
painter: 7 da Vinci (Leonardo) 8 Leonardo (da Vinci)

lagniappe
3 tip 4 gift, perk 5 bonus 7 cumshaw, largess 8 dividend, gratuity 9 baksheesh, pourboire 10 perquisite

lagomorph
4 hare, pika 6 rabbit

lagoon
4 pond, pool 5 bayou, sound 6 strait 7 channel, narrows

____ La Guardia
8 Fiorello

Lahmi
brother: 7 Goliath
slayer: 7 Elhanan

laid-back
4 cool 6 breezy, casual 7 relaxed 8 carefree, informal 9 easygoing, hang-loose 10 nonchalant

lair
3 den 4 cave 5 haunt, lodge 6 burrow, refuge 7 hideout, retreat 8 hideaway 9 sanctuary

Laius
father: 8 Labdacus
slayer, son: 7 Oedipus
wife: 7 Jocasta

lake
4 loch, mere, pond, pool, tarn 5 lough
6 lagoon
Adriatic: 6 Varano
Alberta: 6 Louise
Algeria: 5 Hodna
Alps: 6 Annecy
Arizona-Nevada: 4 Mead
Armenia: 5 Sevan 6 Gokcha, Sevang 9 Lychnitis
Aswan's: 6 Nasser
Australia: 4 Eyre 5 Carey, Cowan, Frome, Wells 6 Barlee 7 Amadeus, Everard, Torrens 8 Gairdner
Austria: 5 Atter, Traun 6 Kammer 8 Attersee 9 Kammersee
Bolivia: 5 Poopó
Botswana: 5 Ngami
British Columbia: 4 Pitt 5 Atlin
California: 4 Mono, Tule 5 Clear, Eagle, Honey
Cambodia: 8 Tonle Sap
Canada: 4 Dyke 8 Manitoba
central Africa: 4 Kivu 5 Mweru 6 Albert
Central America: 5 Guija
central Europe: 5 Leman 6 Geneva, Lugano 7 Ceresio 8 Bodensee 9 Constance
central North America: 5 Rainy
Chile: 4 Laja 5 Ranco
China: 6 Poyang 8 Dongting
Colorado: 5 Grand
Denmark: 5 Esrum
east Africa: 6 Rudolf 7 Turkana
east Asia: 6 Khanka 7 Xingkai 8 Hsingkai
east central Africa: 8 Victoria 10 Tanganyika
east China: 3 Tai 5 Dalai, Hulun
Ethiopia: 4 Tana, Zwai 5 Abaya, Shala, Shamo, Tsana 8 Stefanie 9 Chew Bahir

Finland: 5 Inari
Florida: 5 Worth 10 Okeechobee
Germany: 5 Ammer, Chiem 8 Ammersee, Chiemsee
Ghana: 5 Volta
Great: 4 Erie 5 Huron 7 Ontario 8 Michigan, Superior
Greece: 5 Bolbe, Volvi
Guatemala: 7 Atitlán
Honduras: 5 Yojoa
Honshu: 3 Omi 4 Biwa, Suwa, Yodo
Hungary: 7 Balaton 10 Plattensee
Idaho: 4 Waha 5 Grays 6 Priest 11 Coeur d'Alene, Pend Oreille
India: 3 Dal 5 Wular 6 Chilka
Indonesia: 4 Poso, Toba 5 Ranau
Iowa: 5 Storm
Iran: 5 Niriz, Shahi, Urmia 8 Matianus, Urumiyeh 9 Bakhtigan
Ireland: 3 Gur, Ree 4 Conn, Derg, Mask 5 Allen, Arrow, Leane
Israel: 12 Bahr Tabariya, Sea of Galilee
Israel-Jordan: 7 Dead Sea
Italy: 4 Como, Iseo, Nemi 5 Garda 6 Albano 7 Bolsena, Perugia 8 Maggiore 9 Trasimene
Japan: 4 Imba 8 Imbanuma
Kazakhstan: 7 Balqash 8 Balkhash
Louisiana: 4 Soda 9 Catahoula 13 Pontchartrain
Maine: 6 Sebago 9 Moosehead
Mali: 4 Debo
Manitoba: 4 Gods 5 Cedar, Moose 8 Winnipeg
Mexico: 7 Chapala
Michigan: 4 Burt
Minnesota: 3 Red 4 Cass, Gull, Swan 5 Leech 6 Itasca 9 Mille Lacs 10 Minnetonka, of the Woods 11 Lac qui Parle
Minnesota-Wisconsin: 5 Pepin
Mongolian: 3 Har 5 Har Us, Khara 8 Khara Usu
Montana: 8 Medicine
mountain: 4 tarn
Myanmar: 4 Inle
Nevada: 4 Ruby 7 Pyramid
New Hampshire: 5 Squam 13 Winnipesaukee
New Jersey: 5 Union

New York: 4 Long 5 Chazy, Keuka 6 Cayuga, George, Oneida, Otsego, Owasco, Placid, Seneca 7 Crooked, Saranac 8 Onondaga, Saratoga 10 Chautauqua 11 Canandaigua, Skaneateles
New Zealand: 4 Ohau 5 Hawea, Taupo 6 Pukaki, Wanaka 8 Wakatipu
Nicaragua: 7 Managua
North Africa: 4 Chad
Northern Ireland: 5 Neagh
Northwest Territories: 4 Gras 5 Baker, Garry, Pelly 9 Great Bear 10 Great Slave
Norway: 5 Mjosa
Nova Scotia: 7 Bras d'Or
Ontario: 4 Rice, Seul 5 Trout
Oregon: 5 Abert 6 Crater 7 Malheur, Wallowa
Paraguay: 4 Ypoá
Peru: 5 Junín 13 Chinchaycocha
Philippines: 4 Bato, Taal 5 Lanao 6 Bombon
Poland: 5 Mamry, Mauer
Quebec: 5 Minto, Payne
Russia: 3 Seg 5 Chany, Ilmen, Lacha, Onega 6 Baikal, Ladoga 7 Rybinsk 10 Eltonskoye 11 Ladozhskoye
Saskatchewan: 4 Cree 5 Ronge
Scotland: 3 Ard, Awe 4 Doon, Earn, Ness, Oich, Shin, Sloy 5 Leven, Lochy, Maree, Morar, Shiel 6 Lomond
Siberia: 6 Baikal, Baykal
South Africa: 4 Kosi
South America: 5 Merin, Mirim 8 Titicaca
South Carolina: 7 Wateree
South Dakota: 5 Andes
southeast Africa: 5 Nyasa 6 Nyassa
southwest Europe: 5 Ohrid 7 Okhrida
Sweden: 5 Asnen, Roxen 6 Siljan, Vänern, Vetter 7 Malaren, Vattern
Switzerland: 3 Zug 4 Biel, Joux 5 Zuger 6 Bieler, Bienne, Brienz, Sarnen, Sarner, Zurich 7 Lucerne, Lungern 8 Brienzer, Züricher 9 Neuchâtel, Zürichsee

Tajikistan: 7 Karakul
Tanzania: 5 Rukwa
Texas-Louisiana: 5 Caddo
Tibet: 4 Na-mu 6 Nam Tso, Tengri
Turkey: 3 Tuz, Van 4 Bafa, Nice 5 Iznik, Sugla 6 Nicaea
Uganda: 5 Kyoga
Utah: 6 Powell, Sevier 9 Great Salt
Wales: 4 Bala
Washington: 4 Omak 5 Moses 6 Chelan 9 Wenatchee
western China: 4 Ai-pi 6 Ebinur
western United States: 4 Bear 5 Tahoe
Wisconsin: 5 Green 9 Winnebago
Yellowstone National Park: 5 Heart, Lewis 8 Shoshone
Zaire: 5 Tumba
Zambia: 9 Bangweolo, Bangweulu

lake group
central North America: 5 Great
Connecticut: 4 Twin
Egypt: 5 Balah
Maine: 8 Rangeley
New Hampshire: 11 Connecticut
New York: 6 Finger
Saskatchewan: 5 Quill
Twin: 8 Washinee 9 Washining
Wisconsin: 4 Four

lake herring
5 cisco

Lake poet
7 Southey (Robert) 9 Coleridge (Samuel Taylor) 10 Wordsworth (William)

Lake Wobegon Days author
7 Keillor (Garrison)

Lakmé
aria: 8 Bell Song
composer: 7 Delibes (Léo)

Lakshmi
husband: 6 Vishnu
son: 4 Kama

lam
3 hit 4 beat, blow, bolt, drub, flay, flee, flog, pelt, skip, whip 5 baste, paste, pound, scram, smack, split, whale 6 batter, beat it, buffet, cut

lamb
4 cade 5 sheep 6 cosset 8 yeanling
leg of: 5 gigot

lambaste
3 pan 4 beat, drub, flay, flog, lash,
lick, pelt, slam, slap, trim, whip
5 paste, pound, roast, scold, score,
slash, smear 6 assail, attack, berate,
cudgel, hammer, pummel, scathe,
scorch, thrash, wallop 7 assault,
blister, censure, clobber, reprove,
scourge, shellac, upbraid 8 bludgeon, denounce, harangue, lash
into 9 castigate, criticize, excoriate
10 tongue-lash

lambent
5 aglow 6 ardent, bright, lucent
7 beaming, glowing, radiant, shining
8 gleaming, luminous, lustrous
9 brilliant, effulgent, refulgent, twinkling 10 flickering, glittering, shimmering 12 incandescent

lamblike
4 meek 6 docile

lamb of God
5 Jesus 6 Christ 8 Agnus Dei

Lamb's pseudonym
4 Elia

lame
4 gimp, halt, limp 5 gimpy, stiff
6 feeble, flimsy 7 cripple, disable,
halting, limping 8 crippled, disabled,
hobbling, inferior 10 inadequate
11 ineffectual 12 contemptible,
unconvincing 13 incapacitated

lamebrain
3 oaf 4 dolt, dope, goof, mutt, simp,
yo-yo 5 chump, dummy, dunce, idiot,
moron, ninny, noddy, stupe 6 dimwit,
donkey, dum-dum, nitwit, noodle

7 airhead, dullard, pinhead, schnook
8 bonehead, clodpoll, dumbbell,
dumbhead, imbecile, lunkhead,
meathead, numskull 9 blockhead,
ignoramus, numbskull, simpleton,
thickhead 10 dunderhead, hammerhead, nincompoop 11 chowderhead,
chucklehead, knucklehead

Lamech
daughter: 6 Naamah
father: 10 Methuselah
son: 4 Noah 5 Jabal, Jubal 9 Tubalcain
wife: 4 Adah 6 Zillah

lament
3 cry, rue 4 keen, moan, pine,
wail, weep 5 dirge, elegy, mourn
6 bemoan, bewail, grieve, plaint,
regret, repent, sorrow 7 deplore,
elegize, wailing 8 jeremiad, threnody
9 complaint, ululation

lamentable
6 rueful, woeful 7 doleful, pitiful
8 dolorous, grievous, mournful
9 plaintive, sorrowful 10 afflictive,
deplorable, lugubrious, melancholy
11 distressing, regrettable, unfortunate 13 heartbreaking

lamentation
5 elegy, grief 7 anguish, remorse,
wailing 8 grieving, mourning, threnody 9 sorrowing, ululation 13 mortification

Lamerok
father: 9 Pellinore
lover: 8 Margawse
slayer: 6 Gawain

lamia
3 hag, hex 5 witch 7 hellcat, vampire 9 sorceress 11 enchantress,
necromancer

Lamia
country: 5 Libya
form: 7 serpent
lover: 4 Zeus

lamina
5 blade, flake, layer, plate, scale

lamp
3 arc 4 bulb 5 klieg, light, torch
7 lantern 10 candelabra 11 candelabrum
floor: 8 torchère 9 torchiere
hanging: 10 chandelier

lampblack
4 soot 6 carbon

Lampetia
father: 6 Apollo, Helios
husband: 9 Asclepius
mother: 6 Neaera
sister: 9 Phaethusa

lampoon
4 mock 5 roast, spoof, squib 6 parody, satire, send-up 7 take off
8 ridicule, satirize 9 burlesque
10 caricature, pasquinade

lamprey
3 eel

lanai
5 patio, porch 6 piazza 7 terrace,
veranda

lance
4 gash, hurl 5 slash, spear 6 impale,
pierce, skewer 7 javelin 8 transfix

Lancelot, Launcelot
father: 3 Ban
lover: 6 Elaine 9 Guinevere
son: 7 Galahad
victim: 6 Gawain

lancer
10 cavalryman
Prussian: 5 uhlan

lancet
4 arch 5 blade, knife 6 cutter,
window 7 scalpel

land
4 dirt, dock, gain, soil 5 acres, berth,
earth, light, manor, shore, terra, tract
6 alight, estate, ground, obtain, pick
up, secure 7 acquire, acreage,
country, expanse, grounds, procure,
set down, terrain, terrene 9 touch
down 10 terra firma
alluvial: 5 delta
barren: 5 waste 6 desert
cultivated: 4 farm 5 tilth 7 tillage

for grazing: 3 lea, ley 5 range
6 meadow 7 pasture
high: 4 hill, mesa 7 plateau 8 mountain
level: 4 mesa 5 plain 7 plateau
low: 4 vale 6 valley 9 intervale
measure: 3 rod 4 acre
open: 3 lea 5 field, green, plain
6 meadow 7 pasture
piece: 3 lot 4 plot 5 tract 6 estate,
parcel
reclaimed: 6 polder
sloping: 6 cuesta
strip: 7 isthmus
wet: 3 bog, fen 5 marsh, swamp
6 marish

land east of Eden
3 Nod

landed
4 alit

landlord
6 lessor, squire 9 innkeeper 10 freeholder

landmark
5 cairn, guide 9 benchmark, milestone, watershed 11 achievement
12 breakthrough, turning point

Land of Enchantment
9 New Mexico

Land of Lakes
8 Michigan

Land of Opportunity
3 USA 8 Arkansas 12 United States

Land of the Midnight Sun
6 Norway

landowner
6 squire, yeoman
Anglo-Saxon: 5 thane, thegn
Dutch: 7 patroon
Scottish: 5 laird

landscape
5 scene, vista 7 scenery, setting,
terrain 8 backdrop, prospect

lane
3 way 4 path, road 5 aisle, alley,
byway, track 6 street 7 pathway,
roadway 8 footpath 10 passageway

lang syne

4 past, yore **10** yesteryear

language

4 cant **5** argot, idiom, lingo, prose, slang **6** jargon, patois, speech, tongue **7** dialect, lexicon, palaver **10** vernacular, vocabulary **11** terminology

ambiguous: 8 newspeak **10** double-talk

ancient: 5 Greek, Latin **6** Hebrew **8** Etruscan, Sanskrit

artificial: 3 Ido **7** Volapük **9** Esperanto

classical: 5 Greek, Latin

combining form: 5 gloss, glott **6** glosso, glotto

expert: 8 linguist

informal: 4 jive **5** lingo, slang

meaningless: 6 babble, jabber **7** blather **9** gibberish **10** mumbo-jumbo

mixed: 6 creole, pidgin

pretentious: 7 bombast, fustian **8** claptrap

regional: 7 dialect

relating to: 10 linguistic

Romance: 6 French **7** Catalan, Italian, Spanish **8** Romanian, Rumanian **10** Portuguese

secret: 4 cant, code **5** argot

structure: 6 syntax **7** grammar

suffix: 3 ese

written: 5 prose

languid

4 lazy, limp **5** inert **6** draggy, supine, torpid **8** drooping, flagging, inactive, listless, slothful, sluggish **9** apathetic, enervated, impassive, lethargic **10** languorous, phlegmatic, spiritless **13** lackadaisical

languish

4 fade, fail, pine, tire, wilt **5** brood, droop **6** weaken **7** decline **9** waste away

languishing

4 limp, weak **6** feeble, pining **7** languid **8** fainéant, indolent, listless, weakened **9** depressed, enervated, enfeebled **10** dispirited, languorous, spiritless **11** debilitated, devitalized **13** lackadaisical

languor

3 kef, kif **5** ennui **6** stupor, tedium, torpor **7** fatigue **8** doldrums, dullness, hebetude, lethargy **9** heaviness, inertness, lassitude, torpidity, weariness **10** exhaustion

languorous

4 lazy, limp **5** inert **6** draggy, supine, torpid **7** laggard, languid, passive, relaxed **8** dilatory, drooping, fainéant, flagging, inactive, indolent, indulged, listless, pampered, slothful, sluggard **9** apathetic, enervated, impassive, lethargic **10** phlegmatic, spiritless **11** languishing **13** lackadaisical

lank

4 bony, lean, thin **5** rangy, spare **6** gangly **7** angular, scraggy, slender **8** gangling **10** attenuated

lanky

4 lean, thin **5** gaunt, spare **6** gangly **7** scrawny **8** gangling, rawboned

lanyard

4 cord, line, rope **7** cordage

Laocoön

city: 4 Troy

killer: 8 serpents

Laodamia

father: 7 Acastus

husband: 11 Protesilaus

Laomedon

daughter: 7 Hesione

father: 4 Ilus

kingdom: 4 Troy

mother: 8 Eurydice

slayer: 8 Heracles, Hercules

son: 5 Priam **8** Tithonus

Laos

capital: 9 Vientiane

city: 11 Savannakhet

ethnic group: 5 Hmong

monetary unit: 3 kip

neighbor: 5 Burma, China 7 Myanmar, Vietnam 8 Cambodia, Thailand 9 Kampuchea
river: 6 Mekong

lap
3 sip 4 fold, join, wind 6 cuddle, splash, swathe 7 circuit, control, custody, shingle 9 imbricate

lapidary
6 cutter 7 elegant, jeweler 8 engraver, polisher

lapillus
4 lava 6 cinder

lapin
6 rabbit

Lapiths
foes: 8 centaurs
king: 5 Ixion

lappet
4 flap, fold 5 lapel

Lapsang
3 tea 6 Fujian

lapse
3 err, gap, sin 4 fall, flub, goof, sink, slip, vice 5 boner, cease, error, fluff, gaffe, slide 6 breach, bungle, expire, foible, miscue 7 blooper, blunder, decline, descend, failing, failure, faux pas, forfeit, frailty, mistake, screwup, subside 8 apostasy, interval, trespass 9 backslide, deviation, oversight, violation 10 apostatize 11 backsliding, impropriety 12 indiscretion, interruption 13 retrogression, transgression

lapsed
4 sunk 5 ended 6 ceased 7 expired 8 obsolete 9 forfeited

Laputan
6 absurd 9 visionary

Lar
3 god 6 spirit

larboard
4 left, port 8 leftward

larcenist
5 thief 6 bandit, robber 7 burglar, filcher, stealer 8 pilferer 9 embezzler, plunderer, purloiner 10 pickpocket, shoplifter

larcenous
7 robbing 8 thieving 9 pilfering 10 plunderous 13 light-fingered

larceny
5 theft 7 looting, robbery 8 burglary, stealing, thievery, thieving
kind: 5 grand, petty

lard
3 fat 6 fatten, grease 10 shortening

larder
6 pantry

large
3 big, fat 4 bull, huge, vast 5 ample, bulky, giant, grand, great, gross, hefty, husky, jumbo, major 6 goodly 7 copious, extreme, immense, mammoth, massive, outsize, sizable 8 colossal, enormous, gigantic, king-size, oversize, spacious, whopping 9 capacious, excessive, extensive, humongous, monstrous 10 exorbitant, immoderate, inordinate, large-scale, monumental, prodigious, stupendous, tremendous, voluminous 11 extravagant, substantial
combining form: 4 macr, mega 5 macro 6 megalo

largesse
4 alms, gift 6 bounty 7 bequest, charity, cumshaw, gifting, present 8 donation, gratuity 9 endowment, pourboire 10 almsgiving, generosity, liberality 11 benefaction, benevolence, beneficence, magnanimity, munificence 12 philanthropy

largo
4 slow 5 broad, tempo

lariat
4 rope 5 lasso, noose, reata, riata
user: 6 cowboy, drover 10 cowpuncher

lark

4 bird, dido, romp 5 antic, caper,
prank, shine, stunt, trick 6 frolic
7 rollick 8 escapade, songbird
9 diversion 10 tomfoolery 11 distraction, shenanigans 12 monkeyshines

larrup

3 tan 4 beat, cane, drub, dust, flay,
flog, hide, lash, lick, whip, whup
5 pound, spank, whale 6 cudgel,
lather, paddle, thrash, wallop 7 clobber, scourge, shellac, trounce 8 lambaste 10 flagellate

larva

3 bot 4 grub, worm 6 dobson,
maggot 8 cercaria, hornworm,
mealworm 10 casebearer 11 caterpillar 12 hellgrammite
amphibian: 7 tadpole
crustacean: 4 zoea
flatworm: 5 redia
free-swimming: 7 planula
mollusk: 7 veliger
moth: 8 leafworm
tapeworm: 6 measle

larynx

7 trachea 8 voice box

lasagna

5 pasta 7 noodles

lascivious

4 lewd 5 bawdy, loose, randy 6 carnal, coarse, rakish, wanton 7 fleshly,
goatish, immoral, lustful, satyric
8 depraved, prurient 9 lecherous,
libertine, lickerish, salacious 10 libidinous, licentious, lubricious, profligate
12 concupiscent

lash

4 beat, bind, dash, flay, flog, hide, whip
5 baste, birch, fling, pound, scold,
slash, whale 6 assail, berate, buffet,
pummel, scathe, strike, stripe, switch,
thrash 7 blister, scarify, scourge,
upbraid 8 lambaste 9 castigate,
excoriate, horsewhip 10 flagellate

lass

3 gal 4 girl, maid 5 wench 6 damsel, maiden 7 colleen

lassitude

5 ennui, sloth 6 apathy, stupor,
tedium, torpor 7 fatigue, languor
8 debility, doldrums, dullness, hebetude, laziness, lethargy 9 indolence,
tiredness, torpidity, weariness 10 exhaustion 11 disinterest, insouciance
12 heedlessness, indifference,
listlessness, sluggishness

lasso

see **lariat**

last

3 end, lag 5 abide, final 6 endure,
latest, latter, utmost 7 closing,
extreme, perdure, persist 8 continue, crowning, eventual, farthest,
furthest, hindmost, rearmost, remotest, terminal, ultimate 9 umpteenth,
uttermost 10 concluding, conclusive
11 terminating
French: 7 dernier
next to: 6 penult 11 penultimate

last-ditch

5 final 7 defiant 8 ultimate 9 desperate 10 concluding

lasting

6 stable 7 abiding, durable, undying
8 enduring, lifelong, long-term,
longtime 9 continual, indelible,
perennial, permanent, unceasing
10 continuing, continuous, perdurable, persisting 12 indissoluble,
long-standing

Last of the Mohicans, The

5 Uncas
author: 6 Cooper (James Fenimore)
character: 4 Cora 5 Alice, Magua,
Uncas 11 Natty Bumppo 12 Chingachgook

Last Supper, The

painter: 7 da Vinci (Leonardo)

latch

4 bolt, hasp, hook 5 catch 6 fasten,
secure 8 fastener
British: 5 sneck

latchet

4 band, cord, lace 5 strap, thong
8 shoelace

late
4 dead, past, slow 5 tardy 6 former, recent, whilom 7 defunct, delayed, onetime, overdue, quondam 8 deceased, departed, sometime 9 preceding

Late George Apley, The
author: 8 Marquand (John P.)

latent
4 idle 5 inert 6 covert, fallow, hidden, innate, unripe 7 abeyant, dormant, lurking 8 immature, inactive, inherent 9 concealed, intrinsic, potential, quiescent

later
4 anon, soon 5 after, infra 6 behind 7 by and by, ensuing 9 afterward, following, posterior 10 subsequent, succeeding 12 subsequently

lateral
4 pass, side 6 branch 8 crabwise, flanking, sidelong, sideward, sideways, sidewise

laterally
8 crabwise, sideward, sideways, sidewise

latest
6 newest, red-hot 7 current 8 contempo 9 au courant 10 dernier cri 13 up-to-the-minute

latex
6 balata 8 emulsion
product: 5 paint 6 chicle, rubber

lath
4 slat 5 board, frame, stave, stick, strip

lather
4 flap, flog, foam, hide, lash, soap, stew, suds, whip 5 froth, spume, tizzy, yeast 6 dither, hoopla, pother, thrash, welter 7 scourge, turmoil 8 soapsuds

Latin
5 Roman 7 Italian 8 Hispanic
after: 4 post
always: 6 semper
before: 4 ante, prae

book: 5 liber
boy: 4 puer
brother: 6 frater
but: 3 sed
day: 4 dies
dog: 5 canis
foot: 3 pes
friend: 6 amicus
god: 4 deus
goddess: 3 dea
grammarian: 7 Donatus (Aelius)
hand: 5 manus
is: 3 est
law: 3 ius, jus, lex
light: 3 lux
love: 3 amo 4 amas, amat, amor
peace: 3 pax
pronoun: 3 ego, nos, vos
road: 3 via
see: 4 vide
that is: 5 id est
thing: 3 res
this: 3 hic, hoc 4 haec
thus: 3 sic
war: 6 bellum
wife: 4 uxor
woman: 6 femina
year: 5 annus

Latin American
country: 4 Cuba, Peru 5 Chile 6 Belize, Brazil, Guyana, Mexico, Panama 7 Bolivia, Ecuador, Uruguay 8 Colombia, Honduras, Paraguay, Suriname 9 Argentina, Costa Rica, Guatemala, Nicaragua, Venezuela 10 El Salvador
revolutionary: 6 Castro (Fidel) 7 Bolívar (Simón), Guevara (Ché), Hidalgo (Father Miguel) 8 O'Higgins (Bernardo) 9 San Martín (José de)

Latinus
daughter: 7 Lavinia
father: 6 Faunus 8 Odysseus
son-in-law: 6 Aeneas
wife: 5 Amata

latitude
4 play, room 5 range, scope, space, width 6 leeway, margin 7 breadth, compass, freedom, liberty, license 9 elbowroom 10 discretion 12 independence

latke
7 pancake 13 potato pancake

Latona
4 Leto
daughter: 5 Diana 7 Artemis
father: 5 Coeus
mother: 6 Phoebe
son: 6 Apollo

Latter-day Saint
6 Mormon

lattice
4 grid, mesh 5 grate, grill 7 grating, network, trellis 12 reticulation

Latvia
capital: 4 Riga
city: 7 Liepaja 10 Daugavpils
gulf: 4 Riga
monetary unit: 3 lat
neighbor: 6 Russia 7 Belarus, Estonia 9 Lithuania
river: 7 Daugava 12 Western Dvina
sea: 6 Baltic

Latvian
4 Lett 7 Lettish

laud
5 adore, bless, cry up, extol, glory, honor 6 admire, praise, revere 7 acclaim, flatter, glorify, magnify, worship 8 eulogize, venerate 9 celebrate, reverence

laudable
6 worthy 9 admirable, deserving, estimable 11 commendable, meritorious, thankworthy 12 praiseworthy

laudatory
7 glowing 9 adulatory, approving 10 eulogistic, flattering 11 approbative, encomiastic, panegyrical 12 commendatory 13 complimentary

laugh
3 yuk 4 ha-ha, roar, yuck 5 tehee, whoop 6 cackle, giggle, guffaw, hee-haw, titter 7 chortle, chuckle, snicker 10 cachinnate

laughable
4 rich 5 comic, droll, funny, goofy, witty 6 absurd, jocose 7 amusing, comical, jocular, mocking, risible 8 derisive, derisory, farcical, humorous 9 ludicrous 10 ridiculous

laughing
5 merry, riant 6 blithe 8 mirthful 9 sparkling

laughingstock
4 butt, dupe, fool, jest, joke, mark, mock 5 sport 6 target 7 mockery 8 derision

launch
4 boat, cast, fire, hurl 5 begin, debut, fling, heave, pitch, sling, start, throw 6 get off 7 jump off, kick off, lift off, release, take off, usher in 8 blast off, catapult, commence, embark on, initiate 9 inception, institute, introduce, motorboat, set afloat 10 inaugurate, initiation 12 inauguration

launder
4 wash 5 clean 6 trough 7 cleanse 8 sanitize, transfer

Laura's lover
8 Petrarch

laurels
4 bays, fame 5 award, honor, kudos, prize 6 awards, badges, honors, prizes, renown 7 acclaim 8 accolade, citation 9 accolades, citations 10 decoration, reputation 11 decorations, distinction 12 achievements, distinctions

laurel-tree nymph
6 Daphne

lava
4 slag 5 magma 6 scoria 8 andesite, trachyte
fragment: 8 lapillus
stream: 4 flow 6 coulee

lavalava
5 cloth, skirt

lavaliere
7 pendant 8 necklace

lavatory
4 head, john 5 basin, potty, privy 6 johnny, toilet 7 latrine 8 bathroom, restroom, washroom 11 water closet

lave
4 pour, wash 5 bathe

Lavinia
father: 7 Latinus
husband: 6 Aeneas
mother: 5 Amata

Lavinium's founder
6 Aeneas

lavish
4 lush, pour 5 plush, spend, waste
6 swanky 7 liberal, opulent, profuse
8 effusive, prodigal, splendid, squander 9 bountiful, excessive, exuberant, luxuriant, luxurious, sumptuous
10 immoderate, inordinate, munificent 11 extravagant

law
3 act, lex 4 bill, code, rule 5 axiom,
canon, edict, Torah 6 assize, decree,
equity 7 dictate, justice, mandate,
precept, statute, theorem 8 exigency
9 enactment, ordinance, principle
10 principium, regulation 11 commandment, fundamental 12 prescription
body of: 4 code 7 pandect 12 constitution
degree: 3 LLB, LLD
expert: 5 judge 6 jurist 7 justice
practitioner: 6 lawyer 7 counsel
8 attorney 9 barrister, solicitor
relating to: 5 jural, legal 7 canonic
8 forensic, juristic 9 judiciary
violation of: 4 tort 5 crime 6 felony
11 misdemeanor

law-abiding
6 decent 7 duteous, dutiful, orderly,
upright 8 obedient, obliging, straight
9 compliant, peaceable 10 forthright,
respectful 11 respectable, wellbehaved

lawbreaker
3 con 4 hood, thug 5 crook, felon
6 outlaw, sinner 7 convict, hoodlum,
mobster 8 criminal, gangster, hooligan, jailbird, offender, scofflaw,
violator 9 desperado, wrongdoer
10 malefactor, trespasser 12 transgressor

lawful
3 due 4 just 5 legal, legit, licit, valid
6 kosher 7 condign 8 bona fide,
innocent, mandated, ordained
9 allowable, canonical, juridical,
legalized 10 authorized, legitimate
11 permissible

lawgiver
5 Draco, Moses, solon 7 senator
8 alderman 10 councilman, legislator 11 congressman

lawlessness
5 chaos 6 strife 7 anarchy, discord,
misrule, turmoil 8 conflict, disorder
9 mobocracy 10 illegality, misconduct, ochlocracy, unruliness, wrongdoing 11 criminality, pandemonium

lawman
7 marshal, officer, sheriff 9 policeman

Lawrence novel
7 Rainbow (The) 8 Kangaroo, Lost
Girl (The) 9 Aaron's Rod 11 Women
in Love 13 Sons and Lovers

lawsuit
4 case 5 cause, claim 6 action
8 replevin 9 assumpsit 10 litigation,
proceeding 11 presentment, prosecution

lawyer
6 jurist, legist 7 counsel, pleader
8 advocate, attorney 9 barrister,
counselor, solicitor
dishonest: 7 shyster 11 pettifogger
fictional: 7 Matlock (Ben) 10 Perry
Mason
French: 6 avocat

lax
5 loose, slack 6 casual, remiss,
sloppy 7 lenient 8 careless, derelict,
lacrosse 9 deficient, forgetful, negligent 10 neglectful 11 inattentive

lay
3 bet, put, set 5 apply, hatch, place,
wager 6 assert, assign, ballad,
charge, credit, devise, impute, settle,
spread 7 amateur, arrange, ascribe,
concoct, deposit, prepare, present
11 nonclerical

lay by

4 keep, save 5 amass, hoard, store 7 deposit, discard, store up 8 preserve, salt away, set aside 10 accumulate

lay down

3 set 4 rule 5 order, store, yield 6 assert, decree, define, give up, impose, ordain, record, resign 7 abandon, command, dictate, specify 8 hand over, preserve, proclaim 9 establish, prescribe, surrender 10 relinquish

layer

3 hen, ply 4 coat, film, seam, tier 5 paver, sheet 6 folium, lamina, veneer 7 coating, stratum 8 covering, laminate, membrane, sandwich, stratify
inner: 6 lining
of skin: 6 dermis 9 epidermis
outer: 4 skin 6 veneer

lay for

6 ambush 8 surprise

lay in

see **lay by**

layman

6 novice 7 amateur, secular 11 parishioner

lay off

4 halt, quit, stop 5 avoid, cease, let go, lie by 6 desist 7 dismiss, measure, release 9 discharge, terminate 10 inactivity 11 discontinue

lay out

3 pay 4 give, plan 5 chart, dummy, place, spend 6 design, expend 7 arrange, display, exhibit, prepare 8 disburse

lay waste

4 ruin 6 ravage 7 destroy 8 desolate 9 devastate

lazar

5 leper

Lazarus' sister

4 Mary 6 Martha

laze

3 bum, lag 4 bask, hang, idle, loaf, loll 5 chill 6 dawdle, loiter, lounge, slouch 7 goof off, hang out 8 chill out 9 goldbrick 10 hang around

laziness

5 sloth 6 torpor 7 inertia, languor, laxness, loafing 8 idleness, lethargy, otiosity 9 indolence, lassitude, loitering, slackness 10 inactivity 11 languidness 12 listlessness

lazy

3 lax 4 idle 5 inert, slack 6 droopy, remiss, supine, torpid 7 languid, loafing, passive 8 fainéant, inactive, indolent, listless, slothful, sluggish 9 lethargic, negligent, shiftless, slowgoing 10 languorous

lazy Susan

4 tray 9 turntable

leach

4 drip, leak, ooze, perk, seep, suck, weep 5 bleed, drain, exude, issue 7 draw out, dribble, trickle 8 filtrate, perspire 9 discharge, lixiviate, percolate

lead

3 tip 4 head, hint, show, star 5 guide, metal, plumb, route, steer, trace, usher 6 bullet, ceruse, direct, escort, leader 7 captain, conduct, precede, preface 8 graphite, persuade, shepherd 10 bellwether
combining form: 5 plumb 6 plumbo
ore: 6 galena 9 anglesite
oxide: 6 sinter
sounding: 5 plumb 7 plummet

lead astray

6 seduce 7 corrupt

leaden

4 drab, dull, flat, gray 5 heavy, inert 6 gloomy, somber 7 languid, weighty 8 dragging, lifeless, sluggish 9 ponderous

leader

4 boss, dean, duce, guru, head, jefe, lord 5 chief, guide, pilot 6 despot,

honcho, rector **7** captain, foreman,
general, headman, manager, warlord
8 chairman, director, hierarch, superior **9** chieftain, commander, conductor, demagogue, harbinger, precursor, president, principal, straw boss
10 bellwether, forerunner, pacesetter
authoritarian: **10** Big Brother
Cossack: **6** ataman, hetman
German: **6** führer **7** fuehrer
Japanese: **6** shogun
military: **7** admiral, general, warlord
9 commander **12** field marshal
Muslim: **3** aga **4** agha, emir **6** caliph, mullah
national: **7** premier **9** president
12 chief of state

leading
4 arch, head, main **5** chief, first,
major **6** famous, master **7** premier,
primary **8** champion, foremost,
headmost, peerless **9** paramount,
principal, prominent, well-known
10 preeminent

lead on
3 con **4** bait, dupe, fool, gull, hoax,
lure, scam, tole, toll, wile **5** cozen,
flirt, tempt **6** allure, betray, cajole,
coquet, delude, entice, entrap,
humbug, seduce, suck in, take in,
trifle **7** beguile, deceive, toy with
8 coquette, hoodwink, inveigle
9 bamboozle **11** string along

leaf
4 flip, foil, page, riff, scan, skim
5 blade, bract, folio, frond, petal,
scale, sepal, thumb **6** browse,
glance, riffle, spathe
aperture: **5** stoma
axis: **6** rachis
combining form: **5** phyll **6** phyllo
7 phyllum
edge: **9** crenation
lily: **3** pad
part: **4** lobe, vein **5** blade, costa,
stoma **7** petiole, stipule, tendril
pine: **6** needle
vein: **5** costa

leafage
7 foliage, umbrage, verdure

leaflet
5 flier, flyer, pinna, sheet, tract
6 folder **7** handout **8** circular, handbill, pamphlet

leafy
4 lush **5** green, shady **6** shaded,
wooded **7** foliate, verdant **8** foliated,
laminate **9** verdurous

league
4 band, bond, club, crew **5** class,
grade, group, guild, order, union,
unite **6** circle **7** circuit, combine,
society **8** alliance, category, division, grouping, sodality **9** coalition **10** conference, consortium,
federation, fellowship, fraternity
11 association, brotherhood, confederacy **13** confederation

Leah
daughter: **5** Dinah
father: **5** Laban
husband: **5** Jacob
sister: **6** Rachel
son: **4** Levi **5** Judah **6** Reuben,
Simeon **7** Zebulun **8** Issachar

leak
4 drip, ooze, seep **5** break, crack,
spill **6** escape, get out, reveal,
source **7** come out, divulge, seepage **8** disclose **9** discharge **10** make
public

leaky
6 broken, faulty, porous **7** cracked,
damaged

lea, ley
4 veld **5** field, veldt **6** fallow, meadow **7** pasture **9** grassland, pasturage

lean
3 sag, tip **4** bend, bony, cant, heel,
lank, list, slim, thin, tilt **5** gaunt,
lanky, shift, slant, slope, spare
6 meager, meagre, skinny, slight,
wasted **7** angular, deviate, haggard, incline, pinched, scraggy,
scrawny, slender, stringy, wizened
8 gradient, rawboned **9** deficient
11 inclination

Leander's beloved
4 Hero

Leaning Tower site
4 Pisa

lean-to
3 hut 4 shed 5 shack 6 shanty
7 bivouac, shelter

leap
3 hop 4 buck, jump, loup, rise,
soar 5 bound, caper, clear, mount,
vault 6 ascend, gambol, hurdle,
spring 7 saltate 8 capriole, surmount
ballet: 4 jeté 9 entrechat
by a horse: 7 gambado

Lear, King
daughter: 5 Regan 7 Goneril
8 Cordelia
servant: 4 Kent

learn
3 con 4 hear 5 grasp, study 6 attain,
detect, master, pick up 7 acquire,
catch on, discern, find out, realize,
uncover, unearth 8 discover, memorize 9 ascertain, determine 10 comprehend, understand 11 stumble
onto

learned
4 sage, wise 6 expert, versed
7 bookish, erudite, sapient, studied
8 abstruse, academic, cultured,
educated, esoteric, highbrow, lettered, pedantic, well-read 9 recondite, scholarly 10 cultivated,
scholastic 12 intellectual

learner
4 tyro 5 pupil 6 novice, rookie
7 student, trainee 8 beginner, disciple, initiate, neophyte 9 greenhorn,
postulant 10 apprentice, catechumen 11 abecedarian

learning
4 lore 6 wisdom 7 science, tuition
8 booklore, pedantry 9 education,
erudition, knowledge 11 scholarship
person of: 7 egghead, scholar
9 professor 12 intellectual

lease
3 let 4 hire, rent 6 sublet 7 charter,
compact 8 contract, covenant,
document 11 continuance

leash
3 tie 4 bind, cord, curb, rein, rope
5 strap 6 bridle, fetter, hamper,
tether 7 shackle, trammel 8 restrain
9 entrammel

least
6 fewest 7 minimal, minimum
8 smallest

leather
3 tan 4 hide, skin, whip 6 thrash
kind: 3 kid, kip, oak 4 bock, buff,
calf, roan 5 crown, grain, mocha,
strap, suede, whang 6 castor, latigo,
oxhide, patent, roller, saddle, skiver
7 buffalo, chamois, morocco, ostrich,
peccary 8 capeskin, cordovan,
cordwain, shagreen
maker: 5 tawer 6 tanner 7 tannery
piece: 4 welt 5 strap, thong
prepare: 3 tan, taw 5 curry
soft: 5 mocha, suede 8 cabretta

leatherneck
6 marine

Leatherstocking Tales, The
author: 6 Cooper (James Fenimore)
hero: 5 Natty (Bumppo)
title: 7 Prairie (The) 8 Pioneers
(The) 10 Deerslayer (The), Pathfinder (The) 17 Last of the Mohicans
(The)

leave
3 fly, let 4 blow, cede, exit, flee,
move, part, quit, will 5 allow, scram,
split 6 assent, assign, beat it, commit, cut out, decamp, depart, desert,
devise, escape, get off, legate,
permit, resign, retire, set out, vacate
7 abandon, abscond, absence,
consent, consign, entrust, forsake,
get away, liberty, pull out, take off,
vamoose 8 bequeath, clear out,
farewell, furlough, hand down,
transmit, vacation, withdraw 9 departure, disappear, surrender, terminate 10 permission, relinquish,
sabbatical 13 authorization

leaved
5 green 7 foliate, verdant 8 foliated

leaven
5 imbue, steep, yeast 6 infuse, invest, modify, temper, vivify 7 enliven, ingrain, lighten, suffuse 8 moderate 9 alleviate, inoculate, sourdough 12 baking powder

leave of absence
8 furlough

leave off
3 end 4 halt, quit, stop 5 cease 6 desist, give up 7 abstain 8 give over, surcease 9 terminate 11 discontinue

leave out
4 omit, skip 5 elide 7 exclude

Leaves of Grass author
7 Whitman (Walt)

leavings
4 lees, orts, rest 5 dregs, scrap 6 debris, grouts 7 balance, remains, remnant, residue, rubbish 8 discards, oddments, remnants, residual, residuum 9 fragments, leftovers, remainder

Lebanon
capital: 6 Beirut
city: 4 Tyre 5 Sidon 6 Zahlah 7 Tripoli
language: 6 Arabic, French
monetary unit: 5 pound
mountain: 6 Hermon
neighbor: 5 Syria 6 Israel
river: 6 Litani 7 Orontes
sea: 13 Mediterranean
valley: 5 Bekáa

Le Carré, John
character: 6 Smiley (George)
novel: 11 Russia House (The) 17 Little Drummer Girl (The) 22 Tinker, Tailor, Soldier, Spy 23 Spy Who Came in from the Cold (The)

lecher
4 rake, roué, wolf 7 Don Juan, seducer 8 Casanova, lothario 9 debauchee, reprobate, libertine, womanizer 10 degenerate, profligate, voluptuary 11 philanderer

lecherous
4 lewd 5 bawdy, loose, randy 6 carnal, coarse, rakish, wanton 7 fleshly, goatish, immoral, lustful, satyric 8 depraved, prurient, scabrous 9 debauched, libertine, lickerish, salacious 10 lascivious, libidinous, licentious, lubricious, profligate 11 promiscuous 12 concupiscent

lectern
4 desk 5 stand

lecture
4 talk 5 chide, scold, speak 6 berate, preach, rebuke, sermon, speech 7 address, declaim, expound, oration, reproof, reprove, upbraid 8 admonish, briefing, harangue, scolding 9 chalk talk, criticism, criticize, discourse, hold forth, reprimand, talking-to 10 allocution 12 disquisition, dressing-down

lecturer
3 don 6 docent, fellow, master, orator, reader 7 scholar, speaker, teacher, trainer 9 pedagogue, preceptor, professor 10 instructor 11 academician

Leda
daughter: 5 Helen 12 Clytemnestra
father: 8 Thestius
husband: 9 Tyndareus
lover: 4 swan, Zeus
son: 6 Castor, Pollux

ledge
3 bar, rim 4 berm, lode, reef, sill, vein 5 bench, ridge, shelf 6 mantle 7 bedrock, molding 10 projection

ledger
4 book 5 tally 6 record 7 account, balance 8 register 9 reckoning

lee
5 haven 7 shelter 9 protected, sheltered

leech
4 milk, worm 5 bleed, drain 6 sponge, sucker 7 exhaust, sponger 8 barnacle, hanger-on, parasite 10 freeloader 11 bloodsucker 12 lounge lizard

leer

3 eye 4 ogle 5 fleer, gloat, smirk,
sneer, stare 6 glance, goggle, squint
7 grimace

leery

4 wary 5 chary 6 unsure 7 dubious,
guarded 8 cautious, doubtful, doubting 10 suspicious 11 circumspect,
distrustful, mistrustful

lees

5 dregs 6 grouts, refuse 7 deposit,
grounds, residue 8 leavings, residual, residuum, sediment 9 settlings
11 precipitate

leeward

8 downwind
opposite: 8 windward

leeway

4 play, room 5 scope, space 6 margin 7 breadth, compass, freedom,
liberty 8 latitude 9 elbowroom,
tolerance

left

4 port 7 liberal, radical 8 departed,
deserted, larboard, residual, sinister
9 abandoned, discarded, remaining,
sinistral

left-handed

5 inept 6 clumsy, gauche 7 awkward, dubious 8 fumbling, southpaw
9 ambiguous, equivocal, insincere,
maladroit 10 morganatic

left-hand page

5 verso

leftover

5 extra, spare 6 excess, unused
7 remnant, reserve, residue, surplus,
uneaten, vestige 8 residual, unneeded 9 redundant, remainder,
remaining 10 unconsumed 11 superfluous

leftovers

see **leavings**

leftward

4 levo 5 aport
go: 3 haw

leg

3 gam 4 limb 5 shank 7 support,
upright 8 cabriole 9 appendage,
drumstick
bone: 4 shin 5 femur, tibia 6 fibula
7 patella
part: 4 calf, crus, foot, knee, shin
5 ankle, thigh

legacy

4 gift 5 trust 6 devise, estate 7 bequest 8 heirloom, heritage 9 endowment, patrimony, tradition 10 birthright 11 benefaction, inheritance

legal

5 legit, licit 6 lawful 7 allowed
8 innocent 9 juridical, statutory
10 legitimate, sanctioned
matter: 3 res 4 case, suit
order: 4 writ 7 summons 8 subpoena
party: 6 suitor 8 litigant 9 defendant, plaintiff
restraint: 8 estoppel

legal tender

3 wad 4 cash 5 bread, dough,
money, moola, notes 6 moolah,
specie 7 coinage 8 banknote,
currency 9 long green

legate

4 will 5 endow, envoy, grant, leave
6 bestow, commit, devise, deputy,
devise, pass on 7 entrust, leave to
8 bequeath, delegate, emissary,
hand down, transmit 10 ambassador

legatee

4 heir 7 devisee 9 inheritor

legato

5 fluid 6 smooth 7 flowing

legend

3 key 4 lore, myth, saga, tale, yarn
5 fable, motto, story 6 mythos
7 caption, fiction 8 epigraph, folklore, folktale 9 mythology, tradition
11 inscription

legendary

5 famed 6 fabled, famous, mythic
7 fabular, fancied, fictive, storied
8 fabulous, mythical, renowned,

supposed **9** well-known **10** apocryphal, celebrated **11** illustrious, traditional **12** mythological

legerdemain
5 magic **8** trickery **9** chicanery, conjuring, deception **13** sleight of hand

leggings
5 chaps **7** puttees **9** gambadoes

leghorn
3 hat **4** fowl **5** straw **7** chicken

legible
5 clear **8** distinct, readable **12** decipherable, intelligible

legion
4 army, host, many, mass, rout **5** cloud, crowd, drove, flock, horde **6** myriad, scores, sundry, throng **7** phalanx, various **8** numerous, populous **9** countless, multitude **10** numberless

legislate
5 enact, order **6** codify, decree, ordain, permit, ratify **7** empower, mandate **8** legalize, regulate, sanction **9** establish

legislation
3 act, law **4** acts, bill, code, laws **5** bills, codes, rules **6** edicts **7** statute **8** charters, dictates, statutes **9** enactment, lawmaking **10** enactments, ordinances, regulation **11** regulations **12** codification

legislator
5 solon **7** senator **8** alderman, lawgiver, lawmaker **10** councilman **11** assemblyman, congressman

legislature
4 diet **5** house, junta **6** senate **7** council **8** assembly, congress **10** parliament
Communist: 6 soviet **9** politburo, presidium
czarist Russian: 4 duma
Danish: 9 Folketing
Finnish: 9 Eduskunta
German: 9 Bundesrat, Bundestag

Iceland: 7 Althing
Israel: 7 Knesset
Norway: 8 Storting
one-house: 10 unicameral
Poland: 4 Sejm
Spain: 6 Cortes
Sweden: 7 Riksdag
two-house: 9 bicameral

legitimate
4 fair, just, true **5** legal, licit, sound, usual, valid **6** kosher, lawful, normal, proper **7** genuine, regular, typical **8** accepted, innocent, orthodox, rightful **9** allowable, authentic, canonical, customary **10** admissable, authorized, reasonable, recognized **11** justifiable, well-founded

Le Guin novel
7 Telling (The) **18** Left Hand of Darkness (The)

legume
3 pea, pod **4** bean, guar, seed **5** pulse **6** clover, lentil **7** soybean

leg up
3 aid **4** edge, lift **5** boost **6** assist **9** advantage, head start

lei
6 wreath **7** garland **8** necklace

Leibniz's invention
8 calculus

Leif Eriksson
discovery: 7 Vinland
father: 4 Eric, Erik (the Red)

leisure
4 ease, rest, time **6** casual, chance, repose **7** freedom, liberty **10** relaxation **11** opportunity

leisurely
4 easy, slow **6** lazily, slowly **7** relaxed, restful **8** laid-back **9** unhurried

leitmotiv
4 idea **5** theme, topic **6** burden, motive, thesis **7** subject

lemma
5 bract, theme **7** heading, premise, theorem **8** argument **11** proposition

lemon

3 dud 4 bomb, bust, flop 5 fruit,
loser, scent 6 flavor, yellow 7 failure

lemur

5 indri, loris, potto 6 aye-aye, colugo,
galago 7 tarsier 8 bush baby

lend

4 give, loan 5 allow, grant 6 afford,
oblige, supply 7 advance, furnish,
provide 11 accommodate

length

4 span 5 ambit, range, reach, realm,
scope 6 extent, radius 7 compass,
expanse, measure, purview, section,
stretch, yardage 8 distance, duration

lengthen

6 expand, extend, let out 7 draw out,
prolong, spin out, stretch 8 elongate,
increase, protract 9 string out
Scottish: 3 eke

lengthy

4 long 8 dragging, drawn-out,
extended, overlong 9 elongated,
prolonged 10 long-winded, protracted, voluminous 12 interminable

leniency

5 mercy 7 quarter 8 clemency
9 tolerance 10 indulgence, toleration
11 forbearance

lenient

4 easy, kind, mild, soft 6 benign,
gentle, kindly 7 amiable, clement
8 merciful, obliging, tolerant 9 benignant, forgiving, indulgent 10 forbearing, permissive

lenity

5 mercy 7 quarter 8 clemency
9 tolerance 10 humaneness, indulgence 11 forbearance

lens

5 glass 6 lentil 8 meniscus
kind: 5 toric 6 convex 7 bifocal,
concave 8 trifocal

lento

4 slow 5 tempo

Leofric's wife

6 Godiva

Leoncavallo opera

9 Pagliacci (I) 10 Chatterton

leonine

8 lionlike

Leonora

7 heroine
alias: 7 Fidelio
husband: 9 Florestan

leopard

3 cat 4 pard 5 ounce 7 panther

leper

6 pariah 7 Ishmael, outcast 8 castaway, derelict 9 incurable 10 Ishmaelite 11 untouchable

Leper Priest

6 Damien (Father)

lepers' hospital

9 lazaretto

lepers' island

7 Molokai

lepidoptera

5 moths 8 skippers 11 butterflies
12 caterpillars

Leporello's master

11 Don Giovanni

leprechaun

3 elf 5 dwarf, fairy 6 sprite 7 brownie
trade: 8 cobbling

Lesage hero

7 Gil Blas

Lesbos poet

6 Sappho 7 Alcaeus

_____ LeShan

3 Eda

lesion

3 cut 4 boil, flaw, harm, sore 5 ulcer,
wound 6 injury 7 blister

Lesotho

capital: 6 Maseru
ethnic group: 5 Sotho
former name: 10 Basutoland
language: 5 Sotho
monetary unit: 4 loti
mountain: 9 Ntlenyana
neighbor: 11 South Africa
river: 6 Orange 7 Caledon

lessen

3 cut 4 clip, crop, ease, thin, wane 5 abate, erode, lower, taper 6 dilute, impair, minify, recede, reduce, shrink, weaken 7 abridge, assuage, curtail, degrade, dwindle, lighten, relieve, subside 8 decrease, diminish, minimize, mitigate, taper off 9 attenuate

lessening

4 drop, fall 5 letup 8 decrease, slowdown 9 abatement, reduction 10 curtailing, diminution 11 degradation

lesser

5 lower, minor 7 smaller 8 inferior 9 secondary, small-time, subjacent 11 minor-league, subordinate 13 insignificant

lesson

4 text 5 chide, moral, study 6 rebuke 7 example, lecture, reading, reprove, warning 8 admonish, exercise, homework, reproach 9 reprimand 10 admonition, assignment 11 instruction

lessor

8 landlady, landlord 9 landowner 10 freeholder

let

4 make, rent 5 allow, grant, lease, leave 6 assign, permit, suffer 9 authorize 11 obstruction

letdown

5 slump 6 defeat 7 decline, descent, failure, reverse, setback 10 anticlimax, depression, misfortune 11 frustration

let go

3 can 4 boot, fire, free, sack 5 remit 6 unhand 7 dismiss, neglect, release, set free 8 liberate 9 discharge, terminate

lethal

4 fell 5 fatal 6 deadly, mortal, poison 7 baleful, deathly 8 poisoned, virulent 9 murderous, poisonous 11 destructive, devastating

lethargic

4 dull, idle, slow 5 dopey, heavy, inert 6 draggy, supine, torpid 7 dormant, laggard, languid, passive 8 comatose, dilatory, inactive, listless, slothful, sluggish 9 apathetic, impassive 10 languorous, phlegmatic, spiritless 11 indifferent 12 hebetudinous 13 lackadaisical

lethargy

5 sloth 6 apathy, phlegm, stupor, torpor 7 inertia, languor, slumber 8 dullness, hebetude, idleness, laziness 9 disregard, inanition, indolence, inertness, lassitude, torpidity 10 inactivity, supineness 11 impassivity, passiveness 12 listlessness

lethe

7 amnesia 8 oblivion 13 forgetfulness

Leto

see **Latona**

let off

5 spare 6 excuse, exempt 7 absolve, relieve 8 dispense 9 discharge

let on

3 own 5 admit, allow, grant, own up, spill 6 betray, fess up, reveal 7 concede, confess, confirm, divulge, pretend 8 disclose, give away

let out

5 blurt, loose 6 exhale 7 release, set free, unloose 8 lengthen, liberate, set loose 9 discharge, turn loose

letter

3 bee, cee, cue, dee, ess, gee, jay, kay, pee, tee, vee, wye, zed, zee 4 line, mail, memo, note, rune 5 aitch, print, vowel 6 report, screed, symbol 7 epistle, message, missive 8 dispatch, inscribe 9 consonant
airmail: 8 aerogram
Anglo-Saxon:
(see **Anglo-Saxon**)
Arabic:
(see **alphabet**)
Greek:
(see **alphabet**)

lettuce

Hebrew:
(see **alphabet**)
kind: 5 chain, roman 6 italic, uncial 8 Dear John
large: 7 capital 9 majuscule, uppercase
small: 9 lowercase, minuscule

lettuce

3 cos 4 Bibb, head 6 Boston 7 iceberg, romaine, Simpson 10 butterweed

let up

3 ebb 4 fall, stop, wane 5 abate, cease 6 lessen, relent 7 die away, die down, ease off, slacken, subside 8 decrease, diminish, moderate, taper off

letup

4 lull 5 break, pause 7 respite 9 abatement, cessation, lessening, reduction 10 slackening

levee

4 dike, dock, pier, quay 5 jetty, ridge, wharf 7 seawall 8 assembly, function 9 reception 10 breakwater, embankment, riverfront

level

3 aim, lay, par 4 calm, even, flat, raze, same, tier 5 equal, floor, flush, grade, plane 6 direct, ground, smooth, status, steady 7 aligned, flatten, mow down 8 balanced, bulldoze, demolish, equalize, parallel, smoothen, standing 9 bring down, intensity, knock down, magnitude 10 equivalent, horizontal, reasonable 11 equilibrium

lever

3 bar, pry 4 jack, tool 5 jimmy, peavy, prize 6 peavey, tappet 7 crowbar

leverage

5 clout, power 7 exploit 9 advantage, dominance, influence 11 superiority 13 effectiveness

leveret

4 hare

Levi

father: 5 Jacob
mother: 4 Leah
son: 6 Kohath, Merari 7 Gershon

leviathan

4 huge 5 giant, jumbo, large, titan, whale 7 Goliath, immense, mammoth, massive, monster, titanic 8 behemoth, colossal, colossus, enormous, gigantic 9 cyclopean, monstrous 10 formidable, gargantuan 11 elephantine, monstrosity

Leviathan author

6 Hobbes (Thomas)

levitate

4 lift, rise 5 float, raise 7 elevate, suspend

levity

5 folly, humor 8 buoyancy 9 absurdity, flippancy, frivolity, giddiness, lightness, silliness 10 jocularity, volatility

levy

3 tax 4 duty, toll, wage 5 exact, lay on 6 assess, charge, custom, enlist, impose, impost, tariff 7 carry on, collect 9 conscript 10 assessment, enlistment 12 conscription

lewd

5 bawdy, gross 6 coarse, ribald, smutty, vulgar 7 fleshly, goatish, lustful, obscene, satyric 8 depraved, improper, indecent, prurient, unchaste 9 debauched, lecherous, libertine, lickerish, salacious 10 indelicate, lascivious, libidinous, licentious, lubricious

Lewis and Clark interpreter

9 Sacagawea

Lewis novel

7 Babbitt 9 Dodsworth 10 Arrowsmith, Main Street 11 Elmer Gantry

Lewis work

18 Chronicles of Narnia (The)

lexicographer

8 compiler

American: 6 Porter (Noah)
7 Webster (Noah) 9 Worcester
(Joseph)
English: 4 Wyld (Henry) 6 Fowler
(Francis, Henry), Murray (James),
Onions (Charles) 7 Craigie (William),
Johnson (Samuel) 9 Partridge (Eric)
French: 6 Littré (Paul-Emile) 8 La-
rousse (Pierre)
German: 5 Grimm (Jakob, Wilhelm)

lexicon
4 cant 6 jargon 8 glossary, language, wordbook 9 inventory,
word-hoard 10 dictionary, repertoire, vocabulary 11 terminology

liable
3 apt 4 open 5 given, prone 6 likely
7 exposed, subject 8 inclined
9 sensitive 10 answerable, assailable, vulnerable 11 accountable,
responsible, susceptible

liaison
4 bond, link 5 amour, fixer 6 affair,
broker, hookup 7 contact, romance
8 intrigue 9 go-between 10 connection 12 entanglement, intermediary,
relationship 13 communication

liana
4 vine

liar
6 fibber 7 Ananias 8 fabulist, per-
jurer 9 falsifier 12 prevaricator
female: 8 Sapphira

libation
5 drink 6 liquid, liquor 7 potable
8 beverage, oblation, offering, potation

libel
4 slur 5 smear 6 defame, malign,
vilify 7 asperse, calumny, obloquy,
slander, traduce 8 bad-mouth,
tear down 9 aspersion, denigrate
10 calumniate, defamation, scandalize 11 denigration

libelous
6 untrue 9 injurious, invidious,
maligning, traducing, vilifying
10 backbiting, calumnious, defama-

tory, derogative, derogatory, detracting, detractive, malevolent, pejorative, scandalous, slanderous

liberal
4 full, open 5 ample, broad, loose
6 lavish 7 copious, profuse, radical
8 abundant, generous, prodigal,
tolerant 9 bounteous, bountiful,
indulgent, plentiful, unsparing 10 benevolent, bighearted, charitable,
freehanded, munificent, openhanded,
permissive, unorthodox 11 broad-
minded

liberate
4 free 5 loose 7 manumit, release,
unchain 9 discharge, unshackle
10 commandeer, emancipate 11 appropriate, expropriate

liberator
6 savior 7 messiah 9 deliverer
of Argentina: 9 San Martín (José de)
of Chile: 8 O'Higgins (Bernardo)
of Ecuador: 5 Sucre (Antonio José
de)
of Scotland: 5 Bruce (Robert the)
of South America: 7 Bolívar (Simón)

Liberia
capital: 8 Monrovia
coast: 3 Kru 5 Grain
language: 7 English
neighbor: 6 Guinea 10 Ivory Coast
11 Sierra Leone

Liberian
language: 3 Kwa
native: 3 Kru, Vai 4 Gola, Toma
5 Bassa, Grebo 6 Kruman

libertine
4 lewd, rake, roué 5 bawdy, loose,
randy 6 carnal, rakish, wanton
7 lustful, raffish, satyric 9 debauched,
debauchee, dissolute, lecherous,
salacious 10 degenerate, dissipated,
lascivious, libidinous, licentious,
profligate 11 promiscuous

liberty
4 risk 5 leave 6 chance 7 freedom,
license 8 autonomy 9 franchise,
privilege 10 permission 11 familiarity 12 emancipation, independence

libidinous

4 lewd 5 bawdy, loose, randy 6 carnal, rakish, wanton 7 fleshly, goatish, lustful, satyric 8 depraved, prurient 9 debauched, lecherous, libertine, lickerish, salacious 10 lascivious, licentious, lubricious, profligate 11 promiscuous 12 concupiscent

librarian

5 Dewey (Melvil)

library

7 archive 8 atheneum 9 athenaeum 11 bibliotheca
desk: 6 carrel

Libya

capital: 7 Tripoli
city: 8 Benghazi
desert: 6 Sahara
gulf: 5 Sidra
language: 6 Arabic 7 Hamitic
leader: 7 Gadhafi, Qaddafi (Mu'ammar)
monetary unit: 5 dinar
neighbor: 4 Chad 5 Egypt, Niger, Sudan 7 Algeria, Tunisia
sea: 13 Mediterranean

lice

7 cooties

license

3 let, tag 5 allow, grant, leave 6 enable, laxity, permit, suffer, ticket 7 certify, empower, freedom, go-ahead, liberty 8 accredit, document, sanction, variance 9 authority, authorize, slackness 10 permission, profligacy 11 certificate, impropriety 12 carte blanche 13 authorization

licentious

4 lewd 5 bawdy, loose, randy 6 amoral, carnal, rakish, wanton 7 fleshly, goatish, immoral, lustful, satyric 8 depraved, prurient, scabrous 9 abandoned, debauched, dissolute, lecherous, libertine, salacious 10 lascivious, libidinous, lubricious, profligate 11 promiscuous 12 concupiscent

lichen

4 moss 6 archil, litmus 7 oakmoss
genus: 5 Usnea

licit

4 okay 5 legal 6 lawful 7 allowed 8 approved, innocent, licensed 9 allowable, permitted 10 admissible, authorized, legitimate, sanctioned 11 permissible

lick

3 bit, dab, dig, hit, lap, rap, tan 4 beat, dash, deck, down, drub, hint, swat, whip, wipe 5 cream, pinch, pound, smack, smear, spank, taste, touch, trace, whiff 6 defeat, master, punish, thrash, tongue, wallop 7 clobber, conquer, shellac, trounce 8 lambaste, outstrip, overcome, surmount 9 overwhelm

lickerish

see **libidinous**

lickety-split

4 fast 5 apace 6 presto, pronto 7 flat out, hastily, quickly, rapidly, swiftly 8 chop-chop, full tilt, headlong, pell-mell, speedily 9 posthaste 13 expeditiously, precipitately

licorice

4 root 5 candy
pill: 6 cachou

lid

3 cap, top 5 cover 8 covering
moss: 9 operculum

lie

3 fib 4 rest, tale 5 exist, fable, libel 6 belong, canard, covert, delude, extend, inhere, remain, repose, reside 7 consist, falsify, falsity, perjure, recline, untruth 8 misspeak, misstate 9 dissemble, falsehood, fish story, mendacity 10 inaccuracy, taradiddle 11 prevaricate 12 misstatement

Liechtenstein

capital: 5 Vaduz
language: 6 German
monetary unit: 4 euro
mountain range: 4 Alps
neighbor: 7 Austria 11 Switzerland
river: 5 Rhein, Rhine

lied
4 song 7 art song

lief
4 fain, soon 6 freely, gladly 7 happily, readily 9 willingly 11 contentedly

liege
4 lord, true 5 loyal 6 ardent, master, vassal 7 abiding, staunch 8 constant, enduring, faithful, reliable, resolute, stalwart 9 dedicated, steadfast 10 dependable

lien
5 claim 6 charge, demand 8 interest, mortgage 10 imposition

lieu
5 place, stead

lieutenant
4 aide 6 backup, deputy 7 officer 9 assistant, coadjutor 10 aide-de-camp, coadjutant 11 subordinate

life
3 vim 4 brio, dash, élan, soul 5 verve 6 energy, esprit, spirit 8 vitality 9 animation, existence
animal: 5 fauna
animal and plant: 5 biota
combining form: 3 bio
plant: 5 flora
relating to: 5 vital 8 biologic 10 biological
science: 7 biology

life jacket
7 Mae West

lifeless
4 dead, drab, dull 5 inert 6 asleep, barren, torpid, wasted 7 defunct, extinct 8 comatose, deceased, departed 9 inanimate, inorganic, insensate 10 lackluster

lifelike
5 exact 7 natural, precise 8 accurate, faithful, veristic 9 realistic

life of _____
5 Riley 8 the party

Life with Father author
3 Day (Clarence)

lift
4 heft, hike, jack, load, rear, rise 5 boost, exalt, filch, heave, hoist, pinch, raise, steal, swipe, theft 6 assist, pick up, pilfer, repeal, revoke, snitch, take up 7 elevate, purloin, rescind, reverse, support 8 levitate, stealing, thievery 10 plagiarize

lift-off
6 ascent, launch 7 takeoff 9 launching

ligament
3 tie 4 band, bond, link, yoke 5 nexus 8 ligature, vinculum 10 connection

ligature
see **ligament**

Ligeia author
3 Poe (Edgar Allan)

light
4 airy, dawn, deft, easy, fair, fire, lamp, land, luck, neon 5 blond, flash, minor, perch, roost, sunny, torch 6 beacon, blithe, bright, candle, casual, facile, flimsy, fluffy, ignite, kindle, settle, simple, slight, strobe 7 lantern, sunrise, trivial 8 cheerful, daybreak, enkindle, illumine, luminous, trifling 9 frivolous, touch down 10 chandelier, effortless, illuminate
combining form: 4 luci, phos, phot 5 lumin, photo 6 lumini, lumino
measure: 3 lux 4 phot 5 lumen 6 candle 7 candela
refractor: 5 prism
relating to: 6 photic
ring: 4 halo 6 corona 7 aureola, aureole
science: 6 optics
source: 3 sun 4 lamp

light-emitting
6 lucent 7 fulgent, lambent, shining 8 luminous 9 effulgent, refulgent

lighten
4 dawn, ease, fade 5 allay, cheer 6 bleach, lessen, reduce 7 assuage, gladden, hearten, mollify, relieve 8 decrease, mitigate, unburden 9 alleviate, attenuate, extenuate 11 disencumber

light-headed

5 dizzy, faint, giddy, silly   6 swimmy
7 flighty   9 frivolous, slaphappy
10 unbalanced   11 disoriented,
vertiginous

lighthearted

3 gay   4 glad   5 happy, jolly, merry,
sunny   6 blithe, jocund, jovial, joyful, joyous, lively, upbeat   7 buoyant, festive, gleeful, playful, winsome   8 carefree, cheerful, mirthful, spirited, volatile   9 easygoing,
expansive, resilient, sprightly, vivacious   10 blithesome, insouciant
12 effervescent, happy-go-lucky,
high-spirited

lighthouse

6 beacon   7 warning

lightless

4 dark   5 unlit   7 aphotic, stygian
9 tenebrous, pitch-dark   10 caliginous, pitch-black   11 unillumined

lightness

6 bounce, gaiety, levity   8 buoyancy, vivacity   9 animation, frivolity
10 cheeriness, liveliness, resiliency,
volatility   12 cheerfulness   13 effervescence

lightning bug

7 firefly

lignite

4 coal   9 brown coal

likable

4 nice   6 genial   7 affable, amiable,
popular, winning, winsome   8 charming, engaging, friendly, pleasant,
pleasing   9 agreeable, appealing,
congenial   10 attractive, personable
11 good-natured

like

3 à la, dig   4 akin, same, such
5 close, enjoy, equal, match   6 admire, agnate, allied, prefer, relish
7 approve, cognate, kindred, related,
similar, uniform   8 parallel, selfsame
9 analogous, consonant, identical
10 appreciate, comparable, comprehend, equivalent, resembling

likelihood

6 chance   8 prospect   11 eventuality,
possibility, presumption, probability

likely

3 apt   5 given, prone   6 liable,
odds-on   7 assumed   9 credible,
inclined, possible, presumed, probable, probably, reliable, suitable
9 doubtless, plausible, promising
10 achievable, attractive, believable,
presumably

liken

5 match   6 equate   7 compare
8 parallel   10 assimilate

likeness

4 copy, twin   5 clone, image   6 double, effigy   7 analogy, picture, replica
8 affinity, portrait, sameness   9 depiction, facsimile, look-alike, semblance   10 appearance, photograph,
similarity, similitude, uniformity
11 resemblance

likewise

3 and, too   4 also   6 as well, withal
7 besides   8 moreover   9 similarly
10 in addition   11 furthermore

liking

4 bent   5 fancy, taste   6 desire
8 affinity, appetite, fondness, penchant, pleasure, soft spot, weakness
9 affection   10 attraction, partiality
11 inclination   12 appreciation,
predilection

Lilith

husband: 4 Adam
successor: 3 Eve

lilliputian

3 wee   4 runt, tiny   5 dwarf, petty,
pygmy, small   6 bantam, little,
midget, peanut, peewee, shrimp
7 manikin   8 pint-size, Tom Thumb
9 miniature, pint-sized, undersize
10 diminutive, homunculus

lilt

3 air   4 flow, purl, sing, song, tune
5 carol, pulse, swing, tempo   6 melody, rhythm   7 cadence   8 buoyancy

lily
3 pad 4 aloe, sego 5 calla, tiger, yucca 6 flower 7 leopard 8 mariposa

lily-livered
5 sissy, wimpy 6 craven, yellow 7 caitiff, chicken, fearful, gutless 8 cowardly, cowering, poltroon, recreant, timorous 9 spineless, spunkless, weak-kneed 12 faint-hearted, poor-spirited 13 pusillanimous

lily-white
4 pure 7 upright 8 innocent, virtuous 9 blameless, estimable, exclusive, exemplary, guiltless, righteous, untainted 10 inculpable 11 uncorrupted

limb
3 arm, fin, gam, leg 4 lobe, twig, wing 5 bough, shoot, spray, sprig 6 branch, member, pinion 7 flipper 8 offshoot 9 appendage, dismember, extremity

limber
4 spry 5 agile, lithe, loose 6 nimble, pliant, supple 7 elastic, lissome, pliable, springy 8 flexible 9 lithesome, resilient

limbo
5 dance 7 neglect 8 oblivion 9 detention, purgatory 11 confinement, uncertainty

lime
4 tree 5 color, fruit, green 6 citrus, linden 7 calcium

limen
8 doorsill, doorstep 9 threshold

limerick
4 poem 5 verse
writer: 4 Lear (Edward)

limestone
4 tufa, tuff 5 chalk 6 marble, oolite 7 coquina 10 travertine

lime tree
6 linden

limit
3 bar, cap, end, fix, set 4 curb 5 check, quota 6 border, bounds, curfew, define, extent, hinder, lessen 7 confine, curtail, enclose, extreme, mark out, measure 8 boundary, deadline, restrain, restrict 9 constrict, demarcate, determine, extremity, prescribe 12 circumscribe

limitless
4 vast 7 endless 8 infinite, wide-open 9 boundless, unbounded 10 indefinite 11 illimitable, innumerable, measureless 12 immeasurable, incalculable 13 inexhaustible

limn
4 draw 5 image, paint 6 depict, render, sketch 7 outline, picture, portray 8 describe 9 delineate, interpret, represent

Limoges product
9 porcelain

limp
3 lax 4 bent, halt, lame, wilt 5 hitch, loose, slack, spent, weary 6 dodder, droopy, falter, hobble 7 flaccid, languid, shamble, shuffle, slumped 8 drooping 9 enervated, exhausted 10 spiritless

limpid
4 pure 5 clear, lucid 6 glassy, serene 8 pellucid 10 see-through, untroubled 11 crystalline, translucent, transparent, unambiguous 12 crystal clear

limping
4 halt, lame 5 gimpy 7 halting 8 hobbling, lameness 9 faltering 12 claudication

linchpin
8 backbone, mainstay

Lincoln
assassin: 5 Booth (John Wilkes)
biographer: 8 Sandburg (Carl)
debater: 7 Douglas (Stephen)
law partner: 7 Herndon (William)
mother: 5 Nancy (Hanks)
nickname: 9 Honest Abe 12 Rail-splitter
photographer: 5 Brady (Mathew)

line

secretary of state: 6 Seward (William)
secretary of war: 7 Stanton (Edwin)
wife: 8 Mary Todd

line
3 row 4 file, rank, rope 5 array, goods, queue, route 6 border, column, series, strain, string 7 contour, descent 8 business, pedigree, sequence 10 employment, occupation, succession
curved: 3 arc
mathematical: 6 vector
metrical: 5 verse 6 verset 8 versicle
weather map: 6 isobar

lineage
3 kin 4 clan, folk, race 5 birth, blood, breed, house, stirp, stock, tribe 6 family, origin, strain 7 descent, kindred 8 ancestry, breeding, pedigree 9 forebears, genealogy 10 derivation, extraction, succession 11 forefathers, progenitors

lineal
6 direct 8 familial 9 ancestral, inherited 10 bequeathed, hereditary

lineament
4 form 6 figure, relief 7 contour, feature, outline, profile 10 figuration, silhouette

lined
5 drawn, ruled 7 aligned, striate, striped 8 streaked, wrinkled

linen
4 lawn 5 cloth, toile 6 byssus, damask, fabric, napery, sheets 7 batiste, bedding, cambric, taffeta 8 cretonne, lingerie
fiber: 3 tow
source: 4 flax

linger
3 lag 4 bide, drag, loll, mope, poke, stay, wait 5 abide, dally, delay, mosey, tarry 6 dawdle, loiter, put off, remain 7 saunter 10 dillydally 11 stick around 13 procrastinate

lingerie
8 negligee

lingo
4 cant 5 argot, idiom, slang 6 jargon, patois, patter, speech, tongue 7 dialect 10 vernacular, vocabulary

linguist
8 polyglot 11 philologist

linguistics
9 philology

liniment
3 oil 4 aloe, balm 5 salve 6 lotion 7 anodyne, unction, unguent 8 aloe vera, lenitive, ointment 9 demulcent 11 embrocation

lining
6 facing, insert 8 wainscot

link
3 tie 4 bind, bond, join, knot, ring, yoke 5 hitch, nexus, unite 6 attach, copula, couple, hookup, relate, splice 7 bracket, combine, conjoin, connect, contact, joining 8 catenate, division, vinculum 9 associate, conjugate 10 attachment, connection 11 association 12 relationship

linksman
6 golfer

linnet
5 finch

lint
3 fur, nap 4 down, fuzz, pile 5 floss, fluff 9 ravelings

lion
3 cat 4 puma 6 cougar 7 notable 8 eminence, luminary 9 carnivore, personage
group: 5 pride
young: 3 cub

lionhearted
4 bold 5 brave 6 heroic 7 valiant 8 fearless, intrepid, stalwart, unafraid, valorous 9 dauntless 10 courageous

lionize
4 fete 5 exalt, extol, honor 7 glorify 8 venerate 9 celebrate

lion monkey
7 tamarin 8 marmoset

Lion of Judah
8 Selassie (Haile)

lip
3 rim 4 brim, edge, guff, sass 6 labium, labrum, margin 8 back talk
relating to: 6 labial

lipid
3 fat, wax

lipped
7 labiate 9 bilabiate

liquefy
3 run 4 flux, melt, thaw 5 smelt
6 render 8 dissolve 10 deliquesce

liqueur
4 arak, ouzo, raki 5 crème 6 brandy,
Kahlua, kirsch, kummel, pastis,
Pernod 7 cordial, curaçao, ratafia,
sambuca, sloe gin 8 absinthe,
amaretto, anisette, Drambuie,
Galliano 10 Chartreuse, pousse-
café

liquid
5 drink, fluid, sauce, water 6 watery
7 flowing 8 beverage, emulsion
11 mellifluous
container: 3 cup, jug, keg, mug
4 vial 5 glass 6 bottle, goblet
7 pitcher, tumbler
flammable: 3 gas, oil 5 ether, furan
6 butane, toluol 7 alcohol, toluene
8 gasoline, pyridine
measure: 3 cup, gal 4 pint 5 liter,
ounce, quart 6 gallon
thick: 5 syrup 8 molasses

liquidate
3 pay 4 do in, kill 5 pay up, purge
6 murder, remove, rub out, settle,
square 7 bump off, convert, gun
down, satisfy 8 amortize, dispatch,
dissolve, knock off 9 eliminate,
terminate 10 annihilate 11 assassinate

liquor
5 booze, drink, hooch 7 alcohol,
potable, spirits 8 potation 9 firewater, inebriant 10 intoxicant
add: 4 lace 5 spike
Asian: 4 arak 6 arrack

homemade: 9 moonshine 10 bathtub gin
inferior: 5 hooch 6 red-eye, rotgut
Japanese: 4 sake, saki
kind: 3 gin, rum, rye 5 vodka
6 brandy, geneva, scotch 7 aqua-
vit, bourbon, schnaps, whiskey
8 schnapps, vermouth 9 aqua vitae
10 barley-bree
malt: 3 ale 4 beer 5 nappy, stout
6 porter
measure: 4 dram, shot 6 jigger
7 shooter
Mexican: 5 sotol 6 mescal 7 tequila

lissome
5 agile, lithe 6 limber, nimble, supple, svelte 7 slender 8 flexible,
graceful

list
3 tip 4 book, cant, file, heel, lean,
menu, note, post, roll, tilt 5 arena,
count, index, slant, slate, slope, tally
6 agenda, census, docket, lineup,
record, roster 7 catalog, incline,
itemize, specify 8 calendar, glossary,
manifest, register, roll call, schedule,
tabulate 9 chronicle, enumerate,
inventory 13 particularize

listen
4 hark, hear, heed, note 5 audit
6 attend, harken 7 hearken, monitor
8 overhear 9 eavesdrop

listeners
8 audience

listless
4 dull, limp, weak 5 inert, slack
6 torpid, vacant 7 languid 8 indolent, sluggish 9 apathetic, enervated, lethargic, lymphatic 10 languorous, phlegmatic, spiritless
11 indifferent, languishing 13 lackadaisical

listlessness
6 apathy, stupor, torpor 7 fatigue,
inertia, languor 8 doldrums, lethargy
9 indolence, lassitude, torpidity
10 enervation

litany
4 list 5 chant 6 prayer 7 account,

listing, recital, refrain **8** petition, rogation **9** catalogue **10** invocation, recitation **11** enumeration **12** supplication

literal
4 bald, bare **5** blunt, exact, stark **6** actual, simple, strict **7** precise **8** accurate, bona fide, faithful, verbatim **9** authentic **11** unvarnished, word-for-word **13** unembellished

literally
5 truly **6** direct, indeed, openly, simply **7** plainly, totally, utterly **8** candidly, directly, verbatim **9** genuinely, virtually **11** word for word

literary
7 bookish, erudite, learned **8** lettered, well-read **9** authorial, scholarly **12** belletristic

literary work
4 book, opus, play, poem **5** drama, essay, novel **10** short story

literature
5 prose **6** poetry **7** fiction **13** belleslettres

lithe
4 lean, slim **5** agile, spare **6** limber, supple, svelte **7** lissome, pliable, slender **8** flexible, graceful

lithographer
4 Ives (James Merritt) **7** Currier (Nathaniel)

Lithuania
capital: 7 Vilnius
city: 6 Kaunas **8** Klaipeda
monetary unit: 5 litas
neighbor: 6 Latvia, Poland, Russia **7** Belarus
river: 5 Neman, Venta **7** Lielupe
sea: 6 Baltic

litigant
4 suer **6** suitor **9** defendant, disputant, plaintiff

litigate
3 sue **6** indict **7** arraign, contest, dispute **9** prosecute

litigation
4 case, suit **7** lawsuit **11** prosecution, proceedings

litter
3 bed **4** cubs, junk **5** brood, couch, issue, strew, trash, waste, young **6** clutch, debris, refuse **7** bedding, clutter, garbage, kittens, piglets, progeny, puppies, rubbish, scatter **8** detritus **9** offspring, stretcher **10** scattering

little
3 bit, dab, toy, wee **4** dash, hint, mean, puny, tiny **5** brief, dinky, minor, petty, pinch, short, small, taste, trace, young **6** bantam, meager, meagre, minute, narrow, paltry, petite, skimpy **7** limited, trivial **8** dwarfish, slightly, smallish, trifling **9** miniature, small-beer **10** diminutive, short-lived, undersized **11** microscopic, unimportant

Little Bighorn
state: 7 Montana
victim: 6 Custer (George Armstrong)
victor: 11 Sitting Bull

little by little
6 slowly **8** inchmeal, steadily **9** gradually, piecemeal

Little Dipper
constellation: 9 Ursa Minor
star: 5 North **7** Polaris

Little Women
author: 6 Alcott (Louisa May)
character: 3 Amy, Meg **4** Beth **6** Laurie, Marmee
surname: 5 March

littoral
5 beach, coast, shore **6** strand **7** coastal, seaside **8** seaboard, sea front, seashore **9** shoreline **10** oceanfront

liturgy
4 rite **6** ritual **7** service **8** ceremony **9** sacrament **10** ceremonial, observance, repertoire

livable

6 viable **8** adequate, bearable, passable **9** endurable, habitable, tolerable **11** inhabitable, supportable

live

4 fare, stay **5** abide, dwell, exist, vital, vivid **6** actual, reside, thrive **7** breathe, current, subsist, survive

livelihood

3 job **4** game, keep, work **5** craft, trade **7** support **8** business, vocation **10** employment, handicraft, occupation, profession, sustenance **11** subsistence

liveliness

3 pep, zip **4** brio, élan, zing **5** verve, vigor **6** energy, hustle, spirit **8** dispatch, vibrance, vibrancy, vitality, vivacity **9** animation

lively

3 gay **4** busy, keen, pert, spry, yare **5** agile, alert, brisk, fresh, jazzy, jolly, merry, peppy, zippy **6** active, bouncy, bright, chirpy, frisky, jocund, nimble **7** animate, buoyant, chipper, intense, rousing **8** animated, bustling, hustling, spirited, vigorous, volatile **9** energetic, resilient, sparkling, sprightly, vivacious **11** stimulating

liven

5 pep up **6** jazz up, vivify **7** animate, freshen, quicken **8** energize, inspirit, vitalize **10** invigorate

liver

7 denizen **8** habitant, occupant, resident **10** inhabitant
combining form: 5 hepat **6** hepato
disease: 9 cirrhosis, hepatitis
French: 4 foie
lobster's: 8 tomalley

liverwort

8 hepatica **9** bryophyte

livestock

4 cows, hogs, pigs **5** bulls, goats, sheep **6** beasts, calves, cattle **7** animals
feed: 6 silage **8** ensilage

live wire

6 dynamo **7** hustler, rustler **8** go-getter, promoter **9** energizer, generator **11** self-starter

livid

3 hot, mad, wan **4** ashy, pale **5** ashen, lurid, waxen **6** fuming, leaden, pallid, sultry **7** boiling, bruised, enraged, furious, reddish **8** blanched, contused, incensed **9** colorless **10** discolored, infuriated **12** black-and-blue **13** beside oneself

living

5 means, vital **6** extant, income **8** animated, existent **10** livelihood, sustenance

living room

6 parlor **10** lebensraum

lizard

3 eft **4** gila, newt **5** anole, gecko, skink, teiid **6** dragon, geanna, iguana **7** monitor, reptile, saurian **8** basilisk, mosasaur, slowworm, squamate, whiptail **9** alligator, blindworm, chameleon, crocodile **10** chuckwalla, salamander
combining form: 4 saur **5** saura, sauro

llama

6 alpaca, vicuña **7** camelid, guanaco
country: 4 Peru
habitat: 5 Andes

Lloyd's business

9 insurance

lo

4 hark, heed, look, mark, mind **6** attend **7** observe

load

3 tax **4** bias, copy, fill, haul, heap, lade, onus, pack, pile, task **5** cargo, laden, swamp, weigh **6** burden, debase, doctor, dope up, eyeful, lading, saddle, weight **7** freight **8** encumber, shipment, transfer **9** liability, millstone, transport **11** consignment, encumbrance

loaded

4 full, high, rich **5** awash, doped

loaf

6 aboard, biased, filled, packed, stoned 7 boarded, brimful, brimming, wealthy 8 affluent, brimming, chock-ful, tripping, turned on 9 chock-full

loaf

3 bum, bun 4 idle, laze, lazy, loll 5 bread, dough 6 dawdle, lounge 7 goof off 8 lollygag 9 bum around, goldbrick 10 fool around

loafer

3 bum 4 shoe, slug 5 idler 6 slouch 7 goof-off, lounger 8 deadbeat, dolittle, fainéant, slugabed, sluggard 9 do-nothing, goldbrick, lazybones 11 beachcomber, lollygagger

loam

4 clay, dirt, sand, silt, soil 7 topsoil **deposit:** 5 loess

loan

3 pay 4 lend 6 credit 7 advance, imprest 9 grubstake

loan shark

6 lender, usurer 7 Shylock 10 pawnbroker 11 moneylender

loath

6 afraid, averse 8 hesitant 9 reluctant, unwilling 10 indisposed 11 disinclined 12 antipathetic

loathe

4 hate 5 abhor, scorn, spurn 6 detest, refuse, reject 7 despise 8 execrate 9 abominate

loathsome

4 foul, ugly, vile 5 gross, nasty 6 odious 7 beastly, hateful, hideous 8 horrible 9 abhorrent, execrable, obnoxious, offensive, repellent, repugnant, repulsive, revolting 10 abominable, deplorable, detestable, disgusting, nauseating

lob

4 loft, toss 5 chuck, fling, heave, pitch, sling, throw 6 propel

lobby

4 hall 5 foyer 7 promote 8 anteroom, corridor 9 influence, vestibule 10 passageway 11 waiting room

lobe

4 flap 7 pendant

lobo

4 wolf 8 gray wolf 10 timber wolf

lobster

8 crawfish 10 crustacean **claw:** 5 chela 6 pincer **female:** 3 hen **male:** 4 cock **trap:** 3 pot 5 creel

local

6 native 7 endemic, insular, topical 9 parochial 10 provincial

locale

4 area, belt, site, turf, ward 5 place, scene, venue 6 milieu, parish, region, sector 7 commune, quarter, setting 8 district, precinct, vicinage, vicinity 9 community, territory 11 mise-en-scène 12 neighborhood

locality

4 area, belt, city, site, turf, zone 5 block, field, haunt, place, tract 6 county, domain, hamlet, region, sector, sphere, square 7 habitat, section 8 district, environs, precinct, province, purlieus, township, vicinage, vicinity 9 bailiwick, situation, territory 12 neighborhood

localize

4 mass 5 amass, focus 7 cluster, collect 8 coalesce, pinpoint 10 accumulate 11 concentrate, consolidate 12 conglomerate

locate

3 fix, spy 4 espy, find, site, spot 5 dwell, place, trace 6 detect, reside, settle 7 nose out, situate, station, uncover 8 come upon, discover, pinpoint, position 9 establish, ferret out, search out 10 come across

location

4 area, site, post, spot 5 locus, place, point, scene, venue, where 7 bearing, habitat, setting 8 position 9 situation 11 mise-en-scène, whereabouts

loch
3 bay 4 lake

lock
4 bolt, curl, hank, hold, tuft 5 latch, tress 6 fasten, secure 7 ringlet 8 fastener 9 enclosure, fastening

lockjaw
7 tetanus, trismus

lockup
3 jug, pen 4 brig, cell, coop, jail, stir, tank 5 clink, pokey, pound 6 cooler, prison 7 slammer 8 bastille

loco
3 ape, mad 4 nuts 5 balmy, batty, crazy, kooky, loony, nutty 6 crazed, insane, screwy 7 bananas, berserk, bonkers, cracked, flipped, lunatic 8 demented, deranged, frenzied, unhinged 10 flipped out

locomotive
5 cheer, dolly, train 6 engine
small: 5 dinky 6 dinkey
type: 5 steam 6 diesel 8 electric

locum tenens
3 sub 5 proxy 6 backup, fill-in, supply 7 stand-in 9 alternate, auxiliary, surrogate 10 substitute 11 pinch hitter, replacement, succedaneum

locus
3 hub 4 seat, site 5 focus, heart, stage 6 center 7 setting 8 cynosure, location, polestar 10 focal point 11 nerve center 12 headquarters

locust
4 tree, wood 5 carob 6 cicada, insect 11 grasshopper

locution
4 word 5 argot, idiom, lingo 6 jargon, patois, phrase 7 dialect 8 parlance, phrasing 9 utterance 10 expression 11 phraseology

lode
4 seam, vein 5 store 6 source, supply 7 deposit

lodestar
4 guru 5 gauge, guide, ideal, model 6 beacon, leader, mentor 7 epitome 8 exemplar, paradigm 9 archetype, guidepost 11 inspiration

lodestone
6 magnet 9 magnetite

lodge
3 den, fix, inn 4 bunk, camp, club, file, lair, nest, root, stay 5 abide, abode, board, cabin, couch, dwell, embed, guild, hotel, house, motel, order, put up 6 billet, burrow, hostel, league, remain, shanty, tavern, wigwam 7 auberge, contain, cottage, deposit, hospice, quarter, receive, shelter 8 domicile, hostelry, sodality 9 gatehouse 10 fellowship 11 accommodate, brotherhood, caravansary, public house

lodger
5 guest 6 renter, roomer, tenant 7 boarder, resider

lodging
3 inn, pad 4 dorm, room 5 abode, hotel, motel, place 7 shelter 8 chambers, diggings, domicile, dwelling, quarters 9 apartment, residence 10 pied-à-terre 13 accommodation

loess
4 clay, loam, marl 7 deposit

loft
4 rise 5 attic, raise 6 dormer, garret, propel 7 gallery

loftiness
5 pride 6 height 7 disdain, hauteur, stature 8 altitude, eminence 9 aloofness, arrogance, elevation, pomposity, sublimity 11 haughtiness, superiority 13 condescension

lofty
4 airy, epic, high, tall 5 grand, noble, proud 6 aerial, august, raised, remote, superb 7 exalted, haughty, soaring, stately, sublime, utopian 8 arrogant, cavalier, elevated, eloquent, imposing, insolent, majestic, superior, towering 9 ambitious,

log

grandiose, visionary **10** disdainful
11 overbearing, pretentious, sky-scraping **12** supercilious

log

5 diary, tally **6** record, timber **7** journal **8** register
mover: 5 peavy **6** peavey **7** cant dog

loge

3 box **5** booth, stall **7** balcony
9 mezzanine

logger

9 lumberman **10** lumberjack, wood-cutter
legendary: 10 Paul Bunyan

loggerhead

6 shrike, turtle

loggia

6 arcade **7** balcony, gallery, veranda

logic

6 reason **9** reasoning **10** syntactics
specious: 7 sophism **9** sophistry

logical

5 sound, valid **6** cogent **8** analytic, sensible **9** deducible, deductive, plausible **10** analytical, compelling, convincing, diagnostic, reasonable, scientific, systematic

logjam

5 crowd **7** impasse **8** blockage, deadlock, stoppage **11** obstruction

logo

5 badge, brand, motto **6** cipher, device, emblem, symbol **8** colophon, hallmark, monogram **9** trademark

logograph

6 puzzle **7** anagram

logroll

4 birl

logy

4 dull, slow **5** dopey, heavy **6** drowsy, groggy, torpid **8** listless, sluggish

Lohengrin

composer: 6 Wagner (Richard)
father: 8 Parsifal, Parzival
wife: 4 Elsa

loincloth

5 dhoti **11** breechcloth, breechclout

Loire city

5 Blois, Tours **6** Nantes **7** Orléans

loiter

3 bum, lag **4** drag, idle, laze, lazy, loaf, loll, poke **5** dally, delay, tarry, trail **6** dawdle, diddle, linger, lounge, put off, putter **8** lollygag **10** dilly-dally, fool around, hang around
11 screw around **13** procrastinate

Loki

father: 8 Farbauti
mother: 3 Nal **6** Laufey
offspring: 3 Hel **4** Hela **6** Fenris **7** Midgard
slayer: 8 Heimdall
victim: 6 Balder
wife: 5 Sigyn **9** Angurboda

Lolita author

7 Nabokov (Vladimir)

loll

3 bum, lag **4** drag, idle, laze, lazy, loaf, poke **5** chill, dally, delay, droop, slump, tarry, trail **6** dawdle, diddle, linger, lounge, putter, slouch **8** chill out **10** dillydally, fool around, hang around **13** procrastinate

Lollards' leader

8 Wycliffe (John)

lollygag

4 idle, loaf, loll, poke, drag **6** dawdle, diddle, loiter, piddle, putter **10** dilly-dally, fool around **11** horse around **12** monkey around

Lombard

6 banker **11** moneylender
king: 5 Cleph **6** Alboin, Audoin **7** Aistulf, Aripert, Authari **9** Liudprand

London

borough: 5 Brent **6** Barnet, Bexley, Ealing, Harrow, Sutton **7** Barking, Bromley, Chelsea, Croydon, Enfield, Hackney, Lambeth **8** Haringey, Havering, Hounslow, Lewisham **9** Greenwich, Islington, Redbridge **10** Kensington **11** Westminster
cathedral: 7 St. Paul's
clock: 6 Big Ben

district: 4 Soho 5 Acton 7 Chelsea, Mayfair 9 Belgravia, Southwark
gallery: 4 Tate
policeman: 5 bobby
prison: 7 Newgate
river: 6 Thames
square: 9 Leicester, Trafalgar
street: 4 Bond 5 Fleet 6 Strand 7 Downing 9 Whitehall 10 Piccadilly
subway: 4 tube

London novel
7 Sea Wolf (The) 8 Iron Heel (The) 9 White Fang 10 Martin Eden 13 Call of the Wild (The)

lone
4 only, sole, solo 5 alone 6 single, unique 8 deserted, forsaken, isolated, secluded, separate, singular, solitary 13 unaccompanied

lonely
4 left, lorn 5 alone 7 forlorn 8 deserted, forsaken, homesick, lonesome, rejected, solitary 9 abandoned

loneness
8 solitude 9 isolation 10 detachment 12 separateness, solitariness

loner
6 hermit 7 isolate, outcast, recluse 8 outsider, solitary 13 individualist

Lone Ranger, The
creator: 7 Striker (Fran)
companion: 5 Tonto
horse: 6 Silver
trademark: 4 mask 12 silver bullet

Lone Star State
5 Texas

long
3 far, yen 4 ache, itch, lust, pine, sigh, tall 5 large, wordy, yearn 6 hanker, hunger, prolix, strong, thirst 7 endless, lengthy, tedious 8 dragging, drawn-out, extended, unending 9 extensive 10 full-length, protracted

long-drawn-out
7 endless, lengthy 8 dragging, unending 10 protracted 12 interminable

Longfellow poem
8 Christus, Hiawatha, Hyperion, Kavanagh 10 Evangeline 11 My Lost Youth, Psalm of Life (A)

long for
4 want 5 covet, crave, mourn 6 desire 8 aspire to

longing
3 yen 4 itch, lust, urge, wish 5 greed 6 desire, hunger, thirst 7 avidity, craving, passion 8 appetite

longshoreman
9 stevedore 10 roustabout

long-suffering
7 patient, stoical 8 enduring, resigned 9 compliant 10 forbearing, submissive 13 accommodating, uncomplaining

long suit
3 bag 4 gift 5 forte, thing 6 métier, talent 8 strength 9 specialty

long-winded
5 wordy 6 prolix 7 diffuse, lengthy, verbose 8 rambling 9 garrulous, redundant 10 loquacious

look
3 air, eye 4 gape, gawk, leer, mien, ogle, peek, peep, peer, seem, view 5 glare, stare, watch 6 admire, appear, aspect, behold, expect, eyeful, glance, glower, goggle, regard, squint, survey, visage 7 bearing, examine, eyeball, glimpse, observe 8 demeanor, once-over 10 appearance, expression, rubberneck 11 countenance, physiognomy

look after
4 mind, tend 5 nurse, serve, watch 6 attend, wait on 7 care for, husband 8 wait upon 9 watch over 10 provide for

look-alike
4 twin 5 clone 6 double 7 similar 8 matching 9 duplicate

look at
3 eye, see 4 face, ogle, scan, view 5 check 6 behold, ponder 7 examine, inspect 8 confront, consider 11 investigate

look back
6 recall, review 7 reflect 8 remember 9 reminisce

look down on
5 abhor, scorn, scout, spurn 7 contemn, despise, disdain 8 dominate 9 tower over 10 tower above

looker
6 beauty, eyeful, lovely, vision 7 stunner, witness 8 knockout, ornament 9 bystander, sightseer, spectator 10 eyewitness

looker-on
5 gaper 6 viewer 7 watcher, witness 8 beholder, observer 9 bystander, spectator 10 eyewitness 12 rubbernecker

look for
4 seek 5 await 6 expect, plan on 9 search out 10 anticipate

looking glass
6 mirror 9 reflector

look into
5 check, probe, study 6 pursue, survey 7 examine, explore, inspect 8 check out, question, research 10 scrutinize 11 investigate

look out
4 mind 6 beware

lookout
4 view 5 guard, scout, tower, vista, watch 6 affair, cupola, picket, sentry 7 spotter 8 panorama, prospect, sentinel, watchman 9 belvedere, crow's nest, firetower 10 watchtower, widow's walk 11 observatory, perspective

look over
3 vet 4 read 5 check 6 review, size up 7 examine, inspect 8 appraise, evaluate

loom
4 brew, bulk, near, rear 5 hover, mount, tower 6 appear, come on, emerge, gather, impend 7 portend 8 approach, overhang, stand out, threaten 9 take shape

part: 6 heddle 7 harness, shuttle, treadle, trundle

loon
3 nut, oaf 4 bird, clod, dodo, dolt, goof, lout, yo-yo 5 chump, dummy, dunce, ninny, noddy, stupe, yokel 6 dimwit, dum-dum, nitwit 7 airhead, buffoon, dullard, pinhead 8 bonehead, dumbbell, crackpot, imbecile, lunkhead, meathead, numskull 9 birdbrain, blockhead, ignoramus, lamebrain, numbskull, simpleton 10 dunderhead, nincompoop 11 chowderhead, chucklehead

loony
3 nut 5 balmy, batty, crazy, daffy, dippy, goofy, inane, nutty, silly, wacky 6 absurd, insane, madman, maniac, screwy 7 fatuous, foolish, idiotic, lunatic 8 demented, reckless 9 bedlamite, half-baked, ludicrous, senseless 10 ridiculous 11 harebrained 12 preposterous

loony bin
6 asylum, bedlam 8 bughouse, madhouse, nuthouse 9 funny farm 10 booby hatch, crazy house

loop
3 arc, eye 4 ring 5 curve, noose, picot 6 circle, eyelet, league, staple 7 circlet, circuit 13 circumference

looped
4 high 5 bowed, drunk, stiff 6 blotto, bombed, curved, juiced, loaded, potted, stewed, tanked, zonked 7 crocked, pickled, pie-eyed, sloshed, smashed 9 plastered 10 inebriated 11 curvilinear, intoxicated

loophole
3 out 6 escape, outlet 7 opening

loopy
4 daft, nuts, wavy 5 arced, batty, bowed, crazy, daffy, dotty, flaky, nutty, silly, snaky, wacky 6 arched, curved, freaky, fruity, screwy, swirly 7 bizarre, idiotic, lunatic, offbeat, sinuous, touched 8 demented 9 eccentric 10 flipped out, off-the-wall, outlandish

loose

3 lax **4** easy, fast, free, lewd, limp
5 baggy, slack, vague **6** flabby,
wanton **7** flaccid, relaxed **8** flexible
9 debauched, desultory, dissolute,
imprecise **10** disjointed, dissipated,
ill-defined, licentious, unattached,
unconfined **12** disconnected, unrestrained

loose end

6 detail **8** fragment

loose-lipped

see **loquacious**

loosen

4 ease, free, undo **5** relax, slack,
untie **6** unbind **7** ease off, manumit,
release, slacken, unchain **8** liberate,
unbuckle, unfasten **10** emancipate

loosen up

5 relax **6** unbend, unwind **7** ease
off, stretch

loot

3 rob **4** haul, lift, pelf, raid, sack,
swag **5** boost, booty, dough, lucre,
money, moola, reave, rifle, spoil
6 boodle, moolah, ravish, spoils
7 despoil, pillage, plunder, ransack,
stick up **9** knock over

looter

5 thief **7** brigand **8** marauder

lop

3 cut **4** chop, clip, crop, trim **5** prune,
sever **6** excise **8** amputate, truncate
9 dismember **10** guillotine

lope

3 jog, run **4** gait, romp, trot **5** amble
6 canter

lopsided

4 awry **5** askew **6** uneven **7** crooked,
leaning, tilting **8** top-heavy **10** asymmetric, off-balance, unbalanced
12 asymmetrical **13** unsymmetrical

loquacious

5 gabby, talky, wordy **6** chatty,
mouthy, prolix **7** verbose, voluble,
yakking **8** babbling **9** garrulous,
jabbering, talkative **10** blathering,
chattering, long-winded **11** loose-
lipped **12** motormouthed

lord

3 sir **4** boss, duke, earl, peer **5** noble,
ruler **6** master **7** marquis **8** governor, marquess, nobleman, viscount
9 sovereign, tyrannize
feudal: 5 liege **8** seigneur, suzerain
Muslim: 6 sayyid

Lord High Executioner

4 Koko

Lord Jim author

6 Conrad (Joseph)

lordly

5 grand, lofty, noble, proud **6** august,
uppity **7** exalted, haughty, pompous,
stately, swollen **8** affected, arrogant,
cavalier, gracious, imposing, insolent,
majestic, princely, snobbish, superior
9 dignified, egotistic, grandiose
10 disdainful, high-handed **11** dictatorial, magisterial, magnificent, overbearing, patronizing **12** aristocratic,
supercilious **13** authoritarian, high-
and-mighty

Lord of the Flies

author: 7 Golding (William)
character: 4 Jack **5** Piggy, Ralph

Lord's Prayer

9 Our Father **11** Paternoster

lore

6 mythos, wisdom **7** history **8** folkways, learning **9** knowledge, mythology, tradition **11** information **12** superstition

Lorelei

5 siren **9** temptress **10** seductress
11 femme fatale
poet: 5 Heine (Heinrich)
river: 5 Rhein, Rhine
victim: 6 sailor **7** mariner

lorgnette

10 eyeglasses, spectacles **12** opera
glasses

Lorna Doone

author: 9 Blackmore (Richard)
hero: 4 Ridd (John)

_____ Lorraine
6 Alsace

lorry
3 rig, van 4 semi 5 truck

lose
4 miss 5 evade, shake, waste, yield
6 escape, give up, mislay 7 destroy,
forfeit, succumb 8 misplace, shake
off, throw off 9 sacrifice, surrender

lose it
7 crack up, flip out, go crazy 8 freak
out

loser
3 dud 4 bomb, bust, flop 5 lemon
6 bummer, fiasco, misfit, turkey
7 also-ran, debacle, failure, washout
8 deadbeat 11 incompetent

loss
4 harm, ruin 5 waste 6 damage,
defeat, injury 7 deficit, failure, forfeit 8 casualty, decrease, fatality
9 depletion, privation, sacrifice,
shrinkage 10 divestment, forfeiture, misfortune, misplacing 11 bereavement, deprivation, destruction
13 disappearance

lost
4 dead, gone, rapt 6 absent, astray,
bygone, damned, doomed, futile,
hidden, wasted 7 defunct, faraway, lacking, mislaid, missing
8 absorbed, departed, distrait, helpless, hopeless, vanished 9 condemned, desperate, destroyed
10 abstracted, insensible, overlooked 11 irrevocable, preoccupied
12 irredeemable, unregenerate

Lost Horizon
author: 6 Hilton (James)
character: 6 Conway (Hugh)
land: 9 Shangri-La

lot
3 cut, ilk, set 4 doom, fate, give,
heap, kind, mass, part, plat, sort,
type, yard 5 allow, batch, block,
bunch, field, group, misfira, patch,
quota, share, slice, tract, weird
6 assign, barrel, bundle, clutch,

kismet, parcel, stripe 7 acreage,
cluster, destiny, fortune, mete out,
portion, species 8 allocate, clearing,
frontage 9 aggregate, allowance,
apportion

Lot
father: 5 Haran
sister: 5 Iscah 6 Milcah
son: 4 Moab 5 Ammon
uncle: 7 Abraham

lothario
4 stud, wolf 5 letch, Romeo 6 lecher,
tomcat 7 amorist, Don Juan, gallant,
seducer 8 Casanova, paramour
9 debaucher, womanizer 10 lady-
killer 11 philanderer

lotion
3 oil 4 balm 5 cream, salve 6 cerate
7 unguent 8 ablution, cosmetic, lenitive, liniment, ointment 9 demulcent
11 embrocation

lottery
6 raffle 7 drawing 11 sweepstakes

lotus-eater
7 dreamer 8 escapist, romantic
10 daydreamer 13 castle-builder

loud
5 forte, gaudy, noisy, showy 6 brassy,
brazen, flashy, garish, glitzy, tawdry,
vulgar 7 blaring, blatant, booming,
chintzy, glaring, pealing, raucous,
roaring 8 piercing, resonant, sonorous, strident 9 clamorous, deafening, obnoxious, obtrusive, offensive,
tasteless 10 bigmouthed, boisterous, flamboyant, resounding, stentorian, thunderous, vociferous 12 earsplitting

loudmouth
6 ranter 7 stentor 8 blowhard,
braggart 9 blusterer

loudspeaker
6 woofer 7 tweeter 9 amplifier

Louisiana
capital: 10 Baton Rouge
city: 10 New Orleans, Shreveport
college, university: 6 Tulane

county: 6 parish
lake: 13 Pontchartrain
nickname: 7 Pelican (State)
river: 11 Mississippi
state bird: 12 brown pelican
state flower: 8 magnolia
state tree: 11 bald cypress

lounge
3 bar, bum, lie, pub, tap 4 idle, laze,
loaf, loll, sofa 5 couch, dally, drift,
lobby, relax 6 dawdle, loiter, parlor,
repose, saloon 7 barroom, goof off,
lie down, recline, taproom 8 restroom, kill time 10 living room

lounge lizard
3 fop 4 rake, toff 5 blade, dandy,
leech 6 gigolo, sponge 9 ladies'
man

Lourdes saint
10 Bernadette

louse
3 cur, dog, rat 4 toad 5 aphid,
creep, skunk, snake 6 cootie, psylla,
rotter, slater, wretch 7 stinker
egg: 3 nit

louse up
4 blow, flub, muff, ruin 5 botch,
spoil, wreck 6 bobble, bollix, bumble, bungle, fumble

lousy
3 ill 4 poor, rife 5 awful 6 shoddy,
rotten 7 replete, teeming 8 crawling,
horrible, inferior, infested, terrible
9 miserable, repulsive 10 despicable
12 contemptible

lout
3 oaf 4 boob, boor, dolt, gawk, hick,
rube 5 brute, chuff, churl, klutz,
looby, scorn, yokel 6 galoot, lubber,
lummox, rustic 7 bumpkin, hayseed,
palooka 9 simpleton 10 clodhopper

Louvre masterpiece
8 Mona Lisa 11 Venus de Milo

lovable
4 dear 5 sweet 6 cuddly 7 winning,
winsome 8 adorable 9 appealing,
endearing 11 embraceable

love
4 zeal 5 adore, ardor, crush, Cupid,
exalt, prize, value 6 desire, dote on,
fervor, revere 7 adulate, cherish,
idolize, passion, romance, worship
8 devotion, fondness, idolatry, treasure, venerate, yearning 9 adoration, adulation, affection, delight in,
sentiment 10 allegiance, appreciate,
attachment, enthusiasm 11 amorousness, infatuation
combining form: 5 phily 6 philia
French: 5 amour
Italian: 5 amore

love apple
6 tomato

lovebird
6 budgie, parrot 10 budgerigar

love feast
5 agape

love god
4 Amor, Eros, Kama 5 Bhaga, Cupid

love goddess
5 Athor, Freya, Venus 6 Hathor,
Inanna, Ishtar 7 Astarte 9 Aphrodite,
Ashtoreth

love letter
8 mash note 9 valentine 10 billet-
doux

lovely
4 fair 5 sweet, swell 6 comely,
dainty, pretty 7 elegant 8 adorable,
alluring, charming, delicate, engaging, graceful, knockout 9 beauteous,
beautiful, exquisite 10 attractive,
delightful, enchanting, entrancing
11 captivating, good-looking

love potion
7 philter, philtre 11 aphrodisiac

lover
3 fan 4 beau, buff 5 flame, leman,
Romeo, swain 6 addict, steady,
suitor, votary 7 amorist, darling,
devotee, Don Juan, gallant, habitué,
squeeze 8 fancy man, lothario,
mistress, paramour 9 boyfriend,
inamorata, inamorato 10 aficionado,
girlfriend, sweetheart

lovey-dovey
5 mushy 6 doting 7 amorous
12 affectionate

loving
4 dear, fond 6 ardent, erotic, tender
7 amatory, amorous, cordial, devoted, fervent 8 attached, enamored, faithful 10 benevolent, infatuated, passionate, solicitous
11 impassioned 12 affectionate

low
3 moo 4 base, blue, dead, deep,
down, flat, mean, neap, poor, weak
5 cheap, short 6 abject, ailing,
humble, hushed, lesser, nether,
poorly, sickly, sordid, sparse, unwell
7 cut-rate, reduced, scrubby 8 cast
down, dejected, depleted, downcast, inferior, mediocre, wretched
9 declining, depressed, miserable,
subnormal, woebegone 10 economical, inadequate, indisposed,
marked down, spiritless 11 crestfallen, downhearted, substandard,
unfavorable

lowbred
4 base, rude 6 coarse, oafish,
vulgar 7 boorish, brutish, loutish,
uncouth 8 churlish, cloddish, lubberly 11 uncivilized

low-cost
5 cheap 6 budget, cheapo 7 bargain, cut-rate 10 affordable, reasonable 11 inexpensive

low-down
4 base, mean, ugly, vile 6 odious,
scurvy 7 ignoble 8 shameful,
wretched 9 abhorrent, worthless
10 despicable, disgusting 11 ignominious 12 contemptible

lowdown
4 dope, info 5 facts, scoop, specs
6 skinny 8 briefing 11 information

lower
3 cut 4 clip, drop, fall, sink 5 frown,
gloom, scowl, shave, slash, under
6 debase, demean, demote, humble,
lesser, menace, nether, reduce 7 cut
down, deflate, degrade, demerit,

depress, descend, devalue, let down
8 inferior, mark down, overcast,
submerge, threaten 9 devaluate,
downgrade
prefix: 5 infra

Lower Depths author
5 Gorki, Gorky (Maksim, Maxim)

lowest point
5 nadir
in the U.S.: 11 Death Valley
on earth: 7 Dead Sea

low-grade
4 hack 5 junky, lousy 6 cheesy,
cruddy, shabby, shoddy, sleazy,
tawdry 8 below par, déclassé, inferior, mediocre 9 deficient 10 second-
rate 11 second-class, substandard
12 second-drawer

low-key
4 soft 5 muted, quiet 7 relaxed,
subdued 8 laid-back, softened,
tasteful 9 easygoing, minimized,
temperate, toned down 10 played
down, restrained 11 understated

lowland
4 flat, sump, vale 5 basin 6 bottom,
slough, valley 7 bottoms
Scottish: 6 lallan 7 lalland

lowlife
4 fink, heel 5 knave, rogue 6 no-
good, outlaw, rascal, wretch 7 hoodlum, ruffian, villain 9 miscreant,
reprobate, scoundrel 10 blackguard,
black sheep, sleazeball 11 rapscallion, slimebucket 12 bottom-feeder

lowly
4 base, mean, meek 6 abject,
humble, menial, modest 7 ignoble,
mundane, obscure, prosaic, servile
8 baseborn, plebeian, unwashed

low-pressure
4 calm 6 casual, dégagé, folksy,
mellow 7 relaxed 8 flexible, informal, laid-back 9 easygoing 10 nonchalant

low-spirited
3 sad 4 blue, down, glum 6 abject,
droopy, gloomy, morose 7 doleful

8 cast down, dejected, downcast, saddened **9** bummed out, cheerless, depressed, woebegone **10** dispirited, melancholy **11** discouraged, downhearted **12** disheartened, heavyhearted

low tide
3 ebb **4** neap

loyal
4 firm, true **5** liege **6** ardent, trusty **7** devoted, dutiful, staunch **8** constant, faithful, resolute, true-blue **9** allegiant, steadfast, unfailing **10** dependable **11** trustworthy

loyalist
4 Tory **7** patriot **8** partisan **10** countryman **11** nationalist

loyalty
6 fealty **8** adhesion, devotion, fidelity **9** adherence, constancy **10** allegiance, attachment, dedication **11** staunchness **12** faithfulness **13** dependability, steadfastness

lozenge
4 pill **6** troche **7** diamond, rhombus **8** pastille

LSD
4 acid
user: **8** acidhead

lubricate
3 oil **6** grease, smooth **7** moisten

lubricious
4 lewd, oily **5** slick **6** carnal, greasy, slippy, wanton **8** prurient, slippery, slithery, ticklish **9** lecherous, salacious **10** lascivious, libidinous **12** concupiscent

lucent
5 clear **6** bright, limpid **7** beaming, crystal, glowing, lambent, radiant, shining **8** clear-cut, luminous, pellucid **9** brilliant, effulgent, refulgent **11** unambiguous

Lucia di Lammermoor
character: **7** Edgardo
composer: **9** Donizetti (Gaetano)
novelist: **5** Scott (Walter)

lucid
4 sane **5** clear **6** bright, limpid **7** crystal, lambent, radiant **8** clear-cut, knowable, luminous **9** brilliant, effulgent, graspable, refulgent, unblurred **10** articulate, fathomable **11** translucent, transparent, unambiguous **12** compos mentis, incandescent, intelligible, transpicuous **13** apprehensible

lucidity
6 acumen, sanity **7** clarity **8** sagacity, saneness **9** clearness, plainness, soundness **10** cognizance, perception **12** clairvoyance

Lucifer
5 devil, fiend, Satan, Venus **7** Old Nick **8** Apollyon **9** archfiend, Beelzebub **10** Old Scratch **13** Old Gooseberry

Lucinde
beloved: **7** Leandre **9** Clitandre
father: **7** Geronte **10** Sganarelle

luck
3 hap, hit **4** juju, meet **5** fluke, light **6** chance, happen, hazard, kismet **7** fortune, godsend, stumble **8** fortuity, occasion, windfall **9** advantage **11** opportunity
token: **5** charm **6** amulet, clover, fetish, mascot **8** talisman **9** horseshoe **11** rabbit's foot

luckless
7 adverse, hapless, unhappy **8** ill-fated, untoward, wretched **9** miserable **10** ill-starred **11** star-crossed, unfavorable, unfortunate **12** misfortunate, unpropitious

lucky
6 golden, timely **7** favored **9** favorable, fortunate **10** auspicious, beneficial, felicitous, fortuitous, propitious **12** advantageous, providential **13** serendipitous
Scottish: **5** canny

Lucky Jim author
4 Amis (Kingsley)

lucrative
6 paying **7** gainful **8** fruitful **10** high-income, productive, profitable,

well-paying, worthwhile **11** money-making **12** advantageous, remunerative

lucre
3 pay **4** cash, gain, jack, loot **5** dough, green, money, moola **6** dinero, do-re-mi, moolah, profit, wampum **7** cabbage, revenue **9** long green **10** greenbacks

Lucrezia _____
6 Borgia

ludicrous
4 zany **5** antic, comic, droll, funny, goofy, nutty, silly **6** absurd **7** amusing, bizarre, comical, foolish, risible **8** farcical **9** fantastic, grotesque, laughable **10** off-the-wall, outlandish, ridiculous **11** incongruous **12** preposterous

Ludlum novel
14 Bourne Identity (The) **15** Bourne Supremacy (The) **16** Holcroft Covenant (The) **19** Prometheus Deception (The)

lug
3 nut, oaf, tow, tug **4** bear, buck, drag, draw, haul, hump, jerk, pull, tote **5** carry, ferry, shlep **6** convey, schlep **9** transport

luggage
4 bags, gear **7** baggage

lugubrious
3 sad **4** blue, dour, down, glum **5** bleak **6** dismal, dreary, gloomy, morose, rueful, somber, sullen, woeful **7** doleful, joyless **8** cast down, dejected, dolesome, downcast, mournful **9** cheerless, depressed, plaintive, saturnine, sorrowful, woebegone **10** depressing, despondent, lamentable, melancholy, oppressive **11** discouraged, dispiriting, downhearted **12** disconsolate

lukewarm
5 blasé, tepid **7** dubious, offhand **8** hesitant **9** uncertain, undecided **10** wishy-washy **11** halfhearted, indifferent

lull
3 ebb **4** balm, calm, hush, wane **5** letup, pause, quiet, still **6** becalm, pacify, soothe, temper **7** compose, decline, ease off, slacken **8** abeyance, interval **9** stillness **10** quiescence **11** tranquilize

lullaby
8 berceuse **10** cradlesong

lulu
3 ace **5** dandy, doozy, dream **6** doozie, wonder **7** delight **8** knockout **9** sensation

lumber
3 tax **4** clog, lade, load, logs, plod, slog, wood **5** barge, clump, stump, weigh **6** burden, charge, rumble, saddle, timber, trudge **8** encumber

lumberjack
see **logger**

luminance
10 brightness

luminary
3 sun, VIP **4** lion, name, star **5** celeb, light, nabob **6** leader, worthy **7** big name, notable **8** big-timer, eminence, somebody **9** celebrity, dignitary, superstar **10** notability **12** leading light

luminous
5 clear, lucid **6** bright, lucent **7** beaming, crystal, fulgent, lambent, radiant, shining **8** clear-cut, lustrous, pellucid **9** brilliant, effulgent, refulgent **11** illustrious, translucent, transparent **12** enlightening, incandescent

lummox
3 oaf **4** boor, clod, gawk, lout **5** klutz, looby **6** lubber **7** palooka

lump
3 gob, lot, oaf, wad **4** blob, bulk, chip, clod, gawk, glob, heap, hunk, lout, mass, pile, welt **5** abide, batch, block, brook, bulge, bunch, chunk, hunch, klutz, knurl, looby, piece, scrap, stand, tumor **6** digest, endure, entire, lubber, morsel, nugget **7** handful, palooka, portion, stomach,

swallow **8** swelling, totality **9** aggregate **10** protrusion, tumescence **12** protuberance

lumpy
5 crude, gawky, rough **6** choppy, clumsy, coarse, oafish **8** clumpish, unformed **9** roughhewn

lunacy
5 folly, mania **6** idiocy **7** fatuity, foolery, inanity, madness **8** delirium, dementia, insanity **9** absurdity, craziness, silliness, stupidity **10** imbecility **11** derangement, foolishness **13** senselessness

lunar
dark area: 4 mare **5** maria (plural)
valley: 4 rill **5** rille

lunatic
3 mad, nut **4** daft, kook, loco, yo-yo, zany **5** balmy, batty, crank, crazy, nutty, raver, wacko, wacky **6** absurd, crazed, cuckoo, insane, madman, maniac, nitwit, psycho, screwy **7** bonkers, cracked, foolish **8** crackpot, demented, demoniac, deranged, frenzied, maniacal, paranoid, schizoid, unhinged **9** bedlamite, ding-a-ling, fruitcake, harebrain, screwball **10** crackbrain **11** nonsensical

lunch
3 eat **4** meal, nosh **5** snack

luncheonette
4 café **5** diner **6** bistro, eatery **7** beanery, canteen, tearoom **8** snack bar **9** cafeteria **10** coffee shop, restaurant **11** greasy spoon

lune
3 bow **5** curve **6** sickle **8** crescent, meniscus

lung
combining form: 5 pneum, pulmo **6** pneumo, pulmon
disease: 9 emphysema, pneumonia **10** byssinosis **12** tuberculosis

lunge
3 jab **4** dash, dive, stab **5** bound, drive, pitch, surge **6** charge, plunge, pounce, thrust

lunkhead
3 oaf **4** boob, clod, dodo, dolt, goof, yo-yo **5** booby, chump, dummy, dunce, idiot, moron, ninny, noddy, stupe **6** dimwit, dum-dum, nitwit **7** dullard **8** dumbbell, imbecile, numskull **9** birdbrain, ignoramus, lamebrain, numbskull, simpleton **10** nincompoop

lupine
5 feral **6** brutal, fierce **7** wolfish **8** ravening **9** predatory, rapacious **10** bluebonnet, sanguinary

lurch
3 bob, yaw **4** jerk, lean, list, reel, rock, roll, sway, tilt, toss **5** heave, pitch, slide, swing **6** bumble, careen, falter, plunge, seesaw, swerve, teeter, totter **7** blunder, stagger, stumble **8** flounder

lure
3 bag **4** bait, call, draw, fake, hook, pull, rope, toll, trap, wile **5** blind, catch, charm, decoy, snare, tempt, trick **6** appeal, cajole, come-on, draw in, draw on, entice, entrap, invite, lead on, seduce **7** attract, beguile, bewitch, capture, con game, enchant, ensnare, gimmick, wheedle **8** blandish, delusion, illusion, inveigle **9** captivate, fascinate, incentive, seduction, siren song **10** attraction, camouflage, enticement, inducement, seducement, temptation
fishing: 3 fly **4** worm **5** spoon **6** minnow **8** bucktail

lurid
3 wan **4** ashy, gory, gray, grim, pale **5** ashen, fiery, gross, livid, waxen **6** doughy, grisly, malign, sultry, yellow **7** baleful, ghastly, graphic, hideous, macabre, malefic, tabloid **8** blanched, gruesome, horrible, shocking, sinister, terrible **9** colorless **10** horrifying, maleficent, terrifying **11** sensational **12** melodramatic

Lurie novel
14 Foreign Affairs **18** War Between the Tates (The)

lurk

4 hide, slip 5 creep, prowl, skulk, slide, slink, sneak, snoop, steal 9 pussyfoot

luscious

4 rich, sexy 5 sapid, sweet, tasty, yummy 6 delish, divine, ornate, savory 7 opulent, piquant, sensual 8 sensuous 9 ambrosial, epicurean, exquisite, flavorful, luxurious, seductive, sumptuous, toothsome 10 delectable, delightful, flamboyant, flavorsome, voluptuous 11 scrumptious 13 mouth-watering

lush

3 sot 4 rank, rich, wino 5 dense, drink, drunk, yummy 6 bibber, boozer, deluxe, lavish, savory 7 fertile, opulent, profuse, sensual, teeming, tippler 8 abundant, drunkard, palatial, prodigal, sensuous, thriving 9 ambrosial, delicious, epicurean, exuberant, inebriate, luxuriant, luxurious, plentiful, sumptuous, toothsome 10 boozehound, delectable, delightful, profitable, prosperous, voluptuous 11 extravagant, flourishing

Lusitania

8 Portugal

lust

3 rut, yen 4 ache, itch, pine, urge, wish, zeal, zest 5 ardor, crave, drive, greed, letch, yearn 6 desire, fervor, hanker, hunger, libido 7 avidity, craving, lechery, longing, passion 8 appetite, coveting, cupidity, lewdness, priapism, salacity, satyrism, yearning 9 carnality, eagerness, eroticism, lubricity, prurience, pruriency 10 enthusiasm, excitement, satyriasis, wantonness 11 nymphomania 13 concupiscence, lecherousness, salaciousness

luster

4 glow 5 glaze, gleam, glint, gloss, sheen, shine 6 polish 7 burnish, shimmer 8 lambency, radiance 9 afterglow 10 brightness, brilliance, brilliancy, effulgence, luminosity, refulgence 11 candescence, iridescence

lusterless

3 dim, wan 4 blah, drab, dull, flat, gray, matt 5 brown, dingy, dusky, faded, matte, muddy, muted, vapid 6 boring 10 uninspired

lustful

3 hot 4 lewd 5 bawdy, horny 6 carnal, erotic, wanton 7 burning, goatish, itching, ruttish, satyric 8 prurient 9 debauched, lecherous, libertine, lickerish, salacious 10 hot-blooded, lascivious, libidinous, licentious, lubricious, passionate 12 concupiscent

lustrate

5 purge 6 purify 7 cleanse

lustration

6 ritual 8 ablution 9 catharsis, cleansing, purgation 10 sprinkling 12 purification

lustrous

5 nitid, shiny 6 bright, gleamy, glossy, sheeny 7 fulgent, glowing, lambent, radiant, shining 8 gleaming, luminous, polished, splendid 9 brilliant, burnished, effulgent, refulgent 10 glimmering, glistening 11 resplendent 12 incandescent

lusty

4 hale 5 hardy, vital 6 brawny, hearty, mighty, potent, robust, strong, virile 7 dynamic, healthy, rousing 8 vigorous 9 energetic, strapping, strenuous 10 prodigious, red-blooded 12 enthusiastic

lute

4 clay, seal 5 grout 6 cement 7 bandora 8 mandolin 10 chitarrone, instrument
Arabic: 3 oud
two-necked: 7 theorbo

lutenist

5 Bream (Julian) 7 Dowland (John) 8 Gaultier (Denis)

Lutetia
5 Paris

Luxembourg
capital: 10 Luxembourg
monetary unit: 4 euro
mountain range: 8 Ardennes
neighbor: 6 France 7 Belgium,
Germany
river: 4 Sûre 7 Alzette

luxuriant
4 lush, rank, rich 5 dense 6 fecund,
lavish 7 copious, fertile, opulent,
profuse, rampant, riotous, teeming
8 abundant, fruitful, luscious, prodigal, prolific 9 excessive, exuberant,
sumptuous

luxuriate
4 bask 5 bloom, enjoy, feast, revel
6 abound, relish, thrive, wallow
7 delight, indulge 8 flourish

luxurious
4 lush, posh, rich 5 fancy, grand,
plush, ritzy, showy 6 costly, deluxe,
lavish, plushy 7 opulent, sensual,
stately 8 imposing, majestic, palatial,
splendid 9 elaborate, epicurean,
expensive, grandiose, sumptuous
10 impressive 11 extravagant,
magnificent
situation: 7 fat city 10 bed of roses,
easy street

luxury
5 frill, treat 6 dainty 7 amenity, comfort 8 delicacy, opulence 9 abundance, affluence 10 indulgence
11 superfluity 12 extravagance

lycée
6 school 10 high school

lyceum
4 hall 6 school 7 academy, chamber
9 institute

Lycidas author
6 Milton (John)

Lycomedes
daughter: 8 Deidamia
victim: 7 Theseus

Lycus
brother: 7 Nycteus
father: 7 Pandion
slayer: 6 Zethus 7 Amphion
wife: 5 Dirce

Lydian
king: 5 Gyges 7 Croesus 8 Alyattes
queen: 7 Omphale

lye
7 caustic 9 hydroxide

lynch
4 hang 5 scrag 6 gibbet, murder
7 execute 8 string up

Lynette
see **Line**

lynx
4 puma 6 bobcat, cougar 7 caracal,
wildcat 9 catamount

Lyra star
4 Vega

lyre
4 harp

lyric
3 ode 4 odic, poem 5 melic, verse
6 poetic 7 melodic, musical 8 operatic 9 exuberant, rhapsodic

lyrical
7 lilting, melodic, musical, songful,
tuneful 8 operatic

lyricist
4 poet 10 librettist

Lysander's beloved
6 Hermia

M

Maacah
father: 5 Nahor 6 Talmai 7 Absalom
husband: 5 David 6 Jehiel, Machir 8 Rehoboam
son: 5 Hanan 6 Abijam, Achish 7 Absalom 10 Shephatiah

macabre
4 grim 5 lurid 6 grisly, horrid, morbid 7 deathly, ghastly, hideous 8 ghoulish, gruesome, horrible 9 deathlike 10 horrifying

macadam
3 tar 7 asphalt, roadway 8 pavement

macaque
6 monkey, rhesus

macaroni
3 fop 4 beau, buck, dude, toff 5 dandy, pasta, swell 7 coxcomb, gallant

macaw
6 parrot

Macbeth
character: 4 Ross 5 Angus 6 Hecate, Lennox 7 Fleance
slayer: 7 Macduff
successor: 7 Malcolm
title: 5 thane
victim: 6 Banquo, Duncan

mace
4 club 5 baton, staff 6 cudgel, nutmeg 8 bludgeon

Macedonia
capital: 6 Skopje
city: 6 Tetovo
monetary unit: 5 denar

neighbor: 6 Greece, Serbia 7 Albania 8 Bulgaria
part of: 7 Balkans
peninsula: 6 Balkan

macerate
4 soak 5 steep 6 drench, soften 7 immerse, suffuse 8 saturate

machete
4 bolo 5 knife 6 scythe

Machiavellian
4 wily 6 shrewd 7 cunning, devious 8 guileful, scheming 9 conniving, deceitful, insidious 10 conspiring 11 duplicitous, treacherous 12 unscrupulous

Machiavelli work
6 Prince (The) 8 Mandrake (The) 10 Mandragola (La)

machinate
4 plot 6 scheme 7 connive, finagle 8 conspire, intrigue, maneuver

machination
4 plot, ploy, ruse 5 cabal, dodge 6 gambit, scheme 8 artifice, intrigue, maneuver, scheming, trickery 9 chicanery, collusion, deception, dirty work, expedient, stratagem 10 hanky-panky, subterfuge 11 contrivance, skulduggery 12 gamesmanship, skullduggery

machine
6 device, engine, gadget 9 apparatus, appliance, automaton 11 contraption

machine-gun
4 rake 6 strafe 8 enfilade 9 rapid-fire

machine-gun inventor
7 Gatling (Richard)

machinery
5 works 9 apparatus, equipment, mechanism

machismo
7 swagger 8 virility 9 manliness 11 masculinity

macho
5 manly 6 virile 9 masculine

Machu Picchu resident
4 Inca

mackinaw
4 coat 5 cover, trout 7 blanket

mackintosh
7 slicker 8 raincoat

macrocosm
5 world 6 cosmos 8 creation, universe

mad
4 daft, nuts, rash, sore, wild 5 angry, crazy, irate, irked, kooky, livid, loony, nutty, rabid, wacky 6 absurd, crazed, cuckoo, heated, insane, ireful, screwy 7 berserk, bonkers, cracked, enraged, foolish, frantic, furious, lunatic 8 choleric, demented, deranged, frenetic, frenzied, incensed, offended, outraged, unhinged, worked up, wrathful 9 delirious, fanatical, fantastic, hilarious, illogical, senseless 10 distracted, infuriated, irrational, unbalanced

Madagascar
capital: 12 Antananarivo
channel: 10 Mozambique
city: 9 Mahajanga, Toamasina
language: 6 French 8 Malagasy
monetary unit: 5 franc
mountain range: 9 Ankaratra

madame
3 Mrs. 4 wife 6 milady, missus

Madame Bovary
author: 8 Flaubert (Gustave)
character: 4 Emma (Bovary)
7 Charles (Bovary) 8 Rodolphe

Madame Butterfly
character: 9 Cho-Cho-San, Cio-Cio-San, Pinkerton, Sharpless
composer: 7 Puccini (Giacomo)

madcap
4 rash, wild 5 antic 7 foolish 8 reckless 9 frivolous, hotheaded 10 capricious, incautious

Mad Cavalier
6 Rupert (Prince)

madden
3 ire, vex 4 goad 5 anger, craze 6 enrage 7 derange, incense, inflame, outrage, possess, steam up, unhinge 9 infuriate, unbalance

Madeira Islands
capital: 7 Funchal
export: 4 wine
part of: 8 Portugal

mademoiselle
4 girl, Miss 6 maiden 9 governess 10 yellowtail 11 silver perch

made-to-order
6 custom 7 bespoke 10 customized 11 custom-built

made-up
5 bogus, false 7 painted 8 invented, mythical, specious 9 fictional, imaginary, pretended, trumped-up 10 fabricated, fictitious 11 make-believe 12 cosmeticized

madhouse
6 asylum, bedlam 8 loony bin 9 funny farm 10 booby hatch

madman
3 nut 4 kook, loon 5 loony, raver 6 cuckoo, maniac, psycho 7 lunatic, nutcase 8 bedlamite, psychotic, fruitcake

madness
4 rage 5 folly 6 lunacy 8 insanity 9 psychosis 11 derangement

Madonna initials
3 BVM

Madras
9 Tamil Nadu
founder: 3 Day (Francis)

Madrid museum
5 Prado

madrigal
4 glee, poem, song 8 part-song

madrigalist
English: 4 Byrd (William) 6 Morley
(Thomas), Wilbye (John) 7 Tomkins
(Thomas), Weelkes (Thomas)
Flemish: 8 Willaert (Adriaan)
Italian: 8 Marenzio (Luca) 10 Mon-
teverdi (Claudio)

maelstrom
4 eddy 5 whirl 6 vortex 7 turmoil
9 whirlpool

maenad
9 bacchante, priestess

maestro
see **conductor**

Mafia
3 mob 4 ring 6 clique 7 rackets
8 gangland 9 Black Hand, syndicate
10 Cosa Nostra, underworld

mafioso
4 goon 6 hit man 7 mobster 8 gangster 9 racketeer

magazine
4 dump 5 cache, depot, organ, store
6 armory, digest, review, weekly
7 arsenal, gazette, journal, monthly
8 biweekly 9 bimonthly, quarterly,
warehouse 10 depository, periodical,
repository, storehouse 11 publication

mage
6 priest 8 magician, sorcerer

maggot
4 grub, whim 5 fancy, larva 6 vagary
7 caprice, conceit

Magi
6 Caspar, Gaspar 8 Melchior 9 Balthasar, Balthazar
gift: 4 gold 5 myrrh 7 incense
12 frankincense

Magian
see **magus**

magic
4 juju 5 wicca 6 hoodoo, voodoo
7 alchemy, devilry, sorcery 8 satanism, witchery, witching, wizardry
9 conjuring, diablerie, diabolism,
occultism, sortilege 10 hocus-pocus,
mumbo jumbo, necromancy, witchcraft 11 abracadabra, bewitchment,
enchantment, legerdemain, thaumaturgy

magical
6 occult 8 wizardly 10 bewitching,
entrancing 11 necromantic 12 thaumaturgic

Magic Flute composer
6 Mozart (Wolfgang Amadeus)

magician
5 brujo, witch 6 shaman, wizard
7 Houdini, warlock 8 conjurer,
satanist, sorcerer 9 diabolist, enchanter, trickster, voodooist 11 medicine man, necromancer, thaumaturge
Arthurian: 6 Merlin
Shakespearean: 8 Prospero
stage: 5 Randi (James) 11 Copperfield (David), illusionist
Tolkien's: 7 Gandalf

Magic Mountain, The
author: 4 Mann (Thomas)
character: 7 Castorp (Hans)

magisterial
6 lordly 7 pompous 8 dogmatic
9 imperious, masterful 10 high-
handed 11 doctrinaire, domineering,
overbearing 13 authoritative, self-
important

Magister Ludi author
5 Hesse (Hermann)

magistrate
5 court, judge 7 bencher, justice
8 official
ancient Greek: 5 ephor 6 archon
ancient Roman: 6 aedile 7 duumvir,
praetor, questor 8 quaestor
Italian: 7 podesta
Scottish: 6 bailie

Magna Carta
king: 4 John
place signed: 9 Runnymede

magnanimous
5 noble 7 liberal 8 generous, princely 9 forgiving, unselfish 10 benevolent, bighearted, charitable, chivalrous, high-minded, munificent

magnate
5 baron, mogul, nabob 6 fat cat, prince, tycoon 9 personage, plutocrat

magnet
9 lodestone 10 attraction

magnetic
8 alluring 9 appealing, seductive 10 attractive 11 captivating, charismatic, fascinating 12 irresistible
substance: 4 iron 7 ferrite

magnetism
4 draw, lure, pull 5 charm 6 allure, appeal 7 glamour 8 charisma 10 attraction 11 fascination

magnetize
4 draw, lure, wile 5 charm 7 attract, bewitch, enchant 9 captivate, fascinate

magnification unit
8 diameter

magnificence
4 pomp 7 majesty 8 grandeur, splendor 9 pageantry 13 sumptuousness

magnificent
5 grand, noble, regal, royal 6 august, lavish, lordly, superb 7 exalted, opulent, stately, sublime 8 glorious, imposing, majestic, palatial, princely, splendid 9 brilliant, grandiose, luxurious, sumptuous 11 extravagant, resplendent, splendorous 13 splendiferous

magnifier
4 lens 9 telescope
jeweler's: 5 loupe

magnify
4 hymn, laud 5 add to, boost, cry up, exalt, extol, honor, swell 6 expand, extend, praise 7 amplify, augment, enhance, enlarge, ennoble, glorify, inflate 8 eulogize, heighten, increase, maximize, multiply, overplay 9 aggravate, celebrate, embellish, embroider, intensify, overstate 10 aggrandize, exaggerate, panegyrize 13 overemphasize

magniloquent
5 tumid, windy 6 florid, turgid 7 aureate, flowery, fustian, orotund, pompous, swollen 8 sonorous 9 bombastic, high-flown, overblown, rhapsodic 10 euphuistic, rhetorical 11 declamatory

magnitude
4 size 5 order, range 6 extent, import, number, volume 7 bigness, caliber, measure, quality 8 enormity, hugeness, quantity, vastness 9 greatness, immensity, largeness 10 dimensions, importance, proportion 11 consequence

Magnolia State
11 Mississippi

magnum opus
7 classic 10 masterwork 11 chef d'oeuvre, masterpiece, tour de force

Magog's king
3 Gog

magpie
3 jay 4 bird 6 gabber, prater 7 blabber, hoarder 8 jabberer, prattler 9 chatterer, collector 10 chatterbox 12 blabbermouth

maguey
5 agave, fiber 7 cantala
relative: 4 aloe

magus
6 wizard 7 diviner, warlock 8 conjurer, sorcerer 9 enchanter 10 astrologer 11 necromancer

Magyar
9 Hungarian

Mahalath
father: 7 Ishmael 8 Jerimoth
husband: 4 Esau 8 Rehoboam

mah-jongg piece
4 tile

Mahlon
father: 9 Elimelech
mother: 5 Naomi
wife: 4 Ruth

Maia
father: 5 Atlas
mother: 7 Pleione
sisters: 8 Pleiades
son: 6 Hermes 7 Mercury

maid
4 girl, lass, miss 5 biddy, bonne,
wench 6 au pair, damsel, lassie,
live-in, virgin 7 servant 8 domestic
9 charwoman, hired girl 10 au pair
girl
Indian: 4 ayah
lady's: 7 abigail
stage: 9 soubrette

maiden
3 gal 4 girl, lass, miss 5 first, fresh,
missy, prime, wench 6 damsel,
lassie, unused, virgin 7 initial,
pioneer, primary 8 earliest, original,
spinster, virginal 10 spinsterly
Norse mythological: 8 valkyrie

maidenhair tree
6 ginkgo

maidenhead
5 hymen 6 purity 9 virginity

maidenhood
9 virginity

Maid of Astolat
6 Elaine

Maid of Orleans, The
4 Joan (of Arc) 7 Pucelle (La)
author: 8 Schiller (Friedrich von)

mail
4 post 5 armor 7 hauberk, letters
8 messages

_____ mail
3 air 5 chain

maim
4 maul 6 mangle 7 cripple, disable
8 mutilate, paralyze 9 disfigure

main
3 sea 5 chief, great, major, ocean,
prime, trunk, vital 7 central, high
sea, leading, premier, primary 8 cardinal, foremost, high seas 9 essential, paramount, principal 10 preeminent, prevailing 11 fundamental,
outstanding, predominant

Maine
capital: 7 Augusta
city: 6 Bangor 8 Lewiston, Portland
college, university: 5 Bates, Colby
7 Bowdoin
lake: 6 Sebago
motto: 6 Dirigo
mountain: 8 Cadillac, Katahdin
nickname: 8 Pine Tree (State)
park: 6 Acadia
river: 8 Kennebec 9 Penobscot
state bird: 9 chickadee
state flower: 22 white pine cone
and tassel
state tree: 9 white pine

mainly
6 mostly 7 chiefly, largely 8 above
all 9 primarily 10 especially 11 principally 13 predominantly

mainstay
4 prop 5 brace 6 pillar 7 bulwark,
standby, support 8 backbone,
buttress 9 supporter, sustainer

Main Street author
5 Lewis (Sinclair)

maintain
4 aver, avow 5 argue, claim 6 affirm,
allege, assert, back up, defend,
insist, keep up, manage, stress,
uphold 7 care for, carry on, contend,
declare, justify, persist, profess,
support, sustain, warrant 8 continue,
preserve 9 cultivate, emphasize,
look after 10 provide for

maintenance
4 care, keep 6 living, upkeep 7 alimony, support 10 livelihood 11 subsistence 12 alimentation
worker: 7 janitor 9 custodian

maize
4 corn, milo 10 Indian corn

majestic

5 grand, noble, regal, royal **6** august, kingly, lordly, superb **7** exalted, stately **8** elevated, imperial, imposing, princely, splendid **9** dignified, grandiose, sumptuous **11** ceremonious, magnificent

majesty

4 pomp **5** glory **8** eminence, grandeur, splendor **9** greatness, loftiness **11** stateliness **12** magnificence

major

3 big **4** main, star **5** chief, grave, large **6** higher, larger **7** capital, greater, notable, primary, serious, sizable **8** sizeable, superior **9** principal, prominent **10** large-scale, preeminent **11** outstanding, predominant, significant **12** considerable

Major Barbara author

4 Shaw (George Bernard)

majority

4 bulk, edge **6** margin **13** preponderance

make

3 act, net, set **4** earn, form, gain, mold **5** build, cause, erect, forge, frame, hatch, shape, spawn **6** compel, create, derive, draw up, effect, output, parent **7** achieve, bring in, compose, fashion, prepare, produce **8** comprise, conclude, draw down, generate **9** construct, establish, fabricate, originate **10** constitute **11** manufacture, put together
amends: 5 atone
believe: 7 pretend
certain: 6 assure **8** convince
fast: 3 fix **4** gird **6** secure
good: 7 succeed **9** indemnify
known: 3 air **6** expose, reveal, spread **7** declare, divulge, uncover **8** announce, disclose, proclaim
use of: 6 employ

make-believe

4 mock, sham **7** charade, feigned, fiction **8** disguise, pretense **9** fictional, imaginary, insincere, pretended, simulated **10** fictitious

make do

4 cope **5** get by, get on, shift **6** endure, fake it, manage, wing it **7** survive **8** get along **9** improvise **11** extemporize **13** muddle through

make off

3 fly, run **4** flee, skip **5** leave, scoot, scram **6** decamp, depart, escape **7** abscond, run away **9** skedaddle

make out

3 see **4** fare, neck **5** grasp, infer **6** accept, deduce, derive, follow, gather, manage, take in, thrive **7** discern, prosper, succeed **8** conclude, flourish, get along, perceive **9** apprehend, determine, establish, interpret **10** comprehend, understand

make over

4 cede, deed **6** assign, convey, reform **7** remodel, reshape **8** renovate, transfer

maker

7 builder, creator **8** borrower, designer, inventor, producer **10** originator **11** constructor **12** manufacturer

makeshift

6 resort **7** stopgap **8** recourse, resource **9** expedient, temporary **10** expediency, substitute **11** provisional **13** quick-and-dirty, rough-and-ready

make up

4 form **5** atone **6** devise, invent **7** arrange, compile, compose, concoct, fashion, prepare **8** comprise, contrive **9** apologize, construct, fabricate, formulate, improvise, reconcile **10** compensate

makeup

4 cast, form, kohl, mold **5** blush, fiber, gloss, grain, paint, rouge, shape, stamp, style **6** design, nature, powder, stripe, temper **7** blusher, mascara **8** lip gloss, war paint **9** character, formation **10** complexion, maquillage **11** arrangement, composition, disposition,

greasepaint, personality, temperament 12 architecture, constitution,
construction, organization

maladroit
5 inept 6 clumsy, gauche, klutzy
7 awkward, unhandy 8 bumbling,
bungling, tactless 9 ham-handed,
impolitic 10 blundering, ungraceful
11 heavy-handed 12 undiplomatic

malady
3 ill 7 ailment, disease, illness
8 disorder, sickness, syndrome
9 complaint, condition, infirmity
10 affliction

malaise
4 funk 5 dumps, ennui 8 debility,
doldrums 10 enervation

Malamud, Bernard
novel: 5 Fixer (The) 7 Natural (The)
9 Assistant (The)
story: 11 Magic Barrel (The)

malapert
4 rude 5 brash, fresh, nervy, sassy,
saucy, smart 6 brassy, brazen,
cheeky 7 forward 8 impudent,
insolent 12 presumptuous

Malaprop creator
8 Sheridan (Richard Brinsley)

malapropos
5 inapt, undue 8 improper, unseemly, untimely 10 unsuitable
11 inopportune 13 inappropriate,
inopportunely

malaria
4 ague 6 miasma
medicine: 7 quinine 8 cinchona
mosquito: 9 anopheles

malarkey
4 guff 5 bilge, hokum, hooey, tripe
6 bunkum, drivel 7 hogwash, rubbish, twaddle 8 nonsense 9 poppycock 10 balderdash 12 blatherskite

Malawi
capital: 8 Lilongwe
city: 8 Blantyre
explorer: 11 Livingstone (David)
former name: 9 Nyasaland
lake: 5 Nyasa 6 Malawi

language: 7 English 8 Chichewa
monetary unit: 6 kwacha
neighbor: 6 Zambia 8 Tanzania
10 Mozambique
river: 5 Shire

Malaysia
capital: 11 Kuala Lumpur
city: 4 Ipoh 6 Penang 11 Johor
Baharu
island: 6 Borneo
monetary unit: 7 ringgit
neighbor: 8 Thailand 9 Indonesia
peninsula: 5 Malay
sea: 10 South China
strait: 7 Malacca

malcontent
5 rebel 6 griper, grouch, unruly
8 agitator, factious, frondeur, grumbler, mutinous, restless 9 alienated
10 bellyacher, complainer, rebellious
11 disaffected, disgruntled, disobedient, ungratified 12 contumacious,
dissatisfied

mal de mer
6 nausea 8 vomiting 10 queasiness
11 seasickness

Maldives
capital: 4 Male
language: 6 Divehi
monetary unit: 7 rufiyaa

male
3 guy, tom 4 gent 5 macho, manly
6 manful, virile 7 manlike 9 masculine, staminate

malediction
4 jinx, oath 5 curse 7 malison
8 anathema 10 execration 11 imprecation

malefactor
5 felon, knave, rogue 6 sinner
8 criminal, evildoer, offender 9 miscreant, reprobate, scoundrel, wrongdoer 10 blackguard, lawbreaker

maleficent
4 evil, vile 5 toxic 6 malign, sinful,
wicked 7 baleful, baneful, beastly,
harmful, noxious, vicious 8 damnable, sinister, virulent 9 execrable,
injurious, nefarious, repugnant

10 pernicious, villainous 11 destructive

malevolence
4 evil 5 spite 6 grudge, malice, spleen 7 ill will 9 hostility, malignity 12 spitefulness 13 maliciousness

malevolent
4 evil 6 malign, wicked 7 baleful, hateful, hurtful, vicious 8 sinister, spiteful, venomous 9 injurious, malicious, malignant, poisonous

malfunction
6 glitch 7 misfire

Mali
capital: 6 Bamako
city: 5 Mopti, Ségou 7 Sikasso 8 Timbuktu 10 Tombouctou
desert: 6 Sahara
former name: 11 French Sudan
language: 6 French
monetary unit: 5 franc
neighbor: 5 Niger 6 Guinea 7 Algeria, Senegal 10 Ivory Coast, Mauritania 11 Burkina Faso
river: 5 Niger

malice
4 bile, hate 5 spite, venom 6 animus, enmity, grudge, hatred, poison, spleen 7 ill will 8 meanness 9 animosity, antipathy 10 bitterness, resentment 11 hatefulness, malevolence 12 spitefulness 13 invidiousness

malicious
4 evil, mean 5 nasty, petty 6 wicked 7 baneful, hateful, heinous, jealous 8 spiteful, vengeful, venomous, virulent 9 poisonous, poison-pen, rancorous 10 malevolent

maliciousness
see **malevolence**

malign
4 evil, soil 5 abuse, decry, libel, smear, stain, sully, taint 6 befoul, defame, defile, revile, smirch, vilify, wicked 7 asperse, baleful, baneful, blacken, detract, hateful, hostile, noxious, slander, tarnish, traduce, vicious 8 besmirch, derogate,

inimical, sinister, spiteful, tear down, virulent 9 denigrate, disparage, injurious, rancorous 10 calumniate, depreciate, maleficent, malevolent, pernicious, scandalize, vituperate 11 deleterious, opprobiate 12 antagonistic, antipathetic

malignant
4 evil 5 fatal 6 deadly, lethal, wicked 7 baleful, hateful, vicious 8 devilish, fiendish, spiteful 9 injurious, rancorous 10 diabolical, malevolent

malison
5 curse 8 anathema 11 commination, imprecation, malediction

mall
4 lane 5 alley, plaza, strip 7 passage 9 concourse, esplanade, promenade 10 passageway 11 median strip

malleable
6 pliant, supple 7 ductile, plastic, pliable 8 flexible 9 adaptable

mallet
6 hammer

malodorous
4 foul, gamy, rank 5 fetid, fuggy, funky, fusty, musty, stale 6 frowsy, putrid, rancid, rotten, smelly, stinky 7 noisome, noxious, reeking, spoiled 8 mephitic, stinking 9 offensive 10 nauseating 11 ill-smelling 12 pestilential

Malta
capital: 8 Valletta
city: 5 Qormi 10 Birkirkara
island: 4 Gozo 6 Comino
language: 6 French 7 Maltese
monetary unit: 4 lira
sea: 13 Mediterranean

Maltese Falcon, The
actor: 5 Astor (Mary), Lorre (Peter) 6 Bogart (Humphrey) 11 Greenstreet (Sydney)
author: 7 Hammett (Dashiell)
detective: 5 Spade (Sam)
director: 6 Huston (John)

maltreat
5 abuse 6 ill-use, misuse, molest

mama

4 dame, doll, wife 5 broad, femme, hussy, madam, woman 6 matron, mother

Mamet play

7 Oleanna 14 Boston Marriage 15 American Buffalo 17 Glengarry Glen Ross

mammal

3 ass 5 camel, hippo, hyrax 6 alpaca, colugo, dassie, rabbit 7 primate 8 elephant 12 hippopotamus
African: 5 okapi, zebra 8 aardvark, aardwolf
aquatic: 6 dugong, sea cow 7 cowfish, manatee, narwhal, platypi (plural) 8 cetacean, platypus, porpoise, sirenian
arboreal: 5 lemur 6 sifaka 7 opossum 8 kinkajou
Australian: 5 koala 8 kangaroo
burrowing: 8 starnose
carnivorous: 3 cat, dog, fox 4 bear, lion, mink, seal, wolf 5 genet, hyena, otter, panda, ratel, sable, tiger 6 badger, grison, marten, racoon, walrus 7 linsang, polecat, raccoon 8 mongoose
catlike: 5 civet
doglike: 6 jackal
extinct: 6 quagga 8 mastodon, stegodon
feline: 4 lion 5 tiger, tigon 6 ocelot, tiglon 7 leopard, lioness, tigress
flying: 3 bat
gnawing: 3 rat 6 beaver, rodent 8 squirrel
goatlike: 4 tahr 5 takin
harelike: 5 hyrax 7 hyraces (plural)
hoofed: 3 cow, pig 4 deer, goat, oxen (plural) 5 camel, sheep, tapir 6 alpaca 7 peccary 8 ruminant, ungulate 12 hippopotamus
horned: 4 goat
insect-eating: 4 mole 5 shrew 6 tenrec 8 hedgehog
long-necked: 7 giraffe
marine: 4 orca, seal 6 walrus 7 dolphin, grampus
marsupial: 9 bandicoot
nocturnal: 6 wombat
raccoon-like: 10 cacomistle
ruminant: 4 deer 5 llama, moose, sheep 6 vicuña
small: 4 pika 8 hedgehog, hedgepig
South American: 7 guanaco
toothless: 5 sloth 8 edentate, pangolin 9 armadillo
tropical: 5 coati
unweaned: 8 suckling
with flippers: 8 pinniped
wolflike: 5 hyena

mammon

4 pelf 5 lucre 6 riches, wealth 8 treasure 9 abundance, affluence 10 prosperity 11 possessions

mammoth

4 huge, vast 5 giant, jumbo 6 mighty 7 immense, massive, monster, titanic 8 colossal, enormous, gigantic 9 leviathan, monstrous 10 gargantuan, mastodonic, monumental 11 elephantine

man

3 guy 4 buck, chap, cuss, dude, gent 5 being, bloke 6 fellow, mister, mortal, person 7 husband 8 creature, paramour 9 boyfriend, mortality, personage 10 individual 11 Homo sapiens
castrated: 6 eunuch
combining form: 4 andr 5 andro, homin 6 homini
French: 5 homme
Italian: 4 uomo
Latin: 3 vir 4 homo
old: 6 codger, geezer
Spanish: 6 hombre
Yiddish: 6 mensch
young: 3 boy, lad 6 shaver 9 stripling

manage

3 run 4 cope, fare, head, keep 5 get by, get on, guide, shift 6 afford, direct, effect, govern, handle 7 achieve, carry on, conduct, control, execute, finagle, operate, oversee, succeed 8 carry out, contrive, cope with, deal with, dominate, engineer, get along, maintain 9 cultivate,

supervise **10** accomplish, administer, bring about **11** superintend

manageable
6 docile **8** amenable, bearable, biddable, passable **9** agreeable, compliant, endurable, tractable **10** responsive **11** cooperative, supportable, sustainable **13** accommodating

management
4 care **5** brass **6** charge **7** conduct, control, running **8** guidance, handling **9** direction, oversight **10** conducting **11** front office, supervising, supervision

manager
4 boss, exec **6** gerent **7** handler, officer **8** director, official, overseer, producer **9** conductor, executive **10** impresario, supervisor **13** administrator
museum: **7** curator

mañana
7 someday **8** sometime, tomorrow

Man and Superman author
4 Shaw (George Bernard)

Manassas battle
7 Bull Run

Manasseh, Manasses
brother: **7** Ephraim
father: **6** Hashum, Joseph **8** Hezekiah **10** Pahathmoab
grandfather: **5** Jacob
grandson: **6** Gilead
mother: **7** Asenath
son: **6** Machir

man-at-arms
7 fighter, soldier, warrior **10** serviceman

Mandalay author
7 Kipling (Rudyard)

mandarin
5 elder **6** orange **8** official **9** tangerine **10** bureaucrat, panjandrum

mandate
4 fiat, word **5** edict, order, ukase

6 behest, charge, decree **7** bidding, command, dictate **9** authority, directive **10** imperative, injunction **13** authorization

mandatory
6 forced **7** binding **8** required **9** de rigueur, necessary, requisite **10** compulsory, imperative, obligatory **11** involuntary

mandible
3 jaw **8** lower jaw

man-eater
4 lion, ogre **5** shark, tiger **8** cannibal **13** mackerel shark

Manette's daughter
5 Lucie

maneuver
3 ply **4** move, plan, plot, ploy, step **5** feint, trick, wield **6** design, device, gambit, handle, jockey, scheme, tactic, wangle **7** exploit, finagle, finesse **8** artifice, démarche, engineer, exercise, intrigue, movement, navigate **9** machinate, procedure, stratagem **10** manipulate, proceeding, subterfuge **11** contrivance, machination **12** manipulation

maneuvering room
8 latitude

Man for All Seasons, A
author: **4** Bolt (Robert)
subject: **4** More (Thomas)

manganese
ore: **10** pyrolusite

manger
4 rack **6** cratch, feeder, trough

mangle
3 mar **4** iron, maim, maul **5** press **6** damage, deface, deform, impair, injure **7** butcher, contort, distort **8** lacerate, mutilate **9** disfigure

mangy
5 seedy **6** ragtag, shabby **7** scruffy, squalid **8** decrepit, tattered **9** motheaten **10** down-at-heel, threadbare

manhandle
5 abuse 6 batter 7 rough up 8 maltreat, mistreat 10 push around, slap around

Manhattan
building: 11 Empire State
district: 4 Soho 6 Harlem 7 Chelsea, Tribeca
entertainment district: 11 Times Square
financial district: 10 Wall Street
museum: 7 Whitney 10 Guggenheim 12 Metropolitan
opera house: 12 Metropolitan
purchaser: 6 Minuit (Peter)
river: 4 East 6 Hudson
school: 3 NYU 8 Columbia 9 Juilliard

mania
4 rage, zeal 5 craze, fancy 6 frenzy, lunacy 7 madness, passion 8 fixation, idée fixe, insanity 9 cacoëthes, obsession 10 compulsion, enthusiasm 11 infatuation

maniac
3 bug, nut 4 loon 5 fiend, freak 6 madman, psycho, zealot 7 fanatic, lunatic, nutcase 8 crackpot 9 bedlamite 10 enthusiast

manifest
4 show 5 clear, overt, plain, shown, utter, voice 6 appear, embody, evince, expose, patent, reveal 7 display, evident, evinced, exhibit, express, invoice, obvious, visible 8 apparent, distinct, evidence, palpable, proclaim, revealed 9 evidenced, incarnate, objectify, prominent 10 illustrate, noticeable, observable 11 demonstrate, exteriorize, externalize, perceptible, unambiguous

manifestation
4 show, sign 5 proof 7 display, symptom 8 epiphany 10 appearance, revelation

manifesto
4 fiat, rule, writ 5 credo, creed, edict, ukase 6 decree, dictum, gospel, notice, policy, ruling 7 mandate, statute 8 doctrine, document, platform 9 affidavit, directive, statement, testament, testimony, ultimatum 10 deposition, indictment, injunction, regulation, resolution 11 declaration 12 announcement, denunciation, notification, proclamation 13 pronouncement

manifold
7 diverse, various 8 compound, multiple, multiply, numerous 9 multiform, multiplex 10 multiphase 12 multifarious

manikin
4 runt 5 dummy, dwarf, gnome, model, pygmy 6 midget, peewee 8 Tom Thumb 10 homunculus

Manila
founder: 7 Legazpi (Miguel López de)
site: 11 Phillipines
victor: 5 Dewey (George)

manipulate
3 ply, rig 4 play 5 steer, swing, wield 6 direct, doctor, handle, jockey, juggle, manage 7 beguile, conduct, control, exploit, finagle, finesse, massage 8 engineer, maneuver 9 machinate 10 tamper with

Man, Isle of
capital: 7 Douglas
cat: 4 Manx
possession of: 7 Britain
sea: 5 Irish

Manitoba
capital: 8 Winnipeg
lake: 8 Winnipeg 12 Winnipegosis
mountain: 5 Baldy
provincial flower: 13 prairie crocus
river: 6 Nelson 9 Churchill

mankind
6 humans, people 8 humanity 11 Homo sapiens

manlike
4 male 6 virile 8 hominoid, humanoid 9 masculine 10 anthropoid

manly
4 male 5 macho 6 virile 9 masculine

man-made
9 synthetic 10 artificial, factitious
object: 8 artefact, artifact

Mann character
6 Joseph 10 Aschenbach (Gustav von), Felix Krull 11 Hans Castorp, Tonio Kröger

manner
3 air, use, way 4 form, kind, look, mien, mode, sort, vein, wont 5 habit, modus, style, usage 6 aspect, custom, method 7 bearing, conduct, fashion, p's and q's 8 behavior, demeanor, habitude, practice, presence 9 demeanour, etiquette, technique 10 consuetude, deportment 11 affectation, comportment, peculiarity 12 idiosyncrasy

mannered
7 stilted 8 affected 10 artificial 13 self-conscious

mannerism
3 tic 4 pose 5 quirk 10 preciosity 11 affectation, peculiarity, singularity 12 eccentricity, idiosyncrasy 13 artificiality

mannerless
4 rude 6 coarse 7 boorish, ill-bred, uncivil, uncouth 8 impolite 12 discourteous

mannerly
5 civil 6 polite 7 genteel, refined 8 decorous, gracious, well-bred 9 civilized, courteous 10 respectful

Manon composer
8 Massenet (Jules)

Manon Lescaut
author: 7 Prévost (Abbé)
composer: 7 Puccini (Giacomo) 8 Massenet (Jules)
lover: 9 des Grieux

manor
5 villa 6 estate, quinta 7 château, demesne 12 landed estate

manservant
5 valet 6 butler

mansion
4 hall 5 villa 6 palace 7 château

manslayer
6 killer 8 homicide, murderer

manta
3 ray 5 cloak, cloth, shawl 7 blanket

manteau
4 coat, robe, wrap 5 cloak 6 capote, mantle, tabard

mantic
5 vatic 7 Delphic, fatidic 8 Delphian, oracular 9 prophetic, sibylline, vaticinal 10 divinatory

mantilla
4 cape, wrap 5 cloak, fichu, scarf, shawl

mantle
4 cope, glow, pink, robe, rose 5 blush, cloak, color, cover, flush, rouge 6 capote, casing, pinken, redden 7 crimson

man-to-man
4 open 5 frank, plain 6 candid, direct, honest 10 forthright, unreserved 11 openhearted

mantra
5 chant, motto 6 prayer, slogan 9 watchword 10 invocation 11 incantation

manual
4 text 5 guide 6 primer 8 Baedeker, handbook, hornbook, textbook 9 guidebook, vade mecum 10 compendium 11 abecedarium, enchiridion
religious: 9 catechism
worker: 6 menial 7 laborer

manufacture
4 form, make 6 create, invent 7 fashion, produce 8 assemble 9 fabricate 11 put together

manumit
4 free 6 unbind 7 release, set free, unchain 8 liberate 9 unshackle 10 emancipate

manure

4 dung 6 ordure 7 excreta 9 excrement 10 fertilizer

manuscript

4 hand 6 scrawl 8 longhand 9 autograph 10 penmanship 11 calligraphy, handwriting
ancient: 5 codex 6 scroll 7 codices (plural)
red part: 6 rubric

Man Without a Country, The

author: 4 Hale (Edward Everett)
character: 5 Nolan

many

5 scads 6 divers, legion, myriad, sundry 7 copious, diverse, umpteen, various 8 abundant, manifold, multiple, numerous 9 abounding, bounteous, bountiful, countless, multitude, plentiful 12 multifarious 13 multitudinous
combining form: 4 poly 5 multi, pluri

many-sided

7 diverse 8 all-round, talented 9 all-around, versatile 10 variegated 11 diversified 12 multifaceted, multifarious 13 comprehensive

Mao's successor

3 Hua (Guofeng, Kuo-feng) 4 Deng (Xiaoping), Teng (Hsiao-p'ing)

map

4 plan, plat 5 chart, draft, globe, graph 6 design, lay out, set out, sketch, survey 7 arrange, diagram, drawing, outline, tracing 9 delineate
collection: 5 atlas
line: 6 isobar 7 contour, isogram, isohyet 8 isogloss, isogonic, isopleth, isotherm
maker: 12 cartographer
making: 11 cartography

maple

genus: 4 Acer
product: 5 syrup
type: 3 red 5 sugar 8 box elder

map projection

5 conic 8 Mercator 9 polyconic
10 sinusoidal 12 orthographic
13 stereographic

maquillage

6 makeup

mar

4 ding, harm, hurt, scar, warp 5 spoil, stain 6 bruise, damage, deface, deform, impair, injure 7 blemish, scratch, tarnish, vitiate 9 disfigure

marabou

5 stork

Marat/Sade author

5 Weiss (Peter)

Marat, Jean-Paul

colleague: 6 Danton (Georges)
11 Robespierre (Maximilien)
slayer: 6 Corday (Charlotte)

maraud

4 loot, raid, sack 5 foray, harry 6 harass, ravage, ravish 7 despoil, pillage, plunder, ransack

marauder

6 bandit, pirate 7 brigand, spoiler, wrecker 9 buccaneer, desperado 10 freebooter

marble

3 mib, mig, taw 4 immy, migg 5 agate, aggie, alley, rance 6 blotch, miggle, mottle, streak 7 cipolin, glassie, steelie 9 limestone

marbled

6 veined 7 dappled, flecked, mottled 8 speckled, streaked

Marble Faun, The

author: 9 Hawthorne (Nathaniel)
character: 5 Hilda 6 Kenyon, Miriam 9 Donatello
setting: 4 Rome

marcel

4 wave

march

3 hem, rim 4 abut, file, line 5 skirt 6 adjoin, border, parade 7 advance, headway, proceed 8 anabasis, boundary, frontier, outlands, progress, traverse 9 periphery 10 borderland

March
date: 4 ides
mother: 6 Marmee
sisters: 3 Amy, Meg 4 Beth

March Hare creator
7 Carroll (Lewis)

March King
5 Sousa (John Philip)

Mardi Gras
8 carnival 10 Fat Tuesday
city: 10 New Orleans

Marduk
city: 7 Babylon
consort: 8 Zarbanit, Zarpanit
victim: 5 Kingu 6 Tiamat

mare
3 sea 5 horse 6 equine

mare's nest
3 con, din 4 hoax, scam 5 babel,
cheat, fraud, put-on, spoof 6 bedlam, clamor, hubbub, humbug, racket,
ruckus, tumult, uproar 7 swindle,
turmoil 8 brouhaha, flimflam, illusion
9 confusion, imposture 10 hullabaloo 11 pandemonium

margarine
4 oleo

margin
3 hem, rim 4 brim, edge, join, line,
play, room, side 5 bound, brink,
frame, scope, shore, skirt, verge
6 border, fringe, leeway 7 minimum,
outline, selvage 8 boundary, latitude, selvedge, surround, trimming
9 elbowroom, perimeter, periphery
13 circumference
tiny: 4 hair

marginal
5 minor 7 limited, minimal 9 bordering 10 borderline, negligible,
peripheral, subsidiary 13 insignificant

Marguerite's lover
5 Faust

Maria ____
5 Elena 7 Stuarda

Marianas
discoverer: 8 Magellan (Ferdinand)
island: 4 Guam, Rota 5 Pagan
6 Guguan, Saipan, Tinian 7 Agrihan,
Aguijan

marijuana
3 pot 4 hash, hemp, weed 5 bhang,
grass 6 reefer 7 hashish 8 cannabis

marina
4 dock, pier, quay 5 basin, berth,
wharf 8 boatyard

marinate
4 soak 5 steep 6 drench, pickle
7 immerse 8 macerate

marine
5 naval 7 abyssal, aquatic, deep-
sea, oceanic, pelagic 8 nautical,
seagoing 9 seafaring, thalassic
10 oceangoing 12 hydrographic
13 oceanographic
crustacean: 6 shrimp 7 lobster
8 barnacle
deposit: 5 coral
plant: 4 kelp, nori 5 dulse 6 wakame
7 seaweed

mariner
3 gob, tar 4 jack, salt, swab 5 limey
6 hearty, rating, sailor, sea dog,
seaman 7 jack-tar, old salt, swabbie
8 seafarer 9 sailorman, shellback,
tarpaulin 10 bluejacket

marital
6 wedded 7 married, nuptial, spousal
8 conjugal, hymeneal 9 connubial

maritime
7 oceanic, pelagic 8 nautical 9 thalassic 12 navigational

mark
3 aim, jot, sap 4 butt, dupe, fool,
goal, gull, heed, look, nick, note,
pick, show, sign, view 5 blaze,
bound, brand, chart, chump, elect,
grade, label, notch, stamp, token,
trait 6 behold, choose, denote,
evince, lay off, notice, object, opt for,
rating, record, select, sucker, target,
victim, virtue 7 betoken, delimit,
discern, exhibit, fall guy, feature,

gudgeon, indicia, initial, measure, observe, qualify, scratch, signify, symptom **8** function, indicate, perceive, register **9** attribute, character, designate, objective, single out **10** indication **11** differentia, distinction, distinguish **12** characterize
distinctive: 7 indicia **8** indicium
identifying: 4 logo, seal **6** emblem, signet, symbol **8** colophon, logotype
of insertion: 5 caret
of omission: 8 ellipsis **10** apostrophe
over a vowel: 5 breve **6** accent, macron
over n: 5 tilde
punctuation: 4 dash **5** brace, colon, comma, slant, slash **6** hyphen, period **7** bracket, solidus **9** backslash, guillemet, semicolon **10** apostrophe
under a letter: 7 cedilla

Mark
6 Gospel
cousin: 8 Barnabas
mother: 4 Mary

mark down
3 cut **4** pare **5** shave, slash **6** reduce **7** devalue **8** discount **9** devaluate **10** depreciate, undervalue

marked
5 noted **6** patent, signal **7** evident, notable, obvious, pointed, salient **8** distinct, manifest, striking **9** arresting, prominent **10** noticeable, remarkable **11** conspicuous, outstanding **12** considerable **13** distinguished
man: 4 Cain

market
4 fair, mall, sell, shop, vend **5** store **6** bazaar, outlet, retail **8** emporium, exchange, showroom **9** advertise, traffic in, wholesale **11** merchandise
kind: 4 flea **5** money, stock

marketable
5 sound **7** salable **8** vendible **10** commercial

marketplace
4 mall, souk **5** agora **6** bazaar, rialto **8** emporium

marksman
4 shot **7** deadeye, shooter **12** sharpshooter

marl
4 clay, silt

marlin
8 billfish **9** spearfish

Marlowe play
8 Edward II **9** Dr. Faustus **10** Jew of Malta (The) **11** Tamburlaine **13** Doctor Faustus

marmot
6 rodent **9** woodchuck **10** prairie dog

maroon
3 red **6** claret, desert, strand **7** abandon, crimson, forsake, isolate, outcast **8** burgundy, castaway

Marquand character
4 Gray (Charles), Moto (Mr.) **5** Apley (George), Wayde (Willis) **6** Pulham (H.M.) **7** Goodwin (Melville)

Marquis, Don
cat: 9 Mehitabel
cockroach: 5 Archy

marriage
5 match, union **6** bridal **7** nuptial, spousal, wedding, wedlock **8** coupling, espousal, monogamy, nuptials, polygamy **9** matrimony **11** conjugality **12** connubiality
combining form: 4 gamy **6** gamous
notice: 5 banns
outside a group: 7 exogamy
within a group: 8 endogamy

marriageable
6 nubile **8** eligible

marriage broker
9 go-between **10** matchmaker

Marriage of Figaro composer
6 Mozart (Wolfgang Amadeus)

marrow
4 core, meat, pith, soul 5 heart, stuff
6 kernel 7 essence 12 quintessence

marry
3 tie, wed 4 join, link, mate, wive,
yoke 5 hitch, merge, unite 6 couple,
splice, spouse 7 combine, conjoin,
espouse 9 conjugate

Mars
4 Ares 6 planet
lover: 5 Venus
mission: 6 Viking 7 Mariner
10 Pathfinder
moon: 6 Deimos, Phobos
relating to: 7 martian
(see also **Ares**)

Marseillaise composer
13 Rouget de Lisle (Claude-Joseph)

marsh
3 bog, fen 4 mire, ooze, quag
5 bayou, glade, swale, swamp 6 morass, muskeg, slough 7 wetland
8 quagmire 9 swampland

marshal
5 align, array, guide, order, rally,
usher 6 deploy, direct, escort,
muster 7 arrange, officer, round up
8 assemble, mobilize, organize,
shepherd 9 methodize, systemize

Marshall Islands
atoll: 6 Bikini 8 Enewetak 9 Kwajalein
capital: 6 Majuro
ethnic group: 11 Micronesian
island chain: 5 Ralik, Ratak 6 Sunset 7 Sunrise
language: 7 English 11 Marshallese
monetary unit: 6 dollar

marsupial
5 koala 6 possum, wombat 7 opossum 8 kangaroo 9 bandicoot

marten
6 fisher, weasel

Martha
brother: 7 Lazarus
sister: 4 Mary

martial
7 warlike 8 militant, military, spirited
9 bellicose, combative, soldierly
11 belligerent 12 militaristic

martial art
4 judo 5 kendo 6 aikido, karate,
kung fu, tai chi 7 shaolin 8 capoeira,
jiujitsu 9 tae kwon do 11 tai chi
chuan
school: 4 dojo

Martial's forte
7 epigram

Martin Chuzzlewit author
7 Dickens (Charles)

Martinique
capital: 12 Fort-de-France
department of: 6 France
discoverer: 8 Columbus (Christopher)
island group: 8 Windward
location: 10 West Indies
neighbor: 8 Dominica 10 Saint
Lucia
volcano: 5 Pelée

martyr
4 Paul, rack 5 Agnes, Alban, James,
Peter, saint, wring 6 George, harrow,
Justin 7 afflict, agonize, Clement,
crucify, Cyprian, Stephen, torment,
torture 8 Ignatius, Lawrence, Poly-
carp, sufferer 9 Joan of Arc, Sebastian 10 excruciate, Thomas More
Protestant: 6 Ridley (Nicholas)
7 Cranmer (Thomas), Latimer (Hugh)

marvel
4 gape 6 wonder 7 miracle, portent,
prodigy, stunner 9 curiosity, sensation 10 phenomenon 12 astonishment

marvelous
5 super, swell 6 divine 7 amazing,
awesome, ripping 8 glorious, striking, stunning, superior, terrific,
wondrous 9 excellent, wonderful
10 astounding, incredible, miraculous, phenomenal, prodigious, remarkable, staggering, stupendous,

Marx brother

surprising **11** astonishing, exceptional, sensational, spectacular **12** awe-inspiring, supernatural **13** extraordinary

Marx brother
5 Chico, Harpo, Zeppo **7** Groucho

Marxist
9 socialist **9** communist

Marx, Karl
book: **7** Kapital (Das)
collaborator: **6** Engels (Friedrich)

Mary
husband: **6** Clopas, Joseph **8** Alphaeus
kinswoman: **9** Elisabeth
son: **4** Mark **5** James, Jesus

Maryland
bay: **10** Chesapeake
capital: **9** Annapolis
city: **9** Baltimore, Frederick
college, university: **6** Towson **7** Goucher **9** Annapolis **12** Johns Hopkins **12** Naval Academy (U.S.)
fort: **7** McHenry
nickname: **7** Old Line (State)
river: **7** Potomac **8** Patuxent
state bird: **15** Baltimore oriole
state flower: **14** black-eyed Susan
state tree: **8** white oak

mascot
4 juju **5** charm **6** amulet, fetish, symbol **8** talisman

masculine
4 male **5** macho, manly **6** manful, virile **7** manlike

masculinity
8 machismo, virility **9** manliness

mash
4 pulp **5** crush, smash **6** squish **8** macerate **9** pulverize

masher
4 wolf **5** flirt **6** chaser **7** Don Juan, seducer **8** Casanova **9** ladies' man, womanizer **10** lady-killer **11** philanderer

mash note
10 billet-doux, love letter

mask
4 hide, pose, sham, veil **5** cover, front, guard, guise, visor **6** facade, screen, vizard **7** dress up, frisket, pretext **8** coloring, disguise, pretense **9** dissemble, semblance **10** appearance, camouflage, false front, simulation **11** dissimulate **13** dissimulation

masonry
9 brickwork, stonework
in a frame: **7** nogging

masquerade
4 pose **6** facade **7** costume, posture **8** carnival, disguise **10** camouflage, masked ball **11** costume ball

mass
3 lot, sum, wad **4** bank, body, bulk, clot, core, glob, heap, hill, lump, pack, peck, pile **5** clump, group, mound **6** corpus, volume **7** expanse, globule, wadding **8** assemble **9** aggregate, great deal, stockpile, substance **11** aggregation **12** conglomerate
for the dead: **7** requiem
of individuals: **3** mob **4** host **5** crowd, crush, flock, horde, swarm **6** throng **12** congregation **13** agglomeration
part: **6** proper **8** ordinary

Massachusetts
cape: **3** Ann, Cod
capital: **6** Boston
city: **6** Lowell, Quincy **9** Cambridge, Worcester **10** New Bedford **11** Springfield
college, university: **3** MIT **5** Clark, Smith, Tufts **6** Boston **7** Amherst, Berklee, Harvard **8** Brandeis, Williams **9** Hampshire, Radcliffe, Wellesley **12** Mount Holyoke, Northeastern
island: **9** Nantucket **15** Martha's Vineyard
mountain, range: **8** Greylock **9** Berkshire
nickname: **3** Bay (State) **9** Old Colony (State)
river: **11** Connecticut

state bird: 9 chickadee
state flower: 9 mayflower
state tree: 3 elm (American)

massacre
4 kill 6 mangle, murder, pogrom
7 butcher, carnage 8 butchery,
decimate, genocide, mangling,
mutilate 9 bloodbath, bloodshed,
slaughter 10 annihilate, blood purge,
decimation, mutilation 11 exterminate 12 annihilation

massage
3 rub 5 knead 7 flatter, rubdown
8 blandish 10 manipulate

Massenet opera
5 Le Cid, Manon, Sapho, Thaïs
7 Werther

massive
4 huge, vast 5 bulky, giant, jumbo,
solid 6 mighty 7 hulking, immense,
mammoth, weighty 8 colossal, cumbrous, enormous, gigantic, towering
9 humongous, monstrous 10 gargantuan, monumental, prodigious,
stupendous, tremendous 11 elephantine, mountainous

master
4 best, boss, guru, head, lick, rule,
tame 5 adept, bwana, chief, crack,
learn, ruler, sahib, tutor 6 artist,
expert, genius, honcho, leader,
subdue, victor 7 captain, conquer,
headman, maestro, padrone, prevail,
skilled, triumph 8 dominant, dominate, employer, governor, overcome,
overlord, overseer, regulate, skeleton, skillful, superior, surmount,
virtuoso 9 authority, chieftain,
conqueror, dominator, paramount,
principal, sovereign 10 proficient
11 predominant

masterful
4 deft 5 adept, bossy 6 adroit,
expert 7 skilled 8 despotic, skillful
9 imperious 10 autocratic, high-
handed, proficient, tyrannical 11 dictatorial, domineering, magisterial,
overbearing 13 authoritarian, authoritative, high-and-mighty

masterly
5 adept, crack 6 adroit, expert
7 skilled 8 skillful 9 dexterous
10 proficient 11 crackerjack 12 accomplished

Master of Ballantrae, The
6 Durrie
author: 9 Stevenson (Robert
Louis)

masterpiece
7 classic 10 magnum opus 11 chef
d'oeuvre, tour de force

mastery
5 knack, skill 7 ability, command,
control, know-how, prowess 8 dominion 9 authority, expertise 10 ascendancy, domination, expertness,
virtuosity 11 proficiency, superiority

masticate
4 chaw, chew, pulp 5 champ, chomp,
crush, munch 6 crunch 7 scrunch
8 macerate, ruminate 9 break down

mat
3 rug 4 felt 6 border, carpet

matador
6 torero 8 toreador 11 bullfighter
adjunct: 6 muleta
move: 4 pase 5 faena 8 veronica

Mata Hari
3 spy

match
3 pit 4 bout, game, like, meet, peer,
suit, twin 5 array, equal, liken, rival,
touch, union 6 double, equate,
oppose 7 compare, compeer, contest, counter, opposer, paragon, play
off 8 alliance, analogue, marriage,
opponent, parallel 9 adversary,
correlate, duplicate, encounter,
measure up, partake of 10 antagonist, complement, coordinate,
engagement, equivalent, reciprocal,
supplement, tournament 11 counterpart 12 correspond to 13 correspondent, harmonize with
a bet: 3 see
friction: 7 lucifer

matchless

6 unique 7 supreme 8 peerless, singular 9 nonpareil, unequaled, unrivaled 10 inimitable 12 incomparable, unparalleled

matchmaker

see **marriage broker**

mate

3 pal, tie, wed 4 chum, pair, twin 5 amigo, breed, buddy, crony, equal, hitch, marry 6 cohort, couple, double, fellow, friend, helper, splice, spouse 7 compeer, comrade, consort, partner 8 confrere, sidekick 9 associate, companion, copartner, duplicate, procreate 10 complement, equivalent, reciprocal 11 concomitant

maté

3 tea 5 holly 8 beverage

mater

3 mom, mum 6 mother 9 matriarch

_____ mater

4 alma

material

4 real, true 5 cloth, stuff 6 actual, fabric, matter, object 7 earthly, element, germane, worldly 8 apposite, palpable, physical, relevant, sensible, tangible 9 component, corporeal, equipment, essential, important, objective, pertinent, substance 10 applicable, individual, ingredient, meaningful, phenomenal 11 appreciable, constituent, fundamental, perceptible, significant, substantial 12 considerable 13 consequential

building: 5 adobe, brick 6 stucco 7 lagging, plaster, plywood, shingle 8 concrete

materialistic

7 secular, worldly 11 acquisitive

materialize

4 loom, rise 5 arise, issue, reify 6 appear, embody, emerge, evolve, show up, typify 7 develop, surface 8 manifest 9 come about, incarnate, objectify, take shape 11 exteriorize 12 substantiate

matériel

4 gear 5 stock 8 supplies 9 apparatus, equipment, machinery 10 provisions 13 accouterments, accoutrements, paraphernalia

maternal

8 motherly

matey

5 pally, tight 6 clubby 7 affable 8 amicable, familiar, friendly, intimate, sociable 9 congenial

mathematician

American: 5 Wiles (Andrew) 6 Peirce (Charles S.), Veblen (Oswald), Wiener (Norbert)
Austrian: 5 Gödel (Kurt)
British: 6 Stokes (George)
Dutch: 7 Huygens (Christiaan)
English: 6 Newton (Isaac), Taylor (Brook), Turing (Alan), Wallis (John) 7 Pearson (Karl), Russell (Bertrand) 8 Hamilton (James Rowan) 9 Sylvester (James Joseph), Whitehead (Alfred North, Henry)
French: 5 Borel (Emile), Comte (Auguste), Viète (François) 6 Galois (Evariste), Pascal (Blaise), Picard (Charles-Emile) 7 Fourier (Jean-Baptiste), Laplace (Marquis de), Vernier (Pierre) 8 Painlevé (Paul), Poincaré (Jules-Henri) 9 Descartes (René)
German: 5 Gauss (Carl), Wolff (Freiherr von) 6 Staudt (Karl von) 7 Leibniz (Gottfried Wilhelm), Riemann (Georg) 11 Weierstrass (Karl)
Greek: 6 Euclid 10 Archimedes, Pythagoras
Hungarian: 5 Erdos (Paul)
Italian: 8 Volterra (Vito) 10 Torricelli (Evangelista)
Norwegian: 7 Stormer (Fredrik)
Russian: 11 Lobachevsky (Nikolay)
Scottish: 4 Tait (Peter) 6 Napier (John) 8 Stirling (James)
Swiss: 5 Euler (Leonhard), Sturm (Jacques) 7 Steiner (Jakob)

mathematics

branch: 4 trig 7 algebra 8 calculus, geometry, topology 10 arithmetic, statistics 12 trigonometry
proven statement in: 7 theorem

_____ Mather
6 Cotton 7 Richard 8 Increase

matriarch
4 dame 6 mother 7 dowager
10 grande dame

matriculate
4 join 5 enter 6 enroll, sign on
8 register

matrimonial
6 bridal, wedded 7 marital, married,
nuptial, spousal 8 conjugal, hymeneal 9 connubial 11 epithalamic

matrimony
7 wedlock 8 marriage 11 conjugality
12 connubiality

matrix
3 die, net, web 4 grid, mesh 5 array
6 cradle, gangue 7 complex, network 10 groundmass, truth table

matron
4 dame 7 dowager 8 chaperon
9 chaperone 10 grande dame

Mattathias
father: 5 Simon 6 Ananos 7 Absalom, Boethus 10 Theophilus
son: 8 Josephus

matter
4 body, core, gist, meat, pith, text
5 being, cause, order, point, sense,
stuff, theme, thing, topic, value,
weigh 6 affair, amount, burden,
entity, import, object 7 concern,
signify, subject 8 argument, material
9 grievance, magnitude, substance
11 constituent 12 circumstance

matter-of-fact
3 dry 4 plain, prose, prosy, sober,
stoic 6 stolid 7 prosaic 9 impassive,
objective, practical, pragmatic, realistic 10 hard-boiled, hardheaded,
impersonal, phlegmatic, unaffected
11 cold-blooded, down-to-earth,
emotionless 13 unimpassioned,
unsentimental

mattress
3 pad 4 sack
case: 4 tick
fabric: 7 ticking
straw: 6 pallet

mature
3 age, due 4 grow, ripe 5 adult,
grown, owing, ready, ripen 6 flower,
grow up, mellow, season, unpaid
7 advance, blossom, decline, develop, grown-up, overdue, payable,
ripened 8 progress 9 developed,
full-blown, full-grown 11 full-fledged

maudlin
5 gushy, mushy, silly, sappy, soppy
6 slushy, sticky 7 cloying, gushing,
mawkish 8 bathetic 11 sentimental,
tear-jerking

Maugham character
4 Kear, Liza 5 Carey, Rosie, Sadie
7 Mildred 8 Ashenden, Craddock
10 Strickland

maul
4 bang, bash, beat, club, drub, flog,
whip 5 abuse, flail, pound 6 batter,
bruise, buffet, cudgel, hammer,
injure, mangle, molest, pummel,
sledge, thrash 7 clobber, rough
up 8 bludgeon, lambaste, maltreat
9 manhandle

Mauna _____
3 Kea, Loa

maunder
3 bat, gad 4 rove 5 drift, mooch,
range 6 mumble, mutter, ramble,
wander 7 blather, digress, traipse
8 divagate

Mauritania
capital: 10 Nouakchott
desert: 6 Sahara
language: 5 Wolof 6 Arabic, Fulani
7 Soninke
monetary unit: 7 ouguiya
neighbor: 4 Mali 6 Guinea 7 Senegal 7 Algeria 13 Western Sahara
river: 7 Senegal

Mauritius
capital: 9 Port Louis
island group: 9 Mascarene
language: 6 Creole 7 English
monetary unit: 5 rupee

Maurois biographee
4 Hugo (Victor), Sand (George)
5 Byron (Lord), Dumas (Alexandre)

mauve

6 Balzac (Honoré de), Proust (Marcel) 7 Shelley (Percy Bysshe) 8 Disraeli (Benjamin)

mauve

5 lilac 6 purple, violet

maven

3 ace 4 buff, whiz 5 adept, freak, shark 6 addict, expert, master, savant 7 devotee, fanatic, hotshot 8 virtuoso 9 authority 10 enthusiast 11 connoisseur

maverick

5 stray 7 heretic 8 unmarked 9 dissident, unbranded 10 iconoclast 11 independent 13 nonconformist

maw

4 crop 5 chasm, mouth 6 cavity, gullet 7 stomach

mawkish

5 gushy, mushy, sappy, soppy 6 sloppy, slushy, sticky, syrupy 7 cloying, gushing, insipid, maudlin 8 bathetic, romantic 9 schmaltzy, sickening 10 lovey-dovey, nauseating 11 sentimental, tear-jerking

maxilla

3 jaw 4 bone

maxim

3 law, saw 4 rule 5 adage, axiom, gnome, moral, motto, tenet, truth 6 byword, dictum, saying, truism 7 precept, proverb, theorem 8 aphorism, apothegm 9 platitude, prescript, principle 11 commonplace

maximal

3 top 6 utmost 7 highest, largest, supreme, topmost 8 complete, greatest, ultimate 9 paramount

maximum

3 top 6 utmost 7 highest, largest, supreme, topmost 8 extremum, greatest, ultimate 9 paramount

may

5 might, shrub 6 spirea 8 hawthorn

maybe

7 perhaps 8 possibly 9 perchance 11 conceivably, uncertainty

Mayflower

document: 7 Compact
passengers: 8 Pilgrims

mayhem

4 maim, riot 5 chaos, havoc 7 cripple, dislimb 8 mutilate 9 dismember 10 mutilation

mayor

11 burgomaster
Chicago (former): 5 Daley (Richard)
New York (former): 4 Koch (Edward) 6 Walker (Jimmy) 7 Lindsay (John) 8 Giuliani (Rudolph) 9 La Guardia (Fiorello)
Spanish: 7 alcalde

Mayor of Casterbridge, The

author: 5 Hardy (Thomas)
character: 8 Henchard (Michael)

maze

3 web 4 knot, mesh 5 skein, snarl 6 jungle, morass, tangle 7 confuse, network, perplex 8 bewilder, mishmash 9 labyrinth

Mazel _____!

3 tov

McCarthy novel

8 Crossing (The) 16 Cities of the Plain 18 All the Pretty Horses

McCullers, Carson

novel: 18 Ballad of the Sad Cafe (The) 18 Member of the Wedding (The) 20 Heart Is a Lonely Hunter (The) 23 Reflections in a Golden Eye

McCullough novel

10 Thorn Birds (The)

McMurtry novel

12 Buffalo Girls, Lonesome Dove 14 Horseman Pass By 15 Last Picture Show (The) 17 Terms of Endearment

McTeague author

6 Norris (Frank)

MD

3 doc 6 doctor, medico 8 sawbones 9 physician

mea culpa
5 error, fault 7 apology 9 admission
10 concession, confession

meadow
3 lea, ley 5 green 7 pasture 9 grassland
historic: 9 Runnymede
low-lying: 5 haugh

meadow mushroom
6 agaric

meager
4 bare, bony, lean, mere, thin
5 gaunt, lanky, scant, short, spare
6 paltry, scanty, shabby, skimpy,
skinny, slight, sparse 7 angular,
minimum, scraggy, scrawny, scrimpy
8 exiguous, rawboned 9 deficient,
miserable 10 inadequate 12 insufficient

meal
4 chow, fare, feed, grub 5 board,
feast, lunch, snack 6 brunch, dinner,
farina, picnic, repast, spread, supper
7 high tea, nooning 8 victuals
9 breakfast, collation, refection
army: 4 mess

mealy
6 spotty, uneven 11 farinaceous

mean
3 low, mid, par 4 base, fair, hint,
norm, poor, want, wish 5 cheap,
cruel, imply, lousy, lowly, mingy,
petty, rough, small, snide, spell, tight,
weigh 6 attest, center, common,
denote, design, humble, intend,
matter, medial, medium, middle,
paltry, scummy, scurvy, shabby,
shoddy, sleazy, stingy, unwell 7 average, betoken, connote, express,
lowborn, miserly, pitiful, portend,
propose, purport, signify, suggest,
vicious 8 déclassé, indicate, inferior,
mediocre, middling, midpoint, moderate, ordinary, pitiable, plebeian,
stand for 9 designate, penurious,
represent, symbolize 10 despicable,
second-rate 11 closefisted, tightfisted 12 contemptible, intermediary,
intermediate

meander
4 roam, rove, turn, wind 5 amble,
drift, range, snake, stray, twist
6 ramble, wander 7 traipse, winding
8 vagabond 9 gallivant, labyrinth

meandering
5 snaky 7 sinuous 8 flexuous,
tortuous 10 convoluted, serpentine
11 anfractuous

meaning
3 aim 4 gist, pith 5 drift, force, point,
sense 6 effect, import, intent 7 essence, message, purport 9 intention,
substance 10 definition, denotation,
intimation 11 connotation, implication 12 significance 13 signification

meaningful
5 valid 7 pointed, serious, weighty
8 eloquent, material 9 important,
momentous 10 expressive 11 sententious, significant, substantial
13 consequential

meaningless
5 empty, inane 6 absurd, futile,
hollow 7 trivial 8 nugatory 11 nonsensical 13 insignificant

meanings
diverse: 8 polysemy
study of: 9 semantics

means
5 funds, money 6 agency, assets,
avenue, income 7 backing, capital
8 finances, holdings, property, reserves 9 apparatus, equipment,
resources, substance 10 instrument
11 wherewithal

meantime
7 interim 8 interval

measly
4 poor, puny 5 petty, scant 6 meager, meagre, paltry, scanty 7 pitiful,
trivial 8 niggling, pathetic, picayune,
piddling, trifling 9 miserable 10 picayunish 13 insignificant

measure
3 bar 4 bill, size, step, test 5 bound,
gauge, index, quota, scale, share,

shift, weigh 6 amount, bounds, degree, effort, extent, figure, ration, reckon, resort, size up, survey 7 caliper, compute, delimit, mark out, portion, stopgap 8 calliper, estimate, regulate, resource, standard 9 allotment, benchmark, calculate, calibrate, criterion, demarcate, determine, expedient, magnitude, yardstick 10 dimensions, indication, proceeding, proportion, touchstone 11 proposition 13 apportionment

area: 4 acre 7 hectare

capacity: 4 gill, peck, pint 5 liter, minim, quart 6 bushel, gallon 8 fluidram 9 fluid dram 10 fluid ounce, milliliter

cloth: 3 ell

combining form: 6 metric 8 metrical

depth: 5 plumb, sound

dry: 4 peck 6 bushel

electrical: 3 amp 4 watt 6 ampere 7 coulomb

horse height: 4 hand

interstellar space: 6 parsec

length: 3 rod 4 foot, inch, link, mile, yard 5 chain, cubit, meter 6 league 7 furlong 9 kilometer 10 centimeter

liquid: 4 gill, pint 5 minim, quart 6 gallon

mixed drinks: 6 jigger

of comparison: 8 standard

paper: 4 ream

printer's: 4 pica 5 point

radioactive decay: 8 halflife

rotation: 5 angle

strength of solution: 7 titrate

surface: 3 are

thermodynamic: 7 entropy 8 enthalpy

measured

7 regular, stately 8 metrical 9 regulated, temperate, unhurried 10 calculated, controlled, deliberate, restrained 13 proportionate

Measure for Measure

character: 6 Angelo, Juliet 7 Claudio, Mariana 8 Isabella 9 Vincentio

setting: 6 Vienna

measurement

4 area 6 degree 8 capacity, quantity 9 dimension, magnitude 11 calibration, mensuration

measure up to

3 tie 4 meet 5 equal, match, rival, touch 7 emulate 10 qualify for

measuring device

4 gage 5 buret, gauge, scale 7 burette, caliper, sextant, venturi 8 calipers 8 dipstick 9 altimeter, barometer, dosimeter, pedometer 11 tensiometer, velocimeter

meat

4 core, food, gist, pith, pork, veal 5 flesh, jerky, steak 6 thrust, upshot 7 edibles 8 victuals 9 foodstuff, provender, substance 10 provisions 11 comestibles

broth: 8 bouillon

cake: 6 búrger 9 hamburger

cured: 7 biltong

cut: 3 rib 4 loin, rump 5 chuck, flank, plate, round, shank 7 brisket, sirloin 8 rib roast 9 club steak, rump roast, short loin, short ribs 10 blade roast, flank steak, round steak, T-bone steak 12 boneless neck, pinbone steak, sirloin steak 13 blade rib roast, crosscut shank

dealer: 7 butcher

deer: 7 venison

dried: 5 jerky

fastening pin: 6 skewer

holding rod: 4 spit 10 rotisserie

juices: 5 gravy

packer: 5 Swift 6 Armour

raw: 6 gobbet

roasted: 8 barbecue

roasting shop: 10 rotisserie

seasoned: 7 sausage 8 pastrami, scrapple

sheep: 6 mutton

side: 8 sowbelly

skewered: 5 kebab, kebob

slice: 6 cutlet, rasher

small portion: 6 collop

tough part: 7 gristle

meat-eating

11 carnivorous

meathead

3 lug, oaf 4 clod, dodo, dolt, gawk,
goon, lout 5 chump, klutz, looby
6 dimwit, lubber 7 bungler, palooka
8 dumbbell, numskull 9 birdbrain,
ignoramus, lamebrain, numbskull
10 nincompoop

Mebd

husband: 6 Ailill
victim: 10 Cuchulainn

Mecca

4 goal
country: 11 Saudi Arabia
pilgrimage: 4 hadj, hajj
port: 5 Jedda, Jidda 6 Jeddah,
Jiddah
shrine: 5 Kaaba

mechanic

7 artisan 9 machinist

mechanical

4 cold 7 cursory, robotic 8 lifeless
9 automated, automatic, unfeeling
10 impersonal 11 emotionless,
instinctive, involuntary, perfunctory,
unemotional

mechanism

4 gear 5 gizmo, means, works
6 agency, doodad, jigger, medium,
widget 7 whatsit 8 dohickey 9 apparatus, appliance, procedure,
technique, thingummy 10 instrument
11 contraption, contrivance, thingamabob, thingamajig, thingumajig

medal

5 badge, honor, prize 6 reward
7 laurels 8 accolade 10 decoration
13 commemoration

meddle

3 pry 4 fool, nose 5 snoop 6 butt
in, dabble, horn in, kibitz, monkey,
putter, tamper, tinker 7 intrude,
obtrude 8 trespass 9 interfere,
interlope, intervene 10 mess around

meddler

5 snoop, yenta 7 snooper 8 busybody, intruder, kibitzer 9 buttinsky
12 troublemaker

meddlesome

4 busy, nosy 6 prying 9 intrusive,
obtrusive, officious 11 impertinent,
interfering

Medea

5 witch 9 sorceress 11 enchantress
aunt: 5 Circe
brother: 8 Absyrtus
father: 6 Aeëtes
husband: 5 Jason 6 Aegeus
sister: 5 Circe
son: 6 Medeus
victim: 6 Creusa, Glauce, Glauke

medial

3 mid 4 mean 6 center, middle
7 average, central, halfway, midmost
8 middling, moderate 10 centermost,
middlemost 11 equidistant 12 intermediary, intermediate

median

see medial

mediate

5 judge 6 broker, convey, liaise,
settle, step in, umpire 7 adjudge,
referee, resolve 8 moderate, transmit 9 arbitrate, intercede, interfere,
interpose, intervene, negotiate
10 conciliate

mediator

5 judge 6 broker, umpire 7 arbiter,
liaison, referee 9 go-between,
middleman 10 interceder, negotiator,
peacemaker 11 intercessor

medical instrument

6 needle 7 forceps, scalpel, scanner,
syringe 8 otoscope, speculum
9 endoscope 11 cardiograph,
stethoscope

medical practitioner

3 doc 5 nurse 6 doctor, intern
7 surgeon 9 physician

medicament

4 cure, pill 6 elixir, physic, remedy
7 nostrum 8 antidote, curative
10 palliative
inert: 7 placebo

medicate
4 cure, dose, drug, heal 5 treat

medicinal
8 curative, remedial, salutary, sanative 9 healthful 12 health-giving, pharmaceutic

medicine
4 cure, pill 5 bromo 6 physic, remedy 7 anodyne, nostrum 8 busulfan, poultice 11 antipyretic
bottle: 4 vial
branch: 7 surgery 8 oncology 9 neurology, pathology 10 bariatrics, cardiology, geriatrics, gynecology, nephrology, obstetrics, pediatrics, psychiatry
cathartic: 8 evacuant 9 purgative
combining form: 5 iatro 8 pharmaco
quantity of: 4 dose 6 dosage
shell: 7 capsule
soothing: 7 anodyne 8 lenitive, narcotic, sedative 9 calmative, soporific

medicine man
6 doctor, kahuna, shaman 9 curandero

medieval study
5 logic 7 grammar, trivium 8 rhetoric 10 quadrivium

mediocre
4 dull, fair, hack, so-so 6 common 7 average, fairish 8 inferior, middling, moderate, ordinary, passable 9 tolerable 10 pedestrian, uninspired 11 commonplace, indifferent 12 run-of-the-mill 13 unexceptional

meditate
4 mull, muse 5 weigh 6 intend, ponder 7 purpose, reflect, revolve 8 cogitate, consider, mull over, ruminate, turn over 9 reflect on 10 deliberate 11 contemplate

meditative
6 broody 7 pensive 8 brooding 10 reflective, ruminative, thoughtful

meditator
4 yogi

Mediterranean
11 Mare Nostrum 12 Mare Internum
coastal region: 7 Riviera
eastern shores: 6 Levant
island:
(see at **island**)
wind: 7 mistral, sirocco

medium
3 par 4 fair, mean, so-so 5 agent, organ 6 agency, métier, milieu, normal 7 ambient, average, channel, climate, culture, neutral, vehicle 8 ambience, middling, moderate, passable, standard 9 tolerable 10 atmosphere 11 clairvoyant, environment 12 run-of-the-mill
of exchange: 5 money 8 currency 11 legal tender

medley
4 brew, olio 5 combo, gumbo 6 jumble, ragout 7 farrago, mélange, mixture 8 mishmash, pastiche 9 pasticcio, patchwork, potpourri 10 assortment, hodgepodge, miscellany, salmagundi 11 gallimaufry

Medusa
6 Gorgon
father: 7 Phorcus, Phorcys
hair: 6 snakes
mother: 4 Ceto
offspring: 7 Pegasus 8 Chrysaor
sister: 6 Stheno 7 Euryale
slayer: 7 Perseus

medusa
9 jellyfish

meed
3 due 4 part 5 quota, share 6 amount, desert, ration, return, reward 7 guerdon, measure, portion 8 dividend 9 allotment, allowance 10 recompense 13 apportionment

meek
3 shy 4 mild, tame 5 lowly, timid 6 docile, gentle, humble, modest 7 patient 8 tolerant 10 submissive, unassuming 11 deferential 13 long-suffering

meerschaum
4 pipe 9 sepiolite

meet
3 apt, fit 4 face, fair, fill, find, join,
just, open, spot 5 cross, event, hit on,
match, right, touch, unite 6 answer,
chance, engage, oppose, proper,
settle, take on, useful 7 contest,
convene, fitting, fulfill, hit upon, satisfy, stumble, undergo 8 approach,
assemble, come upon, concours,
conflict, confront, converge, suitable
9 encounter, impinge on, measure up
10 congregate, provide for 11 appropriate, competition
a bet: 3 see
a need: 7 suffice
athletic: 8 gymkhana 10 tournament
by appointment: 10 rendezvous

meeting
4 moot, talk 5 tryst 6 huddle, parley,
powwow 7 session 8 assembly,
conclave, concours, congress,
junction 9 concourse, encounter,
gathering, rencontre 10 conference,
confluence, convention, rendezvous
11 competition, convocation, get-
together 12 intersection
Anglo-Saxon: 5 gemot 6 gemote
place: 5 forum
spiritual: 6 séance

Mefistofele composer
5 Boito (Arrigo)

Megaera
see **Erinyes**

megaphone
8 bullhorn 10 mouthpiece

Megara
father: 5 Creon
husband: 8 Heracles, Hercules
king: 5 Nisus

megillah
5 story 7 account

megrim
4 urge, whim 5 fancy, freak, humor
6 notion, vagary, whimsy 7 caprice,
conceit, impulse, vertigo 8 crotchet,
migraine 9 dizziness

Mehitabel
3 cat

creator: 7 Marquis (Don)
friend: 5 Archy

Mein Kampf author
6 Hitler (Adolf)

meiosis
7 litotes 12 cell division

Meissen
5 china 8 ceramics 9 porcelain

Meistersinger
5 Sachs (Hans) 9 Frauenlob

Meistersinger, Die
beloved: 3 Eva
composer: 6 Wagner (Richard)
hero: 6 Walter
mentor: 5 Sachs (Hans)

melancholia
5 gloom 6 sorrow 7 despair, sadness 9 dejection, morbidity 10 depression, desolation, gloominess
11 despondency, dolefulness

melancholic
3 low, sad 4 blue, glum 6 gloomy,
morose, triste 7 joyless 8 dejected,
downcast, mournful 9 depressed,
saddening 10 depressing, despondent, dispirited

melancholy
3 low, sad 4 blue, funk, glum 5 blues,
dumps, ennui, gloom 6 dismal,
dreary, gloomy, misery, morose,
rueful, somber, tedium, triste, woeful 7 boredom, despair, doleful,
joyless, pensive, sadness, unhappy
8 dejected, dolorous, downcast,
funereal, mournful, saddened 9 black
bile, dejection, depressed, plaintive,
saddening, sorrowful 10 depressing,
depression, despondent, dispirited,
lachrymose, lamentable, lugubrious,
reflective, thoughtful 11 despondency, unhappiness 12 heavyhearted, wretchedness

mélange
see **medley**

Melanippus
father: 7 Theseus
slayer: 10 Amphiaraus
victim: 6 Tydeus

Melchior
companion: 6 Caspar, Gaspar
9 Balthasar, Balthazar
gift: 4 gold

Melchizedek's kingdom
5 Salem

meld
3 mix **4** fuse **5** blend, merge **6** mingle
7 combine, mixture **8** compound
9 commingle, interfuse **10** amalgamate **11** intermingle

Meleager
beloved: 8 Atalanta
father: 6 Oeneus
mother: 7 Althaea
victim: 4 boar

melee
3 row **4** fray, riot **5** brawl, broil,
clash, fight **6** affray, fracas, ruckus,
rumpus **7** scuffle **8** skirmish
9 scrimmage **10** donnybrook,
free-for-all

meliorate
4 help **5** amend **6** better, soften
7 improve **8** mitigate, palliate

Mélisande's lover
7 Pelléas

melisma
7 cadenza, descant

mellifluous
5 sweet **6** dulcet, fluent, golden,
liquid, smooth **7** flowing, honeyed,
silvery **8** euphonic, soothing **10** euphonious **13** silver-tongued

mellow
3 age **4** aged, ripe **5** ripen **6** genial,
golden, grow up, mature, season,
smooth **7** honeyed, matured, ripened **8** laid-back, pleasant, seasoned **9** agreeable

melodic
5 sweet **6** dulcet **7** musical, songful,
tuneful **8** canorous, euphonic
10 euphonious

melodious
5 lyric, sweet **6** dulcet **7** musical,
songful, tuneful **8** euphonic **9** cantabile **10** euphonious

melody
3 air, lay **4** aria, song, tune **5** canto,
music, theme **6** chorus, strain,
warble **7** descant, refrain **11** tune-
fulness

melon
4 pepo **5** gourd **6** casaba, profit
8 crenshaw, honeydew, windfall
10 cantaloupe

Melpomene
see **Muse**

melt
3 run **4** flux, fuse, thaw **6** relent,
soften **7** liquefy **8** dissolve, liquesce,
unfreeze **9** disappear **10** deliquesce
down: 6 render
together: 4 fuse

Melville, Herman
character: 3 Pip **4** Ahab, Toby
5 Bembo, Chase **6** Cereno (Benito),
Jermin, Pierre **7** Fayaway, Ishmael **8** Bartleby, Queequeg, Starbuck
work: 4 Omoo **5** Mardi, Typee
6 Pierre **7** Redburn **8** Moby Dick
11 White-Jacket **12** Benito Cereno
13 Confidence-Man (The)

member
3 cut **4** part **5** piece **6** clause,
parcel **7** portion, section, segment
8 division **9** appendage, component
10 ingredient
political party: 4 Tory, Whig **7** Liberal **8** Democrat, Laborite **9** La-
bourite **10** Republican **12** Conservative
service club: 4 Lion **8** Kiwanian,
Rotarian

membrane
4 film **6** pleura **7** pleurae (plural)
bodily: 6 serosa
brain: 3 pia
diffusion through: 7 osmosis
dividing: 5 septa (plural) **6** septum
ear: 8 tympanum
enclosing: 8 indusium
thin: 6 lamina **7** lamella, laminae
(plural) **8** lamellae (plural)
wing: 8 patagium

memento
5 relic, token, trace 6 trophy 7 vestige 8 keepsake, reminder, souvenir 11 remembrance

Memnon
father: 8 Tithonus
mother: 3 Eos 6 Aurora
slayer: 8 Achilles

memoir
3 bio 4 life 5 diary 6 record, report, thesis 7 account, journal 8 anecdote 9 biography 11 confessions 12 recollection, reminiscence 13 autobiography

memoirist
7 Boswell, diarist 10 biographer

memorable
7 lasting, notable 8 historic 9 deathless, indelible, momentous, red-letter 10 noteworthy 11 significant 13 distinguished

memorandum
4 chit, note 6 minute, notice, record 7 tickler 8 notation, reminder 12 announcement

memorial
4 note 5 relic, token, trace 6 record, trophy 7 relique 8 keepsake, monument, reminder, souvenir 10 dedicatory 11 celebrative, remembrance 12 consecrative, remembrancer 13 commemoration, commemorative
mound: 5 cairn

memorial park
see **cemetery**

memorize
3 con, get 6 retain 8 remember

memory
6 recall 8 mind's eye, souvenir 9 anamnesis, awareness, flashback, retention 10 reflection 11 remembrance 12 recollection, reminiscence 13 retentiveness, retrospection
assisting: 8 mnemonic
loss: 7 amnesia

menace
4 risk 5 alarm, peril, scare 6 danger, hazard, threat 7 imperil, jeopard,

torment 8 endanger, frighten, jeopardy, threaten 9 terrorize 10 intimidate, jeopardize

ménage
4 clan 5 house 6 family 8 quarters 9 household 12 housekeeping

menagerie
3 zoo 7 mixture

mend
3 fix, sew 4 cure, darn, heal 5 patch, renew 6 cobble, doctor, look up, perk up, reform, remedy, repair, revamp 7 correct, improve, patch up, rebuild, rectify, redress, restore 8 overhaul, renovate 9 condition, refurbish 10 ameliorate, convalesce, recuperate 11 recondition, reconstruct

mendacious
5 false, lying 6 shifty 7 fibbing 9 deceitful, deceptive, dishonest, paltering 10 untruthful 11 dissembling 13 prevaricating

mendacity
3 lie 6 deceit 9 deception, duplicity, falsehood 10 dishonesty 12 equivocation 13 truthlessness

mendicancy
7 beggary, begging, bumming, cadging 8 mooching, sponging 11 panhandling

mendicant
5 friar 6 beggar 7 begging

Mending Wall author
5 Frost (Robert)

Menelaus
brother: 9 Agamemnon
father: 6 Atreus
kingdom: 6 Sparta
mother: 6 Aerope
wife: 5 Helen

menial
4 dull 5 lowly 6 humble 7 servant, servile, slavish 8 obeisant, retainer 9 unskilled 10 obsequious 11 subservient, undignified

meniscus
4 lens 9 cartilage

Menlo Park inventor
6 Edison (Thomas Alva)

menopause
11 climacteric 12 change of life

menorah
10 candelabra

Menotti, Gian Carlo
character: 5 Amahl
opera: 6 Consul (The), Medium
(The) 9 Telephone (The)

men's store
12 haberdashery

mental
5 inner 7 psychic 8 cerebral, rational, thinking 9 reasoning, spiritual
10 immaterial, telepathic 11 intelligent 12 intellective, intellectual
13 psychological
faculty: 6 memory

mentality
3 wit 5 sense 6 brains 7 mindset,
outlook 9 intellect, mother wit
10 brainpower 12 intelligence

mention
4 cite, name, note 7 refer to, specify
8 advert to, allude to, citation, instance 9 reference

mentor
4 guru 5 coach, guide, tutor 7 teacher
9 counselor 10 counsellor

Mentor's pupil
10 Telemachus

menu
4 card, diet 5 carte 10 bill of fare
11 carte du jour
item: 4 soup 5 salad 6 entrée
7 dessert 9 appetizer

Mephibosheth
father: 4 Saul 8 Jonathan
mother: 6 Rizpah

Mephistophelian
7 satanic 8 devilish, diabolic 10 diabolical

mephitic
4 rank 5 fetid, funky, musty 6 putrid,
smelly 7 noisome, noxious, reeking
8 stinking 9 poisonous 10 malodorous

Merab
father: 4 Saul
husband: 6 Adriel

mercenary
4 hack 5 venal 6 greedy 7 corrupt,
soldier 8 hireling

merchandise
4 line, sell 5 cargo, goods, stock,
trade, wares 6 deal in, job lot,
market, retail 7 effects, promote,
staples, traffic 8 products 9 publicize, vendibles 11 commodities

merchandiser
6 dealer, trader, vendor 8 retailer
9 tradesman 10 wholesaler 11 businessman 13 businesswoman

merchant
5 buyer 6 dealer, jobber, seller,
trader, vendor 7 peddler 8 purveyor,
retailer 9 tradesman 10 trafficker,
wholesaler 11 businessman, storekeeper
guild: 5 Hansa, Hanse
League: 9 Hanseatic
ship: 5 oiler 6 argosy, coaler,
galiot, packet, tanker, trader 7 collier, galliot, steamer 8 Indiaman
9 freighter
wine: 7 vintner

Merchant of Venice, The
7 Antonio
character: 6 Portia 7 Jessica,
Lorenzo, Nerissa, Shylock 8 Bassanio

merciful
4 kind 6 benign, humane, kindly
7 clement, lenient 8 tolerant 9 forgiving, indulgent 10 charitable,
forbearing 11 softhearted 13 compassionate

merciless
4 grim 5 cruel, harsh 6 brutal,
savage, wanton 9 cutthroat, ferocious, unfeeling 10 gratuitous,
implacable, ironfisted, unyielding
11 hardhearted, unrelenting 12 unappeasable

mercurial
5 flaky 6 fickle, mobile 7 erratic
8 unstable, variable, volatile 9 impulsive 10 capricious, changeable, inconstant 13 temperamental, unpredictable

mercury
5 azoth 11 quicksilver
ore: 8 cinnabar

Mercury
6 planet
(see also **Hermes**)

Mercutio
friend: 5 Romeo
slayer: 6 Tybalt

mercy
4 pity, ruth 5 grace 6 lenity 7 caritas, charity 8 clemency, goodwill, kindness, leniency 9 benignity, tolerance 10 compassion, generosity, kindliness 11 benevolence, forbearance 13 commiseration
petition for: 5 kyrie 8 miserere

mere
4 bare, lake, pool, pure 8 boundary, landmark 9 undiluted

merely
4 just, only 6 simply, solely, wholly

meretricious
4 loud, sham 5 gaudy, phony, showy 6 flashy, garish, glitzy, sleazy, tawdry, tinsel, trashy 7 chintzy 8 delusive, delusory, illusory 9 contrived, deceptive 10 misleading 11 counterfeit, pretentious

merganser
4 duck, smew

merge
3 mix 4 fuse, join 5 blend, unify, unite 6 mingle 7 combine 8 coalesce, compound 9 commingle, interfuse 10 amalgamate, assimilate 11 consolidate, intermingle

merger
5 union 6 fusion 7 melding 8 alliance, takeover 9 coalition 10 absorption 11 combination, unification 12 amalgamation 13 consolidation

meridian
4 acme, apex, peak 6 apogee, climax, summit, zenith 8 pinnacle

merit
3 due 4 earn, rate 5 arete, value, worth 6 virtue 7 caliber, deserts, deserve, entitle, justify, quality, stature, warrant 10 excellence, perfection, recompense 11 achievement

merited
3 due 4 fair, just 5 right 7 condign, fitting 8 deserved, rightful, suitable 9 justified, requisite 11 appropriate

meritorious
6 worthy 8 laudable 9 admirable, deserving, estimable, honorable 10 creditable 11 commendable, thankworthy 12 praiseworthy

Merlin
4 seer 5 augur, magus 6 shaman, wizard 7 prophet 8 magician 10 soothsayer 11 necromancer, thaumaturge

merlin
6 falcon 10 pigeon hawk

mermaid
3 nix 5 Ariel, nixie 7 manatee 8 sirenian 10 water nymph 11 water sprite

Merope
father: 5 Atlas 8 Oenopion
husband: 7 Polybus 8 Sisyphus 11 Cresphontes
lover: 5 Orion
mother: 7 Pleione
sisters: 8 Pleiades
son: 7 Aepytus, Glaucus

merriment
4 glee 5 mirth, revel 6 gaiety 7 jollity, revelry, whoopee 8 hilarity, reveling 9 festivity, jocundity, joviality 10 jocularity, jubilation 13 entertainment

merry
3 gay 4 glad 5 happy, jolly 6 blithe, jocund, jovial, joyful, joyous, lively

7 festive, gleeful **8** animated, cheerful, mirthful **9** hilarious, sprightly, vivacious **12** high-spirited, lighthearted

merry-andrew
4 fool, zany **5** clown, joker **6** jester, madcap **7** buffoon **9** harlequin **10** mountebank

merrymaker
7 partyer, reveler **8** carouser

merrymaking
5 party, revel **6** frolic, gaiety **7** jollity, revelry, whoopee **8** hilarity **9** festivity **12** conviviality

Merry Widow composer
5 Lehár (Franz)

Merry Wives of Windsor, The
character: 3 Nym **4** Ford, Page **5** Caius **6** Fenton, Pistol **7** Slender **8** Falstaff

mesa
5 bench, butte **7** plateau **9** tableland

mescal
5 agave **6** cactus, liquor, maguey, peyote

mesh
3 net, web **4** jibe, maze **5** skein, snare, snarl **6** engage, morass, tangle **7** netting, network **8** dovetail, entangle **9** harmonize, interlock, labyrinth **10** coordinate **12** reticulation

meshuga
3 mad **4** nuts **5** crazy, goofy, kooky, loony, nutty, wacky **6** insane, screwy **7** foolish

mesmeric
8 alluring, hypnotic **9** glamorous **10** bewitching, enchanting **11** captivating

mesmerize
4 vamp **6** dazzle, seduce **7** bewitch **8** ensorcel, enthrall, entrance **9** captivate, ensorcell, fascinate, hypnotize, spellbind

Mesopotamia
4 Iraq
civilization: 4 Elam **5** Akkad, Sumer **7** Assyria, Elamite **8** Akkadian, Assyrian, Sumerian **9** Babylonia **10** Babylonian
river: 6 Tigris **9** Euphrates

mess
4 hash **5** botch, snafu **6** fright, jumble, muddle **7** eyesore **8** botchery, disarray, disorder, shambles, wreckage **9** confusion **10** hodgepodge, miscellany
around: 4 idle **5** chill, dally **6** dawdle, doodle, fiddle, potter, putter **7** goof off, hang out **8** chill out, lollygag **10** dilly-dally
up: 4 blow, flub, muff, ruin **5** botch, fluff, fudge, spoil, touse **6** bungle, fumble, tousle **7** butcher

message
4 note **5** sense, theme **6** letter, report **7** epistle, meaning, mission, missive, purport **8** bulletin, dispatch, telegram **9** directive, telegraph **10** communiqué **12** significance **13** communication, signification

Messalina's husband
8 Claudius

mess around
4 fool, idle **5** flirt **6** dabble, dawdle, fiddle, meddle, monkey, potter, putter, tamper, tinker **8** womanize **9** associate, interfere, interlope, philander

messenger
4 post **5** envoy **6** herald, runner **7** apostle, courier **8** emissary **9** gobetween, harbinger **10** ambassador **11** internuncio **12** intermediary
God's: 5 angel
of the gods: 6 Hermes **7** Mercury
Turkish: 6 chiaus

messiah
6 savior **7** saviour **8** defender **9** deliverer, liberator

Messiah composer
6 Handel (George Frideric)

messy
6 frowsy, frowzy, sloppy, unneat, untidy 7 chaotic, rumpled, unkempt 8 careless, confused, ill-kempt, slapdash, slipshod, slovenly 10 disheveled, disorderly 11 dishevelled
abode: 3 sty 6 pigpen, pigsty

mestizo
5 métis 6 ladino 10 mixed-blood

Mestor
father: 7 Perseus
mother: 9 Andromeda

metal
4 gold, iron 5 steel 6 bronze
alloy:
(see **alloy**)
casting mold: 5 ingot
corrosion: 4 rust
fuse: 6 solder
in mass: 7 bullion
layer: 7 plating
lump: 6 nugget
magnetic: 4 iron
refuse: 4 slag 5 dross 6 scoria
sheath: 5 armor
thin: 4 foil, leaf 5 plate
worker: 5 smith 10 blacksmith

metallic element
3 tin 4 gold, iron, lead, zinc 6 barium, cobalt, copper, nickel, radium, silver, sodium 7 arsenic, bismuth, cadmium, calcium, lithium, mercury, uranium 8 aluminum, chromium, platinum, titanium, tungsten, vanadium 9 magnesium, manganese, potassium, strontium 10 molybdenum

metamere
6 somite 7 segment

metamorphic rock
5 slate 6 gneiss, marble, schist 9 quartzite, soapstone

metamorphose
6 change, mutate 7 convert, develop 9 transform, translate, transmute 11 transfigure 12 transmogrify

metamorphosis
6 change 8 changing, mutation 9 evolution, sea change 10 changeover 13 transmutation

Metamorphosis author
5 Kafka (Franz)

_____ me tangere
4 noli

metaphor
5 trope 6 simile, symbol 7 analogy 8 allegory 10 comparison, similitude

metaphorical compound
7 kenning

metaphysical
8 bodiless, numinous 9 unearthly, unfleshly 10 immaterial, suprahuman 12 supermundane, supramundane, supranatural, transcendent 13 preternatural
poet: 5 Donne (John) 6 Cowley (Abraham) 7 Crashaw (Richard), Herbert (George), Marvell (Andrew), Vaughan (Henry) 9 Cleveland (John)

mete
4 deal, dole, give 5 allot, bound 6 border, parcel, ration 7 portion 8 allocate, boundary, disburse, dispense 9 apportion 10 distribute

meteor
8 fireball 12 shooting star
exploding: 6 bolide
shower: 5 Lyrid 6 Leonid, Taurid 7 Aquarid, Geminid, Orionid, Perseid 10 Quadrantid

meteorite
8 aerolite 10 siderolite

meter
4 beat, scan 6 rhythm 7 cadence, measure, pattern

metheglin
4 mead 8 beverage
ingredient: 5 honey

method
3 way 4 mode, modi (plural), plan 5 means, modus, order, style 6 course, design, manner, schema, scheme, system 7 fashion, formula, pattern, process, routine, wrinkle

8 practice 9 procedure, technique
11 orderliness 13 modus operandi
careful: 8 strategy
of employing troops: 6 tactic
7 tactics
of procedure: 4 game

methodical
5 exact 7 careful, logical, orderly,
precise, regular 9 efficient, organized 10 deliberate, scrupulous,
systematic, systemized 12 system-
atized

Methuselah
father: 5 Enoch
grandson: 4 Noah
son: 6 Lamech

meticulous
5 exact, fussy, picky 6 strict 7 careful, finicky, precise 8 detailed, thorough 10 fastidious, nitpicking, pernickety, scrupulous 11 microscopic,
painstaking, persnickety, punctilious
13 conscientious

métier
4 work 5 craft, field, forte, trade
7 calling, pursuit 8 business, strength,
vocation 9 specialty 10 employment, occupation, profession

metrical foot
4 iamb 5 ionic, paeon 6 cretic,
dactyl, iambic, iambus 7 anapest,
pyrrhic, pyrrhus, spondee, triseme,
trochee 8 bacchius, choriamb,
dactylic, spondaic, tribrach, trochaic
9 anapestic 10 tribrachic

metric unit
area: 3 are 7 hectare
capacity: 5 liter, litre 9 decaliter,
deciliter, kiloliter 10 centiliter, hecto-
liter, milliliter
length: 5 meter 9 decameter,
decimeter, dekameter, kilometer
10 centimeter, hectometer, millimeter
mass and weight: 4 gram 7 quintal
8 decagram, decigram, dekagram,
kilogram 9 centigram, hectogram,
metric ton, milligram

metro
4 tube 6 subway 11 underground

metropolis
4 city 7 capital

metropolitan
5 urban 6 urbane 7 primate 9 municipal 10 archbishop

mettle
4 fire, grit, guts 5 heart, moxie,
nerve, pluck, spunk, steel, valor,
vigor 6 daring, spirit, starch, temper
7 cojones, courage, resolve, stamina
8 backbone, boldness, tenacity,
vitality 9 fortitude 10 resolution

mettlesome
4 bold, game 5 brave, fiery, gutsy
6 plucky, spunky 7 staunch, valiant
8 intrepid, resolute, spirited, vigorous
9 tenacious 10 courageous, determined

mew
3 hem, pen 4 cage, coop, gull
5 alley, fence 6 corral, immure, shut
in, stable 7 enclose 8 hideaway

mewl
4 moan, pule 5 whine 6 snivel
7 whimper

Mexican
crop: 5 sisal
estate: 8 hacienda
food: 4 masa, taco 5 chili, salsa
6 tamale 7 burrito, panocha, penuche, tostada 8 frijoles, tortilla
9 enchilada, guacamole 10 quesadilla 11 chimichanga
house: 5 jacal
liquor: 7 tequila

Mexico
ancient city: 12 Tenochtitlán
ancient culture: 4 Maya 5 Aztec,
Mayan, Olmec 6 Toltec
bay: 8 Campeche
capital: 10 Mexico City
city: 4 León 6 Juárez, Mérida,
Oaxaca, Puebla 7 Nogales, Tijuana
8 Acapulco, Mexicali, Saltillo 9 Chihuahua, Matamoros, Monterrey
10 Cuernavaca 11 Guadalajara
12 Ciudad Juárez
conqueror: 6 Cortés (Hernán,
Hernando)

discoverer: 7 Córdoba (Fernández de)
emperor: 10 Maximilian
gulf: 10 California
island: 7 Cozumel
island group: 13 Revillagigedo
lake: 7 Chapala, Cuitzeo, Texcoco 9 Pátzcuaro
language: 7 Spanish
leader: 4 Díaz (Porfirio) 6 Juárez (Benito) 8 Carranza (Venustiano)
monetary unit: 4 peso
mountain, range: 8 Malinche 11 Sierra Madre
neighbor: 6 Belize 9 Guatemala
peninsula: 4 Baja 7 Yucatán
port: 7 Tampico 8 Ensenada, Mazatlán, Veracruz
resort: 6 Cancún 8 Acapulco
revolutionist: 5 Villa (Pancho) 6 Zapata (Emiliano) 7 Hidalgo (Padre Miguel)
river: 4 Mayo 5 Bravo, Yaquí 6 Balsas, Grande, Pánuco 7 Conchos 8 Grijalva, Río Bravo, Santiago 9 Rio Grande 10 Usumacinta
ruined city: 5 Uxmal 7 Mayapán 8 Palenque 11 Chichén Itzá
sea: 9 Caribbean
volcano: 6 Colima 9 Paricutín 11 Ixtacihuatl 12 Citlaltépetl, Ixtaccíhuatl, Popocatépetl

mezzanine
5 story 7 balcony 8 entresol

mezzo
4 half 6 singer 7 soprano

mezzo-soprano
American: 5 Elias (Rosalind), Horne (Marilyn), Jones (Sissieretta) 6 Bumbry (Grace), Graves (Denyce) 7 Stevens (Risë), Verrett (Shirley) 8 Troyanos (Tatiana), von Stade (Frederica)
Austrian: 6 Ludwig (Christa)
English: 5 Baker (Janet)
Italian: 7 Bartoli (Cecilia) 8 Cossotto (Fiorenza)

Miami
bowl: 6 Orange
chief: 12 Little Turtle
county: 4 Dade
stadium: 9 Joe Robbie
team: 4 Heat 7 Marlins 8 Dolphins, Panthers

miasma
3 fog 4 haze, mist, murk, smog 5 brume, vapor 9 effluvium

mica
7 biotite 8 silicate 9 isinglass, muscovite

Michelangelo Buonarotti
painting: 10 Holy Family (The) 12 Last Judgment (The)
statue: 5 David, Moses, Pietà 7 Bacchus

Michener novel
5 Space, Texas 6 Hawaii, Poland, Source (The) 8 Caravans, Covenant (The), Drifters (The), Sayonara 10 Centennial, Chesapeake 13 Fires of Spring (The) 15 Bridges at Toko-Ri (The)

Michigan
capital: 7 Lansing
city: 5 Flint 7 Detroit, Lansing, Pontiac 8 Ann Arbor, Dearborn 9 Kalamazoo 11 Grand Rapids 13 Sault Ste. Marie 16 Sault Sainte Marie
college, university: 6 Calvin 9 Kalamazoo 10 Wayne State
lake: 4 Erie 5 Huron 8 Michigan, Superior
nickname: 9 Wolverine (State) 10 Great Lakes (State)
state bird: 5 robin
state flower: 12 apple blossom
state tree: 9 white pine

mickey
5 flask, split

microbe
3 bug 4 germ 5 virus 8 bacillus, pathogen 9 bacterium 13 microorganism

microfilm sheet
5 fiche

Micronesia
capital: 7 Palikir

microorganism
island, island group: 3 Yap 5 Chuuk
6 Kosrae 7 Pohnpei 8 Caroline
language: 7 English

microorganism
4 germ 5 virus 6 aerobe 7 bacilli
(plural), microbe, protist 8 bacillus,
bacteria (plural), pathogen, protozoa
(plural) 9 bacterium, protozoan,
protozoon

microphone
3 bug 4 mike
shield: 4 gobo

microscope
9 magnifier
inventor: 11 Leeuwenhoek (Antoni
van)
part: 5 stage 6 mirror 8 eyepiece
9 objective

microscopic
4 tiny 5 small 6 minute

Mid-Atlantic state
7 New York 8 Delaware, Maryland,
Virginia 9 New Jersey 12 Pennsylvania, West Virginia

midday
4 noon, sext 8 high noon, noontide,
noontime

middle
4 core, mean 5 mesne, waist 6 center, medial, median 7 average,
central, halfway 8 interior 10 centermost 11 equidistant, intervening
12 intermediary, intermediate

Middle American country
4 Cuba 5 Haiti 6 Belize, Mexico,
Panama 7 Bahamas, Grenada,
Jamaica 8 Barbados, Dominica,
Honduras 9 Costa Rica, Guatemala,
Nicaragua 10 El Salvador

middlebrow
7 Babbitt

middle class
11 bourgeoisie

middle-class
9 bourgeois

middle ear
bone: 5 incus 6 stapes 7 malleus
membrane: 7 eardrum 8 tympanum

Middle Eastern country
4 Iran, Iraq, Oman 5 Egypt, Qatar,
Sudan, Syria, Yemen 6 Cyprus,
Israel, Jordan, Kuwait, Turkey
7 Bahrain, Lebanon 11 Saudi
Arabia

Middle Kingdom
5 China

middleman
5 agent 6 broker 8 mediator 9 go-
between 11 intercessor 12 intermediary, intermediate

Middlemarch author
5 Eliot (George), Evans (Mary Ann)

middle-of-the-road
7 neutral 8 moderate 9 impartial
11 nonpartisan

middling
4 fair, okay, so-so 6 fairly, medium,
rather 7 average, fairish, typical
8 adequate, mediocre, moderate,
ordinary, passable 9 tolerable
10 moderately, second-rate 11 indifferent 12 intermediate, run-of-the-
mill

midge
3 fly 6 punkie 7 no-see-um 8 dip-
teran 10 chironomid
larva: 9 bloodworm

midget
4 runt 5 dwarf, pygmy 6 bantam,
peewee 7 manikin 8 Tom Thumb
10 homunculus 11 hop-o'-my-
thumb, Lilliputian

Midian
father: 7 Abraham
mother: 7 Keturah

midpoint
3 par 4 mean, norm 6 center,
median, middle 7 average, centrum,
halfway 8 bull's-eye, standard

midwife
6 granny, Lucina 10 accoucheur

mien
3 air, set 4 look 6 aspect, manner
7 address, bearing 8 carriage,
demeanor, presence 9 mannerism
10 appearance, deportment, expression 11 comportment

miff
3 fit, irk, vex 4 beef, flap, spat 5 annoy, pique, run-in, upset 6 bother,
fracas, nettle, offend, put out 7 dispute, provoke, quarrel, rhubarb
8 irritate, squabble 10 conniption,
falling-out 11 altercation

might
3 may 4 sway 5 brawn, clout, force,
means, power 6 energy, muscle
7 ability, command, control, mastery,
potency 8 capacity, strength 9 authority, resources 12 forcefulness

mighty
4 huge, very 5 grand, great 6 heroic,
potent, strong 7 eminent, immense,
massive, titanic 8 enormous, forceful, gigantic, imposing, powerful,
puissant 10 impressive, monumental, prodigious, stupendous, tremendous 11 illustrious 13 extraordinary

Mignon composer
6 Thomas (Ambroise)

mignonette
4 herb 5 sauce 6 annual 6 reseda

migrant
5 exile, mover, nomad 7 drifter,
nomadic, refugee 8 traveler, wanderer 9 itinerant, transient 10 expatriate

migrate
4 move, trek 5 drift, range, shift
6 wander 8 transfer

migration
6 exodus 8 diaspora
of professionals: 10 brain drain

migratory
5 nomad 6 errant, mobile, moving,
roving 7 nomadic, ranging 9 wandering

Mikado, The
composer: 8 Sullivan (Arthur)
librettist: 7 Gilbert (W. S.)

milady
6 madame 10 noblewoman 11 gentlewoman

Milan
family: 6 Sforza 8 Visconti
opera house: 7 La Scala

Milcah
brother: 3 Lot
father: 5 Haran 10 Zelophehad
husband: 5 Nahor
son: 7 Bethuel

mild
4 calm, easy, meek, soft, tame
5 balmy, bland, faint, tepid 6 benign, docile, gentle, placid, serene,
smooth, tender 7 amiable, clement,
equable, insipid, lenient, patient,
subdued 8 moderate, obliging 9 benignant, temperate 10 forbearing,
submissive

mildew
4 mold, rust 6 fungus, growth

_____ mile
7 statute 8 nautical

mileage recorder
8 odometer

milestone
5 event 6 marker 8 landmark,
occasion

milieu
5 scene 6 medium, sphere 7 ambient, climate, setting 8 ambience
10 atmosphere, background 11 environment, mise-en-scène 12 surroundings

militant
7 fighter, martial, warlike, warrior
8 activist, fighting 9 assertive,
bellicose, combatant, combative,
truculent 10 aggressive, pugnacious
11 belligerent, contentious, quarrelsome 12 gladiatorial

military
5 troop 6 forces, troops 7 martial,

warlike **8** soldiery **9** soldierly
10 servicemen **11** armed forces,
soldierlike
alliance: 4 NATO
base: 4 camp, fort, post **5** depot,
field **6** billet **8** barracks, garrison,
quarters **10** encampment
officer: 5 major **7** captain, colonel,
general **9** brigadier **10** lieutenant
prisoner: 3 POW
school: 3 OCS, OTS **4** ROTC,
USMA **9** Annapolis, West Point
sector: 10 combat zone, front lines
11 battlefront
store: 10 commissary
storehouse: 5 depot **6** armory
7 arsenal
supplies: 8 matériel, ordnance
unit: 5 corps, squad, troop **7** company, platoon **8** division, regiment
9 battalion **11** battle group
vehicle: 4 jeep, tank **6** Abrams,
Humvee **7** Bradley **9** Blackhawk,
half-track

militate
4 tell **5** count, weigh **6** matter
11 carry weight

militia
7 reserve

milk
4 pump, rook, suck **5** drain, educe,
empty, evoke, exact, mulct, nurse,
wring **6** elicit, extort, fleece **7** exhaust, exploit, extract
coagulated: 4 curd
combining form: 4 lact **5** lacti,
lacto
curdled: 7 clabber
fermented: 5 kefir **6** kumiss, yogurt
7 koumiss, yoghurt
liquid part: 4 whey
store: 5 dairy
sugar: 7 lactose

milk shake
6 frappe **7** frosted

milky
4 fair, meek, mild, pale, tame **5** white
6 chalky, cloudy, gentle **7** lacteal,
whitish **8** timorous

mill
5 grind, plant, shape, works **7** factory, machine **9** circulate, pulverize
11 manufactory

millenary
8 thousand

Miller, Arthur
film: 7 Misfits (The)
play: 5 Price (The) **9** All My Sons
8 Crucible (The) **12** After the Fall
16 Death of a Salesman **17** View
from the Bridge (A)
salesman: 5 Loman (Willy)

milliner
6 hatter

million
combining form: 3 meg **4** mega

millionth
combining form: 4 micr **5** micro

Mill on the Floss author
5 Eliot (George), Evans (Mary Ann)

millstone
4 duty, load, onus **6** burden, charge,
weight **9** albatross **10** affliction,
deadweight

Milne bear
4 Pooh

milord
8 nobleman **9** gentleman, patrician
10 aristocrat **12** silk stocking

Milquetoast, Caspar
creator: 7 Webster (Harold Tucker)
(see also **milksop**)

Miltiades' victory
8 Marathon

Milton work
5 Comus **7** Lycidas **8** L'Allegro
12 Areopagitica, Paradise Lost

mime
3 act **5** actor **6** act out **7** Marceau
(Marcel) **9** performer, represent
11 impersonate **12** impersonator

mimic
3 act, ape **4** copy, mock, play
5 actor, enact **6** mummer, parody,

parrot, player **7** copycat, imitate
8 resemble, simulate, travesty
9 burlesque, pantomime **11** impersonate **12** impersonator

mimicry

4 echo **6** parody **8** travesty **9** imitation, parroting **10** caricature **13** impersonation

minatory

4 dire, grim **7** baleful, baneful, direful, hostile, malefic, ominous
8 menacing, sinister **9** ill-boding
10 forbidding, foreboding, maleficent
11 frightening, threatening **12** intimidating

mince

4 chop, dice, hash **5** cut up, strut
6 prance, sashay, soften **8** moderate, restrain, tone down **9** euphemize

mincing

5 fussy **6** dainty, la-di-da, too-too
7 finical, finicky, stilted **8** affected, delicate **10** fastidious, pernickety
11 persnickety

mind

3 wit **4** mood, obey, soul, tend, will, wits **5** brain, fancy, watch, weigh
6 attend, belief, beware, brains, follow, memory, notice, psyche, reason, senses, spirit **7** care for, discern, dislike, feeling, observe, oversee, purpose **8** consider
9 intellect, intention, mentality, supervise **10** brainpower, gray matter
11 disposition, temperament
12 intelligence **13** consciousness
combining form: 5 psych **6** psycho

mindful

5 alert, awake, aware **7** knowing
8 sensible, vigilant **9** attentive, cognizant, conscious, observant
10 conversant **13** conscientious

mindless

4 rash **5** silly **6** simple, stupid
7 asinine, foolish, unaware, vacuous
9 nitwitted, oblivious **10** irrational, unthinking **13** unintelligent

mine

3 dig, pit, sap **4** fund, lode, vein, well
5 delve, drill, hoard, stock, store
6 burrow, quarry, spring **7** bonanza, deposit, extract **8** eldorado, excavate, Golconda **10** excavation, wellspring **13** treasure trove
coal: 8 colliery
entrance: 4 adit

miner

6 pitman **7** collier

mineral

5 beryl, topaz, trona **6** augite, barite, garnet, iolite, pinite, rutile, sphene, spinel, sulfur, zircon **7** apatite, azurite, bornite, calcite, citrine, coesite, cyanite, jadeite, kernite, kunzite, olivine, zeolite **8** boracite, cinnabar, dolomite, epsomite, fayalite, feldspar, fluorite, hematite, lazulite, lazurite, siderite, sodalite, stibnite, triplite, wellsite **9** aragonite, celestite, cerussite, danburite, fosterite, kaolinite, lawsonite, magnetite, malachite, muscovite, phenakite, scapolite, tridymite, turquoise, wulfenite **10** chalcedony, orthoclase, pyrrhotite, tourmaline **11** alexandrite, chrysoberyl, melanterite **12** brazilianite, chalcopyrite, tincalconite
13 rhodochrosite
flaky: 4 mica
greasy: 4 talc **10** serpentine
hard: 6 spinel **7** diamond **8** corundum
iridescent: 4 opal
nonmetallic: 5 boron **6** gypsum, halite **8** asbestos, graphite
shiny: 4 gold **6** galena, pyrite, silver
soft: 4 talc **6** gypsum **8** graphite
transparent: 6 quartz

mineral water

7 seltzer **8** club soda

Minerva

see **Athena**

mingle

3 mix **4** meld **5** blend, merge
6 commix **7** combine **8** intermix
9 associate, socialize

mingy

4 mean 5 cheap, tight 6 stingy
7 chintzy, miserly, scrimpy 8 grudging, ungiving 9 niggardly, penurious
10 pinchpenny 11 closefisted,
tightfisted

miniature

3 wee 4 tiny 5 small, teeny, weeny
6 little, minute, petite, teensy 9 itsy-bitsy, itty-bitty 10 diminutive, small-scale, teeny-weeny 11 Lilliputian
12 illumination

minify

4 trim 6 lessen, shrink 7 abridge,
curtail 8 decrease, diminish 10 abbreviate

minim

3 bit, jot 4 atom, iota 5 grain, speck
7 modicum, smidgen 8 particle
music: 8 half note

minimal

5 basic, least, token 6 lowest 7 nominal 8 littlest, smallest 9 slightest

minimize

5 decry 6 reduce 7 run down
8 belittle, derogate, discount, downplay, play down 9 disparage, soft-pedal, underrate 10 depreciate
13 underestimate

minimum

3 dab, jot 4 iota, whit 5 least,
speck 6 lowest, margin 7 smidgen
8 particle, pittance, smallest

minion

4 idol 5 toady 6 flunky, lackey,
vassal, yes-man 7 darling, devotee,
spaniel 8 creature, favorite, follower,
parasite, truckler 9 sycophant,
toadeater, underling 10 bootlicker
11 lickspittle, subordinate

minister

4 tend 5 agent, clerk, serve 6 cleric,
curate, divine, parson 8 clerical,
preacher, reverend 9 churchman,
clergyman 10 ambassador 12 ecclesiastic
of state: 10 chancellor
plenipotentiary: 5 envoy 6 consul
8 diplomat, emissary

ministry

5 agent, organ 6 agency, clergy,
medium 7 cabinet 10 department,
instrument 11 bureaucracy

Minnehaha's husband

8 Hiawatha

Minnesota

capital: 6 St. Paul
city: 5 Edina 6 Duluth 9 Rochester
11 Minneapolis
college, university: 8 Carleton
9 Saint Olaf 10 Macalester
nickname: 6 Gopher (State) 9 North
Star (State)
park: 9 Voyageurs
river: 7 St. Croix 9 Minnesota
11 Mississippi
state bird: 4 loon (common)
state flower: 12 lady's slipper
state tree: 7 red pine

minor

5 lower, petty, small, youth 6 casual,
lesser, little, paltry, slight 7 trivial
8 inferior, mediocre, piddling, small-fry, trifling, underage 9 dependent,
secondary, small-beer, small-time
10 bush-league, second-rate, shoe-string 11 indifferent, unimportant
13 insignificant

minority

5 youth 6 nonage 7 infancy 9 child-hood 10 immaturity

minor-league

5 small 6 lesser 9 secondary,
small-time 11 unimportant

Minos

daughter: 7 Ariadne, Phaedra
father: 4 Zeus 7 Jupiter
kingdom: 5 Crete
monster: 8 Minotaur
mother: 6 Europa
son: 9 Androgeos
wife: 8 Pasiphaë

Minotaur

father: 4 bull
home: 9 labyrinth
mother: 8 Pasiphaë
slayer: 7 Theseus

minstrel

4 bard, wait 6 harper, singer 7 glee-
man 8 jongleur 9 balladist 10 troubadour
end man: 5 Bones (Mr.), Tambo
(Mr.)
instrument: 4 lute, lyre 5 rebec,
shawm, tabor 8 crumhorn, psaltery
9 krummhorn 10 tambourine

mint

3 pot 4 cast, coin, heap, pile, sage
5 basil, bugle, forge, issue, stamp,
trove 6 boodle, bundle, create,
intact, packet, savory, strike, unused
7 fortune, like-new, menthol, perfect,
produce 8 brand-new, lavender,
marjoram, original 9 blue curls,
bugleweed, undamaged

Minuit's purchase

9 Manhattan

minus

4 flaw, lack, less, sans 6 absent,
defect 7 lacking, missing, wanting,
without 8 drawback, negative,
subtract 10 deficiency

minuscule

4 tiny 5 small 6 letter, little, minute
7 trivial 9 lowercase, miniature
10 negligible, small-scale 11 meaningless, microscopic 13 imperceptible, inappreciable, insignificant

minute

3 wee 4 jiff, memo, note, tiny 5 draft,
flash, jiffy, small, teeny, weeny
6 little, moment, record, teensy
7 careful, instant, precise, trivial
8 detailed, itemized, thorough, trifling
itsy-bitsy, itty-bitty, miniature,
minuscule 10 diminutive, memorandum, meticulous, scrupulous, teeny-
weeny 11 Lilliputian, punctilious
13 infinitesimal

minutes

3 log 6 annals, record 7 summary
10 transcript 11 proceedings

minutiae

6 trivia 7 details 10 fine points,
triviality 11 particulars

minx

4 bawd, moll, slut, tart 5 bimbo,
tramp, wench, whore 6 floozy, harlot,
hooker 7 hustler, trollop 8 strumpet
10 prostitute

miracle

4 boon, feat 6 marvel, wonder
7 godsend, portent, prodigy, stunner
8 windfall 9 sensation 10 phenomenon

miraculous

7 amazing 8 wondrous 9 marvelous,
unearthly, wonderful 10 astounding,
prodigious, superhuman 11 astonishing, spectacular 12 inexplicable,
supernatural 13 preternatural

mirage

6 vision, wraith 8 delusion, illusion,
phantasm 11 fata morgana, ignis
fatuus 13 hallucination

Miranda

father: 8 Prospero
lover: 9 Ferdinand

mire

3 bog, fen, mud 4 muck, ooze, sink,
trap 5 delay, marsh, slush, swamp
6 detain, enmesh, entrap, hang up,
morass, slough, tangle 7 bog down,
embroil, ensnare, involve, set back
8 entangle 9 imbroglio, implicate,
quicksand

Miriam's brother

5 Aaron, Moses

mirror

5 glass 6 embody, typify 7 reflect
8 speculum 9 exemplify, personify,
reflector, represent 10 illustrate
11 cheval glass 12 looking glass
signaling: 10 heliograph

mirth

3 fun, joy 4 glee 5 cheer 6 gaiety,
levity 7 jollity, revelry 8 gladness,
hilarity 9 festivity, frivolity, happiness, jocundity, joviality, merriment
10 jocularity 11 merrymaking
12 cheerfulness

mirthful

3 gay 5 jolly, merry, riant 6 jocund,

jovial **7** festive **9** exuberant, hilarious **12** lighthearted

miry
4 oozy **5** boggy, mucky, muddy **6** marshy, slushy, swampy

misadventure
4 slip **5** boner, error, lapse **6** howler, mishap **7** blunder, faux pas **8** accident, calamity, casualty, disaster **9** cataclysm **10** misfortune **11** catastrophe

misanthrope
5 cynic, grump, loner **6** grinch **7** killjoy, recluse, scoffer **10** curmudgeon

misanthropic
7 cynical **10** antisocial

misappropriate
5 filch, steal **6** pilfer **7** purloin **8** embezzle, peculate **9** defalcate

misbegotten
7 bastard, illicit, natural **8** baseborn, deformed, spurious **10** fatherless, unfathered **12** contemptible, disreputable, ill-conceived, illegitimate

misbehave
5 act up, cut up, lapse, rebel, stray **6** act out, offend **7** carry on, disobey **8** trespass **10** roughhouse, transgress

misbehavior
7 misdeed **8** rudeness **9** high jinks **10** misconduct, wrongdoing **11** delinquency, dereliction, naughtiness **13** transgression

miscalculate
3 err **8** miscount, misgauge

miscarry
4 fail, flop **5** abort **6** fizzle **7** go wrong

miscellaneous
3 odd **5** mixed **6** motley, sundry, varied **7** diverse **8** assorted **9** different, disparate, scrambled **13** heterogeneous

miscellany
3 ana **4** hash, olio, stew **5** salad **6** jumble, medley, motley, muddle **7** farrago, mélange, mixture, omnibus **8** mixed bag, pastiche **9** anthology, congeries, pasticcio, patchwork, potpourri **10** assortment, hodgepodge, hotchpotch, salmagundi **11** aggregation, gallimaufry, odds and ends, olla podrida, smorgasbord

mischance
6 mishap **7** bad luck, tragedy **8** accident, casualty **9** adversity **10** misfortune **11** contretemps

mischief
3 ill **4** evil, harm **5** prank **6** damage, strife **7** devilry, roguery, trouble, waggery **8** deviltry, sabotage **9** devilment, diablerie, vandalism **10** wrongdoing **11** naughtiness, shenanigans **12** monkeyshines

mischief-maker
3 imp **4** puck **5** devil, knave, rogue, scamp **6** rascal **7** villain **8** agitator, scalawag **9** prankster, trickster **11** rapscallion **12** rabble-rouser

mischievous
3 sly **4** arch, foxy **5** antic, saucy **6** artful, bratty, impish, tricky, vexing **7** harmful, irksome, larkish, naughty, playful, puckish, roguish, tricksy, waggish **8** annoying, damaging, perverse, prankish, rascally, sportive **9** injurious, malicious **10** bothersome, frolicsome, ill-behaved

misconception
5 error **7** fallacy, mistake **8** delusion, illusion

misconduct
8 adultery **10** wrongdoing **11** dereliction, impropriety, malfeasance, malpractice, misbehavior **12** malversation **13** transgression

miscreant
4 heel **5** felon, knave, rogue **6** outlaw, rascal, sinner, wretch **7** corrupt, culprit, heretic, hoodlum, infidel, lowlife, vicious, villain **8** apostate, criminal, depraved, infamous, perverse **9** heretical, nefarious, scoun-

drel, unhealthy, wrongdoer **10** black-guard, degenerate, delinquent, un-believer, villainous

miscue
4 goof, miss, slip, trip **5** error, fluff, lapse **6** slipup **7** blooper, blunder, mistake

misdeed
3 sin **5** crime, wrong **6** breach **7** offense **9** violation **10** infraction **13** transgression

misdoubt
4 fear **5** dread **7** suspect

mise-en-scène
3 set **4** site **6** locale, medium, milieu **7** ambient, climate, context, scenery, setting **8** ambience, stage set **10** atmosphere, background **11** environment **12** stage setting, surroundings

miser
5 piker **7** hoarder, niggard, scrooge **8** tightwad **9** skinflint **10** cheapskate, pinchpenny

miserable
6 gloomy, meager, meagre, paltry, rueful, sordid, woeful **7** doleful, forlorn, piteous, pitiful, squalid **8** desolate, dolorous, downcast, hopeless, shameful, tortured, wretched **9** afflicted, destitute, sorrowful, worthless **10** despairing, despondent, melancholy **12** contemptible

Miserables, Les
author: 4 Hugo (Victor)
character: 6 Javert (Inspector) **7** Cosette, Fantine, Valjean (Jean)

miserly
4 mean **5** close, tight **6** greedy, stingy **7** scrimpy **8** covetous, grasping **9** niggardly, penurious, scrimping **10** avaricious **11** closefisted, tight-fisted **12** cheeseparing, parsimonious **13** penny-pinching

misery
3 woe **5** agony, dolor, grief **6** sorrow **7** anguish, squalor **8** calamity, dis-tress **9** adversity, dejection, suffering **10** affliction, depression, desolation **11** despondency **12** wretchedness

misfit
6 oddity, weirdo, zombie **7** oddball **8** maverick **9** eccentric, screwball

misfortune
3 woe **4** blow, harm, loss **5** cross, trial **7** reverse, setback, tragedy, trouble **8** accident, calamity, casualty, disaster, hardship **9** adversity, cataclysm **10** affliction, visitation **11** catastrophe, contretemps, tribulation

misgiving
4 fear **5** doubt, dread, qualm **6** unease **7** anxiety **8** distrust **9** suspicion **10** foreboding **11** premonition, trepidation **12** apprehension, presentiment

misguided
5 wrong **9** erroneous **10** ill-advised **11** injudicious **12** short-sighted

mishandle
4 flub **5** abuse, botch **6** bungle, fumble, mess up **7** rough up **8** maltreat **10** knock about, slap around

mishap
7 bad luck, tragedy **8** accident, casualty **9** adversity **11** contretemps

mishmash
6 jumble, litter, medley, muddle **7** clutter, mélange, mixture, rummage **8** pastiche, scramble **9** pasticcio, patchwork, potpourri **10** hodge-podge, hotchpotch

misidentify
5 mix up **7** confuse **8** confound

misinterpret
7 confuse, misread

mislay
4 lose

mislead
4 dupe, fool, gull, lure **5** bluff, cheat **6** betray, delude, entice, seduce, take in **7** beguile, deceive **8** hoodwink, inveigle **11** double-cross

misleading

misleading
5 false, wrong 8 delusive, delusory, specious 9 deceitful, deceptive 10 fallacious, inaccurate 11 casuistical, sophistical

mismatch
3 jar 5 clash 6 jangle 7 discord 8 conflict

misplace
4 lose

misprint
4 typo

misprision
5 scorn 7 despite, disdain, neglect 8 contempt, sedition 9 contumely, disregard 10 misconduct, negligence 11 concealment, dereliction, impropriety, malpractice

misrepresent
4 warp 5 twist 6 garble 7 distort, falsify, varnish 8 disguise 9 embellish, embroider 10 camouflage 11 counterfeit

misrepresentation
3 fib, lie 4 tale 5 story 6 canard 7 falsity, untruth 9 falsehood 10 distortion

miss
3 err, gal 4 fail, girl, lass, maid, omit, skip 5 avoid 6 damsel, escape, forget, ignore, lassie, maiden 7 failure, misfire, neglect 8 discount, leave out, overlook 9 disregard

Missa Solemnis composer
9 Beethoven (Ludwig van)

misshape
4 warp 6 deform 7 contort, distort, torture 9 disfigure

missile
4 bolt, dart 5 arrow, shell, spear 6 bullet, rocket 10 cannonball, projectile
underwater: 7 torpedo
(see also **guided missile**)

missing
4 AWOL 6 absent

mission
3 aim, job 4 duty, goal, task 5 quest 6 charge, errand, object 7 calling, embassy, purpose 8 legation, lifework, ministry, vocation 9 objective 10 assignment

missionary
7 apostle 8 emissary 10 evangelist, revivalist 12 propagandist, proselytizer

Mississippi
capital: 7 Jackson
city: 6 Biloxi 8 Gulfport 10 Greenville
college, university: 12 Jackson State 8 Millsaps
nickname: 8 Magnolia (State)
river: 5 Pearl 11 Mississippi
state bird: 11 mockingbird
state flower: 8 magnolia
state tree: 8 magnolia

missive
4 memo, note 6 letter, report 7 epistle, message 8 dispatch

Miss Julie author
10 Strindberg (August)

Miss Lonelyhearts author
4 West (Nathanael)

Missouri
capital: 13 Jefferson City
city: 7 St. Louis 10 Kansas City 11 Springfield 12 Independence
college, university: 10 Washington
lake: 15 Lake of the Ozarks
nickname: 6 Show Me (State)
river: 8 Missouri 11 Mississippi
state bird: 8 bluebird
state flower: 8 hawthorn
state tree: 7 dogwood

misstate
4 warp 5 color, twist 6 garble 7 distort, falsify

misstatement
3 fib, lie 4 tale 7 falsity, untruth 9 falsehood 13 prevarication

misstep
4 flub, goof, slip 5 boner, error, fluff,

gaffe, lapse 6 slipup 7 blooper,
blunder, faux pas

mist
3 dim, fog 4 blur, film, haze, murk
5 befog, brume, cloud 7 becloud,
obscure

mistake
4 flub, slip 5 boner, error, fluff, folly,
gaffe, lapse 6 boo-boo, bungle,
howler, slipup 7 blooper, blunder,
confuse, faux pas, take for 8 confound 10 inaccuracy

mistaken
5 false, wrong 6 all wet, faulty,
flawed, untrue 7 invalid 8 specious
9 defective, incorrect, misguided,
unfounded 10 fallacious, fraudulent,
inaccurate 11 misinformed

mister
3 sir 7 husband
French: 8 monsieur
German: 4 Herr
Italian: 6 signor
Spanish: 5 señor

Mister Roberts author
6 Heggen (Thomas)

mistreat
5 abuse 6 ill-use, molest 7 rough up
9 brutalize, manhandle

mistress
4 doxy, moll 5 lover, woman 7 hetaira 8 dulcinea, ladylove, paramour
9 concubine, courtesan, inamorata,
kept woman 10 chatelaine, girl
friend
of Charles II: 4 Gwyn (Nell) 8 Villiers (Barbara)
of Edward III: 7 Perrers (Alice)
of Henry II (England): 8 Clifford
(Rosamund)
of Henry II (France): 9 de Poiters
(Diane)
of Louis XV: 9 Pompadour (Madame de)

mistrust
5 doubt 7 concern, dispute, dubiety, surmise, suspect 8 wariness
9 apprehend, misgiving, suspicion

10 foreboding, skepticism 11 incertitude, uncertainty 12 apprehension

mistrustful
4 wary 5 leery 6 uneasy 7 dubious,
jealous 8 doubting 9 skeptical
10 disquieted, suspicious 12 apprehensive

misty
3 dim 4 hazy 5 foggy, vague
6 cloudy, vapory 7 blurred, obscure,
tearful, unclear 8 confused, nebulous, vaporous 10 indistinct

misunderstanding
4 rift, spat, tiff 5 mix-up 6 breach
7 dispute, quarrel, rupture 8 squabble
10 falling-out 12 disagreement

misuse
5 waste
of a word: 8 malaprop 11 malapropism

mite
3 bit, jot 4 atom, iota 5 grain,
minim, ounce, speck 6 acarid,
tittle 7 chigger, modicum, smidgen
8 molecule, particle
family: 8 oribatid

miter
5 crown, joint 9 headdress

mitigate
4 ease 5 abate, allay, relax, slake
6 lessen, soften, subdue, temper
7 assuage, lighten, mollify, relieve
8 palliate, moderate, tone down
9 alleviate, extenuate, meliorate

mitigation
4 ease 6 relief 8 easement

mitosis
12 cell division, karyokinesis
stage: 8 anaphase, prophase
9 metaphase, telophase

mix
4 fuse, link, lump, meld, stir 5 blend,
merge, unite 6 fusion, jumble,
mingle, tangle, work in 7 amalgam,
combine, concoct, confuse, conjoin 8 coalesce, compound, confound 9 associate, commingle,

mixed

interfuse **10** amalgamate, crossbreed **11** intermingle **12** amalgamation

mixed

6 hybrid, impure, motley, sundry, varied **7** diluted, diverse, mongrel **8** assorted, compound **9** composite, interbred, irregular **12** multifarious **13** heterogeneous, miscellaneous

mixed bag

4 olio **5** salad **6** jumble, medley **7** mélange **8** mishmash, pastiche **9** potpourri **10** assortment, hodgepodge, miscellany **11** gallimaufry

mixed-up

5 fazed **7** jumbled **8** confused **9** flustered, perplexed **10** bewildered, disjointed, distracted, incoherent, nonplussed **12** disconcerted

mixologist

6 barman **7** tapster **9** barkeeper, bartender

mixture

4 brew, hash, olio, stew **5** alloy, blend, fusion, hybrid, jumble, medley **7** amalgam, farrago, mélange **8** compound, mishmash, solution **9** composite, potpourri **10** concoction, confection, miscellany, salmagundi **11** combination **12** amalgamation

mix up

5 addle **6** fuddle, jumble, muddle **7** confuse, fluster, mistake **8** befuddle, bewilder, confound **10** disarrange, discompose **11** disorganize, misidentify

mix-up

4 hash, mess, muss **5** botch, chaos, error, melee **6** muddle, tangle **7** mistake **8** shambles **9** commotion, confusion

mks unit

3 lux, ohm **4** mole, volt, watt **5** farad, henry, hertz, joule, lumen, meter, metre, tesla, weber **6** ampere, kelvin, newton, pascal, second **7** candela, coulomb, siemens **8** kilogram

Mnemosyne

6 Memory
daughters: **5** Muses
father: **6** Uranus
lover: **4** Zeus
mother: **4** Gaea

Moabite

city: **3** Kir
god: **7** Chemosh
king: **5** Eglon, Mesha

Moab's father

3 Lot

moan

4 wail, weep **5** gripe, groan, whine **6** bewail, grieve, grouse, lament **7** deplore **8** complain

mob

3 jam **4** clan, gang, herd, pack, push, ring, riot **5** crowd, crush, horde, mafia, press, swarm **6** jostle, masses, rabble, throng **8** canaille, riffraff **9** hoi polloi, multitude **11** proletariat

mobile

5 fluid **6** moving **7** migrant, movable, protean **8** cellular, moveable, unstable, unsteady, variable **9** adaptable, changeful, itinerant, mercurial, migratory, unsettled, versatile **10** ambulatory, capricious, changeable, inconstant **11** peripatetic

mobile home

6 camper **7** trailer **9** Airstream

mobile-phone area

4 cell

mobilize

5 drive, impel, rally, ready, rouse **6** arouse, call up, muster, prompt, propel **7** actuate, animate, marshal **8** activate, assemble, organize **9** circulate

mobster

4 goon, thug **6** hit man **7** mafioso **8** criminal, gangster **9** godfather, racketeer

Moby Dick

5 whale **10** white whale

author: 8 Melville (Herman)
character: 3 Pip 6 Daggoo, Parsee
7 Ishmael 8 Queequeg, Starbuck,
Tashtego
pursuer: 4 Ahab
ship: 6 Pequod

moccasin
6 loafer 7 slipper 8 larrigan

mock
3 ape 4 defy, fake, gibe, jape, jeer,
razz, twit 5 bogus, chaff, dummy,
false, feign, mimic, phony, quasi,
sneer, taunt, tease 6 deride, ersatz,
parody, pseudo, send up 7 deceive,
feigned, imitate, lampoon, mislead
8 ridicule, satirize, so-called, spurious 9 imitation, simulated 10 artificial 11 counterfeit

mockery
4 sham 5 farce, scorn, sport 6 jap-
ery, parody, satire 7 take-off 8 contempt, derision, raillery, ridicule,
travesty 9 burlesque, imitation
10 caricature 13 laughingstock

mocking
8 derisive, sardonic, scornful 9 sarcastic

mode
3 fad, way 4 chic, rage 5 state,
style, vogue 6 custom, manner,
method, status, system 7 fashion
9 condition, procedure, situation,
technique 10 convention, dernier cri

model
4 copy, type 5 dummy, ideal, shape
6 design, effigy, mirror, mockup,
symbol 7 classic, epitome, example,
imitate, manikin, paragon, pattern,
perfect, replica, typical 8 ensample,
exemplar, flawless, mannikin, ma-
quette, nonesuch, paradigm, standard 9 archetype, beau ideal, blueprint, classical, criterion, exemplary,
miniature, nonpareil 10 apotheosis,
embodiment, prototypal, touchstone
12 paradigmatic, prototypical, reproduction

moderate
3 ebb 4 calm, cool, curb, even, fair,

mild, slow, so-so, wane 5 abate,
bland, let up, sober 6 gentle, lessen,
medium, paltry, reduce, relent, slight,
soften, steady, subdue, temper
7 average, chasten, control, cushion, die away, die down, ease off,
equable, lighten, limited, neutral,
relieve, slacken, subside, trivial
8 centrist, constant, decrease, diminish, discreet, mediocre, middling,
mitigate, restrain 9 alleviate, constrain, temperate 10 abstemious,
controlled, reasonable, restrained
11 indifferent 12 conservative

moderation
7 control, measure 9 restraint
10 abstinence, constraint, limitation,
temperance 13 temperateness

moderator
5 judge 7 arbiter 8 chairman, examiner, governor, mediator 10 peacemaker 11 chairperson

modern
3 new 5 fresh, novel 6 recent
7 current 8 neoteric, up-to-date
10 newfangled, present-day 12 contemporary

modernize
5 renew 6 update 8 renovate 9 refurbish 10 rejuvenate

modest
3 coy, shy 4 meek, prim 5 lowly,
plain, timid 6 decent, demure, humble, prissy, proper, seemly, simple
7 bashful, prudish 8 decorous,
discreet, moderate, priggish, reserved, reticent, retiring 9 diffident
10 unassuming 11 puritanical,
straitlaced, unassertive, unelaborate
12 self-effacing, unornamented
13 unembellished, unembroidered,
unpretentious

Modest Proposal author
5 Swift (Jonathan)

modesty
7 decency, reserve 8 chastity,
humility, timidity 9 propriety, reticence 10 diffidence

modicum

3 bit, jot **4** atom, iota, mite, whit
5 grain, minim, ounce, pinch, scrap,
speck, trace **7** smidgen, soupçon
8 particle

modify

4 vary **5** adapt, alter, amend, limit,
tweak **6** adjust, change, mutate,
revise, rework, temper **7** qualify
8 mitigate, moderate, restrain **9** refashion

modish

4 chic **5** smart, swank **6** chichi,
trendy, with-it **7** dashing, stylish
11 fashionable

Modred

father: **6** Arthur
mother: **8** Margawse
slayer, victim: **6** Arthur

modulate

4 vary **5** tweak **6** adjust, attune,
temper **8** fine-tune, regulate, restrain

modus _____

7 vivendi **8** operandi

modus operandi

5 style **6** custom, manner, method,
system **7** process, program, routine **8** approach, practice, strategy
9 procedure, technique

mogul

4 czar, king, lord **5** baron, nabob,
ruler **6** bigwig, prince, sachem,
tycoon **7** kingpin, magnate **9** plutocrat, potentate

Mohammed

see **Muhammad**

Mohawk chief

5 Brant (Joseph) **8** Hiawatha

Mohican chief

5 Uncas

moiety

3 cut **4** half, part **5** piece **7** element,
portion, section, segment **8** division
9 component

moil

3 tug, wet **4** grub, to-do, work

5 churn, dirty, drive, grind, labor, swirl
6 bustle, clamor, drudge, hubbub,
lather, seethe, strain, strive, uproar
7 ferment, travail, trouble, wrangle
8 drudgery **9** agitation, commotion,
confusion **10** hurly-burly, turbulence

moist

3 wet **4** damp, dank, dewy **5** humid
6 clammy, steamy, sticky **7** dampish,
maudlin, tearful, wettish

moisten

3 wet **6** dampen **8** humidify, saturate

moisture

4 damp **5** vapor **7** wetness **8** humidity **13** precipitation

mojo

3 hex **4** jinx **5** charm, magic, power,
spell **6** hoodoo, whammy

molar

5 tooth **7** grinder
neighbor: **6** canine

molasses

7 treacle **10** blackstrap

mold

3 die **4** cast, form, sort, type **5** forge,
knead, shape, stamp **6** design,
fungus **7** fashion, pattern **8** template
9 construct **11** description

moldable

6 pliant, supple **7** ductile, plastic,
pliable **9** adaptable, malleable

molder

3 rot **5** decay, waste **7** crumble
9 break down, decompose **11** deteriorate **12** disintegrate

molding

4 bead, ogee **5** congé, ogive, talon,
torus **6** reglet **7** annulet, beading,
cavetto, cornice, reeding **8** cincture
9 baseboard
compound: **4** beak, cyma, ogie
10 serpentine
edge: **5** arris
flat: **5** bevel, splay **6** fascia, fillet,
listel, regula **7** chamfer
simple curve: **4** roll **5** flute, ovolo,
torus **6** scotia **8** astragal

Moldova
  capital: 8 Chisinau, Kishinev
  former name: 8 Moldavia
  language: 8 Romanian
  monetary unit: 3 leu
  neighbor: 7 Romania, Ukraine
  river: 8 Dniester

moldy
  5 dated, fusty, musty, passé 6 bygone, old hat 7 ancient, antique, archaic, outworn 8 mildewed, outdated 9 crumbling, moth-eaten 10 antiquated 12 old-fashioned

mole
  3 spy 4 pier, quay 5 jetty, nevus 6 burrow, tunnel 9 birthmark 10 breakwater

molecule
  3 bit, jot 4 iota 5 minim, speck 7 modicum 8 particle

molest
  3 vex 4 bait 5 abuse, annoy, harry, tease 6 badger, bother, harass, heckle, hector, pester, plague 7 disturb, torment, trouble 9 persecute

Moll Flanders author
  5 Defoe (Daniel)

mollify
  4 calm, ease 5 allay 6 pacify, soften, soothe, temper 7 appease, assuage, lighten, placate, relieve, sweeten 8 mitigate 9 alleviate 10 ameliorate, conciliate, propitiate

mollusk
  6 chiton
  bivalve: 4 clam 6 cockle, mussel, oyster, teredo 7 geoduck, scallop 8 shipworm
  cephalopod: 5 squid 7 octopus 8 argonaut, nautilus 10 cuttlefish
  part: 6 mantle, radula, siphon
  tooth shell: 9 dentalium
  univalve: 4 slug 5 conch, cowry, murex, snail, whelk 6 cowrie, limpet, triton 7 abalone 10 nudibranch, periwinkle

Molly ____
  7 Maguire, Pitcher

mollycoddle
  3 pet 4 baby 5 humor, spoil 6 cocker, cosset, dandle, pamper 7 cater to, indulge

Moloch's pit
  6 Tophet

molt
  4 cast, shed, slip 6 change, slough 7 cast off, discard, ecdysis 9 slough off

molted skins
  7 exuviae

molten
  6 melted 7 glowing 9 liquefied

molten rock
  4 lava 5 magma

moment
  5 flash, jiffy, point, shake, trice 6 import, minute, second 7 instant 8 juncture, occasion 9 magnitude 10 importance 11 consequence, split second 12 significance

momentary
  5 brief, quick 8 fleeting, fugitive 9 ephemeral, fugacious, transient 10 evanescent, short-lived, transitory

momentous
  5 grave 7 epochal, fateful, serious, weighty 9 important 10 meaningful 11 significant, substantial 12 considerable 13 consequential

momentousness
  6 import, weight 9 magnitude 10 importance 11 consequence, weightiness 12 significance

momentum
  5 drive 6 energy, thrust 7 impetus, impulse 10 propulsion

Momo author
  4 Ende (Michael)

momus
  6 carper, critic, mocker 7 caviler 8 caviller 9 detractor 11 faultfinder

Monaco
  commune: 10 Monte Carlo

monad

language: 6 French
monetary unit: 4 euro
neighbor: 6 France
prince: 6 Albert 7 Rainier
princess: 5 Grace

monad

3 one 4 atom, unit 8 zoospore
9 protozoan

Mona Lisa

10 La Gioconda
painter: 7 da Vinci (Leonardo)
8 Leonardo (da Vinci)

monarch

4 czar, king, raja, tsar, tzar 5 queen,
rajah, ruler 6 kaiser, prince 7 emperor, empress, majesty 9 butterfly,
potentate, sovereign

monarchical

5 regal, royal 6 kingly 8 imperial,
kinglike, majestic 9 sovereign

monarch's daughter

8 princess
Portuguese, Spanish: 7 infanta

monarch's son

6 prince
French: 7 dauphin
Portuguese, Spanish: 7 infante

monarchy

4 rule 5 realm, reign 7 kingdom
8 kingship 9 autocracy, monocracy
11 sovereignty

monastery

5 abbey 6 friary, priory 7 convent,
nunnery 8 cloister
Buddhist: 8 lamasery
Eastern Orthodox: 5 laura
head: 5 abbot, prior

monastic

4 abbé, monk 7 ascetic, brother
8 isolated, secluded 9 reclusive
10 cloistered 11 sequestered

_____ Mondrian

4 Piet

monetary

6 fiscal 9 financial, pecuniary
10 numismatic

monetary rate

7 millage

monetary unit

see at individual countries

money

4 cash, coin, gelt, jack, kale, loot,
pelf, swag 5 bread, chips, dough,
funds, lucre, moola, rhino 6 boodle,
change, dinero, do-re-mi, mammon,
moolah, riches, specie, wampum,
wealth 7 cabbage, capital, coinage,
lettuce, needful, scratch, stipend
8 bankroll, currency, finances, treasure 9 resources 10 greenbacks
11 filthy lucre, legal tender

moneyed

4 rich 5 flush 6 loaded 7 opulent,
wealthy, well-off 8 affluent, well-to-
do 10 prosperous, well-heeled

money-grubber

5 miser 7 hoarder, niggard, scrooge
8 tightwad 9 skinflint 10 cheapskate
12 penny-pincher

moneymaking

6 paying 7 gainful 9 lucrative
10 profitable, well-paying, worthwhile
12 advantageous, remunerative

monger

4 hawk, sell, vend 6 broker, dealer,
hawker, peddle, trader, vendor
7 higgler, packman, peddler 8 huckster

Mongol conqueror

9 Tamerlane 10 Kublai Khan
11 Genghis Khan, Tamburlaine

Mongolia

capital: 9 Ulan Bator
11 Ulaanbaatar
conqueror: 6 Ögödei 11 Genghis
Khan
desert: 4 Gobi
lake: 6 Baikal
monetary unit: 6 tugrik
mountain range: 5 Altai, Altay
6 Kentai 7 Hentiyn 9 Altai Shan,
Altay Shan
neighbor: 5 China 6 Russia
river: 5 Orhun 7 Selenga

mongrel
3 cur 4 mule, mutt 5 cross 6 hybrid 7 bastard, mixture 8 half-bred 9 crossbred, half blood, half-breed 10 crossbreed

moniker
3 tag 4 name 6 handle 8 cognomen, nickname 9 sobriquet 11 appellation, designation

monish
4 warn

monition
6 caveat 7 caution, portent, warning 11 forewarning

monitor
4 test 5 check, watch 6 screen 7 adviser, observe, oversee 8 watchdog 11 keep track of

Monitor
designer: 8 Ericsson (John)
opponent: 8 Virginia 9 Merrimack

monitory
7 warning 8 advisory 10 cautionary

monk
4 abbé 5 friar 7 brother 8 cenobite, monastic 9 anchorite
Buddhist: 4 lama 5 bonze
Hindu: 8 sannyasi
Roman Catholic: 8 Capuchin, Salesian, Trappist 9 Carmelite, Dominican 10 Carthusian, Cistercian, Franciscan 11 Augustinian
room: 4 cell
shaven crown: 7 tonsure
title: 3 Dom, Fra 5 Padre

monkey
3 imp 4 mess 5 gamin 6 meddle, simian, tamper, urchin 8 busybody 9 interfere, interlope
New World: 4 titi 6 howler, spider, uakari, woolly 7 sapajou, tamarin 8 capuchin, marmoset, squirrel 11 douroucouli
Old World: 5 Diana, drill 6 guenon, langur, rhesus, vervet 7 colobus, hanuman, macaque 8 mandrill, mangabey 9 proboscis 10 Barbary ape

monkeyshine
3 gag 4 dido, jape, lark 5 antic, caper, prank, stunt, trick 6 frolic 10 shenanigan, tomfoolery

monocratic
8 absolute, despotic 9 arbitrary, autarchic, tyrannous 10 autocratic, tyrannical

monogram
8 initials

monograph
5 study 6 thesis 8 tractate, treatise 9 discourse 12 disquisition, dissertation

monopolize
3 hog 5 sew up 6 absorb, corner 7 control, engross 8 dominate, take over

monopoly
5 trust 6 cartel, corner 7 control 9 ownership, syndicate 10 consortium, domination 11 exclusivity

monotone
5 drone

monotonous
4 blah, dull 6 boring, dreary 7 droning, humdrum, one-note, uniform 8 singsong, unvaried 9 unvarying 10 pedestrian, repetitive 11 repetitious

monotony
6 tedium 7 humdrum 8 flatness, sameness 10 uniformity

monsoon
6 deluge 8 downpour 9 rainstorm 10 cloudburst

monster
4 ogre 5 beast, freak, giant, whale 6 mutant, ogress 8 behemoth, bogeyman, colossus, giantess 9 hellhound, leviathan, manticore
biblical: 5 Rehab 8 Behemoth 9 Leviathan
female: 6 Gorgon, Medusa, Scylla
fire-breathing: 6 dragon, Typhon 7 Chimera 8 Chimaera
fowl-dragon: 10 cockatrice

French: 8 Tarasque
horse-fish: 11 hippocampus
hundred-armed: 9 Enceladus
hundred-eyed: 5 Argus
hundred-handed: 8 Briareus
lion-eagle: 7 griffin
serpent-headed: 6 gorgon
study of: 10 teratology
three-bodied: 6 Geryon
three-headed dog: 8 Cerberus
two-headed dog: 6 Orthos
water: 6 kraken
woman-bird: 5 Harpy
woman-lion: 6 Sphinx
woman-serpent: 7 Echidna
(see also **dragon**)

_____ monster
4 Gila

monstrosity
4 mess 5 freak 6 fright, horror
7 eyesore, outrage, prodigy 8 atrocity, enormity 11 abomination 12 malformation

monstrous
4 huge, vast 5 awful, giant, large
7 glaring, heinous, hellish, hideous, immense, mammoth, massive, titanic
8 aberrant, abnormal, colossal, deformed, dreadful, enormous, fiendish, freakish, gigantic, godawful, gruesome, horrible, infamous, shocking, towering 9 atrocious, egregious, fantastic, frightful, grotesque, loathsome, malformed, unnatural 10 diabolical, flagitious, gargantuan, horrendous, impressive, monumental, outrageous, prodigious, scandalous, stupendous, tremendous 11 elephantine

montage
6 jumble, medley 7 mélange, mixture 9 composite, patchwork, potpourri 10 assortment, miscellany
12 conglomerate

Montagues' enemies
8 Capulets

Montaigne's forte
5 essay

Montana
capital: 6 Helena
city: 5 Butte 7 Bozeman 8 Billings, Missoula 10 Great Falls
lake: 8 Flathead
motto: 9 Oro y plata
mountain: 7 Granite (Peak)
nickname: 8 Treasure (State)
park: 7 Glacier
river: 8 Missouri 11 Yellowstone
state bird: 10 meadowlark
state flower: 10 bitterroot
state tree: 13 ponderosa pine

Monteverdi opera
5 Orfeo 7 Arianna

Montezuma
capital: 12 Tenochtitlán
conqueror: 6 Cortés, Cortéz (Hernán, Hernando)
people: 6 Aztecs
revenge: 8 diarrhea

month
Hindu: 3 Pus 4 Asin, Jeth, Magh
5 Aghan, Chait, Sawan 6 Asargh, Bhadon, Kartik, Phagun 7 Baisakh
Jewish: 4 Adar, Elul, Iyar 5 Nisan, Sivan, Tebet 6 Kislev, Shebat, Tammuz, Tishri 7 Heshvan
Muslim: 4 Rabi 5 Rajab, Safar
6 Jumada, Sha'ban 7 Ramadan; Shawwal 8 Muharram 9 Dhu'l-Hijja, Dhu'l-Qa'dah

Montmartre church
10 Sacré Coeur

Montserrat
capital: 8 Plymouth
discoverer: 8 Columbus (Christopher)
location: 10 West Indies
territory of: 7 Britain
volcano: 9 Soufrière

monument
5 cairn, stela, stupa 7 memento, tribute 8 archives, cenotaph, document, memorial 9 footstone, headstone, tombstone 10 gravestone
11 grave marker, testimonial
prehistoric: 6 dolmen, menhir
8 cromlech, megalith

monumental

4 huge, vast 6 mighty, mortal
7 awesome, immense, mammoth,
massive 8 enormous, gigantic,
historic, majestic, towering 9 monstrous 10 prodigious, stupendous,
tremendous 11 mountainous, outstanding 12 overwhelming

mooch

3 bat, beg, bum 4 grub, roam,
rove 5 amble, cadge, drift, range,
slink, sneak, steal, stray 6 ramble,
sponge, wander 7 maunder, meander, saunter 8 freeload, scrounge
9 panhandle

mooching

7 beggary 9 mendicity 10 mendicancy

mood

3 air 4 aura, feel, tone, whim 5 fancy,
humor 6 spirit, temper, vagary 7 caprice, emotion, feeling, mind-set
8 ambiance, ambience 9 character,
semblance 10 atmosphere 11 disposition, personality, temperament

moody

4 glum 5 mopey 6 fickle, gloomy
7 pensive 8 unstable 9 mercurial,
whimsical 10 capricious, changeable, depressive, inconstant, melancholy 13 temperamental

moola

4 cash, coin, pelf, swag 5 bread,
dough, money 6 dinero, specie,
wampum 7 cabbage, scratch 9 long
green

moon

4 gape, mope 5 dream 6 dawdle
8 languish 9 satellite
dark area: 4 mare 5 maria (plural)
7 farside
god: 3 Sin 5 Nanna 6 Meztli
goddess: 4 Luna 5 Diana, Tanit
6 Hecate, Hekate, Selena, Selene,
Tanith 7 Artemis, Astarte
valley: 4 rill
vehicle: 3 LEM
(see also **satellite**)

Moon and Sixpence author

7 Maugham (W. Somerset)

mooncalf

4 dolt, fool 5 dunce, ninny 7 jackass, tomfool 9 simpleton

Moon River composer

7 Mancini (Henry)

moonshine

4 bosh, jake 5 hokum 6 bunkum,
humbug 7 bootleg, eyewash, hogwash 8 homebrew, malarkey, nonsense, tommyrot 9 poppycock
10 balderdash, bathtub gin, contraband, flapdoodle 11 mountain dew
12 blatherskite

Moonstone, The

author: 7 Collins (Wilkie)
detective: 4 Cuff

moonstruck

4 daft, nuts 5 batty, corny, flaky,
kooky, mushy, nutty, sappy, wacko,
wacky 6 crazed, cuckoo, fruity,
insane, screwy 7 berserk, bonkers,
lunatic, maudlin, touched 8 romantic
9 nostalgic, schmaltzy 10 loveydovey, saccharine, unbalanced
11 sentimental

moor

3 bog, fen 4 dock, fell 5 berth,
catch, tie up 6 anchor, Berber,
fasten, Muslim, secure, tether 7 peat
bog 8 make fast, Moroccan
fictional: 7 Othello

moose

6 cervid
female: 3 cow
male: 4 bull
relative: 3 elk 4 deer

moot

5 argue, plead 6 broach, debate
7 agitate, bring up, canvass, discuss,
dispute, dubious, suggest, suspect
8 abstract, academic, arguable,
disputed, doubtful 9 debatable,
introduce, thrash out, uncertain,
unsettled, ventilate 10 disputable,
unresolved 11 problematic 12 questionable 13 controversial

mop
4 swab, wipe

mope
4 fret, idle, moon, pine, pout, sigh, stew, sulk 5 brood, drift, mosey 6 dawdle, linger 7 maunder, meander, saunter 8 languish

mopes
4 funk 5 blues, dumps, ennui, slump 7 dismals, malaise, sadness 8 dolefuls 10 depression, melancholy 11 unhappiness

mopey
3 low 4 blue, down, glum 6 broody, droopy, morose 7 doleful 8 cast down, dejected, downcast 9 depressed 10 dispirited, melancholy, spiritless

moppet
3 kid, tot 4 tyke 5 chick, child 7 toddler 8 juvenile 9 youngster

mop up
4 beat, drub, dust, lick, whip 6 absorb, garner, gather 7 shellac, trounce 8 complete, lambaste 9 overwhelm

moral
3 saw 4 good, just, pure, rule 5 adage, axiom, gnome, maxim, noble, right 6 chaste, decent, dictum, honest, lesson, proper, saying, truism 7 epigram, ethical, preachy, precept, proverb, upright, virtual 8 aphorism, apothegm, didactic, elevated, sermonic, virtuous 9 honorable, righteous 10 high-minded, principled, scrupulous, upstanding 11 rightminded 13 conscientious

morale
4 mood 5 heart 6 esprit, mettle, spirit, temper 7 resolve 10 confidence 13 esprit de corps

moralistic
5 noble, pious 7 canting, ethical 8 didactic, virtuous 9 righteous 10 principled 11 pharisaical, rightminded 13 sanctimonious

morality
5 ethic, honor, mores 6 purity, virtue 7 decency, probity 8 goodness 9 integrity, rectitude, rightness 11 saintliness, uprightness 13 righteousness

moralize
6 preach 7 lecture 9 preachify, sermonize 11 pontificate

morals
5 mores 6 ethics, ideals 8 scruples 9 integrity, standards 10 principles

morass
3 bog, fen, web 4 knot, maze, mesh, mire, quag, trap 5 marsh, skein, snarl, swamp 6 jungle, muddle, tangle 8 quagmire 9 imbroglio

moratorium
3 ban 5 delay 8 interval 10 suspension

moray
3 eel

morbid
4 dark, sick 5 moody 6 gloomy, grisly, morose, sickly, sullen 7 unsound 8 diseased, gruesome 9 saturnine, unhealthy 11 melancholic, unwholesome 12 pathological

mordancy
7 acidity 8 acerbity, acridity, acrimony, asperity, pungency 9 harshness, sharpness 10 causticity, trenchancy 11 astringency, sardonicism 12 incisiveness

mordant
4 keen 5 acrid, salty, sharp 6 biting 7 burning, caustic, cutting, pungent 8 incisive, sardonic, scathing 9 sarcastic, trenchant

Mordecai
cousin: 6 Esther
father: 4 Jair
mother: 6 Esther

more
3 new, too 4 also, else, plus 5 added, again, along, extra, fresh, older, other, spare 6 as well, better, nearer,

withal **7** another, besides, farther, further, greater **8** likewise, moreover **9** increased **10** additional

More book
6 Utopia

more or less
5 about **7** roughly **13** approximately

moreover
3 and, too **4** also **6** as well, withal **7** besides, further **8** likewise **10** in addition **11** furthermore **12** additionally

mores
6 ethics, habits, values **7** beliefs, customs, manners **8** folkways **9** amenities, etiquette **10** civilities **11** proprieties

Morgana's brother
6 Arthur

Morgan le Fay
9 sorceress
brother: 6 Arthur (King)

moribund
5 dying **6** ebbing, fading **7** dormant, outworn **8** decaying, expiring, inactive **9** declining **11** obsolescent **13** deteriorating

Mormon Church
administrative unit: 4 ward **5** stake
founder: 5 Smith (Joseph)
leader: 5 Young (Brigham)
priest: 5 elder

Mormon State
4 Utah

morning
4 dawn **5** sunup **6** aurora **7** dawning, sunrise **8** cockcrow, daybreak, daylight, forenoon
moisture: 3 dew **8** dewdrops
song: 6 aubade

Morocco
capital: 5 Rabat
city: 3 Fès **6** Meknès **9** Marrakech, Marrakesh **10** Casablanca
coast: 7 Barbary
language: 6 Arabic, Berber
monetary unit: 6 dirham

mountain: 7 Toubkal
mountain range: 3 Rif **5** Atlas
neighbor: 5 Spain **7** Algeria **13** Western Sahara
sea: 13 Mediterranean

moron
4 dodo, dolt, dope, fool **5** dummy, dunce, idiot **6** cretin, dimwit, stupid **7** dullard, half-wit **8** dumbbell, imbecile, numskull **9** ignoramus, lamebrain, numbskull, simpleton

moronic
4 dull, dumb **6** simple, stupid **8** backward, retarded **9** brainless, dim-witted, imbecilic **10** half-witted, slow-witted **12** feebleminded, simpleminded

morose
4 dour, glum, sour **5** moody, sulky **6** cranky, crusty, gloomy, morbid, sullen **7** crabbed, unhappy **9** depressed, saturnine **10** depressive, ill-humored, melancholy

morph
6 change, mutate **7** convert **9** transform, transmute **12** metamorphose, transmogrify

Morpheus
father: 6 Hypnos
god of: 5 sleep

Morrison novel
4 Jazz, Love, Sula **7** Beloved **9** Bluest Eye (The) **13** Song of Solomon

Morse code
dash: 3 dah
dot: 3 dit

morsel
3 bit **4** bite **5** crumb, goody, piece, scrap, snack, taste, treat **6** dainty, nibble, tidbit **7** soupçon **8** delicacy, fragment, kickshaw, mouthful

mortal
3 man **5** awful, being, fatal, frail, human, party **6** deadly, lethal, person **7** deathly, earthly, extreme, fleshly, tedious, worldly **8** creature, ruthless, temporal **9** merciless,

mortality

personage 10 implacable, individual, perishable 11 conceivable

mortality

5 flesh 7 mankind 8 fatality, humanity 9 death rate, humankind, lethality 10 deadliness

mortar

5 grout 6 binder, cannon, cement, vessel 7 plaster, sealant 8 howitzer, ordnance

Morte d'Arthur author

6 Malory (Thomas)

mortgage

4 hock, lien, pawn 6 pledge 10 obligation

mortician

8 embalmer 10 undertaker

mortified

6 shamed 7 ascetic, ashamed, austere 8 red-faced 9 chagrined 10 humiliated, shamefaced 11 embarrassed

mortify

5 abash, shame 6 dismay 7 chagrin, perturb 8 disgrace 9 discomfit, embarrass, humiliate

mortuary

8 funereal 10 sepulchral 11 funeral home

mosaic

5 inlay 7 chimera 8 terrazzo 9 composite, patchwork 12 tessellation
piece: 6 smalto 7 tessera 8 tesserae (plural)

Moscow

cathedral: 11 Saint Basil's
citadel: 7 Kremlin
resident: 9 Muscovite

Moses

brother: 5 Aaron
brother-in-law: 5 Hobab
deathplace: 4 Nebo
father-in-law: 6 Jethro
sister: 6 Miriam
son: 7 Eliezer, Gershom
spy: 5 Caleb
successor: 6 Joshua
wife: 8 Zipporah

mosey

4 mope 5 amble, drift 6 dawdle, linger, ramble, stroll, wander 7 maunder, meander, saunter

mosh

4 slam 9 slam-dance

Moslem

see **Muslim**

mosque

6 masjid
niche: 6 mihrab
prayer caller: 7 muezzin
turret: 7 minaret

mosquito

5 culex
genus: 5 Aëdes, Culex 9 Anopheles

moss

9 bryophyte
kind: 4 peat 8 sphagnum
part: 4 seta 7 capsule, rhizoid
study of: 8 bryology

mossback

4 fogy 6 fossil 10 fuddy-duddy 11 reactionary 12 antediluvian, conservative 13 stick-in-the-mud

mostly

6 mainly 7 chiefly, largely, overall, usually 9 generally, primarily 11 principally 13 predominantly

mote

3 bit, dot, jot 4 iota, whit 5 grain, point, speck, trace 8 flyspeck, particle

moth

immature: 5 larva 6 larvae (plural) 11 caterpillar
kind: 4 luna 7 codling, tussock 8 Cecropia, silkworm 9 browntail
order: 11 Lepidoptera

moth-eaten

4 worn 5 dated, dingy, faded, mangy, moldy, musty, passé, ratty, seedy 6 bygone, old hat, patchy, shabby 7 antique, archaic, raggedy, rundown, unkempt 8 decrepit, outdated, outmoded, tattered, timeworn 10 antiquated, down-at-heel, threadbare 11 dilapidated

mother
3 dam, mom 4 mama, root 5 fount,
mammy, mater, momma, mommy,
mummy, nurse 6 origin, source
7 care for, nurture 9 prototype,
rootstock 10 provenance, wellspring
combining form: 4 matr 5 matri,
matro

mother country
8 homeland 10 fatherland

Mother Courage author
6 Brecht (Bertolt)

motherly
8 maternal 9 nurturing 10 protective

mother-of-pearl
5 nacre

Mother of Presidents
8 Virginia

Mother of the Gods
3 Ops 4 Rhea 6 Cybele

motif
4 idea, text 5 point, theme, topic
6 design, device, figure, matter
7 pattern, subject 13 subject matter

motion
4 stir, sway 6 signal 7 gesture
8 movement, proposal, stirring
9 agitation

motionless
5 fixed, inert, still 6 frozen, static
7 stalled 8 becalmed, immobile,
stagnant, unmoving 9 immovable,
steadfast 10 stationary, stock-still

motion picture
see **movie**

motivate
4 fire, goad, move, spur 5 impel,
pique, rouse 6 arouse, excite, incite,
induce, prompt 7 actuate, inspire,
provoke, quicken, trigger 8 inspirit,
persuade 9 galvanize, influence,
stimulate

motivation
4 spur 5 drive 7 impetus, impulse
8 ambition, catalyst, stimulus 9 impulsion, incentive, stimulant 10 incitation, incitement 11 inspiration,
instigation, provocation

motive
3 aim, end 4 spur 5 cause, point,
theme, topic 6 design, device,
figure, intent, matter, object, reason,
spring 7 impulse, pattern, purpose,
subject 8 stimulus 9 incentive,
intention, rationale 10 incitement,
inducement 11 inspiration

motley
5 mixed, salad 6 jumble, medley,
varied 7 dappled, diverse, piebald
8 assorted, pastiche 9 disparate,
multihued 10 assortment, hodgepodge, miscellany, multicolor, variegated 11 gallimaufry, varicolored
12 conglomerate, multicolored,
multifarious, parti-colored 13 heterogeneous, miscellaneous, polychromatic

motor
3 car 4 auto, ride 5 buggy, drive
6 cruise, engine 7 machine 10 automobile

motorboat
6 launch 7 cruiser, inboard 8 outboard, runabout 12 cabin cruiser

motorcycle
7 chopper 8 minibike 9 trail bike
adjunct: 7 sidecar

Motown
7 Detroit

mottle
4 spot 5 fleck 6 blotch, dapple,
marble 7 spatter, speckle, stipple,
splotch

mottled
5 tabby 7 blotchy, dappled, flecked,
spotted 8 blotched, brindled, speckled 9 checkered 10 variegated

motto
3 cry 5 adage, axiom, maxim 6 byword, saying, slogan, war cry 7 precept, proverb 8 aphorism 9 battle
cry, catchword, watchword 10 shibboleth 11 catchphrase

moue
3 mow, mug 4 face, pout 7 grimace

mound

4 bank, cock, heap, hill, hump, mass,
pile 5 cairn, drift, knoll, shock, stack
6 barrow, tumuli (plural) 7 bulwark,
hillock, rampart, tumulus 9 elevation
10 embankment
Buddhist: 5 stupa
burial, Eastern Europe: 6 kurgan
of detritus: 4 kame
of sand: 4 dune
of stones: 5 cairn

mount

3 alp, wax 4 lift, peak, rise, show,
soar 5 arise, build, climb, frame,
horse, put on, raise, rouse, scale,
set up, stage, steed, swell 6 ascend,
aspire, deepen, expand, launch,
uprear 7 advance, augment, display,
enhance, enlarge, install, magnify,
produce, support, upsurge 8 bestride, escalade, escalate, heighten,
increase, multiply, redouble 9 aggravate, intensify 10 promontory

mountain

3 alp, lot 4 bank, crag, dome, heap,
hill, hulk, lump, mass, mesa, much,
peak, pile, slew 5 bluff, butte, drift,
mound, shock, stack 6 height
Alaska: 4 Bona 6 Denali 7 Fora-
ker, Sanford 8 McKinley, Wrangell
Alberta: 6 Castle 10 Eisenhower
Alps: 4 Rosa (Monte) 5 Blanc,
Eiger 8 Jungfrau 10 Matterhorn
Angola: 4 Moco
Antarctica: 4 Mohl 6 Vinson
(Massif) 7 Gardner 9 Elizabeth
Appalachians: 8 Mitchell 10 Kitta-
tinny 10 Washington 13 Clingmans
Dome
Argentina: 9 Aconcagua
Australia: 4 Ziel 5 Bruce 6 Cradle
9 Kosciusko
biblical: 5 Horeb, Tabor 6 Hermon
8 Har Tavor
Black Hills: 6 Harney (Peak)
Bolivia: 6 Sorata 8 Illimani
Borneo: 8 Kinabalu, Kinabulu
California: 5 Guyot 6 Shasta,
Sonora (Peak) 7 Palomar, Whitney
8 Tuolumne 10 Buena Vista, Stanis-
laus

Canada: 5 Logan
China: 4 Emei, Song
Colorado: 5 Pikes (Peak) 9 Pur-
gatory (Peak)
Costa Rica: 6 Blanco 14 Chirripó
Grande
Cyprus: 7 Olympus, Troodos
depression: 3 col
Dominican Republic: 6 Duarte
8 Trujillo
Egypt: 4 Musa 5 Sinai
Fiji: 8 Victoria 9 Tomaniivi
foot: 8 piedmont
France: 5 Blanc (Mont)
Gabon: 8 Iboundji
Georgia: 8 Springer 10 Oglethorpe
Germany: 7 Zollern 9 Zugspitze
11 Fichtelberg
Greece: 3 Ida 5 Athos, Levka
7 Helicon, Olympus 9 Parnassus,
Psiloriti 10 Pendelikon, Pentelicus
Greenland: 9 Gunnbjorn
Himalayas: 6 Lhotse 7 Everest
9 Annapurna
India: 5 Japvo
Indonesia: 4 Lawu 5 Kwoka,
Lawoe, Raung 6 Raoeng, Semeru
7 Kerinci
Israel: 5 Meron 6 Carmel
Ivory Coast: 5 Nimba
Japan: 4 Fuji 5 Iwate 7 Fujisan
8 Fujiyama
Java: 5 Liman
Jordan: 3 Hor 5 Hārūn
Maine: 8 Katahdin
Malaysia: 5 Ophir, Tahan 6 Ledang
Mediterranean entrance: 5 Calpe
9 Gibraltar
Mexico: 7 Orizaba (Pico de)
New York: 4 Bear 5 Marcy
North America's highest: 6 Denali
8 McKinley
North Carolina: 8 Mitchell
Oman: 4 Sham
Oregon: 4 Hood
Pakistan: 9 Tirich Mir
Papua New Guinea: 7 Wilhelm
Pennine Alps: 4 Rosa (Monte)
Philippines: 3 Apo, Iba 4 Labo
5 Silay
ridge: 4 spur 5 arête, crest 7 saw-
buck

Romania: 11 Moldoveanul
South America: 7 Roraima 9 Aconcagua
South Dakota: 6 Custer (Peak)
Switzerland: 3 Dom 4 Rosa (Monte) 5 Eiger 8 Jungfrau 10 Matterhorn
Syria: 4 Druz 5 Duruz
Tanzania: 11 Kilimanjaro
Tasmania: 4 Ossa
Tennessee: 13 Clingmans Dome
Togo: 4 Agou
Utah: 5 Kings
Vermont: 9 Mansfield
Vietnam: 8 Ngoo Linh
Virginia: 6 Rogers
Western Hemisphere's highest: 9 Aconcagua
world's highest: 7 Everest
Wyoming: 5 Cloud 7 Gannett (Peak)
(see also **peak**)

mountain climbing
　equipment: 3 axe, nut 5 piton 7 crampon 9 carabiner
　maneuver: 6 rappel 10 rappelling

mountain dew
　see **moonshine**

mountain formation
　7 orogeny 10 orogenesis

mountainous
　4 huge, vast 6 alpine, mighty 7 immense, mammoth, massive 8 enormous, gigantic, towering 10 monumental, prodigious

mountain pass
　3 col
Afghanistan-Pakistan: 6 Khyber
Alps: 5 Gries
California: 4 Muir 6 Sonora
China-Myanmar: 5 Namni
Colorado: 3 Ute 5 Mosca, Muddy, Music, Raton
Europe: 8 Moravian
Greece: 5 Rupel
Hindu Kush Mts.: 5 Dorah, Durah
Pakistan: 5 Bolan, Gomal, Gumal
Sierra Nevada: 4 Mono
Switzerland: 5 Furka, Gemmi 7 Grimsel 8 Lötschen

Tunisia: 4 Faïd
Ukrainian: 5 Uzhok
Wyoming: 5 Union

mountain range
Asia: 5 Altai, Altay 8 Himalaya, Tien Shan 9 Altai Shan, Altay Shan, Himalayan, Himalayas, Hindu Kush
Australia: 8 Flinders
Europe: 4 Alps 10 Carpathian
Germany: 4 Harz 5 Hartz
Greece: 4 Oeta
India: 5 Ghats
Iran: 6 Zagros
Italy: 9 Apennines
Mexico: 11 Sierra Madre
North Africa: 5 Atlas
North America: 5 Rocky 7 Rockies 11 Appalachian
Russia: 4 Ural
Scotland: 9 Grampians
Sinai: 9 Gebel Musa
Slovakia: 5 Tatra, Tatry 9 High Tatra
South America: 5 Andes
Turkey: 6 Taurus
United States: 5 Rocky, White 6 Brooks 7 Cascade, Olympic, Rockies, Sawatch, Wasatch 8 Absaroka, Aleutian, Catskill, Wrangell 9 Blue Ridge, Wind River 10 Adirondack, Bitterroot, Black Hills, Clearwater, Grand Teton
Zimbabwe: 6 Matopo (Hills) 7 Matoppo (Hills)

Mountain State
　7 Montana 12 West Virginia

mountebank
　5 quack 6 con man 8 swindler 9 charlatan 11 flimflammer, quacksalver 13 confidence man

Mount St. Helens
　7 volcano

mourn
　3 rue 6 bemoan, bewail, grieve, lament, sorrow 7 deplore, protest

mournful
　3 sad 6 dismal, gloomy, rueful, somber, triste, woeful 7 doleful, forlorn, joyless, unhappy 8 dejected,

desolate, dolorous, funereal, grievous, wretched **9** dirgelike, plaintive **10** depressing, despondent, dispirited, lugubrious, melancholy **11** distressing, melancholic, regrettable, unfortunate **12** heavyhearted

mournfulness
5 blues, dumps, gloom **7** dismals, sadness **9** dejection **10** depression, melancholy

mourning
5 grief **7** keening, remorse, wailing, weeping **8** grieving **9** lamenting, morbidity, sorrowing, ululation **10** heartbreak **11** bereavement, lamentation

Mourning Becomes Electra
author: **6** O'Neill (Eugene)

mourning period, Jewish
5 shiva **6** shivah

mourning symbol
7 armband

mouse
6 rodent, shiner **8** black eye

mousy
3 shy **4** drab, dull **5** plain, quiet, timid **7** bashful **8** retiring, timorous **9** colorless, diffident, shrinking **11** unassertive **12** self-effacing

mouth
3 gob **4** trap **5** chops **6** kisser **8** entrance **10** embouchure

mouthlike opening
5 stoma **7** stomata (plural)

mouthpiece
5 organ **6** puppet **7** speaker **8** front man **9** spokesman **10** figurehead **11** spokeswoman **12** spokesperson

mouthwatering
5 sapid, tasty, yummy **6** savory, toothy **8** tasteful **9** delicious, palatable, succulent, toothsome **10** appetizing, delectable **11** good-tasting

mouthy
4 glib **5** gabby, talky, windy **7** verbose, voluble **8** effusive **9** bombastic, garrulous, talkative

movable
5 loose **6** mobile, motile, roving **8** portable **10** changeable

movables
5 goods **7** effects **8** chattels **10** belongings **11** furnishings

move
3 act **4** lead, spur, stir, sway **5** bring, budge, carry, drive, impel, leave, march, rouse, shift, start, touch **6** affect, convey, depart, excite, incite, induce, kindle, prompt, propel **7** actuate, advance, animate, conduct, impress, inspire, migrate, proceed, propose, provoke, request, suggest **8** activate, dislodge, displace, evacuate, get along, maneuver, motivate, persuade, progress, relocate, resettle, transfer, withdraw **9** dislocate, galvanize, influence, instigate, stimulate, transport

movement
4 flow, stir **5** tempo, trend **6** action, motion **7** crusade **8** activity, campaign, dynamism, maneuver, progress, stirring, tendency, velocity **9** migration
music: 4 moto
reflex: 5 taxis
stimulated: 7 kinesis

movie
4 cine, film, show **5** flick **6** cinema, talkie **7** picture **9** photoplay **11** picture show **13** motion picture
cowboy: 5 oater **7** western
short: 4 clip **8** newsreel

movie director
American: 3 Lee (Spike), Ray (Nicholas) **4** Coen (Joel), Ford (John), Hill (George Roy), Mann (Anthony), Penn (Arthur), Ritt (Martin), Ross (Herbert), Sirk (Douglas), Wise (Robert) **5** Allen (Woody), Ashby (Hal), Brown (Clarence), Capra (Frank), Cukor (George), Demme (Jonathan), Donen (Stanley), Fosse (Bob), Hawks (Howard), Ivory (James), Jonze (Spike), Kazan

(Elia), LeRoy (Mervyn), Logan (Joshua), Lucas (George), Lumet (Sidney), Lynch (David), Moore (Michael), Roach (Hal), Stone (Oliver), Vidor (King), Walsh (Raoul), Whale (James), Wyler (William), Zwick (Ed) **6** Altman (Robert), Beatty (Warren), Benton (Robert), Brooks (Richard), Burton (Tim), Cimino (Michael), Curtiz (Michael), Fuller (Samuel), Gibson (Mel), Hanson (Curtis), Howard (Ron), Huston (John), Kramer (Stanley), Malick (Terrence), Pakula (Alan), Parker (Alan), Welles (Orson), Wilder (Billy) **7** Borzage (Frank), Cameron (James), Chaplin (Charlie), Coppola (Francis Ford, Sofia), Costner (Kevin), De Mille (Cecil B.), De Palma (Brian), Fleming (Victor), Gilliam (Terry), Jewison (Norman), Kubrick (Stanley), McCarey (Leo), Nichols (Mike), Pollack (Sydney), Redford (Robert), Siodmak (Robert), Stevens (George), Sturges (Preston), Van Sant (Gus), Wellman (William) **8** Avildsen (John), Eastwood (Clint), Flaherty (Robert), Friedkin (William), Griffith (David Wark), Jarmusch (Jim), Levinson (Barry), Lubitsch (Ernst), Marshall (Penny), Minnelli (Vincente), Mulligan (Robert), Scorsese (Martin), Zemeckis (Robert) **9** Carpenter (John), Hitchcock (Alfred), Milestone (Lewis), Peckinpah (Sam), Preminger (Otto), Spielberg (Steven), Sternberg (Josef von), Streisand (Barbra), Tarantino (Quentin), Zinnemann (Fred) **10** Cassavetes (John), Heckerling (Amy), Mankiewicz (Joseph), Soderbergh (Steven) **11** Bogdanovich (Peter) **13** Frankenheimer (John)

Australian: 4 Weir (Peter) **6** Noonan (Chris) **9** Armstrong (Gillian), Beresford (Bruce)

Austrian: 4 Lang (Fritz) **8** Stroheim (Erich von) **9** Sternberg (Josef von)

British: 4 Lean (David), Reed (Carol) **5** Leigh (Mike), Losey (Joseph), Reisz (Karel), Scott (Ridley) **6** Figgis (Mike), Frears (Stephen), Jordan

(Neil), Newell (Mike), Parker (Alan), Powell (Michael) **7** Boorman (John), Branagh (Kenneth), Forsyth (Bill) **8** Anderson (Lindsay) **9** Hitchcock (Alfred) **10** Richardson (Tony) **11** Schlesinger (John)

Chinese: 3 Lee (Ang) **4** Chen (Kaige) **5** Zhang (Yimou)

French: 4 Demy (Jacques), Tati (Jacques), Vigo (Jean) **5** Malle (Louis) **6** Godard (Jean-Luc), Ophüls (Marcel), Renoir (Jean), Rohmer (Eric) **7** Bresson (Robert), Chabrol (Claude), Cocteau (Jean), Resnais (Alain), Rivette (Jacques) **8** Truffaut (François)

German: 6 Herzog (Werner), Ophüls (Max) **7** Winders (Wim) **8** Petersen (Wolfgang) **10** Fassbinder (Rainer Werner) **11** Riefenstahl (Leni), Schlöndorff (Volker)

Italian: 5 Leone (Sergio) **6** De Sica (Vittorio) **7** Fellini (Federico) **8** Pasolini (Pier Paolo), Visconti (Luchino) **9** Antonioni (Michelangelo) **10** Bertolucci (Bernardo), Rossellini (Roberto), Wertmüller (Lina), Zeffirelli (Franco)

Japanese: 3 Ozu (Yasujiru) **5** Itami (Juzo) **8** Kurosawa (Akira), Miyazaki (Hayao) **9** Mizoguchi (Kenji)

New Zealand: 7 Campion (Jane)

Polish: 5 Wajda (Ardrzej) **7** Holland (Agñieszka) **8** Polanski (Roman)

Russian: 9 Tarkovsky (Andrei) **10** Eisenstein (Sergei)

Spanish: 6 Buñuel (Luis) **9** Almodóvar (Pedro)

Swedish: 7 Bergman (Ingmar) **10** Zetterling (Mai)

movie producer
American: 3 Fox (William) **4** Cohn (Jack) **5** Lasky (Jesse), Mayer (Louis B.), Zukor (Adolph) **6** Warner (Jack L.), Zanuck (Darryl, Richard) **7** Goldwyn (Samuel), Laemmle (Carl) **8** Selznick (David O.)

Austrian: 9 Reinhardt (Max)

moving
5 astir **6** mobile **7** emotive, rousing **8** arousing, exciting, gripping,

pathetic, poignant, stirring, touching
9 affecting, emotional, inspiring,
transient **11** stimulating

moving stairs
9 escalator

mow
3 cut **4** clip, crop, fell, heap, moue,
pile, raze, rick **5** level, shave, shear,
stack **7** grimace **9** knock down

moxie
3 pep, vim, zip **4** grit, guts **5** brass,
heart, nerve, oomph, pluck, savvy,
spunk, vigor **6** energy, mettle, spirit,
starch **7** cojones, courage, know-
how **8** backbone **9** fortitude **10** get-
up-and-go, resolution **13** determination

Mozambique
capital: 6 Maputo
language: 5 Bantu **7** Swahili
10 Portuguese
monetary unit: 7 metical
neighbor: 6 Malawi, Zambia
8 Tanzania, Zimbabwe **9** Swaziland
11 South Africa
river: 6 Ruvuma **7** Limpopo, Zambezi

Mozart, Wolfgang Amadeus
birthplace: 8 Salzburg
cataloger: 6 Köchel (Ludwig)
deathplace: 6 Vienna
opera: 8 Idomeneo **10** Magic Flute
(The) **11** Don Giovanni, Il Rè Pas-
tore **12** Cosí Fan Tutte **16** Marriage
of Figaro (The)

MP's prey
4 AWOL **8** deserter

Mr. Moto star
5 Lorre (Peter)

Mrs. Grundy
4 prig **5** prude **7** puritan **8** bluenose

much
3 oft **4** long, many, most **5** often
6 highly, hugely, plenty **7** greatly,
notably **8** abundant **9** eminently,
extremely, great deal **10** frequently,
oftentimes, repeatedly
combining form: 4 poly **5** multi

Much Ado About Nothing
character: 4 Hero **7** Claudio, Don
John **8** Beatrice, Benedick, Dogberry

muck
3 goo, mud **4** crap, crud, dirt, dung,
gook, goop, grub, gunk, junk, mess,
mire, murk, plod, slog, slop, soil, toil
5 dirty, dreck, filth, grime, gumbo,
slave, slime, swill, trash, waste
6 drudge, litter, manure, meddle,
putter, sleaze, sludge, smirch, tinker
7 garbage, rubbish **8** nonsense
9 interfere

muckety-muck
3 VIP **5** nabob **6** bigwig, fat cat
7 big shot, kingpin, notable **8** kingfish, somebody **9** dignitary

mucky
4 foul **5** dirty, grimy, muddy, muggy,
murky, nasty, soggy **6** cruddy, filthy,
grubby, grungy **7** squalid, unclean

mucous
5 slimy **6** viscid

mud
4 dirt, mire, muck, ooze **5** dregs,
slime **6** depths, sludge

muddle
3 mix **4** hash, mess, muck, rile,
roil **5** addle, botch, mix up, snarl
6 ataxia, bungle, drivel, foul up,
fumble, jumble, jungle, litter, mess
up, tangle, tumble **7** clutter, confuse,
fluster, perplex, rummage, shuffle,
snarl up, stumble, stupefy **8** befuddle, bewilder, confound, disarray,
disorder, distract, entangle, mishmash, scramble, shambles, throw off,
unsettle **9** confusion, throw away
10 complicate, disarrange, discompose **11** disorganize

muddled
5 drunk, tight, tipsy, vague **7** mixed-
up **8** inchoate **10** disjointed, disordered, incoherent, inebriated
11 intoxicated, unorganized

muddle through
4 cope, fare **5** get by, get on **6** man-

age **7** carry on, make out **8** get along

muddy

3 dim, fog **4** base, blur, drab, dull, fade, foul, hazy, oozy, roil, soil **5** befog, cloud, dingy, dirty, grime, grimy, murky **6** cloudy, gloomy, grubby, sordid, turbid **7** becloud, begrime, confuse, obscure, squalid, tarnish, unclean, unclear **8** confused

muff

4 blow, flub **5** botch, fluff **6** bobble, bollix, bungle, fumble, goof up, mess up **7** louse up, misplay, screw up **9** mishandle

muffle

4 dull, mute, veil **5** shush **6** dampen, deaden, lessen, shroud, soften, stifle, subdue, wrap up **7** envelop, repress, silence, smother, squelch **8** bundle up, suppress, tone down

muffled

5 muted **6** dulled **7** stifled, subdued **8** deadened, obscured, silenced **9** distorted, enveloped **10** indistinct, suppressed

muffler

4 mask, veil **5** cloak, scarf

mug

3 cup, ham, mop, mow, rob **4** boob, dolt, dope, face, fool, moue, phiz, punk, puss, thug **5** dunce, idiot, mouth, rowdy, stein, tough **6** ambush, dimwit **7** assault, grimace, tankard **8** bullyboy, dumbbell, features, numskull **9** blockhead, bushwhack, ignoramus, roughneck

mugger

4 thug **6** robber **9** assailant, crocodile

muggy

4 damp **5** humid, moist **6** sticky, sultry **7** dampish

Muhammad

adopted son: **3** Ali
birthplace: **5** Mecca
camel: **5** Kaswa
daughter: **6** Fatima
deathplace: **6** Medina
deity: **5** Allah
father: **8** Abdallah, Abdullah
father-in-law: **7** Abu Bakr
flight: **6** hegira, hejira
follower: **6** Moslem, Muslim
horse: **5** Buraq **7** Alborak
religion: **5** Islam
son: **7** Ibrahim
son-in-law: **3** Ali
successor: **6** caliph **7** Abu Bakr
tribe: **7** Koreish, Quraysh
uncle: **8** Abu Talib
wife: **5** Aisha **6** Ayesha **7** Khadija

mulatto

5 métis, mixed **7** mestizo **9** half-breed, half-caste **10** crossbreed

mulberry

3 fig **10** breadfruit
type: **6** banyan **11** India rubber, osage orange

mulct

4 fine, milk, rook **5** bleed, cheat, gouge **6** extort, fleece **7** deceive, defraud, forfeit, penalty, swindle **8** penalize **9** blackmail

mule

5 cross, scuff **6** bagman, hybrid **7** bastard, courier, mongrel **8** smuggler **9** crossbred, half blood, half-breed **10** crossbreed

mulish

8 contrary, perverse, stubborn **9** obstinate, pigheaded **10** bull-headed, headstrong, inflexible, refractory, unyielding **11** stiff-necked

mull

4 hash, muse **5** brood, think, weigh **6** ponder **7** reflect **8** cogitate, consider, meditate, ruminate, turn over **9** pulverize **10** deliberate **11** contemplate

multicolored

4 pied **6** motley **7** dappled **9** prismatic **10** variegated **13** polychromatic

multifarious

5 mixed **6** motley, sundry, varied

multiform 858

7 diverse, various **8** assorted, manifold **13** heterogeneous, miscellaneous

multiform
6 sundry, varied **7** diverse, various **8** assorted, manifold **9** disparate **12** multifarious

multilateral
9 many-sided

multiple
4 many **6** shared, sundry **7** diverse, several, various **8** assorted, manifold, numerous **9** composite

multiplicity
3 lot **4** heap, load, mass, peck **5** flood, hoard, horde **6** barrel **7** variety **8** mountain, plethora **9** diversity, great deal, profusion

multiply
3 wax **4** rise **5** boost, breed, build, mount **6** expand, extend, spread **7** amplify, augment, enlarge, magnify **8** generate, heighten, increase **9** procreate, propagate, reproduce **10** aggrandize **11** proliferate

multitude
3 mob **4** army, herd, host, mass, slew **5** crowd, crush, drove, flock, horde, swarm **6** legion, myriad, public, throng **8** populace

multitudinous
4 many **6** legion, myriad, sundry **7** copious, various **8** abundant, manifold, numerous, populous **9** countless **10** numberless, voluminous **11** innumerable

mum
4 dumb, mute **5** quiet **6** silent **8** wordless **10** speechless, tongue-tied

mumble
6 murmur, mutter **7** maunder

mumbo jumbo
4 juju **6** fetish **9** gibberish **10** hocus-pocus **11** abracadabra **12** gobble-dygook, superstition

mummer
4 mime **5** actor, mimic **12** impersonator

mummify
5 dry up, wizen **6** embalm, wither **7** shrivel **9** desiccate

munch
3 eat **4** chaw, chew **5** champ, chomp, snack **6** crunch **9** masticate

mundane
5 lowly **6** earthy, normal **7** earthly, humdrum, prosaic, routine, terrene, worldly **8** banausic, day-to-day, everyday, familiar, ordinary, telluric, workaday **9** practical, sublunary, tellurian **11** commonplace, terrestrial, uncelestial **13** materialistic

municipal
5 civic, local, urban **12** metropolitan

munificent
6 lavish **7** liberal **8** generous, handsome **9** bounteous, bountiful **10** benevolent, freehanded, open-handed **11** magnanimous **13** philanthropic

munitions maker
5 Krupp

muralist
4 Sert (José María) **6** Benton (Thomas Hart), Giotto, Orozco (José Clemente), Rivera (Diego) **7** La Farge (John) **9** Siqueiros (David Alfaro) **12** Michelangelo (Buonarotti)

murder
3 hit, off **4** do in, kill, slay **5** blood, lynch, scrag, snuff, waste **6** rub out **7** bump off, execute, garrote, killing, smother, take out **8** foul play, homicide, knock off, strangle **9** eradicate, liquidate, slaughter **10** annihilate, asphyxiate, decapitate, extinguish **11** assassinate, electrocute, exterminate **12** manslaughter
brother: **10** fratricide
father: **9** patricide
king: **8** regicide
mother: **9** matricide

parent: 9 parricide
sister: 10 sororicide

murderer
6 hit man, killer, slayer 7 butcher
8 assassin, homicide 9 cutthroat,
manslayer 11 slaughterer

Murder in the Cathedral
author: 5 Eliot (Thomas Stearns)
character: 5 Henry (II) 6 Becket
(Thomas à)

murderous
6 deadly, lethal 10 sanguinary
12 bloodthirsty

murk
3 fog 4 haze, mist 5 brume, gloom
6 miasma 8 darkness 9 obscurity

murky
3 dim 4 dark, dull, foul, gray 5 dirty,
dusky, foggy, misty, muddy, roily,
vague 6 cloudy, gloomy, opaque,
somber, turbid 7 obscure 8 nebulous 9 ambiguous, equivocal,
tenebrous 10 caliginous

murmur
3 hum 4 buzz, purr 5 drone, rumor 6 grouch, grouse, mumble,
mutter, rumble 7 grumble, whisper
8 complain 9 grumbling, undertone
11 scuttlebutt, susurration

Muscat sultanate
4 Oman

muscle
4 beef, thew 5 brawn, force, might,
power, sinew 6 energy 7 potency
8 strength 9 strong arm
abdomen: 7 abdomen
arm: 6 biceps 7 triceps
back: 7 trapezius
calf: 6 soleus
chest: 10 pectoralis
jaw: 8 masseter
kind: 6 flexor, tensor 7 dilator,
evertor, levator, rotator 8 abductor,
adductor, extensor
loin: 5 psoas
neck: 8 platysma
shoulder: 7 deltoid 10 deltoideus
study of: 7 myology
thigh: 8 gracilis 9 sartorius

muscle-bound
5 rigid, stiff 6 wooden

muscular
4 ropy 5 beefy, burly, husky 6 brawny,
mighty, robust, sinewy, strong, sturdy
8 athletic, forceful, powerful, resolute,
stalwart, vigorous 9 Herculean,
strapping, well-built

muse
5 angel, brood, guide, think 6 genius,
ponder, trance 7 reflect, reverie
8 cogitate, meditate, mull over,
ruminate, turn over 10 deliberate
11 contemplate

Muse
father: 4 Zeus 7 Jupiter
mother: 9 Mnemosyne
of astronomy: 6 Urania
of choral song: 11 Terpsichore
of comedy: 6 Thalia
of dancing: 11 Terpsichore
of epic poetry: 8 Calliope
of history: 4 Clio
of love poetry: 5 Erato
of lyric poetry: 5 Erato
of music: 7 Euterpe
of pastoral poetry: 6 Thalia
of sacred poetry: 8 Polymnia
10 Polyhymnia
of tragedy: 9 Melpomene

museum
5 salon 7 archive, exhibit, gallery
8 atheneum 10 collection, repository

mush
4 slop 5 grits, gruel, hokum 6 bathos,
drivel, hominy 8 porridge, schmaltz

mushroom
4 grow 6 expand, spread 7 burgeon, explode, inflate 8 snowball
11 proliferate
combining form: 3 myc 4 myco
5 mycet 6 myceto
edible: 5 enoki, morel 6 bolete
7 cremini, crimini, porcini 8 shiitake
9 mousseron 10 champignon, porta-
bella, portabello, portobello 11 chan-
terelle
kind: 6 agaric, bolete 7 inky cap,
russula

mushy

part: 3 cap 4 gill, ring 5 stipe, volva 6 pileus 7 annulus 8 mycelium
poisonous: 7 amanita 8 death cap 9 fly agaric, toadstool

mushy

4 soft 5 pulpy, soppy, vague 6 quaggy, spongy 7 amorous, maudlin, mawkish, squashy, squishy 8 bathetic, effusive, romantic, squooshy 9 schmaltzy 10 lovey-dovey, saccharine 11 sentimental

music

abbreviation: 3 fff, ppp, sfz 5 cresc
bass staff lines: 5 GBDFA
bass staff spaces: 4 ACEG
characteristic phrase: 9 leitmotif, leitmotiv
chord: 5 major, minor, tonic 7 harmony 8 dominant 9 augmented 10 diminished
embellishment: 3 run 4 turn 5 trill 7 cadenza, mordent, roulade 8 arpeggio, flourish 9 grace note
for eight: 5 octet
for five: 7 quintet
for four: 7 quartet
for nine: 5 nonet
for one: 4 solo
for seven: 6 septet
for six: 6 sextet
for three: 4 trio
for two: 3 duo 4 duet
god: 6 Apollo
hall: 7 cabaret, theater
instrumental form: 3 jig 4 jazz, reel 5 étude, fugue, gigue, march, polka, rondo, suite, swing, waltz 6 minuet, pavane, sonata 7 bourrée, gavotte, mazurka, prelude, ragtime, toccata 8 chaconne, concerto, courante, fantasia, galliard, nocturne, overture, rhapsody, ricercar, saraband, serenade, symphony, tone poem 9 allemande, polonaise 11 rock and roll
medley: 4 olio
morning: 6 aubade
Muse: 7 Euterpe
night: 8 nocturne, serenade
note: 4 half 5 breve, minim, neume, whole 6 eighth, quaver 7 quarter 8 crotchet 9 sixteenth 10 semiquaver
patron saint: 7 Cecilia
period: 6 Modern, Rococo 7 Baroque 8 Medieval, Romantic 9 Classical
symbol: 3 bar, key 4 clef, flat, note, rest, slur, turn 5 sharp, staff 7 fermata, mordent 9 alla breve 10 accidental
treble staff lines: 5 EGBDF
treble staff spaces: 4 FACE
vocal form: 3 air 4 aria, hymn, lied, mass, song 5 chant, motet, opera, round 6 anthem, ballad 7 cantata, chanson, chorale 8 cavatina, madrigal, operetta, oratorio, serenade 9 cabaletta

musical

4 show 5 revue 6 choral 7 lyrical, melodic, songful, tuneful 8 harmonic, operetta, zarzuela 9 melodious, symphonic 10 euphonious, harmonious

musical composition

4 aria, hymn, lied, opus, song, trio 5 chant, canon, carol, étude, fugue, march, motet, opera, rondo, suite 6 anthem, ballad, sextet, sonata 7 cantata, chanson, chorale, prelude, quartet, quintet, requiem, scherzo, toccata 8 concerto, fantasia, madrigal, nocturne, operetta, oratorio, overture, postlude, serenade, sonatina, symphony 9 bagatelle, cabaletta, interlude 10 intermezzo, recitative

musical direction

accented: 7 marcato 8 sforzato 9 sforzando
all: 5 tutti
brisk: 4 vivo 6 vivace 7 allegro, animato
connected: 6 legato
detached: 8 spiccato, staccato
dignified: 8 maestoso
disconnected: 8 staccato
emotional: 12 appassionato
emphatic: 7 marcato
excited: 7 agitato

fast: 4 vite, vivo 6 presto, veloce, vivace 7 allegro
faster: 7 stretto 11 accelerando
fluctuating tempo: 6 rubato
forcefully: 7 furioso
freely: 9 ad libitum
gay: 7 giocoso
gentle: 5 dolce 7 amabile, amoroso 10 affettuoso
graceful: 8 grazioso
half: 5 mezzo
heavy: 7 pesante
held firmly: 6 tenuto
less: 4 meno
little: 4 poco
little by little: 9 poco a poco
lively: 4 vite 6 vivace 7 allegro, animato, giocoso
loud: 5 forte
louder: 9 crescendo
majestic: 8 maestoso
moderate: 7 andante 8 moderato
moderately loud: 10 mezzo forte
moderately soft: 10 mezzo piano
playful: 10 scherzando
plucked: 9 pizzicato
quick: 4 vite, vivo 6 presto, veloce, vivace 7 allegro
quickening: 11 affrettando
repeat: 3 bis 6 da capo
run: 8 arpeggio 9 glissando
sad: 7 dolente 8 doloroso
separate: 6 divisi
silent: 5 tacet
singing: 9 cantabile
sliding: 9 glissando
slow: 5 grave, largo 6 adagio 7 andante 9 larghetto
slowing: 3 rit 6 ritard 10 ritardando 11 rallentando
smooth: 5 legato
soft: 5 dolce, piano
softening: 10 diminuendo 11 decrescendo
solemn: 5 grave
spirited: 4 vivo 6 vivace 7 animato 9 spiritoso
stately: 7 pomposo 8 maestoso
sustained: 6 tenuto 9 sostenuto
sweet: 5 dolce
tender: 7 amabile, amoroso 10 affettuoso

together: 4 a due 5 tutti
very: 5 assai
very fast: 11 prestissimo
very loud: 10 fortissimo
very soft: 10 pianissimo

musical drama
5 opera 8 operetta, zarzuela 9 singspiel

musical group
4 band, trio 5 choir, combo 6 chorus, sextet 7 quartet, quintet 8 ensemble, glee club 9 orchestra

musical instrument
African: 5 mbira 7 kalimba
ancient: 4 lyre, rote 5 crwth 6 syrinx 7 cithara, kithara, panpipe, sistrum
Arabic: 3 oud
bagpipe: 7 musette, pibroch
biblical: 6 cymbal 7 timbrel 8 psaltery
brass: 4 horn, tuba 5 bugle 6 cornet 7 althorn, clarion, helicon, saxhorn, trumpet 8 trombone 10 French horn
Indian: 4 vina 5 sarod, sitar, tabla
Japanese: 4 biwa, koto 7 samisen 8 shamisen 10 shakuhachi
keyboard: 5 organ, piano 6 spinet 7 celesta, cembalo, clavier 8 calliope, melodeon, virginal 9 accordion 10 clavichord, concertina, pianoforte 11 harpsichord
medieval: 4 lute 5 naker, rebab, rebec, shawm, tabor 7 gittern, mandola, panpipe 8 cornetto, dulcimer, gemshorn, hornpipe, Jew's harp, oliphant, recorder 9 monochord 10 clavichord, hurdy-gurdy
percussion: 4 bell, drum 5 anvil, güiro, piano 6 cymbal, maraca 7 marimba, timbrel, timpani, tympani 8 bass drum, castanet, triangle 9 snare drum, xylophone 10 kettledrum, tambourine, vibraphone
Persian: 6 santir
pipe: 6 syrinx 7 bagpipe, musette, panpipe
reed: 4 oboe 7 bassoon 8 clarinet 9 harmonica, saxophone 11 English horn

musical interval

Renaissance: 4 viol 5 regal, shawm
6 curtal, spinet 7 bagpipe, bandora,
cittern, rackett, sackbut, serpent, theorbo, vihuela, violone 8 crumhorn,
recorder, virginal 10 chitarrone,
colascione 11 harpsichord
Russian: 9 balalaika
stringed: 3 oud 4 harp, lute, lyre,
vina, viol 5 banjo, cello, piano,
rebec, sitar, viola 6 fiddle, guitar,
violin, zither 7 bandora, cittern,
gittern, kantele, pandura, ukulele
8 autoharp, dulcimer, mandolin
10 contrabass, double bass 11 harpsichord, violoncello
toy: 5 kazoo 7 ocarina
two-necked: 7 theorbo
woodwind: 4 oboe 5 flute 7 bassoon, piccolo 9 flageolet, saxophone
11 English horn

musical interval

5 fifth, major, minor, sixth, third
6 fourth, octave, second 7 perfect,
seventh, tritone

musical syllable

3 sol

musician

4 bard 5 piper 6 player 7 jazzman,
maestro 8 minstrel, virtuoso 9 performer 10 troubadour

muskeg

3 bog, fen 4 mire, quag 5 marsh,
swamp 6 morass, slough 8 quagmire

musket

5 fusil 9 flintlock, matchlock 12 muz-
zleloader

Musketeer

5 Athos 6 Aramis 7 Porthos
author: 5 Dumas (Alexandre)
friend: 9 d'Artagnan

muskmelon

10 cantaloupe

Muslim

ascetic: 4 Sufi 5 fakir 7 dervish
8 marabout
body of scholars: 5 ulama, ulema
branch: 4 Shia 5 Sunni 6 Shiite

caller to prayer: 7 muezzin
decree: 5 fatwa, irade
devil: 5 Iblis
garment: 6 chador
god: 5 Allah
holy city: 5 Mecca 6 Medina
holy war: 5 jihad
judge: 5 mufti
leader: 3 aga 4 agha, amir, emir
5 ameer
mendicant: 5 fakir
messiah: 5 Mahdi
month:
(see at **month**)
month of fasting: 7 Ramadan
mosque: 6 masjid
mystic: 4 Sufi
pilgrim: 5 hajji
pilgrimage: 4 hajj
prayer: 5 salat
priest: 4 imam
prophet: 8 Mohammed, Muhammad
religion: 5 Islam
scripture: 5 Koran, Quran
shrine: 5 Kaaba
temple: 6 mosque
title: 3 aga 4 emir 6 caliph
tradition: 5 sunna
(see also **mosque; Muhammad**)

muss

3 row 4 mess 5 botch, chaos,
mix-up, upset 6 jumble, mess-up,
muddle, rumple, tousle 7 disrupt,
rummage 8 disarray, dishevel,
disorder, shambles 9 confusion
10 disarrange 11 disorganize

mussel

5 naiad
genus: 4 Unio 7 Mytilus 8 Ano-
donta
larva: 9 blackhead

Mussolini, Benito

4 Duce (II)
son-in-law: 5 Ciano (Galeazzo)

mussy

6 sloppy, untidy 7 tousled, unkempt
8 slovenly 9 cluttered 10 disheveled

must

4 duty, mold, need, want 5 juice,

ought 6 devoir, should 9 condition, essential, necessity, requisite 10 obligation, sine qua non 11 requirement 12 precondition, prerequisite

muster

4 call, roll 5 crowd, group, raise, rally, rouse 6 enlist, enroll, gather, induce, invoke, join up, roster, sample, sign on, sign up, summon, work up 7 collect, convene, develop, include, marshal, produce 8 assemble, assembly, comprise, congress, generate, mobilize, organize, roll call, specimen 9 gathering, inventory, nose count 10 accumulate, assemblage, collection, congregate, rendezvous 12 accumulation, congregation

muster out

5 demob, let go 9 discharge 10 demobilize

musty

4 dank, dull, sour 5 funky, moldy, stale, tired, trite 6 frowsy, frowzy, old hat, smelly 7 airless, antique, mildewy, squalid 8 shopworn, timeworn 10 antiquated, malodorous, threadbare

Mut

husband: 4 Amen, Amon
son: 5 Chons 6 Chonsu, Khonsu

mutable

5 fluid 6 fickle, mobile, shifty 7 erratic, protean 8 slippery, unstable, unsteady, variable, volatile, wavering 9 changeful, mercurial, unsettled 10 capricious, changeable, inconstant 11 fluctuating, vacillating 12 inconsistent

mutate

4 vary 5 alter, morph 6 change, modify 9 refashion, transform, transmute 11 transfigure 12 metamorphose, transmogrify

mutation

5 sport 6 change 7 novelty 9 deviation, variation 10 alteration 11 vicis-

situde 12 modification 13 metamorphosis

mute

3 mum 4 dumb 5 quiet 6 dampen, deaden, muffle, muzzle, reduce, silent, soften, stifle, subdue 7 silence 8 silencer, wordless 9 voiceless 10 speechless, tongue-tied

muted

3 dim, mat 4 dull 6 low-key, silent 10 speechless

mutilate

3 mar 4 maim 6 damage, deface, injure, mangle 7 cripple 9 disfigure, dismember

mutineer

5 rebel

mutinous

6 unruly 8 factious 9 insurgent, seditious, turbulent 10 rebellious 12 contumacious 13 insubordinate

mutiny

5 rebel 6 revolt, rise up 8 uprising 9 rebellion 12 insurrection

mutt

3 cur, dog 4 mule 5 cross 6 hybrid 7 mixture, mongrel 9 half blood, half-breed 10 crossbreed

Mutt and _____

4 Jeff

mutter

5 growl 6 grouch, grouse, mumble, murmur 7 grumble 9 undertone

muttonchops

9 burnsides, sideburns 10 sideboards 11 dundrearies 12 sidewhiskers

mutual

5 joint 6 common, public, shared, united 7 related 8 communal, conjoint, conjunct 9 bilateral, connected 10 associated, reciprocal, respective
prefix: 5 inter

muumuu

6 caftan

muzzle
3 gag 4 hush, mute, nose, phiz
5 snout 7 silence, squelch

muzzy
3 dim 4 dull, hazy 5 faint, vague
6 blurry, gloomy 7 blurred, muddled,
unclear 8 confused, nebulous
9 imprecise

myalgia
4 ache, pain 5 cramp 6 strain
8 soreness

Myanmar
5 Burma
bay: 6 Bengal
capital: 6 Yangon 7 Rangoon
monetary unit: 4 kyat
neighbor: 4 Laos 5 China, India
8 Thailand 10 Bangladesh
peninsula: 9 Indochina
river: 7 Salween 9 Irrawaddy
sea: 7 Andaman

My Antonia author
6 Cather (Willa)

My Last Duchess author
8 Browning (Robert)

My Lost Youth author
10 Longfellow (Henry Wadsworth)

Myra Breckenridge author
5 Vidal (Gore)

myriad
3 lot 4 heap, host, raft, slew 5 flood,
horde, swarm 6 throng 9 countless,
multitude 10 infinitude, numberless
11 innumerable 12 incalculable
13 multitudinous

myrmecology subject
3 ant 4 ants

myrmidon
6 minion 8 follower, retainer 9 attendant, underling 11 subordinate

Myron's statue
10 Discobolos, Discobolus 13 Discus
Thrower (The)

Myrrha's son
6 Adonis

mysterious
6 arcane, mystic, occult, secret
7 cryptic, obscure, strange 8 abstruse, esoteric, numinous 9 ambiguous, enigmatic, equivocal, recondite 10 cabalistic, unknowable
11 inscrutable 12 impenetrable,
inexplicable, unfathomable 13 unaccountable

mystery
5 poser 6 enigma, puzzle, riddle,
secret 7 arcanum, problem, stumper
8 whodunit 9 conundrum 10 closed
book, perplexity, puzzlement 13 Chinese puzzle

mystic
4 seer 6 arcane, medium, occult,
oracle, secret 7 obscure 8 anagogic, esoteric, hermetic, numinous
9 enigmatic, visionary 10 cabalistic,
unknowable 11 inscrutable, necromantic 12 impenetrable, thaumaturgic 13 unaccountable

mystical
4 holy 6 arcane, covert, divine,
occult, orphic, sacred, secret 7 cryptic, sub-rosa 8 anagogic, esoteric,
hermetic, oracular, profound 9 recondite, spiritual 10 miraculous,
symbolical 11 clandestine 12 supernatural, supranatural

mysticism
7 Orphism 8 cabalism, quietism
11 hermeticism

mystify
6 baffle, puzzle 7 confuse, obscure,
perplex 8 befuddle, bewilder, confound 9 obfuscate

mystifying
7 cryptic, delphic 8 Delphian 9 enigmatic

mystique
5 charm, magic 7 glamour 8 charisma 9 magnetism

myth
4 lore, saga, tale 5 fable, story

6 legend 7 fiction, figment, parable 8 allegory, folklore 9 tradition 11 fabrication

mythical
6 fabled, made-up, unreal 7 created, fictive 8 fabulous, fanciful, invented 9 fantastic, fictional, imaginary, legendary 10 apocryphal, fictitious

mythologist
4 Jung (Carl Gustav), Ovid 5 Tylor (Edward Burnett) 6 Eliade (Mircea), Frazer (James George), Müller (Friedrich Max) 8 Campbell (Joseph) 9 Euhemerus 10 Malinowski (Bronislaw)

mythology
see myth

N

Naamah
  brother: **9** Tubalcain
  father: **6** Lamech
  husband: **7** Solomon
  mother: **6** Zillah
  son: **8** Rehoboam

nab
  4 grab **5** catch, pinch, run in, seize
  6 arrest, clutch, collar, pick up, pull
  in, snatch **7** capture **9** apprehend

nabob
  3 VIP **5** mogul, noble **6** bigwig, fat
  cat, tycoon **7** big shot, magnate, notable **8** big chief, eminence, governor **9** big cheese, dignitary, personage **10** notability

Nabokov novel
  3 Ada **4** Gift (The), Pnin **6** Lolita
  7 Defense (The), Despair **8** Pale
  Fire **14** King Queen Knave

nacre
  13 mother-of-pearl

nada
  3 nil, zip **5** zilch **6** naught **7** nothing,
  nullity **11** nothingness

nadir
  4 base, foot **5** depth **6** bottom **8** low
  point
  opposite: **6** zenith

nag
  3 irk, vex **4** bait, carp, goad, ride
  5 annoy, chivy, harry, horse, hound,
  worry **6** badger, bother, carp at,
  harass, heckle, hector, needle,
  peck at, pester, plague **7** henpeck,
  torment **8** complain, harangue,
  irritate

naiad
  5 nymph

naïf
  7 ingenue

nail
  3 bag, get, nab **4** brad, grab, stud,
  tack, trap **5** catch, clone, spike, sprig
  6 arrest, collar, secure **7** capture
  9 apprehend

naive
  6 simple **7** artless, natural **8** gullible,
  innocent, wide-eyed **9** childlike,
  credulous, guileless, ingenuous,
  unstudied **10** self-taught, unaffected,
  unschooled **11** susceptible

naked
  3 raw **4** bald, bare, mere, nude, pure
  5 clear, sheer **6** peeled, scanty,
  simple, unclad **7** denuded, evident,
  exposed, obvious **8** revealed,
  stripped **9** au naturel, disclosed,
  unclothed, uncovered, undressed
  combining form: **4** gymn **5** gymno

Naked and the Dead author
  6 Mailer (Norman)

namby-pamby
  4 weak **5** banal, bland, inane, sissy,
  vapid **6** effete, jejune **7** insipid
  8 nebbishy, weakling **9** spineless
  10 effeminate, indecisive, pantywaist,
  wishy-washy **12** milk-and-water
  13 characterless

name
  3 dub, nom, tab, tag, tap **4** call, cite,
  race, term **5** alias, label, nomen,
  quote, state, style, title **6** byword,
  finger, handle, report, repute, rubric

7 appoint, baptize, declare, entitle, epithet, mention, moniker, publish, specify **8** announce, christen, identify, instance, nominate **9** advertise, character, designate, incognito, recognize, sobriquet, stipulate **10** denominate, reputation **11** appellation, appellative, designation
ancient Rome: **7** agnomen **8** prenomen
assumed: **5** alias **9** sobriquet
family: **8** cognomen
fictitious: **9** pseudonym
giver: **6** eponym

nameless
6 unsung **7** obscure, unknown **9** anonymous **11** indefinable, unutterable **12** uncelebrated, unidentified

namely
3 viz. **5** to wit **6** that is **8** scilicet **9** expressly, specially, videlicet **10** especially **12** particularly, specifically

Namibia
capital: **8** Windhoek
city: **8** Oshakati, Rehoboth
desert: **5** Namib **8** Kalahari
language: **5** Bantu **6** German **9** Afrikaans
neighbor: **6** Angola **8** Botswana **11** South Africa
river: **6** Cunene, Orange **8** Okavango

nana
7 grandma **11** grandmother

Nana
author: **4** Zola (Emile)
mother: **8** Gervaise

Nanna
brother: **6** Nergal, Ninazu
father: **5** Enlil
husband: **6** Balder
mother: **6** Ninlil
son: **3** Utu
wife: **6** Ningal

nanny
5 nurse **9** caregiver, governess, nursemaid

Naomi
4 Mara
daughter-in-law: **4** Ruth **5** Orpah
husband: **9** Elimelech
son: **6** Mahlon **7** Chilion

nap
4 doze, pile, rest, shag, wale, warp, weft, woof **5** sleep, weave **6** drowse, nod off, siesta, snooze **7** drop off, surface **10** forty winks

nape
6 scruff

Naphtali
brother: **3** Dan
father: **5** Jacob
mother: **6** Bilhah
son: **4** Guni **5** Jezer **7** Jahzeel, Jahziel, Shallum

naphtha
7 solvent **9** petroleum

napkin
5 cloth, doily, towel **9** serviette

napoleon
4 boot **6** pastry **8** card game **9** solitaire
bid: **7** blucher **10** wellington

Napoleon
adversary: **6** Nelson (Horatio) **7** Kutuzov (Mikhail) **10** Wellington (Duke of)
birthplace: **7** Ajaccio, Corsica
brother: **5** Louis **6** Jérome, Joseph, Lucien
brother-in-law: **5** Murat (Joachim)
deathplace: **8** St. Helena
defeat: **7** Leipzig **8** Waterloo **9** Trafalgar
father: **5** Carlo
island of exile: **4** Elba **8** St. Helena
marshal: **3** Ney (Michel) **5** Murat (Joachim), Soult (Nicolas-Jean) **6** Suchet (Louis-Gabriel)
sister: **5** Maria **8** Carlotta, Carolina
victory: **3** Ulm **4** Jena, Lodi **5** Ligny **6** Abukir, Abu Qir, Arcole, Wagram **7** Bautzen, Dresden, Marengo **8** Borodino **10** Austerlitz
wife: **9** Josephine **11** Marie Louise

narcissism

6 egoism, vanity 7 conceit, egotism
8 self-love, vainness 9 vainglory
11 egocentrism, self-conceit 13 conceitedness

narcissistic

4 vain 7 stuck-up 9 conceited,
egotistic 10 self-loving 11 egotistical
12 self-absorbed, self-admiring,
self-centered, vainglorious

Narcissus

admirer: 4 Echo
father: 9 Cephissus
mother: 7 Liriope

narcotic

3 hop 4 dope, drug, junk 5 opium
6 heroin, opiate 7 anodyne, cocaine,
hashish 8 hypnotic, morphine,
nepenthe 9 somnolent, soporific
10 somnorific 11 somniferous
peddler: 6 dealer, pusher

narrate

4 tell 5 state 6 depict, detail, recite,
relate, report 7 express, outline,
portray, recount 8 describe, rehearse 9 chronicle, delineate

narrative

4 epic, myth, saga, tale, yarn 5 fable,
story 6 legend, report 7 account,
history, recital, version 8 anecdote
9 chronicle
medieval French: 5 roman 7 romance
prose: 5 novel 7 novella

narrator

6 teller 7 reciter 8 reporter 9 describer, performer 10 chronicler

narrow

5 close, small, taper 6 lessen, strait
7 bigoted, limited, precise, slender
8 contract, decrease, straiten 9 confining, constrict, hidebound, illiberal
10 brassbound, inflexible, intolerant,
prejudiced, restricted

narrowly

6 barely 7 closely 8 scarcely, strictly

narrow-minded

5 petty 7 bigoted, insular 9 hidebound, illiberal 10 brassbound,
intolerant, prejudiced, provincial

nasal

6 rhinal, twangy 9 nosepiece
combining form: 4 rhin 5 rhino

nascency

5 birth 6 origin 7 genesis 8 birthing,
creation, nativity 9 inception 11 parturition

nascent

7 budding, growing, newborn 8 emergent 9 beginning, embryonic, fledgling, incipient, sprouting 10 blossoming, burgeoning, initiative,
initiatory

Naseby victor

7 Fairfax (Thomas) 8 Cromwell
(Oliver)

_____ Nastase

4 Ilie

nasty

4 evil, foul, icky, mean, vile 5 awful,
dirty, gross, snide 6 coarse, filthy,
grubby, horrid, malign, odious,
wicked 7 beastly, harmful, hateful,
ill-bred, painful, raunchy, squalid,
vicious 8 god-awful, improper,
indecent, spiteful 9 hazardous,
loathsome, malicious, malignant,
obnoxious, offensive, repugnant,
repulsive, vexatious 10 disgusting,
malevolent 11 distasteful 12 disagreeable

natant

8 floating, swimming

Nathan

father: 4 Bani 5 Attai, David
son: 5 Zabad

nation

4 race 5 realm, state, tribe 6 domain, people, polity 7 country,
kingdom, society 8 dominion,
populace, republic 11 sovereignty
12 commonwealth, principality

national

6 native 7 citizen, federal, subject 8 resident 10 countryman
11 countrywide

National Basketball Association

Atlanta: 5 Hawks
Boston: 7 Celtics
Charlotte: 7 Hornets
Chicago: 5 Bulls
Cleveland: 9 Cavaliers
Dallas: 9 Mavericks
Denver: 7 Nuggets
Detroit: 7 Pistons
Golden State: 8 Warriors
Houston: 7 Rockets
Indiana: 6 Pacers
Los Angeles: 6 Lakers 8 Clippers
Miami: 4 Heat
Milwaukee: 5 Bucks
Minnesota: 12 Timberwolves
New Jersey: 4 Nets
New York: 6 Knicks
Orlando: 5 Magic
Phoenix: 4 Suns
Portland: 12 Trail Blazers
Sacramento: 5 Kings
San Antonio: 5 Spurs
Seattle: 11 SuperSonics
Toronto: 7 Raptors
Utah: 4 Jazz
Vancouver: 9 Grizzlies
Washington: 7 Bullets

National Football League

Arizona: 9 Cardinals
Atlanta: 7 Falcons
Baltimore: 6 Ravens
Buffalo: 5 Bills
Carolina: 8 Panthers
Chicago: 5 Bears
Cincinnati: 7 Bengals
Cleveland: 6 Browns
Dallas: 7 Cowboys
Denver: 7 Broncos
Detroit: 5 Lions
Green Bay: 7 Packers
Houston: 6 Oilers
Indianapolis: 5 Colts
Jacksonville: 7 Jaguars
Kansas City: 6 Chiefs
Miami: 8 Dolphins
Minnesota: 7 Vikings
New England: 8 Patriots
New Orleans: 6 Saints
New York: 4 Jets 6 Giants
Oakland: 7 Raiders
Philadelphia: 6 Eagles
Pittsburgh: 8 Steelers
St. Louis: 4 Rams
San Diego: 8 Chargers
Seattle: 8 Seahawks
Tampa Bay: 4 Bucs 10 Buccaneers
Tennessee: 6 Oilers
Washington: 8 Redskins

national historical park

Alaska: 5 Sitka
Idaho: 8 Nez Percé
Kentucky-Tennessee: 13 Cumberland Gap
Maryland-West Virginia: 12 Harpers Ferry
Massachusetts: 9 Minute Man
New York: 8 Saratoga

National Hockey League

Anaheim: 11 Mighty Ducks
Atlanta: 9 Thrashers
Boston: 6 Bruins
Buffalo: 6 Sabres
Calgary: 6 Flames
Carolina: 10 Hurricanes
Chicago: 10 Blackhawks
Colorado: 9 Avalanche
Columbus: 11 Blue Jackets
Dallas: 5 Stars
Detroit: 8 Red Wings
Edmonton: 6 Oilers
Florida: 8 Panthers
Los Angeles: 5 Kings
Minnesota: 4 Wild
Montreal: 9 Canadiens
Nashville: 9 Predators
New Jersey: 6 Devils
New York: 7 Rangers 9 Islanders
Ottawa: 8 Senators
Philadelphia: 6 Flyers
Phoenix: 7 Coyotes
St. Louis: 5 Blues
San Jose: 6 Sharks
Tampa Bay: 9 Lightning
Toronto: 10 Maple Leafs
Vancouver: 8 Canucks
Washington: 8 Capitals

nationalism

8 jingoism 10 chauvinism, patriotism

National League
Arizona: 12 Diamondbacks
Atlanta: 6 Braves
Chicago: 4 Cubs
Cincinnati: 4 Reds
Colorado: 7 Rockies
Florida: 7 Marlins
Houston: 6 Astros
Los Angeles: 7 Dodgers
Milwaukee: 7 Brewers
New York: 4 Mets
Philadelphia: 8 Phillies
Pittsburgh: 7 Pirates
St. Louis: 9 Cardinals
San Diego: 6 Padres
San Francisco: 6 Giants
Washington: 9 Nationals

national military park
Alabama: 13 Horseshoe Bend
Arkansas: 8 Pea Ridge
Mississippi: 9 Vicksburg
Pennsylvania: 10 Gettysburg
South Carolina: 13 Kings Mountain
Tennessee: 6 Shiloh

national monument
Alabama: 11 Russell Cave
Alaska: 9 Aniakchak
Arizona: 5 Tonto **6** Navajo **7** Saguaro, Wupatki **8** Tuzigoot **10** Chiricahua, Pipe Spring, Tumacacori **11** Hohokam Pima **12** Sunset Crater, Walnut Canyon
California: 8 Cabrillo, Lava Beds **9** Muir Woods, Pinnacles **10** Joshua Tree **11** Death Valley
Colorado: 10 Yucca House
Colorado-Utah: 8 Dinosaur **9** Hovenweep
Florida: 12 Fort Matanzas **13** Fort Jefferson
Georgia: 8 Ocmulgee **11** Fort Pulaski **13** Fort Frederica
Iowa: 12 Effigy Mounds
Louisiana: 12 Poverty Point
Maryland: 11 Fort McHenry
Minnesota: 9 Pipestone **12** Grand Portage
Nebraska: 9 Homestead **11** Scotts Bluff
New Mexico: 5 Pecos **7** El Morro
9 Bandelier, El Malpais, Fort Union **10** Aztec Ruins, White Sands
New York: 11 Fort Stanwix **13** Castle Clinton
South Carolina: 10 Fort Sumter **13** Congaree Swamp
South Dakota: 9 Jewel Cave
Utah: 11 Cedar Breaks **13** Rainbow Bridge
Wyoming: 11 Devils Tower, Fossil Butte

national park
Alaska: 6 Denali, Katmai **9** Lake Clark **10** Glacier Bay **11** Kenai Fjords, Kobuk Valley
Angola: 4 Iona, Mupa
Arizona: 11 Grand Canyon
Arkansas: 10 Hot Springs
Botswana: 5 Chobe
California: 7 Redwood, Sequoia **8** Yosemite **11** King's Canyon
Chad: 5 Manda
Colombia: 5 Uraba
Colorado: 9 Mesa Verde **13** Rocky Mountain
eastern Africa: 10 Mount Kenya
Florida: 8 Biscayne **10** Everglades
Hawaii: 9 Haleakala
India: 5 Kanha
Japan: 5 Nikko
Kentucky: 11 Mammoth Cave
Kenya: 4 Meru **5** Tsavo **10** Royal Tsavo
Lake Superior: 10 Isle Royale
Maine: 6 Acadia
Malaysia: 8 Kinabalu
Minnesota: 9 Voyageurs
Montana: 7 Glacier
Nevada: 10 Great Basin
Oregon: 10 Crater Lake
Poland: 5 Ojcow, Tatra
South Africa: 6 Kruger
South Dakota: 8 Badlands, Wind Cave
Sri Lanka: 4 Yala
Sweden: 5 Sarek
Tanzania: 5 Ruaha **9** Serengeti
Texas: 7 Big Bend
Utah: 4 Zion **6** Arches **11** Bryce Canyon, Canyonlands, Capitol Reef
Virginia: 10 Shenandoah

Washington: 7 Olympic 12 Mount Rainier 13 North Cascades
Wyoming: 10 Grand Teton
Wyoming-Idaho-Montana: 11 Yellowstone
Zambia: 5 Kafue
Zimbabwe: 13 Rhodes Inyanga, Victoria Falls

native
3 raw 4 wild 5 local 6 inborn, innate 7 connate, endemic, natural 8 domestic, indigene, inherent, internal, national 9 inherited 10 aboriginal, congenital, connatural, indigenous, unacquired
Acadian Louisiana: 5 Cajun
China: 3 Han 9 Celestial
India: 5 sepoy
Japan: 9 Nipponese
London: 7 Cockney
New England: 4 Yank 6 Yankee
New York: 13 Knickerbocker

Native Son author
6 Wright (Richard)

Nativity
4 Noel, Xmas, yule 8 yuletide 9 Christmas

nativity
5 birth, start 6 origin, outset 7 genesis 8 delivery 9 beginning, horoscope, inception 11 parturition

natter
3 gab, jaw, yak, yap 4 blab, buzz, chat, go on 5 prate, run on 6 babble, gabble, gossip, tattle 7 chatter, prattle, twaddle 8 chitchat, converse

natty
4 neat, tidy, trim 5 doggy, sassy, smart, swank 6 classy, dapper, jaunty, snazzy, spiffy, spruce, sprucy, swanky 7 bandbox, doggish, stylish 9 turned out 11 well-groomed

natural
4 pure, wild 5 naive, usual 6 candid, inborn, innate, native, normal, simple 7 artless, connate, organic 8 homespun, inherent, innocent 9 childlike, ingenuous, ingrained, primitive
10 congenital, indigenous, legitimate, unaffected 11 commonplace, instinctive, spontaneous

naturalist
American: 4 Muir (John) 5 Hyatt (Alpheus) 7 Audubon (John James), Verrill (Addison, Alpheus)
English: 3 Ray (John) 5 White (Gilbert) 6 Darwin (Charles) 7 Wallace (Alfred) 10 Williamson (William)
French: 5 Fabre (Jean-Henri) 7 Lamarck (Chevalier de), Réaumur (René-Antoine)
Scottish: 6 Wilson (Alexander) 10 Richardson (John)

nature
3 ilk, way 4 kind, sort, type 6 makeup, manner, stripe, temper 7 essence, scenery 8 creation, tendency, universe 9 character, landscape 10 complexion 11 description, disposition, personality, temperament 12 constitution

naught
3 nil, zip 4 love, nada, zero 5 zilch 6 cipher 7 nothing, nullity 8 goose egg 11 nothingness

naughty
3 bad 4 lewd 5 bawdy 6 unruly, ribald, risqué, smutty, vulgar 7 froward, obscene, raunchy, wayward, willful 8 contrary, improper, perverse, rascally 10 ill-behaved 11 disobedient, mischievous 12 obstreperous, recalcitrant

Nauru
capital: 5 Yaren
former name: 8 Pleasant (Island)
monetary unit: 6 dollar

nauseate
5 repel 6 offend, sicken 7 disgust, repulse

nauseated
6 queasy 7 carsick 8 qualmish 9 disgusted, squeamish 10 grossed out

nauseating

6 putrid 7 noisome 9 loathsome, offensive, repellant, repugnant, repulsive, revolting, sickening 10 disgusting

Nausicaa

father: 8 Alcinous
mother: 5 Arete

nautical

5 naval 6 marine 7 oceanic 8 maritime 12 navigational
instrument: 3 aba 7 compass, pelorus, sextant

Navajo dwelling

5 hogan

naval hero

5 Jones (John Paul), Perry (Matthew, Oliver Hazard) 8 Farragut (David, George), Lawrence (James)

navel

6 middle 7 nombril 9 umbilicus 11 belly button
combining form: 6 omphal 7 omphalo

navigate

4 helm, plot, sail 5 guide, pilot, steer 6 cruise 8 maneuver, traverse

navigation

8 piloting 10 seamanship 12 helmsmanship

navigational system

5 loran

navigator

5 flyer, pilot 6 airman 7 copilot
Danish: 6 Bering (Vitus)
Dutch: 6 Tasman (Abel) 7 Barents (Willem)
English: 4 Cook (Captain James) 5 Cabot (John, Sebastian), Drake (Francis) 6 Hudson (Henry) 7 Gilbert (Humphrey), Raleigh (Walter) 9 Vancouver (George)
French: 7 Cartier (Jacques) 9 La Perouse (Comte de)
Italian: 6 Caboto (Giovanni) 8 Columbus (Christopher), Vespucci (Amerigo) 9 Verrazano (Giovanni) 10 Verrazzano (Giovanni)

Norwegian:

4 Eric (the Red) 8 Ericsson (Leif) 12 Leif Ericsson, Leif Eriksson
Portuguese: 4 Dias (Bartolomeu, Dinis) 6 Cabral (Pedro Alvares), da Gama (Vasco) 8 Magellan (Ferdinand)
Spanish: 9 Fernández (Juan)

navy

4 blue 5 fleet 6 argosy, armada 8 flotilla

Nazi

9 Hitlerite 10 brownshirt
admiral: 6 Dönitz (Karl), Raeder (Erich) 7 Doenitz (Karl)
air force: 9 Luftwaffe
armed forces: 9 Wehrmacht
collaborator: 5 Laval (Pierre) 8 Quisling (Vidkun)
concentration camp: 6 Belsen, Dachau 9 Auschwitz, Treblinka 10 Buchenwald, Nordhausen
field marshal: 5 Model (Walter) 6 Keitel (Wilhelm), Paulus (Friedrich), Rommel (Erwin) 9 Rundstedt (Karl von) 10 Kesselring (Albert)
greeting: 4 heil
leader: 3 Ley (Robert) 4 Hess (Rudolf), Röhm (Ernst) 5 Roehm (Ernst) 6 Führer, Göring (Hermann), Hitler (Adolf) 7 Fuehrer, Goering (Hermann), Himmler (Heinrich) 8 Goebbels (Joseph), Heydrich (Reinhard) 9 Rosenberg (Alfred)
police: 7 Gestapo
propagandist: 8 Goebbels (Joseph)
submarine: 5 U-boat
surrender signer: 4 Jodl (Alfred) 6 Keitel (Wilhelm)
symbol: 6 fylfot 8 swastika
tactic: 10 blitzkrieg
tank: 6 Panzer

NCO

3 cpl, sgt 8 corporal, sergeant

neap

3 low 4 tide

near

4 nigh 5 about, circa, close, round 6 almost, around 7 close by, close on

8 adjacent, approach 9 immediate, proximate 11 approximate

nearby
4 nigh 5 about, aside, close, handy 6 around, beside 8 adjacent 9 adjoining, proximate 10 contiguous, convenient 11 neighboring

nearest
4 next 7 closest 8 adjacent, proximal 9 proximate 10 contiguous

nearsighted
6 myopic

neat
4 deft, nice, prim, snug, tidy, trig, trim 5 clean, clear, kempt 6 clever, smooth, spruce 7 orderly, precise, unmixed 8 straight, well-kept 9 shipshape, undiluted 10 methodical, systematic 11 spic-and-span, uncluttered, well-groomed 12 spick-and-span 13 unadulterated

neb
3 tip 4 beak, bill, nose, prow 5 snoot, snout 9 proboscis

Nebraska
capital: 7 Lincoln
city: 5 Omaha
college, university: 9 Creighton
nickname: 10 Cornhusker (State)
river: 6 Platte 8 Missouri
state bird: 10 meadowlark
state flower: 9 goldenrod
state tree: 10 cottonwood

nebula
6 galaxy

nebulous
4 hazy 5 vague 6 cloudy, turbid 7 clouded, obscure, unclear 9 ambiguous, amorphous, uncertain 10 indefinite, indistinct 13 indeterminate

necessary
5 basic, vital 6 needed 7 crucial, needful 8 cardinal, integral, required 9 de rigueur, essential, mandatory, requisite 10 compulsory, imperative, inevitable, obligatory, undeniable 11 fundamental, ineluctable,

inescapable, unavoidable 12 all-important, prerequisite 13 indispensable

necessitate
5 cause, exact, force 6 compel, demand, entail 7 call for, involve, require 8 occasion

necessity
4 must, need 6 crisis, duress 7 poverty 8 exigency 9 essential, privation, requisite 10 compulsion, imperative, obligation, sine qua non 11 dire straits, needfulness, requirement 12 precondition, prerequisite

neck
3 pet 4 kiss 6 fondle, smooch
back of: 4 nape 5 nucha 6 scruff
ornament: 6 gorget, torque

necklace
5 chain 6 choker 7 rivière 8 carcanet

necktie
5 ascot 6 cravat 10 four-in-hand

necrology
4 obit 8 obituary

necromancy
4 juju 5 magic, vodun 6 hoodoo, voodoo 7 devilry, sorcery 8 witchery, wizardry 9 conjuring, diabolism, magicking 10 black magic, witchcraft 11 bewitchment, conjuration, enchantment, incantation, thaumaturgy

necropolis
8 boneyard, boot hill, cemetery, God's acre 9 graveyard 10 churchyard 12 memorial park, potter's field

necropsy
7 anatomy, autopsy 10 dissection, postmortem

née
4 born 10 originally

need
3 use 4 call, duty, lack, must, want 5 crave 6 demand, devoir, hunger, penury, thirst 7 poverty, require 8 distress, exigency, occasion,

shortage 9 indigence, necessity, privation, requisite 10 compulsion, deficiency, obligation 11 deprivation, destitution, requirement

neediness

4 want 6 penury 7 poverty 9 indigence, privation 11 deprivation, destitution 13 insufficiency

needle

3 rib 5 annoy, tease 6 harass, pester, plague 7 bedevil, hagride, obelisk, pricker, syringe 10 hypodermic
case: 4 etui
hole: 3 eye

needlefish

3 gar 8 pipefish

needlelike

7 styloid 8 belonoid
part: 7 acicula

needlepoint

4 lace 7 alençon, crochet, tatting 8 bargello 10 embroidery 11 cross-stitch

needlework

4 lace 6 sewing 7 alençon, crochet, sampler, tatting 8 bargello, knitting 9 stitching 10 crocheting, embroidery 11 cross-stitch

needy

4 poor 5 broke 6 hard up 8 beggared, dirt-poor, indigent, strapped 9 destitute, penniless, penurious 10 down-and-out 11 impecunious, necessitous 12 impoverished

ne'er-do-well

3 bum, dud 5 loser 6 loafer, no-good 7 failure, wastrel 8 derelict 9 shiftless 10 profligate, scapegrace

nefarious

4 evil, vile 6 savage, wicked 7 heinous, impious, noxious 8 depraved, dreadful, flagrant, infamous, perverse 9 execrable, miscreant, monstrous, offensive 10 abominable, degenerate, detestable, iniquitous, outrageous, villainous 11 opprobrious 13 reprehensible

negate

4 deny, undo, void 5 annul, quash, rebut 6 cancel, impugn, refute, vacate 7 abolish, gainsay, nullify, redress, vitiate 8 abrogate, disallow, disprove, overturn, traverse 9 cancel out, disaffirm, repudiate 10 contradict, contravene, counteract, invalidate, neutralize 12 countercheck

negative

3 nix 4 deny, kill, veto 5 annul, cross, minus 6 impugn 7 adverse, gainsay, nullify, redress, refusal 8 abrogate, disprove, traverse 9 cancel out, frustrate 10 contradict, contravene, counteract, invalidate, neutralize 11 detrimental, unfavorable
battery terminal: 5 anode
ion: 5 anion
Scottish: 3 nae
sign: 5 minus

neglect

4 fail, omit 5 let go, shirk 6 forget, ignore, laxity, slight 7 failure, laxness 8 omission, overlook, overpass, pass over 9 avoidance, disregard, oversight, pretermit 10 negligence 11 dereliction, inattention 12 carelessness 13 pretermission

neglectful

see **negligent**

negligee

4 gown 5 teddy 7 chemise, nightie 8 camisole, peignoir 9 nightgown

negligent

3 lax 5 slack 6 remiss 8 careless, derelict, heedless 9 forgetful, imprudent 10 delinquent, neglectful, nonchalant, regardless, unthinking 11 inattentive, pococurante, unconcerned 12 disregardful, lackadaisical

negligible

4 puny, slim 5 minor, petty, small 6 meager, meagre, minute, remote, paltry, skimpy, slight 7 minimal, slender, trivial 8 nugatory, picayune,

trifling 9 minuscule 11 meaningless, unimportant 13 imperceptible, insignificant

negotiable
8 passable 11 convertible 12 transferable

negotiate
4 cash 6 confer, dicker, hurdle, manage, parley, settle 7 arrange, bargain, develop, mediate, work out, wrangle 8 contract, covenant, moderate, surmount, transact, transfer 9 arbitrate 10 horse-trade

neigh
6 nicker, whinny

neighbor
4 abut 5 flank, frame, skirt 6 adjoin, border 7 abutter 8 border on

neighborhood
4 area, turf, ward 5 block, range 6 parish 8 district, locality, precinct, purlieus, vicinage, vicinity 9 community, proximity

neighborly
6 genial 7 amiable, cordial, helpful 8 amicable, friendly, obliging, sociable 9 congenial 10 gregarious, hospitable 11 considerate, cooperative, good-natured 13 accommodating

nematode
4 worm 7 eelworm 9 roundworm

Nemean predator
4 lion

nemesis
4 bane, doom 5 curse, enemy, rival 8 opponent 9 bête noire 11 retribution

neologism
7 coinage, new word

neophyte
see **newcomer**

Neoptolemus
7 Pyrrhus
father: 8 Achilles
slayer: 7 Orestes
victim: 5 Priam
wife: 8 Hermione

neoteric
6 modern, recent

Nepal
capital: 8 Katmandu 9 Kathmandu
city: 7 Pokhara 8 Lalitpur
monetary unit: 5 rupee
mountain, range: 7 Everest 8 Himalaya 9 Himalayan, Himalayas 10 Dhaulagiri 11 Gauri Sankar 12 Kanchenjunga
neighbor: 5 China, India
river: 6 Ganges

nepenthe
6 opiate, potion 7 anodyne 8 lenitive, narcotic 9 analgesic 10 anesthetic, painkiller

Nephthys
brother, husband: 3 Set 4 Seth

nepotism
10 favoritism, partiality

Neptune
6 planet
satellite: 6 Nereid, Triton
(see also **Poseidon**)

nerd
4 drip, geek 6 misfit 7 egghead, nebbish, oddball 10 pointy-head

Nereid
6 Thetis 7 Galatea 10 Amphitrite
father: 6 Nereus
mother: 5 Doris

Nereus
daughters: 8 Nereides
emblem: 7 trident
father: 6 Pontus
mother: 4 Gaea
wife: 5 Doris

Nergal
brother: 5 Nanna 6 Ninazu
father: 5 Enlil
mother: 6 Ninlil

Nero
birthplace: 4 Rome
mother: 9 Agrippina
successor: 5 Galba
tutor: 6 Seneca
victim: 5 Lucan 6 Seneca 7 Octavia, Poppaea 9 Agrippina
wife: 7 Octavia, Poppaea

Nero Wolfe creator
5 Stout (Rex)

nerve
4 face, gall, grit, guts 5 brass, cheek, crust, heart, moxie, spunk 6 daring 7 sciatic 8 audacity, backbone, boldness, chutzpah, temerity 9 assurance, brashness, fortitude, hardihood, hardiness 10 confidence, effrontery 11 presumption
cell: 6 neuron
cell group: 7 ganglia (plural) 8 ganglion
combining form: 4 neur 5 neura, neuro
cranial: 4 vagi (plural) 5 optic, vagus 8 abducens
ending: 8 receptor
lesion: 8 neuritis

nerve center
3 hub 4 core, seat 5 focus, heart, locus 7 capital 8 cynosure, polestar 10 crossroads, focal point 12 headquarters

nerve gas
5 sarin, soman, tabun

nervous
4 edgy 5 jerky, jumpy, tense, timid 6 fitful, goosey, on edge, spooky, uneasy 7 erratic, fidgety, fretful, jittery, restive, twitchy, uptight 8 aflutter, agitated, forcible, skittery, skittish, spirited, twittery, unsteady, vigorous, volatile 9 excitable, irregular, irritable 10 high-strung 12 apprehensive

nervy
4 bold, edgy, pert 5 brash, cocky, fresh, jerky, jumpy, sassy, tense 6 brassy, cheeky, goosey, plucky, spooky, uneasy 7 fidgety, forward, jittery, restive, twitchy, uptight 8 impudent, intrepid, twittery 9 excitable 10 high-strung 11 smart-alecky

ness
4 cape 8 foreland, headland 9 peninsula 10 promontory

Nessus' victim
8 Heracles, Hercules

nest
3 den 4 aery, home, lair, nidi (plural) 5 aerie, eyrie, nidus 7 hangout, shelter 11 aggregation
eagle's: 4 aery 5 aerie, eyrie
wasp's: 8 vespiary

nest egg
5 cache, funds, hoard, kitty, stash 6 assets 7 reserve

nestle
4 snug 6 bundle, burrow, cuddle, huddle, nuzzle 7 snuggle

Nestor
father: 6 Neleus
kingdom: 5 Pylos

net
4 gain, gist, mesh 5 basic, catch, clear, seine, tulle, yield 6 maline 7 clean up, essence, malines
conical: 5 trawl
fishing: 5 seine
hair: 5 snood

Nethanel
brother: 5 David
father: 5 Jesse 7 Pashhur 8 Obededom
son: 8 Shemaiah

nether
3 low 4 down 5 below, lower, under 6 lesser 8 chthonic, inferior 9 subjacent 10 underworld 11 underground 12 subterranean

Netherlands
7 Holland
capital: 9 Amsterdam
city: 5 Hague (The) 7 Utrecht 8 The Hague 9 Rotterdam
former inlet: 9 Zuider Zee
island group: 11 West Frisian
lake: 10 IJsselmeer
language: 5 Dutch
monetary unit: 4 euro
monetary unit, former: 7 guilder
neighbor: 7 Belgium, Germany
river: 4 Maas 5 Meuse, Rhein, Rhine 8 Scheldt
sea: 5 North

Netherlands Antilles
capital: 10 Willemstad
discoverer: 8 Columbus (Christopher)
former name: 7 Curaçao
island: 4 Saba 7 Bonaire 7 Curaçao
location: 10 West Indies
part of: 11 Netherlands

netherworld
3 pit 4 hell 5 abyss, hades, Sheol
6 blazes, Tophet 7 Gehenna, inferno
8 hellfire 9 perdition 10 no-man's-land, underworld 11 underground

netlike
9 reticular 10 reticulate

nettle
3 nag, vex 4 gall, huff, rile, roil
5 annoy, chafe, peeve, pique, upset
6 abrade, badger, harass, incite, put
out, pester, ruffle, stir up 7 agitate,
disturb, perturb, provoke 8 irritate
10 exasperate

nettle rash
5 hives 9 urticaria

nettlesome
5 pesky 6 vexing 7 galling, irksome,
prickly 8 annoying, rankling 9 irritable, upsetting, vexatious 10 irritating

network
3 web 4 mesh 8 gridiron 9 reticulum
anatomical: 4 rete 5 retia (plural)

neurotic
6 phobic, touchy 7 anxious 8 abnormal, unstable 9 disturbed, obsessive
10 compulsive, disordered

neuter
3 fix 4 geld, spay 5 alter, unsex
7 sexless 8 castrate, mutilate 9 sterilize 11 desexualize 12 intransitive

neutral
7 hueless 8 detached, middling,
unbiased 9 colorless, impartial,
unaligned 10 achromatic, disengaged, even-handed, impersonal,
nonaligned, pokerfaced 11 indifferent, nonpartisan 13 disinterested,
dispassionate

neutralize
4 undo 5 annul 6 negate, offset
7 balance, nullify, redress, reverse
9 cancel out 10 counteract, invalidate 11 countervail 12 countercheck, counterpoise

Nevada
capital: 10 Carson City
city: 4 Elko, Reno 8 Las Vegas
dam: 6 Hoover 7 Boulder
lake: 4 Mead 5 Tahoe
mountain: 8 Boundary (Peak)
nickname: 6 Silver (State)
river: 8 Humboldt
state bird: 8 bluebird (mountain)
state flower: 9 sagebrush
state tree: 5 piñon 6 pinyon 15 bristlecone pine

névé
4 firn, snow

never-ending
7 eternal 8 immortal 9 ceaseless
11 everlasting

Never-Ending Story author
4 Ende (Michael)

nevertheless
3 but, yet 5 still 6 anyhow, anyway,
though, withal 7 howbeit, however
8 after all 10 regardless 11 nonetheless, still and all

nevus
4 mole 9 birthmark

new
5 fresh, novel 6 modern, recent
7 another, revived 8 neoteric,
pristine 10 additional, unfamiliar
11 modernistic 12 contemporary
combining form: 3 neo, nov 4 novo
word: 7 coinage 9 neologism

New Brunswick
capital: 11 Fredericton
city: 6 St. John 7 Moncton
mountain: 8 Carleton
provincial flower: 12 purple violet
river: 9 Miramichi, Saint John
10 Nepisiguit 11 Restigouche

New Caledonia
capital: 6 Nouméa

newcomer

department of: 6 France
discoverer: 4 Cook (Capt. James)
island: 7 Loyalty, Walpole 11 Isle of
Pines

newcomer

4 colt, tyro 6 novice, rookie 8 beginner, freshman, initiate, neophyte
9 greenhorn, immigrant, novitiate
10 apprentice, tenderfoot

New Deal agency

3 CCC, NRA, SEC, TVA, WPA
4 FDIC, NLRB

Newfoundland and Labrador

capital: 7 St. John's
mountain: 8 Caubvick
provincial flower: 12 pitcher plant
river: 6 Gander 8 Exploits 9 Churchill

New Hampshire

capital: 7 Concord
city: 6 Nashua 10 Manchester,
Portsmouth
college, university: 9 Dartmouth
motto: 13 Live Free or Die
mountain, range: 5 White 10 Washington
nickname: 7 Granite (State)
river: 9 Merrimack 11 Connecticut
state bird: 11 purple finch
state flower: 11 purple lilac
state tree: 10 white birch

New Jersey

capital: 7 Trenton
city: 6 Camden, Newark 7 Cape
May 8 Paterson 9 Elizabeth
10 Jersey City
college, university: 4 Drew
7 Rutgers 9 Princeton, Seton Hall
18 Fairleigh Dickinson
nickname: 6 Garden (State)
river: 6 Hudson 7 Raritan 8 Delaware
state bird: 9 goldfinch
state flower: 6 violet
state tree: 6 red oak

New Mexico

capital: 7 Santa Fe
caverns: 8 Carlsbad
city: 4 Taos 7 Roswell 9 Las
Cruces, Los Alamos 10 Farmington
11 Albuquerque

mountain, range: 7 Wheeler (Peak)
14 Sangre de Cristo
nickname: 17 Land of Enchantment
river: 5 Pecos 9 Rio Grande
state bird: 10 roadrunner
state flower: 5 yucca
state tree: 5 piñon 6 pinyon

news

4 dope, poop, word 5 rumor 6 advice, gossip, report, tattle 7 low-
down, tidings 9 knowledge, speer-
ings 11 information, scuttlebutt
12 announcement, intelligence
4 TASS 7 Reuters 8 ITAR-TASS

newspaper

5 daily, organ 6 review 7 journal,
tabloid 8 magazine 10 periodical
publisher: 6 Hearst (William
Randolph) 7 Murdoch (Rupert)
11 Beaverbrook (Lord)

newt

3 eft 6 triton
green: 5 ebbet

New Testament
see at Bible

New York

capital: 6 Albany
city: 4 Rome, Troy 5 Utica 6 Elmira,
Ithaca 7 Buffalo, Yonkers 8 Saratoga, Syracuse 9 Rochester 11 New
York City
college, university: 3 RPI 4 Pace,
CUNY, SUNY 5 Pratt, Siena 6 CW
Post, Hunter, Vassar 7 Adelphi,
Barnard, Colgate, Cornell, Fordham,
Hofstra, St. Johns, Yeshiva 8 Columbia, Skidmore, Syracuse 9 Juilliard, West Point 13 Sarah Lawrence
island: 4 Long, Fire
lake, lake group: 4 Erie 6 Cayuga,
Finger, Oneida 7 Saranac 9 Champlain
motto: 9 Excelsior
mountain, range: 5 Marcy 8 Catskill 10 Adirondack
nickname: 6 Empire (State)
river: 6 Hudson 7 Niagara 10 St.
Lawrence
state bird: 8 bluebird
state flower: 4 rose
state tree: 10 sugar maple

New York City
6 Gotham   8 Big Apple
borough: 5 Bronx   6 Queens
8 Brooklyn, Richmond   9 Manhattan
12 Staten Island

New Zealand
capital: 10 Wellington
city: 8 Auckland   12 Christchurch
ethnic group: 5 Maori
explorer: 4 Cook (Capt. James)
6 Tasman (Abel)
island: 5 North, South   7 Chatham,
Stewart
island group: 4 Cook   8 Manihiki
12 Northern Cook
lake: 5 Taupo
language: 5 Maori   7 English
monetary unit: 6 dollar
mountain, range: 4 Cook   6 Egmont
12 Southern Alps
native: 4 Kiwi
strait: 4 Cook
volcano: 7 Ruapehu   9 Ngauruhoe

next
4 then   5 after, later   6 behind,
beside, second   7 closest, ensuing,
nearest   8 abutting, adjacent, touching   9 adjoining, afterward, alongside, following, proximate   10 contiguous, subsequent, succeeding
11 neighboring

next to
4 near   6 almost, beside   7 abreast,
close by   8 abutting, adjacent, opposite, touching   9 adjoining, alongside,
bordering   11 neighboring

nexus
3 tie   4 bond, knot, link, yoke   5 focus
6 center   8 ligament, ligature, vinculum   10 connection

Nez Percé chief
6 Joseph

Niagara
5 flood, spate   6 deluge   7 torrent
8 alluvion, cataract, flooding, overflow
9 cataclysm, waterfall   10 inundation

nib
3 neb, tip   4 beak, bill, nose, prow
5 prong, snoot, snout, tooth   8 pen
point   9 proboscis

nibble
3 eat, nip   4 bite, chew, crop, gnaw,
nosh, peck, pick   5 graze, munch,
snack, taste   6 morsel, tidbit

Nicaragua
capital: 7 Managua
city: 4 León   6 Masaya
coast: 8 Mosquito
ethnic group: 4 Maya   5 Mayan
discoverer: 8 Columbus (Christopher)
language: 7 Spanish
monetary unit: 7 córdoba
neighbor: 8 Honduras   9 Costa Rica
sea: 9 Caribbean

nice
4 fine, good, kind, mild, neat   5 right
6 benign, comely, dainty, decent,
polite, proper, seemly   7 affable,
clement, cordial, correct, fitting,
refined   8 becoming, charming,
decorous, obliging, pleasant, pleasing, suitable, virtuous, well-bred
9 admirable, agreeable, courteous,
congenial, enjoyable, favorable,
judicious   10 attractive, personable
11 appropriate, respectable

niche
4 nook   6 alcove, corner, cranny,
recess   7 calling   8 vocation   9 cubbyhole   11 compartment

Nicholas Nickleby author
7 Dickens (Charles)

nick
3 cut   4 chip, gash   5 cheat, notch,
score   6 groove, record   10 overcharge   11 indentation

nickname
3 tag   5 label   6 byword, handle
7 agnomen, epithet, moniker   8 cognomen   9 sobriquet   10 diminutive,
hypocorism

Nicomede
conquest: 10 Cappodocia
dramatist: 9 Corneille (Pierre)
half-brother: 6 Attale
stepmother: 7 Arsinoë

nictitate
3 bat   4 wink   5 blink   7 flutter, twinkle

nifty

4 cool, keen, neat 5 dandy, ducky, super, swell 6 clever, groovy, peachy 7 stylish 8 jim-dandy, splendid, terrific 9 ingenious

Niger

capital: 6 Niamey
city: 6 Maradi, Zinder
desert: 5 Sahel 6 Sahara
ethnic group: 5 Hausa
language: 5 Hausa 6 Arabic, French
monetary unit: 5 franc
neighbor: 4 Chad, Mali 5 Benin, Libya 7 Algeria, Nigeria 11 Burkina Faso
river: 5 Niger

Nigeria

capital: 5 Abuja, Lagos
city: 4 Kano 6 Ibadan, Ilorin 7 Oshogbo 9 Ogbomosho
ethnic group: 4 Igbo 5 Hausa 6 Fulani, Yoruba
gulf: 6 Guinea
lake: 4 Chad
language: 5 Hausa 7 English
monetary unit: 5 naira
neighbor: 4 Chad 5 Benin, Niger 8 Cameroon
river: 5 Benue, Niger 6 Kaduna

niggard

5 churl, miser, piker, screw 7 hoarder, scrooge 8 tightwad 9 skinflint 10 cheapskate, curmudgeon 12 money-grubber, penny-pincher

niggardly

5 tight 6 scanty, stingy 7 chintzy, miserly 9 penurious 10 begrudging 11 closefisted, tightfisted 12 cheeseparing, parsimonious 13 penny-pinching

niggling

5 minor, petty 6 measly, paltry, two-bit 7 trivial 8 picayune, piddling, tiresome, trifling 9 small-time 10 bothersome, picayunish 11 small-minded

nigh

4 near 5 about, close, round 6 all but, almost, around, beside, nearby, nearly 7 close to 8 approach 9 immediate, just about, proximate, virtually 10 near at hand, pretty much 11 practically

night blindness

10 nyctalopia

nightclub

5 disco 6 bistro, casino 7 cabaret 9 honky-tonk, speakeasy 11 discotheque

nightfall

3 eve 4 dusk, even 6 sunset 7 evening, sundown 8 eventide, gloaming, twilight

nighthawk

6 petrel 7 bullbat 10 goatsucker

nightjar

9 nighthawk 10 goatsucker 12 whip-poor-will

nightly

9 nocturnal

nightmare

5 dream, fancy, worry 6 fright, horror, ordeal, vision 7 bugbear, fantasy, incubus, torment 8 phantasm, phantasy, succubus 12 apprehension 13 hallucination

nightshade

6 tomato 7 henbane 10 belladonna 11 bittersweet

nightstick

3 bat 4 club, mace 5 baton, billy, staff 6 cudgel 8 bludgeon 9 billy club, blackjack, truncheon 10 shillelagh

Nike

father: 6 Pallas
goddess of: 7 victory
mother: 4 Styx

nil

3 nix, zip 4 love, wind, zero 5 zilch 6 naught 7 nothing

Nile

6 Al-Bahr
dam: 5 Aswan 6 Makwar 10 Gebel Aulia

explorer: 5 Baker (Sir Samuel),
Bruce (James), Grant (James
Augustus), Speke (John Hanning)
queen: 4 Cleo 9 Cleopatra
section: 4 Abay 5 Abbai

nilgai
8 antelope

nimble
4 deft, spry, yare 5 agile, alert, fleet,
handy, light, quick, zippy 6 adroit,
limber, lively 7 lissome 9 dexterous,
sprightly 10 responsive 11 quick-
witted

Nimrod
6 hunter
father: 4 Cush

Ninazu
brother: 5 Nanna 6 Nergal
father: 5 Enlil
mother: 6 Ninlil

nincompoop
3 oaf 4 boob, clod, dodo, fool, goof,
mutt, simp, yo-yo 5 chump, dummy,
dunce, idiot, moron, ninny, noddy,
stupe 6 dimwit, donkey, dum-dum,
nitwit 7 airhead, dullard, pinhead,
schnook, tomfool 8 bonehead,
clodpoll, dumbbell, dumbhead,
imbecile, lunkhead, meathead,
numskull 9 birdbrain, blockhead,
ignoramus, lamebrain, numbskull,
simpleton, thickhead 10 dunderhead, hammerhead 11 chowderhead, chucklehead, knucklehead

nine
12 baseball team
combining form: 3 non 4 nona
goddesses: 5 Muses
group: 6 ennead
inches: 4 span
instruments: 5 nonet

Nine Worlds
3 Hel 6 Asgard 7 Alfheim, Midgard
8 Niflheim, Vanaheim 10 Jotunnheim
12 Muspellsheim 13 Svartalfaheim

ninny
see **nincompoop**

Ninsum's son
9 Gilgamesh

Nintu
consort: 4 Enki
son: 6 Ninsar

Ninurta
father: 5 Enlil
victim: 3 Kur

Ninus
father: 5 Belus
wife: 9 Semiramis

Niobe
brother: 6 Pelops
father: 8 Tantalus
husband: 7 Amphion
sister-in-law: 5 Aedon

nip
3 bit, nab, sip 4 bite, dart, dash,
dram, drop, jolt, peck, shot, slug,
swig 5 chill, clamp, hurry, pinch,
sever, snort, steal 6 imbibe, snatch,
thwart, tipple 7 cabbage, snifter,
swallow 9 frustrate

nipper
3 kid 4 tyke 5 child 6 moppet,
shaver 7 pincers 8 young one
9 youngling, youngster

nipple
3 pap 4 teat

Nippon
5 Japan

nippy
3 icy, raw 4 cold, cool 5 algid,
chill, crisp, sharp 6 arctic, biting,
bitter, chilly, frosty, wintry 7 caustic,
glacial, numbing, shivery 8 chilling,
freezing

nirvana
5 bliss, dream 6 heaven 7 Elysium
8 empyrean, oblivion, paradise
9 Shangri-la

Nisus
betrayer, daughter: 6 Scylla
father: 7 Pandion

nitid
6 bright, glossy, lucent 7 fulgent,

glowing, shining **8** gleaming, glinting, luminous, lustrous, polished
9 burnished

nitpick
4 carp **5** cavil **7** quibble **10** split hairs

nitrogen
5 azote
combining form: 3 azo

nitwit
3 oaf **4** boob, clod, dodo, dolt, dope, goof, mutt, simp **5** chump, cluck, dummy, dunce, idiot, moron, ninny, noddy, stupe **6** donkey, dum-dum **7** airhead, dullard, pinhead, schnook **8** bonehead, clodpoll, dumbbell, imbecile, lunkhead, meathead, numskull **9** birdbrain, blockhead, ignoramus, lamebrain, numbskull, simpleton, thickhead **10** dunderhead, hammerhead, nincompoop **11** chowderhead, chucklehead, knucklehead

nix
3 nay, zap **4** kill, nope, veto **5** quash **6** cancel, naught, reject, scotch, sprite **7** call off, nothing, nullify

Njord, Njorth
daughter: 5 Freya
son: 4 Frey
wife: 6 Skadhi, Skathi

no
3 nay, nix **6** denial **7** refusal **8** negative **10** thumbs-down
German: 4 nein

no-account
see **no-good**

Noachian
3 old **4** aged **5** fusty, hoary **6** ageold **7** ancient, antique, archaic **8** timeworn **9** venerable **10** antiquated, oldfangled **12** antediluvian, old-fashioned **13** superannuated

Noah
father: 6 Lamech **10** Zelophehad
grandson: 4 Aram **6** Canaan
great-grandson: 3 Hul
landing place: 6 Ararat
son: 3 Ham **4** Shem **6** Canaan
7 Japheth

Nobel Prize winner
chemistry:
1901: 8 van't Hoff (Jacobus)
1902: 7 Fischer (Emil)
1903: 9 Arrhenius (Svante)
1904: 6 Ramsay (William)
1905: 9 von Baeyer (Adolf)
1906: 7 Moissan (Henri)
1907: 7 Buchner (Eduard)
1908: 10 Rutherford (Ernest)
1909: 7 Ostwald (Wilhelm)
1910: 7 Wallach (Otto)
1911: 5 Curie (Marie)
1912: 8 Grignard (François), Sabatier (Paul)
1913: 6 Werner (Alfred)
1914: 8 Richards (Theodore)
1915: 11 Willstatter (Richard)
1918: 5 Haber (Fritz)
1920: 6 Nernst (Walther)
1921: 5 Soddy (Frederick)
1922: 5 Aston (Francis)
1923: 5 Pregl (Fritz)
1925: 8 Zsigmondy (Richard)
1926: 8 Svedberg (Theodor)
1927: 7 Wieland (Heinrich)
1928: 7 Windaus (Adolf)
1929: 6 Harden (Athur) **12** Euler-Chelpin (Hans von)
1930: 7 Fischer (Hans)
1931: 5 Bosch (Karl) **7** Bergius (Friedrich)
1932: 8 Langmuir (Irving)
1934: 4 Urey (Harold)
1935: 11 Joliot-Curie (Frédéric, Irene)
1936: 5 Debye (Peter)
1937: 6 Karrer (Paul) **7** Haworth (Walter)
1938: 4 Kuhn (Richard)
1939: 7 Ruzicka (Leopold) **9** Butenandt (Adolf)
1943: 6 Hevesy (Georg de)
1944: 4 Hahn (Otto)
1945: 8 Virtanen (Artturi)
1946: 7 Sumner (James) **7** Stanley (Wendell) **8** Northrop (John Howard)
1947: 8 Robinson (Robert)
1948: 7 Tiselius (Arne)
1949: 7 Giauque (William)
1950: 5 Alder (Kurt), Diels (Otto)

1951: 7 Seaborg (Glenn) 8 Mc-
Millan (Edwin)
1952: 5 Synge (Richard) 6 Martin
(Archer)
1953: 10 Staudinger (Hermann)
1954: 7 Pauling (Linus)
1955: 10 du Vigneaud (Vincent)
1956: 7 Semenov (Nikolay)
11 Hinshelwood (Cyril)
1957: 4 Todd (Alexander)
1958: 6 Sanger (Frederick)
1959: 9 Heyrovsky (Jaroslav)
1960: 5 Libby (Willard)
1961: 6 Calvin (Melvin)
1962: 6 Perutz (Max) 7 Kendrew
(John)
1963: 5 Natta (Giulio) 7 Ziegler
(Karl)
1964: 7 Hodgkin (Dorothy)
8 Woodward (Robert)
1966: 8 Mulliken (Robert)
1967: 5 Eigen (Manfred) 6 Porter
(George) 7 Norrish (Ronald)
1968: 7 Onsager (Lars)
1969: 6 Barton (Derek), Hassel
(Odd)
1970: 6 Leloir (Luis)
1971: 8 Herzberg (Gerhard)
1972: 5 Moore (Stanford), Stein
(William) 8 Anfinsen (Christian)
1973: 7 Fischer (Ernst) 9 Wilkinson (Geoffrey)
1974: 5 Flory (Paul)
1975: 6 Prelog (Vladimir) 9 Corn-
forth (John)
1976: 8 Lipscomb (William)
1977: 5 Prigogine (Ilya)
1978: 8 Mitchell (Peter)
1979: 5 Brown (Herbert) 6 Wittig
(Georg)
1980: 4 Berg (Paul) 6 Sanger
(Frederick) 7 Gilbert (Walter)
1981: 5 Fukui (Kenichi) 8 Hoffmann (Roald)
1982: 4 Klug (Aaron)
1983: 5 Taube (Henry)
1984: 10 Merrifield (R. Bruce)
1985: 5 Karle (Jerome) 8 Haupt-
man (Herbert)
1986: 3 Lee (Yuan) 7 Polanyi
(John) 10 Herschbach (Dudley)
1987: 4 Cram (Donald), Lehn (Jean-
Marie) 8 Pedersen (Charles)

1988: 5 Huber (Robert) 6 Michel
(Hartmut) 11 Deisenhofer
(Johann)
1989: 4 Cech (Thomas) 6 Altman
(Sidney)
1990: 5 Corey (Elias)
1991: 5 Ernst (Richard)
1992: 6 Marcus (Rudolph)
1993: 5 Smith (Michael) 6 Mullis
(Kary)
1994: 4 Olah (George)
1995: 6 Molina (Mario) 7 Crutzen
(Paul), Rowland (F. Sherwood)
1996: 4 Curl (Robert) 5 Kroto
(Harold) 7 Smalley (Richard)
1997 4 Skou (Jens) 5 Boyer (Paul)
6 Walker (John)
1998: 4 Kohn (Walter) 5 Pople
(John)
1999: 6 Zewail (Ahmed)
2000: 6 Heeger (Alan) 9 Shira-
kawa (Hideki) 10 MacDiarmid
(Alan)
2001: 6 Noyori (Ryoji) 7 Knowles
(William) 9 Sharpless (K. Barry)
2002: 4 Fenn (John) 6 Tanaka
(Koichi) 8 Wüthrich (Kurt)
2003: 4 Agre (Peter) 9 MacKinnon
(Roderick)
2004: 4 Rose (Irwin) 7 Hershko
(Avram) 11 Ciechanover (Aaron)
economics:
1969: 6 Frisch (Ragnar) 9 Tinbergen (Jan)
1970: 9 Samuelson (Paul)
1971: 7 Kuznets (Simon)
1972: 5 Arrow (Kenneth), Hicks
(John)
1973: 8 Leontief (Wassily)
1974: 5 Hayek (Friedrich von)
6 Myrdal (Gunnar)
1975: 8 Koopmans (Tjalling)
11 Kantorovich (Leonid)
1976: 8 Friedman (Milton)
1977: 5 Meade (James), Ohlin
(Bertil)
1978: 5 Simon (Herbert)
1979: 5 Lewis (Arthur) 7 Schultz
(Theodore)
1980: 5 Klein (Lawrence)
1981: 5 Tobin (James)
1982: 7 Stigler (George)
1983: 6 Debreu (Gerard)

1984: 5 Stone (Richard)
1985: 10 Modigliani (Franco)
1986: 8 Buchanan (James)
1987: 5 Solow (Robert)
1988: 6 Allais (Maurice)
1989: 8 Haavelmo (Trygve)
1990: 6 Miller (Merton), Sharpe (William) 9 Markowitz (Harry)
1991: 5 Coase (Ronald)
1992: 6 Becker (Gary)
1993: 5 Fogel (Robert), North (Douglass)
1994: 4 Nash (John) 6 Selten (Reinhard) 8 Harsanyi (John)
1995: 5 Lucas (Robert)
1996: 7 Vickrey (William) 8 Mirrlees (James)
1998: 3 Sen (Amartya)
1999: 7 Mundell (Robert)
2000: 7 Heckman (James) 8 Mc-Fadden (Daniel)
2001: 6 Spence (Michael) 7 Akerlof (George) 8 Stiglitz (Joseph)
2002: 5 Smith (Vernon) 8 Kahne-man (Daniel)
2003: 5 Engle (Robert) 7 Granger (Clive)
2004: 7 Kydland (Finn) 8 Prescott (Edward)

literature:
1901: 9 Prudhomme (Sully)
1902: 7 Mommsen (Theodor)
1903: 8 Bjornson (Bjornstjerne)
1904: 7 Mistral (Frédéric) 9 Eche-garay (José)
1905: 11 Sienkiewicz (Henryk)
1906: 8 Carducci (Giosue)
1907: 7 Kipling (Rudyard)
1908: 6 Eucken (Rudolf)
1909: 8 Lagerlof (Selma)
1910: 5 Heyse (Paul)
1911: 11 Maeterlinck (Maurice)
1912: 9 Hauptmann (Gerhart)
1913: 6 Tagore (Rabindranath)
1915: 7 Rolland (Romain)
1916: 10 Heidenstam (Verner von)
1917: 9 Gjellerup (Karl) 11 Pon-toppidan (Henrik)
1919: 9 Spitteler (Carl)
1920: 6 Hamsun (Knut)
1921: 6 France (Anatole)

1922: 9 Benavente (Jacinto)
1923: 5 Yeats (William Butler)
1924: 7 Reymont (Wladyslaw)
1925: 4 Shaw (George Bernard)
1926: 7 Deledda (Grazia)
1927: 7 Bergson (Henri)
1928: 6 Undset (Sigrid)
1929: 4 Mann (Thomas)
1930: 5 Lewis (Sinclair)
1931: 9 Karlfeldt (Erik Axel)
1932: 10 Galsworthy (John)
1933: 5 Bunin (Ivan)
1934: 10 Pirandello (Luigi)
1936: 6 O'Neill (Eugene)
1937: 12 Martin du Gard (Roger)
1938: 4 Buck (Pearl)
1939: 9 Sillanpää (Frans Eemil)
1944: 6 Jensen (Johannes)
1945: 7 Mistral (Gabriela)
1946: 5 Hesse (Hermann)
1947: 4 Gide (André)
1948: 5 Eliot (Thomas Stearns)
1949: 8 Faulkner (William)
1950: 7 Russell (Bertrand)
1951: 10 Lagerkvist (Pär)
1952: 7 Mauriac (François)
1953: 9 Churchill (Winston)
1954: 9 Hemingway (Ernest)
1955: 7 Laxness (Halldór)
1956: 7 Jiménez (Juan Ramón)
1957: 5 Camus (Albert)
1958: 9 Pasternak (Boris)
1959: 9 Quasimodo (Salvatore)
1960: 5 Perse (Saint-John)
1961: 6 Andric (Ivo)
1962: 9 Steinbeck (John)
1963: 7 Seferis (George)
1964: 6 Sartre (Jean-Paul)
1965: 9 Sholokhov (Mikhail)
1966: 5 Agnon (Shmuel Yosef), Sachs (Nelly)
1967: 8 Asturias (Miguel Angel)
1968: 8 Kawabata (Yasunari)
1969: 7 Beckett (Samuel)
1970: 12 Solzhenitsyn (Alexander)
1971: 6 Neruda (Pablo)
1972: 4 Böll (Heinrich)
1973: 5 White (Patrick)
1974: 7 Johnson (Eyvind) 9 Mar-tinson (Edmund)
1975: 7 Montale (Eugenio)
1976: 6 Bellow (Saul)

1977: 10 Aleixandre (Vicente)
1978: 6 Singer (Isaac Bashevis)
1979: 6 Elytis (Odysseus)
1980: 6 Milosz (Czeslaw)
1981: 7 Canetti (Elias)
1982: 13 García Márquez (Gabriel)
1983: 7 Golding (William)
1984: 7 Seifert (Jaroslav)
1985: 5 Simon (Claude)
1986: 7 Soyinka (Wole)
1987: 7 Brodsky (Joseph)
1988: 7 Mahfouz (Naguib)
1989: 4 Cela (Camilo José)
1990: 3 Paz (Octavio)
1991: 8 Gordimer (Nadine)
1992: 7 Walcott (Derek)
1993: 7 Morrison (Toni)
1994: 2 Oe (Kenzaburo)
1995: 6 Heaney (Seamus)
1996: 10 Szymborska (Wislawa)
1997: 2 Fo (Dario)
1998: 8 Saramago (José)
1999: 5 Grass (Günter)
2000: 3 Gao (Xingjian) 11 Gao
  Xingjian
2001: 7 Naipaul (V. S.)
2002: 7 Kertész (Imre)
2003: 7 Coetzee (J. M.)
2004: 7 Jelinek (Elfriede)
peace:
  1901: 5 Passy (Frédéric) 6 Dunant
    (Jean-Henri)
  1902: 5 Gobat (Charles Albert)
    8 Ducommun (Elie)
  1903: 6 Cremer (William)
  1905: 7 Suttner (Bertha von)
  1906: 9 Roosevelt (Theodore)
  1907: 6 Moneta (Ernesto) 7 Re-
    nault (Louis)
  1908: 5 Bajer (Fredrik) 9 Arnold-
    son (Klas Pontus)
  1909: 6 Beernaert (Auguste)
    13 d'Estournelles (Paul)
  1911: 5 Asser (Tobias), Fried
    (Alfred)
  1912: 4 Root (Elihu)
  1913: 10 La Fontaine (Henri)
  1919: 6 Wilson (Woodrow)
  1920: 9 Bourgeois (Léon)
  1921: 9 Lange (Christian Louis)
    8 Branting (Karl Hjalmar)
  1922: 6 Nansen (Fridtjof)

1925: 5 Dawes (Charles) 11 Chamberlain (Austen)
1926: 6 Briand (Aristide) 10 Stresemann (Gustav)
1927: 6 Quidde (Ludwig) 7 Buis-
  son (Ferdinand)
1929: 7 Kellogg (Frank)
1930: 7 Soderblom (Nathan)
1931: 6 Addams (Jane), Butler
  (Nicholas Murray)
1933: 6 Angell (Norman)
1934: 9 Henderson (Arthur)
1935: 9 Ossietzky (Carl von)
1936: 13 Saavedra Lamas (Carlos
  de)
1937: 5 Cecil (Robert)
1945: 4 Hull (Cordell)
1946: 4 Mott (John) 5 Balch (Emily
  Greene)
1949: 3 Orr (John Boyd)
1950: 6 Bunche (Ralph)
1951: 7 Jouhaux (Léon)
1952: 10 Schweitzer (Albert)
1953: 8 Marshall (George)
1957: 7 Pearson (Lester)
1958: 4 Pire (Dominique Georges)
1959: 9 Noel-Baker (Philip)
1960: 7 Luthuli (Albert John)
1961: 12 Hammarskjold (Dag)
1962: 7 Pauling (Linus)
1964: 4 King (Martin Luther)
1968: 6 Cassin (René)
1970: 7 Borlaug (Norman)
1971: 6 Brandt (Willy)
1973: 8 Le Duc Tho 9 Kissinger
  (Henry)
1974: 4 Sato (Eisaku) 8 MacBride
  (Sean)
1975: 8 Sakharov (Andrey)
1976: 8 Corrigan (Mairead),
  Williams (Betty)
1978: 5 Begin (Menachem), Sadat
  (Anwar el-)
1979: 12 Mother Teresa
1980: 8 Esquivel (Adolfo Pérez)
1982: 6 Myrdal (Alva) 12 García
  Robles (Alfonso)
1983: 6 Walesa (Lech)
1984: 4 Tutu (Desmond)
1986: 6 Wiesel (Elie)
1987: 12 Arias Sánchez (Oscar)
1989: 9 Dalai Lama

1990: 9 Gorbachev (Mikhail)
1991: 13 Aung San Suu Kyi
1992: 6 Menchú (Rigoberta)
1993: 7 de Klerk (F. W.), Mandela (Nelson)
1994: 5 Peres (Shimon), Rabin (Yitzhak) 6 Arafat (Yasir)
1995: 7 Rotblat (Joseph)
1996: 10 Ramos-Horta (José) 11 Ximenes Belo (Carlos Felipe)
1997: 8 Williams (Jody)
1998: 4 Hume (John) 7 Trimble (David)
2000: 3 Kim (Dae-jung) 10 Kim Dae-jung
2001: 5 Annan (Kofi)
2002: 6 Carter (Jimmy)
2003: 5 Ebadi (Shirin)
2004: 7 Maathai (Wangari)
physics:
1901: 8 Roentgen (Wilhelm)
1902: 6 Zeeman (Pieter) 7 Lorentz (Hendrik Antoon)
1903: 5 Curie (Marie, Pierre) 9 Becquerel (Antoine-Henri)
1904: 6 Strutt (John) 8 Rayleigh (Lord)
1905: 6 Lenard (Philipp von)
1906: 7 Thomson (Joseph)
1907: 8 Michelson (Albert)
1908: 8 Lippmann (Gabriel)
1909: 5 Braun (Karl) 7 Marconi (Guglielmo)
1910: 11 van der Waals (Johannes)
1911: 4 Wien (Wilhelm)
1912: 5 Dalen (Nils)
1914: 5 Laue (Max von)
1915: 5 Bragg (William)
1917: 6 Barkla (Charles)
1918: 6 Planck (Max)
1919: 5 Stark (Johannes)
1920: 9 Guillaume (Charles)
1921: 8 Einstein (Albert)
1922: 4 Bohr (Niels)
1923: 8 Millikan (Robert)
1924: 8 Siegbahn (Karl)
1925: 5 Hertz (Gustav) 6 Franck (James)
1926: 6 Perrin (Jean-Baptiste)
1927: 6 Wilson (Charles) 7 Compton (Arthur)

1928: 10 Richardson (Owen)
1929: 7 Broglie (Louis-Victor de)
1930: 5 Raman (Chandrasekhara)
1932: 10 Heisenberg (Werner)
1933: 5 Dirac (Paul) 11 Schrödinger (Erwin)
1935: 8 Chadwick (James)
1936: 4 Hess (Victor) 8 Anderson (Carl)
1937: 7 Thomson (George) 8 Davisson (Clinton)
1938: 5 Fermi (Enrico)
1939: 8 Lawrence (Ernest)
1943: 5 Stern (Otto)
1944: 4 Rabi (Isidor Isaac)
1945: 5 Pauli (Wolfgang)
1946: 8 Bridgman (Percy)
1947: 8 Appleton (Edward)
1948: 8 Blackett (Patrick)
1949: 6 Yukawa (Hideki)
1950: 6 Powell (Cecil)
1951: 6 Walton (Ernest) 9 Cockcroft (John)
1952: 5 Bloch (Felix) 7 Purcell (Edward)
1953: 7 Zernike (Frits)
1954: 4 Born (Max) 5 Bothe (Walther)
1955: 4 Lamb (Willis) 5 Kusch (Polykarp)
1956: 7 Bardeen (John) 8 Brattain (Walter), Shockley (William)
1957: 3 Lee (Tsung Dao) 4 Yang (Chen Ning)
1958: 4 Tamm (Igor) 5 Frank (Ilya) 9 Cherenkov (Pavel)
1959: 5 Segrè (Emilio) 11 Chamberlain (Owen)
1960: 6 Glaser (Donald)
1961: 9 Mossbauer (Rudolf) 10 Hofstadter (Robert)
1962: 6 Landau (Lev)
1963: 5 Mayer (Maria) 6 Jensen (J. Hans), Wigner (Eugene)
1964: 5 Basov (Nikolay) 6 Townes (Charles) 9 Prochorov (Alexander)
1965: 7 Feynman (Richard) 8 Tomonaga (Shinichiro) 9 Schwinger (Julian)
1966: 7 Kastler (Alfred)
1967: 5 Bethe (Hans)
1968: 7 Alvarez (Luis)

1969: 8 Gell-Mann (Murray)
1970: 4 Néel (Louis) 6 Alfven (Hannes)
1971: 5 Gabor (Dennis)
1972: 6 Cooper (Leon) 7 Bardeen (John) 10 Schrieffer (John)
1973: 5 Esaki (Leo) 7 Giaever (Ivar) 9 Josephson (Brian)
1974: 4 Ryle (Martin) 6 Hewish (Antony)
1975: 4 Bohr (Aage) 9 Mottelson (Ben), Rainwater (L. James)
1976: 4 Ting (Samuel) 7 Richter (Burton)
1977: 4 Mott (Nevill) 8 Anderson (Philip), Van Vleck (John)
1978: 6 Wilson (Robert) 7 Kapitsa (Pyotr), Penzias (Arno)
1979: 5 Salam (Abdus) 7 Glashow (Sheldon) 8 Weinberg (Steven)
1980: 5 Fitch (Val) 6 Cronin (James)
1981: 8 Schawlow (Arthur), Siegbahn (Kai) 11 Bloembergen (Nicholaas)
1982: 6 Wilson (Kenneth)
1983: 6 Fowler (William) 13 Chandrasekhar (Subrahmanyan)
1984: 6 Rubbia (Carlo) 11 van der Meere (Simon)
1985: 8 Klitzing (Klaus von)
1986: 5 Ruska (Ernst) 6 Binnig (Gerd), Rohrer (Heinrich)
1987: 6 Müller (K. Alex) 7 Bednorz (J. Georg)
1988: 8 Lederman (Leon), Schwartz (Melvin) 11 Steinberger (Jack)
1989: 4 Paul (Wolfgang) 6 Ramsey (Norman) 7 Dehmelt (Hans)
1990: 6 Taylor (Richard) 7 Kendall (Henry) 8 Friedman (Jerome)
1991: 8 De Gennes (Pierre-Gilles)
1992: 7 Charpak (Georges)
1993: 5 Hulse (Russell) 6 Taylor (Joseph)
1994: 5 Shull (Clifford) 10 Brockhouse (Bertram)
1995: 4 Perl (Martin) 6 Reines (Frederick)
1996: 3 Lee (David) 8 Osheroff (Douglas) 10 Richardson (Robert)

3 Chu (Steven) 8 Phillips (William) 14 Cohen-Tannoudji (Claude)
1998: 4 Tsui (Daniel) 7 Störmer (Horst) 8 Laughlin (Robert)
1999: 6 't Hooft (Gerardus) 7 Veltman (Martinus)
2000: 5 Kilby (Jack) 7 Alferev (Zhores), Kroemer (Herbert)
2001: 6 Wieman (Carl) 7 Cornell (Eric) 8 Ketterle (Wolfgang)
2002: 5 Davis (Raymond) 7 Koshiba (Masatoshi) 8 Giacconi (Riccardo)
2003: 7 Leggett (Anthony) 8 Ginzburg (Vitaly) 9 Abrikosov (Alexei)
2004: 5 Gross (David) 7 Wilczek (Frank) 8 Politzer (David)
physiology or medicine:
1901: 7 Behring (Emil von)
1902: 4 Ross (Ronald)
1903: 7 Finsen (Niels Ryberg)
1904: 6 Pavlov (Ivan)
1905: 4 Koch (Robert)
1906: 5 Golgi (Camillo) 11 Ramón y Cajal (Santiago)
1907: 7 Laveran (Alphonse)
1908: 7 Ehrlich (Paul) 11 Metchnikoff (Elie)
1909: 6 Kocher (Emil)
1910: 6 Kossel (Albrecht)
1911: 10 Gullstrand (Allvar)
1912: 6 Carrel (Alexis)
1913: 6 Richet (Charles)
1914: 6 Barany (Robert)
1919: 6 Bordet (Jules)
1920: 5 Krogh (August)
1922: 4 Hill (Archibald) 8 Meyerhof (Otto)
1923: 7 Banting (Frederick), Macleod (John)
1924: 9 Einthoven (Willem)
1926: 7 Fibiger (Johannes)
1927: 13 Wagner-Jauregg (Julius)
1928: 7 Nicolle (Charles)
1929: 7 Eijkman (Christiaan), Hopkins (Frederick)
1930: 11 Landsteiner (Karl)
1931: 7 Warburg (Otto)
1932: 6 Adrian (Edgar) 11 Sherrington (Charles)
1933: 6 Morgan (Thomas)

1934: 5 Minot (George) 6 Murphy (William) 7 Whipple (George)

1935: 7 Spemann (Hans)

1936: 4 Dale (Henry) 5 Loewi (Otto)

1937: 12 Szent-Györgyi (Albert)

1938: 7 Heymans (Corneille)

1939: 6 Domagk (Gerhard)

1943: 3 Dam (Henrik) 5 Doisy (Edward)

1944: 6 Gasser (Herbert) 8 Erlanger (Joseph)

1945: 5 Chain (Ernst) 6 Florey (Howard) 7 Fleming (Alexander)

1946: 6 Muller (Hermann)

1947: 4 Cori (Carl, Gerty) 7 Houssay (Bernardo)

1948: 7 Mueller (Paul)

1949: 4 Hess (Walter) 5 Moniz (Antonio)

1950: 5 Hench (Philip) 7 Kendall (Edward) 10 Reichstein (Tadeus)

1951: 7 Theiler (Max)

1952: 7 Waksman (Selman)

1953: 5 Krebs (Hans) 7 Lipmann (Fritz)

1954: 6 Enders (John), Weller (Thomas) 7 Robbins (Frederick)

1955: 8 Theorell (Hugo)

1956: 8 Cournand (André), Richards (Dickinson) 9 Forssmann (Werner)

1957: 5 Bovet (Daniel)

1958: 5 Tatum (Edward) 6 Beadle (George) 9 Lederberg (Joshua)

1959: 5 Ochoa (Severo) 8 Kornberg (Arthur)

1960: 6 Burnet (Macfarlane) 7 Medawar (Peter)

1961: 6 Bekesy (Georg von)

1962: 5 Crick (Francis) 6 Watson (James) 7 Wilkins (Maurice)

1963: 6 Eccles (John), Huxley (Andrew) 7 Hodgkin (Alan)

1964: 5 Bloch (Konrad), Lynen (Feodor)

1965: 5 Jacob (Francois), Monod (Jacques) 5 Lwoff (André)

1966: 4 Rous (Francis) 7 Huggins (Charles)

1967: 4 Wald (George) 6 Granit (Ragnar) 8 Hartline (H. Keffer)

1968: 6 Holley (Robert) 7 Khorana (H. Gobind) 9 Nirenberg (Marshall)

1969: 5 Luria (Salvador) 7 Hershey (Alfred) 8 Delbruck (Max)

1970: 4 Katz (Bernard) 5 Euler (Ulf von) 7 Axelrod (Julius)

1971: 10 Sutherland (Earl)

1972: 6 Porter (Rodney) 7 Edelman (Gerald)

1973: 6 Frisch (Karl von), Lorenz (Konrad) 9 Tinbergen (Nikolaas)

1974: 4 Duve (Christian) 6 Claude (Albert), Palade (George)

1975: 5 Temin (Howard) 8 Dulbecco (Renato) 9 Baltimore (David)

1976: 8 Blumberg (Baruch), Gajdusek (D. Carleton)

1977: 5 Yalow (Rosalyn) 7 Schally (Andrew) 9 Guillemin (Roger)

1978: 5 Arber (Werner), Smith (Hamilton) 7 Nathans (Daniel)

1979: 7 Cormack (Allan) 10 Hounsfield (Godfrey)

1980: 5 Snell (George) 7 Dausset (Jean) 10 Benaceraf (Baruj)

1981: 5 Hubel (David) 6 Sperry (Roger), Wiesel (Torsten)

1982: 4 Vane (John) 9 Bergstrom (Sune) 10 Samuelsson (Bengt)

1983: 10 McClintock (Barbara)

1984: 5 Jerne (Niels) 7 Koehler (Georges) 8 Milstein (Cesar)

1985: 5 Brown (Michael) 9 Goldstein (Joseph)

1986: 5 Cohen (Stanley) 14 Levi-Montalcini (Rita)

1987: 8 Tonegawa (Susumu)

1988: 5 Black (James), Elion (Gertrude) 9 Hitchings (George)

1989: 6 Bishop (J. Michael), Varmus (Harold)

1990: 6 Murray (Joseph), Thomas (E. Donnall)

1991: 5 Neher (Erwin) 7 Sakmann (Bert)

1992: 5 Krebs (Edwin) 7 Fischer (Edmond)

1993: 5 Sharp (Phillip) 7 Roberts (Richard)

1994: 6 Gilman (Alfred) 7 Rodbell (Martin)

1995: 5 Lewis (Edward) 9 Wieschaus (Eric) 15 Nüsslein-Volhard (Christiane)
1996: 7 Doherty (Peter) 11 Zinkernagel (Rolf)
1997: 8 Prusiner (Stanley)
1998: 5 Murad (Ferid) 7 Ignarro (Louis) 9 Furchgott (Robert)
1999: 6 Blobel (Günter)
2000: 6 Kandel (Eric) 8 Carlsson (Arvid) 9 Greengard (Paul)
2001: 4 Hunt (Tim) 5 Nurse (Paul) 8 Hartwell (Leland)
2002: 7 Brenner (Sydney), Horvitz (Robert), Sulston (John)
2003: 9 Lauterbur (Paul), Mansfield (Peter) 4 Axel (Richard), Buck (Linda)

Nobel's invention
8 dynamite

nobility
6 virtue 7 dignity, peerage, royalty 8 eminence, noblesse 9 loftiness 10 exaltation, excellence, worthiness 11 aristocracy, superiority, uprightness

noble
4 peer 5 grand, lofty, moral 6 august, lordly, titled, worthy 7 courtly, eminent, exalted, notable, stately, sublime, upright 8 baronial, elevated, generous, gracious, heroical, highborn, highbred, imposing, magnific, majestic, princely, sterling, virtuous, wellborn 9 dignified, estimable, excellent, grandiose, honorable, righteous 10 high-minded, impressive, principled 11 illustrious, magnanimous, magnificent, outstanding, right-minded 12 aristocratic

nobleman
4 duke, earl, peer 5 baron, count 6 prince 7 baronet, marquis 8 marquess, viscount
French: 5 comte 7 vicomte
German: 4 Graf 8 margrave 9 landgrave
Indian: 6 sardar, sirdar 8 maharaja 9 maharajah

Italian: 8 marchese
Japanese (former): 6 daimyo
Scandinavian: 4 jarl
Spanish: 7 hidalgo

noblewoman
4 lady 7 baronne, duchess, peeress 8 baroness, countess, princess 11 marchioness, viscountess
French: 8 marquise
Italian: 8 marchesa

nobody
4 zero 6 cipher 7 nothing, nullity, upstart 9 nonentity 11 lightweight, small potato

nocturnal
7 nightly 9 nighttime

nocuous
3 bad 6 nocent 7 harmful, hurtful 8 damaging 9 injurious 11 deleterious, destructive, detrimental, mischievous

nod
3 bob, err 4 doze, okay 5 agree, droop, slump 6 assent, invite, signal 7 approve 8 approval 10 acceptance

nodding
6 casual, slight 7 passing 8 drooping 9 pendulous 11 superficial

noddle
3 nob, nut 4 bean, head, pate, poll 6 noggin

noddy
3 oaf 4 boob, clod, dodo, dolt, dope, fool, goof, mutt, simp, yo-yo 5 chump, dummy, dunce, moron, ninny, stupe 6 dimwit, donkey, dum-dum 7 airhead, dullard, pinhead, schnook 8 bonehead, clodpoll, dumbbell, dumbhead, imbecile, lunkhead, meathead, numskull 9 birdbrain, blockhead, ignoramus, lamebrain, numbskull, simpleton, thickhead 10 dunderhead, hammerhead, nincompoop 11 chowderhead, chucklehead, knucklehead

node

4 bump, burl, knob, knot, lump, mass
5 bulge, point 6 growth, vertex
8 swelling 11 enlargement, predicament 12 entanglement, protuberance

Noel

4 Xmas 5 carol 9 Christmas

nog

3 ale 4 beer, brew, malt, suds
5 lager, stout

noggin

3 cup, mug, nip, nob, nut 4 bean,
gill, head, pate, poll 6 noddle,
noodle

no-good

3 bum, dud 4 base, vile, worm
5 loser 6 scurvy, wretch 7 dirtbag,
inutile, lowlife, rounder, wastrel
8 deadbeat, shameful, unworthy,
wretched 9 no-account, valueless,
worthless 10 ne'er-do-well, profligate, scapegrace 11 ignominious 12 contemptible, disreputable
13 reprehensible

noise

3 din 4 blab, talk 5 babel, rumor,
sound 6 clamor, gossip, hubbub,
racket, ruckus, rumpus, tattle, uproar 7 ruction, sonance, stridor
8 resonant 11 pandemonium

noiseless

4 hush, mute 5 muted, quiet, still,
whist 6 hushed, silent, stilly 9 soundless

noisemaker

4 horn 6 rattle 7 clapper

noisome

4 foul, rank, vile 5 fetid, funky, fusty,
musty, nasty 6 filthy, horrid, putrid,
rancid, smelly 7 harmful, noxious,
squalid 8 stinking 9 obnoxious,
offensive, repulsive, revolting, sickening 10 disgusting, malodorous,
nauseating

noisy

4 loud 5 rowdy 7 blatant, booming,
clamant, rackety, raucous, squeaky
8 clattery, strident 9 clamorous,
deafening, turbulent 10 boisterous,
chattering, clangorous, tumultuous,
uproarious, vociferous 11 conspicuous 12 earsplitting, obstreperous

nomad

5 gypsy, rover 7 migrant, rambler
8 vagabond, wanderer
Arabic: 7 bedouin

nomadic

5 gypsy 6 roving 7 roaming, vagrant
8 drifting, vagabond 9 itinerant,
migratory, wandering, wayfaring
11 peripatetic 13 perambulatory

nom de plume

see **pen name**

nomen

4 name 7 moniker 11 appellation,
designation

nomenclature

4 list, name 7 catalog 8 glossary,
taxonomy 11 appellation, designation, phraseology, terminology
12 codification

nominal

3 low 5 given, named, rated, small
6 formal, puppet 7 alleged, minimal, seeming, titular 8 apparent,
so-called, trifling 9 pretended,
professed 10 ostensible 11 approximate, inexpensive 12 satisfactory,
substantival 13 insignificant

nominate

3 tap 4 call, name 5 offer, put up
7 appoint, propose, suggest 9 designate, recommend

nominee

6 choice 8 aspirant 9 candidate,
contender 10 contestant

nonage

5 youth 7 infancy 8 minority 9 childhood 10 immaturity, juvenility

nonchalant

4 cool, easy 5 blase 6 casual,
mellow, serene 7 offhand 8 care-

free, careless, cheerful, composed, laid-back 9 collected, easygoing, incurious, unruffled 10 effortless, insouciant, untroubled 11 indifferent, unconcerned, unflappable, unperturbed 12 lighthearted 13 dispassionate, imperturbable, lackadaisical

noncommittal
7 neutral 8 reserved 9 impassive 10 disengaged

nonconformist
5 rebel 7 beatnik, heretic, oddball, offbeat, radical 8 bohemian, maverick 9 dissenter, dissident, eccentric, heretical, heterodox, protester, sectarian 10 schismatic, separatist, unorthodox 11 misbeliever, schismatist

nonconformity
6 heresy, schism 7 dissent 9 misbelief, recusancy 10 dissidence, heterodoxy, opposition 11 unorthodoxy 12 disaffection 13 individualism, noncompliance

nonentity
4 zero 5 aught, zilch 6 cipher, nobody 7 nothing, nullity, whiffet 8 unperson 10 figurehead, mouthpiece

nonesuch
5 ideal 7 epitome, paragon, pattern 8 exemplar, paradigm, standard 9 archetype, matchless, nonpareil, unequaled, unrivaled

nonetheless
3 yet 5 still 6 anyway, though, withal 7 howbeit, however 8 although, after all 10 regardless 11 still and all

nonexistence
4 nada, void 7 nullity, vacuity 11 nothingness

nonflammable
9 fireproof 10 unburnable 13 incombustible

non-Hawaiian
5 haole

non-Jewish
3 goy 6 goyish 7 gentile

non-Muslim
6 giaour

no-nonsense
5 grave, sober 6 solemn 7 earnest, serious 8 resolute 9 pragmatic, realistic 10 determined, hardheaded, sobersided 11 plainspoken 12 businesslike 13 unsentimental

nonpareil
see nonesuch

nonpartisan
7 neutral 8 unbiased 9 equitable, impartial, objective, uncolored 10 nonaligned 11 independent 12 unprejudiced

nonplus
4 faze 5 stump 6 baffle, boggle, muddle, puzzle, rattle, stymie 7 buffalo, confuse, dilemma, flummox, fluster, mystify, perplex, stagger 8 bewilder, confound, distract, overcome, paralyze, quandary 9 discomfit, dumbfound, frustrate 10 disconcert

nonresistant
6 docile, pliant 7 passive, pliable 8 resigned, yielding 9 complying, tractable 10 conforming, submissive 11 acquiescent, conformable 13 accommodating

nonsense
3 rot 4 blah, bosh, bull, bunk, crap, gook, guff, jazz, punk, tosh 5 bilge, crock, drool, folly, fudge, Greek, hokum, hooey, trash 6 babble, blague, bunkum, drivel, hot air, humbug, jabber, piffle 7 baloney, blather, eyewash, flubdub, foolery, fooling, hogwash, inanity, rubbish, trifles, twaddle 8 buncombe, claptrap, falderal, folderol, flimflam, malarkey, pishposh, slipslop, tommyrot, trumpery 9 gibberish, moonshine, poppycock 10 applesauce, balderdash, double-talk, flapdoodle, tomfoolery 11 jabberwocky

nonsensical

12 blatherskite, fiddle-faddle, fiddle-sticks **13** horsefeathers
British: 10 codswallop

nonsensical

5 crazy, daffy, flaky, goofy, inane, kooky, loony, nutty, silly, wacky
6 absurd, screwy **7** foolish, idiotic, risible **9** illogical, laughable, ludicrous, senseless **10** irrational
12 preposterous, unreasonable

nonviolent

6 irenic **7** pacific **8** pacifist **9** peaceable **10** pacifistic

noodle

3 oaf **4** bean, boob, clod, dodo, dope, goof, head, mutt, poll, simp, yo-yo **5** chump, dummy, dunce, idiot, moron, ninny, noddy, stupe **6** dimwit, donkey, dum-dum, nitwit, noggin **7** airhead, dullard, pinhead, schnook **8** bonehead, clodpoll, dumbbell, dumbhead, imbecile, lunkhead, meathead, numskull **9** birdbrain, blockhead, ignoramus, lamebrain, numbskull, simpleton **10** dunderhead, hammerhead, nincompoop **11** chowderhead, chucklehead, knucklehead

nook

3 bay **4** cove **5** hutch, niche **6** alcove, cavity, corner, cranny, recess **9** cubbyhole **11** compartment

noose

3 tie **4** bait, bind, hang, loop, lure, trap **5** lasso, snare **6** entrap, secure

norm

3 par **4** mean, rule, type **5** gauge, maxim, model **6** median **7** average, measure, pattern **8** paradigm, standard **9** benchmark, criterion **10** touchstone

Norma

composer: 7 Bellini (Vincenzo)
librettist: 6 Romani (Felice)

normal

4 sane **5** usual **6** common **7** average, general, natural, regular, typical **8** ordinary, standard **9** customary, prevalent **11** commonplace, traditional **12** conventional **13** perpendicular

Normandy's capital

5 Rouen

Norns

5 fates, Skuld, Urdur **9** Verthandi

Norris novel

3 Pit (The) **4** Blix **7** Octopus (The) **8** McTeague

Norse

abode of the dead: 8 Niflheim
alphabet: 5 Runic
archer: 4 Egil
bard: 5 scald, skald
chieftain: 4 jarl, Rolf **5** Rollo
demon: 4 Mara, Surt **5** Surtr
dragon: 6 Fafnir **8** Nithhogg
epic: 4 Edda
explorer: 4 Erik, Leif **8** Ericsson (Leif), Eriksson (Leif)
first man: 3 Ask **4** Askr
first woman: 5 Embla
giant: 4 Egil, Wade, Wate, Ymer, Ymir **5** Aegir, Egill, Hymir, Jotun, Mimir **6** Fafnir, Jotunn
giantess: 4 Egia, Norn, Nott
god: 3 Asa, Ass **4** Surt, Vali, Vili **5** Aesir (plural), Surtr, Vanir (plural) **6** Hoenir, Vithar **7** Vitharr
  blind: 4 Hoth **5** Hoder, Hodur, Hothr
  chief: 4 Odin **5** Othin, Wodan, Woden, Wotan
  guardian: 7 Heimdal **8** Heimdall **9** Heimdallr
  messenger: 6 Hermod **7** Hermodr
  of beauty: 5 Baldr **6** Balder, Baldur
  of evil: 4 Loke, Loki
  of fertility: 4 Frey **5** Freyr
  of justice: 7 Forsete, Forseti
  of light: 3 Dag
  of peace: 5 Baldr **6** Balder, Baldur
  of poetry: 5 Brage, Bragi
  of the hunt: 3 Ull **4** Ullr
  of the seas: 5 Njord **6** Njoerd, Njorth **4** Hler **5** Aegir, Gymir
  of the sky: 4 Odin **5** Othin

of thunder: 4 Thor 5 Donar
of war: 3 Tiu, Tiw, Tyr, Zio, Ziu
wolf: 6 Fenrir
goddess: 3 dis 4 Saga 5 disir
(plural) 7 Asynjur
 of fate: 3 Urd 4 Norn, Urth, Wyrd
 5 Skuld 9 Verthandi
 of healing: 3 Eir
 of love: 5 Freya
 of marriage: 5 Frigg 6 Frigga
 of night: 4 Natt, Nott
 of storms: 3 Ran
 of the earth: 5 Joerd, Jorth
 of the moon: 5 Nanna
 of the sea: 3 Ran
 of the sky: 5 Frigg 6 Frigga
 of the underworld: 3 Hel 4 Hela
 of youth: 4 Idun 5 Ithun 6 Ithunn
gods' abode: 6 Asgard
hall of heroes: 7 Valhalla
king: 4 Atli, Olaf
nobleman: 4 jarl
patron saint: 4 Olaf
poem: 4 rune
poet: 5 scald, skald
rainbow bridge: 7 Bifrost
sea serpent: 4 Wade, Wate 6 kraken 7 Midgard
smith: 6 Völund
tale: 4 saga
toast: 5 skoal
watchdog: 4 Garm 5 Garmr
world's destruction: 8 Ragnarok
world tree: 8 Ygdrasil 10 Yggdrasill

north
 combining form: 4 arct 5 arcto

North African
 country: 5 Egypt, Libya 7 Algeria,
 Morocco, Tunisia
 fruit: 3 fig 4 date
 garment: 4 haik
 grass: 4 alfa 7 esparto
 jackal: 4 dieb
 language: 6 Arabic, Berber
 Muslim sect: 6 Sanusi 7 Senussi
 people: 6 Berber, Hamite 7 bedouin
 seaport: 4 Oran, Sfax 6 Annaba
 7 Tangier 10 Casablanca

North America
 country: 6 Canada, Mexico,
Panama 8 Honduras 9 Costa Rica,
Guatemala, Nicaragua 10 El Salvador 12 United States

North Carolina
 capital: 7 Raleigh
 city: 6 Durham 9 Asheville, Charlotte 10 Greensboro 12 Winston-Salem
 college, university: 4 Duke, Elon
 10 Wake Forest
 mountain, range: 8 Mitchell 9 Blue
 Ridge 10 Great Smoky
 nickname: 7 Tar Heel (State)
 state bird: 8 cardinal
 state flower: 7 dogwood
 state tree: 4 pine

North Dakota
 capital: 8 Bismarck
 city: 5 Fargo, Minot 10 Grand
 Forks
 nickname: 5 Sioux (State) 11 Flickertail (State)
 river: 3 Red 8 Missouri
 state bird: 10 meadowlark
 state flower: 11 prairie rose
 state tree: 3 elm (American)

northern
 4 pike 6 boreal 11 hyperborean

Northern Mariana Islands
 commonwealth of: 12 United
 States
 discoverer: 8 Magellan (Ferdinand)
 island: 4 Rota 6 Saipan, Tinian

North Star State
 9 Minnesota

Northwest Passage author
 7 Roberts (Kenneth)

Northwest Territories
 capital: 11 Yellowknife
 gulf: 8 Amundsen
 island: 5 Banks 8 Victoria
 lake: 9 Great Bear 10 Great Slave
 river: 9 Mackenzie
 sea: 8 Beaufort

north wind
 see at **wind**

Norway
 Arctic region: 7 Lapland

cape: 7 Nordkyn
capital: 4 Oslo
city: 6 Bergen 9 Stavanger, Trondheim
inlet: 9 Skagerrak
island: 5 Senja 6 Sørøya 8 Magerøya, Steinsøy 8 Nord-Kvaløy, Ringvassøy 10 Nord-Kvaløy, Ringvassøy
island group: 7 Lofoten 10 Vesterålen
lake: 5 Mjøsa
monetary unit: 5 krone
mountain range: 6 Kjølen 11 Jotunheimen
neighbor: 6 Russia, Sweden 7 Finland
part of: 11 Scandinavia
port: 5 Vardø 6 Tromsø 8 Kirkenes 10 Hammerfest
river: 4 Tana 5 Glåma, Lågen 9 Dramselva
sea: 5 North

Norwegian

goblin: 5 nisse
language: 5 Norse 6 Bokmal 7 Bokmaal, Nynorsk, Riksmal 8 Landsmal, Riksmaal 9 Landsmaal

nose

3 pry 4 beak, bent, bump, gift, head, poke 5 aroma, flair, knack, scent, smell, sniff, snift, snoop, snoot, snout, snuff 6 genius, muzzle, nuzzle, talent 7 aptness, faculty, smeller, sneezer 8 smell out 9 olfaction, proboscis, schnozzle
French: 3 nez
kind: 3 pug 5 Roman 8 aquiline
lengthener: 3 lie
opening: 7 nostril

nosebleed

9 epistaxis

nosedive

4 drop, fall 6 header, plunge 7 plummet

nosegay

4 posy 6 flower 7 bouquet, corsage 11 boutonniere

nosh

4 bite 5 graze, munch, snack 6 nibble

Nostradamus

7 prophet

Nostromo author

6 Conrad (Joseph)

nostrum

4 cure 6 elixir, remedy 7 cure-all, panacea 8 antidote, medicine 10 catholicon, corrective 11 restorative

nosy

6 prying, snoopy 7 curious, peeping 8 snooping 9 intrusive 11 inquisitive, inquisitory

notability

3 VIP 4 lion, star 5 celeb, chief 6 leader, worthy 7 big name, big shot 8 big-timer, eminence, luminary, presence, somebody 9 celebrity, chieftain, dignitary, personage, superstar 11 personality

notable

3 VIP 4 star 5 celeb, chief, famed, mogul, nabob, power 6 big boy, biggie, big gun, bigwig, famous, fat cat, leader, prince 7 big name, big shot, eminent, magnate, pooh-bah 8 big chief, big-timer, big wheel, eminence, luminary, renowned, somebody, striking 9 big cheese, celebrity, character, dignitary, distingué, personage, prominent, superstar 10 celebrated, celebrious, noteworthy, remarkable 11 conspicuous, heavyweight, illustrious, muckety-muck, personality 13 distinguished, high-muck-a-muck

notarize

7 certify, endorse 8 validate 12 authenticate

notch

3 cut, gap, jag 4 gash, mark, nick, nock, rung, slit, step 5 cleft, grade, score, stage 6 degree, groove, indent, rabbet, record 7 achieve, scratch 8 incision, undercut 11 indentation

note

3 jot 4 bond, chit, heed, mark, memo, show, sign, tone 5 catch,

sound, token **6** letter, notice, record, regard **7** comment, discern, jotting, missive, observe, promise, set down **8** eminence, indicate, perceive, reminder **9** attention, knowledge **10** cognizance, commentary, memorandum, observance, reputation **11** distinction, distinguish, observation

notebook
3 log **5** diary **7** journal

noted
6 famous **7** eminent, leading, popular **8** esteemed, renowned, striking **9** acclaimed, prominent, well-known **10** celebrated, recognized, remarkable **11** illustrious **13** distinguished

noteworthy
7 salient **8** singular, striking **9** arresting, bodacious, memorable, prominent, red-letter **10** impressive, meaningful, remarkable **11** conspicuous, exceptional, high-profile, major-league, outstanding, significant **12** considerable **13** extraordinary

nothing
3 nil, nix **4** zero **5** aught, nihil, zilch **6** cipher, naught, nobody, nought, trifle **7** nullity, whiffet **8** goose egg, whipster **9** no-account, nonentity
French: 4 rien
German: 6 nichts
Latin: 5 nihil
Spanish: 4 nada

nothingness
4 nada, void **5** death **6** vacuum **7** nullity, vacuity **9** emptiness **12** nonexistence

notice
3 see **4** espy, heed, mark, memo **5** catch, sight **6** descry, regard, review **7** discern, observe, respect **8** handbill, perceive **9** attention, directive, recognize **10** cognizance, evaluation **11** declaration, information, observation **12** announcement, proclamation **13** communication

noticeable
6 marked, patent, signal **7** evident, obvious, pointed, salient **8** apparent, manifest, striking **9** arresting, prominent **10** noteworthy, observable, remarkable **11** appreciable, conspicuous, eye-catching, outstanding, perceptible, significant **12** unmistakable

notify
3 cue **4** tell, warn **5** alert, brief **6** advise, clue in, fill in, inform **7** apprise **8** acquaint **9** enlighten

notion
4 clue, hint, idea, whim **5** fancy **6** belief, maggot, theory, vagary **7** caprice, conceit, concept, inkling, thought **8** crotchet **10** conception, impression, intimation, perception **11** inclination

notional
5 ideal **6** unreal **7** fancied, fictive **8** fanciful, illusory, imagined **9** imaginary, visionary, whimsical **10** capricious, conceptual **11** speculative, theoretical **12** hypothetical

notoriety
4 fame **6** infamy, renown **7** obloquy **9** disrepute **10** opprobrium, prominence **11** recognition

notorious
5 noted **6** famous **8** ill-famed, infamous **9** prominent, well-known **10** outrageous, scandalous **12** disreputable

Notus
6 Auster
brother: 5 Eurus **6** Boreas **8** Zephyrus
father: 6 Aeolus **8** Astraeus
mother: 3 Eos

noun
4 name **7** nominal **11** substantive
inflectional form: 4 case
verbal: 6 gerund

nourish
4 feed, rear **5** nurse, raise **6** foster **7** bring up, build up, nurture, promote, support **8** maintain **9** cultivate, encourage **10** provide for, strengthen

nourishment
3 pap 4 diet, eats, feed, food, grub
6 viands 7 aliment, pabulum, vittles
8 victuals 9 nutriment, provender
10 sustenance

_____ nous
5 entre

nouveau riche
7 parvenu, upstart 9 arriviste

Nova Scotia
capital: 7 Halifax
city: 9 Dartmouth
island: 10 Cape Breton
lake: 7 Bras D'Or
provincial flower: 9 mayflower

novel
3 new, odd 5 fresh 6 unique 7 offbeat, unusual 8 atypical, original,
peculiar, singular, uncommon 9 different, narrative 10 avant-garde,
innovative, newfangled

novelist
see **author**

novelty
5 curio 6 bauble, gewgaw, oddity,
trifle 7 bibelot, gimmick, newness,
trinket, whatnot 8 gimcrack, souvenir
9 bagatelle, curiosity, objet d'art
10 innovation, knickknack

novice
3 cub 4 colt, punk, tyro 6 rookie
7 amateur, learner, recruit, student,
trainee 8 aspirant, beginner, freshman, neophyte, newcomer, prentice
9 fledgling, greenhorn, novitiate,
postulant 10 apprentice, tenderfoot
11 probationer

Novum Organum author
5 Bacon (Francis)

now
3 PDQ 4 soon 5 today 6 at once,
pronto 7 anymore, present 8 directly, first off, promptly 9 forthwith,
instanter, instantly, presently, right
away, sometimes 11 immediately,
straightway 12 straightaway

now and then
7 at times, betimes 9 sometimes

12 infrequently, occasionally, periodically, sporadically

Nox
brother: 6 Erebus
daughter: 3 Day 4 Eris 5 Light
father: 5 Chaos
husband: 6 Erebus
son: 6 Charon, Hypnos 8 Thanatos

noxious
4 foul 5 fetid, toxic 6 deadly, putrid 7 baneful, harmful, noisome
8 stinking 9 dangerous, pestilent,
poisonous, unhealthy 10 corrupting,
pernicious 11 deleterious, destructive, detrimental, pestiferous 12 disagreeable, pestilential

nozzle
4 nose, vent 5 spout 7 channel

nuance
4 hint 5 shade, tinge, touch, trace
6 nicety 7 shading, soupçon 8 overtone, subtlety 9 gradation, suspicion
10 refinement, suggestion 11 distinction

nub
4 core, crux, gist, knob, knot, lump,
meat, node, pith 5 bulge, point,
short 6 kernel, upshot 8 swelling
9 substance 10 projection 12 protuberance

Nubian
5 Mahas 6 Birked, Kenuzi, Midobi
7 Dongola 8 Cushitic 9 Chari-Nile

nubile
4 ripe 10 attractive 12 marriageable

nuchal
4 nape

nuclear agency
3 AEC, NRC

nuclear particle
5 meson 6 proton 7 neutron

nucleus
3 bud 4 core, germ, head, kern, ring,
seed 5 focus, spark 6 embryo
material: 8 karyotin

nude

3 raw 4 bald, bare 5 naked, stark
6 barren, peeled, unclad 8 disrobed,
stripped 9 au naturel, buck naked,
unattired, unclothed, uncovered,
undressed 10 stark naked

nudge

3 dig, jab, jog 4 near, poke, prod,
push 5 elbow, punch, shove 8 approach

nudnik

4 bore, drip, pill, twit 8 nuisance

nugatory

4 idle, vain 5 empty, inane, vapid
6 futile, hollow, otiose 7 invalid,
vacuous 8 trifling 9 fruitless, worthless 11 inoperative, meaningless

nugget

3 gob, wad 4 hunk, lump, plum
5 chunk 6 tidbit

nuisance

4 pain, pest, pill 6 bother, nudnik
8 headache, irritant, pesterer, vexation 11 botheration

nuke

4 bomb 5 crush, smash 6 attack
7 destroy 8 demolish 9 eradicate,
microwave 10 annihilate 11 exterminate

null

4 void, zero 5 annul, empty 6 futile 7 invalid, useless 8 nugatory
9 worthless 10 invalidate, obliterate,
unavailing 11 ineffective, ineffectual,
inoperative

nullify

3 zap 4 undo, veto, void 5 abate,
annul, limit, quash, scrub, trash
6 cancel, efface, negate, offset,
repeal, revoke, squash 7 abolish,
rescind, scratch, take out, wipe out
8 abrogate 10 annihilate, compensate, counteract, invalidate, neutralize 11 countervail

nullity

4 nada, zero 5 zilch 6 cipher,
nobody 7 nothing, vacuity, whiffet

9 annulment, nonentity 11 nothingness 12 nonexistence

numb

5 chill, dazed 6 deaden, freeze
7 callous 8 deadened, detached
9 insensate, paralyzed, stupefied,
unfeeling 10 insensible, insentient 11 desensitize, indifferent
12 anesthetized, desensitized

number

5 add up, count, digit, run to, sum to,
tally, total 6 amount, cipher, come
to, figure 7 chiffer, include, integer,
numeral, ordinal, run into, several,
sum into 8 cardinal, numerate,
paginate 9 aggregate, enumerate
added to another: 6 augend
resulting from division: 8 quotient
resulting from multiplication:
7 product
resulting from subtraction: 10 difference
science: 11 mathematics

number one

4 best, main 5 chief, major 6 finest,
Grade A, top dog 7 capital, highest,
leading, primary, stellar 8 dominant,
five-star, foremost, superior 9 excellent, first-rate, front-rank, numero
uno, principal, top-drawer 10 blue-
ribbon, first-class, preeminent
11 first-string, outstanding, predominant

numbness

5 shock 6 stupor 10 anesthesia
12 stupefaction
combining form: 4 narc 5 narco

numeral

5 digit 6 cipher, figure, number
7 integer 11 whole number

numerate

4 list 5 count, tally 6 number 7 compute, itemize, tick off 8 tabulate
9 calculate

numerous

4 many 6 legion 7 profuse, umpteen
8 abundant, populous 9 plentiful
10 voluminous 13 multitudinous

Numitor

brother: 7 Amulius
daughter: 9 Rea Silvia 10 Rhea Silvia
grandson: 5 Remus 7 Romulus

numskull

3 oaf 4 boob, clod, dodo, dolt, dope, goof, mutt, simp 5 chump, dummy, dunce, idiot, moron, ninny, noddy, stupe 6 dimwit, donkey, dum-dum, nitwit 7 airhead, dullard, pinhead, schnook 8 bonehead, clodpate, clodpoll, dumbbell, dumbhead, imbecile, lunkhead, meathead 9 birdbrain, blockhead, ignoramus, lamebrain, simpleton, thickhead 10 dunderhead, hammerhead, nincompoop 11 chowderhead, chucklehead, knucklehead

nun

6 sister
headcloth: 6 wimple

Nunavut

capital: 7 Iqaluit
island: 5 Devon 6 Baffin 9 Ellesmere 11 Southampton
mountain: 7 Barbeau (Peak)
peninsula: 7 Boothia 8 Melville
provincial flower: 11 Arctic poppy

nunnery

7 convent 10 sisterhood
head: 8 superior

nuptial

6 bridal, wedded 7 marital, married, spousal, wedding 8 conjugal, espousal, hymeneal, marriage 9 connubial 11 matrimonial

nurse

4 feed, nana, rear, suck 5 nanny, serve 6 attend, foster, pamper, suckle 7 care for, cherish, nourish, nurture 9 cultivate 10 minister to
children's: 5 nanny
English: 11 Nightingale (Florence)
Indian: 4 ayah
Chinese: 4 amah

nursemaid

4 nana 5 nanny 6 minder, sitter 9 governess 10 babysitter
Indian: 4 ayah
Chinese: 4 amah

nursery

6 crèche 7 brooder 8 hothouse 9 fosterage 10 greenhouse 12 conservatory

nurture

4 care, feed, rear, tend 5 nurse, raise, train 6 cradle, foster 7 bring up, care for, develop, educate, nourish, rearing 8 breeding, instruct, training, tutelage 9 cultivate 10 upbringing

nut

3 bug 4 kook, loon 5 acorn, crank, fiend, freak, loony, pecan 6 almond, cashew, cuckoo, madman, maniac, zealot 7 fanatic, filbert, hickory, lunatic 8 crackpot 9 bedlamite, ding-a-ling, macadamia, pistachio, screwball 10 enthusiast, Tom o' Bedlam
of a violin bow: 4 frog, heel

Nut

consort: 3 Geb, Keb
daughter: 4 Isis 8 Nephthys
son: 6 Osiris

nuthouse

6 asylum, bedlam 8 loony bin 9 funny farm 10 booby hatch 11 institution 12 insane asylum

Nutmeg State

11 Connecticut

nutria

5 coypu

nutriment

4 diet, fare, food, grub, keep 6 viands 7 aliment, pabulum 8 victuals 9 provender 10 provisions, sustenance 11 comestibles, nourishment, subsistence

nutrition

4 diet 7 vittles 8 victuals 10 sustenance 11 nourishment

nutritious

9 healthful, wholesome 10 alimentary, nourishing

nuts

3 mad 4 daft, keen, wild 5 batty, crazy, kooky, loony, rabid, wacky 6 absurd, cuckoo, insane, screwy 7 bonkers, cracked, excited, foolish, idiotic 8 animated, demented, deranged 9 exuberant, fanatical, screwball 10 passionate, unbalanced 12 enthusiastic

nutty

see **nuts**

nuzzle

3 rub 4 root, snug 5 nudge 6 burrow, cuddle, nestle 7 snuggle

Nycteus

brother: 5 Lycus
daughter: 7 Antiope

nymph

3 nix 5 dryad, larva, naiad, nixie, sylph 6 kelpie, maiden, sprite 7 mermaid
changed into a bear: 8 Callisto
changed into a laurel: 6 Daphne
changed into a rock: 4 Echo
mountain: 5 oread
sea: 6 Nereid 7 Calypso
water: 5 naiad 6 undine
wood: 5 dryad

Nyx

see **Nox**

O

oaf
4 boob, boor, bull, clod, dodo, dolt, goof, goon, hulk, lout, lump, slob **5** booby, chump, clown, dummy, dunce, klutz **6** dum-dum, galoot, lubber, lummox **7** fathead, palooka **8** bonehead, lunkhead, meathead **9** blockhead, blunderer, lamebrain, simpleton

oafish
5 dense **6** clumsy, klutzy, rustic **7** boorish, doltish, loutish **8** bungling, churlish, clownish, lubberly

oak
African: 7 turtosa
fruit: 5 acorn
genus: 7 Quercus
kind: 3 bur, pin, red **4** bear, cork, holm, ilex, live **5** black, holly, roble, white **6** barren, cerris, encina **7** durmast, English, moss-cup, valonia **9** blackjack
Mexican: 8 chaparro
young: 8 flittern

oar
3 row **4** pole, pull **5** rower, scull **6** paddle **7** paddler
part: 4 loom, palm **5** blade, shaft **6** button, collar
pin: 5 thole

oarsman
3 bow **5** rower **6** stroke **7** sculler
director: 3 cox **8** coxswain

oasis
3 spa **4** wadi **6** refuge, relief
ancient: 4 Merv

Egypt: 4 Siwa **5** Gafsa **6** Dakhla **7** Farafra **8** Ammonium
Libya: 5 Mizda, Sebha `6** Sabhah **7** Gadames **8** Ghudamis
Niger: 5 Bilma
Saudi Arabia: 5 Hofuf, Taima **7** Al-Hufuf

oast
4 kiln, oven

oat
5 grain, grass **6** cereal
genus: 5 Avena
Scottish: 3 ait

oater
7 western **10** horse opera

oath
3 vow **4** cuss **5** curse, swear **6** pledge **7** promise **8** cussword **9** expletive, profanity, swearword
mild: 3 gee **4** darn, drat, egad, geez, gosh, jeez **5** golly **6** jiminy **7** gee whiz

oatmeal
5 gruel **6** burgoo **8** porridge
Scottish: 8 drammock

obdurate
3 set **4** firm, hard **5** harsh, rigid, stony **6** dogged, mulish **7** adamant, callous **8** stubborn **9** heartless, immovable, unbending, unfeeling **10** hard-boiled, inflexible, unshakable, unyielding **11** coldhearted, hardhearted, insensitive, unemotional **12** intransigent, stonyhearted **13** unsympathetic

obeah
5 charm, magic

Obed
father: 4 Boaz 6 Ephlal
8 Shemaiah
mother: 4 Ruth
son: 5 Jesse 7 Azariah

obedient
5 loyal 6 docile 7 devoted, duteous,
dutiful, willing 8 amenable, biddable, obliging, yielding 9 compliant,
tractable 10 law-abiding, manageable, respectful, submissive 11 acquiescent, cooperative, deferential,
subservient

obeisance
3 bow 5 honor 6 curtsy, esteem,
fealty, homage, kowtow, salaam
7 gesture, loyalty, respect 9 deference, reverence 10 allegiance,
submission

obelisk
6 dagger, pillar, symbol

Oberon
messenger: 4 Puck
wife: 7 Titania

Oberto composer
5 Verdi (Giuseppe)

obese
3 fat 5 bulky, gross, heavy, tubby
6 fleshy 7 adipose, outsize, porcine
9 corpulent 10 overweight

obey
3 bow 4 heed, keep, mind 5 agree,
defer, serve, yield 6 accede, accept,
assent, comply, follow, regard,
submit 7 abide by, conform, execute,
fulfill, observe, satisfy 8 adhere to,
carry out 9 acquiesce

obfuscate
4 blur 5 cloud, muddy 6 darken
7 becloud, conceal, confuse, cover
up, obscure 9 adumbrate

obi
4 sash

obiter dictum
4 note 6 remark 7 comment, opinion 10 commentary, incidental
11 observation

obituary
9 necrology 11 death notice

object
3 aim, end, use 4 goal, idea, item,
kick, view, wish 5 being, cause,
demur, focus, frown, point, thing
6 design, entity, except, intent,
matter, motive, oppose, target
7 article, dissent, protest, purpose
8 complain, disagree, function,
material 9 criticize, intention, something 10 disapprove

objection
5 demur 7 protest 8 argument,
demurral, demurrer, question 9 challenge, complaint, exception 10 difficulty, opposition 11 disapproval
12 disagreement, remonstrance
13 remonstration

objectionable
5 unfit 8 unwanted 9 abhorrent,
invidious, loathsome, obnoxious,
offensive, repellent, repugnant,
repulsive, revolting, unwelcome
10 ill-favored, unpleasant 11 displeasing, distasteful, undesirable
12 disagreeable

objective
3 aim, end 4 fair, goal, just, lens,
mark 6 actual, design, intent, target 7 mission, purpose 8 ambition,
function, material, physical, sensible,
unbiased 9 corporeal, equitable,
impartial, intention 10 impersonal
11 independent, substantial 12 unprejudiced 13 dispassionate

objet d'art
5 curio, virtu (plural) 7 bibelot,
novelty 10 knickknack

objurgate
5 chide, decry, scold 6 rebuke
7 censure, reprove, upbraid

oblate

8 admonish, reproach 9 castigate, reprimand

oblate

7 lay monk 9 flattened, religious

oblation

4 gift 6 corban 8 holy gift, offering 9 sacrifice 12 presentation

obligate

4 bind 7 require 8 encumber, restrict 9 constrain

obligated

5 bound, owing 6 liable 8 beholden, indebted 11 accountable, responsible

obligation

3 IOU, vow 4 bond, call, debt, dues, duty, need, oath 5 cause 6 burden, charge, pledge 7 promise 8 business, contract 9 committal, liability, necessity, restraint 10 commitment, compulsion, constraint 11 requirement 12 indebtedness

obligatory

7 binding 8 required 9 essential, mandatory, necessary, requisite 10 compulsory, imperative 11 unavoidable

oblige

3 aid 4 bind, help, make 5 avail, favor, force 6 assist, coerce, compel, please, profit 7 benefit, command, gratify, require 9 constrain 10 contribute 11 accommodate, necessitate

obliged

4 made 5 bound 6 forced 8 beholden, grateful, indebted, thankful 11 constrained 12 appreciative

obliging

4 kind 5 civil 7 amiable, helpful, willing 8 friendly, pleasant 11 complaisant, considerate, cooperative, good-humored, good-natured 12 good-tempered

oblique

6 sloped, tilted 7 devious, leaning, obscure, sloping, tilting 8 inclined, indirect 9 inclining 10 roundabout

obliterate

4 raze, x out 5 erase 6 cancel, delete, efface, remove, rub out 7 blot out, destroy, expunge, wipe out 8 black out, cross out 10 annihilate

oblivion

5 lethe, limbo 7 amnesia, nirvana, nowhere 9 emptiness 11 nothingness 13 forgetfulness, insensibility

oblivious

4 lost 5 blind 7 unaware 8 absorbed, heedless, ignorant 9 forgetful, unknowing, unmindful, unwitting 10 unfamiliar, uninformed 11 inattentive, incognizant, unconscious

oblong

4 oval 5 ovate 7 ellipse 8 elongate 9 elongated, rectangle 11 rectangular

obloquy

4 slam, slur 5 abuse, odium, shame 6 infamy, rebuke 7 calumny, censure 8 disgrace, dishonor, ignominy 9 aspersion, contumely, discredit, disrepute, invective, stricture 10 defamation, opprobrium, scurrility 11 disapproval 12 billingsgate, condemnation, vituperation

obnoxious

4 vile 5 awful 6 odious, rotten 7 hateful 9 abhorrent, invidious, loathsome, offensive, repellent, repugnant, revulsive, sickening 10 abominable, detestable, disgusting

oboe

4 reed 7 hautboy 8 hautbois, woodwind 10 double reed
early: 5 shawm
relative: 7 bassoon 11 English horn

O'Brian character

6 Aubrey (Jack) 7 Maturin (Stephen)

obscene

4 foul, lewd, rank, vile 5 bawdy, crass, crude, dirty, gross, lurid, taboo 6 coarse, filthy, impure, ribald, risqué, smutty, vulgar 7 immoral, noisome, profane, raunchy

8 indecent, scabrous **9** abhorrent, appalling, excessive, offensive, repellent, repugnant, repulsive, salacious **10** disgusting, lascivious, scurrilous **11** foulmouthed, unprintable **12** pornographic, scatological

obscure

3 dim **4** blur, hide, mask, veil **5** blind, cloak, cloud, cover, dusky, faint, minor, murky, shade, shady, vague **6** cloudy, darken, hidden, opaque, remote, screen, secret, shadow, shroud, veiled **7** clouded, conceal, cryptic, eclipse, removed, shadowy, unclear, unknown, unnoted **8** disguise, nameless, overcast, puzzling, secluded, shrouded **9** ambiguous, enigmatic, tenebrous, uncertain, undefined **10** camouflage, ill-defined, indefinite, indistinct, mysterious, overshadow **11** out-of-the-way, unimportant **12** inaccessible, unnoticeable **13** inconspicuous

obscurity

3 fog **4** haze, mist, murk **5** gloom **6** enigma, miasma, puzzle **7** dimness, mystery, shadows **8** darkness **9** ambiguity

obsequies

4 rite **5** rites **7** funeral **10** burial rite

obsequious

4 oily **6** abject **7** fawning, servile, slavish **8** obedient, obeisant, toadying, unctuous **9** parasitic **10** flattering, submissive **11** deferential, subservient, sycophantic

observance

4 rite, rule **6** custom, notice, regard, ritual **7** liturgy, service **8** ceremony, practice **9** adherence, attention, formality **10** ceremonial

observant

4 keen **5** alert, awake, aware, sharp **7** heedful, mindful **8** watchful **9** advertent, attentive **10** perceptive

observation

4 note **6** notice, record, regard, remark **7** comment, finding, opinion **8** judgment, notation **9** attention,

inference **10** commentary **12** obiter dictum

observatory

5 tower **7** lookout, outlook **8** overlook
famous: 4 Lick **6** Wilson, Yerkes **7** Palomar
instrument: 9 telescope

observe

3 see **4** espy, keep, look, mark, mind, note, obey, twig, view **5** honor, opine, sight, state, study, watch **6** behold, comply, follow, look at, notice, remark **7** abide by, comment, conform, discern, respect **8** perceive **9** celebrate, solemnize **10** comply with **11** commemorate

obsess

5 beset, haunt, hound, rivet **6** absorb, plague **7** consume, possess **9** captivate, preoccupy

obsessed

6 dogged, driven, hipped, hooked **7** gripped, haunted, plagued **8** overcome, troubled **9** dominated, possessed **11** preoccupied **12** prepossessed

obsession

5 craze, mania **6** fetish, hang-up **8** fixation, idée fixe **11** infatuation **13** preoccupation

obsessive

5 rabid **8** frenetic, maniacal, neurotic **9** fanatical, possessed **10** passionate **11** preoccupied

obsolete

3 old **5** dated, passé, stale **6** old hat **7** disused, worn-out **8** outmoded, time-worn **9** out-of-date **10** antiquated, superseded **12** antediluvian, old-fashioned

obstacle

3 bar **4** bump, clog, snag **5** block, catch, check, crimp, hitch **6** hurdle **7** barrier **8** handicap, hardship **9** hindrance, impedance, roadblock **10** difficulty, impediment **11** encumbrance, vicissitude **12** interference

obstinate

4 deaf, firm **5** balky, fixed **6** dogged, mulish **7** staunch, willful **8** obdurate, perverse, resolute, stubborn **9** pigheaded, resistant, unbudging, immovable **10** hardheaded, headstrong, inflexible, persistent, refractory, unyielding **11** intractable, opinionated, stiff-necked, wrongheaded **12** intransigent, pertinacious, recalcitrant

obstreperous

4 loud **5** noisy, rowdy **6** unruly **7** blatant, raucous **8** strident **9** clamorous, insistent **10** boisterous, disorderly, vociferant, vociferous **11** disobedient, loudmouthed **12** rambunctious

obstruct

3 bar, dam **4** clog, hide, plug, stop **5** block, check, choke, close **6** cut off, hamper, hinder, impede, stymie, thwart **7** congest, occlude, prevent, shut off, shut out, trammel **9** interfere

obstruction

3 bar **4** snag **5** hitch **6** hamper, hurdle **7** barrier **8** blockage, obstacle, stoppage **9** hindrance, impedance **10** impediment

obtain

3 buy, get, win **4** earn, gain, have, reap **5** annex, reach **6** pick up, secure **7** achieve, acquire, chalk up, procure **8** purchase

obtrude

5 cut in **6** butt in, horn in, impose, meddle **7** presume, push out **8** chisel in, infringe **9** interfere, thrust out

obtrusive

4 nosy **5** pushy **6** prying **7** forward **8** meddling **9** bumptious, officious **10** meddlesome, protruding **11** impertinent, interfering

obtuse

4 dull, dumb, slow **5** blunt, dense, thick **6** stupid **7** rounded, unclear **11** insensitive

obverse

4 face, side **5** front **8** opposite **9** other side **10** complement **11** counterpart

obviate

4 ward **5** avert, deter, block **7** forfend, prevent, rule out **8** preclude, stave off **9** forestall, interfere, interpose, intervene **10** anticipate

obvious

5 clear, overt, plain **6** patent, simple **7** blatant, evident, glaring **8** apparent, clear-cut, distinct, manifest, palpable **10** undeniable **11** conspicuous, self-evident, transparent, unambiguous, unequivocal

oca

5 tuber **6** sorrel

O'Casey, Sean

9 dramatist **10** playwright **plays: 17** Juno and the Paycock, Plough and the Stars (The)

occasion

4 call, need, shot, show, time **5** basis, break, cause, event **6** chance, demand, effect, excuse, ground, lead to, moment, reason **7** episode, instant, opening, produce **8** ceremony, incident, instance **9** condition, happening, necessity **10** bring about, foundation, obligation, occurrence **11** celebration, determinant, opportunity **12** circumstance **13** justification

occasional

3 few, odd **4** rare **6** casual, random, scarce, seldom **7** special, unusual **8** specific, sporadic, uncommon **9** irregular **10** incidental, infrequent

Occidental

7 Western **8** European **9** Westerner

occlude

4 clog, fill, hide, plug, stop **5** block, choke, close, cover **6** screen, stop up **7** close up, conceal, congest **8** block off, obstruct

occult
  5 eerie, magic 6 arcane, orphic, secret 8 abstruse, esoteric, hermetic, mystical 9 recondite, unearthly 10 cabalistic, mysterious 12 supernatural

occupant
  5 liver 6 inmate, tenant 7 denizen, dweller, resider 8 habitant, resident 10 inhabitant

occupation
  3 job, use 4 line, work 5 trade 6 career, métier, office 7 calling, control, pursuit, seizure 8 activity, business, position, vocation 9 occupancy, residence 10 employment, habitation, possession, settlement

occupy
  3 use 4 busy, fill, hold, take 5 seize, tie up 6 absorb, employ, engage, live in, people, take up, tenant 7 control, engross, immerse, inhabit, involve, possess 8 populate, reside in, take over

occur
  3 hap 4 pass 5 arise, ensue, pop up 6 appear, befall, betide, chance, dawn on, happen, result, strike 7 come off, develop 9 take place, transpire

occurrence
  3 hap 4 pass 5 event, state 7 episode 8 exigency, incident, juncture, occasion 9 adventure, condition, emergency, happening, situation

ocean
  3 sea 4 blue, deep, main 5 brine, drink 6 Arctic, Indian 7 Pacific 8 Atlantic 9 Antarctic
  movement: 4 tide, wave

Oceania
  country: 4 Fiji 5 Belau, Nauru, Palau, Samoa, Tonga 6 Tuvalu 7 Vanuatu 8 Kiribati 9 Australia 10 New Zealand
  territory: 7 Tokelau 12 New Caledonia 13 American Samoa
  ethnic group: 6 Fijian, Papuan, Samoan 10 Melanesian, Polynesian 11 Micronesian
  language: 5 Maori 6 Fijian, Papuan, Pidgin, Samoan 10 Melanesian

oceanic
  4 huge, vast 5 great 6 marine 7 immense, pelagic 8 enormous, maritime 9 saltwater, thalassic

Ocean State
  11 Rhode Island

Oceanus
  daughter: 5 Doris 7 Oceanid 8 Eurynome
  father: 6 Uranus
  mother: 4 Gaea
  sister: 6 Tethys
  son: 6 Peneus 7 Alpheus
  wife: 6 Tethys

ocellus
  3 eye 7 eyespot

ocelot
  3 cat 7 wildcat

octave
  5 eight, scale 6 eighth, stanza 8 interval

Octavia
  brother: 8 Augustus
  grandson: 8 Caligula
  husband: 4 Nero 6 Antony

octopus
  7 mollusc, mollusk 9 devilfish 10 cephalopod
  arm: 8 tentacle
  genus: 7 Polypus
  kin: 5 squid 10 cuttlefish

ocular
  4 seen 5 optic 6 visual 7 eyelike, optical, visible 8 eyepiece, viewable 9 perceived

Odalisque painter
  6 Ingres (Jean-Auguste-Dominique) 7 Matisse (Henri)

odd
  4 lone, rare 5 extra, fluky, queer, rummy, weird 6 casual, chance, single, uneven 7 curious, erratic,

strange, unusual **8** peculiar, singular **9** eccentric, unmatched
13 idiosyncratic

oddball

4 kook **5** kooky, weird **6** weirdo
7 bizarre, curious, offbeat, strange,
unusual **8** original, peculiar **9** character, eccentric **10** outlandish
13 idiosyncratic

oddity

5 freak, quirk **6** weirdo **7** anomaly
9 character, curiosity, departure,
deviation, eccentric, weirdness
10 aberration, difference **11** abnormality, peculiarity, strangeness
12 eccentricity, idiosyncrasy, irregularity

odds

4 edge **5** favor, ratio **7** benefit,
chances **8** handicap, variance
9 advantage, allowance, disparity
10 difference, likelihood, partiality
11 probability **12** disagreement

odds and ends

4 bits, olio **6** jumble, medley, motley,
scraps **7** mélange, mixture **8** remnants, sundries **9** etceteras, leftovers, potpourri **10** assortment,
hodgepodge, miscellany **13** paraphernalia

ode

4 hymn, poem **5** lyric, psalm, verse
part: 5 epode **7** strophe **11** anti-
strophe

Odets play

9 Golden Boy **11** Country Girl (The)
12 Awake and Sing **15** Waiting for
Lefty

odeum

4 hall **7** theater **11** concert hall

Odin

brother: 4 Vili
daughter-in-law: 5 Nanna
father: 3 Bor
hall: 8 Valhalla
horse: 8 Sleipnir
maiden: 8 Valkyrie
mansion: 9 Gladsheim

mother: 6 Bestla
raven: 5 Hugin, Munin
ring: 8 Draupnir
son: 3 Tyr **4** Thor, Vali **6** Balder
spear: 7 Gungnir
sword: 4 Gram
wife: 4 Fria, Rind **5** Frigg **6** Frigga
wolf: 4 Geri **5** Freki

odious

4 foul, vile **6** horrid **7** hateful **8** horrible **9** abhorrent, execrable, invidi-
ous, loathsome, malicious, repellent,
repugnant **10** abominable, despicable, detestable

odium

4 hate, onus **5** shame **6** hatred,
infamy, stigma **7** censure, obloquy
8 contempt, disgrace, dishonor,
ignominy, loathing **9** disrepute
10 abhorrence, opprobrium **11** detestation **12** condemnation

odor

4 funk **5** aroma, scent, smell, stink,
whiff **6** stench **7** bouquet, perfume
9 fragrance, redolence

odorous

5 heady, sweet **6** smelly, strong
7 pungent, scented **8** aromatic,
fragrant, perfumed, redolent, unsavory **9** offensive

Odysseus

7 Ulysses
dog: 5 Argos
enchantress: 5 Circe
father: 7 Laertes
friend: 6 Mentor
harasser: 8 Poseidon
herb: 4 moly
kingdom: 6 Ithaca
mother: 8 Anticlea
son: 9 Telegonus **10** Telemachus
swineherd: 7 Eumaeus
voyage: 7 odyssey
wife: 8 Penelope

odyssey

4 trek **5** quest **6** voyage **7** journey
9 wandering **13** peregrination

Odyssey author

5 Homer

Oedipus
  brother-in-law: 5 Creon
  daughter: 6 Ismene **8** Antigone
  father: 5 Laius
  foster father: 7 Polybus
  foster mother: 8 Periboea
  kingdom: 6 Thebes
  mother: 7 Jocasta
  son: 8 Eteocles **9** Polynices
  10 Polyneices
  victim: 5 Laius
  wife: 7 Jocasta

Oeneus
  kingdom: 7 Calydon
  son: 8 Meleager
  wife: 7 Althaea

Oenomaus
  charioteer: 8 Myrtilus
  daughter: 10 Hippodamia
  kingdom: 4 Pisa
  slayer: 6 Pelops

Oenone
  husband: 5 Paris
  rival: 5 Helen

oeuvre
  4 work **6** corpus, output **8** lifework
  10 collection **11** compilation

of
  German: 3 aus, von
  Italian: 5 degli, della, delle

off
  4 away, kill **5** aside **6** depart, murder, remote, slight **7** seaward,
spoiled **9** eccentric, incorrect

offal
  4 guts **4** junk **5** gurry, trash, waste
6 debris, litter, refuse, spilth **7** carrion, garbage, innards, rubbish,
viscera **8** entrails **9** sweepings
10 intestines

offbeat
  3 odd **5** fresh, outré, weird **6** way
out **7** bizarre, oddball, strange,
unusual **8** bohemian, peculiar,
singular, uncommon **9** different,
eccentric, whimsical **10** outlandish,
unorthodox **11** distinctive **13** idiosyncratic

off-color
  3 ill, low **4** blue, racy **5** bawdy,
broad, salty, shady **6** ailing, peaked,
poorly, risqué, sickly, unwell **7** dubious, naughty **8** improper, indecent
10 indisposed, suggestive

offend
  3 sin, vex **4** gall, hurt, miff, pain
5 anger, annoy, pique, repel, shock,
upset **6** appall, breach, insult, nettle
7 affront, disturb, provoke, violate
8 aggrieve, distress, irritate **9** displease **10** antagonize, transgress

offender
  5 felon **6** sinner **7** culprit **8** criminal,
violator **9** wrongdoer **10** lawbreaker,
malefactor **12** transgressor

offense
  3 sin **4** huff, hurt, miff, tort, vice
5 crime, fault, pique, wrong **6** attack,
breach, felony, injury, insult **7** affront,
assault, dudgeon, misdeed, mis-
take, outrage, umbrage **9** indignity,
onslaught, violation **10** aggression,
infraction, resentment **11** displeasure, indignation, misdemeanor

offensive
  3 bad **4** foul, rank, vile **5** drive,
onset **6** attack, odious **7** assault,
noisome, obscene, painful **8** nauseous, unsavory **9** loathsome,
obnoxious, onslaught, repellent,
repugnant, repulsive, sickening
10 aggression, aggressive, disgusting, nauseating, unpleasant
11 uncongenial, unpalatable, unwholesome **12** disagreeable, unappetizing **13** objectionable

offer
  3 bid, try **4** seek, show **5** assay,
essay, pitch, put up **6** afford, extend,
submit, tender **7** advance, attempt,
display, exhibit, hold out, present,
propose, provide, suggest **8** endeavor, proposal, threaten **9** sacrifice **10** submission **11** proposition

offering
  4 alms, gift **5** grant **6** course, corban

7 charity, present 8 donation, oblation 9 sacrifice 11 benefaction, beneficence 12 contribution

offhand

5 ad-lib 6 blithe, breezy, casual 8 informal 9 extempore, impromptu, unstudied 10 improvised, nonchalant, unprepared 11 extemporary, spontaneous, unrehearsed

office

3 job 4 duty 5 berth, suite 6 agency, billet, bureau 7 station 8 business, cube farm, function, province 9 situation, workplace 10 department
head: 4 boss 7 manager
machine: 3 fax 6 copier 7 printer 8 computer 10 calculator, fax machine 11 photocopier
seeker: 9 candidate 10 politician
worker: 5 clerk 6 typist 9 file clerk, secretary 10 bookkeeper

officer

3 cop 4 exec 6 noncom, police 7 John Law, manager 8 official 9 executive
abbreviation: 3 Adm., Col., Ens., Gen., Maj. 4 Capt., Cmdr. 5 Comdr., Lieut.
army: 5 major 7 captain, colonel, general 10 lieutenant
British: 9 brigadier
court: 7 bailiff
king's: 11 chamberlain
law-enforcement: 3 cop 6 deputy, police 7 marshal, sheriff 9 constable, patrolman, policeman
naval: 4 mate 6 ensign 7 admiral, captain 9 commander, commodore 10 lieutenant
noncommissioned: 5 sarge 8 corporal, sergeant
petty: 5 bosun 6 yeoman 9 boatswain
prison: 5 guard 6 warden

official

4 exec 7 cleared, manager 8 approved, bona fide, endorsed 9 authentic, canonical, cathedral, certified, executive 10 accredited, authorized, ex cathedra, magistrate, sanctioned 13 administrator, authoritative
city or town: 5 mayor 8 alderman 9 councilor, selectman 10 councillor
diplomatic: 5 envoy 6 consul 7 attaché 10 ambassador
governmental: 6 syndic
parish: 6 beadle
sports: 3 ref, ump 6 umpire 7 referee 8 linesman
university: 4 dean 6 bursar 7 provost 9 registrar 10 chancellor

officiate

5 chair, serve 6 direct, umpire 7 conduct, oversee, preside, referee 9 supervise 11 superintend

officious

4 busy, nosy 5 pushy 7 forward 8 meddling 9 assertive, intrusive, obtrusive 10 meddlesome 11 impertinent 13 self-important

offing

6 future 7 by-and-by 9 aftertime, hereafter 10 near future

off-key

3 odd 4 sour 7 jarring 9 anomalous, dissonant, unnatural 10 discordant 12 inharmonious

off-putting

8 daunting 9 dismaying, offensive, repellent 10 forbidding, foreboding 11 distasteful 12 disagreeable, discouraging 13 disconcerting, disheartening, objectionable

offscouring

5 trash 6 pariah, refuse, reject 7 outcast 8 castaway, derelict 11 untouchable

offset

6 square 7 balance 8 equalize 10 balance out, compensate, neutralize 11 counterpose, countervail 12 counterpoise, displacement

offshoot

4 twig 5 scion 6 branch 7 product, spin-off 9 affiliate, by-product, outgrowth 10 derivative, descendant

offspring
3 kid 4 kids, seed 5 brood, child, hatch, issue, scion, spawn, swarm, young 7 produce, product, progeny 8 children 9 posterity 10 descendant 11 progeniture

off-the-wall
3 odd 5 kooky, weird 6 far-out, way-out 7 bizarre, oddball, unusual 8 freakish 9 eccentric, fantastic, grotesque 10 outlandish

off-white
4 bone 5 cream, ivory 6 oyster, vellum 9 parchment

Of Human Bondage author
7 Maugham (W. Somerset)

Of Mice and Men
author: 9 Steinbeck (John)
character: 6 George (Milton), Lennie (Small)

often
9 generally 10 frequently, habitually, repeatedly 11 recurrently

ogee
3 ess 4 arch 5 curve 7 molding

Ogier the _____
4 Dane

ogive
3 rib 4 arch 5 graph

ogle
3 eye 4 gape, gaze, leer, look 5 stare 6 goggle 10 rubberneck

ogre
5 bogey, giant 7 bugbear, monster 8 bogeyman 9 boogeyman
Algonquian: 7 windigo

ogress
5 harpy, scold, shrew, vixen 6 amazon, virago 8 fishwife 9 termagant, Xanthippe

O'Hara novel
7 Pal Joey 12 Butterfield 8 17 Ten North Frederick

Ohio
capital: 8 Columbus

city: 5 Akron, Xenia 6 Canton, Dayton, Toledo 9 Cleveland 10 Cincinnati
college, university: 5 Miami 6 Kenyon 7 Antioch, Denison, Oberlin 9 Kent State 12 Bowling Green
nickname: 7 Buckeye (State)
river: 4 Ohio 6 Maumee 8 Sandusky
state bird: 8 cardinal
state flower: 16 scarlet carnation
state tree: 7 buckeye

Oholibamah
father: 4 Anah
husband: 4 Esau

oil
3 fat, gas 4 balm, fuel, lube, oleo 5 oleum, slick 6 anoint, grease, pomade 7 blarney, incense, lanolin 8 flattery, soft soap 9 adulation, lubricant, lubricate, petroleum
combining form: 3 ole 4 olei, oleo
consecrated: 6 chrism
fragrant: 5 attar 6 neroli
fuel: 3 gas 6 petrol 8 gasoline, kerosene
relating to: 5 oleic
ship: 6 tanker
source: 5 olive, shale
well: 6 gusher

Oil! author
8 Sinclair (Upton)

oilbird
8 guacharo

oily
5 fatty, slick, soapy, suave 6 greasy, smarmy, smooth 7 fulsome 8 slippery, unctuous 10 lubricious, obsequious, oleaginous

ointment
4 balm 5 cream, salve 6 lotion 7 unction, unguent 8 calamine, liniment 9 emollient 11 embrocation

Okinawa capital
4 Naha

Oklahoma
capital: 12 Oklahoma City

city: 3 Ada 4 Enid 5 Tulsa 6 Norman
college, university: 11 Oral Roberts
mountain: 9 Black Mesa
nickname: 6 Sooner (State)
river: 3 Red 8 Arkansas, Canadian
state bird: 10 flycatcher
state flower: 9 mistletoe
state tree: 6 redbud

OK, okay

3 aye, yea, yes 4 fine, good, safe, well 5 agree, allow, favor 6 agreed, assent, decent, permit 7 approve, certify, endorse, support 8 accredit, adequate, all right, approval, blessing, high sign, passable, sanction, thumbs-up 9 authorize, hunky-dory 10 acceptable, permission 11 endorsement 12 satisfactory

okra

4 herb, soup 5 gumbo 6 mallow

old

4 aged, gray, late, past 5 dated, hoary, passé, stale 6 bygone, démodé, former, mature, senior, whilom 7 ancient, antique, archaic, elderly, lasting, onetime, overage, quondam, veteran 8 enduring, lifelong, Noachian, outmoded, timeworn 9 erstwhile, geriatric, long-lived, perennial, perpetual, primitive, venerable 10 antiquated, inveterate 13 superannuated
Scottish: 4 auld

old age

6 dotage 8 caducity 10 senescence 11 decrepitude, elderliness, senectitude

Old Bailey

5 court

Old Colony State

13 Massachusetts

Old Curiosity Shop author

7 Dickens (Charles)

Old Dominion State

8 Virginia

Old Faithful

6 geyser

old-fashioned

4 aged 5 dated, dowdy, fusty, moldy, passé, stale, tired 6 bygone, démodé, quaint, stodgy 7 ancient, antique, archaic, outworn, vintage 8 cocktail, obsolete, outdated, outmoded 9 out-of-date, unstylish 10 antiquated

old hand

3 pro, vet 6 expert, master 7 veteran 9 authority 10 past master, specialist

old hat

5 dated, passé, stale, tired, trite 6 démodé 7 antique, clichéd, vintage 8 outmoded, timeworn, wellworn 9 hackneyed, out-of-date 10 antiquated

Old Ironsides

12 Constitution (U.S.S.)
poet: 6 Holmes (Oliver Wendell)

Old Line State

8 Maryland

old maid

6 fusser 7 fusspot 8 card game, spinster 10 fussbudget

Old North State

13 North Carolina

Old Rough and Ready

6 Taylor (Zachary)

Olds' car

3 Reo

old-time

5 dated 6 bygone 7 antique, vintage 10 antiquated 12 long-standing

old-timer

3 vet 5 elder 6 senior 7 ancient, antique, veteran

Old World

6 Europe

oleaginous

see **oily**

oleaster

5 shrub 12 Russian olive

olecranon

9 funny bone

oleo
9 margarine

oleoresin
10 turpentine

oleum
3 oil

olfaction
5 sense, smell 8 smelling

olid
4 rank 5 fetid 6 putrid, rancid, rotten
7 stenchy 8 stinking 9 offensive
10 malodorous

olio
3 mix 4 stew 5 umble 6 medley
7 mélange, mixture 8 mishmash,
mixed bag 9 potpourri 10 assortment, collection, hodgepodge,
miscellany

Oliver Twist
author: 7 Dickens (Charles)
character: 5 Fagin, Nancy, Sikes
(Bill) 6 Bumble (Mr.) 12 Artful
Dodger

Ollie's partner
4 Stan

Olympian
3 god 5 lofty, noble 6 lordly 7 athlete, exalted, godlike 8 majestic,
superior 10 competitor

Olympics
5 games 6 sports 9 athletics
place of origin: 6 Greece
symbol: 5 flame, torch

Oman
capital: 6 Masqat, Muscat
language: 6 Arabic 7 Baluchi
monetary unit: 4 rial
mountain range: 7 Al-Hajar
neighbor: 5 Yemen 11 Saudi Arabia
peninsula: 7 Arabian
sea: 7 Arabian

Omar
4 poet 7 Khayyém
country: 6 Persia
father: 7 Eliphaz
poem: 8 Rubaiyat

omega
3 end 6 ending, finale, letter
kin: 3 zed, zee

omen
4 sign 5 augur, token 6 augury,
boding 7 auspice, portent, presage,
warning 8 bodement, prophecy
9 foretoken 10 foreboding, prediction, prognostic

ominous
4 dark, dire, grim 6 dismal 7 baleful,
direful, doomful, fateful 8 alarming,
lowering, menacing, sinister 9 ill-
boding, prophetic 10 forbidding,
foreboding, portentous 11 frightening, threatening 12 inauspicious,
unpropitious

omission
3 cut, gap 4 lack, skip, slip 5 blank,
break, chasm, error, lapse 6 hiatus,
lacuna 7 elision, failure 8 eclipsis,
ellipsis, overlook 9 exclusion
mark: 5 caret 8 ellipsis 10 apostrophe

omit
4 drop, fail, skip 5 elide 6 except,
forget, ignore, slight 7 exclude,
neglect 8 leave out, overlook, pass
over 11 leave undone

omnibus
3 ana 4 posy 5 album 7 garland
8 analects, treasury 9 anthology
10 miscellany 11 florilegium

omnipotent
6 divine 7 godlike, supreme 8 almighty 9 unlimited 11 all-powerful

omnipresent
7 allover, endless 8 infinite, unending 9 boundless, limitless, universal
10 ubiquitous

omniscient
4 wise 7 learned 9 know-it-all
10 all-knowing

omnium-gatherum
see **olio**

Omphale
domain: 5 Lydia
slave: 8 Heracles, Hercules

omphalos

3 hub 5 navel 9 umbilicus 10 focal
point

on

4 atop, over 5 above, along 7 working 9 operating 11 functioning

onager

3 ass 5 kiang 8 catapult

Onan's father

5 Judah

once

4 ever, late, past 5 at all 6 before,
bygone, former, whilom 7 already,
earlier, long ago, onetime, quondam
8 formerly, sometime

once-over

4 look 5 check 6 gander, glance,
survey 10 inspection 11 examination

one

4 lone, only, sole, unit 5 monad
6 single, unique 7 numeral 8 separate, singular, solitary 9 undivided
10 individual, particular
combining form: 4 mono
French: 3 une
German: 3 ein 4 eine
prefix: 3 uni
Scottish: 3 ane
Spanish: 3 una, uno

one and a half

combining form: 6 sesqui

one-eyed giant

7 Cyclops 10 Polyphemus

one-handed god

3 Tiu, Tyr

one-horse town

4 burg 6 hamlet, Podunk 11 whistle-
stop

one hundred

6 centum
years: 7 century

O'Neill, Eugene

heroine: 4 Anna, Nina
play: 3 Ile 4 Gold 8 Hairy Ape
(The) 12 Ah Wilderness, Anna

Christie, Emperor Jones, Iceman
Cometh (The) 13 Great God Brown
(The), Marco Millions 16 Strange
Interlude 18 Desire Under the Elms
22 Mourning Becomes Electra
24 Long Day's Journey into Night

oneiric

6 dreamy 8 anagogic 9 dreamlike

oneness

3 all 5 union, unity, whole 7 harmony
8 entirety, identity, sameness, totality
9 integrity, unanimity 10 singleness,
uniformity 11 singularity, unification
13 individuality

onerous

4 hard 5 heavy, tough 6 taxing,
trying 7 arduous, exigent, wearing,
weighty 8 exacting, grievous, imposing, pressing, toilsome 9 demanding, difficult, laborious 10 burdensome, cumbersome, oppressive
11 troublesome

one-sided

6 biased, uneven 7 colored, partial, unequal 8 inclined, partisan,
weighted 10 prejudiced, unbalanced, unilateral

onetime

3 old 4 once, past 6 bygone, former,
whilom 7 quondam 8 previous
9 erstwhile

ongoing

7 current, growing 8 evolving
9 advancing, in process 10 continuing, continuous, developing, in
progress, unfinished 11 progressing

on hand

4 here 5 ready 6 nearby 7 pending,
present 9 available

onion

4 bulb 7 shallot
bulb: 3 set
genus: 6 Allium
kin: 4 leek 6 garlic
kind: 7 Bermuda, Danvers, Spanish
roll: 5 bialy
young: 8 scallion

online
5 wired 9 connected
business: 5 e-tail
guffaw: 3 LOL
system: 3 Web 8 Internet

onlooker
6 viewer 7 watcher, witness 8 beholder, kibitzer, observer 9 bystander, spectator 10 eyewitness
12 rubbernecker

only
3 but, few, one, yet 4 just, lone,
mere, save, sole, solo 5 alone
6 and yet, at most, except, merely,
simply, single, solely, unique 7 however, utterly 8 entirely, singular,
solitary 11 exclusively

onomasticon
7 lexicon 8 wordbook

onomatopoeic
5 mimic 6 echoic 7 mimetic 9 emulative, imitative 10 simulative

onset
4 dawn, rush 5 birth, start 6 attack,
coming, origin 7 arrival, assault,
dawning, offense, opening 8 invasion 9 beginning, inception,
offensive 10 aggression 12 commencement

onslaught
5 blitz 6 attack, charge, deluge
7 assault, barrage, offense, torrent
8 invasion 9 offensive 10 aggression

on-target
5 exact, right 7 correct, perfect,
precise 8 accurate 11 appropriate

Ontario
bay: 8 Georgian
capital: 7 Toronto
city: 4 York 6 London, Ottawa
7 Markham, Windsor 8 Hamilton
9 Etobicoke, Kitchener, North York
10 Thunder Bay 11 Mississauga,
Scarborough 13 Sault Ste. Marie
lake: 4 Erie 5 Huron 7 Nipigon,
Ontario 8 Superior

provincial flower: 13 white trillium
river: 5 Moose 6 Albany, Severn,
Winisk

on the house
4 free 6 gratis 13 complimentary

on the nose
5 bingo 6 dead-on, spot-on 7 exactly
8 accurate 9 precisely 10 accurately

on the other hand
3 but 7 however

on the rocks
4 iced 7 with ice, wrecked

on the whole
6 mainly, mostly 7 usually 8 all in all
9 generally, in general, typically
10 altogether, by and large

onus
3 tax 4 duty, load, task 5 blame,
brand, fault, guilt, odium, stain
6 burden, charge, stigma, weight
8 black eye 9 liability 10 obligation,
oppression

onward
5 ahead, along, forth 7 forward
9 advancing

onyx
5 agate 10 chalcedony

oodles
4 gobs, lots, tons 5 heaps, loads,
rafts, scads 6 plenty

oolong
3 tea

oomph
3 pep, vim, zip 4 brio, dash, élan,
life, push, zest, zing 5 charm, drive,
punch, verve, vigor 6 esprit, pizazz,
spirit 7 glamour, pizzazz 8 strength,
vitality 9 magnetism, sex appeal

ooze
3 goo, mud 4 emit, goop, leak, seep,
weep 5 bleed, exude, issue, marsh,
slime, sweat 7 secrete, seepage
8 transude

opacity
8 dullness 9 murkiness, obscurity
10 obtuseness

opal
3 gem 5 jewel, stone 6 silica 7 girasol, hyalite, mineral 8 gemstone

opaque
3 dim 4 dull, hazy 5 dense, filmy, murky, vague 6 cloudy 7 clouded, obscure, unclear 8 abstruse

OPEC nation
3 UAE 4 Iran, Iraq 5 Libya, Qatar 6 Kuwait 7 Algeria, Nigeria 9 Indonesia, Venezuela 11 Saudi Arabia

open
4 ajar, bare, free, wide 5 frank, naked, overt 6 broach, candid, expand, expose, public, reveal, spread, unfold, unlock, unseal, unveil 7 convene, outdoor, uncover, unlatch 8 disclose, outdoors, stripped, unclothe, unlocked, unsealed 9 available, uncovered 10 out-of-doors, unfastened 11 susceptible, unconcealed, undisguised 12 unrestricted

open-air
7 outdoor, outside 8 alfresco, outdoors 9 out-of-door 10 out-of-doors

open-and-shut
4 easy 5 clear, plain 6 patent, simple 7 evident, obvious

openhanded
6 giving, lavish 7 liberal 8 generous 9 bounteous, bountiful, unselfish, unsparing 10 beneficent, bighearted, charitable, munificent 11 magnanimous

openhearted
4 kind, warm 5 frank, plain 6 candid, honest 8 generous 10 responsive 11 sympathetic

opening
3 gap 4 dawn, door, gate, hole, pass, pore, slit, slot, vent 5 break, chasm, chink, cleft, crack, debut, mouth, onset, start, stoma 6 breach, chance, lacuna, outlet, outset 7 crevice, dawning, fissure, orifice, pinhole 8 aperture, overture 9 beginning 11 opportunity

ship's: 5 hatch 8 hatchway, porthole

open-minded
7 liberal 8 tolerant, unbiased 9 receptive 12 freethinking, unprejudiced

openmouthed
4 agog, awed, rapt 5 agape 6 amazed, gaping 7 stunned 9 astounded, surprised 10 astonished, speechless

open sesame
3 key 5 charm 6 ticket 8 passport, password

open up
4 fire, talk 5 shoot 6 reveal 7 cut into, divulge 8 disclose 9 make plain, spread out 11 communicate

opera
comic: 5 buffa 6 bouffe
glasses: 9 lorgnette
kind: 4 soap 5 comic, grand, horse, space
part: 3 act 4 aria 5 scena
solo: 4 aria
star: 4 diva 10 prima donna
text: 8 libretto
(see also individual titles and composers)

operant
8 behavior 9 effective 10 measurable, observable, productive 12 conditioning

operate
3 act, cut, run, use 4 work 5 drive, exert, steer 6 behave, direct, effect, handle, manage 7 carry on, conduct, control, perform, produce 8 function, maneuver 9 influence 10 bring about, manipulate

operation
3 use 4 step 6 action 7 concern, mission, process, surgery 8 activity, business, exercise, exertion, function, maneuver 9 procedure 10 employment, engagement, enterprise 11 performance, transaction

operative
3 key 4 hand, live, open 5 agent,
alive 6 active, artisan, moving,
usable, worker 7 dynamic, in force,
laborer, running, working, workman
8 mechanic, relevant 9 effective,
essential, important 10 functional
11 efficacious, influential, secret
agent, significant

operator
5 agent, fixer, pilot 6 doctor, driver
7 schemer, surgeon 9 conductor

operculum
3 lid 4 flap 8 covering

operetta composer
5 Friml (Rudolf), Lehár (Franz),
Suppé (Franz von) 6 Straus (Oscar)
7 Gilbert (William S.), Herbert
(Victor), Romberg (Sigmund),
Strauss (Johann) 8 Sullivan (Arthur)
9 Offenbach (Jacques)

operose
4 dull 6 boring, tiring 7 tedious
8 tiresome, toilsome, weariful 9 difficult, laborious, wearisome

Ophelia
beloved: 6 Hamlet
brother: 7 Laertes
father: 8 Polonius

ophidian
5 snake 9 snakelike

opiate
4 dope, drug 7 anodyne 8 hypnotic,
narcotic, nepenthe, sedative 9 analgesic, soporific 10 anesthetic, painkiller 11 somniferous 12 somnifacient, tranquilizer
type: 7 codeine 8 morphine

opine
4 deem, hold, view 5 judge, state,
think 6 advise, assert 7 believe,
express, suppose 8 point out
9 recommend

opinion
4 idea, view 5 tenet 6 belief, notion,
theory 7 feeling, thought 8 attitude,
estimate, judgment, reaction 9 sentiment 10 assumption, conclusion,

conjecture, conviction, estimation,
hypothesis, persuasion 11 speculation, supposition
express an: 4 vote 5 judge 9 criticize

opium
4 dope, drug 8 narcotic
derivative: 6 heroin 7 codeine
8 laudanum, morphine 9 paregoric
source: 5 poppy

opossum
9 marsupial
kin: 8 kangaroo

opponent
3 con, foe 4 anti 5 enemy, rival
6 muscle 7 nemesis 9 adversary,
assailant, combatant 10 antagonist,
challenger, competitor 12 counteragent

opportune
3 apt, fit 6 timely 8 suitable 9 favorable, well-timed 10 auspicious,
convenient, felicitous, propitious
11 appropriate

opportunity
4 turn 5 break, space, spell 6 chance
7 opening 8 juncture, occasion,
prospect 12 circumstance

oppose
4 buck, defy, deny, duel 5 cross,
fight, repel 6 attack, combat, debate,
differ, object, refute, resist 7 assault,
contest, counter, dispute, prevent,
protest 8 confront, contrast, disagree, obstruct 9 withstand 10 contradict, contravene, controvert,
disapprove

opposite
4 foil 5 polar 6 contra, facing
7 antonym, counter, inverse, obverse, opposed, reverse 8 antipode,
antipole, contrary, contrast, converse
9 antipodal, diametric 10 antipodean, antithesis 11 contrasting,
counterpole 12 antithetical, counterpoint 13 contradictory
prefix: 3 dis 5 retro 6 contra
7 counter

opposition
3 con, foe **5** enemy **7** rivalry **8** conflict, defiance **9** adversary, animosity, hostility, other side **10** antagonism, antithesis, resistance **11** contrariety, disapproval

oppress
5 abuse, crush, wrong **6** burden, injure, sadden, subdue **7** afflict, torment, torture, trouble **8** aggrieve, distress, overload **9** persecute, subjugate, weigh down

oppressive
5 harsh, heavy **6** brutal, dismal, gloomy, severe, somber, sombre, taxing **7** exigent, onerous, weighty **8** crushing, exacting, grievous, stifling **9** demanding **10** burdensome, depressing, tyrannical **11** dispiriting, overbearing, suffocating **12** discouraging, overwhelming

oppressive force
4 onus, yoke **6** burden, weight

oppressor
5 bully **6** despot, tyrant **8** autocrat, dictator **9** strongman

opprobrious
4 evil, vile **6** odious, vulgar **7** abusive, hateful **8** infamous **9** notorious, truculent **10** despicable, scurrilous **11** disgraceful, ignominious **12** contemptible, contumelious, vituperative

opprobrium
5 abuse, blame, odium, scorn, shame **6** infamy **7** obloquy **8** contempt, disgrace, dishonor, ignominy, reproach **9** discredit, disesteem, disrepute **10** scurrility **12** vituperation

oppugn
5 argue, fight **6** battle, combat **7** contend, contest, dispute **8** question

Ops
4 Rhea
consort: 6 Cronus, Saturn
daughter: 5 Ceres **7** Demeter

opt
3 tap **4** pick **5** elect, favor **6** choose, decide, prefer, select

optical
6 ocular, visual **8** visional
instrument: 4 lens **5** scope **7** transit **9** magnifier, periscope, telescope **10** microscope

optimal
4 best **5** ideal **6** choice, finest **7** perfect **8** choicest, superior

optimist
5 hoper **7** dreamer **8** idealist, Micawber **9** Pollyanna **10** positivist

optimistic
4 rosy **5** happy, merry, sunny **6** bright, hoping, upbeat **7** assured, buoyant, hopeful **8** cheerful, positive, sanguine, trusting **9** confident, promising **11** rose-colored **12** Pollyannaish

option
4 pick **5** claim, extra, grant, right **6** choice **7** license **8** contract, election **9** accessory, privilege, selection **10** preference **11** alternative, prerogative

optional
4 free **5** extra **8** elective **9** voluntary **11** alternative **13** discretionary
item: 5 add-on, extra

opulence
6 bounty, luxury, plenty, riches, wealth **7** fortune **9** abundance, affluence, plenitude, profusion

opulent
4 lush, rich **5** plush, showy, swank **6** deluxe, lavish **7** moneyed, profuse, wealthy **8** affluent, palatial **9** luxuriant, luxurious, plentiful, sumptuous **11** extravagant **12** ostentatious

opuntia
6 cactus

opus
4 work **5** piece **6** oeuvre **7** product **8** creation **11** composition

or

4 else, gold 6 golden, yellow 9 otherwise

oracle

4 sage, seer 5 augur, sibyl 6 augury, medium, Pythia, vision 7 prophet 8 haruspex, prophecy 10 apocalypse, revelation, soothsayer
site: 4 Claros, Delphi, Didyma, Dodona 7 Olympia 9 Epidaurus

oracular

5 vatic 6 mantic, orphic 7 cryptic, Delphic, fatidic, obscure 8 Delphian, dogmatic 9 ambiguous, arbitrary, prophetic, sibylline, vaticinal

oral

4 exam 5 vocal 6 spoken, verbal, voiced 8 narrated, viva voce 9 unwritten 11 examination

orange

6 citrus
brownish: 6 Titian
deep: 11 bittersweet
genus: 6 Citrus
kin: 4 lime 5 lemon 7 kumquat, satsuma 8 mandarin 9 tangerine 10 grapefruit
kind: 4 sour 5 blood, chino, navel, Osage, sweet 7 Seville 8 bergamot, mandarin, Valencia
oil: 6 neroli
seed: 3 pip
skin: 4 rind

orangutan

3 ape 6 pongid 7 primate 10 anthropoid

orate

4 rant 5 mouth, speak, spiel 6 preach 7 address, declaim, lecture 8 bloviate, harangue, perorate 9 discourse, sermonize, speechify 11 pontificate

oration

6 homily, sermon, speech 7 address, lecture 9 discourse
funeral: 6 eulogy

orator

7 speaker
American: 4 Clay (Henry) 5 Bryan (William Jennings), Henry (Patrick)
7 Calhoun (John C.), Douglas (Stephen), Webster (Daniel)
British: 5 Burke (Edmund) 8 Disraeli (Benjamin) 9 Churchill (Winston), Gladstone (William)
French: 8 Mirabeau (Comte de)
Greek: 5 Corax 8 Pericles 11 Demosthenes
Roman: 6 Cicero

oratory

6 chapel, speech 7 bombast 8 rhetoric 9 discourse, elocution, eloquence 10 expression 11 exhortation, speechcraft

orb

3 eye 4 ball 5 globe, round 6 circle, sphere

orbit

4 path 5 ambit, range, reach, scope, sweep, track 6 extent, radius 7 ellipse
farthest point: 5 apsis 6 apogee 8 aphelion
nearest point: 5 apsis 7 perigee 10 perihelion

orchard

5 trees 10 plantation

orchestra

4 band 7 gamelan 8 ensemble, symphony 12 philharmonic
leader: 9 conductor
section: 5 brass 6 string 7 brasses, strings 8 woodwind 9 woodwinds 10 percussion

orchestrate

5 blend, score, unify 6 manage 7 arrange, compose 8 organize 9 harmonize, integrate 10 coordinate

orchid

kind: 7 calypso, pogonia 8 cattleya, oncidium 9 cymbidium 11 cypripedium
petal: 3 lip 8 labellum
product: 5 salep
tuber: 5 salep

ordain

4 will 5 enact, order 6 decree,

ordeal

direct, impose, invest **7** appoint, command, conduct, destine, dictate, install, lay down **9** establish, prescribe, pronounce **10** predestine

ordeal

4 test **5** agony, cross, trial **7** calvary, torment, trouble **8** crucible **9** suffering **10** affliction, difficulty, visitation **11** tribulation

order

4 book, rank **5** array, caste, class, genre, range **6** decree, lineup, method, scheme, series, system **7** command, harmony, mandate, marshal, pattern, reserve **8** classify, neatness, position, shipment, tidiness **9** directive, hierarchy, procedure, structure **10** injunction, regularity **11** progression

lack of: 5 chaos **6** ataxia **7** anarchy, clutter **9** confusion **11** pandemonium

of business: 6 agenda, docket

of preference: 8 priority

orderly

4 aide, calm, neat, tidy, trim **6** batman **7** correct, precise, regular, soldier, uniform **8** methodic, peaceful **9** attendant, organized, peaceable, regulated, shipshape **10** methodical, systematic **11** uncluttered, well-behaved **12** businesslike

ordinance

3 law **4** code, rule **5** edict **6** decree **7** precept, statute **9** direction, prescript **10** regulation

ordinary

4 so-so **5** banal, cheap, judge, plain, trite, usual **6** common, normal **7** average, humdrum, mundane, natural, popular, prelate, prosaic, regular, routine, typical **8** everyday, familiar, inferior, mediocre, workaday **9** clergyman, customary, quotidian **10** uneventful, unoriginal **11** commonplace **12** unnoteworthy

ordnance

4 arms, guns **6** cannon **7** weapons **8** armament, supplies, weaponry **9** artillery, munitions **10** ammunition

ore

4 gold, rock **5** metal **6** copper, silver **7** mineral **8** platinum

analysis: 5 assay

deposit: 4 lode, vein

excavation: 5 stope

iron: 5 ocher, ochre **8** goethite, hematite, limonite

lead: 6 galena

process: 8 leaching, smelting

refuse: 4 slag **5** dross, matte **6** scoria

smelted: 7 regulus

oread

5 nymph

Oregon

capital: 5 Salem

city: 4 Bend **6** Eugene **7** Coos Bay, Medford **8** Portland

college, university: 4 Reed

lake: 6 Crater

mountain, range: 4 Hood **7** Cascade

nickname: 6 Beaver (State)

river: 5 Snake **8** Columbia

state bird: 10 meadowlark

state flower: 11 Oregon grape

state tree: 10 Douglas fir

Orestes

father: 9 Agamemnon

friend: 7 Pylades

mother: 12 Clytemnestra

sister: 7 Electra **9** Iphigenia

victim: 9 Aegisthus **12** Clytemnestra

wife: 8 Hermione

organ

5 agent, means **6** agency, medium, review **7** channel, journal, vehicle **8** magazine, ministry **9** newspaper **10** instrument, periodical

ancient: 9 hydraulus

barrel: 10 hurdy-gurdy

bodily: 3 ear, eye **4** lung, nose, skin **5** gland, heart, liver **6** kidney, larynx, spleen, tongue, tonsil, viscus **9** intestine

mouth: 9 harmonica

part: 4 pipe, reed, stop **5** pedal, valve **6** blower **7** console, tremolo **8** keyboard **9** wind chest

reed: 8 melodeon 9 harmonium
stop: 4 oboe, sext 5 gamba, quint, viola 6 dulcet 7 bassoon, celesta, melodia, subbass, tertian 8 carillon, diapason, dulciana, gemshorn
tactile: 6 feeler 8 tentacle

organ cactus
7 saguaro

organic
5 basic 6 innate 7 natural, primary 8 inherent, integral 9 essential 10 structural 11 fundamental

organism
5 being, plant 6 animal
disease-producing: 4 germ 5 virus 8 pathogen 9 bacterium
single-celled: 5 monad 6 amoeba 9 protozoan

organist
American: 3 Fox (Virgil) 5 Biggs (E. Power) 6 Newman (Anthony)
Dutch: 9 Sweelinck (Jan)
English: 6 Wesley (Samuel) 7 Gibbons (Christopher, Edward, Ellis, Orlando)
French: 5 Alain (Marie-Claire), Widor (Charles) 6 Franck (César) 8 Messiaen (Olivier) 10 Schweitzer (Albert)
German: 4 Bach (Johann Sebastian) 6 Handel (George Frideric), Walcha (Helmut) 7 Richter (Anton, Ernst, Ferdinand, Johann, Karl)
Swiss: 4 Rogg (Lionel)

organization
4 body, club, unit 5 group, guild, setup 6 agency, system 7 pattern 9 framework, structure 11 arrangement, association, corporation, institution 13 establishment
college: 4 frat 8 sorority 10 fraternity
criminal: 4 gang 5 Mafia
fraternal:
(see **fraternal society**)
government:
(see **government agency**)
lack of: 5 chaos
political: 4 bloc 5 party 7 apparat, machine

organize
4 form 5 array, group, order, rally, set up, start 6 create, line up 7 arrange 8 classify, unionize 9 construct, establish, institute, integrate 10 constitute, coordinate 11 put together

orgulous
5 proud

orgy
4 rite 5 binge, revel, spree 7 blowout, carouse, debauch, rampage, revelry, splurge 8 carousal 9 bacchanal 10 indulgence, saturnalia 11 bacchanalia

oriel
3 bay 6 window

orient
3 set 4 face 5 adapt, align, pearl, sheen 6 adjust, direct, inform, locate, luster 7 arrange 8 acquaint, lustrous 9 sparkling 11 accommodate, familiarize

Orient
4 Asia, East 7 Far East

Oriental
3 rug 5 Asian 6 carpet 7 Eastern 10 Far Eastern

orientation
7 bearing 8 location, position 9 alignment, direction 10 adjustment 11 arrangement

orifice
see **opening**

oriflamme
4 flag 5 ideal 6 banner, pennon, symbol 7 pendant, pennant 8 standard, streamer

origami
12 paper folding
bird: 5 crane

origin
4 root, seed, well 5 birth, blood, start 6 source 7 descent, genesis, lineage 8 ancestry, fountain, pedigree 9 beginning, inception, maternity, parentage, paternity 10 derivation, extraction, provenance, wellspring

original

3 new 5 first, model, novel, prime
6 native, unique 7 initial, pattern,
pioneer, primary 8 creative, earliest
9 archetype, ingenious, innovator,
inventive, precursor, primitive, prototype 10 archetypal, forerunner,
innovative

originally

5 first 7 at first 8 formerly 9 initially,
primarily

originate

4 coin, flow, hail, make, rise, stem
5 arise, begin, found, hatch, issue,
set up, start 6 create, derive, invent,
launch, spring 7 emanate, proceed,
produce, think up 8 commence,
generate, initiate, innovate 9 institute, introduce

originator

5 maker 6 author 7 creator, founder, planner 8 inventor, producer
9 initiator, innovator 10 institutor,
introducer

oriole

4 bird 8 troupial
European: 6 loriot
genus: 7 Icterus
golden: 6 loriot
kind: 6 golden 7 orchard 8 Bullock's 9 Baltimore

Orion

6 hunter 13 constellation
beloved: 3 Eos
belt: 7 Ellwand
father: 7 Hyrieus 8 Poseidon
slayer: 5 Diana 7 Artemis
star: 5 Rigel 9 Bellatrix 10 Betelgeuse

orison

6 prayer 8 entreaty, petition 12 supplication

Orithyia

lover: 6 Boreas
son: 5 Zetes 6 Calais

Orlando author

5 Woolf (Virginia)

Orlando Furioso author

7 Ariosto (Ludovico)

Orléans heroine

9 Joan of Arc

orlop

4 deck

ormolu

5 brass 6 bronze

ornament

3 gem 4 bead, deck, trim 5 adorn,
jewel 6 bedeck, finial, tassel 7 dress
up, garnish, jewelry, pendant, whatnot 8 beautify, decorate, filigree
9 embellish, embroider, lavaliere
Christmas tree: 4 bulb 5 angel
6 tinsel
lip: 6 labret
shoulder: 7 epaulet

ornamental case

4 etui

ornate

4 lush, rich 5 fancy, gaudy, showy
6 florid, frilly, gilded, glitzy, rococo
7 baroque, flowery, opulent 8 overdone 9 elaborate, luxuriant, sumptuous 10 flamboyant

ornery

5 balky, cross, testy 6 crabby, cranky,
crusty, grumpy 7 bearish, froward,
grouchy 8 contrary, perverse, stubborn, vinegary 9 crotchety, difficult,
irascible, irritable 10 inflexible, vinegarish 12 cantankerous

ornithic

5 avian 8 birdlike

ornithologist

American: 4 Bond (James) 7 Au-
dubon (John James), Bartram
(William) 8 Peterson (Roger Tory)
English: 5 Gould (John)
Scottish: 6 Wilson (Alexander)

orotund

4 full, loud 5 round 7 flowery,
pompous, ringing 8 resonant,
sonorous 9 bombastic, high-flown,
overblown 10 euphuistic, oratorical,
resounding, rhetorical, stentorian

11 declamatory 12 magniloquent
13 grandiloquent

Orpah
husband: 7 Chilion
sister-in-law: 4 Ruth

orphan
4 waif 5 Annie, gamin, stray 6 bereft,
gamine, urchin 7 cast-off, ignored
8 forsaken, homeless 9 abandoned,
foundling, neglected 10 motherless,
parentless

Orpheus
father: 6 Apollo 7 Oeagrus
home: 6 Thrace
instrument: 4 lyre
mother: 8 Calliope
wife: 8 Euridice

orphic
6 arcane, mystic, occult 7 cryptic,
Delphic, obscure 8 abstruse, Delphian, esoteric, hermetic, mystical,
oracular, profound 9 enigmatic,
recondite

ort
3 bit 4 bite 5 crumb, piece, scrap
6 morsel 7 remnant 8 leftover

orthodox
6 proper 8 accepted, approved,
official, received, standard 9 canonical, customary 10 conformist,
recognized, sanctioned 11 established, traditional 12 acknowledged,
conservative, conventional 13 authoritative

orthography
7 writing 8 spelling

ortolan
7 bunting

Orwell novel
10 Animal Farm 18 Nineteen Eighty-
four

oryx
7 gemsbok 8 antelope

os
3 ora (plural) 4 bone, ossa (plural)
5 mouth 7 orifice

Osborne play
15 Look Back in Anger

oscillate
4 sway, vary 5 swing, waver
6 change, seesaw 7 vibrate 9 alternate, fluctuate

oscillation
4 sway 5 swing 9 variation, vibration 10 undulation 11 fluctuation,
periodicity

osculate
3 lip 4 buss, kiss, peck 5 smack
6 smooch

osier
3 rod 6 willow 7 dogwood

Osiris
brother: 3 Set 4 Seth
father: 3 Geb, Keb, Seb
mother: 3 Nut
scribe: 5 Thoth
sister: 4 Isis
slayer: 3 Set 4 Seth
son: 5 Horus 6 Anubis
wife: 4 Isis

osmosis
4 flow 8 transfer 9 diffusion 10 absorption 12 assimilation 13 incorporation

osprey
4 hawk 8 fish hawk

osseous
4 bony 8 bonelike

ossicle
4 bone 5 incus 6 stapes 7 malleus

ossify
3 set 6 harden 7 stiffen 8 solidify
9 fossilize

osso _____
4 buco

ossuary
4 tomb 5 vault 8 boneyard, cemetery 9 sepulcher, sepulchre

ostensible
6 stated 7 alleged, seeming 8 apparent, asserted, illusive, illusory,

ostentation
so-called, supposed **9** pretended,
professed, purported, semblable
11 superficial

ostentation
4 show **5** flash, swank **7** display
9 pomposity, showiness, vainglory
10 flashiness, pretension **11** flamboyance

ostentatious
4 loud **5** gaudy, showy, swank
6 flashy, garish, swanky **7** pompous,
splashy **8** overdone, peacocky
10 flamboyant, peacockish **11** pretentious **12** vainglorious

ostiole
4 pore **7** orifice **8** aperture

ostracism
5 exile **7** removal **9** exclusion
10 banishment, relegation **11** deportation

ostracize
3 bar, cut **4** shun, snub **5** exile
6 banish, deport **7** exclude, keep
out, shut out **8** throw out **9** blackball
10 expatriate **12** cold-shoulder

ostrich
6 ratite

Ostrogoth king
9 Theodoric

otalgia
7 earache

Otello composer
5 Verdi (Giuseppe) **7** Rossini
(Gioacchino)

O tempora! O _____!
5 mores

Othello
author: **11** Shakespeare (William)
ensign: **4** Iago
lieutenant: **6** Cassio
maid: **6** Emilia
victim, wife: **9** Desdemona

others
4 rest **9** remainder
and: **4** et al **6** et alia, et alii **7** et
aliae

other than
3 but **4** save **6** except **7** besides
9 apart from, aside from, except for,
excepting, excluding

otherwise
3 not **5** if not **6** or else **7** changed
9 differently **11** differently **12** anything
else **13** alternatively

otic
5 aural **8** auditory **9** auricular

otiose
4 idle, vain **5** empty **6** futile, hollow
7 surplus, useless **8** nugatory
9 fruitless, pointless, worthless
11 ineffective, purposeless, superfluous **12** functionless **13** supernumerary

Ottawa chief
7 Pontiac

ottoman
4 seat **5** couch **6** fabric **9** footstool

Ottoman
4 Turk **7** Turkish
ruler: **5** Osman, Selim **8** Suleiman,
Süleyman

Otus
5 giant
brother: **9** Ephialtes
father: **6** Aloeus **8** Poseidon
mother: **9** Iphimedia
slayer: **6** Apollo

ouch
3 cry **5** bezel, jewel **6** brooch,
buckle **7** setting **8** ornament **11** exclamation

ounce
3 bit, cat **4** dram **5** pinch, scrap,
shred **6** amount, splash, weight
7 measure, modicum, smidgen
8 fraction, particle **11** snow leopard

our
French: **5** notre
Italian: **6** nostra

Our Town author
6 Wilder (Thornton)

oust
4 fire, sack 5 eject, evict, expel
6 banish, deport, remove, topple,
unseat 7 boot out, cast out, deprive,
dismiss, kick out 8 displace, drive
out, force out, relegate, supplant,
take away, throw out 10 dispossess

ouster
7 removal 8 ejection, eviction
9 discharge, dismissal, expulsion
10 banishment

out
4 away, exit 5 forth, loose 6 absent,
excuse
of control: 4 wild 7 chaotic
of gas: 5 tired 7 drained 9 exhausted
of line: 4 awry, rude 5 askew, fresh
of place: 13 inappropriate
of sorts: 5 cross 7 grouchy, peevish
9 irritable
of the ordinary: 3 odd 7 bizarre,
strange, unusual

outage
4 loss 5 break 7 failure 8 blackout
12 interruption

out-and-out
5 gross, sheer, total, utter 7 perfect
8 absolute, complete, positive
9 downright 10 consummate 11 unmitigated, unqualified 13 thoroughgoing

outback
4 bush 6 sticks 7 boonies 9 boondocks 10 hinterland, wilderness

outboard
4 boat 5 motor 6 engine

outbreak
4 rash, rise, rush 5 burst, flare,
spike, surge 6 attack, blowup,
plague, revolt 7 flare-up 8 epidemic, eruption, increase, uprising
9 rebellion 12 insurrection

outburst
3 fit 4 gush, gust 5 flare, sally,
scene, spasm, storm, surge 6 frenzy,
tirade 7 flare-up, tantrum, torrent
8 eruption, paroxysm, upheaval
9 explosion

outcast
4 hobo 5 exile, leper, tramp 6 pariah
7 Ishmael, vagrant 8 castaway,
derelict, vagabond 9 reprobate
10 expatriate, Ishmaelite 11 offscouring, untouchable

outclass
3 top 4 best 5 excel 6 exceed
7 surpass

outcome
3 end 5 event, fruit, issue 6 effect,
result, sequel, upshot 9 aftermath
10 conclusion 11 aftereffect, consequence, development

outcrop
4 rock 5 ledge 6 appear 7 project
8 protrude 10 projection, protrusion
12 protuberance

outcry
4 yell 5 noise, shout 6 clamor,
tumult, uproar 7 auction, ferment,
protest 8 upheaval 9 commotion,
objection 11 exclamation

outdated
3 old 5 passé 6 démodé, old hat
7 antique 12 old-fashioned

outdistance
3 top 4 beat, best, pass 5 trump
6 better 7 eclipse, surpass

outdo
3 top 4 beat, best 5 excel, trump
6 better, defeat, exceed 7 eclipse,
surpass, triumph 8 overcome
9 transcend

outdoor
7 open-air 8 alfresco

outer
6 remote 7 surface 8 exoteric,
exterior, external 9 extrinsic 10 extraneous 11 superficial

outermost
4 last 5 final 6 far-off 7 distant,
extreme 8 farthest, furthest, remotest

outfit
3 kit, rig, set 4 band, firm, gear, suit,
team, togs, unit 5 corps, dress,
equip, getup, group, squad, troop

outflank

6 clothe, supply, tackle, troupe
7 appoint, company, concern, costume, furnish 8 accouter, accoutre, business, clothing, ensemble, matériel, tackling 9 equipment, provision 10 enterprise 12 organization 13 accouterments, accoutrements, establishment

outflank

5 evade 6 bypass 9 get around 10 circumvent

outflow

6 efflux 8 drainage, effluent 9 effluence

out-front

4 open 5 frank 6 candid, honest 10 forthright

outgoing

4 open 7 affable 8 friendly, sociable 9 departing, expansive 10 gregarious, responsive 11 extroverted

outgrowth

6 effect, result 7 product, spin-off 8 offshoot 9 by-product, offspring 10 derivative 11 aftereffect, consequence

outhouse

5 jakes, privy 7 latrine

outing

4 spin, trip 5 drive, jaunt, sally 6 junket, picnic 9 excursion 10 appearance, disclosure

outlandish

3 odd 4 wild 5 alien, outré, ultra, weird 6 exotic, quaint, remote, vulgar 7 bizarre, curious, extreme, foreign, offbeat, strange, uncouth, unusual 8 peculiar, singular 9 eccentric, fantastic, tasteless 10 ridiculous, unorthodox 11 extravagant

outlast

6 endure 7 survive, weather 9 withstand

outlaw

3 ban, con 4 wild 5 crook 6 bandit, banned, enjoin, forbid 7 exclude, illegal 8 criminal, disallow, fugitive, prohibit, renegade, restrict 9 desperado, illegalize, interdict, proscribe 10 rebellious

outlay

3 pay, tab 4 cost, give 5 spend 6 amount, expend 7 expense, payment 8 disburse 11 expenditure 12 disbursement

outlet

4 exit, hole, mart, shop, vent 5 issue, store 6 avenue, egress, escape, market 7 channel, opening, passage, release 8 aperture 10 discounter, receptacle

outline

4 edge, form, limn, plan 5 brief, draft, shape, trace 6 bounds, border, précis, schema, sketch 7 contour, profile, summary 8 abstract, boundary, skeleton, syllabus, synopsis 9 delineate, summarize 10 figuration, silhouette 11 skeletonize

outlive

7 survive, weather

outlook

4 side, view 5 angle, scope, sight, slant, vista 6 aspect, future 7 promise 8 attitude, forecast, position, prospect 9 direction, viewpoint 10 standpoint 11 expectation, observatory, perspective, point of view

outlying

3 far 6 far-off, remote 7 distant, faraway, removed 8 far-flung

outmoded

4 dead 5 dated, passé, tired 8 obsolete 9 moth-eaten, unstylish 10 oldfangled 11 obsolescent 12 old-fashioned

Out of Africa author

7 Dinesen (Isak)

out-of-date

3 old 4 past 5 passé, stale 6 démodé, old hat, square 7 antique, archaic, old-time, vintage 8 obsolete 9 unstylish 10 antiquated 12 old-fashioned

out of it
4 lost 5 dazed 7 muddled 8 confused 10 bewildered

out-of-the-way
4 rare 6 remote 7 distant, obscure, removed, unusual 8 secluded, uncommon

outpost
4 base 6 branch, colony 8 foothold 10 detachment, settlement

outpouring
4 flow, gush, rush 5 burst, flood, spate, spurt 6 deluge, stream 7 torrent 8 effusion

output
4 crop, gain, take 5 power, yield 6 amount, profit 7 harvest, produce, product 10 production 11 achievement, information

outrage
4 fury, rape 5 abuse, shock, wrong 6 injury, insult, offend 7 affront, incense, violate 8 aggrieve, atrocity, ill-treat, mischief, violence 9 brutality, infuriate 10 resentment, scandalize

outrageous
5 awful, gross 6 horrid, insane, odious, unholy, wicked 7 beastly, ghastly, heinous, ignoble, obscene 8 dreadful, flagrant, horrible, shocking, terrible 9 atrocious, egregious, excessive, fantastic 10 abominable, inordinate, scandalous 11 intolerable

outré
3 odd 5 ultra 6 far-out 7 bizarre, extreme, off-beat, strange 8 peculiar 9 eccentric

outrigger
4 boat, beam, prau, proa, spar

outright
4 pure 5 total, utter, whole 6 entire 7 perfect 8 absolute, complete, entirely, positive 9 on the spot 10 completely, consummate 11 unequivocal, unmitigated, unqualified 13 thoroughgoing

outrun
3 top 4 beat, pass 6 exceed 7 surpass

outset
4 dawn 5 birth, start 7 opening 9 beginning, inception 12 commencement

outshine
3 top 4 beat, best 5 excel 6 exceed 7 surpass

outside
5 alien 7 foreign, open-air 8 alfresco, exterior, external

outsider
5 alien 7 inconnu 8 newcomer, stranger 9 foreigner

outsmart
see **outwit**

outspoken
4 free, open 5 blunt, frank, plain, vocal 6 candid, direct, honest 7 up front 8 explicit, forthright, point-blank, unreserved 11 unequivocal

outstanding
3 due 4 star 5 noted, owing 6 signal, superb, unpaid 7 capital, eminent, notable, salient, stellar 8 dominant, striking, superior 9 arresting, excellent, prominent, unsettled 10 noticeable, preeminent, remarkable, unresolved 11 conspicuous, distinctive, exceptional, magnificent, superlative, uncollected 13 extraordinary

outstrip
3 top 4 beat, best, pass 5 excel 6 better, exceed 7 surpass 8 distance, go beyond, overtake 9 transcend 11 leave behind

outward
5 overt 7 evident, visible 8 apparent, exterior, external 10 noticeable, ostensible 11 superficial

outweigh
6 exceed 8 overbear 10 overshadow 11 overbalance 12 preponderate

outworn
see **outmoded**

ouzel
6 dipper, thrush **9** blackbird

oval
5 track **6** oblong **7** ellipse **8** elliptic
9 egg-shaped, racetrack **10** elliptical
11 ellipsoidal

ovation
5 kudos **6** homage, praise **7** acclaim, tribute **8** applause, approval,
cheering, clapping, plaudits **11** acclamation

oven
4 kiln, oast **5** range, stove

over
4 anew, atop, done, past, upon
5 above, again, aloft, ended **6** across,
beyond **8** finished, once more
French: 3 sur
German: 4 über
prefix: 3 epi, sur **5** extra, hyper,
super, supra
Spanish: 5 sobre

overabundance
4 glut **6** excess **7** surfeit, surplus
8 plethora **10** surplusage **11** superfluity

overact
3 ham, mug **4** rant **5** emote **10** exaggerate

overage
6 excess **7** surplus

overall
5 smock, total **6** global, mainly,
mostly **7** chiefly, general, largely
8 as a whole, sweeping **9** generally,
inclusive, in general, primarily **10** far
and wide **11** principally **13** comprehensive, predominantly

overalls
5 pants **8** trousers

over and above
4 also **6** as well, beyond **7** besides
8 as well as **10** in addition

over and over
3 oft **5** often **8** ofttimes **10** frequently, oftentimes, repeatedly
11 continually, recurrently

overbearing
5 bossy **6** lordly **7** haughty, pompous **8** absolute, arrogant, despotic,
dogmatic, dominant, imperial, insolent, scornful, superior **9** imperious,
tyrannous **10** autocratic, disdainful,
dominating, high-handed, oppressive, peremptory, tyrannical **11** dictatorial, domineering, magisterial
12 supercilious **13** high-and-
mighty

overblown
6 turgid **7** flowery, hyped up, orotund, pompous **8** inflated **9** bombastic, excessive, high-flown
10 euphuistic, oratorical, rhetorical
11 declamatory, exaggerated, pretentious **12** magniloquent **13** grandiloquent

overcast
3 sew **4** dull, gray, hazy **5** cloud,
cover **6** cloudy, darken, shadow
7 becloud, blanket, clouded, obscure
8 covering, lowering **9** adumbrate

overcharge
3 pad **4** bilk, clip, skin, soak **5** cheat,
stick **6** fleece **7** inflate

overcoat
5 paint **6** capote, raglan, ulster
7 surtout **9** balmacaan, outerwear
12 chesterfield

overcome
4 beat, best, lick **5** drown, throw
6 defeat, hurdle, master **7** conquer,
prevail, triumph **8** surmount **9** prostrate

overconfident
4 rash **5** brash, cocky, pushy **8** arrogant, cocksure, reckless **9** hubristic,
presuming **12** presumptuous

overdo
7 exhaust, fatigue, wear out **9** embellish **10** exaggerate

overdue
4 late **5** owing, tardy **6** behind,
unpaid **7** belated, delayed, payable

8 dilatory 9 unsettled 10 behindhand, delinquent, unpunctual 11 outstanding

overemphasize
7 magnify 8 heighten 9 dramatize, embellish 10 exaggerate

overflow
4 pour 5 cover, drown, flood, slosh, spate, spill, swamp 6 deluge, engulf, excess, outlet 7 surfeit, surplus, torrent 8 flooding, inundate, spillage, submerge 10 inundation, surplusage 11 superfluity

overgrown
4 lush 5 dense, thick 6 brushy 7 hulking 8 ungainly 9 excessive, ponderous 10 junglelike

overhang
3 jut 4 loom 5 bulge 6 beetle, extend, impend 7 project 8 protrude, stick out, threaten 10 projection

overhaul
3 fix 4 mend, redo 5 patch, renew 6 doctor, remake, repair, revamp, revise 7 rebuild, restore 8 renovate 11 recondition, reconstruct

overhead
4 atop 5 above, aloft, smash 7 ceiling, expense 8 expenses

overheated
5 fiery 7 fervent 8 inflated 9 perfervid 11 impassioned

overindulgence
6 excess 7 surfeit 8 gluttony 11 dissipation 12 immoderation, intemperance

overjoyed
6 elated 7 gleeful 8 ecstatic, euphoric, exultant, jubilant, thrilled 9 rapturous 11 transported

overkill
4 glut 6 excess 7 surfeit, surplus, too much 8 plethora 10 obliterate, redundancy, surplusage 11 superfluity

overlap
7 shingle 9 imbricate

overlay
3 cap 4 coat 5 cover, glaze 6 finish, veneer 7 blanket, coating, lacquer, varnish 8 covering 11 superimpose 12 transparency

overload
4 glut 5 stuff 6 burden, excess, pile on, strain 7 surfeit

overlook
4 fail, miss, omit, skip 5 check, let go 6 excuse, forget, ignore, pass by, slight, slip up, survey, wink at 7 blink at, condone, forgive, inspect, let pass, neglect 8 discount, dominate, surmount 9 disregard, supervise 11 superintend

overlord
4 czar, tsar, tzar 5 chief, mogul, ruler 6 tycoon 7 magnate 8 suzerain 9 potentate, sovereign

overly
3 too 6 unduly 11 exceedingly, excessively 12 immoderately, inordinately

overpass
5 cross 6 bridge 8 crossing, traverse 9 traversal 11 interchange

overplay
4 hype 6 expand 7 enlarge, inflate, magnify, point up, stretch 8 maximize 9 dramatize 10 exaggerate 11 hyperbolize

overpower
4 rout 5 crush, swamp, whelm 6 defeat, master, subdue 7 conquer 8 vanquish 9 prostrate, subjugate

overreach
3 con 4 beat, bilk 5 cheat, outdo 6 defeat, outfox, outwit 7 defraud 8 flimflam, outsmart 10 exaggerate 11 outmaneuver

override
4 veto 5 annul 6 cancel 7 nullify 10 counteract, neutralize

overriding
3 key 4 main 5 chief, major, prime, vital 7 central, crucial, pivotal, primary, supreme 8 cardinal, dominant, foremost 9 paramount, principal

overrule

4 undo, veto 5 upset 6 negate, revoke 7 reverse 8 set aside 11 countermand

overrun

4 beat, raid, teem, whip 5 swamp, swarm 6 defeat, excess, infest, invade, occupy, ravage, spread, thrash 7 clobber, conquer

overseas

6 abroad 11 transmarine, ultramarine 12 transoceanic

oversee

3 run 4 boss 5 watch 6 direct, manage, survey 7 command, examine, inspect 9 supervise 11 superintend

overseer

4 boss, exec, head 5 chief 7 foreman, manager 8 director 9 executive 10 supervisor 13 administrator

overshadow

4 veil 5 cloud, dwarf, shade 6 darken, exceed 7 becloud, eclipse, obscure, surpass 8 dominate, outshine, outweigh 9 adumbrate

overshoe

4 boot 6 arctic, galosh, patten, rubber

oversight

4 care, slip 5 aegis, check, error, lapse 6 charge, slip-up 7 control, failure, mistake, neglect 8 omission 10 intendance, management 11 supervision

overspread

3 cap 5 beset, cover, flood, swarm 6 infest, invade 7 blanket, obscure, pervade 8 permeate

overstate

3 pad 7 amplify, enlarge, magnify 9 embellish, embroider 10 exaggerate

overstep

6 exceed, offend 7 surpass, violate 8 infringe, trespass 10 transgress

overstock

4 glut 5 extra 6 excess 7 surplus 9 remainder 10 surplusage

overstress

7 magnify 8 maximize 10 exaggerate

overt

4 open 5 clear 6 patent 7 evident, obvious, outward, visible 8 apparent, manifest 10 observable

overtake

4 pass 5 catch 6 pass by 7 outpace, surpass 8 come upon, outstrip 11 outdistance

Over the Rainbow

composer: 5 Arlen (Harold) 7 Harburg (E. Y.)
singer: 7 Garland (Judy)

over there

3 yon 6 yonder

over-the-top

7 extreme 8 reckless 9 egregious, excessive 10 exorbitant, flamboyant, outrageous 11 extravagant

overthrow

4 fell, oust, rout 5 purge, upset 6 defeat, depose, remove, topple, unseat 7 conquer 8 dethrone, downfall 9 bring down

overtone

4 hint 5 sense 8 coloring, harmonic 9 inference 10 suggestion 11 association, connotation, implication 12 undercurrent

overture

3 bid 5 proem 7 advance, preface, prelude, present 8 approach, foreword, preamble, prologue, proposal 9 prelusion 10 initiative 11 proposition 12 introduction, presentation

overturn

3 tip 4 flip, void 5 upend, upset 6 topple, tumble 7 capsize, nullify, reverse 8 set aside 10 invalidate

overused

5 stale, tired, trite 7 clichéd, worn-out 9 hackneyed

overview
6 aperçu, précis, survey 7 epitome, summary 10 conspectus

overweening
5 brash, pushy 6 lordly, uppish, uppity 7 forward 8 arrogant 9 conceited, presuming 10 immoderate 11 exaggerated 12 presumptuous

overweight
3 fat 5 beefy, burly, dumpy, gross, heavy, husky, obese, plump, pudgy, stout 6 chubby, chunky, flabby, fleshy, portly, rotund 7 outsize 8 heavyset, thickset 9 corpulent

overwhelm
4 beat, bury, rout, ruin, sink, whip 5 crush, drown, flood, swamp, upset, wreck 6 defeat, deluge, engulf, thrash 7 conquer, destroy, oppress, shatter, shellac, smother 8 inundate, submerge 9 devastate, prostrate 10 demoralize 11 subordinate

overwhelmed
6 aghast 7 shocked, stunned, touched 8 defeated, helpless 10 distressed 13 thunderstruck

overwhelming
4 huge 5 great 7 extreme 8 numerous

overwrought
5 hyper, upset 7 anxious, frantic, wound up 8 agitated, frenetic, stressed, troubled 9 disturbed, emotional 10 distracted, freaked out, high-strung, hysterical 11 discomposed

Ovid work
5 Fasti 6 Amores 7 Tristia 8 Heroides 13 Metamorphoses

ovine
5 sheep 9 sheeplike

ovoid
4 oval 5 ovate 9 egg-shaped

ovule
3 egg
fertilized: 4 seed

ovum
3 egg 6 gamete 7 egg cell 11 macrogamete

owing
3 due 6 in debt, mature, unpaid 7 overdue, payable 9 unsettled 11 outstanding

owing to
4 over 7 through 9 because of 10 by reason of 11 on account of

owl
cry: 4 hoot
genus: 4 Otus
kind: 3 elf 4 barn, gray, lulu 5 eagle, gnome, madge, pygmy, snowy 6 barred, horned 7 saw-whet, screech 9 long-eared 10 short-eared 11 great horned

Owl and the Pussycat author
4 Lear (Edward)

own
4 avow, have, hold 5 admit, allow, enjoy, grant, let on 6 accept, fess up, retain 7 concede, confess, possess 8 disclose 9 recognize 11 acknowledge

owner
6 holder 8 landlady, landlord 9 possessor, purchaser 10 proprietor

ownership
4 hand 5 title 8 dominion, property 10 possession 11 proprietary
perpetual: 8 mortmain

ox
3 yak 4 anoa, gaur, musk, zebu 5 bison, steer 6 bovine 7 banteng, buffalo
Asian: 4 zebu
attachment: 4 yoke
extinct: 4 urus 7 aurochs
family: 7 Bovidae
relating to: 6 bovine
wild: 4 anoa, gaur 7 banteng

oxeye
5 daisy 6 flower

oxford
4 shoe 5 cloth, sheep 6 cotton, fabric

oxide

oxide
  calcium: **4** lime **9** quicklime
  ferric: **4** rust
  sodium: **4** soda

oxidize
  4 rust

oxygen
  3 air, gas **5** ozone **7** element
  discoverer: **9** Lavoisier (Antoine)
  form: **5** ozone
  liquid: **3** lox

oyster
  7 bivalve, mollusc, mollusk
  bed: **4** park **6** claire, cultch
  eggs: **5** spawn
  genus: **6** Ostrea
  Long Island: **9** bluepoint

product: **5** pearl
shell: **4** test **5** shuck
young: **4** spat

oyster plant
  7 salsify

Oz
  creator: **4** Baum (L. Frank)
  inhabitant: **8** Munchkin
  princess: **4** Ozma

Ozark State
  8 Missouri

Ozem
  brother: **5** David
  father: **5** Jesse **9** Jerahmeel

Ozymandias author
  7 Shelley (Percy Bysshe)

P

pabulum
3 pap **4** food **7** aliment **8** nutrient
9 blandness, nutriment **10** insipidity,
sustenance **11** nourishment

paca
4 cavy

pace
3 set **4** beat, clip, gait, lead, rate,
step, time, walk **5** speed, tempo,
tread, troop **6** motion, stride, timing
7 example, fluency, measure, precede, proceed, routine, step off
8 ambulate, antecede, movement,
progress, regulate

pachyderm
8 elephant

pacific
4 calm, mild **6** gentle, irenic, placid,
serene **8** dovelike, peaceful, soothing, tranquil **9** peaceable, temperate
12 conciliatory

Pacificator, Great
4 Clay (Henry)

Pacific nation
5 Belau, Japan, Nauru, Palau, Tonga
6 Tuvalu **7** Vanuatu **8** Kiribati

Pacific Ocean discoverer
6 Balboa (Vasco Núñez de)

pacifist
4 dove **6** irenic **8** appeaser, peaceful, peacenik **9** peaceable **10** nonviolent **11** peacemonger

pacify
4 calm, cool, ease, lull **5** allay, quell,
quiet, still **6** disarm, settle, soften,
soothe, subdue, temper **7** appease,

assuage, mollify, placate **9** subjugate **10** conciliate, propitiate

pack
3 jam, kit, lot, lug, ram, set, wad
4 band, bear, cram, deck, fill, gang,
heap, load, lump, mass, pile, stow,
tamp, tote, unit **5** bunch, carry,
cover, crowd, ferry, group, store,
stuff, troop **6** bundle, charge, clique,
convey, depart, gather **7** possess
8 assemble, compress, knapsack
9 container, equipment, influence,
transport **10** collection, congregate

package
3 box **4** deal, unit, wrap **5** array,
combo, whole **6** bundle, parcel
7 enclose, present, wrapper **8** shipment **9** container **10** collection
11 combination

pack animal
3 ass **4** mule **5** burro, camel, horse,
llama **6** donkey **7** jackass **13** beast
of burden

packed
4 full **5** awash, dense, flush **6** filled,
jammed **7** brimful, crowded, stuffed
8 brimming **9** chock-full **10** compressed

packet
3 wad **4** boat, mass, pile **5** group
6 bundle, parcel **7** cluster

pact
4 bond, deal **6** accord, treaty
7 bargain, concord **8** alliance, contract, covenant **9** agreement

pad
3 bed, mat, wad **4** foot, mute **5** fudge,

guard, paper, stuff **6** buffer, expand, muffle, shield, tablet **7** augment, bolster, cushion, stretch **8** dressing, increase **9** embellish, embroider, overstate **10** exaggerate, overcharge

paddle
3 oar, row **4** beat, stir **5** spank **6** propel, thrash

paddock
5 field **7** pasture **9** enclosure

paddy wagon
10 Black Maria

padre
3 Fra **6** father, priest **8** chaplain, minister **9** clergyman, confessor

paean
4 hymn, song **6** anthem, eulogy, praise **7** tribute **8** accolade, encomium **9** panegyric

page
4 book, call, leaf **5** folio, sheet **6** locate, summon **7** bellhop, equerry
left-hand: 5 verso
right-hand: 5 recto

pageant
4 sham, show **7** charade, display, tableau **8** pretense **9** spectacle **10** exhibition

pageantry
4 pomp, show **7** display, panoply **8** flourish, splendor **9** spectacle **10** exhibition **11** flamboyance, ostentation **12** magnificence

Pagliacci, I
character: 5 Canio, Nedda, Tonio **6** Silvio
composer: 11 Leoncavallo (Ruggero)

pagoda
6 temple

pail
6 bucket, piggin, vessel

pain
3 irk **4** ache, care, hurt, pang **5** agony, cramp, grief, throe, upset **6** grieve, harass, stitch, twinge **7** afflict, anguish, torture, travail, trouble **8** aggrieve, distress **9** suffering **10** affliction, discomfort
back: 7 lumbago
muscular: 7 myalgia

painful
3 raw **4** hard, sore **5** acute, sharp **6** aching, trying **7** arduous, irksome **8** annoying, piercing, stinging **9** agonizing, difficult, laborious, torturous, upsetting, vexatious **10** afflictive, tormenting

painkiller
4 drug **6** opiate **7** anodyne, codeine **8** morphine, narcotic **9** analgesic **10** anesthetic

painstaking
5 exact **7** careful, heedful **8** diligent, exacting, thorough **9** assiduous, diligence, laborious **10** meticulous, scrupulous **11** punctilious

paint
4 coat, daub, limn, swab, tint **5** adorn, brush, color, cover, horse, pinto, rouge, stain **6** depict, makeup **7** coating, pigment, portray, produce, touch up **8** cosmetic, decorate **9** delineate, represent **10** maquillage

painter
6 artist
American: 4 Cole (Thomas), Haas (Richard), West (Benjamin), Wood (Grant) **5** Abbey (Edwin Austin), Davis (Stuart), Gorky (Arshile), Grosz (George), Henri (Robert), Hicks (Edward), Homer (Winslow), Johns (Jasper), Kline (Franz), Kroll (Leon), Marin (John), Marsh (Reginald), Moses (Grandma), Peale (Anna, Charles Willson, James, Raphaelle, Rembrandt, Sarah, Titian), Ryder (Albert Pinkham), Shahn (Ben), Sloan (Eric, John), Weber (Max), Wyeth (Andrew, Jamie, Newell Convers) **6** Albers (Josef), Benton (Thomas Hart), Catlin (George), Church (Frederick Edwin), Coburn (Alvin Langdon), Copley (John Singleton), Durand (Asher), Eakins (Thomas), Hassam (Childe), Hopper (Edward), Inness (George),

Leutze (Emanuel), Martin (Agnes, Homer), Newman (Barnett), Rivers (Larry), Rothko (Mark), Stella (Frank), Stuart (Gilbert), Tanguy (Yves), Thorpe (Thomas), Warhol (Andy) **7** Allston (Washington), Bearden (Romare), Bellows (George), Bingham (George Caleb), Cassatt (Mary), Duchamp (Marcel), Harnett (William), Hartley (Marsden), Kinkade (Thomas), La Farge (John), O'Keeffe (Georgia), Parrish (Maxfield), Pollock (Jackson), Sargent (John Singer), Sheeler (Charles), Tiffany (Louis Comfort), Tworkov (Jack), Wiggins (Carleton) **8** Melchers (Gari), Rockwell (Norman), Sullivan (Patrick), Trumbull (John), Whistler (James McNeill) **9** Bierstadt (Albert), de Kooning (Willem), Feininger (Lyonel), Reinhardt (Ad), Remington (Frederic), Twachtman (John Henry), Vanderlyn (John) **10** Motherwell (Robert), Whittredge (Thomas) **12** Lichtenstein (Roy), Rauschenberg (Robert)

Austrian: 5 Klimt (Gustav) **9** Kokoschka (Oskar)

Belgian: 5 Ensor (James) **6** Campin (Robert) **8** Magritte (René)

Canadian: 4 Kane (Paul) **6** Harris (Lawren), Watson (Homer) **7** Jackson (Alexander Young), Thomson (Tom) **9** MacDonald (James Edward Hervey)

Chinese: 4 Wu Li **6** Ma Yüan **7** Wang Wei **9** Yen Li-pen

Dutch: 3 Dou (Gerrit) **4** Hals (Frans), Lely (Peter), Maas (Nicolas) **5** Bosch (Hieronymus), Hooch (Pieter de), Steen (Jan) **6** Potter (Paul) **7** de Hooch (Pieter), de Witte (Emanuel), Hobbema (Meindert), van Gogh (Vincent), Vermeer (Jan) **8** Mondrian (Piet), Ruisdael (Jacob van, Salomon), Ruysdael (Salomon), Terborch (Gerard) **9** de Kooning (Willem), Rembrandt (van Rijn), Wouwerman (Philips) **11** Terbrugghen (Hendrik)

English: 4 John (Augustus), Lear (Edward) **5** Bacon (Francis), Blake (William), Brown (Ford Madox),

Lewis (Wyndham), Watts (George Frederick) **6** Romney (George), Turner (Joseph Mallord William), Wilson (Richard) **7** Hogarth (William), Kneller (Godfrey), Millais (John) **8** Lawrence (Thomas), Reynolds (Joshua), Rossetti (Dante Gabriel) **9** Constable (John), Nicholson (Ben, William) **12** Gainsborough (Thomas)

Finnish: 9 Järnefelt (Edvard)

Flemish: 4 Eyck (Hubert van, Jan van), Goes (Hugo van der) **6** Rubens (Peter Paul), Weyden (Rogier van der) **7** Memling (Hams), Teniers (David), Van Dyck (Anthony), van Eyck (Hubert, Jan) **8** Breughel, Brueghel (Abraham, Ambrose, Jan, Pieter)

French: 4 Doré (Gustave), Dufy (Raoul), Erté **5** Corot (Camille), David (Jacques-Louis), Degas (Edgar), Léger (Fernand), Manet (Edouard), Monet (Claude), Redon (Odilon), Vouet (Simon) **6** Braque (Georges), Breton (André), Claude (of Lorrain), Clouet (François, Jean), Gérôme (Jean-Léon), Greuze (Jean-Baptiste), Ingres (Jean-Auguste-Dominique), Le Brun (Charles), Le Nain (Antoine, Louis, Mathieu), Millet (Jean-François), Renoir (Pierre-Auguste), Seurat (Georges), Sisley (Alfred), Tanguy (Yves), Vernet (Carle, Horace, Joseph) **7** Balthus, Bonheur (Rosa), Bonnard (Pierre), Boucher (François), Cézanne (Paul), Chardin (Jean-Baptiste), Courbet (Gustave), Daumier (Honoré), Duchamp (Gaston, Marcel), Gauguin (Paul), Matisse (Henri), Morisot (Berthe), Poussin (Nicolas), Rouault (Georges), Utrillo (Maurice), Watteau (Antoine) **8** Dubuffet (Jean), Magritte (René), Pissarro (Camille), Rousseau (Henri, Théodore), Vlaminck (Maurice de), Vuillard (Edouard) **9** Delacroix (Eugène), Fragonard (Jean-Honoré), Géricault (Théodore), Laurencin (Marie) **10** Bouguereau (William), Meissonier (Jean-Louis) **11** Caillebotte (Gustave) **13** Claude Lorrain

German: 5 Dürer (Albrecht), Ernst (Max), Grosz (George), Nolde (Emil) 6 Albers (Josef), Müller (Friedrich "Maler") 7 Cranach (Lucas), Holbein (Hans), Lochner (Stefan), Schwind (Moritz von), Zoffany (Johann) 8 Kirchner (Ernst), Kollwitz (Käthe) 9 Grünewald (Matthias), Kandinsky (Wassily) 10 Schongauer (Martin), Wohlgemuth (Michael)

Greek: 6 Zeuxis 7 Apelles 10 Polygnotus

Irish: 5 Yeats (Jack, John Butler)

Italian: 4 Reni (Guido), Rosa (Salvator), Tura (Cosme) 5 Campi (Antonio, Bernardino, Giulio, Vincenzo), Lippi (Fra Filippo, Filippino, Lorenzo), Piero (della Francesca, di Cosimo), Sarto (Andrea del) 6 Andrea (del Sarto), Cosimo (Agnolo di, Piero di), Giotto, Romano (Giulio), Sodoma (II), Titian, Vasari (Giorgio) 7 Bellini (Gentile, Giovanni, Jacopo), Chirico (Giorgio De), Cimabue, da Vinci (Leonardo), Fiesole (Giovanni da), Martini (Simone), Orcagna, Peruzzi (Baldassare), Raphael, Tiepolo (Giovanni), Uccello (Paolo), Zuccari (Taddeo) 8 del Sarto (Andrea), Fabriano (Gentile da), Giordano (Luca), Leonardo (da Vinci), Mantegna (Andrea), Masaccio, Montagna (Bartolommeo), Perugino, Pontorno (Jacopo da), Severini (Gino), Veronese (Paolo), Vivarini (Alvise, Antonio, Bartolomeo) 9 Carpaccio (Vittore), Correggio, Francesca (Piero della) 10 Caravaggio, Modigliani (Amedeo), Signorelli (Luca), Tintoretto, Verrocchio (Andrea del), Zuccarelli (Francesco) 11 Ghirlandaio (Domenico), Ghirlandajo (Domenico) 12 Michelangelo (Buonarotti), Parmigianino

Japanese: 5 Korin 6 Sesshu

Lithuanian: 7 Soutine (Chaim)

Mexican: 6 Orozco (Jose), Rivera (Diego), Tamayo (Rufino) 9 Siqueiros (David)

Norwegian: 5 Munch (Edvard)

Russian: 7 Chagall (Marc), Roerich (Nikolay) 9 Kandinsky (Wassily)

Scottish: 6 Ramsay (Allan) 7 Nasmyth (Alexander), Raeburn (Henry)

Spanish: 4 Dalí (Salvador), Goya (Francisco), Gris (Juan), Miró (Joan), Sert (José Maria) 6 Ribera (José), Rincón (Antonio del), Tapiés (Antonio) 7 El Greco, Herrera (Francisco de), Murillo (Bartolomé Esteban), Picasso (Pablo), Zuloaga (Ignacio) 8 Zurbarán (Francisco de) 9 Velázquez (Diego)

Swedish: 4 Zorn (Anders) 6 Roslin (Alexander)

Swiss: 4 Klee (Paul), Witz (Konrad)

painting

3 oil 7 acrylic, picture 10 watercolor

circular: 5 tondo

one-color: 8 monotint 10 monochrome

plaster: 5 secco 6 fresco

style: 4 Dada 5 fauve 6 cubism, cubist, Gothic, pop art, rococo 7 baroque, Bauhaus, dadaism, fauvism, fauvist, realism, realist 8 Barbizon, futurism, futurist, romantic 9 Byzantine, geometric, mannerism, mannerist 10 classicism, classicist, surrealism, surrealist 11 romanticism 13 expressionism, expressionist, impressionism, impressionist

technique: 3 oil 6 fresco, pastel 7 gouache, polymer, tempera 9 encaustic 10 watercolor

tool: 5 brush, easel, knife, paint 6 canvas 7 palette

wall: 5 mural

pair

3 duo, two 4 dyad, join, mate, span, team, twin, yoke 5 brace, match, twins, unite 6 couple 7 doublet, twosome 8 geminate

Pakistan

capital: 9 Islamabad

city: 6 Lahore, Multan 7 Karachi 9 Hyderabad 10 Faisalabad, Rawalpindi

language: 4 Urdu

leader: 6 Bhutto (Benazir)

monetary unit: 5 rupee

mountain, range: 8 Himalaya
9 Himalayan, Himalayas 11 Nanga
Parbat
neighbor: 4 Iran 5 China, India
11 Afghanistan
sea: 7 Arabian

pal
4 chum, mate 5 amigo, buddy, crony
6 comate, friend 7 comrade, partner
9 companion

palace
5 court, manor, manse 6 castle
7 alcazar, château, mansion

paladin
6 leader 8 advocate, champion,
defender, official

Palamedes
brother: 6 Sforza 8 Achilles
father: 8 Nauplius
slayer: 7 Corinda, Ulysses 8 Odysseus

palatable
5 sapid, tasty 6 savory 8 pleasing,
savorous, tasteful 9 agreeable,
appealing, delicious, toothsome
10 acceptable, appetizing 12 satisfactory

palate
5 taste 6 liking 6 relish

palatial
4 rich 5 grand, large, noble, plush,
regal 6 deluxe, ornate 7 opulent,
stately 8 imposing, majestic, splendid 9 grandiose, luxuriant, luxurious,
sumptuous 10 impressive 11 magnificent

Palau
capital: 5 Koror
former name: 5 Pelew
island: 5 Koror 6 Angaur 7 Eli Malk
10 Babelthuap, Urukthapel
language: 7 English, Palauan

palaver
3 gas, yak 4 blab, cant, chat, guff,
talk 6 babble, cajole, hot air, jargon,
parley, powwow, speech 7 chatter,
prattle 8 colloquy, converse, dialogue 10 conference, discussion,
rap session 12 conversation

pale
3 dim, wan 4 area, ashy, dull, fade,
sick, weak 5 ashen, faded, faint,
fence, field, light, livid, pasty, stake,
waxen 6 anemic, blanch, chalky,
doughy, feeble, pallid, picket, sallow,
sickly, weaken, whiten 7 enclose,
ghastly, insipid 8 blanched, district,
encircle 9 bloodless, colorless,
enclosure

palinode
10 retraction 11 recantation

pall
4 bore, cloy, damp, jade, sate, tire
5 cloak, cloth, cloud, drape, ennui,
gloom, weary 6 coffin, damper,
mantle, shadow 7 dwindle, satiate,
surfeit 8 covering

palladium
9 safeguard

Pallas
6 Athena
brother: 6 Aegeus
father: 7 Pandion
slayer: 7 Theseus
wife: 4 Styx
(see also **Athena**)

palliate
4 ease, help 5 cover, salve 6 excuse, lessen, reduce, soften, soothe,
temper 7 assuage, cover up, lighten
8 mitigate, moderate 9 alleviate,
sugarcoat, whitewash 10 ameliorate

pallid
3 wan 4 ashy, dull, pale, weak
5 ashen, pasty, waxen 6 anemic,
doughy, sickly 8 blanched, lifeless
9 bloodless, colorless

pallor
8 lividity, paleness 9 pastiness,
whiteness 10 etiolation 12 glaucousness

pally
4 cozy 5 close, matey 6 chummy
7 devoted 8 familiar, friendly, intimate

palm
5 prize, steal, swipe 6 trophy 7 conceal, triumph, victory
beverage: 4 nipa
fiber: 4 bass, bast 8 piassava
fruit: 4 date 7 coconut 11 coquilla nut
kind: 3 fan, wax 4 coco, date, doom, hemp, nipa, sago 5 areca, betel, ivory, royal 6 raffia, rattan 7 cabbage, feather, palmyra 8 carnauba, palmetto, piassava 12 Washingtonia
leaf: 4 olla 5 frond
starch: 4 sago
vine: 6 rattan

palmer
7 pilgrim

Palmetto State
13 South Carolina

palmistry
6 augury 8 prophecy 10 divination 11 soothsaying

palm off
5 foist 7 deceive, pretend 8 disguise

palmy
6 golden 7 booming, halcyon, opulent 8 affluent, thriving 10 prospering, prosperous 11 flourishing

Palmyra's queen
7 Zenobia

palooka
3 oaf 4 boob, dolt, goon, lout, lump 5 boxer, klutz 6 baboon, galoot, lummox 7 bruiser

palpable
4 real, sure 5 clear, plain 6 patent 7 certain, concrete, evident, obvious, tactile 8 apparent, definite, distinct, manifest, material, positive, tangible 10 noticeable 11 discernible, perceptible, unequivocal

palpate
4 feel 5 touch 6 finger 7 examine

palpitate
4 beat 5 pulse, throb 6 quiver 7 flutter, pulsate 12 pitter-patter

palsy-walsy
4 cozy 5 close, thick, tight 6 chummy 8 intimate 10 buddy-buddy

palter
3 fib, lie 5 evade 6 dicker, haggle 7 bargain, chaffer, deceive, falsify, wrangle 10 equivocate 11 prevaricate 12 misrepresent

paltry
3 low 4 base, mean, poor, puny, vile 5 cheap, petty, tatty 6 meager, measly, narrow, shabby, shoddy, sleazy, trashy 7 low-down, pitiful, trivial 8 beggarly, inferior, picayune, piddling, rubbishy, trifling 9 worthless 10 despicable, picayunish 11 unimportant 12 contemptible 13 insignificant

paludal place
3 fen 5 marsh

Pamela author
10 Richardson (Samuel)

pampa
5 plain 7 prairie 9 grassland

pamper
3 pet 4 baby 5 humor, spoil 6 caress, cocker, coddle, cosset, cuddle, dandle, fondle 7 cater to, cherish, gratify, indulge 9 spoon-feed 11 mollycoddle

pamphlet
5 flier, flyer, tract 6 folder 7 leaflet 8 brochure, circular 9 throwaway 10 broadsheet

pan
3 pot, rap 4 slam, wash 5 basin, knock, roast, trash 6 attack, vessel 7 censure, condemn, skillet 8 denounce, ridicule 9 betel leaf, container, criticism, criticize 10 receptacle

Pan
5 Inuus 6 Faunus
father: 6 Hermes
invention: 6 syrinx
lower part: 4 goat
mother: 8 Penelope

pipe: **6** syrinx
seat of worship: **7** Arcadia
son: **7** Silenus

panacea
4 cure **6** remedy **7** cure-all, nostrum
10 catholicon

Panacea's father
9 Asclepius **11** Aesculapius

panache
4 brio, dash, élan, tuft, zest **5** ardor,
crest, flair, style, verve, vigor **6** esprit,
polish, spirit **8** aigrette, flourish,
vivacity **11** flamboyance

panama
3 hat

Panama
capital: **10** Panama City
discoverer: **6** Balboa (Vasco Núñez
de) **8** Columbus (Christopher)
gulf: **7** San Blas **8** Mosquito
language: **7** Spanish
leader: **7** Noriega (Manuel)
monetary unit: **6** balboa
neighbor: **8** Colombia **9** Costa Rica
peninsula: **6** Azuero
sea: **9** Caribbean
volcano: **8** Chiriquí

pancake
8 flapjack, slapjack
French: **5** crepe
Jewish: **5** latke **6** blintz **7** blintze
Russian: **5** blini

Pandarus
6 archer **8** procuror
father: **6** Lycaon
slayer: **8** Diomedes

pandect
4 code, laws **8** treatise **10** compendium **11** compilation

pandemic
4 rife **7** general, rampant **9** contagion, extensive, prevalent **10** contagious, widespread **11** wide-ranging

pandemonium
3 din **5** babel, chaos, furor **6** bedlam, clamor, hubbub, tumult, uproar
7 anarchy, discord, inferno, misrule,
turmoil **8** disorder **9** confusion
10 hullabaloo

pander
4 pimp **5** cater **9** exploiter, go-
between

Pandion
daughter: **6** Procne **9** Philomela
son: **6** Pallas

Pandora
creator: **10** Hephaestus
husband: **10** Epimetheus

pane
4 side **5** sheet **7** section

panegyric
6 eulogy, praise **7** tribute **8** citation,
encomium **9** laudation **10** compliment **12** commendation

panegyrical
8 praising **9** laudative, laudatory
10 eulogistic **11** encomiastic **12** commendatory **13** complimentary

panel
4 jury **5** board, frame **6** hurdle
7 section **9** dashboard

panfry
5 sauté

pang
4 ache, pain, stab **5** agony, prick,
spasm, throe **6** stitch, twinge **7** anguish, torment **8** distress

Pangloss's pupil
7 Candide

panhandle
3 beg, bum, tap **5** cadge, hit up,
touch **6** hustle **7** solicit

panhandler
6 beggar

panic
4 fear, riot, rush **5** alarm, scare
6 dismay, frenzy, fright, horror, terror
7 anxiety, terrify **8** frighten, hysteria,
stampede

pannier
4 hoop, pack **6** basket, hamper
9 overskirt

panoply
4 pomp, show **5** armor, array **6** attire **7** display, fanfare **9** trappings

panorama
4 view **5** range, reach, scene, scope, sweep, vista **7** display, expanse, picture, purview **12** presentation

panoramic
8 sweeping, synoptic **12** all-inclusive, unobstructed **13** comprehensive

pan out
4 work **5** click, prove, score **7** come off, succeed

pant
4 blow, gasp, gulp, huff, puff **5** chuff, heave **6** wheeze

Pantagruel
5 giant
companion: 7 Panurge
father: 9 Gargantua
mother: 7 Badebec

pantaloon
7 buffoon, trouser

Pantaloon's daughter
9 Columbine

pantheon
4 gods **5** Aesir **6** temple **9** hierarchy **10** hall of fame

panther
4 pard, puma **6** cougar, jaguar **7** leopard **12** mountain lion

pantomime
5 drama, mimic **6** act out, ballet, dancer **7** charade **12** harlequinade
clown: 7 Pierrot

pantry
6 closet, larder **7** buttery **9** storeroom

pants
5 jeans **6** slacks **7** drawers, garment **8** breeches, britches, knickers, trousers

Panurge's companion
10 Pantagruel

Paolo's lover
9 Francesca

pap
4 food, mash, mush **7** aliment, pabulum **8** soft food **9** blandness, nutriment **10** sustenance **11** nourishment

papal
8 pontific **9** apostolic **10** pontifical
court: 5 Curia
decree: 8 decretal
envoy: 6 nuncio
letter: 4 bull **10** encyclical

paper
5 essay, sheet, theme **6** letter, report **7** article **8** document **9** monograph, newsprint **10** memorandum **11** composition, publication **12** dissertation
measure: 4 ream **5** quire
roll: 6 scroll
scrap: 4 chad
size: 3 cap **5** atlas, crown, folio, legal, royal, sexto, sixmo **6** octavo, quarto **7** emperor **8** elephant, foolscap, imperial
stiff: 7 bristol **9** cardboard **12** bristol board
strong: 5 kraft **6** manila
thin: 6 tissue **9** onionskin
transparent: 8 glassine
writing: 3 rag **6** vellum **9** parchment

paper folding
7 origami

paperwork
7 red tape

papillon
7 spaniel **9** butterfly

Papua New Guinea
archipelago: 8 Bismarck
capital: 11 Port Moresby
city: 3 Lae
island: 12 Bougainville
language: 4 Motu **8** Tok Pisin
monetary unit: 4 kina
neighbor: 9 Indonesia, Irian Jaya

par
4 mean, norm **5** equal, score, usual **6** median, normal **7** average, typical **8** equality, standard

parable
4 myth, tale 5 fable, moral, story
7 example 8 allegory

parachute
7 bailout, skydive
part: 5 riser 6 canopy 7 harness,
ripcord

Paraclete
9 Holy Ghost 10 Holy Spirit

parade
4 brag, pomp, show 5 array, boast,
flash, march, shine, strut 6 expose,
flaunt, ground, reveal, review 7 display, disport, exhibit, fanfare, marshal, panoply, show off, trot out
8 brandish, ceremony, movement,
proclaim 9 advertise, cavalcade,
pageantry, promenade 10 exhibition,
masquerade, procession 11 demonstrate

paradigm
5 ideal, model 6 mirror 7 example,
pattern 8 exemplar, standard 9 archetype, beau ideal, framework,
prototype

paradise
4 Eden, Zion 5 bliss 6 heaven,
utopia 7 arcadia, elysium, nirvana
8 empyrean 9 Shangri-la 10 wonderland 12 New Jerusalem, promised land

Paradise Lost author
6 Milton (John)

paragon
3 gem 4 tops 5 champ, cream,
ideal, jewel, match, model, peach,
saint 6 beauty 7 compare, epitome
8 champion, exemplar, last word,
nonesuch, parallel, ultimate 9 archetype, beau ideal, nonpareil 10 apotheosis

Paraguay
capital: 8 Asunción
lake: 4 Ypoá
language: 7 Guarani, Spanish
monetary unit: 7 guarani
neighbor: 6 Brazil 7 Bolivia 9 Argentina
river: 9 Pilcomayo

parallel
4 akin, copy, even, like 5 agree,
align, alike, along, equal, liken,
match 6 double, equate, line up
7 aligned, compare, similar 8 analogue 9 alongside, analogous,
companion, consonant, corollary,
correlate, duplicate 10 comparable,
comparison, correspond, equivalent,
similarity 11 coextensive, counterpart, duplication, resemblance
13 correspondent, corresponding

parallelogram
5 rhomb 6 oblong, square 7 rhombus
8 rhomboid 9 rectangle 13 quadrilateral

paralysis
5 palsy 7 inertia 9 impotence

paralyze
3 awe 4 daze, numb, stun 6 benumb, deaden, dismay 7 cripple,
disable, nonplus, petrify, stupefy
8 shut down 10 immobilize 12 incapacitate

paramount
5 chief, ruler 6 master 7 capital,
leading, primary, regnant, supreme
8 cardinal, crowning, dominant,
foremost, headmost, superior 9 principal, sovereign, uppermost 10 commanding, preeminent 11 predominant

paramour
5 lover, Romeo 7 Don Juan, gallant
8 Casanova, lothario, mistress
9 courtesan, inamorata, inamorato

parapet
4 wall 7 bastion, bulwark, rampart
10 battlement, breastwork
part: 6 merlon 12 crenellation

paraphernalia
4 gear 5 items 6 outfit, tackle
7 effects 8 property 9 equipment,
trappings 10 belongings 11 accessories, furnishings 13 accouterments,
accoutrements, appurtenances

paraphrase
6 reword 7 restate, version 9 interpret, rendering, translate 11 restatement, translation

parasite

5 leech, toady 6 sponge, sucker
7 sponger 8 barnacle, deadbeat,
hanger-on 9 dependent, exploiter,
sycophant 10 freeloader, self-seeker
11 bloodsucker

parasitic

8 sponging, toadying 9 leech-
like 11 freeloading, sycophantic
12 bloodsucking

parasol

8 umbrella

_____ paratus

6 semper

Parcae

5 Fates, Norns 6 Moirai
name: 4 Nona 5 Morta 6 Decuma

parcel

3 box, cut, lot 4 body, deal, land,
mete, pack, part, plot, wrap 5 allot,
array, batch, bunch, group, piece,
share, tract 6 assign, bundle, divide,
packet, ration 7 package, partial,
portion, prorate, section, segment
8 allocate, disburse, disperse,
division, part-time 9 apportion,
partition 10 distribute

parch

3 dry 4 burn, sear 5 dry up, roast,
toast 6 dry out, scorch 7 shrivel
9 dehydrate, desiccate

parched

3 dry 4 arid, sere 5 dusty 7 bone-
dry, thirsty 8 scorched, withered
9 shriveled, waterless 10 dehydrated

parchment

4 skin 5 paper 6 vellum 7 diploma
8 document

pardon

4 free 5 remit, spare 6 excuse, let
off 7 absolve, amnesty, condone,
forgive, release 8 liberate, reprieve,
tolerate 9 acquittal, exculpate,
indemnity, remission 10 absolution,
indulgence 11 exculpation, exoneration, forgiveness

pardonable

6 venial 9 allowable, excusable
11 permissible

pare

3 cut 4 clip, crop, peel, trim 5 lower,
prune, shave 6 reduce, remove
7 curtail, cut back, cut down, trim off,
whittle 8 diminish

parent

4 make, rear 5 beget, cause, hatch,
raise, spawn 6 author, create, father,
mother, origin 7 bring up, care
for, produce 8 begetter, generate
9 originate, procreate 10 progenitor

parenthetically

7 by the by 8 by the bye, by the way
9 in passing 12 incidentally

parentless

6 orphan 8 orphaned

par excellence

3 top 5 prime 7 premier, supreme
8 foremost, peerless, superior
9 number one, unmatched 10 first-
class, preeminent 11 outstanding

pariah

5 leper 7 Ishmael, outcast 8 castaway 10 Ishmaelite 11 offscouring,
untouchable
Japanese: 3 eta

Paris

ancient name: 7 Lutetia
avenue: 13 Champs-Elysées
basilica: 10 Sacré Coeur
cathedral: 9 Notre Dame
city hall: 12 Hôtel de Ville
college: 8 Sorbonne
garden: 9 Tuileries 10 Luxembourg
island: 11 Île de la Cité
museum: 5 Cluny 6 Louvre
palace: 6 Louvre 7 Bourbon
patron saint: 9 Geneviève
racecourse: 7 Auteuil
river: 5 Seine
section: 8 Left Bank 9 Right Bank
10 Montmartre 12 Latin Quarter
stock exchange: 6 Bourse
subway: 5 Métro
tower: 6 Eiffel

Paris
  beloved: **5** Helen
  betrothed: **6** Juliet
  father: **5** Priam
  mother: **6** Hecuba
  slayer: **11** Philoctetes
  wife: **6** Oenone

parish
  6 county **8** district **9** community
  12 congregation, neighborhood

Parisina
  author: **5** Byron (Lord)
  husband: **3** Azo
  lover: **4** Hugo
  slayer: **3** Azo

parity
  8 equality, sameness, symmetry
  10 similarity, similitude **11** equivalence, equivalency, parallelism

park
  4 stop **5** green, plaza **7** deposit,
  funfair, reserve **8** carnival, preserve
  9 esplanade **11** reservation

parka
  6 anorak, jacket **7** garment **8** pullover **9** outerwear

park designer
  4 Vaux (Calvert) **6** Paxton (Joseph)
  7 Alphand (Jean), Le Nôtre (André),
  Olmsted (Frederick Law)

parlance
  4 talk **5** idiom, style, usage **6** phrase,
  speech **7** wording **8** language,
  locution, phrasing **9** verbalism
  11 phraseology

parlay
  3 bet **4** risk **5** bid up, boost, stake,
  wager **6** expand, extend, hazard
  7 build up, enhance, enlarge, exploit, venture **8** increase, leverage
  9 transform

parley
  4 talk **5** speak **6** confab, confer,
  huddle, powwow **7** discuss, meeting
  8 colloquy, converse, dialogue
  9 discourse, negotiate **10** conference, discussion **11** confabulate
  12 conversation **13** confabulation

parliament
  see **legislature**

parlor
  4 room **5** salon **11** drawing room
  13 reception room

parlous
  5 hairy, risky **6** chancy, unsafe
  8 critical **9** dangerous, hazardous
  10 precarious

Parnassian
  4 poet **6** poetic

parochial
  5 local **6** narrow **7** insular, limited
  9 sectarian, small-town **10** provincial, restricted

parody
  3 rib **4** mock **5** mimic, spoof **6** satire
  7 imitate, lampoon, mockery, takeoff
  8 ridicule, travesty **9** burlesque,
  imitation **10** caricature

parole
  4 free, word **6** let out, pledge **7** promise, release **9** discharge, probation,
  watchword **11** performance

paronomasia
  3 pun **11** play on words

paroxysm
  3 fit **4** bout **5** spasm, throe **6** attack,
  frenzy **7** flare-up, seizure **8** eruption, outbreak, outburst **9** explosion
  10 conniption, convulsion

parrot
  3 ape **4** aper, copy, echo **5** mimic
  6 repeat **7** chatter, copycat, imitate
  kind: **3** ara, kea **4** kaka, lory **5** macaw **6** Amazon, budgie, kakapo
  8 cockatoo, lorikeet, lovebird, parakeet **9** cockatiel **10** budgerigar

parrot fever
  11 psittacosis

parry
  4 duck, fend **5** avert, avoid, block,
  dodge, elude, evade **7** counter,
  deflect, evasion, fend off, prevent,
  respond, ward off **8** sidestep, stave
  off **9** turn aside **10** circumvent

parse

4 scan 7 analyze, dissect, examine, resolve 8 construe 9 anatomize, explicate, interpret

Parsi

11 Zoroastrian

Parsifal

composer: 6 Wagner (Richard)
magician: 8 Klingsor
quest: 5 Grail
son: 9 Lohengrin
temptress: 6 Kundry

parsimonious

4 mean 5 cheap, close, tight 6 frugal, stingy 7 chintzy, miserly, sparing, thrifty 9 penurious 10 restrained 11 closefisted, tightfisted 13 penny-pinching

parsley

4 herb 7 garnish
family: 6 carrot
piece: 5 sprig

parson

6 cleric, pastor, rector 8 clerical, minister, preacher, reverend 9 clergyman 12 ecclesiastic

parsonage

5 manse 7 rectory

part

3 bit, cut 4 chip, unit 5 chunk, piece, quota, scrap, sever, share, slice 6 detail, divide, member, moiety, ration, sector 7 element, measure, portion, quantum, quarter, section, segment 8 division, fraction, fragment, function, separate 9 component

partake

3 eat 5 savor, share 6 accept, sample 7 acquire, consume, receive 9 enter into 11 participate

Parthenon

sculptor: 7 Phidias 8 Pheidias
sculpture: 6 frieze
site: 9 Acropolis

partial

6 biased, unfair, warped 7 colored, half-way 8 inclined, one-sided 9 jaundiced 10 fractional, incomplete, prejudiced 11 fragmentary, predisposed

partiality

4 bent, bias 5 favor, taste 6 liking 7 leaning 8 affinity, fondness, tendency 10 favoritism, preference 11 inclination 12 one-sidedness, predilection

participant

5 party 6 fellow, member, player, sharer 7 partner, sharing 11 contributor, shareholder

participate

4 join, play 5 share 6 engage, join in 7 partake 8 take part

particle

3 ace, bit, dot, jot, tad 4 atom, doit, dram, drop, hint, hoot, iota, mite, mote, spot, whit 5 atomy, crumb, fleck, grain, minim, ounce, scrap, shred, speck 6 morsel, tittle 7 granule, modicum, smidgen, soupçon 8 fragment 9 scintilla
atomic: 3 ion 5 anion 6 cation
elementary: 3 psi, tau 4 kaon, muon, pion 5 boson, meson 6 baryon, hadron, lambda, lepton, photon, proton 7 fermion, hyperon, neutron, nucleon, upsilon 8 electron, mesotron, neutrino, positron
hypothetical: 5 gluon, quark 6 parton 8 graviton
virus: 6 virion
with negative charge: 8 electron
with positive charge: 6 proton 8 positron

particular

3 one 4 fact, full, item, lone 5 exact, fussy, picky, point, thing 6 detail, marked, minute, single, unique 7 careful, correct, element, feature, finicky, notable, precise, several, special, unusual 8 accurate, concrete, detailed, distinct, especial, exacting, itemized, separate, solitary, specific, uncommon 10 blow-by-blow, fastidious, individual, meticu-

lous, pernickety, scrupulous **11** distinctive, exceptional, persnickety, punctilious **12** circumstance

particularize
4 list **6** detail **7** catalog, itemize, specify **8** spell out **9** enumerate, inventory **13** individualize

parting
4 last **5** adieu, break, congé, final **6** good-by **7** good-bye **8** division, farewell **10** divergence, separation **11** leave-taking, valedictory

partisan
6 backer, biased, warped **7** devotee, die-hard, fanatic, patriot, sectary **8** adherent, advocate, disciple, follower, one-sided, stalwart, upholder **9** factional, guerrilla, irregular, satellite, sectarian, supporter

partition
4 wall **6** divide, screen **7** divider, section, wall off **8** disunion, division, fence off, separate **10** separation

partner
4 ally, chum, mate **5** buddy, crony **6** cohort, fellow **7** comrade **8** confrere, sidekick **9** assistant, associate, colleague, companion **10** accomplice **11** confederate

partnership
4 firm **5** union **7** cahoots, company, sharing **8** alliance, business, marriage, relation **11** affiliation, association, combination **12** consociation, togetherness **13** participation

parturient
6 gravid, parous **8** enceinte, pregnant **9** expecting

parturition
5 birth **8** delivery **10** childbirth **12** childbearing

party
4 ball, band, bash, bevy, bloc, crew, fete, gala, orgy, side **5** actor, corps, covey, feast, group, revel, troop **6** fiesta, frolic, kegger, mortal, person, social, soiree, troupe **7** blowout,

carouse, faction, roister, shindig **8** carousal, litigant, wingding **9** bacchanal, gathering, make merry, raise hell **10** detachment, individual, saturnalia **11** bacchanalia, celebration, participant

parvenu
7 upstart **9** arriviste **12** nouveau riche

Pascal essay
6 Pensée

Pasiphaë
daughter: **7** Ariadne, Phaedra
husband: **5** Minos
son: **8** Minotaur

pass
3 die, end **4** fare, hand **5** cease, lapse, occur, relay, spend, while **6** crisis, depart, elapse, exceed, expire, hand on, happen, permit, push on, slight, slip by, strait **7** come off, develop, journey, proceed, succumb **8** bequeath, fork over, hand down, juncture, outshine, outstrip, transmit **9** while away
Afghanistan: **5** Murgh
Afghanistan-Pakistan: **6** Khyber
Alaska: **5** White
Alps: **3** col **5** Cenis, Loibl **7** Brenner, Ljubelj, Simplon **9** St. Bernard
California: **5** Cajon
China-India: **9** Karakoram
Colorado: **3** Ute
Pakistan: **5** Kilik
Russian: **12** Caspian Gates
Tennessee: **10** Cumberland
Turkey: **13** Cilician Gates

passable
4 okay, open, so-so **6** decent **8** adequate, all right **9** tolerable, unblocked **10** accessible, good enough **12** satisfactory

passably
6 enough **8** all right, somewhat **10** moderately

passage
3 way **4** exit, fare, hall, path, text **5** route, shift **6** access, arcade, avenue, course, egress, strait, travel,

tunnel, voyage **7** channel, excerpt, hallway, journey, transit **8** corridor, transfer, traverse **9** enactment, quotation **10** transition **11** transmittal **12** transference, transmission
air: **7** windway
arched: **6** arcade
Atlantic-Pacific: **9** Northwest
roofed: **6** arcade **9** breezeway

Passage to India author
7 Forster (E. M.)

pass away
3 die, end **6** demise, depart, elapse, expire, perish **7** decease, succumb **9** disappear

pass by
4 miss, omit **6** forget, ignore **7** neglect **8** overlook **9** disregard

passé
4 dead **5** dated, stale **6** démodé, old hat **7** demoded, disused, extinct, outworn **8** obsolete, outdated, outmoded **9** out-of-date **10** antiquated, superseded **12** old-fashioned

passel
3 lot **4** heap, pack **5** bunch **6** bundle **9** multitude

passing
5 brief, death, quick **6** demise, highly **7** cursory, decease **8** fleeting **9** ephemeral, fugacious, extremely, momentary, transient **10** evanescent, short-lived, transitory **11** exceedingly, superficial **12** satisfactory

passion
4 fire, fury, heat, itch, love, lust, rage, urge, zeal **5** agony, amour, anger, ardor, craze, crush, drive **6** desire, fervor, hunger **7** avidity, craving, ecstasy, emotion, feeling, rapture **8** appetite, devotion, outburst, yearning **9** affection, eagerness, suffering, transport **10** enthusiasm, excitement, heartthrob **11** amorousness, infatuation

passionate
3 hot **5** angry, fiery **6** ardent, fer-

vid, heated **7** amorous, aroused, blazing, burning, excited, fervent, furious, intense **8** incensed, vehement **9** impetuous, steamed up **10** hot-blooded, stimulated **11** hot-tempered **12** enthusiastic **13** quick-tempered

passive
4 idle **5** inert **6** docile, latent **8** enduring, immobile, inactive, listless, resigned, yielding **9** apathetic, compliant, lethargic, quiescent **10** motionless, nonviolent, phlegmatic, submissive **11** acquiescent, complaisant, indifferent, unresistant

pass out
3 die **5** faint, swoon **7** divvy up **8** disburse, keel over **10** distribute

pass over
4 miss, omit, skip **6** forget, ignore **7** dismiss, neglect **8** discount, leave out **9** disregard

Passover
5 Pasch **6** Pesach
bread: **5** matzo **6** matzoh
meal: **5** seder

pass up
5 forgo **6** refuse, reject **7** decline

past
3 ago, old **4** gone, late, once, yore **5** above, after, prior **6** beyond, bygone, former, whilom **7** onetime, quondam **8** anterior, foretime, lang syne, previous, sometime **9** antiquity, erstwhile, foregoing, precedent, preceding, yesterday **10** antecedent, yesteryear

pasta
5 dough
kind: **4** ziti **7** gnocchi, lasagna, ravioli **8** linguine, linguini, macaroni, rigatoni **9** canneloni, fettucine, fettucini, manicotti, spaghetti **10** cannelloni, fettuccine, fettuccini, tortellini, vermicelli **11** cappelletti

paste
3 fix, hit **4** beat, clay, drub, food,

glue, sock **5** affix, dough, pound, stick, stuff **6** adhere, attach, cement, defeat, fasten, thrash, wallop **7** trounce **8** adhesive, material

Pasternak hero
7 Zhivago (Dr.)

pastiche
4 olio **6** jumble, medley **7** farrago, mélange, mixture **8** mishmash **9** potpourri **10** assortment, hodgepodge, hotchpotch, miscellany, salmagundi **11** gallimaufry

pastime
4 game **5** hobby, sport **9** amusement, diversion **10** recreation **13** entertainment

past master
4 whiz **5** adept, maven **6** expert, wizard **9** authority

pastor
5 padre **6** cleric, parson **8** minister, preacher, reverend, sky pilot **9** clergyman

pastoral
5 idyll, rural **6** rustic **7** bucolic, country, crosier, idyllic **8** agrarian, clerical, innocent, peaceful **10** campestral

pastor's assistant
6 curate

pastry
3 bun, pie **4** baba, cake, flan, tart **5** torte **6** cornet, Danish, éclair, gâteau, pirogi **7** baklava, beignet, bouchée, dariole, fritter, gâteaux (plural), palmier, savarin, strudel, tartlet **8** napoleon, papillon, piroshki, pirozhki, turnover **9** barquette, cream puff, madeleine, petit four, vol-au-vent **10** cheesecake **11** profiterole **12** millefeuille
kind: 4 filo, puff **5** flaky **6** phyllo
shell: 7 timbale **8** meringue

pasture
3 lea, ley **4** feed, land **5** field, grass, graze **6** browse, meadow **9** grassland

pasty
3 wan **4** pale **6** doughy, pallid, sickly **7** meat pie **8** turnover **9** unhealthy

pat
3 apt, dab, set **4** firm **5** fixed, slice, stiff, trite **6** dead-on **7** apropos, fitting **8** apposite, standard, suitable **9** contrived, pertinent, rehearsed

patch
3 bit, fix **4** area, fill, mend, plot **5** cover, piece, scrap, spell **6** doctor, emblem, fill up, repair, shield **7** connect, plaster **8** material **10** connection

patchwork
4 olio **5** quilt **6** jumble **7** mixture **8** covering, mishmash, mixed bag **10** assortment, hodgepodge, hotchpotch, miscellany, salmagundi

patchy
6 fitful, random, spotty, uneven **7** erratic **8** sporadic **9** haphazard, hit-or-miss, irregular **12** intermittent

pate
4 bean, dome, head, poll **5** brain, crown **6** noddle, noggin, noodle

pâté de _____
8 foie gras

patella
7 kneecap, kneepan

patent
4 open **5** clear, plain, right **6** secure **7** evident, license, obvious, visible **8** apparent, distinct, manifest, unclosed **9** exclusive, privilege, prominent, protected **11** proprietary **12** intelligible, unobstructed

paternal
8 fatherly
relative: 6 agnate

paternity
7 lineage **8** ancestry **10** fatherhood, provenance **11** progenitors

Pater Noster
9 Our Father

path
3 way 4 lane, line, road, tack, walk
5 byway, orbit, route, track, trail
6 avenue, bridle, course 7 passage,
walkway 9 direction 10 trajectory

pathetic
3 sad 4 poor 5 sorry 6 absurd,
moving, paltry, rueful 7 piteous,
pitiful, risible, useless 8 inferior,
pitiable, poignant, touching 9 affecting, laughable, miserable 10 inadequate, lamentable, ridiculous

Pathfinder
author: 6 Cooper (James Fenimore)
hero: 6 Bumppo (Natty)

pathogen
4 germ 5 virus 9 bacterium

pathological
7 deviant 8 aberrant, abnormal,
diseased, maniacal, schizoid 9 psychotic

pathos
4 pity 7 emotion 8 sympathy 9 poi-
gnance, poignancy

pathway
4 line, walk 5 route, track, trail
6 course 7 channel, conduit, network, passage

patience
4 cool 8 calmness, stoicism 9 composure, endurance 10 equanimity,
sufferance 11 forbearance, resignation, self-control

Patience
composer: 8 Sullivan (Arthur)
librettist: 7 Gilbert (W. S.)

patient
4 case, meek 8 enduring 9 easygoing 10 persistent 11 susceptible
13 long-suffering
man: 3 Job

patina
4 aura, coat, film 6 finish, polish
7 coating 8 covering 10 appearance, coloration

patio
5 court 6 atrium 7 terrace 9 courtyard

patois
4 cant 5 argot, lingo, slang 6 jargon 7 dialect 10 colloquial, vernacular

patriarch
4 sire 6 father 7 creator, founder
9 architect, graybeard
biblical: 5 David, Isaac, Jacob
7 Abraham

patrician
5 noble 6 aristo 9 blue blood,
gentleman 10 aristocrat, upper-class

patriciate
5 elite 6 gentry 9 blue blood, gentility 10 upper crust 11 aristocracy

patrimony
6 estate, legacy 8 heritage 9 endowment 10 birthright 11 inheritance

patriot
5 jingo 8 jingoist, loyalist 9 flag-
waver 10 chauvinist 11 nationalist

patriotism
8 jingoism 10 chauvinism 11 nationalism

Patroclus
friend: 8 Achilles
slayer: 6 Hector

patrol
5 guard, round, scout, troop, watch
7 protect 8 sentinel 9 keep watch

patrolman
3 cop 5 guard 6 police 7 officer

patrol wagon
see **paddy wagon**

patron
5 angel 6 backer, client 7 sponsor
8 customer, guardian 9 protector,
supporter 10 benefactor

patronage
4 help 5 aegis, trade 6 custom
7 backing, subsidy, support, traffic
8 activity, advocacy, auspices, business, cronyism 9 clientage, clientele, influence 10 pork barrel, protection 11 benefaction, sponsorship
12 guardianship

patronize
3 aid, use **4** back **5** deign, favor **6** assist, shop at **7** protect, support **8** frequent **10** condescend

patron saint
of beggars, cripples: 5 Giles
of children: 8 Nicholas
of England: 6 George
of fishermen: 5 Peter
of France: 5 Denis
of Ireland: 7 Patrick
of lawyers: 4 Ives
of musicians: 7 Cecilia
of Norway: 4 Olaf
of physicians: 4 Luke
of sailors: 4 Elmo **8** Nicholas
of Scotland: 6 Andrew
of shoemakers: 7 Crispin
of Spain: 5 James **8** Santiago
of Wales: 5 David
of winegrowers: 7 Vincent
of workers: 6 Joseph

patsy
3 sap **4** dupe, fool, mark **5** chump **6** pigeon, sucker, victim **8** easy mark, pushover

patter
4 cant **5** argot, lingo, slang, spiel **6** babble, jargon, patois **7** chatter, prattle

pattern
4 copy, form, plan **5** guide, ideal, model, motif, order, shape **6** design, figure, follow, method, mirror, system **7** diagram, emulate, example, imitate **8** exemplar, grouping, paradigm, standard, template **9** archetype, incidence, prototype **10** flight path **11** arrangement, orderliness **12** distribution **13** configuration

paucity
4 lack, want **6** dearth **7** poverty **8** scarcity, shortage **9** scantness, smallness **10** deficiency, meagerness, meagreness **13** insufficiency

_____ Paulo
3 São

Paul the Apostle
birthplace: 6 Tarsus

companion: 5 Silas, Titus **7** Artemas, Timothy **8** Barnabas
original name: 4 Saul
place of conversion: 8 Damascus
prosecutor: 9 Tertullus
teacher: 8 Gamaliel
tribe: 8 Benjamin

paunch
3 gut, pot **5** belly, tummy **7** abdomen, stomach **8** potbelly **9** bay window, beer belly **11** breadbasket

paunchy
3 fat **5** beefy, plump, tubby **6** chunky, portly, rotund **8** thickset **10** overweight, potbellied

pauper
6 beggar **7** have-not **8** bankrupt, indigent **9** mendicant

pauperism
4 need, ruin, want **6** penury **7** beggary, poverty **9** indigence, neediness, privation **11** destitution

pause
3 gap **4** halt, hush, lull, rest, stop, wait **5** break, comma, delay, lapse, letup **6** hiatus, linger, recess **7** caesura, respite, time out **8** breather, hesitate, inaction, interval, take five **9** cessation, interlude **10** hesitation, suspension **12** intermission, interruption

pave
3 lay, tar **5** cover **7** asphalt, surface **8** blacktop, concrete

pavement
6 tarmac **7** asphalt, macadam, surface **8** concrete, sidewalk

pavilion
4 tent **5** kiosk **6** canopy, gazebo **9** belvedere **11** summerhouse

paw
4 feel, foot, grab, hand **5** grope, touch **6** fondle, handle, molest, scrape

pawn
4 hock, tool **6** pledge, puppet, stooge, victim **7** deposit, hostage, warrant **8** guaranty, security **9** guarantee **10** chess piece, instrument

pax
5 peace 6 tablet

Pax _____
3 Dei 6 Romana 10 Britannica

pay
3 fee 4 wage 5 clear, offer, remit, serve, spend 6 answer, defray, employ, expend, kick in, lay out, pony up, profit, render, return, salary, settle, square, tender, reward 7 benefit, bring in, cough up, forfeit, fork out, requite, satisfy, stipend 8 defrayal, disburse, earnings, shell out 9 discharge, emolument, indemnify, liquidate, reimburse 10 compensate, recompense, remunerate 12 compensation, remuneration

payable
3 due 4 owed 5 owing 6 mature, unpaid 7 overdue 9 unsettled 10 obligatory 11 outstanding, uncollected

paycheck
5 wages 6 salary

payload
4 haul 5 cargo, goods 6 burden, lading, weight 7 freight, tonnage 8 shipment

payment
3 fee 4 dues 5 award, money 6 amends, outlay, return, reward 7 penance 8 defrayal, requital 11 restitution 12 compensation, remuneration, satisfaction

payoff
3 fix 5 bribe 6 climax, profit, result, reward, upshot 7 outcome 8 clincher, decisive 10 conclusion, conclusive, denouement 11 retribution

payola
5 bribe

PDQ
4 ASAP 6 at once, pronto 8 directly, right now, right off 9 forthwith, instanter, instantly, right away 11 immediately, straightway 12 straightaway

peace
3 pax 4 calm, ease, pact 5 amity, order, quiet 6 accord, repose 7 concord, harmony, silence 8 serenity 11 tranquility 12 tranquillity

peaceable
6 dovish, irenic 7 amiable, pacific 8 amicable, friendly, pacifist, tranquil 10 nonviolent 11 complaisant 12 conciliatory

peaceful
4 calm 5 still, quiet 6 irenic, placid, serene 7 equable, pacific 8 composed, tranquil 9 unruffled 10 harmonious, nonviolent, untroubled

peacemaker
7 arbiter 8 mediator, pacifier, placater 10 arbitrator, negotiator 11 conciliator, pacificator

peace officer
3 cop 6 police 9 policeman 11 policewoman

peach
3 rat 4 blab, tree 5 fruit 6 betray, inform, reveal, snitch, squeal 9 freestone, humdinger, nectarine 10 clingstone 11 crackerjack
family: 4 rose

Peach State
7 Georgia

peachy
4 fine, good, nice 5 dandy, nifty, super, swell 8 pleasant, pleasing 9 excellent, hunky-dory, marvelous, wonderful

peacockish
5 showy, swank 6 chichi, flashy, swanky 7 splashy 8 show-offy 10 flamboyant 11 pretentious 12 ostentatious

peak
3 alp, top, tor 4 acme, apex, bill, crag, roof 5 crest, crown, mount, visor 6 apogee, summit, vertex, zenith 8 capsheaf, capstone, meridian, mountain, pinnacle
Adirondack: 9 Whiteface

Africa's highest: 4 Kibo
Alaska-Canada: 12 Mt. Saint Elias
Andes: 4 Ruiz 5 Torrá
Apennines: 5 Amaro
Argentina: 4 Azul 5 Negra, Payún
Bavaria: 5 Arber
Berkshires: 8 Greylock
Black Hills: 8 Rushmore
Bolivia: 5 Cuzco, Tahua, Ubina
6 Sajama
Borneo: 4 Raja
California: 6 Shasta, Sonora
7 Palomar, Whitney 8 Half Dome
9 Excelsior
Canada: 5 Keele
Canaries: 5 Teide 8 Tenerife
Carpathian: 4 Rysy
Cascades: 7 Rainier
Catskill: 6 Pisgah
Caucasus: 5 Ushba 6 Elbrus
Chile: 4 Mayo, Pili 5 Paine, Pular
Colombia: 4 Tama 5 Neiva
Colorado: 3 Ute 5 Pikes 9 Purgatory
Cuba: 8 Turquino
Ecuador: 10 Chimborazo
England: 11 Scafell Pike
Ethiopia: 4 Guna 5 Holla
France: 5 Pilat
French Guiana: 5 Amana
Georgia: 8 Springer
Glacier National Park: 8 Kootenai
Greece: 4 Ossa 5 Pelion
Himalayas: 3 Api 5 Kamet 6 Lhotse
10 Gasherbrum
Honshū: 4 Yari 10 Yarigatake
Idaho: 11 Pend Oreille
Iran: 8 Damavand
Italy: 4 Etna 8 Vesuvius
Japan: 4 Sobo 5 Oyama 7 Sobozan
Java: 6 Slamet
Jordan: 6 Gilead
Karakoram Range: 7 Dapsang
10 Masherbrum 12 Godwin Austen
Maine: 8 Katahdin 10 Saddleback
Montana: 8 Gallatin
Nevada: 3 Ely
Newfoundland: 9 Gros Morne
New Hampshire: 9 Monadnock
New Zealand: 3 Una 4 Cook
7 Aorangi 8 Aspiring

Oahu: 5 Kaala
Oregon: 4 Hood
Papua New Guinea: 8 Victoria
Pennine Alps: 10 Matterhorn, Mont Cervin
Philippines: 4 High
Pyrenees: 11 de Vignemale
Russia's highest: 6 Elbrus
Scotland: 8 Ben Nevis
Sicily: 4 Etna
Spain: 5 Yelmo 8 Mulhacén
Switzerland: 3 Dom 4 Dôle, Tödi
5 Eiger, Mönch 6 La Dôle, Rusein
7 Pilatus 8 Jungfrau
Tanzania: 11 Kilimanjaro
Utah: 5 Kings
Venezuela: 5 Icutú
Vermont: 8 Haystack, Stratton
8 Ascutney 9 Mansfield
Washington: 7 Olympus, Rainier
11 Saint Helens
White Mts.: 10 Washington
Wyoming: 3 Elk 10 Grand Teton
Yukon: 4 King 5 Logan

peaked
3 ill, wan 4 ashy, pale, sick 5 acute,
ashen, drawn, sharp 6 ailing, pallid,
sickly 7 pointed 9 emaciated

peal
4 bell, bong, ring, toll 5 chime, knell,
sound 7 ringing 8 ding-dong

peanut
6 goober, legume 10 foam pellet

pear
4 Bosc 5 Anjou, Hardy 6 Comice,
Garber, Seckel 7 Kieffer, LeConte
8 Bartlett
cider: 5 perry

pearl
3 gem 4 dear 5 jewel 7 paragon
8 treasure

Pearl Mosque site
4 Agra

pearly
8 lustrous, nacreous, precious
10 iridescent, opalescent

pear-shaped
8 pyriform

peasant
4 carl, kern, peon, serf 5 churl
6 rustic 7 bumpkin, hayseed, villein
Arab: 6 fellah
Latin-American: 9 campesino
Russian: 6 muzhik

peccary
8 javelina
genus: 7 Tayassu

peck
3 lot, nag 4 buss, carp, fuss, heap,
kiss, load, mess, pile, poke 6 carp
at, nibble, pick at, pick up, pierce,
strike 8 quantity

pecking order
6 ladder 7 pyramid 9 food chain,
hierarchy

peculate
5 steal 8 embezzle 9 defalcate
11 appropriate

peculiar
3 odd 4 rare 5 queer, weird 6 unique
7 bizarre, curious, oddball, offbeat,
special, strange, unusual 8 abnormal, singular, specific, uncommon
9 eccentric 10 individual, particular
11 distinctive

peculiarity
4 mark 5 quirk, trait 6 oddity 7 feature, quality 8 property 9 attribute,
character, mannerism 12 eccentricity, idiosyncrasy

pecuniary
6 fiscal 8 economic, monetary
9 financial

pedagogue
5 tutor 6 pedant 7 teacher 8 educator 12 schoolmaster

pedagogy
8 teaching 9 education

pedal
5 lever 7 bicycle, treadle
digit: 3 toe

pedant
7 teacher 9 formalist 10 school-
marm 12 precisionist

pedantic
3 dry 4 arid, dull 6 stodgy 7 bookish, donnish, erudite, learned, tedious 8 academic, didactic, priggish
9 ponderous 10 pedestrian, scholastic 11 pedagogical 13 unimaginative

peddle
4 hawk, push, sell, vend 5 pitch
6 monger 8 huckster

peddler
6 coster, dealer, hawker, monger,
vendor 8 huckster, merchant, promoter 9 tradesman 12 costermonger

pedestal
4 base, foot 5 stand 7 footing,
support 10 foundation 12 underpinning
part: 4 dado 6 plinth 7 subbase

pedestrian
4 blah, dull 5 banal 6 dreary,
stodgy, walker 7 humdrum, mundane, prosaic 8 everyday, ordinary
11 commonplace 13 unimaginative

pedigree
6 origin, purity 7 descent, history, lineage 8 ancestry, purebred
9 bloodline, genealogy 10 background, extraction, family tree

peduncle
4 stem 5 stalk 7 pedicel

peek
3 spy 4 look 6 glance 7 glimpse

peel
4 bark, pare, rind, skin 5 flake,
scale, strip 7 take off 8 flake off
9 break away, exfoliate

peeled
4 bare, open 5 naked 7 denuded,
exposed 8 stripped 9 uncovered

peep
3 see, spy 4 look 5 chirp, tweet,
watch 6 glance, squeak 7 glimpse,
twitter 9 sandpiper

Peeping Tom
5 snoop 6 voyeur 7 prowler, snooper

peer
3 pry 4 gaze, lord 5 equal, glare, noble, stare 6 goggle, squint 9 associate
British: 4 duke, earl 5 baron 7 marquis 8 marquess, viscount

Peer Gynt
author: 5 Ibsen (Henrik)
beloved: 7 Solveig
composer: 5 Grieg (Edvard)
mother: 3 Ase 4 Aase

peerless
4 best 6 unique 7 perfect, supreme 8 superior 9 matchless, nonpareil, paramount, unequaled, unmatched, unrivaled 12 incomparable, unparalleled

peeve
3 bug, irk, vex 4 miff, rile 5 anger, annoy, pique 6 bother, nettle, put out 7 disturb, provoke 8 irritate, nuisance, vexation 9 aggravate, annoyance, grievance 10 exasperate 11 aggravation

peevish
4 sour 5 cross, testy 6 cranky, grumpy, ornery 7 fretful, whining 8 petulant 9 fractious, irritable, obstinate, querulous 11 ill-tempered

peewee
4 runt, tyke 5 dwarf, pygmy, small 6 midget, shaver, shrimp, squirt 9 miniature 10 diminutive, flycatcher 11 lilliputian

Peewee _____
5 Reese

peg
3 fix, pin 4 hold, mark, plod, plug, step, work 5 dowel, place, prong, stake, throw 6 attach, degree, fasten, hustle, marker, reason 7 pin down, pretext, support 8 identify, restrict

Pegasus
5 horse, steed
rider: 11 Bellerophon

pejorative
7 adverse 8 critical, debasing 9 slighting 10 belittling, derogatory, detractive 11 denigrating, deprecatory, disparaging, opprobrious, unfavorable 12 depreciatory

pelagic
6 marine 7 oceanic 8 maritime

Peleus
brother: 7 Telamon
father: 6 Aeacus
half brother: 6 Phocus
son: 8 Achilles
victim: 8 Eurytion
wife: 6 Thetis

pelf
4 loot, swag 5 booty, money, moola 6 boodle, moolah, riches, spoils 7 plunder

Pelias
country: 6 Iolcus
father: 8 Poseidon
half brother: 5 Aeson
son: 7 Acastus

Pelican State
9 Louisiana

Pelléas
beloved: 9 Mélisande
brother, slayer: 6 Golaud

Pelles
daughter: 6 Elaine
grandson: 7 Galahad

pellet
3 wad 4 ball, shot 6 sphere 10 projectile

Pellinore
slayer: 6 Gawain
son: 5 Torre 6 Dornar 7 Lamerok 8 Percival 9 Agglovale

pell-mell
5 chaos, snarl 6 muddle, rashly 7 chaotic, clutter, hastily 8 confused, disarray, disorder, headlong, reckless 9 confusion, haphazard, hurriedly 10 carelessly, heedlessly 11 hurryscurry 13 helter-skelter

pellucid
5 clear, plain, sheer 6 limpid 7 crystal, evident, obvious 8 clear-cut,

luminous **9** unblurred **10** see-through **11** crystalline, transparent

Pelops
  father: 8 Tantalus
  son: 6 Atreus **8** Pittheus, Thyestes
  wife: 10 Hippodamia

pelota
  4 ball **7** jai alai

pelt
  3 fur, run **4** beat, blow, dash, drub, hide, hurl, rush, skin, whop **5** hurry, pound, scoot, speed, strip, throw, whack **6** assail, batter, pepper, pummel, strike, wallop **7** bombard, hotfoot

pen
  3 sty **4** cage, coop, jail, swan **5** pound, quill, write **6** cooler, corral, indite, prison, shut in, stylus, writer **7** close in, confine, enclose, fence in **9** ballpoint, enclosure

penal
  8 punitive **12** correctional, disciplinary

penalize
  4 dock, fine **5** mulct **6** punish **7** deprive **8** handicap **10** discipline **12** disadvantage

penalty
  4 fine, loss **5** mulct **7** damages, forfeit **8** hardship **10** amercement, forfeiture, punishment **12** disadvantage

penance
  4 rite **7** penalty **8** hardship **9** atonement **10** punishment

penchant
  4 bent **5** taste **6** liking **7** leaning **8** affinity, fondness, tendency **9** inclining **10** partiality, proclivity, propensity **11** inclination **12** predilection

pendant
  4 flag, jack, rope **7** fixture **8** ornament **10** supplement

pendent
  7 hanging **9** suspended, undecided, unsettled **11** overhanging **12** undetermined

pending
  6 during **8** awaiting, imminent **9** undecided, unsettled **12** undetermined

_____ Pendragon
  5 Uther

pendulous
  7 hanging **8** dangling, drooping, wavering **9** faltering, suspended, tentative, uncertain **10** hesitating, indecisive **11** vacillating

Penelope
  father: 7 Icarius
  father-in-law: 7 Laertes
  husband: 7 Ulysses **8** Odysseus
  mother: 8 Periboea
  son: 10 Telemachus
  suitor: 7 Agelaus

penetrable
  6 porous **8** pervious **9** permeable

penetrate
  3 jab **4** bore, go in, stab **5** break, drive, enter, probe, touch **6** affect, charge, invade, pierce **7** pervade **8** discover, encroach, perceive, permeate, puncture, saturate **9** percolate, perforate **10** understand

penetrating
  4 keen **5** acute, sharp **6** astute, shrewd **8** incisive, piercing **9** trenchant **10** discerning, insightful, perceptive **11** quick-witted, sharp-witted **12** sharp-sighted

Peneus
  daughter: 6 Daphne
  father: 7 Oceanus
  mother: 6 Tethys

penguin type
  6 Adélie

_____ Penh
  5 Phnom

peninsula
  4 neck **10** chersonese
  Alaska: 5 Kenai **6** Seward
  Australia: 6 Tasman
  Barents Sea: 5 Kanin
  British colony: 9 Gibraltar

Canada: 8 Labrador
Chile: 5 Swett
Costa Rica: 3 Osa
Croatia: 6 Istria
Denmark: 7 Jutland
eastern United States: 8 Delmarva
Estonia: 5 Sorve
Florida: 8 Pinellas 9 Canaveral
France: 5 Giens
Greece: 4 Acte 10 Chalcidice
11 Peloponnese 12 Peloponnesus
Guam: 5 Orote
Hong Kong: 7 Kowloon
Honshu: 3 Izu 5 Miura
Massachusetts: 7 Cape Ann, Cape
Cod
Mexico: 7 Yucatan 14 Baja Califor-
nia
Michigan: 8 Keweenaw
Middle East: 5 Sinai
New Guinea: 4 Huon
New Jersey: 9 Sandy Hook
New Zealand: 5 Banks, Mahia
Nunavut: 7 Boothia 8 Melville
Ontario: 5 Bruce
Persian Gulf: 9 Ras Tanura
Quebec: 5 Gaspé
Russia: 4 Kola 5 Taman, Yamal
6 Kolski, Taimyr 9 Kamchatka
Scotland: 7 Kintyre
South Australia: 4 Eyre 5 Yorke
Southeast Asia: 5 Malay 9 Indo-
china
southeastern Europe: 6 Balkan
southwestern Asia: 6 Arabia
7 Arabian
southwestern Europe: 7 Iberian
Texas: 9 Matagorda
Tierra del Fuego: 5 Mitre
Turkey: 8 Anatolia 9 Asia Minor
Ukraine: 5 Kerch
Wales: 5 Gower, Lleyn
Washington: 7 Olympic
Wisconsin: 4 Door

Peninsular State
7 Florida

penitence
3 rue 4 ruth 6 regret, sorrow 7 anguish, remorse 8 distress, humbling
10 contrition, repentance 11 compunction, self-reproof 12 self-
reproach

penitent
5 sorry 6 rueful 8 contrite 9 regretful, repentant 10 apologetic,
remorseful

penitentiary
see **prison**

penman
5 clerk 6 author, scribe, writer
7 copyist 9 scrivener 12 calligrapher

penmanship
4 hand 5 style 6 script 7 writing
11 calligraphy, chirography, handwriting

pen name
6 anonym 9 pseudonym 10 nom de
plume
Addison, Joseph: 4 Clio
Arouet, François-Marie: 8 Voltaire
Beyle, Marie-Henri: 8 Stendhal
Blair, Eric: 12 George Orwell
Brontë, Anne: 9 Acton Bell
Brontë, Charlotte: 10 Currer Bell
Brontë, Emily: 9 Ellis Bell
Clemens, Samuel: 9 Mark Twain
Dickens, Charles: 3 Boz
Dodgson, Charles Lutwidge:
12 Lewis Carroll
Dupin, Amandine-Aurore:
10 George Sand
Evans, Mary Ann: 11 George Eliot
Faust, Frederick: 8 Max Brand
Franklin, Benjamin: 11 Poor
Richard
Geisel, Theodore: 7 Dr. Seuss
Glidden, Frederick: 9 Luke Short
Lamb, Charles: 4 Elia
Munro, Hector Hugh: 4 Saki
Poquelin, Jean-Baptiste: 7 Molière
Porter, William Sidney: 6 O. Henry
Ramé, Maria Louise: 5 Ouida
**Thibault, Jacques-Anatole-
François:** 13 Anatole France
Viaud, Louis-Marie-Julien:
10 Pierre Loti

pennant
4 flag, jack 5 color 6 banner, ensign
8 standard, streamer 9 banderole
12 championship

penniless
4 poor 5 broke, needy 8 bankrupt,

pennon

indigent **9** destitute, insolvent **11** impecunious

pennon

4 flag, jack, wing **5** color **6** banner, ensign **8** bannerol, gonfalon, streamer **9** banderole, oriflamme

Pennsylvania

capital: 10 Harrisburg
city: 4 Erie **7** Reading **8** Scranton **9** Allentown **10** Pittsburgh **12** Philadelphia
college, university: 6 Drexel, Lehigh, Temple **7** LaSalle **8** Bryn Mawr, Bucknell **9** Dickinson, Lafayette, Penn State, Villanova **10** Swarthmore **14** Carnegie Mellon
mountain range: 6 Pocono
nickname: 8 Keystone (State)
river: 9 Allegheny **10** Schuylkill **11** Monongahela, Susquehanna
state bird: 12 ruffed grouse
state flower: 14 mountain laurel
state tree: 7 hemlock

penny-pincher

5 miser **7** niggard, scrooge **8** tightwad **9** skinflint **10** cheapskate

penny-pinching

4 mean **6** frugal, stingy, thrift **7** miserly, thrifty **9** frugality, niggardly, parsimony, penurious **11** tightfisted **12** cheeseparing, parsimonious

penny-wise

5 canny, tight **6** frugal, stingy **7** prudent, sparing, thrifty **9** provident **10** economical **12** parsimonious

pen point

3 neb, nib

pension

3 inn **5** hotel, lodge **6** hostel, reward **7** annuity, auberge, payment, stipend **8** gratuity **9** allowance **12** room and board, roominghouse **13** boardinghouse

pensioner

7 retiree

pensive

3 sad **6** dreamy, musing **7** wistful **10** meditative, melancholy, reflective, ruminative, thoughtful **11** preoccupied **13** contemplative

Pentateuch

5 Torah
books: 6 Exodus **7** Genesis, Numbers **9** Leviticus **11** Deuteronomy

Penthesilea

queen of: 7 Amazons
slayer: 8 Achilles

Pentheus

grandfather: 6 Cadmus
king of: 6 Thebes
mother: 5 Agave

penumbra

4 veil **5** cover, shade **6** fringe, screen, shadow, shroud **7** curtain

penurious

4 mean, poor **5** needy, tight **6** frugal, stingy **7** miserly **8** indigent, stinting **9** destitute, niggardly **11** impecunious, tightfisted **12** impoverished, parsimonious **13** pennypinching

penury

4 need, want **7** beggary, poverty **8** distress **9** indigence, privation, pauperism **11** destitution, needfulness

peon

4 serf **5** slave **6** drudge, toiler **7** laborer, peasant **11** galley slave
Anglo-Saxon: 4 esne

peonage

4 yoke **6** thrall **7** bondage, helotry, serfdom, slavery **9** servitude, thralldom, villenage **11** enslavement

people

3 kin **4** folk **5** plebs **6** public **7** society **8** populace **9** commoners, community, plebeians **10** commonalty **11** inhabitants, rank and file, third estate

pep

3 vim **4** brio, dash **5** moxie, punch, verve, vigor **6** energy **7** sparkle **8** vitality, vivacity **10** get-up-and-go, liveliness **11** high spirits

pepo
5 gourd, melon 6 squash 7 pumpkin 8 cucumber

pepper
4 pelt 5 chili 6 season, shower 7 cayenne, paprika, pimento, tabasco 8 capsicum, cascabel, chipotle, habanero, jalapeño, pimiento, sprinkle 9 condiment, seasoning 12 Scotch bonnet

peppery
3 hot 5 cross, fiery, sharp, spicy, testy, zesty 6 biting, lively, snappy, touchy 7 piquant, pungent 8 choleric, poignant, seasoned, stinging 9 irascible, irritable 11 hot-tempered 13 quick-tempered

peppy
5 alert, perky 6 active, bright, lively 7 vibrant 8 animated, spirited, vigorous 9 energetic, sprightly, vivacious

_____ Pepys
6 Samuel

Pequod
cabin boy: 3 Pip
captain: 4 Ahab
harpooner: 6 Daggoo 8 Queequeg, Tashtego
mate: 8 Starbuck

per
3 via 4 a pop, each, with 6 apiece 7 by way of, for each, through 9 by means of 12 individually

perambulate
4 walk 6 ramble, stroll 8 traverse 9 promenade

per capita
4 each 6 apiece, by each 7 equally, for each

perceive
3 see 4 espy, feel, know, mark, note 5 grasp, seize, sense 6 detect, notice, remark 7 discern, observe, realize 8 identify 9 apprehend, recognize 10 comprehend, understand

percentage
3 cut 4 part 5 piece, share, slice 6 profit 7 portion 9 advantage 10 commission, proportion 11 probability

perceptible
5 clear 6 marked 7 visible 8 apparent, definite, distinct, palpable, sensible, tangible 10 detectable, noticeable, observable 11 appreciable, discernible 12 recognizable

perception
4 idea 5 grasp, image 6 acumen, notion 7 concept, feeling, insight, thought 9 awareness, cognition 10 impression 11 discernment, observation 12 appreciation 13 understanding

perceptive
4 keen, sage, wise 5 acute, alert, aware, sharp 7 knowing 9 intuitive, observant, sagacious, sensitive 10 discerning, insightful, responsive 13 understanding

perch
3 bar, peg, set 4 fish, land, rest, seat 5 light, roost, sit on 6 alight, settle 7 set down, sit atop, sit down

perchance
5 maybe 7 perhaps 8 possibly 11 conceivably

percipience
6 acumen 8 keenness 9 cognition, intuition 10 astuteness 11 discernment 12 appreciation, perspicacity 13 comprehension

percolate
4 drip, ooze, seep 5 exude 6 charge, filter, simmer, spread 7 pervade, trickle 9 penetrate

percussion
3 jar 4 bump, jolt 5 clash, crash, shock 6 impact 9 collision 10 concussion
instrument:
(see at **musical instrument**)

Perdita
father: 7 Leontes
mother: 8 Hermione

perdition
4 hell 5 hades 7 inferno 9 damnation 10 underworld 11 netherworld

Père Goriot author
6 Balzac (Honoré de)

peregrination
4 trek, trip, walk 7 journey, travels 9 traversal 10 expedition

peremptory
5 bossy, final 7 haughty 8 absolute, arrogant, decisive, dogmatic, imperial 9 imperious, masterful 10 autocratic, commanding, disdainful, high-handed, imperative 11 dictatorial, domineering, magisterial, overbearing

perennial
7 durable 8 constant, enduring, lifelong 9 continual, long-lived, permanent, perpetual, recurrent, unceasing 10 continuing, persistent, persisting, unchanging 11 long-lasting

Perez
brother: 5 Zerah
father: 5 Judah
mother: 5 Tamar

perfect
4 full, pure 5 exact, ideal, model, right, sound, total, utter, whole 6 entire, expert, intact, polish, proper, refine 7 correct, improve, precise 8 absolute, accurate, complete, finished, flawless, outright, peerless, spotless, unbroken, unflawed 9 downright, excellent, faultless, matchless, stainless, unalloyed, undamaged, undiluted 10 consummate, impeccable, proficient 11 unequivocal, unmitigated, unqualified

perfection
4 acme 5 ideal 6 purity, virtue 7 paragon 9 integrity, wholeness 10 excellence, excellency 11 saintliness 12 completeness, flawlessness, transcendence 13 faultlessness

perfectly
5 fully, quite 6 wholly 7 to a turn, utterly 8 entirely 10 altogether, completely, thoroughly

perfidious
5 false 6 untrue 8 disloyal 9 deceitful, dishonest, faithless 10 treasonous, traitorous, unfaithful, unreliable 11 treacherous

perfidy
6 deceit 7 falsity, sellout, treason 8 betrayal 9 falseness, treachery 10 disloyalty, infidelity 13 faithlessness

perforate
3 pit 4 bore 5 drill, prick, punch 6 pierce 8 puncture 9 penetrate

perform
3 act 4 play, work 5 enact 6 behave, comply, effect 7 achieve, execute, fulfill, operate, playact, present, satisfy 8 bring off, carry out, complete, function 9 discharge, entertain, implement 10 accomplish

performance
3 act 4 deed, feat, show, work 6 acting, action 7 conduct, display 8 behavior, efficacy, exercise 9 discharge, execution, operation 10 efficiency, exhibition 11 achievement, fulfillment 12 presentation

performer
4 doer, mime 5 actor, mimic 6 mummer, player 7 actress, artiste, trouper 8 thespian 9 playactor 12 impersonator

perfume
4 balm 5 aroma, cense, scent, smell, spice 6 sachet 7 bouquet, incense, odorize 9 aromatize, fragrance, redolence
source: 4 musk 5 attar, myrrh, orris 8 bergamot

perfumer
6 Chanel (Coco)

perfunctory
7 cursory, routine 8 careless 9 automatic 10 impersonal, mechanical 11 superficial

pergola
5 arbor, bower 7 trellis

perhaps
5 maybe 8 feasibly, possibly 9 perchance 11 conceivably

periapt
see **amulet**

Pericles
father: 10 Xanthippus
mistress: 7 Aspasia
mother: 8 Agariste

peril
4 risk 6 danger, hazard, menace 8 exposure, jeopardy 9 liability 12 endangerment

perilous
5 hairy, risky 6 chancy, unsafe 7 unsound 9 dangerous, desperate, hazardous, uncertain 11 treacherous

_____ **Perilous**
5 Siege

perimeter
4 edge 5 limit, verge 6 border, bounds, margin 8 boundary

period
3 age, end, era 4 span, stop, term, time 5 cycle, phase, point, spell, stage 6 extent 8 division, duration, interval, sentence

periodic
6 cyclic, fitful 7 regular 8 cyclical, repeated, sporadic 9 recurrent, recurring 10 occasional 11 fluctuating 12 intermittent

periodical
5 organ 6 cyclic, review 7 journal 8 cyclical, magazine 9 alternate, newspaper, recurrent, recurring 10 isochronal 11 isochronous, publication 12 intermittent

peripatetic
6 moving, roving 7 nomadic, walking 8 ambulant, vagabond 9 itinerant, traveling, wayfaring 10 ambulatory, pedestrian, travelling 13 perambulatory

peripheral
6 remote 7 lateral, surface 8 far-flung, marginal, outlying 9 auxiliary, secondary 10 borderline, tangential 11 out-of-the-way 13 supplementary

perish
3 die, end 4 pass 5 cease 6 be lost, demise, depart, expire, vanish 7 decease, decline, go under, succumb 8 collapse, pass away 9 disappear

perjure
3 lie 6 delude 7 deceive, distort, falsify, mislead 8 forswear 9 misinform 10 equivocate 11 prevaricate

perk
4 gain, mend, plus 5 cheer, extra 7 benefit, freshen, improve, refresh, smarten 8 brighten

perky
5 alert, cocky, happy 6 bouncy, bubbly, cheery, chirpy, frisky, jaunty, lively, upbeat 7 buoyant, chipper 8 animated, cheerful, spirited, sportive 9 energetic, sparkling, sprightly, vivacious 12 effervescent, high-spirited

permanent
5 fixed 6 stable 7 abiding, durable, lasting 8 constant, enduring, hair wave 9 continual, perennial 10 changeless, invariable, unchanging 11 established, everlasting 12 imperishable

permeable
6 porous, spongy 8 pervious 9 diffusive 10 penetrable

permeate
5 imbue 6 drench, infuse, spread 7 diffuse, pervade, suffuse 8 saturate 9 penetrate, percolate 10 impregnate, infiltrate 11 pass through

permissible
4 okay 5 legal 7 allowed 8 approved 9 allowable, tolerable, tolerated 10 acceptable, authorized, sanctioned

permission

5 leave 6 assent, permit 7 consent, license 8 approval, sanction 9 agreement, allowance 11 approbation, endorsement 12 acquiescence 13 authorization

permissive

3 lax 4 open 7 lenient, liberal 8 tolerant 9 easygoing, forgiving, indulgent 10 forbearing 11 acquiescent, complaisant

permit

3 let 4 okay, pass 5 agree, allow, grant, leave 6 accede, enable, say yes, suffer 7 consent, license, warrant 8 sanction, tolerate 9 allowance, authorize, give leave 10 permission 13 authorization

permutation

6 change 7 variety, version 9 variation 10 alteration, innovation 11 arrangement, vicissitude 12 modification

pernicious

4 evil 5 fatal, toxic 6 deadly, lethal, malign, wicked 7 baleful, baneful, harmful, hurtful, killing, malefic, noxious, ruinous 8 damaging, sinister, virulent 9 injurious, malignant, offensive, poisonous 10 maleficent 11 deleterious, destructive, detrimental, devastating

Pernod flavor

5 anise 8 licorice

perorate

5 speak 7 declaim, lecture 8 bloviate, harangue, proclaim 9 hold forth

perpend

5 study, weigh 6 ponder 7 examine, reflect 8 consider, think out 9 reflect on, think over 10 excogitate, think about 11 contemplate

perpendicular

5 plumb, sheer, steep 7 upright 8 straight, vertical 11 precipitate, precipitous

perpetrate

6 commit, effect 7 inflict, execute, perform 8 carry out 10 bring about

perpetual

7 endless, eternal, undying 8 constant, unending 9 ceaseless, continual, incessant, perennial, recurrent, unceasing 10 continuous 11 everlasting, unremitting

perpetuate

7 sustain 8 conserve, continue, eternize, maintain, preserve 9 keep alive 10 eternalize 11 immortalize

perplex

5 befog, mix up, stump 6 baffle, bemuse, muddle, puzzle 7 buffalo, confuse, mystify, nonplus, perturb 8 befuddle, bewilder, confound, distract, entangle 9 dumbfound 10 discompose

perquisite

3 tip 4 gain 5 right 6 profit 7 benefit, payment 8 gratuity 9 privilege

per se

6 as such, solely 8 in itself 11 essentially 13 intrinsically

persecute

4 bait, ride 5 annoy, harry, hound, worry, wrong 6 badger, harass, hector, injure, molest, pester, pick on, plague, punish, pursue 7 afflict, oppress, torment, torture 8 aggrieve

Persephone

4 Kore 10 Proserpina
father: 4 Zeus 7 Jupiter
husband: 5 Hades, Pluto
mother: 5 Ceres 7 Demeter

Perseus

father: 4 Zeus 7 Jupiter
grandfather: 8 Acrisius
mother: 5 Danaë
victim: 6 Medusa 8 Acrisius
wife: 9 Andromeda

perseverance

8 tenacity 9 diligence, endurance 10 dedication 11 persistence 13 steadfastness

persevere
see **persist**

Persia
4 Iran

Persian
ancient: 4 Mede
fairy: 4 peri
governor: 6 satrap
language: 5 Parsi
mystic: 4 sufi
poet: 5 Hafez, Hafiz 7 Firdusi
8 Ferdowsi, Firdausi, Firdawsi,
Firdousi 11 Omar Khayyám
prophet: 9 Zoroaster
robe: 6 caftan
sacred books: 6 Avesta
sun-god: 7 Mithras
title: 4 shah
writing: 9 cuneiform

persiflage
6 banter, joking 7 jesting, kidding,
ribbing 8 badinage, raillery, repartee

persist
4 go on, last 5 abide 6 endure,
hang on, keep on, linger 7 carry on,
prevail 8 continue 9 persevere

persistence
8 duration 9 endurance 10 continuity 11 continuance 12 continuation

persistent
6 dogged 7 lasting 8 enduring,
obdurate, stubborn 9 continual,
steadfast, tenacious 10 continuing,
determined, relentless, unshakable
11 persevering, unremitting

persnickety
5 fussy, picky 6 choosy 7 finicky
8 exacting 10 fastidious, particular

person
3 guy 4 self, soul 5 being, human
6 entity, mensch, mortal 8 creature,
specimen 10 individual

personable
4 nice 6 genial 7 affable, amiable
8 charming, friendly, pleasant, pleasing 9 appealing, congenial 10 attractive

personage
3 VIP 5 human 6 bigwig, figure
7 big shot, notable 8 creature,
luminary, somebody 9 celebrity,
character, dignitary 10 individual

personal
3 own 5 privy 7 private, special
8 peculiar 10 individual, particular

personal effects
5 stuff 10 belongings 11 possessions

personality
3 ego, VIP 4 self 6 makeup, nature,
temper, traits 7 notable 8 identity,
selfhood, selfness 9 celebrity, character, dignitary, qualities 10 complexion 11 disposition, singularity,
temperament 13 individualism,
individuality

personate
3 act 4 play 5 enact 6 embody,
typify 7 perform 9 epitomize, exemplify, represent 10 illustrate

personify
6 embody, typify 8 stand for 9 actualize, epitomize, exemplify, incarnate,
represent, symbolize 11 emblematize

perspective
4 view 5 angle, scene, slant, vista
7 outlook 8 position, prospect
9 viewpoint 10 standpoint 11 point
of view

perspicacious
4 keen 5 acute, quick, savvy, sharp
6 astute, clever, shrewd 9 observant, sagacious 10 discerning,
insightful, perceptive 11 penetrating

perspicacity
6 acumen 7 insight 8 keenness
10 astuteness, shrewdness 11 discernment, penetration, percipience

perspicuous
5 clear, lucid, plain 6 lucent, simple
7 crystal, precise 8 clear-cut, pellucid 11 unambiguous

perspiration
5 sweat

perspire
see **sweat**

persuadable
4 open 7 willing 9 receptive 11 suggestible, susceptible

persuade
3 win 4 coax, lead, sell, sway, urge 5 argue 6 entice, induce, prompt 7 convert, impress, win over 8 convince 9 influence, prevail on 11 bring around

persuasion
4 kind, mind, sort, type, view 5 group 6 belief, school 7 faction, opinion 8 argument 9 character, prejudice, sentiment 10 connection, conviction 11 affiliation, description

Persuasion author
6 Austen (Jane)

persuasive
6 cogent 7 telling, winning 8 credible 10 compelling, convincing 11 influential

pert
4 bold, chic, flip, trim 5 alert, cocky, fresh, sassy, saucy, smart 6 brazen, bright, cheeky, jaunty, lively 7 forward 8 animated, flippant, spirited 9 audacious, sprightly, vivacious

pertain
5 apply, refer 6 affect, bear on, belong, regard, relate 7 concern 8 bear upon 9 touch upon

pertinacious
4 firm 5 fixed 6 dogged, mulish 7 willful 8 resolute, stubborn 9 obstinate, tenacious 10 inflexible, persistent, unshakable, unyielding

pertinent
3 apt, fit 5 ad rem 7 apropos, fitting, germane 8 apposite, material, relevant 10 applicable 11 appropriate

perturb
5 upset, worry 6 bother 7 agitate, disturb, fluster, trouble 8 disorder, disquiet, unsettle 10 discompose, disconcert

Peru
ancient civilization: 4 Inca
capital: 4 Lima
city: 5 Cusco, Cuzco 6 Callao 8 Arequipa, Trujillo
conqueror: 7 Pizarro (Francisco)
ethnic group: 7 Quechua
lake: 8 Titicaca
language: 6 Aymara 7 Quechua, Spanish
leader: 8 Fujimori (Alberto)
monetary unit: 3 sol
mountain, range: 5 Andes 9 Huascarán
neighbor: 5 Chile 6 Brazil 7 Bolivia, Ecuador 8 Colombia
river: 6 Amazon 7 Marañón
volcano: 5 Misti 7 El Misti 8 Yucamani

peruse
4 read, scan 5 study 6 survey 7 examine 8 consider, look over, pore over

pervade
5 imbue 6 spread 7 diffuse 8 permeate, saturate 9 penetrate, percolate, transfuse 10 impregnate

perverse
5 balky 6 cranky, mulish, ornery 7 corrupt, deviant, froward, peevish, wayward, willful 8 contrary, depraved, improper, stubborn 9 incorrect, irritable, obstinate 10 degenerate, headstrong, refractory 11 stiff-necked, wrongheaded 12 cross-grained, unreasonable

pervert
4 ruin, skew, warp 5 abuse, twist 6 debase, divert, garble, misuse 7 corrupt, debauch, deprave, distort, deviant, falsify, vitiate 8 misstate, mistreat 9 misdirect 11 misconstrue 12 misinterpret, misrepresent

pervious
4 open 6 porous 9 permeable 10 accessible, penetrable

pesky
6 vexing 7 irksome 8 annoying 9 vexatious 10 bothersome 11 troublesome

pessimist
5 cynic 9 Cassandra, defeatist, doomsayer, worrywart 11 misanthrope

pessimistic
6 gloomy, morose 7 cynical 10 despairing 11 distrustful 12 misanthropic

pest
4 bane 5 trial, worry 6 bother, plague, vermin 7 nudnick, trouble 8 irritant, nuisance, vexation 9 annoyance, tormentor

pester
3 bug, irk, nag 4 ride 5 annoy, harry, tease, worry 6 badger, bother, harass, hassle, plague 7 bedevil, disturb, torment 8 irritate

pestiferous
7 baneful, noxious 8 annoying, infected 9 infective, pestilent 10 pernicious 11 troublesome 12 pestilential

pestilence
5 curse 6 plague 7 scourge

pestilential
5 fatal 6 deadly, lethal, vexing 7 baneful, deathly, noxious, ruinous 8 annoying 10 pernicious

pestle
4 mano 6 muller
vessel: 6 mortar

pet
3 cat, dog, hug 4 dear, kiss, love, neck, pout, sulk 5 loved 6 caress, cosset, dandle, fondle, pamper, stroke 7 beloved, cherish, darling, indulge 9 favorite, treasure 9 cherished, endearing, sulkiness

petcock
3 tap 5 valve 6 faucet, spigot

Peter Grimes composer
7 Britten (Benjamin)

peter out
4 fade, wane 5 abate, cease 6 lessen, recede, run dry 7 dwindle 8 decrease, diminish, taper off 9 drain away

Peter Pan
author: 6 Barrie (James)
character: 5 Wendy 7 Michael 9 Tiger Lily 10 Tinker Bell
dog: 4 Nana
pirate: 4 Hook, Smee

Peter the Apostle
brother: 6 Andrew
father: 5 Jonah
original name: 5 Simon

Peter the Great
father: 6 Alexis
wife: 7 Eudoxia 9 Catherine

petite
5 small 6 little 8 smallish 10 diminutive

petition
3 ask 4 plea 5 plead 6 appeal 7 beseech, entreat, implore, request, solicit 8 entreaty 10 supplicate 11 application 12 supplication

Petrarch's beloved
5 Laura

Petrified Forest author
8 Sherwood (Robert)

petrify
4 daze, numb, stun 5 chill, scare 6 benumb, deaden, harden 7 startle 8 confound, frighten, paralyze

Petruchio's wife
9 Katharina, Katharine

pettifogger
7 shyster 8 quibbler 9 nitpicker

petty
4 mean 5 minor, small 6 measly, narrow, paltry 7 trivial 8 niggling, picayune, piddling, trifling 9 frivolous, secondary 10 irrelevant, negligible 11 small-minded, subordinate, unimportant 13 insignificant

petty officer
6 noncom

petulant
5 huffy, moody, sulky, testy, whiny 6 touchy 7 grouchy, peevish 8 snappish 9 irascible, irritable, querulous 10 ill-humored

pew
3 row 4 seat 5 bench

peyote
6 cactus, mescal
drug: 9 mescaline

Phaedra
father: 5 Minos
husband: 7 Theseus
mother: 8 Pasiphaë
sister: 7 Ariadne
stepson: 10 Hippolytus

Phaëthon's father
6 Helios 7 Phoebus

phalanx
4 army, host, mass 5 horde 6 myriad,
throng 6 troops

phantasm
5 dream, fancy, ghost 6 spirit, vision
7 fantasy, fiction, figment, specter,
spectre 8 daydream, delusion,
illusion 9 invention 10 apparition
11 fabrication 13 hallucination

phantom
5 dummy, ghost, shade, spook
6 goblin, shadow, spirit, vision
7 bugbear, chimera, eidolon, specter,
spectre 8 illusory 9 imaginary
10 apparition, fictitious 12 will-o'-the-
wisp

pharaoh
3 Tut 4 Seti 5 Menes, ruler 6 Ah-
mose, Ramses, tyrant 7 Harmhab
8 Ikhnaton, Thutmose 9 Amenhotep,
Merneptah 11 Tutankhamen

pharisee
9 hypocrite

pharmacist
8 druggist 10 apothecary
British: 7 chemist

pharos
6 beacon 10 lighthouse

Pharsalus, battle of
vanquished: 6 Pompey
victor: 6 Caesar (Julius)

phase
4 part, side, view 5 point, stage,
state 6 adjust, aspect 7 conduct
8 carry out, position 9 condition,
situation, viewpoint 10 appearance

PhD exam
5 orals

Phèdre author
6 Racine (Jean)

phenomenal
6 actual 7 unusual 8 material,
physical, sensible, singular, tangible,
uncommon 9 corporeal, fantastic,
objective 10 remarkable 11 exceptional, outstanding, perceivable,
perceptible, substantial 13 extraordinary

phenomenon
4 fact 5 event 6 marvel, object,
rarity, wonder 7 miracle, reality
9 actuality, sensation 10 experience,
uniqueness 11 peculiarity, singularity

Phi ____ Kappa
4 Beta

philander
8 womanize

philanthropic
6 giving, humane 8 generous 10 altruistic, benevolent, bighearted,
charitable 11 magnanimous 12 eleemosynary, humanitarian

philanthropist
American: 5 Gates (Bill) 6 Cooper
(Peter), Girard (Stephen), Mellon
(Andrew) 7 Cornell (Ezra), Eastman
(George), Packard (David), Whitney
(Gertrude Vanderbilt) 8 Carnegie
(Andrew), Stanford (Leland) 9 Ro-
senwald (Julius) 10 Vanderbilt
(Cornelius) 11 Rockefeller (J. D.)
English: 11 Wilberforce (William)
Swedish: 5 Nobel (Alfred)

Philemon's wife
6 Baucis

philharmonic
8 symphony 9 orchestra, symphonic

Philip of Macedonia
father: 7 Amyntas
son: 9 Alexander

philippic
6 tirade 8 diatribe, harangue, jeremiad 12 condemnation

Philippics author
6 Cicero

Philippines
capital: 6 Manila
city: 4 Cebu 5 Davao 10 Quezon City
discoverer: 8 Magellan (Ferdinand)
island: 4 Cebu 5 Leyte, Luzon, Panay, Samar 6 Negros 7 Masbate, Mindoro, Palawan 8 Mindanao
language: 7 Ilocano, Tagalog 8 Filipino, Pilipino
leader: 6 Aquino (Corazon), Marcos (Ferdinand)
liberator: 9 MacArthur (Douglas)
patriot: 5 Rizal (José)
monetary unit: 4 peso
sea: 4 Sulu 5 Samar 7 Celebes, Sibuyan, Visayan 8 Mindanao 10 Philippine, South China
volcano: 4 Taal 5 Mayon

Philippi victor
6 Antony (Marc, Mark) 8 Octavian

Philip the Tetrarch
father: 5 Herod
mother: 9 Cleopatra

philistine
4 boob 7 Babbitt 9 bourgeois, vulgarian 10 capitalist 11 materialist

Philistine
champion: 7 Goliath
city: 4 Gath, Gaza 5 Ekron 6 Ashdod 8 Ashkelon
foe: 5 David 6 Samson
god: 5 Dagon

Philoctetes
father: 5 Poeas
victim: 5 Paris

Philomela
11 nightingale
father: 7 Pandion
ravisher: 6 Tereus
sister: 6 Procne

philosopher
American: 5 Adler (Mortimer), Dewey (John), James (William), Quine (Willard), Rorty (Richard), Royce (Josiah) 6 Langer (Susanne), Peirce (C. S.) 7 Marcuse (Herbert), Mumford (Lewis), Strauss (Leo) 9 Santayana (George)
Arab: 8 Averroës, Avicenna
Austrian: 6 Popper (Karl) 12 Wittgenstein (Ludwig)
Chinese: 5 Laoxi 6 Lao-tsu 7 Dai Zhen, Mencius, Tai Chen 9 Confucius
Danish: 11 Kierkegaard (Soren)
Dutch: 7 Erasmus (Desiderius), Spinoza (Baruch de)
English: 4 Ayer (A. J.), Mill (John Stuart), More (Henry, Thomas), Watt (James) 5 Bacon (Francis), Burke (Edmund), Locke (John), Moore (G. E.), Occam (William of), Paine (Thomas) 6 Berlin (Isaiah), Hobbes (Thomas), Huxley (Thomas), Ockham (William), Popper (Karl) 7 Bentham (Jeremy), Russell (Bertrand), Spencer (Herbert), Whewell (William) 9 Whitehead (Alfred North) 12 Wittgenstein (Ludwig)
Finnish: 11 Westermarck (Edward)
French: 4 Weil (Simone) 5 Comte (Auguste), Taine (Hippolyte) 6 Pascal (Blaise), Sartre (Jean-Paul), Valéry (Paul) 7 Abelard (Peter), Bergson (Henri), Derrida (Jacques), Diderot (Denis), Fourier (Charles) 8 Foucault (Michel), Maritain (Jacques), Rousseau (Jean-Jacques), Voltaire 9 Descartes (René), Montaigne (Michel de) 10 Saint-Simon (Comte de) 11 Montesquieu (Baron de) 12 Merleau-Ponty (Maurice)
German: 4 Kant (Immanuel), Marx (Karl) 5 Frege (Gottlob), Hegel (Georg Wilhelm Friedrich), Wolff (Christian von) 6 Carnap (Rudolf), Fichte (Immanuel, Johann), Herder (Johann von) 7 Husserl (Edmund), Jaspers (Karl), Leibniz (Gottfried) 8 Spengler (Oswald) 9 Heidegger (Martin), Nietzsche (Friedrich),

Schelling (Friedrich von) 12 Schopenhauer (Arthur) 14 Albertus Magnus
Greek: 4 Zeno 5 Plato, Timon 6 Thales 7 Gorgias, Proclus 8 Diogenes, Epicurus, Longinus, Socrates 9 Aristotle, Epictetus 10 Anaxagoras, Democritus, Empedocles, Heraclitus, Parmenides, Protagoras, Pythagoras, Xenocrates, Xenophanes 11 Anaximander 12 Theophrastus
Irish: 8 Berkeley (George)
Italian: 5 Croce (Benedetto) 6 Ficino (Marsilio) 11 Machiavelli (Niccolo)
Jewish: 5 Buber (Martin), Philo 10 Maimonides (Moses) 12 Philo Judaeus
Roman: 6 Seneca (Lucias Annaeus) 8 Boethius (Anicius), Plotinus 9 Lucretius
Scottish: 4 Hume (David), Mill (James), Reid (Thomas) 7 Stewart (Dugald)
Spanish: 6 Suárez (Francisco) 7 Unamuno (Miguel de) 13 Ortega y Gasset (José)
Swedish: 10 Swedenborg (Emanuel)

philosopher's stone
3 key 6 elixir

philosophical
4 calm 7 stoical 8 composed, rational, resigned 9 unruffled 10 thoughtful

philosophy
6 system, theory, values 7 beliefs, inquiry 8 attitude, calmness 10 discipline
component: 5 logic 6 ethics 10 aesthetics 11 metaphysics 12 epistemology

philter
4 drug 5 charm, tonic 6 potion 9 stimulant 10 love potion 11 aphrodisiac, restorative

Phineas
beloved: 9 Andromeda
tormentors: 7 Harpies
wife: 9 Cleopatra

phlegm
5 humor, mucus 6 apathy 8 calmness, coolness, dullness 9 composure, sangfroid 10 equanimity 11 impassivity, nonchalance 12 indifference

phlegmatic
4 calm, cool, dull 5 aloof, stoic 6 stolid 8 detached 9 apathetic, impassive, lethargic 11 indifferent, unconcerned

Phlegyas
daughter: 7 Coronis
father: 4 Ares, Mars
son: 5 Ixion

phobia
see **fear**

Phobos
4 moon 9 satellite
brother: 6 Deimos
father: 4 Ares, Mars

Phocus
father: 6 Aeacus 8 Ornytion
half brother: 6 Peleus 7 Telamon
mother: 8 Psamathe
slayer: 6 Peleus 7 Telamon
wife: 7 Antiope

Phoebe
5 Diana 7 Artemis
daughter: 4 Leto
father: 9 Leucippus
mother: 4 Gaea

Phoebus
see **Apollo**

Phoenician
city: 4 Acre, Tyre 5 Sidon
colony: 8 Carthage
god: 4 Baal 6 Eshmun
goddess: 6 Baltis 7 Astarte

Phoenix
pupil: 8 Achilles
sister: 6 Europa
team: 4 Suns 7 Coyotes 9 Cardinals 12 Diamondbacks

phony
4 fake, sham 5 bogus, cheat, faker, false, fraud 6 humbug, pseudo 8 impostor, specious, spurious

9 charlatan, dishonest, pretender
10 ficticious, suspicious **11** counterfeit **12** hypocritical

photograph
3 pic **4** film, snap **5** shoot **6** glossy
7 picture, tintype **8** snapshot
three-dimensional: 8 hologram

photographer
8 photoist **9** cameraman **10** shutterbug
famous: 3 Ray (Man) **4** Capa
(Cornell, Robert), Haas (Ernst), Hine
(Lewis), Penn (Irving), Riis (Jacob)
5 Adams (Ansel), Arbus (Diane),
Atget (Eugène), Brady (Mathew),
Evans (Frederick, Walker), Horst
(Horst Peter), Karsh (Yousuf), Lange
(Dorothea), Model (Lisette), Nadar,
Parks (Gordon), Ritts (Herb), Smith
(W. Eugene), Weber (Bruce), White
(Clarence, Minor) **6** Abbott (Berenice), Avedon (Richard), Beaton
(Cecil), Brandt (Bill), Coburn (Alvin),
Curtis (Edward S.), Newton (Helmut),
Porter (Eliot), Rowell (Galen), Siegel
(Eliot), Strand (Paul), Talbot (William
Henry Fox), Weegee, Wegman
(William), Weston (Brett, Edward)
7 Brassaï, Cameron (Julia Margaret),
Emerson (Peter), Halsman (Philippe),
Jackson (William Henry), Kertész
(André), Salomon (Erich), Siskind
(Aaron), Snowdon (Earl of), Thomson (John), Watkins (Carleton)
8 Callahan (Harry), Cosindas (Marie),
Daguerre (Louis-Jacques-Mandé),
Kasebier (Gertrude), Scavullo (Francesco), Steichen (Edward), Steinert
(Otto) **9** Caponigro (Paul), Feininger
(Andreas), Leibovitz (Annie), Meyrowitz (Joel), Muybridge (Eadweard),
O'Sullivan (Timothy), Rejlander
(Oscar), Rothstein (Arthur), Stieglitz
(Alfred), Winogrand (Garry) **10** Cunningham (Imogen), Heartfield (John),
Moholy-Nagy (Laszlo) **11** Bourke-
White (Margaret), Eisenstaedt
(Alfred) **12** Mapplethorpe (Robert)

photographic
5 exact, vivid **7** graphic **8** accurate,
detailed **9** pictorial **11** picturesque

solution: 4 hypo **5** fixer, toner
7 reducer **9** developer

phrase
5 couch, frame, idiom **6** slogan
7 diction, express, styling, wording
8 locution, verbiage **9** catchword,
formulate, verbalism, watchword
10 expression

Phrygian
god: 4 Atys **5** Attis
goddess: 6 Cybele
king: 5 Midas **7** Gordius

phylactery
5 charm **6** amulet **7** periapt **8** talisman

physic
4 cure, heal **5** purge **6** remedy
8 medicine **9** cathartic, purgative
10 medication

physical
4 real **5** lusty, rough **6** actual, bodily,
carnal, sexual **7** fleshly, natural,
somatic **8** concrete, corporal, material, sensible, tangible **9** corporeal,
objective **10** phenomenal **11** perceivable, perceptible, substantial

physician
3 doc **5** medic **6** doctor, medico
7 surgeon **8** sawbones
American: 4 Rush (Benjamin), Salk
(Jonas) **5** Minot (George), Spock
(Benjamin), Still (Andrew) **6** Jarvik
(Robert), Murphy (John), Weller
(Thomas) **7** Huggins (Charles),
Robbins (Frederick), Theiler (Max)
8 Richards (Dickinson) **9** Sternberg
(George Miller)
Arab: 8 Avicenna
Canadian: 5 Osler (William)
English: 4 Ross (Ronald) **6** Harvey (William), Jenner (Edward,
William), Willis (Thomas) **8** Sydenham (Thomas)
French: 5 Widal (Fernand) **7** Laveran (Charles) **10** Schweitzer
(Albert)
German: 7 Sylvius (Franciscus)
Greek: 5 Galen **11** Hippocrates
Italian: 7 Galvani (Luigi)

physicist

South African: 7 Barnard (Christiaan)
Swiss: 10 Paracelsus
(see also **Nobel Prize winner physiology or medicine; surgeon**)

physicist

American: 4 Rabi (I. I.), Ting (Samuel) 5 Fermi (Enrico), Gibbs (J. Willard), Kusch (Polykarp), Mayer (Maria-Goeppert), Pauli (Wolfgang), Pupin (Michael), Segré (Emilio), Smyth (Henry DeWolf), Stern (Otto) 6 Teller (Edward), Townes (Charles), Wigner (Eugene) 7 Alvarez (Luis), Feynman (Richard), Goddard (Robert), Purcell (Edward) 8 Einstein (Albert), Gell-Mann (Murray), McMillan (Edwin), Millikan (Clark, Robert), Mulliken (Robert), Shockley (William), Van Allen (James) 9 Michelson (Albert), Schwinger (Julian) 11 Oppenheimer (J. Robert)
Austrian: 4 Mach (Ernst) 7 Doppler (Christian) 11 Schrödinger (Erwin)
British: 4 Snow (C. P.) 5 Dirac (B. A. M.), Jeans (James), Joule (James) 6 Dalton (John), Kelvin (Baron), Newton (Isaac), Powell (Cecil), Stokes (George) 7 Faraday (Michael), Hodgkin (Dorothy), Thomson (George, Joseph, William) 7 Tyndall (John) 8 Rayleigh (Lord), Robinson (Robert), Thompson (Benjamin, Silvanus) 9 Wollaston (William) 10 Richardson (Owen), Rutherford (Ernest), Wheatstone (Charles)
Chinese: 4 Yang (Chen-Ning)
Danish: 4 Bohr (Aage, Niels)
Dutch: 6 Zeeman (Pieter) 7 Huygens (Christian), Lorentz (Hendrik), Zernike (Frits) 11 Van der Waals (Johannes)
French: 4 Néel (Louis) 5 Arago (François) 6 Ampère (André-Marie), Perrin (Jean-Baptiste) 7 Coulomb (Charles-Augustin de), Kastler (Alfred), Réaumur (René-Antoine de) 8 Lippmann (Gabriel)
German: 3 Ohm (Georg) 4 Laue (Max von), Wien (Wilhelm) 5 Hertz (Gustav, Heinrich), Stark (Johannes)

6 Jensen (Hans), Lenard (Philipp), Nernst (Walther), Planck (Max) 7 Meitner (Lise) 8 Roentgen (Wilhelm) 9 Helmholtz (Hermann von), Kirchhoff (Gustav), Mossbauer (Rudolf) 10 Fahrenheit (Daniel), Hofstadter (Robert)
Indian: 5 Raman (Chandrasekhara)
Irish: 6 Walton (Ernest)
Italian: 5 Rossi (Bruno), Volta (Alessandro) 7 Galileo (Galilei), Galvani (Luigi) 10 Torricelli (Evangelista)
Japanese: 6 Yukawa (Hideki) 8 Tomonaga (Shinichiro)
Mexican: 8 Vallarta (Manuel)
Russian: 4 Tamm (Igor) 6 Landau (Lev) 9 Prokhorov (Aleksandr)
Scottish: 4 Tait (Peter) 6 Wilson (Charles) 7 Maxwell (James Clerk)
Swedish: 7 Rydberg (Johannes) 8 Angstrom (Anders), Siegbahn (Kai, Karl)
Swiss: 6 Zwicky (Fritz) 7 Piccard (Auguste)
(see also **Nobel Prize winner physics**)

physiognomy

3 mug 4 face 5 front 6 aspect, visage 7 profile 8 features 9 character 10 lineaments 11 countenance, temperament

physiologist

English: 8 Starling (Ernest)
German: 5 Weber (Ernst), Wundt (Wilhelm) 7 Schwann (Theodor) 9 Helmholtz (Hermann von)
Italian: 11 Spallanzani (Lazzaro)
(see also **Nobel Prize winner physiology or medicine**)

physique

4 body, form 5 build, shape 6 figure, makeup 7 anatomy 9 structure 12 constitution

pianist

American: 4 Nero (Peter), Wild (Earl) 5 Arrau (Claudio), Janis (Byron), Watts (André) 6 Duchin (Peter), Joplin (Scott), Serkin (Peter, Rudolf) 7 Cliburn (Van), Istomin

(Eugene), Ohlsson (Garrick), Perahia (Murray), Winston (George) **8** Graffman (Gary), Horowitz (Vladimir), Pennario (Leonard) **9** Fleischer (Leon) **10** Johannesen (Grant), Rubinstein (Arthur)
Argentinian: 8 Argerich (Martha)
Austrian: 6 Czerny (Karl) **7** Brendel (Alfred) **8** Schnabel (Artur)
Bulgarian: 11 Weissenberg (Alexis)
Canadian: 5 Gould (Glenn)
Cuban: 5 Bolet (Jorge)
English: 4 Hess (Myra) **5** Ogdon (John) **6** Curzon (Clifford)
French: 6 Cortot (Alfred) **7** Cziffra (Gyorgy) **9** Casadesus (Robert), Entremont (Philippe) **10** Saint-Saëns (Camille)
German: 6 Kempff (Wilhelm) **8** Schumann (Clara) **9** Gieseking (Walter)
Hungarian: 5 Liszt (Franz) **7** Cziffra (Gyorgy)
Italian: 6 Busoni (Ferruccio) **7** Pollini (Maurizio) **8** Clementi (Muzio)
Japanese: 6 Uchida (Mitsuko)
Polish: 6 Chopin (Frédéric) **7** Hofmann (Josef) **10** Paderewski (Ignacy), Rubinstein (Arthur)
Romanian: 4 Lupu (Radu) **7** Lipatti (Dinu)
Russian: 6 Berman (Lazar), Gilels (Emil), Kissin (Evgeny) **7** Richter (Sviatoslav) **8** Horowitz (Vladimir), Pachmann (Vladimir von) **9** Ashkenazy (Vladimir) **10** Rubinstein (Anton) **12** Rachmaninoff (Sergey)
Spanish: 6 Iturbi (José) **8** Granados (Enrique) **10** de Larrocha (Alicia)
Swiss: 4 Anda (Geza)

piano

5 grand **6** softly, spinet **7** quietly, upright **9** baby grand
builder: 5 Knabe (William), Stein (Johann), Zumpe (Johann) **7** Baldwin (Dwight) **8** Steinway (Henry) **9** Bechstein (Friedrich) **10** Chickering (Jonas), Silbermann (Johann)
inventor: 10 Cristofori (Bartolomeo)
pedal: 6 damper **9** sostenuto

piazza

5 patio, plaza, porch **6** square **7** balcony, gallery, portico, terrace, veranda **9** courtyard

picaroon

5 rogue, rover, thief **6** pirate **7** brigand, corsair **8** sea rover **9** buccaneer **10** freebooter

picayune

5 petty **6** measly, paltry, trifle **7** trivial **8** piddling **11** small-minded **13** insignificant

pick

3 rob, tap **4** best, carp, cull, open, pull, take, tool **5** elect, pluck, probe, prize **6** choice, choose, chosen, option, pierce, pilfer, remove, select, unlock **7** harvest, provoke **8** selected **9** exclusive, single out

picket

4 pale, post **5** fence, guard, stake, watch **6** sentry, tether **7** enclose, lookout, protest **8** palisade, sentinel, watchman **11** demonstrate

pickle

3 fix, jam **4** dill, spot **5** brine, treat **6** plight, scrape **7** dilemma, gherkin, trouble **8** marinate, preserve **10** difficulty **11** predicament

pick on

5 bully, harry, taunt, tease **6** hector, pester **9** criticize, single out

pick out

4 espy, name, spot **6** choose, descry, detect, select, take in **7** discern **8** identify, perceive **9** apprehend, ascertain, recognize **11** distinguish

pickpocket

3 dip **5** thief **6** dipper **8** cutpurse

pick up

3 buy, get **4** cull, gain, earn, land, lift, tidy **5** catch, glean, hoist, learn, raise, run in **6** arrest, detain, gather, notice, obtain, pull in, resume, revive **7** acquire, clean up, collect, restart **8** perceive **9** apprehend **10** appreciate, understand

pickup

5 truck 9 detention 10 hitchhiker
11 improvement 12 acceleration

picky

5 fussy 6 choosy 7 finicky 10 fastidious, particular, pernickety 11 persnickety

picnic

4 snap 5 cinch 6 breeze, outing
7 cookout 8 cakewalk 11 piece of cake

picture

4 limn, show 5 image, photo, pinup
7 drawing, tableau 8 describe, painting, portrait 9 depiction, portrayal 10 simulacrum 11 delineation, description 13 spitting image
stand: 5 easel

picturesque

5 vivid 6 quaint, scenic 8 artistic, charming

piddling

4 puny 5 petty 6 meager, meagre, measly, paltry 7 trivial 8 picayune, trifling 11 Mickey Mouse, unimportant 13 insignificant

pie

4 flan, tart 5 pasty 6 pastry 7 cobbler, dessert 8 turnover

piebald

5 mixed 6 motley 7 mottled 10 multicolor

piece

4 part 5 patch, slice 6 member, parcel 7 firearm, portion, section, segment 8 division, fraction, fragment 9 allotment 10 allocation

pièce de résistance

8 main dish 9 showpiece 11 centerpiece, chef d'oeuvre, masterpiece

piecemeal

5 apart 6 slowly 7 gradual 8 bit by bit 9 by degrees, gradually 11 fragmentary

pied

6 motley 7 blotchy, brindle, dappled, mottled 8 brindled, speckled
9 multihued 10 variegated 11 varicolored 12 parti-colored

pier

4 anta, dock, quay, slip 5 berth, jetty, levee, wharf 6 column, pillar 8 pilaster
architectural: 4 anta

pierce

3 cut 4 stab 5 probe, spear 6 impale, incise, skewer 8 puncture
9 penetrate, perforate 10 run through

piercing

4 high, keen 5 acute, sharp 6 piping, shrill 8 shooting, stabbing, strident 9 knifelike 12 earsplitting
tool: 3 awl

piety

6 fealty 7 loyalty 8 devotion, fidelity, sanctity 9 reverence 10 allegiance, dedication, devoutness 12 faithfulness

piffle

4 bosh, bunk 5 hooey 6 drivel
7 baloney, rubbish, twaddle 8 malarkey, nonsense 10 balderdash

pig

3 hog 4 slob 5 shoat, swine 6 farrow, piglet, porker 7 casting, glutton
breed: 5 Duroc 8 Tamworth 9 Berkshire, Hampshire, Yorkshire
female: 3 sow 4 gilt
feral: 9 razorback
litter: 6 farrow
male: 4 boar 6 barrow
meat: 3 ham 4 pork 5 bacon
7 sausage 8 chitlins 12 chitterlings
wild: 7 peccary, warthog 8 babirusa

pigeon

3 sap 4 dupe, fool, gull, mark
5 chump, decoy, patsy 6 culver, stooge, sucker 7 fall guy 8 rock dove
genus: 7 Columba
house: 4 cote, loft
kind: 4 barb, rock 5 homer 6 homing, pouter, roller 7 carrier, crowned, fantail, tumbler
relative: 4 dove
young: 5 squab

pigeon hawk
6 merlin

pigeonhole
4 slot, sort 5 class, cubby, grade, group, niche 6 recess, shelve 7 catalog 8 category, classify, grouping 10 categorize 11 compartment

piggish
6 greedy 7 selfish, swinish 10 gluttonous

pigheaded
5 rigid 6 dogged, mulish 7 willful 8 contrary, perverse, stubborn 9 obstinate 10 inflexible, unyielding

piglet
5 shoat

pigment
3 dye 4 tint 5 color, paint, stain 8 colorant, dyestuff, tincture
black: 9 lampblack
blue: 4 cyan 5 azure, smalt 6 indigo 7 cyanine 8 cerulean 9 verdigris 11 ultramarine
brown: 5 sepia
umber: 6 bister, sienna
combining form: 5 chrom 6 chromo
dark: 7 melanin
green: 7 celadon 8 viridian 10 biliverdin
orange: 7 realgar 8 carotene
red: 4 lake
toxic: 8 gossypol
yellow: 5 ocher, ochre 6 flavin, lutein 7 flavine, xanthin

pigpen
3 sty 4 dump, mess 5 hovel

pigskin
6 saddle 8 football

pike
4 dive, fish 5 spear 7 highway 8 pickerel

oiker
5 miser 7 scrooge 8 tightwad 9 skinflint 10 cheapskate 12 pennypincher

pilaster
4 pier 6 column, pillar

pilchard
7 herring, sardine

pile
3 fur, lot, nap 4 coat, fill, heap, hill, load, mass, much, pack, peck, pyre 5 amass, crowd, drive, stack 6 bundle, column, jumble 7 collect, fortune, reactor 8 quantity 9 great deal 10 assemblage, collection 11 aggregation 12 accumulation

pileup
4 mass 5 crash, smash 8 accident 9 collision 12 accumulation

pilfer
3 rob 4 lift, take 5 filch, pinch, steal, swipe 6 finger, snitch, thieve 7 purloin 11 appropriate

pilgarlic
4 butt 8 baldhead 13 laughingstock

Pilgrim
5 Alden (John) 6 Carver (John) 7 Puritan, Winslow (Edward) 8 Bradford (William), Brewster (William), Standish (Myles)

pilgrim
5 hadji, hajji 6 palmer 8 traveler, wanderer, wayfarer

pilgrimage
4 hajj, trip 7 journey

Pilgrims' interpreter
7 Squanto

Pilgrim's Progress
8 allegory
author: 6 Bunyan (John)
hero: 9 Christian

pill
4 ball, bore, pain, pest 5 bolus 6 pellet 7 capsule, lozenge 8 medicine, nuisance 9 annoyance

pillage
4 lift, loot, sack 5 booty, prize, spoil, steal 6 maraud, ravage, thieve 7 despoil, plunder, purloin 8 spoliate 9 depredate, desecrate

pillar
4 pier, post, prop 5 pylon, shaft, stela, stele 6 column, stelae (plural)

pillory

7 obelisk, support, upright 8 backbone, mainstay, pedestal, pilaster

pillory

6 stocks

pillow

3 pad 4 rest 7 bolster, cushion, support

pilot

4 lead, show, tool 5 drive, flier, guide, steer 6 airman, direct, leader 7 aviator, conduct, guiding, tracing 8 aviatrix, helmsman, shepherd

pimple

3 dot, zit 4 acne, boil, spot, stud 6 papule 7 blemish, blister, pustule, speckle 8 sprinkle, swelling

pin

3 leg, peg 4 clip, hold, join 5 affix, blame, stake 6 attach, broach, brooch, cotter, emblem, fasten, secure, trifle 8 fastener, hold down, ornament, restrain

pinafore

5 apron, dress, frock

pinch

3 bit, nab, nip 4 dash, lift, pain, take 5 filch, press, prune, run in, skimp, steal, swipe, taper, theft, tweak 6 arrest, crisis, narrow, pilfer, snatch, stress 7 confine, deficit, larceny, squeeze, straits 8 compress, exigency, hardship, juncture, pressure, stealing, straiten 9 apprehend, constrict, emergency, privation, tight spot 10 substitute

pinchbeck

4 fake, sham 5 alloy, bogus, false, phony 6 pseudo 8 spurious 9 brummagem 11 counterfeit

pinch hitter

3 sub 6 backup, fill-in, relief 7 standin 9 alternate, surrogate 10 substitute 11 alternative, replacement

pinchpenny

4 mean 5 cheap, close, mingy, tight 6 stingy 7 chintzy, costive, miserly, scrimpy 9 niggardly, penurious

11 closefisted, tightfisted 12 parsimonious

Pindar

home: 6 Thebes
poem: 3 ode

pine

4 ache, long, mope, sigh, tree, wish, wood 5 brood, crave, dream, yearn 6 desire, grieve, hanker, hunger, lament, thirst 7 conifer 8 languish 9 evergreen

Pine Tree State

5 Maine

pinhead

4 dolt, dope, fool 5 dunce 6 dimwit, nitwit 7 dullard 8 dumbbell 9 birdbrain

pinion

3 cog 4 bind, gear, wing 5 quill, tie up, truss 6 fetter, tether 7 disable, feather, shackle 8 cogwheel, restrain 9 hamstring

pink

3 cut 4 best, peak, stab 5 blush 6 flower, height, pierce 7 excited, paragon 9 perforate

pinna

3 ear, fin 4 wing 7 feather, leaflet

pinnacle

3 top, tor 4 acme, apex, peak 5 crest, crown, serac, spire 6 apogee, climax, height, summit, zenith 7 steeple 8 capsheaf, meridian 11 culmination

pinniped

4 seal 6 walrus

Pinocchio author

7 Collodi (Carlo) 9 Lorenzini (Carlo)

pinochle

card: 3 ace, ten 4 jack, king, nine 5 queen
term: 4 meld 5 widow 7 auction
two-handed: 7 goulash

pinpoint

3 aim, fix 4 spot, tiny 5 exact, place 6 locate 7 precise 8 identify, stand

out 9 determine, highlight, recognize
11 distinguish

Pinter play
8 Betrayal 9 Caretaker (The)
10 Homecoming (The)

pinto
4 pied, pony 5 horse, paint 7 mottled, piebald 8 skewbald

pint-size
3 wee 5 dwarf, small 6 midget,
pocket 9 miniature 10 diminutive

pioneer
5 first, prime 6 maiden 7 explore,
founder, initial, primary, settler
8 colonist, earliest, explorer, original
9 innovator 10 avant-garde, pathfinder 11 trailblazer 12 frontiersman
famous: 5 Boone (Daniel), Bowie
(Jim), Clark (William), Lewis (Meriwether) 6 Carson (Kit), Colter (John)
7 Bridger (Jim), Chapman (John),
Frémont (John C.), Whitman (Marcus) 8 Crockett (Davy)

pious
4 holy 5 godly 6 devout, worthy
7 devoted, dutiful 8 reverent, virtuous 9 hypocrite, pietistic, prayerful,
religious 10 devotional 12 hypocritical

pip
3 dot 4 blip, peep, seed, spot
5 speck 9 break open

pipe
3 keg, tun 4 butt, cask, duct, hose,
tube 6 barrel, convey, funnel, siphon
7 channel, conduct, conduit 8 aqueduct, hogshead
ceremonial: 7 calumet
part: 4 bowl, stem

pipe down
4 hush 5 dry up, quiet 6 shut up
7 be quiet

pipe dream
4 wish 7 chimera, fantasy 8 illusion

pipeline
5 works 6 system 7 channel, conduit, process 8 activity, supplier
10 connection

pipsqueak
6 shaver, squirt 7 tadpole 8 halfpint, small fry

piquant
4 tart 5 sharp, spicy, tangy, zesty
6 biting, lively, savory, snappy
7 peppery, pungent 8 poignant,
spirited 9 flavorful, sparkling 10 appetizing 11 provocative, stimulating

pique
3 irk, vex 4 huff, miff, move 5 anger,
annoy, peeve, pride, rouse 6 arouse,
excite, nettle, offend, put out 7 dudgeon, offense, provoke, quicken
8 irritate, motivate, vexation 9 aggravate, annoyance, challenge, stimulate 10 exasperate, irritation, resentment

piracy
5 theft 7 lifting, looting, pillage,
plunder, robbery 8 stealing, thievery
10 plagiarism

piranha
6 caribe

pirate
5 rover 6 looter, raider, robber, sea
dog 7 brigand, corsair, sea wolf
8 marauder, picaroon, pillager, sea
rover 9 buccaneer, plunderer, privateer, sea robber 10 freebooter
English: 4 Read (Mary) 5 Bonny
(Anne), Teach (Edward) 6 Morgan (Henry) 7 Dampier (William)
10 Blackbeard
flag: 10 Jolly Roger
French: 7 Laffite (Jean), Lafitte
(Jean)
Scottish: 4 Kidd (William)

Pirates of Penzance, The
composer: 8 Sullivan (Arthur)
librettist: 7 Gilbert (W. S.)

pirogue
5 canoe 6 dugout

pirouette
4 spin, turn 5 twirl, whirl

piscator
6 angler 9 fisherman

pismire
3 ant

pistol
3 gat, rod 4 Colt 5 Glock, Luger
6 Magnum, Mauser, roscoe 7 bulldog, handgun 8 revolver, small arm
9 derringer, pepperbox
case: 7 holster

pit
3 vie 4 dent, hell, hole, scar 5 arena,
hades, match, shaft, stone 6 cavity,
hollow, oppose 7 counter, play off
8 pockmark 11 indentation

Pit and the Pendulum author
3 Poe (Edgar Allan)

pitch
3 dip, set 4 buck, dive, drop, fall,
hurl, line, play, plug, tilt, tone, toss
5 erect, fling, heave, lurch, put up,
resin, slant, sling, slope, spiel, throw
6 encamp, go down, plunge 7 discard, incline, present, promote
8 distance 9 advertise, declivity
13 advertisement

pitch-dark
3 jet 4 ebon, inky 5 black, ebony,
jetty

pitcher
4 ewer, olla, toby 5 cruse 6 beaker,
flagon 7 creamer
area: 5 mound
handle: 3 ear 4 ansa
see also **baseballer**

pitch in
3 aid 4 help 5 begin, set to, start
6 fall to 8 commence, get going,
start off 9 subscribe, volunteer
10 contribute

piteous
3 sad 4 poor 8 pathetic 9 affecting
10 lamentable 11 distressing

pitfall
4 risk, snag, trap 5 catch, peril,
snare 6 danger, hazard 9 booby
trap 10 difficulty 12 entanglement

pith
3 nub 4 core, kill, meat, pulp 5 focus,
heart 6 center, import, kernel 7 essence, nucleus 9 substance 10 importance 12 significance

pith helmet
5 topee

pithy
5 brief, crisp, meaty, short, terse
6 cogent 7 compact, concise,
pointed 8 succinct 12 epigrammatic
13 short and sweet

pitiable
4 poor 5 cheap, sorry 8 shameful
10 deplorable, lamentable 12 contemptible

pitiful
3 sad 4 mean, poor 5 cheap, sorry
6 meager, meagre, paltry, shabby
7 forlorn 8 beggarly, pathetic,
wretched 9 miserable 10 despicable, inadequate 12 contemptible
13 heartbreaking

pitiless
4 cold, hard 5 cruel, harsh, stony
6 brutal 8 inhumane, uncaring
9 barbarous, unfeeling 10 unmerciful
11 coldhearted, hardhearted

pittance
4 wage 5 scrap, trace 6 trifle
7 modicum, peanuts 9 allowance

pity
3 rue 4 ache, ruth 5 mercy 6 regret,
sorrow 7 empathy, feel for, sadness 8 distress, sympathy 10 compassion, condolence, sympathize
11 commiserate 13 commiseration

pivot
3 pin 4 turn 5 hinge, shaft, swing,
wheel 6 center, swivel

pivotal
3 key 5 chief, vital 7 central, crucial
8 critical, decisive 9 essential,
important

pixie
3 elf, fay, imp 5 antic, fairy, scamp

6 elvish, impish, rascal, sprite
7 brownie, coltish, playful, puckish
8 prankish 11 mischievous

pixilated
3 fey 7 bemused, erratic, flighty,
muddled, touched 9 eccentric,
whimsical 10 capricious

Pizarro, Francisco
brother: 7 Gonzalo
city founded: 4 Lima
conquest: 4 Peru
victims: 5 Incas 9 Atahualpa
10 Atahuallpa

pizzazz
3 pep, vim, zip 4 bang, brio, dash,
snap, zest, zing 5 éclat, flair, flash,
gusto, moxie, oomph, punch, verve
6 dazzle, energy, hoopla, sizzle, spirit
7 glamour, panache 8 vitality 10 excitement

placard
4 bill, post 6 notice, plaque, poster
7 affiche 8 handbill

placate
4 calm, ease 6 pacify, soothe 7 appease, assuage, comfort, mollify,
satisfy, sweeten, win over 10 conciliate, propitiate

place
3 lay, put, set 4 area, lieu, loci
(plural), post, rank, site, spot, zone
5 locus, point, stead, tract 6 region,
status 7 situate, station 8 district,
identify, locality, location, pinpoint,
position, standing 9 establish,
recognize
combining form: 3 top 4 loco,
topo, topy

placid
4 calm, easy, mild 5 quiet, still
6 gentle, serene 7 halcyon 8 composed, peaceful, tranquil, waveless,
windless 9 unruffled 10 complacent,
unagitated, untroubled 11 undisturbed 13 imperturbable

plagiarize
4 copy, crib 5 steal 6 pirate 11 appropriate

plague
3 vex 4 bane, evil, pest 5 annoy,
beset, curse, harry, hound, smite,
trial, worry 6 blight, bother, infest,
harass, hassle, hector, pester
7 afflict, bedevil, disease, disturb,
scourge, torment, trouble 8 calamity,
distress, epidemic, invasion, irritant,
irritate, nuisance, outbreak, pandemic 9 annoyance, beleaguer
10 affliction, black death, pestilence
11 infestation

plaid
6 tartan

plain
3 lea 4 bald, bare, open, pure
5 blunt, clear, field, frank, usual
6 candid, common, homely, modest, patent, severe, simple, tundra
7 expanse, evident, obvious, prairie,
savanna 8 apparent, distinct, everyday, homespun, manifest, ordinary,
straight 9 outspoken, unadorned
10 absolutely, forthright, unaffected
11 undecorated, unvarnished 13 uncomplicated

plainclothesman
4 dick 6 shamus, sleuth 7 gumshoe
8 hawkshaw 9 detective 12 investigator

_____ Plaines
3 Des

plainness
6 candor, purity 7 clarity, honesty
8 lucidity 10 simplicity

plainsong
5 chant 12 cantus firmus

plainspoken
4 open 5 frank 6 candid, direct,
honest 8 straight, truthful 10 forthright 11 undisguised, unvarnished

plaintive
3 sad 4 glum 6 woeful 7 doleful,
piteous, pitiful 8 dolorous, downcast,
mournful 9 sorrowful 10 dispirited,
lamentable, lugubrious, melancholy

plait
4 fold 5 braid, pleat, weave 7 pigtail
10 intertwine, interweave

plan

3 aim, map, way **4** cast, goal, idea, mean, plot **5** chart, frame **6** design, devise, intend, intent, lay out, map out, method, scheme, set out **7** arrange, diagram, drawing, outline, pattern, program, project, propose, purpose, work out **8** contrive, engineer, organize, strategy, think out **9** blueprint, formulate, intention, procedure **11** arrangement, formulation

plane

3 fly, jet **4** even, flat, tool, tree **5** flush, level **6** smooth **8** aircraft, airliner

planet

4 Mars **5** Earth, Pluto, Venus **6** Saturn, Uranus **7** Jupiter, Mercury, Neptune
path: **5** orbit
satellite: **4** moon
shadow: **5** umbra
small: **8** asteroid

planetary

4 vast **6** global **7** erratic, immense **8** colossal, enormous **9** universal, wandering, worldwide **11** terrestrial

plangent

7 orotund, ringing, vibrant **8** resonant, sonorous **9** consonant, plaintive **10** expressive, resounding **11** reverberant

plank

4 item, wood **5** board, floor **6** lumber, timber **7** article, support

plant

3 fix, pot, set, sow **4** bury, grow, hide, mill, park, root, seed, tomb **5** cache, cover, imbed, inter, place, plunk, put in, stash, works **6** entomb, inhume, occult, screen, conceal, factory, install, lay away, put away, secrete **8** colonize, populate **9** cultivate
angiosperm: **5** dicot **7** monocot
aquatic: **4** reed **5** lotus, sedge **7** awlwort, cattail, fanwort, papyrus **8** duckweed, eelgrass, hornwort, pondweed **9** water lily **10** watercress **11** bladderwort **12** pickerelweed
Australian: **6** mallee **7** banksia **8** blackboy **10** eucalyptus
body: **4** stem **7** thallus
bulbous: **4** lily **5** camas, onion, tulip **7** jonquil **8** hyacinth **9** narcissus
carnivorous: **6** sundew **10** butterwort **12** pitcher plant, Venus flytrap
cell layer: **7** phellem
climbing: **3** ivy **4** vine **5** betel, liana, vetch **6** bryony, derris, smilax **7** creeper, jasmine **8** bignonia, fumitory, moonseed, scammony, wisteria **12** morning glory
coloring agent: **8** carotene **11** chlorophyll, xanthophyll
combining form: **4** phyt **5** phyto
cone-bearing: **3** fir, yew **4** pine **5** cedar, cycad **6** ginkgo, spruce **7** conifer, cypress, redwood **10** arborvitae, gymnosperm
desert: **4** aloe **5** agave **6** cactus, cholla **8** mesquite, ocotillo **9** paloverde **11** brittlebush
disease: **3** rot **4** gall, mold, rust, scab, smut, wilt **5** ergot **6** blight, mildew, mosaic **7** blister **8** clubroot **9** black spot **10** black heart
extinct: **8** calamite
flowerless: **4** alga, fern, kelp, moss **5** algae (plural), fungi (plural) **6** fungus, lichen **7** seaweed **8** clubmoss **9** bryophyte, equisetum, horsetail, liverwort
fluid: **3** gum, sap **4** milk **5** latex, resin
gland: **7** nectary
hallucinogenic: **4** hemp **5** poppy **6** mescal **8** cannabis **9** marijuana
largest: **7** sequoia
life: **5** flora
marine: **4** kelp, nori **5** dulse, fucus **6** wakame **7** seaweed **8** gulfweed **10** sea lettuce
marsh: **4** reed **5** carex, sedge **7** bogbean, bulrush, calamus, cattail **8** red maple, sphagnum **11** loosestrife
medicinal: **4** aloe, sage **5** poppy, senna, tansy **6** catnip, fennel, garlic, hyssop, ipecac, nettle **7** aconite, boneset, burdock, camphor, comfrey,

ginseng, hemlock, henbane, juniper, lobelia, mullein, mustard, parsley **8** camomile, capsicum, cinchona, feverfew, licorice, pilewort, plantain, wormwood **9** asafetida, chamomile, dandelion, echinacea, fenugreek, monkshood **10** asafoetida, goldenseal, peppermint

microscopic: 4 mold **6** diatom **7** euglena **8** bacteria (plural) **9** bacterium

oldest: 11 bristlecone

onion-like: 4 leek **5** chive **7** shallot **8** scallion

opening: 5 stoma **7** stomata (plural)

parasitic: 6 dodder, fungus **7** pinesap **8** gerardia **9** broomrape, mistletoe, rafflesia, witchweed **10** beechdrops

part: 3 bud, nut, sap **4** bark, bulb, cell, cone, corm, leaf, pome, root, seed, stem, wood **5** drupe, fruit, grain, spore, thorn, tuber, xylem **6** catkin, flower, nectar, phloem, raceme **7** rhizome **8** lenticel **9** cellulose, cotyledon **11** chlorophyll, chloroplast **13** inflorescence

pest: 5 aphid, scale **6** chafer, thrips, weevil **7** cutworm **8** fruit fly, wireworm **9** gypsy moth **10** cankerworm, leafhopper, phylloxera **11** codling moth

poisonous: 4 poke, upas **5** sumac **6** castor, croton, datura **7** amanita, cassava, cowbane, henbane, lobelia, tobacco **8** foxglove, larkspur, locoweed, mayapple, oleander, pokeweed **9** baneberry, monkshood **10** belladonna, jimsonweed, manchineel, nightshade

saprophytic: 5 fungi (plural) **6** fungus **7** pinesap **9** pinedrops, snow plant **10** beechdrops, Indian pipe

succulent: 4 aloe **5** agave **6** cactus **10** bitterroot

thorny: 4 rose **5** briar **6** cactus, nettle, teasel **7** caltrop, thistle **9** cocklebur

tissue: 5 xylem **6** phloem **7** cambium, medulla **8** meristem

young: 5 scion, shoot **6** sprout **7** cutting **8** seedling

plantain
5 fruit **6** banana

plantation
5 manor **6** colony, estate, quinta **7** acreage, demesne **8** hacienda **10** encampment, habitation, settlement

plant louse
5 aphid

plaque
4 film **5** badge, patch **6** brooch, lesion, tablet **7** tribute **8** bacteria, memorial **13** commemoration

plaster
3 dab **4** coat **5** affix, cover, gesso **6** stucco **7** coating, conceal, overlay **8** dressing
of paris: 5 gesso **6** gypsum

plastered
3 lit **4** high **5** drunk, lit up, oiled **6** bashed, blotto, bombed, juiced, potted, soaked, soused, stewed, stoned, tanked, wasted, zonked **7** crocked, drunken, pickled, pie-eyed, sloshed, smashed, sottish **10** inebriated, liquored up **11** intoxicated

plastic
4 soft **5** vinyl **6** pliant, supple **7** ductile, pliable **8** creative, flexible, moldable, workable **9** adaptable, formative, malleable, synthetic **10** artificial, credit card, sculptural

plat
3 lot, map **4** plan **5** chart, tract **6** parcel **7** quadrat

plate
4 base, coat, disc, dish, disk, gild, tile **5** layer, paten, scute, slice **6** enamel, fascia, lamina, plaque **7** anodize, lamella, overlay

plateau
4 mesa **5** table **6** upland **9** altiplano, tableland
arid: 4 puna
barren: 5 field **6** paramo
dry: 5 karoo **6** karroo

platform

3 map 4 bank, base, dais, deck, plan 5 bimah, forum, ledge, riser, shelf, stage, stump 6 design, perron, podium, pulpit, scheme 7 balcony, pattern, rostrum 8 hustings, scaffold 9 banquette, manifesto 11 declaration

temporary: 7 staging 8 scaffold
wooden: 9 boardwalk

Plath, Sylvia

novel: 7 Bell Jar (The)
poem: 5 Ariel, Daddy

platitude

6 cliché, truism 7 bromide 8 banality, prosaism 10 shibboleth

Plato

father: 7 Ariston
literary form: 6 dialog 8 dialogue
original name: 10 Aristocles
school: 7 Academy
work: 3 Ion 4 Meno 5 Crito, Lysis 6 Laches, Phaedo 7 Apology, Gorgias 8 Phaedrus, Republic (The) 9 Charmides, Symposium

platter

5 plate 6 record 8 trencher

platypus

8 duckbill

plaudits

5 kudos 6 cheers, praise 7 acclaim, ovation 8 applause, approval, encomium 9 accolades 11 acclamation

plausible

8 credible, specious 10 believable, convincing, creditable, persuasive, reasonable

play

3 act, fun 4 game, jest, joke, romp 5 drama, feint, serve, sport, treat, trick, wager 6 cavort, comedy, fiddle, frolic, gambit, gambol, leeway, margin 7 delight, disport, perform, twiddle 8 latitude, maneuver, pleasure 9 amusement, diversion, enjoyment, stratagem 10 manipulate, recreation

kind: 5 farce 6 comedy 7 musical, tragedy 8 one-acter 9 melodrama, pantomime
part: 3 act 5 scene 8 epilogue, prologue

playact

5 put on 7 perform, posture, pretend 9 personate 11 impersonate, make believe

playboy

4 rake, roué 8 hedonist 9 bon vivant

play down

8 minimize 9 deprecate, soft-pedal, underrate 11 de-emphasize

player

5 actor 6 mummer 7 actress, athlete, trouper 8 musician, thespian 9 contender, performer 10 competitor, contestant 11 participant

playful

5 antic, jolly, merry, pixie 6 elvish, frisky, impish, jocund, joking, jovial, lively 7 coltish, jocular, puckish, waggish 8 humorous, sportive 9 kittenish, sprightly 10 frolicsome

play off

3 pit, vie 5 match 6 oppose 7 counter 8 contrast

plaything

3 toy

play up

6 stress 7 feature 9 dramatize, emphasize, highlight, overstate, underline 10 accentuate, exaggerate, underscore

playwright

9 dramatist 10 dramaturge (see also **dramatist**)

plaza

6 circus, common, square, zocalo 9 carrefour 11 marketplace

plea

4 suit 5 alibi 6 appeal, excuse, orison, prayer 7 apology, defense, pretext, request 8 entreaty, overture, petition 11 application, imploration 12 supplication

defendant's: **4** nolo **6** guilty **8** innocent **9** not guilty

plead
3 beg **4** pray **5** argue **6** allege, answer, appeal **7** beseech, entreat, implore **8** advocate, maintain **9** importune **10** supplicate

pleasant
4 fair, fine, good, nice **5** clear, sunny, sweet **6** cheery, genial, pretty **7** amiable, clarion, likable, welcome **8** amicable, charming, cheerful, engaging, gracious, grateful, likeable, pleasing, sunshine, sunshiny **9** agreeable, appealing, cloudless, congenial, convivial, enjoyable, favorable, unclouded **10** delightful, gratifying

pleasantry
3 fun **4** jest, joke **6** banter, levity **8** badinage, repartee **9** wittiness **10** jocularity

please
4 like, suit, wish **5** agree, amuse, enjoy, serve **6** choose **7** content, delight, gladden, gratify, indulge, satisfy
French: **12** s'il vous plait
German: **5** bitte
Spanish: **8** por favor

pleasing
4 good, nice **6** pretty **7** welcome **8** suitable **9** agreeable, congenial, favorable, palatable **10** attractive, delightful, gratifying **12** satisfactory

pleasure
3 fun, joy **4** will **5** bliss, fancy **6** desire, liking, relish **7** delight, gladden, gratify **8** felicity, gladness, hedonism **9** amusement, diversion, enjoyment, happiness, merriment **11** inclination

pleat
4 fold **5** crimp **6** crease

plebe
5 frosh **8** freshman

plebeian
3 low **4** base **5** crude, lowly **6** coarse, common, humble, menial **8** commoner, everyday, ordinary **10** lower-class

plectrum
4 pick

pledge
3 vow **4** bail, bind, bond, gage, hock, oath, pawn, seal, sign, word **5** drink, swear, toast, token **6** parole, plight, surety **7** chattel, earnest, promise, warrant **8** bailment, contract, covenant, guaranty, security, warranty **9** agreement, assurance, certainty, guarantee, undertake

pledget
3 pad **8** compress

Pleiades
4 Maia **6** Merope **7** Alcyone, Celaeno, Electra, Sterope, Taygeta **8** Asterope
brightest star: **7** Alcyone

plenary
4 full **5** whole **6** entire **7** general **8** absolute, complete **9** inclusive **11** unqualified **12** unrestricted

plenitude
4 glut **6** excess **7** satiety, surfeit **8** fullness **9** abundance, profusion, repletion **11** copiousness, sufficiency, superfluity **12** completeness

plenteous
7 fertile **8** abundant, fruitful, prolific **9** abounding **10** productive

plentiful
4 full, rich **5** ample, flush **7** copious, profuse **8** abundant, affluent, generous **9** abounding, bounteous, unstinted **10** sufficient

plenty
3 lot **4** heap, pack, peck, pile **6** stacks, wealth **8** adequacy, fullness, mountain **9** abundance, affluence, great deal **10** cornucopia

pleonasm
8 verbiage **9** prolixity, tautology, verbosity, wordiness **10** redundancy **11** periphrasis, superfluity

plethora
4 glut 5 flood 6 excess 7 overrun,
surfeit, surplus 8 fullness, overflow
9 abundance, profusion, repletion
11 superfluity 13 overabundance

plexus
4 rete 7 network

pliable
6 supple 7 plastic 9 adaptable
10 adjustable 11 complaisant, manipulable

pliant
5 lithe 6 limber, supple 7 ductile,
plastic, springy 8 flexible, moldable,
workable, yielding 9 adaptable,
malleable, tractable 10 manageable

plica
4 fold 6 crease, groove

plight
3 fix, jam, vow 4 hole, spot, word
5 swear 6 engage, pickle, pledge,
scrape 7 betroth, dilemma, promise
8 quandary 9 betrothal 10 difficulty,
engagement 11 predicament

plod
4 slog, toil 5 grind, slave, tramp,
tread, tromp 6 drudge, lumber,
trudge 8 plug away

plot
3 map 4 area, land, mark, note, plan
5 cabal, chart, story, tract 6 design,
devise, invent, lay out, locate, parcel,
scheme 7 collude, compact, connive, diagram, outline 8 conspire,
contrive, intrigue, scenario 9 collusion, conniving, machinate 10 complicity, connivance, conspiracy
11 machination

plover
5 pewit, stilt 6 peewit 7 lapwing
8 dotterel, killdeer
relative: 9 sandpiper, turnstone

plow
3 dig 4 till, turn 5 break 6 furrow,
harrow, trench 8 turn over 9 cultivate
part: 4 beam, frog 5 share 7 coul-
ter 8 landside 9 moldboard

ploy
4 ruse, scam, wile 5 feint, trick
6 device, frolic, gambit, tactic 7 gimmick 8 artifice, escapade, maneuver
9 stratagem 11 contrivance

pluck
3 rob, tug 4 grit, guts, pick, pull,
yank 5 cheek, grasp, heart, moxie,
nerve, spunk 6 daring, fleece,
mettle, remove, snatch, spirit, tweeze
7 bravery, courage, pull out 8 game-
ness 10 resolution

plucky
4 bold, game 5 brave 6 feisty,
spunky 7 doughty 8 fearless, spirited, unafraid 9 dauntless 10 courageous

plug
3 tap 4 bung, clog, core, cork, fill,
hype, pack, push, stop, tout 5 block,
blurb, boost, choke, close, cry up,
shoot 6 device, remedy 7 congest,
fitting, hydrant, promote, stopper
8 obstruct 9 advertise, publicity,
publicize 10 connection

plug-ugly
4 thug 5 bully, rowdy, tough 7 hoodlum, ruffian 9 roughneck

plum
5 prize 6 purple, reward 7 guerdon,
premium 8 dividend
dried: 5 prune
kind: 6 damson 7 bullace 9 green-
gage
spiny: 10 blackthorn

plumage
8 feathers
early: 4 down

plumb
5 delve, probe, sound 6 fathom,
weight 7 exactly, examine, explore,
install, measure 8 absolute, complete, thorough, vertical 10 absolutely, vertically 11 immediately
13 perpendicular

plume
4 tail 5 array, preen, pride, prize
6 column 7 feather 8 aigrette

plummet

4 dive, drop, fall 5 crash 6 plunge, tumble 8 collapse, nose-dive 11 precipitate

plump

3 fat 4 drop, fall, full 5 ample, buxom, favor, pudgy, round, stout, tubby 6 chubby, portly, rotund 7 rounded, support 8 abundant, directly, roly-poly 10 Rubenesque

plumply

7 frankly, plainly 8 candidly 12 forthrightly

plunder

3 rob 4 loot, sack, swag, take 5 booty, prize, seize, spoil, steal, strip 6 boodle, rapine, spoils 7 despoil, pillage, ransack, relieve, stick up 9 pillaging

plunge

3 bet, ram, run 4 dive, drop, fall, jump, rush, sink, stab, swim 5 drive, lunge, pitch, stick 6 charge, gamble, hasten, hurtle, thrust, topple, tumble 7 descend, immerse, plummet 8 nose-dive, submerge 9 penetrate

plus

3 and 4 more, perk 5 added, asset, bonus, boost, extra 6 excess 7 benefit 8 addition, increase, positive

plush

4 full, rich 6 deluxe, fabric, lavish, velvet 7 opulent 8 luscious, palatial 9 expensive, luxuriant, luxurious, sumptuous

Pluto

3 Dis 5 Hades
brother: 4 Zeus 7 Jupiter, Neptune 8 Poseidon
father: 6 Cronus, Saturn
mother: 3 Ops 4 Rhea
wife: 10 Persephone, Proserpina

plutocrat

5 mogul 6 fat cat, tycoon 7 magnate 9 financier, moneybags 10 capitalist

plutonian

8 infernal 10 underworld

Plutus

father: 6 Iasion
god of: 6 riches, wealth
mother: 5 Ceres 7 Demeter

ply

3 use 4 bias, sail 5 apply, exert, layer, wield 6 employ, handle, strand, supply, travel, voyage 7 furnish, perform 8 maneuver, practice 11 inclination

pneuma

4 soul 5 anima 6 psyche, spirit

pneumatic

4 airy 5 ample, buxom, plump 6 aerial, zaftig 9 spiritual 10 curvaceous 11 atmospheric

poach

4 cook 5 steal 6 coddle, simmer 7 intrude 8 encroach, trespass 9 interlope 11 appropriate

Pocahontas

father: 8 Powhatan
husband: 5 Rolfe (John)

pock

3 pit 4 hole, spot 7 pustule

pocket

3 bag 4 lift, sack 5 filch, pinch, pouch, purse, steal, swipe 6 cavity 7 capsule, dead end, impasse 8 culde-sac 9 condensed 10 blind alley
billiards: 4 pool

pocketbook

3 bag 4 poke 5 purse 6 clutch, income, wallet 7 handbag 8 billfold 9 clutch bag

pocket bread

4 pita

pocket money

6 change 9 petty cash 11 small change

pocket-size

4 tiny 5 small 9 miniature 10 diminutive

pod

3 bag, gam, sac 4 boll, case, hull, husk, skin 5 shell, shuck 6 cocoon 7 capsule, silique 8 seedcase

pod-bearing tree

plant: 3 pea 4 bean, okra 5 chili, gumbo 6 cassia, cowpea, legume, lentil, peanut, pepper 8 capsicum, mesquite, milkweed 9 lespedeza

pod-bearing tree
5 carob 6 locust 7 catalpa

podiatry
9 chiropody

podium
4 dais 6 pulpit 7 lectern, rostrum 8 platform

_____ podrida
4 olla

Poe, Edgar Allan
detective: 5 Dupin (C. Auguste)
poem: 5 Bells (The), Raven (The) 6 Lenore 7 Israfel, To Helen, Ulalume 8 Eldorado, For Annie 10 Annabel Lee
tale: 6 Ligeia, Shadow 7 Gold-Bug (The), Morella, Silence 8 Black Cat (The) 13 Tell-tale Heart (The) 15 Purloined Letter (The) 17 Cask of Amontillado (The), Pit and the Pendulum (The) 19 Masque of the Red Death (The) 21 Fall of the House of Usher (The)

poem
3 ode 4 epic, epos, idyl, rime, rune, song 5 ditty, elegy, epode, idyll, lyric, rhyme, verse 6 ballad, epopee, jingle, rondel, sonnet 7 eclogue, rondeau 9 limerick, madrigal
closing: 5 envoi, envoy
division: 4 foot, line 5 canto, epode, stich, verse 6 stanza 7 refrain 8 epilogue, prologue
Japanese: 5 haiku, tanka
of eight lines: 6 octave 7 triolet
of four lines: 8 quatrain
of fourteen lines: 6 sonnet
of three lines: 7 triplet
pastoral: 7 eclogue, georgic
short: 5 ditty 7 epigram

poet
4 bard, muse, scop 5 skald 6 lyrist 7 elegist 8 idyllist, lyricist 9 balladist, sonneteer 10 Parnassian

American: 3 Poe (Edgar Allan) 4 Dove (Rita), Hass (Robert), Nash (Ogden), Read (Thomas), Rich (Adrienne), Tabb (John Banister), Tate (Allen) 5 Auden (Wystan Hugh), Benét (Stephen Vincent), Crane (Hart), Field (Eugene), Frost (Robert), Guest (Edgar), Moore (Marianne), Plath (Sylvia), Pound (Ezra), Riley (James Whitcomb), Wylie (Elinor) 6 Barlow (Joel), Bishop (Elizabeth), Brooks (Gwendolyn), Bryant (William Cullen), Ciardi (John), Dickey (James), Dunbar (Paul Laurence), Hughes (Langston), Kilmer (Joyce), Lanier (Sidney), Lowell (Amy, James Russell, Robert), McKuen (Rod), Millay (Edna St. Vincent), Pinsky (Robert), Ransom (John Crowe), Seeger (Alan), Strand (Mark), Taylor (Edward), Warren (Robert Penn), Wilbur (Richard) 7 Angelou (Maya), Ashbery (John), Emerson (Ralph Waldo), Freneau (Philip), Halleck (Fitz-Greene), Jeffers (Robinson), Lindsay (Vachel), Markham (Edwin), Merrill (James), Nemerov (Howard), Roethke (Theodore), Shapiro (Karl), Stevens (Wallace), Whitman (Walt) 8 Berryman (John), Cummings (E. E.), Ginsberg (Allen), MacLeish (Archibald), Robinson (Edwin Arlington), Sandburg (Carl), Teasdale (Sara), Wheatley (Phillis), Whittier (John Greenleaf), Williams (C. K., William Carlos) 9 Dickinson (Emily), Santayana (George) 10 Bradstreet (Anne), Longfellow (Henry Wadsworth) 12 Wigglesworth (Michael)
Anglo-Saxon: 7 Caedmon, Cynwulf 8 Cynewulf, Kynewulf
Arab: 5 Jarir 6 Hariri 8 al-Hariri
Australian: 8 Paterson (Andrew Barton)
Belgian: 11 Maeterlinck (Maurice)
Canadian: 5 Pratt (Edwin John) 6 Hébert (Anne) 7 Roberts (Charles G. D.), Service (Robert) 8 Drummond (William Henry) 9 Fréchette (Louis-Honoré)
Chilean: 6 Neruda (Pablo) 7 Mistral (Gabriela)

Chinese: 4 Li Po, Tu Fu 7 Wang Wei

Danish: 4 Rode (Helge) 5 Ewald (Johannes)

English: 3 Gay (John) 4 Gray (Thomas), Owen (Wilfred), Pope (Alexander), Rowe (Nicholas), Tate (Nahum), Wyat (Thomas) 5 Blake (William), Byron (Lord), Carew (Thomas), Clare (John), Donne (John), Eliot (Thomas Stearns), Gower (John), Hardy (Thomas), Keats (John), Noyes (Alfred), Wilde (Oscar), Wyatt (Thomas), Young (Edward) 6 Arnold (Matthew), Austin (Alfred), Belloc (Hilaire), Brooke (Rupert), Butler (Samuel), Clough (Arthur Hugh), Cowper (William), Dryden (John), Graves (Robert), Larkin (Philip), Milton (John), Savage (Richard), Sidney (Philip), Surrey (Earl of), Symons (Arthur), Waller (Edmund), Warton (Thomas), Watson (William), Wotton (Henry) 7 Bridges (Robert), Campion (Thomas), Chaucer (Geoffrey), Gilbert (W. S.), Herbert (George), Herrick (Robert), Hopkins (Gerard Manley), Housman (A. E.), Kipling (Rudyard), Layamon, Marvell (Andrew), Patmore (Coventry), Quarles (Francis), Shelley (Percy Bysshe), Skelton (John), Southey (Robert), Spender (Stephen), Spenser (Edmund) 8 Betjeman (John), Browning (Elizabeth Barrett, Robert), de la Mare (Walter), Langland (William), Lovelace (Richard), Meredith (George), Rossetti (Christina, Dante Gabriel), Suckling (John), Tennyson (Alfred Lord), Thompson (Francis) 9 Coleridge (Samuel Taylor), Masefield (John), Swinburne (Algernon Charles) 10 Chatterton (Thomas), FitzGerald (Edward), Wordsworth (William) 11 Shakespeare (William)

Finnish: 8 Runeberg (Johan Ludvig)

French: 5 Marot (Clément) 6 Musset (Alfred de), Valéry (Paul), Villon (François) 7 Bourget (Paul), Chénier (André de, Marie-Joseph), Gautier (Théophile), Rimbaud (Arthur), Ronsard (Pierre de) 8 Malherbe (François de), Mallarmé (Stéphane), Verlaine (Paul) 9 Lamartine (Alphonse de) 10 Baudelaire (Charles) 11 Apollinaire (Guillaume)

German: 5 Heine (Heinrich), Rilke (Rainer Maria), Sachs (Hans), Storm (Theodor) 6 Brecht (Bertolt), Goethe (Johann Wolfgang von), Uhland (Ludwig) 7 Walther (von der Vogelweide), Wolfram (von Eschenbach) 8 Schiller (Friedrich von) 9 Klopstock (Friedrich Gottlieb)

Greek: 5 Arion, Homer 6 Elytis (Odysseus), Erinna, Hesiod, Pindar, Ritsos (Yannis), Sappho 7 Agathon, Alcaeus, Orpheus, Seferis (George), Thespis 8 Anacreon 9 Simonides 10 Apollonius, Theocritus

Hindu: 5 Naidu (Sarojini) 6 Tagore (Rabindranath) 8 Kalidasa, Tulsidas

Hungarian: 6 Petofi (Sandor), Zrinyi (Miklos)

Irish: 5 Moore (Thomas), Wolfe (Charles), Yeats (William Butler) 6 Heaney (Seamus) 7 Dunsany (Lord) 8 Drummond (William Henry), MacNeice (Louis)

Italian: 4 Rosa (Salvator), Vida (Marco) 5 Dante (Alighieri), Tasso (Torquato) 7 Ariosto (Ludovico), Manzoni (Alessandro), Montale (Eugenio) 8 Carducci (Giosuè), Leopardi (Giacomo), Petrarch 9 Boccaccio (Giovanni), D'Annunzio (Gabriele), Marinetti (Filippo Tommaso), Quasimodo (Salvatore), Ungaretti (Giuseppe)

Japanese: 5 Basho 6 Matsuo

medieval: 8 minstrel, trouvère 10 troubadour

Mexican: 3 Paz (Octavio)

nonsense: 4 Lear (Edward)

Norwegian: 6 Bjornson (Bjornstjerne), Welhaven (Johan) 9 Wergeland (Henrik)

Persian: 4 Sadi 5 Attar, Hafez, Hafiz 11 Omar Khayyám

Roman: 4 Ovid 6 Horace, Vergil, Virgil 7 Juvenal, Martial, Statius 8 Catullus, Tibullus 9 Lucretius

Russian: 4 Blok (Aleksandr)
7 Brodsky (Joseph), Pushkin (Aleksandr), Yesenin (Sergey) 9 Akhmatova (Anna), Kheraskov (Mikhail), Pasternak (Boris), Tsvetaeva (Marina) 10 Mandelstam (Osip), Mayakovsky (Vladimir) 11 Yevtushenko (Yevgeny)
Saint Lucian: 7 Walcott (Derek)
Scottish: 4 Hogg (James), Muir (Edwin) 5 Burns (Robert), Scott (Alexander, Walter) 6 Dunbar (William), Ramsay (Allan) 7 Thomson (James) 10 MacDiarmid (Hugh)
Spanish: 5 Lorca (Federico García) 7 Jiménez (Juan Ramón) 8 Figueroa (Francisco) 10 Aleixandre (Vicente) 11 García Lorca (Federico)
Swedish: 5 Sachs (Nelly) 6 Tegner (Esaias) 8 Snoilsky (Carl Johan) 9 Karlfeldt (Erik Axel)
Swiss: 5 Amiel (Henri Frédéric) 9 Spitteler (Carl)
Welsh: 6 Thomas (Dylan) 7 Aneurin, Watkins (Vernon)

poetic
5 lyric 6 dreamy 8 romantic 9 aesthetic, beautiful

poet laureate
British: 3 Pye (Henry) 4 Rowe (Nicholas), Tate (Nahum) 6 Austin (Alfred), Cibber (Colley), Dryden (John), Hughes (Ted), Jonson (Ben), Motion (Andrew) 7 Bridges (Robert), Southey (Robert) 8 Betjeman (John), Davenant (William), Day-Lewis (Cecil), Shadwell (Thomas), Tennyson (Alfred) 9 Masefield (John), Whitehead (William) 10 Wordsworth (William)
American: 4 Dove (Rita), Hass (Robert) 5 Glück (Louise) 6 Kooser (Ted), Kunitz (Stanley), Merwin (W. S.), Pinsky (Robert), Strand (Mark), Warren (Robert Penn), Wilbur (Richard) 7 Brodsky (Joseph), Collins (Billy), Nemerov (Howard), Van Duyn (Mona)

Pogo creator
5 Kelly (Walt)

poi
4 taro

poignancy
6 pathos 7 emotion, sadness 9 sentiment

poignant
3 sad 4 keen 5 acute, sharp 6 biting, moving 7 painful, piquant, pointed, pungent 8 incisive, piercing, stirring, touching 9 affecting, emotional 11 penetrating, stimulating

point
3 aim, bit, dot, end, jag, nib, tip 4 apex, barb, crux, goal, item, mark, show, site, spot, step, tine, turn, unit 5 brink, motif, place, stage, theme, topic, trace, verge 6 credit, detail, direct, intent, moment, motive, object, period, reason 7 cogency, decimal, element, essence, feature, instant, meaning, purpose, sharpen, subject 8 headland, juncture, locality, location, particle, position 9 direction, emphasize, punctuate 10 promontory 12 significance

Point Counter Point author
6 Huxley (Aldous)

pointed
5 acute, sharp 6 barbed, marked, signal 7 salient 8 incisive, striking 9 arresting, pertinent, prominent 11 conspicuous, penetrating

pointer
3 dog, tip 4 clue, hint 5 arrow, guide 6 gundog 9 indicator 10 suggestion

pointillist
6 Seurat (Georges), Signac (Paul) 8 Pissarro (Camille)

pointless
4 idle, vain 5 inane, silly 6 futile 7 useless 8 bootless 9 fruitless, senseless, worthless 10 immaterial, irrelevant, unavailing, unfruitful 11 meaningless 12 unprofitable

point of view
5 angle, slant 7 outlook 8 position, prospect 11 perspective

poise
4 ease, hang, tact 5 brace, grace, hover, skill 6 aplomb, steady 7 address, balance, bearing, dignity, support, suspend 8 calmness, carriage, elegance, serenity 9 assurance, composure, diplomacy 10 confidence, equanimity 11 delicatesse, equilibrium, savoir faire, tactfulness

poised
4 calm 6 at ease, serene, steady 7 assured, equable 8 composed, tranquil 9 collected, confident 13 self-possessed

poison
4 bane, upas 5 toxin, venom 6 toxoid 7 arsenic, botulin, cyanide, envenom 8 toxicant 9 botulinum, contagion 10 strychnine 13 contamination
arrow: 4 inée, upas 6 curare 7 ouabain
combining form: 3 tox 4 toxi, toxo 6 toxico

poisoning
food: 8 botulism
lead: 8 plumbism

poisonous
5 toxic 7 baneful, miasmal, nocuous, noxious 8 mephitic, venomous, virulent 9 pestilent 10 pernicious

poke
3 dig, hit, jab, jut, lag, pry 4 cuff, nose, prod, push, sock, stab, stir, urge 5 bulge, dally, delay, elbow, nudge, punch, snoop, tarry 6 dawdle, meddle, pierce, putter, thrust 7 intrude, project, rummage 8 stick out 9 interfere, interject, interpose

poker
bet total: 3 pot
form: 4 stud
hand: 4 pair 5 flush 8 straight 9 full house 10 royal flush 13 straight flush
stake: 4 ante
term: 3 see 4 call, draw, open 5 raise
token: 4 chip

poker-faced
5 blank, staid 7 deadpan, neutral 9 impassive 11 inscrutable, noncommital 12 inexpressive

pokey
3 can, jug, pen 4 brig, coop, jail, stir 5 clink 6 cooler, prison 7 slammer 9 calaboose

poky
4 slow 5 dingy, seedy 6 dreary, shabby 7 cramped, laggard, rundown 8 dilatory, plodding, sluggish

Poland
capital: 6 Warsaw
city: 4 Lódz 6 Gdansk, Kraków, Poznan 7 Wroclaw 8 Katowice, Szczecin
leader: 6 Walesa (Lech)
monetary unit: 5 zloty
mountain range: 10 Carpathian
national hero: 10 Kosciuszko (Thaddeus)
neighbor: 6 Russia 7 Belarus, Germany, Ukraine 8 Slovakia 9 Lithuania 13 Czech Republic
river: 4 Oder 7 Vistula
sea: 6 Baltic

polar
6 arctic 7 pivotal 8 opposite 9 diametric

pole
4 punt, spar 5 shaft, staff, stick, stilt
Indian: 5 totem
Scottish: 5 caber

polecat
5 fitch, skunk 6 ferret 7 fitchet

polemic
6 attack, debate, screed, tirade 7 defense, dispute 8 argument, diatribe, harangue, jeremiad 9 assertion, philippic 10 contention, refutation 11 controversy, disputation 12 denunciation, remonstrance

polemical
7 scrappy 10 pugnacious 11 contentious, opinionated 12 disputatious 13 argumentative, controversial

polestar
3 hub 5 focus, guide 10 focal point

police
3 cop, law, man 4 fuzz, heat 6 copper, govern, lawman, patrol 7 control, monitor, trooper 8 bluecoat, flatfoot, gendarme, regulate 9 patrolman 12 peace officer

police officer
3 cop 4 fuzz, heat 5 bobby 6 copper, peeler 7 John Law, sheriff, trooper 8 bluecoat, Dogberry, flatfoot, gendarme 9 constable, patrolman
Italian: 11 carabiniere
Parisian: 4 flic 8 gendarme

policy
4 plan 6 course, method, number 7 lottery, program 8 contract, practice 9 procedure 10 management

polio vaccine developer
4 Salk (Jonas) 5 Sabin (Albert)

polish
3 rub, wax 4 buff 5 glaze, glint, gloss, sheen, shine 6 luster, refine, smooth, soften 7 burnish, culture, enhance, improve, perfect, touch up 8 brighten 10 refinement

Polish
dumpling: 7 pierogi
leader: 6 Walesa (Lech)
patriot: 9 Kosciusko (Thaddeus)
pope: 8 John Paul
sausage: 8 kielbasa
soldier: 7 Pulaski (Casimir)

polish off
5 eat up 6 devour 7 consume, put away 8 dispatch 9 dispose of

polite
5 civil 7 courtly, genteel, refined 8 cultured, mannerly, polished, well-bred 9 attentive, courteous 10 thoughtful 11 considerate 12 well-mannered

politeness
7 manners 8 civility, courtesy 10 refinement

politic
4 wise 5 suave 6 adroit, shrewd, smooth 7 prudent, tactful 8 tactical 9 advisable, expedient, judicious, sagacious 10 diplomatic

political
meeting: 6 caucus
party: 3 GOP 10 Democratic, Republican
system: 7 fascism 9 communism, democracy, socialism

poll
4 cast, clip, crop, head, nape 5 count, shear, tally, votes 6 record, sample, survey 7 canvass, pollard 8 question 9 interview 10 canvassing

pollack
4 fish 6 saithe 8 bluefish
family: 3 cod

pollard
3 top 4 crop, tree 7 cut back

pollen-producing organ
6 stamen

pollex
5 thumb

_____ polloi
3 hoi

pollster
5 Zogby (John) 6 Gallup (George), Harris (Lou)

pollute
4 foul, soil 5 dirty, spoil, stain, sully, taint 6 befoul, damage, debase, defile 7 corrupt, profane 10 adulterate 11 contaminate

pollution
4 smog 5 abuse 8 impurity 10 defilement

Pollux
10 Polydeuces
brother: 6 Castor
father: 4 Zeus
mother: 4 Leda
sister: 5 Helen 12 Clytemnestra

Pollyanna
8 optimist
author: 6 Porter (Eleanor)

Pollyannaish
6 blithe, cheery, upbeat 8 cheerful, positive 10 optimistic 11 rose-colored

pollywog
7 tadpole

Polonius
daughter: 7 Ophelia
slayer: 6 Hamlet
son: 7 Laertes

poltergeist
5 ghost 6 spirit

poltroon
6 coward, craven, yellow 7 chicken, dastard, gutless 8 cowardly 9 dastardly 11 lily-livered

Polydorus
father: 5 Priam 6 Cadmus
mother: 6 Hecuba 8 Harmonia
slayer: 8 Achilles 10 Polymestor 11 Polymnestor

polygon
eight-sided: 7 octagon
five-sided: 8 pentagon
four-sided: 8 tetragon
nine-sided: 7 nonagon
seven-sided: 8 heptagon
six-sided: 7 hexagon
ten-sided: 7 decagon
three-sided: 8 triangle
twelve-sided: 9 dodecagon

Polyhymnia
4 Muse
invention: 4 lyre

Polynesian
5 Maori 6 Samoan, Tongan 8 Hawaiian, Tahitian 9 Marquesan

Polynices
brother: 8 Eteocles
father: 7 Oedipus
mother: 7 Jocasta
wife: 5 Argia 6 Argeia

polyp
5 tumor, zooid 6 growth 7 hydroid
freshwater: 5 hydra

Polyphemus
7 Cyclops

beloved: 7 Galatea
father: 8 Poseidon
victim: 4 Acis

pome
4 pear 5 apple, fruit

pommel
4 knob 6 handle

pomp
4 show 5 array 6 parade, ritual 7 display, fanfare, panoply 8 ceremony, grandeur, splendor 9 pageantry, vainglory 11 ostentation

pompano
4 fish 8 carangid 10 butterfish

Pompeii's volcano
8 Vesuvius

pompous
4 vain 5 proud, showy 6 lordly, ornate, stuffy 7 stuck-up 8 arrogant, boastful, inflated 9 bombastic, conceited, important, overblown 10 egocentric, flamboyant, pontifical 11 magisterial, pretentious· 12 ostentatious, vainglorious

pond
4 mere, pool, tarn 5 stank 6 lagoon

ponder
4 mull, muse 5 study, think, weigh 6 reason 7 examine, perpend, reflect 8 appraise, cogitate, consider, evaluate, meditate, mull over, ruminate 9 reflect on, speculate 10 deliberate, think about 11 contemplate

ponderous
4 dull 5 heavy 6 clumsy, dreary, stodgy, wooden 7 labored, massive, weighty 8 cumbrous, lifeless, plodding, unwieldy 9 lumbering 10 burdensome, cumbersome, oppressive

poniard
6 dagger

Ponte Vecchio
city: 8 Florence
river: 4 Arno

Pontiac
5 chief
tribe: 6 Ottawa

pontiff
4 pope

pontifical
7 pompous 8 dogmatic 9 episcopal
11 magisterial

pony
4 crib, trot 5 horse 6 bronco, cayuse
7 mustang
breed: 6 Exmoor 8 Shetland

pony up
3 pay 6 lay out, pay out 7 dish out,
dole out, fork out 8 hand over, shell
out, turn over 10 compensate, remunerate

pooch
3 dog, pup 4 tyke 5 hound, puppy
6 bowwow, canine

Pooh
creator: 5 Milne (A. A.)
illustrator: 7 Shepard (Ernest)

pooh-bah
3 VIP 4 czar, king, star, tsar, tzar
5 baron, heavy, mogul 6 big gun,
bigwig, honcho, kahuna, prince,
worthy 7 big name, big shot, kingpin,
magnate, notable 8 big wheel,
eminence, luminary 9 big cheese,
personage, superstar 11 heavyweight

pooh-pooh
5 scorn 6 deride 7 disdain, dismiss,
sneer at 8 minimize, play down

pool
3 pot 4 mere, pond, tarn 5 chain,
group, kitty, merge, trust 6 cartel,
lagoon, laguna, puddle 7 combine,
jackpot 9 syndicate
player: 7 Mosconi (Willie) 13 Minnesota Fats

poop
4 dirt, info, tire 7 fatigue

poor
4 base, mean 5 broke, needy, scant,
skimp, spare 6 humble, meager,
meagre, paltry, scanty, skimpy,
sparse 8 bankrupt, beggarly, indigent, strapped 9 destitute, insolvent,
penniless, penurious 10 down-and-
out, pauperized, stone-broke 11 impecunious, necessitous

poorly
3 ill, low 4 sick 5 badly 6 ailing,
sickly, unwell 10 indisposed 11 imperfectly

pop
3 dad, dot, gun, hit, try 4 dada, dart,
ding, shot, slap, slog, sock, soda
5 catch, crack, daddy, drink, fling,
shoot, whack, whirl 6 attack, bug
out, effort, father, strike 7 assault,
attempt, explode 8 backfire

pop artist
5 Blake (Peter), Johns (Jasper)
6 Warhol (Andy) 7 Hockney (David),
Indiana (Robert) 9 Oldenburg
(Claes), Wesselman (Tom) 10 Ros-
enquist (James) 12 Lichtenstein
(Roy)

pope
3 Leo 4 John, Mark, Paul, Pius
5 Caius, Conon, Donus, Felix, Gaius,
Lando, Linus, Peter, Soter, Urban
6 Adrian, Agatho, Fabian, Julius,
Lucius, Martin, Sixtus, Victor 7 An-
terus, Clement, Damasus, Gregory,
Hadrian, Hyginus, Marinus, Paschal,
Pontian, Romanus, Sergius, Stephen,
Zosimus 8 Agapetus, Anicetus,
Benedict, Boniface, Calixtus, Euge-
nius, Eusebius, Formosis, Gelasius,
Hilarius, Honorius, Innocent, John
Paul, Liberius, Nicholas, Pelagius,
Siricius, Theodore, Vigilius, Vitalian
9 Adeodatus, Alexander, Anacletus,
Callistus, Celestine, Cornelius,
Densdedit, Dionysius, Eutychian,
Evaristus, Hormisdas, Marcellus,
Miltiades, Severinus, Silverius,
Silvester, Sisinnius, Sylvester,
Symmachus, Valentine, Zacharias
10 Anastasius, Melchiades, Sa-
binianus, Simplicius, Zephyrinus
11 Christopher, Constantine, Eleu-
therius, Eutychianus, Marcellinus,
Telesphorus

Pope poem
7 Dunciad (The) 10 Essay on Man
(An) 13 Rape of the Lock (The)

Popeye
accessory: 4 pipe
baby: 7 Swee'Pea 8 Sweet Pea
energizer: 7 spinach
friend: 5 Wimpy 8 Olive Oyl
occupation: 6 sailor
rival: 5 Bluto

pop in
4 call 5 visit 6 drop by, look up, stop
by 8 come over

popinjay
3 fop 4 toff 5 dandy, swell 7 peacock 8 macaroni

poplar
5 abele, alamo, aspen 6 balsam
9 tulip tree 10 cottonwood 12 balm
of Gilead

Poppaea's husband
4 Nero

poppycock
3 rot 4 bosh, bunk, guff 5 bilge,
hokum 6 bunkum 7 baloney 8 malarkey, nonsense 10 balderdash

populace
5 plebs 6 masses, people, public
9 citizenry, commonage, commoners,
plebeians 10 commonalty 11 com-
monality, rank and file, third estate

popular
5 cheap, noted 6 common, famous
7 admired, current, favored, general,
leading 8 accepted, approved,
favorite, ordinary 9 preferred, prevalent, prominent, well-known, well-
liked 10 democratic, prevailing,
widespread 11 inexpensive

populate
6 occupy, people, settle 7 inhabit

populous
6 packed 7 crowded, teeming
8 numerous 9 congested 13 multitudinous

porcelain
Chinese: 9 Lowestoft
English: 3 Bow 5 Derby, Spode

6 Minton 7 Aynsley, Belleek, Bristol,
Chelsea 8 Caughley, Wedgwood
French: 6 Sèvres 7 Limoges
German: 7 Dresden, Meissen
ingredient: 6 kaolin
Italian: 6 Doccia
Japanese: 5 Imari

porch
4 deck 5 lanai 6 piazza 7 gallery,
veranda 8 verandah

porcupine
8 hedgehog

pore
6 outlet 7 opening, orifice, reflect
8 meditate 10 interstice

pore over
4 read, scan 5 study 6 peruse
10 scrutinize

porgy
4 fish, scup 6 sparid 8 menhaden

Porgy and Bess
composer: 8 Gershwin (George)
librettist: 7 Heyward (DuBose)
8 Gershwin (Ira)

Po River city
5 Milan, Padua, Turin 6 Milano,
Padova, Torino, Verona 7 Brescia

pork
3 ham, pig 5 bacon, swine 8 sowbelly
cut: 3 ham 4 jowl, loin, side 7 fat-
back 8 forefoot, hind foot, spare rib
9 picnic ham 10 Boston butt

pork-barreling
9 patronage

pornographic
7 obscene

porous
5 leaky 6 spongy 8 pervious 9 permeable 10 penetrable

porpoise
5 whale 7 dolphin

porridge
4 mush 5 gruel, kasha 6 burgoo,
cereal, congee, pablum, sowens
7 oatmeal, pabulum 8 flummery
loblolly 9 stirabout

port

port
4 hole, jack, left, wine 5 cover,
haven 6 harbor, refuge, retreat, shelter 8 larboard,
opening, retreat, shelter 8 larboard,
left side 9 anchorage, harborage,
roadstead, sanctuary 11 comportment
opposite: 9 starboard

portable
5 handy 6 mobile, wieldy

portal
4 door, gate 5 entry 7 doorway,
gateway 8 approach, entrance,
entryway

portcullis
4 gate 7 grating, lattice

portend
4 bode 5 augur 6 signal 7 betoken,
predict, presage, promise, signify
8 forebode, forecast, foretell, indicate, prophesy 9 adumbrate, foretoken 10 foreshadow, vaticinate

portent
4 omen, sign 6 augury, boding
7 presage, prodigy 9 foretoken,
sensation 10 foreboding, indication
11 premonition

portentous
5 grave 6 solemn 7 ominous, pompous, serious, weighty 8 inflated
9 marvelous, momentous, ponderous
10 prodigious

porter
5 hamal, stout 6 bearer, redcap,
skycap 7 bellboy, bellhop, carrier
9 transport 10 doorkeeper

Portia
6 lawyer
husband: 6 Brutus 8 Bassanio
maid: 7 Nerissa

portico
4 stoa 9 colonnade

portion
3 cut, lot 4 bite, part 5 dower, moira,
piece, quota, share, slice 6 moiety,
parcel 7 measure, quantum, segment 8 division

largest: 10 lion's share
unused: 8 leftover

portly
3 fat 5 bulky, heavy, large, stout
6 fleshy 7 rotound, stately, weighty
8 imposing 9 corpulent 10 overweight

portmanteau
8 carryall, suitcase

portrait
4 bust 5 image 6 figure, statue
7 picture 8 painting 9 depiction

portray
4 draw, limn, play 5 enact, paint
6 depict, render 7 picture 8 describe
9 delineate, interpret, represent

portrayal
5 image 7 account, picture 8 likeness, painting 9 depiction 11 delineation, description, performance
12 illustration

Portugal
capital: 6 Lisbon
city: 5 Porto 6 Oporto 7 Amadora
former name: 9 Lusitania
island group: 6 Azores 7 Madeira
leader: 7 Salazar (Antonio de)
monetary unit: 4 euro
monetary unit, former: 6 escudo
neighbor: 5 Spain
peninsula: 7 Iberian
river: 5 Tagus

pose
3 act, air, ask, set, sit 4 airs, fake,
role, sham 5 feign, front, offer, place,
stand, state, strut 6 affect, assume,
pass as, stance 7 pass for, pass off,
present, pretend, show off, suggest
8 attitude, pretense, set forth 9 mannerism 10 pretension 11 affectation

Poseidon
7 Neptune
brother: 4 Zeus 5 Hades, Pluto
7 Jupiter
consort: 4 Tyro 6 Medusa 7 Demeter
father: 6 Cronus

mother: 4 Rhea
offspring: 7 Pegasus
son: 5 Orion **6** Neleus, Pelias,
Triton **7** Antaeus **10** Polyphemus
weapon: 7 trident
wife: 10 Amphitrite

poser
  6 puzzle, riddle **7** problem **9** conundrum **11** brainteaser

poseur
  4 fake **5** bluff, decoy, fraud, phony,
quack **7** bluffer **8** deceiver, imposter
9 charlatan, hypocrite, pretender
10 mountebank **11** masquerader
12 impersonator

posh
  4 chic, rich, tony **5** fancy, grand,
smart, swank **7** elegant, stylish
9 exclusive, expensive, luxurious
11 fashionable, highfalutin, pretentious

posit
  3 fix **5** offer **6** affirm, assert, assume
7 premise, present, presume, propose, suggest **9** postulate

position
  3 job **4** rank, site, spot **5** locus,
place, point, situs, stand, state
6 belief, locate, stance **7** emplace,
footing, stature **8** attitude, capacity,
location, prestige, standing **10** standpoint

positive
  4 firm, real, sure **5** clear, sound
6 actual, useful **7** assured, certain,
decided, factual, genuine, helpful,
reality **8** absolute, complete, constant, definite, forceful, outright
9 confident, doubtless, downright,
effective, favorable, realistic **10** beneficial, inarguable, optimistic, prescribed, undeniable **11** categorical,
irrefutable, unequivocal, unmitigated,
unqualified **12** indisputable, unmistakable **13** incontestable

possess
  3 own **4** have, hold, keep **5** carry
6 retain **7** acquire, control

possessed
  3 mad **6** crazed, hooked **8** frenzied
9 bewitched

possession
  7 control **8** property **9** occupancy,
ownership **10** occupation

possessive
  7 jealous **8** watchful **10** protective
11 proprietary

possibility
  4 odds **6** chance **8** instance **9** potential **10** likelihood **11** contingency,
feasibility

possible
  6 doable, likely, viable **7** earthly
8 feasible **9** expedient, potential
10 imaginable, realizable **11** practicable

possibly
  5 maybe **7** perhaps **8** by chance
9 perchance **11** conceivably

post
  3 set **4** camp, mail, pole, ride, spot,
task **5** affix, hurry, newel, place, put
up, score, stage, stake **6** advise, column, fill in, inform, notify, office,
pillar **7** apprise, express, placard,
publish, station **8** announce, denounce, position **9** advertise
10 assignment

poster
  4 bill, sign **6** notice **7** affiche, placard **9** broadside, signboard **12** announcement **13** advertisement

posterior
  4 back, hind, rear, rump, seat, tail
5 after, fanny, later **6** behind, caudal,
dorsal, hinder **7** ensuing, rear end,
tail end **8** backside, buttocks, derriere, hindmost, rearward **9** following
10 subsequent

posterity
  6 future **7** progeny **8** children
9 offspring **11** descendants

posthaste
  4 fast **6** at once, pronto **7** fleetly,
quickly, rapidly, swiftly **8** promptly,
speedily **11** immediately

Postimpressionist painter
6 Seurat (Georges) 7 Cezanne (Paul), Gauguin (Paul), Van Gogh (Vincent) 8 Pissarro (Camille), Rousseau (Henri)

postmortem
7 autopsy 8 necropsy

postpone
5 defer, delay, table 6 hold up, put off, shelve 7 hold off, lay over, suspend 8 hold over, prorogue

postulate
5 axiom, claim 6 assert, assume, demand, thesis 7 premise, suppose 10 assumption, hypothesis, presuppose 11 hypothesize, presumption, supposition

posture
4 mode, pose 5 state 6 affect, assume, manner, stance, status 7 bearing, outlook 8 attitude, carriage, position 9 condition, situation 12 attitudinize

posy
5 bloom 6 flower 7 blossom, bouquet, corsage, nosegay 9 sentiment

pot
3 bet, pan, wad 4 ante, hemp, olla 5 grass, kitty, stake, wager 6 boodle, bundle, pipkin 8 cannabis 9 marijuana

potable
5 clean, drink, fresh 6 liquid, liquor 8 beverage 9 drinkable

potassium ore
7 sylvite

potato
3 yam 4 spud 5 tater
bud: 3 eye

pot-au-____
3 feu

potbelly
3 gut 5 stove 6 paunch 9 bay window, spare tire

potency
3 pep 5 force, might, power, vigor 6 energy, muscle 8 strength 9 influence, puissance 10 capability 13 effectiveness

potent
4 rich 6 mighty, robust, strong, virile 7 dynamic 8 forceful, forcible, powerful 9 effective 10 persuasive 11 influential

potential
6 latent, likely 7 ability, promise 8 capacity, possible 9 plausible, promising 10 imaginable 11 conceivable, possibility

pother
3 ado 4 flap, fret, fuss, stir, to-do 5 furor, whirl, worry 6 bustle, flurry, furore, hassle, hubbub, tumult, uproar 7 fluster, turmoil 9 agitation, annoyance, commotion, confusion

potion
6 liquid 7 mixture, philter, philtre 8 medicine 10 concoction

Potiphar's slave
6 Joseph

Potiphera
daughter: 7 Asenath
son-in-law: 6 Joseph

Potok novel
6 Chosen (The) 16 My Name Is Asher Lev

potpourri
4 olio 5 blend 6 medley 7 grab bag, mélange, variety 8 mishmash, pastiche 10 assortment, collection, hodgepodge, miscellany, salmagundi

potshot
3 cut, dig 4 gibe, jibe 5 crack, shoot, swipe 6 attack, insult 9 criticism

potter
see **putter**

Potter character
5 Mopsy, Mr. Tod 6 Flopsy, Jemima (Puddleduck) 10 Cotton-tail, Hunca Munca 11 Peter Rabbit 12 Jeremy Fisher

potter's field
8 cemetery, God's acre 9 graveyard

pottery
4 raku 5 delft 7 redware 8 ceramics, clayware, slipware 10 lusterware, terra-cotta, yellowware 11 earthenware

pouch
3 bag, sac 4 sack 5 bulge, bursa, burse 6 pocket 7 saccule 8 sacculus

pouf
5 quilt 7 ottoman 9 comforter

poultry
4 fowl
type: 4 duck, swan 5 goose, quail 6 grouse, pigeon, turkey 7 chicken, ostrich, peacock 8 pheasant 9 partridge

pounce
5 seize, swoop, talon 6 attack, powder 7 assault, stencil

pound
4 bang, bash, beat, slam, slug, sock 5 drive, money, stamp, throb, thump, tramp 6 batter, buffet, hammer, pummel, strike, thrash, wallop 7 belabor, impress, pulsate 9 enclosure

Pound work
6 Cantos (The)

poupée
4 doll

pour
4 flow, gush, rain, rill, rush, teem 5 flood, issue, skink, spate, surge, swarm 6 decant, deluge, drench, sluice, spring, stream 7 cascade, torrent 8 inundate, overflow

pourboire
3 tip 7 cumshaw 8 gratuity

pout
3 pet 4 fish, moue, sulk 5 grump 8 protrude 10 expression, protrusion

poverty
4 need, want 6 dearth, penury 7 beggary, paucity 8 hardship, poorness, scarcity, shortage 9 indigence, neediness, pauperism, privation 10 mendicancy, scarceness 11 destitution 13 pennilessness

POW camp
6 stalag

powder
4 bray, dust, talc 5 crush 6 talcum 8 sprinkle 9 comminute, pulverize, triturate 10 besprinkle

power
3 vis 4 sway 5 force, might, sinew, steam, vigor, vires (plural) 6 energy, muscle 7 command, ability, control, potency, voltage 8 dominion, dynamism, imperium, strength 9 authority, influence, privilege, puissance, strong arm 10 ascendancy, domination 11 prerogative, sovereignty, superiority 12 jurisdiction, potentiality
combining form: 5 dynam 6 dynamo
unit: 4 watt

powerful
5 great 6 mighty, potent, strong 7 dynamic 8 dominant, puissant, vigorous 9 energetic, strenuous 10 convincing, impressive, invincible, persuasive 11 efficacious, influential, prestigious 13 authoritative

powerless
4 weak 5 inert 6 feeble, unable 7 passive 8 impotent 9 incapable 11 incompetent, ineffective

powwow
4 chat, talk 6 confab, confer, huddle, parley 7 discuss, meeting 8 ceremony 9 gathering 10 discussion 11 confabulate, get-together

practicable
5 utile 6 doable, likely, usable, useful 8 feasible, possible 9 operative 10 functional

practical
5 handy, utile 6 active, useful, versed 7 applied, skilled, trained, virtual 8 sensible 9 pragmatic, realistic 10 functional 11 down-to-earth, experienced 12 businesslike

practically
5 about 6 all but, almost, near to, nearly 7 close to 8 in effect 9 in essence, just about

practice
3 use, way 4 form, mode, wont 5 drill, habit, usage 6 custom, manner, method, repeat, system, tryout, warm up 7 perform, process 8 drilling, engage in, exercise, habitude, rehearse 9 procedure, rehearsal 10 convention

pragmatic
7 factual, logical 8 rational 9 practical, realistic 11 down-to-earth

prairie
4 veld 5 plain, veldt 7 plateau 9 grassland

prairie chicken
6 grouse

prairie wolf
6 coyote

praise
4 hail, hymn, laud, puff 5 bravo, cry up, exalt, extol, honor, kudos 6 belaud, kudize 7 acclaim, adulate, applaud, commend, enhance, flatter, glorify, hosanna, magnify, ovation, plaudit, puffery, sublime 8 accolade, applause, approval, citation, encomium, eulogize, flattery 9 celebrate, laudation, panegyric, recommend 10 aggrandize, compliment, panegyrize 11 acclamation 12 commendation

praiseworthy
8 laudable 9 admirable, deserving, estimable 11 commendable, meritorious

prance
4 step 5 mince, strut 6 sashay, spring 8 cakewalk

prank
3 gag 4 deck, dido, lark, whim 5 adorn, antic, caper, fancy, spiff, sport, trick 6 doll up, frolic, gambol, levity, shavie, vagary, whimsy 7 caprice, deck out, doll out, dress up, garnish, rollick, spiff up 8 beautify, decorate, escapade, ornament, spruce up 9 embellish, frivolity, horseplay, smarten up 10 shenanigan, tomfoolery 11 monkeyshine

prankster
3 wag 5 cutup, joker

prate
3 gab, jaw, yak 4 blab, chat, go on 5 run on 6 babble, gabble, jabber 7 blabber, blather, chatter 9 yakety-yak

prater
6 gossip, magpie 10 chatterbox 12 blabbermouth

pratfall
6 mishap, tumble 7 blunder, stumble 11 humiliation

prawn
6 shrimp 11 langoustine
French: 8 crevette

praxis
5 habit 6 action, custom, manner 7 conduct 8 exercise, habitude, practice

Praxiteles statue
5 Satyr 6 Hermes 9 Aphrodite

pray
3 ask, beg 5 plead 6 appeal 7 beseech, entreat, implore, request 8 petition 10 supplicate

prayer
4 plea, suit 6 appeal, litany, orison 7 angelus, begging, worship 8 blessing, devotion, entreaty, petition, pleading, rogation 9 adoration 11 application, imploration, imprecation 12 supplication
beads: 6 rosary
ending: 4 amen
for the dead: 7 requiem
Jewish: 7 kaddish, kiddush
period: 6 novena 7 triduum
shawl: 7 tallith

prayer book
6 missal, siddur 8 breviary

prayerful
4 holy 5 godly, pious 6 devout
7 earnest, sincere

preach
4 urge 6 exhort 7 address, deliver,
lecture 8 admonish, advocate,
moralize 9 sermonize 10 evangelize

preacher
5 padre 6 cleric, divine, parson,
pastor 8 chaplain, clerical, minister,
reverend 9 churchman, clergyman
10 evangelist, sermonizer 12 ecclesiastic

preaching friar
9 Dominican

preachy
4 smug 7 donnish 8 didactic, sermonic, unctuous 9 homiletic, hortative, pedagogic, pietistic 10 moralizing 11 exhortative, sermonizing
13 sanctimonious, self-righteous

preamble
5 intro, proem 8 exordium, foreword,
overture, prologue 12 introduction

precarious
4 iffy 5 dicey, risky, shaky 6 chancy,
touchy, tricky, unsafe 7 dubious
8 delicate, doubtful, insecure, ticklish,
unstable 9 dangerous, hazardous,
sensitive, uncertain 10 unreliable

precaution
4 care 8 prudence 9 foresight,
insurance, provision, safeguard
11 forethought

precede
4 lead, rank 5 usher 6 herald
7 forerun, outrank, surpass 8 announce, antedate, go before 9 introduce

precedence
5 order 8 priority 9 seniority

precedent
4 past, rule 5 model, prior 6 former
7 earlier, example 8 anterior 9 foregoing 10 convention

preceding
4 past 5 prior 6 before, former

7 ahead of, prior to 8 anterior,
hitherto 9 erstwhile 10 heretofore
11 in advance of
prefix: 4 ante

precept
3 law 4 rule 5 axiom, edict, order,
tenet 6 behest, decree 7 bidding,
command 8 doctrine 9 principle
10 injunction, regulation 11 fundamental

preceptive
8 didactic

preceptor
4 head 5 tutor 7 teacher 9 principal
10 headmaster

precinct
4 area 6 domain, region, sector,
sphere 7 quarter, section 8 district,
division, township 9 bailiwick, enclosure

precious
3 pet 4 dear, nice, rare, rich, very
5 fussy, great, loved, showy 6 adored,
choice, costly, la-di-da, prized 7 beloved, darling 8 affected, esteemed,
favorite, valuable 9 cherished,
exquisite, extremely, priceless
10 invaluable

precipice
5 brink, cliff 8 overhang

precipitancy
4 rush 5 haste, hurry 9 hastiness
10 abruptness, suddenness 11 hurriedness

precipitate
4 fall, hurl 5 hasty, sheer, steep,
throw 6 abrupt, madcap, result,
sudden, upshot 7 bring on, deposit,
falling, flowing, grounds, hurried,
outcome, product 8 condense,
headlong, sediment, separate
9 breakneck, impatient, impetuous,
impulsive 10 unexpected, unforeseen 11 consequence

precipitation
4 hail, mist, rain, snow 5 sleet
7 deposit 8 sediment

precipitous

4 rash 5 hasty, sheer, steep 6 abrupt, sudden 7 hurried, rushing 8 headlong, heedless, plunging 9 breakneck 13 perpendicular

précis

6 digest, survey 7 summary 8 abstract, overview, syllabus 10 abridgment, compendium 11 abridgement 12 condensation

precise

4 nice 5 exact, fixed, right 6 narrow, strict 7 correct, limited 8 accurate, clear-cut, definite, rigorous, specific 9 clocklike, stringent 10 particular

precisely

4 just 5 right 7 exactly 8 strictly

precision

4 care 5 rigor 8 accuracy 9 exactness 10 exactitude, refinement 11 correctness

preclude

5 avert, deter 7 forfend, obviate, prevent, rule out 8 prohibit, stave off 9 forestall

precocious

5 smart 6 brainy, bright, mature 7 forward 8 advanced

precondition

4 must, need 7 proviso 9 essential, necessity, provision, requisite 10 sine qua non 11 requirement, stipulation

precursor

6 herald 8 ancestor, forebear 9 harbinger, indicator, prototype 10 antecedent, forerunner

predator

6 hunter, preyer, raptor 7 stalker 8 devourer 9 destroyer 10 bird of prey

predatory

6 greedy 9 pillaging, rapacious 10 plundering 12 exploitative

predecessor

8 ancestor, forebear 9 precursor, prototype 10 antecedent, forerunner

predicament

3 fix, jam 4 bind, hole, spot 5 pinch, state 6 corner, muddle, pickle, plight, puzzle, scrape, strait 7 dilemma, impasse, trouble 8 hardship, nuisance, quagmire 9 condition, situation 10 difficulty

predicate

4 aver, avow, base, rest 5 found, imply 6 affirm, assert, avouch 7 declare, profess 9 establish

predict

5 augur, guess, infer 6 expect 7 forbode, foresee, portend, surmise 8 announce, conclude, forebode, forecast, foretell, indicate, prophesy, soothsay 10 conjecture, vaticinate 13 prognosticate

prediction

6 augury 8 forecast, prophecy 9 prognosis 10 expectancy 11 expectation

predilection

4 bent, bias 5 fancy, taste 6 liking 7 leaning 8 fondness, penchant, tendency 9 inclining 10 partiality, proclivity, propensity 11 inclination

predispose

4 bend, bias, tend, sway 5 prime 6 affect 7 incline 9 influence

predisposed

5 prone, ready 6 biased 7 partial, willing 8 inclined 11 susceptible

predisposition

4 bent, bias 7 leaning 8 penchant, tendency 9 inclining 10 partiality, proclivity, propensity 11 inclination

predominant

4 main 5 chief, major 6 master, ruling 7 capital, general, leading, primary 8 reigning, superior 9 number one, paramount, principal, sovereign 10 prevailing 11 outstanding

predominate

4 rule 5 reign 6 govern, master 7 command, control, prevail 8 outweigh

preeminence
6 renown 7 primacy 8 dominion, prestige 9 supremacy 10 ascendancy, domination, excellence, importance 11 distinction, superiority

preeminent
4 main 5 chief 7 capital, stellar, supreme 8 dominant, foremost, peerless, towering, ultimate 9 matchless, number-one, paramount, principal, unrivaled 10 surpassing, unrivalled 11 outstanding, unmatchable 12 incomparable, transcendent
prefix: 4 arch

preempt
4 bump, take 5 annex, seize, usurp 6 assume 7 acquire, replace 8 arrogate 9 forestall 10 confiscate, substitute 11 appropriate, expropriate

preen
5 gloat, groom, pride, primp, swell 6 smooth

preface
4 lead, open 5 begin, proem, usher 6 herald 8 exordium, foreword, overture, preamble, prologue 9 introduce 11 preliminary 12 introduction

prefatory
7 opening 8 proemial 12 introductory

prefect
7 head boy, monitor 8 head girl 10 magistrate

prefer
5 elect, favor 6 choose, opt for, select 7 advance, elevate, promote, upgrade

preferable
5 finer 6 better 8 superior, worthier

preference
4 pick 6 choice, option 8 election, priority 9 advantage, elevation, promotion, selection, upgrading 10 favoritism, partiality

prefigure
4 hint 7 foresee 8 indicate 9 adumbrate 10 foreshadow

pregnancy
9 gestation, gravidity

pregnant
4 full, rich 5 heavy 6 gravid, parous 7 teeming, weighty 8 eloquent, enceinte, profound 9 expectant, expecting, gestating, inventive, momentous, with child 10 expressive, meaningful, parturient 11 significant

prehensile
8 grasping

prejudice
3 mar 4 bias, harm, hurt, sway 5 color, favor 6 damage, injure, injury, racism, sexism 7 bigotry, leaning 8 aversion 9 antipathy, hostility, influence 10 partiality 11 intolerance 12 one-sidedness

prejudicial
6 biased 7 bigoted 8 damaging 9 injurious 11 deleterious, detrimental

prelate
5 abbot 6 bishop 7 primate 8 cardinal, diocesan 9 patriarch 10 archbishop 12 ecclesiastic

preliminary
4 heat 5 basic, match, trial 7 initial, opening 8 proemial 9 beginning 10 qualifying 11 fundamental 12 introductory

prelude
5 intro, proem 8 exordium, foreword, overture, prologue 12 introduction, prolegomenon

premature
5 early 8 untimely 10 beforehand

premeditated
5 set up 7 planned, studied, willful 8 designed, intended 9 conscious 10 calculated, considered, deliberate, thought-out 11 intentional

premier
4 head, main 5 chief, first 7 leading, primary 8 earliest, foremost, original 9 principal 13 prime minister

premiere

premiere
5 debut 7 opening 8 earliest, original 9 beginning 10 first night

premise
4 base 5 posit 6 assume, thesis 8 building, property, set forth 9 postulate 10 assumption 11 postulation, proposition, supposition

premium
5 bonus, extra, prize 6 reward 8 dividend, superior 9 excellent 10 recompense 11 exceptional

premonition
4 omen 9 misgiving, suspicion 10 foreboding 11 forewarning 12 apprehension, presentiment

preoccupied
4 deep, lost, rapt 6 absent, intent 7 engaged, faraway, worried 8 absorbed, immersed 9 concerned, engrossed, wrapped up 10 abstracted, distracted 11 inattentive 12 absentminded

prep
5 basic, coach, drill, equip, groom, prime, ready, train, trial 8 get ready 11 preliminary 12 introductory

preparation
4 base, plan 5 study 7 fitness, measure 8 compound, medicine, training 9 alertness, foresight, readiness 10 background, concoction

preparatory
5 basic 11 preliminary, rudimentary 12 introductory

prepare
3 fit, fix 4 gird 5 draft, prime, ready, train 6 draw up, make up, outfit 7 fortify, furnish 9 formulate

prepared
3 set 4 up on 5 fixed, ready 6 primed 7 treated 9 processed

preponderance
4 bulk 8 dominion, majority, main part 9 ascendant, dominance, supremacy 10 ascendancy, domination 11 superiority

preponderant
7 supreme 8 dominant, superior 9 paramount 10 prevailing

preponderate
4 rule 5 reign 6 exceed 7 command, dictate, outrank, prevail 8 dominate, outweigh

prepossess
4 bias, sway 5 favor 6 absorb, engage, occupy 7 engross, immerse, involve 9 influence

prepossessing
7 likable 9 appealing 10 attractive

preposterous
4 wild 5 crazy, wacky 6 absurd, insane 7 asinine, foolish, idiotic 9 fantastic, laughable, senseless 10 irrational, ridiculous 11 harebrained 12 unreasonable

prerequisite
4 must, need 5 vital 8 required 9 condition, essential, mandatory, necessary, necessity 10 imperative, sine qua non 11 requirement 13 indispensable

prerogative
5 power, right 8 appanage, immunity 9 authority, exemption, privilege 10 birthright, perquisite

presage
4 bode, omen, warn 5 augur, sense 6 augury, boding, herald, intuit 7 portend, portent, predict, promise, warning 8 announce, forebode, forecast, foretell, forewarn, indicate, prophesy, soothsay 9 foretoken, harbinger, intuition, misgiving 10 foreboding, foreshadow, prediction, prognostic, vaticinate

presbyter
5 elder 6 priest

prescience
9 foresight 12 anticipation, clairvoyance 13 foreknowledge

prescribe
3 fix, set 4 rule 5 guide, order 6 assign, choose, decide, decree,

define, direct, impose, ordain, select
7 dictate, lay down, pick out, require, specify **9** designate, determine, stipulate

prescript
3 law **4** rule **5** edict, order **6** decree **10** regulation

prescription
4 drug, rule **5** claim, right, title **6** custom, remedy **8** medicine **9** direction **10** medication

presence
3 air **4** look, mien **5** poise **6** aspect, spirit **7** address, bearing **8** carriage, demeanor **9** composure

present
3 act, aim, now **4** boon, gift, give, here, pose, show **5** award, bring, favor, offer, point, stage, tense, today **6** at hand, bestow, confer, convey, direct, donate, extend, in view, modern, submit, tender **7** hand out, largess, perform, proffer **8** existing, nominate **9** introduce **12** contemporary

presentable
3 fit **6** decent, proper **8** becoming **9** befitting **10** acceptable **11** appropriate **12** satisfactory

present-day
6 living, recent **7** current, ongoing, popular, topical **8** contempo, existent, existing, pressing, up-to-date **9** prevalent, surviving **10** prevailing **12** contemporary

presently
3 now **4** anon, soon **5** today **6** in time, one day **7** by and by **9** forthwith, these days **10** before long

preservation
4 care **6** saving, shield **7** defense, keeping **8** pickling **10** husbanding, protection **11** conservancy, maintenance, safekeeping

preserve
3 can, jam **4** save **5** jelly, put up **6** keep up, pickle **7** protect, shelter, sustain **8** keep safe, maintain **9** confiture

preside
3 run **4** head, lead **5** chair **6** direct, handle, manage **7** conduct, control, operate, oversee **8** moderate **9** officiate

president
United States: 4 Bush (George, George W.), Ford (Gerald R.), Polk (James K.), Taft (William H.) **5** Adams (John, John Quincy), Grant (Ulysses S.), Hayes (Rutherford B.), Nixon (Richard M.), Tyler (John) **6** Arthur (Chester A.), Carter (Jimmy), Hoover (Herbert), Monroe (James), Pierce (Franklin), Reagan (Ronald), Taylor (Zachary), Truman (Harry S.), Wilson (Woodrow) **7** Clinton (Bill), Harding (Warren), Jackson (Andrew), Johnson (Andrew, Lyndon), Kennedy (John F.), Lincoln (Abraham), Madison (James) **8** Buchanan (James), Coolidge (Calvin), Fillmore (Millard), Garfield (James), Harrison (Benjamin, William Henry), McKinley (William), Van Buren (Martin) **9** Cleveland (Grover), Jefferson (Thomas), Roosevelt (Franklin D., Theodore) **10** Eisenhower (Dwight D.), Washington (George)

presidio
4 fort **7** bastion, citadel **8** fastness, fortress, garrison **10** stronghold **13** fortification

press
3 hug, jam, ram **4** cram, iron, mass, pack, pile, push, rush, urge **5** clasp, crowd, crush, drive, force, horde, hurry, media, shove **6** demand, hustle, insist, jostle, propel, squash, stress, throng, thrust **7** beseech, entreat, imprint, printer, squeeze **9** constrain, influence, multitude

pressing
5 acute, vital **6** urgent **7** crucial, earnest, exigent, serious **8** critical **9** immediate, important, insistent **10** compelling, imperative

pressure

4 push, rush 5 drive, impel 6 burden, strain, stress 7 tension 10 constraint
combining form: 5 piezo
instrument: 9 barometer
unit: 3 bar 6 pascal

prestige

4 fame, rank, sway 5 power 6 cachet, credit, esteem, regard, renown, repute, status, weight 7 dignity, stature 8 eminence, position, standing 9 authority, influence 10 importance, prominence 11 consequence, distinction

prestigious

5 famed, great 6 famous 7 eminent, honored, notable 8 esteemed, renowned 9 prominent, respected 10 celebrated 11 influential 13 distinguished

presto

4 fast 7 hastily, quickly, rapidly 8 suddenly 9 posthaste 11 immediately

presumably

6 likely, surely 8 probably 9 doubtless

presume

4 dare 5 guess, imply, infer, think, trust 6 expect, gather, impose, reason 7 believe, intrude, suppose, surmise, venture 8 infringe 9 postulate 10 conjecture

presumption

4 gall 5 brass, cheek, nerve 6 belief, daring, ground, reason, thesis 7 conceit 8 audacity, chutzpah, evidence 9 brashness, inference, postulate 10 confidence, effrontery

presumptuous

4 bold, smug 5 brash, fresh, pushy 6 cheeky, uppity 7 forward 8 arrogant 9 audacious, confident 11 overweening, self-assured

presuppose

5 posit 6 assume, expect 7 imagine, require, surmise 9 postulate

pretend

3 act 4 fake, pose, sham 5 bluff, claim, false, feign, guess, put on 6 affect, assume, delude, invent 7 deceive, imitate, mislead, playact, profess, purport, suppose, surmise 8 simulate 9 imaginary 11 counterfeit, make-believe

pretender

4 fake, sham 5 actor, faker, fraud, phony 6 humbug 8 claimant, impostor 9 hypocrite

pretense

3 act, air 4 face, fake, mask, pose, sham 5 claim, cloak, cover, front, guise 6 deceit, facade, humbug 7 charade, fiction 8 disguise 9 deception, false show, imposture 10 masquerade, simulation 11 affectation, make-believe, ostentation

pretension

5 claim, right 6 vanity 8 ambition 10 allegation, aspiration 11 affectation

pretentious

5 lofty, put-on, showy 6 chichi, la-di-da, too-too 7 pompous, stilted 8 affected, inflated, puffed up, snobbish, specious 9 bombastic, conceited, grandiose, overblown 10 euphuistic, rhetorical 11 highfalutin 12 high-sounding, magniloquent, vainglorious

preternatural

7 psychic, unusual 8 abnormal, atypical 9 anomalous, unearthly, untypical 10 mysterious 12 inexplicable, supernatural 13 extraordinary

pretext

4 mask, ploy 5 alibi, cloak, cover, front, guise 6 device, excuse 7 apology 10 subterfuge

pretty

3 apt, pat 4 cute, fair, nice, some 5 bonny, quite 6 adroit, artful, clever, comely, fairly, kind of, lovely, mainly, rather, seemly, sort of 7 cunning, darling 8 graceful, handsome,

pleasant, pleasing, skillful, somewhat **9** appealing, beautiful **10** attractive, moderately, more or less **11** good-looking **12** considerable

prevail
4 beat, rule **5** reign **6** master **7** conquer, impress, persist, triumph **8** convince, dominate, domineer, overcome, override, persuade **9** influence

prevalent
4 rife **6** ruling **7** favored, popular, regnant **8** accepted, dominant, superior **9** ascendant, customary, paramount, sovereign **10** accustomed, widespread

prevaricate
3 fib, lie **5** avoid, evade **6** palter **7** confuse, deceive, distort, falsify, quibble **12** misrepresent

prevarication
3 fib, lie **4** tale **5** lying, story **6** canard, deceit **7** falsity **9** deception, falsehood

prevent
3 bar, dam **4** balk, foil, ward **5** avert, avoid, block, check, debar, deter **6** arrest, baffle, forbid, hinder, impede, thwart **7** forfend, head off, inhibit, obviate **8** obstruct, prohibit, stave off **9** forestall, frustrate, interdict **10** anticipate

previous
4 fore, past **5** early, prior **6** before, former **7** earlier, onetime **8** anterior **9** erstwhile, foregoing, in advance **10** antecedent, beforehand

previously
4 once **5** afore, ahead **6** before **7** already, earlier **8** formerly **9** erstwhile **10** heretofore

prewar
10 antebellum

prey
4 feed, game, mark **5** chase **6** quarry, target, victim **8** casualty, distress

Priam
daughter: 6 Creusa **8** Polyxena **9** Cassandra
father: 8 Laomedon
grandfather: 4 Ilus
kingdom: 4 Troy
slayer: 7 Pyrrhus **11** Neoptolemus
son: 5 Paris **6** Hector, Lycaon **7** Helenus, Troilus **9** Deiphobus, Polydorus
wife: 6 Arisbe, Hecuba

Priapus
father: 7 Bacchus **8** Dionysus
mother: 5 Venus **9** Aphrodite

price
3 fee, fix, tab **4** cost, fare, rate, toll **6** amount, assess, charge, figure, outlay, reward, tariff **7** expense, payment **8** appraise

priceless
4 rare, rich **5** droll, funny, witty **6** absurd, costly, prized, valued **7** amusing **8** precious, valuable **9** cherished, treasured **10** invaluable

pricey
4 dear **5** steep **6** costly **9** expensive

prick
3 jab **4** goad, mark, prod, spur, urge **5** egg on, point, sting, thorn **6** affect, excite, exhort, pierce, prompt **7** pinhole **8** puncture **9** perforate

prickly
5 burry, sharp, spiny **6** briary, thorny, tingly, touchy, trying **7** brambly, waspish **8** annoying, nettling, snappish, stinging **9** difficult, fractious, irritable, vexatious **10** bothersome, irritating, nettlesome **11** troublesome

pride
3 ego, top **4** best, brag, pack, pick **5** boast, cream, elite, exult, group, preen, prime, prize, vaunt **6** choice, egoism, vanity **7** conceit, delight, elation, dignity, disdain, egotism **8** smugness, treasure **9** arrogance, cockiness, vainglory **10** self-esteem, self-regard **11** self-respect **12** congratulate

Pride and Prejudice author
6 Austen (Jane)

prideful
6 elated 7 haughty 8 exultant
10 disdainful

prier
5 snoop 7 meddler 8 busybody,
quidnunc 9 buttinsky

priest
6 cleric, divine, rector 8 chaplain
9 clergyman, presbyter
ancient Roman: 6 flamen 8 ponti-
fex
Buddhist: 4 lama
Celtic: 5 druid
French: 4 abbé, curé
Muslim: 4 imam
tribal: 6 shaman

priestly
8 clerical, hieratic 10 sacerdotal

prig
5 prude, thief 6 pedant 8 bluenose
9 Mrs. Grundy 10 goody-goody

priggish
5 fussy 6 stuffy 7 genteel, pompous, prudish 8 affected, pedantic
11 puritanical, straitlaced

prim
4 neat, nice, snug, tidy, trig 5 stiff
6 formal, proper, strict, stuffy, wooden
7 correct, genteel, orderly, precise, prudish 8 decorous, priggish
11 straitlaced

prima donna
4 diva, snob, star 7 artiste 9 chanteuse 10 narcissist 11 leading lady

prima facie
4 true 5 valid 8 apparent 11 self-
evident

primal
5 basic 6 age-old 7 ancient, premier
8 cardinal, original 9 atavistic,
paramount, primitive 10 preeminent
11 prehistoric

primary
4 main 5 basal, basic, chief, first
6 direct 7 initial, pioneer, radical
8 cardinal, earliest, original 9 elemental, essential, firsthand, immediate, number-one, paramount,
principal 10 aboriginal, underlying 11 fundamental, rudimentary
12 foundational, introductory
combining form: 4 prot 5 proto
prefix: 4 arch 5 archi

primate
3 ape, man 5 human, lemur, loris
6 aye-aye, bonobo, monkey 7 gorilla
10 anthropoid, chimpanzee, human
being 11 Homo sapiens
nocturnal: 5 loris 7 tarsier
small: 6 galago

prime
3 top 4 best, dawn, fill, load, morn,
peak, pick, rate 5 coach, cream,
elite, first, paint, sunup, tonic, youth
6 choice, excite, height, spring,
symbol 7 capital, highest, initial,
morning, prepare, provoke, quicken
8 earliest, motivate, original, superior
9 excellent, first-rate, principal,
stimulate 10 first-class

primer
4 book 5 guide 6 manual, reader
8 hornbook

primeval
7 ancient 8 earliest, original 10 aboriginal

primitive
3 raw 4 rude 5 basic, crude, early
6 savage 7 archaic, Spartan 8 barbaric, original, primeval 9 atavistic,
barbarian, barbarous, elemental,
essential, unevolved 10 elementary,
primordial, underlying 11 fundamental, preliterate, uncivilized, undeveloped 12 uncultivated
combining form: 5 palae, paleo
6 archae, archeo, palaeo 7 archaeo
prefix: 4 arch 5 arche, archi

primogenitor
8 ancestor, forebear 9 precursor
10 forefather

primordial
5 basic, early, first 7 ancient 8 earliest, original

primp
4 fuss 5 adorn, dress, fix up, preen
7 dress up

prince
Anglo-Saxon: 8 atheling
Arab: 4 amir, emir
Austrian: 8 archduke
Ethiopian: 3 ras
Indian: 4 raja 5 rajah
of demons: 9 Beelzebub
of Monaco: 7 Rainier
of the church: 8 cardinal
of Wales: 7 Charles

Prince and the Pauper author
5 Twain (Mark) 7 Clemens (Samuel)

Prince _____ Coast, Antarctica
4 Olav

Prince Edward Island
capital: 13 Charlottetown
provincial flower: 12 lady's slipper

Prince Igor composer
7 Borodin (Aleksandr)

princely
5 grand, noble, royal 8 generous,
imposing, majestic 9 dignified
11 magnificent

princess
7 infanta
mythical: 3 Ino
of Monaco: 5 Grace

Prince Valiant
artist: 6 Foster (Hal)
son: 3 Arn
wife: 5 Aleta

principal
4 arch, dean, head, main, star
5 chief, first, major, prime 6 assets
7 capital, leading, premier, primary, stellar 8 cardinal, champion,
dominant, foremost 9 paramount
10 headmaster, preeminent 11 outstanding, predominant
combining form: 4 prot 5 proto
prefix: 4 arch 5 archi

principium
3 law 5 axiom, basis 7 element,
theorem 10 foundation 11 fundamental

principle
3 law 4 code, form, rule 5 axiom,
basis, canon, ethic, tenet 6 ground,
origin, source 7 conduct, faculty,
precept 8 doctrine, polestar, rudiment 10 assumption, convention, foundation 11 fundamental

principled
5 moral, noble 6 honest 7 ethical,
upright 8 virtuous 9 righteous
10 moralistic

print
4 type 5 issue, litho, stamp, write
7 engrave, impress, publish, typeset
10 impression
style: 4 bold 5 roman 6 italic
7 cursive 8 boldface

printer
English: 6 Caxton (William)
German: 9 Gutenberg (Johann,
Johannes)
Italian: 6 Bodoni (Giambattista)
8 Manutius (Aldus)

printing
7 edition, reissue 10 impression
measure: 4 pica 5 agate
process: 4 roto 7 gravure

priority
4 lead 5 order 8 ordering 9 supremacy 10 importance, precedence, preference

prison
3 can, pen 4 brig, coop, jail, keep
5 clink 6 cooler, lockup 7 dungeon,
slammer 8 bastille, big house,
stockade 9 calaboose 11 reformatory 12 penitentiary
California: 8 Alcatraz 10 San
Quentin
New York: 6 Attica 8 Sing Sing
12 Rikers Island
Northern Ireland: 4 Maze
resident: 6 inmate 7 convict 8 jailbird

prisoner
7 captive, convict, hostage 8 criminal, detainee, jailbird

prissy

5 picky **7** finicky, precise, prudish
8 exacting **10** fastidious, particular
11 straitlaced

pristine

4 pure **5** clean, fresh **8** earliest,
original **9** unspoiled

privacy

6 secret **7** retreat, secrecy **9** seclusion **11** concealment

private

5 inner **6** secret **7** soldier **8** eyes-
only, hush-hush, intimate, personal
9 concealed **10** closed-door, restricted, unofficial **11** independent,
sequestered **12** confidential

privateer

4 ship **7** gunship **9** mercenary

private eye

3 spy **4** G-man, tail **6** sleuth,
shamus **7** gumshoe **9** detective
12 investigator

privately

7 sub rosa **8** covertly, in camera, in
secret, secretly

privation

4 lack, loss, need, want **6** dearth,
penury **7** absence, poverty **8** distress **9** indigence, neediness,
suffering

privilege

4 boon **5** favor, grant, right **7** license
8 appanage **9** allowance, exemption
10 birthright, concession, perquisite
11 entitlement, opportunity, prerog-
tive
pope-granted: 6 indult

privy

3 can, loo **4** head, john **5** jakes
6 secret, toilet **7** latrine **8** bathroom,
informed, lavatory, outhouse, per-
sonal **9** concealed, withdrawn
11 water closet

prize

3 pry, top **4** best, loot, pick, plum, rate,
swag **5** award, booty, cream, elite,
force, lever, spoil, value **6** choice,
esteem, reward, spoils, trophy
7 capture, cherish, jackpot, plunder,
premium **8** treasure **10** appreciate
11 outstanding

prizefighting

6 boxing **8** pugilism

pro

3 for **6** expert, master **8** skillful
9 authority, in favor of **11** affirmative

probable

6 likely **7** seeming **8** apparent,
credible, expected, feasible, rational,
reliable **10** reasonable

probe

4 poke, quiz, test **5** query, study
6 search **7** dig into, examine, explore, feel out, inquest, inquire,
inquiry **8** check out, look into, research, sound out **9** delve into,
penetrate **11** exploration, investigate, reconnoiter **13** investigation

probity

5 honor **6** virtue **7** honesty **8** fairness, goodness **9** integrity, rectitude
11 uprightness

problem

4 mess **5** hitch, issue, poser
6 enigma, puzzle, riddle **7** dilemma,
example, mystery, puzzler, trouble
8 hardship, headache, question
10 difficulty

problematic

4 iffy, moot, open **7** dubious **8** arguable, doubtful **9** debatable, uncertain, unsettled **10** precarious
12 questionable

proboscis

4 beak, nose **5** snoot, snout, trunk

procedure

4 plan, step **6** course, custom,
method, policy, system **7** formula,
measure, routine **8** protocol **9** operation **11** instruction

proceed

4 flow, move, rise, stem, wend **5** arise,
get on, issue, segue **6** emerge, push
on, spring, travel **7** advance, carry
on, emanate, journey **8** continue, get
along **9** originate **10** derive from

proceedings
  8 goings-on
  recorded: 4 acta 6 annals 7 minutes

proceeds
  4 gain, take 5 yield 6 profit, result, return 8 earnings

process
  3 way 4 mode, wise 5 modus, treat 6 handle, manner, method, refine, system 7 fashion, prepare, recycle, routine 8 workings 9 evolution, operation, outgrowth, procedure, technique 11 development

procession
  5 march, order, train 6 parade, series, string 7 caravan, cortege 8 sequence 9 cavalcade, marchpast, motorcade 11 consecution

proclaim
  5 extol 6 assert, insist 7 declare, exhibit, glorify, publish 8 announce, evidence, manifest 9 advertise, broadcast, make known 10 annunciate, bruit about

proclivity
  4 bent 6 liking 7 leaning 8 penchant 9 proneness 11 inclination

Procne
  father: 7 Pandion
  husband: 6 Tereus
  sister: 9 Philomela
  son: 4 Itys

procrastinate
  5 dally, delay 6 dawdle

procreate
  5 beget, breed 7 produce 8 conceive, generate, multiply 9 reproduce

Procris' husband
  8 Cephalus

Procrustean ____
  3 bed

proctor
  7 monitor, oversee 9 supervise 10 supervisor

procure
  3 buy, get 4 gain 6 obtain, pick up 7 achieve, acquire 8 purchase 10 bring about

prod
  3 dig, jab, jog 4 goad, poke, push, spur, stir, urge 5 elbow, nudge, point, prick, rouse 6 excite, exhort, incite, thrust 8 motivate 9 stimulate 10 incitement

prodigal
  4 lush 6 lavish 7 opulent, profuse, riotous, spender, wastrel 8 reckless, wasteful 9 exuberant, luxuriant 10 profligate, squanderer 11 extravagant, spendthrift

prodigious
  4 huge, vast 6 mighty, unreal 7 amazing, immense, mammoth, massive, strange, unusual 8 colossal, enormous, gigantic 9 fantastic, marvelous, wonderful 10 astounding, impressive, monumental, phenomenal, remarkable, staggering, stupendous, surprising 11 astonishing 13 extraordinary

produce
  4 bear, form, grow, make, show, sire 5 beget, breed, build, cause, erect, frame, hatch, mount, put on, raise, spawn, stage, yield 6 create, effect, father, output, parent, secure, work up 7 deliver, fashion, turn out 8 engender, generate, multiply 9 construct, fabricate, originate, procreate, propagate 10 bring about 11 manufacture, put together

product
  5 fruit, issue, yield 6 effect, legacy, output, result, upshot 7 harvest, outcome, turnout 8 artifact, creation, multiple, offshoot 9 handiwork, outgrowth 11 consequence, manufacture

production
  5 fruit, yield 6 output 7 staging, turnout 8 artifact, assembly, creation 9 execution, handiwork, rendering 11 achievement, manufacture, realization

productive

4 rich 6 fecund, useful 7 fertile
8 abundant, fruitful, prolific 9 rewarding 10 beneficial

proem

7 preface, prelude 8 exordium,
foreword, overture, prologue 11 preliminary

profane

3 lay 4 damn, foul 5 abuse, dirty,
pagan 6 coarse, debase, defile,
filthy, impure, unholy, vulgar 7 impious, obscene, secular 8 indecent,
temporal, unsacred 9 desecrate
10 irreverent, unhallowed 11 blasphemous, irreligious 12 sacrilegious,
unsanctified

profanity

4 oath 5 abuse, curse 7 cursing,
cussing 8 swearing 9 blasphemy,
sacrilege 10 execration 11 imprecation, irreverence

profess

4 aver, avow 5 claim, teach 6 affirm,
allege, assert, avouch 7 declare,
pretend, protest, purport 8 maintain,
practice

profession

3 art, job, vow 5 craft, trade 6 avowal,
career, métier 7 calling 8 business,
vocation 9 assertion, specialty,
statement, testimony 10 handicraft,
occupation 11 affirmation

professional

4 paid 6 expert, master 7 learned,
skilled 9 authority 10 proficient,
specialist 11 experienced 12 businesslike

professor

3 don 6 expert 7 teacher 8 academic, educator

proffer

4 give, pose 6 extend, submit,
tender 7 hold out, present, suggest
10 invitation, suggestion

proficiency

5 savvy, skill 7 ability, advance
8 progress 9 adeptness, expertise,
knowledge 10 competence

proficient

4 able 5 adept 6 expert 7 capable,
skilled 8 advanced, masterly, skillful
9 authority, competent, effective,
masterful, qualified 11 crackerjack,
experienced 12 accomplished

profile

5 chart 6 sketch, survey 7 contour,
diagram, outline 8 exposure, portrait, side view 9 biography 10 silhouette 11 description

profit

3 net 4 gain, take 5 serve, yield
6 excess, income, payoff, return
7 benefit, receipt 8 earnings, proceeds 10 percentage 12 compensation

profitable

6 paying, useful 7 gainful 8 fruitful
9 lucrative, rewarding 10 beneficial,
well-paying, worthwhile 11 moneymaking 12 advantageous, remunerative

profligate

4 wild 6 waster 7 immoral, spender,
wastrel 8 prodigal, reckless, wasteful 9 abandoned, dissolute, indulgent, reprobate 10 dissipated, immoderate, licentious, squanderer
11 extravagant, promiscuous, spendthrift 13 self-indulgent

profound

4 deep, wise 5 heavy, total, utter
7 abysmal, intense 8 absolute,
abstruse, complete, esoteric, thorough 9 intensive 10 deep-seated,
insightful

profundity

5 depth 6 wisdom 7 insight 8 deepness 12 abstruseness

profuse

4 lush 6 lavish 7 copious, fulsome,
liberal, opulent 8 abundant, generous, prodigal 9 abounding, bounteous, bountiful, excessive, exuberant, luxuriant, plentiful 10 munificent
11 extravagant

profusion
4 glut, riot 5 flood, spate, surge
6 bounty, deluge, excess, wealth
7 nimiety, satiety, surfeit, surplus,
torrent 8 overflow, overload, plethora
9 abundance, plenitude 10 lavishness, luxuriance, oversupply, plenti-
tude, redundancy 11 copiousness,
prodigality, sufficiency, superfluity
12 extravagance 13 overabundance

progenitor
4 sire 6 author, father, mother
8 ancestor, forebear 9 initiator,
precursor 10 antecessor, forefather,
forerunner, originator 11 predecessor

progeny
4 line 5 issue 6 litter, result, scions
7 outcome, product 8 children
9 offspring, posterity 11 descendants

prognosis
8 estimate, forecast, prophecy
9 prevision 10 estimation, prediction
11 expectation 12 anticipation

prognostic
4 omen, sign 6 augury 7 portent,
presage 10 foreboding, indication

prognosticate
6 divine 7 foresee, predict, presage
8 forecast, foretell, prophesy

program
4 bill, book, plan, show 5 plans,
slate 6 agenda, course, docket,
lineup, policy 7 listing 8 calendar,
playbill, schedule, syllabus 9 broadcast, procedure, timetable 10 bill of
fare, curriculum

progress
4 fare, gain, grow 5 get on, march
6 course, growth 7 advance, headway, passage, proceed 8 anabasis,
get along, momentum 9 evolution,
flowering, unfolding 11 advancement, development, improvement
planned: 7 telesis

progressing
5 afoot 7 en route 8 under way

progression
5 chain 6 course, growth, series
7 advance 8 sequence 9 evolution,
unfolding 11 development

progressive
6 modern 7 growing, liberal, radical
8 advanced, tolerant 9 advancing
10 developing, increasing

prohibit
3 ban, bar 4 stop 5 block, debar
6 enjoin, forbid, outlaw 7 prevent
8 preclude 9 interdict

prohibited
5 taboo 6 banned, barred 7 illegal,
illicit 8 verboten 9 forbidden

prohibition
3 ban, bar 5 taboo 7 embargo
8 sanction 9 interdict 10 constraint,
forbidding, injunction 12 disallowance, interdiction, proscription

prohibitive
5 steep 6 costly 7 sky-high 9 excessive 10 exorbitant, forbidding
11 restrictive

project
3 jut 4 cast, feat, plan 5 bulge
6 affair, design, devise, extend,
intend, scheme, vision 7 arrange,
concern, emprise, exploit, feature,
imagine, propose, purpose, venture
8 business, conceive, envisage,
envision, game plan, overhang,
protrude, stand out, stick out, strategy 9 blueprint, visualize 10 enterprise 11 proposition, undertaking

projection
3 jut 4 bump, knob, view 5 bulge
7 display 8 estimate, forecast,
overhang, scheming, swelling 9 extension 10 jutting out, perception
11 expectation

proletariat
6 masses 7 workers 8 laborers
9 commoners, hoi polloi 12 working
class

prolific
4 rich 6 fecund, gifted, lavish 7 fertile 8 abundant, creative, fruitful

9 abounding, bountiful, inventive
10 generating, generative 11 reproducing 12 reproductive

prolix

4 long 5 windy, wordy 7 diffuse, lengthy, tedious, verbose 8 drawn out, rambling, tiresome 9 redundant, wearisome 10 long-winded

prologue

7 opening, preface, prelude 8 exordium, foreword, overture, preamble 9 beginning 12 introduction

prolong

6 extend 7 drag out, draw out, spin out, stretch 8 continue, elongate, lengthen

prolonged

7 lasting, lengthy 8 drawn-out 9 lingering 10 continuing, persistent, persisting

prom

4 ball, fete, gala 5 dance 6 formal

promenade

4 deck, walk 6 parade, stroll 9 boardwalk

Prometheus

brother: 5 Atlas 9 Menoetius 10 Epimetheus
creation: 3 man 7 mankind
father: 7 Iapetus
gift: 4 fire
mother: 7 Clymene
rescuer: 8 Heracles, Hercules
tormentor: 5 eagle

prominence

4 crag, fame, rise, spur 5 bulge 6 height, renown, status 8 eminence, headland, prestige, salience, standing 9 celebrity, elevation 10 importance, projection 11 distinction

prominent

5 famed, great, noted 6 famous, marked, signal 7 eminent, jutting, leading, notable, popular, salient 8 renowned, striking 9 arresting, notorious, well-known 10 celebrated, noticeable, pronounced, remarkable 11 conspicuous, eye-catching, illustrious, outstanding 13 distinguished
person: 3 VIP 4 BMOC, lion 5 mogul, nabob 6 bigwig, honcho 7 big shot, grandee 8 luminary, mandarin, somebody 9 dignitary 13 high-muck-a-muck

promiscuous

5 mixed 6 casual, random, varied 7 immoral 8 careless 9 haphazard, hit-or-miss, irregular 10 licentious 11 unselective 12 unrestrained

promise

3 vow 4 bode, bond, oath 5 agree, augur, swear, vouch 6 assure, engage, ensure, expect, insure, parole, pledge, plight 7 betroth, compact, consent, declare, outlook, portend, presage, suggest 8 contract, covenant, indicate 9 assurance, betrothal, potential, undertake 11 declaration, expectation

promised land

4 Zion 6 Canaan, heaven 8 paradise 11 kingdom come

promising

6 likely 7 hopeful 9 favorable 10 auspicious 11 encouraging

promissory note

3 IOU

promontory

4 beak, bill, cape, head, ness 5 bulge, point 8 foreland, headland

promote

3 aid 4 help, plug, puff, push, sell, tout 5 boost, favor, raise 6 foster, launch, prefer 7 advance, build up, elevate, endorse, forward, further, nurture, present, support 8 advocate, champion 9 advertise, encourage, publicize, recommend

promotion

6 step up 7 advance, buildup, puffery 9 elevation, publicity, upgrading 10 preference, preferment 11 advancement, advertising, improvement 13 advertisement

prompt

3 apt, cue, jog 4 fast, goad, help, hint, move, spur, urge 5 alert, quick, rapid, ready 6 assist, incite, induce, on time, remind, speedy, stir up, timely 7 suggest 8 convince, persuade, punctual, reminder 10 responsive

promulgate

5 issue 6 decree 7 declare, publish 8 announce, proclaim 9 advertise, broadcast 10 annunciate 11 disseminate

prone

3 apt 4 flat, open 5 given, level 6 liable, likely, supine 7 subject, tending, willing 8 disposed, facedown, inclined 9 lying down, reclining, recumbent 10 horizontal 11 predisposed, susceptible

prong

4 barb, fang, fork, spur, stab, tine 5 point, thorn 6 pierce

pronghorn

8 antelope

_____ pro nobis

3 ora

pronoun

archaic: 3 thy 4 thou 5 thine
demonstrative: 4 that, this 5 these, those
indefinite: 3 all, any, few, one 4 both, each, none, some 5 no one, other 6 anyone, either, nobody 7 another, anybody, neither, nothing, someone 8 anything, somebody 9 everybody, something 10 everything
personal: 3 her, him, she, you 4 them, they
possessive: 3 her, his, its, our 4 hers, mine, ours, your 5 their, yours 6 theirs
reflexive: 6 itself, myself 7 herself, himself, oneself, ourself 8 yourself 9 ourselves 10 themselves, yourselves
relative: 3 who 4 that, what, whom 5 which, whose, whoso 6 whomso

7 whoever 8 whatever, whomever 9 whichever, whosoever 10 whatsoever, whomsoever 11 whichsoever

pronounce

3 say 5 judge, sound, speak, utter 6 affirm, assert, decree, recite 7 declare 9 enunciate 10 articulate

pronounced

5 clear 6 marked, strong 7 assured, decided, evident, obvious 8 clearcut, definite, distinct 12 unmistakable

pronouncement

5 edict 6 decree 9 manifesto, statement 11 declaration, publication 12 notification

pronto

3 now, PDQ 4 ASAP, fast, stat 6 at once 7 quickly 8 directly 9 forthwith, posthaste, right away 11 immediately

pronunciation

distinctive: 4 burr, lilt 5 drawl, twang 6 accent, brogue
study: 8 orthoepy 9 phonetics

proof

4 test 5 facts, goods 6 galley 8 argument, evidence 9 testament, testimony 10 impression 11 attestation 12 confirmation

proofreaders' mark

4 dele, stet 5 caret

prop

4 stay 5 brace, shore 6 buoy up, hold up 7 bolster, shore up, support, sustain 8 buttress 10 strengthen 12 underpinning

propaganda

4 hype 8 agitprop, lobbying

propagandize

4 tout 5 boost, extol 7 advance, promote, trumpet 9 brainwash, catechize, inculcate 10 promulgate 11 proselytize 12 indoctrinate

propagate

5 beget, breed, raise, strew 6 extend, spread 7 diffuse, publish,

propel

radiate 8 disperse, generate, increase, multiply, transmit 9 circulate, cultivate, publicize, reproduce 10 distribute 11 disseminate

propel

4 goad, move, push, spur, urge 5 drive, egg on, power, shoot, shove 6 exhort, launch, thrust 7 actuate 8 activate

propellant

3 gas 4 fuel, spur 7 impetus, impulse 8 catalyst, stimulus 9 explosive, incentive, stimulant 10 motivation

propensity

7 leaning 8 penchant 10 preference 11 inclination

proper

3 apt, due, fit 4 good, just, meet, nice, prim, true 5 exact, happy, right 6 au fait, decent, prissy, seemly, useful 7 correct, desired, fitting, genteel, precise 8 accurate, becoming, decorous, peculiar, priggish, rightful, rigorous, suitable 9 befitting 10 applicable, convenient, felicitous, individual 11 appropriate, comme il faut, distinctive
combining form: 4 orth 5 ortho

property

4 land, mark 5 acres, trait, worth 6 assets, estate, realty, riches, virtue, wealth 7 acreage, chattel, effects, feature, fortune, quality 8 chattels, dominion, hallmark, holdings, premises 9 attribute, ownership, resources, substance 10 belongings, possession, real estate
conveyor: 7 alienor
recipient: 7 alienee
seller: 7 Realtor
transfer: 8 alienate

prophecy

6 vision 8 forecast 10 divination, prediction 11 foretelling

prophesy

5 augur 6 divine, preach 7 foresee, portend, predict, presage 8 forecast, foretell, instruct, soothsay

9 adumbrate, prefigure 10 vaticinate 13 prognosticate

prophet

4 seer 5 augur, sibyl 6 auspex, oracle 7 diviner, seeress 8 foreseer, haruspex 9 predictor 10 forecaster, foreteller, prophesier, soothsayer 11 Nostradamus 13 fortune-teller
Arthurian: 6 Merlin
Major: 6 Daniel, Isaiah 7 Ezekiel 8 Jeremiah
Minor: 4 Amos, Joel 5 Hosea, Jonah, Micah, Nahum 6 Haggai 7 Malachi, Obadiah 8 Habakkuk 9 Zechariah, Zephaniah

Prophet author

6 Gibran (Khalil)

prophetess

5 sibyl 7 Deborah 9 Cassandra

prophetic

5 vatic 6 orphic 7 Delphic 8 Delphian, oracular 9 presaging, prescient, sibylline, vaticinal 10 predictive, revelatory 11 apocalyptic, foretelling

propinquity

7 kinship 8 nearness 9 closeness, proximity 10 contiguity

propitiate

5 adapt, atone 6 adjust, pacify, soothe 7 appease, assuage, gratify, mollify, placate, satisfy 9 intercede, reconcile 10 conciliate

propitious

4 good, rosy 5 lucky 6 benign, bright 7 benefic, helpful 8 favoring 9 favorable, fortunate, opportune, promising 10 auspicious, beneficent, beneficial, benevolent 12 advantageous

proponent

6 backer 8 advocate, champion, defender 9 expounder, supporter 10 enthusiast

proportion

4 rate, size 5 allot, ratio, quota, share 6 adjust, divide 7 balance,

conform, harmony **8** symmetry
9 dimension **10** percentage **12** relationship

proportional

5 scale **7** in scale **8** relative **9** equalized **10** contingent, equivalent, reciprocal **11** correlative, symmetrical **12** commensurate **13** commensurable, corresponding

proposal

3 bid **4** idea, plan **6** motion, scheme **7** outline, proffer, project **8** scenario **10** invitation, suggestion **11** proposition
final: 9 ultimatum

propose

3 aim, ask, put **4** name, plan, pose **5** offer **6** design, intend, submit, tender **7** advance, move for, present, request, solicit, suggest **8** nominate, put forth, set forth, theorize **9** recommend **10** put forward

proposition

4 plan **5** offer **6** scheme, thesis **7** premise, suggest, theorem **10** invitation, suggestion

propound

3 put **4** pose **5** offer **7** present, suggest **8** put forth

proprietor

5 owner **8** landlord **9** possessor

propriety

7 aptness, decency, decorum, manners **8** behavior, civility, good form **9** etiquette, rightness **10** seemliness **11** correctness, fittingness, suitability **12** decorousness

propulsion

4 fuel, push **5** drive, force, power **6** energy, thrust

prorate

5 allot, divvy, quota, share, split **6** assess, divide, parcel, ration **7** divvy up, portion **9** apportion, partition **10** distribute

prorogue

3 end **4** rise, stay **5** defer, delay

6 hold up, put off, recess, shelve **7** adjourn, hold off, suspend **8** dissolve, hold over, postpone **9** terminate

prosaic

4 dull, flat **5** banal, prose, prosy, trite, vapid **6** boring, common **7** factual, literal, mundane, tedious **8** everyday, lifeless, ordinary, workaday **9** colorless **10** lackluster, uneventful **11** commonplace **13** unimaginative

proscenium

5 frame, stage **9** forestage **10** foreground

proscribe

3 ban **4** damn **6** enjoin, forbid, outlaw **7** condemn **8** prohibit, sentence **9** interdict

proscription

3 ban **5** taboo **11** prohibition **12** condemnation, interdiction

prosecute

3 sue **4** wage **5** press **6** charge, indict, pursue **7** carry on, perform **8** continue **9** bring suit, persevere

proselyte

7 convert, recruit **8** neophyte

proselytize

5 draft **6** enlist, enroll, sign up **7** convert, recruit, win over **8** convince **9** brainwash, catechize **11** prevail upon **12** indoctrinate

—— prosequi

5 nolle

prospect

4 mine, view **5** scene, vista **6** chance, survey, vision **7** dig into, explore, lookout, outlook **8** customer, exposure **9** candidate **10** expectancy **11** expectation, possibility **12** anticipation

prospective

6 coming, future, likely **7** awaited, ensuing, nearing, pending, planned, would-be **8** destined, eventual, expected, hoped-for, intended, proposed, soon-to-be **9** impending,

looked-for, potential, scheduled
10 consequent, succeeding **11** anticipated, approaching, predestined, forthcoming

prospectus

4 list, plan **6** design, layout, précis **7** epitome, outline, program, summary **8** bulletin, synopsis **9** catalogue, timetable **10** projection **11** description **12** announcement

prosper

5 score, yield **6** arrive, do well, thrive **7** make out, produce, succeed, turn out **8** flourish, grow rich

prosperity

4 ease **6** riches, wealth **7** success **8** thriving **9** abundance, advantage, affluence, well-being

Prospero

daughter: 7 Miranda
servant: 5 Ariel
slave: 7 Caliban

prosperous

4 rich, well **5** happy, lucky **6** robust, strong **7** booming, halcyon, opulent, wealthy, well-off **8** affluent, thriving, well-to-do **9** desirable, favorable, fortunate, promising, well-fixed **10** auspicious, successful, well-heeled **11** comfortable, flourishing

prostitute

4 bawd, doxy, drab, moll **5** abuse, B-girl, madam, quean, whore **6** callet, debase, floozy, harlot, hooker, misuse, wanton **7** chippie, cocotte, corrupt, cyprian, floozie, hustler, Paphian **8** call girl, meretrix, strumpet **9** courtesan, party girl **11** fille de joie, nightwalker **12** camp follower, streetwalker
reformed: 8 magdalen **9** magdalene

prostitution

8 harlotry, whoredom **13** streetwalking
house of: 4 crib, stew **6** bagnio **7** brothel, lupanar **8** bordello, cathouse **10** bawdy house **13** sporting house

prostrate

4 fell, flat **5** abase, level, prone **6** humble, lay low, submit, supine **7** exhaust, wear out **8** helpless, overcome **9** decumbent, exhausted, overpower, overwhelm, powerless, recumbent **10** procumbent, submissive

protagonist

4 hero, lead, star **5** actor **6** leader **7** heroine, sponsor **8** advocate, champion **9** principal

protean

6 mobile, varied **7** diverse, mutable **8** variable **9** adaptable, versatile **10** changeable

protect

4 save **5** cover, guard **6** defend, screen, secure, shield **7** shelter **8** preserve, restrict **9** safeguard

protection

4 care **5** aegis, armor, bribe, graft, guard **6** safety, shield **7** bulwark, defense, shelter, support **8** armament, coverage, immunity, security **9** extortion, insurance, safeguard **11** supervision

protector

5 armor, guard **6** patron, regent, shield **8** guardian **9** caretaker

protégé

4 ward **5** pupil **7** student, trainee **8** disciple

protein

4 zein **5** actin, opsin **6** avidin, enzyme, fibrin, globin **7** albumin, elastin, fibroin, histone, keratin, legumin, sericin **8** creatine, globulin, glutelin, prolamin, protamin, proteose, vitellin
complex: 6 mucoid
derivative: 7 peptone
poisonous: 5 abrin, ricin

pro tem

6 acting **7** interim **9** ad interim, temporary

protest

4 aver, avow, beef **6** affirm, assert,

avouch, except, object, oppose, picket, resist **7** declare, profess **8** maintain **9** challenge, complaint, objection **10** disapprove **11** demonstrate, disapproval **13** demonstration

Protestant
5 Amish **6** Mormon, Quaker, Shaker **7** Baptist, Lollard, Pilgrim, Puritan **8** Anglican, Lutheran, Moravian **9** Adventist, Mennonite, Methodist, Unitarian **11** Pentecostal **12** Episcopalian, Presbyterian
Bohemian: 7 Hussite
French: 8 Huguenot

protocol
4 code, form, rule **6** custom, ritual **7** compact, conduct, decorum, manners **8** courtesy **9** concordat, etiquette, politesse, propriety **11** conventions, formalities

prototype
4 norm **5** model **6** design **7** example, pattern **8** original, paradigm, standard

prototypical
5 ideal, model **7** classic **9** classical, exemplary **10** archetypal

protozoan
4 cell **5** ameba **6** amoeba **7** ciliate, stentor **10** flagellate, paramecium

protract
6 drag on, extend **7** drag out, draw out, prolong, stretch **8** continue

protrude
3 jut **4** poke, pout **5** bulge **6** jut out **7** project **8** overhang, stand out, stick out

protrusion
3 jut, nub **4** bump **5** bulge **8** swelling **10** projection

protuberant
5 bulgy **7** bulging **9** prominent **11** conspicuous

proud
4 vain **5** huffy, lofty, noble **6** lordly, stuffy, superb **7** haughty, pleased, pompous, stuck-up, stately **8** arro-

gant, exultant, glorious, scornful, snobbish, spirited, splendid, superior, vigorous **9** conceited, delighted, imperious **10** disdainful, high-handed **11** magnificent, pretentious, resplendent **12** ostentatious, supercilious

Proulx novel
9 Postcards **12** Shipping News (The)

prove
3 try **4** show, test **5** argue, check **6** attest, pan out, verify **7** bear out, certify, confirm, examine, explain, turn out **8** document, indicate, validate **9** determine, establish **11** corroborate, demonstrate **12** substantiate

provenance
4 root, well **6** origin, source **7** history **9** inception **10** derivation

provender
4 feed, food **8** victuals **10** provisions

proverb
3 saw **5** adage, axiom, maxim **6** byword, saying **7** epigram **8** aphorism

provide
4 give, hand **5** endow, equip, serve, state **6** afford, outfit, supply **7** deliver, furnish, prepare, specify, support **8** dispense, hand over, maintain **9** stipulate

provided
5 given **6** if only **8** equipped, supplied

providence
4 care **6** thrift **7** caution, economy **8** prudence **9** foresight, frugality **11** forethought, thriftiness

provident
5 canny, chary **6** frugal, saving **7** careful, prudent, sparing, thrifty **8** prepared **10** economical, unwasteful **11** foresighted

providential
5 happy, lucky **9** benignant, fortunate **10** auspicious, fortuitous

province

4 area, duty, role, work 5 field, shire
6 canton, county, domain, office,
region, sphere 7 demesne, pursuit,
terrain 8 district, dominion, function
9 bailiwick, champaign, territory
10 department 12 jurisdiction

provincial

5 local, rural 6 narrow, rustic, simple
7 country, insular, limited 8 pastoral
9 parochial, sectarian, small-town
11 countrified

provision

5 stock, store 6 supply 9 condition
11 preparation, requirement, reservation, stipulation

provisional

5 stamp 6 acting, pro tem 9 temporary 10 contingent 11 conditional

provisions

4 feed, food, grub 5 stock 6 viands
7 aliment, edibles, nurture, vittles
8 supplies, victuals 9 provender
10 sustenance 11 comestibles
dealer: 8 chandler

proviso

6 clause 7 article 9 condition
11 stipulation

provocation

5 cause, wrong 7 offense 8 stimulus,
vexation 9 annoyance, incentive
10 incitement 11 instigation

provocative

5 heady 8 alluring, annoying, arousing, exciting 9 offensive 10 intriguing 11 challenging, stimulating

provoke

3 bug, irk, vex 4 abet, rile, stir, wake
5 anger, annoy, cause, evoke, pique,
rouse, upset, waken 6 arouse,
awaken, bother, excite, foment,
harass, incite, induce, kindle, nettle,
stir up, whip up 7 incense, inflame,
inspire, outrage, quicken 8 generate, irritate, motivate, occasion
9 challenge, galvanize, instigate,
stimulate

provost

4 head 6 keeper 7 marshal 8 director 10 magistrate 13 administrator

prow

3 bow 4 stem 5 front 10 projection

prowess

5 skill, valor 7 bravery, command,
courage, heroism, mastery 9 expertise, gallantry 10 excellence

prowl

4 hunt, roam 5 skulk, slink, sneak,
steal 6 search, wander

proximate

4 near, next 5 close 6 nearby
8 adjacent, imminent 9 following,
immediate, preceding 10 near-at-
hand 11 forthcoming

proximity

8 nearness, vicinity 9 adjacency,
closeness, immediacy 10 contiguity
11 propinquity

proxy

5 agent 6 deputy 7 stand-in 8 attorney 9 surrogate 10 substitute

pro ____

3 tem 4 bono, rata 5 forma 7 tempore

prude

4 prig 7 old maid, Puritan 8 bluenose 9 Mrs. Grundy

prudence

4 care 5 skill 6 acumen, reason,
thrift, wisdom 7 caution, economy
8 sagacity 9 foresight, frugality
10 astuteness, discretion, expediency, precaution, providence,
shrewdness 11 calculation, forethought, thriftiness

prudent

4 sage, sane, wary, wise 5 canny,
chary 6 frugal 7 careful, politic
8 cautious, discreet, sensible 9 expedient, judicious 11 circumspect

prudish

4 prim 5 stern 6 narrow, prissy,
proper, severe, strict, stuffy 7 aus-

tere, genteel **8** affected, decorous, priggish **11** puritanical, straitlaced

prune
3 cut, lop **4** clip, crop, pare, plum, thin, trim **5** shear **6** cut off, reduce, remove **7** cut away, cut back, shorten **8** pare down, truncate

prurience
4 lust **6** desire, libido **7** lechery, passion **8** cupidity **9** carnality, eroticism **11** lustfulness **13** concupiscence

prurient
4 lewd **5** bawdy **6** erotic **7** goatish, lustful, satyric, sensual **9** lickerish **10** lascivious, libidinous, passionate **12** concupiscent

pruritic
5 itchy

Prussian
aristocrat: **6** Junker **12** Hohenzollern
prime minister: **8** Bismarck (Otto von)
ruler: **7** Wilhelm **9** Frederick (the Great)

pry
4 nose, open, poke **5** jimmy, lever, snoop **6** meddle **7** inquire **9** interfere

prying
4 nosy **6** snoopy **7** curious **8** meddling, snooping **9** intrusive, obtrusive, officious **10** meddlesome **11** impertinent, inquisitive

psalm
3 ode **4** hymn, poem, song **5** paean
book: **7** psalter
selection: **6** Hallel
word: **5** selah

psalmist
4 poet **5** Asaph, David **6** cantor

pseudo
4 fake, mock, sham **5** bogus, false, phony **7** pretend **8** spurious **9** imitation **10** artificial **11** counterfeit

pseudonym
5 alias **7** pen name **9** false name, stage name **10** nom de plume **11** nom de guerre

psyche
4 mind, soul **5** anima **6** animus, pneuma, spirit
part: **3** ego **8** superego

Psyche's beloved
4 Eros **5** Cupid

psychiatrist
6 shrink **8** alienist **11** neurologist
American: **3** May (Rollo) **5** Reich (Wilhelm) **6** Kramer (Peter), Rogers (Carl) **7** Erikson (Erik) **8** Sullivan (Harry Stack) **9** Menninger (Karl)
Austrian: **5** Adler (Alfred), Freud (Anna, Sigmund), Reich (Wilhelm)
British: **5** Laing (R. D.)
French: **5** Lacan (Jacques)
German: **5** Fromm (Erich) **6** Horne' (Karen)
Swiss: **4** Jung (Carl) **9** Rorschach (Hermann)

psychic
4 seer **6** medium, mental, occult **8** cerebral **9** mentalist, prophetic, spiritual **10** mind reader, telepathic **11** clairvoyant, telekinetic **12** intellectual, supersensory
American: **5** Cayce (Edgar), Dixon (Jeane) **10** Montgomery (Ruth)
power: **3** ESP

psycho
3 nut **5** crazy, sicko, wacko **6** madman, maniac, mental, schizo, weirdo **7** berserk, haywire, lunatic, nutcase **8** crackpot, demented, deranged, head case **9** fruitcake, screwball, sociopath

psychoanalyst
4 Jung (Carl Gustav), Rank (Otto) **5** Adler (Alfred), Freud (Sigmund), Fromm (Erich), Klein (Melanie), Kohut (Heinz), Lacan (Jacques) **6** Horney (Karen) **7** Erikson (Erik) **8** Ferenczi (Sandor)

psychologist
6 shrink 9 therapist
American: 5 James (William)
6 Terman (Lewis), Watson (John),
Yerkes (Robert) 7 Skinner (B. F.)
9 Thorndike (Edward L.)
English: 4 Ward (James) 8 Spear-
man (Charles), Tichener (Edward)
German: 5 Wundt (Wilhelm)
6 Müller (Georg), Stumpf (Carl)
10 Wertheimer (Max)

psychotic
3 mad 5 crazy 6 insane 8 demented,
deranged, schizoid 13 schizophrenic

ptarmigan
6 grouse

ptomaine
6 poison

pub
3 bar, inn 4 dive 5 joint 6 tavern
7 barroom, gin mill, taproom 8 grogshop 9 roadhouse 11 rathskeller

puberty
11 adolescence

public
4 open 5 civic, civil, state 6 common, mutual, people, shared, social
7 general, popular, society 8 communal, national, populace 9 community, municipal, universal 10 accessible, government

publican
7 barkeep 8 landlord, licensee,
taverner 9 bartender, collector,
innkeeper 12 tax collector

publication
4 book 7 article, journal 8 magazine, pamphlet 9 broadside, newspaper 10 periodical
list: 12 bibliography

public house
3 bar, inn 6 hostel, saloon, tavern
7 auberge, hospice 8 hostelry

publicity
3 ink 4 hype, plug 5 blurb, press,
promo 6 hoopla, notice 7 billing,
write-up 8 ballyhoo 9 attention,
promotion 11 advertising 12 announcement 13 advertisement

publicize
4 bill, hype, plug, puff, push, tout
5 boost 7 promote, trumpet 8 announce 9 advertise, broadcast
10 press-agent, promulgate

publish
3 air 5 issue, print 6 get out, inform,
put out, report 7 release 8 announce, bring out, proclaim 9 advertise, broadcast, make known
10 distribute, promulgate 11 disseminate

Puccini, Giacomo
opera: 5 Tosca 7 Le Villi 8 La
Bohème, Turandot 12 Manon
Lescaut 15 Madame Butterfly

puck
3 elf, imp 4 disk 5 fairy 6 spirit,
sprite 9 hobgoblin, prankster

pucker
4 fold 5 purse 6 cockle, crease
7 wrinkle 8 compress, contract
9 constrict

puckish
5 antic, elfin, larky, pixie 6 elvish,
impish 7 playful 8 prankish 9 whimsical 11 mischievous

Puck's master
6 Oberon

pudding
4 duff 6 burgoo 7 custard, tapioca
baked: 5 kugel 10 brown Betty

pudgy
3 fat 5 plump, round, stout, tubby
6 chubby, chunky, flabby, rotund
8 plumpish, roly-poly

pueblo
4 town 7 village 8 dwelling
ceremonial room: 4 kiva

puerile
5 inane, silly 6 jejune 7 foolish
8 childish, immature, juvenile

Puerto Rico
  capital: 7 San Juan
  city: 5 Ponce 7 Bayamon 8 Mayagüez
  discoverer: 8 Columbus (Christopher)
  language: 7 Spanish
  location: 10 West Indies

puff
  3 pad 4 blow, brag, crow, drag, emit,
  huff, pant, plug, pouf, push, tout, waft
  5 blurb, boast, boost, elate, expel, quilt, swell, vaunt, whiff 6 exhale, pastry, praise 7 flatter, inflate
  8 swelling 9 advertise, comforter,
  publicize 10 exaggerate

puffer
  8 blowfish 9 globefish, swellfish

puffery
  4 hype, plug 9 promotion, publicity
  11 advertising 12 exaggeration,
  press-agentry

puffin
  4 bird 7 seabird 9 sea parrot
  10 shearwater
  cousin: 3 auk

puffy
  7 swollen 8 inflated

pug
  3 bun, dog 4 nose 5 boxer, track
  9 footprint

pugilism
  6 boxing 13 prizefighting

pugilist
  5 boxer 7 fighter 12 prizefighter

pugnacious
  7 defiant, scrappy 8 brawling,
  fighting, militant 9 bellicose, combative, truculent 10 aggressive,
  rebellious 11 belligerent, contentious, quarrelsome 13 argumentative

pugnacity
  9 hostility 10 aggression, truculence,
  truculency 12 belligerence 13 combativeness

puisne
  6 junior 8 inferior

puissance
  5 force, might, power 6 energy
  7 potency 8 strength

puissant
  6 mighty, potent, strong 8 forceful,
  powerful

pukka
  4 real, tops 7 genuine 8 bona fide
  9 authentic 10 first-class

pule
  3 cry 4 mewl 5 whine 7 whimper

Pulitzer Prize fiction winner
  1918: 5 Poole (Ernest)
  1919: 10 Tarkington (Booth)
  1921: 7 Wharton (Edith)
  1922: 10 Tarkington (Booth)
  1923: 6 Cather (Willa)
  1924: 6 Wilson (Margaret)
  1925: 6 Ferber (Edna)
  1926: 5 Lewis (Sinclair)
  1927: 8 Bromfield (Louis)
  1928: 6 Wilder (Thornton)
  1929: 8 Peterkin (Julia)
  1930: 7 La Farge (Oliver)
  1931: 6 Barnes (Margaret)
  1932: 4 Buck (Pearl)
  1933: 9 Stribling (T. S.)
  1934: 6 Miller (Caroline)
  1935: 7 Johnson (Josephine)
  1936: 5 Davis (Harold)
  1937: 8 Mitchell (Margaret)
  1938: 8 Marquand (John)
  1939: 8 Rawlings (Marjorie Kinnan)
  1940: 9 Steinbeck (John)
  1942: 7 Glasgow (Ellen)
  1943: 8 Sinclair (Upton)
  1944: 6 Flavin (Martin)
  1945: 6 Hersey (John)
  1947: 6 Warren (Robert Penn)
  1948: 8 Michener (James)
  1949: 7 Cozzens (James Gould)
  1950: 7 Guthrie (A. B.)
  1951: 7 Richter (Conrad)
  1952: 4 Wouk (Herman)
  1953: 9 Hemingway (Ernest)
  1955: 8 Faulkner (William)

1956: 6 Kantor (MacKinlay)
1958: 4 Agee (James)
1959: 6 Taylor (Robert Lewis)
1960: 5 Drury (Allen)
1961: 3 Lee (Harper)
1962: 7 O'Connor (Edwin)
1963: 8 Faulkner (William)
1965: 4 Grau (Shirley Ann)
1966: 6 Porter (Katherine Anne)
1967: 7 Malamud (Bernard)
1968: 6 Styron (William)
1969: 7 Momaday (N. Scott)
1970: 8 Stafford (Jean)
1972: 7 Stegner (Wallace)
1973: 5 Welty (Eudora)
1975: 6 Shaara (Michael)
1976: 6 Bellow (Saul)
1978: 9 McPherson (James Alan)
1979: 7 Cheever (John)
1980: 6 Mailer (Norman)
1981: 5 Toole (John Kennedy)
1982: 6 Updike (John)
1983: 6 Walker (Alice)
1984: 7 Kennedy (William)
1985: 5 Lurie (Alison)
1986: 8 McMurtry (Larry)
1987: 6 Taylor (Peter)
1988: 8 Morrison (Toni)
1989: 5 Tyler (Anne)
1990: 8 Hijuelos (Oscar)
1991: 6 Updike (John)
1992: 6 Smiley (Jane)
1993: 6 Butler (Robert Olen)
1994: 6 Proulx (E. Annie)
1995: 7 Shields (Carol)
1996: 4 Ford (Richard)
1997: 10 Millhauser (Steven)
1998: 4 Roth (Philip)
1999: 10 Cunningham (Michael)
2000: 6 Lahiri (Jhumpa)
2001: 6 Chabon (Michael)
2002: 5 Russo (Richard)
2003: 9 Eugenides (Jeffrey)
2004: 5 Jones (Edward P.)

pull
3 oar, row, tow, tug 4 drag, draw, haul, lure, root, yank 5 clout, draft, drive, force, pluck, put on 6 appeal, assume, entice 7 attract, draw out, extract, stretch 9 advantage, influence 10 attraction

pull back
6 rein in 7 retreat 8 withdraw

pull down
4 draw, earn, raze, ruin 5 lower, wreck 6 reduce 7 depress, destroy 8 demolish, overcome 9 dismantle

pullet
3 hen 5 chick 7 chicken

pulley
5 wheel 6 sheave
watch's: 5 fusee

pull in
3 nab 4 stop 5 check, pinch 6 arrest, arrive, collar, detain, pick up 7 inhibit 8 hold back, restrain 9 apprehend

pulling
6 towage 7 draught, haulage 8 traction
cable: 7 towline

Pullman
3 car 7 sleeper 8 suitcase 11 railroad car

pull off
6 attain, manage 7 achieve, succeed 8 carry out 10 accomplish

pull out
4 exit, quit 5 leave 6 depart 7 abandon, retreat, take off 8 shove off, withdraw

pull through
5 rally 7 get over, recover, ride out, survive, weather 9 get better

pullulate
4 teem 5 breed, crawl, swarm 6 abound, sprout 7 produce 9 germinate

pull up
4 halt, stop 5 check 6 rebuke 8 draw even 9 reprimand

pulp
4 mash, pith 5 crush 6 bruise, squash 7 tabloid 8 soft part

pulpit
4 ambo, dais 6 podium 7 lectern, rostrum 8 ministry, platform

pulpy
4 soft 5 cheap, juicy, lurid, mushy
6 spongy 11 sensational

pulsate
4 beat, pump 5 pound, throb 7 vibrate 9 oscillate, palpitate

pulse
4 beat 5 throb 6 rhythm

pulverize
4 beat, ruin 5 crush, grind, smash,
wreck 6 crunch, powder 7 atomize,
destroy 8 demolish 9 micronize
10 annihilate

puma
3 cat 6 cougar 7 panther 12 mountain lion

pumice
5 glass, stone 8 polisher

pummel
3 hit 4 beat, drub 5 pound, punch
6 batter, buffet, hammer, thrash,
wallop 7 belabor

pump
4 draw, shoe, quiz 5 exert, grill,
heart, raise 6 device, elicit 7 operate 8 energize, question

pumpernickel
3 rye 5 bread

pumpkin
4 pepo 6 orange, squash 12 jack-o'-
lantern
family: 5 gourd

pump up
4 fill 6 excite, expand 7 enthuse,
inflate 8 energize, increase, motivate 9 stimulate

pun
4 joke 11 paronomasia, play on
words 13 double meaning

punch
3 box, cut, die, dig, hit, jab, jog, pep
4 bang, blow, cuff, poke, prod, push,
snap, sock 5 clout, drive, notch,
smack, vigor 6 buffet, emboss,
energy, impact, pummel, strike,
thrust 8 uppercut, vitality 9 emphasize, perforate

punch bowl
8 monteith

punch-drunk
5 dazed, dizzy, woozy 6 addled,
groggy 8 unsteady 9 befuddled,
slaphappy 10 staggering 11 disoriented

puncheon
3 log 4 cask, slab, tool 6 timber

puncher
5 boxer 6 cowboy

Punch's wife
4 Judy

punchy
5 dazed, dizzy, vivid 6 addled, lively
7 dynamic, vibrant 8 forceful, spirited, vigorous 9 befuddled, energetic, slaphappy 11 light-headed

punctilious
5 exact, fussy 7 careful, precise
9 attentive, observant 10 meticulous, particular, scrupulous 11 painstaking

punctual
5 ready 6 on time, prompt, timely

punctuate
4 mark 5 point 6 accent, divide,
stress 8 separate 9 emphasize,
interrupt 10 accentuate

punctuation mark
4 dash 5 brace, colon, comma,
slant, slash 6 hyphen, parens,
period 7 bracket, solidus, virgule
8 diagonal, ellipsis 9 backslash,
guillemet, semicolon 10 apostrophe
11 parenthesis

puncture
3 jab 4 bore, flat, hole, stab 5 burst,
drill, prick, punch 6 blow up, debunk,
riddle 7 deflate, explode 8 disprove 9 discredit, perforate 11 perforation

pundit
4 guru, sage 5 maven, swami
6 critic, expert 7 teacher, wise man
9 authority

pungency
4 bite 5 sting 8 piquancy 9 intensity, sharpness

pungent
5 acrid, acute, harsh, sharp, spicy, tangy, zesty 6 barbed, biting 7 caustic, cutting, intense, mordant, painful, peppery, piquant, pointed 8 exciting, incisive, poignant, stinging 9 trenchant 10 irritating 11 provocative, stimulating

punish
4 fine, hurt 5 mulct, spank 6 amerce, avenge 7 chasten, correct, put down, reprove, revenge, scourge, torture 8 chastise, penalize 9 castigate, criticize 10 discipline

punishment
3 rod 4 fine 5 lumps, mulct 7 penalty, reproof 10 amercement, chastening, correction, discipline 11 castigation, comeuppance, just deserts 12 chastisement

punitive
5 penal 11 castigating, vindicative 12 correctional, disciplinary

punk
4 hood, thug 5 rowdy, tough 6 novice, rookie, tinder 7 hoodlum, ruffian, toughie 8 beginner, gangster, inferior 9 roughneck 10 delinquent

punkah
3 fan

punt
4 boat, boot, kick, play 6 gamble, propel

Punta del ____
4 Este

puny
4 weak 5 dinky, petty, small 6 feeble, little, measly, paltry, slight 7 trivial 8 inferior, niggling, picayune, piddling, trifling

pupa
9 chrysalid, chrysalis

pupil
5 cadet, tutee 7 learner, scholar, student 8 disciple 9 schoolboy 10 apprentice, schoolgirl
French: 5 élève

puppet
4 doll, dupe, pawn, tool 6 figure, stooge 10 figurehead, marionette

puppy
3 dog 5 whelp

Purcell opera
13 Dido and Aeneas

purchase
3 buy 4 hold 6 obtain, pay for 7 acquire, procure 9 advantage 11 acquisition

pure
5 clean, fresh, plain, sheer, total, utter 6 chaste, decent 7 a priori, genuine, perfect, unmixed 8 absolute, abstract, innocent, spotless, virtuous 9 authentic, continent, exemplary, inviolate, stainless, unalloyed, undiluted, untainted 10 immaculate 11 theoretical, unblemished, unmitigated, unqualified 13 unadulterated

purebred
8 pedigree 9 full-blood, pedigreed 10 registered 11 full-blooded

puree
4 soup 5 paste

purely
4 just 5 quite 6 merely, simply, wholly 7 exactly, totally, utterly 8 entirely 10 altogether, completely 11 exclusively

purfle
4 trim 6 border 8 decorate, ornament

purgation
9 catharsis, cleansing 10 lustration

purgative
5 jalap 7 lustral 9 cathartic

purge
3 rid 4 oust 5 clear, expel 6 purify, remove 7 cleanse, wipe out 8 get rid of, lustrate 9 eliminate, liquidate

purification

8 ablution 9 catharsis, cleansing, expiation, purgation 10 absolution, lustration 11 expurgation 12 regeneration
sacrament: 7 baptism

purify

5 clean, purge 6 filter, refine 7 clarify, cleanse

Purim

11 Feast of Lots
queen: 6 Esther

puritan

4 prig 5 prude 8 bluenose 9 Mrs. Grundy

puritanical

4 prim 5 rigid 6 severe, strict 7 ascetic, austere, prudish 8 priggish 9 bluenosed 11 straitlaced

purity

8 chastity 9 innocence

purl

4 eddy, edge, knit 5 swirl, whirl 6 border, murmur, stitch 9 embroider

purlieu

5 haunt 7 hangout

purlieus

6 bounds, limits 7 suburbs 8 boundary, confines, environs 9 outskirts, precincts 12 neighborhood

purloin

3 nip 4 lift, take 5 filch, pinch, steal, swipe 6 pilfer, remove, rip off, snitch 11 appropriate

purloiner

5 crook, thief 8 larcener 9 larcenist

purple

4 plum, robe 5 cloth, grape, lilac, mauve, regal 6 florid, maroon, orchid, ornate, turgid, violet 7 flowery, pigment, pompous 8 imperial, lavender 9 bombastic, high-flown, overblown 10 rhetorical

Purple Heart

5 award, medal 10 decoration

purport

4 gist, mean 5 claim, drift, sense, tenor 6 allege, intend, thrust 7 meaning, message, profess, purpose 8 maintain 9 substance 11 connotation, implication 12 significance, significancy

purported

7 alleged, reputed, seeming 8 apparent, so-called, supposed 9 professed 10 ostensible

purpose

3 aim, end, use 4 goal, plan 5 point 6 action, design, intent, object 7 meaning, mission, resolve, subject 8 ambition, function, proposal 9 direction, intention, objective 10 aspiration, resolution 13 determination

purposeful

6 driven, intent 7 earnest, planned, studied, willful 8 resolute 9 conscious, dedicated 10 calculated, considered, deliberate, determined 11 intentional 12 premeditated

purposeless

6 random 9 desultory, haphazard, hit-or-miss, irregular, unplanned

purposely

9 expressly 10 explicitly 12 deliberately 13 intentionally

purr

3 hum 6 murmur

purse

3 bag, sum 4 knit 5 money, pouch, prize 6 pucker, wallet 7 handbag 8 reticule 9 clutch bag 10 pocketbook, prize money
Scottish: 7 sporran

pursue

3 woo 4 hunt, seek 5 chase, haunt, hound, stalk, track, trail 6 badger, follow 7 afflict, go after, proceed 8 continue, engage in 9 persecute, persevere

pursuit

3 job 4 hunt, work 5 chase, quest, trade 6 search 8 activity, business, vocation 9 avocation, following

purvey
10 employment, occupation, profession

purvey
6 obtain, peddle, supply 7 furnish, provide 9 provision

purview
3 ken 5 ambit, limit, orbit, range, reach, scope, sweep 6 extent 8 boundary

push
3 pep 4 goad, plug, prod, sell, spur, urge 5 boost, drive, elbow, exert, force, impel, press, punch, shove, vigor 6 attack, effort, energy, expand, peddle, propel, throng, thrust 7 advance, assault, impetus, promote 8 ambition, pressure, vitality 9 incentive, influence, offensive 10 enterprise, get-up-and-go, initiative

Pushkin, Alexander
novel: 12 Eugene Onegin
play: 10 Stone Guest (The) 12 Boris Godunov
story: 13 Queen of Spades (The)

push off
4 exit 5 leave, start 6 depart, set out

push on
6 travel 7 advance, journey, proceed 8 continue, progress

pushover
4 snap 5 chump, cinch, softy 6 breeze, picnic, stooge, sucker 9 soft touch

pushy
4 bold 5 brash, nervy 7 forward 8 forceful 9 assertive, obnoxious 10 aggressive 12 presumptuous

pusillanimous
5 timid 6 coward, craven 7 chicken, gutless 8 cowardly, poltroon, timorous 9 spineless 11 lily-livered

puss
3 cat, mug 4 face 6 kisser, kitten

pussycat
5 sissy, softy 6 softie 8 pushover,

weakling 9 soft touch 10 namby-pamby 13 bleeding heart

pussyfoot
5 creep, dodge, evade, glide, skulk, slink, sneak, steal 6 tiptoe 10 equivocate

pustule
4 boil 6 pimple 7 abscess, blister 8 furuncle 9 carbuncle

put
3 lay, set 4 park 5 place 8 position

putative
7 assumed, reputed 8 accepted, believed, presumed, supposed 11 conjectural 12 hypothetical

put away
3 eat 4 stow 5 eat up, swill 6 commit, devour, lock up 7 confine, consume 9 polish off 11 incarcerate

put by
4 save 5 lay in, store 7 lay away 8 lay aside, salt away

put down
5 crush, quash, quell 6 demean, demote, depose, squash, subdue 7 squelch 8 belittle, suppress 9 criticize, disparage, downgrade, humiliate

put forth
5 issue 6 assert 7 present, propose

put off
5 defer, delay 7 suspend 8 hold over, postpone

put on
3 act, don, kid 4 fake 5 apply, bluff, feign, mount, stage 6 affect, assume 7 mislead, perform, pretend, produce

put-on
3 act 4 fake, sham, show 5 faked, phony, spoof 6 parody 7 assumed, feigned 8 affected, disguise 9 pretended 10 artificial, false front

put out
3 vex 4 gall 5 annoy, douse, issue,

upset **6** bother, quench **7** disturb, produce, publish, trouble **8** irritate **9** aggravate, displease, embarrass **10** disconcert, exasperate, extinguish **13** inconvenience

putrefy
3 rot **5** decay, spoil, taint **6** molder **7** corrupt **9** break down, decompose

putrid
4 foul **5** fetid **6** rancid, rotten **7** corrupt, decayed, noisome, spoiled

putsch
4 coup **6** revolt **8** takeover, uprising **9** coup d'état, overthrow, rebellion **10** usurpation

putter
4 club, idle **6** fiddle, golfer, tinker **8** golf club

putting area
5 green

putto
6 cherub **8** amoretto

put together
4 form, join, make **5** build, unite **7** combine, connect, fashion, produce **8** assemble **9** construct, fabricate

putty
3 mud **4** clay **6** cement

put up
4 bunk **5** board, build, erect, house, lodge, raise **6** billet, harbor **7** quarter **8** domicile **9** construct

put up with
4 bear **5** stand **6** endure **8** tolerate

Puzo novel
6 Omerta **7** Last Don (The) **8** Fools Die, Sicilian (The) **9** Godfather (The)

puzzle
3 why **4** foil **5** poser, rebus **6** baffle, enigma, fuddle, muddle, riddle **7** anagram, confuse, mystery, mystify, nonplus, perplex, problem,

tangram **8** acrostic, befuddle, bewilder, confound **9** conundrum, crossword, dumbfound, frustrate **10** disconcert **11** brainteaser

puzzle out
5 solve **6** answer, decode **7** clarify, clear up, explain, unravel **8** decipher, unriddle

puzzling
6 knotty **7** cryptic **8** baffling **9** confusing, difficult, enigmatic **10** mystifying, perplexing **11** bewildering, paradoxical **12** inexplicable

Pygmalion
beloved: **7** Galatea
father: **5** Belus
playwright: **4** Shaw (George Bernard)
sister: **4** Dido
victim: **8** Sichaeus

pygmy
4 tiny **5** dwarf **6** bantam, little, midget **8** dwarfish **10** diminutive, homunculus **11** lilliputian

Pylades
companion: **7** Orestes
father: **9** Strophius
wife: **7** Electra

pylon
4 post **5** tower **6** marker **7** gateway

Pym's creator
3 Poe (Edgar Allan)

Pynchon novel
15 Gravity's Rainbow

pyramid builder
5 Khufu **6** Cheops

Pyramus' beloved
6 Thisbe

pyre
4 heap, pile

pyretic
3 hot **7** burning, febrile, fevered **8** feverish

pyromaniac
5 torch 8 arsonist 10 incendiary

pyrosis
9 heartburn

pyrotechnics
7 display 9 fireworks, spectacle

Pyrrha's husband
9 Deucalion

Pyrrhonist
7 doubter, skeptic 10 unbeliever

Pyrrhus
kingdom: 6 Epirus
victory: 7 Asculum

Pythias' friend
5 Damon

python
3 boa 5 snake
slayer: 6 Apollo

pyx
3 box 4 case 6 vessel 9 container
10 receptacle

Q

Qatar
  capital: **4** Doha
  gulf: **7** Persian
  language: **6** Arabic
  monetary unit: **5** riyal
  neighbor: **11** Saudi Arabia
  peninsula: **7** Arabian

QED word
  4 erat, quod **13** demonstrandum

q.t., on the
  8 covertly, secretly **13** under the table

quack
  3 cry **4** honk, sham **6** con man, humbug **7** shammer **9** charlatan **10** mountebank **12** saltimbanque

quackery
  4 hoax, scam **5** fraud, hokum **6** deceit **8** flimflam, pretense **9** deception, duplicity, imposture **11** dissembling

quad
  see **quadrangle**

quadrangle
  4 yard **5** close, court, patio **6** square **7** polygon **9** courtyard, curtilage, enclosure

quadrant
  3 arc **6** fourth **9** one-fourth **10** instrument

quadratic
  4 boxy **5** square **7** boxlike **10** four-square

quadriga
  7 chariot

quadrille
  5 dance, ombre **8** card game

quadrivium subject
  5 music **8** geometry **9** astronomy **10** arithmetic

quaestor
  6 bursar **8** official **9** paymaster, treasurer

quaff
  3 sip **4** swig, toss **5** drink, sup up **6** guzzle, imbibe, sup off **7** carouse, swallow

quagga
  3 ass

quaggy
  4 soft **5** boggy, mushy, pulpy **6** flabby, marshy, spongy **7** flaccid, squashy, squishy **8** squooshy, yielding

quagmire
  3 bog, fen, fix, jam **4** mire **5** marsh, pinch, swamp **6** morass, pickle, plight, scrape, slough **7** dilemma **8** quandary **9** imbroglio, marshland, swampland **11** predicament

quahog
  4 clam **7** mollusc, mollusk **9** shellfish **11** cherrystone

quail
  5 cower, wince **6** blanch, blench, cringe, flinch, recoil, shrink **7** shudder, squinch, tremble **8** bobwhite
  flock of: **4** bevy

quaint
  3 odd **5** funny, queer **7** antique, archaic, curious, oddball, strange, unusual **8** peculiar, singular **9** different, eccentric, whimsical **10** antiquated, unfamiliar **12** old-fashioned

quake

5 shake, waver 6 dither, quaver,
quiver, shiver, tremor 7 shudder,
temblor, tremble, twitter, vibrate
8 trembler

Quaker

6 Friend
city: 12 Philadelphia
colonizer: 4 Penn (William)
founder: 3 Fox (George)
poet: 6 Barton (Bernard) 8 Whittier
(John Greenleaf)
State: 12 Pennsylvania

qualification

6 caveat 7 ability, fitness 8 adequacy, aptitude, capacity, standard
9 condition, criterion 10 capability,
competence 11 requirement, restriction, stipulation

qualified

3 fit 4 able 6 au fait, proper, proved,
proven, tested 7 capable, limited,
partial, skilled, trained 8 eligible,
modified, reserved 9 competent
10 restricted 11 conditional 12 accomplished

qualify

3 fit 5 limit 6 lessen, modify, reduce,
soften, temper 7 certify, entitle,
license, mollify, prepare 8 describe,
mitigate, moderate 9 authorize
12 characterize

quality

4 rank 5 class, elite, grade, merit,
prime, savor, state, trait, value, worth
6 factor, flower, gentry, status, virtue
7 caliber, element, feature, stature
8 position, property, standing 9 attribute, blue blood, character, gentility, parameter 10 excellence, patriciate, perfection

qualm

4 fear 5 demur, doubt 6 nausea,
unease 7 illness, scruple 8 mistrust
9 faintness, misgiving, objection
10 conscience, foreboding, reluctance, uneasiness 11 compunction,
nervousness, uncertainty 12 apprehension, remonstrance 13 unwillingness

qualmish

3 ill 4 sick 6 queasy, uneasy, unwell
8 hesitant, nauseous 9 nauseated,
reluctant, squeamish, uncertain
10 scrupulous 12 apprehensive

quandary

3 fix, jam 4 bind, hole, spot 5 pinch
6 pickle, plight, scrape 7 dilemma
8 quagmire 10 difficulty 11 predicament

quantity

4 body, bulk, dose 5 total 6 amount,
degree, volume 9 abundance,
aggregate, magnitude
fixed: 8 constant
small: 3 bit 7 modicum, smidgen

Quantrill's _____

7 Raiders

quantum

5 quota, share, total 6 amount,
budget, ration 7 measure, portion
9 aggregate, allotment, allowance,
increment 13 apportionment
of gravity: 8 graviton
of radiant energy: 6 photon
of vibrational energy: 6 phonon
theory originator: 6 Planck (Max)

quarantine

6 detain 7 confine, isolate 8 restrain
9 isolation, restraint 10 detainment
11 confinement

quarrel

3 row 4 beef, bolt, dust, feud, fray,
fuss, miff, spar, spat, tiff 5 argue,
arrow, brawl, broil, clash, fight,
melee, run-in, scrap, set-to 6 affray,
battle, bicker, differ, dustup, fracas,
ruckus, squall, strife 7 brabble,
discord, dispute, dissent, fall out,
rhubarb, ruction, scuffle, wrangle
8 argument, catfight, conflict, disagree, skirmish, squabble 9 altercate, bickering, brannigan, disaccord,
lock horns, imbroglio, scrimmage
10 contention, difference, dissension,
donnybrook, falling-out, free-for-all
11 altercation, battle royal, embroilment 12 disagreement

quarrelsome

6 brawly 7 adverse, counter, hostile,

scrappy, warlike **8** brawling, choleric, inimical, militant **9** bellicose, combative, irascible, irritable, rancorous, truculent **10** pugnacious **11** bad-tempered, belligerent, contentious **12** cantankerous, disputatious **13** argumentative

quarry
3 dig, pit **4** game, mine, pane, prey **5** chase, delve **6** source, victim **8** excavate **10** excavation

quarter
4 area, bunk, part **5** board, house, lodge, mercy, put up **6** barrio, billet, canton, fourth, ghetto, harbor, sector **7** barrack, section, shelter **8** clemency, district, division, locality, precinct, quadrant
circle: 8 quadrant
note: 8 crotchet
pint: 4 gill
ship's: 6 fo'c'sle **10** forecastle

quarterback
4 boss, head, lead **6** direct, leader, player **7** athlete, oversee **8** director, overseer **9** supervise **10** footballer, supervisor

quartet
4 four **5** group **6** tetrad **8** ensemble, foursome **10** quadruplet, quaternion **11** composition

quart, metric
5 liter, litre

quartz
4 onyx, sard **5** agate **6** jasper **7** citrine, mineral **8** amethyst, sardonyx **9** cairngorm, carnelian **10** chalcedony

quash
4 undo, void **5** annul, crush, quell **6** defeat, negate, quench, stifle, subdue **7** abolish, nullify, put down, repress, smother, squelch **8** abrogate, dissolve, suppress **10** extinguish, invalidate

quasi
6 almost **7** nominal, seeming, virtual **8** apparent

Quasimodo
9 hunchback
creator: 4 Hugo (Victor)
occupation: 10 bell ringer
residence: 9 Notre Dame

quaver
4 note **5** quake, shake, trill, waver **6** dither, shiver, tremor **7** shudder, tremble, twitter **10** eighth note

quay
4 dock, pier, slip **5** berth, jetty, levee, wharf **6** marina **7** moorage

quean
4 bawd, slut, tart **5** tramp, wench, whore **6** harlot, hooker **7** chippie, hustler **8** strumpet **9** courtesan **10** prostitute **12** streetwalker

queasy
3 ill **4** sick **6** qualmy, uneasy, unwell **7** dubious **8** delicate, doubtful, hesitant, nauseous, qualmish, troubled **9** hazardous, nauseated, reluctant, squeamish

Quebec province
capital: 6 Quebec
city: 5 Laval **8** Montreal **9** Longueuil
island: 9 Anticosti
mountain: 9 Tremblant **10** D'Iberville
peninsula: 5 Gaspé
provincial flower: 10 fleur-de-lys **11** madonna lily
river: 10 St. Lawrence

Queeg's ship
5 Caine

queen
Austria-Hungary: 12 Maria Therésa
Belgian: 6 Astrid
Danish: 8 Margaret, Margrete
Egyptian: 9 Cleopatra **10** Hatshepsut
English: 4 Anne, Mary **8** Victoria **9** Elizabeth
French and English: 7 Eleanor
Netherlands: 7 Beatrix, Juliana **10** Wilhelmina
of heaven: 4 Mary, moon **7** Astarte
of Isles: 6 Albion
of Ithaca: 8 Penelope

of Navarre: 8 Margaret
of Scots: 4 Mary
of Sheba: 6 Balkis
of the Adriatic: 6 Venice
of the Antilles: 4 Cuba
of the East: 7 Zenobia
of the fairies: 3 Mab 7 Titania
of the gods: 4 Hera, Juno, Sati
of the Nile: 9 Cleopatra
of the North: 9 Edinburgh
of the underworld: 3 Hel 4 Hela
10 Persephone, Proserpina
Spanish: 8 Isabella
Swedish: 9 Christina

Queen Anne's lace
6 carrot 10 wild carrot

Queen of Spades
author: 7 Pushkin (Alexander)
composer: 11 Tchaikovsky (Peter
Ilyich)

Queensland
capital: 8 Brisbane
explorer: 4 Cook (Captain James)

queer
3 odd 4 ruin 5 bogus, droll, funny,
spoil, weird 6 qualmy, queasy,
unwell 7 bizarre, curious, dubious,
oddball, strange, touched, unusual
8 doubtful, obsessed, peculiar,
qualmish, singular 9 eccentric,
squeamish, worthless 10 outlandish,
suspicious 11 counterfeit 12 questionable

quell
4 calm, stop 5 check, crush, quash,
quiet 6 pacify, quench, squash,
subdue 7 conquer, put down, squelch
8 overcome, suppress, vanquish
9 overwhelm, subjugate 10 extinguish

Quemoy's neighbor
4 Amoy 5 Matsu

quench
4 sate 5 allay, douse, quash, quell,
slake 6 lessen, put out, reduce
7 appease, assuage, gratify, lighten,
put down, relieve, satiate, satisfy
8 mitigate, suppress 9 alleviate,
eliminate 10 extinguish

quenelle
8 dumpling, meatball 9 forcemeat

quern
4 mill

querulous
5 whiny 7 fretful, peevish, pettish,
whining 8 petulant 9 lamenting
10 whimpering 11 complaining

query
3 ask 4 quiz 5 doubt, grill 7 dubiety,
inquire, inquiry 8 question 9 catechize 11 interrogate 13 interrogation

quest
4 hunt 5 probe 6 pursue, search
7 delving, inquire, inquiry, probing,
pursuit, seeking 8 research 9 pursuance 11 inquisition 13 investigation

question
3 ask, pry 4 poll, pump, quiz 5 doubt,
grill, issue, probe, query 6 chance,
matter 7 debrief, dispute, examine,
inquire, inquiry, problem, suspect
8 distrust, mistrust 9 catechize,
challenge, objection 10 difficulty,
puzzle over 11 interrogate, possibility 13 interrogation, interrogatory

questionable
4 iffy, moot 5 shady, vague 6 unsure 7 dubious, obscure, suspect
8 arguable, doubtful, unproven
9 debatable, equivocal, refutable,
uncertain 10 disputable, fly-by-night,
improbable, unreliable 11 problematic 12 undependable

questioning
5 probe, query 6 show-me 7 delving,
dubious, inquiry, probing 8 doubtful,
grilling 9 inquiring, quizzical, skeptical, uncertain 11 incredulous, inquisitive, unbelieving 12 disbelieving
13 interrogation, interrogatory, inves-
tigative

quetzal
4 bird, coin 6 trogon

queue
3 row 4 file, line, rank, wait 5 braid
6 column 8 sequence

quibble
4 carp **5** argue, cavil **6** argufy, bicker, niggle, object **7** dispute, evasion, nitpick, wrangle **8** squabble **9** criticism, criticize, objection **10** split hairs

quick
4 core, deft, fast, keen, pith, root **5** acute, agile, brisk, fleet, hasty, rapid, sharp, smart, swift **6** abrupt, clever, nimble, prompt, speedy, sudden **7** hurried **9** breakneck, impetuous **10** harefooted **11** expeditious **12** lickety-split
combining form: 5 tachy

quick bread
6 muffin **7** biscuit

quicken
4 goad, grow, move, spur, stir, wake **5** hurry, liven, pique, rouse, speed **6** arouse, awaken, excite, hasten, incite, induce, kindle, revive, step up, vivify **7** actuate, animate, enliven, provoke, shake up, sharpen, speed up **8** activate, energize, motivate, vitalize **9** galvanize, stimulate **10** accelerate, exhilarate, invigorate

quickly
5 apace **6** at once, pronto **9** forthwith, posthaste **12** straightaway

quickness
5 haste, speed **8** alacrity, celerity, dispatch, legerity, rapidity, velocity **9** fleetness, rapidness, swiftness **10** promptness

quicksand
3 bog **4** mire **6** morass

quicksilver
7 mercury **9** mercurial **10** inconstant

quick-tempered
5 cross, fiery, ratty, testy **6** cranky, touchy **7** peppery **8** choleric, petulant **9** irascible, irritable, splenetic **10** passionate

quick-witted
3 apt **4** keen **5** acute, agile, alert, canny, ready, sharp, smart **6** astute, brainy, bright, clever, prompt **9** brilliant **10** perceptive **11** intelligent, penetrating

quid
3 cut, wad **4** chew, coin **5** money, pound **9** sovereign

quiddity
3 nub **4** gist, meat, pith **6** trifle **7** essence, quibble **8** crotchet **12** eccentricity, quintessence

quidnunc
see **rumormonger**

quiescent
4 calm **5** quiet, still **6** benign, hushed, latent, placid, serene, stilly **7** abeyant, dormant, halcyon, lurking **8** inactive, tranquil **10** untroubled

quiet
4 calm, hush, idle, lull, mute, stop **5** abate, allay, inert, muted, shush, still, whist **6** asleep, becalm, gentle, hushed, lessen, placid, serene, settle, silent, sleepy, soothe, subdue **7** compose, halcyon, pacific, passive, restful, silence, subdued **8** decrease, inactive, peaceful, reserved, secluded, taciturn, tranquil **9** cessation, easygoing, noiseless, soundless, stillness, unruffled **10** restrained, untroubled **11** tranquility, tranquilize, unobtrusive **12** tranquillity

quietus
3 end **5** death, sleep **6** damper, demise, finish **7** decease, passing, silence **8** curtains **10** inactivity, settlement **11** termination

quill
3 pen **5** float, shaft, spine, spool **6** bobbin **7** feather, spindle

quilt
4 pouf, puff **5** duvet **8** coverlet **9** comforter, eiderdown **11** counterpane
design: 8 trapunto

quintessence
4 gist, meat, pith, soul **5** ideal,

model, stuff **6** marrow **7** epitome
8 exemplar, last word, quiddity,
ultimate **9** substance **10** apotheosis
12 essentiality

quintessential
5 ideal, model **7** classic, typical
8 ultimate **9** classical, exemplary
10 archetypal, consummate, prototypal **12** prototypical

quintuple
8 fivefold

quip
3 dig, gag, kid **4** gibe, gird, jape,
jeer, jest, jibe, joke **5** crack, fleer,
sally, scoff, sneer, tease **6** banter,
oddity, retort **7** quibble **8** drollery,
repartee **9** wisecrack, witticism
12 equivocation

quipster
3 wag, wit **4** card **5** clown, comic,
droll, joker **6** jester **8** comedian,
funnyman, humorist, jokester
11 wisecracker

quirk
3 tic **4** bend, kink, quip, whim
5 crook, curve, twist **6** groove,
oddity, vagary **7** caprice **8** accident,
crotchet **9** mannerism **11** peculiarity
12 idiosyncrasy

quirky
3 odd **7** erratic, offbeat **8** peculiar
9 eccentric, irregular, whimsical
10 capricious **13** idiosyncratic

quirt
4 lash, whip

quisling
5 Judas, rebel **7** traitor **8** apostate,
betrayer, defector, turncoat **10** copperhead **11** backstabber **12** collaborator

quit
3 end, pay **4** drop, free, halt, stop
5 cease, chuck, leave **6** depart,
desert, desist, give up, resign, retire,
settle **7** abandon, drop out, forsake,
release, relieve, satisfy **8** knock off,

leave off, released, renounce, withdraw **9** discharge, liquidate, surrender, terminate **10** relinquish
11 discontinue

quite
3 all **4** just, very, well **5** fully, in
all **6** in toto, purely, rather, wholly
7 exactly, totally, utterly **8** entirely
9 perfectly **10** absolutely, altogether,
completely, positively, thoroughly
12 considerably

quittance
6 amends **7** redress **8** reprisal,
requital **9** atonement, discharge,
expiation, repayment **10** recompense, reparation **11** restitution
12 compensation

quitter
4 funk **6** coward, craven **7** chicken,
dastard **8** poltroon, recreant **9** defeatist **11** yellowbelly

quiver
4 beat, case **5** pulse, quake, shake,
throb, waver **6** arrows, dither, jitter,
quaver, shiver, tremor **7** pulsate,
shudder, tremble, twitter, vibrate
9 palpitate, vibration

Quixote
see **Don Quixote**

quixotic
7 foolish **8** fanciful, illusory, romantic
9 fantastic, imaginary, visionary
10 capricious, chimerical, idealistic
11 impractical **13** unpredictable

quiz
3 ask **4** exam, test **5** grill, query
7 examine, inquire **8** question
9 catechize **11** interrogate **12** cross-
examine

quizzical
3 odd **5** queer **6** quaint, show-me
7 curious, dubious, mocking, probing,
puzzled, teasing **8** doubtful, doubting, sardonic **9** inquiring, skeptical
11 incredulous, inquisitive, questioning, unbelieving **12** disbelieving

quodlibet
5 issue, point 6 debate, medley
7 mélange 8 fantasia, question
11 disputation

quoin
5 angle, block, wedge 6 corner
8 keystone, voussoir

quoit
4 game, ring 6 circle

quoits peg
3 hob

quondam
4 late, once, past 6 bygone, former,
whilom 7 defunct, onetime 8 sometime 9 erstwhile 10 occasional

quorum
4 body 5 group 7 council 8 majority

quota
3 cut, lot 4 bite, meed, part 5 share,
slice, whack 6 amount, parcel, ration
7 measure, portion, quantum 9 allotment, allowance 10 allocation,
percentage, proportion

quotation
3 bid 5 offer, price 7 excerpt,
extract, passage 8 citation

quotation mark, French
9 guillemet

quote
3 bid 4 cite, list 5 offer, price, refer
6 adduce, borrow, repeat 7 excerpt,
extract, passage 8 citation

quotidian
5 daily, plain, usual 6 common
7 average, diurnal, prosaic, regular,
routine, vanilla 8 day-to-day, everyday, ordinary, workaday 9 circadian
11 commonplace 12 unremarkable

quotient
5 ratio, share 7 caliber, portion
9 allotment, magnitude 10 percentage, proportion

Quo Vadis
author: 11 Sienkiewicz (Henryk)
character: 4 Nero 5 Lygia, Peter
8 Vinicius 9 Petronius

R

Ra
son: 6 Khonsu
wife: 3 Mut

Raamah
father: 4 Cush
son: 5 Dedan, Sheba

Rabbi Ben Ezra author
8 Browning (Robert)

rabbit
4 cony, hare 5 bunny, coney
female: 3 doe
fictional: 5 Fiver, Hazel, Mopsy,
Peter 6 Flopsy, Harvey 7 Thumper
8 Crusader, Ricochet 9 Bugs Bunny
10 Cotton-tail 11 Easter Bunny
food: 5 salad 6 carrot 7 lettuce
neutered: 5 lapin
tail: 4 scut

rabble
3 mob 4 mass, rout 5 crush, horde
6 masses 8 canaille, populace,
riffraff, unwashed 9 hoi polloi
10 lower class 11 proletariat, rank
and file

rabble-rouser
7 inciter 8 agitator, fomenter 9 demagogue 10 incendiary 12 troublemaker

Rabelais character
7 Panurge 9 Gargantua 10 Pantagruel

rabid
3 mad 4 wild 5 crazy, ultra 6 crazed,
insane 7 extreme, fanatic, frantic,
furious, radical, zealous 8 demented,
deranged, frenetic, frenzied, obsessed, ultraist 9 delirious, extremist
10 corybantic 11 hydrophobic

rabies
11 hydrophobia

raccoon
8 ringtail
dog: 6 tanuki
relative: 5 civet, coati, panda 8 civet
cat, kinkajou 10 cacomistle, coati-
mundi

race
4 bolt, dart, dash, gill, lash, meet,
rush, tear, type 5 brook, chase,
creek, fling, hurry, match, rally, relay, shoot, speed, spurt 6 charge,
course, gallop, runnel, scurry, sprint,
stream 7 channel, contest, rivalry, rivulet, scamper 8 marathon
9 grand prix 11 competition, watercourse

racecourse
4 oval, turf 5 track

racehorse
5 Alsab, Kelso 6 Forego 7 Assault,
Man O' War 8 Affirmed, Citation
9 Riva Ridge, War Emblem 10 War
Admiral 11 Forward Pass, Seattle
Slew, Secretariat, Smarty Jones
12 Native Dancer

Rachel
father: 5 Laban
husband: 5 Jacob
servant: 6 Bilhah
sister: 4 Leah
son: 6 Joseph 8 Benjamin

rachis
4 back 5 chine, spine 8 backbone
12 spinal column

rachitic
5 shaky 6 wobbly 7 rackety, rickety, tenuous 9 tremulous 10 ramshackle, rattletrap

_____ Rachmaninoff
6 Sergei, Sergey

racing enthusiast
8 railbird

racism
7 bigotry, jim crow 9 apartheid, prejudice 11 segregation

racist
4 nazi 5 bigot 7 bigoted 10 intolerant, prejudiced 11 supremacist

rack
3 bed 4 buck, bunk, pace, pain, sack, scud 5 frame, wring 6 harass, harrow, martyr, strain, wrench 7 afflict, agonize, antlers, crucify, ratchet, sawbuck, stretch, torment, torture 8 distress, sawhorse 9 framework, persecute 10 excruciate

racket
3 con, din 4 game 5 babel, fraud, hoo-ha, noise 6 clamor, hubbub, rattle, scheme, tumult, uproar 7 pursuit, swindle 8 ballyhoo, brouhaha, foofaraw 10 hullabaloo 11 pandemonium

racketeer
7 mafioso, mobster 8 extorter, gangster 9 godfather

rack up
3 win 4 gain 5 reach, score 6 attain 7 achieve, realize 10 accomplish

raconteur
11 storyteller

racy
4 blue, gamy 5 bawdy, broad, juicy, salty, spicy, vampy, zesty 6 purple, risqué, smutty, snappy, vulgar, wicked 7 piquant, pungent 8 indecent, off-color, vigorous 10 suggestive

Radames' beloved
4 Aïda

radar image
3 pip 4 blip, spot 5 trace

Raddai
brother: 5 David
father: 5 Jesse

radiance
3 ray 4 glow 5 glory, shine 6 luster 7 aureola, aureole 8 splendor 10 brightness, brilliance

radiant
4 glad 5 beamy, shiny 6 bright, cheery, lucent 7 beaming, fulgent, glowing, lambent 8 cheerful, luminous, lustrous 9 brilliant, effulgent 10 effulgence 12 incandescent

radiate
4 beam, glow 5 gleam, shine, strew 6 spread 7 diverge 8 illumine 10 illuminate

radiation unit
3 rad, rem, rep 7 langley, sievert 8 roentgen

radiator
6 cooler, heater 9 convector 11 transmitter 13 heat exchanger

radical
4 acyl, root 5 basal, basic, rebel, ultra 7 extreme, fanatic, primary 8 agitator, cardinal, inherent, militant, ultraist 9 anarchist, essential, extremist, intrinsic 10 subversive, underlying 11 fundamental 12 foundational, iconoclastic 13 revolutionary
mathematical: 4 surd

radicle
4 root 5 radix 9 hypocotyl

radio
8 wireless
frequency range: 8 waveband

radioactive
3 hot 7 nuclear

radius
5 ambit, orbit, range, reach, sweep
6 extent 7 compass, purview 9 extension

radix
4 base, root 6 source

raffish
6 coarse, jaunty, rakish, sporty, vulgar 9 dissolute 12 devil-may-care

raffle
7 drawing, lottery

raft
3 lot, ton 4 heap, mess, pile, scad, slew 5 balsa, float 6 bundle

rafter
4 balk, beam, viga

rag
3 jaw, kid, rib 4 bait, jive, josh, rail, razz, rock 5 baste, cloth, scold, tease 6 berate, harass, hector, needle, pester 7 tabloid, torment
9 newspaper

ragamuffin
3 bum 4 hobo, waif 5 gamin, tramp
6 beggar, gamine, orphan, urchin
7 wastrel 8 vagabond 9 scarecrow
11 guttersnipe

rage
3 cry, fad, ire, mad, wax 4 chic, fume, fury, mode, rant 5 anger, craze, fancy, furor, mania, storm, style, vogue, wrath 6 blow up, frenzy, furore, seethe 7 fashion, madness, passion 8 boil over, hysteria, violence 10 dernier cri
11 indignation

ragged
4 rent, torn 5 seedy 6 frayed, jagged, shabby, uneven 7 unkempt, worn-out 8 frazzled, straggly, tattered 10 threadbare

raging
4 wild 6 stormy 7 furious, extreme,

intense, violent 8 blustery 9 ferocious, turbulent 10 blustering
11 tempestuous

ragout
4 stew 5 salmi 6 burgoo, jumble, medley 7 farrago, goulash, mélange, mixture 8 mishmash 9 potpourri
10 hodgepodge, salmagundi 11 gallimaufry

rags
4 duds, garb 5 dress 6 attire, shreds 7 apparel, clothes, raiment, threads 8 clothing 10 attirement
11 habiliments

ragtag
see rabble

ragwort
7 senecio 9 cineraria, groundsel
10 butterweed

raid
4 bust, loot, sack 5 foray, harry
6 attack, forage, harass, inroad, invade, maraud, ravage, sortie
7 assault, despoil, overrun, plunder
8 invasion, spoliate 9 incursion, onslaught

raider
6 pirate 10 freebooter

rail
3 bar, jaw 5 fence, scold, track
6 berate, revile 7 barrier, inveigh, upbraid 8 banister 10 tongue-lash, vituperate

rail bird
4 sora 5 crake 7 clapper 8 marsh hen, water hen

railing
8 banister 10 balustrade
part: 8 baluster

raillery
5 scorn 6 banter 7 mockery, teasing
8 badinage, derision, ridicule, taunting 10 lampoonery, persiflage

railroad
branch: 6 siding
car: 5 coach, diner, stock 6 hopper
7 caboose, gondola, Pullman

engine: 10 locomotive
locomotive: 9 iron horse
station: 5 depot
underground: 4 tube 5 metro
6 subway
worker: 6 porter 7 fireman 8 brakeman, engineer 9 conductor 11 gandy dancer

raiment
4 duds, garb, gear, togs 5 array, dress 6 attire 7 apparel, clothes, threads, vesture 8 clothing, garments, glad rags, vestiary 9 caparison 10 attirement 11 habiliments

rain
6 deluge, mizzle, shower 7 drizzle 8 downpour, sprinkle 10 cloudburst 13 precipitation

rainbow
3 arc 4 iris 5 array, gamut 7 fantasy 8 illusion, spectrum 9 pipe dream
bridge: 7 Bifrost
chaser: 9 visionary
goddess: 4 Iris

rainbow fish
5 guppy, trout 6 wrasse

raincoat
3 mac 4 mack 6 poncho, trench 7 oilskin, slicker 10 mackintosh

rain leader
9 downspout

rain tree
9 monkeypod

raise
4 ante, grow, hike, jack, jump, lift, pump, rear 5 boost, breed, erect, exalt, hoist, put up 6 foment, incite, jack up, muster 7 augment, bring up, collect, elevate, enhance, inflate, produce 8 heighten, increase 9 construct, cultivate, increment, propagate

raisin
5 grape 7 currant, sultana 10 dried grape

Raisin in the Sun author
9 Hansberry (Lorraine)

raison d' _____
4 état, être

raja
4 king 5 chief, ruler 6 prince 9 dignitary

rake
3 rip 4 comb, roué 5 angle, blood, pitch, rifle, scamp, scour, slope 6 forage, glance, lecher, rascal, scrape, search, strafe 7 incline, playboy, ransack, rummage, scratch 8 enfilade, lothario 9 debauchee, libertine 10 profligate

rakehell
4 fast, wild 5 blood 6 rascal, sporty 7 playboy, raffish 8 lothario, rascally 9 debauchee, dissolute, lecherous, libertine 10 licentious, profligate

rake-off
3 cut 4 bite, take 5 chunk, share 7 portion 9 baksheesh, lagniappe 10 commission, percentage

rake's look
4 leer, ogle

Rake's Progress artist
7 Hogarth (William)

rakish
see rakehell

rally
4 race, stir, wake 5 harry, renew, rouse, waken 6 arouse, awaken, bestir, kindle, muster, perk up, pick up, repair, volley 7 convene, enliven, marshal, rebound, recover 8 assemble, clambake, comeback, mobilize, recovery 9 challenge, re-collect 10 invigorate, reorganize

rallying cry
5 motto 6 byword, slogan 9 watchword 10 shibboleth 11 catchphrase

ram
5 Aries, crash, crowd, drive, pound, sheep, stuff 6 batter, plunge, strike, thrust 7 warship

Rama's wife
4 Sita

ramble

3 gad 4 roam, rove 5 drift, range,
stray, troll 6 stroll, wander 7 blather,
digress, diverge, maunder, meander,
saunter, traipse 8 divagate, straggle
9 gallivant

rambler

4 rose 5 gypsy, hiker, nomad, rover
6 roamer, walker 7 drifter, vagrant
8 stroller, vagabond, wanderer
9 itinerant 10 ranch house

rambunctious

5 rowdy 6 unruly 7 raucous, willful
10 boisterous, headstrong 11 intractable 12 recalcitrant, ungovernable

ramification

5 shoot 6 branch, offset 8 offshoot
9 outgrowth, offspring 11 consequence

ramify

6 branch, divide, extend 7 develop,
radiate 9 branch out, propagate
11 proliferate

Ramona author

7 Jackson (Helen Hunt)

ramose

8 branched

ramp

5 apron 7 incline

rampage

4 rage, riot, tear 5 binge, fling,
spree, storm

rampageous

4 wild 6 unruly 7 riotous

rampant

4 rank, rife, wild 7 rearing, regnant
9 prevalent, unbridled 10 widespread 12 uncontrolled, unrestrained

rampart

4 wall 5 ridge 7 bulwark, parapet
9 barricade 10 breastwork

ramshackle

6 flimsy 7 rickety, run-down 8 decrepit 10 tumbledown 11 dilapidated

ram's mate

3 ewe

ranch

5 finca 8 estancia, hacienda
worker: 6 cowboy, gaucho 7 cow-
girl, cowhand, cowpoke 10 cowpuncher

rancher

6 cowboy 7 breeder 9 cattleman

rancid

4 high, rank, sour 5 fetid 6 putrid,
skunky, smelly 7 noisome, spoiled
8 stinking 9 offensive 10 malodorous

rancor

4 gall 6 animus, enmity, hatred 7 ill
will 9 animosity, antipathy, hostility
10 antagonism, bitterness

rancorous

6 bitter 7 hateful, hostile 8 spiteful,
venomous 9 malicious, malignant,
vitriolic 10 malevolent 11 acrimonious 12 antagonistic

Rand, Ayn

novel: 6 Anthem 12 Fountainhead
(The) 13 Atlas Shrugged

random

6 casual 7 aimless 8 slapdash
9 arbitrary, desultory, haphazard, hit-
or-miss, unplanned 10 accidental,
contingent, hit-and-miss, incidental
11 purposeless

randy

4 lewd 5 bawdy, lusty 7 lustful,
satyric 9 lecherous, libertine, lickerish, salacious 10 lascivious, libidinous, licentious

range

3 row, run 4 area, band, roam, rove,
shot, site, sort, span, vary 5 align,
ambit, carry, drift, field, gamut, orbit,
order, reach, realm, ridge, scale,
scope, space, stove, stray, sweep,
width 6 assort, domain, extent,
length, limits, ramble, sierra, sphere,
spread, wander 7 compass, earshot,
expanse, eyeshot, habitat, meander,

purview, stretch **8** confines, distance, latitude, locality, panorama, province, stovetop, traverse, vicinity **9** amplitude, extension, gallivant, magnitude, territory **12** distribution

range finder
9 telemeter

ranger
3 spy **5** scout **6** lawman, patrol, warden **8** overseer **9** caretaker, protector

rangy
4 lean **5** lanky **6** gangly **7** spindly **8** gangling

rani's mate
4 raja **5** rajah

rank
3 row **4** file, foul, lush, rate, sort, tier **5** class, fetid, funky, grade, gross, humid, order, place, queue **6** assort, cachet, coarse, filthy, lavish, putrid, rancid, rating, smelly, status **7** arrange, dignity, echelon, footing, noisome, perfect, profuse, rampant, reeking, station, stature **8** absolute, classify, evaluate, flagrant, outright, position, standing, stinking **9** downright, egregious, loathsome, luxuriant, overgrown, repulsive **10** consummate, malodorous **11** conspicuous, outstanding, unmitigated

rank and file
5 plebs **6** people, plebes **8** populace **9** commonage, commoners, plebeians **10** commonalty **11** enlisted men

rankle
3 irk, vex **4** rile **5** annoy **6** bother, fester, nettle, seethe **8** embitter, irritate **9** aggravate **10** exasperate

ransack
3 rob **4** comb, grub, loot, rake **5** rifle, scour **6** forage, ravage **7** plunder, rummage

Ran's husband
5 Aegir

ransom
3 buy **4** free **6** redeem, regain, rescue **7** deliver, recover **8** liberate **13** consideration

rant
3 jaw, rag **4** huff, rage, rail, rate, rave **5** mouth, scold **7** bluster, bombast, declaim, fustian **8** bloviate, harangue, perorate **10** vituperate **11** rodomontade

ranula
4 cyst

rap
3 hit, tap **4** blow, chat, swat, talk, wipe **5** blame, chide, knock, swipe **6** charge, patter, rebuke **7** censure, condemn, reproof **8** causerie, denounce, reproach, sentence **9** criticize, criticism, reprehend, reprimand, reprobate **10** discussion **12** conversation

rapacious
6 greedy **8** covetous, grasping, ravening, ravenous **9** predatory, raptorial, voracious **10** gluttonous, predaceous

rapacity
5 greed **7** avarice, avidity **8** cupidity, voracity **10** greediness **12** covetousness, ravenousness

rape
4 ruin **5** colza, force, spoil **6** canola, defile, ravage, ravish **7** assault, debauch, despoil, outrage, plunder, violate **9** violation **10** ravishment, spoliation

Rape of the Lock, The
author: **4** Pope (Alexander)
heroine: **7** Belinda

Raphael
birthplace: **6** Urbino
subject: **7** Madonna
teacher: **8** Perugino

rapid
4 fast **5** brisk, chute, fleet, hasty, quick, swift **6** speedy **7** hurried **9** breakneck **11** expeditious

rapidity
5 haste, hurry, speed 8 celerity, velocity

rapids
5 chute 8 cataract 10 white water

rapine
4 loot, swag 5 booty, prize, spoil 6 boodle, spoils 7 pillage, plunder 10 spoliation

Rappaccini's Daughter
8 Beatrice
author: 9 Hawthorne (Nathaniel)

rapport
5 unity 6 accord 7 concord, harmony 8 affinity 9 communion 13 communication

rapscallion
see rascal

rap session
6 confab, parley 7 palaver 8 colloquy 10 discussion

rapt
6 intent 7 engaged 8 absorbed, immersed 9 engrossed 11 carried away, preoccupied, transported

raptor
3 owl 4 hawk 5 eagle 6 condor, falcon, merlin, osprey 7 kestrel, vulture 9 gyrfalcon 10 bird of prey 11 deinonychus

rapture
5 swoon 6 heaven 7 delight, ecstasy, nirvana 9 transport 10 exaltation 13 seventh heaven

rara _____
4 avis

rare
3 few, red 4 pink, thin 6 choice, dainty, exotic, scarce, seldom, select 7 elegant, unusual 8 delicate, singular, sporadic, superior, uncommon, unwonted 9 exquisite, recherché, underdone 10 infrequent, occasional 11 distinctive, exceptional 13 extraordinary

rarefied
4 fine, thin 7 tenuous 8 esoteric 10 attenuated

rarefy
4 thin 6 refine 9 attenuate

rarely
6 little, seldom 9 extremely, unusually 12 infrequently

raring
4 avid, keen 5 eager 6 gung-ho 12 enthusiastic

rarity
5 curio 6 oddity 7 curiosa 8 scarcity 9 curiosity 10 aberration 11 collectible

rascal
3 imp 4 rake 5 devil, knave, rogue, scamp 7 lowlife, villain, wastrel 8 scalawag 9 miscreant, reprobate, scoundrel, skeezicks 10 blackguard 11 rapscallion
Irish: 8 spalpeen

rash
5 hasty, heady 6 abrupt, daring, madcap, plague, sudden, unwary, unwise 7 foolish 8 careless, epidemic, eruption, headlong, heedless, outbreak, reckless 9 audacious, daredevil, foolhardy, hotheaded, impetuous, imprudent, impulsive 10 ill-advised, incautious, indiscreet, unthinking 11 injudicious, precipitate, temerarious, thoughtless

rasp
4 file, fret 5 annoy, chafe, grate 6 abrade, scrape 7 scratch 8 irritate

raspberry
7 catcall 8 blackcap 10 Bronx cheer

raspy
3 dry 5 harsh, rough 6 hoarse 7 grating, jarring, raucous 8 scrabbly, scratchy

rat
4 fink, heel, scab 5 louse 6 defect, desert, inform, rodent, snitch, squeak, squeal, tattle 7 stoolie 8 apostate,

defector, informer, recreant, renegade, squealer, turncoat **9** bandicoot, repudiate, turnabout **11** stool pigeon **12** tergiversate
female: 3 doe

rate
3 fee, set, tab **4** cost, earn, rank
5 assay, class, grade, merit, price, scale, set at, value **6** amount, assess, charge, degree, esteem, regard, survey, tariff **7** apprize, deserve, valuate **8** appraise, classify, consider, estimate, evaluate, price tag **9** valuation **10** proportion

rather
4 a bit **5** quite **6** fairly, in lieu, kind of, pretty, sort of **7** instead **8** somewhat **9** tolerably **10** moderately, more or less, preferably **11** alternately **12** considerably **13** alternatively

rathskeller
3 bar, inn, pub **4** dive **6** saloon, tavern **7** barroom, taproom **8** alehouse, basement

ratify
4 seal **5** enact **7** approve, certify, confirm, endorse, license **8** accredit, sanction, validate

rating
4 mark, rank **5** class, grade **6** number **8** estimate, standing

ratio
5 scale **7** percent **8** fraction, quotient **10** percentage, proportion

ratiocination
8 judgment, sequitur **9** inference, reasoning **10** conclusion

ration
4 dole, food, meal, mete **5** allot, divvy, quota, share **6** divide, parcel **7** measure, mete out, prorate **8** allocate **9** allotment, allowance **10** provisions **13** apportionment

rational
4 calm, cool, sane **5** lucid, sober,

sound **6** stable **7** logical, prudent **8** sensible, thinking **9** judicious **10** consequent, reasonable **11** circumspect, intelligent, level-headed **12** intellectual

rationale
5 basis, logic **6** reason **7** grounds **9** reasoning **11** explanation **13** justification

rationalize
7 explain, justify **10** account for **11** externalize

ratite
3 emu, moa **4** kiwi, rhea **7** ostrich

rattail
3 cod **9** grenadier

rattan
4 cane, palm **6** switch **7** malacca

Rattigan play
10 Winslow Boy (The) **14** Separate Tables

rattle
3 gab, jaw, yak **4** chat, faze **5** abash, addle, clack, noise, rouse, run on, upset **6** babble, gabble, jangle, racket **7** chatter, clatter, confuse, disturb, flummox, perplex **8** bewilder, confound, distract **9** discomfit, embarrass **10** noisemaker

rattlebrained
5 dizzy, giddy, silly **7** flighty **8** skittish **9** frivolous

rattling
4 very **5** brisk, quick **6** damned, lively, mighty **8** whacking, whopping **9** energetic, extremely **11** exceedingly

ratty
4 mean **5** dowdy, dumpy, tacky **6** cheesy, scurvy, shabby **7** unkempt **8** slovenly **10** despicable **11** treacherous **12** contemptible

raucous
4 loud **5** harsh, noisy, rough, rowdy **6** hoarse, unruly **7** grating, jarring,

squawky **8** rowdyish, strident
9 termagant, turbulent **10** boisterous, disorderly, stridulent, stridulous, tumultuous **11** cacophonous
12 rambunctious

raunchy
4 foul **5** dirty, nasty **6** coarse, filthy,
sloppy, smutty, vulgar **7** obscene
8 indecent **9** salacious

ravage
4 loot, raze, ruin, sack **5** foray, harry,
spoil, strip, waste, wreck **6** forage,
invade, ravish **7** despoil, overrun,
pillage, plunder, ransack, scourge
8 desolate, spoliate **9** depredate,
desecrate, devastate

rave
4 gush, rant **5** storm **6** babble,
jabber **7** enthuse **10** rhapsodize

ravel
3 run **4** fray **5** snarl **6** muddle,
tangle **7** perplex, untwine **8** entangle **9** extricate **10** complicate
11 disentangle

ravelings
4 lint **7** threads

Ravel work
6 Boléro **7** La Valse **14** Daphnis et
Chloé **17** Rapsodie espagnole

raven
3 jet **4** ebon, inky, prey **5** black,
ebony, jetty, sable **7** despoil, plunder
9 pitch-dark **10** pitch-black
relative: 3 jay **4** crow **6** magpie
7 blue jay

Raven, The
author: 3 Poe (Edgar Allan)
lost love: 6 Lenore
refrain: 9 Nevermore

ravenous
6 greedy, hungry **7** starved **8** edacious, famished, starving **9** rapacious, voracious **10** gluttonous

ravine
3 cut, gap **4** gulf, pass **5** abyss,
chasm, cleft, clove, flume, gorge,
gulch, gully, notch **6** arroyo, canyon,

clough, coulee, defile, gutter, nullah
7 crevice, fissure **8** barranca, crevasse
Mt. Washington's: 9 Tuckerman

raving
3 mad **5** manic, rabid, upset **6** crazed
7 frantic, lunatic, unglued **8** demented, deranged, frenetic, frenzied,
maniacal, obsessed, unhinged,
worked up **9** ravishing **10** distraught, flipped out, hysterical,
irrational **11** overwrought

ravish
4 rape **5** force, spoil **6** defile **7** assault, despoil, outrage, pillage,
plunder, violate **8** deflower, entrance, overcome **9** enrapture,
transport

raw
4 cold, nude, rude **5** bleak, chill,
crass, crude, fresh, green, naked,
rough, young **6** callow, coarse,
impure, native, unclad, unripe, vulgar
7 uncouth **8** immature, uncooked,
unformed **9** au naturel, inelegant,
irritated, run-of-mine, unbridled,
unclothed, undressed, unrefined
10 unfinished, unpolished **13** inexperienced

rawboned
4 bony, lank, lean **5** gaunt, gawky,
lanky, spare **6** skinny **7** angular,
scraggy, scrawny

ray
4 beam **5** gleam, manta, shaft,
skate, trace **6** radius, streak, stream
7 radiate, sawfish, sunbeam, torpedo
8 moonbeam **9** devilfish, thornback
10 guitarfish

raze
4 ruin **5** level **7** destroy **8** demolish,
pull down, tear down

razor
6 shaver

razz
3 rag, rib **4** bait, josh, mock, twit
5 scout, taunt **6** badger, banter, deride, heckle, hector **8** ridicule
(see also **raspberry**)

RBI
11 run batted in 12 runs batted in

re
4 as to 5 as for 7 apropos 9 apropos of, as regards, regarding 10 as respects, concerning, relating to, respecting 12 with regard to 13 with respect to

reach
4 beat, gain, pass, span, tack 5 carry, get at, get to, grasp, level, range, scope, sweep, touch 6 arrive, attain, extend, extent, rack up, thrust 7 achieve, horizon, project, stretch 9 encompass, influence 10 accomplish, get through

____ reaction
4 dark 5 alarm, chain, light 7 nuclear 8 chemical

reactivate
5 renew 6 revive 8 rekindle, revivify 9 resurrect 10 revitalize 11 resuscitate

read
4 scan, skim 6 peruse 8 pore over
inability to: 8 dyslexia

readable
7 legible

reader
6 lector, primer 7 proofer, scanner 8 bookworm 9 anthology

readily
4 well 6 easily, freely 7 lightly 9 willingly 12 effortlessly

readiness
4 ease 5 skill 7 aptness 8 alacrity, dispatch, facility 9 dexterity, quickness 10 promptness 11 inclination, promptitude 12 preparedness

reading
6 lesson 7 lection, version, vulgate 9 rendition 10 recitation

ready
3 set 4 prep, ripe 5 equip 6 active, gear up, make up, primed, prompt 7 prepare 8 prepared 9 available, inclined

real
4 true, very 5 pukka, sound, valid 6 actual, honest 7 certain, genuine, sincere 8 bona fide, concrete, existent, tangible 9 authentic, undoubted, veridical 10 sure-enough, undeniable 11 substantive 12 indisputable

realism
6 verism 7 verismo 10 naturalism, pragmatism 11 objectivism, objectivity

realistic
4 sane 5 sober, sound 7 genuine, natural 8 lifelike, rational, sensible, veristic 9 practical, pragmatic 10 bottom-line, hard-boiled, hardheaded, reasonable, unromantic 11 down-to-earth 12 matter-of-fact 13 unsentimental

reality
4 fact, true 5 being, sooth, truth 9 actuality, existence, substance 13 flesh and blood

realize
4 gain 5 grasp, reach, score 6 attain, rack up 7 achieve, feature, imagine, reflect 8 conceive, envisage, envision 9 actualize, recognize 10 accomplish, comprehend

really
4 very 5 truly 6 indeed, verily 7 awfully, clearly 8 actually, honestly 9 assuredly, certainly, decidedly, genuinely 10 definitely, positively 11 exceedingly, indubitably, undoubtedly 12 unmistakably

realm
5 orbit, range, scope, sweep 6 domain, empire, estate, extent, radius, sphere 7 compass, demesne, kingdom, purview 8 dominion

ream
4 load, scad 5 widen 7 enlarge 11 countersink

reanimation
7 rebirth, revival 10 renascence, resurgence 11 reawakening, renaissance 12 risorgimento

reap

3 cut 4 earn, gain 5 glean, shear
6 garner, gather, obtain, sickle,
thresh 7 harvest

rear

3 aft 4 back, butt, hind, lift, ramp,
rump, seat, tail 5 after, breed, build,
erect, fanny, hoist, nurse, put up,
raise, set up 6 behind, bottom,
fledge, foster, uphold 7 bring up,
caboose, elevate, nurture 8 backside, buttocks, hindmost 9 construct,
posterior

rear end

3 bum, bun, can 4 duff, moon,
rump, seat, tail, tush 5 booty, fanny
6 behind, bottom, heinie 7 caboose,
keister, tail end 8 backside, buttocks, derriere 9 posterior

rearmost

3 end 4 last 5 final 8 terminal,
ultimate

rearrange

see readjust

rearward

3 aft 4 back 6 behind 8 backward
9 posterior 10 retrograde

Rea Silvia

father: 7 Numitor
son: 5 Remus 7 Romulus

reason

3 why, wit 4 mind, nous 5 basis,
cause, infer, proof, think 6 excuse,
ground, motive, sanity, senses
7 account, reflect 8 argument,
cogitate, conceive, persuade 9 inference, intellect, rationale, soundness, speculate, wherefore 10 antecedent, deliberate 11 determinant,
explanation 12 intelligence 13 consideration, justification, ratiocination,
understanding

reasonable

4 fair, just 5 cheap, level, sound
6 modest 7 logical, low-cost, tenable
8 credible, feasible, moderate, rational, sensible 9 equitable, plausible
10 acceptable, affordable, restrained
11 inexpensive, intelligent

reasoning

4 case 5 logic 8 argument 9 deduction

reasonless

7 invalid 8 baseless 9 illogical,
senseless, unfounded 10 fallacious,
groundless, irrational 11 meaningless, purposeless

reawaken

5 renew 6 revive 7 refresh 8 revivify 9 reanimate 10 regenerate
12 reinvigorate

rebate

6 lessen, refund, return 8 decrease,
diminish, give back 9 deduction,
reduction

Rebecca

beloved: 7 Ivanhoe
father: 5 Isaac

Rebekah

brother: 5 Laban
father: 7 Bethuel
husband: 5 Isaac
nurse: 7 Deborah
son: 4 Esau 5 Jacob

rebel

6 anarch, mutiny, resist, revolt 7 disobey 8 frondeur, mutineer 9 insurgent 10 malcontent 13 revolutionary,
revolutionist

rebellion

6 émeute, mutiny, revolt, rising
8 defiance, intifada, sedition, uprising
10 insurgence, insurgency, resistance, revolution 12 insurrection

rebellious

6 unruly 8 mutinous, stubborn
9 insurgent 10 refractory 11 disaffected, disobedient 12 contumacious, unmanageable 13 insubordinate

rebirth

7 revival 9 awakening 10 conversion, renascence, resurgence
11 reanimation, reawakening, renaissance 12 resurrection, risorgimento

rebound

5 rally 6 bounce, reecho, recoil, re-

peat **7** recover **8** comeback, recovery, ricochet, snap back **10** convalesce

rebozo
   5 scarf, shawl

rebuff
   4 slap, snub **5** repel **6** reject **7** fend
   off, repulse, ward off **8** turn away

rebuild
   6 repair, revamp **7** remodel, restore
   8 overhaul, renovate, retrofit **9** modernize, refurbish **11** recondition,
   reconstruct **12** rehabilitate

rebuke
   3 rap **4** snub **5** chide, scold, scorn
   6 berate, earful, lesson, rebuff
   7 bawl out, lecture, reproof, reprove
   8 admonish, call down, reproach,
   scolding **9** reprimand, talking-to
   10 tongue-lash **11** comeuppance,
   objurgation **12** admonishment,
   dressing-down **13** tongue-lashing

rebut
   5 repel **6** refute, reject **7** confute,
   fend off, repulse, ward off **8** confound, disprove, stave off **10** controvert, disconfirm

rebuttal
   5 reply **6** answer, retort **7** defense,
   riposte **8** argument, comeback,
   response **9** rejoinder **10** refutation
   11 repudiation

recalcitrant
   6 unruly **7** froward, willful **8** contrary,
   perverse, stubborn, untoward **9** fractious, obstinate, resistant **10** headstrong **11** intractable **12** ungovernable, unmanageable

recall
   4 stir **5** evoke, renew, rouse, waken
   6 arouse, awaken, cancel, memory,
   remind, repeal, revive, revoke
   7 bethink, rescind, restore, retract,
   reverse **8** callback, remember, resemble, take back, withdraw **9** anamnesis, recollect, reinstate, reminisce, represent, reproduce
   10 revocation **11** bring to mind,

countermand, remembrance
12 recollection, reminiscence

recant
   5 unsay **6** abjure, revoke **7** retract
   8 forswear, renounce, take back,
   withdraw **9** backtrack, repudiate

recap
   5 sum up **6** précis, résumé **7** reprise, retread, summary **8** overview
   9 summarize **10** retrograde

recapitulate
   5 sum up **6** resume **9** summarize
   10 retrograde

recapitulation
   5 sum-up **6** précis, résumé **7** epitome, reprise, summary **9** summing-
   up

recede
   3 ebb **4** back **5** abate, taper **6** lessen,
   reduce, retire **7** dwindle, regress,
   retract, retreat **8** decrease, diminish,
   fall back, withdraw **10** retrograde,
   retrogress

receipts
   4 gate, take **5** sales **6** income
   7 revenue, takings **8** earnings,
   proceeds

receive
   4 host **5** admit, catch, greet **6** accept, endure, suffer, take in **7** acquire, sustain, welcome **10** experience

received
   5 plain, sound **6** common **7** popular
   8 accepted, familiar, ordinary, orthodox **12** acknowledged, conventional

receiver
   4 dish **5** donee, fence, pager **6** aerial
   7 antenna, catcher, scanner **9** recipient, treasurer

recent
   3 new **4** late **5** fresh, novel **6** latest,
   modern **8** neoteric

receptacle
   6 hamper, holder, hopper, trough,
   vessel **9** container **10** repository

receptive

4 open 7 passive 8 amenable 9 sensitive 10 accessible, hospitable, open-minded, responsive 11 persuadable, persuasible, suggestible, susceptible

recess

4 cove, nook 5 break, cleft, niche 6 alcove, grotto, hiatus 7 adjourn 8 prorogue 9 prorogate, terminate 11 indentation

Recessional author

7 Kipling (Rudyard)

recessive

3 shy 8 retiring 9 reclusive, withdrawn 10 unsociable

recherché

4 rare 5 novel 6 choice, dainty, exotic, select 7 elegant, unusual 8 affected, delicate, original, superior, uncommon 9 exquisite 11 pretentious

recipe

7 formula 9 procedure 12 prescription

reciprocal

4 mate, twin 5 match 6 double, fellow, mutual 8 requited 9 companion, duplicate 10 coordinate 11 interactive
prefix: 5 inter

reciprocate

5 repay 6 retort, return 7 requite 8 exchange 9 retaliate 10 compensate, recompense 11 interchange

recital

5 story 6 soiree 7 concert, reading 9 discourse, narration 10 recounting 11 enumeration, performance

recite

4 tell 5 chant, count, state 6 detail, number, relate, repeat, report, set out 7 declaim, narrate, recount, reel off 8 describe, rehearse 9 pronounce

reckless

4 rash, wild 5 brash, hasty 6 daring, madcap 8 carefree, heedless 9 audacious, daredevil, foolhardy, hotheaded 10 ill-advised, incautious 11 harebrained, temerarious, thoughtless 12 devil-may-care 13 irresponsible

reckon

3 sum 5 count, gauge, guess, judge, tally, total 6 cipher, figure, number, regard 7 account, compute, suppose, surmise 8 consider, estimate 9 calculate, enumerate 10 conjecture 11 approximate

reckoning

3 tab 4 bill 5 tally, score 7 account, invoice 9 statement 10 arithmetic, estimation 11 calculation, computation

reclaim

4 save, tame 6 redeem, reform, rescue 7 deliver, recover, restore 9 restitute 11 recondition, reconstruct 12 rehabilitate

recline

3 lie 4 rest, tilt 5 couch, slant, slope 6 lounge, repose 7 lie down 10 stretch out

reclining

4 flat 5 prone 6 supine 9 decumbent, prostrate, recumbent

recluse

5 loner 6 hermit, shut-in 7 eremite 8 cenobite, solitary 9 anchorite
female: 7 ancress 9 anchoress

reclusive

8 eremitic, hermetic, reserved, solitary 9 withdrawn 10 antisocial, eremitical, unsociable 12 misanthropic

recognition

6 credit, esteem, notice 9 attention, awareness, gratitude 10 cognizance, perception 11 realization 12 appreciation

recognize

4 note, spot 5 admit 6 notice 7 observe, realize 8 diagnose, identify 9 apprehend 10 appreciate 11 acknowledge, determinate, distinguish

recoil
4 balk, kick **5** cower, dodge, quail, start, wince **6** blench, cringe, flinch, shrink **7** rebound, retract, squinch **8** reaction

recollect
5 evoke **6** recall, remind, revive **7** bethink **8** remember **9** reminisce

recollection
6 memory, recall **9** anamnesis, flashback **11** remembrance **12** reminiscence

recommence
5 renew **6** pick up, reopen, resume, take up **7** restart **8** continue

recommend
4 tout **6** advise, praise, prefer **7** acclaim, commend, counsel, endorse, entrust, propose, suggest **8** advocate

recommendation
4 plug **5** pitch **6** advice **7** counsel **11** endorsement, testimonial

recompense
3 pay **4** wage **5** repay **6** amends, reward **7** guerdon, premium, redress, requite **8** gratuity, requital **9** indemnify, indemnity, quittance, reimburse, repayment **10** compensate, remunerate, reparation **11** reciprocate, restitution, retribution **12** compensation, remuneration **13** consideration, gratification

reconcile
4 suit, tune **5** adapt **6** accept, accord, adjust, attune, make up, resign, settle, square, submit, tailor **7** conform, get over, resolve **9** harmonize, integrate **10** conciliate, coordinate **11** accommodate

recondite
4 deep **6** hidden, mystic, occult, orphic, secret **7** cryptic, erudite, learned, obscure **8** abstruse, academic, esoteric, hermetic, profound **9** concealed, difficult, enigmatic, scholarly

recondition
3 fix **4** mend **6** doctor, repair, revamp **7** rebuild, restore **8** make over, overhaul, retrofit **9** restitute **10** rejuvenate **12** rehabilitate

reconnoiter
5 scout **6** survey

reconsider
6 review, revise **7** rethink, reweigh **8** reassess **9** reexamine **10** reevaluate **13** think better of

reconstruct
6 recast, re-form, remake, revamp **7** rebuild, reclaim, remodel, restore **8** make over, overhaul, readjust, renovate **9** refashion, restitute **10** reassemble, reorganize

record
4 disc, disk **5** album **6** annals, enroll **7** archive, journal, platter **8** archives, document, register **9** chronicle **10** transcript
of a meeting: 7 minutes
of proceedings: 4 acta
ship's: 3 log **7** logbook

recorder
5 flute **9** registrar
flight: 8 black box

record player
5 phono **8** Victrola **9** turntable **10** gramophone, phonograph

recount
4 tell **5** state **6** recite, relate, report, retail **7** narrate **8** describe, rehearse **9** enumerate

recoup
6 regain **7** get back, reclaim, recover **8** retrieve **9** repossess

recourse
6 backup, refuge, resort **7** standby, stopgap, support **8** resource **9** expedient, makeshift

recover
4 heal, mend **5** evict, rally, renew **6** recoup, redeem, regain, revive **7** get back, get over, improve, rebound, reclaim, recycle, restore

recreant

8 retrieve, snap back 9 come round, reacquire, recapture, re-collect, repossess, restitute 10 bounce back, convalesce, recuperate

recreant

3 rat 5 false 6 coward, craven, untrue 7 chicken, dastard, unloyal 8 apostate, cowardly, defector, deserter, disloyal, poltroon, renegade, turncoat 9 dastardly, faithless, turnabout 10 perfidious, traitorous, unfaithful 13 pusillanimous

recreate

4 play 5 evoke, renew 7 freshen, refresh, restore 11 reconstruct

recreation

4 play 5 hobby, sport 7 leisure, pastime 8 activity 9 avocation, diversion 10 relaxation 13 entertainment

recrudesce

5 recur 6 return, revert, revive 7 reoccur 8 break out

recruit

4 boot, hire 5 raise 6 engage, enlist, enroll, muster, novice, rookie 7 draftee 8 beginner, enlistee, freshman, headhunt, neophyte, newcomer 9 conscript, fledgling, reinforce, replenish 10 apprentice, tenderfoot

rectifier

4 tube 5 diode 8 detector, ignitron

rectify

3 fix 4 mend 5 amend, emend 6 adjust, remedy, repair 7 correct

rectitude

6 virtue 7 honesty, probity 8 morality 9 rightness 11 uprightness 13 righteousness

rector

6 parson, pastor, priest 9 clergyman 10 headmaster

rectory

5 manse 8 benefice 9 parsonage

recumbent

4 flat 5 prone 6 supine 7 leaning, resting 8 reposing 9 lying down, prostrate, reclining

recuperate

4 heal, mend 5 rally 6 regain, revive 7 rebound, recover 8 snap back 10 convalesce

recur

5 cycle, haunt 6 repeat, resort, return 7 iterate, revolve 8 turn back

recurring

7 chronic 8 periodic 10 continuous, isochronal, periodical, persistent 11 isochronous 12 intermittent

red

4 puce, ruby 5 coral, gules, rouge, ruddy 6 cerise, claret, florid, maroon 7 carmine, crimson, flushed, glowing, magenta, oxblood, scarlet, vermeil 8 burgundy, sanguine 9 vermilion **combining form:** 4 rhod 5 rhodo

Red

6 Bolshy, commie 7 Bolshie, comrade 9 Bolshevik, Communist

redact

4 edit 6 censor, revise

Red and the Black author

8 Stendhal

red ape

9 orangutan

red arsenic

7 realgar

red-backed sandpiper

6 dunlin

Red Badge of Courage

author: 5 Crane (Stephen) **hero:** 7 Fleming (Henry)

red-bellied snipe

9 dowitcher

redbird

7 tanager 8 cardinal 13 summer tanager

red blood cell

11 erythrocyte

red-blooded

5 juicy, lusty, manly 6 hearty, robust, virile 8 vigorous 9 energetic

redbreast
4 knot 5 robin 7 sunfish

red-breasted snipe
9 dowitcher

Redburn author
8 Melville (Herman)

red carp
8 goldfish

red cobalt
9 erythrite

red copper ore
7 cuprite

Red Cross
founder: 6 Barton (Clara)
Knight: 6 George

redden
5 blush, color, flush, rouge 6 mantle, ruddle 11 incarnadine

red dog
5 blitz

redecorate
4 redo 5 fix up 9 refurbish

redeem
4 free, save 5 atone, loose, renew 6 offset, pay off, ransom, reform, rescue 7 expiate, reclaim, recover, restore 9 exonerate

redeemer
5 Jesus 6 Christ, savior 7 messiah, saviour

redemption
6 ransom 7 release 9 atonement, expiation, salvation 11 deliverance

red-eye
5 hooch 6 flight, rotgut 7 whiskey 8 rock bass 9 moonshine

red-faced
5 ruddy 6 florid, shamed 7 abashed, flushed, glowing 8 blushing, rubicund, sanguine, sheepish 9 mortified 11 embarrassed

redfish
4 bass, drum 5 perch 6 salmon 10 ocean perch 11 channel bass

red hickory
6 pignut

red-hot
5 fiery 6 ardent, fervid 7 blazing, boiling, burning, fervent, flaming, glowing 8 brand-new, scalding, sizzling 9 scorching 10 blistering, passionate, sweltering 11 impassioned

red Indian paint
9 bloodroot 11 sanguinaria

red ink
7 arrears, deficit 8 shortage

red inkberry
8 pokeweed

red ironbark
8 eucalypt 10 eucalyptus

red iron ore
5 ocher, ochre 8 hematite

red lauan
8 mahogany

red-legged crow
6 chough

red-legged sandpiper
9 turnstone

red-letter
7 notable 8 historic 9 important, memorable 10 noteworthy, observable, remarkable 11 significant

red-light district
5 stews 10 tenderloin

red mite
7 chigger

redneck
4 clod, hick, rube 5 Bubba, yahoo, yokel 6 rustic 7 bumpkin, hayseed 9 hillbilly 10 olodhopper, good old boy, good ole boy

redo
5 renew 6 repeat, revamp 7 remodel, restyle 8 make over, overhaul, refinish, renovate 9 refurbish 10 redecorate

red ocher
8 hematite

redolence
4 balm, odor 5 aroma, attar, scent,
spice 7 bouquet, incense, perfume
9 fragrance

redolent
5 balmy, spicy, sweet 7 odorous,
scented 8 aromatic, fragrant, perfumed 9 ambrosial, evocative
10 suggestive 11 reminiscent

redouble
4 dupe 7 dualize, enhance, magnify
8 heighten 9 duplicate, intensify,
reinforce 10 strengthen

redoubt
4 fort 7 bastion, citadel 8 fastness,
fortress 10 stronghold

redoubtable
5 famed, great 6 famous, mighty
7 awesome, eminent 8 imposing,
puissant, renowned 9 prominent
10 celebrated, formidable, impressive 11 illustrious 12 intimidating,
overwhelming 13 distinguished

redound
6 accrue, recoil 7 conduce, reflect
10 contribute

red pigment
5 ocher, ochre 6 ruddle

Red Planet
4 Mars

redpoll
5 finch 6 linnet

redraft
6 revamp, revise, rework 7 restyle,
rewrite 8 make over, overhaul,
rescript, revision, work over 9 recen-
sion

redress
4 heal 6 amends, avenge, negate,
offset, relief, remedy 7 correct
8 reprisal, requital 9 cancel out,
indemnity, quittance, vindicate
10 compensate, counteract, correction, neutralize, recompense,
reparation 11 restitution, retribution
12 compensation

red roe
5 coral 6 caviar

redroot
7 alkanet, pigweed 9 bloodroot
12 New Jersey tea

red sable
8 kolinsky

red silver ore
9 proustite

red squirrel
9 chickaree

reduce
3 cut 4 cull, diet, melt, pare 5 abate,
force, lower, shade, shave, slash,
smelt 6 humble, lessen, recede,
weaken 7 abridge, curtail, cut back,
cut down, dwindle, liquefy, squeeze
8 boil down, compress, contract,
decrease, diminish, discount, mark
down, minimize, simplify, taper off
10 depreciate, slenderize 11 consolidate

reductio ad _____
8 absurdum

reduction
6 digest, précis, rebate 7 cutback,
cutdown, epitome, summary 8 abstract, discount, markdown, synopsis
9 abatement 10 shortening 11 curtailment 12 condensation

redundancy
6 excess 7 nimiety, surfeit 8 pleonasm 9 abundance, profusion,
prolixity, tautology 10 repetition
11 periphrasis, reiteration, superfluity
13 supernumerary

redundant
5 extra, spare, windy, wordy 6 prolix
7 surplus, verbose 9 duplicate,
excessive, iterative 11 duplicative,
reiterative, repetitious, superfluous,
tautologous 13 supernumerary

redux
7 revived 8 restored

redwing
6 thrush 9 blackbird

redwood
7 amboyna, sequoia 8 mahogany

reed
4 pipe 5 arrow, grass

reedy
4 thin 6 skinny, stalky, twiggy
7 spindly

reef
3 bar, cay, key 4 lode, vein 5 atoll,
ledge 6 reduce, skerry 7 sandbar

reek
4 funk 5 fetor, smell, stink 6 stench
9 effluvium

reeking
4 rank 5 fetid, funky, fusty 6 putrid,
rancid, smelly, stinky 7 noisome,
stenchy 10 malodorous

reel
4 spin, sway, turn 5 lurch, spool,
weave, whirl 6 bobbin, careen,
teeter, totter, waggle, wobble 7 stagger, stumble 8 fall back

reestablish
5 renew 6 revive 7 restore 9 reinstate 10 reinscribe 11 reintroduce

reevaluate
6 review 7 rethink, reweigh 8 reassess 9 reexamine 10 reconsider

reeve
4 ruff 6 thread 9 sandpiper 10 magistrate

reexamine
see reevaluate

refashion
5 alter 6 change, modify, recast,
remake, revamp 7 remodel 8 make
over, overhaul 9 transmute

refection
4 feed, meal 6 repast 11 nourishment, refreshment

refectory
10 dining hall

refer
6 advert, allude, assign, relate,
submit 7 ascribe 9 attribute

referee
3 ump 5 judge 6 umpire 7 adjudge,
arbiter, mediate 8 mediator 9 arbitrate, officiate 10 adjudicate, arbitrator

reference
5 atlas 6 credit, source 7 almanac,
meaning, mention 8 allusion, citation, innuendo, relation, resource
9 directory 10 dictionary 11 testimonial 12 encyclopedia

reference book
5 atlas, bible, guide 6 manual
7 almanac 8 handbook 9 guidebook
10 dictionary 11 enchiridion 12 encyclopedia

reference guide
5 index 12 bibliography

referendum
4 poll, vote 10 plebiscite

refine
5 prune, smelt 6 polish, purify,
smooth 7 elevate, improve, perfect,
process 8 civilize 9 cultivate

refined
4 pure 6 subtle, urbane 7 elegant,
genteel, raffiné 8 cultured, elevated,
ladylike, raffinée, well-bred 9 civilized
10 cultivated, fastidious 13 sophisticated

refinement
5 couth, grace, taste 6 finish, polish
7 culture, finesse, suavity 8 breeding,
civility, courtesy, elegance, subtlety,
urbanity 9 politesse 10 politeness
11 cultivation 12 civilization, distillation, purification 13 clarification

reflect
4 echo, pore, show 5 weigh
6 bounce, mirror, ponder, reason,
return 7 redound 8 chew over,
cogitate, consider, ruminate 9 cerebrate 10 deliberate, retrospect
11 contemplate, demonstrate

reflection
4 slur 5 image 6 musing 7 replica,
thought 8 reproach 9 aspersion
10 cogitation, meditation, rumination,

simulacrum 11 cerebration 12 deliberation, reproduction 13 animadversion, consideration, contemplation

reflective
7 pensive 9 reflexive 10 cogitative, indicative, meditative, ruminative, thoughtful 12 deliberative 13 contemplative

reflux
3 ebb 4 GERD 8 backflow

reform
5 amend, emend 6 redeem, revise 7 correct, improve, reclaim, shape up 8 make over 10 correction, house-clean, regenerate

Reformation leader
4 Knox (John) 6 Calvin (John), Luther (Martin) 7 Zwingli (Huldrych)

reformatory
3 pen 6 prison 7 borstal 8 big house, remedial 10 corrective 12 penitentiary

refractory
6 mulish, unruly 7 froward, restive 8 contrary, perverse, stubborn 9 obstinate 10 bullheaded, head-strong, rebellious, unyielding 11 intractable, stiff-necked 12 unmanageable

refrain
4 keep, stop 6 burden, chorus, shrink 7 abstain, forbear 8 hold back

refresh
5 renew 6 revive 7 animate, enliven, quicken, restore 8 irrigate, recreate, renovate 9 replenish, stimulate 10 rejuvenate

refresher
5 drink, tonic 6 bracer 8 reminder 9 stimulant 11 restorative

refreshing
5 brisk, tonic 7 bracing 8 reviving 9 analeptic, animating 10 delightful, energizing 11 restorative, stimulating 12 invigorating, rejuvenating

refrigerant
3 ice 5 freon 7 coolant, cryogen 12 fluorocarbon 13 sulfur dioxide

refrigerator
6 cooler, fridge, icebox, walk-in 9 condenser 10 Frigidaire

refuge
4 lair, port 5 cover, haven 6 asylum, covert, harbor, resort 7 hideout, protect, retreat, shelter 8 hideaway, recourse, resource 9 expedient, harborage, sanctuary, safe house

refugee
5 exile 6 émigré 7 evacuee 8 emigrant, fugitive 10 boat person, expatriate

refulgent
6 bright 7 glowing, radiant 8 luminous 9 brilliant

refund
5 repay 6 rebate 8 give back 9 reimburse, repayment, restitute 11 restitution

refurbish
4 redo 5 fix up, renew 6 revamp 7 restore 8 make over, overhaul, renovate 10 redecorate, rejuvenate 11 recondition

refusal
4 veto 6 denial 7 regrets 8 negative, negation 9 disavowal 10 abnegation 11 declination, repudiation

refuse
3 jib, nix 4 deny, junk, scum 5 dreck, dross, offal, spurn, swill, trash, waste 6 debris, litter, reject, scraps, spilth 7 decline, garbage, residue, rubbish 8 disallow, leavings, remnants, turn down, withhold 9 reprobate, repudiate, sweepings 10 disapprove

refutation
8 disproof, elenchus, rebuttal

refute
4 deny 5 rebut 7 confute 8 confound, disprove 10 controvert, disconfirm

regain
6 recoup 7 get back, recover 8 re-occupy, retrieve 9 recapture, repossess

possession: 7 replevy 8 replevin

regal
5 grand 6 august, kingly, purple 7 queenly, stately, sublime 8 glorious, imperial, imposing, kinglike, majestic, princely, splendid 9 monarchal, sovereign 10 monarchial 11 magnificent, monarchical, resplendent

regale
4 feed 5 amuse, feast 6 dinner, divert, spread 7 banquet 9 entertain

regalia
5 array 6 finery 8 frippery, insignia 9 caparison, full dress, trappings 10 decoration 11 habiliments

Regan
father: 4 Lear
husband: 8 Cornwall
sister: 7 Goneril 8 Cordelia

regard
4 deem, heed, mark, note, rate, view 5 assay, favor, honor, judge, value 6 admire, assess, esteem, homage, liking, notice, reckon, repute 7 account, concern, respect 8 approval, consider, devotion, estimate, fondness 9 attention 10 admiration, cognizance, estimation, observance, solicitude 11 approbation, contemplate, observation 12 appreciation, satisfaction 13 consideration

regardful
7 heedful 8 watchful 9 advertent, attentive, observant 10 perceptive, respectful

regarding
4 as to, in re 5 about, anent, as for 7 apropos 8 touching 9 apropos of 10 as respects, concerning, relative to, respecting 11 in respect to 13 with respect to

regatta
4 race

regenerate
5 renew 6 reform, revive 7 rebirth, restore 8 recreate 9 reproduce

regent
5 ruler 6 warden 8 governor 9 protector

regicide's victim
4 king

regime
4 rule, term 5 reign 6 empire, tenure 7 dynasty 10 government, leadership

regimen
4 diet, plan, rule 6 course 10 government

region
4 area, belt, part, zone 5 field, tract 6 domain, locale, sector, sphere 7 demesne, terrain 8 locality, province, vicinity 9 bailiwick, territory 12 neighborhood

regional
5 local 9 localized, sectional 10 provincial 11 territorial

register
4 file, list, note, roll, till 5 enter, range, tally 6 annals, docket, enroll, ledger, record, roster 7 catalog, check in, express 8 indicate 9 catalogue

regnant
4 rife 6 ruling 7 current, popular 8 dominant, reigning 9 paramount, prevalent, sovereign 10 prevailing, widespread

regress
6 revert 9 backslide 10 retrograde

regret
3 rue, woe 4 care 5 grief, mourn 6 bemoan, bewail, excuse, grieve, lament, repent, sorrow 7 anguish, apology, deplore, remorse 9 heartache, penitence 10 contrition, heartbreak 11 compunction

regretful
5 sorry 6 rueful 8 contrite, mournful,

regrettable
penitent **9** repentant, sorrowful
10 apologetic, remorseful **11** penitential

regrettable
3 sad **6** too bad, woeful **8** grievous
10 lamentable **11** distressing, unfortunate **13** heartbreaking

regular
3 due, set **4** even **5** fixed, usual
6 common, normal, steady **7** average, equable, general, natural,
orderly, typical, uniform **8** complete,
constant, everyday, methodic, ordinary, standard **9** clocklike, customary,
prevalent **10** methodical, systematic
11 commonplace **12** run-of-the-mill

regulate
5 order, scale **6** adjust, direct,
govern, police, square, temper
7 arrange, control **8** organize **9** methodize, systemize **11** systematize

regulation
3 law **4** rule **5** canon, edict, order
6 decree **7** precept, statute **9** ordinance, prescript **11** restriction
12 codification

regulator
8 governor

rehabilitate
4 cure, heal **7** reclaim, recover,
restore **8** renovate **9** reeducate,
restitute **11** recondition

rehash
5 reuse **6** repeat, review, rework
7 restate, version **8** chew over,
rehearse, talk over **9** rendering,
rendition, rewording **11** restatement
12 recapitulate

rehearse
5 drill, train **6** repeat **7** run over
8 exercise, practice **10** run through

Rehoboam
father: **7** Solomon
kingdom: **5** Judah **6** Israel
mother: **6** Naamah

reign
4 rule, sway **6** govern **7** prevail

8 dominate, dominion **11** predominate, sovereignty

reimburse
3 pay **5** repay **6** recoup, refund
7 requite **9** indemnify **10** compensate, remunerate

rein
4 curb, stem **5** check **6** bridle
7 compose, control, repress **8** hold
back, restrain, suppress

reinforce
4 prop **5** brace **7** augment, bolster,
enlarge, fortify, recruit, sustain
8 buttress, increase, redouble **10** invigorate, strengthen

reinstate
6 recall **7** restore **11** reestablish,
reintroduce **12** rehabilitate

reintroduce
6 recall, revive **7** restore **9** reinstate
11 reestablish

reinvestment
4 DRIP **8** plowback

reiterate
5 renew, resay **6** repeat, resume,
retell **7** reprise

reject
3 nix **4** jilt, junk, shed **5** debar,
scorn, scrap, spurn **6** abjure, pariah,
pass up, rebuff, refuse **7** cashier,
castoff, decline, discard, dismiss,
exclude, outcast, repulse, shut out
8 castaway, jettison, throw out, turn
away, turn down **9** eliminate, repudiate, shoot down, throw away **10** disapprove

rejoice
5 cheer, exult, glory **7** delight,
gladden **8** jubilate

rejoinder
5 reply **6** answer, retort **8** comeback, rebuttal, repartee, response

rejuvenate
5 green, renew **7** refresh **8** renovate
9 modernize **10** revitalize

rekindle

5 renew 6 revive 7 restart 8 reawaken, reignite, revivify 10 reactivate, revitalize

relate

4 link, tell 5 apply, refer 6 assign,
detail, recite, report 7 connect,
express, pertain, recount 8 describe,
disclose, interact, rehearse 9 appertain, chronicle

related

4 akin 5 alike, enate 6 agnate, allied
7 cognate, connate, germane, kindred 8 incident 9 analogous, connected, identical, pertinent 10 associated, connatural, homologous
11 consanguine

relation

3 kin 6 agnate 7 hinship, kinsman
8 affinity 9 kinswoman, reference
11 propinquity

relationship

3 tie 4 bond, link 5 ratio, tie-in,
union 6 affair 7 analogy, contact,
liaison 8 affinity, alliance 10 connection 11 affiliation, association
13 confederation, consanguinity

relative

3 mom, sib, sis, son 4 aunt, mama,
papa 5 blood, madre, mamma,
momma, niece, pappy, pater, poppa,
uncle 6 agnate, cousin, father,
mother, nephew, parent, sister
7 apropos, brother, cognate, germane, kinsman, sibling 8 ancestor,
daughter, grandson, relation, relevant
9 ascendant, dependent, kinswoman,
pertinent 10 applicable, collateral,
descendant, grandchild 11 comparative, conditional, grandfather, grandmother, grandparent 13 grand-
daughter

relatives

3 kin 4 kith 5 folks 7 kindred,
kinfolk 8 kinfolks 9 relations

relax

4 bask, ease, loll, rest 5 chill, let go,
loose, remit 6 loosen, lounge, modify, unkink, unwind 7 slacken 8 chill

out, kick back, loosen up, unbuckle,
wind down 9 untighten 10 de-
compress

relaxation

3 fun 4 ease, rest 5 hobby 6 repose
7 leisure, pastime 9 amusement,
diversion, enjoyment 10 recreation

relaxed

5 loose, slack 6 casual, dégagé,
mellow 8 informal 9 easygoing
11 low-pressure

release

4 emit, free, vent 5 issue, loose,
untie, yield 6 acquit, loosen, pardon,
ransom, unbind, uncage 7 give off,
give out, manumit, set free, unchain,
unleash 8 liberate, unfetter 9 acquittal, discharge, exculpate, exonerate, surrender 10 emancipate
11 manumission 12 emancipation
conditional: 6 parole

relegate

5 exile, expel 6 assign, banish,
charge, commit, demote, resign
7 commend, confide, consign,
entrust 8 delegate, hand over,
transfer, turn over

relent

3 ebb 4 cave, ease, wane 5 abate,
let up, yield 6 give in, submit 7 die
away, die down, ease off, slacken,
subside 8 moderate 9 acquiesce
10 capitulate

relentless

5 cruel, rigid, stern 6 dogged 7 adamant, nonstop 8 constant, obdurate,
rigorous, unabated 9 ferocious,
incessant, stringent 10 implacable,
inexorable, inflexible, unyielding
11 remorseless, unfaltering

relevant

3 apt, fit 5 ad rem 6 cogent 7 apropos, germane 8 apposite, material,
relative 9 pertinent 10 admissible,
applicable 11 applicative, appropriate 12 proportional

reliable

4 safe, sure 5 solid, sound, tried,

reliance

valid **6** proven, secure, trusty **7** bedrock, certain **8** constant, verified **9** foolproof, validated **10** dependable **11** trustworthy **12** tried-and-true

reliance

4 hope **5** faith, stock, trust **10** dependence

relic

5 token **6** corpse **7** antique, memento, remains, remnant, vestige **8** artifact, fragment, keepsake, memorial, reminder, souvenir **11** remembrance

relict

5 widow **8** survivor

relief

3 aid **4** ease, fret, hand, help, lift **5** break, cameo **6** assist, raised, remedy, succor **7** comfort, redress, respite, support, welfare **8** breather, fretwork, repoussé **9** abatement, diversion **10** assistance, mitigation **11** alleviation, deliverance
pitcher: 6 closer **7** fireman, stopper

relieve

3 rid **4** calm, ease, free, help, quit, vent **5** allay, relax, spell **6** assist, exempt, lessen, loosen, reduce, remedy, soften, solace, soothe, succor, supply **7** absolve, assuage, comfort, deprive, lighten, mollify, release **8** diminish, dispense, mitigate, moderate, palliate, unburden **9** alleviate

religion

4 cult, sect **5** cause, creed, dogma, faith **6** belief, church **8** devotion, doctrine

religious

3 nun **4** holy, monk **5** friar, godly, pious **6** devout, priest, sacred, votary **7** staunch, upright **8** cenobite, faithful, monastic, priestly, reverent **9** pietistic, prayerful, spiritual, steadfast **10** scriptural, scrupulous, worshipful

relinquish

4 cede, quit, shed **5** forgo, leave, waive, yield **6** desert, give up, resign

7 abandon, discard, lay down, release **8** abdicate, hand over, renounce **9** quitclaim, sacrifice, surrender

relish

4 like, tang, zest **5** enjoy, fancy, flair, gusto, savor, taste **6** flavor, liking, palate **7** delight **8** fondness, penchant, pleasure, sapidity **9** appetizer, condiment, enjoyment **10** appreciate **11** delectation, hors d'oeuvre

relucent

6 bright **7** glaring, radiant, shining **10** reflecting

reluctant

3 shy **4** wary **5** chary, loath **6** afraid, averse **8** cautious, grudging, hesitant **9** unwilling **10** indisposed **11** disinclined
prophet: 5 Jonah

rely

3 bet **4** bank, plan **5** count **6** depend, gamble, reckon

rely on

5 trust **6** expect **10** anticipate

remain

4 bide, last, live, stay, wait **5** abide, tarry **6** endure, linger, loiter **7** persist, survive **8** continue **10** hang around **11** stick around

remainder

4 rest **5** dregs, trace **6** excess **7** balance, residue, remnant, surplus, vestige **8** leavings, leftover, residual, residuum

remains

4 body **5** ashes, bones, ruins **6** corpse, debris, relics **7** balance, cadaver, carcass, flotsam **8** leavings, remnants **9** reliquiae

remand

8 send back

remark

4 gibe, note **5** aside, crack **7** comment, mention **9** utterance, wisecrack, witticism **10** annotation **11** observation **12** obiter dictum

remarkable
4 rare 5 great 6 signal, unique 7 salient, strange, unusual 8 singular, striking, uncommon 9 arresting, bodacious, momentous, prominent 10 impressive, noteworthy, noticeable 11 conspicuous, exceptional, outstanding, significant 13 extraordinary

—— **Remarque**
5 Erich (Maria)

remedial
8 curative, salutary, sanative 9 medicinal 10 corrective 11 restorative, therapeutic 12 recuperative

remedy
3 fix 4 cure, drug, heal 5 salve, solve 6 elixir, relief, repair 7 correct, cure-all, nostrum, panacea, rectify, redress, relieve 8 antidote, medicine, specific 9 alleviate, treatment 10 corrective, medicament, medication

remember
5 educe, evoke 6 recall, record, relive, retain, reward 7 bethink 9 flash back, recollect, reminisce 10 bear in mind 11 commemorate, memorialize

remembrance
4 gift 5 favor, relic, token 6 memory, recall, trophy 7 memento, present, thought 8 keepsake, memorial, reminder, souvenir 9 anamnesis, flashback 12 recollection, reminiscence

remind
6 advise, prompt 7 bethink 8 admonish

reminder
4 hint, memo 5 relic, token 6 prompt, trophy 7 memento 8 keepsake, memorial, monument, souvenir 9 refresher 10 admonition, memorandum 11 remembrance

reminisce
see **remember**

reminiscence
6 memory, recall 8 anecdote 9 anamnesis, flashback 11 remembrance 12 recollection

remise
4 cede, deed 5 alien, grant 6 assign, convey 8 make over, transfer 9 quitclaim

remiss
3 lax 4 lazy 5 slack 8 careless, derelict, heedless, indolent, slothful 9 negligent 10 delinquent, neglectful, slatternly 11 inattentive

remit
4 send, ship, stay, stop 5 abate, defer, delay, relax 6 desist, hold up, pardon, put off, remand, shelve 7 condone, consign, forgive, forward, hold off 8 dispatch, moderate, postpone

remnant
3 end 4 heel, husk, part, rest, rump 5 relic, trace, wrack 6 fag end, relict 7 balance, oddment, residue 8 leavings, leftover, residuum 9 remainder

remodel
4 redo 6 recast, revamp 8 make over, overhaul, redesign 9 refashion 11 reconstruct

remonstrance
5 demur 7 protest 8 demurral, demurrer 9 challenge, objection

remonstrate
5 argue, demur, plead 6 combat, object, oppose, reason 7 protest 9 challenge

remora
4 clog, drag 6 sucker 9 hindrance 10 impediment 11 encumbrance, shark sucker

remorse
3 rue 4 ruth 5 guilt, smart 6 regret, sorrow 9 penitence 10 contrition, repentance 11 compunction 12 self-reproach

remorseful
see **regretful**

remote

3 far, off 4 slim 5 aloof 6 far-off, slight 7 distant, faraway, obscure, outside, slender 8 detached, far-flung, frontier, isolated, lonesome, off-lying, outlying, secluded 9 backwoods, withdrawn 10 negligible 11 godforsaken, out-of-the-way

combining form: 3 tel 4 tele

remotest

6 utmost 7 extreme, outmost 8 farthest 9 outermost, uttermost 11 furthermost

remove

4 doff, skim 5 purge 6 unseat 7 extract, take off, take out 8 dislodge, evacuate, take away, withdraw 9 clear away, eliminate

from office: 6 depose

hair: 8 depilate

surgically: 6 resect

removed

5 aloof, apart 6 far-off, remote 7 devious, distant, faraway, obscure 8 detached, far-flung, isolated, outlying, separate 10 distracted 11 unconnected

remunerate

3 pay 5 repay 7 requite 9 indemnify, reimburse 10 compensate, recompense

remunerative

6 paying 7 gainful, payable 9 lucrative 10 productive, profitable 11 moneymaking

Remus

brother: 7 Romulus

father: 4 Mars

mother: 9 Rea Silvia 10 Rhea Silvia

slayer: 7 Romulus

renaissance

see rebirth

renal

7 nephric 9 nephritic

rend

3 rip 4 rive, tear 5 split 6 cleave, divide

render

3 pay 4 cede, limn 5 yield 6 depict, give up, impart, return, submit 7 deliver, execute, pay back, picture, portray, provide, restore 8 carry out, describe, hand over, turn over 9 delineate, interpret, represent, translate, transpose 10 administer, relinquish 12 administrate

rendering

4 copy 7 version 9 depiction 10 paraphrase 11 description, performance, restatement, translation 12 reproduction

rendezvous

4 date 5 haunt, tryst 6 gather, muster 7 collect, hangout, meeting 8 assemble 10 congregate, engagement 11 appointment, assignation, get-together

rendition

7 reading, version 10 adaptation 11 performance, translation

renegade

3 rat 5 rebel 6 outlaw 7 heretic 8 apostate, defector, deserter, maverick, recreant, turncoat 9 turnabout 10 schismatic

renege

4 deny 5 welsh 6 cry off, recall, recant, revoke 7 back off, back out, retract 8 renounce, withdraw 9 backpedal

renew

6 redeem, reform, revamp, revive 7 freshen, refresh, remodel 8 make over, overhaul, recharge, recreate, rekindle, renovate, revivify 9 refurbish, resurrect 10 reactivate, recommence, regenerate, rejuvenate, revitalize

rennet

8 abomasum

renounce

4 deny, quit 5 demit 6 abjure, defect, desert, give up, recant, renege, resign 7 abandon, decline,

forsake, put away, retract **8** abdicate, abnegate, disclaim, forswear, swear off **9** repudiate, sacrifice **10** apostatize

renovate
4 redo **5** renew **6** remake, repair, revamp, revive **7** furbish, refresh, restore **8** overhaul, revivify **9** modernize, refurbish, resurrect **10** rejuvenate, revitalize **12** rehabilitate

renown
4 fame **5** éclat, glory, kudos **6** repute **7** acclaim **8** eminence, prestige **9** celebrity, notoriety **10** prominence, reputation **11** distinction

renowned
5 famed, great, noted **6** fabled, famous **7** eminent, notable **8** extolled **9** acclaimed, legendary, notorious, prominent, well-known **10** celebrated **11** illustrious, outstanding **13** distinguished

rent
3 let, rip **4** hire, rift, tear, torn **5** lease, split **6** breach, sublet **7** charter, fissure, rupture **8** fracture

rental
4 hire **7** tenancy

renter
6 lessee, tenant **11** leaseholder

renunciation
6 denial **7** refusal **8** apostasy, eschewal, forgoing **9** disavowal, sacrifice, surrender **10** abdication, abnegation, disclaimer, self-denial **11** abandonment, forswearing, repudiation, resignation

reorder
5 shift **7** permute **9** rearrange, reshuffle

reorganization
7 shake-up **8** turnover

repair
3 fix **4** mend **5** patch **6** cobble, doctor **7** fitness, service **8** overhaul **9** condition **11** recondition

reparations
6 amends **7** redress **9** indemnity, quittance **10** recompense, settlement **11** restitution **12** satisfaction

repartee
4 quip **6** banter, retort **7** riposte **8** backchat, badinage, comeback **9** cross talk, rejoinder **10** persiflage

repast
3 eat **4** feed, meal **5** feast **9** refection

repay
6 offset, return, reward **7** requite **9** indemnify, reimburse **10** compensate, recompense, remunerate **11** get even with

repeal
4 lift, void **5** annul **6** recall, revoke **7** abandon, abolish, nullify, rescind, reverse **8** abrogate, renounce

repeat
4 copy, echo **5** recap, recur, rerun, resay **6** go over, parrot, reecho, recite, rehash, relate, retell **7** imitate, iterate, reprise, restate **9** duplicate, reiterate, replicate **11** reduplicate **12** recapitulate

repeater
7 firearm **10** recidivist

repeating
7 iterant **9** perennial, recurrent **11** reiterative, repetitious

repel
5 rebut **6** rebuff, reject, revolt, sicken **7** disgust, fend off, hold off, repulse, ward off **8** nauseate, stave off

repellent
4 foul, vile **5** nasty **7** noisome **8** aversive **9** abhorrent, loathsome, obnoxious, offensive, repulsive, revolting **10** forbidding, disgusting, off-putting **11** rebarbative

repent
3 rue **6** regret

repentance
3 rue **4** ruth **6** sorrow **7** remorse **10** contrition **11** compunction

repentant

repentant
see **regretful**

repetition
4 copy, echo 5 rerun 7 recital, reprise 11 duplication

rephrase
6 recast, reword 7 restate

repine
4 beef, fuss, kick, long, moan, wail 5 gripe, yearn 6 grouse, hanker, murmur 7 grumble 8 complain

replace
7 put back, restore 8 exchange, supplant 9 supersede 10 substitute

replacement
3 sub 6 fill-in, makeup 7 stand-in 9 alternate, surrogate, temporary 10 substitute 11 locum tenens, pinch hitter, succedaneum

replenish
4 fill 5 renew, stock 6 refill 7 refresh, restore

replete
4 full, rife 5 awash, lousy 7 brimful, crammed, stuffed 8 brimming 9 chock-full 11 overflowing

replica
4 copy, dupe, fake 5 clone, ditto 6 carbon 9 duplicate, facsimile, imitation 10 carbon copy, simulacrum 12 reproduction

replicate
4 copy 5 clone 6 repeat 9 reproduce

reply
4 echo 6 answer, rejoin, retort 7 respond 8 comeback, repartee, response 9 rejoinder

report
4 bang, boom, news, tell 5 crack, relay, rumor, study 6 record, relate, return, review, show up 7 account, article, check in, hearsay, narrate, recount, rundown 8 advisory, bulletin, describe, dispatch 9 broadcast, chronicle, narrative, statement 11 compte rendu

reporter
7 newsman 8 pressman 9 newshound, newswoman 10 journalist
Inexperienced: 3 cub

repose
3 lie 4 calm, rest 5 peace, poise, quiet, sleep 7 lie down, recline 8 quietude 9 composure, stillness 10 inactivity, quiescence, relaxation 11 restfulness, tranquility 12 tranquility

repository
3 ark 5 depot, store 7 archive, arsenal 8 magazine, treasury 10 storehouse

repossess
see **regain**

reprehend
3 rap 4 rate, skin 5 blame, chide, fault, knock, scold 6 berate, rebuke 7 censure, condemn, upbraid 8 admonish, denounce 9 criticize 10 denunciate

reprehensible
4 base, evil 6 guilty, sinful, unholy, wicked 8 blamable, criminal, culpable 10 censurable 11 blameworthy, disgraceful

represent
3 act 6 denote, depict, embody, mirror, recall, relate, render, sketch, typify 7 display, exhibit, express, hold out, imitate, make out, narrate, outline, picture, portray, present, protest, realize, signify, suggest 8 describe, stand for 9 delineate, epitomize, exemplify, interpret, personify, symbolize 10 constitute, illustrate, substitute 11 emblematize, impersonate

representation
5 draft, image 6 effigy, symbol 7 picture 8 likeness 9 portrayal, statement 10 caricature, delegation

representative
5 agent, envoy, model, proxy 6 deputy, sample 7 burgess, example, typical 8 delegate, emissary, sampling, specimen 9 exemplary,

spokesman **10** ambassador, legislator, prototypal, substitute **11** congressman **12** illustrative, prototypical **13** congresswoman

repress
4 curb **5** check, sit on **6** bridle, muffle, stifle, subdue **7** smother, squelch, swallow **8** keep down, restrain, suppress

repression
4 curb **7** amnesia, control **8** stifling **9** clampdown, crackdown, restraint **10** constraint

reprieve
4 stay **5** grace **7** respite, suspend

reprimand
3 rap **4** rate, ream, task **5** chide, scold **6** rebuke **7** bawl out, censure, chew out, reproof, reprove **8** admonish, call down, reproach, scolding **9** reprimand, talking-to **10** admonition **12** admonishment, dressing-down **13** tongue-lashing

reprisal
7 redress, revenge **8** revanche **9** vengeance **11** counterblow, retaliation, retribution

reprise
5 recap **6** repeat **9** reiterate **10** recurrence, repetition

reproach
3 rap **4** rail **5** blame, chide, scold **6** berate, rebuke **7** bawl out, censure, chew out, remorse, reprove, upbraid **8** admonish, call down **9** reprimand **10** admonition, opprobrium **12** admonishment

reprobate
3 rap **4** skin **5** blame, scamp, spurn **6** refuse, reject, sinner **7** censure, condemn, lowlife, villain **8** denounce, scalawag **9** miscreant, scoundrel **10** blackguard, degenerate

reproduce
4 bear, copy **5** beget, breed, spore **7** imitate **8** multiply **9** duplicate, procreate, propagate, replicate **10** regenerate **11** reduplicate

reproduction
see **replica**

reproductive cell
3 egg **4** ovum **5** sperm, spore **6** gamete **12** spermatozoid, spermatozoon

reproof
3 rap **6** rebuke **7** censure, lecture **8** scolding **9** criticism, reprimand **10** admonition **11** castigation **12** admonishment, reprehension **13** remonstration

reprove
5 chide, scold **6** rebuke **7** censure, chasten **8** admonish, call down, lambaste, reproach **9** criticize, dress down, reprimand

reptile
5 snake **6** caiman, cayman, gavial, iguana, lizard, turtle **7** tuatara **8** tortoise **9** alligator, crocodile, sphenodon
combining form: 6 herpet **7** herpeto
extinct: 8 dinosaur

republic
5 state **6** nation **9** democracy

Republican Party
3 GOP
mascot: 8 elephant

Republic author
5 Plato

repudiate
4 deny **5** spurn **6** abjure, disown, recant, refuse, reject **7** decline, disavow, dismiss **8** disclaim, renounce **9** disaffirm **10** apostatize, disapprove

repugnance
6 horror **7** disgust **8** aversion, loathing **9** repulsion, revulsion **10** abhorrence, antagonism, odiousness **11** abomination, detestation

repugnant
4 foul, vile **5** nasty, yucky **6** creepy, horrid, skanky **7** noisome **8** aversive, gruesome **9** abhorrent, loathsome, obnoxious, offensive, repulsive, revolting **10** disgusting

repulse
5 rebut, repel, spurn 6 rebuff, reject, revolt, sicken 7 disgust, fend off, hold off, ward off 8 nauseate, stave off

repulsion
see repugnance

repulsive
see repugnant

reputable
7 eminent, upright 8 esteemed 9 estimable, honorable 10 creditable, legitimate, recognized, sanctioned 11 respectable, trustworthy 13 well-thought-of

reputation
4 fame, name, note 5 éclat, honor 6 esteem, renown, report 8 position, prestige, standing 9 celebrity, character, notoriety

reputed
6 honest 7 alleged 8 putative, supposed 9 estimable, purported 10 creditable, ostensible 11 respectable 12 hypothetical

request
3 ask, dun, sue 4 pray, seek 5 plead, press 6 appeal, demand, invite 7 entreat, solicit 8 entreaty, petition 10 invitation

Requiem for a Nun author
8 Faulkner (William)

require
3 ask, beg 4 lack, need, want 5 claim, crave 6 demand, desire 7 call for, dictate, mandate, solicit 11 necessitate

required
3 due 5 vital 7 crucial 9 essential, mandatory, necessary, requisite 10 compulsory, obligatory 11 fundamental

requirement
4 must, need, want 5 claim 6 charge, demand 9 condition, essential, necessity, requisite 10 imperative, sine qua non 11 stipulation

requisite
3 due 4 must 5 vital 7 crucial, needful 8 cardinal 9 condition, essential, necessity, sine qua non 10 imperative, sine qua non 11 fundamental 12 precondition 13 indispensable

requisition
4 call 5 claim, exact 6 demand 7 solicit 11 application

requite
3 pay 5 repay 6 return 7 revenge, satisfy 9 indemnify, reimburse 10 compensate, recompense, remunerate 11 reciprocate

reredos
6 screen 9 partition

rescind
4 lift 5 annul 6 cancel, recall, repeal, revoke 7 retract, reverse 8 roll back, take back

rescue
4 free, save 6 ransom, redeem 7 bailout, deliver, reclaim, recover, release, salvage 8 liberate, preserve 9 extricate 11 deliverance

rescuer
6 savior 7 saviour

research
5 probe, study 7 inquest, inquiry 8 look into 9 delve into 10 experiment 11 examination, inquisition, investigate 13 investigation

resect
6 cut out, excise 8 amputate 9 extirpate

resemblance
7 analogy 8 likeness 9 alikeness 10 comparison, similarity, similitude 11 parallelism

resemble
5 favor 6 recall 8 look like, simulate 9 take after 11 approximate

resembling
4 like 6 akin to

resentful
4 sore 6 bitter, piqued, sullen 7 envious

resentment
 5 pique 6 animus, grudge, malice, rancor 7 dudgeon, offense, umbrage 9 animosity 11 indignation

reservation
 5 doubt 7 booking, proviso 8 homeland, preserve 9 condition, misgiving, sanctuary 10 limitation

reserve
 4 book, fund, hold, keep 5 hoard, put by, stash, stock, store, tract 6 retain, supply 7 nest egg, savings, standby 8 contract, distance, fallback, hold back, postpone, set aside, squirrel, withhold 9 inventory, restraint, reticence, stockpile 10 constraint, discretion, diffidence 13 qualification

reserved
 4 cool 5 aloof, stiff 6 demure, formal, remote 7 distant 8 reticent, retiring, taciturn 9 diffident, reclusive, secretive, withdrawn 10 unsociable 11 tight-lipped 12 closemouthed 13 self-contained

reservoir
 5 hoard, stock, store 6 supply 7 nest egg 9 inventory, stockpile

reside
 3 lie 4 live, stay 5 dwell, exist 6 inhere 7 consist

residence
 4 home, stay 5 abode, house 7 address 8 domicile, dwelling 9 occupancy 10 habitation

resident
 5 liver 6 inmate, lodger, native, tenant 7 citizen, denizen, dweller, present 8 inherent, occupant 10 inhabitant 11 householder

residential area
 9 community 12 neighborhood

residual
 7 balance, payment, remnant 8 leavings, leftover 9 remainder

residue
 3 ash 4 heel, lees, rest, silt, slag 5 ashes, dregs, grout 6 debris, excess, scraps 7 balance, grounds, remains, remnant, surplus 8 leavings, remnants, residuum 9 leftovers, remainder, scourings

resign
 4 cede, quit 5 demit, leave, yield 6 give up, retire, submit 7 abandon, consign 8 abdicate, hand over, relegate, renounce, step down 9 reconcile, surrender 10 relinquish

resignation
 8 meekness 9 demission, surrender 10 abdication, compliance, submission 12 acquiescence, renunciation

resigned
 9 compliant 10 submissive 11 acquiescent, complaisant

resile
 6 recede, recoil, spring 7 rebound, retract, retreat 8 draw back, snap back

resilient
 6 bouncy, supple, whippy 7 buoyant, elastic, springy 8 flexible, stretchy 9 adaptable

resin
 4 balm 5 copal, damar, roset 6 dammar 7 acrylic, copaiba
 aromatic: 6 balsam, mastic 8 sandarac
 fragrant: 5 elemi 6 storax, styrax 7 ladanum 8 labdanum
 gum: 5 myrrh 7 benzoin
 medicinal: 6 guaiac 8 guaiacum
 of an insect: 3 lac
 synthetic: 8 phenolic
 used by bees: 8 propolis

resist
 4 buck, defy, kick 5 rebel 6 baffle, combat, oppose, revolt 7 contest, counter, gainsay 8 traverse 10 contradict, contravene

resistance
 7 dissent 8 defiance, variance 10 dissension, dissidence, opposition 11 contrariety, obstruction

resistance unit
3 ohm

resistor
8 rheostat, varistor 10 thermistor

resolute
3 set 4 bent, bold, fast, firm, true
6 intent, steady, sturdy 7 decided,
staunch 8 constant, decisive, faithful, intrepid, stubborn 9 obstinate,
steadfast, tenacious, undaunted
10 determined, persistent 12 pertinacious, single-minded

resolution
4 guts 5 heart, nerve, pluck, spunk
6 mettle, spirit 7 courage, outcome 8 decision, firmness, tenacity
10 conclusion 12 perseverance
13 determination, steadfastness

resolve
5 clear, crack 6 decide, settle
7 clear up, iron out, unravel, work
out 8 boldness, conclude, decipher,
firmness 9 breakdown, determine,
intention, reconcile 10 unscramble
13 determination, steadfastness

resonant
4 deep, full, rich 6 silver 7 booming,
echoing, orotund, vibrant 8 powerful,
sonorous 11 reverberant

resonate
4 echo, peal, ring 7 resound, vibrate
11 reverberate

resort
3 spa 5 haven, hotel, lodge, shift
6 harbor, refuge 7 retreat, riviera,
stopgap 8 recourse 9 expedient,
makeshift 10 substitute

resound
4 boom, echo, peal, ring 11 reverberate

resounding
7 booming, echoing, orotund, vibrant
8 emphatic, sonorous 10 clangorous, resonating, thunderous 11 unequivocal

resource
3 aid 5 asset, means, shift 6 supply
7 standby

resourceful
5 adept 6 adroit, artful, clever,
shrewd 7 capable, cunning 8 creative, skillful 9 ingenious, inventive
10 innovative 11 imaginative 12 enterprising

resources
5 funds, means, purse 6 assets,
riches, wealth 7 capital, fortune,
reserve 8 bankroll, finances,
property, reserves 9 substance
11 wherewithal

respect
3 awe 5 favor, honor, props 6 admire, detail, devoir, esteem, homage,
regard, revere 7 account, concern
8 venerate 9 deference 10 admiration, estimation, particular, veneration

respectable
4 fair 5 ample 6 decent, proper,
worthy 8 adequate 9 admirable,
estimable, honorable 10 sufficient
11 appropriate, presentable 12 satisfactory 13 well-thought-of

respectful
5 civil 6 polite 8 obeisant, reverent
9 courteous 11 deferential, reveren-
tial

respecting
3 per 4 as to, in re 5 about 7 apropos 9 as regards, regarding 10 as
concerns, concerning, relating to
11 considering

respire
7 breathe

respite
4 lull, rest 5 break, delay, pause,
spell, truce 6 hiatus, recess, relief
8 breather, reprieve, surcease
12 intermission

resplendent
5 regal 7 glowing, shining 8 glorious, gorgeous 9 brilliant, refulgent
11 magnificent

respond
5 react, reply 6 answer, rejoin, retort
8 come back

response

5 reply 6 answer, retort, return
7 riposte 8 antiphon, comeback,
reaction 9 rejoinder
involuntary: 6 reflex 7 tropism

responsibility

4 buck, duty, onus 5 blame, brief,
fault 6 burden, charge, devoir
10 obligation 11 reliability

responsible

6 liable 8 amenable, reliable 10 answerable, chargeable, dependable
11 accountable, trustworthy

responsive

4 open 8 sentient 9 sensitive
11 susceptible, sympathetic

rest

3 sit 4 calm, ease, loaf, loll, lull, stay
5 let up, pause, peace, quiet, relax,
spell 6 depend, excess, lounge,
repose 7 balance, leisure, lie down,
recline, remains, remnant, surplus
8 breather, leavings, vacation 9 interlude, predicate, remainder

restate

4 echo 6 reword 8 rephrase 9 translate 10 paraphrase 12 recapitulate

restatement

10 paraphrase 11 translation

restaurant

4 café 5 diner 6 eatery 7 beanery
9 brasserie, cafeteria 10 coffee shop
11 coffeehouse, greasy spoon
price: 8 à la carte, prix fixe 10 table
d'hôte
worker: 4 chef, cook 6 busboy,
server, waiter 7 maître d', waitron
8 waitress 10 dishwasher, head-
waiter, waitperson 12 maître d'hôtel

_____ Restaurant

6 Alice's

restful

4 calm 5 quiet 6 placid 8 peaceful,
tranquil

restitute

6 refund, return 7 reclaim, recover,
restore 8 give back 11 recondition,
reconstruct 12 rehabilitate

restitution

6 amends, refund, return 7 redress
8 reprisal 9 indemnity, quittance
10 recompense, reparation 11 restoration 12 remuneration, satisfaction

restive

4 edgy 5 balky, nervy, tense 6 ornery,
uneasy 7 fidgety, froward, uptight,
wayward 8 contrary, perverse,
skittish

restiveness

7 anxiety, ferment, turmoil 8 disquiet
9 balkiness 10 inquietude, perversity
11 contrariety, disquietude, wayward-
ness 12 contrariness

restless

5 antsy, itchy, jumpy 6 fitful, uneasy
7 anxious, fidgety, fretful, jittery,
nervous, unquiet 8 agitated, troubled
9 disturbed, perturbed, unsettled
12 discontented, dissatisfied

restorative

4 balm 5 tonic 7 healing 8 curative,
remedial, sanative 12 recuperative

restore

4 cure, heal, mend 5 amend, remit,
renew, right 6 recall, recoup, reform,
remedy, render, repair, return, revive
7 get back, improve, reclaim, recover, rectify, refresh, replace 8 give
back, recreate, renovate, revivify
9 refurbish, reinstate, replenish,
restitute 10 regenerate, rejuvenate
11 recondition, reestablish 12 rehabilitate

restrain

3 bit, gag 4 curb, rein 5 check,
leash 6 arrest, bridle, halter, hamper,
hinder, hold in, impede, muzzle,
temper 7 collect, control, harness,
inhibit, repress 8 hold back, hold
down, moderate, suppress
trade: 7 embargo

restrained

4 cool 6 low-key 5 canny, quiet
6 modest 7 subdued 8 discreet,
reserved, reticent, retiring, tasteful
9 contained, inhibited, temperate
10 controlled, reasonable

restraint

6 bridle 7 durance, embargo, reserve 8 estoppel, pullback 9 hindrance 10 deterrence, inhibition, limitation, moderation 11 confinement, forbearance 12 straitjacket

restrict

3 bar, tie 4 bind, curb 5 hem in, limit 6 hamper, hobble, impede, narrow, shrink 7 confine, curtail, delimit, inhibit, trammel 8 hold back, prelimit 10 delimitate 12 circumscribe
a will: 6 entail

restriction

4 curb 5 check, limit, stint 7 control 9 restraint 10 constraint, limitation, regulation 11 confinement, prohibition 12 proscription 13 qualification

restyle

4 redo 6 revamp, revise, rework 8 make over

result

3 end 4 flow, stem 5 close, ensue, fruit, issue 6 effect, emerge, finish, follow, payoff, sequel, upshot 7 outcome, product 8 sequence, solution 9 aftermath, come about, eventuate 10 conclusion, denouement, production 11 aftereffect, consequence, eventuality
incidental: 7 spinoff

resume

4 go on 5 renew 6 pick up, reopen 7 carry on, proceed, restart 8 continue 10 recommence

résumé

4 vita 5 sum-up 7 summary 9 summation, summing-up

resurgence

5 rally 7 rebirth, revival 8 comeback, recovery 10 renascence 11 renaissance 12 risorgimento

resurrect

5 raise, renew 6 come to, revive 8 retrieve, revivify 10 reactivate

resurrection

7 rebirth, revival 10 renascence 11 renaissance 12 risorgimento

resuscitate

see **resurrect**

retail

4 sell, tell, vend 6 market 7 narrate 11 merchandise

retailer

6 dealer, seller, trader, vendor 8 merchant 9 tradesman 10 shopkeeper 11 storekeeper 12 merchandiser

retain

3 own 4 hire, hold, keep 6 detain 7 reserve 8 hold over, preserve, remember, withhold

retainer

3 fee 6 lackey, menial, minion, yeoman 7 deposit, servant 8 bite plate, dependent, pensioner

retaliate

7 get back, get even

retaliation

see **reprisal**

retaliatory

8 punitive, vengeful 10 vindictive

retard

4 clog, mire, slow 5 delay, stunt 6 detain, fetter, hamper, hang up, hinder, impede, slow up 7 set back, slacken 8 decrease, hold back, restrain 10 decelerate

retarded

3 dim 4 dull, dumb, slow 6 opaque, simple, stupid 8 backward 9 dimwitted 10 half-witted, slow-witted 11 exceptional

retch

3 gag 4 barf, hurl, puke, spew 5 heave, vomit 6 spit up 7 bring up, throw up, upchuck 8 disgorge

retention

6 memory 7 storage

reticent

see **reserved**

reticulate

4 vein 5 veiny 6 meshed, netted 7 netlike 10 crisscross

retinue
4 band, tail 5 suite, train 6 livery
7 company, cortege 9 entourage,
following

retire
4 exit, quit 5 leave, yield 6 bow out,
depart, recede, resign, turn in 7 dismiss, pension 8 step down, withdraw 9 discharge, strike out, terminate 10 relinquish

retired person
7 emerita 8 emeritus 9 pensioner

retiree
9 pensioner 10 golden-ager 13 senior citizen

retirement allowance
3 SEP 7 pension

retiring
3 shy 5 mousy, timid 6 demure,
modest 7 bashful 8 reserved 9 diffident, withdrawn 11 unassertive

retool
7 reequip 10 reengineer

retort
5 reply, sally 6 answer, rejoin
7 counter, respond, riposte 8 comeback, repartee, response 9 rejoinder, retaliate, wisecrack

retouch
5 alter, emend, renew 6 repair
7 correct, enhance, improve, restore

retract
4 deny 5 unsay 6 abjure, recall,
recant, recede, renege, resile, revoke
7 disavow, rescind, retreat, swallow
8 forswear, renounce, take back,
withdraw

retreat
3 den, ebb 4 flee, quit 5 cover,
haven, leave 6 ashram, asylum, bow
out, covert, decamp, depart, escape,
recede, recoil, refuge, shrink, vacate
7 abandon, back off, back out, pull
out, shelter 8 back down, draw
back, evacuate, fall back, hideaway,
withdraw 9 backtrack, climb down,
sanctuary 10 give ground, withdrawal

retrench
3 cut 4 pare 5 slash 6 excise,
lessen, reduce 7 abridge, curtail
9 economize

retribution
6 return, reward 7 deserts, revenge
8 avenging, reprisal, requital, revanche 9 vengeance 10 punishment, recompense 11 counterblow,
retaliation
goddess of: 3 Ate 4 Fury 7 Nemesis

retrieve
5 fetch 6 recall, recoup, redeem,
rescue 7 get back, recover, restore,
salvage 9 resurrect

retro
7 antique, revival, vintage 9 nostalgic 12 old-fashioned

retrograde
4 back 7 inverse, reverse 8 backward, inverted, rearward

retrogress
see revert

retrospect
9 hindsight 12 recollection 13 reexamination

retrospective
6 review 8 backward 10 exhibition,
reflective, ruminative

return
5 recur, repay, reply, yield 6 answer,
rebate, regain, rejoin, render, repeat,
retort, revert 7 bring in, get back,
rebound, recover, reprise, requite,
respond, reverse, riposte 8 comeback, dividend, earnings, give back,
proceeds, reappear, response
9 rejoinder, repayment, reversion
10 recompense, recurrence 11 reciprocate, restitution

Return of the Native
author: 5 Hardy (Thomas)
character: 4 Clym 8 Eustacia

Reuben
brother: 6 Joseph
father: 5 Jacob
mother: 4 Leah

son: **5** Carmi **6** Hanoch, Hezron, Phallu

Réunion
capital: **7** St.-Denis
city: **6** St.-Paul **7** St.-Louis **8** St.-Pierre
department of: **6** France
ethnic group: **6** Creole
former name: **7** Bourbon **9** Bonaparte
island group: **9** Mascarene

revamp
4 redo **5** renew **6** remake, repair, revise, rework **7** remodel, restyle, rewrite **8** make over, overhaul, redesign, renovate **9** refurbish **11** recondition

reveal
4 bare, blab, jamb, leak, open, show, tell **5** admit, let on, peach, spill **6** betray, evince, expose, impart, unmask, unveil **7** confess, declare, display, divulge, exhibit, publish, uncover, undress **8** announce, decipher, disclose, discover, give away, unclothe **9** broadcast **11** acknowledge, communicate **12** bring to light

revel
4 bask, orgy, riot **5** binge, feast, party, spree **6** boogie, frolic, gaiety, hoopla, wallow **7** carouse, delight, indulge, jollity, roister, rollick, wassail, whoopla **8** carnival, carousal, festival **9** bacchanal, celebrate, festivity, luxuriate, merriment, whoop-de-do **11** bacchanalia, celebration, merrymaking

revelation
6 kicker **8** epiphany, giveaway, prophecy, surprise **9** discovery **10** apocalypse, disclosure **13** manifestation

reveler
7 orgiast **8** bacchant, carouser **9** bacchante, wassailer **10** merrymaker

revelry
4 orgy, riot **6** gaiety **7** carouse,

jollity, wassail, whoopee, whoopla **8** carousal, partying **9** festivity, high jinks, merriment, whoop-de-do **10** whoop-de-doo **11** merrymaking

revenant
5 ghost, haunt, shade, spook **6** shadow, spirit, wraith, zombie **7** phantom, specter, spectre **8** phantasm, prodigal, visitant **10** apparition

revenge
5 right **6** defend **7** get back, get even, redress, requite **8** reprisal, requital, revanche **9** retaliate, vindicate **11** retaliation, retribution

revenue
4 rent **5** gains, issue, yield **6** income, profit, return **7** comings **8** earnings, interest, proceeds, receipts, taxation

reverberant
6 hollow **7** booming, echoing **8** resonant **10** resounding

reverberate
4 echo, ring **6** reecho **7** resound

revere
4 laud **5** adore, exalt, extol, honor, prize, value **6** admire, esteem, regard **7** cherish, magnify, respect, worship **8** treasure, venerate **10** appreciate

revered
9 venerable

reverence
3 awe **5** adore, dread, honor, piety **6** esteem, fealty, homage **7** loyalty, respect, worship **8** devotion, venerate **9** deference, obeisance, solemnity **10** veneration
gesture of: **3** bow **6** kowtow **8** kneeling **12** genuflection

reverend
4 abbé, holy **5** clerk, vicar **6** clergy, cleric, deacon, divine, parson, rector **8** chaplain, clerical, minister, preacher **9** churchman, clergyman **11** clergywoman **12** ecclesiastic

reverent
5 godly 6 devout 7 dutiful 9 prayerful 10 God-fearing, respectful, worshipful

reverie
4 muse 5 dream 6 trance, vision 7 fantasy 8 daydream 10 absorption, brown study, meditation 11 abstraction 13 woolgathering

reversal
4 turn 5 U-turn 6 double, switch 7 setback, undoing 8 backfire, flip-flop 9 about-face, inversion, turnabout, volte-face 10 switcheroo 12 solarization 13 change of heart

reverse
4 lift 6 change, contra, defeat, invert, recall, repeal, revoke 7 capsize, counter, rescind, setback 8 antipode, backward, contrary, disaster, exchange, opposite, overrule, overturn 9 about-face, backwards, diametric, overthrow, transpose, turnabout, volte-face 10 antithesis, misfortune

reversion
4 turn 5 lapse 6 return 7 atavism, escheat 9 about-face, throwback, turnabout, volte-face 10 regression, succession

revert
4 turn 6 return 7 decline, devolve, escheat, inverse, regress 8 turn back 9 backslide 10 degenerate, retrograde, retrogress

revetment
6 bunker, riprap 9 barricade, earthwork 10 embankment

review
4 scan 5 audit, recap, study 6 assess, go over, parade, report, revise, survey 7 analyze, journal, rethink 8 analysis, critique, magazine, revision, scrutiny, talk over 9 criticism, reexamine, refresher 10 evaluation, inspection, periodical, reconsider, reevaluate 11 examination 13 reexamination, retrospective

revile
4 rail, rate 5 abuse, scold 6 attack, berate, defame, malign, vilify 7 asperse, bawl out, chew out, upbraid 8 belittle, disgrace, execrate 9 blaspheme 10 tongue-lash, vituperate

revise
4 edit 5 alter, amend, emend, proof, renew 6 change, polish, redraw, reform, retool, revamp, rework 7 correct, improve, redraft, restore, restyle, rewrite 8 overhaul, redesign, work over 9 red-pencil 10 blue-pencil

revision
6 change, revamp, update 7 redraft 8 facelift, overhaul, updating 10 alteration, correction, emendation 11 overhauling 12 modification

revitalize
see revive

revival
7 rebirth, renewal 8 comeback 10 renascence, resurgence 11 reanimation, renaissance, restoration 12 regeneration, rejuvenation, resurrection, risorgimento 13 recrudescence, resuscitation

revive
4 wake 5 rally, renew, rouse 6 arouse, awaken, come to, recall 7 bring to, enliven, freshen, quicken, refresh, restore 8 reawaken, rekindle, renovate, retrieve 9 reanimate, resurrect 10 reactivate, recuperate, regenerate, rejuvenate 11 bring around, reintroduce, resuscitate 12 reinvigorate

revoke
4 lift, void 5 annul, erase 6 abjure, cancel, recall, recant, renege, repeal 7 abolish, nullify, rescind, retract, reverse 8 abrogate, call back 10 invalidate 11 countermand

revolt
4 riot 5 rebel, repel, shock 6 mutiny, resist, sicken 7 disgust, repulse 8 nauseate, outbreak, uprising

revolter

9 jacquerie, rebellion 10 insurgence, insurgency 12 insurrection

revolter

5 rebel 6 anarch 8 frondeur, mutineer 9 anarchist, insurgent 10 malcontent

revolting

4 foul, ugly, vile 5 nasty 6 horrid 7 hideous, noisome, obscene 8 shocking 9 atrocious, loathsome, repellent, repugnant, repulsive 10 disgusting, nauseating

revolution

4 gyre, reel, riot, roll, spin, turn 5 cycle, orbit, twirl, wheel, whirl 6 mutiny 7 circuit 8 gyration, rotation, uprising 9 pirouette, rebellion 10 barrel roll, changeover, somersault 12 insurrection

revolutionary

5 rebel, ultra 7 extreme, radical 8 mutineer, rotating, ultraist 9 extremist, insurgent
American: 4 Reed (John) 5 Shays (Daniel)
French: 5 Marat (Jean-Paul) 6 Danton (Georges) 8 Mirabeau (Comte de) 9 Saint-Just (Louis) 11 Robespierre (Maximilien)
Irish: 4 Tone (Wolfe) 6 Pearse (Padraig, Patrick) 7 Collins (Michael), Parnell (Charles Stewart) 8 Casement (Roger), de Valera (Eamon), Griffith (Arthur), O'Connell (Daniel)
Mexican: 5 Villa (Pancho) 6 Zapata (Emiliano) 7 Hidalgo (Padre Miguel)
Russian: 5 Kirov (Sergey), Lenin (Vladimir Ilyich) 7 Trotsky (Leon) 8 Kerensky (Aleksandr) 9 Kropotkin (Pyotr)

revolutionize

9 transform 11 transfigure

revolve

4 spin, turn 5 twirl, wheel, whirl 6 circle, gyrate, rotate

revolver

3 gun, rod 4 Colt 5 Glock, Luger, Ruger 6 Magnum, pistol, six-gun 7 firearm, handgun, shooter, sidearm 10 six-shooter

revue

4 show 9 burlesque 10 production, vaudeville 13 entertainment

revulsion

4 hate 6 hatred, horror 7 disgust 8 aversion, loathing 10 abhorrence, repugnance 11 abomination, detestation

reward

5 bonus, booty, crown, medal, price, prize 6 bounty, carrot, payoff, trophy 7 guerdon, jackpot, premium 8 dividend 10 compensate, honorarium, recompense, remunerate 12 compensation, remuneration

rewarding

7 gainful 8 edifying, fruitful, valuable 9 lucrative 10 beneficial, fulfilling, gratifying, productive, profitable, satisfying, worthwhile 12 advantageous, remunerative

reword

see **restate**

rework

6 revamp, revise 7 restyle, rewrite

Reynard

3 fox

rhadamanthine

3 due 4 just 5 right 6 strict 7 condign, fitting, merited 8 deserved, rigorous, rightful, suitable 9 requisite, stringent 11 appropriate

Rhadamanthus

5 judge
brother: 5 Minos
father: 4 Zeus 7 Jupiter
mother: 6 Europa

rhapsodic

5 lyric 8 ecstatic, effusive 9 emotional, exuberant

rhapsodize

4 gush, rave 5 drool 6 effuse 7 enthuse

Rhea

3 Ops
daughter: 4 Hera, Juno 5 Ceres, Vesta 6 Hestia 7 Demeter

father: 6 Uranus
husband: 6 Cronus, Saturn
mother: 4 Gaea
son: 4 Zeus 5 Hades, Pluto 7 Jupiter, Neptune 8 Poseidon

Rheingold, Das
character: 4 Loki 5 Freya, Wotan 6 Fafner, Fafnir, Fasolt 8 Alberich
composer: 6 Wagner (Richard)

rheostat
8 resistor

rhesus
6 monkey 7 macaque

rhetoric
4 rant 6 speech 7 bombast, fustian, oratory 8 rhapsody 9 elocution, eloquence, verbosity 11 rodomontade, speechcraft
term: 6 aporia, simile 7 litotes 8 metaphor 10 apostrophe, digression 12 alliteration, onomatopoeia

rhetorical
4 glib 5 gassy, grand, tumid, windy 6 florid, fluent, ornate, purple, turgid 7 aureate, flowery, orotund, pompous, stilted 8 eloquent, forensic, inflated, overdone, sonorous 9 bombastic, grandiose, high-flown, overblown, tumescent 10 euphuistic, flamboyant, oratorical 11 declamatory, highfalutin, overwrought, pretentious 12 high-sounding, magniloquent 13 grandiloquent

rhetorician
6 orator, writer 7 speaker
Roman: 10 Quintilian

Rhine River
city: 4 Bonn, Köln 5 Basel, Mainz 7 Coblenz, Cologne, Koblenz 8 Duisburg, Mannheim 9 Rotterdam, Weisbaden 10 Düsseldorf
nymph: 7 Lorelei
tributary: 3 Aar, Ill, Lek 4 Aare, Lahn, Main, Ruhr, Waal

rhizome
4 root 5 tuber

Rhode Island
bay: 12 Narragansett
capital: 10 Providence

city: 7 Newport, Warwick 9 Pawtucket
college, university: 4 RISD 5 Brown
island: 5 Block
nickname: 5 Ocean (State) 11 Little Rhody
river: 8 Pawtuxet
state bird: 14 Rhode Island red
state flower: 6 violet
state tree: 8 red maple

Rhodesia
8 Zimbabwe

rhombus
7 diamond, lozenge 13 parallelogram

rhonchus
5 snore

Rhône River
city: 4 Lyon 5 Arles, Lyons 6 Geneva 7 Avignon
lake: 6 Geneva
mountain range: 4 Jura
tributary: 5 Isère, Saône

rhubarb
3 row 4 flap 5 run-in 6 ruckus, tangle 7 dispute, quarrel, wrangle 8 argument, pieplant 11 altercation, controversy

rhyme
4 poem, song 5 agree, ditty, verse 6 accord, jingle, poetry 7 conform 8 dovetail 9 harmonize 10 coordinate, correspond

rhymer
4 bard, poet 5 odist 7 metrist 9 poetaster, rhymester, sonneteer, versifier

rhythm
4 beat, flow, lilt, time 5 meter, pulse, swing 6 accent, groove 7 cadence, measure, pattern 8 sequence

rhythmic
7 pulsing, regular 8 measured, metrical

rialto
6 market 8 district, exchange 11 marketplace

riant

3 gay **5** jolly, merry **6** blithe, bright, jocund, jovial **7** buoyant, gleeful **8** cheerful, mirthful **10** blithesome

riata

4 rope **5** lasso **6** lariat

rib

3 fun, kid, rag **4** band, bone, dike, fool, jape, jest, joke, josh, purl, razz, stay, wale **5** chaff, costa, ridge, tease **6** banter, costae (plural), lierne, needle

ribald

3 raw **4** blue, racy, rude **5** bawdy, crude, dirty **6** coarse, earthy, filthy, purple, risqué, smutty, vulgar **7** obscene, profane, raunchy **8** indecent, off-color **9** offensive, reprobate **10** suggestive

ribbon

3 bow **4** band, tape **5** braid, shred, strip **6** cordon, fillet, stripe, tatter **7** bandeau

rice

7 arborio, risotto
dish: 5 pilaf **6** congee **7** risotto **9** jambalaya
drink: 4 sake, saki **5** mirin **6** arrack
field: 5 paddy
husk: 5 lemma

rich

4 dear, lush, oily, posh **5** ample, fatty, flush, grand, heavy, plush, swank, vivid **6** costly, creamy, deluxe, fecund, gilded, lavish, loaded, monied, ornate, potent, rococo **7** baroque, copious, elegant, fertile, filling, moneyed, opulent, orotund, profuse, wealthy, well-off **8** abundant, affluent, eloquent, fruitful, palatial, well-to-do **9** abounding, bountiful, elaborate, luxuriant, luxurious, plentiful, sumptuous, well-fixed **10** productive, prosperous, well-heeled **11** extravagant
person: 5 Midas, mogul, nabob **6** fat cat **7** Croesus, magnate **9** moneybags, plutocrat

Richardson work

6 Pamela **8** Clarissa

Richelieu's successor

7 Mazarin

riches

4 gold, pelf **5** booty, lucre, worth **6** mammon, wealth **7** fortune **8** opulence, property, treasure **9** resources
demon of: 6 Mammon

rick

4 cock, heap, pile **5** shock, stack

rickety

4 weak **5** shaky **6** wobbly **7** unsound **8** decrepit, insecure, rachitic, unstable, unsteady **10** ramshackle, rattletrap

ricochet

4 ping, skim, skip **5** carom **6** bounce, glance **7** rebound **9** boomerang

rid

6 divest **7** relieve **8** unburden **11** disencumber

riddle

5 rebus **6** enigma, puzzle **7** mystery, perplex, problem **9** conundrum, perforate **10** closed book, puzzlement **11** brainteaser

ride

4 spin, tour, trip **5** drive, jaunt, mount **7** journey **8** carousel **9** excursion

ride out

6 endure **7** outlast, survive, weather **9** withstand

rider

6 clause, cowboy, jockey **7** codicil **8** addendum, addition, appendix, horseman, reinsman **9** amendment **10** equestrian, horsewoman, supplement

ridge

3 rib, top **4** bank, brow, fold, keel, reef, roll, ruck, seam, wave **5** arête, arris, chine, crest, knurl, plica, spine **6** crease, divide, furrow, rimple, saddle, summit **7** annulet, breaker, crinkle, hogback, wrinkle **8** shoulder **9** razorback **11** corrugation
gravelly: 5 esker
on the skin: 4 welt
sharp: 7 hogback

ridicule

3 pan 4 gibe, haze, jape, jeer, mock, razz, ride, twit 5 chaff, flout, mimic, roast, scoff, scout, sneer, squib, taunt 6 deride, satire 7 lampoon, mockery, pillory, sarcasm 8 derision, raillery, satirize, travesty 9 burlesque 10 caricature

god of: 5 Momus
object of: 4 butt 13 laughingstock

ridiculous

5 comic, daffy, dotty, goofy, silly, wacky 6 absurd, insane 7 bizarre, comical, foolish, risible 8 derisory, farcical 9 cockamamy, fantastic, grotesque, laughable, ludicrous, monstrous 10 cockamamie, outrageous 11 for the birds, harebrained 12 preposterous, unbelievable

riding

academy: 6 manège
costume: 5 habit
pants: 8 jodhpurs
whip: 4 crop 5 quirt

Rienzi composer

6 Wagner (Richard)

rife

4 full 5 flush 6 common 7 replete, teeming 8 abundant, swarming 9 abounding, plentiful, prevalent 10 widespread 11 overflowing

riff

4 flip, leaf, scan, skim 5 thumb 6 browse 8 ostinato

riffle

4 flip, leaf, fret, scan, skim, wave 5 shoal, thumb 6 browse, sluice 7 shallow, shuffle 10 interstice

riffraff

3 mob 5 trash, waste 6 debris, kelter, litter, masses, rabble, refuse 7 garbage, rubbish 8 canaille, unwashed 11 proletariat

rifle

3 arm, gun, rob 4 loot, sack 5 steal 6 burgle, groove, weapon 7 carbine, despoil, firearm, pillage, plunder, ransack, rummage 9 chassepot

accessory: 6 ramrod
kind: 6 Garand, Mauser 7 Enfield 8 Browning 9 Remington 10 Winchester 11 Springfield

rift

3 gap 4 rent 5 break, chasm, chink, cleft, crack, fault, space, split 6 breach, cleave, divide, hiatus, schism 7 fissure, opening, rupture 8 crevasse, division, fracture, interval 9 fault line 10 separation 12 estrangement

rig

3 arm, fit, fix 4 fake, gear 5 dress, equip, getup, trick 6 adjust, clothe, doctor, outfit, tackle 7 apparel, arrange, costume, derrick, furnish, turn out 8 accouter, accoutre, clothing, equipage 9 apparatus, construct, equipment 10 manipulate

rigging

3 net 4 duds, gear, togs 5 dress, lines, ropes 6 attire, chains, tackle, things 7 apparel, clothes, raiment 8 clothing 9 apparatus, equipment

right

3 apt, due, fit 4 fair, just, sane, true, well 5 amend, amply, claim, droit, emend, exact, sound, title 6 at once, common, decent, dexter, direct, equity, honest, lawful, proper, square, strict 7 condign, correct, exactly, fitting, freedom, genuine, healthy, liberty, license, merited, old-line, rectify, redress 8 accurate, becoming, bona fide, decorous, easement, faithful, interest, orthodox, smackdab, straight, suffrage, suitable 9 authentic, befitting, equitable, forthwith, honorable, privilege, requisite, veracious, veritable 10 altogether, applicable, felicitous, perquisite, scrupulous 11 appropriate, correctness, prerogative

combining form: 4 orth, rect 5 dextr, ortho, recti 6 dextro
feudal: 4 soke
legal: 5 droit 8 usufruct
royal: 7 regalia (plural)

right away

3 now 6 at once, pronto 8 directly, promptly 9 forthwith, instanter, instantly 11 immediately, straight off, straightway 12 then and there

righteous

4 good, holy, just, pure 5 godly, moral, noble, pious 6 devout, worthy 7 ethical, genuine, sinless, upright 8 innocent, virtuous 9 blameless, guiltless 10 inculpable, principled

righteousness

6 equity, virtue 7 justice, probity 8 holiness, morality 9 rectitude

rightful

3 apt, due, fit 4 fair, just, true 5 legal 6 honest, lawful, proper 7 condign, fitting 8 deserved, suitable 9 befitting, equitable, impartial 10 applicable, legitimate 11 appropriate

right-handed

6 dexter 7 dextral 9 clockwise

right-hand page

5 recto

rightist

4 tory 11 reactionary 12 conservative

right-minded

5 moral, noble 6 decent, honest 7 ethical 8 virtuous 10 upstanding

Rights of Man author

5 Paine (Thomas)

rigid

3 set 4 firm, hard, taut 5 fixed, stiff, tense 6 severe, strict 7 austere, precise, hard-set 8 cast-iron, ironclad, obdurate, rigorous 9 draconian, immovable, inelastic, rockbound, stringent, unbending 10 adamantine, brassbound, inflexible, relentless, unyielding 11 unbudgeable 13 rhadamanthine

rigidity

6 turgor 7 buckram 8 hardness 9 stiffness
muscular: 8 myotonia

rigmarole

6 bunkum, drivel, ramble 8 nonsense 9 gibberish, procedure 10 balderdash, mumbo jumbo

Rigoletto

composer: 5 Verdi (Giuseppe)
daughter: 5 Gilda

rigor

7 cruelty 8 asperity, hardness, hardship, severity 9 austerity, exactness, harshness, roughness, sharpness, sternness 10 affliction, difficulty, exactitude, strictness 11 tribulation 13 inflexibility

rigorous

5 exact, harsh, rigid, rough, stern, stiff 6 bitter, brutal, proper, rugged, severe, strict 7 ascetic, drastic, onerous, precise 8 accurate, exacting 9 draconian, ironbound, stringent 10 burdensome, inflexible, ironhanded, oppressive 13 rhadamanthine

rile

3 bug, rub, vex 4 roil 5 anger, annoy, grate, muddy, peeve, pique, upset 6 muddle, nettle, put out, rankle 7 agitate, disturb, fluster, inflame, perturb, provoke 8 disorder, disquiet, irritate 9 aggravate 10 discompose, exasperate

rill

3 run 4 burn, purl 5 bourn, brook, creek 6 runnel, stream, valley 7 freshet, rivulet 8 brooklet 9 streamlet 11 watercourse

rim

3 hem, lip 4 bank, boss, brim, edge, ring 5 bezel, bezil, bound, brink, skirt, verge 6 border, flange, fringe, margin, shield 7 annulus, horizon, outline 8 boundary, surround 9 perimeter, periphery
of a basket: 4 hoop
of a cask: 5 chime
of an insect's wing: 6 termen
of a spoked wheel: 5 felly 6 felloe

rime

3 ice 4 hoar 5 crust, frost 7 coating,

encrust **9** hoarfrost, Jack Frost
12 incrustation

Rinaldo
beloved: 8 Angelica
cousin: 7 Orlando
father: 5 Aymon
horse: 6 Bayard
mother: 3 Aya
sister: 10 Bradamante
uncle: 11 Charlemagne

rind
4 bark, husk, peel, skin **5** crust
9 crackling

ring
3 eye, hem, rim **4** band, bloc, bong,
echo, gird, gyre, hoop, loop, peal,
toll **5** arena, bezel, cabal, chime,
clang, cycle, group, knell, knoll,
round, sound **6** circle, clique, collar, girdle, staple **7** annulus, clangor, combine, compass, resound,
vibrate **8** bracelet, cincture, encircle, surround **9** coalition, encompass **11** combination, reverberate
around sun or moon: 6 corona
curtain: 3 eye
for a compass: 6 gimbal
harness: 3 dee **6** button, terret
heraldic: 7 annulet
in a hinge: 7 gudgeon
of chain: 4 link
of color: 8 stocking
of leaves or flowers: 6 wreath
7 garland
of light: 4 halo **5** glory **6** corona,
nimbus **7** aureole **8** halation
of rope or metal: 4 hank **6** becket
7 garland, grommet, thimble
of two hoops: 6 gimmal
relating to: 7 annular
used as a valve or diaphragm:
5 wafer
wedding: 4 band

Ring and the Book author
8 Browning (Robert)

ringed
8 annulate, bordered **9** encircled
10 surrounded

ringer
4 fake, spit **5** clone, image **6** double
7 clapper, picture **8** impostor, portrait
10 simulacrum **13** spitting image

ringing
7 orotund, vibrant **8** decisive, emphatic, plangent, resonant, sonorous
10 clangorous, resounding **11** reverberant, unequivocal

ringleader
4 boss **5** chief **6** honcho **7** kingpin
9 godfather **10** head honcho, instigator, mastermind

ringlet
4 curl, lock **5** crimp, tress **7** circlet,
earlock, tendril

Ring of the Nibelung composer
6 Wagner (Richard)

rinse
4 dunk, lave, wash **5** bathe, douse,
swill **6** shower, sluice **7** cleanse
the mouth: 6 gargle

riot
5 brawl, melee, revel, spree **6** bedlam, émeute, jumble, revolt, tumult, uproar **7** carouse, debauch,
rampage, revelry, roister, wassail
8 carousal, disorder, uprising **9** commotion **10** debauchery, donnybrook,
revolution **11** disturbance

riotous
4 lush, wild **6** stormy, unruly, wanton
7 bacchic, profuse **8** abundant
9 abounding, clamorous, exuberant,
luxuriant, plentiful, turbulent **10** boisterous **11** saturnalian, tempestuous
12 unrestrained

rip
4 gash, hole, rend, rent, rive, spit,
tear **5** shred, slash, split **6** attack,
cleave **7** current, sputter **8** lacerate,
undertow **9** criticize, disparage
12 undercurrent
into: 5 go for **6** assail, attack
8 lambaste
off: 3 con, rob **4** copy **5** cheat,
steal, theft **7** defraud, imitate, swindle **9** imitation

ripe

4 aged, full, late 5 adult, grown, ready, ruddy, plump 6 mature, mellow, smelly, timely 7 grown-up 8 prepared, suitable 9 developed, full-blown, full-grown, offensive, opportune 10 seasonable 11 appropriate, full-fledged

ripen

3 age 4 cure, grow 6 better, grow up, mature, mellow, season 7 develop, enhance, improve, perfect 8 heighten, maturate

riposte

5 parry, reply 6 retort, return, thrust 8 back talk, comeback, repartee 13 counterattack

ripping

4 fine 5 grand, nifty, super, swell 6 divine, peachy 7 capital 8 glorious, splendid, terrific 9 admirable, delicious, excellent, fantastic, marvelous, wonderful 10 delightful, delectable, remarkable 11 scrumptious, sensational

ripple

3 lap 4 curl, fret, riff, wave 6 cockle, dimple, lipper, popple, ruffle, spread, wimple 7 crinkle, wavelet, wrinkle 8 undulate

rip-roaring

5 noisy 6 lively 8 exciting 9 hilarious 10 boisterous, rollicking, uproarious

ripsnorter

5 dandy 6 hummer 8 jim-dandy 9 humdinger 11 crackerjack

riptide

7 current 8 undertow 12 undercurrent

Rip Van Winkle

author: 6 Irving (Washington)
dog: 4 Wolf

rise

3 wax 4 flow, grow, lift, rear, soar, stem, well 5 awake, begin, climb, get up, issue, mount, rouse, stand, surge, swell, tower 6 ascend, ascent, awaken, emerge, expand, growth, spring, thrive, uprear 7 advance, augment, develop, emanate, enhance, enlarge, stand up, succeed, surface, upsurge 8 eminence, heighten, increase 9 ascension, increment, intensify, originate, terminate
above: 8 surmount
again: 7 resurge 9 resurrect
against: 5 rebel 6 mutiny, revolt
and fall: 4 tide 5 heave 6 welter
and shine: 5 get up
gradually: 4 loom

Rise and Fall of the Third Reich author

6 Shirer (William)

Rise of Silas Lapham author

7 Howells (William Dean)

riser

4 step 8 platform

risible

4 rich 5 comic, droll, funny, jokey 6 absurd 7 comical 8 farcical 9 laughable, ludicrous 10 ridiculous

risk

4 ante, dare, defy 5 peril, stake, throw, wager 6 chance, danger, gamble, hazard, menace, stakes 7 imperil, jeopard, venture 8 endanger, exposure, jeopardy 9 adventure, encounter, liability 10 jeopardize

risky

4 bold 5 dicey, hairy 6 chancy, daring, touchy, tricky 7 parlous, unsound 8 delicate, perilous, ticklish 9 dangerous, hazardous, unhealthy 10 jeopardous, precarious 11 adventurous, speculative, treacherous

risqué

4 blue, lewd, racy, sexy 5 broad, crude, dirty, salty, spicy, vampy 6 coarse, daring, earthy, purple, ribald, vulgar 7 naughty, obscene, raunchy 8 indecent, off-color, scabrous 9 salacious 10 indecorous, indelicate, suggestive

rite
6 office 7 liturgy, mystery, service 8 ceremony 9 formality, ordinance, sacrament, solemnity 10 ceremonial, initiation, observance 11 celebration, sacramental
funeral: 6 exequy 7 obsequy 8 exequies 9 obsequies
Jewish: 4 bris
of initiation or purification: 7 baptism
of knighthood: 8 accolade
(see also **sacrament**)

ritual
see **rite**

ritzy
4 posh 5 fancy, swank 6 chichi, classy, modish, snazzy, swanky 7 elegant, high-hat, stylish 9 au courant, exclusive, expensive, luxurious 11 fashionable 12 ostentatious

rival
3 tie, try, vie 4 even, peer, side 5 equal, match 6 strive 7 attempt, compete, contend, contest, emulate 8 approach, opponent 9 adversary, competing, contender, measure up 10 antagonist, competitor, contending, contestant 11 comparative, competition

rivalry
6 strife 7 contest, warfare 8 conflict, jealousy, tug-of-war 9 emulation 10 contention, opposition 11 competition

rive
3 rip 4 rend, tear 5 break, burst, crack, sever, smash, split 6 cleave, divide, shiver, sunder 7 fissure, shatter 8 fracture, fragment, lacerate, separate, splinter

river
Africa: 4 Bomu, Juba 5 Chari, Congo, Shari, Tsavo, Zaire 6 Atbara, Mbomou, Songwe, Ubangi 7 Aruwimi, Limpopo, Zambesi, Zambezi 9 Astaboras, Crocodile
Alabama: 5 Coosa 6 Mobile

7 Conecuh, Perdido 9 Tombigbee 10 Tallapoosa
Alaska: 5 Kobuk 6 Copper, Noatak, Tanana 7 Koyukuk, Susitna 9 Kuskokwim
Albania: 4 Drin 5 Drini
Argentina: 5 Negro 6 Paraná 7 Matanza
arm: 6 branch 9 tributary
Asia: 3 Ili 4 Amur, Oxus 5 Indus 6 Jayhun, Sutlej 7 Oedanes 8 Amu Darya 9 Dyardanes 11 Brahmaputra
Australia: 4 Daly 5 Roper, Yarra 6 Barwon, Culgoa, Dawson, DeGrey, Murray 7 Darling, Fitzroy, Lachlan 8 Victoria 10 Yarra Yarra
Austria: 4 Enns
bank: 5 levee
Belgium: 5 Rupel, Senne, Weser 6 Dender, Dindar, Ourthe 8 Visurgis
Bolivia: 4 Beni 5 Abuná 6 Mamoré
Borneo: 5 Kajan
bottom: 3 bed
Brazil: 3 Ica 4 Pará, Paru 5 Negro, Xingu 6 Paraná 7 Madeira, Tapajos, Tapajoz
British Columbia: 6 Skeena 10 Bella Coola
California: 3 Eel, Pit 4 Kern, Yuba 6 Merced 7 Feather, Salinas, Trinity 8 Tuolumne
Cambodia: 8 Tonle Sap
Canada: 3 Bow 4 Back 5 Moose, Peace, Slave 6 Beaver, Fraser, Nelson 8 Gatineau, Saguenay 9 Athabasca, Great Fish, Mackenzie, Richelieu 11 Assiniboine
Carolinas: 7 Catawba
central United States: 3 Fox 5 Grand 6 Neosho, Platte, Wabash 8 Keya Paha, Missouri, Niobrara 9 Tennessee, Verdigris 10 Republican, Saint Croix 11 Mississippi
channel: 6 alveus
Chile: 3 Loa 5 Itata, Maule 6 Bío-Bío 8 Valdivia
China: 3 Bei, Hun, Wei 4 Dong 5 Baihe, Chang, Huang, Tarim 6 Yellow 7 Kashgar, Yangtze
China-North Korea: 4 Yalu
Colombia: 4 Tomo 6 Atrato 9 Magdalena

Colorado: 5 Yampa   8 Gunnison

Connecticut: 6 Thames   7 Niantic, Shepaug   9 Naugatuck   10 Farmington, Housatonic, Quinnipiac   11 Willimantic

crossing: 4 ford

current: 4 eddy   6 rapids

Czech Republic: 4 Iser   6 Jizera, Moldau, Vltava

dam: 4 weir

Denmark: 4 Stor

dried bed: 4 wadi

East Asia: 4 Yalu   5 Amnok   7 Oryokko

Ecuador: 4 Napo   10 Esmeraldas

England: 3 Esk, Exe, Nen, Ure   4 Aire, Avon, Eden, Nene, Ouse, Tees, Tyne, Wear, Yare   5 Swale, Trent   6 Mersey, Ribble, Thames

Ethiopia: 3 Omo   4 Baro, Dawa

Europe: 4 Eger, Elbe, Labe, Oder, Ohre   5 Albis, Saale   6 Danube, Ticino

Florida: 6 Indian   9 Kissimmee   10 Saint Johns   12 Apalachicola

France: 3 Ain, Lot, Var   4 Aire, Aude, Cher, Eure, Gers, Loir, Oise, Orne, Saar, Tarn, Yser   5 Adour, Aisne, Drôme, Indre, Isère, Loire, Marne, Rhône, Saare, Sâone, Seine, Somme, Yonne   6 Allier, Ariège, Scarpe, Vienne   7 Durance, Garonne, La Riège   8 Charente, Dordogne

Georgia: 6 Etowah, Oconee   8 Altamaha, Ocmulgee   13 Chattahoochee

Germany: 3 Ems, Rur   4 Eder, Eger, Elbe, Isar, Main, Rems, Ruhr   5 Hunte, Lippe, Rhine, Spree, Werra, Weser   6 Neckar

Germany-Poland: 4 Oder

Ghana: 5 Volta

god: 7 Alpheus, Inachus   8 Achelous

Greece: 3 Iri   4 Arta   5 Lema, Lerne   7 Alpheus, Eurotas   8 Achelous   9 Arakhthos

Honduras: 4 Ulúa   5 Aguán   6 Patuca

Iberian: 5 Douro, Duero

Idaho: 5 Lemhi

Illinois: 8 Mackinaw

India: 4 Sind   5 Sindh, Tapti   6 Chenab, Ganges, Jhelum, Kaveri, Kistna   7 Cauvery, Krishna   8 Acesines, Godavari

inlet: 5 bayou   6 slough

Iran: 3 Kor   4 Mand, Mund   5 Karun   8 Safid Rud, Sefid Rud

Ireland: 3 Lee   4 Deel, Erne, Suir   5 Boyne, Clare, Foyle   6 Barrow, Liffey   7 Shannon

Italy: 4 Adda, Arno, Liri, Nera   5 Adige, Arnus, Etsch, Liris, Oglio, Padus, Piave, Tiber   6 Ollius, Rapido, Tevere, Trebia   7 Athesis, Rubicon, Secchia, Tiberis, Trebbia   8 Rubicone, Volturno

Kansas: 6 Pawnee

Kazakhstan-Russia: 4 Ural   5 Tobol   6 Irtysh

Kenya: 4 Athi, Tana

Kubla Khan's: 4 Alph

land: 4 holm   5 flats   7 bottoms

Latvia: 5 Gauja

Latvia-Lithuania: 7 Lielupe

Lebanon: 4 Litani

Little Rock's: 8 Arkansas

living on the bank of: 8 riparian

longest: 4 Nile

Louisiana: 11 Atchafalaya

Maine: 8 Kennebec   9 Aroostook, Penobscot

Malaysia: 9 Trengganu

Maryland: 8 Monocacy, Patapsco, Patuxent   9 Nanticoke

Massachusetts: 7 Charles, Taunton   9 Westfield   10 Housatonic

Mexico: 6 Pánuco, Sonora   7 Tabasco   8 Grijalva

Michigan: 4 Cass   5 Huron   7 Saginaw   8 Manistee, Muskegon   9 Cheboygan, Kalamazoo   10 Michigamme, Shiawassee

Mississippi: 5 Pearl, Yazoo   10 Pascagoula

Moldova-Ukraine: 8 Dneister

Missouri: 5 Osage

mouth: 5 delta

Myanmar (Burma): 4 Pegu   8 Chindwin, Irrawady

Nebraska: 4 Loup   6 Nemaha, Platte   7 Elkhorn

Netherlands: 4 Waal 5 Issel, Yssel 6 IJssel 7 Vahalis
New England: 4 Saco 6 Nashua 9 Merrimack 10 Blackstone 11 Connecticut 12 Androscoggin
New Jersey: 6 Rahway 7 Passaic, Raritan 8 Tuckahoe
New York: 5 Tioga 6 Hudson, Mohawk, Oneida, Oswego, Seneca 7 Chemung, Niagara 8 Chenango
New Zealand: 7 Waikato
Nicaragua: 6 Coco 7 Segovia
Nigeria: 5 Benin
North Carolina: 3 Haw, Tar 5 Neuse 6 Chowan 8 Alamance
northeast United States: 4 Ohio 6 Hoosic 7 Genesee, Hocking 8 Delaware, Mahoning 9 Allegheny 11 Monongahela, Susquehanna
Northern Ireland: 4 Bann 6 Mourne
North Korea: 5 Daido 7 Taedong
northwest United States: 5 Snake 7 Klamath 8 Columbia 11 Pend Oreille
Norway: 4 Tana, Teno
nymph: 5 naiad
of fire: 10 Phlegethon
of forgetfulness: 5 Lethe
of ice: 7 glacier
of woe: 7 Acheron
Ohio: 5 Miami 8 Cuyahoga, Sandusky 9 Muskingum 10 Tuscarawas
Oklahoma: 8 Cimarron
Oregon: 5 Rogue 6 Owyhee 7 Malheur 8 McKenzie 9 Clackamas, Deschutes 10 Willamette
Panama: 5 Tuira 7 Chagres
Papua New Guinea: 3 Fly 5 Sepik
Paraguay: 3 Apa 9 Pilcomayo
Pennsylvania: 6 Lehigh 10 Schuylkill
Peru: 5 Rímac, Santa 7 Marañón 8 Apurímac, Huallaga, Urubamba
Philippines: 4 Abra, Agno 5 Pasig 7 Cagayan 8 Cotabato, Mindanao, Pampanga
Poland: 3 San 7 Vistula
Portugal: 4 Sado 7 Mondego
relating to: 7 fluvial
Rhode Island: 7 Seekonk 8 Sakonnet 10 Providence

Romania: 5 Arges
Russia: 3 Don, Oka, Ufa, Usa 4 Kama, Kara, Lena, Msta, Neva, Sura, Svir 5 Onega, Terek, Volga 6 Anadyr, Angara, Belaya, Kolima, Kolyma, Ussuri, Vyatka 7 Dnieper, Pechora, Yenisey 8 Barguzin, Kostroma, Voronezh, Vychegda
Russia-Ukraine: 6 Donets
sacred: 6 Ganges
Scotland: 3 Dee, Don, Esk, Tay 4 Doon, Nith, Spey, Tyne 5 Afton, Annan, Clyde, Forth, Tweed 6 Teviot 7 Deveron 8 Findhorn
Shanghai's: 7 Huangpu, Hwang Pu
Sicily: 5 Salso 6 Simeto
siren: 7 Lorelei
Slovakia: 3 Vag, Vah 4 Gran, Hron, Waag 5 Garam, Nitra 6 Neutra, Nyitra
South Africa: 4 Vaal 6 Orange
South America: 3 Apa 6 Amazon 8 Amazonas, Orellana 9 Pilcomayo
South Carolina: 6 Saluda, Santee 7 Wateree 8 Congaree
South Dakota: 3 Bad
Southeast Asia: 6 Dza-chu, Mekong 7 Salween 8 Lan-ts'ang
southeast United States: 6 Pee Dee 7 Noxubee, Washita 8 Escambia, Ouachita, Suwannee 10 Okanoxubee
southern United States: 6 Sabine
South Korea: 3 Kum
southwest United States: 4 Gila, Zuni 5 Pecos 8 Colorado
Spain: 4 Ebro 8 Aragon 12 Guadalquivir
Sweden: 4 Göta 5 Kalix
Switzerland: 3 Aar 4 Aare 5 Reuss
Syria: 6 Khabur 7 Orontes
Tasmania: 4 Huon
Tbilisi's: 4 Kura
Texas: 5 Llano 6 Brazos, Nueces 7 San Saba, Trinity 9 Guadalupe
Texas-Mexico: 8 Rio Bravo 9 Rio Grande
tidal: 7 estuary
Tokyo's: 6 Sumida
Turkey: 4 Aras 5 Araks 6 Seihun, Seyhan
Ukrainian: 3 Bug 4 Alma

underworld: 4 Styx 5 Lethe
7 Acheron, Cocytus 10 Phlegethon
Uruguay: 5 Negro
Utah: 5 Provo, Uinta, Weber 6 Jordan, Sevier
valley: 6 strath
Venezuela: 5 Apure, Caura 6 Caroní 7 Orinoco
Vermont: 3 Mad 5 Onion, White
8 Winooski
Virginia: 3 Dan 5 James 7 Rapidan 9 Nansemond 10 Appomattox, Shenandoah 12 Chickahominy, Rappahannock
wailing: 7 Cocytus
Wales: 4 Dyfi 5 Clwyd, Dovey, Teifi
Washington: 6 Skagit, Yakima
9 Klickitat, Snohomish, Wenatchee
West Africa: 5 Niger 6 Gambia
7 Senegal
western United States: 7 Laramie
8 Columbia, Flathead 11 Yellowstone
West Virginia: 7 Kanawha
Wisconsin: 8 Kickapoo 9 Menominee
Wyoming: 8 Shoshone 10 Gros Ventre 11 Medicine Bow

_____ Rivera
5 Diego

river duck
4 teal 6 wigeon 7 dabbler, mallard, widgeon 8 shoveler 9 greenwing

river horse
5 hippo 12 hippopotamus

riverine
8 riparian

river island
3 ait

rivet
3 fix, pin 4 bolt, brad, stud 5 affix
6 absorb, attach, clinch, fasten 7 engross 8 fastener

Riviera city
4 Nice 6 Cannes, Monaco 7 Antibes, San Remo 8 St. Tropez
10 Monte Carlo

rivulet
3 run 4 beck, burn, gill, race, rill

5 bourn, brook, creek 6 runlet, runnel, stream 9 streamlet

Rizpah
father: 4 Aiah
lover: 4 Saul
son: 6 Armoni 12 Mephibosheth

roach
3 hog 6 shiner 7 sunfish

road
3 way 4 fare, lane, line, path 5 drive, going, route, track 6 artery, avenue, career, causey, course, street
7 highway, journey, passage 8 causeway, chaussée, crossway, highroad, pavement, speedway, turnpike 9 boulevard 12 thoroughfare
along a cliff: 8 corniche
around a city: 6 bypass 7 beltway
bend: 7 hairpin
edge: 4 berm 8 shoulder
French: 6 chemin
Irish: 6 boreen
machine: 5 paver 6 grader 9 bulldozer
Roman: 3 via 4 iter
side: 6 branch 8 shunpike
Spanish: 6 camino
surface: 3 tar 6 gravel 7 macadam
8 pavement

roadblock
7 barrier 8 blockade 9 barricade
11 obstruction

road book
3 map 5 atlas 9 gazetteer, itinerary

roadhouse
3 bar, inn 4 dive 5 hotel, lodge
6 tavern 9 nightclub

roadrunner
6 cuckoo 13 chaparral cock

road rut
6 kettle 7 pothole 9 chuckhole

roam
3 bat, bum, gad, run 4 rove, walk
5 drift, prowl, range, stray 6 ramble, stroll, travel, wander 7 meander, traipse 8 straggle, vagabond 9 gallivant

roamer

3 bum 5 gipsy, gypsy, nomad, rover 6 ranger, walker 7 drifter, prowler, rambler, vagrant 8 marauder, stroller, traveler, vagabond, wanderer 11 nightwalker

roar

3 din 4 bawl, bell, boom, bray, howl, yell 5 shout 6 bellow, clamor, outcry 7 bluster 10 vociferate
bullring: 3 olé

roast

4 bake, mock, rack, sear 5 broil, grill, joint, parch 6 scathe, scorch 7 banquet, blister, mockery, swelter 8 barbecue, ridicule 9 criticize

rob

3 cop, mug 4 lift, loot, nick, raid, roll, sack 5 boost, filch, heist, pinch, pluck, reave, steal 6 burgle, fleece, hijack, hold up, pilfer, rip off, snitch, thieve 7 defraud, deprive, despoil, pillage, plunder, purloin, ransack, stick up, swindle 8 knock off 9 knock over 10 burglarize

robber

4 yegg 5 crook, thief 6 bandit, looter, mugger, pirate, reiver 7 brigand, burglar, footpad, rustler 8 hijacker, swindler 9 holdup man 10 cat burglar, highwayman, sandbagger, stickup man 12 housebreaker
grave: 5 ghoul

robbery

5 heist, theft 6 holdup, piracy 7 larceny, mugging, stickup 8 banditry

robe

3 aba 4 cape, gown, wrap 5 cloak, habit 6 caftan, mantle 7 garment, manteau 8 covering, dalmatic, vestment
baptismal: 7 chrisom
bishop's: 7 chimere
of Roman emperors: 6 purple
Turkish: 6 dolman

Robinson Crusoe

author: 5 Defoe (Daniel)
character: 6 Friday

robot

5 golem 7 android 8 automata (plural) 9 automaton

Rob Roy author

5 Scott (Walter)

robust

4 hale, rude 5 hardy, husky, lusty, rough, sound, stout 6 hearty, potent, rugged, sinewy, strong, sturdy 7 healthy 8 athletic, muscular, vigorous 9 strapping 10 boisterous, red-blooded, full-bodied, prosperous

robustious

4 rude 5 lusty, rough, rowdy, wooly 6 rugged 7 boorish, ill-bred, loutish 8 churlish, clownish 9 unrefined 10 boisterous, unpolished

rock

4 crag, reel, roll, sway, toss 5 geode, pitch, quake, shake, swing 6 totter 7 boulder, breccia 8 astonish, convulse, undulate 9 oscillate
basaltic: 5 wacke
cavity: 3 vug
combining form: 4 lite, lith, lyte, petr 5 clast, petri, petro
decomposed: 6 gossan
fissile: 5 shale
formation: 5 nappe 6 pluton 7 rimrock, terrane 8 isocline, syncline
fragment: 8 xenolith
igneous: 4 lava 6 basalt, gabbro, pumice 7 diabase, diorite, granite 8 eruptive, felstone, obsidian, porphyry, traprock 10 travertine
layer: 10 mantlerock
mass: 5 scree 9 batholith
metamorphic: 5 slate 6 gneiss, marble, schist 9 quartzite, soapstone
molten: 4 lava
sedimentary: 4 clay, coal 5 chalk, chert, coral, flint, shale 8 mudstone 9 limestone, sandstone, siltstone
volcanic: 4 tuff 6 basalt

rock bass

7 sunfish

rock-bottom

4 root 6 lowest 8 cheapest 9 lowermost 11 fundamental

rocket

3 fly, zip **4** soar, whiz, zoom **5** mount
6 ascend, bullet **7** missile, shoot up
8 firework, starship **10** projectile
landing: 7 reentry **10** splashdown
launcher: 7 bazooka
launching: 7 liftoff **8** blastoff
scientist: 5 Braun (Wernher von)
7 Goddard (Robert)

rockfish

4 cony, hind **5** coney **7** grouper,
jewfish, sea bass **8** bocaccio
10 scorpaenid **11** striped bass

Rockies resort

4 Vail **5** Aspen **8** Snowmass **9** Telluride

_____ Rockne

5 Knute

rock rabbit

4 cony, pika **5** coney, hyrax **6** dassie

rock-ribbed

5 rigid **8** dogmatic, obdurate **9** unbending **10** inflexible, unyielding

rockweed

5 algae, fucus **7** seaweed **12** bladder wrack

rocky hill

3 tor **5** kopje

rococo

4 busy **5** showy **6** florid, frilly, ornate
7 baroque, elegant, opulent **9** elaborate, intricate **10** decorative, flamboyant **11** overwrought

rod

3 bar **4** cane, pole, wand **5** baton,
dowel, spoke, staff, stave, stick
6 pistol **7** scepter **8** revolver **10** correction, discipline, punishment
11 castigation **12** chastisement
bundle of: 6 fasces

rodent

3 rat **4** cavy, cony, mole, paca, pika,
vole **5** cavie, coney, coypu, mouse,
shrew **6** agouti, beaver, gerbil,
gopher, jerboa, marmot, murine,
nutria, rabbit **7** hamster, lemming,
leveret, muskrat **8** capybara, chip-

munk, dormouse, squirrel, tuco
tuco, viscacha, vizcacha, water rat
9 guinea pig, porcupine **10** chinchilla, field mouse, prairie dog
11 kangaroo rat, meadow mouse,
pocket mouse **12** pocket gopher
aquatic: 5 coypu **6** beaver, nutria
7 muskrat **8** musquash
burrowing: 6 gerbil, gopher **7** hamster **8** viscacha, vizcacha
family: 5 murid **6** murine **7** sciurid
genus: 3 Mus **5** Lepus

rodeo

7 contest, roundup **9** enclosure
10 exhibition **11** competition
animal: 5 horse, steer **10** Brahma
bull
event: 10 calf roping **11** bulldogging **12** bronco riding
performer: 5 clown **6** cowboy

_____ Rodin

7 Auguste

rodomontade

4 blow, brag, rant **5** boast, swash,
vaunt **7** bluster, swagger **9** gasconade **11** braggadocio

Rodomonte

beloved: 8 Doralice
slayer: 8 Ruggiero

Rodrigo Díaz de Bivar

5 El Cid

rod-shaped

7 virgate **8** bacillar **9** bacillary

roe

4 deer, eggs **6** beluga, caviar, osetra
7 sevruga

Roentgen's discovery

4 X-ray

rogation

6 litany, prayer **8** entreaty, petition
10 beseeching **12** supplication

_____ Rogers

3 Roy **4** Carl, Fred, Will **6** Ginger,
Robert

rogue

5 cheat, gypsy, knave, scamp **6** rascal **7** lowlife, sharper, villain **8** pica-

roon, scalawag, swindler **9** defrauder, miscreant, reprobate, scoundrel, skeezicks, trickster **10** blackguard, mountebank **11** rapscallion
relating to: **10** picaresque

roguery
5 fraud **7** devilry, knavery, waggery **8** deviltry, mischief, trickery **9** devilment, diablerie **11** waggishness **12** sportiveness

roguish
3 sly **4** arch **6** impish, wicked **7** knavish **8** devilish, espiègle, scampish **10** picaresque **11** mischievous

roil
3 mud, vex **4** foul, rile, romp **5** annoy, dirty, grate, muddy, peeve, upset **6** befoul, muddle, nettle, stir up **7** agitate, disturb **8** disorder, irritate **9** aggravate **10** exasperate

roily
5 muddy, riley **6** turbid **9** turbulent

roister
4 riot **5** revel **6** frolic **7** carouse, reveler, wassail **9** wassailer

Roland
7 Orlando
beloved: **4** Aude
betrayer: **4** Gano **7** Ganelon
friend: **6** Oliver **7** Olivier
horn: **7** Olivant
sword: **8** Durandal, Durendal
uncle: **11** Charlemagne

role
3 bit **4** duty, lead, part, pose **5** cameo, cloak, guise, niche **6** aspect, office **7** quality **8** capacity, function, position **9** character **13** impersonation

roll
3 bun, rob **4** bolt, coil, flow, furl, gyre, list, pour, rock, toss, turn, wind, wrap **5** heave, pitch, surge **6** bundle, roster, rotate, stream, swathe, wallow, wrap up **7** biscuit, brioche, envelop, revolve, swaddle, trundle **8** involute, register, schedule, turn over

roll about
6 wallow, welter

roll back
5 lower **6** reduce, repeal **7** curtail, rescind

roller
3 rod **4** bowl, drum, wave **6** canary, caster, platen **7** breaker, carrier, tumbler **8** cylinder

Roller-Derby round
3 jam

rollick
4 lark, play, romp **5** caper, frisk, party, revel, sport **6** cavort, frolic, gambol **7** disport, skylark **8** escapade **9** merriment

rollicking
4 wild **5** antic, merry **6** frisky, lively **8** sportive **10** boisterous, frolicsome **12** high-spirited

rolling stock
4 cars **7** coaches, engines **8** cabooses, Pullmans, sleepers, trailers **11** locomotives

rolling stone
5 rover **6** roamer **7** drifter, rambler, vagrant **8** wanderer, vagabond

roly-poly
see rotund

Roman
5 Latin **7** Italian
amphitheater: **9** Colosseum
assembly: **5** forum **6** senate **7** comitia
building: **5** Forum **6** Circus **8** basilica, Pantheon
clan: **4** gens
comedy writer: **7** Plautus (Titus), Terence
conspirator: **6** Brutus (Marcus Junius) **7** Cassius (Gaius) **8** Catiline
date: **4** Ides **7** calends, kalends
emperor: **4** Nero, Otho **5** Galba (Servius Sulpicius), Nerva (Marcus Cocceius), Titus, Verus (Lucius Aurelius) **6** Julian, Trajan **7** Hadrian, Maximus (Magnus Clemens, Marcus

Clodius, Petronius), Severus (Lucius
Septimius) **8** Augustus, Caligula,
Claudius, Commodus (Lucius
Aelius), Domitian, Tiberius, Valerian
9 Caracalla, Vespasian **10** Diocletian, Theodosius **11** Constantine,
Valentinian
entrance hall: 5 atria (plural)
6 atrium
epic: 6 Aeneid
epigrammatist: 7 Martial
family: 7 Gracchi
Fates: 4 Nona **5** Morta **6** Decuma,
Parcae
founder: 5 Remus **7** Romulus
fountain: 5 Trevi **6** Triton
garment: 4 toga **5** tunic
general: 5 Sulla (Lucius Cornelius),
Titus **6** Antony (Marc), Marius
(Gaius), Scipio (Publius Cornelius)
8 Agricola (Gnaeus Julius)
god: 4 deus
  blind: 6 Plutus
  chief: 4 Jove **7** Jupiter
  messenger: 7 Mercury
  of agriculture: 6 Saturn
  of animals: 6 Faunus
  of death: 4 Mors
  of dreams: 8 Morpheus
  of fire: 6 Vulcan
  of gates and doors: 5 Janus
  of healing: 9 Asclepius **11** Aescu-
    lapius
  of heaven: 6 Uranus
  of households: 5 Lares **7** Pe-
    nates
  of love: 4 Amor **5** Cupid
  of medicine: 9 Asclepius **11** Aes-
    culapius
  of mirth: 5 Comus
  of regeneration: 7 Priapus
  of sleep: 6 Somnus
  of the sea: 6 Pontus **7** Neptune,
    Proteus
  of the sun: 3 Sol **6** Apollo
  of the underworld: 3 Dis **5** Orcus,
    Pluto **8** Dispater
  of the wind: 5 Eurus, Notus
    6 Aeolus, Aquilo, Auster, Boreas
    8 Favonius, Zephyrus
  of war: 4 Mars **8** Quirinus
  of wealth: 6 Plutus

of wine: 7 Bacchus
of woods: 6 Faunus
two-faced: 5 Janus
goddess: 3 dea
  of agriculture: 5 Ceres
  of beauty: 5 Venus
  of dawn: 6 Aurora
  of flowers: 5 Flora
  of handicrafts: 7 Minerva
  of harvests: 3 Ops
  of health: 7 Minerva
  of hope: 4 Spes
  of hunting: 5 Diana
  of justice: 7 Astraea
  of love: 5 Venus
  of marriage: 4 Juno
  of night: 3 Nox
  of peace: 3 Pax
  of springs: 7 Juturna
  of strife: 9 Discordia
  of the earth: 6 Tellus
  of the hearth: 5 Vesta
  of the moon: 4 Luna
  of the sea: 10 Amphitrite
  of the underworld: 10 Proserpina
  of victory: 6 Vacuna
  of war: 7 Bellona
  of wisdom: 7 Minerva
  of womanhood: 4 Juno
greeting: 3 ave
hero: 6 Caesar (Julius) **11** Cincinnatus (Lucius Quinctius)
hill: 7 Caelian, Viminal **8** Aven-
  tine, Palatine, Quirinal **9** Esquiline
  10 Capitoline
historian: 4 Livy **5** Nepos **7** Sallust, Tacitus **9** Suetonius
king: 7 Romulus, Servius, Tullius
  12 Ancus Martius **13** Numa Pom-
  pilius
marketplace: 5 agora
military formation: 3 ala **6** alares
  (plural) **7** phalanx
miltary unit: 6 cohort, legion
  7 maniple
officer: 9 centurion
official: 5 augur, edile **6** aedile,
  censor, consul, lictor **7** praetor,
  prefect, tribune **8** quaestor
people: 5 Laeti, plebs **6** populi
  (plural) **7** populus, Sabines **9** plebeians

philosopher: 4 Cato **6** Seneca
8 Apuleius **9** Epictetus, Lucretius
physician: 9 Asclepius **11** Aesculapius
port: 5 Ostia
procurator: 6 Pilate (Pontius)
racecourse: 6 circus
road: 4 iter
slave: 9 Spartacus
statesman: 4 Cato **5** Pliny **6** Caesar, Cicero, Pompey, Seneca
7 Agrippa **8** Augustus, Gracchus, Maecenas **9** Flaminius
symbol of authority: 6 fasces

roman à ____
4 clef

romance
3 woo **4** gest, love **5** amour, court, fling, geste, novel **6** affair **7** fantasy, fiction **8** stardust **10** love affair
12 bodice ripper

Romance language
6 French **7** Catalan, Italian, Spanish
8 Romanian, Rumanian **9** Sardinian
10 Portuguese

Romania
capital: 9 Bucharest
city: 4 Iasi **6** Brasov, Galati **7** Craiova **9** Constanta, Timisoara
monetary unit: 3 leu
mountain range: 10 Carpathian
neighbor: 6 Serbia **7** Hungary, Moldova, Ukraine **8** Bulgaria
part of: 7 Balkans
peninsula: 6 Balkan
river: 5 Tisza **6** Danube
sea: 5 Black

romantic
5 gauzy, ideal, idyll, mushy **6** ardent, dreamy, exotic, gothic, poetic, unreal
7 amorous, maudlin, mawkish **8** fanciful, quixotic **9** fantastic, imaginary, visionary **10** idealistic, lovey-dovey
11 sentimental

Romany
5 Gipsy, Gypsy

Romeo
7 amorist, Don Juan, gallant **8** Casanova, lothario, paramour

beloved: 6 Juliet
enemy: 6 Tybalt
father: 8 Montague
friend: 8 Mercutio

Rommel, Erwin
9 Desert Fox

romp
4 lark, play **5** caper, frisk, sport
6 cavort, frolic, gambol, hoyden
7 rollick, runaway, skylark **8** escapade

Romulus
brother: 5 Remus
father: 4 Mars
mother: 9 Rea Silvia **10** Rhea Silvia
victim: 5 Remus

rondure
3 arc, orb **4** arch, ball, ring **5** curve, globe, round **6** circle, sphere **9** curvature

rood
5 cross **8** crucifix

roof
3 hip, top **4** apex, peak **5** cover, crest, crown **6** summit **7** ceiling
8 covering, housetop
material: 3 tar, tin **4** tile **5** slate, straw, terne **6** copper, thatch **7** shingle
of a cavern: 4 dome
of the mouth: 6 palate
part: 3 hip **4** eave
structure: 9 penthouse
type: 5 gable **7** gambrel, mansard
9 butterfly
vaulted: 4 dome

roofer
5 tiler

rook
4 bilk, colt, crow, scam, tyro **5** cheat, mulct, raven, stick **6** castle, fleece, novice **7** amateur, defraud, recruit, swindle, trainee **8** beginner, flimflam, freshman, neophyte, newcomer
10 apprentice, tenderfoot

rookery
5 roost **6** colony

rookie

4 colt, tyro 6 novice 7 amateur, recruit, trainee 8 beginner, freshman, neophyte, newcomer 10 apprentice, tenderfoot

room

3 den 4 cell, hall, play, rein 5 divan, house, lodge, put up, salon, scope, space 6 alcove, billet, leeway, margin, reside, studio 7 chamber, cubicle, expanse, gallery, lodging 9 clearance

ancient Roman: 5 atria (plural) 6 atrium

eating: 4 nook 6 alcove 7 commons, kitchen 8 mess hall 9 refectory

food storage: 6 larder, pantry

for paintings: 7 gallery

in a monastery: 4 cell 9 refectory 11 calefactory

in a prison: 4 cell

on a ship: 5 cabin 6 galley

round: 7 rotunda

roomer

5 guest 6 lodger, renter, tenant 7 boarder

roomy

4 wide 5 ample, broad, large 8 spacious 9 capacious 10 commodious

Roosevelt, Franklin D.

birthplace: 8 Hyde Park

dog: 4 Fala

message: 12 fireside chat

mother: 4 Sara

predecessor: 6 Hoover (Herbert)

program: 7 New Deal

successor: 6 Truman (Harry)

wife: 7 Eleanor

roost

3 sit 4 land, nest, rest 5 perch 6 alight, settle 7 rookery 8 dovecote

rooster

4 cock 5 capon 8 cockerel, gamecock 10 cockalorum 11 chanticleer

root

3 dig, fix 4 base, bulb, core, grub, pith, stem, well 5 basis, cheer, embed, grout, lodge, plant, radix, tuber 6 bottom, etymon, ground, marrow, origin, settle, source 7 applaud, bedrock, essence, footing, radical 8 radicate 9 beginning, establish, inception 10 foundation

aromatic: 7 ginseng

edible: 3 oca, yam 4 beet 6 carrot, daikon, ginger, jicama, potato, radish, turnip 7 burdock, parsnip, salsify 8 celeriac, kohlrabi, rutabaga, tuckahoe 11 horseradish

fragrant: 5 orris 7 vetiver

main: 7 taproot

medicinal: 5 jalap 7 ginseng

relating to: 7 radical

starch: 4 arum

tropical: 4 taro

word: 6 etymon

rootlet

7 radicle, rhizoid

root out

4 grub 9 eradicate, extirpate 10 deracinate

Roots author

5 Haley (Alex)

rope

3 guy, tie 4 bind, cord, line, stay 5 belay, bight, brace, cable, chord, lasso, riata, sheet 6 binder, fasten, halter, hawser, lariat, marlin, shroud, strand, string, tether 7 halyard, lashing, marline, painter, towline 8 buntline, lifeline

loop: 7 cringle

mooring: 6 hawser

ship's: 6 marlin, parral, parrel 7 lanyard, marline, ratline

ropedancer

11 funambulist

rope off

6 cordon

ropes

10 ins and outs, procedures, techniques

ropy

4 wiry 6 sinewy 7 stringy, viscous 8 muscular

roque
7 croquet

rorqual
5 whale 7 finback 8 fin whale
11 baleen whale

Rosalind's beloved
7 Orlando

rosary
5 beads 7 chaplet 8 beadroll,
devotion 11 prayer beads

rose
4 glow, pink 5 blush, color, flush,
rouge 6 mantle, pinken, redden
7 crimson 10 erysipelas
Chinese: 8 Cherokee
cotton: 7 cudweed
feature: 5 thorn
kind: 4 moss 5 Peace, Vogue
6 Circus, damask 7 Fashion,
Granada, Iceberg, New Dawn,
Pascali, Tiffany 8 Rubaiyat 9 Flo-
radora, Montezuma, polyantha,
Tropicana 10 Floribunda 11 grandi-
flora, Mount Shasta 12 Crimson
Glory

roseate
3 red 4 pink 5 sunny 6 bright, upbeat 7 beamish 8 cheerful, sanguine 10 optimistic

rose-colored
see **roseate**

Rosenkavalier composer
7 Strauss (Richard)

rose of _____
6 Sharon

rose oil
5 attar

Rose Tattoo author
8 Williams (Tennessee)

rosette
7 cockade 8 ornament

Rosinante's master
7 Quixote (Don)

Rosmersholm author
5 Ibsen (Henrik)

_____ Rossetti
5 Dante (Gabriel) 9 Christina
work: 8 Sing-Song 11 Annus
Domini, House of Life (The), Seek
and Find, Sister Helen 12 Beata
Beatrix, Goblin Market

Rossini opera
6 Otello 8 Tancredi 11 Cenerentola
(La), William Tell 14 Siege of Corinth
(The) 15 Barber of Seville (The)

Rostand hero
6 Cyrano (de Bergerac)

roster
4 list, roll, rota 5 slate 6 muster,
scroll 8 register, roll call, schedule
9 honor roll 10 muster roll 11 waiting list

rostrum
4 dais 5 bimah 6 pulpit 7 lectern,
tribune 8 platform

rosy
see **roseate**

rot
4 bosh, bull, mold 5 decay, hooey,
spoil, taint, trash 6 fester, molder
7 corrupt, crapola, crumble, garbage,
hogwash, putrefy, rubbish 8 gangrene, nonsense 9 break down,
decompose, poppycock 10 balderdash, degenerate 11 deteriorate,
putrescence 12 disintegrate, putrefaction 13 decomposition

rotary
6 circle 8 gyratory, spinning, whirling
10 roundabout 11 vertiginous
13 traffic circle

rotate
4 gyre, roll, spin, turn 5 pivot, twirl,
wheel, whirl 6 gyrate, swivel 7 revolve, trundle 9 alternate, pirouette
a log: 4 birl

rotation
4 gyre, loop, turn 5 cycle, orbit,
pivot, round, wheel, whirl 7 circuit,
turning 8 gyration 10 revolution,
succession

rote
5 crowd, grind 6 custom, groove,

Roth novel
memory 7 routine 8 practice 9 automatic, treadmill 10 mechanical, repetition 12 memorization

Roth novel
11 Call It Sleep 15 Goodbye Columbus 16 American Pastoral 17 Portnoy's Complaint

rotten
4 foul 5 fetid, lousy 6 crummy, putrid 7 corrupt, decayed, spoiled, tainted 9 nefarious, offensive, putrefied 10 decomposed, degenerate, putrescent

rotter
3 cad, cur 4 lout 5 creep, louse 7 bounder 9 scoundrel 10 blackguard

rotund
3 fat 5 obese, plump, podgy, pudgy, round, stout, thick, tubby 6 chubby, chunky, portly, stocky 7 rounded 8 heavyset, roly-poly, thickset 9 corpulent 10 potbellied

roué
4 lech, rake, wolf 6 lecher 7 Don Juan, seducer, swinger 8 Casanova, lothario, sybarite 9 bon vivant, debauchee, libertine, womanizer 10 sensualist, voluptuary 11 philanderer

rouge
3 red 4 glow, pink, rose 5 blush, color, flush 6 mantle, pinken, redden 7 crimson

rough
3 raw 4 rude, wild 5 brute, bumpy, crass, crude, hairy, harsh, raspy, rowdy, yahoo 6 choppy, coarse, craggy, crusty, hoarse, jagged, rugged, stormy, uneven 7 cragged, grating, jarring, rasping, raucous, ruffian, scraggy, uncivil, uncouth 8 bullyboy, churlish, impolite, scabrous, unformed 9 difficult, imperfect, strenuous, turbulent, unrefined 10 boisterous, tumultuous, unfinished, unpolished 11 approximate, tempestuous

rough-and-ready
5 crude 6 make-do 7 stopgap 8 slapdash 9 expedient, impromptu, makeshift 10 improvised 11 provisional 13 quick-and-dirty

rough-hewn
4 rude 5 crude, plain 10 unfinished, unpolished 12 uncultivated

roughly
5 about 9 virtually 10 more or less 13 approximately

roughneck
see **ruffian**

rough out
5 block, chalk, draft 6 sketch 7 outline 9 adumbrate 11 skeletonize

rough up
4 beat, maul 6 batter, pummel 8 maltreat 9 brutalize, manhandle 10 slap around

round
4 gyre, tour, turn 5 bowed, cycle, globe, wheel 6 circle, curved, rotund 7 annular, circuit 8 circular, globular, roly-poly, rotation 9 orbicular, spherical 10 conglobate

roundabout
6 circle, detour, rotary 7 circuit, compass, curving, devious, oblique, winding 8 circular, indirect 10 circuitous, meandering 13 traffic circle

rounded
5 bowed, plump 6 arched, convex, curved, zaftig 7 concave 9 developed 10 curvaceous, Rubenesque 13 well-developed

rounder
4 rake, roué, waif 6 no-good, waster 7 wastrel 8 vagabond 9 libertine 10 profligate

roundly
4 well 5 fully, quite 6 widely, wholly 7 bluntly, sharply, smartly, utterly 8 candidly, entirely 9 brusquely 10 altogether, completely, rigorously, scathingly, thoroughly, vigorously

round off
3 cap, top 5 crown 6 climax, finish
8 conclude 9 culminate

round-robin
6 appeal, letter, series 7 protest
8 petition, sequence 9 statement
10 tournament

round trip
4 tour 7 circuit 9 excursion

round up
4 herd 5 drive, group 6 gather
7 cluster, collect 8 assemble

rouse
3 jog 4 call, goad, rock, stir, wake,
whet 5 alarm, awake, pique, rally,
roust, waken 6 awaken, bestir,
excite, foment, incite, kindle, muster,
rattle, recall, revive, vivify, work up
7 agitate, animate, commove, disturb, enliven, provoke, quicken
8 motivate 9 aggravate, challenge,
galvanize, instigate, stimulate

rousing
5 brisk, peppy 6 lively 8 animated,
exciting, spirited, stirring 9 inspiring
11 stimulating 12 exhilarating, intoxi-
cating

Rousseau work
5 Émile

roustabout
4 hand 6 worker 7 laborer, workman 8 deckhand 10 workingman 12 longshoreman, troublemaker

route
3 way 4 path, road, send, ship
5 guide, pilot, steer, track, trail 6 avenue, bypass, course, detour, direct,
divert, escort, flyway, seaway, sky-
way 7 channel, circuit, conduct,
consign, forward, highway, journey,
passage, portage, sea-lane 8 corridor, dispatch, transmit, traverse
9 direction, itinerary

routine
3 act, bit, rut 4 dull, pace, rote
5 chore, drill, grind, habit, ho-hum,
plain, round, trial, usual 6 course,
groove, improv, shtick, wonted 7
chronic, formula, program, regular,
utility 8 accepted, everyday, habitual, ordinary, standard, workaday
9 customary, procedure, quotidian,
treadmill 10 accustomed, donkeywork, mechanical, monologue
11 commonplace, cut-and-dried,
housekeeping, perfunctory 12 unremarkable

rove
3 gad 4 roam 5 drift, range, stray
6 ramble, wander 7 meander,
traipse 8 straggle, vagabond 9 gallivant

rover
5 stray 6 pirate, roamer, viking
7 corsair, drifter, floater, rambler,
vagrant 8 picaroon, runabout,
traveler, wanderer 9 buccaneer,
meanderer 10 freebooter 12 rolling
stone

roving
6 errant, mobile 7 movable, nomadic, vagrant 8 straying, vagabond
9 itinerant, migratory, wayfaring
11 peripatetic

row
3 oar, way 4 bank, crew, file, fray,
fuss, line, muss, rank, spat, tier, tiff
5 align, brawl, broil, chain, fight,
melee, order, queue, range, run-in,
scrap, scull, strip, swath 6 bicker,
clamor, column, dustup, fracas,
kickup, paddle, propel, ruckus, series, string, stroke 7 brabble, dispute, quarrel, rhubarb, wrangle 8 argument, diagonal, sequence,
squabble 9 commotion 10 falling-
out, single file, succession 11 altercation, disturbance, progression

rowdy
4 punk, rude 5 bully, crude, rough,
yahoo 6 unruly 7 hoodlum, rackety,
raffish, raucous, ruffian 8 bullyboy,
hooligan 9 roughneck 10 boisterous, disorderly, robustious 11 rumbustious 12 rambunctious

Rowena
father: **7** Hengist
guardian: **6** Cedric
husband: **7** Ivanhoe **9** Vortigern

Rowling character
11 Harry Potter

Roxana
husband: **9** Alexander
rival: **7** Statira

royal
5 grand, noble, regal **6** kingly, lordly
7 stately **8** glorious, imperial, imposing, majestic, princely, splendid
9 grandiose, monarchal, sovereign
10 monarchial **11** magnificent,
monarchical

rub
4 buff **5** chafe, grate, shine **6** abrade,
polish, smooth, stroke **7** burnish,
massage

Rubaiyat author
4 Omar (Khayyám)

rubber
4 buna **5** crepe **6** eraser **10** caou-
tchouc
basis: **5** latex
hard: **7** ebonite
synthetic: **8** neoprene
tree: **4** Para

Rubber City
5 Akron

rubberneck
3 eye **4** gape, gawk, gaze **5** snoop,
stare **6** goggle **8** sightsee

rubber-stamp
7 approve, certify, endorse **9** authorize

rubbish
3 rot **4** bosh, crap, crud, junk, muck,
slop **5** bilge, dreck, hooey, offal,
trash, truck, waste **6** debris, litter,
refuse, raffle, rubble, spilth **7** crapola, garbage, hogwash **8** nonsense,
riffraff, tommyrot **9** poppycock,
sweepings **11** foolishness

rubbishy
5 cheap, tatty **6** paltry, shoddy,
sleazy, trashy **9** worthless

rubble
5 ruins, scree **6** debris, litter **8** detritus, wreckage

rube
4 boor, hick, naïf **5** churl, cluck, swain,
yahoo, yokel **6** rustic **7** bumpkin,
hayseed, redneck **9** greenhorn,
hillbilly **10** clodhopper **12** apple-
knocker, backwoodsman

rubicund
3 red **5** flush, ruddy **6** florid **7** glowing, reddish **8** sanguine **11** full-
blooded, incarnadine

_____ Rubik
4 Erno

rub out
3 ice, off, zap **4** do in, kill, slay
5 erase, smoke, waste, whack **6** finish, murder **7** bump off, destroy, put
away **8** dispatch, knock off **9** liquidate, terminate **10** extinguish,
obliterate **11** assassinate

rubric
4 name, rule **5** canon, class, gloss,
style, title **6** custom **7** concept,
heading **8** category, headline **9** tradition **11** appellation, designation
13 interpolation

ruck
3 mob **4** fold, heap, mass, pile
5 crimp, crowd, group, purse, ridge
6 cockle, crease, furrow, gather,
jumble, pucker, rumple **7** crinkle,
crumple, scrunch, wrinkle **10** gener-
ality **11** corrugation

rucksack
4 pack **6** kit bag **7** musette **8** backpack

ruckus
3 row **4** fuss, to-do **5** brawl, melee,
scrap **6** fracas, furore, hassle,
pother, rumpus, shindy, uproar **7** dispute, quarrel, rhubarb, shindig, wrangle **8** squabble **9** commotion
10 falling-out **11** altercation, controversy, disturbance

ruddle
see redden

ruddy

3 red 4 ripe, rosy 5 flush 6 blowsy, florid 7 flushed, glowing 8 rubicund, sanguine 11 full-blooded, incarnadine

rude

3 raw 4 curt 5 crass, gross, gruff, harsh, rough, rowdy, surly 6 abrupt, callow, clumsy, coarse, crusty, robust, rugged, rustic, sturdy, unhewn, vulgar 7 boorish, brusque, ill-bred, loutish, lowbred, uncivil, uncouth 8 arrogant, churlish, clownish, impolite, tactless 9 barbarian, barbarous, elemental, inelegant, primitive, rough-hewn, unrefined 10 ungracious, unmannered, unmannerly, unpolished 11 ill-mannered, impertinent, uncivilized 12 discourteous, uncultivated 13 disrespectful

rudimentary

5 basal, basic 6 simple 7 initial, primary 8 simplest 9 beginning, elemental, vestigial 10 elementary 11 fundamental, undeveloped 12 introductory

rudiments

6 basics 10 essentials 12 fundamentals

rue

3 woe 4 pity, ruth 5 dolor, grief, mourn, prick 6 grieve, lament, regret, repent, sorrow 7 anguish, deplore, remorse 8 sympathy 9 heartache, penitence 10 affliction, compassion, contrition, heartbreak, repentance 11 compunction

rueful

5 sorry 6 woeful 8 contrite, penitent 9 regretful, sorrowful 10 remorseful

ruff

5 frill, perch, trump 6 collar, fringe 9 sandpiper 11 pumpkinseed
female: 5 reeve

ruffian

4 goon, hood, punk, thug 5 beast, brute, bully, rowdy, tough, yahoo 6 Apache, hector 7 gorilla, hoodlum 8 bullyboy, hooligan 9 muscleman, roughneck, swaggerer

ruffle

3 bug, irk, rub, vex 4 fret, gall, wear 5 annoy, brawl, chafe, frill, graze, jabot, pleat, ruche 6 abrade, bother, nettle, ripple 7 agitate, bristle, disturb, flounce, provoke, trouble, wrinkle 8 drumbeat, furbelow, irritate, skirmish 9 commotion

rug

3 mat 6 carpet, runner 7 laprobe
kind: 3 rag, rya 6 hooked 7 braided, dhurrie, flokati, Persian 8 Aubusson, bearskin, Oriental 10 Savonnerie

rugby

formation: 5 scrum 9 scrummage
goal: 7 dropped, penalty
period: 4 half
player: 6 center, hooker, winger 8 standoff 9 scrum half
scoring: 3 try 4 goal 10 conversion
team: 7 fifteen
term: 4 heel 5 match 7 convert, dribble, hand off, knock on 9 fair catch
time-out: 8 stoppage
version: 5 union 6 league

rugged

5 burly, hardy, harsh, heavy, husky, rough, tough 6 brawny, coarse, craggy, jagged, robust, severe, stable, stormy, strong, sturdy, uneven 7 arduous, austere, scraggy 8 leathery, muscular, rigorous, scabrous, stalwart, vigorous 9 difficult, inclement, strenuous, unrefined, weathered 10 formidable, unpolished 11 tempestuous

Ruggiero

guardian: 7 Atlante
sister: 7 Marfisa
slayer: 11 Tisaphernes
wife: 10 Bradamante

rug rat

3 tot 4 tyke 6 moppet 7 toddler

Ruhr industrial city

5 Essen

ruin

4 bane, bust, dash, do in, doom, fall, loss, rape, raze, sack, undo 5 decay,

havoc, smash, spoil, trash, use up, waste, wrack, wreck **6** beggar, finish, pauper, perish, ravage **7** corrupt, deplete, despoil, destroy, exhaust, failure, nemesis, pillage, shatter, undoing, wipe out **8** bankrupt, collapse, decimate, demolish, downfall, depredate, devastate, disrepair, overthrow, pauperize, shipwreck **10** desolation, impoverish **11** destruction, devastation, dissolution **12** degeneration **13** deterioration

ruination
4 bane, loss, rack **5** havoc **7** undoing **8** calamity, disaster, downfall **10** decimation **11** destruction, devastation

ruinous
5 fatal **7** baneful **10** calamitous, disastrous, pernicious **11** destructive **12** catastrophic

rule
3 law **4** lead, sway **5** axiom, bylaw, canon, edict, habit, judge, maxim, moral, order, reign **6** assize, custom, decree, deduce, dictum, direct, govern, regime, truism **7** brocard, command, control, precept, prevail, regency, regimen, resolve, statute **8** decretum, doctrine, dominate, domineer, dominion **9** authority, determine, etiquette, ordinance, principle, procedure **10** regulation **absolute: 7** autarky **8** autarchy **by a god: 8** theonomy

Rule Britannia composer
4 Arne (Thomas)

rule out
3 bar **5** block, debar **6** forbid, refuse, reject **7** exclude, forfend, head off, obviate, prevent **8** preclude, prohibit, stave off **9** eliminate

ruler
4 king, lord **5** queen **6** archon, dynast, ferule, gerent, prince, regent, satrap, sultan **7** emperor, monarch, viceroy **8** governor, hierarch, oligarch, pentarch, princess, theocrat **9** dominator, imperator, matriarch, patriarch, potentate, sovereign **12** straightedge
absolute: 6 despot, tyrant **8** autocrat, dictator, overlord
Arab: 4 amir, emir **5** sheik **6** sharif, sheikh, sultan
Asian: 4 khan
Byzantine Empire: 6 exarch
Egyptian: 7 pharaoh
family: 7 dynasty
Iranian: 4 shah
one of four: 8 tetrarch
one of seven: 8 heptarch
one of three: 7 triarch **8** triumvir
Persian: 6 satrap
Russian: 4 czar, tsar, tzar
Turkish: 3 bey, dey

ruling
3 law **4** call **5** chief, edict, order, ukase **6** decree **7** current, finding, popular, regnant, verdict **8** decision, judgment **9** directive, judgement, prevalent, statement **10** prevailing, widespread **11** predominant **12** adjudication

Rumania
see **Romania**

rumble
4 buzz, roar, roll **5** brawl, drone, fight, growl, rumor **6** murmur, report **7** hearsay, quarrel, resound, thunder **8** feedback **9** complaint **11** altercation, disturbance, reverberate, scuttlebutt

ruminant
3 cow, yak **4** deer, goat, tahr **5** bison, camel, okapi, serow, sheep, takin **6** alpaca, cattle, musk ox, vicuña **7** buffalo, chamois, chewing, giraffe, guanaco **8** antelope
stomach: 5 rumen **6** omasum **8** abomasum **9** reticulum

ruminate
4 chew, mull, muse **5** champ, chomp, weigh **6** ponder **7** reflect **8** cogitate, consider, meditate **9** masticate **10** deliberate **11** contemplate

ruminative

7 pensive 8 thinking 9 pondering 10 cogitative, meditative, reflective, thoughtful 11 speculative 13 contemplative, introspective

rummage

4 comb, fish, grub, hash, hunt, poke, rake, rout, seek 5 delve, scour 6 ferret, forage, jumble, litter, search 7 clutter, ransack 8 mishmash 9 potpourri 10 hodgepodge, hotchpotch, miscellany

rummy

3 gin, odd, sot 4 lush, soak, wino 5 drunk, souse, toper 6 boozer 7 bizarre, canasta, curious, guzzler, strange, swiller, tippler, tosspot 8 drunkard, peculiar 9 eccentric, inebriate 10 boozehound

rumor

4 blab, buzz, talk 5 bruit, story 6 canard, gossip, murmur, mutter, report, rumble, tattle 7 hearsay, tidings, whisper 9 grapevine 11 scuttlebutt, susurration

rumormonger

6 gossip 8 gossiper, informer, quidnunc, telltale 9 whisperer 10 talebearer, tattletale

rump

3 can 4 beam, butt, duff, hind, rear, tush 5 fanny 6 behind, bottom, breech, heinie 7 keister, rear end 8 backside, buttocks, derriere, haunches 9 posterior

rumple

4 fold, muss, ruck 5 crimp, screw, touse 6 pucker, tousle 7 crimple, crinkle, scrunch, wrinkle 8 dishevel, disorder

rumpus

see **ruckus**

run

3 fly, hie, jog 4 bolt, dart, dash, flee, flow, race, rush, scud, tear 5 chase, haste, hurry, scoot, skirr, speed 6 career, gallop, hasten, scurry, sprint, streak, stream 7 scamper, scuttle, smuggle 9 skedaddle

run across

4 meet 8 bump into, discover 9 encounter, stumble on

runagate

4 hobo 5 tramp 6 outlaw 7 drifter, floater, lamster, vagrant, wastrel 8 bohemian, fugitive, rapparee, vagabond, wanderer 11 guttersnipe

run along

5 leave, scram 6 beat it, begone, cut out, depart 7 get lost, skiddoo, take off, vamoose 8 shove off 9 skedaddle 10 make tracks

runaround

4 duck, slip 5 dodge 7 elusion, evasion

run away

4 bolt, flee, skip 5 elope, leave, scram, skirr, split, steal 6 depart, desert, escape 7 abscond, make off 8 clear out, light out, stampede 9 skedaddle 10 make tracks

runaway

4 wild 5 loose 6 outlaw 7 escapee, lamster 8 deserter, fugitive 10 delinquent 12 uncontrolled

run down

3 hit, ram, tag 5 catch, knock, trace 6 pursue 7 decline 8 belittle, derogate, diminish 9 apprehend, disparage 10 depreciate 11 catch up with

run-down

5 dingy, seedy, tacky, tired 6 beatup, bushed, shabby 7 rickety, ruinous, worn-out 8 decrepit, tattered, untended 9 burned-out, exhausted, neglected 10 bedraggled, down-atheel, ramshackle, uncared-for 11 dilapidated

rundown

4 dope, poop 5 recap, scoop 6 report, review, skinny, update 7 outline, summary 8 briefing, synopsis

runes

4 ogam 5 ogham 7 futhark

rung

3 bar 4 step 5 grade, notch, round,

run-in

spoke, staff, stage, stair, tread
6 degree, rundle 10 crosspiece

run-in

3 row 4 tiff 5 brush, fight, set-to
6 hassle, scrape, tangle 7 dispute,
quarrel, rhubarb, wrangle 8 skirmish,
squabble 9 encounter 10 falling-out
11 altercation

run into

3 hit, ram 4 meet 9 encounter,
stumble on 11 collide with

runner

3 rug 5 miler, racer 6 carpet, stolon
7 carrier, courier 8 smuggler, sprinter
9 go-between, messenger 10 mara-
thoner 11 ballcarrier

running

6 active, fluent 7 cursive, dynamic,
flowing, working 9 operative 10 continuous 11 functioning

run-of-the-mill

4 dull, so-so 5 usual 6 common,
normal 7 average, humdrum, regular, typical 8 everyday, familiar,
mediocre, middling, moderate,
ordinary 9 prevalent 10 monotonous 11 commonplace, indifferent
12 intermediate 13 unexceptional

run on

3 gab, yak 4 blab 5 clack 6 babble,
cackle, gabble, jabber, rattle 7 chatter, prattle 8 continue

run out of

5 use up 6 finish 7 exhaust

run over

5 spill 6 exceed, repeat 7 examine
8 overfill, overflow, rehearse

runt

5 dwarf, pygmy 6 midget, peanut,
peewee, shrimp, squirt 7 manikin
8 Tom Thumb 10 homunculus
11 hop-o'-my-thumb, lilliputian

run through

3 jab 4 blow, gore, read, scan, stab
5 spend, use up, waste 6 expend,
finish, impale, pierce 7 consume,
examine, exhaust 8 rehearse,
squander, transfix

runty

3 wee 4 puny 6 peewee 7 stunted
8 dwarfish 10 diminutive, undersized

run up

5 build, erect, mount 6 expand
7 augment, enlarge 8 increase,
multiply 9 construct 10 accumulate

runway

4 duct, path 5 strip, track, trail
6 sluice, tarmac 7 channel, conduit
8 airstrip, platform

rupture

4 rend, rent, rift, rive 5 break, burst,
cleft, sever, split 6 breach, cleave,
hernia, schism, sunder 7 blowout,
break up, disrupt, divorce, fissure,
parting, split-up 8 division, fracture,
separate 9 partition 10 separation
11 dissolution 12 estrangement

R.U.R.

author: 5 Capek (Karel)
character: 5 robot

rural

6 rustic 7 bucolic, country, idyllic
8 agrarian, arcadian, down-home,
pastoral 10 campestral 11 countrified

ruse

3 con, jig 4 hoax, ploy, wile 5 dodge,
feint, fraud, stall, trick 6 deceit,
gambit 7 gimmick, swindle 8 artifice, maneuver, trickery 9 deception,
stratagem 10 subterfuge 13 double-
dealing

rush

3 fly, rip, run 4 boil, bolt, dart, dash,
flit, flow, hurl, lash, race, roar, scud,
tear, tide, whiz 5 blitz, break, carry,
chase, court, daily, flash, haste,
hurry, lunge, onset, sally, scoot,
shoot, spate, speed, storm, surge
6 attack, barrel, beat it, bustle, career, charge, course, hasten, hurtle,
hustle, irrupt, plunge, streak, stream,
thrill, whoosh 7 assault, cattail, current, rampage, torrent 8 stampede
9 whirlwind, wire grass 13 precipitation

Rushdie novel
5 Shame **13** Satanic Verses (The)
17 Midnight's Children

rushing
5 hasty **6** abrupt, sudden **7** hurried
8 headlong **9** impetuous **11** precipitate, precipitous

rusk
7 biscuit **8** biscotto

Russia
capital: 6 Moscow
city: 3 Ufa **4** Omsk, Perm'
5 Kazan', Kursk **6** Grozny, Samara
7 Groznyy, Izhevsk, Ivanovo **8** Murmansk **9** Leningrad, Volgograd
10 Stalingrad **11** Chelyabinsk,
Novosibirsk, Vladivostok **12** St. Petersburg **13** Yekaterinburg
emperor: 5 Boris (Godunov), Peter
(the Great) **7** Godunov (Boris),
Michael (Romanov), Romanov
(Michael) **8** Nicholas
empress: 4 Anna (Ivanovna)
9 Catherine (the Great), Elizabeth
(Petrovna)
ethnic group: 7 Cossack
island: 8 Sakhalin
island group: 5 Kuril **6** Kurile
lake: 5 Il'men', Onega **6** Baikal,
Ladoga
leader: 5 Lenin (Vladimir), Putin
(Vladimir) **6** Stalin (Joseph) **7** Trotsky (Leon) **8** Brezhnev (Leonid)
10 Khrushchev (Nikita)
monetary unit: 5 ruble
mountain, range: 4 Ural **5** Altai,
Altay, Sayan **6** Elbrus, Kolyma,
Koryak **8** Caucasus, Stanovoy
neighbor: 5 China **6** Latvia, Norway **7** Belarus, Estonia, Finland,
Georgia, Ukraine **8** Mongolia **9** Kazakstan **10** Azerbaijan, Kazakhstan,
North Korea
peninsula: 4 Kola **5** Gydan, Kanin,
Yamal **6** Taymyr **7** Chukchi **9** Kamchatka
region: 7 Siberia **9** Circassia
11 Golden Horde
revolution: 9 Bolshevik
river: 3 Don **4** Amur, Lena, Ural

5 Desna, Dvina, Vitim, Volga **6** Belaya, Kolyma, Vilyui, Vilyuy **7** Pechora, Yenisey **9** Indigirka
sea: 4 Azov, Kara **5** Black, White
6 Laptev, Okhotsk **7** Barents, Caspian, Chukchi
strait: 6 Bering

Russian
aristocrat: 5 boyar
family: 7 Romanov **9** Stroganov
grandmother: 8 babushka
monk: 8 Rasputin
peasant: 5 kulak, mujik **6** moujik,
muzhik
ruler:
(see **czar**)
saint: 15 Alexander Nevsky
urn: 7 samovar
vehicle: 6 troika
villa: 5 dacha

rustic
4 hick, rube, rude **5** churl, clown,
plain, rough, rural, swain, yokel
6 farmer **7** bucolic, bumpkin, country, granger, hayseed, peasant, plow-
boy, plowman, red-neck, uncouth
8 agrarian, pastoral **9** chawbacon,
hillbilly **10** campestral, clodhopper,
countryman, husbandman **11** countrified **12** apple-knocker, backwoodsman

rustle
5 haste, hurry, speed, steal, swish
6 forage, swoosh **7** crackle, crinkle
8 susurrus

rustler
5 thief **6** duffer, robber **7** forager
8 marauder

Rustum's son
6 Sohrab

rusty
4 slow **6** bygone, creaky **7** outworn
8 outdated, outmoded **10** antiquated, discolored **12** old-fashioned

rut
5 gouge, grind, track **6** furrow,
groove **7** channel, routine **9** treadmill

rutabaga

5 swede 6 turnip

ruth

3 rue, woe 4 pity 5 grief, mercy
6 regret, sorrow 7 anguish, remorse,
sadness 8 distress, sympathy 9 attrition, penitence 10 compassion,
contrition, repentance 11 compunction 13 commiseration

Ruth

husband: 4 Boaz 6 Mahlon
mother-in-law: 5 Naomi
son: 4 Obed

ruthful

6 woeful 7 doleful 8 dolorous,
wretched 9 miserable, sorrowful

ruthless

4 hard 5 cruel, harsh 6 brutal,
savage 7 inhuman 8 pitiless 9 barbarous, cutthroat, dog-eat-dog,
ferocious, heartless, merciless,
unsparing 10 implacable, ironfisted

ruttish

4 lewd 5 lusty, randy 6 wanton
7 goatish, lustful, satyric 9 lecherous, lickerish, salacious 10 lascivious, libidinous 12 concupiscent

Rwanda

city: 6 Kigali
ethnic group: 4 Hutu 5 Tutsi
language: 6 French, Rwanda
monetary unit: 5 franc
neighbor: 5 Congo 6 Uganda
7 Burundi 8 Tanzania

S

_____ Saarinen
4 Eero 5 Eliel

Sabatini novel
11 Scaramouche 12 Captain Blood

sabbatical
4 rest 5 leave 7 time off 8 vacation

saber
5 sword 7 cutlass 8 scimitar

sabertooth
3 cat 5 tiger

sable
3 fur 4 dark, inky 5 black, ebony, raven 6 gloomy, somber, sombre, weasel 8 mourning

sabot
4 clog, shoe 10 wooden shoe

sabotage
5 wreck 6 damage, hamper, hinder 7 cripple, disable, subvert, torpedo 8 obstruct, wreckage, wrecking 9 frustrate, undermine, vandalize 10 subversion 11 undermining

Sabra
father: 7 Ptolemy
rescuer: 8 St. George
son: 3 Guy 5 David 9 Alexander

sac
4 caul, cyst 5 pouch 7 vesicle

saccharine
5 mushy, sweet 6 sugary, syrupy 7 candied, cloying, honeyed, maudlin, mawkish, sugared 9 oversweet, schmaltzy 11 sentimental, sugarcoated 12 ingratiating

sacerdotal
8 hieratic, pastoral, priestly 10 priestlike 11 ministerial

sachem
4 boss 5 chief 6 leader

sachet
3 bag 6 powder 7 perfume 9 potpourri

sack
3 bag, bed, can 4 bunk, drop, fire, loot, raid, wine 5 expel, pouch, strip, waste 6 pocket, ravage 7 boot out, cashier, despoil, dismiss, hammock, kick out, pillage, plunder 8 desolate, spoliate 9 container, depredate, desecrate, devastate, white wine

sackbut
8 trombone

sacque
6 jacket

sacrament
4 rite 6 ritual 7 baptism, penance 8 ceremony, marriage 9 Communion, Eucharist, matrimony 10 holy orders 12 confirmation

sacrarium
6 chapel, shrine 7 oratory, piscina 8 sacristy 9 sanctuary

sacred
4 holy 5 godly 6 divine, immune 7 angelic, blessed, saintly 8 hallowed, numinous 9 inviolate, spiritual 10 inviolable, sacrosanct, sanctified 11 consecrated, sacramental

sacrifice

combining form: 4 hagi, hier, sacr 5 hagio, hiero, sacro
monkey: 6 baboon, rhesus 7 hanuman
place: 7 sanctum
weed: 7 vervain

sacrifice

4 bunt, cede, lose, loss 5 forgo, yield 6 devote, donate, eschew, give up, martyr, victim 7 forfeit, offer up 8 dedicate, hecatomb, immolate, oblation, offering 12 renunciation

sacrilege

6 heresy 7 impiety, offense 9 blasphemy, violation 11 desecration, irreverence, profanation

sacrilegious

7 impious, profane, ungodly 10 irreverent 11 blasphemous

sacristan

6 sexton

sacristy

6 vestry

sacrosanct

9 inviolate 10 inviolable

sad

4 blue, down 5 sorry 6 dismal, dreary, gloomy, morose, triste, woeful 7 doleful, joyless, piteous, pitiful, unhappy 8 dejected, desolate, dolorous, downbeat, downcast, grieving, mournful, pathetic, pitiable 9 depressed, sorrowful, woebegone 10 depressing, dispirited, lamentable, melancholy 11 melancholic 12 heavyhearted

sadden

7 depress, oppress, trouble 8 aggrieve, dispirit 9 weigh down 10 discourage

saddle

3 tax 4 lade, load, task 5 weigh 6 burden, charge, hamper, impede, impose, weight 7 aparejo, inflict 8 encumber, restrict
adjunct: 7 stirrup
part: 6 cantle, pommel
strap: 5 cinch, girth 6 latigo 7 harness

sadness

3 woe 4 funk 5 blues, dolor, dumps, gloom, grief, mopes 6 misery, sorrow 7 dismals, megrims 8 doldrums, glumness, mourning 9 dejection, dysphoria, heartache 10 blue devils, depression, desolation, melancholy 11 despondency, melancholia, unhappiness

safari

4 hunt, trek, trip 7 caravan, journey 10 expedition

safe

4 snug, wary 5 chary 6 secure, unhurt 7 careful, guarded 8 cautious, defended, shielded, unharmed 9 innocuous, protected, sheltered, uninjured, unscathed 10 inviolable, sheltering 11 impregnable 12 invulnerable, unassailable

safecracker

4 yegg 8 picklock 9 cracksman

safeguard

4 ward 6 convoy, defend, escort, shield, surety 7 bulwark, defense, protect 8 armament, preserve 10 precaution, protection

safety

6 asylum, refuge 7 defense, shelter 8 immunity, security 9 assurance, sanctuary 10 protection 13 inviolability

sag

3 dip 4 bend, drop, flag, flap, flop, hang, sink, slip, wilt 5 droop, slide, slump 6 dangle, hollow, slouch 7 decline, drop off, falloff, sinkage, sinking 8 downturn, settling, sinkhole 9 concavity, downswing 10 depression

saga

4 edda, epic, myth, tale 5 story 6 legend 9 chronicle, narrative 12 Heimskringla

sagacious

4 keen, wise 5 acute, smart 6 astute, clever, shrewd 7 knowing, prudent, sapient 8 critical 9 far-

seeing, judicious 10 discerning, insightful, perceptive 11 intelligent 13 perspicacious

sagacity
5 grasp 6 acuity, acumen, wisdom 7 insight 8 judgment, keenness, prudence, sapience 10 perception, shrewdness 11 discernment, penetration, percipience, perspicuity 12 perspicacity 13 comprehension, judiciousness, understanding

sagamore
5 chief 6 sachem

Sagan work
6 Cosmos 16 Bonjour tristesse

sage
4 guru, mint, wise 6 expert, master, nestor, pundit, savant, shrewd 7 gnostic, knowing, learned, prudent, sapient, scholar, wise man 8 polymath, profound, sensible 9 judicious 10 discerning, insightful, perceptive 11 penetrating, philosophic
Hindu: 6 pandit 7 mahatma

Sage
of Chelsea: 7 Carlyle (Thomas)
of Concord: 7 Emerson (Ralph Waldo)
of Emporia: 5 White (William Allen)
of Ferney: 8 Voltaire
of Monticello: 9 Jefferson (Thomas)
of Pylos: 6 Nestor

Sagebrush State
6 Nevada

Sagittarius
6 archer 7 centaur 13 constellation

sago
4 palm 6 starch

saguaro
6 cactus

sahib
3 sir 6 master 9 gentleman

sail
3 fly 4 dart, flit, scud, skim, wing 5 fleet, float, shoot, skirr, sweep 6 cruise, mizzen 7 spencer 9 spinnaker
triangular: 3 jib 5 genoa

sailboat
4 bark, yawl 5 ketch, skiff, sloop, yacht 6 dinghy 8 schooner, skipjack

sailing vessel
4 bark, brig 5 xebec 6 barque 7 frigate, galleon 8 schooner 10 barkentine, brigantine 11 barquentine

sailor
3 gob, tar 4 jack, mate, salt, swab 6 hearty, sea dog, seaman 7 jacktar, mariner, matelot, old salt, swabbie 8 flatfoot, seafarer, shipmate, water dog 9 shellback, tarpaulin, yachtsman 10 bluejacket
British: 5 limey
fictional: 6 Sinbad
patron saint: 4 Elmo
song: 6 chanty 7 chantey 9 barcarole

saint
7 paragon
biography: 11 hagiography
list: 9 hagiology
(see also patron saint)

Saint, The
12 Simon Templar
creator: 9 Charteris (Leslie)

Saint Anthony's cross
3 tau

Saint Elmo's Fire
9 corposant

Saint Helena
capital: 9 Jamestown
colony of: 7 Britain
island: 9 Ascension

Saint Joan author
4 Shaw (George Bernard)

Saint John's bread
5 carob

Saint Kitts and Nevis
capital: 10 Basseterre
island group: 7 Leeward
language: 7 English
location: 10 West Indies
monetary unit: 6 dollar

Saint Lucia
capital: 8 Castries

island group: 8 Windward
language: 6 French 7 English
location: 10 West Indies
monetary unit: 6 dollar
volcano: 8 Quilabou

saintly
4 holy, pure 5 godly, pious 6 devout, worthy 7 angelic, blessed, upright 8 beatific, seraphic, virtuous 9 righteous

Saint Paul's architect
4 Wren (Christopher)

Saint Peter's Basilica
architect: 7 Bernini (Gian Lorenzo) 12 Michelangelo (Buonarotti)
sculpture: 5 Pietà

Saint-Pierre and Miquelon
capital: 8 St.-Pierre
department of: 6 France

Saint Vincent and the Grenadines
capital: 9 Kingstown
island group: 8 Windward
language: 6 French 7 English
location: 10 West Indies
monetary unit: 6 dollar
volcano: 9 Soufrière

Saint Vitus' dance
6 chorea

sake
3 end 4 good 5 drink 7 benefit, purpose, welfare

Saki
5 Munro (H. H.)

salaam
3 bow 6 kowtow 8 greeting 9 obeisance

salacious
4 fast, lewd 5 bawdy 6 erotic, ribald, risqué 7 lustful, satyric 8 indecent, prurient 9 lecherous, libertine 10 lascivious, libidinous, licentious

salad
item: 3 egg 4 bean, cuke, herb 5 cress, olive, onion 6 carrot, celery, cheese, endive, pepper, potato, radish, tomato 7 anchovy, cabbage, crouton, lettuce, parsley, spinach 8 chickpea, coleslaw, cucumber, garbanzo, mushroom, scallion 10 watercress
type: 5 chef's 6 Caesar

salamander
3 eft 4 newt 7 urodele 8 mud puppy, water dog 10 hellbender
Mexican: 7 axolotl

salary
3 pay 4 take, wage 6 income 7 stipend 8 earnings 9 emolument 10 recompense 12 compensation, remuneration

sale
6 bazaar, demand 7 auction 8 closeout, disposal, transfer 9 clearance 11 transaction

salient
6 marked, signal 7 obvious, weighty 8 striking 9 arresting, important, obtrusive, pertinent, prominent 10 impressive, noticeable, projecting, pronounced, remarkable 11 conspicuous, outstanding, significant

saline
5 briny, salty 8 brackish

Salinger, J. D.
character: 4 Esmé 6 Holden (Caulfield)
novel: 14 Franny and Zooey 15 Catcher in the Rye

saliva
4 spit 6 slaver, sputum 7 spittle

salivate
5 drool 6 drivel, slaver 7 slobber

_____ Salk
5 Jonas

sallow
3 wan 4 pale, waxy 5 pasty 6 pallid, sickly, willow, yellow 7 bilious 9 jaundiced

sally
3 gag 4 gust, jape, jest, joke, quip 5 blast, burst, crack, jaunt 6 depart, junket, outing, set out, sortie, volley 7 barrage, flare-up 8 drollery, erup-

tion, outbreak, outburst, paroxysm
9 discharge, excursion, explosion,
wisecrack, witticism

salmagundi
see **hodgepodge**

salmon
4 parr, pink **5** smolt **6** grilse **7** sockeye **9** brandling
cured: 7 gravlax **8** gravlaks
male: 6 kipper
smoked: 3 lox

Salome
composer: 7 Strauss (Richard)
father: 5 Herod
husband: 6 Philip **7** Zebedee
11 Aristobulus
mother: 8 Herodias
son: 4 John **5** James
victim: 4 John (the Baptist)

salon
4 hall, shop **5** suite **6** parlor **7** gallery **9** apartment, reception **10** exhibition

saloon
3 bar, pub **6** tavern **7** barroom,
cantina, gin mill, taproom **9** beer
joint **12** watering hole

salt
3 tar **4** jack, keep, NaCl **5** brine
6 sailor, saline, seaman **7** jack-tar,
mariner **8** salinize **9** sailorman

salt away
4 bank, save **5** hoard, lay by, lay up,
put by, stash, store **7** deposit **8** lay
aside, squirrel

saltpeter
5 niter, nitre

salty
4 blue, racy **5** briny, crude, spicy,
tangy **6** earthy, purple, risqué, saline
7 caustic, mordant, pungent **8** brackish, off-color, scathing **9** trenchant

salubrious
5 tonic **7** bracing, healthy **8** hygienic, salutary **9** healthful, wholesome **10** beneficial **11** restorative
12 invigorating

Salus
see **Hygeia**

salutary
5 tonic **6** benign **7** bracing, healing **8** curative, remedial, sanative
9 analeptic, healthful, vulnerary,
wholesome **10** beneficial, salubrious
11 restorative, therapeutic **12** advantageous, health-giving

salutation
4 hail **5** hello, howdy **7** welcome
8 greeting
Arab: 6 salaam
French: 5 salut
Hawaiian: 5 aloha
Italian: 4 ciao
Latin: 3 ave
Spanish: 4 hola

salute
4 hail **5** greet, honor **6** praise
7 address, commend **8** greeting
12 congratulate

salvage
4 save **6** ransom, recoup, redeem,
regain, rescue **7** deliver, reclaim,
recover **8** retrieve

salvation
6 saving **7** keeping **10** redemption
11 deliverance **12** conservation,
preservation

Salvation Army founder
5 Booth (General William)

salve
4 balm **5** cream, quiet **6** cerate,
chrism, lotion, remedy **7** assuage,
unction, unguent **8** ointment **9** emollient

salver
4 tray

salvo
4 hail **5** burst, spray, storm **6** attack,
shower, volley **7** barrage, proviso
9 broadside, cannonade, discharge,
fusillade **11** bombardment

Samaritan
6 helper **10** benefactor

same

4 idem, like, very 5 equal, exact
7 coequal, similar 8 constant 9 duplicate, identical, unvarying 10 consistent, equivalent, invariable, unchanging

Samoa

capital: 4 Apia
island: 5 Upolu 6 Savai'i
language: 6 Samoan 7 English
monetary unit: 4 tala

samovar

3 urn

samp

6 cereal, hominy

sampan

4 boat 5 skiff

sample

3 try 4 case, part, test, unit 5 piece, taste 7 element, example, excerpt, portion, segment 8 fragment, instance, specimen 10 indication 11 case history, constituent 12 illustration

Samson

betrayer: 7 Delilah
birthplace: 5 Zorah
deathplace: 4 Gaza
father: 6 Manoah
tribe: 3 Dan

Samson Agonistes author

6 Milton (John)

Samuel

father: 7 Elkanah
grandson: 5 Heman
mother: 6 Hannah

samurai code

7 Bushido

San Antonio

team: 5 Spurs
landmark: 5 Alamo

sanatorium

3 spa 8 hospital, rest home

sanctify

5 bless 6 hallow, ordain, purify
8 dedicate 10 consecrate

sanctimonious

5 pious 7 canting, preachy 8 unctuous 9 pharisaic 11 pharisaical
12 hypocritical, Pecksniffian 13 self-righteous

sanction

4 fiat, okay 5 bless, leave 6 assent, decree, permit, ratify 7 approve, backing, boycott, certify, consent, embargo, endorse, license, penalty, support 8 accredit, approval 9 allowance, authorize 10 commission, permission, sufferance 11 approbation, endorsement 12 confirmation, ratification 13 authorization, encouragement

sanctity

8 holiness 9 godliness 11 saintliness, uprightness 13 inviolability, righteousness

sanctuary

5 haven, oasis 6 asylum, covert, harbor, refuge, shrine, temple 7 reserve, retreat, shelter 8 preserve
9 holy place

sanctum

4 lair 6 shrine 7 retreat, shelter
9 holy place, sanctuary

sand

3 tan 4 buff, ecru, fawn, grit 5 beach, beige, camel, grind, khaki, scour, shore 6 gravel, polish, smooth
7 burnish 8 granules

sandal

4 clog, zori 5 sabot, thong 6 patten
8 flip-flop, huarache 10 espadrille

sandbag

6 ambush, waylay

sandbar

4 reef, spit 7 tombolo

Sand County Almanac author

7 Leopold (Aldo)

sandpiper

4 knot, ruff 5 reeve 6 dunlin 9 shorebird

sandstone deposit

6 flysch

sandwich
3 BLT, sub 4 club, gyro, roti 5 butty,
Cuban 6 Denver, hoagie, Reuben
7 grinder, Western 9 submarine
10 muffuletta
shop: 4 deli

sandy
4 fair 5 blond 6 blonde, grainy, gritty

sane
3 fit 4 good, hale, sage, well, wise
5 lucid, right, sober, sound 6 cogent,
normal 7 healthy, logical, prudent,
sapient 8 all there, balanced, ori-
ented, rational, sensible 9 judicious,
wholesome 10 reasonable 11 level-
headed 12 compos mentis

San Francisco
hill: 3 Nob 7 Russian
tower: 4 Coit

sangfroid
4 calm 5 poise 6 aplomb, phlegm
9 composure 10 equanimity 11 self-
control

sanguinary
4 gory 6 bloody 9 homicidal, murdering, murderous 12 bloodstained,
bloodthirsty

sanguine
4 gory 5 flush, ruddy 6 bloody,
florid, secure, upbeat 7 assured,
buoyant, flushed, glowing, hopeful
8 bloodred, cheerful, rubicund
9 confident, homicidal, murdering,
murderous 10 optimistic 11 self-
assured 12 blood-stained, bloodthirsty, Pollyannaish 13 self-confident

sanitary
5 clean 7 sterile 8 hygienic
9 healthful 10 antiseptic, salubrious

sanitize
5 clean, purge 6 bleach, censor,
purify 7 cleanse, launder 8 black
out 9 disinfect, expurgate, sterilize
10 bowdlerize

sanity
6 health, reason 7 balance 8 lucidity, prudence 9 normality, soundness, stability

San Marino
capital: 9 San Marino
monetary unit: 4 euro
monetary unit, former: 4 lira
neighbor: 5 Italy

sans
7 lacking, missing, wanting, without

Sanskrit
dialect: 4 Pali
epic: 8 Ramayana
Scripture: 4 Veda

Santa Lucia composer
5 Denza (Luigi)

São Tomé and Príncipe
capital: 7 São Tomé
language: 10 Portuguese
location: 12 Gulf of Guinea
monetary unit: 5 dobra

sap
4 dupe, fool, gull, mark 5 chump,
drain 6 pigeon, sucker, weaken
7 cripple, deplete, disable, exhaust,
fall guy 8 enervate, enfeeble 9 attenuate, schlemiel, undermine
10 debilitate

sapid
5 tasty 6 savory 9 delicious, flavorful, palatable, toothsome 10 appetizing 11 scrumptious

sapience
see sagacity

sapient
see sagacious

sapling
4 tree 5 child, youth 9 youngster

Sapphira's husband
7 Ananias

Sappho
forte: 6 poetry
island: 6 Lesbos

sappy
5 ditzy, flaky, mushy, silly, soupy
6 drippy, slushy, sticky, syrupy
7 cloying, foolish, maudlin, mawkish
8 bathetic 11 sentimental

Saracen hero
9 Rodomonte

Sarah
husband: 7 Abraham
maid: 5 Hagar
son: 5 Isaac

sarcasm
3 wit 4 gibe 5 irony, scorn 6 satire
7 mockery 8 acerbity, mordancy,
ridicule, sneering 10 causticity

sarcastic
4 acid, tart 5 acerb, sharp 6 biting,
ironic 7 acerbic, caustic, cutting,
cynical, jeering, mocking, mordant,
satiric 8 sardonic, scathing, scornful,
stinging 9 corrosive

sarcophagus
4 tomb 6 coffin

sardine
4 sild 7 anchovy, herring 8 pilchard

Sardinia's capital
8 Cagliari

sardonic
3 wry 6 ironic 7 caustic, cynical,
jeering, mocking, satiric 8 derisive,
scornful, sneering 9 corrosive,
sarcastic 10 disdainful 12 contemptuous

sarong
5 skirt 7 garment

Sarpedon
brother: 5 Minos 12 Rhadamanthus
father: 4 Zeus 7 Jupiter
mother: 6 Europa 8 Laodamia

Sartor _____
8 Resartus

Sartre work
4 Wall (The) 5 Flies (The) 6 Nausea, No Exit 8 Huis Clos 10 Saint
Genet

sash
4 belt 6 girdle 8 ceinture, cincture
9 waistband 10 cummerbund

sashay
5 mince, strut 6 prance 7 flounce,
saunter, swagger

Saskatchewan
capital: 6 Regina
city: 8 Moose Jaw 9 Saskatoon
12 Prince Albert
mountain range: 12 Cypress Hills
provincial flower: 7 red lily 11 prairie lily
river: 9 Churchill 11 Assiniboine

sass
3 lip 4 guff 5 brass, cheek, mouth,
sauce 8 back talk 9 impudence,
insolence 12 impertinence

sassy
4 bold, flip, pert, wise 5 fresh, lippy,
nervy, smart 6 brazen, cheeky
7 forward 8 flippant, impudent,
insolent, malapert 9 audacious,
unabashed 11 smart-alecky

Satan
5 demon, devil, fiend 6 diablo
7 Lucifer, Old Nick, serpent, villain
9 archfiend, Beelzebub 10 Old
Scratch

satanic
4 evil 6 wicked 7 demonic, hellish
8 demoniac, devilish, diabolic,
fiendish, infernal

satanism
9 diabolism

satchel
3 bag 4 case, tote 5 pouch 6 valise
7 handbag 9 briefcase

sate
4 cloy, fill, glut, jade, pall 5 gorge,
stuff 6 stodge 7 appease, overeat,
placate, surfeit 8 overfill 9 overstuff
10 conciliate

sated
4 full 6 filled, gorged 7 glutted,
overfed, replete, stuffed 8 appeased,
chockful 9 chock-full, surfeited

satellite
4 moon 5 toady 6 cohort, minion
7 Sputnik 8 adherent, disciple,
follower, henchman, partisan 9 attendant, supporter, sycophant,
tributary
of Jupiter: 6 Europa 8 Callisto,
Ganymede

of Mars: 6 Deimos, Phobos
of Neptune: 6 Nereid, Triton
of Saturn: 4 Rhea 5 Dione, Janus,
Mimas, Titan 6 Phoebe, Tethys
7 Iapetus 8 Hyperion 9 Enceladus
of Uranus: 5 Ariel 6 Oberon 7 Miranda, Titania, Umbriel

satiate
see sate

satire
3 wit 5 irony, spoof, squib 6 parody 7 lampoon, mockery, takeoff
8 raillery, ridicule, spoofery, travesty
9 burlesque 10 caricature, lampoonery, pasquinade, persiflage

satiric
6 ironic 7 mocking 8 farcical,
ironical

satirist
English: 5 Swift (Jonathan) 7 Marston (John)
French: 8 Rabelais (François),
Voltaire
Greek: 8 Menippus
Italian: 7 Aretino (Pietro)
Roman: 6 Horace 7 Juvenal,
Martial, Persius 9 Petronius

satirize
4 mock 5 spoof 6 parody, send up
7 lampoon 8 ridicule 10 caricature

satisfaction
6 amends 7 redress 8 pleasure,
serenity 9 atonement 10 reparation
11 contentment, fulfillment, restitution, vindication 12 propitiation
13 gratification

satisfactory
4 fair, good, okay 5 sound 6 decent
8 adequate, all right, passable
9 competent, tolerable 10 acceptable, sufficient 13 unexceptional

satisfy
3 pay 4 fill, meet, sate, suit 5 clear,
humor, pay up, serve 6 answer,
assure, dispel, pacify, please, settle,
square 7 appease, content, fulfill,
gladden, gratify, indulge, placate,
satiate, suffice, win over 8 convince,
persuade 9 conform to, discharge,
indemnify 10 comply with

satori
12 illumination 13 enlightenment

satrap
5 ruler 6 cohort 7 viceroy 8 governor, henchman, sidekick 11 subordinate

saturate
3 sop, wet 4 fill, soak 5 bathe, douse,
imbue, souse, steep 6 charge,
drench, infuse 7 pervade, suffuse
8 permeate, waterlog 9 transfuse

Saturn
moon: 4 Rhea 5 Dione, Janus,
Mimas, Titan 6 Phoebe, Tethys
7 Iapetus 8 Hyperion 9 Enceladus
see also **Cronus**

saturnalia
4 orgy 5 party, revel 6 excess
7 debauch 9 bacchanal 11 bacchanalia, dissipation

saturnine
4 dour, glum, grim 5 sulky, surly
6 gloomy, moping, morose, somber,
sombre, sullen 7 crabbed 8 funereal, sardonic

satyr
4 goat, rake, wolf 6 lecher 9 butterfly

satyric
4 lewd 5 randy 6 wanton 7 goatish,
lustful 8 prurient 9 lecherous, libertine, lickerish, salacious 10 lascivious, libidinous, licentious, lubricious
11 promiscuous 12 concupiscent

sauce
4 guff, sass 5 mouth 6 relish 7 topping 8 back talk 9 condiment,
impudence
kind: 3 soy 4 hard, mole 5 chili,
curry, gravy, melba, pesto, salsa
6 Mornay, panada, tamari, tartar
7 chutney, marengo, Newburg,
piquant, soubise, tartare, velouté
8 béchamel, duxelles, marinara,
matelote, noisette, normande 9 béarnaise, lyonnaise, rémoulade 10 bordelaise, Provençale 11 hollandaise,
vinaigrette

saucy
see **sassy**

Saudi Arabia
capital: 6 Riyadh
city: 5 Jedda, Jidda, Mecca 6 Jeddah, Jiddah, Medina
desert: 7 Arabian 10 Rub Al-Khali 12 Empty Quarter
gulf: 7 Persian
monetary unit: 5 riyal
neighbor: 3 UAE 4 Iraq, Oman 5 Qatar, Yemen 6 Jordan
peninsula: 7 Arabian
sea: 3 Red

Saul
concubine: 6 Rizpah
cousin: 5 Abner
daughter: 5 Merab 6 Michal
father: 4 Kish
son: 8 Jonathan
successor: 5 David
uncle: 3 Ner
wife: 7 Ahinoam

saunter
4 mope, roam, rove 5 amble, drift, mosey 6 loiter, ramble, sashay, stroll, wander 7 meander, traipse

sausage
5 wurst 6 banger, kishke, salami, Vienna, wiener 7 baloney, bologna, boloney, chorizo, saveloy 8 cervelat, kielbasa 9 andouille, bratwurst, frankfurt, pepperoni, Thuringer 10 knackwurst, knockwurst, liverwurst, mortadella 11 frankfurter

sauté
3 fry 4 sear 5 brown, grill 6 sizzle 7 frizzle

savage
4 grim, wild 5 brute, cruel, feral 6 bloody, brutal, fierce, Gothic, rugged 7 bestial, brutish, inhuman, untamed, vicious, wolfish 8 barbaric, inhumane, primeval, ravenous, unbroken 9 barbarian, barbarous, ferocious, heartless, murderous, primitive, rapacious, truculent, voracious 10 implacable, relentless 11 uncivilized 12 bloodthirsty, uncontrolled, uncultivated, unsocialized

savagery
7 cruelty 8 atrocity 9 barbarity, brutality, depravity 10 bestiality, inhumanity 11 abomination, monstrosity, viciousness 12 ruthlessness

savanna
5 plain 9 grassland

savant
4 sage 7 scholar, thinker, wise man

save
3 bar, but, yet 4 bank, keep, only, stow 5 amass, avoid, cache, guard, hoard, lay by, lay in, lay up, put by, set by, skimp, spare, store 6 defend, except, gather, keep up, manage, ransom, redeem, rescue, scrimp, shield, unless 7 barring, besides, collect, deliver, deposit, however, husband, lay away, protect, reclaim, reserve, salvage, set free, store up 8 conserve, lay aside, liberate, maintain, preserve, salt away, set aside, squirrel 9 aside from, economize, excluding, safeguard, stash away, stockpile 10 accumulate

savior
7 messiah, paladin, rescuer 8 defender 9 deliverer, liberator, preserver, protector, salvation 11 white knight

savoir faire
4 tact 5 grace, poise 6 aplomb 7 address, dignity, finesse, manners 8 urbanity 10 confidence, refinement 13 self-assurance

savor
4 odor, tang 5 enjoy, scent, smack, smell, spice, taste, tinge 6 flavor, relish, season 8 sapidity

savory
5 sapid, spicy, tangy, tasty 7 piquant 9 flavorful, palatable, toothsome 10 appetizing

savvy
4 deft 5 adept, craft, handy, knack, skill 6 clever, talent 7 ability, know-

how, skilled **8** deftness **9** adeptness, expertise, handiness, ingenuity **10** capability, cleverness, competence

saw
3 cut, hew **5** adage, axiom, maxim **6** byword, cliché, saying **7** precept, proverb **8** aphorism, apothegm

___ saw
3 bow, jig, pit, rip **4** band, buck, buzz, fret, hack, whip **5** chain, crown, saber **6** coping, scroll **7** compass, keyhole **8** circular, crosscut

sawbones
3 doc **6** doctor **7** surgeon **9** physician

sawbuck
6 tenner **7** trestle

sawhorse
see **sawbuck**

saw-toothed
7 serrate, serried **8** serrated **11** denticulate

Saxon
assembly: 4 moot **5** gemot **6** gemote
nobleman: 8 atheling
serf: 4 esne
warrior: 5 thane

say
4 talk, tell **5** mouth, speak, state, utter, voice **6** affirm, assert, assume, recite, remark **7** comment, declare, express **8** announce, proclaim **9** enunciate, pronounce **10** articulate

Sayers character
6 Wimsey (Lord Peter)

saying
3 mot, saw **5** adage, axiom, maxim **6** byword, dictum, truism **7** precept, proverb **8** apothegm

scab
5 crust **6** eschar **13** strikebreaker

scabbard
6 sheath

scabrous
4 lewd **5** harsh, rough, salty, scaly **6** craggy, grubby, jagged, knobby, knotty, rugged, scabby, scurfy, sordid, uneven **7** bristly, prickly, scraggy, squalid **8** indecent **10** scandalous

scads
4 gobs, lots, wads **5** loads, piles, reams **6** oodles **8** slathers **10** quantities

scaffold
5 stage, truss **7** staging **8** platform **9** framework

Scala, La
city: 5 Milan
production: 5 opera

scalawag
see **scamp**

scald
4 boil, burn **6** scorch

scale
4 peel, rate, skin **5** climb, flake, gamut, gauge, mount, ratio, scute, strip **6** ascend, degree, extent, ladder, lamina, scutum, squama **7** measure, ranking **8** escalade, flake off, spall off **9** exfoliate, hierarchy **10** desquamate, proportion **11** decorticate
auxiliary: 7 vernier
earthquake: 7 Richter
temperature: 6 Kelvin **7** Celsius **10** centigrade, Fahrenheit
wind: 8 Beaufort

scallion
4 leek **5** onion **7** shallot **10** green onion

scalp
4 flay, skin **5** cheat **6** resell, trophy

scam
3 con, gyp **4** bilk, dupe, fool, hoax **5** cheat, fraud, stick, trick **6** delude, diddle, take in **7** beguile, deceive, defraud, swindle **8** flimflam, hoodwink **11** double-cross

scamp
3 imp **4** brat, rake, tyke **5** devil,

joker, knave, rogue 6 rascal, urchin
7 hellion 8 scalawag, slyboots
9 prankster, skeezicks 11 rapscallion

scamper
3 run 4 dash, skip 5 scoot 6 scurry
7 scuttle

scan
3 eye 4 skim, view 5 audit, check
6 browse, review, survey 7 examine,
eyeball, inspect 8 glance at 10 run
through, scrutinize

scandal
5 rumor 6 gossip, infamy 7 calumny, obloquy, offense, slander
8 disgrace, dishonor, reproach
9 aspersion, discredit, disrepute
10 backbiting, defamation, detraction, opprobrium

scandalize
5 libel, shock, smear 6 defame,
malign 7 asperse, slander 9 denigrate 10 calumniate

scandalmonger
6 gossip 8 busybody, gossiper,
quidnunc, telltale 9 backbiter, muck-
raker 10 talebearer

scandalous
7 heinous 8 infamous, libelous,
shameful, shocking 9 notorious,
offensive 10 defamatory, outrageous, scurrilous 11 disgraceful

Scandinavian
see **Norse**

Scandinavian country
6 Norway, Sweden 7 Denmark,
Finland, Iceland

scant
5 short, skimp, spare, stint, tight
6 meager, meagre, paltry, scarce,
scrimp, skimpy, slight, sparse
7 scrimpy, wanting 8 exiguous
10 inadequate 12 insufficient

scantiness
4 lack 6 dearth 7 deficit, paucity
8 scarcity, shortage, sparsity 10 deficiency, inadequacy, scarceness,
sparseness 13 insufficiency

scanty
see **scant**

scapegoat
6 target, victim 7 fall guy 9 sacrifice
11 whipping boy

scapegrace
5 knave, rogue, scamp 6 bad egg,
rascal 7 ruffian, varmint, villain
8 hooligan, recreant, scalawag
9 miscreant, reprobate, scoundrel
10 blackguard, black sheep, delinquent 11 rapscallion

Scapin
5 rogue, valet 6 rascal
author: 7 Molière
employer: 7 Léandre

scar
3 mar 4 flaw 5 score 6 deface,
defect, keloid 7 blemish, scratch
8 cicatrix, pockmark 9 cicatrize,
disfigure
on a seed: 5 hilum

scarab
6 beetle

scaramouch
see **scamp**

scarce
3 few 4 rare 5 scant 6 barely,
hardly, scanty, sparse 7 limited,
wanting 8 sporadic, uncommon
9 deficient 10 inadequate, infrequent, occasional 12 insufficient

scarcity
see **scantiness**

scare
5 alarm, panic, spook 6 fright
7 horrify, petrify, shake up, startle,
terrify 8 frighten, paralyze 9 terrorize

scaredy-cat
4 wimp, wuss 5 mouse, sissy 6 coward 7 chicken, dastard 8 alarmist,
poltroon 11 milquetoast, yellowbelly

scare up
4 find, snag 5 rally 6 corral, gather,
locate, obtain, secure 7 acquire,
collect, procure, unearth 8 smoke
out 9 ferret out, track down

scarf
4 gulp, wolf 5 ascot, fichu, plaid, shawl, stole 6 cravat, devour, gobble, inhale 8 babushka, liripipe, mantilla, puggaree 10 lambrequin
Mexican: 6 rebozo

Scarlet Letter, The
author: 9 Hawthorne (Nathaniel)
character: 5 Pearl 6 Hester (Prynne) 10 Dimmesdale (Arthur) 13 Chillingworth (Roger)

Scarlet Pimpernel author
5 Orczy (Baroness Emmuska)

Scarlett's home
4 Tara

scary
6 creepy, spooky 8 chilling 9 frightful

scathe
4 burn, flay, flog, harm, lash, sear 5 roast, slash 6 assail, berate, scorch, thrash 7 blister, scarify, scourge, upbraid 8 lambaste 9 castigate, excoriate

scathing
6 biting, brutal 7 caustic, mordant 8 stinging 9 trenchant

scatter
3 sow 4 cast, part, shed 5 strew 6 divide, spread 7 bestrew, break up, diffuse, disband, diverge 8 disperse, sprinkle 9 broadcast, dissipate 10 besprinkle, distribute 11 disseminate

scatterbrained
5 dizzy, giddy, silly 7 flighty, foolish 8 heedless 9 frivolous

scattering
8 diaspora 10 dispersion

scavenger
5 hyena 6 jackal 7 vulture

scenario
4 plot 6 script 7 outline 8 libretto, synopsis 10 screenplay

scene
3 row, set 4 fuss, site, spot, view 5 arena, field, place, sight, vista

6 locale, milieu, sphere 7 episode, outlook, setting, tableau, tantrum 8 backdrop, locality, location, stage set 9 commotion, landscape, situation 10 background 11 environment 12 stage setting

scenery
3 set 5 decor, props 7 setting 8 stage set 10 properties 11 furnishings 12 stage setting

scent
4 nose, odor 5 aroma, smell, sniff, snuff, whiff 7 bouquet, essence, incense, odorize, perfume 9 aromatize, fragrance, redolence

scepter
4 mace 5 baton, staff 11 sovereignty

schedule
4 list, roll 5 chart, slate, table 6 agenda, docket, record, roster 7 catalog, program, reserve 8 calendar, register, roll call 9 catalogue, timetable

scheme
4 plan, plot, ploy, ruse 5 cabal, order 6 design, device, devise 7 collude, connive, diagram, program, project 8 cogitate, conspire, contrive, game plan, intrigue, proposal, strategy 9 blueprint, expedient, machinate 10 conspiracy 11 arrangement, contrivance, machination

schism
4 rent, rift 5 break, chasm, cleft, split 6 breach, heresy 7 discord, dissent, fissure, rupture 8 cleavage, division, fracture 10 disharmony, dissidence, divergence, falling-out, heterodoxy, separation 11 unorthodoxy 12 estrangement

schlemiel
4 fool 5 chump, klutz 7 bungler

schlep
3 lug, tow 4 drag, haul, hump, plod, pull, slog, tote 5 carry, truck 6 trudge 7 shamble, shuffle 8 straggle

schlock

4 junk, mean 5 cheap, dreck, gaudy, junky, tacky, tatty 6 cheesy, common, kitsch, shoddy, sleazy, tawdry, trashy 8 inferior, low-grade 11 second-class, substandard

schmaltzy

5 mushy, soppy 6 drippy 7 maudlin, mawkish 11 sentimental

schmo

4 dolt, dope, dork, fool, goof, jerk, mutt, simp, twit, yo-yo 5 brute, chump, idiot, moron, ninny, noddy, scamp 6 dimwit, donkey, dumdum, nitwit, noodle, nudnik, rascal 7 dullard, halfwit, jackass, schmuck, schnook 8 bonehead, clodpoll, imbecile, lunkhead, meathead, numskull 9 birdbrain, blockhead, ignoramus, lamebrain, numbskull, thickhead 10 dunderhead, hammerhead, nincompoop 11 chowderhead, chucklehead, knucklehead

schmooze

3 gab, yak 4 chat 6 chat up 8 converse

schnoz

4 beak, nose 6 honker

scholar

4 sage, wonk 5 pupil 6 savant 7 bookman, egghead, student, wise man 8 bookworm, polymath 12 intellectual
Hindu: 6 pandit, pundit
Muslim: 5 ulama, ulema

scholarly

7 bookish, erudite, learned 8 academic, educated, studious 10 scholastic 12 intellectual

scholarship

5 award, grant 7 stipend 8 learning 9 education, erudition, knowledge 11 learnedness

scholastic

7 bookish, erudite, learned 8 academic, lettered, literary, pedantic 9 scholarly
life: 8 academia

school

3 gam, pad 5 shoal, teach, train, tutor 7 academy, borstal, college, educate 8 instruct 9 alma mater, institute 10 discipline, university
French: 5 école, lycée
grounds: 6 campus
Jewish: 5 heder 7 yeshiva
judo: 4 dojo
organization: 3 PTA, PTO
religious: 8 seminary
term: 7 quarter 8 semester 9 trimester

schoolbook

4 text 6 primer, reader 7 speller

School for Scandal author

8 Sheridan (Richard Brinsley)

schooner

4 ship 5 stoup 6 goblet, seidel 7 tumbler 8 sailboat

Schubert forte

4 lied, song

science

of agriculture: 8 agronomy
of animals: 7 zoology
of armorial bearings: 8 heraldry
of criminal punishment: 8 penology
of environment: 7 ecology
of fermentation: 8 zymology
of health: 7 hygiene 9 hygienics
of heredity: 8 genetics
of human behavior: 10 psychology
of measuring time: 8 horology 11 chronometry
of motion: 8 kinetics
of mountains: 7 orology
of plants: 6 botany
of projectiles: 10 ballistics
of the earth: 7 geology

scientific classification

8 taxonomy

sci-fi writer

3 Lem (Stanislaw) 4 Card (Orson Scott), Dick (Philip K.), Pohl (Frederik) 5 Disch (Thomas M.), Lewis (C. S.), Niven (Larry), Verne (Jules), Wells (H. G.) 6 Aldiss (Brian), Asimov (Isaac), Bester (Alfred), Bishop

(Michael), Butler (Octavia), Clarke (Arthur C.), Delany (Samuel), Farmer (Philip José), Gibson (William), Le Guin (Ursula), Leiber (Fritz), Miller (Walter) **7** Ballard (J. G.), Clement (Hal), Ellison (Harlan), Herbert (Frank), Hubbard (L. Ron), Van Vogt (A. E.), Zelazny (Roger) **8** Anderson (Poul), Bradbury (Ray), Heinlein (Robert A.), Sterling (Bruce), Sturgeon (Theodore), Vonnegut (Kurt) **9** Gernsback (Hugo), Kornbluth (C. M.) **10** Silverberg (Robert)

scimitar
5 saber, sabre, sword **7** cutlass

scintilla
3 bit, jot **4** iota, whit **5** grain, spark, speck, trace **8** particle

scintillate
5 flash, gleam, glint, spark **6** glance **7** glimmer, glisten, glitter, shimmer, sparkle, twinkle **9** coruscate

scion
4 heir **5** child, graft, issue **7** progeny **8** offshoot **9** inheritor, offspring, successor **10** descendant

scoff at
4 mock, twit **5** fleer, scorn **6** deride **7** contemn, disdain **8** belittle, pooh-pooh, ridicule

scold
3 rag **4** chew, lash, rail, rant **5** baste, blame, chide, grill, harpy, hound, shrew, vixen **6** berate, grouch, grouse, harass, murmur, mutter, rebuke, revile, virago **7** bawl out, blister, censure, chasten, chew out, grumble, lecture, reprove, tell off, upbraid **8** admonish, execrate, fishwife, lambaste, reproach, Xantippe **9** criticize, dress down, excoriate, objurgate, reprehend, reprimand, termagant, Xanthippe **10** tongue-lash, vituperate

scoop
3 dig, dip **4** bail, beat, lift **5** gouge, ladle, spade **6** dig out, pick up, shovel **8** excavate **9** exclusive

scoot
3 fly, run, zip **4** dash, flee, race, rush, skip **5** hurry, scram, skirr, slide **6** hustle, scurry, sprint **7** scamper **9** skedaddle

scope
4 area, room **5** ambit, gamut, orbit, range, reach, sweep **6** extent, leeway, margin, radius **7** breadth, compass, purview **8** capacity, fullness, latitude **9** amplitude, extension

Scopes trial lawyer
5 Bryan (William Jennings) **6** Darrow (Clarence)

scorch
4 bake, burn, char, flay, sear **5** broil, roast, singe **6** scathe **7** blacken, blister, scarify, scourge, swelter **8** lambaste **9** castigate, excoriate

score
3 cut, tab, win **4** bill, gain, goal, line, mark, nick, slit **5** cleft, count, notch, reach, tally, total **6** attain, furrow, groove, grudge, rack up, record, thrive, twenty **7** account, achieve, invoice, prosper, scratch, succeed **8** flourish **9** reckoning **10** accomplish

scorn
4 gibe, jeer, mock **5** abhor, flout, scoff, spurn, taunt **6** deride **7** contemn, despise, despite, disdain, jeering, mockery **8** contempt, derision, ridicule, scoffing, taunting **9** contumely

Scorpius star
7 Antares

Scotch cocktail
6 Rob Roy **9** Rusty Nail

scoter
7 sea coot, sea duck

Scotland
capital: 9 Edinburgh
city: 6 Dundee **7** Glasgow **8** Aberdeen **9** Inverness **11** Dunfermline
firth: 5 Clyde, Forth, Moray **6** Solway

Scott, Sir Walter

former capital: 5 Perth
island, island group: 4 Iona, Jura,
Mull, Skye, Uist 5 Arran, Islay
7 Orkneys 9 Shetlands 8 Hebrides
lake: 8 Loch Ness 10 Loch Lomond
mountain, range: 8 Ben Nevis
9 Grampians
patron saint: 6 Andrew
river: 3 Dee, Esk

Scott, Sir Walter

novel: 5 Abbot (The) 6 Rob Roy
7 Ivanhoe 8 Talisman (The), Waverley 9 Woodstock 10 Kenilworth
11 Redgauntlet 12 Old Mortality
14 Quentin Durward
poem: 7 Marmion 13 Lady of the
Lake (The)

_____ Scott case
4 Dred

Scottish

cap: 3 tam 9 glengarry 11 tam-o'-
shanter
child: 5 bairn
dance: 4 reel 5 fling 10 strathspey
guide: 6 gillie
hero: 5 Bruce (Robert) 7 Wallace
(William)
hill: 4 brae
lake: 4 loch
landowner: 5 laird
outlaw: 6 Rob Roy
patron saint: 6 Andrew
plaid: 6 tartan
pudding: 6 haggis
skirt: 4 kilt
spirit: 6 kelpie 7 banshee
sword: 8 claymore
trousers: 5 trews

scoundrel
see **scamp**

scour
4 comb, rake 5 erode, purge, range,
scrub 6 forage, search 7 corrode,
eat away, ransack, rummage 8 wear
away 9 ferret out

scourge
4 bane, flay, flog, hide, lash, whip,
whop 5 curse, flail, slash, whale
6 plague, ravage, scathe, stripe,
thrash 7 afflict, blister, despoil,

pillage, scarify 8 chastise, lambaste
9 castigate, depredate, desecrate,
devastate, excoriate 10 affliction,
flagellate, pestilence

Scourge of God
6 Attila

scout
3 spy 6 ranger, survey 7 explore,
lookout 8 searcher, watchman
11 investigate, reconnoiter

scouting group
3 BSA, GSA

scow
3 hoy 5 barge 6 garvey 7 lighter

scowl
5 frown, glare, lower 6 glower

scrabble
5 grope 6 scrawl 7 clamber 8 flounder

scraggly
6 ragged, shaggy, uneven 7 unkempt 9 irregular

scraggy
4 bony, lank, lean 5 gaunt, harsh,
lanky, rocky, rough 6 jagged, rugged, skinny, uneven 7 angular,
scrawny, spindly, unlevel 8 gangling,
rawboned, scabrous

scram
5 scoot, split 6 beat it, get out
7 buzz off, get lost, skiddoo, take off,
vamoose 8 clear out 9 skedaddle

scramble
4 hash 6 jumble, jungle, muddle,
scurry, tumble 7 clamber, clutter,
rummage, scuttle, shuffle 8 mishmash, scrabble, straggle 9 confusion

scrambled
7 chaotic, jumbled, mixed-up 8 confused 9 corrupted 10 disordered,
disorderly

scrap
3 bit, jot, row 4 chip, dump, fray,
junk, spat, tiff, whit 5 brawl, chuck,
crumb, fight, melee, piece, set-to,
shred, speck 6 bicker, fracas, reject, sliver, tittle 7 brabble, cutting,

discard, fall out, quarrel, scuffle, smidgen, wrangle 8 fragment, jettison, leftover, particle, squabble, throw out 9 throw away

scrape

3 fix, jam, rub 4 mess, rasp, spot 5 chafe, fight, grate, graze, pinch, scour, scuff, shave, skimp, spare, stint 6 abrade, pickle, plight, scrimp 7 dilemma, scratch, trouble 8 abrasion, struggle 11 predicament

scrappy

6 feisty 8 brawling 9 combative, truculent 10 pugnacious 11 belligerent, contentious, quarrelsome

scratch

4 claw, rake, rasp 5 grate, score, scrup 6 scotch, scrape, scrawl 7 call off 8 scrabble, scribble

scratchy

5 rough 6 gritty 7 itching, prickly, rasping 8 abrasive, granular, tingling 10 irritating

scrawl

6 doodle 7 scratch 8 scrabble, scribble

scrawny

4 bony, lank, lean 5 gaunt, lanky 6 skinny 7 scraggy 8 rawboned

scream

3 cry 4 yell, yowl 5 shout 6 screak, shriek, shrill, squeal 7 screech

screech

6 screak, scream, shriek, shrill, squeal

screed

5 level, spiel 6 letter, tirade 8 diatribe, harangue, jeremiad 9 discourse, philippic 11 disputation 12 disquisition

screen

4 cull, sift, veil 5 blind, sieve 6 facade, filter, movies, shroud, winnow 7 conceal, obscure, pick out 9 partition 10 camouflage
Japanese: 5 shoji

screw

9 propeller

screwball

3 nut, wag 4 kook, zany 5 clown, crazy, cutup, flake, flaky, freak, gonzo, joker, kooky, loony, nutty, silly, wacko, wacky 6 madcap, weirdo 7 buffoon, dingbat, farceur 8 crackpot, jokester 9 ding-a-ling, eccentric, fruitcake, whimsical

Screwtape Letters author

5 Lewis (C. S.)

screwy

3 mad 4 daft, nuts 5 batty, crazy, goofy, loony, nutty, wacky 6 absurd, insane 7 bizarre, cracked, lunatic 9 eccentric 10 unbalanced

scribble

5 write 6 scrawl 7 scratch 8 squiggle

scribe

5 clerk, write 6 author, writer 7 copyist 9 scrivener, secretary

scrimmage

4 fray 5 brawl, broil, clash, fight, melee, scrap, set-to 6 battle, fracas, ruckus, rumpus 7 scuffle 8 skirmish 10 donnybrook, free-for-all

scrimp

4 save 5 stint 6 save up, scrape 8 conserve 9 economize

script

4 hand, text 5 write 8 longhand, scenario 10 penmanship, screenplay 11 calligraphy, chirography, handwriting, orchestrate

scrivener

6 notary, scribe, writer 7 copyist

scrooge

5 miser 7 niggard 8 tightwad 9 skinflint 10 cheapskate 12 moneygrubber

scrounge

3 beg, bum, tap 4 grub, hunt, loot 5 cadge, filch, mooch, pinch, steal, swipe, touch 6 forage, hustle, pilfer, snitch, sponge, thieve 7 finagle, solicit, wheedle 8 freeload 9 panhandle

scroungy

5 dirty, seedy **6** grubby, grungy, scurvy, scuzzy, shabby, sleazy, sordid **7** scruffy, squalid, unkempt **8** slovenly **10** slatternly

scrub

3 rub **4** buff, drop, wash **5** abort, brush, scour **6** cancel, mallee, maquis, polish **7** abandon, call off, cleanse, scratch **9** chaparral, eliminate

scrubby

4 drab, mean **5** dingy, dowdy, runty **6** paltry, ragged, shabby, shoddy **7** rundown, runtish, stunted **8** inferior **9** neglected **10** bedraggled, broken-down

scruff

4 nape, neck

scruffy

5 mangy, seedy, tacky **6** frowsy, frowzy, shabby, shaggy **7** run-down, scrubby, unkempt **8** slovenly, tattered **10** down-at-heel, threadbare

scrumptious

5 tasty, yummy **8** heavenly, luscious **9** ambrosial, delicious, succulent, toothsome **10** delectable, delightful **13** mouthwatering

scruple

3 bit, jot **4** balk, iota **5** demur, doubt, grain, qualm, scrap, shred, worry **7** concern, modicum **8** particle, question **9** hesitancy **11** compunction

scrupulous

5 exact, fussy **6** honest, minute, strict **7** careful, heedful, upright **8** critical, punctual, rigorous **9** honorable **10** fair-minded, fastidious, meticulous, principled, upstanding **11** painstaking, punctilious **12** conscionable **13** conscientious

scrutinize

4 comb, scan **5** audit, probe, study **6** peruse **7** analyze, canvass, dig into, dissect, examine, eyeball, inspect **8** look over, pore over **9** check over **11** contemplate, investigate

scrutiny

4 scan **5** audit **6** review, survey **7** perusal **8** analysis **10** inspection **11** examination **12** surveillance

scuba diver

7 frogman **8** aquanaut

scud

3 fly **4** race, rain, rush, sail, skim **5** brume, froth, scoot, speed, spray, spume **6** clouds, scurry, shower

scuff

6 scrape **7** scratch, shamble, shuffle

scuffle

3 row **4** fray **5** brawl, broil, fight, scrap, set-to **6** affray, fracas, hubbub, tussle **7** bobbery, grapple, shamble, shuffle, wrestle **10** roughhouse

scull

3 oar, row **4** boat **5** shell **6** propel

sculpt

3 hew **5** carve, shape **6** chisel

sculptor

American: 3 Lin (Maya) **4** Gabo (Naum), Taft (Lorado) **5** Andre (Carl), Koons (Jeff), Pratt (Bela), Segal (George), Serra (Richard), Smith (David), Story (William) **6** Aitkin (Robert), Calder (Alexander), French (Daniel Chester), Powers (Hiram), Zorach (William) **7** Borglum (Gutzon), Cornell (Joseph), Noguchi (Isamu) **8** Lachaise (Gaston), Lipchitz (Jacques), Nadelman (Elie), Nevelson (Louise) **9** Bourgeois (Louise), Mestrovic (Ivan), Oldenburg (Claes), Remington (Frederic) **12** Saint-Gaudens (Augustus) **Czech: 6** Stursa (Jan) **Danish: 11** Thorvaldsen (Bertel), Thorwaldsen (Bertel) **Dutch: 6** Sluter (Claus) **English: 5** Moore (Henry), Watts (George) **7** Epstein (Jacob), Flaxman (John) **8** Hepworth (Barbara)

French: 3 Arp (Hans, Jean) 4 Bloc (André) 5 Rodin (Auguste) 6 Dubois (Paul), Houdon (Jean-Antoine) 7 Maillol (Aristide), Pevsner (Antoine) 9 Bartholdi (Frédéric-Auguste), Roubillac (Louis-François)
Greek: 5 Myron 7 Phidias 8 Pheidias 10 Polyclitus, Praxiteles 11 Polycleitus
Italian: 5 Leoni (Leone), Salvi (Niccolò, Nicola) 6 Canova (Antonio), Pisano (Andrea, Nino), Robbia (Andrea, Giovanni, Girolamo, Luca della) 7 Bernini (Gian Lorenzo), Cellini (Benvenuto), da Vinci (Leonardo), Orcagna, Quercia (Jacopo della) 8 Ghiberti (Lorenzo), Leonardo (da Vinci), Vittoria (Alessandro) 9 Donatello, Sansovino (Jacopo) 10 Verrocchio (Andrea del) 12 Michelangelo (Buonarroti)
Rhodian: 9 Polydorus
Romanian: 8 Brancusi (Constantin)
Russian: 7 Zadkine (Ossip)
Swedish: 6 Milles (Carl) 9 Oldenburg (Claes)
Swiss: 10 Giacometti (Alberto)

scum
5 algae, dregs, dross 6 refuse, vermin 8 riffraff

scummy
3 low 4 base, mean, vile 5 dirty, mucky, slimy 6 grubby, odious, sleazy, sordid 7 squalid 10 despicable 12 contemptible

scurrilous
4 foul 5 dirty, gross, nasty 6 coarse, filthy, vulgar 7 abusive, obscene, profane 8 indecent 9 insulting, offensive 10 outrageous 11 opprobrious 12 contumelious, vituperative

scurry
3 run 4 dart, dash 5 scoot, shoot 6 bustle 7 scamper, scuffle, scuttle

scurvy
see **scummy**

scut
4 tail

scuttlebutt
4 buzz, talk 5 rumor 6 gossip, report 7 chatter, hearsay 9 grapevine

Scylla
4 rock
counterpart: 9 Charybdis
father: 5 Nisus
lover: 5 Minos

scythe handle
5 snath 6 snathe

sea
4 blue, deep, main 5 brine, drink, ocean
Antarctica: 4 Ross 5 Davis 7 Weddell 8 Amundsen
Arctic: 4 Kara 7 Chukchi 8 Beaufort, Karskoye 9 Chuckchee, Norwegian 11 Chukotskoye 12 East Siberian
Asia-Europe: 5 Black
Asia Minor: 7 Icarian
Atlantic: 5 North 7 Weddell 9 Caribbean
Australia-Indonesia: 7 Arafura
Balkan Peninsula-Italy: 8 Adriatic
Bay of Bengal: 7 Andaman
China-Korea: 5 Huang, Hwang 6 Yellow
combining form: 3 mer 4 mari 5 pelag 6 pelago 7 thalass 8 thalasso
Corsica-Italy: 10 Tyrrhenian
Denmark-Norway: 9 Skagerrak
Denmark-Sweden: 8 Kattegat
England-Ireland: 5 Irish
Fiji: 4 Koro
France-Italy: 8 Ligurian
Greece: 5 Crete
Greece-Italy: 6 Ionian
Greece-Turkey: 6 Aegean 8 Thracian
Honshu: 6 Sagami
Indian Ocean: 5 Timor 7 Arabian
Indonesia: 4 Bali 6 Flores
inland: 3 Red 4 Aral 7 Caspian
Japan: 3 Suo 6 Inland
Malay Archipelago: 5 Banda
Mexico: 6 Cortés
Netherlands: 6 Wadden
North Atlantic: 8 Sargasso

Northern Europe: 6 Baltic, Ostsee 8 Suevicum
North Pacific: 6 Bering
off Scotland: 8 Hebrides
off Sweden: 5 Aland
Pacific: 4 Java 5 China, Coral 6 Maluku 7 Celebes, Eastern, Molucca, Solomon 9 East China 10 South China
Philippine: 4 Sulu
Russia: 5 White 7 Okhotsk
Russia-Ukraine: 4 Azov
South Pacific: 4 Ross 6 Tasman 8 Amundsen
Turkey: 7 Marmara 9 Propontis
West Pacific: 5 Ceram, Japan 8 Bismarck 10 Philippine

sea anemone
5 polyp

seabird
see **bird aquatic**

seacoast
5 beach, coast, shore 6 strand 8 littoral 9 shoreline

sea cucumber
7 trepang 11 holothurian

sea dog
see **sailor**

sea duck
5 eider, scaup 6 scoter 9 merganser

sea eagle
4 erne 6 osprey 8 fish hawk

seafarer
3 tar 4 salt 5 sailor 7 jack-tar, mariner

seafood dish
4 clam, crab 5 clams, squid 6 mussel, oyster, shrimp 7 lobster, mussels, oysters, scallop 8 calamari, scallops

seagoing
8 maritime, nautical

seal
5 sigil, stamp 6 cachet, signet 7 sticker
female: 3 cow
herd: 3 pod 5 patch
young: 3 pup

sealant
4 lute 5 caulk, grout 6 luting, mastic 8 caulking

sea lily
7 crinoid

seam
4 bond 5 joint, union 8 coupling, juncture 10 connection

seaman
see **sailor**

sea monster
3 Orc 6 kraken 9 leviathan

seamount
5 guyot

seamy
5 dirty, rough, seedy 6 sordid 7 squalid 12 disreputable

séance
7 meeting, session, sitting
holder: 6 medium

seaport
Alaska: 6 Juneau 9 Anchorage
Albania: 5 Vlorë 6 Durres, Valona
Algeria: 4 Bône, Oran 6 Annaba
Angola: 6 Lobito, Luanda 7 Cabinda 8 Benguela
Argentina: 11 Buenos Aires, Mar del Plata
Australia: 4 Eden 5 Bowen, Perth 6 Darwin, Hobart, Sydney 8 Brisbane 9 Melbourne 10 Wollongong
Azores: 5 Horta
Balearic: 5 Ibiza
Belgium: 6 Ostend 7 Antwerp
Benin: 7 Cotonou 9 Porto-Novo
Black Sea: 5 Varna 6 Burgas, Odessa 8 Constanta
Brazil: 3 Rio 4 Pará 5 Bahia, Belém, Natal 6 Recife, Santos 7 Vitoria 8 Salvador 9 Fortaleza 10 Pernambuco 11 Pôrto Alegre, São Salvador 12 Rio de Janeiro
Bulgaria: 5 Varna 6 Burgas
Cameroon: 6 Douala
Canaries: 8 Arrecife 9 Las Palmas
Chile: 5 Arica 8 Coquimbo 10 Valparaíso
China: 4 Amoy 6 Dalian, Fuzhou, Lüshun, Xiamen 7 Foochow, Hsia-

men, Qingdao, Tianjin **8** Shanghai, Tientsin, Tsingtao **9** Guangzhou, Zhenjiang **10** Chen-chiang, Port Arthur

Colombia: 6 Lorica **9** Cartagena **12** Barranquilla
Corsica: 5 Calvi **7** Ajaccio
Costa Rica: 5 Limón **10** Puntarenas
Crimean: 5 Kerch, Yalta **10** Sebastopol, Sevastopol
Croatia: 5 Rieka, Split **6** Rijeka **9** Dubrovnik
Cuba: 6 Havana **8** Matanzas, Santiago
Cyprus: 9 Famagusta
Denmark: 5 Arhus **6** Aarhus, Alborg **7** Aalborg **8** Elsinore **10** Copenhagen
Ecuador: 9 Guayaquil
Egypt: 4 Said **10** Alexandria
England: 4 Hull **5** Dover **9** Liverpool **10** Portsmouth **11** Southampton
Equatorial Guinea: 4 Bata
Eritrea: 4 Aseb
Estonia: 5 Pärnu **7** Tallinn
Finland: 3 Abo **4** Kemi, Oulu, Pori, Vasa **5** Hango, Kotka, Rauma, Turku, Vaasa **6** Vyborg
Florida: 5 Miami, Tampa **9** Pensacola **12** Apalachicola, Jacksonville
France: 4 Nice **5** Brest, Havre **6** Calais, Cannes, Toulon **7** Dunkirk, Le Havre **8** Bordeaux, Boulogne **9** Cherbourg, Dunkerque, Marseille **10** Marseilles
French Polynesia: 7 Papeete
Georgia: 8 Savannah **9** Brunswick
Georgia, Republic of: 8 Pot'i
Germany: 4 Kiel **5** Emden **6** Bremen, Lübeck, Wismar **7** Hamburg, Rostock **8** Cuxhaven **11** Bremerhaven
Ghana: 4 Tema **5** Accra
Greece: 5 Pylos, Syros, Volos **7** Piraeus
Guatemala: 7 San José **10** Livingston
Haiti: 5 Cayes **10** Cap Haitien
Honduras: 7 La Ceiba **8** Trujillo
India: 3 Goa **4** Puri **5** Marud **6** Bombay, Madras, Mumbai, Old

Goa **7** Calicut, Chennai **8** Calcutta **9** Jagannath **10** Trivandrum
Iran: 4 Jask **7** Bushehr
Iraq: 5 Basra
Ireland: 4 Cork **5** Sligo **6** Dingle, Dublin, Galway, Tralee **8** Drogheda, Limerick **9** Waterford **10** Balbriggan
Israel: 4 Acre, Akko, Elat, Yafo **5** Accho, Eilat, Haifa, Jaffa, Joppa **6** Ashdod **8** Ashqelon
Italy: 4 Bari **5** Anzio, Gaeta, Genoa **6** Naples, Pesaro, Rimini, Venice **7** Leghorn, Livorno, Marsala, Messina, Rapallo, Salerno, Taranto, Trieste **8** Brindisi, Sorrento, Syracuse
Ivory Coast: 5 Tabou **7** Abidjan
Jamaica: 8 Kingston **10** Montego Bay
Japan: 4 Kobe **5** Kochi, Osaka, Rumoi, Ujina, Uraga **6** Sasebo **7** Fukuoka **8** Nagasaki, Yokohama **9** Hiroshima
Java: 5 Tegal, Tuban **7** Cilacap, Jakarta **8** Semarang, Surabaya
Jordan: 5 Aqaba, Elath **6** Aelana
Latvia: 4 Riga
Lebanon: 4 Tyre **5** Saida, Sidon **6** Beirut **7** Tripoli
Libya: 6 Tobruk **7** Tripoli **8** Benghazi
Lithuania: 5 Memel **8** Klaipeda
Madagascar: 8 Tamatave
Maine: 7 Belfast **8** Portland
Malaysia: 4 Miri, Weld **5** Pekan **6** Melaka, Pinang **7** Malacca **10** George Town
Massachusetts: 6 Boston **9** Fall River **10** New Bedford
Mauritius: 9 Port Louis
Mediterranean: 4 Gaza, Oran **5** Genoa, Haifa, Jaffa **6** Beirut, Naples, Venice **7** Algiers, Bizerte, Catania, Palermo, Piraeus, Tripoli **8** Benghazi, Port Said **9** Barcelona, Marseille **10** Alexandria, Marseilles
Mexico: 7 Tampico **8** Acapulco, Mazatlán, Veracruz
Minorca: 5 Mahón
Moluccas: 5 Ambon
Montenegro: 5 Kotor
Morocco: 4 Safi, Salé **5** Ceuta **6** Agadir **7** Tangier, Tétouan **10** Casablanca

Mozambique: 5 Beira, Pemba
6 Amelia, Maputo, Xai Xai 11 Porto
Amelia
New Hampshire: 10 Portsmouth
New Zealand: 8 Auckland 10 Wellington
Nicaragua: 5 Brito
Nigeria: 5 Lagos 8 Harcourt
Niger mouth: 5 Bonny
North Korea: 4 Yuki 5 Nampo,
Unggi 6 Wonsan
Norway: 4 Bodo, Moss 5 Vadso
6 Bergen, Tromso 9 Stavanger,
Trondheim 11 Fredrikstad
Oman: 6 Masqat, Muscat
Pakistan: 5 Pasni 6 Gwadar
7 Karachi
Papua New Guinea: 3 Lea
Peru: 3 Ilo 4 Eten 5 Paita, Pisco
6 Callao
Philippines: 4 Cebu 5 Davao,
Laoag 6 Aparri, Cavite, Iloilo, Manila
7 Legaspi 8 Tacloban 9 Zamboanga
Poland: 6 Danzig, Gdansk, Gdynia
7 Stettin 8 Szczecin
Portugal: 4 Faro 5 Porto 6 Oporto
7 Funchal
Puerto Rico: 5 Ponce 7 Arecibo,
San Juan 8 Mayagüez
Russia: 6 Vyborg 8 Murmansk
11 Kaliningrad, Vladivostok
Ryukyu: 4 Naha, Nawa
Sakhalin Island: 8 Korsakov
Saudi Arabia: 5 Jedda, Jidda,
Yanbu, Yenbo 6 Jeddah, Jiddah
Scotland: 3 Ayr 5 Leith, Leven
6 Dundee 7 Glasgow 8 Aberdeen
Sicily: 7 Catania, Marsala, Messina,
Palermo 8 Syracuse
Slovenia: 5 Kopar, Koper, Piran
Somalia: 7 Berbera 9 Mogadishu
South Africa: 5 Natal 6 Durban
8 Cape Town
South Carolina: 8 Savannah
10 Charleston
South Korea: 5 Masan, Mokpo,
Pusan 6 Inchon 7 Incheon, Masampo
Spain: 5 Cádiz, Gijón 6 Abdera,
Málaga 8 Alicante 9 Algeciras,
Barcelona, Cartagena, Las Palmas

Sri Lanka: 7 Colombo 10 Batticaloa
Sumatra: 5 Medan 6 Padang
9 Banda Aceh
Sweden: 4 Umea 5 Gavle, Lulea,
Malmö, Pitea, Ystad 8 Göteborg
9 Stockholm 10 Gothenburg 11 Helsingborg
Tanzania: 5 Lindi, Tanga 8 Zanzibar 11 Dar es Salaam
Thailand: 4 Trat 8 Bang Phra
Tunisia: 4 Sfax 5 Gabès 6 Sousse
7 Bizerta, Bizerte
Turkey: 4 Rize 5 Izmir, Sinop
6 Samsun, Smyrna 7 Antalya
8 Istanbul
Ukraine: 5 Kerch, Yalta 6 Odessa
7 Kherson
Vanuatu: 4 Vila 8 Port-Vila
Vietnam: 4 Hue 6 Da Nang 7 Tourane 8 Haiphong, Nha Trang
Virginia: 7 Norfolk 10 Portsmouth
Yemen: 4 Aden 5 Mocha

seaport capital
4 Aden, Apia, Dili, Lomé, Suva 5 Accra, Adana, Dakar, Lagos 6 Banjul,
Belize, Bissau, Dublin, Havana,
Kuwait, Lisbon, Maputo, Masqat,
Muscat, Roseau 7 Algiers, Batavia,
Colombo, Jakarta, Moresby, San
Juan 8 Castries, Djakarta, Freetown,
Hamilton, Helsinki, Honolulu, Kingston, Monrovia, Valletta 9 Mogadishu,
Nuku'alofa, Porto-Novo, Reykjavík,
Singapore 10 Bridgetown, Daressalem, Libreville, Mogadiscio, Paramaribo 11 Dar es Salaam, Port of
Spain 12 Port-au-Prince

sear
3 dry 5 parch, singe 6 burn up,
scorch, sizzle 7 shrivel 9 cauterize,
dehydrate, desiccate

search
4 beat, comb, grub, hunt, scan, seek
5 chase, check, delve, frisk, grope,
quest, rifle, scour 6 ferret, forage
7 fossick, hunting, manhunt, pursuit, ransack, rummage, run down
8 finecomb, scavenge, scout out
9 cast about, ferret out 10 scrutinize

searing
3 hot 5 harsh 6 severe 7 blazing, burning, intense 8 scathing 9 agonizing, scorching 10 blistering 12 excruciating

sea robber
5 rover 6 pirate 7 corsair 8 picaroon 9 buccaneer 10 freebooter

seasickness
6 nausea 8 mal de mer

season
3 fit 4 fall, term, time 5 spice, train, treat 6 autumn, harden, pepper, period, school, spring, summer, winter 7 prepare, toughen 8 marinade, marinate 9 acclimate 10 caseharden, discipline 11 acclimatize

seasonable
3 apt 6 timely 7 welcome 9 favorable, opportune, pertinent, well-timed 10 auspicious, convenient, propitious 11 appropriate

seasoned
6 inured, mature, tested, versed 7 adapted, matured, veteran 8 flavored, hardened 9 flavorful, practiced 10 acclimated, habituated 11 experienced 12 acclimatized, accomplished

seasoning
3 bay 4 dill, herb, mace, sage, salt 5 anise, basil, chili, clove, cumin, spice, thyme 6 cloves, fennel, garlic, ginger, nutmeg, pepper, savory 7 cayenne, chervil, mustard, oregano, paprika, parsley, saffron 8 allspice, cardamom, cinnamon, rosemary, tarragon, turmeric 9 condiment, coriander

seat
3 hub 4 base, beam, duff, rear, rest, rump 5 basis, chair, place, usher 6 behind, bottom, center, settee 7 fulcrum 8 backside, buttocks, derriere 9 fundament, posterior 10 foundation
church: 3 pew
on a camel or elephant: 6 howdah
upholstered: 9 banquette

sea urchin
7 echinus 8 echinoid

seaweed
4 kelp, nori, ulva 5 dulse, fucus, kombu 6 fucoid, wakame 8 sargasso 9 carrageen, Irish moss 12 bladder wrack

Sea Wolf, The
author: 6 London (Jack)
captain: 10 Wolf Larsen
ship: 5 Ghost

Sebastian
brother: 6 Alonso
sister: 5 Viola

secco
3 dry 8 painting, staccato

secede
4 quit 5 leave 8 separate, withdraw

seclude
4 hide 6 closet, immure, retire, screen 7 confine, enclose, isolate, shut off 8 cloister, separate, withdraw 9 sequester

secluded
6 hidden, remote 7 private, recluse, shut off 8 hermetic, isolated, screened, solitary 9 concealed, reclusive, withdrawn 10 cloistered, tucked away 11 out-of-the-way, quarantined, sequestered

seclusion
7 privacy 8 solitude 9 isolation 10 separation, withdrawal

second
4 wink 5 flash, jiffy, trice 6 moment 7 endorse, instant, support 9 twinkling

secondary
3 sub 6 lesser 7 derived 8 borrowed, inferior 9 resultant, tributary 10 collateral, derivative, subsequent 11 subordinate, subservient

second-class
6 common 8 déclassé, inferior, low-grade, mediocre

secondhand
4 used, worn 7 derived 8 borrowed 10 derivative

second-string
3 sub 6 backup 9 alternate 10 substitute

secrecy
7 silence, stealth 10 covertness, subterfuge 11 concealment, furtiveness

secret
5 sneak 6 arcane, closet, covert, hidden, occult 7 cryptic, furtive, obscure, sub-rosa 8 abstruse, backdoor, discreet, hermetic, hush-hush, stealthy 9 concealed, recondite 10 classified, restricted, undercover 11 clandestine, out-of-the-way, underhanded 12 confidential, hugger-mugger 13 surreptitious, under-the-table
combining form: 5 crypt, krypt 6 crypto, krypto

secret agent
3 spy 8 emissary

secretary
4 aide, desk 5 clerk 6 scribe 9 assistant 10 amanuensis, escritoire
king's: 10 chancellor

secrete
4 bury, emit, hide 5 cache, exude, plant, stash 6 screen 7 conceal, deposit, emanate

secretive
7 furtive 8 reticent, taciturn 10 backstairs, buttoned-up 11 tight-lipped 12 close-mouthed 13 unforthcoming

secretly
7 sub rosa 9 furtively 10 stealthily

secret society
3 KKK 4 tong 5 cabal, Mafia, Triad 6 Mau Mau, Yakuza 7 camorra 9 camarilla, Carbonari 10 Cosa Nostra, Freemasons, Ku Klux Klan

sect
4 cult 5 creed, party 7 faction 8 division, religion 12 denomination

sectarian
5 local 8 splinter 9 dissident, heretical, heterodox, parochial 10 provincial, schismatic, unorthodox 13 nonconformist

sectary
5 rebel 7 heretic 8 adherent, disciple, follower, partisan 9 dissenter, dissident 10 schismatic, separatist 13 nonconformist, revolutionary

section
3 cut 4 area, belt, part, zone 5 chunk, piece, slice, tract 6 member, moiety, parcel, region, sector, sphere 7 portion, quarter, segment 8 district, division, locality, precinct 11 subdivision

sector
4 area, zone 7 quarter, section 8 district, precinct 11 subdivision

secular
3 lay 7 earthly, profane, worldly 8 temporal, unsacred 11 nonclerical, terrestrial 12 nonreligious

secure
3 fix 4 bind, fast, firm, gain, land, lock, moor, nail, safe 5 catch, cinch, clamp, cover, fixed, guard, solid, sound, tried 6 anchor, assure, cement, clinch, defend, effect, ensure, fasten, insure, obtain, shield, stable 7 acquire, assured, capture, procure, protect, tie down 8 reliable, sanguine 9 confident, safeguard 10 batten down, bring about 11 established, impregnable

security
4 bail, bond, pawn 5 guard, token 6 pledge, safety, shield, surety 7 defense, earnest, warrant 8 guaranty, immunity, warranty 9 assurance, guarantee, safeguard, soundness, stability 10 collateral, protection, steadiness 13 certification

sedate
4 calm 5 grave, sober, staid 6 placid, proper, seemly, serene, steady 7 earnest, serious 8 composed, decorous, tranquil 9 collected, dignified, unruffled 10 sobersided 13 dispassionate, imperturbable

sedative
4 balm 6 downer, Valium 7 calmant, Librium, Miltown, Seconal 8 barbital, hyoscine, Nembutal 9 calmative 10 depressant 11 barbiturate 12 sleeping pill, tranquilizer

sedentary
4 lazy 6 seated 7 settled, sitting 8 inactive 10 stationary

sediment
4 lees, silt 5 dregs, dross 7 bottoms, deposit, grounds, heeltap, residue 8 residuum 9 settlings 11 precipitate
layer: 5 varve

sedition
4 coup 6 mutiny, putsch, revolt, strike 7 protest, treason 8 intrigue, uprising 9 coup d'état, rebellion 10 revolution 12 insurrection

seditious
8 disloyal, factious, mutinous 9 dissident, insurgent 10 rebellious, traitorous 11 treacherous

seduce
4 bait, coax, lure 5 decoy, tempt 6 allure, betray, delude, entice, entrap, lead on, ravish 7 corrupt, debauch, deceive 8 entrance, inveigle

seducer
4 roué, vamp 7 Don Juan, playboy 8 lothario 9 libertine

seduction
4 lure 8 conquest 9 siren song 10 allurement, attraction, ravishment, temptation

seductive
5 siren 8 alluring, magnetic, tempting 9 beguiling 10 attractive, bewitching, enchanting 11 captivating

seductress
5 siren 7 Lorelei 9 temptress 11 femme fatale

sedulous
8 diligent, tireless 9 assiduous, laborious 10 persistent 11 industrious, persevering, unremitting

see
4 call, date, espy, gape, gaze, look, mark, peer, scan, view 5 grasp, sight, visit, watch 6 behold, come by, descry, divine, drop by, drop in, go with, look in, notice, stop by, stop in, take in 7 discern, examine, find out, glimpse, imagine, make out, observe, realize 8 conceive, consider, envisage, envision, perceive 9 apprehend, ascertain, determine, recognize, visualize 10 comprehend, scrutinize, understand

seed
3 sow 4 core, germ 5 brood, grain, issue, ovule, plant, spark, spawn 6 embryo, kernel, notion 7 concept, nucleus, progeny 8 children 9 offspring 11 descendants
aromatic: 6 fennel
coating: 5 testa 6 testae (plural)
covering: 4 aril
of a bean: 7 haricot
of a vine: 6 peanut
poisonous: 10 castor bean
vessel: 3 pod 5 fruit, pyxis 7 silicle, silique

seedcase
3 pod

seedy
5 dingy, faded, mangy, ratty, tired 6 droopy, frowsy, frowzy, shabby, used up, wilted 7 run-down, scruffy, squalid, unkempt, wilting 8 decaying, decrepit, drooping, flagging, inferior, slovenly, tattered 9 neglected, overgrown 10 bedraggled, down-at-heel, threadbare 12 disreputable

seek
3 try 4 fish, hunt, root 5 assay, delve, essay, offer, quest, sniff 6 pursue, strive 7 attempt, inquire, look for, request 8 endeavor, smell out 9 search for, search out, undertake

seem
3 act 4 look 5 imply 6 appear, behave 7 suggest 8 resemble

seemly
3 fit 6 decent, proper, suited 7 apropos, correct, fitting 8 becoming,

seep

decorous, suitable **9** befitting, congenial, congruous **10** compatible, conforming **11** appropriate, comme il faut

seep

4 drip, leak, ooze, weep **5** bleed, exude, leech, sweat **6** filter, strain **7** diffuse, dribble, trickle **8** transude **9** percolate

seer

5 augur, sibyl **6** oracle **7** diviner, prophet **8** foreseer, haruspex **9** predictor **10** forecaster, foreteller, soothsayer **11** clairvoyant, Nostradamus

seesaw

3 yaw **4** rock, veer **5** lurch, pitch, swing **6** teeter **7** bascule **8** flip-flop **9** alternate, fluctuate, oscillate **11** teeterboard

seethe

3 sop **4** boil, burn, foam, fret, fume, rage, soak, stew **5** churn, erupt, froth, souse, steam, steep **6** bubble, drench, simmer, sizzle **7** bristle, ferment, parboil, smolder **8** saturate, smoulder, waterlog

see-through

5 clear **6** limpid **8** pellucid **11** translucent, transparent

segment

3 cut **4** part **5** piece **6** divide, member, moiety **7** portion, section **8** division, separate **10** categorize

sego

4 lily

segregate

6 enisle, select **7** isolate **8** separate **9** sequester **10** disconnect

segregation

9 apartheid, isolation **10** jim crowism, separatism **13** ghettoization

segue

7 proceed **8** continue **10** transition **11** progression

seidel

5 stoup **8** schooner

seine

3 net **5** trawl

Seine tributary

4 Oise **5** Marne, Yonne

seismologist

7 Richter (Charles)

seize

3 bag, nab **4** grab, take **5** annex, catch, clasp, grasp, usurp **6** abduct, arrest, clinch, clutch, kidnap, occupy, secure, snatch **7** capture, grapple, impound **8** arrogate, carry off **9** apprehend, sequester **10** commandeer, confiscate **11** appropriate, expropriate

seizure

3 fit **4** turn **5** spasm, spell, throe **6** access, attack, taking **7** capture **8** paroxysm, takeover **9** breakdown **10** annexation, convulsion, usurpation **12** confiscation

seldom

6 hardly, rarely **8** scarcely **10** hardly ever **12** infrequently, occasionally, sporadically

select

4 best, cull, fine, pick, rare **5** cream, elite, prime **6** choice, choose, chosen, culled, opt for, picked **7** favored, pick out **8** screened, superior **9** exclusive, exquisite, preferred, recherché, single out

selection

6 choice **7** culling, excerpt, picking **8** choosing **10** assortment, preference

selective

5 fussy, picky **6** choosy **7** choosey, finicky **8** specific **10** discerning, particular, scrupulous **11** persnickety

Selene

4 Luna **6** Hecate **7** Artemis
beloved: 8 Endymion
brother: 6 Helios
father: 8 Hyperion
mother: 4 Thea

self
3 ego
combining form: 3 aut 4 auto

self-absorbed
4 smug 8 egoistic 9 conceited,
egotistic 10 complacent, egocentric
11 egotistical, introverted 12 narcissistic 13 inner-directed

self-acting
9 automatic

self-assertive
4 bold 5 brash, pushy 6 cheeky
7 forward 8 cocksure, militant
9 audacious, obtrusive, officious
10 aggressive 11 impertinent,
overweening 12 presumptuous

self-assurance
5 poise 6 aplomb 8 coolness
9 composure, sangfroid 10 confidence, equanimity 13 collectedness

self-assured
4 smug 6 poised 8 sanguine 9 confident

self-centered
9 conceited, egotistic 10 egocentric
11 egotistical 12 narcissistic

self-composed
4 calm 6 poised, serene 7 assured
9 collected, confident, possessed
10 controlled

self-confidence
5 poise 6 aplomb 9 assurance

self-confident
5 cocky 6 jaunty, poised 7 assured
8 sanguine

self-conscious
4 prim 5 stiff 6 formal, uneasy
7 awkward, stilted, studied 8 affected, mannered 9 contrived, ill at
ease 10 artificial

self-contained
6 closed, formal 7 built-in 8 composed, enclosed, reserved, reticent
9 exclusive 10 restrained 11 independent

self-control
7 balance, dignity, reserve 9 restraint, stability, willpower 10 abstinence, constraint, discipline, temperance 11 forbearance

self-defense art
4 judo 6 aikido, karate, kung fu
7 jujitsu 9 tai kwan do

self-destruction
7 suicide 8 felo-de-se, hara-kiri

self-discipline
4 will 8 stoicism 9 willpower 10 abstinence

self-educated
12 autodidactic

self-effacing
3 shy 5 timid 6 modest 7 bashful
8 retiring, sheepish 9 diffident,
unassured 11 unassertive

self-esteem
5 pride 6 vanity 7 conceit, dignity,
egotism 10 narcissism 11 amour
propre

self-evident
5 clear, plain 6 patent 7 obvious
8 manifest, palpable 10 prima facie,
undeniable 12 demonstrable, unmistakable

self-explanatory
5 clear, plain 7 evident, obvious
8 manifest 11 perspicuous, transparent

self-governing
7 popular 9 sovereign 10 autonomous, democratic

self-importance
3 ego 5 pride 6 egoism, hubris
7 conceit, egotism 9 arrogance,
pomposity, vainglory

self-important
4 smug, vain 6 lordly 7 bloated,
haughty, pompous 8 arrogant
9 conceited, egotistic 10 pontifical
11 magisterial, pretentious

self-indulgent
9 libertine, sybaritic 10 hedonistic

self-interest
6 egoism

selfish
6 stingy 8 egoistic 9 egotistic
10 egocentric, ungenerous 11 ego-
maniacal 12 self-centered 13 self-
indulgent

selfless
8 generous 10 altruistic, benevolent,
charitable

self-love
6 egoism, vanity 7 conceit, egotism
8 vainness 9 vainglory 10 narcissism 11 amour propre 13 conceitedness

self-possessed
4 calm 6 poised, serene 7 equable
8 composed, sanguine 9 collected,
unruffled 11 unflappable 13 imperturbable

self-proclaimed
8 so-called 9 soi-disant 10 self-
styled

Self-Reliance author
7 Emerson (Ralph Waldo)

self-respect
5 pride 7 dignity 11 amour propre

self-restraint
8 chastity, sobriety 9 willpower
10 abnegation, abstention, abstinence, continence, discipline 11 forbearance

self-righteous
5 pious 7 canting, preachy 8 unctuous 9 pharisaic 10 complacent,
goody-goody 11 pharisaical 12 hypocritical, pecksniffian 13 sanctimonious

self-sacrificing
8 generous, selfless 9 unselfish

self-satisfied
4 smug 8 priggish 10 complacent

self-seeking
6 greedy 7 selfish 8 egoistic 9 egotistic 10 egocentric 11 egotistical

self-serving
see **self-seeking**

self-starter
7 hustler 8 go-getter

self-styled
7 nominal, would-be 8 so-called
9 soi-disant

self-taught
12 autodidactic

sell
4 hawk, vend 5 trade 6 barter, deal
in, hustle, market, peddle, retail,
unload 7 auction 8 exchange

sell out
4 dump, move 6 betray, turn in,
unload 7 deceive 8 inform on
11 double-cross

selvage, selvedge
3 hem 4 edge 6 border

semblance
3 air 4 face, look, mask, pose, show,
veil 5 front, guise, image 6 aspect,
facade, simile, veneer 7 analogy,
feeling, modicum 8 affinity, disguise,
likeness, pretense 10 apparition,
appearance, comparison, false front,
masquerade, similarity, similitude,
simulacrum 11 countenance

Semele
father: 6 Cadmus
mother: 8 Harmonia
sister: 3 Ino 5 Agave 7 Autonoë
son: 7 Bacchus 8 Dionysus

semi
3 rig 4 demi, half, hemi 5 truck
6 partly

seminar
5 forum 8 colloquy 10 colloquium,
conference, roundtable

Seminole chief
7 Osceola

Semiramis
husband: 5 Ninus
kingdom: 7 Babylon

Semite
3 Jew 4 Arab 6 Hebrew 7 Moabite
8 Akkadian, Assyrian 9 Canaanite
10 Babylonian, Phoenician

Senapo
daughter: 8 Clorinda
kingdom: 8 Ethiopia

senate
> 7 chamber, council 8 assembly
> 11 legislature

senator
> 5 solon 8 lawmaker 10 legislator

send
> 4 mail, post, ship 5 relay, remit,
> route 6 commit, export, launch
> 7 address, advance, airmail, consign,
> forward, traject 8 dispatch, transmit
> **back:** 6 remand

Sendak book
> 17 In the Night Kitchen 21 Where
> the Wild Things Are

send in
> 6 submit

send-up
> 5 roast, spoof 6 parody, satire
> 7 lampoon, takeoff 9 burlesque
> 10 caricature, pasquinade

Senegal
> **capital:** 5 Dakar
> **enclave:** 6 Gambia
> **ethnic group:** 5 Wolof 6 Fulani
> 7 Malinke
> **language:** 6 French
> **monetary unit:** 5 franc
> **neighbor:** 4 Mali 6 Guinea
> 10 Mauritania 12 Guinea-Bissau
> **river:** 6 Gambia 7 Senegal

senescence
> 6 old age 8 caducity 11 elderliness,
> senectitude

senior
> 5 doyen, elder, older, prior 7 ancient,
> doyenne, oldster 8 higher-up,
> old-timer, superior 10 golden-ager

Sennacherib
> **domain:** 7 Assyria
> **father:** 6 Sargon
> **kingdom:** 7 Assyria
> **slayer, son:** 8 Sharezer 11 Adram-
> melech

sensation
> 4 bomb 6 marvel, tingle, wonder
> 7 feeling, miracle, prodigy, stunner
> 8 response 9 bombshell 10 impres
> sion, perception, phenomenon
> 13 consciousness

sensational
> 3 hot 5 boffo, juicy, lurid 6 purple,
> vulgar 7 tabloid 8 dramatic, exciting,
> fabulous, glorious, slambang, smash-
> ing, stunning 9 hunky-dory, mar-
> velous, thrilling 10 astounding,
> impressive, incredible, remarkable,
> scandalous 11 astonishing, extrava-
> gant, outstanding, spectacular
> 12 electrifying

sense
> 3 wit 4 feel 5 sight, smell, taste,
> touch 6 divine, discern, intuit, pick up 7 be-
> lieve, discern, feeling, hearing,
> meaning, message, realize 8 con-
> sider, judgment, perceive, prudence
> 9 awareness, foresight, intuition
> 10 anticipate, cognizance, discretion,
> perception 12 intelligence, signifi-
> cance 13 comprehension, con-
> sciousness, understanding
> **sixth:** 3 ESP

Sense and Sensibility author
> 6 Austen (Jane)

senseless
> 4 cold, numb 5 silly 6 absurd,
> numbed, simple, stupid 7 fatuous,
> foolish, idiotic, moronic, trivial, witless
> 8 benumbed, comatose, deadened,
> mindless 9 brainless, pointless
> 10 irrational 11 meaningless, pur-
> poseless, unconscious

senselessness
> 5 folly 7 inanity 8 insanity 9 ab-
> surdity, stupidity 12 illogicality

sense organ
> 3 ear, eye 4 nose, skin 6 tongue
> 8 receptor

sensibility
> 5 taste 7 emotion, feeling, insight
> 8 judgment, keenness 9 affec-
> tion, awareness, sensation 11 dis-
> cernment, penetration 12 apprecia-
> tion

sensible
> 4 sage, sane, wise 5 solid, sound
> 6 astute, shrewd 7 logical, prudent,
> sapient 8 rational 9 judicious,
> objective, sagacious 10 reasonable

sensitive

4 keen, sore 5 aware, prone 6 liable, tender, touchy, tricky 7 feeling, nervous 8 delicate, sensible, sentient, ticklish 9 emotional 10 highstrung, perceptive, precarious, responsive 11 susceptible 13 understanding

sensitive plant

6 mimosa
family: 3 pea

sensual

4 lush 6 animal, carnal, earthy 7 fleshly, mundane, worldly 8 temporal 9 epicurean, luxurious, sybaritic 10 hedonistic, voluptuous 11 irreligious, unspiritual

sensuality

4 lust 6 desire, luxury 7 lechery, license 8 hedonism, lewdness, pleasure 9 carnality, depravity, eroticism, prurience 10 debauchery, degeneracy, immorality, indulgence, perversion, profligacy, sybaritism 11 dissipation 12 incontinence 13 dissoluteness, gratification, salaciousness

sensuous

4 lush 6 carnal 7 fleshly 8 luscious 9 epicurean, luxurious, sybaritic 10 hedonistic, voluptuous 13 selfindulgent

sentence

3 rap 4 damn, doom 5 blame, judge 6 dictum, ordain, punish 7 adjudge, condemn, convict, verdict 8 decision, denounce, judgment, penalize 10 adjudicate, punishment

sententious

5 crisp, pithy, terse 7 concise, piquant, pointed 8 eloquent, pregnant, succinct 10 aphoristic, expressive, meaningful, moralistic, moralizing

sentient

5 alert, aware, savvy 7 knowing 8 sensible 9 attentive, cognizant, conscious, receptive, sensitive 10 conversant, discerning, perceptive, percipient, responsive 12 appreciative

sentiment

4 view 6 belief 7 emotion, feeling, leaning, opinion, passion, posture 8 penchant, position, tendency 9 affection, inclining, sensation 10 conception, conviction, partiality, persuasion, propensity 11 disposition, inclination, sensibility

sentimental

4 soft 5 corny, gooey, gushy, mushy, sappy, soupy, sweet 6 dreamy, drippy, slushy, sticky, sugary, syrupy, tender 7 cloying, gushing, insipid, maudlin, mawkish 8 bathetic, effusive, romantic 9 misty-eyed, nostalgic, schmaltzy 10 idealistic, loveydovey, moonstruck, namby-pamby, saccharine, soft-boiled 11 tearjerking 12 affectionate

sentimentality

4 mush 8 schmaltz

sentinel

see **sentry**

sentry

5 guard, watch 6 picket 7 lookout 8 sentinel, watchman

separate

4 comb, only, part, sift, sole, sort 5 apart, sever, split 6 cut off, detach, divide, single, sunder, unique, winnow 7 asunder, disjoin, diverse, divided, divorce, isolate, several, split up, unravel, various 8 alienate, detached, discrete, disjoint, disperse, distinct, insulate, isolated, solitary, splinter, uncouple 9 different, divergent, extricate, segregate, sequester 11 compartment, distinctive, distinguish, independent, unconnected 12 disconnected, discriminate 13 differentiate

separation

3 gap 4 rift 5 break, split 6 schism 7 breakup, divorce, parting, rupture, split-up 8 disunion, disunity, division 9 apartheid, dichotomy, partition 11 disjunction, dissolution, segrega-

tion **12** dissociation, estrangement
13 disconnection, sequestration

separatism
  9 apartheid **11** segregation

separatist
  10 schismatic **12** secessionist·

sepia
  3 ink **5** brown, umber **6** sienna

sepulchral
  4 grim **5** bleak, grave **6** dismal,
gloomy, solemn, somber **7** doleful,
macabre **8** funereal, ghoulish,
mortuary **9** tenebrous

sepulchre
  4 tomb **5** grave, vault **9** mausoleum

sequel
  3 end **5** close **6** effect, ending,
finish, result, upshot **7** closing,
outcome **8** epilogue **9** aftermath
10 succession **11** aftereffect, consequence, development, eventuality,
progression, termination **12** continuation

sequence
  3 row, run, set **4** flow **5** chain,
order, train **6** course, series, string
8 disposal, ordering **9** placement
10 procession, succession **11** arrangement, disposition, progression
12 distribution

sequential
  6 serial **9** succedent **10** continuous,
succeeding, successive **11** consecutive **12** successional **13** chronological

sequester
  4 hide, take **5** annex, seize **6** attach, cut off, enisle **7** impound,
isolate, preempt, seclude, secrete
8 accroach, arrogate, cloister, close
off, insulate, separate, set apart,
withdraw **9** segregate **10** commandeer, confiscate, dispossess **11** appropriate, expropriate

sequoia
  7 big tree, redwood **12** coast redwood

seraglio
  5 harem

serape
  5 shawl

seraph
  5 angel **8** guardian **9** messenger

seraphic
  4 pure **7** angelic, sublime **8** beatific,
cherubic, ethereal

Serbia and Montenegro
  capital: 8 Belgrade
  city: 3 Bar **5** Kotar, Tivat **7** Novi
Sad, Pancevo **9** Podgorica **11** Pris-
tinauzi
  monetary unit: 4 euro **5** dinar
  neighbor: 6 Bosnia, Kosovo **7** Albania, Croatia, Hungary, Romania
8 Bulgaria **9** Macedonia
  part of: 7 Balkans
  peninsula: 6 Balkan
  province: 9 Vojvodina
  province, former: 6 Kosovo
  river: 4 Sava **6** Danube
  sea: 8 Adriatic

sere
  3 dry **5** dried **7** parched, thirsty
8 withered **9** shriveled, unwatered

serenade
  7 lullaby **8** shivaree **9** charivari

serene
  4 calm **5** quiet, still **6** limpid, placid,
poised, sedate **7** halcyon **8** composed, tranquil **9** unruffled **10** untroubled

serenity
  4 calm **5** peace **8** calmness, quietude **9** composure, placidity, stillness **10** equanimity **11** contentment, tranquility **12** peacefulness,
tranquillity

serf
  4 esne, peon **5** churl, helot, slave
6 thrall **7** bondman, villein
  freeborn: 7 colonus

serial
  10 sequential, successive **11** consecutive, installment

series

3 row, run, set 4 list, tier 5 chain, range, scale, train 6 catena, column, parade, sequel, string 8 sequence 9 cavalcade, gradation 10 procession, succession 11 progression 12 continuation

serious

4 grim, hard 5 grave, heavy, major, sober, staid, stern, tough 6 intent, sedate, severe, solemn, somber, sombre, steady 7 austere, earnest, intense, pensive, sincere, unfunny, weighty 8 funereal, menacing, resolute, sobering 9 difficult, humorless, important, laborious, strenuous, unamusing 10 determined, formidable, meditative, no-nonsense, pokerfaced, purposeful, reflective, sobersided, thoughtful, unhumorous 11 significant, threatening 12 businesslike 13 contemplative

sermon

6 homily, speech, tirade 7 address, lecture, oration 8 harangue 9 preaching 10 preachment 11 exhortation

sermonize

5 orate 6 dilate, exhort, preach 7 dissert, lecture 8 moralize 9 discourse, expatiate, preachify 10 dissertate, evangelize 11 pontificate

serpent

5 fiend, Satan, snake
fabled: 8 basilisk
mythical: 10 cockatrice
sound: 4 hiss

serpentine

4 rock, wily 5 snaky 7 cunning, devious, mineral, sinuous, winding 8 flexuous, tempting, tortuous 9 snakelike 10 circuitous, convoluted, meandering

serrated

7 notched, toothed 8 saw-edged, sawtooth 10 saw-toothed 11 denticulate

servant

4 maid, peon 5 slave, valet 6 butler, flunky, helper, lackey, menial 7 family.

ulus, footman 8 domestic, handmaid, hireling, houseboy 9 attendant 11 chamberlain, chambermaid
India: 4 syce
kitchen: 8 scullion
Wodehouse: 6 Jeeves

serve

3 act, fit, use 4 help, make, play, suit, work 5 nurse, spend, treat 6 foster, handle, wait on 7 advance, benefit, care for, present, promote, provide, satisfy, suffice, work for 8 deal with, function 9 encourage, officiate 10 minister to

service

3 use 4 duty, help, rite 5 favor 6 employ, repair, ritual 7 account, benefit, fitness, liturgy 8 ceremony, courtesy, disposal, maintain 10 active duty, assistance, ceremonial, observance, usefulness 11 maintenance 12 dispensation

serviceable

5 handy, utile 6 decent, usable, useful 7 durable, helpful 8 adequate, suitable 9 efficient, practical 10 acceptable, beneficial, convenient, dependable, functional 11 utilitarian 12 satisfactory

servile

6 abject, craven, humble, menial 7 fawning, slavish 8 obedient, obeisant 9 groveling 10 obsequious, submissive 11 subservient

servility

7 bondage, helotry, peonage, serfdom, slavery 9 thralldom 11 enslavement

serving

6 dollop 7 helping, portion

servitude

5 labor 6 corvée, thrall 7 bondage, helotry, peonage, serfdom, slavery 9 captivity, indenture, thralldom, villenage 10 subjection 11 enslavement 12 enthrallment

sesame

3 til
grass: 4 gama

sessile
5 fixed 6 rooted 7 settled 8 attached 11 established

session
6 assize, séance 7 meeting, sitting

set
3 aim, dry, fix, gel, lay, lot, put 4 firm, jell 5 array, batch, bunch, fixed, group, place, put on, ready, rigid, scene 6 belong, harden, impose, placed, rooted, secure, stated 7 arrange, certain, cluster, congeal, decided, deposit, dictate, jellify, lay down, located, prepare, scenery, situate, specify, station 8 prepared, resolute, resolved, situated, solidify, specific 9 confirmed, designate, establish, prescribe, specified, stipulate, tenacious 10 assortment, determined, gelatinize, inflexible, positioned, prescribed, stipulated 11 established, mise-en-scène
a gem: 6 collet
right: 7 redress

set aside
4 void 5 annul 7 discard, dismiss, reserve 8 overrule

set back
4 mire 5 delay 6 detain, hang up, hinder, retard, slow up

setback
5 check, hitch 6 defeat, rebuff 7 reverse 8 obstacle, reversal 9 hindrance 10 impediment, regression

set down
4 land 5 light, perch, roost 6 alight, record 9 establish, touch down

set fire to
4 burn 6 ignite 7 emblaze, inflame 8 enkindle, touch off

set forth
4 cite 5 state 6 adduce, affirm, allege, avouch, depart, embark, launch, submit 7 advance, declare, express, present, proffer, propose, take off 8 proclaim, spell out 9 introduce 10 account for

set free
5 loose 6 redeem, rescue, unbind 7 deliver, manumit, unchain, unloose 8 liberate, unloosen 9 unshackle 10 emancipate

Seth
brother: 4 Abel, Cain
father: 4 Adam
mother: 3 Eve
son: 4 Enos

set out
5 start 6 embark, intend 7 take off 9 undertake

Set's victim
6 Osiris

settee
4 seat, sofa 5 bench, divan 6 lounge

setting
5 scene 7 context, scenery 8 ambience 10 background 11 mise-en-scène
for a stone: 4 ouch

settle
3 fix, lay, pay, put 4 calm 5 allay, judge, light, pay up, perch, place, quiet, roost, still 6 alight, clinch, decide, soothe, square, verify, wind up 7 arrange, compose, confirm, dispose, install, mediate, resolve, satisfy, work out 8 colonize, conclude, ensconce, nail down 9 determine, discharge, establish, negotiate, reconcile, touch down

settlement
4 deal 6 colony, hamlet 7 outpost, quietus, village 8 decision 9 agreement 10 conclusion, encampment, habitation, resolution 11 arrangement 13 determination
Israeli: 6 moshav

settler
7 pioneer 8 colonist, squatter 9 colonizer

set-to
3 row 4 fray, spat 5 brawl, broil, brush, fight, run-in, scrap 6 affray, blowup, fracas, tussle 7 dispute,

set up

quarrel, rhubarb, scuffle **8** argument, skirmish **9** encounter **10** falling-out **11** altercation

set up

4 open **5** erect, found, raise, start **6** create, launch **7** arrange, install **8** assemble, generate, initiate, organize **9** construct, establish, institute, originate

setup

4 plan **5** array, trick **6** layout, scheme, shoo-in **7** pattern, project, setting **8** assembly, carriage, position, slam dunk **9** alignment, apparatus, structure, sure thing **11** arrangement, preparation **12** constitution

seven

combining form: 4 hept, sept **5** hepta, septi
group of: 6 heptad **8** hebdomad

seventeenth century

8 seicento

sever

3 cut, lop **4** part, rend **5** slice, split **6** cleave, cut off, detach, divide, sunder **7** break up, divorce **8** amputate, disjoint, separate

several

4 a few, many, some **6** divers, plural, sundry, varied **7** certain, diverse, various **8** assorted, discrete, distinct, manifold, numerous, separate, specific **9** different **10** respective

severe

4 dour, grim, hard **5** acute, grave, harsh, heavy, rigid, sober, stern, tough **6** bitter, brutal, rugged, strict **7** arduous, ascetic, austere, extreme, intense, onerous, serious, weighty **8** exacting, pitiless, rigorous **9** demanding, difficult, laborious, strenuous, stringent, unbending **10** forbidding, implacable, inflexible, iron-willed, oppressive, unyielding **11** disciplined, heavy-handed

severity

5 rigor **7** gravity, urgency **8** exigency, grimness, obduracy, rigidity **9** austerity, harshness, intensity, plainness, privation, restraint, spareness, starkness, sternness **10** strictness, stringency **11** seriousness

sew

4 darn, mend, seam **5** baste **6** needle, stitch, suture

sewer

4 duct **5** ditch, drain **6** tailor **7** cesspit, conduit **8** cesspool, stitcher

sewing

aid: 7 thimble
case: 4 etui
kit: 9 housewife

sewing-machine inventor

4 Howe (Elias)

sexless

6 neuter **7** epicene **8** neutered

sex manual

9 Kama-sutra

sexton

6 deacon **9** custodian, sacristan

sexual

4 blue, lewd, racy **6** carnal, erotic, ribald, risqué, smutty **7** obscene **8** venereal **9** salacious **12** pornographic

sexual desire

4 eros, lust **6** libido

sexy

4 blue, racy **5** bawdy, spicy **6** erotic, purple, ribald, risqué, steamy, sultry **7** naughty **8** alluring, off-color, sensuous **9** appealing, salacious, seductive **10** attractive, suggestive

Seychelles

capital: 8 Victoria
island: 4 Mahé **7** La Digue, Praslin
language: 6 Creole, French
monetary unit: 5 rupee

Sganarelle

brother: 6 Ariste
daughter: 7 Lucinde
ward: 7 Leonore **8** Isabelle
wife: 7 Martine

shabby
5 dingy, dowdy, faded, mangy, ratty, seedy, sorry, tacky, tired **6** frayed, scurvy, shoddy, sleazy, sordid **7** outworn, rickety, run-down, scrubby, scruffy, squalid, worn-out **8** beggarly, decaying, decrepit, dog-eared, tattered **9** miserable, moth-eaten, neglected, worm-eaten **10** bedraggled, down-at-heel, ramshackle, threadbare **11** dilapidated **12** deteriorated, disreputable **13** deteriorating, unrespectable

shack
3 cot, hut **4** camp, shed **5** cabin, hovel, lodge **6** shanty **7** cottage

shackle
4 gyve **5** bilbo, chain, leash, strap **6** fetter, hobble, hog-tie, impede, pinion, secure **7** enchain, leg-iron, manacle, trammel **8** handcuff **9** entrammel

shad
7 clupeid, herring

shade
3 hue **4** cast, tint, tone, veil **5** ghost, tinge, trace, umbra **6** awning, darken, nuance, screen **7** dimness, eclipse, phantom, shelter, specter, spectre, umbrage **8** darkness, penumbra, phantasm, tincture **9** gradation, intensity, obscurity **10** apparition **11** distinction

shadow
3 dim, dog, tag **4** haze, hint, tail **5** cloud, shade, tinge, touch, trace, trail, umbra **6** screen, spirit, wraith **7** eidolon, obscure, phantom, specter, umbrage, vestige **8** overcast, penumbra, phantasm, revenant, tincture **9** inumbrate, overcloud, suspicion **10** apparition, intimation, suggestion **11** adumbration

shadowy
3 dim **4** dark **5** dusky, faint, murky, vague **6** gloomy, shaded **7** ghostly, obscure **9** tenebrous **10** indistinct

shady
4 dark **5** bosky, dusky, fishy **6** purple, shabby, shoddy **7** clouded, dubious, suspect **8** doubtful, screened **9** equivocal, sheltered, uncertain **10** suggestive, suspicious, umbrageous, unreliable **12** disreputable

Shaffer play
5 Equus **7** Amadeus

shaft
3 jab, ray, rod **4** axle, barb, beam, dart, pole, stem **5** arrow, lance, shoot, spear, stalk, thill **6** thrust **7** chimney, spindle **8** short end

shag
3 nap, rug **4** pile **5** chase, fetch **7** thicket, tobacco **9** cormorant

shaggy
5 bushy **7** unkempt **8** uncombed

shake
3 jar, jog, rid **4** deal, jerk, jolt, lose, rock, roil, sway **5** avoid, churn, daunt, elude, jiffy, quail, quake, shock, upset, waver, worry **6** escape, frappe, jiggle, joggle, outwit, quaver, quiver, rattle, ruffle, shimmy, shiver, stir up, tremor **7** agitate, chatter, disturb, perturb, shingle, shudder, temblor, tremble, unnerve, vibrate **8** brandish, convulse, throw off, unsettle **9** oscillate, palpitate **10** earthquake

shake down
5 frisk, gouge, screw, wrest, wring **6** coerce, extort, fleece, search **7** squeeze **9** blackmail

shakedown
3 bed **4** test **5** dance, trial **6** pallet, search, tryout **7** pursuit, testing **8** exaction **9** blackmail, extortion **10** inspection

Shakers leader
3 Lee (Ann) **9** Mother Ann

Shakespearean actor
4 Kean (Edmund) **5** Booth (Edwin), Dench (Judi), Evans (Maurice), Terry (Ellen) **6** Irving (Henry) **7** Branagh (Kenneth), Burbage (Richard), Garrick (David), Gielgud (John), Olivier (Laurence), Siddons (Sarah)

8 Ashcroft (Peggy), Macready (William), Redgrave (Michael), Scofield (Paul) **9** Barrymore (Ethel, John, Lionel, Maurice) **10** Richardson (Ralph)

Shakespeare, William

mother: **9** Mary Arden
play: **6** Hamlet, Henry V **7** Henry IV, Henry VI, Macbeth, Othello, Tempest (The) **8** King John, King Lear, Pericles **9** Cymbeline, Henry VIII, Richard II **10** Coriolanus, Richard III **11** As You Like It, Winter's Tale (The) **12** Julius Caesar, Twelfth Night **13** Timon of Athens **14** Comedy of Errors (The), Romeo and Juliet **16** Love's Labour's Lost, Merchant of Venice (The), Taming of the Shrew (The) **17** Measure for Measure **18** Antony and Cleopatra **19** Much Ado About Nothing **20** All's Well That Ends Well, Midsummer Night's Dream (A)
theater: **5** Globe
wife: **12** Anne Hathaway

shaky

4 weak **6** infirm, unsure, wobbly **7** aquiver, dubious, jittery, quaking, rackety, rickety, suspect, trembly, unsound **8** doubtful, insecure, rachitic, unstable, unsteady, wavering **9** quivering, tottering, trembling, tremulous, uncertain, unsettled **10** indecisive, precarious, rattletrap, unreliable **11** problematic, vacillating

shale

4 rock **5** slate

shallot

4 herb **5** onion **10** green onion

shallow

4 idle, vain **5** petty, shoal **7** cursory, sketchy, trivial **8** trifling **9** depthless, frivolous **11** perfunctory, superficial

shallows

6 lagoon, shoals

Shallum

father: **5** Shaul, Zadok **6** Jabesh, Josiah, Sismai, Tikvah **8** Colhozeh, Naphtali **9** Hallohesh

mother: **6** Bilhah
nephew: **8** Jeremiah
slayer: **7** Menahem
son: **6** Mibsam **7** Hilkiah **8** Maaseiah
victim: **9** Zechariah

shalom

5 peace

sham

3 act, ape **4** fake, hoax, mock **5** bluff, bogus, bunco, cheat, dummy, false, farce, feign, fraud, phony, put on, spoof **6** deceit, ersatz, facade, fakery, forged, invent, pseudo **7** assumed, feigned, forgery, imitate, mislead, mockery, pretend **8** affected, flimflam, simulate, spurious, travesty **9** brummagem, burlesque, deception, hypocrisy, imitation, imposture, pinchbeck, simulated **10** artificial, caricature, false front, fictitious, fraudulent, sanctimony, substitute **11** counterfeit, make-believe **12** pecksniffery
combining form: **5** pseud **6** pseudo

shaman

6 healer, priest, wizard **7** diviner **8** conjurer, conjuror, magician, sorcerer **9** enchanter, priestess **10** high priest, soothsayer **11** faith healer, necromancer, thaumaturge, witch doctor

Shamash

6 sun-god
father: **3** Sin
sister: **6** Ishtar
wife: **3** Aya

shamble

see **shuffle**

shambles

4 mess **5** chaos **6** jumble, muddle **8** disarray, disorder, wreckage **9** confusion

shame

4 pity **5** abash, guilt, odium **6** infamy, stigma **7** chagrin, mortify, obloquy, remorse, scandal **8** disgrace, dishonor, ignominy **9** disrepute, embarrass, humiliate, ill repute **10** opprobrium **11** humiliation **12** self-reproach **13** embarrassment, mortification

shamefaced
7 abashed **8** blushing, sheepish **9** mortified **10** humiliated **11** crestfallen, embarrassed

shameless
6 arrant, brazen, wanton **7** blatant, immoral **8** depraved, flagrant, immodest, impudent **9** abandoned, bald-faced, barefaced, dissolute, unabashed **10** outrageous, profligate, unblushing **11** brazen-faced, disgraceful **12** presumptuous

Shammah
brother: 5 David
father: 4 Agee **5** Jesse, Reuel
grandfather: 4 Esau **7** Ishmael
son: 7 Jonadab **8** Jonathan

Shammua
father: 5 David, Galal **6** Bilgah, Zaccur
mother: 9 Bathsheba
son: 4 Abda

shamus
3 cop **4** dick, tail **6** copper, shadow, sleuth **7** gumshoe **8** flatfoot, sherlock **9** constable, detective, operative, policeman **10** private eye **12** investigator **13** police officer

shanghai
6 abduct, hijack, kidnap

Shangri-la
5 Tibet **6** utopia **7** arcadia **8** paradise **9** Cockaigne, fairyland **10** wonderland

shank
3 leg **4** shin, stem **5** stalk, tibia

shanty
3 cot, hut **4** camp, shed **5** cabin, hovel, lodge, shack **7** cottage

shape
3 fit **4** case, cast, form, mold, plan, trim **5** forge, frame, state, whack **6** aspect, devise, fettle, figure, kilter, repair, sculpt, tailor, work up **7** contour, fitness, outline, pattern, profile **8** assemble **9** condition, construct, fabricate, semblance **10** appearance, silhouette **12** conformation **13** configuration
combining form: 5 morph **6** morpho

shapeable
6 pliant, supple **7** ductile, plastic, pliable **8** flexible **9** tractable

shapeless
8 inchoate, unformed **9** amorphous

shapely
4 trim **5** buxom **9** Junoesque **10** curvaceous, statuesque, well-turned **11** clean-limbed

shard
4 chip **5** chunk, scale, scrap, shell **6** sliver **7** elytron **8** carapace, fragment

share
3 cut, lot **4** part **5** chunk, claim, quota, slice, stake **6** divide, parcel, ration **7** dole out, give out, helping, partake, portion, prorate, quantum **8** dispense, fraction, interest, quotient **9** allotment, allowance, apportion **10** experience, percentage, proportion **11** participate

shared
5 joint **6** common, mutual, public **8** communal, conjoint, conjunct **9** concerted **10** collective **11** cooperative

Sharezer
father, victim: 11 Sennacherib

shark
5 cheat **8** swindler
kind: 4 mako, sand, tope **5** nurse, tiger **7** basking, dogfish, leopard **8** mackerel, man-eater, thresher **9** porbeagle **10** great white, hammerhead
skin: 8 shagreen

sharp
3 sly **4** acid, keen, tony, trig **5** acrid, acute, alert, canny, crisp, honed, quick, slick, smart, swank **6** biting,

sharpen

bitter, brainy, bright, clever, jagged, nimble, peaked, shrewd, shrill, snappy **7** caustic, dashing, intense, pointed, prickly, stylish, whetted **8** clean-cut, clear-cut, incisive, piercing, shooting, stabbing, stinging **9** agonizing, brilliant, ingenious, knifelike, vitriolic **10** astringent, perceptive **11** intelligent, penetrating, quick-witted, resourceful **12** excruciating, nimble-witted

sharpen

4 edge, file, hone, whet **5** grind, strop

sharper

6 con man **7** diddler **8** chiseler, swindler **9** defrauder, trickster **10** mountebank **12** double-dealer

sharp-eyed

4 keen **5** alert **8** vigilant, watchful **9** attentive, observant **10** discerning, perceptive

sharpie

see **sharper**

sharpness

4 edge **6** acumen **9** precision

sharpshooter

8 marksman

sharp-sighted

8 hawk-eyed, lynx-eyed **9** eagle-eyed

sharp-witted

4 keen **5** acute, canny, quick, smart **6** astute, clever, shrewd **11** intelligent

shatter

4 dash **5** break, burst, crush, smash **6** shiver **8** demolish, fragment, splinter **9** pulverize **10** annihilate **11** fragmentize **12** disintegrate

shatterable

7 brittle, fragile **9** breakable, frangible

shave

3 cut **4** clip, crop, pare, peel, skim, trim **5** lower, prune, shear, skive **6** barber, cut off, deduct, reduce, scrape, sliver **7** cut back, whittle **8** mark down

shaveling

3 boy, kid, lad, tad **6** laddie, squirt **9** stripling, youngster

shaver

3 boy, kid, lad, tad **5** child, razor **6** barber, laddie, squirt **9** stripling, youngster

shawl

4 wrap **5** fichu, manta **6** chador, serape **7** tallith **8** mantilla

shawm's descendant

4 oboe

Shawnee chief

8 Tecumseh, Tecumtha **9** Cornstalk

Shaw play

6 Geneva **7** Candida **9** Pygmalion, Saint Joan **11** Misalliance **12** Major Barbara **13** Arms and the Man

shay

6 chaise **8** carriage

shear

3 cut, mow **4** clip, crop, pare, snip, trim **5** prune, shave, skive **6** barber

shears

8 scissors

shearwater

4 bird **6** petrel **7** skimmer

sheath

4 case, skin **5** cover **7** holster **8** scabbard

sheathe

4 case, clad, face, side, skin, wrap **5** cover, panel **6** encase, jacket

Sheba

father: **6** Bichri
queen: **6** Balkis

shebang

4 mess **6** affair **7** schmear **8** business, caboodle **9** ball of wax, enchilada

shed

3 hut **4** cast, doff, drop, emit, molt **5** exude, hovel, hutch, scrap, shack, stall **6** divest, lean-to, reject, slough **7** cast off, diffuse, discard, radiate, take off **8** jettison, throw out **9** throw away

sheen

5 glaze, gleam, glint, gloss, shine
6 finish, luster, lustre, polish 7 burnish, glitter, shimmer 8 radiance
9 shininess 10 brightness

sheeny

see **shiny**

sheep

5 ovine
breed: 5 Tunis 6 Dorper, Dorset, Merino, Navajo, No-Tail, Oxford, Panama, Romney 7 Cheviot, Colbred, Karakul, Lincoln, Ryeland, Suffolk 8 Columbia, Cotswold, Polwarth 9 Hampshire, Leicester, Montadale, Southdown 10 Corriedale, Debouillet 11 Rambouillet
coat: 4 wool 6 fleece
disease: 3 gid
female: 3 ewe
male: 3 ram 6 wether
meat: 6 mutton
relating to: 5 ovine
Scottish: 9 blackface
sound: 5 bleat
tender: 8 shepherd
wild: 5 urial 6 aoudad, argali, bharal 7 bighorn, mouflon
young: 4 lamb

sheepish

4 meek 5 timid 7 abashed, ashamed, bashful 8 timorous 9 diffident
10 shamefaced 11 embarrassed

sheepskin

4 roan 6 mouton 7 diploma 9 parchment
prepare: 3 taw

sheer

4 pure, skew, thin, turn, veer 5 filmy, gauzy, steep, utter 6 abrupt, arrant, flimsy, simple, swerve 7 chiffon, deflect, deviate, perfect, unmixed 8 absolute, complete, gossamer, outright 9 out-and-out, unalloyed, undiluted 10 diaphanous, seethrough 11 precipitate, precipitous, transparent, unmitigated

sheet

3 ply 4 film, leaf, page, sail, slab
5 cover, linen, paper 6 lamina, veneer 8 membrane 9 newspaper

sheet _____

3 ice 4 film 5 glass, metal, music
6 anchor

shelf

3 hob 4 bank, edge, reef, sill 5 ledge, shoal 6 mantel 7 counter 8 sandbank

shell

3 pod 4 boat, bomb, case, hull, husk, rake, skin 5 blitz, conch, shuck 6 pepper 7 bombard, capsule, grenade, mollusc, mollusk 8 carapace 9 cannonade, cartridge
defective: 3 dud
explosive: 4 bomb
layer: 5 nacre
ornamental: 6 cowrie
study: 10 conchology

shellac

4 beat, drub, flay, lick, rout, trim, whap, whip, whop, whup 5 resin, smear, whomp 6 defeat, thrash
7 clobber, smother, trounce 8 lambaste, vanquish

Shelley, Percy Bysshe

poem: 5 Cloud (The) 7 Adonais, Alastor 8 Queen Mab 10 Ozymandias, To a Skylark 16 Ode to the West Wind

shellfish

4 clam, crab 5 conch, cowry, prawn, snail, whelk 6 cockle, limpet, mussel, oyster, quahog, triton 7 abalone, crawdad, geoduck, lobster, mollusc, mollusk, scallop 8 barnacle, crayfish, escargot 10 crustacean, periwinkle

shell out

3 pay 4 give 5 spend 8 fork over, hand over

shell-shaped

6 spiral 9 cochleate

shelter

3 den, hut, lee 4 cote, fold, hide, port, roof, shed, tent 5 arbor, bower, cloak, cover, haven, house, shack, tower 6 asylum, burrow, covert, defend, harbor, refuge, shield

7 chamber, defense, foxhole, hide-out, hospice, housing, lodging, pergola, pillbox, protect, retreat **8** hideaway, hidy-hole, security **9** dwellings, hermitage, hidey-hole, sanctuary **10** retirement
for aircraft: 6 hangar
for cows: 4 barn, byre
toward: 4 alee

shelve
4 dish, drop, stay, tilt **5** defer, delay, slope, stock, waive **6** freeze, give up, hold up, put off **7** hold off, suspend **8** hold over, mothball, postpone, prorogue, set aside

Shem
brother: 3 Ham **7** Japheth
father: 4 Noah

Shema's father
4 Joel **6** Hebron

Shemida's father
6 Gilead

shenanigan
4 dido, lark **5** antic, caper, prank, stunt, trick **6** frolic **8** escapade, mischief **10** tomfoolery **11** monkey-shine

Sheol
see **hades**

shepherd
4 lead, show, tend **5** guide, pilot, route, steer, watch **6** direct, escort, leader **7** conduct **8** guardian
dog: 6 collie **12** border collie
stick: 5 crook, staff

Sheridan play
6 Critic (The), Rivals (The) **7** Pizarro **16** School for Scandal (The)

sheriff
5 reeve **6** lawman **7** marshal, officer
aide: 6 deputy

sherlock
4 dick, tail **5** snoop **6** shadow, shamus, sleuth **7** gumshoe **8** hawkshaw **9** detective **10** private eye **12** investigator

Sherlock Holmes
creator: 5 Doyle (Arthur Conan)
sidekick: 6 Watson (Dr.)

sherry
4 fino, wine **7** oloroso **10** manzanilla **11** amontillado

Sherwood play
10 Road to Rome (The) **13** Idiot's Delight **14** Waterloo Bridge **15** Petrified Forest (The)

shibboleth
3 saw, tag **5** axiom, maxim **6** byword, cliché, phrase, saying, slogan, truism **7** bromide **8** banality, chestnut, password, prosaism **9** catchword, platitude, watchword **11** catchphrase, commonplace

shield
4 fend, roof, ward **5** aegis, armor, cover, guard, haven, house **6** buffer, defend, harbor, screen, secure **7** buckler, bulwark, defense, protect, shelter **8** defilade **9** safeguard **10** escutcheon
band: 4 fess
bullfighter's: 9 burladero
light: 5 targe
part: 4 boss, umbo **7** bordure
Roman: 7 testudo

shield-like
7 peltate

shift
3 yaw **4** bend, bout, move, stir, tack, time, tour, turn, vary, veer **5** alter, budge, get by, spell, stint, trick **6** change, make do, manage, remove, resort, swerve **7** deviate, replace, shuffle, stopgap **8** get along, relocate, resource, transfer **9** deviation, expedient, fluctuate **10** alteration, changeover, conversion, transition **11** fluctuation

shiftless
4 idle, lazy **5** inept **8** feckless, indolent, slothful **11** inefficient

shifty
3 sly **4** foxy, wily **5** cagey, lying, shady, slick **6** crafty, sneaky, tricky

7 cunning, devious, elusive, evasive, furtive **8** guileful, slippery, sneaking **9** conniving, deceitful, deceptive, dishonest, insidious, underhand **10** inconstant, untruthful **11** duplicitous, underhanded **12** equivocating

shill
5 blind, decoy, pitch **6** capper **8** promoter **10** accomplice, sales pitch

shillelagh
3 bat **4** club, cosh, mace **5** baton, billy, stick **6** cudgel **8** bludgeon **9** bastinado, billy club, blackjack, truncheon **10** nightstick

shilling
3 bob

shilly-shally
5 fudge, hedge, stall, waver **6** dawdle, dither, waffle **7** whiffle **8** hesitate **9** temporize, vacillate **11** prevaricate **12** tergiversate

Shimea
brother: **5** David
father: **5** David, Jesse
son: **7** Jonadab **8** Jonathan

shimmer
5 flash, gleam, glint, sheen **6** luster, lustre **7** glimmer, glisten, glitter, spangle, sparkle, twinkle **9** coruscate **11** coruscation, scintillate **13** scintillation

shimmy
5 dance, shake **6** quiver, shiver, tremor **7** chemise, shudder, tremble, vibrate **9** vibration

shin
3 run **4** dash **5** scoot, tibia **6** scurry, sprint **7** scamper

shindig
4 ball, bash, fête, gala **5** binge, dance, party, revel **6** affair, frolic **7** blowout **8** wingding

shine
3 ray, rub **4** beam, buff, burn, glow **5** blaze, flare, flash, glare, glaze, gleam, glint, gloss, sheen **6** luster,

lustre, polish **7** burnish, glimmer, glisten, glitter, radiate, shimmer, sparkle, twinkle **9** luminesce **10** incandesce

shiner
4 fish **8** black eye, cyprinid

shingle
5 beach, coast, shore **7** haircut, overlap, overlay **8** detritus **9** signboard

shiny
6 bright, glossy **7** fulgent, radiant **8** dazzling, gleaming, lustrous, polished **9** burnished, effulgent **10** glistening

ship
4 boat, send **5** remit, route **6** export **7** consign, forward, freight **8** dispatch, transfer, transmit
ancient: **6** galley **7** galleon, trireme
attendant: **7** steward
beam: **7** keelson
berth: **4** dock, slip
boat: **6** dinghy
body: **4** hull
cabin: **9** stateroom
commercial: **5** liner, oiler **6** argosy, tanker, trader **9** freighter
crew member: **4** hand, mate **6** sailor
deck: **4** boat, main, poop **5** orlop **6** bridge **10** forecastle
fishing: **6** lugger **7** trawler
fleet: **6** armada
floor: **4** deck
front: **3** bow **4** prow, stem **8** cutwater
hoister: **4** boom **5** davit **7** capstan
kitchen: **6** galley
left side: **4** port **8** larboard
military: **6** cutter, PT boat **7** carrier, cruiser **9** destroyer, submarine
officer: **4** mate **5** bosun **6** purser **7** captain, steward **9** boatswain
part: **3** bow **4** beam, deck, helm, hold, hull, keel, mast, stem **5** bilge, hatch, stern **6** bridge, rudder **7** scupper
partition: **7** bulwark **8** bulkhead
personnel: **4** crew

platform: 9 crow's nest, gangboard, gangplank
post: 4 mast 7 bollard
prison: 4 brig
projection: 7 sponson
rear: 5 stern
record: 3 log
right side: 9 starboard
room: 4 brig 5 cabin 6 galley
rope: 4 line 5 sheet 7 halyard
sailing: 3 hoy 4 brig, dhow, prau, proa, yawl 5 ketch, sloop, xebec, yacht 6 lugger 7 caravel, galleon 8 schooner
steerer: 4 helm 6 tiller
storage area: 4 hold
to the rear of: 3 aft 5 abaft 6 astern
valve: 7 seacock
window: 4 port 8 porthole

shipment
5 cargo 6 lading 7 freight, payload 8 delivery 11 consignment

Ship of Fools author
6 Porter (Katherine Anne)

Shipping News author
6 Proulx (Annie)

ships, group of
4 navy 5 fleet, flota 6 armada 8 flotilla

shipshape
4 neat, snug, tidy, trig, trim 7 orderly 11 spic-and-span, uncluttered 12 spick-and-span

shipworm
6 teredo

shire
5 horse 6 county 8 district 10 draft horse

shirk
4 duck, lurk, shun 5 avoid, creep, dodge, elude, evade, skulk, slink, sneak, steal 8 sidestep

shirker
see **slacker**

shirt
4 polo, sark 5 dress, kurta, sport 6 blouse, jersey 9 guayabera

shirty
3 mad 5 angry, cross, irate 6 heated, ireful 7 annoyed 8 choleric, incensed, offended 9 indignant, irritated

shiv
5 blade, knife, shank 6 dagger 8 stiletto

Shiva
consort: 3 Uma 4 Devi, Kali 5 Durga, Gauri 6 Ambika, Chandi 7 Parvati 9 Haimavati
son: 6 Ganesa, Skanda 7 Ganesha 10 Karttikeya

shiver
5 burst, quake, shake, smash 6 quaver, quiver, tremor 7 shatter, shudder, tremble, twitter 8 fragment, splinter, splitter

shoal
3 bar 4 bank, hook, reef, spit 6 school 7 barrier, sandbar, shallow, tombolo 8 sandbank, sand reef

shoat
3 hog, pig 5 swine 6 piglet, porker

Shobab
father: 5 Caleb, David
mother: 6 Azubah 9 Bathsheba

shock
3 jar 4 blow, bump, daze, jolt, pile, rick, stun 5 amaze, clash, crash, mound, quake, shake, sheaf 6 appall, dismay, impact, insult, offend, trauma, tremor 7 astound, disgust, horrify, outrage, stagger, startle, stupefy, temblor 8 astonish, surprise 9 collision, electrify 10 concussion, earthquake, percussion, scandalize, traumatize 11 flabbergast 12 stupefaction

shock absorber
6 spring 7 dashpot, snubber

shocker
4 blow 7 stunner 8 surprise, thriller 9 bombshell, eye-opener, sensation 11 showstopper

shocking
5 awful, lurid **6** horrid **7** glaring, heinous **8** dreadful, horrible, horrific, shameful, terrible **9** appalling, atrocious, frightful, monstrous, revolting **10** outrageous, scandalous **11** disgraceful, distressing, unspeakable

shoddy
4 base, mean, poor **5** cheap, dingy, gaudy, junky, seedy, tacky, tatty **6** cheesy, common, paltry, shabby, sleazy, tawdry, trashy **7** run-down, scruffy **8** inferior, rubbishy, shameful **9** makeshift **10** broken-down, down-at-heel **11** dilapidated, disgraceful, ignominious, pretentious **12** dishonorable, disreputable **13** discreditable

shoe
4 boot, clog, geta, mule, pump **5** sabot, wedge **6** brogan, brogue, buskin, gaiter, galosh, gillie, loafer, oxford, patten, sandal **7** chopine, ghillie, slipper, sneaker **8** balmoral, moccasin, platform, plimsoll **10** clodhopper, espadrille
armored: 8 solleret
athlete's: 7 sneaker
form: 4 last, tree
kind: 8 elevator, open-toed **10** high-heeled
part: 3 tip, toe **4** arch, heel, lace, lift, sole, vamp **5** shank, upper **6** box toe, collar, foxing, insole, lining, throat, tongue **7** counter, outsole **8** backstay
protective: 6 galosh, rubber
shiner: 6 polish **9** bootblack
wooden: 5 sabot **7** chopine

shoelace tip
5 aglet

shoeless
6 unshod **8** barefoot **9** discalced

shoemaker
7 cobbler
patron saint: 7 Crispin
Scottish: 6 souter

Shogun author
7 Clavell (James)

Sholem Aleichem character
5 Tevye

shoo
4 scat **5** drive, leave, scare, scram, split **6** beat it, begone, bug off, skidoo **7** buzz off, get lost, skiddoo, vamoose **8** clear out **9** skedaddle, take a hike **10** hit the road

shoo-in
6 winner **7** sure bet **8** slam dunk **9** sure thing

shoot
3 bud, fly, gun, ray **4** beam, bolt, dart, dash, fire, lash, race, rush, sail, scud, skim, spew, tear **5** blast, chase, fling, photo, shaft, skirr, snipe, spurt **6** branch **7** project **9** discharge **10** photograph

shoot down
3 pan, rap **4** bash, kill, slam **5** blast, decry, knock, scorn, trash **6** assail, deride, dump on, reject, squash **7** deflate, squelch, torpedo **8** badmouth, belittle, derogate, discount, disprove, puncture, ridicule **9** discredit

shooting
4 keen **5** acute, sharp **7** gunplay **8** piercing, stabbing

shooting star
6 meteor **8** fireball

shoot up
4 soar **6** inject, rocket **7** burgeon **8** mushroom **9** skyrocket

shop
4 hunt **5** store **6** browse, market, outlet, search **8** boutique, emporium, showroom

shoplift
3 bag, cop **4** lift, palm **5** filch, pinch, steal, swipe **6** pilfer, rip off, snitch

shop owner
8 merchant, retailer **9** tradesman **10** proprietor

shopworn
5 banal, faded, stale, tired, trite

shore
6 cliché, soiled 7 clichéd 8 over-used 9 hackneyed 10 threadbare

shore
4 bank, prop, stay 5 beach, brace, brink, coast 6 bear up, strand, uphold 7 bolster, shingle, support, sustain 8 buttress, littoral, seacoast 9 coastland, coastline, riverbank, riverside, waterside 10 embankment, waterfront

shorebird
see at **bird**

short
3 shy 4 curt 5 blunt, brief, crisp, scant, skimp, spare, squat, stint, terse 6 abrupt, meager, meagre, scanty, scarce, skimpy, stubby 7 brusque, compact, concise, lacking, laconic, stunted, wanting 8 abridged, succinct 9 deficient 10 inadequate 11 abbreviated 12 insufficient

shortage
4 lack 5 pinch 6 dearth, ullage 7 deficit, paucity 8 scarcity 10 deficiency, inadequacy, scantiness

shortcoming
3 bug, sin 4 flaw, lack 5 fault, lapse 6 defect 7 demerit, failing 8 weakness 9 weak point 10 deficiency 12 imperfection

shortcut
6 bypass, cutoff

shorten
3 bob, cut 4 clip, dock 5 elide, slash 6 lessen, reduce, shrink 7 abridge, curtail, cut back, cut down, excerpt 8 boil down, compress, condense, contract, decrease, diminish, minimize, truncate 10 abbreviate

shorthand
11 stenography
method: 5 Gregg 6 Pitman

shorthanded
7 wanting 11 undermanned 12 understaffed

short-lived
5 brief 7 passing 8 fleeting 9 ephemeral, fugacious, momentary, temporary 10 evanescent, transitory

shortly
4 anon, soon 6 pronto 7 briefly, by and by, in brief, quickly, tersely 8 directly 9 concisely, presently 10 succinctly 11 laconically

shortness
7 brevity 9 concision

shortsighted
6 myopic 8 heedless, reckless 10 astigmatic

short-spoken
4 curt 5 bluff, blunt, brief, gruff, terse 6 abrupt, crusty, snippy 7 brusque 8 snippety

short-tempered
5 testy 6 touchy 7 prickly 8 snappish 9 irascible, irritable

Shoshone chief
8 Washakie 9 Pocatello

shot
3 nip, pop, try 4 dose, dram, drop, jolt, stab 5 blast, break, carom, crack, fling, guess, ounce, photo, range, reach, snort, swipe, whack, whirl 6 chance, effort, stroke 7 attempt, snifter 8 marksman, occasion 9 discharge 11 opportunity

shoulder
4 bear, edge, push, side 5 elbow, press, shove 6 assume, hustle, jostle, take on 8 bulldoze
bone: 7 scapula 8 clavicle
covering: 6 tippet 8 scapular
muscle: 7 deltoid
relating to: 7 humeral 8 scapular

shoulder blade
7 scapula

shout
3 cry 4 bark, bawl, bray, call, roar, yell 5 blare, whoop 6 bellow, clamor, holler, scream 7 exclaim 10 vociferate

shove
3 dig, jab, jam 4 cram, prod, push 5 crowd, drive, elbow, press 6 jostle, propel, thrust 8 bulldoze, shoulder

shovel
3 dig 4 grub 5 delve, scoop, spade
6 dig out, dredge, trowel 8 excavate

shoveler
4 duck 9 broadbill

shove off
3 git 4 blow, exit 5 leave, scoot,
scram, split 6 beat it, cut out, decamp, depart, move on 7 move out,
pull out, vamoose 8 clear out, run
along

show
4 fair, film, lead, pomp, sham 5 array, flick, front, guide, mount, movie,
offer, prove, revue, sport, stage
6 appear, arrive, direct, effect, evince,
expose, flaunt, lay out, parade,
reveal, set out, submit, unveil 7 conduct, display, divulge, exhibit, explain, fanfare, panoply, picture,
present, produce, project, trot out
8 brandish, disclose, evidence,
illusion, indicate, instruct, manifest,
proclaim 9 determine, establish,
pageantry, represent, semblance,
spectacle 10 appearance, exhibition,
exposition, illustrate, production
11 demonstrate, materialize, performance 13 demonstration, manifestation

Show Boat
  author: 6 Ferber (Edna)
  composer: 4 Kern (Jerome)
  lyricist: 11 Hammerstein (Oscar)

showcase
6 flaunt, parade 7 cabinet, exhibit,
feature, vitrine

shower
4 hail, rain, wash 5 bathe, burst,
party, salvo, spray, storm 6 deluge,
lavish, volley 7 barrage, cascade,
shatter, spatter 8 cataract, downpour, fountain, rainfall 9 broadside,
cannonade, fusillade 10 cloudburst
11 bombardment

showman
8 producer, promoter 10 impresario
  famous: 4 Cody (William F.) 6 Barnum (Phineas T.)

Show Me State
8 Missouri

show off
4 brag 5 boast, flash, model, vaunt
6 expose, flaunt, hotdog, parade
7 display, exhibit, swagger, trot out
8 brandish 10 grandstand

show-off
3 ham 6 hotdog 7 boaster, hotshot,
peacock 8 blowhard, braggart
9 swaggerer 13 exhibitionist ·

showpiece
3 gem 5 jewel, prize 10 magnum
opus, masterwork 11 chef d'oeuvre,
masterpiece

show up
4 come 6 appear, arrive, debunk,
expose, reveal, unmask 8 discover
9 discredit, embarrass 10 invalidate
11 materialize

showy
4 loud 5 gaudy, jazzy 6 flashy,
garish, ornate, sporty, tawdry 7 opulent, splashy 8 gorgeous, overdone,
striking 9 luxurious, sumptuous
10 flamboyant 11 overwrought,
pretentious, resplendent, sensational
12 meretricious, orchidaceous,
ostentatious

shred
3 bit, dag, jot, rag 4 iota, whit
5 crumb, grain, grate, ounce, scrap,
shave, speck, trace 6 sliver, tatter
7 modicum, smidgen, snippet 8 demolish, fragment, particle 9 scintilla

shrew
3 nag 4 mole 5 harpy, scold, vixen,
witch 6 dragon, gorgon, ogress,
rodent, virago 7 hellcat 8 battle-ax,
fishwife, harridan, she-devil, spitfire,
Xantippe 9 battle-axe, termagant,
Xanthippe

shrewd
3 sly 4 foxy, keen, wily, wise 5 acute,
cagey, canny, savvy, sharp, slick,
smart 6 artful, astute, clever, crafty,
smooth 7 knowing, prudent 8 sensible 9 ingenious, judicious, sagacious

10 discerning 11 intelligent, penetrating, quick-witted 13 perspicacious

shrewish

5 cross, testy 6 cranky, snappy 7 peevish, peppery 8 choleric, petulant 9 crotchety, fractious, irascible, splenetic 10 ill-natured 11 contentious, intractable, quarrelsome 12 disputatious 13 quick-tempered, short-tempered

shriek

3 cry 4 yell 6 screak, scream, shrill, squawk, squeal 7 screech

shrill

4 keen 5 acute, sharp 6 piping 8 piercing, strident 9 deafening 12 earsplitting

shrimp

4 runt 5 prawn 6 peanut, scampi 10 crustacean

shrine

5 altar 6 temple 7 sanctum 9 reliquary, sacrarium, sanctuary
Buddhist: 5 stupa 7 chorten

shrink

3 shy 4 wane 5 cower, quail, slink, start, wince 6 blench, boggle, cringe, flinch, huddle, recede, recoil, wither 7 analyst, dwindle, refrain 8 compress, condense, contract, draw back, withdraw 9 constrict, shrivel up, therapist, waste away 12 psychiatrist, psychologist

shrinking

3 shy 5 mousy, timid 7 bashful 8 retiring, skittish 9 withdrawn

shrive

5 purge 6 pardon, purify 7 absolve, confess, expiate 8 lustrate

shrivel

4 wilt 5 dry up, parch, wizen 6 shrink, wither 7 dwindle, wrinkle 9 dehydrate, desiccate

Shropshire Lad author

7 Housman (A. E.)

shroud

4 hide, rope, veil, wrap 5 cloak, cover, shade 6 enfold, enwrap, screen 7 conceal, enclose, envelop, obscure 8 cerement, obstruct 9 cerecloth 12 winding-sheet

shrouded

5 privy 6 covert, hidden, secret 7 obscure 10 mysterious

shrub

4 bush 5 elder, erica, hazel 6 muskit, privet 7 arboret, dyeweed, guayule 8 barberry, bluewood, boxthorn, inkberry, ironweed, rosebush 9 bearberry 10 bladdernut
Asian: 4 bago 6 kerria 8 caragana, japonica
desert: 7 ephedra
dwarf: 6 bonsai
East Indian: 3 aal 4 sunn
European: 4 cade 8 woodbine
evergreen: 3 box, kat, yew 4 ilex, khat, titi 5 furze, heath, holly, pyxie, savin, taxus 6 kalmia, laurel, myrtle, nandin, protea, sabine, savine 7 boxwood, heather, jasmine, juniper, rosebay 8 lambkill, oleander, rosemary, tamarisk
flowering: 5 ribes, tiara, wahoo 6 daphne, laurel, myrtle, spirea 7 chamise, chamiso, mahonia, maybush, rhodora, spiraea, weigela 8 magnolia, mezereon, nineback, oleander, oleaster, shadblow, shadbush, snowball, snowbush, tornillo, viburnum, wisteria
genus: 4 Inga, Itea 7 Solanum 8 Euonymus
hardwood: 6 cornel
Mexican: 8 ocotillo
ornamental: 6 privet 7 syringa 9 bluebeard
pasture: 8 cowberry
prickly: 5 briar, chico, furze, gorse 7 bramble 8 hawthorn, mesquite 9 buckthorn
thicket: 6 maquis 7 macchia 9 chaparral
tropical: 4 kava 5 henna 7 lantana 8 buddleia 10 frangipani
West Indian: 4 anil 7 acerola

shrug off
8 belittle, downplay, minimize

shtick
3 act, bag, bit 5 spiel 6 number
7 routine 9 specialty · 11 performance

Shuah
father: 7 Abraham
mother: 7 Keturah

shuck
3 pod 4 case, cast, hull, husk, junk,
peel, shed, skin 5 ditch, scrap, shell,
strip 6 reject, remove, slough 7 discard, peel off, take off 8 jettison
11 decorticate

shudder
5 quake, shake 6 quaver, quiver,
shimmy, shiver, tremor 7 frisson,
tremble, twitter, vibrate

shuffle
3 mix 4 hash 5 dodge, evade,
hedge, scuff, shift 6 jumble, mess
up, muddle, weasel 7 clutter, reorder, rummage, shamble 8 disarray,
disorder, intermix, mishmash 9 rearrange · 10 disarrange, equivocate
11 disorganize

shun
3 cut 4 duck, snub 5 avoid, dodge,
elude, evade, scorn 6 escape,
eschew, refuse, reject 7 decline,
disdain

shunt
4 turn 5 avert, shift 6 change, divert,
switch 7 deflect, shuttle 8 transfer
9 sidetrack

shush
4 hush 5 quiet, still 6 muffle, muzzle, shut up, stifle 7 repress, silence,
squelch 8 suppress

shut
3 bar 4 lock, seal, slam 5 close
6 fasten 9 close down 10 batten
down

Shute novel
10 On the Beach

shut in
3 hem, mew, pen 4 cage, coop, wall
5 fence 6 coop up, immure 7 confine, enclose 8 imprison

shut-in
7 invalid 8 confined 9 withdrawn
12 convalescent

shut out
3 bar 6 screen 7 exclude 9 ostracize

shutter
5 blind 6 screen

shuttle
5 ferry, shunt 6 bobbin 7 commute,
spindle 9 alternate

shuttlecock
4 bird 5 bandy

shut up
3 gag, mew, pen 4 cage, hush, jail,
mute 5 burke, choke, quiet, shush,
still 6 muzzle, stifle 7 confine, enclose, impound, silence, squelch
8 choke off, imprison, pipe down, suppress 9 quiet down 11 incarcerate

shy
3 coy 4 balk, duck, meek, shun,
wary 5 avoid, chary, elude, evade,
mousy, quail, scant, short, timid
6 averse, blench, demure, modest,
recoil, scanty, scarce, shrink 7 bashful, fearful, lacking, wanting 8 hesitant, reserved, reticent, retiring,
sheepish, timorous 9 diffident
11 introverted, unassertive 12 apprehensive, insufficient, self-effacing
13 self-conscious

Shylock
6 usurer 9 loan shark
daughter: 7 Jessica

shyster
11 pettifogger

Siam
see **Thailand**

sib
3 bro, kin, sis 4 akin 6 sister
7 brother, kindred, kinsman, related
8 relation, relative 9 relatives

Sibelius composition
9 Finlandia 11 Valse Triste

Siberian
dog: 5 husky 7 Samoyed
native: 5 Tatar, Yakut 6 Tartar,
Tungus 7 Chukchi 9 Mongolian
plain: 6 steppe
tent: 4 yurt

sibilate
4 buzz, fizz, hiss, whiz 6 fizzle,
sizzle 7 whisper

sibling
3 bro, sis 6 sister 7 brother

sibyl
4 seer 6 oracle 7 prophet 10 prophetess, soothsayer 13 fortune-teller

sic
3 set 4 thus 5 chase 6 attack

Sicilian
secret organization: 5 Mafia
volcano: 4 Etna

Sicily
capital: 7 Palermo
city: 7 Catania, Messina 8 Siracusa, Syracuse, Taormina
volcano: 4 Etna

sick
3 ill 5 fed up, tired, weary 6 ailing,
laid up, morbid, peaked, rotten,
unwell, wobbly 7 fevered, invalid
8 confined, diseased 9 bedridden,
defective, disgusted, unhealthy
10 indisposed 11 debilitated

sicken
5 upset 7 afflict, disgust, fall ill
8 nauseate

sickle
5 blade, mower 6 scythe 8 crescent

sickle-shaped
7 falcate

sickly
3 ill, low, wan 4 puny, weak 5 frail
6 ailing, anemic, feeble, infirm,
morbid, peaked, poorly, unwell
8 delicate, diseased 9 unhealthy
10 indisposed 11 unhealthful,
unwholesome 12 insalubrious

sickness
3 bug 6 malady 7 ailment, disease,
illness 8 disorder, syndrome 9 complaint, condition, infirmity 10 affliction 13 indisposition

sic transit gloria ____
5 mundi

side
4 clad, team 5 angle, facet, flank
6 aspect 9 direction 10 standpoint
combining form: 5 later 6 lateri,
latero
exposed: 8 windward
sheltered: 3 lee

sideboard
5 table 6 buffet 8 credence, credenza
for wine: 8 cellaret 10 cellarette

sideburns
9 burnsides 10 sideboards 11 dundrearies, muttonchops

sidekick
3 pal 4 chun 5 buddy, crony 7 partner 9 assistant, companion 10 accomplice

sideline
5 eject, hobby 6 injure 7 disable,
pastime, take out 9 avocation,
diversion 10 recreation 11 distraction 12 incapacitate

sidereal
6 astral, starry 7 stellar

side road
5 byway 8 bystreet, shunpike

sideshow
9 diversion 11 distraction

sidestep
4 duck 5 avoid, burke, dodge,
evade, hedge, skirt 6 bypass,
swerve, weasel 10 circumvent,
equivocate 12 tergiversate

sideswipe
5 brush, carom, graze, shave
6 glance, scrape

sidetrack
5 shunt 6 divert, switch 7 deflect

sidewhiskers
see **sideburns**

side with
4 back 5 favor 6 second, uphold
7 endorse, support 8 backstop,
champion

sidle
4 edge, slip

siege
4 bout 5 spell 6 attack 7 assault,
seizure 8 blockade 9 onslaught

Siegfried
composer: 6 Wagner (Richard)
lover: 8 Brunhild
mother: 9 Sieglinde
slayer: 5 Hagen
sword: 7 Balmung
vulnerable spot: 4 back 8 shoulder
wife: 9 Kriemhild

Sienkiewicz novel
8 Quo Vadis

sierra
3 saw 4 fish 5 range 8 mackerel
13 mountain range

Sierra Leone
capital: 8 Freetown
ethnic group: 5 Mende, Temne
language: 4 Krio 7 English
monetary unit: 5 leone
neighbor: 6 Guinea 7 Liberia

Sierra Nevada lake
5 Tahoe

Sierra ____
5 Ancha, Leone, Madre 6 Blanca,
Nevada

siesta
3 nap 4 doze 5 sleep 6 catnap,
snooze 10 forty winks

sieve
4 sift 6 filter, screen, winnow 8 colander, filtrate, strainer

Sif's husband
4 Thor

sift
3 pan 4 comb, cull, sort 5 glean,
sieve 6 filter, screen, strain, winnow
8 filtrate, separate

sigh
3 sob 4 gasp, long, moan, pine
5 groan, sough, whine, yearn
6 exhale, grieve, hanker, murmur
7 breathe, respire, suspire

sight
3 aim, eye, spy 4 espy, view 5 scene,
vista 6 notice, vision 7 make out,
outlook
relating to: 5 optic 6 ocular, visual
7 optical

sightseer
7 tourist 10 rubberneck 12 rubbernecker

sign
3 cue, ink 4 flag, hint, mark, omen
5 index, proof, token, trace 6 motion,
signal, symbol 7 endorse, gesture,
indicia, initial, symptom, vestige,
warning 8 evidence, exponent,
reminder 9 autograph, indicator
10 expression, indication, suggestion
directional: 5 arrow
of the zodiac:
(see **zodiac sign**)

signal
3 cue, nod 4 flag 5 alarm, alert
6 beckon, wigwag 7 gesture 8 high
sign 9 indicator
distress: 3 SOS 6 Mayday

signature
4 name 9 autograph 11 John
Hancock
flourish: 6 paraph

signet
4 ring, seal 5 stamp 6 device
8 hallmark, intaglio

significance
4 pith 5 merit, point, sense 6 credit,
import, moment, weight 7 gravity,
meaning 9 authority, magnitude
10 importance 11 consequence,
weightiness

significant
5 sound, valid 7 notable, telling,
weighty 8 material, powerful 9 important, momentous 10 compelling,
convincing, meaningful, noteworthy

11 substantial 12 considerable
13 consequential

signification
4 gist 5 point, sense 6 import
7 essence, meaning, message,
purport 9 substance 10 intendment
11 implication 12 notification 13 understanding

signify
4 mean, show 5 count, imply, spell,
weigh 6 convey, denote, intend,
matter 7 add up to, bespeak, connote, express, purport, suggest
8 indicate

sign on
4 book, hire, join 5 draft 6 engage,
enlist, enroll, induct, join up, retain,
secure 7 recruit 9 conscript

sign over
4 cede, deed 5 alien, grant 6 assign, convey, remise 7 consign
8 alienate, transfer

sign up
4 join 5 enter 6 enlist, enroll, muster

Sigurd
horse: 5 Grani
slayer: 5 Hogni
victim: 6 Fafner, Fafnir
wife: 6 Gudrun

Sigyn's husband
4 Loki

Sikhism
deity: 4 Akal
founder: 5 Nanak 9 Guru Nanak
leader: 5 Arjan 9 Guru Arjan
11 Gobind Singh
scripture: 9 Adi Granth
shrine: 12 Golden Temple

silage
6 fodder

silence
3 gag 4 calm, hush, lull, mute
5 quash, quell, quiet, shush, still
6 dampen, deaden, muffle, muzzle,
shut up, squash, stifle 7 secrecy,
squelch 8 choke off, muteness,
quietude, suppress 9 quietness,
reticence, stillness

silent
3 mum 4 dumb, mute 5 muted,
quiet, still, tacit, whist 6 hushed,
stilly 8 reticent, taciturn, unspoken,
wordless 9 noiseless, soundless,
voiceless 10 speechless 11 close-
lipped, tight-lipped 12 closemouthed,
tight-mouthed

silhouette
6 shadow 7 contour, outline, profile
9 lineament, lineation 10 figuration
11 delineation

Silicon Valley city
8 Palo Alto

silk
5 fiber 7 foulard 8 sarcenet, sarsenet
fabric: 4 gros 5 caffa, ninon, Pekin,
satin, surah, tulle 6 mantua, pongee,
samite, sendal, tussah 7 taffeta
factory: 8 filature
hat: 6 topper
maker: 4 worm
raw: 6 greige
source: 6 cocoon
waste: 4 noil 5 floss
wild: 6 tussah

sill
5 bench, ledge, shelf 9 threshold

silliness
5 folly 6 idiocy 7 inanity 9 absurdity,
stupidity

silly
4 daft 5 balmy, crazy, daffy, dippy,
dizzy, funny, giddy, inane, loony,
sappy, wacky 6 absurd, simple
7 asinine, fatuous, flighty, foolish,
idiotic, vacuous, witless 9 brainless, frivolous, ludicrous, nitwitted,
senseless 10 irrational, ridiculous,
weak-minded 11 empty-headed,
harebrained, light-headed 12 preposterous, simpleminded 13 rattlebrained

silt
5 dregs 7 deposit, residue 8 alluvium, sediment

silver
4 coin 5 money, shiny 6 argent,

dulcet **7** bullion, element **8** flatware, lustrous, sterling **9** argentine, tableware
relating to: 9 argentine

silverfish
6 insect, tarpon

silversmith
6 Revere (Paul) **11** metalworker

silver-tongued
4 glib **6** fluent **7** voluble **8** eloquent

silvery
6 argent **7** shining **9** argentine, brilliant **10** glittering, shimmering

Silvia's beloved
9 Valentine

_____ Simbel
3 Abu

Simenon character
7 Maigret (Inspector)

Simeon
father: 5 Jacob
mother: 4 Leah
son: 4 Ohad **6** Nemuel

simian
3 ape **5** chimp, lemur, loris **6** baboon, bonobo, galago, monkey **7** apelike, gorilla, primate, tarsier **9** orangutan **10** anthropoid, chimpanzee, monkeylike

similar
4 akin, like **5** alike **6** agnate **7** uniform **8** parallel, suchlike **9** analogous, consonant **10** comparable, reciprocal **11** correlative **13** complementary, corresponding

similarity
6 parity **7** analogy, harmony, kinship **8** affinity, likeness, parallel, sameness **9** alikeness, closeness, congruity, semblance **10** conformity, congruence **11** coincidence, correlation, homogeneity, parallelism, resemblance

similarly
8 likewise

simile
7 analogy **8** affinity, likeness, metaphor **9** alikeness, semblance **10** comparison **11** correlation, resemblance
word: 4 like

similitude
4 copy **5** image **6** double **7** analogy, kinship, replica **8** affinity, likeness, metaphor, relation, sameness **9** alikeness, congruity, semblance **10** comparison, similarity **11** correlation, counterpart, equivalence, resemblance

simmer
4 boil, fret, fume, stew, stir **5** churn **6** bubble, seethe **7** ferment, smolder

simmer down
5 relax

Simon
brother: 5 Jesus **6** Andrew
father: 5 Jonah
new name: 5 Peter
son: 5 Judas, Rufus **9** Alexander

Simon _____
5 Magus **6** Legree **8** of Cyrene **9** the Zealot

Simon Maccabaeus
father: 10 Mattathias
nickname: 6 Thassi
slayer: 7 Ptolemy

Simon play
9 Odd Couple (The) **10** Chapter Two, Plaza Suite **11** Biloxi Blues **12** Sunshine Boys (The) **13** Lost in Yonkers **16** Come Blow Your Horn **17** Barefoot in the Park **20** Brighton Beach Memoirs **21** Last of the Red Hot Lovers **22** Prisoner of Second Avenue (The)

simp
4 dope **5** dunce, idiot, moron **6** dimwit, nitwit **7** pinhead **8** bonehead, imbecile, lunkhead, numskull **9** blockhead, lamebrain, numbskull **10** nincompoop

simple
4 easy, mere, pure **5** basic, lucid,

naive, plain, sheer **6** modest **7** artless, natural, unmixed **8** absolute, trusting **9** childlike, credulous, ingenuous, unadorned **10** effortless, elementary, unaffected **11** fundamental, undecorated, unelaborate **13** unpretentious
combining form: 4 hapl **5** haplo

simpleminded
4 dull, slow **5** naive **6** stupid **7** foolish, idiotic, moronic **8** gullible, retarded **9** dim-witted, imbecilic **10** half-witted, slow-witted

simpleton
4 dolt, dope, fool **5** dummy, dunce, idiot, moron **6** cretin, dimwit, nitwit **7** dullard, half-wit, pinhead **8** bonehead, dumbbell, imbecile, lunkhead **9** blockhead, ignoramus, lamebrain **10** nincompoop

simplify
4 ease **7** clarify, clear up **8** boil down **10** facilitate, streamline, unscramble **11** disentangle **13** straighten out

simply
4 just, only **6** merely

simulacrum
4 copy **5** clone, ditto, guise, image, trace **6** double, ersatz, mirror, ringer **7** picture, replica **8** likeness, portrait **9** facsimile, imitation, semblance **10** appearance **12** reproduction **13** impersonation, spitting image

simulate
3 ape **4** fake, sham **5** feign, mimic **6** embody, mirror, parody, parrot **7** imitate **8** resemble **9** incarnate **11** counterfeit

simulated
4 fake, mock, sham **5** bogus, dummy, false, phony **6** ersatz **8** spurious **9** imitation, insincere, pretended **10** artificial, fictitious, substitute **11** counterfeit

simultaneous
6 coeval **10** coexistent, coexisting, coincident, coinciding, concurrent, synchronic **11** synchronous **12** contemporary

simultaneously
6 at once **7** jointly **8** together **9** meanwhile

sin
3 err **4** debt, evil, tort, vice **5** crime, fault, guilt, lapse, stray, wrong **6** offend **7** demerit, misdeed, offense **8** hamartia, iniquity, trespass **10** deficiency, peccadillo, transgress, wickedness, wrongdoing **11** shortcoming **12** imperfection
deadly: 4 envy, lust **5** anger, greed, pride, sloth **8** gluttony **12** covetousness

Sin
7 moon-god
daughter: 6 Ishtar
son: 7 Shamash
wife: 6 Ningal

since
3 ago **5** after **6** behind **7** because, whereas **8** as long as **9** following **10** inasmuch as **11** considering
Scottish: 4 syne

sincere
4 real, true **5** frank, plain **6** actual, candid, devout, honest **7** artless, earnest, genuine, serious **8** bona fide, truthful **9** authentic, heartfelt, ingenuous, unfeigned **10** aboveboard, forthright **12** wholehearted **13** unpretentious

sincerity
6 candor **7** honesty **8** goodwill, openness **9** frankness, good faith **11** artlessness, earnestness

sine qua non
4 must **9** condition, essential, necessity, requisite **11** requirement **12** precondition, prerequisite

sinew
6 tendon

sinewy
4 ropy, wiry **5** tough **6** brawny **7** fibrous, stringy **8** muscular

sinful
3 bad **4** base, evil, vile **5** wrong **6** guilty, unholy, wicked **7** immoral,

peccant, vicious **8** blamable, culpable, damnable, depraved, shameful **9** reprobate **10** iniquitous **11** blameworthy, disgraceful **13** reprehensible

sing
3 rat **4** fink, hymn **5** carol, chant, chirp, croon, troll, yodel **6** inform, intone, snitch, squeal, warble **7** confess, descant, lullaby **8** serenade, vocalize **10** cantillate

Singapore
capital: 9 Singapore
language: 5 Malay, Tamil **8** Mandarin
monetary unit: 6 dollar

singe
4 burn, char, sear **6** scorch

singer
4 alto, bass **5** mezzo, tenor **6** canary **7** crooner, soloist, soprano **8** baritone, choirboy, songbird, songster, vocalist **9** balladeer, chorister, contralto **10** troubadour
cabaret: 11 chansonnier
female: 9 chanteuse
opera: 4 diva **10** cantatrice
religious: 6 cantor

singing
exercise: 7 solfège
group: 3 duo **4** trio **5** choir **6** chorus **7** chorale, quartet, quintet
voice: 4 alto, bass **5** mezzo, tenor **7** soprano **8** baritone **9** contralto **12** mezzo-soprano

single
3 hit, odd, one **4** free, lone, only, sole **5** unwed **6** maiden, unique **7** base hit, unitary **8** distinct, isolated, separate, solitary, specific **9** exclusive, unmarried **10** individual, particular, unattached
combining form: 3 mon **4** hapl, mono **5** haplo
prefix: 3 uni

single-minded
5 rigid **6** dogged, driven, intent **7** adamant, devoted, diehard **8** hellbent, obdurate, resolute, resolved, stubborn **9** dedicated, steadfast,

unbending **10** brassbound, determined, inexorable, inflexible, purposeful, relentless, unyielding

single out
4 cull, mark, pick **5** elect, favor **6** choose, opt for, select **9** designate **11** distinguish

singular
3 odd **4** lone, only, rare, sole, solo **5** weird **6** unique **7** bizarre, oddball, strange, unusual **8** peculiar, solitary, uncommon **9** exclusive **10** individual, outlandish, particular, unexampled **11** exceptional **13** extraordinary

singularity
5 quirk, unity **6** oddity **7** anomaly, oneness **8** identity **9** exception **11** peculiarity, personality **12** idiosyncrasy **13** individuality, particularity

singularize
4 mark **11** distinguish, individuate **12** characterize **13** differentiate, individualize

sinister
4 dark, dire, evil, left **6** creepy, malign **7** baleful, fateful, malefic, ominous **8** lowering, menacing **9** ill-omened, malicious **10** foreboding, maleficent, portentous **11** apocalyptic, threatening **12** inauspicious, unpropitious

sink
3 dip, pit, sag **4** bore, bury, dive, drop, fall, sump, wane **5** basin, drill, droop, lower, sewer, slope, slump, stoop, swamp **6** hollow, invest, plunge, settle, thrust, worsen **7** capsize, cesspit, decline, depress, descend, founder, go under, immerse, let down, scuttle, subside, torpedo **8** cesspool, hellhole, submerge, submerse **9** concavity, disappear **10** depression

sinker
3 bob **5** plumb **6** weight **8** doughnut, fastball, plumb bob

sinkhole
3 dip, sag **4** bowl **5** basin **6** hollow **8** cesspool **9** concavity **10** depression

sinless
4 pure **6** chaste **8** innocent **9** righteous **10** impeccable

sinner
5 rogue, scamp **6** bad egg, outlaw, rascal, wretch **7** lowlife, villain **8** criminal, evildoer, offender **9** libertine, miscreant, reprobate, scoundrel, wrongdoer **10** black sheep, delinquent, profligate, malefactor **11** rapscallion

Sinn ____
4 Fein

sinuous
4 wavy **5** lithe, snaky **7** winding **8** flexuous, tortuous **10** convoluted, meandering, serpentine **11** anfractuous, snake-shaped

sinus
6 cavity, hollow, recess

Sioux
6 Dakota
chief: 8 Red Cloud **10** Crazy Horse **11** Sitting Bull
people: 3 Ofo **4** Crow **6** Biloxi, Tutelo **7** Catawba, Hidatsa **9** Winnebago

sip
5 drink, savor, taste **6** imbibe

siphon
3 tap **4** draw, pipe, pump **5** draft, drain **6** convoy, divert, funnel **7** channel, conduct, draw off **8** transmit

sir
4 lord **5** title **6** knight, mister **9** gentleman

sire
4 lord **5** beget, breed, hatch, spawn **6** father, parent **7** founder **8** engender **9** patriarch, procreate, propagate **10** forefather

siren
4 vamp **5** alarm **7** Lorelei **9** temptress **10** seductress **11** femme fatale
film: 4 Bara (Theda)

Siren
5 Ligea **8** Leucosia **10** Parthenope
German: 7 Lorelei

sirenian
6 dugong, sea cow **7** manatee

siren song
4 lure **5** decoy, snare **6** come-on **10** allurement, enticement, temptation

Sirius
7 Dog Star

sister
3 nun **7** sibling
French: 5 soeur
Latin: 5 soror
Spanish: 7 hermana

Sister Carrie author
7 Dreiser (Theodore)

sisterly
7 sororal

Sisyphus
brother: 7 Athamas **9** Salmoneus
father: 6 Aeolus
mother: 7 Enarete
son: 7 Glaucus

sit
4 pose **5** perch, roost

Sita
abductor: 6 Ravana
husband, rescuer: 4 Rama

sitarist
7 Shankar (Ravi)

site
3 dig **4** home, spot **5** haunt, locus, place, point, scene, venue **6** locale **7** station **8** locality, location, position

sit-in
7 protest

sitting
6 séance **7** session
prolonged: 8 sederunt

Sitting Bull's tribe
　5 Sioux

sitting duck
　4 butt, mark　6 target

situate
　3 put, set　5 place　6 locate　7 install
　8 position

situation
　3 job　4 post, rank　5 point, state
　6 plight, status　7 footing, setting,
　station　8 location, position, standing
　9 condition　13 circumstances

situs
　5 place, venue　6 locale

Siva
　see Shiva

six
　combining form: 3 hex, sex　4 hexa,
　sexi　5 sexti
　group of: 6 sestet, sextet　9 sex-
　tuplet
　relating to: 6 senary

sixfold
　8 sextuple

six-shooter
　3 gun　6 pistol　8 revolver

sixth sense
　3 ESP　7 insight　9 intuition, telep-
　athy　12 clairvoyance

sizable
　3 big　5 ample, hefty, large, major,
　roomy　8 spacious　9 capacious,
　extensive　10 commodious, large-
　scale　11 substantial　12 consider-
　able

size
　4 area, bulk, mass　5 range, scope,
　width　6 extent, height, length,
　spread, volume　7 bigness, breadth,
　caliber, expanse, measure, stature
　9 amplitude, dimension, extension,
　greatness, largeness, magnitude
　10 dimensions, proportion　11 mea-
　surement, proportions

size up
　3 peg　4 rate, read　5 assay, gauge,
　judge, value　6 assess, review, sur-
　vey　7 adjudge, dope out　8 appraise,
　estimate, evaluate　9 figure out

sizzle
　3 fry　4 buzz, fizz, hiss, whiz　5 grill
　6 hoopla, seethe　7 pizzazz　8 sibi-
　late　10 excitement

sizzling
　3 hot　6 red-hot, torrid　7 burning
　8 scalding, white-hot　9 scorching

skald
　4 bard, poet

Skanda
　6 war-god
　brother: 6 Ganesa　7 Ganesha
　father: 4 Siva　5 Shiva

skate
　3 nag, ray　4 skid, skim　5 glide, skirr,
　slide　8 glissade　11 Rollerblade
　blade: 6 runner
　kind: 6 figure, hockey

skating site
　3 ice　4 rink

skedaddle
　3 run　4 bolt, flee, skip　5 scoot,
　scram, split　6 beat it, begone, bug
　off, cut out, decamp, get out　7 make
　off, run away, scamper, skiddoo, take
　off, vamoose　8 clear out　10 make
　tracks

skein
　4 coil　5 flock, snarl, twist　6 tangle
　12 entanglement

skeletal
　4 bony　5 gaunt　6 wasted　7 angular,
　scraggy, starved　8 rawboned　9 ema-
　ciated　10 cadaverous

skeleton
　5 bones, draft, frame　6 sketch
　7 diagram, outline　9 bare bones,
　framework
　marine: 5 coral, shell

skeptic
　5 cynic　7 doubter, scoffer　8 agnostic
　10 Pyrrhonist, questioner, unbeliever
　11 disbeliever

skeptical
4 wary 5 leery 6 show-me 7 cynical, dubious 8 doubtful, doubting 9 quizzical 10 dissenting, suspicious 11 mistrustful, questioning, unbelieving 12 disbelieving, freethinking

skepticism
5 doubt 7 dubiety 8 distrust, mistrust, wariness 9 dubiosity, misgiving, suspicion 11 incertitude, uncertainty

skerry
4 isle, reef 6 island

sketch
4 draw, plot 5 draft, rough, trace 6 depict, design, doodle, lay out, map out, précis 7 develop, diagram, outline, portray 8 block out, chalk out, rough out 9 blueprint, delineate 12 characterize

sketchy
4 iffy 5 crude, rough, vague 6 skimpy, slight 7 cursory, shallow 8 skeletal 10 incomplete 11 preliminary, superficial 12 questionable

skew
4 bias, veer 5 angle, fudge, slant, slide 6 swerve 7 distort

skewer
3 rod 4 spit 5 lance, spear, spike 6 impale, pierce 8 puncture, ridicule, transfix 9 brochette, criticize

ski
5 glide, slide
lift: 4 J-bar, T-bar 5 chair 7 gondola

skid
5 glide, skate, slide 6 pallet, runner 7 spinout 8 sideslip

skiddoo
4 scat 5 leave, scram, split 6 beat it, begone, bug off, decamp, depart, vacate 7 buzz off, take off, vamoose 8 clear out, shove off 9 skedaddle, take a hike 10 hit the road, make tracks

skid row
6 bowery

skier
American: 3 Moe (Tommy) 4 Kidd (Billy) 5 Mahre (Phil, Steve) 6 Miller (Bode) 7 Johnson (Bill)
Austrian: 5 Maier (Hermann) 6 Proell (Annemarie), Sailer (Toni) 7 Klammer (Franz), Schranz (Karl) 10 Girardelli (Marc) 11 Moser-Proell (Annemarie)
French: 5 Killy (Jean-Claude)
Italian: 5 Tomba (Alberto) 6 Thoeni (Gustavo)
Luxembourg: 10 Girardelli (Marc)
Swedish: 8 Stenmark (Ingemar)
Swiss: 10 Zurbriggen (Pirmin)

skiff
4 boat 7 rowboat

skiing
area: 3 run 5 slope
cross-country: 7 touring
event: 6 schuss, slalom 8 downhill 11 giant slalom
horse-drawn: 9 skijoring
kind: 6 Alpine, Nordic
position: 7 vorlage
technique: 6 wedeln 8 snowplow, traverse
turn: 7 christy 8 christie

skill
3 art 5 craft, knack 7 ability, address, command, cunning, finesse, know-how, mastery, prowess, sleight 8 deftness, facility 9 dexterity, expertise, ingenuity, readiness, technique 10 adroitness, competence 11 proficiency

skilled
3 apt 4 able 5 adept 6 expert 7 capable, trained 8 masterly, talented 9 competent, masterful, practiced 10 proficient 12 accomplished

skillet
3 pan 6 spider 9 frying pan

skillful
4 deft 5 adept, crack, handy 6 adroit, clever, daedal, expert 7 skilled 8 masterly 9 competent, dexterous,

masterful, practiced, workmanly
10 proficient **11** crackerjack, work-
manlike **12** accomplished

skim
4 sail, scan, scud, skip **5** brush,
carom, glide, graze, skirr **6** browse
8 embezzle, ricochet

skimp
4 save **5** pinch, scant, spare, stint
6 meager, scanty, scrape, sparse
7 slender **8** begrudge, conserve,
retrench, withhold **9** economize

skimpy
5 scant, spare **6** meager, meagre,
paltry, scanty, scarce, sparse **7** limited, wanting **8** exiguous **9** deficient
10 inadequate **12** insufficient

skim through
4 scan **6** browse

skin
3 fur, gyp, pod, rap **4** clad, clip,
husk, hide, pare, peel, pelt, rind,
soak **5** blame, cheat, cover, scale,
shell, stiff, strip **6** fleece, sheath,
slough **7** censure, condemn, sheathe
8 denounce **9** epidermis, sheathing
10 integument, overcharge **11** decorticate
animal: **4** coat, hide, pelt **6** hackle,
peltry
combining form: **3** cut **4** cuti, derm
5 derma, dermo, dermy **6** dermat,
dermia, dermis **7** cutaneo, dermata
(plural), dermato, epiderm **8** epi-
dermo
depression: **6** dimple
disease: **4** acne **5** hives, mange
6 eczema **10** dermatitis
dry: **5** scurf
fold: **5** plica
layer: **5** derma **6** corium, dermis
7 cuticle **9** epidermis
opening: **4** pore
protuberance: **3** tag, wen **4** mole,
wart **6** pimple
rabbit: **5** coney
relating to: **6** dermal **9** cuticular,
epidermal
spot: **7** freckle

skin-deep
7 shallow, trivial **11** superficial

skinflint
5 miser **7** niggard, scrooge **8** tightwad **10** cheapskate, pinchpenny

skin game
3 con **4** scam **5** bunco, bunko,
cheat, fraud, sting, trick **6** hustle,
racket **7** swindle **8** flimflam

skink
6 lizard

skinny
4 bony, dope, info, lank, lean, thin
5 gaunt, lanky, scoop, spare, weedy
6 twiggy **7** angular, lowdown, scraggy,
scrawny **8** rawboned, skeletal
9 emaciated

Skin of Our Teeth author
6 Wilder (Thornton)

skip
3 hop, run **4** flee, jump, leap, omit,
trip **5** bound, caper, carom, frisk,
leave, scoot, skirr **6** cavort, gambol,
pass up, spring **7** misfire, scamper,
skitter **8** leave out, overlook, pass
over, ricochet **9** skedaddle

skipjack
4 boat, fish, tuna **8** bluefish, ladyfish,
sailboat

skipper
5 pilot **6** leader **7** captain **9** butterfly, commander

skirmish
3 row **4** fray **5** broil, brush, clash,
melee, run-in, scrap, set-to **6** affray,
battle, fracas **7** assault, dispute
8 conflict, struggle **9** encounter,
scrimmage

skirr
3 run **4** bolt, flee, sail, scud, skim,
skip **5** float, scoot, shoot **7** make off,
scamper **9** skedaddle

skirt
3 hem, rim **4** brim, duck, edge
5 avoid, bound, brink, burke, dodge,
elude, evade, hedge, verge **6** border, bypass, define, detour, escape,

fringe, ignore, margin **8** sidestep, surround **9** perimeter, periphery **10** circumvent
ballet: 4 tutu
feature: 3 hem **4** slit
long: 4 maxi
Scottish: 4 kilt
short: 4 mini
style: 5 A-line **6** sheath

skit
6 shtick, sketch **9** burlesque

skitter
3 hop **4** flit, skip, trip **6** scurry, spring **7** scamper

skittery
see **skittish**

skittish
3 coy, shy **4** edgy, wary **5** chary, dizzy, jumpy, leery **6** fickle **7** bashful, fidgety, flighty, nervous, rabbity, restive **8** unstable, volatile **9** excitable, frivolous, impulsive, mercurial, whimsical **10** capricious, unreliable

skive
4 pare **5** carve, shave, slice

skivvies
9 underwear

skoal
5 toast **6** health

skua
4 bird **6** jaeger **7** seabird

skulduggery
5 fraud **8** foul play, trickery **9** chicanery, duplicity **10** hanky-panky

skulk
4 lurk, slip **5** creep, prowl, shirk, slink, sneak, steal

skull
4 head, mind **5** brain **7** cranium **8** brainpan **9** braincase
back of: 7 occiput
bone: 5 vomer **6** zygoma **7** ethmoid, frontal **8** parietal, sphenoid, temporal
jawless: 9 calvarium
joint: 6 suture
part: 3 jaw **5** inion

skullcap
6 beanie, pileus **7** calotte **8** yarmulke **9** calvarium, zucchetto

skunk
4 beat, drub, lick, scum, whip, whup **6** thrash, wallop **7** clobber, polecat, shellac, stinker, trounce **8** civet cat, lambaste **9** overwhelm, slaughter
genus: 8 Mephitis

sky
5 azure **6** heaven, welkin **7** heavens **8** empyrean **9** firmament

sky-blue
5 azure **8** cerulean

skylarking
5 revel **7** revelry, whoopee **9** high jinks, horseplay, rowdiness, whoop-de-do **10** roughhouse **12** roughhousing

skylight
6 window

skyline
7 horizon, outline

sky pilot
5 padre **6** cleric, parson, pastor **8** chaplain, minister, preacher **9** churchman, clergyman

skyrocket
4 rise, soar **7** shoot up **8** catapult

sky sighting
3 UFO

slab
5 block, chunk, slice, strip **8** pavement

slack
3 lax **4** lazy, slow, soft **5** inert, loose, relax **6** remiss **7** ease off, laggard, passive, relaxed **8** careless, derelict, dilatory, inactive, indolent, slothful, sluggish, stagnant **9** leisurely, lethargic, negligent **10** neglectful

slacken
3 ebb, lax **4** ease, slow, wane **5** abate, let up, loose, relax **6** detain, ease up, lessen, loosen, relent, retard, slow up **7** die down, dwindle, ease off, subside **8** diminish, moder-

ate, slow down **9** untighten **10** decelerate

slacker

3 bum **4** slug **5** idler, sloth **6** loafer **7** goof-off, shirker, wastrel **8** deadbeat, layabout, slugabed, sluggard **9** goldbrick, lazybones **10** delinquent **11** couch potato

slag

4 lava **5** dross **6** cinder, debris, scoria

slake

5 allay **6** deaden, quench **7** crumble, hydrate, relieve, satisfy **9** alleviate

slam

3 bat, hit, jab, pan, rap **4** bang, bash, beat, belt, blow, boom, dash, drub, flay, slug, slur, swat, wham **5** blast, crack, crash, fling, knock, pound, slash, smack, smash, swipe, whack **6** batter, cudgel, hammer, scathe, strike, thwack, wallop **7** clobber, potshot **8** lambaste **9** castigate

slam-dance

4 mosh

slam dunk

5 cinch, setup **6** shoo-in **7** safe bet **9** certainty, sure thing

slammer

3 can, jug, pen **4** brig, coop, jail, stir **5** clink, pokey **6** cooler, lockup, prison **9** calaboose **12** penitentiary

slander

4 slur, tale **5** libel, slime, smear, sully **6** defame, malign, smirch, vilify **7** calumny, scandal, tarnish, traduce **8** besmirch, denigrate **10** backbiting, calumniate, defamation, detraction, scandalize **11** mud-slinging **12** back-stabbing

slang

4 cant, jive **5** argot, lingo **6** jargon, patois, patter **7** dialect **10** vernacular

slant

3 tip **4** bank, bias, cant, heel, lean, list, skew, tilt, veer, warp **5** angle,

aside, bevel, grade, slope, splay **7** distort, incline, leaning, outlook **8** gradient **9** prejudice, viewpoint **10** standpoint **11** inclination **12** predilection

combining form: 4 clin **5** clino

slap

3 hit, pop **4** bash, blow, cuff, shot, slam, swat **5** clout, smack, spank, whack **6** buffet, insult, rebuff, strike **7** affront, putdown **8** brickbat, lambaste, penalize **9** castigate

slapdash

5 hasty, messy **6** random, sloppy **7** cursory **8** careless, slipshod **9** half-baked, haphazard, hit-or-miss, makeshift

slap down

5 quell **6** kibosh **7** squelch **8** prohibit, suppress

slaphappy

5 dazed, dizzy, woozy **6** punchy **10** punch-drunk

slash

3 cut **4** clip, gash, hack, pare, slit **5** lower, shave, slice **6** reduce, scathe, scorch **7** abridge, blister, curtail, cut back, cut down, scarify, scourge, shorten **8** lacerate, lambaste, mark down **9** castigate, excoriate **10** abbreviate

slat

4 lath **5** board, stave, strip **6** louver, louvre **7** airfoil

slate

4 gray, list, rock, tile **6** lineup, record, tablet, ticket **7** shingle **8** schedule **9** designate

slather

5 smear **6** spread **8** squander

slattern

4 bawd, moll, slut, tart **5** hussy, tramp, wench **6** floozy, harlot **7** chippie, jezebel, trollop **8** strumpet **10** prostitute **11** painted lady **12** scarlet woman, streetwalker

slaughter

4 kill, slay **6** murder **7** butcher,

carnage, killing, wipe out **8** butchery, decimate, demolish, hecatomb, massacre **9** bloodbath, bloodshed, liquidate **10** annihilate, butchering **11** destruction, exterminate, liquidation **12** annihilation

slaughterhouse
8 abattoir

Slav
4 Pole, Serb, Sorb, Wend **5** Croat, Czech **6** Bulgar, Slovak **7** Russian, Serbian, Slovene **8** Bohemian, Croatian, Moravian **9** Bulgarian, Ruthenian, Ukrainian

slave
4 grub, help, peon, plod, serf, slog, toil **5** grind, helot, swink **6** drudge, menial, thrall, toiler, vassal **7** bondman, chattel, servant
feudal: 4 serf
harem: 9 odalisque
liberated: 8 freedman
Muslim: 6 Mamluk **8** Mameluke
Spartan: 5 helot

slave driver
6 tyrant **7** foreman **8** martinet, overseer **10** taskmaster **11** Simon Legree

slaver
4 spit **5** drool, froth **6** drivel, saliva **7** dribble, slobber, spittle **8** salivate

slavery
6 thrall **7** bondage, helotry, peonage, serfdom **9** indenture, servitude, thralldom **11** subjugation

Slavic apostle
5 Cyril **9** Methodius

slavish
6 abject, menial **7** servile **8** obeisant, wretched **9** groveling, imitative, laborious **10** obsequious, unoriginal **11** subservient

slay
4 do in, kill **6** murder **7** bump off, butcher, execute, put away **8** dispatch, knock off **9** liquidate, slaughter **11** assassinate

slayer
7 butcher **11** executioner

sleazy
3 low **5** cheap, dingy, seedy, tacky, tatty **6** cheesy, flimsy, shabby, shoddy, trashy **7** run-down, squalid **8** gimcrack **10** down-at-heel **11** dilapidated **12** disreputable

sled
4 luge, pung **6** sleigh **7** coaster, travois **8** toboggan
Russian: 6 troika

sled dog
5 husky **8** malamute

sledge
4 maul **6** hammer, sleigh
Eskimo: 7 komatik

sleek
4 oily **6** glassy, glossy, smooth **7** elegant, stylish **8** lustrous, polished **10** glistening

sleep
3 nap **4** doze, rest **6** catnap, repose, siesta, snooze **7** shut-eye, slumber **11** slumberland
bringer: 7 sandman
combining form: 4 hypn, narc **5** hypno, narco, somni
god: 6 Hypnos, Somnus

sleeper
4 beam, mole **7** Pullman **8** long shot **11** double agent, stringpiece

sleeping
7 dormant **8** comatose
disease: 10 narcolepsy

sleepless
7 wakeful **8** vigilant **9** insomniac

sleeplessness
8 insomnia

sleepwalker
12 somnambulist

sleepy
4 dozy **6** drowsy **7** nodding **9** somnolent **10** slumberous

sleigh
4 pung **6** sledge

sleight
4 ploy, ruse, wile 5 skill, trick 7 gimmick, prowess 8 artifice, deftness, maneuver 9 dexterity, stratagem 10 adroitness

sleight of hand
11 legerdemain

slender
4 lean, slim, thin, trim 5 lithe, reedy, spare 6 skinny, slight, svelte, twiggy 7 spindly, willowy

sleuth
4 dick, Drew (Nancy) 5 Brown (Encyclopedia, Father), Kojak, Morse, Queen (Ellery), Saint (The), snoop, Spade (Sam), Tracy (Dick), Wolfe (Nero) 6 Hammer (Mike), Holmes (Sherlock), Marple (Miss), Poirot (Hercule), shamus, Wimsey (Peter) 7 Cadfael (Brother), Columbo, Fansler (Kate), gumshoe, Maigret, Marlowe (Philip) 8 hawkshaw, Millhone (Kinsey), Rockford (Jim), sherlock 9 Dalgliesh (Adam), detective, Scarpetta (Kay) 10 private eye 12 investigator

slew
3 lot, mob, ton 4 army, heap, host, load, mess, pile, raft, skid, turn, veer 5 batch, bunch, crowd, flock, pivot, twist 6 myriad, passel, swerve, throng 9 abundance, multitude

slice
3 cut 4 gash, slit 5 allot, carve, divvy, quota, sever, share, slash, split, wedge 6 cleave, divide, incise, sample 7 dissect, portion, segment 8 allocate 9 allotment, allowance

slick
4 film, glib, oily, slip, wily 5 sharp, sleek, soapy 6 crafty, glossy, greasy, shrewd, smarmy, smooth, tricky 7 cunning 8 slippery, slithery, unctuous 10 lubricious, oleaginous

slicker
4 dude 5 dandy, shark 6 con man 7 cheater, diddler, grifter, oilskin, sharper 8 raincoat, swindler 9 trickster 11 flimflammer

slide
3 dip, sag 4 flow, ramp, skid, slip 5 chute, coast, chute, drift, glide, skate, slump, spill 6 scooch, stream 7 decline, slither 8 downturn 9 downswing, downtrend 12 transparency

slight
4 omit, skip, slim, snub, thin 5 frail, reedy, scorn, small 6 flimsy, ignore, meager, meagre, modest, offend, paltry, remote, skinny 7 contemn, neglect, outside, put-down, slender, tenuous, trivial 8 brush-off, delicate, discount, overlook, smallish, trifling 9 disregard, pint-sized 10 disrespect, negligible

slim
4 thin 5 lithe, reedy, small, spare 6 meager, meagre, minute, narrow, paltry, remote, skinny, slight, svelte, twiggy 7 lissome, outside, slender, tenuous 9 lithesome 10 negligible

slim down
4 diet, fast 6 reduce 10 slenderize

slime
3 goo, mud 4 glop, gunk, muck, ooze, scum 5 filth 6 sleaze, sludge 7 slander

slimy
4 oozy 6 mucous 7 viscous

sling
3 lob 4 cast, fire, hang, hurl, sock, toss 5 chuck, heave, march, pitch, throw 6 dangle, launch 7 suspend 8 catapult

slink
4 lurk 5 creep, prowl, skulk, slide, sneak, steal 7 gumshoe

slinky
4 sexy 5 lithe, sleek 6 svelte 7 furtive, lissome, sinuous, slender, willowy 8 graceful, sensuous, stealthy

slip
3 sag 4 dock, drop, fall, flow, flub, goof, lurk, shed, sink, skid 5 berth, boner, creep, error, fluff, gaffe, glide,

lapse, slide, slink, slump, sneak, steal **6** escape **7** blooper, blunder, decline, drop off, fall off, faux pas, mistake, slither **8** downturn, throw off **9** downswing, downtrend

slipper
4 mule, shoe **5** scuff **6** bootee, bootie, sandal **8** flip-flop, pantofle

slippery
3 icy **4** eely, oily **5** slick **6** greasy, shifty, smooth **7** devious, evasive **8** illusive, slithery **10** lubricious

slipshod
6 blowsy, blowzy, frowsy, frowzy, shabby, shoddy, sloppy, untidy **7** rumpled, scrubby, scruffy, unkempt **8** careless, ill-kempt, slapdash, slovenly, tattered **9** haphazard, negligent **10** bedraggled, disheveled, down-at-heel

slipup
4 goof **5** boner, error, fluff, lapse **6** bungle, glitch, miscue, mishap **7** blunder, faux pas, misstep, mistake, setback, stumble **8** accident **9** mischance, oversight **10** misfortune **11** misjudgment

slit
3 cut, gap **4** gash, rent **5** chink, crack, slash, slice **6** cranny, incise **7** crevice, fissure, opening

slither
4 slip **5** creep, glide, sidle, slide, slink, snake, sneak, steal **7** wriggle **8** undulate

slithery
see **slippery**

sliver
5 scrap, shard, shave, shred, slice **6** paring **7** shaving, snippet **8** splinter

slob
3 oaf **4** boor, clod, goon, lout **6** galoot, sloven

slobber
4 gush **5** drool, froth **6** drivel, effuse, slaver **7** dribble, enthuse **8** salivate

sloe
4 plum **10** blackthorn

slog
4 grub, moil, plod, plug, toil **5** chore, grind, labor, slave, sweat **6** drudge, schlep, trudge **7** schlepp

slogan
5 motto **6** byword **9** catchword, watchword **10** shibboleth **11** catchphrase

sloop
4 boat **8** sailboat

slop
3 mud, pap **4** gush, muck **5** douse, dreck, dregs, offal, slosh, slush, spill, swill **6** guzzle, pablum, refuse, splash, sludge **7** garbage, pabulum, rubbish **8** splatter

slope
3 tip **4** bend, cant, heel, lean, list, rise, skew, swag, sway, tilt **5** grade, pitch, scarp, slant **6** ascent, glacis **7** descent, incline, leaning, recline **8** gradient **9** acclivity, declivity, obliquity **11** inclination
combining form: 5 cline **6** clinal

sloppy
5 dowdy, gushy, messy **6** slushy, untidy **7** gushing, unkempt **8** careless, effusive, ill-kempt, slapdash, slipshod, slovenly **10** bedraggled, disheveled **11** dishevelled

slosh
4 gush, slop, wash **5** churn, swash **6** gurgle, splash **8** flounder, splatter

slot
4 vent **5** niche, notch **6** groove, keyway **7** keyhole, opening, passage **8** aperture **10** pigeonhole

sloth
4 laze **5** idler **6** acedia, apathy, idling, lazing, loafer, slouch, torpor **7** goof-off, languor, loafing, slacker **8** idleness, laziness, lethargy **9** heaviness, indolence, lassitude, lazybones, torpidity **11** couch potato **12** listlessness, sluggishness **13** shiftlessness

slothful
4 idle, lazy 8 fainéant, indolent
9 shiftless

slouch
3 bum, oaf, sag 4 laze, loaf, loll, lout,
mope, slug 5 droop, idler, sloth,
slump, stoop 6 loafer, loiter, lounge
7 saunter, shamble, shuffle 8 fainéant, slugabed, sluggard 9 do-
nothing, lazybones

slough
3 bog, fen 4 cast, mire, molt, quag,
shed, sump 5 inlet, marsh, scrap,
swamp 6 morass, reject 7 discard
8 jettison, quagmire, throw out
9 backwater, marshland, swampland, throw away

Slovakia
capital: 10 Bratislava
city: 6 Kosice
monetary unit: 6 koruna
mountain range: 10 Carpathian
neighbor: 6 Poland 7 Austria, Hungary, Ukraine 13 Czech Republic
river: 3 Váh 4 Hron 6 Danube,
Morava

Slovenia
capital: 9 Ljubljana
city: 7 Maribor
monetary unit: 5 tolar
neighbor: 5 Italy 7 Austria, Croatia,
Hungary
part of: 7 Balkans
peninsula: 6 Balkan

slovenly
5 dingy, messy, mussy, seedy, slack
6 frowsy, frowzy, grubby, grungy,
scuzzy, shabby, skanky, sleazy,
sloppy, untidy 7 squalid, unkempt
8 careless, slapdash, slipshod
10 bedraggled, slatternly

slow
4 late, poky 5 brake, check, lento,
tardy 6 adagio, hinder, impede,
leaden, retard, torpid 7 halting,
lagging, slacken 8 dilatory, dragging, plodding, sluggish, stagnant
9 leisurely, snaillike, unhurried
10 decelerate, snail-paced, strag-
gling

slowpoke
5 snail 6 lagger 7 dawdler, laggard
8 lingerer, loiterer 9 straggler

sludge
3 mud 4 crud, gunk, mire, muck,
ooze, slop 5 slime 6 sewage 8 sediment

slug
3 bum, hit, nip, tot 4 bash, belt,
dram, drop, jolt, shot, slam, swat
5 blast, clout, idler, larva, pound,
punch, smack, smash, snail, snort,
thump 6 buffet, loafer, slouch,
thwack, wallop 7 clobber, goof-off,
slacker 8 fainéant, toothful 9 do-
nothing, lazybones 11 couch potato
genus: 5 Limax

slugfest
4 bout 5 brawl, set-to 6 rumble
8 dogfight 10 donnybrook, prizefight

sluggard
3 bum 5 idler 6 loafer, slouch
7 dawdler, goof-off, laggard, shirker,
slacker 8 deadbeat, fainéant, slowpoke, slugabed 9 do-nothing, goldbrick, lazybones

slugger
5 boxer 6 batter, hitter 7 palooka

sluggish
4 lazy, logy, slow 5 inert, slack
6 draggy, leaden, stupid, torpid
7 lumpish 8 dragging, indolent,
listless, slothful 9 apathetic, lethargic

sluice
4 duct, flow, gush, pour, race, wash
5 flush, surge 6 trough 7 channel
8 spillway 9 floodgate

slum
6 ghetto 7 skid row

slumber
3 nap 4 doze 5 sleep 6 catnap,
drowse, snooze, stupor, torpor
8 dormancy, hebetude, lethargy
9 lassitude, torpidity

slumberous
see **sleepy**

slumgullion
4 stew 6 burgoo, ragout 7 goulash

slump
3 dip, sag 4 drop, fall, flag, funk, loll, sink, slip 5 droop, hunch, slide 6 slouch, trough 7 decline, drop off, falloff 8 collapse, downturn 9 downslide, downswing, downtrend, recession 10 depression, stagnation

slur
4 blot, blur, lisp, onus, slam, spot 5 brand, knock, libel, odium, smear, stain 6 befoul, defame, insult, malign, stigma, vilify 7 blacken, calumny, obloquy, obscure, slander, spatter, traduce 8 black eye, brickbat, innuendo, tear down 9 aspersion, bespatter, denigrate, discredit, disparage 10 accusation, calumniate

slurp
3 lap 4 gulp, suck 5 lap up, swill 6 guzzle

slush
3 mud 4 mire, muck, slop 6 drivel 8 schmaltz

sly
4 foxy, wily 5 cagey, saucy, shady, slick 6 artful, clever, crafty, shifty, shrewd, smooth, sneaky, subtle, tricky 7 cunning, devious, furtive, roguish, vulpine 8 guileful, scheming, slippery, stealthy 9 designing, insidious, underhand 11 mischievous, underhanded

slyboots
see **scamp**

slyness
4 wile 5 guile 7 cunning 8 caginess, foxiness, wiliness 9 canniness 10 craftiness

smack
3 bat, bop, box 4 bang, bash, belt, biff, blow, buss, chop, clip, cuff, dash, hint, kiss, peck, reek, slam, slap, sock, tang, whop 5 clout, crack, plumb, punch, right, savor, smell, spank, stink, taste, tinge, trace, whack 6 buffet, heroin, relish, smooch, square, strike, thwack 7 clobber, soupçon

smack-dab
4 bang, just 5 plumb, right 7 exactly 8 squarely 9 perfectly, precisely

small
3 wee 4 mean, mini, puny, tiny 5 bitty, dinky, dwarf, micro, minor, petty, runty, short, teeny 6 bantam, little, meager, meagre, minute, monkey, narrow, paltry, petite, slight, teensy 7 cramped, stunted, trivial 8 picayune, piddling, pint-size, trifling 9 miniature, minuscule, pint-sized 10 diminutive, negligible, undersized 11 ineffectual, unimportant
combining form: 4 micr, mini 5 micro

small fry
4 kids, tots 8 children 10 youngsters

small-minded
4 mean 5 petty 6 narrow 7 bigoted 9 hidebound, illiberal, parochial 10 brassbound, intolerant, provincial

smallpox
7 variola

small talk
4 chat 6 banter 7 chatter, palaver, prattle 8 badinage, chitchat, raillery, repartee 10 persiflage

small-time
5 minor, petty 6 paltry, two-bit 7 trivial 8 picayune, piddling, trifling 10 bush-league, negligible, shoestring 11 minor-league, unimportant 13 insignificant

smalt
4 blue

smarmy
4 glib, oily 5 slick 6 sleazy 7 buttery, fawning, fulsome 8 unctuous 10 obsequious, oleaginous 12 ingratiating

smart
3 apt 4 ache, chic, keen 5 acute, alert, canny, fresh, natty, quick, sassy, saucy, sharp, slick, sting, swank, throb 6 brainy, bright, cheeky, clever, dapper, shrewd, spruce,

suffer **7** dashing, stylish **8** impudent
11 fashionable, intelligent, quick-
witted, ready-witted, sharp-witted

smart aleck
7 show-off, wise guy **8** wiseacre
9 know-it-all **11** wisecracker, wisenheimer

smart-alecky
4 wise **5** fresh, sassy, saucy **6** cheeky
8 impudent, insolent **9** bold-faced
11 impertinent

smart set
5 elect, elite **6** bon ton, gentry **7** in
crowd, quality, society, who's who
9 beau monde, haut monde **10** blue
bloods, upper crust **11** aristocracy,
Four Hundred, high society

smarty-pants
7 wise guy **9** know-it-all, swellhead
11 wisenheimer

smash
3 hit, jar **4** bang, bash, belt, blow,
boom, clap, jolt, raze, ruin, slam,
slug, sock, wham, whop **5** blast,
burst, clash, crack, crash, crush,
pound, shock, whack, wreck **6** batter, impact, pileup, shiver, wallop
7 clobber, crack-up, debacle, destroy,
shatter, smashup, success **8** collapse, decimate, demolish, fragment,
knockout, overhand, splinter, tear
down **9** breakdown, collision, pulverize, sensation, succès fou **10** annihilate **12** disintegrate

smashup
5 crash, wreck **6** fiasco, pileup
7 crack-up, debacle **8** accident,
collapse, disaster **9** breakdown,
collision

smattering
3 few **7** handful **10** sprinkling

smear
3 dab, tar **4** beat, coat, daub, drub,
lick, slur, soil, whip **5** cover, libel,
stain, sully, taint **6** befoul, defame,
defile, malign, smirch, smudge,
spread, thrash, vilify **7** asperse,
blacken, calumny, plaster, shellac,

slander, tarnish, traduce **8** besmirch
9 bespatter, denigrate **10** calumniate

smell
4 funk, nose, odor, reek **5** aroma,
scent, sense, smack, sniff, snuff,
stink, trace, whiff **6** detect, stench
7 bouquet, perfume **9** fragrance,
redolence

smell, sense of
9 olfaction

smelly
4 rank **5** fetid, funky, reeky **6** foetid,
putrid, rancid, stinky **7** noisome,
reeking, stenchy **8** mephitic, stinking
10 malodorous

smelt
4 flux, fuse, slag **6** reduce, refine,
tomcod **8** sparling **9** sand lance,
whitebait

smidgen
see **particle**

smile
4 beam, grin **5** smirk **6** simper

smirch
see **smudge**

smirk
4 grin, leer **5** fleer, sneer **6** simper
7 grimace

smite
3 hit **4** belt, kill, sock **5** clout, whack
6 assail, attack, strike **7** afflict,
assault, clobber, torment

smithereens
4 bits **6** pieces **9** fragments, parti-
cles

smitten
5 taken **6** hooked **8** besotted,
enamored **9** enamoured, enchanted,
entranced **10** captivated, enraptured, infatuated **11** intoxicated

smock
5 apron, dress, frock **8** pinafore

smoke
4 cure, fume **5** fumes, vapor **8** fastball, fumigate **9** cigarette

smoky

4 fumy, gray, hazy 5 murky, sooty
6 turbid 7 reeking 10 caliginous,
smoldering

smolder

4 glow 5 churn 6 bubble, seethe,
simmer 7 ferment 9 fulminate

smooch

4 buss, kiss, neck, peck 5 smack
8 osculate

smooth

4 easy, even, flat 5 fluid, flush, level,
plane, sleek, slick, suave 6 facile,
fluent, glassy, glossy, polish, urbane
7 cursive, flatten, flowing, running
8 glabrous, hairless, soothing,
unbroken 10 effortless, unwrinkled

smooth-spoken

4 glib 6 fluent 8 eloquent 10 articulate 13 silver-tongued

smorgasbord

4 hash, olio 6 buffet, jumble, medley
7 farrago, mélange 8 mishmash,
mixed bag, pastiche 9 potpourri
10 hodgepodge, miscellany, salmagundi 11 gallimaufry

smother

5 choke, douse, quell 6 hush up,
muffle, quench, stifle 7 blanket,
repress, squelch 8 inundate, restrain, suppress 9 overwhelm,
suffocate 10 asphyxiate

smudge

3 dab 4 blot, blur, daub, foul, soil
5 dirty, smear, stain, sully, taint
6 bedaub, blotch, defile, smirch
7 begrime, besmear, blacken, blemish, splotch, tarnish 8 besmirch

smug

8 priggish 9 conceited 10 complacent 13 self-satisfied

smuggle

3 run 7 bootleg

smut

4 porn 5 filth 9 obscenity 11 pornography

smutty

4 blue, foul, lewd, racy 5 bawdy,
dirty, nasty, sooty 6 coarse, filthy,
risqué, vulgar 7 obscene, raunchy
8 indecent, off-color, prurient 9 salacious 12 pornographic, scatological

Smyrna

5 Izmir

snack

3 tea 4 bite, nosh, tapa 6 morsel,
nibble 11 refreshment

snaffle

3 bit, cop 4 lift 5 filch, pinch, swipe
6 pilfer, pocket 7 purloin

snafu

5 botch, error, mix-up, snarl 6 bungle, foul up, mess up, muddle 7 chaotic, screwup 9 confusion

snag

3 nab 4 curb, grab, hook, nail, tear
5 catch, hitch 6 glitch, holdup,
hurdle, obtain, secure 7 capture
8 drawback, obstacle 9 apprehend
10 impediment 11 obstruction

snail

5 whelk 6 limpet 7 mollusc, mollusk
8 escargot, ramshorn, slowpoke
9 gastropod 10 periwinkle

snake

3 boa 4 fink 5 crawl, creep, racer,
slide 6 python, writhe 7 hognose,
serpent, slither 8 anaconda, ophidian, undulate
poisonous: 3 asp 5 adder, cobra,
coral, krait, mamba, viper 6 elapid,
taipan 7 rattler 8 pit viper 10 bushmaster, copperhead, fer-de-lance
11 cottonmouth 13 water moccasin

snakebird

6 darter 7 anhinga

snake-eater

8 mongoose 13 secretary bird

snakelike

7 sinuous 8 ophidian 10 serpentine

snakeroot

7 bugbane 10 wild ginger 11 blazing star

snakeweed
7 bistort 13 poison hemlock

snaky
7 sinuous, winding 8 flexuous, tortuous 10 convoluted, meandering, serpentine 11 anfractuous

snap
4 bang, bark 5 break, cinch, crack 6 breeze, picnic 7 crackle 8 duck soup, kid stuff, pushover 10 child's play

snap back
6 revive 7 rebound, recover 10 convalesce, recuperate

snappy
4 edgy, fast, tart 5 brisk, hasty, huffy, natty, quick, rapid, sharp, smart, swank, swift, testy 6 lively, prompt, speedy, touchy 7 dashing, stylish, waspish 8 animated, petulant, vigorous 9 breakneck, fractious, irritable, vivacious

snare
3 bag 4 bait, hook, lure, trap 5 catch, decoy, tempt 6 come-on, enmesh, entice, entrap, seduce, tangle 7 capture, catch up, chicane, embroil, ensnare, ensnarl, involve, pitfall, trammel 8 entangle, inveigle 9 chicanery, deception 10 enticement, temptation

snarl
3 jam, web 4 bark, knot, maze, mesh 5 chaos, growl, ravel, skein 6 jungle, morass, muddle, tangle 7 perplex 8 disarray, disorder, entangle, mishmash 9 confusion, labyrinth 10 complexity, complicate 12 complication, entanglement

snatch
3 bit, nab 4 grab, jerk, take, yank 5 catch, pluck, seize, swipe 6 abduct, clutch, kidnap, wrench 8 fragment

snazzy
4 chic 5 fancy, gaudy, jazzy, nobby, ritzy, sassy, sharp, smart, showy, swank 6 chichi, classy, flashy, garish, glitzy, jaunty, spiffy, swanky 7 elegant

sneak
3 cur, pad 4 lurk, slip, worm 5 crawl, creep, glide, mooch, prowl, shirk, skulk, skunk, slide, slink, steal 6 covert, secret, tiptoe, weasel 7 furtive, gumshoe, slither, smuggle 8 hush-hush, slyboots, stealthy 9 pussyfoot, scoundrel 10 undercover 11 clandestine

sneaky
4 foxy 6 shifty, tricky 7 devious, furtive 8 guileful, indirect, slippery, stealthy 9 underhand 11 duplicitous, underhanded

sneer
4 gibe, jeer 5 fleer, scoff, smirk 7 grimace, snigger

snicker
5 laugh 6 giggle, titter 7 chortle, chuckle

snide
4 mean 5 nasty 8 spiteful 9 malicious 11 insinuating

sniff
4 jeer, nose 5 scent, scoff, smell, snoop 6 inhale

sniffy
4 smug 5 aloof, lofty 6 lordly, snooty, uppity 7 haughty, pompous, stuck-up 8 scornful, superior 10 disdainful, hoity-toity 12 contemptuous, supercilious

snifter
3 nip, sip, tot 4 dram, drop, jolt, shot, slug 5 glass, snort 6 finger, goblet

snip
3 bit, cut 4 clip, crop, trim 5 notch, scrap 8 fragment

snipe
4 carp 9 sandpiper

sniper
6 gunman, killer 7 shooter 8 marksman, rifleman 12 sharpshooter

snippety
see **snippy**

snippy

4 curt 5 bluff, blunt, brief, gruff, short, terse 6 abrupt, crusty 7 brusque 8 snappish

snit

3 fit 4 flap, fume, huff, stew 5 panic, pique, sweat, tizzy 6 dither, frenzy, lather, pother, swivet 10 conniption

snitch

3 cop, nip, rat 4 beak, fink, hook, lift, palm, sing, tell 5 filch, peach, pinch, spill, steal, swipe 6 inform, pilfer, pocket, squeal, tattle 7 purloin, rat fink, tattler, tipster 8 betrayer, informer, squealer 11 stool pigeon

snivel

3 sob 4 weep 5 cower, whine 6 cringe, whinge 7 blubber, snuffle, whimper

snob

5 snoot 6 poseur 7 parvenu

snobbish

6 snooty, uppity 7 haughty, high-hat, stuck-up 10 hoity-toity 11 patronizing, pretentious 12 supercilious 13 condescending

snook

5 cobia 6 robalo 12 sergeant fish

snooker

3 con 4 dupe, fool, hoax, pool 5 trick 6 delude 7 beguile, deceive, defraud 8 flimflam, hoodwink 9 bamboozle 11 hornswoggle

snoop

3 pry, spy 4 nose, peek, peep, peer, poke 5 prier, pryer 6 ferret, meddle, sleuth 7 gumshoe, intrude, meddler 8 busybody, quidnunc 9 detective, inspector, interfere 10 rubberneck

snooper

3 spy 9 detective, inspector 12 investigator

snoopy

4 nosy 6 prying 7 curious 8 meddling 9 intrusive 10 meddlesome 11 inquisitive

snoot

see **snout**

snooty

see **snobbish**

snooze

3 kip, nap 4 doze 5 sleep 6 catnap, drowse, nod off, siesta 7 drop off, slumber 10 forty winks

snore

8 rhonchus

snort

3 nip, tot 4 dram, drop, jolt, shot, slug 5 scoff, snarl 6 exhale, inhale 7 snifter

snout

4 beak, nose 6 muzzle 9 proboscis

snow

glacial: 4 firn, névé
melted: 5 slush
pellet: 7 graupel
ridge: 8 sastruga

snow apple

8 mushroom

snowball

5 mount, run up 6 expand 7 augment, burgeon, explode, inflate 8 increase, multiply, mushroom, viburnum 10 accumulate 11 proliferate

snowbird

5 finch, junco 6 thrush 7 bunting 9 fieldfare, ivory gull

Snow-Bound author

8 Whittier (John Greenleaf)

snow finch

9 brambling

snow grouse

9 ptarmigan

snow leopard

5 ounce

Snow Leopard author

11 Matthiessen (Peter)

snowstorm

8 blizzard

snub

3 cut 4 shun 5 blunt, scorn, spite, spurn 6 rebuff, rebuke, slight, stubby 7 put down 9 ostracize, repudiate 12 cold-shoulder

snuff
3 ice, off 4 kill, nose 5 pinch, scent, smell 6 murder, rappee 7 execute 10 extinguish 11 exterminate

snug
4 cozy, neat, taut, tidy, trim 5 comfy, cushy, tight 6 burrow, cuddle, nestle, nuzzle, secure 7 orderly 9 sheltered, shipshape 11 comfortable

snuggle
5 spoon 6 burrow, cuddle, curl up, huddle, nestle, nuzzle

so
3 sae 4 ergo, then, thus 5 hence 6 indeed 9 similarly, therefore 11 accordingly 12 consequently

soak
3 sot, wet 4 bilk, clip, lush, skin, swig, wino 5 douse, drink, gouge, imbue, souse, steep 6 boozer, drench, fleece, infuse, seethe 7 drinker, guzzler, immerse 8 drunkard, permeate, saturate, submerge 9 alcoholic, penetrate 10 boozehound, impregnate, overcharge
flax: 3 ret

soap
4 suds 6 stroke 7 flatter, wheedle 8 blandish, butter up, inveigle 9 sweet-talk
hard: 7 castile
ingredient: 3 lye

soapbox
4 dais 6 podium 7 rostrum 8 hustings, platform, scaffold

soap plant
5 amole

soapstone
8 steatite

soapwort
7 cowherd 11 bouncing bet

soar
3 fly 4 lift, rise 5 arise, climb, glide, hover, mount, shoot 6 ascend, rocket 7 shoot up 8 increase 9 skyrocket

sob
3 cry 4 bawl, blub, wail, weep 7 blubber, whimper

sober
4 calm, cool 5 grave, sedate, staid 6 low-key, proper, sedate, serene, solemn 7 austere, earnest, serious, subdued 8 composed, decorous, low-keyed, moderate, rational, reserved 9 abstinent, collected, practical, pragmatic, realistic, temperate 10 abstaining, abstemious, controlled, forbearing, hardheaded, no-nonsense, reasonable, restrained 11 disciplined, down-to-earth 12 matter-of-fact 13 imperturbable, self-possessed, unimpassioned

sobriety
7 gravity 10 abstinence, continence, sedateness, temperance 11 seriousness

sobriquet
3 tag 5 alias 6 byname 7 epithet, moniker 8 cognomen, nickname 10 hypocorism

so-called
6 formal 7 alleged, nominal, titular 8 supposed 9 pretended, professed, purported 10 ostensible, self-styled

soccer
cup: 5 World
official: 7 referee 8 linesman
player: 6 booter, goalie, kicker, winger 7 forward, link man, striker, sweeper 8 defender, fullback, halfback 10 goalkeeper
star: 4 Hamm (Mia), Pelé 5 Akers (Michelle) 7 Beckham (David), Ronaldo 8 Maradona (Diego) 11 Beckenbauer (Franz)
term: 3 net 4 boot, chip, kick, trap 6 corner, header, tackle, volley 7 dribble, kickoff, throw-in 8 backheel, free kick, goal kick, goal line 9 touchline 10 center spot, corner flag, corner kick 11 dropped ball, halfway line, penalty kick, penalty spot

sociable
5 close 6 genial 7 affable, amiable,

cordial **8** familiar, gracious **9** clubbable, congenial, convivial **10** gregarious, hospitable **11** good-natured

social

5 civic, civil **8** communal **9** clubbable, convivial **10** collective, gregarious, hospitable **11** extroverted **13** companionable
class: 5 caste

Social Contract author
8 Rousseau (Jean-Jacques)

socialist
American: 4 Debs (Eugene) **6** Ripley (George), Thomas (Norman)
British: 4 Owen (Robert, Robert Dale), Webb (Beatrice, Sidney) **6** Morris (William)
French: 7 Fourier (Charles), Viviani (René) **10** Saint-Simon (Henri de)
German: 4 Marx (Karl) **6** Engels (Friedrich) **9** Luxemburg (Rosa) **10** Liebknecht (Wilhelm)

socialize
3 mix **5** party **6** hobnob, mingle **7** consort **9** associate **10** fraternize

social worker
4 Riis (Jacob), Wald (Lillian D.) **6** Addams (Jane) **7** Alinsky (Saul), Lathrop (Julia C.)

society
4 club **5** elite, guild **6** gentry, league, people, public **7** company, quality, who's who **8** populace, sodality **9** beau monde, community, haut monde **10** fellowship, fraternity, upper class, upper crust **11** aristocracy, association, brotherhood **13** companionship

sociologist
American: 4 Bell (Daniel), Ward (Lester Frank) **5** Balch (Emily Green), Whyte (William H.) **6** Du Bois (W. E. B.), Glazer (Nathan), Sumner (William Graham) **7** Johnson (Charles Spurgeon), Riesman (David)
English: 7 Spencer (Herbert)
French: 8 Durkheim (Emile)
German: 5 Weber (Max)

Italian: 6 Pareto (Vilfredo)
Swedish: 6 Myrdal (Alva, Gunnar)

sock
3 bop, box, hit **4** bash, belt, blow, chop, cuff, ding, slap, slog **5** clout, punch, smack, smash, whack **6** argyle, buffet, strike, thwack **8** stocking

sock away
4 bank, save, stow **5** cache, hoard, lay by, put by, stash **8** lay aside

socks
4 hose **7** hosiery

Socrates
birthplace: 6 Athens
poison: 7 hemlock
pupil: 5 Plato
wife: 8 Xantippe **9** Xanthippe

Socratic
8 maieutic

sod
4 land, peat, turf **5** earth, grass **6** ground

soda
3 pop **4** cola **5** tonic **7** seltzer

sodality
4 club **5** guild, lodge, order, union **6** league **7** society **9** community **10** fellowship, fraternity **11** association, brotherhood

sodden
3 wet **5** soggy, soppy **6** soaked, soused **7** soaking, sopping **8** drenched, dripping **9** saturated **11** waterlogged, wringing-wet

Sodom and ____
8 Gomorrah

sofa
5 couch, divan **7** ottoman **9** banquette, davenport

so far
3 yet **5** as yet, still **6** to date **7** till now **8** hitherto, until now **10** heretofore

Sofia native
6 Bulgar **9** Bulgarian

soft

4 cozy, easy, mild, snug 5 balmy, comfy, cushy, downy, faint, mushy, silky 6 doughy, flabby, gentle, low-key, pliant, satiny, silken, simple, smooth, spongy, tender 7 cottony, lenient, pillowy, pliable, squashy, squishy, subdued, velvety 8 cushiony, workable, yielding 9 malleable 11 comfortable

softcover

9 paperback

soften

4 ease, tame 5 abate, allay, blunt, relax 6 dampen, lessen, mellow, soothe, subdue, temper, weaken 7 assuage, lighten, mollify 8 diminish, enfeeble, mitigate, moderate, palliate, tone down, turn down 9 alleviate

soft hail

7 graupel

softhearted

4 kind, warm 6 humane, kindly, tender 7 lenient 10 responsive 11 sympathetic 13 compassionate

soft palate

5 velum

soft-pedal

4 mute 6 dampen, hush up, muffle, subdue 8 minimize, play down, suppress, tone down 9 underplay 11 de-emphasize

soft-soap

3 con 4 coax 6 cajole, soothe, wangle 7 blarney, flatter, wheedle 8 blandish, butter up, inveigle 9 sweet-talk

soggy

3 wet 6 doughy, soaked, sodden 7 soaking, sopping 8 drenched, dripping 9 saturated 10 bedraggled 11 waterlogged

Sohrab and Rustum author

6 Arnold (Matthew)

soi-disant

7 alleged 8 putative, so-called, supposed 9 pretended, professed, purported 10 ostensible, self-styled

soil

3 mud, tar 4 daub, dirt, foul, land, loam, mess, muck, murk 5 dirty, earth, grime, muddy, smear, stain, sully, taint 6 defile, ground, smirch, smudge 7 blacken, country, pollute, tarnish 8 besmirch, discolor, homeland 10 fatherland, motherland, terra firma 11 contaminate

aggregate: 3 ped
clay: 5 gault
dark: 9 chernozem
deposit: 5 loess 7 eluvium
infertile: 6 podzol
layer: 4 gley, sola (plural) 5 solum
rich: 6 hotbed
tropical: 7 latosol

soiree

4 fete, gala 5 party 6 affair, social 7 shindig 8 function 9 festivity, reception 11 celebration 13 entertainment

sojourn

4 bide, stay, stop 5 abide, lodge, tarry, visit 6 linger 7 layover 8 stopover

Sol

3 sun 7 daystar, phoebus
horse: 4 Eous 5 Ethon 9 Erythreos (see also **Helios**)

solace

5 allay, amuse, cheer 6 buck up 7 comfort, console, hearten 8 inspirit 10 condolence

solar disk

4 Aten, Aton

solarium

7 sunroom

solder

4 fuse, weld 5 braze

soldier

5 grunt, sepoy 7 dogface, draftee, fighter, private, recruit, trooper, veteran, warrior 8 bluecoat, doughboy, fusilier, rifleman 9 free lance, guerrilla, man-at-arms, mercenary 10 carabineer, carabinier, serviceman 11 condottiere, infantryman
ancient Greece: 7 hoplite

sole

British: 5 Tommy 7 redcoat
cavalry: 6 hussar 8 chasseur
Confederate: 3 reb
French: 5 poilu 6 Zouave
German: 5 jerry
irregular: 8 guerilla 9 guerrilla
Prussian: 5 uhlan
Turkish: 9 janissary

sole

3 one 4 lone, only 5 alone 6 bottom, single, unique 8 flatfish, singular 9 exclusive

solecism

4 goof, slip 5 boner, error, gaffe, lapse 6 misuse 7 blooper, blunder, faux pas, mistake 9 barbarism, indecorum, vulgarism 11 impropriety

solemn

5 grand, grave, sober, staid, stern 6 august, formal, ritual, sedate, somber, sombre 7 earnest, plenary, serious, stately, weighty 8 funereal, imposing, majestic 9 dignified 10 ceremonial, impressive, nononsense, sobersided 11 ceremonious, magnificent

solemnize

4 keep 5 bless, honor 6 hallow 7 dignify, observe 8 venerate 9 celebrate, ritualize 10 consecrate 11 commemorate

solicit

3 ask, beg 4 lure, tout, urge 5 apply 6 demand, drum up, entice 7 beseech, bespeak, canvass, entreat, implore, request 8 petition 9 importune 11 proposition, requisition

solicitor

6 jurist, lawyer, suitor 7 pleader 8 advocate, attorney 9 counselor

solicitous

4 avid, keen 5 eager, fussy 6 ardent, tender 7 anxious, careful, devoted, fearful, finicky, worried 8 rigorous 9 assiduous, attentive, concerned, impatient 10 fastidious, meticulous, scrupulous 11 considerate, punctilious, sympathetic 12 apprehensive 13 conscientious

solicitude

4 care, heed 5 qualm, worry 6 unease 7 anxiety, concern, scruple 9 attention, vigilance 10 uneasiness 11 compunction 12 watchfulness 13 consideration

solid

4 firm, hard 5 dense, sound, valid 6 cogent, secure, stable, sturdy, united 7 compact 8 reliable, unbroken 9 steadfast, unanimous, undivided 10 convincing 11 substantial

solidarity

5 union, unity 6 esprit 7 concord, oneness 8 cohesion 9 integrity 10 singleness 12 cohesiveness, togetherness 13 esprit de corps

solidify

3 dry, fix, gel, set 4 cake, jell 6 freeze, harden, secure 7 compact, congeal 8 compress, contract, indurate 11 consolidate

solitary

4 lone, lorn, only, solo 5 alone 6 hermit, lonely, single, unique 7 recluse 8 derelict, deserted, desolate, eremitic, forsaken, isolated, lonesome, separate, singular 9 abandoned, reclusive, withdrawn 10 antisocial, particular, unsociable 11 standoffish 12 misanthropic 13 unaccompanied

solitude

7 privacy 8 loneness 9 aloneness, isolation, seclusion 10 detachment, loneliness, quarantine, retirement, withdrawal 11 confinement 12 separateness

solo

4 lone 5 alone 6 single 7 unaided 8 solitary 13 independently, unaccompanied

Solomon

brother: 8 Adonijah
daughter: 7 Taphath 8 Basemath
father: 5 David
kingdom: 6 Israel
mother: 9 Bathsheba
son, successor: 8 Rehoboam
victim: 4 Joab 8 Adonijah

Solomon Islands
capital: 7 Honiara
ethnic group: 10 Melanesian
island: 7 Florida, Malaita, Rennell
8 Choiseul 11 Guadalcanal, Santa
Isabel 12 San Cristóbal
language: 5 Pijin 7 English
monetary unit: 6 dollar

solon
8 lawgiver 10 legislator

so long
4 by-by, ciao, ta-ta 5 adieu, adios
6 bye-bye 7 cheerio, goodbye,
toodles 8 farewell, Godspeed,
toodle-oo

solution
6 answer, result
salt: 6 saline

solve
3 fix 5 break, crack 6 decode,
reveal, settle 7 clarify, clear up, dope
out, explain, unravel, work out
8 construe, decipher, unriddle,
untangle 9 elucidate, figure out,
interpret, puzzle out 11 disentangle

Somalia
capital: 9 Mogadishu
gulf: 4 Aden
language: 6 Arabic, Somali
location: 12 Horn of Africa
monetary unit: 8 shilling
neighbor: 5 Kenya 8 Djibouti,
Ethiopia

somatic
6 bodily, carnal 7 fleshly 8 corporal,
parietal, physical 9 corporeal

somber
3 dim 4 dark, drab, dull, grim 5 bleak,
dusky, grave, heavy, murky, staid
6 dismal, dreary, gloomy, sedate,
solemn 7 doleful, joyless, obscure,
serious, weighty 8 funereal, mournful 9 tenebrous 10 caliginous,
depressing, depressive, lugubrious,
melancholy, sepulchral, sobersided,
tenebrific 11 dispiriting

somewhat
5 quite 6 fairly, kind of, rather, sort of
7 a little 8 slightly 9 partially, tolerably 10 moderately

sommelier's offering
4 wine

somniferous
see **sleepy**

somnolent
see **sleepy**

Somnus
brother: 4 Mors
god of: 5 sleep
mother: 3 Nox

son
French: 4 fils
Italian: 6 figlio
Spanish: 4 hijo

song
3 air, lay 4 aria, glee, hymn, lied,
tune 5 carol, chant, ditty, lyric, paean
6 ballad, melody, number 7 chanson
8 madrigal
biblical: 8 canticle
boat: 9 barcarole 10 barcarolle
French: 7 chanson
German: 4 lied 6 lieder (plural)
lamentation: 5 dirge 8 threnode,
threnody
medieval: 8 sirvente 9 sirventes
morning: 6 aubade
of joy: 5 paean
operatic: 4 aria 8 cavatina 9 cabaletta
Portuguese: 4 fado
sacred: 5 psalm
sailor's: 6 chanty, shanty 7 chantey
short: 8 canzonet
wedding: 8 hymeneal

song and dance
5 pitch, spiel

songbird
see at **bird**

Song of Myself author
7 Whitman (Walt)

Song of Solomon
9 Canticles

songwriter
8 composer, lyricist

Sonja ____
5 Henie

Sonnambula composer
7 Bellini (Vincenzo)

sonnet
developer: 8 Petrarch
part: 5 octet 6 octave, sestet

sonorous
7 ringing, vibrant 8 resonant 10 oratorical, resounding, rhetorical 11 declamatory 12 magniloquent 13 grandiloquent

Sontag novel
9 In America 12 Volcano Lover (The)

soon
4 anon 6 any day, pronto 7 betimes, quickly, rapidly, shortly 8 directly, promptly, speedily 9 forthwith, presently, right away 10 before long

Sooner State
8 Oklahoma

soothe
4 balm, calm, ease, hush, lull 5 allay, quiet, salve, still 6 becalm, pacify, settle, solace, subdue 7 appease, assuage, comfort, compose, console, massage, mollify, placate, relieve 8 calm down, reassure 9 alleviate 10 conciliate, propitiate 11 tranquilize

soothsay
5 augur 8 prophesy 9 adumbrate 10 vaticinate 13 prognosticate

soothsayer
4 seer 5 sibyl 6 oracle 7 diviner, prophet 8 foreseer 9 predictor 10 forecaster, foreteller
ancient Roman: 5 augur 6 auspex 8 haruspex
blind: 8 Tiresias
(see also **prophet**)

sop
3 wet 4 gift, soak 5 bribe, douse, goody, souse, steep 6 deluge, drench, reward, seethe 7 douceur 8 gratuity, saturate, waterlog 9 incentive, lagniappe, sweetener 10 enticement

sophism
see **sophistry**

sophistic
5 false, phony 7 invalid, seeming, unsound 8 delusive, illusory, spurious 9 beguiling, casuistic, deceptive, plausible 10 fallacious, fraudulent, misleading, ostensible

sophisticated
5 blasé, jaded, suave 6 smooth, svelte, urbane 7 complex, knowing, refined, worldly 8 cultured, involved, schooled, seasoned 9 Byzantine, elaborate, intricate, practiced 10 world-weary 11 complicated, worldly-wise 12 cosmopolitan

sophistry
9 casuistry 12 equivocation 13 dissimulation, prevarication

Sophocles play
4 Ajax 7 Electra 8 Antigone 10 Oedipus Rex

Sophonisba
brother: 8 Hannibal
father: 9 Hasdrubal
husband: 6 Syphax

soporific
4 dozy 6 drowsy, opiate, sleepy 7 anodyne, calming, numbing 8 hypnotic, narcotic, sedative 9 calmative, deadening, somnolent 10 anesthetic, slumberous 11 somniferous 12 somnifacient 13 tranquilizing

soprano
American: 4 Pons (Lily) 5 Costa (Mary), Gluck (Alma), Moffo (Anna), Moore (Grace), Price (Leontyne), Sills (Beverly) 6 Arroyo (Martina), Battle (Kathleen), Callas (Maria), Curtin (Phyllis), Donath (Helen), Farrar (Geraldine), Garden (Mary), Munsel (Patrice), Norman (Jessye), Peters (Roberta), Piazza (Marguerite), Resnik (Regina) 7 Farrell (Eileen), Fleming (Renée), Kirsten (Dorothy), Stevens (Risë), Traubel (Helen) 8 Ponselle (Rosa)
Australian: 5 Melba (Nellie) 10 Sutherland (Joan)

Austrian: 4 Popp (Lucia) 7 Rysanek (Leonie) 8 Sembrich (Marcella)
Canadian: 7 Stratas (Teresa)
French: 7 Crespin (Régine)
German: 6 Leider (Frida) 7 Lehmann (Lilli, Lotte) 11 Schwarzkopf (Elisabeth)
Italian: 5 Freni (Mirella), Grisi (Giuditta, Giulia), Patti (Adelina) 6 Scotto (Renata) 7 Bartoli (Cecilia), Tebaldi (Renata) 10 Tetrazzini (Luisa) 11 Ricciarelli (Katia)
Korean: 6 Sümi Jo
Mexican: 8 Cruz-Romo (Gilda)
New Zealand: 8 Te Kanawa (Kiri)
Norwegian: 8 Flagstad (Kirsten)
Romanian: 8 Cotrubas (Ileana)
Spanish: 7 Caballé (Montserrat) 8 Berganza (Teresa) 12 de los Angeles (Victoria)
Swedish: 4 Lind (Jenny) 7 Nilsson (Birgit)
(see also **mezzo-soprano**)

sorcerer
4 mage 5 magus 6 wizard 7 warlock 8 conjurer, conjuror, magician 9 enchanter 11 necromancer, thaumaturge 13 thaumaturgist

sorceress
3 hag, hex 5 Circe, witch

sorcery
5 magic 8 diablery, wizardry 9 conjuring 10 necromancy, witchcraft 11 bewitchment, enchantment, thaumaturgy
West Indian: 5 obeah

sordid
3 low 4 base, foul, mean, vile 5 dirty, nasty, seamy, shady, venal 6 blowsy, blowzy, filthy, frowsy, frowzy, grubby, scurvy, shabby, sleazy 7 ignoble, low-down, squalid, unclean 8 degraded, shameful, wretched 9 loathsome, mercenary 10 despicable, scandalous, slatternly 11 disgraceful 12 contemptible, disreputable 13 reprehensible

sore
3 raw 4 boil 5 angry, irked, ulcer,

upset, vexed 6 aching, bitter, canker, peeved, tender 7 abscess, chancre, hurting, painful 8 inflamed, smarting 9 chilblain, irritated, rancorous, resentful, sensitive 10 affliction

sorehead
4 crab 5 grump 6 griper, grouch 7 grouser 8 grumbler, sourpuss 10 bellyacher, complainer, crosspatch, malcontent

sorrel
4 dock 8 chestnut, sourwood

sorrow
3 rue, sob, woe 4 moan, ruth 5 dolor, grief, mourn 6 grieve, lament, misery, regret 7 anguish, remorse, sadness 8 distress, grieving, mourning 9 dejection, heartache, suffering 10 affliction, heartbreak, melancholy 11 lamentation, unhappiness 12 mournfulness

sorrowful
3 sad 6 rueful, triste, woeful 7 doleful, forlorn, piteous, ruthful, unhappy 8 dolorous, downcast, grieving, mournful, tristful, wretched 9 afflicted, miserable, plaintive, woebegone 10 lamentable, lugubrious, melancholy 11 heartbroken 12 disconsolate

sorry
3 bad, sad 4 mean, poor 5 cheap 6 cheesy, paltry, scummy, scurvy, shabby, shoddy 7 scruffy, unhappy 8 beggarly, contrite, mournful, penitent, pitiable, saddened, trifling, wretched 9 miserable, regretful, repentant 10 apologetic, despicable, inadequate, melancholy, remorseful 11 disgraceful, penitential 12 contemptible, heavyhearted

sort
3 ilk, lot, set 4 comb, cull, kind, pick, sift, type 5 class, order 6 choose, screen, select, stripe, winnow 7 arrange, catalog, species, variety 8 classify, separate 9 catalogue, character 10 categorize, pigeonhole

sortie
4 dash, raid 5 foray, sally 7 assault, mission 9 excursion 10 expedition

sortilege
6 augury 7 sorcery 8 divining, witchery 10 divination, necromancy, witchcraft 11 thaumaturgy

so-so
4 fair, okay 6 decent, enough, fairly, medium, rather 7 average, fairish 8 adequate, mediocre, middling, moderate, passable, passably 9 tolerably 10 moderately 11 indifferent 12 run-of-the-mill

sot
4 lush, wino 5 drunk, souse 6 bibber, boozer 7 guzzler, tippler, tosspot 8 drunkard 9 alcoholic, inebriate 10 boozehound

sotto voce
3 low 5 aside 6 softly 7 faintly, mutedly, quietly 9 privately

souchong
3 tea

sough
4 sigh 7 suspire, whisper

soul
4 pith 5 anima, being, heart, stuff 6 animus, breast, marrow, pneuma, psyche, spirit 7 essence 9 élan vital, substance 10 conscience, vital force 12 quintessence
combining form: 5 psych 6 psycho

soulful
6 moving, tender 7 emotive, fervent 8 poignant, stirring, touching 9 affecting, emotional 11 impassioned, sentimental

soul singer
4 Gaye (Marvin) 5 Bland (Bobby), Brown (James), Cooke (Sam), Flack (Roberta), Green (Al), Hayes (Isaac) 6 Butler (Jerry), Knight (Gladys), Sledge (Percy) 7 Charles (Ray), Pickett (Wilson), Redding (Otis) 8 Franklin (Aretha), Mayfield (Curtis)

sound
3 fit 4 firm, hale, safe, sane 5 audio, legit, noise, plumb, probe, right, sober, solid, valid, whole 6 cogent, fathom, intact, secure, stable, sturdy, unhurt 7 correct, earshot, healthy, logical, prudent 8 rational, reliable, sensible, unharmed 9 judicious, resonance, undamaged, vibration, wholesome 10 convincing, reasonable 11 well-founded 12 satisfactory, well-grounded 13 reverberation
combining form: 3 son 4 phon, soni, sono 5 audio, audit, phone, phony 6 audito, phonia
high-pitched: 4 ping, ting
pleasant: 7 euphony
quality: 6 timbre
repeating: 7 rat-a-tat 8 rataplan 10 rat-a-tat-tat
science: 6 sonics 7 phonics 9 acoustics

Sound
Alaska: 5 Cross
Antarctica: 7 McMurdo
Australia: 4 King 5 Broad
Bahamas: 5 Exuma
Canada: 4 Howe 6 Nansen
Connecticut-New York: 10 Long Island
English Channel: 8 Plymouth
Georgia: 8 Altamaha
Greenland: 5 Smith
Gulf of Mexico: 8 Suwannee 11 Mississippi
Massachusetts: 8 Vineyard 9 Nantucket
New England: 11 Block Island
North Carolina: 4 Core 5 Bogue 7 Pamlico, Roanoke 9 Albemarle, Currituck
Northwest Territories: 4 Peel 8 Melville 9 Lancaster 12 Prince Albert
Norwegian Sea: 8 Scoresby
Ontario: 4 Owen
Scotland: 3 Hoy 4 Jura, Mull 5 Inner
Spitsbergen: 4 Bell
Washington: 5 Puget

Sound and the Fury, The
author: 8 Faulkner (William)
character: 5 Benjy (Compson),
Caddy (Compson), Jason (Compson)
6 Dilsey 7 Quentin (Compson)

soundness
6 health, sanity 7 balance 8 lucidity,
prudence, security, solidity, strength
9 integrity, stability 11 reliability
12 practicality

sound off
7 speak up 8 speak out

soup
beet: 6 borsch 7 borscht
bowl: 6 tureen
clear: 5 broth 8 bouillon, consommé, julienne
cold: 8 gazpacho 11 vichyssoise
curry: 12 mulligatawny
okra: 5 gumbo
seafood: 7 chowder
thick: 5 gumbo, puree 6 bisque,
burgoo
vegetable: 10 minestrone

soupçon
see **particle**

soupy
5 foggy, gooey, gushy, murky, mushy
6 drippy, slushy, smoggy 7 cloying, maudlin, mawkish 8 cornball
9 schmaltzy 10 saccharine 11 sentimental, tear-jerking

sour
4 acid, dour, tart 5 acerb, acrid,
tangy, testy 6 acidic, bitter, crabby,
cranky, curdle, grumpy, morose,
rancid, rotten, sullen, turned 7 acerbic, grouchy, peevish, prickly, spoiled,
unhappy 8 embitter, vinegary 9 acidulous, fermented 12 disagreeable

source
4 font, root, well 5 basis, cause,
fount, model, onset, start 6 mother,
origin, spring 7 dawning, genesis
8 begetter, fountain, wellhead 9 beginning, inception, informant, precursor, prototype, reference, rootstock
10 antecedent, authorship, birthplace, derivation, originator, progeni-

tor, provenance, wellspring 11 origination, provenience 12 fountainhead

sourness
7 acidity 8 acerbity, asperity

sourpuss
4 crab 5 crank, grump 6 griper,
grouch 7 grouser, killjoy 8 grumbler,
sorehead 10 bellyacher, complainer,
crosspatch, curmudgeon 11 misanthrope

souse
3 dip, sop, sot 4 lush, soak, wino
5 binge, drown, steep 6 boozer,
drench, pickle, plunge, seethe
7 immerse 8 drunkard, inundate,
marinate, preserve, saturate, submerge, submerse 9 alcoholic,
immersion, inebriate 10 boozehound, intoxicate 11 dipsomaniac

soused
3 lit 4 high 5 drunk, lit up, oiled
6 bashed, blotto, bombed, juiced,
potted, soaked, soused, stewed,
stoned, tanked, wasted, zonked
7 crocked, drunken, pickled, pie-
eyed, sloshed, smashed, sottish
8 polluted 9 plastered 10 inebriated,
liquored up 11 intoxicated

south
combining form: 5 austr 6 austro
French: 3 sud
Spanish: 3 sur

South Africa
capital: 8 Cape Town, Pretoria
12 Bloemfontein
city: 6 Durban 12 Johannesburg
desert: 8 Kalahari
enclave: 7 Lesotho
grassland: 4 veld 5 veldt
language: 5 Bantu 7 English
9 Afrikaans
monetary unit: 4 rand
mountain range: 11 Drakensberg
neighbor: 7 Namibia 8 Botswana
9 Swaziland, Zimbabwe 10 Mozambique
plateau: 5 Karoo 6 Karroo
river: 6 Molopo, Orange
settlers: 5 Boers

South America

country: 4 Peru 5 Chile 6 Brázil, Guyana 7 Bolivia, Ecuador, Uruguay 8 Colombia, Paraguay, Suriname 9 Argentina, Venezuela
ethnic group: 6 Aymara, Creole, Indian 7 mestizo, mulatto, Quechua, Spanish 10 Amerindian, Portuguese
language: 6 Aymara 7 Guaraní, Quechua, Spanish 10 Portuguese

South Carolina

capital: 8 Columbia
city: 10 Charleston, Greenville
college, university: 7 Citadel, Clemson
fort: 6 Sumter
island, island group: 3 Sea 6 Edisto, Parris 10 Hilton Head
nickname: 8 Palmetto (State)
river: 6 Edisto, Pee Dee, Santee 7 Tugaloo 8 Savannah
state bird: 12 Carolina wren
state flower: 13 yellow jasmine
state tree: 8 palmetto

South Dakota

capital: 6 Pierre
city: 9 Rapid City 10 Sioux Falls
mountain: 6 Harney (Peak) 8 Rushmore 10 Black Hills
nickname: 6 Coyote (State) 10 Mt. Rushmore (State)
park: 8 Badlands, Wind Cave
river: 8 Missouri 11 Belle Forche
state bird: 18 ring-necked pheasant
state flower: 12 pasqueflower
state tree: 6 spruce

southerly

7 austral

South-West Africa

7 Namibia

south wind

see at **wind**

souvenir

5 relic, token 6 trophy 7 memento 8 keepsake, memorial, reminder 11 remembrance

sovereign

4 coin, czar, free, king, tsar 5 queen, regal, royal, ruler 6 kingly, ruling 7 emperor, empress, highest, monarch, regnant, supreme 8 absolute, autarkic, autocrat, dominant, imperial, kinglike, majestic 9 ascendant, autarchic, monarchal, number one, paramount, potentate 10 autonomous, monarchial 11 independent, monarchical, predominant 12 self-governed

soviet

7 council 9 committee

sow

4 seed, toss 5 drill, fling, plant, strew 7 bestrew, scatter 9 broadcast 11 disseminate

spa

5 baths, hydro, wells 6 hot tub, resort, spring, waters 7 springs 13 watering place
Czech: 6 Bilina 8 Karlsbad
English: 4 Bath 6 Buxton 9 Harrogate
French: 3 Dax 5 Evian
German: 3 Ems 5 Baden 6 Bad Ems 9 Kissingen

space

3 gap 4 area, room 5 blank, scope 6 cavity, extent, spread, volume 7 breadth, expanse, stretch 8 capacity, distance, interval, universe 9 amplitude, expansion

spaced-out

4 high 5 doped 6 stoned, zonked 7 drugged 8 hopped-up, turned on

spacious

3 big 4 vast, wide 5 ample, large, roomy 7 immense 8 enormous, extended 9 boundless, capacious, cavernous, expansive, extensive 10 commodious, voluminous

spade

3 dig 4 grub 5 dig up, scoop 6 dig out, shovel 8 excavate

Spade, Sam

4 dick 6 shamus, sleuth 7 gumshoe 9 detective 10 private eye
creator: 7 Hammett (Dashiell)
novel: 13 Maltese Falcon (The)

Spain
ancient name: 8 Hispania
capital: 6 Madrid
city: 6 Málaga 7 Seville 8 Valencia, Zaragoza 9 Barcelona, Saragossa
island group: 6 Canary 8 Balearic
king: 10 Juan Carlos
leader: 6 Franco (Francisco)
monetary unit: 4 euro
monetary unit, former: 4 real 6 peseta
mountain: 8 Mulhacén 11 Pico de Aneto
mountain range: 8 Pyrenees
neighbor: 6 France 8 Portugal
peninsula: 7 Iberian
region: 8 Valencia 9 Catalonia
river: 4 Ebro 12 Guadalquivir
sea: 13 Mediterranean
strait: 9 Gibraltar

spall
4 chip 5 flake 7 shaving 8 fragment 9 exfoliate

spam
8 junk mail

span
4 arch, term, time 5 cross, reach 6 extent, length, period, spread 7 compass, measure, stretch 8 duration, interval, lifetime, straddle, traverse

spangle
4 trim 5 flash, gleam 6 sequin 7 glitter, shimmer, sparkle, twinkle 9 coruscate 11 scintillate

Spaniard
9 Castilian

Spanish
boss: 7 cacique
chaperone: 6 duenna
combining form: 7 hispano
dictator: 8 caudillo
folksong: 6 tonada
fortress: 7 alcazar
garrison: 8 presidio
hors d'oeuvre: 4 tapa
inn: 6 posada
mayor: 7 alcalde
national hero: 3 Cid (El) 5 El Cid

nobleman: 7 grandee
operetta: 8 zarzuela
penal settlement: 8 presidio
plain: 5 llano, pampa
plantation: 8 hacienda
princess: 7 infanta
ranch: 5 finca 8 estancia
saint: 7 Dominic 8 Ignatius
scarf: 8 mantilla
shawl: 6 serape
title: 3 don 4 doña 5 señor 6 señora 8 señorita
wine: 4 sack 6 sherry

Spanish fly
9 cantharis

spank
4 cane, flog, lash, slap 5 smack 6 larrup, paddle, punish, thrash 7 scourge 8 chastise

spar
3 box, vie 4 pole 5 joust, stall 7 dispute, wrangle 8 longeron
ship's: 4 boom, gaff, mast, yard 7 yardarm 8 bowsprit

spare
4 lank, lean, pity, save, slim 5 avoid, extra, gaunt, lanky 6 backup, excess, excuse, exempt, let off, meager, meagre, pardon, scanty, scrape, scrimp, skimpy, skinny, slight, unused 7 absolve, relieve, reserve, scrawny, scrimpy, surplus 8 leftover 10 additional 11 superfluous

sparing
4 bare, wary 5 canny, chary, tight 6 frugal, meager, meagre, saving, stingy 7 prudent, thrifty 9 provident 10 economical, restrained, unwasteful 11 tightfisted 12 parsimonious

spark
3 woo 5 court, ember, glint 6 foment, incite, kindle, set off 7 provoke, trigger 8 activate, touch off 9 instigate, scintilla

sparkle
4 zing 5 flash, gleam, glint, verve 7 glimmer, glisten, glitter, shimmer,

twinkle **8** vivacity **9** animation, coruscate **10** effervesce, liveliness **11** coruscation, scintillate **13** scintillation

sparkling
6 bubbly, lively **8** animated, bubbling **9** brilliant **12** effervescent

Spark novel
11 Memento Mori **21** Prime of Miss Jean Brodie (The)

sparse
4 rare, thin **5** scant **6** meager, meagre, scanty, scarce, skimpy **7** limited, scrimpy **8** exiguous, sporadic, uncommon **9** dispersed, scattered **10** inadequate, infrequent, occasional **12** insufficient

Sparta
10 Lacedaemon
country: **7** Laconia
king: **8** Leonidas
opponent: **6** Athens

Spartacus
author: **4** Fast (Howard)
slayer: **7** Crassus

spasm
3 fit, tic **4** pang **5** burst, crick, throe **6** twitch **8** paroxysm **10** convulsion
muscular: **6** clonus

spasmodic
5 jerky **6** fitful, spotty **7** erratic **8** sporadic **9** desultory, excitable **10** convulsive **12** intermittent

spat
3 row **4** flap, miff, tiff **5** fight, scene, scrap **6** bicker, gaiter, hassle, oyster **7** brabble, dispute, fall out, quarrel, rhubarb, wrangle **8** argument, outburst, squabble **10** falling-out **11** altercation

spate
4 flow, flux, gush, pour, rain, rush, tide **5** flood, river, spurt, surge **6** deluge, series, shower, stream **7** current, freshet, torrent **8** cataract, outburst, overflow **10** inundation, outpouring

spatter
4 slop, slur, spit **5** douse, fleck, plash, slosh, smear, spray, spurt, swash **6** befoul, defame, malign, splash, splosh, vilify **7** asperse, blacken, handful, slander, speckle, splurge, stipple, traduce **8** besmirch, sprinkle **9** denigrate, disparage

spawn
4 eggs, sire **5** beget, breed, brood, hatch, issue **6** create, father, parent **7** produce, product, progeny, provoke **8** engender, generate **9** offspring, originate, procreate, propagate, reproduce, stimulate

speak
3 gab, jaw, say, yak **4** blab, chat, chin, talk **5** blurt, drawl, mouth, orate, spiel, spout, utter, voice **6** assert, convey, intone, mumble, murmur, mutter, parley **7** address, declaim, declare, lecture, phonate, whisper **8** converse, dilate on, perorate, vocalize **9** discourse, enunciate, expatiate, hold forth, verbalize
confusedly: **7** stammer, stutter **8** splutter
for: **7** testify

speaker
5 voice **9** spokesman **10** mouthpiece **12** spokesperson

spear
3 gig **4** pike, spit **5** gouge, lance, spike **6** impale, pierce, skewer **7** harpoon, leister, trident **8** puncture, transfix **9** penetrate

special
4 rare **6** unique **7** express, notable, unusual **8** peculiar, uncommon **10** designated, individual, noteworthy, particular **11** distinctive, exceptional, outstanding

species
4 kind, sort, type **5** breed, class, order

specific
3 set **5** exact **6** strict, unique **7** express, limited, precise, special

8 clean-cut, clear-cut, definite, distinct, especial, explicit 10 individual, particular 11 categorical, unambiguous

specify
3 fix, set 4 cite, list, name 6 detail 7 itemize, mention, pin down, tick off 8 instance, spell out 9 determine, enumerate, establish, inventory, stipulate 13 particularize

specimen
4 case, sort, type 6 sample 7 example, neotype, variety 8 exemplar, holotype, instance, sampling 12 illustration

specious
5 empty, false 6 hollow 8 spurious 9 casuistic, plausible, sophistic 10 misleading, ostensible 11 sophistical

speciousness
7 sophism 9 casuistry, sophistry

speck
3 bit, dot, jot 4 atom, iota, mite, mote, spot, tick, whit 5 crumb, fleck, grain, point, shred, trace 7 freckle, smidgen 8 molecule, particle, pinpoint

speckle
3 dot 4 spot 5 flake, fleck 6 dapple, pepper 7 stipple 8 sprinkle

spectacle
4 pomp, show 5 drama, sight 6 parade 7 display, pageant, panoply, tableau 10 exhibition, exposition 12 extravaganza

spectacular
5 stagy 7 amazing, pageant 8 dazzling, dramatic, striking, wondrous 9 marvelous, thrilling, wonderful 10 astounding, eye-popping, histrionic, miraculous, phenomenal, prodigious, staggering, stupefying, stupendous, theatrical 11 astonishing, sensational 12 extravaganza

spectator
5 gazer 6 viewer 7 watcher, witness 8 beholder, observer, onlooker 9 bystander 10 eyewitness

Spectator author
6 Steele (Richard) 7 Addison (Joseph)

specter
5 ghost, shade 6 shadow, spirit, wraith 7 eidolon, phantom 8 phantasm, revenant, visitant 10 apparition

spectral
6 spooky 7 ghastly, ghostly, phantom 9 ghostlike, unearthly 10 shadowlike 11 disembodied, phantomlike

spectrum
5 ambit, gamut, range, scale, sweep 7 compass 8 diapason 9 continuum

speculate
4 muse 5 study, think, weigh 6 ponder, reason, review, wonder 7 reflect 8 cogitate, consider, meditate, ruminate, theorize 9 cerebrate 10 conjecture, deliberate 11 contemplate

speculation
5 guess, hunch 6 gamble, review, theory 7 surmise 9 brainwork 10 conjecture

speculative
7 curious, pensive 8 academic 10 thoughtful 11 conjectural, theoretical 12 hypothetical

speech
4 talk 5 idiom, spiel, voice 6 debate, homily, parley, sermon, tirade, tongue 7 address, dialect, diction, lecture, oration, palaver 8 dialogue, diatribe, harangue, language, parlance, rhetoric 9 discourse, monologue, utterance 10 allocution, expression, vernacular 11 declamation 12 articulation, disquisition, vocalization 13 verbalization
defect: 4 lisp 7 stutter

speechcraft
7 oratory 8 rhetoric 9 elocution

speechless
3 mum 4 dumb, mute 6 silent 7 aphonic 10 dumbstruck, tongue-tied

speed

3 fly, run, zip **4** clip, gait, pace, race, rush, tear, whiz **5** chase, haste, hurry, tempo **6** barrel, burn up, career, hasten, hustle, whoosh **7** quicken **8** alacrity, celerity, dispatch, expedite, highball, legerity, momentum, rapidity, velocity **9** fleetness, quickness, swiftness **10** accelerate, cannonball, facilitate, promptness

speedway

5 track **8** turnpike **9** racetrack **10** racecourse

speedy

4 fast **5** brisk, fleet, hasty, quick, rapid, swift **6** nimble, prompt **8** headlong **9** breakneck **11** expeditious

spell

3 hex **4** bout, jinx, mojo, time, tour, turn **5** charm, hitch, shift, stint, throe, while **6** attack, period, streak, voodoo **7** relieve, stretch **11** conjuration, incantation

spellbind

3 hex **4** grip, vamp **5** charm **7** bewitch, catch up, enchant **8** enthrall, entrance **9** enrapture, fascinate, hypnotize, mesmerize

spelling

11 orthography
bad: 10 cacography

spell out

7 clarify, explain, expound **8** construe, set forth **9** elucidate, explicate, interpret

spend

3 pay **4** blow, drop, pass **5** use up, waste **6** lavish, lay out, outlay **7** consume, exhaust, fork out, hand out, splurge **8** disburse, shell out, squander **9** dissipate, go through, throw away, while away **10** contribute, run through

spender

7 wastrel **8** prodigal **10** high roller, profligate, squanderer **11** scattergood

spendthrift

see **spender**

spent

4 shot **5** all in **6** effete, pooped, used-up, wasted **7** drained, worn-out **8** burnt out, consumed, depleted, washed-up **9** exhausted, washed-out

spew

4 gush, ooze **5** belch, eject, eruct, erupt, expel, exude, flood, heave, shoot, spray, vomit **6** irrupt, spit up, squirt **7** throw up, upchuck **8** disgorge

sphagnum

4 moss

sphere

3 orb **4** area, ball, star, turf, zone **5** arena, field, globe, range, realm, round, scope **6** circle, domain, planet **7** demesne, rondure, terrain **8** dominion, province **9** bailiwick, territory **12** jurisdiction

spherical

5 round **6** global **7** globose **8** globular **9** orbicular

Sphinx

builder: 6 Khafre
father: 6 Typhon
mother: 7 Echidna
query: 6 riddle
site: 4 Giza **6** Thebes

spice

3 pep, zip **4** kick, mace, tang, zest **5** anise, aroma, clove, cumin, poppy, savor, scent, smack, smell, taste **6** cloves, fennel, ginger, nutmeg, pepper, relish, sesame **7** bouquet, caraway, perfume **8** cardamom, cinnamon, piquancy **9** fragrance, redolence, seasoning

Spice Islands

8 Moluccas

spick-and-span

3 new **4** mint, neat, snug, tidy, trig, trim **5** clean, fresh **6** spruce **7** orderly **8** brand-new, spotless **9** shipshape **10** immaculate **11** wellgroomed

spicy

3 hot **4** racy **5** bawdy, fiery, salty, tangy, zesty **6** lively, purple, ribald, risqué, savory, snappy, wicked **7** gingery, peppery, piquant, pungent, scented, zestful **8** aromatic, fragrant, off-color, perfumed, redolent, seasoned, spirited **9** flavorful, salacious **10** scandalous, suggestive **11** titillating

spider

6 frypan **7** skillet **8** arachnid **9** frying pan **10** black widow

spiel

4 jive, line **5** pitch **6** patter **12** song and dance

spieler

4 tout **6** barker, hawker, talker **8** huckster

spigot

3 tap **4** cock, gate **5** valve **6** faucet **7** hydrant, petcock, shutoff **8** stopcock

spike

3 pin **4** heel, nail **5** lance, piton, spear **6** antler, impale, needle, skewer **7** spindle **8** increase, mackerel, puncture, transfix

spile

4 bung **5** spout

spill

4 blab, drip, drop, fall, flow, slop, tell **5** spray **6** betray, inform, reveal, splash, squeal, tattle **7** divulge, dribble, run over, spatter **8** disclose, overflow

Spillane detective

10 Mike Hammer

spilth

5 dregs, dross, swill, trash, waste **6** debris, refuse, scraps **7** garbage, rubbish **8** leavings

spin

4 gyre, reel, ride, swim, turn **5** dizzy, swirl, twirl, wheel, whirl **6** gyrate, rotate **7** revolve **8** rotation **9** pirouette, whirligig **10** revolution
a log: 4 birl

spin

out: 4 draw **6** extend **7** prolong, stretch **8** elongate, lengthen, protract **10** prolongate

spinal column

5 chine **6** rachis
curvature: 8 lordosis
part: 8 vertebra
(see also **spine**)

spindle

3 pin, rod **5** newel, shaft, spike **6** impale, rachis

spindly

5 frail, lanky, rangy, shaky, weedy **6** flimsy, gangly, skinny, twiggy, wobbly **7** fragile, rickety, tottery **8** gangling, skeletal, unsteady **9** emaciated **10** jerry-built

spine

4 back **6** rachis **7** spicule **8** backbone **9** vertebrae

spineless

5 timid **8** cowardly, timorous **9** weak-kneed **10** weak-willed **12** invertebrate

spin-off

8 offshoot **9** by-product, outgrowth **10** derivative, descendant

———— Spinoza

6 Baruch

spinster

7 old maid **10** maiden lady

spiny

6 barbed, thorny **7** prickly **8** echinate **10** nettlesome

spiral

4 coil, curl, wind **5** helix, twine, twist **6** volute **7** helical, helices (plural) **8** gyroidal, volution **9** cochleate, corkscrew
combining form: 3 gyr **4** gyro **5** helic **6** helico

spire

4 coil **5** twist, whorl **7** steeple **8** pinnacle

spirit

3 pep, vim, zip **4** brio, dash, élan, gimp, grit, guts, life, mood, snap, soul, zeal, zest, zing **5** anima, ardor, drive, force, heart, moxie, oomph, pluck, shade, spunk, tenor, verve, vigor **6** animus, daimon, energy, esprit, fervor, ginger, mettle, morale, pneuma, psyche, starch, temper, wraith **7** passion, phantom, specter, spectre **8** phantasm, revenant, vitality **9** animation, élan vital, substance **10** apparition, enthusiasm, get-up-and-go, liveliness

away: 6 abduct, kidnap, snatch
evil: 5 afrit, demon **6** afreet **7** erlking, shaitan
female: 5 nymph **7** banshee
Hopi: 7 kachina
Persian: 4 peri

spirited
4 bold, game, keen **5** eager, fiery, peppy **6** ardent, gritty, lively, plucky, spunky **7** chipper, fervent, gingery, peppery, valiant, zealous **8** animated, cheerful, intrepid, resolute **9** audacious, dauntless, energetic, sprightly, vivacious **10** courageous, mettlesome, passionate **12** enthusiastic

spirits
5 booze, drink **6** liquor, tipple **9** aqua vitae, firewater
low: 5 blues, dumps, ennui **8** doldrums **10** blue devils, depression, melancholy

spiritual
6 sacred **7** saintly **8** churchly, mystical, numinous, platonic **9** religious **10** high-minded, immaterial, unphysical **11** disembodied, incorporeal, nonmaterial, nonphysical **12** metaphysical, supernatural, transcendent

spiritualist
6 medium, mystic **7** psychic

spit
5 spear **6** impale, saliva, skewer, slaver, sputum **7** spatter, sputter **8** splutter **9** brochette **11** expectorate

spite
5 venom **6** grudge, malice, rancor,

spleen **7** ill will, revenge **9** pettiness, vengeance **11** malevolence **13** maliciousness

spiteful
4 mean **5** catty, nasty, snide **6** malign, wicked **7** vicious, waspish **8** venomous **9** malicious, malignant, rancorous **10** malevolent, vindictive

spitfire
4 fury **5** harpy, shrew, vixen **6** dragon, virago **7** hellcat, tigress **8** fishwife, harridan **9** termagant

spitting image
4 twin **5** clone **6** double, ringer **9** duplicate **10** carbon copy, dead ringer, simulacrum

spittoon
8 cuspidor

splash
3 sop, wet **4** slop, soak **5** douse, slosh, spray, swash **6** drench **7** spatter **8** sprinkle

splashy
5 gaudy, jazzy, showy **6** flashy, garish, glitzy, tawdry **7** blatant, dashing **8** colorful, dazzling, striking **10** flamboyant, theatrical **11** sensational **12** meretricious, ostentatious

splatter
4 slop **5** douse, plash, slosh, spray, swash **6** splash **8** sprinkle

splay
4 cant, tilt **5** angle, bevel, gawky, slant, slope **6** clumsy, extend, spread **7** awkward, incline **8** ungainly **9** expansion **11** inclination

spleen
see **spite**

splendid
4 fine **5** grand, showy **6** superb **7** shining **8** glorious, gorgeous **9** brilliant, excellent, marvelous, wonderful **10** first-class, impressive **11** illustrious, magnificent, outstanding **12** transcendent

splendor
4 pomp 5 glory 6 dazzle 7 panoply
8 grandeur, richness 9 pageantry,
spectacle 10 brilliance, brilliancy
12 magnificence

splenetic
5 cross, surly 6 fuming 8 incensed,
spiteful 9 malicious 10 ill-natured,
malevolent 11 ill-tempered

splice
3 tie 4 join, mate, mesh 5 braid,
graft, plait, unite

splint
5 brace, strip 7 support 10 immobilize

splinter
4 rive 5 burst, smash 6 shiver, sliver
7 faction, shatter 8 fragment 12 disintegrate

split
3 rip 4 part, rend, rent, rift, rima,
rime, rive, tear 5 break, carve,
chasm, chink, cleft, crack, sever,
slice 6 breach, cleave, cloven,
divide, schism, sunder 7 break up,
disjoin, dissect, diverge, divorce,
divvy up, fission, fissure, rupture
8 cleavage, dissever, fracture,
separate 11 dichotomize
combining form: 5 schiz 6 schizo
7 schisto

splotch
4 blob, blot, spot 5 fleck, stain
6 smudge

splurge
4 orgy 5 binge, fling, spree 7 blowout, rampage 10 indulgence 12 extravagance

splutter
4 spit 6 babble, jabber 7 stammer

spoil
3 mar, rob, rot 4 baby, harm, prey,
ruin, sack 5 decay, humor, taint,
waste, wreck 6 coddle, cosset,
curdle, damage, defile, impair,
molder, pamper, ravish 7 blemish,
cater to, destroy, indulge, pillage,

putrefy, tarnish, vitiate 8 demolish
9 break down, decompose 11 mollycoddle

spoiled
4 rank, sour 6 putrid, rancid, rotten,
ruined 7 coddled, decayed 8 impaired, indulged, pampered 9 indulgent

spoils
4 haul, loot, swag 5 booty 7 pillage,
plunder

spoilsport
7 killjoy

spoken
4 oral, said, told 6 verbal, voiced
7 uttered 8 phonetic, viva voce
9 delivered, unwritten 11 articulated

sponge
4 grub 5 cadge, leech, mooch
7 moocher 8 freeload, parasite,
scrounge 10 freeloader
material: 8 mesoglea
opening: 6 oscula (plural) 7 oscu-
lum, ostiole

sponger
5 leech 7 moocher 8 parasite
10 freeloader

spongy
4 soft 5 mushy, pulpy 6 porous,
quaggy 7 squashy, squishy 9 absorbent

sponsor
4 back, fund 5 angel, stake 6 backer,
patron, surety 7 endorse, finance
8 advocate, bankroll, champion,
Maecenas, mainstay, promoter,
vouch for 9 grubstake, guarantee,
guarantor, patronize, subsidize,
supporter 10 benefactor, underwrite
11 underwriter

sponsorship
5 aegis 7 backing, support 8 advocacy, auspices 9 patronage

spontaneous
5 ad-lib 7 natural, offhand 8 ad-
libbed, unforced 9 automatic, extempore, impromptu, impulsive,

unstudied **10** improvised, off-the-cuff, unprompted **11** instinctive, unmeditated **13** unconstrained

spontoon
4 pike **5** lance, spear

spoof
4 sham **5** farce, put-on **6** parody, satire, send-up **7** lampoon, takeoff **8** travesty

spook
3 spy **5** agent, alarm, ghost, haunt, scare **7** specter, spectre, startle, terrify **8** frighten

spooky
5 eerie, weird **6** creepy **7** ghostly, ominous, uncanny **9** unearthly

spool
4 wind **6** bobbin

spoon
3 pet, woo **4** neck **5** court, ladle, scoop **6** cuddle

spoonbill
4 ibis **8** shoveler **9** ruddy duck **10** paddlefish

Spoon River poet
7 Masters (Edgar Lee)

spoony
5 mushy, silly **6** simple, slushy, syrupy **7** fatuous, foolish, mawkish, smitten, witless **9** schmaltzy **10** saccharine **11** sentimental

spoor
5 scent, trace, track, tract, trail **7** vestige **8** footstep **9** droppings, footprint

sporadic
4 rare **6** catchy, fitful, random, scarce, sparse, spotty **7** erratic **8** episodic, isolated, uncommon **9** desultory, irregular, scattered, spasmodic **10** infrequent, occasional

sport
3 fun **4** game, jest, joke, mock, play **6** frolic, racing, trifle **7** mockery, show off **9** diversion, high jinks, horseplay **10** recreation

indoor: 6 boxing, hockey, squash **7** bowling **8** handball **9** wrestling **10** acrobatics, basketball, gymnastics **11** racquetball, table tennis
Olympic: 4 judo **6** boxing, diving, hockey, rowing **7** archery, cycling, fencing, shot put **8** canoeing, football, high jump, long jump, marathon, shooting, swimming, yachting **9** decathlon, pole vault, water polo, wrestling **10** basketball, gymnastics, pentathlon, triple jump, volleyball **11** discus throw, hammer throw **12** javelin throw, steeplechase **13** weightlifting
water: 6 diving, rowing **7** sailing, surfing **8** canoeing, swimming, yachting
winter: 4 luge **6** hockey, skiing **7** curling, lugeing, skating **8** biathlon, sledding **10** ski jumping **11** bobsledding, tobogganing

sporting house
6 bagnio **7** brothel **8** bordello

sportive
5 antic **6** frisky, impish **7** playful, roguish, waggish **10** frolicsome **11** mischievous

sportiveness
7 devilry, roguery, waggery **8** deviltry, mischief **9** devilment, rascality

sporty
4 fast **5** peppy **6** breezy, casual, jaunty, lively **7** dashing, relaxed **8** debonair, informal **10** insouciant **11** streamlined

spot
3 fix, jam, nip, see **4** espy, post, site **5** fleck, hit on, locus, place, point, speck **6** blotch, detect, pickle, plight, scrape **7** dilemma, smidgen, spatter, speckle **8** diagnose, flyspeck, identify, location, pinpoint, position **9** recognize, situation **11** predicament

spotless
4 pure **5** clean **6** chaste **8** hygienic, sanitary, unsoiled **9** undefiled, unstained, unsullied **10** immaculate **11** unblemished

spotlight
5 focus 6 notice 7 feature, point up 8 interest, point out 9 attention, emphasize, public eye, publicity 10 illuminate 12 illumination

spotted
4 seen 6 motley 7 brindle, dappled, piebald 8 brindled, speckled, stippled

spouse
4 mate, wife 5 bride, groom, hubby 7 consort, husband

spout
3 jet 4 gush 5 chute, eject, spray, spurt 6 nozzle, squirt

sprain
4 pull, tear, turn 5 twist 6 wrench 7 stretch

sprawl
4 flop, loll 5 drape, slump 6 extend, lounge, slouch, spread 7 stretch 11 spread-eagle

spray
3 fog 4 hose, mist 6 shower, spritz 7 aerosol, atomize, diffuse, spatter 8 atomizer, droplets, fumigate, nebulize 9 spindrift

spread
3 jam, lay, set, sow 4 deal, oleo, open, pâté, push 5 apply, feast, jelly, space, splay, strew, sweep 6 butter, expand, extend, fan out, pass on, retail 7 banquet, breadth, diffuse, expanse, overrun, pervade, radiate, scatter, slather, stretch, suffuse 8 bedcover, coverlet, dispense, disperse, mushroom, permeate 9 amplitude, broadcast, circulate, diffusion, dissipate, expansion, extension, profusion, propagate, radiation 10 dispersion, distribute, outstretch 11 counterpane, disseminate 12 transmission 13 proliferation

spree
3 jag 4 bash, bust, lark, orgy, riot, tear 5 binge, drunk, fling, revel 6 bender, frolic 7 blowout, carouse, rampage, splurge 8 carousal, wingding 10 indulgence 11 bacchanalia

sprig
4 brad, heir, twig 5 scion, shoot 7 pintail 9 ruddy duck

sprightly
3 gay 4 keen, spry, yare 5 agile, alert, antic, brisk, peppy, perky, zesty, zingy, zippy 6 active, breezy, chirpy, frisky, jaunty, lively, nimble 7 animate, chipper, coltish, piquant, playful, pungent 8 animated, cheerful, spirited, sportive 9 energetic, vivacious 10 frolicsome, rollicking 13 scintillating

spring
3 hop 4 flow, jump, leap, lope, rise, root, skip, stem, trip, well 5 arise, begin, bound, cause, fount, issue, start 6 appear, bounce, emerge, hurdle, reason, source, uncoil, vernal 7 come out, emanate, proceed, rebound, startle 8 commence, fountain, stimulus, wellhead 9 originate 10 incitement, resilience 12 fountainhead
back: 6 resile

springe
4 trap 5 noose, snare 7 pitfall 9 booby trap

springlike
6 vernal

springy
6 supple 7 elastic 8 flexible, stretchy 9 recoiling, resilient

sprinkle
3 dot 4 rain, spot 5 shake, speck, spray, strew 6 pepper, powder, spritz 7 asperse, drizzle, freckle, scatter, speckle, stipple 9 bespeckle

sprint
3 run 4 dart, dash, race, shin, tear 5 scoot 6 gallop, hurtle, scurry 7 scamper

sprite
3 elf, fay, nix 4 puck 5 dryad, fairy, naiad, nixie, nymph, pixie, sylph 6 kelpie 7 brownie 9 hamadryad

spritz
3 jet 5 spray, spurt 6 shower, squirt

sprout
3 bud 4 grow 5 scion, shoot 6 ratoon, sucker 7 burgeon 8 offshoot 9 germinate

spruce
4 trim 5 natty, sassy, spiff 6 dapper, spiffy 11 well-groomed

spry
4 yare 5 agile, brisk, sound, zesty, zippy 6 active, lively, nimble, robust 7 healthy 8 animated, spirited, vigorous 9 energetic, vivacious

spud
6 potato

_____ Spumante
4 Asti

spume
4 fizz, foam, head, scum, suds 5 froth, spray, yeast 6 lather

spunk
4 grit, guts 5 heart, moxie, nerve, pluck 6 mettle, spirit, tinder 7 cojones, courage 8 backbone, gumption 9 fortitude, toughness 10 liveliness, resolution

spunky
4 bold 5 brave, fiery 6 daring 7 doughty, gingery, peppery 8 fearless, spirited 9 dauntless 10 courageous, mettlesome 12 high-spirited

spur
4 goad, prod, stir, urge 5 egg on, impel, prick, rally, rouse, spine 6 arouse, branch, exhort, motive, prompt, propel 7 impetus, impulse 8 buttress, catalyst, excitant, stimulus 9 actuation, incentive, instigate, stimulant, stimulate 10 incitement, inducement, motivation, projection
part: 5 rowel

spurious
4 fake, mock, sham 5 bogus, dummy, false, phony, put-on 6 ersatz, pseudo 7 assumed, feigned, pretend 8 affected 9 brummagem, imitation, pinchbeck, pretended, simulated 10 apocryphal, artificial, substitute 11 counterfeit, make-believe 12 illegitimate
combining form: 5 pseud 6 pseudo

spurn
4 snub 5 flout, scoff, scorn, scout, sneer 6 rebuff, refuse, reject 7 contemn, decline, despise, disdain, dismiss, repulse 8 turn down 9 disregard, reprobate, repudiate 10 disapprove 12 cold-shoulder

spurt
3 jet 4 gush, jump 5 burst, expel, spout, surge 6 shower, spritz, squirt 7 upsurge 8 eruption, increase 9 discharge

sputter
4 fizz, fume, rage, rant, rave, spew, spit 6 gibber, jabber 7 bluster, stammer

spy
5 agent, scout, snoop, spook 6 beagle, sleuth 7 gumshoe 8 informer, saboteur 9 detective 12 investigator 13 undercover man
name: 4 Ames (Aldrich), Boyd (Belle), Hari (Mata) 5 André (John), Blunt (Anthony), Fuchs (Klaus) 6 Philby (Kim), Smiley (George) 7 Burgess (Guy), Hanssen (Robert), Maclean (Donald), Pollard (Jonathan)

spyglass
9 telescope

spying
9 espionage

Spyri's heroine
5 Heidi

squab
5 couch 6 pigeon 7 cushion

squabble
see **spat**

squalid
3 low 4 base, foul, mean, vile 5 dingy, dirty, nasty, seedy 6 filthy, frowsy, frowzy, grubby, scurvy,

shabby, shoddy, sleazy, sordid
7 ignoble, low-down, run-down, scrubby, unclean, unkempt **8** slovenly, wretched **10** despicable, disheveled **11** dilapidated **12** disreputable

squall

3 caw, row, yap, yip **4** bark, bawl, beef, feud, fuss, gust, howl, roar, tiff, wail, yawp, yell, yelp, yowl **5** brawl, fight, hoo-ha, shout **6** bellow, clamor, flurry, fracas, hubbub, ruckus, rumpus, scream, shriek, squeal, yammer **7** dispute, flare-up, quarrel, rhubarb, screech **8** brouhaha, squabble **9** bickering, caterwaul, commotion **10** falling-out, hullabaloo **11** altercation

squalor

5 filth **6** misery **7** neglect, poverty **8** baseness, iniquity **9** depravity, dirtiness **10** sordidness **11** degradation **12** wretchedness

squander

4 blow **5** spend, waste **7** consume, exhaust, fritter, scatter **9** dissipate, throw away **10** trifle away **11** fritter away

squanderer

see **spender**

square

3 fit, fix **4** bang, boxy, even, fair, jibe, just, tied **5** adapt, agree, align, clear, equal, exact, fit in, match, pay up, plaza, right, sharp, spang, tally **6** accord, adjust, settle **7** balance, conform, exactly, satisfy, settled **8** check out, coincide, dovetail, orthodox, quadrate, smack-dab, straight, unbiased **9** discharge, equitable, harmonize, impartial, liquidate, objective, precisely, quadratic, reconcile, rectangle **10** accurately, correspond

squash

3 jam **4** cram, mash, pepo, pulp **5** crush, gourd, press, quell **7** flatten, put down, squeeze, squelch **8** suppress

variety: 5 acorn **6** cushaw, Sibley, turban **7** Hubbard, scallop **8** pattypan, zucchini **9** butternut, crookneck **10** Marblehead

squat

3 low **5** dumpy, hunch, stoop, stout, thick **6** chunky, crouch, hunker, stocky, stubby **8** heavyset, thickset **10** hunker down **11** thick-bodied

squawfish

4 chub **8** cyprinid **10** pikeminnow

squawk

3 caw, yap, yip **4** beef, crab, fuss, yawp **5** bleat, gripe **6** yammer **7** protest, screech **8** complain **9** bellyache, complaint

squeak

3 rat **4** blab, fink, peep, pipe, sing **5** cheep, creak **6** escape, inform, snitch, tattle **10** tattletale

squeal

3 rat, yip **4** blab, howl, sing, yell, yelp, yowl **5** bleat, creak, grate, gripe, peach **6** inform, screak, scream, shriek, shrill, snitch, squawk, tattle **7** protest, screech **8** complain **10** tattletale

squealer

3 rat **4** fink **6** canary, snitch, weasel **7** ratfink, stoolie, tattler, tipster **8** betrayer, informer **10** talebearer, tattletale **11** stool pigeon

squeamish

5 fussy, upset **6** queasy **7** finical, finicky **8** nauseous **9** nauseated **10** fastidious, particular, pernickety **11** persnickety

squeeze

3 hug, jam **4** bind, cram, grip, milk, pack, push **5** clasp, crowd, crush, exact, gouge, juice, pinch, press, screw, wring **6** clutch, coerce, compel, crunch, eke out, enfold, extort, jostle, squash, squish **7** dilemma, embrace, extract **8** compress, contract, pressure, quandary **9** shake down **11** compression, predicament

squelch
5 quell, shush, sit on 6 muffle, muzzle, squash, squish, stifle, subdue 7 repress, silence, smother 8 strangle, suppress 10 extinguish

squib
4 fire 6 filler 7 lampoon 8 shoot off 9 detonator 11 firecracker

squid
7 mollusc, mollusk 8 calamari, calamary 10 cephalopod
kin: 7 octopus 10 cuttlefish

squiggle
4 worm 6 doodle, scrawl, squirm, writhe 7 scratch 8 curlicue, scrabble, scribble

squinch
5 quail, start, wince 6 blench, crouch, recoil, shrink

squint
4 peek, peep, peer 10 hagioscope, strabismus

squire
6 attend, escort, lawyer 7 consort, gallant 8 cavalier, chaperon 9 accompany, landowner

squirm
4 worm 6 fidget, wiggle, writhe 7 wriggle

squirrel
4 stow 5 cache, hoard, stash 7 secrete
red: 9 chickaree

squirt
3 jet, kid, pup, tot 4 brat, tyke 5 sprat, spray, spurt, twerp 6 shaver, shrimp, splurt, spritz 7 spatter

squish
3 jam 4 cram, mash, mush, pack, push 5 crush, press, quash, smash 7 flatten, scrunch, squeeze, squelch, trample

squishy
4 soft 6 flabby, quaggy, slushy, spongy

Sri Lanka
bay: 6 Bengal

capital: 7 Colombo
city: 8 Moratuwa
ethnic group: 9 Sinhalese
former name: 6 Ceylon
language: 5 Tamil 9 Sinhalese
monetary unit: 5 rupee
shoals: 11 Adam's Bridge
strait: 4 Palk

SRO
7 sellout

SS chief
7 Himmler (Heinrich)

S-shaped
7 sigmoid

stab
3 dig, pop, try 4 pang, poke, shot 5 crack, drive, fling, prick, spear, stick, whack, whirl 6 effort, pierce, thrust, twinge 7 attempt 8 puncture 9 penetrate

Stabat _____
5 Mater

stabile
6 steady 9 sculpture 10 stationary

stabilize
3 fix, set 4 prop 5 brace, poise 6 cement, firm up, fixate, prop up, secure, settle, steady 7 balance, ballast, support, sustain 8 solidify 9 reinforce

stable
3 set 4 barn, fast, firm, mews, safe, sure 5 fixed, solid, sound 6 secure, steady, sturdy 7 abiding, durable, lasting, staunch 8 balanced, constant, enduring, resolute 9 immutable, permanent, steadfast, unvarying 10 perdurable, stationary, unchanging, unshakable

stack
4 cock, heap, hill, load, mass, pile, pipe 5 mound, sheaf 7 chimney, pyramid

stack up
3 add 5 equal, total 6 equate, gather 7 compare, measure

stadium
4 bowl, rink, ring 5 arena 6 garden
8 coliseum 10 hippodrome 12 amphitheater

staff
3 rod 4 club, prop, rung, team, wand
5 baton, billy 6 cudgel 7 faculty,
support 9 personnel
bishop's: 7 crosier, crozier
medical: 8 caduceus

stage
3 lot 4 play, rung, show, step 5 grade,
level, mount, notch, phase, put on
6 degree, period, status 7 execute,
perform, present, produce
direction: 4 exit 5 enter 6 exeunt
scenery: 3 set 8 backdrop
show: 4 play 5 drama, revue
7 musical 9 burlesque 10 vaudeville
signal: 3 cue
whisper: 5 aside

stage set
5 decor, scene 7 scenery 8 backdrop 11 mise-en-scène

stagger
4 daze, reel, stun, sway 5 amaze,
floor, lurch, pitch, stump, waver,
weave 6 boggle, careen, dither,
falter, teeter, topple, totter, wobble,
zigzag 7 astound, nonplus, perplex,
shatter, stumble, stupefy 8 astonish,
bowl over 9 dumbfound, overwhelm,
vacillate 11 flabbergast

stagnant
5 musty, stale 6 static 8 immobile,
unmoving 10 motionless, stationary

stagnate
4 idle 5 stall 6 fester 8 languish,
stultify, vegetate

stagy
10 artificial, histrionic, theatrical
11 pretentious 12 melodramatic

staid
5 grave, sober 6 formal, sedate,
solemn, somber, sombre, stuffy
7 earnest, serious, starchy 8 composed, decorous, priggish 9 dignified

stain
3 dye, tar 4 blot, daub, onus, slur,
soil, spot 5 brand, color, odium,
shame, smear, sully, taint, tinge
6 blotch, defile, embrue, imbrue,
smirch, smudge, stigma 7 blemish,
pigment, tarnish 8 besmirch, colorant, discolor, dishonor, dyestuff,
tincture

staircase
handrail: 8 banister
outdoor: 6 perron
post: 5 newel 8 baluster

stake
3 bet, lay, pot, set 4 ante, back,
game, pale, play, post, risk 5 claim,
put on, share, wager 6 gamble,
paling, picket, pledge, tether 7 finance 8 bankroll, interest 10 capitalize, investment

stalag
7 POW camp 10 prison camp

stale
5 banal, dusty, faded, fusty, moldy,
musty, passé, tired, trite 7 clichéd,
tedious, worn-out 8 overused,
shopworn, timeworn 9 hackneyed,
tasteless 11 commonplace, stereotyped

stalemate
3 tie 4 draw 7 impasse 8 deadlock,
gridlock, standoff

stalk
4 hunt, prey 5 chase, track 6 ambush, follow, pursue, stride 8 flush
out
flower: 8 peduncle
leaf: 7 petiole
short: 5 stipe

stall
3 bay, pew 4 halt 5 booth, brake,
check, delay, hedge, kiosk, stand
6 arrest, put off 7 conk out, counter,
hold off 8 obstruct 9 stonewall
10 filibuster 11 compartment, prevaricate

stalwart
4 bold 5 brave, gutsy, husky, stout,

stamen part

tough **6** brawny, robust, sinewy, strong, sturdy **7** valiant **8** fearless, intrepid, unafraid, valorous, vigorous **9** dauntless, tenacious, undaunted **10** courageous

stamen part

6 anther **8** filament

stamina

8 tenacity **9** endurance, fortitude, tolerance **11** persistence **12** staying power

stammer

6 gibber, jabber **7** sputter, stutter **8** hesitate, splutter

stamp

3 ilk, lot **4** etch, kind, mark, mint, mold, seal, sort, type **5** clomp, clump, pound, print, tromp **6** hammer, stripe **7** impress, imprint, trample **8** hallmark, inscribe **9** character **10** impression **12** characterize

stampede

4 bolt, dash, rout, rush, tear **5** crush, panic, rodeo **6** charge

stamps

7 postage

stance

4 pose **7** bearing, posture **8** attitude, carriage, position **10** deportment

stanch

4 stem, stop **5** check **6** stop up **8** hold back

stanchion

4 post, prop **5** brace **7** support

stand

4 bear **5** abide, booth, brook, kiosk, stall, treat **6** endure, handle, suffer **7** counter, stomach, swallow, weather **8** attitude, platform, position, tolerate
artist's: 5 easel
three-legged: 6 tripod, trivet
ornamental: 7 étagere

standard

3 law, par **4** flag, jack, mean, norm, rule **5** color, gauge, ideal, model, stock, usual **6** banner, belief, common, ensign, median, normal, pennon **7** average, classic, example, general, measure, pattern, pennant, regular, typical, uniform **8** accepted, everyday, exemplar, familiar, ordinary, orthodox, paradigm **9** archetype, benchmark, criterion, customary, principle, yardstick **10** definitive, prevailing, recognized, regulation, touchstone **11** established, fundamental

standardize

6 adjust **7** conform **8** regulate **9** reconcile

stand for

4 bear, mean **5** allow **6** denote, permit **7** signify **8** indicate, tolerate **9** put up with, represent, symbolize

stand-in

3 sub **5** proxy **6** backup, second **9** alternate, surrogate **10** substitute, understudy **11** pinch hitter, replacement **12** impersonator

standing

4 rank, term **5** erect, fixed, place **6** cachet, credit, repute, status **7** dignity, footing, station, stature, upright **8** capacity, duration, eminence, position, prestige, stagnant **9** character, permanent, situation **10** estimation, reputation **11** consequence, established

standoff

see **stalemate**

standoffish

5 aloof **6** chilly **7** distant, haughty **8** detached, reserved **9** reclusive, withdrawn **10** unfriendly, unsociable **12** misanthropic

stand out

3 jut **4** bulk, loom **5** bulge **7** project **8** protrude

standpatter

4 fogy, tory **7** diehard **8** mossback **11** bitter-ender **12** conservative

standpoint

4 side **5** angle, slant **7** outlook **9** direction **11** perspective

standstill
4 halt, stop 5 check, pause 7 impasse 8 deadlock, dead stop 9 cessation, stalemate

Stanford site
8 Palo Alto

Stanley Kowalski's wife
6 Stella

Stanleys' car
7 steamer

Stan's partner
5 Ollie

stanza
7 strophe
combining form: 5 stich
of eight lines: 6 octave
of four lines: 6 ballad 8 quatrain
of six lines: 6 sestet
of three lines: 6 tercet 7 triplet
Persian: 8 rubaiyat

star
4 icon, idol, lead, main, nova 5 actor, chief, major 6 étoile 7 actress, capital 8 asterisk, dominant, luminary 9 celebrity, headliner, principal 10 preeminent 11 outstanding
bright: 4 Vega 5 Deneb, Rigel, Spica 6 Altair, Pollux, Sirius 7 Antares, Canopus, Capella, Procyon 8 Arcturus 9 Aldebaran, Archernar, Fomalhaut 10 Beta Crucis, Betelgeuse 11 Alpha Crucis 12 Beta Centauri 13 Alpha Centauri
combining form: 4 astr 5 aster, astro 6 astero, sidero
five-pointed: 8 pentacle 9 pentagram
giant: 10 Betelgeuse
six-pointed: 8 hexagram

starch
3 pep 4 push, snap 5 drive, moxie, punch, spunk, vigor 7 stiffen 8 gumption, vitality 9 formality
combining form: 4 amyl 5 amylo

starchy
4 prim 5 aloof, stiff 6 doughy, formal, wooden 7 stilted

star-crossed
6 doomed 7 hapless, unlucky 8 ill-fated, luckless 10 ill-starred 11 unfortunate 12 misfortunate

Stardust composer
10 Carmichael (Hoagy)

stare
3 eye 4 gape, gawk, gaze, ogle, peer 6 goggle 10 rubberneck

stark
3 raw 4 bare, nude, pure 5 bleak, blunt, clear, harsh, naked, quite, rigid, sheer, utter 6 barren, strict, unclad, vacant, wholly 8 absolute, complete, desolate, stripped 9 au naturel, out-and-out 10 absolutely

starry
6 astral 7 stellar 8 sidereal

starry-eyed
6 dreamy, unreal 7 utopian 8 ecstatic 9 rapturous, visionary 11 impractical, unrealistic 13 impracticable

Star-Spangled Banner writer
3 Key (Francis Scott)

start
4 bolt, dawn, draw 5 arise, begin, crank, found, issue, onset, quail, react, set up, wince 6 blench, create, embark, flinch, launch, outset, recoil, shrink, spring, take up 7 actuate, genesis, infancy, kickoff, opening, trigger 8 activate, commence, embark on, initiate, organize, reaction 9 beginning, establish, institute, originate 10 inaugurate 12 commencement

startle
4 jolt, jump 5 alarm, scare, shock, spook 8 astonish, frighten, surprise

starved
6 hungry 8 famished, ravenous, underfed

stash
4 bury, hide 5 cache, hoard, plant, store 7 conceal, lay away, nest egg, secrete 8 lay aside, sock away, squirrel 9 stockpile

stasis

7 balance, inertia **9** equipoise **10** immobility, stagnation **11** equilibrium

state

3 air, put, say **4** aver, mode, rank, tell, vent **5** utter **6** affirm, assert, recite, relate, report **7** declare, dignity, explain, expound, express, posture, recount **8** attitude, capacity, describe, position, set forth, standing **9** condition, enunciate, situation, ventilate

subdivison: 6 county

state

easternmost: 5 Maine
largest: 6 Alaska
smallest: 11 Rhode Island
southernmost: 6 Hawaii

state abbreviation

Alabama: 3 Ala.
Alaska: 4 Alas.
Arizona: 4 Ariz.
Arkansas: 3 Ark.
California: 3 Cal. **5** Calif.
Colorado: 3 Col. **4** Colo.
Connecticut: 4 Conn.
Delaware: 3 Del.
Florida: 3 Fla.
Idaho: 3 Ida.
Illinois: 3 Ill.
Indiana: 3 Ind.
Kansas: 3 Kan. **4** Kans.
Kentucky: 3 Ken.
Massachusetts: 4 Mass.
Michigan: 4 Mich.
Minnesota: 4 Minn.
Mississippi: 4 Miss.
Montana: 4 Mont.
Nebraska: 3 Neb. **4** Nebr.
Nevada: 3 Nev.
New Mexico: 4 N. Mex.
North Carolina: 4 N. Car.
North Dakota: 4 N. Dak.
Oklahoma: 4 Okla.
Oregon: 3 Ore. **4** Oreg.
Pennsylvania: 4 Penn. **5** Penna.
South Carolina: 4 S. Car.
South Dakota: 4 S. Dak.
Tennessee: 4 Tenn.
Texas: 3 Tex.

Vermont: 4 Verm.
Virginia: 4 Virg.
Washington: 4 Wash.
West Virginia: 3 W. Va.
Wisconsin: 3 Wis. **4** Wisc.
Wyoming: 3 Wyo.

stately

5 grand, lofty, noble, regal, royal **6** august, formal, kingly, lordly, solemn **7** courtly, elegant, gallant, haughty **8** gracious, imperial, imposing, majestic, palatial, princely **9** dignified **10** ceremonial, impressive, monumental **11** ceremonious, magnificent

statement

3 tab **4** bill **5** score **6** avowal, charge, dictum, remark, report **7** account, comment, invoice, recital **8** averment **9** affidavit, assertion, manifesto, narrative, reckoning, testimony, utterance **10** deposition, expression **11** description

introductory: 7 preface **8** foreword, prologue

stateroom

5 cabin

statesman

10 politician
American: 3 Hay (John Milton) **4** Clay (Henry), Hull (Cordell), Otis (James), Root (Elihu) **5** Adams (Samuel), Henry (Patrick), Lodge (Henry Cabot), Vance (Cyrus) **6** Bunche (Ralph), Bunker (Ellsworth), Dulles (John Foster), Kennan (George F.), Morris (Gouverneur), Powell (Colin), Sumner (Charles) **7** Acheson (Dean), Hancock (John), Kellogg (Frank B.), Lansing (Robert), Sherman (John, Roger), Stimson (Henry L.), Webster (Daniel) **8** Franklin (Benjamin), Hamilton (Alexander), Harriman (Averell), Pinckney (Charles, Thomas), Randolph (Edmund Jennings, John, Payton), Rutledge (John), Trumbull (Jonathan, Joseph) **9** Kissinger (Henry), Stevenson (Adlai) **10** Stettinius (Edward Reilly)

Australian: 9 Wentworth (William Charles)

Austrian: 6 Renner (Karl) 7 Kaunitz (Wenzel von) 8 Dollfuss (Engelbert) 10 Metternich (Klemens von) 13 Schwarzenberg (Felix zu)

Canadian: 4 King (W. L. Mackenzie) 7 Laurier (Wilfrid) 8 Thompson (John Sparrow) 9 Macdonald (John Alexander, John Sandfield), Mackenzie (Alexander, William Lyon)

Chinese: 3 Yen (Hsishan) 4 Deng (Xiaoping), Kung (Hsiang-hsi), Teng (Hsiao-p'ing), Wang (Anshih, Chingwei), Yuan (Shih-kai) 9 Sun Yat-Sen

Dutch: 6 de Witt (Johan de) 7 Grotius (Hugo), Stikker (Dirk)

East German: 8 Ulbricht (Walter)

English: 3 Fox (Charles, Henry) 4 Eden (Anthony, George, William), More (Thomas), Peel (Arthur, Robert, William), Pitt (William), Vane (Henry) 5 Cecil (Robert, William), North (Francis, Frederick, Roger) 6 Morley (John), Sidney (Algernon, Henry, Philip, Robert), Temple (Henry, William), Wolsey (Thomas) 7 Halifax (Earl of), Reading (Marquis of), Russell (John, William), Stanley (Edward George, Edward Henry), Stewart (Robert), Warwick (Earl of) 8 Cromwell (Oliver, Thomas), Disraeli (Benjamin), Robinson (George Frederick Samuel), Villiers (George) 9 Cavendish (Spencer, William), Churchill (Randolph, Winston), Gladstone (William), Salisbury (Earl, Marquis of), Strafford (Earl of), Wellesley (Arthur, Richard Colley) 10 Palmerston (Lord), Rockingham (Marquis of), Sunderland (Earl of), Walsingham (Francis), Wellington (Duke of) 11 Chamberlain (Austen, Joseph, Neville), Shaftesbury (Earl of) 12 Chesterfield (Earl of)

Finnish: 9 Stahlberg (Kaarlo Juho)

French: 5 Sully (Duc de) 6 Guizot (François-Pierre-Guillaume), Thiers (Louis-Adolphe), Turgot (Anne-Robert-Jacques) 7 Herriot (Edouard), Mazarin (Jules), Schuman (Robert), Viviani (René) 8 Hanotaux (Gabriel) 9 Lafayette (Marquis de), Millerand (Alexandre), Richelieu (Duc de) 10 Clemenceau (Georges) 11 Tocqueville (Alexis de)

German: 5 Wirth (Joseph) 10 Stresemann (Gustav)

German-Danish: 9 Struensee (Johann Friedrich)

Greek: 6 Zaimis (Alexandros) 8 Pericles 9 Aristides 11 Cleisthenes, Demosthenes 12 Themistocles

Israeli: 4 Eban (Abba) 5 Begin (Menachem), Dayan (Moshe)

Italian: 6 Cavour (Conte di), Crispi (Francesco) 7 Orlando (Vittorio Emanuele) 11 Machiavelli (Niccolo)

Japanese: 5 genro, Kanoe 6 Kanoye

Norwegian: 6 Nansen (Fridtjof)

Polish: 7 Zaleski (August) 9 Pilsudski (Jozef) 10 Paderewski (Ignacy)

Prussian: 5 Stein (Karl)

Roman: 4 Cato (Marcus Porcius) 6 Cicero (Marcus Tullius), Pompey, Seneca (Lucius Annaeus) 7 Agrippa (Marcus Vipsanius) 8 Gracchus (Gaius, Tiberius), Maecenas (Gaius) 9 Symmachus (Quintus Aurelius)

Russian: 5 Witte (Sergey) 7 Molotov (Vyacheslav) 8 Potemkin (Grigory) 9 Vyshinsky (Andrey)

Scottish: 4 Knox (John)

South American: 7 Bolívar (Simón) 9 San Martín (José de)

Swiss: 4 Ador (Gustave) 5 Welti (Emil)

static

5 fixed, inert 6 stable, steady 7 stabile, stalled, stopped 8 constant, immobile, inactive, stagnant, unmoving 9 immovable, unvarying 10 changeless, unchanging

station

4 post, rank, site, spot 5 depot, locus, place, point 6 assign 7 footing 8 capacity, standing 9 character 10 white noise

stationary

5 fixed 6 static 8 immobile, stagnant, unmoving 9 immovable 10 motionless, stock-still

statue
base: 6 plinth 8 pedestal
gigantic: 8 Colossus
Greek: 5 atlas 7 telamon 8 caryatid
religious: 5 Pietà
small: 8 figurine

stature
see **status**

status
4 rank 5 merit, place, worth 6 cachet, rating, renown 7 caliber, dignity, footing, posture, quality 8 capacity, eminence, position, prestige, standing 9 character, condition, situation 10 prominence 11 consequence, distinction

statute
3 act, law 4 bill 5 canon, edict 9 enactment, ordinance

staunch
4 fast, firm, sure, true 5 liege, loyal, solid, sound 6 secure, stable, strong, trusty 8 constant, faithful, reliable, resolute, stalwart 9 steadfast 10 dependable 11 substantial, trustworthy

stave off
4 foil 5 avert, block, deter, dodge, elude, parry, rebut, repel 6 rebuff, thwart 7 forfend, obviate, prevent, repulse 8 preclude 9 forestall 10 circumvent

stay
3 guy, lag 4 bide, halt, prop, rest, stop, wait 5 abide, brace, check, defer, delay, dwell, lodge, tarry, visit 6 linger, put off, remain 7 sojourn, support, suspend 8 hold over, postpone, stop over 9 interrupt 10 suspension 11 stick around

steadfast
4 firm, sure, true 5 fixed, liege, loyal 7 abiding, adamant, patient, staunch 8 constant, enduring, faithful, immobile, reliable, resolute, stubborn 9 immovable, unbending, unmovable 10 dependable, unwavering, unyielding 11 unfaltering, unflinching 12 never-failing, single-minded, wholehearted 13 unquestioning

steady
3 set 4 even, fast, firm, sure 5 fixed, liege, loyal, sober 6 stable, static 7 abiding, ballast, certain, durable, equable, nonstop, regular, stabile, staunch, uniform 8 constant, enduring, faithful, habitual, reliable, resolute, unbroken, unshaken 9 ceaseless, incessant, stabilize, unvarying 10 changeless, consistent, continuous, dependable, persistent, sweetheart, unchanging, unswerving, unwavering 11 unfaltering 12 unchangeable, wholehearted

steak
4 club, cube, loin 5 chuck, flank, round, T-bone 6 rib eye 7 brisket, sirloin 9 Delmonico, hamburger, Salisbury 10 tenderloin 11 filet mignon, London broil, porterhouse 13 chateaubriand

steal
3 bag, cop, nab, nip, rob 4 grab, hook, kite, lift, loot, lurk, slip, take 5 creep, filch, glide, heist, pinch, poach, prowl, seize, shirk, sidle, skulk, slide, slink, sneak, swipe 6 burgle, fleece, hijack, pilfer, pocket, snatch, snitch, thieve, tiptoe 7 bargain, pillage, plunder, purloin 8 embezzle, shanghai, shoplift 9 pussyfoot 10 burglarize, plagiarize 11 appropriate
a vehicle: 6 hijack 8 highjack

stealing
5 theft 6 piracy 7 larceny, robbery 8 burglary

stealthy
3 sly 4 wily 6 covert, crafty, feline, secret, shifty, silent, slinky, sneaky 7 catlike, cunning, furtive, sub-rosa 8 hush-hush, skulking, slinking, sneaking 9 noiseless 10 undercover 11 clandestine 13 surreptitious

steam bath
5 sauna

steamboat structure
5 texas

steamer
  4 boat, clam, ship

steam organ
  8 calliope

steed
  5 horse, mount 7 charger

steel
  4 gird 5 brace, nerve, rally 6 buck up, harden 7 fortify, hearten, stiffen 8 embolden, inspirit 9 reinforce 10 strengthen

steep
  3 sop 4 high, soak 5 bathe, dizzy, imbue, sheer 6 abrupt, drench, infuse 7 arduous, extreme, immerse, suffuse 8 elevated, marinate, saturate 9 excessive 10 exorbitant, immoderate, impregnate, inordinate 11 precipitate, precipitous

steeple
  5 spire, tower 6 flèche

steer
  4 helm, lead 5 guide, pilot, point, route 6 direct, escort, tip-off 7 channel, conduct, skipper 8 shepherd
  a ship: 4 conn, helm, luff

Stegner novel
  13 Angle of Repose, Spectator Bird (The) 20 Big Rock Candy Mountain (The)

stein
  3 mug 5 stoup 6 goblet 7 tankard

Steinbeck novel
  5 Pearl (The) 10 Cannery Row, East of Eden 12 Of Mice and Men, Tortilla Flat 13 Grapes of Wrath (The)

Stein's companion
  6 Toklas (Alice B.)

Steinway product
  5 piano

stellar
  6 astral, starry 7 leading, shining 8 sidereal, standout, starlike 10 preeminent 11 outstanding, predominant, superlative

stem
  4 flow, head, rise, stop 5 arise, check, issue 6 arrest, derive, spring, stanch 7 control, develop, emanate, proceed 8 peduncle 9 originate
  plant: 5 haulm
  underground: 5 tuber 7 rhizome

stench
  4 funk, reek 5 smell, stink

stentorian
  4 loud 7 blaring, booming, orotund, raucous, roaring 8 sonorous, strident 9 clamorous, deafening 10 thundering 12 earsplitting

step
  4 hoof, pace, rung, walk 5 grade, level, notch, stage, stair, track, tread 6 degree 7 measure, traipse 8 footfall 9 gradation
  dance: 3 pas

step-by-step
  7 gradual 9 piecemeal

steppe
  5 plain 6 tundra

Steppenwolf author
  5 Hesse (Hermann)

stereotype
  4 mold 7 pattern 10 categorize, pigeonhole 11 standardize

stereotypical
  4 hack 5 banal, stale, trite 7 clichéd 8 shopworn, timeworn 9 hackneyed 11 commonplace

sterile
  4 arid, bare, vain 6 barren, fallow 7 aseptic, worn-out 8 desolate, hygienic, impotent, lifeless, sanitary 9 fruitless, infertile 10 antiseptic, unfruitful, uninspired 11 disinfected 12 unproductive

sterilize
  3 fix 4 geld, spay 5 alter 6 neuter, purify 7 cleanse 8 sanitize 9 disinfect 10 emasculate

sterilized
  7 aseptic

sterling
4 pure, true 5 noble 6 worthy
8 virtuous 9 estimable, exemplary,
honorable

stern
4 grim 5 harsh, rigid, sober, stony
6 gloomy, severe, strict 7 ascetic,
austere 8 obdurate 10 forbidding,
implacable, inexorable, inflexible
11 unrelenting

sternward
3 aft

Sterope
father: 5 Atlas
mother: 7 Pleione
sisters: 8 Pleiades

Stevenson novel
9 Kidnapped

stew
4 boil, brew, flap, fret, fume, fuss,
hash, olio, olla, snit 5 daube, salmi,
sweat, tizzy, worry 6 burgoo, dither,
jumble, lather, medley, pother, ragout, seethe, simmer, swivet, tumult
7 brothel, goulash, mélange, mixture,
parboil, swelter, turmoil 8 bordello,
mishmash, mulligan, pot-au-feu
9 Brunswick, cassoulet, commotion,
confusion, pasticcio, potpourri
10 hodgepodge, hotchpotch, miscellany, turbulence 11 olla podrida,
ratatouille, slumgullion 13 bouillabaisse

steward
6 manage 7 manager 8 overseer
10 supervisor

stewed
3 lit 4 high 5 drunk, lit up, oiled
6 bashed, blotto, bombed, cooked,
juiced, potted, soaked, soused,
stewed, stoned, tanked, wasted,
zonked 7 crocked, drunken, pickled,
pie-eyed, sloshed, smashed, sottish
8 simmered 9 plastered 10 inebriated, liquored up 11 intoxicated

Stheno
see **Gorgon**

stick
3 put, rod 4 glue, pole, stab 5 affix,
baton, cling 6 adhere, attach, cleave,
cohere, fasten 7 scruple 10 overcharge

stick around
4 bide, stay, wait 5 abide, dally, tarry
6 linger, remain

sticker
3 pin 4 barb, seal, shiv, spur 5 point,
prong, shank, spike, spine, stamp
6 dagger 8 stiletto

stick-in-the-mud
4 fogy 6 fossil 8 mossback 10 fuddy-
duddy

stick out
3 jut 5 bulge 6 beetle 7 project
8 overhang, protrude

stick up
3 mug, rob 6 waylay 7 project
8 protrude

sticky
5 gluey, gooey, gummy, humid,
muggy, mushy, soggy, tacky
6 clammy, knotty, slushy, sultry,
thorny, viscid 7 awkward, cloying,
maudlin, mawkish, viscous 8 adhesive, bathetic, clinging, romantic
9 difficult 11 problematic, sentimental, tear-jerking

stiff
3 guy, lit, set 4 body, firm, hard, lush
5 cheat, drunk, harsh, oiled, proud,
rigid, stark, steep, stick, tense, tight,
tipsy 6 buzzed, corpse, frozen,
jelled, juiced, person, plowed, potent,
potted, severe, soused, stewed,
wooden 7 cadaver, carcass, sloshed,
starchy, stilted 8 hardened, reserved, stubborn 9 cardboard,
excessive, inelastic, obstinate,
petrified, plastered, unbending
10 exorbitant, inebriated, inflexible,
mechanical, unyielding 11 intoxicated, intractable

stiffen
5 tense 6 harden 7 thicken 8 rigid-
ify, solidify 9 stabilize 10 immobilize

stifle
3 gag 4 hush, mute 5 burke, choke, deter 6 dampen, deaden, hush up, muffle, muzzle 7 repress, silence, smother, squelch 8 stultify, suppress 9 suffocate 10 asphyxiate, discourage

stigma
4 blot, onus, spot 5 brand, odium, shame, stain, taint 6 smudge, smutch 8 black eye, disgrace, dishonor, petechia, tainting

stigmatize
5 brand, label, stamp

still
3 yet 4 calm, even, hush, lull 5 allay, inert, quiet, shush, whist 6 becalm, hushed, placid, serene, settle, silent, though, withal 7 halcyon, however, silence 8 after all, likewise, peaceful, stagnant, tranquil 9 noiseless, quietness, soundless 10 motionless, stationary 11 furthermore, nonetheless, tranquility 12 nevertheless

stilt
4 bird, pile, pole 8 longlegs 9 shorebird

stilted
4 prim 5 stiff 6 formal, wooden 7 pompous, starchy 8 affected 9 cardboard

stilt-like bird
6 avocet

stimulant
4 goad, spur 5 tonic 7 impetus, impulse 8 caffeine, catalyst, excitant 9 analeptic, energizer, incentive 10 incitement, motivation

stimulate
4 fire, goad, move, prod, spur, urge, whet 5 impel, pique, rouse, set up, spark 6 arouse, excite, fire up, foment, incite, prompt, vivify, work up 7 agitate, enliven, inspire, provoke, quicken, trigger 8 activate, energize, motivate, vitalize 9 galvanize 10 exhilarate

stimulus
4 goad, kick, push, spur 5 boost, cause 6 charge, motive 7 impetus, impulse 8 catalyst 9 incentive 10 incitement, inducement, motivation 11 instigation, provocation 13 encouragement

sting
3 con 4 trap 5 cheat, prick, smart, snare 6 hustle, tingle 7 con game 8 skin game

stinging
8 aculeate

stingy
4 mean 5 close, tight 6 frugal, narrow, paltry, skimpy 7 chintzy, costive, miserly, niggard, scrimpy, sparing, thrifty 8 grudging 9 niggardly, penny-wise, penurious 10 economical, ironfisted, pinchpenny, ungenerous 11 tightfisted 12 cheeseparing, parsimonious 13 penny-pinching

stink
4 flap, funk, fuss, reek 5 smell 6 stench

stinker
3 dog, dud 4 bomb, bust, flop 5 lemon, skunk 6 petrel

stinking
see **smelly**

stinky
see **smelly**

stint
3 job 4 bout, task, time, tour, turn 5 chore, cramp, pinch, scant, share, shift, skimp, spare, spell 6 amount, scrape, scrimp 8 quantity, restrict 9 allotment, stricture 10 assignment, limitation 11 restriction

stipend
3 fee, pay 4 hire, wage 5 award 6 salary 7 payment 9 allowance, emolument 13 consideration

stipple
3 dot 5 fleck, speck 6 pepper 7 freckle, speckle 8 sprinkle

stipulate
5 state 6 detail 7 specify 8 contract, spell out 13 particularize

stipulation
5 limit, terms 7 proviso, strings 9 condition, provision 11 requirement

stir
3 ado, din, mix 4 beat, fuss, rout, to-do, wake, whet 5 awake, blend, budge, churn, evoke, impel, raise, rally, rouse, roust, set on, spark, waken, whirl 6 arouse, awaken, bustle, excite, flurry, foment, hubbub, incite, kindle, pother, seethe, simmer, tumult, whip up 7 actuate, agitate, disturb, ferment, inspire, provoke, quicken 8 activate, activity, energize 9 agitation, commotion, galvanize, stimulate 11 disturbance

stirrup
6 stapes 8 footrest

stithy
5 anvil

stoat
6 ermine, weasel

stock
4 butt, fund, hope, race 5 brace, carry, faith, goods, hoard, store, trunk, trust 6 family, supply 7 furnish, lineage 8 pedigree, reliance 9 inventory, selection 10 confidence, dependence 11 merchandise

stockade
4 jail 5 fence 6 paling, prison 8 palisade 9 enclosure, guardroom

stock exchange
6 bourse

stockings
4 hose 5 socks 7 hosiery

stockpile
4 bank, heap, mass 5 amass, cache, hoard, lay up, store 6 garner, supply 7 backlog, collect, nest egg, reserve, store up 9 inventory, reservoir 10 accumulate, repository

stocky
3 fat 5 beefy, burly, dumpy, husky, plump, pudgy, squat, stout, thick 6 chunky, stubby, stumpy 8 heavy-set, thickset 9 corpulent

stodge
4 fill, sate 5 gorge, stuff 7 overeat, surfeit

stodgy
5 fusty 6 stuffy 9 hidebound, out-of-date 12 old-fashioned

stogie
4 shoe 5 cigar 6 brogan

stoic
6 stolid 7 Spartan 9 apathetic, impassive 10 phlegmatic 11 indifferent, unconcerned

stoicism
9 stolidity 11 impassivity
founder: 4 Zeno

stoke
3 fan 4 feed, fuel, poke, stir, tend 6 supply

Stoker novel
7 Dracula

stolid
3 dry 4 dull, flat 5 stoic 6 wooden 8 rocklike 9 apathetic, impassive, unruffled 10 phlegmatic 11 unemotional

stomach
3 gut 4 bear, craw 5 abide, belly, brook, stand, taste, tummy 6 digest, endure, paunch, venter 7 abdomen, swallow 8 appetite, tolerate
combining form: 5 gastr 6 gastro, ventri, ventro
enzyme: 6 pepsin, rennin
muscle: 7 pylorus
ruminant: 6 omasum 8 abomasum 9 reticulum
Scottish: 4 kyte

stomachache
5 colic, gripe 12 collywobbles

stomp
5 clomp, clump, pound, tramp, tromp 7 trample

stone
3 gem 4 rock 5 lapis 6 pebble
7 boulder
base: 6 plinth
block of: 8 monolith
chip: 5 spall
combining form: 4 lite, lith, lyte
cosmic: 6 meteor 9 chondrite,
meteorite
for grinding grains: 6 metate
fruit: 5 drupe
memorial: 7 obelisk
monument: 8 megalith
of a fruit: 3 pit

_____ Stone
7 Blarney, Rosetta

Stone novel
11 Lust for Life 18 Agony and the
Ecstasy (The)

stonecrop
5 sedum

stoned
3 lit 4 high 5 boozy, doped, drunk,
fried, oiled, tight, tipsy 6 buzzed,
canned, juiced, loaded, plowed,
potted, soused, stewed, tanked,
wasted, zonked 7 crocked, drugged,
muddled, pickled, pie-eyed, sloshed,
smashed 8 hopped-up, turned on,
wiped out 9 pixilated, plastered,
spaced-out, strung out 10 inebriated, tripped out 11 intoxicated

stooge
3 act, sap 4 dupe, foil, gull, mark,
pawn, tool 5 chump, dummy, patsy,
proxy 6 puppet, sucker, victim 7 fall
guy 8 sidekick 9 represent 11 stool
pigeon, straight man 12 second
banana

Stooge
3 Moe (Howard) 5 Curly (Howard),
Larry (Fine)

stool pigeon
3 rat 4 fink, nark 5 decoy 6 canary,
snitch 7 ratfink, tipster 8 informer

stoop
3 dip 4 bend, duck, sink 5 deign,

hunch, porch, slump 6 resort, slouch
7 descend, portico, veranda 8 stair-
way 10 condescend

stop
3 bar, can, dam, end 4 clog, fill, halt,
plug, quit, stay, stem 5 block, brake,
cease, check, close, stall, tarry
6 arrest, cut off, desist, draw up,
ending, kibosh, stanch 7 disrupt,
occlude, prevent, shut off, sojourn,
suspend, turn off 8 knock off, leave
off, obstruct 9 cessation, interrupt,
terminate 10 conclusion, standstill
11 discontinue, refrain from, termination
up: 4 cork, plug 7 occlude

stopgap
5 shift 6 resort 8 recourse, resource
9 expedient, makeshift 10 expediency, substitute

stopover
4 stay 5 visit 7 sojourn

stoppage
4 halt 6 cutoff, strike 7 walkout
8 shutdown 10 standstill 11 obstruction

stopper
4 bung, cork, fill, plug 5 close

store
3 bin 4 fund, mart, pack, shop, tank
5 amass, cache, depot, hoard, lay
up, stash 6 ensile, garner, market,
outlet, shoppe, supply 7 arsenal,
backlog, bootery, deposit, reserve
8 boutique, cumulate, emporium,
mothball, showroom, squirrel 9 abundance, chandlery, inventory, reservoir, stockpile, warehouse 10 accumulate, depository, five-and-ten,
repository 11 five-and-dime 12 accumulation

storehouse
5 depot 7 arsenal, granary 8 magazine 9 stockpile 10 depository,
repository

storekeeper
8 merchant, retailer 9 tradesman

storeroom
6 larder, pantry 7 buttery

storm
3 row 4 fury, gale, hail, rage, rant, rave, roar, rush, to-do 5 beset, blast, blitz, burst, furor, onset, salvo 6 assail, attack, charge, clamor, fall on, flurry, furore, hubbub, outcry, pother, racket, rumpus, shower, squall, strike, tumult, volley 7 assault, barrage, bluster, cyclone, monsoon, ruction, tempest, thunder, tornado, turmoil, twister, typhoon 8 blizzard, downpour, drumfire, fall upon, outbreak, outburst, paroxysm, upheaval 9 broadside, cannonade, commotion, discharge, fusillade, hurricane, nor'easter, onslaught 10 blitzkrieg, cloudburst, hurly-burly 11 bombardment, northeaster, northwester

storm trooper
10 brownshirt

stormy
4 foul 5 rainy, rough 6 raging 7 furious 8 blustery 9 turbulent 10 tumultuous 11 tempestuous, threatening

story
3 fib, lie 4 epic, saga, tale, yarn 5 conte, fable 6 canard, legend, report 7 account, fiction, märchen, parable, version 8 allegory, anecdote, folktale, megillah, tall tale 9 chronicle, fairy tale, narration, narrative 11 description, fabrication

storyteller
4 liar 6 fibber 8 fabulist 9 raconteur

stoup
4 font 5 basin 6 flagon, goblet 7 chalice, tankard

stout
3 ale, fat 4 brew 5 beefy, bulky, burly, heavy, husky, obese, plump, thick 6 fleshy, portly, strong, sturdy 9 corpulent 10 overweight

Stout detective
5 Wolfe (Nero)

stouthearted
4 bold, game 5 brave, gutsy 7 doughty, valiant 8 fearless, intrepid, resolute, stalwart, stubborn, unafraid 9 audacious, dauntless, undaunted 10 courageous

stove
4 kiln, oven 5 range 8 Franklin, potbelly

stow
4 load, pack 5 stash, store 7 deposit

stower
9 stevedore

Stowe work
4 Dred

strabismus
6 squint

straddle
4 span 6 sprawl 8 bestride 11 spread-eagle

strafe
4 rake 6 attack 8 enfilade 10 machine-gun

straggle
3 lag 4 poke, roam, rove 5 drift, range, stray 6 dawdle, loiter, ramble, wander 7 maunder, meander 8 trail off 9 string out

straight
4 even, fair, neat, pure, true 5 erect, plain, plumb, right 6 at once, candid, direct, honest, linear, square 7 unmixed, upright 8 orthodox 9 bourgeois, forthwith, undiluted 10 aboveboard, button-down, forthright 12 conventional 13 unadulterated
combining form: 4 orth, rect 5 ortho, recti

straightaway
3 now 6 at once 7 stretch 8 directly, first off, promptly 9 forthwith, instanter 11 immediately

straighten
4 even, tidy 5 align 6 neaten, unbend, uncurl 7 rectify

straightforward
5 frank, lucid 6 candid, direct,

honest **7** genuine, precise, sincere **8** clear-cut **9** outspoken **10** forthright **11** undeviating

strain

3 air, tax, try **4** hint, kind, pull, sort, toil, tune, vein **5** exert, stock, sweat, tinge, touch, trace, twist **6** filter, melody, screen, streak, stress, strive, wrench **7** lineage, overtax, tension, trouble **8** ancestry, exertion, overwork, pedigree, pressure, struggle **9** overexert

strait

4 bind, pass **5** pinch **6** crisis, plight **7** channel, dilemma, narrows, squeeze **8** exigency, hardship, juncture **9** crossroad, emergency **10** difficulty **11** contingency
Adriatic Sea-Ionian Sea: 7 Otranto
Alaska: 3 Icy
Alaska-Russia: 6 Bering
Albania-Greece: 5 Corfu
Asia-Europe: 11 Dardanelles
Atlantic-Baffin Island: 5 Davis
Atlantic-Mediterranean: 9 Gibraltar
Atlantic-Nantucket Sound: 8 Muskeget
Atlantic-North Sea: 7 English
Atlantic-Pacific: 5 Drake **8** Magellan
Atlantic-Saint Lawrence: 5 Cabot
Baffin Island-Quebec: 6 Hudson
Bering Sea-Sea of Okhotsk: 5 Kuril **6** Kurile
Bismarck Sea-Solomon Sea: 6 Vitiaz
Canada: 3 Rae **5** Dease
East China Sea: 5 Korea **8** Tsushima
East China-South China: 6 Taiwan **7** Formosa
England-France: 5 Dover
Flores Sea-Indian Ocean: 4 Sape
Flores Sea-Savu Sea: 4 Alor
Indian Ocean-Java Sea: 5 Sunda
India-Sri Lanka: 4 Palk
Indonesia: 4 Alas, Alor, Bali **5** Tioro **6** Lombok **7** Dampier **8** Macassar, Makassar, Surabaya
Inner Hebrides: 5 Tiree
Iran-Oman: 6 Hormuz

Italy: 7 Messina
Japan: 4 Yura **5** Bungo, Kitan **7** Hayasui
Japan-Sakhalin Island: 4 Soya
Lake Huron: 10 Mississagi
Lake Huron-Lake Michigan: 8 Mackinac
Malay Archipelago: 5 Wetar
Malaysia-Singapore: 6 Johore
Malay-Sumatra: 7 Malacca
New Jersey-Staten Island: 7 van Kull
New South Wales-Tasmania: 4 Bass
New Zealand: 4 Cook
Northwest Territories: 6 Barrow **8** Franklin, Victoria **13** Prince of Wales
Nova Scotia: 5 Canso
Pacific-San Francisco Bay: 10 Golden Gate
Pacific-South China Sea: 5 Luzon
Philippines: 5 Bohol, Tanon **6** Iloilo **7** Basilan
Russia: 4 Kara
Suvu Sea-Timor Sea: 4 Roti
Sea of Azov-Black Sea: 5 Kerch **7** Enikale
Sea of Japan: 5 Tatar
Solomon Islands: 12 Bougainville
South China Sea: 7 Mindoro **9** Singapore
Turkey: 8 Bosporus **9** Bosphorus, Karadeniz
Vancouver-Washington: 10 Juan de Fuca
Wales: 5 Menai
Washington Sound: 4 Haro

straitened

7 lacking, pinched, wanting **8** deprived, strapped **9** deficient, destitute **10** distressed, inadequate **12** impoverished

straitlaced

4 prim **5** staid, stiff **6** formal, narrow, prissy, strict, stuffy **7** genteel, prudish, starchy, stilted **8** priggish **9** hidebound, Victorian **11** puritanical

strand

4 bank **5** beach, coast, fiber, leave,

shore, wreck **6** desert, maroon, thread **7** abandon, shingle **8** cast away, littoral, seacoast, seashore **9** shipwreck **10** run aground, waterfront

strange
3 odd **5** alien, crazy, fishy, funny, kinky, kooky, nutty, outré, queer, weird **6** exotic, far-out, freaky **7** bizarre, curious, oddball, offbeat, uncanny, unknown, unusual **8** aberrant, abnormal, atypical, peculiar, singular, wondrous **9** eccentric, fantastic, grotesque **10** mysterious, off-the-wall, outlandish, surprising, unfamiliar **11** exceptional **12** unaccustomed

Strange Interlude author
6 O'Neill (Eugene)

stranger
5 alien, guest **7** visitor **8** newcomer, outsider, wanderer **9** auslander, foreigner, immigrant, transient

strangle
5 burke, choke, shush **6** muffle, quelch, stifle **7** garotte, garrote **8** suppress, throttle **10** asphyxiate

strap
4 band, beat, belt, bind **5** leash **6** attach, punish, secure, suffer **7** binding, leather **8** distress **9** constrict

strapping
5 beefy, burly, hardy, husky **6** brawny, robust, rugged, sturdy **8** muscular, vigorous **10** able-bodied

stratagem
4 play, plot, ploy, ruse, wile **5** feint, trick **6** device, gambit, scheme, tactic **8** artifice, intrigue, maneuver **10** conspiracy, subterfuge **11** machination

strategy
4 plan **6** design, method, scheme **7** project, tactics **8** game plan **9** blueprint

stratum
3 bed **4** rank **5** class, grade, layer, level

Strauss, Richard
opera: 6 Salome **7** Elektra **13** Rosenkavalier (Der) **15** Ariadne auf Naxos **16** Frau ohne Schatten (Der) **tone poem: 7** Don Juan **10** Don Quixote **11** Heldenleben (Ein) **20** Thus Spake Zarathustra **23** Death and Transfiguration

straw
3 hay **5** blond **6** flaxen, golden, thatch **braided: 6** sennit **mat: 6** tatami **plaited: 7** leghorn

stray
3 err, gad **4** lost, roam, rove, waif **5** drift, range **6** depart, errant, ramble, random, wander **7** deviate, digress, diverge, erratic, meander, runaway, traipse, vagrant **8** divagate, homeless, sporadic **9** gallivant

streak
4 hint, vein **5** fleck, tinge, trace **6** dapple, marble, mottle, strain, stripe **7** striate **8** tincture **9** suspicion, variegate **10** intimation, suggestion

streaked
5 upset **7** brindle, marbled, striped **8** brindled, grizzled **9** disturbed

stream
3 run **4** beck, burn, flow, flux, gill, gush, pour, race, rill, rush, sike, tide **5** bourn, brook, creek, spate, surge **6** bourne, branch, rindle, runnel, sluice **7** current, freshet, rivulet, torrent **8** affluent

streamer
4 flag, jack **6** banner, burgee, ensign, pennon **7** pennant **8** banderol, bannerol, standard **9** banderole

streamline
7 contour **8** organize, simplify **9** modernize

street
3 way **4** drag, road, wynd **5** alley, drive **6** artery, avenue **7** roadway **9** boulevard **12** thoroughfare

border: 4 curb 7 curbing
material: 6 cobble 7 asphalt, macadam 11 cobblestone

streetcar
4 tram 7 trolley

Streetcar Named Desire, A
author: 8 Williams (Tennessee)
character: 6 Stella (Kowalski)
7 Blanche (DuBois), Stanley (Kowalski)

Street Scene author
4 Rice (Elmer)

strength
5 brawn, force, might, power, sinew, vigor 6 energy, muscle 7 potency 8 firmness, security 9 fortitude, intensity, soundness, stability, toughness 10 steadiness, sturdiness

strengthen
4 gird 5 brace, steel 6 anneal, harden, prop up 7 bolster, enhance, fortify, support, toughen 8 buttress, embolden, energize 9 intensify, reinforce, undergird 10 invigorate, rejuvenate

strenuous
4 hard 5 tough 6 taxing, uphill 7 arduous, operose 9 demanding, difficult, effortful, Herculean, laborious 12 backbreaking

Strephon
8 shepherd
beloved: 5 Chloe 6 Urania

stress
6 accent, burden, import, play up, strain, weight 7 anxiety, feature, tension, trouble, urgency 8 emphasis, emphasize, italicize, underline 10 accentuate, underscore 12 accentuation
in poetry: 5 ictus

stretch
4 area, draw, time 5 range, reach, scope, space, spell, sweep, tract, while 6 extend, extent, length, limber, region, spread 7 breadth, compass, draw out, expanse, magnify, prolong, purview, spin out, tighten 8 distance, elongate, lengthen, protract 9 embellish, embroider, expansion, overstate 10 exaggerate
on a frame: 6 tenter
out: 6 sprawl 7 lie down, recline

stretchable
7 ductile, elastic, tensile

stretched
4 taut

stretcher
4 yarn 6 gurney, litter 8 tall tale

strew
3 sow 4 dust 5 cover 6 pepper, spread 7 scatter 8 disperse, sprinkle 9 broadcast, circulate, propagate 10 distribute 11 disseminate

stricken
3 hit, ill 4 hurt, sick 7 injured, wounded 9 afflicted 11 overwhelmed

strict
4 firm 5 exact, harsh, rigid, stern, tough 6 narrow, severe 7 precise 8 exacting, faithful, rigorous 9 draconian, stringent, unsparing 10 inflexible, ironhanded, meticulous, scrupulous 11 punctilious

stricture
5 cramp, stint 7 censure, reproof 8 reproach 9 aspersion, criticism, reprimand 10 constraint, limitation 11 restriction 13 animadversion

stride
4 gait, pace, step 5 march, stalk 7 advance 8 straddle

strident
4 loud 5 harsh 6 shrill 7 grating, jarring, rasping, raucous, squawky 8 piercing 9 clamorous, insistent, obtrusive 10 boisterous, discordant, stentorian, vociferous 11 loudmouthed 12 earsplitting, obstreperous

strife
4 fray 5 broil, fight 6 battle, combat 7 discord, dispute, dissent, quarrel, rivalry, warfare, wrangle 8 argument, conflict, disunity, friction, struggle,

strike

tug-of-war **10** contention, difference, dissension, dissidence **11** altercation, competition, controversy

strike

3 hit, pop, rap **4** bash, beat, find, poke, slam, slap, slug, sock, swat, whap, whop **5** clout, knock, punch, smack, smite, swipe, thump, whack **6** affect, assail, attack, cudgel, delete, hammer, pummel, thrash **7** assault, impress, inflict, inspire **8** discover, stoppage

striking

5 showy, vivid **6** cogent, marked, signal **7** salient, telling **8** forceful **9** arresting, prominent **10** compelling, noticeable, remarkable **11** conspicuous, outstanding

Strindberg play

6 Easter, Father (The) **8** Comrades **9** Creditors (The), Dream Play (A), Miss Julie **10** Master Olaf **11** Ghost Sonata (The) **12** Dance of Death (The), Gustavus Vasa

string

3 row **4** file, line, rank, tier **5** chain, order, queue, train, twine **6** sequel, series **7** echelon **8** recourse, resource, sequence **10** succession
up: **4** hang **5** noose, scrag **6** gibbet

stringent

see **strict**

stringy

4 lean, ropy, wiry **6** sinewy **7** fibrous **8** muscular

strip

4 band, bare, doff, flay, husk, peel, sack, skin **5** scale **6** billet, denude, divest, expose, fillet, ravage, ribbon **7** bandeau, deprive, disrobe, pillage, uncover, undress **8** unclothe
leather: **5** thong
of wood: **4** lath, slat
skin: **6** flense

stripe

3 ilk **4** band, kind, lash, sort, type **5** order **6** strake, streak **7** banding, chevron, lineate, striate, variety

stripling

3 boy, lad **5** youth **9** youngster **10** adolescent

stripper

6 peeler, teaser **9** ecdysiast

stripteaser

see **stripper**

strive

3 try, vie **4** seek **5** labor **6** strain **7** attempt, contend **8** endeavor, struggle **9** undertake

stroke

3 fit, hit, pet, rub **4** blow, hone, whet **5** swing **6** attack, caress, fondle, soothe **7** flatter **8** apoplexy, ischemia **9** heartbeat

stroll

4 rove, turn, walk **5** amble, drift, mosey, paseo **6** cruise, linger, ramble, wander **7** saunter, traipse **9** promenade

stroller

4 pram **6** go-cart **8** carriage **12** baby carriage, perambulator

strong

4 fast, firm, hard **5** burly, hardy, lusty, solid, sound, stout, tough **6** brawny, hearty, heroic, mighty, potent, robust, rugged, secure, sinewy, stable, sturdy **7** durable, intense, staunch **8** forceful, muscular, powerful, stalwart, vigorous **9** resilient, strapping, tenacious **10** able-bodied, full-bodied, spirituous **12** concentrated

strong-arm

5 bully **6** bounce, hector, lean on **7** assault, dragoon **8** browbeat, bulldoze, bullyrag **9** terrorize **10** intimidate

strongbox

4 safe **5** chest **6** coffer **13** treasure chest

stronghold

4 fort **7** bastion, bulwark, citadel, redoubt **8** fastness, fortress

strong point

5 forte **6** métier

strong suit
see **strong point**

strophe
5 verse 6 stanza

structure
4 form 5 frame 6 format, makeup, system 7 anatomy, complex, edifice, network 8 building, erection, skeleton 9 framework 10 morphology 11 arrangement, composition

struggle
3 try, vie 4 agon 5 trial 6 battle, effort, hassle, strain, strife, strive, tussle 7 attempt, compete, contest, grapple, scuffle 8 endeavor, exertion, flounder, skirmish, striving 9 undertake 11 undertaking

strumpet
4 bawd, jade, slut, tart 5 hussy, tramp, trull, wench 6 floozy, harlot, hooker, wanton 7 jezebel, trollop 8 slattern

strut
6 flaunt, parade, prance, sashay 7 flounce, peacock, show off, swagger

stub
3 end 4 butt, tail 5 stump 6 put out, strike 7 remnant 10 extinguish

stubborn
5 balky, rigid 6 cussed, dogged, mulish, ornery 7 adamant, lasting, willful 8 obdurate, perverse 9 obstinate, pigheaded, steadfast, unbending 10 bullheaded, determined, headstrong, inexorable, inflexible, persistent, rebellious, refractory, relentless, unyielding 11 intractable 12 cantankerous, contumacious, pertinacious, single-minded

stubby
5 dumpy, short, squat, stout 6 stocky, stumpy 8 heavyset, thickset

stuck
5 clung, glued 6 jammed, wedged 7 adhered, baffled, blocked, saddled, stabbed, stopped, stumped 8 attached, held fast 11 overcharged

stuck-up
4 vain 6 sniffy, snippy, snooty 7 haughty 8 snobbish 9 conceited 12 narcissistic, supercilious

stud
3 guy 4 dude, hunk, male, nail, post 5 cleat 6 button, pillar 7 earring, speckle, upright 8 sprinkle, stallion

student
5 pupil 6 novice 7 protégé, scholar 8 disciple 10 apprentice
college: 9 undergrad 13 undergraduate
female: 4 coed
first-year: 5 frosh 8 freshman
fourth-year: 6 senior
French: 5 élève 8 étudiant
military: 5 cadet, middy 10 midshipman
second-year: 9 sophomore
third-year: 6 junior
wandering: 7 goliard

studio
4 shop 7 atelier 8 workroom, workshop

studious
7 bookish, learned 9 scholarly

Studs Lonigan creator
7 Farrell (James T.)

study
3 con, den, vet 4 cram, muse 6 ponder, survey 7 analyze, examine, inspect, reverie 8 consider 9 attention, think over 10 excogitate, scrutinize 11 application

stuff
3 jam, ram 4 cram, fill, glut, junk, pack, sate, tamp 5 crowd, gorge, shove 6 matter, things 7 essence, jam-pack, squeeze, surfeit 8 material, overfill 9 substance 11 possessions

stuffy
4 dull, prim 5 close, fuggy, heavy, humid, stale, thick 6 narrow, stodgy 7 airless, bloated, genteel, humdrum, pompous, prudish, stilted 8 priggish, stagnant, stifling 9 hidebound,

Victorian **10** oppressive, pontifical **11** puritanical, suffocating **12** narrow-minded **13** self-important, self-righteous

stultify
4 dull **6** deaden, impair, stifle, weaken **7** inhibit, nullify, repress, smother, trammel **8** restrain, stagnate, suppress **9** suffocate **10** discourage, invalidate

stumble
3 err **4** reel, slip, trip **5** error, fluff, gaffe, lapse, lurch **6** falter, muddle, slipup, totter **7** blunder, faux pas, mistake, stagger, stammer **8** flounder

stump
3 end **4** beat, butt, dare, defy, plod, stub **5** barge, clomp, clump, stick **6** baffle, outwit, puzzle, stymie, trudge **7** buffalo, flummox, galumph, mystify, nonplus, perplex **8** bewilder, campaign, confound, hustings, politick **9** barnstorm, challenge **11** electioneer

stun
4 daze **5** amaze, floor, shock **6** dazzle **7** astound, nonplus, stagger, stupefy **8** astonish, bewilder, bowl over, knock out, paralyze **9** dumbfound **11** flabbergast

stunning
6 superb **7** amazing, awesome **8** gorgeous, striking **9** excellent, wonderful **10** astounding, impressive, remarkable, staggering, surprising **11** astonishing

stunt
4 curb, feat **5** antic, caper, check, dwarf, prank, trick **6** hinder, impair, retard **8** escapade, hold back, suppress

stupefy
4 daze, dull, faze, stun **5** addle, amaze **6** muddle, rattle **7** astound, nonplus, petrify, stagger **8** astonish, bewilder, paralyze **9** disorient, dumbfound **11** flabbergast

stupendous
7 amazing, awesome, massive, titanic **8** colossal, enormous, gigantic, stunning, towering, wondrous **9** fantastic, marvelous, monstrous, wonderful **10** astounding, miraculous, monumental, phenomenal, prodigious, staggering, tremendous **11** astonishing, spectacular **12** breathtaking, mind-boggling, overwhelming

stupid
3 dim **4** dull, dumb, slow **5** dense, dopey, inane, silly, thick **6** oafish, obtuse, simple, torpid **7** asinine, doltish, fatuous, foolish, idiotic, moronic, witless **8** backward, ignorant, mindless, retarded **9** brainless, fatheaded, imbecilic, laughable, ludicrous, pinheaded, senseless **10** half-witted, slow-witted **11** blockheaded, thickheaded, thick-witted **13** chuckleheaded

stupor
6 torpor **7** languor **8** dullness, hebetude, lethargy, narcosis **9** lassitude, torpidity **10** anesthesia, somnolence **13** insensibility
combining form: 4 narc **5** narco

sturdy
5 hardy, solid, sound, stout, tough **6** robust, rugged, secure, strong **7** durable, healthy, staunch **8** stalwart, vigorous **9** strapping

sturgeon
6 beluga
roe: 6 caviar

Sturm und Drang
5 angst **6** unease, unrest **7** anxiety, ferment, turmoil **8** disquiet **9** agitation **10** inquietude, turbulence **11** disquietude, restiveness **12** restlessness

St. Vitus' ____
5 dance

sty
3 pen **4** coop, cyst **6** pigpen **7** piggery

stygian
  4 dark **6** gloomy **7** hellish, sunless
  8 infernal, plutonic **9** Cimmerian,
  plutonian

style
  3 fad, way **4** élan, mode, rage, vein
  5 craze, decor, flair, trend, vogue
  6 manner **7** fashion, panache
  10 dernier cri **11** savoir-faire
  hair: 4 coif **8** coiffure

stylish
  3 mod **4** chic, posh, tony, trig
  5 doggy, natty, ritzy, sassy, sharp,
  showy, sleek, slick, smart, swank,
  swell **6** chichi, dapper, dressy,
  modern, modish, snappy, snazzy,
  spiffy, trendy, with-it **7** à la mode,
  dashing, doggish **8** spiffing, up-to-
  date **10** newfangled **11** fashionable

stymie
  4 stop **5** block **6** hamper, hinder,
  impede, thwart **7** flummox, prevent
  8 confound, obstruct **9** frustrate,
  hamstring

Stymphalides' slayer
  8 Heracles, Hercules

Styron novel
  13 Sophie's Choice **22** Confessions
  of Nat Turner (The)

Styx
  father: 7 Oceanus
  ferryman: 6 Charon
  location: 5 Hades
  mother: 6 Tethys

Styx's counterpart
  5 Lethe **7** Acheron, Cocytus
  10 Phlegethon

suave
  4 oily **5** slick **6** smooth, urbane
  7 cordial, courtly, gallant, politic,
  refined, tactful, worldly **8** debonair,
  gracious, polished, unctuous, well-
  bred **9** courteous **10** cultivated,
  diplomatic **12** ingratiating **13** sophisticated

sub
  5 below, proxy, under **6** backup,
  fill-in **7** stand-by, stand-in **8** pinch-hit

  9 alternate, secondary, surrogate
  10 understudy **11** locum tenens,
  pinch hitter, replacement

subaltern
  8 inferior **9** secondary, underling

subdue
  4 curb, tame **5** crush, quash, quell
  6 defeat, master, quench **7** conquer,
  control, put down, repress, squelch
  8 beat down, overcome, suppress,
  tone down, vanquish **9** overpower,
  overthrow, subjugate

subdued
  4 soft, tame **5** muted, quiet, sober
  6 low-key, mellow, subtle **7** neutral,
  serious **8** low-keyed, softened,
  tasteful, tempered **9** moderated,
  toned down **10** controlled, restrained, submissive **11** unobtrusive

subjacent
  3 low **5** lower, under **6** lesser,
  nether **8** inferior

subject
  3 apt **4** core, open **5** motif, point,
  prone, theme, topic **6** expose, liable,
  likely, matter, motive, vassal **7** citizen, exposed, lay open, problem
  8 argument, inferior, material, question **9** dependent, leitmotif, secondary, sensitive, subjugate, substance, tributary **11** subordinate,
  subservient, susceptible

subjective
  6 biased **10** prejudiced

subjugate
  see **subdue**

sublime
  4 holy **5** ideal, lofty, noble, proud
  6 august, divine, sacred, superb
  7 blessed, exalted **8** elevated, glorious, heavenly, majestic, splendid
  9 celestial, spiritual **11** magnificent,
  resplendent **12** transcendent

submarine
  4 hero **5** po'boy, U-boat **6** hoagie
  7 grinder
  detector: 5 sonar

submerge

3 dip 4 duck, dunk, sink 5 drown, flood, swamp 6 deluge, engulf, plunge 7 founder, go under, immerse 8 inundate, overflow

submerse

see **submerge**

submissive

4 meek, tame 6 abject, docile, pliant 7 servile, slavish, subdued 8 amenable, obedient, obeisant, yielding 9 compliant, tractable 10 obsequious 11 acquiescent, deferential, subservient, unresisting 12 nonresisting

submit

3 bow 4 cave, fold, obey 5 defer, offer, yield 6 accede, comply, give in, hand in, relent, send in, tender 7 concede, deliver, go under, present, proffer, provide, subject, succumb, suggest 9 acquiesce, surrender 10 capitulate 11 buckle under 12 knuckle under

subordinate

5 minor, scrub, under 6 junior 7 adjunct, subject 8 inferior 9 accessory, ancillary, auxiliary, dependent, secondary, subaltern, tributary, underling 10 collateral, submissive, subsidiary 11 subservient

sub rosa

6 covert, secret 7 furtive, private 8 covertly, in camera, secretly, stealthy 9 by stealth, furtively, privately, secretive, underhand 10 stealthily 11 clandestine, underhanded 13 clandestinely, surreptitious

subscribe

3 ink 4 sign 5 agree 6 accede, adhere, assent, attest, pledge 7 approve, consent, endorse, support 8 sanction 9 acquiesce

subsequent

4 next 5 after, later 6 serial 7 ensuing 9 following, resultant, resulting 10 sequential, succeeding, successive 11 consecutive
prefix: 4 post

subsequently

4 next, then 5 after, later 9 afterward 10 afterwards, thereafter

subservient

6 abject, docile 7 fawning, ignoble, servile, slavish 8 adjuvant, obeisant 9 accessory, ancillary, auxiliary, compliant, truckling 10 collateral, obsequious, submissive 11 acquiescent, deferential, subordinate, sycophantic

subside

3 ebb 4 ease, fall, lull, sink, wane 5 abate, let up, taper 6 ease up, recede, settle 7 decline, descend, die away, die down, dwindle, ease off, slacken 8 decrease, diminish, moderate

subsidiary

5 minor 6 backup, branch 7 subject 8 adjuvant 9 accessory, ancillary, auxiliary, secondary, tributary 10 collateral 11 subordinate 12 supplemental 13 supplementary

subsidize

4 back, fund 5 endow, stake 7 finance, promote, sponsor, support 8 bankroll 9 grubstake 10 underwrite

subsidy

4 gift 5 grant 6 reward 10 subvention 13 appropriation

subsistence

4 keep, salt 5 bread, means 6 income, living 7 support 9 resources 10 livelihood, sustenance 11 maintenance, wherewithal 12 alimentation

substance

3 nub 4 bulk, core, crux, gist, mass, meat, pith, soul 5 being, drift, focus, heart, point, sense, stuff, tenor 6 amount, burden, entity, import, kernel, marrow, matter, nubbin, object, thrust, upshot, wealth 7 essence, meaning, nucleus, purport 8 material, property, sum total 9 resources 12 essentiality, quintessence

substantial

3 big 4 full 5 ample, hefty, large, solid 6 strong, sturdy 7 massive, sizable, weighty 8 abundant, concrete, material, physical, sensible, tangible 9 corporeal, important, objective 10 meaningful, phenomenal 11 significant 12 considerable

substantiate

5 prove 6 embody, evince, verify 7 bear out, confirm, justify 8 evidence, manifest, validate 9 establish, incarnate, objectify, vindicate 11 corroborate, demonstrate 12 authenticate

substantive

4 firm, noun, real 5 solid 8 definite 9 essential

substitute

4 mock, sham, swap 5 dummy, locum, proxy, trade 6 acting, backup, deputy, double, ersatz, fill-in, refuge, resort, second, switch 7 replace, reserve, standby, stand-in, stopgap 8 exchange, recourse, resource, spurious 9 alternate, expedient, imitation, makeshift, simulated, surrogate, temporary 10 artificial, expediency, understudy 11 alternative, locum tenens, pinch hitter, replacement, succedaneum

substratum

4 base 5 basis 6 bottom, ground 7 bedrock, footing 10 foundation, groundwork 12 underpinning

substructure

4 base, seat 5 basis 6 bottom 7 footing 10 foundation, groundwork 12 underpinning

subsume

6 embody, take in 7 contain, embrace, include, involve 8 comprise 9 encompass 10 comprehend

subterfuge

4 ploy, ruse, sham 5 cheat, feint, fraud 6 deceit, dupery 7 chicane 8 trickery 9 chicanery, deception 10 dishonesty

subterranean

11 underground

subtle

4 fine 5 faint 6 artful, astute 7 cunning, refined 8 delicate, finespun, guileful, skillful 9 insidious 10 indistinct 13 inconspicuous

subtract

6 deduct, remove 7 take off 8 discount, knock off, take away, withdraw, withhold

subtraction

6 rebate 8 discount 9 abatement, deduction 10 diminution, withdrawal **term:** 7 minuend 9 remainder 10 subtrahend

suburb

8 edge city

suburbs

7 fringes 8 environs, purlieus 9 outskirts

subversion

8 sabotage 11 undermining 12 undercutting

subvert

5 upset 6 debase 7 corrupt, deprave, vitiate 8 overturn, sabotage 9 overthrow, undermine

subway

British: 4 tube 11 underground **French:** 5 métro

succeed

3 win 4 boom 5 click, ensue, score 6 arrive, follow, go over, make it, pan out, thrive, win out 7 catch on, come off, make out, prevail, prosper, replace, triumph 8 displace, flourish, get ahead, make good, supplant 9 supervene

succes _____

3 fou 7 d'estime

success

3 hit 5 smash 7 arrival, fortune, killing, triumph, victory 8 fruition 10 attainment, prosperity 11 achievement, fulfillment

successful

5 smash 7 booming 8 fruitful, thriving 9 effective, lucrative 10 prosperous, triumphant, victorious 11 flourishing

succession
3 row 5 chain, cycle, march, order, round, suite, train 6 course, sequel, series, string 8 sequence 11 progression

successive
4 next 7 ensuing 9 following 10 subsequent

successor
4 heir 8 claimant, follower 9 inheritor 11 beneficiary

succinct
4 curt 5 blunt, brief, pithy, short, terse 7 brusque, compact, concise, laconic, summary 11 compendious

succor
3 aid 4 help, lift 6 assist, relief 7 comfort, relieve, support 10 assistance, sustenance

succulent
5 juicy 8 luscious

succumb
3 bow, die 4 cave, fold, wilt 5 defer, yield 6 accede, buckle, cave in, expire, give in, perish, relent, resign, submit 7 give out, go under, knuckle 8 collapse 9 break down, surrender 10 capitulate 11 buckle under 12 knuckle under

sucker
3 con, gyp, sap 4 bilk, dupe, fool, gull, mark, rook 5 cheat, chump, patsy, shoot 6 diddle, pigeon 7 defraud, fall guy, swindle 8 hoodwink, pushover 9 bamboozle

suckle
5 nurse 7 nourish, nurture 10 breastfeed

Sudan
capital: 8 Khartoum
desert: 6 Libyan
language: 6 Arabic
monetary unit: 5 dinar
neighbor: 4 Chad 5 Congo, Egypt, Kenya, Libya 6 Uganda 7 Eritrea 8 Ethiopia
river: 4 Nile
sea: 3 Red

sudden
4 rash 5 hasty, swift 6 abrupt, prompt 7 hurried 8 headlong 9 impetuous, impromptu, impulsive 10 unexpected, unforeseen 11 precipitant, precipitate, precipitous

suddenly
5 aback 7 hastily, shortly, unaware 8 abruptly, promptly, unawares 10 by surprise 12 unexpectedly

suds
4 beer, fizz, foam, head, soap 5 froth, spume 6 lather

sue
8 litigate

suer
8 litigant

suet
3 fat 4 lard 6 tallow

Suez Canal
builder: 7 Lesseps (Ferdinand de)
city: 8 Ismailia, Port Said

suffer
4 ache, bear, lump 5 abide, admit, allow, brook, leave, stand, yield 6 accept, endure, permit, submit 7 agonize, anguish, stomach, sustain, swallow, undergo 8 tolerate 10 experience 11 countenance

sufferer
6 victim

suffering
4 ache 5 agony, dolor 6 misery, ordeal 7 anguish, passion, torment, torture 8 distress 10 affliction, misfortune

suffice
5 avail, serve

sufficient
3 due 5 ample 6 common, decent, enough, plenty 8 adequate, all right 9 competent, tolerable 10 acceptable 11 comfortable 12 commensurate, satisfactory 13 commensurable, proportionate
poetic: 4 enow

suffocate
5 burke, choke 6 stifle 7 smother
8 snuff out, strangle 10 asphyxiate

suffrage
4 vote 5 voice 6 ballot 9 franchise

suffragist
4 Catt (Carrie Chapman), Howe
(Julia Ward), Mott (Lucretia), Paul
(Alice) 5 Stone (Lucy) 7 Anthony
(Susan B.), Bloomer (Amelia),
Stanton (Elizabeth Cady) 8 Wood-
hull (Victoria Claflin) 9 Pankhurst
(Emmeline)

suffuse
4 fill 5 flush, imbue, steep 7 pervade 8 permeate, saturate 10 impregnate

sugar
6 aldose, fucose, xylose 7 glucose,
lactose, maltose, mannose, pentose,
sorbose, sucrose, sweeten 8 fructose, furanose, levulose 10 saccha-
rose
combining form: 4 gluc, glyc, sucr
5 gluco, glyco, sucro 7 sacchar
8 sacchari, saccharo
from palm sap: 7 jaggery
Mexican: 7 panocha, penuche
source: 4 beet, cane, corn 5 maple

sugarcane refuse
7 bagasse

sugarcoat
5 candy 6 veneer 7 sweeten,
varnish 8 palliate 9 extenuate, gloss
over, gloze over, whitewash

sugary
6 syrupy 7 cloying, honeyed, mawkish 10 saccharine 11 sentimental

suggest
4 hint 5 evoke, imply 6 submit
7 connote, propose, signify 8 indicate, intimate 9 adumbrate, insinuate

suggestion
3 cue 4 clue, hint 5 shade, smack,
tinge, trace 6 advice 7 inkling
8 allusion, innuendo, overtone,
proposal, reminder 9 suspicion,
undertone 10 indication, intimation
11 implication, insinuation

suggestive
4 racy 5 salty, spicy 6 ribald, risqué
8 off-color 9 evocative 10 indicative
11 reminiscent

suicidal pilot
8 kamikaze

suicide
8 felo-de-se, hara-kiri 10 self-murder
13 self-slaughter
Japanese: 7 seppuku

suit
3 fit 4 case, jibe, plea 5 adapt,
agree, befit, cause, check, serve,
tally 6 accord, action, adjust, appeal,
become, go with, please, prayer,
square, tailor 7 conform, enhance,
flatter, lawsuit, request, satisfy
8 entreaty, petition 9 agree with,
reconcile 10 go together 11 accommodate, application, imploration,
imprecation 12 solicitation, supplication
type: 4 zoot 6 monkey, vested
9 paternity 10 pin-striped 11 class-
action

suitable
3 apt, due, fit 4 just, meet 5 right
6 proper, seemly, useful 7 condign,
fitting 8 apposite, becoming, deserved, eligible 9 pertinent, qualified,
requisite 10 acceptable, felicitous
11 appropriate

suitcase
3 bag 4 grip 6 valise 7 carry-on,
holdall 8 carryall

suite
3 lot, row, set 4 flat 5 array, group,
rooms, staff, train 6 sequel, series,
string 7 lodging, retinue 8 chambers, sequence 9 apartment, entourage, following

suitor
4 beau 5 lover, spark, swain, wooer
7 admirer, gallant, sparker 8 cavalier, paramour 9 boyfriend 10 petitioner

sulfur
9 brimstone

sulk
4 mope, pout 5 brood, gloom

sulky
4 cart, dour, glum 5 moody 6 gloomy, morose, sullen 7 crabbed 9 saturnine

sullen
4 dour, glum, mean, sour 5 moody, pouty, surly 6 crabby, dismal, gloomy, grumpy, morose, somber, sombre 7 crabbed, pouting 8 lowering, scowling 9 glowering, saturnine 10 ill-humored 11 pessimistic

Sullivan's partner
7 Gilbert (William Schwenk)

sully
3 tar 4 soil 5 dirty, shame, smear, stain, taint 6 defame, defile, malign, vilify 7 asperse, blacken, pollute, slander, tarnish, traduce 8 besmirch, disgrace, dishonor 9 denigrate

Sultan of Swat
8 Babe Ruth

sultry
3 hot 4 sexy 5 close, humid, muggy 6 steamy, sticky, stuffy, torrid 7 airless 8 stifling 9 seductive 10 passionate, sweltering, voluptuous

sum
3 add, all, tot 4 mass, tote 5 gross, total, whole 6 amount, digest, entity, figure, resumé 7 epitome 8 entirety, integral, nutshell, totality 9 aggregate, epitomize

Sumatra
country: 9 Indonesia
highest peak: 7 Kerinci 8 Kerintji
largest city: 5 Medan
shrew: 4 tana

Sumerian
city: 4 Umma
dragon: 3 Kur
god: 3 Abu, Kur, Utu 4 Enki 5 Enlil, Lahar, Nanna, Nintu 6 Dumuzi, Nergal, Ninazu 7 Enkimdu
goddess: 6 Ningal, Ninlil

summarize
5 recap 6 digest 7 abridge, outline 8 boil down, condense 9 epitomize, synopsize 11 encapsulate 12 recapitulate

summary
5 recap 6 aperçu, digest, précis, résumé, review, wrap-up 7 compend, epitome, outline, roundup, rundown 8 abstract, overview, scenario, synopsis 9 inventory 10 abridgment, compendium, conspectus 12 condensation

summer
French: 3 été

summerhouse
6 alcove, gazebo, pagoda 9 belvedere

summery
7 estival

summit
3 top 4 acme, apex, peak, roof 5 crest, crown 6 apogee, climax, height, vertex, zenith 8 capstone, meridian, pinnacle 11 culmination

summon
3 bid 4 call, cite 5 evoke, order 6 beckon, call in, invite, muster 7 arraign, command, conjure, convene, convoke, send for 8 assemble, subpoena

sump
4 sink 8 cesspool

sumptuous
4 lush, rich 5 grand 6 costly, deluxe, lavish, superb 7 opulent 8 gorgeous, luscious, palatial, splendid 9 grandiose, luxurious 11 extravagant, resplendent 12 awe-inspiring

sun
3 orb, Sol 4 bask, star 7 daystar, phoebus 8 daylight, luminary, radiance 9 radiation
combining form: 4 heli 5 helio
disk: 4 Aten
god: 3 Lug, Sol, Tem, Utu 4 Amen, Atmu, Atum, Inti, Lleu, Llew, Lugh,

Utug 5 Horus, Sunna, Surya
6 Apollo, Babbar, Helios, Marduk
7 Khepera, Ninurta, Phoebus,
Shamash 8 Hyperion, Merodach

Sun Also Rises, The
  author: 9 Hemingway (Ernest)
  character: 6 Ashley (Brett), Barnes
  (Jake)

sunder
  3 cut 4 rend, rive 5 break, sever,
  slice, split 6 cleave, divide 8 dissever, disunite, separate

sundial part
  6 gnomon

sundown
  4 dusk 7 evening 8 eventide,
  gloaming, twilight

sundries
  7 notions 8 oddments 9 etceteras
  11 odds and ends

sundry
  4 many, some 6 varied 7 diverse,
  several, various 8 assorted, manifold, numerous 9 different, disparate
  12 multifarious 13 miscellaneous,
  multitudinous

sunfish
  4 opah 7 pompano 8 bluegill
  11 pumpkinseed

Sunflower State
  6 Kansas

sun-god
  see at **sun**

Sun King
  8 Louis XIV

sunny
  4 fair, fine, warm 5 clear, happy
  6 blithe, bright, cheery, chirpy, golden
  7 beaming, clarion, radiant 8 cheerful, pleasant, rainless 9 brilliant,
  cloudless, unclouded 10 optimistic

sunrise
  4 dawn, morn 6 aurora 7 dawning,
  morning 8 cockcrow, daybreak,
  daylight
  goddess: 3 Eos 6 Aurora

sunroom
  8 solarium

sunset
  3 eve 4 dusk 7 evening 8 gloaming, twilight

Sunset State
  6 Oregon

Sunshine State
  7 Florida

sunup
  see **sunrise**

sup
  3 eat 4 dine 5 feast

super
  4 very 5 great 8 powerful, splendid,
  terrific 9 excellent, extremely, fantastic, first-rate, wonderful 11 outstanding

superannuated
  4 aged 5 hoary, passé 6 bygone
  7 ancient, archaic, elderly, outworn
  8 obsolete, outdated, outmoded
  9 out-of-date 10 antiquated 11 obsolescent 12 old-fashioned

superb
  4 rich 5 grand, lofty, noble, prime,
  super 7 elegant, exalted, optimal,
  optimum, opulent, stately, sublime,
  supreme 8 glorious, gorgeous,
  imposing, majestic, peerless, splendid, standout 9 excellent, marvelous,
  matchless, wonderful 11 magnificent, outstanding, resplendent,
  sensational, splendorous, superlative
  13 splendiferous

supercilious
  5 lofty 6 lordly, sniffy, snippy
  7 haughty, stuck-up 8 cavalier,
  snobbish, superior 10 disdainful
  11 patronizing 13 condescending,
  high-and-mighty

superficial
  5 hasty 6 casual, slight 7 cursory,
  shallow, sketchy, trivial 8 external,
  skin-deep 9 depthless 11 perfunctory

superfluity

4 glut 5 frill 6 excess 7 nimiety, overrun, surfeit, surplus 8 overflow, overkill, overload, overmuch, overplus, plethora 10 oversupply, redundancy, surplusage 11 prodigality 12 extravagance 13 overabundance

superfluous

5 extra, spare 6 de trop, excess 7 surplus 8 needless 9 excessive, redundant 10 gratuitous 11 uncalled-for, unnecessary

superintend

4 boss 6 direct, manage 7 control, oversee 10 administer

superintendence

4 care 6 charge 7 conduct, running 8 handling 9 authority, direction, oversight 10 management

superior

4 rare 5 above, lofty, major, prime, proud, upper 6 better, choice, higher, lordly, select, senior, sniffy, snippy, snooty 7 capital, greater, haughty, premium, stuck-up 8 arrogant, brass hat, cavalier, dominant, higher-up, insolent 9 excellent, first-rate, marvelous 10 disdainful, first-class, noteworthy, preeminent, preferable, remarkable 11 exceptional, overbearing, patronizing, predominant 13 condescending, high-and-mighty

superiority

9 advantage, dominance, seniority, supremacy, upper hand 10 ascendancy

superjacent

4 over 6 higher 7 greater 9 overlying

superlative

4 best 8 peerless, standout 10 consummate 11 magnificent, outstanding

Superman

9 Clark Kent
cartoonist: 7 Shuster (Joe)
girlfriend: 8 Lois Lane

supernatural

5 magic 6 divine, mystic 7 magical, psychic, uncanny 8 heavenly 9 celestial, unearthly 10 miraculous, paranormal, phenomenal 12 metaphysical, transcendent 13 extraordinary

supernatural being

3 elf, fay, god, hob, imp, nix 4 jinn, ogre, peri, puck 5 afrit, angel, bogle, deity, demon, fairy, gnome, jinni, lamia, naiad, nixie, nymph, pixie, satyr, sylph, Titan, troll 6 afreet, goblin, kelpie, seraph, spirit, sprite 7 banshee, brownie, bugbear, goddess, incubus, silenus, vampire 8 bogeyman, demiurge, succubus 9 hobgoblin 10 leprechaun

supernumerary

5 extra, spare 6 de trop, excess, walk-on 7 reserve, surplus 8 leftover 9 redundant

supersede

5 usurp 7 replace, succeed 8 displace, supplant

supervene

5 ensue, occur 6 befall, follow, result 7 succeed 9 eventuate, transpire

supervise

3 run 4 boss 5 steer 6 direct, govern, manage 7 conduct, control, monitor, oversee, proctor, referee 8 chaperon, overlook 10 administer

supervision

4 care 6 charge 7 control, running 8 auspices, handling 9 direction, oversight 10 intendance, management 11 stewardship

supervisor

7 foreman, manager 8 director, overseer 13 administrator

supine

5 inert, prone, slack 7 passive 8 inactive, indolent 9 prostrate, recumbent 10 horizontal 12 outstretched

supper club

6 nitery 7 cabaret 9 night spot

supplant

4 oust **5** usurp **6** cut out, unseat
7 replace, succeed **8** crowd out,
displace, force out **9** overthrow,
supersede

supple

5 agile, lithe, withy **6** limber, nimble,
pliant, whippy **7** ductile, elastic,
lissome, plastic, pliable, springy,
willowy **8** flexible, graceful, moldable
9 adaptable, malleable, resilient

supplement

3 add, pad **5** rider **6** append, beef
up, enrich, extend, sequel **7** adjunct,
augment, codicil, enhance, fill out,
fortify **8** addendum, addition, appendix, buttress, increase **9** accessory,
reinforce **10** postscript, strengthen

suppliant

5 asker **6** beggar, suitor **9** solicitor
10 petitioner

supplicant

see **suppliant**

supplicate

3 ask, beg, sue **4** pray **5** crave,
plead **6** appeal, invoke **7** beseech,
entreat, implore, solicit **8** petition
9 importune

supplication

4 plea, suit **6** appeal, orison, prayer
8 entreaty, petition **11** application

supplies

6 stores **8** matériel **9** equipment,
materials **10** provisions

supply

3 man **4** fund, hand, help **5** cache,
equip, hoard, stock, store **6** afford,
outfit, purvey **7** deliver, fulfill, furnish,
provide, reserve, satisfy, surplus
8 dispense, hand over, transfer, turn
over **9** inventory, provision, reservoir,
stockpile **10** contribute **12** accumulation

support

3 aid **4** back, base, bear, hand, help,
lift, prop, root, side, stay **5** abide,
adopt, boost, brace, bread, brook,
carry, favor, shore, strut, truss **6** anchor, assist, bear up, buoy up, column, crutch, defend, endure, girder,
pillar, second, suffer, uphold, verify
7 alimony, applaud, approve, backing, bolster, comfort, confirm, embrace, endorse, espouse, fortify,
fulcrum, nourish, nurture, pull for,
shore up, stiffen, sustain **8** abutment, advocate, backstop, buttress,
champion, mainstay, maintain, sanction, side with, underpin **9** encourage, reinforce, underprop **10** assistance, foundation, livelihood, provide
for, strengthen, sustenance **11** corroborate, maintenance, subsistence
12 underpinning

supporter

4 ally **6** patron **7** booster, sectary
8 adherent, advocate, champion,
disciple, exponent, follower, henchman, partisan **9** proponent

suppose

4 deem **5** allow, guess, infer, opine,
posit, think **6** assume, expect,
gather, reckon **7** believe, imagine,
presume, pretend, surmise, suspect
8 consider **9** postulate, speculate
10 conjecture **11** hypothesize

supposed

7 alleged, seeming **8** apparent,
putative **10** ostensible

supposition

5 guess, hunch, posit **6** notion,
theory, thesis **7** premise, surmise
9 postulate **10** assumption, conjecture, hypothesis **11** postulation,
presumption, speculation

supposititious

6 unreal **7** dubious, fictive, reputed
8 doubtful, fanciful, illusory, putative, spurious **9** fantastic, fictional,
imaginary, pretended, simulated
10 chimerical, fictitious, fraudulent
11 conjectural **12** hypothetical,
illegitimate, questionable

suppress

4 curb, stop **5** burke, check, choke,
crush, drown, quash, quell, shush,

spike, stunt **6** arrest, censor, cut off, hush up, muffle, muzzle, quench, retard, squash, stifle, subdue **7** abolish, collect, conceal, control, prevent, put down, silence, smother, squelch, swallow **8** prohibit, restrain, snuff out, withhold **9** overthrow **10** extinguish

suppurate
6 fester

supra
5 above

supremacy
7 control, mastery **8** dominion **9** authority, dominance **10** ascendancy, domination, mastership, prepotency **11** preeminence, sovereignty **12** predominance **13** preponderance

supreme
4 best **5** chief, final, prime **6** superb, utmost **7** highest, leading, maximum, perfect **8** absolute, cardinal, crowning, foremost, greatest, peerless, towering, ultimate **9** matchless, paramount, principal, sovereign, unequaled, unmatched, unrivaled **10** preeminent, surpassing **11** culminating, predominant, superlative, unmatchable, unsurpassed **12** incomparable, transcendent, unparalleled **13** unsurpassable

Supreme Being
3 God **5** Allah **7** creator, Jehovah **8** Almighty

surcease
3 end **4** halt, quit, rest, stay, stop **6** desist **7** refrain, respite, suspend **8** knock off, leave off, postpone, stoppage **9** cessation, remission **10** suspension **11** discontinue **12** postponement

sure
3 set **4** fast, firm, safe **5** fixed **6** indeed, secure, stable, steady, strong **7** certain, staunch **8** absolute, definite, enduring, positive, reliable, unerring **9** confident, convinced,

steadfast **10** convincing, dependable, inevitable, infallible, undeniable, unshakable, unwavering **11** indubitable, trustworthy, unequivocal, unfaltering **12** indisputable **13** incontestable, unquestioning

surefire
7 assured, certain **8** reliable **10** dependable, guaranteed

sure thing
6 shoo-in, winner **9** certainty

surety
4 bail, bond **5** angel **6** backer, patron, pledge **7** sponsor **8** guaranty, security, warranty **9** certainty, certitude, guarantee, guarantor **10** confidence, conviction

surface
3 top **4** face, pave, rise, skin **5** cover **6** appear, come up, facade, facing, finish, patina, show up, veneer **7** outside **8** covering, exterior **11** superficial

surfeit
4 cloy, fill, glut, jade, pall, sate **5** gorge, stuff **6** excess **7** replete, satiate, surplus **8** overfill, overflow, overkill, overmuch, overplus, plethora **10** surplusage **11** overindulge, superfluity **13** overabundance

surge
4 flow, gush, pour, rise, roll, rush, tide, wave **5** flood, swell **6** billow, deluge, sluice, stream **7** torrent

surgeon
8 sawbones
American: **4** Mayo (Charles, William), Reed (Walter) **6** Thorek (Max) **7** Cushing (Harvey), DeBakey (Michael) **8** McDowell (Ephraim)
British: **6** Hunter (John)
English: **5** Paget (James) **6** Lister (Joseph)
French: **4** Paré (Ambroise) **5** Broca (Paul)
South African: **7** Barnard (Christiaan)
Swiss: **6** Kocher (Emil Theodor)

surgery
9 operation
instrument: 5 clamp, curet, lance, laser, probe 6 gorget, lancet, splint, stylet, trocar 7 forceps, scalpel

surgical removal
8 ablation
combining form: 6 ectomy

Suriname
capital: 10 Paramaribo
former name: 11 Dutch Guiana
language: 5 Dutch, Hindi 6 Sranan
monetary unit: 7 guilder
mountain range: 10 Tumac-Humac
neighbor: 6 Brazil, Guyana
12 French Guiana
river: 6 Maroni 8 Suriname
10 Courantyne

surly
4 dour, glum 5 cross, gruff, sulky 6 crusty, grumpy, morose, sullen 7 bearish, crabbed, grouchy 8 churlish, menacing, snappish 9 irritable, saturnine 10 ungracious 11 illmannered, threatening 12 discourteous

surmise
see **suppose**

surmount
3 cap, top 4 best, down, leap, lick 5 clear, climb, crest, crown, excel, outdo, vault 6 better, hurdle, master 7 conquer, surpass 8 outstrip, overcome, vanquish 9 negotiate, transcend

surpass
3 cap, top 4 beat, best 5 excel, outdo, trump 6 better, exceed, outrun 7 eclipse, outpace 8 go beyond, outclass, outshine, outstrip, outweigh, overstep 9 transcend 10 overshadow 11 outdistance

surplice
5 cotta, ephod 8 vestment

surplus
5 extra, spare 6 excess 7 overage, overrun, reserve, surfeit 8 leftover, overflow, overkill, overmuch, plethora 9 overstock, remainder 10 oversupply 11 superfluity, superfluous 13 overabundance, supernumerary

surprise
4 faze, stun 5 amaze, floor 6 ambush, dismay, rattle, waylay, wonder 7 astound, capture, nonplus, stagger, startle, stupefy 8 astonish, bewilder, bowl over 9 amazement, dumbfound, overpower, take aback 11 flabbergast 12 astonishment, stupefaction

surreal
5 weird 7 bizarre 9 dreamlike, fantastic 10 outlandish 12 unbelievable

surrender
4 cave, cede, fold 5 waive, yield 6 cave in, give in, give up, resign, submit 7 abandon, concede, succumb 8 cry uncle, hand over 10 abdication, capitulate, relinquish, submission 12 capitulation, renunciation
sign: 7 hands up 9 white flag

surreptitious
see **stealthy**

surrogate
3 sub 5 proxy 6 acting, deputy, fill-in 7 stand-in, stopgap 9 alternate, makeshift 10 substitute 11 alternative, locum tenens, pinch hitter, replacement, succedaneum

surround
3 hem, rim 4 edge, gird, loop, ring 5 beset, bound, hem in, limit, round, skirt, verge 6 border, circle, fringe, girdle, margin 7 besiege, compass, confine, enclose, envelop, outline 8 encircle 9 encompass 12 circumscribe

surrounding
5 about 7 ambient 12 circumjacent
prefix: 4 peri 6 circum

surroundings
6 milieu 7 ambient 8 ambience 11 environment, mise-en-scène

surveillance

3 eye, tab   4 tail   5 vigil, watch
7 lookout   8 scrutiny, stakeout
9 vigilance   11 supervision

survey

3 con, vet   4 case, scan, view
5 assay, audit   6 assess, précis,
review, size up   7 canvass, examine,
inspect, pandect, perusal, preview
8 analysis, appraise, estimate,
evaluate, look over, overlook, overview, scrutiny, syllabus   9 check
over   10 inspection, scrutinize
11 reconnoiter, superintend

survive

4 keep, last   6 endure   7 carry on,
hold out, outlast, outlive, outwear,
persist, recover, ride out, weather
8 continue, live down   9 withstand
11 come through, live through, pull
through

Surya

6 sun-god
son: 4 Manu, Yama   5 Karna
6 Asvins   7 Sugriva
temple site: 7 Konarak

susceptible

4 open   5 naive, prone   6 liable
7 exposed, pliable, subject   8 disposed, inclined, sensible   9 malleable, receptive, sensitive   10 responsive, vulnerable   11 impressible,
persuadable, predisposed   12 nonresistant

suspect

5 doubt, fishy, guess   6 assume,
unsure   7 believe, dubious, imagine,
suppose, surmise   8 distrust, doubtful, mistrust   9 doubtable, uncertain
10 disbelieve   11 problematic
12 questionable

suspend

3 bar   4 bate, halt, hang, stay, stop
5 debar, defer, delay, hover, sling
6 dangle, depend, hold up, put off,
shelve   7 adjourn, hold off   8 intermit,
postpone, prorogue   9 eliminate
11 discontinue

suspended

6 frozen   7 hanging, pendant, pendent, stopped   8 dangling, swinging
9 pendulous

suspenders

6 braces   8 galluses

suspense

7 anxiety, mystery, tension   10 expectancy   11 expectation, uncertainty
12 apprehension

suspension

4 halt, stay, stop   5 delay, letup,
pause   6 cutoff, freeze   7 latency,
respite, time-out   8 abeyance,
dormancy, stoppage   9 remission
10 moratorium, quiescence   11 cold
storage, withholding   12 intermission,
interruption, postponement

suspicion

4 hint   5 doubt, dread, guess, hunch,
qualm, shade, smell, tinge, touch,
trace, whiff   7 concern, dubiety,
surmise   8 distrust, mistrust, wariness   9 chariness, misgiving   10 foreboding, intimation, skepticism,
suggestion   11 incertitude, premonition, supposition, uncertainty

suspicious

4 wary   5 chary, fishy, leery   7 dubious, jealous, suspect   8 doubtful,
watchful   9 doubtable, skeptical
11 distrustful, mistrustful, problematic
12 apprehensive, questionable

suspire

4 sigh   5 sough

sustain

4 bear, feed, prop, save   5 brace,
carry, stand   6 bear up, buoy up,
endure, foster, hold up, keep up,
succor, suffer, uphold   7 bolster,
confirm, nourish, nurture, prolong,
relieve, shore up, support, undergo
8 buttress, preserve, tolerate   9 withstand   10 experience, strengthen

sustenance

3 pap   4 food, keep, meat   5 bread,
means   6 living, viands   7 aliment,
alimony, pabulum, support   8 victuals

9 nutriment, provender **10** livelihood, provisions **11** maintenance, nourishment, subsistence, wherewithal **12** alimentation

susurration
4 purr **6** mumble, murmur, mutter, rustle **7** whisper **9** undertone

suture
3 sew **4** seam **6** stitch

suzerain
5 ruler **8** overlord **9** sovereign

svelte
4 slim **5** lithe, sleek, suave **6** smooth, urbane **7** elegant, slender **8** graceful

swab
3 mop **5** clean **6** sponge

swaddle
4 roll, wrap **5** drape **6** enfold, enwrap, swathe, wrap up **7** blanket, envelop **8** enshroud, enswathe

swag
3 yaw **4** loot, tilt **5** booty, droop, lurch, money, pitch, prize **6** boodle, seesaw, spoils **7** cluster, festoon, garland, pillage, plunder, profits **10** contraband

swagger
4 brag **5** boast, bully, strut, swank, swash, swell **7** bluster, bravado, peacock, saunter **9** arrogance, cockiness, gasconade **11** braggadocio, swashbuckle

swagman
4 hobo **5** rover, tramp **7** drifter, vagrant **8** vagabond, wanderer

swain
4 beau **5** lover, spark, wooer **6** rustic, suitor **7** admirer, peasant, sparker **8** shepherd **9** boyfriend

swallow
3 buy, sip **4** bear, belt, bolt, down, gulp, swig, take, toss, wolf **5** abide, brook, drink, quaff, slurp, stand, swill **6** absorb, accept, digest, endure, guzzle, imbibe, ingest, inhale **7** believe, consume, fall for, repress, retract, stomach **8** chugalug, take back, tolerate **11** ingurgitate

swamp
3 bog, fen **4** holm, mire, moss, muck, quag **5** drown, flood, glade, marsh, whelm **6** deluge, engulf, morass, muskeg, slough **7** bottoms **8** inundate, overcome, overflow, quagmire, submerge **9** everglade, marshland, overwhelm
Everglades: **10** Big Cypress
Georgia: **10** Okefenokee
North Carolina-Virginia: **6** Dismal

Swamp Fox
6 Marion (Francis)

swan
female: **3** pen
male: **3** cob **4** cobb
young: **6** cygnet

Swanhild
father: **6** Sigurd
mother: **6** Gudrun

swank
4 posh, tony, trig **5** boast, fancy, ritzy, sharp, showy, smart, swell, swish **6** chichi, classy, dapper, deluxe, lavish, plushy, snappy, trendy **7** elegant, peacock, show off, splashy, stylish, swagger **8** peacocky **9** glamorous, luxurious **10** flamboyant, peacockish **12** orchidaceous, ostentatious

swap
5 trade, truck **6** barter, change, switch **7** bargain, traffic **8** exchange **10** substitute

swarm
3 jam, mob **4** army, bevy, herd, host, mass, pack, push, shin, teem **5** crawl, crowd, crush, drove, flock, group, horde, mount, press **6** abound, gather, myriad, throng **7** climb up, cluster, overrun **9** multitude, pullulate **10** congregate

swarthy
4 dark **5** dusky, sooty **6** brunet **8** bistered **11** dark-skinned

swash

3 lap 4 brag, dash, gush, rush, slop
5 boast, churn, douse, froth, plash,
slosh 6 bubble, burble, gurgle,
seethe, splash 7 bluster, channel,
saunter, spatter, splurge, swagger
8 splatter

swat

3 bat, box, hit, rap 4 bash, belt,
blow, cuff, lick, slap, slog, slug, sock
5 blast, clout, homer, knock, smack,
smash, smite, swipe, whack 6 buffet,
larrup, strike, wallop 7 clobber,
home run

swath

4 belt, path 5 strip, sweep 6 stroke

swathe

see **swaddle**

sway

4 bend, bias, rock, rule 5 lurch,
might, power, range, reach, reign,
scope, sweep, swing, waver, weave
6 affect, direct, govern, induce, totter,
wobble 7 command, control, dispose, impress, incline, mastery, stagger, win over 8 dominate, dominion,
overrule, persuade, undulate 9 authority, dominance, fluctuate, influence, oscillate, prevail on, vacillate
10 domination, predispose 11 fluctuation

Swaziland

capital: 7 Lobamba, Mbabane
city: 7 Manzini
language: 5 Swazi 7 English
monetary unit: 9 lilangeni
neighbor: 10 Mozambique 11 South
Africa
river: 5 Usutu 6 Komati 8 Um-
beluzi

swear

3 vow 4 avow, bind, cuss, damn,
oath, rail, rant 5 abuse, curse, vouch
6 adjure, affirm, assert, attest,
depone, depose, pledge, plight
7 declare, promise, testify, warrant
8 covenant, maintain 9 blaspheme,
imprecate 10 asseverate, vituperate

swearword

4 cuss, oath 5 curse 9 expletive,
obscenity 10 scurrility

sweat

4 emit, glow, moil, ooze, seep, toil,
weep 5 exude, grind, labor 6 strain,
swivet 7 excrete 8 perspire, transude 12 perspiration

sweater

8 cardigan, pullover, slipover 10 tur-
tleneck

sweaty

6 clammy, sticky 7 glowing 10 per-
spiring

Sweden

Arctic region: 7 Lapland
capital: 9 Stockholm
city: 5 Malmö 8 Göteborg
gulf: 7 Bothnia 8 Kattegat
island: 5 Öland 7 Gotland
lake: 6 Vänern 7 Mälaren, Vättern
9 Hjälmaren
monetary unit: 5 krona
mountain range: 5 Kölen
neighbor: 6 Norway 7 Finland
part of: 11 Scandinavia
river: 3 Dal
sea: 6 Baltic

Swedish Nightingale

4 Lind (Jenny)

sweep

3 arc, fly, mop, win 4 flit, sail, scud,
skim, wing 5 ambit, broom, brush,
clean, clear, curve, drive, orbit,
range, reach, scope, surge, whisk
6 extent, radius, search 7 compass,
purview, victory 9 extension

sweeping

5 broad 6 all-out 7 blanket, general,
overall, radical 8 thorough, whole-
hog 9 extensive, inclusive, out-and-
out, universal, wholesale 12 all-
embracing 13 comprehensive,
thoroughgoing

sweepings

4 dust 5 trash, waste 6 debris, litter,
refuse 7 garbage, residue, rubbish
8 detritus

sweet
5 candy, honey **6** bonbon, dulcet, lovely, sugary, syrupy **7** angelic, cloying, dessert, melodic, scented, sugared, winning, winsome **8** aromatic, fragrant, heavenly, luscious, perfumed **9** ambrosial, delicious **10** delectable, saccharine
combining form: 4 glyc **5** glyco

Sweet ——
7 Adeline, Charity **8** Caroline

sweeten
5 candy, honey, sugar **6** soften **7** appease, assuage, enhance, mollify, placate **9** sugarcoat, sugar over **10** conciliate, propitiate

sweet potato
3 yam

sweet-talk
4 coax **5** charm **6** banter, cajole, wangle **7** blarney, flatter, wheedle **8** blandish, butter up, inveigle, soft-soap

swell
4 fine, grow, keen, neat, pout, puff **5** bloat, bulge, dandy, nifty, pouch, super, surge, swank **6** abound, billow, blow up, dilate, expand, groovy **7** amplify, augment, balloon, distend, inflate, peacock, swagger, upsurge **8** increase, terrific **9** crescendo, marvelous, wonderful
British: 3 nob **4** toff

swelled head
5 pride **6** egoism, vanity **7** conceit, egotism **8** smugness **9** arrogance, vainglory **10** narcissism **11** amour propre, self-conceit **13** conceitedness

swelling
3 sty **4** boil, bubo, bump, corn, gall, node **5** bulge, edema, tumid, tumor **6** bunion, growth, nodule **7** gibbous **8** tubercle **9** carbuncle, chilblain, expansion, tumescent **10** tumescence **11** excrescence **12** inflammation, protuberance

sweltering
3 hot **5** fiery **6** baking, sultry, torrid **7** burning, searing **8** broiling, roasting, sizzling, tropical **9** scorching

swerve
4 skew, turn, veer **5** sheer, shift, stray, waver **6** depart, wander **7** deflect, deviate, digress, diverge

swift
4 fast **5** fleet, hasty, quick, rapid, ready **6** prompt, snappy, speedy, sudden **8** full-tilt, headlong **9** breakneck

—— Swift
3 Tom **8** Jonathan
character: 8 Gulliver

swiftness
4 gait, pace **5** haste, hurry, speed **6** hustle **8** celerity, dispatch, legerity, rapidity, velocity **9** quickness, rapidness **10** expedition, speediness

swig
4 belt, down, drag, gulp, pull, slug **5** booze, draft, drain, drink, quaff, swill **6** guzzle, imbibe, tipple **7** swallow, swizzle

swill
4 bolt, gulp, slop, swig, tope, wolf **5** booze, draft, drink, gorge, scarf, scoff, slops, trash, waste **6** debris, gobble, guzzle, ingest, inhale, refuse, spilth, tank up, tipple **7** consume, garbage, hogwash, put away, rubbish, swizzle **8** chow down **9** polish off

swim
3 dip **4** reel, spin, turn **5** bathe, crawl, float, swoon, whirl **9** dizziness, dog-paddle

swimmingly
6 easily **8** smoothly **10** splendidly

swimming stroke
5 crawl **7** dolphin, trudgen **9** butterfly, dog paddle

swindle
3 con, gyp **4** bilk, clip, dupe, fake, hoax, rook, scam, sell, sham, skin,

swindler

soak 5 bunco, bunko, cheat, cozen, fraud, gouge, phony, rogue, shaft, skunk, sting 6 chouse, diddle, fleece, humbug, hustle, take in 7 defraud 8 flimflam, hoodwink 9 bamboozle, imposture, victimize 11 hornswoggle

swindler

5 cheat, crook, ganef, gonif, shark 6 con man, goniff 7 sharper, shyster 8 deceiver 9 charlatan, defrauder 10 mountebank

swine

see **hog**

swing

4 sway, veer 5 flail, lurch, pivot, twirl, waver, weave, whirl, wield 6 dangle, divert, rhythm, rotate, seesaw, stroke, swerve, switch 7 revolve, suspend 8 brandish 9 alternate, fluctuate, oscillate, vacillate

swinish

5 feral 6 animal, coarse 7 beastly, bestial, porcine

swipe

3 cop, hit, nab, rap 4 blow, clip, conk, grab, hook, lick, lift, nick, sock, swat, wipe 5 clout, filch, heist, knock, pinch, smack, steal 6 pilfer, snatch, snitch, strike, wallop

swirl

4 eddy, purl, roil 5 curve, twist, whirl, whorl 6 swoosh, vortex 9 whirlpool 11 convolution

swish

4 buzz, chic, fizz, hiss, posh, tony, whiz 5 ritzy, smart, swank, whisk 6 classy, dressy, sizzle, trendy, whoosh 7 elegant, stylish 8 sibilate 9 exclusive

Swiss Family Robinson author

4 Wyss (Johann David)

switch

3 rod, wag 4 beat, flay, flog, lash, swap, veer, wand, whip 5 shift, shunt, trade, whisk 6 change, strike, waggle 7 scourge 8 exchange,

flip-flop, reversal 9 about-face, sidetrack 10 substitute 12 substitution

Switzerland

capital: 4 Bern
city: 5 Basel 6 Geneva, Zürich 8 Lausanne
lake: 6 Geneva, Wallen 7 Lucerne 9 Constance, Neuchâtel, Thunersee, Zürichsee
language: 6 French, German 7 Italian
monetary unit: 5 franc
mountain, range: 4 Alps, Jura 9 Monte Rosa
neighbor: 5 Italy 6 France 7 Austria, Germany 13 Liechtenstein
resort: 5 Davos, Vevey 7 Zermatt 8 Montreux, St. Moritz 10 Interlaken
river: 4 Aare 5 Rhine, Rhône
state: 6 canton

swivel

4 spin, turn 5 pivot, swing, twirl, whirl 6 rotate 7 revolve 9 pirouette

swivet

see **snit**

swizzle

see **swig**

swollen

5 puffy, tumid 6 turgid 7 bloated, bulbous, bulging, pompous 8 enlarged, inflated, varicose 9 bombastic, distended, tumescent 10 rhetorical 12 magniloquent 13 grandiloquent

swoon

4 coma, daze, fade 5 droop, faint 6 torpor 7 pass out, rapture, syncope 8 black out

swoosh

4 eddy, gush, purl, rush 5 swirl, whirl, whorl

sword

4 épée, foil 5 saber, sabre 6 barong, bilboa, rapier, Toledo 7 cutlass 8 claymore, falchion, scimitar, yataghan

sword of _____
  8 Damocles

sword-shaped
  8 ensiform

sworn
  6 avowed 7 devoted 8 affirmed
  9 committed, confirmed 10 deep-
  rooted, deep-seated, entrenched,
  inveterate

sybarite
  7 epicure 8 hedonist 9 libertine
  10 sensualist, voluptuary

sybaritic
  6 carnal 7 sensual 8 sensuous
  9 epicurean, libertine, luxurious
  10 hedonistic, voluptuous 13 self-
  indulgent

sycophancy
  7 fawning 8 flattery, toadying
  9 truckling 11 bootlicking

sycophant
  5 leech, toady 6 flunky, lackey,
  minion, yes-man 8 groveler, hanger-
  on, parasite, truckler 9 easy rider,
  flatterer, toadeater 10 bootlicker,
  self-seeker 11 lickspittle 13 applepolisher

sycophantic
  7 fawning, servile, slavish 8 toadying, unctuous, kindly, kowtowing, parasitic, truckling 10 obsequious 11 bootlicking

Sycorax's son
  7 Caliban

syllable
  deletion: 7 apocope
  last: 6 ultima
  lengthening of: 7 ectasis
  next to last: 6 penult
  shortening: 7 elision, systole
  stressed: 5 arsis

syllabus
  6 aperçu, digest, précis, sketch,
  survey 7 epitome, outline, pandect,
  summary 8 abstract, headnote,
  synopsis 10 compendium

sylph
  5 fairy, nymph 6 sprite

sylvan
  5 bosky, woody 6 rustic, wooded
  deity: 3 Pan 4 Faun 5 dryad, satyr
  6 Faunus 7 Silenus 8 Arethusa,
  Silvanus, Sylvanus

symbol
  4 logo, mark, sign 5 badge, motif,
  stamp, token 6 design, device,
  emblem, mascot 9 attribute 10 indication
  chemical:
  see individual element
  musical: 4 clef, flat, hold, note,
  rest, turn 5 shake, sharp, trill 7 fermata, mordent, natural 8 arpeggio
  9 crescendo 10 diminuendo 11 decrescendo

symbolic
  5 token 10 emblematic 11 allegorical

symbolist poet
  7 Rimbaud (Arthur) 8 Mallarmé
  (Stéphane), Verlaine (Paul)

symbolize
  4 mean 6 embody, mirror, typify
  7 signify 8 stand for 9 epitomize,
  exemplify, personify, represent
  10 illustrate 11 emblematize

symmetrical
  5 equal 7 regular 8 balanced
  12 commensurate, proportional
  13 commensurable

symmetry
  5 order 6 parity 7 balance, harmony
  8 equality, evenness 9 agreement,
  congruity 10 conformity, proportion,
  regularity 11 arrangement

sympathetic
  4 kind, warm 6 benign, caring,
  humane, kindly, tender 8 amenable,
  friendly 9 agreeable, approving,
  benignant, congenial, congruous,
  consonant, favorable, receptive
  10 compatible, consistent, responsive 11 consistent, kindhearted, softhearted, warmhearted

sympathize
12 well-disposed 13 compassionate, understanding

sympathize
4 pity 7 condole 11 commiserate 13 compassionate

sympathy
4 pity, ruth 5 heart 6 accord, solace, warmth 7 comfort, harmony, rapport 8 affinity, kindness 9 agreement 10 benignancy, compassion, condolence, kindliness, tenderness 11 consolation, sensitivity 13 commiseration

symphonic
10 orchestral

symphony
9 orchestra 12 philharmonic

symposium
5 forum 7 meeting, seminar 9 gathering 10 conference, discussion

symptom
4 mark, sign 5 index, token 8 evidence 10 indication

symptoms
7 indicia 8 syndrome

synagogue
6 temple

sync
4 jibe 5 agree, match 7 harmony 8 coincide 9 harmonize 10 concurrent 12 simultaneous

synchronize
5 agree 6 concur 8 coincide

synchronous
6 coeval 10 coetaneous, coexistent, coexisting, coincident, concurrent 11 concomitant 12 contemporary, simultaneous 13 geostationary

syncope
4 coma 5 faint, swoon 8 blackout

syndicate
3 mob 4 pool 5 chain, group, mafia, trust, union 6 cartel, league 7 combine 11 association, partnership 12 conglomerate, organization 13 confederation

syndrome
3 ill 6 malady 7 ailment, disease 8 disorder, sickness 9 complaint, condition, infirmity

synergic
5 joint 6 shared 8 coacting, coactive, conjoint 9 collusive, concerted 11 cooperating, cooperative, coordinated

synod
4 body, diet 7 council, meeting 8 assembly, conclave, congress 10 conference, convention 11 convocation

synopsis
5 brief, recap 6 aperçu, digest, précis, review 7 capsule, epitome, outline, rundown, summary 8 abstract, breviary, syllabus 10 abridgment, compendium, conspectus 12 condensation

synopsize
5 recap, sum up 6 digest 7 outline, summate 8 abstract, boil down, compress, condense 9 epitomize, inventory, summarize 11 encapsulate

synthesis
5 blend, union 6 fusion, merger 7 amalgam 8 blending, compound 9 composite 11 combination 12 amalgamation 13 incorporation

synthesize
4 fuse, meld 5 blend, merge, unify 7 combine 8 compound 9 harmonize, integrate 10 amalgamate 11 incorporate

synthetic
6 ersatz 7 man-made 9 unnatural 10 artificial, fabricated 11 counterfeit

Syria
capital: 8 Damascus
city: 4 Homs 6 Aleppo
desert: 6 Syrian
language: 6 Arabic, French
monetary unit: 5 pound
mountain range: 7 Lebanon
neighbor: 4 Iraq 6 Israel, Jordan, Turkey 7 Lebanon

plain: **11** Mesopotamia
river: **9** Euphrates
sea: **13** Mediterranean

syringe
6 needle

Syrinx
5 nymph
pursuer: **3** Pan

syrinx
7 panpipe **8** panpipes

syrup
6 orgeat **9** grenadine

syrupy
5 gooey, mushy, sappy, sweet
6 drippy, dulcet, slushy, sticky, sugary **7** cloying, maudlin, mawkish
9 schmaltzy **10** saccharine **11** sentimental

system
3 way **4** mode, plan **5** modus, order,
setup **6** entity, manner, method,
scheme **7** complex, network, pattern, process, regimen, routine
8 strategy **9** procedure, structure,
technique **10** regularity **11** arrangement, disposition, orderliness

systematic
7 logical, ordered, orderly, regular
8 arranged **9** organized **10** analytical, methodical **12** businesslike

systematize
5 array, order **6** codify **7** arrange,
catalog, dispose, marshal **8** classify,
organize, regiment **9** catalogue,
methodize

system of weights
4 troy **11** avoirdupois **12** apothecaries

T

tab
4 bill, cost, flap, list, loop, rate
5 check, count, price, score 6 charge,
record 7 account, invoice 8 eagle
eye, price tag, scrutiny 9 appendage, designate, extension, reckoning,
statement 12 surveillance

tabard
4 cape, coat 5 tunic 10 coat of arms

tabby
3 cat 6 feline, cement 8 brindled

tabernacle
4 tent 5 hovel 6 church, temple

tabes
7 atrophy, wasting 12 degeneration

Tabitha's Greek name
6 Dorcas

table
4 fare, list 5 bench, board, chart,
defer, stand 6 buffet, put off, record,
shelve, teapoy 7 counter 8 mahogany, postpone 9 sideboard
ornament: 7 epergne
11 centerpiece
writing: 4 desk 9 secretary 10 escritoire

table d' _____
4 hôte

tableland
4 mesa 5 butte 6 upland 7 plateau
Alabama-West Virginia: 10 Cum-
berland
Arizona: 5 Kanab 6 Kaibob
England: 8 Dartmoor
India: 5 Malwa
(see also **plateau**)

tablet
3 bar, pad 4 cake, disk, pill, slab
5 panel, slate 6 pellet, plaque,
troche 7 lozenge, notepad 8 steno
pad

Table Talk author
6 Selden (John)

tableware
4 cups 5 bowls, china, forks
6 dishes, knives, plates, silver,
spoons 7 glasses, saucers 8 set-
tings, utensils 9 stainless

tabloid
3 rag 5 lurid, pulpy 6 digest 7 summary 9 condensed, newspaper
11 sensational 12 scandal sheet

taboo
3 ban 4 no-no 6 banned, enjoin,
forbid 7 inhibit, obscene 9 forbidden, ineffable, interdict, off-limits,
restraint 10 inhibition 11 restriction,
unspeakable 12 interdiction

tabor
4 drum

tabulate
4 list 5 count, order 6 codify, figure,
record 7 arrange 9 enumerate
11 systematize

tabulation
4 list 5 chart, tally 6 record 7 account

tabula _____
4 rasa

tacit
6 silent, unsaid 7 assumed, implied
8 implicit, inferred, unspoken 9 inti-

mated, suggested **10** subtextual, undeclared, underlying, understood **11** acquiescent, unexpressed **12** inarticulate

taciturn
4 dumb **6** silent **7** laconic **8** reserved, reticent, wordless **9** secretive **11** tight-lipped **12** closemouthed

Tacitus work
7 Annales **8** Dialogus, Germania **9** Historiae

tack
3 pin, yaw **4** beat, brad, gear, join, nail, stay, turn **5** baste, reach, shift **6** attach, double, stitch, swerve, turn up, zigzag **7** tangent **8** put about **9** come about, deviation **10** alteration, deflection, digression, sea biscuit **11** ship biscuit **12** pilot biscuit

tackle
3 cat, rig **4** gear, sack **6** outfit, take on, take up **7** halyard, lineman, rigging **8** set about **9** apparatus, equipment, machinery, undertake **10** footballer, linebacker, plunge into **13** paraphernalia

tacky
5 cheap, crude, dingy, dowdy, gaudy, messy, seedy, ratty, tatty **6** blowsy, frowsy, frumpy, kitsch, shabby, sleazy, sloppy, sticky, frumpy, tawdry, untidy, vulgar **7** run-down, unkempt **8** adhesive, frumpish, slovenly **9** inelegant, tasteless, unstylish **10** broken-down, down-at-heel, threadbare

tact
5 poise, touch **6** acumen **7** address, finesse, suavity **8** civility, courtesy, delicacy, urbanity **9** diplomacy, politesse **10** adroitness, politeness, smoothness **11** savoir faire, sensitivity

tactful
5 civil, suave **6** adroit, urbane **7** politic **8** delicate, discreet, polished **9** courteous, sensitive **10** diplomatic, perceptive, thoughtful **11** considerate

tactical
7 politic, prudent **9** advisable, expedient, strategic

tactics
4 plan **6** method, scheme **8** maneuver, playbook, strategy **9** stratagem

tactile
8 palpable, tangible **9** touchable

taction
4 feel **5** touch **7** contact **9** palpation

tactless
4 rude **5** blunt, crude, inept **6** candid, clumsy, gauche **7** awkward **8** impolite **9** impolitic, maladroit **10** indiscreet **11** insensitive

tad
3 bit, boy, lad, son **4** lick, mite, snap, spot, whit **5** child, crumb, sonny, speck **6** laddie, nipper, shaver **7** smidgen **8** fraction

tadpole
8 polliwog, pollywog

taffy
5 candy **8** flattery

tag
3 bit, dog, end **4** cost, flag, game, logo, mark, name, tail **5** aglet, brand, label, price, trail **6** append, charge, follow, select, shadow, slogan, tassel, tatter, ticket **7** license, run down **8** graffito, identify, insignia

Tahiti
city: **7** Papeete
painter: **7** Gauguin (Paul)

tail
3 dog, end, tag **4** butt, rear **5** hound, stalk **6** follow, pursue, shadow **7** hind end, rear end **8** backside, buttocks **9** posterior
bone: **6** coccyx
relating to: **6** caudal
short: **4** scut

tailed
7 caudate

tailor

3 fit, sew 4 suit 5 alter 8 clothier, seamster 11 haberdasher

tailor-made

6 fitted, suited 7 bespoke, fitting 8 suitable 10 well-suited 11 appropriate

taint

3 rot 4 blot, blur, foul, harm, hurt, smut, soil, spot, turn, vice 5 brand, cloud, color, decay, dirty, fault, smear, spoil, stain, sully, touch 6 befoul, darken, defile, poison, smudge, smutch 7 blacken, blemish, corrupt, pollute, putrefy, tarnish 8 besmirch, discolor 9 discredit 10 adulterate, stigmatize 11 contaminate

taipan

5 snake 8 merchant 11 businessman

Taiwan

7 Formosa
capital: 6 Taipei
channel: 5 Bashi
city: 6 T'ai-nan 8 Pan-ch'iao, T'ai-chung 9 Kao-hsiung
language: 8 Mandarin
leader: 13 Chiang Kai-shek
monetary unit: 6 dollar
mountain: 6 Yü Shan

Tajikistan

capital: 8 Dushanbe
monetary unit: 5 ruble
mountain, range: 6 Pamirs 9 Communism (Peak), Trans Alai 10 Revolution (Peak)
neighbor: 5 China 10 Kyrgyzstan, Uzbekistan 11 Afghanistan
river: 8 Amu Dar'ya, Syr Dar'ya

Taj Mahal

9 mausoleum
builder: 9 Shah Jahan
site: 4 Agra

take

3 get, nab 4 grab 5 annex, catch, seize 6 gather, obtain, secure 7 capture, receive 8 proceeds, receipts
account of: 6 notice
advantage of: 5 abuse 7 exploit
after: 6 follow 8 resemble
apart: 7 analyze, dissect 9 dismantle
care: 6 beware
care of: 3 fix 4 tend 5 nurse 6 attend
exception: 6 object
five: 4 rest
from: 7 deprive, detract 8 subtract
it easy: 5 relax
on the: 7 corrupt
part: 4 join 5 share 11 participate
place: 5 occur 6 happen
to task: 5 scold 7 reprove
turns: 9 alternate
unawares: 8 surprise

take away

4 grab 5 wrest 6 arrest, commit, deduct, detach, detain, remove 7 deprive, detract 8 diminish, discount, minimize, subtract, withdraw

take back

5 unsay 6 abjure, recall, recant, return 7 replace, restore, retract, swallow 8 forswear, withdraw 9 repossess

take down

4 note 5 lower, write 6 humble, record, reduce 7 deflate 8 dismount 9 dismantle 11 disassemble

take in

3 con 4 dupe, fool, furl, jail 5 admit, bluff, board, house, trick 6 absorb, accept, arrest, attend, betray, delude, embody 7 beguile, compass, contain, deceive, embrace, include, involve, mislead, observe, receive, shelter, snooker, subsume 8 flimflam, hoodwink, perceive 9 apprehend, bamboozle, encompass, four-flush 10 assimilate, comprehend, understand 11 doublecross

take off

4 doff, exit, quit 5 leave, scram 6 begone, deduct, depart, remove, set out 7 pull out, skiddoo, vamoose 8 clear out, discount, hightail, light out, subtract, withdraw 9 skedaddle

takeoff
5 spoof 6 launch, parody, satire, send-up 7 lampoon 8 travesty 9 burlesque 10 caricature
area: 3 pad 6 runway

take on
3 don 4 face, hire, meet 5 adopt, annex, fight 6 accept, append, assume, attack, battle, employ, engage, strike, tackle 7 contest, embrace, espouse, venture 8 endeavor, set about 9 encounter, undertake

take out
4 date, kill, omit 5 loose 6 deduct, remove 7 destroy, release, unleash 8 discount, knock off, separate, subtract, withdraw, withhold 9 eliminate 10 annihilate

take over
5 seize, spell, usurp 6 assume 7 capture, relieve

take up
3 use 4 fill, open 5 adopt, begin, enter, raise, renew, set to, start 6 absorb, accept, assume, gather, occupy, resume, shrink, tackle 7 embrace, espouse, kick off, restart, shorten, tighten 8 commence, continue, initiate 10 recommence

talc
6 powder 8 steatite 9 soapstone

tale
3 fib, lie 4 myth, saga, yarn 5 fable, rumor, story 6 canard, legend 7 fiction 8 anecdote 9 narration, narrative

talebearer
3 rat 4 fink 6 canary, gossip, snitch 7 rat fink, tattler 8 busybody, gossiper, informer, quidnunc, squealer, telltale 9 informant 10 newsmonger, tattletale 11 rumormonger, stool pigeon 12 blabbermouth 13 scandalmonger

talent
4 bent, gift, head, nose 5 craft, dowry, flair, forte, knack, skill 6 genius 7 ability, aptness, faculty 9 endowment, expertise

talented
4 able 6 clever, expert, gifted 8 skillful

Tale of Two Cities, A
author: 7 Dickens (Charles)
character: 5 Lucie (Manette) 6 Carton (Sidney), Darnay (Charles) 7 Defarge (Madame), Manette (Alexander)

Tales of a Traveller author
6 Irving (Washington)

Tales of a Wayside Inn author
10 Longfellow (Henry Wadsworth)

Tales of Hoffman composer
9 Offenbach (Jacques)

talisman
4 juju, luck 5 charm 6 amulet, fetish, mascot, scarab 7 periapt 10 phylactery

Talisman author
5 Scott (Walter)

talk
3 gab, rap, yak 4 blab, buzz, chat, chin, yarn 5 prate, rumor, run on, speak, utter, voice 6 babble, gabble, gossip, parley, patter, report, speech 7 address, chatter, declaim, hearsay, lecture, prattle 8 colloquy, converse, dialogue, harangue 9 discourse, utterance 10 discussion 12 conversation
about: 7 discuss
back: 4 sass
foolish: 4 bunk 6 babble 7 chatter, palaver
indistinctly: 6 mumble, mutter
over: 7 discuss
slowly: 5 drawl
small: 8 chitchat
wildly: 4 rant, rave

talkative
4 glib 5 gabby, vocal 6 chatty, fluent 7 gossipy, voluble 9 garrulous 10 loquacious 13 communicative

talk over
6 debate 7 discuss, hash out 8 consider 9 thrash out 10 deliberate

talky
5 gabby, windy, wordy 6 chatty, prolix 7 verbose, voluble

tall
4 high, long 5 lanky, large, lofty, rangy 6 absurd 7 pompous 8 towering 9 high-flown 10 far-fetched 11 skyscraping 12 altitudinous

tallow
3 fat 4 lard, suet 6 grease

tally
3 tab 4 jibe, list, tale 5 agree, count, match, score, total 6 accord, census, number, reckon, square 7 account, balance, catalog, compute, conform, itemize 8 check off, register, tabulate 9 agreement, catalogue, enumerate, harmonize, inventory, reckoning 10 complement, correspond

talon
4 claw, hand 5 stock 6 finger

talus
5 ankle, scree, slope 9 anklebone 10 astragalus

tam
3 cap

Tamar
brother: 7 Absalom
father: 5 David 7 Absalom
father-in-law: 5 Judah
half brother: 5 Amnon
seducer: 5 Amnon
son: 5 Perez, Zerah

tamarisk
9 salt cedar

tambour
3 cup 4 drum 9 embroider 10 embroidery

Tamburlaine the Great author
7 Marlowe (Christopher)

tame
4 bust, dull, meek, mild 5 break, train, vapid 6 bridle, docile, gentle, humble, soften, subdue 7 harness, insipid, reclaim, subdued 8 domestic, familiar, obedient 9 tractable

10 housebreak, submissive 11 domesticate, housebroken 12 domesticated

Taming of the Shrew, The
character: 6 Bianca 8 Baptista 9 Katharina, Petruchio

Tammany boss
5 Tweed (William)

Tammuz's lover
6 Ishtar

tam-o'-shanter
3 cap

tamp
3 ram 4 pack 5 pound, press, stuff

tampion
4 plug 5 cover

tan
3 sun, taw 4 beat, ecru, flog, whip 5 beige, brown, tawny, toast 6 bronze, darken, thrash 7 biscuit

Tan novel
11 Joy Luck Club (The) 15 Kitchen God's Wife (The) 19 Bonesetter's Daughter (The)

tanager
7 redbird

Tancred, Tancredi
beloved: 8 Clorinda
father: 3 Odo
mother: 4 Emma
victim: 8 Clorinda

tandem
4 pair 7 bicycle, concert 8 carriage

tang
3 nip 4 bite, fang, odor, ring, zest 5 aroma, clang, prong, sapor, savor, shank, smack, taste, trace 6 flavor, relish 8 piquancy, pungency, sapidity 9 spiciness

tangible
4 real 7 tactile 8 concrete, material, palpable, physical, sensible 9 corporeal, touchable 10 detectable, observable, phenomenal 11 appreciable, discernible, perceptible, substantial

tangle
3 mat, web 4 foul, knot, maze, mesh, shag 5 clash, ravel, skein, snare, snarl 6 entrap, foul up, hamper, jumble, jungle, morass, muddle, pileup, raffle 7 dispute, embroil, ensnare, ensnarl, involve, perplex, seaweed, thicket 8 obstruct 9 embarrass, implicate 10 complicate 11 altercation, predicament 12 bewilderment, complication

Tanglewood Tales author
9 Hawthorne (Nathaniel)

tango
5 dance 8 circuity 11 indirection 13 deceitfulness

tangy
5 sharp 6 lively 7 piquant, pungent, zestful 9 flavorful

tank
3 vat 5 basin 7 cistern 8 aquarium 9 reservoir
American: 6 Abrams 7 Bradley, Sherman
German: 6 panzer
part: 6 turret

tankard
3 mug 5 stoup 6 flagon 9 blackjack

tanked
3 lit 4 high, lost 5 drunk, lit up, oiled 6 bashed, blotto, bombed, failed, gave up, juiced, potted, soaked, soused, stewed, stoned, tanked, wasted, zonked 7 crocked, drunken, pickled, pie-eyed, sloshed, smashed, sottish 9 collapsed, plastered 10 inebriated, liquored up 11 intoxicated

tanker
4 ship 5 oiler

Tannhäuser composer
6 Wagner (Richard)

tantalize
3 rag 4 bait, lure 5 tease, tempt 6 entice, needle 7 torment 9 frustrate

Tantalus
daughter: 5 Niobe
father: 4 Zeus
son: 6 Pelops

tantamount
4 same 5 alike, equal 8 parallel, selfsame 9 duplicate, identical 10 equivalent 12 commensurate

tantara
5 blare 7 fanfare

tantivy
3 run 6 gallop

tantrum
3 fit 6 blowup 8 outburst, paroxysm 9 hysterics 10 conniption

Tanzania
capital: 6 Dodoma 11 Dar es Salaam
city: 6 Arusha
former name: 10 Tanganyika
island: 5 Mafia, Pemba 8 Zanzibar
lake: 5 Rukwa 6 Malawi 8 Victoria 10 Tanganyika
language: 7 English, Swahili
monetary unit: 8 shilling
mountain: 11 Kilimanjaro
neighbor: 5 Congo, Kenya 6 Malawi, Rwanda, Uganda, Zambia 7 Burundi 10 Mozambique
plain: 9 Serengeti
river: 6 Kagera, Rufiji, Ruvuma 7 Pangani
volcano: 6 Lengai

Taoism founder
5 Laozi 6 Lao Tzu

tap
3 hit, pat 4 cock, draw, flap, name, plug, tick 5 chuck, draft, drain, nudge, touch, valve 6 faucet, select, siphon, spigot, strike 7 appoint, draw off, hydrant, percuss, petcock 8 drumbeat, half sole, nominate, stopcock 9 designate

tape
4 band, belt, bind 5 strip 6 fillet, ribbon 7 bandage
kind: 5 inkle 6 ferret 7 masking 8 adhesive
machine: 4 deck 8 recorder

taper

4 wane, wick 5 abate, close, draft, pinch, spire 6 candle, lessen, narrow, reduce 7 dwindle, glimmer 8 decrease, diminish

tapering

5 conic, spiry 6 spired, terete 7 conical 8 ensiform, fusiform, napiform, subulate 9 acuminate, attenuate 10 lanceolate

tapestry

5 arras, kilim 6 dossal 7 curtain, Gobelin, hanging
pattern: 7 cartoon

Taphath's father

7 Solomon

tapioca

4 yuca 5 yucca 6 manioc 7 cassava, farinha, pudding

taproom

3 bar, pub 4 café 6 bodega, saloon, tavern 7 cantina 8 dramshop 9 roadhouse

tapster

6 barman 7 barkeep, barmaid, skinker 9 barkeeper, bartender 10 mixologist

tar

3 gob 4 jack, salt, soil, swab 5 pitch, smear, stain, sully, taint 6 defile, hearty, sailor, seaman 7 asphalt, besmear, mariner, shipman 8 besmirch, creosote, deckhand, flatfoot 9 shellback

taradiddle

3 fib, lie 5 hooey, story, trash 6 bunkum, canard 7 baloney, falsity 8 claptrap, nonsense 9 falsehood 10 balderdash 13 prevarication

tarantella

5 dance

tarantula

6 spider 10 wolf spider

Taras Bulba author

5 Gogol (Nikolai)

tarboosh

3 fez, hat

tardy

4 dull, late, lazy, slow 7 belated, delayed, laggard, overdue 8 dilatory, sluggish 10 behindhand, delinquent, unpunctual

tare

4 seed 5 vetch, weigh 6 weight 11 undesirable 13 counterweight

target

3 aim 4 butt, goal, mark, prey 5 aim at 6 object, quarry, victim 9 objective 11 sitting duck
center: 8 bull's-eye
shooter's: 10 clay pigeon

Tar Heel State

13 North Carolina

tariff

3 tax 4 cost, duty, levy, rate 5 price 6 charge, impost 7 tribute 10 assessment

Tarkington character

6 Penrod

tarn

4 lake, pool

tarnish

3 dim, mar 4 dull, foul, harm, hurt, soil 5 dirty, muddy, smear, spoil, stain, sully, taint 6 damage, darken, defile, injure, smirch, smudge, smutch 7 begrime, besmear, blemish, vitiate 8 besmirch, discolor

taro

5 aroid 6 yautia 7 dasheen, malanga
product: 3 poi

tarpaulin

3 gob 4 jack, salt, swab 5 cover, sheet 6 hearty, sailor, seaman 7 mariner, shipman 9 shellback

tarpon

8 ladyfish 10 silverfish

tarry

3 lag 4 bide, drag, stay, wait 5 abide, dally, delay, visit 6 dawdle, linger, loiter, pitchy, remain 7 sojourn

tarsus

5 ankle

tart

3 pie 4 acid, bawd, moll, slut, sour
5 acerb, quean, sharp, tramp, trull,
whore 6 biting, harlot, pastry 7 acerbic, cutting, piquant, pungent, tootsie
8 chess pie, strumpet 10 prostitute

tartar

5 argol 6 plaque 8 calculus

Tartar

6 Mongol, Turkic 7 Turkish 9 Mongolian

Tartuffe author

7 Molière

Tarzan

chimpanzee: 7 Cheetah
creator: 9 Burroughs (Edgar Rice)
mate: 4 Jane

task

3 job 4 duty, lade, load, post, slog,
toil, work 5 chare, chore, labor, stint
6 assign, burden, charge, detail, devoir 7 mission, project 8 business,
encumber, function 9 challenge,
dress down, reprimand 10 assignment, commission 11 undertaking
12 dressing-down

Tasmanian

4 wolf 5 devil
capital: 6 Hobart
pine: 4 Huon

tassel

3 tag 4 tuft 5 adorn 6 fringe 7 pendant, tzitzit 8 ornament 13 inflorescence

Tasso, Torquato

patron: 4 Este (Alfonso II d')
work: 6 Aminta 7 Rinaldo 18 Jerusalem Delivered

taste

3 eat, sip, try 4 tang, zest 5 savor,
smack 6 flavor, liking, palate, relish
7 stomach 8 appetite, elegance,
fondness, sapidity, soft spot, weakness 10 experience, partiality,
refinement 11 inclination
kind: 4 salt, sour 5 sweet 6 bitter
organ: 3 bud

tasteful

4 fine 7 elegant, genteel, refined,
stylish 8 artistic, becoming 9 aesthetic

tasteless

4 dull, flat 5 bland, crass, gaudy,
showy, stale, tacky, vapid 6 vulgar
7 insipid 8 off-color, unsavory
9 inelegant, savorless, unrefined
10 flavorless

tasty

5 sapid, yummy 6 dainty, delish,
savory 8 luscious 9 delicious,
flavorful, palatable, succulent, toothsome 10 appetizing, delectable,
flavorsome

tattered

4 torn 5 dingy, seedy 6 frayed,
ragged, ripped, shabby 7 raggedy,
run-down, worn-out 10 bedraggled,
threadbare 11 dilapidated

tattle

3 wag, yak 4 blab, buzz, dish, talk
5 clack, prate, rumor 6 gossip,
inform, report, snitch, squeal 7 chatter, hearsay, prattle 8 chitchat
9 grapevine 11 scuttlebutt

tattletale

see **talebearer**

tatty

5 cheap, dingy, dowdy, dumpy, seedy,
tacky 6 beat-up, cheesy, paltry,
scuzzy, shabby, shoddy, sleazy,
trashy 7 run-down, scrubby 8 rubbishy 10 threadbare 11 dilapidated

taunt

3 jab 4 gibe, jeer, mock, quip, razz,
skit, twit 5 scout, tease 6 deride,
insult 7 affront, provoke 8 reproach,
ridicule 9 challenge

taurine

6 bovine 8 bull-like

Taurus

4 bull
star: 9 Aldebaran

taut

4 firm, snug, trim 5 rigid, tense, tight
6 corded 10 high-strung

tautology

8 iterance, pleonasm **9** iteration
10 redundancy, repetition

tavern

3 bar, inn, pub **4** café, dive **6** bistro, bodega, saloon **7** barroom, cantina, gin mill, taproom **8** alehouse, pothouse, wineshop **9** roadhouse **11** public house, rathskeller **12** watering hole **13** watering place

taverner

7 barkeep **8** boniface, publican **9** barkeeper, bartender, innkeeper **12** saloonkeeper

taw

3 tan **6** marble **7** partner

tawdry

4 loud **5** cheap, gaudy, tacky **6** brazen, flashy, garish, tinsel **7** chintzy, glaring, ignoble **9** brummagem, dime-store **12** meretricious

tawny

3 tan **4** buff **5** beige, brown, sandy **6** copper, tanned

tax

4 duty, lade, levy, load, onus, scot, toll **5** drain, tithe **6** assess, burden, cumber, impost, saddle, strain, tariff, weight **7** tribute **8** encumber **10** imposition
agency: 3 IRS
feudal: 7 scutage, tallage
kind: 4 geld **5** sales, tithe **6** excise, income **9** property **9** surcharge
on salt: 7 gabelle
rate: 10 assessment

taxi

3 cab, car **4** hack **5** cyclo

taxing

5 tough **6** trying **7** exigent, onerous, wearing **8** exacting, grievous, grueling **9** demanding, difficult **10** burdensome, oppressive

Taygeta

father: 5 Atlas
mother: 7 Pleione
sisters: 8 Pleiades

tazza

3 cup **4** vase

Tchaikovsky, Pyotr Ilyich

ballet: 8 Swan Lake **10** Nutcracker (The) **14** Sleeping Beauty
opera: 12 Eugene Onegin **13** Queen of Spades (The)

tea

5 party **6** repast **8** beverage **9** reception
black: 5 bohea, pekoe **8** souchong
cake: 6 cookie
genus: 4 Thea
kind: 4 herb, Java **5** Assam, black, bohea, green, hyson, pekoe **6** Ceylon, congou, oolong **7** cambric **8** Earl Grey, souchong **9** sassafras **10** Darjeeling

teach

5 coach, edify, guide, train, tutor **6** impart, school **7** educate, instill, profess **8** instruct **9** enlighten, inculcate **12** indoctrinate

teacher

4 guru, prof **5** coach, guide, tutor **6** docent, master, mentor, pedant **7** maestro, trainer **8** educator **9** pedagogue, preceptor, professor **10** instructor **12** schoolmaster
Hindu: 5 swami
Jewish: 5 rabbi, rebbe
Muslim: 6 mullah
organization: 3 NEA
religious: 9 catechist **10** mystagogue

Tea for Two composer

7 Youmans (Vincent)

team

4 band, club, crew, gang, join, pair, side, yoke **5** group, squad, troop, wagon **6** stable, troupe **8** carriage
baseball: 4 nine
basketball: 4 five **7** quintet
football: 6 eleven
kind: 6 jayvee **7** varsity

teamster

6 driver **7** trucker

tear
3 cry, cut, fly, rip, run 4 bolt, claw, dash, drop, flaw, gash, hole, lash, pull, race, rend, rift, rive, rush, slit, snag, weep 5 chase, hurry, shoot, shred, slash, speed, split, spree 6 career, charge, course, sunder, tatter, wrench 7 droplet, fissure, rupture 8 lacerate 10 laceration

tear down
4 raze, ruin, slur 5 knock, smash, smear, wreck 6 defame, malign, vilify 7 asperse, traduce, destroy, shatter, slander 8 demolish 9 denigrate, disparage, take apart 10 annihilate, calumniate 11 disassemble

tearful
3 sad 5 misty, moist, weepy 6 crying, watery, woeful 7 bawling, sobbing, weeping 8 mournful, pathetic 9 lamenting, sniveling, sorrowful 10 blubbering, lachrymose

tear-jerking
5 mushy 6 drippy, sticky 7 maudlin, mawkish 8 touching 9 schmaltzy 11 sentimental

teary-eyed
5 blear, moist

tease
3 bug, kid, rag, rip 4 bait, coax, comb, gibe, jive, josh, ride, tear, twit 5 annoy, chaff, chivy, harry, shred, taunt, worry 6 cajole, harass, needle, pester, pick on, plague 7 bedevil, torment 8 ridicule 9 tantalize

teaser
5 promo 7 preview

teched
3 mad 4 daft 5 batty, crazy 6 insane 7 cracked, lunatic 8 demented

technicality
6 detail 8 loophole

technique
4 mode 5 modus 6 method, system 8 approach 9 procedure 13 modus operandi

ted
5 strew 6 spread 7 scatter

tedious
3 dry 4 dull 5 ho-hum, stale 6 boring, dreary 7 irksome, operose 8 drudging, tiresome 9 dryasdust, wearisome 10 monotonous 11 mind-numbing 13 uninteresting

tedium
4 yawn 5 ennui 7 boredom 8 doldrums, dullness, monotony, sameness

teem
4 flow, pour 5 crawl, empty, swarm 6 abound, bustle 7 produce 9 pullulate

teeming
4 lush, rife 5 alive 6 aswarm 7 replete 8 abundant, swarming, thronged 9 abounding 11 overflowing

teen
5 youth 10 adolescent

tee off
4 open 5 begin, drive, enter, start 8 commence, initiate

teeter
4 rock, sway 5 waver 6 falter, seesaw, wobble 9 vacillate

telamon
5 atlas
counterpart: 8 caryatid

Telamon
brother: 6 Peleus
father: 6 Aeacus
half-brother: 6 Phocus
son: 4 Ajax 6 Teucer

Telegonus
father: 7 Ulysses 8 Odysseus
mother: 5 Circe

telegraph
4 wire 5 cable 6 signal
code: 5 Morse

Telemachus
father: 7 Ulysses 8 Odysseus
mother: 8 Penelope

telephone

4 buzz, call, dial, ring 5 phone
6 ring up
inventor: 4 Bell (Alexander Graham)

Telephus

father: 8 Heracles, Hercules
mother: 4 Auge

telescope

5 glass 6 finder 7 compact 8 compress, condense, contract, spyglass
9 reflector, refractor

television

4 tube 5 video 8 boob tube, idiot
box
antenna: 10 rabbit ears
award: 4 Emmy
British: 5 telly
children's: 6 kidvid
frequency: 3 UHF, VHF
interference: 4 snow
network: 3 ABC, BBC, CBS, Fox,
NBC, NET, PBS
pioneer: 5 Baird (John Logie) 8 De
Forest (Lee), Zworykin (Vladimir)
program: 4 news 5 rerun 6 series,
sitcom 7 western 8 game show, talk
show 9 broadcast, docudrama, soap
opera 11 infomercial 12 infotainment
tube: 9 kinescope

tell

3 say 4 blab, clue, warn 5 break,
count, crack, mound, order, spill,
state, utter 6 advise, betray, fill in,
inform, notify, relate, report, retail,
reveal 7 confess, declare, divulge,
narrate, recount, reel off 8 describe,
disclose, give away 9 come clean

teller

5 clerk 6 banker 7 cashier, counter
8 informer, narrator 12 communicator

telling

5 solid, sound, valid 6 cogent
7 weighty 8 powerful 9 effective
10 convincing, expressive

tell off

4 flay, rate, ream 5 chide, scold
6 berate, rebuke 7 bawl out, chew
out, reprove, upbraid 8 admonish,
call down 9 dress down, excoriate,
reprimand 10 take to task, tongue-
lash, vituperate

tell on

6 inform, snitch, tattle

telltale

3 cue 4 clue, fink, lead, sign 5 proof
6 canary, gossip, signal, snitch, tip-
off 7 rat fink, tattler 8 evidence,
gossiper, informer, quidnunc, signpost, squealer 9 indicator 10 indication, newsmonger 12 blabbermouth,
gossipmonger 13 scandalmonger

telluric

6 earthy 7 earthly, mundane, terrene, worldly 9 sublunary 11 terrestrial

temblor

5 quake, shake, shock 6 tremor
8 upheaval 10 aftershock, earthquake

temerarious

4 rash 6 daring 8 heedless, reckless 9 audacious, daredevil, foolhardy, venturous 11 adventurous,
venturesome 13 adventuresome

temerity

4 gall 5 cheek, nerve 6 daring
8 audacity, chutzpah, rashness
9 assurance, brashness, hardihood,
hardiness 10 effrontery 12 recklessness 13 foolhardiness

temper

4 heat, mean, mind, mood, tone, vein
5 admix, alloy, anger, blood, grain,
humor, trend 6 anneal, attune, dander, dilute, govern, hackle, makeup,
medium, season, soften, spirit, strain
7 courage, mollify, passion, quality,
toughen 8 hardness, moderate,
modulate, restrain 9 character,
composure, condition 10 resilience, resiliency 11 disposition,
personality

temperament

4 mood 5 humor 6 manner, makeup,
mettle, nature 9 character 10 complexion 11 disposition, personality

temperamental
5 moody 6 ornery, touchy 7 erratic
8 contrary, ticklish, unstable, variable, volatile 9 mercurial 10 capricious, changeable, high-strung,
inconstant 13 unpredictable

temperance
8 sobriety 9 austerity, restraint
10 abstinence, continence, moderation, self-denial 11 self-control
advocate of: 6 Nation (Carry)
7 Willard (Frances)

temperate
4 calm, even, mild, soft 5 balmy,
sober 6 modest, steady 7 clement
8 discreet, moderate 9 abstinent,
continent 10 abstemious, controlled,
reasonable, restrained 11 abstentious

temperature
4 heat, mood 5 fever 6 degree,
warmth 7 hotness 8 coldness
9 intensity

tempered
7 diluted, treated 8 adjusted, hardened, softened 9 mitigated, moderated, qualified 12 strengthened

tempest
3 din 4 blow, gale, rage, wind
5 furor, hurly, storm 6 hubbub,
squall, tumult, uproar 8 brouhaha,
foofaraw 9 commotion, hurricane
10 hullabaloo, hurly-burly

Tempest, The
character: 5 Ariel 6 Alonso 7 Caliban, Miranda 8 Prospero 9 Ferdinand

tempestuous
4 wild 5 roily, rough 6 raging, stormy
7 furious, moiling, violent 8 blustery
9 turbulent 10 tumultuous

temple
4 fane 6 church 9 synagogue
10 tabernacle
ancient: 8 pantheon
Aztec: 8 teocalli
Buddhist: 3 wat
Eastern: 6 pagoda

Greek: 9 Parthenon
sanctuary: 5 cella 6 adytum
10 penetralia

tempo
4 pace, rate, time 5 speed 6 rhythm
fast: 6 presto, vivace 7 allegro
moderate: 7 andante
slow: 5 grave, lento 6 adagio

temporal
3 lay 5 civil 6 carnal 7 earthly,
mundane, profane, secular, worldly
13 chronological, synchronistic

temporary
6 acting 7 Band-Aid, interim 8 fleeting 9 ad interim, makeshift, transient
10 short-lived, substitute, transitory
11 provisional

temporize
5 delay, stall, yield 6 palter 7 draw
out 8 gain time 10 equivocate
11 prevaricate

tempt
3 woo 4 bait, lure, risk, sway 5 court,
decoy 6 allure, entice, entrap, invite,
lead on, seduce 7 provoke 8 inveigle 9 tantalize

temptation
4 bait, lure, trap 5 decoy, siren,
snare 6 allure, come-on 9 seduction
10 attraction, enticement

tempting
8 alluring 9 appealing, delicious,
seductive 10 attractive, come-hither

temptress
4 vamp 5 siren 7 Lorelei 10 seductress 11 femme fatale

ten
cents: 4 dime
combining form: 3 dec, dek 4 deca,
deka 5 decem
dollars: 7 sawbuck
mills: 4 cent
thousand: 6 myriad
years: 6 decade

tenable
5 sound 8 rational 10 defendable,
defensible, reasonable 12 main-
tainable

tenacious

3 set 4 fast, firm, true 5 fixed, stout
6 dogged, secure, sturdy 8 adhesive, clinging, resolute, stalwart, stubborn 9 obstinate, steadfast
10 persistent 11 persevering

tenacity

4 grit, guts 5 moxie, pluck, spunk
6 mettle, spirit 7 courage 8 firmness
10 resolution 11 persistence 13 determination

tenant

6 holder, lessee, lodger, renter
7 boarder, dweller 8 occupant
feudal: 6 vassal

tenantable

7 livable 9 habitable 11 inhabitable

Ten Commandments

9 Decalogue

tend

4 lean, mind, till, work 5 guard, labor, nurse, serve, watch 6 foster
7 babysit, care for, conduce, incline, nurture, oversee 8 minister 9 cultivate, look after, watch over

tendency

4 bent, bias 5 drift, tenor, trend
7 current, leaning 8 penchant
10 partiality, proclivity, propensity
11 disposition, inclination 12 predilection

tendentious

6 biased 7 colored, partial 8 one-sided, partisan 10 prejudiced

tender

3 bid 4 fond, mild, soft, sore, warm
5 green, money, mushy, offer, young
6 callow, extend, gentle, humane, loving, submit, touchy 7 fragile, hold out, lenient, painful, present, proffer, propose 8 delicate, immature, proposal 9 sensitive, succulent
10 benevolent, solicitous 11 considerate, warmhearted 12 affectionate 13 compassionate

tenderfoot

4 colt, punk, tyro 6 novice, rookie
7 amateur 8 beginner, freshman, neophyte, newcomer 9 cheechako, fledgling, greenhorn, novitiate 10 apprentice

tenderhearted

6 kindly 11 sympathetic 13 compassionate

Tender Is the Night author

10 Fitzgerald (F. Scott)

tendon

4 band, cord 5 nerve, sinew 6 leader
9 hamstring

tendril

4 curl, vine 6 cirrus, spiral 7 ringlet

tenebrific

4 dark, glum, gray, grim 5 black, bleak, sable 6 dismal, dreary, gloomy, somber, sombre 8 desolate, funereal
10 depressing, oppressive 11 dispiriting

tenebrous

3 dim 4 dark, deep, dusk, hazy
5 dusky, foggy, muddy, murky, vague
6 cloudy, gloomy 7 cryptic, obscure, shadowy, unclear 9 ambiguous, lightless 10 caliginous

tenement

4 flat 6 rental, walk-up, warren
7 lodging, rookery 8 building
9 apartment, residence

tenet

3 ism 5 canon, creed, dogma 6 belief
7 paradox 8 doctrine 9 principle
10 empiricism

tenfold

7 decuple

Tennessee

capital: 9 Nashville
city: 7 Memphis 9 Knoxville
11 Chattanooga
college, university: 10 Vanderbilt
mountain, range: 7 Lookout
10 Great Smoky 13 Clingmans
Dome
nickname: 9 Volunteer (State)
public works: 3 TVA 9 Norris Dam
river: 9 Tennessee 11 Mississippi
state bird: 11 mockingbird

state flower: 4 iris
state tree: 11 tulip poplar

tennis
award: 8 Davis Cup
item: 3 net 4 ball 6 racket 7 racquet
kind: 5 table 7 doubles, singles 8 platform
score: 4 love 5 deuce
serve: 3 ace
shoe: 7 sneaker
stroke: 3 cut, lob 4 chop, drop 5 serve, slice 6 volley 8 backhand, forehand
term: 3 let, set 5 court, fault 7 service 9 advantage, backcourt

tennis champ
4 Ashe (Arthur), Borg (Bjorn), Cash (Pat), Graf (Steffi), King (Billie Jean), Noah (Yannick), Wade (Virginia) 5 Budge (Don), Chang (Michael), Court (Margaret Smith), Evert (Chris), Gómez (Andres), Laver (Rod), Lendl (Ivan), Perry (Fred), Seles (Monica), Stich (Michael), Vilas (Guillermo), Wills (Helen) 6 Agassi (André), Austin (Tracy), Becker (Boris), Casals (Rosie), Edberg (Stephan), Fraser (Neale), Gibson (Althea), Hewitt (Lleyton), Hingis (Martina), Kramer (Jack), Muster (Thomas), Pierce (Mary), Stolle (Fred), Tilden (Bill) 7 Connors (Jimmy), Courier (Jim), Emerson (Roy), Federer (Roger), Lacoste (Rene), McEnroe (John), Nastase (Ilie), Novótna (Jana), Sampras (Pete) 8 Connolly (Maureen), González (Pancho), Martínez (Conchita), Newcombe (John), Rosewall (Ken), Sabatini (Gabriela), Wilander (Mats), Williams (Serena, Venus) 9 Davenport (Lindsay) 10 Mandlikova (Hana) 11 Navrátilova (Martina) 14 Sánchez Vicario (Arantxa)

Tennyson poem
4 Maud 7 Ulysses 8 Princess (The), Tiresias 10 Enoch Arden, In Memoriam 12 Locksley Hall 23 Charge of the Light Brigade (The)

tenor
4 mood, tone 5 drift, voice 6 singer 7 meaning, purport 8 tendency 9 substance
American: 5 Lanza (Mario) 6 Hadley (Jerry), Peerce (Jan), Tucker (Richard) 8 Melchior (Lauritz) 9 McCormack (John), McCracken (James)
Canadian: 7 Vickers (Jon)
Czech: 6 Slezak (Leo)
German: 10 Wunderlich (Fritz)
Italian: 5 Gigli (Beniamino) 6 Alagna (Roberto), Caruso (Enrico) 7 Bocelli (Andrea), Corelli (Franco) 8 Bergonzi (Carlo) 9 del Monaco (Mario), di Stefano (Giuseppe), Pavarotti (Luciano)
Spanish: 5 Kraus (Alfredo) 7 Domingo (Plácido) 8 Carreras (José)
Swedish: 5 Gedda (Nicolai) 8 Björling (Jussi) 9 Bjoerling (Jussi)

tenpins
7 bowling

tense
4 edgy, taut 5 nervy, rigid, tight, wired 6 uneasy 7 anxious, jittery, nervous, restive, uptight 8 strained, stressed 10 high-strung
grammatical: 4 past 6 future 7 perfect, present 8 preterit 9 preterite 10 pluperfect 11 progressive

tension
5 state, steam 6 nerves, strain, stress, unease 7 anxiety, balance 8 edginess, pressure, tautness 9 agitation, hostility, stiffness 10 discomfort, opposition, uneasiness 11 nervousness, uptightness

tent
4 camp 6 canopy, encamp, laager 7 bivouac, shelter
kind: 3 pup 4 yurt 5 Baker, tepee 6 wigwam 7 marquee 8 pavilion, umbrella
maker: 4 Omar
material: 6 canvas
part: 3 fly, guy, peg 4 pole

tentacle
3 arm 6 barbel, feeler

tentative
4 test 5 chary, loath, probe, trial
6 averse 7 halting 8 hesitant, insecure 9 diffident, makeshift, reluctant,
uncertain, undecided, unsettled
10 irresolute 11 conditional, disinclined, problematic, provisional

tenth
5 tithe
combining form: 4 deci

tenuous
4 slim, thin, weak 5 reedy, shaky
6 feeble, flimsy, slight, stalky 7 fragile, sketchy, slender 8 gossamer
10 precarious 11 implausible 13 insubstantial, unsubstantial

tenure
4 term 6 estate 10 incumbency
feudal: 7 burgage

tepid
4 mild, warm 7 warmish 8 lukewarm
9 apathetic 11 halfhearted, indifferent

tequila source
5 agave

Terentia's husband
6 Cicero

Tereus
son: 4 Itys
wife: 6 Procne

tergiversate
3 haw, hem, rat 5 dodge, evade,
hedge 6 defect, desert, waffle,
weasel 7 abandon, shuffle 8 renounce, sidestep 9 pussyfoot,
repudiate 10 apostatize, equivocate

term
3 dub, end 4 call, name, span, tour,
word 5 label, spell, stint, title 6 detail, period, tenure 7 quarter, session
8 duration, semester 9 designate
10 conclusion, denominate, expression, limitation, particular 11 appellation, designation

termagant
5 harpy, scold, shrew, vixen 6 ogress,
virago 8 fishwife, harridan 9 Xanthippe

terminable
6 finite

terminal
3 end, lag 4 last 5 depot, fatal, final
6 finial, latest, latter, lethal 7 closing,
extreme, station 8 eventual, hindmost, junction, ultimate 9 extremity
10 concluding
negative: 7 cathode
positive: 5 anode

terminate
3 end 4 boot, drop, fire, halt, kill,
quit, sack, stop 5 abort, cease,
close, issue, leave 6 cut off, finish,
wind up 7 abolish, dead-end, dismiss 8 complete, conclude, dissolve
9 determine, discharge 10 extinguish 11 assassinate, discontinue

terminology
4 cant 5 argot, idiom, lingo 6 jargon,
patois 7 lexicon 8 language, shop-
talk 10 vernacular, vocabulary
12 nomenclature

termite
5 alate 8 white ant

ternary
5 third 6 triple 9 threefold

Terpsichore
see **Muse**

terrace
4 bank, deck, mesa, park, roof,
step 5 bench, porch, shelf 6 street
7 balcony, sundeck 8 platform
9 promenade

terra-cotta
4 clay 7 pottery

terra firma
4 dirt, land, soil 5 earth 6 ground

terrain
4 area, land, turf 5 field 6 domain,
ground, milieu, sphere 8 province
9 bailiwick, territory 10 topography
11 environment

terrapin
6 turtle

terrestrial
4 land 6 earthy, ground 7 earthly, mundane, worldly 8 everyday, ordinary, telluric, workaday 9 earthlike, planetary, sublunary 10 earthbound

terrible
4 dire 5 awful, dread 6 fierce, grisly, horrid, severe 7 dreaded, fearful, furious, ghastly, hideous, intense, macabre, vicious, violent 8 dreadful, gruesome, horrible, horrific, shocking, vehement 9 abhorrent, appalling, atrocious, desperate, frightful, harrowing, laborious, loathsome, monstrous, strenuous 10 disastrous, formidable, horrendous, horrifying

terrier
3 dog
kind: 3 fox 4 blue, bull, Skye 5 cairn, Irish, Welsh 6 Boston 8 Airedale, Lakeland 9 Yorkshire

terrific
5 super, swell 6 superb 7 amazing, awesome 8 dreadful, dynamite, glorious 9 appalling, frightful, marvelous, upsetting, wonderful 10 formidable 11 magnificent, sensational 13 extraordinary

terrify
5 alarm, scare 7 scarify, startle 8 affright, frighten 10 intimidate

terrifying
4 grim 5 scary 6 grisly, horrid 7 ghastly, hideous, macabre 8 alarming, dreadful, fearsome, gruesome, horrible, terrible 9 frightful 10 formidable, horrifying

territory
4 area, belt, land, turf, zone 5 field, route, state, tract 6 domain, region, sphere 7 country, demesne, terrain 8 conquest, district, dominion, province 9 bailiwick 10 borderland 12 jurisdiction

terror
4 brat, fear 5 alarm, dread, panic, worry 6 dismay, fright, horror 7 scourge 9 nightmare 11 fearfulness, trepidation

terrorize
3 cow 5 alarm, bully, scare 6 coerce, fright, menace 7 scarify 8 browbeat, bulldoze, frighten, threaten 9 strongarm 10 intimidate

terry
4 loop 5 cloth 6 fabric 12 Turkish towel

terse
4 curt 5 brief, crisp, pithy, short 6 abrupt 7 brusque, compact, concise, elegant, laconic, summary 8 polished, succinct 11 compendious, sententious, telegraphic 12 monosyllabic

tertiary
5 third

terza _____
4 rima

tessera
3 die 4 tile 6 tablet, ticket

test
3 try 4 exam, quiz 5 assay, check, essay, final, proof, prove, shell, taste, touch, trial, try on 6 sample, tryout, verify 7 confirm, examine, midterm 8 evaluate, gut check, sounding, trial run 9 benchmark, criterion 10 evaluation, experiment, touchstone 11 demonstrate, examination 12 experimental

testa
6 cupule 7 coating 8 envelope, seed coat, tegument 10 integument

testament
4 will 5 credo, creed, proof 7 tribute, witness 8 evidence 9 scripture 11 attestation 12 confirmation

tester
4 coin 6 canopy, prover 7 analyst, assayer 8 examiner 12 investigator

testifier
7 witness 8 deponent

testify
5 prove, swear **6** affirm, attest, depone, depose, evince **7** certify, witness **11** certificate

testimonial
5 proof **6** salute **7** tribute, witness **8** evidence, memorial, monument **9** affidavit, character, reference **11** attestation **12** appreciation, commendation, confirmation **13** commemoration

testimony
5 proof **6** avowal **7** witness **8** evidence **9** affidavit, authority **10** deposition, profession **11** affirmation, attestation, declaration **12** confirmation **13** corroboration, documentation

testy
4 edgy **5** cross, fussy, hasty **6** cranky, ornery, tetchy, touchy **7** fretful, grouchy, peevish **8** choleric **9** crotchety, irascible, irritable **10** ill-humored, out of sorts **12** cantankerous **13** quick-tempered

tetanus
7 lockjaw, trismus

tetchy
see **testy**

tête-à-tête
4 chat, talk **5** à deux **7** private, vis-à-vis **8** causerie **10** face-to-face **12** conversation

tether
3 tie **4** bind, rope **5** cable, chain, stake **6** fasten, fetter, lariat, picket **8** restrain **9** restraint

Tethys
daughters: 9 Oceanides
father: 6 Uranus
husband: 7 Oceanus
mother: 4 Gaea **5** Terra

tetrad
4 four **7** quartet **8** foursome **10** quaternion

Teutonic
6 German **8** Germanic

language:
5 Dutch **6** Danish, German, Gothic **7** English, Flemish, Frisian, Swedish **9** Afrikaans, Norwegian

Texas
capital: 6 Austin
city: 4 Waco **6** Dallas, El Paso **7** Houston **8** Amarillo **9** Arlington, Fort Worth **10** San Antonio
college, university: 3 SMU **4** Rice **5** Lamar **6** Baylor **9** Texas Tech **15** Sam Houston State
island: 5 Padre
mountain: 9 Guadalupe (Peak)
nickname: 8 Lone Star (State)
park: 7 Big Bend
river: 3 Red **5** Pecos **6** Brazos **8** Colorado **9** Rio Grande
state bird: 11 mockingbird
state flower: 10 bluebonnet
state tree: 5 pecan

text
6 script

textbook
6 primer

textile
5 cloth **6** fabric
dealer: 6 mercer
machine: 8 calender
shop: 7 mercery
treat: 9 mercerize

texture
3 web **4** feel, hand, wale, woof **5** weave **6** fabric

Thackeray novel
9 Pendennis **10** Vanity Fair **11** Barry Lyndon, Henry Esmond

Thailand
capital: 7 Bangkok
city: 9 Chiang Mai
former name: 4 Siam
island: 6 Phuket
monetary unit: 4 baht
neighbor: 4 Laos **5** Burma **7** Myanmar **8** Cambodia, Malaysia
river: 10 Chao Phraya
sea: 7 Andaman

Thaïs
7 hetaera, hetaira **9** courtesan

author: 6 France (Anatole)
composer: 8 Massenet (Jules)
husband: 7 Ptolemy
lover: 9 Alexander (the Great)

thalassic
6 marine 7 oceanic 8 maritime

Thalia
see Graces; Muse

Thanatopsis author
6 Bryant (William Cullen)

Thanatos
5 death
brother: 6 Hypnos
mother: 3 Nyx

thankful
4 glad 8 grateful 12 appreciative

thanks
5 grace 8 blessing 9 gratitude
11 benediction 12 appreciation,
gratefulness

Thanksgiving
5 feast 7 holiday
first celebrant: 6 Indian 7 Pilgrim
food: 6 turkey

thatch
3 mop 4 hair, roof 5 cover

that is
Latin: 5 id est

Thaumas
daughter: 4 Iris 5 Aello, Harpy
7 Celaeno, Ocypete
daughters: 7 Harpies
father: 6 Pontus
mother: 4 Gaea
wife: 7 Electra

thaumaturgic
5 magic 6 Magian, mystic, witchy
7 magical 8 wizardly 9 marvelous
10 miraculous 11 necromantic
12 supernatural

thaumaturgy
5 magic 7 sorcery 8 cabbalah,
kabbalah, witchery, wizardry 10 necromancy

thaw
4 melt 5 deice, relax 6 unbend
7 defrost, liquefy 8 dissolve, unfreeze 10 condescend, deliquesce

the
7 article
French: 3 les
German: 3 das, der, die
Spanish: 3 las, los

Thea
daughter: 6 Selene
father: 6 Uranus
husband: 8 Hyperion
mother: 4 Gaea

theater
4 nabe 5 drama, stage 6 boards
9 playhouse 10 footlights
award: 4 Tony
district: 6 rialto
entrance: 5 foyer, lobby
Greek: 5 odeum
movie: 6 cinema 8 cineplex, mega-
plex 9 multiplex
outdoor: 7 drive-in
part: 3 box, pit 4 loge 5 apron,
stage, wings 7 balcony, parquet
8 parterre 9 greenroom, mezzanine,
orchestra 10 proscenium

theatrical
5 stagy 6 staged 8 dramatic, thespian 10 artificial, flamboyant, histrionic 11 dramaturgic 12 melodramatic
agent: 6 Morris (William)
device: 4 prop
group: 6 troupe

Theban Eagle
6 Pindar

Thebes
founder: 6 Cadmus
king: 5 Laius 7 Oedipus
queen: 7 Jocasta

theft
5 heist, pinch 6 holdup, piracy
7 break-in, larceny, robbery 8 burglary, stealing, thievery 9 pilferage
combining form: 5 klept 6 klepto

theme
4 stem, text, tune 5 essay, lemma,
motif, paper, point, topic, topos
6 burden, matter, melody, mythos,
thesis 7 article, conceit, message,
subject 8 argument 11 composition
12 dissertation

Themis
father: 6 Uranus
goddess of: 3 law 7 justice
husband: 4 Zeus 7 Jupiter
mother: 4 Gaea

then
4 also, anon, ergo, next, thus, when
5 again, hence, later 7 besides,
further 8 moreover 9 therefore,
thereupon 10 in addition 11 accordingly, furthermore 12 additionally,
consequently

thence
4 away 7 thereof 9 from there,
therefrom

Theogony poet
6 Hesiod

theologian
American: 6 Merton (Thomas)
7 Edwards (Jonathan), Niebuhr
(Reinhold), Tillich (Paul), Walther
(Carl)
Dutch: 6 Jansen (Cornelis)
English: 4 Bede (Venerable)
5 Pusey (Edward), Watts (Isaac)
6 Alcuin, Wesley (John) 7 Langton
(Stephen) 8 Pelagius, Wycliffe
(John)
French: 6 Calvin (John) 7 Abelard
(Peter), William (of Auvergne, of
Auxerre) 8 Maritain (Jacques),
Sabatier (Auguste), Teilhard (de
Chardin, Pierre)
German: 6 Rahner (Karl) 7 Eckhart
(Meister) 8 Albertus (Magnus)
9 Niemöller (Martin) 10 Bonhoeffer
(Dietrich)
Greek: 9 Zygomalas (Theodore)
Italian: 6 Thomas (Aquinas) 7 Aqui-
nas (Thomas), Socinus (Fausto,
Laelius)
Scottish: 10 Duns Scotus (John)
Spanish: 6 Suárez (Francisco)
7 Vitoria (Francisco de) 8 Servetus
(Michael)
Swedish: 9 Soderblom (Nathan)
Swiss: 4 Küng (Hans) 5 Barth
(Karl), Vinet (Alexandre-Rodolphe)

theological
school: 8 seminary
virtue: 4 hope 5 faith 7 charity

_____ Theologica
5 Summa

theorbo
4 lute

theorem
3 law 4 rule 5 axiom 7 formula,
inverse, stencil 8 converse 9 principle 10 principium 11 fundamental,
proposition

theoretical
4 pure 5 ideal 8 abstract, academic,
notional, unproved 11 conjectural,
speculative 12 hypothetical 13 problematical, suppositional

theorize
5 guess 6 submit 7 suggest 9 formulate, postulate, speculate 10 conjecture 11 hypothesize

theory
7 perhaps, premise, surmise 8 supposal 10 conjecture, hypothesis
11 speculation, supposition
astronomical: 7 big bang
suffix: 3 ism

therapeutic
5 tonic 7 healing, helpful 8 curative,
remedial, salutary, sanative 9 healthful, medicinal, vulnerary, wholesome
10 beneficial, corrective 11 restorative 12 health-giving

therapy
9 treatment

therefore
4 ergo, then, thus 5 hence 6 thence
11 accordingly 12 consequently

therefrom
4 away 6 thence

thereupon
4 ergo, then, thus 6 at once, at that,
thence 8 directly 9 right away,
therefore, wherefore 11 accordingly,
straightway 12 consequently

thermal unit
3 Btu 6 degree 7 calorie

thermometer
5 gauge 9 indicator
kind: 7 Celsius, Réaumur 10 centigrade, Fahrenheit

thermos
5 dewar 10 Dewar flask

Theroux work
9 Saint Jack 13 Mosquito Coast
(The) 14 Half Moon Street 18 Great
Railway Bazaar (The)

Thersites' slayer
8 Achilles

thesaurus editor
5 Roget (Peter Mark)

Theseus
beloved: 7 Ariadne
father: 6 Aegeus
mother: 6 Aethra
slayer: 9 Lycomedes
son: 10 Hippolytus
victim: 6 Sciron 8 Minotaur 10 Procrustes
wife: 7 Phaedra

thesis
5 essay, point, theme 6 belief 7 premise 8 downbeat, position, tractate,
treatise 9 discourse, monograph,
postulate, synthesis 10 contention,
exposition 11 postulation, proposition, supposition 12 disquisition,
dissertation

thespian
5 actor 6 mummer, player 7 actress,
trouper 8 dramatic 9 performer
10 histrionic, theatrical 11 dramaturgic 12 impersonator, melodramatic

Thespis' forte
5 drama 7 tragedy

Thessalian hero
5 Jason 8 Achilles

_____ the Terrible
4 Ivan

Thetis
6 Nereid
father: 6 Nereus
husband: 6 Peleus
mother: 5 Doris
son: 8 Achilles

theurgist
5 witch 7 warlock 8 magician,
sorcerer 12 wonder-worker

thew
4 beef 5 brawn, might, power,
sinew, vigor 6 muscle 8 strength,
vitality

thick
3 fat 4 wide 5 broad, bulky, burly,
close, dense, dumpy, husky, squat,
stout 6 chummy, chunky, packed,
stocky 7 compact, crammed,
crowded, viscous 8 familiar, heavyset, intimate 11 inspissated

thicken
3 set 4 blur, clot, jell 6 curdle
7 broaden, compact, congeal 8 condense 9 coagulate 10 inspissate
11 concentrate, consolidate

thicket
4 bosk, bush, shaw, wood 5 clump,
copse, grove, hedge 6 bosket,
covert, mallee, tangle 7 boscage,
bosquet, coppice, spinney 8 hedgerow, quickset 9 brushwood, cane-
brake, chaparral

thickness
3 ply 4 loft 5 depth, gauge, layer,
sheet 7 density 8 dullness 9 stupidity, viscosity

thickset
5 bulky, burly, husky, pudgy, stout
6 chunky, portly, stocky, sturdy
7 compact 9 corpulent

thief
3 dip 4 prig 5 ganef 6 bandit,
lifter, looter, pirate, rascal, robber
7 booster, burglar, filcher, stealer
8 hijacker, larcener, pilferer, water rat
9 larcenist, purloiner 10 cat burglar,
highwayman, pickpocket, shoplifter
12 housebreaker

thieve
3 rob 4 hook, lift, pick, roll 5 filch,
pinch, pluck, steal, swipe 6 hijack,
hold up, pilfer, rip off, snitch 7 purloin
8 knock off 9 knock over

thievery
see **theft**

thievish
9 larcenous 13 light-fingered

thigh
3 ham   5 flank   6 gammon
bone: 5 femur
relating to: 6 crural   7 femoral

thimble
3 cup   5 cover

thin
4 fine, lank, lean, slim   5 gaunt, lanky, reedy, scant, sharp, spare   6 dilute, flimsy, meager, meagre, rarefy, scanty, skimpy, skinny, slight, sparse, stalky, treble, twiggy, watery   7 diluted, scraggy, scrawny, slender, spindly, squinny, subtile, tenuous   8 rarefied, skeletal   9 attenuate; extenuate   10 attenuated   11 watered-down   13 unsubstantial

thing
4 item   5 being, event   6 entity, matter, object   7 article, concern, element   8 business, incident, material, occasion   9 existence, happening   10 occurrence, phenomenon
in law: 3 res

thingamajig
5 gizmo   6 dingus, doodad, gadget, jigger, widget   7 whatsit   9 doohickey

things
4 gear   5 goods, stock, stuff   7 baggage, clothes, effects, luggage   8 chattels, clothing, matériel, movables, property, supplies   10 belongings, provisions   11 impedimenta, merchandise   13 accoutrements, paraphernalia

think
4 mull, muse   5 brood, study, weigh   6 ideate, ponder, reason   7 believe, imagine, reflect, suppose, surmise   8 cogitate, consider, meditate, ruminate   9 cerebrate, speculate   10 conjecture, deliberate, excogitate   11 contemplate

Thinker sculptor
5 Rodin (Auguste)

third
8 tertiary
combining form: 3 tri
power: 4 cube

third degree
7 torture   8 grilling   11 inquisition, questioning   13 interrogation

third estate
5 plebs   6 people, plebes   8 populace   9 commonage, commoners, plebeians   10 commonalty   11 rank and file

Third Man author
6 Greene (Graham)

Third of May painter
4 Goya (Francisco)

thirst
3 yen   4 itch, long, lust, pine   5 crave, yearn   6 desire, hanker, hunger   7 craving, dryness, longing   8 appetite

thirsty
3 dry   4 arid, avid   5 eager   6 ardent   7 anxious, bone-dry, parched   8 droughty   9 absorbent, waterless

this and that
8 oddments, sundries   9 etceteras   11 miscellanea, odds and ends

Thisbe's lover
7 Pyramus

This Side of Paradise author
10 Fitzgerald (F. Scott)

thistle
4 weed   7 caltrop
Russian: 10 tumbleweed

thistlebird
9 goldfinch

thither
3 yon   5 there   6 yonder

thole
3 peg, pin   6 endure

Thomas à ____
6 Becket, Kempis

Thomas's Greek name
7 Didymus

Thomas opera
6 Mignon

Thompson
4 Emma   5 Sadie   6 Hunter   7 Dorothy, Francis, J. Walter   8 Benjamin

thong
4 band, lace, lash, rein, zori 5 lasso, strap, strip, whang 6 sandal 7 latchet 8 flip-flop

Thor
5 Donar
father: 4 Odin 5 Wotan
god of: 7 thunder
hammer: 8 Mjollnir
mother: 5 Jordh, Jorth

thorax
5 chest, trunk 6 pereon

Thoreau, Henry David
friend: 7 Emerson (Ralph Waldo)
town: 7 Concord
work: 6 Walden

thorn
4 barb 5 briar, spike, spine 7 prickle, spinule 9 annoyance 10 irritation

thorny
5 sharp, spiny 6 briary, touchy, tricky 7 awkward, prickly, spinous 8 ticklish 9 difficult, vexatious 10 nettlesome 11 troublesome

thorough
4 full 6 minute 7 careful, in-depth 8 complete, detailed, diligent, whole-hog 9 downright 10 blow-by-blow, exhaustive, meticulous 11 painstaking 13 conscientious

thoroughbred
8 pedigree, purebred 9 pedigreed, pureblood 10 bloodstock 11 full-blooded

thoroughfare
3 way 4 road 5 track 6 artery, avenue, street 7 highway, parkway 8 corridor 9 boulevard

thoroughgoing
5 utter 6 all-out 7 extreme 8 absolute, complete, outright, whole-hog 9 out-and-out 10 consummate, exhaustive 11 straight-out, unmitigated 13 dyed-in-the-wool

thou
3 you 5 grand
French: 5 mille

though
3 yet 5 still, while 6 albeit 7 however, whereas 8 after all 11 nonetheless 12 nevertheless

thought
4 idea 6 notion, reason 7 concept, opinion 8 ideation 9 brainwork 10 cogitation, conception, meditation, reflection, rumination 11 cerebration, speculation 12 deliberation, intellection 13 contemplation

thoughtful
6 polite 7 careful, gallant, heedful, mindful, pensive, serious, studied 8 gracious, studious, thinking 9 attentive, courteous, pondering, regardful 10 cogitative, meditative, reflective, ruminative, solicitous 11 considerate 12 deliberative, intellectual 13 contemplative

thoughtless
4 rash, rude 5 brash, hasty 6 madcap 7 selfish 8 careless, feckless, heedless, impolite, reckless, uncaring 9 insensate 10 incautious, ungracious 12 discourteous 13 inconsiderate

thousand
combining form: 4 kilo
dollars: 5 grand
years: 10 millennium

thousandth
10 millesimal
combining form: 5 milli

thrall
4 peon, serf, yoke 5 helot, slave 7 bondage, bondman, helotry, peonage, serfdom, slavery, villein 9 servitude, villenage 10 absorption 11 enslavement

thrash
3 tan 4 beat, belt, drub, flog, hide, lash, lick, maul, pelt, trim, whip 5 baste, flail, pound, smear, swing, thump, whale, whang 6 batter, buffet, larrup, pummel, stripe, wallop 7 scourge, shellac, trounce 8 flounder, lambaste, work over 10 flagellate

thrash out
4 moot **5** argue **6** debate **7** discuss
10 deliberate, kick around

thread
4 line, vein, yard **5** fiber, trail, weave
6 strand, stream, string **8** filament
ball of: 4 clew
dental: 5 floss
holder: 6 bobbin
kind: 4 silk, yarn **5** floss, lisle
6 cotton **8** surgical
loose: 8 raveling **9** ravelling
surgical: 6 catgut, suture

threadbare
4 hack, worn **5** dingy, faded, seedy,
stale, tacky, tatty, tired, trite **6** beat-
up, cheesy, cliché, frayed, ragged,
shabby, shoddy **7** clichéd, run-down,
tedious, worn-out **8** shopworn, slipshod, tattered, timeworn, well-worn
9 destitute, hackneyed **10** down-at-
heel **11** commonplace, dilapidated, down-at-heels, stereotyped
13 down-at-the-heel

threadlike
11 filamentous

threads
4 duds **7** clothes **8** clothing, garments

threat
6 danger, duress, menace **7** assault, warning **8** big stick, coercion
11 thunderbolt

threaten
3 cow **4** warn **5** augur **6** coerce,
menace **7** caution, portend, presage
8 endanger, forebode, forewarn,
overhang **10** intimidate

three
4 trey **5** crowd
combining form: 3 ter, tri

threefold
5 trine **6** thrice, treble, trinal, triple
7 triplex

Three Musicians artist
7 Picasso (Pablo)

Three Musketeers
5 Athos **6** Aramis **7** Porthos
author: 5 Dumas (Alexandre)
friend: 9 D'Artagnan

Threepenny Opera, The
author: 6 Brecht (Bertolt)
music: 5 Weill (Kurt)

threescore
5 sixty

Three Sisters, The
4 Olga **5** Irina, Masha
author: 7 Chekhov (Anton)

threesome
4 trio **5** triad, trine **6** triple, triune,
troika **7** trinity **8** triangle **11** triumvirate

three-wheeler
5 cycle, trike **7** pedicab **8** tricycle
10 velocipede

threnody
5 dirge, elegy **6** lament

thresh
3 lam, tan **4** beat, belt, drub, flog,
hide, lash, lick, pelt, trim, wave, whip
5 baste, forge, flail, pound, slate,
smear, swing, thump, whale, whang
6 batter, buffet, larrup, pummel, strike,
stripe, wallop, winnow **7** scourge,
shellac, trounce **8** lambaste, work
over **10** flagellate

threshold
3 eve **4** door, edge, gate, sill **5** brink,
limen, verge **6** outset **8** boundary

thrift
6 saving **7** economy, sea pink
8 prudence **9** frugality, parsimony

thrifty
5 canny **6** frugal, saving **7** sparing
9 provident **10** economical **12** parsimonious

thrill
3 wow **4** bang, boot, kick, rush, send
5 blast, throb **6** charge, excite, shiver,
tingle, wallop **7** frisson, tremble,
vibrate **9** electrify **10** excitement
11 titillation

thriller
6 gothic 7 chiller, mystery, shocker
8 whodunit 9 dime novel 10 hair-
raiser 13 penny dreadful

thrive
4 boom, grow 7 advance, burgeon,
develop, prosper, succeed 8 flourish, get ahead

throat
3 maw 4 tube 5 gorge 6 groove,
gullet 7 channel, weasand
inflammation: 5 croup 6 angina,
quinsy 10 laryngitis
relating to: 8 guttural
warmer: 5 scarf

throaty
5 gruff, husky, thick 6 hoarse
8 gravelly, guttural

throb
4 ache, beat, drum 5 pound, pulse
6 thrill 7 pulsate, vibrate 9 palpitate

throe
3 fit 4 pain, pang 5 agony, spasm
6 attack 7 seizure 9 suffering
10 convulsion 11 contraction

thrombus
4 clot 8 blockage, coagulum

throne
4 seat 5 chair, crown, power, reign
8 cathedra, dominion 11 sovereignty

throng
3 jam, mob 4 host, pack, push, rout
5 bunch, crowd, crush, drove, flock,
group, horde, press, scrum, shoal,
swarm 9 resort 9 multitude 10 assemblage

throttle
3 gun 5 choke 6 throat 7 garrote,
trachea 8 strangle, suppress 11 ac-
celerator, strangulate

through
3 per, via 4 done, past 5 due to,
ended 6 direct 7 by way of, done
for, nonstop, owing to 8 by dint of,
complete, finished, washed-up
9 because of, by means of, com-

pleted, concluded 10 by virtue of,
terminated, throughout
prefix: 3 dia, per

throughout
3 mid 4 amid 5 midst 6 during 7 all
over, overall 10 everywhere, far and
near, far and wide, high and low

Through the Looking Glass
author: 7 Carroll (Lewis)
character: 5 Alice

throve
9 burgeoned, prospered 10 flour-
ished

throw
3 lob, peg, put 4 cast, fire, hurl, toss
5 chuck, fling, heave, pitch, sling
6 launch, propel 7 buck off, project
in the towel: 4 quit 6 give up

throw away
4 blow, cast, junk, shed 5 scrap,
waste 7 discard, fritter 8 jettison,
squander

throwback
7 atavism 9 reversion

throw down the gauntlet
4 defy 8 confront 9 challenge

throw off
4 lose, shed 5 addle, shake 7 confuse, fluster 8 befuddle, bewilder,
distract
the track: 6 derail 7 confuse,
mislead

throw out
4 emit, junk, shed 5 chuck, eject,
evict, scrap 6 reject 7 discard
8 jettison

throw up
4 barf, cast, hurl, lose, puke, quit,
spew, toss 5 heave, retch, vomit
7 upchuck 8 disgorge 11 regurgitate

thrush
5 mavis, ouzel, robin, veery 6 mistle
8 bluebird 9 blackbird, fieldfare,
mistletoe 11 nightingale

thrust
3 dig, jab, ram 4 barb, butt, core,

cram, dash, dive, duck, gist, hurl,
kick, pith, poke, prod, push, stab, tilt
5 barge, crowd, cut in, drive, force,
lunge, press, punch, sense, shoot,
shove, spear, stick, stuff **6** burden,
extend, insert, pierce, plunge, propel,
upshot **7** assault, obtrude, project,
purport, riposte **8** pressure **9** substance

thud
3 jar **4** bump, jolt, plop **5** clunk,
throb, thump **6** impact **10** concussion

thug
3 mug **4** goon, hood, punk **5** bully,
rough, rowdy, tough **6** Apache,
Capone, gunman, hit man **7** hoodlum, mobster, ruffian **8** enforcer,
gangster, hooligan, plug-ugly **9** cutthroat, roughneck

thumb
4 leaf, turn **5** digit, hitch, ovolo
6 pollex, riffle **8** pollices (plural)
9 hitchhike

thumbs-up
3 AOK, nod **4** okay **7** go-ahead
10 green light

thumb through
4 scan **6** browse, riffle **7** dip into

thump
3 bop, hit **4** bash, beat, belt, blow,
drub, jolt, pelt, whip **5** knock, paste,
pound, punch, shock, smack, sound,
whack **6** batter, buffet, impact,
pummel, strike, thrash, thwack,
wallop **7** clobber, endorse, promote,
shellac, trounce **8** advocate

thunder
4 bang, boom, clap, peal, roar
6 rumble **7** resound **8** rumbling
9 fulminate

thunderbolt
9 lightning

thunder lizard
11 apatosaurus **12** brontosaurus

thunderstruck
5 agape **6** amazed **7** shocked,
stunned **8** dismayed **9** astounded,
staggered **10** astonished, bewildered, confounded **11** dumbfounded
13 flabbergasted

Thurber character
5 Mitty (Walter)

thus
3 sic **4** ergo, then **5** hence **9** therefore **11** accordingly **12** consequently
French: 5 ainsi

Thus Spake Zarathustra author
9 Nietzsche (Friedrich)

thwack
3 bop **4** belt, biff, blow, pelt, sock,
whop **5** crack, pound, smack, thump,
whack

thwart
4 balk, beat, dash, foil **5** bench
6 baffle, hinder, oppose, scotch,
stymie **9** checkmate, frustrate
10 circumvent, contravene, disappoint

Thyestes
brother: 6 Atreus
daughter: 7 Pelopia
father: 6 Pelops
mother: 10 Hippodamia
son: 9 Aegisthus

Tiamat
husband: 4 Apsu
slayer: 6 Marduk

tiara
5 crown **6** diadem **8** headband

Tibetan
animal: 3 yak **5** takin
capital: 5 Lhasa
coin: 5 tanga
monk: 4 lama
people: 6 Bhotia, Sherpa

tibia
8 shinbone

tic
5 quirk, spasm **6** twitch **9** twitching

tick
5 check **8** arachnid, parasite
9 checkmark **11** bloodsucker

ticker
4 bomb 5 clock, heart, watch

ticket
3 key, tag 4 comp, pass, vote
5 slate 6 ballot 7 receipt 8 passport, password 10 open sesame
seller: 7 scalper

tickle
4 stir 5 amuse, tease, touch
6 arouse, excite, please, tingle
7 delight, gratify, provoke 9 stimulate, titillate

tickled
5 happy 6 amused 7 pleased
9 delighted

ticklish
6 tender, thorny, touchy, tricky
8 delicate, unstable 9 sensitive
10 precarious 13 oversensitive

tick off
3 ire, irk 5 anger 6 rankle 7 incense, provoke 9 aggravate

tidal flood
4 bore

tidbit
4 bite 5 goody, treat 6 dainty, morsel, nugget

tide
4 flow, flux, rush 5 drift, flood, spate, surge 6 stream 7 current, holiday
type: 3 ebb, low 4 high, neap
5 flood 6 spring

tidings
4 news, word 6 advice 7 message
11 information 12 intelligence

tidy
4 fair, neat, smug, snug, trim 5 kempt
6 pick up 7 clean up, orderly, precise
9 shipshape 10 acceptable, methodical 11 respectable, spic-and-span, substantial, uncluttered, well-groomed 12 satisfactory, spick-and-span

tie
3 rod 4 band, bind, bond, cord, draw, gird, join, knit, knot, lash, link, moor, rope, yoke 5 equal, leash, match, truss 6 attach, cravat, fasten, fetter, hamper, oxford, ribbon, secure 7 connect, harness, shackle
8 dead heat, deadlock, fastener, ligament, ligature, restrain, shoelace, standoff, vinculum 9 constrain, stalemate 10 attachment, four-in-hand

tied
5 bound 6 joined, united 8 attached, fastened 9 connected

tier
3 row 4 bank, deck, file, line, rank
5 class, grade, group, story 6 league
7 echelon 8 category, grouping

tie-up
3 jam 4 snag 5 crimp, delay, hitch
6 glitch 7 problem 8 gridlock, slowdown, stoppage 10 connection, traffic jam 11 association

tiff
3 row 4 fuss, spat 5 run-in, scrap
6 bicker 7 brabble, dispute, quarrel, wrangle 8 argument, squabble
10 falling-out 11 altercation 12 disagreement

tiffany
5 gauze 11 cheesecloth

tiger
3 cat 6 feline 9 carnivore
young: 3 cub

tight
4 fast, firm, snug, taut, trim 5 cheap, close, drunk, fixed, tipsy 6 firmly, secure, stingy 7 compact, crowded, drunken, miserly 8 intimate 9 tenacious 10 inebriated 11 closefisted, intoxicated 12 cheeseparing, parsimonious 13 penny-pinching

tighten
4 bind 5 choke, close, cramp, pinch, screw 6 clench, fasten, narrow, secure, shrink 8 compress, restrict
9 clamp down, constrict

tightfisted
see **stingy**

tight-lipped
6 silent 8 reserved, reticent, taciturn
12 closemouthed

tightwad
5 miser, piker 7 niggard, scrooge
9 skinflint 10 cheapskate 12 penny-
pincher

tile
5 plate, slate 6 domino 7 tessera
8 linoleum

till
3 hoe, sow 4 disk, plow, tend, turn,
up to, work 6 before, harrow 7 prior
to 9 cultivate 11 in advance of
12 cash register

tillable
6 arable 10 cultivable 12 cultivat-
able

tillage
4 farm, land 5 tilth 7 culture 11 cultivation

tiller
4 helm 5 stalk 6 farmer, sprout
7 planter, steerer 9 sodbuster
10 cultivator

tilt
3 tip 4 bank, bent, bias, cant, cock,
heel, lean, list, toss 5 grade, joust,
level, lurch, pitch, slant, slope, speed
6 attack, charge, thrust 7 dispute,
incline, leaning, recline 8 gradient
11 inclination

timbal
4 drum 10 kettledrum

timber
3 log 4 balk, beam, stud, tree,
wood 5 board, joist, plank, trees,
woods 6 forest, girder, lumber, rafter
8 woodland
uncut: 8 stumpage
wolf: 4 lobo

timbre
4 tone 6 temper 7 quality 9 resonance, tone color

timbrel
4 drum 10 tambourine

time
3 age, era 4 bout, date, hour, pace,
span, term 5 clock, epoch, shift,
space, spell, stint, tempo, while
6 moment, period, season 7 instant,
stretch 8 duration, occasion 11 opportunity
combining form: 5 chron 6 chrono
gone by: 4 past 9 yesterday
long: 3 age, eon, era 4 aeon
of day: 4 dawn, dusk, noon 5 night
6 sunset 7 evening, morning, sunrise 8 daybreak, twilight 9 afternoon
olden: 4 yore 10 yesteryear
period: 3 age, day, eon, era 4 aeon,
hour, week, year 5 epoch, month
6 decade, minute, moment, second
7 century, instant 9 fortnight 10 millennium
present: 3 now
relating to: 8 temporal
short: 5 jiffy 6 moment, second
7 instant
to come: 6 future 8 tomorrow
waste: 4 loaf 5 dally 6 loiter

time and again
3 oft 5 often 6 hourly 8 commonly,
ofttimes 10 constantly, frequently,
oftentimes, repeatedly 11 continually, over and over 12 periodically

Time founder
4 Luce (Henry R.) 6 Hadden (Briton)

timeless
7 ageless, eternal, unaging 8 un-
ageing 9 atemporal, perpetual
11 everlasting

timely
5 early 6 prompt, proper 8 punctual,
suitable 9 opportune 10 seasonable
11 appropriate

Time Machine author
5 Wells (H. G.)

Time of Your Life author
7 Saroyan (William)

time-out
4 rest 5 break, pause 6 hiatus,
recess 7 respite 8 breather
9 interlude 12 interruption

timepiece
5 clock, watch 7 sundial 8 horologe 9 clepsydra, stopwatch 10 water clock 11 chronograph, chronometer

timetable
6 agenda, docket 7 program 8 calendar, schedule

timeworn
3 old 4 aged, hack 5 hoary, stale, trite 6 age-old 7 ancient 8 dog-eared, Noachian 9 hackneyed 10 threadbare

time zone
7 Central, Eastern, Pacific 8 Mountain

timid
3 shy 4 wary 5 chary, mousy 6 afraid, yellow 7 bashful, chicken, fearful, halting, nervous, panicky 8 cowardly, retiring, timorous 9 diffident, tentative, trepidant, uncertain 11 unassertive 12 apprehensive, fainthearted

timidity
4 fear 7 modesty, shyness 8 meekness 9 hesitancy, reticence 10 diffidence, hesitation

Timon's servant
7 Flavius

timorous
4 wary 5 timid 6 afraid 7 fearful 8 retiring 9 shrinking, tremulous 12 apprehensive

Timothy's associate
4 Paul

tin
3 box, can 5 metal 7 element 9 container
mining region: 8 stannary
relating to: 7 stannic 8 stannous
sheet: 6 latten

tincture
3 dye 4 cast, hint, tint 5 color, shade, smack, stain, tinge, touch, trace 6 iodine, streak 8 colorant, dyestuff, laudanum 9 paregoric 10 intimation, suggestion

tinder
4 punk 5 spunk 8 kindling

tine
5 point, prong, spike 6 branch

tinge
3 dye, hue 4 cast, hint, tint, tone 5 color, imbue, shade, stain, tinct, touch 8 tincture 10 intimation

tingle
5 sting 6 thrill 7 prickle 9 sensation

tinker
3 fix 4 mend, mess, muck, play 5 gypsy 6 adjust, diddle, fiddle, mender, potter, putter, repair 7 bungler, twiddle 9 repairman

tinkle
4 ring, ting 5 chink, clink, plink 6 jingle

tinny
4 thin 5 cheap, harsh 8 metallic

Tin Pan Alley acronym
3 BMI 5 ASCAP

tinsel
5 gaudy 6 flashy, garish, tawdry 7 chintzy, glaring, trinket 8 ornament, specious 9 clinquant 11 superficial 12 meretricious

tint
3 dye, hue 4 cast, tone, wash 5 color, shade, tinge, touch 8 tincture 10 coloration 12 pigmentation

tiny
3 wee 5 bitsy, bitty, elfin, pygmy, teeny, weeny 6 minute, peewee, pocket, teensy, weensy 8 pint-size 9 itsy-bitsy, itty-bitty, miniature, minuscule 10 diminutive, pocket-size, teeny-weeny 11 lilliputian, microscopic 12 teensy-weensy 13 infinitesimal

tip
3 cap, cue, top 4 apex, cant, clue, cusp, heel, hint, lean, list, peak, perk, tilt 5 point, slant, slope, steer, upset 6 advice, topple 7 cumshaw, incline 8 gratuity, overturn, turn over 9 baksheesh, lagniappe, pourboire 11 information

tip-off
4 clue, hint, sign   6 advice   7 pointer, warning   8 giveaway, jump ball
10 indication

Tippecanoe and ____ too
5 Tyler

tippet
4 cape   5 scarf   8 liripipe

tipple
3 bib, sip   4 swig, tope   5 booze, drink   6 guzzle, imbibe   7 swizzle
8 liquor up

tippler
3 sot   4 lush, soak   5 drunk, toper
6 bibber, boozer   7 tosspot   8 drunkard   9 inebriate

tipstaff
7 bailiff

tipster
4 fink   6 canary, snitch   7 adviser, rat fink, stoolie, tattler   8 informer, squealer   11 stool pigeon

tipsy
3 lit   4 high   5 askew, drunk, lit up, oiled, tight   7 drunken, fuddled
8 unsteady   10 inebriated   11 intoxicated

tiptoe
5 creep, steal   9 pussyfoot

tirade
4 rant   6 screed   8 diatribe, harangue, jeremiad   9 philippic   12 denunciation, vituperation   13 tongue-lashing

tire
3 sap   4 bore, fail, flag, jade, pall, poop, wear   5 drain, droop, ennui, weary, wheel   6 tucker, weaken
7 exhaust, fatigue, wear out   8 enervate, wear down
airless: 4 flat   7 blowout
kind: 4 bias, snow   6 radial   7 retread
9 whitewall

tired
4 worn   5 spent, weary   6 done in
7 drained, run-down, worn out

8 fatigued, flagging   9 enervated, exhausted

tiredness
7 fatigue   8 collapse   9 lassitude
10 exhaustion   11 prostration

tireless
10 unflagging   13 indefatigable, inexhaustible

Tiresias
4 seer   10 soothsayer

tiresome
4 dull   5 stale   6 boring   7 irksome, lumpish, operose, tedious

Tirol
capital: 9 Innsbruck
country: 7 Austria
mountains: 4 Alps

Tisiphone
see **Erinyes**

tissue
3 web   4 film, mesh   5 fiber, gauze, paper   6 fabric
anatomical: 4 tela   5 fiber   6 diploe
8 ganglion   10 epithelium
connective: 6 stroma, tendon
9 cartilage
kind: 3 fat   5 nerve   6 muscle
7 nervous   8 muscular   10 connective
layer: 6 dermis   7 stratum
plant: 4 bast, wood   5 xylem
6 phloem

titan
5 giant   8 colossus

Titan
father: 6 Uranus
female: 4 Rhea   6 Tethys, Themis
male: 6 Cronus   7 Iapetus, Oceanus
mother: 4 Gaea

Titan author
7 Dreiser (Theodore)

Titania's husband
6 Oberon

titanic
4 huge, vast   5 great   6 mighty
7 immense, mammoth, massive
8 colossal, enormous, gigantic

9 cyclopean, Herculean, monstrous
10 gargantuan, tremendous

tithe
3 tax 4 levy 5 tenth 12 contribution

Tithonus
beloved by: 3 Eos
father: 8 Laomedon

Titian painting
5 Danaë 8 Ecce Homo 10 Assumption (The), Holy Family (The)
12 Rape of Europa (The) 13 Maltese Knight, Medea and Venus, Venus and Cupid 14 Worship of Venus (The) 17 Bacchus and Ariadne

titillate
6 arouse, excite, stir up, thrill, tickle
9 stimulate

title
3 dub, due 4 call, deed, dibs, name, term 5 claim, merit, nomen 7 baptize, caption, heading 8 christen, cognomen, pretense 9 designate
10 denominate, pretension 11 appellation, appellative, designation
12 championship, compellation, denomination
Dutch: 7 mynheer
ecclesiastic: 8 reverend
feminine: 3 Mrs. 4 dame, lady, ma'am, miss 5 madam 6 madame, milady, missus 8 mistress
French: 6 madame 8 monsieur
12 mademoiselle
German: 4 Frau, Herr 8 Fräulein
holder: 5 noble 8 champion
Indian: 3 sri 5 sahib
Islamic: 5 hajji 6 sayyid 9 ayatollah
Italian: 5 donna 6 signor 7 signora
9 signorina
monk's: 3 fra 7 brother
of nobility: 3 sir 4 duke, earl, king, lady, lord, sire 5 baron, count, queen
6 prince 7 baronet, duchess, marquis 8 Archduke, baroness, countess, marchesa, marchese, marquise, princess, viscount 11 marchioness, viscountess
Oriental: 4 khan
Persian: 5 mirza

Portuguese: 3 dom 4 dona 6 senhor 7 senhora 9 senhorita
Spanish: 3 don 4 doña
Turkish: 3 bey

titmouse
4 bird 6 tomtit 7 bushtit 9 chickadee

Tito
4 Broz (Josip)

titter
5 laugh 6 giggle 7 chortle, chuckle, snicker, snigger

tittle
3 bit, jot 4 atom, iota, mite 5 minim, speck 7 smidgen 8 particle 9 diacritic

titular
5 legal 6 titled 7 nominal 8 so-called
11 designative

Tityus
father: 4 Zeus
slayer: 6 Apollo

Tiu
see **Tyr**

tizzy
4 flap, fume, snit, stew 5 sweat
6 dither, swivel, uproar

T-man
5 agent 8 revenuer

to
be sure: 6 indeed 7 granted 9 certainly
Scottish: 3 tae
wit: 3 viz 6 namely, that is 8 scilicet

toad
6 anuran, peeper 8 truckler 9 amphibian, brownnose, sycophant
10 batrachian, bootlicker 11 lickspittle
genus: 4 Bufo

toady
4 fawn 5 cower, leech 6 cringe, flunky, grovel, kowtow, lackey, sponge 7 truckle 8 bootlick, parasite, truckler 9 brownnose, sycophant 10 bootlicker 11 apple-polish, lickspittle

toast
5 bread, drink, skoal 6 cheers,
health, l'chaim, pledge, prosit, salute
7 wassail 8 mazel tov
kind: 5 melba 6 French 8 zwieback

toastmaster
5 emcee

To a Waterfowl author
6 Bryant (William Cullen)

tobacco
4 leaf, weed
cask: 8 hogshead
chewing: 4 chaw, quid
ingredient: 3 tar 8 nicotine
juice: 6 ambeer
kind: 4 shag 5 snuff 6 burley
7 caporal, perique, Turkish 9 broad-
leaf, mundungus
pipe: 4 heel 6 dottle
rolled: 5 cigar 9 cigarette
Turkish: 7 latakia

Tobacco Road author
8 Caldwell (Erskine)

to be
Latin: 4 esse

Tobias
father: 5 Tobit
son: 8 Hyrcanus

toby
3 jug, mug 7 pitcher

tocsin
3 SOS 5 alarm, alert 6 signal

today
3 now 9 currently, presently

toddler
3 tot 4 tyke

to-do
4 fuss, rout, stir 5 hoo-ha, rouse,
stink, whirl 6 bother, bustle, clamor,
furore, hubbub, hurrah, pother,
ruckus, rumpus, uproar 7 turmoil
8 foofaraw 9 agitation, commotion
10 hurly-burly 11 disturbance

toe
5 digit
big: 6 hallux
combining form: 6 dactyl

toehold
7 footing

toff
3 fop 4 beau 5 blade, dandy, swell
7 coxcomb, peacock 8 macaroni,
popinjay 9 exquisite 12 clotheshorse

toga
4 gown, robe, wrap

together
6 at once, joined, united 7 jointly
8 mutually 10 conjointly 11 con-
certedly 12 coincidently, collectively,
concurrently
prefix: 3 col, com, con, cor, sym, syn

togetherness
5 union 7 cahoots 8 alliance 10 connection, solidarity 11 affiliation,
association, combination, conjunction, partnership

toggle
3 pin 6 fasten, switch 9 alternate
10 crosspiece

Togo
capital: 4 Lomé
language: 3 Ewe 6 French
monetary unit: 5 franc
neighbor: 5 Benin, Ghana 11 Burkina Faso

togs
3 rig 4 duds, suit 5 dress 6 attire,
outfit 7 apparel, clothes, raiment,
rigging 8 clothing, ensemble, garments

To His Coy Mistress author
7 Marvell (Andrew)

toil
3 fag, net, tug 4 grub, plod, plug,
slog, trap, work 5 grind, labor, slave,
snare, sweat 6 drudge 7 slavery,
travail 8 drudgery

toiler
4 peon 5 slave 6 drudge, slavey
9 workhorse

toilet
3 loo 4 head, john 5 bidet, potty,

privy **6** johnny **7** latrine **8** bathroom, lavatory **11** water closet

toilsome
4 hard **5** heavy **6** uphill **7** arduous, labored **9** difficult, effortful, laborious, strenuous

Tokay
4 wine

token
4 buck, chip, gift, mark, note, sign **5** badge, check, favor, index, piece, plume, prize, relic, scrip **6** copper, emblem, pledge, symbol, ticket, trophy **7** earnest, gesture, memento, symptom, warrant **8** evidence, keepsake, memorial, reminder, security, souvenir **9** indicator **10** expression, indication **11** perfunctory, remembrance

To Kill a Mockingbird author
3 Lee (Harper)

Tokyo
formerly: 3 Edo
island: 6 Honshu

tolerable
4 fair **6** common, decent **7** livable **8** adequate, all right, bearable, passable **9** endurable **10** acceptable, sufferable **11** respectable **12** satisfactory

tolerably
4 so-so **5** quite **6** fairly, pretty, rather **8** passably **9** averagely **10** moderately

tolerance
6 leeway **8** patience **9** allowance, endurance, deviation, fortitude, variation **10** indulgence, resistance, sufferance **11** forbearance, habituation

tolerant
4 easy **5** broad **7** lenient, liberal **8** placable **9** easygoing, eurytopic, forgiving, indulgent, tractable **10** open-minded, permissive **11** broad-minded, progressive, sympathetic **13** understanding

tolerate
4 bear, bide, hack **5** abide, allow, brook, stand **6** accept, endure, pardon, permit, suffer **7** condone, stomach, swallow **8** bear with, live with **9** put up with **11** countenance

Tolkien creature
3 Ent, Orc **5** Ainur **6** Balrog, Hobbit, Nazgul, Shelob **9** Oliphaunt

toll
3 fee, tax **4** bell, bong, cost, levy, peal, ring **5** chime, knell, price, sound **6** charge, summon, tariff **7** expense **8** casualty **10** assessment

tollbooth
11 customhouse

Tolstoy novel
8 Cossacks (The) **11** War and Peace **12** Anna Karenina **16** Death of Ivan Ilich (The)

tomato
9 love apple

tomb
5 crypt, grave **6** burial **9** mausoleum, sepulcher, sepulchre, sepulture
ancient Egyptian: 7 mastaba
empty: 8 cenotaph

tomboy
6 gamine, hoyden

tombstone
4 slab **8** memorial, monument **11** grave marker
inscription: 3 RIP **8** hic jacet

tome
4 book **6** volume

_____ Tomé and Príncipe
3 Sao

tomfool
3 ass **4** dolt, fool, jerk **5** crazy, idiot, loony, ninny, silly, wacky **6** absurd, donkey, stupid **7** doltish, foolish, jackass **8** clodpoll, dummkopf, imbecile **9** blockhead, fantastic,

horse's ass, thickhead **10** dunderhead, nincompoop **11** chowderhead, chucklehead, harebrained **12** preposterous

tomfoolery
4 dido, lark **5** antic, caper, prank, shine, trick **6** frolic **8** escapade, fandango **9** high jinks **10** shenanigan **11** monkeyshine

Tom Jones author
8 Fielding (Henry)

tommyrot
4 bull **5** hooey, trash **7** baloney, hogwash, rubbish **8** claptrap, nonsense **10** balderdash **13** horsefeathers

Tom o'Bedlam
3 nut **4** loon **5** loony **6** madman, maniac **7** lunatic **9** bedlamite

tomorrow
6 future, mañana

Tom Sawyer
author: 5 Twain (Mark) **7** Clemens (Samuel)
character: 5 Becky (Thatcher) **8** Huck Finn, Injun Joe **9** Aunt Polly **10** Muff Potter

Tom Thumb
4 runt **5** dwarf, pygmy **6** midget, peanut, peewee **7** manikin **8** halfpint **10** homunculus **11** lilliputian

ton
3 lot **4** chic **5** bunch, style, trend, vogue **6** bundle **7** fashion

tone
3 hue **4** cast, mode, mood, note, tint, vein **5** color, pitch, shade, style, tinge **6** accent, manner, spirit, strain, temper, timbre **7** fashion **10** inflection

toned down
4 mute, soft **5** sober **6** low-key, mellow **7** subdued **8** laid-back, low-keyed, softened

Tonga
capital: 9 Nuku'alofa
ethnic group: 10 Polynesian
explorer: 4 Cook (Capt. James) **6** Tasman (Abel)
island group: 5 Vava'u **6** Haapai **9** Tongatapu
language: 6 Tongan **7** English
monetary unit: 6 pa'anga

tongue
4 lick, pole, tang **6** glossa, lingua, speech **7** clapper, dialect, languet **8** language **10** vernacular
combining form: 4 glot **5** gloss, lingu **6** glossa, glosso, lingua, lingui, linguo **7** glossia

tongue-lash
4 lash, rail **5** chide, scold **6** berate, rebuke, revile **7** bawl out, chew out, tell off, reprove, upbraid **8** admonish, call down, reproach **9** castigate, reprimand **10** vituperate

tongue-lashing
6 rebuke, tirade **7** censure, reproof **8** scolding **9** reprimand, talking-to **11** castigation **12** dressing-down

tongue-tied
3 mum, shy **4** mute **6** silent **7** bashful **9** diffident **10** speechless **12** inarticulate

tonic
3 pop **4** cola, soda **5** brisk **7** bracing, soda pop **8** curative, salutary **10** refreshing **11** restorative, stimulating **12** exhilarating, invigorating
extract: 4 cola **9** berberine

tons
4 gobs, lots **5** heaps, loads, piles, scads

tony
4 chic, posh **5** smart, swank, swish **6** classy, modish, uptown **7** à la mode, elegant, stylish **9** exclusive **11** fashionable

too
4 also, ever, over, very **5** along **6** as well, overly, unduly, withal **7** awfully, besides, further, greatly **8** likewise, moreover, overmuch **9** extremely, immensely **10** in addition, remark-

ably, strikingly **11** exceedingly, excessively, furthermore **12** additionally, exorbitantly, immoderately, inordinately **13** exceptionally

tool

4 pawn **5** means **6** puppet, rimmer, stooge **7** cat's-paw, hayfork, machine, rounder, utensil **8** picklock **9** appliance, implement, mechanism **10** instrument
axlike: 4 adze
boring: 5 auger, drill
carving: 6 veiner
cleaving: 4 froe
cobbler's: 3 awl
cutting: 3 axe, saw **4** adze **5** knife **6** shears **8** billhook
digging: 4 pick **5** spade **6** shovel **7** mattock
engraving: 5 burin
farm: 6 seeder
filing: 4 rasp **7** riffler
garden: 3 hoe **4** rake **5** spade **6** trowel, weeder
grasping: 6 pincer **7** tweezer **8** tweezers
mining: 6 trepan
prehistoric: 6 eolith
pruning: 6 shears **8** secateur
rubbing: 9 burnisher
scooping: 6 router
toothed: 3 saw **7** rippler
woodworking: 3 saw **5** bevel, plane **6** chisel, hammer

toot

3 bat, jag **4** bout, bust, tear **5** binge, blast, drunk, snort, sound, souse, spree **6** bender **7** carouse

tooth

5 molar **7** incisor **8** bicuspid, premolar
combining form: 4 dent **5** denti, dento
cuspid: 6 canine **8** dogtooth, eyetooth
cutting: 10 carnassial
decay: 6 caries
doctor: 7 dentist
pointed: 4 fang **6** canine, cuspid
small: 8 denticle

toothless

7 useless **8** edentate **10** edentulous **11** ineffective, ineffectual

toothsome

5 sapid, tasty **6** delish, savory **8** luscious, pleasant, pleasing, tasteful **9** agreeable, delicious, palatable, succulent **10** appetizing, attractive

too-too

6 la-di-da **7** extreme **8** affected, overdone, overmuch, precious **9** excessive **10** hoity-toity, inordinate **11** exaggerated, overrefined, pretentious

tootsie

3 pet **4** dear **5** honey **7** beloved, darling, sweetie **10** sweetheart

top

3 cap, tip **4** acme, apex, best, cusp, head, peak, pick, roof **5** cream, crest, crown, elite, point, prime, prize **6** apical, choice, climax, height, summit, utmost, vertex **7** capital, highest, maximal, maximum, surface **8** five-star, loftiest, pinnacle, superior **9** first-rate, uppermost **10** first-class **11** culmination

tope

3 nip **4** soak **5** booze, drink, shark, stupa **6** guzzle, imbibe, tipple **7** swizzle **8** liquor up

toper

3 sot **4** lush, soak, wino **5** drunk, rummy, souse **6** bibber, boozer **7** tippler, tosspot **8** drunkard **9** inebriate

Tophet

4 hell **5** hades, Sheol **6** blazes **7** Gehenna, inferno **9** perdition **10** underworld

topic

4 talk, text **5** issue, motif, point, score, theme **6** burden, matter, motive, thread **7** content, subject **8** argument **11** proposition

topical

5 local **7** current, nominal **8** regional **9** temporary **11** superficial

topmost

7 highest, leading, supreme
8 crowning, ultimate **9** paramount,
principal **10** consummate, preeminent **11** culminating

top-notch

5 prime **6** choice **7** capital **8** five-
star, superior **9** excellent, first-rate
10 first-class **11** first-string

top off

3 cap **5** crown **6** climax, finish, refill
8 complete, conclude, resupply
9 culminate

topography

7 surface, terrain **8** features

topple

3 tip **4** drop, fall **5** crash, lurch,
pitch, slump, upset **6** defeat, falter,
plunge, totter, tumble **8** collapse,
keel over, overturn **9** overthrow

tops

4 best **5** primo **6** at most **7** highest
8 peerless, superior **9** at the most,
first-rate, matchless **11** outstanding

topsy-turvy

7 chaotic, jumbled, mixed-up **8** cockeyed, confused, inverted **10** disjointed, disordered, upside down

toque

3 cap, hat

tor

4 crag, hill, peak **5** butte, cliff, mound,
talus

Torah

10 Pentateuch

torch

4 fire **5** flame, light **6** ignite **7** firebug **8** arsonist, flambeau, guidance
10 flashlight, incendiary

toreador

6 torero **7** matador **11** bullfighter

torero

7 matador **11** bullfighter

torment

3 rag, try, vex **4** bait, bane, hell, hurt,
pain, pang, rack **5** abuse, agony,
curse, grill, harry, tease, worry, wring
6 harass, harrow, heckle, misery,
molest, needle, plague **7** afflict,
agonize, anguish, crucify, distort,
hagride, torture, travail, trouble
8 distress **9** persecute, tantalize
10 affliction, excruciate

torn

4 rent **5** split **6** ragged, ripped,
unsure **7** mangled **8** tattered,
wrenched **9** lacerated, uncertain,
undecided

tornado

6 funnel **7** cyclone, twister **9** wind-
storm, whirlwind

toro

4 bull

torpedo

3 gun, ray **4** mine, thug **5** blast,
bravo, smash, wreck **6** gunman,
gunsel, hit man, killer, weapon
7 destroy, nullify, scuttle **8** assassin,
firework **9** explosive, shoot down
10 hatchet man, projectile, triggerman **11** electric ray

torpid

4 dull, lazy, numb **5** dopey, inert
6 sodden, stupid **7** dormant **8** comatose, inactive, sluggish **9** apathetic,
lethargic **12** hebetudinous

torpor

4 coma, daze **5** swoon **6** apathy,
stupor **7** languor **8** dopiness,
dullness, hebetude, lethargy **9** lassitude, passivity, stolidity **10** stagnation **12** listlessness

torque

5 twist

torrent

4 rush **5** flood, spate **6** deluge,
stream **7** cascade, Niagara **8** cataract, flooding **9** cataclysm **10** inundation, outpouring

torrid

3 hot **5** fiery **6** ardent, fervid, heated,
red-hot, sultry **7** boiling, burning,

flaming, parched **8** broiling, white-hot **9** scorching **10** hot-blooded, passionate, sweltering **11** impassioned

tort
5 crime, wrong **7** offense **10** wrong-doing

tortilla dish
4 taco **6** flauta **7** burrito, chalupa, tostada **9** enchilada **10** quesadilla **11** chimichanga

Tortilla Flat author
9 Steinbeck (John)

tortoise
6 turtle **8** terrapin **9** chelonian
beak: 3 neb
shell: 8 carapace

tortuous
5 snaky **6** cranky, tricky **7** crooked, devious, sinuous, winding **8** flexuous, indirect, involute, involved **9** meandrous **10** circuitous, convoluted, meandering, serpentine **11** anfractuous, vermiculate **12** labyrinthine

torture
4 pain, rack, warp **5** agony, wring **6** harrow, martyr **7** afflict, agonize, anguish, crucify, torment **9** martyrdom **10** excruciate **11** third degree

tortured
4 bent **6** racked, warped **7** twisted **8** deformed **9** distorted

tory
5 right **7** old-line **8** loyalist, old guard, orthodox, rightist, royalist **12** conservative

Tosca
character: 5 Mario (Cavaradossi) **7** Scarpia (Baron)
composer: 7 Puccini (Giacomo)

_____ Toscanini
6 Arturo

tosh
3 rot **4** bosh, bunk **5** bilge, hooey **6** bunkum, drivel, humbug **7** baloney, eyewash, hogwash, twaddle **8** malarkey, nonsense, tommyrot, trumpery

toss
4 cast, flap, flip, hurl, rock, roll **5** chuck, drink, fling, heave, match, pitch, quaff, sling, surge, throw, vomit **6** imbibe, tumble, welter, writhe **7** discard **9** knock back, throw away

tosspot
see **tippler**

tot
3 add, kid, nip, sum **4** dram, shot, slug, tyke **5** child, snort **6** figure, infant, nipper, shaver, squirt **7** snifter, toddler

total
3 add, all, sum **4** foot, full **5** add up, equal, gross, run to, smash, sum to, utter, whole, wreck, yield **6** all-out, amount, budget, entire, figure, number **7** crack up, destroy, full-out, overall, perfect, plenary, quantum **8** absolute, complete, demolish, entirety, outright, positive, quantity **9** aggregate, full-blown, full-scale, inclusive, out-and-out, unlimited **10** consummate, unreserved **11** unmitigated **13** comprehensive, thoroughgoing

totalitarian
8 absolute, despotic **10** autocratic **11** dictatorial **13** authoritarian

totality
3 all, sum **4** lump **5** whole **7** oneness **8** entirety **9** aggregate, wholeness **12** completeness

totalize
3 add, sum **5** sum up **6** figure **7** summate

tote
3 lug **4** cart, haul, load, pack **5** carry, ferry, sum up **6** burden, convey, figure **7** summate **9** transport **10** pari-mutuel

totem
6 emblem, symbol

To the Lighthouse author
5 Woolf (Virginia)

totter
4 reel, sway 5 lurch, shake, waver
6 falter, toddle, topple, wobble
7 stagger

touch
4 abut, feel, meet, move, stir 5 brush,
graze 6 adjoin, border, caress,
finger, stroke 7 contact, palpate
9 palpation, tactility

touchable
7 tactile 8 palpable, tangible

touch down
4 land 5 light, perch, roost 6 alight,
settle

touched
3 odd, off 5 batty, crazy, moved
7 stirred 8 affected 9 emotional

touching
4 as to, in re 5 about, anent, as for
6 moving, tender 7 against, apropos,
emotive, meeting, piteous, pitiful,
tangent 8 abutting, adjacent, pathetic, pitiable, poignant, stirring
9 adjoining, affecting, apropos of,
as regards, bordering, immediate,
impinging, regarding 10 as respects,
back-to-back, concerning, contiguous, respecting, tangential 11 coterminous 12 conterminous

touch off
5 erupt, spark, start 6 ignite, incite,
kindle 7 explode, inflame, provoke,
trigger 8 initiate 9 instigate 11 precipitate

touchstone
4 test 5 check, gauge, proof, trial
7 measure 8 standard 9 barometer,
benchmark, criterion, yardstick

touch up
3 fix 5 patch 6 rework 7 improve,
perfect

touchy
5 dicey, huffy, risky, testy 6 tender,
tricky 7 peppery 8 delicate, ticklish
9 explosive, hazardous, irascible,

irritable, sensitive 10 precarious
11 inflammable, quarrelsome, thin-
skinned 13 oversensitive, temperamental, unpredictable

tough
3 bad, mug 4 goon, hard, hood, lout,
punk, stud, thug 5 bully, hardy, harsh
6 rugged, severe, sturdy, unruly
7 arduous, hoodlum, onerous, ruffian
8 bullyboy, exacting, hooligan, obdurate 9 arbitrary, demanding, difficult,
effortful, hard-nosed, hidebound,
immutable, laborious, resistant,
roughneck, strenuous 10 hard-
bitten, hard-boiled, hardheaded,
inflexible, refractory, unyielding
11 intractable, unbreakable 12 pertinacious

toughen
5 inure 6 anneal, harden, season,
temper 9 acclimate, habituate
10 strengthen 11 acclimatize

toughie
4 goon, hood, lout, punk, thug
5 poser, rowdy 7 hoodlum, ruffian,
stumper 8 bullyboy, hooligan, plug-
ugly 9 roughneck

toupee
3 rug, wig 6 peruke, wiglet 7 periwig
8 postiche 9 hairpiece

tour
4 bout, trip, turn 5 jaunt, round, shift,
spell, stint 6 junket, period, travel,
troupe 7 circuit, journey 8 progress
9 barnstorm, excursion 10 expedition, rubberneck

tour de force
4 deed, feat 7 classic, display,
exploit 10 magnum opus, masterwork 11 achievement, chef
d'oeuvre, masterpiece

tour guide
8 cicerone

tourist
7 tripper, visitor 8 traveler 9 sightseer, traveller 10 day-tripper, rubberneck, vacationer 12 excursionist,
globe-trotter

tournament
4 open, tilt 5 pro-am 6 jousts, series
7 contest, tourney 8 carousel
10 round-robin 11 competition
12 championship

tourney
4 meet 5 event, games, match
7 compete, contest 8 concours
11 competition

tousle
4 mess, muss 6 rumple 8 dishevel,
disorder

tout
3 spy, tip 4 brag, laud, plug 5 watch
6 blow up, peddle, praise, talk up
7 acclaim, crack up, promote, solicit
8 ballyhoo, persuade, proclaim
9 publicize

tovarich
7 comrade

tow
3 lug, tug 4 drag, draw, haul, pull,
rope, yarn 5 chain, trail 6 hawser
truck: 7 wrecker

towel word
3 his 4 hers

tower
4 loom 5 spire 6 turret 8 overlook
on a mosque: 7 minaret

towering
4 high, tall 5 grand, great, lofty
6 aerial, mighty 7 extreme, soaring,
stately 8 imposing, majestic 9 excessive, grandiose 10 exorbitant,
immoderate, inordinate, monumental,
prodigious 11 extravagant, magnificent, skyscraping 12 altitudinous,
overwhelming

towhee
5 finch 7 chewink

to wit
3 viz 6 namely 8 scilicet 9 c'est-à-
dire, videlicet

town
4 burg 6 hamlet, podunk 7 borough,
village
medieval: 5 bourg

town and _____
4 gown 7 country

townsman
7 burgher, citizen

town square
5 plaza
Italian: 6 piazza

toxic
6 poison 7 harmful 8 venomous,
virulent 9 poisonous 10 infectious

toxin
5 venom 6 poison

toy
4 fool, play 5 antic, curio, dally, flirt,
knack, mouse, tease 6 bauble,
caress, coquet, diddle, fiddle, gewgaw, trifle 7 bibelot, novelty, pastime,
trinket, whatnot 8 gimcrack 9 plaything 10 diminutive, knickknack

trace
3 jot, ray, run, tug 4 blip, echo, hint,
iota, mark, path, scan, wisp 5 relic,
shade, tinge, trail, tread 6 derive,
detect, nuance, shadow, strain,
streak 7 outline, remains, remnant,
run down, soupçon, symptom, vestige 8 discover, tincture, traverse
9 delineate, footprint, remainder,
scintilla, suspicion 10 intimation,
suggestion

trachea
6 larynx, throat, vessel 7 weasand
8 throttle, windpipe

track
3 way 4 drag, path, road, sign, step,
tail 5 chase, cover, print, spoor,
trace, trail, tread 6 artery, follow,
pursue, shadow, travel 7 footway,
imprint, monitor, pathway, vestige
8 footpath, footstep 9 footprint

track-and-field event
4 dash 5 relay 6 discus 7 javelin,
hurdles, shot put 8 footrace, high
jump, long jump 9 broad jump,
decathlon, pole vault 10 hep-
tathlon, triple jump 11 discus throw
12 steeplechase

tract

3 lot **4** area, belt, farm, land, plat, plot, zone **5** block, claim **6** parcel, region **7** leaflet, portion, terrain **8** pamphlet, preserve **9** territory

tractable

4 tame **6** docile, gentle, pliant **7** ductile, plastic, pliable **8** amenable, biddable, flexible, obedient, workable **9** adaptable, breakable, malleable **10** manageable

tractate

5 summa **6** memoir, thesis **7** pandect **8** hornbook, monument, treatise **9** discourse, monograph **10** commentary **12** disquisition, dissertation, introduction

traction

4 drag, pull **5** force **7** drawing, tension **8** friction

tractor maker

5 Deere (John)

trade

4 deal, sell, swap **5** craft, truck **6** barter, change, custom, market, métier, peddle, switch **7** bargain, calling, pursuit, traffic **8** business, commerce, exchange, industry, vocation **10** employment, occupation, profession, substitute **11** merchandise, transaction
illicit: **11** black market

trademark

3 tag **4** logo **5** brand, label, stamp **6** patent, symbol **8** colophon, logotype **9** brand name

trader

4 ship **6** broker, dealer, vendor **8** merchant

trade route

7 sea-lane

tradition

4 lore, myth **5** habit **6** belief, custom, legacy, legend, mythos, rubric **7** folkway **8** folklore, heredity, heritage, practice **9** mythology **10** convention **12** old wives' tale

traditional

4 oral **5** usual **6** common, spoken, verbal **7** classic, old-line, popular **8** habitual, orthodox **9** classical, customary, old-school, unwritten **10** button-down **11** established **12** acknowledged, buttoned-down, conservative, conventional

traditionalist

6 purist **12** conservative

traditionalistic

4 tory **7** die-hard, old-line **8** orthodox, standpat **12** conservative

traduce

4 slur **5** libel, smear, wrong **6** betray, breach, defame, malign, vilify **7** asperse, slander, violate **8** disgrace, tear down **9** denigrate **10** calumniate

Trafalgar commander

6 Nelson (Horatio)

traffic

4 deal **5** cargo, fence, trade, truck **6** barter, custom **7** bootleg, freight **8** commerce, dealings, exchange, movement **9** patronage, transport **11** black-market
circle: **6** rotary **10** roundabout
cone: **5** pylon
jam: **5** tie-up **6** holdup **8** gridlock **10** bottleneck

trafficker

6 dealer, trader

tragedy

3 woe **6** mishap, plague **8** calamity, disaster **9** cataclysm, mischance **10** misfortune **11** catastrophe **12** misadventure

trail

3 dog, lag, tag **4** drag, flag, path, plod, poke **5** chase, dally, delay, tarry, trace, track **6** dawdle, follow, linger, pursue, shadow **7** draggle, gumshoe, pathway, traipse **8** footpath, footwalk **10** bridle path
emigrant: **6** Oregon
Florida: **7** Tamiami
Georgia-Maine: **11** Appalachian
Indian: **5** Great

trailer
  5 truck 7 preview 9 motor home, transport 10 mobile home

trailer truck
  4 semi

train
  3 row 4 file, tame 5 coach, drill, teach, track 6 column, convoy, course, school, sequel, series, thread 7 caravan, cortege, educate, prepare, retinue 8 exercise, instruct, sequence 9 cultivate, entourage, following, habituate 10 succession 11 progression

trainee
  6 novice 7 learner, new hire 8 beginner 10 apprentice

training
  7 tuition 8 teaching, tutelage 9 education, schooling 11 instruction **horses:** 6 manège

traipse
  3 gad 4 hoof, pace, roam, rove, step, walk 5 amble, range, trail, tramp, tread 6 ramble, stroll, wander 7 maunder, meander 8 ambulate 9 gallivant

trait
  4 mark 5 point, quirk, trace 6 oddity 7 feature, quality 8 hallmark, property, specific 9 attribute

traitor
  5 Judas 8 apostate, betrayer, defector, deserter, quisling, renegade, turncoat 9 turnabout

traitorous
  5 Punic 8 apostate, disloyal, mutinous, recreant, renegade 9 faithless 10 perfidious, rebellious, unfaithful 11 treacherous

traject
  4 beam, pass, pipe, send 5 carry 6 convey, render 7 conduct, forward, impress 8 hand down, transfer, transmit 9 broadcast, transfuse

tram
  3 car 7 trolley 9 streetcar

trammel
  3 tie 4 bind, curb 5 check, gauge, leash 6 fetter, hamper, hobble 7 compass, confine, ensnare, manacle, pothook, shackle 8 entangle, handcuff 9 restraint

tramontane
  8 outsider 9 foreigner, outlander 11 transalpine

tramp
  3 bum 4 hike, hobo, jade, plod, slog, thud 5 bimbo, caird, clump, gypsy, march, stamp, stiff, stomp, tread 6 ramble, stroll, travel, trudge, wander 7 chippie, clochard, drifter, floater, saunter, stroller, traipse, vagrant 8 derelict, footslog, homeless, vagabond 10 prostitute

trample
  4 mash 5 crush, pound, stamp, stomp, tread, tromp

trance
  4 daze, muse 5 swoon 7 ecstasy, rapture, reverie 8 hypnosis 9 catalepsy, enrapture 10 absorption, brown study 11 abstraction

tranquil
  4 calm, easy 5 quiet, still 6 dreamy, placid, poised, serene 7 restful 8 composed, peaceful 10 untroubled 13 self-possessed

tranquilize
  4 calm, hush, lull 5 quiet, relax, still 6 becalm, pacify, sedate, settle, soothe, subdue 7 compose, mollify

tranquilizer
  6 downer 8 diazepam, pacifier, sedative 10 depressant 11 barbiturate

tranquillity
  4 calm 5 peace, quiet 8 calmness, serenity 9 composure, placidity

transaction
  4 deal 5 trade 7 bargain, dealing 8 contract, covenant 9 agreement

transcend
3 top **4** beat, best **5** excel, outdo **6** better, exceed **7** surpass **8** outshine, outstrip, overcome, surmount

transcendent
5 ideal **7** perfect, sublime, supreme **8** abstract, immanent **10** consummate, surpassing

Transcendentalist
6 Alcott (Bronson), Fuller (Margaret) **7** Emerson (Ralph Waldo), Thoreau (Henry David)

transcribe
4 copy **5** write **6** record **8** transfer **9** translate, write down **13** transliterate

transfer
4 cede, deed, hand, pass, ship **5** carry, grant, shift **6** assign, convey, remove, supply **7** consign, convert, deliver, devolve, dispose **8** alienate, hand over, make over, relocate, turn over **9** carry over **10** assignment, conveyance **11** disposition

transfix
4 spit **5** lance, spear, spike, stick **6** impale, skewer **7** spindle **8** entrance **9** fascinate, hypnotize, mesmerize

transform
5 alter, morph **6** change, mutate **7** commute, convert **12** metamorphose

transformation
8 reaction **10** changeover, conversion **13** metamorphosis

transfuse
5 endue, imbue **7** pervade, suffuse, traject **8** permeate, saturate **9** penetrate, percolate **10** impregnate

transgress
3 err, sin **6** breach, exceed, offend **7** violate **8** infringe, overpass, overstep, trespass **10** contravene

transgression
3 sin **5** crime, error, wrong **6** breach **7** misdeed, offense **9** violation **12** infringement

transient
4 hobo **5** brief, tramp **7** drifter, migrant, passing **8** fleeting, flitting, fugitive, volatile **9** ephemeral, fugacious, momentary, temporary **10** evanescent, fly-by-night, short-lived **11** impermanent

transit
7 passage **8** traverse **10** conveyance

transition
4 leap **5** segue, shift **6** change **7** passage **10** conversion **13** metamorphosis

transitory
see **transient**

translate
6 render **7** convert **9** interpret, reproduce **10** paraphrase

translation
9 rendition **10** conversion, paraphrase

transmarine
7 oversea **8** overseas

transmission
7 gearbox **8** handover **9** broadcast, infection

transmit
3 air **4** beam, hand, pass, pipe, send **6** convey, hand on, impart, pass on, render, signal **7** channel, conduct, consign, diffuse, forward, traject **8** bequeath, dispatch, hand down **9** broadcast

transmogrify
see **transform**

transmute
see **transform**

transoceanic message
4 wire **5** cable **9** cablegram

transparent
5 clear, filmy, gauzy, sheer **6** limpid **7** crystal **8** clear-cut, gossamer, pellucid **10** diaphanous, see-through **11** crystalline

transpire
3 hap 4 leak 5 exude, occur, sweat 6 chance, emerge, happen 7 develop 9 come about, take place 11 come to light

transplant
8 relocate, resettle

transport
3 bus, fly, lag, lug, wow, zap, zip 4 haul, hump, lift, pack, pass, send, ship, taxi, tote 5 carry, ferry, motor, truck 6 convey, excite, ravish, remove, thrill 7 delight, ecstasy, freight, rapture, sealift, trundle, vehicle 8 carriage, displace, railroad, rhapsody 9 carry away, chauffeur, troopship 10 conveyance, helicopter

transportation
6 moving 7 freight, hauling, removal, vehicle 8 carriage, carrying 10 conveyance 12 displacement

transpose
6 invert 7 convert, permute, reorder, reverse 9 rearrange 11 interchange

transude
4 ooze, reek, seep, weep 5 bleed, sweat 7 diffuse, give off 8 permeate 9 transfuse

transverse
5 cross 6 across, thwart 8 crossbar, crossing 9 crossbeam, crosswise 10 crosspiece

trap
3 bag, net 4 bait, snag 5 catch, decoy, set up, snare 6 ambush, enmesh, tangle 7 ensnare, pitfall 8 birdlime, deadfall, entangle, quagmire 9 ambuscade

trappings
4 gear 5 dress 6 finery 8 equipage, ornament 9 adornment, caparison, equipment 10 decoration 11 habiliments 13 accouterments, accoutrements, embellishment, paraphernalia

Trappist
4 monk
writer: 6 Merton (Thomas)

trash
3 rag, rot 4 bosh, junk, ruin, scum, slop 5 bilge, blast, dreck, dregs, hokum, offal, spoil, tripe, waste, wreck 6 bunkum, debris, insult, litter, refuse, rubble 7 clutter, destroy, garbage, hogwash, put down, rubbish 8 claptrap, malarkey, nonsense 9 disparage, throw away, vandalize 10 balderdash 11 guttersnipe, proletariat

trash can
7 dustbin

trashy
5 bawdy, cheap, tatty 6 cruddy, shoddy, sleazy, smutty, vulgar 8 rubbishy 9 third-rate

trauma
4 blow, pain 5 shock, upset, wound 6 crisis, injury, stress 8 collapse 9 suffering

travail
4 grub, moil, task, toil, work 5 grind, labor, pains 6 drudge, effort 7 slavery, torment 8 drudgery, struggle

travel
4 fare, pass, roam, tour, trek, trip, wend 5 jaunt, tramp 6 junket, push on, voyage 7 explore, journey, passage, proceed, traffic, transit 8 movement, traverse 9 gallivant 10 hit the road

traveler
5 gypsy 7 drummer, tourist 8 salesman, vagabond 9 itinerant, sightseer 10 journeyman 11 peripatetic

traveling library
10 bookmobile

traverse
4 ride, walk 5 cover, cross, march, route, trace, track 6 course, thwart, travel, voyage 7 transit 8 crossing, navigate, pass over 10 crisscross 11 perambulate, peregrinate

travesty
3 ape 4 mock, sham 5 farce, mimic, spoof 6 parody 7 imitate, lampoon,

mimicry, mockery, take off **8** ridicule
9 burlesque **10** caricature, distortion
satanic: **9** Black Mass

Traviata, La
character: 7 Alfredo (Germont),
Germont **8** Violetta (Valéry)
composer: 5 Verdi (Giuseppe)

trawl
3 net **4** fish **7** setline

tray
6 salver, server **7** platter **8** teaboard
revolving: 9 lazy Susan

treacherous
5 false, Punic, risky **6** chancy, tricky
7 unsound **8** disloyal, perilous,
recreant **9** dangerous, deceptive,
faithless, hazardous, insidious
10 perfidious, traitorous, unfaithful,
unreliable

treachery
7 perfidy, treason **8** bad faith,
betrayal **9** disloyalty, infidelity
11 double-cross **13** dastardliness,
double-dealing, faithlessness

treacle
4 mush **5** slush, syrup **8** molasses,
schmaltz **11** golden syrup

tread
4 hoof, pace, plod, step, walk
5 dance, march, stamp, stomp, trace,
track, tramp, tromp, troop **6** follow,
stride **7** footing, traipse, trample
8 footstep

treadle
5 lever, pedal

treadmill
3 rut **4** rote **5** chore, grind **6** groove
7 routine **8** drudgery, turnspit

treason
7 perfidy **8** betrayal, sedition
9 treachery **10** disloyalty, misprision

treasure
4 haul, save **5** adore, cache, hoard,
pearl, prize, trove, value **6** esteem,
revere, riches, wealth **7** apprize,
cherish, idolize, worship **8** conserve,
preserve, venerate **9** reverence
10 appreciate

Treasure Island
author: 9 Stevenson (Robert Louis)
character: 7 Ben Gunn **8** Long
John (Silver)
narrator: 10 Jim Hawkins

treasurer
6 bursar, purser **7** curator **8** receiver
11 chamberlain

Treasure State
7 Montana

treasure trove
4 find, mine **7** bonanza, pay dirt **8** El
Dorado, Golconda, gold mine

treasury
4 fisc, mine **5** cache, chest, hoard
6 argosy, coffer, museum **7** bonanza, gallery, omnibus **8** archives,
El Dorado, Golconda, gold mine,
war chest **9** anthology, exchequer
10 depositary, depository, repository,
storehouse

treat
5 goody, nurse **6** bonbon, dainty,
doctor, goodie, handle, manage,
morsel, tidbit **7** care for **8** deal with,
delicacy, medicate **10** minister to
animals: 3 vet
leather: 3 tan, taw **7** tanning

treatise
6 thesis **8** tractate **9** discourse,
monograph **10** exposition **12** disquisition, dissertation

treatment
4 care **7** therapy

treaty
4 pact **6** accord **7** charter, compact,
concord **8** alliance, contract, covenant **9** agreement, concordat
10 convention

treble
4 high **6** shrill, triple **7** descant,
soprano **9** threefold **11** high-pitched

tree
African: 4 akee, cola, shea **5** limba,
sassy **6** baobab **7** avodire, bubinga
8 sasswood **9** berberine
Asian: 4 dhak, upas **6** banyan,
kamala

Australian: 7 blue gum **8** lacewood, quandong **9** casuarina
branch: 5 bough
Brazilian: 3 apa, ule **7** arariba, seringa, wallaba
Chinese: 4 tung **5** yulan **6** ginkgo, lychee **7** kumquat
citrus: 4 lime **5** lemon **6** orange **8** bergamot
combining form: 3 dry **4** dryo **5** arbor, dendr **6** arbori, dendra (plural), dendro
coniferous: 3 fir, yew **4** pine **5** alder, cedar, larch **6** spruce **7** cypress, hemlock, juniper, redwood, sequoia
dwarf: 8 arbuscle **10** chinquapin
East Indian: 4 neem, poon, teak, toon **6** banyan, deodar **7** deodara
elm: 4 wych
Eurasian: 5 abele, rowan **6** medlar
European: 5 osier **8** bourtree
European oak: 7 murmast
evergreen: 3 fir, yew **4** atle, pine, titi **5** athel, carob, cedar, piñon, taxus **6** arbute, loquat, mallee, sapota **7** arbutus, camphor, conifer, inkwood, juniper, lentisk, madrona, madrone, redwood, sequoia **8** loblolly, longleaf, tamarisk **9** balsam fir **12** balm of Gilead
evergreen oak: 6 encina
fig: 5 pipal
flowering: 5 sumac **6** acacia **7** dogwood **8** sourwood
hardwood: 3 oak **5** beech, birch, ebony, maple **6** cherry, cornel, walnut **7** hickory **8** chestnut, mahogany
Japanese: 4 kaki **7** zelkova
linden: 8 basswood
mulberry: 8 sycamine
North African: 5 babul
nut-bearing: 4 cola, kola **5** hazel, pecan, piñon **6** almond, cashew **7** buckeye, filbert, hickory **8** pistachio
oak: 5 roble **8** bluejack
ornamental: 3 box **5** holly **6** ginkgo, mimosa, myrtle, redbud **8** laburnum, magnolia **9** poinciana **12** rhododendron
palm: 4 coco, nipa **5** ratan **6** pinang, raffia, rattan **7** coquito **8** carnauba

Peruvian: 8 cinchona
Philippine: 4 dita, pili **6** bataan **10** calamondin
resinous: 10 candlewood
rubber: 3 ule
shade: 3 elm, oak **5** maple **6** linden **8** sycamore **10** chinaberry
softwood: 5 alamo **6** tupelo **8** black gum, corkwood
(see also **coniferous**)
South American: 3 apa **4** ombu **7** wallaba **9** Brazil nut
swamp: 11 bald cypress
tropical: 4 akee, ohia, palm, sago, teak **5** areca, assai, balsa, cacao, ceiba, lehua, mamey **6** acajou, balata, baobab, citrus **7** genipap, logwood, majagua, palmyra, quassia, soursop **8** allspice, barbasco, mahogany, mangrove, milkwood, palmetto, rosewood, soapbark, sweetsop, tamarind **9** candlenut, jacaranda **10** breadfruit, manchineel **11** candleberry, coconut palm
trunk: 4 bole
willow: 5 osier, sauch, saugh **6** poplar
young: 7 sapling

trefoil
4 leaf **6** clover
part: 3 arc

trek
4 hike, trip **6** travel, trudge **7** journey **9** migration **10** expedition

trellis
5 arbor **6** screen **7** lattice, pergola **8** espalier **11** latticework

tremble
5 quake, shake **6** dither, quaver, quiver, shiver **7** shudder, twitter, vibrate

tremblor
see **temblor**

tremendous
4 huge, vast **6** mighty, raging **7** awesome, immense, massive, titanic **8** colossal, enormous, fearsome, gigantic, terrific, towering

tremolo
9 fantastic, monstrous 10 formidable, gargantuan, incredible, monumental, prodigious, stupendous 13 extraordinary

tremolo
7 vibrato

tremor
5 quake, shock 6 quaver, quiver, shiver 7 shudder, temblor 10 earthquake
muscular: 8 dystaxia

tremulous
5 shaky, timid 6 afraid 7 aquiver, fearful, quaking, shivery 8 timorous 9 quivering, shivering

trench
4 sink 5 ditch, fosse, gully, verge 6 border, furrow, trough
Caribbean: 6 Cayman

trenchant
4 keen 5 crisp, sharp 6 biting 7 caustic, cutting, mordant, probing, satiric 8 clear-cut, distinct, incisive, sardonic, scathing 9 sarcastic 11 penetrating

trencher
4 tray 7 platter

trencherman
7 glutton

trend
3 fad, run 4 flow, mode 5 curve, drift, shift, style, swing, tenor, vogue 6 course, temper 7 current, fashion, incline 8 approach, movement, tendency 9 direction

trendy
3 hep, hip, hot 4 cool, tony 5 faddy 6 groovy, modish, with-it 7 à la mode, faddish, stylish 8 downtown, nouvelle, up-to-date 11 fashionable, ultramodern

trepang
10 bêche-de-mer

trepidation
4 fear 5 alarm, dread 6 dismay 7 anxiety 12 apprehension 13 consternation

trespass
3 err, sin 4 debt 5 lapse, poach 6 breach, invade, offend 7 impinge, intrude 8 encroach, entrench, infringe 9 interlope, violation 10 infraction, transgress 12 encroachment, infringement 13 transgression

tress
4 curl, lock 5 braid, plait

trestle
4 buck 6 bridge 7 sawbuck 8 sawhorse

trey
5 three

triad
4 trio 5 chord 6 triple, troika 7 harmony, trinity 9 threesome 11 triumvirate

trial
3 woe 4 care, test 5 agony, cross, essay, grief, rigor, worry 6 dry run, hassle, misery, ordeal, sorrow, tryput 7 anguish, attempt, contest, trouble 8 crucible, distress, endeavor, gauntlet, hardship, struggle, vexation 9 adversity, rehearsal, suffering 10 affliction, coup d'essai, difficulty, experiment, misfortune, proceeding, temptation 11 preliminary, tribulation 12 experimental

trial balloon
6 feeler, tryout

trial run
4 test 5 essay 7 break-in 10 experiment

triangle type
5 acute, right 6 obtuse 7 scalene 9 isosceles 11 equilateral

tribal unit
6 moiety 7 phratry

tribe
4 clan, folk, race 5 house, stock 6 family 7 kindred, lineage

tribulation
3 woe 5 cross, trial 6 burden, ordeal 9 adversity 10 affliction, oppression, visitation 11 persecution

tribunal

3 bar 4 dais 5 bench, court 8 platform 10 consistory 12 court of honor

tributary

5 bayou, creek 6 branch, feeder, stream 7 subject 8 affluent, influent 9 backwater, confluent, dependent, satellite 12 contributory

tribute

5 paean 6 eulogy 8 citation, encomium 9 panegyric 10 salutation 11 recognition, testimonial 12 appreciation

trice

4 lash, wink 5 blink, flash, jiffy, shake 6 moment, second, secure 7 instant 8 eyeblink 9 twinkling 11 split second

trick

3 jig 4 dido, dupe, fool, gull, hoax, lark, play, ploy, ruse, sham 5 antic, caper, dodge, feint, fraud, prank, stunt 6 gambit, outwit, scheme 7 chicane, finagle, gimmick, sleight 8 escapade, flimflam, hoodwink 9 bamboozle, deception, stratagem, victimize 10 red herring, shenanigan, tomfoolery 11 hornswoggle, monkeyshine 13 practical joke

trickery

4 scam, wile 5 cheat, fraud 6 deceit 7 chicane, dodgery 8 jugglery 9 chicanery, deception 10 subterfuge 11 double cross 13 doubledealing, jiggery-pokery, sharp practice

trickle

4 drip, seep 5 creep, trill 7 dribble

trickster

5 cheat, shark 7 cheater, diddler, grifter, sharper 8 conjurer, deceiver, magician, swindler 9 defrauder 11 flimflammer, illusionist 12 doubledealer

tricksy

5 rough 6 trying 7 arduous 8 prankish

tricky

3 sly 4 foxy, wily 5 dodgy 6 catchy, clever, crafty, shifty, sticky, thorny, touchy, trying 7 cunning, knavish 8 delusive, guileful, slippery, ticklish, tortuous, unstable 9 deceptive, difficult, dishonest, ingenious, intricate 10 misleading, nettlesome, precarious, unreliable 11 complicated, treacherous, troublesome 12 undependable

trident

5 spear

tried

6 proved, proven, secure, tested, trusty 7 staunch 8 approved, faithful, reliable, true-blue 9 certified, steadfast 10 dependable 11 trustworthy

tried and true

6 proven, secure, tested, trusty 8 reliable 10 dependable 11 trustworthy

trifle

3 bob, fig, pin, toy 4 doit, fool, mess, play 5 curio, dally, flirt, sport, waste 6 bauble, coquet, diddle, doodle, fiddle, fidget, footle, frivol, gewgaw, monkey, niggle 7 bibelot, conceit, fribble, fritter, novelty, trinket, twiddle, whatnot 8 folderol, gimcrack, kickshaw, nonsense, cream puff, dalliance 10 knickknack, triviality 11 small change

trifling

4 tiny 5 petty 6 measly, paltry 7 trivial 8 niggling, picayune, piddling 9 frivolous, worthless 10 negligible 11 unimportant 13 insignificant

trifolium

6 clover 8 shamrock

trig

4 chic, neat, prim, snug, tidy, trim 5 sharp, smart, swank, trick 6 classy, modish, snappy 7 chipper, dashing, orderly, precise, stylish 9 shipshape

trigger
4 fire 5 cause, spark, start 6 ignite, kindle, set off 7 actuate, release 8 activate, initiate, touch off

triggerman
3 gun 5 bravo 6 gunsel, killer 7 torpedo 8 assassin 9 cutthroat, pistolero

trigonometric function
see at **function**

trill
4 burr, drop, roll 5 chirr, shake, twirl 6 quaver, warble 7 dribble, revolve, trickle, twitter, vibrato

trillion
combining form: 4 tera, treg 5 trega

trillionth
combining form: 4 pico

trim
3 cut, fit 4 clip, crop, deck, neat, pare, snug, tidy, trig 5 adorn, order, prune, shape, shave, shear, skive 6 barber, dapper, fettle, kilter, repair, spruce 7 chipper, dress up, garnish, orderly, shapely 8 clean-cut, decorate, manicure 9 shipshape 11 spic-and-span, streamlined, well-groomed 12 spick-and-span
a tree: 5 prune 7 pollard

Trinidad and Tobago
capital: 11 Port of Spain
language: 7 English
monetary unit: 6 dollar
sea: 9 Caribbean

trinity
see **triad**

trinket
3 toy 5 curio, jewel 6 bauble, doodad, gewgaw, trifle 7 bibelot, novelty, whatnot 8 gimcrack, kickshaw 9 bagatelle, plaything, tchotchke 10 knickknack

trinkets
10 bijouterie

trio of goddesses
5 Fates 6 Furies, Graces

trip
3 hop, run 4 fall, ride, skip, slip, step, tour, trek 5 boner, caper, dance, error, lapse 6 bungle, junket, outing, sashay, travel, tumble, voyage 7 blooper, blunder, journey, mistake, misstep, stumble 9 excursion 10 expedition

tripe
4 guts 5 bilge, trash 6 waffle, viscus 7 innards, viscera (plural) 8 entrails, stuffing 9 internals

triple
4 trio 5 triad, trine 6 treble, triune, troika 7 triform, trilogy, trinity 8 trifecta 9 threefold, threesome 11 three-bagger, triumvirate

Triple Crown winner
1919: 9 Sir Barton
1930: 10 Gallant Fox
1935: 5 Omaha
1937: 10 War Admiral
1941: 9 Whirlaway
1943: 10 Count Fleet
1946: 7 Assault
1948: 8 Citation
1973: 11 Secretariat
1977: 11 Seattle Slew
1978: 8 Affirmed

tripped out
4 high 5 doped 6 stoned, zonked 7 drugged 8 hopped-up, turned on, wiped out 9 spaced-out 10 freaked-out

Tristan's beloved
6 Iseult, Isolde

Tristan und Isolde composer
6 Wagner (Richard)

triste
3 sad 5 sorry 7 doleful, pensive, wistful 8 mournful 9 depressed, sorrowful 10 melancholy 11 melancholic

Tristram Shandy author
6 Sterne (Laurence)

trite
3 pat, set 4 dull, flat, hack 5 banal,

corny, musty, slick, stale, stock, tired, vapid 6 cliché, common, jejune, old-hat 7 prosaic, worn-out 8 bathetic, bromidic, flyblown, ordinary, shopworn, timeworn, well-worn 9 hackneyed 10 threadbare 11 commonplace, stereotyped 13 platitudinous, stereotypical

triton
5 conch 7 mollusc, mollusk 9 shellfish

Triton
6 merman
attribute: 5 conch
father: 7 Neptune 8 Poseidon
mother: 10 Amphitrite

triturate
4 bray 5 crush, grind 6 powder 9 comminute, pulverize

triumph
3 joy, win 4 crow, palm 5 exult, glory, vaunt 6 master 7 conquer, prevail, succeed, success, victory 8 conquest, overcome, surmount 10 exultation, jubilation

triumphant
8 exultant, exulting, jubilant 10 conquering, victorious

triumvirate
see **triad**

Triumvirate, First
member: 6 Caesar (Julius), Pompey (the Great) 7 Crassus (Marcus Licinius)

Triumvirate, Second
member: 6 Antony (Marc) 7 Lepidus (Marcus Aemilius) 8 Octavius (Gaius)

trivet
4 rack 5 stand 6 tripod

trivia
8 factoids, minutiae 9 small beer 11 small change 13 small potatoes

trivial
5 light, minor, petty, small 6 casual, measly, paltry, piddly, slight 8 pic-ayune, piddling, piffling, trifling 9 small-beer 10 negligible 11 Mickey Mouse, unimportant 13 insignificant

troche
6 tablet 7 lozenge 8 pastille 9 cough drop

troglodyte
6 hermit 7 caveman, recluse 11 cave dweller

Troilus
beloved: 8 Cressida, Criseyde
father: 5 Priam
mother: 6 Hecuba
slayer: 8 Achilles

Trojan
horse builder: 5 Epeus
king: 5 Priam
priest: 7 Laocoon
soothsayer: 7 Helenus 9 Cassandra
warrior: 5 Paris 6 Aeneas, Agenor, Hector 9 Euphorbus

Trojan Horse builder
5 Epeus 6 Epeius

troll
4 fish, lure, sing, spin 5 angle, dwarf, prowl 6 goblin, search

trolley
3 car 4 cart, tram 8 carriage 9 streetcar

Trollope novel
10 Claverings (The) 11 Ayala's Angel, Phineas Finn 12 Phineas Redux 12 Way We Live Now (The) 15 Eustace Diamonds (The) 16 Barchester Towers

trombone
7 sackbut

tromp
4 beat, drub, hike, pelt, slog, walk 5 pound, stamp, stomp, stump, tramp, tread 6 batter, buffet, pummel, thrash, trudge 7 belabor, trample 8 lambaste

troop
4 army, band, crew, host, pace, step,

trooper

walk **5** corps, crowd, flock, tread **6** legion, outfit **7** brigade, company, soldier, traipse **8** assembly **9** associate, battalion, gathering, multitude **10** collection

trooper

3 cop **5** actor, horse **7** soldier **9** policeman **10** cavalryman

trope

6 cliché, simile **8** metaphor, metonymy **10** synecdoche

Trophonius

brother: **8** Agamedes
temple site: **6** Delphi

trophy

3 cup **5** award, prize, relic, scalp, token **6** spoils **7** memento **8** hardware, keepsake, memorial, reminder, souvenir **9** loving cup **11** remembrance

tropical

3 hot **4** lush, warm **5** balmy, humid **6** jungly, steamy, sultry, torrid **10** equatorial

tropical storm

see typhoon

Tropic of Cancer author

6 Miller (Henry)

Tros' son

4 Ilus **8** Ganymede

trot

3 jog **4** gait, lope, pony, rack **5** amble, hurry **7** setline **11** translation

troth

6 commit, engage, pledge **7** loyalty **8** affiance, contract, espousal, fidelity **10** engagement **12** faithfulness

trot out

4 show **6** expose, parade **7** display, disport, exhibit, show off

Trotsky, Leon

associate: **5** Lenin (Vladimir)
rival: **6** Stalin (Joseph)

troubadour

4 bard, poet **6** singer **8** jongleur, minstrel, musician **9** balladist **10** folksinger

trouble

3 ado, ail, ill, irk, try, vex, woe **4** care, fret, fuss, pain **5** annoy, beset, Dutch, grief, harry, haunt, pains, trial, upset, worry **6** bother, doo-doo, effort, harass, impose, kiaugh, misery, pester, plague, put out, ruffle, strain, stress, unrest **7** afflict, agitate, ailment, bedevil, concern, disturb, oppress, perturb, torment **8** aggrieve, disquiet, distress, exertion, hardship, hot water, irritate, vexation **9** beleaguer, importune, suffering **10** difficulty, disconcert **11** disturbance, predicament

troubled

6 uneasy **7** anxious, worried **9** concerned, disturbed **10** distressed

troublemaker

7 hellion **8** agitator **9** firebrand **10** instigator **11** provocateur **12** rabble-rouser

troublesome

5 pesky **6** thorny, tricky, trying, vexing **7** carking, onerous, prickly **8** annoying **9** difficult, upsetting, vexatious **10** bothersome, burdensome, cumbersome, disturbing **11** disquieting, importunate, pestiferous

troublous

5 pesky **6** rugged, stormy **7** onerous **9** turbulent, vexatious **10** tumultuous **11** tempestuous

trough

3 hod **4** bowl, tank **5** basin, drain **6** vessel **7** channel

trounce

4 beat, drub, lick, rout, whip, whup **5** whomp **6** defeat, larrup, punish, thrash, thresh, wallop **7** clobber, shellac **9** overwhelm

troupe

4 band **5** corps, party **6** outfit **7** company

trouper

4 mime **5** actor, mimic **6** mummer, player **7** actress, artiste **8** thespian **9** performer **11** entertainer

trousers
　5 pants　6 slacks　7 drawers
　8 breeches, britches
　tartan:　5 trews

trout
　kind:　3 sea　4 char, lake　5 brook,
　brown, river　7 rainbow　8 speckled
　9 steelhead

Trovatore, Il
　character:　7 Azucena, Leonora,
　Manrico　11 Count di Luna
　composer:　5 Verdi (Giuseppe)

trove
　4 find, haul　5 hoard, store　8 trea-
　sure　10 collection　11 aggregation
　12 accumulation

Troy
　5 Ilium
　epic of:　5 Iliad
　excavator:　10 Schliemann (Hein-
　rich)
　founder:　4 Ilus
　modern site:　9 Hissarlik
　(see also **Trojan**)

truant
　4 idle　5 shirk　7 shirker, slacker
　8 shirking　10 delinquent

truce
　4 lull　5 letup, pause, peace　6 accord
　7 respite　9 armistice, cease-fire

truck
　3 van　4 semi, swap　5 lorry, trade
　6 barter, handle, peddle, retail
　7 bargain, traffic　8 commerce,
　dealings, exchange
　military:　6 camion

Truckee River city
　4 Reno

truckle
　4 fawn　5 cower, defer, toady　6 cringe,
　grovel, kowtow　8 bootlick　11 apple-
　polish

truckler
　5 leech, toady　6 lackey, sponge
　7 spaniel　8 parasite　9 sycophant
　10 bootlicker　11 lickspittle　13 apple-
　polisher

truculent
　4 fell, grim　5 cruel, harsh, rough,
　sharp　6 brutal, deadly, fierce, sav-
　age, severe　7 abusive, warlike
　9 barbarous, bellicose, combative,
　ferocious　10 pernicious, pugnacious
　11 belligerent, contentious, destruc-
　tive, opprobrious, quarrelsome

trudge
　4 plod, slog, trek　5 march, tramp,
　tromp　8 footslog

true
　4 real, very　5 valid　6 actual, honest,
　trusty　7 factual, genuine, staunch,
　upright　8 accurate, bona fide, con-
　stant, faithful, resolute, rightful
　9 authentic, honorable, steadfast,
　undoubted, veracious, veritable
　10 dependable, legitimate, undeni-
　able　11 indubitable, trustworthy
　12 indisputable　13 authoritative

true-blue
　5 loyal　6 proven, steady　7 gen-
　uine　8 bona fide, constant, faithful
　9 steadfast　10 unswerving

truism
　3 saw　4 rule　5 adage, axiom, gnome,
　maxim, moral　6 cliché, dictum,
　gospel, saying, verity　8 aphorism,
　apothegm　9 platitude　10 shibboleth
　11 commonplace

Truk Island
　3 Tol　4 Moen, Udot, Uman　5 Fefa.ι
　6 Dublon

truly
　4 well　6 easily, indeed, really, surely,
　verily　7 de facto　8 actually　9 doubt-
　less, genuinely, sincerely, veritably
　10 absolutely, definitely, positively,
　truthfully, undeniably　11 confidently,
　doubtlessly, undoubtedly

Truman, Harry S
　birthplace:　5 Lamar (Missouri)
　predecessor:　3 FDR
　successor:　3 DDE

trump
　3 cap, top　4 beat, best, pass, ruff
　5 excel, outdo　6 better　7 manille,

trumpery

surpass **8** clincher, jew's harp, outstrip, override, spadille
up: 6 invent **7** concoct **9** fabricate **11** manufacture

trumpery

4 bosh, junk, muck, slop, tosh **5** bilge, cheap, dreck, hokum, trash **6** bunkum, cheesy, common, humbug, paltry, piffle, shoddy, trashy **7** baloney, twaddle **8** claptrap, flimflam, malarkey, nonsense, rubbishy, tommyrot **10** double-talk

trumpet

4 horn, tout **6** herald **8** ballyhoo
call: 6 sennet
ram's horn: 6 shofar

trumpeter

4 Hirt (Al), swan **5** André (Maurice), Baker (Chet), Brown (Clifford), Davis (Miles), James (Harry) **6** Alpert (Herb), Bolden (Buddy), Farmer (Art), Voisin (Roger) **7** Schwarz (Gerard) **8** advocate, Eldridge (Roy), eulogist, Marsalis (Wynton), Masekela (Hugh) **9** Armstrong (Louis), encomiast, Gillespie (Dizzy), spokesman **10** mouthpiece, panegyrist, Severinsen (Doc)

truncate

3 lop, top **4** crop, trim **5** prune, shear **6** cut off **7** abridge, shorten **10** abbreviate

truncheon

3 bat **4** club **5** baton, billy **6** cudgel, warder **8** bludgeon **9** billy club **10** nightstick, shillelagh

trundle

3 bed, tub **4** cart, haul, roll, spin **5** churn, wheel **6** rotate **7** revolve **9** transport

trunk

3 box **4** body, case, stem **5** chest, torso **7** channel, circuit, luggage
elephant: 9 proboscis
tree: 4 bole **5** stump

truss

3 tie **4** band, bind **5** brace **7** bandage, bracket, support **9** framework, supporter **10** strengthen

trust

4 hope, pool, rely **5** faith, stock **6** assume, bank on, belief, cartel, charge, commit, credit, rely on **7** build on, combine, confide, consign, count on, custody, keeping, presume **8** bank upon, credence, depend on, reckon on, reliance, rely upon **9** assurance, certainty, certitude, syndicate **10** confidence, conviction, dependence, depend upon **11** safekeeping **12** conglomerate

trustee

8 guardian **9** custodian, protector **10** supervisor

trustworthy

4 sure, true **5** tried, valid **6** honest, proven, secure **8** accurate, credible, faithful, reliable **9** authentic, realistic, veracious **10** dependable **11** responsible **12** tried and true **13** authoritative

trusty

4 true **5** tried **6** proven, secure, stable, steady **7** certain, convict **8** faithful, reliable **9** truepenny **10** dependable **11** responsible **12** tried and true

truth

5 axiom, maxim, sooth **6** candor, gospel, verity **7** lowdown, reality, veritas **8** veracity **9** rightness **11** genuineness **12** authenticity
goddess: 4 Maat
serum: 11 scopolamine

truthful

5 frank **6** candid, honest **7** factual, sincere **8** accurate **9** realistic, veracious, veridical

truthfulness

6 candor, verity **7** honesty **8** veracity

try

3 aim, tax, vex **4** seek, shot, stab, test **5** annoy, assay, essay, judge, offer, prove, study, whack, whirl, worry **6** aspire, harass, harrow, strain, stress, strive **7** afflict, adjudge, attempt, trouble **8** endeavor, struggle **9** undertake **10** adjudicate, experiment

trying
6 taxing, thorny, tricky, vexing **7** arduous, onerous **8** annoying, exacting, grueling **9** demanding, difficult, strenuous, vexatious **10** irritating **11** aggravating, troublesome

try out
8 audition

tryst
4 date **7** meeting **10** engagement, rendezvous **11** appointment, assignation

tsunami
9 tidal wave

tub
3 vat **4** boat **9** container
hot: 3 spa **7** Jacuzzi

tuba
7 helicon **9** bombardon, euphonium **10** sousaphone

Tubalcain
father: 6 Lamech
mother: 6 Zillah

tubby
3 fat **5** plump, podgy, porky, pudgy **6** chubby, chunky, rotund **8** roly-poly

tube
4 duct, hose, pipe **5** buret **6** siphon, subway, tunnel, vessel **7** burette, conduit, cuvette, pipette, syringe **8** pipeline
anatomical: 3 vas **4** duct, vasa (plural) **7** salpinx **9** salpinges (plural)

tuber
3 set **4** bulb, corm, root, stem **6** potato **7** rhizome **10** prominence

tuberculosis
8 phthisis, scrofula **11** consumption **12** Pott's disease

tucker out
4 do in, poop, tire **5** drain, weary **7** exhaust

tuft
5 clump, mound **7** cluster
of feathers: 7 panache
ornamental: 6 pom-pom
vascular: 6 glomus

tufted
7 crested

tug
3 tow **4** drag, draw, haul, moil, pull, toil **5** labor **6** strain, strive

tug-of-war
5 match **6** strife **7** contest, grapple, rivalry **8** conflict, struggle **10** contention **11** competition

tuition
3 fee **6** charge **8** teaching, training, tutelage **9** education, schooling **11** instruction

tumble
4 drop, fall, trip **5** upset **6** plunge, topple **8** collapse, keel over **9** bring down, overthrow **10** somersault

tumbledown
8 decrepit **10** ramshackle **11** dilapidated

tumbler
5 glass **6** roller **7** acrobat, gymnast **11** cartwheeler

tumbrel
4 cart **5** wagon **7** tipcart

tumescent
6 turgid **7** aureate, bloated, bulging, flowery, swollen **8** inflated, swelling **9** bombastic, dropsical, overblown **10** euphuistic, rhetorical **12** magniloquent **13** grandiloquent

tummy
3 gut **5** belly **6** paunch **7** abdomen, stomach **8** potbelly **9** bay window **11** breadbasket

tumult
3 din **4** flap, riot, to-do **5** babel, broil, hoo-ha, hurly, noise, whirl **6** clamor, dither, hubbub, lather, outcry, pother, racket, strife, uproar **7** ferment, tempest, turmoil **8** disorder, foofaraw, outburst, paroxysm, upheaval

tumultuous

9 agitation, commotion, confusion, kerfuffle, maelstrom **10** convulsion, hullabaloo, hurly-burly, turbulence **11** disturbance, pandemonium

tumultuous

5 rowdy **6** stormy, unruly **7** raucous, riotous **9** clamorous, turbulent **10** boisterous, disorderly **11** rumbustious, tempestuous **12** rambunctious

tumulus

5 grave, knoll, mound **6** barrow **7** hillock

tun

3 keg, vat **4** butt, cask, pipe **6** barrel **8** hogshead, puncheon

tuna

3 ahi **4** pear **6** bigeye, bonito **7** bluefin **8** albacore, skipjack **9** scombroid, yellowfin

tune

3 air **4** dial, lilt, song **5** theme **6** accord, adjust, amount, attune, extent, jingle, melody, strain, temper **7** descant **8** modulate, regulate **9** harmonize **10** coordinate, intonation
out: 6 ignore

tuneful

5 sweet **6** dulcet **7** melodic **9** melodious **10** euphonious

tungsten

7 wolfram **9** scheelite **10** wolframite

tunic

5 jupon **6** kirtle
Greek: 6 chiton

tunicate

4 salp **8** ascidian, chordate **9** sea squirt **11** urochordate

Tunisia

capital: 5 Tunis
city: 4 Sfax **6** Ariana
island: 5 Jerba
language: 6 Arabic
monetary unit: 5 dinar
neighbor: 5 Libya **7** Algeria
ruins: 8 Carthage
sea: 13 Mediterranean

tunnel

4 tube **6** burrow **7** conduit **8** crawlway
Alps: 7 Simplon
France: 4 Rove
Hudson river: 7 Holland, Lincoln
Nevada: 5 Sutro
railroad: 6 Hoosac **7** Cascade

Turandot

character: 3 Liu **5** Calaf
author: 5 Gozzi (Carlo)
composer: 6 Busoni (Ferruccio) **7** Puccini (Giacomo)

turban

7 bandana, pugaree **8** bandanna **9** headdress

turbid

4 dark **5** dense, mucky, muddy, murky, riley, roily, smoky, thick **6** cloudy, opaque, roiled **7** clouded, obscure

turbot

8 flatfish

turbulence

3 din **4** flap, stew **5** babel, fight, hoo-ha **6** dither, fracas, lather, pother, tumult, uproar **7** turmoil **8** foofaraw **9** agitation, commotion, confusion **11** pandemonium

turbulent

4 wild **5** bumpy, roily, rough, rowdy **6** raging, stormy, unruly **7** furious, moiling, raucous, riotous, roaring **8** agitated, blustery, brawling, mutinous, rowdyish, swirling **9** clamorous **10** boisterous, disorderly, tumultuous **11** rumbustious, tempestuous **12** rambunctious

tureen

3 pot **4** bowl **5** crock **6** vessel **9** casserole

turf

3 sod **4** area, peat **5** grass, sward, track **6** domain, region **7** terrain **9** racetrack, territory **11** horse racing **12** neighborhood

turgid

see **tumescent**

Turkey
capital: 6 Ankara
city: 5 Adana, Bursa, Izmir, Konya
8 Istanbul 9 Gaziantep
enclave: 8 Naxçivan
lake: 3 Van
leader: 7 Atatürk (Kemal)
monetary unit: 4 lira
mountain, range: 6 Ararat, Taurus
neighbor: 4 Iran, Iraq 5 Syria
6 Greece 7 Armenia, Georgia
8 Bulgaria
part of: 7 Balkans
peninsula: 6 Balkan 9 Asia Minor
river: 6 Tigris 8 Menderes 9 Euphrates 10 Kizil Irmak
sea: 6 Aegean 7 Marmara 13 Mediterranean

turkey
buzzard: 7 vulture
disease: 9 blackhead
female: 3 hen
head growth: 5 snood 7 dewbill
male: 3 tom 7 gobbler
throat pouch: 6 wattle
young: 5 poult

Turkey in the ____
5 Straw

Turkish
cavalryman: 5 spahi
empire: 7 Ottoman
governor: 4 vali
inn: 4 kahn 6 imaret
measure: 3 ohe
music: 9 janissary
soldier: 5 nizam 9 janissary
sultan: 5 Ahmed, Selim 7 Bajazet,
Bayezid, Ilderim
sword: 8 yataghan
title: 3 aga, bey 4 agha 5 pasha
6 vizier 7 effendi

Turkmenistan
capital: 8 Ashgabat 9 Ashkhabad
city: 9 Chardzhou, Dashhowuz
desert: 7 Kara-Kum
monetary unit: 5 manat
neighbor: 4 Iran 10 Kazakhstan,
Uzbekistan 11 Afghanistan
river: 6 Murgab 7 Murghab 8 Amu
Dar'ya
sea: 7 Caspian

Turks and Caicos Islands
capital: 9 Grand Turk
location: 10 West Indies
passage: 6 Caicos 8 Mouchoir
territory of: 7 Britain

turmeric
3 dye 4 herb 5 spice 6 ginger
8 dyestuff

turmoil
4 coil, flap, moil, riot, stew, stir, to-do
5 chaos, whirl 6 clamor, dither, hassle, hubbub, lather, pother, strife,
tumult, unease, unrest, uproar, welter
7 anxiety, ferment 8 disorder, disquiet, distress, upheaval 9 agitation,
commotion, confusion 10 disruption,
hurly-burly, inquietude, storminess,
turbulence, uneasiness 11 anx-
iousness, disquietude, hurry-scurry,
pandemonium, restiveness 12 restlessness 13 helter-skelter, Sturm
und Drang

turn
3 yaw, zag, zig 4 bend, bias, bout,
cast, grow, gyre, reel, spin, tack, tour,
veer, whip, wind 5 angle, curve,
pivot, refer, shunt, spell, stint, swirl,
train, twirl, whirl 6 detour, divert,
gyrate, mutate, revert, rotate, switch,
swivel 7 circuit, convert, deflect,
deviate, digress, diverge, reverse,
revolve 8 gyration, rotation 9 about-
face, deviation, pirouette, volte-face
10 deflection, revolution, tergiverse
11 changeabout 12 tergiversate
to stone: 8 lapidify

turnabout
3 rat 6 coward 7 reverse 8 apostate, defector, recreant, renegade,
reversal 9 about-face, reversion,
volte-face 11 retaliation 12 merry-
go-round 13 tergiversator

turn aside
4 veer, shun, sway, veer 5 avert,
repel, shunt, stave 6 divert, refuse,
reject, swerve 7 deflect, deviate,
digress, dismiss, diverge, fend off,
reflect, ward off 8 alienate, estrange,
separate 9 sidetrack

turncoat
  3 rat, spy 5 Judas 7 traitor 8 apostate, betrayer, defector, deserter, quisling, recreant, renegade 9 traitress, turnabout 13 tergiversator

turn down
  4 jilt, veto 5 spurn 6 rebuff, refuse, reject 7 decline, dismiss 9 repudiate 10 disapprove

turned on
  4 high 5 doped 6 stoned, zonked 7 aroused, drugged, excited 8 hopped-up, tripping 9 activated, spaced-out, zonked-out 10 passionate 12 enthusiastic

turn in
  5 crash, rat on 6 betray, inform, rat out, retire 7 deliver, produce, sack out 8 hand over 10 hit the sack, relinquish

turning point
  4 cusp 5 pivot 6 climax, crisis 8 landmark 11 climacteric

turnip
  5 swede 8 rutabaga
  Scottish: 4 neep

turnip-shaped
  8 napiform

turnkey
  6 jailer

turn left
  3 haw

Turn of the Screw, The
  author: 5 James (Henry)
  character: 5 Flora, Miles 10 Peter Quint
  composer: 7 Britten (Benjamin)

turn on
  5 start 6 excite, ignite 7 start up 8 activate, motivate 9 stimulate, titillate

turn over
  4 plow, roll 5 upend, upset 6 assign, commit, give up, rotate 7 capsize, consign, deliver, entrust, furnish, provide, revolve 8 delegate, transfer 9 overthrow, surrender 10 relinquish

turnpike
  7 highway

turn right
  3 gee

turn up
  4 find 6 appear, arrive, reveal 7 uncover, unearth 8 discover 9 encounter 11 materialize

Turnus
  beloved: 7 Lavinia
  slayer: 6 Aeneas

Turow work
  4 One L 13 Burden of Proof 14 Pleading Guilty 16 Personal Injuries, Presumed Innocent

turpentine
  7 galipot, solvent, thinner
  ingredient: 6 pinene
  tree: 4 pine 9 terebinth

turret
  5 tower 6 cupola, louver, louvre 7 mirador 8 bartizan 9 belvedere

turtle
  8 terrapin, tortoise 9 chelonian
  edible part: 7 calipee 8 calipash
  sea: 6 ridley 8 hawkbill
  shell: 8 carapace
  shell part: 8 plastron

Tuscany
  city: 4 Pisa 8 Florence
  river: 4 Arno
  tower: 4 Pisa
  wine: 7 chianti

tusk
  4 fang 5 ivory, tooth

tusker
  6 dugong, walrus 7 mammoth, muntjac, narwhal, warthog 8 elephant, musk deer 11 barking deer

tussle
  4 spar 5 scrap, scrum 6 hassle, scrape 7 scuffle, wrangle, wrestle 8 argument, skirmish, struggle 9 scrimmage 11 controversy

tussock
  4 tuft 5 clump, mound 7 cluster

tutelage
see **tuition**

tutor
3 don 5 coach, teach 6 docent,
mentor 7 teacher 9 pedagogue,
preceptor 10 instructor

Tut's tomb discoverer
6 Carter (Howard)

tutti
3 all

Tuvalu
capital: 9 Fongafale
ethnic group: 10 Polynesian
former name: 6 Ellice (Islands)
monetary unit: 6 dollar

twaddle
3 jaw, yak 4 bosh, bull, bunk, chat,
guff, muck, talk, tosh 5 clack, drool,
hooey, prate, run on 6 babble,
bunkum, burble, drivel, gabble, hot
air, humbug, jabber, tattle 7 baloney,
blabber, blarney, blather, chatter,
hogwash, prattle, rubbish 8 claptrap,
malarkey, nonsense, tommyrot,
trumpery 9 poppycock 10 applesauce, balderdash 12 blatherskite
13 horsefeathers

tweak
4 jerk, mock, pull, zing 5 annoy,
pinch, pluck 6 adjust, bother, twitch
8 fine-tune 9 poke fun at

tweet
4 call, note 5 cheep, chirp 7 chirrup,
twitter

Twelfth Night character
5 Viola 6 Olivia, Orsino (Duke)
7 Antonio, Cesario 8 Malvolio
9 Sebastian, Toby Belch

twelve
combining form: 5 dodec 6 dodeca

twenty
combining form: 4 icos 5 icosa,
icosi

twerp
4 brat, drip, fool, jerk, nerd, twit
6 squirt

twice
3 bis 7 twofold
combining form: 3 bis
prefix: 3 dis

twice a day
3 b.i.d. 8 bis in die 11 semidiurnal

twice a year
8 biannual 10 semiannual, semi-
yearly

Twice-Told Tales author
9 Hawthorne (Nathaniel)

twig
5 shoot, sprig 6 branch
bundle of: 5 fagot 6 faggot

twiggy
4 slim, thin 5 reedy 6 slight, stalky
7 slender 9 sticklike

twilight
3 eve 4 dusk 5 gloam, gloom
6 sunset 7 decline 8 gloaming
9 nightfall 10 crepuscule

Twilight of the Gods
8 Ragnarok
composer: 6 Wagner (Richard)

twill
5 chino, cloth, serge, toile, tweed,
weave 6 fabric 7 cheviot 8 dungaree 9 bombazine, gabardine
11 herringbone

twin
4 dual, like, mate 5 clone, match
6 bifold, binary, double, fellow,
paired 7 matched, similar, twofold
8 matching 9 companion, duplicate,
identical 10 coordinate, reciprocal

Twin Cities
6 St. Paul 11 Minneapolis

twine
4 coil, cord, curl, wind, wrap 5 twist,
weave 6 spiral, string 7 embrace,
meander, wreathe 8 entangle
9 interlace 10 interweave

twinge
4 ache, pain, pang 5 pluck, shoot,
throe, tweak 6 stitch

twinkle
3 bat 4 flit, wink 5 blink, flash, flirt, gleam, glint, light, shake, shine, trice 6 moment, second, winkle 7 flicker, flutter, glimmer, glisten, glitter, instant, shimmer, sparkle 9 coruscate, nictitate 11 coruscation, scintillate, split second

twin stars
6 Castor, Pollux

twirl
4 coil, gyre, spin 5 pitch, trill, whirl, whorl 6 gyrate 7 revolve 9 pirouette

twist
3 wry 4 coil, curl, turn, warp, wind 5 belie, gnarl, pivot, twine, twirl, wring 6 garble, spiral, sprain, squirm, torque, wrench, writhe 7 contort, distort, entwine, falsify, pervert, wriggle 8 misstate 9 corkscrew 12 misrepresent

twisted
3 wry 4 awry, sick 5 askew, kinky 6 swirly, warped 9 perverted

twister
6 funnel 7 tornado 9 dust devil, whirlwind 10 waterspout

twit
4 dolt, fool, gibe, jeer, jive, josh, mock, quiz, razz 5 chide, rally, scout, taunt, tease, twerp 6 deride 8 bonehead, numskull, ridicule 9 blockhead, numbskull 10 nincompoop

twitch
3 tic 4 jerk, pang, pull, yank 5 pluck, spasm, throe, tweak 6 quiver 10 quack grass 11 contraction

twitter
4 chat, peep 5 cheep, chirp, quake, tweet 6 cackle, giggle, jargon, quiver, shiver, titter, tremor, warble 7 chatter, chirrup, chitter, flicker, flitter, flutter, tremble 9 vibration

twittery
6 giggly 8 chattery 9 flustered, tremulous

two
3 duo 4 duet, pair 5 twain 6 couple
combining form: 3 bis, duo, dyo
divide into: 4 fork 6 bisect 9 bifurcate
prefix: 3 twi

two-faced
9 deceitful, dishonest, insincere 11 duplicitous 12 hypocritical 13 double-dealing
god: 5 Janus

twofold
4 dual, twin 5 binal, duple 6 binary, double, duplex, dyadic, paired 9 dualistic

Two Gentlemen of Verona
author: 11 Shakespeare (William)
character: 5 Julia 6 Silvia, Thurio 7 Proteus 9 Valentine

twosome
3 duo 4 dyad, pair 5 brace 6 couple 7 doublet

two-time
4 dupe 6 betray, delude, humbug, take in 7 beguile, cheat on, deceive, mislead 9 bamboozle 11 double-cross

two-wheeler
4 bike 5 cycle 7 bicycle, scooter 10 motorcycle

Two Years Before the Mast
author
4 Dana (Richard Henry)

Tybalt
cousin: 6 Juliet
family: 7 Capulet
slayer: 5 Romeo
victim: 8 Mercutio

Tyche
goddess of: 7 fortune

tycoon
5 mogul, nabob 7 magnate

tyke
3 dog, kid 5 child, hound, puppy 6 canine, moppet, nipper, shaver 7 mongrel

Tyler novel
16 Breathing Lessons 17 Accidental Tourist (The) 29 Dinner at the Homesick Restaurant

tympanum
7 eardrum 9 middle ear

Tyndareus
kingdom: 6 Sparta
wife: 4 Leda

type
3 cut, ilk, lot, way 4 cast, form, kind, mold, sort 5 breed, class, genre, order, print, serif, stamp 6 kidney, nature, stripe 7 feather, species, variety 8 category 9 character 10 persuasion 11 description
bar: 4 slug
measure: 4 pica 5 point
set: 7 compose
setter: 10 compositor
size: 4 pica 5 agate, pearl
stroke: 5 serif
style: 4 bold 5 roman 6 Gothic, italic 7 Fraktur 8 boldface 9 lightface, sans serif
tray: 6 galley

Typee
author: 8 Melville (Herman)
character: 4 Toby

typewriter
part: 3 key 6 platen, spacer
type size: 4 pica 5 elite

Typhon
3 Set 7 monster 8 Typhoeus
offspring: 6 Sphinx 7 Chimera 8 Cerberus, Chimaera
wife: 7 Echidna

typhoon
7 cyclone 9 hurricane 13 tropical storm

typical
5 ideal, model, usual 6 common, normal 7 classic, general, natural, regular 8 symbolic

typify
6 embody, mirror 9 epitomize, exemplify, personify, represent, symbolize 10 illustrate 11 emblematize 12 characterize

typo
5 error 7 erratum 8 misprint 11 corrigendum

typographer
7 printer 10 compositor

Tyr
3 Tiu
brother: 4 Thor
father: 4 Odin
god of: 3 war
mother: 5 Jordh, Jorth

tyrannical
8 absolute, despotic 9 arbitrary 10 absolutist, autocratic, oppressive 11 dictatorial 12 totalitarian

tyrannize
7 oppress 8 dominate, domineer, overbear 9 terrorize

tyrannous
5 harsh 6 brutal, severe 8 absolute, despotic 9 arbitrary, fascistic 10 autocratic 11 dictatorial 12 totalitarian

tyranny
7 cruelty, fascism 9 autocracy, despotism, monocracy 10 absolutism, domination, oppression 12 dictatorship

tyrant
4 czar, duce, tsar, tzar 5 ruler 6 despot, führer 7 fuehrer, pharaoh, usurper 8 autocrat, dictator 9 oppressor, strongman 10 absolutist 12 totalitarian

Tyrian ___
6 purple

tyro
4 punk 6 novice, rookie 7 amateur, dabbler, student 8 beginner, freshman, neophyte, newcomer 9 novitiate 10 apprentice, dilettante, tenderfoot 11 abecedarian

Tyrol
see **Tirol**

tzar
see **czar**

tzigane
3 Rom 5 gypsy 6 Romany

U

übermensch
8 superman

ubiquitous
7 allover **9** pervasive, universal
10 everywhere, wall-to-wall, widespread **11** omnipresent

U-boat
3 sub **7** pigboat **9** submarine

Uganda
capital: 7 Kampala
falls: 5 Ripon
lake: 5 Kyoga **6** Albert, Edward, George **8** Victoria
language: 7 English, Swahili
leader: 4 Amin (Idi)
monetary unit: 8 shilling
mountain: 5 Elgon
mountain range: 9 Ruwenzori
neighbor: 5 Congo, Kenya, Sudan **6** Rwanda **8** Tanzania
river: 4 Nile

ugly
4 vile **7** hideous **8** deformed **9** loathsome, misshapen, offensive, repugnant, repulsive, unsightly **10** disfigured **12** unattractive

Ugly Duckling author
8 Andersen (Hans Christian)

ukase
4 fiat **5** edict, order **6** decree, dictum, ruling **7** command, dictate, mandate **9** directive **10** injunction **12** proclamation **13** pronouncement

Ukraine
capital: 4 Kiev
city: 4 Lviv, Lvov **5** Yalta **6** Odessa **7** Kharkiv **9** Chernobyl
ethnic group: 7 Cossack
monetary unit: 6 hryvny
mountain range: 10 Carpathian
neighbor: 6 Poland, Russia **7** Belarus, Hungary, Moldova **8** Slovakia
peninsula: 5 Kerch **6** Crimea **7** Crimean
river: 3 Bug **5** Tisza **6** Donets **7** Dnieper **8** Dniester
sea: 4 Azov **5** Black

Ulalume author
3 Poe (Edgar Allan)

ulcer
4 sore **6** fester **7** corrupt
kind: 6 peptic **8** duodenal
mouth: 10 canker sore

ulna
7 forearm

Ulster hero
6 Fergus **7** Deirdre **9** Conchobar, Cuchulain, Cuchullin **10** Cú Chulainn

ulterior
5 privy **6** covert, future, hidden, latent **7** further, obscure, remoter **9** ambiguous, concealed **10** subsequent, succeeding **11** undisclosed

ultimate
3 end **4** acme, last, peak **5** basic, final **6** summit, utmost, zenith **7** closing, epitome, extreme, maximum, primary, supreme, topmost **8** absolute, deciding, decisive, eventual, farthest, furthest, greatest, original, terminal **9** elemental, paramount **10** apotheosis, concluding, conclusive, consummate,

preeminent **11** categorical, fundamental, furthermost, indivisible
12 incomparable, quintessence

ultimatum
5 order **6** demand, threat **7** mandate **9** challenge **12** notification

ultra
5 kinky, outré, rabid **6** beyond,
far-out, too-too **7** extreme, fanatic,
radical **9** excessive, extremist,
fanatical **10** outlandish **11** extravagant

ultraconservative
11 reactionary

ultraist
5 rabid **6** zealot **7** extreme, fanatic,
radical **9** extremist

ultramarine
7 oversea, sea-blue **8** overseas
11 lapis lazuli

ululate
3 bay **4** howl, wail, yowl

Ulysses
author: 5 Joyce (James)
character: 5 Bloom (Leopold), Molly
(Bloom) **6** Blazes (Boylan) **7** Dedalus
(Stephen)
(see also **Odysseus**)

umber
5 brown, sepia, shade **6** darken,
shadow

umbilicus
3 hub **4** core **5** heart, hilum, navel
6 center

umbra
5 shade **6** shadow

umbrage
4 hint, huff **5** anger, pique, shade
6 shadow **7** chagrin, dudgeon,
foliage, leafage, offense **9** annoyance, suspicion **10** irritation, resentment **11** displeasure, indignation
12 exasperation

umbrageous
5 shady **6** shaded, touchy **7** shadowy **8** shadowed **9** defensive,
sensitive

umbrella
5 cover, guard, shade **6** brolly,
pileus, screen **7** parasol, protect,
shelter **8** sunshade **10** protection
11 bumbershoot

umph
see **oomph**

umpire
3 ref **5** judge **6** decide, settle **7** arbiter, referee **9** arbitrate **10** arbitrator
call: 3 out **4** balk, ball, safe **6** strike

unabashed
5 blunt, brash, frank, naked, overt
6 arrant, brassy, brazen, candid
7 blatant, forward **8** outright **9** audacious, barefaced, shameless,
undaunted **10** unblushing **11** undisguised, unmitigated **12** unapolo-
getic

unabbreviated
see **unabridged**

unable
5 inept, unfit **8** helpless, impotent
9 incapable, maladroit, powerless,
unskilled **10** unequipped **11** incompetent, unqualified **13** incapacitated

unabridged
5 uncut, whole **6** entire, intact
8 complete **10** full-length **11** uncondensed **13** unabbreviated

unacceptable
8 unwanted **9** unwelcome **10** unsuitable **11** intolerable, undesirable
12 inadmissible **13** exceptionable,
inappropriate, insupportable, objectionable

unaccompanied
4 lone, sole, solo, stag **5** alone,
apart **6** single **8** detached, solitary
9 a cappella **10** unattended, un-
escorted

unaccountable
6 arcane, mystic **7** strange **8** baffling, puzzling **9** enigmatic **10** mysterious, mystifying, unknowable,
unreliable **12** impenetrable, inexplicable, undependable, unfathomable
13 irresponsible, unexplainable

unaccustomed

3 new 5 alien, novel 6 unused
7 strange, unusual 8 singular, uncommon, unwonted 10 unexpected, unfamiliar

unadorned

4 bald, bare 5 naked, plain, spare, stark 6 rustic, severe, simple 7 artless, austere, natural, spartan 11 undecorated 13 unembellished, unembroidered, unpretentious

unadulterated

4 neat, pure 5 sheer, utter 7 genuine, unmixed 8 absolute, straight 9 unalloyed, undiluted 11 unmitigated, unqualified

unaffected

5 naive 6 candid, simple 7 artless, callous, genuine, natural, sincere, unmoved 9 guileless, impassive, ingenuous, unaltered, unchanged, unstudied, untouched 10 hardboiled, impervious 13 unpretentious

unalloyed

4 pure 5 sheer, total 7 genuine, unmixed 8 absolute, straight 9 authentic, out-and-out, undiluted 11 unmitigated, unqualified 13 thoroughgoing, unadulterated

unalterable

5 fixed 7 binding, bounden, certain, decided 8 constant, required 9 immutable, mandatory, necessary 10 compulsory, invariable 12 unchangeable 13 predetermined

unambiguous

5 clear, lucid, plain 6 patent 7 evident, express, obvious, precise 8 apparent, clean-cut, clear-cut, decisive, definite, distinct, explicit, manifest, specific, univocal 10 definitive, forthright 11 categorical, translucent, transparent, unequivocal 12 transpicuous

unanimous

6 united 8 communal, univocal 9 unopposed 10 collective 11 uncontested 13 consentaneous

unanimously

5 as one, wholly 7 en masse 10 altogether

unanticipated

9 unplanned 10 surprising, unexpected, unforeseen 12 out of the blue

unappeasable

4 grim 7 adamant 8 obdurate, resolute 9 insatiate, unbending 10 implacable, insatiable, relentless, unyielding 11 unrelenting 12 unquenchable

unappetizing

4 icky 5 gross, yucky 7 insipid 8 unsavory 9 repugnant 11 unappealing, unpalatable 12 unattractive

unapproachable

5 aloof 6 remote, offish 7 distant 8 reserved 10 unfriendly, unsociable 11 standoffish, unreachable 12 inaccessible, unattainable

unasked

7 willing 8 unbidden, unsought, unwanted 9 uninvited, unwelcome, voluntary 10 gratuitous, unprompted 11 spontaneous, uncalled-for, unrequested, voluntarily

unassailable

6 secure 8 airtight 10 invincible, inviolable, undeniable 11 impregnable, irrefutable 12 indisputable, invulnerable 13 incontestable, unconquerable

unassertive

3 shy 4 meek 5 mousy, timid 6 modest, mousey 7 bashful 8 backward, reticent, retiring, sheepish, timorous 9 diffident, shrinking 10 submissive 12 self-effacing

unassuming

3 shy 6 humble, modest, simple 8 ordinary, retiring 9 diffident 11 unassertive 12 self-effacing 13 unpretentious

unattached

4 free 5 loose 6 single 8 separate 9 unmarried 10 unassigned 11 un-

committed, unconnected **12** disconnected, freestanding, unassociated

unattainable
7 elusive **10** impossible **12** inaccessible

unattractive
4 drab, dull, ugly **5** dowdy, plain **6** homely **8** frumpish **10** unalluring, unsuitable **11** unappealing, undesirable **12** unflattering

unauthentic
4 fake, mock, sham **5** bogus, dummy, faked, false, phony **6** ersatz, forged, pseudo **7** feigned **8** affected, spurious **9** contrived, imitation, pretended, simulated **10** apocryphal, artificial **11** counterfeit, make-believe **12** illegitimate

unavailable
4 busy **6** absent, tied up **7** missing **8** occupied

unavailing
4 idle, vain **5** empty **6** barren, futile **7** useless **8** abortive, bootless **9** fruitless, pointless **11** ineffective, ineffectual **12** unproductive

unavoidable
5 fated **7** certain **8** destined **9** impending, necessary **10** compulsory, inevitable, obligatory **11** ineluctable, inescapable

unavoidably
8 perforce **10** helplessly, inevitably, willy-nilly **11** inescapably, necessarily, whether or no

unaware, unawares
5 aback **7** unready **8** abruptly, heedless, ignorant, off guard, suddenly **9** oblivious, unknowing, unmindful, unwitting **10** by surprise, unfamiliar, uninformed, unprepared **12** unacquainted, unexpectedly

unbalance
11 destabilize

unbalanced
3 mad **4** daft **5** batty, nutty **6** crazed, insane, uneven, wobbly **7** unequal, unsound **8** demented, deranged, lopsided, unhinged, unstable **9** psychotic **10** disordered, moonstruck

unbearable
11 intolerable, unendurable **12** excruciating, insufferable

unbeautiful
4 ugly **5** plain **6** homely **8** uncomely, unlovely **9** unsightly **10** illfavored, unbecoming, uninviting **12** unattractive

unbecoming
8 improper, unlovely, unseemly, untimely, untoward, unworthy **9** inelegant, tasteless, unfitting **10** indecorous, indelicate, malapropos, unsuitable **11** disgraceful **12** unattractive **13** inappropriate

unbelievable
7 amazing, awesome **8** fabulous **9** fantastic **10** astounding, improbable, incredible, phenomenal, staggering, stupendous **11** astonishing, implausible, spectacular **12** unconvincing, unimaginable **13** extraordinary, inconceivable

unbeliever
5 pagan **6** giaour **7** atheist, doubter, gentile, heathen, heretic, infidel, scoffer, skeptic **8** agnostic **10** Pyrrhonist **11** freethinker

unbelieving
5 leery **6** show-me **8** agnostic, apostate, doubting **9** quizzical, skeptical **10** dissenting, suspicious **11** incredulous, mistrustful, questioning

unbending
5 rigid, stern, stiff **8** hard-line, obdurate, resolute **9** inelastic **10** brassbound, inexorable, inflexible, unyielding

unbiased
4 fair, just **5** equal **7** neutral **8** detached, tolerant **9** equitable, impartial, objective, unbigoted **10** even-handed, open-minded

11 broad-minded, uncommitted
12 unprejudiced 13 disinterested,
dispassionate

unbidden

7 unasked, willing 8 unsought,
unwanted 9 impromptu, uninvited,
unwelcome, voluntary 10 gratuitous,
unprompted 11 spontaneous,
unrequested

unbind

4 free, undo 5 loose, untie 6 detach,
loosen 7 manumit, release, unchain,
unloose 8 dissolve, liberate, unfasten, unloosen 9 discharge, disengage, unshackle 10 emancipate

unblemished

4 pure 7 perfect 8 flawless, spotless, unmarred, virtuous 9 exemplary, faultless, stainless, undefiled,
unspotted, unsullied 10 immaculate
11 untarnished

unbosom

4 bare, open, tell 6 betray, expose,
reveal, unveil 7 divulge, express,
uncover 8 disclose

unbound

4 free 5 freed, loose 6 loosed
10 unattached, unconfined, unfastened

unbounded

4 open 6 untold 7 endless 8 infinite, unending 9 excessive, limitless, unchecked, unlimited 10 immoderate, indefinite, inordinate
11 extravagant, measureless 12 immeasurable, incalculable, uncontrolled, unrestrained

unbreakable

7 durable, lasting 10 unyielding
11 everlasting

unbridled

4 free 5 loose 6 madcap 8 reckless, uncurbed 9 dissolute, unchecked 10 immoderate, licentious,
unconfined, unfettered, ungoverned
11 spontaneous, uninhibited, unrepressed 12 uncontrolled, unrestrained, unrestricted 13 unconstrained

unbroken

5 solid, sound, whole 6 entire, intact,
single 8 complete, constant, enduring 9 ceaseless, steadfast, unceasing, undamaged, undivided, un-
subdued, unvarying 10 continuous,
unimpaired 13 uninterrupted

unburden

3 rid 4 dump, ease, lose 5 shake
6 reveal, unload 7 cast off, confess,
confide, off-load, relieve 8 shake off,
throw off 9 discharge 10 relinquish
11 disencumber

uncalled-for

8 baseless, needless 9 officious,
unfounded 10 gratuitous, groundless
11 unessential, unjustified, unnecessary, unwarranted 13 unjustifiable

uncanny

5 eerie, weird 6 creepy, spooky
7 ghostly, strange 9 unearthly,
unnatural 10 mysterious, mystifying,
superhuman 11 supernormal, supra-
normal 12 supernatural

uncared-for

5 dingy 6 beat-up, shabby 7 rickety,
run-down, worn-out 8 decrepit,
derelict, deserted, desolate, forsaken, tattered, untended 9 neglected 10 broken-down, down-at-
heel, ramshackle, tumble-down
11 dilapidated

uncaring

4 cold 7 callous 9 heartless, negligent, oblivious, unfeeling, unheeding
11 coldhearted, hard-hearted, indifferent, insensitive, thoughtless,
unconcerned 13 inconsiderate,
unsympathetic

unceasing

7 abiding, endless, eternal, nonstop,
undying 8 constant, enduring,
unbroken, unending 9 continual,
perennial, perpetual 10 continuous
11 amaranthine, everlasting, unremitting 12 imperishable, interminable
13 uninterrupted

unceremonious

4 curt, rude 5 bluff, blunt, frank,

hasty, sharp, short, terse **6** abrupt, breezy, casual, sudden **7** brusque, hurried, offhand **8** familiar, informal **10** ungracious **11** precipitate, precipitous

uncertain
4 hazy, iffy, moot **5** vague **6** chancy, fitful, unsure, wobbly **7** dubious, erratic, halting, unclear **8** arguable, doubtful, insecure, slippery, unstable, unsteady, variable **9** ambiguous, debatable, undecided, unsettled **10** ambivalent, disputable, inconstant, indefinite, precarious **11** problematic, speculative **12** questionable, undependable **13** indeterminate, problematical, unforeseeable, unpredictable, untrustworthy

uncertainty
5 doubt **7** dubiety **8** distrust, mistrust **9** ambiguity, suspicion **10** indecision, perplexity, puzzlement, skepticism, uneasiness **11** ambivalence **12** doubtfulness, irresolution

unchain
4 free **5** loose **6** loosen, unbind **7** manumit, release **8** liberate, unfasten, unfetter **9** discharge, unshackle **10** emancipate **11** disenthrall

unchangeable
3 set **4** firm **5** fixed **7** settled **8** constant **9** immutable, permanent **10** continuing, inflexible, invariable **11** established, inalterable

unchanging
5 fixed **6** stable, static, steady **7** abiding, equable, eternal, settled, stabile, uniform **8** constant, enduring **9** immutable, steadfast, unvarying **10** consistent, continuing, invariable

unchaste
4 easy, lewd **5** bawdy, loose **6** impure, vulgar, wanton **7** immoral, lustful, obscene, scarlet, unclean **8** depraved, prurient **9** debauched, dissolute, lecherous, salacious **10** adulterous, lascivious, libidinous, licentious, profligate **11** promiscuous

unchecked
5 loose **7** rampant **9** spreading, unbounded, unbridled **10** widespread **11** uninhibited **12** unrestrained, unrestricted

uncivil
4 rude **5** crass, crude **6** coarse, savage, vulgar **7** boorish, ill-bred, uncouth **8** barbaric, impolite **9** barbarous **10** indecorous, uncultured, ungracious **11** ill-mannered, uncourteous **12** discourteous **13** disrespectful

uncivilized
4 rude, wild **5** crude **6** brutal, coarse, Gothic, savage **7** boorish, Hunnish, ill-bred, loutish, lowbred, uncouth **8** barbaric, churlish **9** barbarian, barbarous, primitive, unrefined **10** mannerless, uncultured, unmannerly, unpolished **12** uncultivated **13** unenlightened

unclad
see **unclothed**

uncle
cry: **6** give up **9** surrender
Scottish: **3** eme
Spanish: **3** tío
U.S. symbol: **3** Sam

unclean
4 foul **5** dingy, dirty, grimy **6** filthy, grubby, grungy, impure, soiled, sordid **7** corrupt, defiled, immoral, obscene, squalid, stained, sullied, tainted **8** befouled, indecent, polluted, unchaste **9** tarnished **10** besmirched, desecrated **12** contaminated

unclear
3 dim **4** hazy **5** murky, vague **6** bleary, blurry, cloudy, opaque, unsure **7** clouded, cryptic, dubious, obscure, shadowy **8** doubtful, nebulous, overcast, puzzling **9** ambiguous, enigmatic, tenebrous, unsettled **10** ill-defined, indistinct, indefinite, inexplicit **13** indeterminate

Uncle Remus creator
6 Harris (Joel Chandler)

Uncle Tom's Cabin
  author: **5** Stowe (Harriet Beecher)
  character: **5** Eliza, Topsy **6** Legree
    (Simon) **9** Little Eva

Uncle Vanya author
  7 Chekhov (Anton)

unclothe
  5 strip **6** denude, divest, expose,
  unveil **7** display, disrobe, uncloak,
  uncover, undress

unclothed
  4 bare, nude **5** naked **6** peeled,
  unclad **7** denuded, exposed **8** in the
  raw, stripped **9** au naturel, buck-
  naked, undressed **10** stark naked

unclouded
  4 fair **5** clear, lucid, sunny **6** bright
  7 halcyon **8** rainless, sunshiny

uncluttered
  4 neat, tidy, trig, trim **7** orderly
  9 organized, shipshape **11** spic-and-
  span, well-ordered **12** spick-and-
  span

uncombed
  5 messy, mussy **6** matted, mussed
  7 ruffled, snarled, tangled, tousled,
  unkempt **10** disheveled

uncommon
  3 odd **4** rare **5** novel **6** choice,
  scarce, unique **7** special, unusual
  8 esoteric, especial, singular, sporadic, unwonted **10** infrequent,
  noteworthy, remarkable **11** distinctive, exceptional **12** unaccustomed **13** extraordinary

uncommunicative
  3 mum **4** dumb **5** aloof **6** offish,
  silent **7** distant, guarded, private
  8 reserved, reticent, taciturn **9** reclusive, secretive, withdrawn
  10 antisocial, poker-faced, speechless, tongue-tied, unsociable **11** inscrutable, standoffish, tight-lipped
  12 closemouthed, tight-mouthed,
  unresponsive **13** unforthcoming

uncompassionate
  4 cold, hard **5** stony **7** callous **8** ob-

durate, pitiless, uncaring **9** heartless, unfeeling **10** hard-boiled
11 coldhearted, hardhearted, insensitive **12** stonyhearted **13** unsympathetic

uncomplicated
  4 easy **5** basic, clear, plain **6** simple
  8 clear-cut **10** effortless, elementary,
  manageable, uninvolved

uncomplimentary
  7 adverse **8** critical **9** degrading
  10 belittling, derogatory, pejorative
  11 deprecatory, disparaging, unfavorable **12** depreciative, depreciatory,
  unflattering

uncompromising
  4 firm **5** rigid **8** hard-line, obdurate,
  resolute, stubborn **9** hard-nosed,
  immovable, insistent, unbending
  10 brassbound, determined, inexorable, inflexible, unshakable, unyielding **12** intransigent, single-
  minded

unconcealed
  4 bald, bare, open **5** frank, naked,
  overt, plain **6** candid **7** blatant,
  evident, exposed, express, obvious,
  visible **8** apparent, explicit, manifest,
  palpable **10** forthright **11** openhearted, transparent, undisguised,
  unvarnished

unconcern
  6 apathy **7** neglect **9** aloofness,
  disregard **10** alienation, detachment,
  dispassion **11** disinterest, inattention, insouciance, nonchalance
  12 carelessness, heedlessness,
  indifference **13** preoccupation

unconcerned
  4 cool **6** remote **7** unmoved **8** careless, detached, heedless **9** alienated, apathetic, oblivious, unmindful,
  unruffled **10** insouciant, neglectful,
  untroubled **11** inattentive, indifferent,
  unperturbed **12** uninterested **13** disinterested, dispassionate

unconditional
  5 sheer, total, utter **8** absolute,

definite, explicit, outright **9** down-right, out-and-out **10** unreserved **11** unequivocal, unqualified **12** un-restricted **13** thoroughgoing

unconfined
4 free, vast **5** loose **7** at large **9** at liberty, boundless, limitless, unlimited **12** unrestrained, unrestricted

uncongenial
6 at odds **8** unfitted **9** repellent, repugnant, unlikable **10** discordant, unsociable, unsuitable **11** conflicting, displeasing **12** antipathetic, disagreeable, incompatible, unattractive **13** unsympathetic

unconnected
5 alone, apart **8** discrete, detached, disjoint, disjunct, distinct, inchoate, rambling, separate **9** unrelated **10** unattached **11** independent **12** unassociated **13** discontinuous, noncontinuous

unconquerable
10 invincible, inviolable, unbeatable **11** bulletproof, impregnable, indomitable, insuperable **12** invulnerable, unassailable

unconscionable
5 undue **6** unfair, unholy, unjust, wanton, wicked **7** immoral, ungodly **8** barbaric, criminal **9** barbarous, unethical **10** exorbitant, inordinate, outrageous **11** inexcusable, uncivilized **12** unprincipled, unscrupulous

unconscious
3 out **6** asleep, chance **7** out cold, stunned, unaware **8** comatose **9** insensate, passed out, unplanned, unwitting **10** blacked out, insensible, knocked out **11** inadvertent, instinctual, involuntary **12** uncalculated **13** unintentional

unconsciousness
4 coma **5** faint **6** stupor, torpor, trance **7** syncope **13** obliviousness

unconsidered
4 rash **5** brash, hasty **6** casual **7** offhand **8** careless, reckless,

slapdash **9** desultory, haphazard, hit-or-miss, hotheaded, impetuous, unplanned **10** ill-advised, incautious, unthinking **11** thoughtless

unconstrained
4 free, open **6** blithe, dégagé, wanton **7** buoyant, gushing, relaxed **8** animated, carefree, effusive, informal, outgoing **9** easygoing, expansive, liberated **10** expressive, nonchalant, unreserved

uncontrollable
4 wild **6** unruly **7** wayward, willful **9** fractious **10** headstrong, refractory, self-willed **11** intractable **12** overwhelming, recalcitrant, ungovernable, unmanageable **13** irrepressible, undisciplined

uncontrolled
4 free, wild **5** loose **6** wanton **9** automatic, excessive, unbounded, unlimited, unmanaged **10** autonomous, immoderate, licentious, ungoverned **11** independent, instinctual, involuntary, unconscious, uninhibited, unregulated **12** disorganized, unrestrained **13** self-governing

unconventional
3 odd **4** beat **5** kinky, kooky, outré **6** casual, far-out, freaky, quirky, unique, way-out, weirdo **7** bizarre, deviant, oddball, offbeat, unusual, wayward **8** aberrant, abnormal, atypical, bohemian, freakish, original, peculiar **9** anomalous, eccentric, irregular **10** avant-garde, unexpected, unorthodox **11** uncustomary **13** idiosyncratic

unconvinced
5 leery **6** unsure **7** dubious **8** doubtful **9** skeptical, undecided **10** suspicious

unconvincing
4 lame **6** feeble, flimsy, forced **7** dubious, suspect **8** doubtful, strained **10** farfetched, improbable, incredible **11** implausible, unrealistic **12** unbelievable **13** unsubstantial

uncooked
3 raw

uncouple
4 part 6 detach, divide 7 disjoin, divorce, unhitch 8 separate, unfasten 9 disengage 10 disconnect, dissociate 12 disaffiliate

uncouth
3 odd, raw 4 rude 5 crass, crude, gross, rough 6 clumsy, coarse, rugged, vulgar 7 awkward, bizarre, boorish, ill-bred, loutish, strange, uncivil 8 barbaric, clownish, impolite, ungainly 9 eccentric, graceless, inelegant, unrefined 10 outlandish, uncultured, unpolished 11 ill-mannered, uncivilized 12 discourteous, uncultivated
person: 3 oaf 4 boor, dolt, lout 5 clown 6 bumpkin 9 barbarian

uncover
4 bare 5 strip 6 betray, detect, divest, expose, remove, reveal, unmask, unveil 7 display, divulge, unearth 8 disclose

uncritical
5 naive 9 credulous 11 perfunctory

unction
3 oil 4 balm 5 cream, salve 6 balsam, cerate, chrism 7 suavity, unguent 8 liniment, ointment 9 emollient 11 embrocation

unctuous
4 oily 5 fatty, slick, soapy, suave 6 greasy, smarmy 7 cloying, fawning, fulsome 8 slippery 9 wheedling 10 flattering, oleaginous, saccharine 11 sycophantic

uncultivated
4 wild 5 crass, crude, gross 6 coarse, desert, fallow, savage, vulgar 7 boorish, lowbrow, uncouth 8 barbaric, unplowed, untilled 9 barbarian, barbarous, inelegant, unrefined 10 unpolished 11 uncivilized

uncultured
3 raw 4 rude 5 crass, crude, gross, rough 6 coarse, vulgar 7 artless, boorish, ill-bred, loutish, lowbred, lowbrow, natural, uncouth 8 barbaric, churlish, cloddish 9 barbarian, barbarous, benighted, inelegant, unrefined 10 unpolished 11 uncivilized 13 unenlightened

uncustomary
4 rare 7 special, strange, unusual 8 aberrant, abnormal, atypical, singular, uncommon 9 anomalous 10 surprising, unfamiliar, unorthodox 11 exceptional 13 extraordinary

uncut
5 whole 6 entire, intact 8 complete 9 undiluted 10 full-length, unabridged 11 uncondensed 13 unabbreviated

undamaged
5 sound, whole 6 intact, unhurt 8 unbroken, unmarred 9 uninjured, unscathed 10 unimpaired 11 unblemished

undaunted
4 bold 5 brave 6 daring, heroic 7 doughty, Spartan, valiant 8 fearless, intrepid, resolute, unafraid, valorous 9 audacious 10 courageous 11 lionhearted, unconquered, unflinching 12 stouthearted

_____ und Drang
5 Sturm

undeceive
8 disabuse 11 disillusion

undecided
4 iffy, moot, open 6 unsure 7 dubious, pending 8 doubtful, wavering 9 equivocal, tentative, uncertain, unsettled 10 ambivalent, indefinite, unresolved 12 undetermined

undeclared
5 tacit 6 unsaid 7 assumed, implied 8 accepted, implicit, inferred, presumed, unspoken, unstated 10 understood

undecorated
4 bare 5 plain, stark 6 homely, severe, simple 8 no-frills 9 un-

adorned **12** unornamented **13** unembellished, unembroidered

undefiled
4 pure **6** chaste, intact, vestal, virgin **8** innocent, spotless, virginal, virtuous **9** stainless, unstained, unsullied, untainted **10** immaculate **11** unblemished, untarnished

undefined
3 dim **4** hazy **5** faint, vague **6** bleary **7** obscure, shadowy, unclear **8** inchoate, nebulous, unformed **9** amorphous, shapeless **10** indistinct **12** undetermined

undemonstrative
4 calm, cold, cool **5** aloof, chill **7** aseptic, distant, laconic **8** reserved, retiring **9** contained, inhibited, shrinking, withdrawn **10** restrained, unsociable **11** emotionless, passionless, standoffish, unemotional **12** matter-of-fact, unresponsive **13** self-contained

undeniable
6 patent **7** certain, evident, genuine, obvious **8** manifest **9** veridical **10** inarguable **11** indubitable, irrefutable, unequivocal **12** indisputable **13** incontestable

undependable
6 fickle, tricky, unsafe **7** erratic **10** capricious, fly-by-night, inconstant, unreliable **12** inconsistent, questionable **13** irresponsible, unpredictable, untrustworthy

under
3 low, sub **4** down, less **5** below, lower, short **6** lesser **7** beneath, covered, subject **8** downward, inferior **9** dependent, receiving, secondary, subjacent **11** subordinate
prefix: 3 hyp, sub **4** hypo

undercarriage
5 frame **9** framework **11** landing gear

undercover
6 covert, hidden, secret **7** furtive, stealth, sub-rosa **8** hush-hush, stealthy **11** clandestine **12** confidential **13** surreptitious
person: 3 spy **4** mole **5** agent, spook **6** sleuth **9** detective, operative **10** counterspy **11** double agent, secret agent **12** counteragent

undercroft
5 crypt, vault **7** chamber **8** catacomb

undercut
7 subvert **8** sabotage

underdeveloped
4 poor **7** dwarfed, stunted **8** backward, immature **9** unevolved **10** third-world

underdog
5 loser **6** victim **7** also-ran, fall guy **9** dark horse

underdone
3 raw, red **4** rare

underestimate
6 slight **7** dismiss **8** belittle, discount, disprize, minimize **9** deprecate, disparage, sell short **10** depreciate

undergarment
3 bra **4** BVDs, slip **5** teddy **6** bikini, bodice, briefs, corset, girdle, shorts, undies **7** chemise, drawers, panties, stammel, step-ins **8** lingerie, pretties, Skivvies, woollies **9** brassiere, jockstrap, long johns, petticoat, underwear **10** foundation

undergo
4 bear, face **5** abide, brave, brook **6** endure, suffer **7** sustain, weather **8** submit to, tolerate **9** withstand **10** experience

undergraduate
4 coed **5** frosh **6** junior, senior **8** freshman **9** collegian, sophomore

underground
4 tube **5** metro, train **6** buried, hidden, nether, secret, subway **7** illegal, off-beat, railway **8** hypogeal, hypogean **10** undercover **11** alternative, clandestine **12** subterranean **13** surreptitious

underhanded

3 sly 4 wily 5 shady 6 covert, crafty, secret, shifty, sneaky, tricky 7 cunning, devious, elusive, evasive, furtive, sub-rosa 8 guileful, sneaking, stealthy 9 deceitful, deceptive 10 circuitous 11 clandestine, duplicitous 13 surreptitious

underlie

4 bear 6 prop up 7 subtend, support 8 buttress

underline

4 mark 6 play up, stress 9 emphasize, italicize 10 accentuate, underscore

underling

4 aide, peon, serf 5 gofer, scrub, slave 6 flunky, gopher, lackey, menial, minion 7 fall guy 8 inferior 9 assistant, attendant, subaltern 11 subordinate

underlying

4 root 5 basal, basic 7 primary 8 implicit 9 elemental, essential 11 fundamental

Under Milk Wood author

6 Thomas (Dylan)

undermine

3 sap 4 foil 5 blunt, erode 6 impair, thwart, weaken 7 cripple, disable, subvert 8 sabotage 9 attenuate, frustrate 10 debilitate, demoralize

undermost

6 bottom, lowest 9 lowermost 10 bottommost, nethermost, rock-bottom

underneath

4 sole 5 below, lower 6 bottom 7 covered

underpin

4 back, base, prop, root 5 brace 6 uphold 7 bolster, justify, shore up, support 8 buttress, validate 10 strengthen 11 corroborate

underpinning

4 base, prop, root, stay 5 basis, brace 7 bedrock, footing, seating, support 8 buttress 10 foundation, groundwork 12 substructure

underprivileged

4 poor 5 needy 7 hapless, unlucky 8 deprived 11 handicapped, unfortunate 13 disadvantaged

underrate

7 devalue 8 discount, mark down, minimize, write off 9 devaluate, write down 10 depreciate

underscore

6 accent, play up, stress 9 emphasize, italicize 10 accentuate

underside

4 sole 6 bottom 7 reverse

undersized

3 toy 4 baby, mini, puny 5 dinky, dwarf, pygmy, runty, short, small 6 bantam, little, pocket, slight 7 scrubby, stunted 9 miniature 10 diminutive 11 Lilliputian

understand

3 con, ken, see 4 know 5 grasp, guess, infer, savvy, sense, think 6 accept, assume, deduce, expect, fathom, figure, follow, gather, reason, reckon, take in, take it 7 believe, discern, imagine, presume, realize, suppose, surmise, suspect 8 conceive, conclude, consider, perceive 9 apprehend, interpret 10 appreciate, comprehend, conjecture

understandable

5 clear, lucid, plain 8 clear-cut, coherent, knowable 9 excusable, graspable, plausible 10 articulate, believable, defensible, fathomable, reasonable 11 justifiable, perceivable, unambiguous 12 intelligible 13 apprehensible

understanding

3 ken, wit 4 deal, pact 5 grasp, sense 6 accord, humane, kindly 7 compact, empathy, entente, insight, mastery 8 sympathy 9 agreement, awareness, knowledge, tolerance 10 acceptance, impression, perception 11 considerate, discernment, explanation, sympathetic 12 apprehension, relationship 13 comprehension

understatement
7 litotes

understood
5 tacit 7 assumed, implied 8 accepted, implicit, inferred, unspoken

understudy
6 double, backup, fill-in 7 standby, stand-in 9 surrogate 10 substitute 11 replacement

undertake
3 try 4 dare 5 assay, begin, essay, start 6 accept, assume, pledge, strive, tackle, take on, take up 7 attempt, certify, execute, perform, promise, warrant 8 commence, contract, covenant, endeavor, set about, set forth, shoulder 9 guarantee

undertaker
8 embalmer 9 mortician

undertaking
3 job 4 task 6 affair, charge, effort 7 calling, emprise, exploit, mission, project, pursuit, venture 8 endeavor 9 adventure, guarantee, operation 10 enterprise 11 proposition, transaction

under-the-table
6 covert, hidden, secret, sneaky 7 furtive, sub-rosa 8 hush-hush, stealthy 9 concealed, underhand 10 undercover 11 clandestine 13 surreptitious

undertone
3 hue, hum 4 cast, hint, tint 5 shade 6 mumble, murmur, mutter 7 inkling 10 suggestion 11 association, connotation, implication

undertow
4 eddy 7 current, riptide, sea puss

undervalue
see **underrate**

underwater
9 submarine 10 subaquatic, subaqueous
breathing apparatus: 5 scuba
captain: 4 Nemo
chamber: 7 caisson
device: 8 paravane
missile: 7 torpedo
sound detector: 5 sonar

underwear
see **undergarment**

underwood
5 brush, copse, hedge, scrub 7 boscage, coppice, thicket 9 shrubbery

underworld
4 hell 5 hades, Sheol 6 Erebus, Tophet 7 Gehenna, inferno 8 gangland 9 antipodes 11 Pandemonium
boatman: 6 Charon
deity: 3 Dis 4 Bran 5 Pluto 6 Osiris
goddess: 6 Hecate 10 Persephone
organization: 5 Mafia
relating to: 8 chthonic
watchdog: 8 Cerberus

underwrite
4 back, fund, sign 5 endow, stake 6 assure, insure, pay for, secure 7 agree to, endorse, finance, sponsor, support 8 bankroll 9 grubstake, guarantee 11 subscribe to

undesigning
5 frank 6 candid, honest 7 artless, earnest, genuine, sincere 9 guileless, ingenuous, unfeigned 10 aboveboard, forthright

undesirable
8 annoying, unwanted 9 offensive, unwelcome 10 ill-favored, unpleasant, unsuitable 11 displeasing, inadvisable, troublesome 12 disagreeable, unacceptable, unattractive 13 inappropriate, objectionable

undesired
8 needless, unsought, unwanted 9 uninvited, unwelcome 10 gratuitous 11 uncalled-for, unnecessary 12 nonessential

undetermined
5 vague 7 dubious, obscure, pending, unclear 8 doubtful 9 ambiguous, equivocal, uncertain, undecided, undefined, unsettled 10 ill-defined, indefinite, indistinct 12 inconclusive

undeveloped
5 crude, green, rough 6 latent

8 backward, immature, inchoate
9 embryonic, incipient, primitive, unevolved **10** unfinished

undiluted

4 neat, pure **5** sheer, utter **7** genuine, unmixed **8** absolute, straight **9** authentic, unalloyed **11** unmitigated, unqualified **13** unadulterated

undiplomatic

4 rash, rude **5** brash, cocky **6** brazen, cheeky **8** impudent, tactless **9** audacious, hotheaded, impolitic, impulsive, maladroit, untactful **10** ill-advised, indiscreet **11** impertinent, injudicious, insensitive, thoughtless **12** presumptuous

undisciplined

4 wild **6** unruly, wanton **7** froward, restive, wayward, willful **8** contrary, untoward **9** fractious **10** disorderly, rebellious, refractory **11** intractable **12** contumacious, noncompliant, obstreperous, recalcitrant, ungovernable, unmanageable

undisclosed

6 hidden, sealed, secret **7** unknown, unnamed **8** ulterior, withheld **9** anonymous **10** unreported, unrevealed **11** clandestine, unmentioned, unspecified **12** confidential, undesignated, unidentified

undisguised

4 bald, open, pure **5** frank, naked, overt, sheer, stark **6** candid, patent **7** obvious **8** apparent, explicit, manifest, palpable **9** barefaced **11** openhearted, unconcealed, unvarnished

undistinguished

5 cheap, stock **6** common **7** humdrum, obscure, routine **8** déclassé, everyday, inferior, low-grade, mediocre, middling, ordinary, workaday **10** second-rate **11** commonplace, nondescript, second-class **12** run-of-the-mill **13** insignificant

undivided

3 one **4** full **5** fixed, total, whole **6** entire, intact, united **8** complete, unbroken **9** unanimous **10** continuous, unswerving **11** indivisible **12** concentrated, undistracted

undo

4 free, open, ruin **5** annul, loose, untie, upset, wrack, wreck **6** cancel, defeat, loosen, negate, stymie, unbind, unsnap **7** abolish, destroy, nullify, release, reverse, vitiate, wipe out **8** abrogate, unfasten, unloosen **9** disengage **10** invalidate **11** disentangle, outmaneuver

undoing

4 bane, doom, ruin, slip **5** shame **7** misstep **8** downfall, reversal **9** destroyer, overthrow, ruination **10** misfortune **11** destruction, humiliation

undoubted

4 real, sure, true **7** certain, genuine **8** definite, positive **9** authentic **10** undisputed

undoubtedly

5 truly **6** indeed, really, surely **7** clearly **8** of course **9** assuredly, certainly **10** definitely, positively, presumably, undeniably **11** indubitably

undress

see **unclothe**

undressed

4 nude, rude **5** naked **6** unclad **7** exposed **8** in the raw, stripped **9** au naturel, unclothed

undue

5 inapt **7** extreme **8** ill-timed, improper, needless, untimely **9** excessive, unfitting **10** immoderate, indecorous, inordinate, unsuitable **11** extravagant, uncalled-for, unnecessary, unwarranted **12** unreasonable **13** inappropriate, unjustifiable

undulant fever

11 brucellosis

undulate

4 roll, swag, sway, wave **5** heave, snake, swell, swing **6** billow, ripple **7** slither **9** fluctuate, oscillate

unduly
3 too 6 overly 9 extremely, immensely 11 excessively 12 immoderately, inordinately, unreasonably 13 unnecessarily

undying
7 abiding, ageless, endless, eternal 8 enduring, immortal, unending 9 continual, deathless, perennial, perpetual, unceasing 10 continuing 11 amaranthine, everlasting 12 imperishable, unquenchable

unearth
4 find, show 5 dig up, learn 6 exhume, expose, reveal 7 exhibit, find out, root out, uncover 8 come upon, disclose, discover, dredge up, excavate 9 ascertain, determine 10 come across

unearthly
5 eerie, weird 6 absurd, insane, spooky 7 awesome, ghostly, uncanny, ungodly 8 abnormal, ethereal, heavenly, numinous, spectral 9 appalling, fantastic 10 miraculous, mysterious, outlandish, superhuman, suprahuman 12 preposterous, supermundane, supernatural 13 preternatural

unease
4 care, fear 5 angst, worry 6 strain, stress, unrest 7 anxiety, concern, tension 8 disquiet, distress 9 abashment, confusion, misgiving 10 discomfort, discontent, solicitude 11 disquietude, fretfulness, nervousness, uncertainty, uptightness 12 apprehension, discomfiture, discomposure 13 embarrassment

uneasy
4 edgy 5 jumpy, tense 6 afraid 7 anxious, awkward, fearful, fidgety, fretful, nervous, restive, unquiet, uptight, worried 8 agitated, doubtful, insecure, restless, unstable 9 ambiguous, concerned, difficult, disturbed, perturbed, uncertain, unsettled 10 disquieted, precarious, solicitous 11 embarrassed 12 apprehensive 13 uncomfortable

uneducated
5 crude, rough 8 ignorant, untaught 9 benighted, untutored 10 illiterate, unlettered, unschooled 12 uncultivated, uninstructed

unembellished
4 bald, bare 5 blunt, plain, spare, stark 6 severe 7 austere 9 essential, unadorned 11 undecorated, unelaborate, ungarnished, unvarnished 12 unornamented 13 unembroidered, unpretentious

unemotional
4 cold, cool 5 chill, stoic, stony 6 frigid, sedate, serene 7 deadpan, equable, glacial, stoical 8 composed, obdurate, reserved, reticent 9 apathetic, impassive 10 hardboiled, phlegmatic 11 insensitive, passionless, unexcitable 12 intellectual, thick-skinned, unresponsive 13 dispassionate

unemployed
4 idle 5 fired 6 otiose, unused 7 jobless, laid off, loafing 8 inactive, leisured, workless 10 unoccupied

unending
7 eternal, undying 8 constant, immortal, infinite, timeless 9 boundless, ceaseless, continual, incessant, limitless, perennial, perpetual, unceasing 10 continuous 11 amaranthine, everlasting, unremitting 12 interminable 13 uninterrupted

unenlightened
5 naive 6 unread 7 heathen, unaware 8 backward, ignorant, nescient 9 benighted, unknowing 10 uneducated, uninformed 11 uninitiated 12 uncultivated

unenthusiastic
4 cool 5 tepid 8 grudging, listless, lukewarm 9 apathetic, unexcited 10 lackluster, lacklustre, spiritless 11 halfhearted, indifferent, perfunctory 12 uninterested

unequal
3 odd 6 uneven, unfair 7 diverse

unequaled

8 inferior, lopsided, one-sided 9 different, disparate, divergent, irregular 10 asymmetric, dissimilar, inadequate, mismatched, off-balance 12 insufficient

unequaled

6 unique 7 supreme 8 foremost, nonesuch, peerless 9 matchless, paramount, unmatched, unrivaled 10 preeminent, surpassing 12 incomparable, transcendent, unparalleled 13 unprecedented

unequivocal

5 clear 6 direct, patent 7 certain, evident 8 apparent, definite, distinct, explicit, manifest, palpable 10 undeniable 11 categorical, indubitable, unambiguous 12 indisputable, undisputable

unerring

5 exact 6 dead-on 7 certain, correct, perfect, precise 8 accurate, reliable 9 faultless, unfailing 10 dependable, infallible 11 trustworthy

unessential

8 marginal, needless, unneeded 9 redundant 10 expendable, gratuitous, irrelevant, peripheral, unrequired 11 dispensable, superfluous, uncalled-for, unimportant, unnecessary 13 insignificant, insubstantial

unethical

5 venal, wrong 7 corrupt, crooked, immoral 9 dishonest, reprobate 12 disreputable, unprincipled, unscrupulous

uneven

3 odd 4 wavy 5 bumpy, erose, harsh, jaggy, rough 6 craggy, jagged, patchy, ragged, random, rugged, spotty 7 scraggy, unequal, varying 8 lopsided, scabrous, scraggly, variable 9 haphazard, hit-or-miss, irregular 10 asymmetric, imbalanced, unbalanced

unevenness

4 bump, wave 7 anomaly 8 asperity, imparity 9 disparity, imbalance, roughness, variation 10 inequality 12 irregularity, lopsidedness 13 disproportion

uneventful

5 usual 6 placid 7 humdrum, prosaic, routine 8 ordinary 10 unexciting 11 commonplace 12 unremarkable

unexampled

4 lone, only, sole, solo 5 alone 6 unique 8 singular, solitary 9 matchless, unequaled, unmatched, unrivaled 10 consummate, inimitable, sui generis, unequalled, unrivalled 12 incomparable, unparalleled 13 unprecedented

unexcited

4 calm 5 blasé, stoic 6 placid, sedate, serene 7 relaxed, stoical 8 composed, tranquil 9 apathetic, collected, unruffled 10 nonchalant 11 indifferent 12 uninterested 13 dispassionate

unexciting

4 arid, dull, tame 5 banal, bland, ho-hum 6 boring, stodgy 7 humdrum, insipid, prosaic, tedious 8 lifeless, tiresome 10 monotonous 11 commonplace 13 uninteresting

unexpected

10 surprising, unforeseen 11 unpredicted 13 unanticipated

unexpectedly

5 aback, short 6 sudden 7 unaware 8 abruptly, suddenly, unawares 9 forthwith 11 unwittingly 12 accidentally 13 inadvertently

unexpended

5 saved 7 reserve, surplus 8 left over, reserved 9 remaining

unexpired

5 valid 9 operative

unexpressed

5 tacit 6 silent, unsaid 7 assumed, implied 8 implicit, presumed, unspoken, wordless 9 unuttered 10 undeclared, understood

unfailing
4 fast, sure 7 certain, devoted
8 constant, faithful, reliable, resolute,
surefire, unerring 9 steadfast, unvarying 10 consistent, dependable,
infallible, invariable, persistent,
unchanging, unflagging, unwavering
11 everlasting, persevering, unrelenting 12 tried-and-true 13 inexhaustible

unfair
4 foul 5 wrong 6 biased, shabby,
uneven, unjust 7 unequal 8 wrongful 9 arbitrary, dishonest, unethical
10 prejudiced 11 inequitable, underhanded, unrighteous

unfaithful
5 false 6 untrue 8 cheating, disloyal,
recreant, turncoat 9 faithless, two-
timing 10 adulterous, inaccurate,
perfidious, traitorous 11 treacherous
13 untrustworthy

unfaltering
3 set 4 firm 6 steady 7 abiding
8 constant, enduring, resolute, tireless 9 steadfast, unfailing 10 continuous, unflagging, unwavering
11 persevering 12 never-failing,
wholehearted

unfamiliar
3 new 5 alien, novel 6 exotic
7 foreign, strange, unaware, unknown 8 peculiar 11 incognizant,
out-of-the-way 12 unaccustomed,
unacquainted

unfashionable
5 dated, dowdy, passé, stale 6 bygone, démodé, old-hat, shabby
7 outworn 8 outdated, outmoded
9 out-of-date, unstylish 10 antiquated, oldfangled

unfasten
4 free, open, undo 5 loose, unbar,
unfix, unpin, untie 6 detach, loosen,
unbind, unbolt, unlace, unlock,
unsnap 7 release, unclasp, unhitch,
unlatch, unleash, unloose, unstrap
8 unbuckle, unfetter, unloosen,
untether 9 disengage

unfathomable
7 abysmal, obscure 8 profound
9 boundless, enigmatic, unplumbed
10 bottomless, fathomless, unknowable 11 inscrutable 12 immeasurable, impenetrable

unfavorable
3 bad, ill 4 poor 6 averse, unfair,
unkind 7 adverse, hostile, opposed
8 contrary, damaging, inimical,
negative 9 disliking, troubling
11 detrimental, displeasing 12 antagonistic, disapproving, inauspicious
prefix: 3 dys

unfavorably
4 awry 5 amiss, badly 6 astray,
poorly 7 wrongly 10 negatively,
unsuitably 13 unfortunately

unfeasible
8 quixotic 9 visionary 10 chimerical,
impossible, unworkable 11 impractical, speculative, theoretical,
unrealistic 12 unattainable, unrealizable 13 impracticable

unfeeling
4 cold, hard, numb 5 cruel, harsh,
stern, stony 6 brutal, leaden, marble,
numbed, severe, stolid, unkind
7 callous 8 benumbed, deadened,
hardened, obdurate, pitiless, ruthless, uncaring 9 apathetic, heartless,
indurated, insensate, senseless
10 hardboiled, insensible, insentient
11 cold-blooded, coldhearted, hard-
hearted, insensitive, unemotional
12 anesthetized 13 unsympathetic

unfeigned
4 real, true 6 actual, hearty, honest
7 artless, earnest, genuine, natural,
sincere 8 innocent 9 guileless,
heartfelt, ingenuous 11 undesigning
12 wholehearted

unfinished
3 raw 5 crude, rough 7 sketchy
9 imperfect, roughhewn, undressed
10 incomplete, unpolished

**Unfinished Symphony
composer**
8 Schubert (Franz)

unfit

4 sick, weak 5 inapt, inept 6 faulty
7 deprive, disable, unsound, useless
8 disabled, improper, unsuited 9 ill-
suited, incapable, maladroit 10 disqualify, ill-adapted, inadequate, ineligible, unsuitable 11 incompetent,
unqualified 12 disqualified, incompatible 13 inappropriate, incapacitated

unfitting

5 inapt 8 improper, unseemly 9 imprudent 10 ill-advised, inapposite,
malapropos, unbecoming, unsuitable
11 inadvisable 13 inappropriate

unfix

4 part, undo 5 loose, sever 6 cut off,
detach, loosen, sunder, unbind
7 unloose 8 uncouple, unfasten,
unloosen 9 disengage 10 disconnect, dissociate

unflagging

6 steady 7 staunch 8 constant,
tireless, untiring 9 unceasing,
unfailing, unwearied 11 persevering,
unfaltering, unrelenting, unremitting
13 indefatigable, inexhaustible

unflappable

4 calm 6 poised, serene 7 assured,
equable 8 composed, laid-back
9 collected, unruffled 10 deliberate,
nonchalant 11 self-assured 13 imperturbable, self-possessed

unfledged

5 green, young 6 callow, jejune,
unripe 7 puerile 8 immature, juvenile 10 unseasoned 11 undeveloped, unfeathered 13 inexperienced

unflinching

4 firm, grim 6 dogged 7 doughty,
staunch, valiant 8 intrepid, resolute
9 dauntless, steadfast 10 relentless,
unwavering, unyielding 11 unfaltering, unrelenting 12 stouthearted

unfold

4 open 6 deduce, evolve, expand,
expose, extend, flower, mature,
reveal, unwrap 7 blossom, burgeon,
clear up, develop, display, dope out,

exhibit, explain, resolve 8 decipher,
disclose, evidence, manifest 9 elaborate, explicate, figure out, puzzle
out, transpire 10 effloresce, outstretch 11 come to light

unforced

4 easy 7 natural, willing, witting
8 elective, optional 9 available,
easygoing, voluntary 10 deliberate,
volitional 11 intentional 12 unpre-
scribed 13 discretionary, noncompulsory

unforeseeable

9 uncertain, unplanned 10 accidental

unforeseen

6 chance 8 surprise 10 accidental,
surprising, unexpected 11 unlooked-
for, unpredicted 13 unanticipated

unforgivable

9 untenable 10 censurable, inexpi-
able, outrageous 11 blameworthy,
inexcusable, intolerable 12 indefensible, unacceptable, unpardonable 13 insupportable, reprehensible, unjustifiable

unformed

4 rude 5 crude, rough, vague 6 callow 8 immature, inchoate, nebulous,
unshaped 9 amorphous, roughhewn, shapeless 10 indefinite,
unfinished, unpolished 11 undeveloped, unfashioned 12 unstructured
13 indeterminate

unfortunate

3 bad, sad 4 dire, poor 6 woeful,
wretch 7 adverse, awkward, hapless, unhappy, unlucky 8 grievous,
ill-fated, luckless, untoward, wretched
9 desperate, graceless, ill-chosen,
miserable 10 afflictive, calamitous,
deplorable, disastrous, ill-starred,
lamentable, unsuitable 11 distressing, regrettable, star-crossed,
unfavorable 12 disagreeable, inauspicious, infelicitous, unsuccessful
13 heartbreaking

unfounded

4 idle, vain 5 false 8 baseless,
spurious, unproven 9 deceptive,

dishonest, untenable **10** fabricated, fallacious, gratuitous, groundless, mendacious, misleading, untruthful **11** uncalled-for, unsupported, unwarranted

unfriendly

4 cold, cool **5** alien, aloof, chill, gruff, surly **6** chilly, frosty, remote **7** distant, grouchy, hostile, opposed, warlike **8** inimical, unsocial **10** antisocial, censorious, inimicable, unsociable **11** ill-disposed, uncongenial **12** antagonistic, disagreeable, inhospitable, misanthropic, unneighborly **13** unsympathetic

unfruitful

4 arid, idle **5** empty, waste **6** barren, desert, effete, fallow, futile, wasted **7** parched, sterile, useless **8** abortive, bootless, depleted, impotent **9** infertile, pointless **10** unavailing **11** ineffective, ineffectual **12** impoverished, unproductive, unprofitable

unfurl

4 open **6** expose, reveal, spread, unfold, unroll, unwind **7** develop, display, exhibit, uncover **8** disclose **9** elaborate, spread out

unfurnished

4 bare **5** empty **6** vacant

unfussy

5 loose **6** breezy, casual, common, dégagé, folksy, mellow **7** cursory, relaxed **8** familiar, informal, laid-back **9** easygoing **10** unreserved **11** low-pressure, pococurante, unconcerned **12** unparticular **13** unceremonious, uncomplicated

ungainly

5 gawky, lanky, splay **6** clumsy, klutzy, oafish **7** awkward, boorish, hulking, loutish, lumpish, uncouth **8** bungling, clownish, lubberly, unwieldy **9** lumbering, maladroit **10** blundering

ungarnished

5 plain **6** modest, simple **9** un-

adorned **11** undecorated, unelaborate **12** unornamented **13** unembellished, unembroidered

ungenerous

4 mean **5** petty, tight **6** paltry, shabby, skimpy, stingy **7** chintzy, miserly **8** grudging, picayune, ungiving **9** illiberal, niggardly, penurious **11** closefisted, tightfisted **12** parsimonious **13** penny-pinching

ungodly

see **unholy**

ungovernable

4 wild **6** unruly **7** froward, lawless, willful **8** mutinous, untoward **9** fractious, turbulent, unbridled **10** disorderly, headstrong, rebellious, refractory, tumultuous **11** intractable **12** recalcitrant, uncontrolled, unmanageable **13** irrepressible, undisciplined

ungraceful

5 crude, gawky, inept, stiff **6** clumsy, gauche, klutzy, oafish, wooden **7** artless, awkward, halting, labored, stilted **8** bumbling, bungling, ungainly, untoward **9** all thumbs, inelegant, lumbering, maladroit **10** blundering

ungracious

4 rude **5** gruff **6** crusty **7** brusque, uncivil **8** churlish, impolite **9** offensive **10** unmannerly **11** disobliging, ill-mannered, impertinent, thoughtless, uncalled-for **12** disagreeable, discourteous **13** disrespectful, inconsiderate, unceremonious

ungraspable

6 opaque **7** obscure **8** baffling **9** enigmatic **10** unknowable **12** impenetrable, inexplicable, unfathomable

ungrateful

9 thankless

unguarded

5 frank, hasty **6** candid, direct, unwary **7** offhand **8** careless, heedless, reckless **9** impolitic, imprudent,

unguent

4 balm 5 cream, salve 6 balsam, cerate, chrism, lotion 8 ointment 9 emollient, lubricant 11 embrocation

ungulate

3 hog, pig 4 deer 5 horse, tapir 6 hoofed 8 elephant 10 rhinoceros

unhallowed

4 evil 6 impure, unholy, wicked 7 immoral, impious, profane, ungodly 8 infernal 9 nefarious 10 desecrated, iniquitous, irreverent 13 unconsecrated

unhampered

4 free, open 5 frank, loose 6 direct 8 uncurbed 9 unbridled, unchecked, unimpeded, unlimited 10 unhindered 11 uninhibited, untrammeled 12 unrestrained, unrestricted, unobstructed 13 unconstrained

unhand

5 let go 7 release

unhandy

5 bulky, inept 6 clumsy, gauche, klutzy 7 awkward, halting, hulking 8 bumbling, bungling, cumbrous, unwieldy 9 all thumbs, ham-handed, maladroit, ponderous 10 cumbersome, unskillful 12 inconvenient

unhappiness

3 woe 5 blues, dolor, dumps, gloom, grief, worry 6 misery, mishap, sorrow 7 anxiety, sadness 8 distress 9 dejection 10 depression, desolation, discontent, heartbreak, melancholy 11 despondency, dolefulness 12 mournfulness, wretchedness 13 cheerlessness

unhappy

3 sad 4 down, grim 5 sorry 6 dismal, dreary, gloomy 7 joyless 8 dejected, downcast, mournful, saddened, troubled, wretched 9 cheerless, depressed, sorrowful, woebegone 10 despondent, dispir-

ited, melancholy 11 melancholic, unfortunate 12 disconsolate, heavyhearted

unharmed

4 safe 5 sound 6 intact, secure, unhurt 8 unbroken, unmarred 9 protected, undamaged, undefiled, uninjured, unscathed 10 unimpaired 11 unblemished

unhealthiness

7 ailment, disease, illness, malaise 8 debility, sickness 9 infirmity 10 affliction, sickliness 11 decrepitude 13 indisposition

unhealthy

3 ill 4 sick 5 ailing, infirm, sickly, unwell 7 baneful, noisome, noxious, unsound 8 diseased 9 injurious 11 deleterious, unwholesome 12 insalubrious

unheard-of

3 new 6 unique 7 obscure, unknown, unnoted 8 nameless 10 phenomenal, unrenowned 12 uncelebrated 13 extraordinary, unprecedented

unhesitating

7 assured, earnest 8 decisive, positive, resolute 9 confident, immediate, unchecked 10 determined, forthright, purposeful 11 unflinching 12 wholehearted

unhinge

5 addle, craze 6 madden, ruffle 7 derange 9 unbalance

unhinged

3 mad 4 daft, loco, nuts 5 balmy, crazy, loony, wacky 6 insane 7 lunatic, unglued 8 demented, deranged 9 disturbed 10 unbalanced

unholy

4 base, evil, vile 6 impure, sinful, wicked 7 heinous, immoral, impious, profane, ungodly 8 dreadful, fiendish, god-awful, shocking 9 atheistic, barbarous 10 iniquitous, irreverent, outrageous, scandalous, unhallowed 11 irreligious, unbelieving 12 sacrilegious, unsanctified 13 reprehensible

unhorse
  5 pitch, throw **6** topple, tumble, unseat **7** buck off **8** dislodge, dismount, overturn, unsaddle **9** overthrow

unhurried
  4 easy, slow **7** laggard, relaxed **8** dilatory, laid-back **9** easygoing, leisurely **10** deliberate **11** low-pressure

unhurt
  4 safe **5** sound, whole **6** entire, intact **7** perfect **8** unbroken, unharmed, unmarred **9** undamaged, uninjured, unscathed, untouched **10** unimpaired **11** unblemished

unification
  5 union **6** fusion, hookup, merger **7** amalgam, joining, linkage, melding, merging **8** alliance, coupling **9** coalition **10** connection, federation **11** affiliation, coalescence, combination **12** amalgamation **13** confederation, consolidation

uniform
  4 even, like, suit **5** alike, dress, equal, level **6** attire, outfit, stable, steady **7** ordered, orderly, regular, similar, stabile **8** constant, unvaried **9** consonant, unvarying **10** comparable, consistent, invariable, unchanging **11** homogeneous **13** unfluctuating
  combining form: 3 iso
  type: 5 blues, habit, khaki **6** livery, whites

uniformity
  6 parity **7** oneness **8** equality, evenness, identity, monotony, sameness **9** agreement, congruity, constancy **11** consistency **13** invariability

uniformly
  6 always, evenly **7** equally **8** smoothly **10** comparably **11** analogously, identically **12** equivalently

unify
  3 tie, wed **4** bind, bond, fuse, knit, link, mesh **5** blend, marry, merge, unite **6** cement, couple **7** combine, conjoin **8** coalesce, compound, federate **9** integrate **10** amalgamate, centralize, synthesize **11** concatenate, consolidate

unimaginable
  10 incredible, unknowable **11** unthinkable **12** mind-boggling, unbelievable **13** extraordinary, inconceivable, indescribable

unimaginative
  4 dull, flat **5** banal, bland, trite, vapid **6** common **7** literal, prosaic, routine, vanilla **8** bromidic **10** derivative, pedestrian, uncreative, uninspired **11** commonplace

unimpaired
  4 safe **5** sound **6** intact, unhurt **7** perfect **8** unbroken, unharmed, unmarred **9** undamaged, uninjured, unscathed **11** unblemished

unimpassioned
  4 calm, cool **5** sober, stoic **6** placid, remote, stolid **7** deadpan **8** detached, lukewarm, reserved, tranquil **9** impassive, temperate **10** phlegmatic, spiritless **11** cold-blooded, emotionless **12** matter-of-fact

unimpeachable
  5 valid **7** correct **8** flawless, reliable, virtuous **9** blameless, exemplary, faultless, unspotted, unsullied **10** conclusive, impeccable, undisputed **11** unblemished, untarnished **13** authoritative

unimportant
  5 minor, petty **6** casual, minute, paltry **7** trivial **8** piddling **9** smallbeer, worthless **10** expendable, immaterial, irrelevant, negligible **11** dispensable, meaningless, superfluous **13** insignificant

uninformed
  7 unaware **8** ignorant, nescient **9** oblivious, unknowing, unwitting **10** unfamiliar **11** incognizant, superficial **12** unacquainted, undiscerning

uninhabited
  5 empty, waste **6** barren, vacant **7** vacated **8** deserted, desolate, forsaken **9** abandoned, evacuated **10** unoccupied

uninhibited
3 lax **4** free **5** loose **8** uncurbed **9** expansive, fancy-free, liberated, unbridled **10** boisterous, ungoverned, unhampered, unreserved **11** spontaneous, unrepressed, untrammeled **12** unrestrained, unsuppressed **13** unconstrained

uninjured
4 safe **5** sound, whole **6** intact, unhurt **8** unharmed, unmarred **9** undamaged, undefiled, unscathed, untouched **10** unimpaired **11** unblemished

uninspired
4 blah, drab, dull **5** banal, stock, trite, vapid **6** boring, leaden, old-hat, stodgy **7** humdrum, insipid, plastic, sterile, vanilla **8** bromidic, lifeless, ordinary **9** colorless **10** lackluster, lacklustre, pedestrian, uncreative, unoriginal **11** commonplace **13** unimaginative

unintelligent
4 dumb **5** dense **6** obtuse, stupid **7** asinine, brutish, doltish, fatuous, foolish, moronic, vacuous, witless **8** mindless **9** brainless, ludicrous **10** half-witted, ill-advised, irrational, ridiculous, weak-minded **11** harebrained, lamebrained **12** feeble-minded

unintentional
6 chance, random **9** haphazard, unplanned, unwitting **10** accidental, fortuitous, incidental, unexpected, unforeseen, unthinking **11** inadvertent, unconscious, unlooked-for **12** adventitious, coincidental **13** unanticipated

uninterested
5 aloof, blasé, bored, jaded **9** apathetic, incurious, unexcited **10** uninvolved **11** indifferent, unconcerned

uninteresting
3 dry **4** arid, blah, drab, dull, flat **5** banal, dusty, ho-hum, stale **6** boring, jejune **7** humdrum, insipid, prosaic, tedious **8** bromidic, plodding, tiresome **9** colorless, dryasdust,

wearisome **10** monotonous, pedestrian, uneventful, unexciting **11** uninspiring

uninterrupted
6 direct **7** endless, nonstop **8** constant, unbroken, unending **9** ceaseless, continual, incessant, perpetual, sustained, unceasing **10** continuous **11** undisturbed, unremitting **12** interminable

uninvited
7 unasked **8** unbidden, unsought **9** intruding **10** gratuitous **11** uncalled-for, unrequested, unsolicited **12** presumptuous

union
4 bloc, bond, club **5** alloy, group, guild, joint **6** fusion, league, merger **7** amalgam, joining, melding, merging, society **8** alliance, congress, coupling, junction, juncture, marriage, sodality **9** coalition **10** connection, federation, fellowship **11** association, brotherhood, coalescence, combination, confederacy, cooperative, unification **13** confederation, consolidation
labor: 3 AFL, CIO, UAW, UMW **5** ILGWU

unique
3 odd, one **4** lone, only, sole, solo **5** alone, novel **6** single **8** peculiar, peerless, singular, solitary, uncommon, unwonted **9** anomalous, exclusive, matchless, unequaled, unmatched, unrivaled **10** inimitable, particular, sui generis, unequalled, unexampled, unrivalled **11** distinctive, exceptional **12** incomparable, unparalleled, unrepeatable **13** extraordinary, idiosyncratic, unprecedented

uniqueness
8 identity **10** singleness **11** singularity **13** individuality

———-Unis
5 Etats

unit
3 arm, one **4** area, item, part, wing

5 digit, group, monad, piece, whole
6 entity **7** element, measure **8** molecule **9** component **10** individual
11 constituent
administrative: 6 agency, bureau, sector **8** district
boy scout: 5 troop
educational: 6 course
military:
(see at **military**)
of acceleration: 3 gal
of action: 7 episode
of advertising space: 4 line
6 column
of an element: 4 atom **8** molecule
of angular measure: 6 radian
of area: 3 are **4** acre **6** morgen
7 hectare **9** square rod **10** square mile, square yard
of astronomical distance: 6 parsec
9 light-year
of brightness: 7 lambert
of capacity: 3 cup, tun **4** cord, dram, gill, peck, pint **5** liter, litre, minim, ounce, quart **6** barrel, bushel, firkin, gallon
of computer information: 3 bit, gig, meg **4** byte **8** gigabyte, megabyte
of conductance: 3 mho **7** siemens
of distance: 4 mile, yard **5** meter
6 league **7** furlong
of electricity: 3 amp **4** volt, watt
6 ampere **7** coulomb
of energy: 3 erg **5** joule **7** quantum
8 watt-hour
of explosive force: 7 megaton
of fineness: 5 carat, karat
of force: 4 dyne **6** newton **7** poundal
of frequency: 5 hertz **7** fresnel
of grain: 5 sheaf
of heat: 3 BTU **5** therm **7** calorie
of illumination: 3 lux **5** lumen
of inductance: 5 henry
of length: 3 mil, rod **4** foot, hand, inch, mile, rood, yard **5** chain, fermi, meter **6** fathom, micron **7** furlong
9 kilometer
  historic: 5 cubit
of loudness: 4 sone **7** decibel
of lumber: 9 board foot
of magnetic flux: 5 gamma, gauss, tesla, weber **7** maxwell

of magnetic intensity: 7 oersted
of magnetomotive force: 7 gilbert
of pressure: 3 bar **4** torr **6** pascal
10 atmosphere
of radiation: 3 rad **8** roentgen
of radioactivity: 5 curie
of resistance: 3 ohm
of solar radiation: 7 langley
of sound absorption: 5 sabin
of speech: 4 word **6** toneme
7 phoneme **8** morpheme, syllable
of speed: 3 CPS, MPH, RPM
4 knot
of temperature: 6 degree, kelvin
of time: 3 day **4** beat, bell, hour, week, year **5** month **6** minute, season, second **8** svedberg
of viscosity: 5 poise
of volume: 9 cubic foot, cubic yard
10 cubic meter
of weight: 3 cwt, ton **4** dram, gram, tael **5** carat, grain, ounce, pound, tonne **6** drachm **7** gigaton, kiloton, quintal, scruple **8** kilogram, millieme
9 metric ton, microgram, milligram
  historic: 3 tod **5** gerah, libra
  Indian: 4 tola
  Russian: 4 pood
of work: 3 erg **5** ergon, joule
social: 4 clan **5** tribe **6** family
7 chapter

unite
3 mix, tie, wed **4** ally, band, bind, bond, fuse, join, knit, link, meld, pool, weld **5** blend, graft, marry, merge, unify **6** cement, couple, gather, league, mingle, splice **7** combine, conjoin, connect **8** assemble, coadjute, coalesce, compound, federate
9 affiliate, aggregate, commingle
10 amalgamate, federalize **11** confederate, incorporate

united
3 one, wed **5** joint **6** allied, linked, merged, wedded **7** made one
8 agreeing, combined, in accord
10 harmonious

United Arab Emirates
  capital: 8 Abu Dhabi
  city: 5 Dubai **6** Dubayy
  coast: 6 Pirate **7** Trucial

United Kingdom

emirate: 5 Dubai 6 Dubayy 8 Abu Dhabi
former name: 13 Trucial States
gulf: 4 Oman 7 Persian
monetary unit: 6 dirham
neighbor: 4 Oman 11 Saudi Arabia
peninsula: 7 Arabian
strait: 6 Hormuz

United Kingdom

capital: 6 London
city: 3 Ely 4 Bath 5 Derby, Dover, Leeds 6 Exeter, Oxford 7 Bristol, Cardiff, Glasgow, Paisley 8 Bradford, Brighton, Coventry, Plymouth 9 Cambridge, Edinburgh, Leicester, Liverpool, Newcastle, Sheffield 10 Birmingham, Manchester, Nottingham 11 Bournemouth
colony: 8 Falkland (Islands)
component: 5 Wales 7 England 8 Scotland 12 Great Britain
conqueror: 6 Caesar (Julius) 7 William (the Conqueror)
island: 3 Man 4 Jura, Skye 5 Islay, Lewis, Wight 6 Jersey 8 Anguilla, Guernsey, Mainland
island group: 6 Orkney 7 Channel 8 Hebrides, Shetland
language: 5 Welsh 6 Gaelic 7 English
leader: 8 Cromwell (Oliver) 9 Churchill (Winston)
monarch: 4 Anne, Mary 5 Henry, James 6 Alfred (the Great), Edward, George 7 Charles, Richard, William 8 Victoria 9 Elizabeth
monetary unit: 5 pence, penny, pound
monetary unit, former: 3 bob 5 crown, groat 6 florin, guinea 7 ha'penny 8 farthing, shilling, sixpence 9 halfpenny 10 threepence
mountain, range: 7 Scafell (Peak), Snowdon 8 Ben Nevis, Cumbrian, Grampian 12 Cheviot Hills
peninsula: 7 Kintyre
prehistoric site: 7 Avebury 9 Skara Brae 10 Stonehenge
river: 3 Dee, Exe, Wye 4 Aire, Avon, Ouse 5 Clyde 6 Mersey, Severn, Thames
sea: 5 Irish, North 6 Celtic
territory: 8 Anguilla

United Nations

secretary-general: 3 Lie (Trygve) 5 Annan (Kofi), Thant (U) 8 Waldheim (Kurt) 12 Boutros-Ghali (Boutros), Hammarskjöld (Dag) 14 Pérez de Cuéllar (Javier)

United States

desert: 6 Mojave 7 Sonoran 8 Colorado
highest point: 6 Denali (Mt.) 8 McKinley (Mt.)
island: 6 Hawaii, Kodiak, Unimak 7 Nunivak 9 Admiralty, Chichagof 10 St. Lawrence 13 Prince of Wales
island group: 3 Fox 6 Hawaii 8 Aleutian, Pribilof, Thousand
lowest point: 11 Death Valley
mountain range: 5 Coast, Green, Ozark, Rocky, White 7 Cascade, Olympic 9 Blue Ridge, Catskills 10 Adirondack, Great Smoky 11 Appalachian 12 Sierra Nevada
national park: 4 Zion 6 Denali 7 Glacier, Olympic, Redwood, Sequoia 8 Badlands, Carlsbad, Wind Cave, Yosemite 9 Mesa Verde, Mt. Rainier 10 Everglades, Grand Teton, Hot Springs, Isle Royale, Shenandoah 11 Dry Tortugas, Grand Canyon, Kenai Fjords, Mammoth Cave, Yellowstone
possession: 10 Puerto Rico
state: 4 Iowa, Ohio, Utah 5 Idaho, Maine, Texas 6 Alaska, Hawaii, Kansas, Nevada, Oregon 7 Alabama, Arizona, Florida, Georgia, Indiana, Montana, New York, Vermont, Wyoming 8 Arkansas, Colorado, Delaware, Illinois, Kentucky, Maryland, Michigan, Missouri, Nebraska, Oklahoma, Virginia 9 Louisiana, Minnesota, New Jersey, New Mexico, Tennessee, Wisconsin 10 California, Washington 11 Connecticut, Mississippi, North Dakota, Rhode Island, South Dakota 12 New Hampshire, Pennsylvania, West Virginia 13 Massachusetts, North Carolina, South Carolina
territory: 4 Guam 13 American Samoa, Virgin Islands

unity
5 union 6 accord 7 concord, harmony, oneness 8 identity, soleness 9 agreement, consensus 10 continuity, singleness, solidarity

universal
3 all 5 broad, total, whole 6 common, cosmic, entire, global 7 general, generic 8 catholic 9 extensive, planetary, unlimited, worldwide 10 ecumenical, ubiquitous 11 omnipresent 12 all-embracing, all-inclusive, cosmopolitan 13 comprehensive
combining form: 4 omni

universe
3 all 5 whole, world 6 cosmos, system 8 creation 9 macrocosm

unjust
5 wrong 6 biased, shabby, unfair 7 partial, unequal 8 one-sided, improper, wrongful 9 inequable 10 prejudiced, undeserved 11 inequitable, unrighteous

unjustifiable
5 undue 7 invalid 8 baseless 9 unfounded, untenable 10 groundless 11 inexcusable, unsupported, unwarranted 12 indefensible

unkempt
5 messy 6 frowsy, frowzy, shaggy, sloppy, untidy 7 ruffled, rumpled, scruffy, tousled 8 scraggly, slipshod, slovenly, uncombed 10 bedraggled, disarrayed, disheveled, disordered, unpolished 11 disarranged

unkind
4 mean, vile 5 cruel, harsh, rough, stern 6 severe 7 callous 8 uncaring 9 inclement, malicious 10 ungenerous, ungracious 11 insensitive, thoughtless, unfavorable 12 uncharitable 13 unsympathetic

unknowable
6 arcane, hidden, mystic, occult, secret 7 cryptic 8 mystical, numinous 9 enigmatic, recondite 10 mysterious 11 inscrutable, ungraspable 12 impenetrable, unfathomable

unknowing
6 unwary 7 unaware 8 heedless, ignorant 9 oblivious, unmindful, unwitting 10 insensible, unfamiliar, uninformed 11 incognizant 12 unsuspecting

unknown
6 hidden, nobody, secret 7 obscure, strange 8 nameless 9 anonymous, incognito

unlawful
6 banned 7 bootleg, corrupt, crooked, illegal, illicit, immoral 8 criminal, outlawed, wrongful 9 forbidden, felonious, nefarious 10 contraband, flagitious, indictable, iniquitous, prohibited, proscribed, unlicensed 11 black-market 12 illegitimate, unauthorized

unlearned
5 naive 6 unread 7 unaware 8 ignorant, nescient, untaught 10 illiterate, uneducated, unlettered, unschooled 11 instinctive 13 unenlightened

unleash
4 free, vent 5 let go, loose, untie, visit, wreak 6 unbind 7 inflict, release 8 carry out, liberate 10 bring about

unless
3 but 4 save 6 except, saving 7 barring, but that, without 9 excepting, excluding

unlettered
see **uneducated**

unlikable
9 obnoxious, offensive, repellent 10 unpleasant 11 displeasing, distasteful 12 disagreeable

unlike
5 mixed 7 diverse, unequal, various 8 assorted 9 different, disparate, divergent 10 dissimilar 11 distinctive, diversified 13 heterogeneous

unlikely
5 faint, unfit 6 remote, slight 7 distant, dubious 8 doubtful 10 farfetched, improbable, unsuitable

11 implausible, unpromising **12** questionable

unlimited
4 full, vast **5** total **6** untold **7** endless, immense **8** absolute, infinite, wide-open **9** boundless, countless, unbounded, universal **10** unconfined, unfettered **11** unqualified, untrammeled **12** immeasurable, interminable, unrestrained, unrestricted **13** comprehensive, unconditional, unconstrained

unlit
4 dark, inky **6** gloomy **9** lightless

unload
4 drop, dump, junk **5** chuck, ditch, empty **6** debark, remove **7** confess, confide, deep-six, deliver, discard, divulge, lighten, relieve **8** disclose, disgorge, jettison **9** disburden, discharge, disembark, eighty-six, stevedore **11** disencumber

unloose
4 free, undo **5** let go, relax, untie **6** detach, unbind **7** break up, manumit, release, set free, slacken **8** liberate, uncouple, unfasten **9** disengage, extricate, untighten **10** disconnect

unlucky
6 jinxed **7** hapless, ominous **8** ill-fated, untoward **9** ill-boding **10** ill-starred **11** detrimental, inopportune, regrettable, star-crossed, unfavorable, unfortunate **12** inauspicious, unpropitious

unmanageable
4 wild **5** balky, bulky **6** unruly **7** awkward **8** contrary, cumbrous, perverse, stubborn, unwieldy **9** fractious, obstinate **10** cumbersome, disorderly, headstrong, inflexible, rebellious, refractory **11** intractable **12** obstreperous, recalcitrant, ungovernable **13** uncooperative, undisciplined

unmannered
4 rude **5** crude, rough **6** coarse,

gauche **7** boorish, ill-bred, loutish **8** impolite **10** indecorous, ungracious **12** discourteous **13** disrespectful

unmarred
5 sound, whole **6** intact, unhurt **7** perfect **8** pristine, unflawed, unharmed **9** undamaged, undefiled, unscathed, unstained **10** unimpaired **11** unblemished, untarnished

unmask
6 debunk, detect, expose, reveal, show up, unveil **7** deflate, uncover **8** disclose, discover, disprove **9** demystify

unmatched
3 odd **4** only **5** alone **6** unique **8** peerless, singular **9** unequaled, unrivaled **10** inimitable, unequalled, unrivalled **11** exceptional **12** incomparable, unparalleled

unmerciful
5 cruel, harsh **6** brutal **7** callous, extreme **8** inhumane, pitiless, ruthless, uncaring, vengeful **9** heartless, unfeeling, unsparing **10** relentless

unmindful
7 unaware **8** careless, heedless **9** forgetful, negligent, oblivious, unheeding, unwitting **10** abstracted, distracted, neglectful **11** inattentive

unmistakable
5 clear, frank, plain **6** patent **7** certain, decided, evident, express, obvious **8** apparent, definite, distinct, explicit, manifest, palpable **11** unambiguous, unequivocal

unmitigated
4 pure, rank **5** gross, sheer, utter **6** arrant **7** perfect, unmixed **8** absolute, clearcut, complete, outright **9** downright, out-and-out, unalloyed, undiluted **10** consummate, unmodified, unrelieved **11** straight-out, unqualified **12** unalleviated **13** thoroughgoing, unadulterated

unmixed
4 mere, neat, pure **5** plain, sheer,

utter **6** simple **7** perfect, sincere **8** absolute, straight **9** unalloyed, unblended, undiluted, undivided **11** unmitigated, unqualified **13** unadulterated

unmoved

4 calm, cool, firm **5** aloof, stony **6** stolid **7** adamant, callous, stoical **8** obdurate **9** impassive, untouched **10** insensible, untroubled **11** unconcerned, unemotional, unimpressed **12** unresponsive

unnamed

5 incog **6** secret **7** obscure, unknown **9** anonymous, incognito **11** unspecified **12** unidentified

unnatural

7 uncanny **8** aberrant, abnormal **9** anomalous, contrived, irregular, synthetic **10** artificial, fabricated, factitious

unnecessary

6 excess **7** surplus **8** needless, optional, prodigal **9** redundant **10** expendable, extraneous, gratuitous, unrequired **11** dispensable, inessential, superfluous, uncalled-for, unessential **12** nonessential

unnerve

5 daunt, shake, throw, upset **6** dismay, rattle **7** agitate, fluster, perturb, unhinge **8** bewilder, confound **9** undermine **10** demoralize, disconcert, discourage, dishearten, intimidate

unobstructed

4 open **5** clear **8** passable **9** unblocked, unimpeded **10** unhampered, unhindered **12** unrestricted

unobtrusive

5 quiet **6** modest **7** subdued **8** reserved, retiring, tasteful **10** restrained **13** inconspicuous

unoccupied

4 free, idle **5** empty **6** vacant **7** jobless, vacated **8** deserted **9** abandoned, available **10** employable, unemployed **11** uninhabited

unofficial

7 pirated, private, wildcat **8** informal **9** irregular **10** unapproved, unorthodox **12** unauthorized, unsanctioned

unorganized

7 aimless, chaotic, muddled **8** confused, inchoate, nebulous, rambling, unformed **9** amorphous, arbitrary, haphazard, shapeless, unplanned **10** disjointed, disordered, incoherent, incohesive **11** spontaneous

unoriginal

5 banal, stock **6** copied, old-hat **7** clichéd, humdrum, prosaic, sterile **8** borrowed, ordinary **9** hackneyed, imitative **10** derivative, uninspired **11** commonplace, plagiarized, uninventive **12** conventional **13** unimaginative

unornamented

4 bare **5** plain, spare, stark **6** chaste, modest, severe, simple **7** austere **9** unadorned **11** unelaborate, ungarnished **13** unembellished, unembroidered

unorthodox

3 odd **5** kinky, novel, weird **6** far-out **7** strange, unusual **8** abnormal **9** different, dissident, eccentric, heretical, irregular, sectarian **10** schismatic, unexpected **13** nonconformist

unorthodoxy

6 heresy, schism **7** dissent **8** variance **9** disbelief, ingenuity, recusancy **10** contention, dissidence, innovation **13** nonconformism, nonconformity

unpaid

3 due **5** owing **6** mature **7** donated, overdue, payable, pro-bono **8** freewill, honorary, wageless **9** unsettled, voluntary, volunteer **10** delinquent, gratuitous, receivable, unsalaried **11** contributed, outstanding **13** uncompensated, unremunerated

unpalatable

8 unsavory **10** flavorless **11** distasteful **12** unappetizing

unparalleled

6 unique 8 peerless, singular
9 matchless, unequaled, unmatched,
unrivaled 10 inimitable, unequalled,
unrivalled 11 exceptional 12 incomparable

unplanned

5 fluky 6 chance, random 7 aimless
9 desultory, haphazard, hit-or-miss
10 accidental, unexpected, unforeseen, unintended 11 inadvertent
12 adventitious, coincidental, uncon-
sidered 13 unintentional

unpleasant

4 sour 5 seamy 7 painful 8 annoying 9 offensive, troubling 10 disturbing, irritating 11 displeasing, distasteful, distressing 12 disagreeable
13 objectionable

unpolished

4 rude 5 crude, gruff, rough 6 crusty,
unhewn, vulgar 7 brusque, uncivil,
uncouth 8 homespun, unworked
9 inelegant, roughhewn, unrefined
10 amateurish, uncultured, unfinished, ungracious 11 ill-mannered,
uncivilized 12 discourteous

unpredictable

4 iffy 5 dicey, fluky 6 chancy, fickle,
random, touchy 7 erratic, mutable
8 unstable, variable, volatile 9 arbitrary, mercurial, uncertain, whimsical
10 capricious, changeable 13 unforeseeable

unprejudiced

4 fair, just 5 equal 8 balanced,
unbiased 9 equitable, impartial,
objective, unbigoted, uncolored
10 even-handed, fair-minded, open-
minded 11 nonpartisan 12 un-
influenced 13 disinterested, dispassionate

unpressed

7 rumpled, wrinkly 8 crinkled, puckered, wrinkled

unpretentious

5 frank, plain 6 candid, honest,
modest, simple 7 genuine 8 ordinary 9 unadorned 10 forthright,
unaffected, unassuming 11 plainspoken

unprincipled

5 venal 7 corrupt, crooked, immoral
9 deceitful, dishonest, dissolute,
mercenary, reprobate, unethical
10 inconstant, iniquitous, profligate,
unfaithful 11 underhanded 12 unscrupulous

unproductive

4 vain 6 barren, futile 7 sterile,
useless 8 bootless, depleted, feckless, impotent 9 fruitless, infertile
10 unavailing 11 ineffectual 12 hardscrabble

unprofitable

4 idle, vain 6 barren, futile 7 useless
8 bootless 9 fruitless 10 unavailing
11 ineffective 12 unproductive,
unsuccessful

unprogressive

8 orthodox 9 illiberal 11 traditional
12 conservative

unpropitious

4 grim 5 bleak 7 ominous, unlucky
9 ill-boding, ill-omened 10 foreboding
11 inopportune, threatening, unfavorable 12 discouraging 13 disheartening

unprosperous

4 poor 5 needy 8 strapped 9 penurious 11 impecunious

unprotected

6 unsafe 7 exposed 8 helpless,
insecure 9 unguarded 10 endan-
gered, undefended, unshielded,
vulnerable 11 defenseless, susceptible, unsheltered

unproved

7 untried 8 untested 10 postulated
11 conjectural, preliminary, provisional, speculative, theoretical
12 experimental, hypothetical

unpunctual

4 late 5 tardy 6 remiss 7 belated,
delayed, overdue 10 behindhand,
delinquent

unqualified
4 firm, rank 5 sheer, total, unfit, utter
7 express 8 absolute, explicit,
unfitted 9 incapable, out-and-out,
steadfast, unalloyed, undiluted,
unskilled 10 ineligible, unequipped,
unreserved, unsuitable 11 ill-
equipped, incompetent, unmitigated
12 wholehearted 13 unadulterated,
unconditional

unquenchable
6 crying 7 buoyant, exigent 8 pressing, yearning 9 demanding, insatiate,
insistent 10 insatiable 12 effervescent, unrestrained 13 irrepressible, unconstrained

unquestionable
4 real, sure, true 7 certain, genuine
8 absolute, bona fide 9 authentic,
undoubted 10 sure-enough, undeniable 11 established, indubitable,
self-evident, well-founded 12 indisputable, well-grounded 13 authoritative, incontestable, unimpeachable

unquestioning
4 firm, sure 5 fixed 6 steady 7 abiding 8 enduring, gullible, resolute,
trusting, unshaken 9 accepting,
believing, credulous, steadfast
10 uncritical, undoubting, unshakable, unwavering 11 unfaltering,
unqualified 12 never-failing, unhesitating, unsuspecting, unsuspicious,
wholehearted

unravel
5 break, solve 6 answer, decode,
unknit, unwind 7 clear up, dope out,
explain, resolve, unsnarl 8 decipher, dissolve, untangle 9 elucidate,
extricate, figure out, interpret, puzzle
out, translate 11 disentangle

unreadable
7 deadpan 9 illegible 10 poker-
faced 11 inscrutable 12 hieroglyphic
13 cacographical

unreal
4 fake 5 false 6 fabled 7 fictive
8 chimeric, fanciful, illusory, mythical
9 fantastic, fictional, imaginary, imitation 10 artificial, chimerical, fictitious,

improbable, incredible 11 non-
existent 12 unbelievable
combining form: 5 pseud 6 pseudo

unrealistic
7 blue-sky, idyllic, utopian 8 fanciful,
quixotic, romantic 9 distorted, idealized, overblown 10 farfetched,
ivory-tower, overstated, starry-eyed,
unworkable 11 exaggerated, extravagant, impractical, sensational

unreasonable
5 undue 6 absurd 7 invalid 9 arbitrary, excessive, illogical, senseless,
sophistic 10 exorbitant, fallacious,
headstrong, immoderate, inordinate,
irrational, peremptory, ridiculous
11 extravagant, incongruous, nonsensical, uncalled-for, unwarranted
12 preposterous 13 unjustifiable

unreasoned
7 invalid, unsound 9 deceptive,
illogical, sophistic, unfounded 10 fallacious, ill-founded, irrational, misleading, ungrounded 11 nonrational

unrefined
3 raw 4 rude 5 crass, crude, rough,
tacky 6 coarse, earthy, impure,
vulgar 7 natural, uncouth 9 graceless, inelegant, maladroit, roughhewn
10 uncultured, unpolished 11 ill-
mannered, uncivilized, unprocessed
12 uncultivated

unreflective
6 casual 7 offhand 8 careless,
feckless, heedless, mindless 9 imprudent, impulsive, oblivious, unheeding 10 indiscreet, nonchalant,
unthinking 11 inadvertent, perfunctory, thoughtless 13 ill-considered

unrehearsed
7 offhand 8 informal 9 extempore,
impromptu, unstudied 10 improvised, off-the-cuff, unprepared
11 extemporary, spontaneous
12 extemporized

unrelated
8 discrete, separate 9 different,
disparate 10 dissimilar, extraneous,
irrelevant 11 independent

unrelenting

3 set **4** grim **5** stern **7** adamant, endless **8** constant, resolute, ruthless, tireless **9** ceaseless, continual, hard-nosed, incessant, tenacious, unbending, unsparing **10** continuous, determined, implacable, inexorable, inflexible, persistent, unflagging, unshakable, unwavering, unyielding **12** unappeasable

unreliable

6 fickle, shifty, tricky, unsafe **7** dubious **8** fallible, slippery, two-faced **9** deceitful, deceptive, faithless, trustless, unassured, uncertain **10** capricious, fly-by-night, inaccurate, inconstant, perfidious, unfaithful **11** vacillating **12** falsehearted, questionable, unconvincing, undependable **13** irresponsible; unpredictable, untrustworthy

unremarkable

4 so-so **5** plain, usual **6** common, decent, normal **7** average, mundane, prosaic, routine, vanilla **8** adequate, everyday, familiar, habitual, mediocre, ordinary, workaday **9** customary, quotidian, tolerable **11** commonplace, nondescript **12** run-of-the-mill **13** unexceptional

unremitting

7 abiding, chronic, endless, lasting, nonstop **8** constant, enduring, unending **9** ceaseless, continual, incessant, perennial, perpetual, sustained, unceasing **10** continuous, persistent, persisting, relentless **12** interminable **13** uninterrupted

unrepentant

10 impenitent **11** remorseless **12** unregenerate

unrepresentative

7 deviant, unusual **8** aberrant, abnormal, atypical **9** anomalous, divergent, eccentric, irregular, untypical **11** exceptional, heteroclite **13** nonconforming

unreserved

4 open **5** frank, plain **6** candid **7** sincere **8** effusive, explicit, informal, outgoing, outright **9** expansive, talkative **10** definitive **11** forthcoming, openhearted, unconcealed, undisguised, unqualified, unvarnished **13** demonstrative, unconstrained

unresolved

4 moot **7** pending **8** hesitant, wavering **9** faltering, tentative, uncertain, undecided, unsettled **10** ambivalent, hesitating, indecisive, irresolute, unanswered **11** vacillating

unrespectable

3 low **5** shady **6** shabby, shoddy **8** shameful, unworthy **10** inglorious **11** disgraceful, ignominious **12** dishonorable, disreputable **13** discreditable

unresponsive

4 cold **5** aloof, stoic **6** frigid, remote, stolid **7** distant, passive **8** detached, reserved **9** inhibited, withdrawn **10** forbidding, insentient **11** insensitive, passionless, unemotional **12** uninterested **13** insusceptible, unsusceptible

unrest

6 strife, tumult **7** anarchy, anxiety, ferment, tension, turmoil **8** disorder, disquiet, distress, edginess, upheaval **9** agitation, commotion, confusion **10** inquietude, turbulence, uneasiness **11** disquietude, disturbance, instability **12** perturbation **13** Sturm und Drang

unrestrained

5 bluff, blunt, frank **6** candid, wanton **7** rampant **8** outgoing, uncurbed **9** audacious, excessive, expansive, indulgent, unbridled **10** forthright, immoderate, implacable, inordinate, ungoverned, unhampered **11** extravagant, impassioned, intemperate, overwrought, plainspoken, spontaneous, uninhibited, untrammeled **12** uncontrolled **13** demonstrative, irrepressible, overindulgent

unrestricted

4 free, full, open **9** boundless, extensive, unlimited **10** accessible, unconfined, unfettered, unhampered **11** far-reaching, unqualified, wide-ranging **12** unobstructed **13** unconditional

unripe

3 raw **5** green, young **6** callow, jejune **7** untried **8** emergent, immature, juvenile, unformed, youthful **9** unfledged, untrained **10** unprepared, unseasoned **11** undeveloped **13** inexperienced

unrivaled

4 only, sole **5** alone **6** unique **7** leading, stellar, supreme **8** champion, foremost, greatest, peerless **9** matchless, paramount, principal, unequaled, unmatched **10** inimitable, preeminent, unequalled **11** outstanding, predominant, unsurpassed **12** incomparable, transcendent, unparalleled

unroll

6 expose, extend, reveal, unfurl, unwind **7** exhibit, open out **8** disclose **9** spread out

unromantic

5 sober **8** sensible **9** practical, pragmatic, realistic **10** hard-boiled, hardheaded **11** down-to-earth, level-headed, utilitarian **12** businesslike, matter-of-fact **13** unsentimental

unruffled

4 calm, cool **6** poised, placid, serene, smooth **7** equable, unmoved **8** composed, tranquil **9** collected, unexcited **10** nonchalant, untroubled **11** unconcerned, undisturbed, unflappable **13** imperturbable, self-possessed

unruly

4 wild **5** rowdy **7** froward, naughty, raucous, wayward, willful **8** contrary, perverse, untoward **9** fractious, obstinate, turbulent **10** boisterous, disorderly, headstrong, ill-behaved, rebellious, refractory, tumultuous **11** disobedient, indomitable, intractable **12** contumacious, incorrigible, obstreperous, rambunctious, recalcitrant, ungovernable, unmanageable **13** undisciplined

unsafe

5 risky, shaky **6** chancy **7** erratic, harmful, parlous, rickety, tottery, unsound **8** insecure, perilous, slippery, unstable **9** dangerous, hazardous, uncertain **10** precarious, ramshackle, unreliable, vulnerable **11** threatening, treacherous **12** undependable

unsaid

5 known, tacit **6** silent **7** assumed, implied **8** accepted, implicit, indirect, inferred, presumed, unspoken, unstated, wordless **9** customary, unuttered **10** insinuated, undeclared, understood **11** traditional, unexpressed

unsatisfactory

3 bum **4** lame **5** amiss **8** mediocre **9** defective, deficient **10** inadequate **11** displeasing, substandard **12** unacceptable **13** disappointing

unsavory

4 rank **5** gross, shady **6** rancid **7** insipid **9** repugnant, repulsive, sickening, tasteless **10** disgusting, flavorless **11** distasteful, ill-flavored, unpalatable **12** disagreeable, unappetizing

unsay

4 lift, void **6** abjure, cancel, disown, recall, recant, revoke **7** nullify, rescind, retract, reverse, suspend **8** abnegate, abrogate, disclaim, forswear, renounce, take back, withdraw **11** countermand

unscathed

4 safe **5** sound, whole **6** intact, unhurt **8** unharmed **9** uninjured, unscarred, untouched **11** unscratched

unscented

8 odor-free, odorless

unschooled

5 naive **7** artless, natural, vacuous **8** ignorant, untaught **9** ingenuous, unstudied, untrained, untutored **10** illiterate, unaffected, uneducated, unlettered **11** empty-headed **12** unartificial, uninstructed

unscramble

5 solve, untie 6 unwind 7 clarify,
resolve, restore, sort out, unravel,
untwine 8 untangle 9 extricate
11 disentangle 12 disembarrass

unscrupulous

5 shady, venal 7 corrupt, crooked,
knavish 8 scheming, wrongful
9 deceitful, dishonest, mercenary,
shameless, underhand, unethical
11 underhanded 12 dishonorable,
exploitative, unprincipled

unseasonable

8 ill-timed, untimely 12 inconvenient

unseasoned

3 raw 4 flat 5 bland, fresh, green,
young 6 callow 7 untried 8 immature 9 credulous, tasteless,
unfledged, untrained 10 flavorless
11 unpracticed 13 inexperienced

unseat

3 axe, can 4 boot, buck, fire, oust,
sack 5 eject, pitch, purge, throw
6 depose, recall, remove 7 buck off,
dismiss, unhorse 8 dethrone, dislodge, displace 9 ostracize

unseemliness

5 gaffe 7 blunder, faux pas 8 solecism 9 barbarism, gaucherie, im-
modesty, impudence, indecency,
vulgarity 10 coarseness, imprudence, incivility, indelicacy 11 impropriety 12 indiscretion

unseemly

8 improper, untoward 9 inelegant,
unrefined 10 indecorous, indelicate,
malapropos, unbecoming, unsuitable
11 unbefitting 13 inappropriate

unseen

6 hidden 9 concealed, invisible,
unnoticed 10 overlooked, unob-
served 11 unsuspected

unsentimental

see unromantic

unserviceable

7 useless 10 inoperable, unfeasible,
unworkable 11 impractical, unrealistic 13 impracticable, nonfunctional

unsettle

3 vex 4 faze 5 spook, upset 6 bother,
flurry, jumble, rattle, ruffle 7 agitate,
disturb, fluster, perturb, trouble,
unhinge, unnerve 8 bewilder, confound, disarray, disorder, disquiet
9 discomfit 10 disarrange, discompose, disconcert 11 disorganize

unsettled

3 due 4 open 5 fluid, owing, shaky
6 mobile, queasy, shaken, uneasy,
unpaid 7 anxious, dubious, mutable,
overdue, payable, pending, restive
8 agitated, bothered, doubtful, frontier, restless, troubled, unstable,
unsteady, variable 9 disturbed,
uncertain, undecided 10 changeable, indecisive, unbalanced, unresolved 11 outstanding, problematic
12 undetermined

unsex

3 fix 4 geld, spay 5 alter 6 change,
neuter 8 castrate 9 sterilize
10 emasculate

unshackle

4 free 5 loose 6 loosen, unbind
7 manumit, release, unchain 8 liberate, unfetter 10 emancipate

unshakable

4 firm, sure 5 fixed 6 stable, steady
7 abiding, adamant, settled, staunch
8 resolute 9 steadfast, tenacious,
unbending 10 determined, persistent, unwavering, unyielding 11 unfaltering, unrelenting 12 never-failing
13 unquestioning

unshaped

5 vague 7 nascent 8 formless,
inchoate, unformed 9 amorphous,
embryonic 11 preliminary, undeveloped 13 indeterminate

unshared

4 sole 6 single, unique 7 private
8 singular 9 exclusive, undivided
10 individual 11 distinctive

unshod

8 barefoot, shoeless 9 discalced
10 barefooted

unsightly
4 ugly 5 gross 6 grisly 7 hideous
9 repulsive 10 ill-favored 12 unattractive

unskillful
5 inept 6 clumsy, gauche 7 awkward, unhandy 8 bumbling, bungling,
inexpert 9 ham-handed, incapable,
maladroit, stumbling, untrained
11 unpracticed 13 unworkmanlike

unsnarl
see **untangle**

unsociable
3 shy 4 cold, cool 5 aloof, timid
6 offish, remote, shut-in 7 distant
8 reserved, secluded, solitary 9 diffident, reclusive, unbending, withdrawn 10 unfriendly 11 introverted,
standoffish 12 inaccessible, unneighborly

unsoiled
5 clean 8 spotless 9 unspotted,
unstained, unsullied, untainted
10 immaculate 11 unblemished,
untarnished

unsophisticated
5 corny, green, naive 6 callow,
folksy, rustic, simple 7 artless,
natural, sincere, uncouth 8 gullible,
innocent 9 childlike, ingenuous,
unrefined, unworldly

unsorted
5 mixed 6 divers, motley, sundry,
varied 7 diverse, jumbled, mingled
8 ungraded 9 disparate, scrambled,
unmatched, unrefined 10 variegated
11 diversified 12 multifarious 13 heterogeneous, miscellaneous

unsought
7 unasked, willing 8 unbidden,
unwanted 9 undesired, uninvited,
unwelcome, voluntary 10 gratuitous,
unprompted 11 spontaneous, unrequested, unsolicited

unsound
3 mad 4 weak 5 false, frail, shaky,
wrong 6 faulty, flawed, flimsy, infirm,
insane, sickly, untrue, weakly

7 cracked, damaged, fragile, invalid
8 decrepit, demented, deranged,
specious 9 defective, erroneous,
imperfect, incorrect, unhealthy
13 insubstantial

unsparing
5 ample, harsh, stern, tough 6 lavish,
severe, strict 7 copious, liberal,
onerous, profuse 8 abundant, exacting, generous, prolific, rigorous,
ruthless 9 bounteous, bountiful,
demanding, plenteous 10 freehanded, munificent, openhanded,
unmerciful 11 magnanimous

unspeakable
4 dire, evil 5 awful 6 grisly 7 beastly,
ghastly, hateful, heinous, hideous
8 dreadful, ghoulish, gruesome,
horrific, shocking 9 appalling, atrocious, execrable, frightful, loathsome,
monstrous, obnoxious, repugnant,
repulsive, revolting 10 abominable,
detestable, disgusting, horrendous,
outrageous, scandalous 11 unutterable 13 inexpressible

unspoiled
5 ideal 6 intact, virgin 7 halcyon,
idyllic, perfect, untamed 8 arcadian,
pastoral, pristine, virginal 9 idealized,
undamaged, undefiled, untouched
10 unimpaired 11 unblemished,
uncorrupted

unspoken
4 mute 5 tacit 6 hinted, silent, unsaid 7 assumed, implied 8 implicit,
inferred, presumed, unstated, wordless 9 intimated, suggested, unuttered 10 undeclared, understood
11 unexpressed

unstable
5 fluid, shaky 6 fickle, shifty, tricky,
wobbly 7 dubious, protean, rickety,
suspect 8 insecure, rootless, slippery,
ticklish, unsteady, variable, volatile,
wavering 9 ambiguous, changeful,
fluctuant, irregular, mercurial, teetering, uncertain, unsettled 10 capricious, inconstant, precarious
11 vacillating 13 temperamental,
unpredictable

unstated

5 tacit 6 latent, unsaid 7 assumed,
implied 8 implicit 10 understood

unsteady

5 rocky, shaky, tippy 6 uneven,
wobbly 7 erratic, mutable, rickety,
varying 8 shifting, unstable, variable
9 changeful, irregular, tottering
10 changeable, inconstant
British: 5 wonky

unstudied

5 naive 6 casual, improv, simple
7 artless, natural, offhand 8 careless, informal, unforced, unversed
9 extempore, guileless, impromptu,
ingenuous, makeshift, unlabored,
unlearned, unplanned, untutored
10 improvised, nonchalant, unaffected, unpolished, unschooled
11 extemporary, spontaneous,
uncontrived, unrehearsed 13 im-
provisatory

unstylish

4 drab, dull 5 dated, dowdy, fusty,
passé, ratty, tacky 6 démodé,
frumpy, old-hat, shabby, stodgy
7 vintage 8 outdated, outmoded
9 inelegant, moth-eaten, out-of-date
10 antiquated, oldfangled 12 old-
fashioned 13 unfashionable

unsubstantial

4 thin 5 frail, shaky 6 feeble, flimsy,
infirm 7 fragile, shadowy, tenuous, unsound 8 ethereal, illusory
9 dreamlike, imaginary, spiritual,
unearthly 10 immaterial, impalpable,
intangible 11 implausible, incorporeal, nonmaterial, nonphysical
12 metaphysical

unsuitable

5 inapt, undue, unfit 7 awkward,
jarring 8 ill-timed, improper, unfitted,
unseemly, untimely 9 ill-suited
10 ill-adapted, inadequate, inapposite, malapropos, mismatched,
unbecoming 11 inadvisable, inopportune, unbefitting, unqualified
12 incompatible, infelicitous, unacceptable, unseasonable 13 inappropriate

unsullied

4 pure 5 clean 6 chaste 8 flawless,
spotless, unsoiled 9 blameless,
exemplary, guiltless, stainless, taint-
less, undefiled 10 immaculate
11 unblemished, untarnished

unsure

5 dicey, shaky 6 wobbly 7 dubious,
unclear 8 doubtful, insecure, unstable, wavering 9 fluctuant, skeptical,
uncertain, undecided 10 ambivalent,
indecisive, irresolute, unreliable
11 unconvinced, vacillating 12 questionable, undependable 13 indeterminate, untrustworthy

unsurpassable

7 supreme 8 ultimate 9 matchless 10 consummate, preeminent
12 transcendent

unsusceptible

6 immune, inured 8 hardened
9 impassive, resistant 10 impervious
11 insensitive 12 invulnerable,
unresponsive

unsuspecting

5 naive 6 unwary 8 gullible, trustful,
trusting 9 confiding, credulous,
imprudent 10 incautious

unswerving

see **unfaltering**

unsympathetic

4 cold, cool 5 chill, stony 6 averse
7 callous, haughty, unmoved 8 detached, lukewarm 9 apathetic,
unfeeling, unpitying 10 disdainful,
hard-boiled 11 coldhearted, hard-
hearted, indifferent, insensitive,
unconcerned, uncongenial 12 contemptuous, stonyhearted, unresponsive 13 disinterested

untactful

4 flip, rash, rude 5 brash, nervy
6 brazen 8 flippant, insolent 9 audacious, impolitic, imprudent, maladroit 10 indiscreet 11 impertinent,
thoughtless 12 presumptuous,
undiplomatic

untamed

4 wild 5 brute, feral 6 carnal, fierce,

savage **7** bestial, brutish **8** barbaric
9 primitive **11** uncivilized

untangle
5 solve **7** clear up, explain, resolve,
unravel, unsnarl, untwine, untwist
9 elucidate, extricate, interpret
10 disembroil, disentwine, straighten,
unscramble **11** disencumber **12** disembarrass

untaught
5 naive **7** natural **8** ignorant, nescient **9** intuitive, untrained, untutored **10** uneducated, unlettered,
unschooled **11** empty-headed,
instinctive, instinctual, spontaneous
12 uncultivated, uninstructed

untempered
6 wanton **7** extreme **9** excessive
10 gratuitous, immoderate, inordinate
11 extravagant **12** unrestrained

untenable
5 wrong **6** faulty, flimsy **10** inadequate **12** indefensible

untended
5 seedy **7** rickety, run-down **8** decrepit, derelict, deserted, forsaken,
tattered **9** neglected **10** ramshackle,
tumbledown, uncared-for **11** dilapidated

Unter den _____
6 Linden

untested
6 intact, unused **7** untried **8** unproved, unproven **11** unpracticed

unthinkable
10 impossible, incredible, outlandish
12 preposterous, unimaginable
13 extraordinary, inconceivable,
unprecedented

unthinking
8 careless, feckless, habitual, heedless, knee-jerk, uncaring **9** automatic, reflexive, unheeding, unmindful **10** distracted, unintended
11 inattentive, inadvertent, instinctive, instinctual, involuntary, perfunctory, spontaneous, thoughtless
12 unreflective

unthrifty
6 lavish, wanton **7** ruinous **8** prodigal, wasteful **9** imprudent **10** profligate **11** extravagant, improvident
12 uneconomical

untidy
5 messy **6** sloppy **7** chaotic, jumbled, unkempt **8** confused, littered,
slapdash, slipshod, slovenly **9** cluttered **10** disheveled, disordered,
disorderly, topsy-turvy **11** disarranged, dishevelled **12** disorganized, unsystematic

untie
5 let go **6** loosen, unbind, unknot,
unlace, unlash **7** release, resolve,
set free **8** unstring **9** extricate
11 disencumber, disentangle **12** disembarrass

until
4 up to **6** before **7** prior to **11** in
advance of

untimely
5 early, undue **9** premature **10** malapropos **11** ill-seasoned, inopportune **12** unseasonable **13** inappropriate

untiring
7 devoted, patient **8** diligent, enduring **9** assiduous, ceaseless, dedicated, energetic, unceasing **10** determined, persistent, unflagging,
unwavering, unwearying **11** persevering, unfaltering **13** indefatigable, inexhaustible

untold
4 huge, vast **7** immense **8** enormous,
gigantic **9** countless **10** prodigious
11 innumerable, uncountable **12** incalculable **13** indescribable

untouchable
5 leper **6** pariah **7** outcast **8** outcaste

untouched
4 pure **5** sound, whole **6** intact,
virgin **7** unmoved **8** flawless, pristine, unharmed, unmarred, untapped,
virginal **9** undamaged, unspoiled
10 unaffected **11** unblemished,
unconcerned, unimpressed

untoward

6 unruly **7** adverse, awkward, froward, ungodly, unhappy, unlucky **8** ill-fated, improper, indecent, luckless, unseemly **9** fractious, unfitting, vexatious **10** ill-starred, indecorous, indelicate, refractory, unbecoming **11** detrimental, intractable, starcrossed, troublesome, unfortunate **12** inconvenient, recalcitrant, ungovernable, unmanageable, unpropitious

untrained

see **unskilled**

untrammeled

8 uncurbed **9** unimpeded **10** unconfined, unfettered, ungoverned, unhampered **11** uninhibited **12** unobstructed, unrestrained, unrestricted

untried

3 raw **5** fresh, green **6** callow, rookie **8** unproved, untested **10** innovative, pioneering, unseasoned **11** unpracticed **13** inexperienced, unprecedented

untroubled

4 calm **5** still **6** blithe, placid, serene **7** halcyon **8** carefree, composed, peaceful, tranquil **9** easygoing, unruffled **10** insouciant, nonchalant **11** unconcerned, unperturbed **12** lighthearted

untrue

4 fake **5** false, wrong **7** inexact **8** disloyal, specious **9** erroneous, faithless, imprecise, incorrect **10** fictitious, inaccurate, unfaithful
combining form: 5 pseud **6** pseudo

untrustworthy

5 shady **6** shifty, unsafe, unsure **7** devious, dubious **8** disloyal, slippery, two-faced **9** deceptive, negligent, two-timing **10** fly-by-night, unreliable **11** duplicitous **12** questionable, undependable **13** doubledealing, irresponsible

untruth

3 fib, lie **4** sham **5** error **6** canard, deceit **7** blarney, fallacy, falsity, fiction, hogwash **9** deception, duplicity, falsehood, falseness, hypocrisy, mendacity **11** fabrication, insincerity **12** misstatement **13** prevarication

untruthful

4 sham **5** bogus, false, lying, phony **7** knavish **8** specious **9** deceitful, dishonest, erroneous, incorrect **10** fictitious, inaccurate, mendacious

untutored

see **unschooled**

unusable

7 outworn, useless **8** obsolete **9** worthless **10** inoperable, unavailing, unworkable **11** impractical, unrealistic **12** inapplicable **13** nonfunctional

unused

3 new **4** idle **5** fresh **6** excess **7** dormant, surplus **8** leftover, residual **9** untouched

unusual

3 odd **4** rare **6** quaint, unique **7** bizarre, curious, special, strange **8** aberrant, abnormal, peculiar, singular, uncommon, atypical, unwonted **9** anomalous, different, eccentric, irregular **11** exceptional **13** extraordinary

unusually

4 very **5** extra **6** rarely, seldom **8** markedly **9** curiously, extremely, strangely **10** abnormally, especially, peculiarly, remarkably, strikingly, uncommonly **11** exceedingly **12** infrequently, particularly

unutterable

5 taboo **7** awesome **9** ineffable **11** unspeakable **13** indescribable, inexpressible

unvaried

4 like, same **5** alike **7** uniform **9** identical **10** consistent, unchanging **11** undeviating

unvarnished

see **undisguised**

unvarying
see **unchanging**

unveil
see **uncover**

unversed
3 raw 5 fresh, green 6 callow
7 untried 8 inexpert 9 unfledged
10 unfamiliar, unseasoned 11 uninitiated, unpracticed 12 unaccustomed 13 inexperienced

unwanted
see **unwelcome**

unwarranted
5 undue 8 baseless 9 misguided,
unfounded 10 gratuitous, groundless, immoderate, unprovoked
11 extravagant, inexcusable, injudicious, uncalled-for, unjustified
12 indefensible, unreasonable
13 insupportable, unjustifiable,
unsupportable

unwary
5 brash, hasty 8 careless, gullible,
heedless, reckless 9 credulous,
impetuous, imprudent, unguarded
10 ill-advised, incautious, indiscreet
11 thoughtless 12 unsuspecting

unwavering
see **unfaltering**

unwelcome
7 unasked 8 unsought, unwanted
9 undesired, uninvited 11 undesirable 12 unacceptable 13 objectionable

unwell
3 ill 4 sick 5 frail, shaky 6 ailing,
feeble, infirm, offish, peaked, queasy,
sickly, wobbly 8 diseased, stricken
9 afflicted, enfeebled, unhealthy
10 indisposed 11 debilitated

unwholesome
4 foul 5 toxic 6 sickly 7 adverse,
baneful, corrupt, harmful, immoral,
noisome, noxious, obscene, ruinous,
unsound 8 diseased 9 injurious,
loathsome, offensive, unhealthy
10 disgusting, pernicious, subversive
11 deleterious, detrimental, unhealthful 12 insalubrious

unwieldy
5 bulky 7 awkward, massive 8 cumbrous 9 ponderous 10 burdensome, cumbersome 12 unmanageable

unwilling
5 loath 6 averse 8 grudging, hesitant 9 obstinate, reluctant 10 indisposed 11 disinclined

unwind
4 rest, undo 5 let go, relax 6 loosen,
unbend, uncoil, unfold, unreel, unroll
7 ease off, slacken, unravel 8 calm
down, kick back, loosen up

unwise
4 rash 5 silly 6 stupid 7 asinine,
fatuous, foolish, idiotic, witless
8 reckless 9 brainless, foolhardy,
ill-judged, imbecilic, impolitic, imprudent, ludicrous, misguided, senseless 10 ill-advised, indiscreet,
ridiculous 11 impractical, injudicious,
thoughtless, undesirable, unfortunate
13 unintelligent

unwitting
6 chance 7 unaware 8 ignorant,
innocent 9 haphazard, oblivious,
unknowing, unmindful, unplanned
10 unfamiliar, uninformed, unintended 11 inadvertent 12 unacquainted

unwonted
4 rare 6 signal, unique 7 notable, unusual 8 singular, uncommon 10 remarkable, unexpected
11 exceptional 12 unaccustomed
13 extraordinary

unworkable
7 useless 8 quixotic 9 half-baked
10 impossible, infeasible, inoperable,
unfeasible 11 impractical, unrealistic
12 inapplicable 13 impracticable,
nonfunctional

unworldly
5 naive 6 astral, dreamy, simple
7 artless, natural 8 ethereal, innocent, trusting 9 celestial, ingenuous,
spiritual, unearthly, visionary 11 impractical 13 inexperienced

unworthy

6 no-good 7 ignoble 8 shameful, unseemly 9 no-account, unmerited, worthless 10 unbecoming 11 disgraceful, inexcusable, undeserving

unwrap

see **uncover**

unwritten

4 oral 5 blank, tacit 6 latent, spoken, verbal 7 assumed 8 accepted, implicit 10 understood 11 traditional, word-of-mouth 12 conventional

unyielding

4 firm, grim, hard 5 fixed, rigid, stern, stiff, tough 6 dogged, mulish 7 adamant 8 hard-core, obdurate, stubborn 9 hard-nosed, insistent, obstinate, pigheaded, steadfast, unbending 10 determined, headstrong, implacable, inexorable, inflexible, persistent, relentless 11 intractable, unrelenting 12 pertinacious, single-minded, unappeasable

up

4 hike, jump, lift, rise 5 above, ahead, arise, boost, built, mount, raise, risen 6 ascend, arisen, lifted, versed 7 abreast, promote 8 familiar, increase, informed, positive 9 au courant, northward 10 acquainted, conversant
prefix: 3 ana, sur

up-and-coming

7 go-ahead, hot-shot 8 aspiring 9 promising 11 presumptive, prospective 12 enterprising

upbeat

4 rosy 6 cheery 7 buoyant, hopeful 8 cheerful, positive, sanguine 9 confident, expectant, promising 10 heartening, optimistic 12 Pollyannaish

upbraid

4 lash, rate 5 chide, scold 6 berate, rail at, rebuke, revile, scorch 7 bawl out, censure, chasten, chew out, reprove, scourge, tell off 8 admonish, chastise, reproach 9 castigate, criticize, dress down, reprimand 10 tongue-lash, vituperate

upbringing

7 nurture, rearing 8 training 9 schooling

upchuck

4 barf, hurl, puke, spew 5 heave, retch, vomit 6 spit up 7 bring up, throw up 8 disgorge 11 regurgitate

upcoming

7 looming, nearing, pending 8 expected, foreseen, imminent 9 advancing, impending, onrushing 11 anticipated, approaching, forthcoming, prospective

up-country

4 bush 6 inland, sticks, upland 7 outback 8 backland, frontier, interior, outlying, woodland 9 backwater, backwoods, boondocks 10 hinterland, timberland

update

5 amend, brief, renew 6 inform, revamp, revise, revive 7 apprise, enhance, improve, refresh, restore, rundown, upgrade 8 renovate 9 modernize, refurbish 10 rejuvenate

upend

4 beat, best, drub, flip, lick, skin, trim, whip 5 cream, crush, upset 6 invert, subdue, thrash, topple, unseat, wallop 7 capsize, clobber, conquer, overrun, shellac, trounce 8 dethrone, lambaste, overcome, overturn, vanquish 9 overpower, overwhelm, subjugate

upgrade

4 hike, rise 5 boost, raise 6 prefer 7 advance, elevate, enhance, improve, promote 8 increase 9 promotion 10 betterment 11 advancement, improvement 12 breakthrough

upheaval

6 clamor, outcry, tumult, upturn 7 ferment, turmoil 8 churning, disaster, disorder 9 cataclysm, commotion 10 alteration, convulsion, disruption 11 catastrophe

uphill

4 hard 6 rising, rugged, taxing 7 arduous, labored, operose, tedious

8 climbing, grueling, toilsome **9** ascending, difficult, effortful, gruelling, laborious, punishing, strenuous, wearisome

uphold
3 aid **4** back, help, lift, prop **5** brace, carry, hoist, raise **6** assist, back up, bear up, buoy up, defend, second **7** bolster, elevate, justify, shore up, support, sustain **8** advocate, backstop, buttress, champion, maintain, side with **9** vindicate

upkeep
4 cost **7** expense **8** overhead **11** expenditure, maintenance

upland
4 mesa **5** table **7** plateau

uplift
4 buoy **5** cheer, hoist, raise **6** take up **7** animate, elevate, enliven, gladden, hearten **8** brighten, embolden, inspirit **9** encourage **10** exhilarate, strengthen

upon
4 atop
prefix: 3 epi

upper class
4 rank **5** elite **6** gentry **7** peerage, quality, society, who's who **8** affluent, nobility, noblesse, well-to-do **9** blue blood, gentility, haut monde **10** patricians, patriciate **11** aristocracy **13** carriage trade, Establishment

upper hand
4 edge, sway **5** leg up **7** control, mastery **8** leverage **9** advantage, dominance **10** ascendancy **11** superiority **12** predominance

uppermost
3 top **6** apical **7** highest **8** loftiest

uppity
4 smug **5** aloof, brash **6** lordly, sniffy, snippy, snooty, snotty **7** forward, haughty, pompous **8** arrogant, cavalier **9** conceited, egotistic, imperious, know-it-all, presuming **10** disdainful, high-handed **11** overweening, pretentious **12** contemptuous, presumptuous, supercilious **13** self-asserting, self-assertive, self-important

upright
4 fair, good, just, pure, true **5** erect, moral, noble, piano **6** honest, raised **7** correct, ethical **8** elevated, goalpost, standing, vertical, virtuous **9** equitable, exemplary, honorable, impartial **10** principled, scrupulous **13** conscientious, perpendicular

uprightness
5 honor **6** repute, virtue **7** honesty, probity **8** morality, nobility **9** character, integrity, rectitude **13** righteousness

uprising
4 riot **6** mutiny, revolt **8** upheaval **9** rebellion **10** insurgence, revolution **12** insurrection

uproar
3 din, row **4** coil, fuss, to-do, riot **5** babel, brawl, broil, chaos, furor, hoo-ha, melee, whirl **6** bedlam, clamor, fracas, furore, hassle, hubbub, mayhem, pother, racket, ruckus, rumpus, shindy, tumult **7** shindig, turmoil **8** brouhaha, disorder, foofaraw **9** commotion, confusion **10** hullabaloo, hurly-burly, turbulence **11** pandemonium

uproarious
5 noisy, rowdy **7** comical, rackety, raucous, riotous **8** brawling, clattery, mirthful, strident **9** clamorous, hilarious **10** clangorous, hysterical, resounding, rollicking, tumultuous **12** obstreperous **13** sidesplitting

uproot
4 grub, move, weed **8** displace, overturn, supplant **9** eradicate, extirpate, overthrow, supersede **10** annihilate, transplant **11** exterminate

upset
3 ail, ill **5** worry **6** bother, defeat, dismay, invert, jumble, muddle, topple, tumble **7** afflict, agitate, capsize, disturb, fluster, invalid,

jittery, jumbled, muddled, perturb,
rattled, reverse, tip over, toppled,
trouble, unnerve, worried **8** agitated,
bewilder, bothered, confound, confused, disarray, dismayed, disorder,
distress, overturn, troubled, turn over,
unnerved **9** afflicted, confusion,
disturbed, flustered, knock over,
overthrow, perturbed **10** bewildered,
confounded, disconcert, disordered,
distracted, distressed, indisposed,
invalidate, overthrown, overturned,
tipped over **11** overwrought **12** apprehensive, disconcerted

upshot
5 issue **6** burden, climax, effect,
ending, finish, result **7** outcome,
purport **9** substance **10** conclusion,
denouement **11** consequence,
culmination, termination **12** significance

upside-down
7 chaotic, haywire, jumbled **8** backward, confused, inverted, pell-mell,
reversed **10** disordered, overturned,
topsy-turvy **13** helter-skelter

upstanding
see **upright**

upstart
5 comer **7** parvenu **8** outsider
9 arriviste, pretender **12** nouveau
riche **13** social climber

upsurge
4 gain, jump, rise, wave **5** boost,
spurt **6** growth **7** advance **8** increase

uptight
4 edgy **5** riled, tense **6** uneasy
7 anxious, nervous, restive, worried

up to
4 till **5** until **6** before **11** in advance of

up-to-date
6 modern, modish, timely, trendy
7 abreast, à la mode, current, stylish
8 advanced, brand-new, contempo
9 au courant **10** avant-garde **11** cutting-edge, fashionable **12** contemporary **13** state-of-the-art

upturn
4 jump, rise **6** growth **8** increase
11 improvement

Urania
see **Muse**

Uranus
6 planet
mother, wife: 4 Gaea
offspring: 6 Titans **8** Cyclopes
overthrower, son: 6 Cronus

urban
9 municipal **12** metropolitan

urbane
5 suave **6** poised, smooth **7** elegant, genteel, politic, refined **8** cultured, debonair, gracious, polished
9 civilized, distingué **10** cultivated,
diplomatic **12** cosmopolitan **13** sophisticated

urbanize
6 citify

urchin
3 imp **4** brat **5** child, gamin, scamp
10 ragamuffin

Urdur
see **Norn**

urge
3 egg, sic, yen **4** coax, goad, itch,
lust, prod, push, spur, wish **5** drive,
egg on, impel, press, prick, set on,
tar on **6** adjure, cajole, compel,
demand, desire, exhort, incite, induce, needle, prompt, propel **7** beseech, conjure, craving, entreat,
implore, impulse, inspire, longing,
passion, promote, propose, provoke,
solicit, wheedle **8** advocate, appetite, blandish, pressure, yearning
9 encourage, instigate, stimulate
12 high-pressure

urgency
6 duress, stress **8** exigence, exigency, pressure **9** necessity **10** compulsion, insistence

urgent
5 vital **6** crying **7** burning, clamant,
crucial, driving, exigent, instant,

present **8** critical, pressing **9** clamorous, demanding, immediate, impelling, insistent, momentous **10** compelling, imperative **11** importunate

Uriel
9 archangel

Uris novel
3 Haj (The) **5** QB VII **6** Exodus **7** Trinity **9** Battle Cry, Mitla Pass **10** Angry Hills (The), Redemption

urn
4 vase **6** vessel **7** samovar
Greek: 7 amphora

Ursa Major
9 Great Bear **11** Great Dipper

Ursa Minor
10 Little Bear **12** Little Dipper
star: 7 Polaris **8** polestar **9** North Star

Uruguay
capital: 10 Montevideo
language: 7 Spanish
monetary unit: 4 peso
neighbor: 6 Brazil **9** Argentina
river: 7 La Plata **8** Río Negro

usable
6 liquid **7** running, working **9** adaptable, available, operative **10** accessible, applicable, employable, expendable, functional, marketable, negotiable **11** exploitable, operational, serviceable

usage
3 way **4** form, mode, wont **5** habit, sense **6** action, amount, custom, manner, method, praxis **7** process **8** habitude, practice **9** formality, procedure **10** convention

use
3 ply **4** wont, work **5** apply, avail, habit, serve, treat, value, wield, worth **6** custom, demand, employ, handle, liking, manage, manner **7** benefit, exploit, operate, purpose, service, utility, utilize **8** deal with, exercise, exertion, function, impose on, occasion, practice, regulate **9** advantage,

habituate, objective, relevance **10** employment, manipulate **11** application

used
8 pre-owned, shopworn **10** secondhand

used up
5 all in, spent **6** bleary, effete, sapped, wasted **7** drained, emptied, far-gone, worn-out **8** consumed, depleted **9** exhausted, washed-out

useful
3 fit **4** meet **5** handy, utile **7** helpful **8** fruitful, suitable, valuable **9** favorable, practical **10** beneficial, convenient, functional, productive, profitable, propitious, worthwhile **11** appropriate, practicable, serviceable, utilitarian **12** advantageous

usefulness
5 value, worth **7** fitness, service, utility **8** function **9** advantage, relevance, substance **10** expedience, expediency **12** practicality **13** applicability

useless
4 idle, vain **5** inept **6** futile **7** inutile **8** bootless, hopeless, unusable **9** fruitless, pointless, worthless **10** unavailing, unworkable **11** impractical, ineffective, ineffectual, inoperative **12** unproductive, unprofitable **13** impracticable, nonfunctional

user
5 buyer **6** addict **8** consumer, customer, utilizer

use up
5 drain, spend **6** devour, expend **7** consume, deplete, exhaust **8** draw down **10** run through

usher
4 lead, seat **5** guide **6** escort **7** conduct, precede **9** conductor **10** doorkeeper

usher in
5 begin, greet, start **6** launch **7** kick off, trumpet, welcome **8** announce,

commence, initiate, proclaim **9** institute, introduce, originate **10** inaugurate

usual

5 stock, typic **6** common, kosher, normal, wonted **7** average, regular, routine, typical, vanilla **8** accepted, everyday, expected, familiar, habitual, ordinary, orthodox, standard, workaday **9** customary, prevalent, quotidian **10** accustomed, prevailing **11** commonplace, established **12** conventional, unremarkable

usually

6 mainly, mostly **7** as a rule **8** commonly, normally **9** generally, routinely **10** habitually, ordinarily **11** customarily

usurer

7 Shylock **9** loan shark **11** moneylender

usurp

5 wrest **6** assume **7** preempt **8** arrogate, displace, supplant **10** commandeer **11** appropriate

Utah

capital: 12 Salt Lake City
city: 4 Orem **5** Ogden, Provo
college, university: 12 Brigham Young
lake: 6 Powell **9** Great Salt
motto: 8 Industry
mountain: 5 Kings (Peak)
nickname: 7 Beehive (State)
park: 4 Zion **5** Bryce **6** Arches **11** Canyonlands
river: 5 Green **6** Sevier
state bird: 14 California gull
state flower: 8 sego lily
state tree: 10 blue spruce

utensil

3 pan, pot **4** fork, tool **5** knife, spoon **6** device, vessel **8** saucepan, teaspoon **9** implement **10** instrument

uterus

4 womb

Uther Pendragon

son: 6 Arthur
wife: 6 Ygerne **7** Igraine

utile

5 handy **6** useful **7** working **9** available, operative, practical **10** accessible, convenient, dependable, functional **11** practicable, serviceable

utilitarian

6 useful **9** practical, pragmatic **10** functional
philosopher: 4 Mill (John Stuart) **7** Bentham (Jeremy)

utility

3 use **7** benefit, fitness, service **8** function **9** advantage, relevance **10** efficiency, usefulness **12** practicality **13** applicability

utilize

3 use **5** apply, spend **6** bestow, deploy, employ, handle, occupy **7** exploit **8** exercise **11** appropriate

utmost

3 top **4** acme, apex, best, peak **6** height, zenith **7** extreme, highest, maximal, maximum, supreme **8** farthest, furthest, greatest, pinnacle, remotest, ultimate **9** damnedest, extremity

utopia

4 Eden, Zion **5** bliss **6** heaven **7** Elysium **8** paradise **9** Cockaigne, dreamland, Shangri-la **10** dreamworld **12** promised land **13** Elysian fields

Utopia author

4 More (Thomas)

utopian

5 ideal, lofty **6** edenic **7** dreamer **8** arcadian, fanciful, idealist, quixotic **9** grandiose, ideologue, visionary **10** chimerical, idealistic, impossible, millennial, unfeasible **11** impractical **12** otherworldly **13** castle-builder, impracticable

utter

3 say **4** damn, dang, darn, rank, talk, tell **5** sheer, speak, stark, state, total, voice **6** arrant, dashed, deuced, reveal **7** blasted, blessed, declare, deliver, divulge, flat-out **8** absolute, bring out, complete, crashing, dis-

close, infernal, outright, positive,
throw out **9** downright, out-and-out,
pronounce, verbalize **10** confounded,
consummate **11** come out with,
straight-out, unmitigated, unqualified
13 thoroughgoing

utterance

4 rant, vent, word **5** voice **6** speech
7 oration **8** delivery, speaking
9 assertion, discourse, statement
10 expression, revelation **11** declaration **12** announcement, articulation **13** pronouncement, verbalization

utterly

4 just **5** plumb, quite **6** in toto
7 totally **8** entirely **9** perfectly
10 absolutely, altogether, completely,
thoroughly

uttermost

4 last **5** final **7** extreme, outmost
8 farthest, furthest, remotest

Utu

see **Shamash**

Uzbekistan

capital: 8 Tashkent
city: 7 Bokhara, Bukhara **9** Samarkand, Samarqand
desert: 8 Kyzyl Kum
enclave: 10 Karakalpak
monetary unit: 3 sum
neighbor: 9 Kazakstan **10** Kazakhstan, Kyrgyzstan, Tajikistan **11** Afghanistan **12** Turkmenistan
river: 8 Amu Dar'ya, Syr Dar'ya
9 Zeravshan
sea: 4 Aral

V

vacancy
4 void 6 vacuum 7 opening 8 idleness 9 blankness, emptiness

vacant
4 bare, free, idle, open, void 5 blank, clear, empty, inane, stark 6 unused 7 deadpan, vacuous 8 deserted, unfilled 9 abandoned, impassive 10 tenantless, unoccupied 11 empty-headed 12 inexpressive

vacate
4 quit, void 5 annul, clear, empty, leave 6 bow out, give up, repeal, revoke 7 abandon, rescind, retract, reverse 8 abrogate, check out, dissolve, evacuate 9 discharge 10 relinquish

vacation
4 rest, trip 5 break, leave 6 recess 7 holiday, leisure, respite, time off 8 furlough, interval 10 sabbatical 12 intermission

vacationer
7 tourist, tripper 9 weekender 10 rubberneck 12 holidaymaker

vaccination
4 shot 7 booster 9 injection 11 inoculation

vaccine
4 shot 5 serum 9 antiserum 11 preparation
Inventor: 6 Jenner (Edward)

vacillate
4 sway, yo-yo 5 waver 6 dither, falter, teeter, waggle 7 swither, whiffle 8 hesitate 9 alternate, fluctuate, oscillate 10 equivocate 12 shilly-shally

vacillating
4 weak 6 fickle, unsure, wobbly 8 hesitant, shifting, unstable, unsteady 9 fluctuant, tentative, uncertain, undecided, unsettled 10 changeable, inconstant, indecisive, irresolute 12 shilly-shally

vacillation
5 doubt 8 to-and-fro, wavering 9 hesitancy 10 fickleness, indecision 12 irresolution, shilly-shally

vacuity
4 hole, void 6 cavity, hollow, vacuum 7 inanity 9 black hole, blankness, ditsiness, ditziness, emptiness, stupidity 10 hollowness 11 nothingness

vacuous
4 idle, void 5 blank, empty, inane, silly 6 stupid, vacant 7 foolish, shallow 11 birdbrained, empty-headed, superficial

vacuum
4 void 5 space 7 suction 9 emptiness 11 nothingness
bottle: 5 dewar 7 thermos

vacuum tube
5 diode 6 triode 7 tetrode
casing: 4 bulb

vade mecum
5 guide 6 manual 8 Baedeker, handbook 9 guidebook 11 enchiridion

_____ Vadis
3 Quo

vagabond
3 bum 4 hobo 5 gypsy, idler, rogue,

rover, tramp **6** picaro, roamer
7 drifter, migrant, nomadic, vagrant,
wastrel **8** bohemian, clochard,
picaroon, runabout, runagate, traveler, wanderer **9** itinerant, transient,
wandering **11** peripatetic

vagarious

6 fickle **7** erratic, flighty, mutable,
wayward **8** unstable, volatile **9** impulsive, mercurial, whimsical **10** capricious, inconstant **13** unpredictable

vagary

3 bee **4** whim **5** crank, fancy, freak,
humor, quirk **6** megrim, whimsy
7 caprice, fantasy **8** crotchet

vagrancy

6 roving **7** roaming **8** drifting, no-
madism, rambling **9** wandering
10 itinerancy

vagrant

see **vagabond**

vague

3 dim **4** hazy **5** blear, faint, foggy,
fuzzy, gauzy, misty, muddy, woozy
6 bleary, blurry, cloudy, dreamy,
slight, vacant **7** inexact, obscure,
shadowy, unclear **8** confused,
nebulous, vaporous **9** ambiguous,
dreamlike, enigmatic, imprecise, uncertain **10** diaphanous, indefinite, indistinct **13** indeterminate, unsubstantial

vain

4 idle **5** empty, proud **6** futile,
hollow, otiose **7** foppish, haughty,
stuck-up, trivial, useless **8** abortive,
arrogant, boastful, bootless, nugatory
9 conceited, fruitless, valueless,
worthless **10** egocentric, profitless,
sophomoric, unavailing **11** egotistical, ineffective, ineffectual **12** narcissistic, unproductive, unprofitable,
unsuccessful **13** self-important

vainglorious

8 arrogant, boastful, bragging,
puffed-up, vaunting **9** conceited,
egotistic **10** swaggering **11** egotistical **12** supercilious

vainglory

4 pomp **5** pride **6** egoism, vanity
7 conceit, egotism **9** arrogance
10 pretension **11** haughtiness
12 boastfulness

valance

5 drape **6** pelmet **7** curtain, drapery
10 lambrequin

vale

4 dale, dell, glen **5** combe **6** dingle,
hollow, valley

valediction

5 adieu **7** good-bye **8** farewell
11 leave-taking

valedictory

see **valediction**

valentine

4 card, dear, love **7** beloved, darling,
tribute **10** sweetheart

valet

7 servant **9** attendant **10** manservant

valiant

4 bold **5** brave **6** heroic, plucky
7 doughty, gallant, valiant **8** fearless,
intrepid **10** chivalrous, courageous
11 lionhearted **12** greathearted,
stouthearted

valid

4 just, true **5** legal, solid, sound
6 cogent, lawful, potent, proven
7 binding, in force, logical, telling
8 attested, bona fide, credible,
forceful **9** effective, effectual, operative **10** acceptable, compelling,
convincing, legitimate, persuasive
11 justifiable, trustworthy **12** well-
grounded

validate

5 prove **6** affirm, ratify, verify **7** approve, bear out, certify, confirm,
endorse, justify, probate **8** legalize,
sanction **10** legitimate, legitimize
11 corroborate, rubber-stamp **12** authenticate, substantiate

validity

5 force, proof **7** cogency, potency
8 efficacy **9** soundness **10** lawfulness **13** effectiveness

valise

3 bag 4 grip 6 kit bag, suiter
7 handbag, Pullman 8 gripsack,
suitcase 9 gladstone, two-suiter
10 weekend bag 11 portmanteau
12 overnight bag, traveling bag
13 traveling case

Valjean's pursuer

6 Javert

Valkyrie

6 maiden 8 Brynhild

valley

4 dale, dell, glen, vale, wadi 5 basin,
combe, gulch, gully, swale 6 canyon,
dingle, hollow, ravine 10 depression
Africa-Asia: 4 Rift 9 Great Rift
Alps: 11 Grindelwald
ancient Greece: 5 Nemea
Asia: 7 Fergana
California: 4 Napa 5 Death, Squaw
7 Central 8 Imperial, Yosemite
11 San Fernando
Dead Sea area: 6 Arabah
Dominican Republic: 5 Cibao
Egypt: 6 Kharga
England: 5 Doone
Germany: 4 Ruhr
Greece: 5 Tembi, Tempe
India: 4 Kulu 7 Kashmir (Vale of)
Ireland: 5 Avoca, Ovoca
Israel: 4 Elah
Lebanon: 4 Biqa 5 Bekaa
moon: 4 rill 5 rille
New York: 12 Sleepy Hollow
Pennsylvania: 7 Nittany
Scotland: 7 Glen Roy
Switzerland: 5 Hasli 8 Engadine
11 Grindelwald
Virginia: 10 Shenandoah
Washington: 11 Grand Coulee

Valmiki's epic

8 Ramayana

valor

4 guts 6 mettle, spirit, virtue 7 bravery, courage, heroism, prowess,
stomach 8 chivalry, valiance, valiancy 9 fortitude, gallantry 10 resolution

valorous

see **valiant**

valse

5 waltz

valuable

4 dear 6 costly, prized, useful,
worthy 8 precious 9 expensive,
important, rewarding, treasured
10 satisfying, worthwhile

valuate

4 rate 5 assay, price 6 assess,
survey 7 adjudge 8 appraise,
estimate

valuation

4 cost, rate 5 price, worth 6 rating
7 opinion 8 estimate, judgment
9 appraisal 10 assessment, estimation 12 appreciation

value

4 cost, rate 5 assay, gauge, judge,
price, prize, scale, worth 6 assess,
assign, charge, esteem, figure,
reckon, regard, return, survey
7 account, apprize, care for, cherish,
compute, quality, respect, utility
8 appraise, estimate, evaluate,
quantity, treasure 9 appraisal,
principle 10 appreciate, assessment,
equivalent, importance 11 market
price 12 denomination

valve

3 tap 4 cock, flap, gate 6 device,
faucet, poppet, spigot 7 hydrant,
petcock, shutoff 8 stopcock 9 regulator
cardiac: 6 mitral 8 bicuspid

vamoose

3 git 4 scat 5 leave, scram, split
6 beat it, begone, cut out, decamp,
depart, get out 7 run away, skiddoo,
take off 8 clear out 9 skedaddle

vamp

3 fix 4 fake, lure, mend, wile 5 ad-
lib, flirt, intro, patch, siren, tempt
6 cook up, entice, groove, lead-in,
make up, repair, seduce 7 beguile,
charmer, rebuild 8 inveigle 9 fabricate, formulate, improvise, refurbish,
temptress 10 gold digger, seductress 11 enchantress, extemporize,
femme fatale

vampire
3 bat 5 lamia 6 undead 7 Dracula
9 Nosferatu 11 bloodsucker

van
3 car 4 head, lead, wing 5 front,
truck, wagon 7 minibus 11 cutting
edge, leading edge

vandal
3 Hun 5 yahoo 6 looter 8 pillager
9 despoiler, destroyer, plunderer,
spoliator

vandalize
5 smash, trash, wreck 6 damage,
deface, ravage, tear up 7 destroy
8 demolish, sabotage

Vandal king
8 Gaiseric, Genseric

Vandyke
5 beard 6 border, collar, edging,
goatee

vane
3 web 7 feather, wind tee 8 vexillum
10 bellwether 11 weathercock

vanguard
4 lead 5 front 9 forefront 11 cutting
edge, leading edge

vanilla
4 tame 5 beige, cream, plain
7 extract 8 ordinary 9 innocuous
10 white-bread 12 conventional
13 garden-variety

vanish
3 die, fly 4 fade, flee, melt 5 clear
8 dissolve, evanesce 9 disappear,
dissipate, evaporate 13 dematerialize

vanity
3 ego 5 pride 6 egoism 7 conceit,
egotism 8 self-love, smugness
9 vainglory 10 narcissism, pretension 13 dressing table

Vanity Fair author
9 Thackeray (William Makepeace)

vanquish
4 beat, best, drub, lick, rout 5 cream,
crush, quell 6 defeat, humble,

subdue, thrash 7 clobber, conquer,
destroy, smother, trounce 8 surmount 9 overpower, overthrow,
subjugate 10 annihilate

vantage
4 edge, odds 8 handicap 9 head
start, upper hand
point: 3 POV 5 perch 7 lookout,
outlook 8 position 10 watchtower

Vanuatu
capital: 8 Port-Vila
ethnic group: 10 Melanesian
explorer: 4 Cook (Capt. James)
former name: 11 New Hebrides
island: 3 Epi 5 Efate, Maéwo,
Tanna 6 Ambrim 8 Aneityum, Male-
kula 9 Erromango, Pentecost
13 Espíritu Santo
language: 6 French
monetary unit: 4 vatu

vapid
4 dull, flat, weak 5 banal, bland,
ditsy, ditzy, inane, silly 6 jejune
7 fatuous, insipid, sapless, vacuous
9 brainless, colorless, innocuous
10 namby-pamby, wishy-washy
13 uninteresting

vapor
3 fog, gas 4 brag, haze, mist, smog
5 brume, cloud, smoke, steam
6 breath, miasma, nimbus 7 bluster
8 phantasm
condensed: 3 dew
frozen: 4 hoar, rime 5 frost 9 hoarfrost

vaporize
5 steam 6 ablate 8 disperse, dissolve, evanesce 9 dissipate, evaporate

vaporous
4 airy, hazy 5 foggy, misty, vague,
wispy 6 cloudy, unreal 7 gaseous
8 ethereal, illusory, volatile 10 evanescent 13 unsubstantial

vaquero
5 waddy 6 cowboy, gaucho, herder,
waddie 7 cowpoke 8 buckaroo,
herdsman, wrangler 10 cowpuncher

varia

6 medley 7 mélange, mixture,
omnibus 8 treasury 9 anthology
10 compendium, miscellany 11 compilation

variable

5 fluid 6 fickle, fitful, mobile, symbol
7 mutable, protean 8 unstable,
unsteady, volatile 9 irregular, mercurial, uncertain, unsettled, versatile
10 capricious, changeable, inconstant 13 temperamental

variance

3 war 4 odds 6 change, strife
7 discord, dispute, dissent 8 conflict, disunity, division 9 variation
10 contention, difference, dissension,
dissidence 11 fluctuation 12 disagreement

variation

4 riff 5 shade, shift 6 change,
nuance 7 partita 8 mutation 9 disparity 10 alteration, difference,
divergence 11 fluctuation, declination, discrepancy, oscillation
12 modification 13 dissimilarity

varicolored

see variegated

varicose

7 bulging, dilated, swollen

varied

5 mixed 6 motley, sundry 7 diverse,
various 8 assorted 9 different,
disparate, divergent 10 dissimilar
12 multifarious 13 heterogeneous,
kaleidoscopic, miscellaneous

variegated

4 pied 5 mixed, pinto 6 calico,
motley 7 checked, dappled, diverse,
mottled, piebald, spotted 8 skewbald, stippled, streaked 9 checkered, multihued 10 multicolor, particolor, polychrome 12 multicolored,
parti-colored 13 kaleidoscopic,
polychromatic

variety

3 ilk 4 kind, mode, sort, type
5 array, breed 6 flavor, medley,
nature, stripe 8 mixed bag 9 diversity, variation 10 assortment, collection, miscellany, subspecies 12 multiformity, multiplicity

various

4 some 5 mixed 6 divers, sundry,
unlike 7 diverse, several, unalike
8 assorted, separate 9 different,
disparate, divergent, unsimilar
10 dissimilar 12 multifarious 13 heterogeneous, miscellaneous

varlet

3 cur 4 page 5 knave, rogue, skunk
6 menial, rascal, wretch 8 coistrel
9 attendant, miscreant, scoundrel
10 blackguard

varmint

4 pest 5 knave, rogue, scamp,
skunk, sneak 6 rascal 7 critter
9 scoundrel

varnish

4 coat 5 adorn, cover, glaze, gloss,
japan 6 veneer 7 coating, conceal,
cover up, shellac 8 covering 9 embellish, gloss over, sugarcoat, whitewash
component: 5 resin

vary

5 alter, range 6 change, depart,
differ, modify, mutate 7 deviate,
digress, diverge 8 modulate 9 diversify

vase

3 urn 5 tazza 6 crater, krater, vessel
7 amphora

Vashni's father

6 Samuel

Vashti's husband

6 Xerxes 9 Ahasuerus

vassal

4 leud, serf 5 helot, liege, slave
6 tenant 7 bondman, homager,
peasant, servant, subject 8 bondsman, liege man 9 dependent, underling 11 subordinate 12 feudal tenant
high-ranking: 7 vavasor 8 vavasour

vast

4 huge, mega 5 giant, great, jumbo
6 untold 7 immense, mammoth,
oceanic, titanic 8 colossal, enormous, gigantic, spacious, whopping
9 boundless, expansive, humongous
10 gargantuan, tremendous, widespread 12 astronomical

vastness

5 sweep 8 enormity, hugeness
9 immensity, magnitude 13 expan-
siveness

vat

3 tub, tun 4 beck, butt, cask, kier,
tank 5 keeve, kieve 6 barrel, liquor,
vessel 7 cistern 8 cauldron
cheese: 7 chessel

vatic

6 mantic 7 fatidic 8 oracular 9 fa-
tidical, prophetic, sibylline 10 predictive 11 apocalyptic

Vatican City

10 papal state
army: 11 Swiss Guards
chapel: 7 Sistine
church: 11 Saint Peter's
ruler: 4 Pope
site: 4 Rome

vaticinal

see **vatic**

vaticinate

5 augur 6 divine 7 portend, predict,
presage 8 forebode, forecast, foretell, prophesy, soothsay 9 adumbrate 13 prognosticate

vaudeville

5 revue 9 burlesque, music hall
11 variety show 12 song and dance

vaudevillian

11 entertainer

vault

3 pit, sky 4 arch, cave, dome, jump,
leap, room, safe, tomb 5 bound,
crypt 6 cavern, cellar, cupola, hurdle, spring, welkin 7 archway,
dungeon 8 catacomb, overleap
9 firmament 10 undercroft

vaulting

4 arch, dome 7 emulous 8 aspiring
9 ambitious 12 enthusiastic 13 opportunistic

vaunt

4 blow, brag, crow, puff, rant 5 boast,
strut 6 flaunt, parade 7 bluster,
display, exhibit, show off 8 brandish
9 gasconade 11 rodomontade

veal

4 calf
cutlet: 9 schnitzel
roasted: 10 fricandeau
shank: 8 osso buco

vector

5 agent 7 carrier 9 direction 10 pol-
linator

Vedic religion

country: 5 India
god: 4 Agni, deva, Soma 5 Indra
6 Varuna
language: 8 Sanskrit
priest: 7 Brahman
treatise: 9 Upanishad
writing: 7 Rig Veda, Samhita

veer

3 yaw 4 cast, chop, slew, sway, turn
5 fetch, sheer, shift, trend 6 depart,
swerve 7 deflect, deviate, digress,
diverge

vegetable

3 pea, soy, yam 4 bean, beet, corn,
kale, leek, okra, soya, taro, wort
5 chard, chive, cress, green, onion,
plant 6 carrot, celery, cowpea,
endive, garlic, legume, lentil, peanut, pepper, potato, radish, sorrel,
squash, tomato, turnip 7 cabbage,
chayote, dullard, lettuce, mustard,
parsley, parsnip, pumpkin, rhubarb,
salsify, shallot, soybean, spinach
8 broccoli, collards, cucumber, egg-
plant, kohlrabi, lima bean, rutabaga,
scallion, snap bean 9 artichoke,
asparagus, muskmelon 10 water-
melon 11 cauliflower, horseradish,
sweet potato
bog: 6 muskeg
dish: 5 salad
mold: 5 humus

seller: 6 grocer 7 grocery 12 costermonger
sponge: 5 luffa 6 loofah
spread: 4 oleo 9 margarine

vegetarian
9 herbivore 11 herbivorous

vegetate
4 idle, laze, loaf, loll 5 chill, slack 6 loiter, lounge 7 goof off, hang out 8 languish, lollygag, slack off, stagnate 9 goldbrick, hibernate

vegetation
5 flora 6 growth, plants 7 verdure 8 greenery 9 plant life
floating: 4 sudd 8 pleuston

vehement
3 hot 4 wild 5 fiery, rabid 6 ardent, bitter, fervid, fierce, heated 7 excited, fervent, vicious, violent, zealous 8 forceful, powerful 9 perfervid 10 passionate 11 impassioned 12 antagonistic

vehicle
3 ATV, bus, cab, car, SUV, van 4 auto, bike, taxi, tool 5 agent, buggy, means, organ, plane, sedan, train, truck, wagon 6 agency, binder, medium, vector 7 bicycle, carrier, channel, machine, solvent, travois 8 airplane, ministry 9 ambulance, implement, motor home, transport 10 automobile, conveyance, instrument, motorcycle
baby's: 4 pram 8 carriage, stroller 9 baby buggy
child's: 5 trike 7 scooter 8 tricycle
farm: 4 wain 9 tractor
horse-drawn: 4 cart, dray 5 buggy, lorry, sulky, wagon 6 hansom, landau, troika 7 calèche, phaeton 8 carriage 9 buckboard
military: 4 jeep, tank 6 Humvee
one-wheeled: 8 unicycle
passenger: 3 bus, cab, car 4 auto, taxi 7 ricksha 8 cable car, rickshaw
public: 3 bus 4 tram 5 train 6 subway 7 omnibus, trolley
Roman: 7 chariot
winter: 4 sled 6 sleigh 8 snowplow 10 snowmobile

veil
4 caul, hide, mask, wrap 5 cloak, cloth, cloud, cover, velum 6 mantle, screen, shield, shroud 7 conceal, cover up, curtain, obscure, secrete 8 covering, disguise, enshroud 10 camouflage, false front
Muslim: 7 yashmak
netting: 6 maline 7 malines

vein
3 bed, way 4 line, lode, mind, mode, mood, seam, tone, tube 5 style, tenor 6 manner, nature, spirit, strain, streak, vessel 7 channel, fashion, pattern, quality, stratum 8 aptitude 11 blood vessel
combining form: 3 ven 4 veni, veno
deposit: 3 ore
fluid: 5 blood
heart: 8 vena cava
leaf: 3 rib
leg: 7 saphena 9 saphenous
neck: 7 jugular
small: 6 venule
varicose: 5 varix

velar
8 guttural

veld
7 prairie 9 grassland

velleity
4 bent, wish 5 fancy 6 desire, liking 7 leaning 10 propensity 11 inclination

velocipede
4 bike 5 cycle, trike 6 tandem 7 bicycle, pedicab 8 tricycle

velocity
4 pace 5 haste, speed, tempo 7 headway 8 celerity, rapidity 9 quickness, swiftness 12 acceleration

velum
4 caul, veil 8 membrane 10 soft palate

velvet
4 gain, mild, rich, soft 5 cloth 6 fabric, profit, smooth 8 winnings 10 antler skin

velvety
4 mild, soft 5 plush 6 smooth

venal
4 paid 6 sordid 7 corrupt 8 bribable
9 mercenary, unethical 11 corrupt-
ible, purchasable 12 unprincipled,
unscrupulous

vend
4 hawk, sell, toot 6 market, monger,
peddle, retail 8 huckster 9 advertise, broadcast

vendee
5 buyer 6 client 8 customer 9 purchaser

vendetta
4 feud 7 rivalry 9 blood feud

vendible
7 salable 8 sellable 10 marketable
12 merchantable

vendor
6 dealer, duffer, hawker, seller
7 packman, peddler 8 huckster,
merchant, retailer, salesman

vendue
4 sale 7 auction 10 public sale

veneer
3 ply 4 burl, coat, face, mask, show,
veil 5 cover, front, gloss, layer, plate
6 facade, facing 7 conceal, overlay
8 disguise

venerable
3 old 4 aged 5 hoary 6 sacred
7 ancient, antique, elderly, honored,
revered, stately 8 esteemed 9 admirable, dignified, estimable, honorable, respected

venerate
5 adore, honor, prize 6 admire,
esteem, revere 7 cherish, idolize,
respect, worship 8 treasure 9 reverence

veneration
3 awe 5 honor 6 esteem, homage
7 respect, worship 9 adoration,
reverence 10 admiration 11 hero
worship

venery
3 sex 4 game, prey 5 chase
7 hunting

venesection
10 phlebotomy

Venetian
boat: 7 gondola
boatman: 9 gondolier
product: 5 glass 9 glassware
ruler: 4 doge
school: 6 Titian 7 Bellini, Tiepolo
8 Veronese 9 Giorgione 10 Tintoretto
street: 5 canal
suburb: 6 Murano

Venezuela
capital: 7 Caracas
city: 8 Valencia 9 Maracaibo
12 Barquisimeto
island: 9 Margarita
lake: 8 Valencia 9 Maracaibo
language: 7 Spanish
monetary unit: 7 bolívar
mountain, range: 5 Andes 6 Parima
(Serra, Sierra) 7 Bolívar (Pico)
9 Pacaraima 11 Pico Bolívar, Serra
Parima 12 Sierra Parima
neighbor: 6 Brazil, Guyana 8 Colombia
peninsula: 9 Paraguaná
river: 7 Orinoco
sea: 9 Caribbean
waterfall: 10 Angel Falls

Venezuelan
herdsman: 7 llanero
liberator: 7 Bolívar (Simón)
people: 5 Carib 6 Timote

vengeance
6 payoff 7 payback, redress, revenge
8 reprisal, revanche 9 repayment
10 punishment 11 retaliation, retribution

vengeful
8 punitive 10 vindictive 11 retalia-
tory

venial
5 minor 7 trivial 8 harmless, trifling
9 allowable, excusable, tolerable

10 condonable, forgivable, pardonable, remissible, remittable 13 insignificant

Venice of the East
7 Bangkok, Udaipur

Venice of the North
6 Bruges, Brugge 9 Amsterdam,
Stockholm 12 St. Petersburg

Veni, Creator _____
8 Spiritus

venison
4 deer

veni, vidi, _____
4 vici

venom
4 bane, hate 5 spite 6 malice,
poison, rancor 7 ill will, vitriol 8 embitter 9 contagion, malignity, virulence 11 malevolence

venomous
5 toxic 6 deadly, malign, poison
7 baneful, malefic, noxious 8 spiteful, viperish, viperous, virulent
9 malicious, malignant, poisonous
10 malevolent, pernicious 12 vituperative

vent
3 air 4 emit, flue, hole, pipe, pour,
slit 5 burst, expel, issue, loose, utter,
voice 6 broach, nozzle, outlet
7 chimney, exhaust, express, give
off, opening, orifice, release, take
out, unleash, volcano 8 breather,
fumarole, spiracle 9 discharge
11 black smoker

venter
3 gut 5 belly 6 paunch 7 abdomen,
stomach

ventilate
3 air 5 state, utter 6 aerate, expose
7 discuss, express 9 advertise,
broadcast, circulate, verbalize
11 investigate

ventral area
7 abdomen, stomach

ventricle
6 cavity 7 chamber

ventriloquist
9 performer 11 entertainer
companion: 5 dummy
famous: 6 Bergen (Edgar)

venture
3 bet, try 4 dare, face, feat, gest,
risk 5 brave, peril, stake, wager
6 chance, expose, gamble, hazard
7 attempt, daresay, emprise, exploit
8 endanger, jeopardy, long shot,
make bold 9 challenge, crapshoot, speculate 10 enterprise
11 speculation, undertaking

venturesome
4 bold, rash 5 brave 6 daring
8 reckless 9 audacious, daredevil,
foolhardy 11 adventurous, temerarious

venue
4 site 5 arena, forum, place, scene
6 locale, outlet 7 setting 8 locality

Venus
6 planet, Vesper 7 daystar, Lucifer
8 Hesperus
(see also **Aphrodite**)

Venus de _____
4 Milo

_____ vera
4 aloe

veracious
4 just, true 5 exact, frank, right, valid
6 candid, honest 7 correct, factual,
sincere 8 accurate, truthful

veracity
4 fact 5 truth 6 candor 7 honesty
8 accuracy, trueness 9 actuality,
exactness 11 correctness 12 truthfulness

veranda
5 lanai, porch, stoop 6 piazza
7 gallery, portico

verb
auxiliary: 3 are, can, did, had, has,
may, was 4 have, must, were, will,
word 5 could, might, shall, would
6 should
form: 6 active, gerund 7 passive
10 infinitive, participle

kind: 10 transitive 12 intransitive
linking: 6 copula
mood: 8 optative 10 imperative,
indicative 11 subjunctive
tense: 4 past 6 aorist, future
7 perfect, present 9 predicate
10 pluperfect

verbal
4 oral 5 wordy 6 gerund, spoken
7 literal 9 unwritten 10 infinitive,
participle, rhetorical 11 word-for-
word

verbalism
4 term 6 phrase 7 wording 8 phrasing 9 prolixity, windiness, wordiness
11 phraseology

verbalization
4 talk 6 speech 8 speaking 9 discourse, utterance 12 articulation,
vocalization

verbalize
3 air, say 4 talk 5 speak, state, utter,
voice, write 6 broach 7 express
8 bloviate, vocalize 9 ventilate

verbatim
5 exact 6 direct 7 exactly, literal,
precise 8 directly 9 literally, lit-
eratim, precisely 10 accurately
11 word-for-word

verbiage
4 talk 6 phrase 7 diction, wording
8 parlance, phrasing, pleonasm
9 wordiness 10 redundancy
11 phraseology

verbose
5 gassy, windy, wordy 6 prolix
7 diffuse 9 garrulous, redundant,
talkative 10 loquacious, pleonastic
11 tautologous

verbosity
9 prolixity, windiness, wordiness
10 redundancy

verboten
5 taboo 6 banned 7 illegal 8 outlawed 9 forbidden 10 prohibited

verdant
4 lush 5 green, leafy, naive 6 grassy,
unripe

verdict
6 assize, ruling 7 finding, opinion
8 decision, judgment 9 judgement

Verdi opera
4 Aïda 6 Ernani, Oberto, Otello
7 Nabucco 8 Don Carlo, Falstaff,
Lombardi (I), Traviata (La) 9 Don
Carlos, Rigoletto, Trovatore (II)
15 Simon Boccanegra

verdure
7 foliage 8 greenery 9 greenness
10 vegetation

verge
3 hem, lip, rim 4 abut, cusp, edge,
sink 5 bound, brink, skirt, staff, touch
6 adjoin, border, fringe, margin
7 selvage 8 approach, shoulder
9 threshold 10 borderline

veridical
see **veracious**

verifiable
4 true 6 proven 7 certain 8 provable 9 undoubted

verification
5 proof 10 validation 11 attestation
12 confirmation 13 corroboration

verify
4 aver, test 5 check, prove, vouch
6 attest, settle 7 bear out, confirm
8 document, validate 9 establish,
fact-check 11 corroborate, demonstrate 12 authenticate, substantiate

verily
5 truly 6 indeed 7 in truth 9 assuredly, certainly 11 confidently,
undoubtedly

veritable
4 real, true 6 actual 7 factual,
genuine 8 bona fide 9 authentic,
undoubted 10 sure-enough 11 indubitable

verity
5 truth 6 gospel, truism 7 honesty,
reality 9 actuality 12 truthfulness

vermiform
8 wormlike

vermilion
3 red

vermin
4 lice, mice, pest, rats, scum 5 fleas, pests, trash 7 bedbugs, varmint

Vermont
capital: 10 Montpelier
city: 7 Rutland 10 Burlington
college, university: 7 Norwich 8 Marlboro 10 Bennington, Middlebury
mountain, range: 5 Green 9 Mansfield
nickname: 13 Green Mountain (State)
river: 11 Connecticut
state bird: 12 hermit thrush
state flower: 9 red clover
state tree: 10 sugar maple

vernacular
4 cant 5 argot, idiom, lingo, slang 6 common, jargon, patois, patter, speech, tongue, vulgar 7 dialect, vulgate 8 language 9 dialectal 10 colloquial 12 mother tongue

vernal
5 fresh, green 6 spring 8 youthful 10 springlike

Verne, Jules
character: 4 Fogg (Phileas), Nemo 12 Passepartout
submarine: 8 Nautilus
work: 16 Mysterious Island (The) 21 From the Earth to the Moon 26 Around the World in Eighty Days

versant
see **conversant**

versatile
5 handy 6 adroit, facile 7 protean 8 variable 9 all-around, competent, many-sided 10 changeable 11 well-rounded 12 ambidextrous

verse
3 lay, ode 4 epic, poem, rune 5 lyric, poesy, rhyme 6 ballad, jingle, poetry, sonnet, stanza 7 passage 8 acquaint 11 composition, familiarize
analysis: 8 scansion

four-line: 8 quatrain
free: 5 blank 8 unrhymed
six-line: 6 sestet
three-line: 6 tercet
two-line: 7 couplet
writer: 4 poet

versed
5 adept 6 au fait 7 abreast, skilled, veteran 8 familiar, informed, seasoned 9 au courant, competent, practiced 10 acquainted 11 experienced 13 knowledgeable

versifier
4 bard, poet 6 rhymer 9 poetaster, rhymester, sonneteer

version
4 copy 5 draft, model 6 flavor, remake 7 account, edition, reading, variant 8 revision 9 iteration, narrative, redaction, rendition, rewording 10 adaptation, paraphrase 11 arrangement, description, incarnation, restatement, translation

versus
4 anti 6 contra 7 against, vis-à-vis 11 over against

vertebra
7 segment
kind: 6 dorsal, lumbar, sacral 8 cervical, thoracic 9 coccygeal

vertebrae
4 back 5 spine 6 coccyx, rachis, sacrum 8 backbone, tailbone 12 spinal column

vertebrate
6 animal
characteristic: 5 spine 7 cranium 12 spinal column
kind: 4 bird, fish, frog 6 mammal 7 reptile 9 amphibian

vertex
3 cap, top 4 acme, apex, peak 5 crest, crown 6 apogee, summit, tip-top, zenith

vertical
5 erect, plumb, sheer, steep 7 upright 8 straight 10 lengthwise, straight-up 13 perpendicular

vertiginous
5 dizzy, giddy, woozy 6 fickle, rotary 11 light-headed

vertigo
6 megrim 9 dizziness, giddiness

verve
3 pep, vim, zip 4 brio, dash, élan, fire, life, zest, zing 5 flair, gusto, moxie, oomph, style, vigor 6 bounce, energy, spirit, spring 7 panache 8 vitality, vivacity 10 enthusiasm, liveliness 13 sprightliness

very
3 too 4 bare, mere, most, much, pure, real, same, true 5 exact, ideal, model, plain, quite, sheer, super, truly, utter 6 actual, ever so, highly, hugely, mighty, really, simple 7 awfully, genuine, greatly, notably, perfect, precise, special 8 absolute, actually, bona fide, selfsame, terribly 9 authentic, extremely, genuinely, identical, undoubted 10 absolutely, particular 11 exceedingly
French: 4 très
German: 4 sehr
Italian: 5 molto
Scottish: 3 gey
Spanish: 3 muy

vesicle
3 sac 4 cell, cyst 5 bulla 6 cavity 7 blister, vacuole

vespers
8 evensong

_____ Vespucci
7 Amerigo

vessel
3 can, cup, jar, pan, pot, tub, urn 4 boat, bowl, cask, drum, duct, ewer, pail, ship, tank, tube, vase, vein 5 canal, craft, cruse 6 artery, barrel, bottle, bucket, firkin, flagon, kettle, krater, pottle 7 cresset, pitcher 8 crucible 9 container 10 receptacle, watercraft
combining form: 3 vas 4 angi, vaso 5 angio
drinking: 3 cup, mug 4 toby 5 flask, glass, gourd, stein, stoup 6 goblet, seidel 7 tankard, tumbler
Indian: 4 lota 5 lotah
Scottish: 6 quaich, quaigh

vest
6 weskit 9 waistcoat

Vesta
see **Hestia**

vestal
4 pure 6 chaste, virgin 8 celibate, virginal, virtuous

vestibule
5 entry, foyer, lobby 6 cavity 7 hallway, narthex, passage 8 anteroom, entrance, entryway 10 antechapel 11 antechamber

vestige
4 echo 5 dregs (plural), relic, scrap, stump, trace, track 6 shadow 7 memento, remains, remnant 8 leftover 9 remainder 10 hide or hair 11 hide nor hair

vestment
3 alb 4 cope, garb, gown, robe 5 amice, cotta, dress, habit, stole, tunic 6 attire, rochet 7 apparel, cassock, garment, maniple, pallium, tunicle 8 chasuble, cincture, clothing, covering, dalmatic, parament, surplice
ancient Hebrew: 5 ephod 11 breastplate

vestry
6 closet 8 sacristy 9 sacrarium

vesture
4 robe 6 clothe 7 apparel, garment 8 clothing 10 habiliment

Vesuvius
7 volcano

vet
5 check 6 go over, review 7 analyze, examine, inspect 8 appraise, check out, evaluate, look over 10 old soldier

vetch
4 herb, tare 6 legume

type: 4 milk (vetch) 5 crown (vetch), hairy (vetch)

veteran
4 ex-GI 5 adept 6 expert, master 7 old hand, skilled 8 old-timer, warhorse 9 practiced, shellback 10 past master 11 experienced

veto
3 nix 4 kill 6 defeat, forbid, refuse, reject 7 decline 8 disallow, negative, prohibit 9 blackball 10 disapprove 11 prohibition 12 interdiction

vex
3 bug, irk 4 fret, gall, itch, roil 5 annoy, chafe, gripe, harry, rowel, tease, worry 6 badger, baffle, bother, harass, harrow, nettle, pester, plague, puzzle, rankle, ruffle 7 chagrin, torment, trouble 8 bullyrag, distress, irritate

vexation
4 fret, sore 5 chafe, trial 6 bother 7 problem, torment 8 distress, headache 9 annoyance, troubling 10 affliction, harassment, irritation 11 aggravation, bedevilment, provocation

vexatious
5 pesky 7 prickly 8 annoying, tiresome 10 troublous 10 bothersome, irritating 11 distressing, troublesome 12 exasperating

vexed
6 sticky, touchy 7 debated, weighty 8 ticklish 9 difficult, discussed, troubling

vexing
5 tough 7 irksome 8 annoying 9 difficult, harassing, upsetting 10 bothersome, irritating 11 distressing, troublesome

via
3 per 4 over, with 5 along 7 by way of, through 9 by means of

viable
6 doable 7 capable 8 feasible, possible, workable 11 practicable, sustainable

vial
6 ampule 7 ampoule

viands
4 eats, fare, feed, food, grub 7 aliment, edibles, vittles 8 victuals 9 provender 10 provisions 11 comestibles

vibrant
5 alive, vital, vivid 6 bright, lively, punchy 7 ringing 8 resonant 9 consonant, pulsating 10 resounding 11 oscillating 12 effervescent

vibrate
3 jar 4 ring 5 quake, shake, swing, throb, waver 6 quiver, shimmy, thrill, tremor 7 flutter, pulsate 8 undulate 9 fluctuate, oscillate, vacillate

vibration
4 aura 5 quake, shake, trill 6 motion, quaver, quiver, shimmy, spirit, tremor 7 flutter, shaking 8 fremitus, wavering 9 emanation, trembling 11 fluctuation, oscillation, vacillation

vicar
6 pastor, priest 8 minister, reverend 9 clergyman

Vicar of Wakefield, The
author: 9 Goldsmith (Oliver)
character: 8 Primrose

vice
3 sin 4 evil, flaw 5 crime, fault 6 defect 7 devilry, failing, frailty, offense, scandal 8 iniquity 9 deformity, depravity, indecency 10 corruption, debauchery, immorality, perversion, wickedness 11 shortcoming

vice-president
4 veep 6 deputy 7 officer 9 executive
American: 4 Burr (Aaron), Bush (George), Ford (Gerald), Gore (Albert), King (William) 5 Adams (John), Agnew (Spiro), Dawes (Charles), Gerry (Elbridge), Nixon (Richard), Tyler (John) 6 Arthur (Chester), Cheney (Richard), Colfax (Schuyler), Curtis (Charles), Dallas

(George), Garner (John Nance), Hamlin (Hannibal), Hobart (Garret), Morton (Levi), Quayle (Dan), Truman (Harry), Wilson (Woodrow) **7** Barkley (Alben), Calhoun (John Caldwell), Clinton (George), Johnson (Andrew, Lyndon Baines, Richard Mentor), Mondale (Walter), Sherman (James Schoolcraft), Wallace (Henry), Wheeler (William) **8** Coolidge (Calvin), Fillmore (Millard), Humphrey (Hubert Horatio), Marshall (Thomas), Tompkins (Daniel), Van Buren (Martin) **9** Fairbanks (Charles), Hendricks (Thomas), Jefferson (Thomas), Roosevelt (Theodore), Stevenson (Adlai) **11** Rockefeller (Nelson) **12** Breckinridge (John)

viceroy
5 nabob **6** exarch, satrap **7** khedive **8** alderman, governor **9** butterfly **11** stadtholder

vice versa
10 conversely **12** contrariwise

vicinity
4 area **5** range **6** extent, locale, region, shadow **7** suburbs **8** ballpark, district, environs, locality, nearness, precinct **9** closeness, magnitude, proximity **12** neighborhood

vicious
4 evil, mean, vile **5** cruel **6** fierce, malign, savage, sinful, wicked **7** brutish, corrupt, hateful, immoral, noxious, violent **8** depraved, horrible, perverse, spiteful **9** barbarous, ferocious, malicious, malignant, monstrous, nefarious, reprobate **10** degenerate, flagitious, iniquitous, malevolent, villainous, vindictive

vicissitude
5 rigor, trial **6** chance, change **7** weather **8** hardship, mutation, reversal **9** adversity, mischance **10** affliction, difficulty, misfortune, mutability **11** permutation, progression, tribulation

victim
4 butt, dupe, gull, mark, prey

5 chump, patsy **6** pigeon, martyr, quarry, sucker **7** fall guy **8** casualty, fatality, offering, underdog **9** sacrifice

victimize
4 dupe, fool, gull, hoax **5** cheat, cozen, trick **7** deceive, swindle **8** flimflam, hoodwink **9** bamboozle, sacrifice **11** hornswoggle

victor
5 champ **6** top dog, winner **7** subduer **8** champion **9** conqueror **10** vanquisher

Victorian
4 prim **6** prissy, stuffy **7** prudish **8** priggish **11** puritanical, straitlaced **12** old-fashioned

Victoria, Queen
family: **7** Hanover
father: **6** Edward
husband: **6** Albert
prime minister: **8** Disraeli (Benjamin) **9** Gladstone (William), Melbourne (Lord)
son: **6** Edward

victory
3 win **5** sweep **6** defeat **7** mastery, success, triumph **8** conquest, walkaway, walkover **10** overcoming **11** superiority
costly: **7** Pyrrhic
easy: **8** cakewalk, walkaway
monument: **4** arch **13** Arc de Triomphe
reward: **6** spoils
sign: **3** vee
symbol: **4** flag **6** laurel, wreath

Victory author
6 Conrad (Joseph)

victuals
4 chow, eats, feed, food, grub, prog **6** viands **7** edibles, vittles **9** provender **10** provisions **11** comestibles

_____ Vidal
4 Gore

videlicet
3 viz **5** to wit **6** namely, that is **8** scilicet **11** that is to say

vie

3 pit 5 match 6 oppose, strive
7 compete, contend, contest, counter
8 struggle

Viennese

city hall: 7 Rathaus
family: 8 Habsburg, Hapsburg
palace: 7 Hofburg
park: 6 Prater
river: 6 Danube

Vietnam

capital: 5 Hanoi
city: 3 Hue 6 Da Nang, Saigon
8 Haiphong 13 Ho Chi Minh City
delta: 6 Mekong
gulf: 6 Tonkin 8 Thailand
monetary unit: 4 dong
mountain: 8 Fan-si-pan
neighbor: 4 Laos 5 China 8 Cambodia 9 Kampuchea
river: 3 Red 6 Mekong
sea: 10 South China

Vietnamese New Year

3 Tet

view

3 eye, see 4 espy, look, plan, scan
5 scene, sight, vista, watch 6 behold, belief, look at, notice, notion,
regard, review, survey 7 close-up,
examine, inspect, lookout, observe,
opinion, outlook, picture, scenery,
vantage 8 judgment, panorama,
perceive, prospect, scrutiny, snapshot 10 conviction, inspection,
scrutinize 11 contemplate, examination

viewer

7 witness 8 looker-on, onlooker
9 bystander, spectator 10 eyewitness

viewing instrument

5 glass, scope 6 binocs 7 glasses
9 telescope 10 binoculars, microscope 12 field glasses
combining form: 5 scope

viewpoint

3 eye 5 angle, slant, stand 6 stance
7 outlook 8 attitude, position 9 direction 11 perspective

vigil

4 wake 5 watch 7 lookout, prayers
9 devotions 10 deathwatch 11 wakefulness 12 surveillance, watch and
ward

vigilance

5 watch 9 alertness 12 surveillance,
watchfulness

vigilant

4 keen, wary 5 alert, awake, aware,
chary, sharp 7 careful, jealous, on
guard 8 cautious, open-eyed, watchful 9 attentive, sharp-eyed, wideawake

vignette

5 scene 6 sketch 7 glimpse, picture
8 ornament

vigor

3 pep, vim, zip 4 brio, push, snap,
tuck 5 ardor, drive, force, gusto,
moxie, oomph 6 energy, mettle,
muscle, spirit, starch 7 potency
8 dynamism, strength, tonicity,
virility, vitality 9 hardihood, lustiness,
puissance 10 get-up-and-go, robustness, sturdiness

vigorous

5 brisk, hardy, lusty, stout, tough,
vital 6 active, hearty, lively, potent,
robust, strong, sturdy, virile 7 dashing, driving, dynamic, healthy 8 athletic, forceful, muscular, powerful,
spirited, youthful 9 energetic, strenuous 10 mettlesome, red-blooded

Viking

see **Norse**

vile

4 base, evil, foul, mean, ugly 5 gross,
nasty, slimy 6 filthy, horrid, sordid,
vulgar, wicked 7 low-down, noisome,
obscene, squalid 8 depraved,
wretched 9 abhorrent, loathsome,
obnoxious, offensive, perverted,
repugnant, repulsive, revolting
10 despicable, disgusting 12 contemptible

vilify

5 abuse, libel, smear 6 assail,
attack, berate, defame, malign

7 asperse, run down, slander, spatter, traduce **8** denounce, tear down **9** denigrate, disparage **10** calumniate

villa
5 dacha, manor **6** estate, quinta **7** château, mansion **9** residence

village
4 burg, town **5** bourg, thorp **6** hamlet **7** townlet
African: 4 dorp **5** kraal
Indian: 6 pueblo
Japanese: 4 mura
Jewish: 6 shtetl
Malay: 7 kampong
Russian: 3 mir

Village Blacksmith author
10 Longfellow (Henry Wadsworth)

villain
4 boor, heel **5** demon, devil, heavy, knave, rogue **6** rascal, sinner **7** lowlife **8** antihero, criminal, evildoer, offender, scalawag **9** character, miscreant, reprobate, scoundrel **10** blackguard, malefactor
classic: 4 Iago **5** Judas (Iscariot) **6** Brutus (Marcus Junius) **8** Quisling (Vidkun)

villainous
4 evil **6** rotten, wicked **7** corrupt, debased, heinous, vicious **8** depraved, wretched **9** atrocious, felonious, miscreant, nefarious **10** detestable, diabolical, flagitious, iniquitous, perfidious, traitorous **11** treacherous

villainy
4 vice **5** crime **8** evilness **9** depravity, treachery, turpitude **10** corruption, wickedness

villein
7 peasant **8** villager

villenage
4 yoke **6** tenure, thrall **7** bondage, serfdom **9** servitude, thralldom

vim
3 zip **4** brio, dash, élan, gimp, zing **5** gusto, oomph, verve, vigor **6** bounce, energy, esprit, spirit **7** vinegar **9** animation **10** enthusiasm, razzmatazz

_____ vincit omnia
4 Amor

vinculum
3 tie **4** bond, knot, link, yoke **5** nexus **8** ligament, ligature

vindicable
7 tenable **9** excusable **10** condonable, defendable, defensible, pardonable **11** justifiable, warrantable

vindicate
4 free **5** clear, guard, prove, right **6** acquit, avenge, defend, excuse, refute, shield, uphold, verify **7** absolve, bear out, confirm, deliver, justify, redress, revenge, support, warrant **8** maintain **9** exculpate, exonerate, safeguard **11** corroborate **12** substantiate

vindictive
5 catty, nasty **6** malign **7** hateful, hurtful, vicious **8** punitive, spiteful, vengeful, venomous **9** malicious, malignant, poisonous

vine
3 hop, ivy, pea **5** grape, kudzu, liana, liane, maile, plant **6** maypop **7** chayote, climber, creeper **8** catbrier, clematis **11** bittersweet
Asian: 6 pikake

vinegar
3 vim **6** liquid **8** ill humor, sourness **9** condiment **12** preservative
relating to: 10 acetic acid
steep in: 6 pickle

vinegarish
4 sour **6** bitter, cranky, ornery **7** bearish, waspish **8** snappish **9** crotchety, irascible **12** cantankerous, cross-grained, disagreeable

Vinegar Joe
8 Stilwell (Joseph)

vineyard
French: 3 cru **7** château, domaine

Vinland discoverer
4 Leif (Ericsson, Eriksson) 12 Leif
Ericsson, Leif Eriksson

vintage
3 age, old 4 crop, wine 5 yield
7 antique, classic, harvest 8 outdated 9 classical 10 antiquated
12 old-fashioned

Viola
brother: 9 Sebastian
husband: 6 Orsino
play: 12 Twelfth Night

viola da ____
5 gamba

violate
4 rape 5 break, wrong 6 breach,
defile, offend, ravish 7 disturb,
outrage, profane, traduce 8 fracture,
infringe, trespass 9 desecrate,
disregard 10 contravene, transgress

violation
4 foul, rape 5 break, crime, wrong
6 breach, injury 7 offense, outrage,
perjury, scandal 8 trespass 9 blasphemy, injustice, sacrilege 10 illegality, infraction, ravishment 11 desecration, disturbance, misdemeanor,
profanation 12 encroachment,
infringement, interruption 13 contravention, transgression

violence
4 fury, riot 5 clash 6 frenzy, mayhem
7 assault, outrage, rampage 8 foul
play, savagery 9 onslaught 10 distortion, roughhouse

violent
5 cruel, harsh, rabid 6 fierce, raging,
savage, stormy 7 berserk, furious,
intense, vicious 8 slam-bang, vehement 9 explosive, ferocious 10 hel-
lacious 11 acrimonious, destructive

violet
5 mauve 6 purple 8 amethyst,
lavender 10 heliotrope

violin
6 fiddle 10 instrument
kind: 5 Amati, Strad 8 Guarneri
10 Guarnerius, Stradivari 12 Stradivarius

part: 3 bow, nut, peg 4 neck
6 bridge, scroll, string 8 chin rest
9 tailpiece 10 soundboard 11 finger-
board
precursor: 5 rebec 6 rebeck

violinist
American: 4 Hahn (Hilary) 5 Elman
(Mischa), Fodor (Eugene), Ricci
(Ruggiero), Stern (Isaac) 6 Midori,
Powell (Maud) 7 Heifetz (Jascha),
Menuhin (Yehudi), Szigeti (Joseph)
8 Kreisler (Fritz), Milstein (Nathan)
9 Zimbalist (Efrem)
Belgian: 5 Ysaÿe (Eugene) 8 Gru-
miaux (Arthur)
Czech: 3 Suk (Josef)
English: 7 Menuhin (Yehudi)
French: 12 Francescatti (Zino)
German: 6 Mutter (Anne-Sophie)
Hungarian: 7 Joachim (Joseph)
Israeli: 7 Perlman (Itzhak) 8 Zuker-
man (Pinchas)
Italian: 6 Viotti (Giovanne Battista)
7 Corelli (Arcangelo), Vivaldi (Anto-
nio) 8 Paganini (Niccolo) 9 Gemi-
niani (Francesco)
Romanian: 6 Enescu (George)
Russian: 8 Oistrakh (David)

violin maker
4 Salò (Gasparo da) 5 Amati (An-
drea, Antonio, Girolamo, Nicolo)
7 Maggini (Giovanni Paolo), Stainer
(Jacob) 8 Guarneri (Andrea, del
Gesù, Giuseppe, Pietro) 10 Guar-
nerius (Andrea, Giuseppe, Pietro),
Stradivari (Antonio, Francesco,
Omobono) 12 Stradivarius (Antonio,
Francesco, Omobono)

VIP
4 BMOC, lion 5 mogul, nabob
6 big gun, biggie, bigwig, fat cat,
honcho 7 big shot, notable, someone 8 big wheel, luminary, mandarin,
somebody 9 big cheese, dignitary
10 panjandrum 13 high-muck-a-
muck

viper
3 asp 5 adder, snake 7 serpent
10 bushmaster, copperhead, fer-de-
lance 11 rattlesnake 13 water
moccasin

virago

5 harpy, scold, shrew, vixen 6 amazon, dragon, gorgon, ogress 8 battle-ax, fishwife, harridan, Xantippe
9 battle-axe, termagant, Xanthippe

Virgil

4 poet 5 guide 6 orator 8 cicerone
epic: 6 Aeneid
poems: 8 Eclogues, Georgics

virgin

3 new 4 pure 5 first, fresh, unwed
6 chaste, intact, maiden, modest,
unused, vestal 7 initial 8 celibate,
innocent, primeval, pristine, spotless
9 abstinent, undefiled, unmarried,
unspoiled, unsullied, untouched
10 immaculate

virginal

4 pure 5 fresh 6 chaste, intact,
maiden, spinet 8 pristine, virtuous
9 undefiled, unspoiled, unsullied,
untouched

Virgin Goddess

5 Diana 6 Hestia 7 Artemis

Virginia

capital: 8 Richmond
city: 7 Norfolk, Roanoke 10 Alexandria 11 Newport News 13 Virginia
Beach
college, university: 3 VMI 7 Hampton 10 Sweet Briar 11 George
Mason, Old Dominion 12 James
Madison 13 Randolph-Macon
14 William and Mary
historical site: 10 Monticello
11 Mount Vernon 12 Williamsburg
mountain, range: 6 Rogers 9 Blue
Ridge
nickname: 11 Old Dominion
river: 5 James 7 Potomac 10 Shenandoah
state bird: 8 cardinal
state flower: 7 dogwood (American)
state tree: 7 dogwood (American)

Virginian, The

author: 6 Wister (Owen)
character: 7 Trampas

Virgin Island

5 Peter 6 Norman, St. John 7 Anegada, St. Croix, Tortola 8 St. Thomas

Virgin Islands (U.S.)

capital: 15 Charlotte Amalie
island: 6 St. John 7 St. Croix
8 St. Thomas
location: 10 West Indies
territory of: 12 United States

Virgin Islands, British

capital: 8 Road Town
island: 5 Peter 6 Norman 7 Anegada, Tortola 11 Jost Van Dyke,
Virgin Gorda
location: 10 West Indies

virginity

6 purity 8 celibacy, chastity
10 chasteness, maidenhead, maidenhood

Virgin Queen

9 Elizabeth

Virgo star

5 Spica

virgule

5 comma, slant, slash 7 solidus
8 diagonal

viridity

5 green 7 naïveté 9 freshness,
greenness, innocence

virile

4 male 5 macho, manly 6 manful,
potent, robust 7 manlike 8 forceful,
vigorous 9 energetic, masculine

virtual

5 moral, tacit 7 de facto 8 implicit
9 essential, practical 10 electronic
11 fundamental

virtuality

4 core, pith, soul 5 being, juice, stuff
6 effect, marrow, nature 7 essence,
makings 8 quiddity 9 substance
10 capability 12 essentiality, quintessence, potentiality

virtually

4 nigh 6 all but, almost, fairly, nearly,
next to 7 morally 8 as good as,
in effect, well-nigh 9 basically,
in essence, literally 10 implicitly
11 effectively, essentially, practically
13 approximately, fundamentally,
substantially

virtue

5 merit, power, right, trait, valor, value, vigor, worth **7** courage, feature, potency, probity, quality **8** chastity, goodness, morality, strength **9** attribute, character, puissance, rectitude, rightness **10** excellence, excellency, perfection **11** uprightness
cardinal: 4 hope, love **5** faith **7** charity, justice **8** prudence **9** fortitude **10** temperance

virtuosic

5 showy **6** expert, flashy **7** hotshot, skilled **9** brilliant, masterful **10** consummate, prodigious **12** razzle-dazzle

virtuoso

4 whiz **6** expert, master, savant, wizard, wonder **7** artiste, hotshot, maestro, prodigy **10** past master, wunderkind

virtuous

4 good, pure **5** moral, noble, pious, right **6** chaste, decent, modest, proper **7** ethical, sinless **8** innocent, spotless **9** blameless, faultless, guiltless, righteous, unsullied, untainted **10** inculpable, moralistic **11** respectable, right-minded, untarnished

virulent

5 harsh, toxic **6** biting, bitter, malign, poison **7** cutting, hateful, hostile **8** scathing, spiteful, venomous **9** malicious, malignant, pestilent, poisonous, rancorous, vitriolic **10** pathogenic

virus

3 bug **8** pathogen **9** contagion, infection

vis

5 force, might, power

visage

3 mug, pan **4** cast, face, look, mien, phiz, puss **6** aspect, kisser **8** features **9** semblance **10** expression **11** countenance

vis-à-vis

4 date **6** escort, facing, toward **7** against **8** fronting, opposite, together **9** tête-à-tête **10** face-to-face **11** counterpart

visceral

3 gut **4** deep **5** inner **8** internal, intimate **9** intuitive **10** intestinal **11** instinctive, instinctual

viscid

see **viscous**

viscount

4 lord, peer **8** nobleman

viscous

4 limy, ropy **5** gluey, gooey, gummy, limey, slimy, thick **9** glutinous, semifluid **10** gelatinous **12** mucilaginous

vise

5 clamp, screw **7** squeeze

Vishnu

4 Hari
avatar: 4 Rama **5** Kurma **6** Buddha, Matsya, Vamena, Varaha **7** Krishna **9** Narasinha
consort: 3 Sri **4** Shri **7** Lakshmi
home: 4 Meru

visible

6 patent **7** obvious **8** apparent, viewable **9** available, well-known **10** detectable **11** conspicuous, discernible, perceivable, perceptible **12** recognizable

Visigoth

conquest: 4 Rome
king: 6 Alaric

vision

3 eye **5** dream, fancy, image, sense, sight **6** beauty, seeing **7** concept, fantasy, feature, picture, specter **8** daydream, eyesight, phantasm, presence, prophecy **9** foresight, nightmare **10** apparition, perception, phenomenon, revelation **13** manifestation
combining form: 4 opto **5** opsis
deceptive: 6 mirage
relating to: 5 optic **6** visual **7** optical

visionary

4 seer **5** ideal, lofty, noble **6** unreal
7 blue-sky, dreamer, utopian **8** fanciful, idealist, illusory, quixotic, romantic **9** ambitious, ideologue, imaginary
10 abstracted, daydreamer, idealistic, starry-eyed **11** impractical

visionless

5 blind

Vision of Sir Launfal author

6 Lowell (James Russell)

visit

3 gam, see **4** call, chat, stay, talk, tour **5** pop in, run in **6** call on, come by, drop by, drop in, look in, look up, stay at, stop by, stop in **7** force on, sojourn **8** come over, converse, stay with, stopover **10** social call

visitation

3 woe **4** wake **5** cross, trial **6** misery, ordeal, plague **8** calamity **9** martyrdom **10** affliction **11** tribulation

visitor

5 alien, guest **6** caller, drop-in
7 company, invitee **8** stranger, visitant **9** transient **10** houseguest

visor

4 bill, mask **6** domino **8** eyeshade, disguise, face mask, sunshade

vista

4 view **5** scene, sight **7** lookout, outlook **8** panorama, prospect
9 landscape **11** perspective

visual

5 optic **6** ocular **7** graphic, optical, seeable **8** viewable **9** pictorial
11 discernible, perceivable, perceptible

visualize

3 see **4** view **5** fancy, image **6** call up **7** feature, imagine, picture
8 conceive, envisage, envision
9 conjure up

vital

4 dire **5** alive **6** lively, living, mortal, urgent **7** animate, crucial, pivotal
8 animated, cardinal, critical, decisive, integral, pressing, required, vigorous **9** essential, important, necessary, requisite **10** imperative, red-blooded **11** fundamental, life-or-death **12** invigorating **13** indispensable

vitality

see **vigor**

vitalize

5 liven **6** arouse, excite, infuse, perk up, spirit, vivify **7** animate, enliven, quicken **8** energize **9** encourage, galvanize, stimulate **10** invigorate

vitals

see **viscera**

vitamin

6 biotin, niacin **7** choline, folacin, retinal, retinol **8** thiamine **9** carnitine, cobalamin, folic acid **10** calciferol, pyridoxine, riboflavin, tocopherol **12** ascorbic acid

Vita Nuova author

5 Dante (Alighieri)

vitelline

5 yolky **6** yellow

vitiate

3 mar **4** harm, soil, undo **5** annul, spoil, sully, taint **6** damage, debase, defile, impair, negate **7** blemish, corrupt, debauch, deprave, nullify, pervert, tarnish **8** abrogate **9** undermine **10** bastardize, demoralize, invalidate

vitreous

6 glassy

vitriol

4 bile **5** spite, venom **6** malice, rancor **7** sulfate **8** acrimony **9** virulence **12** sulfuric acid

vitriolic

4 acid **5** acrid **7** acerbic, caustic, cutting, mordant **8** scathing, stinging, virulent **9** rancorous, truculent

vituperate

3 rag **4** lash, rail, rant, rate **5** abuse, baste, curse, scold, score **6** berate, malign, revile, scorch **7** asperse, bawl out, chew out, condemn, cuss out, upbraid **8** lambaste **9** castigate **10** tongue-lash

vituperation

5 abuse **6** rebuke **7** censure, obloquy, reproof **8** scolding **9** contumely, invective **10** scurrility **11** fulmination, mudslinging **12** billingsgate **13** tongue-lashing

vituperative

7 abusive, railing, scurril **8** scathing, scolding, scurrile, venomous, viperish **9** invective **10** censorious, scurrilous **11** opprobrious **12** contumelious

vivace

5 brisk **6** lively **8** animated, spirited

vivacious

3 gay **4** airy, pert **5** perky, spicy, sunny, zesty **6** bouncy, breezy, bubbly, jaunty, lively, sparky **7** buoyant, chipper **8** animated, pixieish, spirited **9** ebullient, sprightly **12** effervescent, high-spirited

vivacity

see **verve**

Vivaldi epithet

9 red priest (the)

_____ vivant

3 bon

vivarium

9 terrarium

viva voce

4 oral **6** orally, spoken **11** word-of-mouth

vivid

5 alive, sharp **6** bright, garish, lively, punchy, visual **7** graphic, intense, vibrant **8** animated, colorful, eloquent, lifelike **9** chromatic, pictorial **10** expressive **11** picturesque

vivify

5 liven, renew **6** excite, infuse, kindle, revive **7** animate, enliven, quicken, refresh, restore **9** stimulate

vixen

3 fox, nag **5** harpy, scold, shrew **6** ogress, virago **8** fishwife, harridan, Xantippe **9** termagant, Xanthippe

viz

5 to wit **6** namely, that is **8** scilicet **9** videlicet **12** in other words

vizard

4 face, mask **5** guise, visor **6** domino **8** disguise

vocabulary

4 cant **5** argot, lingo, slang, words **6** jargon, patois **7** lexicon **8** glossary **9** word-hoard **10** vernacular **11** terminology

vocal

4 oral **5** blunt, frank **6** phonic, spoken, voiced **7** uttered **8** eloquent **9** outspoken **10** articulate, expressive, free-spoken

vocalic

5 vowel

vocalist

4 diva **6** belter, canary, singer **7** crooner, warbler, yodeler **8** minstrel, songbird **9** balladeer, chanteuse, chorister **10** cantatrice, prima donna

vocalization

4 song **5** voice **6** speech **7** diction **8** speaking **9** utterance **11** enunciation **12** articulation **13** pronunciation

vocalize

3 air, hem **4** sing, talk **5** chant, croon, speak, state, utter, voice **6** warble **7** express **9** enunciate, pronounce

vocal organ

6 larynx **8** voice box
bird: 6 syrinx

vocation

3 art, job **4** call, work **5** craft, trade **6** career, métier **7** calling, mission, pursuit **8** business, lifework **10** employment, handicraft, occupation, profession

vociferate

3 bay, cry **4** bark, bray, call, roar, yawp, yell **5** shout **6** bellow, clamor, holler **7** thunder

vociferous

4 loud **5** noisy **6** shrill **7** blatant, clamant, raucous **8** strident **9** clamorous **11** openmouthed **12** obstreperous

vogue

3 cry, fad, ton **4** chic, mode, pose, rage **5** craze, favor, furor, style, trend **6** furore **7** fashion **10** dernier cri, popularity **11** stylishness

voice

3 put, say **4** part, talk, tell, vent **5** say-so, sound, speak, state, utter **6** assert, choice, medium, singer, speech **7** declare, express, opinion, present **8** vocalize **9** condition, enunciate, formulate, pronounce, statement, utterance, verbalize **10** articulate, expression, instrument
female: **4** alto **5** mezzo **7** soprano **9** contralto
high: **5** tenor **7** soprano **8** falsetto
in grammar: **6** active **7** passive
Latin: **3** vox
male: **4** bass **5** tenor **8** baritone
quality: **5** pitch **6** timbre
quiet: **7** whisper
relating to: **5** vocal **8** phonetic
without: **4** dumb, mute

voice box

6 larynx

voiced

4 oral **5** vocal **6** sonant, spoken **7** uttered **8** phonated **9** expressed

voiceless

3 mum **4** dumb, mute, surd **6** silent **8** breathed **12** inarticulate

void

3 gap, nix **4** emit, hole, idle, lack, null, undo **5** abyss, annul, blank, clear, empty, inane, quash **6** bereft, cancel, cavity, hollow, negate, remove, vacant, vacate, vacuum **7** absence, give off, negated, nullify, rescind, reverse, vacuity, vacuous **8** abrogate, deserted, evacuate **9** black hole, discharge, eliminate, emptiness **10** extinguish **11** nothingness

volant

4 fast, spry, yare **5** agile, fleet, quick, zippy **6** flying, lively, nimble **9** dexterous, sprightly

volar

6 palmar

volatile

5 flaky **6** fickle, flying, lively **7** erratic, essence, flighty **8** fleeting, fugitive, skittery, skittish, unstable, variable, volcanic **9** ephemeral, explosive, fugacious, mercurial, momentary, transient **10** capricious, changeable, evanescent, inconstant, short-lived, transitory **11** impermanent **13** temperamental

volatility

10 fickleness **11** flightiness, inconstancy, instability **13** changeability

volcanic

7 violent **8** volatile **9** explosive
explosion: **8** eruption
glass: **8** obsidian
matter: **3** ash **4** lava, tufa, tuff **5** magma **6** scoria
mound: **4** cone
passage: **6** throat **7** conduit
vent: **8** fumarole **9** solfatara

volcano

4 hill, vent **8** mountain
Alaska: **6** Katmai (Mount) **8** Wrangell (Mount) **9** Aniakchak (Crater)
Andes: **5** Omate **12** Huaina Putina
Antarctica: **6** Erebus (Mount)
Azores: **4** Alto (Pico)
California: **6** Lassen (Peak)
Canaries: **5** Teide (Pico de), Teyde (Pico de) **8** Tenerife (Pico de)
Colombia: **5** Huila (Nevado del), Pasto **6** Purace **7** Galeras
Costa Rica: **4** Poás **5** Barba, Irazú
Ecuador: **6** Sangay **8** Antisana, Cotopaxi
extinct: **4** Popa (Mount) **5** Iriga,

Kenya (Mount) **8** Mauna Kea
9 Haleakala (Crater)
Guatemala: 4 Agua **5** Fuego
7 Atitlán
Hawaii: 7 Kilauea **8** Mauna Loa
Honshu: 4 Nasu **5** Asama, Azuma
6 Bandai **8** Nasudake **9** Asama-
yama
Iceland: 5 Askja, Hecla, Hekla
Indonesia: 3 Awu (Gunung)
5 Agung (Gunung) **7** Tambora
(Gunung)
island: 5 Thera, Thira **8** Krakatau,
Krakatoa, Santorin **9** Santorini
Italy: 8 Vesuvius **9** Stromboli
Iwo Jima: 9 Suribachi (Mount)
Japan: 3 Aso **5** Unzen **6** Asosan
Java: 4 Gede (Gunung) **5** Bromo,
Gedeh (Gunung), Kelud (Gunung),
Salak (Gunung)
Madeira: 5 Ruivo (Pico)
Martinique: 5 Pelée (Mount)
Mexico: 6 Colima **7** Orizaba
9 Paricutín **12** Popocatepetl
New Zealand: 7 Ruapehu (Mount)
9 Ngauruhoe, Tongariro
Peru: 5 Misti (El)
Philippines: 3 Apo (Mount) **4** Taal
5 Mayon (Mount) **8** Pinatubo (Mount)
Sicily: 4 Etna
Solomons: 5 Balbi
South America: 5 Lanín, Maipo,
Maipu
Sumatra: 5 Dempo (Gunung)
7 Kerinci **8** Kerintji
type: 6 shield **10** cinder cone
Washington: 11 Saint Helens
(Mount)
West Indies: 9 Soufrière

_____ **volente**
3 Deo

volition
4 will **6** choice, desire, intent, option
8 decision, election **9** selection
10 preference

volley
4 hail, shot **5** burst, round, salvo,
storm **6** return, shower **7** barrage
8 drumfire **9** broadside, cannonade,
discharge, fusillade

volplane
5 glide

Volpone
3 Fox (The)
author: 6 Jonson (Ben)
servant: 5 Mosca

Volsung
grandson: 6 Sigurd **9** Siegfried
great-grandfather: 4 Odin
son: 7 Sigmund

voltage
5 power **6** energy **9** intensity

Voltaire
drama: 5 Zaïre **6** Alzire, Brutus,
Mèrope, Oedipe **7** Mahomet **8** Tan-
crède
novel: 5 Zadig **7** Candide
real name: 6 Arouet (François
Marie)

volte-face
5 U-turn **8** flip-flop, reversal, turnover **9** about-face, inversion, turnabout **10** switcheroo **13** change of
heart

voluble
4 glib **5** gabby, talky, windy **6** chatty,
fluent, mouthy, prolix **7** verbose
8 effusive, vocative **9** garrulous,
talkative **10** long-winded, loquacious

volume
4 body, book, bulk, mass, size,
tome **5** album, flood, folio, space
6 amount, scroll **7** content **8** capacity, loudness, quantity **9** aggregate
12 displacement

voluminous
4 full **5** bulky **6** legion, prolix **7** copious **8** numerous, prolific **9** capacious **10** convoluted **13** multitudinous

Volumnia's son
10 Coriolanus

voluntary
4 free **7** willful, willing, witting
8 elective, freewill, optional **10** autonomous, deliberate, volitional
11 independent, intentional, spontaneous **13** discretionary

volunteer
5 offer 6 enlist, join up, sign up
7 present, propose, suggest
hospital: 12 candy striper

Volunteer State
9 Tennessee

voluptuous
4 sexy 5 ample, buxom 6 wanton
7 languid, sensual 8 luscious,
sensuous 9 bodacious, luxurious
10 curvaceous

volute
5 helix, shell 6 scroll, spiral 7 mollusc, mollusk 8 curlicue

vomit
3 gag 4 barf, cast, gush, hurl, lose,
puke, spew, toss 5 expel, retch
6 spit up 7 bring up, throw up,
upchuck 8 disgorge 11 regurgitate

vomiting
6 emesis

Vonnegut work
9 Galapagos, Timequake 10 Cat's
Cradle, Hocus Pocus 11 Player
Piano 13 Sirens of Titan (The)
18 Slaughterhouse Five 20 Breakfast of Champions 22 Happy Birth-
day Wanda June

voodoo
3 hex 4 jinx, juju, mojo 5 charm,
magic, spell 6 amulet, whammy
7 bewitch, enchant, sorcery 8 ensorcel, wizardry 9 ensorcell 10 hocus-
pocus, mumbo jumbo, necromancy,
witchcraft 11 abracadabra, implausible, unrealistic

voracious
4 avid 5 eager 6 ardent, greedy,
hungry 7 piggish, starved 8 edacious, famished, ravenous, starving
9 rapacious 10 gluttonous, insatiable, omnivorous, quenchless

vortex
4 eddy, gyre 5 swirl 7 tornado
9 hurricane, maelstrom, whirlpool,
whirlwind 11 tourbillion

votary
3 bug, fan, nut 4 buff 5 lover 6 addict, zealot 7 admirer, advocate,
apostle, devotee, groupie, habitué
8 adherent, believer, disciple, follower 9 worshiper 10 aficionado,
enthusiast, worshipper

vote
3 opt 4 poll 5 elect, judge, offer
6 ballot, choice, choose, decide,
ratify, select, ticket 7 adjudge,
declare, endorse, express, opinion,
propose, suggest, verdict 8 election,
suffrage 9 franchise 10 expression
affirmative: 3 aye, nod, yea, yes
6 placet
kind: 5 proxy, straw, voice 6 secret
7 write-in 8 absentee 10 plebiscite,
referendum
negative: 3 nay
right to: 8 suffrage 9 franchise

votive
8 grateful 10 devotional

vouch
5 prove 6 affirm, assert, assure,
attest, uphold, verify 7 certify, confirm, support, witness 8 accredit
9 guarantee 11 corroborate 12 substantiate

voucher
3 IOU 4 chit 5 proof 6 coupon,
surety 7 receipt 9 affidavit, indenture 10 credential 11 certificate
13 authorization

vouchsafe
4 give 5 award, favor, grant 6 accord, bestow, confer, oblige 7 concede, furnish

vow
4 aver, oath, word 5 swear, troth
6 assert, attest, pledge, plight 7 confirm, declare, promise, warrant
8 covenant 9 assertion, guarantee
10 obligation 11 declaration

vowel
6 letter, symbol 11 speech sound
kind: 4 high, long 5 glide, schwa,
short 9 diphthong 11 monophthong
omission: 7 aphesis 11 contraction
variation: 6 ablaut, umlaut

voyage

4 sail, trek, trip 5 jaunt 6 cruise,
junket, outing, travel 7 journey,
odyssey, set sail 8 traverse 9 excursion 10 expedition, pilgrimage

voyeur

6 peeper 10 peeping Tom

Vronski's lover

12 Anna Karenina

Vulcan

see **Hephaestus**

vulgar

3 low, raw 4 base, lewd, rude, vile
5 crass, crude, gaudy, gross, rough,
tacky 6 coarse, earthy, flashy, garish, ribald, sordid, tawdry 7 kitschy,
lowbred, lowbrow, obscene, profane,
uncouth 8 churlish; improper,
indecent, off-color, unseemly 9 barbarous, graceless, low-minded,
offensive, tasteless, unrefined 10 indecorous, indelicate, scurrilous,
unpolished, vernacular 11 pretentious

vulgate

10 vernacular

Vulgate translator

6 Jerome

vulnerability

8 exposure, soft spot, weakness
10 underbelly 12 Achilles' heel

vulnerable

4 open, weak 6 liable 7 exposed
10 assailable 11 susceptible

vulnerary

4 balm 5 salve, tonic 7 healing,
unguent 8 curative, ointment, remedial, salutary, sanative 9 medicinal,
wholesome 10 salubrious 11 restorative, therapeutic 12 health-
giving

vulpine

3 sly 4 foxy, wily 5 slick 6 artful,
astute, crafty, shrewd, tricky 7 cunning, foxlike 8 guileful

vulture

4 bird 6 condor 11 lammergeier,
lammergeyer
food: 7 carrion
relative: 4 hawk 5 eagle 6 falcon
7 buzzard

vulturine

8 ravenous 9 predatory, rapacious,
raptorial 10 predaceous, predacious,
scavenging

W

wacky
3 fey, mad 4 daft, nuts 5 batty, daffy, crazy, flaky, kooky, loony, loopy, silly 6 absurd, fruity, insane, screwy 7 bonkers, cracked, foolish, idiotic, lunatic, offbeat 8 crackers, demented 9 eccentric 10 irrational 11 harebrained 12 preposterous

wad
3 gob 4 lump, mint, pile, plug, quid, roll, swab 5 chunk, stuff 6 boodle, bundle, packet, pellet 7 fortune 8 bankroll

waddle
6 toddle

waddy
4 club, cosh 6 cowboy, cudgel 7 rustler 8 bludgeon

wade
4 ford, plod 5 labor 6 drudge, trudge
into: 5 set to 6 attack, plunge, tackle 9 undertake

wadi
3 bed 4 wash 5 gully 6 arroyo, coulee, course, ravine 9 streambed 10 depression 11 watercourse

wafer
4 chip, disk, host 5 matzo, slice 6 matzoh 7 cracker

waffle
4 yo-yo 5 tripe, waver 6 dither, drivel, seesaw 7 blather 8 flip-flop 9 fluctuate, vacillate 10 equivocate

waft
4 flag, gust, puff, wave 5 drift, float, hover 7 pennant

wag
3 bob, nod, wit 4 card, lash, wave 5 clown, cutup, joker, shake, swing, whisk 6 kidder, switch, twitch, waddle 8 brandish, comedian, funnyman, jokester

wage
3 fee, pay 6 income, reward, salary 7 carry on, payment, stipend 8 earnings, pittance, receipts 9 emolument 10 recompense 12 compensation, remuneration

wager
3 bet, lay, pot 4 ante, game, risk 5 stake 6 chance, gamble, hazard 7 venture

waggery
3 gag 4 jest, joke 5 prank, sport 7 devilry, kidding, roguery 8 deviltry, drollery, mischief 10 impishness, pleasantry 11 roguishness 12 sportiveness 13 practical joke

waggish
4 arch, pert 5 antic, comic, droll, saucy, witty 6 impish, jocose 7 comical, jocular, playful, puckish, roguish 8 humorous, prankish, sportive 9 facetious 10 frolicsome 11 mischievous

waggle
3 bob 4 reel, sway

Wagner, Richard
birthplace: 7 Leipzig
father-in-law: 5 Liszt (Franz)
festival site: 8 Bayreuth
opera: 4 Ring 6 Rienzi 8 Parsifal 9 Lohengrin, Rheingold (Das),

Siegfried **10** Die Walküre, Tannhäuser **12** Das Rheingold **13** Meistersinger (Die) **14** Flying Dutchman (The) **15** Götterdämmerung **16** Tristan und Isolde **17** Ring of the Nibelung (The)
recurring theme: 9 leitmotif, leitmotiv
wife: 5 Minna **6** Cosima

wagon
3 van **4** cart, dray, tram, trek, wain **7** caravan, coaster, hayrack

wahoo
3 ono **8** mackerel **9** winged elm **11** burning bush

waif
5 gamin, stray **6** gamine, orphan, urchin **8** wanderer **9** foundling **10** ragamuffin **11** guttersnipe

wail
3 bay, cry **4** bawl, blub, fuss, howl, keen, weep, yowl **5** mourn, whine **6** bemoan, lament, plaint, repine **7** blubber, ululate **8** complain **9** complaint **11** lamentation

wain
5 wagon **9** Big Dipper

waistband
3 obi **4** belt, sash **6** girdle **8** ceinture, cincture **10** cummerbund

waistcoat
4 vest **6** jerkin, weskit

wait
4 bide, idle, stay **5** abide, dally, delay, serve, tarry, watch **6** expect, hold on, linger, remain **8** hang fire, mark time, sit tight **10** anticipate **11** stick around

waiter
4 tray **6** garçon, salver, server **7** servant **9** attendant

Waiting for ____
5 Godot, Lefty

wait on
4 tend **5** serve **6** attend, tend to **7** care for, cater to **9** look after

waive
4 cede, stay **5** allow, defer, delay, forgo, table, yield **6** give up, hold up, put off, shelve **7** abandon, concede, dismiss, hold off, suspend **8** hand over, hold over, postpone **9** surrender **10** relinquish

wake
4 path, stir, wash **5** alert, arise, get up, rally, rouse, track, vigil, watch **6** arouse, bestir, excite, kindle, stir up **7** roll out **8** backwash **9** aftermath, stimulate

wakeful
5 alert **8** restless, vigilant **9** insomniac, sleepless

waken
see **wake**

Walden author
7 Thoreau (Henry David)

wale
3 rib **4** bend, welt **5** brace, ridge **6** strake

walk
3 pad **4** gait, hike, hoof, pace, path, plod, roam, slog, step, trip **5** alley, amble, clump, mince, paseo, stave, strut, stump, trail, tramp, tread, troop **6** prance, ramble, sashay, stride, stroll, toddle, trudge, waddle, wander **7** saunter, shamble, shuffle, stumble, swagger, traipse **8** ambulate, traverse **9** promenade **11** base on balls, perambulate, peregrinate

walkaway
4 romp, rout

walking shorts
8 Bermudas

walking stick
4 cane **5** staff **6** crutch, insect **7** phasmid, whangee

walk out
5 leave **6** strike

walk out on
5 leave **6** desert **7** abandon, forsake

Walküre composer
6 Wagner (Richard)

walkway
4 path 7 passage 9 promenade

wall
3 bar, hem 4 side, stop 5 block,
close, fence, hedge 6 immure
7 barrier, close in, enclose 8 blockade, surround 9 barricade, enclosure, roadblock, structure
bearing: 7 support
hanging: 8 tapestry
painting: 5 mural
protective: 7 parapet, rampart
top of: 6 coping

wallaby
8 kangaroo

wallet
5 funds 6 folder 8 billfold 9 accessory, resources 10 pocketbook

Wallis and Futuna Islands
capital: 7 Mata-Utu
island: 4 Uvéa
territory of: 6 France

wallop
3 bop, hit 4 bang, bash, beat, belt,
blow, boil, bust, clip, drub, lick, pelt,
slam, slug, sock, whip, whop, whup
5 baste, paste, pound, punch,
smack, whack 6 buffet, pummel,
thrash, thwack 7 shellac, trounce
8 lambaste

walloping
4 huge 5 giant 7 immense, mammoth, monster 8 colossal, enormous, gigantic, smashing 10 gargantuan, impressive, incredible,
prodigious

wallow
4 bask, roll 5 enjoy, revel 6 billow,
welter 7 delight, indulge 9 luxuriate

_____ Walpole
4 Hugh 6 Horace

_____ Walton
3 Sam 5 Izaak

waltz
5 dance, valse

Waltz King
7 Strauss (Johann)

Wampanoag chief
9 Massasoit, Metacomet 10 King
Philip

wampum
5 beads, money 6 shells

wan
3 dim 4 ashy, gray, pale, waxy,
weak, worn 5 ashen, faint, livid,
lurid, pasty, waxen 6 anemic,
doughy, feeble, infirm, pallid, peaked,
sallow, sickly 7 ghastly, languid
8 blanched 9 bloodless, colorless,
washed-out 10 cadaverous, white-
faced

wand
3 rod 4 pole, tube 5 baton, staff

wander
3 bat, bum, gad 4 mill, roam, rove,
swan 5 amble, dally, drift, float,
gypsy, mooch, prowl, range, stray,
tramp 6 ramble, stroll 7 deviate,
digress, diverge, maunder, meander,
saunter, traipse 8 divagate, straggle,
vagabond 9 expatiate, gallivant
10 kick around

wanderer
4 waif 5 gypsy, nomad, rover, stray
7 pilgrim, vagrant 8 runabout,
vagabond

wandering
7 erratic, migrant, nomadic, vagrant
8 vagabond 9 itinerant, migratory,
walkabout, wayfaring 10 roundabout
11 peripatetic

wane
3 dim, ebb 4 fail, fall 5 abate, let up
6 lessen, recede, reduce, relent,
shrink, weaken 7 decline, dwindle,
slacken, subside 8 decrease, diminish, moderate, slack off, taper off

wangle
6 scheme 7 finagle, wheedle 8 inveigle, scrounge 10 manipulate

wannabe
5 clone 7 also-ran, copycat, hopeful,
wishful 8 apparent, aspiring, desiring, desirous 9 ambitious, look-alike,
potential

want

4 lack, like, need, void, wish **5** covet, crave, fault **6** dearth, desire, penury **7** absence, poverty, require **8** exigency **9** indigence, necessity, neediness, privation **10** deficiency, desiderate, inadequacy, scantiness **11** destitution, requirement **13** insufficiency

wanting

4 away, less, sans **5** minus, scant, short **6** absent, scanty, scarce **7** lacking, missing, without **9** deficient **10** inadequate, incomplete **12** insufficient

wanton

4 doxy, jade, lewd, minx, rank, slut **5** bawdy, cruel, hussy, loose, tramp, trull, wench **6** coquet, floozy, harlot, lavish, trifle, unruly **7** baggage, cyprian, immoral, jezebel, lustful, obscene, Paphian, sensual, trollop, wayward **8** inhumane, pitiless, ruthless, slattern, spiteful, sportive, strumpet **9** dissolute, luxuriant, malicious, merciless **10** gratuitous, lascivious, malevolent, outrageous, prostitute **11** extravagant, mischievous, uncalled-for

wapiti

3 elk **7** red deer

war

4 feud, odds **5** fight **6** battle, combat, strife **7** contest **8** conflict, struggle, variance **9** hostility **10** antagonism **11** competition
German: **5** Krieg **10** blitzkrieg
god: **3** Tiu, Tyr **4** Ares, Mars, Odin **5** Woden, Wotan
goddess: **4** Enyo **5** Anath **6** Inanna, Ishtar **7** Bellona
Latin: **6** bellum
Muslim: **5** jehad, jihad
relating to: **7** martial

War and Peace

author: **7** Tolstoy (Leo)
composer: **9** Prokofiev (Sergey)

warble

4 sing **5** carol, chirp, trill, tweet **6** gadfly, maggot, quaver **7** descant, melisma, twitter

warbler

4 bird **6** singer **7** kinglet **8** songster **9** blackpoll **11** gnatcatcher
European: **10** chiffchaff

war cry

5 motto **6** slogan
Greek: **5** alala
Japanese: **6** banzai

ward

4 care **5** aegis, stave **6** barrio, charge **7** custody, defense, keeping **8** district, division, precinct, security **9** bishopric **10** protection **11** safekeeping **12** guardianship

warden

6 jailer, keeper, regent **7** provost **8** governor, guardian, official **9** castellan, constable, custodian, protector **10** commandant, supervisor

ward off

5 avert, parry, rebut, repel **6** divert **7** deflect **8** turn away **9** forestall

wardrobe

5 trunk **6** closet **7** apparel, armoire, clothes **8** clothing **9** garderobe **12** clothespress

warehouse

4 stow **5** depot, lodge, stock, store **7** confine, deposit, shelter, storage, stowage **8** building **9** stockroom, storeroom **10** depository, repository **11** accommodate
oriental: **6** godown

wares

4 line **5** goods, stock **9** vendibles **11** commodities, marketables, merchandise

warfare

6 battle, combat, strife **8** conflict, struggle **10** operations **11** hostilities
type: **4** germ **6** trench **10** biological

warhorse

4 hack **7** charger, courser, veteran **8** chestnut, standard

warlike

7 hawkish, martial **8** militant, military **9** bellicose, combative, truculent **10** aggressive, pugnacious **11** belligerent

warlock
3 wiz 4 mage 5 magus 6 wizard
8 conjurer, conjuror, magician, satanist, sorcerer 9 diabolist, enchanter
11 necromancer

warm
4 bask, heat, kind 5 angry, fresh
6 ardent, genial, heated, heat up,
loving, reheat, secure, tender 7 affable, cordial, excited, fervent,
sincere 8 friendly, gracious, spirited
9 heartfelt 10 passionate, responsive 11 kindhearted, sympathetic
12 affectionate, enthusiastic, wholehearted 13 compassionate
air: 7 thermal

warmed-over
5 banal, stale, tired, trite 6 old-hat
7 cliched 8 shopworn, timeworn
9 hackneyed

warmhearted
4 kind 6 benign, kindly, loving,
tender 7 cordial 8 generous 9 benignant, unselfish 10 benevolent
11 magnanimous, sympathetic
12 affectionate 13 compassionate

warmth
4 glow, heat 7 comfort 8 fondness
9 affection 10 cordiality

warn
3 tip 4 clew, clue 5 alert 6 advise,
inform, notify, tip off 7 apprise,
caution, counsel 8 admonish

warning
3 tip 4 hint 5 alarm, alert 6 caveat,
notice, signal, tip-off 7 caution,
counsel, summons 8 monition,
monitory 10 admonition, cautionary
12 admonishment
legal: 6 caveat

War of the Worlds author
5 Wells (H. G.)

warp
4 base, bend, cast, kink, rope, wind
5 color, curve, twist 6 buckle, debase, deform, wrench 7 confuse,
contort, corrupt, deflect, distort,
pervert, torture, vitiate 10 bastardize
12 misrepresent

warrant
4 pawn, writ 5 proof, prove, token
6 affirm, assert, assure, attest,
avouch, ensure, ground, insure,
pledge, secure 7 certify, contend, declare, justify, precept 8 guaranty,
maintain, mittimus, sanction, security
9 assurance, authority, authorize,
guarantee 10 foundation 11 certificate 12 confirmation 13 justification

warranty
4 bail, bond 6 surety 8 covenant,
security 9 guarantee

warren
4 maze 7 network, rabbits
8 tenement

warrior
4 hero 7 battler, fighter, soldier
8 champion 9 combatant 10 serviceman
female: 6 Amazon
Japanese: 7 samurai

Warsaw
castle: 5 Zamek
river: 7 Vistula

wart
4 flaw 6 defect, growth 7 blemish,
verruca 11 excrescence

wary
5 alert, cagey, canny, chary, leery
7 careful, dubious, guarded, mindful
8 cautious, skittish, vigilant, watchful
10 suspicious 11 circumspect,
distrustful

wash
3 lap, pan, tub 4 hose, lave, suds,
wadi 5 bathe, clean, creek, douse,
drift, float, flush, marsh, scrub, slosh,
swill 6 drench, shower, sluice,
splash 7 cleanse, coating, launder,
laundry, shampoo, suffuse
8 backwash

washed-out
4 beat 5 all in, faded, spent, tired,
weary 6 bushed, effete, sapped,
used-up, wasted 7 drained 8 depleted 9 exhausted

washed-up
4 beat, done 5 kaput, spent 6 done

in **7** also-ran, defunct, done for, through **8** finished

washing
4 bath **6** lavage **7** laundry **8** ablution, lavation
ceremonial: 6 lavabo

Washington
capital: 7 Olympia
city: 6 Tacoma **7** Seattle, Spokane **9** Vancouver **10** Walla Walla
college, university: 7 Gonzaga, Whitman **9** Evergreen
dam: 11 Grand Coulee
mountain, range: 7 Cascade, Olympic, Rainier **8** St. Helens
nickname: 9 Evergreen (State)
river: 6 Yakima **8** Columbia
state bird: 9 goldfinch
state flower: 12 rhododendron
state tree: 7 hemlock

Washington, D.C., designer
7 L'Enfant (Pierre-Charles)

Washington, George
home: 11 Mount Vernon
wife: 6 Martha

Washington Square author
5 James (Henry)

wasp
5 mason **6** digger, hornet, vespid **9** ichneumon, mud dauber **12** yellow jacket

waspish
5 testy **6** snappy, snarky, snippy, touchy **7** peevish, vespine **8** petulant, snappish, vinegary **9** crotchety, fractious, irritable, querulous **10** vinegarish **12** cantankerous, cross-grained

wassail
5 binge, carol, drink, revel, spree, toast **6** bender **7** carouse, revelry, roister **8** carousal, drinking

Wasserstein play
15 Heidi Chronicles (The) **17** Sisters Rosenzweig (The)

waste
4 arid, fail, kill, loss, ruin, sack, wild **5** empty, offal, scrap, trash **6** barren, damage, debris, desert, devour, litter, ravage, refuse, sewage, shrink, weaken **7** badland, consume, despoil, destroy, fritter, garbage, pillage, plunder, rubbish **8** decrease, desolate, emaciate, enfeeble, misspend, prodigal, spoilage, squander, wear away, wildland **9** devastate, dissipate, excrement, sweepings, throw away **10** desolation, wilderness **11** prodigality **12** extravagance, extravagancy
maker: 5 haste
time: 5 dally **6** dawdle, footle, piddle, trifle

waste away
4 fade, fail **6** molder, shrink **7** atrophy, decline, dwindle, shrivel **10** degenerate

wasted
3 lit **4** high **5** drunk, gaunt **6** peaked, sickly, stoned **7** elapsed, ravaged **8** skeletal **9** emaciated **10** cadaverous, skeletonic **11** intoxicated

wasteful
6 lavish **8** prodigal **9** throwaway **10** profligate, thriftless, uneconomic **11** extravagant, improvident, inefficient, spendthrift

wastefulness
6 excess **10** lavishness **11** prodigality **12** extravagance, immoderation

wasteland
4 wild **5** heath **6** barren **10** desolation, wilderness

Waste Land author
5 Eliot (T. S.)

wastrel
3 rip **4** rake, roué **7** rounder, spender **8** prodigal **9** fritterer, libertine **10** dissipater, high roller, ne'er-do-well, profligate, squanderer **11** scattergood, spendthrift

watch
3 eye, see, spy **4** bide, look, tend, tout, wait, wake, ward **5** guard, shift,

vigil **6** attend, follow, look at, notice, sentry **7** care for, lookout, monitor, observe, surveil **8** bulletin, eagle eye, scrutiny, sentinel, watchman **9** attention, timepiece, vigilance **10** duty period, observance **11** chronometer, observation **12** surveillance
chain: **3** fob
maker: **10** horologist

watchdog
5 guard **6** keeper **8** Cerberus, guardian **9** custodian, protector

watcher
6 viewer **7** guarder, lookout **8** beholder, follower, guardian, observer, onlooker **9** spectator

watchful
4 wary **5** alert, chary **7** on guard, wakeful **8** cautious, vigilant **9** attentive, observant, sleepless, wide-awake **10** unsleeping
Scottish: **5** tenty **6** tentie

watchman
5 guard, scout **6** patrol, picket, sentry, warder **7** lookout **8** sentinel

watch out
6 beware **8** take care

watchtower
6 turret **7** lookout **8** barbican, bartizan **10** lighthouse

watchword
3 cry **5** motto **6** mantra, parole, signal, slogan **8** password **9** principle **10** shibboleth **11** catchphrase, countersign

water
4 soak, thin, tide **5** drink, fluid, spray **6** dilute, liquid, supply **7** moisten **8** irrigate, moisture, snowmelt, sprinkle **10** excellence **13** amniotic fluid
body: **3** bay, sea **4** gulf, lake, pond **5** ocean **6** lagoon, strait **9** reservoir
combining form: **4** aqui, aquo, hydr **5** hydro
French: **3** eau
goddess: **4** Nina **7** Anahita, Anaitis
Latin: **4** aqua
Spanish: **4** agua

water buffalo
4 arna **5** bovid **7** carabao
female: **5** arnee

water clock
9 clepsydra

water closet
3 loo **4** head, john **5** privy **6** toilet **7** latrine **8** bathroom, lavatory

watercourse
4 dike, duct **5** bayou, canal, ditch **6** arroyo **7** channel, conduit **8** aqueduct, headrace, tailrace **9** streambed

water cow
6 dugong **7** manatee

watered-down
5 washy **6** dilute **7** diluted

waterfall
5 chute, sault, shoot **7** cascade **8** cataract
Brazil: **6** Iguaçú (Falls), Iguazú (Falls)
California: **8** Yosemite (Falls)
Canada: **5** Grand (Falls) **8** Takkakaw **9** Churchill (Falls)
Canada-U.S.: **7** Niagara (Falls)
Congo: **6** Boyoma (Falls) **7** Stanley (Falls)
former Nile: **4** Owen (Falls) **5** Ripon (Falls)
Kentucky: **10** Cumberland (Falls)
New Zealand: **10** Sutherland (Falls)
Niagara: **8** American, Canadian **9** Horseshoe
Norway: **6** Rjukan (Falls)
Oregon: **9** Multnomah (Falls)
South Africa: **6** Tugela (Falls)
Snake River: **4** Twin (Falls) **8** Shoshone (Falls)
Venezuela: **5** Angel (Falls)
Washington: **10** Snoqualmie (Falls)
world's highest: **5** Angel (Falls)
Wyoming: **11** Yellowstone (Falls)
Zambezi River: **8** Victoria

water finder
6 dowser **11** divining rod

waterfront
8 seacoast **9** lakeshore, riverside

water hole
5 oasis

watering hole
3 bar, pub 4 café 5 oasis 6 lounge, nitery, resort, saloon, tavern 7 barroom, cabaret 9 nightclub, nightspot, roadhouse 10 supper club

waterless
3 dry 4 arid, sere 7 bone-dry 8 droughty 9 anhydrous 10 dehydrated

waterlog
8 saturate

waterloo
4 ruin 6 defeat 7 failure 8 disaster, downfall

water nymph
4 lily 5 naiad 6 mayfly, Nereid 7 Oceanid 9 dragonfly
female: 3 nix 5 nixie

water oscillation
6 seiche

water pipe
4 bong 5 spout 6 hookah 8 narghile, nargileh 12 hubble-bubble

water plant
7 aquatic, seaweed 8 duckweed, wild rice 9 arrowhead, tape grass 10 hydrophyte, manna grass 11 bladderwort

water rat
6 nutria

watershed
6 crisis, divide 12 turning point

water spirit
3 nix 5 nixie, nymph 6 sprite, undine

water tank
7 cistern

watery
4 pale, thin, weak 5 banal, bland, vapid, washy 6 dilute, serous 7 diluted, insipid

wattle
4 gill, grid, jowl 5 frame 8 caruncle 9 framework, interlace 10 interweave

wattle and ___
4 daub

wave
3 wag 4 flag, flap 5 heave, ridge, surge, sweep, swell 6 comber, influx, marcel, motion, period, ripple, signal, waggle 7 breaker, dismiss, flutter, gesture, upsurge 8 activity, brandish, flourish, undulate 9 disregard
large: 7 tsunami

waver
4 reel, sway 5 swing, weave 6 dither, falter, quaver, quiver, teeter, totter, wobble 7 flicker, stagger, whiffle 8 hesitate, undulate 9 oscillate, vacillate 12 shilly-shally

wavering
4 weak 5 shake, shaky 6 unsure, wobbly 7 halting 8 doubtful, insecure, to-and-fro, unstable 9 equivocal, faltering, fluctuant, hesitancy, undecided, vibration, whiffling 10 hesitating, hesitation, indecision, irresolute 11 fluctuating, vacillating, vacillation 12 irresolution, shilly-shally

Waverly author
5 Scott (Walter)

wavy
7 rolling 8 rippling, swelling 9 fluctuant 10 undulating 11 fluctuating

wavy pattern
5 moiré 8 squiggle 10 undulation 11 crenulation

wax
4 come, grow, rise 5 boost, build, mount 6 become, expand, record 7 augment, enlarge 8 heighten, increase, multiply, paraffin, simonize 9 secretion, substance

waxen
3 wan 4 ashy, pale 5 ashen, livid 6 pallid, smooth 7 pliable 8 blanched, moldable 9 colorless

way
3 ilk 4 door, kind, mode, much, path,

road, sort, type, very **5** entry, habit, means, order, route, state, style, usage **6** access, artery, action, avenue, course, custom, degree, manner, method, street **7** ability, fashion, feature, ingress, opening, outcome, respect **8** distance, entrance, practice **9** boulevard, condition, direction, procedure, technique **11** opportunity, possibility **12** thoroughfare

wayfarer
5 gypsy, hiker, nomad, tramp **8** traveler **9** itinerant, journeyer

wayfaring
6 roving **7** nomadic, vagrant **8** vagabond **9** itinerant, traveling, wandering **10** travelling **11** peripatetic **13** perambulatory

waylay
5 brace **6** ambush, attack **8** surprise **9** bushwhack, still-hunt

Way of All Flesh author
6 Butler (Samuel)

Way of the World author
8 Congreve (William)

wayward
5 balky **6** fickle, unruly **7** froward, restive, vagrant **8** contrary, perverse, untoward **9** whimsical **10** capricious, headstrong **11** intractable, wrongheaded **12** ungovernable **13** unpredictable

we
French: 4 nous
German: 3 wir
Italian: 3 noi
Spanish: 8 nosotros

weak
3 dim, wan **4** puny, soft, thin **5** faint, frail, shaky, timid **6** dilute, feeble, flimsy, infirm, sickly, unsure, watery, wobbly **7** brittle, diluted, fragile, rickety, spindly, tenuous, unsound **8** decrepit, delicate, helpless, impotent, inferior, insecure, timorous, unstable, wavering **9** deficient, enfeebled, inaudible, powerless, spineless, uncertain **10** improbable, inadequate, unreliable, unstressed **11** debilitated, implausible, ineffective, ineffectual, vacillating, watered-down **12** unconvincing, undependable **13** insubstantial, unsubstantial

weaken
3 lag, sap **4** fail, flag, thin, wane **5** abate **6** damage, dilute, impair, lessen, reduce, soften **7** corrode, decline, disable, dwindle, subvert, unbrace **8** enervate, enfeeble, moderate **9** attenuate, grind down, honeycomb, undermine **10** debilitate, demoralize, invalidate

weak-kneed
5 timid **6** wobbly **7** gutless **8** cowardly, wavering **9** faltering, uncertain, whiffling **10** irresolute **11** lily-livered, vacillating **12** fainthearted, shilly-shally **13** pusillanimous

weakling
4 wimp, wuss **5** mouse, sissy **7** doormat, milksop, sad sack **8** pushover **9** jellyfish **10** namby-pamby **11** milquetoast, mollycoddle **12** invertebrate

weakness
4 flaw, hole, vice **5** crack, fault, taste **6** defect, desire, liking, relish **7** failing, frailty **8** appetite, debility, fondness, soft spot **9** infirmity **10** feebleness **11** decrepitude, shortcoming **12** Achilles' heel

weal
4 welt **5** ridge **7** welfare **9** well-being

weald
5 woods **6** forest **8** woodland **10** timberland, wilderness

wealth
5 goods, worth **6** assets, estate, plenty, riches **7** capital, fortune **8** holdings, opulence, property **9** abundance, affluence, profusion, resources **11** possessions

Wealth of Nations author
5 Smith (Adam)

wealthy
4 rich 5 flush 6 loaded 7 moneyed, opulent, well-off 8 affluent, well-to-do 9 well-fixed 10 prosperous, well-heeled 12 silk-stocking

wean
4 free, part 5 alien 6 detach 8 accustom, estrange, separate

weapon
3 bow, gun 4 bill, bolo, bomb, club, dart, dirk, mace, nuke, pike 5 A-bomb, arrow, H-bomb, knife, lance, prick, rifle, saber, sabre, sling, spear, steel, sword 6 dagger, Magnum, musket, pistol, poleax, rapier, rocket 7 bazooka, broadax, car bomb, carbine, firearm, gisarme, halberd, javelin, machete, missile, shotgun, sidearm, stun gun, torpedo, war club 8 battle-ax, bludgeon, broadaxe, catapult, crossbow, death ray, nerve gas, nunchaku, partisan, partizan, petronel, revolver, spontoon, tomahawk 9 battle-axe, blackjack, boomerang, derringer, slingshot 10 atomic bomb, machine gun, projectile 11 blunderbuss, depth charge, nuclear bomb 12 quarterstaff 13 brass knuckles

weapons
4 arms 7 arsenal, battery 8 ordnance 9 armaments, artillery, munitions 13 armamentarium

wear
3 rub 4 fray, tire 5 chafe, dress, erode, grind 6 abrade, attire, endure, impair 7 corrode, exhibit, fatigue, fashion 8 abrasion, clothing
and tear: 12 depreciation
thin: 4 fray 5 chafe 6 tatter 7 hackney

wear down
5 drain, erode, grind 6 abrade, weaken 7 corrode, degrade, exhaust, fatigue

weariness
5 ennui 7 boredom, fatigue, languor 8 lethargy 9 lassitude 10 enervation, exhaustion 12 taedium vitae

wearing
6 taxing, tiring, trying 9 difficult, fatiguing

wearisome
see **tiresome**

wear out
3 fag 4 bust, do in, fray, poop, tire 5 drain 6 efface, tucker 7 consume, deplete, exhaust, frazzle 8 overstay

weary
4 beat, jade, limp, tire, worn 5 drain, jaded, spent, tired 6 bushed, done in, pooped, tucker, wasted 7 drained, fatigue, worn-out 8 dog-tired, fatigued, tiresome 9 apathetic

weasand
6 gullet, throat 7 trachea 8 windpipe 9 esophagus

weasel
5 dodge, evade, hedge, slink, sneak, stoat 6 ermine, escape, ferret, mammal 7 sneaker 8 sidestep 9 pussyfoot 10 equivocate
Scottish: 8 whittret

weather
4 rain 5 storm 6 bear up, endure, expose 7 climate, ride out, undergo 9 withstand
forecasting: 11 meteorology

weathercock
4 vane

weathered
8 hardened, seasoned, tempered

weave
4 cane, lawn, leno, spin, sway 5 braid, cloth, lurch, twine, waver 6 careen, fabric, pleach, raddle, wobble, zigzag 7 pattern, stagger, textile, texture 8 contrive 9 interlace 10 crisscross, intertwine

web
3 net 4 mesh, vane 5 snare, snarl 6 enmesh, fabric, tangle 7 ensnare, netting, network 8 entangle 10 enmeshment 12 entanglement

Weber opera
6 Oberon 9 Euryanthe 10 Freischütz (Der)

_____ Webster
4 Noah 6 Daniel

wed
4 join, link, mate, yoke 5 hitch, marry, merge, unite 6 splice 7 combine, conjoin, connect, espouse 10 tie the knot

wedded
7 marital, nuptial 8 conjugal, hymeneal 9 connubial 11 matrimonial

wedding
6 bridal 7 spousal 8 espousal, marriage, nuptials

wedding anniversary
fifteenth: 7 crystal
fifth: 6 wooden
fiftieth: 6 golden
first: 5 paper
seventy-fifth: 7 diamond
tenth: 3 tin
twentieth: 5 china
twenty-fifth: 6 silver

wedge
4 shim 5 chock, stuff 8 golf club, golf shot, keystone 10 force apart

wedge-shaped
7 cuneate 8 cottered, sphenoid 9 cuneiform

wedlock
4 knot, yoke 8 espousal, marriage 9 matrimony 11 conjugality 12 connubiality

wee
4 tiny 5 bitsy, bitty, early, small, teeny 6 little, minute, teensy 9 itty-bitty, miniature 10 diminutive, teeny-weeny 11 Lilliputian, little bitty 12 teensy-weensy

weed
4 dock, tare 5 chess, clear, plant 6 cockle, darnel, dodder, nettle, remove 7 burdock, burseed, ragweed, ruderal 8 amaranth, charlock, purslane 9 chickweed, cocklebur, dandelion, knotgrass, marijuana, poison ivy, poison oak, stickseed 10 cheatgrass, lady's thumb, sow thistle

European: 6 spurry 7 spurrey
killer: 8 paraquat 9 herbicide
Western: 4 loco

weedy
4 lean, thin 5 lanky 6 skinny 7 scrawny, stringy, willowy 8 untended 9 overgrown

week
6 period 8 hebdomad
two weeks: 9 fortnight

weep
3 cry, sob 4 drip, moan, ooze, tear, wail 5 bleed, exude, sweat 6 lament 7 blubber, dribble, trickle 8 transude

weepy
5 misty, moist, teary 7 tearful 10 lachrymose

weevil
7 billbug 8 curculio

weft
3 web 4 pick, woof, yarn 6 fabric, thread

weigh
3 way 4 heft, rate, tare 5 count, judge, scale, study 6 burden, ponder 7 balance, measure, oppress, perpend 8 appraise, bear down, consider, evaluate, militate 11 contemplate

weigh down
4 load 5 press 6 burden, sadden 7 depress, oppress 8 encumber 10 discourage, overburden

weight
3 tax 4 heft, lade, load, mass, onus, task 5 class, force, power 6 amount, assign, burden, charge, credit, import, moment, saddle 7 oppress, potency, quality 8 encumber, poundage, pressure, prestige, quantity 9 authority, influence, magnitude 10 corpulence, importance 11 consequence 12 significance
allowance: 4 tare
apothecary: 4 dram 5 grain, pound 7 scruple

Asian: 6 cattie
gem: 5 carat
measure of: 3 ton **4** dram, gram
5 grain, ounce, pound **7** long ton,
scruple **8** kilogram, short ton **9** metric ton
system: 3 net **4** troy **6** metric
10 apothecary **11** avoirdupois

weightiness

4 pith **6** import, moment **7** dignity,
gravity **9** heaviness, magnitude,
solemnity **10** importance **11** consequence, massiveness **12** significance **13** momentousness

weight lift

4 pull **5** clean, press, shrug **6** snatch
12 clean and jerk

weighty

3 fat **5** grave, gross, heavy, hefty,
obese, sober, staid **6** fleshy, portly,
sedate, severe, solemn, somber
7 massive, serious, telling **8** cumbrous, grievous, powerful **9** corpulent, effective, important, momentous, ponderous **10** burdensome,
convincing, cumbersome **11** significant, substantial **12** considerable
13 consequential

weir

3 dam **5** stank

weird

3 odd **5** eerie, queer **6** creepy,
freaky, spooky **7** bizarre, curious,
oddball, strange, uncanny **8** freakish,
peculiar, singular, sinister **9** eccentric, fantastic, unearthly **10** mysterious **11** inscrutable **12** supernatural **13** preternatural

weirdo

4 geek, kook **5** freak **7** nutcase,
oddball **8** crackpot **9** eccentric,
screwball

welcome

4 hail **5** cheer, greet, hello, howdy
6 accept, invite, salute **7** embrace,
invited, receive **8** greeting, pleasant,
pleasing **9** agreeable, favorable,
reception **10** gratifying, hospitable
11 hospitality, pleasurable

weld

4 bond, fuse, join **5** braze, joint,
merge, unite **6** solder

welfare

3 aid **4** dole, help, weal **5** pogey
6 health, relief, succor **7** benefit,
fortune, success, support **8** interest
9 advantage, happiness, well-being
10 assistance, commonweal, prosperity

welkin

3 sky **5** ether, vault **6** heaven
7 heavens **8** empyrean **9** firmament

well

3 far, fit, pit **4** easy, emit, hale, hole,
pool, rise, sane **5** amply, clear,
cured, fully, quite, shaft, sound,
truly **6** easily, freely, healed, indeed,
justly, kindly, likely, nicely, origin,
rather, really, source, spring, wholly
7 clearly, healthy, perhaps, readily,
rightly **8** entirely, expertly, pleasing,
possibly, probably, properly, sensibly,
smoothly, suitably **9** advisable,
correctly, desirable, elegantly, favorably, fittingly, fortunate, perfectly,
wholesome **10** acceptably, adequately, affluently, becomingly,
completely, pleasantly, pleasingly,
prosperous, reasonably, thoroughly
11 attentively, comfortable, compartment, fortunately, substantial
12 considerably, prosperously, satisfactory, successfully **13** appropriately, significantly

well-being

4 weal **6** health **7** welfare **8** thriving
9 happiness **10** prosperity

well-bred

6 urbane **7** genteel, refined **8** cultured, highborn, polished **9** civilized,
patrician **10** cultivated **11** blueblooded, gentlemanly

well-built

4 buff **5** hunky, solid **8** muscular
9 strapping

well-developed

5 curvy **7** fulsome, rounded, shapely
8 advanced **9** Junoesque **10** curvaceous

well-disposed
7 amiable 8 friendly 9 favorable, receptive 11 sympathetic 13 understanding

Welles movie
5 Trial (The) 7 Macbeth, Othello 8 Jane Eyre, Stranger (The), Third Man (The) 11 Citizen Kane, Touch of Evil 15 Journey into Fear 16 Chimes at Midnight, Lady from Shanghai (The) 20 Magnificent Ambersons (The)

well-favored
4 fair 6 comely, lovely, pretty 8 gorgeous, handsome 9 beauteous, beautiful 10 attractive 11 good-looking

well-fixed
see **well-to-do**

well-founded
5 sound, valid 6 cogent 8 rational 9 justified 10 convincing

well-groomed
4 neat, snug, tidy, trig, trim 5 natty, smart 6 dapper, snappy, spiffy, spruce, sprucy 7 orderly 8 clean-cut 9 shipshape

well-heeled
see **well-to-do**

Wellington
4 duke 7 general 8 Iron Duke
horse: 10 Copenhagen
original name: 9 Wellesley (Arthur)
victory: 7 Vitoria 8 Talavera, Waterloo 9 Salamanca

well-known
5 noted 6 famous 7 big-name, eminent, popular 8 renowned 9 notorious, prominent 10 celebrated 11 illustrious

well-liked
7 beloved, favored, popular 8 favorite 9 cherished, preferred

well-mannered
5 civil, suave 6 poised, polite, proper, urbane 7 genteel, tactful 9 courteous 10 diplomatic

well-nigh
6 all but, almost, fairly, nearly, next to 8 as good as 9 just about, virtually 11 essentially, practically

well-off
see **well-to-do**

well-paying
7 gainful 9 lucrative, rewarding 10 profitable, worthwhile 11 money-making 12 advantageous, remunerative

wellspring
4 font, root 5 fount 6 origin, source 7 genesis 8 fountain 10 provenance 11 provenience 12 fountainhead

well-thought-of
6 valued, worthy 7 admired, reputed 9 estimable, reputable 10 creditable 11 respectable

well-timed
6 timely 7 apropos, fitting, timeous 9 favorable, opportune 10 auspicious, felicitous, fortuitous, propitious, seasonable

well-to-do
4 rich 5 flush 6 loaded 7 moneyed, upscale, wealthy 8 affluent 10 prosperous 11 comfortable

well-turned
4 trim 5 plump 7 rounded, shapely 10 curvaceous, felicitous, Rubenesque, statuesque 11 clean-limbed

well-worn
5 banal, musty, stale, stock, tired, trite 6 frayed, old-hat, shabby 7 clichéd 8 bromidic, cobwebby, dog-eared, overused 9 hackneyed 10 threadbare 11 commonplace, stereotyped

Welsh
see **Cymric**

welsh
5 dodge 6 renege, resile 7 back out, default

welt
4 blow, edge, seam, wale, weal 5 ridge, wheal, whelk 6 insert

welter

4 coil, moil, toss 5 chaos, churn,
steep, surge 6 flurry, hassle, hubbub, jumble, lather, ruckus, seethe,
thrash, wallow, writhe 7 ferment,
turmoil 8 disorder 9 confusion

_____ Welty

6 Eudora

wen

4 bleb, cyst 5 blain 6 growth 7 vesicle 11 excrescence

wench

3 gal 4 girl, jade, lass, maid, minx,
miss, puss, slut, tart 5 hussy, nymph,
tramp, trull, whore, woman 6 damsel, gamine, harlot, hoyden, lassie,
maiden, wanton 7 jezebel, servant,
trollop 8 slattern, strumpet

wend

3 hie 4 fare, pass 6 direct, push on,
repair, travel 7 journey, proceed

werewolf

9 loup-garou 11 lycanthrope

Werther's beloved

5 Lotte 9 Charlotte

Wesleyan

9 Methodist

West

8 Occident

western

5 oater 9 Hesperian 10 horse
opera, occidental
hemisphere: 8 Americas, New
World

Western novelist

4 Grey (Zane), Ross (Dana Fuller)
5 Brand (Max), Faust (Frederick),
Short (Luke) 6 Judson (E. Z. C.),
L'Amour (Louis), Patten (Lewis),
Wister (Owen) 7 Guthrie (A. B.),
Leonard (Elmore) 8 Buntline (Ned),
McMurtry (Larry)

West Indies

country: 4 Cuba 5 Haiti 7 Bahamas, Grenada, Jamaica 8 Barbados, Dominica 10 Guadeloupe,
Martinique, Puerto Rico, Saint Lucia
17 Dominican Republic
island group: 6 Virgin (Islands)
7 Bahamas, Leeward (Islands)
8 Antilles (Greater, Lesser), Windward (Islands)

West Point

father of: 6 Thayer (Sylvanus)
freshman: 5 plebe
student: 5 cadet

West Side Story

composer: 9 Bernstein (Leonard)
heroine: 5 Maria
lyricist: 8 Sondheim (Stephen)

West Virginia

capital: 10 Charleston
city: 8 Wheeling 10 Huntington
mountain: 10 Spruce Knob
nickname: 8 Mountain (State)
river: 4 Ohio
state bird: 8 cardinal
state flower: 12 rhododendron
state tree: 10 sugar maple

west wind

see at wind

wet

3 sop 4 damp, dank, rain, soak,
wash, weak 5 douse, drown, drunk,
humid, moist, rainy, soggy, soppy,
souse, water 6 dampen, drench,
soaked, sodden, soused, sweaty,
watery 7 moisten, raining, soaking,
sopping 8 drenched, dripping,
humidify, irrigate, moisture, saturate,
slippery 9 saturated, spineless
combining form: 4 hygr 5 hygro

wet blanket

6 grinch 7 killjoy 8 sourpuss 9 pessimist 10 spoilsport 11 party pooper

wether

4 goat 5 sheep

wetland

3 bog, fen 4 mire, quag 5 marsh,
swamp 6 morass, muskeg, slough

whack

3 bat, hit, pop, try 4 bash, belt, biff,
blow, chop, cuff, kill, pelt, shot, sock,

stab, wham, whap, whop **5** crack,
punch, smack, smash **6** attack,
defeat, murder, strike, wallop **7** bump
off **8** knock off, lambaste
up: 4 part **5** divvy, split **6** divide
7 portion **9** apportion

whale

3 hit **4** beat, flog, hide, lash, whip
5 giant **6** defeat, strike, stripe, thrash
7 mammoth **8** cetacean, behemoth
9 leviathan **10** flagellate
arctic: 7 bowhead
group: 3 pod
killer: 4 orca
kind: 3 sei **4** blue **5** right, sperm
6 baleen, beluga, killer **7** narwhal,
rorqual **8** cachalot
tale: 8 Moby Dick
toothed: 5 pilot (whale) **9** blackfish
young: 4 calf

whalebone

9 scrimshaw

wham

3 hit **4** bang, beat, blow, boom, clap,
slam **5** blast, burst, crack, crash,
smash, whack **6** impact, propel,
strike **7** explode

whammy

3 hex, zap **4** jinx, juju **5** curse, spell
6 hoodoo, voodoo **7** evil eye

wharf

4 dock, pier, quay **5** jetty, levee

Wharton novel

10 Buccaneers (The), Ethan Frome
12 House of Mirth (The) **14** Age of
Innocence (The) **18** Custom of the
Country (The)

whatnot

7 étagère

wheal

4 lump, welt **5** ridge, whelk

wheat

4 crop **5** emmer, flour, grain, grass,
spelt **6** cereal **7** einkorn
beard: 3 awn
beat: 6 thresh
chaff: 4 bran

crushed: 6 bulgur
disease: 4 rust, smut
type: 4 club **5** durum

wheedle

3 con **4** coax **5** cozen **6** cajole,
entice, seduce **7** blarney, flatter
8 blandish, inveigle, scrounge,
soft-soap **9** sweet-talk

wheel

3 VIP **4** auto, gyre, move, reel, spin,
turn **5** cycle, drive, motor, pilot, pivot,
round, whirl **6** bigwig, circle, gyrate,
league, rotate, totter, travel **7** big
shot, circuit, revolve **8** rotation
9 about-face, volte-face
part: 3 hub, rim **4** tire **5** felly, spoke
spoke: 6 radius
toothed: 3 cog **4** gear

wheeze

3 saw, yuk **4** gasp, hiss, joke, puff,
rasp **5** adage, cough **6** saying
7 proverb, whistle **8** chestnut, rhonchus

whelk

4 wale, weal, welt **5** wheal

whelm

4 bury, sink **5** cover, drown, flood,
swamp **6** deluge, engulf **8** bear
down, inundate, overbear, overcome,
submerge **9** devastate

whelp

3 cub, kid, pup **4** bear **5** child,
puppy **9** youngster

whereas

5 since, while **6** seeing, though
7 howbeit **8** although **11** considering

wherefore

3 why **4** thus **5** proof **6** ground,
reason, whence **8** argument **11** explanation

wherewithal

5 funds, means, money **9** resources

wherry

4 boat **5** barge, scull **7** lighter,
rowboat

whet
4 edge, goad, hone **5** drink, rally, rouse, waken **6** arouse, awaken, excite, kindle **7** sharpen, starter **8** aperitif **9** appetizer, challenge, stimulate **10** incitement **11** hors d'oeuvre

whiff
3 fan **4** blow, gust, hint, puff, waft **5** expel, smoke, tinge, trace **6** breath, exhale, inhale **7** soupçon, whisper **9** strikeout **10** indication, inhalation

whiffet
6 nobody, squirt **9** nonentity

whiffle
4 blow, gust, puff **5** waver **6** dither, falter **9** fluctuate, vacillate **12** shilly-shally

while
4 pass, time, when **5** spell **6** albeit, moment, though **7** howbeit, stretch, whereas **8** although, as long as, so long as

whilom
6 bygone, former **7** onetime, quondam **8** formerly, previous, sometime **9** erstwhile

whim
3 bee **4** idea, kink **5** dream, fancy, freak, humor **6** maggot, megrim, notion, vagary **7** caprice, capstan, conceit, thought **8** crotchet

whimper
3 cry **4** fret, mewl, pule, wail **5** bleat, whine **6** snivel

whimsical
4 iffy, zany **5** droll, fancy, flaky **6** chancy, fickle, fitful, quirky, random **7** erratic, flighty, mutable, puckish, wayward **8** fanciful, freakish, volatile **9** eccentric, impulsive, pixilated, screwball, uncertain, vagarious **10** capricious **13** unpredictable

whimsy
3 bee **4** play **5** dream, fancy, freak, humor **6** levity, maggot, megrim, notion, vagary **7** caprice, conceit, fantasy **9** capriccio, frivolity

whim-wham
4 dido **5** curio, fancy, frill **6** bauble, gewgaw, ruffle, trifle **7** bibelot, flounce, trinket **8** furbelow, gimcrack, kickshaw **9** objet d'art **10** knick-knack

whine
3 cry **4** cant, fret, fuss, kick, moan, pule, wail **5** bleat, gripe **6** grouse, repine, snivel, whinge, yammer **7** grumble, snuffle, whimper **8** complain **9** bellyache

whinny
5 neigh **6** nicker **7** whicker

whiny
5 fussy **7** fretful, grouchy, peevish **8** petulant **9** irritable, querulous

whip
3 cut, hem, set **4** beat, cane, crop, dash, flog, hide, jerk, lash, lick, pull, rout, wind, wrap **5** abuse, mop up, quirt, spank, sting, whale, whisk **6** defeat, lather, snatch, strike, stroke, subdue, switch, thrash, urge on **7** agitate, dessert, provoke, rawhide, shellac, trounce, utensil **8** coachman, lambaste, overcome, vanquish **9** instigate, overwhelm **10** flagellate **13** cat-o'-nine-tails
braided: 10 blacksnake

whippersnapper
see **whiffet**

whipping boy
4 goat **5** patsy **7** fall guy **9** scapegoat

whippy
6 supple **7** elastic, springy **8** flexible **9** resilient

whir
3 fly, hum **4** burr, buzz, whiz **5** chirr, churr, drone, whizz **7** revolve, vibrate **9** bombinate

whirl
3 ado, gig, pop, try **4** eddy, flit, fuss, gyre, moil, reel, shot, spin, stab, stir, swim, turn, veer **5** hurry, pivot, swirl, whack, wheel **6** bustle, circle, gyrate, hassle, hubbub, pother, rotate **7** cir-

cuit, dervish, turmoil **8** ballyhoo, gyration, rotation **9** commotion, pirouette **10** revolution

whirligig
4 gyre, spin **6** beetle, gyrate **8** carousel **9** pirouette **12** merry-go-round

whirlpool
3 ado **4** eddy, fuss **6** bustle, flurry, furore, tumult, vortex **7** turmoil **8** vortices (plural) **9** commotion, maelstrom

whirlwind
4 rush, stir, to-do **5** hasty, spout, swift **6** bustle **7** cyclone, tornado, twister, typhoon **8** headlong **9** commotion, dust devil, dust storm, hurricane **10** waterspout **11** tourbillion

whish
4 fizz, hiss **6** fizzle **8** sibilate

whisk
3 mix, nip, wag, zip **4** beat, flit, whip **5** broom, brush, fluff, hurry, speed **6** switch

whisker
4 hair **7** bristle **8** filament, vibrissa **9** outrigger **11** hairbreadth

whiskered
5 hairy **6** pilose **7** bearded, bristly, hirsute **8** stubbled, unshaven

whiskers
5 beard **6** goatee **7** stubble, weepers **8** bristles **9** burnsides, peach fuzz, sideburns **11** muttonchops

whiskey
3 rye **6** liquor, Scotch **7** alcohol, bourbon
with beer chaser: 11 boilermaker

whisper
4 buzz, hint, hiss, whiz **5** rumor, shade, tinge, touch, trace, whiff **6** breath, gossip, murmur, mutter **8** sibilate, susurrus **9** suspicion, undertone **11** susurration

whist
4 game, hush **5** quiet, still **6** silent **9** noiseless, soundless

whistle
4 pipe, toot **5** flute, whiff **6** signal, tootle, wheeze

whistle-stop
5 stump **8** campaign, politick **9** barnstorm **11** electioneer

whit
3 bit, fig, jot, rap **4** atom, damn, hoot, iota, mite **5** crumb, scrap, shred, speck, whoop **7** dribble, modicum, smidgen **8** molecule, particle

white
4 pure **5** livid, milky, snowy **6** albino, blanch, bleach, pallid **7** silvery **9** colorless
combining form: 4 leuc, leuk **5** leuco, leuko
egg's: 5 glair **6** glaire **7** albumen

White novel
12 Stuart Little **13** Charlotte's Web

white cliffs of _____
5 Dover

White Fang author
6 London (Jack)

White House
designer: 5 Hoban (James)
first occupant: 5 Adams (Abigail, John)

white lightning
5 hooch **7** bootleg, whiskey **9** moonshine **10** bathtub gin **11** mountain dew

whiten
4 fade, pale **5** frost **6** blanch, bleach, blench **8** etiolate **10** decolorize

white plague
8 phthisis **11** consumption **12** tuberculosis

whitewash
6 parget **7** cover up **9** gloss over, gloze over, sugarcoat

whither
5 where **7** whereto **9** whereunto

whiting
3 cod **4** hake **10** silver hake

Whitsunday
9 Pentecost

Whittier poem
9 Snow-Bound 10 Maud Muller
11 Barefoot Boy 16 Barbara Frietchie

whittle
4 chip, form, fret, pare, trim 5 carve, shape, shave, skive 6 reduce, sculpt 8 diminish

whiz
3 fly, hum, zip 4 buzz, flit, hiss, zoom 5 hurry, speed, swish, whirl 6 expert, fizzle, genius, phenom, rotate, whoosh 8 virtuoso 10 wunderkind

whoa
3 hey 4 slow, stop 6 hold up

whole
3 all, fit, sum 4 full, hale, sane 5 sound, total, uncut, unity 6 entire, entity, healed, intact, system, unhurt 7 healthy, perfect, plenary 8 complete, entirely, entirety, flawless, restored, totality, unbroken, unmarred 9 recovered, undamaged, undivided, uninjured, untouched 10 unimpaired, unmodified 11 unblemished 12 concentrated, undistracted
combining form: 3 hol, pan 4 holo

wholehearted
6 ardent 7 devoted, earnest, fervent, sincere 8 bona fide 9 committed, heartfelt, steadfast, unfeigned 10 passionate, unwavering 11 impassioned 12 enthusiastic 13 unquestioning

whole-hog
6 all-out, gung-ho 8 complete, thorough 9 full-scale 11 straight-out 13 thoroughgoing

wholeness
7 oneness 8 entirety, totality 9 integrity, soundness 10 intactness, perfection

whole note
9 semibreve

whole number
5 digit 6 cipher 7 integer, numeral

wholesome
3 fit 4 good, hale, safe, sane, well 5 right, sound 6 benign 7 healthy 8 hygienic, salutary 9 favorable, healthful' 10 beneficial, salubrious

wholly
3 all 4 only 6 in toto, singly, solely, purely 7 totally 8 entirely 10 altogether, completely 11 exclusively

whomp
3 hit 4 beat, drub, slap, whip, whup 5 crash, thump 6 crunch, strike, thrash, wallop 7 clobber, shellac, trounce 8 lambaste

whomp up
4 stir 5 rouse, spark 6 arouse, excite, foment

whoopee
3 fun 5 revel, yahoo 6 gaiety, hoopla, yippee 7 jollity, revelry, wassail, whoopla 8 hilarity 9 festivity, high jinks, merriment 10 hurly-burly 11 merrymaking

whoopla
see **hoopla**

whop
3 bat, bop 4 bash, beat, biff, blow, drub, lick, sock 5 baste, pound, smack, thump, whack 6 batter, buffet, defeat, hammer, pummel, strike, thrash, thwack, wallop 7 trounce 8 lambaste

whopping
4 huge, vast 6 mighty 7 amazing, immense, massive 8 colossal, enormous, gigantic, whacking 9 bodacious, humongous, monstrous 10 gargantuan, incredible, prodigious 13 extraordinary

whorl
4 coil, eddy, turn 5 swirl 6 spiral

why
5 cause 6 enigma, motive, puzzle, reason, riddle 7 mystery, problem, what for 9 conundrum, rationale,

therefore, wherefore **10** puzzlement
11 explanation

wicked

4 evil, mean, very, vile **5** awful,
black, wrong **6** fierce, malign, sinful,
unholy **7** corrupt, hateful, heinous,
immoral, naughty, ungodly, vicious
8 depraved, devilish, fiendish
9 atrocious, barbarous, dangerous,
extremely, hazardous, injurious,
malicious, malignant, nefarious
10 iniquitous, malevolent, outrageous **11** treacherous

wickedness

3 sin **4** evil, vice **7** devilry **8** enormity, iniquity, satanism **9** depravity
10 corruption, immorality **12** devil-
ishness, fiendishness

wicker

4 twig **5** osier, withe **6** branch

wicket

4 arch, door, gate, hoop **6** window
sticky: 3 fix, jam **4** knot **7** toughie
9 conundrum, tight spot

wide

4 vast **5** broad, fully **8** extended,
spacious, straying, sweeping **9** deviating, expansive, extensive, inclusive **10** completely **13** comprehensive

widen

4 ream **6** dilate, expand, extend,
open up, spread **7** broaden, distend,
enlarge

widespread

4 rife, vast **6** common **7** current,
general, popular, rampant, regnant
8 far-flung **9** extensive, pervasive,
prevalent **10** far-ranging, ubiquitous

widget

5 gizmo **6** device, dingus, doodad,
gadget, hickey, jigger **7** gimmick,
whatsit **9** doohickey, thingummy
11 contraption, thingamabob, thingamajig, thingumajig

width

4 gape, kerf, span **5** depth, range
6 spread **7** breadth **9** extension

wield

3 use **5** exert **6** handle **7** control
8 exercise **10** manipulate
the gavel: 7 preside

wiener

3 dog **5** frank **6** hot dog **7** sausage
11 frankfurter **13** Vienna sausage

wife

3 Mrs. **4** mate **5** bride, woman
6 female, matron, missis, missus,
spouse **7** consort, partner **8** helpmate, helpmeet
Latin: 4 uxor
of a rajah: 4 rani **5** ranee

wifely

7 uxorial

wig

3 jaw, rap, rug **4** flip, rail, rate **5** chide,
freak, scold **6** berate, peruke, rebuke,
revile, toupee **7** bawl out, chew out,
reproof, upbraid **8** postiche, reproach
9 hairpiece, reprimand **10** tongue-
lash

wiggle

4 jerk **5** shake, twist **6** fidget, squirm,
writhe
Scottish: 5 hotch

wight

3 man **5** human **6** animal, mortal,
person **7** critter **8** creature **10** human being, individual

wild

3 mad **4** fast **5** crazy **6** barren,
raging, savage, stormy, unruly
7 erratic, frantic, furious, natural,
untamed, vicious **8** barbaric, blustery, desolate, frenetic, frenzied,
reckless **9** barbarian, barbarous,
delirious, fantastic, turbulent, wasteland **10** incautious, outlandish
11 extravagant, intractable, sensational, tempestuous, uncivilized,
uninhabited **12** preposterous,
uncontrolled, uncultivated, ungovernable, unmanageable **13** irresponsible, undisciplined

wild ass

5 kiang **6** onager

Wild Duck author
5 Ibsen (Henrik)

wildebeest
3 gnu

wilderness
4 bush 5 heath, waste 6 barren, desert 9 backlands, wasteland 10 hinterland 11 backcountry

Wilder play
7 Our Town 10 Matchmaker (The) 14 Skin of Our Teeth (The)

wild-eyed
6 raving 7 blue-sky, radical 9 visionary

wile
4 ploy, ruse, vamp 5 charm, feint, guile, trick 6 allure, deceit, entice, gambit 7 attract, beguile, bewitch, chicane, cunning, enchant, gimmick 8 artifice, inveigle, maneuver, trickery 9 captivate, chicanery, fascinate, magnetize, stratagem 10 subterfuge

wiliness
5 guile 7 cunning

will
4 like, wish 5 cause, elect, leave, order 6 choice, choose, decree, desire, direct, intend, intent, liking, option, ordain, please 7 bequest, consent, control, passion, purpose 8 appetite, bequeath, pleasure, volition 9 intention, testament 10 discipline 11 disposition, inclination, self-control 13 determination, self-restraint
addition: 7 codicil
maker: 8 testator 9 testatrix
without: 9 intestate

willful
5 heady 6 dogged, mulish, unruly 8 perverse, stubborn 9 obstinate, pigheaded, voluntary 10 deliberate, hardheaded, headstrong, purposeful, self-willed 11 intentional, intractable, wrongheaded 12 contumacious, pertinacious, ungovernable

Williams play
10 Camino Real, Rose Tattoo (The) 14 Glass Menagerie (The), Summer and Smoke 16 Cat on a Hot Tin Roof, Night of the Iguana (The), Sweet Bird of Youth 18 Suddenly Last Summer 20 Streetcar Named Desire (A)

William Tell composer
7 Rossini (Gioacchino)

willies
6 creeps, shakes 7 jimjams, jitters, shivers 9 whim-whams 10 goose bumps 13 heebie-jeebies

willing
3 apt 4 fain, game, glad, open 5 prone, ready 6 minded 7 forward, witting 8 amenable, disposed, inclined, obliging, unforced 9 agreeable, compliant, favorable, receptive, voluntary 10 deliberate, volitional 11 intentional, predisposed

williwaw
4 gust, wind 5 blast 8 outburst, paroxysm 9 commotion

will-o'-the-wisp
7 fantasy, figment, phantom 8 daydream, delusion 11 ignis fatuus

willow
5 osier, salix 6 sallow 10 cricket bat
flower cluster: 6 catkin
kind: 5 crack, pussy, white 6 basket 7 weeping

willowy
4 tall 5 lithe 6 pliant, supple, svelte 7 lissome, pliable, slender 8 graceful

Wilson play
6 Fences 11 Piano Lesson (The) 12 Talley's Folly 13 Hot l Baltimore (The) 20 Ma Rainey's Black Bottom

wilt
3 sag 4 swag 5 droop, dry up, wizen 6 wither 7 shrivel 8 languish

wily
3 sly 4 foxy 5 cagey, canny, slick 6 artful, astute, clever, crafty, shrewd, tricky 7 cunning, devious, vulpine 8 guileful, scheming 10 serpentine

wimble
4 bore 5 auger, borer, brace, drill 6 gimlet

Wimbledon's game
6 tennis

wimp
4 nerd, wuss 5 sissy 7 doormat, nebbish 9 jellyfish 11 milquetoast

wimple
4 bend, veil, wrap 5 cover, curve 6 ripple
wearer: 3 nun

wimp out
6 beg off, cave in, give in 8 back down

wimpy
4 lame, puny, weak 5 dinky, inept, timid 6 craven, feeble 7 gutless 8 cowardly, feckless, impotent, pathetic 9 spineless 10 namby-pamby, wishy-washy 11 ineffective, ineffectual

win
3 get 4 beat, earn, gain 5 reach, score 6 attain, defeat, obtain, secure 7 achieve, acquire, conquer, procure, produce, realize, succeed, success, triumph, victory 8 conquest, persuade 9 influence 10 accomplish
over: 6 disarm, induce 8 convince, persuade, talk into 9 prevail on

wince
5 cower, quail, start 6 blanch, blench, cringe, flinch, recoil, shrink 7 squinch

wind
3 air, dry, fan, gas 4 bend, blow, clue, coil, curl, gale, gird, gust, haul, hint, reel, rest, talk, turn, warp, wrap 5 cover, crank, curve, force, hoist, raise, sound, spool, twine, twist 6 breath, breeze, circle, enlace, girdle, notion, zephyr 7 enclose, entwine, envelop, inkling, involve, monsoon, nothing, tighten 8 easterly, encircle, entangle, surround, tendency, westerly 9 direction, idle words, influence, insinuate 10 indication, intimation, suggestion
cold: 4 bora 7 mistral, pampero 8 williwaw
combining form: 4 anem 5 anemo, venti, vento

gentle: 6 breeze, zephyr
god: 6 Boreas (north) 8 Favonius, Zephyrus (west)
hot: 6 simoom 7 sirocco
instrument: 3 sax 4 horn, oboe, tuba, vane 5 flute 7 bassoon, trumpet 8 trombone 9 saxophone 10 anemometer 11 weather vane
into: 8 aweather
measure of speed: 4 knot
Mediterranean: 7 sirocco 8 levanter, libeccio
scale: 8 Beaufort
stormy: 4 gale 7 cyclone, tornado, twister 9 hurricane 11 northeaster
warm: 4 föhn 5 foehn 7 chinook

windbag
6 gabber 7 blabber 8 bigmouth, blowhard, braggart

windfall
4 boon, gain 5 break 7 jackpot 8 fortuity

winding
4 curl, kink 5 snaky 6 spiral 7 coiling, curving, devious, sinuous 8 flexuous, indirect, tortuous, twisting 9 meandrous 10 circuitous, convoluted, meandering, roundabout, serpentine 11 anfractuous 12 labyrinthine

windmill
4 spin 5 wheel 7 machine
fighter: 10 Don Quixote

window
3 bay, eye 4 pane 5 oriel 6 dormer 7 opening 8 aperture, casement, jalousie
cover: 5 blind 7 curtain, shutter
French: 7 fenêtre
over a door: 7 transom 8 fanlight
part: 4 pane, sash, sill 5 frame
projecting: 3 bay 5 oriel
roof's: 6 dormer 7 lucarne 8 skylight
Scottish: 7 winnock
ship's: 4 port 8 porthole

windpipe
7 trachea
combining form: 6 trache 7 tracheo

windrow
4 bank, heap, hill, mass, pile
5 mound, ridge, stack

wind up
3 end 4 halt 5 close 6 finish, settle
8 complete, conclude 9 terminate

windup
3 end 5 close 6 ending, finale, finish
9 backswing 10 completion, conclusion 11 termination

windy
4 airy 5 blowy, gassy, gusty, inane, tumid, wordy 6 breezy, prolix, stormy, turgid 7 diffuse, orotund, pompous, verbose 8 blustery, inflated 9 bombastic, overblown
11 tempestuous 13 grandiloquent

wine
4 vino 5 drink, juice 8 beverage
aromatized: 8 vermouth 9 hippocras
beverage: 5 negus, punch 6 bishop, cooler 7 sangria 8 sangaree, spritzer 9 hippocras
bottle: 6 fiasco, magnum 8 decanter, jeroboam 10 methuselah
cabinet: 8 cellaret
cask: 3 tun, vat 4 butt, pipe
cellar: 6 bodega
combining form: 3 eno, oen 4 oeno
discoverer: 4 Noah
distillate: 6 brandy, cognac
dry: 3 sec 4 brut
flavor: 4 mull
fortified: 4 port 6 Malaga, sherry 7 Madeira, marsala, oloroso 8 muscatel
fragrance: 4 nose 7 bouquet
lover: 9 oenophile 11 oenophilist
maker: 7 vintner 8 vigneron 10 winegrower 13 viticulturist
merchant: 7 vintner
red: 4 port 5 Gamay, Macon, Medoc, Rioja 6 Barolo, Beaune, claret, Shiraz 7 Chianti 8 Bordeaux, Burgundy, cabernet 9 Lambrusco, Pinot Noir, St. Emilion, zinfandel 10 Beaujolais, Sangiovese 11 Petite Sirah 12 Valpolicella

relating to: 6 vinous
residue: 4 marc
rice: 4 sake
richness: 4 body
sediment: 4 lees 5 dregs
shop: 6 bistro, bodega, tavern
sparkling: 8 cold duck, sparkler, Spumante 9 champagne, Lambrusco
specialist: 9 enologist 10 oenologist
spiced: 6 mulled (wine) 9 hippocras
steward: 9 sommelier
study of: 7 enology 8 oenology
sweet: 4 port 5 Tokay 6 canary, Malaga, muscat 7 Catawba, Madeira, malmsey, marsala, oloroso, Vouvray 8 Malvasia, muscatel, sauterne 9 Sauternes 11 scuppernong
sweeten: 4 mull
vessel: 7 chalice
white: 4 hock 5 Rhine, Soave 7 Catawba, Chablis, Moselle, Orvieto, Vouvray 8 Bordeaux, Riesling, Semillon, vermouth 9 champagne, Hermitage, Meursault 10 chardonnay, Montrachet 11 Chenin Blanc, scuppernong 13 liebfraumilch 14 sauvignon blanc
year: 7 vintage

wing
3 ala, arm, ell, fly 4 sail, unit, vane 5 annex, flank, fleet, pinna, wound 6 flight 7 airfoil, faction, flanker, section 9 appendage, expansion, extension, improvise
combining form: 3 ali 4 pter 5 ptero
relating to: 4 alar 5 alary

wingding
4 bash, fete, gala 5 binge, party 7 blowout, shindig 9 festivity

winged
5 alate, fleet, rapid, swift 7 soaring 8 elevated
deity: 4 Amor, Eros, Nike 5 Cupid 6 Hermes 7 Mercury
horse: 7 Pegasus
monster: 5 harpy

wingless
8 apterous

winglike
4 alar 5 alary
part: 3 ala 4 alae (plural)

wink
3 bat, nap 5 flash, jiffy, shake, trice
6 moment, second, signal 7 connive,
flicker, instant, twinkle 9 nictitate,
twinkling 11 split second

winner
3 ace 4 lulu 5 doozy 6 doozie, top
dog, victor 7 success 8 champion
9 conqueror 11 titleholder

Winnie-the-Pooh
author: 5 Milne (A. A.)
character: 3 Roo 5 Kanga 6 Piglet,
Tigger

winning
8 charming, engaging, pleasing
9 agreeable 10 delightful, successful, triumphant, victorious 11 captivating 13 prepossessing

winnow
3 fan 4 blow, cull, pare, sift, sort
6 delete, filter, narrow, reduce,
remove, screen, select 8 separate

winsome
5 sweet 6 dulcet, lovely 8 charming,
cheerful, engaging, pleasing 9 easygoing 12 lighthearted

winter
6 season 9 hibernate
French: 5 hiver
Spanish: 8 invierno

Winter's Tale, A
author: 11 Shakespeare (William)
character: 7 Camillo, Leontes,
Paulina, Perdita 8 Florizel, Hermione 9 Antigonus, Autolycus,
Polixenes

wintry
3 icy 4 cold 5 bleak, hoary, nippy,
snowy 6 frigid, frosty 8 chilling,
freezing, hibernal 12 bone-chilling

wipe
3 dry, rub 4 swab 5 towel, whisk
6 napkin, smudge, sponge 8 squee-
gee

wipe out
4 rout 5 crash, erase, smear, sweep
7 blot out, destroy, expunge 8 decimate 9 eradicate, extirpate 10 annihilate, obliterate

wipeout
4 fall, rout 5 crash 8 drubbing
11 destruction 12 annihilation

wire
3 rod 4 cord, line, send 5 cable,
metal 6 thread 7 message 8 mesh-
work, telegram 9 cablegram, telegraph 10 finish line
measure: 3 mil 5 gauge

wiry
4 lean, ropy 6 sinewy, supple
7 fibrous, stringy

Wisconsin
capital: 7 Madison
city: 6 Racine 7 Kenosha 8 Green
Bay 9 Milwaukee
college, university: 5 Ripon 6 Beloit
9 Marquette
lake: 7 Mendota
motto: 7 Forward
nickname: 6 Badger (State)
peninsula: 4 Door
river: 7 St. Croix 9 Menominee,
Wisconsin 11 Mississippi
state bird: 5 robin
state flower: 6 violet
state tree: 10 sugar maple

wisdom
5 sense 7 insight, science 8 judgment, learning, sagacity, sageness,
sapience 9 good sense, knowledge
10 horse sense 11 common sense,
information

wise
3 hep, hip 4 bold, keen, sage, sane,
tell, warn, wily 5 alert, aware, brash,
cagey, canny, cocky, fresh, learn,
nervy, quick, sassy, sharp, smart
6 artful, astute, bright, cheeky, clever,
crafty, fill in, inform, notify, shrewd,
sophic, tricky 7 cunning, gnostic,

knowing, politic, prudent, sapient
8 discreet, flippant, impudent, insolent, sensible, tactical **9** advisable,
bold-faced, expedient, judicious,
sagacious, scholarly **10** discerning, insightful, perceptive, reflective, thoughtful **11** foresighted,
impertinent, intelligent, quick-witted,
sharp-witted, smart-alecky **13** contemplative, knowledgeable, perspicacious
old man: 6 Nestor
person: 4 sage **6** savant **7** scholar

wiseacre
see **wise guy**

wisecrack
3 dig, gag **4** gibe, jape, jest, joke,
quip **5** sally **9** witticism

wise guy
6 smarty **7** mobster **8** gangster,
smart-ass **9** know-it-all, swellhead
10 smart aleck **11** smarty-pants,
wisenheimer

wise man
4 guru, sage **5** magus **6** savant

Wise Men
see **Magi**

wish
3 bid **4** care, goal, like, long, lust,
want **5** covet, crave, fancy, foist,
order, yearn **6** desire, impose
7 request **10** desiderate

wishbone
7 furcula

wishful
5 eager **7** anxious, hopeful, longing
8 desirous

wishy-washy
4 lame, weak **5** banal, bland, vapid,
wimpy **6** jejune, watery **7** insipid,
languid **10** namby-pamby **11** ineffective, ineffectual **13** characterless

wisp
3 bit **5** shred, strip, trace **6** sliver,
snatch, streak **7** smidgen, snippet
8 fragment **9** scintilla

wispy
4 slim **5** frail **6** flimsy, slight **7** slender, tenuous **8** fleeting, nebulous
10 evanescent

Wister novel
9 Virginian (The)

wistful
3 sad **6** dreamy, triste **7** longing,
pensive **8** yearning **9** nostalgic
10 melancholy

wit
3 wag **5** brain, comic, droll, humor,
irony, joker **6** banter, esprit, jester,
reason, satire, wisdom **7** farceur,
punster **8** banterer, comedian,
funnyman, judgment, humorist,
jokester, quipster, repartee **9** alertness, ingenuity, intellect **10** cleverness, persiflage

witch
3 hag, hex **5** dowse, spell **6** voodoo,
Wiccan **7** charmer **8** magician,
sorcerer **9** sorceress **11** enchantress
companion: 3 cat
group: 5 coven
male: 6 wizard **7** warlock
meeting: 6 sabbat
town: 5 Endor
vehicle: 5 broom

witchcraft
5 magic, wicca **6** hoodoo, voodoo
7 devilry, hexerei, sorcery **8** wizardry
9 diablerie, sortilege, voodooism
10 black magic, hocus-pocus, mumbo
jumbo, necromancy **11** abracadabra,
thaumaturgy

witch hazel
5 shrub **6** lotion

witchy
6 Wiccan **7** magical **8** wizardly
9 sorcerous **11** necromantic
12 thaumaturgic

with
3 for, per, pro, via **4** over, upon
5 about **6** having **7** against, by way
of, through **8** as well as **9** by means
of, in favor of **10** by virtue of

French: 4 avec
German: 3 mit
Italian, Spanish: 3 con
Latin: 3 cum

withal
3 too, yet **4** also **5** still **6** as well, though **7** besides, howbeit, however **8** after all, moreover **11** furthermore, nonetheless **12** additionally, nevertheless

withdraw
4 exit, quit **5** demit, leave, unsay **6** depart, bow out, call in, cash in, desert, detach, recall, recant, recede, recoil, retire, secede, shrink **7** back out, drop out, pull out, retract, retreat, scratch, take off, take out **8** back down, evacuate, fall back, pull away, push back, separate, take back, turn away **9** disengage, stand down **10** disconnect, give ground

withdrawal
4 exit **6** exodus **7** exiting, pullout, removal, retreat **9** departure **10** alienation, detachment, retirement, retraction, revocation

withdrawn
4 cool **5** aloof **6** casual, remote **7** distant, removed **8** detached, isolated, reserved, retiring, solitary **9** incurious, unaffable, uncurious **10** unsociable **11** indifferent, introverted, standoffish, unconcerned, unexpansive **12** uninterested, unresponsive

wither
3 age, dry **4** fade, sear, wilt **5** dry up, parch, quail, wizen **6** scorch **7** mummify, shrivel

withered
4 sere **7** sapless **8** shrunken, wrinkled **9** shriveled

withhold
4 deny **5** check **6** deduct, detain, refuse, retain **7** abstain, deprive, forbear, inhibit, refrain, reserve **8** restrain, subtract **9** constrain

within
4 into **5** among **6** inside **7** indoors, inwards **8** enclosed, interior, inwardly **10** inner place
prefix: 5 infra, intra, intro

with-it
6 modern, modish, trendy **7** à la mode, current, faddish, stylish **8** up-to-date **11** fashionable **12** contemporary

without
4 open, past, sans **5** minus **6** absent **7** lacking, open air, outside, wanting **8** outdoors **10** externally, out-of-doors
Latin: 4 sine

with respect to
4 as to, in re **5** as for **7** apropos **8** touching **9** as regards, regarding **10** concerning

withstand
4 bear, buck, defy **5** fight, repel **6** endure, oppose, resist, suffer **7** hold off, survive, sustain **8** tolerate, traverse

withy
4 twig **5** osier **6** branch, willow **8** flexible **9** resilient

witless
3 mad **4** daft, nuts **5** crazy, daffy, dotty, nutty, silly **6** insane, simple, stupid **7** asinine, cracked, foolish, idiotic **8** demented, deranged, mindless **9** bedlamite, brainless, senseless **10** weak-minded, unbalanced

witlessness
5 folly **6** idiocy, lunacy **7** inanity **8** insanity **9** absurdity, stupidity

witness
3 see **4** note, sign, view **5** proof, vouch **6** attest, depone, depose, notice, viewer **7** bear out, confirm, betoken, certify, testify, watcher **8** attester, beholder, deponent, evidence, looker-on, observer, onlooker **9** bystander, spectator, testament, testifier, testimony **11** affirmation, attestation, corroborate, testimonial **12** confirmation

witticism

3 dig, gag, mot **4** gibe, jape, jest,
jibe, joke, quip **5** crack, sally **6** bon
mot **8** one-liner, repartee **9** throwaway, wisecrack

witting

5 aware **7** knowing, willful **8** sensible, sentient **9** cognizant, conscious, voluntary **10** deliberate
11 intentional

witty

5 funny **6** clever, jocose **7** amusing,
jocular **8** humorous **9** facetious
13 scintillating

wiz

3 ace **5** adept, fiend **6** artist, expert,
phenom **7** artiste **8** virtuoso

wizard

3 ace **4** mage **5** adept, druid, fiend,
magus **6** expert, phenom **7** warlock
8 conjurer, magician, sorcerer, virtuoso **9** enchanter **10** past master
11 necromancer, thaumaturge
13 thaumaturgist

wizardly

5 magic **6** mystic, witchy **7** magical
9 sorcerous **10** mysterious **11** necromantic **12** thaumaturgic

Wizard of Menlo Park

6 Edison (Thomas Alva)

Wizard of Oz

author: **4** Baum (L. Frank)
character: **7** Dorothy **9** Scarecrow
10 Tin Woodman **12** Cowardly Lion
dog: **4** Toto

wizardry

5 magic **6** voodoo **7** sorcery
8 witchery **9** diablerie, sortilege
10 black magic, necromancy, witchcraft **11** bewitchment, conjuration,
enchantment

wizen

3 dry **4** sere, wilt **5** dry up **6** shrink,
wither **7** dried-up, shrivel, wrinkle

wizened

4 aged, sere **5** dried **6** shrunk
7 pinched **8** shrunken, withered,
wrinkled

wobble

4 reel, rock, sway **5** quake, shake,
waver, weave **6** dither, falter, quaver,
teeter, totter **7** stagger, stumble,
tremble **8** nutation **9** vacillate

wobbly

4 weak **5** rocky, shaky **6** unsure
7 rackety, rickety **8** insecure, rachitic,
unstable, unsteady, wavering **9** faltering, teetering, tottering **10** nuta-
tional **11** vacillating

Wodehouse, P. G.

castle: **9** Blandings
character: **6** Bertie (Wooster),
Gussie (Fink-Nottle), Jeeves, Psmith
7 Wooster (Bertie) **8** Emsworth
(Lord), Mulliner (Mr.) **10** Threepwood
(Clarence, Freddie) **12** Lord Emsworth
club: **6** Drones

Woden

see **Odin**

woe

3 rue **4** bale, bane, care **5** grief
6 misery, regret, sorrow **7** anguish, sadness, trouble **8** calamity
9 heartache **10** affliction, heartbreak **11** lamentation, unhappiness
12 wretchedness

woebegone

3 low, sad **4** blue, down, worn
6 shabby **7** doleful, forlorn, ruthful
8 dejected, dolorous, downcast,
wretched **9** depressed, miserable,
sorrowful **10** despondent, melancholy **11** crestfallen, downhearted,
low-spirited **12** disconsolate

woeful

3 sad **5** heavy, sorry **6** dismal,
rueful, tragic, triste **7** ruthful **8** dejected, dolorous, downcast, grievous,
mournful, stricken, tortured, wretched
9 afflicted, aggrieved, depressed,
heartsick, miserable, plaintive,
sorrowful **10** deplorable, lamentable, lugubrious, melancholy
11 distressing, downhearted, low-
spirited **12** disconsolate **13** heartbreaking

wolf

4 bolt, lobo, rake, roué **5** canid **6** canine, coyote, devour, gobble, masher **7** Don Juan, poverty **8** Casanova, lothario **10** starvation
genus: 5 Canis
group: 4 pack
young: 5 whelp

Wolfe novel

17 Look Homeward Angel, Of Time and the River **18** You Can't Go Home Again **20** Bonfire of the Vanities (The)

wolfish

4 wild **5** cruel, feral **6** fierce, lupine, savage **7** bestial, brutish, vicious **9** ferocious

wolverine

European: 7 glutton
genus: 4 Gulo

Wolverine State

8 Michigan

woman

4 dame, lady **5** madam **6** female, matron **8** mistress **10** girlfriend
attractive: 5 belle **6** beauty, eyeful, looker **7** stunner **8** knockout
combining form: 4 gyny **5** gynec **6** gynaec, gyneco, gynous **7** gynaeco
courageous: 7 heroine
dignified: 6 matron **7** dowager **10** grande dame
dowdy: 5 frump
English: 6 milady
first, biblical: 3 Eve
first, mythological: 7 Pandora
French: 5 femme
German: 4 Frau **8** Fräulein
Hawaiian: 6 wahine
Indian: 5 squaw
Italian: 5 donna **7** signora
old: 3 hag **4** dame **5** crone **6** beldam, carlin, gammer, granny
pregnant: 7 gravida
resembling: 8 gynecoid
royal: 5 queen **8** princess
sailor: 4 Wave
servant: 4 maid
soldier: 3 Wac
Spanish: 4 doña **6** señora

strong: 6 amazon, virago
unmarried: 4 miss **6** maiden **8** spinster
young: 4 girl, lass **6** lassie, maiden

womanize

4 wolf **9** gallivant, philander **10** fool around, mess around

womanizer

4 stud, wolf **6** masher **7** Don Juan, gallant, playboy **8** Casanova, lothario **9** ladies' man **10** lady-killer **11** philanderer

womb

6 uterus
combining form: 6 hyster **7** hystero

women

hatred of: 8 misogyny
organization of: 3 DAR, NOW **8** sorority

Women in Love author

8 Lawrence (D. H.)

wonder

3 awe **4** muse **5** doubt **6** marvel **7** dubiety, miracle, portent, prodigy **8** mistrust, question **9** amazement, speculate, suspicion **10** admiration, skepticism **11** incertitude, uncertainty **12** astonishment

wonderful

4 keen **5** grand, great, nifty, super, swell **6** divine, groovy, peachy, spiffy **7** amazing, strange, too much, topping **8** dynamite, fabulous, glorious, spiffing, terrific **9** admirable, excellent, marvelous, wunderbar **10** astounding, delightful, miraculous, out-of-sight, stupendous **11** astonishing, outstanding

wondrous

6 mystic **7** amazing, awesome, strange **9** marvelous **10** astounding, formidable, miraculous, portentous, prodigious, remarkable, stupendous, surprising **11** astonishing, spectacular **13** extraordinary

wonky

4 awry **5** geeky, nerdy, shaky **7** bookish **8** unsteady

wont

3 apt **4** used **5** habit, usage **6** custom, manner **8** accustom, habitude, inclined, practice **10** accustomed, consuetude

wonted

5 usual `7 routine **8** habitual, ordinary **9** customary **10** accustomed

woo

3 sue **5** court **6** pursue **7** address, entreat, solicit

wood

5 weald **6** forest, lumber, timber **8** golf club **10** timberland
combining form: 3 xyl **4** lign, xylo **5** ligni, ligno
decayed: 4 punk
eater: 7 termite
for burning: 5 fagot **6** tinder **8** kindling
golf: 6 driver
hard: 3 elm, oak **4** ebon, rata, teak **5** beech, birch, ebony, maple **6** cherry, walnut **8** chestnut, mahogany, sycamore
imperfection: 4 knot **5** gnarl
light: 5 balsa
made of: 5 treen
pattern in: 5 grain **6** figure
product: 3 tar **5** paper **10** turpentine
soft: 4 pine

wood alcohol

6 methyl **8** carbinol, methanol

woodchuck

6 marmot **9** groundhog

wood coal

7 lignite

wooded

5 bosky, treed **6** sylvan **8** forested, timbered

wooden

5 rigid, stiff **6** clumsy **7** awkward, stilted **8** ligneous **10** inflexible

woodland

5 copse, taiga, weald **6** forest, pinery **7** coppice **10** rain forest

wood nymph

5 dryad

woodpecker

4 bird **7** flicker, wryneck **9** sapsucker
genus: 5 Picus
kind: 5 downy, green, hairy **8** imperial, pileated **9** redheaded **11** ivory-billed

woodsman

6 logger **8** forester **10** bushranger **11** bushwhacker

wood sorrel

3 oca **6** oxalis **8** shamrock **9** carambola

woodsy

6 rustic, sylvan

woodwind

4 oboe, reed **5** flute, shawm **7** bassoon, piccolo **8** clarinet **9** saxophone **10** instrument **11** English horn **13** contrabassoon

woodworker

9 carpenter **12** cabinetmaker

woody

8 ligneous **12** station wagon

wooer

4 beau **5** lover, spark, swain **6** suitor **7** admirer, gallant, sparker

woof

4 bark, crow, weft, yarn **5** boast, weave **6** fabric, thread **7** texture

wool

3 fur **4** coat, hair **6** fabric, fleece
cut: 5 shear
fabric: 4 felt **5** baize, crepe, serge, tweed **6** covert, kersey, mohair, poplin, shoddy, velour **7** flannel, worsted **8** cashmere, chenille **9** gabardine **10** broadcloth
fat: 7 lanolin
kind: 4 hogg **6** angora, hogget, virgin
low-quality: 5 mungo **6** shoddy
musk-ox: 6 qiviut
process: 7 carding
source: 4 goat, lamb **5** camel, llama, sheep **6** alpaca

woolly

5 fuzzy, hairy, nappy   6 fleecy, shaggy
7 blurred, hirsute   9 roughness
10 indistinct

woozy

4 hazy, sick, weak   5 dazed, dizzy,
faint, fuzzy, muzzy, vague   6 addled,
blurry, groggy, punchy   8 confused,
nauseous   9 nauseated, slaphappy
11 light-headed

word

3 vow   4 buzz, news, oath, term
5 logos, order, rumor   6 advice,
gospel, gossip, phrase, pledge,
plight, remark, report, saying, signal
7 command, message, promise
8 locution   9 assurance, directive,
discourse, guarantee, statement,
utterance   10 commitment, expression   11 declaration, information
12 announcement, conversation,
intelligence
connective: 11 conjunction
group: 6 clause, phrase   8 sentence
misused: 8 malaprop   11 malapropism
naming: 4 noun
new: 7 coinage   9 neologism
of action: 4 verb
of honor: 4 oath   7 promise
origin: 9 etymology
part: 8 syllable
root: 6 etymon
scrambled: 7 anagram
shortened: 11 contraction   12 abbreviation
square: 10 palindrome
with opposite meaning: 7 antonym
with same meaning: 7 synonym
with same pronunciation: 7 homonym   9 homophone
with same spelling: 7 homonym
9 homograph

wordbook

5 vocab   7 lexicon   8 glossary
9 thesaurus   10 dictionary, vocabulary

word-for-word

7 literal   8 ad verbum, verbally,
verbatim

wordiness

8 verbiage   9 logorrhea, prolixity, verbosity   10 bloviation

word-of-mouth

4 oral   6 spoken, verbal   8 viva voce
9 unwritten

wordy

5 windy   6 prolix, verbal   7 diffuse,
verbose   9 dictional, garrulous,
iterative, redundant, vocabular
10 long-winded, logorrheic, loquacious, rhetorical

work

3 act, fix, job, run, tug, use   4 duty,
line, make, opus, take, task, tend, till,
toil   5 chore, craft, drive, forge, grind,
guide, labor, shape, solve, sweat,
trade   6 create, effect, effort, energy,
excite, métier, result, strain, strive
7 arrange, calling, control, exploit,
fashion, operate, perform, product,
provoke, pursuit, resolve, succeed,
travail   8 activity, business, contrive,
drudgery, exertion, function, operate,
slogging, striving, vocation   9 cultivate, embroider, execution   10 assignment, employment, handicraft,
occupation, profession
together: 9 cooperate   11 collaborate
unit: 3 erg   5 joule

workaday

5 plain, usual   7 mundane, prosaic,
routine   8 ordinary   9 quotidian
11 commonplace   12 run-of-the-mill

worker

4 doer, hand, serf   5 prole   6 toiler,
wallah   7 artisan, laborer   8 employee, mechanic, operator   9 craftsman, operative   10 roustabout, wage
earner   11 proletarian
fellow: 7 comrade, partner   9 colleague
group: 4 crew, gang   5 shift, staff,
union
hard: 5 slave   6 beaver, drudge
insect: 3 ant, bee   4 wasp   7 termite
itinerant: 6 boomer   7 migrant
slow: 7 plodder
unskilled: 4 peon   7 jackleg, laborer

working

4 busy, live **6** active, useful, viable
7 dynamic, engaged, running
8 employed, occupied **9** operative
11 functioning
not: 5 kaput **6** broken

workman

see **worker**

work out

3 fix **5** solve, train **6** devise, settle
7 arrange, develop, resolve **8** exercise

workout

4 test **5** drill **8** exercise, practice
10 daily dozen

work over

4 beat, redo **5** scrag, study **6** beat
up, mess up, redraw, rehash, revamp, revise **7** examine, redraft,
restyle, rewrite, rough up **9** manhandle

workroom

3 lab **4** shop **6** studio **7** atelier
10 laboratory

works

4 mill **5** plant **7** factory **8** workshop
11 manufactory

Works and Days author

 6 Hesiod

world

5 class, earth, globe, realm **6** career,
cosmos, nature, planet, public,
sphere, system **7** kingdom, society
8 creation, division, everyone,
renowned, universe **9** human race,
macrocosm, microcosm **13** distinguished
combining form: 4 cosm **5** cosmo

worldly

5 blasé **6** carnal, earthy, urbane
7 earthly, fleshly, mundane, profane,
secular, sensual, terrene **8** material,
telluric, temporal **9** sublunary **11** terrestrial **12** cosmopolitan **13** sophisticated

worldly-wise

12 cosmopolitan **13** sophisticated

World War I

battle: 5 Aisne, Marne, Somme,
Ypres **6** Isonzo, Verdun **7** Jutland
9 Caporetto **10** Tannenberg **11** Dardanelles
battle line: 9 Siegfried
general: 4 Foch (Ferdinand), Haig
(Douglas) **7** Allenby (Edmund)
8 Pershing (John) **10** Hindenburg
(Paul von), Ludendorff (Erich)
hero: 4 York (Alvin) **8** Red Baron
(The) **10** Richthofen (Manfred von)
12 Rickenbacker (Eddie)
treaty: 10 Versailles

World War II

admiral: 6 Halsey (William "Bull"),
Nimitz (Chester)
alliance: 4 Axis **6** Allies
battle: 4 St.-Lô **5** Anzio, Bulge
6 Bataan, Midway, Tarawa, Warsaw
7 Britain, Iwo Jima, Okinawa, Saint-
Lô **8** Coral Sea, Normandy **9** El
Alamein, Leyte Gulf **10** Stalingrad
11 Guadalcanal
general: 6 Patton (George), Rommel (Erwin), Zhukov (Georgy)
7 Bradley (Omar) **9** MacArthur
(Douglas) **10** Eisenhower (Dwight
David), Montgomery (Bernard)
hero: 6 Murphy (Audie)
journalist: 4 Pyle (Ernie)
vehicle: 4 jeep
weapon: 5 A-bomb **6** rocket **8** buzz
bomb

worldwide

6 cosmic, global **8** catholic **9** planetary, universal **10** ecumenical
12 cosmopolitan

worm

3 cad, cur **4** grub, lout **5** borer,
creep, fluke, leech, louse, screw,
treat **6** edge in, maggot, no-good,
squirm, thread, wiggle, wretch, writhe
7 extract, lowlife, serpent, triclad,
wriggle **8** helminth, nematode,
squiggle **9** insinuate, planarium,
trematode **10** infiltrate
marine: 6 nereid **7** annelid, tubifex
parasitic: 5 fluke, leech **7** ascarid,
ascaris, cestode, filaria **8** helminth,
trichina **9** strongyle

worn
3 old, wan **4** aged, beat **5** drawn, jaded, tatty, tired, weary **6** eroded, frayed, ragged, shabby **7** haggard **8** fatigued **9** woebegone **10** threadbare

worn-out
4 beat **5** all in, spent, tired, weary **6** bleary, bushed, ragged, used-up **7** drained, run-down **8** decrepit, depleted, fatigued, overused **9** exhausted, worm-eaten **10** broken-down, threadbare, tumbledown **11** debilitated, dilapidated

worried
6 afraid, on edge **7** anxious, nervous **8** bothered, distrait, troubled **9** concerned, tormented **10** distracted, distraught, distressed **12** apprehensive

worry
3 nag, try, vex **4** care, fret, fuss, gnaw, goad, pain, stew, test **5** annoy, beset, shake, tease, trial, upset **6** assail, attack, bother, harass, needle, pester, plague, pull at, unease **7** afflict, anguish, anxiety, concern, disturb, oppress, torment, trouble **8** aggrieve, distress, irritate **9** agitation, annoyance, misgiving **10** irritation, uneasiness

worrywart
7 fusspot **9** Cassandra, doomsayer, pessimist **10** fussbudget

worse
8 inferior

worsen
4 sink **7** decline **10** degenerate **11** deteriorate

worship
4 love **5** adore, honor **6** admire, dote on, homage, revere **7** idolize, lionize, liturgy, respect **8** devotion, idolatry, venerate **9** adoration, affection, reverence **10** admiration, veneration **11** idolization
object of: 3 god **4** icon, idol
place of: 5 altar **6** church, mosque, shrine, temple **9** cathedral, synagogue

worshipper
3 fan **6** votary **7** admirer, devotee **8** adherent, believer, disciple **10** enthusiast

worsted
4 yarn **5** stuff **6** caddis, fabric **7** cheviot, etamine, flannel, lasting **8** shalloon **9** bombazine, sharkskin **10** broadcloth

worth
4 rate **5** merit, price, value **6** regard, riches, wealth **7** caliber, calibre, fortune, quality, stature **9** resources, substance, valuation **10** excellence

worthless
4 vain **6** futile, no-good **7** inutile **8** nugatory **9** no-account

worthwhile
6 paying **7** gainful **9** estimable, honorable, lucrative **10** profitable, well-paying **11** meritorious, money-making **12** advantageous, remunerative

worthy
4 good **5** noble **8** laudable, standout **9** admirable, deserving, desirable, estimable, honorable **10** acceptable, creditable **11** commendable, meritorious

Wotan
see **Odin**

Wouk novel
4 Hope (The) **5** Glory (The) **10** Winds of War (The) **11** Caine Mutiny (The) **19** Marjorie Morningstar

would-be
7 hopeful, wishful **8** apparent, aspiring, desiring, desirous **9** ambitious, potential

wound
3 cut **4** blow, harm, hurt, pain, rift **6** damage, injure, injury, insult, lesion, trauma **8** lacerate **10** laceration
discharge: 3 pus
sign: 4 scab, scar **5** blood **7** blister

wow

3 hit 4 boff, grab 5 amaze, boffo,
smash 6 dazzle 7 astound, impress,
success 8 bedazzle

Wozzeck composer

4 Berg (Alban)

wrack

4 kelp, raze, ruin 5 smash, total
7 destroy, flotsam, remnant, seaweed 8 decimate, demolish, shambles, wreckage 11 destruction

wraith

5 ghost, shade, spook 6 double,
shadow, spirit 7 phantom, specter,
spectre 8 phantasm 10 apparition

wrangle

3 row 4 spar, spat, tiff 5 argue,
brawl, fight, scrap 6 bicker, fracas,
haggle, hassle 7 brabble, dispute,
fall out, finagle, quarrel, quibble
8 squabble 11 altercation

wrangler

6 cowboy 8 buckaroo 9 ranch hand

wrap

3 fur 4 bind, cape, coat, roll 5 cloak,
drape, shawl, stole 6 bundle, clothe,
enfold, invest, jacket, mantle, muffle,
parcel, shroud, swathe 7 bandage,
blanket, conceal, dress up, embrace,
enclose, engross, envelop, involve,
package, swaddle 8 bundle up,
enshroud, surround

wrapped up

4 deep 6 intent 7 engaged 8 absorbed, consumed, immersed 9 engrossed 11 preoccupied

wrapper

5 cover 6 jacket 10 dust jacket
12 dressing gown

wrap up

6 muffle 8 close out, complete,
conclude 9 summarize

wrap-up

4 coda 5 close 6 capper, closer,
finale, report 7 closing 8 epilogue
9 summation 10 denouement

wrath

3 ire 4 fury, rage 5 anger 6 choler
8 ferocity 9 vengeance 10 punishment 11 retribution 12 chastisement

wrathful

3 mad 5 angry, irate 6 heated,
raging 7 enraged, furious 8 choleric,
incensed, inflamed 10 infuriated

wreak

5 cause, exact, visit 6 effect, impose
7 inflict 10 bring about

wreath

3 bay, lei 5 crown 6 anadem, laurel
7 chaplet, circlet, coronal, coronet,
garland, laurels

wreathe

4 coil, curl, wind 5 twine, twist
6 spiral 7 entwine 9 corkscrew
10 interweave

wreck

4 do in, heap, hulk, raze, ruin 5 beach,
crack, crash, cream, smash, total
6 beater, damage, jalopy, junker,
pileup, ravage, strand 7 clunker,
crack-up, destroy, scuttle, smashup,
torpedo 8 decimate, demolish
9 vandalize 11 destruction

wreckage

5 wrack 6 debris 7 flotsam 8 detritus, shambles 11 destruction

wrecker

8 salvager, tow truck

wrench

4 jerk, pull, rack, tool, turn, warp,
yank 5 force, twist, wrest, wring
6 change, injure, injury, snatch,
socket, sprain, strain 7 disable,
distort, pervert, squeeze 8 distress,
twisting
kind: 6 monkey 7 ratchet

wrest

4 rend, rive 5 exact, twist, wring
6 elicit, extort, snatch, wrench
7 extract, squeeze

wrestle

6 combat, strain, strive, tussle
7 contend, grapple, scuffle 8 struggle

wrestling
hold: 4 lock 6 nelson 8 headlock, scissors
kind: 4 sumo
term: 3 pin 4 fall 5 throw 8 take-down

wretch
3 cur, dog 4 scum, toad, worm
5 devil, knave, louse, rogue, skunk, snake 6 rascal, rotter 7 caitiff, hangdog, lowlife, outcast, rat fink, stinker, villain 8 scalawag, stinkard
9 scoundrel 10 blackguard, sleaze-ball 11 rapscallion

wretched
3 low, sad 4 base, foul, mean, vile
6 abject, dismal, horrid, scurvy, sordid, woeful 7 abysmal, doleful, forlorn, ignoble, ruthful, servile, squalid, un-happy 8 dejected, dolorous, hope-less, inferior 9 afflicted, execrable, miserable, sorrowful 10 despairing, despicable, deplorable, despondent, melancholy, villainous

wretchedness
3 woe 6 misery 7 anguish 8 distress

wriggle
4 worm 5 slink 6 squirm, writhe

wring
3 wry 5 choke, exact, screw, twist, wrest 6 extort, squirm, wrench, writhe 7 afflict, draw out, extract, squeeze, torment
the neck: 5 scrag

wringing-wet
5 soppy 6 soaked, sodden, soused
7 soaking, sopping 8 drenched, dripping 9 saturated

wrinkle
4 fold, ruck, ruga, seam 5 crimp, crisp, plica, ridge, wizen 6 cockle, crease, fillip, furrow, pucker, rumple
7 crumple, novelty, scrunch, shrivel
8 contract 9 corrugate, crow's-foot, worry line 10 innovation 11 corruga-tion 12 imperfection, irregularity

wrinkled
5 lined 6 rugose, rumply 7 creased
8 puckered, rugulose

Wrinkle in Time author
6 L'Engle (Madeleine)

wrist
5 joint 6 carpus
bone: 6 carpal, hamate 8 pisiform

writ
5 brief, order 6 assize, capias, decree, elegit, extent 7 mandate, process, summons, warrant 8 de-tainer, document, mandamus, mit-timus, praecipe, replevin, subpoena
9 execution 10 attachment, certio-rari, court order, injunction 11 fieri facias, scire facias, supersedeas
12 habeas corpus, venire facias
13 sequestration

write
3 ink, jot, pen 4 note 5 chalk, draft, print, score, spell 6 answer, author, byline, draw up, indite, ordain, pencil, record, scrawl, scribe 7 compose, dissert, engross, fire off, put down, scratch, set down 8 inscribe, scrib-ble, spell out 9 autograph, transpose
10 correspond, underwrite

write down
4 note 6 record, reduce 10 tran-scribe

write off
6 cancel 7 dismiss, expense 8 am-ortize, discount 9 eliminate 10 de-preciate

write-off
4 debt, loss 7 expense 8 donation
9 allowance, deduction, reduction

writer
4 poet 6 author, penman, scribe
8 composer, novelist 9 scribbler, wordsmith
bad: 4 hack

write-up
5 blurb, story 7 account, article

writhe
4 curl, worm 5 twist 6 squirm, suf-fer, wallow, welter, wiggle, wrench
7 agonize, contort, distort, wriggle
8 convolve, squiggle 10 intertwine

writing

4 book, hand, note **5** essay, paper, print, prose, style, words **6** letter, notice, record, script **7** epistle **8** document, longhand **9** signature **10** authorship, literature, manuscript, penmanship **11** calligraphy, composition, inscription, publication

character: 6 letter **9** cuneiform **10** hieroglyph
combining form: 4 gram **6** grapho, graphy
for the blind: 7 braille
instrument: 3 pen **5** chalk, quill **6** pencil, stylus
kind: 5 prose, verse **6** poetry
sacred: 5 Bible, Koran **6** Talmud, Tantra **9** scripture
secret: 4 code
surface: 5 board, paper, slate **6** scroll **9** parchment

wrong

3 bad, ill, off, sin **4** awry, evil, harm, hurt, tort **5** abuse, amiss, badly, crime, false, inapt, unfit **6** afield, astray, injure, injury, malign, offend, sinful, unfair, unjust, untrue **7** defraud, immoral, oppress, outrage, violate **8** aggrieve, ill-treat, improper, inequity, iniquity, maltreat, mistaken, mistreat, opposite **9** discredit, erroneous, grievance, incorrect, injustice, misguided, persecute, unethical, unfitting, violation **10** inaccurate, iniquitous, mistakenly, unfairness, unjustness, unsuitable, wickedness **11** erroneously, incorrectly, unfavorably **12** inaccurately, infelicitous **13** inappropriate

wrongdoer

5 felon **6** sinner **8** criminal, offender **9** miscreant, reprobate **10** accomplice, delinquent, malefactor **12** transgressor

wrongdoing

3 sin **4** evil **5** crime **7** misdeed, offense **8** iniquity **10** misconduct **11** malefaction, malfeasance, misbehavior

wrongful

6 unjust, unfair **7** illegal, illicit, lawless **8** criminal, improper, unlawful **12** illegitimate

wrongheaded

6 mulish **7** froward **8** contrary, perverse **9** obstinate

wrought

4 made **6** formed, shaped, worked **7** created **8** finished, hammered **9** decorated, fashioned, processed **10** ornamented **11** embellished **12** manufactured
up: 7 excited, stirred

wry

4 bent **5** askew, twist, wrest **6** ironic, wrench **7** crooked, twisted **8** humorous, sardonic **11** wrongheaded

wryneck

10 woodpecker **11** torticollis

wurst

7 sausage

Wuthering Heights

author: 6 Brontë (Emily)
character: 5 Cathy **9** Catherine **10** Heathcliff
family: 6 Linton **8** Earnshaw

Wycliffite

7 Lollard

Wyoming

capital: 8 Cheyenne
city: 6 Casper **7** Laramie
mountain, range: 5 Rocky **7** Gannett (Peak) **9** Wind River **10** Grand Teton
nickname: 8 Equality (State)
river: 5 Green, Snake **6** Powder **7** Bighorn **11** Yellowstone
state bird: 10 meadowlark
state flower: 16 Indian paintbrush
state tree: 10 cottonwood

X

x
3 chi, ten 4 kiss 5 annul, cross, erase, error, times, wrong 6 cancel, delete, efface 7 mistake, unknown 8 abscissa 9 signature

Xanthippe
3 nag 5 scold, shrew 6 nagger 9 termagant
husband: 8 Socrates

Xenophon work
8 Anabasis 9 Cyropedia, Hellenica

xerophyte
6 cactus

Xerxes
crossing site: 10 Hellespont
defeat: 7 Plataea, Salamis
father: 6 Darius
kingdom: 6 Persia
mother: 6 Atossa
victory: 11 Thermopylae

Xmas
4 Noel, yule 8 Nativity, yuletide

X-ray
discoverer: 8 Roentgen (Wilhelm)
science: 9 radiology

xylophone relative
7 marimba

Y

yacht
4 race, sail 6 cruise 7 cruiser 8 sailboat 12 cabin cruiser

yahoo
3 hun, yay 4 boor, clod, dolt, hood, lout, punk, thug 5 brute, chuff, churl, clown, rough, rowdy, tough 6 hoorah, hooray, hurrah, savage, terror, vandal, yippie 7 buffoon, bumpkin, hoodlum, ruffian, toughie 8 bullyboy, hooligan 9 roughneck 10 clodhopper

Yahweh
3 God 6 Adonai, Elohim 7 Jehovah

yak
3 gab, jaw 4 blab, chat 5 clack, prate 6 babble, gabble, jabber, natter, yammer 7 blabber, blather, chatter, palaver, prattle 11 confabulate

Yalta participant
6 Stalin (Joseph) 9 Churchill (Winston), Roosevelt (Franklin Delano)

yam
7 boniato 11 sweet potato

yammer
3 cry 4 bawl, crab, fuss, moan, wail, yawp, yell 5 bleat, gripe, whine 6 babble, bellow, clamor, gabble, grouch, grouse, jabber, natter, snivel, squawk 7 blather, prattle, whimper 8 complain 9 bellyache, caterwaul

yank
3 tug 4 grab, jerk, pull, tear 5 hoick 6 snatch, wrench 7 extract

yap
3 gab 4 bark, hick 5 mouth, prate 6 babble, bowwow, gabble, jabber, natter, rustic, yammer 7 blather, bumpkin, chatter, hayseed, prattle 9 hillbilly 10 clodhopper

yard
3 pen 4 herd, quad, spar, unit 5 court, garth, glass 6 length 7 grounds, measure 9 curtilage, enclosure 10 playground, quadrangle
five and one-half: 3 rod
part of: 4 foot
two hundred and twenty: 7 furlong

yardstick
4 norm, test 5 basis, gauge, model 7 measure, pattern 8 paradigm, standard 9 barometer, benchmark, criterion, guideline 10 touchstone

yare
4 deft, spry 5 agile, brisk, handy, lithe, quick, ready, zippy 6 lively, nimble, volant 7 lissome 9 sprightly

yarn
4 tale, talk 5 fiber, story 6 caddis, cotton, crewel, strand, thread 7 account, caddice 8 anecdote, tall tale 9 adventure, narration, narrative
ball of: 4 clew
coil: 5 skein 6 skeane
cotton: 10 candlewick
for fastening a sail: 6 roband
woolen: 6 crewel 7 worsted 8 shetland

yaw
4 rock, swag, veer 5 lurch 6 swerve 7 deviate 9 alternate, deviation 10 deflection

yawn
3 gap 4 bore, gape 5 ennui 6 cavity, tedium 7 boredom, bromide 10 dullsville

yawning
4 deep 5 agape 6 gaping 7 abyssal
9 cavernous

yawp
3 bay, cry, nag 4 bark, bawl, beef,
crab, fuss, gape, wail 5 bleat, gripe
6 clamor, outcry, squall, squawk,
yammer 8 complain 9 bellyache

yaws
9 frambesia

yclept
5 named 6 called

yea
3 aye, too 4 also, amen, even, more,
okay 5 truly 6 agreed, assent, as
well, indeed, really, verily 7 besides,
granted 8 likewise, moreover, positive 9 certainly 10 definitely 11 affirmation, affirmative 12 additionally

yeanling
3 kid 4 lamb

year
4 time 5 cycle 6 period
academic division: 4 term 7 quarter, session 8 semester 9 trimester
French: 5 année
kind: 4 leap 5 solar 6 fiscal 8 academic, calendar, sidereal
Latin: 5 annus
Scottish: 7 towmond
Spanish: 3 año

yearbook
5 annal 6 annual 7 almanac

yearling
4 colt, foal 5 filly

Yearling, The
author: 8 Rawlings (Marjorie Kinnan)
character: 4 Jody
fawn: 4 Flag

yearly
6 annual 8 annually

yearn
4 ache, burn, itch, long, lust, pant,
pine, sigh, wish 5 dream, spoil
6 hanker, hunger, thirst

yearning
4 wish 5 ardor, drive, eager 6 desire,
thirst 7 craving, wistful 8 appetite
10 aspiration

years
3 age, era
five: 7 lustrum 12 quinquennial,
quinquennium
four: 11 quadrennial, quadrennium
one hundred: 7 century
9 centenary 10 centennial
one thousand: 10 millennium
ten: 6 decade 9 decennial, decen-
nium
three: 9 triennial, triennium
two: 8 biennial, biennium

yeast
4 barm, foam, suds 5 froth, spume
6 lather, leaven 7 ferment

yeasty
5 dizzy, giddy, light 6 frothy 7 flighty
8 immature, restless, seething
9 exuberant, frivolous, unsettled
11 light-headed

Yeats, William Butler
beloved: 9 Maud Gonne
birthplace: 6 Dublin
play: 7 Deirdre 9 Herne's Egg (The)
16 Countess Cathleen (The)
poetry: 5 Tower (The) 10 Easter
1916 12 Second Coming (The)
16 Wild Swans at Coole (The)
18 Sailing to Byzantium
theater: 5 Abbey

yegg
5 thief 6 robber 7 burglar 8 picklock
11 safecracker

yell
3 cry 4 call, howl, roar, wail 5 cheer,
hallo, hollo, shout, whoop 6 bellow,
clamor, holler, outcry, scream, shriek,
squall 10 vociferate

yellow
3 age 4 buff, mean, weak, yolk
5 amber, blond, color, lemon, straw,
tawny, topaz 6 coward, craven,
flaxen, golden, sallow 7 gutless,
ignoble, mustard, saffron 8 cowardly,
discolor 9 dastardly, jaundiced,
spunkless 11 sensational 12 dishonorable 13 pusillanimous

brownish: 3 dun 5 amber, ocher
dye: 7 annatto
greenish: 5 olive 6 acacia 10 chartreuse

yellowhammer
5 finch 7 bunting, flicker

yelp
3 cry, yap 4 bark 6 outcry, squeal

Yemen
capital: 4 Sana 5 Sanaa
city: 4 Aden 5 Ta'izz
desert: 10 Rub' al-Khali
gulf: 4 Aden
island: 7 Socotra
island group: 7 Kamaran
language: 6 Arabic
monetary unit: 4 rial
neighbor: 4 Oman 11 Saudi Arabia
peninsula: 7 Arabian
sea: 3 Red 7 Arabian

yen
4 ache, itch, long, lust, pine, sigh,
urge 5 taste, yearn 6 desire, hanker, hunger, thirst 7 craving, longing,
passion 8 appetite, yearning 9 hankering

yeoman
5 clerk 6 farmer 7 freeman 8 retainer 9 attendant, beefeater, landowner 10 freeholder 11 homesteader

yeomanly
5 loyal 6 sturdy 8 faithful

yes
3 aye, yea, yeh, yep, yup 4 okay,
yeah 5 agree 6 agreed, assent,
gladly 7 consent, exactly 8 all right
9 assuredly, certainly, willingly
11 affirmation, affirmative, undoubtedly
French: 3 oui

yeshiva
6 school 8 seminary

yes-man
5 toady 6 minion, stooge 7 spaniel
8 groveler, truckler 9 flatterer, sycophant 10 bootlicker 13 applepolisher

yesterday
4 past, yore 8 recently 10 recent
time
French: 4 hier
Spanish: 4 ayer

yesteryear
4 past, yore 7 history 8 foretime,
lang syne

yet
3 but, too 4 also, even, more, only,
save 5 so far, still 6 as well, though,
withal 7 besides, earlier, finally, howbeit, however, someday, thus far
8 after all, hitherto, moreover, sometime 10 eventually, ultimately 11 furthermore, nonetheless, still and all
12 additionally, nevertheless

Yevtushenko poem
7 Babi Yar, Baby Yar

Ygerne
see **Igraine**

yield
3 bow, net, pay 4 bear, bend, cave,
cede, crop, fold 5 defer, grant, waive
6 accede, bounty, buckle, comply,
impart, output, profit, relent, render,
resign, return, reward, submit, supply, tender 7 abandon, bring in,
concede, consent, deliver, furnish,
harvest, produce, product, proffer,
provide, revenue, succumb 8 abdicate, collapse, generate, hand over
9 acquiesce, surrender 10 bring
forth, capitulate, production, relinquish

yielding
4 soft 6 pliant, supple 7 bearing,
passive, pliable 8 flexible 9 adaptable, tractable 10 manageable,
productive, submissive 11 acquiescent, unresistant

yin and _____
4 yang

yip
3 cry 4 bark, yelp

yippee
6 hoorah, hooray, hurrah, hurray

yoga posture
5 asana

yoke
3 bar, tie, wed 4 bond, join, link, pair, span, team 5 clamp, frame, hitch, marry, unite 6 attach, couple, inspan 7 bondage, connect, control, harness, peonage, serfdom, slavery 8 marriage 9 servitude 10 crosspiece, oppression
combining form: 3 zyg 4 zygo
part: 5 oxbow

yokel
3 oaf 4 boor, clod, hick, rube 5 churl, swain 6 rustic 7 bucolic, bumpkin, hayseed 9 chawbacon, hillbilly 10 clodhopper, countryman

yolk
4 food 6 yellow 10 ovum center

yon
see yonder

yonder
5 there 7 farther, further, thither 8 outlying

yore
3 old 7 history 8 foretime, lang syne 9 antiquity, yesterday 10 yesteryear

you
3 one 4 thee, thou
French: 4 vous
German: 3 Sie
Spanish: 5 usted 7 ustedes

young
3 fry, new 4 baby, tyro 5 brood, fresh, green 6 babies, callow, infant, junior, litter, tender, unripe 7 untried 8 childish, immature, juvenile, unformed, youthful 9 unfledged 10 unfinished, unseasoned 11 unpracticed 13 inexperienced
animal: 3 cub, fry, kid, kit, pup

4 calf, colt, fawn, foal, joey 5 puppy 6 kitten, heifer, piglet
bird: 5 chick 7 gosling
hare: 7 leveret
sheep, goat: 4 lamb 8 yeanling

younger
6 junior

youngster
3 boy, cub, kid, lad, tad, tot 4 girl, lass, tike 5 chick, child 6 moppet, shaver 8 juvenile 9 fledgling

youth
5 prime 6 period, spring 8 juvenile, preadult, teenager 9 stripling 10 adolescent, springtide, springtime 12 inexperience
ancient Greek: 6 ephebe 7 ephebus
goddess of: 4 Hebe
mythological: 6 Adonis, Apollo, Icarus 8 Ganymede
time of: 9 salad days

youthful
5 fresh, green, young 6 boyish, callow, maiden, unripe 7 puerile 8 immature, juvenile, virginal 9 beardless, unfledged

yowl
3 bay, cry 4 bawl, howl, wail 6 scream, squall, squeal 7 ululate 9 caterwaul

yucca
7 cassava 9 bear grass

Yukon
bay: 9 Mackenzie
capital: 10 Whitehorse
city: 6 Dawson
mountain: 5 Logan
river: 5 Yukon 8 Klondike

yule
4 Noel, Xmas 8 Nativity 9 Christmas 13 Christmastide

Z

Zambia
capital: 6 Lusaka
city: 5 Kitwe, Ndola 11 Livingstone
lake: 5 Mweru 9 Bangweulu
10 Tanganyika
language: 7 English
monetary unit: 6 kwacha
mountain range: 8 Muchinga
neighbor: 5 Congo 6 Angola,
Malawi 7 Namibia 8 Tanzania,
Zimbabwe 10 Mozambique
river: 5 Kafue 7 Luangwa, Zambezi
waterfall: 13 Victoria Falls

zany
3 nut, wag 4 card, fool, kook 5 antic,
campy, clown, comic, crazy, cutup,
dotty, goofy, idiot, joker, kooky, loony,
nutty, wacky 6 jester, madcap 7 buffoon, farceur, half-wit 8 clowning,
clownish, comedian, funnyman, jokester 9 harlequin, prankster, screwball, simpleton, trickster 11 merry-
andrew

zap
3 hit 4 blow, kill, nuke 5 blast,
snuff 6 attack 7 destroy, wipe out
8 dissolve 9 eliminate, irradiate,
liquidate 10 annihilate

Zauberflöte composer
6 Mozart (Wolfgang Amadeus)

zeal
4 brio, fire, zest 5 ardor, drive, mania
6 desire, energy, esprit, fervor, spirit
7 avidity, passion, urgency 8 devotion, dynamism, keenness 9 eagerness, intensity, vehemence 10 enthusiasm, fanaticism, fierceness

zealot
3 bug, fan, nut 4 buff 5 fiend, freak
6 maniac, votary 7 devotee, fanatic,
sectary 8 partisan 10 aficionado,
enthusiast 12 true believer

zealous
4 avid, keen 5 afire, eager, fiery,
fired, nutty, rabid 6 ardent, fervid,
gung-ho 7 devoted, fanatic, fervent
8 frenetic, obsessed, wild-eyed
9 dedicated, fanatical, possessed
10 passionate 11 impassioned
12 enthusiastic

zebra
6 equine 7 referee 9 crosswalk
extinct: 6 quagga
type: 6 Grevy's 8 mountain
9 Burchell's

zebu
4 oxen

Zebulun
9 lost tribe
brother: 4 Levi 5 Judah 6 Simeon
father: 5 Jacob
mother: 4 Leah

zecchino
6 sequin

Zechariah
7 prophet

Zedekiah
9 Mattaniah
father: 6 Josiah

zenana
5 harem, serai 8 seraglio

zenith
3 top 4 acme, apex, peak 6 apogee, height, summit, vertex 8 capstone, pinnacle 11 culmination 12 highest point
opposite: 5 nadir

Zenobia
husband: 9 Odenathus
kingdom: 7 Palmyra

Zeno follower
5 Stoic

Zephaniah
7 prophet 9 Sophonias

zephyr
6 breeze 8 west wind

Zephyrus
father: 8 Astraeus
mother: 3 Eos 6 Aurora

zeppelin
5 blimp 7 airship 9 dirigible

zero
3 aim, nil, zip 4 love, nada, none, null, void 5 aught, nadir, zilch 6 cipher, naught, nobody 7 nothing, nullity 8 goose egg 9 nonentity

zest
4 élan, peel, tang, zeal 5 ardor, gusto, taste 6 fervor, flavor, relish 7 delight, ecstasy, elation, passion, sparkle 8 appetite, dynamism, piquancy, pleasure 9 eagerness, enjoyment 10 enthusiasm 11 delectation 12 exhilaration, satisfaction

zesty
4 racy, tart 5 sharp, spicy, tangy 6 biting, lively, savory, snappy 7 peppery, piquant, pungent 8 exciting, poignant, seasoned, spirited 9 flavorful

Zetes
brother: 6 Calais
father: 6 Boreas
mother: 8 Orithyia
slayer: 8 Heracles, Hercules

Zethus
brother: 7 Amphion
father: 4 Zeus 7 Jupiter
mother: 7 Antiope

Zeus
7 Jupiter
brother: 5 Hades 8 Poseidon
daughter: 3 Ate 4 Hebe 5 Helen 6 Athena 7 Artemis 9 Aphrodite 10 Persephone, Proserpina
father: 6 Cronus
home: 7 Olympus (Mt.)
lover: 4 Leda, Leto, Maia 5 Danae, Dione, Metis 6 Aegina, Europa, Latona, Semele, Themis 7 Alcmene, Antiope, Demeter 8 Callisto, Eurynome
mother: 4 Rhea
nurse: 9 Almathaea
oracle: 6 Dodona
shield: 5 aegis
sister: 4 Hera, Juno
son: 4 Ares 5 Arcas, Argus, Minos 6 Aeacus, Apollo, Hermes, Zethus 7 Amphion, Perseus 8 Dionysus, Heracles, Hercules, Sarpedon, Tantalus
tree: 3 oak
wife: 4 Hera, Juno
weapon: 11 thunderbolt

zigzag
4 tack, turn 5 angle, crank, weave 6 jagged 7 chevron 8 flexuous, indirect, serrated

zilch
3 nil, zip 4 zero 5 aught, squat 6 cipher, naught, nobody 7 nothing, nullity 8 goose egg 9 nonentity 11 diddly-squat

Zimbabwe
capital: 6 Harare
city: 5 Gweru 6 Kwekwe, Mutare 8 Bulawayo, Maxvingo 11 Chitungwiza
ethnic group: 5 Shona 7 Ndebele
former name: 8 Rhodesia
lake: 6 Kariba
language: 5 Bantu 7 English
monetary unit: 6 dollar
neighbor: 6 Zambia 8 Botswana 10 Mozambique 11 South Africa
river: 4 Sabi 7 Limpopo, Zambezi
waterfall: 13 Victoria Falls

zinc
7 element
ingot: 7 spelter
ore: 6 blende 10 sphalerite

zing
3 pan, pep, rap, vim, zap, zip 4 brio,
dash, élan, slam, snap, zeal 5 ardor,
flair, oomph, verve, vigor 6 energy,
esprit, fervor, spirit 7 panache,
passion, sparkle 8 dynamism,
vitality 9 animation, eagerness
10 ebullience, enthusiasm

Zion
5 bliss 6 heaven, Israel 7 Elysium
8 eternity, paradise 12 New Jerusalem, promised land

Zionist
American: 5 Szold (Henrietta)
English: 7 Sokolow (Nahum)
8 Zangwill (Israel)
German: 6 Nordau (Max Simon)
Hungarian: 5 Herzl (Theodor)
Israeli: 5 Buber (Martin) 8 Weiz-
mann (Chaim)

zip
3 fly, nil, nix, pep, run, vim 4 brio,
dash, hiss, rush, nada, snap, tear,
whiz, zero, zest, zing, zoom 5 drive,
gusto, hurry, oomph, speed, squat,
whisk, zilch 6 bustle, energy, hasten,
hustle 7 nothing 8 vitality 10 excitement, liveliness 11 diddly-squat

zippy
4 keen, spry, yare 5 agile, alert,
brisk, peppy, quick, ready 6 lively,
nimble, snappy, speedy 7 dynamic
8 spirited 9 sprightly

zircon
6 jargon 7 jargoon, mineral
variety: 7 jacinth 8 hyacinth

zit
6 pimple

zither
10 instrument
Chinese: 3 kin 4 ch'in
Japanese: 4 koto
relative: 8 autoharp, dulcimer

zodiac sign
3 Leo (the Lion) 5 Aries (the Ram),
Libra (the Balance), Virgo (the Virgin)
6 Cancer (the Crab), Gemini (the
Twins), Pisces (the Fishes), Taurus
(the Bull) 7 Scorpio (the Scorpion)
8 Aquarius (the Water Bearer)
9 Capricorn (the Goat) 11 Sagittarius (the Archer)

Zola, Emile
work: 4 Nana 7 J'accuse 8 Drunkard (The), Germinal 9 La Débâcle
10 L'Assommoir 13 Thérèse
Raquin

zombie
5 robot 8 cocktail 9 automaton

zone
4 area, band, belt 5 layer, tract
6 region, sector 7 portion, quarter,
section, segment, stretch 8 district,
division, encircle, surround 9 partition, territory

zonked
4 high 5 dazed, doped, drunk, tight
6 ripped, stoned 7 drugged, drunken,
smashed 8 hopped-up, tripping,
turned on, wiped out 9 spaced-out,
strung out, stupefied 10 inebriated,
tripped out 11 intoxicated

zoologist
American: 5 Clark (Eugenie), Hyatt
(Alpheus) 6 Carson (Rachel), Fos-
sey (Dian), Osborn (Henry Fairfield),
Yerkes (Robert) 7 Agassiz (Alexan-
der), Ditmars (Raymond), Merriam
(Clinton) 8 Hornaday (William)
Austrian: 6 Frisch (Karl von)
British: 6 Darwin (Charles), Huxley
(Julian, Thomas) 7 Goodall (Jane),
Medawar (Peter) 9 Lankester (Ed-
win)
Dutch: 10 Swammerdam (Jan)
French: 6 Buffon (G.-L. Leclerc),
Cuvier (Georges)
German: 7 Haeckel (Ernst)
Norwegian: 6 Nansen (Fridtjof)
South African: 5 Broom (Robert)
Swedish: 8 Linnaeus (Carolus)

zoom
3 hum, zip 4 buzz, dash, whiz, zero
5 focus, speed, whizz 6 streak
7 shoot up 9 skyrocket

zoophyte
5 coral 6 sponge 8 bryozoan 9 gorgonian 10 sea anemone

Zoroastrian
demon: 4 deva
god: 10 Ahura Mazda
sacred writings: 6 Avesta

zounds
3 gad 4 egad 8 gadzooks 11 odd's bodkins

zucchetto
7 calotte 8 skullcap

zwieback
5 toast 7 biscuit

zygomatic bone
5 malar 9 cheekbone

zygote
4 cell 6 oocyst